Understanding Social Psychology

FIFTH EDITION

Understanding Social Psychology

Stephen Worchel
Texas A & M University

Joel Cooper
Princeton University

George R. Goethals
Williams College

Brooks/Cole Publishing Company
Pacific Grove, California

Brooks/Cole Publishing Company
A Division of Wadsworth, Inc.

Printed in the United States of America

10   9   8   7   6   5   4   3   2   1

Library of Congress Cataloging-in-Publication Data
Worchel, Stephen.
   Understanding social psychology / Stephen Worchel, Joel Cooper,
George R. Goethals. — 5th ed.
      p.   cm.
   Includes bibliographical references and indexes.
   ISBN 0-534-13626-5
   1. Social psychology.   I. Cooper, Joel.   II. Goethals, George R.
   III. Title.
   HM251.W76   1990   90-47466/
   302—dc20   CIP/

Sponsoring Editor: *Philip L. Curson, Claire Verduin*
Project Development Editor: *Patricia P. Gadban*
Editorial Assistant: *Heather L. Riedl*
Production Editor: *Marjorie Z. Sanders*
Manuscript Editor: *Barbara Salazar*
Permissions Editor: *Mary Kay Hancharik*
Interior and Cover Design: *E. Kelly Shoemaker*
Cover Illustration: *Harry Briggs*
Art Coordinator: *Cloyce J. Wall*
Interior Illustration: *Graphic Typesetting Service, Inc.*
Photo Editor: *Ruth Minerva*
Photo Researcher: *Marion Paone*
Typesetting: *Graphic Typesetting Service, Inc.*
Cover Printing: *The Lehigh Press, Inc.*
Printing and Binding: *Rand McNally & Company*

(Credits continue on p. 581.)

To our parents,
who were our first teachers of psychology;

to Jack W. Brehm and Edward E. Jones,
who imparted to us a respect
for the field of psychology;

to our children, Leah, Jessica, Elise, Hannah,
Jason, Aaron, Grant, Jefferson, and Andrew,
who have shown us how much more
psychology we still have to learn;

and to our wives, Frances, Barbara, and Marion,
who have worked so hard
at creating the type of environment
that allows us to continue our own learning.

Preface

When we sat down to begin writing this Fifth Edition, it struck us that we had been working on *Understanding Social Psychology* for almost twenty years. After agreeing that the field had gotten older, but we had not aged, we began reflecting on the changes in social psychology and how we could present those changes in this edition. Our intention with this edition, as in past editions, is to show the life and vitality of social psychology by exploring its historical roots, reviewing the present state of the field, and anticipating future directions. As in our own classes, we have attempted to help students understand social psychology by presenting the unique balance of theory, research, and application. Anniversaries always present an opportunity to take stock of the past and speculate about the future.

Exploring the boundaries of social psychology

One of the first points that struck us was the tremendous extension of the boundaries of social psychology. Unlike some areas of psychology such as clinical, child, or developmental, the discipline of social psychology has not been defined by a specific population of study. Social psychology studies "people," whether old or young, male or female, black, white, or other racial group, and adjusted or maladjusted. Over the years social psychology has made use of this license to roam, and as you will see in the text, research in the field touches many populations. In another sense, this license has allowed social psychologists to cross the boundaries of many other disciplines. More than at any time in its history, social psychologists are working on problems relevant to almost every area of psychology and other social sciences. Accordingly, we have included social psychology research that is relevant to clinical psychology, personality, cognitive psychology, developmental

psychology, sociology, political science, and business. Overall, this approach has led us to demonstrate that social psychology is a field increasingly open to including new ideas and issues, rather than narrowing its focus and building artificial boundaries.

In addition to moving outward, social psychology has also increased its "inward" focus. When we began writing the first edition, the focus of social psychology was largely on the relationship between people and peoples. Over the years, social psychologists have been increasingly concerned with perceiving, processing, and interpreting these interactions. Accordingly, this edition has a greater coverage of social cognition and the self than any previous edition. We have attempted to show the close relationship between cognitive and motivational approaches and how each approach helps us understand the other. In a sense, this edition shows most clearly the role of the self in the relationship between people and peoples.

A concern for social issues

While the science of social psychology has developed, the field has retained deep concerns and roots in social and world problems. Indeed, these concerns were the foundation on which the field was built. Since the last edition, the world has undergone rapid change. The political map of the world becomes obsolete almost as quickly as it is drawn. The Eastern Europe of the 1990s only faintly resembles the Eastern Europe of the 1980s. Political change is taking place in China. The world is holding its breath, and protecting its oil reserves, as violence and conflict dominate the Middle East. In the United States, abortion has become the leading issue in political campaigns. There are increasing concerns about the fair treatment of individuals regardless of their gender, race, and physical ability. This concern has renewed attention on how groups are portrayed in the media.

We have attempted to be sensitive to the relationship between social psychology and social issues in this edition. Within the chapters, we have increased our coverage of gender issues; attitudes regarding such issues as abortion, AIDS, equal rights, and interpersonal and intergroup conflict; media effects on behavior; and terrorism. We added a separate chapter on aggression and violence and expanded coverage of the environment. Throughout the text we have retained commitment to showing how social psychology can be applied to understanding (and helping to solve) everyday problems.

Examining the past and the present

Looking back at social psychology, as well as examining the present and future, made us realize how important a historical perspective is of the field. It is one thing to know the nature of the field today; understanding its history gives important insight into the present. Seeing the conditions that led to a particular experiment being performed helps bring that study to life. In addition, looking at the old and the new shows how the field has developed and how new ideas have been incorporated. In this edition we have paid particular attention to presenting both the new and contemporary work and the classic studies and showing how they are related.

Helping students learn

We have also attempted to make the book more friendly to the reader. At key points in the chapter, we have raised questions that you should be able to answer. These "Stop, Think, & Understand" questions offer you a chance to check whether or not you are picking up the important points. We have added a running glossary, so that important words and phrases, boldfaced in text, are defined on the page where they appear.

Once again, we have placed the study of social psychology in the context of real incidents, which begin each chapter. You may also use these incidents to help add meaning and coherence to the various studies and theories within each chapter. Beyond this, however, these incidents can help demonstrate a lesson we learned twenty years ago when we began writing this text: Learning about and doing social psychology is fun and challenging.

Supplementary materials

To assist the student, the Study Guide, written by Fred Rhodewalt, University of Utah, includes learning devices such as a review of the learning objectives, answers to the "Stop, Think, & Understand" questions, multiple-choice questions, and matching exercises using key terms from the text.

To assist the instructor, a Test Bank is available. It contains at least 50 multiple-choice questions per chapter. Also available is an Instructor's Manual, written by John Fleming, University of Minnesota, that contains chapter outlines, lecture suggestions, key terms, and suggested films. These items are available under one cover.

Acknowledgments

The writing of this textbook was an exercise in applied social psychology. While the authors must assume the ultimate responsibility for the product, the text is truly a group effort. We received excellent reviews and suggestions from a large number of reviewers; we'd like to thank all of the people who contributed in this manner: Ann H. Baumgardner, Michigan State University; Kim Daubman, Williams College; Charles Dufour, Colby College; David Dunning, Cornell University; Michael E. Enzle, University of Alberta; John Fleming, University of Minnesota; Grace Galliano, Kennesaw State College; Jeff Greenberg, University of Arizona; Jack Hautaluoma, Colorado State University–Fort Collins; and Suzanne R. Pallak, Georgetown University.

In addition to those who had the official title of "reviewer," we received valuable input from the following people: Joshua Aronson, Jason Cooper, Dawna Coutant-Sassic, Bill Crano, Karen Duffy, John Fleming, Michelle Grossman, Lori Nelson, Jeff Simpson, Bill Webb, Frank Wong, and Wendy Wood.

The team at Brooks/Cole played a vital and crucial role throughout the project. Paul Curson, the editor, alternated between being a resource person, motivator, referee, and team leader. He started the ball rolling and kept it on course throughout the project. We received tremendous support and advice from Marjorie Sanders, Ruth Minerva, Pat Gadban, Kelly Shoemaker, and Cloyce Wall. In addition to their help, these people made us feel a special part of the Brooks/ Cole family.

Closer to home, the following people contributed to our efforts throughout the project: Dink Asano, Theresa Bradbury, Vicky Corrington, Ann Faranetta, Angie Giusti, Joan Hall, Elaine James, Lorie Lapaglia, Fran Rosenfeld, Vera Sohl, Elizabeth Stanton, and Karen Ware.

We'd also like to thank the scores of students at our own institutions and other schools who took the time to give us comments on the book. We are writing the book for the students, and their comments have been of great help in keeping to this goal. We also invite you to write us with your comments (we've included a questionnaire and reply card at the back of the book) so that we can continue to keep improving our efforts to develop a student-friendly text.

Stephen Worchel
Joel Cooper
George R. Goethals

Contents

Understanding
Social Psychology

Chapter One

Social Psychology: What, Why, and How

O n Halloween eve, 1938, a radio program of Spanish music was interrupted by a "newscast" reporting
explosions on Mars. Sometime later, Roman
Raquello and his orchestra were again interrupted, this time with the information that a huge
flaming object had landed in the small town of
Grover's Mill, near Princeton, New Jersey. The
radio network sent reporter Carl Phillips to the
scene. This is part of the report heard by millions
of listeners on the CBS network:

[Phillips] Well, I . . . I hardly know where to begin,
to paint for you a word picture of the strange
scene before my eyes, like something out of a
modern *Arabian Nights*. Well, I just got here. I
haven't had a chance to look around yet. I guess
that's it. Yes, I guess that's the . . . thing, directly
in front of me, half buried in a vast pit. Must have
struck with terrific force. The ground is covered
with splinters of a tree it must have struck on its
way down. What I can see of the . . . object itself
doesn't look very much like a meteor, at least not
the meteors I've seen. It looks more like a huge
cylinder. . . . (Hadley Cantril in *The Panic Broadcast: Portrait of an Event* by Howard Koch [copy-
right © 1940 by Princeton University Press, copyright renewed, copyright © 1968 by Howard Koch],
reprinted by permission of International Creative
Management, Inc.)

After Phillips has gone into a more detailed
description, he gasps:

[Phillips] Just a minute! Something's happening!
Ladies and gentlemen, this is terrific! This end of
the thing is beginning to flake off! The top is
beginning to rotate like a screw! The thing must
be hollow! . . . Ladies and gentlemen, this is the
most terrifying thing I have ever witnessed. . . .
Wait a minute! Someone's crawling out of the hollow top. Someone or . . . something. I can see
peering out of that black hole two luminous disks
. . . are they eyes? It might be a face. It might be
. . . Good heavens, something's wriggling out of
the shadow like a gray snake. Now it's another one,
and another. They look like tentacles to me. There,
I can see the thing's body. It's large as a bear and
it glistens like wet leather. But that face. It . . . it's
indescribable. I can hardly force myself to keep
looking at it. The eyes are black and gleam like a
serpent. The mouth is V-shaped with saliva drip-
ping from its rimless lips that seem to quiver and
pulsate. . . .

Phillips then moves to find a better position
from which to view the strange happenings. Once
in position, he reports:

[Phillips] A humped shape is rising out of the pit.
I can make out a small beam of light against a
mirror. What's that? There's a jet of flame spring-
ing from that mirror, and it leaps right at the
advancing men. It strikes them head on! Good
Lord, they're turning into flame! Now the whole
field's caught fire. [Explosion] The woods . . . the
barns . . . the gas tanks of automobiles . . . it's
spreading everywhere. It's coming this way. About
20 yards to my right. . . .
    [Announcer Two] Ladies and gentlemen, due
to circumstances beyond our control, we are unable to continue the broadcast from Grover's Mill.
Evidently there's some difficulty with our field
transmission. (Koch, 1968)

When communication with the scene was
restored, forty people, including six troopers, were
reported dead, burned beyond all recognition.
Martial law was declared in central New Jersey.
Captain Lansing of the armed forces took to the
air to announce that the feared object was surrounded by eight infantry battalions.

A few seconds later, the radio audience was
exposed to sounds of gunfire, the shouting of
orders, and general pandemonium. Silence fell,
only to be broken by a bulletin read by a news-
man in the New York studio:

[Announcer Two] Ladies and gentlemen, I have
a grave announcement to make. Incredible as it
may seem, both the observations of science and
the evidence of our eyes lead to the inescapable
assumption that those strange beings who landed
in the Jersey farmlands tonight are the vanguard
of an invading army from the planet Mars. The
battle which took place tonight at Grover's Mill
has ended in one of the most startling defeats ever
suffered by an army in modern times; seven thousand men armed with rifles and machine guns
pitted against a single fighting machine of the
invaders from Mars. One hundred and twenty
known survivors. The rest strewn over the battle
area from Grover's Mill to Plainsboro, crushed
and trampled to death under the metal feet of the
monster, or burned to cinders by its heat ray. The
monster is now in control of the middle section
of New Jersey and has effectively cut the state
through its center. (Koch, 1968)

On Halloween eve, 1938, millions of Americans heard their radio program of Spanish music interrupted by a special newscast reporting explosion on Mars. Many of these listeners were soon to believe that the Earth was being invaded by monsters from Mars.

As the drama continued, the listeners were addressed by the U.S. secretary of the interior, whose advice to the worried citizens was that they should place their faith in God. Residents of New York were urged to evacuate and were told which routes to take and which to avoid. It was reported that communication with New Jersey had been broken and that the smoke was descending upon New York as reports were being received of Martian landings in Buffalo, Chicago, and St. Louis. "This is the end now," exclaimed the reporter. "People are trying to run from it, but it's no use. They're falling like flies. Now the smoke's crossing Sixth Avenue . . . Fifth Avenue . . . 100 yards away . . . it's 50 feet. . . ."

It is estimated that at least six million people heard Orson Welles's Mercury Theater broadcast based on H. G. Wells's *War of the Worlds* and that well over one million people believed that it was a legitimate newscast and that the Earth was being invaded by Martians. Before the hour-long program had ended, hundreds of thousands of Americans were seized with panic as they tried to flee the monsters from the planet Mars. People cried, screamed, gathered loved ones, huddled together, or drove to flee the attacking onslaught. A male college student reported:

One of the first things I did was to try to phone my girl but the lines were all busy, so that just confirmed my impression that the thing was true. We just started driving. We had heard that Princeton was wiped out and gas was spreading over New Jersey . . . we figured our friends and families were all dead. . . . (*The Invasion from Mars: A Study in the Psychology of Panic* by Hadley Cantril [copyright 1940, © 1968 by Princeton University Press], p. 52. Reprinted by permission of Princeton University Press)

Orson Welles stands in the CBS studio with the cast and orchestra during the broadcast of *War of the Worlds*. What was intended as an entertainment special led millions of listeners to fear for their lives and seek out social support from friends.

The "invasion from Mars" stimulated a variety of responses and created a fertile ground for the study of numerous social phenomena. Hadley Cantril, a Princeton social psychologist, conducted 135 interviews in an effort to catalog people's reactions. One that occurred with regularity was a tendency to seek the company of other people, to confront the stressful situation as a member of a group. People huddled in stores, storm cellars, apartments, and houses, and groups crowded into cars. One hysterical New Jersey woman phoned her local police department, which informed her that the danger was probably not "immediate." "We all kissed one another," she reported, "and felt we would all die. When I heard the gas was in the streets of Newark, I called my brother and his wife and told them to get in their car and come right over so we could all be together." Another of Cantril's respondents spoke of "gathering her friends and driving as far as she could," and coeds recalled that "the girls in the sorority houses and dormitories huddled around their radios, trembling and weeping in each other's arms."

Defining Social Psychology

The *War of the Worlds* broadcast had a profound and far-reaching effect on the people who turned on their radios that Halloween eve. Assume for the moment that you are part of a group whose class project is to describe and explain the effects of the broadcast. This is clearly a mammoth task; six million people heard the broadcast. How would your group go about working on this project?

One way would be for each group member to take a slightly different approach in examining the audience and its reactions. For example, you could examine the impact on individuals who heard the broadcast and on those who did not. You could then compare the attitudes, behaviors, and emotions of the people in these two categories. Another member of your group could focus on the effects of the broadcast on groups. This person could investigate how families or social groups were influenced by the events of that evening. Still a third member of your group might focus on specific individuals. This student might identify four people who heard the broadcast and compare each person's reaction to the reactions of the other three. Each of these perspectives would add to our understanding of the event by taking a slightly different approach.

In laying out these approaches, we have roughly identified the focuses of social psychology, sociology, and personality psychology. **Social psychology** can be defined as a discipline that uses scientific methods to "understand and explain how the thought, feeling, and behavior of individuals are influenced by the actual, imagined, or implied presence of others" (Allport, 1985, p. 3).

An important point to remember is that the focus of social psychology is on the *individual* rather than on the group or some other unit. It is individuals who think, feel, and behave. As social psychologists we want to learn how the individual is affected by social events. It is this concern with the individual that ties social psychology to the family of psychology rather than to some other branch of social science. Having said this, we need to take one additional step to capture the flavor of social psychology. While the focus is on the individual, the goal is to understand how *most* people act in a given situation. We are not so concerned about the unique personal characteristics of individuals that may cause them to act differently from each other. Our aim is to understand the general tendencies in the actions, feelings, and thoughts of individuals.

If you took this approach to your class project, you might ask whether most people were frightened by the broadcast (emotions); whether most people tried to be with others or stayed alone (behavior), and whether most people believed the

While social psychologists acknowledge that everyone does not act the same in any given situation, their primary concern is how *most* people would act in a given situation. Given that premise, what kind of question would a social psychologist be likely to ask about the situation shown here?

Martians were coming to their area (attitudes). Carrying your role as a social psychologist further, you would be interested in explaining why people reacted as they did: Was it fear that caused people to want to be with others, and if so, why? And you might conclude your presentation with predictions about how people would respond in similar situations.

Your classmate who was interested in the effects of the broadcast on groups would be tak-

---

social psychology A discipline that employs scientific methods to understand and explain how the thought, feeling, and behavior of individuals are influenced by the actual, imagined, or implied presence of others.

TABLE 1-1

Reactions of people to various social situations

	Meeting a friend at dinner	Listening to a frightening broadcast	Encountering two friends arguing
Mary	Ignores him	Seeks a friend	Ignores them
John	Acts politely	Seeks a friend	Breaks up argument
Sue	Gets into argument	Seeks a friend to argue with	Joins argument
George	Races to cafeteria line	Seeks a friend	Listens to argument

Social psychology approach: Identify the most likely responses within the situation and examine how the situation affects the most likely response.
Personality approach: Compare each person with the others to identify how each is unique.

ing the sociological perspective. In general, sociologists are interested in the structure and functioning of groups. The groups can be small (a family), of moderate size (a sorority or fraternity), or large (a society). The focus here might be on the rules that the group has developed to deal with the crisis created by the *War of the Worlds;* or on what groups (social or work) were most strongly affected by the broadcast.

The student who researched a single individual represents the approach of personality psychologists. The interest here is in identifying *individual differences* that guide behavior. In this case, we would be concerned with how a single individual (Mary) reacted to various situations and how Mary's response differed from that of another person (John). To illustrate this approach, consider Table 1-1. The personality psychologist, who is interested primarily in identifying consistencies within people, will be most concerned with the horizontal axis: How does Mary (John, Sue, or George) act across situations? The social psychologist, who considers the effects of situations on persons, is interested in investigating the vertical consistencies in Table 1-1. We know that Mary, John, Sue, and George differ in many ways. They will react to situations with some differences, and we may come to recognize them as having different personalities. But personality differences are not what concern social psychologists; they are interested in determining the way *most* people react.

From the table, it appears that being frightened causes most people to affiliate—to seek other persons. Though Mary generally seems to be more reclusive than John and less argumentative than Sue, this does not alter the fact that all of the individuals in the sample react to the social situation of the frightening broadcast by wanting to affiliate. As social psychologists, we know that if we continue to sample individuals, we will find someone who will not affiliate when afraid; differences among people will lead some to behave differently from the way the majority act.

Having examined these differences, we must point out that we are referring to the *emphasis* of the fields and not to clear disciplinary boundaries: while these distinctions may help us understand the focus of social psychology, personality, and sociology, they do not exclude considerable overlap. No sharp boundaries separate these fields; instead, interest and approach overlap among these and other fields (Figure 1-1).

Serge Moscovici, a French social psychologist, characterizes social psychology as a "bridge" between other branches of knowledge (Moscovici, 1989). The field recognizes the importance of the individual in a larger social system and therefore draws on sociology, political science, anthropology, and economics. It acknowledges the wide range of human activities and the influence of culture and of the past on human behavior. In taking this focus, social psychology intersects with philosophy, history, art, and music. In addition to this broad perspective, social psychology understands the relevance of internal human activities to social behavior. Social psychologists may ask, for example, how being with other people after a frightening incident affects levels of physiological arousal, such as blood pressure and heart rate. Because of this perspective, you will find us discussing such issues as

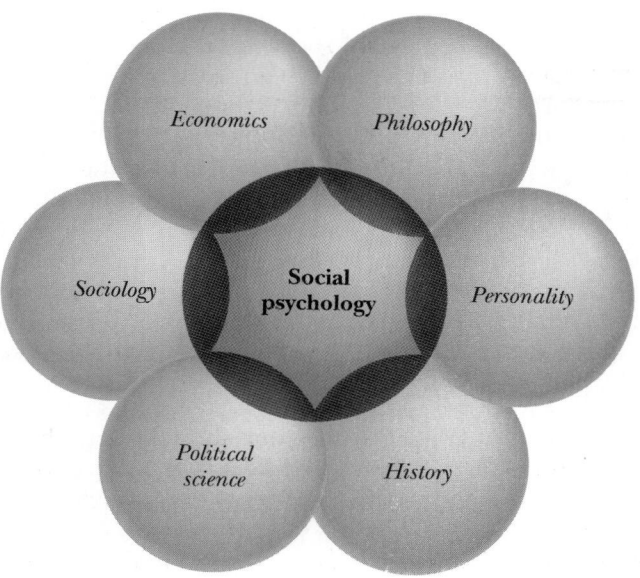

FIGURE 1-1 Social psychology and its relatives
NOTE: In addition to these disciplines, social psychology is developing close relationships with business, education, architecture, medicine, and law.

perception, cognition, and physiological responses in our descriptions of research in social psychology. Therefore, although social psychology has its own exciting, unique identity, it is fair to characterize it as a close cousin of many other disciplines in the humanities, social sciences, and natural sciences. Indeed, our hope is that after reading this text, you not only will be motivated to learn more about social psychology, but also will develop a greater interest in learning about human social behavior from other perspectives.

The History of Social Psychology

Now that we have identified social psychology and its next of kin, let us take a quick look at its roots. This is actually a rather easy task because social psychology is really a child of the 20th century. In fact, it has been estimated that 90% of all social psychologists who ever lived were alive in 1979 (Cartwright, 1979)!

In addition to being localized in time, social psychology is rather localized in place. The field has been largely a product of the Western world. Although modern social psychology had some early European architects, the field was confined to the United States until fairly recently (Jones, 1985; Graumann, 1988).

As we read the history of the field, let us keep one interesting point in mind. Possibly more than any other science, social psychology has been shaped by world events, political currents, and social issues (Harris, 1986). Important events of the day have been the impetus for many of its themes and areas of study. And, of equal importance, the findings of this young science can be used to influence the course of social events.

The year 1897 is generally celebrated as the year of the first social psychology experiment. Norman Triplett (1897; see Chapter 12) examined official records of bicycle races and noticed that a rider's maximum speed was approximately 20% faster when he raced in the presence of other riders than when he raced alone. Triplett then devised a laboratory study to demonstrate this effect further. In that study, children were given the task of winding line on a fishing reel either alone or in the presence of other children performing the same task. The effect of the presence of others on individual task performance was essentially the only issue studied experimentally for the first three decades of social psychology (Allport, 1985).

Soon after the turn of the century, two social psychology textbooks were published. One, titled *Social Psychology,* was written by E. A. Ross (1908), a sociologist, who argued that social behavior was caused by imitation or suggestion. Ross was interested in crowd psychology and the behavior of collectives. His work set the tone for the development of the study of social psychology within sociology (Pepitone, 1981). A second text, by William McDougall (1908), suggested that much of human behavior resulted from instincts. Instincts are innate, unlearned behavior tendencies that are common to members of a species. Hence McDougall viewed much of human social behavior as internally derived or motivated. McDougall focused more squarely on the individual than Ross did; this is the focus of social psychology. Although the two decades that followed the publication of McDougall's book were a time of growth for social psychology, it remained a discipline devoid of its own theoretical approach. Its methodology was also derivative, its techniques borrowed from the study of memory, learning, and education.

In 1929 Louis L. Thurstone and E. J. Chave published *The Measurement of Attitudes.* With this work an entire new field was born. As we shall see in Chapter 5, Thurstone and Chave's work meant that attitudes could be conceptualized and measured. Soon new techniques were added (by Rensis Likert [1932], among others) and the 1930s became an era for measuring and studying the functions of attitudes. The first public opinion polling institute was founded in 1934 and spawned the giant industry that today tells us what we think about everything from toothpaste to presidential candidates.

The events of the 1930s played an important role in setting the stage for social psychology in the United States. The Great Depression found many young psychologists out of work. These psychologists banded together and found that unemployment was not their only common bond;

they believed that psychologists should study important social issues, such as the fascism that was developing in Europe and the labor problems that were common in the United States (Finison, 1986; Stagner, 1986). This group of psychologists, which included such people as Ross Stagner, David Krech, Gordon Allport, Ernest Hilgard, and Gardner Murphy, formed the Society for the Psychological Study of Social Issues (SPSSI) in 1936. Although the society included psychologists from all areas of the discipline, a large proportion of the members were social psychologists.

Research in social psychology was still very different from what it is today until Kurt Lewin came on the scene. Lewin came from a tradition of applied psychology. During World War I he developed a test for wireless operators in Germany and his interests were on means for increasing group productivity (John, Eckardt, & Hiebsch, 1989). While this interest clearly fitted the focus of those psychologists in SPSSI, Lewin had a broader agenda that established him as the founder of modern social psychology. Lewin, who emigrated from Hitler's Germany in 1933, introduced theory into social psychology. An unabashed proponent of the deductive method in science, he believed that general propositions that linked human behavior with social situations could and should be developed (Lewin, 1935). Moreover, he felt that these general propositions could be tested with the aid of experimentation. Under the influence of Lewin and his colleagues, social psychology began to view research not just as investigations into separate and unconnected phenomena, but also as a way of testing general theories on human behavior (Lewin, 1935). With this new outlook, social psychology entered its modern age.

Lewin was also noteworthy for setting the tone for social psychology as a science that investigated social phenomena of the time and that then used its data to influence those social issues. For example, the beginning of World War II raised the issue of how people in the United States could be persuaded to conserve materials and food that were needed for the war effort. Lewin (1943) conducted a study on the effectiveness of various methods of social influence (see Chapter 12) in getting homemakers to serve different and read-

During World War II social psychological research was used to develop ways to influence citizens in aiding the war effort, for example by recycling scrap iron. Social psychological researchers conducted numerous studies to examine how the message and its source affected persuasion. What kinds of studies might be designed today to understand how to motivate citizens to recycle to preserve the environment?

ily available foods. The war also created increased interest in the United States in what type of government was most effective: dictatorship or democracy. Lewin (Lewin, Lippitt, & White, 1939) took advantage of the war climate to compare the effects of different styles of leadership on group performance and dynamics (see Chapter 13). Lewin and his students also initiated a series of studies on group dynamics that served as one of the foundations for industrial/organizational psychology. In an effort to study group development, Lewin developed the participant-observation method, which gave rise to the use of T-groups in research and industry.

World War II was also the stimulus for the development of the Yale Communication Research Program. National leaders' concern about the effects of propaganda and their desire to construct effective, persuasive propaganda campaigns led this group of researchers to apply learning theory to the area of attitude change (Lott & Lott, 1985). These investigators conducted dozens of studies to find out who should say what and how in order to persuade an audience to believe a message or adopt a position (see Chapter 5).

The 1950s and early 1960s saw social psychology leave the starting gate and enter the race with a vengeance. The atrocities of the war created concern about the extent to which people would obey the orders of authority figures and conform to group patterns. Social psychologists initiated studies on conformity (Asch, 1956; see Chapter 12) and obedience (Milgram, 1965; see Chapter 12). Growing world tension, the arms race, and a war of words and nerve between Eastern and Western powers that was known as the cold war focused attention on the issues of conflict and conflict resolution. Social psychologists combined their talents with those of sociologists, mathematicians, political scientists, and economists to develop theories and research methodologies for the study of conflict and decision making (Deutsch & Krauss, 1960; see Chapter 10).

While these efforts focused on the *relationship* between individuals, the theory that fanned the glowing embers of social psychology into a blaze emphasized the effect of *social situations* on individuals. Leon Festinger began his work by questioning how people evaluate themselves, including their efforts, attitudes, appearances, and behavior. He argued that in the absence of objective measures, people compare themselves with others (Festinger, 1954; see Chapter 3). The concern with the evaluation process led Festinger to examine what happened when people were faced with inconsistencies between their behaviors, their attitudes and behaviors, and their attitudes. He proposed the theory of cognitive dissonance (Festinger, 1957; see Chapter 6), in which he argued that people strive for consistency in their cognitions (beliefs, attitudes, and information about their behaviors and those of others). The discovery of inconsistency creates a state of cognitive dissonance and motivates individuals to restore consistency. Research on cognitive dissonance filled the social psychology journals for the next fifteen years, and the theory was used to improve understanding of such issues as consumer behavior, interpersonal attraction, school desegregation, and learning.

The ten years from the mid-1960s to the mid-1970s found social psychology increasingly concerned with the way the individual perceived and interpreted social events. The attribution process (Kelley, 1967; Jones & Davis, 1965; see Chapter 2) captured the imagination of social psychologists and was applied to further explain emotions, self-evaluation, and the perception of other people. This period also witnessed another change in emphasis in social psychology. If the field was truly to be taken seriously as a science, it had to develop study methods that could be replicated and reported, and that could stand the rigorous scrutiny demanded by other sciences. Hence social psychologists turned their attention to refining their methods, embracing new techniques for recording and observing human behavior, and applying more advanced statistical tools for analyzing and interpreting their data (Kenny, 1985). Technological advances allowed researchers to incorporate physiological measures and precise video recordings in their studies and to use increasingly sophisticated computer software to conduct research and analyze data. In addition to refining their methodology, social scientists were able to refine their theories, thanks to the new vistas that the technological advances opened up to them.

This concern with housekeeping was viewed with alarm by some social psychologists (Elms, 1975). Was social psychology losing its dedication to social issues and was it destined to become a science preoccupied with minutiae and irrelevant details? Indeed, this was not a new concern; it had been expressed by J. F. Brown, one of Lewin's students, in the early 1930s (Minton, 1984). The alarm was unfounded, however, as the 1970s saw social psychology incorporate its more sophisticated methodologies and theories in the study of women's issues, the environment, the law and legal process, and peace and conflict resolution. And with their unique training in behavioral theories and methodology, social psychologists have been sought for positions in government, law firms, and industry. And the field expanded its geographical boundaries. The European Association of Experimental Social Psychology was founded and important European research in such areas as social influence and group behavior (Tajfel, 1970) became widely known.

The last decade has also seen a change in the emphasis of social psychological theory and research. There is an increasing fascination with the way people perceive and process social information (cognition). Emphasis on the cognitive approach (Markus & Zajonc, 1985; see Chapter 2) has shown that people are not merely passive pawns who react to their social environment; rather, they organize and interpret events. The work on social cognition is directed at identifying how people process this information, and at making more precise predictions about the relationship between people and their social world.

Thus present-day social psychology is neither myopically focused on practical issues nor concerned solely with basic theoretical ones. Rather, the social psychology of today represents the coexistence of the applied and basic approaches—and a new excitement characterizes both. Although debates—sometimes heated—rage about which approach is the true social psychology (Gergen, 1989; Zajonc, 1989), a new, more vigorous field may grow out of this philosophical conflict. The basic research is gleaning new ideas and areas of study from the virgin territory being opened by investigators in the areas of applied research. And conversely, the psychologist whose interest is carrying the torch of social psychology into the arena of social issues is able to draw on a rapidly expanding store of knowledge. As we will see throughout this text, social psychology today is represented by a diversity of concerns, approaches, and methods, each with the potential to complement and strengthen the other.

Elliot Aronson (1989) recently likened the field of social psychology to

> a large circus tent, where a lot of different acts are going on simultaneously, and the acts occasionally cross, intermingle, and overlap. In this circus-tent world, we frequently bump into one another, challenge one another, influence one another, and sharpen one another's thinking to the overall betterment of the final product. (p. 510)

Methods of Social Psychology

Now that we have clearly identified the field of social psychology, let us turn from the question of *what* to that of *how*. We can begin by returning to the panic created by the *War of the Worlds* broadcast.

Hadley Cantril's account of the events following the broadcast provides us with detailed illustrations of human behavior during a crisis. Our first response to the 135 interviews, however, might be dismay and confusion. We would find that some people screamed, some wept, some gathered their families together, and some ran to be with friends. We would find that some people panicked while others calmly stood their ground and waited for the Martian onslaught. Still others did not believe the broadcast and went

STOP, THINK, & UNDERSTAND

1. Define social psychology in terms of its focus and the general aim of its approach to understanding behavior.

2. What is meant when social psychology is characterized as a "bridge" between other branches of knowledge?

3. What was the state of the field of social psychology in the 1890s? 1930s? 1940s? 1950s? 1970s? 1980s?

4. How did Kurt Lewin influence the field of social psychology?

5. How have social issues affected the development of social psychology?

on with their normal routine. This is quite an array of events, and we would be hard pressed to give an accurate description of human behavior in crisis after a cursory glance at Cantril's interviews.

Investigators in almost every field of knowledge are often faced with similarly imposing tasks: they must make sense of vast amounts of data and communicate their conclusions to other investigators. In an effort to achieve consistency in the investigating and reporting of events, researchers develop a standardized set of rules governing these procedures. It is this set of rules for inquiry that constitutes a **science**. Whether we talk about the study of chemistry, physics, or social behavior, the common ground that leads each of these fields of inquiry to be labeled a science is adherence to the scientific method—a standardized set of rules for investigating events and communicating findings.

Many of us are intimidated by the term *science*. The word sends chills down our spine as we think of a gang of bespectacled individuals in laboratory coats working on some complex, almost mysterious problem and speaking in long,

---

science A set of rules guiding the inquiry and study of events.

There were many different reactions to Welles's broadcast. In Grover Mills, New Jersey, for example, William Dock, age 76, stood ready to meet the Martians, while others fled in panic. The task for a social scientist would be to choose a method to study these reactions and to develop a theory to explain them.

incomprehensible sentences. There is, however, nothing mysterious about science. It is a process that aims to (1) describe, (2) predict, and (3) explain events. Achieving these objectives allows the scientist to control conditions so the desired event can be produced. In a sense, we can view science as a never-ending quest for understanding in accordance with an agreed-upon set of rules. The excitement for many people, and the frustration for others, is that each answer we find raises new questions and challenges for scientific inquiry. The philosopher George Santayana captured this process in his description of William James:

> I think it would have depressed him if he had to confess that any important question was finally settled. He would still have hoped that something might turn up on the other side, and that, just as the scientific hangman was about to dispatch the poor convicted prisoner, an unexpected witness would ride up in hot haste, and prove him innocent. (Santayana, 1920, p. 84; see also Viney, 1989)

In an effort to expedite these goals and to guide inquiry, scientists develop theories and hypotheses. A **theory** is a systematic statement that seeks to explain *why* two or more events are related. Theories may be of broad scope, such as Copernicus's theory of the heliocentric motion of the planets, or they may be more focused, seeking to explain, for example, why people become fearful in a given situation, why particular attitudes are formed, or why people act aggressively toward others.

Scientists also develop **hypotheses,** which express educated guesses about the relationship between events. Unlike theories, hypotheses do not attempt to explain why two events are related; they express *what* the relationship between two events will be. Hypotheses can be derived from theories, or they can be formed from existing data. One hypothesis suggested by Cantril's interview data, for example, is that people tend to affiliate when they are anxious, nervous, or afraid. This statement is a hypothesis rather than

Chapter One   Social Psychology: What, Why, and How

a theory because it simply states a relationship and does not attempt to explain why this relationship exists. The hypothesis may be correct or incorrect; testing hypotheses is a major task of science. Social psychology, like other sciences, is involved in explaining, predicting, understanding, and verifying the relationships between events.

In using the scientific method, the social psychologist becomes a detective. The social psychologist may have a theory or a hypothesis about a certain type of human behavior, just as a detective may have a hunch about the perpetrator of a certain crime. The task of both is to track down information that will verify or refute the theory or hunch. Just as a detective must collect information that is clear enough to convince a judge or a jury that a hunch is correct "beyond a reasonable doubt," so the social psychologist must obtain enough clear support for a theory to convince critics and other social psychologists of its correctness. Carrying the analogy one step farther, just as detectives have developed methods for tracking down leads, so social psychologists have devised procedures for following through on their hunches and testing their theories.

Social psychologists use a variety of methods to test theories and track down leads. Hence part of the social psychologist's detective work is to select the best strategy for investigating a particular problem. With this point in mind, we will examine the methodologies of social psychology. In order to illustrate their use, we will focus on the reactions of people to the *War of the Worlds* broadcast. If we want to pursue the hypothesis that fear, such as that aroused by the broadcast, causes people to affiliate with others, how can we go about obtaining evidence to support the hypothesis?

Whether the object of study is plants or people, the nature of the scientific method is the same: describing, predicting, and explaining events using a standard procedure to collect data and report observations.

chapter. Such testimony is valuable, but are we certain that we have learned much that is reliable about the way most people behave? We do not know whether the reports are representative of the population at large or are unique to the few individuals whose statements were recorded. Most of Cantril's reports were gathered in the state of New Jersey, the reputed site of the Martians' landing. The imminent disaster may have led people there to behave very differently from people in more distant areas. Other case histories were obtained from people who learned of Cantril's investigation and took the trouble to write to him. Such reports are interesting, but they represent a very select portion of the population, those who felt the desire or need to relate their stories. Consequently, we tend to use case histories as ways of generating, not testing, hypotheses.

Case History

One method of testing hypotheses, the **case history,** uses a few respondents and analyzes their reactions in depth. In one part of Cantril's work, for example, people who admitted that they had been scared by the broadcast were interviewed at length about their reactions; several excerpts from those interviews have been presented in this

case history method A method of inquiry that examines the responses of a few individuals and analyzes their reactions in depth.

hypothesis A statement that expresses the nature of the relationship between events; expresses *what* relationship exists between the events, not *why* they are related.

theory A systematic statement that seeks to explain *why* two or more events are related.

The case history method involves making systematic observations and/or interviewing people involved in a single event. This method offers insight into that event, but it is often difficult to generalize the results to other events, and the method does not yield a cause-and-effect relationship. Anthropologists who do in-depth studies of a single group or tribe are using a version of the case history method.

Archival Search

Rather than focus on one incident, as in the case history method, one could, by engaging in **archival research,** examine historical accounts of a broad variety of incidents that had one or more features in common and try to identify common responses to these events. If we were interested in studying the effects of fear on behavior, we could search through newspapers, magazines, and books to identify instances when groups faced fearful situations. Our search would uncover natural disasters, such as volcanic eruptions and hurricanes; industrial catastrophes, such as the nuclear accident at Chernobyl and the chemical leak at Bhopal, India; and the crisis of a community that learned that its food supply had been poisoned. We would study these reports to map out people's reactions under the various circumstances and to see if we could identify behavior patterns common to all the incidents. This approach would yield rich information because we would not be dealing with only one type of fear-arousing situation. If we found common behavior patterns, we could **generalize** beyond a specific case—that is, use the information collected from our sample of situations to predict and explain behavior in similar situations. In other words, we could be more confident that people's responses were due to fear rather than to concern about a Martian invasion. However, we would still be faced with many nagging doubts. How accurate were these random accounts of the incident and people's responses? Were people experiencing fear or reacting to some other emotion? Were the reports of the incident tainted by the reporters' own feelings and interpretations? These types of issues limit the value of the archival method for developing precise theories and testing hypotheses.

Survey

One way of getting into people's heads and making a better determination of what they thought and felt would be to devise a questionnaire; select a large sample that represents the geographical, socioeconomic, and educational background of the population; and ask questions of persons in the sample about their fear and their desire to

Archival research involves examining many incidents that have a common feature. We would be using this method if we examined people's reactions to earthquakes that occurred at different times in different locations.

affiliate. This is the **survey method** (Schuman & Kaulton, 1985).

The survey is useful because it attempts to uncover how people react to a real situation. In addition, a representative sample of respondents can be chosen to participate. A survey is used to describe people's attitudes, feelings, and reported behaviors in regard to a particular event. There are problems with a survey, however. First, people often do not remember exactly what they did in a particular situation. Second, respondents may try to slant their answers to a survey in order to appear in a better light. A man who panicked and ran screaming from his house when he heard that the Martians were coming may tell the interviewer that he quickly ran outside to see whether he could help his neighbors. In short, the responses on a survey questionnaire may not be completely accurate. Finally, some people are not willing to be interviewed.

A point in common: Relation, not causation

As you look over the three methods we have discussed, what do you think they have in common? Indeed, they seem very different: one involves reading newspaper accounts, while another

---

archival research A method of study by which the investigator examines historical accounts of events that have one or more features in common and identifies common responses to those events.

generalization The process of deriving from a sample of situations information that predicts and explains behavior in other situations of a similar sort.

survey method A method of research by which the investigator asks questions of a large sample of subjects.

---

requires us to ask people questions. The common point is that each method gives us information about the *relationship* between events, but none of them tells us clearly which event is the cause and which is the effect. In statistical terms, we are dealing with a **correlation,** which is a statistical measure of the degree of association between events. A correlation can range between 1.00 and -1.00. If we found a positive correlation between fear and affiliation, it would mean that an increase in fear was associated with an increase in affiliation. Conversely, a negative correlation would indicate that an increase in fear was accompanied by a decrease in affiliation.

The degree of relationship between two variables is a valuable piece of information. If we know that two events are positively correlated, we know that when one of the two events occurs, the other is also likely to occur. However, we probably also want to know which event *caused* the other; that is, does fear *cause* people to affiliate, or does affiliation *cause* people to become fearful? A correlation does not provide this answer. A correlation between two variables can have one of three meanings:

1. A difference in the first variable causes a difference in the second variable.
2. A difference in the second variable causes a difference in the first variable.
3. A third, unspecified variable causes differences in both the first and the second variables.

Suppose that Cantril found the following data:

1. Seventy-five percent of the people who reported feeling a great deal of fear after hearing the broadcast spent time with other people after the broadcast.
2. Fifteen percent of the people who reported feeling little fear after hearing the broadcast spent time with other people after the broadcast.

What do these data mean with regard to the hypothesis that fear causes people to affiliate? One possible meaning is the one suggested by the hypothesis—fear causes people to affiliate. However, a second possible interpretation is that affiliation leads to fear. This is a plausible explanation, since we can easily imagine that people may have congregated and discussed the *War of*

the Worlds program and that this discussion may have generated fear. Finally, it is also possible that a third variable that is not even measured in the correlation could be responsible for the results. For example, we might find that individuals who score high on some personality dimension, say gregariousness, are motivated to be with other people and also tend to frighten easily. Thus the correlation may not mean that fear leads to affiliation or that affiliation leads to fear. It may simply result from the fact that the third variable, the personality trait, was responsible for both fear and affiliation.

Thus surveys, case studies, and archival research can be used to achieve the aim of prediction since they tell how closely related two variables are. In most cases, however, they do not enable the researcher to achieve the second scientific goal of understanding or explanation. That is, they do not enable the researcher to uncover a cause-and-effect relationship between variables.

Experiment

To examine cause-and-effect relationships, the researcher must have some control over the variables he or she wishes to study and must be able to eliminate the possibility that some unspecified variable is systematically affecting the results. The method that is designed to allow the necessary control so that cause-and-effect relationships can be uncovered is the experiment.

The **experiment** is a procedure for testing the validity or correctness of a hypothesis. The basic design of an experiment is quite simple. The experimenter manipulates the **independent variable** and studies the effects of the manipulation on the **dependent variable.** The independent variable gets its name from the fact that it is not under the control of the subject. The experimenter determines which level of the independent variable the subject will receive. The dependent variable is the subject's response. The hypothesis is stated in terms of the independent variable causing the dependent variable (fear causes affiliation). Thus the aim of the experiment is to investigate the causal relationship

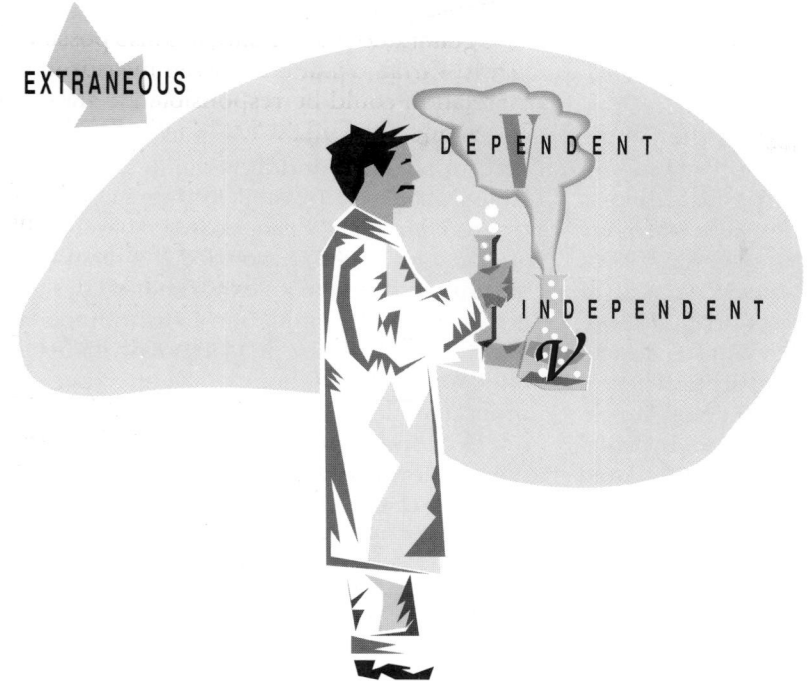

EXTRANEOUS

DEPENDENT

INDEPENDENT

An experiment involves manipulating the *independent variables* and studying the effects on the *dependent variables*. The experimenter's goal is to be able to say that the independent variables *caused* the dependent variables. In order to achieve this certainty, he or she must eliminate or control any *extraneous variables* that could affect the results.

between the independent variable and the dependent variable.

To be able to say that a particular independent variable did cause the dependent variable, the experimenter must be sure that no **extraneous variables** were present in the experiment. An extraneous variable is a factor that may influence people's reactions in a systematic way, although it has nothing to do with the relationship between the independent and dependent variables. Let us assume that you set up an experiment to test whether fear causes people to affiliate. You decide to use two levels of fear (high and low). You manipulate high fear by running into a room and telling people that the building is on fire. In the low-fear condition, you run into a room and tell people that a building in the next town is on fire. Hence the degree of fear is your independent variable and you have control over it. Your dependent variable is affiliation, which is measured by how often people in the room

talk to one another after they hear the news. So far, so good. You run the experiment, and you find that high fear leads to greater affiliation than does low fear. Can you be confident that you have obtained evidence that fear causes affiliation?

It is possible that in reviewing your procedure you may find that all of your efforts were

---

correlation   The degree of association between two events; a statistical measure.

dependent variable   The subject's response in an experiment.

experiment   A method of study aimed at determining the cause-and-effect relationship between events; the experimenter exercises control over the independent variable.

extraneous variable   A factor that may influence the dependent variable, though it has nothing to do with the independent variable.

independent variable   A variable manipulated by the experimenter to study its effect on the dependent variable.

for naught. Even though you manipulated and controlled your independent variable and carefully observed your dependent variable, extraneous variables may have affected your results. For example, you may discover that the people who happened to be in the rooms where you manipulated high fear were all friends, whereas the people in the low-fear rooms were strangers to one another. Thus the extraneous variable of prior acquaintance may have "caused" your affiliation results. Further, you may find that all of your high-fear conditions were run after lunch, when people naturally wanted to affiliate, whereas the low-fear conditions were run just before lunch, when people tended to be grumpy and wished isolation. Thus, even though you manipulated your independent variable and found the predicted results, the existence of these extraneous variables would not allow you to believe that your study demonstrated that fear causes affiliation.

A "clean" experiment must eliminate or control the extraneous variables. To ensure that the extraneous variable of preexisting subject characteristics is not the cause of the results in an experiment, subjects are randomly assigned to the various conditions. By **random assignment** we mean that each subject has an equal opportunity of being in each experimental condition. Through random assignment, the experimenter ensures that the characteristics of the subjects assigned to any particular experimental condition are the same as those of subjects in the other experimental conditions. One way to illustrate the procedure of random assignment is to imagine a blindfolded individual whose task is to divide 100 pennies, half of which are colored red and half green, into two equal piles. The chances are that when the task is finished, each pile will have a similar distribution of red and green pennies. Thus the reason for randomly assigning subjects to conditions is to get similar groups of subjects into the different experimental conditions so that preexisting subject characteristics cannot be the cause of differences in the results. In addition to randomly assigning subjects to conditions, we can eliminate other extraneous variables by randomly assigning the order of conditions. In the earlier example, we could eliminate the alternative explanation based on hunger by not running all high-fear conditions after lunch and all low-

fear conditions just before lunch. This can be done by randomly choosing a condition to run at a particular time.

As you can see, much of experimentation is an exercise in control. We must have control to determine when and how the independent variable will be manipulated, and we must have control to eliminate extraneous variables. Campbell and Stanley (1963) have used the term **internal validity** to describe an experimental design that is free from contamination by extraneous variables. As they phrase it, "Internal validity is the basic ingredient without which an experiment is uninterpretable" (p. 5).

To summarize, an experiment involves varying the levels of the independent variable and studying the effects of this manipulation on the dependent variable. The aim of the experiment is to say that the independent variable caused the dependent variable results. To say this, the experimenter must ensure internal validity by eliminating extraneous variables from his or her experiment.

Constructing an Experiment

We have discussed the aims and some of the possible pitfalls of experimentation. You may be able to think of a way to conduct an experiment to test the hypothesis that fear leads to affiliation. The important points to remember are:

1. You must create at least two levels of the independent variable (that is, conditions of high fear and low fear).

2. Participants must be randomly assigned to the conditions (that is, you would not want to assign all smart people or all poor people or all Northerners to one condition).

3. The dependent variable (affiliation) must be measured.

An experiment that was designed to demonstrate that high fear causes people to affiliate was reported by Stanley Schachter (1959). Suppose that you are a volunteer who has been randomly assigned to the high-fear condition. You will encounter a serious-looking man in horn-rimmed glasses who is intent on giving you a good scare. For effect, he is dressed in a white lab coat with a stethoscope dribbling conspicuously from his pocket, and he is standing in front of an array of elaborate-looking electrical equipment. He introduces himself to you as Dr. Gregor Zilstein, and he informs you that you are in an experiment that is concerned with the effects of electric shock. Pausing slightly, so that his words will have maximum impact, Zilstein says:

> We would like to give each of you a series of electric shocks. Now, I feel I must be completely honest with you and tell you exactly what you are in for. These shocks will hurt, they will be painful. As you can guess, it is necessary that our shocks be intense. What we will do is put an electrode on your hand, hook you into apparatus such as this, give you a series of shocks, and take various measures. . . . Again, I do want to be honest with you and tell you that these shocks will be quite painful but, of course, they will do no permanent damage. (Schachter, 1959, p. 13)

You probably would have been more fortunate, or at least less frightened, if you had been randomly assigned to the low-fear condition. You would still have been greeted by Dr. Zilstein, but the pile of electrical equipment would not have been displayed. With a much more pleasant demeanor, Dr. Zilstein would tell you (as he does in the high-fear condition) that this is an experiment involving the effects of electric shock. But this time he would qualify this statement by saying, "I hasten to add, do not let the word *shock* trouble you; I am sure that you will enjoy this experiment." He would continue:

> We would like to give each of you a series of very mild electric shocks. I assure you that what you will feel will not in any way be painful. It will resemble more a tickle than anything unpleasant. We will put an electrode on your hand, give you a series of very mild shocks and measure such things as your pulse rate . . . which I am sure you are all familiar with from visits to your family doctor. (pp. 13–14)

In this manner Schachter manipulated the independent variable into two levels: low fear and high fear. Did he successfully create two levels of fear in the minds and feelings of his subjects? One way to find out is to ask. So Schachter gave each participant a printed form to be filled out that asked: "How do you feel about taking part in this experiment and being shocked?" The par-

ticipant was asked to respond along a five-point scale ranging from "I dislike the idea very much" to "I enjoy the idea very much." When the questionnaires were examined, subjects who had met the stern Dr. Zilstein in the high-fear condition were much less inclined to be shocked than were those who had met the benign and reassuring Dr. Zilstein. This procedure, which is known as a **check on the manipulation,** allows investigators to feel secure that the variable they thought they were manipulating with elaborate staging was accurately perceived by the participants.

Schachter's experiment was designed to test the hypothesis that fear leads to affiliation. Once he had successfully induced two levels of fear, the next step was to get a measure of the desire to affiliate (dependent variable). Schachter decided to solve this problem by giving the participants a choice of waiting together or alone for the shock portion of the study. In both fear conditions, Dr. Zilstein stated:

> Before we begin with the shocking proper there will be about a 10-minute delay while we get this room in order. We have several pieces of equipment to bring in and get set up. . . . Here is what we will ask you to do for this 10-minute period of waiting. We have on this floor a number of additional rooms so that each of you, if you would like, can wait alone in your own room. These rooms are comfortable and spacious; they all have armchairs and there are books and magazines in each room. It did occur to us, however, that some of you might want to wait for these 10 minutes together with some of the other girls here. If you would prefer this, of course, just let us know. We'll take one of the empty classrooms on the floor and you can wait together with some of the other girls there. (pp. 13–14)

---

check on the manipulation   A procedure that ensures that the variable investigators intended to manipulate was accurately perceived by participants in the experiment.

internal validity   Freedom of an experimental design from contamination by an extraneous variable; allows the investigator to state that manipulations of the independent variable are responsible for changes in the dependent variable.

random assignment   Assignment of subjects to experimental conditions in such a way that all subjects have equal opportunities to be in each experimental condition.

TABLE 1-2

Relationship of fear to the affiliative tendency

	Number choosing		
	Waiting together	*Don't care*	*Waiting alone*
High fear	20	9	3
Low fear	10	18	2

SOURCE: Adapted from Schachter (1959).

Participants were then given a chance to state whether they preferred waiting alone or waiting with others or had no preference. This constituted the measurement of the dependent variable. What Schachter hoped to find was that women assigned to the high-fear condition would want to wait together more than women in the low-fear condition. Schachter's results are presented in Table 1-2.

The table makes it quite clear that subjects in the high-fear condition wanted to wait together much more than subjects in the low-fear condition did. Thus the hypothesis was supported by the data.

The Advantages of Experiments

As you can see, Schachter expended a great deal of time and effort to test the rather simple hypothesis that fear leads to affiliation. Was it worth it? Why go to such lengths to set up an experiment? The answer is that there are many important advantages to experiments that justify their use. In fact, the vast majority of data collected in social psychology come from laboratory research.

A number of advantages of experimentation should be clear. First and most important, experimentation provides a way of determining the direction of causation. Because the experimenter controls the independent variable and assigns people to different levels of that variable on a random basis, the question of which variable is cause and which is effect can be answered.

Another advantage of experimentation is that extraneous elements that might otherwise influence the results can be well controlled. For example, some of the people in Cantril's survey may have listened during a thunderstorm, tuned in late, or heard the program on a crackling radio. It is unknown whether any of these factors could have influenced fear or affiliation. We do know, though, that such factors are extraneous to the relationship in question. Some individuals were exposed to one or more of them; others to none. The factors remain uncontrolled. By contrast, the experiment controls for such events. The variables are usually manipulated in the confines of a small unit of space and time. All subjects are generally treated identically, with the exception of the one event that serves as the independent variable.

Yet another advantage of experimentation is that the experimenter can devise *numerous levels* of an independent variable and study trends in the data. For example, Schachter used only two levels of fear arousal (high and low). The experimenter might hold the hypothesis that very fearful subjects would not want to affiliate. An experiment could then be developed so that there were three conditions of fear (low, high, and very high). Such systematic variation of the fear variable would present a clear relationship between fear and affiliation.

Issues of Concern in Experimentation

Mark Twain once remarked that a common characteristic of everything developed by humans is imperfection. This statement clearly describes experimentation: while the experiment represents an excellent method for collecting data and determining cause and effect, it is not perfect. You have probably already identified many problems with the experimental method.

One of the basic problems that plagues research is generalization beyond the laboratory: How far can we go in applying the results we collect in an experiment? For example, we would like to be able to argue that the Schachter study supported the position that *fear* causes *people* to *affiliate*. This desire to generalize raises a number of questions. One is that we want to describe the behavior of people in general, while the study used only college students as subjects. In raising this issue, we do not wish to imply that college students are not people; rather, college students may be special people in that they possess characteristics that are not common to the population as a whole. For example, Schachter's subjects were white, female, mostly from the Northeast, most probably from middle-class families, and had some years of college education. Would respondents of different backgrounds or educational levels behave as Schachter's subjects did? We can take this question of generalization further by asking whether (1) studies of females can predict males' behavior, (2) studies of whites can predict the behavior of blacks or Hispanics, (3) studies of 18-to-22-year-olds can predict the behavior of older or younger people, (4) studies of college students can predict the behavior of less educated people, and so on. If these generalizations are to be made with some degree of confidence, additional experiments with different subjects must be conducted.

Another generalization question concerns the setting and specific manipulations that we use in the experiment. Are people who are afraid of having a university scientist place electrodes on them experiencing the same kind of fear that people experience in a natural ongoing situation? Is the fear of Schachter's laboratory the same as the fear we would experience if we encountered a burglar in our house, a lion in the jungle, or a Martian in the New Jersey meadowland? When we raise these questions, we are referring to the **external validity** of an experiment (Carlsmith, Ellsworth & Aronson, 1976).

The best way to deal with questions of external validity is to test the relationship in a series of similar but not identical ways. If Schachter's participants were really scared and if fear leads to affiliation, then other studies using different fear manipulations should yield the same result. Indeed, several other studies that use different methods of fear arousal and affiliation measurement have produced very similar results (e.g., Darley & Aronson, 1966; Gerard, 1963). This fact makes us more confident that we can generalize from our experimental results to fear and affiliation as they occur in the natural environment.

Another concern with experimentation is that of realism. We must actually consider two types of realism. The first, **experimental realism,** concerns the impact the experiment has on subjects. "An experiment is realistic if the situation is involving to the subjects, if they are forced to take it seriously, if it has impact on them" (Aronson, Brewer & Carlsmith, 1985, p. 482). It is vital for a study to have high experimental realism if we wish to argue that the independent variable caused the dependent response. It is not hard to see that Schachter's study had a high degree of experimental realism; the ominous-looking Dr. Zilstein who gravely explained the painful shocks certainly captured the subjects' attention. The second type of realism is **mundane realism.** An experiment is high in mundane realism to the extent that the situation that subjects encounter is similar to what they face in the normal course of their lives. While a high degree of mundane realism may increase a study's impact, its presence is not a necessary research requirement. For example, Schachter's study was quite low in mundane realism. (How often are we approached in our everyday lives by a Dr. Zilstein who threatens to shock us?) Yet Schachter's study did manipulate the fear that subjects experienced, as well as allowing him to study the relationship between fear and affiliation. Having high mundane realism in our study gives us greater latitude to generalize beyond the specific experimental setting.

The Social Psychology of the Subject and the Experimenter

Thus far our concern has been the design and manipulation of the experimental setting.

---

experimental realism   The degree to which experimental manipulations have impact and involve the subjects in the experimental situation.
external validity   The degree to which research findings may be generalized to situations outside the laboratory.
mundane realism   The degree to which the experimental setting approximates a real-life setting.

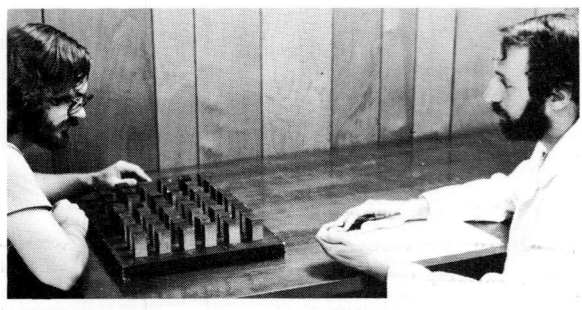

Experiments can be viewed as a social relationship, where the experimenter is interested in confirming a hypothesis and the subject is concerned with being evaluated. In order to minimize the possibility that the results of a study are not determined by this relationship, investigators take many precautions to reduce experimental demand characteristics and the possibility of experimenter bias.

Experiments, however, involve more than just a setting; they are also the stage for the interaction of the subjects and the experimenter. Let us quickly examine how the psychology of subject and experimenter can influence the results of a study. The subject's role in a study is unique. Martin Orne (1962) has demonstrated people's willingness to do the "right thing" in an experiment, that is, to do what they think the experimenter wants them to do. You do not want to appear silly, obstinate, or recalcitrant. You want to be cooperative and to be seen as a "good subject." In some of his demonstrations, Orne showed that people will use a variety of bizarre behaviors to be good subjects. For example, Orne asked people whether they would be willing to copy numbers in the school library, although he told them that doing so would not be very useful to anyone. Not only were subjects willing to comply with the request, but they stayed after the investigator and librarian had left and after the library was closed and locked!

The significant implication of such behavior is clear. If people who want to be good subjects can know the purpose of an experiment or if they have a notion about what the experimenter wants them to do, they are likely to cooperate. If the subjects in Schachter's study had known that he hoped they would affiliate in the high-fear condition and remain alone in the low-fear condition, they might have cooperated. When peo-ple act in a particular way not because it is their typical reaction to the situation but because they are trying to do what the experimenter desires, we say that they are acting in accord with the experiment's **demand characteristics.**

Several methods can be used to guard against demand characteristics in an experiment. A popular method, though not necessarily the most effective one, is **deception.** In this case, the experimenter gives the subject a false but plausible hypothesis, so that if the subject's behavior is affected by this hypothesis, the effects will not be in any way systematic. Further, through this deception or cover story the experimenter prevents subjects from discovering the true hypothesis. Schachter used deception in his study. He told subjects that he was interested in studying the effects of actual electric shocks on his subjects, when in fact he was interested only in the effects of fear on affiliation.

Another way to reduce the problem of demand characteristics is to measure the dependent variable in a context apart from the independent variable and to use **unobtrusive measures.** For example, after telling a subject that she would be shocked, Schachter could have followed through with the story he gave the subject. He might have told his subject that he would not be able to run her immediately and that she should wait in the experimental waiting room until the study was ready. When the subject arrived at the waiting room, she could find two or three other subjects who had been given similar instructions. Unknown to the subjects, an experimenter could be observing through a one-way mirror whether or not the subjects affiliated and interacted with one another. The advantage of this method is that the dependent measure is examined apart (in time and place) from the independent manipulation. Further, the measure is unobtrusive; the subjects do not know that their responses are being studied. Thus precautions can be taken to reduce the role of demand characteristics in an experiment.

A final problem involves the unique psychology of the experimenter in a research effort. Experimenters have hypotheses: they think that they *know* what a subject will do; they know what they *want* a subject to do to confirm their hypotheses. Robert Rosenthal and his colleagues have shown that such expectations may actually influence the behavior of subjects in experiments. In one study, Rosenthal and Fode (1963) used photographs of faces that had previously been rated as neutral with regard to success and failure. They gave these pictures to students who were serving as assistant experimenters and asked the students to obtain ratings from subjects as to whether the people in the pictures appeared successful or unsuccessful. Rosenthal and Fode told half of the assistant experimenters that they were trying to duplicate a "well-established" finding that people generally rated the persons photographed as successful. The other half of the experimenters were told that the "well-established" finding was that people generally rated the persons photographed as unsuccessful.

Armed with identical photographs, two sets of assistant experimenters set out to collect evidence. They were instructed about what to say and how to collect the ratings. Both groups were supposed to behave in precisely the same fashion. Yet the results were dramatically different. Every experimenter who was led to expect that people generally rated the persons photographed as successful obtained higher success ratings than the experimenters who expected to obtain failure ratings. Most assuredly the experimenter's influence on the subject's rating was unintentional, yet his expectation was somehow communicated to the subject, who behaved accordingly. The influence of a subject's performance as a function of an investigator's expectation has been called **experimenter bias.**

Experimenter bias is a troublesome problem, and investigators are now more careful to make certain that their hypotheses do not become self-fulfilling prophecies because of bias. The best way to keep an experimenter's expectancy from influencing people's behavior is to keep the experimenter unaware of the experimental treatment to which the subject has been exposed. Often two experimenters are used to obtain this result. In Schachter's research, for example, any possibility of experimenter bias could have been eliminated if someone other than Dr. Zilstein had asked the subjects whether they wished to wait together or alone. Only Zilstein would know whether a particular participant had been subjected to high-fear or low-fear treatment. There-

STOP, THINK, & UNDERSTAND

1. What is science?
2. What is the relationship between theory and hypothesis?
3. Why are social psychologists often dissatisfied with correlations?
4. What is the role of the following concepts in the experiment: independent variable, dependent variable, random assignment of subjects, internal validity, external validity?
5. What are the advantages and disadvantages of the experiment?
6. How can the problems of demand characteristics and experimenter bias be reduced?

fore, only his expectations could affect the final measure. Anyone else who collected that final measure would not know what to expect on the measure of affiliation.

The Field Experiment

One common criticism of laboratory experiments is that because the setting is unlike anything experienced in the real world, it is difficult to create an impactful experience for subjects. While we could successfully argue that the Schachter study certainly made an impact on its subjects, it could equally well be argued that the

---

deception (in an experiment) The practice of giving subjects false information about the reasons for the study or the manipulations.

demand characteristics Cues in the experimental setting that communicate to subjects the behavior that is expected of them.

experimenter bias Influence on subjects' behavior as a function of the investigators' expectations.

unobtrusive measures Experimental methods that permit subjects' behavior to be measured without their awareness.

There is no one best method. The experimenter must fit the method to the problem he or she wishes to study, remembering the limitations of each method. Some events must be studied in their natural setting.

manipulation was not as successful as it could have been because the subjects knew they were in an experiment; they may have reduced their fear by telling themselves that Dr. Zilstein couldn't really do anything too terrible because this was only an experiment. To achieve a real-world effect, we might want to run a field experiment.

In theory, the **field experiment** is similar to the laboratory experiment except that the location has changed. The field experiment is run in a natural setting, and subjects often do not know that they are in an experiment. The experimenter varies the independent variables and examines the effects of the manipulation on the dependent variable. The added realism of the setting should allow greater generalization of results from the field experiment.

Earlier we discussed one way in which the fear-affiliation hypothesis can be tested as a field experiment. The experimenter can randomly select people in a building and tell them either that their building is on fire or that a building in another town is on fire. The experimenter can then record the behavior of the subjects.

This method includes the randomization of subjects to conditions, and it has control over the independent variable. It also has the advantage of studying subjects in their natural habitat. These advantages are responsible for the increasing popularity of the field experiment in social psychology.

Before field experimentation is adopted, however, it is important to examine the weaknesses of the method. First, control over some types of extraneous variables is more difficult to obtain in the field than in the laboratory. In the laboratory, we can ensure that the setting is the same for each subject; we cannot do this in the field. For example, if we were to run our "building on fire" experiment, we might find that some of our subjects were run when other people were in sight, whereas other subjects were run when no other people were around. Some subjects might have been run when there was a lot of distracting noise, such as elevators opening or airplanes flying overhead, whereas other subjects might have been run without these distractions. Although such extraneous variables might not influence the results of our study in any systematic manner, they would reduce the precision of our experiment. Hence the laboratory setting permits a more precise test of our hypothesis because of the increased control that this setting makes possible.

Another drawback to field experimentation is that in the field it is often difficult to manipulate complex variables or to manipulate a number of variables simultaneously. For example, it would be difficult to conduct a field experiment that tests the hypothesis that tired people have a stronger desire than well-rested people to affiliate when they are fearful. To test this hypothesis we would have to manipulate both fear and tiredness. In the field it would be nearly impossible to assign people randomly to a restful or tired condition. We could, however, do this in the laboratory, where before manipulating fear we could

TABLE 1-3

Research methods: Strengths and weaknesses *Study*

Method	Strengths	Weaknesses
Case history	Involves a real event: high mundane realism; in-depth study of a single event; generates hypotheses	Cannot determine cause and effect; no control over independent variables; no randomization of subjects; relies on recall, which may be faulty
Archival research	Involves real events: high mundane realism; involves many incidents, so increases generalizability; easy and cheap to collect data; generates hypotheses	Cannot determine cause and effect; no control over independent variables; no randomization of subjects; relies on secondhand reports; possible bias in reports; often very incomplete accounts of events and responses
Survey	Collects much information from a wide variety of subjects; can deal with a variety of events; easy to collect data	Cannot determine cause and effect; no control over independent variables; relies on people's memory, which may be faulty
Experiment	Allows determination of cause and effect; random assignment of subjects to condition; maximum control over independent variables; high control over extraneous variables	Often low mundane realism; difficult to achieve high generalizability; time-consuming; limits type and intensity of independent variables
Field experiment	Allows cause and effect to be determined; high mundane realism; some control over independent variable; permits study of wide range of subjects	Difficult to control extraneous variables; may be impossible to test some complex hypotheses in such settings

have some subjects go one night without sleep while providing other subjects with a restful night.

Hence the field experiment has the advantage of generalization of results, but may achieve this advantage at the sacrifice of control over extraneous variables. Further, some hypotheses are difficult to test in the field setting because of the complexity of the required manipulations.

Choosing a Method

Earlier we pointed out that social psychology often requires a great deal of detective work. Not only must social psychologists observe behavior and develop theories to explain that behavior; they must also determine the best method for testing their theories. As you can see in Table 1-3, there is no single right or wrong method; each method offers both advantages and disadvantages. The researcher must determine the goal of his or her investigation and select the method that will best fit that goal. In most cases, the social psychologist is interested in establishing a cause-and-effect

relationship and therefore uses the laboratory experiment.

The ideal modus operandi, however, would be to use a mix of methods to study a problem. That is, the same hypothesis could be tested by means of a survey, a laboratory experiment, and a field experiment. If the hypothesis were tested and supported by each of these methods, a great deal more confidence could be placed in its correctness than if it were tested and supported by only one method. This multiple-method approach requires considerable time, and it is rarely used by a single investigator. Later in this book, however, we will examine instances in which a hypothesis has been tested by several investigators who used a variety of methods.

One other point should be made clear: an experiment, whether it is carried out in the laboratory or in the field, can be no better than the

---

field experiment An experiment that is run in a natural setting, and subjects often do not know that they are in an experiment; the realism should allow greater opportunity for generalization and more mundane realism.

Although many students are often confused and frightened by statistics, statistical formulas tell psychologists whether they are looking at real differences.

idea it is testing. As Leon Festinger (1980) points out: "Precision of measurement and precision of experimental control are a means to an end—the discovery of new knowledge. Too much emphasis on precision can lead to research which is barren" (p. 252). Like a hammer used to build a house, experimental methods are only tools used to expand knowledge. The success of an experiment is measured less by the precision of its execution than by the knowledge that results from it. Therefore, careful planning and thought about the idea to be tested are vital steps to be taken before a method is chosen.

Beyond a Reasonable Doubt: Statistical Significance

To obtain a guilty verdict, a prosecuting attorney must convince the members of the jury that a defendant is guilty beyond a reasonable doubt.

This does not mean that the prosecutor must positively prove guilt—it only means that the jury must believe it highly probable that the defendant is guilty. The social psychologist, too, works with probabilities. The aim of an experiment is not to prove that a hypothesis is correct. Rather, the aim is to demonstrate that it is highly probable that the hypothesis is correct. Researchers ask the question in the following way: "What is the probability that the results I have obtained could have been found by chance alone?" Hence social psychology, like most other sciences, deals with probabilities rather than absolutes.

As a means of demonstrating this point, let us reexamine the Schachter experiment. Schachter found that approximately 63% of the high-fear subjects wanted to wait together, whereas only 33% of the low-fear subjects wanted to do so. What does this difference mean? Is it reliable, or is it simply a chance finding? With the Schachter study we must ask whether highly fearful people really want to affiliate more than low-fear people do. Is the difference large enough to make us believe that if more and more people participated in the study, the same connection between fear and affiliation would be found? Or would we discover that the difference was found only by chance and that the addition of more people washes out the difference?

To answer these questions, investigators apply statistical tests that are designed to estimate the likelihood that a difference found in the data would continue to be manifested if everyone in the population participated in the study. By convention, we agree that we will accept a difference as **statistically significant** (reliable) if the likelihood of its having occurred by chance (that is, the likelihood that the difference would disappear if the entire population were tested) is less than 1 in 20. In other words, the result could have occurred by chance less than 5% of the time. The difference reported in the Schachter study was tested with one statistical procedure, and it was found that the likelihood that the difference had occurred by chance was less than 1 in 20. We therefore refer to the result as statistically significant. Thus social psychologists assume that a finding that could have occurred by chance less than 5% of the time is reliable beyond a reasonable doubt.

Of all the aspects of experimentation, students probably fear statistics the most. There is nothing magical or mysterious about them. If we ask subjects in an experiment to indicate on a scale how much they want to be with other subjects, our data will have two properties of major concern to us. First, we will have a **mean,** or average, of all the scores. Second, we will have a measure of **variability** around the mean. For example, if our scores averaged 5 on a 7-point scale, we might find that all our subjects checked point 4, 5, or 6. This would indicate rather low variability. On the other hand, we could have gotten our mean of 5 if various numbers of subjects checked each of the points on the scale. This would indicate high variability. The **analysis of variance test,** a popular statistical procedure used to analyze experimental data, takes into account both the mean and the variability to determine the statistical significance of our results. This is not the place to enter into an extended discussion of statistical procedures. We simply want to point out that these procedures are tools that allow sci-entists to examine their data and communicate their findings.

Questions of Ethics

We have discussed some of the methods that are used in social psychology and have examined how the hypothesis that fear leads to affiliation could be tested. The suggestion that we could test the hypothesis by telling people that the building they are in is burning may have made you uncomfortable. You may even have winced as you thought about the fear experienced by the subjects in Schachter's high-fear condition. Finally, you may have felt that we were a little callous when we suggested that the method used in a study should be chosen on the grounds of how well it fits the goals of the experimenter. In all of these cases we seem to have been overlooking one important ingredient in the experiment—the subject.

Shouldn't some concern be shown for the subject who is terribly frightened? Shouldn't some attention be given to choosing a method that will protect the subject? The answer to both of these questions is an emphatic yes. Almost from the time social psychologists began conducting experiments, they expressed deep concern for the physical and psychological safety of their subjects. Before our newspapers reported secret CIA experiments with LSD and before the Kennedy Committee on Human Experimentation began its hearings, social psychologists were discussing the problems of ethics in research and developing guidelines to protect subjects in psy-

---

analysis of variance test A statistical procedure that takes into account both the mean and the variability of experimental data to determine the statistical significance of the results.

mean Average, computed by dividing the sum of the terms by the number of terms.

statistically significant Reliable; a finding is considered statistically significant if a statistical test indicates that the event could have occurred by chance fewer than 5 times out of 100 ($p < .05$).

variability The extent to which scores vary about the mean. The closer the scores cluster about the mean, the lower the variability.

chological experimentation. The American Psychological Association (1982) published a comprehensive guideline outlining ethical precautions that should be taken when research is conducted.

Let us review quickly some of the ethical problems that social psychologists have identified. The first problem is *invasion of privacy*. Although this may not have been a serious problem in the Schachter study because little "sensitive" information was asked of the subject, it does become a problem when sensitive information is requested. Some studies ask subjects questions about their sex lives or about criminal activities they may have participated in. Other studies give subjects personality and intelligence tests. In all of these cases, the experimenter is obtaining private information from the subject. Is this ethical? That is a difficult question to answer. Psychologists have attempted to safeguard the privacy of subjects by keeping responses anonymous or by letting no one but the experimenter have access to them. Further, they attempt to follow the principle of **informed consent**: subjects are given the choice of participating or not participating in an experiment after they have been told of the procedures that will be used. In practice, however, this principle is often difficult to follow because some experiments require the subject to be unaware of what is really being studied.

A second problem is the use of deception. Deception is practiced when the experimenter tells subjects something other than the truth. In the Schachter study, the subjects were deceived about the purpose of the study and they were told that they would receive an electric shock even though they were never actually shocked. Such deception is often necessary to prevent the subjects from focusing on the true nature of the interaction being studied. In an effort to make the deception only temporary, experimenters carry out elaborate debriefing sessions at the conclusion of studies. At these sessions, subjects are told exactly what did happen in the study, what problem was being investigated, and why they had been deceived. In this way, the experiment and debriefing become an educational experience for the subjects.

A third problem is the *harmful consequences* that the subject may suffer in the course of the study. Subjects may be given drugs that have unpleasant side effects or may have to suffer painful shocks. Other harmful consequences may be psychological rather than physical. In the Schachter study, the subjects suffered stress and fear. In other studies, the subjects may be degraded or insulted and suffer depression. Again the question can be asked: Is this ethical? There has been a great deal of discussion about this matter. The answer is to try to find procedures that do not create negative consequences for the subject.

Another ethical problem is that *subjects may be taught something about themselves that they do not wish to know*. For example, a subject in the Schachter study could become so fearful that she cries and begs to be let out of the study. In this case, the subject is being shown that she has little tolerance for stress. One might argue that the experimenter is only showing the subject something true about herself. However, the subject did not come to the experiment asking to learn about herself. She came to be a subject in an experiment.

The question of ethics is a difficult and controversial one; what is ethical to one person may not be ethical to another. And while it is important to consider ethical issues in every experiment, it is also important not to become paralyzed by these issues. Festinger (1980) argues that a valuable experiment must be both involving for the subject and considerate of ethical issues. An experiment that slights either of these concerns in favor of the other loses value for the subject, the experimenter, and our store of knowledge on human behavior.

Social psychologists are well aware of the ethical problems connected with research and have spent a great deal of time pondering those problems. Despite the value of social-psychological research, such research will have a bitter taste if it is achieved at the expense of the subjects involved in it. In an effort to protect the rights of subjects, universities and many psychology departments have set up **institutional review boards (IRBs),** committees in which a cross section of professionals considers the risks and benefits of research to participants.

These IRBs review proposed experimental procedures before psychologists are allowed to proceed with their studies. The IRBs determine whether subjects' rights will be protected. The boards may not allow an experimenter to run a study, or they may suggest alternative methods that offer better safeguards for the subjects. The system is not perfect, however, because ethics is a very subjective concept. One study asked IRBs at several universities to review a research proposal (Ceci, Peters & Plotkin, 1985). Although all the IRBs reviewed the same proposal, their responses varied widely. This finding may be disturbing, but other researchers who had subjects and psychologists evaluate research proposals found that psychologists were more likely than subjects to declare a study ethically unacceptable (Sullivan & Deiker, 1973). In other words, psychologists may be their own harshest critics.

The bottom line, then, is that research is actually guided by three principles: the desire for maximum control, the desire to create impactful situations, and the desire to protect the subjects in the study. As you read the remainder of this text, you will see how these three guidelines have been skillfully combined to create settings that yield valuable knowledge about human social behavior.

Learning About Social Psychology

We are now ready to guide you through the halls of social psychology. Our aim in this text is to introduce you to the variety of areas studied by social psychologists and to show you some of the more important theories and research findings. We've included the older classic studies as well as the newer findings. There is a great deal of material here, but it should be viewed as only the beginning chapter in your lesson on social psychology.

Our students often ask us, "How can I really get to know the field of social psychology?" A first step is to take a class on the subject and read the text and other books in the area. However, there are many other things you can do to supplement your understanding of the field. One is simply to *observe* other people in their day-to-day activities. Who do these people talk to? What do they talk about? How do they interpret events? How do they justify their actions? What are the

STOP, THINK, & UNDERSTAND

1. What are the advantages of the field experiment over the laboratory experiment? What are its disadvantages?

2. Is there a *best method* for studying human behavior in all situations?

3. Why do we perform statistical tests on data collected in research?

4. What are some of the ethical issues of concern in experimentation?

5. How can you learn about the field of social psychology?

similarities and differences in people's behavior? In conducting your observations, don't forget to look at yourself. The beauty of social psychology is that the world is its storehouse of information and its source of ideas. Your observations should encourage you to develop your own hypotheses and stimulate you to seek out research on the topics you find interesting.

A second step is to *become part of social psychology research.* At most universities you can volunteer to be a subject in ongoing research. But your involvement shouldn't stop there. Talk to professors to learn about the research they are conducting. When you find a professor studying a topic of interest to you, volunteer to work with him or her as a research assistant. You will find that many faculty members are delighted to have you participate in planning and conducting research. At many universities you can receive course credit for this activity. You may even find a professor willing to hire you as a research assis-

---

informed consent   Consent given to participate in an experiment after the procedures to be used have been explained and the subject has been given an opportunity to withdraw from the experiment.

institutional review boards (IRBs)   Committees in which a cross section of professionals considers the risks and benefits of research to participants and ensures that proposed research methods protect subjects' safety and rights.

tant. This experience will help you appreciate the time, effort, and thought that goes into research. You'll experience the excitement of obtaining significant results and the frustration associated with nonsignificant results. But above all, you'll leave with a better understanding of the science of social psychology. Learn social psychology by doing social psychology.

Finally, *take a broad range of courses* both in psychology and in other fields. Courses in history, philosophy, political science, sociology, economics, and anthropology not only will show you exciting areas to study, but also will reveal how other disciplines approach and study human behavior. Learning about social psychology should increase your appreciation of these other disciplines. Likewise, the information you get from these other disciplines should help you better understand the value of social psychology and its approach to human behavior.

With this introduction, we will return to Aronson's metaphor of the circus and invite you into the big tent of social psychology.

Summary

Social psychology is a discipline that employs scientific methods to understand and explain how the thoughts, feelings, and behaviors of individuals are influenced by the actual, imagined, or implied presence of others. Social psychologists are interested in discovering how most people behave most of the time. Sociologists generally focus on the structure and functioning of groups, while personality psychologists are most concerned with differences between individuals.

Social psychology is a twentieth-century science that developed in the United States and has recently been expanding in Western Europe. World and social events have played a major role in influencing the themes and issues studied by its practitioners. The first social psychology study, in 1897, examined the effects of performing alone and performing in front of a group. The first social psychology textbooks were published in 1908. In the 1930s, social psychology was concerned with measuring and studying the functions of attitudes. During that decade, Kurt Lewin (1935) presented his field theory and demonstrated the importance of conducting controlled research on social phenomena. World War II influenced the direction of Lewin's research; Lewin examined social influence, leadership, and group dynamics. The war also gave rise to the study of attitude and attitude change by the Yale Communication Research Program. The postwar period of the 1950s and 1960s found social psychologists studying conformity, obedience, and conflict. Leon Festinger introduced the theory of cognitive dissonance in 1957; this theory captured the attention of social psychologists for the next fifteen years. In the late 1960s and early 1970s, attribution theory was a much-researched topic. In addition, social psychologists developed new methods for gathering and analyzing data. Social cognition has been the field's major focus in recent years.

Science is a set of rules for investigating events and communicating findings. The goals of any science include (a) the description of events, (b) the prediction of events, and (c) the explanation of why events occur. Scientists generally work with *theories*, which explain why events are related, and with *hypotheses*, which are educated guesses about the nature of the relationship between events.

Social psychologists use numerous methods in conducting their inquiry into human behavior. The *case history, archival search,* and *survey* are correlational methods for making predictions about the relationship between events. The *laboratory experiment* and the *field experiment* are methods for determining cause-and-effect relationships. In an experiment, the experimenter controls the *independent variable* and examines changes in the *dependent variable*. *Extraneous variables* must be eliminated if the experimenter is to be able to determine that the manipulation of the independent variable caused the observed changes in the dependent variable. The experiment is a valuable scientific tool because it allows the experimenter to randomly assign subjects to conditions and hence to arrive at the cause-and-effect relationship between variables. Laboratory experiments are often criticized because it is sometimes difficult to generalize beyond the laboratory, because they may lack *external validity* and *mundane realism*, and because they may allow *demand characteristics* and *experimenter bias* to affect the results. The field experiment generally has more external validity and mundane realism than the laboratory experiment. The field experiment's major drawback is that the experimenter loses some control over extraneous variables. Each method has advantages and disadvantages. The research method chosen must fit the experimental question and the aims of the experimenter.

Statistical tests are used to determine whether the results obtained in a study are reliable. Social psychologists have adopted the 5% chance level as the acceptable measure of significance of results. An important consideration in all research is the protection of subjects' psychological and physical safety. Ethical concerns in research center on invasion of privacy, the use of deception, potential harmful consequences, and the fact that subjects are often the unwilling recipients of a lesson about themselves. Strict guidelines have been developed to protect human subjects in social psychology research studies. Most institutions have *institutional review boards* that examine research proposals to ensure protection of subjects.

You can learn about social psychology by taking classes on the subject, observing people in their day-to-day activities, getting involved in experimentation, and taking a broad range of courses in the social sciences, the natural sciences, and the humanities.

Key Terms

analysis of variance test
archival research
case history
check on the manipulation
correlation
deception
demand characteristics
dependent variable
experiment
experimental realism

experimenter bias
external validity
extraneous variable
field experiment
generalization
hypothesis
independent variable
informed consent
institutional review boards (IRBs)
internal validity
mean

mundane realism
random assignment of subjects
science
social psychology
statistically significant
survey
theory
unobtrusive measures
variability

Suggested Readings

Allport, G. W. (1985). The historical background of social psychology. In G. Lindzey and E. Aronson (Eds.), *Handbook of social psychology* (Vol. 1, 3rd ed., pp. 1–46). New York: Random House.

Aronson, E., Brewer, M., & Carlsmith, S. M. (1985). Experimentation in social psychology. In G. Lindzey and E. Aronson (Eds.), *Handbook of social psychology* (Vol. 1, pp. 441–486). New York: Random House.

Campbell, D. T., & Stanley, J. C. (1963). *Experimental and quasi-experimental designs for research.* Chicago: Rand McNally.

Deutsch, M., & Krauss, R. M. (1965). *Theories of social psychology.* New York: Basic Books.

Festinger, L. (1980). *Retrospections on social psychology.* New York: Basic Books.

Lindzey, G., & Aronson, E. (1985). *Handbook of social psychology* (Vol. 1, 3rd ed.). New York: Random House.

Parker, I. (1989). *The crisis in modern social psychology—and how it ended.* London: Routledge & Kegan Paul.

Selltiz, C., Wrightsman, L. S., & Cook, S. W. (1976). *Research methods in social relations.* New York: Holt, Rinehart & Winston.

Chapter Two

Social Cognition

Not satisfied with Dan Quayle's earlier answers, Tom Brokaw put the question again. In his debate with Lloyd Bentsen during the 1988 U.S. presidential campaign, Quayle had been asked repeatedly what he would do if he were vice president and had to step in and take over for President George Bush. Quayle had responded by listing his qualifications to be vice president, but didn't say enough to satisfy Brokaw about what he would actually do. Brokaw, anchor of NBC *Nightly News*, did not want to hear more about qualifications, he wanted to hear about actions. He pushed ahead: "I hate to beat this drum until it has no more sound left in it, but . . . surely, you must have some plan in mind about what you would do if it fell to you to become president of the United States as it has to so many other vice presidents just in the last twenty-five years or so."

Senator Quayle expressed his irritation at having to deal with this issue again, but began to answer. He said that he would meet with the cabinet and other advisers to the president, and that he would be prepared to carry out the duties of the presidency. He said that he had "far more experience than many others that sought the office of the vice president of this country." Then he made his mistake. "I have as much experience in the Congress as Jack Kennedy did when he sought the presidency. I will be prepared to deal with the people in the Bush administration if that unfortunate event should ever occur."

Lloyd Bentsen, the senior senator from Texas, shook his head when Quayle mentioned the late John F. Kennedy. His manner expressed exasperation with Quayle's presuming to compare himself with the fallen president, long a hero to many Democrats. Bentsen began like a kindly and patient uncle explaining some fundamental facts of life to a wayward young nephew, and then he leveled Dan Quayle: "Senator, I served with Jack Kennedy. I knew Jack Kennedy. Jack Kennedy was a friend of mine. Senator, you're no Jack Kennedy."

The audience's response was immediate and intense. Many, obviously Democrats, cheered lustily. But the Republicans in the auditorium seemed to feel that Bentsen's comment was unfair, a low blow. Bentsen tried to rise above the uproar to finish his rebuttal to Quayle while the moderator tried to quiet the crowd. When the audience had quieted some, but before Bentsen could proceed, Dan Quayle fought back. With a firm and indignant look on his face, he said, "That was really uncalled for, Senator." Quayle's comment brought forth more reaction, both positive and negative, but Bentsen got in the last word. He said, "You're the one that was making the comparison, Senator, . . . and frankly I think you're so far apart in the objectives you choose for your country that I did not think the comparison was well taken."

Lloyd Bentsen's memorable putdown, "You're no Jack Kennedy," was one of the harshest retorts that has ever been made in a political debate, and certainly its impact was one of the most telling. Dan Quayle was a controversial figure from the moment George Bush chose him to be his running mate, just before the Republican convention in August 1988. Many people, Republicans as well as Democrats, felt that Quayle was too young, too immature, and too naive to be second in command of the United States, just a heartbeat away from the presidency. He was ridiculed with the nickname "Bush Lite," and some people cracked that he had "a third less credentials than the regular candidates." There was a great deal of controversy about Quayle's service in the National Guard during the war in Vietnam, his undistinguished college academic record, and whether he had used powerful family connections to gain admission to law school. The scrutiny that Quayle was subjected to was so intense that there was a backlash against the media for the grilling that they seemed to be administering. While many people felt that the media were too rough on Quayle, they still had lingering doubts about his qualifications and his stature. Democratic vice-presidential candidate Lloyd Bentsen, by contrast, was a model of experience, maturity, and wisdom.

In light of the doubts about Quayle, it was no surprise that reporters pressed him about his qualifications and the way he would handle the job of president if he had to succeed George Bush in an emergency. His answers failed to allay the serious doubts of many viewers. Because of these continuing concerns about Quayle's abilities, Lloyd Bentsen's comment touched a raw nerve in voters on both sides of the political fence. And even

During the 1988 vice-presidential debate, Lloyd Bentsen and Dan Quayle each tried to present himself in the best possible light while hoping to maneuver his opponent into a less favorable position. As voters watched, they had to make inferences about each man's personal qualities and his qualifications to be vice-president and, perhaps, president.

more important, it seemed to crystallize many of the doubts that people had about Quayle. "You're no Jack Kennedy" summarized in one slashing comment what many people felt but couldn't quite articulate. Dan Quayle simply wasn't presidential timber.

Presidential and vice-presidential debates present candidates with both opportunity and danger. Candidates get a chance to present themselves to the American public in a positive light. They can get their message across. But at the same time, they must withstand attacks and criticism by their opponents, as well as reporters' questions designed to be difficult and to get them away from their canned, memorized answers. The press tries to catch the candidates off guard and make them show something revealing and spontaneous. For example, Bernard Shaw opened the second presidential debate in 1988 by asking candidate Michael Dukakis, "If Kitty Dukakis were raped and murdered, would you favor the death penalty for the assailant?" Dukakis showed no reaction to the idea of his wife's rape and murder; he unflinchingly said he would not favor the death penalty, and began to explain that what the country needed was an effective war on drugs. By not acknowledging the horror he surely felt at the idea of his wife lying dead in a morgue, Dukakis confirmed the "iceman" image the Republicans had been trying to tag him with throughout the campaign.

In the face of these struggles between the candidates and the press, viewers must sift through all the information that is transmitted over a period of 90 minutes and construct their own assessments of the candidates. Because some of their evaluations will decisively tilt the balance on election day, the stakes are high.

For Dan Quayle the stakes were particularly high. He had to present himself as mature and competent. He had to reassure voters that at 41 years of age he was prepared to assume command of the government at a moment's notice. The issues he dealt with gave him the opportunity to do that. However, he was frustrated by the panel's relentless questioning of his plan of action for an emergency presidential transition. And finally he gave Lloyd Bentsen the kind of opening Democrats hoped they might get. While Quayle performed well in many respects, it was hard for him to shake the devastating putdown "You're no Jack Kennedy."

Social Cognition: Making Sense of People

Throughout a presidential campaign, citizens try to understand and make sense of the candidates' behavior. They try to understand specific behaviors, remember who said and did what, and form a general impression of each candidate's character and qualifications. This whole social understanding process goes into high gear during a presidential or vice-presidential debate. We watch the candidates behave, we hear what they say, and we form opinions about their competence, their decisiveness, their drive and energy, and other important leadership traits. While debates may have more to do with personality than with issues, this doesn't mean that they are all style and no substance: they give voters a chance to see the candidates in action in a competitive stressful setting, which enables people to make important inferences about whether the candidates will be good leaders. In this chapter we will consider just how people form impressions and make inferences about others. In Chapter 3 we will consider the closely related topics of self-perception and self-understanding.

We call the process of understanding or making sense of people **social cognition.** Two key components of social cognition are making attributions about why people act as they do, and interpreting their behavior in light of our general knowledge of them as individuals and as members of groups.

Making Attributions: Understanding Why

In our everyday experience we encounter a wide range of behaviors in other people. First thing in the morning we may run into grumpy, sour, barely conscious roommates who grunt more than talk but still manage to act unhappy and unfriendly. An hour or so later we may meet people in class who seem much cheerier and much more pulled together. They've obviously had a shower and a cup of coffee. As we proceed through the afternoon and evening, we will have to interact with people who are friendly and helpful, rude and incompetent, or funny and energetic. During the evening we may watch a political debate and see one candidate appear unconcerned about his wife and another become flustered by a sarcastic putdown. How do we sort out all of this information about the way people act?

Psychologists who study the way we form impressions of other people have shown that one way we make sense of the vast array of behaviors we observe is by trying to determine what qualities in each person explain their actions and make them act as they do. What is it that makes one individual act optimistic and extraverted and another behave cautiously and industriously? The personal qualities or traits that distinguish one person or group from another are called **dispositions,** and we infer their existence by making **attributions** about the causes of people's actions. Basically, we make attributions by inferring whether a particular behavior is caused by a personal disposition or by something in the situation. If we decide that a personal disposition caused a behavior, we are making an **internal attribution.** If we decide that the behavior reflects something in the environment or the situation, we are making an **external attribution.** For example, when Dan Quayle scolded Lloyd Bentsen for his Jack Kennedy comment ("That was uncalled for, Senator"), voters had to decide whether the scolding was attributable to a petulant streak in Dan Quayle's personality (internal attribution) or to the fact that Lloyd Bentsen was out of line in his putdown ("You're no Jack Kennedy") and deserved to be straightened out (external attribution). Their attributions were likely to have a significant impact on their votes on election day.

Attribution theory in social psychology originated with the work of Fritz Heider (1944, 1958) and classic papers by Jones and Davis (1965) and Kelley (1967). Heider pointed out that people attribute behavior to either internal or external causes but prefer to make internal attributions because a person's dispositions are likely to guide his or her behavior over time, and thus serve as useful reference points. Attributing Dan Quayle's scolding to his petulance not only permits us to explain one particular incident but tells us how he is likely to act in other situations. If we can identify people's dispositions, we can predict and perhaps control their behavior in the future. Thus knowing a person's dispositions or personal traits not only helps us understand the social environment, it also allows us, through prediction and control, to act effectively in it.

How do people make attributions? How do we decide whether Michael Dukakis is an unemotional iceman or just reserved in the setting of a formal debate? Here we will discuss the principles people typically follow in making such attributions. First we will discuss how we make internal or external attributions on the basis of observing just a single action. Then we will consider how people take information about someone's behavior over a longer period of time and compare it with the actions of others to make internal or external attributions. Later we will outline the ways people violate some of the basic principles of attribution.

In assessing a situation we make both internal and external attributions. If you were at this party, would you attribute these persons' behavior to the fact that it was a victory party or to the probability that they all had exuberant personalities?

One-Shot Attributions:
Interpreting a Single Behavior

Suppose you go to a party and meet a fellow student named Carole. You and Carole chat for a while and then, seeing a nearby Ping-Pong table, the two of you pick up a pair of paddles and begin to hit the ball back and forth. You aren't sure whether Carole will just try to keep the ball in play or start to hit hard shots that you can't return. That is, will her play be cooperative or competitive? You would just as soon hit the ball casually and try to keep it in play, and it turns

out that that is what Carole does. Her behavior is clearly cooperative. But you want to go beyond noting Carole's behavior, you want to make an attribution and see if you can infer that she has a cooperative disposition. Her behavior may reflect a personal disposition or it may be caused by something in the situation. Perhaps Carole is just

---

attribution   An inference about the cause of a person's action.
disposition   A quality or trait that distinguishes one person or group from another.
external attribution   An inference that a person's behavior is caused by an environmental or situational factor.
internal attribution   An inference that a person's behavior is caused by a personal disposition.
social cognition   The processing, organizing, and retrieval of information about other people.

Study from here

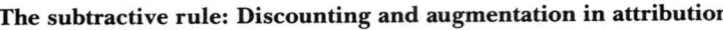

TABLE 2-1

The subtractive rule: Discounting and augmentation in attribution

Example 1, positive inducement for behavior and discounting:
A person behaves in a cooperative manner in a situation that calls for cooperative behavior.

Behavior: Cooperative

Disposition implied by the behavior: Cooperativeness

Situational inducement: Positive for cooperation

Application of subtractive rule: The subtractive rule says that the contribution of situational inducements should be subtracted from the personal disposition implied by the behavior. Since the inducement is positive for the disposition implied by the behavior, cooperativeness, the attribution of cooperativeness should be reduced.

Attribution: The situation caused the behavior. The person may not have a cooperative disposition. Cooperativeness is discounted as a cause of the behavior.

Example 2, negative inducement for behavior and augmentation:
A person behaves in a competitive manner in a situation that calls for cooperative behavior.

Behavior: Competitive

Disposition implied by the behavior: Competitiveness

Situational inducement: Negative for competition

Application of subtractive rule: The subtractive rule says that the contribution of situational inducements should be subtracted from the personal disposition implied by the behavior. Since the inducement is negative for the disposition implied by the behavior, competitiveness, the attribution of competitiveness should be increased. That is, the negative inducement is subtracted, with the effect that it is added to the attribution of competitiveness.

Attribution: The disposition caused the behavior. The person probably has a strongly competitive disposition. Competitiveness is augmented as a cause of the behavior.

following your lead, perhaps she thinks it's more appropriate to play casually rather than competitively at a party, or perhaps she is following a traditional norm that tells her that women should be cooperative and supportive rather than competitive and assertive.

In trying to make such an attribution, perceivers often follow what is known as the **subtractive rule**: "the contribution of situational inducements should be subtracted from the personal disposition implied by the behavior itself" (Trope, Cohen & Moaz, 1988). Thus if the party situation provides an inducement for Carole to be cooperative, that inducement should be subtracted from the cooperative disposition that may be inferred from her behavior. Another way of saying this is that you should follow the **discounting principle**, and discount a cooperative disposition as the cause of Carole's behavior if the party situation is also a plausible cause (Kelley, 1972). Thus if you follow the subtractive rule,

you won't know whether Carole is really a cooperative person. She may be, but maybe not.

On the other hand, suppose that in this friendly party atmosphere Carole begins to overwhelm you with an assortment of slams, spinning backhands, and unreturnable drop shots. Her behavior is competitive but the situational inducements toward competitive behavior are negative. Again you follow the subtractive rule and subtract these negative inducements. As you may remember from elementary algebra, when you subtract a negative you actually add. Thus you *augment* your perception of Carole's competitiveness, because you figure she must be a competitive person indeed to play so hard when the situation really calls for cooperation (Kelley, 1972). In short, the subtractive rule sometimes leads you to discount the role of a disposition and sometimes it leads you to follow the **augmentation principle** and augment your perception of its strength (see Table 2-1).

In many cases following the subtractive rule means deciding what is socially desirable in a particular situation. If a person does what is socially desirable, we have to subtract the positive inducement of acting in a socially desirable way and discount the disposition implied by the behavior (Jones & Davis, 1965). However, if the person goes against the norm—dresses sloppily when the situation calls for formal wear, for example—the norm is seen as a negative inducement toward sloppy dress and we would attribute the person's dress to some dispositional factor.

Several studies have shown that people can and do follow the logic of the subtractive rule. In one study subjects judged Dan, who behaved in an angry fashion, in one of two situations (Trope, Cohen & Moaz, 1988). In one situation subjects read: "When Dan came to the city hall and was told by the clerk he couldn't be helped because of a strike, Dan was very itchy and almost screamed at the clerk." In the other situation subjects read: "As Dan came home, his little son jumped on him and hung onto his neck. Dan was very itchy and almost screamed at him." In the first situation the subtractive rule says that we should discount the angry disposition implied by Dan's behavior. His behavior can be attributed to a frustrating situation. In accord with this principle, Dan is seen as having a personality that is only slightly more angry than average. In the latter situation the subtractive rule says that we should augment the angry disposition implied by Dan's behavior. The situation calls for Dan to be happy, not angry, and in accordance with the subtractive rule, Dan is seen as having a personality that is much more angry than average in this situation.

Another important experiment that illustrates the subtractive rule was conducted with subjects who heard tape recordings of a person's behavior in a job interview (Jones, Davis & Gergen, 1961). Half of the subjects believed that the applicant was applying for a job as an astronaut, and the other half thought that he was applying for a job as a member of a submarine crew. In the second case, the subjects heard the job interviewer describe the ideal candidate as one who was outgoing, friendly, and cooperative—in short, outer-directed. Subjects who listened to the astronaut job interview heard the ideal candidate

TABLE 2-2

Summary of conditions in experiment on behavior and role conformity

Behavior	Job	Role conformity
Inner-directed	Submariner	Out of role
Outer-directed	Submariner	In role
Inner-directed	Astronaut	In role
Outer-directed	Astronaut	Out of role

SOURCE: Jones, Davis, and Gergen (1961).

described as one who was inner-directed. As the interview proceeded, the subjects heard the job candidate act either consistently or inconsistently with his role requirement. Half of the astronaut candidates and half of the submariner candidates acted in a friendly and outer-directed fashion. The other half of them acted in an introverted, inner-directed manner. The inner-directed astronauts and the outer-directed submariners were acting consistently with their role requirements; the inner-directed submariners and the outer-directed astronauts were acting in an out-of-role fashion. The conditions are summarized in Table 2-2.

After listening to the tape-recorded interview, the subjects were asked to judge the way they thought the candidate *really* was. That is, they were asked to make inferences about the true dispositions of the job candidates. The result showed that the two in-role candidates were rated near the neutral point on all personality dimensions and that the degree of confidence that subjects had in these ratings was quite low. On the other hand, the outer-directed astronaut was seen as being outgoing, friendly, and so on, while the inner-directed submariner was seen as being truly

augmentation principle   In attribution theory, the principle that situational inducements against a behavior tend to lead perceivers to attribute the behavior to a personal disposition.

discounting principle   The tendency to discount a cause to which a behavior might be attributed when other plausible explanations are available.

subtractive rule   In attribution theory, the principle that perceivers should subtract the contribution of situational inducements from the personal disposition implied by the behavior.

[Hamlet] "fell into a sadness, then into a fast, thence to a watch, thence to a weakness thence to a lightness, and by this declension into the madness wherein he now raves." What kinds of attributions would you make about Hamlet's personality as his depression became more global and consistent?

quiet and reserved. Moreover, subjects were quite confident about their judgments of the out-of-role candidates. In sum, subjects followed the subtractive rule in discounting dispositions as causes for the in-role candidates and augmenting dispositional attribution for the out-of-role candidates. So the next time a politician shakes your hand at a rally and acts as though she's your close friend, remember to apply the subtractive rule in deciding whether her disposition toward you is really one of high regard and affection.

Attributions Over Time: Observing Multiple Behaviors

Our earlier example about the party Ping-Pong player considers how we make inferences when all we know is a single behavior of a single person in a single situation. Very often, however, we know

about more than just a single instance of behavior. We can interpret an action of our roommate in the context of his or her behavior in a variety of situations, the behavior of a brother or sister in the context of years of experience, and the reactions of a boyfriend or girlfriend in the context of many dates in many places. And very important, we know how other people in general react in many of the same situations in which we have seen the behavior of our roommate, brother, or date.

Attribution theorists have identified several key variables we consider in deciding whether someone we know a lot about is acting as a result of an internal disposition (a **person attribution**) or some external person, object, or situation in the environment (an **entity attribution**). Specifically, we consider three such factors: whether the response is consistent, whether it is unique or distinctive for that person, and whether the consensus for the response among other people is high or low (Kelley, 1967, 1972). Suppose your friend Paul came home from his physics class in a gloomy, frustrated mood. Should you make an internal attribution and infer that Paul's blue mood is attributable to a depressive or gloomy personal disposition, or should you make an external attribution and decide that that physics class is a bad entity and is responsible for Paul's bad humor? Let's consider how you might use information about consistency, distinctiveness, and consensus to make the attribution.

Of first importance is *consistency*. If the response is not consistent, we can't really attribute it to either Paul or the physics course. If Paul likes the physics class on some days but not on others, we can't say that Paul has a gloomy disposition or that the course is frustrating. Paul's gloomy reaction can be attributable only to specific circumstances, perhaps the winter weather or a particular topic in physics. This *circumstance attribution* doesn't tell us much about Paul or about the course.

If Paul's response is high in consistency, we may then think about its uniqueness or *distinctiveness*. Is Paul generally gloomy or is his response unusual and distinctive? If Paul is gloomy a great deal of the time, the response has low distinctiveness. If it is unusual—that is, Paul is generally quite upbeat—we refer to his response as having high distinctiveness. In the case of a low-distinctiveness response (Paul is often gloomy), we should attribute his gloominess to his personal disposition. In the case of a high-distinctiveness response (it's unusual for Paul to be gloomy), we may suspect the physics class.

The final variable we need to consider is *consensus*. How do other people react to the physics class? If Paul's response has low consensus—that is, it makes few people as gloomy as Paul—we tend to attribute the response to Paul's disposition. If consensus is high (most people get frustrated and depressed by the class), we tend to think there is something wrong with the class.

Putting consistency, distinctiveness, and consensus information together, we can predict the following attributions. When consistency is low, we simply make a circumstance attribution. When consistency is high but distinctiveness and consensus are low, we can make a person attribution and infer that Paul is a gloomy person. He consistently reacts that way in physics class, it's not just the physics class that makes him feel that way, and no one else is bothered by the class. On the other hand, when consistency is high and distinctiveness and consensus are also high, we suspect the entity. Something's wrong with the class. It almost always puts Paul in a funk, though he reacts to most things in a cheerful, easygoing manner, and almost everyone else gets upset by it as well.

Do people really use information about consistency, distinctiveness, and consensus in making internal and external attributions? When the question was put to an experimental test, the answer was clearly yes. Participants in a study by McArthur (1972) were given information about a fictitious person. They were told about a particular behavior and then read three pieces of information designed to manipulate the degrees of consensus, distinctiveness, and consistency. For example, subjects may have learned that "John laughed at the comedian." They were then told that *either:*

Consensus
a. Almost everyone who hears the comedian laughs at him; *or*

b. Hardly anyone who hears the comedian laughs at him.

Distinctiveness
a. John does not laugh at almost any other comedian; *or*

b. John also laughs at almost any other comedian.

Consistency
a. In the past, John has almost always laughed at the same comedian; *or*

b. In the past, John has almost never laughed at the same comedian.

In this way, either high- or low-consensus information could be combined with either high- or low-distinctiveness information and with either high- or low-consistency information to allow

---

entity attribution An inference that a behavior is caused by some external person, object, or entity.
person attribution An inference that a person's behavior is caused by an internal disposition.

As you look at Tiffany Chin executing this mid-air split, what kinds of attributions are you making? Do you think she has a gift, or is it that she's worked hard? Is it a lucky jump, or is this just plain easy?

subjects to form an impression of John's behavior. In the end, subjects were asked to attribute the source of John's laughter either to (1) something about John, (2) something about the comedian, (3) something about the particular circumstances, or (4) some combination of factors.

The results of such a study are bound to be complex because of the eight possible combinations produced by the three informational factors. However, the results of McArthur's study were generally supportive of Kelley's model. Internal attributions (something about John) were facilitated by low distinctiveness, low consensus, and high consistency. External attributions (something about the comedian) were facilitated by high distinctiveness, high consensus, and high consistency. Of the three types of information, distinctiveness played the most important role in determining whether the attribution should be internal or external. Finally, attribution to fleeting circumstances was created by low consistency. When John laughed once at this comedian but had almost never laughed at him in the past, the attribution was neither to John nor to the comedian, but rather to the circumstances.

There is also evidence that consistency, distinctiveness, and consensus information affect not only our attributions but also the way we interact with other people. Experimental subjects watched a videotape of a young woman who behaved rudely in an interview. A female interviewer asked her how often she took the initiative in her interactions with men and whether she was willing to be the aggressor in relationships, "even in the sexual domain." The woman refused to answer. She said, "Do I really have go through this again? It's none of your business about my sex life. I'm not answering that question. Go on to the next one." Some subjects were given attributional information implying an internal cause. They were told that the woman had refused to answer that question in a previous interview (high consistency), that she didn't answer several other questions either (low distinctiveness), and that all the other women who were asked that question answered it (low consensus). These subjects rated the woman as dispositionally rude and during a meeting with her they kept at a distance and didn't talk to her very much. In contrast, other subjects were given information that implied an external cause. They were told that the woman had not answered that question in a previous interview (high consistency) but that she had answered all other questions (high distinctiveness) and that a lot of other women had refused to answer the question (high consensus). The subjects with this information attributed the woman's response to the question, they did not perceive her as rude, and they were much friendlier when they interacted with her (Hazlewood & Olson, 1986).

Beyond Internal vs. External Attributions: Assessing Causal Stability, Controllability, and Specificity

Thus far we have seen that when we encounter people whose behavior is cooperative or competitive, rude or friendly, we make attributions about the causes of their behavior. These attributions affect not only the judgments we make about the people but how we interact with them as well. But in many cases attribution goes further than deciding whether behavior is caused by something in a person or something in the situation, particularly when we judge success and failure. Consider the following example. We turn on the television on a Sunday in November and see a football player make a diving catch in the end zone. "Lucky!" shouts someone in the room. "Whaddaya mean?" another responds angrily. "He's the best receiver in the league." A third, more intellectual-looking viewer explains that the success was due not to the player's luck or skill but to the unusual amount of effort that he expended to catch this particular pass. The fourth person in the room responds, "Aw, it was easy anyway."

What these people are arguing about is both whether the cause of the catch was internal or external and whether it is stable or unstable; that is, whether the football player could make that kind of catch again, or is likely to do so infrequently. Only when attributions of internality-externality *and* attributions of stability-instability are made can a final attribution for the success or failure be made.

Table 2-3 summarizes the view of Weiner and his colleagues (1971) as to how the factors are combined to form a final attribution. We can judge that the football player made his catch because he is good (a stable, internal attribution), because making such a catch is easy (a stable, external attribution—he could do it again and again; anyone could; it has to do with the kind of catch, not his ability), because he tried hard (an unstable, internal attribution—he couldn't do that again and again; it was his tremendous effort), or because of luck (an unstable, external attribution—he couldn't do that many times; it was lucky that his hands and the ball happened to wind up in the same place).

An interesting study that provides data relevant to the football player situation was conducted by Frieze and Weiner (1971). They told subjects of the success or failure that a hypothetical person had experienced at a task. They then told the subjects of the success or failure that that person had had at similar tasks and the percentage of other people who had succeeded or failed at that task. In this way, Frieze and Weiner established the basic conditions that would enable attribution of internality or externality. Then the subjects were informed that the actor had done the task one more time, and some subjects were told that he had succeeded, whereas other subjects were told that he had failed.

TABLE 2-3

Classification scheme for the perceived determinants of achievement behavior

Stability \ Locus of control	Internal	External
Stable	Ability	Task difficulty
Unstable	Effort	Luck

SOURCE: Weiner, Frieze, Kukla, Reed, Rest, and Rosenbaum (1971).

To what did subjects attribute the most recent success or failure? The answers generally confirmed the predictions of the model of Weiner and his colleagues. Performance that was inconsistent with the person's past performance (whether he succeeded or failed) and different from the performance of other persons was attributed to effort (he tried extra-hard in the case of success; he didn't try very hard in the case of failure). Performance that was consistent with the person's past performance and similar to the performance of other persons was attributed to task difficulty (success = easy task; failure = hard task). Performance that was consistent with the person's past performance and different from the performance of other persons was attributed to ability (success = high ability; failure = low ability).

Thus the questions we would have to ask about the football player in order to make an attribution for the success we observed on TV become clear. First, was it a catch that anyone could make—that is, was consensus high or low? Second, was the success a stable phenomenon—that is, was it something that was consistent or inconsistent with the player's past behavior as a pass receiver? We would conclude that he is a player of high ability if we rated the pass catching to be internal and his success in receiving to be stable.

Attributions that we make first to internal or external factors and then to stable or unstable factors have important consequences. Typically our evaluation of a person depends on whether we make internal or external attributions. We evaluate people positively when we make internal attributions for their successes (high ability or effort) and external attributions for their failures (a difficult task or bad luck). Negative evaluations follow from internal attributions for failure (low ability or effort) and external attributions for success (an easy task or good luck). While internal and external attributions affect evaluation, stable and unstable attributions affect expectancies. If the cause of a success or failure is stable (ability or task difficulty), we expect to see more of it in the future. If the cause is unstable (effort or luck), we aren't so likely to expect the same success or failure in the future.

More recently, attribution theorists have discussed causal dimensions beyond internality and stability which also have important consequences. One such dimension is *controllability* (Weiner, 1985, 1986). Suppose a person failed a test because she hadn't put effort into studying. Lack of effort is an internal-unstable cause, and we might evaluate the person negatively and expect that her future performance might improve. But our reaction will be affected by whether the lack of effort was due to something the person could control, such as choosing to go sailing on Sunday afternoon, versus one that she could not control, such as being required to serve on a jury.

In general, if people fail because of causes beyond their control, we feel pity rather than anger, and we are inclined to try to help them. We have the opposite reactions when someone fails because of factors he or she can control. These reactions were shown in a study of people with a stigma; that is, some characteristic that marks them as "deviant, flawed, limited, spoiled or generally undesirable" (Jones et al., 1984, p. 6). People with stigmas that were perceived to be uncontrollable, such as blindness, cancer, or delayed stress reactions to fighting in Vietnam, elicited feelings of pity and inclinations to help. People with stigmas that were seen as controllable, such as obesity, AIDS, and drug addiction, elicited reactions of anger and inclinations toward neglect (Weiner, Perry & Magnusson, 1988). A key factor here seems to be that we hold people responsible for stigmas or failures that are controllable and could have been prevented, and we react to them with anger. When people cannot control their stigmas or failures, they are not held responsible. Consequently, we feel pity and we want to help them.

A final dimension of attribution is *globality*. We often judge whether causes are very specific in their effects or are global; that is, whether they affect just a few outcomes or a wide range of them (Abramson, Seligman & Teasdale, 1978). If Tom failed a math test, for example, we might think he had some kind of ability deficit. On the one hand, we might infer that he cannot take timed multiple-choice math tests, a very specific shortcoming, but that he is generally competent in math and is basically quite intelligent. A more global attribution would be that Tom just doesn't have any math aptitude, although he is competent in other areas. An even more global attribution is that Tom has a deficit that will affect a great many performances and a wide range of experiences—he just isn't very bright.

In sum, when we make attributions we identify causes that are internal or external and that vary in their stability, controllability, and globality. In Chapter 3 we will see that people make attributions about their own behaviors and their own successes and failures as well as about other people's. We will also see that people's feelings and expectations about their behaviors and performances are strongly affected by these self-attributions.

Making Biased Attributions: Misunderstanding Why

We have seen that people can follow several essentially rational principles of attribution in forming impressions of others. All these principles require is a little elementary logic. People can use the subtractive rule either to discount or to augment the dispositional attribution implied by a behavior, and they can use information about an action's consistency, distinctiveness, and consensus to infer whether the behavior is attributable to the person or the entity.

Consider, for example, people trying to decide whether Michael Dukakis is really cold and unemotional on the basis of his cool reaction to the question about his wife's being raped and murdered. They might follow the subtractive rule and decide that the unemotionality implied by his behavior should be discounted because the formal setting of a debate demands that people behave in a reserved, unemotional manner. Or they might apply the principles of consistency, distinctiveness, and consensus. Thus they might ask whether Dukakis consistently is unemotional in debates, whether he is unemotional in other situations, and how much emotion other candidates show when they are dealing with such questions in debates. They might use these principles, but *will* they?

In fact, attribution theorists have shown that in many instances people do not follow the simple logic of basic attributional principles. Indeed, there are a number of pitfalls in applying these principles, and a number of biases that can sidetrack logical attribution. Some of these biases are due to our shortcomings in processing information and some of them come from motives that lead us to prefer to make a particular kind of attribution that may not be implied by the available information. We don't want to imply that people are either rational or irrational. They are clearly both, and it depends on the person and on the situation whether they will be rational in any given instance. Here we will consider three specific obstacles to accurate attribution: the correspondence bias, the saliency bias, and defensive attribution.

The Correspondence Bias

As noted earlier, the psychologist Fritz Heider (1944, 1958) was the first to write about the processes of attribution. He explained that while it is perfectly possible to attribute behavior to external factors, we tend to be more comfortable with internal attributions. We prefer to know the dispositions of the people with whom we interact because this knowledge helps us to predict and perhaps control their behavior. As a result of the preference for knowing dispositions, when we make attributions we often underestimate the role of situational forces in causing behavior. That is, we overestimate the role of personal dispositions, and assume that people's behavior simply reflects their dispositions. For example, we might decide that Michael Dukakis is cold and unemotional because that's how he behaved. We ignore the forces in the situation that made him act that way. Because a dispositional attribution requires us to decide that an action corresponds directly to a

disposition, the bias toward making dispositional attributions is called the **correspondence bias** (Gilbert & Jones, 1986). For example, we are falling prey to the correspondence bias when we decide that a person who behaves angrily when provoked is an angry person. Ignoring the provocation, we assume the angry behavior corresponds to an angry disposition. Because it is such a pervasive and important phenomenon, the correspondence bias has also been called the **fundamental attribution error** (Ross, 1977).

The correspondence bias can be seen at work in an experiment in which subjects had to present some information about a case study to a woman who was described as a graduate student in clinical psychology. They were told that the woman was practicing techniques for helping people such as teachers and nurses discuss case study information. In some cases the subjects were told that the woman was practicing a technique that called for her to be as open and spontaneous as possible. Thus her behavior was freely chosen. Other subjects were told either that the graduate student was practicing a technique that required her to be distant and unfriendly, in order to help teachers and nurses develop independence, or that she was practicing a technique that required her to be as friendly and supportive as possible, in order to help her clients feel comfortable. Thus the woman's behavior in these cases was forced, either forced unfriendly behavior or forced friendly behavior. After being given this information about the woman's freely chosen or constrained behavior, the subjects actually read a case study and discussed it with her. The woman's behavior in the discussions was either very friendly or very unfriendly.

How did the subjects perceive the graduate student's personality? The results showed that information about the woman's forced friendly or unfriendly behavior was never taken into account. Subjects thought she was a very friendly person when her behavior was friendly, whether that behavior was freely chosen or forced. When her behavior was unfriendly, she was seen as being

---

correspondence bias (fundamental attribution error)
  The tendency of perceivers to infer that behavior reflects internal dispositions and to ignore external factors that might explain it.

extremely cold and hostile, even when she was just practicing a technique that required her to be unfriendly. In short, subjects showed a strong correspondence bias. They simply did not consider situational inducements when they judged the woman's personality (Napolitan & Goethals, 1979).

A direct application of the subtractive rule would not have produced the attributions made in the forced behavior conditions. Thus we see that the correspondence bias essentially involves the failure to use the subtractive rule—the failure to discount personal disposition when there are situational inducements for behavior. What causes the correspondence bias? Why do people fail to apply the subtractive rule? A number of factors are critical in determining just how much people show the correspondence bias.

As Heider suggested, one important factor may simply be people's desire to identify dispositions and predict behavior. Therefore we take behavior as an indicator of a disposition and overlook the fact that doing so may not be logical. Heider also suggested another important reason. He said that "behavior has such salient properties it tends to engulf the field." By that Heider meant that sometimes behavior is so vivid, and environmental constraints are so subtle in comparison, that we conclude, for example, that Michael Dukakis is a cold fish simply because he seems cold. Certainly subjects in the study with the clinical psychology graduate student encountered behavior that was vivid in its friendliness or unfriendliness. Also, we are all too ready to assume that any single observed behavior is representative of the actor's behavior in general. This is particularly true if the behavior is something we are not sure we would do in a similar circumstance. The behavior then stands out as something we assume to be representative of that person's behavior—something the person might have done even if she or he had not been constrained by the environment.

Several recent experiments have told us a great deal more about the correspondence bias—both what makes it show up and what makes it go away. One important factor is simply that people are busy and have only so much time and energy to think through the logical implications of behavior and situational inducements. There is evidence that inferring traits directly from

behavior is spontaneous, unconscious, and automatic, perhaps because behavior is so salient, and that this process gets slowed down only when we have the time and inclination to sit back, deliberate, and be logical; and that may not happen very often (Uleman, 1987; Winter & Uleman, 1984). From these considerations we would predict that the busier people are, the more they would demonstrate the correspondence bias. This is exactly what was shown in research by Gilbert, Pelham, and Krull (1988).

In this experiment subjects watched seven silent videotape segments of a woman who was having a discussion with another woman she had just met. The first woman's behavior appeared to be extremely anxious. Some subjects were told that many of the topics she was discussing on the taped segments were in fact anxiety-producing, such as embarrassing moments, personal failures, hidden secrets, and sexual fantasies. Other subjects were told that all of the topics were relaxing, such as fashion trends, world travel, ideal vacations, and best restaurants. In addition, half of the subjects in each group were given a task that made them cognitively busy—they had to memorize the list of topics the woman was discussing. The other half of the subjects in each group were not busy. They didn't have to memorize the topics. After watching the tape, all subjects were asked to infer to what extent the woman actually had an anxious disposition.

The results showed that the nonbusy subjects used the subtractive rule perfectly well, and avoided the correspondence bias. Nonbusy subjects who were told that the woman was discussing relaxing topics augmented their dispositional attribution and saw her as highly anxious. She had behaved in an anxious way even though the situation should have made her relaxed. And subjects who thought she was discussing anxiety-provoking topics thought she was a much less anxious person. They subtracted the situational inducement toward anxiety and discounted the anxious disposition implied by her behavior. On the other hand, busy subjects, who had to memorize the discussion topics, showed the correspondence bias. They thought the woman was relatively anxious whether she was discussing anxious or relaxing topics. The situational inducement was not factored into their attributions. It is important to note that the busy sub-

Suppose you had witnessed the incident above. According to the correspondence bias, would you be likely to offer the woman on the left a job as a customer service representative?

jects didn't forget the situational inducements. In fact, they were busy memorizing what they were. But memorizing the topics made subjects unable to think through their logical attributional implications.

Other research shows that when we are interacting with someone, the demands of interacting effectively often keep our minds so busy that we can't apply the subtractive rule as we should, and as a result we fall prey to the correspondence bias. For example, in one study subjects had their hands full trying to be friendly to an unfriendly confederate. These subjects knew that some of the attitudes the confederate expressed were dictated by the experimenter, but they attributed those attitudes to her anyway. Subjects didn't do this when they were being friendly to someone who was friendly in return. They didn't have to work as hard and they were able to think about the situational inducements that caused her to express the attitudes she did. They did not think she believed what she was saying (Gilbert, Krull

& Pelham, 1988). A similar result was found in an experiment in which subjects had to present themselves to another person in a favorable way. Their positive self-presentations elicited similar positive self-presentations from the other person. From these reciprocated positive self-presentations the subjects inferred that the other person had very high self-esteem. Devising their own positive self-presentations kept subjects too busy to think about the fact that the other person's self-presentations were induced by their own behavior and should not have been taken as an indication of high self-esteem (Baumeister, Hutton & Tice, 1989).

Several other studies have shown that nonverbal behavior can be key in helping us to overcome the correspondence bias and apply the subtractive rule. For example, when subjects watch a videotape of someone reading an essay, they tend to think the reader agrees with the attitude expressed in the essay, even though they know he was randomly assigned to read that particular

Sometimes a dimension of a person's behavior or appearance is so salient that it's difficult to focus on any other characteristics in making attributions. Look at this young man. What kinds of attributions are you making based on his appearance?

any stimulus that is vivid or salient in a situation will be seen as the cause of behavior in that situation. They showed that if the attention of perceivers was focused on a particular member of a dyad during a conversation, that member was perceived as more central and causative in directing the course of the conversation. Observers thus fell prey to the **saliency bias.** McArthur and Post (1977) demonstrated that making an actor's environment salient increased the number of attributions that were made to the environment. Taylor and her associates (1978) showed that a novel member of a group, by being more salient, was perceived as greatly influential. Perceivers rated the only black person in a group of whites, for example, as having talked more frequently and as having been more influential in affecting the discussion. His salience affected his availability in perceivers' memories, which in turn affected their memory of how frequently he contributed to the group.

Defensive Attribution

In their debates with George Bush and Dan Quayle, Michael Dukakis and Lloyd Bentsen tried as hard as they could to prove that the Republicans were responsible for everything that had gone wrong during the last eight years. In particular, Dukakis tried to blame Bush for the Iran-Contra affair and for the Reagan administration's inept handling of General Manuel Noriega of Panama. Both of these episodes seriously eroded international respect for the United States. Dukakis may have felt he could blame these fiascoes on Bush on the basis of research in social psychology indicating that we often heap blame on people who are associated with misfortunes that have serious consequences.

The first experiment done on this question required subjects to decide how responsible a person was for causing an automobile accident (Walster, 1966). Surprisingly, the more severe the consequences of the accident became, the more responsible the victim of the accident was held to be. In her study, Walster described the saga of Lennie, who left his car parked at the top of a hill. Unfortunately, the brake cable came loose, and the car rolled down the hill and was damaged. The more damage the car and other people suffered, the more Lennie was held responsible.

essay rather than one expressing the opposite point of view. But if subjects see the person nonverbally express disappointment when he is assigned to read a particular essay—a prochoice essay, say, rather than an antiabortion essay—they don't infer a prochoice attitude corresponding to the prochoice essay. The nonverbal expression of disappointment reminds subjects to think about the situational constraint. When they do this, they avoid the correspondence bias (Fleming & Darley, 1989).

The Saliency Bias

When Heider wrote that behavior engulfs the field, he implied that we may fall prey to the correspondence bias simply because behavior is so salient and vivid in comparison with subtle environmental pressures. Taking this idea one step further, Taylor and Fiske (1975) argued that

Why should Lennie be held virtually blameless when the damage to the car and others was minimal and held responsible when the car and/or others were harmed more severely? Why was Lennie negligent about checking his brake cable in the second case but not in the first? In short, why were observers less than rational in deciding on Lennie's blame?

Research has shown that rational, controllable factors, such as driving speed and previous driving record, will be used in a rational way if they are available (Arkkelin, Oakley & Mynatt, 1979). However, it has been suggested that we become much less the rational observer when we feel that an unfortunate accident *might happen to us*. In these situations we become emotionally aroused and we tend to try to reduce our arousal by making a **defensive attribution**; we hold the victim of an act responsible for his or her fate. For example, in one study female subjects who became emotionally aroused when reading about a rape held the woman who was raped responsible for the assault (Thornton et al., 1986). Returning to Lennie, if we all have cars and if we can see ourselves as potentially in the same predicament as Lennie, then it is safer to attribute responsibility to Lennie. As the consequences become increasingly severe, we would rather think that Lennie caused his own fate by his negligence. Clearly, *we* are not negligent, so such an accident could not happen to us.

Although we often act as impartial observers, in some situations we have definite preferences for the way we would like the results of our attributional search to turn out. In the case of defensive attribution, we are motivated to perceive the causes of events in a way that makes us feel that we could not become the unfortunate victims of undesirable situations. If accidents occur because of chance, luck, fate, or properties of the environment, then it is possible for the same unfortunate events to happen to us. Therefore, we may be motivated to distort events that would lead us to make an external entity or circumstance attribution so that we can arrive at an internal or person attribution instead. All we have to believe, then, is that we are not as evil or as negligent as the victim of the undesired event, for such events happen only to negligent people (cf. Lerner & Matthews, 1967).

In summary, psychologists have identified

several biases that may influence our attributions. The correspondence bias, the saliency bias, and defensive attribution are particularly prominent and important. These biases may result from cognitive distortion in the processing of information, or they may be motivated by the unique needs and desires of the perceivers. In either case, they remind us that while people are often guided by basic logic in their use of attributional principles, sometimes make attributions under the misguidance of basic human frailty.

The Impact of Schemata: Using What We Know

One of the most important concepts in social cognition is that of *schema* (plural, *schemata*). A **schema** is a body of general knowledge about

---

defensive attribution An attribution of causality that is made to reduce the perceiver's anxiety.
saliency bias The tendency to attribute behavior to any stimulus that is most vivid or salient in the situation.
schema A body of general knowledge and expectations about a person, object, or event.

---

any person, object, or event. We have many kinds of schemata stored in memory, including social schemata, which contain our knowledge of particular individuals and of certain kinds of people. The word *schema* is the Greek word for "shape," so that it refers to the shape or general outline of what we know about somebody or something (Crider et al., 1989). Because we use what we know to make guesses about what will happen in the future, our schemata can also be thought of as general expectations or preconceptions about other people (Myers, 1983). During the 1988 presidential campaign, for example, many people were generally aware that Dan Quayle was young and inexperienced in comparison with Lloyd Bentsen. This schema (or general image) of Quayle led many voters to the expectation that he would be overmatched in his debate with Bentsen.

A concept closely related to the concept of schema is that of scripts. A **script** is our knowledge of a particular situation and the way events in that situation unfold (Abelson, 1981; Schank & Abelson, 1977); it can be thought of as an event schema. For example, we know that when people go into a restaurant, they will be seated, given a menu, asked if they would like a cocktail, and so on. Similarly, Bush and Dukakis followed a script at the end of both of their two presidential debates. They walked over and shook each other's hands, turned to kiss their wives, chatted with their advisers, and so on. The most distinctive characteristic of a script is that it includes knowledge of the sequence of events that characterize situations.

How do schemata work? Generally, they provide us with expectations or preconceptions about how people will behave. Consequently, we notice information that is consistent with our schemata, we interpret information that may be ambiguous as fitting our schemata, and we recall information that is related to our schemata better than information that is unrelated to it. Furthermore, we tend to recall information that we interpreted as fitting a schema as being even more consistent with that schema as time passes (Higgins & McCann, 1984). Let us consider how schemata affect our impressions of other people and how they affect our memory for their behavior.

Schemata and Impressions

Schemata provide us with expectations and a tendency to perceive people's behavior as fitting those expectations. The impact of expectations on our perceptions of people can be seen in a classic experiment known as the "warm-cold" study (Kelley, 1950). The subjects in this study were undergraduates taking an introductory economics course at MIT. They were all told that they were to have a guest instructor for a specific class and were then given a little bit of information about the visitor. Students in half the sections were told that the visitor was twenty-nine years old, that he was married, and that people considered him "a rather cold person, industrious, critical, practical, and determined." Students in the other sections were given the same information except that they were told he was said to be "a rather warm person, industrious, critical, practical, and determined." In short, the only difference was that one-half of the subjects were told that the guest lecturer was cold and the other half were told that he was warm. Because warm versus cold is an important "central trait" in the perception of a person (Asch, 1946), this one-word difference created strong expectancy differences in the two subject groups. The impact of this expectancy difference was dramatic. The subjects who were told that the guest was warm had much more positive impressions of him than those who were told the opposite. Both groups of subjects saw the same guest giving the same lecture. And both groups spent a full class period with him. Yet their impressions of him, based on that hour of instruction, were strongly affected by the one-word difference: they interpreted the man's behavior according to their "knowledge" that he was warm or cold.

How can a schema have such a strong effect? As noted, we interpret information that is ambiguous to fit our schemata. For example, when subjects were told that the guest lecturer was a determined person, they probably envisioned his determination as ruthlessness if they thought he was cold but as dedication when they thought he was warm. Also, we remember information that fits our schemata better than information that is unrelated to them. In short, we see things as fitting our schemata and we remember those things.

Schemata and Memory

Schemata affect not only what we remember but how we remember. If we have some general knowledge of a person and form an impression as a result, we will often remember the person's behavior as fitting that impression more than it actually does. For example, if we watched Dan Quayle debate Lloyd Bentsen with a preconception that Quayle was shallow and superficial, we might slightly misrecall what he said in the debate to fit that impression. We might recall that he gave no specific answers to the question of what he would do if he became president in an emergency when in fact Quayle said he would immediately say a prayer and then meet with the cabinet. An interesting recent experiment on memory for conversations shows precisely this kind of error.

In this study subjects read or actually observed a conversation between two businessmen, Robert and Michael. Sometimes they were told that Robert was the boss of a company and that Michael was his employee and sometimes they were told that Robert and Michael were executives of equal status in the company. Two days after reading or listening to the conversation, subjects had to recall what Robert had said in the conversation. If they thought Robert was the boss, they remembered what he said as being considerably more assertive than they did if they thought Robert and Michael had equal status. Subjects' memory of what Robert said fitted their impression of him as the boss or as just another executive (Holtgraves, Srull & Socall, 1989).

While we often remember people as behaving in ways that fit our schemata, at times we also recall very clearly incongruent behaviors that don't fit our schemata (Belmore & Hubbard, 1987). Thus we would recall Dan Quayle's debating points as being vague and imprecise, but if he did say one or two things that were insightful and important, we might well remember those unexpected statements very clearly. Our attention is drawn to novel and unexpected behaviors, and as a result they stick in our minds (Hastie, 1980). The key factor in determining whether we have superior recall for incongruent information is whether we take the time and make the effort to understand it. Voters who expected Dan Quayle to fall on his face in his debate may not have bothered to con-

An entertainer must be very aware of his audience's schema for him and know how to use it. Arsenio Hall, for example, an actor and popular late-night TV show host, displays a warm, exuberant, and intelligent personality for his nightly audience and draws a great deal of support.

sider his strong moments; they may simply have overlooked and forgotten them. On the other hand, if those voters really wanted to understand what was going on, they may have taken the time and effort to explain Quayle's performance. Depending on the explanation, they may have changed their schema about Quayle's skill in debating and perhaps, more generally, his competence.

One clear demonstration that attributions made about incongruent information can affect whether the information is remembered and whether remembering such information changes our schemata comes from a study by Crocker, Hannah, and Weber (1983). Subjects were led to form a schema that someone named John was friendly. They were then given the incongruent

---

script The sequence of events that one has learned to expect in a given situation.

Given what you understand about priming, would you want to administer a test that would measure this person's attitude toward having more children at this moment in time?

Priming: The Impact of What's on Your Mind

As people watch presidential and vice-presidential debates, a variety of things can determine the dispositions they attribute to the candidates, the impressions they form of them, and what they recall about the candidates' performances. Attributions are important determinants, whether they are true to the logic of attribution principles or are undermined by attribution biases. Our schemata exert a significant role as well. Another, often more subtle influence on the impressions we form and the memories we construct is what just happens to be on our minds as we turn on the television.

Suppose, for example, that before watching the debate between Lloyd Bentsen and Dan Quayle, a schoolteacher had been thinking about the difficulties she had been having with some spoiled, immature, and petulant young pupils. These children weren't learning well, and she knew that such children have trouble assuming responsibility when they grow up. When Dan Quayle said, "That was really uncalled for, Senator," in response to Lloyd Bentsen's Jack Kennedy putdown, and attempted to look tough and angry, the teacher might have perceived Quayle's behavior as spoiled, immature, and petulant. Simply because those traits are on her mind, and because Quayle's behavior could potentially have been perceived in that way, she might have attributed these dispositions to Dan Quayle and recalled his behavior as reflecting them. She might also infer that Quayle might have trouble assuming responsibility if he became president. A person who did not have those traits in mind might have perceived Quayle very differently, perhaps as assertive and quick-witted.

The person who has the traits of spoiledness, immaturity, and petulance in mind is said to be *primed* to perceive those traits in others. Ambiguous behavior that might be perceived as reflecting those traits is much more likely to be perceived as in fact indicating them if the observer has been primed for them. **Priming** is the process of somehow bringing certain things, typically behaviors or personal characteristics, to mind, that

information that John had cut in front of a line at the bank. The subjects were also given information that indicated that John's unexpected behavior was attributable to something external (John was being paged for an emergency) or that it was attributable to John's personal characteristics (he didn't care what the other people in line thought about his behavior). When subjects attributed John's incongruous behavior to the emergency, they forgot about it and didn't change their opinion of John. However, if they attributed his rude behavior to his personality, they remembered it well, and the better they remembered it, the worse they thought of John.

In short, we typically interpret information as consistent with our schemata or expectations; we also recall information that is consistent with them. However, we sometimes recall highly incongruent information if we think about its meaning. When we do recall the new information, we change our schemata to accommodate it.

is, *activating* them. In some instances priming is done subconsciously, so that the primed person is unaware that the ideas have been activated.

Psychologists have done a number of studies to demonstrate the impact of priming on perception, behavior, and memory. In one study subjects were primed by having to find four names embedded in a puzzle. For some subjects the four names were of figures thought of as moderately nonhostile (Daniel Boone, Robin Hood, the tennis champion Billie Jean King, and former Secretary of State Henry Kissinger), while for others the names were of figures thought of as relatively hostile (Israeli Prime Minister Menachem Begin, acid rock singer Alice Cooper, heavyweight boxing champion Joe Frazier, and Indiana basketball coach Bobby Knight). Then subjects read an ambiguous description of Donald, a person whose behavior could be characterized as either hostile or nonhostile. When subjects indicated their impressions of Donald, those who had been primed with the list of nonhostile names perceived Donald as less hostile than those who had been primed with the hostile names. When subjects later played a bargaining game with a person they thought was Donald, they played more competitively if they had been primed with hostile names. Thus both their impression of Donald and their behavior toward him were affected by priming (Herr, 1986). A similar study showed that people primed to think of kidnapping by reading a real missing-child poster were more likely to think that an ambiguous videotaped interaction between an adult and a child, which could have been a kidnapping, was actually an emergency situation (James, 1986).

Priming can also affect memory. Primed traits act like a schema and influence the way we recall incoming information that is related to them. In one experiment, subjects read a list of dispositional labels and were urged to hold those labels in memory as part of a study on "information processing." Next, as part of what the subjects thought was a second study, they were asked to read descriptions of behavior that could be interpreted either positively or negatively. If subjects had been primed with a positive label—for example, "adventurous"—they recalled a related behavior, shooting rapids, more positively than they did if they had been primed with a negative

label, "reckless" (Higgins, Rholes & Jones, 1977). In short, what we are thinking about when we receive information about people can have a dramatic effect on what we remember about them and how we evaluate them.

In the studies of priming we have mentioned thus far, subjects were primed with information that was brought into conscious awareness. It is probably the case that the subjects were not actually aware of the primed information when they judged Donald or the kidnapping videotape, though they had previously been made consciously aware of the priming information. A series of studies suggest that sometimes people can be primed without their conscious awareness of the information at any time. Psychologists have developed techniques of subliminal perception, by which they present trait or behavior words to subjects on a screen for very brief flashes. The subjects cannot read the words, cannot recall them, and cannot recognize whether they have seen them or not when the words are presented to them later. Yet those words clearly prime them for certain trait or behavior concepts and affect their impressions.

In one study words related to kindness *(considerate, caring, thoughtful)* were flashed subliminally on a television screen. Then subjects read a 12-sentence description of a person (named Donald again!) whose behavior was ambiguous but could have been perceived as reflecting a kind disposition. Subjects who had been primed with the kindness words thought Donald was kinder than subjects who had been primed with neutral words. The same was true if words related to shyness *(timid, meek, bashful)* were presented before an ambiguously shy behavioral description (Bargh et al., 1986). Another study showed similar results with subjects subliminally primed with words related to honesty and meanness (Erdley & D' Agostino, 1988). In short, studies of priming show that what is on our minds when we receive information about a person can have a dramatic impact on our impressions, our behavior, and our memory.

---

priming The process of bringing certain things, typically behaviors or personal characteristics, to mind, activating them.

Social Inference: Making Judgments About People

Millions of people watch the nationally televised presidential debates every four years. For many, these debates are their major source of information about the candidates and the issues. On the basis of what they perceive and remember about the debates and any information they get from other sources, people must decide for whom to vote. How do they put together the various bits and pieces of information they have and arrive at a judgment about the two candidates? Social cognition research that focuses on inferences attempts to understand these judgment processes. What we have learned from this research is that human beings are not perfect in their judgments and inferences. Whether this imperfection means that people are basically irrational and thus make flawed judgments or that they are pretty sound in their thinking, given the difficulties of meeting perfect standards, has been a matter of considerable debate (Nisbett & Ross, 1980; Markus & Zajonc, 1985). Most of the research that we will describe illustrates people's mistakes and the shortcuts they take in making inferences. These mistakes result from following modes of thinking that work well in most instances; unfortunately, sometimes these modes are inappropriate, and then the results can be serious.

Underusing Base-Rate Information

Imagine an individual, Bob, deciding what kind of car to buy. Since reliability is important to him, Bob has carefully gone through all the data on frequency of repair in consumer magazines and decides that he will buy a Toyota; it has the best repair record. Shortly before Bob makes a final decision, a friend tells him about his neighbor's cousin who bought a 1980 four-door Toyota Tercel that was always in the shop. Bob is impressed by this story and decides he'd better not get tangled up with a Toyota. In this situation, a person ignores the available **base-rate information** on auto repairs and makes a judgment about the most reliable car on the basis of a single, albeit impressive, example.

Good, into

Studies suggest that people make this error frequently. They ignore available general information and pay attention to concrete instances. In one study, for example, subjects were told about a taxi that was involved in a nighttime accident. One of the eyewitnesses said the cab could have been blue. Subjects were also told that 85% of the cabs in the city were green and 15% were blue. Most subjects went with the eyewitness's testimony and guessed that the cab was blue, thereby ignoring the base-rate information, which indicated that the cab was probably green. On the other hand, when the subjects were told that 85% of the cars involved in the city's accidents were green, they did use that base-rate information (Ginosar & Trope, 1980). Furthermore, another study shows that people use base-rate information if they are induced to think scientifically or if they realize the relevance of such information to their goals (Zukier & Pepitone, 1984). Thus people will use base-rate information if they think it is relevant; in many cases, they seem to make the mistake of ignoring its relevance.

The Dilution Effect

Suppose you missed the Quayle-Bentsen debate on television but someone told you that Bentsen ruined Quayle's attempt to look experienced and qualified by saying, "You're no Jack Kennedy." What overall impression would you have of Quayle's success in portraying himself as an experienced, well-qualified candidate for vice president? You might think he failed pretty miserably. Now suppose you were told not only that Bentsen embarrassed Quayle but also that Quayle arrived on time, that he had shrimp scampi for dinner, and that Lloyd Bentsen's wife was wearing a green dress. Would your impression of Quayle's performance be any different? Perhaps you think not, but several studies have shown that an impression can be softened if relevant information (in this case about Quayle's performance) is diluted with irrelevant information (such as what Quayle had for dinner or what Mrs. Bentsen was wearing). You might actually have a less negative view of Quayle's performance in the second case (Zukier, 1982). The tendency to be influenced or distracted by such irrelevant information is called the **dilution effect.** Politicians seem to understand it; they often give out cheerful but irrelevant information to soften the impact of bad news.

Illusory Correlation

Another of the errors that we make in perceiving the world around us is to conclude that a relationship exists between two things when that conclusion simply isn't supported by the available data. For example, a person may believe that "politicians are dishonest" when the available data actually show otherwise. To accurately conclude that there is a unique association between dishonesty and politicians, the person would have to list honest and dishonest politicians and honest and dishonest physicians, bankers, and college professors and then show that dishonesty occurs more frequently among politicians than among members of other occupational groups. A belief that is held even when the data right in front of you don't support that belief is called **illusory correlation.** People seem to make this error because confirming instances (in this case, examples of dishonest politicians) can be highly salient and can obscure all the data that show numerous honest politicians and crooked bankers.

Several studies show that we are likely to form illusory correlations about the performances—both successes and failures—of salient individuals, including ourselves. In particular, we see the salient person as more closely associated with the predominant behavior, success or failure, than other people are, even though that simply isn't true. As a result of this tendency, if several individuals, some salient and some nonsalient, are performing well in a particular situation, we will recall the salient person as performing better, even if all are doing equally well. If the individuals are all equally doing poorly, we will recall the salient one as doing worse. Again, we see the salient person as more closely associated with the predominant behavior than he or she actually is.

There is one exception to this pattern. If the salient person is yourself, and the predominant performance level is low, you will not see yourself as performing more poorly than others. In this case, a bias toward perceiving ourselves positively (see Chapter 3) counteracts the typical illusory correlation (Sanbonmatsu et al., 1987). As

One of these persons is president of a corporation, one is an administrative assistant, and another is a salesperson. Who would you match to each job? On what basis?

we will see in Chapter 11, illusory correlations play a strong and disturbing role in stereotypes. While we don't form illusory correlations if they would lead to negative impressions of ourselves, they often lead us to have negative impressions of others.

The Availability Bias

Suppose a friend of yours asked you how Dan Quayle performed in his debate with Lloyd Bentsen. What comes to mind most readily is Bentsen's use of the Jack Kennedy putdown and

base-rate information Data or information about the frequency of specific events or behaviors in particular groups.

dilution effect The tendency of an inference to be weakened by irrelevant information.

illusory correlation A correlation erroneously perceived between a person or group and a characteristic on the basis of a few coincidences.

Quayle's inept attempt at a comeback. Because this event is so available or accessible to you in memory, you may recall the overwhelming of Quayle as setting the dominant tone of the debate. Making judgments about the frequency or probability of events on the basis of the instances that come easily or quickly to mind is called the **availability bias** (Tversky & Kahneman, 1973). If you think back to illusory correlations, you can see that the availability bias is implicated there as well. Watergate and other instances of political corruption are so readily available to you that you overestimate the frequency of dishonest politicians, thereby inferring an illusory correlation.

The Representativeness Bias

A common rule of thumb used to judge whether a person belongs to a group is called the **representativeness bias.** We tend to leap to the conclusion that a person who shares some characteristics with typical members of a group probably belongs to that group. For example, people reading that Tom is intelligent but not creative, that he is orderly with a corny sense of humor, and that he has little interest in interacting with others are likely to see him as an engineer or computer scientist, even if they know that engineers and computer scientists are relatively rare (Kahneman & Tversky, 1973). He seems representative of the category. To use the representativeness bias to make this judgment when engineers and computer scientists are rare is to make the error of underusing the base-rate information that we discussed earlier. Thus, as you can see from the last two examples, biases in inference often work together.

Order Effects in Person Perception: "The First Time Ever I Saw Your Face"

A friend of yours is going on a job interview tomorrow. He has spent hours choosing the right suit to wear and deciding what brand of aftershave to use. Standing in front of a mirror, he rehearses the words "Hello, it's good to meet you" over and over again. You ask him why he is going through these torturous procedures. He reminds you of the conventional wisdom that first impres-

sions are what count. So, instead of thinking about all the things that he should know for his interview, he is concentrating on what happens up to the time he says hello. You remind him that the popular wisdom also suggests the importance of leaving a favorable impression; the last impression that the interviewer will get about him is based on what happens at the end of the interview. You remind him how, on a recent blind date, he was obsessed with the way he would say goodbye, not hello!

Primacy Effects: The Importance of First Impressions

Social psychologists are extremely interested in how impressions of people are formed. In addition to outlining the rules that a person uses to infer people's dispositions from their behavior, social psychologists are interested in the effect of the order in which the impressions are formed. Whenever the conventional wisdom about a social phenomenon is self-contradictory, we should not be surprised to find evidence supporting both points of view. As we shall see, there is evidence to support the importance that your friend attaches to first impressions, and there is also evidence to support the conventional wisdom of "recency."

In the pioneering investigation in this area, Solomon Asch (1946) used a very simple procedure. Subjects were shown a list of six adjectives that described a hypothetical person. Each of the adjectives was related to a stable disposition of that person, so the subjects did not have to infer disposition from behavior. The hypothetical person was described as (1) intelligent, (2) industrious, (3) impulsive, (4) critical, (5) stubborn, and (6) envious. You might try to do what half of the subjects were asked to do—form an impression of this hypothetical person. The other half of Asch's subjects also had to form an impression of the person, but they were given the list of six adjectives in the *reverse* order: (1) envious, (2) stubborn, (3) critical, (4) impulsive, (5) industrious, and (6) intelligent. Do you see a difference between a person who is described with adjectives that run from good to bad and a person who is described with adjectives that run from bad to good? Asch's subjects did. The order of presentation made an important difference in the impressions that the subjects formed of the hypothetical person. The subjects who read the intelligent → envious list rated the person as more sociable, humorous, and happy than did the subjects who read the envious → intelligent list.

The results were evidence for a **primacy effect** in forming impressions. The adjectives read first seemed to have more weight than the adjectives that came later. Why should this be? Typically, we remember more recent events better than earlier ones. So why should adjectives that are read first be more influential than those that come later? Asch provided an interesting hypothesis. He contended that the order of trait adjectives is important because the meaning of the later adjectives is changed by that of the earlier adjectives. We might call this the *assimilation of meaning* hypothesis. According to this reasoning, an impression is formed by virtue of the early trait descriptions. As soon as we say that a person is intelligent, we are forming a general impression of that person. The later terms *stubborn* and *envious* take on a meaning that is consistent with that first impression. So the intelligent person who is later described as stubborn may be seen as persevering. However, the stubborn person who is later described as intelligent may be viewed more as a spoiled brat than as a persevering intellectual. Again, it is the meaning of the later information that is assimilated to (changed toward) the meaning of the earlier information.

Because Asch provided subjects with a list of adjectives, his study might be viewed as a rather artificial situation that has as much to do with linguistic memory as with the perception of persons. A later study of Luchins (1957b) provided further support for a primacy effect in a different type of situation. Subjects read a story that described the behavior of a boy named Jim. In one paragraph, Jim was described as an outgoing, affable person. For example:

> Jim left the house to get some stationery. He walked out into the sun-filled street with two of his friends. . . . Jim entered the stationery store, which was full of people. Jim talked with an acquaintance while he waited for the clerk to catch his eye. On his way out, he met the girl to whom he had been introduced the night before. They talked for a short while, and then Jim left for school.

Another paragraph described Jim somewhat differently.

After school, Jim left the classroom alone. . . . The street was brilliantly filled with sunshine. Jim walked down the street on the shady side. Coming down the street toward him, he saw the pretty girl whom he had met the previous evening. Jim crossed the street and entered a candy store. . . . Jim waited quietly until the counterman caught his eye and then gave his order. Taking his drink, he sat down at a side table. When he had finished his drink, he went home.

Subjects who read only the first paragraph saw Jim as a highly extraverted, sociable person. Those who read only the second paragraph saw him as a quiet, introverted person. The interesting question was how subjects who read *both* paragraphs would rate him. As we might expect from Asch's (1946) study, the order in which the paragraphs were read made the critical difference. Subjects who read the extravert paragraph and then the introvert paragraph saw Jim as much more outgoing and sociable than did subjects who read the paragraphs in the reverse order.

Luchins believed that the first paragraph does produce a mind-set that affects the reading of the second paragraph. For example, if we formed the first impression that Jim is gregarious, then we might interpret the events of the second paragraph as having more to do with a temporary state of Jim's health (he had a headache) than with Jim's stable disposition.

 ### *Primacy in Success and Failure*

An interesting experiment that was less abstract than either Asch's or Luchins's was conducted by Jones and his colleagues (1968b). Their subjects observed a stimulus person performing a test of intellectual ability. The test that this person was taking looked much like a standard college aptitude test (such as the SAT) and contained 30 multiple-choice items. In all conditions, the stimulus person answered 15 questions correctly. But in

availability bias   The tendency of a stimulus that comes easily or quickly to mind to be seen as the cause of an event.

primacy effect   The tendency of information received first to be more influential than information received later.

representativeness bias   The tendency to assume that a person who shares some characteristics of a group probably belongs to that group.

one condition, after starting off like the proverbial "house on fire" on the first few items, she trailed off into mediocrity. In another condition, the stimulus person started poorly but then improved considerably. The patterning of correct responses in the latter (ascending) condition was the mirror image of the patterning in the former (descending) condition.

At the end of the study, the subjects were asked to predict how well the stimulus person would do on the next series of 30 problems, and to rate the person's intelligence. Although both the ascending and the descending overall performances were the same, the stimulus person in the descending condition (who started well and then trailed off) was rated as more intelligent than the stimulus person in the ascending condition. In addition, subjects predicted that the person with the descending performance would do better on the next set of items than the person with the ascending performance.

This study offers strong evidence of a primacy effect and also indicates the potentially insidious manner in which primacy effects can influence our judgments of people. Both test takers were equal in their overall performance, yet one was seen as brighter than the other. The only difference between them was the way in which the observer processed the information received— that is, by giving more weight to earlier information. Consider the consequences that such a primacy effect might have in a classroom. Students who start poorly at the beginning of a semester but show improvement at the end of the semester may still be rated as less intelligent than students who start well. And consider the implications for a student of whom first impressions are formed before he enters the classroom. Suppose that he is a student from a minority group and that the commonly held stereotype is that members of his group are not intelligent and cannot learn. Suppose, too, that despite the growing evidence that standardized tests unfairly discriminate against minority cultures (see Kamin, 1974), those scores are used to show that the minority group student has less ability than other students in the class. The results of the study by Jones and his associates indicate that it is very difficult for the student to do anything to rectify fully the impression that the teacher may already have. If the student succeeds, to what will the success be attributed? Combining the findings of this study with attribution principles, we can predict that success that is inconsistent with the first impression may be seen as unstable and then attributed either to an unusual expenditure of effort or to luck.

Some Evidence for Recency

It would defy common experience if we did not have evidence that supported the importance of last impressions. On some occasions the powerful effect of primacy can be broken and even reversed. If the idea that later information is tuned out has merit, then asking subjects to recall all of the descriptive traits about a person before forming a final impression should reduce the primacy effect. Anderson and Hubert (1963) led some subjects to believe that their memory for the traits listed would be tested. They found evidence that, under this condition, the more recent traits were more important in forming a final impression. In another study, Stewart (1965) showed that when people were asked to form a separate judgment about a stimulus person after each presentation of a trait adjective, the effect of the undue weight of the early information was eliminated. These studies provide convincing evidence of a **recency effect**; that is, the tendency of an impression based on the information most recently gained to outweigh an impression based on information gained earlier.

In addition, Luchins (1957a) found that a simple instruction (warning of the dangers of first impressions) weakened the primacy effect that had been obtained with the two paragraphs about Jim that we reprinted above. Even more effective in reducing the primacy effect in the story of Jim was increasing the time between the presentation of the two paragraphs. Luchins found that the greater the time that elapsed between the presentation of the two paragraphs, the more the final judgment of Jim depended on the second paragraph rather than the first. As time lengthened, the material presented in the first paragraph was probably increasingly forgotten.

In general, though, the bulk of the evidence appears to be on the side of your friend who was concerned with his first impression in an upcoming job interview. It is certainly not true that later

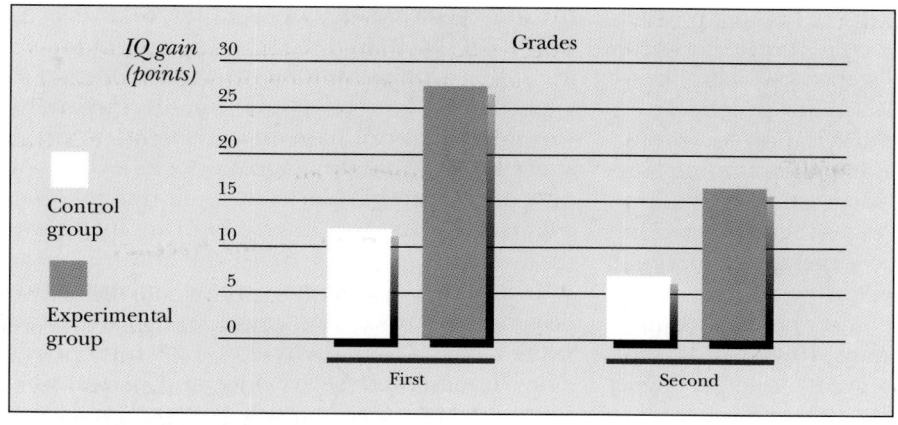

FIGURE 2-1   Gains in total IQ for children in first and second grades.
SOURCE: Rosenthal and Jacobson (1968).

information has *no* effect on the final impression formed, but the evidence does appear to favor the position that early attributions influence total judgments more than later attributions do.

Some Consequences of Forming Impressions: The Self-Fulfilling Prophecy

When we form impressions of people, we tend to act in ways that perpetuate those impressions. In Kelley's (1950) study of warm and cold guest lecturers, students tended to act in a distant fashion to the instructor who they believed would be cold. Undoubtedly, in a situation in which the instructor was not a confederate, the distant manner of the student would have encouraged behaviors in the teacher that would confirm the student's impression that the teacher was a cold person.

Some interesting research has been done on the consequences of believing information about others. In a famous study, Rosenthal and Jacobson (1968) told elementary school teachers that some of the children in their classrooms could be expected to show dramatic spurts in academic performance during the school year. It was alleged

that such information was based on the reliable Harvard Test of Inflected Acquisition. In truth, there was no such test, and approximately one-third of the students were chosen at random to be designated as spurters. At the end of the school year, the children's IQs were measured. Figure 2-1 depicts the results for the children in the first and second grades. Those students who had been designated as spurters actually showed a marked gain in their IQ scores over the year—even though their designation as spurters bore no relation to any legitimate test.

Like Henry Higgins in George Bernard Shaw's play *Pygmalion*, the teachers apparently created the person they expected to find. The possible implications of this research were startling. Is long-term academic achievement largely a function of biased expectations? The Rosenthal and Jacobson study thus drew the attention of many social psychologists and policy makers.

Rosenthal and Jacobson's work has drawn considerable criticism. Questions have been directed at the intelligence instrument they used (Fleming & Anttonen, 1971; Snow, 1969), at the way they used it (Jensen, 1969), and at their analyses of the data they obtained (Elashoff & Snow,

---

recency effect   The tendency of an impression based on the information most recently gained to outweigh an impression based on information gained earlier.

1971). In addition, differences between boys and girls in the various grades and differences between various subtests of the intelligence scale have been embarrassing for the study's major conclusion.

Despite all of these very important problems, Rosenthal and Jacobson's main finding has withstood the test of time. More than 100 studies have examined the effects of teacher expectation (Brophy, 1982). Systematic **expectancy effects,** or **self-fulfilling prophecies,** were found in middle-class schools in the East and West (Conn et al., 1968; Rosenthal & Evans, 1968). Anderson and Rosenthal (1968) observed the expectancy effect in a class of mentally retarded boys, and Michenbaum, Bowers, and Ross (1969) reported it in a study that systematically varied behavioral and academic expectancies in an Ontario training school for female offenders.

What produces these expectancy effects? Recent research suggests that four factors are important: *climate, feedback, input,* and *output* (Harris & Rosenthal, 1985; Rosenthal, 1973). According to the theory that explains these research findings, teachers provide a warmer climate for students whom they expect to do well. The warmth is conveyed both verbally and nonverbally. Second, teachers give more careful, detailed feedback to students for whom they have high expectations. These students are given more guidance about what they should and should not do. Third, teachers give these students more input; that is, more instruction and explanation about learning materials. Finally, high-expectancy students are given more opportunity for output. They have more time to ask and answer questions and more opportunities to learn how to produce.

The characteristics of people who hold either positive or negative expectations are critical in determining whether these expectations become self-fulfilling prophecies. Teachers who are biased against students because of negative expectations tend to "leak" nonverbal negative feelings about such children through face and body signals at the same time that they are communicating positive feelings verbally (Babad, Bernieri & Rosenthal, 1989). In general, people who create self-fulfilling prophecies are highly expressive nonverbally, and, not surprisingly, students who are most sensitive to nonverbal communications are the most affected by them (Cooper & Hazelrigg, 1988).

Other studies have shown that the impact of expectations is not felt only in the classroom. Consider what can happen in a job interview. A study by Word, Zanna, and Cooper (1974) took note of the fact that black job applicants are often reported to perform less well during interviews than white applicants. Using the analysis of the self-fulfilling prophecy, these investigators designed a study in two stages. In the first stage, white subjects took the role of a job interviewer. They interviewed both white and black applicants. Unknown to the subjects, the applicants were carefully trained confederates who had rehearsed their answers to all the questions to be asked during the interview. When the interview took place, therefore, there was no objective difference between the verbal and nonverbal performances of the black and white applicants.

The investigators were actually observing the behavior of the *interviewers.* It was found that their interviews with white applicants lasted longer and that in those interviews there was a significant increase in the behaviors that Mehrabian (1968) has labeled "immediacy." White applicants received greater eye contact, greater forward body lean, and other responses that are usually associated with positive interactions.

In the second phase of the study, white subjects served as applicants and carefully trained confederates served as interviewers. The trained interviewers responded to half of the applicants with precisely the behaviors that had been afforded to the black applicants in the first stage of the study. That is, they responded with low-immediacy behaviors. The other half of the applicants received the high-immediacy behaviors that had been afforded to the white applicants in the first stage.

At the end of the second-stage interview, independent judges rated the performance of the applicants. Those applicants who were treated as the black applicants had been treated in the first stage (low-immediacy behaviors) performed considerably worse in the second-stage interview. And those applicants also reported feeling worse about themselves at the end of the interview. Thus, starting with some assumptions about the way in which blacks would perform on a job interview, the interviewers had acted in a way (with low-immediacy behaviors) that was sufficient to produce poor performance in such an interview.

Expectations also play an important role in everyday interpersonal relationships. They affect not only the behavior of the people who have the expectancies but also the behavior of the people who hold the expectancies. Male and female college students who had been led to believe that another person liked them behaved in a way that led them to be liked. They expressed less dissimilarity, disagreed less, spoke in a more positive tone of voice, and expressed overall a more positive attitude than students who thought the other person disliked them. In short, people who thought that others had positive or negative impressions of them behaved in ways that confirmed those impressions (Curtis & Miller, 1986). Another study has shown that some people who initially believe they rank low in sociability improve their self-perception if they interact with someone who thinks they are high in sociability and acts accordingly (Major et al., 1988).

How can we keep our expectations from becoming self-fulfilling prophecies? If we enter an interaction with the goal of discovering whether the people we are interacting with actually have the characteristics we expect, we will often find that our expectations are incorrect and change them (Darley et al., 1988). Thus we are less likely to make our expectation self-fulfilling. Also, if we simply enter an interaction with the goal of forming an accurate impression, even if we have a negative expectation, we are less likely to behave in ways that elicit negative performances from the other person. When we are open-minded and objective ourselves, we are less likely to convey a negative bias and disrupt the other person's behavior (Neuberg, 1989).

As Darley and Fazio (1980) have noted, the self-fulfilling prophecy is just one of the possible outcomes of our day-to-day social interactions. It is a particularly intriguing phenomenon, however, because the individuals involved are seldom aware that the expectancy of one has substantially influenced the behavior of the other. As the research we have discussed indicates, the potential for misunderstanding and perpetuation of bias among social participants is great.

STOP, THINK, & UNDERSTAND

1. Explain a study showing how schemata affect impressions and a study showing how they affect memory.

2. How can priming affect perception, behavior, and memory?

3. How does the availability bias contribute to the formation of illusory correlations?

4. What two studies show that people often demonstrate primacy effects in perceiving other people?

5. How do teachers' expectations affect students' performances?

Summary

Attribution is the process of deciding whether behavior was caused by a personal disposition of the actor or external situational forces. One of the principles we follow in making attributions is the *subtractive rule,* which states that we should subtract the situational inducements from the personal disposition implied by the behavior. If the situational inducement may have contributed to the behavior, the role of disposition should be discounted. If the situational inducement actually inhibits the behavior, the role of disposition should be augmented.

If we observe multiple behaviors, we can consider other factors necessary for making *internal* (person) or *external* (entity) *attributions* for behaviors. Observers of other people's behavior consider the distinctiveness, the consensus, and the consistency of that behavior. Low distinctiveness,

---

expectancy effect (self-fulfilling prophecy) The tendency of expectations in regard to a person's behavior or performance to be realized because of the climate, feedback, input, and opportunities for output that such expectations create; a self-fulfilling prophecy.

low consensus, and high consistency lead to internal attributions.

Psychologists have stressed the importance of considering factors beyond internal or external causes. In judging success and failure, for example, we often judge whether a cause is stable, controllable, and global. When we consider whether success or failure is caused by internal or external factors, we attribute performance to ability, luck, effort, or the difficulty of the task.

Attribution researchers have discovered a number of biases in the way people make attributions. The *correspondence bias,* or *fundamental attribution error,* is the tendency to attribute behavior to corresponding internal dispositions rather than to external factors. The *saliency bias* is the tendency to attribute behavior to salient or easily noticeable possible causes. *Defensive attribution* occurs when an observer feels threatened by a misfortune that befalls another person and blames that person for his or her misfortune.

A *schema* is a general body of knowledge about a person, object, or event. A closely related concept is that of *script,* the sequence of events we have come to expect in a given situation. We tend to interpret information consistently with our schemata and scripts, and to recall information that is consistent with them. Incongruent information is also well recalled when people take the time to think about its meaning.

Priming occurs when specific ideas are activated through recent or frequent use. When we have been primed by information, so that it is on our minds, it can affect our memory for people's behavior. In making inferences about other people, individuals make many errors. They underuse or ignore *base-rate data,* let irrelevant information affect an inference *(dilution effect),* and perceive *illusory correlations*. In addition, people are prey to the *availability bias,* judging the likelihood of events by the ease with which they come to mind; and the *representativeness bias,* assuming that people belong to a group if they have characteristics similar to those of typical members of the group.

Research on first impressions shows that we are often most affected by the early information we get about other people, thereby showing a *primacy effect*. Other research shows that *recency effects* can occur—that is, information gained recently can more strongly color our impressions than information gained earlier—if we are cautioned about jumping to conclusions or are required to think about and remember all the information we have received.

The impressions that people form of others have implications for the way those others act. Rosenthal and Jacobson are among researchers who have demonstrated the effect of the *expectancy effect,* or the *self-fulfilling prophecy*. In their research, schoolchildren whose teachers expected them to perform well actually performed better than did students for whom teachers had no favorable expectation. This phenomenon has been shown to apply to job applicants of different racial groups.

Key Terms

attribution	*disposition*	*priming*
augmentation principle	*entity attribution*	*recency effect*
availability bias	*expectancy effect (self-*	*representativeness bias*
base-rate information	*fulfilling prophecy)*	*saliency bias*
correspondence bias	*external attribution*	*schema*
(fundamental	*illusory correlation*	*script*
attribution error)	*internal attribution*	*social cognition*
defensive attribution	*person attribution*	*subtractive rule*
dilution effect	*primacy effect*	

Suggested Readings

Fiske, S. T., & Taylor, S. E. (1984). *Social cognition*. Reading, Mass.: Addison-Wesley.

Heider, F. (1958). *The psychology of interpersonal relations*. New York: Wiley.

Higgins, E. T., Herman, C. P., & Zanna, M. P. (1981). *Social cognition. The Ontario Symposium, Volume 1*. Hillsdale, N.J.: Erlbaum.

Jones, E. E., & David, K. E. (1965). "From acts to dispositions: The attribution process in person perception." In L. Berkowitz (Ed.), *Advances in experimental social psychology* (Vol. 22, pp. 219–266). New York: Academic Press.

Kelley, H. H. (1967). "Attribution theory in social psychology." *Nebraska Symposium on Motivation, 15,* 192–238.

Markus, H., & Zajonc, R. B. (1985). The cognitive perspective in social psychology. In G. Lindzey and E. Aronson (Eds.), *The handbook of social psychology* (Vol. 1, pp. 137–230). New York: Random House.

Nisbett, R., & Ross, L. (1980). *Human inference: Strategies and shortcomings of human judgments*. Englewood Cliffs, N.J.: Prentice-Hall.

Ross, M., & Fletcher, G. J. O. (1985). Attribution and social perception. In G. Lindzey and E. Aronson (Eds.), *The handbook of social psychology* (Vol. 2, pp. 73–122). New York: Random House.

Schneider, D., Hastorf, A., & Ellsworth, P. (1979). *Person perception* (2nd ed.). Reading, Mass.: Addison-Wesley.

Chapter Three

Knowing the Self

*B*riefly escaping the Southern California heat, Joan Benoit ran into the chill darkness of the Los Angeles Coliseum tunnel. When she reached the end of the passageway she would run, alone, back into the sun, out onto the track, to be greeted by the cheers of 77,000 spectators. In the cool dimness she thought, "Once you leave this tunnel your life will be changed forever" (Benoit, 1987, p. 192). Though tempted by this realization to stop, she put her head down, completed a lap around the inside of the Coliseum, and claimed a convincing victory in the first women's Olympic marathon. Joan Benoit's 1984 Olympic triumph was a highpoint in a life of achievement, honor, and generosity. While it meant the end of her privacy and solitude, it had been a cherished goal. There simply was no turning away from it.

For more than a dozen years Joan Benoit has been one of the world's top distance runners. While still a student at Bowdoin College, in her home state of Maine, she won her first Boston Marathon, setting an American and course record for women. Four years later, in 1983, she won at Boston again, this time breaking the world record by nearly three minutes. Though she came to the sport of running literally by accident, she has proven to be one of the most courageous and gifted athletes of our time.

Joan grew up in a small town in Maine as the only daughter in an athletics-minded family. Her early love was skiing. While her parents insisted that she make academics her top priority, Joan was consumed by skiing, and wanted to go to a private high school that would allow her to put athletics first. But her parents set the priorities. During World War II her father had been one of the "ski troops," a member of the Tenth Mountain Division, fighting in the Alps. Both he and Joan's mother, also a talented athlete, supported Joan's interest in skiing. At the same time, they felt that she should not let sports crowd out the other priorities in her life. But Joan pushed herself hard. Too hard. One day when she was 15, after hours of training on a slalom course, she made a wrong turn and broke her leg. Her career as a competitive skier was over. But in getting back into shape she found that she could run, and then slowly but surely she rose to the top.

After excelling in both running and field hockey in high school, Joan chose to go to Bowdoin College. Bowdoin is one of the top national liberal arts schools, and it is in her native Maine. Although very happy there, Joan left for three semesters to attend North Carolina State University in Raleigh—in order to concentrate on her running. But after a time there she realized that what her parents and professors told her, that athletics could not be everything, was true for her. She quickly returned home, to Maine and Bowdoin. And during her senior year she proudly wore her Bowdoin uniform in winning the Boston Marathon.

Bowdoin was important for another reason. It was there that she met her husband, Scott Samuelson. Joan describes the fraternity party where she first encountered him. "I saw him right away— he is so tall that I can always find him in a crowd. I can't say it was love at first sight because I know how complicated love is; there was something there, though" (Benoit, 1987, p. 90). Joan and Scott became M.D.s for each other—major distractions. And from their first meeting on, Scott has supported Joan's career, and she his.

Joan most needed support during the tumultuous months leading up to her victory in Los Angeles. After winning the 1983 Boston Marathon, making the 1984 Olympic team became her goal, the gold medal her dream. However, a series of painful and career-threatening injuries put those designs in serious jeopardy. The biggest crisis occurred just a few weeks before the Olympic trials that would select the U.S. team for Los Angeles. Joan had been having severe difficulties with her right knee. It tightened up so much that it was "a real effort to lift my right leg over a twig" (p. 176). "It was as if a spring were unraveling in the joint" (p. 173). After attempting several unsuccessful cures, Joan decided to have arthroscopic surgery on her knee a mere 17 days before she would have to compete in the Olympic trials. The surgery seemed successful, and she worked herself back into shape remarkably swiftly. Still, it was anybody's guess as to whether the knee would hold up under grueling race conditions.

On the day of the trials Joan's knee did hold up. Not only was it well enough for her to race,

Joan Benoit is a woman with a remarkable sense of herself. Her victory in the 1984 Olympic marathon represented the culmination of a life's efforts, training, and personal integrity.

it was well enough for her to win. She was crying with joy as she broke the tape. She had made the team. Then, following a carefully planned training schedule, Joan took off at the gun in the first women's Olympic marathon. The race started in Santa Monica. Joan ran with the pack for the first several miles, and then, feeling strong, raced out ahead and grabbed the lead. For the rest of the race she was alone, following the ABC television truck down the L.A. freeways. There was always

the possibility that her fast early start would break her, but she felt stronger as the race went on. Finally she reached the Coliseum, ran through the tunnel, and won the gold medal.

Despite all efforts to resist change, Joan Benoit's life has been altered by her fame. She has to think even more carefully than before about how to balance her career with the other demands, priorities, and opportunities in her life. A few months after the Olympics she married Scott

Samuelson, her first priority. But her personal life and running career also have to make room for demands by various charitable organizations. She has lent her name to such groups as the Special Olympics and the Big Sisters of Boston. In addition, she has a strong interest in environmental and international issues and gives considerable support to efforts to improve the quality of living on planet Earth.

The quality and integrity of Joan's life, and her commitment to both academics and athletics, led her alma mater to give her its prestigious Bowdoin Prize in 1985, an award given only once every five years for significant contribution. Then in 1987, along with Sir Roger Bannister, the first man to break the four-minute mile, and the late A. Bartlett Giammati, former Yale president and commissioner of baseball, Joan received an honorary degree from Williams College for her contributions to athletics and academics.

While trying to continue her running career and fulfill her ambition to be the first woman to run a marathon in less than two hours and 20 minutes, Joan has also taken on the responsibilities of motherhood. A daughter was born in 1987, and 1990 brought the Samuelsons a second child. Joan is still battling injuries and faces unknown challenges when she decides, sadly for all those who have admired her sportsmanship, to stop running competitively. One day she may go to medical school, though that is uncertain. Whatever the future holds for her, Joan is sustained by a deep faith that God meant it to be. The world is enriched by Joan Benoit, and the authors of this book are grateful for her willingness to discuss with us and with you, our readers, aspects of her own self-concept and the ways she has grown to know herself.

Knowing the Self

In many respects, Joan Benoit has a clear idea of who she is. She is a runner, a wife, a mother, a concerned citizen, and much more. Yet she is uncertain how to balance her various roles, how she will cope with life after competitive athletics, and how she will combine public demands with her strong desire for privacy and peace of mind.

Where does an individual acquire a sense of self? How do we know what we believe, how well we can perform, and, generally speaking, what kind of person we are? In this chapter on self-perception, we will start to answer these questions. Social psychologists have discovered a great deal about the ways we know ourselves and how we evaluate ourselves. We will begin by considering how our self-concept emerges from our interactions with other people. Then we will consider the way we make attributions about ourselves on the basis of our behavior. We will also consider important applications of research on self-perception and the ways in which self-perception can be biased.

Social Interaction and Self-Conception

We learn who we are through all our experiences in the world, especially our interactions with other people. One of the founders of psychology, William James (1890), wrote nearly a century ago of the fact that our sense of who we are, of "me," is derived from our experiences with others. For example, we learn that we are polite when an uncle or aunt compliments our behavior; or that we are a good speller by finding out that we got the highest score in the class. One way we learn about ourselves from social interaction is by finding out what other people think of us. Throughout our lives, we are influenced by other people's opinions about everything from how cold it is outside to whether our national government should allow prayer in the schools. Our self-concepts are no exception. We are impressed by what other people think of us. The process of perceiving what we are like, and feeling that we are good or bad on the basis of what other people think of us, has been called **reflected appraisal** (Gergen, 1971). It is one of the most important processes affecting our self-concept.

Reflected Appraisal

The term *reflected appraisal* refers to the idea that how we appraise ourself reflects, or mirrors, how others appraise us. Charles Horton Cooley (1902) talked about this concept many years ago; he called

We learn to see ourselves as others see us and as we imagine how others see us. Do you think others see the person you see when you look in the mirror?

it the looking-glass self. Cooley said that we always imagine what others think of us, and what we think they think about us affects our own self-evaluation. A few years later, George Herbert Mead (1934) used the same idea. He said that we pay close attention to the opinion of us that is implied in the behavior of "significant others," that is, important other people, such as parents and friends. Furthermore, we come to think of ourselves in terms of the opinion that their behavior implies. Again, our self-concept reflects what others seem to think of us.

A recent study of fourth- through eighth-grade children shows that imagined appraisals of parents do affect self-appraisals, even though these imagined or reflected appraisals are frequently inaccurate (Felson, 1989). That is, what we imagine our parents, or other significant people in our lives, think of us may not be what they actually think. But that reflected appraisal has an impact nevertheless. Furthermore, when another person's appraisal is brought to mind, it can affect our feelings and behavior. Women college students were asked to visualize the faces of either two fellow students or two older members of their families. Then they read a sexually explicit piece of fiction, and indicated how much they

enjoyed it. The students who had been asked to visualize older members of their family, and presumably were imagining how those family members would react to their enjoyment of pornographic material, rated the fiction as much less enjoyable than those who were imagining their peers (Baldwin & Holmes, 1987). Finally, in a study of reflected appraisals and behavior, schoolchildren who were told that they were tidy actually littered less on the school grounds than students who were told nothing or than those who were told that they *should* be neat. Thus people made to feel neat actually *acted* that way. The results were even more impressive when littering was measured after two weeks had passed (Miller, Brickman & Bolen, 1975).

These two studies and other research on reflected appraisal show how much we can be affected by our social interactions with others. Perhaps, though, we would do well to remember that we know a great deal about ourselves that others do not know, and that we shouldn't let ourselves be too greatly affected by what others

reflected appraisal   A view of the self based on other people's appraisals.

For a game to be truly competitive, persons playing must be of comparable ability. Besides ability, on what other dimensions do we compare and evaluate ourselves?

think. Joan Benoit, for example, maintained an independent and modest appraisal of her own abilities as an athlete and a student during her college years, even though responses from others clearly mattered as well. Reflected appraisal is powerful but not all-powerful.

Social Comparison

Another way we learn about ourselves during social interaction is through the **social comparison** process. We can evaluate our ability in math or tennis, for example, by comparing our performances with those of other people, and we can evaluate our opinion of a movie or a presidential candidate by comparing our opinions with those of other people. Joan Benoit evaluates her running capacity in part by the way she compares with other gifted runners, such as Ingrid Kristiansen and Grete Waitz. Leon Festinger, one of our most distinguished social psychologists, developed a theory of social comparison processes that outlines how comparison with other people affects our self-evaluations (Festinger, 1954). Inspired by Festinger's original theory, other researchers have explored social comparison in detail (Goethals & Darley, 1987; Suls & Wills, 1990).

Research on the way people describe themselves illustrates the importance of social comparison. When they are asked to respond to the question "Who am I?" people answer by mentioning ways in which they differ from others, ways in which they are unique. For example, fourth-grade children who were asked to describe themselves mentioned whether they were male or female more often if they came from homes where their gender was in the minority (McGuire & McGuire, 1981). So if you are the only boy in your family, being male makes you distinctive and becomes part of your self-concept. Similarly, people are likely to mention their race or ethnicity if that characteristic makes them distinct; or they are apt to mention being tall or heavy if those qualities are distinctive (McGuire et al., 1978; McGuire & Padawer-Singer, 1976). In short, people's sense of who they are depends on the ways they are distinctive in comparison with others.

Another study shows that our overall self-evaluation (that is, our self-esteem) is affected by social comparison (Morse & Gergen, 1970). Subjects who came to apply for a job as a research assistant in a college research center encountered someone, actually a confederate of the experiment, who posed as another job applicant: the confederate presented himself as either Mr. Clean or Mr. Dirty. Mr. Clean was immaculately dressed, seemed serious and well prepared, and acted sophisticated and well read. Mr. Dirty seemed sloppy, confused, and disinterested. Subjects filled out questionnaires that measured their self-esteem both before and after meeting Mr. Clean or Mr. Dirty. The results showed that people evaluated themselves in comparison with the other applicant. Their self-esteem rose when the other was Mr. Dirty, who seemed less well qualified, and it fell if the other was Mr. Clean, who seemed better qualified. Both the traits or characteristics that we feel define us and how favorably we evaluate ourselves are affected by comparison with other people.

The similarity and related attributes hypotheses

One of the central hypotheses of social comparison theory is the **similarity hypothesis,** which suggests that we choose to compare ourselves with people who are similar to us. For example, if we want to evaluate our tennis-playing ability, we need to compete against other people whose performance level is about the same as our own to find out just how good we are. Research shows that we usually compare ourselves either with similar others or with people who are slightly better than we are. We strive to become better and better (Festinger called this the *unidirectional drive upward*), so we want to see how well we compare with others whose performance level is slightly above ours (Wheeler, 1966; Wheeler, Koestner & Driver, 1982). When she hadn't yet held the world record herself, Joan Benoit always compared her own marathon times with those of the record holder.

It is important to note an exception to the tendency to compare ourselves with similar people. When we evaluate *opinions* we sometimes compare our opinions with those of people who are very different from us (Gorenflo & Crano, 1989). We sometimes feel that if people who do not share our biases agree with us, we must be correct, and we find their agreement extremely gratifying (Goethals, 1972; Orive, 1988).

The **related attributes hypothesis** holds that we compare ourselves not only with others whose performance is similar to ours but also with people whose performance level *should* be similar to ours, given their standing on performance-related attributes (Goethals & Darley, 1977). By comparing ourselves with people who are similar in respect to related attributes, we can most accurately assess our ability. For example, if you wanted to compare your basketball-playing ability, you would learn the most by comparing your playing with that of others of the same sex, of roughly the same age, and with about the same amount of recent practice. In that way, if your performance is better, you know that the reason is your greater ability rather than the fact that you are in better shape or have been working like mad to improve your game. Similarly, Joan Benoit, feeling that having a child could affect her performance, finds Ingrid Kristiansen, also a mother, a more appropriate comparison person than Grete Waitz, who has not had a child.

The related attributes hypothesis also applies to opinion evaluation. We should compare our opinion about President Bush's performance in office with the opinions of other Americans rather than those of Russians, and with Americans who share our political philosophy. Knowing that you disagree with a Russian only tells you that the two of you have dissimilar points of view. You need to know how your opinion compares with that of someone whose opinions should be similar to yours.

A great deal of research supports the related attributes hypothesis (Suls, Gaes & Gastorf, 1979; Wheeler & Koestner, 1984). One study showed that when people felt that sex was related to performance on a test, they wanted to compare their performance with that of other people of the same sex (Zanna, Goethals & Hill, 1975). Men

---

related attributes hypothesis   In social comparison theory, the hypothesis that we evaluate our opinions and abilities by comparing them with those of people whose opinions and performance should be similar to ours, given their standing on characteristics related to opinion and performance.

similarity hypothesis   The hypothesis that we evaluate ourselves by comparing our opinions and abilities with those of other people who are similar to us.

social comparison   The process whereby individuals reduce uncertainty about their opinions, abilities, and emotions by observing those of similar others.

sought to learn the scores of men to assess the adequacy of their performance while women wanted to compare themselves with women.

Although the related attributes hypothesis has strong support, research also shows that we want to compare ourselves with people who are similar to us on such salient characteristics as physical attractiveness and sex even when those characteristics are not specifically related to the ability or opinion being evaluated (Miller, 1982, 1984). Furthermore, we like to compare ourselves with others with whom we share an identity or bond, or those who are similar to us in ways that make us both distinct (Miller, Turnbull & McFarland, 1988). For example, Joan Benoit compares herself with Ingrid Kristiansen not only because they are mothers, and having a child could affect performance, but also because the two of them are very similar and distinct in lifestyle and interests. Unlike many other runners, for example, they both feel that running is important for them, but that it is not everything.

Downward comparison and self-evaluation maintenance

While we generally compare ourselves with people who are similar or slightly superior to us, at times we engage in **downward comparison**: we compare ourselves with people who are inferior to us or worse off than we are. Downward comparison makes us feel better about ourselves because it allows us to feel that even if we have negative traits, others have them to a far greater degree (Wills, 1981). Research shows that when depressed people are feeling especially blue, they compare themselves with people who are suffering, and feel better after they have done so (Gibbons, 1986). Downward comparison is most likely to occur after we have failed or if we have low self-esteem (Smith & Insko, 1987). But we don't always compare ourselves with people whose fate is worse than our own when we want to feel better. One study showed that people facing coronary bypass surgery preferred to have a hospital roommate who had been through the operation rather than one who was waiting for it (Kulik & Mahler, 1989). In a case like this, our desire to believe that we will survive the trauma leads us to compare ourselves with people who have already done so.

The principle of downward comparison shows that not all of our social comparison choices are designed for objective self-evaluation: often we make comparisons to validate ourselves as well (Gruder, 1977). Efforts to show that we are as good as people who are superior and very different from people who are inferior demonstrate the self-validating or **self-serving bias.** They reflect our desire to evaluate ourselves positively. Sometimes that desire leads us to engage in "active" downward comparison, actually denigrating or harming others so that we can feel good in comparison with them (Wills, 1981).

Our desire to evaluate ourselves positively sometimes leads to more constructive behavior than downward comparison. The theory of **self-evaluation maintenance** suggests that people are upset when close friends outperform them on tasks that are important for their self-definitions (Tesser, 1988; Tesser, Millar & Moore, 1988). If your piano-playing ability is less than that of a friend and you pride yourself on that ability, you may try to improve your performance level to maintain your self-evaluation. On the other hand, if piano playing isn't important to your self-definition, you will maintain your self-evaluation by closely associating with your talented friend and basking in her reflected glory. Consistent with the principles of downward comparison, studies on self-evaluation maintenance also show that people don't always try to improve their performance level to maintain their self-evaluation. Sometimes they denigrate the other person's performance or actually try to interfere with it. Thus the desire to compare favorably can lead to both constructive efforts at self-improvement and destructive efforts to undermine others.

False consensus estimates

We sometimes make estimates about how other people's opinions or behaviors compare with our own in ways that make us feel good about ourselves, and we then ignore social comparison information that shows that perhaps we are wrong. For example, several studies show what is known as the **false consensus effect.** *False consensus* refers to a tendency to overestimate the number of people who agree with our opinions or behave as we do (Ross, 1977; Mullen et al., 1985). If we overestimate the number of people who agree with us, we can evaluate our opinion as correct. And if we overestimate the number of people who do what we do, we can feel that our actions are appropriate. One study of false consensus judgments asked college students whether they would be willing to walk around campus wearing a sign that said "Eat at Joe's." Those who agreed to wear the sign thought that most other people would wear it, specifically, 62% of the others. Those who said no thought that only 33% would wear the sign and that 67% would say no (Ross, Greene & House, 1977). Each group felt that it had made the appropriate choice and assumed that others had done the same. Other research shows that when people are given comparison information showing that their consensus estimates are wrong, that other people don't agree as much as they thought, they ignore this information unless it is very clear and simple (Goethals, 1986a).

Not all self-serving consensus estimates inflate the number of people who act as we do. If we do something that isn't clearly good or bad, such as wearing a sign saying "Eat at Joe's," we may be prompted to believe that most other people will do the same. Further, if we do something negative, we may want to think that most others will do the same so that we can feel that we aren't so bad. On the other hand, if we do something positive, we may want to think that our behavior is distinctive (Mullen & Goethals, in press). Hence we may underestimate the number of people who would do the same thing. Several studies show that if people make a desirable choice, such as helping someone in trouble, giving blood, or leaving the larger piece of pizza for their friend, they underestimate the number of others who would do the same (Goethals, 1986a). In general, when it comes to positive traits, people show a **uniqueness bias,** seeing their own strengths and abilities as being unusual (Campbell, 1986; Goethals, Messick & Allison, 1990). One interesting manifestation of people's tendency to see themselves as uniquely good is that sexually active college women see themselves as less likely than similar women to have an unwanted pregnancy. Consequently, they tend not to use effective methods of birth control (Burger & Burns, 1988).

Self-Attribution

Having considered how the processes of reflected appraisal and social comparison affect our self-

concept, let us now explore the important role that attribution processes play in self-knowledge and self-perception. The basic notion behind theories of self-attribution is that we can make attributions about our own behavior in the same ways we make them about other people's behavior. For example, a person might use the criteria of distinctiveness, consistency, and consensus (see Chapter 2) to decide whether his roommate's interest in chemistry is attributable to the roommate's personality or to chemistry itself. You could use the same principle to decide whether your admiration for the movie *Driving Miss Daisy* is attributable to your own unique tastes and interests (you like relaxing, sentimental movies) or to the fact that the movie really was good. You would use the same criteria of distinctiveness (Do you like other movies?), consistency (Did you like the movie as much the second time?), and consensus (Did other people enjoy the movie?).

Another attribution theory that can be applied to your own behavior as well as that of other people is Weiner's theory of attributions of success and failure. People make attributions in regard to their own successes and failures just as they do in regard to others'. They decide that their own success is due to great ability, extra effort, or good luck. Joan Benoit attributed her victory in the Olympics in 1984 to her own hard work but also to the support of her doctors, her husband-to-be, her family, and, to some degree, God's will.

Although the attribution theories we considered earlier can generally be applied to self-attribution, several attribution theories apply *only* to the self. We will consider them now.

---

downward comparison Comparison with people who are worse off than we so that we may feel better by contrast.

false consensus effect The tendency to overestimate the number of people who think and act as we do.

self-evaluation maintenance Upholding of self-evaluation by constructive efforts to improve oneself or destructive efforts to undermine others.

self-perception theory (see p. 76) The theory that people infer their own attitudes and feelings from their behaviors and the situations in which they take place.

self-serving bias A tendency to try to show that we are as good as people who are superior and very different from people who are inferior.

uniqueness bias A tendency to see one's own strengths and abilities as unusual.

Self-Perception Theory

One of the most provocative theories of self-attribution is known as **self-perception theory** (Bem, 1972). Self-perception theory considers the way we perceive our own attitudes and preferences. It argues that just as we would infer that our friend likes rock music because he listens to it whenever he has a chance, so we infer that we like country music from our own behavior. We notice that when we are in the car we are most likely to push the button that brings in the local country station. All this sounds reasonable enough—but isn't something missing? Don't we just *know* whether we like country music? Must we infer that we do? Self-perception theory says we don't "just know," that we don't have a very good idea of how we feel about things on the basis of our feelings alone. We *really* learn what we like or dislike from our behavior.

Here are the basic principles of self-perception theory: First, self-perception is simply a special case of social cognition in which we rather than others are the objects of perception. That is, we perceive ourselves in exactly the same way as we perceive others. Second, we learn about our attitudes, preferences, and feelings by considering two things: our behavior and the situation in which it took place. The most important aspect of the situation that must be taken into account is whether there are situational constraints that explain the behavior. For example, if you listen to the country station because your sister begs you to turn it on, you would not infer that you like country music; your sister's pressure explains your behavior. The discounting principle, discussed in Chapter 2, leads you to discount your own attitude as a cause of your behavior because your sister's begging explains why you listened. Only when our behavior is freely chosen do we infer that it reflects our attitudes or feelings. But the basic idea is the most important one. We infer our attitudes and feelings, internal characteristics, from external information, our behavior, which we consider along with the forces in the situation. As the British novelist E. M. Forster said many years ago, "How can I tell what I think 'til I see what I say?"

Considerable evidence supports self-perception theory. First, we know that people internalize roles. The fact that people actually do define themselves in accordance with the behavior specified by their roles supports self-perception theory. One interesting and subtle example of role internalization is the finding that professional football and ice hockey teams that wear black uniforms actually play more aggressively, as measured by numbers of penalties. (Frank & Gilovich, 1988). Black is associated with evil and death in many cultures, and black uniforms become a cue for athletes to adopt an aggressive role and thereby see themselves as aggressive persons. Second, several experiments illustrate important aspects of inferring feelings and attitudes from behavior. For example, in one study subjects listening to a tape recording were distracted by noises that were too low to notice. They observed that they were not paying attention to the recording and actually experienced boredom (Damrad-Frye & Laird, 1989). Because they didn't realize that their inattention was due to an external distraction, they inferred that it must be due to boredom. In another study subjects had to summarize a description of one individual's personality for a second person who either liked or disliked that individual. Not surprisingly, people responded to the second person's expectations and made their summary more positive or more negative depending on that person's feelings about the first individual. What is surprising is that subjects reported liking the person more if they had described him positively than if they had described him negatively (Higgins & Rholes, 1978). Further, they felt that they had freely chosen to describe the person somewhat positively or negatively and they perceived their attitudes by inferring them from their behavior.

There is also evidence that our descriptions of ourselves can be a basis for inferring what we actually think of ourselves. In one study subjects were induced to describe themselves to an interviewer in either very modest or very flattering terms. On a later test of self-esteem, subjects who had described themselves positively actually felt more positive about themselves while those who had been modest felt more negative. Consistent with self-perception theory, these effects on self-esteem were stronger when subjects felt they had freely chosen the way they described themselves (Jones et al., 1981).

Other studies show fascinating self-perception effects. If subjects are asked to hold the end of a pencil in their teeth, they configure their face in a manner that resembles a smile. If they hold the end of the pencil in their lips, they configure their face in a manner that resembles a frown. If they are then told to rate the humorousness of cartoons, people with the forced smile rate them as funnier than people with the forced frown. It may be that subjects actually infer their enjoyment of the cartoon from the expressions on their faces (Strack, Martin & Stepper, 1988). Similarly, if subjects are induced to adopt facial expressions of fear, anger, disgust, or sadness, or postures typical of feelings of fear, anger, or sadness, they actually feel these emotions (Duclos et al., 1989). In another study, subjects were asked to nod their heads up and down or from side to side to test their headphones while they listened to a speech. Those who nodded up and down (the usual yes gesture), agreed with the speech they had heard more than those who shook their heads in the usual negative fashion (Wells & Petty, 1980).

Even though self-perception effects are remarkably strong and remarkably pervasive, they are not without limits. For example, when people have clearly defined internal attitudes about an issue, they are less likely to infer how they feel about the issue from a single instance of a particular behavior (Chaiken & Baldwin, 1981). Still, self-perception theory has shown interesting and impressive effects. In the remainder of the book, we will see that it has wide applicability. One particularly important application is in the area of what are called "overjustification effects."

Overjustification: Killing a Good Thing

We are deluged by offers of bonuses for buying a particular brand of popcorn, double coupons at a particular supermarket, and so on. In the advertising trade these are known as "come-ons"; their purpose is to get you to come into the store or to try a product. But if you already like the product and do not need the come-on to enter the store, what effect will the added inducement have on your attitude toward the store or the product? An attributional analysis suggests that the come-ons, or the "overjustification," may have the reverse effect of the one intended.

After behavior is committed, the actor asks himself why he behaved that way. A review of the stimuli surrounding the behavior suggests an

When you buy one on Wednesday and get one free, are you more or less likely to come in on the other days to make a purchase?

answer: "I bought Poppy brand popcorn because they offered me a Mickey Mouse ring inside the package." In other words, the behavior is attributed *not* to the actor's preference for that kind of popcorn but rather to the bonus—or overjustification. Now, popcorn brands outlive the bonus come-ons that are offered. When the actor who has already bought Poppy popcorn returns to the supermarket to restock his popcorn supply, he recalls that he purchased that particular brand *because of the extra bonus*. With the bonus removed, there is no reason to purchase the brand anymore. Indeed, after examining consumer behavior in Chicago, Dodson, Tybout, and Sternthal (1978) found an **overjustification effect**: that advertisements featuring come-ons actually resulted in reduced loyalty to the brand offering the come-on.

The last laugh may be on Madison Avenue's advertising and gimmick people in this instance. But a moment's reflection will conjure up less

---

overjustification effect The tendency of inappropriately large rewards to be counterproductive.

In any social situation where psychoactive substances are being taken, participants learn from the other people in the situation how to interpret the substance's effects.

laughable situations in which needless overjustifications can ruin the intrinsic value that an important behavior might hold. In a first-grade classroom, children know that they will receive one gold star for picking up a book and two gold stars for reading it. In a mental hospital, patients know that they will receive better food if they successfully make their beds and put on their clothing (see Ayllon & Azrin, 1968). But adding an attractive inducement may cause the behavior to be attributed not to an interest in reading or in taking care of oneself, but rather to the gold stars and other external rewards. When the rewards are no longer available, when the children are no longer being awarded stars, when the mental patients leave the hospital and try to return to their natural environment, the overjustifications for their original behaviors may result in a lack of interest in continuing those behaviors.

A fascinating study was conducted at Horizon House, a psychiatric rehabilitation center in Philadelphia (Bogart, Loeb & Rittman, 1969). To achieve better attendance at group therapy sessions, the institution offered prizes for good monthly attendance. In one condition, the value of the prizes could reach approximately $8. In a second condition, patients were offered prizes that could reach only $2 in value. During the month in which prizes were offered, attendance increased. In the $8 condition, it rose from 90% before the reward period to 95% during the reward period. After a month, the reward was withdrawn and attendance fell sharply—to 75%. In the small-reward condition, attendance improved from 82% to 88% during the reward period and stayed about there after the reward period ended (90%). A number of technical difficulties with this study make it less than definitive in demonstrating the detrimental effect of overjustification, but it does suggest that the effects of large rewards may often be counterproductive.

Lepper, Greene, and Nisbett (1973) undertook a direct test of the overjustification hypothesis with nursery school children in California. The children were asked to play with new drawing equipment that was so attractive that any child would welcome the opportunity to play with it. Some of the children were told that they were drawing to obtain a "Good Player award," which included a certificate with colored ribbons. Two other groups of children were offered no extrinsic reward for playing with the equipment. Of the last groups, one served as an "unexpected reward" treatment in which a Good Player award

Chapter Three   Knowing the Self

was given at the end, although it had not been anticipated. The other group served as a control, with no reward given or anticipated. Several days later, the children from all groups were allowed to use the drawing materials if they wished, or to play with a variety of other toys. Observers watched from behind a one-way mirror. They noticed that the children who had originally anticipated and received an external reward for playing with the drawing material played with it only about half as much as the children from the other two groups: it appeared that their interest in the art activity had been diminished by the award offer.

Because of its theoretical and practical implications, the concept of overjustification has received considerable attention in recent years (Fazio, 1981). It has been both extended and qualified by more recent research. One interesting extension shows that if people are asked not to cheat in an exam, and are thus given "superfluous deterrence"—that is, more pressure not to cheat than they need—they attribute their noncheating to the deterrence rather than to their own honesty. Hence they are not afforded the opportunity to see themselves as behaving with voluntary honesty. Consequently, they are more likely to cheat in the future (Wilson & Lassiter, 1982).

The overjustification effect presents a serious problem to parents, educators, and others trying to encourage behaviors that they hope will become intrinsically motivated. Consequently we should be careful not to do for a reward something in which we otherwise have no interest, or to encourage others to do so. For example, Joan Benoit anticipated that if she ran races just for prize money, her intrinsic interest in running could be undermined. As a consequence, she has turned down large offers to run in races when she felt that she was not internally motivated to compete.

We should also realize that there are exceptions to the overjustification effect. If rewards are seen as signs of competence rather than efforts to control behavior, they can increase intrinsic interest (Sansone, 1986, 1989). Interestingly, such rewards as praise can either increase or decrease intrinsic motivation, depending on several other variables. For example, there are gender differ-

ences in response to various kinds of praise. A study of fifth- and sixth-grade children showed that for boys praise based on ability increased intrinsic motivation more than praise based on effort. For girls the opposite was true. Their intrinsic motivation increased more after praise based on effort than after praise based on ability (Koestner, Zuckerman & Koestner, 1989). How can this pattern of results be explained? Perhaps boys are socialized to become competent and develop interest in activities in which they can feel competent. Girls may be socialized to try hard, and may like activities at which they feel they will be rewarded for effort.

The Attribution of Emotions

The research on self-perception and overjustification suggests that people often infer their attitudes, their feelings, and even why they didn't cheat from their behavior and the situation in which it took place. Research also suggests that we infer our emotions from external information: we are often unsure about how we feel, and when this is the case, we make attributions about our emotions rather than just experiencing them directly.

Considerable thought about the attribution of emotions has grown out of the work of Stanley Schachter. His classic studies of anxiety and affiliation (discussed in Chapter 1) demonstrated that anxious subjects who had been threatened with electric shock wanted to wait with other people (Schachter, 1959). Follow-up research has shown that they wanted to wait with other people only when those people were also waiting to be shocked. The threatened subjects were somewhat unsure about their own reactions and wanted help from others in understanding and interpreting what they were feeling. They needed to compare their emotions with those of people who were in the same threatening situation as they were.

Schachter (1964) took this insight and ran with it. He proposed that if people are emotionally aroused but aren't sure what they are feeling, they will look for cues in the environment, including the behavior of other people, in an effort to find the correct interpretation for their ambiguous feelings. It should be noted that Schachter's theory emphasizes not only self-attribution but also social comparison. We clarify emotions by comparing our reactions with those of others, specifically, with reactions of people who are similar on related attributes in that they face the same situation as we do. We then attribute to ourselves the same emotions that the others are feeling.

What evidence is there that people experience emotions on the basis of the reactions of other people? In a classic experiment, Schachter and Singer (1962) were the first to demonstrate this phenomenon. Subjects were given injections of epinephrine, or adrenalin, which makes people feel highly physiologically aroused. Some subjects were informed of the drug's effects. They were told that they would experience an increase in heart rate, a flushed face, and occasional trembling. Since they had an explanation or attribution for the arousal they would experience later, they should not have had to compare their reactions with those of others to figure out what they were feeling. Other subjects were misinformed; they were told that they would experience headaches or numb feet. These subjects would need an explanation for the unexpected effects of the epinephrine. And still other subjects were uninformed; they too would need an explanation for their arousal. Finally, for control purposes, some subjects were given a placebo, which does not cause arousal. None of the subjects who received the placebo should have had to compare themselves with others because they would not have had any arousal to explain.

After the subjects were given the injections and were informed, misinformed, or given no information, they were asked to wait with another person who presumably had had the same injection. The other person was a confederate of the experimenters who acted in one of two ways during the waiting period. In some cases, he acted euphoric, throwing paper airplanes, shooting crumpled balls of paper into the wastebasket, and twirling a hula hoop. In other cases, the confederate became angry. He and the subject had to complete a questionnaire that asked extremely intimate and inappropriate questions (With how many men, other than your father, has your mother had extramarital affairs? Four and under, five to nine, or ten and over?); the confederate became angrier and angrier and finally ripped up his questionnaire in a fit of rage. After a few moments, the experimenter returned and asked the subjects to complete a questionnaire about their feelings.

Table 3-1 summarizes the conditions of the Schachter and Singer experiment and the predictions for each condition. Basically, the results were consistent with the predictions. Subjects took on the mood of the confederate when they had received an injection of epinephrine and were either misinformed or uninformed of its effects. The informed subjects, who already had an explanation of the drug's effects, and subjects who had received the placebo and were thus not aroused, did not experience the confederate's emotions to the same degree.

On the basis of these findings, Schachter and Singer developed a **two-factor theory of emotions** that postulates that our emotions are based on two components: physiological arousal and cognitions about what that arousal means. Stated as a formula, E (emotion) = A (arousal) × C (cognition). Both the arousal and the interpretation or cognition are necessary for a specific emotion to be experienced. In their experiment, Schachter and Singer gave subjects the arousal, but in some cases (uninformed and misinformed conditions) they gave them no cognitions to explain the arousal. The subjects who did not have an explanation for their arousal compared themselves with other people in the situation who were experiencing the same arousal and attributed the emotion the other person was obviously experiencing to themselves. We can see the two-factor theory operating in Joan Benoit's description of her feeling of love at first sight when she first met Scott Samuelson. There was immediate arousal ("There was something there, though . . . I stood there with my mouth hanging open"), and the cognitive explanation was "love at first sight."

Schachter and Singer's provocative research has not gone unchallenged. First, several critics have pointed out that while the results are generally supportive, they are not as strong as they should be to give the theory unequivocal support. Other attempts to replicate the study have failed. They have shown that people who experience unexplained arousal do not attribute to themselves whatever emotion others are feeling in the situation. They typically feel uncomfort-

TABLE 3-1

Conditions of Schachter and Singer's experiment

| | Confederate's behavior | |
Arousal information	Angry	Euphoric
Subjects informed	Subjects should not become angry	Subjects should not become euphoric
Subjects uninformed	Subjects should become angry	Subjects should become euphoric
Subjects misinformed	Subjects should become angry	Subject should become euphoric
No arousal control (placebo)	Subjects should not become angry	Subjects should not become euphoric

able and interpret the arousal negatively (Marshall & Zimbardo, 1979; Maslach, 1979). Reviews of the research on Schachter and Singer's theory caution us that the support for the theory is still "soft" (Cotton, 1981). On the other hand, there is enough evidence for us to conclude that in many situations in which feelings are ambiguous, people will use the information in the situation, especially the reactions of other people, to attribute emotions to themselves.

Excitation transfer:
From one emotion to another

Schachter and Singer's theory and later work by Schachter (1964, 1971) shows that arousal needs to be understood before we can experience an emotion. If the cause of arousal is ambiguous, we look to the environment, including other people's feelings, for an explanation. A more recent theory extends Schachter's work and shows that arousal generated by one emotion or experience can be transferred or channeled into another emotion (Zillmann, 1978, 1983, 1984). For example, if you became aroused because you ran to the top of a hill, your arousal could be interpreted as romantic feelings if you had met someone really attractive at the top; or it could be interpreted as anger if a passing motorist had honked at you. In the latter case, your anger could have been fueled by the arousal from running and might therefore have been more intense than otherwise. This theory of **excitation transfer** holds that emotions consist of an excitatory component, in which arousal occurs, and an experien-

tial component, in which the excitation is interpreted and an emotion is attributed. Arousal can be transferred if a person makes a misattribution. If you attribute your arousal from running to the beautiful person you have just met or to the motorist you have just cursed, that arousal increases your emotional reaction of romance or anger, as the case may be. Joan Benoit talked to us about the excitation transfer experiences that she has often had. When she is "wired" for a race, her competitive feelings intensify other feelings of happiness or anger she may be experiencing. As she put it, "The highs feel higher and the lows lower." In later chapters, we will see how sexual arousal can be transferred to aggression and how arousal caused by fear can be transferred to sexual attraction. In short, Zillman's theory explains how we attribute and sometimes misattribute feelings to ourselves in ways suggested by Schachter and Singer.

Imagined arousal and emotions

Both Schachter and Zillman have considered the way we interpret genuine physiological arousal and the way our interpretations lead to the self-attribution of emotions. Some interesting related

---

excitation transfer   The transfer of arousal produced by one source to the energization of an unrelated response.

two-factor theory of emotions   Schachter's theory that emotional experience is based on a combination of physiological arousal and cognitive labeling or interpretation of the causes of arousal.

research suggests that we sometimes attribute emotions when we only *think* we are aroused. We infer that we are responding emotionally to whatever it is we *falsely* believe is arousing us. This kind of self-attribution was seen when male college students were shown several centerfold pictures of nude women from *Playboy* magazine. Fake electrodes placed on the subjects allegedly measured their heart rates as they looked at the pictures. In addition, the subjects were allowed to "overhear their heart rates" as they looked through the pictures. At various intervals, the subjects heard what they believed were their real heart beats markedly increase or decrease. At the end of the experiment, the subjects were told that they could take home any of the nude pictures that they wanted to. Most of the pictures they chose were the ones they had been looking at when their heart rate presumably changed during the experiment (Valins, 1966).

The key point here is that the changes in the heart rate that the subjects heard were not real; all were preprogrammed by the experimenter. Yet subjects inferred that they were responding emotionally to pictures that seemed to cause their heart rates to change, and those were the pictures they decided they liked. In a follow-up study, Valins (1972) repeated the procedure but after giving the subjects the bogus heart-rate feedback he carefully debriefed them, informing them that the heart-rate change was not real. Even after the debriefing, subjects remained more attracted to the nudes that they had initially believed caused their heart rates to change. Apparently the combination of perception of arousal and an inferred attraction created a liking that a simple debriefing could not undo.

Additional recent research suggests that we make attributions about our likes and dislikes on the basis of false arousal feedback only when we don't have to give much thought to our feelings. In one study, after rating photographs of men, college women were given false feedback about their attraction to those men. They were then asked to rerate the photographs. If they expected to meet the men, their second ratings were based more on their first ratings than on the false feedback; if they didn't expect to meet the men, their second ratings were based more on the false feedback. In the first situation, when the subjects expected to meet the men, they had to think

harder about whom they really liked. In that case they didn't let themselves be misled by the false arousal feedback (Taylor, 1975).

Attributions to Self and Others: The Actor-Observer Bias

We noted earlier that attribution principles discussed in Chapter 2, such as those of Kelley and Weiner, could be applied to the self. At times we make attributions about the self just as we make them about other people. Bem's (1972) self-perception theory makes an even stronger claim. He argues that self-perception is just like other-people perception; it's simply the special case in which the actor and the perceiver are the same person. Jones and Nisbett (1971) disagree. They hold that actors and observers view the world quite differently.

Let us consider the following clinical case. Betty and George Barnes seek psychotherapy for problems in their marriage. Both of them agree that Betty often flies into fits of rage, throws dishes, and makes life very difficult for the two of them. Betty claims that her actions are caused by her husband's stupidity. She asserts that she becomes enraged when George forgets to put enough money into the checking account, loses his keys, is unable to get a raise. George asserts that his wife becomes enraged because she is unpleasant, illogical, and irascible.

No doubt there is motivation to this madness. Betty's behavior is attributed to George's actions by Betty, and attributed to Betty by George. He blames her; she blames him. But the analysis must go deeper. Betty, the actor, blames the *situations* that George allegedly causes. George, the observer, blames Betty's *disposition*. Jones and Nisbett (1971) have argued that this **actor-observer bias** is a common tendency. In their terms, "there is a pervasive tendency for actors to attribute their actions to situational requirements whereas observers tend to attribute the actions to stable dispositions" (p. 80).

A study reported by McArthur (1972) supports this proposition. The procedure was elegantly simple. She asked subjects to volunteer for a survey about interpersonal relationships and then asked the subjects why they had agreed to participate. Written accounts of the request and the consent were given to observers. Like the involved subjects, the observers were asked why they thought the subjects had agreed to participate. The results showed that the involved subjects attributed their participation to the importance of the survey (situational attribution). The observers, on the other hand, attributed the actors' participation to a disposition to take part in surveys. Similar differences between actors and observers have been obtained by Nisbett and his colleagues (1973). In addition, consistent with the actor-observer hypothesis, a recent study of letters written to advice columnists "Ann Landers" and "Dear Abby" showed that in describing the sources of their own difficulties, writers blamed the behavior of other people—that is, external factors. They did not show this tendency in explaining other people's difficulties (Fisher, Schoeneman & Rubanowitz, 1987).

Actors and observers: Why are they different?

Jones and Nisbett contend that several factors combine to produce the different attributions of actors and observers. The first is that the actor has access to a greater *history* of behaviors than the observer. The actor knows that she behaved in one way today, in a different way yesterday, and in yet another way last week. Therefore, the actor looks to the environment for an explanation. The observer, on the other hand, has but one act of behavior with which to judge the actor. The observer is apt to generalize and to assume that the actor's behavior is consistent across situations. Consequently, the observer is more prepared to attribute the cause of a behavior to the disposition of the actor.

Second, Jones and Nisbett reason that the actor and the observer approach an act from different perspectives. Each has a different focus and different information is salient to each. As we noted in Chapter 2, people tend to attribute causality to whatever is salient in their environment or whatever they are focusing their attention on (Taylor & Fiske, 1978). Since the actor's attention is focused on the environment, he or she is more likely to attribute causality to things in the environment. The observer's attention is focused on the actor, an important aspect of his or her environment, so the observer is likely to attribute causality to the actor. Thus, the observer will make more internal dispositional attributions for the actor's behavior than the actor will.

Is this child clumsy or did the food spill accidentally? What questions would you need to ask before you could decide whether the situation or the disposition explains the spill?

There is considerable support for this differential focus-of-attention explanation of the actor-observer bias (Ross & Fletcher, 1985). For example, one study showed that attributions to internal versus external causes made by actors and observers could be changed if each was given a different perspective. Two actors, A and B, had a conversation and were watched by two observers, one looking at each actor. After the conversation, A and B and the two observers made attributions consistent with the focus-of-attention explanation. Each actor attributed his own behavior to the situation and the other actor's behavior to his dispositions, while each observer attributed the behavior of the actor he watched

actor-observer bias The tendency of actors to attribute their behavior to situational factors and of observers to attribute it to stable dispositions.

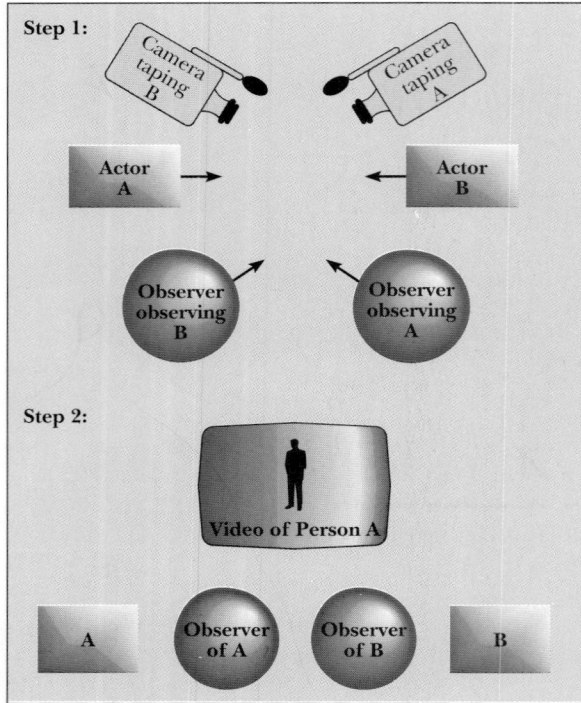

Step 1:

Camera taping B

Camera taping A

Actor A →

← Actor B

Observer observing B

Observer observing A

Step 2:

Video of Person A

A

Observer of A

Observer of B

B

FIGURE 3-1 Testing the perceptual explanation for the actor-observer effect
SOURCE: Fiske and Taylor (1984), after Storms (1973).

1. Explain why at different times we might compare with others who are superior to us, inferior to us, or similar on related attributes.

2. Explain the findings of two studies that support the basic hypothesis of Bem's self-perception theory.

3. Explain the problem of overjustification of intrinsically enjoyable activities. What research findings show that overjustification undermines intrinsic interest?

4. What evidence is there that our emotions are influenced by labeling and attribution processes as well as by physiological arousal?

5. What evidence is there for the actor-observer bias?

to that actor and the behavior of the other actor to the situation. That is, all four subjects attributed causality to the person on whom they were focused. Later in the experiment, the subjects were shown a videotape of actor A participating in the conversation. The subjects who had not paid attention to actor A before—that is, actor A himself and the observer watching actor B—now made more dispositional attributions to actor A; they saw him more as the locus of causality. The subjects who had been paying attention to actor A previously—that is, actor B and the observer watching A—did not change their attributions. As before (see Figure 3-1), they made dispositional attributions for the behavior of actor A (Storms, 1973).

Another factor may be influencing the attributions of actors and observers, one that is closely tied to the way we view ourselves in comparison with others. We like to see ourselves as having the ability to respond appropriately to external circumstances. Thus we typically say that our behavior was caused by an external circumstance

and was the appropriate response to it. Furthermore, we believe that we have the ability to respond appropriately to a wide range of external circumstances because we have many traits. We are multifaceted (Sande, Goethals & Radloff, 1988). We can show an angry side if the situation calls for it, and a gentle side if that is required. We are variable, flexible, and adaptive (Baxter & Goldberg, 1987). But we don't see others this way. As observers of their behavior, we see their actions as caused by the specific traits that dominate their personalities. Again, our own behavior is caused by external factors and reflects a flexibility and adaptiveness that come from having a wide range of traits.

Biases in Self-Perception: The Totalitarian Ego

In Chapter 2 we discussed several biases (such as the correspondence bias) that affect our perceptions of other people. What biases, if any, distort our perceptions of ourselves? Jones and Nisbett's actor-observer concept shows that we don't make

Chapter Three Knowing the Self

How might the woman in these photos rate cartoons? Would she think they were funnier if she was holding the pencil in her teeth rather than between her lips?

attributions about ourselves in exactly the same way we make them about others. It's not surprising, then, to learn that several biases are unique to self-perception. Taken together, they make up what is known as the totalitarian ego (Greenwald, 1980).

The **totalitarian ego** or self is described as an organization of knowledge characterized by cognitive biases. These biases function to preserve our organization of social information and our positive views of ourselves. Greenwald noticed a similarity between the way the ego controls and biases information and the way totalitarian governments control and bias information. The totalitarian ego manages information by means of three biases: egocentricity, beneffectance, and cognitive conservatism.

Egocentricity: Self as the Focus of Knowledge and Attribution

Much of our knowledge about the world around us is autobiographical—we remember people and events in accordance with our role in interacting with them and in influencing them or being influenced by them. Our memory of a city that we visited, for example, centers on where we went and what we saw. Our memory of what happened when we participated in a softball game centers on the hits we made and the balls we caught. This tendency to recall information better if it is related to the self is called **egocentricity.**

One of the consequences of egocentricity is the tendency to exaggerate the importance of one's role in shaping events. Ross (1981) provides numerous examples of this tendency. People who have collaborated on a research project, a newspaper story, or a music composition may try to recall their contributions to the joint product. When order of authorship implies level of contribution, many collaborators sit in disbelief as their partners indicate that they believe they should be named first. Each person, however, tends to remember events through his or her own eyes. A meeting that the authors may have had will be remembered differently by each participant, because each views it with egocentricity. None of the participants may be lying when they all claim that they were the primary contributor to the meeting. Each recalls that part of the event to which he or she contributed, and remembers less well those parts to which others contributed.

Consider husbands and wives who are asked how much they contribute to various household chores. Ross and Sicoly (1979) interviewed married couples and asked them how much each contributed to cleaning house, caring for children,

egocentricity A bias toward perceiving oneself as the central actor and causal agent in events.

totalitarian ego The biased organization of information about the self that functions to preserve a favorable self-impression.

When people argue they often tend to present themselves in a good light, attributing failures and problems to external causes such as other people, and success to internal causes—for example, themselves. What do you suppose these two people are arguing about? Which one is on the defensive?

making important decisions, and causing conflicts. Both husbands and wives claimed to have made the major contribution about 70% of the time. Of course, it is impossible for an activity to be the wife's responsibility 70% of the time and the husband's responsibility 70% of the time. It is not that the partners wish to lie about their roles. The fact is, their judgments of responsibility for everyday activities are self-centered: the bias in processing and recalling information results in the egocentric judgment. When asked to discuss this bias in her own marriage, Joan Benoit recognized it right away. In general, she is extremely aware of how much Scott does for her and for their daughter as she pursues her career, but she did admit that when she is heavily involved in training or feeling emotionally down, she falls prey to the egocentric bias. She gets "nit-picky" because it becomes harder to remember all that Scott has contributed to the family and the household.

Another aspect of the egocentricity bias is the "self as locus of cause and effect." That is, we see ourselves as generating behavior. For example, we think of other people's actions in terms of the effects those actions have on us and we assume they acted to produce those effects. We can see these tendencies in international affairs. Americans tend to see what the Soviet Union does as being caused by our actions. Similarly, we see the Soviets' behaviors as designed to have some effect on us. We may think that they are trying to cooperate with us or to compete with us. The key fact here is that we see ourselves as central causes of their behavior.

Beneffectance: The Self-Serving Bias

People are motivated to see themselves in a good light. We tend to take credit for success and deny responsibility for failure. This bias is referred to as **beneffectance.** The term comes from the fact that we tend to view ourselves positively in two ways: (1) we see ourselves as beneficent, that is, helpful and moral, and (2) as competent, that is, as having "effectance." Beneffectance combines beneficence with effectance. Although this bias is not inconsistent with the actor-observer bias, it does qualify it. While we generally attribute our behavior to the environment, this tendency is much greater when our negative actions are at issue than when our positive actions are under consideration. The beneffectance bias is illustrated in a study in which women college students were made to succeed or fail on an intellectual task. Then they were asked to indicate what causes they thought best explained their success or failure. After success they chose internal causes. After failure they chose external causes that constituted excuses for poor performance (DeJong, Koomen & Mellenbergh, 1988). Joan Benoit told us that she did not want to share the credit for her Olympic success with anyone, though she is clearly grateful for her family's support. She also said that she was tempted to make excuses for her disappointing performance in the 1989 Boston Marathon, even though logically she feels she has to accept responsibility. Her feelings show the strength of the beneffectance bias, even when we try to resist it.

Observers are not likely to share the actor's bias. Johnson, Feigenbaum, and Weiby (1964)

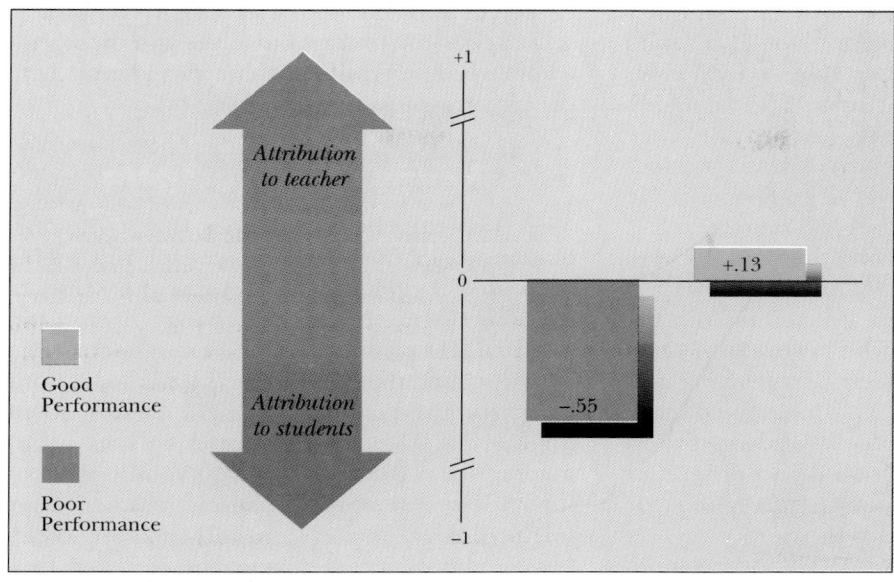

FIGURE 3-2 Teachers' attributions of the success and failure of students
NOTE: A score of +1 equals total attribution to the teacher's effort; a score of −1 equals total attribution to the student.
SOURCE: Johnson, Feigenbaum, and Weiby (1964).

asked women taking educational psychology classes to participate in an experiment in teaching mathematics to nine-year-old boys. Each teacher taught two boys. During the first part of the learning sequence, boy A did well and boy B did poorly. During the second half, A continued to do well. For half of the teachers, B showed improvement so that he was doing as well as A; for the other half, B continued to do poorly. When the teachers were asked to what they attributed the performance of the students, teachers who had an improving B saw themselves as responsible for the performance. The teachers whose B continued to do poorly blamed the performance on the student (see Figure 3-2). In a replication of this study, Beckman (1970) found precisely the same effect. However, she also asked observers to what they attributed the students' performance. In marked contrast to the teachers, the observers saw the teachers as more responsible for B's poor performance and saw B as more responsible for his own good performance.

Reviews of the literature on the self-serving bias generally support it (Fiske & Taylor, 1984;

Riess et al., 1981; Ross & Fletcher, 1985). A review by Bradley (1978) specified that both beneffectance biases—taking credit for success and denying responsibility for failure—are most likely to occur under the following conditions: (a) when the actor is highly *involved* in an activity; (b) when the actor has *choice* in engaging in the activity; and (c) when the actor's performance in the activity is *public*.

This last condition has been explored carefully. Is beneffectance simply a public claim or do people really believe in private that they are responsible for their success but not their failure? Several studies seem to suggest that people genuinely believe in their own beneffectance. For example, in one study (Greenberg, Pyszczynski & Solomon, 1982), subjects took what they believed to be a test of intelligence. In half of the cases, the test results were private. Subjects graded

beneffectance The tendency to take credit for success and deny responsibility for failure; from *beneficence* + *effectance*.

their own tests, they did not put names on their answer sheets, and they were told the tests would not be collected. The other subjects had their tests scored by the instructor with their names attached. All of the subjects learned that they had answered 12 of 20 items correctly, but half were led to believe this was a good score; the other half believed this was a bad score.

After receiving their scores, the subjects were asked to attribute their performance to their ability, their effort, or luck. Consistent with the self-serving bias, subjects who believed they had done well indicated that their performance was due to their effort and ability, while subjects who thought they had done poorly attributed their results to bad luck. And it made no difference whether the test performance was public or private.

Riess and his colleagues (1981) also explored whether beneffectance is a private, self-serving bias designed to bolster self-esteem or a public display of impression management. They used a technique known as the bogus pipeline to measure attributions. With this technique, subjects are convinced that their true attributions are being measured by electronic gadgetry. Their job is to predict what the machine is saying about their real attributions. These predictions are taken as the subjects' attributions. The results showed that the self-serving bias held up under the scrutiny of the bogus pipeline. Subjects took credit for good performance and avoided blame for poor performance, even if they believed that their private perceptions were being measured accurately by the machinery.

Research has also shown what is known as vicarious beneffectance. Married people evidence the beneffectance bias when explaining their spouse's behavior (Hall & Taylor, 1976). People also evidence this bias in explaining poor debate performances by their preferred presidential candidates (Winkler & Taylor, 1979). Similarly, people strengthen their identification with groups to which they belong when a group is doing well. For example, people are more likely to wear their college's sweatshirts following a football victory than after a football loss; they report "We won" and "They lost" after victory and defeat (Cialdini et al., 1976).

In summary, beneffectance seems to be a dis-

tortion of information that is designed to protect self-esteem. We protect ourselves and those with whom we identify, although we may identify with people or groups less after they fail.

Cognitive Conservatism: Resisting Changes in Thinking

The egocentricity bias implies that our information about ourselves is plentiful and highly organized. Evidence indicates that our self-conceptions also are resistant to change. Swann and Read (1981) conducted three experiments that demonstrated that people use social interactions to verify their previously held beliefs about themselves. That is, they prefer to seek information that is consistent with a hypothesis about themselves and avoid situations in which they might discover inconsistent information. When people choose interaction partners, when they choose the topics to talk with their partners about, when they choose the topics to avoid, they do so with the goal of confirming their self-concept. As a result, it is difficult for self-concepts to change. If attribution processes result in the formation of ideas about the self, then we would normally predict that people would be fluid in their self-concept development. But **cognitive conservatism** suggests that we "stack the deck." We tend to put ourselves into social situations in which our behavior leads to attributions consistent with our self-image and in which the information we receive further confirms our view of ourselves.

While we may try hard to resist change, we aren't always successful. When we do change, we try to maintain the belief that our knowledge about ourselves and the world has not actually changed much. We do this through the rewriting of personal history. For example, when we are given information that we didn't know before, we tend to feel that perhaps we actually did know it. This is called the "I knew it all along effect" (Fischoff, 1975). Furthermore, when we change our attitudes or beliefs about the world, we tend to misrecall our earlier attitudes. We remember those earlier attitudes as being essentially the same as our new ones. Thus we perceive our attitudes as consistent over time, and we keep ourselves unaware of having changed them (Goethals & Reckman, 1973).

Self-Perception and Psychological Well-Being

Obviously our psychological well-being is closely tied to our self-perception. Reflected appraisal, social comparison, and self-attribution all affect the way we feel about ourselves. They directly influence whether we evaluate ourselves positively or negatively, and whether we feel good about the person that we are. But beyond their direct impact on self-esteem, self-perception processes play an important role in producing depression, anxiety, and feelings of helplessness. At the same time, these self-perception processes can be used to alleviate such problems. Here we will consider how a variety of self-perception processes, particularly self-attribution, affect our psychological well-being, and how they offer ways to improve it.

Self-Attribution, Feelings of Control, and Learned Helplessness

We have seen that people make many self-attributions, including attributions as to why they succeeded or failed. Generally they attribute their actions or the outcomes of these actions to either internal or external causes. These attributions are often affected by the beneffectance bias, and this bias undoubtedly protects self-esteem. But not all people are protected by the beneffectance bias to the same degree. We vary considerably in our thinking about what causes our successes and failures, and more generally about what causes the outcomes, both good and bad, that we experience in day-to-day living.

Research has shown that different people have consistently different perceptions of the causes of their outcomes (Rotter, 1966; Phares, 1984; Lefcourt, 1982). Some individuals perceive an internal locus of control; they believe that they are the masters of their own destiny and are in control of their own fate. Others believe that their outcomes are determined by external factors— by luck, fate, or chance. Rotter argued that people's experiences lead them to develop generalized expectancies that their outcomes are internally or externally controlled. He went

TABLE 3-2

Sample items from an early version of Rotter's test of internal-external locus of control

I more strongly believe that:

1. a. Many people can be described as victims of circumstance.
   b. What happens to other people is pretty much of their own making.
2. a. The world is so complicated that I just cannot figure things out.
   b. The world is really complicated alright, but I can usually work things out by effort and persistence.
3. a. Most students would be amazed at how much grades are determined by capricious events.
   b. The marks I get in class are completely my own responsibility.
4. a. Promotions are earned through hard work and persistence.
   b. Making a lot of money is largely a matter of getting the right breaks.
5. a. In my case the grades I make are the results of my own efforts; luck has little or nothing to do with it.
   b. Sometimes I feel that I have little to do with the grades I get.
6. a. Getting along with people is a skill that must be practiced.
   b. It is almost impossible to figure out how to please some people.

SOURCE: Adapted from Rotter (1971a).

on to develop a scale that measures whether people perceive an internal or external locus of control (see Table 3-2). You might want to answer the questions in Table 3-2 to see if you tend to perceive an internal or external locus of control.

People who perceive an **internal locus of control,** referred to as "internals," believe that what happens in their lives depends on how hard they work, that nobody is going to give them anything, but anything is within their reach if they exert the effort. Thus internals work. They are aptly characterized by the slogan "We try harder." Joan Benoit is typical of many internals. She believes that she is largely in control of her success in running, and she works hard to make suc-

---

cognitive conservatism   The tendency to seek social situations consistent with one's self-image and in which information received confirms one's self-concept.

internal locus of control   A perception that one's outcomes are due to one's own efforts and actions.

In the aftermath of Hurricane Hugo this woman looks at her destroyed home. Natural disasters tend to leave people with deep feelings of powerlessness that can last long after the disaster has occurred.

cess happen. People with an **external locus of control,** on the other hand, perceive their fate as controlled by factors outside themselves. Since they believe that they have no control over what happens to them, they don't put much effort into their lives. In one study, for example, hospitalized tuberculosis patients' attitudes differed dramatically depending on their perceived locus of control. Internals made efforts to find out what caused their disease and what they could do about it, while externals were more passive (Seeman & Evans, 1962). Langer (1981) has argued that elderly people are passive not because they are senile but because their life difficulties cause them to perceive an external locus of control.

Research on learned helplessness shows that you don't have to be elderly to begin to perceive that your outcomes are beyond your control and thus to become passive and helpless. It also shows that whether people become helpless or not after they have had difficult life experiences depends on the attributions they make in regard to the causes of their difficulties. **Learned helplessness** (discussed further in Chapter 14) is a phenomenon first discovered in animal research by Martin Seligman and his colleagues (Overmier &

Seligman, 1967; Maier, Seligman & Solomon, 1969). It turns out that animals, after being exposed to inescapable shock when they are learning a task, later fail to learn a second task. Not only do animals in this situation fail to learn the second task, they usually cease behaving entirely. Seligman has labeled this state learned helplessness because the animal is learning that there is no relationship between its responding and its reinforcement, and thus it simply stops responding.

The state of learned helplessness has been experimentally produced in humans as well as animals by means of inescapable adversive stimuli (electric shocks and loud noise) or insoluble problems in the first task, or the "helplessness pretraining task" (Hiroto & Seligman, 1975; Thornton & Jacobs, 1971; Roth & Kubal, 1975). In all of these studies, experience with uncontrollability produced deficits in learning, whether the later task was learning to make an avoidance response or solving a cognitive problem. The common occurrence is that subjects with helplessness pretraining make significantly fewer attempts to respond, and adopt a general state of passivity resembling depression.

In what way do attributions relate to this

research? The attributions people make about the causes of their failure on the first task are extremely important. If people attribute failure to their inability to cope with difficult situations, then there is little reason for them to try again in the future. However, if people attribute failure to the task, then that failure may not lead to a state of helplessness and hence their unwillingness to try again.

The importance of attributions was shown in a study by Tennen and Eller (1977). Subjects thought that they were participating in two separate experiments. In the first experiment (the pretreatment stage), they were given either ability (self) or task difficulty (external) explanations for their apparent inability to solve a discrimination problem. The subjects in one insoluble condition were told that the task was becoming more difficult, whereas the subjects in another insoluble condition were told that the task was becoming easier. As you can see, the potential was created for the subjects in one group to attribute failure to task difficulty (the task-harder condition), whereas the subjects in the other group should have attributed failure to their own lack of ability (the task-easier condition). The measure of helplessness was the subject's success at solving anagrams in the second experiment. Subjects in the ability attribution condition solved significantly fewer anagrams than did either subjects without prior helplessness training or subjects who could attribute their previous poor performance to task difficulty. This finding provides strong support for the role of self-attribution in learned helplessness. It is not simply the expectation that responding is unrelated to outcome that is critical. Rather, it is the self-attribution that failure reflects the lack of an ability that causes people to carry the helplessness expectation into other situations.

Let's be more specific about what kinds of attributions lead to learned helplessness. A classic paper by Abramson, Seligman, and Teasdale (1978) presents what is known as the **revised learned helplessness (RLH) model.** Specifically, it suggests that people become helpless when they attribute their failures and other negative outcomes to causes that are internal, stable, and global. For example, suppose you ask someone to go to a dance with you and are turned down. What attributions do you make for being told no?

If you make an internal rather than external attribution, you decide it's something about you, perhaps your appearance or your voice, rather than the fact that the person is busy or doesn't like to dance. If you make a stable rather than unstable attribution, you further decide you were turned down because of something that won't change, such as your height or hair color, rather than the way you asked the question, which can be changed. Finally, if you make a global rather than specific attribution, you decide that whatever caused you to be turned down this one time is going to affect lots of other interpersonal interactions too. You might, for example, decide that your high-pitched voice put the other person off, and is likely to cause trouble with many other people as well, including future prospective dates, casual acquaintances, and employers. These attributions are enough to make anyone stop trying. Why bother? Obviously, then, they can lead to passivity and lack of effort, or what we call learned helplessness.

How much support does this theory have? A great deal of research has shown that the pattern of internal, stable, and global attributions for setbacks can have devastating effects on future performance. A study of college freshmen looked at students' responses to upsetting academic events encountered early in the year. Those who attributed their problems to internal, stable, and global causes ended up with lower grades, despite the fact that they were just as bright. Their lower grades were tied to setting vague academic goals and not taking advantage of academic advisers. In other words, they responded to their problems passively, and got into academic difficulties (Peterson & Barrett, 1987).

Other research shows that the global dimension may be particularly important in learned helplessness. If people fail in one situation and make global attributions (there's something about

---

external locus of control A perception that one's outcomes are due to factors outside of one's control, such as luck, chance, or fate.

learned helplessness A state resulting when the individual perceives no control over his or her environment.

revised learned helplessness (RLH) model The theory that people learn to become helpless, and eventually become depressed, as a result of attributing their negative outcomes to internal, stable, and global causes.

---

me that won't change, *and* it will affect everything I try to do) they are likely to perform poorly in a broad range of situations, not just situations similar to the one in which they initially failed (Mikulincer, 1986). Furthermore, subjects who make global attributions for failures are likely to experience cognitive interference from irrelevant thoughts when they try to work on a task (Mikulincer & Nizan, 1988).

Self-attribution has effects on psychological well-being beyond its impact on learned helplessness. It also affects anxiety and psychological "hardiness" (Kobasa, 1979). For example, anxious people don't take personal credit for success the way their nonanxious counterparts do (Alden, 1987). That is, they don't show the beneffectance bias that protects most people. Also, research shows that psychologically hardy people—people who get highly involved, who like challenges, and who feel in control—tend to make less internal, stable, and global attributions for negative events than their nonhardy counterparts (Hull, Van Treuren & Propsom, 1988). In short, patterns of self-attribution have a significant impact on a range of psychological problems.

We should also recognize that whether people are active or helpless in addressing their problems is affected by more than just attribution processes. One key variable is perceived self-efficacy (Bandura, 1977). Perceived **self-efficacy** is one's confidence in one's ability to produce a positive outcome. People who are high in perceived self-efficacy are likely to take action to solve or get out of stressful or painful situations. They feel that they have control, and they exercise it (Litt, 1988). Similarly, people who view themselves as effective problem solvers feel that they can solve their personal problems by exerting effort (Baumgardner, Heppner & Arkin, 1986). In short, when you have problems to deal with, seeing yourself as having the capacity to cope and be effective may be half the battle.

Self-Attribution and Depression

One of the first applications of the learned helplessness concept was to the psychological disorder of depression. The passivity observed in the early studies of learned helplessness reminded many researchers of depression. More specifically, the revised learned helplessness model,

emphasizing self-attribution, has been extended to suggest that people who make internal, stable, and global attributions for failures and other negative outcomes become depressed. A great deal of research has been done to test this hypothesis in recent years. It has generated considerable support for the model, but it has also suggested further revisions.

A study that is typical of those supporting the RLH model looked at depressive symptoms and attributional style in schoolchildren. The children were studied over the course of a year, and it was found that those who explained negative events in terms of internal, stable, and global causes were more likely to show depressive symptoms throughout the year and to have lower levels of school achievement (Nolen-Hoeksema, Girgus & Seligman, 1986). Another study of college students' responses to low grades on midterm exams showed that immediately after the exam, students' depressive moods were explained simply by their grades. However, their long-term depressive reactions were determined both by the grades and by their internal, stable, and global attributions (Metalsky, Halberstadt & Abramson, 1987). Although some studies do not support the revised learned helplessness model (Follette & Jacobson, 1987, for example), a meta-analytic review of more than 100 studies with nearly 15,000 subjects showed clear support for it (Sweeney, Anderson & Bailey, 1986).

Even though the revised learned helplessness model has clear support, in recent years it has undergone some fine-tuning. One modification argues that attributing negative events to stable and global causes is key in creating "hopelessness" and therefore depression, whereas also attributing such events to internal causes adds in low self-esteem. In addition, it suggests that depression is more likely when the negative events are considered important (Abramson, Alloy & Metalsky, 1986). Another addition to the model suggests that depression is likely only when the internal, stable, and global causes for negative events are also seen as uncontrollable (Brown & Siegel, 1988).

One important question in this research on attributions and depression is how people initially develop the depressive attributional style— seeing negative events as due to internal, stable, and global causes. A recent study suggests that low self-esteem may be a key factor in producing the depressive attributional style (Tennen & Herzberger, 1987). This study is important in tying together the three broad aspects of self-perception we have considered in this chapter—reflected appraisal, social comparison, and self-attribution. The first two processes, reflected appraisal and social comparison, may be critical in establishing high or low self-esteem. Level of self-esteem may, in turn, exert a strong impact on an individual's attributional style.

Two other aspects of self-perception are involved in depression. One is pessimism. Depressed people see negative outcomes as much more likely than positive outcomes. Not that depressed people are biased toward pessimism; it would be truer to say that nondepressed people are biased toward optimism. Nondepressed people see themselves as more likely to experience positive events than similar other people, and less likely to experience negative events. This is a bias that depressed people do not show (Alloy & Ahrens, 1987). These and other findings suggest the existence of a phenomenon that has been called **depressive realism.** It may be that depressed people view themselves and the world quite realistically. Nondepressed people are protected by a range of biases, such as the beneffectance and optimism biases, which support high self-esteem and an active approach to living. Perhaps it isn't good for you to be too honest with yourself, or completely accurate in perceiving both yourself and others. A little self-deception can be protective and adaptive.

A final aspect of self-perception involved in depression is the quickness with which negative thoughts about the self come to mind. When depressed people are busy with a memory task, they can still do another task very quickly, that is, deciding whether negative adjectives apply to them. It takes them more time, however, to decide whether those adjectives apply to other people (Bargh & Tota, 1988). It seems that depressed people find it very easy—it is nearly automatic—to think of themselves in negative terms. Negative thoughts about the self are highly available and accessible in their memory. The easy accessibility of these negative thoughts about the self may be a key contributor to depression.

Young people often attribute the negative events in their lives to factors that will never change. This kind of attribution can lead to depressive symptoms and learned helplessness.

Self-Complexity, Self-Discrepancies, and Psychological Well-Being

In recent years social psychologists have discovered a number of other aspects of self-perception that have a large impact on both physical and psychological well-being. One of the most interesting is self-complexity (Linville, 1987). **Self-complexity** is the condition of perceiving oneself as having many aspects, which differ greatly from one another. A noncomplex person, for example, may perceive herself simply to be a woman,

depressive realism The tendency of depressed people to see themselves and the world realistically, without the self-deceiving biases that protect nondepressed people.

self-complexity The condition of perceiving oneself to have many aspects, which differ greatly from one another.

self-efficacy Confidence in one's ability to produce positive outcomes.

a runner, and a champion. Joan Benoit, who has a highly complex view of herself, is well aware that she is all of those things and many more: a concerned environmentalist, a mother, a loyal family member, an involved citizen of her hometown in Maine, an active Bowdoin alumna, and on and on. In other words, she is a person of high self-complexity.

What difference does self-complexity make? It seems to buffer us against stress-related illness and depression. We all have to deal with stressful life events, but the effects of such events vary with the degree of our self-complexity. Low-complexity individuals respond to high levels of stress with feelings of depression and high rates of flu and other physical illnesses. High-complexity people are buffered or protected from these unhealthy consequences of stress.

How does this work? The key may be that individuals such as Joan Benoit, who have high levels of self-complexity, can throw themselves into other activities or concerns when stress interrupts one part of their lives. If Joan has a debilitating running injury, for example, she turns to other activities and concerns. People who are low in self-complexity suffer both physically and psychologically when stress disrupts one of the few aspects of their lives. They have little else to turn to, and their well-being is impaired.

Another aspect of self-perception that affects psychological well-being consists of self-discrepancies (Higgins, 1989). According to **self-discrepancy theory,** people's psychological well-being is affected not only by their self-concepts or their actual selves but also by the way their self-concepts match or mismatch various "self-guides." There are two kinds of self-guides. One is an *ideal self,* what you hope or aspire to be, or what someone else hopes you will be. The other kind of self-guide is an *ought self,* what you feel duty-bound or obligated to be, or what someone else believes you ought to be.

Self-discrepancy theory predicts that if people have a mismatch or discrepancy between their actual self and their own or someone else's ideal self, and thereby feel that they aren't being all that they *could* be, they will suffer from sadness and dejection, feelings that might lead eventually to depression. On the other hand, the theory predicts that if there is a discrepancy between the actual self and the ought self, so that one feels that one isn't what one *ought* to be, one will suffer agitation and anxiety. Several recent studies have supported these predictions (Strauman & Higgins, 1987; Higgins et al., 1986). In addition, they have shown that people with discrepant self-guides show signs of being in chronic conflict about how to behave, and are muddled, indecisive, distracted, and confused about their identities (Van Hook & Higgins, 1988). Finally, a recent study shows that self-esteem is correlated with the discrepancy between actual self and ideal self, just as the theory predicts (Moretti & Higgins, 1990).

Applying Self-Attribution: Misattribution Therapy

The research on self-attribution and depression shows that the attributions we make about our behaviors and the outcomes of our behaviors can lead to psychological problems. But there is hope in these findings. If we understand what attributions lead to problems, and then learn how we can change those attributions, we may be able to prevent or alleviate the problems such attributions ordinarily cause. Consider anxiety. Anxiety is one of the major problems that bring people to psychotherapists today. Complaints may range from the relatively trivial anxiety associated with insects or snakes to extremely debilitating fears of air travel, of taking tests, of performing in public. The research on self-attribution suggests a unique way for psychotherapists to deal with such fears: try the **misattribution** approach; that is, contrive to make patients misattribute the source of their arousal. If people are given an opportunity to attribute their arousal to an external source rather than to anxiety, perhaps their symptoms can be reduced. For example, telling someone who is afraid of flying that her anxiety attack is due to an airsickness pill could provide a credible explanation for her anxious feelings and might lead her to actually experience less anxiety. Her arousal can be misattributed to the pill.

Several studies show exactly this kind of symptom reduction due to misattribution of arousal. In one study (Ross, Rodin & Zimbardo, 1969), subjects were made anxious by being told that they would be given painful electric shocks.

However, half of the subjects were exposed to a very loud noise piped over a headset and were led to believe that their arousal was due to the loud noise. Subjects were then given a chance to work on two puzzles. Solving one puzzle would enable them to escape the forthcoming shock; solving the other would bring them a cash reward. The investigators found that the subjects who attributed their arousal to the noise abandoned work on the escape-the-shock puzzle and worked significantly more for the cash reward. That is, their behavior indicated less fear of the shock.

The implication of this study is that the psychological disorder known as *phobia,* or irrational fear, is amenable to an attribution approach. Ross and his associates were able to lessen subjects' fear of shock so that they could pursue more positive and productive goals. Presumably such common phobias as fear of heights and fear of closed or open spaces can be alleviated if patients can be persuaded to attribute their emotional arousal (falsely) to other external stimuli.

A study of the misattribution of speech anxiety suggests that under some circumstances people can actually relax and speak more effectively in public if they attribute their speaking errors to "subliminal noise" rather than to anxiety (Olson & Ross, 1988). No real noise was introduced, but subjects were told that they would be exposed to a "subliminal noise"—a noise they could not hear but that would affect their mood. The "noise" improved performance only under certain conditions. First, the subjects had to believe that the noise was causing the arousal that actually came from their anxiety. Second, they had to believe that the arousal was having a strong impact on their performance. If both of these conditions were present, the subjects relaxed and made fewer speech errors.

Another important study of misattribution therapy (Storms & Nisbett, 1970) used the emotional relabeling approach to alleviate a common but sometimes debilitating symptom: insomnia. Under the guise of a drug and fantasy experiment, subjects known to be insomniacs were given a pill (actually a placebo sugar pill with no real physiological effects) to take before going to bed. Since it was assumed that people suffering from insomnia experience a considerable amount of physiological arousal at bedtime, it was predicted that being able to attribute the arousal to a pill would help insomniacs fall asleep.

Subjects in an arousal condition were told that the pill would increase their bodily activity and make them tense and uneasy (in using this explanation of the side effects of the pill, the experimenters were mapping the reports of insomniac victims about how they felt at bedtime). In the relaxation condition, subjects were told that the pill would reduce their heart rates and relax them. In the placebo condition, subjects were told that the pill would have no side effects.

Subjects were then asked to record how long it took them to fall asleep (see Figure 3-3). The subjects in the arousal condition reported that on the nights when they took the pill, they fell asleep almost 12 minutes sooner than on the nights when they did not take the pill. By contrast, the subjects who experienced their normal insomniac arousal but thought that they were supposed to be calmed by the pill took over 15 minutes longer to fall asleep on the nights that they took the pill. The arousal subjects apparently were able to relabel their insomniac arousal on the nights when they took the pill. Thinking that the arousal was attributable to a pill and not to their own psyches, they fell asleep. On the other hand, the subjects who felt that they should be calm (because of the pill) yet still experienced arousal may have become more worried and upset over the tremendous amount of insomniac arousal that they believed they were suffering.

Storms and Nisbett's approach is of interest for more than its relevance to insomnia; it also sheds doubt on what we normally think of as the "placebo effect." We can all conjure up situations in which a physician is tempted to prescribe a sugar pill to a nervous and upset patient while convincing the patient that the pill will effect a cure. The placebo effect implies that patients' symptoms will abate if they believe that the treatment will help.

---

misattribution   The incorrect attribution of causality; generally an incorrect attribution of internal arousal to internal or external causes.

self-discrepancy theory   The theory that one's psychological well-being is affected by the match or mismatch between one's self-concept and one's self-guides: one's ideal self and the self one thinks one ought to be.

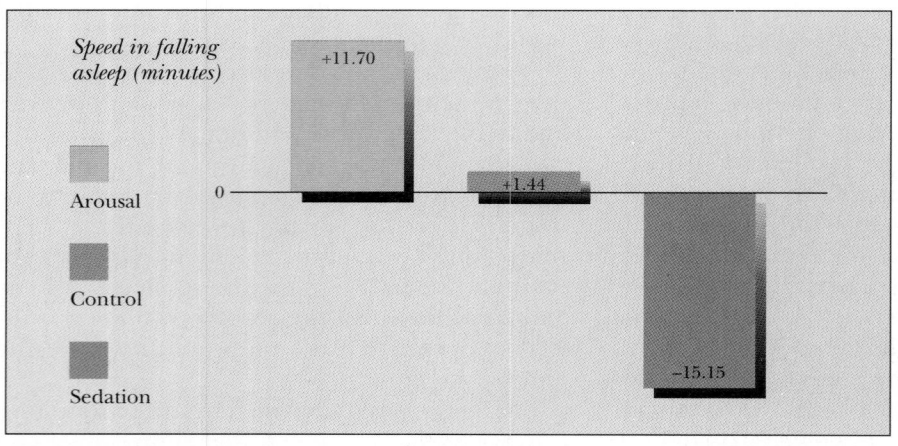

FIGURE 3-2 Teachers' attributions of the success and failure of students
NOTE: A score of +1 equals total attribution to the teacher's effort; a score of −1 equals total attribution to the student.
SOURCE: Johnson, Feigenbaum, and Weiby (1964).

Medical evidence has been accumulating that placebo treatments often have deleterious effects (Rickels & Downing, 1967). The data provided by Storms and Nisbett support this evidence, for it can be said that their procedure produced a "negative placebo effect." Their subjects who believed that the pill would calm them had more, not less, difficulty in falling asleep. In attributional terms, the fact that arousal existed even though an environmental force (the pill) was working against it caused an even greater attribution to a personal disposition ("I must really be a grade-A insomniac"). Therefore, it would seem that if a problem persists in the face of a reason for it to disappear, a greater personal attribution will be made—the patient will feel that he has a greater problem than he originally thought he had.

The provocative results of Storms and Nisbett's study, taken by themselves, seem to indicate that placebo treatments must be run in reverse. The placebo should always be introduced as causing the symptoms that the patient wants alleviated. Then the patient's feeling that her disposition (neurosis) is the cause of the problem can be *discounted* (recall the discussion of Kelley, 1971, in Chapter 2) and the arousal can be misattributed to an external source. However, the research picture is somewhat more complex.

Several studies show that direct placebo effects are common; that is, people seem to accept the direct suggestion that a placebo pill will alleviate their symptoms, and they got better (Kellogg & Baron, 1975; Bootzin, Herman & Nicassio, 1976). It may be that direct suggestion works when people do not have clear internal standards for the way they are feeling and can accept the suggestion that they are experiencing less arousal (Snyder, Schultz & Jones, 1974). There is ongoing controversy about when direct placebo suggestions work and when they produce negative placebo effects (Ross & Olson, 1981). Additional research will be needed to clarify the situation.

Another experiment on misattribution therapy (Wilson & Linville, 1982) shows how widely it can be applied—in this case to improving academic performance. College freshmen who had done less well than they had expected and were worried about their grades were given information that allowed them to attribute their problems to temporary factors that would eventually go away. Specifically, they were told that grades improve after the freshman year, and they saw videotapes of juniors and seniors testifying that their grades had improved over time. Subjects who received this information showed improved academic performance in comparison with subjects who did not. They scored higher a week

STOP, THINK, & UNDERSTAND

1. Distinguish egocentricity from beneffectance. Give some evidence of each of these biases in self-perception.

2. Explain how people with internal vs. external perceived loci of control differ in their attributions and behavior.

3. What is the reformulated learned helplessness theory? How does it explain depression?

4. Explain how self-complexity helps and self-discrepancies hurt psychological well-being.

5. How can misattribution therapy be used to relieve insomnia?

Dweck's reasoning turned out to be correct. Helpless children in her study received either reattribution training or extensive training with only success experiences. Children in the reattribution training condition were told that they had failed on a certain number of the math problems that they had attempted. Each time they failed they were told that they had done so because they had not tried hard enough. In the success-only condition, the children simply worked on the same number of math problems, but they were never made to fail or confronted with failure. Each child received five weeks of training. The results provided strong support for Dweck's proposal. Only the children who received reattribution training could experience later failures in other situations without again giving up and becoming helpless. These are provocative findings that attest not only to the role of self-attribution in the learning and maintenance of helplessness, but also to the possibility of treating people who have expectations of helplessness.

later on a test of academic performance, they got higher grades during the next year, and they were less likely to drop out of school. Clearly, misattribution therapy has great potential. It remains a promising and intriguing extension of experimentation on the attribution of arousal.

Consider finally a study by Dweck (1975) that has intriguing implications for the "cure" of learned helplessness and perhaps of depression. Dweck wanted to investigate possible ways of reducing learned helplessness in children. She chose as her subjects children who showed extreme negative reactions to failure. These children expected to fail, and in the face of failure they would simply stop performing and give up. Dweck reasoned that their expectation of failure stemmed from the fact that they typically attributed their failure either to their own lack of ability or to the fact that they had no control over their environment—both of which were enduring stable factors that should not be expected to change from one situation to the next. Dweck proposed that if these helpless children could be retrained to take responsibility for failure and simultaneously to attribute it to a more temporary self-attribution, such as lack of effort, then the learned helplessness could be alleviated.

Summary

As a result of social interaction, we learn a great deal about ourselves. Our view of ourselves is affected by both *reflected appraisal*—what others think of us—and *social comparison*—the ways in which we appraise ourselves in comparison with others. Usually we compare ourselves with other people who are similar to us on related attributes, though we may compare ourselves with people who are worse (or more negative) than we are to enhance our feelings of well-being. Sometimes people "make up" social comparison information in self-serving ways: they overestimate consensus for many behaviors but underestimate consensus for socially desirable behaviors.

Bem's *self-perception theory* argues that we make attributions about ourselves just as we do for others; that is, we consider our own behavior and the situation in which it takes place. We do not attribute attitudes to ourselves from things we were forced or pressured to do. One application of self-perception theory is understanding the *overjustification* effect, in which high external justification leads to the possibly mistaken attribution that a behavior was engaged in not for its own intrinsic merit but rather for its high external reward.

Schachter and Singer have suggested that emotions are subject to a type of attribution process. In their view, emotions are a function of physiological arousal and cognitive labeling. Schachter and Singer demonstrated that people who were physiologically aroused by a drug but had no adequate explanation for their arousal used the behavior of another person in the same situation to infer their emotion. Zillman has shown that arousal from one source can be transferred to another emotion and make that emotion more intense.

Jones and Nisbett have shown that we do not make attributions about ourselves in exactly the same way as we make them about others. They have demonstrated the *actor-observer bias*: as actors, we attribute our own behavior to external causes, while as observers, we attribute other people's behavior to internal personal causes.

A number of other biases affect our perceptions of ourselves. They operate much like the biases encountered in our discussion of attributions to others. However, the operation of biases in self-perception leads to different outcomes than that of biases in perceiving others. Many of the biases that affect the self have been characterized as part of the *totalitarian ego*—the organization of information in a manner that enables us to form a favorable impression of ourselves. Among these biases are *egocentricity,* or the tendency to process and recall information that is self-rele-

vant; *beneffectance,* or the tendency to see ourselves as responsible for good rather than bad outcomes; and *cognitive conservatism,* or the resistance of self-perceptions to change and the tendency to deny that actual change has taken place.

Different individuals perceive different loci of control for their outcomes. People with an *internal locus of control* perceive their outcomes as being a result of their own behavior and they generally "try harder." People with an *external locus of control* believe that chance controls their outcomes and they are more passive. *Learned helplessness* is a phenomenon whereby people cease to behave adaptively after experiencing uncontrollable events. Learned helplessness is a function of the attributions people make about their failures as well as a function of their perceptions about their degree of control over their outcomes in general. People who attribute their failures and negative outcomes to internal, stable, and global causes are likely to become helpless and depressed.

Studies have shown that if automatic arousal is misattributed, people's anxieties can be lowered. *Misattribution* can take on therapeutic aspects if people's troublesome fears can be attributed to external agents. Using misattribution, Ross, Rodin, and Zimbardo were able to reduce subjects' fears and enable them to work on productive pursuits, and Storms and Nisbett used misattribution to enable insomniacs to fall asleep. Wilson and Linville used misattribution to increase academic performance.

Key Terms

actor-observer bias
beneffectance
cognitive conservatism
depressive realism
downward comparison
egocentricity
excitation transfer
external locus of
    control

false consensus effect
internal locus of
    control
learned helplessness
misattribution
overjustification effect
reflected appraisal
related attributes
    hypothesis

revised learned
    helplessness (RLH)
    model
self-complexity
self-discrepancy theory
self-efficacy
self-evaluation
    maintenance
self-perception theory

self-serving bias   totalitarian ego   uniqueness bias
similarity hypothesis   two-factor theory of
social comparison   emotions

Suggested Readings

Berkowitz, L. (1988). *Advances in experimental social psychology* (Vol. 21). San Diego: Academic Press.

Cotton, J. L. (1981). A review of research on Schachter's theory of emotion and the misattribution of arousal. *European Journal of Social Psychology, 11,* 365–397.

Festinger, L. (1954). A theory of social comparison processes. *Human Relations, 7,* 117–140.

Gergen, K. J. (1971). *The concept of self.* New York: Holt, Rinehart & Winston.

Jones, E. E., & Nisbett, R. (1971). *The actor and the observer: Divergent perceptions of the causes of behavior.* Morristown, N.J.: General Learning Press.

Nisbett, R., & Ross, L. (1980). *Human inference: Strategies and shortcomings of social judgment.* Englewood Cliffs, N.J.: Prentice-Hall.

Schachter, S., & Singer, J. E. (1962). Cognitive, social, and physiological determinants of emotional state. *Psychological Review, 69,* 379–399.

Suls, J., & Miller, R. J. (Eds.). (1977). *Social comparison processes: Theoretical and empirical perspectives.* Washington, D.C.: Hemisphere/Halsted.

Wegner, D. M., & Vallacher, R. R. (1980). *The self in social psychology.* New York: Oxford University Press.

Chapter Four

Presenting the Self

*E*arly in Meryl Streep's film career, the actress had to give her best performances at home. The man she loved and lived with, actor John Cazale, was dying of bone cancer. Although Meryl knew he was near death, she threw herself into the role of being optimistic, cheerful, and supportive. In cheering John up, in behaving as if she had hope and faith, Meryl actually came to believe in his recovery. Not only did she "perform" well enough to keep despair away from Cazale, she kept it from herself as well. Meryl nursed him until his death, eventually moving into the hospital with him for his last two weeks of life. A nurse at the hospital said that Meryl "became his mother, his lover, his buddy. It was the kind of love you read about in poetry books" (Maychick, 1984). Cazale died on March 12, 1978.

Since Cazale's death, Meryl Streep has become known as one of the finest actresses in the world. She has been nominated for eight Academy Awards, most recently in 1989 for her stirring and powerful performance in *A Cry in the Dark,* and she has been the winner twice. Her success is unprecedented but it has created predictable difficulties. Meryl has lost much of her privacy. She longs for the simple anonymous life. But she also works with utmost devotion to be the consummate actress. Most critics believe that this is what she has become.

Meryl Streep was born in 1949 in suburban New Jersey. She was a happy child who concentrated on boys and cheerleading during her high school years. She was voted homecoming queen in her senior year. She was admitted to Vassar College in New York on the basis of her excellent high school record (except in math), a record that reflected superior intelligence more than hard work. Vassar was to have a profound influence on Meryl Streep's life. It was there that she became serious about acting. Her impact as an actress was so stunning that the head of the drama department was persuaded to do a play that he originally thought too difficult for college students after watching Meryl read the part. He saw that she was special, and that the power of her ability alone could carry the most difficult theatrical production. At Vassar, Meryl also learned something that would shape the way she portrayed many of her film characters: she learned that she could have significant intellectual and personal relationships with her women peers. Vassar certainly wasn't all cheerleading.

After college, Meryl pursued her acting career. She worked in summer theaters and spent three years studying at the Yale Drama School. After her graduation from Yale in 1974, she headed for New York to work in the theater and—if the opportunity presented itself—the movies. Her first film role was a small part in the movie *Julia* with Jane Fonda and Vanessa Redgrave. Few people remembered her in that role, but they began to take notice after her performance in the television miniseries *Holocaust* and her subsequent stunning portrayal of Linda, a young woman from a steel town, in the movie *The Deer Hunter.* She was nominated for her first Oscar for her performance in that film.

It was while she was in New York that Meryl met and fell in love with her leading man in Shakespeare's *Measure for Measure.* The man was John Cazale and Meryl began living with him shortly after they fell in love. They starred in *The Deer Hunter* together, but that was to be Cazale's last role; he died before the film was released. Meryl was devastated and exhausted by the effort to keep her acting career moving and Cazale smiling. Despite being emotionally drained after Cazale's death, Meryl kept working. It was not long before she got a key role in the movie *Kramer vs. Kramer* and her first Academy Award. Much of the power of her performance was due to her own rewriting of the script to make her character, who finally chose to relinquish custody of her child, both believable and sympathetic.

Not long after John Cazale's death, Meryl became involved with and soon married a sculptor named Donald Gummer. Like Meryl, Gummer is a devoted artist who prefers a private existence. Although the Gummers are busy raising a family and avoid publicity as much as possible, Meryl's devotion to her craft means that she must be a public figure. She won another Oscar for her role in the film *Sophie's Choice,* and has been nominated for her performances in *The French Lieutenant's Woman, Silkwood, Ironweed,* and *Out of Africa,* as well as *A Cry in the Dark.*

The amount of effort and sacrifice that Streep puts into her work is considerably greater than the general public realizes. For example, Meryl

Meryl Streep has an extremely well-known public self as a result of being an outstanding, Oscar-winning actress. Maintaining that public image can require a great deal of conscious effort.

had to learn German and Polish for *Sophie's Choice.* Learning a language or an accent for a part demands such immersion in a role that it becomes part of a performer's identity during the whole filming period. When Streep was making *The French Lieutenant's Woman,* a lifelong friend couldn't recognize Meryl's voice on the phone. And while she was making *Sophie's Choice,* Meryl's baby son couldn't recognize his mother's voice and cried when she approached him. Meryl must also deal with problems beyond being unrecognizable to close friends and family. For example, in a studio ad for *The French Lieutenant's Woman,* her character was referred to as the "French Lieutenant's whore," a description she knew would be upsetting to her family.

When Meryl gave the commencement address at Vassar in 1983, she spoke of "the intrusion of extreme self-consciousness" that is intrinsic to life as a public figure, but at the same time she encouraged the graduates to "take your heart to work, and ask the best of everybody else too."

Fortunately for those of us who enjoy her work, Meryl Streep gives the best to her craft, and we will enjoy it for years to come.

The Self and Interpersonal Behavior

In his famous play *As You Like It,* William Shakespeare wrote, "All the world's a stage," implying that the way people behave in everyday life is like playing different parts in the theater. Meryl Streep's life—and our own lives as well—shows that there is a big difference between private life and life on the stage. At the same time, however, the *real* optimism that Streep's optimistic acting gave her when John Cazale was dying demonstrates the degree to which we become the way we act. Much of the way we interact with our fellow human beings involves presenting ourselves in ways that we hope will make a certain impression on them, just as actors and actresses do. In fact, as we shall see, many have argued that Shakespeare's comparison of life and the stage is highly instructive, and that we need to understand how much of our everyday behavior involves presenting ourselves as people in the theater do. In this chapter we will consider how people present themselves, and how concerns with the self affect the way they behave in face-to-face interaction.

The Presentation of Self in Everyday Life

The sociologist Erving Goffman (1959, 1967) was one of the keenest observers of human interaction in general and of self-presentation in particular. His approach is often referred to as the *dramaturgical approach* because he compared the way we present ourselves with the way people on the stage present themselves.

Goffman's Dramaturgical Approach

Goffman wrote that when people interact, each person acts out a "line," much like a part in a play. By a **line** Goffman meant all the verbal and non-verbal expressions that people use to convey their view of the situation, the people they are interacting with, and themselves. An important part of the individual's line is what Goffman called his or her **face,** which he defined as the positive social value one claims about him- or herself when interacting with others. For example, when a person walks into a party, her line may convey that she thinks that this is a good place to have a good time, that the people are friendly and interesting, and that she is looking forward to the evening. The face she presents is that of one who enjoys a good time and knows how to have one. Acting out certain lines and claiming a certain face are the heart of self-presentation.

One important way in which people claim face is through the acting out of what Goffman calls **idealized performances.** When we give an idealized performance, we act as though we support and live up to ideal social values and behavioral standards more than in fact we do. For example, we may act as though we have more interest in culture and education than we really do by letting people see our copy of *War and Peace* (largely unread though it is), but keeping our *People* magazine hidden. This idealized performance is part of our line that claims face—that is, positive social value—in the realm of history and literature.

Goffman makes it very clear why people act out lines and present certain faces. One of the realities of social life that we saw in Chapter 2 is that people are constantly forming impressions of each other and making attributions. We need to understand our world, particularly our fellow human beings. In so doing, we quickly realize that just as we are judging others, they are judging us. It then becomes apparent that it is in our interest to control, if we can, other people's impressions so that they will treat us as we would like them to. Thus the basic reason for engaging in self-presentation is to control other people's impressions of us. Trying to control these impressions is referred to as **impression management.** As we shall see, more must be said about the motives behind self-presentation, but the heart of the phenomenon is trying to control what others think of us.

Once an individual has claimed a certain face by acting out a line, how do other people respond? For example, when someone drops hints that he is experienced in dancing and is pretty good at it, what is the reaction from others likely to be? Goffman argues that at least publicly people go along with other people's claims of face, thereby achieving a working consensus or the "veneer of consensus." Thus we would act as though we were impressed by and interested in the person's dancing experience. The agreement may not be genuine but it is carefully maintained by everyone. Goffman also suggests that others expect that we will claim good things about ourselves, just as they expect we will openly agree with the good things they claim about themselves. Furthermore, not only do we initially support other people's faces, but we do all we can to help them when subsequent events embarrass or contradict their claims. For example, if one of your classmates who has presented herself as good in biology gets a poor grade on a test, we will not only go along with *her* excuses, but we are also likely to offer our own ("You really didn't have enough

In her private life Meryl Streep Gummer does the same things the rest of us do, except that there aren't photographers watching us shop at the grocer's. Hers is a problem of continual impression management.

time to study properly with all the noise in the dorm the night before the exam"). In fact, if we think our friend did poorly, we will avoid even asking about her grade to prevent embarrassing her. And similarly, we expect the same treatment from other people. These efforts either to prevent embarrassment or to correct it, and to restore face when someone has lost it are referred to as **face work.**

Why are we so often expected to present ourselves positively and to put so much effort into maintaining faces—our own and others'? Goffman thinks that face work and other "interaction rituals," such as the "How-are-you-fine-thanks" exchange, are necessary conditions for social life to work. They allow people to interact smoothly, if somewhat superficially, and to avoid having to worry about hurt feelings or discomfort. Interaction rituals allow us to transact our business with people in a relatively safe and predictable environment. If something is lost in honesty and authenticity, something is gained in security, simplicity, and efficiency. As you might imagine, psychologists and sociologists have argued at length about whether face work is desirable; but there is considerable agreement that it is necessary, and even more agreement that it is pervasive.

Audience Pleasing, Self-Construction, and Situated Identities

Goffman's theories have inspired much thinking and research about how and why people engage in self-presentation. One general theory of self-presentation by Baumeister (1982; Baumeister & Hutton, 1987) suggests two major self-presentation motives. The first is **audience pleasing.** We want to please other people, either because we have a generally high need for approval (Crowne & Marlow, 1964) or because we want

audience pleasing Self-presentational behavior designed to make an audience happy.

face The positive social value we claim for ourselves in social interaction.

face work In Goffman's theory of self-presentation, behavior designed to maintain other people's faces.

idealized performance Behavior suggesting we live up to ideal standards of social behavior more than in fact we do.

impression management Behavior designed to control what others think, especially so as to maintain power in relation to them.

line The verbal and facial expressions by which we convey our views of ourselves, other people, and the situation.

them to behave in certain ways (Arkin, 1980). Thus, in general, we try to conform to their expectations and preferences. The second important motive in self-presentation is **self-construction.** Here we have an ideal image of the kind of person we would like to be, and we want to come as close to the ideal in our actual behavior as we can; in many respects, however, we are unsure about how close we really come. Therefore, we act as if we have certain desired traits and then see if others view our behavior as supporting our self-image. When others validate our self-presentation, the process of self-construction has occurred. For example, a person may want to see herself as effective in leading a group. In a review session for an exam, she takes the initiative in organizing the discussion. When others go along, she has advanced the construction of her identity as a leader.

An important distinction between audience pleasing and self-construction rests on *whose* ideas and preferences determine self-presentation—the audience's or the actor's. Often these preferences can conflict, as when a student back home from college on vacation doesn't know if he should reveal his new values and tastes—in the hope that they will be accepted—or conform to his parents' expectations.

When we engage in self-construction, we may do so in particular settings. For instance, the young woman who wants to be identified as a leader by her peers may want to be seen as an aspiring musician by her parents and as a witty humorist by her boyfriend. We attempt to get others to accept our view of ourselves in each of these settings, thereby "negotiating" a **situated identity** for each (Alexander & Rudd, 1981). Meryl Streep would like to maintain an identity as an outstanding actress in her professional life and as the quiet and private Mrs. Gummer, wife and mother, in her private life. We try to negotiate the most positive and satisfying situated identity we can in each setting that is important to us.

An interesting study of the difficulties of achieving desired identities indicates that professional sports teams on the verge of winning a championship are more likely to "choke" if they have to win at home (Baumeister, 1985; Baumeister & Steinhilber, 1984). Data from seventh games played in baseball's World Series and basketball's NBA Finals show that the home team often loses in the final game. The pressure of achieving the desired identity plus the pressure and distraction of supportive home-town fans can lead to more fielding errors and missed free throws for the home team. Ironically, home-town support acts to distract players from concentrating on effective performance.

Self-Presentation and the Self-Concept

We saw earlier that when Meryl Streep acted cheerful and optimistic while she was caring for John Cazale, she actually began to feel better. Do our self-presentations often lead to changes in attitude or feeling? Goffman (1959) argued that we are often "taken in by our own act" and hence begin to feel like the person we are portraying. Further, recent research suggests that self-presentation can cause us to adopt attitudes consistent with the way we have presented ourselves (Baumeister & Tice, 1984). That is, once we act as though we believe or feel something, we often internalize our behavior and come to genuinely feel the way we act. Thus Meryl Streep's experience is a common one. Just as we internalize the roles we play (recall Chapter 3), we internalize many of our self-presentations (Baumeister, 1986).

Power and Ingratiation

Implicit in Goffman's self-presentation theory is the idea that in everyday life, power is important. We want to be able to control other people's impressions of us and ultimately the way they treat us, which is why we engage in various forms of impression management. The idea that power is important in social life is much more explicit in two self-presentation theories influenced by Goffman.

Impression Management Theory

Impression management theory (Tedeschi, Schlenker & Bonoma, 1971; Tedeschi, 1981) holds that people try to obtain power in large part because power is important to effective interaction with others. One of the consequences of the desire to have power is that we strive to ensure that we have credibility. That is, if we can't be believed, if people can't depend on us, we rapidly lose power. And if we are to be credible, it is important that other people regard us as consistent in our attitudes and beliefs. Some observers of the presidency in the United States say that Jimmy Carter lost his credibility and power because of his inconsistency in formulating policy: because he sometimes changed his policies and couldn't be depended on, he wasn't always believed. As a result, his power to influence events quickly eroded. Thus, according to impression management theory, one major aspect of self-presentation is that we try to appear consistent in the interest of maintaining our credibility and power.

Strategic Self-Presentation Theory

The principles of ingratiation

Power is also important in Edward E. Jones's theory of ingratiation and strategic self-presentation (Jones, 1964; Jones & Wortman, 1973; Jones & Pittman, 1982). Jones's theory begins by considering the plight of the person in a low-power position. Power is one person's ability to reward or punish, help or hurt another person. The person in the low-power position in a relationship is the one who has less power to reward or punish the other. A factory foreman, for example, may have the power to give a worker a raise or to fire her. The worker, on the other hand, has relatively little ability to affect the actions of the foreman, and thus has less power. In contrast, an actress like Meryl Streep has considerable power in negotiating her salary: she can affect potential employers' profits by making a film with one company or by taking her services elsewhere. Assuming the perspective of the low-power individual, Jones suggests that this person will be motivated to modify the power relationship.

How can a person in a low-power position modify the relationship and thereby reduce the power differential? The answer: If the low-power person can ingratiate himself with the high-power person and induce that person to like him, the power differential can be reduced. What does liking have to do with relative power? Let us consider a student and a professor. Assume that the professor, by virtue of her ability to give grades, has more power than the student, who, whether friendly or unfriendly, has little real impact. If the student can make the professor like him, two things will happen. First, the professor will be less likely to punish the student by giving him a bad grade, thus reducing her power over him. Second, the professor will be more affected by the student's friendliness or unfriendliness and will care more about what the student thinks of her teaching, thus increasing the student's ability to reward or punish the professor. In these two ways, the professor's power advantage is reduced—though she can still flunk the student if she has to!

On the basis of this analysis, Jones (1964) predicts that low-power people will try to curry favor or attempt to ingratiate themselves with those in power and make themselves liked. A great deal of research has been conducted on the various ways in which people try to ingratiate themselves. Most of this research recognizes the difficulty of successful **ingratiation** and how those difficulties can be overcome. Some of these difficulties are summarized in the concept of the **ingratiator's dilemma,** which has two aspects. The first is that the less power one person has in a relationship, the more he or she will want to ingratiate. At the same time, the more powerful person will be increasingly alert to possible ingratiation attempts. The less powerful person's attempts to win the approval of the more powerful person may be seen as ingratiating and thus backfire. For example, the manager of a fast-food restaurant may be aware that certain employees act friendly in an effort to influence their chances for promotion. The dilemma for the employee is that the less power he has, the more he wants

---

ingratiation   Use of a variety of strategies to enhance one's image illicitly in the eyes of others.

ingratiator's dilemma   A problem posed by the fact that a low-power position makes a person want to ingratiate but alerts the target person to the possibility of ingratiation and thus makes it more difficult; also, the problem of wanting to ingratiate but not wanting to see oneself as an ingratiator.

self-construction   Self-presentational behavior designed to confirm a desired view of the self.

situated identity   The conception one has of oneself in a specific situation.

In relationships with a power differential, low-power persons will try to ingratiate themselves with the high-power person. Meanwhile, the high-power person will be on the lookout for ingratiation attempts. In the group of men shown here, who do you think has the highest power? Who is likely to be ingratiating?

Autistic conspiracy

to ingratiate, but the manager's awareness of his ingratiating behavior makes it harder for him to succeed.

The second aspect of the ingratiator's dilemma is that low-power persons, such as employees interacting with a manager or local managers interacting with a regional manager, do not want to view themselves as ingratiating. Ingratiation is considered somewhat demeaning behavior. Ideal behavioral standards dictate that we don't try to get someone to like us for ulterior motives, so we typically give idealized performances, indicating that we concur with that standard. But, as with other idealized performances, we sometimes violate the standard; that is, we ingratiate more than we admit. But the fact remains that people don't like to see themselves as ingratiating, as being a "brownie," and this too is part of the ingratiator's dilemma.

One phenomenon that lessens the ingratiator's dilemma is known as the **autistic conspiracy.** As we have mentioned, the potential ingratiator, the low-power individual, does not want to view himself as such. Further, the target person, the more powerful person toward whom ingratiating behavior is directed, does not want to view the low-power person as an ingratiator either. For example, the manager doesn't want to think that the employee is being nice for ulterior motives. She prefers to see the ingratiator's

behavior as genuine. If the employee compliments the manager's decision, the manager wants to believe that her decision is really a good one and that the employee's compliment is therefore well deserved. Similarly, if a student agrees with a professor's point in class, the professor wants to believe that she was really persuasive and insightful, not that the student was "brownnosing." In short, both persons, the high- and low-power individuals, prefer to look the other way and believe that ingratiation is not taking place. This mutual self-deception about what's really happening is what is meant by autistic conspiracy, a phenomenon that not only lessens the ingratiator's dilemma but also makes it much easier for ingratiation to be successful.

Another way people try to cope with the ingratiator's dilemma is by being subtle. While there are a variety of ingratiation tactics, the general subtlety principle applies to all of them. Since people want their behavior to be believed, ingratiation can't be so blatant that it arouses suspicions of ulterior motives. We will discuss three behaviors that can be ingratiation tactics, all of which require subtlety.

Ingratiation tactics

One ingratiation tactic is conformity to the opinions and values of the high-power person. You can easily imagine a student nodding his head and saying yes when the professor makes a point. You have probably also heard of presidential aides doing the same thing when they talk to the chief executive. Several studies of conformity by Jones and his colleagues indicate how frequently and subtly people conform when they have an opportunity to agree or disagree with the opinions of a high-power person who can control their outcomes. These studies show that lower power leads to both more conformity and more subtlety—just as the ingratiator's dilemma would lead us to predict.

In one study, naval ROTC freshmen conformed a good deal to the opinions expressed by high-status ROTC seniors. However, they seemed to "pick their spots." That is, they would conform on issues that concerned the ROTC program, but they maintained independence on such issues as music and the movies, things having nothing to do with ROTC. In this way they showed that they could think for themselves without challenging the authority of their senior officers (Jones, Gergen & Jones, 1964). In another study, low-power subjects who conformed indicated that they were extremely confident about their opinions, as if to show that the views they were mirroring were their own. When they disagreed, they qualified what they said by indicating that they were not very confident about their opinions (Jones & Jones, 1964). In still another study, subjects who were low in power showed a tendency to conform more on the target person's basic values than on his specific opinions (Davis & Florquist, 1965). In all cases, people tried to indicate that their conformity was not total and that they really meant it when they agreed.

Sometimes conformity is nonverbal. In one study, women subjects who came for a job interview were given information about the opinions of the male interviewer. Some were told that the interviewer valued the traditional emotional and deferential female, while others were told that the interviewer preferred more liberated women. Depending on what they had been told about the interviewer, when the subjects came to the interview they actually dressed and behaved differently, in addition to saying the things they thought the interviewer wanted to hear. When the interviewer allegedly preferred traditional women, the subjects wore more makeup and a lot of feminine jewelry; they also behaved more passively in general. The women who were interviewed by the man who allegedly preferred liberated women talked more and made more eye contact with the interviewer, and generally acted more assertively (Von Baeyer, Sherk & Zanna, 1981). In short, ingratiating conformity can be both verbal and nonverbal and it is usually highly subtle.

Another ingratiation tactic is flattery, or other-enhancement. If we say nice things to other people, indicating that we like or admire them, there is a good chance that they will like us in return. Subtlety is important here as well. Our flattery or building up of the other person must be perceived as sincere and credible. For example, research indicates that we like other people who like us—especially if they appear discerning and discriminating in their judgments. People who are *always* positive aren't liked as much; their enhancing comments about us aren't perceived

as especially significant (Mettee & Aronson, 1974). Other research shows that it is important that the person who says nice things about us doesn't seem to have anything to gain. In general, the more people like us, the more we like them, but this isn't true if the other person has an ulterior motive and is obviously ingratiating (Jones & Wortman, 1973).

There are a number of interesting ways to flatter others. In his famous book *How to Win Friends and Influence People,* Dale Carnegie (1936) talked about ways to show that others are significant to you. One way is simply to call them by name. Army officers sometimes find that soldiers generally respond more favorably when they are called by name. As Carnegie said, our names are the "sweetest sound" we can hear.

We noted earlier that the behavior of "self-construction" (Baumeister & Hutton, 1987) often occurs around personal characteristics that we value highly but are unsure that we possess. For example, a person who values being athletic will see if he can impress others in a game of volleyball. Gaining others' approval results in self-construction. Not surprisingly, flattery often works best when we flatter other people in areas where they are unsure of themselves (Schlenker, 1980). Complimenting a statistics professor on her facility with mathematical expressions won't have much impact; she already knows she's good with numbers. But telling her that you like her witty examples, which she is very insecure about, should lead her to appreciate your discerning appraisal.

Meryl Streep works in a highly competitive profession—acting—where, as we can imagine, conformity and flattery are used frequently, along with a host of other ingratiation tactics designed to get people roles in plays, top billing in a film, and so on. Meryl's remarkable career shows that a third form of ingratiation is often successful—simply presenting oneself as positively as possible. Often this means using self-enhancement, revealing positive information about ourselves. In Meryl's case, it typically means just showing

---

autistic conspiracy The tendency for an ingratiator and a target person to pretend or believe that ingratiation is not occurring, because neither one wants to acknowledge it.

what she can do in reading a role. Meryl is neither overly modest nor self-congratulatory; she is simply direct about how she thinks parts should be played and what she believes she can bring to them. Research shows, however, that people often present themselves very positively, or sometimes modestly, depending on what they consider appropriate to the occasion (Gergen & Taylor, 1969). In short, self-presentation, in the direction of either modesty or self-enhancement, is a third ingratiation tactic, along with conformity and flattery.

Other self-presentation strategies

Thus far, we have considered self-presentation tactics designed for ingratiation—making other people like us. Making others like us gives us more power in our relationships. However, several other important self-presentation strategies (Jones & Pittman, 1982) are used to try to control the way other people view and treat us. While ingratiation aims at getting people to like us, the other strategies are designed to elicit somewhat different perceptions in others, and to induce them to act accordingly. The four we will consider—intimidation, self-promotion, exemplification, and supplication—are used to induce others to fear us, respect our abilities, respect our morals, and feel sorry for us, respectively.

In the case of **intimidation,** a person tries to influence someone else's behavior through fear. The intimidator attempts to appear powerful and willing to use power, and often uses threats of punishment. Jones and Pittman give street robbers or muggers as examples of intimidators who use threats and fear to gain compliance; for example, to force their victims to hand over money. Intimidation is frequently seen in sports. During the introductions and instructions before a boxing match, the fighters glare at each other as menacingly as possible, each trying to strike fear in the other. In football games, the players frequently shout in threatening ways at each other, especially at quarterbacks who have just been tackled. One former football player, Jack Tatum of the Oakland Raiders, wrote a book called *They Call Me Assassin* to discuss the intimidating reputation he had while playing for the NFL, a reputation he carefully cultivated to frighten his opponents and disrupt their play. The word *intimidation* is now used frequently to describe a

One self-presentation strategy is intimidation. We try to convey to other people the idea that we are dangerous and that we should be feared. Iraqi President Saddam Hussein used this strategy successfully when he invaded Kuwait.

tactic for dominating other players in hockey and basketball, as well as in football.

Intimidation can also be used in other domains. When Lyndon Johnson was president of the United States, he often intimidated members of Congress and aides to gain their compliance. Jones and Pittman note that self-presentation strategies can be combined, and Johnson provides a good example of such mixing. Often he mixed intimidation with sweet cajolery and ingratiation. He wanted to be liked as well as feared, so he presented himself as both likable and formidable.

The person who uses **self-promotion** wants to be respected more than liked. Specifically, self-promoters want to be respected for their intelligence and competence. To enhance the credibility of claims that they make about their abilities, self-promoters may acknowledge certain of their minor flaws or shortcomings (Baumeister & Jones, 1978). In so doing, they acknowledge that they have both strengths and weaknesses, but are generally confident about their competencies. Meryl Streep frequently worried that she was not as pretty as she needed to be for romantic parts. After one of her few unsuccessful films, a critic wrote of Meryl and her costar, Roy Scheider, "You can't strike a flame with two metallic matches" (Maychick, 1984). The respect that critics have for Streep's ability and competence is all the more impressive in light of the fact that they do not view her as exceptionally beautiful. Having and admitting a flaw can enhance our claims of competence.

Related to the idea of enhancing the credibility of competence claims by admitting weaknesses is the notion of enhancement (Schlenker, 1980). When we have done something competently, we may try to enhance the amount of ability that went into our successful performance by emphasizing how difficult it was (Quattrone & Jones, 1978). Some of Meryl Streep's performances seem even more impressive when we realize the emotional strain she was under when she gave them—because of John Cazale's fatal illness. Self-promoters may try to take advantage of the enhancement phenomenon by suggesting, for example, that their performance would have been more effective had they not been ill when they gave it.

Another method of self-promotion relies on the principle of association (Cialdini, 1989; Schlenker, 1980): we present ourselves as part of or connected to what is successful or competent. One form of self-promotion by association is "basking in reflected glory" (Cialdini et al., 1976), which is similar to the idea of vicarious beneffectance, discussed in Chapter 3. One way of basking in reflected glory is to wear college sweatshirts after the school's football team has won. Another is for the president of the United States to telephone the locker room of a championship team or a space shuttle after it has safely landed to enjoy being associated with the team's victory or the astronauts' successful flight. By getting as close as they can to the winning team or the successful astronauts, students and presidents bask in and share their glory.

A subtler picture of self-promotion by association comes from a study of students who had

Star of the Week

LEOS have a powerful personality and charisma that can be overwhelming. They have a zest for life and hate boredom. They handle all their roles with success, like Arnold Schwarzenegger (7/30/49), husband, father, actor, businessman and presidential fitness adviser.

If you were born this week, a vacation near water is ideal before the summer ends. During the fall, literary endeavors ought to be pursued. Volunteer work will be recognized during the winter holidays. Ask yourself this next spring—what have I got to lose if I go for it?

Others born this week: Delta Burke (7/30/56); Dom DeLuise (8/01/33); Carroll O'Connor (8/02/25); Martin Sheen (8/03/40); Richard Belzer (8/04/44); Loni Anderson (8/05/45). ■

Astrological readings are a source of self-promotion for many people. They usually give you an uplifting view of your personality and sometimes enhance it by letting you know about famous and successful people born under "your" star.

an opportunity to link themselves to another person by revealing that they have the same birth date (Cialdini & De Nicholas, 1989). Subjects were led to believe that they had done well or poorly on a test of social abilities. They also received information about another person, Douglas, whose personality profile contained information about either his social skills or his intellectual abilities. In some cases Douglas stood high on the trait, in other cases he stood low. The question was: When would subjects hide and when would they reveal that they were born on the same day as Douglas?

intimidation Behavior designed to get others to believe that one is dangerous.

self-promotion Behavior designed to get others to believe that one is competent and talented.

Subject's social abilities	Douglas's social ability		Douglas's intellectual ability	
	High	Low	High	Low
High	50	60	42	30
Low	42	50	70	20

■ Conditions in which subjects are *most likely* to mention birthdate similarity to Douglas

▲ Conditions in which subjects are *least likely* to mention birthdate similarity to Douglas

FIGURE 4-1 Percentage of subjects in each condition who revealed similarity of birth date to Douglas
SOURCE: Adapted from Cialdini and De Nicholas (1989).

The results are complex and subtle (see Figure 4-1). If Douglas had low *intellectual* competence, the subjects very seldom made it known that they had the same birth date, regardless of their own social abilities. They didn't want to suggest that they had anything in common with him—perhaps that they also lacked intellectual competence. But subjects were not always reluctant to reveal the coincidence of birth date when Douglas had low *social* ability. They did hide the coincidence if they were low in social ability themselves, but they were quick to mention it if they had just scored high on social ability. Why? If subjects were low on social ability, they didn't want to be associated with Douglas. That association seemed only to confirm the fact of their own low social ability. However, if they had been certified by a test as high in social ability, then they could reveal their similarity to Douglas. They seemed to be saying, "Despite my high social ability, you should know that I have something in common with a person who has low social ability." By revealing their similarity to Douglas, the subjects are, in effect, showing some modesty about their social ability, but they do this only when that ability has already been demonstrated to the person with whom they are sharing the information.

When Douglas's personality profile showed him to have high social or intellectual ability, only one group of subjects revealed their similarity to him. Specifically, subjects who had done poorly on the social ability test revealed their similarity to Douglas when Douglas had high *intellectual* ability but not high *social* ability. These subjects saw no point in trying to establish similarity to Douglas when he had high social ability. They had already been shown not to have that ability. If Douglas was high on intellectual ability, however, subjects who had done poorly on the test of social ability might compensate by showing that they were similar to someone who had good intellectual ability. When subjects had scored high on social ability and Douglas was described as being high in either social or intellectual ability, they showed no special tendency to reveal or hide their similarity to him. Once their own social ability had been confirmed, they had little reason to try to use the subtleties of self-promotion by association.

A third self-presentation strategy is **exemplification.** Here individuals try to present themselves as being moral and worthy, and as having integrity. The person who works late at the office or gives a great deal to charity is being exemplary in ways that might influence other people to behave in the same manner. Such individuals provide a clear and worthy model for others to follow. Like other self-presentation strategies, exemplification is used to influence both other people's impressions and their behavior.

A final self-presentation strategy, which can be viewed almost as a last resort, is one that Jones and Pittman term **supplication.** In this case, people play on others' sympathies by acting weak and helpless. The goal of the supplicator, quite simply, is to get help. Children who want to stay home from school may act ill or otherwise helpless to get their parents to relent and allow them to stay home. Supplication works best when people convey the fact that their helpless or weak position is not their fault. For example, college students faced with accumulating paper deadlines may ask for help from professors or deans by pleading the overwhelming pressures of assignments that are beyond their control. In short, we often present ourselves as being likable. But we also try to appear threatening, competent, morally exemplary, and needy, all of which can affect people's behavior as effectively as ingratiation.

The Psychology of Self-Handicapping

Others often judge us by the way we perform. It is for this reason that people use the self-promotion strategy of conveying as much information as possible about their competence. Of course, what people claim about their abilities eventually must be put to the test. Surprisingly, it has been observed that people often do things that put obstacles in the way of effective performances. For example, people in Meryl Streep's profession have been known to skip key rehearsals or to be drunk on opening night. And college students frequently stay up all night before exams, sometimes studying but often partying. Sometimes they lose their notebooks or forget to take care of themselves so that they become ill. (At least, on occasion, that is what students have told us at exam time.) Why would people, college students included, put obstacles in the way of successful performance? Why would they engage in what has come to be known as **self-handicapping**?

Self-Handicapping: Discounting Failure

Self-handicapping can easily be seen as a self-presentational strategy that makes clever use of

some of the basic principles of attribution. It is premised on the idea that putting obstacles in our own way provides an excuse for failure (Jones & Berglas, 1978). If we fail in the face of obstacles, an attribution of low ability can be discounted. The failure can be attributed to the obstacles; they provide the excuse. For example, the student who fails after partying can blame the poor grade on being unprepared, not on low ability. Research on self-handicapping suggests that drinking and underachieving are specific strategies that people use to give themselves and others excuses for failure. Thus, having a problem with alcohol and having trouble working to capacity are personal problems that can explain poor performance (Jones & Berglas, 1978).

Studies of self-handicapping have helped to make us aware of the circumstances in which it is most likely to be used. One such circumstance is when people do not have confidence in their abilities; they are therefore likely to be worried about failure and are more apt to engage in excuse-generating self-handicapping. In a study designed to test this hypothesis, subjects participated in an experiment described as a study of the effects of various drugs on performance. One of the drugs was expected to lower performance and the other was expected to raise it. Before taking the drug, one group of subjects was given a form of an intelligence test. For some, the test was easy and they were told that they did well. Other subjects were given insoluble problems but they too were told that they had done well. The first group felt that they had performed well, were told that they had, and felt confident about future success. The second group did well but didn't know why. They were *not* confident about doing well in the future, as they did not feel that they had been in control of the situation.

After receiving the feedback, subjects had the option of taking one of the two drugs before another form of the same intelligence test was administered. As the researchers predicted, those

exemplification   Behavior designed to get others to believe that one is moral and self-sacrificing.
self-handicapping   Putting obstacles in the way of one's own success, for the purpose of providing an excuse for poor performance.
supplication   Behavior designed to make others feel sorry for you and want to help.

subjects who did not feel they had been in control of the situation, those who were told that they had answered the insoluble questions correctly, chose the drug that lowered performance; that is, they handicapped themselves. Those who were confident tried to do even better on the second part of the test; they took the performance-enhancing drug (Berglas & Jones, 1978). These findings suggest that people are likely to handicap themselves when they are unsure of their abilities because then at least they can avoid being *blamed* for failure should it occur.

Self-handicapping takes many forms. One of the most interesting is presenting oneself as ill, or actually feeling ill (Smith, Snyder & Perkins, 1983). A study similar to the one described above shows that people will use—and possibly abuse—alcohol to handicap themselves. Students at Vanderbilt University, in Nashville, were told that they would be taking part in a study of the effects of self-determined quantities of alcohol on intellectual performance. Some subjects were given insoluble problems and either told or not told that they had done well. Subjects who were told that they had done well on the insoluble problems drank more alcohol before taking a second test than subjects who were not told that they had done well. Thus, in a situation where people succeeded but didn't have confidence about future success, they used drinking as a means of self-handicapping (Tucker, Vucinish & Sobell, 1981).

Self-handicapping strategies are not only ways of managing impressions that others form of you. They also provide solutions for the attributions that you make about yourself. Self-handicappers never have to face their own negative attributions about themselves. By self-handicapping, they can always discount the possibility that their abilities are too limited (Smith, Snyder & Handelsman, 1982). Even though self-handicapping can be done for oneself as well as others, research suggests that it is primarily a self-presentational tactic (Baumeister & Tice, 1985; Baumeister & Hutton, 1987). Self-handicapping is particularly likely to be used when other people expect future success from you on the basis of your past success, and it is less likely to occur when people can't observe your self-handicapping actions (Kolditz & Arkin, 1982). It is also most likely to occur when people feel that their performances

are important and they have no other obvious or salient excuse for not performing well (Sheppard & Arkin, 1989a).

Individual Differences in Self-Handicapping

As we have noted before, social behavior is affected by two major factors, the external situation and the personal characteristics of the individuals in those situations. Not surprisingly, recent research has shown that people handicap themselves to different degrees in the same situation. One study shows that individual college students differ in the degree to which they actually use the strategy. Social psychologists at Princeton University developed a scale to measure how much different people are likely to self-handicap. They gave the scale to members of the swimming team, then observed attendance at team practices, and asked the coaches to rate how hard individual swimmers worked at each practice. The psychologists predicted that the tendency to self-handicap might be greatest just before a big important meet, at which time swimmers might want an excuse for failure. The results showed that before unimportant meets, the high and low self-handicapping swimmers did not differ in their behavior at practice. However, the low self-handicappers increased their attendance at practices and worked harder before *important* meets, while the high self-handicappers did not. The combination of an individual's tendency to self-handicap and a difficult situation produced self-handicapping behavior. Similar results were found for professional golfers (Rhodewalt, Saltzman & Wittmer, 1984).

What kind of people are most likely to handicap themselves? Interesting differences have been found between high and low self-handicappers. One important difference is gender. Researchers have consistently found that men handicap themselves more than women (Berglas & Jones, 1978; Rhodewalt & Davison, 1986). It isn't really clear why this is the case. One plausible explanation is that men tend to make ability attributions more readily than women, and thus may want to deflect attributions of low ability for their own failures by self-handicapping and giving themselves, and others, excuses not linked to their ability if they anticipate failure (Sheppard & Arkin,

1989b). Research also suggests that men who are the most *uncertain* of their self-esteem, even though they may not be *low* in self-esteem, are most likely to handicap themselves (Harris & Snyder, 1986).

Concern about what others think of you is also likely to lead to self-handicapping. Individuals who have a high degree of **public self-consciousness**—that is, concern about how they appear to others and what others think of them—are considerably more likely to fall into the self-handicapping trap (Sheppard and Arkin, 1989b).

One final point. Self-handicapping gives people an excuse for failure. But is also has another effect, one that is related to our earlier concept of enhancement. If a person succeeds after setting up self-handicapping obstacles, he or she can enhance that success. That is, the success looks even more impressive if it occurs *in spite of* obstacles. Thus self-handicapping can be used as a self-promotion tactic if people succeed in spite of it.

Self-Attention

Much of our everyday behavior is fairly routine and automatic. We get up, get dressed, eat breakfast, and read the newspaper in a fairly habitual manner, without giving a lot of thought to what we are doing. Some of this behavior is referred to as mindless (Langer, 1989). Generally we do not think about ourselves very much when we are performing automatic behaviors, nor do we think about what others may be thinking of us (Wicklund & Frey, 1980)—we just go about our business. On the other hand, events in the environment can focus our attention on ourselves and put us in a state that has been called self-focused attention, self-directed attention, or simply self-attention, in which we are self-conscious or self-aware. As we shall see, when this happens we can behave with a great deal of deliberation and thought. We will also see that **self-awareness** is often unpleasant. Meryl Streep makes plain that one of the most difficult parts of her career is losing her anonymity and dealing with the "intrusion of extreme self-consciousness" that is

part of the celebrity role. Like others, Meryl Streep does not enjoy being the focus of attention, even though she understands that in her profession being in the spotlight is inevitable. What happens when people become self-aware, and why is self-awareness so often unpleasant?

Self-Attention, Self-Assessment, and Matching to Standards

Recent theories of self-attention suggest that people can become self-aware whenever they are asked to talk about themselves, when they are in unfamiliar or unstructured settings, when they can see themselves in the mirror or hear themselves on a tape recorder, when television cameras are pointing at them or people are looking at them, or when they are in a minority status in a group and thus stand out. Obviously, being on stage or performing before movie cameras produces self-awareness, so self-awareness must be a large part of Meryl Streep's life. But it is something we *all* deal with at times, so what are its consequences?

Self-attention theorists (Carver & Scheier, 1990; Duval & Wicklund, 1972; Gibbons, 1990; Wicklund & Frey, 1980) argue that when people become self-focused, two things happen. First, our overall self-concept and the various parts of it are brought into consciousness. Second, when the self-concept is on our mind, "self-assessment is inevitable" (Gibbons, 1990, p. 286). That is, we begin to evaluate ourselves. We do this by comparing some aspect of ourselves with standards that the situation makes salient.

Any of four aspects of the self can become the focus of attention. First, we may simply focus on our appearance, and evaluate the way we look in comparison with other people or in comparison with the way we look at other times. Second, we may focus our attention on our physiological or psychological experience. This often happens when we are in a strong mood or have been aroused by exercise, anger, passion, anxiety, dis-

---

public self-consciousness   Awareness of how others react to or evaluate oneself.
self-awareness (self-focused attention)   A state of paying attention to and being aware of oneself.

Many people aspire to an ideal and work hard to attain it. What kinds of expectations and frustrations are involved in trying to "measure up"? How can we tell if our aspirations are attainable?

gust, or some other strong emotion (Hansen, Hansen & Crano, 1989). Then we compare our experience with our normal levels of mood or arousal and precisely assess our emotion. Third, we may focus on our self as a whole, and form an overall evaluation of ourselves. Usually this overall evaluation is made with respect to our ideal self, although it may involve comparison with others. Fourth, and most commonly, we may focus our attention on our specific behavior and compare our actions with relevant rules, norms, or other behavioral standards. In some cases, we may focus attention on more than one of these aspects of self.

Consider, for example, what happens when we see ourselves in the mirror. We are likely to compare the way we look or the way we are acting with ideal standards of appearance or conduct. When we make this comparison, we often find that our behavior falls short of what we perceive as ideal. We may feel that our performance is not as good as we would like it to be, that our appearance isn't as pleasing as that of attractive people we see on television, or that we aren't being as helpful or cooperative as we feel we ought to be.

In other words, comparing behavior with standards is apt to be an unpleasant and painful experience because in all likelihood we will discover that we fall short of *our ideal standards*. What happens when people experience the unpleasant feelings that accompany the self-aware state of mind?

Escaping from Self-Awareness

One obvious method of dealing with an unpleasant situation is simply to try to get out of it. For example, Meryl Streep and other celebrities try to avoid or escape from self-focused attention by wearing inconspicuous clothes and attempting to blend into the crowd. What coping methods do people in psychological experiments on self-awareness use? If they face the unpleasant combination of self-awareness and falling short of standards, they too will escape as soon as they feel they can. In one study, subjects took a test that measured "cleverness," a combination of intelligence and creativity. Some subjects were told that they had done very well (in the upper 10%), and others were told that they had scored very poorly (in the bottom 10%). The subjects were then told to wait in another room for a different experimenter to arrive, but that if the experimenter did not arrive within five minutes, they should leave. For some subjects, the other room had a mirror and a television camera pointed at them, which, of course, induced self-awareness. Others went to a room that had no mirror or camera. According to self-awareness theory, the subjects who were not made self-focused by the mirror and camera should not have wanted to escape; they didn't need to think about themselves or their performance. But the situation was different for subjects who *were* made self-aware. Those who had scored at the top on the cleverness scale should not have minded being self-aware, since they would have felt that they had done well in meeting ideal standards. The subjects who scored poorly, however, should have felt extremely unpleasant when they were self-aware and would have compared their performance with ideal standards; they should have wanted to get out of the situation, to escape. And they did! Subjects in the low-performance/self-aware condition stopped waiting for the absent experimenter and left significantly sooner than subjects in the other three conditions (Duval, Wicklund & Fine, in Duval & Wicklund, 1972).

Although people typically avoid self-focused attention, several studies indicate that there are exceptions. If we expect to compare well with standards and to achieve a desired identity, we may welcome self-focused attention; we may even seek it out (Greenberg & Musham, 1981).

Matching to Standards

Sometimes people cannot run away from self-awareness; escape is impossible. What typically happens here is that people try to change their behavior so that it more nearly meets ideal standards. These attempts are referred to as **matching to standards** (Carver & Scheier, 1981; Mullen, 1983). However, whether or not people attempt to match to standards is influenced by their sense of whether they will be successful, their *outcome expectancy*. If people have a positive outcome expectancy, if they think they will succeed in matching to standards, they will attempt to do so. This process is called **self-regulation.**

For example, people who are self-aware are more likely to be helpful. In one study, subjects who had seen a videotape about a venereal disease epidemic and were made self-aware were more likely to volunteer their services in a prevention program than control-group subjects. The self-aware group attempted to match to social responsibility standards (Duval, Duval & Neely, 1979). Another interesting instance of self-regulation occurred in a study of Halloween trick-or-treaters (Beaman et al., 1979). The trick-or-treaters were told by the owner of a house (actually an experimenter) not to take more than one piece of candy. The candy was put in a bowl and the children were left alone to take what they wanted. Self-awareness was created with a mirror behind the candy bowl. The results showed that without the mirror, well over half the children took more than one piece of candy. But when the mirror stood behind the bowl and the children watched themselves taking candy, the cheating (taking more than one piece of candy) dropped to less than 10%. In general, when people are made self-aware, their efforts to match to standards lead them to socially desirable behavior that matches to social standards.

There are other interesting instances of self-regulation. For example, self-aware individuals are more likely to behave according to their own personal values. College women who were either high or low on guilt about sex were required to read pornographic passages and to rate how much they enjoyed them. Some of the subjects were made self-aware when they participated in the experiment and some were not. For self-aware subjects, there was a much higher correlation between sex-guilt scores and dislike of the passages. That is, when made self-aware, the subjects thought about the extent to which they had negative feelings about sex and reacted to the pornography accordingly (Gibbons, 1978).

While self-regulation or matching to standards is a common response to self-awareness or

---

matching to standards Attempting to meet ideal standards of behavior in a situation; caused or increased by self-awareness.

self-regulation The process by which self-awareness leads to matching to standards if outcome expectancy is positive.

TABLE 4-1

Private self-consciousness and public self-consciousness

Items measuring private self-consciousness:

> I reflect about myself a lot.
> I'm generally attentive to my inner feelings.
> I'm constantly examining my motives.
> I'm alert to changes in my mood.
> I'm aware of the way my mind works when I work through a problem.

Items measuring public self-consciousness:

> I'm concerned about what other people think of me.
> I usually worry about making a good impression.
> I'm concerned about the way I present myself.
> I'm usually aware of my appearance.
> One of the last things I do before leaving my house is look in the mirror.

SOURCE: From Buss (1980).

self-focused attention, people will not self-regulate if they have a low outcome expectancy. If they *expect to fail*, they will simply demonstrate *withdrawal*, a breakdown of normal self-regulation and matching to standards.

A Self-Attention Perspective on Group Behavior

We noted earlier that having a minority status in a group can generate self-awareness (Wicklund & Frey, 1980). A recent theory has taken this insight and considered the consequences of being self-attentive in a group setting (Mullen, 1983, 1987). The application of self-attention theory to groups holds that self-attention and matching to standards increases in a group as the individual and his or her subgroup become outnumbered by people belonging to another subgroup. For example, when performing in a play, Meryl Streep tends to become more self-attentive as the size of the audience (the other subgroup) increases but less self-attentive as the size of the cast (her own subgroup) increases. More specifically, self-attention is proportional to what is known as the *other-total ratio*. In Meryl Streep's case, this ratio translates to the number of people in the audience (other subgroup) divided by the total number of people in the group—both cast and audience. Mullen (1983) has shown that self-attention

and self-regulation increase precisely according to increases in the other-total ratio. Stated simply, the more you feel that you or your group is outnumbered, the more self-attentive you become.

A number of interesting studies demonstrate this effect. For example, in classrooms students are more likely to participate in discussions (matching standards for classroom behavior) as the ratio of teachers (other subgroup) to the teacher-plus-student total increases. As the number of students increases and that ratio decreases, students spend less time participating. Similarly, reports of lynchings in the South show that when the lynch mob is large, the atrocity of the lynching, as measured by shooting, burning, dismemberment of the victim, and so on, increases. Engaging in these kinds of behaviors represents an absence of self-regulation, which is what self-awareness theory predicts will occur when self-attention is low. When mob members vastly outnumber victims, the other-total ratio (number of victims divided by number of victims plus mob members) is low and the predicted absence of self-regulation occurs (Mullen, 1986).

Self-awareness theory is like a theory of the superego or conscience in that people who are a majority in a group have a low other-total ratio, are less self-aware, and show less evidence of being regulated by a conscience. Individuals in a large mob provide an excellent example of lack of self-regulation. Fortunately, self-awareness is generally a civilizing state (Wicklund & Frey, 1980).

The Effects of Public Self-Consciousness

We just saw some of the situational factors that can make people self-aware or self-conscious, for example, mirrors, television cameras, and being outnumbered by people belonging to a different subgroup. However, situational factors are not the only ones that affect self-awareness. Some individuals have a greater tendency to be self-aware than others. Research has shown that people differ in both **private self-consciousness** and public self-consciousness (Fenigstein, Scheier & Buss, 1975). Items from the self-consciousness scale are shown in Table 4-1. You might want to see how you score on them. People who are high on private self-consciousness tend to be more aware of their own internal states and feelings and their own attitudes and opinions. People who are high on public self-consciousness are more aware of themselves as social objects and are very concerned with their appearance and how other people perceive them. The second group is interesting in terms of self-presentation because their concern with making a good impression, with audience pleasing, can lead them to change their behavior to conform to other people's attitudes and expectations (Froming & Carver, 1981; Scheier, 1980).

People who are high on public self-consciousness tend to be more interested in clothing and fashion; this difference between high and low individuals is especially marked among men (Solomon & Schopler, 1982). Perhaps the degree of difference here is due to the fact that women are *typically* interested in fashion, regardless of their degree of public self-consciousness, a phenomenon that does not hold for men. High public self-consciousness individuals are also more sensitive to others in that they can predict how others will react to them (Tobey & Tunnell, 1981). One study of public self-consciousness clearly shows how sensitive people who are high on this characteristic can be to other people's reactions to them. Subjects had to wait for an experiment to begin with two confederates posing as fellow subjects who talked to each other and ignored the subject. Shortly thereafter, the subjects had a chance to indicate whether they wanted to work with the pair they had waited with or another pair. How did the subjects react to being ignored? Those who were low on public self-consciousness chose to work with another pair 50% of the time. Those who were high on public self-consciousness chose to work with another pair 85% of the time: these subjects were very concerned with their shabby treatment by the two confederates (Fenigstein, 1979).

It it important to remember that people can become self-aware either as a result of situational factors such as mirrors or voice recordings or as a result of personal factors such as a high degree of public or private self-consciousness. A study of juror behavior in mock trials shows that individuals who are low in public self-consciousness behave much like high self-consciousness jurors when they are in the presence of a television camera (Kassin, 1985).

Self-Attention and Depression

Generally, though not always, self-attention is not pleasant. People typically find that they do not completely match relevant standards, such as their ideal selves or their standards of ideal behavior in specific situations. As we have noted, when this happens, two responses are to try to escape from self-awareness and to try to behave in a more desirable way. Either of these courses of action reduces self-awareness and its unpleasantness. However, some individuals may consistently focus attention on themselves, with the result that they are consistently unhappy. That is, they may keep thinking about and evaluating themselves, finding that they are not all that they might be. They may feel that they don't measure up to relevant standards and they may be continually aware of that. What is the likely consequence of this chronic self-evaluation and sense of falling short? Several studies suggest that the consequence is depression.

There are a number of findings implicating a high degree of self-attention as a factor in depression. We know, for example, that depressed people have a **negative memory bias** (Blaney, 1986). That is, they typically recall more of the negative things that happen to them than positive things. This tendency to recall the negative can, of course, contribute to depression. What would cause people to have a negative memory bias? One possibility is that it comes from self-attention. When people spend lots of time focusing their attention on themselves, negative personal qualities and events can become salient. In other words, focusing too much attention on yourself can make you depressed! If this is true, one way of reducing the negative memory bias, and consequent depression, is by distracting people from thinking about themselves. A recent study showed that depressed people remembered more recent negative things that happened to them during the past two weeks than nondepressed people when they were self-focused. However, when they were paying attention to

---

negative memory bias   The tendency of depressed people to remember more negative than positive experiences.

private self-consciousness   Awareness of one's own feelings and internal states.

STOP, THINK, & UNDERSTAND

1. Explain Goffman's concepts of face, idealized performance, and face work. Why are they such prominent aspects of social interaction?

2. Why do low-power persons ingratiate themselves with high-power persons? How does the autistic conspiracy make ingratiation more likely?

3. What are common tactics of ingratiation, and what self-presentation strategies are there other than ingratiation?

4. Why do people handicap themselves? Under what conditions are they most likely to do so?

5. Explain the various ways people feel and behave when they are self-aware. Explain specifically the concept of matching to standards.

external objects, depressed people did not show the negative memory bias (Pyszczynski et al., 1989). In other words, it is possible to break the cycle of self-attention leading to negative self-evaluations that in turn lead to depression by getting people to avoid self-attention.

Another study has looked at people's expectations of future events; that is, their optimism or pessimism (Pyszczynski, Holt & Greenberg, 1987). Depressed people are more pessimistic than nondepressed people when they are in a state of self-attention. When they can be distracted from paying attention to themselves, they are not more pessimistic than nondepressed people. Again, the implication is that a high level of self-attention contributes to pessimism and ultimately to depression, and that relief from depression can be found by reducing the degree to which we pay attention to ourselves. Interestingly, other recent research suggests that women tend to have higher levels of self-attention than men, and that these high levels of self-attention may contribute to the well-established finding that women are more

frequently depressed than men (Ingram et al., 1988).

Self-Monitoring

In addition to self-consciousness, another personality difference has important implications for the way people present themselves. Individuals differ greatly in the extent to which they engage in self-monitoring (Snyder, 1974, 1979, 1987). **Self-monitoring** is adjusting one's behavior to situational norms or to the expectations of others. If you are self-monitoring, you control both your verbal and nonverbal self-presentation so that you can respond to those expectations. Being a high self-monitor is similar to being high in public self-consciousness, but self-monitoring is more complete. People who are high on public self-consciousness are concerned about and aware of how others react to them. The high self-monitoring individual is more marked by actively and effectively changing his or her behavior to adjust to others' reactions and expectations.

Snyder and Gangestad (1986) developed a scale to measure the extent to which people self-monitor. It contains such items as "I may deceive people by being friendly when I really dislike them," "I'm not always the person I appear to be," and "I would not change my opinions (or the way I do things) in order to please someone or win his favor." Other items on the self-monitoring scale are shown in Table 4-2. Although recent research suggests that there are not just high and low self-monitors—people may be high, low, or anywhere in the middle (Miller & Thayer, 1989)—it is useful to identify some characteristics of both high and low self-monitors. High self-monitors have been shown to be extraverted, good actors, and willing to change their behavior to suit others (Briggs & Cheek, 1988; Briggs, Cheek & Buss, 1980). They have been described as having a "pragmatic self" (Snyder, 1987). They have also been shown to (1) have a concern for the appropriateness of behavior; (2) give careful attention to others for cues as to what is appropriate; (3) be skillful in presenting many different behaviors in different situations; and (4) be able to change the manner of self-presentation (Gabrenya

TABLE 4-2

Sample items measuring self-monitoring

Answer the following items, true or false.

1. I find it hard to imitate the behavior of other people.   T / F

2. In a group of people, I am rarely the center of attention.   T (F)

3. I may deceive people by being friendly when I really dislike them.   T (F)

4. I can only argue for ideas which I already believe.   T (F)

5. I can make impromptu speeches even on topics about which I have almost no information.   (T) F

6. I am not always the person I appear to be.   T (F)

7. In different situations and with different people, I often act like very different persons.   (T F)

SOURCE: Adapted from Snyder (1974).

In a relationship, a high self-monitoring person would not only be very aware of the other person's expectations, he or she would be very anxious to behave as expected. How is that a useful quality? Might it be disadvantageous as well?

& Arkin, 1980). In short, high self-monitors are interested in adapting to the situation, they are skillful in sensing others' wishes and expectations, and they are able to modify their behavior to meet others' expectations. One interesting example of adapting behavior to the situation is shown in a study in which subjects either did or did not anticipate future interaction with a fellow subject. High self-monitors were more cooperative when they anticipated future interaction than when they didn't. Low self-monitors were equally cooperative whether they anticipated future interaction or not (Danheiser & Graziano, 1982).

Low self-monitors are marked by consistency in behavior across situations. They have a clearer self-image and are truer to that self-image than high self-monitors. They are referred to as having a "principled self" rather than the "pragmatic self" of the high self-monitor (Snyder, 1987). They are more likely to enter situations that are consistent with their self-image and they behave in ways that are consistent with their attitudes (Snyder & Gangestad, 1982). One reason that their behavior is more consistent with their attitudes is that they can access their attitudes from memory more quickly than high self-monitors (Kardes et al., 1986). Values and principles seem more important to low self-monitors than to high self-monitors, and they come to mind faster. In

one study, for example, low self-monitors supported a woman suing a university for sex discrimination to a degree that was predictable from their attitudes about affirmative action. The support of high self-monitors was not consistent with their affirmative action attitudes (Snyder & Swann, 1976). Interestingly, high self-monitors show their adaptability and flexibility by acting more in accordance with their attitudes when the importance of being consistent is made salient (Snyder & Kendzierski, 1982). That is, they can demonstrate the consistency of low self-monitors if that's what's expected.

There are some interesting differences between the ways high and low self-monitors process social information. High self-monitors remember more information about other people and make more confident and extreme inferences about them (Berscheid et al., 1976). The ability to remember other people's actions better has been associated with a capacity on the part of high self-monitors to make more accurate eyewitness identifications (Hosch & Platz, 1984). While this is generally true, recent research suggests that leading questions by a lawyer can inter-

---

self-monitoring Modifying one's behavior to meet the expectations of others.

fere with the accuracy of the memories of high self-monitors more than with those of low self-monitors (Lassiter, Stone & Weigold, 1987). Because they are more sensitive to the lawyer's expectations and beliefs, high self-monitors may be more misled by false information that the lawyer suggests.

Another area of difference between high and low self-monitors lies in the area of intimate and romantic relationships. As we will see in Chapter 7, high self-monitors put more emphasis on physical attractiveness than on personal qualities when they choose romantic partners (Snyder, 1987). Not surprisingly, then, high self-monitors believe compatibility between a man and a woman is determined more by similarity in physical attractiveness than by similarity in personality traits. Low self-monitoring individuals believe the opposite. They predict greater compatibility for couples matched on personality and interests than for those matched on physical attractiveness (Glick, DeMorest & Hotze, 1988).

Finally, a field study of people in organizations shows that high self-monitoring individuals function better in what are known as boundary-spanning positions (Caldwell & O'Reilly, 1982; Snyder, 1987). *Boundary-spanning* means working at the intersection between organizations or with people in several different organizations outside one's own. Such behavior requires flexibility and being open to other people's desires and expectations. This is where the high self-monitor excels.

A century ago William James (1890) wrote about the many different social selves an individual shows to different audiences: "Many a youth who is demure enough before his parents and teachers, swears and swaggers like a pirate among his 'tough' friends. We do not show ourselves to our children as to our club-companions, to our customers as to the laborers we employ, to our own masters and employers as to our intimate friends" (p. 282). The kind of variability in behavior that James suggests is more often found in some individuals than in others. The high self-monitor has the ability and inclination to behave differently with different people in different situations. Low self-monitors are on a straighter track: they know who they are and they act that way without being unduly influenced by the social situation.

Nonverbal Communication

In his book on the presentation of self in everyday life, Erving Goffman (1959) noted that self-presentation involves both verbal and nonverbal behavior. He distinguished expression "given," or verbal expression, from expression "given off," or nonverbal expression, and he suggested that the latter is less controllable than the former. Nonverbal behavior or expression is especially powerful in conveying emotion, and because it is less controllable, it conveys our true feelings even when we wish we could hide them. The feelings that nonverbal behavior expresses are shown with unusual power in one of Meryl Streep's most stirring roles: Sophie in *Sophie's Choice*. In the climactic scene, Sophie is ordered by an officer at a Nazi concentration camp to choose which of her two children will be sent to immediate death and which will survive. The horror of the situation and the emotional wrenching it causes are portrayed with genius. Meryl Streep must control her nonverbal expressions to make it look as though Sophie's feelings are spilling out despite her attempts to contain them. It's a stunning performance.

Nonverbal behavior communicates a great deal of information about feelings, moods, and attitudes. Information about these internal states comes from voice quality, eye contact, facial expressions, gestures, body movements, and touching (Brown, 1986). Nonverbal expression is often called the language of emotion, and many studies report that verbal behavior, by comparison, contributes relatively little to our inferences about a person's feelings (e.g., Archer & Akert, 1977). Brown (1986) has pointed out, however, that words certainly can convey a lot of what we feel. Meryl Streep's moving courtroom speech in *Kramer vs. Kramer*, in which she describes the difficulty of holding her life together, shows the power of words to convey feelings. Nonetheless, nonverbal behavior communicates feelings with great force.

Some Elements of Nonverbal Communication

As we have noted, there are many nonverbal behaviors that communicate. Among the most significant of these behaviors is gaze (which is often referred to as eye contact), facial expression, and gestures and body movements.

The effects of gaze

The way we look at a person says a great deal about our feelings, and it can significantly affect the quality of social interaction. People in love spend a lot of time looking at each other (Rubin, 1970), and looking at another person generally conveys positive feelings and leads to positive reactions (Imada & Hakel, 1977). In addition, gaze is associated with status. Lower-status people tend to gaze more at upper-status people (Exline, Ellyson & Long, 1975). One important exception here is staring or **visual dominance behavior.** Staring or looking at someone while speaking is assertive, dominating behavior. It can be an effective aspect of leadership behavior (Exline, Ellyson & Long, 1975). But staring can also generate uncomfortable feelings (Strom & Buck, 1979). In short, looking into someone's eyes can convey extremely warm feelings, but *staring* conveys feelings of dominance. Thus a high degree of eye contact can intensify any feeling, positive or negative (Ellsworth & Carlsmith, 1968).

Facial expressions

Scientists have been studying facial expression for more than a century. In 1872 Charles Darwin argued in *The Expression of the Emotions in Man and Animals* that particular facial expressions may convey the same emotions in all human societies and in animals as well as people. Recent research provides support for the idea that the same facial expressions are distinguished across cultures and that people in one culture can identify the videotaped emotions of a person in a culture with which they have had no visual contact (Ekman, Friesen & Ellsworth, 1982). Six separate emotions can be reliably identified: fear, anger, disgust, happiness, sadness, and surprise. For example, members of the Fore society in New Guinea who had never had contact with the Western media and had had almost no contact with any white people were shown pictures of Westerners expressing these six emotions: they made the same judgments about the feelings as subjects in the United States. Then the expressions of the New Guinea subjects in various

hypothetical situations such as "Your child has died and you are sad" were videotaped and shown to American subjects. The American subjects, in turn, generally identified the emotions being expressed accurately. In short, the face expresses the same emotions in different cultures, and the emotions felt by people in one culture can be identified via facial expression by those in another.

Some emotions are particularly clearly expressed in the human face. One is pain. A recent study showed very clear facial actions that led observers to infer that a person receiving a high level of shock was experiencing a great deal of pain, even when the person being shocked was trying successfully to tolerate the pain. That is, the person in pain fooled herself but not observers about how much pain she felt. Actions such as brow lowering, narrowing of the opening of the eyes, and blinking clearly revealed pain the person reported not feeling (Patrick, Craig & Prkachin, 1986). Another emotion very clearly identifiable by facial expression is anger. Human beings seem very sensitive to anger in other people's faces, and hostile, threatening faces are much more likely to pop out of crowds than happy, benign faces (Hansen & Hansen, 1988). We are extremely alert to signs of threat, and thus respond very quickly to anger in people's faces.

Gestures and body movements

Even though there appears to be some universality in human emotions and their nonverbal expressions, social psychologists recognize that there are also marked cultural differences in the expression of emotions. Ekman and Friesen (1969) have discussed different **display rules** or norms as to what emotions are appropriate to express in different situations in different cultures. One interesting study of the way feelings are expressed in different cultures showed that people looking at silent films of Mayor Fiorello La Guardia of New York could tell in what language he was giving a speech—English, Italian, or Yiddish—because of the typical gesturing pattern that is

---

display rules Norms as to the emotions that are appropriate to display in particular situations.
visual dominance behavior Staring or other assertive, dominating nonverbal behavior.

Research suggests that there may be universal emotions and universal ways of expressing them. Do you doubt what emotions are being expressed by the people shown here, even though they are from cultures different from our own?

associated with speaking in each of those languages (Birdwhistell, 1952). What are some of the feelings expressed through gestures and body movements in Western culture?

Some gestures are referred to as **emblems** (Johnson, Ekman & Friesen, 1975): they are commonly used in a particular culture or group to express certain feelings or ideas. In our culture, waves convey a warm greeting and a thumbs-up gesture conveys happiness. Other hand gestures, euphemistically termed *uncomplimentary*, convey aggressive contempt; you may be familiar with some of them. Body movements convey not only how positive we feel about someone else, but also how much relative power or status we

feel we have in the relationship. People who like each other lean forward, face each other directly, and assume a relaxed position. Dislike is conveyed by leaning away, looking away, and visible tenseness. High status or dominance is conveyed by relaxing and leaning back; low status is shown by physical rigidity—arms drawn in, feet together, and standing or sitting straight, more or less as if at attention (Mehrabian, 1972).

Deception and Detection

Earlier we noted that self-presentation and ingratiation can be somewhat demeaning. Ingratiation, for example, may involve flattering

Chapter Four   Presenting the Self

someone when you don't mean it, or pretending to agree with his or her opinions. Goffman (1959) recognized the exaggerated or downright deceitful side of self-presentation and suggested that people constantly try to check up on others' self-presentations by observing whether the less controllable aspects of self-presentation, the nonverbal, are congruent with what is being said. In recent years a good deal of research has been done on the nonverbal aspects of deception and its detection (Zuckerman, DePaulo & Rosenthal, 1981).

Central to this research are studies that deal with nonverbal sensitivity (Hall, 1984; Rosenthal & Benowitz, 1985). These studies show that in making judgments about people's emotions from videotaped nonverbal behavior, with voice quality but not actual words preserved, viewers come to the most accurate conclusions when they pay attention to those aspects or *channels* of nonverbal behavior that are the most controllable. The most controllable nonverbal channel is facial expression, which is followed by body movement; the least controllable is voice quality. Words—that is, *verbal* expressions—are the most controllable channel and, if added to the videotapes, convey the most information as long as they are congruent or consistent with the nonverbal behaviors and the nonverbal behaviors are congruent with each other (Blanck & Rosenthal, 1982).

The nonverbal behaviors that are the *least* controllable, voice quality and body movement, have the most "leakage"; that is, they reveal or leak the individual's real feelings, feelings that he or she may be trying to conceal. Therefore, these are the behaviors that are important to note in attempting to detect deception. One can construct a controllability-leakage continuum, with controllable behaviors on one end and uncontrollable leaky behaviors on the other (Brown, 1986; Ekman & Friesen, 1969; see Table 4-3). As we have noted, when the various verbal and nonverbal channels of expression are congruent, the controllable behaviors generally convey the most precise information. Thus, when we are being truthful, words followed by facial expression say the most about our feelings. However, when one person is deceiving another, incongruent messages are likely to be coming through the other channels. This incongruity can alert the target

to the deception. Or the person toward whom deception is aimed may be alerted by specific cues associated with deception such as slow speech, speech slips, and avoidance of eye contact (Zuckerman et al., 1981).

When deception is occurring, it is the leakier rather than the more controllable nonverbal channels that are apt to be most informative, and those are the channels to which people look when they try to detect the deceiver's real thoughts or feelings. Parents can often tell, for example, if their child is lying about a mess in the kitchen by paying attention to voice quality and body movement, as those channels can leak the truth and disconfirm the child's denial. Thus, when deception is being practiced, the controllable and generally informative verbal and facial expressions must be taken with a grain of salt. Although the less controllable channels, voice quality and body movement, are less precise and informative when they are congruent with the other channels, because they leak what is being hidden, they are crucial in detecting deception.

Recent research has started to explore how even the relatively controllable channel of facial expression can be penetrated to detect deceit. For example, people often smile when they are not really happy. We tend particularly to smile when we are engaging in face work. But are the smiles of a person who is not really happy the same as the genuine article? It seems not. Muscular activity around the eyes and lips is more frequent when people are really happy than when

TABLE 4-3

The controllability-leakage continuum

Controllable channels of communication
    Verbal expression, words
    Facial expression
    Body movement
    Voice quality
Leaky channels of communication

NOTE: The communication channels at the top of this list are relatively controllable. The ones at the bottom are relatively leaky.
SOURCE: Adapted from Brown. (1986).

---

emblems Gestures used in particular cultures to express certain ideas or feelings.

they are faking. The facial muscles can reveal disgust, fear, contempt, or sadness to the trained observer, although the muscular activity is very difficult for most people to detect (Ekman, Friesen & O'Sullivan, 1988).

You may wonder what kinds of people are most adept at detection. Not surprisingly, socially skilled people lead the way (Riggio, Tucker & Throckmorton, 1987). People who are expressive and socially tactful deceive the best. Those who are socially anxious are the worst. Apparently socially skilled people convey a much more honest demeanor while socially anxious people convey a deceptive demeanor.

Gender Differences in Nonverbal Communication

Throughout the history of research on nonverbal communication, a number of gender differences have been observed. These differences help us to understand the ways in which men and women differ and the relationships between the sexes.

Gender differences in nonverbal behavior

One difference between men and women is that their nonverbal behaviors are not the same (Henley, 1977). Women typically gaze when someone else is speaking, especially a man, while men typically do not look at women speaking. Women are generally apt to be more tense and formal in their posture and demeanor while men are generally relaxed and informal. Women are more likely to smile. Henley (1977) has argued that these differences between men and women are associated with the high-status, high-power position of men in our society and the lower status and power of women. Men's nonverbal behaviors are those that are performed by people and animals with power. Women's nonverbal behaviors are those of the submissive. Henley argues that by engaging in these inconspicuous, small behaviors many times each day, men and women maintain the power difference between them. For example, although women may behave ingratiatingly, their behavior is so clearly a product of the power difference that it reinforces that difference.

Another particularly pervasive difference between men and women has to do with touch-ing. Men touch but do not generally like being touched (Whitcher & Fisher, 1979). Women generally respond positively to touch, but do not usually initiate touching. In short, in day-to-day interactions, men touch women but women do not touch men (Henley, 1977; Major, 1981). In noting that men assert the right to touch and women acknowledge that right but do not claim it for themselves, we see another example of differences in nonverbal behavior that perpetuate power differences between the sexes.

Gender differences in expressiveness and sensitivity

The difference between men and women in nonverbal expressiveness and sensitivity can be stated succinctly: women are superior both in accurately sending and in understanding nonverbal communication (Hall, 1984; Mayo & Henley, 1981; Rosenthal & Benowitz, 1985; Wagner, MacDonald & Manstead, 1986). While there are occasional exceptions to these generalizations, such as the finding in one recent study of a tendency for men "to be more accurate at recognizing anger" (Wagner MacDonald & Manstead, 1986), they have been very clearly established. Some recent research suggests that women's superiority in conveying nonverbal messages may, in fact, be related more to the masculinity versus femininity phenomenon than to their actual gender. The term *masculinity versus femininity* refers to people's psychological tendencies (measured by a questionnaire) to behave in either a typically masculine or typically feminine manner. Subjects higher on femininity, whether male or female, were superior in using both facial expressions and tone of voice to convey their feelings (Zuckerman et al., 1982). Women's superiority in understanding nonverbal communication is especially evident in their ability to identify negative feelings, with the possible exception, as we have noted, of anger. This heightened ability may be a function of women's less powerful position in relation to men; they may have to develop sensitivity to the leakage of negative feelings (Brown, 1986).

Nonverbal communication of feelings, whether affection, dominance, or a temporary mood, is important in relationships. We know, for example, that nonverbal expressiveness, independent of physical attractiveness, contributes to initial likability (Friedman, Riggio &

Casella, 1988). Such expressiveness contributes to an individual's personal charisma (Friedman & Riggio, 1981). We may not be able to see personal charisma in a photograph, but we know it when we interact with a charismatic person, and feel the charm of that nonverbal expressiveness.

Research has also shown that nonverbal communication of feelings is important in marriage, an obviously special relationship between a man and a woman. One study showed that the nonverbal skill of the wife in both conveying and interpreting nonverbal information was significantly related to marital satisfaction (Sabatelli, Buck & Dreyer, 1982). Another study showed again that women's nonverbal skills were superior to men's and that both the husbands' and wives' ability to communicate with each other nonverbally was related to marital adjustment (Noller, 1980). Nonverbal communication is an important element of both self-presentation and mutual understanding. Its subtlety and pervasiveness makes it a subject worthy of continued research.

Classifications of Interpersonal Behaviors and Styles

Goffman (1955) noted that during self-presentation an individual acts out a line, a total pattern of verbal and nonverbal expression that conveys his or her definition of the situation, other people in the situation, and him- or herself. It might seem that there is an endless set of lines that different people could enact and that the varieties of interpersonal behavior would be infinite. Certainly, if you imagine how different people are, or even the wide range of characters and styles of interpersonal behavior that Meryl Streep has acted out in her film career, you are impressed with the great variety in human behavior. However, psychologists who have studied the varieties and classifications of interpersonal behavior have found that they fall into a surprisingly small number of categories (Bales, 1958; Carson, 1969; Leary, 1957).

Leary's research showed that if the correlations between diverse sets of ratings of **interpersonal style** are subjected to factor analysis (a sta-

tistical technique for determining the basic dimensions that describe the ratings), the basic dimensions number only two. One is a positive versus negative or friendly versus hostile dimension and the other a dominant versus submissive dimension. That is, even though people can be rated on numerous scales, many of the ratings are correlated with each other. There seem to be only two basic sets of correlations, one indicating that behavior is classified according to how friendly or hostile it is and the other indicating that it is classified according to how dominant or submissive it is. From these findings, Leary developed the **circumplex,** the depiction of the varieties of interpersonal behavior shown in Figure 4-2. Each variety differs from others in terms of how friendly it is—anywhere from very friendly to very hostile—and how dominant or submissive it is—from highly dominant through partly dominant and partly submissive to highly submissive.

Subsequent research has supported Leary's representation of interpersonal behaviors in three important ways. First, research shows that Leary's dimensions really do characterize interpersonal behavior. Second, it shows that people are quite consistent in their friendliness and reasonably consistent in their dominance. Third, it shows that each kind of interpersonal behavior provokes a complementary kind, just as Leary predicted (and as Figure 4-2 shows).

Regarding the reality of the dimensions, scales have been developed to measure eight of the major classes of behavior depicted in the circumplex, studies have been done to show that there are two dimensions of interpersonal behavior, and still other research shows that actual interpersonal behavior does in fact vary from one individual to another along the dimensions of dominance and friendliness (Gifford & O'Connor, 1987; McCrae & Costa, 1989; Wiggins, 1979). Regarding consistency, we have recently learned that people tend to be highly consistent in their friendliness from one situation to another but

circumplex Leary's classification scheme for interpersonal behavior, which arrays behaviors in a circle created by crossing a dominant-submissive dimension and a friendly-hostile dimension.

interpersonal style A characteristic style of behaving with other people, categorized by degree of dominance and friendliness.

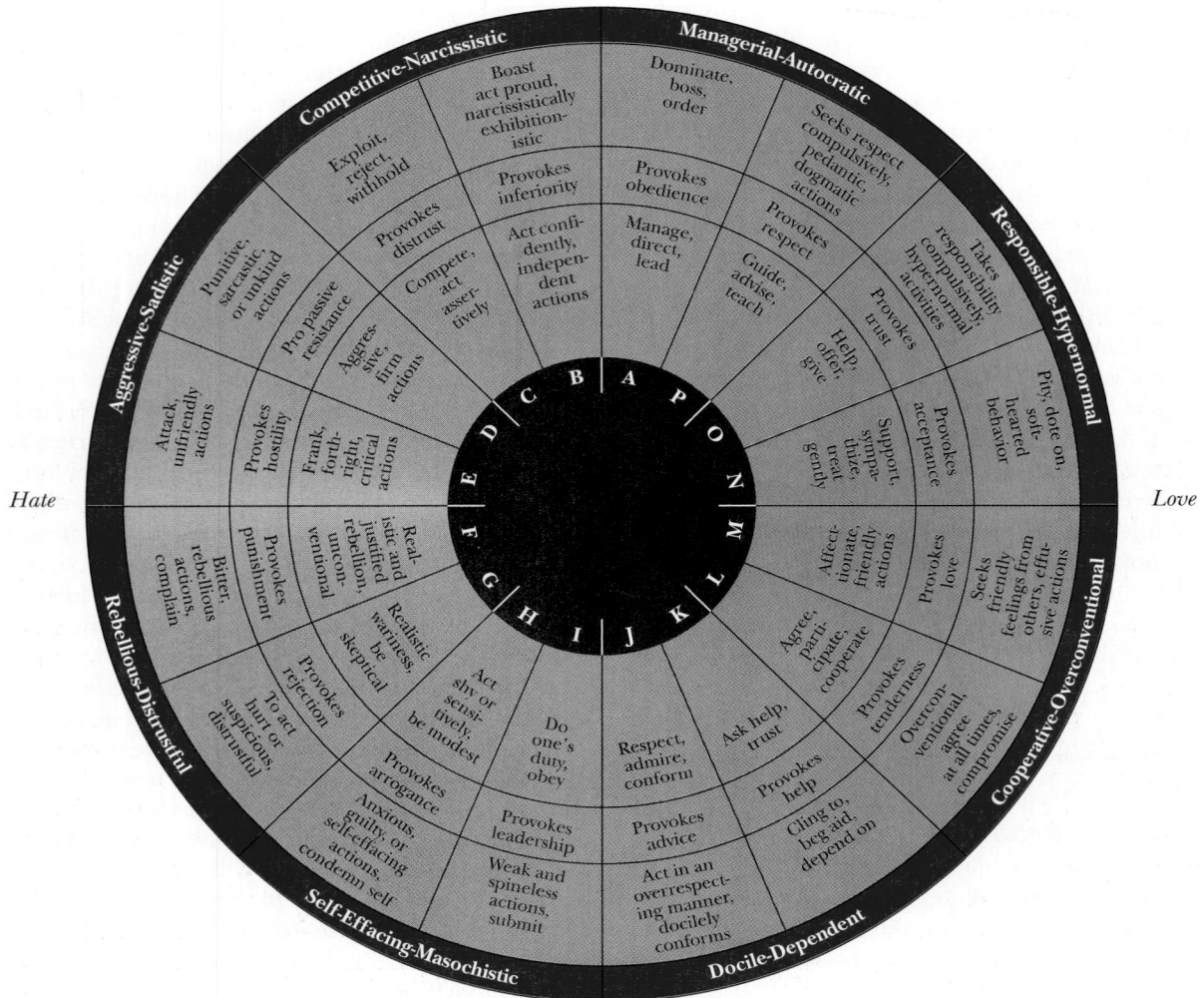

Classification of interpersonal behavior into sixteen mechanisms or reflexes. Each of the sixteen interpersonal variables is illustrated by sample behaviors. The inner circle presents adaptive reflexes; for the variable *A*, for example, *manage*. The center ring indicates the type of behavior that this interpersonal reflex tends to "pull" from the other one. Thus we see that the person who uses the reflex *A* tends to provoke others to *obedience*, and so on. These findings involve two-way interpersonal phenomena (what the subject does and what the "other" does back) and are therefore less reliable than the other interpersonal codes presented in this figure. The next circle illustrates extreme or rigid reflexes; for example, *dominates*. The perimeter of the circle is divided into eight general categories employed in *interpersonal diagnosis*. Each category has a moderate (adaptive) and an extreme (pathological) intensity, such as *managerial-autocratic*.

FIGURE 4-2 Leary Interpersonal Behavior Classification System
SOURCE: Adapted from Leary (1957).

somewhat less consistent in their dominance. When individuals are interacting with other people with whom they are familiar, they are consistent in their dominance. If you are a dominant person, you are likely to be that way consistently with friends, family, teammates, or other people you are well acquainted with. However, you are not so likely to be consistently dominant when you interact with strangers (Moskowitz, 1988).

What about **complementarity?** Leary proposed that friendly behavior would provoke or invite complementary friendly behavior in return and that unfriendly behavior would elicit complementary unfriendliness. That is, friendliness or unfriendliness would invite similar behavior from others. He also suggested that dominance and submissiveness invite their opposites. Dominant behavior provokes complementary submissiveness while submissiveness, in turn, invites dominance. Recent research supports this part of Leary's theory as well (Strong et al., 1988).

Since people tend to behave consistently within and to some extent across situations, we can talk about interpersonal styles in terms of whether people's characteristic interpersonal behaviors are of the friendly versus unfriendly variety and of the dominant versus submissive variety. On stage or in front of the camera, Meryl Streep can adopt any interpersonal style. Off camera, however, her style seems friendly but not exceptionally dominant, though it is certainly not submissive: she can be assertive and has thus held leadership positions, but she is not domineering.

The idea of interpersonal styles is helpful in understanding the different lines that people act out in self-presentation. Although there are many different kinds of lines, all of them can be classified according to one of the interpersonal styles. Thus, in acting out a line a person behaves in a way that is—both verbally and nonverbally—to some degree friendly or hostile and to some degree dominant or submissive. In this way the person conveys what she thinks of herself and how she feels about her relationship with the other person. By acting friendly, she indicates that she sees the relationship as a friendly one. By acting submissive, she indicates that she sees the relationship as one of unequal status in which the other person is dominant. Of the two basic dimensions of a relationship, one runs from friendliness and warmth to hostility and coldness, the other from equal to unequal status (Brown, 1965). These two dimensions are essentially the same as the friendliness and dominance dimensions of interpersonal behavior. The quality of interpersonal behavior that we enact in our lines conveys how we see the quality of our relationship with the other person.

Self-Disclosure

Self-presentation, especially of the audience-pleasing variety, has a somewhat distasteful quality. It is pervasive, but as we saw when we discussed the autistic conspiracy earlier in the chapter, no one likes to admit that it happens. We can distinguish audience pleasing from self-construction (Baumeister, 1982; Baumeister & Hutton, 1987) and realize that sometimes when we present ourselves we are being true to the person we would like to be and hope we are, and that at such times we would like the other person to accept that definition of who we are. One of the kinds of behavior involved in self-construction is self-disclosure. **Self-disclosure** can be defined as talking to another person about private matters; for example, your needs, values, attitudes, background, worries, and aspirations (Archer, 1980). Several items from a scale measuring self-disclosure are shown in Table 4-4, in which people are asked to indicate how much they have talked to their parents, their male and female friends, and their spouses about each topic.

People generally find self-disclosure highly rewarding: it offers the possibility of both self-construction and self-realization. It can also reduce loneliness, although lonely people may be less likely to disclose themselves in the first place (Davis & Franzoni, 1986). In addition, self-disclosure often leads to intimacy with the person with whom we are sharing personal information (Jourard,

complementarity   The quality of eliciting a behavioral response that dovetails with one's own behavior.
self-disclosure   The act of revealing personal information to others.

Talk show hosts and TV interviewers specialize in disclosures, bringing apparently private selves to public presentation. But when the persons disclosing information know they are on TV, are their "private" disclosures really private? Or are they part of the public presentation of self?

1971; Rubin & Schlenker, 1978). In intimate relationships, including marriage, mutual self-disclosure enhances the quality of the relationship (Hendrick, 1981). One important determinant of self-disclosure is **reciprocity** (Cohn & Strassberg, 1983; Cozby, 1972). The more someone discloses to us, the more we disclose to him or her. Reciprocity can produce relationships marked by a high degree of mutual self-disclosure, even though the individuals in it are not generally high self-disclosers (Miller & Kenny, 1986). We don't always like a person who discloses a great deal to us—sometimes it's too much too soon—but even here we follow the reciprocity principle and disclose more in return (Kleinke & Kahn, 1980). We may not match the other's degree of self-disclosure exactly if it doesn't seem appropriate to do so in the situation; instead, we will compromise between the reciprocity principle and a desire to follow the situational norms for appropriate self-disclosure.

If mutual self-disclosure often leads to intimacy but sometimes, if it happens too soon, produces negative reactions, what *is* the right amount at the right time? We prefer people who warm up to us slowly in that their self-disclosures come at the end of a conversation (Jones & Gordon, 1972; Jones & Archer, 1976). One exception to this rule is that we like being told very early in our interaction with someone about a negative event for which that person was responsible (Archer & Burleson, 1980): this seems to clear the air and lead to greater liking. Also, we like it when someone who is ordinarily reserved opens up to us and discloses something that seems to signify that he or she feels unusually open with us (Taylor, Gould & Brounstein, 1981).

Research on self-disclosure shows consistent differences between men and women in both their degree of self-disclosure and what they actually reveal. Women generally disclose more than men, especially about relationships and other personal

Chapter Four   Presenting the Self

TABLE 4-4

Sample items from Jourard's Self-Disclosure Questionnaire

Instructions: The answer sheet you have been given has columns with the headings "Mother," "Father," "Male Friend," "Female Friend," and "Spouse." You are to read each item on the questionnaire and then indicate on the answer sheet the extent that you have talked about that item to each person; that is, the extent that you have made yourself known to that person. Use the rating scale that you see on the answer sheet to describe the extent that you have talked about each item.

1. My personal views on sexual morality—how I feel that I and others ought to behave in sexual matters.

2. What I would appreciate most for a present.

3. What I enjoy most, and get the most satisfaction from in my present work.

4. How I really feel about the people that I work for, or work with.

5. All of my present sources of income—wages, fees, allowance, dividends, etc.

6. The facts of my present sex life—including knowledge of how I get sexual gratification; any problems that I might have; with whom I have relations, if anybody.

7. Things in the past or present that I feel guilty or ashamed and guilty about.

8. My present physical measurements, for example, height, weight, waist, etc.

SOURCE: Jourard (1971).

matters (Cozby, 1972; Davidson & Duberman, 1982). Gender-role stereotypes can also govern self-disclosure. Both men and women who are insecure and socially anxious are likely to disclose themselves in a way that is consistent with gender-role stereotypes, and thus they may reinforce and perpetuate those stereotypes (Snell, 1989). Times may be changing, but recent research shows that men are still evaluated more negatively than women for personal self-disclosure, perhaps because men see disclosing as a sign of weakness (Cunningham, 1981). If this is the case, no wonder men don't self-disclose as much! Jourard (1971) has argued that men's lack of self-disclosure, their tendency to hold everything in, adds stress to their lives. Henley (1977) has argued that men only disclose to women with whom they are intimate, which puts the woman in the position of being an "emotional service station." She argues that such a pattern is not good for either

STOP, THINK, & UNDERSTAND

1. What are high and low self-monitoring individuals like? What are the principal ways in which high and low self-monitoring people differ in their interpersonal behavior?

2. Explain how deception can most easily be detected from nonverbal behaviors.

3. What are the major gender differences in nonverbal behavior? In self-disclosure?

4. According to Leary, what are the two major dimensions of interpersonal behaviors, and what are the eight major categories of interpersonal behavior?

5. What are the determinants of the amount of self-disclosure in interpersonal relationships?

men or women. Given the satisfaction that comes from intimate self-disclosure, it seems regrettable that it should be so difficult for men to take part in it.

Summary

Erving Goffman argued that self-presentation is pervasive in everyday life because we try to control other people's impressions of us by presenting ourselves positively. We do this by claiming *face*. When we claim face, other people generally go along with our claim to form a working consensus that facilitates efficient social interaction. We try to support each other's faces by preventing or ignoring embarrassments or explaining them in a positive way. These mutually supportive behaviors are called *face work*.

Jones's theory of *ingratiation* and strategic self-

reciprocity A mutual exchange of confidences and self-disclosures.

presentation holds that we ingratiate, or try to get other people to like us, to enhance our power in a relationship. We must do this subtly to avoid alerting the other person to our attempts to ingratiate. We can ingratiate by conforming, flattering the other person, or presenting ourselves positively. Other self-presentation strategies include *intimidation, self-promotion, exemplification,* and *supplication.*

Sometimes individuals put obstacles to successful performance in their own way. This behavior is known as *self-handicapping.* Self-handicapping is most likely to happen when people are unsure of their abilities in an area. They handicap themselves so that they can have an excuse for failure and so that failure cannot be attributed to low ability.

When people are not self-aware, their behavior is generally fairly routine and automatic. People can be made self-aware by a variety of external stimuli, such as tape recordings of their own voices and mirrors. Self-aware people compare their behavior with ideal standards and generally find themselves falling short. Therefore, *self-awareness* is usually unpleasant and people will escape it if they can. If they cannot escape, people will respond to self-awareness by attempting to match their behavior to salient standards. In a group, people become more self-attentive if there is a proportionally large number of people in subgroups *other than* their own. Some individuals are more self-aware than others. People who are high on public self-consciousness are especially concerned with how they appear to others and how others evaluate them. Recent research suggests that people who are highly self-focused are likely to become depressed, and that distracting people from self-attention can reduce feelings of depression.

People who are high *self-monitors* are extremely sensitive to other people's expectations and are skilled in modifying their behavior to respond to those expectations. Low self-monitors are consistent across situations and their behavior reflects their clear self-concept.

Nonverbal behaviors convey a great deal about our emotions and our feelings about others. Channels of nonverbal communication include gaze or eye contact, facial expression, body movements and gestures, touch, and voice quality. Much of our nonverbal communication conveys our liking for other people and our feelings of relative power or status in relation to them. Facial expression conveys six different emotions—joy, sadness, anger, surprise, disgust, and fear—and the way people express these emotions seems to be universal. Nonverbal channels vary along a controllability-leakage continuum, with facial expression the most controllable and voice quality the most leaky. Men and women differ in their nonverbal behaviors and abilities. In general, men assert their power in nonverbal behavior while women are submissive in theirs. Women are superior to men in conveying feelings nonverbally and in interpreting nonverbal communications.

Interpersonal behaviors can be classified along the dimensions of friendliness versus hostility and dominance versus submissiveness. Individuals' *interpersonal styles* vary along these same two dimensions.

Self-disclosure is extremely rewarding and can lead to the forming of intimate relationships. While people generally like others who self-disclose, self-disclosure must be timed and limited carefully. Self-disclosure follows a reciprocity principle; that is, we generally disclose as much as others disclose, although we also observe norms about the appropriate degree of self-disclosure in different situations. Women disclose more than men. Men are evaluated less positively when they self-disclose.

Key Terms

audience pleasing	*display rules*	*face work*
autistic conspiracy	*emblems*	*idealized performance*
circumplex	*exemplification*	*impression*
complementarity	*face*	*management*

ingratiation
ingratiator's dilemma
interpersonal style
intimidation
line
matching to standards
negative memory bias
private self-
consciousness
public self-
consciousness
reciprocity
self-awareness (self-
focused attention)
self-construction
self-disclosure
self-handicapping
self-monitoring
self-promotion
self-regulation
situated identity
supplication
visual dominance
behavior

Suggested Readings

Bales, R. F. (1970). *Personality and interpersonal behavior.* New York: Holt, Rinehart & Winston.

Chaikin, A. L., & Derlega, V. L. (1974). *Self-disclosure.* Morristown, N.J.: General Learning Press.

Duval, S., & Wicklund, R. A. (1972). *A theory of objective self-awareness.* New York: Academic Press.

Ekman, P. (Ed.). (1982). *Emotion in the human face* (2nd ed.). Cambridge, England: Cambridge University Press.

Goffman, E. (1959). *The presentation of self in everyday life.* Garden City, N.Y.: Doubleday.

Jones, E. E. (1964). *Ingratiation: A social psychological analysis.* New York: Appleton-Century-Crofts.

Schlenker, B. R. (1980). *Impression management: The self-concept, social identity, and interpersonal behavior.* Pacific Grove, Calif.: Brooks/Cole.

Snyder, M. (1987). *Public appearances/private realities. The psychology of self-monitoring.* New York: Freeman.

Tedeschi, J. T. (Ed.). (1981). *Impression management theory and social psychological research.* New York: Academic Press.

Chapter Five

Forming and Changing Attitudes

On May 24, 1986, the family of Louise and Clifford Ray returned to their home in Arcadia, Florida, to discover their house in flames. The six-room wooden structure was so thoroughly ablaze that there was little chance of saving anything. This culminated an odyssey that had begun several months before, when Rick, Randy, and Robert tested positive for HIV antibodies. A positive test for HIV antibodies indicates the likely presence of HIV, thought to be the precursor of the deadly disease AIDS (Acquired-Immune Deficiency Syndrome).

The three brothers are hemophiliacs, and because the blood products necessary to control their hemophilia may transmit HIV, they are also members of a group at risk for AIDS. Rick, Randy, and Robert were healthy children, however, showing no sign of AIDS. Nonetheless, their journey through childhood, already made difficult by hemophilia, took a turn for the bizarre after the discovery of the HIV antibodies.

Clifford Ray explained to a U.S. Senate panel what happened when the family learned of the boys' positive HIV test. "After learning of our boys' positive test, we went to the pastor of our church seeking counseling. The pastor said it would be a good idea that we no longer go to church." Ray also said that he informed the local school authorities of the positive HIV test. School officials in Arcadia recommended that the Ray children be kept out of school "temporarily." The temporary absence lengthened to more than a year.

Although the Ray children had virtually no chance of communicating any disease to anyone in the community, all attempts to have them educated in the local schools failed. Finally, after a full year of the "temporary" absence, the Rays sued in federal court and succeeded in having the children returned to their community school. For a week, according to Senate testimony, the Rays were subjected to intimidating phone calls and bomb threats. The boys were unsure whether to stay in school. Louise Ray commented, "My husband told [the boys] that we would finish up the week and then make a decision. At the end of the week, the boys decided they wanted to continue. . . . My husband and I were happy. That same night, while we were out, our house burned down. We lost everything we had" (*Boston Globe*, Sept. 12, 1987).

Sagas like that of the Ray family are not unique in today's society. Attitudes toward AIDS victims, coupled with a lack of knowledge about the source of the disease, have caused replications of the Rays' troubles in too many households. A Massachusetts schoolteacher was ordered to take a medical leave and then resign when rumors circulated that he was being treated for AIDS. In New York, a mail carrier refused to deliver mail to an AIDS task force office because he feared catching the disease. And the columnist William F. Buckley, Jr., proposed in the *New York Times* that "everyone detected with AIDS should be tattooed on the upper forearm."

Persuading people of the truth about AIDS has continued to be one of the most difficult problems facing policy makers worldwide. How can attitudes toward AIDS and its victims be changed so that the spread of the disease may be curbed and the rights of its victims protected? The Ray family of Arcadia, Florida, suffered from the ignorance surrounding the spread of AIDS and the discriminatory attitudes of the people in their community. At the same time, thousands more people become victims of the disease while scores of thousands placed themselves at risk because they did not understand, did not believe, or did not care about the means available to protect themselves from it. Changing attitudes and changing behaviors of the population became a public health emergency.

In 1988 U.S. Surgeon General C. Everett Koop sought to correct the lack of knowledge about the disease. He had the U.S. Public Health Service mail a brochure titled *Understanding AIDS* to each of 107 million homes in the United States. According to a Gallup poll released on July 20, 1988, 82% of the people who recall receiving the pamphlet read it. Of those, one-third reported that it increased their knowledge about AIDS. Among the most important functions of the brochure was to persuade people of the inaccuracy of some popularly held beliefs. In 1987, 18% of Americans believed that AIDS could be contracted from toilet seats, 11% believed that they could catch AIDS by working alongside someone with the disease, 25% believed that AIDS could

Sometimes people's attitudes may be based on half-truths and fears, and this can cause people to act in destructive ways. The Rays' home was set on fire by just such actions as people responded to their fear and ignorance of AIDS.

be contracted from a cough or sneeze, and 26% believed that they could catch AIDS from a drinking glass. The barber of the Ray children apparently believed he could catch AIDS from hair, because he refused to serve the children after the discovery of the antibodies. None of these beliefs are true. The booklet also tried to squash another myth: that AIDS could be communicated by the bite of a mosquito.

No direct test of the effectiveness of the *Understanding AIDS* booklet has been carried out. The booklet, however, in combination with massive efforts by the media, has resulted in some striking shifts of public opinion. A subsequent survey conducted by the Gallup organization in 1988 showed some of these changes. In 1988 fewer people believed in the drinking glass, casual contact, and close proximity theories than in 1987, while more people were aware that unprotected sexual encounters were a major means of transmitting the virus.

Perhaps the most important effort in the

campaign to change public attitudes has been directed toward persuading people to take steps to avoid AIDS. The United States emerged from the sexual revolution of the 1960s with a more relaxed attitude toward sex. The ready availability of contraceptives lessened the risk of pregnancy. Homosexuals felt freer to declare their sexual preference and singles bars were crowded. In 1981, when AIDS exploded in the gay community, it caused reverberations in every sexual being. Yet there was little knowledge of the way the disease was transmitted. Despite warnings from health officials, most Americans believed that AIDS was a disease only of homosexuals and saw little risk in heterosexual encounters. Moreover, even sexually active people saw no need to take preventive measures to reduce their own risk. Change in this attitude has come slowly. Advertising campaigns in the media, as well as the surgeon general's AIDS brochure, sought to convince people that anyone can be at risk but that there are ways to reduce that risk. Reducing

What You Should Know About AIDS

In 1988 C. Everett Koop, the U.S. Surgeon General, tried to change attitudes and inform the public about AIDS. As part of his efforts, he openly discussed the use of condoms. Opinion was divided as to whether or not this was his proper sphere of action.

extramarital sexual contacts is one. Knowing a great deal about one's sexual partner is another, and the use of condoms in sexual relations is a third. The condom industry was quick to capitalize on the changing attitudes. In 1986 Life-Styles condoms began a $2.5 million advertising campaign, the first to rely exclusively on the all-important health features of condom use in sexual relations.

The need to persuade people in all countries around the world of the causes, communication, and consequences of AIDS continues to be enormous. The number of lives that could be lost if people are not aware and do not remain cautious is incalculable. And the consequences to people who are merely "at risk" of contracting the dis-

ease, like the three Ray children of Arcadia, Florida, may continue to be disastrous unless attitudes are changed.

How do we go about the process of changing attitudes? Appeals to reason, appeals to emotions, appeals for caution by celebrities and government officials have been seen in the AIDS campaign thus far. New techniques will continue to be introduced. How effective are these efforts? What have social psychologists been able to tell us about the process of attitude change?

Defining the Attitude

What is an **attitude**? People have attitudes toward a wide variety of things: AIDS victims, the practice of safe sex, presidential politics, our friends, our teachers, and so forth. Yet a precise definition of *attitude* has remained elusive. A friend of yours, Mark, may tell you that he believes practicing safe sex is wiser than not. You may have every reason to think that you know Mark's attitude toward safe sex. But wait! He may then tell you that he does not like safe sexual practices. Amazed at this seeming inconsistency, you press him further. He tells you that, although from a purely rational standpoint using condoms makes sense, they bring out a negative feeling in him. Which statement do you take as his attitude? Is he pro–safe sex or anti–safe sex? Before you decide, you should know that Mark is celibate.

Put another way, your friend has a belief, a sentiment, and a behavior in respect to sexual practices. Although on many occasions these three indicators of an attitude are consistent, in this case they are not. Which one represents Mark's true attitude? Not all social psychologists agree on a definition of the term *attitude*. Some view attitudes exclusively as sentiments, statements of feeling or affect. "I like the Reverend Jesse Jackson"; "I feel terrible about war"—these are statements of sentiments or affect. Other social psychologists include beliefs in their definition. "War kills many people"; "George Bush was vice president before he was elected president"; "The HIV retrovirus leads to AIDS." And still others include behaviors as part of their definition. William McGuire (1985), after an extensive search of the literature on attitude change, reported that more than 500 definitions of *attitude* have been used by social psychologists in their research on the subject.

Despite the plethora of definitions, most research has considered sentiment, or affect, to be the most important dimension of an attitude. Therefore, in this book we will adopt a definition of attitude offered by Petty and Cacioppo (1981), which focuses on this dimension of attitudes: a general and enduring positive or negative feeling about some person, object, or issue.

Measuring Attitudes

Imagine that the surgeon general has hired you in your capacity as a social psychologist to study the attitudes of college students toward people with AIDS. You recall that our definition of an attitude has us considering the feeling or affect of people toward the category in question. You will want to have students respond to questions such as "Do you like or dislike people with AIDS?" In addition, you will probably want to know the intensity of this feeling: "How much do you like or dislike people with AIDS?" A good attitude scale will measure both the direction and the intensity of a person's affect. Although investigators are free to create their own ways of asking questions about attitudes, some standard types of scales can be used.

One widely used measurement device is the **Likert scale,** consisting of a list of statements concerning the object of the attitude. For example, one such item might be "People with AIDS should be treated with respect and dignity." Another might be "People with AIDS are morally inferior people." The respondents' task is to indicate whether they agree or disagree with the various statements (the direction of affect) and the intensity with which they agree or disagree. A typical Likert scale consists of five possible positions—two levels of agreement (strongly and slightly), two levels of disagreement, and a neutral position.

Increasing Honesty: The Bogus Pipeline

Occasionally it is difficult to get people to tell us what their true attitudes are on a given question. It is difficult for subjects in an experiment to express negative attitudes toward a colleague; it is difficult for subjects to express unpopular political opinions; it is difficult for subjects to admit to bigoted or other socially unacceptable attitudes, such as negative attitudes toward people who test positive for HIV antibodies. If social scientists are to study problems involving attitudes toward others, however, they need techniques that can overcome the understandable hesitancy of respondents to express opinions that they feel they ought not express.

Jones and Sigall (1971) have reviewed a number of studies that used a form of deception to get people to state their attitudes honestly, even if those attitudes were unpopular. They have called this technique the **bogus pipeline.** The essential feature of the technique is to convince participants that the investigators already know their true attitudes. Typically, elaborate-looking machinery is attached to subjects, who are told that it is capable of measuring their attitudes toward an object. Using an appropriate rationale, the investigators ask subjects to indicate verbally or in writing what they believe the machine has discovered. In this way, subjects tend to disclose their true attitudes, for they believe that those attitudes have already been recorded by the electronic gadgetry and they would prefer not to seem to be dishonest.

Sigall and Page (1971) were among the first to use the bogus pipeline, in their study of racial stereotyping. In an earlier report, Karlins, Coffman, and Walters (1969) found that in the years leading up to their study, white students had adopted more favorable stereotypes of blacks in this country. Although Sigall and Page did not

---

attitude A general and enduring positive or negative feeling about some person, object, or issue.

bogus pipeline A technique by which subjects are induced to state their attitudes honestly in the belief that a machine has already registered their true attitudes.

Likert scale A scale that measures the direction and intensity of attitudes.

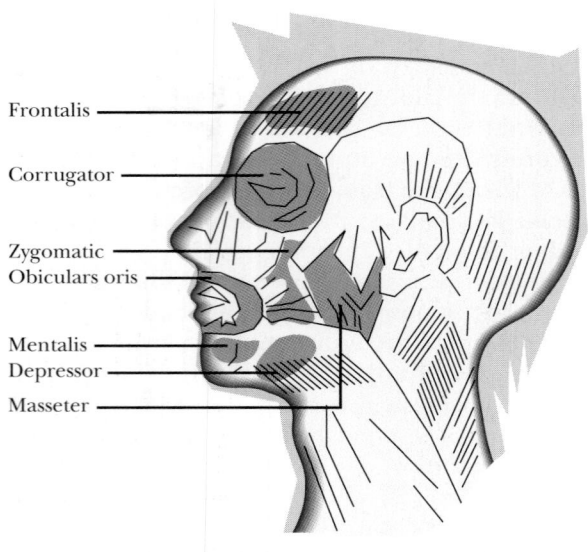

Frontalis

Corrugator

Zygomatic

Obiculars oris

Mentalis

Depressor

Masseter

Muscle groups of the face that are used for EMG recordings when assessing attitudes.

question the notion that stereotypical attitudes had changed over time, they wondered whether some of the changes might be due to reluctance on the part of white students to admit that they held some negative racial attitudes. Consequently, the researchers asked half of their subjects to rate on a questionnaire the degree to which various stereotypical terms applied to black Americans. The other half of the subjects were attached to a bogus pipeline and asked the same questions. Some of the results were dramatic. For example, white students who used the pencil-and-paper approach indicated that they did not think that the term *lazy* really characterized blacks. However, subjects who believed that the investigator was getting an accurate reading of their opinions by means of the bogus pipeline admitted that, to a degree, they did think the term applied to blacks.

Physiological Recordings

If a person's truest and most private attitudes could be recorded on the surface of the skin or by the pounding of the heart or the constriction of the pupils, investigators would have an excellent measure, devoid of many of the problems we have been discussing. Although the task is daunting, significant progress is being made in recording attitudes physiologically. One measure of an attitude that has shown some success is **galvanic skin resistance (GSR).** GSR measures how well the skin conducts electrical current passed between electrodes placed on the skin. The skin's conductance can be used as a measure of emotional arousal, because increases in emotional arousal cause increases in perspiration, which in turn cause the skin to become a better conductor of electricity. Slight changes in the skin's conductance of electrical current can be measured with GSR recording devices. GSR has been used as an indicant of attitudes in many studies, including the assessment of attitudes toward people of different races (Rankin & Campbell, 1955). Increases in pupil size (Hess, 1965) and increases in heart rate (Katz et al., 1965) have also been used as indicants of how much a person or object is liked.

One problem posed by physiological measurement is interpretation of the result. Suppose a person is thinking about her attitude toward a final exam. Her heart pounds, her GSR increases, her pupils dilate. These responses tell us she has a strong attitude toward the exam. But what is the direction of that emotion? Does she fear the exam, hate it, or relish the great opportunity it will give her to show her knowledge? Without some way to assess the direction or type of affect being expressed, the use of physiological recording devices is limited.

Cacioppo and Petty (1979a, 1981b, 1986) are among those who have been advocating greater reliance on physiological techniques and have reported progress with deciphering the direction and meaning of the affect. Cacioppo and his colleagues pointed out (1986) that portions of our faces show greater muscle activity when we are happy and other parts of the face show muscle activity when we are unhappy (see Figure 5-1). Different muscle groups in the face respond during different mood states. If you try frowning, you will become aware that the muscles used to pull your mouth downward, tighten your eyes, and pull your eyebrows together are different from the muscle groups used for smiling.

A piece of equipment that can directly measure facial muscle activity is the **electromyograph (EMG)** (see photo). Cacioppo and his colleagues

(1986) showed that the EMG can be used to measure both the direction and the intensity of attitudes by having subjects view slides that produced either moderately positive or moderately negative responses. As the subjects watched the slides, their facial muscles were monitored with the EMG. By measuring the strength and velocity of muscle movement the machine was able to determine not only whether the subjects had favorable or unfavorable attitudes toward the slides, but also how favorable or unfavorable their responses were. More important, the EMG was able to detect differences that were not noticeable to the eye—emotional responses too subtle or fleeting to be discerned by just a look at the participants' faces.

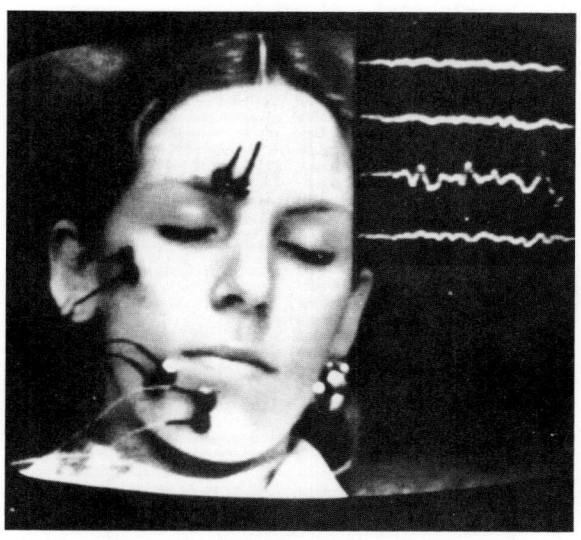

Photograph of the videoscreen showing placement of the four pairs of EMG electrodes and, superimposed electronically next to the face, the oscilloscope tracings of the amplified electromyographic activity from the four facial regions.

Growing Up with Attitudes

Two children grow up in the same town. One becomes a physician, marries, settles in suburbia, and opposes socialized medicine, tax reform, and nuclear disarmament negotiations. The other becomes a political activist for the Peace Now movement and supports disarmament, tax reform, environmental groups, and so forth.

What accounts for the development of different attitudes? The specific roles of heredity and environment are not entirely clear; heredity may play a part—perhaps through differences in physiological characteristics and intelligence. Heredity may also interact with environment in interesting and complex ways to affect attitudes (Scarr & McCartney, 1983; Goldsmith, 1983). Despite the importance of these issues, definite answers about the role of heredity in attitude formation remain elusive (Cavalli-Sforza et al., 1982). We will confine ourselves to the role played by the environment, for it is in this area that social psychologists have sought to find answers.

The Parents: Getting There First with the Most

Parents, of course, are exceedingly important forces in development, and it would be surprising if they were not among the most important determinants of the development of our attitudes and values. The issue is not so much whether parents influence the development of attitudes in children but how they do so.

In our early years, our parents—or the other parental figures who raise us—have control over two important aspects of our lives. First, they control most of our rewards and punishments. They can permit access to the things we like; they can force us to do things we do not want to do. They control access to the candy and the ice cream. Their smiles of approval and their frowns of disappointment are of paramount importance to us. In addition, they control a sizable portion of the information that reaches us. If we wanted to know why the sky is blue, the stars are bright, or the sun is hot, we asked our parents. As many of us realize when we leave the protection of childhood, our parents do not always (and in some

---

electromyograph (EMG) Instrument that has been used to measure the direction and intensity of attitudes by monitoring the activity of facial muscles used in smiling and frowning.

galvanic skin resistance (GSR) A measure of the skin's conductance of an electrical current; an indicant of attitudes.

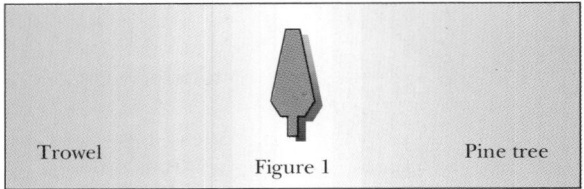

Trowel   Figure 1   Pine tree

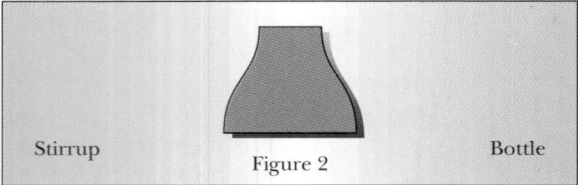

Stirrup   Figure 2   Bottle

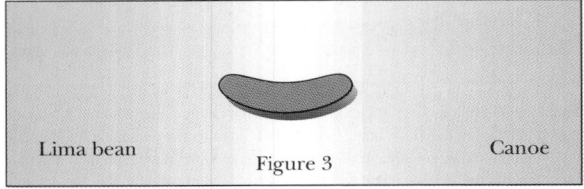

Lima bean   Figure 3   Canoe

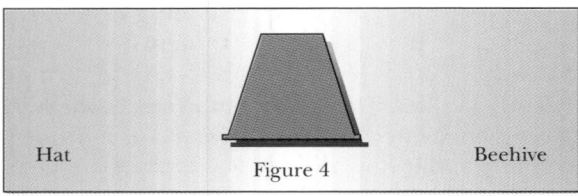

Hat   Figure 4   Beehive

FIGURE 5-2 Stimulus figures used in study of preexisting categories
SOURCE: Bruner, Busiek, and Minturn (1952).

cases not even often) have the correct answers. But they do begin the information flow that results in our forming beliefs and attitudes about things.

Categories are formed in our heads on the basis of early information. For example, a child may form a rudimentary category of "witch" from stories his parents told him. He knows that a witch is ugly and mean, and rides a broomstick. Later he sees *The Wizard of Oz* and discovers that the Witch of the North is beautiful and not at all mean. What happens to the child's original category?

Almost all theorists agree that the new information about the Witch of the North will undergo **assimilation** to the already existing category. That is, it will be distorted to some degree to fit into the established category. At the same time, the category will undergo **accommodation** to the new information (see Piaget, 1932). The child's category of "witch" will show some expansion to incorporate the new information.

So far, so good. The extraordinary influence of the parents in forming attitudes, beliefs, and values arises from the fact that they establish the initial categories and that those categories are resistant to change. That is, the result of the clash between the existing category and any new information is usually resolved more in the direction of assimilation than of accommodation. This tendency may be due to two factors. First, parents are particularly credible sources of information for a young child. Information acquired later, if it is provided by a different source, may not weigh so heavily because the source of the communication may not seem to be as credible as the parents. Second, there is some good evidence that preexisting categories simply exert more influence on stimuli than the stimuli do on the categories.

For example, Bruner, Busiek, and Minturn (1952) had subjects look at line drawings that were quickly flashed on a screen (Figure 5-2). Some subjects were first told that they would see a drawing of a pine tree. Others were told that they would see a drawing of a trowel. When the subjects were asked to reproduce faithfully the pictures they had seen, the pictures were distorted in the direction of the category that had been established by the experimenter's suggestion.

We can imagine how this phenomenon might work in the case of a social attitude. If a child's parents believe in a set of attitudes and communicate those attitudes to their child, the child will establish categories. For example, suppose a parent believes that people with AIDS are morally bad and the child comes to share this attitude. Then, if the child hears a classmate express the attitude that people with AIDS are victims and deserve compassion, the child is more likely to see the classmate as unworthy, evil, or just incorrect than to adopt the classmate's attitude. That is, the preexisting category will shape the subsequent information more than it will be modified by that information.

Indeed, Lord, Ross, and Lepper (1979) showed arguments both in favor of and against capital punishment to subjects who were already committed to a pro-capital-punishment stance. These subjects considered the weight of the evidence to be overwhelmingly in favor of capital punishment—so much so that they became even firmer in their pro-capital-punishment attitudes. The experimenters used the identical arguments with anti-capital-punishment subjects. These subjects considered the weight of the very same evidence to be against capital punishment, and they became still more militant on that side of the issue. As our analysis suggests, the preexisting category regarding attitude toward capital punishment clearly had more influence on the new information than the information had on the cognitive category.

In a different context, the eminent psychiatrist and personality theorist Harry Stack Sullivan observed that the information provided by parents in the earliest stages of life is very difficult to eradicate. Erroneous and maladaptive attitudes molded from parental feedback have tremendous implications for future personality development, precisely because the early categories formed from this information alter a child's view of the events around her more than those events alter her early categories. It remains the extremely difficult task of subsequent stages of development to open the child's horizons to new information about herself, the environment, and the people in it (Sullivan, 1953).

Expanding Horizons: The Influence of Reference Groups

As we grow, the number of influences on our lives increases. Instead of viewing parents as the exclusive bearers of information, we begin to realize that the teacher at school, the police officer on the corner, and the counselor at camp all have information to transmit. Sometimes they agree with our parents and sometimes they do not. One of the most important influences with which we come into contact is that of our peers, who often serve as a reference group against which our attitudes and values can be compared. A **reference group** is a group toward which one orients oneself. Whether or not one actually holds membership in the group, it forms the basis of comparison for attitudes, values, and behaviors. A classic study by Newcomb (1943) demonstrated the power of reference groups to affect our attitudes.

In 1935 Newcomb conducted extensive interviews with the incoming class at Bennington College. The prevailing attitudes of the student body and the faculty were quite liberal, but Bennington was not yet known as an extremely liberal school. Consequently, many upper-crust families of conservative New England were willing to send their daughters there. To attest to the conservatism of the parents of Bennington's incoming class, attitudes were collected about the upcoming election between the liberal Franklin D. Roosevelt and the conservative Alfred M. Landon. Although Roosevelt won the election by a remarkable landslide, carrying over 62% of the popular vote, 60% of the families of the Bennington students favored Landon. The students of the incoming class seemed to echo their parents' attitudes: 62% of them favored Landon.

What influence would Bennington's peer-group structure have on the students' attitudes? One way to study this question would be to compare the attitudes of the incoming freshmen with the attitudes of students in the other classes. It was found that only 43% of the sophomore class favored Landon, and that the proportion dropped to 15% among juniors and seniors. It was conceivable, however, that the members of the incoming class were in fact different from the members of the upper classes in some important ways and would hold to their original beliefs until graduation day. So Newcomb traced an incoming class for four years. He found a conclusive shift toward liberalism among the women in the class of 1939 as they proceeded through Bennington. Moreover, the degree of liberalism that a student expressed was highly correlated with her popularity and prestige on campus. One way to interpret the shift toward liberalism is to see it as an

---

accommodation Expansion of a mental category to incorporate new information.

assimilation Distortion of new information to fit an already existing mental category.

reference group A group toward which one orients oneself; it forms the basis of comparison for attitudes, values, and behaviors.

In the case of ethnic minorities, such as the Native Americans, the influence of reference groups may be one of the few ways of maintaining an ethnic identity.

attitude approved of by the important people in the reference group. Since the seniors in the class of 1936 were far more liberal than the incoming freshmen in 1935, it is likely that interactions with the more prestigious seniors encouraged the incoming freshmen's attitudes toward political and social issues to shift in the direction indicated by those peers. An apparent benefit of the shift toward agreement with the more prestigious peers was an increase in the students' prestige and popularity.

What of the women who did not adopt the attitudes of their reference group? They were less popular with their classmates and less influential on the campus. In addition, Newcomb reported two different subgroups of "uninfluenced" (that is, conservative) students. One subgroup appeared to be unaware that their attitudes were at variance with the Bennington norm. Their friendship groups tended to be quite small and generally included only women who shared their conservative beliefs. We do not know whether these students chose their friends because of their conservatism or whether they remained conservative because of the friends they chose. Newcomb's data suggest the second proposition more

strongly than the first. In other words, this subgroup was uninfluenced by Bennington's liberalism because the members had less opportunity or occasion to interact with a wide cross section of Bennington students.

Another subgroup of uninfluenced students might be called the "family" group. These were women who were well aware of the disparity between their own attitudes and those of the Bennington College community, but they expressed very strong attachment to their families. They either stated that they felt attached to their families or expressed an awareness of the difficulty that they would experience at home if they were to adopt the attitudes prevailing on campus. We might say that for these women, the family rather than the campus of peers served as the relevant reference group.

How long-lasting are attitudes that are formed by close attachments to reference groups? Two follow-up studies conducted by Newcomb and his colleagues are exceedingly interesting. First, recall the power of parental influence before the women entered college. The students who entered in 1935 very closely resembled their parents in their attitudes, despite roughly 18 years of expo-

Chapter Five   Forming and Changing Attitudes

sure to all types of external influences. As most of you will attest, however, living in a residential college community is a powerful experience. Contacts and relationships that have survived for a long time are abruptly pushed into the background, and a large number of strangers have to be relied on for social, physical, and emotional support. So it is not surprising that reference-group pressures on a college campus are strong and, as Newcomb was able to demonstrate, often long-lasting.

In 1960, 25 years after interviewing the Bennington freshmen, Newcomb (1963) reinterviewed the entire class of 1939. The Bennington group was found to be much more liberal than a comparable group of women from the identical socioeconomic class. In addition, he found that the Bennington women had married men who were considerably more liberal than a comparable group of men of equal socioeconomic status. Newcomb and his colleagues (1967) reported that, whereas only 30% of the women of the same socioeconomic class supported John Kennedy over Richard Nixon in the 1960 election, 60% of the Bennington graduates supported Kennedy. As for the uninfluenced conservatives, they had not changed much either: 67% were married to men who had voted for Nixon rather than Kennedy.

The influence of reference groups on sex and drugs

The influence of reference groups on attitudes and behaviors is enormous. Walsh, Ferrell, and Tolone (1976) studied the effect of peer reference groups on attitudes and behaviors in regard to sexual permissiveness. Working with the class of 1971 and the class of 1974 at a Midwestern university, the investigators examined changing attitudes and behaviors from the students' freshman to senior years. Like Newcomb and his colleagues, the investigators found that students' attitudes and behaviors from the beginning of college until the senior year were very much affected by their reference groups. Sexual attitudes and behaviors became much more permissive, provided that the student's reference group consisted of their peers. Students who were still oriented toward their parents did not show this shift.

Finally, the important question of direction-

ality of influence was addressed by Kandel's (1978) study of marijuana use. As we noted in regard to Newcomb's study, it is difficult to assess whether people of similar attitudes come together to form reference groups or whether reference groups cause people's attitudes to become similar. Kandel conducted initial and follow-up interviews with a large group of high school students in New York State. He found convincing evidence that both effects are operative: students with similar patterns of marijuana use tended to form reference groups for each other, and those groups caused attitudes and behavior to become more similar once the reference groups had formed. Given some disparity in the attitudes held by members of a reference group, Kandel's findings showed that when people did not conform to the other members of a reference group, the group was likely to break apart. Although Kandel also found some support for this phenomenon with regard to attitudes toward educational and political issues, the evidence was most striking when the issue was of present and immediate concern: the smoking of marijuana.

Forming Attitudes by Balance

A very popular group of theories concerning the way attitudes are formed are known as **balance theories** (Cartwright & Harary, 1956; Heider, 1946, 1958; Newcomb, 1953, 1968). The earliest of these theories, Heider's theory of psychological balance, was created primarily to explain the way we come to like or dislike other persons, but it has been equally important in the study of attitudes of all kinds.

According to Heider, two kinds of relationships wed people to objects or to other people. One is the **unit relationship.** An example of such

---

balance theories Theories concerning the way attitudes toward persons, objects, and issues are formed, based on the supposition that people prefer orderly, consistent, and harmonious relationships among their cognitions.

unit relationship In Heider's balance theory, a relationship with no emotional content.

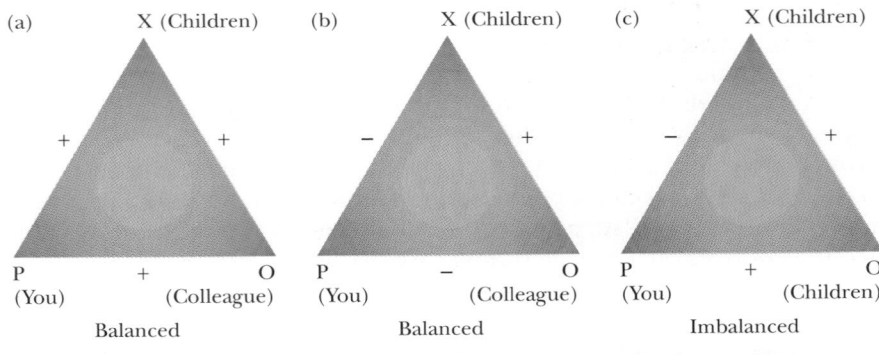

FIGURE 5-3   Balanced and imbalanced triadic relationships

a relationship is seen in the statement "Peter works for Ansell, Incorporated, the manufacturer of LifeStyles condoms." The statement relates Peter to LifeStyles but does not express an emotion. It does not tell us whether Peter likes or dislikes the company. The other type of relationship is known as a **sentiment relationship.** This kind of relationship is seen in the statement "Peter is ecstatic about the company he works for." Love, hate, agreement, and disagreement are all typical of sentiment relationships. An example should make this clear.

Suppose you were a teacher in Arcadia when the Ray children discovered that their HIV antibody tests were positive. Suppose, too, that you had a friend and teaching colleague who felt very strongly that the children should be educated in the public schools. What would your attitude be toward the children? Figure 5-3 expresses the possibilities in terms of balance theory.

Heider's system is essentially an uncomplicated one that involves the relationship of two people and an attitude object. The people, P (you) and O (your colleague), are related to each other and to the attitude object, X (the children), by a sentiment relationship. Heider was a psychologist in the gestalt tradition, which holds that people prefer relationships that "fit well" to relationships that are discordant. Therefore, he felt, people prefer that their relationships be balanced rather than imbalanced.

In Figure 5-3a we can see the most likely outcome of our hypothetical relationship. Feeling positive about O (your colleague), and knowing that O feels positive about X (the children), you will feel better (in a state of balance) if you feel positive toward the children. But if your colleague is someone you do not like, the colleague's positive attitude toward the children will put pressure on you to have a negative attitude toward the children (Figure 5-3b).

There is a relatively simple way to determine when a triadic relationship is balanced or imbalanced (Cartwright & Harary, 1956). In Figure 5-3, a simple algebraic multiplication of the affective signs on the three sides of the triangle should produce the result. If the product is positive, the triangle is balanced. If it is negative, the triangle is imbalanced. Therefore, when P likes O (+) and O likes X (+), it follows that P should come to like X (+):

$$(+) \times (+) \times (+) = +.$$

This is a balanced state. Had P decided that he did not like teaching children with HIV antibodies even though his friend did, as in Figure 5-3c,

$$(+) \times (+) \times (-) = -.$$

This is an imbalanced state.

What happens if a relationship is imbalanced? According to Heider, there will be a "strain" to restore balance. You can restore balance by changing your feeling about your colleague, changing your attitude toward the children, or trying to influence your friend to change her attitude toward the children.

The Conditioning of Attitudes
Operant or Instrumental Conditioning

People (and other organisms) seek to increase their pleasure and decrease their pain. When we behave in a way that increases our pleasure, we are likely to behave in that way again. For example, if we order a roast beef dinner in a particular restaurant and we find it superb, there is every likelihood that we will come back to that restaurant and order roast beef. B. F. Skinner (1938) called this type of learning **operant conditioning.** A behavior (or response) that is emitted in the presence of a situational stimulus (that is, in a particular situation) and is followed by a reinforcing stimulus is likely to be repeated.

In the example of the good roast beef dinner, the restaurant serves as the situational stimulus or location. The response is ordering a roast beef dinner, and the reinforcing stimulus is the delectable taste of the food. That reward reinforces the behavior in the sense that it increases the probability that the behavior will occur again in the same situation.

Now consider the child whose parents believe that condoms should not be advertised on television. One evening during dinner the child repeats what his parents have said—that is, he expresses the attitude that such advertisements are immoral. This precocious statement may be met with smiles and hugs by mommy and daddy. The attitudinal statement, a response made in the presence of a particular stimulus, is reinforced by smiles and hugs. Looking at the situation in another way, we could say that the attitude statement was instrumental in obtaining a reward. Thus this type of learning has been called instrumental as well as operant conditioning. In either case, an attitude has been learned through rewards administered by the parents.

Since parents hold a full house of rewards early in a child's life, it is likely that they make the most ready use of conditioning techniques in shaping the child's attitudes. But the model of operant conditioning is silent as to who is most effective in administering the rewards. Presumably attitudes can be conditioned at any time by virtually anyone who is in a position to bestow rewards.

Insko (1965) conducted an interesting study that showed the persistence of conditioned attitudes over time. He called students at the University of North Carolina by telephone and used a verbal conditioning technique to alter some of their attitudes. Approximately one week later, an instructor handed out an attitude survey in class. Some of the items on the survey were identical to those that had been reinforced with a "Good" on the telephone a week earlier. The students did not realize that all students in the class had been called and that the survey was connected to those phone calls. The results of the survey indicated that even in a different context and after a week's delay, the attitude that had been conditioned on the phone remained conditioned.

Attitudes by Association: Classical Conditioning

A little boy is sitting in a high chair near a window. As his mother begins to bring chopped meat to his mouth, a tremendous clap of thunder is heard. To the mother's astonishment, the child later throws a temper tantrum every time meat is put on his tray. The storm over, his sister is about to eat her vegetables when her mother, delighted by some news announced by her husband, breaks into a smile. From that point on, the child wants vegetables. Both of these children have been **classically conditioned.** They have learned behaviors based on a different kind of conditioning, one that stresses the association between a neutral stimulus, such as chopped meat, and a stimulus that produces an emotional response, such as the thunderclap.

Perhaps the first organisms to be studied while being classically conditioned were the dogs of Ivan Pavlov (1927). Pavlov reasoned that some

---

classical conditioning Modification of behavior by the pairing of a neutral stimulus with another stimulus that produces an unconditioned response.

operant conditioning Modification of behavior by rewards and punishments: behavior that is reinforced (rewarded) is likely to be repeated.

sentiment relationship In Heider's balance theory, a relationship with unconditioned content.

Classical conditioning . . . of the experimenter
By permission of Johnny Hart and Creators Syndicate

responses are inherently connected to certain stimuli. When a hungry dog sees food, for example, it salivates. Such a connection is called an unconditioned reflex, for it links an unconditioned stimulus (food) with an unconditioned response (salivation) in a biologically determined way. What would happen if the stimulus that produced the reflex response were associated with a neutral stimulus? Pavlov sought the answer to this question by sounding a bell just before offering meat powder to a hungry dog. After a few pairings, the dog began to salivate at the bell, though the bell had no logical connection to the powder. The bell was neither a reward for eating nor instrumental in the dog's receiving a reward; it was associated with the meat powder simply because it was contiguous with it in time. Such contiguity with a stimulus that necessarily evokes a reflexive response invests the new stimulus with the capacity to bring about the same response. In the dog's case, the bell came to produce the salivation response. The little boy in the high chair had a reflexive reaction of fear to the stimulus of the thunderclap. The chopped meat was paired contiguously in time with the thunderclap and thus took on the capacity to bring fear to the child. The little girl's vegetables were paired in time with her mother's smile. Since the smile usually evoked pleasure in the girl, the vegetables took on the power to produce pleasure in her. Figure 5-4 demonstrates the pairings of the neutral stimuli with the unconditioned reflexes that

led the dog to salivate at the bell and the little girl to like vegetables.

We are less concerned here with dogs that salivate than with people who form positive and negative attitudes. As our examples have shown, classical conditioning, by focusing on the pairing of a neutral attitude object with a stimulus that evokes an emotional reaction, can account for a variety of attitudes. In one experiment, Staats and Staats (1958) showed that words that have acquired affective meaning can create positive or negative attitudes toward a neutral stimulus if they are merely paired with that stimulus. They chose the names of two nationalities (*Swedish* and *Dutch*) as the neutral words. The affective words were either positive (*happy, gifted*) or negative (*bitter, ugly*). Half of the subjects always had the positive words associated with *Dutch* and the negative words with *Swedish;* the other half had the pairings reversed.

At the end of the study, subjects were asked to rate the pleasantness of the two nationalities. The results are seen in Table 5-1. Even though the experimenter was not indicating that the word *pairings* had any logical connection—he was not saying that *bitter* was paired with *Dutch* because the Dutch are bitter—subjects still rated the nationality that had been paired with positive words more positively than the nationality that had been paired with negative words. Positive and negative attitudes were apparently formed through the association of classical conditioning.

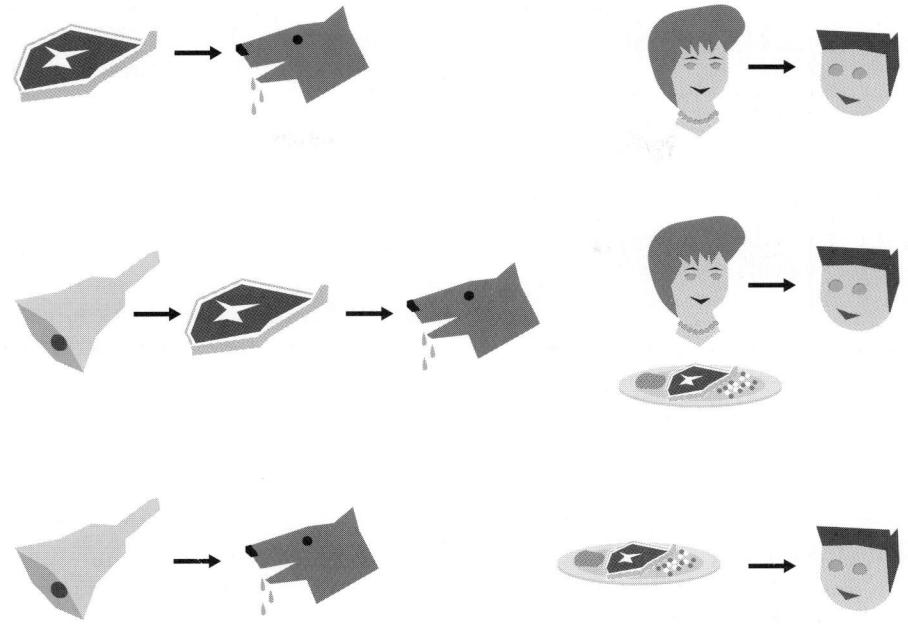

FIGURE 5-4 The classical conditioning paradigm

Changing Attitudes: The Psychology of Persuasion

Perhaps no other area of social psychology has generated so much interest as that of attitude change. William McGuire (1985) points out that interest in the phenomenon has had its peaks and valleys. In the 1930s, social psychologists made attitude change their major area of interest; their concentration was on measurement. Interest declined in the 1940s, only to peak again in a more comprehensive way at the end of the 1950s and in the early 1960s. The 1970s showed another valley in the progression of research on attitude change (Kiesler & Munson, 1975), but McGuire sees the 1980s as a decade in which attitude change regained its preeminence as a focus of study. And even during the supposedly fallow period of the 1970s, 20,209 articles and books were published on the topic (Dawes & Smith, 1985).

If you are trying to convince a friend that he should abandon his Sunday football game and go to the movies, an employer that she should promote you rather than her son, or a teacher that your unpreparedness for class is really a virtue, then you are actively engaged in the process of persuasion or attitude change. The stakes may

TABLE 5-1

Means of conditioned attitude scores in "neutral stimulus" rating

Name positively reinforced	Names	
	Dutch	Swedish
Swedish	2.67	3.42
Dutch	2.67	1.00

NOTE: Higher numbers indicate greater liking.
SOURCE: Adapted from Staats and Staats (1958).

STOP, THINK, & UNDERSTAND

1. What is meant by an attitude? What are the factors that need to be considered in a definition of an attitude?

2. What are the strengths and weaknesses of both physiological and paper-and-pencil measurements of attitudes?

3. What factors make a person's parents very influential in the creation of attitudes?

4. How did Newcomb's study of Bennington College students demonstrate the influence of reference groups in changing attitudes?

5. How can you determine if a person's attitudes are in balance?

6. What is the difference between the instrumental and classical conditioning of attitudes?

be politically high, as in persuading the populace to elect your candidate president of the United States; or they may be high in public health consequences, as in persuading people to engage in safe sexual practices to reduce the risk of exposure to AIDS.

If you were trying to persuade people, what factors would you consider important? You would probably have a great deal of concern about what you said: Do you have the facts? Can you present a well-reasoned argument? You would also have some regard for who was going to deliver the message: someone with a sexy voice, a politician, an actor? Finally, you would have some regard for your audience; you would not want to waste your time selling Pepsi-Cola to the chairman of the board of Coca-Cola, or LifeStyles to men who already use them.

Aristotle was one of the first to construct the basic skeleton of attitude-change inquiries, although modern research has added numerous facets and modifications. In his *Rhetoric* Aristotle states: "Of the modes of persuasion furnished by the spoken word, there are three kinds. The first

depends on the personal character of the speaker; the second on putting the audience into a certain frame of mind; the third on the proof . . . provided by the words of the speech itself." For Aristotle, then, the analysis of communication involved an analysis of the speaker, the message, and the audience.

In more modern times, Carl Hovland and his associates in the Yale Communication and Attitude Change Program (Hovland, Janis & Kelley, 1953) began a systematic inquiry into attitude change processes. Their approach was rooted in the learning theory tradition; that is, they viewed persuasion as a learning process. Consequently, they believed that they could make their efforts at persuasion successful by getting their target to "learn" a new attitude. Harking back to Aristotle's admonition, the Yale group focused on the variables they thought would have the greatest impact on this learning process. They believed they could best study attitude change by examining "who says what to whom with what effect" (Lasswell, 1948). Until quite recently, this approach represented the standard format for organizing and describing persuasion research. In the last few years, however, persuasion theorists have offered a new approach that differs conceptually from the traditional approach.

Overarching Views: The ELM and the Heuristic Model of Persuasion

Suppose we knew a great deal about the effects of attitude change. For example, suppose we knew that a carefully constructed message would lead to greater change than a sloppily worded, poorly organized message. Suppose we knew that a Ph.D. in physics would be more persuasive about the likelihood of nuclear destruction than the first baseman for a minor-league ball club. And what if we knew that the first baseman would be more persuasive than the physicist about the quality of a shortstop? We would probably still be dissatisfied with the level of our knowledge unless we were able to move toward a set of overarching principles to help us understand why a particular factor led to attitude change while another did not. We would want some guidance as to why a factor that is influential on some occasions is ineffective on others.

As a way of dealing with the overarching questions, investigators have been working with models that help to explain the process by which attempts to persuade lead to attitude change (Chaiken, 1980, 1987; Chaiken & Stangor, 1987; Eagly & Chaiken, 1984; Petty & Cacioppo, 1986). Two approaches have become exceptionally useful for organizing research and suggesting new principles. Although they differ in several ways, the **elaboration likelihood model** (known as **ELM**), suggested by Petty and Cacioppo (1986), and the **heuristic processing model,** suggested by Chaiken and her colleagues (e.g., Chaiken, 1980), share some common themes—themes to which we will refer in the remainder of this chapter. First, both models point out that there are at least two distinct ways in which persuasion can be accomplished. We can be convinced via a peripheral route (Petty and Cacioppo's term) or heuristic route (Chaiken's term). Alternatively we may sometimes be convinced by a central or systematic route. In **peripheral/heuristic processing,** persuasion is effected by factors other than the content of the persuasive message. The targets of an attempt to persuade do not attend to the message's content; they are influenced more by the image conveyed by the communicator, the mood they are in, the medium used to convey the message, or some other set of factors besides the actual content of the message itself. Among the many variables that can influence persuasion via the peripheral or heuristic route, those related to the communicator, the audience, and the persuasion context play important roles, and they are frequently independent of the message that the communicator delivers.

Contrasted to the peripheral or heuristic route is the central or systematic route. In **central/systematic processing,** persuasion is effected by the arguments that are actually contained in the message. How strong are the arguments? How consistent are they? How reliable are the facts? The more we are motivated and able to think carefully about the message, the more persuasive it will be; and if the arguments are strong, the persuasion will last longer and be more resistant to change. Petty and Cacioppo use the term *elab-*

oration to refer to the scrutiny a person gives a message's content. Chaiken refers to this kind of scrutiny as *systematic processing*. We will be considering, then, the factors that motivate people to process the content of the message thoughtfully and systematically. We will also consider the factors that make a message more effective as a persuasive device, assuming that people are paying attention to its content. Finally, we will be examining persuasion that results from a combination of peripheral and central variables—perhaps the most active area of investigation in attitude research in the 1990s.

We should point out that the two models of persuasion (the ELM and the heuristic processing model) differ in some interesting details, particularly in what they consider central (systematic) and peripheral (heuristic) processing (see Chaiken & Stangor, 1987, p. 599). Nonetheless, it is our belief that the two models are both innovative, both organizationally rich, and sufficiently parallel that they can be considered in tandem. The basic dichotomy between central and peripheral persuasion will serve as a vantage point from which to examine both classical and contemporary research on attitude change.

These two models will guide us as we examine aspects of the communicator ("Who says?"), the communication ("Says what?"), and the audience ("To whom?") and see how peripheral or central variables make them effective. In all of the research, the dependent variable—the object of study—is the result of the attempt to influence ("With what effect?"). Was the message delivered by a particular communicator to a particular audience successful in producing attitude change?

---

central/systematic processing Persuasion caused by thinking about the arguments contained in the message.

elaboration likelihood model (ELM) A model of attitude change that focuses on the distinction between scrutinizing the content of a message (central route) and the other factors (peripheral route) that affect persuasion.

heuristic processing model A model of attitude change that focuses on the distinction between systematic and heuristic processing of a message.

peripheral/heuristic processing Persuasion effected by factors other than the content of the persuasive message.

This ad tries to persuade via the peripheral or heuristic route. Here, the focus is on Cher, the actress-singer. The message doesn't give out information; it presents the side issue of people's shyness about discussing condoms.

Attitude Change by the Peripheral Route: Factors Affecting Peripheral Processing

The communicator

Tens of billions of dollars are spent each year on attempts to persuade audiences of the mass media. The salaries that various communicators receive to appear on radio and television make it clear that the communicator's characteristics are believed to be influential in attempts to persuade. The campaign to make people aware of AIDS has relied on well-known celebrities, including Jason Robards, who has talked about hypodermic needles, and Tony Danza, who has advocated the use of condoms. Commercial campaigns for products from automobiles to soft drinks rely still more heavily on celebrities to attract people to their products. Pepsi-Cola has perhaps been the most aggressive with this form of persuasion, spending millions to hire celebrities

(Michael Jackson, Michael J. Fox, Lionel Richie) and public figures (the former vice-presidential candidate Geraldine Ferraro) to extol the virtues of its product. Campaigning political figures compete for endorsements from entertainers, scientists, and other political figures. In many cases, the characteristics of the communicators may not be at all related to the message; therefore they are attempting to persuade by the peripheral route. What qualities make a communicator effective in changing attitudes?

Credibility. In most attempts to persuade, a highly credible communicator is preferable to one with low **credibility.** Someone who ought to know what he or she is talking about is preferable to someone who is not qualified to speak on the subject. When George Bush ran for the presidency in 1988, he relied on help from the current president, Ronald Reagan. Who was in a better position to know whether Bush was the right man for the job? Newspaper editorialists who endorse a candidate are (appropriately or inappropriately) adopting the role of the expert in telling us what to do. Countless TV commercials implore us to buy a product because "four out of five doctors recommend . . ." or "the American Council on Dental Therapeutics recommends . . ." or "a study at a leading research university concludes . . . ." Presumably doctors and scientists know the facts and therefore should be effective at changing our attitudes.

"I'm not a doctor but I play one on TV": Incredible credibility. Credibility can also be invested in individuals who do not have it in any real sense. The actor Robert Young, who played Marcus Welby, M.D., on television, made several commercials for Sanka decaffeinated coffee. Apparently his role as a warm and friendly general practitioner was sufficient to induce people to attribute special knowledge to him, even though they knew logically that he had no such qualifications (Cialdini, 1985).

Credibility over time: The sleeper effect. Hovland and Weiss (1952) were among the first to study the effect of the communicator's credibility on attempts to persuade. Subjects received communications on several topics. The source of the communication was made to seem of either high or suspect credibility. For example, a communi-

Chapter Five   Forming and Changing Attitudes

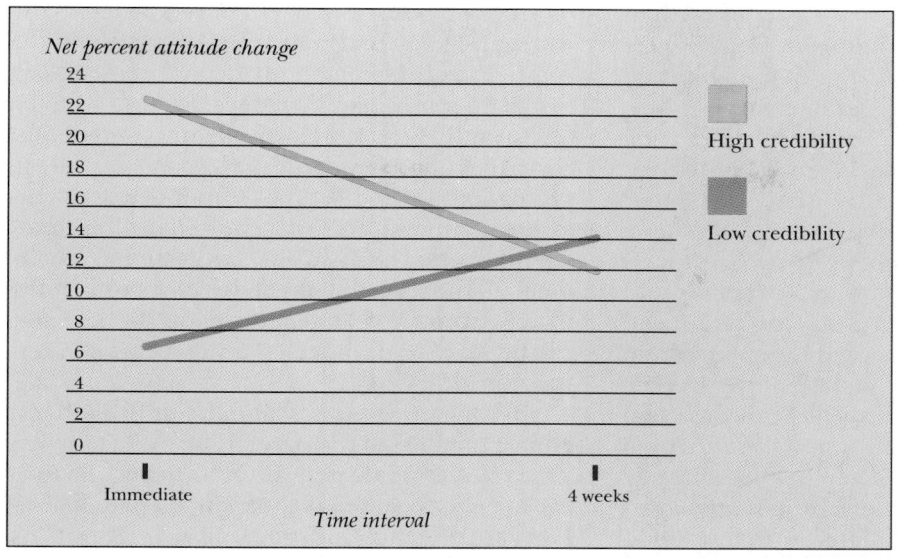

Net percent attitude change

High credibility

Low credibility

Immediate   4 weeks

Time interval

FIGURE 5-5   Immediate and long-term effects of communicators with low and high credibility
SOURCE: Hovland and Weiss (1952).

cation on the advisability of requiring a prescription for the purchase of antihistamine drugs was attributed either to the *New England Journal of Biology and Medicine* or to a mass-circulation pictorial magazine; a message on the practicality of building atomic submarines was attributed either to the eminent scientist J. Robert Oppenheimer or to *Pravda,* the official newspaper of the Communist Party of the Soviet Union. In each case, the communication extolled the virtues of one side of an issue. The communications were identical, regardless of the alleged source. At the left of Figure 5-5 it can be seen that on an immediate measure of attitudes, the highly credible source was significantly more effective in altering opinions than the communicator with low credibility. When the subjects' attitudes after exposure to the communications were compared with their attitudes as measured one week before the experiment, it was found that the highly credible source produced far more attitude change than did the source with low credibility.

What will happen over time, however? Will the words spoken by a believable source continue to be respected and will the same words spoken by a less credible source continue to be derogated? The more complete story told at the right

of Figure 5-5 indicates that the immediate effect of the communicator's credibility does not appear to last very long. When subjects were asked their opinions on the various issues after four weeks had elapsed, the credibility of the communicator ceased to make a significant difference. Not only did the large amount of attitude change induced by the highly credible communicators decrease over time, but the degree of attitude change that the message produced actually increased in the low-credibility condition. The increase in the strength of a communication's persuasiveness over time has been called the **sleeper effect.**

What accounts for the sleeper effect? Kelman and Hovland (1953) suggest that people tend to dissociate the communication from the communicator as time goes by. In other words, subjects in the high-credibility condition, immediately after hearing the communication, were influenced in part by the content of what they had heard and in part by the fact that the com-

credibility   Attribute of a communicator, based on expertise and trustworthiness, that enhances persuasion.
sleeper effect   The increase in the strength of a communication's effectiveness over time.

municator was an expert. It is the latter component that invokes peripheral processing. Robert Oppenheimer, for example, was undoubtedly an expert on nuclear physics and must have known what he was talking about. That fact, without any further analysis of the message, accounted for some of the attitude change that was found immediately after the experiment. As time elapsed, that part of the persuasion process attributable to the communicator's expertise and trustworthiness tended to decay or disappear, since the subjects had dissociated the speech from the speaker. Similarly, at the time of the experiment, subjects in the low-credibility condition also added an influence (but this time a negative one) via the peripheral route. They held an attitude that reflected the content of the message *minus* the effect due to the communicator's low credibility. As dissociation set in, the inhibitory effect of the speaker's low prestige tended to disappear.

The robustness of the sleeper effect has been controversial. Some subsequent studies have found evidence for the sleeper effect (Cook et al., 1979) and others have not (Gillig & Greenwald, 1974; Pratkanis, Greenwald, Leippe & Baumgardner, 1982). More recent research by Pratkanis and his colleagues (1988) supports the notion that the sleeper effect is robust and does rely on differential decay. That is, both the message and the source are taken into memory, but the information about the source decays more rapidly than the arguments that were used in the message. Pratkanis and his colleagues (1988) also have pointed out that if the sleeper effect is to occur, the audience must be told about the low credibility of the source *after* they receive the message. In that case, the message is taken into memory accurately and thought about impartially before it is denigrated by association with the source. If the communicator's low credibility is presented before the message, the meaning of the message may be changed or little attention may be paid to it.

Expertise and trustworthiness. Credibility is a multifaceted concept. Is someone more believable because she is an expert or because she has no ulterior motives for the opinion she offers? In Hovland and Weiss's study, we cannot be certain. Is *Pravda* less credible than Oppenheimer only because it is less expert about atomic sub-

marines or because it is perceived as less trustworthy? The two factors often go together.

It is probable that both factors are necessary to make a source highly credible. Reviews by Eagly (1983) and Hass (1981) have made it abundantly clear that the communicator's expertise affects persuasion. Hass (1981) has shown that such cues as the communicator's level of education, intelligence, social status, and professional attainment all function to enhance **expertise** and, ultimately, attitude change, even though these cues can be very subtle indeed (Hastie, Penrod & Pennington, 1984).

Trustworthiness is a bit more difficult to test. Some gimmicks of the advertising trade may provide a clue to this factor. In 1985, during the early days of the "cola wars" after the introduction of "new Coke" and Coca-Cola Classic, Pepsi-Cola ran a series of TV ads that featured a group of elderly farmers chatting on the front porch. As the camera zooms in, some of the men are discussing soft drinks and are feigning disbelief that new Coke is now old Coke and old Coke is now a classic. In discussing their enthusiasm for Pepsi, they persuade the other members of their little group to drink it. Why does this ad work? It is designed to show that the communicators were not *intending* to persuade us; we just happened on the men as they were conversing. Similarly, in a 1989 advertisement in the campaign to prevent AIDS, the camera just happens in on two women talking about whether to discuss AIDS and the use of condoms with their teenage children. Their credibility as communicators increases precisely because they do not appear to be purposely trying to persuade us.

Walster and Festinger (1962) conducted two studies to assess the effectiveness of "overheard" as opposed to "regular" communications. In one of their studies, students overheard speakers discussing the link between cigarette smoking and cancer: these communicators always took the position that the idea of a causal link between the two was a misconception. In the study's regular condition, it was made clear that the communicators were aware that the subjects were listening to them. In the overheard condition, the subjects believed that their presence was completely unknown to the speakers. Several days later, the subjects (college students) were given a health survey in their classrooms. One question asked how certain they were that cigarette smoking leads to lung cancer. The results showed that for subjects who smoked, the link between smoking and cancer was doubted more strongly (that is, attitudes were changed) when the communication was overheard than when it was supposed to be heard.

We might also expect communicators to be seen as more credible when they take stands that are at odds with the position we might expect them to take given their background, race, religion, or other group affiliations. In other words, communicators who take unexpected stands should generally be seen as more trustworthy. To examine this question, Wood and Eagly (1981) directly manipulated a person's expectation regarding the position that a communicator was likely to take. The issue was the support of pornography. Jim, the communicator, was described to subjects as a member of the Catholic church, as against abortion, and as knowledgeable on the topic of free speech. In an interview he was heard to say, "I very definitely do not think that everyone should have unlimited free speech. There are basic human principles—like the right not to be exploited . . . which are a lot more important than a concept like freedom of speech." With this background Wood and Chaiken established the expectation that Jim would be against pornography. In one experimental condition, this expectation was confirmed. In another condition, the expectation was disconfirmed: Jim claimed to believe that pornography was cathartic and led to a reduction of sex-related crimes. Jim's speech in support of pornography was extremely effective when it stood in contrast to what his background had led the subjects to expect.

One of the factors that has made the former surgeon general effective in the campaign against AIDS may indeed be his credibility, which in turn is a joint function of his expertise and his trustworthiness. The public may assume his expertise from his status and from his M.D. and D.Sc. degrees. His trustworthiness may be derived from his unexpected position on a number of AIDS-related decisions. Take Koop's decision to support condom advertising in the media. This decision was not popular with many religious groups,

including the Catholic church and such fundamentalist groups as the Christian Action Council and the Family Research Council. Such groups formed Koop's chief base of political support when he secured the nomination for the surgeon general's post. As a result of his stand, Koop received a "tremendous amount of hate mail" from conservative Christians (*Christianity Today*, April 3, 1987). Nonetheless, his advocacy of the use and advertisement of condoms was a clear example of the trustworthiness variable that Wood and Eagly (1981) studied in the laboratory. To the extent that Koop's background and allegiances could be expected to incline him in any direction, it would have been directly opposite to the position he advocated.

We can say, then, that a high-credibility communicator is more effective than a low-credibility communicator in producing attitude changes. Credibility seems to be a function of at least expertise and trustworthiness, and seems to be effective along the peripheral route to persuasion. However, research on the sleeper effect has shown that the effect of credibility may be short-lived. The enhancing effect of the high-credibility source may diminish over time and the attitude change produced by the low-credibility source may increase over time. If we wish to preserve the effectiveness of the high-credibility source, we must reinstate the connection between the message and its communicator.

Similarity. Instead of relying on an expert communicator, some persuaders find success with a message that is carried by someone who is just like the communication's target. If you want to sell an automobile to a homemaker, it may be better to get the endorsement of another homemaker rather than that of an automotive expert.

In a paint store in Ohio, Brock (1965) found evidence for the persuasiveness of a similar communicator. Salespeople tried to persuade potential customers to purchase a particular brand of paint. In one condition, a salesman let it be known

---

expertise Special skill or knowledge; a factor in the credibility of a communicator.

trustworthiness The quality of meriting confidence; a factor in the credibility of a communicator.

that he knew very little about paint except that he had bought a quantity of paint similar to that wanted by the customer a short time before. In another condition, the salesman established himself as a paint expert, but the information he provided about his own paint purchase made him quite dissimilar to the customer. The customer's own purchase was the study's dependent variable. It was found that the customer purchased a lot more of the brand of paint being extolled if the communication was delivered by the similar nonexpert salesman.

Why should a communicator who is not an expert be effective in changing our attitudes? Chapter 7 will present research that indicates that similar others are liked better than dissimilar others. In brief, similarity often leads to attraction. And as we have already seen, balance theory predicts that people we like will be persuasive about an attitude issue. If we do not agree with a person whom we like, we feel an unpleasant strain toward balance. Several studies have shown that well-liked communicators are more persuasive than disliked ones. Chaiken (1980), for example, showed that college students were persuaded more by a likable communicator who presented only one strong argument in favor of his position than by an unlikable communicator who presented as many as eight cogent arguments. This effect held for people who were not personally involved in the argument and were therefore not motivated to process the arguments systematically.

The communication
Probably no factor in communication is more straightforwardly central or systematic than the message itself. To the extent that any central processing is done on a message at all, the content of the message will play the major role. How eloquent are the arguments, how well reasoned are they, how well organized are they? All of these considerations must affect a message's acceptance, to the extent that one engages in central, systematic scrutiny of the message. Let us consider here aspects of a message that lie in the heuristic or peripheral modes, saving a discussion of the systematic effects till later.

Details, details. The line between heuristic and systematic processing is a fine one. Imagine a

message that is so rich in its detail that as one mulls over its fine points, one is inescapably persuaded. What student has never written a paper with so many detailed footnotes that he or she feels it cannot help but persuade the professor and earn a high grade? Perhaps, though, the effectiveness of the details lies less in the professor's systematic processing than in his or her heuristic processing. Perhaps the effect of such detailed preparation works as much through the peripheral route as through the central.

A study of courtroom testimony conducted by Bell and Loftus (1989) suggests that a persuasive argument that is full of details—especially unnecessary details—can be more persuasive than one that is not. In that research, subjects serving as mock jurors read court cases including testimony that either did or did not include trivial, irrelevant details. The jurors were generally more persuaded of the defendant's guilt when irrelevant material was included than when it was not. Bell and Loftus offered the explanation that the details make the communicator appear more credible and thus more persuasive. If the communicator can remember tiny details, whether or not they are relevant, he or she is perceived as being more credible and thus more persuasive.

Creating an image: Appeals to emotions. "He says such incredible pap," said one of the major figures in Richard Nixon's 1968 presidential campaign about the man whose candidacy he was selling. "In fact, the radicalness of this [campaign] is in the fact of creating an image without actually saying anything" (McGinniss, 1969). And such was the Nixon campaign that set the precedent for many campaigns to come.

What made the 1968 election of Richard Nixon so important in the history of persuasion in electoral politics was not its use of advertising agencies, mass media, and gimmicks. Its importance lay rather in the fact that it set the stage for campaigns of the future. From Carter to Bush, all successful presidential candidates have relied almost totally on the emotional, value-laden "image" nature of the influence process.

Feeling good. One of the most reliable methods to sell an idea or a product is to create an atmosphere of good feeling. Consider what we are exposed to on television daily: People playing

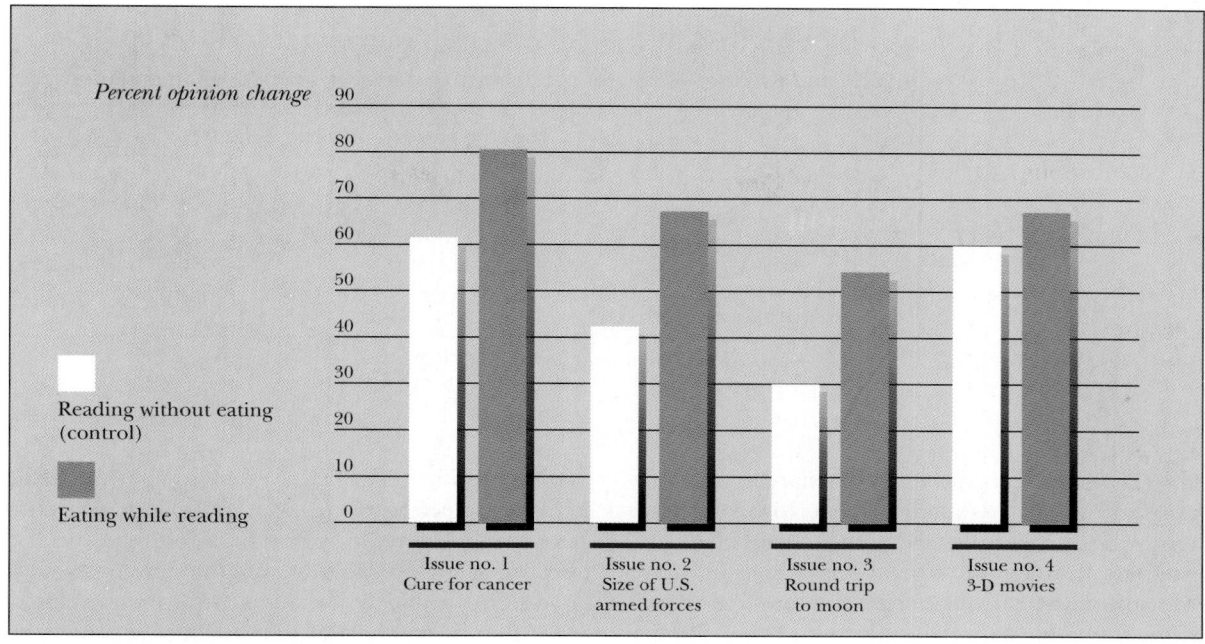

FIGURE 5-6 Effects of eating while reading on the persuasiveness of various messages
SOURCE: Janis, Kaye, and Kirschner (1965).

volleyball on a sunny beach drink Coke. People having a great time at a rock concert drink Pepsi. People seem happy, having made up their minds to vote for a particular candidate. Attitudes can be formed and changed by simple associations with good feelings.

Persuasiveness can be increased by positive feelings that are induced by factors that seem to bear little relation to the persuasion attempt. Consider eating. Janis, Kaye, and Kirschner (1965) asked subjects to read persuasive messages about a series of controversial topics, such as the wisdom of reducing the size of the armed forces. Some of the participants merely read the messages in a typical laboratory room. Others were provided with a snack and soda while they read the messages. At the conclusion of the study, it was found that the people who were snacking while reading were more persuaded by the messages than the people who merely read the messages (Figure 5-6).

Biggers and Pryor (1982) had subjects listen to a speaker giving a talk on automobile safety. The slides that were presented with the speech were selected to create either a very pleasant,

neutral, or unpleasant feeling in the listener. When attitudes were later assessed, it was found that participants who had been put in a pleasant mood were more persuaded by the speech than those who had been put in a neutral mood. Participants who had been placed in an unpleasant mood actually showed negative change—that is, they came to adopt a position opposite to the one taken by the speaker.

Feeling bad: The arousal of fear.   In the standard "protection" racket, a storekeeper is asked whether he would like to insure his property against accidental damage. When a naive storekeeper replies that he does not need insurance because no such accident has ever befallen his property, the "salesmen" turn over cartons, break windows, ruin stock, and perhaps injure the storekeeper. Now protection is called for, and for a fee, the salesmen provide it. This is, and has been, an effective "sales technique."

Arousing an undesired emotion that could be reduced by an appropriate change of attitude was the subject of a study by Janis and Feshbach (1953). Their purpose was to study the relation-

TABLE 5-2

Effect of illustrated talk on conformity to dental hygiene recommendations

Type of change	High-fear group (N = 50)	Moderate-fear group (N = 50)	Low-fear group (N = 50)
Increased conformity	28%	44%	50%
Decreased conformity	20	22	14
No change	52	34	36
Net change in conformity	+ 8	+22	+36

SOURCE: Adapted from Janis and Feshbach (1953).

ship between fear and attitude change, and they chose to try to persuade people to brush their teeth more carefully and to practice better oral hygiene. Could they scare people into a change of attitude and behavior? In the low-fear condition, the subjects were informed of the painful consequences of diseased gums and teeth. Recommendations about improved dental hygiene were offered. In the moderate-fear condition, the pain and diseases were made slightly more vivid, and the same recommendations were made. In the high-fear condition, the investigators really turned it on. The hygiene recommendations were preceded by such comments as "These [gum] infections can spread to your eyes, or your ears, or your joints, and cause paralysis, kidney damage, or total blindness." The messages were accompanied by relevant visual slides that, in the high-fear condition, portrayed disgustingly decayed teeth, results of oral infections, and so on.

Contrary to expectations, the study showed that the old protection racket did not produce significant attitude change. The results can be seen in Table 5-2. Subjects were asked to state their attitudes regarding hygiene practices and to report on their own practices in the week following the study. As the table indicates, only 8% of the subjects who had received a message producing high fear followed the recommendations.

Subsequent research has tended to find a different pattern. Leventhal and his colleagues found that the protection racket is alive and well. In a series of investigations, they found greater influence when subjects were made highly fearful (Leventhal & Niles, 1965; Leventhal, Singer & Jones, 1965; Leventhal, Watts & Pagano, 1967). For example, Leventhal, Watts, and Pagano examined the relationship between fear and the desire to stop smoking. In the moderate-fear condition, subjects saw a lecturer point to charts that demonstrated the relationship between the number of cigarettes sold and the incidence of death from lung cancer. In the high-fear condition, subjects viewed the identical information but also saw a vivid, gory version of a lung operation on a patient suffering from lung cancer. After the films, the subjects were asked about their desire to stop smoking. In this study, unlike Janis and Feshbach's study, the subjects in the high-fear group indicated a much greater desire to stop smoking than the subjects in the moderate-fear group.

How can the differences in these investigations be reconciled? It is difficult to compare conditions between two studies, even if they are both labeled "high fear." It may be that the amount of fear created by Janis and Feshbach's gory pictures was much greater than that inspired by the film in the Leventhal, Watts, and Pagano study. It may then be true that attitude change increases with greater fear—but only up to a point. At some magnitude of fear arousal, we may simply refuse or be unable to cope with the information we receive.

We know from studies such as that of Leventhal, Singer, and Jones (1965) that attitude change will follow a fear-arousing communication only if people know what to do to reduce their fear. If a high degree of fear is aroused by a communication, the panic that is experienced

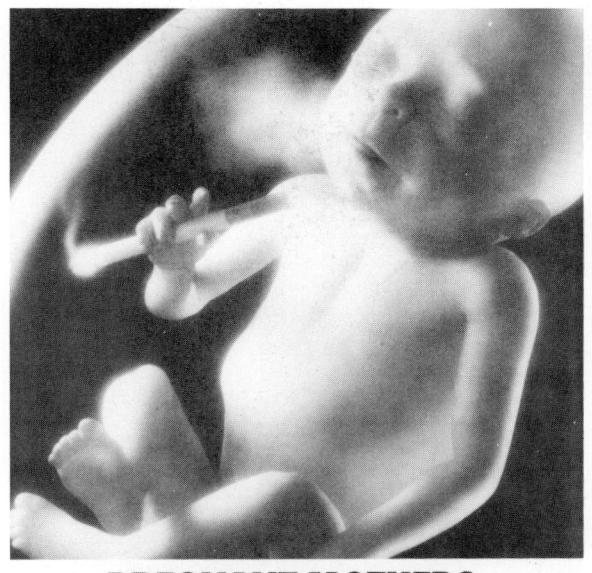

A designated
smoking area
approved
by the American
Cancer Society.

AMERICAN
CANCER
SOCIETY

**PREGNANT MOTHERS:
PLEASE DON'T SMOKE!**

If you are pregnant or planning a family, here are three
good reasons to quit smoking now:
1. Smoking retards the growth of your baby in your womb.
2. Smoking increases the incidence of infant mortality.
3. Your family needs a healthy mother.
Please don't smoke for your baby's sake. And yours.

AMERICAN CANCER SOCIETY

As you can see here, it is possible to deliver the same message many ways. The high-fear ad presents an emotional advertisement whose credibility is bolstered by some detail. The low-fear ad uses humor to gently cajole. Which one do you think has more impact on you?

may interfere with people's ability to take action to make certain that the dreaded event (lung cancer, oral infection) will not happen to them. In that case, attitude change might not be expected to occur.

A graphic depiction of the actual relationship between fear and attitude change may resemble an **inverted U** (as in Figure 5-7). In this view, attitude change increases as fear increases from low to moderate. Arousal may make comprehension of a persuasive message more likely. Arousal may facilitate both comprehension and yielding. However, as fear becomes so intense as to interfere with people's ability to cope with the problem, their response is to avoid or deny the information. They may still comprehend what is presented, but they refuse to believe that it applies to them. Thus attitude change diminishes.

"For reasons of national security . . .": Censorship. Much of the research in the area of persuasion examines how message content and context affect attitude change, but some intriguing evidence suggests that *not* being allowed to listen to a communication can also influence attitudes. Ashmore, Ramchandra, and Jones (1971) told subjects that they would hear a speaker take one of two positions: police should be allowed on university campuses, or they should not. Some subjects were then told that the dean had censored the speech and that they would not hear it. Subjects' attitudes were then measured and the results showed that censorship led subjects to change

inverted U A graphic depiction of the relationship between fear and attitude change.

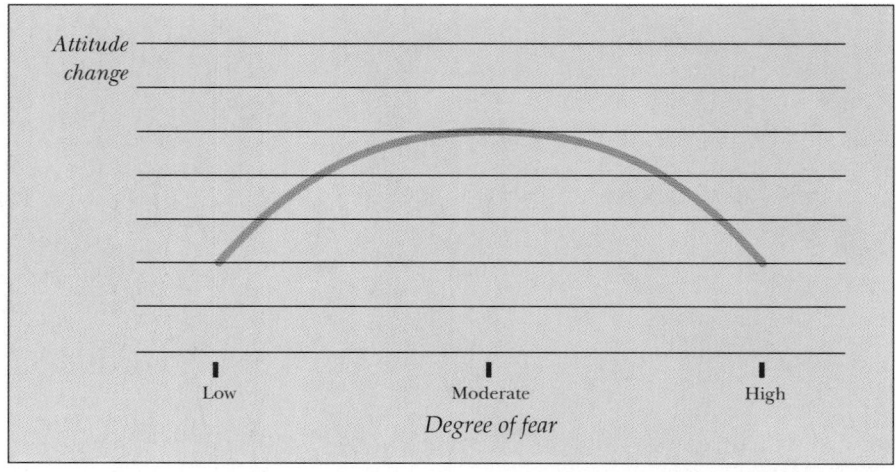

Attitude change

Degree of fear

Low   Moderate   High

FIGURE 5-7   Inverted-U relationship between fear and opinion change

their attitude in the direction of the communication that had been censored.

Worchel and Arnold (1973) investigated the effects of censorship on attitude change by varying the characteristics (positive or negative) of the censor. They too found that censorship of a communication created attitude change in the direction of that communication, and that it did so regardless of the subjects' initial attraction to the censor. In addition to creating attitude change, censoring a communication increased subjects' desire to obtain the communication. In a follow-up study, Worchel, Arnold, and Baker (1975) found that even when the censor was viewed as an expert, prohibiting the airing of a communication increased subjects' desire to hear it and caused attitude change in the direction of the communication.

These findings suggest that a censor's actions are likely to backfire; not allowing a communication to be heard may cause people to change their attitudes in the direction of the censored communication. This effect was evident in 1970, when President Nixon refused to allow the public access to the reports of the National Commission on Obscenity and Pornography (Weaver, 1970). The result of this censorship was that people who had never been interested in the report suddenly demanded to see it. The public clamor was so great that Nixon eventually released the report.

The audience

Cheering or heckling: Audience response as a peripheral cue. Much concern has been expressed about the response of the audience to what candidates have said in televised political debates. The moderator often needs to remind the audience that they are not to cheer and not to heckle. Yet campaign officials often make certain that their candidate has enough fans in the audience to do the right amount of cheering and/or heckling. Does the reaction of the studio audience have any impact on us, the TV and radio audience—that is, the real targets of the communication?

Researchers have shown that audience response is a peripheral cue that people sometimes use when they evaluate a persuasive communication (Axsom, Yates, & Chaiken, 1987). It seems that recipients who hear an audience responding enthusiastically to a persuasive message think, "If other people believe the message is correct, then it probably is valid," and recipients who hear an audience responding hostilely think, "If other people believe the message is incorrect, then it probably is invalid."

Silverthorne and Mazmanian (1975) examined the effect of hecklers by exposing subjects to a communication advocating taxation as a means of population control. The speaker pointed out that the current taxation system favors larger families and suggested that the government should tax large families more heavily than small families. Half of the subjects heard the audience booing and catcalling when the speaker was talking, and half of the subjects heard no audience response. Even though both groups of subjects recalled what the speaker had said, only subjects who did not hear heckling changed their attitudes in the direction of the communication. The subjects who heard boos and hisses were not convinced by the message.

In a study by Axsom and his colleagues (1987), subjects listened to a message arguing that probation should be used more frequently as an alternative to imprisonment. Some subjects heard the audience periodically interrupt the speaker with enthusiastic clapping and cheering, whereas other subjects heard only one or two people clapping and occasional cries of derision from the audience. The results of this study showed that subjects who did not find the issue involving and heard the enthusiastic audience response changed their attitude in the direction of the speaker's position more than did those who heard the unenthusiastic response.

The characteristics of the audience. The most effective communication delivered or written by an effective communicator will not achieve its maximum impact if the characteristics of the audience have not been taken into account. We do not want to say exactly the same thing in the same way to everyone. A bright audience may respond to different types of arguments than those to which a less intelligent audience would respond. An audience with one attitude will respond differently from an audience with another attitude.

Some of the factors that are basically located in the recipient of the communication will be considered here. These factors include the attitudes, intelligence, and personality of the audience, as well as more transient factors such as the audience's attention, mind-set, and commitment.

The attitudes of the audience. To some extent, communications should be tailored to the already existing attitudes of the audience. Richard Nixon, in his successful 1968 presidential campaign, created a unique set of advertisements that make this point. He held a series of seemingly

An audience's laughter is important not only to the comic; it's important to other members of the audience. If no one laughs, you'll be less likely to laugh as well.

impromptu televised question-and-answer sessions. His campaign staff decided beforehand that all such panel programs would be local; for example, the programs taped in Chicago would not be shown in Atlanta, and those taped in Southern California would not be shown in New York City. Thus it made no difference if the answer Nixon gave to a panel member's question varied from state to state. Since no statement would be heard by any audience but the one it was designed for, a question about law and order might evoke one response in New England and a different one in the South (McGinniss, 1969).

This is not to suggest that all communications should be as unprincipled as some political campaigns are. But there is something to be said for tailoring a communication to the initial attitude of the target. On almost every issue, all of us would find some views unacceptable. We might listen politely to such views, but we would be absolutely uninfluenced by them. We might, however, be somewhat influenced by an opinion that was not quite so extreme as the one we found unacceptable. Research that considered the range of opinions that might be acceptable to an audience with a particular attitude was conducted by Hovland, Harvey, and Sherif (1957).

Wets and drys in Oklahoma: Assimilation and contrast of attitudes. At the time of the research by Hovland and his colleagues, Oklahoma was still a dry state with a prohibition statute. But a move to repeal it was under way, and strong feelings had been aroused on both sides of the question. The researchers wished to show (1) that people who feel very strongly about an issue will find few positions other than their own acceptable, and (2) that people will distort opinions other than their own, so that (*a*) opinions that are unacceptable are made to appear more extreme than they really are (**contrast**), and (*b*) opinions that are acceptable are made to appear more similar to their own than they really are (assimilation).

The range of opinions in which assimilation would occur was called the latitude of acceptance, and contrast was said to occur in the latitude of rejection. The **latitude of acceptance** consists of the range of opinions that the individual finds tolerable—those that he or she could consider adopting—and the **latitude of rejection** consists of the range of opinions that the individual could not consider adopting. The investigators also predicted that as some Oklahomans staked out more extreme opinions about prohibition, their latitude of acceptance would become smaller and their latitude of rejection would become larger. On the other hand, people with less extreme attitudes would have a relatively larger latitude of acceptance and a narrower latitude of rejection.

A wide cross section of Oklahoma residents served as subjects. Some held relatively moderate opinions, whereas others, such as members of the Women's Christian Temperance Union, held extreme views. All participants were shown a list of nine opinion statements about prohibition, ranging from "extreme wet" to "extreme dry." They were asked to indicate the statement with which they agreed most, all statements that they did not really object to, and all statements that

they found objectionable. In this way, the participant's own attitudes as well as his or her latitudes of acceptance and rejection were measured.

A week later, all participants returned and were exposed to a communication about prohibition. Some participants heard an "extreme wet" statement, others an "extreme dry" statement, and still others a moderate statement. Then subjects were again asked for their attitudes and their acceptance-rejection latitudes on the nine opinion statements. They were also asked to rate just how wet or dry they considered the communication that they had heard to be. The results showed that (1) extreme wet and extreme dry subjects had much narrower latitudes of rejection than did more moderate subjects, and (2) assimilation and contrast occurred, especially for subjects exposed to the moderate communication. Extreme wets and drys found the moderate position to be in their latitude of rejection. The extreme wets judged the statement to be much more pro-dry than it really was, whereas the extreme drys judged it to be pro-wet (the contrast effect). Moderate subjects, for whom the statement was within the latitude of acceptance, distorted the message to make it more nearly coincide with their own opinion (the assimilation effect).

In summary, three people can hear the same politician and arrive at three different opinions about what was said. Although the talk may truly be moderately liberal, an extremely conservative person may come away shouting, "Radical!"; an extreme left-winger might come away muttering, "Fascist!"; and a middle-of-the-roader might think, "That's what I like, neither too liberal nor too conservative." Positions that are extreme (as we shall see shortly) are less effective in altering opinions than positions that are more mildly discrepant with those of the audience. Hovland, Harvey, and Sherif's study demonstrates that not only is the extremity of a position a function of the spoken or written word, it is also dependent on the judgmental processes of the audience—processes that distort the message's content, depending on the individual's latitudes of acceptance and rejection.

Discrepancy from the opinion of the audience. Regardless of the opinion we express or the way we express it, what we say is bound to be

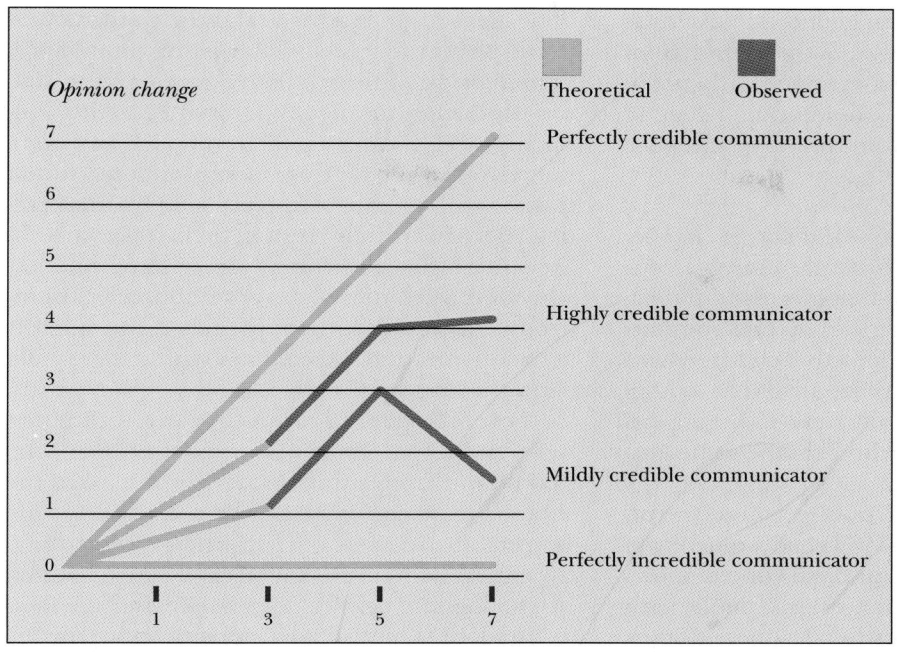

Opinion change

Theoretical   Observed

7 ————————————————————— Perfectly credible communicator

6 —————————————————————

5 —————————————————————

4 ————————————————————— Highly credible communicator

3 —————————————————————

2 —————————————————————

1 ————————————————————— Mildly credible communicator

0 ————————————————————— Perfectly incredible communicator

1   3   5   7

FIGURE 5-8   Opinion change as a function of credibility and the extent of discrepancy (theoretical and observed curves)

moderately deviant from the opinion of some people and extremely deviant from the opinion of others. Just how far can we stray from the initial opinion of the targets of our communication before we lose them? Or will we lose them at all?

Studies have shown that the relationship between discrepancy and attitude change is, in fact, a function of the degree of discrepancy and the perceived expertise of the communicator. In one study, Aronson, Turner, and Carlsmith (1963) asked subjects to rate stanzas of relatively obscure poetry. They then presented the subjects with a communication that advocated ratings that were either widely, moderately, or narrowly discrepant from the subjects' ratings. The communications were attributed to either the famous poet T. S. Eliot or Miss Agnes Sterns, of a local teacher's college. Subjects were then given an opportunity to rerate the stanzas, and this rating served as the measure of the degree to which they were influenced by the communication. The results, shown in Figure 5-8, indicate that subjects were more influenced by a discrepant communication

as a direct function of the size of the discrepancy—but only when the communicator was perceived as a credible expert. Influence peaked at a moderate level of discrepancy when the communicator was seen as lacking in expertise.

In interpreting these findings we could say that it is difficult for people to cope with the fact that their opinions are not shared by all. The wider the discrepancy, the greater our distress about the difference in opinions. As discrepancy grows (perhaps into the latitude of rejection), one easy way to deal with it is to maintain our own opinion and decide that the communicator does not know whereof he or she speaks. The communicator, that is, lacks either expertise or trustworthiness. We deal with the discrepancy by der-

---

contrast   The tendency to distort opinions that are unacceptable so they are made to appear more extreme than they really are.

latitude of acceptance   The range of opinions that one could consider adopting.

latitude of rejection   The range of opinions that one could not consider adopting.

ogating the source: "Only an idiot could take such a far-out position." However, if the source is an expert, such as T. S. Eliot on poetry, then the wide disparity between his opinion and that of the target of communication will still be effective in producing opinion change.

Committing the audience: Making it public. Attitudes that are kept private are more susceptible to change than those that are made public. A person in Arcadia, Florida, who had committed himself publicly to the idea that children with HIV antibodies should not be in public school would have a more difficult time changing his attitude than a neighbor who held the same attitude but kept it to herself.

To test the impact of **public commitment,** Kiesler and her associates (1971) had women who favored the dissemination of birth control information to high school students sign a public petition to that effect. The following day, these women and a control group of women with similar attitudes who had not been asked to sign the petition were exposed to literature advocating that birth control literature not be distributed. When the attitudes of all women were assessed after the attack on their position, the committed women were much more extreme in their support of distributing the birth control literature. Moreover, by a margin of approximately 40% to 10%, the committed women were willing to do volunteer work in support of their position.

Taking action: The foot in the door. Anyone who has tried to sell products from door to door or has had a salesperson appear at the door is probably aware of the **foot-in-the-door technique.** The major aspect of this approach is to have a potential customer commit himself to a very small task or favor. For example, a potential customer might be asked to thumb through an encyclopedia and give his opinion of its new format. After that, he might be given the opportunity to keep the first volume for a mere fraction of its cost. Before he knows it, he could find himself signing on the dotted line for the entire set. The salesperson has put a foot in the door by committing the customer to a position in small incremental steps. Once the customer goes so far, it is easy for him to take the next step, and then the next, and then the next. . . .

In an attempt to see whether the foot-in-the-

door method or a more straightforward request would be more successful in eliciting compliance, Freedman and Fraser (1966) devised a study that was conducted among residents of Palo Alto, California (105 women and 7 men). They were interested in seeing how many residents would comply with a request to place a large, unattractive "Drive Carefully" sign in their front yard. In the straightforward condition, an experimenter who identified himself as representing a citizens' group for safe driving approached the subjects at their homes and asked them whether they would allow the large sign to be installed in their yards.

Several types of foot-in-the-door techniques were employed. In one, an experimenter who said he was from a traffic safety group asked the subjects to place a small sign that read "Be a Safe Driver" in a window of their homes. In another, the experimenter asked subjects to sign a petition promoting safe driving. Two weeks after the foot-in-the-door subjects had been approached by the first experimenter, a second experimenter came to their homes and asked them to place large "Drive Carefully" signs in their front yards. The experimenters were interested in seeing how many subjects would comply with the second request.

The results showed that the foot-in-the-door technique was successful in influencing others. Subjects were more likely to agree to the large request if they had already agreed to comply with a smaller request than if they had not. On the average, 55.7% of the foot-in-the-door subjects agreed, whereas only 16.7% of the subjects who had received a straightforward request agreed.

DeJong (1981) contacted residents of two suburban Massachusetts communities and asked them to participate in a short survey about what it is like to live near Boston. Nearly 80% of those contacted agreed to participate. Two nights later, different researchers, calling from a different civic organization, phoned the same residents and asked them to participate in a time-consuming survey concerning the public's use of state parks. A separate group of subjects who had not been asked to participate in the Boston survey were asked to be interviewed for the parks survey. Only 37% of this group agreed, but more than 55% of the group that had taken the small step of agreeing to participate in the Boston survey agreed to participate.

DeJong (1979) reviewed several dozen studies related to the foot-in-the-door procedure. In general, he concluded that evoking a small behavioral commitment does reliably increase the likelihood of gaining a larger commitment in a wide variety of settings. He concluded that the technique was effective especially when (1) the original request was not so small as to be trivial, and when (2) no compelling extrinsic reason (such as a large financial reward) was offered for engaging in the original behavior.

Why does the foot-in-the-door technique lead to greater compliance? DeJong's review essentially supports Freedman and Fraser (1966). These researchers speculated that by getting a subject to agree with the small request, they had caused the subject to see himself as a "person who agrees to requests made by strangers, who takes action on things he believes in, who cooperates with good causes." Because the subject had changed his self-concept to this "action posture," it was easier to get him to comply with the larger request.

The door in the face. A reversal of the foot-in-the-door technique has also been suggested. Cialdini and his colleagues (1975) reasoned that compliance could also be increased by a **door-in-the-face** approach. They suggested that one way to get an individual to agree to perform a moderately large task is by first asking her to perform a very difficult task. Once she refuses to carry out the very large task, then ask her to comply with the smaller request: "OK, if you won't do that, will you at least do this?" Cialdini and his colleagues conducted a number of studies showing that subjects were more likely to carry out a moderately large request if they had previously refused to comply with a very large request than if they had not been previously asked to comply with the very large request.

Cann, Sherman, and Elkes (1975) tested the door-in-the-face technique in the same experimental design. Subjects were randomly assigned to conditions in which they would either reject a large request or comply with a small one. In addition, the researchers varied the amount of time between that request and the subsequent moderate request. In one set of conditions, the moderate request was made immediately after the initial request; in another set of conditions, it was made seven to ten days later. The results showed that in the immediate condition, both the door in the face and the foot in the door were effective

in producing compliance with the moderate request. In the event of a delay, however, the bargaining posture of the door in the face was ineffective. The results of the study are shown in Figure 5-9.

The low ball. In a maneuver that is similar to the foot in the door, another persuasion technique is to establish commitment by "throwing a low ball." This technique, which has been reported in many consumer magazines, such as *Consumer Reports* (1974), induces a person to make an active decision to engage in a particular action such as making a purchase. The **low ball** is an understatement of the true cost of engaging in the action. When the consumer agrees to pay this cost, he or she is told that the cost has actually risen. However, the consumer is so committed to the decision that he or she is likely to bear the increased cost.

The low-ball technique is, unfortunately, often used in the sale of new cars. A salesperson sparks your interest in a snappy sports car. He extols all of its good features; you really want to buy it. The good news is that he will offer you $1,000 for your 1967 Chevy. Since the net price of the sports car is now low, you decide to buy the car. The salesperson then disappears into the sales manager's office for a signature. Now comes the bad news. The sales manager will not agree to the trade-in. Your Chevy is worth only $135. But you really want the car. You dig deeper into your pocket and pay the added price. You have been low-balled into a behavior that, when you walked into the showroom, you would never have considered.

Cialdini and his colleagues (1978) demonstrated the low-ball effect experimentally. Sub-

---

door-in-the-face technique A persuasion technique whereby the communicator leads the target to comply with a moderately large request by first presenting a request so large that it will be refused.

foot-in-the-door technique A persuasion technique whereby the communicator leads the target to commit him- or herself to the desired position in small incremental steps.

low-ball technique An influence technique whereby the communicator secures the target's commitment to an action by understating its true cost.

public commitment Strengthening of a privately held attitude by making it public, as in signing a petition or making a public statement.

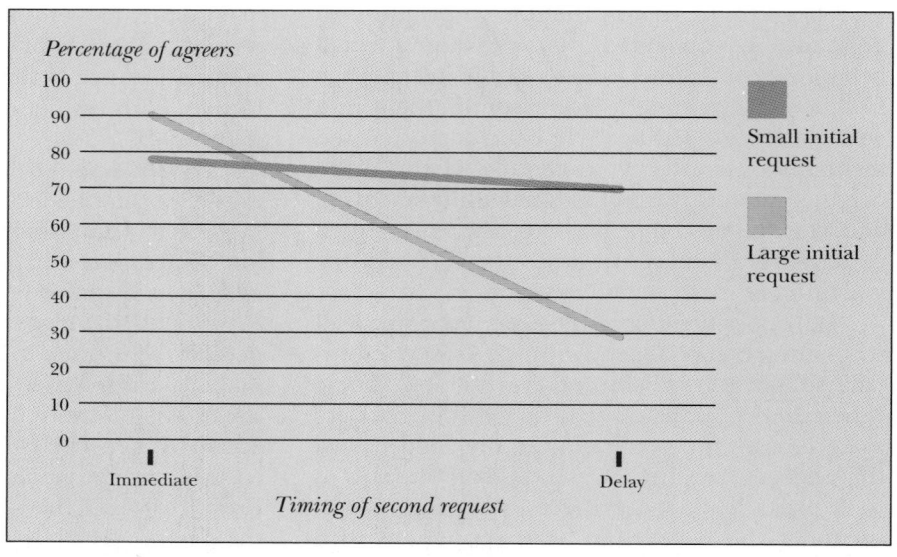

Percentage of agreers

Small initial request

Large initial request

Immediate   Delay

Timing of second request

FIGURE 5-9 The proportion of subjects agreeing to a second request as a function of the time delay and the size of the initial request
SOURCE: Adapted from Cann, Sherman, and Elkes (1975), p. 777.

jects were contacted by phone and asked if they wished to volunteer for an experiment on thinking processes. In the control condition, subjects were informed that the experiment would require them to arrive at the laboratory at 7:00 A.M. This was the "cost" that the student had to incur to participate in the research: it was put to the control subjects in a straightforward fashion. The subjects in the low-ball condition were first asked if they wished to participate. If the subject said yes, the experimenter then revealed the true cost—the experiment would begin at 7:00 A.M. Of the subjects who had been low-balled, 56% agreed to participate; only 31% of the other subjects agreed.

The similarity between the foot-in-the-door technique and the low-ball procedure is that in each case the communicator attempts to gain compliance with a request by first obtaining compliance with a less costly version. The difference is that the foot-in-the-door technique first obtains compliance with a harmless request, leaving the real request hidden. The low-ball technique obtains compliance with the real request; only the costs are hidden. Presumably the low-ball procedure gets its strength from one of two possible sources. First, it may come from the com-

mitment the individual has made to the decision to engage in an activity. Alternatively, its strength may reside in the participant's feeling of an unfulfilled obligation to the person who made the initial request. Does the customer in the car showroom feel committed to the new sports car or to the salesman to whom he made a commitment to purchase a car? Cialdini and his colleagues argue the first position, whereas Burger and Petty (1981) have presented evidence supporting the second. Either way, the commitment implied by the response to the low ball is a powerful inducement to make a more costly behavioral commitment.

The sneak attack: Resistance due to forewarning. Some of the most effective messages are those whose purpose is disguised until virtually the last minute. When we say, "I didn't realize this was an advertisement for Coca-Cola—I thought it was another hit song," the ad has had a head start in changing our attitudes. Indeed, one of the difficulties with political advertisements is that a television viewer can find out from the local newspaper that at 10:25 a station has scheduled a five-minute spot for a political announcement. Such advance notice or **forewarning** can allow the potential target to build her defenses, to think of the myriad reasons why she does not like that candidate or his commercials, or even to move toward the refrigerator for a cold drink.

What do people do during the period of forewarning? As we suggested earlier, one of the things they may do is forearm themselves with arguments to counter the arguments they know they will hear in the communication (Hass & Grady, 1975). We might see this as a form of inoculation or immunization. With the added time to ready arguments contrary to the message, it may be possible to fight off the communication, much as the body fights off a disease. An audience that is distracted or is not forewarned has a more difficult time gathering the necessary counterarguments. A body of literature has grown up around the question whether it is possible to immunize the potential target against attacking arguments.

The medical model: Resistance due to inoculation. When Hawaii was an independent society, it kept itself considerably apart from trade, commerce, or interaction with Western nations. King Kamehameha II decided to become the first of its monarchs (and among the first of its people) to travel abroad. The king and queen traveled to London, where they contracted measles and died. People who are raised in an environment that does not contain a particular germ or virus are extremely susceptible to it if they are ever placed in contact with it. People who are raised in an environment that contains a germ or virus tend to build up an immunity to it, so that the consequences are not so severe. Thus the king and queen of Hawaii, who had never been in contact with the measles (since it had never existed in the islands), were unable to withstand the attack of the virus.

William McGuire and his colleagues have taken the position that the human mind can be immunized against attempted persuasion in much the same way that the body resists attack by disease. Certain of our attitudes, they argued, exist in a relatively "germfree" environment. These are our cultural truisms, which are rarely if ever exposed to attack. For example, we all know that going to bed early is good, that catching a chill is bad, that brushing one's teeth after every meal is advisable. We rarely hear arguments to the

King Kamehameha of Hawaii, the first in a long family line of Hawaiian rulers, was raised in an environment that did not contain the measles virus. Thus his son was very vulnerable to that disease when he traveled to London. Can vulnerability to persuasion be thought of in the same terms?

contrary. Arguing from the disease analogy, we could say that these attitudes are extremely susceptible to attack by arguments for contrary positions.

How can such attitudes be protected against change? One way is to strengthen the already prevalent attitudes by providing additional reasons for holding those beliefs. This method is analogous to providing vitamins, exercise, and a balanced diet with chicken soup to make a per-

forewarning Advance knowledge that a persuasive message is coming, which can allow the potential audience to build defenses against the persuasion.

TABLE 5-3

Beliefs after both immunization and exposure to strong counterarguments

Strong counterarguments only (no immunization)	6.64
Immunization condition	
Supportive	7.47
Refutational	11.51
Control (no immunization or counterarguments)	12.62

NOTE: 15 = absolute agreement; 1 = absolute disagreement.
SOURCE: Adapted from McGuire and Papageorgis (1961).

son strong enough to resist a particular virus. On the other hand, we could expose the person to a weak form of the contrary position by providing a few reasons for believing that going to bed early decays the body, that brushing teeth removes their enamel, and so on. As the body builds resistance to a weak form of the virus that it received in an **inoculation,** the mind can build defenses against the arguments that it may ultimately be exposed to.

In the first study to test the effectiveness of inoculation on resistance to persuasion, McGuire and Papageorgis (1961) collected a set of cultural truisms (mental illness is not contagious; it is good to brush your teeth after every meal). As we have suggested, McGuire and Papageorgis reasoned that such truisms are vulnerable precisely because they are usually considered unassailable and we therefore have virtually no defense against an attack on them. Subjects were given two types of defenses to resist potential attacks against the truisms. For one truism, they were given a "supportive defense" in the form of arguments that upheld the truism. The same subjects received a "refutational defense" in the form of arguments against the truism, followed by a paragraph that refuted those arguments. The refutational defense, of course, was the inoculation analogue. Ostensibly, the attack on the truism helped to generate the kinds of argument that could fight off future attacks.

Two days after the defenses were provided, the subjects heard three counterattitudinal messages. One attacked the truism that had received the supportive defense, one attacked the truism

that had received the refutational defense, and one attacked a truism that had received no defense at all. After the attacks, the subjects' attitudes on all three issues (plus one truism for which they had heard neither a defense nor an attack) were measured.

The results of the study are shown in Table 5-3. It can be seen that both of the two defenses helped the subjects to resist the effects of an attacking message, but that the refutational defense was far more effective than the supportive defense in building resistance to persuasion.

The social-psychological research on audience factors in persuasion is difficult to classify in terms of its systematic or heuristic processing. The factors that we have discussed do have a common thread, however. The factors do not involve the cogency or legitimacy of the persuasive arguments, and we have thus categorized them as heuristic factors in the peripheral route to persuasion. Let us now return to those factors of the persuasion process that more directly relate to the cogency of the arguments in the communication.

Factors Affecting Central Processing

Having investigated some of the ways in which communicators use our emotions to change our attitudes, let us consider attempts to change our attitudes through rational argument. Are the clarity and comprehensibility of a message really important? Are we going to present only our side of the argument, or shall we present and perhaps respond to the arguments of the other side? If we decide to present two sides, which should be presented first? And when we are finished with our well-reasoned argument, do we need to spell out the conclusion to our audiences, or is it better to let the audience reach that conclusion by itself?

The argument: How many sides?

Let us consider a case from the political arena. Imagine that the year is 1988 and George Bush is running for the presidency of the United States. His opponent is Michael Dukakis. Imagine, too, a newspaper editor who would like to endorse Bush for president. The editor knows that some people favor Dukakis and he is aware of the arguments on Dukakis's behalf, but his job is to persuade his readers to vote for Bush. He has at least two options available: (1) he can present a strong one-sided argument that Bush should be elected president, ignoring any reasons why people should not vote for Bush; (2) he can present some anti-Bush arguments and explain why they are overridden by the pro-Bush arguments.

The relative effectiveness of one-sided and two-sided communications was one of the first questions investigated by Carl Hovland's Yale Communication and Attitude Change Program (Hovland, Lumsdaine & Sheffield, 1949). The study used soldiers in the U.S. Army after the fall of Germany in World War II. The government wanted to motivate the soldiers to pursue the war against Japan and to convince them that it would not end quickly or easily. Several hundred soldiers took part in the study. One group was presented with a 15-minute radio broadcast arguing that it would take at least two more years to conclude the war with Japan. A second group heard the identical communication except that a few contradictory arguments were woven into the broadcast. The commentator reminded the last group, for example, of the superiority of the U.S. Navy and the relative ease of fighting a one-front rather than a two-front war. Nonetheless, the broadcast strongly concluded that the war would take a few more years.

At the end of the study, the attitudes of both groups and those of a control group (whose members did not hear either communication) were assessed. Since the attitudes of the subjects had also been measured one week before the session, an index of attitude change was available. When the data obtained from the men were compared, it was found that (1) the experimental groups believed more strongly than the control group that the war would last at least two more years; but (2) there was virtually no difference in attitude change between the group that had heard the one-sided communication and the group that had heard the two-sided communication.

Interesting data emerged when the investigators took the soldiers' initial attitudes into consideration. The one-sided communication was far more effective in strengthening the belief of those who had initially agreed with the communica-

STOP, THINK, & UNDERSTAND

1. In the ELM model of attitude change, what is the difference between the central and peripheral routes to persuasion?

2. What is meant by the "sleeper effect" and what may it be due to?

3. How do factors associated with the communicator affect his or her persuasiveness?

4. What factors associated with a persuasive message (that is, the communication) cause attitude change along the peripheral route?

5. How do the attitudes and behaviors of an audience affect the degree to which the audience may be persuaded by a communication?

tion. However, the two-sided communication held the advantage among those who had initially opposed the point of view of the communication.

Subsequently, R. A. Jones and J. W. Brehm (1970) refined the analysis of one-sided and two-sided communications. These investigators argued that two-sided communications are effective only to the extent that the audience realizes that there are two tenable positions. This is a reasonable interpretation of the experiment by the Yale investigators. Jones and Brehm said that one-sided communications are generally more forceful and convincing since, by definition, they do not raise contradictory issues. On the other hand, individuals who realize that there is a second side to an issue may feel that their freedom to adopt a position is threatened by a communication that insists that there is only one correct stance. To maintain their freedom and independence, such individuals will resist persuasion. (The motivational

---

inoculation A technique for building resistance to persuasion by exposure to weak, easily refuted arguments.

---

aspect of restrictions of freedom is discussed in Chapter 6.)

To test this notion, Jones and Brehm devised a courtroom analogue in which subjects were asked to play the role of jurors. They were informed that they would hear the prosecution's summation of the case and half of the subjects were informed that it was not an open-and-shut case. Then half of the subjects were presented with the prosecution's one-sided argument and the other half read a two-sided statement. The jurors were then asked to assess the guilt of the defendant (that is, to indicate whether or not they agreed with the prosecutor) on an opinion scale. The results indicated that, at least in this situation, the one-sided presentation had an advantage over the two-sided communication. But more important, the advantage of the one-sided communication was greatly diminished when subjects were made aware that a different and defensible position could be taken.

For the newspaper editor, the decision about which type of communication he should use to persuade his audience to vote for Bush would depend on his assessment of the audience. The evidence indicates that one-sided communications may have the advantage over two-sided communications, but only if the audience is not aware that a reasonable case can be made for the other candidate. Thus the editor of an archconservative tabloid might try the one-sided approach, since it is entirely possible that the audience is unfamiliar with Michael Dukakis and other Democrats. However, if the audience is likely to know that there is another candidate whom respectable people are supporting, the two-sided approach would be more effective.

Which side first?
The order of presenting arguments

If you are going to present both sides of an argument, you have to know just how to use the various pro and con statements so that you will be convincing. You might begin with a list of arguments supporting your point of view, develop them fully, and then discuss and perhaps refute the arguments supporting the opposing candidate.

If we consider this approach for a moment, we can think of conventional wisdom, which suggests that everything is not so simple. A good political rally always leaves the audience singing the name of the good guy, not the opposition candidate. And some of the earliest data collected by psychologists (Ebbinghaus, 1885) demonstrate that people do forget rather rapidly what you tell them. Wouldn't you prefer to have people remember the arguments presented about your candidate rather than arguments supporting the opposition?

Miller and Campbell (1959) presented a carefully controlled study to clarify the matter. They argued that presenting your case first is generally more effective. People forget very quickly, however, and if conditions are such that they allow our message to be forgotten while the other message is remembered, the second message will prevail. Since the rate of forgetting is rapid at first and then tapers off, it follows that, if two messages are presented contiguously in time and a long delay follows, there will not be much difference in the amount of each message that is forgotten when attitudes are assessed. But if a long time elapses between messages and attitudes are assessed immediately after the second message, our memory will be greater for the second message.

This type of situation happens most frequently in a courtroom, where the prosecution and the defense—or, in a civil suit, the plaintiff and the defendant—have a chance to give summations to the jury. The prosecutor or plaintiff always presents the first summation. What does vary from trial to trial is the frequency and the duration of recesses in the proceedings. Miller and Campbell (1959) provided subjects with transcripts of an actual court case involving negligence. In one condition, the summation for the plaintiff was followed immediately by the summation for the defense. After one week, the jury was asked to decide the case. In this condition (which we refer to as "Sum_1 Sum_2 . . . Decision"), the argument for the plaintiff was most effective—that is, a primacy effect prevailed: the first information, the summation for the plaintiff, was more influential. In another condition, the summation for the plaintiff was followed by a week's recess. At that point, the defense summarized its case and the jury was asked to decide (Sum_1 . . . Sum_2 Decision). In this condition, a recency effect occurred—that is, the jury was more in favor of the defense.

Two additional conditions were also run. In one, the first summation was immediately followed by the summation for the other side, which was followed closely by the jurors' decision. In the second, a long time delay followed the first summation and the second summation. No advantage was found for the order of presentation in these conditions. The effects found in each of Miller and Campbell's conditions are summarized in Table 5-4.

If we adapt Miller and Campbell's results to the editor's problem, it would appear best for him to present his endorsement first and then deal with the arguments favoring the other candidate, since his situation is most akin to Miller and Campbell's Sum$_1$ Sum$_2$ . . . Decision condition.

When is more better? The multiple source effect

We've already seen conditions under which one- and two-sided communications are most effective. But factors other than the number of sides or the order of the arguments can influence the effectiveness of a communication in changing attitudes. One of these factors is the number of sources that present the persuasive arguments. To put it simply, the **multiple-source effect** is the tendency of information presented by multiple sources to receive greater scrutiny than the same information presented by a single source (Harkins & Petty, 1981a, 1981b, 1983, 1987).

The need for cognition: People who enjoy thinking and people who avoid thinking

A person's **need for cognition** is an individual difference affecting the likelihood that he or she will process a persuasive message centrally, elaborating on the argument contained in the message (Cacioppo & Petty, 1982). The need for cognition is a preference for and tendency to engage in effortful thought. Just as some people enjoy physical exercise and others avoid physical exertion whenever possible, some people really enjoy thinking and others avoid mental exertion whenever they can. The Need for Cognition Scale (Cacioppo & Petty, 1982) measures the tendency to enjoy and seek out situations requiring effortful thought versus the tendency to dislike and avoid such situations.

Cacioppo, Petty, and Morris (1983) examined the influence of the need for cognition on how likely subjects would be to take the central

TABLE 5-4

Conditions and findings of study on primacy and recency effects

Condition	Effect
Summation 1, Summation 2 . . . Decision	Primacy
Summation 1 . . . Summation 2, Decision	Recency
Summation 1, Summation 2, Decision	None
Summation 1 . . . Summation 2 . . . Decision	None

NOTE: . . . indicates a time delay.
SOURCE: Adapted from Miller and Campbell (1959).

route to persuasion. University students who were either low or high in need for cognition read a series of either strong or weak arguments for raising tuition at their university. The investigators found that the quality of an argument had a stronger impact on students who were high in need for cognition; that is, subjects high in need for cognition who read strong arguments became more favorable toward the idea of increasing tuition than subjects who scored similarly high in need for cognition and read weak arguments. The quality of the argument did not have much effect on the attitudes of students who were low in need for cognition. These findings indicate that subjects high in need for cognition were more likely than low need for cognition students to process the message centrally, carefully scrutinizing and elaborating upon its arguments.

Does absence make the heart grow fonder? Mere thought and biased elaboration

What happens to people's attitudes when they just sit and think about an issue? Research by Tesser and his colleagues (1978) has shown that **mere thought** about an attitude object causes atti-

---

mere thought Thought alone, which in the absence of the object contemplated or new information about it, causes preexisting attitudes toward it to become more extreme.

multiple-source effect The tendency of information presented by multiple sources to receive greater scrutiny than the same information presented by a single source.

need for cognition An individual preference for and tendency to engage in effortful thought.

---

tudes to become more polarized; that is, to become more extreme in the direction of the initial attitude. If a person who initially has a positive attitude toward the death penalty contemplates this issue for a while, she will come to feel even more positive about the death penalty. But if a person who has a negative attitude toward the death penalty contemplates the issue, he will develop an even more negative attitude toward the death penalty.

The more time people spend thinking about an object or issue, the more polarized their attitudes become (Tesser & Conlee, 1975). In the absence of any new information, when people think about an object, their thoughts are guided by their preexisting knowledge of the object and attitudes toward it. Such thought biased by preexisting ideas is likely to become more consistent with those ideas. In this way mere thought leads to a polarization of attitudes toward an object. It is important to note, though, that attitude change as a result of thinking about an object occurs *only* when a person already has at least some preexisting notions about that object (Tesser & Leone, 1977).

Tesser (1976) has also shown that the presence of the attitude object acts as a "reality constraint" on the extent of attitude polarization and that thought-induced attitude change is more likely to occur in the absence of the object. He demonstrated this effect by showing that initial attitudes toward a painting did not become as polarized when subjects engaged in thought about the painting while they looked at it. According to Tesser, "absence makes the heart grow fonder" only if the absent person was initially liked and is the object of thought while he or she is absent.

Research on mere thought predicts that if you develop a negative attitude toward your boyfriend, break up with him, and never see him again, you will probably come to feel even more negatively about him. This effect occurs because your initial unfavorable attitude will lead you to remember all kinds of unsavory things about him and to interpret any memories of his ambiguous actions in a negative light. If you see your former boyfriend every once in a while, however, you will be reminded of all aspects of his personality, and, although you may continue to have a negative attitude toward him, reality will probably keep that attitude from becoming extreme.

Which Route to Take?
Factors Limiting Central Processing

Why don't we always use central processing to understand persuasive messages? Why are we not constantly scrutinizing messages, believing the most logical and rejecting the poorly reasoned ones? Systematic central processing requires effort; it requires time. If the message exceeds people's capacity to process, they will use shortcuts, or heuristics. You will recall from our discussion of attribution in Chapter 2 that people frequently resort to heuristic devices when they perceive and evaluate others. These devices are efficient, relatively easy, and more often than not relatively accurate. That is why the expertise of a source generally works to enhance persuasion. If the message is difficult or complex, and if one does not have the time to scrutinize the details, it is convenient to "go with the expert." The experts must know what they are talking about, surely we can trust their word, and so forth. Thus, if you are not in a position to engage in the work of systematic processing, you are likely to use one of the peripheral cues to fix your attitude toward an issue.

Mackie and Worth (1989) provided evidence consistent with the notion that time and capacity limit a person's systematic processing of a message. Some of their subjects read persuasive messages under limited time constraints and others read them with unlimited time. Half of the subjects in each group were shown only strong, powerful arguments; half were shown only weak arguments. When time was limited, the strength of the arguments had no effect on subjects' attitudes; they were influenced only by heuristic cues present in the situation. When time to process the arguments was unlimited, however, subjects were persuaded by the stronger rather than the weaker arguments.

Mackie and Worth (1989) added another variable that has fascinating implications. They put half of their subjects in a positive mood and left the other half in a neutral mood. Mackie and Worth argued that a positive mood was distracting and therefore took away some cognitive capacity to deal with the content of the message. Indeed, the results showed that people who were in a neutral mood and had unlimited time were the ones who used central processing the most.

The wealth of available printed matter can be overwhelming. It is, therefore, not surprising that many people prefer heuristic devices to central processing.

By contrast, people in a good mood used any available heuristic cue and did not process the strength of the arguments presented in the message.

Another important reason for failure to engage in central processing is lack of motivation. As we pointed out, systematic processing takes work. If you are not motivated to engage in it, you may well prefer to take a peripheral route. Take, once again, the expertise of the communicator as a peripheral cue and let us contrast it to the actual strength of the message he or she is presenting. If you are personally involved in an issue, you are more likely to want to know the nature of the arguments pertaining to your final attitude. You will be more motivated to assess the accuracy of a message for yourself. If you had been a schoolteacher in Arcadia, Florida, during the time the Ray children were trying to return to school, you would have been motivated to assess the nature of the claims for and against ostracizing the children because they tested positive for HIV antibodies. On the other hand, if you had

been a resident of another state and had not come across this issue in any personal way, you might have been more likely to use cues such as expertise to determine your attitude. If a highly credible expert had said it was all right to come into contact with HIV-positive individuals, that might have been sufficient to create your attitude.

It should follow, then, that any factor that increases a person's involvement in the issue being presented will decrease the role of such communicator variables as expertise. The degree to which a person is involved in the issue raises his or her motivation to process the arguments in the message and therefore to rely less heavily on the source of the communication.

The role of **personal involvement** in persuasion has been a recurrent theme in recent

---

personal involvement The degree to which a person is involved in an issue, which determines the likelihood that he or she will process the arguments in the message rather than relying on peripheral cues.

---

1. How is systematic or central processing affected by the number of points of view presented in a persuasive message?

2. How is systematic or central processing affected by the order of presentation of the arguments?

3. How does merely thinking about an issue cause attitude change?

4. Why do we not always use systematic or central processing when we hear a persuasive message?

research (Leippe and Elkin, 1987; Petty, Cacioppo & Goldman, 1981; Petty, Cacioppo & Heesacker, 1981; Sivacek and Crano, 1982). Consider the study conducted by Petty, Cacioppo, and Goldman (1981). They had senior undergraduates listen to a communication advocating a policy of compulsory comprehensive examination for graduation from college. Half of the students were highly involved in the issue, since the college in question was their own and the timing was immediate. The other half believed that the exam policy would not be put into effect for ten years, if at all, and therefore the issue was not highly relevant to them. The expertise of the communicator and the strength of the message were also varied. Sometimes the arguments themselves were strong and cogent; at other times they were weak and unconvincing. Finally, the communicator was described as either a professor of education at Princeton University (expert source) or a junior at a local high school (nonexpert).

Who was convinced by the message? Who underwent attitude change? The results showed that the expertise of the source made all the difference if, and only if, the students were not personally involved. When they thought the exam policy was ten years away, they were persuaded that it was a good idea when the communicator was from Princeton. The strength of his argu-

ments was irrelevant. It was his expert status that created the attitude change. This, as we have discussed, is attitude change along the peripheral route.

When subjects were highly involved because of the possibility of an imminent change, the cogency of the arguments created attitude change and the characteristics of the communicator became irrelevant. In this circumstance, strong arguments caused persuasion. This was an example of attitude change along the central route. The relevance created a motivation for elaboration (that is, critical examination) of the arguments.

Attitude Research: Optimism for the Future

The 1980s were a very active decade for attitude research. Social psychologists entered the 1990s amidst predictions that this renewed interest would continue. McGuire (1985) suggests that the optimism is based on newly found conceptual models that treat persuasion as a larger "system" that focuses on the way variables in attitude change interact with one another.

Indeed, the philosophy of attitude research has shifted toward a more comprehensive view. In the past, direct questions about attitude variables could not be answered directly. Sometimes, for example, research on attitude change demonstrated the importance of the communicator's expertise; sometimes it did not. Sometimes evidence pointed to the importance of mood, and sometimes it did not. Because we are now developing more comprehensive theoretical models, we have a better sense of the way variables relate. We are in a better position to make predictions about the relationship among variables and to understand when a variable such as the strength of an argument will be important and when a variable such as the attractiveness of the communicator will overwhelm message strength. Armed with these theoretical advances and searching for new ones, psychologists view the 1990s as a decade when we shall come to understand more about attitude formation and change.

Summary

An *attitude* is a general and enduring positive or negative feeling about some person, object, or issue. In other words, an attitude is a person's liking or dislike for any object, person, or idea. Attitudes are learned during the growing-up process. Some attitudes are learned by *operant* and *classical conditioning*; others may be adopted through contact with *reference groups*. Newcomb's study at Bennington College demonstrated the power of reference groups to shape political attitudes. Other attitudes are generated by the principles of *balance theory*.

Attitudes can be measured in a variety of ways—by paper-and-pencil scales, such as the *Likert scale*; by the *bogus pipeline*, which serves to increase honesty on sensitive issues; by physiological measurements, such as the *GSR* and *EMG*; and by behavioral observations.

Theoretical models try to explain the way in which persuasion occurs. The *elaboration likelihood model* (*ELM*) accounts for attitude change by focusing on the distinction between the central and the peripheral routes. People who take the *central* route scrutinize the content of a message. The *peripheral* route leads to persuasion by other means, such as the attractiveness of the communicator. Similarly, the heuristic processing model posits a *systematic* processing mode and a *heuristic* processing mode, which are generally akin to the central and peripheral routes, respectively.

Early research on attitude change focused on those aspects of the communicator, the communication, and the audience which influence attitudes. Currently more attention is being focused on the factors involved in central versus peripheral processing. In the peripheral mode, Hovland and Weiss (1952) showed that highly credible communicators are more effective in changing attitudes than communicators with low *credibility*. They have also found, however, that with the passage of time, the effectiveness of the highly credible communicator decreases, whereas the effectiveness of a communication delivered by a low-credibility communicator increases. They termed the latter phenomenon the *sleeper effect*. Kelman and Hovland (1953) showed that the sleeper effect was caused by dissociation between the message and its source. Reinstatement of the source eliminates the sleeper effect. Recent research shows that the cause of the dissociation is that memory for the source and memory for the communication decay at different rates.

Expert and trustworthy communicators are more effective in producing opinion change than communicators whose *expertise* and *trustworthiness* are suspect. A person who argues against his or her best interests or whose communication is unintentionally overheard is considered to be especially trustworthy. Communicators who are similar to the target of a persuasive message are more effective in producing changes in value-oriented attitudes, whereas experts are more effective in changing beliefs about facts.

Peripheral or heuristic variables in the message itself include the details it presents. The more details a communication includes, even if they are irrelevant, the more the listener assumes the speaker must know what he or she is talking about. In addition, communications associated with a pleasurable emotion can have enhanced effectiveness in the peripheral mode. Communications associated with fear can be effective if (1) they also provide a way to reduce the fear, and (2) the fear does not reach a debilitating level. It has been suggested that the relationship between fear and attitude change may take the shape of an inverted U.

The audience's behavior and attitudes are influential peripheral-route variables in determining the ability of a persuasive message to change opinions. The perceived heckling or applause of an audience can be convincing to a target. The role of an audience's prior attitude in the persuasion process was first shown by the work of Hovland, Harvey, and Sherif (1957). This work suggests that messages that fall within a target's *latitude of acceptance* will be assimilated to the target's position, whereas messages that fall within the target's *latitude of rejection* will be contrasted, so that they will appear more discrepant than they really are. Aronson, Turner, and Carlsmith (1963) showed that increased discrepancy from a target's position is effective in changing attitudes only if the communicator is highly credible. Committing targets by having them agree to a position in small steps (the *foot-in-the-door technique*) has proved to be effective in changing attitudes, as has asking targets to commit themselves publicly to a position. Such related techniques as the *door in the face* and the *low ball* have also proved to be effective means of persuasion. McGuire and his colleagues have shown that an audience can be helped to resist persuasion by being *inoculated* with small doses of potential arguments. A communication topic for which an audience has developed no counterarguments is subject to successful attack from the opposite point of view. Research has also shown that forewarning about the topic of a speech reduces its effectiveness, probably because the audience has time to think of counterarguments.

Systematic processing is typically enhanced by factors central to the communication itself. Considerable research has been done on whether communications should present only one side of an argument or both sides. Communications are more effective when they present both sides of an argument if the target of the message was initially opposed to the point of view advocated. A one-sided message is more effective for those who were initially in favor of the position advocated. Miller and Campbell (1959) showed that the order of processing arguments in a two-sided message is important. That is, presenting your

side first will be to your advantage if a delay intervenes between the presentations and the attitude measurement. However, a delay between the two presentations will favor the other side if the attitude measurement is taken immediately after its presentation. Allowing an audience to draw its own conclusion from a persuasive message is effective provided that the audience is motivated to reach the conclusion.

Research has also been directed at ascertaining when people will engage in heuristic (peripheral) versus systematic (central) processing of a message. People generally scrutinize a message systematically when they have sufficient time and ability and when they are motivated to do the cognitive work required to elaborate a message fully. When people are personally involved in the situation with which the message is concerned, they tend to scrutinize the message. When they are not personally involved, the lack of motivation to engage in central processing causes the heuristic, peripheral variables to be persuasive.

The development of conceptual models to account for the diversity of findings in regard to attitude change has given this research new energy for the 1990s.

Key Terms

accommodation
assimilation
attitude
balance theories
bogus pipeline
central/systematic
  processing
contrast
classical conditioning
credibility
door-in-the-face
  technique
elaboration likelihood
  model (ELM)
electromyograph
  (EMG)

expertise
foot-in-the-door
  technique
forewarning
galvanic skin
  resistance (GSR)
heuristic processing
  model
inoculation
inverted U
latitude of acceptance
latitude of rejection
Likert scale
low-ball technique
mere thought
multiple-source effect

need for cognition
operant conditioning
peripheral/heuristic
  processing
personal involvement
public commitment
reference group
sentiment relationship
sleeper effect
trustworthiness
unit relationship

Suggested Readings

Chaiken, S. (1987). The heuristic model of persuasion. In M. P. Zanna, J. M. Olson, & C. P. Herman (Eds.), *Social influence: The Ontario Symposium* (Vol. 5). Hillsdale, N.J.: Erlbaum.

Eagly, A. H., & Chaiken, S. (1984). Cognitive theories of persuasion. In L. Berkowitz (Ed.), *Advances in experimental social psychology* (Vol. 17). New York: Academic Press.

Heider, F. (1946). "Attitudes and cognitive organization." *Journal of Psychology* (1964), 107–112.

Hovland, C., Janis, I., & Kelley, H. (1953). *Communication and persuasion.* New Haven, Conn.: Yale University Press.

McGuire, W. J. (1985). Attitudes and attitude change. In G. Lindzey & E. Aronson (Eds.), *The handbook of social psychology* (Vol. 2). New York: Random House.

Newcomb, T. S. (1943). *Personality and social change.* New York: Dryden Press.

Newcomb, T. S., Koenig, K., Flacks, R., & Warwick, D. (1967). *Persistence and change: Bennington College and its students after 25 years.* New York: Wiley.

Petty, R. E., & Cacioppo, J. T. (1981). *Attitudes and persuasion: Classic and contemporary approaches.* Dubuque, Iowa: Brown.

Petty, R. E., & Cacioppo, J. T. (1986). The elaboration likelihood model of persuasion. In L. Berkowitz (Ed.), *Advances in experimental social psychology, 19,* 123–205. New York: Academic Press.

Chapter Six

Relating Actions and Attitudes

The headlights of the little white Honda were almost the only ones on Oklahoma's Highway 74 heading toward Oklahoma City. The driver was late for her meeting, but because she was a careful driver, she kept her speed at 55 miles per hour. Suddenly, whether by accident or by someone's design, the car crossed over to the left side of the highway and went almost 100 yards along the grass shoulder. It flew over one side of a culvert, smashed into the opposite side, and flipped onto its side. Karen G. Silkwood was dead.

Karen was on her way to meet with a representative of the Oil, Chemical, and Atomic Workers Union (OCAW) and a reporter from the *New York Times*. She had with her evidence that the Kerr-McGee plutonium plant where she worked had been falsifying quality-control information and sending out defective plutonium rods. Silkwood had been collecting this evidence secretly for several months, and now, in the middle of contract negotiations between the union and the company, she felt it was time to release the story. It had been dangerous for Karen to acquire the evidence but she believed in the union, so she had acted.

Karen hadn't always been so involved with OCAW. Three months after she was hired by Kerr-McGee in 1972, the union went on strike. Karen had joined the union for the same reason that many others had—out of an interest in protecting her salary and as a defense against one of the largest energy conglomerates in the country. When her local went on strike for higher wages and better working conditions, Karen had joined them—not out of any strong belief in the labor movement, but because she knew it was her responsibility as a union member to do so. Karen had begun the strike feeling somewhat apathetic. But by the time the long and bitter strike ended, Karen was one of a few workers who had stayed away from Kerr-McGee for the duration of the strike. Although she had started out apathetically, she knew at the time of her death that her relationship with the company would never be the same.

In August 1974, with the OCAW local facing a decertification election and new contract negotiations, Karen, though still no union activist, accepted election to the union bargaining com-

mittee. She knew that the union had to negotiate a contract that would call for the company to comply with more stringent safety standards. Plutonium contamination could cause cancer and it could produce genetic defects in the offspring of those who had been contaminated—and more and more Kerr-McGee employees were being contaminated.

Before the local could negotiate a new contract, however, it had to survive a decertification election. If a majority of the workers voted against the union, Kerr-McGee would have a free hand: the workers would have no contract. Karen and the two other members of the union negotiating committee took time off from work and went to Washington to meet with union officials to plan for the election and the contract negotiations. Her involvement in union activities was growing deeper.

The union officials told Karen to collect as much evidence as she could on the quality-control violations and safety problems at the plutonium plant. In the middle of the contract negotiations, the union planned to give the information to the *New York Times* as a way of putting pressure on Kerr-McGee. Karen began to spy on the company. She was becoming increasingly convinced that the union was the only way.

Between the time of her trip to Washington and the beginning of contract negotiations in November, Silkwood's life was busy. She actively tried to persuade workers to support the union in the decertification election, talking to coworkers about the union's importance. The union won. Karen carried around a little notebook and wrote down every safety-standard violation she noticed. And she secretly made copies of quality-control documents and of touched-up X rays of faulty plutonium rods to prove her claims to the newspapers.

This union work took its toll on Karen. Management began to harass her, charging her with neglecting her work and conducting union business on company time. She was getting tired and weak. But Karen worked still harder. Her boyfriend urged her to stop working at the plant. Their relationship was growing more and more difficult as Karen devoted more time to the contract negotiations. But Karen chose to stay on. The union had won the decertification election

Karen Silkwood (played by Meryl Streep in the 1983 movie) involved herself in union activities at the Kerr-McGee plutonium plant where she worked. Each activity led to greater involvement and finally to her investigation of safety standards at the plant. Her activities ended suddenly when her car swerved off the road and crashed . . . no one knows for sure whether by accident or design.

but contract negotiations were still ahead, so Karen continued to collect her evidence.

On November 5, 1974, the day before contract negotiations were to begin, Karen Silkwood discovered that she had been contaminated by plutonium. Readings showed that some parts of her skin had over 20 times the amount of exposure to plutonium than was deemed permissible by the Atomic Energy Commission (AEC). After scrubbing herself with a mixture of Tide and Clorox, she was able to bring the plutonium level down. The next day Karen spent only a few hours in the plant; most of her day was spent at the contract negotiations. But again she found that she was contaminated.

The following morning Karen had a urine sample tested, and learned that the contamination level had shot up overnight. She was not being contaminated at the plant! A team of technicians from Kerr-McGee was sent to Karen's apartment; they found high levels of plutonium in the bathroom and the kitchen. Everything in the apartment was taken and sealed in lead drums and Karen was sent to an AEC hospital in Los Alamos, New Mexico, for more tests. These tests revealed that somehow Karen had swallowed plutonium.

When she got back to Oklahoma, Karen put all of her evidence together. It was time to let the world know about conditions in the Kerr-McGee plant. She believed that she had to do everything she could to help the union, and she knew that this story would do just that. But she never made it to Oklahoma City, and the information about quality control in the Kerr-McGee plutonium plant disappeared.

Who, if anyone, killed Karen Silkwood? The answer has never been found. Was her death planned by Kerr-McGee, the company against whom Karen was going to testify? Was the OCAW in search of a martyr? Or did Karen fall asleep at the wheel of her Honda? The one thing that can be said with certainty is that Karen Silkwood gave her life to the union cause. Whether her union activities caused the fatigue that sent her to a fatal accident or whether she was murdered for what she had allegedly uncovered about Kerr-McGee, her devotion and dedication to the union cause had been complete—and final.

Who could have predicted Karen's dedication to the OCAW? Nothing in her past gave any indication. She had not been involved in union activities before going to work at Kerr-McGee, nor had she ever expressed pro-union sentiments. She hadn't even been particularly liberal in her political attitudes. There was a marked discrepancy between her behaviors and her attitudes. Her relative indifference toward the union seemed inconsistent with her becoming a member of the negotiating team. Her initial apathy toward union activity did not lead anyone to expect that she would devote herself so thoroughly to the union during the decertification election. Nor could anyone have anticipated her behaviors in obtaining evidence about the company's alleged cover-up of its quality-control procedures. All of these behaviors were performed at great personal risk and few of them could have been predicted, given what was known about Karen Silkwood's earlier attitudes.

In this chapter we will discuss the relationship between actions and attitudes. We will deal with the way people's attitudes help to shape or guide their behaviors and vice versa. For example, did Karen Silkwood's attitudes lead to her significant political behavior? Or did her behavior on behalf of the union help to shape her political attitudes? The relationship between attitudes and behaviors has been a major area of study for social psychologists, and it is to this relationship that we now turn.

On the Consistency Between Attitudes and Behaviors

Do we always act in accordance with our beliefs and attitudes? It is a common-sense assumption that people who evaluate an object favorably will behave in a positive way toward that object, and, conversely, that a negative attitude will lead to negative behaviors. Our behavior, we might suspect, is the product of our thoughts and feelings. This may be common sense, but as we shall see, it is not always the case. Consider a fascinating study that was conducted several decades ago. La Pière (1934) investigated the relationship between attitudes and behavior at a time when anti-Chinese feelings were prevalent in this country. He took a Chinese couple on an automobile tour of the United States, covering more than 10,000 miles and stopping at over 250 hotels and restaurants. In only one case did the couple receive anything but full service and courteous treatment. After their travels, La Pière wrote to all of the 250 proprietors who had given service to the couple and asked them whether they would accept members of the Chinese race in their establishments. Despite their behavior (the fact that they had already served the couple), more than 90% of the proprietors who replied stated that they would not serve Chinese.

Other studies tended to corroborate La Pière's findings. Wrightsman (1969) observed the automobiles in a Tennessee parking lot during the 1968 presidential campaign. George Wallace was campaigning for the presidency on a platform arguing for stricter enforcement of the law. Owners of cars that bore bumper stickers promoting Wallace's candidacy were *less* likely to comply with a law that required them to purchase an automobile-tax stamp than supporters of the other candidates. Once again, the correlation between what appeared to be people's attitudes about the law and their actual behavior regarding a specific law was low. Wicker (1969) reviewed the relevant literature at the time and concluded that despite some evidence to the contrary, the relationship between what people say they believe in and what they actually do is not very strong.

Do Attitudes Lead to Behaviors?

The story of Karen Silkwood reveals that attitudes sometimes do and sometimes do not lead to consistent behaviors. Some of Silkwood's behaviors followed quite clearly from her attitudes. When she felt strongly that it was wrong of Kerr-McGee to violate safety standards and submit fraudulent safety-compliance data, her

People's attitudes, represented by their public statements, do not always match their behavior, as LaPière's study illustrated. There are various factors that determine whether an attitude becomes the motivator for our actions.

courageous actions designed to make public her revelations were consistent with her attitudes. On the other hand, like the restaurant owners in La Pière's (1934) study, some of her behaviors did not seem to follow consistently from her attitudes. Her activities on behalf of her union did not seem to follow from the generally apathetic attitude that she had when she first walked into the Kerr-McGee plant.

If it is true that attitudes sometimes predict behavior, the interesting question is: How does it happen? If we understood the *process* by which attitudes were related to behavior, then we could understand and predict the occasions when the two would and would not be related. In fact, at least two processes may be operating to encourage behaviors that are consistent with attitudes. Suppose that we divided people's actions into two categories: (1) those that are carefully planned and (2) those that are spontaneous and automatic. Each of these categories has its own working rules that lead to attitude-consistent behaviors. Let us consider each in turn.

The Theory of Planned Behavior

Do people plan their behaviors carefully? Do they think about their actions and about the relation of their actions to their attitudes and to the situation they are in? Ajzen (1985, 1989) has proposed a **theory of planned behavior** to account for the relationship of attitudes to behaviors. Based on an earlier theory by Ajzen and Fishbein (1980), this model takes the position that people are "usually quite rational and make systematic use of the information available to them" (Ajzen and Fishbein, 1980, p. 5).

Surely you can think of times at which you found it important to think through the way you wanted to behave. For Karen Silkwood, it was important to think very carefully about many of her actions. It was important for her to create a

---

theory of planned behavior   The theory that planned behavior is linked to an attitude toward the specific behavior, subjective norms, and degree of control.

From the bumper stickers on the back of this car, what attitudes might you assume the owner has? Would you expect that person to act in certain ways as well? How sure could you be of that?

plan for acting to turn over her evidence to the *New York Times*. Ajzen (1989) suggests that it is just such a reasoning process that links attitudes to behaviors.

The theory of planned behavior holds that people first consider their *attitude toward the behavior*. Did Karen Silkwood, for example, like gathering evidence for the OCAW union in its fight with management? Did a person in a voting booth on election day in 1988 have a positive attitude toward pulling the lever for George Bush? A person's attitude toward a behavior, then, is the first factor to consider in predicting attitude-behavior consistency. Note that in the theory of planned behavior it is not a general attitude—such as prejudice against Chinese people, as in La Pière's study, or attitudes toward law and order, as in Wrightsman's study—that will predict attitude-behavior consistency, but rather a very specific attitude toward a very specific behavior in which a person may engage.

A study by Davidson and Jaccard (1979) provides evidence for the necessity of matching a specific attitude with specific behaviors. The investigators were interested in predicting whether women would or would not use birth-control pills during a two-year period following the date of an attitude survey. Attitudes relevant to the behavior were assessed in a series of questions ranging from the very general to the very specific. When asked a general question about their attitudes toward birth control, the answers were *not* useful in predicting the women's behavior. As Table 6-1 indicates, the correlation between that general attitude and the specific behavior was near

TABLE 6-1

Correlations between selected attitudinal variables and behavior

Attitudinal variable	
Use of birth control pills during the 2-year-period*	
Attitude toward birth control	.083
Attitude toward birth control pills	.323†
Attitude toward using birth control pills	.525†
Attitude toward using birth control pills during the next 2 years	.572†

*N = 244.
†*p* < .01.

SOURCE: Davidson and Jaccard (1979).

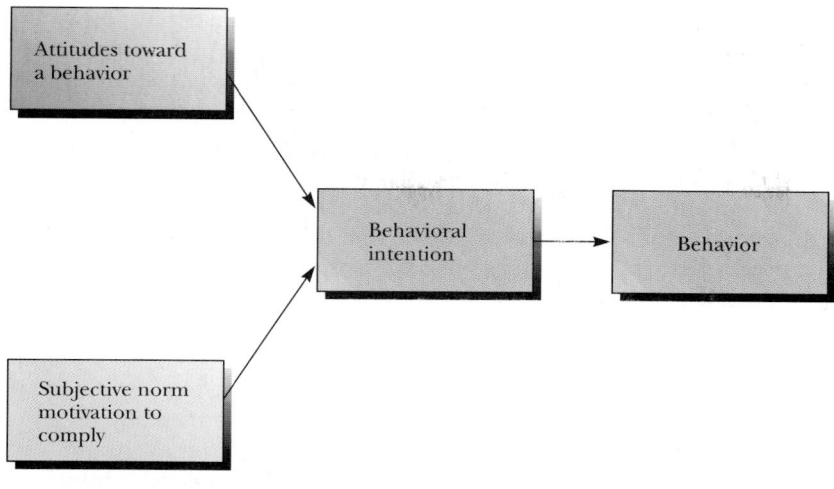

FIGURE 6-1 A diagram of the Theory of Reasoned Action

zero. However, more consistency between attitudes and behavior was found as the attitude became more specific to the behavior in question. As *birth control* became more specifically *birth-control pills,* as the question was increasingly directed toward the *use* of the pills, and as it became set in a relevant time frame, the attitudes and the behavior did become more consistent.

On the basis of this discussion, we can speculate about the relationship of some of Karen Silkwood's attitudes and her behaviors. Karen had attitudes about industry, factories, plutonium factories, and the Kerr-McGee plutonium factory in particular. Since the theory of planned behavior stresses the importance of attitudes that are at the same level of specificity as the behavior that is to follow, we would not have tried to predict Karen Silkwood's behavior at the Kerr-McGee factory from her general attitude toward industry. Her attitude toward Kerr-McGee—in fact, her attitude toward taking action against Kerr-McGee—is the kind of attitude that might predict her behavior. Similarly, we would not try to predict Silkwood's behavior toward her boyfriend, Drew, from her attitude toward men in general. Rather, it is her specific attitude toward Drew that might predict her behavior toward him.

A second factor in the theory of planned behavior, as illustrated in Figure 6-1, is a consideration of the subjective norms that operate in the situation. Behavior occurs in a rich social context. Other people's wishes and desires play an important role in our behavior. **Subjective norms,** in the theory of planned behavior, are what we think others want us to do. For Karen Silkwood, significant others in her environment included her boyfriend, who was vehemently opposed to her union activity; co-workers who were also opposed to her activity; and the people at the OCAW, who clearly wanted her to continue her aggressive behaviors on behalf of the union. After analyzing subjective norms, the individual must determine the *motivation* he or she has for complying with them. If Karen Silkwood had been motivated to please her boyfriend or her co-workers, her behavior might have gone in one direction, while pleasing her union colleagues might have pushed her in another direction.

The behavior of La Pière's subjects may have been inconsistent with their attitudes because of the subjective norms of the situation they were in. Although they may have had a negative attitude toward serving Chinese people in their establishment, the hotel and restaurant owners

---

subjective norms Behavior-guiding rules based on what we think other people want us to do.

may also have seen the norms of the situation they were in as calling for more hospitable behavior. The proprietors may have operated under a norm of hospitality. Did the other patrons of the restaurants and hotels want them to create a scene or act hospitably? If, for economic or any other reasons, the proprietors were motivated to adhere to a hospitality norm, then their behavior would not be consistent with their stated attitudes toward serving Chinese clients.

Finally, the theory of planned behavior considers the degree to which people believe a particular behavior, or behavioral outcome, is under their *control*. Ajzen (1989) points out that people do not take action, even action that is in accordance with their attitudes and subjective norms, if they do not feel they have the resources and opportunities to carry through the behavior. You may want to travel to the reaches of outer space, explore new galaxies, and boldly go where no person has ever gone before, but you may not be in a position to control the resources necessary to do that. Silkwood may have wanted to force Kerr-McGee to switch from producing plutonium to producing food products, but she did not have control over resources to effect such an outcome. In such cases, attitude-consistent behavior is unlikely. Ajzen and Madden (1986) asked college students about their attitudes, subjective norms, and degree of control in regard to getting an A in a course. They found that behaviors designed to achieve an A were correlated with the three variables that are important to the theory of planned behavior: attitudes, norms, and control. People were more likely to intend to engage in behaviors designed to achieve an A if they had (1) a very positive attitude toward those behaviors, (2) viewed others as wanting them to engage in those behaviors, and (3) believed they controlled sufficient resources—such as time and intelligence—to achieve the behavioral goal.

The Automatic Processing Model

Not all behavior is so carefully thought out as the kind described by the theory of planned behavior. Tying your shoes, saying hello to your family, and reaching for the morning paper are all behaviors that take place rather automatically. Without the ability to perform many everyday behaviors more or less automatically, we would find the world a very difficult place to navigate. Having to expend conscious mental effort for all social behavior would be dysfunctional indeed. Acting in a way that Langer (1978) has described as "mindless" is necessary and functional for much of social life. If many of our behaviors occur automatically, then the degree to which they are inconsistent or consistent with our attitudes may have an automatic component as well.

Fazio (1986) has proposed an **automatic processing model** that helps us to understand how attitudes predict behavior. He suggests that people respond relatively automatically to a situation once they interpret what that situation is. Here is where the attitude concept comes into play. Attitudes help us to interpret the situation we are in. Having an attitude that labor unions are good, for example, may help us to interpret an otherwise ambiguous event as one calling for pro-union actions. Therefore, attitudes can lead directly and automatically to behavior because they act to shape our perception of the situation.

You may reasonably argue at this point that we have presented studies such as La Pière's that show that behaviors are not always consistent with attitudes. How can this be, if attitudes automatically help us interpret situations and then bring forth behaviors in accordance with that interpretation? Fazio's model can help us in this regard. He reasons that an attitude will surface and serve as a guide to behavior when that attitude is **accessible** in memory. Not all of our myriad attitudes can possibly be brought into consciousness at the same time. Some are retrieved quickly from storage in memory; others are retrieved with more difficulty. In general, the stronger the association between an object and an evaluation, the more accessible the attitude. Therefore, anything that encourages an attitude to be accessible will lead to behaviors that are consistent with that attitude. Let us consider some of the factors that help to bring attitudes out of memory storage and therefore lead to behaviors consistent with them.

1. *Direct experience.* Attitudes can be formed in a variety of ways. The way a particular attitude is formed may determine how accessible it will be when a person is confronted with a particular object or situation. Your attitude about the value

of labor unions may have been formed by newspaper articles and by a general political orientation. Alternatively, your attitude toward labor unions may have been formed as Karen Silkwood's was, by direct experience in a labor market in which unions were both salient and controversial. We would refer to the latter as an attitude formed through **direct experience.** A direct-experience attitude is more likely to be accessible, to come to mind quickly and automatically, helping us guide our behaviors. Attitudes derived from direct experience are more likely to lead to behaviors that are consistent with those attitudes.

Regan and Fazio (1977) asked students at Cornell University to state their attitudes about a crisis in student housing that had developed at the school. Some of the students had direct experience with the housing crisis. In fact, because of the housing situation, they were currently sleeping in beds set up in dormitory lounges. Other students had been assigned to permanent housing and therefore had no direct experience with the housing crisis. Nonetheless, all students expressed similar attitudes; they were critical of the university's handling of the housing shortage.

All the students in the study were asked if they wished to take some action to help alleviate the crisis. Those who had direct experience with the crisis were more likely to volunteer to behave in ways consistent with their attitude than those who had no such experience.

2. *Relevance of attitudes to behaviors.* An attitude is likely to be more accessible, and therefore to guide behavior, if it is perceived to be relevant to the behavior at hand. The more relevant the attitude, the more likely it is to be retrieved from memory and serve as a road map for action.

Suppose that you are participating in a social psychology experiment. Suppose too that you have a favorable attitude toward being an experimental subject in psychological research. While you are participating, you notice a sign imploring people to volunteer for yet another study. Again you have a favorable attitude, but being a subject does take time and effort. What will you do? Such a situation was arranged by Snyder and Kendzierski (1982) in their study of the role of rele-

Strikers at Eastern Airlines had direct experience with union activity, and they took a hard line against new ownership and management policies that they felt would harm them.

vance in attitude-behavior consistency. Experimental subjects, in a situation like the one just described, read a notice inviting them to donate more of their time to a study that would give them no extra credit for participating. Half of the subjects' attitudes were made relevant to their

accessible An attitude is most easily accessed from memory storage if there exists a strong association between the object of that attitude and the evaluation of the current situation.

automatic processing model The theory that people respond relatively automatically to a situation once they interpret what the situation is.

direct experience An attitude derived from personal contact with the object of the attitude, rather than from hearing or reading about the experience of others.

TABLE 6-2

Proportions of participants volunteering for
extra sessions

	Relevance strategy condition	Comparison condition
Mean attitude toward psychological research	26.65	26.40
Proportion volunteering for extra sessions	0.60	0.25
n	10	10

SOURCE: Adapted from Snyder and Kendzierski (1982).

behavior. They heard another student (actually a confederate of the experimenters) say, "Well, I guess that whether you do or whether you don't is really a question of how worthwhile you think experiments are." In another condition, the confederate merely said, "Beats me. It's up to you."

The results of the research are described in Table 6-2. Clearly, participation was related to whether or not the confederate emphasized the relevance of a person's attitude to the particular behavior. Students were much more likely to behave consistently with their attitudes by volunteering for the research when it had been made relevant by the confederate.

3. *Prototypicality.* When we perceive a situation or an object in the social world, that situation or object has the potential to activate our attitudes. It is more likely to do so if the object is a good exemplar of the category that you have an attitude about. Earlier, when we talked about planned or reasoned behaviors, we noted that attitudes needed to be specific to the behaviors being planned. We are now considering the other side of that coin. Suppose you have an attitude about a broad category of people. That attitude may be activated quickly and automatically if you are interacting with someone who seems to be a good example of people you believe to form the category. More properly, we call this exemplar a prototype. A **prototype** is a standard that incorporates the essential and most characteristic features of a class (Rosch, 1978).

Perhaps the notion of prototypicality can help us to understand the **attitude-discrepant behavior** that LaPière's respondents demonstrated. Lord, Lepper, and Mackie (1984) raise the question whether the "attitude object"—in this case, the Chinese couple—were similar to the respondents' concept of "typical members of the Chinese race." Perhaps a typical Chinese was conceptualized in 1934 as "a barefoot coolie tracking mud across their lobbies" (Lord et al., 1984, p. 1256). The particular Chinese couple who entered their establishment may not have matched their prototype at all. The point here is that people have a prototype in mind when a general attitude is evoked; they have a prototype of a Chinese, a black, an American, a labor union, and so forth. Therefore, when we ask a person what his or her attitudes are toward the Chinese, a particular prototype is evoked and the person responds according to that prototype. It follows, then, that if the person has a chance to behave toward a member of the general class, but that member is not like the person's prototype, the person's behavior may indeed be different from what was expected on the basis of his or her attitude. Thus LaPière's respondents may have acted in a prejudiced manner had the couple matched their prototype. However, because the attitude object (the well-dressed, middle-class Chinese couple in question) did not match the prototype, the behavior and the attitude did not match. Lord, Lepper, and Mackie demonstrated that college students' attitudes toward people described as homosexuals predicted their behavior toward homosexuals only if the homosexual fitted the students' prototype of the "typical" homosexual. Thus, to the extent that the homosexual differed from the prototype, behavior was no longer consistent with attitudes toward homosexuals.

4. *Strength of attitude.* The **strength of an attitude,** in contrast to its extremity, can be measured by the rapidity with which it can be recalled from memory. If, in the days before she died, someone had asked Karen Silkwood how she felt about plutonium contamination or the OCAW, she would most likely have responded very quickly. Had she been asked how she felt about the candidates in the 1972 presidential election, it prob-

In this new era of super fitness, the prototype of an exercise teacher is quite salient in most people's minds. Which of these two women matches the prototype? Is the one who matches the prototype necessarily the better teacher?

ably would have taken her considerably longer to respond. We can say that she had a considerably stronger attitude in the former case than in the latter case.

The automatic processing model predicts that the stronger the attitude, as measured by the amount of time it takes one to state it when one is asked, the more likely one is to act in ways consistent with that attitude. Fazio and Williams (1986) tested this notion in the course of the 1984 presidential election. Three months before election day they phoned people and asked them about their attitudes toward Ronald Reagan. Then they carefully recorded both the direction of the respondents' attitudes and the time it took them to answer. On the day after election day, they called the same people and asked them how they had voted. The results indicated that the subjects' reported behavior (that is, how they voted) was consistent with their earlier attitudes toward Reagan, but primarily among the group who had responded quickly during the first phone call. Those subjects, whose attitudes were strong and accessible, voted for Reagan if they had indicated a preference for Reagan and voted for Walter

Mondale if they had preferred Mondale. The investigators found much less consistency among the group of subjects whose attitudes had been less strong before the election.

Automatic Processing vs. Planned Behavior

We have examined two views of the relationship between attitudes and behavior. We have seen that the theory of planned behavior views people as rational and deliberate. They systematically consider their very specific attitudes toward a behavior. They consider the existing norms and they consider the degree of their personal control before forming an intention to act. In the automatic processing model, we have seen a view of people as perceiving and interpreting the situa-

---

attitude-discrepant behavior Action that is contrary to one's private attitude.
prototype A standard that incorporates the essential and most characteristic features of a category.
strength of an attitude Strong attitudes are easily and quickly recalled from memory; weak attitudes require more effort for recall.

tion they are in through the automatic activation of an attitude. They do not plan the process; rather, the attitude serves as a filter through which an event or an object is perceived, interpreted, and acted upon.

Which view, the automatic processing or the planned behavior model, characterizes human behavior? It is certainly likely that they both do, depending on the situation people find themselves in. Fazio (1986) suggests that the two critical variables that determine whether someone engages in planned or automatic behavior are *motivation* and *opportunity*. When people are highly motivated to behave correctly and fear being wrong, they are motivated to engage in a reasoning mode. But they must also have time. Without ample time to engage in the reasoning process, people are not likely to do so. In that case, their behaviors may be influenced by any accessible attitudes they have about the attitude object. This hypothesis is consistent with the work of Lydon, Jamieson, and Zanna (1988), who found that people who were rushed into reaching a verdict in an affirmative action lawsuit were more consistent with their overall attitude about affirmative action. Presumably they did not have the time to engage in a reasoning process that would have had them consider their specific attitude toward the defendant in the case, their norms, and their perceptions of control.

We began this section by noting the contradiction between what common sense makes us think would be the relationship between attitudes and behaviors and the erratic relationship that seems to exist. In our effort to understand this situation, we have seen two different types of process—the planned and the automatic—each of which can lead to attitude-consistent behaviors if the factors that permit it to operate are present. In the absence of those factors, behavior may be inconsistent with an attitude. If an individual is engaged in planned behavior, an assessment of control or an assessment of norms may cause his or her behavior to differ from an attitude. If an individual is engaged in a spontaneous process, then any factor that serves to decrease or increase attitude strength (such as indirect or direct experience) will determine whether behavior is or is not consistent with attitude.

The conclusion that behaviors are consistent with established attitudes only sometimes still appears to be true (Cooper & Croyle, 1984; Wicker, 1969; Zanna & Fazio, 1982). Theoretical approaches such as we have discussed here make the "sometimes" understandable rather than merely erratic.

Behavior Leads to Attitudes

Even though we are beginning to understand the conditions that lead people to act in ways consistent with their beliefs, the fact remains that in most cases, knowing an individual's attitude toward another person or object is simply insufficient as a basis for predicting how he or she will behave in a given situation. Social behavior is influenced by several factors, attitude being but one of them. In the following chapters of this book we will look at experiments in which people behaved in ways we could not predict by measuring their attitudes. In one case, subjects said things they clearly knew were wrong merely because others had said them too. In another, subjects obeyed a psychologist's commands to administer severe electric shocks to an innocent victim—despite the victim's agonized screams and pleas to be set free. In yet another case, theological students passed by a man bent over and groaning in a doorway without offering help, even though they were on their way to deliver a lecture on the virtue of helping others in need. Clearly, in none of these cases could we have predicted the majority of the subjects' responses from their attitudes. Nor could we have made reliable predictions on the basis of knowledge of each subject's personality (Mischel, 1968). It is not that attitudes and personality simply do not matter, but rather that our behavior is powerfully influenced by situational factors as well.

Again in contrast to our common-sense assumptions, a link that is perhaps more direct and reliable exists between attitudes and behavior when we turn the question around. Does behavior lead to corresponding attitudes? Let's consider once again the case of Karen Silkwood. Silkwood was a person who at the outset of her work at Kerr-McGee did not believe in the labor movement. She described herself as apathetic

Chapter Six   Relating Actions and Attitudes

toward unions. Yet, as we have seen, she became so committed to her union that she endured great personal tragedy and eventually death. As she went through the final years of her life, she became an increasingly avid believer in her union. Her behavior seemed to precede her change in attitude. It seemed that she acted on behalf of the union—first by joining the OCAW, then by striking, then by remaining on strike despite company harassment that led other workers to end their participation, then by working in the decertification election, and finally by obtaining secret company documents. At every turn, her attitudes toward the union and toward her task of exposing cover-ups at the plant seemed to become more positive after she had already taken action.

Is it possible that people's behavior causes their attitudes to change at least as often as attitudes cause behavior to change? One of the social-psychological theories that relates changes in attitudes to changes in actions or behaviors is the theory of cognitive dissonance.

The Theory of Cognitive Dissonance

Cognitive dissonance theory, developed by Leon Festinger (1957), is concerned with the relationships among cognitions. A **cognition,** for the purpose of this theory, may be thought of as a "piece of knowledge." The knowledge may be about an attitude, an emotion, a behavior, a value, and so on. For example, the knowledge that you like the color red is a cognition; the knowledge that you caught a touchdown pass is a cognition; the knowledge that Karen Silkwood died in an automobile crash is a cognition. People hold a multitude of cognitions simultaneously, and these cognitions can be seen as existing in particular relationships with one another—irrelevant, consonant, and dissonant.

Cognitive Irrelevance

Cognitive irrelevance probably describes the bulk of the relationships among a person's cognitions. *Irrelevance* simply means that two cognitions have nothing to do with each other. You know that it is raining outside today, and you know that it is

over 3,000 miles from New York to Paris. These two cognitions exist simultaneously in your head, but neither one has any implication for the other. You have no intention of jumping on a plane to Paris every time it rains in New York, and the rain does not fall because you know the distance between two cities on opposite sides of the Atlantic. Therefore, we may say that two cognitions are irrelevant if one cognition has no psychological bearing on the other.

Consonance

Two cognitions are consonant if one cognition follows from, or fits with, the other. The cognition that it is 3,000 miles from New York to Paris fits with the cognition that you choose to take an airplane to get there. The fact that the Kerr-McGee plutonium plant did not like labor unions fits with the cognition that they fought for the decertification of the OCAW. The fact that you support consumer interests is consonant with the cognition that you contributed to Common Cause.

People like **cognitive consonance** among their cognitions. We do not know whether this inclination stems from the nature of the human organism or whether it is learned during the growing-up process; but we do know that people appear to prefer cognitions that fit together to those that do not, as we saw in Chapter 5. This simple observation gives the theory of cognitive dissonance its interesting form.

Dissonance

Two cognitions are said to be dissonant if one cognition follows from the opposite of the other. Consider these three examples: (1) a person who is apathetic toward labor unions devoted her life to the union; (2) a man who believes in a woman's

---

cognition   An element of knowledge; any thought that an individual has about him- or herself or the environment.

cognitive consonance   A relationship among cognitions such that each fits with or psychologically follows from the others.

cognitive irrelevance   A relationship among cognitions such that one cognition has no psychological implication for the others.

right to terminate her pregnancy makes an anti-abortion speech; (3) a child who dislikes chocolate ice cream buys a chocolate ice cream cone. In each of these examples, the cognitions about the behavior (I just bought a chocolate ice cream cone) follows not from the cognitions about a belief (I hate chocolate ice cream), but rather from the opposite of that cognition (I like chocolate ice cream). In each case **cognitive dissonance** is aroused.

Inside the Head

A person who has dissonant or discrepant cognition is said to be in a psychological state of dissonance that is *experienced as unpleasant psychological tension*. This tension state has drivelike properties that are much like those of hunger and thirst. A person who has been deprived of food for several hours experiences unpleasant tension and is driven to reduce that tension by eating. A person faced with dissonant cognitions will be similarly driven to reduce the tension state that results. Reducing the psychological state of dissonance, however, is not always so simple as eating or drinking.

The Magnitude of Dissonance

To understand the alternatives open to an individual who is in a state of dissonance, we must understand the factors that affect the magnitude of dissonance arousal.

First, in its simplest form, *dissonance increases as the degree of discrepancy among cognitions increases*. The man who delivers the anti-abortion speech will experience more discrepancy between his cognitions if his attitude is strongly in favor of the right to abortion than if it is only marginally so.

Second, *dissonance increases as the number of discrepant cognitions increases*. A child who buys a chocolate ice cream cone experiences some dissonance if she knows that she does not care for chocolate as a flavor. But she experiences greater dissonance if she also has the following cognitions: (1) she is allergic to chocolate; (2) she does not like cones; and (3) she once vowed never to go to this particular store again. Moreover, other discrepancies in the situation may further increase the psychologically tense state of dissonance. For

example, the child may have homework to do, but instead of doing it, she is wasting her time buying ice cream, an activity that is not consistent with getting the work done. Thus dissonance is directly proportional to the number of discrepant cognitions and to the degree of discrepancy among them. As degree and number increase, so does dissonance.

Third, dissonance is inversely proportional to the number of consonant cognitions held. In most life situations, people have cognitions that support certain aspects of an otherwise discrepant situation. The child who eats chocolate ice cream despite the fact that she dislikes it may also know that (1) it is the only flavor in the store, or (2) it is the least expensive ice cream that the store sells. The greater the number of such consonant cognitions, the less the dissonance.

Fourth, to estimate the magnitude of dissonance from the factors listed above, *the importance of the various cognitions must be taken into consideration*. Even glaring discrepancies among cognitions are unlikely to arouse much dissonance if these cognitions are trivial. For example, let us say that the public library on a particular Sunday is giving away hundreds of dollars' worth of free books to people who arrive before 8:00 A.M. Normally you do not like to get up early on Sunday. However, you do so this time to get the books, which you very much want to have. We can consider this situation in terms of dissonance. Your early rising is a cognition that is discrepant with your cognition that you like to sleep late. Your cognition that you will receive free books is consonant with your cognition that you want the books very much. Here the first cognition is trivial in comparison with the last. The magnitude of dissonance would therefore be low, since the relative weights given to the consonant and dissonant cognitions must be adjusted in accordance with their importance in the individual's mind. You should be aware that dissonance researchers rarely make precise predictions about magnitude. Most often only rough estimates as to the magnitude of dissonance are made.

Reducing the Tension

If dissonance is experienced as an unpleasant drive state, the individual is motivated to reduce it. Now that the factors that affect the magnitude of this unpleasant condition have been identified, it should be possible to predict what we can do to reduce the tension associated with it.

1. *Changing cognitions.* If two cognitions are discrepant, we can simply change one to make it consistent with the other. Karen Silkwood could have come to believe, after engaging in pro-union activities, that she really was enthusiastic about the union. She might also have believed that her behavior was not so pro-union as it seemed. Either way, changes of cognitions reduce the inconsistency.

2. *Adding cognitions.* If two discrepant cognitions cause a certain magnitude of dissonance, that magnitude can be reduced by adding one or more consonant cognitions. The pro-choice person who delivers the anti-abortion speech could reduce his dissonance by coming to believe, for example, that he made the speech only because he inadvertently found himself at a right-to-life rally. If he can convince himself that he avoided being harassed or beaten by making the anti-abortion speech, an important consonant cognition can be added to his internal formula, thus reducing the magnitude of the dissonance.

3. *Altering importance.* Since the discrepant and consonant cognitions must be weighted by importance, it may be advantageous to alter the importance of the various cognitions. The girl with the ice cream cone might come to believe that her allergy to and dislike of chocolate are trivial in comparison with the exhilaration she feels when she can buy something on sale. The importance of the consonant cognition (the one-day sale) can be magnified and the importance of the discrepant cognitions (allergy and so forth) can be minimized. When these changes in importance are made, the overall magnitude of dissonance is reduced.

Paradigms Used in Studying the Effects of Dissonant Cognitions

There are, of course, a multitude of situations in which people find themselves with some inconsistency among their cognitions. Social psychologists have employed several paradigms to study the effects of inconsistent or dissonant cognitions. The use of multiple paradigms is one of dissonance theory's strengths, because it not only

illustrates the wide array of situations in which dissonance occurs but successfully predicts behavior in many types of situations in which other theories make either opposite predictions or no predictions at all. The diversity of situations whose outcomes are predicted by dissonance theory will become apparent as we investigate the various paradigms.

The Paradigm of induced compliance: Incentives and threats

In the **induced compliance** paradigm, individuals are persuaded to behave in ways that are inconsistent with their private attitudes. Cognitive dissonance is established by a discrepancy between one's behavioral and attitudinal cognitions. The man whose private attitude is in support of abortion is in the same situation as a subject in the typical induced-compliance experiment. For some unspecified reason, he is induced to make an attitude-discrepant speech opposed to abortion. His true attitude is at variance with the attitude he has expressed in the speech and so dissonance is aroused. What can he do to reduce this uncomfortable state of tension?

As we noted earlier, a change of cognition is a leading possibility. Which cognitions could be expected to change? Typically, dissonance reduction will follow the path of least resistance. Cognitions about behavior are very difficult to change. The behavior is often public and the actor is identified with it. Unless he is particularly adept at outright denial, the man who made the anti-abortion speech will have a great deal of trouble changing the cognition that he has just acted in an attitude-discrepant manner. Privately held attitudes, however, are much easier to change. The man can convince himself that he really isn't pro-choice after all. Since cognitions about one's initial attitudes are less resistant to change, dissonance researchers have typically looked at attitude change as evidence of dissonance reduction.

---

cognitive dissonance   A relationship among cognitions such that one cognition follows from the opposite of another; also, a theory proposed by Leon Festinger that unpleasant psychological tension arises when cognitions are not in harmony.

induced compliance   A paradigm of research in cognitive dissonance in which individuals are persuaded to behave in ways that are discrepant with their private attitudes.

Karen Silkwood seemed to engage in behaviors that were at variance with her attitudes. Her pro-union behavior far exceeded her belief in the union—and each of her behaviors seemed to lead to more attitude change. It may well be that dissonance was aroused in Karen by her counter-attitudinal behavior and was reduced by a change of attitude toward the union.

The best way to get a feel for the psychology of induced compliance is to put yourself in the situation of a college student who has walked into what has become a classic experiment in dissonance research conducted by Festinger and Carlsmith (1959). As you enter the room, you are greeted by an experimenter who introduces the experiment, saying that it involves "measures of performance." You are shown a large board on which you see several rows of square pegs, and you are asked to turn each peg a quarter turn to the left and then a quarter turn to the right. You continue with this task until you are thoroughly bored, and you begin to wonder whether the experimenter is simply teasing you or has a sadistic sense of humor. No, you decide, he is serious. Then, just before you think you will fall asleep on the job, the experimenter stops you and instructs you about your next assignment. This time you have the responsibility of taking spools of thread off a large pegboard, after which you are to replace them on the pegboard. You continue this on-again, off-again project until you can barely stand it.

When you are finished, the experimenter lets you in on a secret that you have probably already guessed. He admits that he has not told you the full design of the experiment and that you really served in a control condition. He further explains that if you had been assigned to the experimental condition, a paid confederate of the experimenter would have joined you in the outer office as you were waiting for this study and would have tried to convince you that the experiment would be exciting, exhilarating, and fun. Then, the experimenter continues, the performance results of subjects in the experimental condition would have been compared with those of control subjects such as yourself.

At this point, you feel fully informed about the experiment, although you may still be scratching your head, wondering why anyone would be interested in the results of such an experiment. What you do not know is that the experimenter has been setting you up for the most important portion of the study, which is still to come. First, he laments that his confederate was not able to come to the lab and that there is another subject who is supposed to be in the experimental (that is, "exciting and fun") condition in the waiting room. But all is not lost; the experimenter has a brainstorm. How would *you* like to play the role of the confederate? All you would have to do, he tells you, is enter the waiting room and convince the student that this experiment is going to be fun. If you do this, you will be paid $1. Would you be willing?

If you agree, you have done what the experimenter was hoping you would do, for your role in the dissonance portion of the experiment is about to begin. You have formed the belief that certain experimental procedures are dull and boring. However, you are about to make a public statement to the effect that they are interesting and fun. Those cognitions do not follow from each other, so the psychological state of dissonance will ensue. In reality, the waiting subject is a confederate of the experimenter who is instructed to listen to your information and accept what you have to say.

How will you reduce your dissonance in this situation? Can you deny that you said the tasks were interesting? That is not a likely possibility. If you really believed that they were interesting and not at all dull, however, your cognitions would be consistent and your dissonance would be reduced.

Now suppose that you are in the identical experimental situation, except that instead of offering you $1 to make an attitude-discrepant statement, the experimenter offers you $20. How then would you reduce your dissonance? We noted earlier that attitude change requires work and effort, and that if there is a convenient cognition that is consistent with one of the cognitions creating the dissonance, it can be added to reduce the total magnitude of dissonance. Accepting $20 is a nice juicy cognition that is consistent with performing the attitude-discrepant behavior. In this condition, it is likely that you will reduce your dissonance by recourse to the $20 incentive and that you will have less need to convince yourself that the task was really interesting.

In all, Festinger and Carlsmith had three

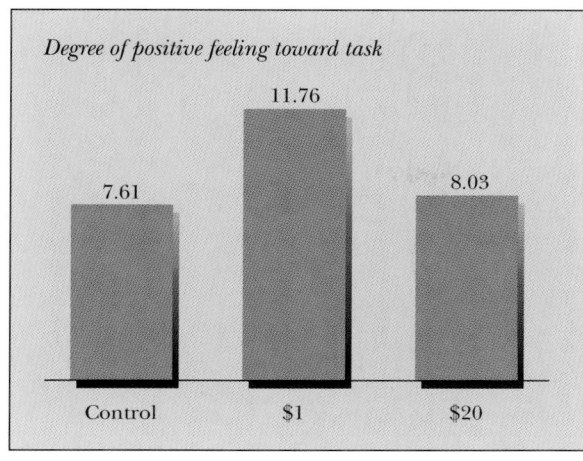

Degree of positive feeling toward task

7.61	11.76	8.03
Control	$1	$20

FIGURE 6-2 Attitude change following induced compliance
SOURCE: Festinger and Carlsmith (1959).

conditions in their study. In addition to the two incentive conditions ($1 and $20), subjects in a control group performed the boring tasks but were not asked to tell the waiting subject that the task was enjoyable.

After an appropriate explanation, all subjects were asked to tell a psychology department secretary how interesting the spool-sorting and peg-turning tasks had been. The results are illustrated in Figure 6-2. The subjects who served in the control condition did indeed think that the tasks were boring, as did the subjects who participated in the experiment for $20. But the subjects who performed the counterattitudinal behavior for only $1 told the secretary that the task was fun and enjoyable. Thus, agreeing to make a counterattitudinal statement for a small incentive led to the greatest degree of attitude change in the Festinger and Carlsmith study.

This study provided astounding support for predictions derived from cognitive dissonance theory. It showed, first, that attitudes could be affected by behavior: statements made contrary to one's attitude could produce changes in attitude. Second, it demonstrated that an inverse relationship exists between the incentive that is offered for the behavior and the degree of attitude change that will take place. As incentive increases, attitude change (and presumably the internal state of dissonance) decreases.

A study conducted at Yale University by Cohen (1962) provides further support for Festinger and Carlsmith's hypothesis. Yale is situated in New Haven, Connecticut, and it is not uncommon for students to become entangled in controversy with the New Haven police department. After one altercation, in which it was alleged that the police had acted with unnecessary aggression in handling a student melee, Cohen realized that he had the right ingredients for a dissonance study. He contacted Yale students in their dormitories and told them that an important research institute wanted them to write forceful essays taking the police side of the question. Further, the students were offered an incentive for writing the essay. Depending on the condition to which the student was assigned, he was offered 50 cents, $1, $5, or $10. After the essay was completed, the subject's attitude toward the police was assessed.[1]

The results of Cohen's study are presented in Figure 6-3. As incentive increased from 50 cents to $10, attitude change decreased. In fact, the $10 condition can be seen to be slightly less favorable to the New Haven police than the control condition (in which no essay was written), although that difference was not meaningfully large.

In summary, the major points to be abstracted from Festinger and Carlsmith's and Cohen's studies are (1) that behavior that is discrepant with one's attitudes can produce changes in those attitudes, and (2) that the amount of attitude change increases as the justification or the inducement for performing the behavior decreases.

Money isn't everything. Induced compliance produces attitude change as an inverse function of justification. Money is not the only justification that can serve as a cognition consonant with

[1] It should be noted that this study, like Festinger and Carlsmith's, is known as an after-only design. Subjects' attitudes are measured only once. In these studies, when a statement is made regarding attitude change, the difference between subjects in a particular condition and subjects under control conditions is being assessed. Since subjects are randomly assigned to the various conditions, it can be assumed that any difference between an experimental group and the control group must be due to a change in the experimental group, as a result of the independent variables of the experiment.

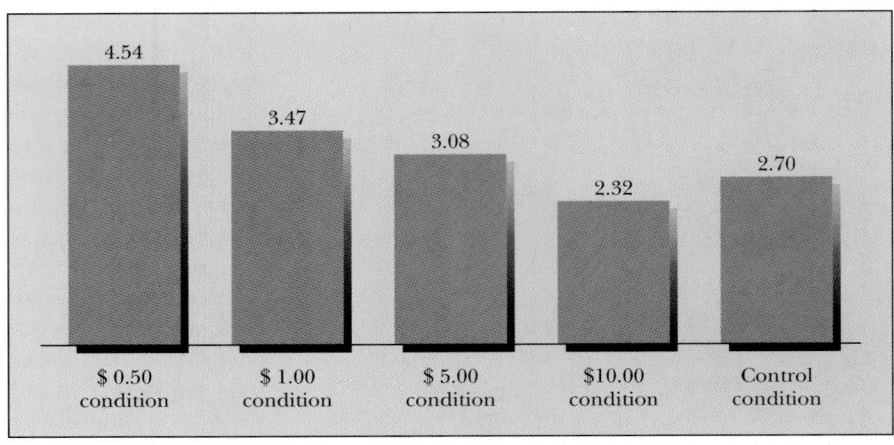

FIGURE 6-3 Mean attitudes toward police actions
NOTE: The higher the mean, the more positive the attitudes toward the New Haven police. The highest value equals 7.00; the lowest value equals 1.00.
SOURCE: Adapted from Cohen (1962).

behavior. Other forms of justification ought to serve the same purpose. For example, if an experimenter asks a subject to do something that is attitude-discrepant, the experimenter is likely to get considerable compliance if he lies on the floor, sobs, and tells the subject that he will suffer a mental breakdown if the subject does not deliver a strong and forceful speech. However, the crying act may also serve as a justification, much like the $20 incentive of the Festinger and Carlsmith study. It may be a large consonant cognition that reduces the magnitude of dissonance and lessens attitude change.

For example, in one study subjects were induced to deliver counterattitudinal speeches. One group was told that their participation in the study would be of great value to the scientific community and how appreciative the experimenter was for their cooperation. A second group received no such justification; they were merely asked to deliver the speech. Those given no justification appeared to change their attitudes in the direction of the speech, whereas those given the song and dance about their contribution to science tended to retain their initial attitude (Rabbie, Brehm & Cohen, 1959). Zimbardo and his colleagues (1965) had an experimenter try to persuade subjects to eat grasshoppers. In one condition, the experimenter was a friendly, affable gentleman. In another condition, he was cold,

abrasive, and decidedly unlikable. Subjects who ate the grasshoppers for the unlikable experimenter (low-justification condition) rated themselves as more favorable toward grasshopper consumption than did those who ate grasshoppers for the likable experimenter. Note that in this case, as in others, dissonance theory makes a rather surprising prediction—all other things being equal, we will come to believe in things we do for people we dislike more than for those we like. It is in part for dissonance theory's ability to make counterintuitive predictions such as these that it has generated so much research over the last thirty years.

In the natural environment outside of the laboratory, people often get involved in situations that are discrepant with their attitudes and that have less than sufficient justification. As the war in Vietnam heated up during the late 1960s, President Nixon introduced the concept of the "draft lottery." Depending on the date of their birth, young men would be given a number at random that indicated the priority with which they would be drafted into the army. By and large, people who received numbers 1–122 could be confident that they would be drafted; people with numbers 245–365 could be confident that they would avoid the draft.

Many male students rushed to join a campus ROTC as a way of avoiding being drafted into

Chapter Six   Relating Actions and Attitudes

service. To be exempt from the draft, it was necessary to join ROTC before receiving a lottery number. Some signed long-term commitments; others joined for one-year intervals. Staw (1974) studied the effect on ROTC membership and attitudes of people once they learned what their draft priority was. Among students who had signed short-term contracts and who received numbers in the 245–365 range, there was a high dropout rate from the ROTC program. This indicates that ROTC membership was counter-attitudinal for a substantial number of students. What justification existed for the behavior of students who had signed long-term contracts? Those who received draft numbers from 1 to 122 had sufficient justification: their ROTC membership was keeping them away from Vietnam. But students who had joined ROTC and then received numbers in the 245–365 range had no such justification. They probably would not have gone to Vietnam regardless of the ROTC.

Dissonance theory would predict that the low justification for ROTC membership among students with 245 + draft numbers would result in attitude change. These students would become more favorable to the ROTC. On the other hand, students with high justification (draft numbers lower than 122) need not change their attitudes about ROTC to make them consistent with their behavior. Staw interviewed the ROTC members and found that the long-term volunteers with the 245 + draft numbers were more favorable toward ROTC and performed better at ROTC drills than people with numbers lower than 122. Since the draft numbers were allocated totally at random and were distributed after all of the students had decided whether or not to join ROTC, the results found by Staw are compelling. Apparently dissonance was created by the high draft number (that is, low justification) and was reduced by attitude change toward ROTC.

In each of the above cases, the drive to reduce dissonance was aroused when people were induced to behave in a counterattitudinal way for minimal rewards or incentives. One particularly exciting line of work applied the psychology of induced compliance to situations in which threats as opposed to incentives were offered to obtain the desired behavior. This work was provocative not only because it once again made predictions that ran counter to both common sense and the prevailing reward-reinforcement theories endorsed by the behaviorists (such as Skinner, 1953), but also because it offered advice to parents on the art of effective child rearing. Aronson and Carlsmith (1963) reasoned that if a child is induced to forgo some desirable behavior (playing with an attractive toy, pummeling little brother, cursing) by way of a parental threat, the degree of severity of the threat will influence the child's attitude toward the desired behavior. If the child is promised a severe spanking if he curses, little if any dissonance will be aroused because there is an abundance of justification for not doing so. The severe threat adds cognitions consonant with those about his behavior—not cursing. But what if the child is given a much less severe threat? What if instead of bodily harm the child is threatened with a statement like "If you curse, I will be disappointed"? In this case, we would expect a good deal more dissonance to be aroused since the mild threat does not provide the child with a great deal of justification for not behaving as he wishes. To reduce this dissonance, the child may have to generate his own justification for not cursing. For example, the child may try to convince himself that cursing isn't so neat after all, or that cursing is for wimps, and so on.

This reasoning was put to the test in what has often been called the "forbidden toy" paradigm. Aronson and Carlsmith had 5-year-olds rate several toys as to their attractiveness. Then they told the children they could play with any of the toys except one they had rated as being highly attractive. Half the children were induced not to play with the toy with a mild threat ("I would be a little angry with you if you played with this toy"). The other half were given a rather severe threat ("I would be very angry; I would take all the toys away and never come back"). The experimenter then left the room. Although all of the children resisted the forbidden toy, the results of the experiment suggested that they did so for different reasons. As predicted, when the children rated the toys a second time, after the play session, those given the mild threat rated the toy as less attractive than before. Those given the severe threat showed no such attitude change—indeed, many of these children actually found the toy more attractive than before.

A subsequent study by Freedman (1965) showed that this change in attitude was a durable one. Freedman conducted essentially the same study as Aronson and Carlsmith, with two critical differences. First, the second measure of the attractiveness of the toy was made several weeks after the threat was made. Second, this measure was made by a different person from the one who had made the threat. Clearly, a meaningful change in the children's attitudes resulted from the dissonance aroused in the mild-threat condition.

Critical factors in induced compliance. In the years since Festinger and Carlsmith (1959) introduced the paradigm, research has shown that the world of induced compliance has grown more complex. Reviewing 20 years in the evolution of research in dissonance theory, Greenwald and Ronis (1978) commented, "Perhaps the only victim of the evolutionary process is the original version of dissonance theory, which has effectively been discarded" (p. 56). It may be more accurate to say that more than 20 years of research has allowed the theory to become more specific, more accurate, and consequently more qualified. It can still be said that behavior discrepant with private attitudes will produce attitude change when the justification is low—if the word *sometimes* is added. We shall now consider the factors that constitute the "sometimes"—that is, the factors that have proved necessary if induced compliance is to lead to dissonance-produced attitude change.

1. *Choice.* One of the most widely investigated factors in induced compliance has been the perception of the individual's freedom to act in a discrepant fashion. If I hold a gun to your head and "request" that you make certain discrepant statements, you will probably have fear—but will you have dissonance? The magnitude of your dissonance will probably be quite low, since the gun serves as the ultimate justification for your attitude-discrepant behavior. *In general terms, coercion, because of its high justification properties, will eliminate any further need for dissonance reduction.*

To see the dramatic difference that perceived freedom makes in creating changes in attitudes, consider an experiment conducted by Linder,

Cooper, and Jones (1967). Students were induced to write essays taking a very unpopular position—that controversial speakers should be banned from the university. Half of the students were *required* to write their attitude-discrepant essays and were then paid either a small or a large amount of money for their participation. The other half of the students were *asked* whether they would be willing to write essays and were promised either the small or the large incentive for their efforts. It was emphasized that the decision to write the essay was completely up to the student.

The results of the study show the dramatic effect of the perception of freedom in determining dissonance-produced attitude change. Figure 6-4 shows that when subjects freely chose to write an attitude-discrepant essay, their attitude change (and presumably their dissonance) decreased as the incentive value increased. This is consistent with the Cohen (1962) and Festinger and Carlsmith (1959) studies reported earlier. But when choice was eliminated, so was cognitive dissonance; only then did some other process begin to operate. In this case we can call the no-choice line in Figure 6-4 a **reinforcement effect.** The more money received, the more positive the attitude toward the task. The process may be akin to serendipitously finding money on a street corner; the person who does so may go back to that spot again and again and come to like that part of town. The more money (the more reinforcement), the more the liking. But the importance of the Linder, Cooper, and Jones study lies in its demonstration that the relationship between justification and eventual attitude change that we have been discussing in the induced compliance paradigm exists only when the individual feels free to comply or not to comply with a request for attitude-discrepant behavior.

The way the concept of freedom is applied in dissonance research is somewhat unusual. Typically a choice is expected to be sometimes accepted and sometimes refused. However, students who serve as subjects in dissonance experiments rarely turn down an experimenter's request. Subjects have been known to undergo undue physical effort (Wicklund, Cooper & Linder, 1967), to eat grasshoppers (Zimbardo et al., 1965), and to shock fellow students (Brock & Buss, 1962), in addition to making counterattitudinal

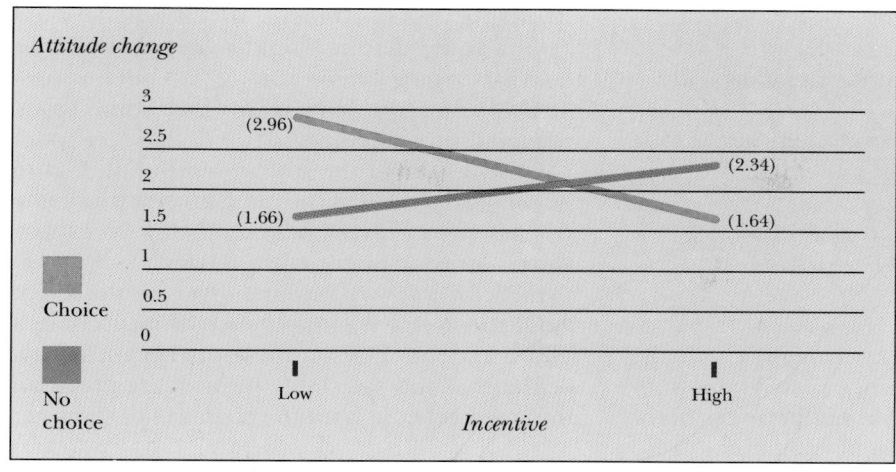

FIGURE 6-4 Changes of attitudes toward speaker ban as a function of choice and incentive
SOURCE: Adapted from Linder, Cooper, and Jones (1967).

statements, even though they had been offered a "choice" for compliance. Rarely do more than 5 to 10% of the subjects reject the experimenter's request. Kelley (1967) has characterized the choice offered to subjects in induced-compliance experiments as an "illusion of freedom." What is important, it can be argued, is not whether the subject has the audacity to refuse the experimenter's request, but whether she feels that she could have refused. As long as people have the illusion that they are free to choose, then induced compliance can lead to dissonance arousal and to attitude change.

2. *Commitment.* Intuitively, it seems likely that we would suffer more dissonance after making a counterattitudinal statement to a group of friends than we would after merely thinking of some statements that are attitude-discrepant. One of the reasons may be the degree of **commitment** to the disliked position (Carlsmith, Collins & Helmreich, 1966). When you are thinking to yourself, no one is a witness to your behavior. If you merely think about a position, you *can* take it back. You are not publicly identified with your attitude-discrepant position, and you can deny to yourself that you ever thought those evil thoughts. When you are speaking to your friends, it is much harder to deny what you said, as you have been clearly and publicly identified with your statements.

An important experiment by Davis and Jones (1960) demonstrates the combined effect of commitment and perceived freedom. Each student subject was asked to serve as an ally of the experimenter and to deliver an untrue evaluation of another student. The experimenter explained that he needed someone to make a hostile and derogatory evaluation of the other student. In half of the cases, the student was told that it was her obligation as an experimental subject to deliver the negative evaluation. In the other half of the cases, the student was merely requested to do so.

In addition to the variation in perceived freedom, the experimenters gave half of the subjects reason to believe that they would meet the other student after the experiment and would have a chance to reveal to her the circumstances behind the negative evaluation. That is, half of the subjects felt that they would be able to take back their evaluation, whereas the other half anticipated no such opportunity.

If a lack of commitment reduces the magnitude of dissonance, and if a lack of perceived freedom reduces dissonance, then only one of

commitment   The degree to which a behavior or decision cannot be undone or rescinded.

reinforcement effect   The tendency of a privately held belief to intensify in proportion to the size of an incentive to state that belief.

The Theory of Cognitive Dissonance   199

TABLE 6-3

Changes in the evaluations of the target person

	Choice	No choice
Commitment	− 7.7	− 1.7
No commitment	− 1.8	− 2.2

SOURCE: Adapted from Davis and Jones (1960).

the conditions of the experiment could be expected to show a difference in attitude. Subjects who delivered their evaluation under high-choice and high-commitment conditions were expected to change their evaluations of the other student in the direction of the negative statements that they had made. The results supported that prediction (see Table 6-3).

3. *Aversive consequences.* Not every attitude-discrepant act produces dissonance. Suppose that a Democrat is induced to make a statement urging a Republican victory in his congressional district. Cooper and Worchel (1970) and Collins and Hoyt (1972) have produced findings that imply that the Democrat would be in a state of dissonance only if he felt that he might have persuaded someone to vote Republican. However, if the speech were made in front of the bathroom mirror with no possibility of convincing anyone of anything, then it would not arouse dissonance. *In general, attitude-discrepant behavior arouses dissonance only if it can have unwanted or* **aversive consequences.**

In Cooper and Worchel's study, subjects participated in the dull peg-turning task of Festinger and Carlsmith's study and were also asked, in return for either a low or a high inducement, to mislead a waiting confederate into thinking that the task was exciting. However, after trying to convince the confederate, half of the subjects in Cooper and Worchel's study heard him say, "You are entitled to your opinion, but every experiment I have ever been in has been dull, and I expect this one to be dull too." The other half of the subjects saw the confederate become enthusiastic and quite excited about participating in an interesting study. In other words, the second group had the unwanted consequence of per-

suading a fellow student to become excited about a study that he would soon find dull. For the first group, there was no aversive consequence, since in this case the confederate remained unpersuaded.

The results of the study (depicted in Figure 6-5) made it clear that the only subjects who came to believe that the task was interesting were those whose attitude-discrepant behavior was performed for a low inducement *and* who brought about the aversive consequence of misleading a fellow student. Thus attitude-discrepant behavior that has the possibility of bringing about an unwanted event may arouse cognitive dissonance.

4. *Personal responsibility.* Wicklund and Brehm (1976) surveyed the entire gamut of research in dissonance theory and concluded that "dissonance as we know it takes place only when the dissonant elements have been brought together through the **personal responsibility** of the individual who experiences dissonance" (p. 7). Cooper (1971) has characterized personal responsibility as the blending of the already introduced concept of *choice* with the concept of **foreseeability.**

As an example, consider a hypothetical person who sees a geographic guide to the United States in a bookstore, buys it, and then finds out that the proceeds of the book are to go to the United Klans of America. Since he despises the KKK and he has just donated money to it, does he experience dissonance? According to the viewpoint that emphasizes personal responsibility, the answer would be no. This viewpoint argues that dissonance results from counterattitudinal behavior only when (a) the behavior was freely chosen and (b) the aversive consequence that follows from that behavior could have been foreseen at the time of the commitment. In the hypothetical example, the book purchase was freely made but the aversive consequence was not foreseeable. If the book buyer can add the cognition, "But I couldn't have known that the money would be used in that way," he can avoid personal responsibility for the inconsistency caused by despising the Klan but contributing money to it.

Goethals, Cooper, and Naficy (1979) conducted research to test the specific prediction that an aversive consequence has to be foreseeable for cognitive dissonance to be aroused. Subjects vol-

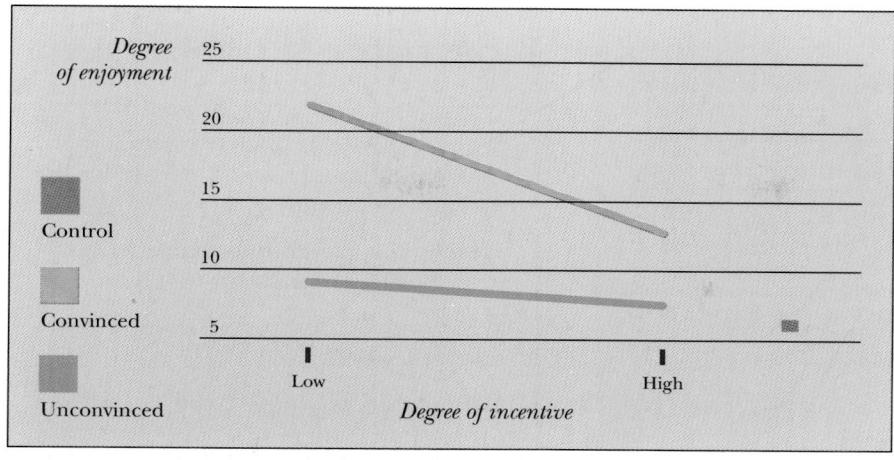

FIGURE 6-5 Mean ratings of enjoyableness
NOTE: Higher numbers represent greater enjoyableness.
SOURCE: Cooper and Worchel (1970).

unteered for what they believed was a study of psycholinguistics. The experimenter explained that the purpose of the study was to assess linguistic devices used in oral communications. This explanation was not exactly accurate but did serve to offer a reason to ask the students to write a counterattitudinal speech—in this case, to advocate doubling the undergraduate enrollment at the university.

Not only was the speech contrary to the subjects' attitudes, but an unwanted consequence might occur as a result of the speech. Recall that the study by Cooper and Worchel (1970) indicated that it was necessary for people to feel that some unwanted event might be caused by the speech. The unwanted consequence in the study by Goethals and his colleagues was that the speech was going to be shown to the Board of Admissions, which was considering a change of policy to allow for the doubling of the student enrollment. Subjects in an *unforeseeable* condition were kept unaware of this consequence. They were not told that the speech would or might be sent to the Board of Admissions. Subjects in this condition, then, thought the speech was for the sole use of the psycholinguistic experiment. Subjects in a *foreseen* condition were told explicitly, before deciding to give their speech, that the Board of Admissions might be sent a copy of the speech. Finally, a *foreseeable* condition was run in which

the possibility that "other interested groups" might hear the speech was mentioned but the Board of Admissions was never explicitly named. When the speech was concluded, the experimenter made it clear to half of the subjects in each condition that their speeches were, in fact, going to be sent to the Board of Admissions. No mention was made to the other half of the subjects of where, if anywhere, the speech was to be sent.

Subjects' attitudes about doubling the size of the freshman class were assessed at the conclusion of the experiment. The results are presented in Table 6-4. They show that when an aversive event was foreseen before subjects decided to engage in the counterattitudinal behavior, attitude change occurred. People who freely wrote essays favoring increasing the size of the student body changed their attitudes in that direction if they knew about the consequence beforehand. Apparently they felt personal responsibility for their actions and therefore

---

aversive consequences Unwanted events that result from a behavior, which lead to cognitive dissonance.
foreseeability Ability to foretell the consequences of a decision before the decision is made; an element of cognitive dissonance.
personal responsibility Accountability for the results of one's behavior, which flows from choice plus foreseeability; a requisite element of cognitive dissonance.

TABLE 6-4

Mean attitudes toward increasing the size of the freshman class

Condition	Foreseen	Foreseeable	Unforeseeable
Informed	7.1	7.4	9.6
Not informed	7.4	10.2	10.1

NOTE: Higher numbers indicate less favorable attitudes toward increasing class size. Low numbers are in the direction of the speech and imply greater attitude change.
SOURCE: Goethals, Cooper, and Naficy (1979).

STOP, THINK, & UNDERSTAND

1. When behavior is planned or reasoned, what are the conditions that make it consistent with attitudes?

2. What are the conditions that make automatic behaviors consistent with attitudes?

3. What is meant by *dissonance, consonance,* and *irrelevance?*

4. Why does receiving a small reward for saying something you do not believe cause dissonance?

5. How do choice, commitment, aversive consequences, and personal responsibility affect cognitive dissonance?

experienced dissonance. Changing their attitudes was their way of reducing that dissonance. However, subjects who had no way of knowing the aversive use to which their essay might be put (unforeseeable condition) did not experience dissonance: their ability to use an "I couldn't have known . . ." cognition eliminated their personal responsibility.

The middle column of Table 6-4 presents the interesting case of people who did not know of the ill use of their essay—but they might have been able to realize it had they thought about it. After all, the Board of Admissions certainly is an "interested group" that might want to hear students' speeches. The results showed that when the subjects were not informed that the Board of Admissions would hear their speech, they did not experience dissonance. But when they were informed, the concept that they *could* have known if they had thought about it was sufficient to invoke personal responsibility and led to the attitude change shown by the low score in the foreseeable-informed condition.

The effort justification paradigm:
To suffer is to love

Closely akin to the psychology of induced compliance is a paradigm that can be called **effort justification.** The observation that people love what they suffer for adequately summarizes this dissonance effect. Normally, we do not like to expend undue effort; we do not like to suffer. But we sometimes find ourselves in a position in which we are volunteering to do just that. The result may be the arousal of dissonance and the need to find a justification for having chosen to suffer.

Aronson and Mills (1959) invited women students to participate in a sexual discussion group. Before the students could join the group, they were required to undergo a screening test to be certain that they would be able to contribute openly to the discussion. It was implied that the test might be embarrassing because of the words that the subject would have to say aloud. Of course, the subject could refuse to undergo the test, but she then would not be allowed to become a member of the group.

Some of the subjects who agreed to take the screening test were assigned to a severe condition in which they were given a list of obscene words and lurid descriptions of sexual activity to read aloud. Other subjects were assigned to the mild condition in which they read ordinary words such as *petting* and *prostitute* for their screening test.

After their initiations, all subjects (plus a control group that received no screening test) were asked to listen to a discussion being held by the group. It was explained that since the subjects had not done the reading for the week's discussion, it would be better if they did not actually join the group now but instead listened to the week's discussion over earphones. The discussion that the girls listened to was dreadful. As Aronson and Mills described it, the discussion concerned "secondary sex behavior in the lower animals. [The participants] inadvertently contradicted themselves and one another, mumbled several non sequiturs, started sentences that they never finished, hemmed, hawed, and in general conducted one of the most worthless and uninteresting discussions imaginable" (p. 179). In fact, the discussion that the subjects were overhearing was actually a tape recording that had been designed to be as boring as possible. At the close of the discussion, the new initiates (the subjects) were asked to rate how interesting they felt the discussion had been.

Now, assume that you were a subject in the severe condition and that you had been embarrassed by the words you had read. Why would you choose to suffer embarrassment? The cognition that you do not like to be embarrassed is dissonant with the cognition that you have chosen to be embarrassed. According to dissonance theory, this arouses an uncomfortable tension that must be reduced. What cognitive changes are possible? You could deny that the embarrassment was severe, but assume that the words and passages were so chosen that this is not a viable alternative. You could decide that you like to suffer. This too is not a likely possibility. Finally, *you could come to like what you suffered for.*

Figure 6-6 depicts the effort justification sequence. If you can come to like the goal for which you suffered, then you will have added a cognition that is consonant with your suffering. In the Aronson and Mills experiment, the goal (the discussion group) was dull. But if you convince yourself that the group is really worth joining, then your dissonance can be reduced.

Many people who strain with pain to achieve physical fitness will come to love their grueling exercise schedule simply because it justifies their efforts.

The results of the Aronson and Mills experiment are presented in Table 6-5. It can be seen that the control group and the mild group rated the discussion and the participants as considerably more boring and less interesting than the group that suffered more severely.

The Aronson and Mills study has been supported by subsequent findings of Schopler and Bateson (1962), who used a very similar procedure, and of Gerard and Mathewson (1966), who conducted a very carefully controlled conceptual

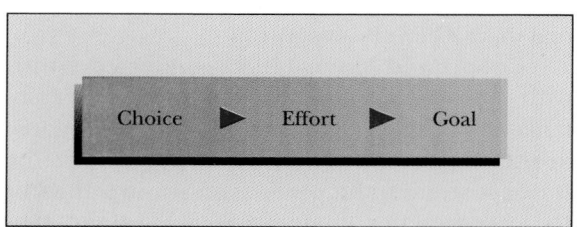

Choice ▶ Effort ▶ Goal

FIGURE 6-6 The effort justification sequence

effort justification Defense of what one has voluntarily suffered for as a means to reduce cognitive dissonance.

TABLE 6-5

Means of the sum of ratings for three experimental conditions

Rating scales	Control	Mild	Severe
Discussion	80.2	81.8	97.6
Participants	89.9	89.3	97.7

SOURCE: Adapted from Aronson and Mills (1959).

replication in a situation involving electric shock rather than embarrassment.

Applications of effort justification. In the effort justification paradigm, the concept of effort is taken in its most generic sense to apply to any situation that an individual would ordinarily prefer to avoid. Thus such noxious events as electric shock (Gerard & Mathewson, 1966), embarrassment (Aronson & Mills, 1959), physical exertion (Wicklund, Cooper & Linder, 1967), and exposure to delayed auditory feedback (Zimbardo, 1965) have all been used as ways to induce effort. Given this broad concept of effort, we can imagine that people may find themselves in many situations that they would ordinarily prefer to avoid. To the extent that they voluntarily place themselves in those situations, dissonance should be aroused. This, in turn, may lead to some interesting and practical consequences.

Let us consider Karen Silkwood. At each turn she had to undergo great emotional hardship for her decision to become involved with the union. Her boyfriend pressured her and Karen became more pro-union; the company harassed her and she became more pro-union; she was poisoned with plutonium and she became even more adamantly pro-union. Under extremely effortful conditions, Karen's attitudes seemed to change, evolve, and become stronger. Might Silkwood have been engaged in an effort justification process, continuing to reduce dissonance by changing her attitudes to justify her suffering?

Now let us turn our effort justification approach to an activity in which many people are involved—the process of psychotherapy. We begin with a hypothetical example.

Mary has trouble losing weight. She cannot seem to sustain a diet or an exercise program.

She wishes to obtain psychotherapeutic help. She can choose from a myriad of therapists and a variety of therapeutic procedures. She can settle on a psychodynamic approach, which emphasizes the hidden or repressed roots of her problem. In this way she can devote several years of her life, spend a considerable amount of money, and dredge up a number of unpleasant traumatic memories to arrive at an understanding of her problem. Alternatively, she can choose a learning approach to therapy. These approaches take less time and are sometimes less of a financial burden than psychodynamic approaches, but they too involve a degree of unpleasant emotional arousal.

Let us assume that Mary decides to enter into a therapeutic situation that is time-consuming, costly, and emotionally draining to achieve her goal: losing weight. Let us also assume that after several sessions, the therapy pays off: Mary begins to reduce. Why has improvement been made? Naturally, Mary's therapist can talk about teaching her to avoid anxiety or about discovering the hidden meaning of her problem. That is, the therapist has a theory of therapy that may account for Mary's improvement. However, a social psychologist will realize that the therapeutic setting has caused Mary to expend *effort* in the broad sense of the term. Whatever the therapist's theoretical bent, Mary has spent money and time and has experienced unpleasant emotions. Consistent with Aronson and Mills's study, Mary experienced dissonance, and to reduce the dissonance she sought to raise her evaluation of the goal, making the cognitions more consonant. Mary's goal was to lose weight. It could be predicted that she would come to like dieting, exercising, and so forth, much as Aronson and Mills's subjects came to like the boring discussion group. "Why did I expend so much effort?" Mary may have asked herself. "Because I really want to diet," may have been the response.

Cooper and Axsom (1982) conducted a study with overweight women who wanted some assistance in losing weight. Each subject participated in the experiment separately. Upon arriving at the first session, the participant was weighed by the experimenter, then informed about the "new experimental procedure" that was being developed to aid weight loss. Using an appropriate rationale, the subject was told about a series of tasks she was to perform. It was clear that each would require a great deal of effort. One task, for example, involved reading tongue twisters and nursery rhymes into a microphone while the subject heard her own voice fed back to her on earphones with a 0.3-second delay. None of the tasks involved any physical exercise, but each was extremely effortful. The tasks lasted about 40 minutes.

Two additional conditions were run. In a low-effort condition, the same tasks were introduced to the participants, but each one was easier and shorter than the parallel tasks in the high-effort condition. Finally, a control group consisting of women who had volunteered for the study were weighed during the initial session, but were not contacted again until it was time to collect the dependent measure. Subjects in the high- and low-effort groups returned to the laboratory for a total of five sessions during a three-week period for the purpose of performing the experimental tasks. At the end of the fifth session, they returned to the scale and were weighed.

The prediction of the research was that subjects who had been in the high-effort condition would lose more weight during the three weeks than either the low-effort or control-group subjects. The first column of Table 6-6 shows that this did occur. After the three-week period, high-effort subjects lost an average of 1.76 pounds compared to the 0.82 pounds lost by the low-effort group and the 0.17 pounds that were gained by the control subjects.

How long-lasting was the weight loss? Without having been informed of this possibility at the outset of the research, each participant was called in to be weighed after an interval of six months. The results after the six-month interval were far more impressive than they were for the earlier weight measure. High-effort subjects had lost nearly nine pounds. In addition, 94% of all subjects in the high-effort condition had lost weight after six months, while only 39% of the low-effort subjects had sustained any weight loss.

In a similar vein, Axsom (1989) has shown that the mere anticipation of high effort is sufficient to arouse enough dissonance to produce therapeutic behavior change. Subjects in this study were interested in overcoming their fear of snakes.

TABLE 6-6

Weight changes in weight control experiment (in pounds)

Effort condition	After 3 weeks	After 6 months	After 1 year
High	− 1.76	− 8.55	− 6.70
Low	− .82	− .07	− .34
Control	+ .17	+ .94	+ 1.86

SOURCE: Cooper and Axsom (1982).

After testing their initial ability to approach a five-foot snake, Axsom had subjects read a description of the therapy they would soon undergo. For subjects in the high-effort (high-dissonance) group, the therapy was described as involving extreme exertion. For the low-effort group, the therapy was described as easy and painless. Axsom also varied the degree of choice, such that half the subjects were told that they would be free to abandon the therapy at any time they wished. Half were not given this choice. As predicted, the greatest amount of dissonance occurred in those who anticipated high effort and perceived that it was their choice to engage in the therapy. In a subsequent test, these subjects came significantly closer to the snake than they had come during the first test, an improvement that did not occur for the low-dissonance subjects.

The free-choice paradigm

Another common way to study cognitive dissonance is by the **free-choice paradigm.** Consider Helen, a woman who has a week's spring vacation. A wide variety of vacation spots is available to her, but she has narrowed the choice to two: she can spend the week tanning her body on the beach at Fort Lauderdale, Florida, or she can schuss down the ski slopes at Whistler Ski Resort, in British Columbia, Canada. Each vacation choice

free-choice paradigm A strategy for research in cognitive dissonance in which an individual is asked to choose one of two or more items. Dissonance is aroused by the choice, owing to rejection of desirable aspects of the rejected item and acceptance of undesirable aspects of the chosen alternative.

Making a difficult choice between going skiing and going sunbathing for spring vacation may induce cognitive dissonance. Whatever decision is made, the alternative will be seen as more attractive than ever as a way to reduce dissonance.

has elements that are very attractive; yet each has drawbacks as well. Since Helen is an ultra-organized soul, she decides to make a list like the one below.

FORT LAUDERDALE

Good	*Bad*
sunny	too hot
relax	possibly boring
get tanned	possibly burned
meet men	

WHISTLER SKI RESORT

Good	*Bad*
exercise	exhausting
invigorating	expensive
sharpen skills	might break leg

If Helen decides to go to Fort Lauderdale, all of the good features of her ski vacation in British Columbia stand in a dissonant relationship with her decision. The same is true for all of the bad features of a trip to the beach. It doesn't make sense for Helen to go to Fort Lauderdale if the weather may be too hot. Nor does it make sense for her to go to Fort Lauderdale if she has

to give up an invigorating time on the slopes. On the other hand, a decision to go skiing would evoke dissonance from the positive features of a potential Fort Lauderdale trip and the negative features of skiing. From the list, it appears that Helen will have to forgo meeting men if she schusses down the slopes of the Canadian Rockies.

In this example, assume that all elements are of equal importance. It follows that our subject will go to Florida since there were more positive elements involved in that choice than there are for the ski vacation. But what will she do with the dissonance? The inconsistency created by all of Florida's unwanted features and all of Canada's beautiful but rejected features creates the tension state of dissonance. Our subject has the same alternatives available to her as we have seen in other dissonance situations. She can change her cognitions, alter their importance, or add new ones that she had not thought of previously. In the present case, she can change her cognitions about skiing and sunbathing. She can peruse her list of good and bad features and decide that she really did not want to sharpen her skills after all (that is, change what used to be a positive feature of the rejected alternative), or she can decide that

Chapter Six Relating Actions and Attitudes

TABLE 6-7

The reduction of postdecision dissonance by changing the attractiveness of items

Condition	Changes from 1st to 2nd rating for		
	Chosen item	Nonchosen item	Net change
Low dissonance (items of disparate value)	+0.11	0.00	+0.11
High dissonance (items of close value)	+0.38	−0.41	+0.79
Gift (control)	0.00		

NOTE: A positive sign indicates an increase in attractiveness; a negative sign indicates a decrease. The "net change" represents the degree of "spreading apart" of the alternatives following a choice.
SOURCE: Adapted from Brehm (1956).

she genuinely likes sweltering heat (that is, change what used to be a negative feature of the chosen alternative). She can alter the importance of cognitions by deciding that her fourth cognition, meeting men, is of such importance that all the others pale by comparison. Finally, she can add a new cognition: traveling to the West at that time of year is so dreadfully dangerous that she might not want to risk life and limb by doing so.

The result of making these changes is that the chosen action is much more appealing after the decision than it was when Helen drew up the list. The two alternatives are further apart after the decision than they were before (Festinger, 1964). That is, the chosen alternative is seen as increasingly attractive; the rejected alternative is seen as increasingly unattractive. In the process, the magnitude of the dissonance is reduced.

The first study to provide data to this effect was conducted by Brehm (1956). Women college students were asked to help a marketing firm to evaluate a number of consumer items, such as a toaster, an electric coffeepot, and a silk-screen print. The women were to rate each item on a scale, and they would then be allowed to choose an item to take home with them in appreciation for their participation in the study.

In the high-dissonance condition, the subjects were allowed to choose between two items that were rated very closely on the rating scale. In the low-dissonance condition, the two items from which the subjects were to choose were rated quite far apart on the scale. Clearly, there is less

dissonance when the chosen alternative is far more attractive than the nonchosen alternative from the start. In the control condition, one of the items was selected by the experimenter and given to the women as a gift.

After having chosen one of the items (or, in the control condition, after having been given one of the items), the women were asked to read some research reports written by the manufacturers of the items and then to rerate all of the items. The measure of interest to Brehm was the degree to which the attractiveness ratings of the two items spread apart after the decision was made.

Table 6-7 presents the results, which strongly support dissonance theory. First, it is clear that the item given as a gift did not change in perceived value (there was no change in the control condition). Second, in the high-dissonance condition, the two items were spread further apart in value than they were in the low-dissonance condition. That is, desirability ratings of the unchosen item decreased and ratings of the chosen item increased.

Free choice at the racetrack and the fair. Knox and Inkster (1968) took to the racetrack to find evidence for free-choice dissonance reduction in a field situation. They reasoned that people who have already placed a bet at the track have made a choice among decision alternatives. However, potential bettors who are on line at the $2 window have declared their intention to bet but have

According to cognitive dissonance, once you've actually placed your bet you'll feel more certain about your choice. (How you feel after the race depends on other factors, of course!)

not yet committed themselves irrevocably to a choice. These two classes of people at the track, then, should be at different stages of the decision process. The first should be more motivated to spread the choice alternatives than the second. Knox and Inkster interviewed people who were returning from the window and people in line at the window. As predicted, the people who had already placed their bets were more confident in their selection and in the outcome of the race than the people who had not yet bet.

Younger, Walker, and Arrowood (1977) replicated the basic design of Knox and Inkster's study at the midway of the Canadian National Exposition. They interviewed as many people as possible who had just placed 25-cent bets on various games of chance (for example, a wheel of fortune and bingo) and those who were on their way to place bets. The interviewers asked the respondents how confident they were that they would win and how lucky they felt that day. Consistent with Knox and Inkster's study, the people who had already placed their bets felt luckier and

more confident than the people who were on their way to bet. Figure 6-7 presents the results of the confidence measure for the subjects in the study by Younger and his colleagues.

A Case Study in Dissonance: Prophecies About the End of the World

Just before the publication of Festinger's cognitive dissonance theory, Festinger, Riecken, and Schachter (1956) read an interesting item in their local newspaper headlined PROPHECY FROM PLANET CLARION CALL TO CITY: FLEE THAT FLOOD! It went on to say that a suburban housewife, Mrs. Marion Keech, had received messages in the form of "automatic writing" from beings on the planet Clarion, who had told her that the world would end in a great cataclysm before dawn on December 21. A clear and definitive prediction had been made by Mrs. Keech and her followers. Moreover, the group of believers headed by Mrs. Keech had taken strong behavioral steps to indicate their degree of commitment to the belief. Some left

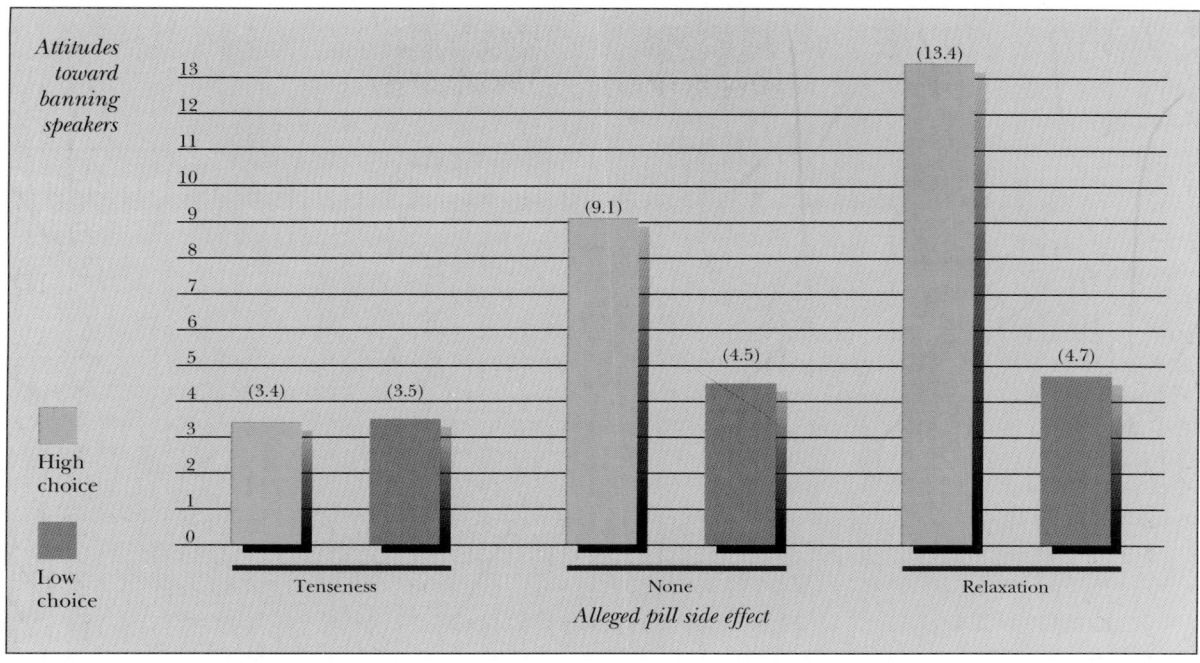

FIGURE 6-8 Attitude change following induced compliance as a function of choice and alleged pill side effects
SOURCE: Adapted from Zanna and Cooper (1974).

drug, attitude change should be viewed as irrelevant to reducing the arousal and should not occur.

To test this hypothesis, Zanna and Cooper had volunteers participate in a study that the volunteers believed was related to the effects of various drugs on memory. The volunteers ingested a pill that, unknown to them, was actually milk powder. But some of the subjects were led to believe that there was a side effect to the pill—that they would become aroused and tense within the next few moments. Other subjects were led to believe that the pill would relax them, and still other subjects were led to believe that the pill would have no side effects at all. After taking the pill, the subjects were asked to participate in "another experiment unrelated to the memory project." They wrote an essay advocating a ban on controversial speakers at their college—a position that was known to be discrepant with their true attitudes. Half of the subjects wrote their essays under high-choice conditions, so that dissonance should have been aroused. The other half wrote their essays without having a choice,

and thus dissonance should have been eliminated (recall Linder et al., 1967).

After writing their essays, participants had their attitudes assessed. Zanna and Cooper predicted that a typical induced compliance effect would occur in conditions in which no side effects were expected from the drug. More favorable attitudes in the direction of the essay under high- rather than low-choice conditions would be consistent with much of the research that we have considered. The middle panel of Figure 6-8 supports this prediction. More important, it was predicted that if subjects believed that they were aroused because of a pill that they had taken, they should not have been motivated to change their attitudes. Consequently, no difference between high- and low-choice essay conditions was expected among this group, and as the left-hand panel of Figure 6-8 indicates, none was found. In contrast, Zanna and Cooper predicted that if subjects believed that they should be relaxed by the pill, then any arousal that they did experience (presumably caused by the writing of the essay) would amplify attitude change. It is as though subjects were to argue: "If I ingested a pill to relax me, but I still feel aroused, I *really* must be upset by the inconsistency between my attitude and my behavior." The right-hand side of Figure 6-8 indicates that high-choice subjects in the relaxation condition did in fact change their attitudes more than any other group in the experiment.

The results found by Zanna and Cooper and supported in further studies reviewed by Kiesler and Pallak (1976) and by Zanna and Cooper (1976) support the view originally suggested by Festinger. Recent investigations have been directed toward specifying the precise form of the arousal and toward making careful distinctions between related concepts such as tension and arousal (e.g., Comer & Rhodewalt, 1979; Cooper, Zanna & Taves, 1978; Higgins, Rhodewalt & Zanna, 1979).

Direct measurements

Croyle and Cooper (1983) have shown direct physiological arousal accompanying the dissonance process. Subjects participated in a study in which they were to write counterattitudinal essays. They wrote persuasive essays on the desirability of having 7:00 A.M. classes at their university, although their own attitudes disagreed with this position. Some of the subjects wrote after freely agreeing to do so. Other subjects were told to write their essays. You undoubtedly recognize the induced compliance paradigm and can predict that dissonance should be experienced under conditions of high choice. What Croyle added to this study was a direct physiological measurement of skin conductance. This measure is related to the degree of perspiration carried on the surface of the skin and can be used as an indicant of physiological arousal. The results indicated that subjects in the high-dissonance (that is, high-choice) condition showed greater skin conductance than subjects in the low-choice condition and than another group of subjects who wrote a statement that was consistent with their attitudes.

Taken as a whole, these results cast doubt on explanations of dissonance phenomena that ignore the role of arousal (for example, impression management and self-perception), making such theories less likely to be accurate accounts of the process that underlies attitude change when behavior and attitudes conflict.

Some Implications of Dissonance and Arousal: On the Effect of Alcohol and Other Agents

We have seen that attitudes change; cognitions are added, eliminated, or changed; and attitudes are altered when dissonance is aroused by such techniques as induced compliance, free choice, and effort justification. If it is true that these cognitive changes come about as a means of reducing the unpleasant tension state, then it may also be true that *any* means of reducing the tension may satisfactorily reduce the dissonance. By and large, the research we have discussed focuses on the way in which people operate on inconsistent cognitions to restore consistency. But it is possible that other stimuli, which have nothing to do with the cognitions involved in the inconsistency, may serve to eliminate the tension. If they do, there may be no need to change or bolster the originally inconsistent cognitions.

A striking example of this reasoning was provided in a study by Steele, Southwick, and Critchlow (1981). They argued that alcoholic beverages may be useful in reducing dissonance. There is ample research (such as McCollam et al., 1980) to support the intuitive belief that, at least during the initial phases of ingestion, small amounts of alcohol lead to positive emotional experiences. "If drinking alcohol . . . eliminates the unpleasantness of dissonance," they argued, "it could also be expected to eliminate dissonance-reducing attitude change" (Steele et al., 1981, p. 833).

In one of the experiments conducted by Steele and his colleagues, subjects were run in three conditions. In the dissonance-alcohol condition, subjects were asked to write a counterattitudinal essay advocating a tuition increase at their university. Then, under the guise of performing a taste discrimination test between different brands of vodka, the subjects were permitted to sip the vodka (with mixers) for a period of ten minutes. After indicating their preferences, subjects were

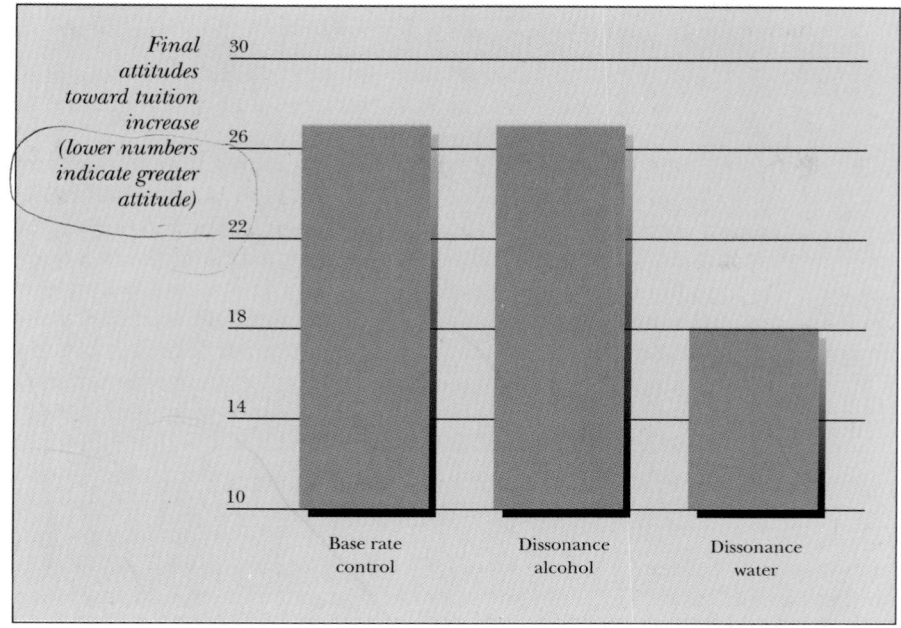

Final attitudes toward tuition increase (lower numbers indicate greater attitude)

FIGURE 6-9 Attitudes toward tuition increase after drinking alcohol or water
SOURCE: Adapted from Steele, Southwick, and Critchlow (1981).

given a questionnaire to assess their attitudes on increasing the tuition fee at their university. Other subjects were run in a dissonance-water condition. The procedure was identical, except that these subjects were given ten minutes to sip various kinds of water rather than vodka. Finally, some subjects were run in a base-rate control condition. These subjects sipped vodka for ten minutes, then responded to the questionnaire. They did not, however, write the counterattitudinal essay.

The results of the study are shown in Figure 6-9. It can be seen that only subjects in the dissonance-water condition showed attitude change. Subjects in the dissonance-alcohol condition indicated attitudes that were virtually identical to the base-rate control group. The results, then, confirmed the prediction that the drinking of alcohol was successful in reducing any need to change discrepant cognitions.

Steele and his colleagues speculate on the meaning of their research by raising the possibility that normal social psychological processes such as dissonance arousal may actually lead to

substance abuse. Inconsistency among cognitions, as we have pointed out, is a common feature of our daily lives. If the appropriate conditions for dissonance are present, the result may be the unpleasant tension state that Festinger (1957) originally proposed. Cognitive changes can reduce the tension; most of our laboratory research demonstrates this. But so may alcohol. By consuming alcohol, even in small quantities, we may experience the positively reinforcing phenomenon of having that unpleasant tension removed. Alcohol use that accomplishes this function, Steele and his associates suggest, may become alcohol abuse.

Revisions and Alternatives to Dissonance Theory

Not everyone agrees that the need to maintain internal consistency is a driving factor in human behavior. In the years since dissonance theory was first proposed (Festinger, 1957), several revisions and alternative explanations for the dissonance phenomena have been made.

Self-Concept

An early revisionist view was proposed by Aronson (1969b). He noticed that in most experimental tests of cognitive dissonance, what was dissonant was not just *any* two cognitions, but cognitions about behavior and the self-concept. In the induced compliance experiments, for example, the original explanation for attitude change after the subject had lied to a waiting confederate about a dull task (Festinger & Carlsmith, 1959) was that he had to reduce the dissonance between the cognitions "I believe the task is dull" and "I told someone that the task is interesting." According to Aronson, however, the dissonance is between the cognitions "I am an honest person" and "I have misled someone." This revision implies that if a person does not think that he is honest and he lies to someone, no dissonance will occur and therefore he will not change his attitude about the boring task.

Self-Affirmation

A similar argument has been offered by Steele, who, like Aronson, claims that dissonance will be aroused only when the self-concept is involved. According to self-affirmation theory, however, one need not deal directly with the inconsistency that threatens the self-concept. Rather, any act or thought that casts the self in a positive light can be harnessed to protect oneself from threatening inconsistencies (Steele, 1988; Steele & Liu, 1983). For example, if I smoke cigarettes although I am aware of the health risks—an inconsistency that threatens my self-image as a rational, intelligent being—I need not convince myself that smoking is really not so bad for me, or that the surgeon general is mistaken. Instead, self-affirmation theory holds that I can reduce the threat to my self-concept by engaging in behaviors that affirm important aspects of my self-concept. Thus, if I believe myself to be a generous, responsible person, I can counteract the threat to my self-concept posed by smoking through giving money to a charity, spending more time with my children, and the like.

In one study Steele and Liu (1983) employed the typical induced compliance procedure of having subjects first write counterattitudinal essays and then measuring their attitudes to note dissonance reduction through attitude change. Before the subjects' final attitudes were measured, however, they were asked to fill out a questionnaire pertaining to their political and economic values. Half of the subjects had been selected to participate in the experiment because they had a strong economic-political orientation and half because they did not have such an orientation. Thus, filling out the value questionnaire would presumably allow one group of subjects to affirm an important aspect of the self, whereas for the other, the questionnaire would have no such effect. Consistent with his reasoning, Steele found that much more attitude change in the direction of the essay occurred among the subjects who did not have a strong economic-political orientation. Those for whom the questionnaire served to affirm their values were better able to tolerate the dissonance aroused by writing the counterattitudinal essay, and thus they did not need to change their attitudes.

A more recent study (Steele, Hopp & Gonzales, 1986) showed that self-affirming behavior reduced the dissonance aroused in a free-choice situation. Half of the subjects had a strong science orientation, the other half a strong business orientation. After rating ten record albums for their attractiveness, subjects were allowed to choose to keep either the fifth- or the sixth-rated album, a behavior that typically results in dissonance, followed by the dissonance-reducing spread of alternatives when subjects are asked to rerate the items after choosing. But before these subjects rerated the ten records, they were asked to put on a white lab coat, ostensibly to prepare for a subsequent experiment. Presumably donning the lab coat served to affirm a central aspect of the self-concept of those subjects with the science orientation. When asked to rerate the ten albums, these subjects made ratings consistent with their earlier ones, indicating that the lab coat had eliminated the dissonance stemming from the choice. In contrast, the business-oriented subjects showed the classic dissonance effect—their ratings reflected increased attractiveness of the chosen album and decreased attractiveness of the non-chosen album.

Responsibility and Dissonance Motivation

Over the years many critics of dissonance theory have claimed that the addition of so many qualifying conditions (such as choice, commitment, aversive consequences, and foreseeability) has turned the theory into a waterlogged explanation of behavior (see Greenwald & Ronis, 1978). However, Cooper and Fazio (1984) attempted to put the preconditions for cognitive dissonance into a coherent framework. They noticed that choice and foreseeability are the necessary conditions to ascribe responsibility for some outcome to an individual. Therefore, they reasoned, dissonance arousal may result not from inconsistencies but rather from a feeling of personal responsibility for some aversive consequences. If this arousal is not misattributed to some other source, it will be converted to **dissonance motivation,** and attitude change will occur. Thus, by changing his or her attitude, a person makes the consequences less aversive and thereby reduces the dissonance.

The three revisions of dissonance that we have discussed (self-concept, self-affirmation, and dissonance motivation) derive directly from Festinger's (1957) original concepts about the theory. The investigators took these concepts and tried to incorporate subsequent findings into them. Some alternative explanations suggest more dramatic differences in their explanations of the findings of dissonance experiments.

Self-Perception

The earliest of these explanations was offered by Darryl Bem (1965, 1972), who claimed that people have no "privileged knowledge" about their attitudes. When pressed to tell someone what your attitude is, according to Bem, you merely look at your own behavior and infer your attitude, using the same techniques that another person would use if asked to judge your beliefs. According to this view, as we saw in Chapter 3, anyone who saw another person freely choose to behave in a certain manner would infer that his or her attitude corresponded to that behavior. Similarly, if you saw yourself giving a speech about an issue, you would infer that your attitude was consistent with the position that you took on the speech. In several experiments, Bem showed that when the subjects' behavior in induced compliance experiments was described to observer-subjects, the observer-subjects' guesses about the attitudes of the original subjects were very close to the *real* attitudes of those subjects in the original experiments.

Although **self-perception theory** offers a simpler explanation for the results obtained in many dissonance studies, this explanation is plausible only when actors are unaware of their previously held attitudes. If I don't have an opinion one way or the other about abortion, knowing that I have just written an anti-abortion speech will arouse no dissonance. If I want to know what my opinion is, I will merely look at my behavior and infer a corresponding attitude. However, if I clearly know that I am not opposed to abortion, it is unlikely that I would, as Bem suggests, simply observe my behavior and conclude that I favor abortion.

Several researchers have employed Bem's technique of having observer-subjects predict the outcome of dissonance experiments—with one crucial addition. The observer-subjects were informed of the subject's attitude before the behavior in question (for example, this person found the peg-turning task tedious and dull). When the observer-subjects had to account for both the behavior and the earlier attitude of the actor, their estimates of the actor's final attitude were not consistent with Bem's findings (Jones et al., 1968a). Self-perception theory, then, may indeed be the better explanation in situations in which we are uncertain or unaware of our atti-

---

dissonance motivation   A drive, leading to attitude change, which originates in the discomforting arousal of cognitive dissonance.

self-perception theory   A theory that people infer their own attitudes and feelings from their behaviors and the situations in which they take place.

---

tudes about something, whereas dissonance theory more accurately captures the process when our attitudes are clear. Additionally, as we mentioned earlier, self-perception theory cannot account for the physiological arousal produced when our actions run counter to our beliefs.

Impression Management

Another alternative explanation to the dissonance findings has been offered under the term **impression management** (Tedeschi, Schlenker & Bonoma, 1971). According to this view, people are motivated to appear consistent because they have been rewarded when it has looked as though they acted consistently, and punished when it has seemed that they acted inconsistently. Consequently, we learn to alter the impressions that we give others to produce the appearance of consistency and reliability. Tedeschi and his colleagues believe that in laboratory situations, people attempt to rationalize or justify inconsistent behavior to the significant other in their immediate environment—that is, the high-status experimenter—just as they would in other situations. Thus they change their attitude not out of some internal need for consistency, but *to appear* consistent.

Schlenker (1982) proposed a revision of the impression management view that he calls the identity-analytic model. According to this model, it is not a need to appear consistent that motivates the attitude change in dissonance experiments, but the desire to avoid appearing responsible for performing some reprehensible behavior.

Baumeister and Tice (1984) addressed the debate between inconsistency and impression management as causes of dissonance. These authors found that dissonance can occur because of self-presentational (impression management) needs *or* because of consistency needs, and when the conditions are right for both of these factors to come into play, attitude change will be maximized.

Conclusions: Dissonance Theory

In general, dissonance theory has had a controversial but productive history. It has led to interesting and sometimes ingenious demonstrations in both laboratory and field settings. Dissonance theory phenomena have not been lacking in controversy, and numerous studies have attempted to provide alternative explanations for findings predicted by dissonance theory (Elms & Janis, 1965; Rosenberg, 1965). Since much of the knowledge gained in any discipline arises out of controversies such as those engendered by dissonance theory, the end product of dissonance research has been a useful accumulation of knowledge.

Dissonance theory has also provided at least partial explanations for events outside the laboratory that on the surface seem to defy explanation when we appeal to common sense. Recall the curious behavior of Mrs. Keech's doomsday group. Or once again the somewhat puzzling actions of Karen Silkwood, whose union activities and changing attitudes, as we noted earlier, would have been very difficult to predict in view of the fact that most people who knew her during her early days at Kerr-McGee described her as an unobtrusive, even apathetic person. Dissonance theory, however, with its emphasis on how behaviors lead to changes in attitudes, can begin to explain such cases.

Psychological Reactance

We have considered the importance of allowing a person to feel at least an illusion of freedom to behave in attitude-discrepant ways if we wish to effect attitude change. From the point of view of dissonance theory, ordering someone to do something that is attitude-discrepant will not evoke the motivational state that culminates in a change of attitude.

History abounds in failed efforts to change people's behaviors through coercion. In a celebrated incident some years ago, a federal court ordered the busing of black and white children to achieve racial balance in the public schools of South Boston. This "do it" order met with extreme resistance and violence from many of the whites in South Boston. Some parents withdrew their children from the public schools and set up their own private schools. This experience suggests that failure to induce feelings of free choice may not only fail to produce the desired changes of opinion; it may even be counterproductive.

Brehm (1966, 1972; Brehm & Brehm, 1981) developed a theory to explain why the use of simple force can backfire in attempts to secure compliance and attitude change. Brehm based his theory on the assumption that each individual has a set of *free behaviors*. A free behavior is an act that the individual feels she can engage in either at the moment or at some time in the future, and that she knows she has the necessary physical or psychological ability to perform. For example, you may feel that going to a movie tonight is one of your free behaviors. The people in South Boston may have felt that choosing what school their child would attend was one of their free behaviors. Free behaviors can vary in importance, with the more important free behaviors being those that satisfy important needs.

According to Brehm, a threat to or elimination of the freedom to perform such behaviors will arouse the individual psychologically. This arousal, which will be aimed at restoring the threatened or eliminated freedom, is called **psychological reactance.** Reactance theory hypothesizes that the strength of psychological reactance will vary with the importance of the free behavior and with the degree of threat to that behavior. For example, your freedom to eat is probably a more important freedom than your freedom to attend a movie tonight. Thus, if a friend told you that you could neither eat nor attend the movie tonight, greater reactance would be aroused by the first threat than by the second.

Research has demonstrated three types of reactions to the arousal of reactance. First, the individual may attempt to reestablish freedom directly by performing the threatened free behavior. For example, Hammock and Brehm (1966) told children that they could choose to have one of several kinds of candy bars. The experimenters then told the children that they should not choose candy bar X. The children reacted to this threat to freedom by choosing candy bar X and thus restoring their freedom to have that particular bar. In a study involving younger children, Brehm and Weintraub (1977) placed a barrier of various sizes between a two-year-old child and an attractive toy. The child could also play with an easily accessible toy in

"I DON'T **WANTA** GO OUTSIDE AN' PLAY..."   UNLESS SHE SAYS I **CAN'T.**"

Restricted behaviors can become more attractive as a result of psychological reactance.
DENNIS THE MENACE used by permission of Hank Ketcham and © by North American Syndicate.

front of the barrier. Brehm and Weintraub varied the importance of the freedom to play with the toy behind the barrier by having it either different from (high importance) or the same as (low importance) the toy in front of the barrier. The investigators found that little boys went behind the barrier to play with the restricted toy if the freedom was important and if the barrier was large rather than small. Thus two-year-old boys, but *not* two-year-old girls, restored their threatened freedom by direct performance of the threatened behavior.

A second reaction is that the threatened freedom increases in attractiveness as a result of the

---

impression management   Behavior designed to control what others think, especially so as to maintain power in relation to them.

psychological reactance   A state of arousal generated by blocking, or the threat of blocking, a person's free behaviors.

Research has shown that people who need a strong sense of control over their environment are more susceptible to heart attacks. In an environment that doesn't allow much control, where conditions fluctuate and clients are demanding, this kind of person could well exhibit patterns of coronary-prone behavior.

increased motivation to perform the threatened behavior. An event that occurred in the state of Florida will serve as an illustration. When social consciousness regarding the environment was being raised in the early 1970s, Dade County (Miami) enacted an ordinance banning the sale of laundry soaps containing phosphates. Mazis (1975) reasoned that delimiting the options of Dade county homemakers would make the restricted product seem more attractive than it had been before. Immediately following the enactment of the ordinance, Mazis asked consumers in Miami and consumers in a similar community (Tampa, Florida) in which phosphate detergents had not been banned to rate the effectiveness of phosphate detergents. In comparison with the Tampa homemakers, Miami residents believed that the restricted product was better for whiteness, freshness, brightness, and virtually any other category that Mazis could generate. Apparently the attractiveness of the product had increased as a function of the threat to the Miami homemakers' freedom to buy it.

Finally, aggression aimed at the threatening agent has been found to follow the arousal of reactance. Worchel (1974) has suggested that aggressing against the threatening agent can

reestablish freedom at the moment and ensure that that agent will not threaten freedom again (see Chapter 9).

Reactance theory provides a basis for a better understanding of the reactions of whites in South Boston in 1974. We have said that before the court's ruling, the South Boston whites may have felt that they were free to decide where their children should attend school. The court order forcing busing eliminated this freedom. The response of many of the whites was to open their own schools so that they could choose to send their children to those schools (direct reestablishment of freedom) and to agress (through riots and acts of violence) against the perceived source of the restriction of their freedom.

Thus reactance theory suggests the need to pay attention to such details as illusions of freedom and the size of the incentives that people are given to adopt certain behaviors. If people feel that they are being forced to adopt a behavior, they are likely to experience reactance and to act against such force. As to the size of the incentive for adopting a behavior, it can be posited that the larger the incentive, the more pressure the individual will feel to perform a particular act. A large incentive may arouse reactance and result in the individual's refusal to adopt the behavior. Brehm and Winer (reported in Brehm, 1966) demonstrated this in a grocery store study. When shoppers entered the store, they were met by an experimenter who asked them to buy brand X bread and then gave them either 25 cents or 35 cents. A loaf of brand X bread cost 25 cents, so the 35-cent payment was a very high incentive. The results showed that over 60% of female shoppers who were given the low incentive (25 cents) bought brand X bread, whereas only 40% of those who were given the high incentive (35 cents) bought brand X bread. According to Brehm and Winer, the high incentive threatened the shoppers' freedom *not* to buy brand X bread, and their response was to resist the pressure and reestablish freedom.

In addition to affecting behavior, the arousal of reactance can affect attitudes. Brehm argues that the freedom to hold a particular attitude may be an important "free behavior" and that a threat to this freedom can arouse reactance. Worchel and Brehm (1970) demonstrated this by having subjects listen to a communication advocating equal treatment for the Communist party in the United States. Subjects in all conditions heard the same communication, except that in the high-threat condition the communication was liberally sprinkled with statements such as "You cannot believe otherwise" or "You have no choice but to believe this." These statements were included to threaten the subjects' freedom to hold the opposite position. The results showed that in the high-threat condition, only 50% of the subjects changed their attitudes in the direction of the communication, whereas 67% of the subjects in the low-threat condition changed their attitudes in the direction advocated by the speech. Further, 40% of the subjects in the high-threat condition actually showed a **boomerang effect** (changed their attitudes in the direction opposite to that of the communication).

An Individual Difference Variable: Coronary-Prone Behavior

Loss of freedom is more important for some people than it is for others. The loss of freedom stems from a dread of having to give up personal control because of environmental constraints (Wortman & Brehm, 1975). Research over the past

STOP, THINK, & UNDERSTAND

1. How might the psychology of effort justification be used to explain the effectiveness of psychotherapy? What evidence supports this link?

2. If you have a choice between a Porsche and a Corvette, why will dissonance occur after you decide?

3. How do Aronson's self-esteem alternative and Steele's self-affirmation view change the motivational basis of dissonance?

4. Can you account for dissonance phenomena by theories that do not invoke the concept of motivation?

5. What is meant by psychological reactance and what evidence supports it?

several years has shown that at least one personality type cannot tolerate giving up control; these are people with so-called coronary-prone behavior patterns.

As the term implies, coronary-prone behavior patterns tend to be associated with heart attacks. Friedman and Rosenman (1959) identified a pattern of behaviors that seemed to be precursors of heart disease. These behaviors included extreme competitiveness and achievement striving, a sense of time urgency, and hostility. People who demonstrate this behavior pattern are referred to as "Type A" personalities. By contrast, noncoronary-prone individuals (called "Type B's") are characteristically laid-back, relaxed, and less aggressive than Type A's.

Rhodewalt and Comer (1982) reasoned that Type A's would be more susceptible to reactance than Type B's. A review of the coronary-prone behavior literature by Glass (1977) reports data showing that Type A's feel that they have a high degree of personal control over their behaviors and outcomes. So it stands to reason that Type

---

boomerang effect Attitude change in a direction opposite to that promoted in a communication.

A's will be extremely upset about anything that restricts their freedom and personal control. Rhodewalt and Comer (1982) subjected Type A and Type B students to pressures not unlike those in the Worchel and Brehm (1970) study. The students' freedom to hold an opinion was threatened by a confederate who virtually told them that they had no choice but to hold a particular attitude. Type B subjects were not terribly upset by this restriction and continued to hold their opinion. Coronary-prone subjects (Type A's), however, experienced reactance at this threat to their freedom and control. Unlike the Type B subjects, they sought to regain their control by altering their attitudes.

Summary

The question of the consistency between attitudes and behaviors has fascinated social psychologists since La Pière (1934) showed that behaviors are not always consistent with privately held attitudes. Two theories help to explain the processes by which behaviors are linked to attitudes. The *theory of planned behavior* suggests that people are reasoning and rational when they decide to act. They consider their attitudes toward the behavior in question, the social norms that operate in the situation, and the degree of control they have in their efforts to reach their behavioral goals. The *automatic-processing model* suggests that people use their attitudes as a filter to help them interpret attitude objects and thereby help to make behaviors consistent with attitudes. Anything that makes attitudes more accessible— that is, makes them come to mind more quickly —increases the likelihood that behavior will be consistent with attitude. Research has shown that some of the factors that increase attitude-behavior consistency are direct experience with the attitude object, perceived relevance of the attitude to the behavior, and the prototypicality of the attitude object. It has been suggested that the motivation to act correctly and the amount of time a person has to consider an action determine whether automatic processing or planned behavior will be engaged.

The theory of *cognitive dissonance* addresses the question of *when* behaviors lead to changes of attitudes. It holds that dissonance is experienced whenever one cognition that a person holds follows from the opposite of at least one other cognition that the person holds. Dissonance has a magnitude that is based on the number and importance of a person's discrepant and consonant cognitions.

According to the theory, dissonance is experienced as an uncomfortable drivelike *state*. People are motivated to reduce any dissonance that they experience. Dissonance can be reduced by (1) changing cognitions, (2) adding cognitions, or (3) altering the importance of the cognitions in

Much of the research in dissonance theory has been conducted on the paradigm of *induced compliance*. In the induced compliance paradigm, a person is persuaded to behave in ways contrary to his or her private beliefs. Research has shown that attitudes are likely to change to restore consistency between attitudes and behavior. Generally, the magnitude of attitude change is inversely proportional to the amount of justification that is provided to engage in the attitude-discrepant behavior. Induced compliance arouses dissonance when (1) the behavior is engaged in *freely*, (2) the actor feels *committed* to his or her attitude-discrepant stance, (3) the behavior results in *aversive consequences*, and (4) the actor feels *personal responsibility* for the unwanted consequences.

Using variations of the induced compliance situation, investigators have identified several interesting phenomena. In the psychology of *effort justification*, it has been shown that people come to love what they have suffered for. For example, a person who enters psychotherapy to overcome a fear of snakes may come to love snakes if the therapy requires a great deal of effort. It has also been shown that *disconfirmed expectations* can arouse dissonance. A cultlike group was able to reduce the dissonance aroused by disconfirmed expectations by gathering social support for their original belief.

The *free-choice paradigm* assumes that dissonance follows any freely exercised choice between cognitive alternatives. The positive features of the rejected alternative and the negative features of the chosen alternative are discrepant with the decision that was reached. Brehm has shown that attitudes change following decisions so that the alternatives will seem more widely discrepant in attractiveness after a decision than they seemed before it.

Some alternative models of dissonance have been proposed based on self-concept, self-affirmation, and personal responsibility. Self-perception and impression management have been offered as theories that compete with dissonance in explaining the experimental phenomena. These theories differ from dissonance theory in that they do not posit that any psychological arousal occurs as a result of inconsistency.

Psychological reactance results when an individual feels that one or more of his or her free behaviors are being threatened. Three types of reactions have been found to follow reactance: (1) the individual may attempt to perform the threatened free behavior; (2) the threatened free behavior increases in attractiveness; and (3) the individual is instigated to aggress against the agent that created the reactance. Reactance theory can be used to explain negative attitude change, or the *boomerang effect.*

Key Terms

attitude-discrepant behavior
automatic-processing model
aversive consequences
boomerang effect
cognitions
cognitive dissonance
cognitive irrelevance
commitment
consonance

direct experience
disconfirmed expectations
dissonance motivation
effort justification
foreseeability
free-choice paradigm
impression management
induced compliance
personal responsibility

prototype
psychological reactance
reinforcement effect
self-perception theory
social support
strength of an attitude
subjective norms
theory of planned behavior

Suggested Readings

Ajzen, I. (1989). Attitude structure and behavior. In A. R. Pratkanis, S. J. Breckler, & A. G. Greenwald (Eds.), *Attitude structure and function. The third Ohio State University volume on attitudes and persuasion* (pp. 241–274). Hillsdale, N.J.: Erlbaum.

Brehm, J. W. (1966). *A theory of psychological reactance.* New York: Academic Press.

Cooper, J., & Fazio, R. H. (1984). A new look at dissonance theory. In L. Berkowitz (Ed.), *Advances in experimental social psychology* (Vol. 17, pp. 229–266). New York: Academic Press.

Fazio, R. H. (1990). Multiple processes by which attitudes guide behavior: The MODE model as an integrative framework. In M. P. Zanna (Ed.), *Advances in experimental social psychology.* New York: Academic Press.

Fazio, R. H., & Cooper, J. (1983). Arousal in the dissonance process. In J. T. Cacioppo & R. E. Petty (Eds.), *Social psychophysiology.* New York: Guilford Press.

Festinger, L. (1957). *A theory of cognitive dissonance.* Palo Alto, Calif.: Stanford University Press.

Steele, C. M. (1988). The psychology of self-affirmation: Sustaining the integrity of the self. In L. Berkowitz (Ed.), *Advances in experimental social psychology* (Vol. 21, pp. 261–302). Orlando, Fla.: Academic Press.

Wicklund, R. A., & Brehm, J. W. (1976). *Perspectives on cognitive dissonance.* Hillsdale, N.J.: Erlbaum.

Zanna, M. P., & Cooper, J. (1974). Dissonance and the attribution process. In J. Harvey, W. Ickes, & R. Kidd (Eds.), *New directions in attribution research* (Vol. 1, pp. 199–217). Hillsdale, N.J.: Erlbaum.

Chapter Seven

Attraction and Close Relationships

A young man of the house of Montague fell deeply in love with the beautiful daughter of the house of Capulet. It was a star-crossed romance, destined to end in the death of the lovers. Romeo, in Shakespeare's classic tragedy *Romeo and Juliet,* was by nature a lover. Impetuous and emotional, he had been deeply in love with another woman, who failed to return his affections. With one glimpse of Juliet, his former love was forgotten and the passionate romance was begun.

Juliet, by contrast, had been untouched by romantic love. Before meeting Romeo, she had been an obedient daughter, unfamiliar with the passions of love. When a marriage to Count Paris was arranged by her parents, she responded in a naive and intellectual fashion: "It is an honour that I dream not of. . . . I'll look to like, if looking move."

The action begins when Romeo, bemoaning his unrequited love, is cajoled by friends to attend a costume ball at the Capulet home. Casting his eyes upon Juliet, he is enthralled by her beauty:

> *Oh, she doth teach the torches to burn bright!*
> *It seems she hangs upon the cheek of night*
> *Like a rich jewel in an Ethiop's ear;*
> *Beauty too rich for use, for earth too dear!*
> (Act I, scene 5)

Juliet, too, is instantly consumed by the passion of romance:

> *My bounty is as boundless as the sea,*
> *My love as deep; the more I give to thee,*
> *The more I have, for both are infinite.*
> (Act II, scene 2)

Both Romeo and Juliet are young and attractive, the offspring of established wealthy families. The impending tragedy has its roots in the longstanding feud between the Montagues and the Capulets. Shakespeare's Prologue states the insurmountable problem:

> *Two households, both alike in dignity,*
> *In fair Verona, where we lay our scene,*
> *From ancient grudge break to new mutiny,*
> *Where civil blood makes civil hands unclean.*
> *From forth the fatal loins of these two foes*
> *A pair of star-crossed lovers take their life.*

When the lovers find themselves attracted to each other, they maintain a sense of the supreme irony of the situation and of the likelihood of impending tragedy. Juliet says:

> *My only love sprung from my only hate!*
> *Too early seen unknown, and known too late!*
> *Prodigious birth of love it is to me,*
> *That I must love a loathed enemy.*
> (Act I, scene 5)

From the time of their initial meeting, events occur with extreme speed. This rapidity accentuates the passion of the romance and the inevitable tragedy. On the following day, the two lovers are married secretly by Friar Laurence. While returning from the marriage vows, Romeo encounters Juliet's cousin, the fiery Tybalt. Although trying to avoid conflict, Romeo is forced into a fight, slays Tybalt, and is banished from Verona. The alternative is a sentence of death. Before leaving Verona, Romeo steals into his new wife's room. There they consummate their love. As fate will have it, they will never see each other alive again.

Angered by the murder of Tybalt, Lord Capulet announces the impending marriage of his daughter to Paris. With Friar Laurence, Juliet devises a plan that will permit her to join Romeo and avoid the bigamous marriage to Paris. The friar prescribes a potion that will put Juliet to sleep, simulating the symptoms of death. After she takes the potion and is believed dead, she is taken to the Capulet's mausoleum.

Though the friar's plan is to let Romeo know of the trick by which Juliet would feign death, fate intervenes. Romeo learns of Juliet's death, but not of the trick that is to return her to his side. Consumed by passion, Romeo races to the mausoleum to join his love. Taking poison from an apothecary, he speaks his last words: "Thus with a kiss I die."

When Juliet awakes from her sleep, she sees her dead lover by her side. Ignoring the friar's exhortation to leave the tomb, Juliet thrusts a knife into her breast and dies.

Personal Relationships: Working Definitions

Personal relationships take many forms. Romeo's relationship with Juliet was passionate. A wom-

Romeo and Juliet's love was passionate and romantic and ended in heartrending tragedy. Were there characteristics of their love that foreshadowed this dismal end?

an's love of her husband of 50 years may take a more compassionate form. A boy's fondness for his third-grade teacher is a different kind of relationship, and his fondness for the man who sells him ice cream may be yet another kind. In each case, we are describing the fondness of one person for another. Some attractions are short-lived; some are enduring; some are passionately hot and some are cool.

In this chapter we will consider the term *personal relationship* to characterize the positive attitudes that two people hold toward each other. When we speak of **attraction,** we will be taking the perspective of a single individual, and referring to a positive attitude held by one person toward another.

Why are we attracted to others? Think about the various relationships in your life. What factors have made you like certain of your friends

or partners? You may find some intriguing contrasts. Some of the people you are attracted to are quite similar to you. You may have thought of going away to college and finding someone who shared your interests, came from a similar town, liked the same music, and so forth. But you can also think of people whom you have been attracted to at least partially because they are intriguingly different. You like rock music; they like classical. You like comedies at the movies; they like serious dramas. You are from a small town; they live in a big city. And the very fact of your differences has made them more appealing. Similarly, you may like people who like you and who always tell you how good you are. You may

---

attraction A positive attitude held by one person toward another.

t x - c -

- x - c +

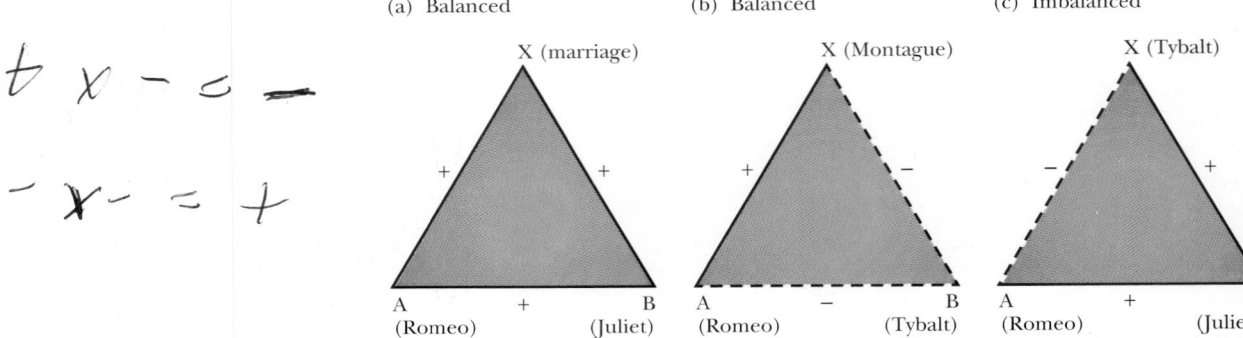

(a) Balanced   (b) Balanced   (c) Imbalanced

X (marriage)   X (Montague)   X (Tybalt)

+   +   +   −   −   +

A   +   B   A   −   B   A   +   B
(Romeo)   (Juliet)   (Romeo)   (Tybalt)   (Romeo)   (Juliet)

FIGURE 7-1   Balance theory representation of relationships in Shakespeare's *Romeo and Juliet*
NOTE: Solid lines represent attraction; broken lines depict disliking.

like other people because they are brutally honest. In romantic relationships, you may be attracted to people who are physically attractive, but at other times you may be attracted to people who fulfill important emotional needs.

Social psychologists have been addressing the question, Why do people come to like and dislike each other? Here we will consider some of the broad theoretical reasons that account for liking and disliking. We will also look at research that deals specifically with the forming of close personal relationships. Why are they formed, how are they maintained, and what factors may lead to their dissolution?

A Cognitive View: Better to Be Balanced

Balance theory has played an important role in many areas of social psychology. Chapter 5 looked at Heider's balance theory as a model of attitude formation and Chapter 6 discussed the related theory of cognitive dissonance. Each of those theories has spawned research on attraction (Darley & Berscheid, 1967; Davis & Jones, 1960; Tyler & Sears, 1977). In this chapter, however, we will consider a variant of balance theory that has been used extensively for understanding some of the issues involved in interpersonal attraction:

Newcomb's symmetry model, often called the **A-B-X model** (Newcomb, 1956, 1961).

Newcomb's theory takes the perspective of person A, who is in a network with another person, B, and an object, X. The system considers the positive and negative bonds that exist between the actor, the other person, and the attitudinal object. In this system, the attitudinal object, X, may be a thing, such as a tree, a pineapple, or a brand of toothpaste; an issue, such as desegregation, population control, or television violence; or another person.

As in Heider's model, systems may be either balanced (symmetrical) or imbalanced (asymmetrical). An example of a balanced system can be seen in Figure 7-1(a). Romeo loves Juliet, and he is also favorable to (likes) marriage. Further, he knows that Juliet favors marriage. "If that thy bent be marriage," she says in the famous balcony scene, "send me word tomorrow. And all my fortunes at thy foot I'll lay." All of these harmoniously positive bonds are shown by the unbroken lines of Figure 7-1(a). As we pointed out in Chapter 5 we can figure out whether a system is balanced by algebraically multiplying the signs of the relationships. In Figure 7-1(a), Romeo's relation to Juliet and to marriage is positive, and he believes that her attitude toward marriage is positive. Since the product of three pluses is plus, the system is balanced.

Figure 7-1(b) shows that balance can also exist when all feelings are less than positive. In this example, Romeo loves his father (Lord Montague); Tybalt (Juliet's cousin) does not. But then again, Romeo does not care much for Juliet's cousin. The product of the three signs is again positive, and the system is balanced. Figure 7-1(c) shows that Romeo loves Juliet, and Juliet loves her cousin Tybalt. But Romeo and Tybalt are enemies. As Tybalt says, "Romeo, the hate I bear thee can afford no better terms than this—thou art a villain." The two positive relationships and the one negative relationship combine to form an imbalanced state. In Newcomb's terms, there is a "strain toward symmetry" such that the perception of asymmetry (or imbalance) will cause activity on the part of actor A to restore symmetry.

How can a person restore symmetry if it does not exist? Your best friend disapproves of your fiancé; your wife or husband disagrees with you about the desirability of having a family; one of your very best friends thoroughly dislikes another of your close friends. Such situations lack equilibrium and attempts must be made to restore symmetry. Consider Romeo's predicament in Figure 7-1(c). He loves Juliet; she loves him—but she also feels positive about Tybalt, and Romeo does not. Romeo (A) could:

1. Try to persuade Juliet (B) to change her attitude about Tybalt (X).
2. Change his own attitude about Juliet (B).
3. Change his own attitude about Tybalt (X).

Changing the signs in the A-B-X system in any of these ways would reduce the tension caused by the disequilibrium. In Shakespeare's play, Romeo did in fact try to alter his attitude about Tybalt. Although he was insulted and prodded by Tybalt, Romeo protested, "I never injured thee, but love thee better than thou canst devise."

There are other possibilities. The strain toward symmetry could be reduced if Romeo could:

4. Reduce the *importance* of the topic about which he and Juliet disagree.
5. Reduce the *common relevance* of the issue.

In the first of these alternatives, Romeo could come to feel that Tybalt is too trivial a person to worry about. In the second, he could feel strongly about both Tybalt and Juliet, but conclude that her opinion about a rivalry between gentlemen

Usually our parents provide our very first rewards, in terms of both praise and attention and material benefits. It is partly because of these rewards that we become attached to our parents and to people like them.

is irrelevant. Her opinion in this situation is not considered germane to areas that are common to him and his wife.

A Reward Model of Attraction

A second model of interpersonal attraction is based on the simple notion that people who are associated with rewards are liked. Such models have been put forth by Albert and Bernice Lott (1968, 1974) and by Byrne and Clore (1970).

Consider a little girl sitting in a high chair

A-B-X model The theory that the relationship between two persons and an attitude object will strain to become symmetrical.

who on this day, unlike every other day, picks up a spoon by herself and brings it to her mouth. Her mother responds with great delight; she smiles, kisses the baby, and gives her a cookie for her efforts. Picking up the spoon has now become a pleasurable response, since it has become associated with the pleasurable feeling generated by the mother's rewards of a kiss and a cookie. From then on, the little girl continues using the spoon to feed herself.

According to the **reward model** of attraction, the very same process is at the root of our interpersonal feelings: Those individuals whom we associate with rewards become preferred and liked.

We should also note that attraction does not occur only when rewards have been received from someone in the past or are associated with them in the present. We also tend to be attracted to those who we believe will be associated with a reward in the *future* (Clore & Kerber, 1981; Tedeschi, 1974). The finding that people are sensitive to rewards that others can give them in the future may help to explain why we sometimes feel attraction to people we have known only briefly or know little about.

We are not surprised by the statement that we like people who give us rewards better than we like people who make us feel unpleasant. We can all think of occasions on which we left a situation fuming at a person who was obnoxious or unpleasant to us—the waiter who spilled soup on our sleeve, the cashier who insisted that the $10 bill we gave her was actually $5—and we can think of as many instances of liking a person who was kind or rewarding to us.

However, the reward model of attraction goes further and indicates that a person who is associated with a pleasant feeling will be liked better than a person who is associated with an unpleasant feeling—whether or not that person was the cause of the feeling.

Griffitt and Guay (1969) conducted an experiment in which an innocent bystander was present when another person administered either a reward or a punishment to a subject. Although that bystander had absolutely nothing to do with the reward or punishment, he was liked better when the subject experienced a reward than when the subject experienced a punishment. In a subsequent study, Griffitt (1970) directly manipu-

lated the pleasantness of an individual's experience by varying the temperature and the humidity of an experimental room. A hypothetical stranger was liked better when the room was comfortable than when the room was hot and humid. Similarly, Veitch and Griffitt (1976) found that after a subject had heard good news on a radio report, the subject liked a stranger more than he did after bad news was broadcast. Apparently the stranger's association with the pleasantness or unpleasantness of the news report made the difference in his rated attractiveness—despite the undeniable fact that he had nothing to do with the temperature or humidity in the first case, or with the nature of the news report in the last case.

Equity: Considering Both Partners' Rewards and Costs

It is time to bring both partners in a relationship into sharper focus. Thus far, we have been discussing the rewards that an individual experiences as a result of a relationship. Now let us consider the importance of what each partner experiences.

Each individual in a two-person relationship receives a certain amount of reward. Each is benefited by pleasant feelings, each may have her or his emotional needs met, each may receive other tangible benefits. But relationships also have costs. As a partner in a relationship, you have to work to maintain that relationship. In addition, you may have to relinquish certain freedoms that you would have had if you had not been in a relationship. You may place certain demands on your partner and your partner places demands on you.

Equity theory (Hatfield and Traupmann, 1980; Walster, Berscheid & Walster, 1978) proposes that satisfaction in a relationship is a function of the ratio of rewards to costs that each member experiences. Consider the formula below:

$$\frac{\text{Your benefits}}{\text{Your costs}} = \frac{\text{Partner's benefits}}{\text{Partner's costs}}$$

Equity theory proposes that relationships are most satisfying when these ratios are equal.

This is an interesting concept. If you are in

Contemporary couples often try to make their relationship more equitable by sharing household tasks. Has the idea of what is equitable in a marital relationship, for example, changed over time?

a relationship with someone, equity theory suggests that your satisfaction does not depend solely upon how much you get out of the relationship—that is, it does not depend on your rewards alone. Nor does it depend on your costs alone. Instead, you will be satisfied if you feel that what you are getting from and contributing to the relationship is similar to what your partner is getting and giving. If your ratio is lower than your partner's, you may feel exploited. If your ratio is higher, you may feel guilty.

This is a provocative hypothesis. But is it true? The data are mixed (Clark & Reis, 1988). In support of equity theory, some investigators have shown that people who feel that their relationships are equitable are happier than people who feel their relationships are inequitable (Sabatelli & Cecil-Pigo, 1985). Furthermore, married people who feel their relationships are equitable are less likely to have extramarital sexual affairs (Hatfield et al., 1985).

On the other hand, Berg and McQuinn (1986) studied couples engaged in romantic relation-

ships at a point early in their relationship and then four months later. Couples who were still dating at the second point showed greater satisfaction, expressed greater love, and did more to maintain the relationship. However, perceptions of equity in the relationship did not predict which couples would and would not be together by the second measuring point. In a study of a different type of interpersonal relationship, Berg (1984) surveyed pairs of same-sex roommates soon after they first met each other and then again at the end of the year. Roommates' perceptions of equity in the relationship did not predict how satisfied they would be at the end of the year. Instead, the total amount of benefit the roommates felt they received was the best predictor of a good relationship.

equity theory The theory that individuals compare their inputs and outcomes with those of the other party to determine the fairness of a relationship.

reward model The theory that we like people whom we associate with rewards.

Equity: Considering Both Partners' Rewards and Costs   229

The questions posed by equity theory are intriguing. Not all of the answers are in. Nonetheless, the work of Hatfield and her colleagues does make us think about the importance of considering others' benefits and contributions to a relationship as well as our own in estimating how satisfying the relationship is likely to be.

Long-Term Relationships
Toward Joint Outcomes

Let's move another step toward considering both people in a close relationship. From the vantage point of equity theory, we saw that people's satisfaction in a relationship depends on how each person perceives his or her own versus the partner's rewards and costs. Kelley and Thibaut (1978), two theorists who have long been analyzing rewards and costs in two-person groups, suggest that lasting *intimate* relationships are based on a transformation of a concern with one's own outcomes ("What's in it for me?") or comparative outcomes ("In view of what we both contribute, am I getting as much as my partner is?") to a concern for joint outcomes ("What's in this for *us*?")

In Kelley and Thibaut's view, then, a long-lasting interpersonal relationship is characterized not by both partners' attempts to maximize their individual payoffs but rather by their attempts to maximize their joint rewards. A couple may choose to attend a football game. One may truly enjoy it; the other may yawn from the first through the fourth quarter. Although one member of the partnership is temporarily pleased, the other is not. The couple is not paying attention to the best joint reward. Ultimately, it is not a pleasing situation for either partner. More durable relationships are characterized by the kind of compromise that pleases both partners equally; for instance, going to the football game one week and to the ballet the next, or skipping both and going to the theater.

An interesting feature of the transformation from a concern with individual rewards to equitable joint rewards is that the partners in the relationship are usually aware of the transformation.

Fleiner and Kelley (1978) interviewed 96 people and had them rate their satisfaction in their personal relationships. They found that in successful partnerships, people did operate under the working rule of maximizing their joint rewards, and that each partner was aware that the other was attempting to do so.

Keeping Track of What You Give and What You Get

Do you always keep track of your rewards and costs in a relationship? Do you always feel put upon if you receive less than your partner or guilty if you receive too much? Do you always expect to receive as much as you give? Clark and her colleagues (Clark, 1984; Clark & Mills, 1979) have proposed that whether you keep track of your rewards and costs depends on the type of interpersonal relationship you are in. She has described two types of relationships, communal and exchange.

An **exchange relationship** is a relationship you have with an acquaintance, a stranger, or someone with whom you do business. In these relationships, there is a concern for equity, by which Clark means "comparable benefit." If you give something in the relationship, you expect something in return. Giving implies a debt assumed by the partner. Clark proposes that people keep track of the benefits they have given so that they can assess the benefits that they are entitled to receive.

A **communal relationship,** on the other hand, is a long-term and deep relationship. We have communal relationships with romantic partners, friends, and family members. Clark suggests that when we desire to establish or maintain communal relationships, we stop counting. We end our record keeping. We do not expect our inputs to be matched by our partners. We are willing to contribute to the relationship, even if we know that our partner has no opportunity to make a similar contribution (Clark, Mills & Powell, 1986).

How might you react if you thought you were in a potentially communal, as opposed to an exchange, relationship? Clark (1984) had students at Carnegie Mellon University enter into a relationship that they either hoped would become communal (in a romantic way) or knew would have to remain of the exchange type. This was accomplished by revealing to male subjects the marital status of their partner, an attractive young woman (actually a confederate of the experimenter). Half the subjects were led to believe the young woman was single, and thus subjects were expected to desire a communal relationship with her. For the other subjects she was presented as being married; subjects were expected to desire an exchange relationship with her, since she was unavailable as a potential romantic partner. In a game situation, the partners were given the task of locating and circling number sequences in a large matrix. As a function of the couple's performance, a reward could be won and divided between them. Clark predicted that subjects in an exchange relation would attempt to keep records—to know just how much each had contributed to the joint product so that each would know exactly how much of the reward he would eventually be entitled to. On the other hand, Clark predicted that those subjects who thought they might share a communal relation would not keep records. Each would refrain from measuring his input into the relationship because the focus would be on the partnership's joint outcome.

The first person to begin the task was always the attractive woman who served as the confederate of the experimenter; she circled numbers with a colored pen. The male subject's turn followed. He could use a pen of the same color as that used by his partner or he could use a pen of a different color. Which would he use? Obviously, if he wanted to keep track of just how many correct solutions he obtained in comparison with those of his partner, he would be motivated to use a different-colored pen. If he did not care about assessing the contributions made by each of them, he would not care very much which pen he used. The results showed that nearly 90% of all subjects in the exchange relationship chose to work with a different-colored pen, while only 12.5% of the people in the communal condition chose the pen of a different color. Apparently Clark was correct in predicting that people are concerned with their individual equity when they are in an exchange relationship, and are concerned only with the joint rewards that the partnership can obtain when they are in a communal relationship.

To see more clearly the distinction between communal and exchange relationships, imagine how you might react in the following situation. Suppose that a stunningly attractive classmate of yours asks to borrow your class notes for some lectures he or she has missed. Grateful for the opportunity to get closer to this person, you readily comply. The next day, your classmate returns your notes and attached you find one of two envelopes. Envelope A contains a warm note of thanks. Envelope B contains a warm note of thanks and a $5 bill. Which of the two envelopes would you rather receive? If you are like the subjects in an experiment conducted by Clark and Mills (1979), you would much rather receive the envelope *without* the $5. The situation staged by Clark and Mills was very similar. In the course of an experimental task, male subjects were given an opportunity to do a favor for an attractive female subject with whom they were told they would be working during a later phase of the experiment. In response to this favor (saving her some work by giving her some of their own experimental materials), the subjects received a thank-you note that this woman had supposedly written. In half of the cases this note was accompanied by the information that the woman was sending one of the credits she had earned during the experiment; in the other half, no such information was given. Additionally, for half of the subjects, background information about the woman indicated she was married; for the other half, she was identified as single. Presumably the subjects who thought their partner was married would desire an exchange relationship whereas those with the single partner would desire a communal one. Of interest to the experimenters was how the male subjects evaluated their female partner. The results were clear. The married woman was liked better when her thank-you note was accompanied by the experimental credit. When the woman was identified as single, however, she was liked better when she gave only the thank-you

---

communal relationship A long-term relationship in which benefits given are not balanced against benefits received.

exchange relationship A relationship in which benefits given are balanced against benefits received.

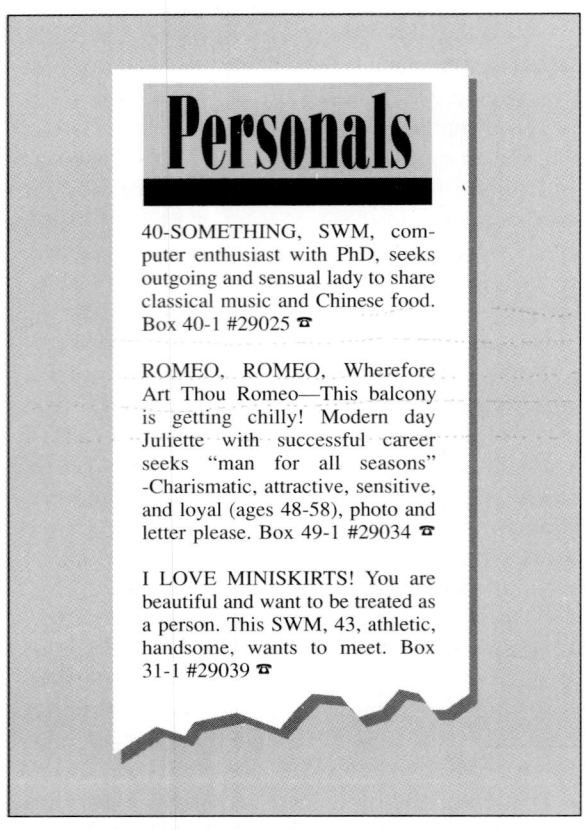

When people place an advertisement in the personals, they are trying to attract a compatible companion. Look at these ads. What do you think these people are looking for, partners who will be similar or those who will be different?

note in return. It appears to be the case that reciprocating kind deeds in a tit-for-tat fashion may work to strengthen relationships that are formal but can actually establish distance between people in more intimate relationships.

Conflict Due to Misperceptions of Joint Rewards

The notion that successful interpersonal relationships depend on the joint-reward rule is also the source of some interpersonal conflict between partners. Fleiner and Kelley (1978) found in their interviews that respondents usually felt that they were following the joint-payoff rule more than their partners. That is, they felt that they were more concerned with paying attention to the best common outcome than their partners were. Orvis,

Kelley, and Butler (1976) asked partners to explain those occasions in which maximum joint rewards were not obtained. The partner who was being interviewed usually blamed the inequity on a dispositional characteristic of the other partner ("He only thinks of himself when sports are on the television"; "He is never honest enough to tell me what he wants"; "She always ignores what I want"). On the other hand, when questioned about their own role in creating an inequity of outcomes, the partner who was interviewed rarely made a dispositional statement but almost always attributed the action to the environment or to circumstances. This, of course, is similar to the general differences between the attributions made by actors and observers when they explain behavior (recall the work of Jones & Nisbett, 1971, discussed in Chapter 2).

In general, research on personal relationships implicates not only the rewards that a person experiences in interaction with another person but also the equity involved in the relationship. Longer-lasting intimate relationships evolve toward a concern for the total partnership. Record keeping diminishes in importance as the partners move toward maximizing the pleasure that the two of them can share.

Similarity and Attraction: I'll Like You if You're Like Me

People tend to like others who have similar attitudes and characteristics. Although there are some important exceptions to this general rule, the evidence linking attitudinal similarity to attraction is considerable. Many of the theoretical positions on attraction predict that similarity should lead to attraction. Consider Newcomb's (1961) version of balance theory. If person A feels positively about an attitude item, X, and B feels the same way about X, then there is a *strain toward balance* that pushes A to feel positively about person B. Reinforcement models of attraction also lead us to believe that similarity leads to attraction, given the reasonable assumption that it is rewarding to hear someone agree with you.

Much of the empirical research that actually links similarity of attitudes to interpersonal attraction has been collected in a systematic series of studies by Donn Byrne and his colleagues (e.g., Byrne, 1971; Byrne, Clore & Smeaton, 1986.) The basic work was conducted exclusively in the laboratory, with a consistent procedure: Subjects were first asked to fill out a 12-item attitude scale. Sometime later, they entered the laboratory and were asked to form judgments about a *hypothetical* person "on the basis of limited information." They were given an attitude scale to read that was supposedly filled out by another person. In fact, the attitude scale was filled out by the experimenter. Depending on the purpose of the particular study, the experimenter could vary the degree of similarity between the hypothetical target person and the subject. At the end of the study, the subject was given a questionnaire to complete, which included two items asking the subject how much he or she liked the target person. The results of many studies reported by Byrne and his colleagues show that people like the target when they share a high proportion of similar attitudes (Byrne and Nelson, 1965). These attitudes can be political, economic, or religious.

What, then, are the variables that can weaken or strengthen the similarity–attraction effect? One of them is the *importance* of the similarity (Clore & Baldridge, 1968). If you are similar to someone on important items, you will be more attracted to that person. Touhey (1972) conducted a study in which he found some interesting differences between men and women in the attitudes they found to be important and, consequently, the attitudes that led to greater interpersonal attraction. He had college students volunteer for computer dates. He purposely matched couples on the basis of the similarity of their religious and sexual attitudes. After the couples interacted, their attraction for each other was measured. Similarity of attitudes did predict attraction. However, women assessed religious attitudes to be most important. They were more attracted to men who shared their religious attitudes and were least attracted to men with dissimilar religious attitudes. For men, sexual attitudes were most important. They were more attracted to women who had similar sexual attitudes and least attracted to women with dissimilar attitudes about sex. The results indicate that similarity of attitudes does lead to attraction, provided the attitudes are the ones the individuals feel are important.

Similarity Outside the Laboratory

In the neat world of the laboratory, the similarity–attraction effect has been fairly robust. The situation is constrained and often, in the paradigm invented by Byrne, the person to whom you are similar is only hypothetical. Does the effect hold up outside the laboratory, where the people are real and the relationships are ongoing? Although there has been some controversy (Rosenbaum, 1986; Wright & Crawford, 1971), there is evidence that the relationship does occur. Kandel (1978) found that similarity did predict the friendship patterns of a large number of adolescents, while Byrne and his colleagues (Byrne, Ervin & Lamberth, 1970; Byrne & Rhamey, 1965) found that similarity successfully predicted dating behavior.

Griffitt and Veitch (1974) studied people living for ten days in a nuclear fallout shelter. Before entering the shelter the participants filled out an attitude questionnaire. After several days they were asked to name the two people whom they would most like to keep in the shelter with them and also to name the two whom they would most like to evict. The results indicated that the people selected to remain in the shelter were more similar to the subject in their attitudes than the people selected for eviction.

From a biosocial point of view, the effect of similarity on attraction is not at all surprising. Kenrick and Trost (1987) argue that bringing together people with similar but not identical genetic characteristics is the most adaptive strategy for the entire human species for purposes of mating. Obviously, the similarity–attraction effect that we have been examining is broader and pertains to more situations than heterosexual mating. Nonetheless, the biosocial point of view argues that the root of this effect—that is, the primary cause for us to prefer similar individuals—may derive from the adaptive evolution of the human species.

Limiting the Effect: Similarity to Whom?

It is apparently true that being in agreement with people makes us feel pleasant and causes us to come to like the people who agree with us. However, this statement may have broader implications than common sense and some data would acknowledge. Might there not be people whose agreement with us would make us feel uncomfortable rather than pleasant? Montague might be chagrined to learn that his attitudes are similar to those of Lord Capulet. Will he come to like Capulet as a result? Novak and Lerner (1968) conducted a study that bears on this question. They showed subjects that their attitudes and general background were similar or dissimilar to those of a mental patient. In comparison with a group who received the same information about a "normal" stranger, people who found that they were similar to the mental patient liked him less than those who found that they were dissimilar to him (cf. Lerner & Agar, 1972). Similarly, when Karuza and Brickman (1981) varied the status of a confederate, they found that subjects liked similar confederates if the confederates were of high status. But subjects did not like being similar to a low-status confederate. In a like vein, Cooper and Jones (1969) showed that subjects took great pains to dissociate themselves from an obnoxious person whose attitudes were similar to their own.

The conclusion that can be drawn from these studies is that attitudinal similarity does not always lead to attraction. The characteristics of the target person also play an important role.

Similarity: Real or Imagined?

In Figure 7-1(c), Romeo liked Juliet and disliked Tybalt. He must have been chagrined to learn that his wife liked Tybalt. In balance-theory terms, this asymmetry could lead to a lessening of the attraction between Romeo and Juliet. In the language of reward models, Juliet's disagreement with her husband might lead Romeo to associate a negative feeling with her, thereby decreasing her attractiveness. But there is an alternative. Romeo merely has to *imagine* that Juliet dislikes Tybalt. Then, as far as he is concerned, there is a state of balance. And if Juliet does not provide evidence to the contrary, Romeo might maintain this blissful distortion, using his *perceived* similarity to his wife to strengthen his attraction to her.

Similarity, then, need not be real; it can be imagined. Good support exists for this possibility. Byrne and Blaylock (1963) found a moderate degree of similarity in the attitudes of married couples. But when they asked the husband or wife to predict the attitudes of his or her partner, the similarity scores increased markedly! The perception that each had of his or her similarity to the partner was much greater than the actual similarity. In a different investigation, Miller and his associates (1966) asked students in dormitory suites at Northwestern University to describe their own personalities. They then asked other residents of the dormitories to describe the personalities of pairs of friends in the dorm. Friends were rated as having very similar personality traits, but when the self-descriptions of the pairs of friends were examined, there was much less actual similarity. From the perception of the outside observer, therefore, there was more perceived similarity than actual similarity.

Don't Opposites Attract?
A Time for Complementarity

In the Broadway show *Fiddler on the Roof,* Yenta the matchmaker says to the father of a homely prospective groom, "The way he looks and the way she sees, it's a perfect match!" We all know of instances in which two people are so dissimilar that they obviously fit well together. Examples from the media are manifold. Comedy teams such as the late Abbott and Costello have used the concept of complementarity. In the comic strip *Peanuts,* the contrast between quiet, naive Charlie Brown and his loud, conniving friend Lucy makes them a perfect match. She is domineering; he is unassuming. He is passive; she is aggressive. It seems there is reason for the notion that attraction can result from complementary characteristics as well as from similar characteristics.

There is evidence to support this observation. Winch (1958) provided data to show that husbands who score high on standard measures of a particular need tend to marry wives who score low on that need or high on complementary needs. For example, a man who has a strong need to dominate is likely to marry a woman who has a need to be submissive and be dominated—though there is no evidence that complementarity leads to happier marriages (Meyer & Pepper, 1977; Katz, Glucksberg & Krauss, 1960).

Kerckhoff and Davis (1962) conducted a study with seriously attached couples, interviewing them at the beginning and end of a seven-month period.

The couples were classified as having "stayed the same" in their relationship over seven months or as having moved "nearer to being a permanent couple." The investigators found that couples who had known each other only a short time showed progress toward permanence if they had similar needs and personalities. For couples who had been going together for a long time, however, complementarity was the best predictor of progress toward permanence.

Similarity, the data suggest, is the best predictor of interpersonal attraction and close personal relationships. By and large, similarity predicts liking inside and outside the laboratory, in dating (Johnson & Ogasawara, 1988), and in marriage. Yet complementarity of needs (Winch, 1958) and of behaviors (Strong et al., 1988) leads to lasting personal relationships as well, though its role is less well understood.

The Reciprocation of Liking: I'll Like You if You Like Me

There is strong pressure to reciprocate liking. In the absence of other information, when someone likes you, you have every reason to like that person. Did Juliet love Romeo only because he loved her? Probably not. But it is not a bad place to start. There is a norm that suggests we should like those who like us, and knowing or anticipating that people like us probably puts us in a frame of mind to like them.

This norm may well help to account for the effect of similarity on attraction. Aronson and Worchel (1966) suggested that the similarity between us and another can cause an implicit assumption that the other person likes us. If we add to this assumption the norm that we should reciprocate liking, then we should like a person who is similar to us.

Aronson and Worchel put their explanation to the test by establishing a situation in which a similar or a dissimilar confederate was said either to like or to dislike the subject. In other words, similarity information was manipulated independently of the stimulus person's evaluation of the subject. The investigators found that attraction to the confederate was affected only by the information that the stimulus person liked or disliked the subject, and not by information regarding similarity. It appears, then, that if we are given explicit information about the way another person feels about us, then that information—rather than the person's similarity to us—is what causes us to like him or her.

Indeed, if we know someone likes us, it may sometimes be more gratifying to know they are dissimilar to us along important dimensions—that they like us *despite* our differences. For example, Jones, Bell, and Aronson (1972) had each of their subjects interact with a confederate for several minutes. During the conversation the confederate expressed attitudes and opinions either opposed to or in agreement with those expressed by the subject. Later the subjects were allowed to overhear the confederate tell the experimenter how she felt about the subject. Half of the subjects heard a uniformly positive evaluation; that is, they heard that the confederate liked them. The other half overheard the confederate confess that she did not like the subject. When the subjects were asked how they felt about the confederate, it was clear that the confederate was liked best when she both *liked* and *disagreed with* the subject. Although we are typically attracted to people with attitudes similar to ours, knowing that others like us despite differences may make us feel particularly good, because the implication is that they see in us qualities that are so positive that they overwhelm the differences in attitudes and opinions.

We mentioned, however, that reciprocal liking was probably only a beginning point in interpersonal attraction. It will not account for an entire relationship—not the passion of Romeo for Juliet, and not even the enduring friendship of two roommates over the course of a year. A study by Backman and Secord (1959) demonstrated the declining impact of the reciprocal-liking effect on a group of subjects who met as strangers. They told each subject that personality tests they had taken indicated that specific members of the group were likely to like them. In fact, this information was bogus. The subjects were to meet six times as informal discussion groups, but the members were told that there was a possibility that each group would be broken into two teams. They were asked to indicate the members with whom they would like to be paired. The data showed that after the first session, the subjects chose the group members who had been designated as likely to like them. But the effect did not last; after a few sessions the pattern broke down. Feedback from group members eventually superseded the information given by the experimenter. Thus initially people were attracted to those who were expected to like them, but many other factors contributed to longer-term attraction. Apparently the "I'll like you if you like me" effect is short-lived.

Ingratiation: A Special Case

Although it is usually true that we enjoy being complimented and react to compliments with liking (Skolnick, 1971), this is not always the case. When we are complimented, we would like to believe that the compliments are attributable to our good nature, our fine qualities, and so on. We are less than happy if we must attribute the compliments to an ulterior motive on the part of the complimenter.

A person who acts in such a way as to enhance his or her image illicitly in the eyes of another may be said to be engaging in **ingratiation** (recall our discussion in Chapter 4). Jones (1964; Jones & Wortman, 1973) and his colleagues have considered the problem of ingratiation at some length. Flattery has been conceived as one tactic that an ingratiator might use to raise his or her esteem in the opinion of others. The question is: Is such a tactic successful?

The answer to this question depends on the perceived dependence of the flatterer on the object of his or her flattery. If you think that someone needs or wants something from you, you are much less likely to feel attracted to that individual as a result of compliments he may pay you than you are to someone who has nothing to gain by complimenting you. Evidence for this point of view can be found in a study in which women students listened to an evaluation of themselves delivered by a graduate student who had been observing them through a one-way mirror (Dickoff, 1961). The graduate student (an accomplice of the experimenter) varied her proportion of compliments, depending on which

experimental condition the subject was in. The subject was (1) complimented excessively, (2) complimented within the bounds of her previously measured self-esteem, or (3) given neutral feedback.

Dickoff manipulated whether the person giving the evaluation had anything to gain by making the subject like her. In the accuracy condition, the subjects were led to believe that the graduate student was trying to be as accurate and honest as possible. In the ulterior-motive condition, the subject was told that the graduate student was going to ask the subject to participate in one of her studies after the current experiment was concluded.

The feedback that the subject received strongly affected her evaluation of the graduate student. As Figure 7-2 shows, increasing the favorableness of the evaluation increases the liking—up to a point. When favorableness turns to flattery, the evaluation of the flatterer depends on the subject's perception of whether the flattery is in the service of ingratiation. When the possibility of an ulterior motive is present, attraction decreases as the favorableness of the compliments increases.

Note that these results present a double-edged dilemma. An ingratiator wishing to increase his esteem must conceal any possible ulterior motivation. If he cannot, it is best to refrain from excessive flattery. On the other hand, a person who genuinely feels that another is worthy of considerable praise may be penalized for the expression of those feelings if the flattery can be misattributed to an ulterior motive.

Propinquity Breeds Attraction— Sometimes

It is most probably true that throughout your life your closest acquaintances will live near you, that you will marry a person who lives close to you, and that the friends you make at work will occupy positions that are physically close to you. Bossard (1932) was one of the first to examine the importance of physical distance in mate selection for marriage. Examining 5,000 marriage license

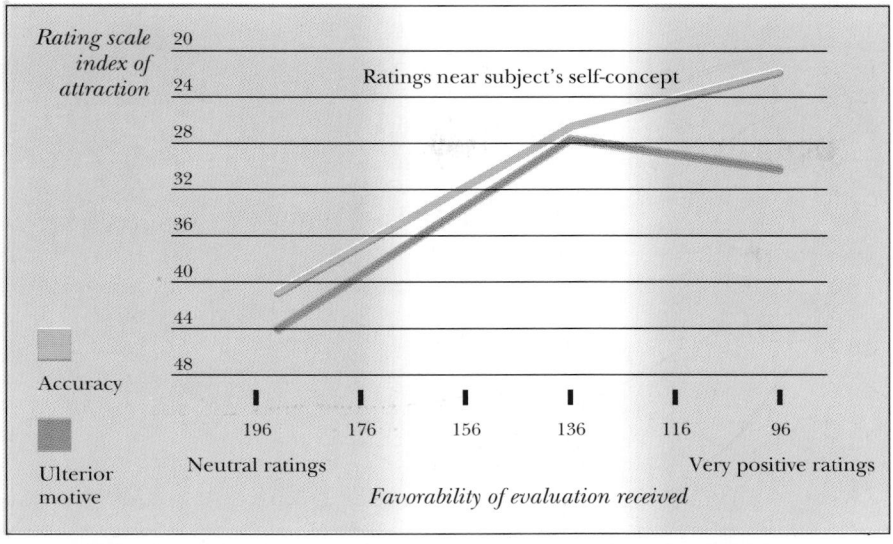

FIGURE 7-2   Mean attraction scores in Dickoff study
SOURCE: Jones (1964).

applications in Philadelphia, he found an inverse relationship between the number of such applications and the physical distance of the addresses of the two engaged partners—as the distance increased, the number of applications sharply decreased.

Perhaps the most systematic investigation of **propinquity** and attraction was conducted by Festinger, Schachter, and Back in 1950. Westgate West, a new housing project for married students, was constructed in the form of small two-story garden apartment complexes. Each unit contained ten apartments. New residents did not have a choice about which apartment to live in; they were assigned on a nearly random basis—that is, apartments were filled as they became vacant. Very few of the tenants knew one another before coming to Westgate West. After some time, all of the residents were asked which members of the complex they saw socially most often. The results are presented in Figure 7-3. The distance between people on the same floor and on different floors was closely related to friendship patterns—the closer two individuals lived to each other, the more likely they were to be friends. Living on different floors (bottom line) reduced the likelihood of friendship because functional distance was increased. It is quite remarkable that

41% of the next-door neighbors (*a* in Figure 7-3) indicated that they got together socially whereas only 10% of the people at opposite ends of the hall (*b*) mixed socially—especially since the maximum difference in distance between the closest and the farthest apartments on the same floor was only 69 feet.

Nahemow and Lawton (1975) examined friendship patterns in an inner-city housing project whose residents were of various age groups and races. Consistent with the findings of Festinger and his colleagues, people of all ages and races showed an overwhelming tendency to have their best friends within the same building (an average of 93%). But within the same building, an interesting pattern emerged. For people whose best friends were of a similar age or the same race, the best friend was no more likely to be on the respondent's floor than on a different floor. In other words, age and racial similarity were more important in predicting friendship than the

---

ingratiation   Use of a variety of strategies to enhance one's image illicitly in the eyes of others.

propinquity   Nearness in space, which tends to lead to liking, under the influence of rewards, expectations, and mere exposure.

The spatial design of the Westgate housing complex lent itself to a study of friendship patterns by Festinger, Schachter, and Back in 1950. Have you ever looked at the spatial designs of your own housing arrangements? Do they facilitate or inhibit social interaction?

floor on which the friends lived. However, if the best friend was of a different race or age, then it was overwhelmingly likely that the person resided on the respondent's floor. Apparently attraction in a housing project can transcend the boundaries of propinquity to some degree if similarity on an important dimension exists. In the absence of such similarity, attraction seems very much a function of physical closeness.

Explaining the Effect of Propinquity: Rewards, Expectations, and Mere Exposure

Rewards

Why should propinquity lead to attraction? Why should people be more attracted to the people next to whom they live and work? One explanation is that we interact more with those who are near us and that such interactions are

rewarding (Davis & Perkowitz, 1979; Werner & Latané, 1974). Newcomb has argued that "when persons interact, the reward-punishment ratio is more often . . . reinforcing" (1956, p. 576). That is, in normal everyday interaction, we are more likely to say nice things to others and to hear compliments in return than we are to say and hear negative things. So the more we interact with others, the more often we may be rewarded by them. Since it is thought that reward leads to greater liking, it would then follow that those who give us the greatest opportunity for frequent interaction would be rewarding to us and therefore would be liked by us.

Expectations

Those who are near us in our jobs, our houses, our dormitories, and so on are likely to be near us tomorrow and the next day as well. That is,

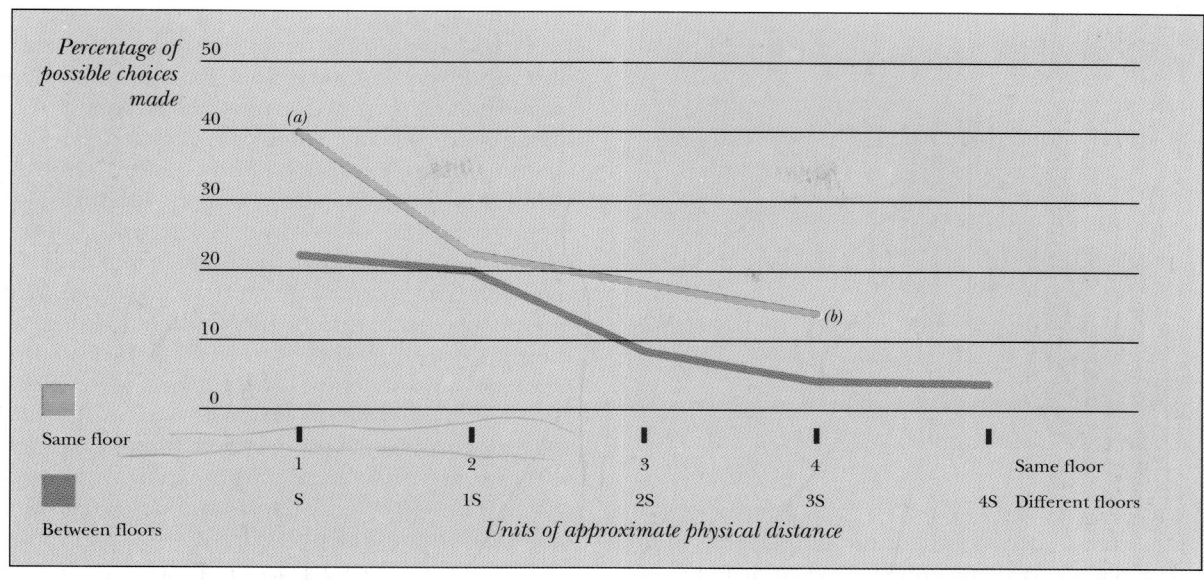

FIGURE 7-3 Relationship between functional distance and liking
SOURCE: Festinger, Schachter, and Back (1950).

we expect to interact with them again and again. As Newcomb's and Heider's balance theories would suggest, there is pressure to form a positive-sentiment relationship with those with whom we constantly interact. Darley and Berscheid (1967) conducted an experiment to demonstrate that a person's expectation of interacting with another person induces a tendency in that person to like the other. College women expected to participate in a study in which they were to discuss sexual standards for female college students. Before beginning the discussion, a subject was shown information about two other women students, one of whom was designated as the subject's partner for the discussion. Although the information about each of the two was of approximately equal attractiveness, the subjects answered the question "How probable is it that you would like this girl better socially?" by picking their prospective partner 70% of the time. In a subsequent study, Berscheid, Boye, and Darley (1968) found that a person with whom a subject was expecting to interact was liked better even when the future interaction was unforeseeably canceled and the person was objectively undesirable.

Mere exposure

Yet a third explanation has received a great deal of attention. Have you ever thought of how fond you become of a familiar possession, such as a sweater? Have you ever thought of how much you like a familiar place or a familiar face? Zajonc and his colleagues have argued that the more familiar we are with almost any object—that is, the more we are merely exposed to an object—the more we seem to like it. To the extent that **mere exposure** truly leads to feelings of attraction, the effect of propinquity can be explained by repeated exposure. The closer we are to someone, the more we interact with that person, the more familiar that person becomes. And familiarity leads to attraction. Let's look at some of the evidence.

In one study, Zajonc (1968) showed that words in a foreign language that subjects saw frequently were given greater positive value than words that were shown infrequently. In another

---

mere exposure Exposure to a person or object which, in the absence of any factor other than familiarity, leads to feelings of attraction.

---

1. What are the various ways of restoring balance in unbalanced relationships?

2. In what circumstances might rewards in a relationship actually undermine satisfaction in that relationship?

3. What are the key differences between communal and exchange relationships?

4. Why does similarity lead to attraction?

study reported by Zajonc (1968), volunteer subjects were shown a number of photographs. Some of the photos were shown often; others were shown infrequently. Later, subjects were asked how much they liked the people depicted in the photographs. People whose pictures were seen frequently were rated as more likable than people whose pictures were seen only once or twice.

Kunst-Wilson and Zajonc (1980) had subjects perform what is known as a "dichotic listening task." Students were given earphones. In one ear they heard a series of words. They had to match those words to words they were reading in a text that had been placed in front of them. In the other ear they heard a series of melodies, although the music was not referred to by the experimenter and seemed to have nothing to do with the task at hand. Later, subjects were asked to listen to a series of melodies, to indicate whether the tunes were familiar, and to indicate how much they liked each one. Subjects could not remember hearing any of the tunes, although several had been played through the earphones during the earlier portion of the experiment. Despite the fact that the students did not consciously recognize the tunes, they liked the familiar ones better. Thus merely being exposed to the music, without being aware of the previous exposure, created greater liking.

Exposure also seems to affect our attractiveness to ourselves! Think about that handsome or beautiful face that you see in the mirror several times each day. There is something a bit unusual about your perspective on your own face. It is the mirror image of what other people see. If Juliet had had a mirror, she would have seen a slightly different image than Romeo saw when he looked at her. Mita, Dermer, and Knight (1977) took note of this fact when they conducted a fascinating mere-exposure study. They showed University of Wisconsin women pictures of themselves that were either their own mirror image (the perspective they had been used to seeing in the mirror) or an actual picture (the perspective that others have when looking at them). They showed the same two pictures to the students' close friends. The subjects were more attracted to their mirror-image photos; the friends were more attracted to the actual photos. Apparently we are affected by mere exposure to ourselves. The view that is most familiar to us is the one we find most attractive.

Propinquity: A Reprise

Propinquity appears to lead to attraction in a variety of situations. This tendency may be attributable to (1) the fact that people near to us have more opportunities to reward us, (2) the expectation of future interaction with those who live and work near us, and/or (3) the phenomenon that mere exposure induces attraction. However, Berscheid and Walster (1978) have pointed out that attraction is not the only result of physical closeness. They cite an FBI report that indicates that one-third of all murders are committed by a member of the victim's family. In addition, the FBI report indicates that "most aggravated assaults occur within family units or between neighbors." Detroit police statistics indicate that the majority of robberies are committed between family members or neighbors, and a recent New York City statistic showed that muggings are more likely to be committed by people who live in the same neighborhood as their victims than by people from different neighborhoods. One reason that social-psychological studies may demonstrate a liking-and-propinquity relationship is that the nature of the studies conducted leads to a high reward/punishment ratio. People in housing projects, for example, do not have to interact in an intimate fashion. Nodding one's head, giving compliments, or politely agreeing with a political comment made by a neighbor while picking up the newspaper may lead to a large number of rewarding situations and an avoidance of negative situations. There is the possibility that one of the things propinquity does is to magnify the intensity of relationships. It may increase attractiveness and hatred, depending on other factors in the situation. Determining those other factors may be the future direction of research in this area.

Physical Attractiveness and Liking

Beauty too rich for use . . . [says Romeo of Juliet].
. . . her eyes in heaven
Would through the airy region stream so bright,
That birds would sing, and think it were not night.

Shakespeare gives Juliet outstanding physical beauty. Surely Romeo's attraction to Juliet is partially based on her striking physical appearance. Social psychologists have studied the effect of physical attractiveness on interpersonal attraction. Their findings have shown that attractive people are liked better than homely people. While some of the effect may be romantic and sexually oriented, not all of it is. Let us consider the evidence.

Walster and his colleagues (1966) arranged dates for subjects at a "Welcome Week" dance. Couples were paired randomly. Each participant was rated on physical attractiveness by a group of judges. At a break in the dance, the participants were asked how much they liked their partners. The researchers found that liking of the partner and desire for a future date were directly related to attractiveness—the more attractive the partner, the greater the liking.

Not all of the evidence indicates that people attempt to date the most attractive member of the opposite sex. The comment "She's out of your league" could be directed to an ordinary-looking man who seeks a date with the town's knockout. In fact, Walster and his colleagues did not expect the desire for a future date to be a function of attractiveness. Instead, they had predicted a "matching" hypothesis: people would choose partners who were about as attractive as they themselves were. However, these investigators realized that arranging the date at the dance did not replicate a setting in which people custom-

arily find themselves. Usually a fear of rejection or failure might accompany an attempt to win the most attractive member of the opposite sex. In a subsequent study by Walster and Walster (1969), subjects were led to believe that they would meet their prospective partners before the dance. They were then asked how attractive a partner they wished to have. With the fear of possible rejection reinstated, people chose potential dates who were about as attractive as they themselves were. Similar data have been collected by Berscheid and her colleagues (1971) and by Huston (1973).

Dating an attractive person, then, is something that is desired but may be tempered by fear of rejection. Kiesler and Baral (1970) showed that men are more likely to make romantic advances to a moderately attractive woman if they have had their self-esteem raised. Yet White (1980) has shown that there may be something beneficial about dating people whose physical attractiveness matches your own. He studied dating couples at UCLA at various points during their relationship. He found that couples who were most similar in their physical appearance were the most likely to have fallen more deeply in love after a nine-month period.

In general, the data support the notion that attractiveness does lead to greater attraction. Perhaps the advances that people make in a romantic situation are tempered by possible fears of rejection (Hustin & Levinger, 1978) or by experience with rejection (Hamilton, 1981), but the general conclusion is that physical beauty does lead to liking.

It would be tempting to attribute the physical-attractiveness phenomenon purely to sexual stimulation. But this is probably not the whole story. Consider some data collected by Dion, Berscheid, and Walster (1972). They presented evidence that physically attractive people are seen as being happier and more successful than less attractive people. They are also rated as having more socially desirable personality traits. And it did not matter whether a respondent was rating a member of the same or the opposite sex. Similar positive feelings have been found in young children who rated other young children (Langlois & Stephan, 1981). In neither case did sexual attraction seem to be involved.

TABLE 7-1

Subjects' ratings of the general quality of the essay in each experimental condition

Essay quality	Writer's physical attractiveness			Total mean
	Attractive	Control	Unattractive	
Good	6.7	6.6	5.9	6.4
Poor	5.2	4.7	2.7	4.2
Total	6.0	5.5	4.3	

NOTE: The higher the rating number, the better the evaluation of the essay.
SOURCE: Adapted from Landy and Sigall (1974).

Beauty and Performance: Altering Our Perceptions of Behavior

We have now seen that we do not always act rationally when physical attractiveness is concerned. We tend to like attractive people more, regardless of their sex or age. Not only do we like them more, we may also evaluate their *behavior* differently. We may be inclined to like the behavior of attractive people more than that of unattractive people or to expect better behavior from them. For example, Clifford and Walster (1973) showed fifth-grade teachers a report card with information about a hypothetical student. Although all of the teachers saw the same information, the photograph of the student that was clipped to the card was varied so that either an attractive or an unattractive boy or girl was pictured. The teacher's assessment of the student's IQ and expected future level of attainment varied as a function of physical attractiveness. Although the test scores did not vary, an attractive child was seen as more intelligent and was expected to do better work than an unattractive child.

In another study, Landy and Sigall (1974) showed college students an essay that had been written by another student. The objective quality of the essay was made either good or bad, and a photograph attached to the essay revealed that the writer was either attractive or unattractive.

(Control group subjects had no photo attached to the essay.) The subjects were asked to rate the quality of the essay. It is true that objectively good essays were rated better than poor essays, but it is also true that essays written by attractive writers were seen as being of better quality than essays written by unattractive writers. And, as the results presented in Table 7-1 indicate, the effect was somewhat stronger for the bad essay than for the good one. That is, an attractive writer who produced a poor essay was given an extra benefit of the doubt by the judges.

There is evidence that the effect of physical attractiveness on our interpretations of behavior occurs at a subtle and basic level. Forgas (1987) had subjects review the case of a female student who was accused of cheating on an exam. In addition to information about the alleged cheating incident, background information about the young woman and a photograph of her were provided. All of the subjects received the same description of the incident and background information. The photograph, however, was cleverly doctored so that half of the subjects saw a rather unattractive student and the other half saw quite an attractive one. Additionally, in half of the photographs the student was shown smiling while in the other half she wore a more neutral expression. Thus each subject saw a photograph of a young woman who was either attractive or unattractive and either smiling or not smiling.

After viewing these materials, the subjects were asked several questions about the young woman, including how blameworthy she was for the cheating incident and how self-confident she appeared. What effects did the woman's attractiveness and facial expression have on these judgments? When the woman was attractive and smiling, she was seen as self-confident. However, the same smile was interpreted as a sign of submissiveness in the unattractive woman. Additionally, the attractive woman was seen as more responsible for the cheating if she smiled, whereas the smiling, unattractive woman was given more lenient treatment than her nonsmiling counterpart. Thus a person's physical attractiveness can serve as a relatively automatic cue that can shape our interpretation of even the most basic acts and gestures—such as smiles.

"The fit's O.K., but does it say 'Not guilty'?"

Drawing by Bernard Schoenbaum; © 1988 *The New Yorker Magazine*, Inc.

The Jury Is Out

Perhaps the most frightening situation in which physical attractiveness can affect judgments is the jury trial. A person's beauty is supposed to be extraneous to the evidence introduced in court. But if beauty affects liking and our attributions of personality and behavior, then it may also affect courtroom judgments. As Clarence Darrow said, "Jurymen seldom convict a person they like or acquit one they dislike. . . . Facts regarding the crime are relatively unimportant."

In a pioneering study, Landy and Aronson (1969) presented a case of negligent homicide to a simulated jury (student subjects pretending to serve as jurors). The defendant was accused of running over a pedestrian on Christmas Eve. The facts were identical in all cases. In half of the cases, however, the defendant was described positively (an insurance man who was going to spend Christmas Eve with his family), and in the other half he was described negatively (a janitor who

was going to spend the evening with his girl-friend). Although the facts did not differ, the janitor was given significantly more years of imprisonment than the positively described defendant.

Landy and Aronson's study did not involve physical characteristics. However, Efran (1974) took this additional step. He asked subjects to decide the fate of a defendant in a college cheating case. Again the facts were held constant, but a photograph of the defendant attached to the written information was varied according to the condition of the subject in the study. Each photograph had been rated by a separate group as either attractive or unattractive. Physically attractive defendants were liked better, were judged less guilty, and received less punishment than defendants who were unattractive.

Why should attractiveness lead simulated juries to confer less guilt and punishment on a defendant? Sigall and Ostrove (1975) suggested that the reason may rest with the jurors' assumption that the attractive defendant is worthier, has

TABLE 7-2

Mean sentence assigned, in years (N = 20 per cell)

Offense	Defendant condition		
	Attractive	Unattractive	Control
Swindle	5.45	4.35	4.35
Burglary	2.80	5.20	5.10

SOURCE: Sigall and Ostrove (1975).

greater potential, and is less likely to transgress in the future than an unattractive defendant. That people make this assumption was demonstrated in an earlier study by Dion (1972). In that study, judges attributed the transgressions of unattractive people to their stable dispositions, whereas they attributed the transgressions of attractive people to momentary circumstances.

If these are the assumptions that jurors make, Sigall and Ostrove argued, the assumptions should apply only to crimes that are not directly related to appearance. That is, if a person uses his or her good looks to put over a con game or a swindle, then the notion that an attractive person will not get involved in such activities again loses its credibility. Sigall and Ostrove established a simulated jury to pass sentence on a defendant who was either attractive or unattractive. In a third condition, no information about attractiveness was provided. For half of the jurors, the crime was described as unrelated to the defendant's attractiveness. In this condition, the defendant burglarized a home of $2,200. For the other half, the defendant "ingratiated herself to a middle-aged bachelor and induced him to invest $2,200 in a nonexistent corporation." Presumably, the defendant's looks may have been a factor in this swindle.

The mean number of years of prison recommended by the jurors is depicted in Table 7-2. As can be seen, the results strongly support Sigall and Ostrove's reasoning. The attractive defendant who committed a burglary was given far less punishment than the unattractive defendant or the defendant about whom no attractiveness information was provided. However, the attractive defendant who had ingratiated herself to commit the swindle was sentenced to more

Why Does Physical Attractiveness Lead to Liking?

Although the phenomenon has some limitations, the effect of physical attractiveness on liking seems robust. People seem to like those who are more attractive; they praise their behaviors and characteristics and find them less culpable for transgressions. What leads to this phenomenon? Why should rational human beings decide that people with more attractive physical characteristics are worthy of such praise?

First, it may be that people like attractive people for the status those people convey. We may have learned throughout our upbringing that people are impressed when we are with others who are attractive. Sigall and Landy (1973), for example, asked subjects to evaluate a man whom they saw seated with either an attractive or an unattractive woman. The man received far more positive ratings when he was seen with the attractive woman than when the woman was unattractive. Kernis and Wheeler (1981) varied both the level of association that a target had with a confederate and the attractiveness of that confederate. When the target was portrayed as being a friend of, rather than someone merely seen with, the confederate, the target was rated as being more likable and more attractive. If we are seen as attractive when we associate with attractive people, then attractive people become very rewarding. It is reasonable to conclude, then, that we would come to evaluate attractive people highly.

A second principle that may govern the high regard given to attractive people comes from a study by Marks, Miller, and Maruyama (1981). These investigators asked people how similar several other people were to them on a variety of traits. Participants rated attractive people as being more similar to themselves. Could it be that there is a general tendency to view ourselves as being more similar to attractive than to unattractive people? Our positive regard for those who are attractive may be due not to their physical appeal but rather to their assumed similarity to us.

A third explanation for the positive evaluations given to physically attractive people is that there may be a kernel of truth in that evaluation. Perhaps physically attractive people do have more pleasing personalities, more varied social contacts, and more interesting friends. Perhaps they do differ from the unattractive in their ability to achieve and to perform. Reis, Nezlek, and Wheeler (1980) collected extensive notes on the social interaction patterns of attractive and unattractive people. Important differences were indeed found between the two groups with regard to the number of friends, the initiation of social contacts, and the number and quality of conversations. The lives of attractive and unattractive people do appear to differ in significant ways. Further research may tell us whether these differences support the hypothesis that there is indeed a good reason for the high ratings given to attractive people.

For Whom Is Physical Attractiveness Most Important? The Role of Self-Monitoring

People differ in the emphasis they put on physical attractiveness, personal attributes, religious affiliation, interpersonal styles, and so forth as they choose the people with whom they interact. Are there systematic differences among people that are related to the degree to which they take physical appearance into account in choosing a potential romantic partner? Snyder, Berscheid, and Glick (1985) examined this question. They suggested that the concept of self-monitoring may provide that systematic difference.

As you may recall from our discussion in Chapter 4, people can be classified on a scale of high to low self-monitoring. Some people pay careful attention to presenting themselves according to what they believe is demanded by the situation. They are particularly responsive to situational cues when they make decisions about appropriate behavior. And they tend to act more in accordance with what they believe is required by the situation than with what they truly believe or feel. Such people are considered high self-monitors. By contrast, low self-monitors are people who base their behaviors in social situations on their dispositions and attitudes, and not on what they think the situation demands. As we

have seen, low self-monitors are more likely to demonstrate attitude-behavior consistency since they are usually more attuned to their own attitudes and less concerned with such distractions as making a good impression.

Since high self-monitors are more influenced by the appearance of a social situation, Snyder and his colleagues reasoned that they would be more inclined than low self-monitors to consider the physical attractiveness of a potential partner. Low self-monitors, on the other hand, would be more interested in discovering a potential partner's true attitudes and personal characteristics.

In a first study, Snyder and his colleagues (1985) gave male subjects at the University of Minnesota a choice of more than 50 files to examine. The files contained information on female students who could serve as potential partners for informal coffee dates at a nearby cafeteria. The subjects were known not to be involved with a steady romantic partner, so it was assumed that they would see the potential date as the possible start of a relationship.

Each file consisted of three pages. The first page consisted of information about the background, attitudes, and preferences of the particular woman; the second page contained some uninterpretable filler information; and the third page contained a photograph of the woman. The participants were able to spend as much time as they liked with as many of the files as they chose. Moreover, they could concentrate on any page of the file that they preferred—the physical information conveyed by page 3's photograph, or the information about personal attributes on page 1. Observers stationed behind a one-way mirror watched the subjects as they examined the files. One dependent measure was the degree to which participants looked at the first (personal information) page or the third (physical information) page. In addition, the subjects had to choose one of the women for a coffee date. Subjects were asked directly whether their choice was made more on the basis of the physical or the personal information.

The results were clear. High self-monitors were much more likely to pay attention to the photographs of the women than low self-monitors. Low self-monitors were more likely to spend

TABLE 7-3

**Reasons for choosing a dating partner:
Investigation 1**

Stated reason	Individuals' self-monitoring category	
	Low	High
Personal attributes	15	3
Photographs	5	10

NOTE: Entries in this table are number of participants in each self-monitoring category who offered each type of stated reason for choosing their dating partner.
SOURCE: Snyder, Berscheid, and Glick (1985).

their time on page 1 information (information on personal attributes). Table 7-3 adds further support to the hypothesis by showing the subjects' stated major reason for their choice of a dating partner. Clearly, high self-monitors stated that they were influenced by physical attractiveness; low self-monitors were affected by personal characteristics.

In a second experiment, Snyder, Berscheid, and Glick (1985) constrained the male subjects' choice of a dating partner to two women. One was very attractive but had a series of unpleasant personal characteristics. The other was physically unattractive but had highly positive personal qualities. Subjects—selected so that they would be either quite high or quite low in self-monitoring—were asked to choose one of the women for an evening date at a local restaurant. Which partner did the subjects select? Of the low self-monitors, 81% chose to date the partner with the desirable personality and the unattractive appearance. Only 31% of the high self-monitors made this choice. By contrast, 69% of the high self-monitors chose the physically attractive woman despite her undesirable personality, while only 19% of the low self-monitors made this choice.

This finding also appears to apply to situations in which people are evaluating the compatibility of *others*. Glick, DeMorest, and Hotze (1988) had male and female subjects examine personality information and photographs of five women and five men from a nearby university. The subjects were asked to pair the men and women into couples that they thought would be "most compatible." They were led to believe that these individuals had agreed to go on a date with the person with whom they were most frequently matched. The results mirrored those of the study by Snyder and his colleagues (1985). The pairings made by the high self-monitors reflected far more concern with physical attractiveness, whereas those made by the low self-monitors were based mainly on the personal characteristics of the target persons. Thus it appears that the differential emphasis placed on physical attractiveness between high and low self-monitors in their own relationships has a marked effect on beliefs about the foundation of compatibility in romantic relationships in general. High self-monitors think along the lines of physical attractiveness, even when they make recommendations for other people.

In summary, we can say that while all people may be interested in the physical attractiveness of a potential partner in a dating situation, high self-monitors are particularly concerned with this dimension. Their preoccupation with presenting an appropriate image in the dating situation leads them to focus on the physical dimension. They also assume that other people would act just as they do, and so their recommendations for dating matches are based on physical attractiveness. Low self-monitors are more concerned with personal qualities and attributes. Given a choice, they will trade physical beauty for inner qualities.

A Candle in the Wind:
Some Negative Consequences of Beauty

The songwriter Elton John speaks of Marilyn Monroe when he says,

*It seems to me you lived your life
Like a candle in the wind,
Never knowing whom to cling to
When the rain sets in.*

Probably no one in recent history has been more glamorous and beautiful than Marilyn Monroe. Her mysterious suicide at the age of 36 shocked the world and continues to intrigue observers. The lamenting lyrics of Elton John's "Candle in the Wind" suggests that beauty, at least in the extreme, has its dark side.

Extremely attractive people are expected to be happier, more socially adept, and better adjusted emotionally than the rest of us (Archer & Cash, 1985). They also receive more positive feedback. But do these expectations have any negative consequences? Are these people under a great deal of pressure to conform, to be as good as such extremely attractive people are supposed to be? Furthermore, is the positive social regard that attractive people receive as believable as the same feedback received by people of more modest appearance? Recall our discussion of *discounting* in Chapter 2. When people are extremely attractive *and* receive positive social feedback, they may discount that feedback. Others who are told positive things have every reason to believe what they are told and can use the feedback to develop a decent sense of self-esteem. It may be that, for highly attractive individuals, the ability to use social feedback, as positive as it may be, is limited. People as attractive as Marilyn Monroe may not be able to trust positive feedback. The ambiguity of the reason for positive feedback may cause anxiety and unstable self-esteem (Summers, 1986).

In one study that shed some light on this proposition, subjects who rated themselves as extremely attractive and those who rated themselves as unattractive were asked to write creative essays (Major, Carrington & Carnevale, 1984). The essays were supposedly rated by judges. The judges' evaluation of the subjects' work was always highly favorable. In half of the cases, however, the judges were said to be observing the subjects through a one-way mirror, while for the other half, the judge was unable to observe. The question raised by Major and her colleagues was: Who would be more likely to believe the favorable feedback? They predicted that attractive subjects whose work was evaluated by a judge who could see them would be less likely to believe the evaluation. This turned out to be true. Attractive men and attractive women were more convinced that they had done good work when their physical attractiveness had not been seen by the judges. Attractive people whose work was praised by a judge who had seen them were less convinced that their work was really of high quality.

It seems that attractive people were less able to rely on feedback, since they believed that the feedback might have been influenced by their

Marilyn Monroe's suicide suggested that her beauty was as much a burden as a gift. She received an enormous amount of adulation—but did she believe it?.

attractiveness. Physically attractive people may have difficulty building a clear, unambiguous image of themselves, and the result may be a sense of anxiety and uncertainty. Extreme physical attractiveness, then, seems to be a mixed blessing. Although it does lead to many social contacts and positive feedback, the very attractive person may be uncertain about the sincerity of that feedback, "never knowing whom to cling to when the rain sets in."

Another pitfall awaits us when we are compared with people more beautiful than we. As we noted earlier, others may perceive us as more physically attractive and likable if we are thought to be friends with someone who is physically attractive (Kernis & Wheeler, 1981). But what if this association is not really close? What if we just happen to be seen in either physical or temporal proximity to attractive others without the

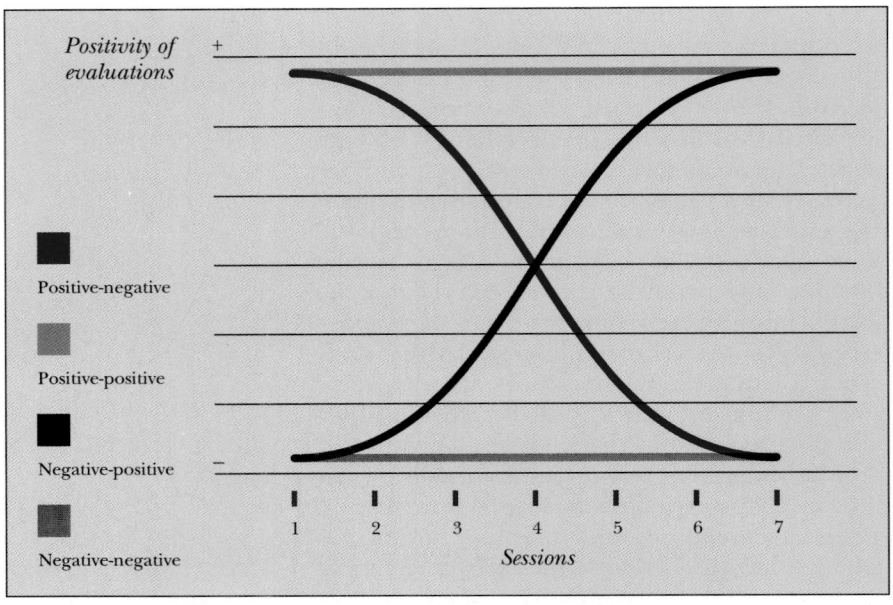

Positivity of evaluations

+

Positive-negative

Positive-positive

Negative-positive

Negative-negative

1 2 3 4 5 6 7

Sessions

FIGURE 7-4   Four conditions of Aronson and Linder's study of the sequence of evaluative comments
NOTE: Positive and negative feedback were systematically varied over seven sessions.
SOURCE: Aronson and Linder (1965).

assumption that we share some kind of interpersonal relationship with them? Chances are, we stand to suffer by comparison. Kenrick and Gutierres (1980) showed their subjects photographs of highly attractive people or rather unattractive people. Later these subjects were asked to rate the attractiveness of average-looking people. The results showed a "contrast effect." That is, the subjects who had been exposed to the attractive targets found the average-looking targets to be less attractive than did the subjects who had viewed the unattractive targets.

In the light of such findings, it seems reasonable to question the popular media's almost exclusive focus on exceptionally attractive and well-proportioned models whose faces and bodies monopolize the pages of such magazines as *Vogue, GQ,* and *Self.* Could such a bombardment of beauty affect the way we see and evaluate the more ordinary people who surround us? The answer appears to be yes. Kenrick, Gutierres, and Goldberg (1989) showed both men and women slides of either beautiful nudes (from *Playboy* and *Playgirl*), average-looking nudes, or works of abstract art. Both sexes showed the expected

contrast effect: average-looking nudes seen later looked uglier to subjects in the *Playboy* and *Playgirl* conditions. Moreover, and somewhat chillingly, the men in a subsequent study reported loving their current mates *less* if they had been exposed to beautiful rather than more plain-looking models. This effect, it should be noted, does not implicate the viewing of erotica per se, since arousal serves mainly to intensify either attraction or revulsion. Rather, these findings seem to implicate the popular media in general, where the majority of the faces and bodies we see look like those of *Charlie's Angels,* Mr. America, and the like.

How to Win Friends and Influence People by Being Insulting and Clumsy

When Dale Carnegie sought to advise people on how to endear themselves to others in *How to Win Friends and Influence People,* he probably never dreamed of some of the less obvious and unusual facets of interpersonal attraction. Elliot Aronson and his colleagues have been active in exploring some of the more interesting situations that lead to attraction.

To insult is divine

Earlier we saw that we generally like people who compliment us better than those who do not (see Skolnik, 1971; Sigall & Aronson, 1969; Tagiuri, Blake & Bruner, 1953). However, this is not always true; after a while compliments can get boring. The doting husband who constantly compliments his wife on her clothing, makeup, and hairdo gets himself into a position where he is expected to be complimentary. His flattering statements, like the knee-jerk reflex, begin to lose their meaning.

Aronson and Linder (1965) sought to investigate the *sequence* of flattering and insulting statements that a person received. The best way to understanding their clever but complicated methodology is to imagine that you are the subject in their experiment. When you enter the laboratory, you are told that a second subject is expected. But since you arrived first, you will serve as the confederate in a study on "verbal conditioning." The experimenter tells you that the other subject will have a conversation with you and that she will then have a discussion with the experimenter, who will ask her what she thought of you. Actually, you are told, the entire purpose of the discussion is to allow the experimenter to "reinforce" with the response "mm-hmm" or "good" all plural nouns that the subject utters. You, serving as the confederate, are to count the number of plural nouns that are used by the subject (which you can hear over a sound system).

You may ask what this has to do with interpersonal perception. The experimenter has not told you the full story. In fact, the other subject is the confederate; you are not. The hoax is designed to force you to "overhear" evaluative comments made about you. The four conditions of the experiment vary only the number and the sequence of the positive and negative evaluations the subject overhears; the positive and negative feedback are systematically varied over seven sessions. As depicted in Figure 7-4, in the positive-positive condition, the seven sessions are devoted to flattering statements that the "other subject" makes about you. In the negative-negative con-

dition, the other subject's statements are all derogatory and insulting ("She seems to be a rather shallow and superficial person"). In the negative-positive (gain) condition, the confederate begins by describing you as dull, ordinary, and so on, but by the fourth session she begins to change her opinion, and at the end she is describing you in very flattering terms. The positive-negative (loss) condition is the mirror image of the negative-positive condition. Here you are described in glowing terms at first; the fourth session marks the change from flattery to insult, and by the end of the study you are described with purely insulting comments.

At the end, the experimenter asks you for your "gut feeling" about the "other subject." The results of this question are shown in Table 7-4. The most-liked person in the study is not the confederate in the positive-positive condition but the one in the negative-positive or gain condition. This is true even though over the course of the seven sessions the positive-positive confederate complimented you 28 times without an insult, and in the gain condition she complimented you only 14 times after delivering 8 insults. The reverse is also true. Subjects liked a person who consistently insulted them better than they liked someone who began by giving them 14 compliments and ended with 8 insults. It should be pointed out that the latter effect was not large enough to be statistically significant.

The Aronson and Linder study and a similar study by Mettee (1971) offer some potent advice about interpersonal attraction over time. The always complimentary husband may wonder why his wife flips for a guy who has always been insulting and belligerent and just once gives her

TABLE 7-5

Mean attraction scores of the interviewee

	Pratfall	No pratfall
Superior ability	30.2	20.8
Average ability	−2.5	17.8

NOTE: The higher the number, the greater the attraction.
SOURCE: Aronson, Willerman, and Floyd (1966).

an approving glance. Moreover, our doting husband should realize the bind that he has gotten himself into. On the one hand, he is at the mercy of the competitor with the one approving glance; but he dare not act disapprovingly himself, for if he does, he could put himself in the loss condition. That is, he would be liked less than if he had always been insulting.

Why should such an effect occur? Aronson and Linder (1965) and Aronson (1969a) have suggested some possibilities, two of which should be mentioned. First, the person in the gain condition may be liked because she is seen as more discriminating. In effect, she establishes her credibility and proves that she is a discerning individual. To earn the praise of such a person who once insulted you indicates that you are really a good person. Second, the insulting person may upset you and cause some uncomfortable uncertainty about your self-esteem. But when she comes around to your side, she reduces that uncertainty. Aronson suggests that this produces a warm and pleasurable feeling—that is, it is rewarding—and therefore it leads to greater attraction.

Clumsiness is attractive: The pratfall

In the early days of his presidency, John F. Kennedy was riding a wave of very positive popular sentiment. But in 1961 came the Bay of Pigs fiasco—a U.S.-supported invasion of Cuba. At the last possible moment, Kennedy withdrew support from the incursion. He advised the American public and shouldered full blame and responsibility for the event, though many analysts believed that he could have legitimately transferred a major portion of the responsibility to his predecessor, President Dwight D. Eisenhower. And a good many of his advisers, with their eye on the 1964 election, wished that he

had. Kennedy's political opponents had their hearts set on the forthcoming opinion polls, which they believed would show a dramatic loss of popularity for the president. The results were indeed dramatic, for they provided Kennedy with the highest ratings he was ever to receive during his presidency.

What could account for this surprising turn of events? Aronson, Willerman, and Floyd (1966) argued that a blunder, mistake, or error of judgment can be endearing in someone of extremely high competence. A man who seems to come from the land of Camelot—born to wealthy and influential parents; possessing superior intelligence, a likable personality, and good looks; and married to a beautiful woman—may be viewed with great admiration, but such a man does not always endear himself to us. He may seem too perfect, too unapproachable. A mistake, however, is something of which we are all capable. A man who commits one has human qualities. If he is otherwise highly competent, a mistake can humanize him in our eyes and serve to increase our liking of him.

Aronson, Willerman, and Floyd (1966) designed a situation in which they could test their hypothesis. Subjects listened to a tape-recorded session in which a stimulus person was being interviewed for a spot on a college team that was to enter a quiz competition (the *College Bowl* television show). In one condition, the stimulus person was of extremely high ability. He was given a series of questions that he answered with a 92% score. During an interview, he said that he had been an honor student in high school, editor of the senior yearbook, and a member of the track team. The stimulus person on a second tape presented quite a different story. He answered only 30% of his questions correctly and said that he had received average grades in high school, that he had been a proofreader on the senior yearbook, and that he had tried out for the track team but failed to make it.

In half of the cases, both the competent and the incompetent stimulus person committed a clumsy pratfall. Near the end of the interview, a lot of shuffling was suddenly heard, and the stimulus person yelled, "Oh, my goodness, I've spilled coffee all over my new suit!" In the other half of the cases, the pratfall did not occur. At

Passion and caring characterize love, and love happens at any age and between many types of people.

iment in which they would have to undergo painful electric shocks. Other subjects anticipated no such shocks. The subjects were later asked how much they would like to date and to kiss the woman they had met. Subjects aroused through anxiety had a more intense desire to kiss the woman than those who had not experienced the arousing anxiety.

In a second study, Dutton and Aron took their research to a 450-foot suspension walkway that hangs some 230 feet above the Capilano River in British Columbia. An attractive woman approached male subjects as they traversed the

450-foot walkway. She asked them to help her fill out a questionnaire for her class. She also wrote down her name and phone number for each subject, inviting him to call. Did the physiological arousal that the subject was experiencing make the woman seem like someone he would like to be with? These subjects' responses were com-

compassionate love A long-term, deep, affectionate attachment between two people.
romantic love A passionately intense attachment to another person.

TABLE 7-6

Passionate Love Scale

In this section of the questionnaire you will be asked to describe how you feel when you are passionately in love. Some common terms for this feeling are passionate love, infatuation, love sickness, or obsessive love.

Please think of the person whom you love most passionately *right now*. If you are not in love right now, please think of the last person you loved passionately. If you have never been in love, think of the person whom you came closest for caring for in that way. Keep this person in mind as you complete this section of the questionnaire. (The person you choose should be of the opposite sex if you are heterosexual or of the same sex if you are homosexual.) Try to tell us how you felt at the time when your feelings were the most intense.

All of your answers will be strictly confidential.

   1. Since I've been involved with _____, my emotions have been on a roller coaster.
• 2. I would feel deep despair if _____ left me.
   3. Sometimes my body trembles with excitement at the sight of _____.
   4. I take delight in studying the movements and angles of _____'s body.
• 5. Sometimes I feel I can't control my thoughts; they are obsessively on _____.
• 6. I feel happy when I am doing something to make _____ happy.
• 7. I would rather be with _____ than anyone else.
• 8. I'd get jealous if I thought _____ were falling in love with someone else.
   9. No one else could love _____ like I do.
• 10. I yearn to know all about _____.
• 11. I want _____—physically, emotionally, mentally.
 12. I will love _____ forever.
 13. I melt when looking deeply into _____s' eyes.
• 14. I have an endless appetite for affection from _____.
• 15. For me, _____ is the perfect romantic partner.
 16. _____ is the person who can make me feel the happiest.
• 17. I sense my body responding when _____ touches me.
 18. I feel tender toward _____.
• 19. _____ always seems to be on my mind.
 20. If I were separated from _____ for a long time, I would feel intensely lonely.
 21. I sometimes find it difficult to concentrate on work because thoughts of _____ occupy my mind.
• 22. I want _____ to know me—my thoughts, my fears, and my hopes.
 23. Knowing that _____ cares about me makes me feel complete.
• 24. I eagerly look for signs indicating _____'s desire for me.
 25. If _____ were going through a difficult time, I would put away my own concerns to help him/her out.
 26. _____ can make me feel effervescent and bubbly.
 27. In the presence of _____, I yearn to touch and be touched.
 28. An existence without _____ would be dark and dismal.
• 29. I possess a powerful attraction for _____.
• 30. I get extremely depressed when things don't go right in my relationship with _____.

Possible responses to each item ranged from:

1	2	3	4	5	6	7	8	9
Not at all true				moderately true			Definitely true	

NOTE: The • indicates items selected for the short version of the Passionate Love Scale.
SOURCE: Hatfield and Sprecher (1986).

pared with those of other men of whom the woman made a similar request on a low, solid bridge. Men approached on the high, wobbly bridge were much more likely to call than men who were approached on the solid bridge. Men whose hearts were beating faster high above the Capilano were likely to interpret their arousal as romantic.

The Nature of Love and Long-Term Relationships

What are the feelings that go into the creation of long-term relationships—that deep compassionate love shared by couples whose bond endures over time? This has been a subject of considerable interest to social psychologists. Sternberg and Grajek (1984) studied the components of love by carefully questioning 85 people in various stages of a love relationship. They found considerable agreement among the people questioned that love comprises several overlapping but important factors. No one factor was so crucial that if it did not exist, love would not be experienced. But overall, love, for each of the people questioned, comprised most of these factors: (1) a deep understanding of the other, (2) sharing of ideas and information, (3) sharing of deeply personal ideas and feelings, (4) receiving and giving emotional support to the other, (5) personal growth through the relationship and helping of the other in his or her personal growth, (6) giving help to the other, (7) making the other feel needed and needing the other, and (8) the giving and receiving of affection in the relationship.

Can the closeness of a relationship predict its duration? Do people who have very close feelings for each other stay with each other longer? Berscheid, Snyder, and Omoto (1989) have created a Relationship Closeness Inventory (RCI). They asked more than 200 University of Minnesota students to respond to this questionnaire as they thought about their very closest relationship. That relationship could be with a romantic partner, a friend, a relative, or anyone whom the participant selected. As it turned out, 59% of the respondents chose a romantic partner, 22% chose family members, and 18% chose close friends. Conceptually, the closeness of a relationship is similar to the magnitude of love between two people. Indeed, Berscheid and her colleagues had their respondents fill out Rubin's liking and loving scales as well. The RCI measure of the strength of the participants' closest relationship showed a significant correlation with Rubin's love scale, but, as we should predict, no correlation with Rubin's liking scale.

Three months after the initial questionnaire,

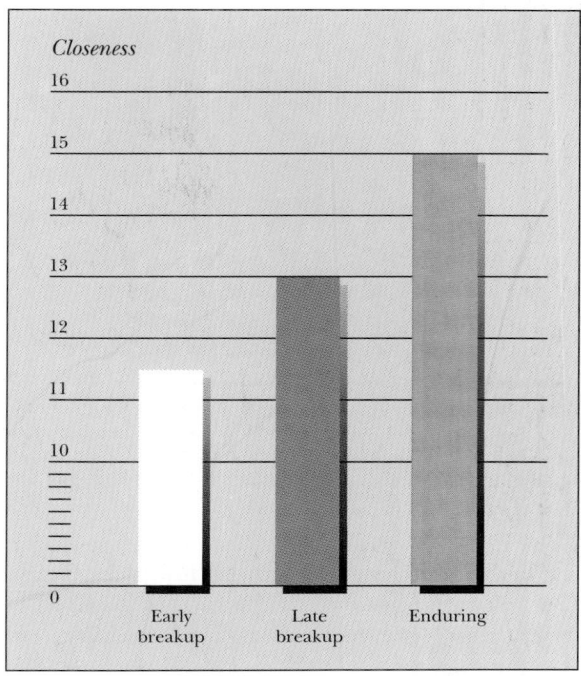

FIGURE 7-5 Mean initial Relationship Closeness Inventory scores as a function of relationship status
SOURCE: Berscheid, Snyder, and Omoto (1989).

Berscheid and her colleagues interviewed all of the respondents who had listed a romantic partner as the person with whom they shared their closest current relationship. Six months after that, the partners were contacted again. Would the initial closeness as measured by the RCI predict the length of time the couples stayed in their relationships? As Figure 7-5 indicates, the answer is yes. Couples still in their relationships nine months after the initial testing were those who scored highest on closeness; low closeness scores successfully predicted early breakups of the relationships. Apparently closeness does help a relationship to endure.

Keith Davis (1985) has reported the results of research identifying what he refers to as the tapestry of love. Love, like very close friendship, includes the partners' enjoyment of each other, their acceptance, trust, respect, mutual assistance, confiding, understanding, and spontaneity. But love has more. Davis's schematic drawing

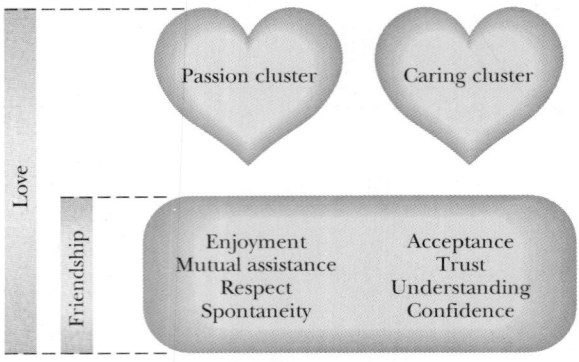

FIGURE 7-6 Love and friendship
The initial model: Love is friendship plus the "passion cluster" and the "caring cluster."
SOURCE: Davis (1985).

of love and friendship can be found in Figure 7-6. In addition to all of the factors involved in friendship, love contains two other clusters of factors: passion and caring. Passion includes the concept of fascination: lovers tend to pay attention to each other even when they should be involved in some other activity. For example, a lover may not be able to concentrate on her or his homework because she or he is able to think only of the other. Passion also includes exclusiveness; that is, giving the romantic relationship priority over all other relationships in one's life. And passion includes sexual desire—wanting physical intimacy with the partner. The desire for physical intimacy may not be acted on if it conflicts with moral or religious values or because of practical considerations (such as fear of pregnancy), but the desire is there nonetheless.

Love, according to Davis's analysis, also includes a caring cluster that has two components. One is "giving the utmost." Davis reminds us to consider O. Henry's famous short story "The Gift of the Magi." In that story, a man pawns his watch to get enough money to give his wife a set of combs for her beautiful long hair. Without her husband's knowledge, the wife has cut her hair and sold it to get enough money to buy her husband a gold chain for his watch. Each has given the utmost—and it is an expression of love. The caring cluster also contains the element of "being an advocate or champion" of the other, which is the notion that lovers will always take their part-

ners' side in all disputes and see them as being able to do little wrong.

The caring cluster, similar to Walster and Walster's notion of compassionate love, plays a very important role in the overall love experience (Davis & Todd, 1982). Fehr (1988) asked subjects to rate the importance of 68 attributes to the experience of love. His subjects rated trust, caring, honesty, and friendship as the most important characteristics of love, while passion was seen as more peripheral. Similar findings were reported by Shaver and his colleagues (1987). As Berscheid (1988) has reminded us, we still have much work to do to see how passion and lust interact with caring and respect to fill out a total picture of love.

The study of love by social psychologists is in its earliest stage. There is need for greater richness and complexity in understanding this basic human emotion. One theorist, who has contributed a great deal to the study of love and attraction, nonetheless warns us that "Love scales seem . . . to do to love what intelligence tests do to intelligence. They leave it emasculated or, at least, bloodless" (Sternberg, 1987). Still, the promise and the hope is that we will continue to make progress toward understanding love now that it has become a more legitimate and serious topic in psychology.

Romeo and Juliet—Alive and Well, for the Time Being

One phenomenon that stands out in the literature on love is the poetic attachment of those who fight against all odds to be together. In Shakespeare's play Romeo is a Montague, Juliet a Capulet. Although there had been an intense and long-lasting hatred between the two households, Romeo and Juliet cast eyes on each other and fall in love. The intensity of the love affair is so great that it causes the lovers to abandon their families, marry in secret, feign death, and ultimately commit suicide.

Neither the balance theories that we have examined nor the research on similarity and attraction would have predicted that a Montague could love a Capulet. We might be tempted to say that their relationship existed despite balance pressures to the contrary. Driscoll, Davis, and

TABLE 7-7

The development of closeness in relationships

As partners grow increasingly closer, the following changes take place in their relationship:

1. They interact more often, for longer periods of time, and in a widening array of settings.
2. They attempt to restore proximity when separated, and feel comforted when proximity is regained.
3. They "open up" to each other, in the sense that they disclose secrets and share physical intimacies.
4. They become less inhibited, more willing to share positive and negative feelings, and to praise and criticize each other.
5. They develop their own communication system, and become ever more efficient in using it.
6. They increase their ability to map and anticipate each other's views of social reality.
7. They begin to synchronize their goals and behavior, and develop stable interaction patterns.
8. They increase their investment in the relationship, thus enhancing its importance in their life space.
9. They begin increasingly to feel that their separate interests are inextricably tied to the well-being of their relationship.
10. They increase their liking, trust, and love for each other.
11. They see the relationship as irreplaceable, or at least as unique.
12. They more and more relate to others as a couple rather than an individuals.

SOURCE: Burgess and Huston (1979).

Lipetz (1972), however, proposed that the intensity of a love relationship may increase *because* of interference from parents to stop it. These investigators employed a love scale much like Rubin's and found that couples scored higher on the scale as their perception of their parents' opposition to the relationship increased. In a similar vein, Rubin found that when lovers were of different religious faiths, the intensity of the love relationship measured by the scale was greater than when they were of the same faith.

Apparently the difficulties and turmoils that couples face—such as parental opposition and religious differences—can be associated with intense love relationships, and indeed those difficulties and turmoils may contribute to the intensity. But the "Romeo and Juliet effect" may not last forever. Rubin found that the strength of interfaith relationships was enhanced for couples who had been going together for less than 18 months, but that among couples who had been together for a longer period, the pattern was reversed—couples of the same faith were higher on the love scale. One reason for the reversal may be that a relationship subjected to external pressures for a long time can begin to crumble.

Kelley and his colleagues (Kelley, 1979; Braiker & Kelley, 1979) have examined the consequences of nonreligious conflict among ongoing couples. They found that conflict, over the short term, was not disruptive to the growth and continuance of intimate relationships. However, unresolved conflict that endures over time does seem to chip away at the strength of the relationship (Rands, Levinger & Mellinger, 1981).

Most social psychologists agree that the concepts that determine interpersonal attraction are relevant for the beginning stage of long-term intimate relationships. Present rewards, anticipation of future rewards, assessments of the costs, and a concern for equity all play roles in initiating and maintaining relationships (Altman, 1974; Levinger, 1980). A number of theorists have gone on to suggest that relationships proceed through a series of orderly stages as they become more and more intimate.

Most people experience loneliness at some point in their lives. It becomes a serious problem when a person lacks intimate social relationships for a long period of time.

Backman (1981) and Secord and Backman (1974) have discussed their view of the stages that a relationship goes through en route to becoming intimate. First, there is an *exploration* stage, in which the possible rewards and costs of a relationship are explored. Second, there is a *bargaining* stage, in which the partners negotiate the terms of the relationship. This is not done in a formal bargaining session, of course, but there is a period of time during which partners must "feel out" the ground rules of the relationship. They learn which behaviors are rewarding, which are costly, and how to maximize the joint benefits. Third, there is a *commitment* stage, characterized by increasing dependency on each other and on the relationship. Finally, Backman posits an *institu-*

tionalization stage, characterized by the emergence of shared expectations. It is also characterized by a recognition both by the partners and by observers that the relationship is exclusive.

Other theorists have discussed slightly different views of the stages through which intimate relationships develop (Levinger, 1980; Scanzoni, 1979). Research has not yet discriminated among the various approaches. But while there may be disagreement about how to characterize the various stages, most theorists do agree on the changes that take place in the way partners act toward each other in deepening relationships (Berscheid, 1985). These changes have been summarized nicely by Burgess and Huston (1979) and are presented in Table 7-7.

Chapter Seven   Attraction and Close Relationships

Loneliness

Intimacy in relationships has a flip side that has been receiving increasing attention from social psychologists (Wheeler, Reis & Nezlek, 1983). People who do not have a reasonable number of relationships or whose relationships are not intimate suffer the damaging unpleasant emotion of loneliness. The experience of loneliness is widespread. Weiss (1973) cites national survey data. When people were asked, "During the past few weeks, did you ever feel very lonely or remote from other people?" 26% indicated that they did.

What is this experience? There is good evidence that it is actually two experiences that share a common core. Weiss (1973, 1974) has called our attention to the two kinds of loneliness. One is **social loneliness.** Here people feel lonely because of a lack of connectedness in a social network; they do not have a sufficient number of friends and companions with whom to share common interests and activities. The other loneliness is **emotional loneliness,** which derives from the lack of an intimate attachment to another person. Emotional loneliness is related to the quality of a person's relationships, while social loneliness is related to the quantity of relationships.

Russell and her colleagues (1984) asked 1,000 students at the University of Iowa about loneliness. They found evidence that, although the experiences of loneliness had a common core, there were two distinct versions, as described by Weiss. They found that social loneliness was evoked when people felt a lack of satisfying friendship patterns, whereas emotional loneliness was evoked in the absence of a satisfying romantic relationship.

ever, are not always so simple. Many factors other than attraction, or the lack of it, dictate whether a relationship will continue to develop or end.

Levinger (1976) has proposed that the continuance of a relationship depends on its "cohesiveness." Cohesiveness has three forces acting on it. The first is the attractiveness of the relationship itself. This is a multifaceted concept but basically involves a consideration of whether the rewards in the relationship are worth the cost. Is the relationship satisfying? Does it make both of the partners feel that their psychological investment is worthwhile? In this regard, we have already seen that an assessment of pleasure in a lasting relationship is not only a function of one's own personal rewards and costs but also a function of perceived equity (Walster, Berscheid & Walster, 1978) and a concern for joint outcomes (Kelley & Thibaut, 1978). The second factor operating on cohesiveness is the potential alternatives to the relationship. Good relationships may be broken if better ones exist or are imagined. Poor relationships may be continued if they provide some minimal satisfaction and there are no alternatives on the horizon. Finally, cohesiveness is a function of the barriers that constrain the partners in the relationship. Barriers are factors that serve as part of the costs of terminating the relationship. They may be institutional—as in the necessity to obtain a divorce to end a marriage; they may be social—as in ridicule or ostracism. These factors not only affect cohesiveness directly, but they may also interact. For example, Berscheid and Campbell (1981) point out that as divorce becomes less difficult to get, more eligible people become available as potential partners in a new relationship. Having more potential partners available increases the likelihood that partners in an existing relationship may find an even more desirable partner outside of their relationship.

Breaking Up: Is It Hard to Do?

Why do relationships end? Logically, it would seem that when two people no longer like each other, their relationship will end. Life and love, how-

emotional loneliness Loneliness caused by lack of an intimate attachment to another person.
social loneliness Loneliness caused by lack of connectedness to a social network.

When Relationships Go Sour: Reacting to Dissatisfaction

Songwriter Paul Simon once wrote, "There must be fifty ways to leave your lover." Actually, recent research has identified two. Rusboldt and her colleagues (Rusboldt & Zembrot, 1983) have embarked on a systematic look at the way in which people respond to the potential dissolution of relationships. In one study, they asked 25 male and 25 female students at the University of Kentucky to describe a time when they became dissatisfied with a romantic relationship. In a second study, the same request was made of 18 residents of Lexington, Kentucky, who ranged in age from 20 to 67. Their responses were analyzed and found to fit into four major categories.

One response to a dissatisfying relationship is to *exit*. Reactions of this type were actively destructive to the relationship. "I told him I couldn't take it any more, and that it was over," and "I slapped her around a bit, I'm ashamed to say," were examples of the exit reaction.

Another way of responding to dissatisfaction was also destructive to the relationship's continuation. Unlike the exit response, this reaction is passive. Rusboldt and Zembrot call it *neglect*. "I guess I just kind of quit—I didn't try to salvage it—I just didn't know what to do," and "Mostly my response was silence to anything he might say, ignoring him," were examples of the neglect approach.

Alternatively, people who are dissatisfied with a relationship may act to salvage that relationship. Some of Rusboldt and Zembrot's respondents used the *voice* reaction. These people took active measures to try to make things better. "We talked it over and worked things out" was typical of this approach. And finally, some people answered with a variety of *loyalty* responses. In general, these were reactions that tried to keep the relationship going, but in a passive manner. "I loved her so much," said one student, "that I ignored her faults." "I prayed a lot," said another, "and left things in God's hands."

Jealousy: Reacting to Threat to a Relationship

Jealousy is a potential emotional consequence whenever a relationship is formed. Losing your partner, or the possibility of losing your partner, creates a complex of emotions, thoughts, and behaviors that can be devastating indeed. What makes jealousy different from similar emotions, such as anger? White (1981) has proposed that romantic jealousy is based on two losses: first, the loss of rewards that a partner enjoys in the relationship; second, the blow to self-esteem that occurs at the idea of rejection by the romantic partner.

Mathes, Adams, and Davies (1985) described five situations to students at Western Illinois University. They were asked to imagine that they had just lost their boyfriend or girlfriend to a rival or to plain rejection (your partner decides he [she] does not love you anymore) or to destiny (your partner moves to a faraway city) or to fate (your partner is killed in an automobile crash). Other students were assigned to a no-loss control condition. Mathes and his colleagues reasoned that all of the loss conditions share one common element: they all deprived the person of the rewards that he or she enjoyed in the romantic partnership. But the rival and rejection conditions should be very damaging to the person's self-esteem. Losing a partner because he or she had to take a job in another city is mildly relevant to self-esteem, whereas the fate condition does not involve self-esteem at all. Mathes and his associates found that the emotion of jealousy was indeed greatest at the loss of a partner to a rival and least at the loss of a partner to fate. Jealousy does seem to depend not only on the loss of the rewards that the relationship held for the person, but also on the magnitude of the blow to self-esteem.

In general, it may be said that social psychologists' interest in studying ongoing relationships is increasing (Berscheid, 1985). Much of the focus has been on the sequence through which casual relationships of liking turn into the more intimate relationship of loving (Backman, 1981;

Levinger, 1980) and in describing the structure of the intimate relationship (Kelley, 1979). Research on the dissolution of intimate relationships is still in its infancy but it will undoubtedly grow and continue.

Summary

Interpersonal *attraction,* the initial step in the formation of personal relationships, is the positive attitude held by one person toward another. Attraction is based on many factors, one of which is our preference for balanced or symmetrical relationships. Newcomb's *A-B-X model* posits a "strain toward symmetry." For example, if A and B like each other, they will both tend to feel similarly toward X.

The *reward model* of attraction considers attraction to be based on associations with positive rewards. Pleasure in an interpersonal relationship depends on the rewards and costs experienced by both partners. *Equity* exists when the ratio of a person's rewards to costs is the same as his or her perception of the partner's rewards-to-cost ratio. Equitable relationships are more pleasurable and last longer than inequitable ones. Also, lasting relationships are characterized by a concern with maximizing the joint outcomes of the two partners. Research has shown that people in short-term *exchange relationships* keep track of their contributions and rewards, whereas people in more meaningful *communal relationships* do not care about keeping such records.

One of the most frequently researched aspects of liking is the relationship between similarity and attraction. In general, Byrne and his colleagues have shown that similarity leads to attraction, especially when the similarity is on important issues.

We feel pressure to reciprocate attraction. We tend to like those who we believe are attracted to us. In addition, *propinquity* (physical closeness) often produces attraction.

There is evidence that physical attractiveness leads to liking. This is true in heterosexual situations, but has other, more surprising effects as well. In simulated jury situations, attractive people are less often judged to be guilty of committing crimes than are unattractive people. In classroom situations, the work of attractive people is judged to be of greater value than that of unattractive people. Physical attractiveness appears to matter more to people who are high self-monitors.

Physical beauty can have negative consequences. First, attractive people may discount much of the positive feedback they receive from others. Second, we may be seen as less attractive than we are when we are viewed in physical or temporal proximity to highly attractive others.

Some research in interpersonal attraction has examined the more unusual features that lead to attraction. Although we tend to like people who compliment us, it has been shown that insults can lead to greater attraction if a pattern of comments about us begins with insults and ends with compliments. Second, people of superior ability who have clumsy accidents can be seen as more attractive because of the accidents.

STOP, THINK, & UNDERSTAND

1. Why do we tend to evaluate physically attractive people more positively than we do people who are not physically attractive?

2. What are the major differences between liking and loving according to both Rubin and Davis?

3. What distinguishes jealousy from other strong emotions?

4. What kind of situational variables might contribute to initial attraction for another person?

5. In terms of underlying features and duration and stability of relationships, what distinguishes passionate and compassionate love?

Attempts have been made to distinguish between liking and love. Rubin is among those who have validated scales that are specifically geared to the emotion of love. He has defined love as involving the components of (1) caring—the feeling that another's satisfactions are as important as your own; (2) attachment—the need to be with the other and to be cared for, and (3) intimacy—the bond between two people. Davis found that love, like friendship, includes partners' enjoyment of each other, their acceptance, trust, respect, understanding, and spontaneity.

In addition, love, as distinct from friendship, includes passion and caring.

Two-factor theories contend that the experience of love is a function of physiological arousal and a cognitive label. If that cognitive label implies love, then the emotion will be experienced as love.

Recent research has also focused on emotions related to love: jealousy and loneliness. Research has also considered the ways in which relationships go sour. The stages of the breakdown of the love relationship have been attracting the attention of social psychologists.

Key Terms

A-B-X model	*compassionate love*	*mere exposure*
attraction	*emotional loneliness*	*propinquity*
balance theory	*equity theory*	*reward model*
communal	*exchange relationship*	*romantic love*
relationships	*ingratiation*	*social loneliness*

Suggested Readings

Berscheid, E. (1985). Interpersonal attraction. In G. Lindzey and E. Aronson (Eds.), *Handbook of social psychology* (3rd ed.). Reading, Mass.: Addison-Wesley.

Berscheid, E., & Walster, E. (1978). *Interpersonal attraction.* Reading, Mass.: Addison-Wesley.

Byrne, D. (1971). *The attraction paradigm.* New York: Academic Press.

Davis, K. E. (1985, February). Near and dear: Friendship and love compared. *Psychology Today,* pp. 22-30.

Jones, E. E., & Wortman, C. B. (1973). *Ingratiation: An attributional approach.* Morristown, N.J.: General Learning Press.

Kelley, H. H. (1979). *Personal relationships: Their structures and processes.* Hillsdale, N.J.: Erlbaum.

Rubin, Z. (1973). *Liking and loving: An invitation to social psychology.* New York: Holt, Rinehart & Winston.

Chapter Eight

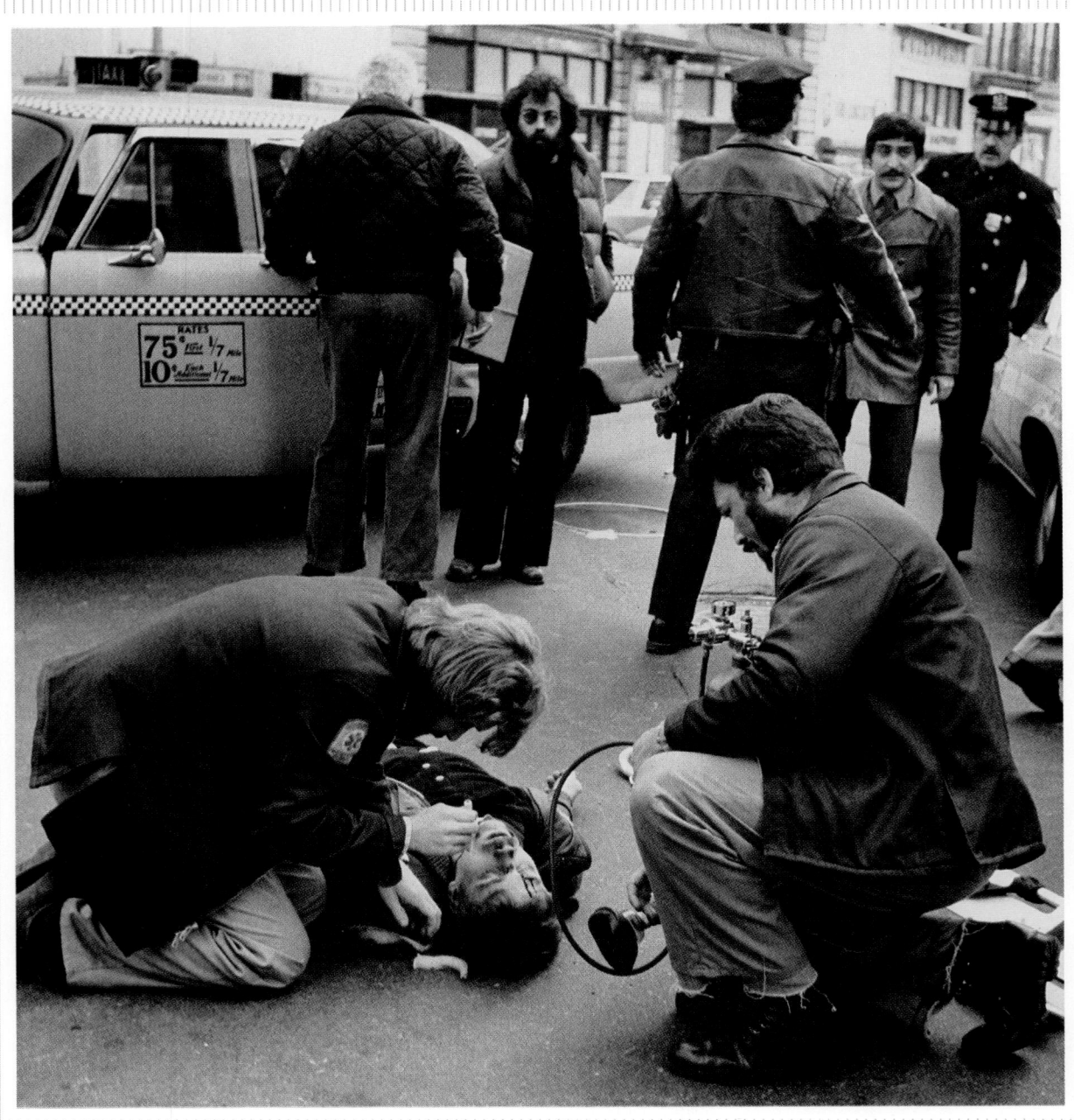

Altruism:
Extending the Self to Others

*J*erry Schemmel worked his way through the dark and noxious smoke of the wreckage. His hands shielded his eyes and mouth as he followed the infant's cry. He did not stop to think of his own safety. Amidst the panic and the confusion of the airplane wreckage, amidst the fire and the smoke, a small human being was in trouble, and Jerry was on his way to help.

It had been a beautiful day in the Midwest that Wednesday. United Airlines flight 232 had taken off from Denver into a cloudless sky on what was supposed to be a routine flight to Chicago. But July 19, 1989, was going to be anything but routine for the 290 passengers and crew aboard the jumbo DC-10 jetliner. About an hour and a half into the flight, the plane was cruising over the state of Iowa. Lunch was being served. Jerry Schemmel and the other passengers were watching an in-flight video. Suddenly they heard a loud bang and the aircraft shuddered. The number 2 engine, mounted in the tail of the aircraft, had exploded, sending jagged debris through the control surfaces of the tail. Flight 232 was at 37,000 feet and it was out of control.

For 30 minutes the pilot and his crew struggled to maneuver the aircraft into position to touch down on the runway at Sioux City. But 500 feet short of the runway, the plane's right wingtip struck the ground. The plane cartwheeled and burst into flames. No one who saw the crash and the gigantic fireball that followed believed anyone could have survived.

Miraculously, the plane struck and burst in such a way that more than half of the passengers survived the impact and the initial explosion. Some climbed out through openings in the plane and walked calmly to safety. But some, such as Jerry Schemmel, had other things on their minds. Although his own route to safety was clearly visible, Schemmel chose not to use it. A baby was crying, and Schemmel was determined to find it. With smoke blanketing the airplane and flames engulfing the craft, it seemed only a matter of minutes before the remaining fuel tanks would catch fire and all remaining passengers would perish in the explosion. Still Schemmel continued his search. He came closer to the sound, searched the floor with his hands, and found 1-year-old Sabrina Michaelson. He whisked up the infant and carried her to safety. Even better news came later. Sabrina's parents had also survived the crash, and the three were reunited by evening.

In all, 170 people survived the crash of United flight 232. Some of them survived because other passengers, strangers just moments before, risked their lives to help people in need.

What motivates people to help others? What makes them risk their lives or safety for the benefit of others? Is altruism a basic human motive, or do people help others to reduce their own tension and anxiety? When we try to answer important questions such as these, it is sometimes helpful to examine situations in which people do not help. And so we come to the story of Kitty Genovese. The year was 1964; the place was Austin Street in the borough of Queens in New York City; the time was 3:20 A.M.

Kitty Genovese was on her way to her apartment building. Suddenly a man appeared, grabbed her, and began to attack her. Kitty screamed, waking some of the neighbors. She struggled to get free and managed to reach a street corner. Here she could be seen and heard by more of her neighbors. She yelled, "He stabbed me! Please help me!"

Lights went on in several apartments overlooking the street. From their windows above, the neighbors could see Genovese escape again, but she was bleeding. She did not get far. The attacker pursued his victim and struck again. Genovese screamed, "I'm dying! I'm dying!" This time the attack was final. This time there were no more screams and no more escapes. Kitty Genovese lay dead of stab wounds in an incident that was thought to have lasted nearly three-quarters of an hour.

What of those neighbors who were awakened that night? Reporters from the *New York Times* sought to determine what the people whose windows faced that part of Austin Street did after they heard the screams. They discovered that at least 38 people heard the screams. At least 38 people had gone to their windows, but not one of them had come to the woman's aid. Not one of them had so much as lifted the telephone to call the police (Rosenthal, 1964). Had even one person done so, Kitty Genovese might have been saved.

Passenger Jerry Schemmel remained in the wreckage of United's flight 232, risking his life while searching for a crying infant, whom he did find. What motivates such pro-social behavior? Can it be learned?

In this chapter we will look at the reasons that people help others and the reasons people refrain from helping. We know that the world has had its heroes who have given freely of themselves for humanity. We know that there are many Jerry Schemmels who have saved people's lives despite threats to their own safety. And we know too well that there have been incidents like that on Austin Street, in which not just one but dozens of people refused to give even the smallest degree of aid to a victim whose life might have been spared had someone helped.

Why Do People Help?

Altruism vs. Egoism

What motivates people like Jerry Schemmel to help others? What motivates so many of us to help our fellow human beings when they are in need? From the proverbial boy scout helping an elderly woman across the street to acts of heroism, people frequently help each other. Why?

There are at least two perspectives on why people help. These perspectives deal with fundamental questions of human nature that philosophers have wrestled with over the centuries. Do we do things for others because human beings are basically good, or must there be some ulterior, self-serving explanation for our apparent helpfulness? Let us examine this distinction. What is a self-serving motive to help others? At a very obvious level, we would not be surprised to find that a person helped an elderly gentleman across the street if that gentleman were known for bestowing lavish tips on people who helped him. If we were to witness this helping incident, we might suspect that the helping was self-serving. Clearly the reward the help-giver might obtain could explain his action. In the absence of a reward, we would probably view the behavior as

What motivates people to help others? Does this child help his grandmother from a sense of altruism or egoism?

selfless—done with genuine regard for the plight of another person. But here we have opened up a fascinating and subtle question. (We will return to the question of rewards later, when we investigate the question "When do people help?") For the present, we will focus our attention on situations in which there is no obvious reward for helpful behavior.

Think about times when you have witnessed someone being helpful. Perhaps a student knew that her roommate was ill and volunteered to attend an important class for her and take notes. One thought you may have had was that this student behaved altruistically. She behaved solely out of regard for her friend's feelings, with no personal satisfactions or rewards involved. Or you may have thought that the student, in a sense, acted to please herself. For example, the student may have been distressed by her friend's illness. To leave her friend without notes for the important class might have contributed even more to the student's distress. So she volunteered to attend the class because that action reduced her own distress. That is, it was rewarding for her to act on behalf of her roommate. No one can argue that she acted in a helpful manner and her roommate benefited from her behavior. In this exam-

ple, she is not attempting to have the favor returned later (although this consideration may sometimes be a cause of helpful behavior). Nonetheless, the question remains: Whom is the helper pleasing? Is she focused on the need of her roommate or is she reducing her own distress?

Auguste Comte, the nineteenth-century philosopher, was one of the first to comment on this distinction. He believed that some helping behavior was based on a person's own sense of self-gratification. He referred to this as **egoism.** At the same time, he believed that people also were motivated to "live for others." To describe this basically unselfish desire, Comte coined the term **altruism.** Why, then, does the helper help? Why did Jerry Schemmel help? If we focus on egoism, we will look for such rewards as self-congratulations ("I am a pretty decent person for doing what I did"), escape from guilt or shame ("I could never live with myself if I didn't help"), and relief from distress ("I felt awful when I saw the person in need; *I* felt better when I helped").

Altruism, on the other hand, has as its ultimate goal a benefit to another person. The focus is solely on the other, without conscious attention focused on one's own self-interest. Daniel Batson and his colleagues (Batson, 1987; Batson et al., 1981; Batson et al., 1987; Batson et al., 1988) have proposed that true altruism comes from **empathy**—feelings that are congruent with the feelings and perceived welfare of another person (Batson and Oleson, 1990). When a person is in need, empathy would suggest the emotions of sympathy, compassion, and tenderness. According to Batson, empathy creates a motivation for altruism, whose ultimate goal is the benefiting of the person in need.

The **empathy-altruism hypothesis** states that empathy gives rise to altruism, and that this is but *one* reason that people help. The empathy-altruism link does not preclude other motivations for acting in a helpful fashion. As Figure 8-1 indicates, Batson and his colleagues believe that the relief of personal distress—that is, egoism—is one motive for helping, but that the more selfless concern for others which we call altruism is yet another.

In order to test the empathy-altruism hypothesis experimentally, Batson and his colleagues have worked out a few standard scenarios

Mother Theresa's ministrations to the poor and dying have often been held up as an example of pure altruism. Would it make any difference if her charity and care were motivated by concern for otherworldly rewards rather than empathy?

in which subjects witness a person in distress and then decide whether or not to offer help. In one of them (Batson et al., 1981) female students were introduced to a person known as Elaine. The subjects were observed in an experiment in which Elaine was considered the worker. Elaine's job was to perform a sequence of recall tasks for two minutes. At random intervals, Elaine was to receive a series of electric shocks. Subjects watched the proceedings on videotape, but believed they were watching live action on closed-circuit TV. The tape made it clear that Elaine was very disturbed by the electric shock. The subjects were then informed that Elaine had had an earlier experience with shocks that made them extremely difficult to bear. Naturally, the subjects were disturbed. The experimenters manipulated the attribution that the subjects made about their feelings. At a prior session Elaine and the participants had filled out a questionnaire to help

the subjects form an impression of Elaine. Elaine's questionnaire was filled out by a confederate of the experimenter so responses were either similar or dissimilar to the subject. Half of the subjects read a similar questionnaire and thus were made to attribute their arousal to empathy, while the other half read a dissimilar questionnaire and were made to attribute their arousal to personal distress.

Subjects were then given an opportunity to help Elaine by trading places with her and receiv-

---

altruism An unselfish desire to help others; an unselfishly helpful act.

egoism A tendency to focus on one's own gratification; behavior directed at self-gratification.

empathy The ability to share in another's feelings.

empathy-altruism hypothesis The hypothesis that helping behavior is based, at least in part, on feelings of empathy with another person.

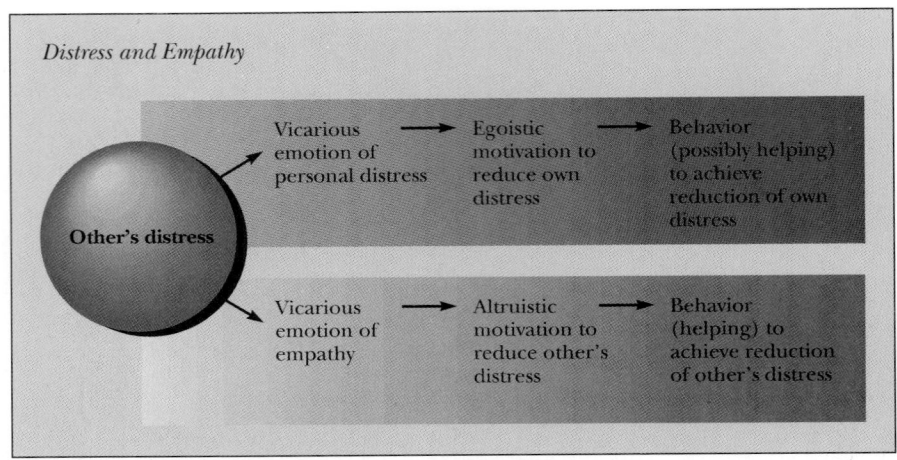

FIGURE 8-1 According to Batson et al. (1987), witnessing another person's distress can lead either to personal distress or to empathy. Each leads to its own motivation and behavioral goal.
SOURCE: Batson, Fultz, and Schoenrade (1987).

ing the shock in her place. Which subjects would help? Batson and his colleagues predicted that both the distressed and the empathic subjects would help. Empathic subjects would help because of their true regard for Elaine. Distressed subjects would help because of the personal, egoistic relief they would experience if they traded places with Elaine. Therefore, Batson and his colleagues introduced a manipulation designed to differentiate between the two approaches. Half of the subjects were led to believe that they were free to leave the experiment whenever they wished. Elaine was given blocks of ten trials on which she was given shocks. Easy-escape subjects were told they could decide whether to switch places with Elaine, stay and watch, or leave. In this condition, then, subjects had an easy alternative way to relieve their personal distress. If it made them uncomfortable to see Elaine suffer, they could leave. The other half of the subjects were in the difficult-escape condition. They had to sit and observe Elaine throughout the ten trials. If these subjects were feeling distressed, they had only one way to relieve their discomfort: they would have to switch places with Elaine.

The results confirmed Batson and his colleagues' predictions. Whether escape was difficult or easy, empathic subjects tended to help Elaine. They seemed to be responding to her suffering, not to their own discomfort. Distressed

subjects, on the other hand, helped Elaine only if that was the only way to relieve their discomfort. If it was easy to leave the situation, distressed subjects chose that route.

Batson and his colleagues (1983) replicated this experiment and obtained further support for the importance of the distinction between empathic and personal-distress arousal. Instead of manipulating what subjects thought they were experiencing after watching Elaine, they asked subjects to describe their emotions after watching Elaine suffer. On the basis of their responses, the subjects were categorized as either personally distressed or empathic. Once again, subjects who were categorized as empathic chose to help whether escape (leaving the situation) was easy or difficult. Distressed subjects helped primarily if leaving was difficult. The data are shown in Figure 8-2.

The Egoism Hypothesis Revised

Does the work we have just described lead to the conclusion that people can help others purely for altruistic reasons? Cialdini and his colleagues (1987) do not think so. They suggest that Batson and his associates may have been taking the wrong view of egoism. Perhaps it is not distress in the sense of tension, agitation, and so forth but rather *sadness* that people experience when they see

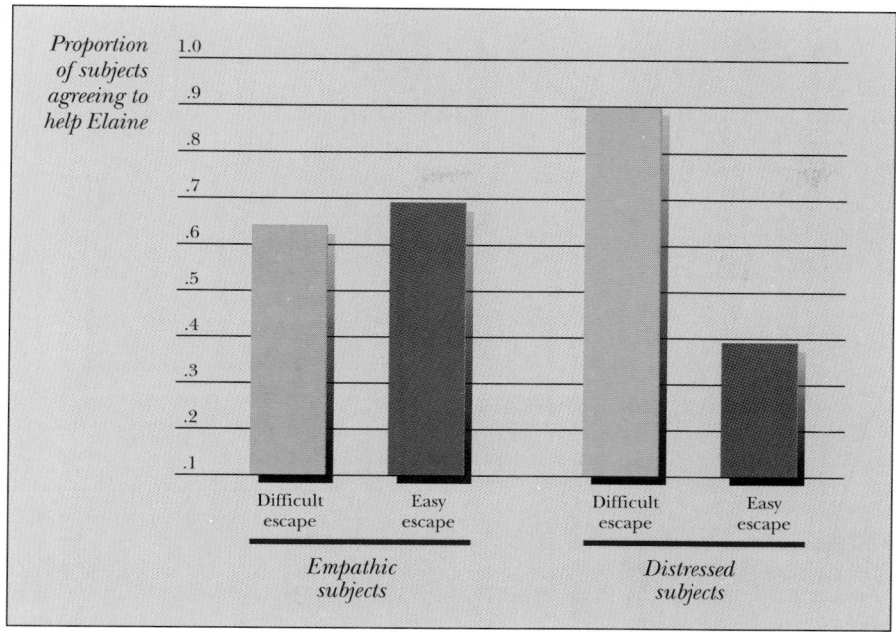

FIGURE 8-2 Results of Batson et al.'s (1983) study comparing empathic versus distressed feelings and ease of escape on the probability of giving help
SOURCE: Batson, O'Quinn, Fultz, Vanderplas, and Isen (1983).

someone in need. They feel sad and depressed. They need to reduce that feeling and elevate their mood. Helping the person in need relieves that sadness in a way that leaving the scene does not. This is an interesting twist on the concept of egoism. It suggests that we help others in order to manage our own mood. Seeing others in a state of need causes us to feel low, and helping is seen as a way of gratifying our own need to feel happy. Therefore, Cialdini and his colleagues are not surprised that empathic subjects help a needy person even when they have the chance to escape. Escape does not accomplish the task; it does not elevate mood, and therefore these subjects continue to help the person in need.

In one study conducted to test this notion, Cialdini and his associates (1987) reasoned that subjects who interpret their emotion as empathy will help a victim under almost all conditions, except when they think that helping will not serve to make them happy. In order to test this hypothesis, the investigators had subjects witness a person in need (named Carol in this study), and then gave them an opportunity to help her. Subjects were instructed either to be objective when par-

ticipating in the research (low empathy) or to imagine how the other person felt (high empathy). The innovative manipulation was to have half of all subjects take a "mood-fixing" drug after observing Carol's plight. Subjects ingested a substance identified as "Mnemoxine" (actually a placebo) and were told, "This is the mood you'll be in for the next 30 minutes or so. . . . It preserves whatever mood you are in when it takes effect." If subjects were saddened when they listened to Carol's difficulties, they could do nothing to elevate their mood—that was the alleged result of the Mnemoxine. To the investigators, this would be the key test. Subjects in the empathy-set condition could still act altruistically; they could still help Carol for her sake (altruism). However, they could not help Carol in order to make themselves feel happier (egoism). Would they nonetheless help?

In support of the revised egoism hypothesis, subjects in the empathy–mood-fixing condition chose not to help Carol under these conditions. Figure 8-3 demonstrates that only subjects in the empathy condition who did not believe their mood had been fixed by the Mnemoxine chose to help

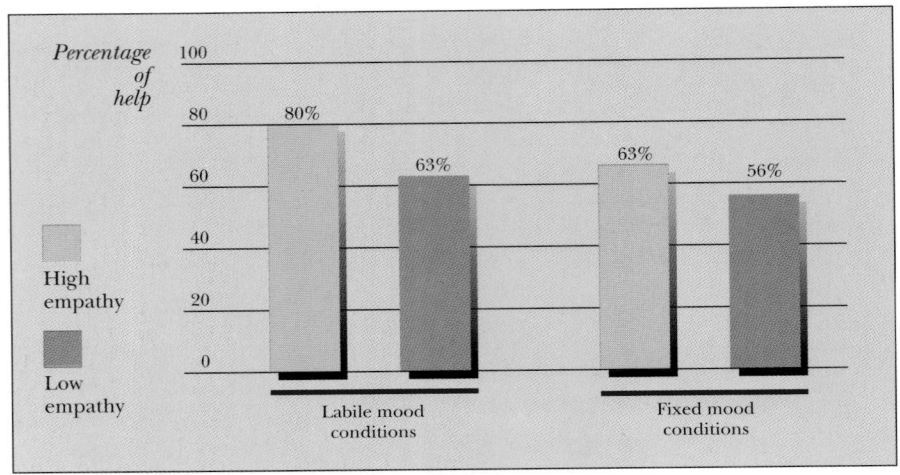

FIGURE 8-3 Proportion of subjects that helped Carol as a function of empathy and the fixedness of their mood
SOURCE: Cialdini et al. (1987).

the person in need. Cialdini and his colleagues (1987) concluded that these subjects decided to help Carol in order to make themselves feel better, and that the decision was not motivated by altruism.

Reprise: The Debate Continues

Why, then, do people help others? The debate between those who believe that people help others—at least sometimes—for altruistic motives and those who believe helping is always motivated by self-interest has been fascinating. A definitive answer remains elusive, however. Batson and Oleson (1990) have taken issue with the Mnemoxine manipulation used by Cialdini and his colleagues on the grounds that the pill may have distracted subjects from the plight of the victim. Using a similar procedure (this time the mood-fixing pill was called "Memorin"), a different group of investigators (Schroeder et al., 1988) found that subjects did help a person in need despite the mood-fixing pill if they were experiencing empathy.

Other investigators (Smith, Keating & Stotland, 1989) have examined this productive debate and concluded that there may be a middle position that can help to disentangle some of the conflicting evidence. They suggest the importance of "empathic joy" in mediating the relation of empathy and altruism. They propose that people will act to help others but are in need of feedback from the victim; that is, some evidence that the victim has been helped by the intervention. Such feedback gives them a feeling of empathic joy. Although this feeling is egoistic in the sense that we all like to feel good, it is also empathic in the sense that we are sharing the good feeling we have imparted to the person we have helped.

Whom Do We Help?
People We Like

Some people are more likely than others to get our help if they need it. It is quite obvious that a member of the family who is in trouble will receive our quick assistance. In most cases, friends will be helped more readily than strangers, although Tesser and Smith (1980) did show that if helping means the helper might be embarrassed, he or she is less likely to help a friend than a stranger.

However, as we have seen, strangers may or may not be helped even if their need seems urgent. It is not surprising, then, that some research efforts have shown that greater help is given to people who are liked than to those who are dis-

    Chapter Eight   Altruism: Extending the Self to Others

liked (Goodstadt, 1971). Benson, Karabenick, and Lerner (1976) conducted a field experiment in an airline terminal to test the effect of physical attractiveness on the likelihood of receiving help. The subjects were persons who used a particular telephone booth in which a completed graduate school application, a photograph, and a stamped envelope had been placed. It was apparent that the application was to be mailed but that the applicant had left it in the booth. Would the subject offer help by placing the application in the envelope and mailing it? Observations of the subjects showed that their responses depended on the attractiveness of the applicant shown in the photograph. The subjects were much more likely to mail the application if the photograph was of an attractive rather than an unattractive person.

Similar Others

A related point is that we appear to be more disposed to helping those we perceive as being like-minded. For example, Emswiller, Deaux, and Willits (1971) had students, dressed either as hippies or in more conservative attire, request a dime for a phone call from passersby. The results indicated that people were far more likely to comply with the request when it came from a similar other. Hippies were significantly more generous to other hippies, and conservatively dressed individuals were more generous to the straight-looking requesters.

Deserving Others

Imagine that the person in line in front of you at the checkout counter at the supermarket turns to you and says, "Excuse me, I seem to be short on cash. Could you give me some money?" Would it make a difference to you if you noticed that the person was buying something that was not essential? A study conducted by Bickman and Kamzan (1973) suggests that it would make a big difference. Subjects in this study were far more likely to give a female shopper a dime when she was buying a carton of milk than when she was buying a package of cookie dough. Fewer than half the subjects helped out the woman when she was buying cookie dough, but two-thirds helped her buy milk. Moreover, the nature of the item

(hence the woman's perceived deservingness) had a considerably larger effect on the subjects' generosity than the race of the requester. Thus we appear to help people whose needs we judge to be legitimate.

When Do We Help? Situations that Promote Helping
When We Are Rewarded

Much of our behavior, our values, and our goals is molded and shaped by the pattern of rewards and punishments that we receive. General patterns of helping behavior are probably shaped in childhood by a myriad of events involving parents, siblings, and peers. In more specific cases, a tendency to help may depend on the way in which similar helping was very recently rewarded. If I try to help a senior citizen cross the street and get kicked in the shins for my efforts, I probably will not try it again soon. On the other hand, if that person responds with great warmth and pleasure and even offers me a tea biscuit in return, I will probably be more inclined to help on the next such occasion.

Using a situation not unlike this one, Moss and Page (1972) set out on the streets of Dayton, Ohio, to find a relationship between rewarded helping and subsequent helping. A passerby was first approached by a stranger and asked directions to a particular part of town. Almost always the passerby willingly gave the stranger directions. The stranger, actually an experimental confederate, responded by saying something positive, such as "Thank you"; or by say something negative, such as grumbling, "I can't understand what you're saying. Never mind, I'll ask someone else"; or by saying something neutral, such as "OK." After being reinforced positively or negatively (or not at all in the control condition), the passerby next saw a woman drop a small bag on the ground and apparently fail to notice it. Who stopped to help the woman in this staged accident? Figure 8-4 shows that people who had been positively reinforced in their earlier encounter with a stranger were much more likely to try to help the woman retrieve her pack-

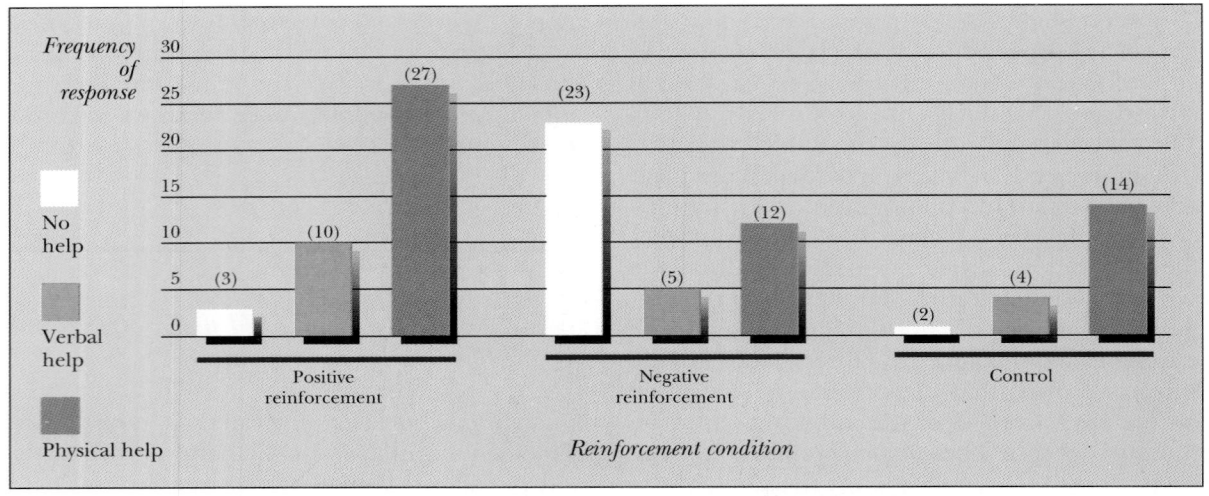

FIGURE 8-4 The frequency and type of helping after being positively or negatively reinforced
NOTE: Physical help = helping to pick up a dropped bag; verbal help = calling attention to dropped bag.
SOURCE: Moss and Page (1972).

age than people who had been negatively reinforced the last time they offered help to someone. Rushton and Teachinan (1978) found support for a similar proposition using children as subjects.

When Our Mood Is Good

Strange things happen when we are in a good mood: we may sing on the street, offer our seat to someone on the bus, maybe even offer help to people who need it. Isen (1970) had teachers in a suburban school system believe that they had done either well or poorly at a task. Afterward a confederate entered the room and asked for a contribution to a fund to purchase air conditioning for the school. Teachers who had done well, and presumably felt happy and successful, contributed more money than teachers who had done poorly. Similarly, Isen and Levin (1972) varied the subjects' happiness by sneaking into a telephone booth and planting dimes in the coin-return slot for subjects to find serendipitously. When such a subject came out of the phone booth, a female confederate dropped a pile of manila folders directly in his or her path. Buoyed by their lucky feeling, the subjects who had found

a coin in the phone booth were much more likely to offer help than the subjects who had not been so fortunate (cf. Isen, Clark, & Schwartz, 1976).

In a more recent field experiment, people emerging from a local movie theater were asked to donate money to the Muscular Dystrophy Foundation. Fewer donations were made to the charity if the moviegoers had seen a sad movie than if they had seen a happy movie (Underwood et al., 1977).

Finally, we should note that on some special occasions a good mood does not lead to greater helping, or a bad mood to less helping. Isen and Simmonds (1978) found that people in a good mood do not wish to interrupt their happiness by taking on helping behavior that is itself unpleasant. And Rosenhan, Salovey, and Hargis (1981) showed that the happiness that does lead to helping is happiness that pertains to oneself. They found that if people were made happy because of someone else's good fortune, the happy mood did not lead to greater helping. On the other side of the coin, people who are in a bad mood because of something that happened to them are indeed less likely to be altruistic. But if they are in a bad mood because of something that happened to someone else (a friend, say), they seem to develop greater empathy for the victim

What motivates the "Good Samaritan"? What kind of person sees himself as his brother's keeper? Under what circumstances would you stop to help this man lying on the street?

and thus increase their helping (Thompson, Cowan & Rosenhan, 1980).

When Someone Else Helps

The concept of modeling has wide use in psychology. Many of the things we do are learned from observing the behavior of a model such as a parent, a teacher, or a friend (Bandura & Walters, 1963). If we observe the model acting in a certain way, we are likely to try that behavior ourselves. Bryan and Test (1967) wanted to see whether male motorists would stop on a highway to assist a woman who was trying to fix a flat tire. They found that motorists were much more likely to stop if they had recently passed a scene in which a male driver had stopped to help another woman change a tire. That is, in the presence of a helping model, people were much more likely to help. Macaulay (1970) has given additional support to Bryan and Test's modeling hypothesis; she found that contributions to a Salvation Army collection box increased markedly when a model was observed making a contribution. The

modeling of charitable behavior is perhaps best seen in TV telethons. There we are asked to contribute both because the charitable organization needs the money and because our neighbor from Teaneck, Seattle, Columbus, or Wichita also contributed.

When Time Permits

You are probably familiar with the parable of the Good Samaritan.

> A man was going down from Jerusalem to Jericho and he fell among robbers, who stripped him and beat him, and departed, leaving him half dead. Now by chance a priest was going down the road, and when he saw him he passed by on the other side. So likewise a Levite. . . . But a Samaritan, as he journeyed, came to where he was; and when he saw him, he had compassion on him and bound his wounds . . . then set him on his own beast and brought him to an inn. (Luke 10:29–37)

According to the parable, the religious outcast—the Samaritan—had more goodwill in his heart than the priest and the Levite, who were hurrying off to Jericho to conduct their business. Darley and Batson (1973) used Jesus' story in considering some of the factors that might affect intervention to help those in need. They set up a situation to show (1) that people who are thinking ethical or moral thoughts are no more likely to help a person in need than people who are thinking other thoughts, and (2) that people who are in a hurry to attend to their business will be less likely to help someone in need than people who are not in a hurry.

Students at a theological seminary volunteered to make short speeches. Half of them were asked to speak on the ethical, moral, and social implications of the parable of the Good Samaritan. The other half were asked to make speeches on interesting employment opportunities open to seminarians. The speeches were to be tape-recorded, and the room with the recording equipment was in another building. Half of the subjects were sent on their way with the knowledge that they were quite late for their appointments; the other half believed that they had ample time.

On the route between the two buildings, each of the subjects encountered a man who was sitting in a doorway, head down, eyes closed, not moving. As the subject walked by, the man coughed and groaned.

Did the subject stop to find out what was wrong or to offer assistance? Did it matter whether the subject was thinking about the parable of the Good Samaritan as he passed by the stranger in need? Did it matter whether he, like the Levite and the priest in the parable, was in a hurry to get to his destination? The victim in need of help carefully rated the reaction of each subject on a 6-point scale, ranging from failing to notice the victim at all to insisting on taking him somewhere for help.

The results supported Darley and Batson's predictions. In their words,

> A person not in a hurry may stop and offer help to a person in distress. A person in a hurry is likely to keep going—even if he is hurrying to give a talk on the parable of the Good Samaritan, thus inadvertently confirming the point of the parable. Indeed, on several occasions a seminary student going to give his talk on the parable of the Good Samaritan literally stepped over the victim as he hurried on his way! (p. 107)

Could it be argued that another interpretation of the parable of the Good Samaritan is possible? Batson and his colleagues (1978) suggested that it is conceivable that the priest and the Levite may have made the decision to bypass the needy person because their business in Jericho was so important that it would result in greater good. In sum, the costs of not helping the needy person may have been less than the costs of failing to arrive in Jericho. Batson and his associates repeated the basic procedure of the Darley and Batson study. Half of the subjects were in a hurry; half were not. In addition, some of the subjects were made to believe that their mission was extremely important; the rest thought their mission less urgent. This time, the parable of the Good Samaritan was replicated only when the subject's hurry was combined with his perception that his mission was extremely important.

A note should be added to Good Samaritan studies. Shortly we will discuss the chain of decisions that must be made if we are to decide to offer help to a victim. This chain begins with noticing that the event is occurring. Darley and Batson report that many subjects who were rushing to combat the time pressure placed on them failed to even look in the direction of the groaning victim and denied ever having heard his coughs and groans. The time pressures of our daily lives may cause us to fail to notice events that, from a more dispassionate perspective, would appear to call out for our attention.

When Making the Attribution of Altruism

People who believe that they are altruistic may be more likely to act in an altruistic manner. Earlier we noted that people use instances of behavior and the cues that situations offer to make attributions about themselves and others. Therefore, people who act altruistically may be more apt to act that way in the future if they attribute the cause of their initial behavior to an altruistic disposition.

Paulhus, Shaffer, and Downing (1977) showed that blood donors who were sensitized to the altruistic nature of donating blood (that is, the humanitarianism and selflessness) indicated a greater willingness to donate again in the future than donors who had been sensitized to the personal benefits of the donation (such as the donor's free use of blood-bank supplies). This was particularly true for first-time donors, who were probably less certain of what attribution to make for their own behavior.

In a related context, Batson and his colleagues (1978) showed that people who behaved altruistically might attribute a low degree of altruism to themselves if possible external causes existed for their behavior. Students who entered the University of Kansas administration building were met by an experimental accomplice who requested help in filling out a questionnaire. Some of the subjects received no payment for their help. Others received payment, but were told about it only after they finished providing assistance. Still other subjects were promised payment before agreeing to help. This situation closely resembles the "overjustification" studies of Lepper and his colleagues (Lepper, Greene & Nisbett, 1973), in which intrinsic motivation was undermined by the promise of an attractive reward (as we saw in Chapter 3). As in those studies, the University of Kansas students rated themselves as less altruistic if they helped while knowing of a reward. Even though the reward was a mere 25 cents, the subjects who behaved altruistically and knew about the reward were less able to convince themselves that they helped because of the kind of persons they were. The subjects who learned of the reward only afterward and the subjects who received no reward saw themselves as altruistic. As the study by Paulhus and his colleagues (1977) suggests, such people are likely to behave more altruistically in the future.

When Norms Direct Us to Help

We have already looked at several norms that prescribe altruistic behavior. The general idea that we should give help to people who need it can be termed a **social responsibility norm.** We saw, too, that helping was part of normative behavior to people we consider our friends. However, it is clear that we do not always behave altruistically and that we can, in fact, tolerate considerable

STOP, THINK, & UNDERSTAND

1. How does the empathy-altruism hypothesis differ from egoism?

2. In Cialdini's revised egoism hypothesis, what role does sadness play?

3. What kinds of people are we likely to help?

4. Make a list of the situations that research has shown prompt people to help others.

5. What point does the parable of the Good Samaritan make for establishing the conditions under which people will help others?

inconsistency between the norms we say we hold and our actual behavior.

The **reciprocity norm** provides a promising approach for understanding conditions under which altruism occurs. People tend to match a partner's intimate self-disclosure with an equally intimate one of their own. Gouldner (1960) believed that the reciprocity norm is more general in its statement that we should help those who help us and not harm those who have helped us. He has argued that the only people exempt from the norm of reciprocity are the old, the very young, and the weak and sick—just those people targeted for aid by the social responsibility norm.

If you ever want someone you know to do you a favor, you may be inclined to remind him of the great number of favors you have done for him: "Remember the time you asked me for a . . ." This folk wisdom is usually effective, as an experiment by Goranson and Berkowitz (1966) demonstrated. The subjects were done a favor by an experimenter who was acting either voluntarily

---

reciprocity norm A rule specifying that people should reciprocate another's self-disclosure and helpful acts to the same degree.
social responsibility norm A general rule specifying that we should give help to people who need it.

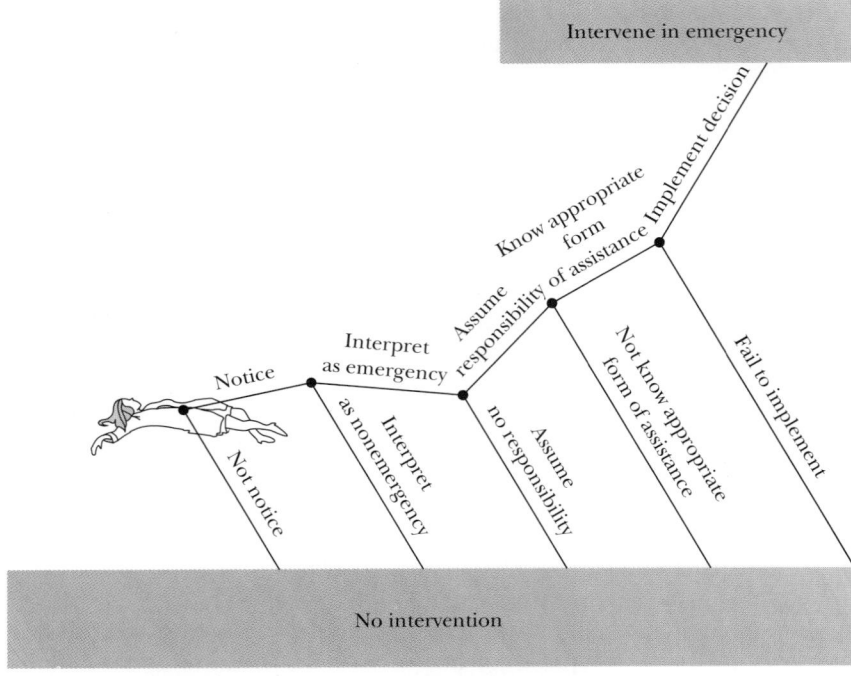

Intervene in emergency

Know appropriate form

Implement decision

Assume responsibility of assistance

Interpret as emergency

Notice

Interpret as nonemergency

Not notice

Assume no responsibility

Not know appropriate form of assistance

Fail to implement

No intervention

FIGURE 8-5 Decision tree analysis of intervention in an emergency
SOURCE: Latané and Darley (1970).

or under compulsion. Later the subjects had a chance to help the experimenter. Even when the subjects did not expect to see the experimenter again, they were inclined to do a favor for him if he had previously done them a favor. This effect was much more pronounced when the experimenter had performed his favor voluntarily (see also Kahn & Tice, 1973).

Why Don't We Help? The Unresponsive Bystander

Bystander Intervention and the Decision Tree

In an emergency situation, altruistic behavior requires us to take an action that will help the person in need. Latané and Darley (1970) pointed out that being altruistic involves not just one decision, but a series of decisions. Only if a per-

son makes an appropriate decision at each decision point will he or she intervene in the emergency. Figure 8-5 outlines these decision points in what has been called a **decision tree.** At each point, branches are available that may cause the bystander to go about his or her business without altruistic intervention.

The first crucial decision is whether to *notice* the incident at all. If a person staggers from the side of the road and waves his arms in front of your car, and your headlights shine directly on him, you have very little alternative but to notice him. A scream at a crowded snack bar at Grand Central Station, however, could go completely unnoticed, and any intervention by passersby would thus be forestalled. Somewhere between these extremes lie most of the situations that call for our intervention.

Second, we have to *interpret* an event as an emergency. Evidence will be presented shortly on just how crucial this decision is. However, we might imagine that the neighbors on Austin Street who heard screams interpreted them as some-

Drawing by Alan Dunn; © 1962, 1990 *The New Yorker Magazine,* Inc.

thing other than calls for help. "I thought I heard hammering noises," explained one of the neighbors. We can see two factors operating here. One is at the level of *perception.* If the screams really sounded like the crash of a hammer, then it might be difficult to make the interpretation necessary for intervention. The second factor is at the level of *motivation.* People may actively want to make a nonemergency interpretation so that they will not be embarrassed by having made a mistake, nor take the risk involved in intervening.

The third decision point is whether we, as bystanders, are *responsible* for helping. If we see two brothers fighting and notice that one of them is getting hurt, we may not view it as our responsibility to intervene if their father is standing there. The factors that may play a role in this decision include whether an appropriate authority who can intervene is present and the number of people who witness the emergency.

Fourth, we must decide on the *appropriate form of assistance.* We may believe that a situation requires direct or indirect intervention. People seeing the Genovese murder may have been loath to intervene directly, yet may have decided that they should contact someone. But who? In the anxiety of the moment, they may not have been able to provide the answer. In short, no one may

intervene because the bystanders cannot decide on the appropriate form of assistance, so they continue to tend to their own business.

Finally, people who notice an event that they interpret as an emergency and decide on the appropriate form of intervention must still decide to *implement the decision.* People who observe a mugging in progress may know what to do but, out of fear, may decide not to implement their decisions. Those who heard the Genovese attack may have felt embarrassed about describing the event to the police or may have been fearful about the consequences of reporting the event if the assailant were not apprehended.

It is clear from the decision tree analysis that intervening in an emergency is a complex act. A series of interlocking decisions must be made, yet the final outcome may have to be achieved in a matter of seconds. Dissecting this speedy decision process is difficult, but research is now accumulating that sheds light on the components that culminate in the final decision regarding intervention.

---

decision tree A model of intervention in emergencies that considers decisions about noticing, interpreting, assessing responsibility, knowing an appropriate form of assistance, and implementing the decision.

Kitty Genovese's death shocked many because it seemed so apparent that her cries signaled an emergency, yet no one responded. Do people in cities have a content of interpretation for cries of help that makes them discredit or downplay emergencies?

Why Doesn't the Bystander Intervene? Diffusing Responsibility

Many factors can account for bystanders' failure to intervene: their personalities, the large city in which they live, the dehumanization of today's technological society, and so on. To shed more light on this social phenomenon, Darley and Latané (1968) set out to isolate the variable that they thought accounted for the witnesses' behavior in the Genovese incident. They reasoned that the *number of persons* watching the crime was primarily responsible for the inaction of the group.

> When only one bystander is present in an emergency, if help is to come, it must come from him. Although he may choose to ignore it . . . any pressure to intervene focuses uniquely on him. When there are several observers present, however, the pressures to intervene do not focus on any one of the observers; instead the responsibility for intervention is shared among all the onlookers and is not unique to anyone. As a result, no one helps. (pp. 377–378)

To test the hypothesis that **diffusion of responsibility** discourages helping, Darley and Latané asked New York University students to participate in an honest discussion about problems they were having in adjusting to college life. Each student was to talk from a separate booth to prevent any possible embarrassment about face-to-face communication; the booths were connected by a sound system. The experimenter also explained that he would not listen to the discussion so that students could have more freedom in their comments.

Actually, only one subject participated in the experiment at a time. Each of the other voices he was to hear was a tape-recorded simulation; no other "discussants" were present. The ruse enabled the experimenters to standardize their procedure for each subject and to set the stage for the emergency.

In the "discussion," the future victim always spoke first. He talked about his difficulties in adjusting to college and then, very hesitantly, mentioned that he was prone to seizures during times of stress. The other prerecorded discussants then took their turns. The actual subject spoke last. When it was the victim's turn to talk again, the emergency took place. The victim began by making a few calm comments and then appeared to be gripped by a seizure. Over the subject's loudspeaker came the following: "I-er-um-I think I-I need-er-if-if—could-er somebody er-er-er-er-er-er-give me a little-er give me a little-er give me a little help here because I-er-I'm . . ." (chokes, then quiet) (p. 379).

The experimenter sat outside the subject's room and recorded the amount of time it took him to seek assistance for the victim. Recall that Darley and Latané were interested in the effect of the number of witnesses to the emergency. Consequently, they systematically varied the alleged size of the discussion group. In some cases, the subject was led to believe that the group consisted of six persons: himself, the victim, and four other witnesses. In another set of cases, the subject believed that the group consisted of three persons. In the remaining cases, the subject believed that he and the victim were the only people in the discussion.

The percentage of subjects who responded to the staged emergency and the speed of their responses are shown in Table 8-1. It took subjects

TABLE 8-1

Effect of group size on the likelihood and speed of response

Group size	Number of subjects	Percent response by end of seizure	Mean time (seconds)
2 (subject and victim)	13	85%	52
3 (subject, victim, and 1 other)	26	62	93
6 (subject, victim, and 4 others)	13	31	166

SOURCE: Adapted from Darley and Latané (1968).

who believed that they were the only witness to the emergency an average of 52 seconds from the beginning of the seizure to swing the door open and attempt to find help. However, as the group became larger, the average amount of time that elapsed before the subject sought help increased to 166 seconds. Moreover, only 31% of the subjects who thought that they were only one of a large group of witnesses ever came out to help, but an overwhelming percentage of the subjects (85%) eventually tried to help the victim if the responsibility for helping rested squarely on their shoulders—that is, if they believed that they were the only person to hear the attack. Thus, by systematically varying one of the factors in the emergency, Darley and Latané could conclude that the number of witnesses to an emergency is a critical determinant of whether any witnesses will take action to intervene.

It is now a well-established finding in quite a variety of situations both inside and outside of the laboratory that the more witnesses present, the less likely that any one will intervene. For example, Latané and Darley (1970) arranged to have a series of thefts occur in a New York discount store. Cases of beer were stolen in front of either one or two customers. Customers who had been lone witnesses were more likely to report the crime to the store clerk than customers who had been one of a pair of witnesses.

Schwartz and Gottlieb (1980) provided the first direct evidence that the number of bystanders had an effect on helping by affecting a witness's feeling of personal responsibility. Subjects observed an emergency situation while they were either alone or in the presence of another bystander. The presence of the bystander inhib-

ited the subject from offering help. Subjects were then asked about their decision to help. Eighty percent of the people who were alone specifically mentioned that they felt it was their responsibility to help; only 17% of the people who were with another bystander felt it was their responsibility to help.

Interpreting the Situation: A Need for Help or a Family Quarrel?

Before we offer help to a person in need, we have to define that person as being in need. Observers may have viewed the Genovese assault as a family quarrel or as a quarrel between two lovers. Given such an interpretation, the scene takes on a different meaning and the appropriate form of action changes. People may feel that it is appropriate to come to the aid of a woman in distress, but not to become involved in an encounter between lovers. In an experimental study, Shotland and Strau (1976) had observers witness a fight in which a woman was attacked by a man. If the woman yelled, "I don't know you," in the course of the fight, 65% of the male bystanders intervened to help. But if she indicated that they knew each other, the same fight was rated as less intense, as less of an emergency, and the rate of intervention dropped to 19%.

The point here is a general one: the context in which an emergency takes place may also affect

---

diffusion of responsibility The sharing of responsibility among several individuals; when no one person can be held accountable, no one may intervene in an emergency.

These two young boys are fighting, yet neither the adults nor the other children are intervening. Do these onlookers perceive the activity as roughhousing or play? Or perhaps as the "natural" activity of boys? Or of these boys?

the way we interpret the event. People may be inclined to interpret situations in a way that does not call for their intervention or help.

DeJong, Marber, and Shaver (1980) examined the effect of a victim's reaction to an emergency in another way. They carried out their study in the engineering and business library at Dartmouth College. Users of the library saw an experimenter drop a $10 bill, which was then snatched up by another person. The experimenter then acted as if he were unaware of the loss, or began to search his pockets and look around. Subjects were more likely to notify the victim of the theft when he appeared to know he was missing the $10. The investigators argue that the reaction of the victim when he knew he had lost the $10 helped witnesses *define the situation* as one that was not ambiguous, but rather as one that called for help.

An intriguing study by Latané and Darley (1970, pp. 81–85) demonstrates in a different way the motivation of bystanders in an emergency to redefine the situation to which they are witnesses. Subjects came to the laboratory individually, ostensibly for a market research study. Each subject was placed in a room and asked to fill out some questionnaires. While alone, he overheard two children playing in an adjacent

room. Soon the play turned into a fight, and an older bully was heard mercilessly beating a younger child. In one condition of the experiment, the subject believed that only he was aware of what was happening in the next room. Therefore, breaking up the fight was the subject's responsibility. In the no-responsibility condition, the subject believed that an adult supervisor was present at the time of the fight.

Only one subject out of eight tried to help in the no-responsibility condition. This is not surprising because an adult was with the children. But could the adult subjects possibly resist going in to break up the fight in the responsibility condition? Yes. Only one of the 12 subjects tried to help. Why was this the case, considering that there was no opportunity for responsibility diffusion? Apparently the answer lay in the subjects' *altered perception* of what was going on. As Table 8-2 points out, three-fourths of the subjects in this condition did not believe that the fight was real. "Children don't really fight like that," said some of the subjects. Of course, they were correct; it was not a real fight. Perhaps the experimenter did a poor job of staging the fight. However, the startling finding in Latané and Darley's study was that in the no-responsibility condition, only one of the eight subjects questioned the authenticity of the

TABLE 8-2

The frequency of believing that the fight was real

Condition	N	Believe	Do not believe
Responsibility (children are alone)	12	25%	75%
No responsibility children are supervised)	8	88	12

SOURCE: Latané and Darley (1970).

fight. The only conclusion that can be reached is that the subjects who felt that they were responsible for taking some helping action were *motivated* to perceive the situation as unreal.

An Analysis of the Costs

In considering people's motivation to avoid helping, we have seen that if people can avoid responsibility, they will do so, and that if they can redefine the situation, they will do so. Why shouldn't people want to help? Why don't people want to get involved? There are no entirely satisfactory answers to these questions, but a model proposed by Piliavin, Piliavin, and Rodin (1975) provides some insight. According to these researchers, witnessing an emergency situation is arousing. Generally this arousal is experienced as uncomfortable tension, and a person is motivated to reduce it. In most cases, the bystander will choose the response to an emergency that most rapidly and completely reduces the arousal.

Intervention in the emergency is not the only behavior that can reduce arousal: interpreting the situation as one that does not call for help, leaving the scene, and failing to notice the situation are other possible reactions. Which behavior will be chosen is a function of the analysis of the net costs of helping. In general, according to the **cost model of helping,** as the costs of helping go up, direct intervention becomes less likely. These costs are of two types. The first is the *cost of intervention to the bystander.* If the attacker on Austin Street was a truly vicious person, then attempting to help could result in a direct physical cost to the bystander (that is, the bystander could be stabbed).

The second type of cost is the *cost to the victim* if the bystander fails to help. How much trouble is the victim in? How much potential benefit can

the bystander provide? A person attacked by a mob may be in genuine jeopardy, but little extra cost to the victim may be involved if the bystander fails to intervene directly, since the bystander simply may not be able to accomplish very much. Table 8-3 shows the schema of the study by Piliavin and his colleagues. Direct intervention is expected to occur when the bystander does not incur high costs in trying to help and the victim will suffer great harm if the bystander fails to act. When the cost to the bystander is high, then the bystander is motivated to reduce arousal by choosing an alternative method. The right-hand column of Table 8-3 suggests some of the alternatives. The most common alternative may be a redefinition of the situation so that it is viewed as a nonemergency or as a situation that does not call for a response by the bystander. The last redefinition is akin to Darley and Latané's concept of diffusion of responsibility. If the situation can be responded to by people other than a particular bystander, that bystander is especially likely to feel little responsibility when the costs of intervention are high.

Testing the costs model

The potential cost of intervention to a bystander can come from a variety of sources. As a bystander, you may incur costs because of the amount of effort you expend to help, because of the risk you run by helping, or because of the lack of internal reward that you derive by being of help. As we pointed out earlier, helping in a situation of physical danger like that of the Genovese case

---

cost model of helping   A model of altruistic behavior that considers the observer's cost of helping and the cost to the victim of not receiving help.

TABLE 8-3

Predicted modal responses of moderately aroused observer as a joint function of costs of direct help and costs of no help to victim

Cost of no help to victim	Cost of direct help	
	Low	*High**
High	(a) Direct intervention	(c) Indirect intervention or Redefinition of situation, disparagement of victim, etc.†
Low	(b) Variable (largely a function of perceived norms in situation)	(d) Leaving scene, ignoring, denial, etc.

*There are some situations, generally those in which victims themselves are very likely to perish, such as severe fires, explosions, cave-ins, and ship accidents, in which the costs for helping become so high that they will be perceived as total, incalculable, or infinite. Under these limiting conditions, the actions and reactions of bystanders will deviate somewhat from those predicted here.

†These responses lower the cost of not helping, leading to (d).

SOURCE: Piliavin, Piliavin, and Rodin (1975).

bears a rather salient cost. According to the model of Piliavin and his associates, this fact should reduce the degree of direct helping.

Consider the situation devised by Allen (in Latané and Darley, 1970, pp. 21–24). In a New York City subway train, a wide-eyed, lost-looking person asks a subway rider whether a particular location is uptown or downtown. In the presence of a second subway rider, the person who has been asked gives the questioner the wrong information. The second subway rider is the real subject in this study. Both the questioner and the respondent are experimental confederates.

What this study varied were events that occurred before the asking of directions. In one condition, the person who gave the misinformation had been sitting with his feet propped up on another seat. When an innocent bystander (another confederate) tripped over the outstretched feet, the seated passenger looked up from his *Muscle* magazine and threatened the bystander with physical violence before letting the incident pass. In a second condition, he looked up and shouted some verbal abuse at the bystander. In a third condition, the bystander was neither threatened nor insulted.

The subject who witnessed these events was aware that the muscle-bound respondent had given the stranger misinformation. It would be easy to help the stranger by correcting the respondent, but what would it cost? As Figure 8-6 indicates, when the costs were small because the stranger had been neither threatened nor insulted, 50% of the subjects corrected the respondent. When the respondent had verbally abused a bystander, only 28% of the subjects corrected him, and when he had physically threatened a bystander, only 16% of the subjects dared to correct him.

Sterling and Gaertner (1984) tested an important assumption of the costs model. Recall that helping is based on the experience of arousal. It is arousal that motivates people to come to the aid of a victim. Sterling and Gaertner argued that if arousal is the basis of the helping response, then increasing arousal in an unambiguous emergency situation should increase the helping rate. They had male subjects perform push-ups as a part of a study that supposedly was investigating physical distraction. Some subjects performed a large number of push-ups (ten) and therefore experienced a heightened degree of physiological arousal; others performed a moderate number (five); and others performed none. The subjects then witnessed an unambiguous emergency. They believed that they heard a female student fall and become pinned under a heavy metal ladder in a room next to theirs. As in Dar-

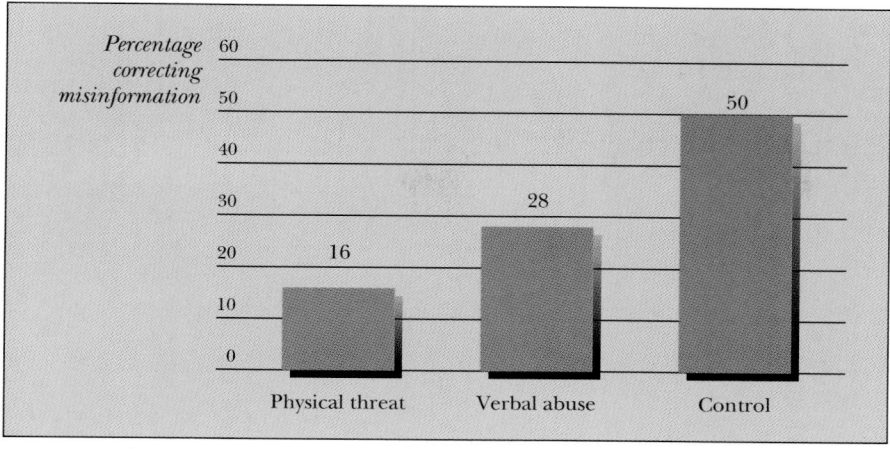

FIGURE 8-6 Correcting a stranger as a function of threat
SOURCE: Adapted from Latané and Darley (1970).

ley and Latané's (1968) experiment, the question was the length of time it took subjects to leave their room to see if they could be of assistance to the female student. The results were clear: when the accident was unambiguous, subjects who had performed ten push-ups and therefore experienced the greatest physiological arousal helped the female confederate more than subjects in either the moderate or no-exercise conditions. Apparently, then, helping *does* seem to be based on a witness's degree of arousal.

The analysis of helping in terms of costs to the helper and the victim has provoked a considerable amount of research and has provided a guide for understanding the motivations of people who choose not to help in an emergency. But any single analysis should not be thought of as sufficient to explain the complex reasons that come together to prevent someone from helping another. For example, a study by Gruder, Romer, and Korth (1978) suggests one limitation. These investigators proposed that the social rules and norms that exist in a situation may alter the effect of the costs-to-the-victim variable in a dramatic way.

Gruder and his colleagues had a female confederate call potential helpers in their homes. Using the "wrong number" technique that had been developed in several previous studies (Gaertner, 1970; Kriss, Indenbaum & Tesch, 1974), the confederate asked for Ralph's Garage.

Of course, the confederate had not reached Ralph's Garage and the subject typically informed the caller that she had the wrong number. The caller then pleaded, "Oh, I'm sorry. Please don't hang up. I'm calling from a pay phone out here on the expressway. . . ."

For half of the phone calls, the confederate indicated her extreme reliance on the subjects' help. She continued by saying, "I don't have any more change for the phone. Do you think you could do me a favor and call Ralph's Garage for me?" For these subjects, it appeared that not being helped would have high costs for the victim. Without any change and stranded on the highway, it is not clear what she could have done. The other half of the subjects received their call from someone for whom the costs of not being helped were low. No mention of lack of money was made, and the subject could presume that the caller would be able to dial Ralph's Garage again.

According to the costs analysis of Piliavin and his colleagues (1975), the subjects should have been considerably more likely to help the caller when their failure to help entailed high costs to the victim. This did not always happen, however. In addition to manipulating the costs, Gruder and his associates manipulated the requester's responsibility for the emergency. For half of her phone calls, the requester added, "I was supposed to take the car into the shop last week to be repaired, but I forgot to. Now it's broken down."

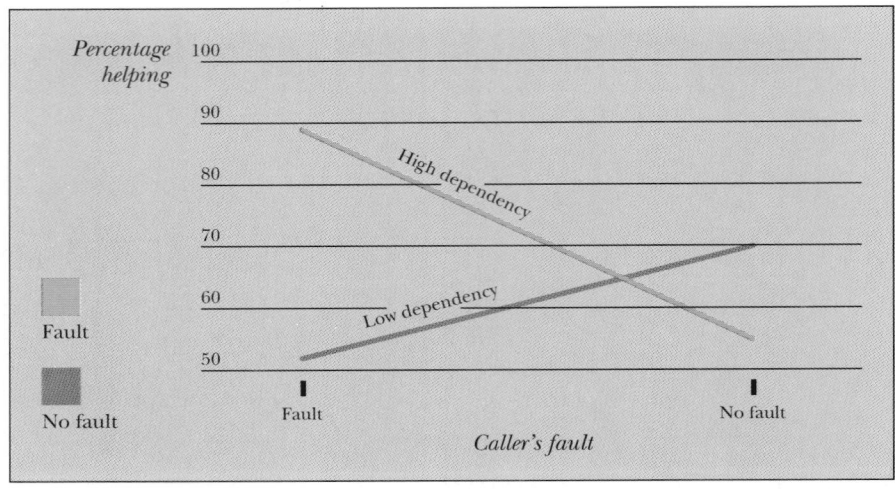

FIGURE 8-7 Percentages of subjects helping in the experimental conditions
SOURCE: Gruder, Romer, and Korth (1978).

For the other half of her phone calls, the requester substituted, "The car was just repaired last week, and it just broke down."

Gruder and his colleagues believed that at least one principle other than the costs to the victim would bear on the decision of the potential helpers. They reasoned that it is embedded in the fabric of our social rules that people are supposed to take care of themselves, to take reasonable precautions, and to avoid negligence. They termed this concept the "norm of self-sufficiency." Clearly, people who forget to take their car into the shop violate this norm. The investigators reasoned that the norm would be invoked to withdraw assistance from its violator if she were not greatly in need of help. Subjects who received the low-dependency call were expected to be more helpful to the caller when the emergency was not the result of the caller's negligence. On the other hand, when the potential costs of a failure to help the caller were high, the caller's negligence was expected to be viewed as just one more illustration of the caller's incompetence and need for help. In this condition, the caller's negligence was expected to strengthen the subject's decision to help.

The results are presented in Figure 8-7. When the costs of not helping the caller were high (high dependency), the subjects made more phone calls for the negligent caller than for the nonnegligent caller. However, when the dependency of the victim was low, the norm of self-sufficiency was apparently invoked and the subjects made significantly more calls to aid the nonnegligent victim than the negligent victim. An analysis purely in terms of the net costs to the victim of the subjects' refusal to help would not have predicted the findings of this study. People's motivations for not getting involved remain complex. Costs are undoubtedly a major component, but future research will most likely uncover further qualifications and components of this process.

We should also be aware that not everyone interprets the costs of a situation in exactly the same way. Some people may look at the cost of saving Sabrina Michaelson from a burning plane as too high; others may think that the cost of not looking for the infant was low because the probability of finding her amidst the wreckage was small. For others, like Jerry Schemmel, the situation may have seemed quite different. For him, and for many others who acted heroically on flight 232, the cost of helping may have seemed lower and the cost of not helping may have been too high to bear. Kerber (1984) provided some research evidence that bears on this point. He found that students at Holy Cross who helped a person in need were much more likely to have perceived the situation's costs favorably than people who did not help. The study makes it difficult to know whether people helped *because* they perceived the costs of helping to be low and the costs of not helping to be high, or whether they held those perceptions because they had decided to help. Nonetheless, Kerber's evidence suggests that people perceive the costs and rewards of a situation differently, and their perceptions may help to determine whether they will help a person in need.

Expanding the costs model

The analysis of helping in terms of its costs to the victim and to the bystander has, as we have seen, attracted a considerable amount of attention. There have also been efforts to expand the model to make it more comprehensive (Lynch & Cohen, 1978). Perhaps the most ambitious of the models was proposed by Piliavin and his colleagues (1982). They suggest that three general factors affect the likelihood that a bystander will intervene in a situation. Costs, they argue, are just one of those factors. First, factors that affect the degree of *empathy* between the bystander and the victim have to be considered. How much does the potential helper feel identified with the victim? Factors that affect feelings of empathy include (1) situational characteristics, such as the ambiguity of the event and the number of bystanders present; (2) bystander characteristics, such as age, sex, and competence to help; and (3) victim characteristics, such as sex, race, and attractiveness.

The bystander's empathy for the victim determines the second factor in the helping process: psychological arousal. Not only must the arousal be experienced, it must also be interpreted as having been caused by the victim's distress. Finally, once arousal has occurred and has been interpreted as being due to the victim's plight, the actual decision to offer direct help, indirect help, or no help at all will be a function of the perceived costs, as specified in the earlier model.

Reactions of the Recipients: Do They Always Love the Helper?

During the first decade of intensive research on helping behavior, almost all attention was focused on the helpers. Their costs, their rewards, their arousal, and their responsibility were the focus of research. The reaction of the recipients of aid

Will someone stop to help this woman? What circumstances would increase the likelihood of her being helped?

was assumed to be positive, as might be predicted by simple reinforcement theories. After all, seeking and receiving help usually results in increased material benefit for the recipient (Gross, Wallston & Piliavin, 1975). More recently, though, attention has been paid to the psychology of receiving help. Several social-psychological theories predict negative reactions by the recipients of help under some conditions. Let us turn to the application of some of these theories (some encountered in earlier chapters and others that will be discussed more fully in later ones) to helping situations.

Equity Theory: Is It as Equal to Give as to Receive?

The heart of equity theory is the proposal that individuals will not only attempt to maximize their rewards in a relationship, they will also try to achieve an equitable relationship. For equity to exist, the ratio of one person's rewards to costs should be equal to his or her partner's rewards-to-costs ratio. People who find themselves in an inequitable relationship will feel distressed. A helping situation is often inequitable, with the recipient of help feeling that he or she is indebted to the helper. Several investigations have demonstrated that the recipient of help may feel negatively toward the helper when the recipient has

1. What are the five steps in the decision tree that indicate whether a bystander will intervene in an emergency?

2. Why does the number of witnesses to an emergency affect the likelihood of offering assistance?

3. What is the cost model of helping? What three variables are included in the "revised" cost model?

4. Sometimes, people who help are appreciated. Sometimes, they are not. How do equity and social exchange considerations affect the recipient's feelings about the helper?

no opportunity to reciprocate (Castro, 1974; Gross & Latané, 1974; Clark, Gotay & Mills, 1974).

Equity theory proposes that in an inequitable relationship, both the individual who has contributed more *and* the individual who has contributed less will be distressed. However, research on helping situations has demonstrated only that the recipient of help is distressed. Helpers often feel good about their actions.

Social Exchange Theories: Helping Is Power

According to **social exchange theories,** any time individuals interact, certain *costs* must be paid and certain *rewards* result. According to Worchel (1984a), an increased sense of power is one of the rewards the helper receives from the interaction. This sense flows from the fact that he or she demonstrated useful abilities and resources and was able to influence other people. This increased sense of power is independent of anything the recipient does to repay the helper, and Worchel (1984a) maintains that often the increased sense of power offsets the cost of helping. From the helper's point of view, this makes the interaction worthwhile. In contrast, an increased sense of powerlessness is a cost that the recipient expe-

riences from the interaction, for the recipient has been forced to acknowledge dependence.

Recipients' Reactions: A Postscript

This discussion should not be taken to mean that help is never appreciated. To the contrary, people who are truly in need of help respond favorably to a person who comes to their aid. But research in the area of helping has identified what might be called the helper's dilemma. The more the helping goes beyond what is absolutely required (Schwartz, 1977), or the more the favor is unsolicited, or the less the opportunity for reciprocation, the more likely that the recipient will react negatively to the help. This may be as true of nations as it is of individuals. So, while partners in a relationship may offer aid as a way of being helpful and getting their partner to like them, the reaction to the assistance may be the opposite of what was desired. Rather than seeming to bring benefit, the assistance may be viewed as a restriction of freedom, the creation of inequity, and a usurpation of power.

Summary

People may come to the aid of other people for altruistic or egoistic reasons. The *empathy-altruism hypothesis* suggests that the emotion of empathy is a motivation for altruism. *Empathy* is the ability to share in another person's feelings. *Altruism* is an unselfish desire to help another person; its ultimate goal is to benefit another's welfare. *Egoism,* on the other hand, is a tendency to focus on one's own gratification. Egoistic helping may be motivated by a desire to relieve one's own distress or sadness. The empathy-altruism hypothesis of Batson and his colleagues does not negate the possibility of egoistic helping but holds that pure altruism is one motivation to help. Cialdini and his colleagues' egoism hypothesis holds that all helping is essentially egoistic. *Empathic joy* has also been held to explain why people choose to help others.

Research on who tends to receive help shows that we are most likely to help people we like, people who are similar to us, and people whose need seems to be most legitimate. Research on the situations that are likely to produce helping behavior has shown that helping increases when (1) we have been positively rewarded for previous helping, (2) we are in a good mood, (3) we observe someone else helping, (4) we are not otherwise preoccupied or hurried, (5) we attribute altruistic motivation to ourselves and (6) norms direct us to help. Among the norms that lead to helping are the *reciprocity* and *social responsibility norms.*

The chapter also considered the factors that cause people to be apathetic when witnessing someone's need for help. The failure of bystanders to help Kitty Genovese led Latané and Darley to study bystander apathy. In their *decision tree* model, bystanders must (1) notice the event, (2) interpret it as an emergency, (3) assume the responsibility to act, (4) know the appropriate form of assistance and (5) implement their decision, in order to help in an emergency.

Much of the research on bystander intervention has revolved about the question of responsibility. Darley and Latané showed that the number of witnesses to an emergency is related to the likelihood of acting: the more witnesses, the less action. The presence of a number of bystanders makes any single bystander feel less responsible for intervening, and therefore less likely to act altruistically.

A cost model of helping has been developed to account for situations that do and do not lead to helping. According to the expanded version of the model, helping increases when empathy and psychological arousal are high. If those conditions are met, the likelihood of intervention increases as the cost to the bystander decreases. Intervention also increases as the cost to the victim for the bystander's failure to help increases. Factors that affect differences in the way people perceive the various costs involved in helping must also be considered.

The recipient's response to helping may not always be positive. Favorable responses depend on the attribution process as the recipient determines the meaning of the helpful action.

---

social exchange theories Theories that view human interaction as a cost-reward transaction.

Key Terms

altruism	*egoism*	*social exchange*
cost model of helping	*empathy*	*theories*
decision tree	*empathy-altruism*	*social responsibility*
diffusion of	*hypothesis*	*norm*
responsibility	*reciprocity norm*	

Suggested Readings

Batson, C. D. (1987). Prosocial motivation: Is it ever truly altruistic? In L. Berkowitz (Ed.), *Advances in experimental social psychology* (Vol. 20, pp. 65–122). Orlando, Fla.: Academic Press.

Krebs, D., & Miller, D. T. (1985). Altruism and aggression. In G. Lindzey & E. Aronson (Eds.), *Handbook of social psychology* (3rd ed.). New York: Random House.

Latané, B., & Darley, J. M. (1970). *The unresponsive bystander: Why doesn't he help?* Englewood Cliffs, N.J.: Prentice-Hall.

Piliavin, J. A., Dovidio, J., Gaertner, S., & Clark, R. D. III (1981). *Emergency interventions.* New York: Plenum.

Rushton, J. P., & Sorrentino, R. M. (Eds.). (1981). *Altruism and helping behavior: Social, personality, and developmental perspectives.* Hillsdale, N.J.: Erlbaum.

Chapter Nine

Aggression: Harming and Hurting Others

Except for the constant drone of the television, the forced silence in the room was broken only by quiet sobbing. No one moved for almost a half hour, until one of the six fraternity men bolted from his chair and turned off the television set, apologizing in a cracked voice, "I can't watch this any more." This statement characterized the feeling of many people who watched live television coverage of the trial of the People versus Steinberg. Indeed, these feelings of sadness, disbelief, depression, anger, and emptiness were rekindled in us as we wrote about the incident.

Joel Steinberg seemed to have everything going for him. He grew up in a well-to-do home in Yonkers, New York. His father was a successful corporate lawyer. Joel was handsome, bright, and self-assured. He had built himself a thriving law practice in New York City and had an impressive list of wealthy clients. In 1975 he met Hedda Nussbaum at a party. Hedda was a tall, attractive woman who worked for a major New York publishing house as an editor of children's books. Although very bright and talented, Hedda lacked faith in herself and her abilities.

Joel supported and encouraged Hedda. As Hedda's self-esteem grew, her work improved, and she received several promotions. The couple seemed to be well on the road to living the American dream when Hedda moved in with Joel in 1976. Life took an unexpected turn, however, when Joel began to criticize Hedda. His criticism was often cruel and harsh, but he convinced her that he was doing it for her own good. Then, after they had lived together for three years, Joel struck her in the face. Both Hedda and Joel were surprised by this action. Hedda, in fact, said later that she was too surprised by the event to be angry. They both thought it wouldn't happen again.

Instead, it became a way of life. The dream quickly became a nightmare. The beatings became more frequent and sadistic. Hedda reported that the violence took many forms; Joel kicked her in the eye, strangled her, broke her nose several times, and even hung her in handcuffs from a chinning bar. One beating was so severe that Hedda had to undergo surgery for a ruptured spleen.

Just when life looked the bleakest, a turn of events promised to rescue the couple. An unmarried woman paid Steinberg to find a good home for her baby. Hedda and Joel took custody of the child. They named her Lisa. Nussbaum reports that life was a joy for about six months, as she and Joel devoted themselves to Lisa. But the beatings began again. This time they were harsher and more frequent.

Hedda's injuries forced her to miss work so often that in 1982 she was fired from her job. She lost weight, going from 125 pounds to 100 pounds. She took on the appearance of a badly beaten prizefighter. She rarely went out in public with Joel. Both Joel and Hedda began to freebase cocaine more frequently, a habit they had begun in 1978. Joel's practice suffered and he was disbarred.

In 1986 the couple was given a baby boy by a physician friend. Few people suspected that anything was wrong in their lives. The arrival of Mitchell marked a short respite in the pattern of beatings. They soon began again. But now Hedda was not the only target; Lisa, too, became a target. Lisa was beaten because she stared too much at Joel.

By late October 1987 Joel was using cocaine almost daily. Hedda told a hushed courtroom that on the evening of November 1, Joel complained that Lisa was staring at him again. He believed she was trying to hypnotize him, and he went into her room to stop her. When Hedda next saw Lisa, she was unconscious. While Lisa lay comatose on the bed, Joel and Hedda smoked cocaine until nearly 4:00 A.M. Hedda consulted a medical dictionary to see what could be done for Lisa, but she felt that Lisa was not critically hurt. About 6:00 A.M. Joel discovered that Lisa had stopped breathing. An ambulance was called and Lisa was taken to a hospital. Four days later Lisa died of a brain hemorrhage.

Initially both Hedda Nussbaum and Joel Steinberg were charged with murder. Charges against Hedda were later dropped, however, on the grounds that she had been so battered that she was incapable of killing Lisa or saving her life. Joel was brought to trial and a shocked world watched and listened as the tragic story unfolded live on television. Joel Steinberg was convicted

Violence has become such a part of our everyday lives that we hardly pay attention to newspaper accounts of people's inhumanity to others. However, the tragic story of Hedda Nussbaum, Joel Steinberg, and their child, Lisa, became a national focus because it symbolized the innocence of many of the victims of violence and our inability to curb human aggression.

of first-degree manslaughter and sentenced to a jail term of 8½ to 25 years.

Aggression: One Definition or Many?

The story of Lisa Steinberg is tragic and dramatic. The senseless violence of one man killed an innocent child and permanently disfigured someone who loved him. What could have caused Joel Steinberg to act with such cruelty? We are immediately tempted to leap in with the simple explanation that Joel Steinberg was nuts. We could build a case for this explanation out of Steinberg's bizarre behavior. But what about the 1 million to 25 million other cases of family violence

(Voice, 1989; Straus, Gelles & Steinmetz, 1980) or the more than a million other violent crimes that are committed in the United States each year? Are all these people crazy? On a less dramatic scale, how do we explain the countless violent confrontations that happen each day?

But we are getting a bit ahead of ourselves. Before we begin to examine the causes of aggression, let's take some time to define what we mean by aggression. As a student preparing for that upcoming exam, you probably have your pen poised to underline a concise and clear definition. Certainly we all know what aggression is. But let's think a minute before we open up the dictionary. We probably all agree that Joel Steinberg's treatment of Lisa and Hedda was aggressive. But what about Hedda's actions on the night

It has been difficult to develop a precise definition of aggression because of such issues as whether to consider the intention of the actor, the emotions of the people involved, or consequences of the action. Research has also shown that victims are more likely to define an act as aggression than are perpetrators.

that Lisa lay comatose on her bed? Hedda did nothing to help the dying child. Her inaction may have contributed to the child's death. Was this aggression? Prosecutors initially thought that her actions opened her to the charge of murder. But later they withdrew this charge.

And what about our agreement that Joel Steinberg's actions were aggressive? Joel argued, and he convinced Hedda, that the beatings he administered to her were aimed at "helping" her. He sounds much like the parent who argues that spanking the child is aimed at making the child a better person: "This hurts me more than it does you."

Thus we reach our first juncture in defining aggression. Do we focus on the act itself, and say that aggression is any behavior that delivers a noxious stimulus to another person (Buss, 1961)? Or do we focus on intention, and define aggression as any act that is *intended* to injure the target (Dollard et al., 1939; Baron, 1977)? Our legal system and many researchers feel that a complete definition of aggression must include intention. If your neighbor shoots you, the action

is aggressive if he or she intended to hurt you, but it is not aggressive if the neighbor was cleaning the gun and it accidentally discharged.

While including intention in our definition makes intuitive sense, it raises new problems for us. How do we determine intention? In an interesting study, subjects were shown videotaped segments of an aggressive encounter between two boys (Mummendey & Otten, 1989). Some observers were told to take the perspective of the initiator and others were instructed to take the perspective of the recipient. Subjects saw the action as more aggressive when they took the perspective of the recipient, and these subjects were most likely to attribute harmful intentions to the aggressor. The point is that it is often difficult to determine the intention behind an act.

Some interesting questions are also raised about the goal of aggression. For some investigators, the goal of aggression is to deliver harm to another person. Other investigators, however, have argued that aggression is an act aimed at influencing the target, demonstrating the power of the aggressor (Boulding, 1989), or, in the case of a male, to show that one is masculine (Segall, 1988). In fact, these various goals are not mutually exclusive, and many acts of aggression may be aimed at achieving some or all of these goals (Carlson, Marcus-Newhall & Miller, 1989). And then we have the distinction between **angry aggression,** which is instigated by anger or hostility, and **instrumental aggression,** whose aim is achieving a goal outside of the aggressive act itself.

By now your own level of anger may be rising as you contemplate what you might do to authors who have confused what should have been a simple issue. Our aim, however, is not to add needless confusion to your life but to point out that there may be varieties of aggression and to illustrate some of the issues that must be considered when we define the concept. We also hope to prepare you for the discussion of theories of aggression. Just as there are numerous types of aggression, so, too, there are many theories about its causes. No one theory may be able to explain all instances of aggression; some may best handle certain types of aggression. With this point in mind, let's now examine some of the theories.

Theories of Aggression

In developing a theory to explain aggression, we have two options. We can look inside the person (or organism) with the view that he or she is *pushed* by some internal force to aggress. The aim, then, becomes to identify that force or seat of aggression. Or we can look to external factors that may *pull* the individual to aggress. Taking this approach, we attempt to identify environmental or social conditions that instigate aggression. Instinct and biological theories take the former view of aggression, while frustration-aggression and social learning theories take the latter approach.

Instinct Theories

Among the oldest and most controversial theories of aggression are those that state that aggression is an *instinct*. This concept implies that a behavior is inherited rather than learned, and that the behavior pattern is common to all members of the species. After witnessing the death and destruction of World War I, Sigmund Freud decided that humans are born with the instinct to aggress. He argued that the drive for violence arises from within people and that human aggression cannot be eliminated. It is therefore important to give people the opportunity to channel their aggression is nondestructive ways.

Another theory of instincts has been proposed by **ethologists,** scientists who study animal behavior. The Nobel Prize–winner Konrad Lorenz (1968) pointed out that the instinct to aggress is common to many animal species. Lorenz, however, differed from Freud in holding that aggressive behavior will not occur unless it is triggered by external cues. Unlike Freud, who saw aggression as destructive and disruptive, Lorenz viewed intraspecies aggression as adaptive and essential for the survival of animal species. An animal protects its territory, and hence its food supply, by attacking other animals that invade the territory. Aggression serves to spread out animal populations and to prevent overcrowding. In addition, as a result of the fights that animals wage over mates, the strongest animals win the mates and reproduce the species. Thus only the fittest members of a species reproduce and the defective members are weeded out.

Instinct theories have been subjected to many attacks. One focuses on the issue of natural releasing mechanisms. Many instinct theories argue that certain animals have built-in releasing mechanisms. However, such mechanisms have not been identified in many animal species or in humans. Zing Yang Kuo (1930) raised some kittens with rat-killing mothers, other kittens in isolation, and a third group of kittens with rats as constant companions. After a period of time, the grown kittens were placed in the presence of rats. Of those that had been raised with the rat-killing

---

angry aggression   An aggressive act instigated by anger or hostility.

ethologist   A scientist who studies animal behavior in natural settings, and may attempt to draw comparisons between animal and human behavior.

instrumental aggression   An act of aggression performed to achieve a goal outside of the aggressive act itself.

mothers, 85% killed the rats, whereas only 17% of those that had been raised with rats attacked them.

A second criticism of instinct theories is most directly concerned with human aggression. If humans are instinctively aggressive, we would expect to find a great deal of similarity in the style and amount of aggression displayed by people. However, one of the main characteristics of human aggression is its diversity. Some people are often violent while others are seldom violent. In 1970, for example, there were 213 homicides in Tokyo, a city of 11 million people. During that same year there were 1,117 homicides in New York, a city of 8 million. Some people use weapons and others wound with words. Some people aggress directly and openly while others engage in passive aggression.

We don't want to ignore the role that instinct can play in aggression. Any animal breeder knows that we can develop a more aggressive animal through selective breeding and that some species of animals are more aggressive than others. But it is difficult to make the leap from here to argue that humans are instinctively aggressive. Or even that some humans are more instinctively aggressive than others. How can an instinct theory help us understand the violence of Joel Steinberg? Steinberg was not always aggressive, nor did he aggress against everyone he met. Therefore, instinct theories do not play a major role in guiding research on human aggression.

Biological Theories

Biological theories also locate the seat of aggression inside the individual. These theories, however, differ from the earlier instinct theories because they attempt to identify specific *biological* mechanisms that excite people to aggression.

Proponents of one biological approach have attempted to locate specific parts of the brain that may trigger aggression. Work in this area often involves either stimulating or severing various parts of an animal's brain and observing the effect of these procedures on aggression. This research has made some headway in identifying certain neural centers that give rise to violent behavior when they are stimulated (Moyer, 1971). However, this approach does not identify the conditions that cause stimulation of these aggression "seats."

A second line of research has focused on the relationship between aggression and hormones. More specifically, this research has suggested that male sex hormones may be responsible for aggressive behavior. Numerous investigators (Maccoby & Jacklin, 1980) have argued that there are definite gender differences in aggressive behavior. These investigators argue that males are more aggressive than females because of hormonal differences. According to this position, the difference is innate. This argument has been vigorously attacked by other researchers, who say that the gender differences in aggressiveness are due to learning and socialization rather than differences in hormones. In addition, there is some evidence that while males are more physically aggressive than females, the gender difference narrows or disappears when we examine verbal aggression (Eagly & Steffen, 1986; Reinish & Sanders, 1986). One of the major battlegrounds for proponents and opponents of the biological predisposition theory centers on whether gender differences in aggression can be found in young children. Presumably, if these gender differences are found only at a later age, learning rather than biological predisposition must play a role in aggressive behavior. At this time, there are no conclusive answers on this issue.

We are left in a position similar to that of the instinct theories. Even if we accept the view that biological mechanisms play a role in instigating violence, we must explain what triggers those mechanisms. To understand aggression fully, we must also look outside the person. We must investigate the ways in which these external conditions affect when and how people aggress.

Frustration-Aggression Theory

In order to understand Joel Steinberg's violence, let's reexamine his life just before he began to abuse Hedda. Steinberg had a thriving practice in the early 1970s, but things were beginning to come unraveled. He was having problems with his associates over such issues as office space and past-due rent. He moved his office at least three times in the 1970s before he began to work out of his home. His law practice started to dwindle just at the time he needed money to support his growing use of drugs. His ambitions were thwarted and he was under increasing stress. Could these conditions have contributed to his violence?

One of the earliest theories to focus on the role of external conditions was the **frustration-aggression theory** (Dollard et al., 1939), which postulates that "aggression is always a consequence of frustration" and that "frustration always leads to some form of aggression" (p. 1). According to this theory, the instigation to aggress should increase as the strength of frustration increases. From these seemingly simple premises, Dollard and his associates attempted to make precise predictions about when people aggress and against whom they direct their aggression. However, the statement that frustration always results in aggression is not as uncomplicated as it appears to be.

Frustration

Dollard and his colleagues included some very formal definitions of the terms used in their theory. **Frustration** was defined as an "interference with the behavior sequence" (p. 7). This statement may be translated to say that we will be frustrated if we cannot have what we want when we want it. A study by Davitz (1952) provides an example of frustration. He gave children candy bars and showed them a very interesting movie. Just before the climax of the movie, he took the candy bars away from the children and escorted them out of the film room. Needless to say, the children were frustrated.

The theory also postulates that the greater the frustration, the greater the resulting aggression. This hypothesis was supported by Harris (1974), who had confederates cut into lines of people waiting in theaters, grocery stores, and movies. The confederates cut in front of either the second person or the twelfth person in line. Observations showed that the second person reacted more aggressively (with verbal abuse) to the line breaker than the twelfth person. Supposedly the frustration was greater for the second person because he or she was closer to the goal than the twelfth person.

Our feelings about ourselves also influence our reaction to frustration. Another variation on this theme is the notion that our feelings about ourselves influence our reaction to frustration. Investigators found that people who had high but unstable self-esteem experienced anger and hostility rather quickly (Kernis, Gannenmann & Barclay, 1989). These people were constantly on guard to protect their self-image, and they experienced simple frustrations as serious threats to their self-esteem.

Although the definition of frustration seems straightforward, there are still questions about what constitutes frustration. Is frustration an external state or an internal feeling? In the Davitz study, is the frustration the experimenter's action in taking the children's candy bars and removing the children from the film room, or is the frustration the feelings that those actions aroused in the children? Dollard and his colleagues (1939) viewed frustration as the entire operation.

Aggression

According to the theory of Dollard and his associates, **aggression** is a behavior whose goal is the "injury of the person toward whom it is directed." Supposedly the aggression may be either physical or verbal.

Displaced aggression. The investigators recognized that one cannot always aggress without reprisal from either the target of the aggression or some other person. Older children are aware of this possibility; parents often mete out punishment when an older child aggresses against a younger one. Dollard and his colleagues stated that although frustration instigates aggression, the actual act of aggression may be inhibited if punishment for aggression is expected. According to frustration-aggression theory, "the strongest instigation, aroused by a frustration, is to acts of aggression directed against the agent per-

---

aggression   Any act that is intended to injure a target (*see also* **angry aggression**; **displaced aggression**; **instrumental aggression**).

frustration   Interference or thwarting of an ongoing behavior.

frustration-aggression theory   The theory that aggression is always a consequence of frustration and that frustration always leads to some form of aggression.

Terrorism involves violence aimed at noncombatants that seeks to intimidate larger groups in order to achieve social, political, or personal goals. This may be viewed as an example of displaced aggression because the immediate targets are not the ones creating the frustration for the terrorist. In August of 1988 in West Germany, Dieter Degowski, a bank robber, took 18-year-old Sylvie Bischoff as hostage when police went in pursuit. The gunmen were captured; Ms. Bischoff was killed.

ceived to be the source of frustration and progressively weaker instigations are aroused to progressively less direct acts of 'aggression.'" Consequently, people who are frustrated should aggress directly against the frustrating agent. However, if the frustrating agent is unavailable or if the aggressor fears punishment for aggressing against the frustrating agent, an aggressor may "displace" aggression to some other target. Using this concept, we might question whether Steinberg's frustration over his business and financial situations led him to displace aggression to Hedda and Lisa.

Identifying the targets of **displaced aggression** has led to some controversy. Miller (1948) hypothesized that the target of displaced aggression will have some similarities with the original frustrating agent. Thus, if the frustrating agent is the father, aggression may be displaced to the mother, since both the mother and the father are parents. However, Miller's hypothesis does not include a clear method for determining the sim-

ilarity dimension. Berkowitz and Knurek (1967) found that aggression may be displaced to a target with a name similar to that of the frustrator. In this study, subjects who were prevented from winning money attributed more unfavorable characteristics to a bystander with the same name as that of the frustrator than to a bystander with a different name.

Frustration-aggression theory also deals with the types of aggression that can be expected to follow frustration. Dollard and his associates suggest that direct physical and verbal aggression will be the most preferred types. However, if the use of direct aggression is inhibited or blocked, an alternative type of aggression, such as spreading rumors about the frustrator or making him or her the butt of jokes, may be employed. Such displacements of aggression can occur in both the target and the type of aggression.

Reducing aggression. Knowing what causes aggression is only partly satisfying. It is also

Chapter Nine   Aggression: Harming and Hurting Others

important to understand how to diminish aggression. Dollard and his colleagues believed that if aggression does not follow frustration, the frustrated person retains a residue of frustration and a readiness to aggress. Each frustration that is not followed by an aggressive response adds to the residue. Finally, the residue builds up to a point at which any further addition sets off a very violent aggressive reaction. A person who is constantly frustrated at work may go home and blow up at a minor offense committed by his or her child. Normally this offense would not upset the person. The situation is analogous to blowing air into a balloon—one breath is not enough to cause the balloon to explode, but one breath can indeed cause an explosion if the balloon is already filled to capacity with air.

Frustration-aggression theory describes two ways of reducing the instigation to aggression after an individual has been frustrated. First, the frustration can be removed, thus removing the motivation to aggress. An interesting demonstration of this effect was provided by an experimenter's assistant who caused subjects to fail on a task (Ohbuchi, Kameda & Agarie, 1989). Anger and aggression were reduced when the assistant apologized and removed the results of the test. As we will see in Chapter 12, apology and removal of negative outcomes are also the steps necessary to restore trust after it has been breached. Second, the individual may be allowed to aggress. **Catharsis** is the term that is applied to the case in which aggression reduces future instigation to aggression. Frustration-aggression theory holds that the act of aggression should remove some of the built-up residual instigation, just as opening a balloon valve removes some of the air inside so that the balloon is less likely to explode.

According to the catharsis hypothesis, two effects should follow aggression. First, the act of aggression should reduce the individual's arousal, and second, the individual should be less likely to aggress in the near future *because* of the reduced arousal. It is important to note that the reduction of future aggression should occur because of the reduced arousal and not because of some other process, such as guilt or the fear of retaliation. The catharsis hypothesis is extremely important because frustration-aggression theory considers catharsis one of the main methods by which future instigations to aggression can be reduced. However, the evidence for the catharsis effect has been far less than compelling.

Some investigators have found evidence supporting the catharsis idea. Hokanson and his colleagues (Hokanson, Burgess & Cohen, 1963; Hokanson & Shelter, 1961) demonstrated that under certain conditions, aggression reduces physiological arousal (systolic blood pressure and heart rate). However, Geen and Quanty (1977) have emphasized that these effects occur only under certain conditions. In their review of the catharsis literature, they point out that aggression does not lead to a reduction of arousal when the target of aggression is of high power or status, when the aggressor feels that his or her aggression is foolish or inappropriately intense, and when a strong possibility of counteraggression exists. Another interesting finding centers on personal style in expressing anger. Engebretson, Matthews, and Scheier (1989) suggest that some of us prefer to express our anger while others prefer to hold it in. Their study showed that people who were allowed to express anger in their preferred way (openly expressing it or holding it in) showed reduced arousal following frustration. Therefore, aggression may reduce arousal for some people but not for others. Thus, while a little aggression can feel good in some situations, it can result in discomfort and guilt in many others.

When we turn to the question whether the expression of aggression reduces the instigation to future aggression, we find the picture even more clouded. Some studies have found that allowing people to participate in controlled real or fantasy aggression does reduce further aggression (Nosanchuk, 1981; Doob & Wood, 1972; Tedeschi, 1979). While these studies suggest that aggression reduces future aggression, other studies have failed to find this catharsis effect. For example, Ryan (1971) allowed some angry subjects to pound on a box with a hammer.

catharsis The reduction in the instigation to aggress following some instances of aggression.

displaced aggression Aggression that varies either in type or in target from that most preferred by the attacker.

The Romanian revolt in the early 1990s may have resulted from years of deprivation combined with the expectation that Romania would be able to obtain the freedoms being accorded the rest of Eastern Europe.

Some of the subjects were competing with a person who had previously angered them whereas others were not. A group of control subjects were not allowed to pound on the box. All of the subjects were then given the opportunity to shock the individual who had angered them. The results showed that the subjects who had pounded on the box were as aggressive as the control subjects. This result would not have been predicted by the catharsis hypothesis.

In our discussion of social learning theory and media violence, we will examine a number of other studies that suggest that aggression leads to more aggression. Taken together, the research shows that the conditions under which a true catharsis of hostility will occur are rather limited. The minimum conditions for catharsis are that the aggressor be angry and be allowed to attack the antagonist directly. Even given these conditions, catharsis may not result; and we shall see later that aggression often leads to more aggression, not less. It is hard to argue for a catharsis effect in the Steinberg incident. Joel's violent behavior increased, rather than decreased, after his first attack on Hedda. Not only was he more violent to Hedda, but he also beat Lisa when she

came into the family. Thus aggression is not a good cure for aggression.

Revolution—Applying and Extending Frustration-Aggression Theory

Before leaving our discussion of frustration, let's switch our focus from individuals to large groups. Most of us watched in awe as events in Eastern Europe and the Soviet Union unfolded during 1989 and 1990. Like dominoes, one communist government after another was overthrown as citizens who endured social and material deprivation for many years demanded more freedom and economic opportunity. In Romania the revolution was accompanied by violence, while in other countries the governments caved in to less violent but equally massive demonstrations of dissatisfaction. In an effort to explain how people are moved to revolt against their leadership, psychologists, political scientists, and sociologists have drawn on the relationship between frustration and aggression.

Ted Robert Gurr (1970) defines **relative deprivation** as "a perceived discrepancy between . . . value expectations and value capabilities" (p. 21). He argues that relative deprivation is loosely

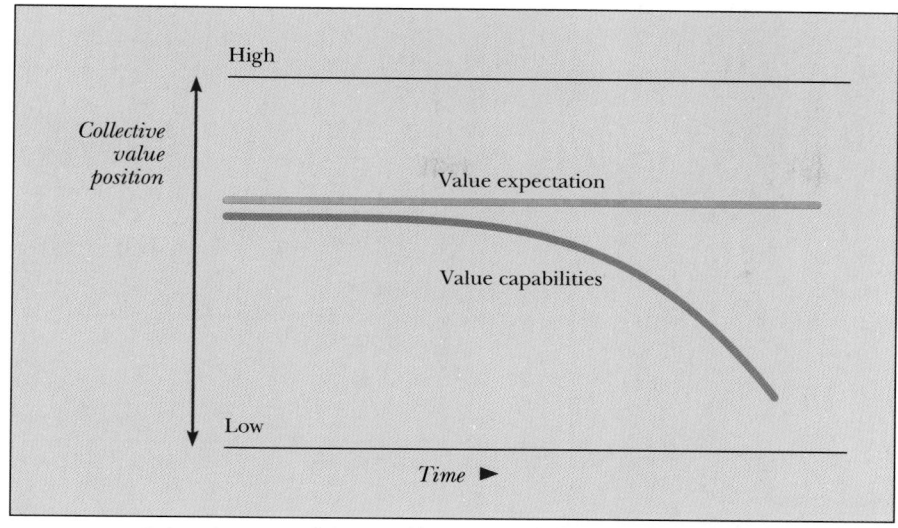

FIGURE 9-1 Decremental deprivation
SOURCE: Gurr (1970).

synonymous with frustration. Gurr describes several causal models of political violence, in all of which relative deprivation plays a key role. There are three distinct patterns of deprivation.

Decremental deprivation is the loss of what people once had thought they could have. They experience deprivation by reference to their own past condition (see Figure 9-1). A variety of situations may lead to decremental deprivation: recession or depression, imposition of foreign rule, a decline in the number of opportunities available to a particular group (such as unskilled labor in an increasingly technological society). Hadley Cantril (1941) did a psychological analysis of the roots of Nazism and concluded that it was able to succeed only because "old norms, old cultural standards, were no longer able to provide the framework necessary for a satisfying adjustment of the individuals who composed the culture." Decremental deprivation occurred for several reasons—many people had suffered reduction in status, economic distress, and personal insecurity as both social structures and normative systems disintegrated in the aftermath of World War I. Another example is seen in the rioting in Argentina when the government had to

make drastic economic changes to repay its foreign debt. Decremental deprivation is credited with being the source of more collective violence historically than any other pattern of relative deprivation.

A second pattern of disequilibrium is **aspirational deprivation.** In this situation people do not feel a loss, but they feel anger at having no means of attaining new or intensified expectations. Their expectations can take one of three forms. One is an increase in the expectation of some commodity in limited supply. The commodity could be a material good, personal freedom, political order, or justice. People can also come to expect some new value they have never had before, such as political participation or equality of classes. And third, people may become

---

aspirational deprivation   Loss of hope of attaining something in limited supply, something one has come recently to value, or something to which one has recently become committed.

decremental deprivation   The loss of what one once had or thought one could have.

relative deprivation   A perceived discrepancy between people's expectations and what they can actually have.

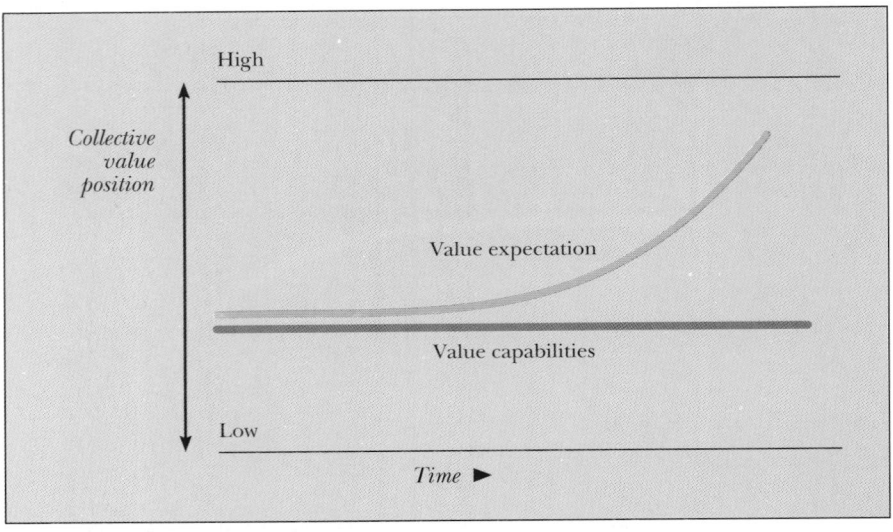

FIGURE 9-2 Aspirational deprivation
SOURCE: Gurr (1970).

intensely committed to something that earlier they gave little thought to. (See Figure 9-2.)

Aspirational deprivation may be seen in Romania's recent revolution. For years the population was deprived of material goods, heat, food, and a variety of personal freedoms, including freedom of expression and freedom to decide whether or not to have children. As nearby Eastern European countries (East Germany, Poland, Hungary) began to obtain more freedom, Romanians began to expect and demand more freedom in their own country. But this freedom was not forthcoming and revolt followed.

The third pattern of relative deprivation is **progressive deprivation,** or the J-curve hypothesis, and is a generalized version of a model proposed by Davies (1962). This work was fundamental in introducing a systematic empirical approach into a field whose mainstay had been the historical approach. The J-curve hypothesis predicts that a revolution is most likely to occur when a prolonged period of objective economic and social development is followed by a short period of sharp reversals. Expectations are generated after a long run of more or less steady improvement in conditions; people come to expect continued improvement. If value capabilities sta-

bilize or decline after such a period, so that improvement is discontinued and conditions stagnate or deteriorate, Davies suggests, progressive deprivation follows (see Figure 9-3). He finds this development to be most common in societies undergoing a great deal of change; "the crucial factor is the vague or specific fear that ground gained over a long period of time will be quickly lost." People marveled at the speed with which radical change transformed East Germany. During the three short weeks in which Egon Krenz held office, borders were opened, the headquarters of the dreaded secret police were opened for inspection, free elections were promised, and, most dramatic, the Berlin Wall was torn down. Despite these rapid changes, the people were unhappy and demanded a new government. Actual change could not keep pace with the rising expectations, and dissatisfaction resulted.

Taking a somewhat different approach, Hopper (1950) proposes a model of stages of a revolution. The preliminary stage of revolution is characterized by a general restlessness, which manifests itself in an increase in drive, suicide, travel, and emigration. People recognize that something is wrong, and the ruling government

302   *Chapter Nine   Aggression: Harming and Hurting Others*

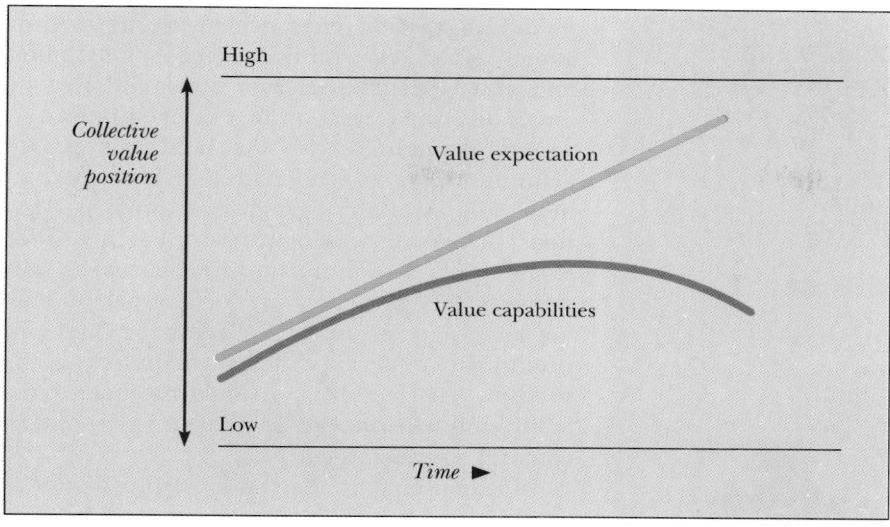

FIGURE 9-3 Progressive deprivation
SOURCE: Gurr (1970).

takes steps to reform. If these efforts are insufficient, the process moves into the popular stage, which is characterized by a spread of discontent and the development of propaganda. In this stage there is conflict between the in-group and the out-group and demand for the abdication of the group in power. Conflict becomes a central theme, supposedly in support of differentiating the in-group from the out-group. Then comes the formal phase. This stage sees the clear identification of attitudes and values. A struggle ensues between radicals, moderates, and conservatives in the revolutionary group. The moderates typically gain control and make an attempt at reform, despite attacks from radicals and conservatives and political inexperience. Norms are formalized and become dogma. The revolution is in full fury at this point; if the reform efforts are unsuccessful, the radicals gain control and the reign of terror begins. The destruction and chaos lead to the institutional stage, in which psychological exhaustion and economic distress signal the need for moderation. The reign of terror ends and amnesty is granted to many prisoners. A new government is established, often with dictatorial powers to put an end to the chaos. People accept the changes in lifestyle and reconcile their attitudes appropriately, and the new group is established.

Extensions, revisions, and new directions
To its credit, frustration-aggression theory was rather clear and straightforward. It stated that frustration always leads to aggression, and that catharsis should follow each aggressive act. Unfortunately, we have seen that the theory is not correct. We do not always react violently to frustration. Catharsis does not always follow aggression. Should we therefore discard the theory and look elsewhere for the cause of aggression? Probably not. It seems that repeated frustrations in many parts of Joel Steinberg's life may have contributed to his violence. If you review your own life, you will probably recall becoming very angry in the face of frustration; you may have yelled at the driver who blocked your way to an important meeting by poking down the road. As we think about the theory, we begin to feel that "they might have something there if they

---

progressive deprivation   Loss of momentum or deterioration of conditions after a prolonged period of steady improvement.

**IN 1988, HANDGUNS KILLED
7 PEOPLE IN GREAT BRITAIN
19 IN SWEDEN
53 IN SWITZERLAND
25 IN ISRAEL
13 IN AUSTRALIA
8 IN CANADA
AND 8,915 IN THE UNITED STATES.**

GOD BLESS AMERICA.

Help stop handgun violence.
Call 1-900-226-4455.

Handgun Control, Inc., 1225 Eye Street, N.W.
Washington, D.C. 20005

STOP HANDGUNS BEFORE THEY STOP YOU.

Is the presence of a weapon a cue for aggression? Does the availability of weapons make aggression more likely? Berkowitz's research would seem to indicate that it does.

had not insisted on such absolute terms as *always.*" We might be willing to buy the position that frustration sometimes causes aggression. In fact, many investigators have taken this position. However, once we start down this road, the obvious question leaps up: When (under what conditions) does frustration lead to aggression?

Aggression cues. One investigator answered this question by suggesting that aggression follows frustration when the environment contains aggression cues that pull the person to aggress. One common aggression cue is a weapon such as a gun or knife. According to Berkowitz (1965), the presence of weapons may well elicit aggression. In fact, he has suggested that it may be the "trigger that pulls the finger." Berkowitz argued that frustration leads to a readiness to aggress, an emotional state that can be labeled *anger.* Actual aggression occurs only when there are appropriate aggression-eliciting cues in the environ-

ment. **Aggression cues,** which are defined as stimuli associated with the source of frustration and with aggressive behavior in general, may be anything from a weapon to a disliked person to a name associated with the frustrator. A cue assumes its aggression-eliciting quality when an individual associates certain instruments, situations, or persons with aggression. Further, since learning plays an important role, an object that serves as an aggression cue for one person may not be an aggression cue for another person. To predict the occurrence of aggression, one needs to know whether the individual has been frustrated and whether the immediate environment contains aggression cues.

To demonstrate the role of aggression cues in eliciting aggression, Berkowitz and his colleagues devised a number of **weapon effect** studies. They reasoned that weapons such as knives and guns would be aggression-eliciting cues and that the presence of a weapon should therefore elicit aggression from an angry individual. In one study, Berkowitz and Le Page (1967) had a confederate either anger or not anger subjects. The subjects were then given an opportunity to administer electric shock to the confederate. In some conditions, a 12-gauge shotgun and a .38-caliber revolver were lying on the table next to the shock apparatus (weapons condition), and in other conditions, two badminton rackets were placed next to the shock apparatus. The results indicated that when the subjects were angry, they gave more shocks to the confederate (aggressed more) in the weapons condition than in the badminton condition. Berkowitz interpreted these results as supporting his hypothesis that the weapons elicited aggression from the angry subjects.

The conclusion derived from the Berkowitz and Le Page study has important implications, but the study has not escaped criticism. Some investigators (Page & Scheidt, 1971; Buss, Booker & Buss, 1972) believed that the subjects may have been thinking about and reacting to demand characteristics in the situation (Chapter 1). The subjects in the weapons condition may have used the presence of weapons not as a cue eliciting aggression in the sense suggested by Berkowitz, but as a cue from the experimenter that it was all right to aggress or that he wanted them to

Chapter Nine   Aggression: Harming and Hurting Others

aggress in this situation. A number of attempts have been made to replicate this study (some successful and others not), and there is still some controversy about exactly what role the weapons do play (aggression cue or demand characteristic).

Berkowitz's cue theory has also been criticized because of its stand that cues are necessary before aggression will occur. In an extensive review of the literature, Rule and Nesdale (1976) cite many examples in which anger alone resulted in aggression. Berkowitz (1969, 1974) incorporated these criticisms into an amended version of his theory by stating that in some cases anger may have aggression-eliciting properties of its own.

In the final analysis, it seems that the presence of aggression cues will increase the likelihood of aggression following anger. However, violence may well occur in the absence of these cues.

Frustration-aggression: Some afterthoughts

Having traveled the rather long road through frustration-aggression theory, we can now ask where we stand. It seems clear that the original theory overstated the case. Frustration can, under some circumstances, lead people to aggress. It is still unclear whether catharsis does follow aggressive actions, or why it occurs. The notion of displaced aggression is intriguing, but it has not been adequately tested.

While the theory may not be correct, it has stimulated a tremendous amount of research on aggression. As we have seen, some of this research has identified the conditions under which frustration leads to aggression, and the conditions under which aggression is not likely to follow frustration. Other research has attempted to reexamine the concept of aggression, arguing that it is not frustration itself that causes people to resort to aggression. One group of researchers suggested that aggression is a behavior aimed at demonstrating control over our own behavior and environment (Allen & Greenberger, 1989). They argue that senseless acts such as vandalism are a means of establishing control; we destroy things to show that we have control over them. Therefore any situation that threatens our sense of control will increase our chances of responding aggressively. In a similar vein, others have suggested that aggression is aimed at impression

management (Tedeschi, Smith & Brown, 1974; Melburg & Tedeschi, 1989). Anything that threatens our self-esteem or casts us in a poor light, be it frustration or something else, will move us to aggression. Still another position is that aggression is a response to threats to our personal freedom (Worchel, 1974). As you can see, each of these views argues for a different focus on the frustration-aggression relationship, but each holds that aggression is instigated by threat or attack on some aspect of the self.

While these approaches are concerned with the causes of aggression, they don't tell us much about the type of aggression a person may use. We can think of many forms of aggression, ranging from insults to violent attacks with knives, guns, or bombs. In fact, as we mentioned earlier, ignoring the needs of someone who is suffering or allowing someone to engage in a destructive activity may be seen as aggression from some points of view. In order to have a more complete understanding of aggressive behavior, we would like to know not only what causes it, but what factors determine how people will aggress.

Social Learning Theory: Learning to Aggress

To obtain a foundation on which to base more specific predictions about the situations in which aggression will be exhibited and the forms that aggression will take, we can turn to a theory that relates aggressive behavior to learning. The major proponents of **social learning theory** (Bandura & Walters, 1963; Bandura, 1973) suggest that children learn when to aggress, how to aggress, and against whom to aggress. Although the bulk of this learning comes from observation of parents, additional learning of aggression comes from peer groups and from mass-media portrayals of aggression and violence. In extreme forms, chil-

---

aggression cues Stimuli associated with the source of frustration and with aggressive behavior in general; when paired with frustration, aggression cues may elicit aggression.
social learning theory The theory that individuals learn behavior by imitating others and receiving rewards.
weapon effect The tendency of people who are frustrated to aggress if a weapon is present.

Popular cartoon features often show violence as an acceptable mode of behavior. How many movies have you seen in the last year that contained a significant amount of violence?

strated that the schedule of reinforcement is important in determining future aggression. Small children were rewarded for hitting a doll. Some of the children were rewarded for every aggressive act (continuous reinforcement) whereas others were rewarded only periodically (partial reinforcement). The hitting behavior of the children increased while they were being rewarded. After a time, the experimenter stopped rewarding the aggressive behavior and studied the children's behavior. Interestingly enough, the children who had been on a partial reinforcement schedule continued to hit the doll longer than the children who had been continuously rewarded. The Cowan and Walters study is important because people are not always rewarded when they act aggressively—their aggression is successful only some of the time. The results of the study show that such partial reinforcement may be enough to sustain continued aggression even without rewards.

Modeling

Bandura and Walters also suggest that aggression is learned through **modeling,** or imitation. People are prone to imitate the behaviors of other persons—especially persons whom they admire or like. A son who sees his father aggress or a boy who sees his favorite television hero wipe out 25 thugs may come to believe that violence must be a good thing because "good" people act violently. Wolfgang and Fenacuti (1967) pointed out that children are surrounded by lessons that violence is good. They are taught that the security of our nation is based on our ability to use violent weapons if we are attacked. Violence permeates our advertising—it is the hero who overcomes obstacles and brings the beer home.

In addition to learning that aggression may be "good" behavior because "good" people aggress, children can learn how to aggress from models. Arnold Schwarzenegger teaches them how to use their fists or tongues to aggress; a teenage mutant ninja turtle gives lessons in karate, and James Bond teaches how to fabricate ingenious weapons. The child will be motivated to try out these new behaviors so he can act like father, or Rambo, or Dirty Harry.

The research on imitative learning has shown that not all models are imitated to the same degree. Bandura, Ross, and Ross (1961, 1963a, 1963b)

dren may actually be schooled in the techniques of aggression by parents or teachers.

Learning to aggress: Reinforcement

People learn to be aggressive by two main mechanisms. The first is **reinforcement.** Children are often rewarded for acting aggressively; the reward may take the form of praise from a father when his son beats up a larger boy or makes a particularly vicious tackle in a football game. The child is also reinforced through the added attention that he or she receives for aggressing. Even when parents and teachers disapprove of a child's aggressive behavior, they make the child the center of attention by scolding him or her or by trying to change the behavior. The child who desires attention from adults may be very willing to suffer such negative sanctions in return for the attention that the aggression brings. Positive reinforcement is also gained directly when the aggressor reaps the fruits of the aggressive acts— when Johnny beats up Jim to get Jim's football and is rewarded by taking possession of the ball. The child can learn from instances such as these that aggression pays.

A great deal of evidence supports the position that individuals learn aggression through reinforcement. Geen and Stoner (1973) found that subjects increased the intensity of aggression when they received verbal reinforcement for violence. Cowan and Walters (1963) demon-

conducted a number of studies in which nursery school children first observed a model aggressively playing with an inflated plastic clown (a "Bobo doll"). The model hit the doll, beat it with a hammer, kicked it, and sat on it. After watching the model, the children were put in a room with some toys—one of the toys being the Bobo doll. Their behavior was carefully observed. By varying the characteristics of the model, Bandura and his associates could study the influence of different types of models. In one study (Bandura et al., 1961), they demonstrated that children are more likely to imitate same-sex models—the boys imitated the male model more than they imitated the female model, and the reverse was true for the girls. Further, imitation is more likely if the model is of high status than of low status (Turner & Berkowitz, 1972).

In another study, Bandura and his colleagues (1963a) found that children imitated a real-life adult, an adult on film, or a cartoon figure that aggressed against a Bobo doll. Thus even cartoons can teach aggression. Myer (1972) found that adults too will imitate the behavior of a model displaying real or staged aggression. In still another example of adult imitation, Arms, Russell, and Sandilands (1979) found that spectators at sporting events involving aggression (wrestling and ice hockey) were more likely to feel hostile and express aggression than people who had watched a competitive but nonaggressive sporting event (swimming). This finding suggests that it is not competition that teaches aggression; it is aggressive acts themselves that teach aggression.

Other studies have focused on the act that the model performs. These studies have shown that subjects are more likely to imitate aggression when the model is rewarded rather than punished for acting violently (Bandura et al., 1963b; Bandura, 1965; Walters & Willows, 1968) and when the model's aggression is justified rather than unjustified (Geen & Stoner, 1973). Bandura (1965) allowed children to observe a model beating the Bobo doll. In one condition, the children observed no consequences to the model for the aggressive action. In a second condition, the children saw the model rewarded and praised by another adult. In a third condition, the children saw the model being punished and being called a bully for acting aggressively. The children were then allowed to play with the Bobo doll. The chil-

dren who observed the punished model played less aggressively than either the children who observed the rewarded model or the children who saw no consequences to the model at all.

Performing aggression
Social learning theory makes an important distinction between learning to aggress and actually committing an aggressive act. People can learn to aggress by being rewarded for this activity or by observing models. However, they will generally express aggression only when there are rewards for doing so in the particular situation. In the Bandura (1965) study, for example, we saw that children did not act aggressively after watching a model being punished for aggressive behavior.

Although these results seem to suggest that watching an aggressive model will not increase aggression if the model is punished, Bandura questioned whether the effect of punishment was on the acquisition of the aggressive behavior or on its performance. That is, did the children who saw the punished model fail to learn aggressive behavior, or did they learn how to aggress but simply inhibit the behavior? To find the answer, Bandura offered all of the children a reward if they could imitate the behavior of the model that they had observed previously. All of the subjects, including those who had seen the punished model, were able to reproduce the aggressive behavior with the same degree of accuracy. This result suggests that the children who observed the punished model had learned how to behave aggressively but had simply inhibited such behavior. When the circumstances were right, they too acted aggressively. This finding is important because it shows that punishing aggressive models will not keep observers from learning aggression. To predict when people will aggress, we need to examine their past learning opportunities *and* conditions in the present situation.

Reducing aggression
The social learning theory of aggression is important for a number of reasons. First, it sup-

---

modeling   Imitation of another person's behavior.
reinforcement   Rewards offered for approved behavior, which tend to increase the probability that the approved behavior will be repeated.

1. Why is aggression so difficult to define?

2. What are some of the weaknesses of instinct theories of aggression?

3. What type of research is often referred to in support and refutation of biological theories of aggression?

4. What are the basic propositions of frustration-aggression theory?

5. According to frustration-aggression theory, how can aggression be reduced?

6. What is an aggression cue and how does it influence the likelihood of aggression following frustration?

7. What are the basic positions of social learning theory?

plies answers to questions that cannot be handled by the frustration-aggression theory. For example, frustration-aggression theory cannot explain why in the same frustrating situation one individual will lash out with fists, another will use a gun, and a third will not aggress at all. According to social learning theory, early experiences and learning determine how an individual will express aggression. We might expect, therefore, that the first individual grew up in an environment where he or she witnessed or was rewarded for fistfighting. The second individual may have been reared in a family in which guns were constantly present and shoot-em-up movies were popular. The third individual may have grown up in an environment in which aggression was discouraged and not rewarded.

In addition to explaining why people aggress as they do, social learning theory provides a foundation on which a program to reduce aggression can be based. Bandura and Walters (1963) point out that parents' use of physical punishment for their children's misdeeds may actually lead to increased aggression. In this case the parents serve as a model for the children.

The children observe the parents' use of aggression (punishment) to obtain what they want (a reduction in the children's aggression). Although the children may not aggress at home because of fear of retaliation, they are likely to use the aggressive responses learned at home in other situations. Sears and his colleagues (1953) found that children who had been severely punished for aggression at home were more likely to act aggressively outside the home than children whose parents had punished them less severely for aggressive acts.

According to social learning theory, aggression can be decreased by the withdrawal of love or withholding of some other desired object as punishment for aggression. In this way, the child receives no reinforcement or attention for aggression and does not witness an aggressive model to imitate in a later situation. Thus social learning theory suggests that when we teach a child not to aggress, we must not use aggression as the deterrent. Brown and Elliott (1965) demonstrated this principle by having nursery school teachers reward children's cooperative and nonviolent behavior and ignore their aggressive behavior. After two weeks of this treatment, there was a significant reduction in the aggressive behavior displayed by the children. The children's aggressive behavior was reduced further when the teachers repeated this program of rewards three weeks later.

Aggression and Social Dilemmas

Aggression and violence create problems at individual, family, and societal levels. Social psychologists have explored several areas of violence in society, seeking answers that can help to shape and explain social policy. We will now look at the research in some of these areas. You should note that in some cases the research has made use of theoretical insights designed uniquely for a particular problem, insights that are less clearly connected to the general theories we have been discussing. In other cases the broad theories of aggression have served as meaningful guides to the research.

Family Violence

It is easy to assume that almost everyone who reads the tragic story of Lisa Steinberg will be shocked by the senseless violence of it. But this assumption may be unfounded, because family violence occurs with disturbing frequency in our society. It is estimated that nearly 20% of all murder victims are killed by members of their families. Women are most often the victims of spouse abuse: more than 1,700 women die annually in the United States as a result of family violence (Steinmetz, 1980). More than 1,000 children were killed by family violence in 1986. Family violence is found in all racial, class, and ethnic groups. These extreme cases represent only the tip of the iceberg, and we can assume that cases of family violence range between 5 and 25 million each year. Therefore, it is likely that a large number of you who are reading this book have been victims of or witnesses to family violence.

How can we explain such a cruel form of human interaction? Do our theories of aggression give us some insight into the problem? In order to answer these questions, let's examine the typical conditions involved in family violence. First, we cannot lay the blame on mental illness; Robert Emery (1989) writes that "if anything conclusive can be said about child abuse research, however, it is that the psychopathological model does not apply to the great majority of abusive parents . . ." (p. 322). The same can be said in regard to spouse abuse. Second, men are most often the abusing spouses; in the case of child abuse there is still disagreement about whether men or women are the most frequent abusers. Third, abuse is often associated with stressful events, such as the loss of a job. Fourth, violence is transmitted through the generations. Finally, many cases of abuse begin as attempts by parents to discipline their children (Parke & Collmer, 1975) or by one spouse to control the other.

Do you begin to see the relevance of family violence to our theories of aggression? In analyzing family violence, Emery (1989) suggests that the pattern involves both frustration-aggression and social learning theories. Some aversive event such as frustration or threat to one's self-esteem sets the stage. The resultant aggression is aimed at a family member because the abuser has learned this pattern as a child. The abusive behavior is reinforced because the individual finds that it is effective in influencing the behavior of other family members and gaining power within the family (Walker, 1989).

While the pattern fits within the framework of our theories, we must add a caution. Though most family violence is perpetuated by individuals who were abused or who witnessed abuse as children, most people who come from abusive families do not become abusers. One survey found that 94% of people who recalled seeing their parents hit each other were reported not to be physically abusive in their marriages (Kalmuss, 1984). Therefore, our theories help us to understand family violence but they are not complete enough to explain the whole picture.

Family violence is notoriously difficult to stop. People are very reluctant to report suspected cases of family violence, and even such victims as Hedda Nussbaum do not report the violence they suffer. Victims often feel that they must have done something to deserve the violence or that the incident was "an unusual case." These assumptions are wrong, because the violence only tends to increase, and the attacks are not the fault of the victim. Programs to treat family violence generally involve temporarily removing the victim from the family situation in order to protect him or her, bringing the family into family therapy, and working to reduce the stress that may have led to the violence (Emery, 1989; Walker, 1989).

Drugs and Aggression

According to Hedda Nussbaum, both she and Joel began using cocaine in 1978. As they increased their use of the drug, the violence began. This set of events is only correlational (remember our discussion in Chapter 1), but it does prompt us to question whether drug use can affect aggression. In fact, we will see that this issue actually involves a number of questions. First, does drug use itself cause people to become more aggressive? Second, do drugs increase people's aggressive behavior when they are thwarted or otherwise angered? And finally, do all drugs have the same effect on aggression? As you might imagine, research on this topic is an ethical minefield. Many of the drugs we might like to study are illegal. The use of even legal drugs, such as

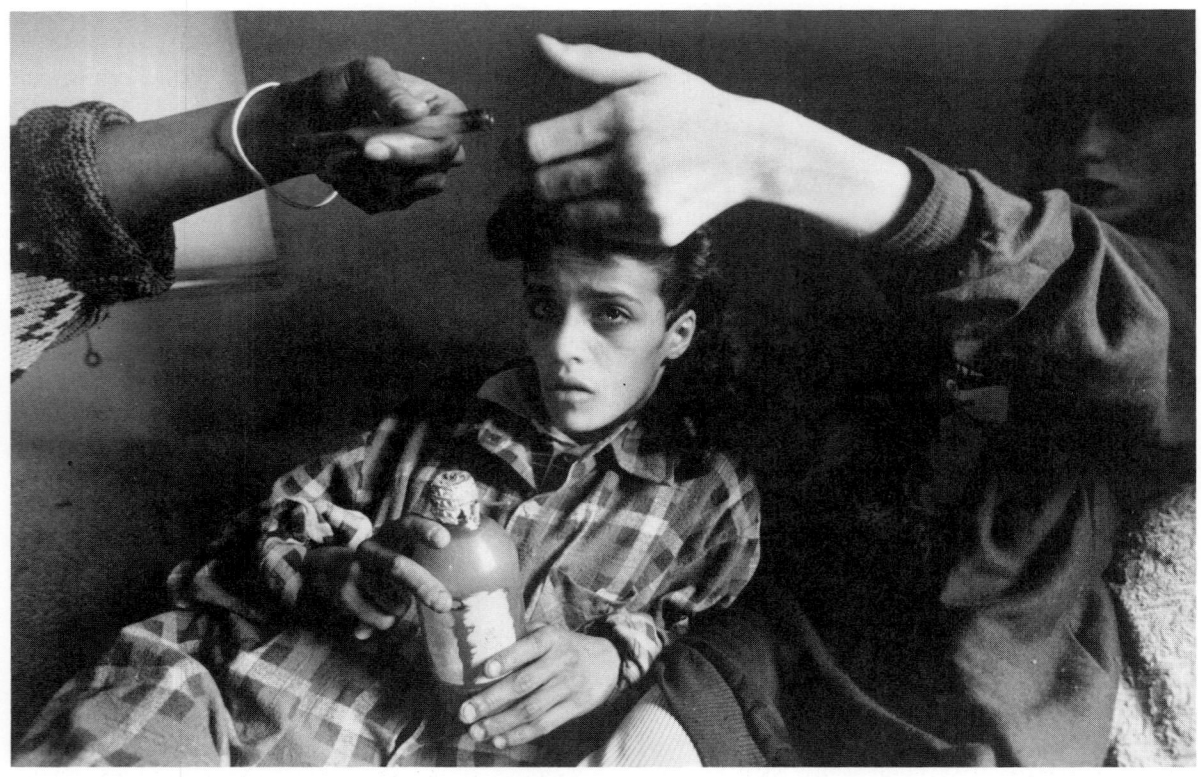

Drugs can have significant effects on aggression, but the direction of this effect is dependent on the type of drug, the dose size, and the existence or absence of frustration. Even drugs such as the depressant diazepam that are used for clinical treatment may influence aggression under some conditions.

alcohol and nicotine, is restricted by state laws to adults. Given these problems and others, we are only just beginning to find answers to these questions.

Taylor and his associates (Taylor & Gammon, 1975; Taylor, Gammon, & Capasso, 1976; Taylor et al., 1976) studied the effects of alcohol and marijuana on aggression. Subjects in the studies were given either alcohol or marijuana, in large or small doses. They were then either angered or not angered by a confederate and given an opportunity to attack the confederate. The results indicated that even in rather large doses, alcohol by itself does not instigate aggression. However, large doses of alcohol do lead to increased aggression if the subject is angered or threatened.

Marijuana, on the other hand, has a different effect. Subjects who have consumed a large dose of marijuana and are later threatened react significantly less aggressively than either subjects who have consumed small doses of the drug or subjects who have not consumed the drug. Further, subjects who have consumed large doses of marijuana are significantly less aggressive than subjects who have consumed large doses of alcohol.

Another interesting effect of alcohol was uncovered when Schmutte and Taylor (1980) placed intoxicated and nonintoxicated subjects in a reaction-time task in which they could shock and be shocked by their opponent. In some conditions, the subjects received little pain feedback from the opponent; in other cases, they heard the opponent express a great deal of pain and discomfort at the shock. The results showed that intoxicated subjects were more aggressive than nonintoxicated subjects and that the aggression of the intoxicated individuals was not influenced

Many X-rated movies have a strong sadomasochistic theme. Studies suggest that viewing such materials stimulates aggression against women.

by the pain cues. On the other hand, the non-intoxicated subjects decreased their aggression in the pain feedback condition. Along a similar line, Zeichner and Pihl (1979) found that feedback about the effects of aggression did not affect the aggressiveness of intoxicated subjects. It did, however, influence the aggression of nonintoxicated subjects. Overall, the results suggest that large quantities of alcohol reduce people's awareness of or concern about situational conditions and the effects of their aggression. More recently, investigators have found that depressant drugs (diazepam) used for the treatment of anxiety affect aggression in a way similar to the effect of alcohol (Gantnot & Taylor, 1988). This finding opens up the important issue of the broad effects of drugs used for the treatment of psychological disorders.

Thus drugs can significantly affect aggressive behavior, but the direction of the effect depends on the type of drug, the size of the dose, and whether or not the subject is threatened.

Erotica, Violent Pornography, and Aggression

Does pornography engender aggressive acts? Does it particularly engender greater aggression by men against women? Pornographic movies, rated with any number of Xs, as well as pornographic pictures and books are abundantly available. In one study, approximately 81% of all males surveyed indicated that they had recently availed themselves of pornographic material and 38% indicated that they had recently viewed violent pornographic material (Demare, Briere & Lips, 1988). To the extent that watching or reading pornographic material is arousing, that arousal may contribute to aggression.

In Chapter 3 we discussed Schachter's work on emotions (Schachter, 1964; Schachter & Singer, 1962). Schachter postulated that emotions are characterized by general, nonspecific arousal and a cognitive label. A person experiences physiological arousal, and then searches the environment for the cause or an explanation. That explanation is the cognitive label that allows us to attribute our arousal to happiness, fear, anger, and so forth.

Dolf Zillmann and his associates (Zillmann, 1971, 1978; Tannenbaum and Zillmann, 1975; Zillmann & Bryant, 1988) adapted Schachter's labeling theory to the aggression paradigm. They reasoned that an angry individual who is further aroused by some other source may label the additional arousal as anger. As a consequence of this misperception, the individual will *feel* even more angry and therefore will be more likely to aggress. According to this **excitation-transfer theory,** what is important is not the real source of arousal but the perceptions that people have in regard to that arousal.

Sexually explicit material should fit the excitation-transfer model proposed by Zillmann. And indeed, several studies have tested this hypothesis. For example, Zillmann (1971) investigated the effects of sexual arousal on aggression. Subjects watched either a sexually arousing film (*The Couch*), a violent boxing film (*Body and Soul*), or an interesting but nonarousing documentary (*Marco Polo's Travels*). The subjects were then either angered or not angered by a confederate. Finally, the subjects were allowed to act as teachers and shock the confederate. The results showed that the subjects who had watched the sexually arousing film were the most aggressive (that is, they delivered the strongest shocks), whereas the subjects who watched the nonarousing documentary were the least aggressive. This finding is consistent with the idea that the sexual arousal created by the erotic film was interpreted by the subjects as anger, and the result was heightened aggression.

Is it possible to conclude that erotic or pornographic material provokes aggression? A second group of studies suggests the opposite. Baron and his colleagues (Baron, 1974; Baron & Bell, 1973; Frodi, 1977) showed that exposure to erotic stimuli can actually reduce subsequent aggression. They argued that aggression and sexuality are intrinsically incompatible. Aroused sexual feelings, they reasoned, would inhibit aggression. Zillmann and Johnson (1973) suggested that sexual arousal, by being absorbing and salient, is distracting, so people who are instigated to aggress will be distracted from their aggression by their sexual feelings.

Clearly, a more comprehensive explanation is necessary to account for the conflicting results. Zillmann and his colleagues (1981), following earlier work by Donnerstein, Donnerstein, and Evans (1975), suggested an **excitation-valence model** of the effects of pornography on aggression. In their research, they found that people who were exposed to unpleasant pornography increased their aggression to a fellow student. Students exposed to pleasant pornography decreased their aggression. Zillmann and his associates (1981) suggested that the likelihood of aggression depends on the degree of excitation caused by the erotic material and its value as pleasure. For example, films of bestiality and sadomasochism produce quite negative reactions in most viewers (Zillmann, Bryant & Carveth, 1981). Such films serve to increase aggression. More pleasing erotic films, however, may serve to reduce aggressive behavior. Thus the same theoretical model may account for both increases and decreases in aggression.

Aggressive pornography

Over the past several years, investigators have been increasingly concerned about aggressive erotica—films that combine sexual arousal with violence. Scenes of forcible rape, sex at gunpoint, and so forth are commonplace in films bearing the X rating. Malamuth and his colleagues have shown that such films have disturbing attitudinal effects on male viewers. They have demonstrated that men who see such films have more fantasies about rape (Malamuth, 1984), have a reduced sensitivity to rape (Malamuth & Check, 1981), and harbor greater feelings that they, too, could commit rape (Malamuth, Haber & Feshbach, 1980).

Linz, Donnerstein, and Adams (1989) monitored the heart rates of undergraduates at the University of California at Santa Barbara while they were viewing film clips of violence being perpetrated by a man against a woman. Before they saw the clips, some subjects had viewed a film containing violent, explicit sex. Other subjects had watched an arousing sex scene that had no violence. Heart rate and attitude measures showed that the violence in the first film desensitized the subjects to the violence against the woman in the second film. In addition, those who had watched the violent sex in the first film attributed less injury to the victim of aggression in the second film. These subjects also saw the male perpetrator of the violence in the second film as less responsible for his aggression than subjects who had initially seen a nonviolent film. This study provides further evidence that violent pornography has both physiological and cognitive effects on viewers.

Why does violent pornography provoke

Chapter Nine   Aggression: Harming and Hurting Others

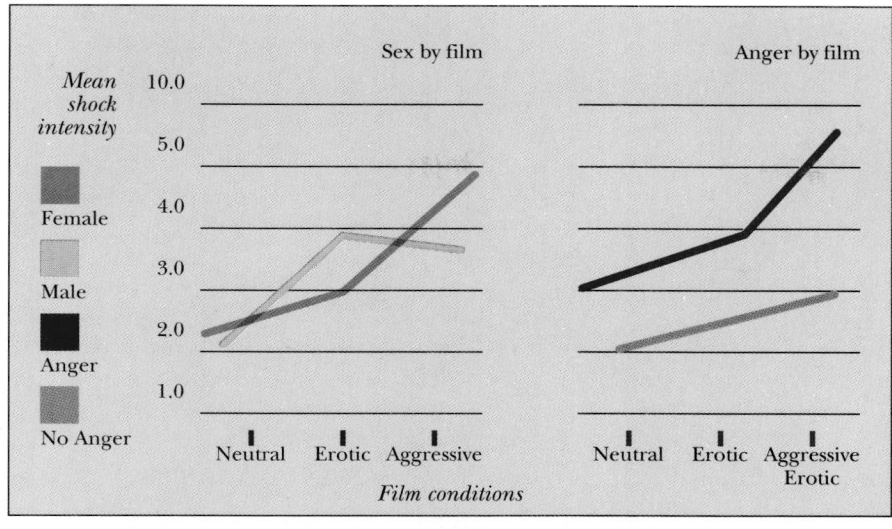

FIGURE 9-4 Mean shock intensity as a function of sex of victim, film, and anger
SOURCE: Donnerstein (1980).

aggression? Donnerstein (1980, 1983) argued that one answer may rest in Berkowitz's (1965) notion of aggressive cues. Watching a woman become the victim of sexual aggression causes arousal in men, and also causes the woman to become associated with aggression. The woman, then, could become an aggressive cue that might trigger aggression by the viewer in a future incident.

Donnerstein (1980) had male subjects angered or treated in a neutral manner by a confederate. They were then given the opportunity to view one of three films. One was a control film that showed neither sex nor violence. The other two films were highly erotic. One of the erotic films was entirely nonaggressive but the other depicted the rape of a woman by a man who broke into her house and forced her into sexual activity at gunpoint. After the film, the subjects had an opportunity to deliver electric shocks to the confederate during what the subject thought was a learning task. The amount of electric shock that the subject wished to administer served as the dependent measure of aggression.

The results are depicted in Figure 9-4. While the erotic film had a mild effect in increasing the amount of electric shock, the aggressive-erotic film had a major effect. The aggressive-erotic film caused a major increase in the amount of aggression shown by the subject, especially when the subject had been angered and when the con-

federate was a woman. In summarizing much of the recent literature, Donnerstein (1983) concludes that a direct causal link has been demonstrated between exposure to aggressive erotica and violence against women.

The response of the witness and the target
Violent pornography tends to lead to aggression against a female target (Hui, 1986). Leonard and Taylor (1983) showed that it makes a difference whether the female target of the aggression approves or disapproves of the pornography. They found that male subjects who viewed sexually explicit slides in the company of a female confederate who expressed approval or pleasure administered shocks of greater intensity than did subjects who received nonpermissive cues.

Now let us consider the target of aggression. Does the level of aggression depend on his or her response to a sexually violent film? In a study by Donnerstein and Berkowitz (1981), some sub-

---

excitation-transfer theory A theory, usually applied to aggression, that holds that arousal from one source can be misperceived and therefore transferred to another source.

excitation-valence model A theory that the likelihood of aggression after viewing pornography depends on the degree of excitation caused by the erotic material and its pleasurableness.

Evidence suggests that children may learn violent behavior by watching aggressive models on television. What kinds of television programming provide nonviolent models for children?

jects were angered by a confederate. Others were not. All of the subjects were male, but half of the confederates were male and half were female. A subject and a confederate then saw a film, and afterward the subject had an opportunity to shock the confederate. The type of film the subject saw and the response of the confederate to that film were varied. The study showed that when subjects were made angry by a male confederate, shocks given to that confederate did not depend on the kind of film the subjects saw or on the confederate's response to the film. On the other hand, subjects angered by a female confederate did show different levels of aggression as a function of the film they saw. When they watched a violently erotic film, they tended to give more painful shocks to the confederate than when they watched a nonviolent film. Apparently the greater

aggression toward women in this condition was fueled by the heightened arousal men experienced as a result of the aggressive erotica. What about the conditions in which the subjects were not previously angered by the confederate? Did they aggress against her as a function of the film they saw? A female confederate was given an intense electric shock when the film had aggressive sexual content and her response to that film was positive. When she seemed to enjoy the film, subjects perceived the film to be less aggressive, they found the film victim to be more responsible for the violence perpetrated against her, and the female confederate received more shocks.

The results of studies such as these point out the perniciousness of aggressive pornography (Donnerstein & Linz, 1986), particularly if there is any indication that the women who are being

Chapter Nine   Aggression: Harming and Hurting Others

victimized—or other women viewing the victimization—experience pleasure. The message conveyed seems to reduce the perception of the seriousness of sexual aggression, justifies the aggression, and reduces inhibitions against aggressive behaviors.

Violent Television and Aggression

Turn on your television set almost any evening and odds are you will be confronted with violence. In 1979, for instance, it was estimated that 70% of all prime-time programs contained physical violence; on the average, 5.7 violent encounters occurred per hour. Weekend daytime shows (mostly for children) were even more violent; 92% of these programs had at least one violent scene and, on the average, 17 violent encounters occurred per hour (Gerbner et al., 1980). Because children watch up to three to four hours of television per day (Lyle & Hoffman, 1972), they almost inevitably are exposed to a heavy dose of violence. Waters and Malamud (1975) estimated that the average 16-year-old has seen 13,000 murders on television.

Because television viewing is one of the most common American pastimes, and violence is one of the most common acts portrayed on television, it should not be surprising that both the public and social psychologists have been interested in the effects of violent television on aggressive behavior. Such groups as Citizens Action for Better Television have called for a decrease in media violence. They assume that such programming leads to increased aggressive behavior in viewers. As we shall see, research has generally supported this contention (Huesmann, 1982). The picture, however, may not be as clear as it is sometimes thought to be.

The two major theories about human aggression (frustration-aggression and social learning) make different predictions about the effects of television violence. On the one hand, the catharsis hypothesis of frustration-aggression theory suggests that participation in an aggressive act will lessen the instigation to future aggression. Thus if people are allowed to play aggressively or if they vicariously experience aggression by watching violence on television, they should be less likely to aggress. From this point of view, it could be argued that violence on tele-

vision (and in other media) should be allowed, if not encouraged. By witnessing violence, viewers can reduce their own needs to act aggressively, since the vicarious experience of violence can lead to catharsis. On the other hand, social learning theory and Berkowitz's cue theory suggest that witnessed aggression should lead to more aggression rather than to catharsis. Portrayed aggression serves as a model for the viewer to imitate, and it can provide aggression cues that are sufficient to release the viewer's aggressiveness. Moreover, in many cases the viewer also sees the aggressor on the screen rewarded for his or her actions. This makes the aggressor an even more attractive model to follow.

Research attempting to resolve this dispute has fallen into two categories. One approach has been correlational. In these studies (see Huesmann, 1982), measures are taken of aggression and of television viewing as they occur naturally. The two measures are then correlated to see if any relationship emerges. What has been consistently found is that violent television viewing and aggressive behavior are mildly but positively related. In other words, the more a person shows a preference for violent television, the more aggressive that person is. This has held true not only in the United States but in Finland, Poland, and Australia as well. This finding poses problems for a catharsis explanation of the effects of violent television; it seems more consistent with social learning theory. However, correlation does not necessarily imply causation. It could be, for instance, that people who are more aggressive to begin with prefer violent television. They may find it more exciting, or a means of justifying their own aggression. If this were true, a positive correlation would be seen between the viewing of violence and aggressive behavior, but *not* because television *caused* the aggressive behavior.

To answer more clearly this question of cause, researchers have turned to experiments as a second avenue of inquiry. Some of the earliest and most influential studies were conducted by Bandura and his colleagues (Bandura, Ross & Ross, 1961, 1963a); we described them earlier. However, as Stein and Friedrich (1975) have observed, it is unclear how far we can generalize from these studies to violence as it is seen on commercial television. Bandura used films constructed specifically for his experiments. These films were brief and simple; the model's aggressive behavior dominated the action. But violence on commercial television may be harder to understand; the shows are longer and more complex. Therefore the person's attention may be less focused and the violence may be less salient. Also, we do not know from Bandura's studies whether the aggression observed in subjects was lasting or more general. Typically, aggression was assessed immediately after the subjects viewed the model's behavior; the subject was given an opportunity to aggress in a similar situation using behaviors similar to the model's. Would the aggression also be observed in a different situation? And more important, would different, even *more* aggressive behaviors be observed in a different context?

Further research has been somewhat contradictory. Some studies report an actual decline in aggressive behavior after witnessing violence. Feshbach (1961) demonstrated that witnessing an aggressive film can lower the viewer's subsequent aggression. He had angry and nonangry subjects watch either an aggressive film (a prizefight scene) or a nonaggressive film. Feshbach found that when given the opportunity to aggress, the angry subjects who had witnessed the aggressive film were less aggressive than the angry subjects who had seen the nonaggressive film. However, the nonangry subjects who saw the aggressive film reported feeling more hostile than the nonangry subjects who saw the nonaggressive film. This finding suggests that witnessing aggression can reduce the instigation to aggression of a viewer who is angry when he sees the film.

In a field study involving 625 boys between the ages of 10 and 17, Feshbach and Singer (1971) found that watching violent movies reduced aggressive behavior. The subjects were upper-class boys at private boarding schools and boys in state institutions for the homeless. They were assigned to watch six weeks (one hour each night) of either aggressive programs or nonaggressive programs. Their behavior was rated for aggressiveness by staff members of the institutions. The results showed that the boys in the state institutions who watched the aggressive movies engaged in only half as many fights as, and were rated as less aggressive than, the boys who watched the nonviolent programs. The type of program was found to have no effect on the behavior of the boys in the private schools. The Feshbach and

Singer study has been cited as supporting the catharsis hypothesis. However, the study has been severely criticized on methodological grounds. For example, boys at the state institution preferred aggressive programs. Thus those boys assigned to view *nonaggressive* programs may have felt deprived and resentful over losing their favorite programs. This in turn may have led them to behave more aggressively.

A second body of research has suggested that violent television increases aggressive behavior. Friedrich and Stein (1973) allowed nursery school children to watch aggressive, neutral, or prosocial programs for a four-week period (see Figure 9-5). The behavior of the children was observed before, during, and after the television period. Interestingly enough, the behavior of the children who had been rated as below-average in aggressiveness before viewing the programs was not affected by them. For children who were initially high in aggressiveness, the results were more complex. Highly aggressive children who saw neutral and prosocial programs *decreased* their aggressiveness over time; those who saw aggressive programs also decreased their aggressiveness, but less. Friedrich and Stein interpreted this to mean that aggressive programs maintained what otherwise would have been a pattern of decreasing aggression, and that such shows thus encouraged aggression. It is important to keep in mind, however, that the aggressive programs did not *increase* subjects' aggressiveness. It is possible that the aggressive shows had little or no impact, and that the neutral and prosocial programs served to decrease aggression. This has been found in several studies with adult subjects (Zillmann & Johnson, 1973; Donnerstein, Donnerstein & Barrett, 1976), and is an interesting finding in its own right.

An experiment that did show an increase in aggression after subjects viewed violent films was reported by Parke and his colleagues (1977). They conducted three extensive studies (two in the United States and one in Belgium) with juvenile delinquents in minimum-custody institutions. The subjects' behaviors were observed for a three-week period to get a baseline measure of general aggressiveness. The subjects were then randomly divided into two groups, and for the next week half of the subjects watched aggressive movies each night and the other half watched nonag-

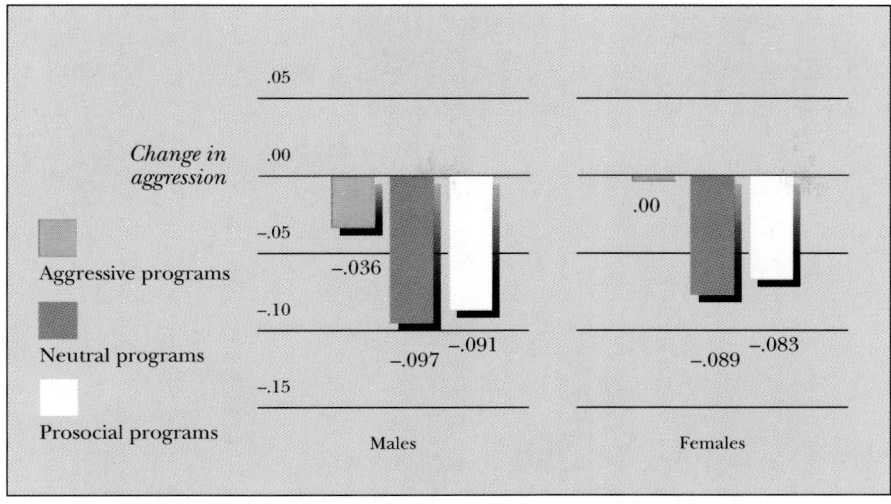

FIGURE 9-5 Mean change scores for interpersonal aggression[1,2]
[1]The lower the score, the greater the reduction in aggression after viewing the programs.
[2]Scores are for subjects high in initial aggression.
SOURCE: Friedrich and Stein (1973).

gressive movies. During the final three-week phase, the subjects were observed in their day-to-day routines and their behavior was evaluated on an aggressiveness dimension. Figure 9-6 presents results from the first study. In each case, the subjects who watched the aggressive movies behaved more aggressively than the subjects who saw the neutral movies. This is consistent with social learning theory. However, the implications of this study for understanding the impact of *television* violence on *typical* individuals is unclear. The films used were unedited, feature-length selections that were much more violent than television fare. Also, the subjects were from institutions for juvenile delinquents. Thus at least one of the problems that Feshbach and Singer were criticized for—the use of an overly aggressive, atypical subject population—was shared by this study. Subjects from this population may have reacted differently from most other people.

An interesting experiment by Josephson (1987) provides further evidence for increased aggression following exposure to violent television. It also addresses the importance of a cue for aggression, which forms the cornerstone of Berkowitz's (1965) theory of aggression cues.

Second- and third-grade boys in Winnipeg, Manitoba, watched either a violent or nonviolent action-oriented program. The action-oriented

program was an exciting motorcycle race. The violent program was an excerpt from a police action series. It began with the coldblooded killing of an off-duty police officer by a group of snipers. As the 14-minute episode proceeded, members of a police SWAT team systematically gunned down or knocked unconscious each member of the gang of snipers. The SWAT team members communicated with each other by walkie-talkies, and aggression was usually preceded by calls on the walkie-talkies.

After watching the violent episode, the boys played a game of floor hockey. Four observers rated the boys' play. Aggression was an index composed of such things as pushing another boy down, elbowing him, insulting him, or hitting him with a hockey stick. Before beginning the game, the boys were interviewed, "just the way real radio announcers interview hockey players." Half of the boys were interviewed with a microphone; the other half were interviewed with a walkie-talkie. The walkie-talkie served as the aggression cue.

Josephson found the greatest amount of aggression in boys who watched the violent episode and had the aggression cue of the walkie-talkie. These youngsters played hockey more aggressively than any other boys in the study. The boys who watched the SWAT program with-

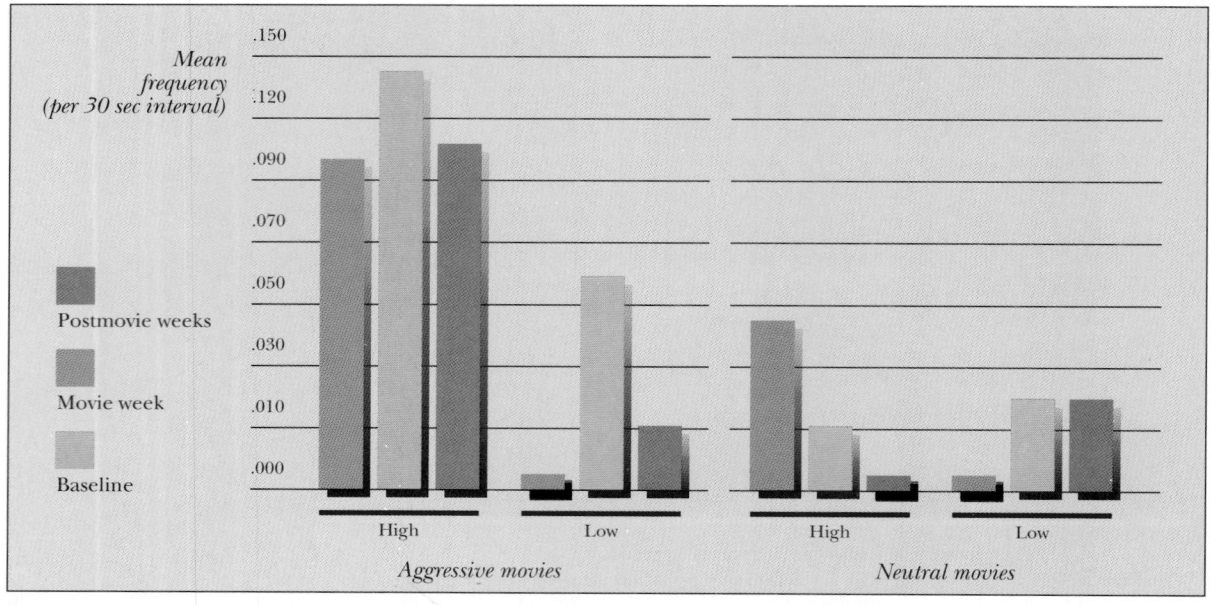

FIGURE 9-6 General aggression index

NOTE: "High" and "low" refer to initial tendencies to aggress.
SOURCE: Parke et al. (1977).

out the aggression cue were less aggressive and the boys who watched the motorcycle race were the least aggressive during the hockey game. These results, while offering support for the aggression cue theory of aggressive behavior, still need to be interpreted with caution. The supportive results were found only for those boys who were rated high on characteristic aggression by their classroom teachers. That is, the aggression cues tended to elicit aggressive behavior in boys *already* predisposed to act aggressively.

On video games

Video games are a multi-billion-dollar industry. It is estimated that video arcades take in approximately $8 billion annually, and billions more are spent on home videos. Anyone who has seen or played such games as Space Invaders and Missile Command knows that the fantasy element in the game is often a violent one, consisting of blowing up the characters, space ships, and planets. Even the popular Pac Man video games contained aggression of a different sort, with characters gobbling each other up as they chased each other around the screen. Do these games affect children and cause them to behave more aggressively? It appears that the answer is yes.

Studies by Cooper and Mackie (1986) and Silvern and Williamson (1987) used experimental paradigms that have become familiar in the TV-and-aggression research. Silvern and Williamson (1987) studied 28 children from 4 to 6 years of age. They observed pairs of children in free play to obtain baseline measures of aggression. Half of the pairs then watched a *Road Runner* cartoon, while the other half played Space Invaders. One child in the pair actually played the game, while the other merely observed. After the game or cartoon, the children were once again observed in free play. Both the violent cartoon and the video game raised the level of aggressive play above the baseline measures. The effect of the games and the TV program were far more pronounced for boys than for girls. It is interesting, too, that observers of video games were affected just as much as the players.

Cooper and Mackie's (1986) research showed similar findings. Their subjects, all 10 and 11 years old, behaved more aggressively after playing Missile Command. These investigators, too, found that observers of video games behaved just as aggressively as the children who actually played them. However, in contrast to Silvern and Williamson (1987), Cooper and Mackie found these effects with girls, but not boys.

Chapter Nine   Aggression: Harming and Hurting Others

What can we conclude?

Policy makers want definitive answers to important questions. Whether television and video games provoke aggression in young people is one of those important questions. We have examined research that has supported the notion that viewing televised aggression causes viewers to increase their aggressive behavior. We have also seen research that supports the opposite position. Most studies find effects for males and not for females; a few studies show that females are more affected by aggressive media than males. Are there any clear and definitive answers?

A report prepared by the National Institute of Mental Health (NIMH) conceded that the television-aggression link has not been established conclusively in any single study (Pearl & Bouthilet, 1982). However, the report did conclude that the "weight of the evidence" suggested that violent television programs increased subsequent aggression by viewers.

This conclusion has not gone unchallenged. Jonathan Freedman (1984, 1986) reviewed "every available published study" and concluded that the weight of the available evidence leads to no conclusion at all—that the evidence at hand is not yet sufficient to prove the hypothesis.

Freedman offered possible reasons for the less than conclusive findings. Suppose that televised aggression tends to lead to aggressive behavior, as has been shown in the laboratory. In the nonlaboratory world, television watching has to be placed in the context of many other behaviors and many other influences. Television viewing itself, even for a person who watches a great deal of televised violence, has to be viewed in relation to other programs in which aggression does not take place. Consequently, the real-world context provides so many other influences that the effect of television viewing may be mitigated by those other influences.

The debate engendered by Freedman's review (Freedman, 1986; Friedrich-Cofer & Huston, 1986) has raised another fascinating point. Perhaps more convincing evidence would be obtained if we paid attention to a *bidirectional* hypothesis (Gunter, 1983; Huesmann, Logerspetz & Eron, 1984). According to this hypothesis, people who watch aggressive television may be those who are characteristically more aggressive, and the watching of the programs may provoke still

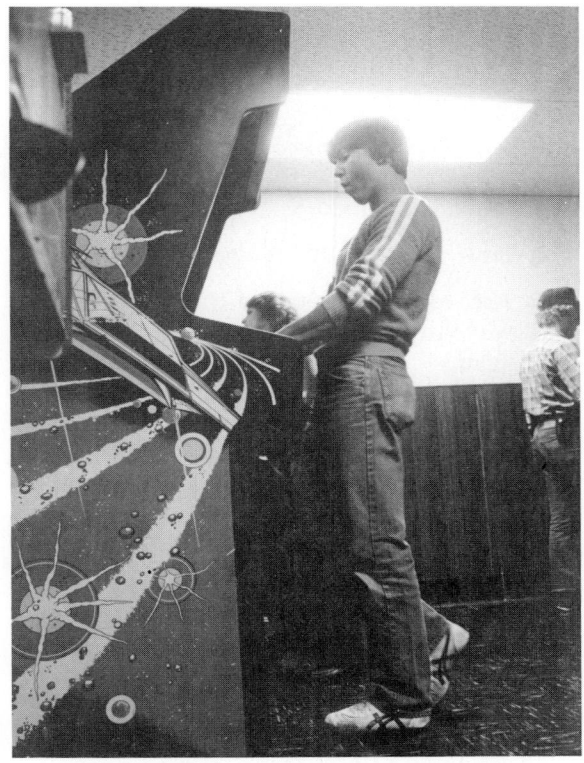

Video games such as Space Invaders and Missile Command involve violent themes. Characters must hit, kick, beat, eat, or in some other way destroy the intruder. Research suggests that both observers and players, especially males, may behave more aggressively as a result of their contact with violent video games.

greater aggression in those people. In other words, instead of seeking to prove that the causal link between TV and aggression goes only in one direction, it may be better and more fruitful to consider TV viewing and aggressive behavior as a two-way street, with each factor affecting the other.

We have placed considerable emphasis on the television-aggression question and the pornography-aggression question for several reasons: (1) they are phenomena of immense social significance; (2) they are phenomena that bring together several theories of social psychology, each of which has received considerable support in the laboratory; and (3) they are areas that demonstrate the rewards and frustrations of bringing basic research to bear on problems of societal significance. We agree with the conclusions of the NIMH, that the weight of the evidence supports

1. How do frustration-aggression and social learning theories help us understand family violence?

2. How do drugs affect aggression?

3. According to excitation-transfer theory, why are men more likely to aggress against women after viewing violent pornography?

4. What evidence supports a link between television violence and aggression? How has it been challenged?

5. What is an aggression cue and how does it influence the likelihood of aggression after viewing violent television or violent pornography?

6. Can social psychologists make social policy? Why not?

the belief that there is a causal link between watching television and behaving aggressively. However, the science of psychology must still refine its hypotheses in these areas and provide more definitive evidence.

Summary

Although *aggression* has been defined as action intended to injure another person, we noted other considerations that suggest several definitions. Aggressive behavior may spring from instinctual or biological origins. We have argued, however, that social psychological theories are necessary if we are to understand when and why aggressive behavior occurs.

One of the most popular theories of aggression regards *frustration* as the root cause of all aggression. According to proponents of the *frustration-aggression hypothesis,* engaging in or witnessing acts of aggression can serve to reduce an individual's frustration via *catharsis.* The frustration-aggression theory also states that if aggression cannot be vented directly upon the frustrating agent, it will be *displaced* onto another target, the most likely targets being those that are highly similar to the source of the frustration. Critics of the theory argue that frustration does not always lead to aggression and that aggression is not always the direct result of frustration. Nevertheless, the frustration-aggression hypothesis has stimulated a tremendous amount of research that has shed light on the conditions under which frustration is likely to lead to aggressive actions.

The concept of revolution may be considered from the perspective of frustration-aggression. When a large group of people experiences frustration, or *relative deprivation,* through the actions of its leaders, the people may be moved to revolt. Their sense of deprivation may result from the loss of freedom or goods they once had (*decremental deprivation*), because they can see no hope of realizing their dreams (*aspirational deprivation*), or if previous improvements in economic and social conditions are suddenly cut back (*progressive deprivation*). Revolution is thought to occur in stages, including the preliminary or *restlessness* stage, the *popular* stage, the *formal* phase, the *reign of terror,* and the *institutional* stage.

Another theoretical approach to aggression suggests that frustration merely produces the readiness to aggress; the presence or absence of aggression cues will determine whether people will actually express aggression. Still other researchers argue that aggressive behavior is a way of expressing the need to exercise control over situations or other people. *Impression management* and the need to maintain self-esteem are also thought to play roles in aggression.

Social learning theory suggests that aggressive behaviors are learned from others. The learning occurs through *reinforcement* and, most important, from *modeling.* Even if an individual learns how to aggress, however, he or she will not necessarily behave aggressively unless rewarded, or at least not punished, for doing so. Research has also shown that people will imitate aggressive models. Thus, social learning theory suggests that aggressive behavior can be diminished by not providing aggressive models for children and not rewarding aggressive behavior.

Theories of aggression allow us to understand a great deal about why people aggress and some ways of reducing aggression. We have seen, however, that theory is helpful to varying degrees when applied to social dilemmas that afflict society. While the application of theory and research is somewhat limited in the areas of family violence and drug abuse, we have a growing body of knowledge on the impact of pornography and violent television programming on aggressive behavior.

Understanding the impact of pornography on aggression has been helped by the use of *excitation-transfer theory.* According to this position, arousal—regardless of its true origin—will increase the likelihood of aggression if people interpret it as anger. Thus excitation from pornography may be transferred to the experience of anger and serve to increase aggression. A more cautious approach is taken by the *excitation-valence model.* This holds that violent and unpleasant pornography will anger men and provoke them to aggress, while pleasant pornography may actually reduce aggression. Other theories question the role of the target's response in provoking aggression related to pornography. Aggression cue theory suggests that men who watch violent sexual acts against women may come to associate the presence of a woman in a similar situation as an *aggressive cue* and thus lead to aggression.

Research on the effects of viewing television violence has generally determined that watching violent programs is associated with increased aggression, although the validity of the research has been controversial through the last several decades. The sex and age of the viewer appear to be important variables influencing the relationship between watching violent programs and engaging in violent behavior. Some research has shown that watching violent acts on television desensitizes the viewer to aggression and reduces empathy toward the victim. Similar links between exposure to violent imagery and aggressive behavior have been demonstrated with video games—both for the player and the spectator. In general, despite serious controversy surrounding both experimental and correlational studies, the weight of the evidence seems to indicate a causal link between violence in the media and aggressive behavior.

Key Terms

aggression	ethologist	instrumental
aggression cues	excitation-transfer	aggression
angry aggression	theory	modeling
aspirational	excitation-valence	progressive
deprivation	model	deprivation
catharsis	frustration	reinforcement
decremental	frustration-aggression	relative deprivation
deprivation	theory	social learning theory
displaced aggression		weapon effect

Suggested Readings

Bandura, A., & Walters, R. H. (1963). *Social learning and personality development.* New York: Holt, Rhinehart & Winston.

Dollard, J., Doob, L., Miller, N. E., Mowrer, O. H., & Sears, R. R. (1939). *Frustration and aggression.* New Haven, Conn.: Yale University Press.

Freedman, J. L. (1984). Effect of television violence on aggressiveness. *Psychological Bulletin, 96*(2), 227–246.

Green, R. G., & Donnerstein, E. I. (Eds.). (1983). *Aggression: Theoretical and empirical reviews* (Volume 1). New York: Academic Press.

Gurr, T. R. (1970). *Why men rebel.* Princeton, N.J.: Princeton University Press.

Lorenz, K. (1968). *On aggression.* New York: Bantam Books.

Chapter Ten

Developing and Resolving Conflict

A haggard-looking pilot leaned out of the window of the solitary jet to speak to reporters standing on the tarmac. "We are continuously surrounded by many, many guards. The gunmen are constantly changing" (*Time,* July 1, 1985, p. 19). TWA flight 847 began as a routine trip from Athens to Rome, but it had now become the focus of international attention and a symbol of the ubiquitous conflicts between people of different nations, different religions, and different cultures.

Soon after flight 847 took off from Athens, two Arab gunmen armed with pistols and grenades seized control of the plane. In a wild frenzy, the terrorists brutally beat and then shot a young U.S. Navy diver who had been a passenger on the plane. For two days the plane crisscrossed the skies between Beirut and Algiers before finally coming to rest at the Beirut airport. About one hundred passengers, mostly women, children, and non-U.S. citizens, had been allowed to leave the plane at earlier stops. Now the remaining thirty-seven American male passengers were hustled off the plane and taken in small groups to hiding places in Beirut. The three American crewmen remained on board the plane along with numerous terrorist gunmen.

These forty men became the bargaining chips of the terrorists, who demanded that Israel release 776 Shi'ites who had been detained during Israel's withdrawal from Lebanon some months before. Some of the concern for the hostages was reduced when the brutal terrorists who had hijacked the plane were replaced by members of the Amal organization, controlled by Nabih Berri. But the resolve of this new group was soon apparent when one of the members told the Beirut flight control tower that if no progress was made on the demands by the next morning, the plane would be loaded with explosives and blown up over Tel Aviv.

The stage was set: the Amal gunmen would hold the American passengers hostage until the United States put pressure on Israel to release the Lebanese detainees. What was to be the response of the United States? The irony of the situation was not lost on the world. The president of the United States, Ronald Reagan, had ridden into office on his criticism of Jimmy Carter's handling of the Iranian hostage crisis, in which fifty Americans were held at the captured U.S. embassy for 444 days; Reagan had publicly blasted Carter for not having been tough enough with the kidnappers. Thus, for President Reagan and his advisers, the task was not only to gain the release of the hostages but also to preserve their image as being tough on terrorism.

Israel, too, was caught in an ironic bind. The Israelis had been planning to release the Shi'ites. The Shi'ites served no purpose and their continued imprisonment was a headache for Israel. But the Israelis now felt that they could not release the prisoners because to do so might damage Israel's reputation as a country that would not capitulate to terrorism.

Even Nabih Berri found himself in an uncomfortable position. As leader of the Amal militia, he faced the difficult task of maintaining control over his followers. Some of the more radical militia members wanted to kill the hostages and wage a suicidal struggle against the United States and Israel. The more moderate members were concerned that such action would result in a serious setback to the group's power in Lebanon. Berri wanted to have his demands met and release the hostages without losing his leadership position; he was like "a man riding a tiger" (*Time,* July 1, 1985, p. 22).

The parties in the conflict may have had some common goals, but these were forgotten during the early days of the crisis. President Reagan made the tough public statement that "Americans will never make concessions to terrorists," but he resisted suggestions that he escalate the conflict by threatening military action. The Israelis also avoided making direct threats against the Amal, but they proclaimed that they would not release the Shi'ites in the face of terrorist demands.

The stalemate continued. After a week had passed, the captors set up a press conference and paraded five of the hostages before an army of media people. The hostages reported that they were getting along, but urged an end to the conflict. Israel attempted to lessen the tension by releasing thirty-one Shi'ites. The Israelis insisted that the release had nothing to do with the hostage crisis, but negotiators suggested that Berri could respond in good faith by releasing some of

Officials from the United States and the Amal group negotiated for days over the fate of the forty hostages. Anger and distrust increased as the conflict wore on. Each side voiced strong demands and each made threats before a compromise was reached.

the hostages. Berri's initial response was "What should we do now? Should we release half a hostage?" (*Time*, July 8, 1985, p. 11). But one hostage who had a heart ailment was later set free.

The negotiation process began to bog down as each side waited for the other to make further concessions. Distrust increased and rumors began to fly. One rumor was that six hostages with Jewish-sounding names had been turned over to a group of radical terrorists.

Convinced that direct negotiations would not work, U.S. officials attempted to find a third party to seek a resolution. This third party had to be someone the terrorists trusted. President Assad of Syria emerged as a candidate. Syria had a history of supporting terrorism, but Assad wanted the hostage crisis ended so he could increase his control over Lebanon. Thus he offered to accept the hostages from the Amal. He also obtained Israel's promise to release the Shi'ite prisoners—but not as a condition of the release of the hostages.

Just when it seemed that the hostages would

be released, Berri halted progress and demanded that President Reagan give assurances that he would not retaliate against Lebanon after the release. These assurances were probably unnecessary, since six other Americans were still being held hostage somewhere in Lebanon.

With the details worked out, the hostages were finally taken to Syria and then sent home. Some days later, Israel released the Shi'ite prisoners. The immediate crisis was over, but mixed with sighs of relief and tears of happiness was the realization that a similar conflict could happen again. And in January 1987 the shadow of flight 847 again loomed over the international scene. One of the terrorists involved in the TWA hijacking was caught in West Germany. Soon afterward four hostages were taken from the American University in Beirut. And in 1989 the world once again held its breath as the captured terrorist was put on trial for his acts. While no major terrorist events followed the trial, the fate of hostages, some held in captivity as long as five years, was still being negotiated in 1990.

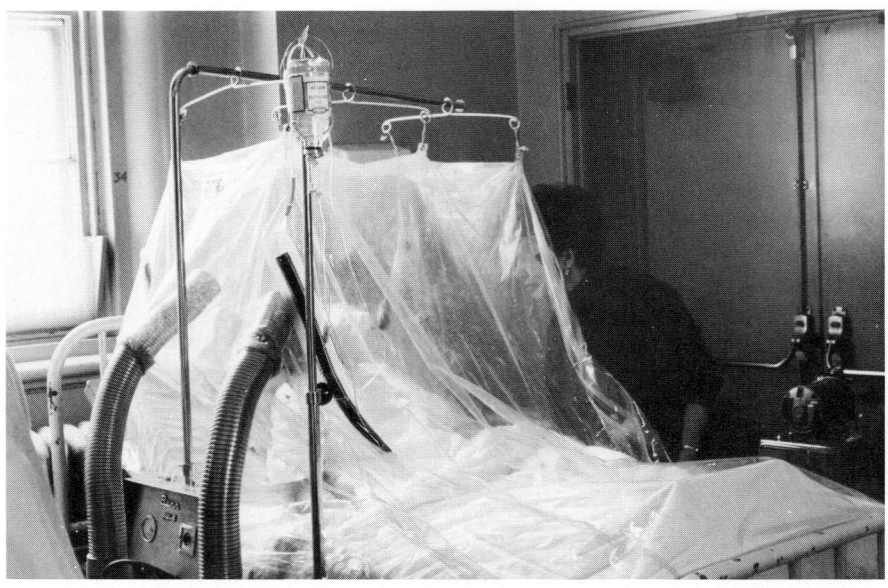

Intrapersonal conflict results when we are motivated to make two or more mutually incompatible responses. With advances in medical science, many of us will face the difficult conflict of deciding when, or if, to remove a loved family member from a life-support system.

Defining Conflict

The plight of TWA flight 847, as well as the broader context of events in the Middle East over the centuries, illustrates a number of social-psychological phenomena. One of the most poignant is conflict.

In an interesting analysis of hostage situations, Merari and Friedland (1988) point out why these incidents are fertile ground for analyzing and discussing conflict. First, conflict unfolds at many levels simultaneously; it is like a play within a play. President Reagan, for example, experienced **intrapersonal conflict** as he tried to decide how to respond to the hijacking: should he negotiate or retaliate with massive force? Showing the effects of this internal struggle, Reagan said, "I'm as frustrated as anyone. I've pounded a few walls myself, when I'm alone, about this" (*Time*, July 1, 1985, p. 8). **Interpersonal conflict** built up between Reagan and Berri, between Berri and members of his Amal militia, and between Reagan and his advisers. And intergroup and inter-

national conflict embroiled the United States, Israel, and the Amal faction.

Second, a single incident of conflict that involves relatively few people directly can have far-reaching consequences and extend well beyond the specific situation. The TWA hostage situation forced officials to weigh the short-term goal (to free the hostages) against the long-term goal (to establish a policy for dealing with terrorists), to debate strategies for reducing conflicts (delay, negotiation, and compromise versus a firm policy of no negotiation with terrorists), and to determine the nature of the conflict. Was it concerned simply with the release of the Shi'ite prisoners or was some larger issue involved, such as an attempt to overthrow the Israeli government, to increase support among the Palestinians, or to create conflict between Israel and the United States? The situation raised issues of trust, coalition formation, bargaining, threat, communication, and self-presentation, all of which we will examine in this chapter.

Conflict is a fascinating topic, not only because it is so common in our everyday lives but because

An increasingly common case of interpersonal conflict occurs in child custody decisions involved in divorce cases. These situations may bring into conflict the parents and the person representing the child or children. It is not uncommon for this conflict to become increasingly bitter as the parties fail to find common ground for agreement. The photo shows a conflict between supporters of "fathers' rights" and "mothers' rights" groups. Missing from this conflict is the group concerned with protecting "children's rights."

it does involve so many areas of human behavior. It is precisely for this reason that conflict plays a central role in almost all social-psychological theories. As a result, views of the concept vary widely. For example, we can look within the individual and define conflict as "a state that obtains for an individual when he is motivated to make two or more mutually incompatible responses" (Jones & Gerard, 1967, p. 709). We can also focus on the relationship between individuals or groups and describe conflict as "tension between two or more social entities (individuals, groups, or larger organizations) which arise from incompatibility of actual or desired responses" (Raven & Kruglanski, 1970, p. 70). A common element in these definitions is opposing forces that create tension and demand a response. Earlier chapters have dealt with the intrapersonal conflict that arises in the course of making attributions (Chapter 3) and decisions (Chapter 6) and in helping behavior (Chapter 8). This chapter will focus on inter-

personal and intergroup conflicts—those that arise between individuals and between groups.

Types of Interpersonal Conflict

Although we can supply a single definition of conflict, there are actually many types of conflict. One type is called **zero-sum conflict** (Table 10-1), indicating that one party's gain is the other party's loss. The zero-sum conflict exemplifies true

interpersonal conflict Tension between two or more individuals or groups resulting from incompatibility of actual or desired responses.

intrapersonal conflict An internal struggle resulting from a wish to make two or more incompatible responses.

zero-sum conflict Pure competition, in which one party's gain is the other party's loss.

TABLE 10-1

A zero-sum or pure conflict situation

Person B	Person A	Response 1	Response 2
Response 1		+4, −4	+1, −1
Response 2		+7, −7	−6, +6

competition; parlor games such as checkers and chess are examples of true competition because one player's gain is the other's loss.

However, most conflict situations do not fit the definition of competition; rather, they fall under the heading of nonzero-sum or **mixed-motive conflict.** As the name implies, mixed-motive conflicts do not present the parties with a situation in which one must win while the other must lose. Rather, these conflicts can be resolved to the benefit of both sides. But a unique twist in mixed-motive conflicts makes it difficult to choose the best solution. The twist is that the solution that offers the best payoff to both sides is not best from any one individual's standpoint. Hence each side must decide whether to work for the best *joint* or the best *individual* payoff. In this situation, concerns about trust, greed, and being double-crossed weigh heavily on the participants. A mixed-motive conflict is difficult to resolve because the tendency to maximize one's own profit is deeply rooted in Western cultures (Grzelak, 1988). Interestingly, research suggests that mixed-motive conflicts between individuals may not be so difficult to resolve in such cultures as the Japanese and the Russian, which stress the good of the group over the good of the individual (Petrovsky, 1985; Triandis et al., 1988).

Because mixed-motive conflict is so common, let us examine two situations that reveal its intriguing characteristics.

Prisoner's Dilemma

President Reagan wanted desperately to catch and punish the terrorists who murdered the navy diver. But he pointed out, "You can't just start shooting without having someone in your sights." In other words, he had to be sure who was responsible for

the murder before he could punish anyone. Let us go on with our scenario and assume that the U.S. officials were able to capture two men who they believed were responsible. These men (we'll call them Abdul and Achmed) are turned over to the attorney general, who must develop the case against them. As it turns out, eyewitness accounts are so vague and contradictory that they will not stand up in court. The attorney general needs a confession, but how can he get these men to confess?

Fortunately, our attorney general is a good student of human behavior. He begins by placing Abdul and Achmed in separate cells where they cannot communicate with each other. He then visits both men and tells them their choices: each can confess to killing the navy diver or each can remain silent and not confess. The attorney general points out that he does not yet have enough evidence to convict either man of murder, but he does have evidence that will convict both of lesser crimes. He now offers each suspect a deal (Table 10-2). If neither man confesses, he will charge each with lesser crimes, such as assault, possession of stolen property, and trespassing, and will fight to get the longest prison sentence possible (four years) for both. On the other hand, if one of the men confesses and testifies against the other, the attorney general will let the confessor go free, but will prosecute the one who did not confess (ninety-nine years in prison). If both confess, however, the attorney general will recommend reduced terms for each (twenty years), since he could not possibly let them both go free. As you can see, our crafty attorney general has set up a conflict between Abdul and Achmed.

This conflict, known as the **prisoner's dilemma,** has the characteristics of the mixed-motive situation. First, one person's gain is not necessarily the other's loss; both men could receive rather short sentences (four years). Second, motives of both cooperation and competition are involved. For example, looking at Table 10-2, we see that a competitive response would be a confession, since a confession by either man hurts the other by increasing the other's sentence. The competitive response is clearly the "safe" response if the person does not trust his partner; it would be disastrous not to confess if the other person confessed. A cooperative response would be not

TABLE 10-2

Matrix representation of the prisoner's dilemma

Achmed \ Abdul	Not confess	Confess
Not confess	4 years, 4 years	99 years, Freedom
Confess	Freedom, 99 years	20 years, 20 years

NOTE: Cooperative responses (not confess) from both parties would lead to relatively light sentences for each, but each party must trust the other before he will make a cooperative response.

to confess. This is a difficult course to follow, however, for two reasons. First, the individual can achieve the best outcome for himself if he acts competitively (confesses) and the partner does not. Hence the person is tempted away from cooperation by greed. Second, we pointed out the risk of cooperation if there is any uncertainty about the partner's willingness to act cooperatively.

Looking at the situation from both players' points of view, we see that their joint payoff will be best if both cooperate and neither confesses. In this way, both will get a light sentence. Thus, on the one hand, the player is motivated to cooperate and obtain a good joint payoff; on the other hand, he is motivated to compete and obtain the best possible payoff for himself.

Social Dilemma

Social dilemma represents another situation in which individuals are faced with the choice of furthering their own immediate self-interest or acting for the long-term good of the group. Robyn Dawes (1980) suggests that all social dilemmas have two basic characteristics: (1) the payoff to each individual for defecting (taking an individualistic approach) is higher than the individual's payoff for cooperating, and (2) all individuals receive a lower payoff if all defect than if all cooperate. The classic social dilemma is represented by the "tragedy of the commons" (Hardin, 1968). Old New England towns were often built next to or around a pasture; this pasture was called the commons because it was used by all the farmers to graze their cattle. The commons served everyone's needs as long as it was not overgrazed. Overgrazing would destroy the grass and ruin

the area for everyone. This situation posed a dilemma for each farmer; adding an extra cow or two to the commons would increase a farmer's personal profit, but if everyone did this the commons would be ruined. If you are a farmer, what do you do in this situation? All too often, the farmers chose to add the extra cattle. The result was the tragedy of the commons (the destruction of the pasture).

In examining the situation, we can see why this outcome occurred. If you were a farmer, two points might come to your mind. First, you might think that adding only one or two cows to the commons would not hurt or be noticed. The problem here is that if all farmers think this way, the result will be disaster. Second, even if you foresee the ultimate disaster, you may suspect that your neighbors will not.

Here we see the two motives that are the foundation of the dilemma. On one hand is the *fear* that one will lose by being the sole cooperator (Rappaport, 1967). On the other hand is the *greed* involved in the temptation to be the only non-cooperator and profit from the others' cooper-

---

competition Interpersonal conflict involving an incompatibility of goals.

mixed-motive conflict A conflict in which both parties may gain by responding in a cooperative manner, but the best joint outcome is not the best outcome for the individuals.

prisoner's dilemma A mixed-motive conflict in which the best individual choice leads to the worst joint payoff; a paradigm used to study trust.

social dilemma Conflict that arises when behaviors bring short-term pleasures but have negative long-term effects, or when one must choose between one's own interest and that of the group.

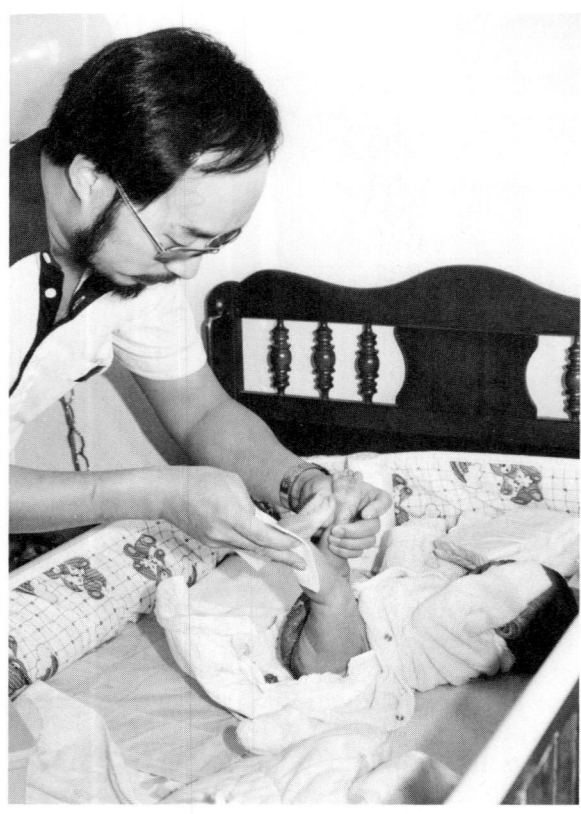

Most parents will be faced with the social dilemma of using disposable plastic diapers or cloth diapers. The plastic diapers are convenient and easy to use, but if everyone uses them, our landfills will soon become clogged. On the other hand, cloth diapers, which can be washed and reused, protect our environment but make the life of the parents more difficult.

ation. Social dilemmas may result when people are faced with the choice of giving resources to the group (giving to charity, for instance, or working on a group project) or taking from the group (perhaps by using more land on the commons or by taking a long trip by car during a gasoline shortage) (Fleishman, 1988). In an interesting study, investigators found that individuals competed (took the self-interested action) when either fear or greed was aroused. Only when fear and greed were inconsequential did individuals work for the collective good (Bruins, Liebrand & Wilke, 1989).

Social dilemmas have proved notoriously difficult to resolve. We could argue that a reward/punishment system could be developed to encourage concern for the group good. However, this would require a complex organization to police individual behavior, and in most common social dilemmas, people know that their behavior cannot be identified. It has been suggested (Lynn & Oldenquist, 1986) that solutions to these dilemmas cannot rely on individual rewards and punishments. Rather, they must be aimed at developing concern for the group by increasing altruistic motives, moral motives, and a deeper sense of identification with the group. Unfortunately, developing these motives may prove as difficult as policing individual behaviors.

Along these lines, research has shown that communication between individuals facing a dilemma can increase the amount of cooperation. However, the cooperation increases only when everyone promises to cooperate. The investigators (Orbell, van de Kragt & Dawes, 1988) suggest that a discussion that commits everyone to cooperate also increases identity with the group. Emphasis on the group rather than on the individual motivates people to sacrifice self-interest for the welfare of the group.

The Escalating Path of Conflict

If we examine a situation such as the social dilemma, we may be tempted to argue that it is an easy one to resolve. It is in everyone's long-term interest to cooperate, and this should be clear. But conflicts do not always follow the most logical path. In the case of the hijacking, for example, Nabih Berri wanted to release the American hostages. President Reagan wanted to get the hostages home *and* he wanted Israel to free the Shi'ite prisoners. The Israelis wanted to release the Shi'ites. But with all these forces pointing toward a speedy resolution of the crisis, the conflict among the parties escalated as threats and counterthreats were hurled with increasing frequency.

Conflict often resembles a snowball rolling downhill; it increases in size and intensity rather than taking a course toward diminution and resolve. This circumstance is referred to as the **conflict spiral** (Deutsch, 1973). As we will see, conflict often leads to increased distrust between the parties, which in turn heightens the conflict. Conflict reaches out and embraces the parties. And people become entrapped in escalating conflict even when they have reasonable and rational means to reduce it (Brockner & Rubin, 1985). They are trapped because they cannot escape heavy costs whether they reduce the conflict or continue it. For an elegant example of this dilemma, consider yourself in the following situation. You and three other students arrive at an experiment and are told that the experimenter will auction off a dollar bill. The rules of the auction are a bit unusual: although the winning bidder will get to keep the dollar, the next highest bidder must pay the amount that he or she bid, even though he or she gets nothing in return. At first this wrinkle seems unimportant to you. The bidding begins; you bid 5 cents, another student bids 10 cents, and so on. After a while, the bidding boils down to you and one other student: you bid 75 cents and he bids 80 cents. Now that insignificant rule applying to the losing bidder takes on new importance. You realize that if you stop here, you will have to pay 75 cents and get nothing in return; therefore, you up the bid to 85 cents. Your opponent has also become aware of the plight that awaits the losing bidder and he bids 90 cents. Now the two of you are trapped in the escalating conflict. How high do you go?

In an experiment using these rules, it was found that the bidding almost always went past the $1 level, and sometimes went as high as $20 (Teger, 1980). As the bids increased in value, all joking and friendly conversation ceased. Anxiety and tension rose and participants showed increasing signs of stress, such as elevated heart rate. The bidders reported that they were forced to remain in the conflict (keep bidding) because of their opponents' bids. And they could not understand why their opponents kept bidding! As the bidding level rose, the participants no longer thought of winning cheap money; now they wanted to beat their opponents and avoid appearing weak or foolish. Was this what prolonged the conflict over the hostages on TWA flight 847?

This process unfolds with alarming regularity every day. In Israel, for example, settlers built a number of towns in the West Bank and Gaza territory occupied by Israel after the 1967 war. The Palestinians are demanding that this territory be returned as part of a peace settlement. But many Israelis now argue that this is too great a price to pay because of the extensive settle-

"It's not a war toy madam. It's a cease fire toy."
Reprinted from *The Wall Street Journal*; permission Cartoon Features Syndicate.

ments that now exist in this territory. Hence the conflict continues to grow.

The Use of Threat

Almost as soon as flight 847 landed in Beirut, threats and counterthreats began to surface. The terrorists threatened to kill the hostages and blow up the plane over Israel. At one point in the negotiations, President Reagan threatened to retaliate against the terrorists; this threat led Berri to delay the hostages' release until he was given assurances that there would be no reprisals. In one of the more bizarre incidents, five hostages were allowed to hold an interview with the media to plead for the parties to stop threatening each other and to work constructively for their release.

conflict spiral The tendency for conflict, once initiated, to increase rather than diminish.

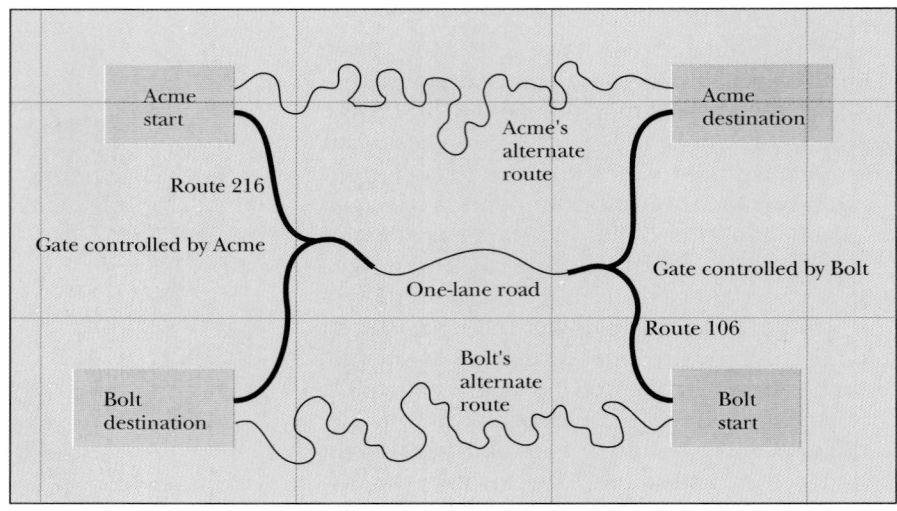

FIGURE 10–1   Road Map in the trucking game
SOURCE: Deutsch and Krauss (1960).

The use of threats by parties to conflict is very common. Does this tactic work or was the advice of many of President Reagan's advisers to avoid any hint of threat wise? What do you think? In an interesting experiment, Rothbart and Hallmark (1988) asked subjects to play the role of a defense minister of a nation involved in a conflict in which both parties were developing threatening weapons. When asked to indicate the tactic that would be most likely to lead to a settlement, subjects reported that their nation would respond most positively if the other nation made some conciliatory response, such as reducing the level of its threatening weapons. However, they believed that the other nation would be most likely to agree to settle the conflict in response to an increased threat. Thus we see others as being influenced by threat, but we see ourselves as most influenced by a reduction in threat! In fact, research suggests that the response to threat is not so one-sided; threat often leads to an increase in conflict.

In one of the earliest experiments on the effects of threat (Deutsch & Krauss, 1960), two subjects were asked to imagine that they were heads of opposing trucking companies (Acme and Bolt). The players' task was to move their truck from the start to the finish as quickly as possible; the quicker the trip, the more money the player

earned. The subjects were then shown a road map (Figure 10-1) that indicated that each player could take two routes to the finish. The longest route was filled with curves, so that a player taking this route was sure to lose money on the trip. The second route was the most direct but had a stretch of one-lane road. If the players' trucks met on this road, neither could proceed unless one of the trucks backed up. Here was the point of conflict: Which player would back up and let the other pass?

To make matters more interesting, Deutsch and Krauss also built in a manipulation of threat. At each end of the one-lane section, there was a gate that was under the control of the player whose starting point was closest to that end. By closing the gate, one player could prevent the other player's truck from reaching its destination by way of the one-lane section. Each player's gate was a threat because the player could close it (thus preventing the other from passing) and then take the alternate route. Deutsch and Krauss ran three conditions by varying the availability of the gates: no threat (no gates), unilateral threat (only one player has a gate), and bilateral threat (both players have gates). After each trial, the experimenter announced how much each player had won or lost. The game was played over twenty trials.

The results indicate quite dramatically that

TABLE 10-3

Payoffs in the Deutsch and Krauss trucking game

	Means		
Variable	No threat	Unilateral threat (Acme has threat)	Bilateral threat
Summed payoffs (Acme and Bolt)	203.31	− 405.88	− 875.12
Acme's payoff	122.44	− 118.56	− 406.56
Bolt's payoff	80.88	− 287.31	− 468.56

NOTE: The highest payoff for each party occurred under the no-threat condition, and the lowest payoff resulted in the bilateral-threat condition.
SOURCE: Deutsch and Krauss (1960).

the quickest resolution (and the best payoff) occurred when neither player had access to a threat and that the slowest resolution occurred when both could threaten. In fact, profit was realized only in the no-threat condition (Table 10-3). Both players received the highest payoffs when neither player had access to a threat. The second highest payoff for each player occurred in the unilateral-threat condition. This was true for the player who had the threat (Acme in Table 10-3) and for the player who had no threat (Bolt). The worst payoff for both players occurred in the bilateral-threat condition. It is interesting to note that the payoff for Bolt was higher when she did not possess the threat capacity that her opponent had than when she did have the capacity to counterthreaten her opponent (bilateral threat). These results suggest that the greater the threat potential in a conflict situation, the more difficult it is to resolve the conflict. The results of several other studies (Deutsch, Canavan & Rubin, 1971; Gallo, 1966; Shomer, Davis & Kelly, 1966) confirmed that threat retards the resolution of conflict. In fact, it has been suggested that the use of threats may be a sign that negotiations are breaking down and the parties are far from achieving a resolution (Barner-Barry & Rosenwein, 1985).

Our discussion has cast doubt on the role of threat and power in the resolution of conflict. Before we leave this important issue, one point should be made. While the ability to threaten an opponent may escalate conflict and result in a poor payoff, lack of power to threaten a powerful opponent may be distressing and damaging to one's self-esteem (Apfelbaum, 1974, 1979). Apfelbaum suggested that, although the actual payoffs may be higher in unequal power relationships, the low-power party may not be happy or satisfied with such a relationship.

Obviously, many questions about the effects of threat on conflict remain unanswered. Continued research in this area is of great importance because people who find themselves in conflict so commonly resort to threat.

The Intrusion of Threat: Two Cases

Research suggests that threat tends to increase conflict and produce few winners. Yet we need merely look at our newspaper, watch our television, or talk to our friends to see how often people in conflict issue threats. With the research in mind, let's look at two cases in which threat dominates thought and action.

Terrorism
A horrified world watched the plight of TWA flight 847. Most people were angered by the terrorists' cowardly actions and hoped for the passengers' safe release; and in the backs of the minds of many of the world's audience was the nagging question "Will it happen to me?" **Terrorism** is actual or threatened violence against noncombatants for avowed political ends (McCauley &

terrorism   actual or threatened violence against noncombatants for avowed political ends.

International terrorism has become a fact of life in contemporary politics. Terrorists, such as those from the Medellin drug cartel who bombed newspaper offices, killing and maiming civilians, wield increasing power as injuries and publicity grow.

Segal, 1987). The threat and violence come in many forms: hostages are taken (as on flight 847), people are kidnapped, embassies are seized, prominent figures are assassinated. And terrorism is increasing. In 1968, 142 incidents of international terrorism were reported (Central Intelligence Agency, 1981); in 1982 there were 794 such incidents (U.S. Department of State, 1983). In 1983 terrorist acts resulted in 720 fatalities and 963 injuries (Cordes et al., 1984). Although these numbers are alarming, they are small in comparison with those of other threats we face routinely. In the United States alone, 45,000 people die in traffic accidents each year. Yet these acts of terrorism had widespread effects: people changed their travel plans, governments changed their policies, millions of dollars were spent to increase security, and countless people lived in fear for their lives and safety (Merari & Friedland, 1985).

In order to understand these effects of terrorism, we must examine its aim. The aim of terrorism, unlike that of the situations we discussed earlier, is not the immediate resolution of conflict. The major goal of terrorists is to achieve worldwide attention and to instill fear (Fried-

land, 1988). Terrorists capture attention by enlisting the unwitting aid of the media. For weeks the world watched the play-by-play actions of the terrorists on flight 847. Their faces were etched in everyone's minds, and we all knew their political goals. Fear results because the act is random, unpredictable, and can happen again in the future. Even as the flight 847 episode ended with the release of the hostages, people were asking themselves, "When will it happen again?"

Beyond the goal of arousing widespread fear, terrorists aim to create conflict within the governments involved. Governments are placed in a no-win situation. Do they take a hard line and refuse to negotiate, thereby jeopardizing the safety of innocent people? Or do they cave in to the demands of the terrorists, thereby presenting themselves as weak and opening themselves up to more such demands in the future? Thus the terrorists create conflict within conflict. In an effort to create this conflict, terrorists often take vulnerable hostages, such as women and children, and make rather modest demands, such as the release of Shi'ite prisoners who are already destined for release. In this way the terrorists enlist the aid of the public to put pressure on governments to negotiate (Merari & Friedland, 1988).

Terrorism is generally a response to conflict by weak groups with few resources. While there have been cases in which terrorists have achieved their political aims (Jewish groups in Palestine, the Mau Mau in Kenya), usually they do not succeed in creating political change or overthrowing governments. This result shows the need to examine both the short-term and long-term effects of conflict and conflict resolution.

The Arms Race

A second area where threat stands out as a response to conflict is seen in the global approach to the buildup of nuclear weapons. For nearly fifty years we lived in a world dominated by the belief that peace can best be achieved through strength and the deterrent force of fear (Gralnick, 1988). And much of this strength and deterrence is achieved through stockpiles of nuclear weapons. Since dropping the atomic bombs on Hiroshima and Nagasaki, the United States has spent more than $750 billion to build 60,000 nuclear warheads for use in 116 weapons systems (*Bulletin of the Atomic Scientists*, 1985). The Soviets have similar stockpiles. The buildup of weapons was accompanied by an increasing lack of trust between the superpowers, and this lack of trust motivated the nations to increase their stockpiles of weapons.

The use of threat to secure peace has had wide-ranging effects on the peoples of the world. Not only has it consumed enormous resources, but it has occupied the minds of young and old alike. In one survey, Soviet young people rated nuclear war as their greatest concern; young Americans ranked it as their second greatest concern, behind worry about the death of a parent (Doctor et al., 1988). And beyond these issues are research data suggesting that an increase in threat is not likely to help resolve basic conflict, and that people who are in a position to make threats are constantly tempted to unleash their power. Added to these points is the fact that nuclear weapons are in effect a double-barreled shotgun with one barrel pointed backward at oneself (Gralnick, 1988): if any country were to unleash its nuclear weapons, the world would probably be rendered uninhabitable for everyone.

Though we have painted a rather grim picture, there is a glimmer of light here. Numerous recent surveys suggest that people see that nuclear war is not survivable by either side (Galperin, Holt & Howells, 1988) and that a majority of people support bilateral freezes on the production and deployment of nuclear weapons, as long as one side is not uniquely advantaged (Gilbert, 1988). The rhetoric and actions of the leaders of both the United States and the Soviet Union have been aimed at reversing the nuclear arms race. Looking at the results of the research, we can expect that reducing the threat levels may open up avenues to conflict reduction.

The Concern with Appearance: Saving Face

One outstanding characteristic of the conflict over flight 847 was the vast amount of media coverage devoted to it. As we pointed out, one of the aims of terrorists is to get attention, and they use the media for this purpose. The terrorists believed that media coverage would increase the pressure on the United States and Israel to capitulate to their demands. Yet the results were not what they expected. The conflict escalated and dragged on. One hostage commented, "It's a bloody circus, all this television stuff. We are just serving their ends, and we wonder sometimes what it is all about" (*Time*, July 8, 1985, p. 15).

If we take a careful look at the feelings of people in conflict, we can understand why this tactic of public display was not successful. Individuals in conflict situations generally have two aims: one is to obtain as much as possible from the conflict; the other is to appear strong and tough. The second goal is often more important than the first, for a number of reasons. First, if the opponent perceives weakness or lack of determination on the part of the other party, he or she may seek out other opportunities for confrontation. A second reason for the concern with appearances is the desire to impress supporters who observe the conflict. Both Nabih Berri and President Reagan wanted to show their supporters that they were strong and in control. Reagan

The U.S.S.R. had opened up many barriers to travel and economic transactions, so Lithuania's declaration of independence, with its rallying cry of "not enough," was a slap in the face to which the U.S.S.R. had to respond to save face. What would the Soviet Union's other choices have been?

had, in fact, implied during the 1980 election campaign that Jimmy Carter had been "too soft" on the terrorists who took Americans hostage in Iran. This "weakness" severely damaged Carter's bid for reelection.

The concern with appearances in conflict situations is referred to as **face saving.** A number of investigators (Brockner & Rubin, 1985; Streufert & Streufert, 1986) have suggested that the desire to save face often motivates people to resort to threats. People feel that yielding is an admission of weakness. Such an admission not only is a blow to one's self-esteem but can lead to embarrassment and distress if other people witness this weakness. B. R. Brown (1968) reasoned that subjects who had been publicly embarrassed would resort to threats as a means of restoring face even if doing so resulted in costs to themselves. He had subjects play against a confederate in a trucking game experiment. The subjects were told that they were being observed by other subjects through a one-way mirror. During the first half of the experiment, the confederate had the greatest power and exploited the subjects. At one point in the experiment, the subjects were given notes that had supposedly been written by the

observers. Half of the subjects received insulting notes saying that they looked like suckers, and the other half received more flattering notes. After receiving the notes, the subjects were given control of the gates and could charge the confederate a high toll to allow him to pass through. The one catch was that using the gates and charging a high toll would also reduce the subject's ability to win. The results showed that subjects who felt that they had lost face during the first part of the study (that is, received insulting notes from the observers) were more likely to use threats than subjects who had not lost face.

Conditions other than public observation can also influence people to attempt to save face in conflicts. The more a person has invested in a conflict, the more he or she will attempt to save face and resist yielding to demands (Teger, 1980). This investment can take the form of time, effort, personal commitment, or material. Realization of this point led U.S. Congressman Edward Markey (1985) to suggest that the incredible cost of military preparedness might actually be prolonging conflict between the United States and the Soviet Union. He pointed out that every four hours, the world's militaries were spending the

Chapter Ten Developing and Resolving Conflict

equivalent of the annual budget of the United Nations Children's Fund (UNICEF). While it can be argued that this money is spent for defense and national safety, it also serves the purpose of increasing the nations' commitment to conflict. A second factor affecting face-saving responses is the possibility of future conflict; the greater the likelihood of future conflict, the greater the efforts to save face in the present conflict (Hiltrop & Rubin, 1981).

Conflict in the Eye of the Beholder: Perceptions of the Other

President Reagan referred to the hijackers as "criminals" whose main purpose was to spread terror. He felt that these acts of terrorism were forcing him to take an aggressive stand against the people who perpetrated them. Nabih Berri, for his part, perceived the United States and Israel as aggressors who had forced the Arabs to take action. He argued that flight 847 would not have been hijacked if Israel had not taken the Shi'ites prisoner. Thus each side saw itself as reasonable and as acting only in response to the aggression of the other.

One point that must be remembered is that conflict is shaped by the parties' perceptions of the situation rather than by what the situation actually is. In other words, perceptions become reality.

Kelley and Stahelski (1970a, 1970b) clearly demonstrated the role of perceptions in the escalation of conflict. They proposed that there are basically two types of individuals: competitive and cooperative. These two types have different views of the way other people intend to respond. The competitive type of person sees other people as being universally competitive, and the cooperative person sees other people as a more diverse lot, some cooperative and some competitive. The manner in which individuals interact with others is partly determined by the intentions they attribute to others. If these propositions are correct, competitive people should always interact competitively because they attribute competitive intentions to others. Cooperative people, how-

STOP, THINK, & UNDERSTAND

1. Identify the various levels on which conflict can occur and define each type of conflict.

2. What are the characteristics of mixed-motive conflicts?

3. How does the use of threat influence the process of conflict?

4. Why does the threat of terrorism have such a profound effect on so many people, when the chance of being a victim of terrorism is so small?

5. If threats are unlikely to resolve conflict, why do parties to conflict so often issue them?

ever, should act cooperatively with a cooperative other and competitively with a competitive other. According to this view, competitive individuals are responsible for setting the tone of a relationship, since they do not adapt to their partner's behavior, whereas cooperative individuals do adapt.

To test their hypothesis, Kelley and Stahelski (1970b) devised a number of experiments using the same paradigm. Generally they began the experiments by showing the subject a modified prisoner's dilemma situation. After identifying subjects who expected to act cooperatively and those who expected to act competitively, they asked the subjects how they expected their opponent in a conflict to respond. As the experimenters expected, competitive individuals overwhelmingly expected their opponents to act competitively. Cooperative players, on the other hand, expected about equal amounts of cooperation and competition from their opponents. Finally, all subjects played a prisoner's dilemma game against an opponent who responded with either cooperative or competitive actions.

---

face saving Behaviors designed to maintain a positive public image.

TABLE 10-4

Percentage of cooperative responses

	Partner					
	First ten trials		Second ten trials		Third ten trials	
Actor	Cooperative	Competitive	Cooperative	Competitive	Cooperative	Competitive
Cooperative	85%	64%	90%	67%	92%	69%
Competitive	34	32	31	18	25	27

NOTE: Competitive individuals gave very few cooperative responses, regardless of the behavior of their partners. The behavior of cooperative players was more affected by the behavior of their partners.
SOURCE: Kelley and Stahelski (1970b).

As Table 10-4 reveals, the competitive players made about the same percentage of cooperative moves throughout the trials, whether the partner was competitive or cooperative. The cooperative players, on the other hand, made significantly more cooperative moves when the partner was cooperative than when he or she was competitive. Thus the results supported the hypothesis that the cooperative players would adapt their behavior to that of their partners more than the competitive players would.

Examining the effects of perceptions in another way, a group of investigators found that competitive individuals tend to interpret the behavior of their opponents in terms of power (strong/weak). Cooperative individuals view the opponent's behavior in terms of evaluation (good/bad) (Liebrand et al., 1986). In another interesting twist, Lanzetta and Englis (1989) led subjects to believe that they would be either cooperating or competing with another person. The subjects then watched as the other person received either a positive response (a reward) or a negative one (a shock). Measures of subjects' emotional reactions showed that they responded with empathy to the cooperative partner (mirrored the other subject's emotions) but showed counterempathy to the competitive opponent (happy when the other person was hurt, distressed when the other person was happy).

The bottom line of all this research is that conflict and our response to it affects the way we perceive others and the situation, and our perceptions affect our behavior (Bar-Tal, 1990). Further, these perceptions serve to reinforce and prolong the conflict.

Trust and Distrust

One of the most significant features of the hostage crisis was the distrust of all the parties involved in it. Berri did not trust the United States, so he moved the hostages to hiding places so that the United States could not attack and free them. The radical element of the Amal group did not trust Berri, so they took a group of hostages, supposedly with "Jewish-sounding" names, to another hiding place so that Berri could not easily give in to demands by the United States and Israel. And it was distrust that delayed the release of the hostages into Syrian custody, as Berri feared that Reagan would order military retaliation once the hostages were freed.

"The perceptions of the other group as untrustworthy is probably a major source of tensions leading to conflict. The history of labor/management strife, interracial violence, war, and revolution demonstrates the significance of distrust" (Webb & Worchel, 1986, p. 213).

The crucial role of trust is driven home in Alexander Gralnick's (1988) harrowing discussion of the possibility of nuclear war.

Trust is the critical link of any policy designed or meant to prevent nuclear holocaust. Without trust there is no safety in the policy of nuclear deterrence. Realism requires trust. Lacking trust there will be nuclear omnicide. . . . The current human condition demands trust. It is an inseparable aspect of any negotiation and human endeavor. (p. 182)

Trust is especially critical to the conflict spiral; the lack of trust helps create conflict, and conflict leads to increased distrust between the parties. Thus we have a vicious circle of distrust→ conflict→increased distrust→increased conflict.

Although **trust** has emerged as a widely used and important concept, there is some question about how to define it. Some investigators (Rotter, 1971b) refer to trust as the expectancy that the word, promise, or verbal or written statement of another can be relied on. Put simply, this means that others will do what they say they will do. Pruitt (1965) adds another dimension to the definition, viewing trust as the expectancy that others will act in a helpful rather than hurtful manner.

Research (Pelton, 1974; Schlenker, Helm & Tedeschi, 1973; Swinth, 1976; Zand, 1972) based on the prisoner's dilemma and similar situations suggests that for trust to develop, one person has to let down his or her guard and become vulnerable to see whether the other person abuses that vulnerability. Many such tests are necessary before a trusting relationship can be established.

Three factors influence the development of trust. One is the individuals' *personalities*. Ainsworth (1979) suggests that people develop the tendency to trust or distrust others during infancy and early childhood; infants who are brought up in a secure environment in which they can rely on consistent and appropriate behavior from their parents (especially the mother) are most likely to develop a readiness to trust. Scales such as the Philosophies of Human Nature Scale (Wrightsman, 1964) and the Interpersonal Trust Scale (Rotter 1971b) have been developed to distinguish between people who have a tendency to trust others and those who tend to distrust. A second influence on trust is the presence of *environmental cues* indicating the probabilities of harmful consequences. These cues include the perception that the opponent has much to gain by betrayal and knowledge that the other has acted in a self-serving way in the past. The final factor that influences the development of trust is the

By having a secure environment where nurturing is consistent and plentiful, an infant learns that the environment and its inhabitants are trustworthy. If the early environment fosters insecurity, the child learns distrust.

individual's motivation for positive outcomes. If one person has little at stake and does not care about the outcome, it is relatively easy for him or her to risk trusting the other person. However, if the stakes are high, as they were in the hostage crisis, trust is more difficult to develop.

Although trust is difficult to develop and a series of positive encounters are often required to develop a trusting relationship, Webb and Worchel (1986) report that it "may take only one betrayal to establish distrust." Further, "once aroused, distrust is extremely resistive to change." Distrust is difficult to change because it leads to the perception that the other person is a threat,

b

trust A general expectancy that another person will respond in a helpful rather than a harmful manner.

and that perception leads to greater distrust. Once an individual has committed one betrayal, it is difficult for him or her to "make up" with another person, because the wronged individual may believe that the betrayal will recur in the future.

We have presented distrust as a rather terminal state; that is, once it develops, it continues. This is certainly true in many cases, but the tide of distrust can be reversed if the wrongdoer confesses the betrayal and convinces the wronged person that he or she is remorseful. Further, if the wrongdoer has gained from the betrayal, he or she must attempt to make restitution. It is interesting that some of the most popular presidents in U.S. history (George Washington, Abraham Lincoln, Harry Truman) made public apologies for events in which they were involved and accepted personal blame. Truman, in fact, had a plaque on his desk that read: "The buck stops here." On the other hand, some presidents who lost popularity while in office failed to take responsibility or show remorse for questionable situations in which they were involved. For example, Lyndon Johnson failed to admit that his judgment on the Vietnam war may have been in error. Richard Nixon has steadfastly refused to admit wrongdoing in the Watergate affair.

Communication

Implied in the concept of trust is communication; trust is built on the communication of intentions and promises, and it develops as people exchange information. Communication is also an important key to determining the development and resolution of conflict. Yet some interesting issues surround communication. The initial tendency of parties in a conflict is to withdraw and cease communication. This response has been called **autistic hostility** (Newcomb, 1947).

The parties soon realize, however, that communication will be necessary if the conflict is to be resolved. And here arises an interesting dilemma (McClintock, Stech & Keil, 1983). On the one hand, neither side wants to give the other information about its strengths, weaknesses, and desires that may be used against it. On the other hand, communication is vital if the parties are to

ascertain the issues and develop solutions to the problem. In addition, both parties are concerned about the type of information to communicate. A party could gain an advantage by misrepresenting its position or concealing information. However, this advantage could be disastrous if the other side believed it was being manipulated or acted on false information. For example, Berri would have gained an advantage if he could have made Reagan believe that the hostages would be killed unless rapid progress was made. On the other hand, if President Reagan believed this, he might have ordered an all-out attack, figuring that he was unlikely to get the hostages back alive, in any case.

Overall, the results of many studies show that communication increases the chances for a positive resolution of conflict (Grzelek, 1988). But people in conflict often must be encouraged or forced to engage in communication (Deutsch & Krauss, 1962; see Table 10-5). Finally, the content and timing of communication are important. For example, Caldwell (1976) found that communications between groups of subjects in a prisoner's dilemma situation increased cooperation when the communications contained information about sanctions that would be applied to subjects who did not cooperate. In addition, it has been found that communication later in the conflict is more likely to have a positive effect than communication early in the conflict (Stech & McClintock, 1981). Late communication may focus attention on cooperative aspects of the relationship and ways to reduce conflict, while early communication often focuses on the conflict and on threats.

Taken together, the results suggest that communication is not a natural event in conflict; it must be encouraged and nurtured. Further, people must be taught constructive ways to communicate. Communicating in the wrong ways can increase distrust and conflict.

Resolving Conflict

By this time, we may have thoroughly depressed you; you may be thinking that conflict is an affliction for which there is no cure. A glance at

TABLE 10-5

Mean joint payoffs (Acme plus Bolt) per trial in modified trucking game

	No threat	Unilateral threat	Bilateral threat
Compulsory communication	6.09	− 5.14	− 41.73
Permissive communication	8.54	− 34.58	− 41.32
No communication	10.41	− 22.13	− 47.44

NOTE: Deutsch and Krauss (1962) replayed the trucking game with three types of communication conditions: a no-communication condition in which the subjects were not given the opportunity to communicate; a permissive-communication condition in which the subjects could communicate if they wished; and a compulsory-communication condition in which the subjects were told that they must communicate. Forced communication had the most dramatic effect in the unilateral condition.
SOURCE: Deutsch and Krauss (1962).

the daily newspaper will reinforce this gloomy picture, as it seems that the world abounds in conflict. It is indeed true that we are confronted by a great deal of competition and conflict in our lives. But we do learn to resolve our disagreements, and often these resolutions lead to progress and deeper understanding. The crisis over flight 847 was resolved and the Shi'ite prisoners were released by Israel (although our relief is only partial, given the brutal murder of the innocent navy diver).

While the many incidents of conflict weigh heavily on us, their existence poses a very real challenge for social scientists: to identify constructive ways to resolve conflict. It is important that conflict be resolved in just and fair ways; resolutions that are viewed as unjust by either side do not result in lasting or stable settlements. In a sense, unjust resolutions perpetuate conflict. Let us now examine some of the factors that influence the resolution of conflict.

Correctly Perceiving the Conflict and the Opponent

It is not unusual for people to perceive their conflicts as pure competition (zero-sum), when in fact the parties share common goals but disagree about the means of achieving them. Filley (1975) suggests that attempts to resolve conflict should begin with a listing of specific goals by both parties; they should refrain from taking positions on how these goals will be met. After specifying their goals, the parties should then discuss methods by which the goals can be achieved. This approach turns the conflict into an **integrative problem-solving** situation rather than a competition. Filley reports that this method leads to a quicker, more lasting resolution to interpersonal conflict than methods that rely on negotiation or compromise.

Other points involving the conflict situation are important. First, negotiation begins when the parties to the conflict recognize that they have interests in common (Barner-Barry & Rosenwein, 1985). Often one common interest is fairness: both profit if the conflict is resolved fairly. Attempts to resolve conflict can begin with this common ground. Second, conflict resolution unfolds over time and requires the conflict to be defined in concrete terms. In fact, it has been argued that the art of bargaining begins with "finding a way of expressing conflict in terms which are concrete and amenable to arbitration" (Morley, Webb & Stephenson, 1988, p. 130). Once the issues are put in concrete terms, the parties can choose the order in which they will deal with them. Several investigators have shown that resolving small issues opens up communication and paves the way for dealing with larger issues (Druckman, Broome & Korper, 1988; Goldberg, 1989).

autistic hostility Withdrawal from a conflict situation and avoidance of interaction.
integrative problem solving Resolution of conflict by identification of common goals rather than a focus on means.

Events in Eastern Europe have been a lesson in how threat reduction can lead to reduced conflict. After decades of threat and increased conflict, the powers in the area began to reduce troop strength and open the way to more direct communication. The destruction of the Berlin Wall is a symbol of the reduced conflict in the area.

Finally, it is important to develop realistic perceptions of the opponent. As we pointed out, people tend to dehumanize their opponents; they believe that an opponent's intentions are the opposite (the mirror image) of their own (Struch & Schwartz, 1989; White, 1985). Remember President Reagan's categorization of the Soviet Union as the "evil empire." These perceptions justify threats and an aggressive approach that will increase conflict. It is therefore important to reverse this tendency by learning about the opponent and understanding his or her perceptions. Viewing the opponent and the conflict situation realistically is an important first step toward reducing conflict.

Reducing Conflict by Reducing Threat

Earlier in this chapter we examined the destructive effects of threat on conflict resolution. Not only does threat escalate conflict, but conflict often motivates the use of threat. Osgood (1962) recognized this and pointed out that negotiations between the United States and the Soviet Union were proceeding on a path directly contrary to conflict resolution. Each side was amassing threat potential, and the huge increase in weapons was making the possibility of accidental war more likely. Osgood suggested a way out of this spiraling increase in conflict. He called his plan the *graduated reciprocation in tension reduction* **(GRIT)** policy. In the first phase, which is aimed at enlisting public support, one party publicly announces that it intends to reduce tension and clearly states the unilateral initiatives that it plans to take to do so. That party should also invite the other party to reciprocate with its own initiatives. The second phase is aimed at establishing the initiator's credibility and authenticity. During this phase the initiator must carry out the announced tension-reducing moves in a way that is unambiguous and open to verification. These steps must be taken even in the absence of reciprocation. The final points of the GRIT strategy relate to the need to have the initiator retain enough power to avoid being exploited by the other party. These steps specify that the initiatives should be risky and create a vulnerability in the initiator; yet they should not be so drastic that the initiator loses the ability to protect itself or to retaliate if the opponent responds aggressively. The idea behind GRIT is that moves by one nation or person to

Warsaw Pact applauds plans to cut U.S. forces

The Associated Press July 9, 1989

BUCHAREST, Romania—The Soviet Union and its Warsaw Pact allies Saturday praised President Bush's NATO proposal for deep cuts in conventional forces and said an accord on reductions could be reached next year.

In remarks at a dinner Friday, Soviet President Mikhail S. Gorbachev said the annual gathering would give a "serious, palpable answer" to Western proposals on cuts in conventional forces announced by Bush May 29 at a NATO summit in Brussels, Belgium.

On behalf of the 16-member North Atlantic Treaty Organization, Bush called for military cutbacks that would fix a ceiling of 275,000 troops in Europe for each superpower and make deep cuts in tanks, combat aircraft and artillery.

In a joint declaration, the Warsaw Pact countries said the Bush plan converged with their proposals, and that rapid progress in negotiating cuts was now possible.

"During the meeting it was noted that the additional proposals regarding conventional armed forces in Europe made at the recent NATO Council summit session met halfway the allied socialist countries's stand," the Eastern alliance said.

The opinion was expressed that the situation of the negotiations is such that the first understandings may be achieved already in 1990, provided that a constructive approach is taken by all," the declaration said.

This article seems to support the GRIT theory—that reduction of threat leads to cooperation by an opponent. The U.S. action demonstrates GRIT's first phase. Bush's decision to cut conventional armed forces is a unilateral public announcement of intent to reduce tension. Time will tell whether the other phases of GRIT will be carried out.

---

reduce threat capabilities would be met with similar reductions by others (Lindskold, 1986).

Overall, the research suggests that GRIT does work; that is, unilateral reductions of threat are often responded to with cooperative efforts on the part of an opponent. Research has found this effect even when the competition is very keen and has lasted for some time (Walters & Lindskold, 1982). Other research has found that GRIT is most likely to be successful when the opponent has equal or less power than the initiator (Lindskold & Aronoff, 1980). High-power people are often slow to give up their advantage.

In a hopeful sign for world peace, the Soviet Union and the United States seem to be adopting a policy similar to GRIT. Instead of a race to build up arms, both sides seem to be trying to outdo the other in reducing weapons and troops in Europe. It is a fragile beginning and the end result is still in doubt, but it has reduced tensions and offered hope.

Negotiation and Bargaining

The hostage crisis on TWA flight 847 offers an opportunity to watch the process of conflict resolution. Each side began by stating its demands,

---

GRIT   Graduated reciprocation in tension reduction; a policy developed by Osgood to reduce international tension through the unilateral reduction of threat capability.

If you are interested in purchasing an automobile, research suggests that it is to your advantage to begin with a rather extreme position and make only moderate concessions in a tit-for-tat manner. Taking a very extreme initial position may lead the other party to break off negotiations. And making unmatched or too-large concessions will invite the other party to take advantage of you.

and then each negotiated to get as many demands met as possible. The process consisted of **overt bargaining,** in which (1) the parties in conflict have divergent interests, (2) some form of communication is possible, and (3) the parties can make provisional offers or concessions (Chertkoff & Esser, 1976). In our everyday lives we often bargain to resolve conflicts. Anyone who has bought an automobile or a home knows that lengthy bargaining is often necessary to settle on a price. Further, anyone who has been in these situations quickly learns that some strategies are more successful than others for achieving a favorable resolution.

The literature on negotiation and bargaining is extensive, and we will only be able to hit the highlights. Negotiation is a process that takes place within a social context. It involves learning, changes in motivation, and the development of perceptions, both of the self and of the opponent. In most cases, bargainers must consider not only the present but the past and the future as well. During the TWA incident, both Nabih Berri and President Reagan had to consider not only the present hostage situation but the fact that

they would probably engage in future discussions about the Middle East situation.

Even within this complex context, research has uncovered some interesting steps that can be taken to enhance one's position.

1. *Initial position.* The advice here seems to be to adopt as extreme an initial position as possible without cutting off negotiation. This approach makes the opponent view you as a hard bargainer, and it sets the boundaries for the negotiation.

In one study (Chertkoff & Conley, 1967), subjects believed that they were either buying or selling an automobile. The subjects could send messages back and forth and were to signal when they had agreed on a price. Actually, the experimenter intercepted the messages that were sent and substituted messages of his own. The first message that the subjects received was either moderately or highly discrepant from the price they wished to get (or pay) for the automobile. When the final price that the subject agreed to receive (or pay) for the automobile was examined, it was found that the subjects were willing

TABLE 10-6

Mean final price for automobile

	Subject's role	
Experimenter's initial offer	Buyer	Seller
Extreme	$1,302.60	$1,221.01
Moderate	$1,189.13	$1,368.78

NOTE: When the subject was the buyer, he ended up paying the highest price when the experimenter's initial offer was extreme. When the subject was the seller, he received the lowest price when the experimenter's offer was extremely low.
SOURCE: Chertkoff and Conley (1967).

to accept less or to pay more for the automobile when the experimenter's initial bid was highly discrepant (Table 10-6). This suggests that from the individual bargainer's point of view, it is better to begin by making highly discrepant offers or very strong demands.

2. *Concessions.* The evidence suggests that concessions made during the bargaining process should be rather small, and that they should be made in accordance with the **tit-for-tat strategy** (Axelrod, 1984; Hirshleifer & Coll, 1988): the opponent who makes a cooperative response is rewarded with concessions, but the opponent's competitive behavior is punished. As this is a very common strategy, it seems especially important to reinforce the cooperative actions of the opponent (Komorita & Barth, 1985).

The tit-for-tat strategy not only develops a reward/punishment contingency but also affects the attributions your opponent may make about you. Subjects who observed a bargaining session rated an opponent who followed a matching strategy as stronger than one who adopted a soft cooperative strategy and fairer than one who took a tough competitive stance (McGillicuddy et al., 1984). Hence, if you always cooperate, your opponent may perceive you as weak (Swingle, 1970) or think you are attempting to manipulate him or her. In bargaining, nice guys (women, groups) do finish last and get exploited.

3. *Using time as a tool.* Bargaining tends to fill up the available time (Kelley, 1966). Procrastination has utility, as each party waits for the

other to make additional concessions. Looking at another side of this issue, numerous studies (Hamner, 1974; Pruitt & Johnson, 1970; Yukl, 1974) have found that time pressure leads to faster concessions from negotiating parties. Taken together, these findings suggest that it is to the advantage of each party to convince the other that it can wait forever for concessions.

Attempts to use time pressure can backfire, however; time pressure may give rise to the use of threat and coercion. Thus the party that feels that time is about to run out may resort to force. In fact, some of Reagan's advisers urged him to use force to end the crisis because they feared that time *was* running out. In addition, while time pressure may facilitate a quick resolution to conflict, it inhibits communication, increases feelings of competitiveness, and often results in poor joint outcomes (Carnevale, Sherer & Pruitt, 1979; Yukl et al., 1978). Thus time can be a valuable weapon, but it can also work against cooperation and problem-solving approaches to conflict resolution.

Depersonalizing Conflict: The Use of Norms

As the crisis continued, focus shifted away from the issues and toward the men involved in the conflict. The conflict began to be viewed as a test of who (Berri or Reagan) was the strongest bargainer, and interest focused on how the outcome would affect these men's standings in the eyes of their supporters. In other words, the conflict quickly became focused on the bargainers, and this personalization of the situation set up additional roadblocks to a resolution.

One way to remove this type of impediment to conflict resolution is to resort to norms to

overt bargaining A situation in which parties with divergent interests have some form of communication and can make provisional offers and concessions.
tit-for-tat strategy A bargaining strategy by which an opponent's cooperative actions receive a cooperative response and his or her competitive responses beget competitive reactions.

resolve differences. **Norms** (see Chapter 12) are rules that determine how behavior should legitimately progress. They are impersonal in that they are concerned with the situation rather than with the personalities of the people in conflict. Efforts at conflict resolution that rely on norms are directed toward identifying a just and fair solution rather than the side that is stronger or more capable. For this reason norms are often used to resolve conflict—especially when both parties can use threats to the same degree and when concern with face saving is high (Thibaut, 1968).

Some norms focus on the distribution of resources. One such norm deals with the *needs* of the two parties. Simply put, this norm states that the more need a person has, the more he or she should receive. A second norm is based on **equality**. According to this norm, resources should be divided equally among the people involved in a social relationship.

The third and most studied norm is *equity*. According to this norm, the amount people receive from a relationship should be determined by how much they put into it. **Equity theory** argues that people are motivated both to maximize their gains *and* to achieve equity in their relationships (Adams, 1963, 1965; Walster, Berscheid & Walster, 1978). A relationship is equitable when a person scrutinizing that relationship can conclude:

$$\frac{(Outcomes_A - Inputs_A)}{Inputs_A} = \frac{(Outcomes_B - Inputs_B)}{Inputs_B}$$

For example, suppose that you work eight hours painting a fence and your friend works two hours. Together you receive $100 for the job. The relationship will be equitable if you receive $80 (80% of the pay for 80% of the work) and your friend receives $20 (20% of the pay for 20% of the work). As can be seen, resolving conflict on the basis of equity can perpetuate differences in power and resources between people.

Norms do have a strong influence on people's behavior. For example, it has been shown that people who feel they are receiving more for a job than is equitable experience uneasiness and will often increase the amount of work to establish equity (Austin & Walster, 1974; Adams, 1965). People become even more uncomfortable and

angry when they receive less than they deserve from a relationship. When people cannot restore actual equity by changing their work or payoffs, they attempt to restore *psychological equity* by changing their perceptions of the relationship (Austin & Hatfield, 1980).

However, the availability of norms does not ensure a smooth resolution of conflict. Disagreement can arise over which norm is most appropriate to use in the situation (Austin, 1986). In some employment settings, for example, men have argued that they should receive more pay than women because they must support families (norm of need). Women have countered by pointing out that they must also support families and that fairness dictates equal pay for equal work (equity). Equality norms are most likely to be used in cohesive groups that enjoy a positive socioemotional climate, whereas equity norms will be most salient in noncohesive groups. Deutsch (1975) argues that equity norms will be used in groups whose greatest concern is productivity, while equality norms will be used when the main concern is developing positive social relations. Another disagreement can arise over the value of inputs or outputs even if there is agreement about the norm to be used in distributing rewards.

As you can see, there are many advantages to using norms to resolve conflict; the norms depersonalize the conflict and make it easier for the parties to make concessions without losing face. However, numerous conditions determine which norm will be used and how the parties will perceive inputs and outcomes. Norms, therefore, do not always prove to be a yellow brick road to conflict resolution.

The Importance of Procedure

In the last section we saw that the use of a norm can dictate the outcome of a conflict. Yet outcome is not the only point to consider in a conflict situation; the procedure used to arrive at the outcome is also very important. For example, Israel had planned to release the Shi'ite prisoners before the hijacking. Yet when the hijackers demanded the prisoners' release, Israel refused, saying that the prisoners would not be released under the conditions established by the hijacking.

Research in the area of **procedural justice** has examined how the procedure used to resolve a conflict affects the parties' perceptions of the fairness of the outcome. Much of the research focuses on procedures used in courts of law (Thibaut & Walker, 1975, 1978). In the **adversary system,** each party has its own lawyers, who present its side in front of a judge. This is the system that is most frequently practiced in U.S. courts. In the *nonadversary system,* a single representative appointed by the court gathers information from both sides and presents findings to the court. This system is often used in British and French courts of law.

In general, the studies suggest that people prefer the adversary procedure and that decisions reached under this procedure are perceived as more fair, satisfying, and unbiased than decisions arrived at by the nonadversary system (Lind et al., 1980). However, there is evidence that the adversary procedure is preferred only in Western cultures, where autonomy and competitiveness are stressed; Chinese students in Hong Kong (with a culture stressing harmony and group solidarity) did not prefer the adversary procedure (Leung & Lind, 1986). Careful examinations of the procedures indicate that the important aspect of the adversarial system is that it allows participants to have a **voice** (Folger & Greenberg, 1985); that is, people feel that their opinions are heard. Active participation generally makes people feel that both the procedure and the outcome are fair. The addition of an appeals process enhances the perceptions of fairness and satisfaction (Sheppard, 1985). Whether or not the appeals procedure is used, its existence is comforting to the participants.

Before concluding this discussion, we must add an important exception. Because participation may raise people's hopes that a certain decision will be reached, they will be especially disappointed when the decision goes against them. The effect of participation is likely to be most negative when the individual receives a negative decision and learns that others also view it as unfair.

As you can see, both the outcome and the procedure used to reach it are important deter-minants of people's satisfaction and of the ultimate success of efforts at conflict resolution.

With a Little Help from Friends and Others: Coalitions, Mediators, and Arbitrators

When it became clear that he had a real crisis on his hands, President Reagan began to recruit support from others to help him settle the conflict. Although the hostages were all United States citizens, Reagan attempted to show leaders of other countries how their interests were involved in this crisis. Israel was quickly involved, but Reagan also tried to get help from France, Great Britain, Egypt, and Switzerland. The development of coalitions to deal with conflict has become a common response to international crises; when the Rome and Vienna airports were bombed by terrorists in December 1985, Reagan again sought the support of allies to put sanctions on Libya. The balance of world power has long rested on an entangled configuration of coalitions, including the North Atlantic Treaty Organization (NATO) countries, the Warsaw Pact countries, and nonaligned countries.

A **coalition** has been defined as "two or more individuals who formally agree to cooperate in order to obtain some mutually desired outcome" (Urruti & Miller, 1984, p. 825). Coalitions are

---

adversary system A system for resolving disputes by which both sides (or their representatives) argue their case before a judge.

coalition A temporary alliance of two or more parties who cooperate and combine their resources to beat an opponent.

equity theory The theory that individuals desire their outcomes to reflect their inputs to determine the fairness of a relationship.

norm A rule that governs a specific behavior and applies to everyone in the group.

norm of equality A means of resolving conflict by which resources are divided equally among the parties, regardless of inputs.

procedural justice Justice and fairness based on the procedure by which resources are allocated.

voice An opportunity for parties in conflict to express their views of the situation.

Conflicts in professional sports are often settled by an arbitrator, who examines the proposals of both sides and chooses one of the proposals as the final solution.

most likely to form when groups are using a "majority wins" decision rule (Thompson, Manniz & Bazerman, 1988). They are less likely when groups have decided to settle their conflicts only when they have reached consensus.

People enter a coalition to beat their adversary. However, once a coalition is formed, the parties are quickly faced with the additional problem of how to divide payoffs should they win. For example, a coalition can divide payoffs in accordance with the amount each party contributes to the coalition (equity); the party who controls the most receives the most. On the other hand, it can be argued that the payoffs should be divided equally because the coalition would not be successful if any of the participants backed out. This is what makes it difficult to predict what coalitions will form and how they will function.

To understand this process, let us examine one popular theory of coalition formation. The bargaining theory of coalitions emphasizes the negotiation process that goes on within coalitions (Komorita & Kravitz, 1983). The theory proposes that each member of a coalition has a maximum expected outcome, a minimum expected outcome, and a most probable expected outcome. For the high-power person in a coalition, the maximum expected outcome is equity (payoffs based on contribution) and the minimum expected outcome is equality (a 50-50 split of the rewards). For the low-power person, the maximum expected outcome is equality and the minimum expected outcome is equity. The most probable expected outcome for both parties is the average of equity and equality. Individuals enter into coalitions because of their desire to establish relationships that will yield the highest possible outcome. Continuing this reasoning, the bargaining theory of coalitions makes the additional prediction that coalitions will often be unstable because those who are excluded from a coalition will entice defectors by offering them higher outcomes than they are getting from the present coalition.

Because of these difficulties with negotiation, coalitions generally form with the smallest number of parties needed to beat the adversary (Gamson, 1961, 1964). People join coalitions that they feel will give them the maximum payoff. The power of any party in a coalition is based on the resources that party controls, the value (or expected profit) of alternative coalitions, and the number of available alternative coalitions that party could enter (Komorita & Miller, 1986). In other words, you can be successful in extracting promises of reward from a coalition if you have many resources to add to that coalition and if there are other coalitions you could enter into. Finally, coalitions are often unstable because their members are constantly tempted to defect to other coalitions that may promise greater rewards.

Thus, rather than offering simple solutions to conflict resolution, coalitions may create new dilemmas. In addition, the inclusion of outside parties that may not be directly involved in the initial conflict often widens the conflict. Coalitions therefore may resolve conflict, or they may encourage the conflict spiral.

Coalitions are not the only means to involve others in conflict resolution. Interest has been growing in the use of mediators and arbitrators to settle conflicts (Carnevale, 1985; Duffy, 1991). A **mediator** generally serves as an adviser, helping the parties identify issues and agree on a solution to the conflict. Although mediators may be neutral third parties, they may also have an interest in seeing the conflict settled. The important characteristic of the mediator is that he or she is trusted by the parties in the conflict (Carnevale, 1985). In the TWA hostage situation, President Assad of Syria served as a mediator. Mediation is now being widely used in labor disputes, divorce cases, and other civil disputes, as well as in international politics. Because the mediator helps the parties develop their own solutions to the conflict, both parties may feel that they have had a voice in the outcome, and they may be more committed to this resolution than they would be to one that was imposed on them.

Under **arbitration,** by contrast, a third party actually decides on the final outcome after hearing the arguments of both sides (Morley et al., 1988). The arbitrator is generally a neutral party who begins with no stake in the conflict. During the process of arbitration, however, the arbitrator may unwittingly become a third party in the conflict. The advantage of arbitration is that a binding solution to the conflict is achieved; mediation may not be successful in achieving a resolution. The disadvantage is that the solution is determined by the arbitrator rather than by the parties involved in the conflict. Further, the parties must agree to have their conflict resolved by an arbitrator and to abide by the outcome; such an agreement is often difficult to obtain.

Both mediation and arbitration have proved their usefulness as means to resolve conflicts. When the principal parties cannot reach agreement, a third party can sometimes bring a conflict to a resolution.

Intergroup Conflict: Some Special Considerations

Thus far we have been examining conflict in a rather general way. Our discussion could apply to conflict between individuals, between an indi-

vidual and a group, or between groups. Many of our conflicts, however, come about because we belong to groups. And intergroup conflict has some special characteristics that make it important to study in its own right (Worchel & Austin, 1986). First, groups tend to be more competitive than individuals (Brown, 1988). Second, the more closely individuals identify with their group, the more likely they are to react aggressively to perceived threats by another group (Struch & Schwartz, 1989). Third, as we will see, the roots for intergroup conflict may lie in the simple existence of groups. Taking this point a step further, Buss (1988) has suggested that the evolutionary basis of the reproductive strategy is responsible for much of the conflict between men and women. Finally, much of our behavior and much of what

---

---

arbitration   A system of dispute resolution by which a third party determines the outcome after hearing the arguments of both sides.

mediator   A third party who helps the principal parties to a conflict develop their own resolution.

---

we observe is based on group membership. Tajfel (1979) makes this point when he states, "Whenever individuals belonging to one group interact collectively or individually with another group or its members, *in terms of their group identification,* we have an instance of intergroup behavior."

A great deal of research has focused on intergroup conflict and its resolution.

The Basis for Intergroup Conflict

Competition

One of the earliest studies in this area examined the hypothesis that competition leads to intergroup hostility. Carolyn and Muzafer Sherif and their colleagues (Sherif et al., 1961) conducted studies at boys' summer camps in Connecticut, New York, and Oklahoma. The same basic design was employed in all of the studies. The subjects at each camp were randomly divided into two groups. The subjects were given a week to become attracted and committed to their group. They lived in bunkhouses, cooked their own meals, cleaned up their own campsites, and organized so that group members could play games with each other. The groups developed their own leadership structures, and some groups gave themselves such names as Pythons, Eagles, and Red Devils.

After this period of group formation, the experimenters brought the two groups together. Each time the groups met, they competed at touch football, tug-of-war, or baseball for attractive prizes. And they competed to see who could put on the best skit, have the cleanest cabin, and pitch a tent faster.

The effects of introducing competition between the groups were striking. The serene camp setting was turned into a miniature battleground as the two groups began to hurl insults and names at each other. *Pigs, dirty bums, jerks,* and several other objectionable words were used to describe the rival team; and the boys made posters showing the other team being bombed or trampled. They engaged in guerrilla tactics; one group raided and vandalized the other group's bunkhouse. There were also incidents of open warfare as food fights erupted between the two groups; often scuffles broke out between rival groups on the camp field; and apples were used as ammunition in full-blown artillery attacks.

The Sherif studies were followed by the work of Blake and Mouton (1961, 1962, 1986). When these investigators examined relations between labor and management, they found that competition resulted in intergroup hostility. They reported that "a 'win' orientation between two groups has a spontaneous, mobilizing effect with a number of predictable consequences."

The Minimal Group Situation

While we know that intergroup competition leads to a dislike of the out-group and a preference for the in-group, we can ask whether or not competition is necessary for the development of intergroup hostility. That is, must competition exist before intergroup hostility will result? The answer is no, competition is not necessary. Research shows that simply placing people in groups leads to in-group favoritism and out-group discrimination.

This point has been clearly demonstrated by Tajfel and his colleagues (Tajfel, 1970, 1972; Tajfel et al., 1971). In these experiments, the investigators assigned schoolboys to groups on the basis of performance on trivial tasks. In one study, for example, subjects believed that they had been assigned to a particular group on the basis of their judgment of two abstract paintings. Following their assignment to the groups, the subjects were asked to divide up a sum of money between the two groups. The results indicated that more money was given to the in-group than to the out-group. In addition to this bias in favor of the in-group, the results indicated that when subjects had the choice of giving money either to increase in-group profit or to maximize the difference in payoff between in-group and out-group, they chose the latter course. They made this choice even when it lowered the in-group's payoff. Thus the boys seemed to be competing rather than following the strategy of maximum gain for the in-group. The in-group bias that results from simple assignment to a group has been referred to as the **minimal group situation** (Tajfel & Turner, 1986).

What causes this effect? An explanation that has received support focuses on the social comparison process (see Chapter 3). According to this theory, people define themselves and develop self-esteem by comparing themselves with others in their own group (Lemyre & Smith, 1985; Turner, 1987). Because of this phenomenon, people want to enhance the status of their own group in comparison with other groups. The effect here is to increase the differences between in-group and out-group and to perceive the in-group in a favorable light. This explanation for the minimal group situation has received support in studies showing that out-group discrimination is greater when group assignment is based on important or personally relevant dimensions than when the assignment is based on irrelevant dimensions (Turner & Brown, 1978).

The Resolution of Intergroup Conflict

Our world is filled with intergroup conflicts. Fighting rages in the Middle East, in India and Sri Lanka, in Central America. Ethnic clashes threaten the stability of the Soviet Union. Racial conflict in South Africa threatens to erupt into revolution. Bickering between Canadians of British and French backgrounds surfaces periodically. The United States is faced with issues of racial conflict and sexism. Indeed, it has been found that conflict between individuals is easier to resolve than conflict between groups; one study (Allison & Messick, 1983) found that individuals do better at resolving social dilemmas than groups do. Despite these problems, however, numerous groups have managed to reduce or resolve their conflicts with other groups. Moreover, the social science literature has been able to identify constructive ways of dealing with this type of conflict.

Contact

Some of the earliest attempts to reduce intergroup and interracial conflict focused on contact (Cook, 1985; Stephan, 1985). It was argued that contact between the groups would lessen conflict and tension. The early results of this approach, however, were not consistently positive. Contact

sometimes reduced conflict but in other situations conflict actually increased. In fact, there is some evidence (Brewer, 1986) that conflict is most likely to erupt between groups that are close together and therefore likely to have frequent contact.

A closer examination of these results identified the conditions under which contact was most likely to have positive effects. First, it was found that *equal status contact* was a key (Amir, 1969); that is, the situation under which the group members have contact must ensure that they have equal status or power. In many attempts to integrate schools, for example, whites who had superior previous schooling were placed in schools with blacks who had previously been forced into inferior schools. The students were then given tasks that the whites were better prepared to handle because of their past history. This contact emphasized the differences between blacks and whites and often increased the conflict. Second, the contact situation must allow group members to interact on a personal basis (Wilder, 1986). Third, the contact should be preceded by positive information about the out-group. An interesting study looked at the attitudes of Israeli tourists in Egypt (Ben-Ari & Amir, 1988). The results showed that the Israelis had the most positive attitudes when they had received information about Egyptians before their visit to Egypt. Neither positive information nor contact alone had much effect on their attitudes. Thus the contact situation must promote perceptions of out-group members as individuals. Fourth, contact is most effective in reducing conflict when the parties do not expect future competition (Wilder & Shapiro, 1989). Fifth, the contact situation must encourage people to see the relationship between the group members with whom they have contact and their group (Wilder, 1986). We tend to perceive out-group members with whom we have positive interactions as "exceptions," people who are not like the others in their group. Here contact may facilitate the personal relationship but it will not reduce the intergroup conflict. Sixth,

minimal group situation Membership in a group based on nothing more than random assignment to it. Research shows that in-group bias results from even this situation.

the contact must encourage cooperation and interdependence.

Cooperation and Interdependence

One of the most productive means for reducing intergroup conflict is cooperation. In the camp studies discussed earlier in this chapter (Sherif et al., 1961) a number of steps were taken to reduce intergroup hostility. Adults at the camp lectured the groups on the necessity of coming together and being friends. This method did not succeed. Then the two groups were united to combat a common enemy—a group from another camp that had been invited to compete against the two warring groups. The two groups did combine and hostility was diminished while they competed against the new group, but after the "common enemy" withdrew, the intergroup hostility recurred. Further, this method merely serves to redirect and widen intergroup conflict and aggression.

The method that proved most effective in reducing intergroup hostility was to have the two warring groups work together toward a superordinate goal. A **superordinate goal** is one that is attractive to the members of two groups but cannot be achieved without cooperation between the groups. To test the hypothesis, a number of tasks were designed that required intergroup cooperation for success. For example, while the boys were on a camping trip, a truck that was to go for their food stalled. The only way to get it started was to push it some distance, and neither group could do this by itself. Thus the two groups were forced to cooperate to get the food. After the two groups had cooperated on a number of tasks, the hostility between them declined significantly.

Elliot Aronson and his colleagues (Aronson, Bridgeman & Geffner, 1978; Aronson et al., 1978) developed a unique method to encourage cooperation between interracial groups in the classroom. The **jigsaw method** involves six-person groups of students who must learn a body of material. Each member of the group is given a part of the lesson that he or she must present to the other group members. Successful group performance is therefore dependent on each member's mastery of his or her part of the lesson.

Under these circumstances, all the group members become motivated to help each other learn their parts of the lesson. Aronson found that when the groups were composed of people of different racial or ethnic groups, the jigsaw method reduced ethnic stereotyping and increased attraction between members of the various ethnic groups.

Follow-up studies on cooperation (Worchel, Andreoli & Folger, 1977) suggested that cooperation is effective if the groups succeed in their effort. However, failure in the cooperative effort may result in scapegoating (blaming the other group) and increased intergroup hostility.

Cooperation is a good means to reduce hostility for a number of reasons. First, it focuses the group members' attention away from their conflict and onto trying to solve the problem that confronts them. Earlier we pointed out the value of transforming conflict into problem-solving efforts. Second, cooperation reduces the salience of the in-group/out-group distinction (Miller & Davidson-Podgorny, 1987; Worchel, 1986b). Groups that work together become more concerned with the task at hand and are less likely to categorize themselves as in-group and out-group. In a sense, all the members are now one group and have increased motivation to see others in a positive light because each person is dependent on all the others.

With this point in mind, it is interesting to note that conflict is not reduced when one party offers to help the other (Worchel, Wong & Skeltema, 1989). Similarly, foreign aid programs often engender bad feelings in the recipients (Taormina & Messick, 1983). It seems that helping, unlike cooperation, draws a distinct boundary between the helper and the recipient and places the helper in a more powerful position. As a result, the group boundary remains salient, and the conflict continues.

As you can see, reducing conflict between groups is no small task, a fact that may explain why we are surrounded by intergroup conflicts. It also helps explain why the conflict over the hostage crisis was so difficult to resolve; the conditions did not promote contact or cooperation between the parties. We may take hope, however, from the knowledge that intergroup conflict *can* be resolved and we *can* identify the steps that are most likely to lead to resolution.

The Other Side of the Coin: The Value of Conflict

Throughout this chapter, and indeed throughout much of our lives, we view conflict as negative; we try to avoid conflict, and when it occurs, we work to reduce it. Clearly, conflict such as that leading to the hostage crisis is negative and can have negative consequences. Yet conflict has another side: it can have a positive influence on people, groups, and relationships.

Conflict often identifies problems and motivates people to work on those problems. The hostage crisis focused attention on the destructiveness of the Middle East situation and emphasized the need to find a solution for the problems there. It also identified problems in airport security around the world and resulted in cooperative efforts to improve that security. Conflict may bring together people who are otherwise separated and offer them a chance to exchange information. The intervention of Syria to gain the release of the hostages was seen as a positive step. Tension between the United States and Syria had been high before the crisis, and President Assad's actions offered fleeting hope that cooperative efforts would be forthcoming in other areas of tension between the two nations. From a group's standpoint, conflict may help to identify its boundaries and establish an identification (Worchel, 1984b). Groups often use and even invite conflict as a way of solidifying membership and establishing an identity. In the hostage crisis, the Amal group became very prominent; the crisis resulted in a clear definition of its boundaries and its membership.

The sociologist George Simmel (1955) suggested two additional positive roles of conflict. First, conflict gives rise to social change. Open conflict between blacks and whites in the United States has led to numerous social changes that have afforded opportunities to increase equality in our society. Simmel also pointed out that conflict between groups may result in a new unity and solidarity within each group: "One unites in order to fight." In the United States, the black power movement that resulted in new solidarity among blacks was a direct result of racial conflict.

STOP, THINK, & UNDERSTAND

1. How does intergroup conflict differ from interpersonal conflict?
2. Is competition necessary before intergroup conflict can arise?
3. What conditions must be met if contact between groups in conflict is to lead to a resolution of that conflict?
4. What are some positive consequences of conflict?

Deutsch (1973) sums up the positive roles of conflict:

> It [conflict] prevents stagnation; it stimulates interest and curiosity; it is the medium through which problems can be aired and solutions arrived at; it is the root of personal and social change. Conflict is often part of the process of testing and assessing oneself and, as such, may be highly enjoyable as one experiences the pleasure of the full and active use of one's capacities. In addition, conflict demarcates groups from one another and thus helps establish group and personal identities; external conflict often fosters internal cohesiveness. (p. 9)

Summary

Interpersonal conflict can be described as tension between two or more social entities that arises from an incompatibility of actual or desired responses. Two major types of interpersonal con-

---

jigsaw method A technique for reducing conflict in a racially mixed group of students by which the group is given a problem to solve such that each member holds a part of the solution; if the group is to succeed, each member must master his or her part.

superordinate goal A goal that is attractive to members of two groups but cannot be achieved without cooperation between the two groups.

---

flict have been defined: *zero-sum* and *mixed-motive*. The zero-sum conflict is a pure competition situation in which one party's loss is exactly equal to the other party's gain. In the mixed-motive situation, the individual player is tempted to compete with the opponent to maximize personal gain and to cooperate with the opponent to maximize the joint payoff. The *prisoner's dilemma* and *social dilemma* are mixed-motive conflicts. Once conflict begins, it has a tendency to spiral because people become entrapped when they realize that costs are associated with reducing conflict as well as with continuing it.

Threat is a common response to conflict. On the whole, research suggests that threat escalates rather than reduces conflict. Terrorists use threat and random violence to create fear. Yet terrorism rarely causes major political change. The arms race is based on the use of threat to gain an advantage. There are hopeful signs that the superpowers are rethinking this approach to conflict. People often remain in conflict because of their concern with saving face and appearing strong. Concern with *face saving* is especially prevalent when people's responses to conflict are public. The perception of others as competitive also feeds the *conflict spiral*; research suggests that some of us tend to view most other people as competitive, while others may see other people as more diverse in their responses.

Distrust widens a conflict. It has been found that *trust* is difficult to develop and requires one party to take risks to see how the other party will respond. It takes only one betrayal for distrust to develop, and once people distrust each other, it is difficult to reestablish trust. While communication may help reduce conflict, people in conflict often do not want to communicate with each other. Communication must contain accurate information to facilitate conflict resolution, but an opponent may use information to gain an advantage in negotiations.

Conflict can be resolved more easily if people clarify their perceptions of the situation. Further, work on *GRIT* (graduated reciprocation in tension reduction) has shown that reducing threat potential helps to reduce conflict.

When people can communicate, they can bargain by exchanging concessions. Bargaining is carried out in a social context over time.

Research suggests that one party in a conflict will achieve the highest payoff if that party takes a very extreme first position and makes only small concessions during the bargaining process. Further, a party who continually responds in a cooperative manner will be taken advantage of by the opponent. Thus unwavering cooperation does not necessarily beget cooperation. The best method is the *tit-for-tat strategy*, by which one matches the opponent's behavior. It is especially important to reward cooperative actions by the opponent. Placing time pressure on an opponent may force concessions, but it may also reduce communication and lead the opponent to resort to threats.

Norms can be used to resolve conflicts because they tend to depersonalize the situation and reduce the need to save face. The *norm of equity* has received the most attention in conflict-resolution research. In addition to outcomes, the procedure used to mediate conflict influences the way people feel. Research has shown that procedures that allow for a great deal of individual participation (*voice*) are most effective in resolving conflict.

A coalition in which two or more parties pool their resources against an opponent may be effective in resolving a conflict. In general, coalitions are formed by parties that have insufficient resources to overcome the opponent alone. A *mediator* is an outside adviser who helps the parties reach a resolution. *Arbitration* involves a third party who actually decides on a resolution of the conflict after gathering information from both principal parties.

Intergroup conflict can result when people are assigned to groups; it is found even when the group assignment is done on a random basis and group members do not interact. Competition heightens the degree of conflict. Groups in conflict tend to view the out-group as bad and see themselves in a positive light. Group members also tend to see more diversity in their own group than in the out-group.

Contact between groups will reduce conflict if the groups meet on an equal footing, if the group members interact at a personal level, if it promotes the perception of a relationship between the individual and the group, if it encourages cooperation and interdependence, and if the groups do not expect future competition. While

Chapter Ten   Developing and Resolving Conflict

helping may reduce conflict between groups that have a history of positive interaction, it may increase conflict between groups that lack trust and have previously competed. Intergroup cooperation that results in a successful outcome reduces intergroup conflict. Cooperation focuses attention on solutions rather than on the conflict and it reduces the salience of the boundary between in-group and out-group.

While conflict can produce negative outcomes, it can also have positive effects. Conflict initiates social change, motivates creative solutions to problems, promotes individual and group identity, and initiates self-evaluation.

Key Terms

adversary system
arbitration
autistic hostility
coalition
competition
conflict spiral
equity theory
face saving
GRIT
integrative problem
    solving

intergroup conflict
interpersonal conflict
intrapersonal conflict
jigsaw method
mediation
mediator
minimal group
    situation
mixed-motive conflict
norm of equality
norms

overt bargaining
prisoner's dilemma
procedural justice
social dilemma
superordinate goal
terrorism
tit-for-tat strategy
trust
voice
zero-sum conflict

Suggested Readings

Bacharach, S., & Lawler, E. (1981). *Bargaining*. San Francisco: Jossey-Bass.

Barner-Barry, C., & Rosenwein, R. (1985). *Psychological perspectives on politics*. Englewood Cliffs, N.J.: Prentice-Hall.

Bar-Tal, D. (1990). *Group Beliefs: A conception for analyzing group structure, process, and behavior*. New York: Springer-Verlag.

Brockner, J., & Rubin, J. Z. (1985). *Entrapment in escalating conflicts*. New York: Springer-Verlag.

Deutsch, M. (1973). *The resolution of conflict*. New Haven, Conn.: Yale University Press.

Druckman, D. (Ed.). (1977). *Negotiations: Social perspectives*. Newbury Park, Calif.: Sage.

Kelley, H., & Thibaut, J. (1978). *Interpersonal relations: A theory of interdependence*. New York: Wiley.

Oskamp, S. (Ed.). *International conflict and national public policy issues*. Applied Social Psychology Annual (Vol. 6). Newbury Park, Calif.: Sage.

Rubin, J., & Brown, B. (1975). *The social psychology of bargaining and negotiations*. New York: Academic Press.

Stroebe, W., Kruglanski, A., Bar-Tal, D., & Hewstone, M. (1988). *The social psychology of intergroup conflict: Theory, research, and applications*. Berlin: Springer-Verlag.

Taylor, D. M., & Moghaddam, F. M. (1987). *Themes of intergroup relations*. New York: Praeger.

Turner, J., & Giles, H. (1981). *Intergroup behavior*. Chicago: University of Chicago Press.

Worchel, S., & Austin, W. (Eds.). (1986). *The psychology of intergroup relations*. Chicago: Nelson-Hall.

Chapter Eleven

Prejudice and Stereotypes

*D*ead silence—not a sound to be heard in the town. The lamps in the street, the lights in the shops and in the houses are out. It is 3:30 A.M. All of a sudden noises in the street break into my sleep, a wild medley of shouts and shrieks. I listen, frightened and alarmed, until I distinguish words: "Get out, Jews! Death to the Jews!" . . . Fists are hammering at the door. The shutters are broken open. . . . I run out of my room, and down the stairs, . . . my eyes looked straight into the guns. . . . "I am hit," stammers my father, before he breaks down on the stairs. I am forced to go on, but I can see blood on the stairs and a dark stain on my father's back. (Bentwich, 1981, p. 84)

These words describe the experience of a 16-year-old Jewish boy in Emden, Germany, on the night of November 9–10, 1938. Similar attacks on Jews were repeated that evening all over Germany, Austria, and parts of Czechoslovakia. As a result of these events, the dark hours of that night have come to be called *Kristallnacht,* or the Night of the Broken Glass. During those hours Adolf Hitler's Nazis went on a rampage against Jews throughout the Third Reich. By the morning of November 11, the dimensions of the attacks were clear. Approximately "100 Jews had been killed, 7,500 Jewish businesses had been destroyed, 275 synagogues had been razed or burned, and 30,000 Jews had been arrested" (U.S. Holocaust Memorial Council, 1989). Streets were blanketed with broken glass from businesses, homes, and synagogues. Most of the people who were arrested were eventually taken to prison camps.

Kristallnacht marked a turning point in the Nazis' persecution of the Jews. It had been designed to look like a spontaneous outbreak of anti-Semitic feeling. In reality, the attacks were carefully organized by two of Hitler's top lieutenants, Josef Goebbels and Reinhard Heydrich, and carried out by the soldiers of the SS disguised as civilians. It was the first time, but not the last, that the German government resorted to organized physical violence against its own Jewish citizens and those of conquered lands.

Why did Kristallnacht occur? To understand the events of that night, and the holocaust that took place during the next six and a half years, we have to understand the madness of Nazi anti-Semitism and Hitler's obsession with the "Jewish problem." Adolf Hitler controlled Germany for 12 years, from 1933 to 1945. Hitler's reign began and ended on nearly the same dates as Franklin Roosevelt's term as president of the United States. He came to power during the Depression, and committed suicide just before Germany finally surrendered at the end of World War II. Hitler expressed a deep anti-Semitism that had been part of German history and culture for centuries. Though Jews made up not more than 1% of the German population, they were often blamed for Germany's problems. As a distinct group whose achievements often aroused envy, they were convenient targets for smoldering frustrations. For years a "Jewish conspiracy" was held responsible for problems ranging from rampant inflation to defeat in World War I. Hitler himself had a deep hatred for Jews and gained political support for his Nazi party by fanning the flames of anti-Semitism among a substantial portion of the German population. Though the Nazis were reviled by many Germans and never received a majority vote in any election, they were able to take power in a badly crippled and divided nation in 1933.

As soon as Hitler became chancellor of Germany, he moved against the Jews. "Non-Aryans" were excluded from the civil service within months. By 1935 Jews had lost their citizenship, and marriage between Jews and German "subjects of the state" was forbidden. Soon Jews were forbidden to fly the German flag. Within a short time they were excluded from all aspects of German economic and cultural life. Concentration camps were established and many Jews were simply locked up. And then, when a 17-year-old Jewish boy shot a Nazi official in Paris, Hitler and his lieutenants had the pretext they needed to organize Kristallnacht, and the attack on Jewish synagogues, businesses, and homes soon followed. Nazi leaders claimed the attacks reflected the nation's "healthy instincts."

After Kristallnacht many Jews committed suicide and many more tried to escape from Germany. Only a third of those who attempted to leave ever succeeded. One 10-year-old boy got out only after being separated from both of his parents. It was a typical story. His mother left him at a friend's home in Berlin until he could

Kristallnacht and the destruction of Jewish lives and property in an allegedly "spontaneous" anti-Semitic outbreak signaled the fact that the Jewish population had become a convenient target for violence.

be transported out of the country. Later he recalled: "My mother had to leave me there, and the last I ever saw of her was in the Berlin street, outside the friend's house, walking backward along the pavement to get a last look at me, until she rounded the corner and we were parted" (Eisenberg, 1981).

World reaction to Kristallnacht was swift and harsh. In the United States, President Roosevelt said he could "scarcely believe that such things could occur in a 20th-century civilization." But although many nations deplored the actions of the German government, none did anything to punish Germany or to stop further persecution of the Jews. Within two days Cabinet Minister Hermann Goering declared that Jews must pay

$400 million for the damage done to their properties by Nazi thugs, and three days later Jewish children were forbidden to attend German schools. In a month ownership of Jewish businesses was transferred to non-Jews. Nothing was done by the international community, and in January 1939, less than three months after Kristallnacht, Hitler predicted the destruction of Jews in Europe in the event of a war.

In the war that soon followed, Hitler saw to it that his prediction came true. Nearly 6 million Jews in Europe were killed by the Nazis, 3.5 million in Poland alone. Today anti-Semitism is still an ugly and explosive problem in Poland. Catholics and Jews recently argued about the right of Catholic nuns to occupy a convent at Auschwitz,

In April 1933 the Nazi government instituted a boycott of Jewish businesses. Shop windows were labeled so shoppers would know which belonged to Jews, and Nazi troops patrolled the streets to enforce the boycott.

the concentration camp where millions of Jews and non-Jews alike were murdered.

Ethnic conflict, racism, and prejudice are endemic throughout the world today. Human beings have made little apparent progress in eradicating intergroup hatred. In fact, racial tensions are at an all-time high in many parts of the United States, and the same is true in such unlikely countries as Norway. How can we understand these hostilities, and what can we do about them? In this chapter we will discuss what social psychologists have taught us about this problem.

The Scope of the Problem

Very often there is nothing subtle about prejudice and racism. When Nazi storm troopers yell "Death to the Jews," or a gang of white youths in Brooklyn kill a young black man because he dared to enter their neighborhood, we know what the problem is, and we know how serious it can be. But prejudice has complex and subtle aspects as well, and a few definitions will help us keep them straight. We need to distinguish prejudice, stereotypes, and discrimination, and clarify their relation to racism and sexism.

Prejudice can be defined as a negative attitude toward, or evaluation of, a person based on his or her membership in a group other than one's own. If one person dislikes another simply because that other person is a member of a different race, sex, or religion, we are dealing with prejudice. We are also confronting prejudice when one person dislikes another because of that person's sexual orientation, social class, hometown, college major, or interest in music, sports, or books. In short, we can be prejudiced against people because of their membership in a wide variety of groups. Here we are most concerned about prejudice based on ethnic background, race, and sex, but we should realize that the dislike and hostility felt toward anyone on the basis of group membership is prejudice.

If prejudices are regarded as attitudes, **stereotypes** are best thought of as beliefs. More precisely, we can define a stereotype as a set of beliefs about the characteristics of the people in a group that is applied to almost all members of that group. We may have stereotypes of white people and black people, men and women, athletes, Jews and Catholics, gay people and straight people, and Volvo drivers. Stereotypes can be thought of as essentially similar to the schemata we discussed in Chapter 2, schemata about groups. They represent our "knowledge" of people in particular groups, true or false.

Very often negative stereotypes or prejudices give rise to **discrimination,** which can be defined as action taken to harm a group or any of its members. It can be thought of as the expression of prejudice in behavior. When discrimination is based on race or sex, and we refer to it as **racism** or **sexism,** and the person who performs it or condones it is called racist or sexist.

Twenty-five years ago prejudice and discrimination seemed to be on the wane in our society. Sexism and racism were firmly opposed by the federal government, and there seemed to be a national consensus that discrimination must be stopped and that racial tolerance would triumph.

Protesters of the killing of black Yusuf Hawkins in the Bensonhurst section of Brooklyn, New York, march to express their anger. Recent outbreaks of racist violence underscore the increase in racial tensions in the United States.

In the 1990s many of these advances have been rolled back. There is more racial tension now than at any time since the 1960s, and the associated problems, particularly on college campuses and in our large cities, seem intractable. In the meantime we have learned a great deal about prejudice and stereotypes, particularly their more subtle and persistent forms. Although we know more about the problem than about the solution, we strongly believe that students must learn all they can about these phenomena, and take responsibility for overcoming them in their own lives. Each of us individually can raise the level of harmony and mutual respect, even if just a little. We hope you will take what you learn in this chapter about prejudice as a challenge to do just that.

spective is widely applicable and can help us understand prejudice against Jews in Germany, against blacks in the United States, and against many other peoples all over the world. The perspectives we consider first emphasize learning and conformity to social norms, competition between groups, the need to maintain high self-esteem and a positive social identity, and the psychological dynamics of displaced aggression. Then we will consider research on cognitive processes implicated in stereotyping and some of the subtleties of modern racism.

All know

discrimination Negative, often aggressive behaviors aimed at the target of prejudice.

prejudice An unjustified negative attitude toward an individual based solely on that individual's membership in a group.

racism Discrimination or prejudice based on race.

sexism Discrimination or prejudice based on sex.

stereotype A set of beliefs about the characteristics of the people in a group, generalized to nearly all group members.

Perspectives on Racial Prejudice

How can we understand racial or ethnic prejudice? Psychologists have pointed out a variety of key factors. You will see, we think, that each per-

Sociocultural Learning

When Hitler espoused his racial theories, blaming Jews for all the problems that confronted Germany, his virulent attitudes easily took root in the soil of the Third Reich. Anti-Semitism, or prejudice against Jews, had been part of German history for centuries. Hitler learned this prejudice himself, and found that his expressions of it appealed to many segments of German society. As a child and young man Hitler was a student of hatred toward Jews. As chancellor of the Reich he was the teacher.

Numerous investigators (among them Kelly, Ferson & Holtzman, 1958) have suggested that prejudice, like other attitudes, is learned. A child may see its parents discriminate against blacks, hear their disparaging remarks about blacks, and find that they will quickly whisk him or her away when black children come out to play. Bird, Monachesi, and Burdick (1952) found that almost half of the white families they interviewed had rules against playing with black children. As the children grew older, they are told by peers that blacks are bad, and they are excluded from peer groups if they are seen playing with blacks. Their parents may point out newspaper stories telling how a gang of blacks raped an innocent white girl. Each of these incidents teaches a child to be prejudiced against blacks. This model of prejudice closely parallels social learning theory. The children have models in their parents, who teach them to dislike blacks. They are positively reinforced by parents and peers for discriminating against blacks, and punished by their parents and peers for associating with blacks. Thus children are neatly taught to hate.

The learning approach can explain why there are such wide variations in the objects of prejudice. Children in different countries, or in different regions of the same country, can be taught to hate different ethnic groups. Interestingly enough, the learning approach allows for the formation of prejudice in children even if they have never seen a member of the group against which they become prejudiced. Parents can instill in their children the idea that they should hate blacks (or some other group) and can tell the children frightening stories about what will happen to them if they interact with blacks. The result

of this schooling will be a child who hates and is afraid of blacks, even though he or she may never have interacted with a black person.

The learning of prejudice can be facilitated by the media. Stories in the newspaper and on television often support stereotypes about groups. For example, blacks are often portrayed as lazy, superstitious, or dangerous, and they are shown holding inferior occupations. Until recently, television commercials were a whites-only club; commercials aimed at portraying glamour and beauty used only white models. The traditional stereotype of women also dominated the media; women were shown as being rather dull, submissive, and inferior to men. These stereotypes were also found in books written for very young children.

There have indeed been many attempts to clean up the media and eliminate the portrayal of blatant prejudices. Further, societal values today stress equality; and discrimination, especially racial discrimination, receives almost universal disapproval. However, Sears and his colleagues (Sears & McConahay, 1973; Kinder & Sears, 1981) argue that blatant racism has been replaced by symbolic racism. We will discuss symbolic racism later in this chapter, and see how much things have actually changed.

Although early learning can implant the seeds of prejudice, Pettigrew (1958, 1959) suggests that discrimination is most likely to surface when the individual is in a group of other prejudiced people. Pettigrew believes that conformity plays an important role in determining prejudice; that is, people see what attitudes their peers hold, and shape their own attitudes to conform. In support of this notion, Pettigrew (1959) found that women, churchgoers, and the individuals who were most concerned about upward social mobility were the most prejudiced people in the South. It was exactly such people who were the most conforming. Other supporting data come from studies such as that of Newcomb (1943), who found that individuals' racial attitudes change when they go to college; the new attitudes come to resemble more closely the attitudes of other college students. Thus individuals do conform to the prevailing racial attitudes of their reference groups, and when people change group membership or move to another part of the country, their racial attitudes are likely to change.

One theory proposes that prejudice and discrimination occur because of a realistic threat of competition. This theory has been used to explain the backlash against women who have entered traditionally male occupations.

The Role of Competition and Conflict

Hitler may have learned and then perpetuated prejudiced attitudes in Germany, but where did those attitudes come from in the first place? Why were Jews discriminated against in Europe for so many centuries? Why have blacks been the objects of so much hatred in the United States? One answer is that at various times in history, minority groups such as Jews and blacks have been in conflict with those in the majority, and have been perceived as a threat. Usually conflict takes the form of competition for scarce economic or natural resources, such as jobs, housing, land, or money. One theory emphasizing the role of conflict and competition over scarce resources in prejudice is known as **realistic conflict theory.** According to this perspective, competition for scarce resources is the key to understanding discrimination.

One early study implicating competition showed that lynching in the southern United States was linked to the price of cotton (Hovland & Sears, 1940). Between 1882 and 1930 the number of lynchings of blacks in the South increased as the price of cotton went down (Hepworth & West, 1988). That is, when things were going well economically, there was less violence against blacks. When the economy was slow and blacks were seen as a threat in competition for scarce goods and resources, lynching increased. Kinder and Sears (1981) have pointed out that some people feel directly threatened by blacks, whom they perceive as wishing to move into their neighborhoods, take their jobs, and displace their children from schools. Perceived threat and competition

realistic conflict theory The theory that discrimination can be traced to competition for scarce resources.

EX: → MEN are scared women will take jobs

may also be part of prejudice against women. Some men may view women's struggle for equality with alarm because they fear that women will be competing directly for jobs once reserved for men.

A recent study done in Israel shows that perceived conflict of interests among religious groups is a strong predictor of discrimination and aggression against out-group members (Struch & Schwartz, 1989). This was especially true for people who were strongly identified with their own in-group and who perceived the out-group as having extremely negative, nearly inhuman traits and highly dissimilar values. Thus when people had a strong preference for their own religious group over the out-group, and perceived the groups to be in conflict, they supported actions that would harm the out-group and opposed actions that would help them. Another study shows that when groups are in competition, the **out-group homogeneity effect**— the tendency to see all members of the out-group as similar or homogeneous—is intensified (Judd & Park, 1988). That is, people have an even greater tendency to say "They're all alike" when they refer to members of an out-group with which their own group is in conflict.

In sum, conflict and competition between groups increase the tendency to discriminate against members of an out-group and to stereotype them. This tendency was very prominent in the early days of Nazi rule in Germany. Many people perceived Jews in terms of competition and conflict during a time of economic hardship. They were a threat. The result was precisely what we have seen in recent studies: negative stereotypes rigidly applied, and a range of hostile and discriminatory actions. However, the hostility that was unleashed did not end when the German economy improved. Only the total defeat of the Nazis and Hitler's death stopped the slaughter.

In-Group Favoritism and Social Identity

Hostility to Jews was part of German culture long before Hitler was born. He learned anti-Semitism and perpetuated it in an extreme form among his followers. Part of the antagonism directed toward Jews in the 1930s can be explained in terms of conflict and perceived threat. But why was anti-Semitism such an integral part of the heritage of Germany? Where did such hatred come from in the first place?

Surely complex factors underlie prejudices that can be traced back hundreds and even thousands of years. However, one very simple factor seems to underlie a great deal of hostility and conflict between groups. That factor is people's basic tendency to divide into groups and to prefer their own group, the in-group, to a different group, the out-group. The theory that most fully explains this phenomenon is known as **social identity theory** (Tajfel & Turner, 1986).

According to the theory of social identity, people are motivated to maintain a positive self-evaluation. Their overall self-evaluation is determined by two components, their personal identity and their social identity. Personal identity depends on one's achievements and how they compare with those of other people. Like social comparison theory (discussed in Chapter 3), social identity theory views comparisons with others as a key determinant of the way we both define and evaluate ourselves. If you find that you are a better writer than most of your classmates, for example, you may define yourself in part as being a writer, and you may use your view of yourself as a good writer as an important source of a positive personal identity.

Social identity theory holds that in addition to forming a personal identity based on individual characteristics and achievements, you will form a social identity based on your membership in a set of groups. That is, group memberships form your social identity. For example, you may define yourself as a woman, a soccer player, a college student, and a psychology major. Your evaluation of each of these groups determines the overall value of your social identity. If psychology majors are held in high regard on your campus, being a psychology major contributes to a positive social identity.

How do we define various social groups, and how do we evaluate them? Like many other social psychologists, Tajfel and Turner believe that we nearly always categorize people, including ourselves, into different groups, on the basis of almost any salient characteristic that makes them different from us (Hamilton & Trollier, 1986). For example, the differences between males and females and between children and adults are very salient, and so we categorize people into one group or the other. In Germany differences between Jews and non-Jews were salient to many people, and so the social categories of "Aryans" and "Jews" were created. Once we have constructed social groups, we evaluate them, as we evaluate individuals, through social comparison. In making these comparisons we are biased, and nearly always assign our own groups the highest value. Thus Aryans in Germany evaluated themselves as better than Jews, and Jews tended to evaluate themselves as better than non-Jews. Why do people categorize and why do they prefer their own group to others?

To ask why people categorize is nearly like asking why they eat and breathe. Categorizing, whether we mean putting people, objects, animals, colors, or sounds into groups, is a basic and automatic cognitive process, which is extremely adaptive in our efforts to perceive and understand a highly complex world. That world would overload our information-processing capacities unless we rendered it comprehensible by grouping things in categories. In other words, we categorize in order to manage the complex flow of information that we must cope with every day. Without categorizing we would be overwhelmed.

But why do we so consistently evaluate the groups in which we include ourselves, our in-groups, more positively than out-groups? The explanation seems simply to be people's desire to achieve and maintain a high level of self-esteem. They want their social identity as well as their personal identity to be as positive as possible. To this end they evaluate the in-group more favorably than the out-group.

But people do more than simply perceive the out-group as inferior. Given an opportunity, they will compete against the out-group to actually make it inferior. One of the most consistent findings of research on social identity is that people show favoritism toward the in-group in the allocation of rewards, a tendency to give their own group more points or money than an out-group. Furthermore, in making these allocations they seem to be concerned primarily with seeing that their own group gets more than the out-group, even when they could get more resources for themselves if they were only willing to let the out-group have just a little more. For example, if sub-

jects in an experiment were confronted with the choice of giving an in-group member 7 points and an out-group member 1 point or an in-group member 19 points and an out-group member 25 points, they would most likely choose the 7-1 combination (Tajfel et al., 1971; see Table 11-1). That is, there is a clear tendency to settle for less, as long as less is more than what the out-group gets. This solution is preferred to getting more for the in-group if the out-group then gets even more. Social identity research shows that people give the in-group more than the out-group because they think it is better and therefore deserves more than the out-group. Allocating the lion's share to the in-group confirms a positive social identity and raises self-esteem (Oakes & Turner, 1980).

What are the implications of social identity theory for understanding prejudice? People have a need to achieve and maintain a high level of self-esteem. One way they can do this is by raising their social identity. They can raise their social identity by perceiving the in-group as better and by actually treating it better. That is, people will derogate and mistreat members of an out-group, and the group as a whole, to maintain a high level of self-esteem, especially when their self-evaluation is threatened (Crocker et al., 1987). Thus the need to maintain a high level of self-esteem can lead people to be prejudiced against and discriminate against members of out-groups. In Nazi Germany the non-Jewish majority categorized the population into the Aryan in-group and the Jewish out-group. Jews were regarded as inferior to the Aryan "master race." As a consequence, they were derogated and discriminated against, eventually to the point of genocide. It seems nearly incredible that the need to maintain a positive social identity could lead to such destructive behavior. Clearly there are other factors that allowed the Holocaust to go so far, but we must live with the fact that the root cause may well have been a concern for self-esteem.

out-group homogeneity effect The tendency to see all members of the out-group as similar or homogeneous.
social identity theory The theory that people evaluate themselves by their membership in groups, and therefore are motivated to evaluate the in-group more positively than the out-group.

TABLE 11-1

Payoff matrices permitting in-group favoritism, fairness, or generosity

These numbers are rewards for:

Member No. 74 of Klee group

Member No. 44 of Kandinsky group

Please select one box:

1	2	3	4	5	6	7	8	9	10	11	12	13	14
14	13	12	11	10	9	8	7	6	5	4	3	2	1

These numbers are rewards for:

Member No. 12 of Kandinsky group

Member No. 50 of Klee group

Please select one box:

1	2	3	4	5	6	7	8	9	10	11	12	13	14
14	13	12	11	10	9	8	7	6	5	4	3	2	1

Maximal in-group favoritism for a member of the Klee group: $\dfrac{14}{1}$ $\dfrac{1}{14}$

Maximal fairness for a member of the Klee group: $\dfrac{7}{8}$ $\dfrac{8}{7}$

Maximal generosity for a member of the Klee group: $\dfrac{1}{14}$ $\dfrac{14}{1}$

SOURCE: Brown (1986).

Authoritarianism and Scapegoating: The Role of Displaced Aggression

Even though an entire culture may be imbued with racism and prejudice, individuals in that culture will vary in the degree to which they subscribe to racist doctrines and participate in discrimination against an out-group. Even in Nazi Germany people varied in how much they helped or hurt Jews. In spite of the danger in protecting Jews, many people did so. We clearly need to understand further why some people accept and act on racist principles and some do not. After World War II the American Jewish Committee supported a large and ambitious study of anti-Semitism in the United States. It was designed to pinpoint why some people accept fascist and racist ideas, and to assess the potential for fascist thinking and behavior in North America. The results of that study were published in a monumental book called *The Authoritarian Personality* (Adorno et al., 1950). Although some of its conclusions have been controversial, it stands as one of the most influential studies in the history of social psychology.

The investigators approached a large number of people who belonged to groups ranging from college fraternities to San Quentin prison

inmates. The respondents, most of whom were white, middle-class Americans, were given a battery of questionnaires, and many of them were interviewed in depth about their feelings toward themselves, their families, and their childhoods. The data from the questionnaires and the extensive clinical interviews provided the material for the investigation.

Respondents filled out an anti-Semitism scale, an ethnocentrism scale, and a political and economic conservatism scale. The anti-Semitism scale tapped respondents' attitudes toward Jews in a variety of situations and circumstances. The ethnocentrism scale measured the degree to which negative, stereotyped attitudes were held toward a variety of other groups. In general, **ethnocentrism** is a tendency to reject people who are culturally dissimilar to one's own in-group while blindly accepting those who are culturally like one's in-group (Sumner, 1906). Adorno and his colleagues found that the correlation between the specific attitude of anti-Semitism and the general quality of ethnocentrism was extremely high: those who were anti-Semitic endorsed similar negative attitudes toward other ethnic, religious, and cultural groups. There was a slight tendency for ethnocentric anti-Semites to express right-wing attitudes on the political and economic con-

Chapter Eleven Prejudice and Stereotypes

accepting
Itlian
people because

servatism scale, but the data were not conclusive in this regard.

Finally, assessments of the respondents' personalities were made by means of a test constructed specially for the occasion (potential for fascism scale, or F scale) and by the clinical interviews. The major findings were extremely interesting from the standpoint of viewing childhood development, personality, and attitudes as inextricably interrelated. The investigators found that people with anti-Semitic and ethnocentric attitudes tended to come from homes in which discipline was severe and threatening. The parents of highly prejudiced subjects tended to have very high aspirations for their children and to measure them in terms of their own needs rather than the children's needs. The products of this upbringing idealized their parents in questionnaire and interview responses; they were more likely to see their fathers as the most influential, likable, and successful person, and their mothers as the most giving and helpful person. Prejudiced subjects saw no weakness in either themselves or their parents, whereas unprejudiced respondents were more apt to admit to some human shortcomings. The irony in the prejudiced subjects' parental adoration is that hostility was found seething beneath the surface. Although it was difficult to find prejudiced subjects who would introspect and examine their feelings, the investigators detected a great deal of hostility directed against authority figures and parents.

How could these findings be explained, and why do people with these characteristics—these **authoritarian personalities**—become so highly prejudiced? Adorno and his associates placed a great deal of emphasis on unconscious defense mechanisms. Because the parents demand perfection, obedience, and respect, and enforce their demands with harsh discipline, authoritarian children repress their negative perceptions of both themselves and their parents, as well as the feelings of hostility that the harsh discipline engenders. The repressed negative perceptions are then projected onto other people, usually members of out-groups. Similarly, the anger and hostility toward the parents is displaced onto those minority group members. Finally, these people rationalize their hostility by thinking that the out-group members deserve discriminatory treat-

ment because of the negative characteristics that they themselves have projected onto them. In the Third Reich, a young boy or girl might project unacceptable sexual and aggressive urges onto Jews and displace hostility toward their parents onto Jews. Then they rationalized such actions as Kristallnacht on the basis of the negative qualities they had assigned to Jews.

We should note that a study of the size and scope of *The Authoritarian Personality* is bound to draw criticism, and this one has drawn its share (see Brown, 1965). Critics have questioned both the way the study's data were collected and the way they were interpreted. Still, a number of studies over the years indicate clearly that there is such an individual as the authoritarian personality and that he or she is likely to be highly racist.

The idea that out-groups, especially minorities, are the targets of displaced aggression is also the central hypothesis of the **scapegoat theory** (Allport, 1954; Hovland & Sears, 1940). This theory holds that a variety of frustrations in everyday life—on the job, in the home, with friends—can lead to displaced aggression, and that ethnic out-groups are convenient targets for such hostility. Berkowitz (1962) argued that they are convenient targets because they typically have the following characteristics:

1. *Safeness:* The target group is so weak that it can be attacked without fear of strong retaliation. Although this may be the case for some prejudices, Berkowitz points out that it cannot be the only factor, as many times the target of prejudice is not the weakest group that could have been chosen.

2. *Visibility:* The group must have qualities that make it visible and make it stand out from

---

authoritarian personality A complex of characteristics that includes ethnocentrism, hostility toward out-groups, and emphasis on obedience, discipline, and respect for authority.

ethnocentrism A tendency to reject people who are culturally dissimilar to one's own ethnic group and to accept without question those who are culturally like one's ethnic group; a characteristic of the authoritarian personality.

scapegoat theory The theory that out-groups are convenient targets for hostility stemming from the frustrations of everyday life.

other groups. Color, physical characteristics, or different customs can make a group visible.

3. *Strangeness:* Berkowitz believes that humans have an instinctive hatred for what is strange to them. He points out that small children become emotionally upset and tend to draw away when a stranger approaches.

4. *Prior dislike for the group:* Berkowitz believes that aggression may be displaced from one disliked person or group to a previously disliked group.

Cognitive Factors: The Impact of Stereotypes

People who are prejudiced against out-groups and who exploit them to displace their pent-up aggressions usually use negative stereotypes of those groups to justify their actions. We have already seen that authoritarians first project their own unacceptable characteristics onto minority groups and then use the negative characteristics that they have assigned as a rationalization for discrimination. A central aspect of the Nazis' campaign against Jews was the propaganda they spread about supposed Jewish traits. This propaganda was used to try to justify the arrest and finally the murder of Jews. In Germany and many other countries, negative stereotypes of Jews provided a foundation for such propaganda. In 1933, the year Hitler took power, American college students at Princeton described Jews as shrewd, mercenary, industrious, and grasping (Katz & Braly, 1933). Nazis assigned other traits as well. Jews were portrayed as conspiratorial, dirty, and lecherous, and not only a threat to peace and prosperity but also a danger to the health and purity of young Aryan women.

Where do such stereotypes come from? How are they maintained? What effect do they have on the way we perceive groups as a whole and individual members of those groups? In considering these questions we will see that very ordinary aspects of information processing, which have nothing to do with negative feelings about members of minority groups, play a central role in both forming and maintaining stereotypes.

Those stereotypes can then have a powerful and disturbing impact on interpersonal behavior.

We defined stereotypes as beliefs about the characteristics of groups that are generalized to nearly all members of those groups. In line with this definition we can also think of stereotypes as schemata of groups (Fiske & Taylor, 1984). For example, if we think of Plymouth owners as quiet, careful, and slow, as people did in the 1950s, we can say that our general knowledge of Plymouth owners is that they are quiet, careful, and slow (Wells, Goi & Seader, 1958). Thinking of stereotypes as schemata about groups reminds us that our stereotypes will have an effect on both our perceptions of group members and what we recall about them, just as schemata of individuals do.

Categorization and the Formation of Stereotypes

The Princeton students who in 1933 believed that Jews were shrewd, mercenary, industrious, and grasping also believed that African-Americans (referred to then as Negroes) were superstitious, lazy, happy-go-lucky, and ignorant. "Americans," though (no doubt meaning white, male, Gentile Americans), were seen as industrious, intelligent, materialistic, and ambitious (Katz & Braly, 1933). Where did these stereotypes come from?

The first process that leads to stereotypes is the simple act of categorizing. As we discussed earlier, **categorization** is one of the most basic human cognitive processes (Hamilton & Trollier, 1986). Just as we categorize objects by groups (animal, mineral, vegetable) and then make finer gradations and groupings, we categorize people according to gender, age, race, occupation, and many other criteria.

When we categorize people into groups, there are some immediate and important cognitive consequences. One is that we magnify or accentuate the differences among people belonging to the various groups (Eiser, 1984). First, we see people belonging to two groups as very different from each other. Second, we minimize differences between individuals belonging to the same group. However, just how much we minimize those in-group differences depends greatly on the group. Our perceptions of the group to which we belong—the in-group—differ from our perceptions of members of groups to which we do not belong—out-groups. The biggest difference is that we minimize differences between members of the out-group much more than we minimize differences between members of our own group (Rothbart, Dawes & Park, 1984). We tend to see "them" as all alike, while we see "us" as considerably more variable (Quattrone, 1986). We especially like to see the group of people that shares our opinions as diverse and heterogeneous. This outlook allows us to believe that our opinions are well considered and not just a reflection of narrow biases (Goethals, Allison & Frost, 1979; Goethals, 1986).

Another difference between our in- and out-group schemata is that the out-group schema is less complex: we know less about the out-group than about the in-group. One consequence of this lowered schematic complexity is that we often have extreme reactions to information about out-group members, as we don't have as much general knowledge with which to combine and moderate the new specific information (Jussim, Coleman & Lerch, 1987). These extreme reactions are known as the **out-group polarization effect** (Linville, 1982). For example, one study showed that white members of admissions committees formed a more favorable impression of a strong black applicant than a similarly qualified white applicant. On the other hand, they assessed a weak applicant described as black more negatively than the same applicant described as white. In other words, the evaluations of the out-group member, the black applicant, were polarized: positive information led to a more favorable impression and negative information led to a less favorable impression than the impressions that were based on equally polarized information about the white applicant (Linville & Jones, 1980).

Why We Believe What We Believe: The Content of Stereotypes

Categorization is only the first step in the formation of stereotypes. It creates various psychological groups but does not by itself create knowledge or belief about what those groups are like. Most of what we know about groups comes from a combination of experience and learning on the

one hand and memory processes on the other.

As individuals and as members of a culture or society we have experiences with people in other groups that form or change our beliefs about them. For example, many Americans characterize English people as conservative, reserved, and sophisticated (Karlin, Coffman & Walters, 1969). This stereotype may reflect the actual experience Americans have had with people from Great Britain. They meet English people when they travel, see them on television, or read about them in books. These contacts, direct or indirect, may provide some knowledge about what the English are like. In short, our stereotypes may reflect what people in certain groups actually seem to us to be like when we have some individual experience with them.

Historical events provide us with another kind of experience with people in different groups. During World War II, for example, Americans had experiences with Germans and Japanese that changed their perceptions of those people dramatically. Before World War II most Americans viewed Germans as scientifically minded, industrious, and intelligent. After the war and their experiences with Hitler, Americans also viewed Germans as extremely nationalistic, aggressive, and arrogant. Nazi behavior during the Third Reich did not go unnoticed. Similarly, Japanese were seen as intelligent, industrious, and progressive before World War II, but after Pearl Harbor they were seen as sly, imitative, and treacherous (Karlins et al., 1969). Thus our stereotypes of people in out-groups are strongly affected by the experiences our own group as a whole has had with those out-groups.

While stereotypes may reflect the behaviors we observe, we should also remember that self-justification and cognitive dissonance (discussed in Chapter 6) can also affect stereotypes. In the 1930s, for example, many Americans viewed blacks as ignorant (Katz & Braly, 1933). This

---

categorization The tendency to conceptualize objects and people as members of groups; a basic human cognitive process.

out-group polarization effect The tendency to have extreme reactions to information about out-group members, overvaluing both positive and negative information.

When groups of people are aroused they may be more easily swayed by illusory correlations, which are only too readily provided by those who would influence the groups.

stereotype may well have been constructed to justify discriminatory treatment of blacks rather than to explain direct experience with them.

While our own experiences can shape stereotypes, what we are taught by others also has a large impact. Every culture has its stereotypes of various groups within that culture and of people in out-groups. These cultural stereotypes are taught to children by parents, siblings, and peers, and sometimes by the mass media, and become lodged in their memories before they can critically evaluate or question them (Devine, 1989). Thus before children are able to think for themselves about what people are like, they are taught the culture's stereotypes.

Although stereotypes may be taught at a very early age, and may affect our perceptions of individual members of out-groups, recent work has pointed out an important distinction between our knowledge of stereotypes and our belief in them. It is possible for us to learn certain stereotypes at an early age but also to reject them as we mature. That doesn't mean we can wipe the stereotypes from our minds. They may always be with us.

But when we think about them consciously, we can reject them. A recent study by Devine (1989), for example, shows that white college students, both those who are prejudiced and those who are not, all know about certain stereotypes of blacks. They realize that whites widely regard blacks as aggressive and unintelligent. But the two groups differ in their own thoughts about blacks. Prejudiced subjects seem to accept many of these beliefs: "Blacks cause problems (e.g., mugging, fights)" while nonprejudiced subjects explicitly reject them: "Blacks and whites are equal"; "My father says all blacks are lazy, I think he is wrong." Later we will see how stereotypes that we know but reject affect our perceptions of individuals.

In addition to experience and learning, stereotypes may be affected by tricks our memory plays on us. It turns out that illusory correlations (discussed in Chapter 2) in regard to the traits that characterize specific groups can be formed by our tendency to recall salient and distinctive information. These illusory correlations can have a strong impact on stereotypes (Hamilton & Sherman, in press). In one study subjects

Chapter Eleven   Prejudice and Stereotypes

TABLE 11-2

Comparison of statements describing and later attributed to groups in Hamilton and Gifford's study of stereotyping

Groups and types of behaviors	Number of statements describing each type of behavior	Number of statements attributed to each group
Variation I		
Group A		
Desirable behaviors	8	5.87
Undesirable behaviors	16	15.71
Group B (minority)		
Desirable behaviors	4	6.13
Undesirable behaviors	8	8.29
Variation II		
Group A		
Desirable behaviors	18	17.52
Undesirable behaviors	8	5.79
Group B (minority)		
Desirable behaviors	9	9.48
Undesirable behaviors	4	6.21

SOURCE: After Hamilton & Gifford (1976).

were told about positive and negative behaviors by members of group A and group B. For instance, subjects heard that John, a member of group A, visited a sick friend in the hospital. While group A always had more members than group B, the proportion of positive and negative behaviors performed by the members of the two groups was constant. Sometimes both groups performed more desirable behaviors and sometimes they performed more undesirable behaviors. However, the results showed that group B members, who were always in the minority, were recalled as having performed more desirable behaviors than they actually did when desirable behaviors were performed less, and more undesirable behaviors when undesirable behaviors were performed less (Hamilton & Gifford, 1976; see Table 11-2). It seems that a person from an underrepresented group performing an unusual behavior is especially salient and memorable. The tendency to remember an unusual combination can lead us to see an illusory correlation between a certain group of people and a certain kind of behavior. For example, to a white person being raised in the suburbs and attending predominantly white schools, blacks may be uncommon. Further, displays of aggressive behavior in either the community or the school may be unusual. In these circumstances, a black person behaving aggressively would be especially unusual and salient and therefore overrecalled, leading to the illusory correlation that blacks are aggressive. In short, noticeable and salient instances of a relationship can lead us to overlook the other relevant data and infer an illusory correlation.

Recent studies tell us more about the role of illusory correlations in forming stereotypes. It turns out that when people are aroused by exercise, they show a greater tendency to recall information that fits illusory correlations, probably because we think less clearly when we are aroused (Kim & Baron, 1988). This finding suggests that young Germans, aroused by the demagoguery of Nazi leaders, might think about Jews even more stereotypically than when they were not aroused. This stereotypic thinking might facilitate their destructive behavior in arousing circumstances, such as the assaults on Jewish stores and synagogues on Kristallnacht. Another study shows that we are less likely to form illusory correlations about groups we belong to ourselves (Schaller & Maass, 1989). In perceiving our own groups, we are likely to recall information that fits our

in-group biases rather than salient and distinctive information.

The Maintenance of Stereotypes

People with stereotypes are bound to encounter people who do not fit those stereotypes. Surely Germans growing up in the 1930s did not find Jews to be lecherous and dirty. How, then, did they maintain their stereotypes? Several of the ideas we discussed in Chapter 2, on social cognition, are relevant here. Our stereotypes are essentially schemata, and we often interpret and recall information in ways that confirm our schemata. A white person who believes that blacks are hostile, for example, may interpret a black person's behavior as reflecting hostility when it may simply reflect shyness or discomfort. Similarly, a German woman may recall a Jewish merchant who drove a hard bargain but forget the same man's generous contribution to a local hospital. Thus the stereotype that Jews are mercenary is irrationally maintained. Another relevant factor we discussed in Chapter 2 is the self-fulfilling prophecy. If a man thinks a woman is beautiful, he is likely to behave in a friendly way that brings out relaxed, socially poised behavior in the woman, thereby confirming his stereotype that attractive women are extraverted and socially skilled (Snyder, Tanke & Berscheid, 1977).

Recent studies have told us more about how some of these processes work, and about some other ones as well. When we get information that is inconsistent with a stereotype, we are likely to process it differently from information that is consistent with the stereotype. One recent study shows that consistent information is processed more extensively than inconsistent information (Bodenhausen, 1988). That is, when we encounter information that fits a stereotype, we think about it long and hard; we give short shrift to information that doesn't fit. Sometimes we do pay careful attention to inconsistent information, but usually when we do so we are trying to figure out how the inconsistency can be explained away (Hastie, 1984). Very rarely does it cause us to change our stereotype (Krueger & Rothbart, 1988).

Not only do we resist changing our stereotypes on the basis of real information; sometimes we support and reinforce those stereotypes with the help of unreal information. A recent study showed that when people were asked to imagine members of groups in specific situations, they tended to create images of them that fit their stereotypes. If they imagined a wealthy person buying a car, for example, they tended to imagine him buying a luxury car. They imagined a poorer person buying a car as looking for basic transportation. After imagining how these individuals might have behaved, subjects then read some information about them. Later they were asked whether or not specific statements about the people had been included in the information they had read. Subjects sometimes remembered reading stereotype-consistent information that they had only imagined. That is, people tended to mistake what they had imagined about the person as information they had read about him (Slusher & Anderson, 1987).

Consider how a Nazi might imagine a Jewish man behaving in a lecherous way toward an Aryan woman. First, he might project his own unacceptable sexual impulses onto the Jewish man. Later he might confuse his own imaginings with his actual experience with Jews, and use those imaginings to confirm his stereotypes. Thus a process of *imaginal confirmation* can perpetuate stereotypes.

Stereotypes and the Perceptions of Individuals

Stereotypes seem to have a life of their own. Real information fails to change them and imagined "information" succeeds in bolstering them. But what impact do these stereotypes have on our perceptions of individuals? Studies show that stereotypes do affect perceptions of individuals, often very subtly—even when we try not to let them influence us. In one study white subjects watched a videotape of either a white or a black individual interacting with another person who was white. As their conversation grew animated, the first person gave the second an "ambiguous shove." When the first person was white, the shove was interpreted as playing around or dramatizing a point. When he was black, it was interpreted as hostile or violent (Duncan, 1976). In a replication of this study, Sagar and Schofield

TABLE 11-3

Mean ratings of both white and black actors' behaviors by both white and black subjects

		Rating scale	
Subject group*	Actor race†	Mean/threatening	Playful/friendly
White	White	8.28	6.43
	Black	8.99	6.24
Black	White	7.38	7.19
	Black	8.40	6.74

Note: Means are based on sums of paired 7-point scales indicating how well the given adjective described the behaviors, from 1 (not at all) to 7 (exactly).
* $n = 40$ for each group.
† Each subject rated two white and two black actors and two white and two black targets. Means are not broken down by target race, since no statistically significant main effects or interactions were found for this variable.
SOURCE: Adapted from Sagar and Schofield (1980).

(1980) showed both white and black schoolchildren pictures of white and black models engaged in aggressive behaviors. As Table 11-3 indicates, both white and black children saw the black model's behavior as more threatening and mean than the same behavior exhibited by a white model.

Another study of social-class stereotypes suggests we can counteract the influence of our prejudices up to a point (Darley & Gross, 1983). Subjects saw slides of a young girl showing where she lived and played, what her parents' backgrounds were, and so on. This information clearly told the subjects that the girl had either an upper- or a lower-class background. When asked to predict how well the girl would do in school, subjects seemed to resist their stereotypes. They did not make different predictions based on social-class information. However, when subjects were shown a videotape of the girl taking some tests in school, those who knew she was lower class perceived her actual performance as worse than those who thought she was upper class. Thus sometimes we can resist making gross inferences about a person from stereotypes, but it is extremely hard to resist perceiving and understanding what we actually see the person doing from the perspective of our schemata and stereotypes.

A final study shows that sometimes a stereotype that we don't even believe can affect our perceptions of an individual without our knowledge. In this study (Devine, 1989) white students

who were prejudiced or nonprejudiced saw words flashed on a screen so rapidly that subjects had no idea what they were. At a later time the subjects couldn't recognize which words they had seen and which ones they had not seen. In one condition most of the words flashed were words that the white students knew were typically associated with blacks, such as *blues, rhythm, ghetto, slavery, busing,* and *welfare.* In a second condition most of the words had no association with blacks. In this way half the subjects were primed with words associated with common black stereotypes and half were not (see Chapter 2). Then all the subjects were asked to read about and form an impression of a person, Donald, whose behavior might or might not have been seen as hostile and aggressive. Donald's race was not mentioned. The results showed that subjects who had been primed with the black stereotype saw Donald's behavior as more aggressive, consistent with the common stereotype of blacks, than those who had not been primed. The results were the same for prejudiced and nonprejudiced subjects. In short, a stereotype was brought to the subjects' minds without their awareness, and it affected their perceptions of Donald.

Do stereotypes or group schemata affect what we remember as much as what we perceive? Do we tend to remember information that is consistent with our stereotypes in the same way we remember information that is consistent with our

1. What are the various traditional approaches to understanding racism?

2. How do people develop authoritarian personalities and how does authoritarianism lead to displaced aggression?

3. What human information-processing tendencies help create stereotypes?

4. How are stereotypes reinforced and maintained?

5. What are the various ways in which stereotypes can affect perception and memory?

schemata of individuals? The answer seems to be yes. In one study subjects watched a videotape of a woman having a birthday dinner with her husband. When the woman was described as a waitress, subjects remembered that she drank beer and had a television set. When she was described as a librarian, they remembered that she wore glasses and listened to classical music (Cohen, 1981). In a similar study Howard and Rothbart (1980) found that subjects were more likely to remember negative information about out-group members and positive information about in-group members.

There is also evidence that people sometimes "remember" information that fits their stereotypes when the information had never been given to them. Subjects received information about an extravert; they were told that such terms as *energetic* and *entertaining* described the person. These words are moderately related to our stereotype of the extravert. Later, subjects were asked what words had been used to describe the person. They tended to remember that highly stereotypic descriptions of extraverts, such as *outgoing,* had been used when in fact they had not (Cantor & Mischel, 1977). As we saw with the study of imaginal confirmation, we remember stereotype-consistent facts about members of groups even when those "facts" never existed.

Although it is clear that our stereotypes influence what we perceive and remember about a person, in some circumstances information about an individual is so clear that it overrides what a stereotype suggests (Krueger & Rothbart, 1988). As we will see shortly, if people are given information that quite clearly indicates that a woman behaved assertively, they will view her as being just as assertive as a man who behaves the same way, despite their stereotype of women as less assertive than men. In other words, if subjects are given individuating information—that is, information about a particular person—they will sometimes put their stereotypes aside and judge the person on the basis of his or her actual behavior rather than their beliefs about the group the person belongs to. Clearly, this does not always happen. Thus we would not generally expect a German official in the Third Reich, imbued with Nazi anti-Semitism, to perceive altruism in a particular Jewish person if the stereotype is that Jews are selfish and miserly. But sometimes when behavior is clear, people will rise above their stereotypes and look at the individual rather than the group.

Modern Racism: The Subtleties of Prejudice Today

There is no question that some progress has been made in reducing racism. When one looks at the changes in stereotypes that white non-Jewish college students in the United States have of Jews and blacks, it is clear that students are less ethnocentric than they were a generation or two ago. That is, they tend less to derogate out-groups and glorify the in-group. In the late 1960s Jews were seen as ambitious, materialistic, and intelligent; these happen to be the same traits applied to "Americans." This stereotype is a big improvement over the old one of shrewd and mercenary. Similarly, blacks were no longer viewed as superstitious, lazy, and ignorant (Karlins et al., 1969). However, it may be that subjects simply fake less ethnocentric responses in stereotyping studies and that ethnocentrism and racism have simply gone underground (Sigall & Page, 1971). Three

In spite of the fact that racism persists in a variety of forms in modern society, more individuals from minority groups achieved significant political status in the last ten years. Among them are Xavier Suarez, mayor of Miami; David Dinkins, mayor of New York; and Dianne Feinstein, former mayor of San Francisco and gubernatorial candidate in 1990.

approaches to modern racism indicate that racism remains a persistent problem for at least some people (Dovidio & Gaertner, 1986).

Symbolic Racism: Prejudice among Conservatives

We noted earlier that several psychologists have argued recently that blatant or "old-fashioned" racism has been replaced by something more subtle, known as symbolic racism or modern racism (Sears & McConahay, 1973; Kinder & Sears, 1981; McConahay, 1986). This more subtle form of racism is thought to be particularly characteristic of people who are politically conservative (Dovidio & Gaertner, 1986). We shall see shortly that other subtle forms of racism are thought to be characteristic of people who are politically liberal.

The concept of symbolic racism has undergone some evolution in the past several years, just as racism itself has. Sears and McConahay defined **symbolic racism** as "a form of resistance to change in racial status, based on moral feelings that blacks violate such traditional American values as individualism and self-reliance, the work ethic, obedience, and discipline." According to this position, people do not learn the traditional racial stereotypes that blacks are lazy or intellectually inferior. Rather, they learn that blacks are a threat to the symbols and values that Americans hold dear. Kinder and Sears conducted a survey of white voters in the Los Angeles area to determine the factors that influenced their decision to vote for a white or black mayoral candidate. They found that symbolic racism rather than direct racial threats to whites' private lives (jobs, neighborhoods, schools) was a major determinant of voting behavior. Because of its roots in moral principles and values, symbolic racism may be more difficult to combat than prejudice based on the perception of direct personal threats.

McConahay's (1986) more recent concept of modern racism is defined slightly differently. Its basic tenets are that discrimination is a thing of the past, that blacks are pushing too hard and too fast, that their demands and tactics are unfair, and that blacks are getting things they don't deserve as a result of their pushing. It is thought that modern racism has its roots in negative feelings about blacks, which stem in part from work-ethic conservatism, combined with a desire to cover over those negative feelings. Modern racism stands in contrast to old-fashioned racism, which held that blacks were less intelligent than whites, that schools and neighborhoods should be segregated by race, and that discrimination against blacks was acceptable. (Table 11-4 shows some items from both old-fashioned and modern racism scales.)

Research by McConahay and his colleagues suggests that people with high scores on the modern racism scale will show their negative feelings about blacks unless they are in a context where doing so may make them look racist. Then they may bend over backward to behave positively toward blacks. This hypothesis was supported by a study (McConahay, 1986) in which white subjects rated undistinguished job applicants who were presented as black less highly than the same applicants who were presented as white. However, when the possibility that subjects might be seen as racist was introduced into the situation, the results were reversed. They actually rated the mediocre black applicant more positively than the mediocre white applicant.

In short, research suggests a subtle and hidden form of racism among people who hold certain conservative political and economic values, and who feel that blacks are a threat to those values. This form of racism may often be suppressed, but it can be detected in votes against black political candidates, negative evaluations of job applicants, opposition to busing, and more subtle forms of resistance to black concerns and demands.

Racial Ambivalence: Conflicts in American Values

Another perspective on modern racism holds that white Americans are ambivalent about blacks (Katz, 1981; Katz, Wackenhut & Hass, 1986). On the one hand, they have positive feelings about blacks. These positive feelings reflect positive stereotypes of blacks and sympathy for the situation that blacks face in American society. On the other hand, they also have negative feelings about blacks. These attitudes grow out of the Protestant ethic, with its emphasis on self-reliance and discipline. To the extent that people perceive blacks as depending too much on government and institutional support rather than on their own efforts, critical perceptions and feelings result.

The source of the ambivalence whites feel toward blacks is a conflict in American values. On the one hand, humanitarianism and egalitarianism are fundamental American values. Many Americans, both black and white, value equality and they value helping people who have been oppressed. These values make whites sympathetic toward blacks and well disposed toward them. On the other hand, many Americans, black and white, support the values represented by the Protestant ethic. This ethic, as we have noted, attaches high value to self-reliance and self-discipline. To the extent that blacks are seen by whites not to share these values, negative feelings result.

Recent research has supported the idea that

Chapter Eleven   Prejudice and Stereotypes

TABLE 11-4

Factor loadings for modern and old-fashioned racism items in 1984 Duke University student sample after maximum likelihood extraction and Oblimin rotation

	Factor loadings[a]	
	Factor 1	Factor 2
Old-fashioned racism items		
I favor laws that permit black persons to rent or purchase housing even when the person offering the property for sale or rent does not wish to rent or sell it to blacks. (Disagree Strongly = 5)	.784	−.130
Generally speaking, I favor full racial integration. (Disagree Strongly = 5)	.678	
I am opposed to open or fair housing laws. (Agree Strongly = 5)	.578	
It is a bad idea for blacks and whites to marry one another. (Agree Strongly = 5)	.562	
Black people are generally not as smart as whites. (Strongly Agree = 5)	.533	
If a black family with about the same income and education as I have moved next door, I would mind it a great deal. (Strongly Agree = 5)	.503	
It was wrong for the United States Supreme Court to outlaw segregation in its 1954 decision. (Strongly Agree = 5)	.444	.157
Modern racism items		
Over the past few years, the government and news media have shown more respect to blacks than they deserve. (Strongly Agree = 5)	.184	.608
It is easy to understand the anger of black people in America. (Strongly Disagree = 5)		.568
Discrimination against blacks is no longer a problem in the United States. (Strongly Agree = 5)		.548
Over the past few years, blacks have gotten more economically than they deserve. (Strongly Agree = 5)	.224	.514
Blacks have more influence upon school desegregation plans than they ought to have. (Strongly Agree = 5)	.409	.403
Blacks are getting too demanding in their push for equal rights. (Strongly Agree = 5)		.359
Blacks should not push themselves where they are not wanted. (Strongly Agree = 5)		.342
Percent of variance	39.0	9.2
Correlation between factors	.59	
Sample N	167	

[a] Standardized regression coefficients for item and factor from the pattern matrix. Loadings below .100 are not shown.
SOURCE: McConahay (1986).

such values lie at the heart of both positive and negative feelings toward blacks. Whites with high humanitarian-egalitarian values have been shown to have pro-black feelings. Whites with high Protestant-ethic values tend to have antiblack feelings. Of course, many whites endorse both values and therefore feel ambivalent about blacks. Furthermore, when humanitarian-egalitarian values are made salient, pro-black feelings increase. When Protestant-ethic values are made salient, antiblack feelings increase (Katz & Hass, 1988).

A second important aspect of the ambivalence formulation holds that in specific situations whites often suppress either their positive or negative feelings about blacks, and that those suppressed feelings actually add strength to the opposite feeling that is not suppressed. For example, if a person is expressing her positive feelings toward blacks and suppressing her negative ones, the negative ones, through a process much like excitation transfer (discussed in Chapter 3), may actually be displaced in the positive direction and amplify the positive response. Thus this theory is called the **ambivalence-amplifi-**

symbolic racism   Hostility to racial minorities based on the belief that they threaten the values of the majority culture.

The banner of equal opportunity and affirmative action has created opposing forces in many areas. Feminist movements, for example, which stress women's and mothers' rights, have generated forces such as the one supporting fathers' rights shown here. Do you see this as backlash in opposition to mothers' rights or as a parallel expression?

cation theory. One can imagine that a German soldier in the Third Reich who was ordered to destroy Jewish homes might actually channel any positive feelings toward Jews into his destructive actions.

Ambivalence-amplification theory holds that people who behave very positively toward blacks, and may seem to overdo it, are doing so because their genuine positive feelings are being amplified by displaced energy from their negative feelings. Both the positive and negative feelings are in fact genuine. There is real ambivalence. Sometimes this ambivalence, combined with amplification, creates extreme behavior in one direction or the other.

Regressive Racism: Backsliding under Duress

A third theory about racism holds that people today, believing in equality, are trying to move beyond historical patterns of racial discrimination. It suggests that whites have new norms for the way they should treat blacks and also that blacks have new norms for the way they should treat whites. In most situations people will act on these new egalitarian norms. Under stress, however, when people are emotionally aroused, they may slip back into the old ways and act in a discriminatory, racist manner. This form of racism—that is, discriminatory behavior elicited under stress or arousal—is called **regressive racism.** The basic idea is that people regress—that is, go back to—their earlier modes of interaction when they feel stress or arousal. Unfortunately, what they regress or return to is an older, historical pattern of discrimination (Griffin & Rogers, 1977; Rogers & Prentice-Dunn, 1981; Wilson & Rogers, 1975).

What are the new norms for whites and for blacks? For whites the new norm is behaving in an egalitarian manner. In fact, white people's desire to suppress earlier forms of interaction and to be egalitarian may lead them to treat blacks more favorably than whites in some situations. For blacks, the old norms of inhibiting aggression toward whites and displacing it to fellow blacks has changed as well. Now a new demand for respect has replaced older subservient modes of behavior. While these new norms and forms of behavior have been demonstrated (e.g., Baron, 1979), it has also been shown that both blacks and whites will regress to older patterns—that is, express more hostility toward blacks than whites—when they have been aroused, frustrated, insulted, or stressed.

One study that illustrates regressive racism showed that white students who were not angered were less aggressive toward blacks than toward whites. On the other hand, when subjects were angered by an experimental confederate who insulted them, subjects retaliated more and expressed more hostility when that confederate was black than when he was white. In short, nonangered subjects treated blacks better than whites, showing the new egalitarianism. Insulted and angry subjects showed regressive racism and were more hostile to blacks (Rogers & Prentice-Dunn, 1981).

Aversive Racism: Racism among the Well-Intentioned

A final perspective on modern racism deals specifically with the attitudes and behavior of liberals who want very much to be nonracist. For these people it is important to be unprejudiced and nondiscriminatory. Their self-concept includes a valued image of themselves as nonracists. Yet they have predominantly negative feelings about blacks and may find contacts with blacks unpleasant or aversive. Thus this type of racism, existing in people who fight racist tendencies in themselves and may not even recognize them, is called **aversive racism** (Gaertner & Dovidio, 1986).

One of the central hypotheses of the aversive racism perspective is that the racist feelings of people who try to see themselves as nonracists will be manifested in subtle and complex ways. When norms against discrimination are clear, they will not treat blacks differently from whites. When norms are less clear, they are likely to show their underlying negative feelings. Furthermore, even when norms against discrimination are clear, aversive racists will discriminate if their negative treatment of blacks can be attributed to something that has nothing to do with race (Dovidio & Gaertner, 1986).

A study illustrating this perspective looked at white subjects' willingness to help a confederate, who was either white or black, in a task at which they worked together as a team (Frey & Gaertner, 1986). The subjects and confederates were physically separated, as each individual was to work on a separate piece of the problem. At one point toward the middle of the experiment, the subject received a request to help the confederate with work on the task. Two aspects of the request were varied. First, it was clear that the confederate needed help either as a result of circumstances beyond his control or because he had been lazy in his work at the task. Second, the request for help came either from a bystander who witnessed the confederate's need for help or from the confederate himself. Did subjects treat black and white confederates differently in any of these situations?

The results are complex. In three of the situations subjects helped the black and white confederates to the same degree. When the confederate's need for help was due to circumstances beyond his control, the subjects helped the black and white confederates equally. Furthermore, under these circumstances it made no difference whether the request for help came from the confederate or from the bystander. When help was needed because of the confederate's laziness, however, the situation varied. Under these circumstances, subjects responded to the bystander's request with the same degree of help for white and black confederates. But when the request came from the confederate himself and he had been lazy, subjects helped the white confederate more than the black one (see Table 11-5). How do we explain these complex results?

---

ambivalence-amplification theory   The theory that when positive and negative attitudes coexist, the negative attitudes may be displaced in the positive direction and amplify the positive response, and vice versa.

aversive racism   An aversion to racial minorities that people hide from other people and to some extent from themselves.

regressive racism   The emergence under stress of racist reactions that one has tried to overcome.

TABLE 11-5

How white college students help their white and black peers in different conditions.

Reason confederate needs help	Person asking for help	
	Confederate	Bystander
Laziness	White confederate helped more than black confederate	White and black confederates helped the same
Factors beyond confederate's control	White and black confederates helped the same	White and black confederates helped the same

SOURCE: Adapted from Frey and Gaertner (1986).

According to Frey and Gaertner, there is only one situation in which it is appropriate not to help the confederate: when the subjects are asked for help by a lazy confederate whom they have no particular obligation to help. On the other hand, help should be granted if the confederate needs it for a good reason. Also, help should be granted when the bystander asks for it, because the bystander is a presumably objective observer who knows what is appropriate. However, when the lazy confederate asks for help, subjects can do as they see fit. What they see fit to do is to help if the confederate is white but not if the confederate is black. These subjects can perceive their lack of helpfulness toward the black confederate as having nothing to do with race. They can tell themselves that they chose not to help because a person should straighten out a mess he gets himself into. In short, subjects think that race has nothing to do with their nonhelping, but we know they're wrong. We know they would help if the confederate were white. Thus subjects will discriminate as long as they don't have to perceive themselves as discriminating. This is the way aversive racism operates.

Common Perspectives on Modern Racism

It is clear that the four perspectives on modern racism have much in common. All of them acknowledge that racism is no longer respected in our society and that people are trying to combat it to one degree or another. They also all argue that whites still have negative feelings about blacks. Thus they all suggest that whites are ambivalent about blacks. However, the theories differ in substance as well as in terminology and emphasis. The theories of symbolic racism, regressive racism, and aversive racism all suggest that whites are still racist to some extent but that racism has simply gone underground. The symbolic racism perspective holds that whites simply hide their racism from others, and present it in more refined forms. The regressive racism perspective assumes that underlying racism, which people hide from themselves and others, will come out under stress. The aversive racism perspective assumes that well-intentioned liberal people hide their racism from themselves but will subtly express it if it can be seen as something other than racism. The ambivalence-amplification perspective is alone in holding that whites do have genuinely positive feelings about blacks, but acknowledges that these feelings are mixed with some degree of negative affect.

We can't say at this point which of these theories is correct. Since they are similar in so many ways, we don't really have to choose among them. It seems clear that ambivalence and the subtle expression of racism is something we have to acknowledge and try harder to overcome. Racism has multiple pernicious effects. One recent study shows that people who overhear a Jewish or black lawyer condemned with derogatory ethnic labels, such as "shyster" or "nigger," subsequently discriminate against Jews or blacks other than the lawyer at whom the slur was originally aimed. These racial epithets spread poison, even

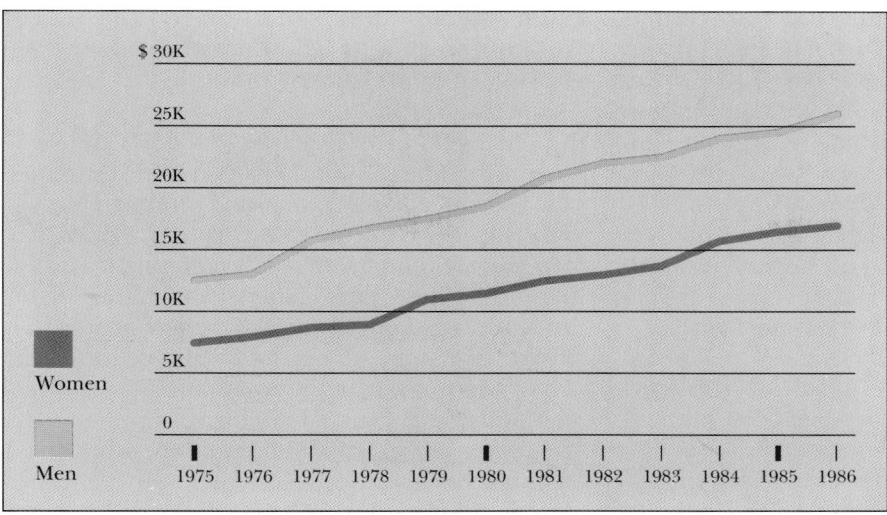

$ 30K

25K

20K

15K

10K

5K

0

Women

Men

1975　1976　1977　1978　1979　1980　1981　1982　1983　1984　1985　1986

Median income of full-time male and female workers, 1975 to 1987.
SOURCE: U.S. Bureau of the Census (1988).

though people seem appalled to hear them in the first place (Kirkland, Greenberg & Pyszczynski, 1987). Have we any reason for optimism? Is there anything that we, and you, can do? We think there are things to be done. After we have discussed sexism we will return to consider how we may usefully combat prejudices and stereotypes of all kinds.

Sexism: Stereotyped Attitudes, Beliefs, and Behaviors

In modern society there have been no organized attacks overtly directed against women. There have been no lynchings or "final solutions." Yet the consciousness of modern society has been raised to the discrimination and prejudice that women have to endure. These experiences have been both violent and nonviolent, behavioral and attitudinal. The incidence of violent rape has been on the rise; date rape on college campuses continues to plague the social environment. It is estimated that 70 to 80% of all rapes are perpetrated by dates, colleagues, or other acquaintances (Chollar, 1989). Until very recently, it was extremely difficult for women to bring a charge of rape to a successful conclusion in the courts

because rules of evidence made it nearly impossible to prove that the woman herself was not responsible for the violence directed against her.

Nonviolent discrimination is a more pervasive fact of women's lives. Although the modern work force is 44% female, women are severely underrepresented in positions of higher authority and salary. The average salary of female workers in the United States is 60% that of men. As Figure 11-1 shows, the salary gap has not decreased over the last several years, and in fact is continuing to widen. In addition, women seem to be blocked by what Robertson (1989) describes as an "invisible ceiling." Women may rise through certain levels of an organization, but proceed no higher. According to the U.S. Bureau of the Census (1981), 95% of the senior executives in the United States are male; only two of the chief executive officers of the 500 leading corporations are female. In every position in which women and men are represented, women make less money and have less authority (Norwood, 1982).

Consider the case of Ann Hopkins. Ms. Hopkins was a junior partner in the giant accounting firm of Price Waterhouse. She was apparently very successful at her job, bringing in $6 million in business, one of the highest records among the class of 88 candidates for promotion to senior partner. She was also the only woman in that cohort. Of the senior partners at Price Waterhouse, fewer than 2% were women. Ms. Hopkins was denied promotion least partially on the grounds that she was a "pushy woman" and an "iron maiden," a person "who was overcompensating for the fact that she was a woman" (*New York Times,* May 2, 1989). These characteristics, her male colleagues judged, would make it unlikely for her to attract clients to the firm. This argument was used despite Ms. Hopkins's proven success in bringing clients to Price Waterhouse.

Ann Hopkins sued Price Waterhouse for violation of her civil rights. In 1986 the U.S. District Court ruled that Ms. Hopkins had been substantially deprived of her rights by sex discrimination. A major portion of her case rested on testimony by psychologists about the reliability of the research that has demonstrated the pervasive and potentially damaging nature of our beliefs about the characteristics and abilities of women.

Gender Stereotypes and Reality

Gender stereotypes are beliefs held about people on the basis of their being either male or female. Clearly there are real and genuine differences between males and females. Differences in chromosomes define the sexes. Differences in hormones are real and lead to anatomical and sexual differences. Differences in anatomy and musculature have determined the roles played by the two sexes for millennia, with men taking on the hunting and protecting functions and women taking on the nurturing functions.

The differences in anatomy, chromosomes, and musculature do not necessarily lead to differences in the characteristics we attribute to the two sexes. Yet there is a pervasive tendency for both men and women to ascribe differences in personality and function as a matter of sex (see Table 11-6).

Men are generally perceived as being independent, dominant, aggressive, assertive, self-confident, and intellectual. Women are perceived as emotional, excitable, home-oriented, and gentle (Spence, Helmreich & Stapp, 1975). While there is nothing wrong with being gentle and all the rest, these are clearly not the characteristics that lead to positions of authority and leadership.

Other studies have found women to be judged incompetent, weak, dependent, passive, and lacking in confidence (American Psychological Association, 1988).

In a very careful review of the psychological literature, Maccoby and Jacklin (1974) examined the evidence for genuine and supportable differences between men and women. They analyzed more than 2,000 studies relating to sex differences in personality and intellectual functioning. They found differences in only four areas: boys tend to act more aggressively than girls, and to have greater mathematical and spatial skills; girls tend to perform better on tasks requiring verbal skills. Subsequently, other investigators have found male-female differences in activity level (Eaton & Enns, 1986), influenceability (Eagly & Carli, 1981), and empathy (Eisenberg & Lennon, 1983). As Ruble (1987) points out, however, the differences that have been found between men and women, even in the areas identified, are quite small.

What, then, accounts for the different treatment of men and women in such important areas as the labor force? Why have women been unable to enter top management? Why have they been paid less for the jobs they do? Observing such differences, Ruble (1987) has commented that "not only do men and women have different roles but they also appear to have different intrinsic worth, at least as measured by financial compensation" (p. 422). In brief, it does not appear that the data on real differences between males and females justify the multifaceted stereotypes that people hold about them.

Origins of Sex Stereotypes

By the age of 3 or 4, children have a decent idea of their gender and are beginning to form ideas of what is appropriate for boys and for girls (Money & Erhardt, 1972). By the age of 7, the idea that one's identity as a boy or girl is stable—that is, it will not change regardless of what one wears or what one is called—has been established (Kohlberg, 1966; Ruble & Ruble, 1982).

From the moment a newborn arrives, parents' expectations depend on whether the child is male or female. In one study of parental atti-

TABLE 11-6

Some views of men and women in major religions

Christian heritage: Old Testament

And God said, Let us make man in our image. . . . So God created man in his own image. (Genesis 1)

And the Lord God said, It is not good that the man should be alone; I will make him a help mate . . . she shall be called Woman because she was taken out of Man. (Genesis 2)

And the Lord God said unto the woman, what is this that thou hast done? And the woman said, the serpent beguiled me. . . . Unto the woman [the Lord God] said, I will greatly multiply thy sorrow . . . and thy desire shall be to thy husband and he shall rule over thee. (Genesis 3)

Christian heritage: New Testament

For a man . . . is the image and glory of God: but the woman is the glory of the man. For the man is not of the woman; but the woman of the man. Neither was the man created for the woman, but the woman for the man. (I Corinthians 11)

Let your women keep silence in the churches: for it is not permitted unto them to speak; but they are commanded to be under obedience. . . . And if they will learn anything, let them ask their husbands at home: for it is a shame for women to speak in the church (I Corinthians 14)

Let the woman learn in silence with all subjugation. But, I suffer not a woman to teach, nor to usurp authority over the man, but to be in silence. For Adam was first formed, then Eve. And Adam was not deceived but the woman being deceived was in the transgression. (I Timothy)

Jewish heritage

Blessed art Thou, O Lord our God, King of the Universe, that I was not born a gentile.

Blessed art Thou, O Lord our God, King of the Universe, that I was not born a slave.

Blessed art Thou, O Lord our God, King of the Universe, that I was not born a woman.

Islamic heritage

Men are superior to women on account of the qualities in which God has given them preeminence.

---

tudes toward newborns within 24 hours after birth, parents were asked to describe their infants to a close friend. Objectively, the babies were of similar size and health, yet boys were described as better coordinated, stronger, more alert, and bigger than girls. Girls were described as smaller, softer, and more finely featured (Rubin, Provenzano & Luria, 1974).

As the child grows, the expectations of parents and others in the environment become stronger. Boys play with trucks, girls play with dolls, and research has shown that they are both encouraged to do so by their parents (Huston, 1983). Fathers tend to play more aggressively with their sons and both parents tend to demand more independence from sons than daughters (Block, 1983; Huston, 1983). Books and texts continue the socialization process, confirming and reinforcing society's expectations.

The gender schema

From our earliest experiences, we learn a set of expectations about what is essentially male and what is essentially female. We learn to encode and organize information using these expectations. Sandra Bem (1981) has referred to this set of expectations as the **gender schema,** a particular instance of the schemata we discussed in Chapter 2. We become set to see girls and boys as having different characteristics. We apply certain dimensions to girls that we do not apply to boys, and vice versa. When we think of a male, we are likely to assess his standing on the strong-weak dimension. It is relevant to the way we see boys; however, it is not so relevant to the way in which society has taught us to see girls. In short,

---

gender schema   A complex of beliefs and expectations about the behavior of males or females.

There are some kinds of sex segregation that we take for granted—for example, in public restrooms. Is this a functional separation or a symbol of institutionalized sexism?

our gender schemata tell us what to expect about males and females, and by what dimensions to measure each.

Moreover, gender schemata give us a means to evaluate people. According to Bem, we evaluate people more highly to the extent that they are perfect examples of their schemata. The strong, successful man and the attractive, nurturing woman are evaluated positively because they match our schemata.

We not only evaluate others by their match to the gender schemata, we also evaluate *ourselves* by those standards. We know what we are supposed to be like as girls or boys, men or women. As we have seen, whether knowingly or unknowingly, our parents began those instructions from our earliest days. So it becomes a measure of our own self-worth to match the stereotype—that is, the gender schema. To the extent that we fail to

measure up to the standard of what we are supposed to be like as men and women, we stand to suffer a loss of self-esteem.

Gender schemata are only one set of schemata; as human beings living in a complex social environment, we have multiple schemata. We may have schemata as students, as children, as parents, as athletes, and so forth. Each of those schemata has its own standards, and we measure ourselves against how well we fit them. Bem points out that the gender schema is particularly important because it is made salient to us again and again in our social environment. We may think about out athletic schema in the gym, about our student schema in the classroom, but the cues in our social world constantly point to the importance of gender. For example, children in a classroom may be asked to line up in a girl's line and a boy's line. The calendar in the nursery and elementary school may be separated for children by silhouetted figures alternately depicting little girls and little boys.

The gist of Bem's argument, then, is that there exist structures by which we encode and organize information. A crucial one for nearly all of us is the gender schema. We rarely think about it, we are rarely aware of it, but it organizes a great deal of information. It tells us what to expect males and females to be like, what we expect them to do, and how we evaluate them. We reach adulthood with the gender schemata we have learned since infancy intact. We are predisposed to see men doing certain things and women doing other things. We are predisposed to think that women have characteristics and abilities that are different from those of men. And we are prepared to see ourselves in the same terms.

A consequence of early experiences: Fear of success

We have learned that people tend to attribute different characteristics to men and to women. We have also learned that many of the characteristics that are attributed to men are ones our society deems important for successful performance. We have also learned that people tend to evaluate themselves in accordance with how well they match the gender schema appropriate for their sex. Both men and women are therefore *motivated* to confirm their sex-role stereotypes.

Matina Horner conducted a series of influential studies to show that women may have actually learned to fear success. Her view is that women are placed in conflict by society's emphasis on success and society's placing of success within the male stereotype. Women deal with this conflict by learning **fear of success** (sometimes called motivation to avoid success), which becomes a stable part of their personalities.

Horner (1970) asked male students to write a story that took the following fact into account: "After first term finals, John finds himself at the top of his medical school class." Female students were shown a story that substituted "Anne" for "John." Such a task is known as a "projective test." Rather than merely writing a fictional story, people generally reveal part of their own personalities in developing the story. How do you think you might respond to such a task? If you had been one of Horner's male subjects, it is likely that you would have written an all-American-boy tale, such as the following:

> John is a conscientious young man who worked hard. He is pleased with himself. John has always wanted to go into medicine and is very dedicated. His hard work paid off. He is thinking that he must not let up now, but must work even harder than he did before. His good marks have encouraged him. . . . He eventually graduates at the top of his class.

If you had been a female subject, however, you might have dealt with the situation as one of Horner's female subjects did:

> Anne has a boyfriend in the same class and they are quite serious. Anne met Carl at college and they started dating. . . . Anne is rather upset and so is Carl. She wants him to be higher in school than she is. Anne will deliberately lower her academic standing next term, while she does all she subtly can to help Carl. His grades come up and Anne soon drops out of medical school. They marry and he goes on in school while she raises their family.

This story is rich in fear-of-success imagery. Other subjects wrote stories that denied that Anne was studying to be a physician and insisted that she was a nurse, stories that dealt with Anne's ultimate decline as a student, and stories that dealt with Anne's social unhappiness as a result of her

success. Some men also wrote fear-of-success stories about John, and of course some women wrote stories about Anne that contained no fear-of-success imagery. But, on average, fear-of-success imagery was found significantly more often in stories written by female students (68%) than in stories by male students (19%). In Horner's view, fear of success forms a stable portion of the personality structure of most women, and may account for women's failure to gain promotions and to rise in competitive fields.

Situational Analysis: Are There Really Personality Differences?

By now you know that social psychologists prefer to look to the social situation in order to understand behavior. If Horner is correct that stereotypical attitudes actually reside in the personality structure of the woman, what role is there for the social psychologist? Not surprisingly, social psychologists have not been satisfied to put the cause of sexism on the personality of the victim. Several investigators, such as Susan Darley (1976), have suggested that we look to the dynamics of the situation in which the woman finds herself to understand the way stereotypes operate.

Does a woman who tells fear-of-success stories actually avoid success in all situations? Probably not. Many activities within the feminine gender schema require a great deal of skill and a great deal of motivation if one is to be successful. Would a person who held a very traditional sex-role stereotype shun success at child care or homemaking? And would a man strive for success in these areas? The situational analysis argues that women do not have fear of success as part of their personalities; rather, it is the situation that calls for behaviors that are consistent with the gender schemata. Some situations call for men to strive for success and others call for women to strive for success. The outcome depends very much on how the task is construed in the situation and whether people expect that success is part of the female or male gender schema.

Howe and Zanna (1975) conducted a study that demonstrates this point nicely. They had male

---

fear of success A fear in women of succeeding in domains traditionally reserved for men.

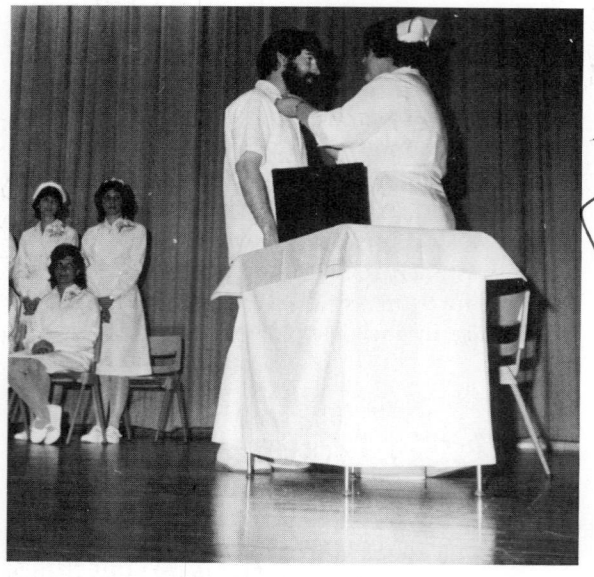

Occupations are still sex stereotyped; a male nurse is the exception rather than the rule. What do you think are the prospects of promotion for this man? Will he be considered inordinately feminine because he is doing "women's" work? Or will he be seen as more capable because he is male?

and female college students solve anagrams. Half of the students were told that success at anagrams is correlated with femininity. After all, they were told, the verbal skills required to perform the task are ones that women usually possess. The other half of the subjects were told that success is usually correlated with masculinity. After all, the spatial component of anagrams is an ability that men possess. Halfway through the test, the investigator called a break, during which the first half of the test was scored. The subjects in the key conditions of the study were told that they were especially successful in the first half of the test.

This information presented half of the subjects with a dilemma. They were succeeding at a task that was supposed to be part of the gender schema of the opposite sex. Subjects then continued with the second half of the anagram test. The results showed that subjects who had been successful on the first half of the test but thought that success was appropriate for the opposite sex actually did worse on the second half. They took a dive in order to avoid being successful at a task

that was appropriate for the opposite gender. Subjects who were succeeding at anagrams and who believed that their sex was supposed to succeed performed as well on the second half as they had on the first half. These findings demonstrate that fear of success does not reside in the personality of either the male or the female, but rather depends on what is socially defined as the sex-appropriateness of a particular behavior in a particular situation.

Situational Analysis: When Does Sexism Happen?

We can now begin to apply what we know about the effects of sexist attitudes on women. We have discussed the development of the stereotypes, the inclusion of those stereotypes in the gender schemata of both males and females, and social psychologists' reluctance to locate the reason for sex-linked behavior in the personality of the victim.

We now need to ask how and when sex-stereotypic schemata come into play in the immediate situation. Let us imagine a hypothetical situation, not unlike Ann Hopkins's situation at Price Waterhouse. Suppose that a woman is applying for a job as supervisor at a large firm in which very few women hold that position. How might sex stereotypes affect the female applicant?

Deaux and Major (1987) have carefully and comprehensively outlined the steps that might lead to prejudicial treatment of the applicant. We shall deal with some of those factors here.

Activating the schema: The perceiver and the situation

As we have pointed out, people have many schemata that help them organize information in the world. Our interviewer (call him the perceiver) has schemata about women, men, successful supervisors, football, lunchtime, and many other things. As he sits at his desk with the candidate (call her the target), what factors might call for the gender schema to be activated? We know that if it is activated—that is, called forth to guide his perceptions, his interactions, and his expectations—it is likely to contain stereotypic beliefs and expectations. But it does have to be activated in order to have these effects.

Several factors can activate the perceiver's set of gender stereotypes, some in the perceiver and some in the situation in which the target and perceiver find themselves. One factor that may tend to activate the stereotyped gender schema is what Higgins and King (1981) have called *chronic accessibility* of the stereotype. This means that for some people, the stereotype is almost always available to be used. It takes very little prompting for some people to invoke their gender stereotypes. Others need many more situational cues to activate the stereotype.

The situation plays an enormous role in bringing forth the stereotyped expectations. One factor is the *uniqueness of gender* in the situation. A perceiver is more likely to be aware of the target's gender if she is applying for a job as a fighter pilot than if she wants office work. There are plenty of female office workers, but very few female pilots. In our hypothetical situation, as in the Price Waterhouse case, there were very few female senior partners and no other women in the group of people applying for the position. So the target's gender was unusual in this regard. Unusualness makes the gender stand out, or become salient (Fiske & Taylor, 1984), and it is the salience that brings forth the stereotypes.

Deaux and Major (1987) point out other features of a situation that can make gender salient. Some contexts are perceived to be sex-linked. A nursery school context, for example, may immediately make people think about female stereotypes; an auto shop may activate masculine stereotypes. Another factor is the target herself. To the extent that she appears feminine, with the cosmetics, clothes, and attractiveness widely thought to be appropriate, she is more likely to invoke the gender stereotype. The proverbial "dumb blonde" may not be at all dumb, but her physical characteristics invoke a set of stereotypic beliefs in almost any situation.

The perceiver behaves

The next step in the process is to consider the behavior of the perceiver. The male interviewer acts in ways that often bring forth the very behavior he is expecting to see. When we discussed the self-fulfilling prophecy in Chapter 2, we noted that when people have an expectation, they tend to do two things: first, they act in ways that make it more likely that other people will act the way they expect them to act, and second, they are likely to interpret ambiguous information as being consistent with their expectations. We can see how this might work in an interview situation. Expecting the target to be like the gender stereotype, the interviewer may ask questions that are related to that stereotype. He may ask about her home life, comment on her clothes, and act in a chivalrous manner. In the end, he is likely to believe that the woman he was interviewing was more interested in her own home life and clothing, and that she acted in too dependent a way to be considered for the administrative position.

As an experimental illustration of this point, Stryphek and Snyder (1982) asked male subjects (perceivers) to engage in a division-of-labor task in which they made decisions about the type of task they would do and the type of task their partner (the target) would do. When a perceiver believed his partner was female, he tended to assign more "feminine" tasks than he did when he believed the partner was male. Thus the behavior differed markedly depending on what the perceiver expected the target to be like.

The target behaves

It is not surprising that people often behave in accordance with the expectation of others. Earlier we noted the finding of Word, Zanna, and Cooper (1974) that black job applicants were treated differently from white applicants, and that this treatment did in fact change the applicants' behavior. Snyder and Swann (1976) showed that people who expected a target to act in a hostile manner actually elicited hostile behavior from the target. We would expect that the behavior of the male interviewer in our hypothetical situation would indeed produce behaviors that conformed to the sex stereotype.

There is another factor to consider. People are generally motivated to act consistently with their own schemata. A woman who holds a stereotyped view of her gender is motivated to act accordingly. We pointed out earlier that Bem's view of the gender schema includes the idea that people evaluate themselves according to how closely they match their schemata. A woman with a traditional view of femininity is not going to evaluate herself well if she comes across as assertive or aggressive. So women with traditional stereotypes, wanting to keep a high sense of self-esteem, are motivated to act in a stereotyped way.

A woman who does not act in accordance with her stereotype not only may evaluate herself poorly but may suffer the same fate in the reactions of others. They may derogate her as well. Brown and Geis (1984) have shown that men who display "manly" traits and women who display "womanly" traits are evaluated more positively and are viewed as more psychologically healthy than those who do not. Bartol and Butterfield (1976) found that female managers were not liked when they were oriented toward the task (generally considered a masculine style) rather than toward interpersonal relations.

The general phenomenon of downgrading people who show behaviors and attitudes that contradict the stereotypes affects men as well as women. One study showed that men who applied for male-oriented positions and women who applied for female-oriented positions were generally well liked. A woman applying for a job traditionally held by a man was not well liked. The person liked least of all was a man who stepped out of role to apply for a job usually thought of as a "woman's job." The problem for women, however, is that the positions that are generally most highly rewarded and that carry most authority are thought of as requiring male characteristics.

The perceiver interprets: The sexism is culminated

Now the perceiver must interpret the behavior of the target. If he has a strong gender schema, if his stereotype is particularly active because of the situation or because of the characteristics of the woman, he is likely to interpret whatever the woman does as evidence in support of his stereotype. There is ample evidence that people interpret information consistently with their expectations (the evidence is reviewed in Darley & Fazio, 1980). This is especially true when the behavior is ambiguous. It is very possible that no hard evidence will emerge in a job interview to confirm or disconfirm a deeply held set of stereotypes. The information will be ambiguous, and that is precisely the kind of information that is readily interpreted as confirming the sex stereotype.

There is also evidence that when the gender stereotype is activated, people make different causal attributions for the same behavior. Even in the face of exactly identical performances at a task, observers are likely to attribute the male's success to his ability while they see the woman's success as being caused by luck or chance (Deaux, 1976; Eagly, 1987). Attributions to ability make it seem likely that the man will be able to succeed again. But attributing any success a woman has to luck or chance means that it is unlikely that she will succeed at another task.

Sexism: Who gets the job?

We have, then, a set of circumstances that come together to produce a sexist decision on a job application. People are likely to believe that the characteristics of men make them better managers. They are assertive, aggressive, strong, task-oriented, and all those good things. Women are expected to be more passive and nurturing, not the stuff that managers are made of. Second, the situation in which the woman finds herself evokes the gender schema. She is a statistical rarity—a female applying for a position in a basically male organization. Third, the interviewer is likely to act toward the woman in a way that will produce evidence that confirms his stereotype. Fourth, the woman in that situation may respond to her own gender schema by producing behaviors that are consistent with that stereotype. Fifth, evidence will be interpreted by the interviewer as meaning that the woman possesses neither the attributes nor the ability for the job.

Who gets the job? Probably not the woman, at least not over an equally qualified man. Yet there is good reason to believe that if you asked the interviewer, he would tell you with all sincerity that he does not discriminate against women. However, the decision is the culmination of a series of events that began as both the interviewer and the applicant developed their own gender schemata about men and women. Both persons were participants in the final outcome. Both brought their expectations to bear: the interviewer his ideas about what he would see in the applicant, and the applicant her own expectations about herself. The social situation they were in activated the schemata and brought the stereotypes to bear on the hiring decision. From that point on, faulty expectations and perceptions led to the final decision. As you will recall, Bem (1981) referred to gender schemas as part of a nonconscious ideology. That ideology is with us so often and pervasively that we fail to recognize it. But it is there nonetheless, having its consequences on the outcomes and satisfaction of women.

Where Do We Go from Here?

Earlier we asked whether we have any reason for optimism. Is there anything we can do about prejudice? Are there ways to overcome it? We think the answer is yes, there is reason for optimism. For one reason, progress has been made and it is continuing. Clearly there is some resistance to change, and we may need to devise more effective approaches to making change happen. Still, we can make further progress. Change is continuing. We think it's up to all of us to make sure that it goes on. Second, we must always remember individual differences. In any situation, some people are more racist or sexist than others, for whatever reason. Several of the perspectives on racism that we have discussed acknowledge individual differences, especially the symbolic or modern racism approach and the ambivalence-amplification approach. Thus the people who are less racist can influence those who are more racist to change their beliefs and their attitudes.

Those of you who think racism or sexism should be combated should use your influence whenever you can, whether by challenging people not to use racist or sexist labels or express racist or sexist views, or by taking the lead in keeping lines of honest communication open. Each of us has a personal responsibility to try to improve our society, and we can do it with just a little effort. In his powerful book of more than twenty years ago, *Soul on Ice,* Eldridge Cleaver (1968) said that if you're not part of the solution, you're part of the problem. We hope you will choose to be part of the solution rather than either an active or a passive part of the problem.

STOP, THINK, & UNDERSTAND

1. Distinguish symbolic racism from aversive racism. Why is one thought to be characteristic of political conservatives and the other characteristic of political liberals?

2. Compare the hypotheses of racial ambivalence and aversive racism.

3. What do we know about the actual differences between human males and females?

4. How can fear of success and situational pressures affect women's performance?

5. What is the process by which gender schemata produce sexist behaviors and outcomes?

We can conclude by referring again to the study by Devine (1989), discussed in connection with stereotypes. Devine found that people who score both high and low on the modern racism scale know current racist stereotypes. She also found that both high and low scorers can be influenced by those stereotypes without being aware of it. But she also found that when people are given an opportunity to take control of their thoughts, high and low scorers act very differently. People who scored high on the modern racism scale simply endorsed and repeated the stereotypes of the culture. People who scored low rejected them. Devine argues that rising above or moving beyond these ingrained stereotypes is like breaking a bad habit. It takes conscious and persistent effort, or, as Devine says, "intention, attention, and time." It won't happen automatically.

Each of you can make a difference. You can take control of your own thoughts, and lift them above the tiresome stereotypes we inherited from an earlier era of our history. And you can try to help other people make progress as well. This is not an easy task, but each of us can make a difference.

Summary

The problem of racial prejudice has been approached from a variety of perspectives. These approaches emphasize the role of cultural learning, competition and conflict, in-group favoritism and social identity, authoritarianism, and displaced aggression. Minority-group and out-group members are often convenient targets for displaced hostility and *scapegoating*.

Recent research on stereotypes emphasizes the purely cognitive factors that lead us to have ethnocentric stereotypes of out-group members. Processes such as *categorization*, the formation of illusory correlations, direct and indirect learning about people in out-groups, and imagined actions on the part of group members are important in the forming of stereotypes. Stereotypes often change as historical forces change the relationship between groups. Stereotypes that we know but do not believe can have automatic and unconscious effects on our perceptions of individuals.

A more subtle form of racism characterizes some segments of American society today, now that racism is widely held to be an evil. We can distinguish modern *symbolic racism,* or racism based on the feeling that blacks threaten important conventional values; racial ambivalence, or mixed positive and negative feelings about blacks; *regressive racism,* or racism that appears under stress; and *aversive racism,* or racism shown in the tendency to discriminate against blacks when such discrimination can be denied.

Research on sex differences and sexism has shown that there are very few differences between human males and females, and the differences that have been found—in aggression, activity level, and verbal, spatial, and mathematical skills—are very small. Stereotypes about sex differences lead to different perceptions of male and female infants and to the reinforcement of gender schemata. Sexism occurs when gender schemata are activated in particular situations, when perceivers interpret behavior to fit their stereotypes and act on the basis of those stereotypes, and when the target of the stereotype responds to the perceiver's actions in ways that reinforce the stereotype.

Key Terms

ambivalence-amplification theory	gender schema	regressive racism
authoritarian personality	out-group homogeneity effect	scapegoat theory
aversive racism	out-group polarization effect	sexism
categorization	prejudice	social identity theory
discrimination	racism	stereotype
fear of success	realistic conflict theory	symbolic racism

Suggested Readings

Allport, G. W. (1954). *The nature of prejudice.* Reading, Mass.: Addison-Wesley.

Bem, S. L. (1981). Gender schema theory: A cognitive account of sex typing. *Psychological Review, 88,* 354–364.

Deaux, K., & Major, B. (1987). Putting gender into context: An interactive model of gender-related behavior. *Psychological Review, 94,* 369–389.

Dovidio, J. F., & Gaertner, S. L. (Eds.) (1986). *Prejudice, discrimination, and racism: Theory and research.* New York: Academic Press.

Jones, J. M. (1972). *Prejudice and racism.* Reading, Mass.: Addison-Wesley.

Pettigrew, T. F. (1981). The ultimate attribution error: Extending Allport's cognitive analysis of prejudice. In E. Aronson (Ed.), *Readings about the social animal* (3rd ed.). San Francisco: W. H. Freeman.

Ruble, D. N., & Ruble, T. L. (1982). Sex stereotypes. In A. Miller (Ed.), *In the eye of the beholder* (pp. 188–252). New York: Praeger.

Chapter Twelve

Social Influence

A rather short, stocky man of 34 ascended a platform in the nation's capital on August 23, 1963. He looked down at a crowd of 250,000 people who were waiting for him to speak. He began slowly, but his voice gained volume and confidence as he spoke:

> I say to you today, even though we face the difficulties of today and tomorrow I still have a dream. It is a dream that is deeply rooted in the American dream. I have a dream that one day this nation will rise up, live out the true meaning of its creed: We hold these truths to be self-evident, that all men are created equal.
>
> I have a dream that one day on the red hills of Georgia the sons of former slaves and the sons of former slaveowners will be able to sit down together at the table of brotherhood. I have a dream that one day even the state of Mississippi, a state sweltering with the heat of oppression, will be transformed into an oasis of freedom and justice.
>
> I have a dream that my four little children one day will live in a nation where they will not be judged by the color of their skin, but by the content of their character.
>
> I have a dream that one day every valley shall be exalted, every hill and mountain shall be made low. The rough places will be made plain and the crooked places will be made straight. This is the faith that I go back to the South with. With this faith we will be able to hew, out of the mountains of despair, the stone of hope. With this faith we will be able to work together, to pray together, to struggle together, to go to jail together, to stand up for freedom together, knowing we will be free one day. (M. L. King, 1963, in C. King, 1969, pp. 239–40)

When the speech ended, the audience sat in awe and then thundered its approval. The "I have a dream" speech became a rallying cry in the drive toward equal rights for blacks in the United States. The speaker, Martin Luther King, Jr., was a strong force in the civil rights movement. He had been characterized as the "moral leader of the nation." He was to receive the Nobel Peace Prize for his courageous leadership of the Black Freedom movement, and his counsel was sought by two presidents.

Martin Luther King, Jr., was born in 1929 in Atlanta, Georgia. He grew up in a middle-class black neighborhood in a relatively secure and uneventful world. His father, a Baptist minister, recalled that "we never lived in a rented house and never rode too long in a car on which payment was due" (Bennett, 1968). Young Martin was a precocious, hard-working student, deferential to his elders and considerate of his peers. He skipped the 9th and 12th grades and entered Morehouse College at the age of 15. He also attended Crozer Seminary, and he received a Ph.D. in philosophy from Boston University. While at Morehouse College, King decided to become a minister, and at the age of 18 he was ordained. In September 1954 he became head pastor at the Dexter Avenue Baptist Church in Montgomery, Alabama. It was there that his crusade for freedom began.

King was the right man in the right place at the right time. World War II had brought blacks and whites into closer contact on a more equal footing than at any other time in the history of this country (Bishop, 1971), and nonwhites were winning independence in other parts of the world—India, Africa, Southeast Asia, and the East Indies. On May 17, 1954, the U.S. Supreme Court, in the case of *Brown* v. *Board of Education of Topeka, Kansas,* ruled that "separate educational facilities are inherently unequal"; and on May 31, 1955, the Court ordered school desegregation "with all deliberate speed."

Then, on December 1, 1955, an incident in Montgomery precipitated King's leadership in the civil rights movement. Rosa Parks, a black seamstress, boarded a crowded bus. She paid her fare and took a seat in the "Negro section" at the back. Six whites boarded the bus at the next stop, and the bus driver then went to the back and ordered the blacks to give up their places so that the whites could be seated. Three blacks yielded to this established custom and immediately rose, but Rosa Parks remained seated. The bus driver repeated his demand, and again she refused. For this act of insubordination she was arrested. This incident provided the catalyst for the unification of the Black Freedom movement under King's leadership.

The black leaders of Montgomery felt that it was time to act—time to protest the treatment of Rosa Parks and of all blacks in the South. King urged that the protest action be nonviolent. A one-day black boycott of the bus line was planned.

Martin Luther King, Jr.'s "I have a dream" speech became a symbol not only of the movement for equal rights but of the man himself. He is remembered today for the strength of his personality and his unique ability to inspire hope.

King and the other leaders expected about 60% cooperation; to their amazement, there was almost 100% participation. Although no direct force was exerted to get people to support the boycott, the "silent pressure of the movement" fueled the action. Blacks who rode on the buses were subjected to hostile stares and scorn by the boycott supporters. These actions were usually enough to bring even the most stubborn person into line.

Encouraged, the black leaders met to plan further action. They elected King to head the Montgomery Freedom movement, and they decided to continue the boycott of buses until three demands were met: "(1) courteous treatment of black riders by the bus operators; (2) passenger seating on a first-come, first-served basis; (3) Negro bus drivers on predominantly Negro routes" (King, 1969).

King proved a vigorous leader. He spoke to crowds of blacks about the purposes of the boycott and about the necessity for nonviolence, and

he arbitrated with Montgomery's mayor, other city officials, and bus company representatives. The boycott continued. Although King's home was bombed, he continued to preach nonviolence. On February 21, 1956, the Montgomery County grand jury declared the boycott illegal, and King and other leaders were arrested. Still the boycott went on, and King's following grew. The one-day boycott evolved into a 382-day struggle that finally ended on November 14, 1956, when the Supreme Court declared illegal the Alabama law requiring segregation on buses. It was a victory for the Black Freedom movement, for its new leader, Martin Luther King, Jr., and for King's doctrine of nonviolent protest.

The year after the Montgomery boycott, King gave 208 speeches and traveled 780,000 miles. In the following years he led drives for black freedom and equality in Georgia, Alabama, Illinois, and Mississippi, always with the goal of achieving freedom through civil disobedience and nonviolence. Despite numerous assassination attempts, he persisted in his advocacy of nonviolence in freedom marches, sit-down strikes, and civil disobedience, and thousands followed his example and his instructions. He earned the respect of blacks and whites alike, and he became a valued adviser to Presidents John F. Kennedy and Lyndon B. Johnson and to Attorney General Robert Kennedy. When King organized the March on Washington to give impetus to the Kennedy Civil Rights Bill, more than 250,000 people turned out, and King was present when the bill was eventually signed into law.

In the years following the passage of the Civil Rights Act of 1964 King became active in opposing the American war in Vietnam and in mobilizing protests against poverty in the United States. He was in Memphis, Tennessee, on April 4, 1968, organizing a march of sanitation workers demanding better working conditions, when he was cut down by an assassin's bullet. He was only 39 years old.

A few years ago the nation decided to honor King properly, and designated January 15, Martin Luther King's birthday, a national holiday. Some members of Congress strongly opposed this change, but most Americans realize the unique contribution to healing and change in their country brought about by Martin Luther King.

The Scope of Social Influence

The story of Martin Luther King and the civil rights movement illustrates many types of social behavior. Among the most central is social influence. People had to be influenced to join the movement, and the nation had to be influenced to adopt the goals of the movement. In its broadest sense, social influence includes almost all of social psychology, since it may be used to describe any change (physiological, attitudinal, emotional, or behavioral) that occurs in one person as the result of the real, implied, or imagined presence of others (Latané, 1981).

In its more limited usage, however, **social influence** involves the exercise of power by a person or group to influence the behavior of others. Social influence is concerned more with behavioral change than with attitudinal or emotional change. King was well aware of this distinction, as he often remarked that, while he would like to change people's attitudes, his main goal was to get people to act in a fair and equitable way toward others, regardless of their race.

The area of social influence is broad and central to social psychology. We are constantly confronted with social influence in our everyday lives; some of this influence is direct and clearly identifiable, while other influence is more indirect and less recognizable. Jones and Pittman (1982) have shown that the desire to influence others even affects the way we present ourselves. In studying the role of social influence in the civil rights movement, we can also become aware of its role in our everyday lives.

Responses to Social Influence

It will be helpful if, at the outset, we identify three distinct types of response to the pressures of social influence (Kelman, 1961). As you will see, different kinds of individual power and group pressure result in different kinds of opinion and behavior change. The first kind of response to social influence is **compliance.** When people comply, they simply go along overtly with certain kinds of social influence; there is no genuine internal or private opinion change in the case of compliance. As a result of peer pressure, for example, a student may participate in a rally demanding that her college hire more minority faculty. The student is demonstrating compliance if she actually believes that her college should not make further efforts to hire minority faculty.

Compliance is public; that is, it does not involve private opinion change. Two kinds of responses to social influence, however, are marked by genuine opinion change. The first is called **identification.** Identification occurs when an individual adopts the standards of a person or group that he or she likes, admires, and wants to establish a relationship with. The individual privately accepts the new standards, but maintains them only as long as he or she continues to admire the other person or group. A student may willingly participate in rallies for more minority faculty, for instance, as long as she likes one of the protest group leaders. When that admiration ends, however, the student may find herself surprisingly disinterested in hiring more minority faculty.

The third response to social influence involves genuine, long-lasting change of opinion based on congruence between a new opinion and the individual's overall value system. This kind of response to social influence is called **internalization.** The student who not only participates in the rally for minority faculty but also believes in that policy because it coincides with her values has internalized the aims of the protest group.

The distinction between compliance and internalization is important, as it enables us to predict how an individual will act when influence pressures have been removed. If the individual is simply complying with individual or group pressures, but retains private attitudes that are inconsistent with those pressures, we would not expect his or her behavior to be the same once the social pressure has been removed. Thus the person whose attendance at the rally only reflects public compliance will not follow through with other actions.

The distinction between compliance and internalization alerts us to the other side of the coin; that is, the fact that influence often results in private acceptance without producing public compliance. Sometimes, for example, people respond to societal minorities by accepting their ideas privately while publicly ignoring them (Nemeth, 1986).

Social Power

As we have seen, power forms the base of an individual's or group's ability to influence others. In fact, **power** is generally defined as the capacity or the potential to influence others and to resist influence by others (Michener & Suchner, 1972). The essential difference between influence and power is that influence actually changes the behavior of another person, whereas power is the ability to bring about such change. A parent may have a great deal of power (the potential to change behavior) over a child, but some parents exercise this power (influence) more than others do.

An important clarification of the power concept was suggested by Cartwright and Zander (1968). They point out that exercising power often brings the actor rewards but may also entail costs. For example, you may have the power to get another individual to wash your automobile. Although getting that individual to wash your car may bring you some rewards (a clean car), it will also have costs for you (money). Although you may have the money to get someone to wash your car (power), the price may be more than you are willing to pay. Hence Cartwright and Zander employ the term *usable power* to describe the power that will bring more rewards than costs. Martin Luther King may have had the power to persuade a group in Rio Hondo, Texas, to carry out a peaceful demonstration. However, this may not have been usable power, because it would have taken King two days of travel by plane, bus, and horse to actually meet and influence the group. Such a trip might not have been worth the benefits.

Types of Power and Their Use

People gain the potential to influence others through many routes. For example, both a policeman and a doctor may be able to influence you to refrain from using certain drugs; however, the bases of their influence are very different. French and Raven (1959) identified five bases from which individuals gain power. They and others (Aries, 1976; Michener & Burt, 1974;

compliance Overt behavioral conformity while maintaining one's own attitude.
identification Adoption of the standards of a person or group that one likes, admires, and wants to establish a relationship with.
internalization The process by which one genuinely accepts an opinion as a result of its good fit with one's other values and opinions.
power The capacity to influence others and to resist influence by others.
social influence The exercise of power by a person or group to change the opinions or behavior of others.

During the civil rights demonstrations in the 1960s coercive power of different types, including police dogs, was used against the demonstrators. Tactics such as these were intended to intimidate activists and those who might be willing to follow them.

Bonoma, 1976) point out that in most cases people derive power from more than one base and that they must decide which type of power to use in a particular situation. Further, the base of power often determines the situations in which it can be used.

Coercive power

The potential to deliver threats and punishment to force another person to change his or her behavior is **coercive power.** A parent uses coercive power when he or she threatens to spank a child if a certain behavior is not carried out. Coercive power was used to stop King's civil rights activities: his house was bombed, he was jailed on several occasions, and there were numerous attempts on his life.

Coercive power is based on access to weapons or other resources that increase strength and the credibility of threat. Two important drawbacks deter the use of coercive power. First, the low-power individual in a coercive relationship is going to be motivated to end the relationship if the opportunity presents itself. Dictatorial governments that rely on coercive power must go to great lengths to keep citizens from leaving the country. Second, the coercive power base requires surveillance of the low-power person (Shaw & Condelli, 1986). The power of coercion is only as effective as the surveillance system. Rarely does a child rush in and announce to its mother, "I just sneaked three cookies from the cookie jar."

The necessity of surveillance is a problem for a number of reasons. First, it is very difficult, if not impossible, to maintain close surveillance. Hijackings continue to occur despite the millions of dollars that have been spent on the surveillance of passengers at airports. Second, surveillance leads to distrust and fosters conflict (Strickland, 1968). Distrust on the part of the high-power individual may occur through a dissonance-reduction process (for example, "I'm spending all this effort on surveillance; therefore that individual I'm having watched must be untrustworthy"). Finally, surveillance does not lead to internalization; it influences individuals only while they are under surveillance. One reason is that the individual does not experience dissonance following behavior performed while under surveillance because he can justify such behavior by saying, "I was only doing that to avoid punishment" (see Chapter 6).

Given these negative aspects of coercive power, one may ask why coercion is ever used. One reason is that it is relatively easy to use; it takes little effort to make a threat. Another reason is that coercion may enhance the self-esteem of its user (Raven & Kruglanski, 1970; Kipnis, 1974). Being able to force another person to act in a prescribed manner leads to a feeling of mastery and superiority. Hence Kipnis reports that supervisors who lack confidence and self-esteem often resort to coercive power. However, coercive power is the type of power that is least likely to sustain change and it is the most difficult to maintain. It is generally used as a last resort.

Reward power

The ability to give positive reinforcement to produce change is **reward power.** The reinforcement may take the form of material commodities, such as money, or it may take a more intangible form, such as praise. Reward power is based on access to commodities that others value. Hence an individual may have reward power over one person but not over another, depending on the value that these people place on the commodities.

Reward power, unlike coercive power, motivates the low-power individual to stay in the relationship. Although surveillance is required for the effective use of reward power, the degree of such surveillance need not be as high as that required by coercive power. It is not uncommon for a child to announce, "Come look, I've just cleaned up my room." When the desired behavior is performed, the actor is likely to call the attention of the high-power individual to that performance. Canavan-Gumpert (1977) found that reward power (praise) is more effective than coercive power (criticism) in increasing performance in children. Hence reward power should be preferred to coercive power.

However, reward power may be costly to the user, especially when the reward is based on material assets, such as money. In addition, because the reward may justify behavior, the exercise of reward power may not result in internalization, or attitude change. Remembering dis-

sonance theory again (see Chapter 6), the actor may say, "I am doing this because of the reward and not because I believe in what I am doing." Thus reward power will be effective only so long as rewards are dispensed.

Legitimate power

The power that one derives from being in a particular role or position is **legitimate power.** Legitimate power is authority, and it is generally limited to a particular domain. For example, your boss may have the legitimate power to influence how you behave at work, but he or she does not have legitimate power to determine how you behave toward your spouse or what you do on your days off. Pruitt (1976) notes that legitimate power is based on the norm of "oughtness"; we are socialized to believe that we should follow the orders of persons in certain positions. For example, the child is taught to "do what your parents say because they are your parents." Martin Luther King, Jr., obtained legitimate power by virtue of the fact that he was the leader of the Black Freedom movement and the president of the Southern Christian Leadership Conference.

Possessors of legitimate power do not have to explain why they want individuals to act in a certain way. People with legitimate power are influential not because they say the right things but because they have the right to influence. Laws may be used to assign legitimate power to certain people. And it is often the case that people who have other bases of power may pass laws to ensure legitimate power for themselves. Hence a dictator who overthrows a government by the use of coercive power may "pass laws" that give him legitimate power.

Expert power

Often people gain power because others see them as being knowledgeable about a particular area. For example, physicians often have **expert power**; they are perceived to have special insight and

---

coercive power The capacity to deliver threats and punishments to force compliance.

expert power Power derived from a reputation for special insight or knowledge about a particular area.

legitimate power Power derived from a particular role or position.

reward power The capacity to give positive reinforcements to achieve compliance.

knowledge about medical problems. If they advise you to have an operation, you will probably have it even if you do not necessarily understand why the operation is necessary. Expert power, like legitimate power, is usually limited to a specific area. Thus your doctor may be able to influence you on health-related issues, but you will not necessarily follow his or her advice about what new car to buy. People often attempt to increase their expert power by the use of diplomas and citations that testify to their knowledge in a certain area. It is not uncommon to walk into a doctor's office and see a whole wall of diplomas. Even garage mechanics may bolster their expert power by displaying diplomas and citations from courses they have taken.

Expert power has some of the advantages and disadvantages of legitimate power. It does not require surveillance; it is clearly vested in the individual; it often covers only a limited domain. It does, however, have the added advantage that internalization of attitudes may follow its use. That is, people not only follow an expert because they are awed by the credentials that he or she possesses, but they also believe that he or she has the correct information.

Referent power

People gain the ability to influence us because we admire and like them. We want to be similar to the people we admire, and hence we often imitate them and try to act as we think they would. **Referent power** was one of the strongest bases of King's power. He was admired by millions for his courage and foresight and his charismatic personality. Hence many people wanted to be like him, and acted as he did.

Given the available evidence, it seems that referent power is the most *usable*. Its use does not require surveillance, and it tends to bring the user and the target closer together rather than force them apart. It is also likely to lead to an internalization of attitudes rather than simply a change in behavior. The belief in the effectiveness of referent power is one of the motivating factors behind group psychotherapy and such behavior-change groups as Weight Watchers and Alcoholics Anonymous. In these cases, peers with similar backgrounds are relied upon as the agents of influence, rather than experts.

Informational power

Raven and Kruglanski (1970) added a sixth basis of power to those suggested by French and Raven (1959). The five types of power that we have discussed are all dependent on the source; the basis of power lies within the particular person. That person's power may be limited to particular situations, but it is independent of the information that the person actually possesses. On the other hand, eyewitnesses to crimes have the power to influence juries solely because of the information they have and not because of their characteristics. This type of independent power has been labeled **informational power.** As Pruitt (1976) points out, "Knowledge is power." It should be noted, however, that once the person who possesses informational power dispenses the information, power is reduced. Once the eyewitness has testified, for example, he or she no longer has the power to influence the behavior of the jury.

Gender Differences in the Use of Power

Although the type of power influences when and how power will be used, many characteristics of the target also influence the way power will be used. One factor is gender.

In an interesting study on the use of power by married couples, Raven, Centers, and Rodrigues (1969) interviewed 776 husbands and wives in the Los Angeles area. They gave examples of behaviors and asked the respondents to tell what type of power would be used by their spouses to influence those behaviors. They found that referent and expert power were used most frequently, and coercive power least frequently. Wives were most likely to attribute expert power ("knew what was best in the case") to their husbands, and husbands saw their wives as using referent power ("both part of the same family") most often. Further, expert power was used more by younger couples than by older ones, and the use of referent power increased with age. Finally, as can be seen in Table 12-1, the use of power was also dependent on the type of behavior being influenced.

Following up on this gender difference, Falbo and Peplau (1980) had subjects write an essay describing "how I get [my intimate partner] to

TABLE 12-1

Percentage attributing each basis of power to the spouse as a function of the domain of power

Domain of power	N	Predominant basis of power attributed to spouse				
		Reward	Coercion	Expert	Legitimate	Referent
"Visit some friend or relative"	768	7%	8%	15%	43%	27%
"Change some personal habit"	758	6	9	35	30	20
"Repair or clean something around house"	766	5	13	28	35	19
"Change station on TV or radio"	766	14	13	8	30	35
"Go somewhere for outing or vacation"	760	10	3	10	37	40
"Go see a doctor"	768	1	2	55	22	20

SOURCE: Raven (1975).

do what I want." These essays were then analyzed to see what power strategy was used. The results indicated that heterosexual men tended to prefer direct and interactive strategies (bargaining, talking, reasoning, and persistence), while heterosexual women tended to use indirect and solitary strategies (withdrawal, negative affect). They also found that the strategies (direct-interactive) used by men were more likely to promote a satisfying relationship. Rather than indicating that men are more socially sensitive than women, Falbo and Peplau argue that because men expect compliance in their relationship, they have the "luxury" of being able to rely on these methods. Women, on the other hand, often see their position as the weaker one in the relationship. As a result, they must resort to the solitary strategies that are used when the goal is important but compliance is not expected.

Leadership

In any group, large or small, some individuals have more power and influence than others. The person with the most influence often assumes a position of prominence in the group and comes to be regarded as the leader. In fact, we can define a **leader** as the person who exerts the most influence in a group (Hollander, 1985; Shaw, 1981). There are many different kinds of leaders and leadership. Martin Luther King was an exceptional leader, and he clearly fits our definition. He had an extremely high degree of influence over other people both within and outside of the Southern Christian Leadership Conference. Many times only his words kept the Black Freedom movement from turning into a violent revolt. For example, on June 30, 1956, a bomb was thrown at his home in Montgomery. A number of police officers, along with the police commissioner and the mayor, arrived on the scene shortly after the blast. A crowd of about 1,000 angry blacks also gathered, armed with guns, rocks, knives, and sticks and ready to do battle with the police. King walked onto the porch and asked the blacks to adhere to the doctrine of nonviolence, reminding them that "he who lives by the sword will perish by the sword." The crowd dispersed

informational power   Power derived from the possession of a specific piece of information.

leader   The person who exerts the most influence in a group.

referent power   Power derived from being admired and liked.

Mikhail Gorbachev, president of the U.S.S.R., has succeeded, in spite of internal opposition, because he has been able to vocalize and actualize the wishes of the Soviet people. As a transformational leader he has exercised not only power but great influence in the Eastern bloc and in the international community.

peacefully. Coretta King recalls hearing a white policeman in the crowd saying, "If it hadn't been for that nigger preacher, we'd all be dead" (King, 1969, p. 130).

Several past presidents of the United States have also been powerful leaders. Psychologists and political scientists who have discussed different kinds of presidential leadership have identified the **transformational leader** as one who senses the unexpressed wants of the populace and tries to bring those desires to expression for the purpose of changing the political system (Burns, 1984). Franklin Roosevelt fit the definition of a transformational leader, as did Ronald Reagan. The current president of the Soviet Union, Mikhail Gorbachev, perhaps exemplifies the concept better than any other recent leader. With his emphasis on *glasnost* (openness) and *perestroika* (restructuring), Gorbachev clearly signals that he wants the desires of the peoples of the Soviet Union and Eastern Europe to be sharply identified and used to reshape their societies. Though leaders around the world differ in many ways, all leaders have the common characteristic

of exerting the most influence in the groups over which they preside. A person may be a leader for only a short time and in a limited situation, but in that time or place he or she has the greatest influence.

The Perception of Leaders

The concept of leadership raises many complex issues. One central question that psychologists have explored actively in recent years is how leaders are perceived (Kinder & Fiske, 1986). Some of the research on leadership perception suggests that people have a generalized **leadership schema** (Simonton, 1986a, 1987). That is, we have an overall image of what a leader is and what a leader does. Studies of presidential leadership show that our general idea of a great leader or an "ideal president" is an individual who has three important characteristics: strength, activity, and goodness. In short, the ideal president, or admired leader of any group, is competent and trustworthy (Kinder et al., 1980; Simonton, 1986a). According to this approach, when people judge

Chapter Twelve   Social Influence

leaders, salient information about their behavior activates to varying degrees this overall image of a strong, active, and good leader. For example, our knowledge of Martin Luther King's dramatic "I have a dream" speech calls to mind the overall leadership schema, and we tend to see him as strong, active, and good.

The leadership schema approach also suggests that people reveal the correspondence bias (discussed in Chapter 2) in judging leaders. That is, they see their leaders' behavior as reflecting their personal traits rather than situational forces. For example, if President Bush were to demonstrate strong leadership in an area of popular concern, such as taking a bold approach to protecting the environment, American citizens might attribute his action to leadership qualities rather than to pressure from environmental groups and the Congress. Then they would attribute to Bush the competence and trustworthiness they associate with leadership.

Consistent with the idea of a leadership schema is a study showing that people tend to make the **halo error** in judging leaders (Saal, Downey & Lahey, 1980). That is, they assume that if leaders have one leadership characteristic, they have them all. The study showed that cadet leaders at the United States Military Academy at West Point rated their own leadership behaviors and skills much more variably than did their subordinates. Subordinates seemed to credit the cadets with a consistent range of leadership qualities, rather than strength in some areas but weakness in others. Consistent with the actor-observer bias (discussed in Chapter 3), the cadets themselves realized that their behavior was affected by the situation as well as by their overall skills as leaders (Frone et al., 1987).

Leadership Behavior

The leadership schema approach shows that perceptions of leadership can be erroneous in several important ways. Therefore, it is important that we clearly identify just what it is that leaders do. Fortunately, this is something we know a good deal about. Psychologists have been doing research on leadership behavior and functions for decades, with the aim of finding out exactly what a leader does in and for a group.

One of the most widely cited studies on leadership was conducted at Ohio State University in the late 1940s. In one phase of that investigation, Halpin and Winer (1952) asked subjects to record what characteristics of a leader they felt were most important. The two most widely mentioned characteristics fell under the headings of *consideration* and *initiating structure*. The consideration category included such characteristics as (1) initiates communication, (2) explains actions, and (3) promotes trust. The initiating structure dimension included the behaviors of directing the actions of the group and group planning. Two minor factors were also found: *production emphasis* (stresses "getting the job done") and *social sensitivity* (flexibility in adjusting plans and listening to others). Lieberman, Yalom, and Miles (1973) point out that these duties of a leader are often contradictory. For example, it is difficult for an individual who is concerned with getting the job done or initiating new tasks to be involved in fraternization or in being "just one of the gang." Similarly, it is difficult to be an evaluator of a member's performance and also to be concerned about that member's feelings.

The duality of leadership and the contradictory pressures that accompany the need to be concerned about both the task and the feelings of the people working on the task would seem to ensure that one could not be an effective leader: it should be almost impossible to perform both functions at the same time. However, Bales and Slater (1955) found that one person does not generally perform both functions; usually, one person leads on task-related issues and another assumes the person-oriented functions. These investigators studied groups of three to six members working on a discussion task. They found an increasing tendency over time for the best-liked individual not to be rated as the person who came up with the best ideas. The tendency was to see the individual with the best ideas as the

---

halo error The assumption that a leader who demonstrates one leadership characteristic has them all.

leadership schema An overall image of what a leader is and does.

transformational leader A leader who can sense and articulate the unexpressed desires of a populace and who expresses those desires to change the political system.

leader because he or she provided suggestions about how the group should solve its problems. Bales and Slater named that leader the *task specialist*—mainly concerned with getting the job done. The best-liked person was called the *socioemotional specialist* by Bales and Slater and the *maintenance specialist* by Thibaut and Kelley (1959). His or her chief concern was to create a good social climate in the group. Zelditch (1955) studied families in 56 societies and found that in most families there was a task specialist and a maintenance specialist. Generally the man was the task specialist and the woman the socioemotional leader.

Thus it is very likely that there are two leaders in many groups: one leader pushes the group members to get the job done and the other works to keep the group members happy. It is probably also true that the two types of leaders use different types of power in their roles. Task leaders use legitimate, expert, and coercive power to get group members to work; socioemotional leaders should be most effective if they use referent and reward power.

A recent study of leadership suggests that in addition to showing consideration and initiating structure, an important and quite general leadership behavior is simply assuming overall responsibility for what happens in the group. This has been shown in an interesting study of intervention in emergencies (Baumeister et al., 1988). You may recall from Chapter 8 that in Darley and Latané's (1968) epileptic seizure study, subjects in groups were much less likely to help than subjects who were alone. Those in groups typically diffused responsibility, assuming someone else should or would help, with the result that few of them took action and the victim was much less likely to receive the aid he needed. In the study by Baumeister and his colleagues, however, people who were designated leaders of a group did not diffuse responsibility. In fact, 80% of group leaders came out of their individual rooms to aid a group member who was having a coughing and choking fit, even though coming out of their rooms ruined the experiment and cost them their leadership position. The 80% rate of helping is comparable to the helping rate of solitary subjects in other experiments, while the 35% helping rate of subordinates in this study is compa-

rable to the rate observed among subjects in groups in those other experiments. People who are leaders find it important to take overall responsibility in their groups, even if their leadership position does not specifically require that they do so.

What Makes a Leader? Theories of Leadership

Thus far we have seen that a leader is an individual who exercises power to influence the direction of group activity. We have seen that there are many leadership behaviors and many ways to measure leadership. We can now ask: Why do some individuals arise as leaders while others do not? Why, for example, did Martin Luther King, Jr., rather than some other individual become the leader of the civil rights movement? Was it some characteristic of King, was it the particular situation, or was it some combination of the two? Hollander (1985) pointed out that the study of leadership has historically progressed by asking these three questions in turn, and that as a result attention focuses first on *trait theories,* next on *situational theories,* and finally on *interactional theories* of leadership.

Trait theories

When we look at powerful leaders such as Martin Luther King, Jr., Mikhail Gorbachev, Franklin Roosevelt, and Margaret Thatcher, we get the impression that these are not ordinary people. There must be, or have been, something special about them that enabled them to become such powerful leaders. The earliest studies of leadership were based on the premise that something sets leaders apart from followers—that leaders are born, not made. If this assumption is correct, it should be possible to identify certain unique traits that characterize leaders. The theory that encompasses these ideas has been labeled the "great person theory of leadership" or the "trait theory." In its simplest form, the theory states that history, or the direction of a group's behavior, is shaped by the particular person in the leadership position, and that the course of events would be completely different if another person were in that position (Jacobs, 1971). In the case of Martin Luther King, Jr., the theory would

Charismatic leaders, such as Franklin Delano Roosevelt and Margaret Thatcher, exert the power of their personalities as well as their offices. They have both been known for their indomitable spirit, unflagging energy, and willingness to surmount great odds.

emphasize the fact that King shaped and determined the direction of the civil rights movement in our country, and that the movement would have had a different look if someone else had been its leader.

Key assumptions of the trait theory have not been supported by empirical studies. First, the same people tend not to be the leaders in all situations and at all times. Second, leaders are not a breed apart. Sometimes they are not so different from followers. That is, many different kinds of people can be both leaders and followers at different times in different places. Still, hundreds of studies of the characteristics of leaders have shown that leaders do tend to have distinctive traits (Stogdill, 1948). Some of the major characteristics, both physical and psychological, that have been associated with leadership include size and strength, sex, intelligence, verbosity, motivation, and the somewhat elusive quality called charisma.

Many years ago Leo Terman (1904) pointed out that primitive tribes chose their leaders on the basis of size, strength, or age. In certain tribes the leader was the individual who could lift the largest beam and carry it longest. In one Colombian tribe, an individual was allowed to lead only after he had passed a test in which he was covered by stinging ants or whipped by other tribe members. Stogdill's data indicate that even in our own culture, leaders tend to be slightly older, taller, heavier, healthier, and more energetic than the average group member. The data on physical traits make sense if one is considering such groups as football teams, exploring expeditions, or hunting parties, where physical prowess is important. However, it is difficult to see why the strongest individual would be the leader of a debate team, where physical strength is irrelevant to the task. Since Stogdill did not differentiate his data according to the task that the group performed, generalizing from these data is somewhat risky. It is interesting to note that such great leaders as Gandhi, King, Napoleon, and Hitler were no stronger, taller, or heavier than most of their followers.

Sex or gender has also been found to be related to leadership, though the picture is rapidly changing. Both men and women expect men to be leaders, and in early studies women were less likely to view themselves as potential leaders (Megargee, 1969). This stereotype of men as more natural leaders than women means that women leaders face an extra handicap in trying to be effective and in being perceived as such. They must "be like gold to be seen as silver" (Hollander, 1985).

However, an interesting group of studies shows that women are more likely to become leaders in small groups now than they were two decades ago. Megargee's study, published in 1969, showed that when a man was low in dominance

Change, while slow, does occur. Once a bastion of male dominance, the West Point Military Academy only admitted women in 1976. Yet in the summer of 1989 they graduated Kristin Baker, who was named overall leader of the corps of cadets, the top honor.

and his female partner was high, only 22% of the women became leaders. In same-sex pairs, by contrast, the high-dominance person became leader about 70% of the time; and in male-female pairs with high-dominance men and low-dominance women, 89% of the men became the leader. Two studies published in 1986 showed change in these figures, one more than the other. Nyquist and Spence (1986) found that 35% of women in pairs made up of a high-dominance woman and a low-dominance man became leaders, while Fleischer and Chertkoff (1986) found that 50% of the women in such pairs became leaders. It is not clear how to explain the divergent findings of the two 1986 studies. The latter study was conducted in the Midwest rather than the Southwest, where Megargee and Nyquist and Spence conducted their studies. Perhaps people in the Mid-

west have become more accustomed to women as leaders than people in the more traditional Southwest. Regardless, both studies show that women are more likely to emerge as leaders now than they were a generation ago.

Two studies of male and female leaders at West Point, where a woman was recently graduated as overall leader of the corps of cadets, give an indication of just how fast concepts of gender and leadership are changing. A 1980 study showed that while women performed as well as men and had equally good morale in their groups, their successes were attributed to luck while men's were attributed to ability. These negative attributions were not found in a 1984 study, although female subordinates still rated female leaders quite negatively (Rice, Bender & Vitters, 1980; Rice, Instone & Adams, 1984).

Studies of men and women in natural leadership positions are beginning to show increasingly fewer differences between the sexes in both their behaviors and their effectiveness. Laboratory studies in which men and women are assigned leadership positions still show lower ratings for women, probably because of enduring schemata suggesting that leaders should be men (Hollander, 1985). As more and more women actually fill leadership positions, we can anticipate that their effectiveness will be the same as men's and that discrimination against them will lessen. Increasing numbers of people may realize that women have been leaders all along and will expect to see more women in leadership positions in the near future. Margaret Thatcher of the United Kingdom is a powerful national leader at present. The first major-party woman candidate for vice president of the United States, Geraldine Ferraro, ran in 1984. The time may not be too distant when women will routinely be on national presidential tickets, including the top spot.

Among the traits most consistently associated with leadership is intelligence. The leader in most groups is somewhat more intelligent than the followers (Gibb, 1969; Mann, 1959; Stogdill, 1948). Simonton (1986b) found that intellectual brilliance is one of the few personality traits consistently linked to greatness ratings among American presidents, with Jefferson, Kennedy, and Wilson being rated the most intelligent. The correlation between intelligence and leadership, however, is not high; Mann reports the median correlation to be around .25, and some studies (for example, Loretto & Williams, 1974) found no relationship between intelligence and leadership. One possible reason for this low correlation is that a leader who is much more intelligent than the other group members will not be able to relate to them.

One kind of intelligence that may help a leader relate to group members is the ability to perceive group members' needs and to behave accordingly (Kenny & Zaccaro, 1983). You may recall from Chapter 4 that individuals who are high self-monitors possess both these abilities. Not surprisingly, it has recently been found that high self-monitors are more likely to emerge as leaders in natural groups (Ellis, 1988). Both their ability to perceive others accurately and their ability to respond to others' expectations allow them to rise to leadership positions. Consistent with these findings are observations by the military historian John Keegan (1987). In his book on heroic leaders, *The Mask of Command*, Keegan argues that leaders must, like high self-monitors, be theatrical, and that "the theatrical impulse will be strong in the successful politician, teacher, entrepreneur, athlete or divine, and will be both expected and reinforced by the audiences to which they perform" (p. 11). Perhaps it is worth remembering that one of America's greatest presidents, Franklin Roosevelt, wanted to be an actor when he was in high school, and that Ronald Reagan, another transformational leader, was one.

Another trait that paves the road for an individual's rise to leadership is verbosity, or talkativeness. A number of investigators (Riecken, 1958; Bass, 1949; McGrath & Julian, 1963) have consistently found evidence supporting the "big mouth" theory of leadership; that is, the most talkative member of the group is seen as the leader.

The relationship between talkativeness and leadership was demonstrated in a study (Bavelas et al., 1965) in which the subjects first met in four-person discussion groups and the observers recorded the amount of time that each member spent talking. After the first discussion, the subjects rated each other on leadership. In the next session, each subject had a box in front of him with a red and green light. The subjects were told that they would receive feedback about how well they performed: a green light would signify good performance; a red light, poor performance. One subject who had been near the bottom in verbosity in the first session was chosen to receive positive feedback for talking. During the second session, he received more green lights than anyone else in the group. This positive reinforcement for talking caused him to more than double his verbal output, and the group then came to view him as the leader. A third session was run without lights. The previously reinforced subject's verbal output remained high, and so did his ratings on leadership. This study strikingly demonstrated the importance of verbosity as a determinant of leadership. In support of these findings, Sorrentino and Boutillier (1975) manipulated both the quantity and quality of a confederate's remarks during a group discussion. While quality had little effect on the confederate's leadership ratings, the more he talked, the higher he was rated on leadership ability by the other group members.

While it seems that talking is a sure road to leadership, there have been some important qualifications of this rule. First, Gintner and Lindskold (1975) found that the amount of talking did not affect leadership ratings of persons introduced to the group as experts on their topic of conversation. Amount of talking, however, was positively related to leadership ratings of nonexperts. Second, talking may be negatively related to leadership if the comments involve negative statements about the group's effectiveness; in other words, if the person rejects the group, the group will reject the person (Morris & Hackman, 1969).

Motives are also important in leadership. Recent research shows that being oriented toward achieving success and being oriented toward affiliating with others are both important in the emergence of a leader in a long-lasting group (Sorrentino & Field, 1986). Other motives may be important in a leader's success. Winter's (1987) studies of American presidents have shown that the presidents who are motivated by power, the ones who are generally energetic, autonomous, self-directed, somewhat narcissistic, and concerned with prestige and having an impact on others, tend to be rated as great presidents and are credited with great decisions. The three presidents with the highest power motive, according to Winter's analyses of themes in their inaugural addresses, are Truman, Kennedy, and Reagan.

One other trait that is often associated with leadership has received little empirical study: **charisma,** a term used to describe the magnetic pull that certain leaders appear to have. It has been applied to such leaders as Martin Luther King, Jr., John F. Kennedy, Adolf Hitler, and Ho Chi Minh. While some leaders seem to have charisma, others do not. Max Weber (1946) used the term to mean the "gift of grace." Charisma has almost supernatural qualities that are difficult to describe and may be impossible to study. Weber felt that a leader's charisma is especially evident in times of crisis and that situational events seem to draw it out. A leader's charisma is also, in part, determined by the followers' needs and emotional states. For this reason, not everyone is affected by the leader in the same way; as a result, a charismatic leader often has a group of strongly devoted followers and a number of strong opponents. This was the case with Martin Luther King, Jr., who had both close followers and vocal antagonists among blacks.

The Zeitgeist theory:
A situational approach to leadership

Psychologists found the trait approach to leadership unsatisfactory because it cannot, by itself, predict who will become a leader or explain why an individual becomes a leader. The emphasis in the study of leadership therefore shifted from traits of individuals to characteristics of particular group situations that might determine who emerges as the leader. This situational or time approach shuns the hypothesis that certain people are born to lead. Situational theorists take the position that the particular time or situation determines who will become the leader:

> At a particular time, a group of people has certain needs and requires the services of an individual to assist it in meeting its needs. Which individual comes to play the role of leader in meeting these needs is essentially determined by chance; that is, a given person happens to be at the critical place at the critical time. (Cooper & McGaugh, 1969, p. 247)

The point has been made that had Hitler espoused his doctrine in the United States rather than in Germany, he would probably have been thrown in jail or committed to a mental institution. In Germany, however, the time and the situation were right for the people to follow the lead of such an individual.

The situation also had a great deal to do with King's rise to leadership. Blacks in the United States had made progress toward achieving a position from which they could wage their fight for freedom and dignity. World War II had been a uniting force. It had also pointed up the inequities that existed: a black man could fight for his country but did not have the freedom to vote, use public restrooms, or sit next to whites on a bus. Coretta King's description of the situation that existed for blacks in 1955 also describes, to a certain extent, the situational theory of leadership:

> There is a spirit and a need and a man at the beginning of every great human advance. Each of these must be right for that particular moment of history, or nothing happens. In Montgomery, what Martin called the "Zeitgeist," or the spirit of the time, was there under the apparent passivity of the Negro people; the hour had struck, and the man was found. Yet what was done there could not have happened without a buildup of forces and an accumulation of suffering. (C. King, 1969, p. 108)

Several situational factors affect leadership, and some that are unsuspected can be highly influential. For example, Howells and Becker (1962) suggested that *seating arrangement* would influence leadership. They suggested that communication would naturally tend to flow across a table. They used five-man groups in which two individuals sat across the table from three. They hypothesized that if communication is important in determining the leader and if communication flows across the table, then people seated on the two-person side of the table would tend to be seen as leaders, since they would be communicating to three other persons. The groups were instructed to work on a number of simple tasks, and the group members were then asked to identify the leader of their group. The results indicated that persons seated on the two-person side

Leadership may also be a function of the match between situational requirements and personality characteristics. Such a match may account for the rise and influence of Lech Walesa and the Solidarity movement in Poland.

of the table were chosen as leaders more than twice as often as persons seated on the three-man side. It has also been found that leaders naturally chose seats at the head of rectangular tables rather than seats along the sides (Lécuyer, 1976).

Seniority is also an important factor in determining who will emerge as leader. Insko and his colleagues (1980) studied experimental groups over a period of time. During the experiment, subjects were removed, one by one, from a group and replaced with new members. The results indicated that groups at the hub of communication had the greatest influence and, within groups, members with the most seniority were accorded leadership roles. While the seniority-leadership norm emerged in all groups, this norm was particularly strong in powerful groups. As you can imagine, having this type of norm allows for orderly change in leadership and reduces the chances of intragroup conflict.

The situation facing the group will also affect leadership. Numerous investigators (Hamblin, 1958; Worchel, Andreoli & Folger, 1977) have found that groups facing threat or competition are more likely to accept an authoritative leader than groups not facing such difficulties. Crisis seems to cause people to rally around their leader. In an interesting series of studies on Dutch subjects, Rabbie and Bekkers (1976) found that leaders who were threatened with losing their positions of leadership tried to engage their groups in competitive and threatening situations. Apparently they felt that they would be less likely to lose their positions if they caused the groups to perceive an external threat than if no such threat existed.

charisma A personal attribute of certain leaders that tends to draw others' support and admiration.

Further, the situational theorists of leadership state that the particular *needs of the group* determine who will emerge as leader. Why did Martin Luther King's "I have a dream" speech have such a tremendous impact on the Black Freedom movement? Situational theorists would say that the speech fitted the needs of the black people at the time; it was a message of hope, not of anger or despair. It expressed the hope for freedom and equality, and that is what the movement was fighting for. The speech also met the need of King's followers for encouragement, and suggested that their goals were attainable.

According to the situational theories, the needs of the group often change, and when this happens the leader of the group will also change. Barnlund (1962) found that when the requirements of the task changed, leadership tended to shift to an individual with more appropriate qualifications. Identification of the leader at a particular time depends on the task on which the group is working. Thus the situational theory argues that there are no general leadership traits and that the traits that make an individual a leader in one situation may not qualify him or her to lead in another situation.

Finally, several psychologists (such as Bem & Funder, 1978; Bem & Lord, 1979) have suggested that a leader's personal characteristics must match the demands of the situation. Studies of presidential leadership in the United States have also shown that the match between the situation and a candidate's personality can have a considerable impact on the candidate's chances of being elected. Barber (1977) argued that at different times the American electorate wants action, reassurance, and high moral purpose from their leader, and that a candidate's election depends partly on his or her ability to project one of those qualities. Winter (1987) found that when the primary motive of a presidential candidate—such as power, achievement, or affiliation—matches the primary motive of the electorate, he tends to get a high percentage of the popular vote, have a large margin of victory, and be reelected.

Interactionist theories

While both the trait and situational theories give us some answers about the emergence of leaders, both are incomplete. Clearly Martin Luther King

had traits that helped him rise to power. However, other people also possessed many of these traits, and they did not become leaders of the movement. On the other hand, it is hard to accept an explanation that does not take into account King as a unique person; King did not become leader simply because he happened to be in the right place at the right time.

Some theorists (Katz & Kahn, 1978; Hollander, 1978) have suggested that the emergence of a leader is the result of characteristics of the leader, the followers, and the situation. Certain traits may make an individual the center of attention. However, if his or her abilities do not satisfy the needs of the members, leadership will not result. The situation influences the needs of the followers and the need of the group for a leader. Thus the leader is influenced by the followers, and the followers are influenced by the leader (see Figure 12-1). As the situation and needs of the followers change, the person who is accepted as leader will change. But the leader must possess certain abilities before he or she will be elevated to a position of leadership. As we will see, the interactionist approach has also been used to predict who will be an effective leader.

The Effective Leader

Having examined research on the emergence of a leader in a group, we can consider the kind of leader who is likely to be effective and the factors that influence that effectiveness. The question of leader effectiveness is distinct from the question of leader emergence, although the two questions are related.

Democratic versus autocratic styles of leadership

One early study on leadership asked: What type of leader will be most effective? Lewin, Lippitt, and White (1939) closely observed four comparable groups of 10-year-old boys under autocratic, democratic, and laissez-faire adult leaders. The leaders were trained to respond in one of these styles and were rotated every six weeks so that each group had each type of leader. The autocratic leader determined the policy of the group, dictated all the steps and techniques for attaining the group goals, assigned tasks and task

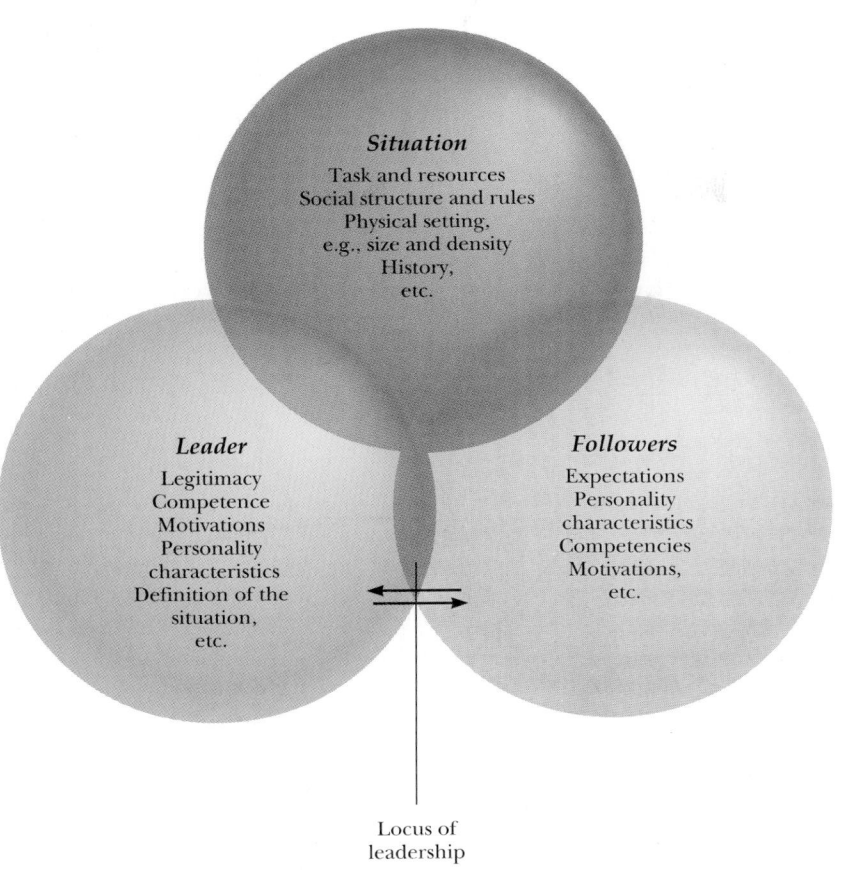

FIGURE 12-1   The elements of leadership

NOTE: The crosshatched area, representing the intersection of three elements of leadership—
the situation, the leader, and the followers—is the locus of leadership. The arrows indicate
the social exchange that occurs there between the leader and the followers.
SOURCE: Hollander (1978).

partners, and remained aloof from the group. The democratic leader allowed the group to determine policy, offered suggestions about procedures and tasks, allowed members to choose their own tasks and task partners, was objective in his praise and criticism, and participated in the group tasks. The laissez-faire leader allowed his group complete freedom and did not participate in the group tasks. The group engaged in such hobbies as making masks and building objects.

The results showed that under the authoritarian leader, the boys were 30 times as hostile and eight times as aggressive as they were under the democratic leader. Subjects under the authoritarian leader tended to pick out scape-goats as the targets of their aggression (two such scapegoats actually left the groups). This behavior did not occur under the democratic leader. Group unity was higher under the democratic leader than under the authoritarian leader. Although the constructiveness of work sharply decreased when the authoritarian leader temporarily left the room, it remained constant in the democratic group. Experimentally induced frustrations were very disruptive to the authoritarian-led group, but the democratic-led group tended to meet these difficulties with organized attacks.

Interesting sequential events occurred when the groups changed leaders. Figure 12-2 shows the effect of leader change in two groups. The

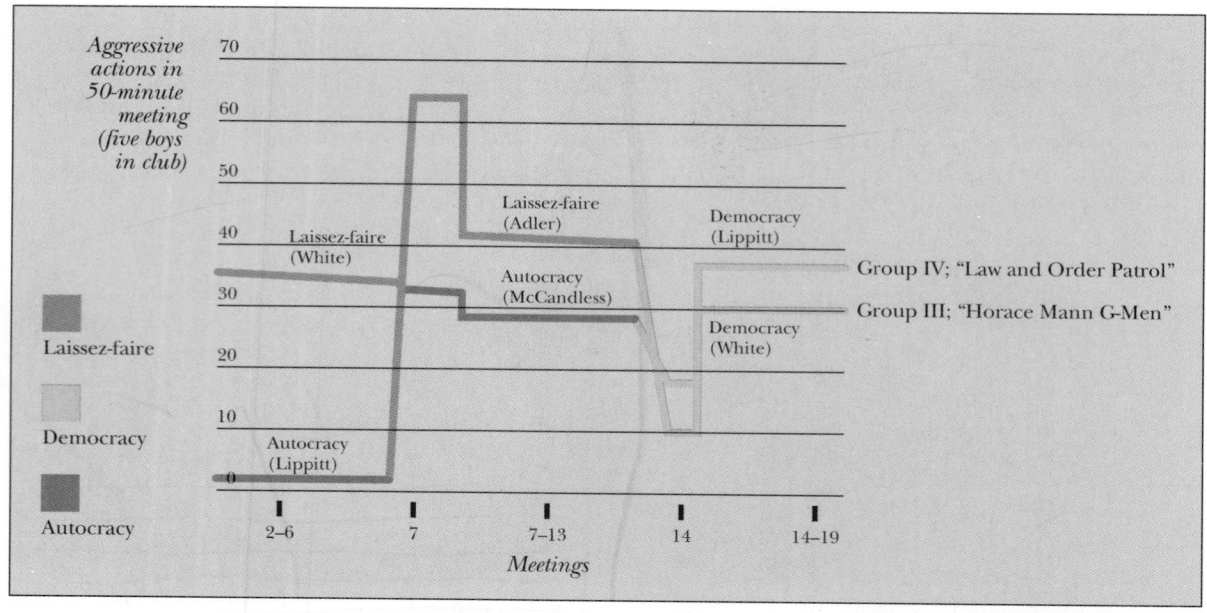

FIGURE 12-2   The effect of different leadership styles on aggressiveness in a group
NOTE: Aggressiveness greatly increases in the group when an autocratic leader is replaced by a laissez-faire leader.
SOURCE: Lewin, et al. (1939).

most noticeable effect is the sharp increase in aggression when the group shifted from an autocratic leader to a laissez-faire leader. This may be the result of repressed aggression under autocratic supervision. The boys may have become angry under the autocratic leader, but they feared the leader and were afraid to disrupt the group by expressing their anger. The laissez-faire leader gave the group a freer atmosphere, which allowed the release of pent-up aggression. It is interesting to note that this type of effect often occurs after the overthrow of an autocratic ruler. In the history of nations, we have often seen a people, liberated after years of autocratic reign, release pent-up hostility and frustration in a bloodbath, such as the one that followed Louis XV's demise in France.

Turning from the psychological atmosphere of the group to the question of productivity, Lewin and his colleagues found that the boys worked longer and turned out more products under the autocratic leader than under the democratic leader. They did, however, tend to turn out products of somewhat better quality under the democratic leader.

Again, however, we find that the effectiveness of the leader is influenced by the situation. Research (Rosenbaum & Rosenbaum, 1971) has found that groups are more productive with an autocratic leader under stressful conditions. But when conditions are nonstressful, groups are more productive with a democratic leader. Thus the most effective style is partly a function of the situation.

The contingency theory of leadership effectiveness
It is clear from the early work that leadership effectiveness is not simply a function of the leader's style. As the interactionist theories imply, the demands of the situation and the interaction between leaders and followers need to be considered as well. For example, to understand Martin Luther King's influence in both the civil rights movement and the peace movement in the 1960s we need to consider his style, the situation facing blacks and peace activists at the time, and the relationship between King and his followers. His effectiveness can be understood in the light of all these factors. A significant step forward in

understanding leadership effectiveness was made by Fiedler (1964, 1978), who developed a theory of leadership effectiveness that considers both personal and situational factors. Fiedler's **contingency model** has been important in combining insights of the trait and situational approaches and in paving the way for other contingency models (Hollander, 1985).

Fiedler identifies two different leadership styles. One is the task-oriented leader who is concerned primarily with getting the job done. The other is the relationship-oriented leader who is more concerned with feelings and relationships in the group. These two styles are similar to Bales and Slater's (1955) task and maintenance specialists. They also remind us of the two broad categories of leadership behavior, initiating structure (getting the task done) and showing consideration (thinking about relationships). The key idea in Fiedler's contingency model is that whether the task-oriented or the relationship-oriented leadership style is most effective will depend on the situation the leader faces.

Situations can be classified according to how favorable they are for the leader. Favorability of the situation depends on three factors. The first is the quality of *leader-group relations*. The situation is favorable to the leader if these relations are good, if he or she is trusted, admired, and respected. The second factor is the *task structure*. Here the situation is favorable to the leader if the task is clear and everyone knows who needs to do what. The third factor is the *leader's position power*. If the leader has a position with a great deal of power (for example, a head of state with no legislature), the situation is more favorable to that leader.

Fiedler hypothesized that the task-oriented leader would be most effective under conditions that were either highly favorable or highly unfavorable to the leader. In the first condition, in which leader-group relations are good, the task is clear, and the leader's position is powerful, it is easy for the leader to be directive and task-oriented without worrying too much about feelings, for everything is going well and people's feelings do not require much attention. In the second condition, in which the situation is chaotic, unpleasant, and ambiguous, a take-charge, task-oriented style will also be more effective; here

the relationship-oriented leader is likely to be swamped by the chaos. On the other hand, when favorability to the leader is in the middle ranges, when people need to be shown consideration, when there is some tension and relations between group members need to be coordinated and clarified, a relationship-oriented leader will do better than a task-oriented leader who tends to overlook interpersonal relations.

Fiedler's theory is a complex and ambitious one. It has been tested in numerous laboratory and field studies with a wide variety of groups, such as Belgian naval officers, postmasters, basketball players, store managers, workers on open-hearth furnaces, B-29 bomber crews, and research chemists. In general, the relationship-oriented leaders were most effective in the moderately favorable situations, whereas the task-oriented leaders were most effective in either very poor or highly favorable situations (Fiedler, 1978; Chemers & Skrzypek, 1972; Hardy, 1976).

The contingency model of leadership effectiveness has generated a great deal of research and, as you might imagine with so complex a theory, a great deal of controversy (Fiedler, 1977; Schreisheim and Kerr, 1977a, 1977b). Reviews of studies of this model suggest that while it has been supported in many ways, a complete understanding of leadership effectiveness will require consideration of factors beyond leadership style and the favorability of the situation to the leader (Rice & Kastenbaum, 1983; Peters, Hartke, & Pohlmann, 1985).

In addition to generating a large body of research and focusing attention on the interaction of personal and situational variables, the contingency theory has had practical impact in the leadership area. The usual approach to finding leaders for businesses and organizations was to rely on personality tests to identify the individual with general potential for leadership. If an individual happened to be in a position of leadership, attempts would be made to train him or her to be a better leader. Millions of dollars were spent on sending people to leadership conferences and training sessions. Essentially, the idea

---

contingency model The theory that the effectiveness of the task-oriented and relationship-oriented leadership styles depends on the situation the leader faces.

1. In what ways do coercive and reward power differ from legitimate, expert, and referent power?

2. How do men and women differ in their use of power?

3. How do task leaders and socioemotional leaders differ in their concerns, their behaviors, and the types of power they use?

4. What are the physical and personality traits that are associated with leadership?

5. What kinds of leaders are most effective? How does leadership effectiveness vary with the situation the leader faces?

was to reshape the person to fit the situation. According to Fiedler, this approach will not succeed. He believes that it is extremely difficult to change a person's leadership style. We should instead change a person's rank, job, or power to fit his or her personality or leadership style (Fiedler, 1964); that is, we should make the environment fit the person instead of trying to make the person fit the environment. Along these lines, Fiedler, Chemers, and Mahar (1976) have developed the LEADERMATCH program, which is aimed at helping leaders to identify and create situations that are most suited to their style of leadership. Here again, the position is that it is easier to change the situation than a person's style of leadership. The LEADERMATCH program has proved successful in preliminary studies (Fiedler, 1978). Like the theory, however, the program has aroused controversy (Kabanoff, 1981; Shiflett, 1981).

Obedience

Martin Luther King commanded through inspiration, rhetoric, energy, and even love. He was not an authoritarian leader who could direct interpersonal behavior by exercising coercive or reward power. By contrast, if we consider the power of an authority figure to command **obedience,** we find chilling examples of the extent to which people will do what their leaders or authorities direct. Perhaps the most vivid example of people's willingness to follow those with authority is seen in the atrocities committed against the Jews by the Nazis during World War II; 6 million men, women, and children were tortured and executed. At the Nuremberg war trials, the Germans who served as executioners in the concentration camps maintained that they were not responsible for the deaths because they were merely following orders. This seemed a poor excuse indeed for their actions, and the executioners who were tried were themselves executed or imprisoned. The general feeling was that no human being could intentionally torture or kill another human being simply because he or she was following orders; anyone with feelings would certainly have resisted or disobeyed such orders.

Although the most common examples of blind faith in following orders occur in emergency or wartime situations, there is nowhere a more striking and, we think, more terrifying example of how blindly people follow orders than in the demonstrations of Stanley Milgram (1963, 1965). Imagine yourself in the following situation:

You arrive at an experimental room, sit down, and begin talking to another subject who has signed up for the same experiment. The experimenter enters and tells you both that the experiment concerns the effects of punishment on learning. You draw straws to see which of you will be the "learner" and which the "teacher," and you draw the teacher straw. The experimenter tells you both that the teacher will ask the learner questions and that the learner will be shocked each time he answers incorrectly. The learner is led away and is supposedly hooked up to a shock apparatus in a small enclosed booth.

You are shown the "teaching machine," which supposedly generates shock. You see a lever and a row of numbers starting at 15 volts and running to 450 volts, with each 15-volt interval labeled. The lower range of numbers is marked "Slight Shock," and the upper end is labeled "Danger: Severe Shock"; 450 volts is marked "XXX." The experimenter tells you that you are

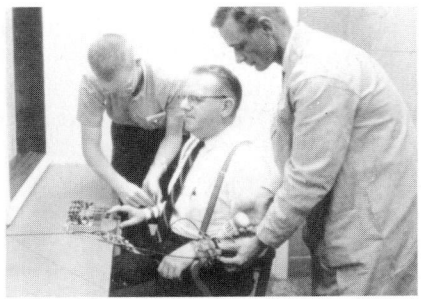

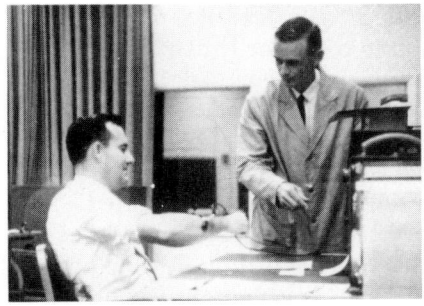

The shock generator in the Milgram experiment, shown in the upper left, was constructed to appear credible and threatening. The learner (upper right) was strapped into the chair and electrodes were attached to his wrists. The "teacher," who was the real subject, was given a sample shock at the beginning of the experiment (lower left). In this case the subject (lower right) refused to continue and left the experiment.

to read a prepared list of questions to the learner, and that if he answers a question incorrectly, you are to shock him. You are to increase the shock by one level after each incorrect answer so that the first shock will be 15 volts, the next 30 volts, and so on.

You begin reading the questions. The learner misses one, then another, and another. After each incorrect answer you increase the voltage by 15 volts, shock the learner, and read the next question. At 90 volts, the learner cries out in pain. At 150 volts, he screams and asks to be let out of the experiment. You look to the experimenter, and he simply says: "Proceed with the next question." At 180 volts, the learner cries out that he can no longer stand the pain and bangs on the wall of the booth. You look at the experimenter and ask to stop the experiment. However, the experimenter calmly tells you: "You have no other choice; you must go on." At 300 volts, the learner refuses to answer any more questions and begs to be let out of the experiment. The experimenter tells

you to continue. From this point on, however, there is no further response from the learner.

What would you do in this situation? Would you continue to administer shock to the 450-volt maximum? What percentage of the people in this experiment do you think would continue to the maximum shock? These were the questions that Milgram wanted to answer. He described the situation to 14 Yale University seniors in psychology and to a group of psychiatrists, and asked them to predict what percentage of subjects would continue to the 450-volt level. They predicted that less than 2 percent of the subjects would "go all the way."

Milgram ran the actual study at Yale University. His subjects were 20 to 50 years old; 40% of them had unskilled jobs, 40% had white-collar sales jobs, and 20% were professionals. He found that 26 of 40 subjects, or 65%, continued to shock

obedience Conformity to direct orders from a person of high status and authority.

until they reached the 450-volt level! Almost two-thirds of the subjects followed orders to directly inflict intense pain on an innocent victim. In actuality, the "victim" was an experimental accomplice who had been trained to make mistakes on the questions and really did not receive any shock. However, the subjects genuinely believed that he was in pain.

The amount of obedience displayed in his studies surprised even Milgram. This was not wartime Nazi Germany; it was New Haven, Connecticut, in 1960. The subjects were not people who had been trained to injure and kill; they were everyday business people. Some critics (Baumrind, 1964; Orne, 1962; Orne & Holland, 1968) argued that the high obedience rate was obtained because the experiment was run at Yale University and because the subjects believed that the experimenter would not let anything bad happen to the victim. Therefore, Milgram moved the experiment to a run-down office building in Bridgeport, Connecticut. The subjects were told nothing of an affiliation with Yale, and the experimenter did not wear a white laboratory coat, as he did in the first study. Although obedience dropped somewhat, the drop was not significant; 48% of the subjects administered maximum shock.

Milgram felt that he had dramatically demonstrated obedience, and he ran a series of additional experiments to determine what variables would affect obedience. In one study, he varied the closeness of the authority figure. Three conditions were run. In one condition, the experimenter sat a few feet away from the subject as the subject was punishing the learner. In a second condition, the experimenter gave his instructions and left the room while the subject shocked. And in the third condition, the subject received his instructions on a tape recorder and never saw the experimenter. Obedience dropped sharply when the authority figure was removed. The number of subjects who obeyed when the experimenter was present was three times as large as the number who obeyed when he was absent. In a follow-up study, Rada and Rogers (1973) found a high degree of obedience if the experimenter gave the orders in person and then left the room.

In another study, Milgram varied the closeness of the learner. In the remote-feedback condition, the learner was placed in an isolation booth and the teacher could neither see nor hear him, except for an occasional pounding on the booth's walls. In a second condition (voice feedback), the teacher could hear the learner but could not see him. In the proximity condition, the learner was in the same room with the teacher so that he would be seen *and* heard. Finally, Milgram introduced a touch-proximity condition in which the learner was seated right next to the teacher and the teacher had to force the learner's hand onto the shock plate when he delivered the shock. Figure 12-3 shows the results of this experiment: the closer the learner, the lower the obedience level.

Although these studies demonstrated a startling degree of obedience, Milgram reported that his subjects suffered even though they obeyed. Many of the subjects became tense; some broke into fits of nervous laughter; and some sweated profusely and begged the experimenter to stop the study.

Although Milgram's experiments are the most often cited studies of obedience, researchers have also found high degrees of obedience in other situations. For example, Hofling and his colleagues (1966) ordered nurses in a hospital to administer unusual doses of drugs to patients. The nurses were telephoned by a doctor who was unfamiliar to them. The doctor ordered the nurses to administer to a patient a drug that was not in common use in the hospital. The doctor also told the nurses to administer the drug in double the amount of the maximum dose stated on the drug box. Of the 22 nurses, 21 followed the doctor's order even though it was in violation of hospital policy and could have had very harmful effects on the patient. Orne and Evans (1965) found that subjects would follow an experimenter's orders to carry out such dangerous tasks as grasping a venomous snake, taking a coin from a jar containing acid, and throwing acid onto another person.

The Milgram studies and similar studies raise a number of questions about obedience. One key question is: Why do subjects obey? Orne (1962) suggested that one reason for the high degree of

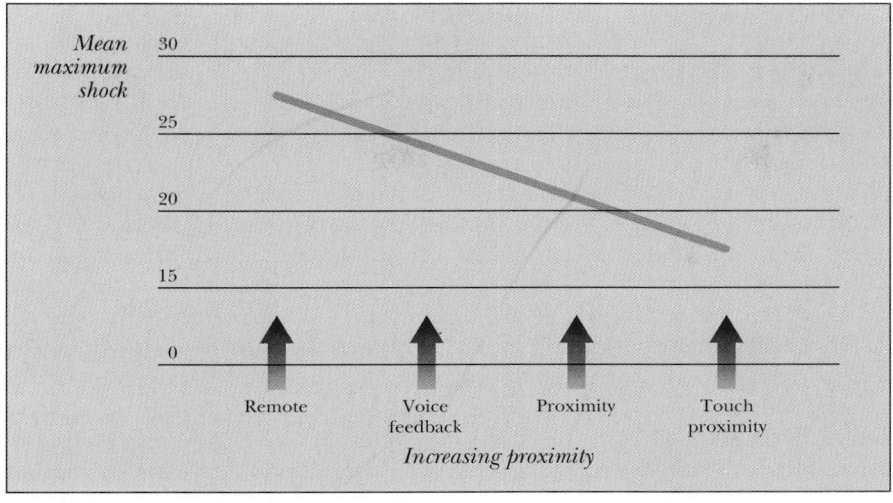

FIGURE 12-3   The effect of the proximity of the "victim" on the average shock delivered
NOTE: The more feedback the subject received from the victim, the less shock he administered to him.
SOURCE: Milgram (1965).

obedience was the experimental procedure itself. The subjects were placed in a situation that was totally unfamiliar to them; they had had little experience with electric shock; and they had no power in the study. Further, they were faced with an experimenter who seemed very familiar with the procedure and showed no signs of concern when the victim was shocked. The experimenter's behavior may have convinced the subjects that there was little need for concern. A second reason for the high degree of obedience may have been that the subjects did not feel responsible for their behavior (Milgram, 1974). The experimenter explicitly told them that the experimenter was the person responsible. A number of studies have shown that when subjects are made to feel responsible for their behavior in the Milgram paradigm, obedience drops sharply (e.g., Tilker, 1970). Further, Milgram (1965) found that obedience decreased when the subjects saw others disobey. It is possible that seeing others disobey caused subjects to feel that if they continued to shock the victim, they would be responsible for their actions.

Ethical questions are also raised by the Milgram studies. Milgram ran his studies in the early

1960s and spent many years responding to criticisms concerning the ethics of his research (see Chapter 1). A number of ethical questions can be leveled at his obedience studies. First, the studies put the unsuspecting subjects through a great deal of psychological pain—they were forced to behave in a way that made them extremely uncomfortable. Second, the subjects learned something about themselves that they may have had no desire to know—that they could be made to follow orders that might lead to the injury, and possibly even the death, of innocent individuals. This is certainly a painful thing to learn about oneself. Critics also chastised Milgram for not stopping the research when he observed the extreme discomfort that the subjects experienced. Milgram was surprised by the degree of criticism he received. He argued: "I'm convinced that much of the criticism, whether people know it or not, stems from the results of the experiment. If everyone had broken off at slight shock or moderate shock, this would be a very reassuring finding and who would protest?" (Milgram, 1977, p. 98). Milgram sent the subjects a follow-up questionnaire. One question asked them how glad they were to have participated. Almost 84%

of the subjects reported that they were glad they had participated.

The question of ethics is a difficult one, especially in regard to the Milgram studies. On the one hand, the results of the studies were valuable, as the studies dramatically demonstrated that an individual would typically obey orders to hurt another individual. The impact of the results would have been lessened had Milgram used a more mundane task, such as asking subjects to write random numbers on paper. On the other hand, the subjects in the study clearly suffered psychological pain and were forced to learn a disturbing fact about themselves (that they would follow orders to hurt another individual). This is a difficult dilemma to resolve, but it should be pointed out that today it would be very difficult to get a departmental ethics committee to approve a study embodying Milgram's methodology.

Conformity

While a great deal of influence is exerted by one person on another, influence is also exerted in groups, and it frequently results in conformity to the group's norms. Often the influence of a group is not so direct as that found in the orders of authority figures. Nonetheless, the influence is often as strong or stronger. Consider the situation that faced many blacks in the Montgomery bus boycott. Many of these people had no other means of transportation, and they had to get to their jobs. Not riding the bus meant a great deal of hardship and possibly the loss of jobs. While these people may have admired King and the other leaders of the civil rights movement, this was not the only influence on their behavior. Many people stated that they joined the boycott because of their friends and neighbors; they were concerned about how their friends and other blacks would react if they rode the bus. Although they were not specifically threatened in most cases, their concern still existed. In this case the group, even a silent group, influenced their behavior.

Conformity is a change in behavior or belief in regard to a group's standards as a result of the group's power. In some cases, conformity results from conflict between the way the individual thinks or acts and the way the group pressures him or her to think or act (Moscovici, 1985). For example, conformity may result when a group pressures a teenage girl into having sex before she feels ready for it. In other cases, conformity results from imagined group pressure (Kiesler & Kiesler, 1969). That is, the teenage girl thinking about whether to have sex may imagine that others want her to conform when that is not really true. In still other cases, conformity results when the individual is uncertain about what is correct or appropriate and adopts the group's standards, believing that they are a reliable guide. In this instance, the teenage girl may not know whether it is good for her to have sex but she goes ahead because the group's standards suggest that doing so is the correct and satisfying way to behave.

The kind of group power that produces conformity varies considerably from case to case. For example, the group may use coercive or reward power to pressure someone into a certain action. In this case, the conformity would be an instance of compliance as we defined it at the beginning of the chapter. Compliance may lead to internalization through cognitive dissonance or self-perception (see Chapter 6), but it is compliance at the outset. In other instances, particularly when the person is uncertain about what is correct, the group's referent or expert power may produce conformity. Referent power is likely to produce identification while expert power may produce internalization.

Why Conform?

Some early theories (Crutchfield, 1955) suggested that certain personality traits made individuals prone to conformity. This approach is of limited value, however, because few people conform all the time, and everyone conforms sometimes. Therefore, we cannot develop a satisfying explanation simply by focusing on individual traits.

For this reason, most investigators began to examine groups to determine how they influenced their members. This research identified the various kinds of influence that groups have. One kind is **informational social influence.** We

Rosa Parks's refusal to give up her seat on a segregated bus in 1955 was a courageous act of nonconformity. It ignited the Alabama bus boycott. The boycott itself was then sustained in part by pressures to conform.

often rely on groups for information about the answer to a question, what to believe, or how to behave (Asch, 1952; Deutsch & Gerard, 1955; Kelley, 1952). This is especially true if we doubt our own judgment (Campbell, Tesser & Fairey, 1986). You might accept an answer supplied by one person, but you are more likely to accept an answer if many people supply it. In other words, a group can influence an individual by supplying that person with information that affects his or her beliefs, attitudes, or behaviors (Festinger, 1950).

While information is power, we also know that groups influence people's behavior even when people are not looking for information. A teenager may know that smoking is bad for his health and he may hate the taste of cigarettes, yet he is quick to light up when he sees his friends smoking. Where does this type of group power come from? Anyone who has been in a group and has wanted to remain part of that group knows the anxiety that is aroused by the thought that he or she may be rejected by the group. This is not an unfounded fear; such rejection is painful. Further, anyone who has been part of a group knows that groups often reject members who act differently from the other group members, who fail to follow the rules of the group, or who consistently hold and express beliefs that are different from those expressed by the group. The group may remove the nonconformist's power by denying him or her the right to vote; it may inflict physical or psychological abuse by beatings or calling out unflattering names; it may see that the nonconformist does not share in any of the rewards that the group obtains.

The individual, believing that deviance from the group may lead to rejection, feels pressure to conform to the group model. This pressure,

conformity A yielding to real or imagined group pressure.

informational social influence Influence based on a group's capacity to supply information.

which is referred to as normative pressure, produces **normative social influence.** We conform because of the group's capacity to reward and punish us. In particular, the group acquires its capacity to exert normative pressure from the individual's fear of the group's response to deviation from its expectations. It should be pointed out that the group may never make it explicit that deviants will receive negative sanctions, and the individual may or may not have seen the group carry out such sanctions. In reality, sanctions for deviation may not even exist. However, the group's normative power results from the fact that the individual believes that deviants will be rejected.

It is interesting to examine how these two types of group pressure lead to different types of conforming behavior. The consensus among psychologists (see Allen, 1965) is that normative pressure is likely to result in public compliance without accompanying private acceptance. An individual who reacts to normative pressure is reacting out of fear or anxiety and will often conform overtly without doing so covertly.

This phenomenon was seen among the prisoners of war during the Korean and Vietnamese wars who openly expressed anti-American views while in the hands of their captors, but held to their private pro-American beliefs and chose to return to the United States when the opportunity was presented to them. They were responding to normative pressures from their captors, but no private acceptance accompanied their public compliance.

On the other hand, an individual who conforms to informational pressures is more likely to evidence private acceptance. This compliance to the group norm is based not on fear but on the desire to do the correct thing. Because the group is used to decide the correct course of action or belief, public compliance is often accompanied by private acceptance. Despite these differences, investigators (Shaw, 1981) point out that in most cases, groups influence individuals by using both types of pressure.

Classic Studies of Conformity

It is interesting to find that one of the earliest studies of conformity was not really aimed at studying conformity at all. Rather, Sherif (1935)

wanted to examine how groups develop norms (see Chapter 13). Using a phenomenon known as the *autokinetic effect,* he demonstrated that groups will establish norms that individuals in the groups will follow. He showed individual subjects a single pinpoint of light in a dark room and asked them to judge how far the light moved. In fact, the light was stationary, but to an individual focusing on a small spot of light in a dark room, the light appears to move. The amount of movement seen varies from one person to another, but it is relatively constant for each individual.

After the individual reported his estimation of the light movement, he was brought together with one or two other naive subjects. The subjects were then asked to continue estimating the light movement and to announce their estimates so that the other group members could hear. Interestingly enough, the estimates of the group members converged so that after a time each person reported that he saw about the same amount of movement as the other group members (see Figure 12-4). Sherif also found that when the individual was later asked to estimate the movement of the light when he was alone, his estimates were very similar to those that he had given by the end of the group estimates.

The Asch Paradigm

Although Sherif's study was not aimed at demonstrating conformity, many people interpreted the results as showing that humans are a conforming breed. Solomon Asch did not believe this. He felt that one reason why subjects conformed in Sherif's study was that the stimulus they were judging was so ambiguous. Asch (1951) devised a unique method for studying conformity. Imagine that you are a subject who has volunteered for an experiment. You enter the experimental room at the appointed time, and you see that six other subjects are already there. You take an empty seat at the table around which everyone is seated. The experimenter enters and tells the subjects that the experiment is concerned with accuracy and visual perception. He shows the group two cards (Figure 12-5). On one card is a single line, and on the other card are three lines labeled A, B, and C. The lone line is actually 10 inches long. Line A is 8¾ inches long,

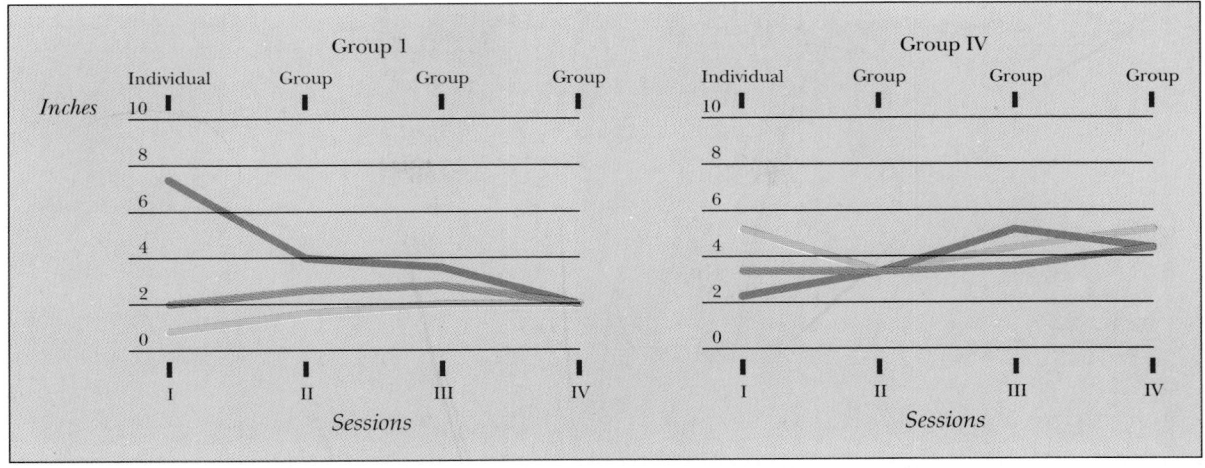

FIGURE 12-4 The convergence of judgments of autokinetic movement in two groups
In session I the subjects judged alone. In sessions II and III they heard the judgments of other group members. In session IV they judged alone. The results show that the subjects' judgments conformed to the group norm and that this conformity continued even when the subjects were alone again in the last session.
SOURCE: Sherif and Sherif (1969).

line B is 10 inches long, and line C is 8 inches long. The experimenter tells the subjects that their task is to match the lone line with the line of equal length from the three-line card. You are to respond next to last.

The experimenter asks each subject in turn to call out the letter of the matching line. The first subject calls out B. This is the line that you also feel is correct. The next four subjects also call out B. When it's your turn, you call out B. The next trial goes the same as the first. The experimenter shows a 2-inch standard line, and everyone before you matches it to another 2-inch line. You do the same, and you wait for the next trial.

On the next trial, the experimenter shows a 3-inch standard line, and the three lines A = 3¾ inches, B = 4¼ inches, and C = 3 inches. You see that line C is the correct answer, and you wait for the first subject to report line C. You may also be thinking that this is really a simple-minded experiment. Suddenly, your whole world begins to collapse! The first subject reports line A. You wonder what's wrong with him; line C is obviously the correct answer. You might even laugh at the obviously incorrect response. You wait for subject two to report line C. Subject two looks the line over carefully and calls out, "Line A is cor-

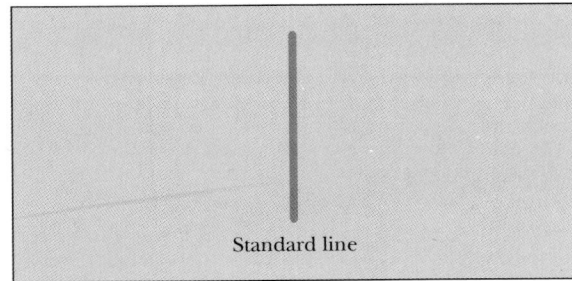

Standard line

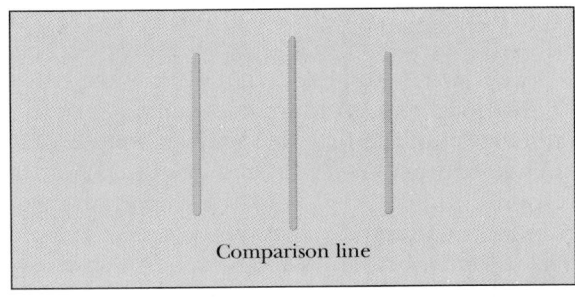

Comparison line

FIGURE 12-5 Stimulus material used by Asch in early conformity research
SOURCE: Adapted from Asch (1955).

normative social influence Influence based on a group's capacity to reward and punish, including the capacity to accept or reject the individual.

Solomon Asch used a group of confederates in a "line judgment" experiment to study conformity to group opinion. In the photo, only subject number six, seated second from the right, is a real subject. The first five "subjects" (the experimenter's confederates) have just given an incorrect response and subject number six must decide whether to give the correct response or the conforming one.

rect." You sit back in disbelief, and you listen while the other subjects who precede you confidently report line A. It's your turn now. What do you do?

This was the question that Asch asked when he devised this procedure for studying conformity. Actually, the first five subjects were experimental confederates who had been told how to respond. On 12 of the 18 trials, they were to respond unanimously with an incorrect answer. The second-to-the-last subject—you in this case—was really the only naive subject, and the experimenter was interested in finding out whether he or she would conform to the group's opinion or stick to the correct answer.

Asch set out to show that people do not conform to group opinion when they know that their own behavior is correct and that the behavior of the group is incorrect. He developed the line-judging task because he found that when people were asked to judge the lines alone, without group influence, they performed almost without error. However, Asch found that his subjects conformed to the group's incorrect opinion over a third of the time, even when they knew that the group was wrong. When faced with the group's unanimous incorrect opinion, most of the subjects conformed at least once, and only about one-fourth of the subjects were able to turn in a completely error-free performance.

Ross, Bierbrauer, and Hoffman (1976) enumerated the pressures on the subject in the Asch situation. First, it is probably clear to everyone that the subject must wonder about his own ability to judge lines. The subject must think, "How can everyone but me see it that way? Is there something wrong with me?" There is, however, an additional pressure on the subjects. If they report the situation as they see it (differently from the group response), are they not challenging the "competence, wisdom, and sanity of the other group members"? By deviating from the group opinion after the other members have stated their judgment, the subject will be telling the other members that they don't have the ability to do a task as simple as judging line lengths. This is a tough position to be in. Despite these pressures, the results obtained by Asch surprised a number of psychologists and created a great deal of interest in studying conformity. We discuss the results of these studies as follows.

Factors Affecting Conformity

Conformity often involves conflict between a person's beliefs or inclinations and the group's norms. The way this conflict is resolved varies a great deal from person to person, from time to time, and from situation to situation. The determinants of conformity versus resistance to group pressure are complex. They range from characteristics of the conformity situation itself to the person's concerns about self-presentation.

Difficulty of the judgments

Let us first consider the way the difficulty of the judgment affects conformity. Asch predicted that there would be more conformity on ambiguous or difficult judgments than on easy ones. Asch found far more conformity than he expected on relatively easy judgments, but conformity does drop when the judgments become easier (Blake, Helson & Mouton, 1956). For example, Asch (1952) found that conformity was greater when the differences between the lengths of the comparison lines were small than when they were large. In Figure 12-6, it is very difficult to determine the correct comparison line for judgment (a) but easy for judgment (b). Asch found greater conformity in the hard judgment than in the easy one. From this finding we can infer that people use the group as a source of information when the task is difficult or ambiguous.

Group size

Another important factor is the size of the group exerting pressure to conform. Asch varied the size of the group that the naive subject confronted, using one, two, three, four, eight, and fifteen confederates. He found that conformity

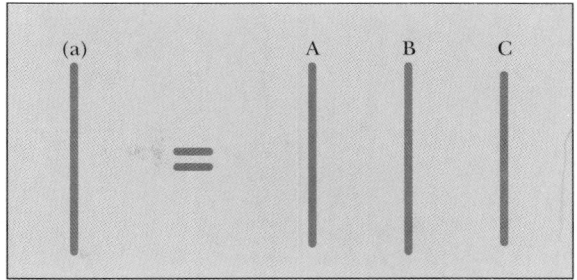

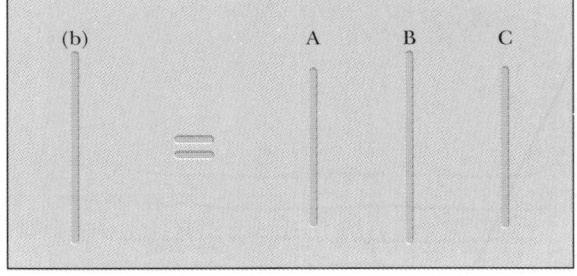

FIGURE 12-6 Examples of difficult (a) and easy (b) line-judging tasks
SOURCE: Asch (1952).

increased with group size until the group consisted of three confederates. Then the amount of conformity leveled off so that there was no more conformity to a group of 15 members than to a group of three (see Figure 12-7). More recent research shows that increasing the majority beyond three does produce more conformity, but the increases are slight (Gerard, Wilhelmy & Conolley, 1968). Three or four people are generally enough to produce very strong conformity effects.

However, other research has shown that the group size under which maximum conformity is achieved is dependent on a number of factors. The type of task may be one factor. For example, Mann (1977) studied queuing behavior (waiting in line). He had groups of two, four, six, and eight people line up at bus stops in Jerusalem, and then observed how many arrivers would conform and get into line. He found that conformity increased as group size increased, with the greatest amount of conformity given to the eight-person group. Thus the relationship between group size and conformity depends on the setting and the task (Shaw, 1981).

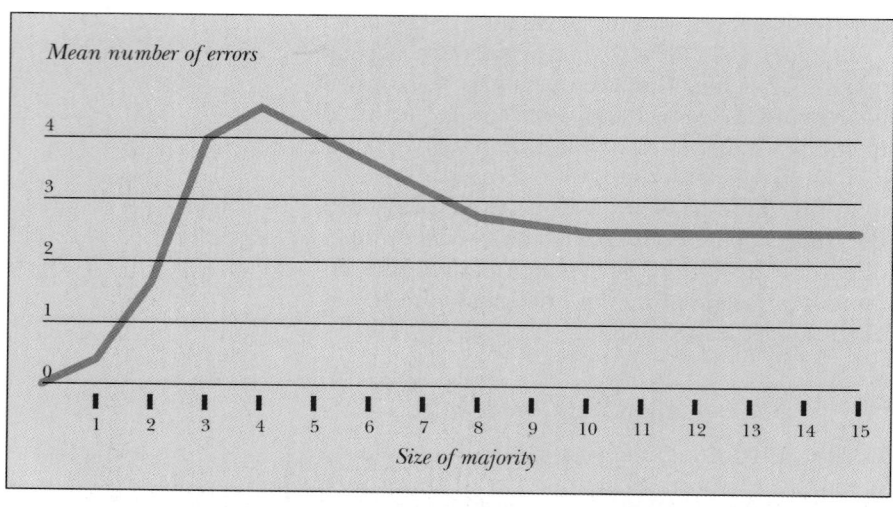

FIGURE 12-7 Errors made by critical subjects to conform with unanimous majorities of various sizes
SOURCE: Asch (1951).

A second issue related to group size is the association among majority members. Wilder (1977) suggests that when people are categorized as belonging to a group, others respond to them as a group rather than as individuals. That is, if three people from the American Red Cross ask you for a donation, you will not respond to the request as if it came from three separate individuals; rather, you will view it as a request coming from "a group from the Red Cross." Wilder argues that as a result of this categorization process, a group may lose some of its ability to influence others. He therefore suggests that instead of counting the number of people in a majority, we should examine the number of subgroups to determine the pressures toward conformity. To illustrate this point, Wilder found more conformity to a majority of four unrelated persons than to a majority of two groups of two persons each (still four people); and more conformity to a majority of six unrelated persons than to two groups of three people. Thus both number and group categorization are important variables influencing conformity.

Recent research also suggests that the two factors we have been looking at separately, difficulty of the judgments and group size, actually interact. It turns out that group size is important when the judgments are easy to make but has relatively little effect when they are hard to make (Campbell & Fairey, 1989). Why should this be? When judgments are easy to make and you know that a group is incorrect, whether you conform or not depends on the amount of normative social influence the group can exert. Informational social influence is not relevant. You already know what's right, because the judgment is clear. But normative social influence is relevant. If the group has a lot of it, you are more likely to conform. Here's where the size of the group is important. The larger it is, the more normative pressure it exerts. Thus the size of the group makes a big difference when people know it is incorrect.

On the other hand, if you are not sure whether the group is correct, you look to them for information, and the amount of conformity they produce is affected relatively little by how many of them there are. When you are uncertain, a small number of other people can influence you, and adding more people doesn't make much difference.

Group unanimity

Asch's (1956) original research also looked at the issue of group unanimity. He studied the effect of having just one person deviate from the unanimous majority and found that deviation by that

The presence of even a single deviant can reduce the amount of conformity within a group. This is one reason people often refuse to permit even minor deviations in expression, dress, or behavior.

one group member reduced the amount of conformity to the group. In one set of conditions, Asch instructed one confederate to give correct judgments on all trials, even when the remainder of the confederates did not. In other conditions, all of the confederates were instructed to agree on their responses. When the group gave a unanimously incorrect answer, conformity occurred about 35% of the time. However, when one deviant gave correct answers, conformity dropped to about one-fourth of that level. Further, it did not seem to matter whether the group size was three or 15—one deviant drastically reduced the amount of conformity. Interestingly enough, conformity by naive subjects decreased even when the deviant gave an incorrect answer.

Why does a single deviant have such a drastic impact on conformity? Allen and Wilder (1980) suggest that a unanimous majority may force the individual to reinterpret the situation; the presence of a deviant, even one, shows the individual that there may be many ways to view the situation and that a reinterpretation is not necessary. While this explanation may apply when there is some doubt about the meaning of events, a broader interpretation focuses on the deviant's effect on normative pressure. If an individual feared group rejection for not conforming, a deviant who was not rejected could alleviate this fear and significantly reduce the amount of normative pressure. The effects of the deviation would quite likely have been very different had the remainder of the group laughed at or threatened the deviant. Then the group's response to the deviant might have actually increased conformity. The group must ensure that the deviant does not "get away with it" lest additional group members decide to act against the desires of the group. One function of brutal public executions is to demonstrate how badly a deviant will be treated by the group. Such penalties cause others to think twice before they try to break away from the group's norms.

Time factors

Time has some interesting effects on conformity. One important consideration is at what point in the development of a group conformity pressure is applied. There is reason to think that it is easier to produce conformity in the early stages of interaction than in later stages. In the early stages the group is attempting to establish norms and individuals are responsive to each other. This is the so-called **norming** stage (Tuckman, 1965). During later periods of group interaction, people are trying to negotiate their position in the group and are less likely to conform. This is the **storming** stage of group development. Consistent with the idea of norming versus storming stages of group development is the finding that conformity can be produced by *either* self-doubt *or* high group pressure in the early stages of interaction. On the other hand, later on *both* self-doubt *and* group pressure are needed to produce conformity (Campbell, Tesser & Fairey, 1986). That is, conformity is easier to come by in the early stages of group interaction.

Another time factor is how long an individual has to think about other people's positions. It may seem surprising, but if people know that the other people they are going to interact with have opinions that differ from their own on an issue, they tend to conform more to those opinions if they are asked to write down their thoughts about the issue before they state their own opinions. When people think about the issue before they say what they think, they try to empathize with the group's opinions, and they open themselves up to those views. If they are simply asked to state their opinions before they are given the chance to think, they simply express their own views and conform less (Tetlock, Skitka & Boettger, 1989). When you interact with people who don't agree with you, you will be more influenced by their views if you think about their position before you simply proclaim your own.

Personal factors

A variety of personal factors affect conformity. One is the individual's concern about his or her position or status in the group, especially when the individual is attracted to the group. Overall, research indicates that people who feel insecure about their position are most likely to conform. For example, Hancock and Sorrentino (1980) found a high degree of conformity in subjects who had received no support from the group in previous meetings and who expected future interaction with the group. The lack of prior support reduced the subjects' self-confidence, and the expectation of future interaction made acceptance as group members an important issue.

Related research has found that conformity is greater when people are attracted to the group (Back, 1951; Brehm & Festinger, 1957) and when the individual has somewhat lower status than other group members (Raven & French, 1958; Stang, 1972).

In these cases, it seems that individuals are responding to normative group pressures and trying to "buy" themselves a secure position in the group by conforming. Hollander (1958), in fact, suggested that people earn *idiosyncrasy credits* when they conform to group expectations. These credits give individuals status in the group and allow them the opportunity to deviate without being rejected by the group. Each time members deviate, they must pay for this action by giving up some of their credits. Therefore, conformity may well help an individual buy a more secure place in the group.

While some research has focused on personal characteristics in isolation, most research has studied how personal and situational variables interact to influence conformity. Let us examine two lines of research that show the value of this approach. The first area is sex differences in conformity. A number of early studies (Gerard, Wilhelmy & Conolley, 1968; Julian, Regula & Hollander, 1968) found that women were more likely to conform than men. These results were often explained by reference to sex roles: men were expected to be independent while women were expected to be "reasonable" and sensitive to others. While this explanation fits many of the earlier results, it does not explain subsequent findings. For example, Sistrunk and McDavid (1971) found that women conformed more than men when the task was one at which men should have been expert. However, when the task involved female-related items, men conformed more than women. Eagly, Wood, and Fishbaugh (1981) found that women conformed more than men when their behavior was being observed, but that there was no sex difference when there was no surveillance. While surveillance did not affect the amount of conformity shown by women, men conformed less under surveillance than under no surveillance conditions. The investigators suggest that surveillance increased concerns with self-presentation: men conformed less than women under these conditions because they were more interested than women in presenting themselves as being independent. Thus sex and sex roles do not necessarily breed conformity; rather, they breed concern with presenting a certain image to others. While there is still some debate about why sex differences in conformity occur (Eagly & Carli, 1981), these studies show that sex alone does not determine conformity; sex interacts with the situation to determine conformity.

Santee and Maslach (1982) also adopt a self-presentation approach to explain conformity. They argue that people vary in the degree to which they want to be seen as distinct and separate from others (this desire can be measured by a number of scales). However, the situation determines when this personality variable will influence conformity. For example, individuals can more readily present themselves as distinct by deviating from a unanimous group as opposed to a nonunanimous group. If other people are already dissenting, an individual who also dissents will not look particularly unusual. Santee and Maslach found, in fact, that desire for distinctiveness had a greater influence on conformity when the group was unanimous than when it was not. Once again, the role of individual characteristics can best be understood in relation to situational variables.

Social Impact Theory

Obedience and conformity are two important consequences of social influence pressures. They can lead to behaviors that few people would have predicted had they not actually been demonstrated in laboratory research. The research on these phenomena helps us to understand a variety of dramatic instances of social influence, including the murder of 6 million Jews under the direction of Adolf Hitler and the mass suicide that took place in Jonestown in 1978 under the direction of the fanatical preacher Jim Jones.

A recent general theory of social influence helps us to understand and relate some of the factors that affect obedience, conformity, and other kinds of social influence. **Social impact theory** (Jackson, 1986, 1987; Latané, 1981) states that the social impact or force felt by a person, or target, is a function of the strength, immediacy, and number of sources of social influence that are present. That is, a person will be more affected when there are stronger sources of influence, when the sources are physically closer or more immediate, and when there are more of them. Social impact works just like physical impact. For example, the amount of light falling on a table is a function of the strength of the lights overhead, their distance from the table, and their number. Let us consider how these basic principles of strength, immediacy, and number might apply to obedience and conformity.

Social impact theory predicts more impact and thus more influence when the source of influence is strong. Thus, in Milgram's procedure, we would predict more obedience when the authority is strong (highly credible, for instance, or distinguished) and more conformity when the group is composed of high-status or physically strong peers. This prediction regarding source strength is supported by research on attitude change showing that more persuasion was produced by credible communicators (Hass, 1981). The theory also predicts more impact and influence when the source is closer. This prediction is directly applicable to Milgram's experiments on obedience, which showed more obedience when the experimenter—one source of social impact—was closer to the subject, but less obedience when the learner—another source of social impact—was closer to the subject (Milgram, 1974).

Third, social impact theory predicts more influence when there are more sources. Consistent with this prediction are the findings showing more conformity with more group members. You may recall that while there was greater conformity when there were more group members, the effect of adding members beyond three or four

---

norming A stage of group development marked by a high degree of conformity, in which members attempt to establish norms.

social impact theory The theory that social influence is a function of the strength, immediacy, and number of sources of influence.

storming A stage of group development marked by a low degree of conformity, in which members negotiate their positions in the group.

The civil rights movement and its leader, Martin Luther King, Jr., capture the spirit of a nation in the march on Washington in 1963. As the number of people in the movement grew, so did its influence.

was relatively small. This finding is consistent with another principle of social impact theory, which says that the mathematical relationship governing all three variables—strength, immediacy, and number—is a power function. This means that initial increases in strength, immediacy, and number have large effects but that additional increases have less and less impact. Not surprisingly, then, adding a few group members at the beginning increases conformity dramatically, but each additional member after that affects conformity relatively little.

It is interesting to think about some of the ways in which Martin Luther King used social impact principles to his advantage. He brought his fight to the heart of segregation (the South) and to Washington, D.C., where the laws were made (immediacy). He worked hard to gather as many people as possible to attend his rallies and marches (number). And, unlike some other black leaders, he invited powerful white political leaders such as President Kennedy to join the movement (strength).

Another principle of social impact theory states that the impact of any source of social influence is diffused as the strength, immediacy, and number of the targets of social influence increase. For example, there should be less impact on a strong target than on a weak one. We just saw that people with less status in a group conform more. As their strength (measured by status) increases, the group's impact is diffused and they conform less. This finding is exactly what social impact theory predicts. The number of targets was explored in one of the variations of Milgram's (1977) research. When two other confederates were posing as real subjects, the experimenter's orders to the actual subject had less impact. These confederates also modeled defiance of the experimenter's orders, so it is unclear if the number of targets *alone* reduces social impact; their behavior also has an effect. However, it is plausible to conclude that their number alone reduces the experimenter's impact (Brown, 1986). The immediacy variable in the case of cotargets of influence suggests that as other people who are also targets of the source are closer to you, the impact of the source will be diffused away from you and onto those cotargets.

While the principles of social impact theory are applicable to obedience and conformity studies, they have also been supported in a number of other contexts. For example, research on stagefright by Jackson and Latané (1981) shows that people singing in front of an audience experience more impact as the size of the audience, which constitutes the source of impact, increases. This study also shows less impact as the number of singers—that is, cotargets—increases. In the last case, the audience's impact is diffused. Research on bystander intervention by Latané and Darley (1970), discussed in Chapter 8, also shows that the impact of a source—for example, a person in distress—is diffused if there are a large number of bystanders.

The research supporting social impact theory is impressive, as is its wide applicability. Similar theories that consider strength, immediacy, and number have also been proposed (Knowles, 1983; Tanford & Penrod, 1984). Their fundamental ideas are compatible with those of social impact theory.

Deviation and Resistance to Social Influence

Our discussion thus far has shown many of the factors that lead people to respond to social influence. Many pressures act on us as targets of social influence, pressures that can be very difficult to resist. Indeed, a person who deviates and refuses to go along with the crowd runs many risks. In one demonstration of such risks, Schachter (1951) set up groups of naive subjects and planted three experimental confederates who acted as subjects in each of the groups. The task of the groups was to discuss how to handle a juvenile delinquent named Johnny Rocco. One of the confederates (the deviant) consistently disagreed with the group's opinion about how to handle Johnny. A second confederate (the slider) began by disagreeing with the majority opinion, but soon switched positions to conform to that of the majority. The final confederate (the mode) agreed with the majority opinion throughout the discussion. Schachter manipulated cohesiveness by making half of the groups believe that they would be working on very attractive tasks (high cohesive) and by making the other half believe

that they would be working on relatively unattractive tasks (low cohesive). After the groups had discussed the Johnny Rocco case, the subjects were asked to rate how much they liked the other members of the group and to nominate group members to serve in various functional positions in the group.

At first the group directed a great deal of its communication and attention to the deviant, apparently in an attempt to persuade him to conform to group opinion. Finally the group members seemed to give up; they stopped talking to him. In essence, they rejected him. When the jobs in the group were divided up, the deviant was consistently given the worst job. Thus he was not only rejected, he was also punished for not conforming to group opinion. Interestingly enough, the rejection of the deviant was greatest in the highly cohesive groups. Schachter also found that the slider, who began by deviating but later switched to a conforming posture, was liked as much as the mode, who consistently agreed with the group. The slider was often assigned popular and attractive jobs, and he received a great deal of the group's attention. Apparently the slider's switch to conformity was interpreted by the group as recognition that he had been wrong and that he was "mature enough" to admit it. Thus consistent deviation from a group is met with rejection whereas conformity is rewarded. It is interesting to note that recent research suggests that the tendency to reject deviants is strongest when the group feels that evaluating an issue is a group goal rather than an individual goal, and when the issue being discussed is a matter of facts rather than values (Earle, 1986). Thus the group that is most likely to reject deviant opinions is one that needs to define reality, not values, for the group as a whole. For example, a labor or management negotiating team trying to predict what the other side will accept in a strike settlement is likely to reject deviant opinion. While this is just the kind of group that may need to hear divergent views, it may be the least likely to tolerate them.

However, despite all the pressures to comply, noncompliance is often as common as, if not more common than, compliance. Every study of conformity found nonconformity by subjects—in fact, nonconformity was more common than conformity in the Asch studies. Many of the great men of history have been nonconformists. Galileo was tortured because he argued that the earth revolved around the sun when the prevailing view was that the earth was the focal point of the universe. Columbus was ridiculed because he believed that the world was round at a time when most people believed that it was flat. Freud was not allowed to publish many of his writings because his theories offended his contemporaries. Why do such men deviate from the majority and risk ridicule and punishment?

Most of the social-psychological work on conformity has studied the conformist, not the deviant or the nonconformist. However, some theories do apply to the question why a person does not conform. One of these is **reactance theory** (Brehm, 1966; West & Wicklund, 1980). As Chapter 6 noted, Brehm hypothesized that an individual whose freedom to perform certain behaviors is threatened or eliminated will experience a motivational arousal that is aimed at regaining the freedom. This motivational arousal is labeled *reactance*. When individuals feel pressure from the group to conform, whether that pressure be normative or informational, they should experience reactance because the pressure threatens their freedom not to conform. Nonconformity should then become a more attractive behavioral option, and individuals should attempt to demonstrate that they are free not to conform. In the reactance view of nonconformity, therefore, pressures from the group to conform cause individuals to experience reactance, and result in their nonconformity.

The desire to be unique is another reason why people resist influence (Maslach, 1974; Snyder & Fromkin, 1980). Most of us believe that we have certain traits or abilities that are different from those possessed by others. Further, in most societies value is placed on being different and standing apart from the crowd. One way of demonstrating uniqueness is by not conforming to the group. Santee and Maslach (1982) found that people who place a high value on uniqueness resist conformity, especially when the rest of the group adopts a unanimous position. Further, being different attracts the attention of others. As we saw in the Schachter (1951) study, early in the group's life the majority of communications were aimed at those people who held deviant atti-

STOP, THINK, & UNDERSTAND

1. How does proximity to the learner affect the degree of obedience in Milgram's study of obedience to authority?

2. Explain the two kinds of social influence that produced conformity in Sherif's studies using the autokinetic effect and in Asch's studies using line judgments.

3. What situational variables affect the amount of conformity?

4. Explain how strength, immediacy, and number affect both the magnitude and the diffusion of social impact.

5. What happens when people deviate from group consensus? Why do people sometimes deviate despite the costs of doing so?

tudes. Thus people may adopt anticonformity as a way of showing their uniqueness and attracting attention.

Summary

Social influence is the exercise of power by a person or group to influence the behavior of others. *Power* is viewed as the potential to influence others. There are many kinds of power, including *coercive, legitimate, expert, referent,* and *informational power.*

A *leader* is the individual who exerts the most influence in a group. Leaders tend to be either task-oriented or relationship-oriented. Often groups have two leaders, each taking a different orientation. One of the earliest theories suggested that leaders have certain traits that make them leaders. This position, however, has received only limited support. The zeitgeist theories argue that the situation determines who will become the group's leader. While some situational factors such as seniority and physical position do influence leadership, this approach has also proved too limited in scope. The most accepted view is that the situation and the personal characteristics of the individual and of the followers interact to determine who will be leader. Research on leadership style shows that while autocratic leaders may have productive groups, members are most happy with a democratic leader. The *contingency model* of leadership suggests that the situation determines what will be the most effective style of leadership.

Obedience is conformity to the direct orders of a person in a position of authority. Milgram's research found that people are surprisingly obedient. One reason is that they feel that the leader will assume responsibility for their behavior.

Conformity is a yielding to the real or imagined pressures of the group. Groups use *infor-*mational and *normative social influence* to get members to conform. Conformity is affected by both situational and personal factors.

Social impact theory states that the impact of a source or sources of influence on a target increases with the strength, immediacy, and number of the sources of influence. Social impact is diffused across targets as the strength, immediacy, and number of the targets of influence increase.

Deviation from group opinion can lead to rejection from the group. Nonconformity may be caused by *reactance* or by a desire to appear unique or to attract attention.

---

reactance theory   The theory that a threat to behavioral freedom arouses a motivation to regain that freedom.

Key Terms

charisma
coercive power
compliance
conformity
contingency model
expert power
halo error
identification
informational power
informational social
    influence

internalization
leader
leadership schema
legitimate power
normative social
    influence
norming
obedience
power

reactance theory
referent power
reward power
social impact theory
social influence
storming
transformational
    leader

Suggested Readings

Cialdini, R. B. (1988). *Influence: Science and practice*. Glenview, Ill.: Scott, Foresman.

Fiedler, F. E., & Chemers, M. M. (1974). *Leadership and effective management*. Glenview, Ill.: Scott, Foresman.

Freeman, J. L., & Doob, A. N. (1968). *Deviancy*. New York: Academic Press.

Hollander, E. P. (1985). Leadership and power. In G. Lindzey and E. Aronson (Eds.), *The handbook of social psychology* (Vol. 2, pp. 485–537). New York: Random House.

Milgram, S. (1977). *The individual in a social world*. Reading, Mass.: Addison-Wesley.

Moscovici, S. (1985). Social influence and conformity. In G. Lindzey and E. Aronson (Eds.), *The handbook of social psychology* (Vol. 2, pp. 347–412). New York: Random House.

Schopler, J., & Layton, B. D. (1972). *Attributions of interpersonal power and influence*. New York: General Learning Corporation.

Tedeschi, J. (Ed.). (1974). *Perspectives on social power*. Chicago: Aldine.

Wheeler, L., Deci, E., Reis, H., & Zuckerman, M. (1978). *Interpersonal influence* (2nd ed.). Boston: Allyn & Bacon.

Chapter Thirteen

The Dynamics of Groups

The museum director smiled at the young man. "That's an interesting theory but it has one major flaw. It would have been impossible for anyone to sail a balsa raft from Peru to the Polynesian islands. Do you realize that the journey is over 4,300 miles?"

Thor Heyerdahl pressed his point. "Look at the similarity between these artifacts found in Peru and on the Polynesian islands. And how do you explain the fact that both the ancient Incas of Peru and the Polynesians have a god named Kon Tiki? The Polynesian islands must have first been settled by peoples from Peru."

"You will never be able to make a strong case by showing similarities in artifacts and gods," responded the director. "These coincidences mean nothing if it is impossible to get from Peru to Polynesia by raft. You have to show that this feat could be done before your theory will be taken seriously."

Thor left this meeting more determined than ever to prove his theory. He would show that it was possible to sail a raft from Peru to Polynesia. He spent weeks in the library studying the type of raft that was used by the Incas during the period between A.D. 500 and 1100. Thor found that they built large rafts out of balsa trees and lashed these logs together with hemp rope. They erected cloth sails and used long rudders to steer the rafts. Could such a raft make a 4,300-mile trip over some of the roughest ocean in the world?

Clearly, Thor could not make the trip by himself. Someone had to man the helm at all times and there were many chores to do on board. With little effort, Thor talked five other men into accompanying him on the trip. Herman would keep the instruments and measure the currents and winds. Erik was an expert at patching sails, splicing ropes, and navigating. Knut and Torstein had experience with wireless radios during World War II, and they would be responsible for communication. Bengt would take scientific notes and act as quartermaster. And Thor would captain the expedition and keep the logbook.

With the crew assembled and financial backing secured, the group set off for Peru to build their raft. They had to go deep into the jungle to find large balsa trees, and with great effort they moved nine gigantic logs to Callao harbor. There they worked on lashing the logs together,

building a small cabin on the deck, and making their sails. They followed drawings of the ancient Inca rafts, and they accepted no help from the curious audience that gathered each day to watch them build their raft. The native Peruvians watched the strange raft take shape, and each day the size of the crowd grew.

Finally the raft was ready. The logs ranged from 30 to 45 feet long. On the large sail they painted a picture of the Tiki and they christened their raft the *Kon Tiki*. Each man had worked with the knowledge that the raft would be only as good as the worst piece of work. Finally, on April 27, 1947, food and water were brought on board and the *Kon Tiki* was ready.

Early the next morning, the raft was towed slowly out to sea. As they waved farewell to the tugboat, the men knew that they would see no other people but each other for at least three months—if all went well.

Three days into their voyage, the men held a meeting to discuss rules. Although each man had been assigned certain duties, all the routine jobs such as steering, watch, and cooking were divided equally. Every man had two hours each day and two hours each night at the steering oar. All meals were to be eaten outside the cabin, and "the 'right place' was only at the farthest end of the logs astern" (Heyerdahl, 1950). Each position also had its rules. For example, the night watch had to be secured by a rope around his waist at all times.

Days wore into weeks, weeks into months. The sturdy raft was battered by high waves and fierce storms, but it always emerged the victor. Each morning the men anxiously checked the ropes to make sure that their raft was holding together.

Coordination of effort was essential if the voyage was to succeed. Each man had to do his part, and they all had to work together during crises such as storms. Life in such close quarters offered little room for bickering, so when trouble arose, the group held a powwow.

Finally, 93 days into their journey, the watch shouted, "Land ahead!" All the men scrambled to the deck and saw the island of Puka Puka in the distance. However, the winds were not in their favor, and they sailed past this island. During the next several days, they passed a number of islands; often the inhabitants rowed out toward the raft.

The *Kon Tiki* crew was formed of men of diverse skills and backgrounds. As they worked together, they developed a strong sense of togetherness and each person learned his role in the group.

On the 101st day, a strong wind blew them onto a reef off a small Polynesian island. They had made it! They had shown that ancient inhabitants of Peru could indeed have been the first settlers of Polynesia. These six men had overcome storms, navigational problems, and interpersonal squabbles. Using only the most primitive means, they had duplicated a trip that may have been made over 1,000 years earlier. They were hailed as heroes throughout the world. President Truman received members of the expedition.

The voyage of the *Kon Tiki* is notable in many respects. One of the most interesting stories of the trip is how six individuals of very different backgrounds could be formed into a closely knit group capable of carrying out such a venture. These men were able to work together and make the complex decisions that ensured success.

What Is a Group?

Let's assume that we wanted to do a closer study of the crew of the *Kon Tiki* to understand how they made this incredible voyage. In beginning our study, we might first ask whether we should focus only on each crew member as an individual or whether we needed to study the unit, the group. This may seem like a rather simple question, but

Thor Heyerdahl, shown here on the deck of the *Kon Tiki*, was its captain. This position defined his duties and responsibilities; he enjoyed privileges that the other men did not have, but he also had responsibilities not shared by them.

The debate refused to die, and in 1952 Solomon Asch offered an interesting analogy. He pointed out that water (H_2O) is composed of hydrogen and oxygen. While it is important to know the characteristics of these two elements, we would not have a good understanding of the nature of water with only this knowledge. He suggested that a group is like water; it helps to understand the individual members, but a clear grasp of group behavior requires an examination of the unit. And to a large degree, recent research has taken Asch's suggestion by studying the behavior of both individual members and the group. And with this position in mind, we can now ask: What is a group?

Today social psychologists view the group as a dynamic whole that is different from the sum of its parts; it is neither greater nor less than these parts, but it is clearly different from the collection of individual members. Although investigators have offered various definitions of the group, most would be comfortable with the idea that a **group** consists of "two or more persons who are interacting with one another in such a manner that each person influences and is influenced by each other person" (Shaw, 1981, p. 8). Group members generally feel that they belong together; they see themselves as forming a single unit. This feeling of self-awareness usually results because the group members share common beliefs and attitudes and accept certain norms of the group. Group members also share at least one common goal.

As we can see, the crew of the *Kon Tiki* fits the definition of a group. They were involved in constant face-to-face interaction during their voyage. They saw themselves as forming a group, and felt that they belonged together. In talking with others, they often referred to themselves as "the *Kon Tiki* crew." In other words, the awareness of being a group became part of their own identity. Finally, they shared the common goal of completing the journey from Peru to Polynesia. We can contrast this group with the collection of people who gathered to watch them build their raft. These people did not interact with each other and had no feeling of belonging together. They simply happened to be in the same place at the same time, and thus engaged in a similar activity. The term **collective** has been used to describe a

social scientists have been asking it for almost 100 years without agreeing on an answer. When we examine the issue more closely, we can see that it is rather complex. It guides the study of group dynamics. Simply stated, we are asking whether the group is greater than the sum of its parts, its members.

Emile Durkheim, the eminent sociologist, had a rather direct answer to the question: "The group thinks, feels, and acts quite differently from the way in which its members would were they isolated. If we begin with the individual, we shall be able to understand nothing of what takes place in the group" (Durkheim, 1898, p. 104).

Floyd Allport (1924) had an equally clear answer about the nature of groups, but he took the opposite position. He stated that "groups" don't think, feel, or act—people do. He capped his argument for of studying individuals with the profound observation that nobody every stumbled over a group, so how could they be real!

A group is not just a collection of individuals like these people standing at the bus stop. A group develops roles and follows norms. It has a recognizable structure and organization.

gathering of individuals who do not have face-to-face interactions but are engaged in a common activity (Milgram & Toch, 1968).

Development of Groups and Their Members

If we examine the *Kon Tiki* crew, one point becomes apparent immediately: the crew and their relationships with each other changed over time. The members thought, acted, and felt differently as they worked together, and the crew functioned differently. In other words, the group was a *dynamic* unit, constantly changing. A great deal of attention has been paid recently to **group development**—the process by which groups form, flourish, and decline, and the changes that take place in the group and in its members over time.

Looking first at the individual, we find that potential group members are faced with an immediate problem: whether to join the group or not (Mackie & Goethals, 1987; Montgomery, 1989). Being a group member clearly has its

advantages. We can accomplish tasks that would be impossible to do alone; a single person could not sail the *Kon Tiki*. Being with other people allows us to evaluate ourselves on several dimensions, as we shall see. You cannot determine how good a tennis player you are by banging a tennis ball against a wall. The protection and sense of security that result from membership in a group tend to make accepted group members healthier and happier than loners (Moreland, 1987). But these and other advantages are balanced by costs. Being a member of a group requires you to give up some of your independence. You may have to change your attitudes and behaviors to become accepted into the group. You must consider the desires of others in addition to your own. Hence

---

collective A gathering of people who have no structure or face-to-face interaction but are engaged in a common activity.

group Two or more persons who are interacting with one another in such a manner that each person influences and is influenced by each other person.

group development The process by which groups form, flourish, and decline, and the changes that take place in the group and in its members over time.

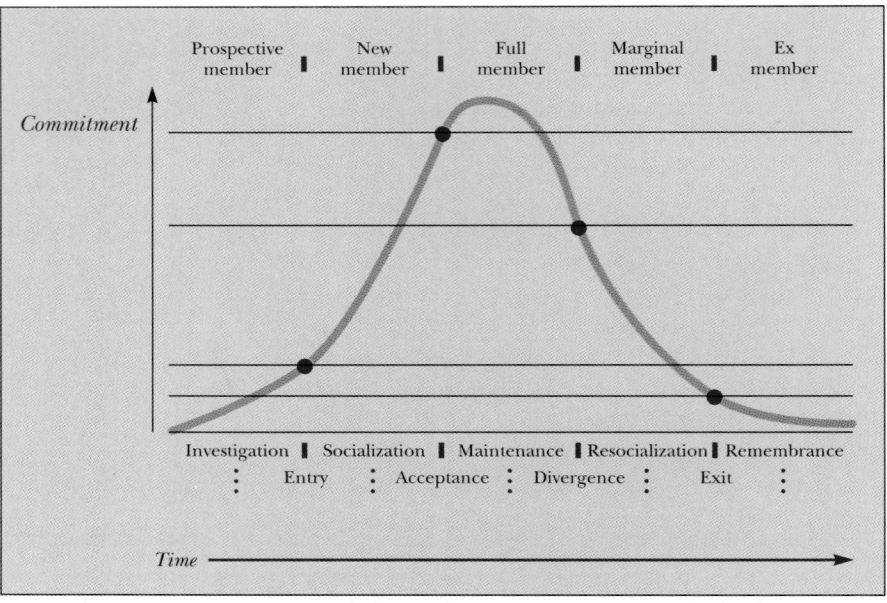

FIGURE 13-1 A model of group socialization
SOURCE: Moreland and Levine (1982).

the first step toward becoming a group member is to decide whether you're prepared to accept the costs of membership in order to reap the benefits.

But the conflict does not end there. Upon entry into the group, the individual steps into the category of new member. The group attempts to change the individual so that he or she can make the maximum contribution to the group (Moreland & Levine, 1982, 1988). At the same time, the new member attempts to change the group so that it will meet his or her needs. We can see this negotiation in the *Kon Tiki* crew when it was formed. As each new member was recruited, the crew stated what was expected of him. And each new member attempted to exact promises and commitments from the crew. Once the person becomes a full member, the focus of negotiations changes somewhat. The group identifies roles or positions it wants the member to occupy, such as navigator or helmsman. And the full member defines the jobs associated with those roles that he or she desires. During the time you belong to a group, you find that the group is not meeting all of your needs. You begin to question

the value of membership in this group, search for other groups, and become a marginal member (see Figure 13-1). If the group does not move to recapture you, you leave the group. The other group members often discuss former members, evaluating their former colleagues' contributions. The ex-member also looks back on the group, remembering the benefits and costs of being a member of the group.

If you examine your own experience in groups, several points may come to mind. First, you may see how you passed through these stages. You may also see that at any one time you are a member of numerous groups, and you may be in a different stage of membership in each of these groups. Finally, in examining any one group to which you belong, you will find that it has members at each of these stages. In this sense, a group is like a highway, with members scattered at various points along the road. The group therefore must deal with members at these various stages at any one time.

While the image of a highway may allow us to visualize members passing through a group, it may be misleading if it causes us to picture groups as stable, unchanging units. Groups, like individual members, are in a constant state of flux. Groups change and develop just as members do. One analysis suggested that new groups begin at a *forming* stage (Tuckman, 1965). During this stage, group members identify a leader and discuss the nature of their task. Groups next enter a *storming* stage, in which members try to change the group to meet their personal needs. Conflict erupts as each member attempts to gain control. In the *norming* stage the group focuses on reducing conflict and works to develop rules to guide members' behavior. At the fourth stage, *performing,* members work together to achieve mutual goals.

Tuckman's analysis focused mostly on small work groups. In an effort to expand this focus, Worchel, Coutant-Sasic, and Grossman (in press) studied larger groups and social movements, such as political parties and the Solidarity Union in Poland. They found that new groups often begin to form when some significant event, such as an assassination of a prominent person or a repressive action by a controlling group, brings people together in a common cause. The new group then enters an *identification* stage, much like the forming stage proposed by Tuckman. During this stage the group is concerned with establishing its identity. It demands conformity from its members and punishes deviants; the group may establish a uniform dress code to define its members; the group often invites conflict with other groups because such conflict establishes group boundaries. During this stage, group members will work for the good of the group, often placing the group's needs ahead of their own. In the next stage, *production,* the group's focus turns from identity to productivity. The group becomes concerned with achieving task goals and meeting the needs of its members. The cooperation of other groups to achieve these goals may be invited. Groups then enter the *individuation* stage, in which the focus is on the individual members. Members begin to examine what they are receiving from the group. They want to be recognized for their individual accomplishments. They may dress to set themselves apart from other members. And they may explore the advantages of membership in other groups. In the final stage, *decay,* members whose needs are not being met by the group

Working in a large restaurant are chefs and sous chefs (subordinates), and within those categories salad chefs and dessert chefs, as well as waitpersons and buspersons. The hierarchy provides direction and personnel to prepare and serve the quantities and varieties of food offered, and it functions to avoid role conflict.

begin to complain and demand changes in leadership and structure. Group cohesion decreases and the stage is set for the forming of new groups.

Several points emerge from this discussion of group and member development. The major point is that any group, such as the *Kon Tiki* crew, is constantly undergoing change and development. A snapshot of the group taken at one time may give a very different picture from a snapshot taken at another time. It is important to discuss groups within the framework of time (McGrath, 1988). Further, the development process of groups and their members does seem to follow a predictable pattern. This is not to say that all groups or all members undergo precisely the same process in a stepwise fashion; but in most cases, there is an order to development. Finally, it is important to recognize that the changes experienced by group members affect the group and the changes in the group affect the members. In order to understand this point, you may want to review your own family. Events such as your going to college probably changed the nature of your family, just as the family's move from one neighborhood to another had effects on you. With this dynamic picture of groups in mind, let's look more closely at the basic properties of the structure of groups.

The Structure of Groups

If we consider the crew of the *Kon Tiki* a group, we begin to see some of the features that characterize groups. First, groups have boundaries; we can determine who is a crew member and who is not. Further, within these boundaries, groups have structure. As we will see, this structure is made up of rules and positions to guide behavior. In this sense, groups can best be viewed as a system of rules and positions as well as a body of distinct members (Von Cranach, Ochsenbein & Valach, 1987). A positive structure can equip the group to respond and adapt to its environment; an inadequate structure can lead to the demise and destruction of the group. In fact, one study found that groups with a rigid structure of leadership and decision-making rules performed more poorly and created more dissatisfaction among the members in stressful (crowded and noisy) environments than groups with more flexible and less defined structures (Worchel & Shackelford, in press). Other investigators found that groups can increase their chances of performing well if they take time to discuss and identify their structure *before* they begin working on tasks (Hackman, Brousseau & Weiss, 1976). It is interesting to note that the crew of the *Kon Tiki* took this precaution; before they set out on their voyage, they met to determine the jobs that each man would perform and how decisions would be made once they set sail.

When we talk of structure, we are most concerned with two concepts: norms and roles.

Norms

As the men developed into the crew, they spent a lot of time discussing their structure and the rules by which they would live. Some of the rules they formed applied to everyone. For example, each person was to spend four hours a day at the helm, and no one was allowed to eat inside the cabin. Each crew member was allowed only one quart of water a day. A **norm,** as we saw in Chapter 10, is a rule that governs a specific behavior and applies to everyone in the group. In other words, a norm specifies "what must or must not be done when" (Steiner, 1972).

Norms are valuable because they allow us to predict the behavior of group members. They help coordinate the activities of group members. Indeed, norms can have a profound and sometimes unrecognized effect on group performance. Consider the groups to which you belong. It is likely that one task facing each of your groups at some point is making a decision. You may not realize it, but the decision made by your group will be a function of the group members' preferences *and* the group norm regarding how decisions will be made (Allison & Messick, 1987). Some groups adopt a majority-wins rule. In other groups a norm allows a few powerful members to make the decisions. Still other groups require unanimity: everyone must agree before a decision is made. The latter two norms may prevent the group from adopting a position that the majority of the members favor. In most cases, the *Kon Tiki* crew used the unanimity norm. This rule allowed one crew member to keep the group from adopting a course of action favored by the other five, and once it saved the crew from making a disastrous decision about the design of their raft.

Some norms may be explicit and develop through group discussions. Others may develop through practice and remain unwritten and unspecified. In either case, group members are expected to follow the norms. Milgram and his colleagues (1986) found that people waiting in line objected when someone broke the unwritten norm about cutting into the line. Interestingly, the highest rate of objection came from the person immediately behind the cutter. Roethlisberger and Dickson (1939) showed the effect of norms in their study of workers at the Western Electric Company in Hawthorne, Illinois. Work teams in this plant were responsible for wiring switchboard panels. Although each worker's pay was determined by the number of boards he wired, the workers developed an informal norm as to the number of panels a worker "should" wire each day. If everyone followed this norm, no individ-

There is no clear answer to the question whether individuals or groups perform better. Even within groups, some tasks can be divided so that each group member has his or her job and the final outcome does not represent a combination of efforts. However, we will see that even on such tasks the group can influence the individual's rate of work.

ual could be singled out as being better or worse than any other. A worker who exceeded ("rate-buster") or failed to meet ("chiseler") these standards was harassed by his fellow workers. Harassment took the form of good-natured but pointed kidding and "binging"—a punch on the upper arm. The bing was hard enough to get the point across, but not so hard that it could injure the individual.

In Chapter 12 we discussed another interesting characteristic of norms. Jacobs and Campbell (1961) demonstrated that groups developed norms as to the amount of movement seen in the autokinetic effect. After the norm was developed, individual group members were replaced one at a time by new people. Even when all the old members had been replaced, the norm regarding the amount of movement seen remained intact. This study demonstrated that norms often outlive the group members who form them. This point can be seen in the laws of many states. An examination will show that there are

still laws about where people may tie their horses, what position may be used during sexual intercourse, and the number of spittoons that must be placed in public places. It seems that old norms die slowly! Fortunately, reasonable norms tend to last longer than unreasonable and arbitrary ones (MacNeil & Sherif, 1976).

Roles

In addition to rules that governed everyone's behavior, the crew of the *Kon Tiki* also had rules that applied only to certain positions, such as the rule that the helmsman was required to wear a safety rope around his waist at night. A **role** defines the obligations and expectations of a per-

---

norm A rule that governs a specific behavior and applies to everyone in the group.

role A set of norms that defines how a particular person in a given position must act.

---

son in a particular position. Roles specify who should do what, when, and how. We may view roles as positions in groups, along with the rules that govern the behavior of people who occupy those positions. For example, Thor Heyerdahl had the role of leader. In this position he had certain responsibilities, such as acting as spokesman for the group and seeing that his men performed the necessary duties. He also had certain privileges, such as dining with dignitaries and accepting honors for the crew.

Numerous studies on a variety of groups identified two roles that often develop (Brown, 1988; Slater, 1955): the **task specialist** functions to keep the group working toward its goals; the **socioemotional specialist** is concerned primarily with the feelings of the group members. The socioemotional specialist, who acts to reduce conflict and ensure that all members feel part of the group, is often the best-liked member of the group. These roles generally develop informally, and different members may occupy them at different times. An interesting finding in studies on families and mixed-gender groups is that a male often occupies the task specialist role and a female takes on the socioemotional role (Bartol & Martin, 1986; Wood, 1987; Zelditch, 1955). However, when the nature of the task is one on which the female member excels, the female often becomes the task specialist and the male the socioemotional specialist. Therefore, the occupant of a role is determined by personal characteristics, task requirements, and group characteristics, as well as by the nature of the role.

In an ideal world, roles and norms should ensure that the group functioned smoothly; not only should members know how to act, but they should also know what to expect from others. But groups are rarely perfect systems, and conflicts often arise to some degree. One of the more common conflicts concerns roles; actually two types of **role conflict** can occur. One type of conflict may reside within the role itself. A role may require a person to perform conflicting behaviors. For example, many parents struggle with the duties of providing warmth and love to their children while also having to punish and discipline them. A second type of conflict arises because we belong to many groups at the same time; the requirements of one role may conflict with those of another. A common form of this conflict is seen in work and family roles. The work role may demand that the person spend large amounts of time at the office or traveling, while the roles of spouse and parent dictate that the person should spend time with the family. It may be interesting for you to examine your own family in this light. Do you see evidence of any role conflict faced by your parents or your spouse?

There are many ways to deal with these role conflicts. One is simply to ignore competing roles or demands within a role (Stryker & Statham, 1986). While this strategy may make life easier for the individual faced with the conflict, it makes his or her behavior more difficult to predict by other group members. A second approach is to choose groups that do not present conflicting roles. For example, a woman may choose a less fulfilling job because it gives her greater freedom to spend time with her family. While this approach reduces the conflict between the roles of work and family, the woman may experience resentment because her job does not meet her needs. As these examples make clear, roles are generally developed to solve the needs of the group rather than those of the individual. For this reason, role conflict is often difficult to resolve and may be a source of considerable tension.

In addition to role conflict, we can identify some other trouble spots with roles and norms. For example, both norms and roles may be ambiguous: people may not know what is expected of them in specific situations or positions. **Role ambiguity** is a major problem in many organizations. Employees' performance is often impaired when they do not know what is expected of them or spend time attempting to clarify their roles (McGee, Ferguson & Seers, 1989). Role ambiguity is likely to result when new employees are added to a group or when new technology is introduced. Another problem is role overload, which afflicts the person of whom too much is expected in the roles that he or she occupies.

In summary, norms and roles give structure to our groups. They are important because they allow us to predict how others will behave. They also relieve us of the need to make a conscious decision for every action we take in the group, thereby playing a vital role in helping the group function smoothly. Finally, they may help avoid or resolve conflict. For example, the crew of the *Kon Tiki* decided that everyone would have equal night duty. If a crew member had attempted to avoid this duty, the other crew members would simply have reminded him of their agreement. In this case, the norm becomes a third party that mediates an agreement and eliminates the need for the use of personal power or coercion (Forsyth, 1990). However, norms and roles that are too rigid can hinder individual creativity and make it impossible for the group to respond to new situations. Likewise, norms and roles that are ambiguous or demand too much can be troublesome for the individual and group.

Now that we have discussed the structure of groups, let us turn our attention to the research and theory on group behavior. We will approach this examination in two ways. First, we will consider the group as a unit and examine how that unit functions. For example, we will discuss conditions that influence how productive the group will be and we will investigate how groups arrive at decisions. Second, we will change our focus to the individual group member and ask how being a member of a group affects that person's behavior, perceptions, and attitudes. Here we will discuss, for example, how being a member of a group affects an *individual's* performance. In several earlier chapters we discussed many of the social processes that occur in groups; for example, in Chapter 12 we examined conformity, leadership, and obedience. In this chapter, therefore, we will focus mainly on how groups influence perceptions, performance, and decisions. Let us begin by considering the group as a unit.

STOP, THINK, & UNDERSTAND

1. Do groups merit study as a unit or should research focus only on individuals?

2. What phases does an individual go through as part of a group?

3. Discuss the process of group development.

4. What factors make up group structure?

5. What are some common problems with roles?

He was faced with the problem of designing his own raft on the basis of these old drawings. How was he to solve this problem? He could study the drawings on his own and arrive at a solution; he could have each crew member arrive at a solution on his own and accept the most common solution; or he could assemble his crew, show them the drawings, and have the group arrive at a plan for the raft.

To advise Heyerdahl on the best strategy to use, we would need to know whether groups are more efficient than individuals at solving problems. This seems like a simple question to answer. One need merely give a group of people a problem to work on and then compare the group's performance with that of an individual. However, the procedure raises some difficult questions. Is it fair to compare a group of six people with an individual working alone? Certainly six

Group Productivity

Some of the earliest studies on groups were concerned with the problem of comparing group and individual productivity. Assuming that there is a problem to be solved or a task to be completed, is it better to have a single individual work on the problem/task or to assemble a group that will work together? Thor Heyerdahl, for example, had numerous drawings of ancient Incan rafts.

role ambiguity   Uncertainty as to what is expected of one in a specific situation or position.

role conflict   The inner struggle that results when incompatible behaviors are demanded either by the various requirements of a role or by the various roles that one person occupies.

socioemotional specialist   A group role; a person who is concerned primarily with the feelings of the group members.

task specialist   A group role; a person who functions to keep the group working toward its goals by focusing on the task demands.

people working on a problem, whether individually or together, should have a better chance of arriving at the correct solution than one person working alone.

Indeed, the question now becomes two questions and we enter an area of central concern to **organizational psychologists,** who focus on the functioning of organizations and work groups. One question involves *effectiveness.* Here we can simply ask whether a group is more likely to find a correct solution than an individual working alone (Pritchard et al., 1988). The second question is one of *efficiency;* this term concerns costs and rewards. We may find that a group is more likely than an individual to arrive at a correct answer, but what is the cost in person-hours devoted to the task? A six-person group would have to identify the correct answer six times as fast as the individual to equal the individual's efficiency. We do not have the time or space to enter into an extended discussion of effectiveness and efficiency. Our interest here is the effectiveness of a given number of people working alone in comparison with the same people working in a group. In other words, does being in a group increase or decrease the chance of producing a good product or finding the correct solution to a problem? How can we go about finding out?

One possibility is to average the work of six people working alone. This arrangement would constitute a **nominal group** (a number of persons working on a problem independently). A comparison of the real group's solution with the nominal group's solution would indicate whether working in a group did aid in problem solving. This is the usual manner in which research in the area of group productivity has proceeded. Looking at a different issue, we could compare the group's product with that of the best of the six individuals working alone. Or we could compare the group's product with the product of the weakest member of the nominal group to see whether a group is more effective than its weakest member. All of these questions are important in determining whether a group is more productive than an individual, and research has been devoted to each of them.

The early research on group productivity proceeded in a haphazard fashion, without theory or structure to guide it. In one early experiment, Marjorie Shaw (1932) asked individuals and groups to arrive at a solution to the following problem:

> On one side of a river are three wives and three husbands. All of the men but none of the women can row. Get them all across the river by means of a boat carrying only three at one time. No man will allow his wife to be in the presence of another man unless he is also there. (p. 492)

Shaw found that 60% of the groups and only 14% of the individuals who worked alone arrived at correct solutions to the problem.

While these early studies suggested that groups were generally more effective than individuals, more recent efforts have focused on explaining the group advantage and identifying when this advantage is most likely to occur.

For example, careful examination of working groups has found that groups are more effective at problem solving than individuals only when one of the group members has known the correct solution (Laughlin & Futoran, 1985). This may seem like a rather insignificant statement, but it adds an important piece to the puzzle of understanding group productivity. Solving a problem involves at least two steps: one is developing the correct solution and the other is recognizing that solution as correct and adopting it. This finding suggests that groups are not necessarily better at generating solutions than individuals working alone, but they are superior at recognizing the correct solution once it has been proposed.

Although we might be tempted to adopt the position that groups are superior at recognizing the correct solution, we must add one caveat to complete this statement: *Groups are superior at recognizing and adopting correct solutions, especially when these solutions are presented by members who have high status in the group.* In a study that examined the problem-solving behavior of B-26 bomber crews, it was found that the crew recognized and adopted the correct solution 94% of the time when it was proposed by the high-status pilots (Torrance, 1954). However, when the correct solution was proposed by a gunner, who had the lowest status in the crew, it was adopted only 62% of the time by permanent crews.

In attempting to identify when groups would be most effective, Steiner (1972, 1976) suggested that the effectiveness of a group is dependent on the **process loss**—the difference between the group's potential and its actual productivity. Two types of process loss can occur in groups. First, **coordination loss** is determined by how well the group can combine and use the individual member's contributions. For example, when the *Kon Tiki* was rowed out to sea, coordination loss would be high if the members all rowed at different times. Along these lines, several investigators have suggested that a crucial task for leaders is to monitor and coordinate group members' actions (Komaki, 1986; Komaki, Desselles & Bowman, 1989). Second, **motivation loss** occurs when members do not put their maximum effort into the task.

As we can see, these approaches to group productivity suggest that resources and adequate membership are not enough to ensure a group's success. The group must blend these talents together and motivate its members to contribute. Many factors influence the group's ability to do this. Two of these factors fall under the heading of task type and group characteristics.

Task Type and Performance

Steiner offered a classification system for tasks. He pointed out that not all tasks have the same requirements, and that performance potential is affected by the requirements of the task. Given this situation, it is important for groups to recognize the type of task and develop an appropriate strategy for working on the task.

Disjunctive Tasks

A **disjunctive task** requires an either-or decision. The problem of the three wives and husbands presented earlier is a disjunctive task. In this problem, the group must decide among a number of alternative answers. It is unlikely that the group will arrive at the correct answer unless at least one of its members offers the correct answer. On disjunctive tasks, the group's maximum potential is dependent on the capacities of its most capable members. There may be motivation losses because the less capable members perceive that their efforts are unimportant.

Conjunctive Tasks

In a **conjunctive task,** all of the group members perform essentially the same subtask, and the overall performance of the group is dependent on the combination of these subtasks. The maximum performance of a team of mountain climbers, for example, is dependent on the capacities of its least capable member; the group of climbers can reach the mountaintop no faster than the slowest climber. On such conjunctive tasks, it is likely that the average performance of the individuals in the group will be better than the group's performance, since a group will be severely penalized by even one bad member. Here, in contrast to the disjunctive task, motivation loss is likely to result because the most capable members reduce their effort.

Additive Tasks

The final group product of an **additive task** is the sum of the efforts of the group members. A tug-of-war is an additive task. The product of a group working on an additive task will almost always be better than the product of the single individual, even if the average individual in the

---

additive task A task whose final product is the sum of group members' efforts.

conjunctive task A task in which all group members perform essentially the same subtask, and the overall performance is dependent on the combination of these subtasks. The maximum effort of the group is defined by the least capable member.

coordination loss Reduced group productivity due to the group's inability to combine and use the individual members' contributions.

disjunctive task A task requiring an either-or decision.

motivation loss Loss of group productivity that occurs when members do not put their maximum effort into the task.

nominal group A number of persons working on a problem independently.

organizational psychologists Psychologists who focus on the functioning of organizations and work groups.

process loss The difference between a group's potential and its actual productivity.

group does not perform as well as the single individual performing alone. Such a case occurred when Ringelmann (1913), a French agricultural engineer, investigated pulling techniques used by farmers. He found that a man pulling on a rope alone exerted an average pull of 63 kilograms, whereas a group of eight individuals exerted an average pull of 248 kilograms. Hence the group was better than the individual even though each member of the group exerted an average of only 31 kilograms of the pull.

Both coordination loss and motivation loss may occur in additive tasks. It is important that the members' efforts be coordinated to get the maximum effort. For example, it does little good for every member to put maximum effort into the rope-pulling task if those efforts are not made simultaneously. As we will see in our discussion of social loafing, motivation loss may occur if members do not feel responsible for the final group product.

Discretionary Tasks

A **discretionary task** requires the group to arrive at a group decision. For example, deciding which route the *Kon Tiki* would follow was a discretionary task. As Steiner points out, this decision does not involve an either-or answer, as the disjunctive task does. Further, the final group decision can be arrived at in a number of ways. The *Kon Tiki* crew could have given a total weight to the estimates of their leader, Thor. Or the group decision could have been reached by taking the average of each member's course. Thus discretionary tasks allow the use of a number of alternative means by which the group can arrive at a decision, and the decision of the group will be strongly affected by the means chosen. For this reason, coordination loss is the major problem faced in this type of task.

Group Characteristics and Productivity

A group's productivity can be as strongly influenced by the group's characteristics as by the type of task in which it is engaged. One important characteristic is the group's size. Would the *Kon Tiki*'s voyage have been accomplished more easily with a larger crew? We can also examine the members' feelings for each other. Heyerdahl chose men who knew and liked each other. Was this factor important for the success of the voyage, or would he have been equally successful if he had chosen people solely on the basis of their expertise? Many other characteristics can be considered, such as the personalities of the group members and the particular structure of the group. Here, however, we will focus on the size, cohesiveness, and composition of the group.

Group Size

Heyerdahl's decision to use a six-man crew was based on space considerations and the amount of provisions that could be taken on the voyage. Assuming that he had adequate space and rations, would he have been wiser to take a larger group?

There are many reasons to expect a large group to perform better than a smaller group. If the task is disjunctive, the larger the group, the greater the likelihood that someone will have the solution. If the task is additive, each additional member will add something to the group, and therefore the large group should perform better than the small group.

However, increasing the size of the group also creates problems. One is coordination loss. On the *Kon Tiki*, it was relatively easy to coordinate the work of the six crew members. If there had been 60 crew members, the problem of seeing that each member performed the correct task at the correct time would have been much more difficult. Time and effort would have been wasted on trying to coordinate members' efforts.

An even more serious problem in large groups is the motivation and dissatisfaction of group members. Numerous studies have found that as group size increases, group members' motivation to work and their satisfaction with the group declines. For example, Wicker and his associates (1976) found greater variability of involvement in large groups than in small groups. In the larger groups, some members were very involved whereas others felt almost no involvement. If you consider large groups in which you have worked, you may recall feeling "lost in the shuffle." This feeling reduces your desire to contribute to the group. On the *Kon Tiki*, each member felt that he played a vital part in the voyage. Had the crew been much larger, it is less likely that the members would have felt the importance of their individual contributions. As a result, the crew might not have tried so hard to make the trip a success.

Another problem is that large group size may cause members to feel inhibited. No one wants to be made a fool of in front of a large group of people. Hence, in large groups, members may withhold suggestions. You have probably experienced such inhibitions when you have considered asking a question in a large class. You raise your hand to ask a question, and the professor calls on you. Suddenly you feel 600 eyes focusing on you. The pressure is on; you'd better ask a "good" question! You may have struggled through such an experience, vowing never to get yourself in that position again.

Overall, there are advantages and disadvantages to increasing the size of the group. Larger groups have more resources to focus on the task, but the increase in size also increases the likelihood of significant process loss. Recalling our earlier discussion of group and member development, we might expect large groups to be particularly difficult when they are newly formed and members do not have clear roles. Likewise, a large group is probably most difficult for new members who are concerned about their acceptance. Later, we will examine juries; here we will see that group size also affects the way in which groups work on tasks.

Cohesiveness

One of the most studied variables in group behavior is cohesiveness. We can best view **cohesiveness** as the desire of members to stay in the group; it is often measured by examining how attracted group members are to each other. One important question that can be asked is: Do highly cohesive groups perform better than less cohesive groups? Our first response to this question might be "Certainly." Imagine how difficult it would have been for the crew of the *Kon Tiki* to work together for more than 100 days if they had disliked each other.

Several studies have suggested that our initial response is correct. In general, group members are happier and more satisfied in cohesive groups (Zander, 1982). Looking at performance, Van Zelt (1952) examined work groups composed of carpenters and bricklayers. In some of the groups, the men all liked one another (high cohesiveness); in other groups, fewer men liked one another. Workers in the high-cohesive groups expressed greater job satisfaction and had lower turnover and less absenteeism. The high-cohesive groups also performed at a higher level. Research on volleyball and baseball teams found that cohesive teams are generally winning teams (Bird, 1977; Long, 1972).

Japanese business firms have gone to great lengths to build cohesive work groups. They have hired friends from the same school and tried to put friends on the same work teams. They sponsor parties and clubs for their employees. To increase commitment to the company, they have promised workers jobs for life, given large bonuses, and even provided economical housing for the workers. One result of these efforts is that Japanese workers seldom change companies.

While this research argues strongly for cohesiveness, there is another side to the issue. First, a number of organizational psychologists have questioned the nature of the relationship between cohesiveness and performance. While a happy group may be a productive group, these investigators suggest that the relationship may also be just the reverse. That is, a productive group may be a happy one. Research (Porter & Lawler, 1968) has found that success increases group cohesiveness. Other research somewhat tarnishes the image of cohesiveness: Terborg, Castore, and DeNinno (1976) found no relationship between cohesiveness and productivity.

There are a number of reasons for this last effect. One of the most important is that *members of cohesive groups are generally more influenced by*

---

cohesiveness   The result of all forces that impel individuals to remain in or leave a group; often measured by how attractive members find their group.

discretionary task   A task that requires group members to agree on a decision that involves several alternatives and different ways to arrive at the decision.

Some groups, such as this rehabilitation organization, work particularly hard to provide cohesiveness, a positive sense of self, and a new social identity for their members.

Group Composition: Gender Differences in Group Performance

The *Kon Tiki* crew was an all-male group. Do you think the results of the voyage would have been different if Heyerdahl had chosen an all-female crew or a mixed-sex crew? Researchers have been interested in comparing groups of men and women for more than 50 years. The issue is particularly important in today's social and economic climate, where equality is the watchword and women are playing increasingly important roles at all levels of the work force.

In addressing the issue of gender differences, we might first ask whether all-male groups perform better than all-female groups. In a review of 52 studies on this question, Wendy Wood concluded that the evidence suggests that all-male groups are more productive than all-female groups on some types of tasks. The research further suggested that males in general are more task-oriented while women are oriented more toward social factors and feelings (Carli, 1982; Amancio, 1989; Wood, 1987). This broad statement, however, tells only part of the story. Many of the tasks used in the research are "male-oriented" problem-solving tasks involving math or mechanical abilities. Men often perform better than women on these tasks when they work alone, so we might well expect a group effect to favor men. Differences between male and female groups decline when their tasks are less sex-typed.

The research raises another interesting issue. In order for most groups to function well, attention must be focused on task behavior and social interactions within the group. Earlier we saw that cohesive groups generally perform better than groups whose members are experiencing conflict and dissatisfaction. If men tend to be predominantly task-oriented and women are concerned with group feelings, we should expect mixed-sex groups to function better than same-sex groups. In fact, the few studies that have been conducted on the topic indicate that mixed-sex groups do perform better than same-sex groups (either all male or all female). While mixed-sex groups have a broader range of styles and abilities, the problem confronting these groups is to make the best use of this variety. An interesting

their groups than members of less cohesive groups (McGrath, 1984). In other words, people who are highly attracted to a group conform to the norms set up by that group. In some cases, as in the Western Electric plant studied by Roethlisberger and Dickson (1939), these norms may set work levels below an individual's capability. When this happens, members of cohesive groups will reduce their productivity to meet the group norm. Another possible effect of cohesiveness is that members will be reluctant to question the direction of the group. In their desire to maintain the positive atmosphere that exists in the group, members may remain quiet even when they feel the group is incorrect. We will see the disastrous consequences that can result from this situation when we examine groupthink.

In the final analysis, we can conclude that cohesiveness usually increases a group's productivity. However, there are exceptions to this rule that must also be considered. Thus it is likely, but not certain, that the camaraderie among the *Kon Tiki* crew contributed to the success of their voyage.

twist to this problem is seen in the effect of gender on the partner's behavior. Carli (1989) found that both male and female subjects showed more positive socially oriented behavior when they were paired with a female work partner and more task-oriented behavior when their partner was male.

Now that we have considered these issues, what would we advise Heyerdahl to do about the composition of his crew? The most important suggestion we could give him would be to consider carefully the task he has set himself. The particular jobs involved in sailing a raft may be best suited to members of one gender or the other. However, assuming that the nature of the tasks and the work setting do not favor men or women, a mixed-sex group should be considered for maximum functioning of the group.

Group Decision Making

Up to this point, our examination of groups has focused mainly on how well or how quickly groups can complete a specific job or make a product. In this light, we could view the voyage of the *Kon Tiki* as a job or product, and ask how well the group performed. If we examine the voyage more carefully, however, we find that the group was called on to perform many tasks. Some involved producing a specific product, such as building the raft or sailing it through a storm. Many others involved making decisions, such as what course to follow and how much food to carry aboard. To produce products, groups must often make decisions about how to work and what the final product should be. The sole task of such groups as juries is to make a decision. Therefore, let us now turn our attention away from questions of material products and focus on a specific type of product: group decisions.

Groupthink

We have many reasons for believing that groups should make better decisions than individuals. Groups have members with different experiences, expertise, and points of view. On the basis

Was the international arms deal called "Iranscam" another example of groupthink? North felt himself to be part of an extremely cohesive government in-group, perhaps seeing himself as invulnerable to the type of public scrutiny that eventually occurred.

of our earlier discussion of cohesiveness, we might further expect that highly cohesive groups would be best able to use the diverse talents of the members and arrive at the best decisions. Indeed, there is evidence that groups often make better decisions than isolated individuals (Shaw, 1981). However, there are so many examples to the contrary that we cannot conclude that groups are always superior decision makers. One of the clearest examples of a situation in which a group made a poor decision occurred on April 17, 1961. On that day 1,400 Cuban exiles landed at the Bay of Pigs in Cuba. Their mission was to establish a beachhead and to join with Cuban rebels in the Escambray Mountains. Together, these forces were expected to unite the Cuban people in a rebellion to overthrow Premier Fidel Castro. The exiles were armed by the United States. Their mission had been planned by one of the best intelligence

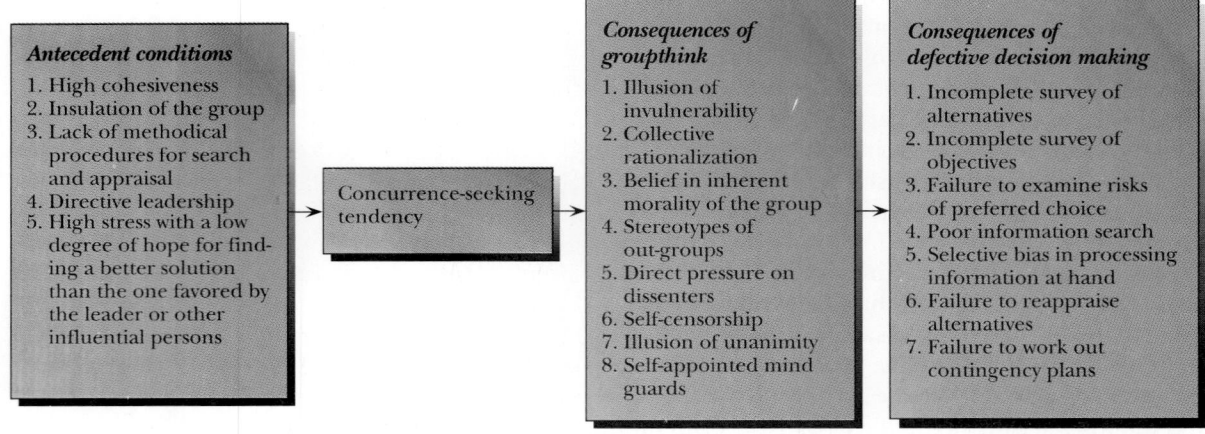

FIGURE 13-2 Analysis of groupthink, based on comparisons of high- and low-quality decisions by policy-making groups
SOURCE: Based on Janis (1972).

organizations in the world, the Central Intelligence Agency (CIA), and approved by one of the most popular leaders of the time, President John F. Kennedy. Despite all of these advantages, the whole plan fell flat on its face. Castro's army was well prepared for the invasion; there was little discontent among the Cuban people; and 80 miles of dense swamp separated the Bay of Pigs from the Escambray Mountains. Within two days of the invasion, the exiles had been surrounded by Castro's army and the entire force either killed or captured. The United States suffered a severe political setback, and it was besieged by cries of outrage and indignation from countries throughout the world.

It is easy to see why the invasion failed. It is not so easy, however, to see how such a misconceived plan could have been devised and set in motion. Janis (1972, 1982) carefully analyzed the decision-making process that produced the Bay of Pigs fiasco and similar blunders (lack of preparedness for the Pearl Harbor attack and increasing U.S. involvement in Vietnam). From these analyses, he concluded that a situation of "groupthink" may develop in cohesive decision-making groups. According to Janis, **groupthink** is "a mode of thinking that people engage in when they are deeply involved in a cohesive group, when members' striving for unanimity overrides their motivation to realistically appraise alter-

native courses of action" (1972, p. 9). In other words, groupthink is excessive concurrence-seeking in groups (t'Hart, 1988).

Janis and his colleagues (Janis & Mann, 1977) developed a model that shows the groupthink process. As Figure 13-2 indicates, groupthink has three causes. One is a highly cohesive group. A second is structural faults in the organization. Groups that are relatively isolated from the scrutiny of others and have members with similar attitudes and backgrounds are most likely to exhibit groupthink. The presence of a strong and respected leader who does not remain impartial is another structural problem that helps set the stage for groupthink. In fact, recent work suggests that the leader's behavior may be more responsible for groupthink than the cohesiveness of the group (t'Hart & Kroon, 1989; Vinokur et al., 1985). The third condition, "provocative situational context," simply means that the group is under a great deal of stress and that the members may have their self-esteem lowered by past failures or the difficulty of their task.

These factors that lead to groupthink have a variety of observable consequences. You can see them in Figure 13-2, so let's briefly review only a few of the more interesting ones.

1. The group develops the illusion of *invulnerability*. As Arthur Schlesinger (1965) reports,

the Kennedy group felt that they had the Midas touch; they had done everything right and won the election against all odds. They were euphoric, and the possibility of failure hardly crossed their minds.

2. The group members view themselves as having a high degree of *morality*. Kennedy's advisers saw themselves as fighting the evil forces of communism.

3. The group members share *common stereotypes*. In the Bay of Pigs case, Kennedy's cabinet members reinforced one another's view that the Cubans were a bunch of unorganized bandits who could not fight.

4. One of the most disastrous consequences is that the group develops an *illusion of agreement and unanimity*. Each person simply assumes that the other group members hold the same opinions and that there is no need to encourage discussion on issues on which everyone agrees.

5. As a result of this illusion, there are strong group *pressures toward conformity* and the group members become *reluctant to express disagreement*. A member or members of the group assume the role of "mind guard" and work to protect the agreement and cohesive feeling of the group.

6. Another possible consequence is the *discussion pattern* that develops in the group and discourages examination of all alternatives. In a careful analysis of group communication, investigators (Stasser & Titus, 1985) found that information is more likely to enter group discussion if it is shared by all or most group members. Groups tend to avoid considering unique information that is not already known by most group members. Further, group discussion is generally biased in favor of preferences that already exist in the group. This tendency suggests that if only one member of Kennedy's cabinet knew of the conditions that existed at the Bay of Pigs site, it is unlikely that the other group members would have given that information much consideration, even if the initial member proposed that they do so. This effect is especially likely if the member has low status in the group.

Having painted a rather dismal picture, we must ask whether groupthink is an inevitable result when cohesive groups with strong leaders are charged with making important decisions. For-tunately, it is not. First, it has been pointed out that groupthink may not necessarily be a phenomenon related solely to groups; an individual who rationalized decisions and failed to carefully examine the risks involved would also make poor decisions (Abelson & Levi, 1985). Group pressures may increase the likelihood of this process, but they are not solely responsible for it. Second, cohesive groups do not always fall prey to groupthink; in fact, such groups can make excellent decisions if they take steps to avoid groupthink. To demonstrate this point, Janis cited another decision made by Kennedy's cabinet. Just over a year after the Bay of Pigs invasion, Kennedy learned that the Soviets were deploying missiles with nuclear warheads in Cuba. Kennedy called a series of meetings of his advisers; many of the advisers were the same men who had planned the Bay of Pigs invasion. This time, however, Kennedy pushed to ensure that numerous proposals for action were discussed and carefully weighed; recommendations were considered and reconsidered. Persons outside the group of advisers were called on to supply information and opinions. Kennedy intentionally excluded himself from many of the meetings so that the discussants would not be unduly influenced by him. In this case, groupthink was avoided and a "good" plan was adopted by the group. A shipping blockade was imposed to prevent the Soviets from delivering additional men and supplies to Cuba. Ensuing events led to the eventual removal of the missiles already in Cuba.

As this incident illustrates, groupthink is most likely to be avoided if the following steps are taken:

1. The leader should avoid stating a preference and should encourage group members to consider all alternatives (Flowers, 1977).
2. Group members should be encouraged to play the role of devil's advocate and force the discussion to focus on unique information.
3. When possible, persons outside the group should be brought in to express opinions and offer suggestions.

---

groupthink   A form of thinking in a decision-making situation in which the group suspends objectivity and careful analysis in an effort to preserve group cohesiveness.

4. New information should be continually reassessed.
5. The group should consist of highly dominant members who are not prone to anxiety about disagreement. Research (Callaway, Marriott & Esser, 1985) has shown that such groups are less likely to show symptoms of groupthink than groups composed of low-dominance members.
6. Individual members should be told that they will be held personally accountable for the group decision and will have to justify their decision (t'Hart & Kroon, 1989).

On this last point, we can wonder if Lt. Col. Oliver North would have acted differently if he had known that he would be held accountable for his actions in the Iran arms deal. Indeed, the publicity surrounding those actions and his eventual trial may serve to reduce the likelihood of groupthink in government decision-making groups.

Groupthink is a very important concept. It is unfortunate that so little research has been done on the topic. Much of the support for the theory comes from case studies. Although the verdict is still out on the theory, the concept of groupthink does caution us to pay attention to the characteristics of the members, structure, and process of decision-making groups.

Who Influences Group Decisions? Majority and Minority Influence

The work on groupthink is concerned with the quality of group decisions. Let's look now at the way groups make decisions. When an issue is first introduced, opinions are often split, with a majority favoring one position and a minority favoring another. Examining the *Kon Tiki* group, we can find numerous instances when the crew initially split 4 to 2 or 5 to 1. Such splits occurred when the crew was deciding how to move the large balsa logs from the jungle to the coast and when they were charting their original sailing plans. In most such instances the group eventually adopted the majority position.

Indeed, this seems to be the case in much of the research: the majority usually wins. Much of the research on this question has examined the decisions made by mock juries. Subjects are given

"evidence" about a case and told to arrive at a verdict. A series of studies (Davis et al., 1975; Davis, Bray & Holt, 1977) found that the majority generally wins; that is, the view held by the majority before discussion begins usually determines the verdict. Thus, if we find that 10 out of 12 jurors believe the defendant is guilty, it is likely that a guilty verdict will be returned if the jury is forced to deliberate to unanimity. On the other hand, there are some important process differences to consider. For example, Foss (1981) formed 12-member mock juries and had them listen to a trial proceeding. Some of the juries were told that they had to reach a unanimous decision before a verdict could be accepted while others were told that a verdict supported by a majority of members (a quorum) could be accepted. The results indicated that the verdicts reached by the two types of juries were roughly the same. However, the quorum juries reached a decision twice as fast and were less likely to be "hung" than the unanimous juries. Further, members of the quorum juries were more cooperative and willing to compromise than the members of the unanimous juries. The individual has much less power in a quorum jury than in a unanimous jury, which can be hung by one member. These findings are important because they may mean that juries required to reach a unanimous verdict are more likely to consider all the evidence carefully than juries under majority rule. (If you were on trial, it would not be very comforting to know that the members of your jury were willing to compromise so that they could reach a quick verdict!)

Some interesting processes help ensure the power of the majority. First, as we discussed in Chapter 12, the majority may simply reject the minority and expel them from the group. However, this is not the case with juries or with the *Kon Tiki* crew. Second, a group with a fixed membership often fails to consider information held by the minority, focusing instead on information known by the majority of the group (Stasser & Titus, 1985). In an interesting study, subjects in groups of three or six members were given information about candidates for student body president (Stasser, Taylor & Hanna, 1989). Some of the information was given to all subjects (shared) and some of the information was known by only one subject in each group (unshared). When the

Research on juries has shown that the majority opinion is generally adopted. However, a minority that takes a clear and uncompromising stand can influence the group. Clearly, a minority is also more likely to be influential if the jury must reach a unanimous as opposed to a majority decision.

subjects met as a group to discuss the candidate, it was found that they more often discussed shared information than unshared information. Further, discussion of shared information was greater in six-person groups than in three-person groups. We might argue that it would be better for groups to seek out the unshared information than to focus on the shared information. Regardless of our views on this matter, we can see that the focus on the shared information favors the adoption of the majority opinion. The minority has an uphill battle if the group refuses to consider and discuss unshared information about a topic.

The majority, then, often determines the position taken by the group. But before accepting this tendency as a general rule, consider the groups in which you have been a member. How often is the group ready to adopt a majority position when someone says, "No, I don't think we should do that. I think we should take this other course of action"? The other group members probably let out an audible groan, but after trying to change the dissenter's mind, the group may well have slowly shifted in his or her direction. In fact, this **minority influence** was the theme of a classic movie, *Twelve Angry Men*, in which

Henry Fonda portrayed one of 12 jurors at a murder trial. After hearing the evidence, the jury retired to the jury room to reach a verdict. Many of the jurors wanted to decide quickly because they had other things planned after the trial. On their first ballot, 11 jurors found the defendant guilty. The one not-guilty vote was cast by Henry Fonda, who believed strongly that there was not enough evidence to prove beyond a reasonable doubt that the defendant was guilty. The remainder of the movie shows how the other jurors tried to get Fonda to change his vote. When he held to his convictions, one by one the other jurors began to agree with him; at the end, the jury voted unanimously for acquittal.

How could Fonda or any other minority change the opinion of the majority? According to investigators (Moscovici & Mugny, 1983), minorities become influential to the extent that they can *become visible* to other group members and *create conflict* and tension within the group. Often the group attempts to silence the minority,

minority influence The ability of a minority opinion to affect the thinking of individual group members.

but the tension may lead others to consider the minority position.

In an interesting display of regionalism in social psychology, while American psychologists focused on the power of the majority, a number of European psychologists have taken the lead in examining the influence of the minority. These investigators argued that the minority can influence the group if it takes a clear and consistent stand (Moscovici, 1976; Moscovici & Nemeth, 1974; Maass & Clark, 1984). The minority must hold to its position in the face of pressure from the majority, but the minority must show that it is willing to compromise if a better alternative is found (Papastamos & Mugny, 1989). This display of openness is necessary to avoid the appearance of rigidity and dogmatism.

With this discussion in mind, you may rush off to a group meeting and adopt a minority position, only to find that you not only fail to sway the group but lose some of your popularity among the members. Were we wrong about minority influence?

The answer is found in the type of influence the minority has on the group. Investigators have found that the influence of the majority is generally direct, immediate, and public. That is, when the majority of group members suggest an alternative, the group may quickly and openly adopt this position. Minority influence is more subtle. The minority is more likely to influence members' *private* beliefs (Mucchi-Faina, 1989). The influence may be *delayed* (Nemeth & Staw, 1989); that is, members will not immediately jump to the alternative suggested by the minority, but they may change their position after thinking about the minority position. And minority influence may show up in *indirect* ways. One study found that a minority message in support of the right to abortion resulted in little change on the abortion issue, but group members did change their formerly negative attitudes toward birth control (Perez & Mugny, 1987). Other studies have shown that hearing a minority position in the group leads members to develop more creative solutions to problems, either related or unrelated to the issue addressed by the minority (Maass & Volpato, 1989; Nemeth & Chiles, 1988).

The suggestion that minorities have a different kind of influence than majorities do is fas-

STOP, THINK, & UNDERSTAND

1. What issues must be examined when we compare group and individual productivity?

2. What factors influence whether groups will perform better than individuals working alone?

3. How does the size of a group affect its performance?

4. Why does groupthink develop and how can it be avoided?

5. Who influences group decisions? What factors affect the influence of majorities and minorities in groups?

cinating. Investigators argue that upon hearing the majority position, people become concerned about how they will be treated if they deviate from it. They feel that the majority must be correct, and focus their attention on the immediate alternatives suggested by the majority and minority. In other words, their thinking *converges* on a few alternatives (Nemeth, 1989). Hearing the minority position sets up a very different process. The minority position gets attention because it is distinctive (Martin, 1989). As we witness the minority hold to its position in the face of pressure from the majority, we view the minority as courageous and as believing in their position; why else would they suffer for it (Moscovici, 1976)? We then try to figure out why the minority would adopt its position, and this leads us to consider the issue from a variety of perspectives. Thus our thoughts *diverge* from the stated alternatives and we may create new alternatives and solutions (Nemeth, 1989). Taking this line of reasoning, we can see that investigators are suggesting that the majority motivates us to quickly adopt a position that favors either the majority or the minority. The minority, on the other hand, does not force us into taking an either-or stand, but instead frees up our thinking so that we can consider a variety of positions.

Therefore, both the majority and the minority influence the group's decisions. We are more likely to see the group quickly and publicly adopt the position of the majority. But the minority will have a more subtle and longer-lasting effect, especially on the private positions accepted by individual group members.

The Group's Effect on the Individual

Thus far we have focused primarily on group behavior; we have investigated how groups perform and make decisions. We will now change our focus and examine how groups influence the individual. With this new focus, we become interested in whether being in a group influences the way individual members perceive, behave, and work. We will therefore be asking whether membership in the *Kon Tiki* crew had an effect on each crew member.

The Influence of Groups on Self-Concept

The crew of the *Kon Tiki* was welcomed to the United States by a large parade. They met with President Truman. A crew member could walk into any sailing club in the world and be greeted with respect. Being a member of the *Kon Tiki* crew became part of each member's self-concept; it gave that person an identity. The groups to which we belong also help form our own self-concepts. If someone asks us to describe who we are, we will include information about the groups to which we belong; we may describe ourselves as a student at Texas A&M University, a member of the band, a Delta Delta Iota, and a Lutheran. Groups, therefore, form the foundation of our **social identity** (Tajfel, 1982; Turner, 1987).

The role of groups in determining our identity sets into motion a number of processes. Most of us want to have a positive view of ourselves. Hence we attempt to join groups that enhance our image. People tend to disassociate themselves from groups that fail, while associating themselves with groups that are successful (Snyder, Lassgard & Ford, 1986). At another level, we want to see the groups to which we belong as good, and the groups to which we do not belong as bad. This desire leads us to perceive and

emphasize the positive aspects of our own group and the negative characteristics of the relevant out-groups (Mackie & Goethals, 1987; Tajfel & Turner, 1986). Further, our desire to be in good groups and to have no part of bad groups causes us to discriminate against the out-groups; we make our own group appear more positive in comparison with the out-group. And the more we identify with our own group, the greater our tendency to discriminate against out-groups (Hinkle et al., 1989).

We should be reminded of the work discussed in Chapter 10, which demonstrated the ease with which people form in-groups and out-groups. People distinguish between their own groups and other groups even when they are assigned to groups randomly or on the basis of a trivial matter, such as a preference for a painting or a political attitude (Hymes, 1986). However, the tendency to identify with the in-group and discriminate against the out-group is greater when we are dependent on our group for outcomes or when our group is threatened (Rabbie, Schot & Visser, 1989). Even within groups, members may make in-group–out-group distinctions on the basis of the most scanty criteria. For example, a distinction between "newcomers" and "oldtimers" may develop and influence the way these members treat and perceive each other (Moreland, 1985). This potentially disruptive distinction, however, diminishes over time.

The Influence of Groups on Perceptions and Evaluations

Belonging to a group not only colors our view of ourselves, but it also has pervasive effects on the way we view others and their products.

In-group = good; out-group = bad

One of the more consistent findings in research is that people perceive their own group and its efforts as good and the out-group and its efforts as bad. This effect is clearly seen in performance ratings. At one point in the study conducted by Sherif and his colleagues (1961; see Chapter 10),

---

social identity An aspect of self-concept that is based on membership in groups.

campers were told to gather as many beans as possible. They were then asked to estimate the number of beans that each boy had collected. The results indicated that the in-group estimated its total as being larger than that of the out-group. Hinkle and Schopler (1986) report a series of studies that also found an overevaluation of in-group performance and an underevaluation of out-group performance. One exception to the tendency to overvalue in-group performance occurs when there is a clear winner in a competition. In this case it was found that group members did not significantly overvalue their group's product when their group won a competition and expected to be competing again in the future (Worchel, Lind & Kaufman, 1975). Further, group members tended to deemphasize the evaluation of a poor performance by their group when they expected to be competing again. It was argued that people use group product evaluations to influence the motivations of other group members. In the first situation (win and expect future competition), group members refrained from giving high ratings to their group's product in an effort to avoid complacency and overconfidence. If group members felt that their group was too good, they might have lessened their efforts in the next round of competition. We often see this effect when coaches discuss a winning effort by their team. In a serious tone of voice, the coach will say, "The win was nice, but [the team] still needs a lot of work to get ready for [to win] the next one." On the other hand, when a group loses a competition and must get ready for another competitive event, members will be motivated to put the best light on their performance to boost group morale. We rarely hear a losing coach proclaim that his team was terrible; rather, these coaches often say that the loss was tough, but there were many bright spots in the team's performance.

The tendency to see the in-group as better than the out-group is not confined to evaluations of performance; it also occurs in the judgment of traits. Investigators have illustrated this point clearly by examining conditions that have led to wars and other conflicts between nations (Burin & Oskamp, 1989; Sande et al., 1989; White, 1966). For example, they point out that as conflict increases, nations form a "diabolical-enemy

image": they view their antagonist as evil and warlike. Hitler saw the Jews as evil and as plotting to take control of Germany. The view of the evil enemy is generally accompanied by a moral and virile self-image. Hitler described Germany and Germans as strong and courageous (virile), and he argued on numerous occasions that his intentions were peaceful. "I wish to point out first that I have not conducted any war; second, that for years past I have expressed my abhorrence of war" (Hitler's speech of April 28, 1939, in White, 1966). This pattern of perceptions repeated itself as the United States and the Soviet Union prepared for a summit meeting in November 1985. President Reagan painted a picture of the United States as peace loving and saw his proposals for arms reduction as positive and constructive. He characterized the Soviets as expansionists bent on world conquest. He saw their arms proposals as hollow and as a trick to gain a propaganda edge. Mikhail Gorbachev presented almost identical views, with the major exception that the names were switched; the Soviets were the good guys while the United States was the threat to world peace. We only need to read the newspapers of 1989 and 1990 to see how a reduction in conflict leads to changes in perceptions. Gorbachev and his supporters are now presented as reformers, and the Soviets see the United States in a more positive light.

Taking research a step further, one study (Howard & Rothbart, 1980) found that people were also more likely to remember the unfavorable behaviors of out-group members than the unfavorable behaviors of in-group members. Therefore, being assigned to a group not only leads us to see our own group more favorably than the out-group, but also structures our memories so that we will be most likely to remember the unfavorable behaviors of the out-group.

In-group members = dissimilar; out-group members = similar

When the *Kon Tiki* arrived in Polynesia, it was met by excited islanders. Heyerdahl discussed the different reactions of each of his crew members to this historic landing. However, he refers to the welcoming party of Polynesians as the collective "they"; they looked this way, or they acted in this manner.

We have a tendency to notice variability within our own groups and to perceive similarities within the out-group. For example, Jones, Wood, and Quattrone (1981) asked members of various eating clubs at Princeton University to indicate how members of their own and other clubs could be described on a number of trait dimensions. There was a significant tendency to indicate greater variability in one's own club than in the other clubs.

If people do see the out-group as being composed of homogeneous members, we might expect them to attribute the same traits to all out-group members. Quattrone and Jones (1980) had subjects watch a target person make decisions regarding a variety of activities. The target person was presented as a member of their own group (from the same college) or as a member of an out-group (from a neighboring college). After watching the target make the decisions, subjects rated the person and indicated how the "average" person from the target person's college would have acted in a similar situation. The results indicated a greater tendency to generalize from the target person's behavior to that of his group if he came from a different college (out-group) than the subject. This effect did not occur if subjects had strong prior expectations about how people would act in the particular setting.

A variety of explanations for this effect have been offered (Quattrone, 1986; and see Chapter 11 on stereotypes). One explanation concerns the frequency of exposure; we have more contact with members of our own groups than with members of out-groups. Therefore, we see more variability in the behavior and attitudes of in-group members than in those of out-group members. A second explanation is that we interact with in-group members over a wider range of situations; our interactions with out-group members are often confined to a narrow range of settings. Therefore, we have information about how the behavior of in-group members varies across situations, but we do not have this information about out-group members. For example, Heyerdahl observed his crew members as they readied for the voyage, as they faced the difficulties at sea, and as they experienced success. He worked, played, and attended formal functions with his crew. On the other hand, he interacted with the Polynesians in only one situation—when they were surprised by the arrival of the strange craft. Finally, Quattrone suggests that because of this limited range of experience with out-group members, we often explain away disconforming information about members of the out-group—that is, we see members of the out-group who do not conform to our expectations as "exceptions." It is relatively easy to ignore these "exceptions" because we have little opportunity to determine the correctness of this assumption. A related explanation is that because of the variety of information we have about the in-group, we have a more complex cognitive image of the in-group. This complex image reduces the extremity of our ratings (Linville, 1982; Linville, Salovery & Fischer, 1986).

Before we leave this discussion, one point should be raised. There is evidence (Worchel, Coutant-Sasic & Grossman, in press) that this effect is most likely to occur in groups that have been well established. Worchel and his colleagues, in fact, found the *opposite* relationship between group and perceptions during the early stages of group formation. That is, people perceived more similarity among in-group members than among out-group members. This perception may reflect people's lack of information about other in-group members early in the group's life. Or it may reflect the individual's desire to see himself or herself as similar to other in-group members. The concern with similarity will be high during this early stage because the person wants to (1) clearly define the in-group and (2) ensure that he or she will be accepted by that group.

In a related study, Brown and Smith (1989) found that members of a minority group perceived more in-group similarity than did members of a majority group. Perhaps minority group members had a greater desire to enhance the status of their group, or perhaps it was more important to them to be accepted by their group.

Group Influence on Individual Performance

We can see the varied effects that groups have on our perceptions and thoughts. Let's now

Many runners crave the excitement and challenge of marathon competition. They often echo Triplett's findings, saying that they run faster when running with others.

examine how groups affect our performance. Remember that earlier we asked about the factors that affect *group* performance. Then we were concerned about the product produced by the group. Now we can shift focus and ask whether being in a group influences your *individual* performance. From your own perspective, you may want to ask whether it would be better for you to work (study, take a test, jog) in a group or alone.

Social Facilitation

Social scientists have been interested in questions such as this since the turn of the century. In 1897, as we saw in Chapter 1, Norman Triplett devised one of the first social psychology experiments when he asked children to wind string on a fishing reel as fast as they could, either alone or in competition with another child. Triplett found

that the children worked faster in competition than they did alone.

Much of the research that followed Triplett's studies also found that people performed better in groups or in front of audiences than alone (Travis, 1925; Allport, 1924). This effect of others has been found with animals and insects. For example, Chen (1937) counted the balls of dirt that ants excavated as they built their tunnels. In some cases he had an ant work alone, and in other cases the ant worked with one or two other ants. Chen found that the individual ant worked harder (removed more balls of dirt) when it worked with other ants than when it worked alone. These results suggest that the presence of others facilitates performance. Since the subjects performed in front of a passive audience in a number of the studies, it seems that the **social facilitation** effects are due to the mere presence of others rather than to direct competition between individuals.

Given these results, we might conclude that groups are good for people (and other animals). Unfortunately, the picture is not quite so clear. At about the same time that the social facilitation results were reported, a number of investigators reported **social inhibition** effects. For example, Pessin and Husband (1933) found that the presence of an audience slowed the learning of a maze task and a nonsense-syllable task. Interestingly, *after* the subjects had learned the maze and nonsense-syllable tasks, they performed better in front of spectators. These contradictory results caution us against indiscriminately using groups to upgrade an individual's performance.

It was not until Zajonc (1965) proposed his theory of social facilitation that some theoretical sense was made of the contradictory results. Zajonc drew a distinction between the learning or acquisition phase of task performance and the performance or emission phase. Zajonc (1965, 1972) proposed that the mere presence of others increases an individual's arousal and drive. He argued that the presence of others in the environment increases alertness. The alertness (or arousal) results because the presence of others may require that the individual act quickly or in novel or unique ways. The arousal is important because it has been shown that an increase in drive increases the likelihood that an individual will perform the dominant response. The dominant response is the one that the individual is most likely to make in a particular situation. Hence Zajonc proposed that the mere presence of others facilitates the performance of the dominant response because it increases drive and arousal. He further pointed out that when an individual is learning a new behavior, the correct behavior has not yet become the dominant response. Thus, according to Zajonc, the mere presence of others should inhibit the learning of new or complicated responses but facilitate the performance of well-learned behaviors.

Overall, psychologists have agreed about the effect groups have on individual performance, but there has been considerable disagreement about why these effects occur (Berger et al., 1982; Guerin & Innes, 1982). One alternative position is that audience effects are due to the performer's concern about being evaluated (Cottrell et al., 1968). According to this position, people learn that others are potential sources of evaluation, and the presence of these others creates an anticipation of positive or negative outcomes. Therefore, social facilitation should occur only when the audience is in a position to evaluate the individual's performance. In support of this position, Henchy and Glass (1968) found greater social facilitation when the audience was perceived as being experts on the task than when the audience knew little about the task. Supposedly the experts were in a better position to evaluate performance than the nonexperts. In an interesting variation on this theme, some psychologists suggest that the effect of an audience on one's performance depends on whether one fears negative evaluation for poor performance or expects positive evaluation for good performance (Paulus, 1983; Wilke & Van Knippenberg, 1988). This hypothesis suggests that a focus on a positive outcome will improve performance on both simple and complex tasks. Concern about a negative outcome, on the other hand, will facilitate performance on simple tasks but inhibit performance on complex tasks. This idea still awaits careful testing.

Other research, however, suggested that concern about evaluation is not necessary to achieve social facilitation. For example, one study (Haas & Roberts, 1975) found that a blindfolded audience that could not evaluate performance did improve the worker's performance, but not as much as an audience that was not blindfolded. More recently, research by Baumeister, Hamilton, and Tice (1985) has found that too much concern about evaluation may lower performance. Results from this study showed that people performed less well in front of an audience that expected success than in front of an audience that did not hold such high expectations.

Another alternative explanation (Sanders, 1981) suggests that the audience serves as a dis-

---

social facilitation An increase in the quality of performance in the presence of an audience or co-actors, whether or not in competition.

social inhibition A restraint on performance effected by the presence of an audience or co-actors.

traction for the performer. In such a situation, the performer is placed in the conflictual position of having to decide whether to pay attention to the audience or to the task. This conflict leads to increased drive and facilitates the performance of simple tasks. In support of this position, a number of studies (Sanders & Baron, 1975) found that low levels of distraction enhanced the performance of simple tasks. Although the distraction/conflict hypothesis has been criticized as being imprecise (Geen, 1981; Markus, 1981) and for failing to account for much of the social facilitation data, it does offer an interesting alternative approach to the area.

It seems that many factors, including arousal, concern for evaluation, and distraction, may enhance social facilitation effects. In fact, all of these processes may occur simultaneously in some situations.

Social Loafing

The findings on social facilitation *seem* quite straightforward and clear. However, as is often the case, human behavior manages to create some interesting wrinkles and challenges for social psychologists. The first hint of such a wrinkle appeared in the Ringelmann (1913) rope-pulling study. Male subjects pulled either alone or in groups of two, three, or eight persons. Ringelmann found that two-man groups pulled 1.9 times as hard as a single individual, that three-man groups pulled 2.5 times as hard, and that eight-man groups pulled 4 times as hard. Hence, the larger the group, the greater the force that was exerted on the rope. As the size of the group increased, however, the output from each individual decreased. In other words, people worked less hard or "loafed" when they worked in the group.

Appropriately, this effect has been called **social loafing,** and research has replicated it many times. For example, it has been found that people clap less loudly in a group than alone. And a result that will interest waiters and waitresses is that individuals leave smaller tips when they are part of a group than when they are tipping alone (Latané, 1981).

Before we scrap everything that we learned about social facilitation, let us examine some of the explanations for the loafing effect. As you will remember, in the studies on social facilitation, subjects performed alone or in front of others: in each case, the person knew that his or her performance could be observed and identified by others. In the social loafing research, on the other hand, the person performs with others and believes that only the group product can be measured (Harkins & Szymanski, 1989). Further, the group product has little personal implication for the individual. In this case, the individual believes that his or her output cannot be specifically identified. In an effort to demonstrate the importance of identifiability, Williams, Harkins, and Latané (1981) had subjects shout either alone or in groups. In some conditions, however, subjects believed that their individual performance was always being monitored (always identifiable); in others, they believed it was identifiable only when they were alone; and in other conditions, they believed their output was never identifiable. As can be seen in Figure 13-3, performance was lower when subjects felt that their efforts were not being identified. Further support for this position comes from research showing that social loafing does not occur if the result of the group performance has clear personal relevance for the individual members (Brickner, Harkins & Ostrom, 1986). Hence one explanation for loafing suggests that the effect results when the individual cannot be identified with a specific output and the output has little implication for the individual.

A second explanation has been termed the **free rider effect** (Kerr & Brunn, 1983). To understand this effect, assume that you are a crew member on the *Kon Tiki*. The job is to pull up the sail. Everyone is pitching in and you see the sail going up nicely. Because all is going well, you may feel that great effort is not needed from you in this situation; you therefore reduce your efforts and become a "free rider." Loafing in this case results because the group members believe that their contributions are dispensable and that the group will succeed without them. From the group's point of view, this is a dangerous situation because if all the members become free riders, the task performance will suffer.

Another interesting explanation for social loafing has been called the **sucker effect** (Kerr, 1983). Again, assume that you are working to

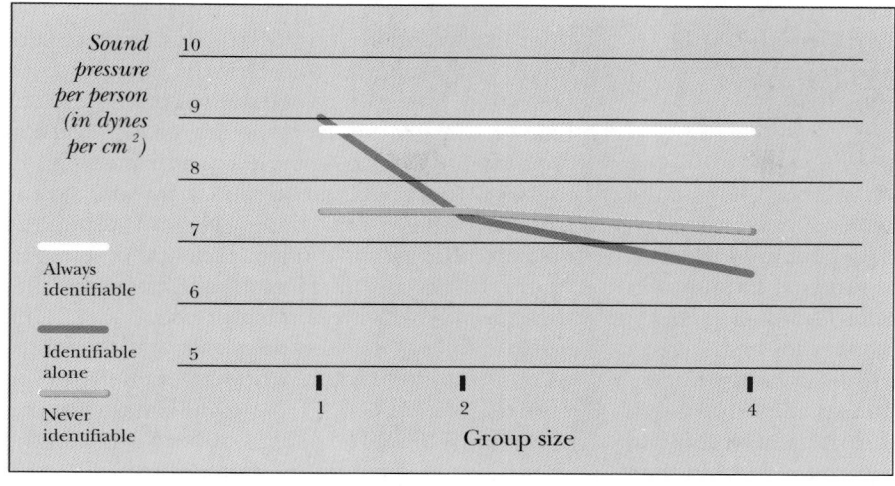

FIGURE 13-3 Sound pressure as a function of group size and identifiability
SOURCE: After Williams et al. (1981).

pull up the sails on the *Kon Tiki*. This time you are working your hardest and turn to see another crew member doing very little. You realize that it is the crew as a whole and not you as an individual that will get credit for getting the job done. This lazy member is therefore playing you for a sucker; you are doing all the work and he will receive as much credit as you. As a result, you may reduce your efforts and not work as hard as you did when you were working alone. In a study demonstrating this effect, subjects worked on a task with another group member who did poorly (Kerr, 1983). The subjects believed that the other member either had or did not have the ability to do better. They reduced their efforts (loafed) to the greatest extent when they felt the other person could do better but simply was not trying. It seems that we especially want to avoid being a sucker for others who can do well but are intentionally acting lazy.

A final point may have occurred to you as you read about the social loafing experiments. Although the subjects worked on their tasks in sight of each other, they had little feeling of being a group. A number of investigators have suggested that loafing is most likely to occur when the workers have little feeling of groupness (Petrovsky, 1985). For example, one study found no loafing when group members were given a

standard and led to believe their group would be evaluated against this standard (Harkins & Szymanski, 1989). In another study, subjects actually worked harder in the group when their interdependence was emphasized by the possibility of a group reward for good performance. In fact, they worked harder for a group reward than for individual rewards (Worchel, Hart & Buttermeyer, 1989). Therefore, loafing may occur in collectives rather than in groups of people who feel bound together by a common fate.

In sum, being in a group enhances individual performance when a person's output is clearly identifiable, the task is easy, and a sense of groupness is emphasized. However, when the output cannot be matched to the individual and people feel little sense of belonging to the group, social loafing may occur.

free rider effect Social loafing as a consequence of a belief that one's contributions to the group are dispensable and that the group will succeed without one's efforts.

social loafing The tendency of individuals to work less hard in a group than alone, perhaps because of lack of individual identifiability or reduced feelings of personal responsibility.

sucker effect Social loafing as a consequence of a belief that other group members are not contributing their maximum effort.

Group Influence on Individual Performance   461

The Influence of Groups on Individual Decisions

One of the critical activities engaged in by the *Kon Tiki* crew was decision making. From the beginning they were faced with a number of tough issues. They had to decide how to build the raft. They had to decide on the kinds and quantities of provisions to take with them. They had to decide who performed which tasks, and they had to make numerous rules to govern their behavior during the voyage. The decisions they made determined the success or failure of the voyage; and some of these decisions would affect their very lives. Often the group would discuss the issues, but the final decisions and actions would rest with the individual crew members. This situation leads to some interesting questions concerning how being a member of a group affects our individual decisions and actions.

Earlier we examined how groups make decisions; now our focus is on the individual. One of the earliest questions to be researched in this area was how making a decision in a group affects the individual's behavior (Lewin, 1943). Kurt Lewin's interest arose out of a practical problem that existed in this country during World War II. The price of foods, especially meats, increased rapidly and supplies ran short. There was no shortage of beef kidneys, brains, and sweetbreads, but the American homemaker was not accustomed to serving such things to her family. The government, interested in getting homemakers to serve these entrails, launched an extensive media campaign to persuade them to do so. Lewin reasoned that this method would not be effective. He believed that, since groups to which the homemakers might belong were responsible for the norm of not serving these products, propaganda attempts should be aimed at the groups, not at the individual.

Lewin felt that it was important to change the group norms regarding these products, and he set up an experiment to demonstrate how this could be done. He brought Red Cross volunteers together in groups of 13 to 17. Half of the groups heard a lecture on the positive values of using these nourishing but unpopular parts and on how their use would help the war effort (lecture condition). The lecturer told how the entrails could be cooked, and even passed out recipes. The other half of the groups were in the group-decision condition, in which a trained group leader summarized the problem briefly and then let the women discuss their feelings about using the entrails. The discussion leader succeeded in getting a 100% vote in favor of the proposal that these meats be served at least once a week. One week later, the women from all of the groups were interviewed to see who had actually served entrails. Ten percent of the women in the lecture condition, compared to 52% of the women in the group-decision condition, had done so.

The Lewin study clearly demonstrates that group discussion and decision can be used to change the norms and the behavior of group members. It is sometimes difficult, however, to have every member of a group involved in the discussion and decision-making process. Hence it would be nice to find that the same change can be achieved by the use of group representatives instead of the whole group. Coch and French (1948) had a chance to investigate this question when they were asked to look at productivity at the Harwood Manufacturing Corporation, a pajama factory. The plant often had to make minor adjustments in the work procedure. Although management expected temporary decreases in productivity after such changes, it found that the declines in productivity were often drastic and long-lasting. Supervisors explained the reasons for the work adjustments to the employees, but these explanations failed to increase productivity. Coch and French designed a study in which some groups of workers (no involvement) were simply told the reasons for the changes and exhorted to work harder. Other groups (total involvement) were given the opportunity to discuss with management the reasons for the changes and how they could improve work conditions. In a third condition, group representatives were brought together to discuss the changes with management. The results indicated that workers in the total-involvement condition adjusted more quickly to the changes than no-involvement workers, and that the productivity of the total-involvement workers rose to a much higher level than that of the no-involvement workers. The performance of the workers in the representative condition was higher than that of the no-involvement groups but did not reach the level of the total-involvement groups. Hence direct involvement in discussions by all group members is the most effective way to bring about group change.

Group Polarization

When Heyerdahl began thinking about the voyage, he proposed his idea to a number of people in the scientific community. He met with disbelief and discouragement that began to shake his commitment to the trip. In somewhat dampened spirits, he had a chance meeting with other sailors and explorers at the New York Explorers' Club. After a long discussion of the pros and cons of the trip, Thor emerged completely committed to making the risky voyage. What could have transformed Thor's growing caution into absolute certainty?

If we were to look at the early literature on group decision making, we would be surprised at this turn of events; we would expect Thor to have emerged from the group in a more cautious frame of mind. William Whyte, in his insightful analysis of business bureaucracies, *The Organization Man* (1956), speculates that the group lowers the creativity and risk-taking behavior of its members to the least common denominator. People rarely risk being creative and innovative because they fear they will be ridiculed by the more conservative power structure.

The view of group effects on individuals was challenged in a dissertation study. Stoner (1961) found that people chose riskier courses of action in groups than when they were alone. Following up on this finding, a group of investigators (Wallach, Kogan & Bem, 1962) asked a large group of college students to fill out a questionnaire consisting of twelve potential dilemmas that a person might face in life, with each choice presenting a risky and a conservative alternative. The risky

alternative had a very high payoff if successful, but if unsuccessful it had dire consequences. Here are four of the dilemmas (Wallach et al., 1962, p. 77):

1. A captain of a college football team, in the final seconds of a game with the college's traditional rival, may choose a play that is almost certain to produce a tie score, or a more risky play that would lead to sure victory if successful, sure defeat if not.

2. The president of an American corporation that is about to expand may build a new plant in the United States where returns on the investment would be moderate, or may decide to build in a foreign country with an unstable political history where, however, returns on the investment would be very high.

3. A college senior planning graduate work in chemistry may enter university X where, because of rigorous standards, only a fraction of the graduate students manage to receive the Ph.D., or may enter university Y which has a poorer reputation but where almost every graduate student receives the Ph.D.

4. A low-ranked participant in a national chess tournament, playing an early match with the top-favored man, has the choice of attempting or not trying a deceptive but risky maneuver that might lead to quick victory if successful or almost certain defeat if it fails.

The students were asked what probability of success they would require before they recommended the risky alternative. When the subjects had completed the questionnaire, they were asked to get together in groups of five to discuss the various dilemmas and arrive at a group consensus—a recommendation that could be agreed to by all members of the group. On 10 of the 12 items, the groups arrived at decisions that were riskier (required less of a probability of success) than the average risk that had been acceptable only moments earlier to the individuals who made up the groups.

In the final step in this study, the subjects were retested individually. The group shift to a risky position may have been one that the individual group members publicly agreed to but did not actually accept; perhaps they had acceded to the will of a few strong individuals. The results showed that the group discussion and decision had caused a change of attitude. The subjects' opinions in the second individual testing remained at the risky position that they had adopted in the group discussion. Some subjects who were tested as much as six weeks after the group session continued to show the shift toward risk.

This and a number of studies with similar results (Muhleman, Bruker & Ingram, 1976; Cartwright, 1973) led investigators to conclude that being in groups led individuals to adopt riskier positions; the term *risky shift* was coined to refer to this effect. But the picture became cloudy when other studies discovered that people in groups adopted more conservative positions than they had had on entering the group. For example, Fraser, Gouge and Billig (1971) were able to identify several items on which the subjects shifted toward caution. McCauley and his colleagues (1973) and Knox and Safford (1976) examined bets on horses at the racetrack. In their field studies, the subjects bet either alone or after group discussion. In both of these cases, groups were more cautious than individuals, as groups bet on the favorite more often than did individuals.

The general picture that emerged was that groups do not necessarily produce a risky shift. Rather, they seem to produce a polarization effect in the direction that was initially preferred. That is, the average postgroup response was more extreme in the same direction as the average pregroup response. If the initial tendency was toward risk, the group response was more risky; if the initial tendency was toward conservatism, the group response was even more conservative. This area of study became known as **group polarization.** Given that groups do lead to polarization in decisions, the next question centered on why this effect occurred. A variety of hypotheses were suggested.

An explanation that focuses on social comparison (see Chapter 3) suggests that people do not want to be seen as taking wishy-washy or neutral positions; they want to appear at least as certain and extreme as others (Myers, 1982). According to this explanation, people use group discussion to compare their position with that of others. As a result of this comparison, they shift their own position until it is at least as extreme

as that of other group members. Along these lines, one study found that people become more confident of their opinion when they perceive consensus in the group and must soon act on their opinion (Orive, 1988). Most group polarization studies find little difference in subjects' initial opinions. Therefore, when you hear other group members agree with your opinion, your confidence in that opinion may increase *and* this increased confidence may cause your opinion to become more extreme.

Social comparison may be responsible for some of the polarization effects, but not all. Studies of the impact of simply exchanging information about preferred positions without group discussion typically show some degree of polarization, but not as much as is found with full discussion. If people simply want to compare their position with that of others, this information exchange should produce complete polarization effects. This finding suggests that social comparison by itself is one factor affecting polarization, but that other factors are important as well.

A second hypothesis (Burnstein & Vinokur, 1977; Burnstein, 1982) suggests that it is not the positions of the other people but the arguments they use to support their positions that create group polarization. According to this hypothesis, members listen to the arguments presented by people during the group discussion, and they shift their opinions in the direction of the position that has the *most persuasive arguments*. Laughlin and Earley (1982) found that the direction of polarization was related to the number of persuasive arguments supporting a position: risky shift occurred when the risky extreme had the most arguments, and conservative shift occurred when the conservative side had the most arguments.

Although the persuasive arguments theory does have support, Sanders and Baron (1977) argue that the theory does not explain why the most compelling arguments favor a particular and relatively extreme position. That is, would it not be just as likely that strong arguments might favor a more neutral and middle-of-the-road stand?

In an effort to reconcile the various positions, several social psychologists (Isenberg, 1986; Brown, 1986) suggested that social comparison and persuasive arguments work together to produce group polarization. According to these investigators, group members first compare their position with that of other group members. This comparison motivates them to present arguments supporting their position. These arguments influence not only the presenter but other members as well. Another intriguing idea is that both social comparison and persuasive arguments affect the extremity of our opinions, but the two forces work in different situations (Kaplan, 1987). According to this position, when the issue involves facts, we will be concerned with the information presented in the arguments. Our position becomes more extreme as we garner information from the discussion. However, on tasks requiring values (for example, the right to abortion), we compare our position with the position (not the reasons for the position) of others. In this case, social comparison plays a strong role in pushing our opinions toward extremity.

Looking back over our discussion of group decision making, we can see that groups may increase the extremity and confidence of our opinions. It is interesting to speculate that this shift toward extremity in individual opinions may increase the possibility of groupthink. The caution here is not that you should avoid making decisions in groups. Indeed, we have seen that groups offer a wealth of information and perspectives that can improve decisions. Rather, it is important to be aware of the influence groups can have on the decision-making process, and guard against the negative dynamics. Using this advice, investigators have found that groups that have received information about group dynamics can perform better than even the best individual member (Hall & Williams, 1970; Michaelson, Watson & Black, 1989).

Deindividuation: Getting Lost in the Group

Before leaving our discussion of group dynamics, we will examine one of the more dramatic effects of groups on individuals. Herman Watzinger, one of the crew members on the *Kon Tiki*, anticipated our discussion when he stated that as the voyage wore on, he lost his concern about himself and focused on "the crew." He felt that his own identity became that of the group. For Watzinger, the effect was enjoyable and enhanced his performance on the voyage. In other cases, the effect has not been positive. In the now infamous "snowball" game between the Denver and San Francisco football teams during the 1985 season, a snowball was hurled from the crowd as San Francisco was preparing to kick a short field goal. The snowball distracted the players and San Francisco missed the goal; Denver won the game by two points. The young man who threw the snowball said he was ashamed of his actions; he had become carried away by the excitement of the crowd, and had acted without thinking of the consequences.

As far back as 1895, the French sociologist Gustave Le Bon observed that individuals often become "lost" in crowds and do things they would not do if they were alone. He observed:

> Whoever be the individuals that compose it, however like or unlike be their mode of life, their occupations, their character, or their intelligence, the fact that they have been transformed into a crowd puts them in possession of a sort of collective mind. (p. 20)

In addition to having a collective mind, a crowd is irrational, and its intellectual level is always below that of the isolated individual. Le Bon also described crowds as emotional and said that when in them, the individual begins to feel and express the emotions of a "primitive being." According to Le Bon, three mechanisms are responsible for creating the monster known as a crowd. First, because the individual is anonymous, he or she loses the sense of individual responsibility and thus participates in acts that he or she would not normally engage in. Second, contagion (see Chapter 12) causes the individual in the crowd to act as he or she likes but would not under other circumstances. Contagion reduces the individual's inhibitions and allows him or her to behave

---

group polarization The tendency of group discussion to cause an individual to make a more extreme decision than he or she would make alone.

Becoming deindividuated—for example, using costumes to conceal one's personal identity and effect a group public identity—makes some people feel they can do things they would not otherwise do. People who are deindividuated do not feel responsible for their actions, and this frees them to not conform to standard social norms.

as the model behaves. Third, people become more suggestible in crowds; the crowd hypnotizes the individual, who then follows the suggestions of other members or the crowd's leader.

Other investigators have expanded the view of the **deindividuation** process, and three models have been proposed. One suggests that conditions such as large groups, anonymity, and a heightened state of arousal are the precursors of deindividuation. These conditions lead individuals to become submerged in the group, losing their own sense of identity (Zimbardo, 1970). When this identity loss occurs, people no longer feel responsible for their behavior; their attention is drawn to the group and behavior becomes regulated by fleeting cues in the immediate situation. When people lose a sense of personal

responsibility for their actions, they are no longer governed by the norms and inhibitions that are present in most situations. Their behavior becomes impulsive, emotional, and difficult to terminate.

At the extreme, this view suggests that deindividuation releases the beast inside each of us. When Watson (1973) studied the warfare patterns of more than 200 cultures, for example, he found that warriors who were deindividuated by masks and paint had a greater tendency to torture captives than warriors in cultures that did not use such devices. Taking a somewhat different approach, Worchel and Andreoli (1978) found that aggressors deindividuated their victims before harming them. This deindividuation of the victim occurred when the aggressor selectively recalled information, thereby removing the victim's identity and uniqueness. It was easier to attack a deindividuated victim than a more individuated one. Finally, Diener and his associates (1976) found that trick-or-treaters were more likely to steal when they wore masks and remained anonymous than when they were clearly identifiable.

A second position also suggests that people lose their personal identity in a crowd. Rather than becoming unrestrained and unrestricted, this position argues, people take on a new identity, one defined by their role in the group (Brown, 1988; Reicher, 1984; Diener, 1979). This new identity then guides their behavior. Consider the following experiment (Johnson & Downing, 1979). Subjects in the study were deindividuated by a uniform. In some cases, however, the experimenter commented that the uniform was similar to that worn by the Ku Klux Klan, a group known for violence. In other cases, the experimenter mentioned the similarity of the uniform to that worn by nurses, a nonviolent group. Subjects were then given the opportunity to shock another person in a learning situation. Aggression increased slightly when the uniform was compared with that of the Ku Klux Klan. The intensity of shocks administered *decreased* significantly when the connection with nurses was salient. When the salience of the individual identity was reduced, the subjects performed more like the group they felt they represented.

In order to understand the third position, consider your own feelings in large groups. Many of us may find losing our identity to the group disturbing or uncomfortable. At many large universities, students complain of being lost in the crowd; they are treated like numbers and no one knows or cares about them. Feeling lost in the crowd may motivate people to do something that makes them stand out from the group, to gain identity, and to be recognized. Hence animated, exaggerated, and sometimes antisocial behavior may represent people's attempts to gain recognition (Maslach, Stapp & Santee, 1985). We might therefore explain the snowball hurler at the football game by focusing on loss of responsibility; being in the group freed him from inhibitions against throwing the snowball. On the other hand, we might argue that being submerged in the crowd motivated him to do something to gain recognition; throwing the snowball separated him from the rest of the crowd.

Clearly, deindividuation is a complex process that may be partially explained by all three hypotheses. Before leaving our discussion of this process, let us point out another side of deindividuation. We have shown that deindividuation can lead to negative antisocial behaviors; but deindividuation can also have positive consequences. As we pointed out in Chapter 12, deindividuation often leads to a reduction in conformity to group norms. In some cases, freeing the individual from the shackles of group norms can give rise to creativity that would otherwise be inhibited. For example, some authors adopt pseudonyms because they feel fewer restraints when they write anonymously. Finally, we find deindividuation in some professions in which individuals must violate social norms to carry out their jobs. For example, surgeons must handle and cut into their patients' bodies. For many years it was believed that surgeons should not become well acquainted with their patients; and when the operation took place, the surgeon was covered from head to foot and the patient was draped with a cloth so that only the affected area was visible. We might speculate that deindividuation here freed the surgeon from concerns and fears that might have interfered with his or her job. However, many patients and doctors complained that they felt uncomfortable with this impersonal transaction; today many doctors spend time getting to know their patients before operations. All

STOP, THINK, & UNDERSTAND

1. Research on social facilitation and social loafing shows that groups sometimes enhance individual performance and sometimes decrease it. How can we reconcile these findings? What factors influence whether social facilitation or social loafing will occur?

2. Describe the group polarization effect and some explanations for it.

3. A dilemma for many people is how to be a member of a group but still retain a personal identity. How has this dilemma been used to explain deindividuation effects?

4. Is deindividuation a positive or negative situation?

the same, though deindividuation has its darker side, it can also have positive effects.

Summary

A *group* may be defined as two or more people who are interacting with one another in such a manner that each person influences and is influenced by each other person. People in groups experience themselves as belonging together and sharing common goals.

From the individual's perspective, joining a group has both positive and negative consequences. Groups allow people to accomplish a variety of tasks that could not be achieved alone, and social comparison is possible in groups. On the other hand, people must give up some freedom and personal identity when they join a group.

deindividuation The loss of individuality that occurs when the individual becomes submerged in the group and feels relatively anonymous.

Group members go through a variety of stages: new member, full member, marginal member, ex-member. Groups, like members, go through a series of stages as they develop and change. These stages affect the dynamics of the group and the behavior of individual group members.

Group structure includes boundaries, norms, and roles. Although the structure is designed to help groups function smoothly, conflict can occur within and between roles.

Groups generally perform better than individuals working alone. Groups are superior at recognizing correct solutions, especially when these solutions are presented by members with high status. The effectiveness of groups is diminished by *process loss*, which includes *coordination* and *motivation loss*. Setting clear group goals and providing performance feedback can enhance group performance. Performance is also influenced by the type of task on which the group is working. For example, large groups may perform better than small groups on *additive tasks*, but may be hindered by motivation loss on *disjunctive* and *conjunctive tasks*. In general, cohesive groups perform better than noncohesive groups unless the cohesive groups develop *norms* that limit production. *Cohesiveness* is promoted by similarity of group members, by threat by another group, by members' sacrifice to the group, and by group success.

Research suggests that men are often more task-oriented than women, while women are more social- and feeling-oriented in groups. It has also been found that partners react with a more social orientation to women and with a task orientation to men. Although there is some indication that all-male groups perform better than all-female groups, a careful analysis suggests that this superiority is found on male-oriented tasks.

Groupthink occurs when group members make a quick and ill-conceived decision in an effort to maintain group harmony. Groupthink is most likely to occur in highly cohesive groups that have a strong and respected leader. The chances that groupthink will occur can be reduced by a careful consideration of proposals, by the leader's avoidance of stating a clear preference, and by solicitation of opinions by people who are not members of the group.

Although the majority usually determines the group's decision, the minority can be effective if it adopts a consistent and unyielding stand. Minorities are effective because they create conflict and challenge the group norm of conformity. Majority influence is generally direct, immediate, and public. *Minority influence* is usually indirect, delayed, and private. The minority often motivates divergent thinking that results in creativity.

Groups influence members' self-concept. Our *social identity* is determined by the groups to which we belong. As a result, people attempt to join "good" groups and perceive their own group as positive. Discrimination results when members attempt to enhance the difference between the in-group and the out-group. Most people perceive in-group members as dissimilar and out-group members as similar. This effect is particularly pronounced in more established groups and majority groups.

Groups may influence the performance of individual members. Research on *social facilitation* shows that people perform simple and well-learned tasks better in groups than alone, but that learning of new material will be inhibited by the presence of others. The last effect seems to occur because others arouse the individual and increase the drive to exhibit the dominant response. Many explanations have been offered for the social facilitation effect, including evaluation apprehension, distraction, and social comparison. *Social loafing* is the tendency of individuals to work less hard in groups than alone. This effect may be the result of reduced feelings of responsibility for the final product and the lack of identifiability of individual performance in a group. Social loafing has also been attributed to the *free rider effect* and the *sucker effect*. Social loafing is reduced when people feel a sense of groupness and a concern that the group product can be evaluated.

Decisions made in groups following group discussion are most likely to influence an individual's behavior. Membership in a group often leads individuals to adopt more extreme positions than they held before they become part of the group. This effect may result from the reduction of responsibility that people feel in group decisions. *Group polarization* has also been explained by social comparison and persuasive argument processes.

Deindividuation occurs when people lose their personal identity and adopt that of the group. It generally occurs in large groups where people feel anonymous and arousal is heightened. People in deindividuated conditions focus on immediate cues. Doing so often lowers inhibitions against performing socially disapproved actions. A second explanation for the deindividuation effect is that people lose their personal identity in a crowd and take on an identity defined by their role in the group. A third explanation for the behaviors of deindividuated people is that they are attempting to gain personal recognition and distinctiveness.

Key Terms

additive task
cohesiveness
collective
conjunctive task
coordination loss
deindividuation
discretionary task
disjunctive task
free-rider effect
group
group development

group polarization
groupthink
minority influence
motivation loss
nominal group
norm
organizational
  psychologists
process loss
role
role ambiguity

role conflict
social facilitation
social identity
social inhibition
social loafing
socioemotional
  specialist
sucker effect
task specialist

Suggested Readings

Brown, R. (1988). *Group processes: Dynamics within and between groups.* Oxford, England: Blackwell.

Forsyth, D. (1990). *An introduction to group dynamics* (2d ed.). Pacific Grove, Calif.: Brooks/Cole.

Hendrick, C. (Ed.). (1987). *Group processes.* Newbury Park, Calif.: Sage.

Janis, I. (1982). *Victims of groupthink.* Boston: Houghton Mifflin.

McGrath, J. (1984). *Groups: Interaction and performance.* Englewood Cliffs, N.J.: Prentice-Hall.

McGrath, J. E. (Ed.). (1988). *The social psychology of time.* Newbury Park, Calif.: Sage.

Moscovici, S., Mugny, G., & van Avermaet, E. (1985). *Perspectives on minority influence.* Cambridge, England: Cambridge University Press.

Mullen, B., & Goethals, G. R. (1987). *Theories of group behavior.* New York: Springer-Verlag.

Petrovsky, A. V. (1985). *The individual and the collective.* Moscow: Progress.

Steiner, I. (1972). *Group process and productivity.* New York: Academic Press.

Turner, J. C. (1987). *Rediscovering the social group: A self-categorization theory.* Oxford, England: Blackwell.

Chapter Fourteen

The Environment

One of the more popular movies of 1985 was *The Gods Must Be Crazy*. Its plot was rather simple but very prophetic. A Coke bottle, tossed from a passing airplane, is found by a tribe of primitive Bushmen in the Kalahari Desert. The Bushmen have been isolated from contact with the modern world. This simple change in their environment drastically alters the tribe's daily routine and social relationships. Outside the theater, the year 1985 offered many real reminders that the environment in which we live strongly influences our lives. In Bhopal, India, a cloud of methyl isocyanate leaked from a Union Carbide chemical plant and killed more than 2,000 people in the crowded neighborhoods around the plant. A drought that had toyed with East Africa for five years tightened its grip.

Concern for the environment was no less dramatic four years later as the *Exxon Valdez*, an oil supertanker, ran aground, spilling 11 million gallons of black goo on the pristine Alaskan coast. Worry about the depletion of the ozone layer gripped the world, leading some people to call for a ban on chlorofluorocarbons. In a symbolic gesture the state of Vermont banned the use of chlorofluorocarbons in automobile air conditioners after 1991. In Europe the Green party, dedicated to protection of the environment, gained increasing popular support in Germany, France, and the Scandinavian countries. In 1990 voices were raised throughout the world to demand protection for the Amazon rainforest. It had become clear that wholesale destruction of the environment in one part of the world affects people everywhere.

These events serve as dramatic reminders of the delicate relationship between people and their environment. They stand out because of their scope and international importance, but they do not stand alone in bringing us this message. In 1975 an energetic sailor, Tristan Jones, dazzled an audience at the Explorers' Club in New York City when he pulled open a curtain to reveal a 19-foot sailboat. Jones was the last of a distinguished panel of speakers that had included the astronaut James Lovell and the industrialist William Rockwell. While these other speakers talked about the wondrous conquests that had been made, Jones spoke of the cost of these conquests, calling for reason and caution. He had just completed a ten-year, 60,000-mile voyage in his small craft, the *Sea Dart*, and had viewed the world from a perspective that few of us have either the patience or opportunity to experience.

He had flown into New York some months earlier marveling that it took seven hours to complete a trip that would have taken him 11 weeks on the *Sea Dart*. But he also noted that the speed of the trip gave him no opportunity to enjoy the seas or land below, or to pause to talk with the people along the way. He noted that in America, unlike Europe, a car is not a luxury; it is an absolute necessity. He found that the public transportation system in the United States was hopelessly inadequate and that the sheer size of the United States made it necessary to own an automobile. Jones observed that travel by car is isolating; in a car people do not have an opportunity to interact with others or to observe their environment closely, as they do on public transportation.

Jones had hoped to find a boat that he could transport to the Caribbean so that he could earn money. While searching for work, he spent a great deal of time walking around New York. He was struck by the enormous diversity of the environment he found and by its effect on the people. One such walking tour particularly stuck in his mind.

Walking through Pelham Park, on the mainland side of the City Island causeway, I was closely surveyed three times by different police cars that slowed down and cruised by me slowly, the cops inside eyeing me suspiciously. I just kept plodding along until I was at Westchester, an urban center. From then on I was seemingly in more criminal surroundings, for I was ignored by passing police.

At first the south side of The Bronx wasn't too bad. Long, long avenues surrounded by boxlike factories and apartment buildings. But further on, closer to Manhattan, there were more and more burned-out buildings, more and more potholes in the road, and more and more an air of sleazy hopelessness. By now just about everyone in the area was black. In the street there was a continual procession of gleaming steel behemoths, Fords, Chevys, Cadillacs, green, blue, red, black, streaming along. The sun reflected hostility from their chrome, their riders were hidden behind tinted windows. On the sidewalks, sitting on bro-

We often overlook our environment and the effect it has on us, until someone or some event captures our attention. In order to force people to pay attention to their environment, Tristan Jones brought his boat, *Sea Dart,* into the Explorers' Club in New York. He talked about his impressions of people's relationship with their environment as he viewed it from the deck of his tiny vessel.

ken door stoops, ambling around and lounging, was group after group of people, most of them staring sullenly at the passing parade. There was a lot of noise, both from the traffic and the locals. Unlike the poor I had seen in many parts of the world, these people did not seem to be hungry or very ill-clad or sick, especially the younger ones. (Jones, 1980, p. 105)

The variety of bars in New York delighted Jones.

There's an extravagant variety of bars in New York. Irish bars and Polish bars, journalists' bars, singles' bars, doubles' bars, theatrical bars, "gay" bars, topless dancing bars, literary bars, painters' bars, sculptors' bars—I suppose there must be an undertakers' bar somewhere. (Jones, 1980, p. 119)

Each bar catered to one type of patron, and those who did not fit the acceptable category were quickly made to feel unwelcome with unkind stares and cold shoulders.

Buckminster Fuller was an early proponent of the view that we must manage human affairs from the perspective of the whole planet rather than any one country. He was an architect who was famous for his construction of the geodesic dome as habitat, for his development of the concept "Spaceship Earth," and for initiating an attempt, called "The World Game," to pool information about the world's resources.

Jones observed that there are great differences in the way seafarers and land dwellers approach their environment. The world of the sailor is unstable and naturally confusing. It does not have the predictability and opportunities for control available to people who live on the land. As a result, the life of a seafarer is aimed at learning skills to aid survival by cooperating with the environment. Land dwellers, on the other hand, view the land and the sea as "an empty wilderness or a promising prairie. They seem to think that if something could not be controlled, it ought to be exploited" (Jones, 1980, p. 281).

In his talk at the Explorers' Club, Jones argued that people who live on the land are losing touch with their environment; they are largely unaware of it and the role it plays in their lives. He observed that

the landsman, at base, is a farmer. He improves the land. He tries to make things grow where they never grew before. . . . Successful agriculture creates comfort for many and it allows capital—in the form of grain, for example—to be accumulated in good years and set aside against setbacks in poor years. (Jones, 1980, p. 231)

As a result of this security, Jones argued, people often fail to pay attention to their environment until disaster or catastrophe strikes.

Jones left a questioning audience at the Explorers' Club that night. Was this unusual man simply a preacher of doom or was he a prophet? Jones seemed to care little what people thought of him. After sailing in all the oceans and seas of the world, he had planned a new trip, one that would allow him to carefully observe the relationship between land dwellers and their environment. But it was also a trip that would allow him to stay tucked away in the *Sea Dart* on the fringes of this relationship that intrigued and frightened him. He planned to sail through the heart of the United States, down the Mississippi River from Minneapolis to New Orleans. As president of the Atlantis Society, he would also devote his efforts to investigating and providing the means for young disabled people to earn their livelihood at sea.

Environmental Psychology: What Is It and Why Study It?

To look at the world through Tristan Jones's eyes is to get a unique picture of our lifestyle. Because he spent so much time isolated from the modern world while sailing on his small boat, Jones's observations give us a chance to explore a question that many of us have asked at one time or another: "What would people from another place or time think about our world if they suddenly arrived on the scene?" It is interesting to note that while Jones commented on the politics and social relationships that he found in the countries he visited, much of his attention was captured by the relationship between people and their physical environment. He was interested not only in how people affected their environment, but in how the environment affected the way people behaved, believed, and interacted.

It is precisely because the environment does affect our behavior that it is an appropriate topic for social psychology. Our physical environment, as we will see, has a strong influence on our attitudes, perceptions, and social interactions. In studying the relationship between people and their environment, we will draw on almost all the theories we have discussed earlier. We'll see the role of attitudes (Chapter 5) in influencing our approach to our environment; we'll see how our self-concept (Chapter 3) is affected by and reflected in our use of the environment; we'll find that attributions and social cognition (Chapter 2) play a major part in determining how we respond to our physical environment; and we'll see how our environment influences our social behavior, such as our attraction to other people (Chapter 7), helping (Chapter 8), frustration and violence (Chapter 9), conflict (Chapter 10), and group behavior (Chapter 13). In a sense, studying the relationship between people and their environment allows us to put many of the theories of social psychology to the test; we have the opportunity to determine whether these theories increase our understanding of this relationship and enable us to create a better relationship between people and their surroundings.

Environmental psychology—the scientific study of the relationship between people and their environment—is a relatively new area of study, tracing its history back only a few decades. The field has a unique character because it has attracted researchers from such diverse areas as architecture, urban planning, engineering, anthropology, and sociology as well as social psychology.

People and Their Environment: A Historical Perspective

Tristan Jones's description of the difference between the seafarers' and land dwellers' views of the environment presents an interesting contrast—interesting in that it not only shows the difference between these two groups but also parallels historical differences in the way people have felt about their environment.

Jones suggested that mariners see their surroundings as uncontrollable and unpredictable; the environment is the master and sailors must learn to survive in it. Altman and Chemers (1980) suggest that this view was characteristic of people early in history; they too saw the environment as master. In early times, people's lives were controlled by nature. It determined the types of homes they built: the Eskimo lived in a home made of ice because the environment supplied only this type of building material. The environment determined where people lived: villages were built close to rivers because people needed water and used the river for travel. When it was hot, people were forced to seek shade for protection; and when it was cold, they shivered together around fires.

According to Jones, land dwellers view themselves as the masters of nature: their aim is to gain complete control of their environment. Jones (1980) protested this approach because he saw it as threatening his domain. "Now [the land dweller] was about to invade the ocean using the same philosophy and methods that had done so much harm ashore" (p. 233). According to Altman and Chemers (1980), the view that people were *above* nature became common during the Industrial Revolution, when people developed many devices to control nature. In time, people could control their climate with air conditioners and heaters. The environment no longer determined where people could build homes; they could dig deep wells for water and level hillsides to make room for houses. Improvements in transportation allowed people to seek out environments that catered to their immediate needs. Their attitude was that the environment was something to be controlled and conquered.

In recent years this view has changed, and a new understanding and respect for the environment has begun to emerge. Pollution and the scarcity of environmental resources have become

---

environmental psychology   The study of the relationship between the environment and behavior.

Native Indian people have traditionally lived in harmony with nature, preserving the balance among human life, animal life, and vegetation. Here Amazonian Indians protest the destruction of forests by developers. These are the same forests they have tapped for centuries without destroying.

matters of major concern. We are slowly realizing that our relationship with the environment is a reciprocal one; we both influence it and are influenced by it. We are once again beginning to see ourselves as part of nature. Research has shown that our environment has a broad effect on a variety of behaviors.

Studying the Environment: Some Unifying Concepts

If you examine your own environment, you will begin to appreciate the enormous task facing environmental psychologists who wish to study the relationship between people and their surroundings. The environment is composed of many variables—the space around you, the shape of the room you are in, the temperature of the air, the amount of noise in the vicinity, the size of the city in which you live. These and many more

variables are part of our environment, and, as we will see, research has shown that each variable can influence our behavior.

The roots of environmental psychology can be traced to the 1940s, when Roger Barker and Herbert Wright (1950) observed the behaviors of people in two small towns in Kansas and Yorkshire, England. Their aim was not only to classify these behaviors but to determine what caused them. They concluded that behaviors take place in ecosettings that include personal and social variables as well as physical and temporal factors. In order to understand behavior, we must examine all of these factors. And so was born **ecological psychology,** which later gave rise to environmental psychology as we know it today (Wicker, 1987).

A concept that consistently crops up in the literature on environmental studies is the **person-environment fit** (Altman, Lawton & Wohlwill, 1984; Holahan, 1982). The heart of this concept is that the relationship between people and their environment is a dynamic one. We cannot simply suggest that a particular environment will have the same effect on all people; the effect of the environment on an individual will be influenced by the individual's characteristics, attitudes, expectations, and personal history.

Investigators have found, for example, that leisure settings are not enjoyable for everyone or even enjoyable for one person at all times. Environments are most enjoyable when they offer us opportunities for action or challenges that are matched to our skills (Csikszentmihalyi & LeFevre, 1989). The most positive environment for some people will be their work setting, because it contains the most comfortable mix of challenge and skill-related action.

Another concept that is frequently relied on is *attribution*, often referred to as *interpretation* or *appraisal* (see Chapter 2). Attribution theories argue that the way people feel and react to others (and their environment) is a function of the interpretation they give to situations and events. For example, Jones got a job to sail a boat, the *Star Rider*, from New York to the West Indies. He took a crew of four men who had little sailing experience. After several days of sailing in light breezes, the wind changed direction and picked up velocity. To the crew this was a welcome change, for it offered them a new challenge and increased the speed at which they sailed. Tristan Jones, however, interpreted the change as a sign that a storm was approaching and he became worried and concerned. The same environment, therefore, led to different interpretations and reactions. Lazarus (1982) argued that the degree to which people will view an event or situation as stressful is determined by their appraisal of that event. Thus it is not only the environment that affects people; their interpretation of the environment plays a major role. This approach forms the heart of a growing area known as environmental cognition, which we shall encounter throughout this chapter (Golledge, 1987; Russel & Snodgrass, 1987).

A third important concept is *control*. Jones felt that people strive to control their surroundings and that a lack of control is very disquieting. Similarly, environmental psychologists have found that control is a central issue in predicting how people will respond to the environment (Bandura & Wood, 1989). People can endure very extreme conditions when they feel that they have control over their environment. On the other hand, seemingly benign environments can become very stressful when people feel that they have no control over their surroundings.

A fourth unifying concept that runs through many environmental studies is **cognitive overload.** According to this theory, people are able to deal with a limited amount of stimulation at any one time. If the environment becomes so complex that people are "overloaded" with stimulation, they will experience stress, their performance will deteriorate, and they will try to reduce the amount of stimulation. This concept is most useful for explaining the effects of urban environments, but it has also been used to explain the circumstances in which people suffer from crowding and experience ill effects from noise.

More than in most areas of social psychology, research on environment and behavior has focused on **arousal.** Investigators are not only interested in how the environment affects an individual's state of arousal; they are also concerned with how arousal then affects the individual's health and performance in that environment (Gatchel, Baum & Krantz, 1989). Arousal has become a key concept because it may explain behavior in a given situation. As we will see, investigators have also been interested in how the environment affects the way people interpret their arousal. It has been argued that two people may experience similar arousal (heart rate, blood pressure, galvanic skin responses [GSR], and so on) but each will interpret that arousal in a way that depends on characteristics of the environment. The interpretations subsequently influence their behavior and their "fit" with their environments.

---

arousal Physiological activity measured by such indices as blood pressure and heart rate.

cognitive overload An excess of stimuli beyond one's ability to process.

ecological psychology The study of human behavior in a social and physical context.

person-environment fit The dynamic relationship between people and their environment, suggesting that the "best" environment must be determined by the needs and characteristics of the people in that environment.

Finally, environmental psychologists are beginning to emphasize that behavior takes place in a **temporal framework** that includes past experience and future expectations (Wicker, 1987). In other words, the influence of a particular setting is determined not only by that particular setting but also by the settings in which we have previously interacted and our expectations about future settings. One study found that employees reacted positively to a move from one office to another, whether the new office was a private cubicle or an open-office design (Oldham, 1988). Another study found that subjects rated a room less crowded when their previous environment had been uncrowded than when their previous environment had been crowded (Worchel, Webb & Reichers, 1989). And Goodman and Garber (1988) found that coal miners who are familiar with their environment have fewer accidents and are absent less frequently than miners who are not familiar with their dangerous work setting. We can imagine how Tristan Jones must have felt when he docked in a large city after sailing alone for weeks. A look at the temporal context of behavior could probably benefit many areas of social psychology that we have studied in earlier chapters. With this background in mind, let us examine some of the specific areas that have been studied by environmental psychologists.

Spatial Features of the Environment

When we think about our environment, one of the first things that comes to mind is space. Do we have too little or too much of it? Are there too many people in it or too few? Can we control what is in that space? Why do we need or want space? What happens when we do not have sufficient space? What qualities make some space more desirable than other space? Because of its prominence, a great deal of research has been done on the way people use and are affected by the space around them. As we will see, this research not only examines such areas as the places in which we live and work but the space that immediately surrounds our bodies.

Personal Space

It was an odd crew that signed on to deliver the 40-foot ketch *Star Rider* to the West Indies. The captain, Tristan Jones, was British. Jerry, the cook, was black and in his early 20s. Johnny, the first mate, was Korean-American and had just turned 20. The two white American crew members could hardly have been more different. Al, the mechanic, was in his early 20s and had been a pipefitter before the voyage. Hank, the navigator, was a middle-aged man who owned a restaurant and was "the image of a suburban American." At the beginning of the voyage, Jones noted that the crew members generally kept to themselves, trying to be very careful not to bump into one another, and apologizing when a sudden lurch brought an unavoidable collision. In a sense, no matter where on the ship a man happened to be, he tried to protect the space around him from uninvited intrusion. As the voyage progressed, however, the concern about close contact abated and the crew often chose to eat together in close quarters; no apology was uttered or discomfort displayed as they crawled over one another while carrying out their daily duties. Each man still viewed the space around him as personal, but the size of that personal space was smaller than it had been at the beginning of the voyage.

The behavior of the *Star Rider*'s crew was not accidental or haphazard. For decades social scientists have observed that animals and people use the space around them in rather predictable ways. This is especially true of the space that directly surrounds the body; we can consider this space "mobile territory" because it is always present and goes wherever we go. Thus each crew member had a zone of personal space whether he was on shore, on the ship's deck, or in the galley.

The existence of personal space was first observed in animals. Hediger (1950) noticed that when animals of the same species are together, they tend to space themselves. The distances they maintain remain constant within species and across situations. Animals will move and attempt to position themselves to keep this normal spacing. Hediger called this distance *personal distance* and noted that it involved interaction between animals of the *same* species.

Edward Hall (1959, 1966), an anthropologist, was fascinated by the way animals used space and wondered whether humans used space in a similar manner. He coined the term **proxemics** to denote the study of the human's use of space. He used the term **personal space** to denote the bubbles of space that people attempt to keep around themselves when they interact. Hall hypothesized that we feel a certain "ownership" of the space around us. He observed people in various cultures and concluded that each culture has its own norm in regard to the distances that persons maintain when they interact. The size of these interaction distances is determined by the culture and by the nature of the interaction.

Hall (1966) characterized individuals in Western societies as having four definite interaction distances, each with a close and far phase:

1. The first is **intimate distance.** In the close phase of intimate distance, the two parties touch each other. This is the distance at which we make love, wrestle, and give protection and comfort. In the far phase, 6 to 18 inches separate the two parties. This phase is used when touching is not permitted and conversation is conducted in very low tones, as in telling secrets.

2. **Personal distance** has a close phase of 18 to 30 inches and a far phase of 30 to 48 inches. Close personal distance is used by close friends or by a married couple when they converse. Hall says that "keeping someone at arm's length" is one way to characterize the far phase of personal distance. This is the distance for ordinary social interactions between friends and acquaintances who wish to discuss matters of personal interest but do not want to engage in physical contact.

3. The close phase (4 to 7 feet) of **social distance** is used for personal business and for conversations at casual social gatherings. The far phase (7 to 12 feet) is used for more formal business and social discourse. Desks in the offices of important people are usually large enough to hold people at the far phase.

4. Formal interactions occur in the close phase (12 to 25 feet) of **public distance**. The far phase (25 feet or more) is the distance that is automatically set around important public figures.

Reviews of hundreds of studies have found that people keep predictable distances between themselves and others (Altman & Vinsel, 1977; Hayduk, 1978, 1983). Violations of personal space cause people to become aroused (McBride, King & James, 1965). When our personal space is violated, we often attempt to restore proper spacing (Sommer, 1969) or reduce the intimacy of the interaction. However, if we perceive the violation of our space as a friendly gesture, we may enjoy and reciprocate the close interaction distance (Schneider & Harsvick, 1977).

One fascinating aspect of spatial behavior is that, despite the regularity involved, people seem unaware of it. Love and Aiello (1980) had pairs of unacquainted women discuss a prearranged topic. After the discussion, the investigators asked the subjects to replicate the spatial behavior they had used during the discussion. Subjects were given dolls to use in indicating their behavior. It turned out that the subjects were unaware of the interaction distances they had kept during their conversation.

Before we become too complacent and accept the image of a world populated by people navigating through their environment encapsulated in perfect bubbles of space, we must caution that the size and shape of personal space are affected by a wide range of factors. Our view of this orderly world must first take into account the fact that the shape of personal space is not necessarily the circle suggested by Hall. Research suggests that frontal distances are often slightly larger than rear distances (Strube & Werner, 1982). However, one caveat here is the finding that violent or delinquent individuals protect larger areas behind them than in front of them (Lothstein, 1972). Other investigators have developed even

---

intimate distance   The distance people use for intimate activities such as making love, offering protection and comfort, and whispering.

personal distance   Space kept between organisms when interacting with a member of the same species.

personal space   The mobile area around an individual of which he or she feels ownership and control.

proxemics   The study of interpersonal space.

public distance   The distance maintained in formal interactions and around public figures.

social distance   The distance used for personal business and at social gatherings.

temporal framework   The context of time, experience, and expectations in which behavior takes place.

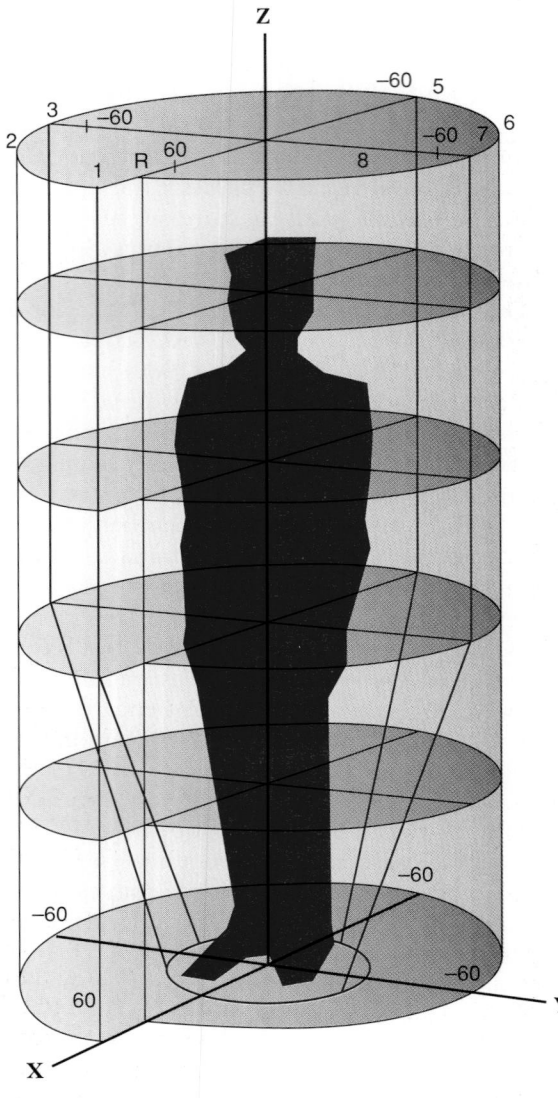

FIGURE 14-1 A three-dimensional view of the shape of personal space
SOURCE: Hayduk (unpublished).

more complex representations of personal space (see Figure 14-1). And while many investigators have focused on the care with which people maintain distance between themselves and others, some researchers have found that people feel discomfort when too much space separates them from people with whom they are interacting

(Aiello, 1987). It seems, therefore, that we have preferred interaction zones; too much space or too little space creates tension and motivates us to establish a proper distance for each interaction.

These observations prompt us to ask what other factors affect the shape and size of personal space. A complete answer to this question would fill at least one volume the size of this text, so let us take a selective look at some of the more interesting variables.

Factors affecting personal space

Gender and age. In general, research has found that the distance kept between interacting males is larger than that kept in female-female interactions and mixed-sex interactions (Brady & Walker, 1978). There is also some support for the hypothesis that greater distance is maintained in mixed-sex interactions than in interactions between females. An exception to this finding is that mixed-sex pairs who have intimate relationships (spouses or lovers) maintain the closest space (Aiello, 1987). Overall, these patterns argue that males have larger personal spaces than females. We can speculate about the reasons for these differences. In Western cultures, there are strong taboos against homosexuality—especially male homosexuality. Children are often punished by their parents for touching or caressing another child of the same sex. However, direct teaching and models inform children that heterosexual touching is acceptable. Hence children's spatial behavior may be partly a response to norms in respect to permissible sexual behavior.

In light of this speculation, it is interesting to note that stable personal space norms do develop around the time the child reaches puberty. Investigations reveal that children do not begin to exhibit consistent spatial behavior before the age of 4 or 5. After that age, the size of personal space increases until the age of 12 or 13 when it stabilizes (Aiello & Aiello, 1974; see Figure 14-2).

Byrne and his colleagues (Byrne, Baskett & Hodges, 1971; Fisher & Byrne, 1975) found another difference between the spatial behaviors of males and females. Males responded most negatively to frontal invasions of their space whereas females reacted most negatively to inva-

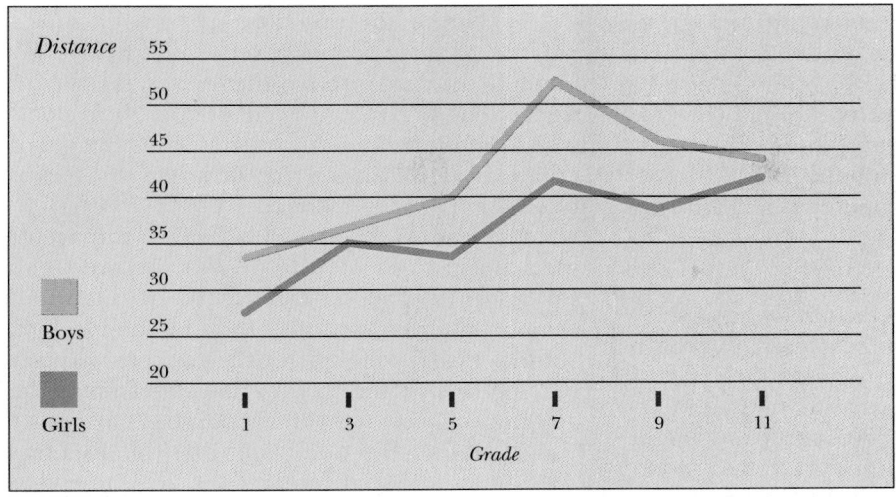

FIGURE 14-2 Mean interaction distances of male and female dyads at six grade levels
SOURCE: Aiello and Aiello (1974).

sions from the side. This finding led Fisher and Byrne to predict that males would be more likely to protect their frontal space than their lateral space, whereas females would be most concerned about protecting their lateral space. To test this hypothesis, observers watched the behavior of males and females in the library. They found that males were most likely to place their books and possessions in front of them on a table, thereby discouraging others from taking a seat across the table. Females, on the other hand, placed their possessions at their side and thus reduced the likelihood of invasion from that direction.

Culture. Culture also affects personal space distances. Latin Americans, French, and Arabs interact at closer distances than people from the United States, England, or Sweden (Hall, 1966). Little (1968) asked subjects from five countries to place dolls in a "comfortable interaction" position. He found that people from Italy and Greece placed the dolls closer than subjects from the United States, Sweden, and Scotland.

Cultural differences in personal space have been the subject of many humorous stories. One such story involves a Latin American and a North American who were conversing at a party. The Latin American continually moved closer and closer to the North American because he was comfortable interacting at a close distance. The North American, on the other hand, felt comfortable with more space and countered the other's approach with movements backward. The result was a "Latin waltz" in which the Latin American moved in and the North American moved back, and the two crossed the room during the course of their conversation.

The cultural variations in personal space norms have some important implications. Inner-city populations represent a mixture of racial and ethnic backgrounds, which may be a source of constant stress. This stress arises not only from differences in language and customs but also from cultural differences in the norms regarding personal space. For example, given that Puerto Ricans like to interact at a close distance, whereas Germans like to maintain rather wide spacing, interactions between members of the two nationalities are likely to be marked by stress. When an interaction occurs between members of two nationalities, each of the two persons involved will attempt to locate himself at a comfortable distance for the interaction. This type of spacing conflict is more acute in North American cities such as New York and Toronto than in such cities as Hong Kong because there is much greater cultural mixing in North America.

It is also interesting to find that the crew of the *Star Rider* was composed of men from different cultural and racial backgrounds. Accordingly, they may have had different requirements for personal space zones, and these differences may have accounted for some of the awkwardness and apologies for unplanned contact during the early stages of the voyage.

Contextual factors. Many factors that are characteristic of the situation in which an interaction takes place are not directly related to the participants (age, sex, race) or the nature of their interaction (friendly, unfriendly, strangers). We might consider these characteristics *contextual factors* (Worchel, 1986a). A wide variety of such factors has been shown to influence the size of personal space zones. For example, people maintain greater distances in small rooms than in large rooms (White, 1975) and in rectangular rooms than in square rooms (Worchel, 1986a). People interacting in inside locations maintain greater distance than people interacting outdoors (Cochran, Hale & Hissam, 1984). When people are in settings that are likely to arouse a great deal of tension (student infirmary, dean's office waiting area), they maintain greater distances than in less anxiety-provoking settings (television lounge, commuter lounge) (Long, 1984). Even ceiling height has an effect; males maintain greater distances when room ceiling heights are low than when they are high (Savinar, 1975). Two other contextual findings are also of interest. First, strangers who are discussing an intimate or potentially embarrassing topic (sexual behavior) keep greater distances than when the topic is less intimate (university classes) (Baker & Shaw, 1980). Finally, people who expect to be interacting over a long period set greater distances than people who expect only a short interaction (Worchel, 1986a).

Why personal space?

Given that spatial behavior is so predictable and that violations of personal space engender such strong responses, we are led to ask why we have a need for personal space. What is the function of the sack of space that we keep around our bodies? Several answers have been offered and all probably have merit.

1. One of the functions of personal space may be to give people a sense of identity. By claiming the space around themselves, people can signal that they are indeed unique individuals who are independent of others. Thus the act of claiming personal space may be a symbolic means of declaring independence.

2. Personal space may be an important mechanism for achieving privacy. According to this argument, people can use the space around them as a buffer to protect their privacy. In fact, Altman (1981) believes that the desire for privacy may be one of the factors that determines the amount of space individuals claim as personal.

3. Hall (1966) points out that the distances used in most social interactions are those that keep others at arm's length. Individuals who have a history of violence or who are angry keep even greater distances. These arm's-length distances allow the individual to see the hands and feet of others and protect against surprise physical assaults.

4. Distance plays an important role in interpersonal communication. The distance at which we interact with others determines the channels of communication that we can use. For example, if we communicate with others at the public distance (12 to 25 feet), we may hear their voices, but it is difficult to determine whether they are maintaining eye contact, frowning, smiling, or expressing anger. As we move closer to such individuals, we can begin to observe more of these nonverbal behaviors; we can distinguish eye contact, smiling, slight changes in the angle of the head, and even sweating. Thus interpersonal distance determines the channels through which communication can take place.

5. Probably the most widely recognized function is the regulation of intimacy. Many studies (Gifford and O'Connor, 1986) have found that people interact at closer distances with others whom they like than with people they dislike. The closer two people are to each other, the more intimate their relationship. But distance is not the only way we communicate intimacy. We can also signal attraction for others by looking into their eyes, smiling, and leaning toward them. We can communicate dislike by moving away from people, reducing eye contact, frowning, turning our shoulder toward them ("giving them the cold

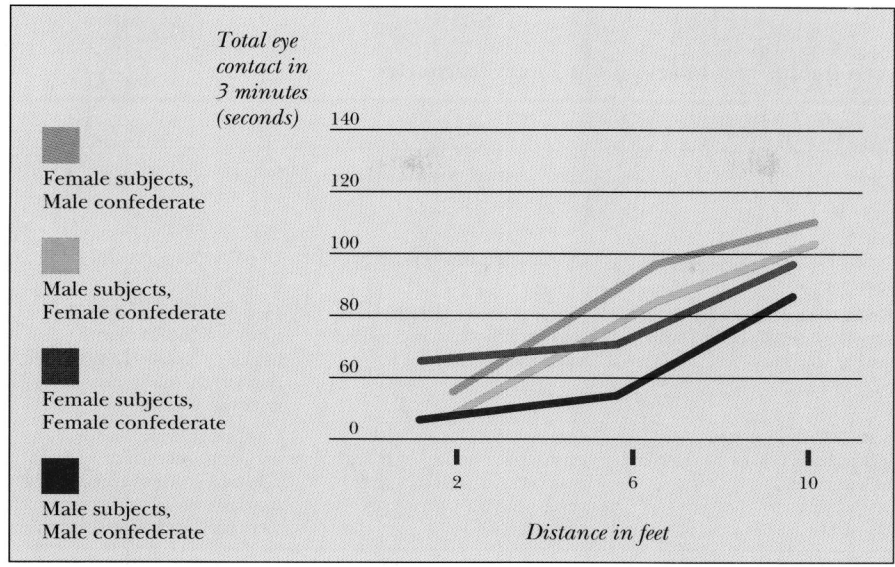

Total eye contact in 3 minutes (seconds)

Female subjects, Male confederate

Male subjects, Female confederate

Female subjects, Female confederate

Male subjects, Male confederate

Distance in feet

FIGURE 14-3   The relation between eye contact and distances for different combinations of confederates and subjects
SOURCE: Argyle and Dean (1965).

shoulder"), and leaning away. Hence Argyle and Dean (1965) suggested that nonverbal behaviors are used to form an equilibrium system through which intimacy is communicated. Individuals form a comfortable level of intimacy, and if that level is upset, the individuals will attempt to compensate and reestablish equilibrium by using any or all of the behaviors associated with intimacy.

Argyle and Dean tested equilibrium theory by having subjects converse with a confederate at distances of 2, 6, and 10 feet. An observer behind a one-way mirror recorded the amount of eye contact maintained by the subject. As the distance between the subject and confederate decreased, so did the amount of eye contact (see Figure 14-3). Patterson (1977) found that as interaction distance decreased, subjects not only reduced eye contact but positioned their bodies to be less open to the confederate (placed their shoulders between themselves and the other person).

Territoriality

Thus far we have been discussing the small bit of mobile territory that immediately surrounds our bodies. Another kind of space that has a strong influence on our behavior is the territory we control. Tristan Jones sailed more than 60,000 miles on a 19-foot boat. He sailed the *Sea Dart* in every ocean in the world and ferried her across continents. He worked at such jobs as janitor to buy rigging and paint for his tiny craft. When he was on the *Sea Dart*, he was king in his own small realm. He decided who could come aboard and who could not. He knew every inch of his boat and he took pride in her appearance. The *Sea Dart* was Jones's territory and he would risk his life to save her.

The desire to possess territory has been observed in both animals and humans. **Territoriality** is persistent attachment to an area or object and defense of it against other persons or groups. Humans have a sense of proprietorship over their territory, in that they can dispose of it as they wish, and they will defend it even to the point of aggression.

territoriality   Persistent attachment to an area or object and defense of it against other individuals or groups.

TABLE 14-1

Dimensional variations between public, secondary, and primary territories

Dimension	Public	Secondary	Primary
Duration	Short	Short, but regular usage common	Long
Centrality	Not central	Somewhat central	Very central
Marking intentions	Intentionally claiming territory	Often claiming territory	Usually personalizing or decorating
Marking range	Few physical markers or barriers; much bodily and verbal marking	Some reliance on physical markers; bodily and verbal marking common	Heavy reliance on a wide range of markers and barriers; bodily and verbal marking usually not necessary
Responses to invasion	Can relocate or use immediate bodily and verbal markers	Can often relocate, use immediate bodily and verbal markers, as well as some reemphasis of physical markers	Cannot relocate easily, can use legal recourse, reestablishment of physical markers and barriers, as well as bodily and verbal markers

SOURCE: Brown and Altman (1981).

Types of territory

An interesting feature of human territorial behavior is that people have many types of territory. Altman (1975) identifies three types of human territories: primary, secondary, and public. As Table 14-1 indicates, people's territorial behaviors depend on the type of territory involved.

Primary territories are exclusively owned and controlled by individuals or groups; they are central to our lives and are generally owned on a permanent basis. We often go to great lengths to mark and protect our primary territories. One's home or apartment or even one's bedroom within a home is a primary territory, as was the *Sea Dart* for Tristan Jones. He often lived on the boat and his life revolved around this craft.

Secondary territories are less central, and it is not usually clear who owns them. They serve as a bridge between the primary territories and the more public areas that can be used by everyone. Often a limited number of persons have access to a secondary territory. One of your secondary territories may be your regular seat in a classroom. You may become accustomed to sitting in a particular seat every time you attend a certain class. If another person sits in "your" seat, you may not throw that person out but you are likely to feel somewhat stressed—the chances are

that you will arrive early at the next meeting of the class to regain control over "your territory." Cavan (1963, 1966) reported that neighborhood bars are typical secondary territories. Patrons who use these bars frequently feel a sense of control over them. Outsiders who wander into them often receive cold stares or insulting questions. The message that strangers do not belong there is made very clear. As we reported in the opening pages of this chapter, Jones observed those behaviors clearly in New York bars; if one wasn't the type to fit into the bar, he or she did not belong in that territory and the patrons gave this message clearly. Thus, while secondary territories are not owned, people usually exercise control over them. Interestingly enough, because secondary territories involve feelings of control but not clear ownership, the potential for conflict and misunderstanding in these areas is very high.

Public territory is open to the public, and individuals or groups do not feel that they have a claim on such territory unless they are occupying it. For example, you may feel that you have exclusive access to a particular spot on the beach while you are occupying that spot; no one should trespass on your spot while you are there. However, you do not feel that you should be entitled to that particular spot if you come back to the beach the next day.

Whether the local corner bar or a well-known rock bar, patrons often view these places as their secondary territory. They do not own the areas, but there is a sense of who "belongs" there and who does not. And whether through hostile stares, body language, or overt physical action, patrons exercise control over "their" territory.

We are most protective of our primary territories and least defensive of public territories. However, the territories that people define as primary, secondary and public may vary from culture to culture (Hagino, Mochizuki & Yamamoto, 1987; Kruse & Graumann, 1987; Küller, 1987). Let us examine a case in which cultural factors affect territorial behavior.

A tourist in Greece is immediately struck by the spectacular landscape dotted with wonderful antiquities—all framed in litter! Trash has invaded the rocky beaches and detracts from the beauty of the ancient ruins. Constant litter campaigns beseech residents to pick up the litter. The distastefulness of the scene gives the casual visitor the impression that Greeks are less concerned about litter than residents of many other countries. This proves to be a shortsighted conclusion, however. Worchel and Lollis (1982) pointed out that Greeks draw a clear distinction between private and public territory; there is very little secondary territory surrounding their residences. Most Greek homes have a fence or hedge separating private property from public property; in fact, in many cases the fence is erected before the home is built. The private-public distinction is not so clear in the United States and Canada. Here people often view the sidewalk and curb in front of the home as a secondary territory. Though other people may pass through these areas, the residents feel that they control the territory. Most homes in the United States and Canada are not surrounded by fences.

To demonstrate how these different perceptions of territory affect behavior, Worchel and Lollis placed plastic bags of litter in three locations near residences in the United States and Greece. Early in the morning, the litter was put either in the front yard, on the sidewalk in front of the house, or on the curb in front of the house. The investigators returned every four hours to see if the litter had been removed. (If the litter had not been removed by the following morning, the experimenters collected it.) As can be seen from Table 14-2, litter in the front yard (private territory) was removed with equal speed in Greece and the United States. However, litter on the sidewalk and street curb was removed significantly more quickly in the United States than in Greece. To determine whether all areas around the home are considered secondary territory in the United States, Worchel and Lollis located

primary territory   An area or object that is exclusively owned or controlled on a permanent basis by an individual or group and is viewed as a central part of the owner's life.
public territory   An area or object that is temporarily controlled by an individual but of which no feeling of ownership exists.
secondary territory   An area or object that is temporarily controlled by an individual or group.

TABLE 14-2

Mean speed for the removal of litter in two countries

Country	Location of drop			
	Yard	Walkway	Street	Across street
Greece	1.53	5.00	5.25	—
	(17)	(15)	(16)	
United States	2.27	2.00	2.25	5.57
	(15)	(15)	(16)	(7)

Scores range from 1 to 6, with lower scores indicating quicker removal. Numbers in parentheses indicate number of houses in the condition.
SOURCE: Worchel and Lollis (1982).

homes with a vacant lot across the street. They placed bags of litter on the curbs in front of these lots, across the street from selected homes. As Table 14-2 shows, the litter was rarely removed in these cases. It therefore seems that secondary territory in the United States does not extend across the street.

The functions of territory

The owning and control of territory play many important roles in our lives.

1. Territoriality helps provide a stable social organization. Rosenblatt and Budd (1975) found that married couples exhibited more territorial behavior than cohabiting couples. Married couples were likely to have a clear understanding about who slept on what side of the bed, to have separate closets or closet areas, and to have specific seating positions at the dinner table. Supposedly, married couples were in a longer-term relationship than cohabiting couples, and social organization was more important to them. You might imagine what your own living situation would be if there were no territorial rules; you would not know what bed you would be sleeping in or what desk you could study at or even which room you would have for the night.

2. Territoriality aids in the regulation of privacy (Ittelson et al., 1974). **Privacy** is "an individual's freedom to choose what he will communicate about himself and to whom he will communicate it in a given circumstance." Thus privacy is a chosen isolation. Usually periods

of privacy are intermingled with periods of social interaction.

Privacy is an important and necessary condition for humans. Four needs that are fulfilled by privacy have been identified (Westin, 1967).

a. It allows us some personal autonomy or self-identity in that it provides a means by which we can control our environment.
b. It provides opportunities for emotional release from the tensions of everyday life.
c. It gives us an opportunity for self-evaluation by allowing us to withdraw and take stock of ourselves.
d. It allows us limited and protected communication by permitting us to decide when and with whom we will share our thoughts and feelings.

By controlling territory, we can achieve privacy whenever we want it. When Tristan Jones wanted privacy, he retreated into the *Sea Dart*; when he really wanted to ensure his privacy, he set sail.

3. A third function of territoriality for humans is analogous to the protection function for animals. Humans seem to have a "home-court advantage"; they perform better on their own territory. Worchel and Sigall (1976) found that Atlantic Coast Conference basketball teams win 88% of their home games and less than 65% of their games on the road. Familiarity with the home territory seems to play some role in these statistics; the basketball player knows how the ball will bounce on the home court and

knows the "action" of the familiar home-court backboards. More recently, however, investigators (Baumeister & Steinhilber, 1984) found that there is actually a slight tendency for home teams to lose decisive championship games. According to the researchers, the pressure to perform well in these decisive games is much greater on the home-court players than on the visitors; the players do not want to make mistakes in front of their own fans. This added pressure may make them self-conscious and cautious, and inhibit their performance.

Moving out of the sports arena, we still find a home-court advantage. A number of studies (Edney, 1975; Taylor & Lanni, 1981) have found that people on their home territory tend to dominate social interactions and play leadership roles. At a more subtle level, observations of people in offices revealed that the officeholder rather than the visitor initiated a handshake (Katovich, 1986) and the visitor often opened the conversation by explaining why he or she had come into the officeholder's territory.

4. A final important function of territory is to establish independence and personal identity. Territory allows people to define who they are and to draw boundaries between themselves and others (Brown, 1987). Territory also lets people advertise their self-identity to others. If you walk through a dormitory or office, you will see that people have decorated their areas to reflect their identity. The skier has pictures of snow-covered mountains; the political activist has pictures of favorite candidates and political slogans.

Before we become completely convinced of the virtues of territorial behavior, let's examine its darker side. While territoriality facilitates the development of order and organization, it also mitigates against change. At the personal level, the fear of giving up territory or changing territory may cause people to forgo opportunities for job advancement and travel. Some people become so attached to territory that they will not part with a possession even after it no longer serves any useful purpose. Most of us know someone whose home is so cluttered with junk that there is hardly any room for people. At the broader social level, rigid adherence to territorial claims and the opportunity to pass on territory to the next generation makes social change very difficult. Today we can witness struggles over territory in the Eastern bloc countries, in India, and in Mexico. Although the conflict may focus on

---

privacy   Freedom to choose what one will communicate about oneself and to whom the information will be communicated; chosen isolation.

FIGURE 14-4 The appearance of a home can influence its chances of being burglarized (left, nonburglarized; right, burglarized)
SOURCE: Brown (1979).

territory, consider the prospect of those people who are stigmatized because of their territory. We may attribute a range of negative characteristics to a person who lives in a "bad neighborhood," for instance. Recently a college administrator confessed his concern about the impression that his students and faculty would get if he drove the expensive sports car his children had given him as a present! Hence our territorial behavior has its functions and dysfunctions.

Establishing and protecting territory

Both animals and humans use markers to define and distinguish their territory so that others will observe that a certain plot is "owned." Some animals, for example, scratch the bark on trees around the boundary. Other animals, such as domestic dogs, will urinate or defecate around the boundaries of their territory. Humans may erect high fences or hedges to protect their territory. Often these **territorial markers** are accentuated with "No Trespassing" signs or even armed guards. People also use nonverbal signals, such as a gaze, an angry stare, or a sprawl of the body over an area to show that it belongs to them and no one should intrude. The adept library patron can manage to claim three seats at a table by spreading body and belongings over the area.

Territorial markings are often very effective in defenses against intrusion. One study (Brown, 1979) found a home was less likely to be burglarized if it had clear territorial markings, such as a fence or name plate, than a home that was not clearly marked (see Figure 14-4). At another level, investigators (Sommer & Becker, 1969) examined the effectiveness of various markers in protecting secondary territory. The experimenters placed various markers on a chair in a crowded study hall and observed how often someone invaded the territory and sat in that chair. The results, presented in Table 14-3, indicate that the greater number of markers and the more personal the markers, the more effective they were in protecting the territory.

It seems, therefore, that people have very clear norms in regard to claiming territory. However, people do not have clear norms as to how to react when territory is invaded. What do you do if you have left your coat to claim a library chair and return to find someone has moved your coat and taken your chair? Some of us might march up and loudly demand our territorial rights. However, Becker and Mayo (1971) found that people seldom resort to confrontation to protect secondary or public territory. Often the individual will retreat and find a new territory.

We know that the situation is very different when primary territory is involved. Although there have been no studies of the protection of primary territory, the newspapers often carry stories of individuals who barricade themselves in their homes and threaten to shoot anyone who attempts to take possession of their territory.

Density and Crowding

Jones came to New York in an effort to find work; his trusty craft, *Sea Dart*, had been impounded in London, and Jones had no money to pay the port tax on her. He had to get her out of bondage and he felt he could find work in New York. When he arrived, he had so little money that he searched through New York for a flophouse where he could find a bed for a few dollars a night. He finally happened on the Uncle Sam, which in "its heyday, had been a medium class full-blown hotel." It was anything but a hotel when Jones found it.

> Now it had the air of being—not just condemned—damned. . . . Upstairs, many of the walls that had once separated rooms had been removed; now there were several big dormitories, each crowded with single beds so that there was only eighteen inches of walkway between them. (p. 188)

Jones vividly remembered trying to sleep in these cramped quarters.

> All night there was muttering in different quarters, coughing, sputtering, wheezing, moaning, a continual going to and from the men's room, the rustle of brown paper bags, the gurgle of "Irish Rose," and the cries of those who even asleep found no peace, no comfort of spirit. There were a half-dozen night-ramblers, mostly very old men who found it impossible to sleep. They spent the night creeping around and around the dormitory. . . . The first night I was exhausted, but I slept only in snatches. (p. 194)

Jones found it terribly stressful being in the center of the room surrounded by people, and he bribed the night attendant with a precious dollar to give him a bed at the side of the room. At least here he did not have a sea of humanity completely around him.

Up to this point, we have been examining personal space—space that contains no other people. Now we turn our attention to space that

TABLE 14-3

Effectiveness of markers in protecting territory

Markers	Percentage of trials in which chair was taken
Sportcoat, textbook, and notebook	0
Sportcoat	20
Textbook and notebook	20
Stacked journals	60
Scattered journals	100
Unmarked chair	100

SOURCE: Sommer and Becker (1969).

other people occupy by right. We will focus on *density* and *crowding*; the two terms are often used interchangeably, but as we will see, the distinction between them is important.

Concern about crowding has many dimensions. First, we all realize that an increasing number of people are sharing our planet. The world's population passed the 5 billion mark in 1988, and a child born today faces the prospect of sharing the world with twice that number of people by age 40 (Schmid, 1988). Added to the population figures is the increasing trend toward urban living; not only are there more of us, but we are living closer together. When we focus on limited areas, we find that the effects of crowding are a matter of concern to people responsible for such institutions as prisons (Ostfeld et al., 1987). The number of people in such institutions is growing at an alarming rate, and inmates are literally stacked in their living quarters. The courts have closed prisons to new inmates until the crowding can be relieved. Even animal rights activists have become concerned about the housing facilities provided for laboratory animals (Novak & Suomi, 1988). What is the effect of putting many animals together in a single cage versus putting them in isolated units? The answers to these and other questions not only have implications for the decent care of such animals but could have profound effects on the results of research conducted with them.

---

territorial markers Devices such as fences and signs used to identify the boundaries of one's territory.

While the density at the rock concert may be similar to that inside the subway, the sense of crowding is remarkably different. The density of the crowd at the concert usually adds to the pleasure and excitement of the event, while the density of the crowd in a rush-hour subway is fatiguing and harrowing.

None of us would be surprised to learn that the more people (or animals) there are in a certain place, the more disease, the more violence, and the more maladaptive behavior results. We would expect such results on the basis of the increasing numbers alone. Yet many of us have enjoyed environments in which many people shared a limited space. Indeed, Tristan Jones had very limited space aboard the *Sea Dart*, but he reported being happiest when he was sailing.

Density and behavior

If we examine the research on **density** (the amount of space available for each individual in a defined area), we find that the data confirm our experiences: high density has negative effects sometimes but not always (Baum & Paulus, 1987). Calhoun (1962) conducted careful observations of a colony of rats that were confined to a limited amount of space. As the rat population and density increased, a number of alarming events ensued. Social order broke down; aggression, homosexuality, cannibalism, and abnormal sexual behavior increased. Female rats failed to build

suitable nests or take care of their young. Health problems dramatically increased; many females developed cancer of their sexual organs and mammary glands, and miscarriages were more frequent. These problems arose despite the fact that the animals had sufficient food, water, and nesting material to maintain a high standard of living. Thus these problems were attributed to the increasing density.

Armed with this evidence, researchers expected to find that density had similarly disastrous effects on humans. In support of this position, Cox, Paulus, and McCain (1984; McCain et al., 1985) found that as the number of inmates in a prison unit increased, so did the number of behavioral and medical problems. Suicide rates at large institutions (population greater than 1,400), for example, were ten times as high as in small units (population less than 1,100), and the number of disciplinary infractions increased as density increased. And it has been found that physiological stress reactions, such as a rise in blood pressure, increase when inmates are placed in high-density dormitories (Ostfeld et al., 1987).

Chapter Fourteen   The Environment

Despite these findings, however, most other carefully controlled research has failed to show that high density, by itself, creates behavioral, performance, or health problems (Sundstrom, 1978). Further, it is difficult to draw general conclusions from research conducted in such settings as prisons, where many aspects of the environment besides density are stressful and the population contains many more violent people than one is likely to encounter elsewhere.

Crowding

The thrust of the density research seems to contradict most people's experience. Most of us would argue that being packed together with other people does affect our mood and performance in some situations. Many investigators were also unsatisfied with the conclusion that people are not affected by spatial restrictions in their environment. These investigators began to search for the factors that determine when people are affected by spatial restrictions.

As a first step, researchers distinguished crowding from density. In most of the earlier research, the two terms had been used interchangeably. However, density is a purely spatial concept. **Crowding,** on the other hand, is a "motivational state aroused through the interaction of spatial, social, and personal factors" (Stokols, 1972, p. 275). We feel crowded: we don't *feel* density.

To understand the distinction between density and crowding, think of a rock concert and a library. At the rock concert, tens of thousands of people may be jammed together on a hillside. This is obviously a high-density situation, yet the music lovers in attendance may not report feeling crowded. On the other hand, an individual in the library may feel crowded when three other people sit at the table where he or she is studying. The density in the library may be far lower than the density at the rock concert, yet the experience of crowding may be greater in the library. This distinction is important because people may be affected more by the experience of crowding than by variations in density. With this distinction in mind, many investigators began to examine the conditions that cause people to feel crowded. Restriction of space was recognized as only one factor in the formula.

Privacy, expectations, and crowding. Altman (1975) suggested that crowding results when "privacy mechanisms" do not function effectively and the individual is subjected to an undesired amount of social contact. Essentially, crowding results when the privacy achieved is less than the privacy desired. As we pointed out earlier, space is an important regulator of privacy.

Taking this reasoning a step further, we find indications that expectations play an important role in determining when a lack of privacy will lead to crowding (Westover, 1989). Visitors to a recreational park are more likely to feel crowded if they expect to find few other visitors than if they expect many other people there. Likewise, subjects who expected to be in a spacious room felt more crowded in a high-density situation than subjects who expected a crowded room (Worchel, Webb & Reichers, 1989). Our needs for and expectations of privacy may serve as a standard by which we evaluate environments.

Crowding and control. There is an ironic inconsistency in Tristan Jones's view of land dwellers and mariners. He complains that "the landsman's society tends toward centralized control" and that people on land are oriented toward controlling their surroundings. Jones, the mariner, had supposedly learned to accept and live with unpredictability and lack of control. But Jones's experience in the Uncle Sam Hotel showed that he was not immune to the need for control. He found it very disturbing that he could not control the noise and the intrusions of the night stalkers, and he went so far as to bribe the attendant to give him a space over which he could exercise more control.

Psychologists have examined the effects of loss of control (Wortman & Brehm, 1975; Seligman, 1975). Seligman postulated that an individual who perceives that he or she has no control over the environment will experience a state of **learned helplessness.** Because of the feeling

---

crowding A motivational state aroused through the interaction of spatial, social, and personal factors.

density The amount of space available for each individual in a defined area.

learned helplessness A state resulting when the individual perceives no control over his or her environment.

---

that they have no control over the environment, such individuals stop trying to affect their surroundings.

Rodin and others (Rodin & Baum, 1978; Baron & Rodin, 1978; Cohen & Sherrod, 1978) applied the concept of loss of control to crowding. They suggested that some high-density situations cause individuals to lose control over social interaction. In these conditions, individuals are forced to interact with one another and have no means to regulate that interaction. According to Rodin, this loss of control leads both to the experience of crowding and to feelings of learned helplessness. High density that does not involve a loss of control will not result in crowding.

It has been demonstrated repeatedly that control does play a central role in the experience of crowding. One study (Rodin, 1976) found that children from high-density homes did show symptoms of learned helplessness. Children who came from homes where a large number of people lived in a small amount of space attempted to exercise less control in a laboratory task than children from less densely populated homes. The children from high-density homes were more willing to let the experimenter or a machine determine what happened to them, even when they had the opportunity to make their own choices.

Arousal, attribution, and crowding. Many events competed for Jones's attention on his first night at the Uncle Sam. The architecture of the building was a fascinating combination of Victorian and Gothic. Jones met some interesting people who became steadfast friends. Yet the feature that stood out in Jones's mind was how crowded he felt there. Given the wide variety of experiences and possible emotions that Jones could have had, why was crowding so prominent?

In an effort to answer such questions, several investigators (Schmidt & Keating, 1979; Worchel & Teddlie, 1976) developed a model of crowding based on social cognition and attribution theory (Chapters 2 and 3). The investigators suggested that crowding results when people become aroused by such events as violations of personal space and then attribute that arousal to a lack of space or to the excessive closeness of other people. People will not feel crowded if they are not aroused or if they do not view their arousal as resulting from violations of their space. As you can see, this model suggests that spatial restrictions or violations of personal space will not always lead to the experience of crowding. Strangers intrude into one another's personal space at basketball games, football games, theaters, and rock concerts. Yet people do not report feeling crowded at these events. In fact, Tuan (1977) reports that in some cases, individuals find that crowds are exhilarating and add to the enjoyment of an experience.

An important factor in the feeling of crowdedness is the salience of others in the environment. When other people are salient (see Chapter 2), we are likely to attribute our arousal to these others and feel crowded. However, if other people are not salient, we may not attribute our arousal to crowding, even though our space has been violated. This model would explain Tristan Jones's experience in the Uncle Sam; when he lay down to sleep, the salient features in his environment were the other people in the room, especially the monk-like figures who often passed quietly by his bed.

In support of this model, one study (Worchel & Teddlie, 1976) found that crowding could be reduced if people's attention were distracted from the others in their environment. Subjects in a densely populated room reported less crowding if there were attention-grabbing pictures on the walls than if there were no pictures. Along similar lines, investigators (Webb et al., 1986) found that crowding could be reduced if people in the environment were categorized in groups rather than identified as individuals. Categorization reduced the attention given to individuals in the environment.

Summing it up. Taken as a whole, the research and theories indicate that high density, by itself, is not always unhealthy or even unpleasant. However, when high density is associated with such factors as overstimulation, loss of personal control, and violations of personal space, the experience of crowding is likely to result. The general conclusion drawn is that we have desired levels of privacy, control, arousal, and stimulation. These levels vary with the individual, the situation, and the background. However, when the environment becomes so dense that spatial factors cause these desired levels to be exceeded, we experience crowding (Baum & Paulus, 1987). Crowding is an uncomfortable state; task performance, interpersonal relationships, and possibly health are negatively affected by it.

If we are interested in improving the quality of human life, this focus on crowding rather than density offers some room for optimism. The world's population is growing rapidly, but the amount of space available is fixed. Hence density will necessarily increase. However, the experience of crowding does not necessarily have to grow at the same rate. If we can structure the environment so that individuals have havens of privacy or feel control over their daily lives, we can reduce crowding and the negative effects associated with it.

STOP, THINK, & UNDERSTAND

1. What is involved in the concept of person-environment fit?

2. How do personal space and territoriality differ?

3. What are Hall's interaction zones and what factors determine the distance at which people interact?

4. Why do people have personal space?

5. What are the functions of territoriality?

6. What factors determine when high density will lead to the experience of crowding?

Nonspatial Environmental Variables

Noise

In addition to complaining about the lack of space at the Uncle Sam, Jones was also made uncomfortable by the noise. All the talking, snoring, and moaning kept him from sleeping at night. The noise inside the hotel, along with the constant rumble of traffic and blaring horns outside, distracted Jones so that he had difficulty writing. In desperation, he commandeered a small closet in which to do his writing. Jones was constantly aware of the changing sounds in New York. One event particularly demonstrated his awareness.

> The first fall of snow in New York is pure magic. I went to bed wrung out after another 12-hour stint of writing. Next morning I was awakened by silence. It was as if the world slept. . . . But the city government seemed to be affronted by this cold charity that like a quiet forgiveness, hid its sins. Soon its henchmen in incredibly rowdy, fume-spouting snow-plough-rigged garbage trucks had restored "normality." (p. 230)

As Jones was well aware, in addition to becoming more crowded, our world is becoming more noisy.

Is this dangerous? Are we being unwittingly affected by the sounds we have created in our environment? In answering this question, envi-

ronmental psychologists begin by making a distinction between sound and noise. **Sound** consists of changes in air pressure that are detected by the ear. It is measured in decibels (dB), with 0 dB being the weakest sound that can be heard by people with good ears. **Noise** is sound that is unwanted by the listener because it is unpleasant and bothersome.

As a general rule, three properties determine when sound will be perceived as noise: volume, predictability, and controllability. The most bothersome sounds are those that are loud, unpredictable, and uncontrollable (Fisher, Bell & Baum, 1984).

Noise has a wide variety of effects on us. At the most basic level, loud noise can damage hearing. As a startling example, it has been found that 70-year-old Sudanese tribesmen who live in a quiet area have the hearing ability of a 20-year-old in America (Rosen et al., 1962). We have all probably complained that noise gives us a headache, but recent research suggests that we'd better not take an aspirin to alleviate that headache

---

noise Sound that is unwanted because it is unpleasant and bothersome.

sound Changes in air pressure that are detected by the ear.

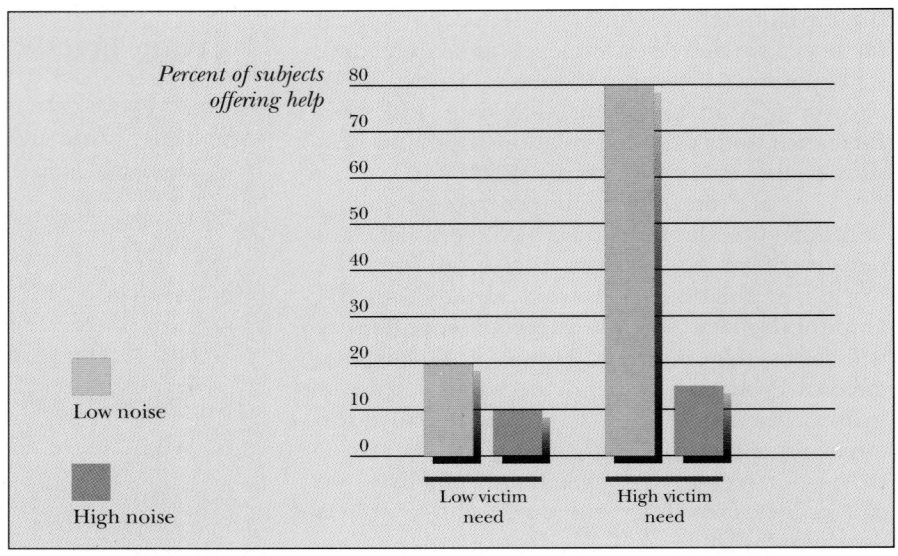

Percent of subjects
offering help

Low noise

High noise

Low victim
need

High victim
need

FIGURE 14-5 Percentages of subjects offering help as a function of noise level and need of victim
SOURCE: Adapted from Mathews and Cannon (1975).

if we are staying in a noisy environment. This research (Raloff, 1982; J. Miller, 1982) suggests that certain drugs such as antibiotics and aspirin may interact with noise to increase the damage caused by that noise.

Noise can also affect our performance; it was not only Jones's imagination that he could not concentrate on his work in the noisy hotel. Studies in Los Angeles found that children in noisy schools made more errors on a puzzle task and were more likely to give up on the task than children in quiet schools (Cohen et al., 1980). Further, the effects of noise were found even after steps were taken to reduce the noise in the classrooms (Cohen et al., 1981). Even over the short term, noise can produce negative aftereffects on performance. In a series of studies, Glass and Singer (1972) found that subjects who had been exposed to uncontrollable and unpredictable noise for a period of less than an hour performed less well on tasks in a quiet room than subjects who had never been exposed to the noise.

Noise can also have negative effects on our social interactions. Studies have shown that we are less attracted to others in a noisy environment. Mathews, Cannon, and Alexander (1974) found that subjects chose greater interpersonal

distances when background noise was piped into the experimental room. We are also less likely to help someone when a loud noise is present (Mathews & Cannon, 1975). As Figure 14-5 indicates, this effect is strongest when the victim of an accident has a high need for help. Apparently we pay less attention to social cues (such as the need for help) in noisy environments than in quieter settings.

These studies show that noise can have wide-ranging effects on human behavior. Interestingly, not all noise has the same effects. Noise that is composed of conversation seems to have the most negative effects on performance (Olszewski, Rotton & Soler, 1976) and is reported to be the most disturbing (Topf, 1985).

Why does noise affect us?

The general picture that emerges from the research on noise is that it can have negative effects, especially when we are working on complex tasks or must use environmental cues such as a victim's need to determine our responses. How do we explain these curious sets of circumstances that influence the effect of noise? Broadbent (1978) argued that exposure to noise causes people to become aroused. Heightened arousal, in turn, causes them to narrow their attention; they focus on important environmental stimuli and neglect ones that they consider unimportant. As a result of this narrowing of attention, performance on some tasks (simple problems or ones requiring visual performance) may actually improve because the individual pays close attention to the task. However, performance becomes impaired on more complex tasks requiring coordination or reasoning. Social interactions may also suffer because people pay less attention to each other and do not discriminate others' needs and desires.

Temperature

One of our favorite topics of conversation when we meet a stranger seems to be the weather. When we don't know where to begin a conversation, we can safely talk about the weather. On his flight from England to the United States, Jones found himself in the awkward situation of wanting to talk with a flight attendant but not knowing what to say. Their conversation settled on the weather and sailing.

The flight attendant asked Jones whether he preferred to sail alone or with a companion. Jones responded, "If the weather is rough then I'm thankful I have no one else to worry about but myself." She asked, "But when it is fine weather and the sun is shining on the sea?" Jones responded with a smile, "Ah, then . . . then I want to *share*" (p. 42).

This conversation shows that the weather is more than something to talk about; it can well influence our moods and social interactions. Investigators have studied almost every aspect of weather, including wind, sunlight, heat, cold, barometric pressure, and moon phases. Because of limited space, let us examine only one component of climate: temperature.

In 1969 the United States Riot Commission observed that a large proportion of civil riots have occurred during the hot summer months. This announcement gave rise to a flurry of studies in efforts to relate temperature to aggression. The studies have taken two forms: archival research and laboratory experimentation. The archival researchers chose a time period, charted temperature and violent acts, and examined the rela-

tionship of these two measures. Although there has been some disagreement as to the exact relationship, the majority of the findings suggest that violence increases as temperature increases (Anderson, 1989). For example, Anderson and Anderson (1984) found that aggressive crimes (murder and rape) in Houston, Texas, tended to increase as the temperature rose (see Figure 14-6).

The relationship between heat and aggression becomes a bit more murky when we examine laboratory studies. In a number of studies in which temperature was manipulated, Baron and his colleagues (Baron & Bell, 1976; Bell & Baron, 1977) found that angry subjects were less aggressive in very hot rooms (92° F to 95° F) than in rooms with more comfortable temperature. On the other hand, nonangry subjects were more aggressive in hot rooms than in comfortable ones. One explanation for these findings is that heat, like other environmental variables, acts as a stressor that arouses people. At moderate levels of arousal, heat leads to anger and aggression. However, at excessively high levels of arousal, people seek to withdraw from social interaction, and aggression is reduced. This high level of arousal is reached when people are angered in a very hot room. This reasoning would lead us to expect a curvilinear relationship between heat and aggression (see Figure 14-7).

How do we reconcile the differences in the results of the laboratory and field research? One possibility is that excessive heat is the salient feature in the laboratory; many people seldom have an occasion to be in a room with a temperature of 95°. However, heat is only one of the outstanding features on a sunny day in Houston; there one's attention is diverted by the traffic, the actions of many other people, and the performance of the Houston Astros. Hence, in the laboratory, arousal will be attributed to the salient feature, heat, and will not be interpreted as anger. In the field setting, however, arousal is less likely to be attributed to heat than to anger (Anderson, 1989). In fact, it is argued that heat increases arousal, and when increased arousal is combined with frustration, it heightens aggression.

The research on temperature and performance has also led to conflicting results. In 1979 the Emergency Building Temperature Restric-

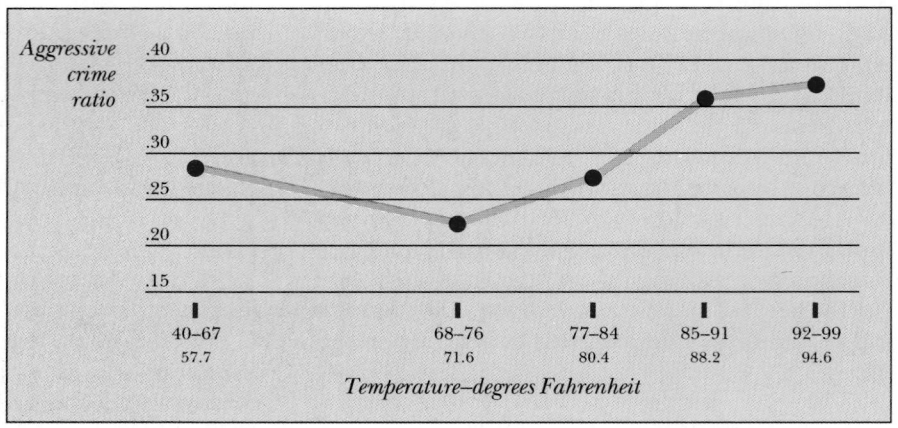

FIGURE 14-6 Aggressive crime ratio as a function of maximum ambient temperatures
NOTE: The aggressive crime ratio is the number of murders and rapes divided by the number of robberies and arsons. (Note that points are plotted at the category-weighted average temperature, as indicated by the small-sized digits. The larger digits indicate the range of temperatures included in each category. The categories were constructed to represent approximately equal numbers of days.)
SOURCE: Anderson and Anderson (1984).

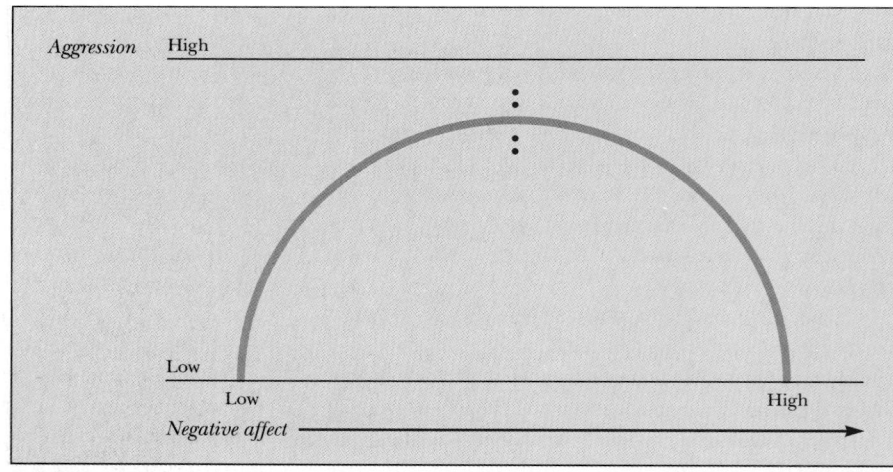

FIGURE 14-7 Theoretical relationship between negative affect and aggression (up to a point, uncomfortable conditions facilitate aggression; past that point, more severe conditions decrease aggression)
SOURCE: Baron and Bell (1976).

tion Plan was put into effect in the United States. The plan required public buildings not to be heated above 65° F in the winter and not to be cooled below 78° F in the summer. A number of reports indicated that the summer temperature restriction caused decreases in performance. A company in Norfolk, Virginia, for example, reported a drop of 15% to 20% in the output of clerical workers (King, 1980). More carefully controlled studies (Mackworth, 1961; Link & Pepler, 1970) also found that performance declined as temperatures rose. Other studies,

TABLE 14-4

Effective temperature (degrees Fahrenheit) at 0% humidity as a function of actual temperature and humidity

Relative humidity	Thermometer reading					
	41°	50°	59°	68°	77°	86°
			Effective temperature			
0%	41	50	59	68	77	86
20	41	50	60	70	81	91
40	40	51	61	72	83	96
60	40	51	62	73	86	102
80	39	52	63	75	90	111
100	39	52	64	79	96	120

SOURCE: Fisher, Bell, and Baum (1984).

however (Provins & Bell, 1970), found that heat led to short-term improvements in performance, which often dissipated over time. At the other end of the thermometer, cold reduces performance on tasks requiring muscle coordination, quick reaction times, and sensitivity to touch (Poulton, 1970). Few studies have been done on the effects of cold on social interaction. But one effect of cold weather is to make people less mobile and cut down on the number and variety of social interactions (Fisher et al., 1984).

Clearly, more research is needed before we can understand the effects of temperature on human behavior. The research on heat, for example, is complicated by the fact that many variables influence the human comfort level. Rohles (1981) listed seven variables: (1) air temperature, (2) relative humidity, (3) radiant temperature (temperature from surfaces such as windows), (4) air velocity, (5) clothing, (6) physical activity, and (7) length of exposure. Table 14-4 shows how humidity affects people's experiences with temperature.

Architecture and Design

We have seen that we cannot make a blanket statement that a certain environmental condition is always bad or always good; much depends on the purpose to which that environment will be put. We saw that crowding, for example, can have negative effects in some cases but positive effects in others. An important factor in the person-environment fit is the activity that will take place in the environment. This principle becomes clear when we investigate architecture and design.

To begin, we can consider Tristan Jones's reactions when he first saw the *Star Rider*. The 44-footer was a Nova Scotia–built wooden vessel fitted with the best sailing gear for a boat her size. But Jones (1980) was not delighted. "I can see she's a fine sea boat, but for charter in the West Indies? Forget it. Look, Tom [her owner], her ventilation hatches are tiny—she's built for the cold North Atlantic—there'll never be any air down here [the berths], and in the island heat . . . she's not built for finicky charterers; they'll mutiny!" (p. 113). As if this were not enough, Jones delivered the final blow when he proclaimed, "The only people who will be happy chartering this vessel are coal miners or circus acrobats. She was built for eight-foot giants and four-foot dwarfs" (p. 113).

With such considerations in mind, let us consider the research on our built environment.

Rooms

Investigators found that variables such as color, the number of windows and doors, and the arrangement of furniture dramatically affect the

In this airline's waiting room the seating arrangement is sociofugal. Is there any reason to either encourage or discourage socializing amongst travelers?

behaviors of the people who use a room. For example, people associate moods with certain colors (Hesselgren, 1975; Wexner, 1954). Wexner asked the subjects to ascribe moods to various colors. With a high degree of agreement the following match was reported:

Blue: secure, comfortable, tender, soothing, calm, serene.
Red: exciting, protective, defending, defiant.
Orange: distressed, upset.
Black: despondent, powerful.
Purple: dignified.
Yellow: cheerful.

Further, Wilson (1966) found that subjects were more physiologically aroused (as measured by GSR) when they viewed red slides than when they viewed green slides. The research suggests that if subdued activities such as reading, sleeping, and studying are to take place in a room, less arousing colors such as blue and green should be used.

The arrangement of furniture is another important design feature that should be taken into account when one plans a room. The layout of a room regulates communication and also communicates the purpose of the environment. When Osmond (1957) conducted an intensive

study of a newly completed geriatric ward, he noted that the design of the environment had marked effects on the patients' behavior. He classified design arrangements into two types. **Sociopetal spaces** are areas arranged to "encourage, foster, and even enforce the development of stable interpersonal relationships." **Sociofugal spaces,** on the other hand, are arrangements that tend to separate people and reduce social interaction. The arrangement of furniture in a room can create either a sociopetal or sociofugal atmosphere.

A study by Sommer and Ross (1958) in a newly remodeled geriatric ward in a Canadian hospital clearly demonstrates the effects of furniture arrangement. The designers of the ward carpeted and painted a dayroom and installed new furniture. They hoped that these improvements would foster social interaction among the women patients and increase their involvement in the hospital routine. The patients' behavior was still apathetic, however, and social interaction was minimal. Sommer observed that the patients were "like strangers in a train station waiting for a train that never came." Sommer and Ross noted that the new furniture had been lined up in long straight rows so that the patients sat shoulder to shoulder and back to back. This arrangement was clearly sociofugal, as it did not foster social interaction. The investigators rearranged the furniture so that four chairs were grouped around small square tables. At first the patients and the staff grumbled about this arrangement; it was unfamiliar to the patients, and it was harder for the staff to keep the room clean. After a few weeks, however, interactions among the patients had nearly doubled. Thus the organization of the furniture in a room can have important effects on the behaviors of the individuals who use the room. The arrangement of room furniture should fit the room's use. Sociopetal arrangements should be used in rooms where interaction will take place (living rooms, dayrooms, dormitory lounges), and sociofugal arrangements should be used in low-interaction rooms (bus stations, airports, libraries).

Offices

Because of its economic implications, the design of offices has aroused considerable interest (Sundstrom, 1986, 1987). The old-style office was an enclosed box. A person's status in the organization could be measured by the size and location of the office (corner or middle, distance from the chief executive, floor of the building) and the number of windows it contained. But changes in building techniques have led to the development of the **open-office design,** in which work spaces are separated by low partitions rather than by floor-to-ceiling walls and doors. The change in office design has had profound effects on work behavior.

Wells (1972) studied an insurance company in Manchester, England, that had two types of office arrangement: small offices and large open office space. He found that people in the small offices tended to form small but cohesive groups, whereas those who worked in the open offices interacted with a larger number of people but did not form close relationships. Studies of open-office design have been conducted (McCarrey et al., 1974), with mixed results. Although workers report that the open office fosters interpersonal contact, they also feel that it offers less privacy and is noisier than the conventional office design.

Once again we are reminded of our person-environment fit. Certain jobs will be facilitated by the open-office design while others will be hindered by it. One study found that although people tend to be more satisfied with private offices, performance on simple tasks improves in the more public open-office setting (Block & Stokes, 1989). Performance on more complex tasks requiring reasoning and problem solving is best in a private office. Going a step further, investigators have found that lighting is an important factor to consider in the design of an office. People involved in arousing activities and work prefer lower levels of lighting than those involved in less arousing activities. Biner and his colleagues (1989) found that high levels of light are arousing, and if the nature of people's work varies, it is important that they have control over the lighting in the office. Hence, for these people the private office that offers maximum control may be the best setting.

The study of offices shows the complex relationship between people and their physical environment. Such physical characteristics as lighting, size, color, and design have been thoroughly investigated. These physical characteristics are found to affect performance, social interactions, and friendship patterns. Beyond these effects are the psychological ones induced by such variables as size, location, and number of windows, which represent status and personal importance in the organization. Any attempt to attain the best person-environment fit must take into account the psychological factors as well as those related to the nature of the job and performance requirements.

Buildings and Institutions

When we walk into a large building such as a bank, department store, or hospital, we often marvel at its imposing exterior design and fancy interior. In our awe, however, we may forget that its design and layout play a major role in determining our behavior in that building. A review

---

open-office design An arrangement whereby work spaces are separated by partitions rather than by floor-to-ceiling walls and doors.

sociofugal space An area arranged in such a way as to separate people and reduce social interaction.

sociopetal space An area arranged in such a way as to foster and encourage social interaction.

Despite winning architectural awards for design, the Pruitt-Igoe complex did not meet the needs of the residents. In fact, they moved out of the complex, and eventually it was demolished. The story of the project stands as a testimony to the importance of person-environment fit.

of the research on hospital design (Reizenstein, 1982) produced a rather impressive list of the behaviors influenced by the hospital design, compiled by Baum and Singer (1982):

Confidentiality
Control over social interaction
Cross-infection
Disclosure
Image
Organizational climate
Perception
Postoperative delirium
Postoperative medication
Travel time

Other investigators have found that design can influence social conflict and friendship patterns.

One of the most troubling examples of the pervasive influence of building design on human behavior was the Pruitt-Igoe complex in St. Louis. In 1954, 43 11-story high-rise apartment build-

ings were erected on a 57-acre tract in St. Louis. Nearly 12,000 people were relocated in these apartments, and the project was hailed as a great advance in low-income housing. Each apartment had all the most modern facilities, and each family was ensured ample living space. Very soon, however, bragging about the Pruitt-Igoe project stopped. Windows were smashed; the elevators became repositories for human waste; gangs roamed the project; and rape and robbery were commonplace. By the early 1970s only 16 of the 43 buildings were occupied, and in April 1972 demolition of the entire project began.

Why was the project such a failure? Could anything be done in the future to ensure against such failures? Several studies indicated that the housing complex, though architecturally well designed, did not fit the needs of the tenants. Yancey (1971) interviewed numerous residents and found that, although they were satisfied with the space and the facilities of the apartments, they were upset because the building design did not foster interactions among neighbors and because they could not supervise their children once the children were out of the apartment. Further, Newman (1972) points out that there was too much **indefensible territory** in the project. According to Newman, when there is no clear way to mark ownership or to patrol territory, vandalism is likely to occur. The stairwells, elevators, and alleyways could not be adequately patrolled, and they were not open to visual inspection. It was impossible to see who lurked in the stairwells or elevators, and as a result the residents were afraid to use these necessary areas. The sheer size of the complex was also a problem. Individuals feel insignificant in such a concentration of large structures and feel little control over their environment.

The importance of person-environment fit is nowhere clearer than in discussions of the design of buildings and institutions. The *Handbook of Environmental Psychology* (Stokols & Altman, 1987) contains chapters on the design of schools, prisons, office buildings, hospitals, and areas for the elderly. No single preferred pattern emerges from these chapters, but a single message is clear: Architects must keep in mind the people who will use the area and the purpose for which they will use it. No simple psychological principle can be the foundation for every design. We have seen in the Pruitt-Igoe complex the devastating effects that lack of control can have on people. Yet there is evidence that too much control can be stressful and disorienting (Thompson, Check & Graham, 1988). The desired amount of control and the types of control that are important to an elderly person in a rest home are very different from the control needed by children in an elementary school (Carp, 1987; Gump, 1987). This rather obvious fact can be overlooked, and the results can be disastrous.

In order to examine some of the factors involved in the design of buildings, let's briefly consider two types of buildings.

Designing space for the mentally retarded

One of the most ambitious studies on the effects of design took place at the Belchertown State School for the mentally retarded in western Massachusetts (Zimring, Weitzer & Knight, 1982). As a result of a court settlement, $2.6 million was designated for renovation of the old institution. The residents had previously lived in large open wards that contained 15 to 20 beds.

Three designs were combined in the renovation. The **module design** retained the ward quality but drew on the open-office plan. Beds in the ward were separated by low (4 1/2-foot) privacy partitions; 12 residents were assigned to a ward that had a small lounge. The **suite design** followed that of many apartments; walls divided the wards into three separate bedrooms and a bathroom with a lounge serving this area. The bedrooms housed two to four residents, who could obtain privacy by closing the bedroom door. The **corridor design** followed that used in many college dormitories. Small one- or two-person bedrooms lined long corridors; each corridor had a common bathroom and lounge area.

Interviews with residents and staff and careful observations of their behavior were conducted over a thirty-month period. A wide range of behaviors was examined. A summary of the results is presented in Figure 14-8. As can be seen, the module design had little effect on the behavior of the residents or the staff. The greatest improvement in the resident's adjustment and interactions was found with the corridor design. Residents became more verbal and alert and their interactions increased dramatically. The staff made fewer undesired intrusions into the residents' private space and residents made more use of their bedroom areas.

The investigators explained the effects by focusing on personal control. They argued that the corridor design gave individuals the greatest control over their space. For example, each person or pair had access to the light switch and

---

corridor design   A design for residence units that locates a large number of private bedrooms along a common hallway.

indefensible territory   An area that is not under the control of any individual or group and cannot easily be regulated, patrolled, or observed.

module design   A design for residence units that separates individual sleeping areas with low partitions.

suite design   A design for a residence unit that locates a limited number of private bedrooms around a common living area.

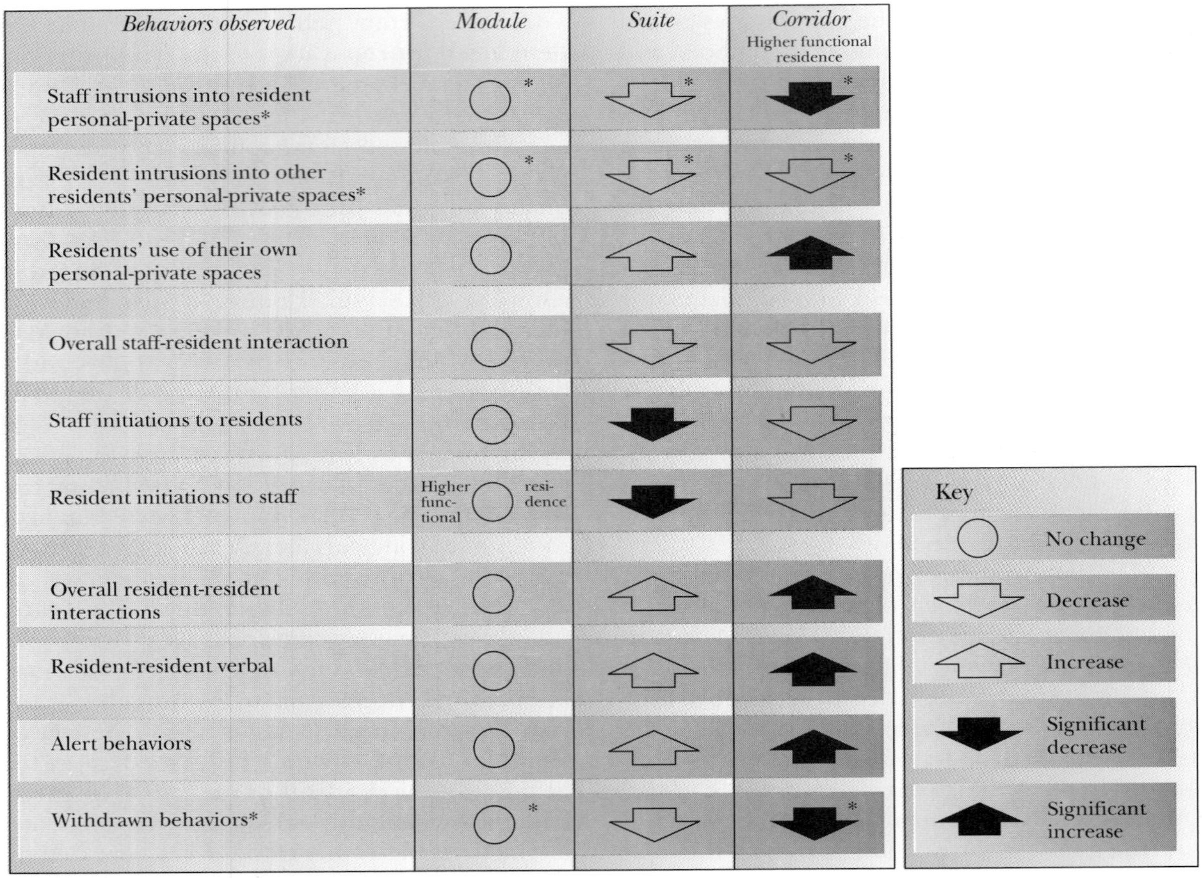

Behaviors observed	Module	Suite	Corridor (Higher functional residence)
Staff intrusions into resident personal-private spaces*	No change*	Decrease*	Significant decrease*
Resident intrusions into other residents' personal-private spaces*	No change*	Decrease*	Decrease*
Residents' use of their own personal-private spaces	No change	Increase	Significant increase
Overall staff-resident interaction	No change	Decrease	Decrease
Staff initiations to residents	No change	Significant decrease	Decrease
Resident initiations to staff	No change (Higher functional residence)	Significant decrease	Decrease
Overall resident-resident interactions	No change	Increase	Significant increase
Resident-resident verbal	No change	Increase	Significant increase
Alert behaviors	No change	Increase	Significant increase
Withdrawn behaviors*	No change*	Decrease	Significant decrease*

Key:
- ○ No change
- ⇩ (open) Decrease
- ⇧ (open) Increase
- ⬇ (filled) Significant decrease
- ⬆ (filled) Significant increase

FIGURE 14-8 Overview of major quantitative results from the institutional design study
SOURCE: Zimring et al. (1982).

could close the door. People could obtain privacy by going into their room and closing the door. This is especially important for mentally retarded people who do not have the verbal or social skills to request privacy in other ways. The renovation also gave the staff private areas where they could work and get their needed "time out."

Additional studies have revealed that design must take into account the programs of the institution (Zimring, Carpman & Michelson, 1987). An institution that has a cooking program, for example, must have adequate kitchen facilities.

The physical design of the institution can often dictate the programs it can and cannot offer. Finally, a forgotten group in many institutional designs is the staff that works there. If institutions are to run smoothly and efficiently, it is vital that the design facilitate the work and adjustment of the staff. Tristan Jones made a similar observation about some pleasure sailboats that were designed to make the passengers comfortable but forced the crew into cramped, unpleasant quarters: "A happy crew," he noted, "makes for a happy voyage."

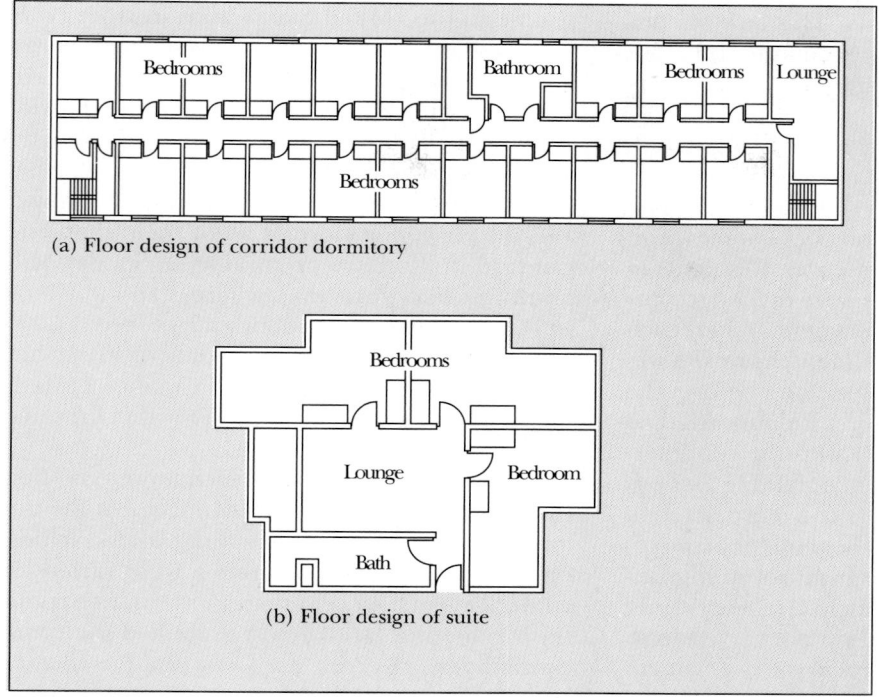

Bedrooms Bathroom Bedrooms Lounge

Bedrooms

(a) Floor design of corridor dormitory

Bedrooms

Lounge Bedroom

Bath

(b) Floor design of suite

FIGURE 14-9   Floor plan of (a) a corridor-style dormitory and (b) a suite-style dormitory
SOURCE: Baum and Valins (1977).

Designing the dormitory

We might be tempted to conclude from the study by Zimring and his colleagues that all institutions should be based on the corridor model. In doing so, however, we would not be paying attention to our caution about person-environment fit: we must design buildings to fit the needs of the people who will use them. Jones's experience with the *Star Rider* made this point very clearly. This position can also be seen in research on college dormitories which also compared the effects of the corridor design and suite design.

In a series of studies, Baum and Valins (1977) examined the behavior of students living in two-person rooms in a corridor-style dormitory with that of students living in suite-type dormitories (see Figure 14-9). The density (space per person) was roughly the same in the two types of dormitories. Baum and Valins predicted, however, that the design would have a marked effect on students' behavior. Unlike the mentally retarded residents in the Belchertown State School, college students are generally skilled in social interaction, are very mobile, and have need for space to study and carry on a wide variety of social interactions. With these factors in mind, Baum and Valins argued that residents in the corridor dormitories have less meaningful control over their environment than do residents in the suite dorms. The former group is often faced with unpredictable and unwanted social interaction in the long corridors, bathrooms, and lounges that are shared by many residents. This lack of control should lead the corridor residents to feel more crowded and less comfortable with social interaction than the suite residents.

These predictions were indeed supported. First, interviews indicated that corridor residents did feel more crowded than suite residents. The effects of the two designs on social interaction were revealed in a more subtle way. Residents in the two types of dormitories were invited to participate in a laboratory experiment. When each resident arrived at the experiment, he or she was asked to wait with a confederate before the experiment began. Corridor residents tried to withdraw from social contact with the confederate by sitting farther away, maintaining less eye contact, and carrying on less conversation than suite residents. Apparently the tendency for corridor residents to withdraw from social interactions generalized beyond their dormitory into other settings. Further, corridor residents attempted to exert less control in the experimental setting than did suite residents.

When we compare the research on the school for the mentally retarded and the studies on the dormitories, we can see why we cannot conclude that one type of building design is always better than another. The design that best fitted the needs of one group did not work best for the other group. At the same time, the underlying principle of control over the environment was important for both groups.

The City

Tristan Jones had a love-hate relationship with large cities. He was consistently attracted to such cities as New York, London, and Buenos Aires for the professional contacts, work, and cultural activities they offered. Yet he found himself easily disoriented in cities and felt that they were an affront to nature. Despite Jones's feelings, cities seem to be attracting and holding an increasing proportion of the world's population.

In 1850 only 2% of the world's population lived in cities. By 1980, over 30% of the world's population lived in urban areas and 70% of the

people in the United States lived in cities (U.S. Bureau of the Census, 1981). This situation makes it important to learn how the cities we have built affect our lives. Large cities present the individual with an enormously complex environment. They offer huge variety in types of housing, types of buildings, types of people, and types of noise, and they have far more of all of them than one can find in a suburb or rural area. Stanley Milgram (1970) reports that, whereas an individual working in a New York suburb might meet 11,000 people within a ten-minute radius of his or her office, an individual working in midtown Manhattan might meet 220,000 people within the same radius of the office.

What are the effects of such an intense and compact environment? People report that the city environment offers fascinating and exciting opportunities. The city offers a wide variety of cultural events, more restaurants than one could try in a lifetime, and almost unlimited shopping possibilities. The city itself is a unique theater where one can gaze in fascination at the varied actions of its very large cast of players.

Although the city has numerous advantages over the less populated rural and suburban areas, the price that its inhabitants pay for these advantages is high. Physical disease is higher in the inner city than in any other area. McHarg (1969) mapped the incidence of eight diseases (heart disease, tuberculosis, diabetes, syphilis, cirrhosis of the liver, salmonellosis, and two types of dysentery) in the Philadelphia area. The highest incidence of all these diseases occurred in the inner city, with a reduction in incidence toward the suburbs. In addition, many people view the city as a hostile environment. City people push and shove and fail to observe the usual social courtesies; they are abrupt and cold; no one seems willing to offer help to a person in need.

The higher disease and crime rates of cities can be traced to a variety of possible causes. Living conditions in the inner city are often woefully inadequate. Harris and Lindsay (1972) surveyed urban welfare families in the United States and found that 24% had no hot and cold running water, that 22.4% had no private use of a bathroom with a shower, and that 30.1% did not have enough space for each member of the family. Also, the inner city is often populated with individuals of widely different cultural backgrounds, who tend to be poorly educated and of low socio-economic status.

Although such conditions may explain the higher urban disease and crime rates, they do not adequately explain why the psychology of the city is often characterized as cold and unfriendly. Milgram (1970) suggested that the seeming aloofness and unfriendliness of the city dweller may be a defensive response to a highly overloaded environment. The city is a place of hustle and bustle—people are constantly moving into and out of view. There are bright lights, things to see in every store window, and different types of vehicles passing by. Since individuals can comprehend and respond to only a limited number of events, they have difficulty accommodating such an overloaded environment.

Milgram hypothesized that individuals give less time to each event or input as the total number of events increases. They either do not respond to unimportant events or they disregard them, and they attempt to devise formal channels through which their interactions with others take place. Above all, Milgram suggests that individuals depersonalize or deindividuate the other people in the environment. Because of the complexity and the huge number of social interactions that take place in the city, it is impossible to respond to each person on an individual basis. Thus, in order to reduce the incoming stimuli to manageable amounts, individuals remove the uniqueness from events and people and respond to them only as classes. They also pay less attention to other people.

This depersonalization results in the "unfriendliness" that the newcomer often perceives in the city. This depersonalization is often blamed for the lack of altruism that is reported in the city. In Chapter 8 we discussed the case in which onlookers failed to respond to Kitty Genovese's cries for help. The depersonalization of other people eliminates empathy, and empathizing with persons in distress is one of the motivating forces behind helping behavior.

This description paints a rather dismal picture of the city dweller. It must be pointed out, however, that no one could function in this overloaded complex environment if it were not possible to organize the incoming stimuli. The depersonalization of other people and the screening out of less important inputs are simply means of coping with such an environment. And it has been pointed out that residents of rural areas can suffer the opposite problem; cognitive underload makes life boring and routine (Krupat, 1985).

Environmental Cognition

It should be obvious by now that we respond to events and people not necessarily as they are but as we see or interpret them. Our reactions to the environment, too, are dictated by our perceptions. And our perceptions of the environment are often selective. One study (Rowles, 1984) found that the elderly make clear distinctions in their perceptions of their environment; they see their environment as a set of zones encircling their home (Figure 14-10). Environmental cognition is one of the most rapidly growing areas of study.

A broad set of issues has been examined under the heading of environmental cognition. For example, how do we store information about our environment in our heads? How do we navigate through our environment? Do you remember that to get to your friend's house you go three blocks down the street and turn left for two blocks? Or do you go as far as the ugly green house on the corner and then turn? If you follow the latter strategy, what happens to your ability to navigate when a convenience store is built on the land once occupied by the ugly green house? Are there ways to change the environment to improve people's memory of it and their ability to travel through it?

In examining how we perceive our environment, researchers have focused much attention on **cognitive maps,** the mental images that we hold of our environments (Golledge, 1987). For example, we use five environmental features to develop a cognitive map of the city we live in (Lynch, 1960).

---

cognitive map   A mental image of a particular area of space.

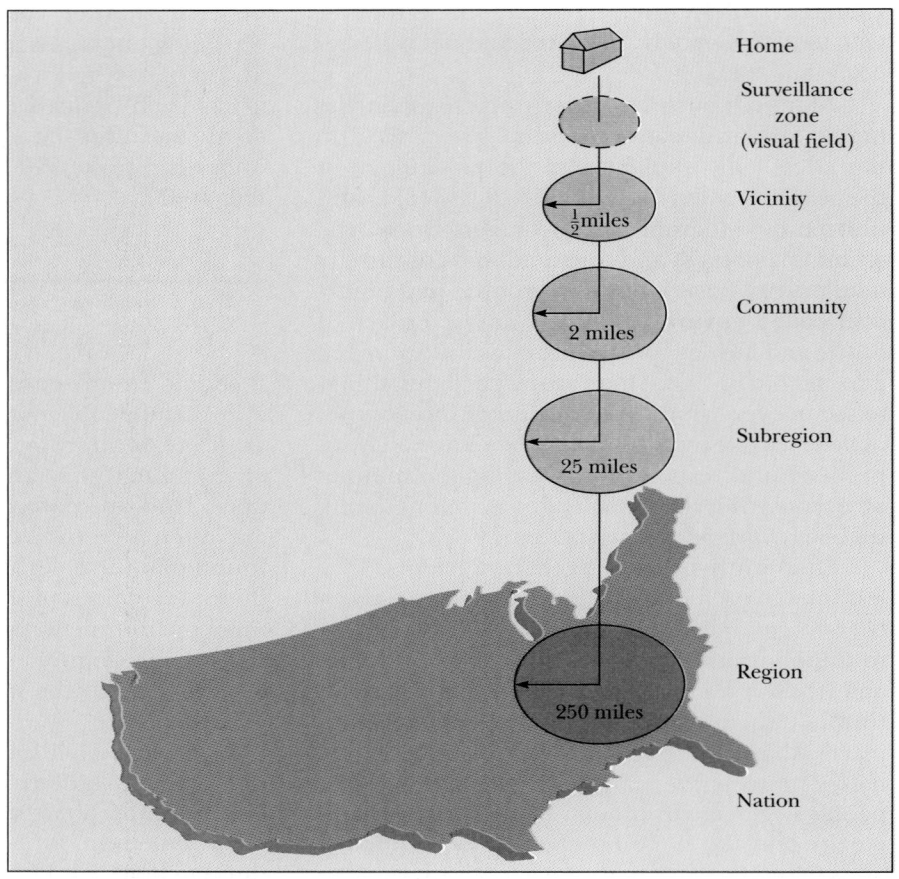

FIGURE 14-10 A hierarchy of environmental spaces
SOURCE: Rowles and Ohta (1983).

1. *Paths:* streets, sidewalks, railroads, and other movement channels.
2. *Edges:* rivers or barriers, such as walls.
3. *Nodes:* intersections or junctions of paths where activity often occurs.
4. *Districts:* regions that are characterized by some common element, such as Chinatown in San Francisco.
5. *Landmarks:* reference points that stand out in the environment, such as the Empire State Building in New York City and the Washington Monument in Washington, D.C.

According to Lynch, some environments are more *legible* than others; the more legible the environment, the easier it is to form a cognitive map of the area. People remember and can function best in environments that have turns of 90°

or none at all rather than turns that take an odd angle (Sadalla & Montello, 1989). But no matter how legible an area is, our cognitive maps are often inaccurate. Three types of error are most often found in our maps (Fisher et al., 1984). First, the maps are generally incomplete; details are left out. Second, we often add to our maps features that are not present in the environment; we may include a house on a lot that is actually vacant, or a sidewalk where none exists. Finally, our map is often distorted; we place objects closer together or farther apart than they actually are. As might be expected, maps of familiar areas tend to be more accurate than maps of unfamiliar areas.

Some interesting things have been found about the way we develop our cognitive maps. Children first learn landmarks and then place them in sequences (Heft & Wohwill, 1987). They

Landmarks are an important part of our environmental cognitive maps. For each of us there is something significant—whether it is a famous landmark such as the St. Louis arch, which draws thousands of tourists each year and is almost the city's sentinel, or a neighborhood store that becomes familiar through the years as an integral part of the community experience.

then encode the paths between these landmarks along with the relative distances between the landmarks. With this information, we can understand why children become so disoriented when a house, a store, or some other landmark is removed or changed.

Cognitive maps play several important roles in our lives. First, we use these maps to navigate through our environment; the more accurate our map, the easier it is for us to deal with our environment. We all have experienced the stress of being lost in a strange area or being unable to find our automobile in a crowded parking lot. Cognitive maps are also used when we communicate about our environment. When Jones wrote about New York, he did not present a road map for his readers to follow; rather, he gave descriptions of certain buildings, major roads, neighborhoods, and waterways. Finally, our maps are used to present our self-identity; they describe our memories, fantasies, beliefs, and feelings about our surroundings.

Because cognitive maps play such a central role in our lives, a legible environment is important for everyone, but it is especially important for the very young and the very old, who may become disoriented in unfamiliar surroundings. Having a clear cognitive map is also becoming increasingly important as we travel at greater speeds through our environment; most of us have experienced panic when we have approached a complicated highway interchange while driving at a high rate of speed. Environments that are clear, are relatively simple, and have prominent features help us to gain a sense of control and facilitate our adjustment to new surroundings (Lynch, 1960). Planners must keep these considerations in mind when they design our environment.

Managing Our Environment: Does Anybody Care?

We've made a number of points in this chapter. First, our physical environment does affect almost every aspect of our behavior, thoughts, and social interactions. Second, much of our environment and our behavior in response to it is under our control. Third, we are destroying and degrading

1. What are sound and noise?

2. Why is noise bothersome?

3. How does the concept of attribution help explain the differences in reactions to heat in laboratory and field settings?

4. Apply the concept of person-environment fit to the choice of the "best" office design.

5. How does the amount of personal control affect people's adjustment to dormitories and other buildings?

6. What are cognitive maps and how do they affect our behavior in physical environments?

our environment at an alarming rate. Psychologists have made these points through research, just as Tristan Jones and others have made them through observations and impassioned pleas. Yet, despite this knowledge, we continue to waste and destroy our surroundings, build buildings and cities that hamper human adjustment, and ignore warnings that these activities cannot continue if we are to survive and thrive. Why does this chain of events continue? What can be done to change these behaviors?

A gap intervenes between research and application in many areas of psychology, but we can use the environment as an arena to examine the problem more closely. Research on managing our environment has taken two approaches. One focuses on ways to change human environmental behavior. Some interesting findings have indeed been made in this area. For example, investigators reasoned that we are often unaware of the rate at which we use our environmental resources, and we feel we have little control over these activities. Therefore, they put meters that monitored the use of electricity in very visible places in a sample of homes. Now residents could see how much electricity they were using each day and how large an effect they could have on

consumption by turning off lights and lowering the thermostat in the winter. This immediate feedback did cause the residents to improve their conservation efforts (Seligman & Darley, 1977). Other investigators have found that they could modify a variety of environmental behaviors, such as littering and energy use, by applying behavioral principles of reward and punishment (Geller, 1989). Carefully constructed campaigns to change specific behaviors through a program of rewards and punishments showed dramatic results.

Though we have the ability to influence people's relationship with their environment, we often fail to use this ability. Understanding this lack of activity has been the second major thrust of work on environmental management. This work has uncovered many explanations that should help us to understand the relationship between science and application. One issue is the difference between a significant event and a meaningful one. If you will recall, in Chapter 1 we saw that investigators search for events that are statistically significant. In other words, is the event observed in an experiment likely to occur by chance fewer than 5 times out of 100? Significance, however, does not necessarily warrant action. People who apply these results ask a second question: Is the significant event a meaningful one? For example, carefully controlled studies in prisons (Ostfeld et al., 1987; Cox et al., 1984) showed that crowding in prisons often results in a significant increase in inmates' blood pressure. However, the next question, whether or not this increase in blood pressure has important negative effects on inmates, is not so clearly addressed. Hence one reason for the slowness of applying research results revolves around the question of the meaning of the results.

A related issue is the ratio of the cost of environmental actions to the benefits to be derived from them. Assume that we could show that prison crowding and the resulting increase in inmates' blood pressure does have negative effects on the inmates. Now the question becomes an economic one (Ruback & Innes, 1989). What is the cost of high blood pressure, in terms of illness and work output, in comparison with the cost of eliminating or reducing the prison crowding? An administrator, especially one who takes a short-term economic view, may decide that the cost of fixing the problem is greater than the cost of the problem itself. This mode of thinking is particularly troublesome when the affected population consists of people who have little power and cannot speak for themselves (inmates, residents of mental institutions, the poor). Going a step further, Ruback and Innes point out that the goals of the administrator may be at odds with those of the researcher. For example, the finding that overcrowding in prisons leads inmates to experience learned helplessness and reduces their efforts to control their environment may be disturbing to many of us. From an administrator's point of view, however, a group of inmates experiencing learned helplessness may be easier to control than inmates who feel not at all helpless. The point is that investigators interested in seeing social science used to solve problems must understand and deal with the needs and views of the people in a position to take action (Syme, Seligman & Macpherson, 1989; Di Mento, 1989). Action requires us to deal with politics and economics as well as research findings.

Another point concerns the psychology of individuals. When we discussed social dilemmas in Chapter 10, we saw that people often do not act for the good of the group because they feel that their actions make little difference. "I can add one more cow to the commons without causing a problem." Or "My piece of trash on the street won't even be noticed." If many people take this view toward the environment, their actions combine to have a dramatic effect: they destroy the environment. If this way of thinking is to change, people must be made aware of their individual impact on the environment and their relation to the community (Heberlein, 1989).

The problem of managing the environment becomes even more complex when we add issues of territoriality and ethics. As you will recall, we examined research showing that people are most likely to protect territory that is central to their lives. Yet the air, the oceans, public lands, and even prisons and institutions are not primary territory for anyone, except the odd person such as Tristan Jones who assumes a general caretaker role. It is therefore very difficult to get people to become concerned enough to use the research findings to protect the environment until the environmental destruction begins to affect them

The celebration of Earth Day 1990 was hailed by many as a way to increase awareness of the environmental problems of the globe and of ways to solve them. Others, though, taking the view that "every day is Earth Day," thought that this kind of one-day event would not do much to actually influence people's attitudes. What position did you take?

directly. Further, there are conflicting views and values in regard to the role of humans in protecting and managing parts of their environment (Seligman, 1989). This conflict was dramatically evident during the massive fires at Yellowstone National Park in 1988. Some people argued that every effort should be made to put out the fires, while others argued against human interference in the domain of nature.

These are indeed tough problems and they have no simple solutions. The problems not only concern the treatment of our environment but illustrate the complex issues involved in applying our research findings. It is very appropriate, then, that we conclude our text by leaving you with this message: Your own thoughts and actions may be those that influence the relationship between research in social psychology and its application.

Summary

Environmental psychology is the scientific study of the relationship between people and their environment. The way in which people view the environment has changed throughout history. The earliest view was that the environment was the master; in the course of the Industrial Revolution, people came to feel that *they* could be the masters. Today the prevailing attitude is that people are partners with the environment. The concept of *person-environmental fit* guides the research and theory on the effects of the environment on people. We can best understand those effects by examining attributions, feelings of control, cognitive overload, arousal, and the temporal context of behavior.

Personal space is the private space that surrounds an individual. Personal space is often conceptualized as a series of concentric circles— although this picture may be misleading. The size of one's personal space is affected by numerous variables, such as one's sex, culture, and age and the nature of the given interaction, as well as such contextual variables as the size and shape of the room one is in. Invasions of personal space may lead to arousal and attempts to restore appropriate spacing. Too large an interaction distance may also lead to discomfort. Depending on how they interpret an invasion, people may enjoy and reciprocate it. Interpersonal distance determines the channels of communication that can be used during an interaction; it can also be used to regulate intimacy and maintain privacy. One of the major messages that people communicate through their spatial behavior is attraction. Equilibrium theory deals with the relationship between spatial communication and other nonverbal modes of communication. *Territoriality* involves the exclusive use of a fixed area by an individual or a group; both humans and animals exhibit territoriality. Humans have three types of territory: *primary, secondary* and *public.* Territory serves many functions: it defines social organization, regulates privacy, and defines personal identity. People establish territory by using *territorial markers* to demonstrate their control of it. Territorial behavior may also have negative effects: it can work against personal and social change and serve to stereotype people.

Density is the amount of space available for each person in a situation. Although demographic and animal research has suggested that high density has negative consequences, laboratory research has failed to confirm this hypothesis.

Crowding is a psychological state rather than a simple spatial measure. Although crowding is related to density, it is a distinct concept. The major theories of crowding hypothesize that lack of privacy, loss of control, *cognitive overload,* and attribution affect people's experience of feeling crowded. In general crowding seems to occur when density makes it impossible for people to obtain their desired levels of control, privacy, arousal, and stimulation. Research has shown that crowding often leads to impaired task performance, discomfort, and stress. The theories in this area imply that the crowding experience can be lessened without any necessary increase in the amount of space.

Noise is sound that is unwanted by the listener because it is unpleasant or bothersome. Loud noises can damage hearing. The most bothersome types of noise are loud, unpredictable, and uncontrollable; research suggests that background conversation is one of the more disruptive types of noise. Noise affects performance and social interactions both immediately and after it has stopped. One reason for these effects is that noise increases arousal and thus makes people focus their attention on a few stimuli.

Research on temperature suggests that within commonly experienced temperature ranges, an increase in heat is associated with an increase in aggression. Excessive cold can impair performance on tasks requiring muscle coordination and quick reaction time. There is some disagreement between field and laboratory studies on the effect of heat on aggression at very high temperatures.

Studies have found that rooms may be designed either to facilitate (sociopetal space) or to inhibit (sociofugal space) social interaction. Other variables, such as the presence of windows and doors, not only affect people's perceptions of a room but also influence behavior inside the room. Buildings that are not designed to fit human behavioral needs may be either misused or not used at all. No single design will be best in all cases; rather, designs must take into account the people who will use the area and the types of activities that will take place there. This effect was clearly evident in studies on institutions for the mentally retarded and college dormitories.

Complex urban environments often lead to cognitive overload. As a result, individuals may depersonalize the environment and exercise selectivity over the stimuli to which they pay attention. Because of the complexity of the urban environment, individuals form *cognitive maps* that aid them to navigate through that environment. Variables such as paths, edges, nodes, districts, and landmarks are the principal features of these cognitive maps. Children develop cognitive maps by first learning landmarks.

People's behavior toward the environment can be changed if they are given feedback about the effects of their actions and subjected to behavioral principles of reward and punishment. However, research is often not applied to solve environmental problems because it often fails to consider political and economic issues, to emphasize meaningful effects of the environment on behavior, and to deal with the question of ethics and values.

Key Terms

arousal	*learned helplessness*	*public territory*
cognitive map	*module design*	*secondary territory*
cognitive overload	*noise*	*social distance*
corridor design	*open-office design*	*sociofugal space*
crowding	*personal distance*	*sociopetal space*
density	*personal space*	*sound*
ecological psychology	*person-environment fit*	*suite design*
environmental psychology	*primary territory*	*temporal framework*
	privacy	*territoriality*
indefensible territory	*proxemics*	*territorial markers*
intimate distance	*public distance*	

Suggested Readings

Altman, I., & Chemers, M. (1980). *Culture and environmental.* Pacific Grove, Calif.: Brooks/Cole.

Baum, A., & Singer, J. E. (1982). *Advances in environmental psychology* (Vol. 4). Hillsdale, N.J.: Erlbaum.

Fisher, C. S. (1984). *The urban experience* (2nd ed.). New York: Harcourt Brace Jovanovich.

Fisher, J., Bell, P., & Baum, A. (1984). *Environmental psychology* (2nd ed.). New York: Holt, Rinehart & Winston.

Glass, D. C., & Singer, J. E. (1972). *Urban stress.* New York: Academic Press.

McGrath, J. (Ed.) (1988). *The social psychology of time: New perspectives.* Newbury Park, Calif.: Sage.

Seligman, C., & Syme, G. J. (Eds.) (1989). Managing the environment. *Journal of Social Issues, 45.*

Stokols, D., & Altman, I. (Eds.) (1987). *Handbook of environmental psychology.* New York: Wiley.

Sundstrom, E. (1986). *Workplaces: The psychology of the physical environment in offices and factories.* Cambridge, England: Cambridge University Press.

Zube, E. (1980). *Environmental evolution: Perception and public policy.* Pacific Grove, Calif.: Brooks/Cole.

Glossary

A-B-X model The theory that the relationship between two persons and an attitude object will strain to become symmetrical.

accessible An attitude is most easily accessed from memory storage if there exists a strong association between the object of that attitude and the evaluation of the current situation.

accommodation Expansion of a mental category to incorporate new information.

actor-observer bias The tendency of actors to attribute their behavior to situational factors and of observers to attribute it to stable dispositions.

additive task A task whose final product is the sum of group members' efforts.

adversary system A system for resolving disputes by which both sides (or their representatives) argue their case before a judge.

aggression Any act that is intended to injure a target (*see also* **angry aggression**; **displaced aggression**; **instrumental aggression**).

aggression cues Stimuli associated with the source of frustration and with aggressive behavior in general; when paired with frustration, aggression cues may elicit aggression.

altruism An unselfish desire to help others; an unselfishly helpful act.

ambivalence-amplification theory The theory that when positive and negative attitudes coexist, the negative attitudes may be displaced in the positive direction and amplify the positive response, and vice versa.

analysis of variance test A statistical procedure that takes into account both the mean and the variability of experimental data to determine the statistical significance of the results.

angry aggression An aggressive act instigated by anger or hostility.

arbitration A system of dispute resolution by which a third party dtermines the outcome after hearing the arguments of both sides.

archival research A method of study by which the investigator examines historical accounts of events that have one or more features in common and identifies common responses to those events.

arousal Physiological activity measured by such indices as blood pressure and heart rate.

aspirational deprivation Loss of hope of attaining something in limited supply, something one has

come recently to value, or something to which one has recently become committed.

assimilation Distortion of new information to fit an already existing mental category.

attitude A general and enduring positive or negative feeling about some person, object, or issue.

attitude-discrepant behavior Action that is contrary to one's private attitude.

attraction A positive attitude held by one person toward another.

attribution An inference about the cause of a person's action.

audience pleasing Self-presentational behavior designed to make an audience happy.

augmentation principle In attribution theory, the principle that situational inducements against a behavior tend to lead perceivers to attribute the behavior to a personal disposition.

authoritarian personality A complex of characteristics that includes ethnocentrism, hostility toward out-groups, and emphasis on obedience, discipline, and respect for authority.

autistic conspiracy The tendency for an ingratiator and a target person to pretend or believe that ingratiation is not occurring, because neither one wants to acknowledge it.

autistic hostility Withdrawal from a conflict situation and avoidance of interaction.

automatic processing model The theory that people respond relatively automatically to a situation once they interpret what the situation is.

availability bias The tendency of a stimulus that comes easily or quickly to mind to be seen as the cause of an event.

aversive consequences Unwanted events that result from a behavior, which lead to cognitive dissonance.

aversive racism An aversion to racial minorities that people hide from other people and to some extent from themselves.

balance theories Theories concerning the way attitudes toward persons, objects, and issues are formed, based on the supposition that people prefer orderly, consistent, and harmonious relationships among their cognitions.

base-rate information Data or information about the frequency of specific events or behaviors in particular groups.

beneffectance The tendency to take credit for success and deny responsibility for failure; from *beneficent + effectance.*

bogus pipeline A technique by which subjects are induced to state their attitudes honestly in the belief that a machine has already registered their true attitudes.

boomerang effect Attitude change in a direction opposite to that promoted in a communication.

case history method A method of inquiry that examines the responses of a few individuals and analyzes their reactions in depth.

categorization The tendency to conceptualize objects and people as members of groups; a basic human cognitive process.

catharsis The reduction in the instigation to aggress following some instances of aggression.

central/systematic processing Persuasion caused by thinking about the arguments contained in the message.

charisma A personal attribute of certain leaders that tends to draw others' support and admiration.

check on the manipulation A procedure that ensures that the variable investigators intended to manipulate was accurately perceived by participants in the experiment.

circumplex Leary's classification scheme for interpersonal behavior, which arrays behaviors in a circle created by crossing a dominant-submissive dimension and a friendly-hostile dimension.

classical conditioning Modification of behavior by the pairing of a neutral stimulus with another stimulus that produces an unconditioned response.

coalition A temporary alliance of two or more parties who cooperate and combine their resources to beat an opponent.

coercive power The capacity to deliver threats and punishments to force compliance.

cognition An element of knowledge; any thought that an individual has about him- or herself or the environment.

cognitive conservatism The tendency to seek social situations consistent with one's self-image and in which information received confirms one's self-concept.

cognitive consonance A relationship among cognitions such that each fits with or psychologically follows from the others.

cognitive dissonance A relationship among cognitions such that one cognition follows from the opposite of another; also, a theory proposed by Leon Festinger that unpleasant psychological tension arises when cognitions are not in harmony.

cognitive irrelevance A relationship among cognitions such that one cognition has no psychological implication for the others.

cognitive map A mental image of a particular area of space.

cognitive overload An excess of stimuli beyond one's ability to process.

cohesiveness The result of all forces that impel individuals to remain in or leave a group; often measured by how attractive members find their group.

collective A gathering of people who have no structure or face-to-face interaction but are engaged in a common activity.

commitment The degree to which a behavior or decision cannot be undone or rescinded.

communal relationship A long-term relationship in which benefits given are not balanced against benefits received.

compassionate love A long-term, deep, affectionate attachment between two people.

competition Interpersonal conflict involving an incompatibility of goals.

complementarity The quality of eliciting a behavioral response that dovetails with one's own behavior.

compliance Overt behavioral conformity while maintaining one's own attitude.

conflict spiral The tendency for conflict, once initiated, to increase rather than diminish.

conformity A yielding to real or imagined group pressure.

conjunctive task A task in which all group members perform essentially the same subtask, and the overall performance is dependent on the combination of these subtasks. The maximum effort of the group is defined by the least capable member.

contingency model The theory that the effectiveness of the task-oriented and relationship-oriented leadership styles depends on the situation the leader faces.

contrast The tendency to distort opinions that are unacceptable so they are made to appear more extreme than they really are.

coordination loss Reduced group productivity due to the group's inability to combine and use the individual members' contributions.

correlation The degree of association between two events; a statistical measure.

correspondence bias (also known as **fundamental attribution error**) The tendency of perceivers to infer that behavior reflects internal dispositions and to ignore external factors that might explain it.

corridor design A design for residence units that locates a large number of private bedrooms along a common hallway.

cost model of helping A model of altruistic behavior that considers the observer's cost of helping and the cost to the victim of not receiving help.

credibility Attribute of a communicator, based on expertise and trustworthiness, that enhances persuasion.

crowding A motivational state aroused through the interaction of spatial, social, and personal factors.

deception (in an experiment) The practice of giving subjects false information about the reasons for the study or the manipulations.

decision tree A model of intervention in emergencies that considers decisions about noticing, interpreting, assessing responsibility, knowing an appropriate form of assistance, and implementing the decision.

decremental deprivation The loss of what one once had or thought one could have.

defensive attribution An attribution of causality that is made to reduce the perceiver's anxiety.

deindividuation The loss of individuality that occurs when the individual becomes submerged in the group and feels relatively anonymous.

demand characteristics Cues in the experimental setting that communicate to subjects the behavior that is expected of them.

density The amount of space available for each individual in a defined area.

dependent variable The subject's response in an experiment.

depressive realism The tendency of depressed people to see themselves and the world realistically, without the self-deceiving biases that protect non-depressed people.

diffusion of responsibility The sharing of responsibility among several individuals; when no one person can be held accountable, no one may intervene in an emergency.

dilution effect The tendency of an inference to be weakened by irrelevant information.

direct experience An attitude derived from personal contact with the object of the attitude, rather than from hearing or reading about the experience of others.

disconfirmed expectations A paradigm of research relevant to cognitive dissonance theory in which dissonance is created by the occurrence of an event that is at variance with one's expectations.

discounting principle The tendency to discount a cause to which a behavior might be attributed when other plausible explanations are available.

discretionary task A task that requires group members to agree on a decision that involves several alternatives and different ways to arrive at a decision.

discrimination Negative, often aggressive behaviors aimed at the target of prejudice.

disjunctive task A task requiring an either-or decision.

displaced aggression Aggression that varies either in type or in target from that most preferred by the attacker.

display rules Norms as to the emotions that are appropriate to display in particular situations.

disposition A quality or trait that distinguishes one person or group from another.

dissonance motivation A drive, leading to attitude change, which originates in the discomforting arousal of cognitive dissonance.

door-in-the-face technique A persuasion technique whereby the communicator leads the target to comply with a moderately large request by first presenting a request so large that it will be refused.

downward comparison Comparison with people who are worse off than we so that we may feel better by contrast.

ecological psychology The study of human behavior in a social and physical context.

effort justification Defense of what one has voluntarily suffered for as a means to reduce cognitive dissonance.

egocentricity A bias toward perceiving oneself as the central actor and causal agent in events.

egoism A tendency to focus on one's own gratification; behavior directed at self-gratification.

elaboration likelihood model (ELM) A model of attitude change that focuses on the distinction between scrutinizing the content of a message (central route) and the other factors (peripheral route) that affect persuasion.

electromyograph (EMG) Instrument that has been used to measure the direction and intensity of attitudes by monitoring the activity of facial muscles used in smiling and frowning.

emblems Gestures used in particular cultures to express certain ideas or feelings.

emotional loneliness Loneliness caused by lack of an intimate attachment to another person.

empathy The ability to share in another's feelings.

empathy-altruism hypothesis The hypothesis that helping behavior is based, at least in part, on feelings of empathy with another person.

entity attribution An inference that a behavior is caused by some external person, object, or entity.

environmental psychology The study of the relationship between the environment and behavior.

equity theory The theory that individuals compare their inputs and outcomes with those of the other party to determine the fairness of a relationship.

ethnocentrism A tendency to reject people who are culturally dissimilar to one's own ethnic group and to accept without question those who are culturally like one's ethnic group; a characteristic of the authoritarian personality.

ethologist A scientist who studies animal behavior in natural settings, and may attempt to draw comparisons between animal and human behavior.

exchange relationship A relationship in which benefits given are balanced against benefits received.

excitation transfer The transfer of arousal produced by one source to the energization of an unrelated response.

excitation-transfer theory A theory, usually applied to aggression, that holds that arousal from one source can be misperceived and therefore transferred to another source.

excitation-valence model A theory that the likelihood of aggression after viewing pornography depends on the degree of excitation caused by the erotic material and its pleasurableness.

exemplification Behavior designed to get others to believe that one is moral and self-sacrificing.

expectancy effect (self-fulfilling prophecy) The

tendency of expectations in regard to a person's behavior or performance to be realized because of the climate, feedback, input, and opportunities for output that such expectations create.

experiment A method of study aimed at determining the cause-and-effect relationship between events; the experimenter exercises control over the independent variable.

experimental realism The degree to which experimental manipulations have impact and involve the subjects in the experimental situation.

experimenter bias Influence on subjects' behavior as a function of the investigators' expectations.

expertise Special skill or knowledge; a factor in the credibility of a communicator.

expert power Power derived from a reputation for special insight or knowledge about a particular area.

external attribution An inference that a person's behavior is caused by an environmental or situational factor.

external locus of control A perception that one's outcomes are due to factors outside of one's control, such as luck, chance, or fate.

external validity The degree to which research findings may be generalized to situations outside the laboratory.

extraneous variable A factor that may influence the dependent variable, though it has nothing to do with the independent variable.

face The positive social value we claim for ourselves in social interaction.

face saving Behaviors designed to maintain a positive public image.

face work In Goffman's theory of self-presentation, behavior designed to maintain other people's faces.

false consensus effect The tendency to overestimate the number of people who think and act as we do.

fear of success A fear in women of succeeding in domains traditionally reserved for men.

field experiment An experiment that is run in a natural setting, and subjects often do not know that they are in an experiment; the realism should allow greater opportunity for generalization and more mundane realism.

foot-in-the-door technique A persuasion technique whereby the communicator leads the target to commit him- or herself to the desired position in small incremental steps.

foreseeability Ability to foretell the consequences of a decision before the decision is made; an element of cognitive dissonance.

forewarning Advance knowledge that a persuasive message is coming, which can allow the potential audience to build defenses against the persuasion.

free-choice paradigm A strategy for research in cognitive dissonance in which an individual is asked to choose from one of two or more items. Dissonance is aroused by the choice, owing to rejection of desirable aspects of the rejected item and

acceptance of undesirable aspects of the chosen alternative.

free rider effect Social loafing as a consequence of a belief that one's contributions to the group are dispensable and that the group will succeed without one's efforts.

frustration Interference or thwarting of an ongoing behavior.

frustration-aggression theory The theory that aggression is always a consequence of frustration and that frustration always leads to some form of aggression.

fundamental attribution error (*See* **correspondence bias**).

galvanic skin resistance (GSR) A measure of the skin's conductance of an electrical current; an indicant of arousal.

gender schema A complex of beliefs and expectations about the behavior of males or females.

generalization The process of deriving from a sample of situations information that predicts and explains behavior in other situations of a similar sort.

GRIT Graduated reciprocation in tension reduction; a policy developed by Osgood to reduce international tension through the unilateral reduction of threat capability.

group Two or more persons who are interacting with one another in such a manner that each person influences and is influenced by each other person.

group development The process by which groups form, flourish, and decline, and the changes that take place in the group and in its members over time.

group polarization The tendency of group discussion to cause an individual to make a more extreme decision than he or she would make alone.

groupthink A form of thinking in a decision-making situation in which the group suspends objectivity and careful analysis in an effort to preserve group cohesiveness.

halo error The assumption that a leader who demonstrates one leadership characteristic has them all.

heuristic processing (*See* **peripheral/heuristic processing**)

heuristic processing model A model of attitude change that focuses on the distinction between systematic and heuristic processing of a message.

hypothesis A statement that expresses the nature of the relationship between events; expresses *what* relationship exists between the events, not *why* they are related.

idealized performance Behavior suggesting we live up to ideal standards of social behavior more than in fact we do.

identification Adoption of the standards of a person or group that one likes, admires, and wants to establish a relationship with.

illusory correlation A correlation erroneously perceived between a person or group and a characteristic on the basis of a few specific coincidences.

impression management Behavior designed to control what others think, especially so as to maintain power in relation to them.

indefensible territory An area that is not under the control of any individual or group and cannot easily be regulated, patrolled, or observed.

independent variable A variable manipulated by the experimenter to study its effect on the dependent variable.

induced compliance A paradigm of research in cognitive dissonance in which individuals are persuaded to behave in ways that are discrepant with their private attitudes.

informational power Power derived from the possession of a specific piece of information.

informational social influence Influence based on a group's capacity to supply information.

informed consent Consent given to participate in an experiment after the procedures to be used have been explained and the subject has been given an opportunity to withdraw from the experiment.

ingratiation Use of a variety of strategies to enhance one's image illicitly in the eyes of others.

ingratiator's dilemma A problem posed by the fact that a low-power position makes a person want to ingratiate but alerts the target person to the possibility of ingratiation and thus makes it more difficult; also, the problem of wanting to ingratiate but not wanting to see oneself as an ingratiator.

inoculation A technique for building resistance to persuasion by exposure to weak, easily refuted arguments.

institutional review boards (IRBs) Committees in which a cross section of professionals considers the risks and benefits of research to participants and ensures that proposed research methods protect subjects' safety and rights.

instrumental aggression An act of aggression performed to achieve a goal outside of the aggressive act itself.

integrative problem solving Resolution of conflict by identification of common goals rather than a focus on means.

internal attribution An inference that a person's behavior is caused by a personal disposition.

internalization The process by which one genuinely accepts an opinion as a result of its good fit with one's other values and opinions.

internal locus of control A perception that one's outcomes are due to one's own efforts and actions.

internal validity Freedom of an experimental design from contamination by an extraneous variable; allows the investigator to state that manipulations of the independent variable are responsible for changes in the dependent variable.

interpersonal conflict Tension between two or more individuals or groups resulting from incompatibility of actual or desired responses.

interpersonal style A characteristic style of behaving with other people, categorized by degree of dominance and friendliness.

intimate distance The distance people use for intimate activities such as making love, offering protection and comfort, and whispering.

intimidation Behavior designed to get others to believe that one is dangerous.

intrapersonal conflict An internal struggle resulting from a wish to make two or more incompatible responses.

inverted U A graphic depiction of the relationship between fear and attitude change.

jigsaw method A technique for reducing conflict in a racially mixed group of students by which the group is given a problem to solve such that each member holds a part of the solution; if the group is to succeed, each member must master his or her part.

latitude of acceptance The range of opinions that one could consider adopting.

latitude of rejection The range of opinions that one could not consider adopting.

leader The person who exerts the most influence in a group.

leadership schema An overall image of what a leader is and does.

learned helplessness A state resulting when the individual perceives no control over his or her environment.

legitimate power Power derived from a particular role or position.

Likert scale A scale that measures the direction and intensity of attitudes.

line The verbal and facial expressions by which we convey our views of ourselves, other people, and the situation.

love (*See* **compassionate love**; **romantic love**).

low-ball technique An influence technique whereby the communicator secures the target's commitment to an action by understating its true cost.

matching to standards Attempting to meet ideal standards of behavior in a situation; caused or increased by self-awareness.

mean Average, computed by dividing the sum of the terms by the number of terms.

mediator A third party who helps the principal parties to a conflict develop their own resolution.

mere exposure Exposure to a person or object which, in the absence of any factor other than familiarity, leads to feelings of attraction.

mere thought Thought alone, which in the absence of the object contemplated or new information about it, causes preexisting attitudes toward it to become more extreme.

minimal group situation Membership in a group based on nothing more than random assignment to it. Research shows that in-group bias results from even this situation.

minority influence The ability of a minority opinion

to affect the thinking of individual group members.

misattribution The incorrect attribution of causality; generally an incorrect attribution of internal arousal to internal or external causes.

mixed-motive conflict A conflict in which both parties may gain by responding in a cooperative manner, but the best joint outcome is not the best outcome for the individuals.

modeling Imitation of another person's behavior.

module design A design for residence units that separates individual sleeping areas with low partitions.

motivation loss Loss of group productivity that occurs when members do not put their maximum effort into the task.

multiple-source effect The tendency of information presented by multiple sources to receive greater scrutiny than the same information presented by a single source.

mundane realism The degree to which the experimental setting approximates a real-life setting.

need for cognition An individual preference for and tendency to engage in effortful thought.

negative memory bias The tendency of depressed people to remember more negative than positive experiences.

noise Sound that is unwanted because it is unpleasant and bothersome.

nominal group A number of persons working on a problem independently.

norm A rule that governs a specific behavior and applies to everyone in the group.

normative social influence Influence based on a group's capacity to reward and punish, including the capacity to accept or reject the individual.

norming A stage of group development marked by a high degree of conformity, in which members attempt to establish norms.

norm of equality A means of resolving conflict by which resources are divided equally among the parties, regardless of inputs.

obedience Conformity to direct orders from a person of high status and authority.

open-office design An arrangement whereby work spaces are separated by partitions rather than by floor-to-ceiling walls and doors.

operant conditioning Modification of behavior by rewards and punishments; behavior that is reinforced (rewarded) is likely to be repeated.

organizational psychologists Psychologists who focus on the functioning of organizations and work groups.

out-group homogeneity effect The tendency to see all members of the out-group as similar or homogeneous.

out-group polarization effect The tendency to have extreme reactions to information about out-group members, overvaluing both positive and negative information.

overjustification effect The tendency of inappropriately large rewards to be counterproductive.

overt bargaining A situation in which parties with divergent interests have some form of communication and can make provisional offers and concessions.

peripheral/heuristic processing Persuasion effected by factors other than the content of the persuasive message.

personal distance Space kept between organisms when interacting with a member of the same species.

personal involvement The degree to which a person is involved in an issue, which determines the likelihood that he or she will process the arguments in the message rather than relying on peripheral cues.

personal responsibility Accountability for the results of one's behavior, which flows from choice plus foreseeability; a requisite element of cognitive dissonance.

personal space The mobile area around an individual of which he or she feels ownership and control.

person attribution An inference that a person's behavior is caused by an internal disposition.

person-environment fit The dynamic relationship between people and their environment, suggesting that the "best" environment must be determined by the needs and characteristics of the people in that environment.

power The capacity to influence others and to resist influence by others.

prejudice An unjustified negative attitude toward an individual based solely on that individual's membership in a group.

primacy effect The tendency of information received first to be more influential than information received later.

primary territory An area or object that is exclusively owned or controlled on a permanent basis by an individual or group and is viewed as a central part of the owner's life.

priming The process of bringing certain things, typically behaviors or personal characteristics, to mind, activating them.

prisoner's dilemma A mixed-motive conflict in which the best individual choice leads to the worst joint payoff; a paradigm used to study trust.

privacy Freedom to choose what one will communicate about oneself and to whom the information will be communicated; chosen isolation.

private self-consciousness Awareness of one's own feelings and internal states.

procedural justice Justice and fairness based on the procedure by which resources are allocated.

process loss The difference between a group's potential and its actual productivity.

progressive deprivation Loss of momentum or deterioration of conditions after a prolonged period of steady improvement.

propinquity Nearness in space, which tends to lead to liking, under the influence of rewards, expectations, and mere exposure.

prototype A standard that incorporates the essential and most characteristic features of a category.

proxemics The study of interpersonal space.

psychological reactance A state of arousal generated by blocking, or the threat of blocking, a person's free behaviors.

public commitment Strengthening of a privately held attitude by making it public, as in signing a petition or making a public statement.

public distance The distance maintained in formal interactions and around public figures.

public self-consciousness Awareness of how others react to or evaluate oneself.

public territory An area or object that is temporarily controlled by an individual but of which no feeling of ownership exists.

racism Discrimination or prejudice based on race.

random assignment Assignment of subjects to experimental conditions in such a way that all subjects have equal opportunities to be in each experimental condition.

reactance theory The theory that a threat to behavioral freedom arouses a motivation to regain that freedom.

realistic conflict theory The theory that discrimination can be traced to competition for scarce resources.

recency effect The tendency of an impression based on the information most recently gained to outweigh an impression based on information gained earlier.

reciprocity A mutual exchange of confidences, self-disclosures, or resources.

reciprocity norm A rule specifying that people should reciprocate another's self-disclosure and helpful acts to the same degree.

reference group A group toward which one orients oneself; it forms the basis of comparison for attitudes, values, and behaviors.

referent power Power derived from being admired and liked.

reflected appraisal A view of the self based on other people's appraisals.

regressive racism The emergence under stress of racist reactions that one has tried to overcome.

reinforcement Rewards offered for approved behavior, which tend to increase the probability that the approved behavior will be repeated.

reinforcement effect The tendency of a privately held belief to intensify in proportion to the size of an incentive to state that belief.

related attributes hypothesis In social comparison theory, the hypothesis that we evaluate our opinions and abilities by comparing them with those of people whose opinions and performance should be similar to ours, given their standing on characteristics related to opinion and performance.

relative deprivation A perceived discrepancy between people's expectations and what they can actually have.

representativeness bias The tendency to assume that a person who shares some characteristics of a group probably belongs to that group.

revised learned helplessness (RLH) model The theory that people learn to become helpless, and eventually become depressed, as a result of attributing their negative outcomes to internal, stable, and global causes.

reward model The theory that we like people whom we associate with rewards.

reward power The capacity to give positive reinforcements to achieve compliance.

role A set of norms that defines how a particular person in a given position must act.

role ambiguity Uncertainty as to what is expected of one in a specific situation or position.

role conflict The inner struggle that results when incompatible behaviors are demanded either by the various requirements of a role or by the various roles that one occupies.

romantic love A passionately intense attachment to another person.

saliency bias The tendency to attribute behavior to any stimulus that is most vivid or salient in the situation.

scapegoat theory The theory that out-groups are convenient targets for hostility stemming from the frustrations of everyday life.

schema A body of general knowledge and expectations about a person, object, or event.

science A set of rules guiding the inquiry and study of events.

script The sequence of events that one has learned to expect in a given situation.

secondary territory An area or object that is temporarily controlled by an individual or group.

self-awareness (self-focused attention) A state of paying attention to and being aware of oneself.

self-complexity The condition of perceiving oneself to have many aspects, which differ greatly from one another.

self-construction Self-presentational behavior designed to confirm a desired view of the self.

self-disclosure The act of revealing personal information to others.

self-discrepancy theory The theory that one's psychological well-being is affected by the match or mismatch between one's self-concept and one's self-guides: one's ideal self and the self one thinks one ought to be.

self-efficacy Confidence in one's ability to produce positive outcomes.

self-evaluation maintenance Upholding of self-evaluation by constructive efforts to improve oneself or destructive efforts to undermine others.

self-fulfilling prophecy (*See* **expectancy effect**).

self-handicapping Putting obstacles in the way of one's own success, for the purpose of providing an excuse for poor performance.

self-monitoring Modifying one's behavior to meet the expectations of others.

self-perception theory A theory that people infer their own attitudes and feelings from their behaviors and the situations in which they take place.

self-promotion Behavior designed to get others to believe that one is competent and talented.

self-regulation The process by which self-awareness leads to matching to standards if outcome expectancy is positive.

self-serving bias A tendency to try to show that we are as good as people who are superior and very different from people who are inferior.

sentiment relationship In Heider's balance theory, a relationship with emotional content.

sexism Discrimination or prejudice based on sex.

similarity hypothesis The hypothesis that we evaluate ourselves by comparing our opinions and abilities with those of other people who are similar to us.

situated identity The conception one has of oneself in a specific situation.

sleeper effect The increase in the strength of a communication's effectiveness over time.

social cognition The processing, organizing, and retrieval of information about other people.

social comparison The process whereby individuals reduce uncertainty about their opinions, abilities, and emotions by observing those of similar others.

social dilemma Conflict that arises when behaviors bring short-term pleasures but have negative long-term effects, or when one must choose between one's own interest and that of the group.

social distance The distance used for personal business and at social gatherings.

social exchange theories Theories that view human interaction as a cost-reward transaction.

social facilitation An increase in the quality of performance in the presence of an audience or co-actors, whether or not in competition.

social identity An aspect of self-concept that is based on membership in groups.

social identity theory The theory that people evaluate themselves by their membership in groups, and therefore are motivated to evaluate the in-group more positively than the out-group.

social impact theory The theory that social influence is a function of the strength, immediacy, and number of sources of influence.

social influence The exercise of power by a person or group to change the opinions or behavior of others.

social inhibition A restraint on performance effected by the presence of an audience or co-actors.

social learning theory The theory that individuals learn behavior by imitating others and receiving rewards.

social loafing The tendency of individuals to work less hard in a group than alone, perhaps because of lack of individual identifiability or reduced feelings of personal responsibility.

social loneliness Loneliness caused by lack of connectedness to a social network.

social psychology A discipline that employs scientific methods to understand and explain how the thought, feeling, and behavior of individuals are influenced by the actual, imagined, or implied presence of others.

social responsibility norm A general rule specifying that we should give help to people who need it.

social support An effort to reduce dissonance by persuading others to adopt a belief system.

socioemotional specialist A group role; a person who is concerned primarily with the feelings of the group members.

sociofugal space An area arranged in such a way as to separate people and reduce social interaction.

sociopetal space An area arranged in such a way as to foster and encourage social interaction.

sound Changes in air pressure that are detected by the ear.

statistically significant Reliable; a finding is considered statistically significant if a statistical test indicates that the event could have occurred by chance fewer than 5 times out of 100 ($p < .05$).

stereotype A set of beliefs about the characteristics of the people in a group, generalized to nearly all group members.

strength of an attitude Strong attitudes are easily and quickly recalled from memory; weak attitudes require more effort for recall.

storming A stage of group development marked by a low degree of conformity, in which members negotiate their positions in the group.

subjective norms Behavior-guiding rules based on what we think other people want us to do.

subtractive rule In attribution theory, the principle that perceivers should subtract the contribution of situational inducements from the personal disposition implied by the behavior.

sucker effect Social loafing as a consequence of a belief that other group members are not contributing their maximum effort.

suite design A design for a residence unit that locates a limited number of private bedrooms around a common living area.

superordinate goal A goal that is attractive to members of two groups but cannot be achieved without cooperation between the two groups.

supplication Behavior designed to make others feel sorry for you and want to help.

survey method   A method of research by which the investigator asks questions of a large sample of subjects.

symbolic racism   Hostility to racial minorities based on the belief that they threaten the values of the majority culture.

symmetrical relationships   In the perception of individuals, a set of relationships that are harmonious and consistent.

systematic processing (*See* **central/systematic processing**)

task specialist   A group role; a person who functions to keep the group working toward its goals by focusing on the task demands.

temporal framework   The context of time, experience, and expectations in which behavior takes place.

territoriality   Persistent attachment to an area or object and defense of it against other individuals or groups.

territorial markers   Devices such as fences and signs used to identify the boundaries of one's territory.

terrorism   Actual or threatened violence against noncombatants for avowed political ends.

theory   A systematic statement that seeks to explain *why* two or more events are related.

theory of planned behavior   The theory that planned behavior is linked to an attitude toward the specific behavior, subjective norms, and degree of control.

tit-for-tat strategy   A bargaining strategy by which an opponent's cooperative actions receive a cooperative response and his or her competitive responses beget competitive reactions.

totalitarian ego   The biased organization of information about the self that functions to preserve a favorable self-impression.

transformational leader   A leader who can sense and articulate the unexpressed desires of a populace and who expresses those desires to change the political system.

trust   A general expectancy that another person will respond in a helpful rather than a harmful manner.

trustworthiness   The quality of meriting confidence; a factor in the credibility of a communicator.

two-factor theory of emotions   Schachter's theory that emotional experience is based on a combination of physiological arousal and cognitive labeling or interpretation of the causes of arousal.

uniqueness bias   A tendency to see one's own strengths and abilities as unusual.

unit relationship   In Heider's balance theory, a relationship with no emotional content.

unobtrusive measures   Experimental methods that permit subjects' behavior to be measured without their awareness.

variability   The extent to which scores vary about the mean. The closer the scores cluster about the mean, the lower the variability.

visual dominance behavior   Staring or other assertive, dominating nonverbal behavior.

voice   An opportunity for parties in conflict to express their views of the situation.

weapon effect   The tendency of people who are frustrated to aggress if a weapon is present.

zero-sum conflict   Pure competition, in which one party's gain is the other party's loss.

References

Abelson, R. P. (1981). The psychological status of the script concept. *American Psychologist, 36,* 715–729.

Abelson, R., & Levi, A. (1985). Decision making and decision theory. In G. Lindzey & E. Aronson (Eds.), *The handbook of social psychology* (3rd ed.). New York: Random House.

Abramson, L. Y., Alloy, L. B., & Metalsky, G. I. (1986). The cognitive diathesis-stress theories of depression: Toward an adequate evaluation of the theories' validity. In L. B. Alloy (Ed.), *Cognitive processes in depression.* New York: Guilford.

Abramson, L. Y., Seligman, M. E. P., & Teasdale, J. D. (1978). Learned helplessness in humans: Critique and reformulation. *Journal of Abnormal Psychology, 87,* 49–74.

Adams, J. S. (1963). Toward an understanding of inequity. *Journal of Abnormal and Social Psychology, 67,* 422–436.

Adams, J. S. (1965). Inequity in social exchange. In L. Berkowitz (Ed.), *Advances in experimental social psychology* (Vol. 2). New York: Academic Press.

Adorno, T. W., Frenkel-Brunswick, E., Levinson, D. J., & Sanford, R. N. (1950). *The authoritarian personality.* New York: Harper.

Aiello, J. (1987). Human spatial behavior. In D. Stokols & I. Altman (Eds.), *Handbook of environmental psychology* (Vol. 1, pp. 533–570). New York: Wiley.

Aiello, J. R., & Aiello, T. (1974). The development of personal space: Proxemic behavior of children 6 through 16. *Human Ecology, 2*(3), 177–189.

Ainsworth, M. (1979). Infant-mother attachment. *American Psychologist, 34,* 932–937.

Ajzen, I. (1982). On behaving in accordance with one's attitudes. In M. P. Zanna, E. T. Higgins, & C. P. Herman (Eds.), *Consistency in social behavior: The Ontario symposium* (Vol. 2). Hillsdale, N.J.: Erlbaum.

Ajzen, I. (1985). From intentions to actions: A theory of planned behavior. In J. Kuhl & J. Beckman (Eds.), *Action-control: From cognition to behavior* (pp. 11–39). Heidelberg: Springer.

Ajzen, I. (1989). Attitude structure and behavior. In A. R. Pratkanis, S. J. Breckler, & A. G. Greenwald (Eds.), *Attitude structure and function. The third Ohio State University volume on attitudes and persuasion* (pp. 241–274). Hillsdale, N.J.: Erlbaum.

Ajzen, I., & Fishbein, M. (1980). *Understanding attitudes and predicting social behavior.* Englewood Cliffs, N.J.: Prentice-Hall.

Ajzen, I., & Madden, T. J. (1986). Prediction of goal directed behavior: Attitudes, intentions and perceived behavioral control. *Journal of Experimental Social Psychology, 22,* (5), 453–474.

Alden, L. (1987). Attributional responses of anxious individuals to different patterns of social feedback: Nothing succeeds like improvement. *Journal of Personality and Social Psychology, 52,* 100–106.

Alexander, C. N., Jr., & Rudd, J. (1981). Situated identities and response variables. In J. T. Tedeschi (Ed.), *Impression management theory and social psychological research.* New York: Academic Press.

Allen, V., & Greenberger. (1989). Destruction and perceived control. In A. Baum & J. Singer (Eds.), *Advances: Environmental Psychology, Vol. 2.* Hillsdale, N. J.: Erlbaum.

Allen, V. L. (1965). Situational factors in conformity. In L. Berkowitz (Ed.), *Advances in experimental social psychology* (Vol. 2). New York: Academic Press.

Allen V. L., & Wilder, D. A. (1980). Impact of group consensus and social support on stimulus meaning: Mediation of conformity by cognitive restructuring. *Journal of Personality and Social Psychology, 39,* 1116–1125.

Allison, S. T., & Messick, D. (1987). From individual input to group outputs, and back again: Group processes and inferences about members. In C. Hendrick (Ed.), *Group processes* (pp. 111–143). Newbury Park, Calif.: Sage.

Allison, S. T., & Messick, D. M. (1983). Effects of experience on performance in replenishable resource trap. *Journal of Personality and Social Psychology, 49,* 943–948.

Alloy, L. B., & Ahrens, A. H. (1987). Depression and pessimism for the future: Biased use of statistically relevant information in predictions for self versus others. *Journal of Personality and Social Psychology, 52,* 366–378.

Allport, F. H. (1924). *Social psychology.* Cambridge, Mass.: Riverside Press.

Allport, G. W. (1954). *The nature of prejudice.* Reading, Mass.: Addison-Wesley.

Allport, G. W. (1985). The historical background of social psychology. In G. Lindzey & E. Aronson (Eds.), *Handbook of social psychology* (3rd ed., Vol. 1, pp. 1–46). New York: Random House.

Altman, I. (1974). The communication of interpersonal attitudes: An ecological approach. In T. L. Huston (Ed.), *Foundations of interpersonal attraction.* New York: Academic Press.

Altman, I. (1975). *The environment and social behavior.* Pacific Grove, Calif.: Brooks/Cole.

Altman, I. (1981). *The environment and social behavior: Privacy, personal space, territory, and crowding.* New York: Irvington.

Altman, I., & Chemers, M. (1980). *Culture and environment.* Belmont, Calif.: Wadsworth.

Altman, I., Lawton, M. P., & Wohlwill, J. (1984). *Elderly people and the environment.* New York: Plenum.

Altman, I., & Vinsel, A. M. (1977). Personal space: An analysis of E. T. Hall's proxemics framework. In I. Altman & J. F. Wohlwill (Eds.), *Human behavior and environment: Advances in theory and research* (Vol. 1). New York: Plenum.

Amancio, L. (1989) Social differentiation between 'dominant' and 'dominated' groups: Toward an integration of social stereotypes and social identity. *European Journal of Social Psychology, 19*, 1–10.

American Psychological Association. (1982). *Ethical principles in the conduct of research with human participants.* Washington, D.C.: APA.

American Psychological Association. (1988). Brief in *Price Waterhouse* v. *Hopkins*, no. 87–1167, U.S. Supreme Court.

Amir, Y. (1969). Contact hypothesis in ethnic relations. *Psychological Bulletin, 71*, 319–341.

Anderson, C. (1989). Temperature and aggression: Ubiquitous effects of heat on the occurrence of human violence. *Psychological Bulletin, 106*, 74–96.

Anderson, C., & Anderson, D. (1984). Ambient temperature and violent crime: Tests of the linear and curvilinear hypotheses. *Journal of Personality and Social Psychology, 46*, 91–97.

Anderson, D., & Rosenthal, R. (1968). Some effects of interpersonal expectancy on institutionalized retarded children. *Proceedings of the 76th Annual Convention of the American Psychological Association,* 479–480.

Anderson, D. C., Crowell, C. R., Doman, M., & Howard, G. S. (1989). Performance posting, goal setting, and activity—Contingent praise as applied to a university hockey team. *Journal of Applied Psychology, 73*, 87–96.

Anderson, N. H., & Hubert, S. (1963). Effects of concomitant recall on order effects of personality impression formation. *Journal of Verbal Learning and Verbal Behavior, 2*, 379–391.

Apfelbaum, E. (1974). On conflicts and bargaining. In L. Berkowitz (Ed.), *Advances in experimental social psychology* (Vol. 7). New York: Academic Press.

Apfelbaum, E. (1979). Relations of domination and movements for liberation: An analysis of power between groups. In W. G. Austin & S. Worchel (Eds.), *The social psychology of intergroup relations.* Pacific Grove, Calif.: Brooks/Cole.

Archer, D., & Akert, R. M. (1977). Words and everything else: Verbal and nonverbal cues to social interpretation. *Journal of Personality and Social Psychology, 35*, 443–449.

Archer, R. L. (1980). Self-disclosure. In D. M. Wegner & R. R. Vallacher (Eds.), *The self in social psychology.* New York: Oxford University Press.

Archer, R. L., & Burleson, J. A. (1980). The effect of timing of self-disclosure on attraction and reciprocity. *Journal of Personality and Social Psychology, 38*, 120–130.

Archer, R. P., & Cash, T. F. (1985). Physical attractiveness and maladjustment among psychiatric in-patients. *Journal of Social and Clinical Psychology, 3*, 170–180.

Argyle, M., & Dean, J. (1965). Eye-contact, distance, and affiliation. *Sociometry, 18*, 289–304.

Aries, D. (1976). Interaction patterns and themes of male, female, and mixed groups. *Small Group Behavior, 7*, 7–18.

Arkin, R. M. (1980). Self-presentation. In D. M. Wegner & R. R. Vallacher (Eds.), *The self in social psychology.* New York: Oxford University Press.

Arkkelin, D., Oakley, T., & Mynatt, C. (1979). Effects of controllable versus uncontrollable factors on responsibility attributions: A single subject approach. *Journal of Personality and Social Psychology, 37*, 110–115.

Arms, R. L., Russell, G. W., & Sandilands, M. L. (1979). Effects on the hostility of spectators of viewing aggressive sports. *Social Psychology Quarterly, 42*, 275–279.

Aronson, E. (1969a). Some antecedents of interpersonal attraction. In W. J. Arnold & D. Levine (Eds.), *Nebraska symposium on motivation* (Vol. 17). Lincoln: University of Nebraska Press.

Aronson, E. (1969b). The theory of cognitive dissonance: A current perspective. In L. Berkowitz (Ed.), *Advances in experimental social psychology* (Vol. 4). New York: Academic Press.

Aronson, E. (1989). Analysis, synthesis, and the treasuring of the old. *Personality and Social Psychology Bulletin, 15*, 493–507.

Aronson, E., Brewer, M., & Carlsmith, J. M. (1985). Experimentation in social psychology. In G. Lindzey & E. Aronson (Eds.), *Handbook of social psychology* (3rd ed., Vol. 1, pp. 1–46). New York: Random House.

Aronson, E., Bridgeman, L., & Geffner, R. (1978). The effects of cooperative classroom structure on student behavior and attitudes. In D. Bar-Tal & L. Saxe (Eds.), *Social psychology of education.* New York: Halsted.

Aronson, E., & Carlsmith, J. M. (1963). The effect of the severity of threat on the devaluation of forbidden behavior. *Journal of Abnormal and Social Psychology, 66*, 584–588.

Aronson, E., & Linder, D. E. (1965). Gain and loss of esteem as determinants of interpersonal attractiveness. *Journal of Experimental Social Psychology, 1*, 156–171.

Aronson, E., & Mills, J. (1959). The effect of severity of initiation on liking for a group. *Journal of Abnormal and Social Psychology, 59*, 177–181.

Aronson, E., Stephan, C., Sikes, J., Blancy, N., & Snapp, M. (1978). *The jigsaw classroom.* Newbury Park, Calif.: Sage.

Aronson, E., Turner, J., & Carlsmith, J. M. (1963). Communicator credibility and communicator discrepancy as determinants of opinion change. *Journal of Abnormal and Social Psychology, 67*, 31–36.

Aronson, E., Willerman, B., & Floyd, J. (1966). The effect of a pratfall on increasing interpersonal attractiveness. *Psychonomic Science, 4*, 227–228.

Aronson, E., & Worchel, P. (1966). Similarity versus liking as determinants of interpersonal attractiveness. *Psychonomic Science, 5*, 157–158.

Asch, S. (1946). Forming impressions on personality. *Journal of Abnormal and Social Psychology, 41*, 258–290.

Asch, S. (1951). Effects of group pressure upon the modification and distortion of judgement. In H. Guetzkow (Ed.), *Groups, leadership, and men.* Pittsburgh: Carnegie Press.

Asch, S. (1952). *Social psychology.* New York: Prentice-Hall.

Asch, S. (1956). Studies of independence and conformity: I. A minority of one against a unanimous majority. *Psychological Monographs, 70*(9).

Ashmore, R., Ramchandra, V., & Jones, R. (1971, April), *Censorship as an attitude change induction.* Paper presented at Eastern Psychological Association convention, New York.

Austin, W. G. (1986). Justice in intergroup conflict. In S. Worchel & W. G. Austin (Eds.), *The psychology of intergroup relations* (pp. 153–176). Chicago: Nelson-Hall.

Austin, W. G., & Hatfield, E. (1980). Equity theory, power, and social justice. In G. M. Kula (Ed.), *Justice and social interaction.* Bern: Hans Huber.

Austin, W. G., & Walster, E. (1974). Participants' reactions to "equity with the world." *Journal of Experimental Social Psychology, 10*, 528–548.

Axelrod, R. (1984). The evolution of cooperation. *In the sciences.* New York: Academy of Sciences.

Axsom, D. (1989). Cognitive dissonance and behavior change in psychotherapy. *Journal of Experimental Social Psychology, 25* (3), 234–252.

Axsom, D, Yates, S., & Chaiken, S. (1987). Audience response as a heuristic cue in persuasion. *Journal of Personality and Social Psychology, 53,* 30–40.

Ayllon, T., & Azrin, N. (1968). *The token economy: A motivational system for therapy and rehabilitation.* New York: Appleton-Century-Crofts.

Babad, E., Bernieri, F., & Rosenthal, R. (1989). Nonverbal communication and leakage in the behavior of biased and unbiased teachers. *Journal of Personality and Social Psychology, 56,* 89–94.

Back, K. W. (1951). Influence through social communication. *Journal of Abnormal and Social Psychology, 46,* 9–23.

Backman, C. W. (1981). Attraction in interpersonal relationships. In M. Rosenberg & R. Turner (Eds.), *Social psychology: Sociological perspectives.* New York: Basic Books.

Backman, C. W., & Secord, P. F. (1959). The effect of perceived liking on interpersonal attraction. *Human Relations, 12,* 379–384.

Baker, E., & Shaw, M. E. (1980). Reaction to interpersonal distance and topic intimacy: A comparison of strangers and friends. *Journal of Nonverbal Behavior, 5,* 80–91.

Baldwin, M. W., & Holmes, J. G. (1987). Salient private audiences and awareness of the self. *Journal of Personality and Social Psychology, 52,* 1087–1098.

Bales, R. F. (1958). Task roles and social roles in problem-solving groups. In E. E. Maccoby, T. M. Newcomb, & E. L. Hartly (Eds.), *Readings in social psychology (3rd ed.).* New York: Holt, Rinehart & Winston.

Bales, R. F., & Slater, P. (1955). Role differentiation in small decision-making groups. In T. Parsons & R. F. Bales (Eds.), *Family, socialization and interaction processes.* Glencoe, Ill.: Free Press.

Bandura, A. (1965). Influences of models' reinforcement contingencies on the acquisition of initiative responses. *Journal of Personality and Social Psychology, 1,* 589–593.

Bandura, A. (1973). *Aggression: A social learning analysis.* New York: Holt, Rinehart & Winston.

Bandura, A. (1977). Self-efficacy: Toward a unifying theory of behavior change. *Psychological Review, 84,* 191–215.

Bandura, A., Ross, D., & Ross, S. A. (1961). Transmission of aggression through imitation of aggressive models. *Journal of Abnormal and Social Psychology, 63,* 575–582.

Bandura, A., Ross, D., & Ross, S. A. (1963a). Imitation of film-mediated aggressive models. *Journal of Abnormal and Social Psychology, 66,* 3–11.

Bandura, A., Ross, D., & Ross, S. A. (1963b). A comparative test of the status envy, social power, and secondary reinforcement theories of identificatory learning. *Journal of Abnormal and Social Psychology, 67,* 527–534.

Bandura, A., & Walters, R. H. (1963). *Social learning and personality development.* New York: Holt, Rinehart & Winston.

Bandura, A., & Wood, R. (1989). Effect of perceived controllability and performance standards on self-regulation of complex decision making. *Journal of Personal and Social Psychology, 56,* 805–814.

Bar-Tal, D. (1990). *Group beliefs: A conception for analyzing group structure, process, and behavior.* New York: Springer Verlag.

Bar-Tal, D., & Geva, N. (1986). A cognitive basis of international conflict. In S. Worchel & W. G. Austin (Eds.), *The psychology of intergroup relations.* Chicago: Nelson-Hall.

Barber, J. D. (1977). *The Presidential character: Predicting performance in the White House.* Englewood Cliffs, N.J.: Prentice-Hall.

Barber, P. J. (1977). Experimenter bias against subliminal perception? A rejoinder. *British Journal of Psychology, 68,* 281–282.

Bargh, J. A., Bond, R. N., Lombardi, W. J., & Tota, M. E. (1986). The additive nature of chronic and temporary sources of construct accessibility. *Journal of Personality and Social Psychology, 50,* 869–878.

Bargh, J. A., & Tota, M. E. (1988). Context-dependent automatic processing in depression: Accessibility of negative constructs with regard to self but not others. *Journal of Personality and Social Psychology, 54,* 925–939.

Barker, R. G., & Wright, H. (1950). *Methods in psychological ecology: A progress report.* Topeka, Kan.: Ray's Printing Service.

Barner-Barry, C., & Rosenwein, R. (1985). *Psychological perspectives on politics.* Englewood Cliffs, N.J.: Prentice-Hall.

Barnlund, D. C. (1962). Consistency of emergent leadership in groups with changing tasks and members. *Speech Monographs, 29,* 45–52.

Baron, R. A. (1974). The aggression-inhibiting influence of heightened sexual arousal. *Journal of Personality and Social Psychology, 30,* 318–322.

Baron, R. A. (1977). *Human aggression.* New York: Plenum.

Baron, R. A. (1979). Effects of victim's pain cues, victim's race, and level of prior instigation upon physical aggression. *Journal of Applied Psychology, 9,* 103–114.

Baron, R. A., & Bell, P. A. (1973). Effects of heightened sexual arousal on physical aggression. *Proceedings of the 81st Annual Convention of the American Psychological Association, 8,* 171–172.

Baron, R. A., & Bell, P. A. (1976). Aggression and heat: The influence of ambient temperature, negative affect, and a cooling drink on physical aggression. *Journal of Personality and Social Psychology, 33,* 245–255.

Baron, R. A., & Rodin, J. (1978). Perceived control and crowding stress. *Advances in Environmental Psychology, 1.*

Baron, L., & Straus, M. A. (1984). Sexual stratification, pornography, and rape in the United States. In N. M. Malamuth & E. Donnerstein (Eds.), *Pornography and sexual aggression.* Orlando, Fla.: Academic Press.

Bartol, K. M., & Butterfield, D. A. (1976). Sex effects in evaluating leaders. *Journal of Applied Psychology, 61,* 446–454.

Bartol, K. M., & Martin, D. C. (1986). Women and men in task groups. In R. Ashmore & F. del Boca (Eds.), *The social psychology of female-male relations.* New York: Academic Press.

Bass, B. M. (1949). An analysis of the leadership group discussion. *Journal of Applied Psychology, 33,* 527–533.

Batson, C. D. (1987). Prosocial motivation: Is it ever truly altruistic? In L. Berkowitz (Ed.), *Advances in experimental social psychology* (Vol. 20, pp. 65–122). Orlando, Fla.: Academic Press.

Batson, C. D., Cochran, P. J., Biederman, M. F., Blosser, J. L, Ryan, M. J., & Vogt, B. (1978). Failure to help when in a hurry. Callousness or conflict? *Personality and Social Psychology Bulletin, 4,* 97–101.

Batson, C. D., & Coke, J. S. (1981). Empathy: A source of altruistic motivation for helping? In J. P. Rushton & R.

M. Sorrentino (Eds.), *Altruism and helping behavior: Social, personality, and developmental perspectives*. Hillsdale, N.J.: Erlbaum.

Batson, C. D., Coke, J. S., Jasnoski, M. L., & Hanson, M. (1978). Buying kindness: Effect of an extrinsic incentive for helping on perceived altruism. *Personality and Social Psychology Bulletin*, 4(1), 86–91.

Batson, C. C., Duncan, B. D., Ackerman, P., Buckley, T., & Birch, K. (1981). Is empathic emotion a source of altruistic motivation? *Journal of Personality and Social Psychology*, 40, 290–302.

Batson, C. D., Dyck, J. L., Brandt, J. R., Batson, J. G., Powell, A. L., McMaster, M. R., & Griffitt, C. (1988). Five studies testing two new egoistic alternatives to the empathy-altruism hypothesis. *Journal of Personality and Social Psychology*, 55, 52–77.

Batson, C. D., Fultz, J., & Schoenrade, P. A. (1987). Distress and empathy: Two qualitatively distinct vicarious emotions with different motivational consequences. *Journal of Personality*, 55, 19–39.

Batson, C. D., & Oleson, K. (1990). Current status of the empathy-altruism hypothesis. *Review of Personality and Social Psychology*, 12.

Batson, C. D., O'Quinn, K., Fultz, J., Vanderplas, N., & Isen, A. M. (1983). Influence of self-reported distress and empathy on egoistic versus altruistic motivation to help. *Journal of Personality and Social Psychology*, 45, 706–718.

Baum, A., & Paulus, P. (1987). Crowding. In D. Stokols & I. Altman (Eds.), *Handbook of environmental psychology* (Vol. 1, pp. 533–570). New York: Wiley.

Baum, A., & Singer, J. E. (1982). *Advances in environmental psychology* (Vol. 4). Hillsdale, N.J.: Erlbaum.

Baum, A., & Valins, S. (1977). *Architecture and social behavior: Psychological studies in social density*. Hillsdale, N.J.: Erlbaum.

Baumeister, R. F. (1982). A self-presentational view of social phenomena. *Psychological Bulletin*, 91, 3–26.

Baumeister, R. F. (1985, April). The championship choke. *Psychology Today*, pp. 48–52.

Baumeister, R. F. (1986). *Public self and private self*. New York: Springer-Verlag.

Baumeister, R. F., Chesner, S. P., Senders, P. S., & Tice, D. M. (1988). Who's in charge here? Group leaders do lend help in emergencies. *Personality and Social Psychology Bulletin*, 14, 17–22.

Baumeister, R. F., Hamilton, J., & Tice, D. (1985). Public versus private expectancy of success: Confidence booster or performance pressure? *Journal of Personality and Social Psychology*, 48, 1447–1457.

Baumeister, R. F., & Hutton, D. G. (1987). A self-presentational perspective on group processes. In B. Mullen & G. R. Goethals (Eds.), *Theories of group behavior*. New York: Springer-Verlag.

Baumeister, R. F., Hutton, D. G., & Tice, D. M. (1989). Cognitive processes during deliberate self-presentation: How self-presenters alter and misinterpret the behavior of their interaction partners. *Journal of Experimental Social Psychology*, 25, 59–78.

Baumeister, R. F., & Jones, E. E. (1978). When self-presentation is constrained by the target's knowledge: Consistency and compensation. *Journal of Personality and Social Psychology*, 36, 608–618.

Baumeister, R. F., & Steinhilber, A. (1984). Paradoxical effects of supportive audiences on performance under pressure: The home field disadvantage in sports championships. *Journal of Personality and Social Psychology*, 47, 85–93.

Baumeister, R. F., & Tice, D. M. (1984). Role of self-presentation and choice in cognitive dissonance under forced compliance: Necessary or sufficient causes. *Journal of Personality and Social Psychology*, 46, 5–13.

Baumeister, R. F., & Tice, D. M. (1985). Toward a theory of situational structure. *Environment and Behavior*, 17, 147–172.

Baumgardner, A. H., Heppner, P. P., & Arkin, R. M. (1986). Role of causal attribution in personal problem solving. *Journal of Personality and Social Psychology*, 50, 636–643.

Baumrind, D. (1964). Some thoughts on ethics of research: After reading Milgram's "Behavioral Study of Obedience." *American Psychologist*, 19, 421–423.

Bavelas, A., Hastorf, A. H., Gross, A. E., & Kite, W. R. (1965). Experiments on the alteration of group structure. *Journal of Experimental Social Psychology*, 1, 55–71.

Baxter, T. L., & Goldberg, L. R. (1987). Perceived behavioral consistency underlying trait attributions to oneself and another: An extension of the actor-observer effect. *Personality and Social Psychology Bulletin*, 13, 437–447.

Beaman, A. L., Klentz, B., Diener, E., & Svanum, S. (1979). Objective self-awareness and transgression in children: A field study. *Journal of Personality and Social Psychology*, 37, 1835–1846.

Becker, F. D., & Mayo, C. (1971). Delineating personal distance and territoriality. *Environment and Behavior*, 3, 375–381.

Beckman, L. (1970). Effects of students' performance on teachers' and observers' attributions of causality. *Journal of Educational Psychology*, 61, 76–82.

Bell, B. E., & Loftus, E. F. (1989). Trivial persuasion in the courtroom: The power of (a few) minor details. *Journal of Personality and Social Psychology*, 56, 669–679.

Bell, P. A., & Baron, R. A. (1977). Aggression and ambient temperature: The facilitating and inhibiting effects of hot and cold environments. *Bulletin of the Psychonomic Society*, 9, 443–445.

Belmore, S. M., & Hubbard, M. L. (1987). The role of advance expectancies in person memory. *Journal of Personality and Social Psychology*, 53, 61–70.

Bem, D. (1965). An experimental analysis of self-persuasion. *Journal of Experimental Social Psychology*, 1, 199–218.

Bem, D. (1972). Self-perception theory. In L. Berkowitz (Ed.), *Advances in experimental social psychology* (Vol. 6). New York: Academic Press.

Bem, D. J., & Funder, D. C. (1978). Predicting more of the people more of the time: Assessing the personality of situations. *Psychological Review*, 85, 485–501.

Bem, D. J., & Lord, C. G. (1979). Template-matching: A proposal for probing the ecological validity of experimental settings in social psychology. *Journal of Personality and Social Psychology*, 37, 833–846.

Bem, S. L. (1981). Gender schema theory: A cognitive account of sex typing. *Psychological Review*, 88, 354–364.

Ben-Ari, R., & Amir, Y. (1988). Intergroup contact, cultural information, and change in ethnic attitudes. In W. Stroebe et al. (Eds.), *The social psychology of intergroup conflict* (pp. 151–166). Berlin: Springer-Verlag.

Bennett, L. (1968). *What manner of man? A biography of Martin Luther King, Jr.* Chicago: Johnson.

Benoit, J. (1987). *Running tide*. New York: Knopf.

Benson, P. L., Karabenick, S. A., & Lerner, R. M. (1976). Pretty pleases: The effect of physical attraction, race and sex on receiving help. *Journal of Experimental Social Psychology, 12,* 409–415.

Bentwich, N. (1981). Kristallnacht: Pogrom in Emden. In A. Eisenberg (Ed.), *Witness to the holocaust.* New York: Pilgrim Press.

Berg, J. H. (1984). Development of friendship between roommates. *Journal of Personality and Social Psychology, 46,* 346–356.

Berg, J. H., & McQuinn, R. D. (1986). Attraction and exchange in continuing and non-continuing dating relationships. *Journal of Personality and Social Psychology, 50,* 942–952.

Berger, S. M., Carli, L. C., Garcier, R., & James, J. B. (1982). Audience effects in anticipatory learning: A comparison of drive and practice inhibition analysis. *Journal of Personality and Social Psychology, 42,* 478–486.

Berglas, S., & Jones, E. E. (1978). Drug choice as a self-handicapping strategy in response to noncontingent success. *Journal of Personality and Social Psychology, 36,* 405–417.

Berkowitz, L. (1962). *Aggression: A social psychological analysis.* New York: McGraw-Hill.

Berkowitz, L. (1965). The concept of aggressive drive: Some additional considerations. In L. Berkowitz (Ed.), *Advances in experimental social psychology* (Vol. 2). New York: Academic Press.

Berkowitz, L. (Ed.) (1969). *Roots of aggression: A reexamination of the frustration-aggression hypothesis.* New York: Atherton.

Berkowitz, L. (1974). Some determinants of impulsive aggression: Role of mediated associations with reinforcements for aggression. *Psychological Review, 81,* 165–176.

Berkowitz, L., & Knurek, D. (1967). Label-mediated hostility generalization. *Journal of Personality and Social Psychology, 5,* 364–368.

Berkowitz, L., & Le Page, A. (1967). Weapons as aggression-eliciting stimuli. *Journal of Personality and Social Psychology, 7,* 202–207.

Berscheid, E. (1985). Interpersonal attraction. In G. Lindzey & E. Aronson (Eds.), *The handbook of social psychology* (3rd ed., Vol. 2). Hillsdale, N. J.: Erlbaum.

Berscheid, E. (1988). Some comments on love's anatomy; or, whatever happened to old-fashioned lust? In R. J. Sternberg & M. L. Barnes (Eds.), *The anatomy of love.* New Haven, Conn.: Yale University Press.

Berscheid, E., Boye, D., & Darley, J. M. (1968). Effects of forced association upon voluntary choice to associate. *Journal of Personality and Social Psychology, 8,* 13–19.

Berscheid, E., & Campbell, B. (1981). The changing longevity of heterosexual close relationships: A commentary and forecast. In M. Lerner (Ed.), *The justice motive in times of scarcity and change.* New York: Plenum.

Berscheid, E., Dion, K., Walster, E., & Walster, G. W. (1971). Physical attractiveness and dating choice: A test of the matching hypothesis. *Journal of Experimental Social Psychology, 7,* 173–189.

Berscheid, E., Graziano, W., Monson, T., & Dermer, M. (1976). Outcome dependency: Attention, attribution, and attraction. *Journal of Personality and Social Psychology, 34,* 978–989.

Berscheid, E., Snyder, M., & Omoto, A. M. (1989). The relationship closeness inventory: Assessing the closeness of interpersonal relationships. *Journal of Personality and Social Psychology, 57,* 792–807.

Berscheid, E., & Walster, E. (1978). *Interpersonal attraction.* Reading, Mass.: Addison-Wesley.

Bickman, L., & Kamzan, M. (1973). The effect of race and need on helping behavior. *Journal of Social Psychology, 89,* 73–77.

Biggers, T., & Pryor, B. (1982). Attitude change: A function of emotion-eliciting qualities of environment. *Personality and Social Psychology Bulletin, 8,* 94–99.

Biner, P., Butler, D., Fischer, A., & Westergren, A. (1989). An arousal optimization model of lighting level preferences. An interaction of social situation and task demands. *Journal of Environment and Behavior, 21,* 3–16.

Bird, A. (1977). Team structure and success as related to cohesiveness and leadership. *Journal of Social Psychology, 103,* 217–223.

Bird, C., Monachesi, E. D., & Burdick, M. (1952). Studies of group tensions: III. The effect of parental discouragement of play activities upon the attitudes of white children toward Negroes. *Child Development, 23,* 295–306.

Birdwhistell, R. L. (1952). *Introduction to kinesics.* Louisville, Ky.: University of Louisville Press.

Bishop, J. (1971). *The days of Martin Luther King, Jr.* New York: Putnam.

Blake, R. R., Helson, H., & Mouton, J. S. (1956). The generality of conformity behavior as a function of factual anchorage, difficulty of task and amount of social pressure. *Journal of Personality, 25,* 294–305.

Blake, R. R., & Mouton, J. S. (1961). Loyalty of representatives to ingroup positions during intergroup competition. *Sociometry, 24,* 177–183.

Blake, R. R., & Mouton, J. S. (1962). The intergroup dynamics of win-lose conflict and problem-solving collaboration in union-management relations. In M. Sherif (Ed.), *Intergroup relations and leadership* (pp. 94–140). New York: Wiley.

Blake, R. R., & Mouton, J. S. (1986). From theory to practice in interface problem-solving. In S. Worchel & W. G. Austin (Eds.), *The psychology of intergroup relations.* Chicago: Nelson-Hall.

Blanck, P. D., & Rosenthal, R. (1982). Developing strategies for decoding "leaky" messages: On learning how and when to decode discrepant and consistent social communications. In R. S. Feldman (Ed.), *Development of nonverbal behavior in children* (pp. 203–229). New York: Springer-Verlag.

Blaney, P. H. (1986). Affect and memory: A review. *Psychological Bulletin, 99,* 229–246.

Block, J. H. (1976). Issues, problems, and pitfalls in assessing sex differences: A critical review of the psychology of sex differences. *Merrill-Palmer Quarterly, 22,* 283–308.

Block, J. H. (1983). Differential premises arising from differential socialization of the sexes: Some conjectures. *Child Development, 54,* 1335–1354.

Block, L., & Stokes, G. (1989). Performance and satisfaction in private versus nonprivate worksettings. *Journal of Environment and Behavior, 21,* 277–297.

Bodenhausen, G. V. (1988). Stereotypic biases in social decision making and memory: Testing process models of stereotype use. *Journal of Personality and Social Psychology, 55,* 726–737.

Bogart, K., Loeb, A., & Rittman, J. D. (1969). *Behavioral consequences of cognitive dissonance.* Paper presented at Eastern Psychological Association.

Bogart, L. (1981). *The press and the public: Who reads what, where, and why in American newspapers.* Hillsdale, N.J.: Erlbaum.

Bonoma, T. V. (1976). Social psychology and social evaluation. *Representative Research in Social Psychology, 7,* 147–156.

Bootzin, R. R., Herman, C. P., & Nicassio, P. (1976). The power of suggestion: Another examination of misattribution and insomnia. *Journal of Personality and Social Psychology, 34,* 673–679.

Bossard, J. (1932). Residential propinquity as a factor in marriage selection. *American Journal of Sociology, 38,* 219–224.

Boulding, K. E. (1989). *Three faces of power.* Newbury Park, Calif.: Sage.

Bradley, G. W. (1978). Self-serving biases in the attribution process: A re-examination of the fact or fiction question. *Journal of Personality and Social Psychology, 35,* 56–71.

Brady, A., & Walker, M. (1978). Interpersonal distance as a function of situationally induced anxiety. *British Journal of Social and Clinical Psychology, 17,* 127–133.

Braiker, H. B., & Kelley, H. H. (1979). Conflict in the development of close relationships. In R. L. Burgess & T. L. Huston (Eds.), *Social exchange in developing relationships.* New York: Academic Press.

Brehm, J. W. (1956). Post-decision changes in desirability of alternatives. *Journal of Abnormal and Social Psychology, 52,* 384–389.

Brehm, J. W. (1966). *A theory of psychological reactance.* New York: Academic Press.

Brehm, J. W. (1972). *Responses to loss of freedom: A theory of psychological reactance.* Morristown, N.J.: General Learning Press.

Brehm, J. W., & Festinger, L. (1957). Pressures toward uniformity of performance in groups. *Human Relations, 10,* 85–89.

Brehm, S. S., & Brehm, J. W. (1981). *Psychological reactance: A theory of freedom and control.* New York: Academic Press.

Brehm, S. S., & Weintraub, M. (1977). Physical barriers and psychological reactance: 2-year-olds' responses to threats to freedom. *Journal of Personality and Social Psychology, 35,* 830–836.

Brewer, M. B. (1979). In-group bias in the minimal intergroup situation: A cognitive-motivational analysis. *Psychological Bulletin, 86,* 307–324.

Brewer, M. B. (1986). The role of ethnocentrism in intergroup conflict. In S. Worchel & W. G. Austin (Eds.), *The psychology of intergroup relations.* Chicago: Nelson Hall.

Brickner, M., Harkins, S., & Ostrom, T. (1986). Effects of personal involvement: Thought-provoking implications for social loafing. *Journal of Personality and Social Psychology, 51,* 763–769.

Briggs, S. R., & Cheek, J. M. (1988). On the nature of self-monitoring: Problems with assessment, problems with validity. *Journal of Personality and Social Psychology, 54,* 663–678.

Briggs, S. R., Cheek, J. M., & Buss, A. H. (1980). An analysis of the self-monitoring scale. *Journal of Personality and Social Psychology, 38,* 679–686.

Broadbent, D. E. (1978). The current state of noise research: Reply to Poulton. *Psychological Bulletin, 85*(S), 1052–1067.

Brock, T. C. (1965). Communicator-recipient similarity and decision change. *Journal of Personality and Social Psychology, 1,* 650–654.

Brock, T. C., & Buss, A. H. (1962). Dissonance, aggression, and evaluation of pain. *Journal of Abnormal and Social Psychology, 65,* 192–202.

Brockner, J., & Rubin, J. Z. (1985). *Entrapment in escalating conflicts.* New York: Springer-Verlag.

Brophy, J. E. (1982). *Research on the self-fulfilling prophecy and teacher expectations.* Paper delivered at annual meeting of the American Educational Research Association, New York.

Brown, B. (1979). *Territoriality and residential burglary.* Paper presented at the American Psychological Association meeting, New York.

Brown, B. B. (1987). Territoriality. In D. Stokols & I. Altman (Eds.), *Handbook of environmental psychology* (Vol. 1, pp. 505–532). New York: Wiley.

Brown, B. R. (1968). The effects of need to maintain face on interpersonal bargaining. *Journal of Experimental Social Psychology, 4,* 107–122.

Brown, J. D., & Siegel, J. M. (1988). Attributions for negative life events and depression: The role of perceived control. *Journal of Personality and Social Psychology, 52,* 316–322.

Brown, P., & Elliott, R. (1965). Control of aggression in a nursery school class. *Journal of Experimental Child Psychology, 2,* 103–107.

Brown, R. (1965). *Social psychology.* New York: Free Press.

Brown, R. (1986). *Social psychology—The second edition.* New York: Free Press.

Brown, R. (1988). *Group process: Dynamics within and between groups.* Oxford, England: Basil Blackwell.

Brown, R., & Smith, A. (1989). Perceptions of and by minority groups: The case of women in academia. *European Journal of Social Psychology, 19,* 61–76.

Brown, V., & Geis, F. L. (1984). Turning lead into gold: Evaluations of men and women leaders and the alchemy of social consensus. *Journal of Personality and Social Psychology, 46,* 811–824.

Bruins, J. J., Liebrand, W. P., & Wilke, H. A. (1989). About the saliency of fear and greed in social dilemmas. *European Journal of Social Psychology, 19,* 155–162.

Bruner, J. S., Busiek, R. D., & Minturn, A. (1952). Assimilation in the immediate reproduction of visually perceived figures. *Journal of Experimental Psychology, 44,* 151–155.

Bryan, J., & Test, M. (1967). Models and helping: Naturalistic studies in aiding behavior. *Journal of Personality and Social Psychology, 6,* 400–407.

Bulletin of the Atomic Scientists. (1985). Note.

Burger, J. M., & Burns, L. (1988). The illusion of unique invulnerability and the use of contraception. *Personality and Social Psychology Bulletin, 14,* 264–270.

Burger, J. M., & Petty, R. E. (1981). The low-ball compliance technique: Task or person commitment? *Journal of Personality and Social Psychology, 40,* 492–500.

Burgess, R. L., & Huston, T. L. (Eds.). (1979). *Social exchange in developing relationships.* New York: Academic Press.

Burn, S. M., & Oskamp, S. (1989). Ingroup bias and the U.S.-Soviet conflict. *Journal of Social Issues, 45,* 73–90.

Burns, J. R. (1984). *The power to God: The crisis of the American presidency.* New York: Simon & Schuster.

Burnstein, E. (1982). Persuasion as argument processing. In M. Brandstatter, J. M. Davis, & G. Stocker-Kreichgauer (Eds.), *Group decision processes.* London: Academic Press.

Burnstein, E., & Vinokur, A. (1977). Persuasive argumentation and social comparison as determinants of attitude polarization. *Journal of Experimental Social Psychology, 9,* 123–137.

Buss, A. H. (1961). *The psychology of aggression.* New York: Wiley.

Buss, A. H. (1980). *Self-consciousness and social anxiety.* San Francisco: W. H. Freeman.

Buss, A. H., Booker, A., & Buss, E. (1972). Firing a weapon

and aggression. *Journal of Personality and Social Psychology, 27,* 296–302.

Buss, D. M. (1988). The evolution of introsexual competition: Tactics of mate selection. *Journal of Personality and Social Psychology, 54,* 616–628.

Byrne, D. (1971). *The attraction paradigm.* New York: Academic Press.

Byrne, D., Baskett, C. D., & Hodges, L. (1971). Behavioral indicators of interpersonal attraction. *Journal of Abnormal and Social Psychology, 1,* 137–149.

Byrne, D., & Blaylock, B. (1963). Similarity and assumed similarity of attitudes between husbands and wives. *Journal of Abnormal and Social Psychology, 67,* 636–640.

Byrne, D., & Clore, G. L. (1970). A reinforcement model of evaluative responses. *Personality: An International Journal, 1,* 103–128.

Byrne, D., Clore, G. L., & Smeaton, G. (1986). The attraction hypothesis. Do similar attitudes affect anything? *Journal of Personality and Social Psychology, 51,* 1167–1170.

Byrne, D., Ervin, C., & Lamberth, J. (1970). Continuity between the experimental study of attraction and real-life computer dating. *Journal of Personality and Social Psychology, 16,* 157–165.

Byrne, D., & Nelson, D. (1965). Attraction as a linear function of proportion of positive reinforcements. *Journal of Personality and Social Psychology, 1,* 659–663.

Byrne, D., & Rhamey, R. (1965). Magnitude of positive and negative reinforcements as determinants of attraction. *Journal of Personality and Social Psychology, 2,* 884–889.

Cacioppo, J. T., & Petty, R. E. (1979a). Attitudes and cognitive response: An electrophysiological approach. *Journal of Personality and Social Psychology, 37,* 2181–2199.

Cacioppo, J. T., & Petty, R. E. (1979b). Effects of message repetition and position on cognitive responses, recall, and persuasion. *Journal of Personality and Social Psychology, 37,* 97–109.

Cacioppo, J. T., & Petty, R. E. (1981a). Effects of extent of thought on the pleasantness ratings of P-O-X triads: Evidence for 3 judgmental tendencies in evaluating social situations. *Journal of Personality and Social Psychology, 40,* 1000–1009.

Cacioppo, J. T., & Petty, R. E. (1981b). Electromyograms as measures of extent and affectivity of information processing. *American Psychologist, 36*(5), 441–456.

Cacioppo, J. T., & Petty, R. E. (1981c). Electromyographic specificity during covert information processing. *Psychophysiology, 18,* 518–523.

Cacioppo, J. T., & Petty, R. E. (1982). The need for cognition. *Journal of Personality and Social Psychology, 42*(l), 116–131.

Cacioppo, J. T., & Petty, R. E. (1986). Stalking rudimentary processes of social influence: A psychophysiological approach. In M. P. Zanna, J. M. Olson, & C. P. Herman (Eds.), *Social influence: The Ontario symposium* (Vol. 5). Hillsdale, N.J.: Erlbaum.

Cacioppo, J. T., Petty, R. E., Losch, M. C., & Kim, H. S. (1986). Electromyographic activity over facial muscle regions can differentiate the valence and intensity of affective reactions. *Journal of Personality and Social Psychology, 50,* 260–268.

Cacioppo, J. T., Petty, R. E., & Morris, K. J. (1983). Effects of need for cognition on message evaluation, recall, and persuasion. *Journal of Personality and Social Psychology, 45*(4), 805–818.

Caldwell, D. F., & O'Reilly, C. A. (1982). Boundary spanning and individual performance: The impact of

self-monitoring. *Journal of Applied Psychology, 67,* 124–127.

Caldwell, M. D. (1976). Communication and sex effects in a five-person prisoner's dilemma game. *Journal of Personality and Social Psychology, 33,* 273–280.

Calhoun, J. B. (1962). Population density and social pathology. *Scientific American, 206*(3), 139–148.

Callaway, M., Marriott, R., & Esser, J. (1985). Effects of dominance on group decision making: Toward a stress-reduction explanation of group think. *Journal of Personality and Social Psychology, 49,* 949–952.

Campbell, D. T., & Stanley, J. C. (1963). *Experimental and quasi-experimental designs for research.* Chicago: Rand McNally.

Campbell, J. D. (1986). Similarity and uniqueness: The effects of attribute type, relevance, and individual differences in self-esteem and depression. *Journal of Personality and Social Psychology, 50,* 281–293.

Campbell, J. D., & Fairey, P. J. (1989). Informational and normative routes to conformity: The effect of faction size as a function of norm extremity and attention to the stimulus. *Journal of Personality and Social Psychology, 57,* 457–468.

Campbell, J. D., Tesser, A., & Fairey, P. J. (1986). Conformity and attention to the stimulus: Some temporal and contextual dynamics. *Journal of Personality and Social Psychology, 51,* 315–324.

Canavan-Gumpert, D. (1977). Generating reward and cost orientations through praise and criticism. *Journal of Personality and Social Psychology, 35,* 501–514.

Cann, A.; Sherman, S. J.; & Elkes, R. (1975). Effects of initial request size and timing of a second request on compliance: The foot in the door and the door in the face. *Journal of Personality and Social Psychology, 32,* 774–782.

Cantor, N., & Mischel, W. (1977). Traits as prototypes: Effects on recognition memory. *Journal of Personality and Social Psychology, 35,* 38–48.

Cantril, H. (1940). *The invasion from Mars: A study in the psychology of panic.* Princeton, N.J.: Princeton University Press.

Cantril, H. (1941). *The psychology of social movements.* New York: Wiley.

Carli, L. (1982). *Are women more social and men more task oriented? A meta-analytic review of sex differences in group interaction, coalition formation, and cooperation in prisoner's dilemma games.* Unpublished manuscript, University of Massachusetts.

Carli, L. (1989). Gender differences in interaction style and influence. *Journal of Personality and Social Psychology, 56,* 565–576.

Carlsmith, J. M., Collins, B. E., & Helmreich, R. L. (1966). Studies in forced compliance: I. The effect of pressure for compliance on attitude change produced by face-to-face role playing and anonymous essay writing. *Journal of Personality and Social Psychology, 4,* 1–13.

Carlsmith, J. M., Ellsworth, P. C., & Aronson, E. (1976). *Methods of research in social psychology.* Reading, Mass.: Addison-Wesley.

Carlson, M., Marcus-Newhall, A., & Miller, N. (1989). Evidence for a general construct of aggression. *Personality of Social Psychology Bulletin, 15,* 377–389.

Carnegie, D. (1936). *How to win friends and influence people.* New York: Simon & Schuster.

Carnevale, P., Sherer, P., & Pruitt, D. G. (1979). *Some determinants of concessions rate and distributive tactics in negoti-*

ation. Paper presented at American Psychological Association, New York.

Carnevale, P. J. (1985). Mediation of international conflict. *Applied Social Psychology Annual, 6,* 87–106.

Carp, F. (1987). Environment and aging. In D. Stokols & I. Altman (Eds.), *Handbook of environmental psychology* (Vol. 1, pp. 329–360). New York: Wiley.

Carson, R. C. (1969). *Interaction concepts of personality.* Chicago: Aldine.

Cartwright, D. (1973). Determinants of scientific progress: The case of research on the risky shift. *American Psychologist, 28,* 222–231.

Cartwright, D. (1979). Contemporary social psychology in historical perspective. *Social Psychology Quarterly, 42,* 82–93.

Cartwright, D., & Harary, F. (1956). Structural balance: A generalization of Heider's theory. *Psychological Review, 63,* 277–293.

Cartwright, D., & Zander, A. (Eds.). (1968). *Group dynamics: Research and theory* (3rd ed.). New York: Harper & Row.

Carver, C. S., & Scheier, M. F. (1981). *Attention and self-regulation: A control-theory approach to human behavior.* New York: Springer-Verlag.

Carver, C. S., & Scheier, M. F. (1990). Self-regulation and the self. In J. Strauss and G. R. Goethals (Eds.), *The self: Interdisciplinary perspectives.* New York: Springer-Verlag.

Castro, M. A. C. (1974). Reactions to receiving aid as a function of cost to donor and opportunity to aid. *Journal of Applied Social Psychology, 4,* 194–209.

Cavalli-Sforza, L. L., Feldman, M. W., Chen, K. H., & Dornbush, S. M. (1982). Theory and observation in cultural transmission. *Science, 218,* 19–27.

Cavan, S. (1963). Interaction in home territories. *Berkeley Journal of Sociology, 8,* 17–32.

Cavan, S. (1966). *Liquor license.* Chicago: Aldine.

Ceci, S. J., Peters, D., & Plotkin, J. (1985). Human subjects review, personal values, and the regulation of social science research. *American Psychologist, 40,* 994–1002.

Central Intelligence Agency. (1981, June). *Research paper.* Washington, D.C.

Chaiken, S. (1980). Heuristic versus systematic information processing and the use of source versus message cues in persuasion. *Journal of Personality and Social Psychology, 39,* 752–756.

Chaiken, S. (1987). The heuristic model of persuasion. In M. P. Zanna, J. M. Olson, & C. P. Herman (Eds.), *Social influence. The Ontario symposium* (Vol. 5). Hillsdale, N.J.: Erlbaum.

Chaiken, S., & Baldwin, M. W. (1981). Affective-cognitive consistency and the effect of salient behavioral information on the self-perception of attitudes. *Journal of Personality and Social Psychology, 34,* 605–614.

Chaiken, S., & Stangor, C. (1987). Attitudes and attitude change. *Annual Review of Psychology, 38,* 575–630.

Chemers, M. M., & Skrzypek, G. J. (1972). Experimental test of the contingency model of leadership effectiveness. *Journal of Personality and Social Psychology, 24,* 172–177.

Chen, S. C. (1937). Social modification of the activity of ants in nest-building. *Physiological Zoology, 10,* 420–436.

Chertkoff, J. M., & Conley, M. (1967). Opening offer and frequency of concession as bargaining strategies. *Journal of Personality and Social Psychology, 7,* 181–185.

Chertkoff, J. M., & Esser, J. K. (1976). A review of experiments in explicit bargaining. *Journal of Experimental Social Psychology, 12,* 464–486.

Chollar, S. (1989). An epidemic of acquaintance rape. *Psychology Today, 23,* 73.

Cialdini, R. B. (1985). *Influence: Science and practice* (pp. 183-188). Glenview, Ill.: Scott, Foresman.

Cialdini, R. B. (1989). Indirect tactics of impression management: Beyond basking. In R. Giacalone & P. Rosenfeld (Eds.), *Impression management in the organization* (pp. 45–56). Hillsdale, N.J.: Erlbaum.

Cialdini, R. B., Borden, R. J., Thorne, A., Walker, M. R., Freman, S., & Sloan, L. R. (1976). Basking in reflected glory: Three (football) field studies. *Journal of Personality and Social Psychology, 34,* 366–375.

Cialdini, R. B., Cacioppo, J. T., Bassett, R., & Miller, J. A. (1978). The low-ball procedure for producing compliance: Commitment, the cost. *Journal of Personality and Social Psychology, 36,* 463–476.

Cialdini, R. B., & De Nicholas, M. E. (1989). Self-presentation by association. *Journal of Personality and Social Psychology, 57,* 626–631.

Cialdini, R. B., Schaller, M., Houlihan, D., Arps, K., Fultz, J., & Beaman, A. L. (1987). Empathy-based helping: Is it selflessly or selfishly motivated? *Journal of Personality and Social Psychology, 52,* 749–758.

Cialdini, R. B., Vincent, J. E., Lewis, S. K., Catalan, J., Wheeler, D., & Darby, B. L. (1975). Reciprocal concessions procedure for inducing compliance: The door-in-the-face technique. *Journal of Personality and Social Psychology, 31,* 206–215.

Clark, M. S. (1984). Record keeping in two types of relationships. *Journal of Personality and Social Psychology, 47,* 549–557.

Clark, M. S., Gotay, C. C., & Mills, J. (1974). Acceptance of help as a function of the potential helper and opportunity to repay. *Journal of Applied Social Psychology, 4,* 224–229.

Clark, M. S., & Mills, J. (1979). Interpersonal attraction in exchange and communal relationships. *Journal of Personality and Social Psychology, 37,* 12–24.

Clark, M. S., Mills, J., & Powell, M. C. (1986). Keeping track of needs in communal and exchange relationships. *Journal of Personality and Social Psychology, 51,* 333–338.

Clark, M. S., & Reis, H. T. (1988). Interpersonal processes in close relationships. *Annual Review of Psychology, 39,* 609–672.

Cleaver, E. (1968). *Soul on ice.* New York: McGraw-Hill.

Clifford, M., & Walster, E. (1973). The effect of physical attractiveness on teacher expectation. *Sociology of Education, 46,* 248.

Clore, G. L., & Baldridge, B. (1968). Interpersonal attraction: The role of agreement and topic interest. *Journal of Personality and Social Psychology, 9,* 340–346.

Clore, G. L., & Kerber, K. W. (1981). *Toward an affective theory of attraction and trait attribution.* Unpublished manuscript.

Coch, L., & French, J. R. P. (1948). Overcoming resistance to change. *Human Relations, 1,* 512–532.

Cochran, C., Hale, W., & Hissam, C. (1984). Personal space requirements in indoor versus outdoor locations. *Journal of Psychology, 117,* 121–123.

Cohen, A. R. (1962). An experiment on small rewards for discrepant compliance and attitude change. In J. W. Brehm & A. R. Cohen (Eds.), *Explorations in cognitive dissonance.* New York: Wiley.

Cohen, C. E. (1981). Person categories and social perception: Testing some boundaries of the processing effects of prior knowledge. *Journal of Personality and Social Psychology, 40,* 441–452.

Cohen, W., Evans, G. W., Krantz, D. S.; & Stokols, D. (1980). Physiological, motivational, and cognitive effects of aircraft noise on children. *American Psychologist, 35*, 231–244.

Cohen, S., Evans, G. W., Krantz, D. S., Stokols, D., & Kelly, S. (1981). Aircraft noise and children: Longitudinal and cross-sectional evidence on adaptation to noise and the effectiveness of noise abatement. *Journal of Personality and Social Psychology, 40*(2), 331–345.

Cohen, S., & Sherrod, D. (1978). When density matters: Environmental control as a determinant of crowding effects in laboratory and residential settings. *Journal of Population, 1*, 189–202.

Cohn, N. B., & Strassberg, D. S. (1983). Self-disclosure reciprocity among preadolescents. *Personality and Social Psychology Bulletin, 9*, 97–102.

Coke tampers with success. (1985, May 6). *Newsweek*, pp. 50–52.

Collins, B. E., & Hoyt, M. G. (1972). Personal responsibility for consequences: An integrating and extension of the "forced compliance" literature. *Journal of Experimental Social Psychology, 8*, 558–593.

Comer, R., & Rhodewalt, F. (1979). Cue utilization in the self-attribution of emotions and attitudes. *Personality and Social Psychology Bulletin, 5*, 320–324.

Conn, L. K., Edwards, C. N., Rosenthal, R., & Crowne, D. (1968). Perception of emotion and response to teachers' expectancy by elementary school children. *Psychological Reports, 22*, 27–34.

Consumer Reports. (1974, April). Making the deal: Old rules in a new ball game, pp. 298–302.

Cook, S. W. (1985). Experimenting on social issues: The case of school desegregation. *American Psychologist, 40*, 452–460.

Cook, T. D., Gruder, C. L., Hennigan, K. M., & Flay, B. R. (1979). History of the sleeper effect: Some logical pitfalls in accepting the null hypothesis. *Psychological Bulletin, 37*, 131–146.

Cooley, C. H. (1902). *Human order and the social order.* New York: Scribner's.

Cooper, H., & Hazelrigg, P. (1988). Personality moderators of interpersonal expectancy effects: An integrative research review. *Journal of Personality and Social Psychology, 55*, 937–949.

Cooper, J. (1971). Personal responsibility and dissonance: The role of foreseen consequences. *Journal of Personality and Social Psychology, 18*, 354–363.

Cooper, J., & Axsom, D. (1982). Effort justification in psychotherapy. In G. Weary & H. Mirels (Eds.), *Integrations of clinical and social psychology.* New York: Oxford University Press.

Cooper, J., & Croyle, R. T. (1984). Attitudes and attitude change. *Annual Review of Psychology, 35*, 395–426.

Cooper, J., & Fazio, R. H. (1984). A new look at dissonance theory. In L. Berkowitz (Ed.), *Advances in experimental social psychology* (Vol. 17). New York: Academic Press.

Cooper, J., & Jones, E. E. (1969). Opinion divergence as a strategy to avoid being miscast. *Journal of Personality and Social Psychology, 13*, 23–30.

Cooper, J., & Mackie, D. (1986). Video games and aggression in children. *Journal of Applied Social Psychology, 16*(8), 726–744.

Cooper, J., & Worchel, S. (1970). Role of undesired consequences in arousing cognitive dissonance. *Journal of Personality and Social Psychology, 16*, 199–206.

Cooper, J., Zanna, M. P., & Taves, P. A. (1978). Arousal as a necessary condition for attitude change following induced compliance. *Journal of Personality and Social Psychology, 36*, 1101–1106.

Cooper, J. E., & McGaugh, J. L. (1969). Leadership: Integrating principles of social psychology. In C. A. Gibb (Ed.), *Leadership.* Baltimore: Penguin.

Cordes, B., Hoffman, B., Jenkins, B., Kellen, K., Moran, S., & Slater, W. (1984). *Trends: International terrorism, 1982 and 1983* (Report No. R-3183–52). Santa Monica, Calif.: Rand Corp.

Cotton, J. L. (1981). A review of research on Schachter's theory of emotion and the misattribution of arousal. *European Journal of Social Psychology, 11*, 365–397.

Cottrell, N., & Wack, D. (1967). The energizing effect of cognitive dissonance and subordinate responses. *Journal of Personality and Social Psychology, 6*, 132–138.

Cottrell, N., Wack, D., Sekerak, G., & Rittle, R. (1968). Social facilitation of dominant responses by the presence of an audience and the mere presence of others. *Journal of Personality and Social Psychology, 9*, 245–250.

Cowan, P. A., & Walters, R. H. (1963). Studies of reinforcement of aggression: I. Effects of scheduling. *Child Development, 34*, 543–551.

Cox, V., Paulus, P., & McCain, G. (1984). Prison crowding research: The relevance for prison housing standards and a general approach regarding crowding phenomena. *American Psychologist, 39*, 1148–1160.

Cozby, P. C. (1972). Self-disclosure, reciprocity, and liking. *Sociometry, 35*, 151–60.

Crider, A. B., Goethals, G. R., Kavanaugh, R. D., & Soloman, P. R. (1989). *Psychology* (3rd ed.). Glenview, Ill.: Scott, Foresman.

Crocker, J., Hannah, D. B., & Weber, R. (1983). Person memory and causal attributions. *Journal of Personality and Social Psychology, 44*, 55–66.

Crocker, J., Thompson, L. L., McGraw, K. M., & Ingerman, C. (1987). Downward comparison, prejudice, and evaluations of others: Effects of self-esteem and threat. *Journal of Personality and Social Psychology, 52*, 907–916.

Crowne, D. P., & Marlow, D. (1964). *The approval motive: Studies in evaluative dependence.* New York: Wiley.

Croyle, R., & Cooper, J. (1983). Dissonance arousal: Physiological evidence. *Journal of Personality and Social Psychology, 45*, 782–791.

Crutchfield, R. A. (1955). Conformity and character. *American Psychologist, 10*, 191–198.

Csikszentmihalyi, M., & LeFevre, J. (1989). Optimal experience in work and leisure. *Journal of Personality and Social Psychology, 56*, 815–822.

Cunningham, J. D. (1981). Self-disclosure intimacy: Sex, sex-of-target, cross-national, and "generational" differences. *Personality and Social Psychology Bulletin, 7*, 314–319.

Curtis, R. C., & Miller, K. (1986). Believing another likes or dislikes you: Behaviors making the beliefs come true. *Journal of Personality and Social Psychology, 51*, 284–290.

Damarad-Frye, R., & Laird, J. D. (1989). The experience of boredom: The role of self-perception of attention. *Journal of Personality and Social Psychology, 57*, 315–320.

Danheiser, P. R., & Graziano, W. G. (1982). Self-monitoring and cooperation as a self-presentational strategy. *Journal of Personality and Social Psychology, 42*, 497–505.

Darley, J. M., & Aronson, E. (1966). Self-evaluation vs. direct anxiety reduction as determinants of the fear-affiliation relationship. *Journal of Experimental Social Psychology, 2*, 66–79.

Darley, J. M., & Batson, C. D. (1973). "From Jerusalem to Jericho": A study of situational and dispositional variables in helping behavior. *Journal of Personality and Social Psychology, 27,* 100–108.

Darley, J. M., & Berscheid, E. (1967). Increased liking caused by the anticipation of personal contact. *Human Relations, 10,* 29–40.

Darley, J. M., & Fazio, R. H. (1980). Expectancy and confirmation processes arising in the social interaction sequence. *American Psychologist, 35,* 867–881.

Darley, J. M., Fleming, J. H., Hilton, J. L., & Swan, W. B. (1988). Dispelling negative expectancies: The impact of interaction goals and target characteristics on the expectancy confirmation process. *Journal of Experimental Social Psychology, 24,* 19–36.

Darley, J. M., & Gross, P. H. (1983). A hypothesis-confirming bias in labeling effects. *Journal of Personality and Social Psychology, 44,* 20–33.

Darley, J. M., & Latané, B. (1968). Bystander intervention in emergencies: Diffusion of responsibility. *Journal of Personality and Social Psychology, 8,* 377–383.

Darley, S. A. (1976). Big-time careers for the "little woman": A dual-role dilemma. *Journal of Social Issues, 32,* 85–98.

Davidson, A. R., & Jaccard, J. (1979). Variables that moderate the attitude-behavior relation: Results of a longitudinal survey. *Journal of Personality and Social Psychology, 37,* 1364–1376.

Davidson, L. R., & Duberman, L. (1982). Friendship: Communication and interactional patterns in same sex dyads. *Sex Roles, 8,* 809–822.

Davies, J. C. (1962). Toward a theory of revolution. *American Sociological Review, xxvii,* 5–19.

Davis, D., & Perkowitz, W. T. (1979). Consequences of responsiveness in dyadic interaction: Effects of probability of response and proportion of content-related responses on interpersonal attraction. *Journal of Personality and Social Psychology, 37,* 534–550.

Davis, J., Bray, R., & Holt, R. (1977). The empirical study of decision processes in juries. In J. Tapp & F. Levine (Eds.), *Law, justice, and the individual in society: Psychological and legal issues.* New York: Holt, Rinehart & Winston.

Davis, J., Kerr, N. L., Atkin, R. S., Holt, R., & Meek, D. (1975). The decision processes of 6- and 12-person mock juries assigned unanimous and two-thirds majority rules. *Journal of Personality and Social Psychology, 32,* 1–14.

Davis, K. E. (1985, February). Near and dear: Friendship and love. *Psychology Today,* pp. 22–30.

Davis, K. E., & Florquist, C. C. (1965). Perceived threat and dependence as determinants of the tactical usage of opinion conformity. *Journal of Experimental Social Psychology, 1,* 219–236.

Davis, K. E., & Jones, E. E. (1960). Changes in interpersonal perception as a means of reducing cognitive dissonance. *Journal of Abnormal and Social Psychology, 61,* 402–410.

Davis, K. E., & Todd, M. (1982). Friendship and love relationships. In K. E. Davis & T. O. Mitchell (Eds.), *Advances in descriptive psychology.* Greenwich, Conn.: JAI Press.

Davis, M. H., & Franzoni, S. L. (1986). Adolescent loneliness, self-disclosure, and private self-consciousness: A longitudinal investigation. *Journal of Personality and Social Psychology, 51,* 595–608.

Davitz, J. R. (1952). The effects of previous training on post-frustrative behavior. *Journal of Abnormal and Social Psychology, 47,* 309–315.

Dawes, R. M. (1980). Social dilemmas. *Annual Review of Psychology, 31,* 169–183.

Dawes, R. M., & Smith, T. L. (1985). Attitude and opinion measurement. In G. Lindzey & E. Aronson (Eds.), *The handbook of social psychology* (3rd ed., Vol. 1, pp. 509–566). New York: Random House.

Deaux, K. (1976). Sex: A perspective on the attribution process. In H. Harvey, W. J. Ickes, & R. F. Kidd (Eds.), *New directions in attribution research.* Hillsdale, N.J.: Erlbaum.

Deaux, K. (1985). Sex and gender. *Annual Review of Psychology, 36,* 49–81.

Deaux, K., & Major, B. (1987). Putting gender into context: An interactive model of gender-related behavior. *Psychological Review, 94,* 369–389.

DeJong, P. F., Koomen, W., & Mellenbergh, C. J. (1988). Structure of causes for success and failure: A multidimensional scaling analysis of preference judgements. *Journal of Personality and Social Psychology, 55,* 718–725.

DeJong, W. (1979). An examination of self-perception mediation of the foot-in-the-door effect. *Journal of Personality and Social Psychology, 37,* 2221–2239.

DeJong, W. (1981). Consensus information and the foot-in-the-door effect. *Personality and Social Psychology Bulletin, 7,* 423–430.

DeJong, W., Marber, S., & Shaver, R. (1980). Crime intervention: The role of a victim's behavior in reducing situational ambiguity. *Personality and Social Psychology Bulletin, 6,* 113–118.

Demare, D., Brier, J., & Lips, H. M. (1988). Violent pornography and self-reported likelihood of sexual aggression. *Journal of Research in Personality, 22,* 140–153.

Dermer, M., & Pyszczynski, T. A. (1978). Effects of erotica upon men's loving and liking responses for women they love. *Journal of Personality and Social Psychology, 36,* 1302–1309.

Deutsch, M. (1973). *The resolution of conflict.* New Haven: Yale University Press.

Deutsch, M. (1975). Introduction. In M. Deutsch & H. A. Hornstein (Eds.), *Applying social psychology: Implications for research, practice, training* (pp. 1–12). Hillsdale, N.J.: Erlbaum.

Deutsch, M., Canavan, D., & Rubin, J. (1971). The effects of size of conflict and sex of experimenter upon interpersonal bargaining. *Journal of Experimental Social Psychology, 7,* 258–267.

Deutsch, M., & Gerard, H. (1955). A study of normative and informational social influences upon individual judgment. *Journal of Abnormal and Social Psychology, 51,* 629–636.

Deutsch, M., & Krauss, R. M. (1960). The effect of threat upon interpersonal bargaining. *Journal of Abnormal and Social Psychology, 61,* 181–189.

Deutsch, M., & Krauss, R. M. (1962). Studies of interpersonal bargaining. *Journal of Conflict Resolution, 6,* 52–76.

Devine, P. G. (1989). Stereotypes and prejudice: Their automatic and controlled components. *Journal of Personality and Social Psychology, 56,* 5–18.

Dickoff, H. (1961). *Reactions to evaluations by another person as a function of self-evaluation and the interaction context.* Unpublished doctoral dissertation, Duke University, Durham, N.C.

Diener, E. (1979). Deindividuation, self-awareness, and disinhibition. *Journal of Personality and Social Psychology, 37,* 1160–1171.

Diener, E., Fraser, S., Beaman, A., & Kelem, Z. (1976). Effects of deindividuation variables on stealing among Halloween trick-or-treaters. *Journal of Personality and Social Psychology, 33,* 178–183.

Di Mento, J. F. (1989). Can social science explain organization noncompliance with environmental law? *Journal of Social Issues, 45,* 109–132.

Dion, K. K. (1972). Physical attractiveness and evaluation on children's transgressions. *Journal of Personality and Social Psychology, 24,* 207–213.

Dion, K. K., Berscheid, E., & Walster, E. (1972). What is beautiful is good. *Journal of Personality and Social Psychology, 24,* 285–290.

Doctor, R. M., Baldenring, J., Chivian, E., Mack, J., Waletzky, J., Lazaroff, C., & Gross, T. (1988). Self-reports of Soviet and American children on worry about the threat of nuclear war. *Political Psychology, 9,* 13–24.

Dodson, J. A., Tybout, A. M., & Sternthal, B. (1978). Impact of deals and deal retraction on brand switching. *Journal of Marketing Research, 15*(1), 72–81.

Dollard, J., Doob, L., Miller, N., Mowrer, O., & Sears, R. (1939). *Frustration and aggression.* New Haven, Conn.: Yale University Press.

Donnerstein, E. (1980). Aggressive erotica and violence against women. *Journal of Personality and Social Psychology, 39,* 269–277.

Donnerstein, E. (1983). Erotica and human aggression. In R. G. Geen & E. Donnerstein (Eds.), *Aggression: Theoretical and empirical reviews* (Vol. 1). New York: Academic Press.

Donnerstein, E., & Berkowitz, L. (1981). Victim reactions in aggressive erotic films as a factor in violence against women. *Journal of Personality and Social Psychology, 41,* 710–724.

Donnerstein, E., Donnerstein, M., & Barrett, G. (1976). Where is the facilitation of media violence: The effects of nonexposure and placement of anger arousal. *Journal of Research in Personality, 10,* 386–398.

Donnerstein, E., Donnerstein, M., & Evans, R. (1975). Erotic stimuli and aggression: Facilitation or inhibition. *Journal of Personality and Social Psychology, 32,* 237–244.

Donnerstein, E., & Linz, D. G. (1986, December). The question of pornography: It is not sex, but violence, that is an obscenity in our society. *Psychology Today,* pp. 56–59.

Donnerstein, E., & Wilson, D. W. (1976). Effects of noise and perceived control on ongoing and subsequent aggressive behavior. *Journal of Personality and Social Psychology, 34,* 774–781.

Doob, A. N., & Wood, L. E. (1972). Catharsis and aggression: Effects of annoyance and retaliation on aggressive behavior. *Journal of Personality and Social Psychology, 22,* 156–162.

Dovidio, J. F., & Gaertner, S. L. (1986). Prejudice, discrimination, and racism: Historical trends and contemporary approaches. In J. F. Dovidio & S. L. Gaertner (Eds.), *Prejudice, discrimination, and racism* (pp. 1–34). New York: Academic Press.

Driscoll, R., Davis, L., & Lipetz, M. (1972). Parental interference and romantic love: The Romeo and Juliet effect. *Journal of Personality and Social Psychology, 24,* 1–10.

Druckman, D., Broome, B., & Korper, S. (1988). Value differences and conflict resolution: Facilitation or delinking? *Journal of Conflict Resolution, 32,* 489–510.

Duclos, S. E., Laird, J. D., Schneider, E., Sexter, M.; Stern, L., & Van Lighten, O. (1989). Emotion-specific effects of facial expressions and postures on emotional experience. *Journal of Personality and Social Psychology, 57,* 100–108.

Duffy, K. (1991). Introduction to community mediation programs: Past, present, and future. In K. Duffy, J. Grosch, & P. Olzak (Eds.), *Issues in community mediation: A handbook for practitioners and researchers.* New York: Guilford Press.

Duncan, D. L. (1976). Differential social perception and attribution of intergroup violence: Testing the lower limits of stereotyping of blacks. *Journal of Personality and Social Psychology, 34,* 590–598.

Durkheim, E. (1898). *The rules of sociological method.* New York: Free Press.

Dutton, D. G., & Aron, A. P. (1974). Some evidence for heightened sexual attraction under conditions of high anxiety. *Journal of Personality and Social Psychology, 30,* 510–517.

Duval, S., Duval, V. H., & Neely, R. (1979). Self-focus, felt responsibility, and helping behavior. *Journal of Personality and Social Psychology, 37,* 1769–1778.

Duval, S., & Wicklund, R. A. (1972). *A theory of objective self-awareness.* New York: Academic Press.

Dweck, C. S. (1975). The role of expectations and attributions in the alleviation of learned helplessness. *Journal of Personality and Social Psychology, 31,* 674–685.

Eagly, A. H. (1983). Gender and social influence: A social psychological analysis. *American Psychologist, 38,* 971–981.

Eagly, A. H. (1987). *Sex differences in social behavior: A social role interpretation.* Hillsdale, N.J.: Erlbaum.

Eagly, A. H., & Carli, L. L. (1981). Sex of researchers and sex-typed communications as determinants of sex differences in influenceability: A meta-analysis of social influence studies. *Psychological Bulletin, 90,* 1–20.

Eagly, A. H., & Chaiken, S. (1984). Cognitive theories of persuasion. In L. Berkowitz (Ed.), *Advances in experimental social psychology* (Vol. 17). New York: Academic Press.

Eagly, A. H., & Steffen, V. J. (1986). Gender and aggressive behavior: A meta-analytic review of the social psychological literature. *Psychological Bulletin, 100,* 309–330.

Eagly, A. H.; Wood, W.; & Fishbaugh, L. (1981). Sex differences in conformity: Surveillance by the group as a determinant of male nonconformity. *Journal of Personality and Social Psychology, 40,* 384–394.

Earle, W. B. (1986). The social context of social comparison: Reality versus reassurance? *Personality and Social Psychology Bulletin, 12,* 159–168.

Eaton, W. O., & Enns, L. R. (1986). Sex differences in human motor activity level. *Psychological Bulletin, 100,* 19–28.

Ebbinghaus, H. (1885). *Memory* (H. A. Ruger & C. E. Bussenius, Trans.). New York: Teachers College, Columbia University. (Original work published 1913; reprint ed., New York: Dover, 1964).

Edney, J. J. (1975). Territoriality and control: A field experiment. *Journal of Personality and Social Psychology, 31,* 1108–1115.

Efran, M. G. (1974). The effect of physical appearance on the judgment of guilt, interpersonal attraction, and severity of recommended punishment in a simulated jury task. *Journal of Experimental Research and Personality, 8,* 45–54.

Ehrlich, P. (1968). *The population bomb.* New York: Ballantine Books.

Eisenberg, A. (Ed.). (1981). *Witness to the holocaust.* New York: Pilgrim Press.

Eisenberg, N., & Lennon, R. (1983). Sex differences in empathy and related capacities. *Psychological Bulletin, 94,* 100–131.

Eiser, J. R. (Ed.). (1984). *Attitudinal judgment.* New York: Springer.

Ekman, P., & Friesen, W. V. (1969). Nonverbal leakage and clues to deception. *Psychiatry, 32,* 88–106.

Ekman, P., Friesen, W. V., & Ellsworth, P. C. (1982). What are the similarities and differences in facial behavior across cultures? In P. Ekman (Ed.), *Emotion in the human race* (Vol. 2, pp. 56–97). Cambridge, England: Cambridge University Press.

Ekman, P., Friesen, W., & O'Sullivan, M. (1988). Smiles when lying. *Journal of Personality and Social Psychology, 54,* 414–420.

Elashoff, J. R., & Snow, R. E. (1971). *Pygmalion reconsidered.* Worthington, Oh.: Charles A. Jones.

Ellis, R. J. (1988). Self-monitoring and leadership emergence in groups. *Personality and Social Psychology Bulletin, 14,* 681–693.

Ellsworth, P. C., & Carlsmith, J. M. (1968). Effect of eye contact and verbal consent on affective response to a dyadic interaction. *Journal of Personality and Social Psychology, 10,* 15–20.

Elms, A. C. (1975). The crisis of confidence in social psychology. *American Psychologist, 30,* 967–976.

Elms, A. C., & Janis, I. L. (1965). Counter-norm attitudes induced by consonant versus dissonant conditions of role-playing. *Journal of Experimental Research in Personality, 1,* 50–60.

Emery, R. E. (1989). Family violence, special issue: Children and their development: Knowledge base, research agenda, and social policy application. *American Psychologist, 44*(2), 321–328.

Emswiller, R., Deaux, K., & Willits, J. (1971). Similarity, sex, and requests for small favors. *Journal of Applied Social Psychology, 1,* 284–291.

Engebretson, T. O., Matthews, K. A., & Scheier, M. F. (1989). Relations between anger expression and cardiovascular reactivity: Reconciling inconsistent findings through a matching hypothesis. *Journal of Personality and Social Psychology, 59,* 513–521.

Erdley, C. A., & D'Agostino, P. R. (1988). Cognitive and affective components of automatic priming effects. *Journal of Personality and Social Psychology, 54,* 741–747.

Engretson, T.O., Matthews, K.A., & Scheier, M. F. (1989). Relations between anger expression and cardiovascular reactivity: Reconciling inconsistent findings through a matching hypothesis. *Journal of Personality and Social Psychology, 59,* 513–521.

Evans, G. W., & Cohen, S. (1987). Environmental stress. In D. Stokols & I. Altman (Eds.), *Handbook of environmental psychology* (Vol. 1, pp. 571–610). New York: Wiley.

Exline, R. V., Ellyson, S. L., & Long, B. (1975). Visual behavior as an aspect of power role relationships. In P. Pliner, L. Krames, & T. Galloway (Eds.), *Nonverbal communication of aggression* (Vol. 2). New York: Plenum.

Falbo, T., & Peplau, L. S. (1980). Power strategies in intimate relationships. *Journal of Personality and Social Psychology, 38,* 618–628.

Fazio, R. H. (1981). On the self-perception explanation of the overjustification effect: The role of the salience of initial attitude. *Journal of Experimental Social Psychology, 17,* 417–426.

Fazio, R. H. (1986). How do attitudes guide behaviors? In R. M. Sorrentino & E. T. Higgins (Eds.), *The handbook of motivation and cognition: Foundations of social behavior.* New York: Guilford.

Fazio, R. H., & Williams, C. J. (1986). Attitude accessibility as a moderator of the attitude-perception and attitude-behavior relations: An investigation of the 1984 presidential election. *Journal of Personality and Social Psychology, 51*(3), 505–514.

Fehr, B. (1988). Prototype analysis of the concepts of love and commitment. *Journal of Personality and Social Psychology, 55,* 557–579.

Felson, R. B. (1989). Parents and the reflected appraisal process. A longitudinal analysis. *Journal of Personality and Social Psychology, 57,* 965–971.

Fenigstein, A. (1979). Self-consciousness, self-attention, and social interaction. *Journal of Personality and Social Psychology, 37,* 75–86.

Fenigstein, A., Scheier, M. F., & Buss, A. H. (1975). Public and private self-consciousness: Assessment and theory. *Journal of Consulting and Clinical Psychology, 43,* 522–527.

Feshbach, S. (1961). The stimulating versus cathartic effects of a vicarious aggressive activity. *Journal of Abnormal and Social Psychology, 63,* 381–385.

Feshbach, S., & Singer, R. D. (1971). *Television and aggression: An experimental field study.* San Francisco: Jossey-Bass.

Festinger, L. (1950). Informal social communication. *Psychological Review, 57,* 271–282.

Festinger, L. (1954). A theory of social comparison processes. *Human Relations, 7,* 117–140.

Festinger, L. (1957). *A theory of cognitive dissonance.* Palo Alto, Calif.: Stanford University Press.

Festinger, L. (1964). *Conflict, decision, and dissonance.* Palo Alto, Calif.: Stanford University Press.

Festinger, L. (1980). *Retrospections on social psychology.* New York: Oxford University Press.

Festinger, L., & Carlsmith, J. M. (1959). Cognitive consequences of forced compliance. *Journal of Abnormal and Social Psychology, 58,* 203–210.

Festinger, L., Pepitone, A., & Newcomb, T. (1952). Some consequences of deindividuation in a group. *Journal of Abnormal and Social Psychology, 47,* 382–389.

Festinger, L., Riecken, H. W., & Schachter, S. (1956). *When prophecy fails.* Minneapolis: University of Minnesota Press.

Festinger, L., Schachter, S., & Back, K. (1950). *Social pressures in informal groups: A study of a housing community.* Palo Alto, Calif.: Stanford University Press.

Fiedler, F. E. (1964). A contingency model of leadership effectiveness. In L. Berkowitz (Ed.), *Advances in experimental social psychology* (Vol. 1). New York: Academic Press.

Fiedler, F. E. (1977). A rejoinder to Schriesheim and Kerr's premature obituary of the contingency model. In J. G. Hunt and L. L. Larson (Eds.), *Leadership: The cutting edge.* Carbondale: Southern Illinois University Press.

Fiedler, F. E. (1978). Recent developments in research on the contingency model. In L. Berkowitz (Ed.), *Group process* (pp. 209–225). New York: Academic Press.

Fiedler, F. E., Chemers, M. M., & Mahar, L. (1976). *Improving leadership effectiveness: The leader match concept.* New York: Wiley.

Filley, A. (1975). *Interpersonal conflict resolution.* Glenview, Ill.: Scott, Foresman.

Finison, L. J. (1986). The psychological insurgency, 1936–1945. *Journal of Social Issues, 42,* 21–34.

Fischer, K., Schoeneman, T. J., & Rubanowitz, D. E. (1987). Attributions in the advice columns. II. The dimensionality of actors' and observers' explanations for interpersonal problems. *Personality and Social Psychology Bulletin, 13,* 458–466.

Fischoff, B. (1975). Hindsight = foresight: The effects of outcome knowledge on judgment under uncertainty. *Journal of Experimental Psychology: Human Perception and Performance, 1,* 288–299.

Fisher, J., Bell, P., & Baum. A. (1984). *Environmental psychology* (Vol. 2). New York: Holt, Rinehart & Winston.

Fisher, J., & Byrne, D. (1975). Too close for comfort: Sex differences in response to invasions of personal space. *Journal of Personality and Social Psychology, 32,* 15–21.

Fiske, S. T., & Taylor, S. E. (1984). *Social cognition.* New York: McGraw-Hill.

Fleiner, S., & Kelley, H. H. (1978). Study cited (but not referenced) in H. H. Kelley, *Personal relationships: Their structures and processes* (p. 5). Hillsdale, N.J.: Erlbaum.

Fleischer, R. A., & Chertkoff, J. M. (1986). Effects of dominance and sex on leader selection in dyadic work groups. *Journal of Personality and Social Psychology, 50,* 94–99.

Fleishman, J. (1988). The effects of decision framing and others' behavior on cooperation in a social dilemma. *Journal of Conflict Resolution, 32,* 162–180.

Fleming, E. S., & Anttonen, R. G. (1971). Teacher expectancy as related to the academic and personal growth of primary-age children. *Monographs of the Society for Research in Child Development, 36* (serial no. 145).

Fleming, J. H., & Darley, J. M. (1989). Perceiving choice and constraint: The effects of contextual and behavioral cues on attitude attribution. *Journal of Personality and Social Psychology, 56,* 27–40.

Flowers, M. L. (1977). A laboratory test of some implications of Janis' groupthink hypothesis. *Journal of Personality and Social Psychology, 35,* 888–896.

Folger, R., & Greenberg, J. (1985). Procedural justice: An interpretive analysis of personnel systems. In K. Rowland & G. Ferris (Eds.), *Research in personnel and human resource management.* Greenwich, Conn.: JAI Press.

Follette, V. M., & Jacobson, N. S. (1987). Importance of attribution as a predictor of how people cope with failure. *Journal of Personality and Social Psychology, 52,* 1205–1211.

Forgas, J. P. (1987). The role of physical attractiveness in the interpretation of facial expression cues. *Personality and Social Psychology Bulletin, 13,* 478–489.

Forsyth, D. (1983). *An introduction to group dynamics.* Pacific Grove, Calif.: Brooks/Cole.

Forsyth, D. (1990). *An introduction to group dynamics* (2nd ed). Pacific Grove, Calif.: Brooks/Cole.

Foss, R. D. (1981). Structural effects in simulated jury decision making. *Journal of Personality and Social Psychology, 40,* 1053–1062.

Frank, M. G., & Gilovich, T. (1988). The dark side of self- and social perception: Black uniforms and aggression in professional sports. *Journal of Personality and Social Psychology, 54,* 74–85.

Frank, R. E., & Greenberg, M. G. (1980). *The public's use of television: Who watches and why.* Newbury Park, Calif.: Sage.

Fraser, S., Gouge, C., & Billig, M. (1971). Risky shifts, cautious shifts, and group polarization. *European Journal of Social Psychology, 1,* 7–29.

Freedman, J. L. (1965). Long-term behavioral effects of cognitive dissonance. *Journal of Experimental Social Psychology, 1*(2), 145–155.

Freedman, J. L. (1984). Effect of television violence on aggressiveness. *Psychological Bulletin, 96*(2), 227–246.

Freedman, J. L. (1986). Television violence and aggression: A rejoinder. *Psychological Bulletin, 100*(3), 372–378.

Freedman, J. L., & Fraser, S. (1966). Compliance without pressure: The foot-in-the-door technique. *Journal of Personality and Social Psychology, 4,* 195–202.

French, J. R. P., Jr., & Raven, B. H. (1959). The bases of social power. In D. Cartwright (Ed.), *Studies in social power* (pp. 150–167). Ann Arbor: University of Michigan Press.

Frey, D. L., & Gaertner, S. L. (1986). Helping and the avoidance of inappropriate interracial behavior: A strategy that perpetuates a nonprejudiced self-image. *Journal of Personality and Social Psychology, 50,* 1083–1090.

Friedland, N. (1988). Political terrorism: A social psychological perspective. In W. Stroebe et al. (Eds.), *The social psychology of intergroup conflict* (pp. 103–116). Berlin: Springer-Verlag.

Friedman, H. S., & Riggio, R. (1981). Effect of individual differences in nonverbal expressiveness on transmission of emotion. *Journal of Nonverbal Behavior, 6,* 96–104.

Friedman, H.S., Riggio, R., & Casella, D. F. (1988). Nonverbal skill, personal charisma, and initial attraction. *Personality and Social Psychology Bulletin, 14,* 203–211.

Friedman, M., & Rosenman, R. H. (1959). Association of specific overt behavior patterns with blood and cardiovascular findings: Blood cholesterol level, blood clotting time, incidence of arcus senilus, and clinical artery disease. *Journal of the American Medical Association, 169,* 1286.

Friedrich, L. K., & Stein, A. H. (1973). Aggressive and prosocial television programs and the natural behavior of preschool children. *Monographs of the Society for Research in Child Development, 38*(4), Whole No. 151.

Friedrich-Cofer, L., & Huston, A. C. (1986). Television violence and aggression: The debate continues. *Psychological Bulletin, 100*(3), 364–371.

Frieze, I., & Weiner, B. (1971). Cue utilization and attributional judgments for success and failure. *Journal of Personality, 39,* 591–606.

Frodi, A. (1977). Sexual arousal, situational restrictiveness, and aggressive behavior. *Journal of Research in Personality, 11,* 48–58.

Froming, W. J., & Carver, C. S. (1981). Divergent influence of private and public self-consciousness in a compliance paradigm. *Journal of Research in Personality, 15,* 159–171.

Frone, M. R., Adams, J., Rice, R. W., & Instone-Noonan, D. (1987). Halo error: A field study comparison of self- and subordinate evaluations of leadership process and leader effectiveness. *Personality and Social Psychology Bulletin, 12,* 454–461.

Gabrenya, W. K., & Arkin, R. M. (1980). Self-monitoring scale: Factor structure and correlates. *Personality and Social Psychology Bulletin, 6,* 12–22.

Gaertner, S. L. (1970). A "call" for help: Helping behavior extended to black and white victims by New York City Liberal and Conservative Party members. *Proceedings of the 78th Annual Convention of the American Psychological Association* (Vol. 5), pp. 441–442.

Gaertner, S. L., & Dovidio, J. F. (1986). The aversive form of racism. In J. F. Dovidio & S. L. Gaertner (Eds.), *Prejudice, discrimination, and racism* (pp. 61–90). New York: Academic Press.

Gallo, P. S. (1966). Effects of increased incentives upon the use of threat in bargaining. *Journal of Personality and Social Psychology, 4,* 14–20.

Galperin, M., Holt, R. R., & Howells, P. (1988). What Soviet emigre adolescents think about nuclear war. *Political Psychology, 9,* 1–12.

Gamson, W. A. A. (1961). A theory of coalition formation. *American Sociological Review, 26,* 373–382.

Gamson, W. A. A. (1964). Experimental studies of coalition formation. In L. Berkowitz (Ed.), *Advances in experimental social psychology* (Vol. 1). New York: Academic Press.

Gantnot, A. B., & Taylor, S. P. (1988). Human physical agression as a function of diazepam. *Personality of Social Psychology Bulletin, 14,* 479–484.

Gatchel, R. J., Baum, A., & Krantz, D. S. (1989). *An introduction to health psychology* (2nd ed.). New York: Random House.

Geen, R. G. (1981). Evaluation apprehension and social facilitation: A reply to Sanders. *Journal of Experimental Social Psychology, 17,* 252–256.

Geen, R. G., & Quanty, M. (1977). The catharsis of aggression: An evaluation of a hypothesis. In L. Berkowitz (Ed.), *Advances in experimental social psychology* (Vol. 10). New York: Academic Press.

Geen, R. G., Rakosky, J. J., & Pigg, R. (1972). Awareness of arousal and its relation to aggression. *British Journal of Social and Clinical Psychology, 11,* 115–121.

Geen, R. G., & Stoner, D. (1973). Context effects in observed violence. *Journal of Personality and Social Psychology, 25,* 145–150.

Geller, E. S. (1989). Applied behavior analysis and social marketing: An integration for environmental preservation. *Journal of Social Issues, 45,* 17–36.

Gerard, H. B. (1963). Emotional uncertainty and social comparison. *Journal of Abnormal and Social Psychology, 66,* 568–573.

Gerard, H. B., & Mathewson, G. (1966). The effects of severity of initiation on liking for a group: A replication. *Journal of Experimental Social Psychology, 2,* 278–287.

Gerard, H. B., Wilhelmy, R. A., & Conolley, E. S. (1968). Conformity and group size. *Journal of Personality and Social Psychology, 8,* 79–82.

Gerbner, G., Gross, L., Morgan, M., & Signorielli, N. (1980). The "mainstreaming" of America: Violence profile no. 11. *Journal of Communication, 30*(3), 10–29.

Gergen, K. J. (1971). *The concept of self.* New York: Holt.

Gergen, K. J., & Taylor, M. G. (1969). Social expectancy and self-presentation in a status hierarchy. *Journal of Experimental Social Psychology, 5,* 79–92.

Gergen, M. (1989). Induction and construction: Teetering between two worlds. *European Journal of Social Psychology, 19,* 431–438.

Gibb, C. A. (1969). Leadership. In G. Lindzey & E. Aronson (Eds.), *The handbook of social psychology* (2nd ed., Vol. 4). Reading, Mass.: Addison-Wesley.

Gibbons, F. X. (1978). Sexual standards and reaction to pornography: Enhancing behavioral consistency through self-focused attention. *Journal of Personality and Social Psychology, 36,* 976–987.

Gibbons, F. X. (1986). Social comparison and depression: Company's effect on misery. *Journal of Personality and Social Psychology, 51,* 140–148.

Gibbons, F. X. (1990). Self-attention and behavior: A review and theoretical update. In L. Berkowitz (Ed.), *Advances in experimental social psychology* (Vol. 23, pp. 249–303). New York: Academic Press.

Gifford, R., & O'Connor, B. (1986). Nonverbal intimacy: Clarifying the role of seating distance and orientation. *Journal of Nonverbal Behavior, 10,* 207–214.

Gifford, R., & O'Connor, B. (1987). The interpersonal circumplex as a behavior map. *Journal of Personality and Social Psychology, 52,* 1019–1026.

Gilbert, D. T., & Jones, E. E. (1986). Perceiver-induced constraint: Interpretations of self-generated reality. *Journal of Personality and Social Psychology, 50,* 269–280.

Gilbert, D. T., Krull, D. S., & Pelham, B. W. (1988). Of thoughts unspoken: Social inference and the self-regulation of behavior. *Journal of Personality and Social Psychology, 55,* 685–694.

Gilbert, D. T., Pelham, B. W., & Krull, D. S. (1988). On cognitive busyness: When person perceivers meet persons perceived. *Journal of Personality and Social Psychology, 54,* 733–740.

Gilbert, R. K. (1988). The dynamics of inaction: Psychological factors inhibiting arms control activism. *American Psychologist, 43,* 755–764.

Gillig, P. M., & Greenwald, A. G. (1974). Is it time to lay the sleeper effect to rest? *Journal of Personality and Social Psychology, 29,* 132–139.

Ginosar, Z., & Trope, Y. (1980). The effects of base rates and individuating information on judgments about another person. *Journal of Experimental Social Psychology, 16,* 228–242.

Gintner, G., & Lindskold, S. (1975). Rate of participation and expertise as factors influencing leader choice. *Journal of Personality and Social Psychology, 32,* 1085–1089.

Glass, D. C. (1977). *Behavior patterns, stress, and coronary disease.* Hillsdale, N.J.: Erlbaum.

Glass, D. C., & Singer, J. E. (1972). *Urban stress.* New York: Academic Press.

Glick, P., DeMorest, J. A., & Hotze, C. A. (1988). Self-monitoring and beliefs about partner compatibility in romantic relationships. *Personality and Social Psychology Bulletin, 14,* 485–494.

Goethals, G. R. (1972). Consensus and modality in the attribution process: The role of similarity and information. *Journal of Personality and Social Psychology, 21,* 84–92.

Goethals, G. R. (1986a). Fabricating and ignoring social reality: Self-serving estimates of consensus. In J. M. Olson, C. P. Herman, & M. P. Zanna (Eds.), *Relative deprivation and social comparison. The Ontario symposium* (Vol. 4, pp. 135–157). Hillsdale, N.J.: Erlbaum.

Goethals, G. R. (1986b). Social comparison theory: Psychology from the lost and found. *Personality and Social Psychology Bulletin, 12,* 261–278.

Goethals, G. R., Allison, S. J., & Frost, M. (1979). Perceptions of the magnitude and diversity of social support. *Journal of Experimental Social Psychology, 15,* 570–581.

Goethals, G. R., Cooper, J., & Naficy, A. (1979). Role of foreseen, foreseeable, unforeseeable behavioral consequences in the arousal of cognitive dissonance. *Journal of Personality and Social Psychology, 37,* 1179–1185.

Goethals, G. R., & Darley, J. M. (1977). Social comparison theory: An attributional approach. In J. M. Suls & R. L. Miller (Eds.), *Social comparison processes: Theoretical and empirical perspectives.* Washington, D.C.: Hemisphere/Halsted.

Goethals, G. R., & Darley, J. M. (1987). Social comparison theory: Self-evaluation and group life. In B. Mullen & G. R. Goethals (Eds.), *Theories of group behavior.* New York: Springer-Verlag.

Goethals, G. R., Messick, D. M., & Allison, S. T. (1990). The uniqueness bias: Studies of constructive social comparison. In J. Suls & T. A. Wills, (Eds.), *Social comparison: Contemporary theory and research.* Hillsdale, N. J.: Erlbaum.

Goethals, G. R., & Reckman, R. F. (1973). The perception of consistency in attitudes. *Journal of Experimental Social Psychology, 9,* 491–501.

Goffman, E. (1955). On face work: An analysis of ritual elements in social interaction. *Psychiatry, 18,* 213–231.

Goffman, E. (1959). *The presentation of self in everyday life.* Garden City, N.Y.: Doubleday/Anchor.

Goffman, E. (1967). *Interaction ritual.* New York: Doubleday/Anchor.

Goldberg, S. (1989). Grievance meditation: A successful alternative to labor arbitration. *Negotiation Journal, 5,* 9–16.

Goldsmith, H. H. (1983). Genetic influences on personality from infancy to adulthood. *Child Development, 54,* 331–355.

Golledge, R. G. (1987). Environmental cognition. In D. Stokols & I. Altman (Eds.), *Handbook of environmental psychology* (Vol. 1, pp. 131–174). New York: Wiley.

Goodman, P. S., & Garber, S. (1988). Absenteeism and accidents in a dangerous environment: Empirical analysis of underground coal mine. *Journal of Applied Psychology, 73,* 81–86.

Goodstadt, M. (1971). Helping and refusal to help: A test of balance and reactance theories. *Journal of Experimental Social Psychology, 7,* 610–622.

Goranson, R. E., & Berkowitz, L. (1966). Reciprocity and responsibility reactions to prior help. *Journal of Personality and Social Psychology, 3,* 227–232.

Gorenflo, D. W., & Crano, W. D. (1989). Judgemental subjectivity/objectivity and locus of choice in social comparison. *Journal of Personality and Social Psychology, 57,* 605–614.

Gouldner, A. (1960). Th norm of reciprocity: A preliminary statement. *American Sociological Review, 25,* 161–178.

Gralnick, A. (1988). Trust, deterrence, realism, and nuclear omnicide. *Political Psychology, 9,* 175–188.

Graumann, C. F. (1988). Introduction to a history of social psychology. In M. Hewstone, W. Stroebe, J. Codol, & G. M. Stephenson (Eds.), *Introduction to social psychology.* Oxford, England: Basil Blackwell.

Greenberg, J., & Musham, C. (1981). Avoiding and seeking self-focused attention. *Journal of Research in Personality, 15,* 191–200.

Greenberg, J., Pyszczynski, T., & Solomon, S. (1982). The self-serving attributional bias: Beyond self-presentation. *Journal of Experimental Social Psychology, 18,* 56–67.

Greenwald, A. G. (1980). The totalitarian ego: Fabrication and revision of personal history. *American Psychologist, 35,* 603–613.

Greenwald, A. G., & Ronis, D. L. (1978). Twenty years of cognitive dissonance: Case study of the evolution of a theory. *Psychological Review, 85,* 53–57.

Griffin, B. Q., & Rogers, R. W. (1977). Reducing interracial aggression: Inhibiting effects of victim's suffering and power to retaliate. *Journal of Psychology, 95,* 151–157.

Griffitt, W. (1970). Environmental effects on interpersonal affective behavior: Ambient effective temperature and attraction. *Journal of Personality and Social Psychology, 15,* 240–244.

Griffitt, W., & Guay, P. (1969). "Object" evaluation and conditioned affect. *Journal of Experimental Research in Personality, 4,* 1–8.

Griffitt, W., & Veitch, R. (1974). Preacquaintance attitude similarity and attraction revisited: Ten days in a fallout shelter. *Sociometry, 37,* 163–173.

Gross, A. E., Wallston, B. S., & Piliavin, I. M. (1975). Beneficiary attractiveness and costs as determinants of responses to routine requests for help. *Sociometry, 38,* 131–140.

Gross, E., & Latané, J. G. (1974). Receiving help, reciprocation, and interpersonal attraction. *Journal of Applied Social Psychology, 4,* 210–223.

Gruder, C. L. (1977). Choice of comparison persons in evaluating oneself. In J. M. Suls & R. L. Miller (Eds.), *Social comparison processes: Theoretical and empirical perspectives.* Washington, D.C.: Hemisphere/Halsted.

Gruder, C. L., Romer, D., & Korth, B. (1978). Dependency and fault as determinants of helping. *Journal of Experimental Social Psychology, 14,* 227–235.

Grzelak, J. (1988). Conflict and cooperation. In M. Hewstone, W. Stroebe, J. Codol, & G. M. Stephenson (Eds.), *Introduction to social psychology* (pp. 288–313). Oxford, England: Blackwell.

Guerin, B., & Innes, J. (1982). Social facilitation and social monitoring: A new look at Zajonc's mere presence hypothesis. *British Journal of Social Psychology, 21,* 7–18.

Gump, P. (1987). School and classroom environments. In D. Stokols & I. Altman (Eds.), *Handbook of environmental psychology* (pp. 691–732). New York: Wiley.

Gunter, B. (1983). Do aggressive people prefer violent television? *Bulletin of the British Psychological Society, 36,* 166–168.

Gurr, T. R. *Why men rebel.* Princeton, N. J.: Princeton University Press.

Haas, D. F., & Deseran, F. A. (1981). Trust and symbolic exchange. *Social Psychology Quarterly, 44,* 3–13.

Haas, J., & Roberts, G. C. (1975). Effect of evaluative others upon learning and performance of a complex motor task. *Journal of Motor Behavior, 7,* 81–90.

Hackman, J. R., Brousseau, K. R., & Wiess, J. A. (1976). The interaction of task design and group performance strategies in determining group effectiveness. *Organizational Behavior and Human Performance, 16,* 350–365.

Hagino, G., Mochizuki, M., & Yamamoto, T. (1987). Environmental psychology in Japan. In D. Stokols & I. Altman (Eds.), *Handbook of environmental psychology* (Vol. 2, pp. 1155–1170). New York: Wiley.

Hall, E. T. (1959). *The silent language.* New York: Fawcett.

Hall, E. T. (1966). *The hidden dimension.* New York: Doubleday.

Hall, J., & Williams, M. S. (1970). Group dynamics training and improved decision making. *Journal of Applied Behavioral Science, 6,* 27–32.

Hall, J. A. (1984). *Nonverbal sex differences: Communication accuracy and expressive style.* Baltimore: Johns Hopkins University Press.

Hall, J. A., & Taylor, S. E. (1976). When love is blind: Maintaining idealized images of one's spouse. *Human Relations, 29,* 751–761.

Halpin, A., & Winer, B. (1952). *The leadership behavior of the airplane commander.* Columbus: Ohio State University Research Foundation.

Hamblin, R. (1958). Leadership and crisis. *Sociometry, 21,* 322–335.

Hamilton, D. L. (1979). A cognitive attributional analysis of stereotyping. In L. Berkowitz (Ed.), *Advances in experimental social psychology* (Vol. 12, pp. 53–84). New York: Academic Press.

Hamilton, D. L. (Ed.), (1981). *Cognitive processes in stereotyping and intergroup behavior.* Hillsdale, N.J.: Erlbaum.

Hamilton, D. L. (1981). Cognitive representations of persons. In E. T. Higgins, C. P. Herman, & M. P. Zanna

(Eds.), *Social cognition: The Ontario symposium* (Vol. 1). Hillsdale, N. J.: Erlbaum.

Hamilton, D. L., & Gifford, R. K. (1976). Illusory correlation in interpersonal perception: A cognitive basis of stereotypic judgments. *Journal of Experimental Social Psychology, 12,* 392–407.

Hamilton, D. L., & Sherman, S. J. (in press). Illusory correlations: Implications for stereotype theory and research. In D. Bar-Tal, C. F. Graumann, A. W. Kruglanski, & W. Stoebe (Eds.), *Stereotypes and prejudice: Changing conceptions.* New York: Springer-Verlag.

Hamilton, D. L., & Trollier, T. (1986). Stereotypes and stereotyping: An overview of the cognitive approach. In J. Dovidio & S. L. Gaertner (Eds.), *Prejudice, discrimination, and racism.* New York: Academic Press.

Hammock, T., & Brehm, J. W. (1966). The attractiveness of choice alternatives when freedom to choose is eliminated by a social agent. *Journal of Personality, 34,* 546–554.

Hamner, W. C. (1974). Effects of bargaining strategy and pressure to reach agreement in a stalemated negotiation. *Journal of Personality and Social Psychology, 30,* 458–467.

Hancock, R. D., & Sorrentino, R. M. (1980). The effects of expected future interaction and prior group support on the conformity process. *Journal of Experimental Social Psychology, 16,* 261–270.

Hansen, C. H., & Hansen, R. D. (1988). Finding the face in the crowd: An anger superiority effect. *Journal of Personality and Social Psychology, 54,* 917–924.

Hansen, C. H., Hansen, R. D., & Crano, W. D. (1989). Sympathetic arousal and self-attention: The accessibility of interceptive and exteroceptive arousal cues. *Journal of Experimental Social Psychology, 25,* 437–449.

Hardin, G. (1968). The tragedy of the commons. *Science, 162,* 1243–1248.

Hardy, R. C. (1976). A test of the poor leader: Member relations cells of the contingency model on elementary school children. *Child Development, 46,* 958–964.

Harkins, S. G., & Petty, R. E. (1981a). The effects of source magnification of cognitive effect on attitudes. An information-processing view. *Journal of Personality and Social Psychology, 40,* 401–413.

Harkins, S. G., & Petty, R. E. (1981b). The multiple source effect in persuasion: The effects of distraction. *Personality and Social Psychology Bulletin, 7,* 627–635.

Harkins, S. G., & Petty, R. E. (1983). Social context effects in persuasion: The effects of multiple sources and multiple targets. In P. Paulus (Ed.), *Basic group processes* (pp. 149–175). New York: Springer-Verlag.

Harkins, S. G., & Petty, R. E. (1987). Information utility and the multiple source effect. *Journal of Personality and Social Psychology, 52,* 260–268.

Harkins, S. G., & Szymanski, K. (1989). Social loafing and group evolution. *Journal of Personality and Social Psychology, 56,* 934–941.

Harris, B. (1986). Reviewing 50 years of the psychology of social issues. *Journal of Social Issues, 42,* 1–20.

Harris, M. B. (1974). Mediators between frustration and aggression in a field experiment. *Journal of Experimental Social Psychology, 10,* 561–571.

Harris, R. F., & Lindsay, D. (1972). *The state of cities.* New York: Praeger.

Harris, M. J., & Rosenthal, R. (1985). Mediation of interpersonal expectancy effects: 31 meta-analyses. *Psychological Bulletin, 97,* 363–386.

Harris, R., & Snyder, C. R. (1986). The role of uncertain self-esteem in self-handicapping. *Journal of Personality and Social Psychology, 51,* 451–458.

Harris, R. F., & Lindsay, D. (1972). *The state of cities.* New York: Praeger.

Hass, R. G. (1981). Effects of source characteristics on cognitive responses and persuasion. In R. E. Perry, T. M. Ostrom, & T. C. Brock (Eds.), *Cognitive responses in persuasion* (pp. 141–172). Hillsdale: N.J.: Erlbaum.

Hass, R. G., & Grady, K. (1975). Temporal delay, type of forewarning, and resistance to influence. *Journal of Experimental Social Psychology, 11,* 459–469.

Hastie, R. (1980). Schematic principles in human memory. In E. T. Higgins, C. P. Herman, & M. P. Zanna (Eds.), *Person memory: The cognition basis of social perception.* Hillsdale, N.J.: Erlbaum.

Hastie, R. (1984). Causes and effects of causal attribution. *Journal of Personality and Social Psychology, 46,* 44–56.

Hastie, R., Penrod, S. D., & Pennington, N. (1984). *Inside the jury.* Cambridge, Mass.: MIT Press.

Hatfield, E., & Sprecher, S. (1986). *Mirror, mirror. . . :The importance of looks in everyday life.* Albany: SUNY Press.

Hatfield, E., & Traupmann, J. (1980). Intimate relationships: A perspective from equity theory. In S. Duck & R. Gilmour (Eds.), *Studying Personal Relationships.* London: Academic Press.

Hatfield, E., Traupmann, J., Sprecher, S., Utne, M., & Hay, J. (1985). Equity and intimate relations: Recent research. In W. Ickes (Ed.), *Compatible and incompatible relationships.* New York: Springer-Verlag.

Hayduk, L. *The vertical profile of personal space.* Unpublished. Edmonton, Canada: University of Alberta.

Hayduk, L. A. (1978). Personal space: An evaluative and orienting overview. *Psychological Bulletin, 85,* 117–134.

Hayduk, L. A. (1983). Personal space: Where we now stand. *Psychological Bulletin, 94,* 293–335.

Hazlewood, J. E., & Olson, J. M. (1986). Covariation information, causal questioning, and interpersonal behavior. *Journal of Experimental Social Psychology, 22,* 276–291.

Heberlein, T. A. (1989). Attitudes and environmental management. *Journal of Social Issues, 45,* 37–58.

Hediger, H. (1950). *Wild animals in captivity.* London: Butterworth.

Heft, H., & Wohwill, J. F. (1987). Environmental cognition in children. In E. Stokols & I. Altman (Eds.), *Handbook of environmental psychology* (Vol. 1, pp. 175–204). New York: Wiley.

Heider, F. (1944). Social perception and phenomenal causality. *Psychological Review, 51,* 358–374.

Heider, F. (1946). Attitudes and cognitive organization. *Journal of Psychology, 21,* 107–112.

Heider, F. (1958). *The psychology of interpersonal relations.* New York: Wiley.

Henchy, T., & Glass, D. C. (1968). Evaluation apprehension and the social facilitation of dominant and subordinate responses. *Journal of Personality and Social Psychology, 10,* 446–454.

Hendrick, S. S. (1981). Self-disclosure and marital satisfaction. *Journal of Personality and Social Psychology, 40,* 1150–1159.

Henley, N. M. (1977). *Body politics: Power, sex, and nonverbal communication.* Englewood Cliffs, N.J.: Prentice-Hall.

Hepworth, J. T., & West, S. G. (1988). Lynchings and the economy: A time-series reanalysis of Hovland and Sears (1940). *Journal of Personality and Social Psychology, 55,* 239–247.

Herr, P. M. (1986). Consequences of priming: Judgment and

behavior. *Journal of Personality and Social Psychology, 51,* 1106–1115.

Hess, E. H. (1965). The pupil responds to changes in attitude as well as to change in illumination. *Scientific American, 212,* 46-54.

Hesselgren, S. (1975). *Man's perception of man-made environment.* Stroudsburg, Pa.: Dowden, Hutchinson & Ross.

Heyerdahl, T. (1950). *Kon-Tiki.* Chicago: Rand McNally.

Higgins, E. T. (1989). Self-discrepancy theory: What patterns of self-beliefs cause people to suffer? In L. Berkowitz (Ed.), *Advances in experimental social psychology* (Vol. 22 pp. 181–227). San Diego: Academic Press.

Higgins, E. T., Bond, R. N., Klein, R., & Strauman, T. (1986). Self-discrepancies and emotional vulnerability: How magnitude, accessibility, and type of discrepancy influence affect. *Journal of Personality and Social Psychology, 51,* 5–15.

Higgins, E. T., & King, G. (1981). Accessibility of social constructs: Information-processing consequences of individual and contextual variability. In N. Cantor & J. F. Kihlstrom (Eds.), *Personality, cognition, and social interaction.* Hillsdale, N.J.: Erlbaum.

Higgins, E. T., & McCann, C. D. (1984). Social encoding and subsequent attitudes, impressions, and memory: Context-driven and motivational aspects of processing. *Journal of Personality and Social Psychology, 47,* 26–39.

Higgins, E. T., Rhodewalt, F., & Zanna, M. P. (1979). Dissonance motivation: Its nature, persistance, and reinstatement. *Journal of Experimental Social Psychology, 15,* 16–34.

Higgins, E. T., & Rholes, W. S. (1978). "Saying is believing": Effects of message modification on memory and liking for the person described. *Journal of Experimental Social Psychology, 14,* 363–378.

Higgins, E. T., Rholes, W. S., & Jones, C. R. (1977). Category accessibility and impression formation. *Journal of Experimental Social Psychology, 13,* 141–154.

Hiltrop, J. M., & Rubin, J. Z. (1981). Position loss and image loss in bargaining. *Journal of Conflict Resolution, 25,* 521–534.

Hinkle, S., & Schopler, J. (1986). Bias in the evaluation of in-group and out-group performance. In S. Worchel & W. Austin (Eds.), *Psychology of intergroup relations.* Chicago: Nelson-Hall.

Hinkle, S., Taylor, L. S., Fox-Cardamone, D. L., & Crook, J. (1989). Intragroup identification and intergroup differentiation: A multi-component approach. *British Journal of Social Psychology, 28,* 305–317.

Hiroto, D. S., & Seligman, M. E. P. (1975). Generality of learned helplessness in man. *Journal of Personality and Social Psychology, 31,* 311–327.

Hirshleifer, J., & Coll, J. (1988). What strategies can support the evolutionary emergence of cooperation? *Journal of Conflict Resolution, 32,* 367–398.

Hofling, C. K., Brotzman, E., Dalrymple, S., Graves, N., & Pierce, C. M. (1966). An experimental study in nurse-physician relationships. *Journal of Nervous and Mental Diseases, 143*(2), 171–180.

Hokanson, J. E., Burgess, M., & Cohen, M. F. (1963). Effect of displaced aggression on systolic blood pressure. *Journal of Abnormal and Social Psychology, 67,* 214–218.

Hokanson, J. E., & Shelter, S. (1961). The effect of overt aggression on physiological arousal level. *Journal of Abnormal and Social Psychology, 63,* 446–448.

Holahan, C. J. (1982). *Environmental psychology.* New York: Random House.

Hollander, E. P. (1958). Conformity, status and idiosyncrasy credit. *Psychological Review, 65,* 117–127.

Hollander, E. P. (1978). *Leadership dynamics: A practical guide to effective relationships.* New York: Free Press/Macmillan.

Hollander, E. P. (1985). Leadership and power. In G. Lindzey & E. Aronson (Eds.), *Handbook of social psychology* (3rd ed., Vol. 2, pp. 485–537). New York: Random House.

Holtgraves, T., Srull, T. K., & Socall, D. (1989). Conversation memory: The effects of speaker status on memory for the assertiveness of conversation remarks. *Journal of Personality and Social Psychology, 56,* 149–160.

Hopper, R. (1950). The revolutionary process. *Social Forces, xxviii,* 270–279.

Horner, M. S. (1970). Femininity and successful achievement: A basic inconsistency. In J. Bardwick, E. L. Douvan, M. S. Horner, & D. Gutmann (Eds.), *Feminine Personality and conflict.* Pacific Grove, Calif.: Brooks/Cole.

Hosch, H. M., & Platz, S. J. (1984). Self-monitoring and eyewitness accuracy. *Personality and Social Psychology Bulletin, 10,* 289–292.

Houseknecht, R. (1977). Reference group support for voluntary childlessness. *Journal of Marriage and the Family, 39,* 285–292.

Hovland, C. I., Harvey, O., & Sherif, M. (1957). Assimilation and contrast effects in communication and attitude change. *Journal of Abnormal and Social Psychology, 55,* 242–252.

Hovland, C. I., Janis, I. L, & Kelley, H. H. (1953). *Communication and persuasion.* New Haven, Conn.: Yale University Press.

Hovland, C. I., Lumsdaine, A., & Sheffield, F. (1949). *Experiments on mass communications* (Studies in social psychology in World War II, Vol. 3, published by Social Science Research Council, 226). Princeton, N.J.: Princeton University Press.

Hovland, C. I., & Sears, R. R. (1940). Minor studies in aggression: VI. Correlation of lynchings with economic indices. *Journal of Psychology, 9,* 301–310.

Hovland, C. I., & Weiss, W. (1952). The influence of source credibility on communication effectiveness. *Public Opinion Quarterly, 15,* 635–650.

Howard, J. W., & Rothbart, M. (1980). Social categorization and memory for in-group and out-group behavior. *Journal of Personality and Social Psychology, 38,* 301–310.

Howe, K. G., & Zanna, M. P. (1975). *Sex appropriateness of the task and achievement behavior.* Paper read at Eastern Psychological Association, New York.

Howells, L. T., & Becker, S. W. (1962). Seating arrangement and leadership emergence. *Journal of Abnormal and Social Psychology, 64,* 148–150.

Huesmann, L. F., Logerspetz, K., & Eron, L. D. (1984). Intervening variables in the TV violence-aggression relation: Evidence from two countries. *Developmental Psychology, 20*(5), 746–775.

Huesmann, L. R. (1982). Television violence and aggressive behavior. In D. Pearl & L. Bouthilet (Eds.), *Television and behavior: Ten years of scientific progress and implications for the 80's.* Washington, D.C.: U.S. Government Printing Office.

Hui, C. H. (1986). Fifteen years of pornography research: Does exposure to pornography have any effects? *Bulletin of the Hong Kong Psychological Society, 16–17,* 41–62.

Hull, J. G., Van Treuren, R. R., & Propsom, P. M. (1988). Attributional style and the components of hardiness. *Personality and Social Psychology Bulletin, 14,* 505–513.

Huston, A. C. (1983). Sex-typing. In P. H. Mussen and E. M.

Hetherinton (Eds.), *Handbook of child psychology.* New York: Wiley.

Huston, T. L. (1973). Ambiguity of acceptance, social desirability, and dating choice. *Journal of Experimental Social Psychology, 9,* 32–42.

Huston, T. L., & Levinger, G. (1978). Interpersonal attraction and relationships. *Annual Review of Psychology, 29,* 115–156.

Hymes, R. W. (1986). Political attitudes as social categories: A new look at selective memory. *Journal of Personality and Social Psychology, 51,* 233–241.

Imada, A. S., & Hakel, M. D. (1977). Influence of nonverbal communication and rater proximity on impressions and decisions in simulated employment interview. *Journal of Applied Psychology, 62,* 295–300.

Ingram, R. E., Cruet, D., Johnson, B. R., & Wisnicki, K. S. (1988). Self-focused attention, gender, gender role, and vulnerability to negative affect. *Journal of Personality and Social Psychology, 55,* 967–978.

Insko, C. A. (1965). Verbal reinforcement of attitude. *Journal of Personality and Social Psychology, 2,* 621–623.

Insko, C. A., Thibaut, J., Moehle, D., Wilson, M., Diamond, W. D., Gilmore, R., Soloman, M. K., & Lipsitz, A. (1980). Social evolution and the emergence of leadership. *Journal of Personality and Social Psychology, 39,* 431–449.

Isen, A. M. (1970). Success, failure, attention, and reactions to others: The warm glow of success. *Journal of Personality and Social Psychology, 15,* 294–301.

Isen, A. M., Clark, M., & Schwartz, M. F. (1976). Duration of the effect of good mood on helping: "Foot-prints on the sands of time." *Journal of Personality and Social Psychology, 34,* 385–393.

Isen, A. M., & Levin, P. F. (1972). The effect of feeling good on helping: Cookies and kindness. *Journal of Personality and Social Psychology, 21,* 284–388.

Isen, A. M., & Simmonds, S. F. (1978). The effect of feeling good on a helping task that is incompatible with good mood. *Social Psychology, 41,* 346–349.

Isenberg, D. J. (1986). Group polarization: A critical review and meta-analysis. *Journal of Personality and Social Psychology, 50,* 1141–1151.

Ittelson, W. H., Proshansky, H. M., Rivlin, L. G., & Winkel, G. (1974). *An introduction to environmental psychology.* New York: Holt, Rinehart & Winston.

Jackson, J. M. (1986). In defense of social impact theory: Comment on Mullen. *Journal of Personality and Social Psychology, 50,* 511–513.

Jackson, J. M. (1987). Social impact theory. In B. Mullen & G. R. Goethals, *Theories of group behavior.* New York: Springer-Verlag.

Jackson, J. M., & Latané, B. (1981). All alone in front of all those people: Stage fright as a function of number and type of co-performance and audience. *Journal of Personality and Social Psychology, 40,* 73–85.

Jacobs, R. C., & Campbell, D. T. (1961). The perpetuation of an arbitrary tradition through several generations of a laboratory misoculture. *Journal of Abnormal and Social Psychology, 62,* 649–658.

Jacobs, T. O. (1971). *Leadership and exchange in formal organizations.* Alexandria, Va.: Human Resources Research Organization.

James, K. (1986). Priming and social categorizational factors: Impact on awareness of emergency situations. *Personality and Social Psychology Bulletin, 12,* 462–467.

James, W. (1890). *Psychology.* New York: Holt.

Janis, I. (1982). *Groupthink* (2nd ed). Boston: Houghton Mifflin.

Janis, I. L. (1972). *Victims of groupthink: A psychological study of foreign policy decisions and fiascoes.* Boston: Houghton Mifflin.

Janis, I. L., & Feshbach, S. (1953). Effects of fear-arousing communications. *Journal of Abnormal and Social Psychology, 48,* 78–92.

Janis, I. L., Kaye, D., & Kirschner, P. (1965). Facilitating effects of "eating-while-reading" on responsiveness to persuasive communications. *Journal of Personality and Social Psychology, 1,* 181–186.

Janis, I. L., & Mann, L. (1977). *Decision making: A psychological analysis of conflict, choice, and commitment.* New York: Free Press.

Jensen, A. R. (1969). How much can we boost IQ and scholastic achievement? *Harvard Educational Review, 39,* 1–123.

John, M., Eckardt, G., & Hiebsch, H. (1989). Kurt Lewin's early intentions (Dedicated to his 100th birthday). *European Journal of Social Psychology, 19,* 163–169.

Johnson, H. G., Ekman, P., & Friesen, W. V. (1975). Communicative body movements: American emblems. *Semiotica, 15,* 335–353.

Johnson, R. C., & Ogasawara, G. M. (1988). Within and across-group dating in Hawaii. *Social Biology, 35,* 103–109.

Johnson, R. D., & Downing, L. L. (1979). Deindividuation and violence of cues: Effects of prosocial and antisocial behavior. *Journal of Personality and Social Psychology, 37,* 1532–1538.

Johnson, R. J., Feigenbaum, R., & Weiby, M. (1964). Some determinants and consequences of the teacher's perception of causation. *Journal of Educational Psychology, 55,* 237–246.

Jones, E. E. (1964). *Ingratiation.* New York: Irvington.

Jones, E. E. (1985). Major developments in social psychology during the past five decades. In G. Lindzey & E. Aronson (Eds.), *Handbook of social psychology* (3rd ed., Vol. 1, pp. 1–46). New York: Random House.

Jones, E. E., & Archer, R. L. (1976). Are there special effects of personalistic self-disclosure? *Journal of Experimental Social Psychology, 12,* 180–193.

Jones, E. E., Bell, L., & Aronson, E. (1972). The reciprocation of attraction from similar and dissimilar others: A study in person perception and evaluation. In C. C. McClintock (Ed.), *Experimental social psychology.* New York: Holt, Rinehart & Winston.

Jones, E. E., & Berglas, S. (1978). Control of attributions about the self through self-handicapping strategies: The appeal of alcohol and the role of underachievement. *Personality and Social Psychology Bulletin, 4(2),* 200–206.

Jones, E. E., & Davis, K. E. (1965). From acts to dispositions: The attribution process in person perception. In L. Berkowitz (Ed.), *Advances in experimental social psychology* (Vol. 2). New York: Academic Press.

Jones, E. E., Davis, K. E., & Gergen, K. (1961). Role playing variations and their informational value for person perception. *Journal of Abnormal and Social Psychology, 63,* 302–310.

Jones, E. E., Farina, A., Hastorf, A. H., Markus, H., Miller, D. T., & Scott, R. A. (1984). *Social stigma: The psychology of marked relationships.* New York: Freeman.

Jones, E. E., & Gerard, H. (1967). *Foundations of social psychology.* New York: Wiley.

Jones, E. E., Gergen, K. J., & Jones, R. G. (1964). Tactics of ingratiation among leaders and subordinates in a status hierarchy. *Psychological Monographs, 77*(3, whole no. 566).

Jones, E. E., & Gordon, E. M. (1972). Timing of self-disclosure and its effects on personal attraction. *Journal of Personality and Social Psychology, 24,* 358–365.

Jones, E. E., & Jones, R. G. (1964). Optimum conformity as an ingratiation tactic. *Journal of Personality, 32,* 436–458.

Jones, E. E., & Nisbett, R. E. (1971). *The actor and the observer: Divergent perceptions of the causes of behavior.* Morristown, N.J.: General Learning Press.

Jones, E. E., & Pittman, T. S. (1982). Toward a general theory of strategic self presentation. In J. Suls (Ed.), *Psychological perspectives on the self.* Hillsdale, N.J.: Erlbaum.

Jones, E. E., Rhodewalt, F., Berglas, S., & Skelton, J. A. (1981). Effects of strategic self-presentation on subsequent self-esteem. *Journal of Personality and Social Psychology, 41,* 407–421.

Jones, E. E., Rock, L., Shaver, K. G., Goethals, G. R., & Ward, L. M. (1968b). Pattern of performance and ability attribution: An unexpected primacy effect. *Journal of Personality and Social Psychology, 10,* 317–340.

Jones, E. E., & Sigall, H. (1971). The bogus pipeline: A new paradigm for measuring affect and attitude. *Psychological Bulletin, 76,* 349–364.

Jones, E. E., Wood G. C., & Quattrone, G. A. (1981). Perceived variability of personal characteristics in in-groups and out-groups: The role of knowledge and evaluation. *Personality and Social Psychology Bulletin, 7,* 523–528.

Jones, E. E., & Wortman, C. (1973). *Ingratiation: An attributional approach.* Morristown, N.J.: General Learning Press.

Jones, R. A., & Brehm, J. W. (1970). Persuasiveness of one and two-sided communications as a function of awareness there are two sides. *Journal of Experimental Social Psychology, 6,* 47–56.

Jones, R. A., Linder, D. E., Kiesler, C. A., Zanna, M., & Brehm, J. W. (1968a). Internal states or external stimuli: Observers' attitude judgements and the dissonance theory-self-persuasion controversy. *Journal of Experimental Social Psychology, 4,* 247–269.

Jones, T. (1980). *Adrift.* New York: Avon.

Josephson, W. (1987). Television violence and children's aggression: Testing the priming, social script, and disinhibition predictions. *Journal of Personality and Social Psychology, 53,* 882–890.

Jourard, S. M. (1971). *The transparent self* (2nd ed.). New York: Van Nostrand Reinhold.

Judd, C. M., & Park, B. (1988). Out-group homogeneity: Judgments of variability at the individual and group levels. *Journal of Personality and Social Psychology, 54,* 778–788.

Julian, J. W., Regula, C. R., & Hollander, E. P. (1968). Effects of prior agreement from others on task confidence and conformity. *Journal of Personality and Social Psychology, 9,* 171–178.

Jussim, L., Coleman, L. M., & Lerch, L. (1987). The nature of stereotypes: A comparison and integration of three theories. *Journal of Personality and Social Psychology, 56,* 536–546.

Kabanoff, B. (1981). A critique of leader match and its implication for leadership research. *Personnel Psychology, 34,* 749–764.

Kahn, A., & Tice, T. (1973). Returning a favor and retaliating harm: The effects of stated intentions and actual behavior. *Journal of Experimental Social Psychology, 9,* 43–56.

Kahneman, D., & Tversky, A. (1973). On the psychology of prediction. *Psychological Review, 80,* 237–251.

Kalmuss, D. (1984). The intergenerational transmission of marital aggression. *Journal of Marriage and Family, 47,* 11–19.

Kamin, L. J. (1974). *The science and politics of I.Q.* Hillsdale, N.J.: Erlbaum.

Kandel, D. (1978). Homophily, selection and socialization in adolescent friendships. *American Journal of Sociology, 84,* 427–436.

Kaplan, M. F. (1987). The influencing process in group decision making. In C. Hendrick (Ed.), *Group processes* (pp. 189–212). Newbury Park, Calif.: Sage.

Kardes, F. R., Sanbonmatsu, D. M., Voss, R. T., & Fazio, R. H. (1986). Self-monitoring and attitude accessibility. *Personality and Social Psychology Bulletin, 12,* 468–474.

Karlins, M., Coffman, J., & Walters, G. (1969). On the fading of social stereotypes: Studies in three generations of college students. *Journal of Personality and Social Psychology, 13,* 1–16.

Karuza, J., Jr., & Brickman, P. (1981). Preference for similarity in higher and lower status others. *Personality and Social Psychology Bulletin, 7,* 504–508.

Kassin, S. M. (1985). Eyewitness identification: Retrospective self-awareness and the accuracy-confidence correlation. *Journal of Personality and Social Psychology, 49,* 878–893.

Katovich, M. (1986). Ceremonial openings in bureaucratic encounters: From shuffling feet to shuffling papers. In N. K. Denzin (Ed.), *Studying in symbolic interaction* (Vol. 6). Greenwich, Conn.: JAI Press.

Katz, D., & Braly, K. W. (1933). Racial stereotypes of 100 college students. *Journal of Abnormal and Social Psychology, 28,* 280–290.

Katz, D., & Kahn, R. L. (1978). *The social psychology of organizations* (2nd ed.). New York: Wiley.

Katz, H., Cadoret, R., Hughes, R., & Abbey, D. (1965). Physiological correlates of acceptable and unacceptable attitude statements. *Psychological Reports, 17,* 78.

Katz, I. (1981). *Stigma: A social psychological analysis.* Hillsdale, N.J.: Erlbaum.

Katz, I., & Hass, R. G. (1988). Racial ambivalence and American value conflict: Correlational and priming studies of dual cognitive structures. *Journal of Personality and Social Psychology, 55,* 893–905.

Katz, I., Wackenhut, J., & Hass, R. G. (1986). Racial ambivalence, value duality, and behavior. In J. F. Dovidio & S. L. Gaertner (Eds.), *Prejudice, discrimination, and racism* (pp. 35–60). New York: Academic Press.

Katz, J., Glucksberg, S., & Krauss, I. (1960). Need satisfaction and Edwards PPS scores in married couples. *Journal of Consulting Psychology, 24,* 205–208.

Keegan, J. (1987). *The mask of command.* New York: Viking.

Kelley, H. H. (1950). The warm-cold variable in first impressions of persons. *Journal of Personality, 18,* 431–439.

Kelley, H. H. (1952). Two functions of reference groups. In G. E. Swanson, T. M. Newcomb, & E. L. Hartley (Eds.), *Readings in social psychology* (2nd ed.). New York: Holt, Rinehart & Winston.

Kelley, H. H. (1966). A classroom study of the dilemmas in interpersonal negotiations. In K. Archibald (Ed.), *Strategic interaction and conflict.* Berkeley: Institution of International Studies, University of California.

Kelley, H. H. (1967). Attribution theory in social psychology. In D. Levine (Ed.), *Nebraska symposium on motivation, 15,* 192–238.

Kelley, H. H. (1972). Attribution in social interaction. In E. E. Jones, D. E. Kanouse, H. H. Kelley, R. E. Nisbett, S. Valins, & B. Weiner (Eds.), *Attribution: Perceiving the causes of behavior.* Morristown, N.J.: General Learning Press.

Kelley, H. H. (1979). *Personal relationships: Their structures and processes.* Hillsdale, N.J.: Erlbaum.

Kelley, H. H. (1982). Love and commitment. In H. H. Kelley, E. Berscheid, A. Christensen, J. Harvey, T. L. Huston, G. Levinger, & D. R. Peterson (Eds.), *The psychology of close relationships.* New York: Academic Press.

Kelley, H. H., & Stahelski, A. J. (1970a). Errors in perception of intentions in a mixed motive game. *Journal of Experimental Social Psychology, 6,* 379–400.

Kelley, H. H., & Stahelski, A. J. (1970b). Social interaction basis of cooperators and competitors' beliefs about others. *Journal of Personality and Social Psychology, 16,* 66–91(6).

Kelley, H. H., & Thibaut, J. W. (1978). *Interpersonal relations: A theory of interdependence.* New York: Wiley Interscience.

Kellogg, R., & Baron, R. S. (1975). Attribution theory, insomnia, and the reverse placebo effect: A reversal of Storms and Nisbett's findings. *Journal of Personality and Social Psychology, 32,* 231–236.

Kelly, J. G., Ferson, J. E., & Holtzman, W. H. (1958). The measurement of attitudes toward the Negro in the South. *Journal of Social Psychology, 48,* 305–312.

Kelman, H. C. (1961). Processes of opinion change. *Public Opinion Quarterly, 25,* 57–78.

Kelman, H. C., & Hovland, C. I. (1953). "Reinstatement" of the communicator in delayed measurement of opinion change. *Journal of Abnormal and Social Psychology, 48,* 326–335.

Kenny, D. A. (1985). Quantitative methods for social psychology. In G. Lindzey & E. Aronson (Eds.), *Handbook of social psychology* (3rd ed., Vol. 1, pp. 1–46). New York: Random House.

Kenny, D. A., & Zaccaro, S. J. (1983). An estimate of variance due to traits in leadership. *Journal of Applied Psychology, 68,* 678–685.

Kenrick, D. T., & Gutierres, S. E. (1980). Contrast effects and judgments of physical attractiveness: When beauty becomes a social problem. *Journal of Personality and Social Psychology, 38,* 131–140.

Kenrick, D. T., Gutierres, S. E., and Goldberg, L. L. (1989). Influence of popular erotica on judgments of strangers and mates. *Journal of Experimental Social Psychology, 25,* 159–167.

Kenrick, D. T., & Trost, M. R. (1987). A biosocial model of heterosexual relationships. In K. Kelley (Ed.), *Males, females, and sexuality: Theory and research.* Albany: SUNY Press.

Kerber, K. W. (1984). The perception of nonemergency helping situations: Costs, rewards, and the altruistic personality. *Journal of Personality, 52,* 177–187.

Kerckhoff, A., & Davis, K. E. (1962). Value consensus and need complementarity in mate selection. *American Sociological Review, 27,* 295–303.

Kernis, M. H., Gannenmann, B. D., & Barclay, L. C. (1989). Stability and level of self-esteem as predictors of anger arousal and hostility. *Journal of Personality of Social Psychology, 56,* 1013–1022.

Kernis, M. H., & Wheeler, L. (1981). Beautiful friends and ugly strangers: Radiation and contrast effects in perception of same-sex pairs. *Personality and Social Psychology Bulletin, 7,* 224–231.

Kerr, N. L. (1983). Motivation loss in small groups: A social dilemma analysis. *Journal of Personality and Social Psychology, 45,* 819–828.

Kerr, N. L., & Brunn, S. (1983). Dependability of member effort and group motivation loss: Free-rider effects. *Journal of Personality and Social Psychology, 44,* 78–94.

Kiesler, C. A., & Kiesler, S. B. (1969). *Conformity.* Reading, Mass.: Addison-Wesley.

Kiesler, C. A., & Munson, P. A. (1975). Attitudes and opinions. In M. R. Rosenzweig & L. W. Porter (Eds.), *Annual Review of Psychology, 26,* 415–456.

Kiesler, C. A., & Pallak, M. S. (1976). Arousal properties of dissonance manipulations. *Psychological Bulletin, 83,* 1014–1025.

Kiesler, C. A., Mathog, R., Pool, P., & Hovenstine, R. (1971). Commitment and the boomerang effect: A field study. Summarized in C. Kiesler (Ed.), *The psychology of commitment: Experiments linking behavior to belief* (pp. 74–85). New York: Academic Press.

Kiesler, S. B., & Baral, R. L. (1970). The search for a romantic partner: The effects of self-esteem and physical attractiveness on romantic behavior. In K. L. Gergen & D. Marlowe (Eds.), *Personality and Social Behavior.* Reading, Mass.: Addison-Wesley.

Kim, H., & Baron, R. S. (1988). Exercise and the illusory correlation: Does arousal heighten stereotypic processing? *Journal of Experimental Social Psychology, 24,* 366–380.

Kinder, D. R., & Fiske, S. T. (1986). Presidents in the public mind. In M. G. Hermann (Ed.), *Political psychology.* San Francisco: Jossey-Bass.

Kinder, D. R., Peters, M. D., Ableson, R. R., & Fiske, S. T. (1980). Presidential prototypes. *Political Behavior, 2,* 315–338.

Kinder, D. R., & Sears, D. O. (1981). Prejudice and politics: Symbolic racism versus racial threats to the good life. *Journal of Personality and Social Psychology, 40,* 414–431.

King, C. (1969). *My life with Martin Luther King, Jr.* New York: Holt, Rinehart & Winston.

King, M. L. (1980, March 11). Turned down thermostats turn off workers who face possible federal extension of the rule. *Wall Street Journal.*

Kipnis, D. M. (1974). Inner direction, other direction and achievement motivation. *Human Development, 17,* 321–343.

Kirkland, S. L., Greenberg, J., & Pyszczynski, T. (1987). Further evidence of the deleterious effects of overheard derogatory ethnic labels: Derogation beyond the target. *Personality and Social Psychology Bulletin, 13,* 216–227.

Kleinke, C. L., & Kahn, M. L. (1980). Perceptions of self-disclosers: Effects of sex and physical attractiveness. *Journal of Personality, 48,* 190–205.

Knowles, E. S. (1983). Social physics and the effects of others: Tests of the effects of audience size and distance on social judgments and behavior. *Journal of Personality and Social Psychology, 45,* 1263–1279.

Knox, R. E., & Inkster, J. A. (1968). Postdecision dissonance at post time. *Journal of Personality and Social Psychology, 8(4),* 319–323.

Knox, R. E., & Safford, R. K. (1976). Group caution at the racetrack. *Journal of Experimental Social Psychology, 12,* 317–324.

Kobasa, S. C. (1979). Stressful life events, personality, and health: An inquiry into hardiness. *Journal of Personality and Social Psychology, 37,* 1–11.

Koestner, R., Zuckerman, M., & Koestner, J. (1989). Attributional focus of praise and children's intrinsic motivation: The moderating role of gender. *Personality and Social Psychology Bulletin, 15,* 61–72.

Kohlberg, L. (1966). A cognitive developmental analysis of children's sex-role concepts and attitudes. In E. Maccoby

(Ed.), *The development of sex differences*. Palo Alto, Calif.: Stanford University Press.

Kolditz, T. A., & Arkin, R. M. (1982). An impression management interpretation of the self-handicapping strategy. *Journal of Personality and Social Psychology, 43*, 492–502.

Komaki, J. L. (1986). Toward effective supervision. *Journal of Applied Psychology, 71*, 270–279.

Komaki, J. L., Desselles, M. L., & Bowman, E. (1989). Definitely not a breeze: Extending an operant model of effective supervision to teams. *Journal of Applied Psychology, 74*, 522–529.

Komorita, S. S., & Barth, J. M. (1985). Components of reward and social dilemmas. *Journal of Personality and Social Psychology, 48*, 364–373.

Komorita, S. S., & Kravitz, D. S. (1983). Coalition formation: A social psychological approach. In P. Paulus (Ed.), *Basic group process* (pp. 179–204). New York: Springer-Verlag.

Komorita, S. S., & Miller, C. (1986). Bargaining strength as a function of coalition alternatives. *Journal of Personality and Social Psychology, 51*, 325–332.

Kriss, M., Indenbaum, E., & Tesch, F. (1974). Message type and status of interactants as determinants of telephone helping behavior. *Journal of Personality and Social Psychology, 30*, 856-859.

Krueger, J., & Rothbart, M. (1988). Use of categorical and individuating information in making inferences about personality. *Journal of Personality and Social Psychology, 55*, 187–195.

Krupat, E. (1985). *People in cities: The urban environment and its effects*. Cambridge, England: Cambridge University Press.

Kruse, L., & Graumann, C. F. (1987). Environmental psychology in Germany. In D. Stokols & I. Altman (Eds.), *Handbook of environmental psychology* (Vol. 2, pp. 1195–1226). New York: Wiley.

Kulik, J. A., & Mahler, H. I. M. (1989). Stress and affiliation in a hospital setting: Preoperative roommate preferences. *Personality and Social Psychology, 15*, 183–193.

Küller, L. (1987). Environmental psychology from a Swedish perspective. In D. Stokols & I. Altman (Eds.), *Handbook of environmental psychology* (Vol. 2, pp. 1243–1280). New York: Wiley.

Kunst-Wilson, W. R., & Zajonc, R. B. (1980). Affective discrimination of stimuli that cannot be recognized. *Science, 207*, 557–558.

Kuo, Zing Yang. (1930). The genesis of the cat's response to the rat. *Journal of Comparative Psychology, 11*, 1–35.

Landy, D., & Aronson, E. (1969). The influence of the character of the criminal and his victim on the decisions of simulated jurors. *Journal of Experimental Social Psychology, 5*, 141–152.

Landy, D., & Sigall, H. (1974). Beauty is talent: Task evaluation as a function of the performer's physical attractiveness. *Journal of Personality and Social Psychology, 29*, 299–304.

Langer, E. J. (1978). Rethinking the role of thought in social interaction. In J. H. Harvey, W. Ickes, & R. E. Kidd (Eds.), *New directions in attribution research* (Vol. 2, pp. 35–58). Hillsdale, N.J.: Erlbaum.

Langer, E. J. (1981). Old age: An artifact? In J. McGaush & S. Kiesler (Eds.), *Aging: Biology and behavior*. New York: Academic Press.

Langer, E. J. (1989). Minding matters: The consequences of mindlessness-mindfulness. In L. Berkowitz (Ed.), *Advances in experimental social psychology* (Vol. 22, pp. 137–173). New York: Academic Press.

Langlois, J. H., & Stephan, C. W. (1981). Beauty and the beast: The role of physical attractiveness in the development of peer relations and social behavior. In S. S. Brehm, S. M. Kassin, & F. X. Gibbons (Eds.), *Developmental social psychology*. New York: Oxford University Press.

Lanzetta, J. T., & Englis, B. G. (1989). Expectations of cooperation and competition and their effects on observers' vicarious emotional responses. *Journal of Personality and Social Psychology, 56*, 543–554.

La Pière, R. T. (1934). Attitudes vs. actions. *Social Forces, 13*, 230–237.

Lassiter, G. D., Stone, J. I., & Weigold, M. F. (1987). Effect of leading questions on the self-monitoring-memory correlation. *Personality and Social Psychology Bulletin, 13*, 537–545.

Lasswell, H. D. (1948). The structure and function of communication in society. In L. Bryson (Ed.), *Communication of ideas*. New York: Harper.

Latané, B. (1981). The psychology of social impact. *American Psychologist, 36*, 343–356.

Latané, B., & Darley, J. M. (1970). *The unresponsive bystander: Why doesn't he help?* Englewood Cliffs, N.J.: Prentice-Hall.

Laughlin, P. R., & Earley, C. (1982). Social combination models, persuasive arguments theory, social comparison theory, and choice shift. *Journal of Personality and Social Psychology, 42*, 273–281.

Laughlin, P. R., & Futoran, G. (1985). Collective induction: Social combination and sequential transition. *Journal of Personality and Social Psychology, 48*, 608–613.

Lazarus, R. S. (1982). Thoughts on the relations between emotions and cognition. *American Psychologist, 37*, 1019–1024.

Le Bon, G. (1903). *The crowd* (Trans.). London: Allen & Unwin.

Leary, T. (1957). *Interpersonal diagnosis of personality*. New York: Ronald Press.

Lécuyer, R. (1976). Man's accommodation to space, man's accommodation of space. *Travail Humain, 39*, 195–206.

Lefcourt, H. M. (1982). *Locus of control: Current trends in theory and research* (2nd ed.). Hillsdale, N.J.: Erlbaum.

Leippe, M. R., & Elkin, R. A. (1987). Issue involvement and response involvement as determinants of persuasion. *Journal of Personality and Social Psychology, 52*, 269–278.

Lemyre, L., & Smith, P. (1985). Intergroup discrimination and self-esteem in minimal group paradigm. *Journal of Personality and Social Psychology, 49*, 660–670.

Leonard, K. E., & Taylor, S. P. (1983). Exposure to pornography, permissive and nonpermissive cues, and male aggression toward females. *Motivation and Emotion, 7*, 291–299.

Lepper, M. R., Greene, D., & Nisbett, R. E. (1973). Undermining children's intrinsic interest with extrinsic reward: A test of the overjustification hypothesis. *Journal of Personality and Social Psychology, 28*, 129–137.

Lerner, M. J., & Agar, E. (1972). The consequences of perceived similarity: Attraction and rejection, approach and avoidance. *Journal of Experimental Research in Personality, 6*, 69–75.

Lerner, M. J., & Matthews, G. (1967). Reactions to suffering of others under conditions of indirect responsibility. *Journal of Personality and Social Psychology, 5*, 319–325.

Leung, K., & Lind, E. A. (1986). Procedural justice and culture: Effects of culture, gender, and investigator status on procedural preference. *Journal of Personality and Social Psychology, 50*, 1134–1140.

Leventhal, H., & Niles, P. (1965). Persistence of influence for varying duration of exposure to threat stimuli. *Psychological Reports, 16*, 223–233.

Leventhal, H., Singer, R., & Jones, S. (1965). The effects of fear and specificity of recommendation upon attitudes and behavior. *Journal of Personality and Social Psychology, 2*, 20–29.

Leventhal, H., Watts, J. C., & Pagano, R. (1967). Effects of fear and instructions on how to cope with danger. *Journal of Personality and Social Psychology, 6*, 313–321.

Levinger, G. (1976). A social psychological perspective on marital dissolution. *Journal of Social Issues, 32*, 21–47.

Levinger, G. (1980). Toward the analysis of close relationships. *Journal of Experimental Social Psychology, 16*, 510–544.

Lewin, K. (1935). *A dynamic theory of personality.* New York: McGraw-Hill.

Lewin, K. (1943). Forces behind food habits and methods of change. *Bulletin of the National Research Council, 108*, 35–65.

Lewin, K. (1948). *Resolving social conflicts: Selected papers on group dynamics.* New York: Harper.

Lewin, K., Lippitt, R., & White, R. (1939). Patterns of aggressive behavior in experimentally created social climates. *Journal of Social Psychology, 10*, 271–299.

Lieberman, M. A., Yalom, I. D., & Miles, M. B. (1973). *Encounter groups: First facts.* New York: Basic Books.

Liebowitz, M. R. (1983). Patient's dramatic mood swings present challenge for therapist. *Hospital and Community Psychiatry, 34*, 305–308.

Liebrand, W. B., Jansen, W. T., Ruken, V. M., & Cuhre, C. J. (1986). Might over morality: Social values and the perception of other players in experimental games. *Journal of Experimental Social Psychology, 22*, 203–215.

Likert, R. (1932). A technique for the measurement of attitudes. *Archives of Psychology, 140*, 1–55.

Lind, E. A., Kutz, S., Musante, L., Walker, L., & Thibaut, J. (1980). Procedural and outcome effects on reactions to adjudicated resolution of conflicts of interest. *Journal of Personality and Social Psychology, 39*, 643–653.

Linder, D. E., Cooper, J., & Jones, E. E. (1967). Decision freedom as a determinant of the role of incentive magnitude in attitude change. *Journal of Personality and Social Psychology, 6*, 245–254.

Lindskold, S. (1986). GRIT: Reducing distrust through carefully introduced conciliation. In S. Worchel & W. G. Austin (Eds.), *The psychology of intergroup relations.* Chicago: Nelson-Hall.

Lindskold, S., & Aronoff, J. R. (1980). Conciliatory strategies and relative power. *Journal of Experimental Social Psychology, 16*, 187–198.

Link, S. M., & Pepler, R. D. (1970). Associated fluctuations in daily temperature, productivity, and absenteeism. *ASHRAE Transactions, 76*(2), 326–337.

Linville, P. W. (1982). The complexity-extremity effect and age-based stereotyping. *Journal of Personality and Social Psychology, 42*, 193–211.

Linville, P. W. (1987). Self-complexity as a cognitive buffer against stress-related illness and depression. *Journal of Personality and Social Psychology, 52*, 663–676.

Linville, P. W., & Jones, E. E. (1980). Polarized appraisals of outgroup members. *Journal of Personality and Social Psychology, 38*, 689–703.

Linville, P. W., Salovery, P., & Fischer, G. W. (1986). Stereotyping and perceived distributions of social characteristics: An application to ingroup-outgroup perception. In J. Dovidio & S. Gaertner (Eds.), *Prejudice, discrimination and racism.* New York: Academic Press.

Linz, D., Donnerstein, E., & Adams, S. M. (1989). Physio-logical desensitization and judgments about female victims. *Human Communication Research, 15*, 509–522.

Litt, M. D. (1988). Self-efficacy and perceived control: Cognitive mediators of pain tolerance. *Journal of Personality and Social Psychology, 54*, 149–160.

Little, K. B. (1968). Cultural variations in social schemata. *Journal of Personality and Social Psychology, 10*, 1–7.

Long, G. (1972). *Cohesiveness of high school baseball teams.* Unpublished master's thesis, Southern Illinois University, Carbondale.

Long, G. (1984). Psychological tension and closeness to others: Stress and interpersonal distance preference. *Journal of Psychology, 117*, 143–146.

Lord, C. G., Lepper, M. R., & Mackie, D. (1984). Attitude prototypes as determinants of attitude-behavior consistency. *Journal of Personality and Social Psychology, 46*, 1254–1266.

Lord, C. G., Ross, L., & Lepper, M. R. (1979). Biased assimilation and attitude polarization: The effects of prior theories on subsequently discovered evidence. *Journal of Personality and Social Psychology, 37*, 2098–2109.

Lorenz, K. (1968). *On aggression.* New York: Harcourt, Brace & World.

Loretto, R., & Williams, D. (1974). Personality, behavioral and output variables in a small group task situation: An examination of consensual leader and nonleader differences. *Canadian Journal of Behavioral Science, 6*, 59–74.

Lothstein, L. (1972). Personal space in assault-prone male adolescent prisoners. *Dissertation Abstracts International, 338*, 1271.

Lott, A. J., & Lott, B. E. (1968). A learning theory approach to interpersonal attitudes. In A. G. Greenwald, T. C. Brock, & T. M. Ostrom (Eds.), *Psychological foundations of attitudes.* New York: Academic Press.

Lott, A. J., & Lott, B. E. (1974). The role of reward in the formation of positive interpersonal attitudes. In T. Huston (Ed.), *Foundations of interpersonal attraction.* New York: Academic Press.

Lott, B. E., & Lott, A. J. (1985). Learning theory in contemporary social psychology. In G. Lindzey & E. Aronson (Eds.), *Handbook of social psychology* (3rd ed., Vol. 1, pp. 1-46). New York: Random House.

Love, K., & Aiello, J. (1980). Using projective techniques to measure interaction distance. *Personality and Social Psychology Bulletin, 6*, 102–104.

Luchins, A. (1957a). Experimental attempts to minimize the impact of first impression. In C. Hovland, W. Mandell, E. Campbell, T. Brock, A. Luchins, A. Cohen, W. McGuire, I. Janis, R. Feierabend, & N. Anderson (Eds.), *The order of presentation in persuasion.* New Haven, Conn.: Yale University Press.

Luchins, A. (1957b). Primacy-recency in impression formation. In C. Hovland, W. Mandell, E. Campbell, T. Brock, A. Luchins, A. Cohen, W. McGuire, I. Janis, R. Feierabend, & N. Anderson (Eds.), *The order of presentation in persuasion.* New Haven, Conn.: Yale University Press.

Lydon, J. E., Jamieson, D. W., & Zanna, M. P. (1988). Interpersonal similarity and the social and intellectual dimensions of first impressions. *Social Cognition, 6*(4), 269–286.

Lyle, J., & Hoffman, H. R. (1972). Explorations on patterns of television viewing by preschool-age children. In E. A. Rubenstein, G. A. Comstock, & J. P. Murray (Eds.), *Television and social behavior. Vol. 4. Television in day-to-day life patterns of use.* Washington, D.C.: U.S. Government Printing Office.

Lynch, J. G., Jr., & Cohen, J. (1978). The use of subjective expected utility theory as an aid to understanding variables that influence helping behavior. *Journal of Personality and Social Psychology, 36,* 1138–1151.

Lynch, K. (1960). *The image of the city.* Cambridge, Mass.: MIT Press.

Lynn, M., & Oldenquist, A. (1986). Egoistic and nonegoistic motives in social dilemmas. *American Psychologist, 41,* 529–534.

Maass, A., & Clark, R. D. (1984). Hidden input of minorities: Fifteen years of minority influence research. *Psychological Bulletin, 95,* 428–450.

Maass, A., & Volpato, C. (1989, June). *Theoretical perspectives on minority influence: Conversion vs. divergence.* Paper presented at the 3rd Workshop on Minority Influence, Perugia, Italy.

McArthur, L. Z. (1972). The how and what of why: Some determinants and consequences of causal attribution. *Journal of Personality and Social Psychology, 22,* 171–193.

McArthur, L. Z., & Post, D. (1977). Figural emphasis and person perception. *Journal of Experimental Social Psychology, 13,* 520–535.

Macaulay, J. (1970). A skill for charity. In J. Macaulay & L. Berkowitz (Eds.), *Altruism and helping behavior: Social psychological studies of some antecedents and consequences.* New York: Academic Press.

McBride, G., King, M. G., & James, J. W. (1965). Social proximity effects on galvanic skin responses in adult humans. *Journal of Psychology, 61,* 153–157.

McCain, G., Cox, V., Paulus, P., Luke, A., & Abadzi, H. (1985). The reduction of crowding in a school environment. *Journal of Applied Social Psychology, 15,* 503–515.

McCarrey, N. W., Peterson, L., Edwards, S., & von Kuniz, P. (1974). Landscape office attitudes: Reflections of perceived degree of control over transactions with the environment. *Journal of Applied Psychology, 59,* 401–403.

McCarty, D., Diamond, W., & Kaye, M. (1982). Alcohol, sexual arousal, and the transfer of excitation. *Journal of Personality and Social Psychology, 42*(6), 977–988.

McCauley, C., Stitt, C. F., Woods, K., & Lipton, D. (1973). Group shift to caution at the race track. *Journal of Experimental Social Psychology, 9,* 80–86.

McClintock, C., Stech, F., & Keil, L. (1983). The influence of communication on bargaining. In P. Paulus (Ed.), *Basic group process* (pp. 205–234). New York: Springer-Verlag.

Maccoby, E. E., & Jacklin, C. N. (1974). *The psychology of sex differences.* Palo Alto, Calif.: Stanford University Press.

Maccoby, E. E., & Jacklin, C. N. (1980). Sex differences in aggression: A rejoinder and reprise. *Child Development, 51,* 964–980.

McCollam, J. B., Burish, T. G., Maisto, S. A., & Sobell, M. B. (1980). Alcohol's effects on physiological arousal and self-reported affect and sensations. *Journal of Abnormal Psychology, 89,* 224–233.

McConahay, J. B. (1986). Modern racism, ambivalence, and the Modern Racism Scale. In J. F. Dovidio & S. L. Gaertner (Eds.), *Prejudice, discrimination and racism* (pp. 91–126). New York: Academic Press.

McCrae, R. R., & Costa, P. T. (1989). The structure of interpersonal traits: Wiggins's circumplex and five-factor model. *Journal of Personality and Social Psychology, 56,* 586–595.

McDougall, W. (1908). *An introduction to social psychology.* London: Methuen.

McGee, G. W., Ferguson, C. E., & Seers, A. (1989). Role conflict and role ambiguity: Do the scales measure these two constructs? *Journal of Applied Psychology, 74,* 815–818.

McGillicuddy, N., Pruitt, D., & Syna, H. (1984). Perceptions of firmness and strength in negotiation. *Personality and Social Psychology Bulletin, 10,* 402–409.

McGinniss, J. (1969). *The selling of the presidency, 1968.* New York: Simon & Schuster/Trident.

McGrath, J. E. (1984). *Groups: Interaction and performance.* Englewood Cliffs, N.J.: Prentice-Hall.

McGrath, J. E. (Ed.). (1988). *The social psychology of time.* Newbury Park, Calif.: Sage.

McGrath, J. E., & Julian, J. W. (1963). Interaction process and task outcome in experimentally created negotiation groups. *Journal of Psychological Studies, 14,* 117–138.

McGuire, W. J. (1985). Attitudes and attitude change. In G. Lindzey & E. Aronson (Eds.), *The handbook of social psychology* (3rd ed., Vol. 2, pp. 233–346). New York: Random House.

McGuire, W. J., & McGuire, C. V. (1981). The spontaneous self-concept as affected by seasonal distinctiveness. In M. D. Lynch, A. Norem-Hebeisen, & K. J. Gergen (Eds.), *Self-concept: Advances in theory and research.* Cambridge, Mass.: Ballinger.

McGuire, W. J., McGuire, C. V., Child, P., & Fujioka, T. (1978). Salience of ethnicity in the spontaneous self-concept as a function of one's ethnic distinctiveness in the social environment. *Journal of Personality and Social Psychology, 36,* 511–520.

McGuire, W. J., & Padawer-Singer, A. (1976). Trait salience in the spontaneous self-concept. *Journal of Personality and Social Psychology, 33,* 743–754.

McGuire, W. J., & Papageorgis, D. (1961). The relative efficacy of various types of prior belief-defense in producing immunity against persuasion. *Journal of Abnormal and Social Psychology, 62,* 317–337.

McHarg, I. (1969). *Design with nature.* Garden City, N.Y.: Natural History Press.

Mackie, D. M., & Goethals, G. R. (1987). Individual and group goals. In C. Hendrick (Ed.), *Review of personality and social psychology* (Vol. 8.) Newbury Park, Calif.: Sage.

Mackie, D. M., & Worth, L. T. (1989). Processing deficits and the mediation of positive affect in persuasion. *Journal of Personality and Social Psychology, 57,* 27–40.

Mackworth, N. H. (1961). Researchers on the measurement of human performance. In H. W. Sinaiki (Ed.), *Selected papers on human factors in the design and use of control systems.* New York: Dover.

MacNeil, M. K., & Sherif, M. (1976). Norm change over subject generations as a function of arbitrariness of prescribed norms. *Journal of Personality and Social Psychology, 34,* 762–768.

Maier, S. F., Seligman, M. E. P., & Solomon, R. L. (1969). Pavlovian fear conditioning and learned helplessness. In B. A. Campbell & R. M. Church (Eds.), *Punishment.* New York: Appleton-Century-Crofts.

Major, B. (1981). Gender patterns in touching behavior. In C. Mayo & N. Henley (Eds.), *Gender, androgyny, and nonverbal behavior.* New York: Springer-Verlag.

Major, B., Carrington, P. I., & Carnevale, P. J. D. (1984). Physical attractiveness and self-esteem. Attributions for praise from an other-sex evaluator. *Personality and Social Psychology Bulletin, 10,* 43–50.

Major, B., Cozzarelli, C., Testa, M., & McFarlin, D. B. (1988). Self-verification versus expectancy confirmation in social interaction: The impact of self-focus. *Personality and Social Psychology Bulletin, 14,* 346–359.

Malamuth, N., Haber, S., & Feshbach, S. (1980). Testing hypotheses regarding rape: Exposure to sexual violence, sex differences, and the "normality" of rapists. *Journal of Research in Personality, 14,* 121–127.

Malamuth, N. M. (1984). Aggression against women: Cultural and individual causes. In N. M. Malamuth & E. Donnerstein (Eds.), *Pornography and sexual aggression.* Orlando, Fla.: Academic Press.

Malamuth, N. M., & Centi, J. (1986). Repeated exposure to violent and nonviolent pornography: Likelihood of raping ratings and laboratory aggression against women. *Aggressive Behavior, 12*(2), 129–137.

Malamuth, N. M., & Check, J. V. P. (1981). The effects of mass media exposure on acceptance of violence against women: A field experiment. *Journal of Research in Personality, 15,* 436–446.

Mann, R. (1959). A review of the relationship between personality and performance in small groups. *Psychological Bulletin, 56,* 241–270.

Mann, S. H. (1977). The use of social indicators in environmental planning. In I. Altman & J. R. Wohlwill (Eds.), *Human behavior and environment* (Vol. 2). New York: Plenum Press.

Markey, E. J. (1985). The politics of arms control: A matter of perception. *American Psychologist, 40,* 557–560.

Marks, G., Miller, N., & Maruyama, G. (1981). Effect of targets' physical attractiveness on assumptions of similarity. *Journal of Personality and Social Psychology, 41*(l), 198–206.

Markus, H. (1978). The effect of mere presence on social facilitation: An unobtrusive test. *Journal of Experimental Social Psychology, 14,* 389–397.

Markus, H. (1981). The drive for integration: Some comments. *Journal of Experimental Social Psychology, 17,* 257–261.

Markus, H., & Zajonc, R. (1985). The cognitive perspective in social psychology. In G. Lindzey & E. Aronson (Eds.), *The handbook of social psychology* (3rd ed., Vol. 1, pp. 137–230). New York: Random House.

Marshall, G. D., & Zimbardo, P. G. (1979). Affective consequences of inadequately explained physiological arousal. *Journal of Personality and Social Psychology, 37,* 970–988.

Martin, R. (1989, June). *Minority influence, majority influence and social identification: Some thought and contradictions.* Paper presented at the 3rd Workshop on Minority Influence, Perugia, Italy.

Maslach, C. (1974). Social and personal bases of individuation. *Journal of Personality and Social Psychology, 29,* 411–425.

Maslach, C. (1979). Negative emotional biasing of unexplained arousal. *Journal of Personality and Social Psychology, 37,* 953-969.

Maslach, C., Stapp, J., & Santee, R. (1985). Individuation: Conceptual analysis and assessment. *Journal of Personality and Social Psychology, 49,* 729–738.

Mathes, E. W., Adams, H. E., & Davies, R. M. (1985). Jealousy: Loss of relationship rewards, loss of self-esteem, depression, anxiety, and anger. *Journal of Personality and Social Psychology, 48,* 1552–1561.

Mathews, K. E., & Cannon, L. K. (1975). Environmental noise level as a determinant of helping behavior. *Journal of Personality and Social Psychology, 32,* 571–577.

Mathews, K. E., Cannon, L. K., & Alexander, K. (1974). The influence of level of empathy and ambient noise on body buffer zones. *Proceedings of the American Psychological Association, 1,* 367–370.

Maychick, D. (1984). *Meryl Streep: The reluctant superstar.* New York: St. Martin's.

Mayo, C., & Henley, N. M. (Eds.), (1981). *Gender and nonverbal behavior.* New York: Springer-Verlag.

Mazis, M. B. (1975). Antipollution measures and psychological reactance theory: A field experiment. *Journal of Personality and Social Psychology, 31,* 654–660.

Mead, G. H. (1934). *Mind, self and society.* Chicago: University of Chicago Press.

Megargee, E. I. (1969). Influence of sex roles on the manifestation of leadership. *Journal of Applied Psychology, 53,* 377–382.

Mehrabian, A. (1968). Relationship of attitudes to seated posture, orientation, and distance. *Journal of Personality and Social Psychology, 10,* 26–30.

Mehrabian, A. (1972). *Nonverbal communication.* Chicago: Aldine-Atherton.

Melburg, V., & Tedeschi, J. T. (1989). Displaced aggression: Frustration or impression management? *Environmental Journal of Social Psychology, 19,* 139–146.

Merari, A., & Friedland, N. (1985). Social psychological aspects of political terrorism. *Applied Social Psychology Annual, 6,* 185–206.

Merari, A., & Friedland, N. (1988). Negotiating with terrorists. In W. Stroebe et al. (Eds.), *The social psychology of intergroup conflict* (pp. 135–150). Berlin: Springer-Verlag.

Metalsky, G. I., Halberstadt, L. J., & Abramson, L. Y. (1987). Vulnerability to depressive mood reactions: Toward a more powerful test of the diathesis-stress and causal mediation component reformulated theory of depression. *Journal of Personality and Social Psychology, 52,* 386–393.

Mettee, D. R. (1971). Rejection of unexpected success as a function of the negative consequences of accepting success. *Journal of Personality and Social Psychology, 17,* 332–341.

Mettee, D. R., & Aronson, E. (1974). Affective reactions to appraisal from others. In T. L. Huston (Ed.), *Foundations of interpersonal attraction.* New York: Academic Press.

Meyer, J. P., & Pepper, S. (1977). Need, compatibility, and marital adjustment in young married couples. *Journal of Personality and Social Psychology, 35,* 331–342.

Michaelson, L. K., Watson, W. E., & Black, R. H. (1989). A realistic test of individual versus group consensus decision making. *Journal of Applied Psychology, 74,* 834–839.

Michenbaum, D. H., Bowers, K. S., & Ross, R. R. (1969). A behavioral analysis of teacher expectancy effects. *Journal of Personality and Social Psychology, 13,* 306–316.

Michener, H. A., & Burt, M. R. (1974). Legitimacy as a base of social influence. In J. Tedeschi (Ed.), *Perspectives on social power.* Chicago: Aldine.

Michener, H. A., & Suchner, R. (1972). The tactical use of social power. In J. Tedeschi (Ed.), *The social influence process.* Chicago: Aldine.

Mikulincer, M. (1986). Attributional processes in the learned helplessness paradigm: Behavioral effects of global attributions. *Journal of Personality and Social Psychology, 51,* 1248–1256.

Mikulincer, M., & Nizan, B. (1988). Causal attribution, cognitive interference, and the generalization of learned helplessness. *Journal of Personality and Social Psychology, 55,* 470–478.

Milgram, S. (1963). Behavioral study of obedience. *Journal of Abnormal and Social Psychology, 67,* 376.

Milgram, S. (1965). Some conditions of obedience and disobedience to authority. *Human Relations, 18,* 57–76.

Milgram, S. (1970). The experience of living in cities. *Science, 167*, 1461–1468.

Milgram, S. (1974). *Obedience to authority.* New York: Harper & Row.

Milgram, S. (1977). *The individual in a social world.* Reading, Mass.: Addison-Wesley.

Milgram, S., Liberty, H. J., Toledo, R., & Wackenhut, T. (1986). Response to intrusion into waiting lines. *Journal of Personality and Social Psychology, 51*, 683–689.

Milgram, S., & Toch, H. (1968). Reply to the critics. *International Journal of Psychiatry, 6*, 294–295.

Miller, C. T. (1982). The role of performance-related similarity in social comparison of abilities: A test of the related attributes hypothesis. *Journal of Experimental Social Psychology, 18*, 513–523.

Miller, C. T. (1984). Self-schemas, gender, and social comparison: A clarification of the related attributes hypothesis. *Journal of Personality and Social Psychology, 46*, 1222–1229.

Miller, D. T., Turnbull, W., & McFarland, C. (1988). Particularistic and universalistic evaluation in the social comparison process. *Journal of Personality and Social Psychology, 55*, 908–917.

Miller, J. (1982). The effects of noise on people. *Journal of the Acoustical Society of America, 56*, 729–764.

Miller, L. C., & Kenny, D. A. (1986). Reciprocity of self-disclosure at the individual and dyadic levels: A social relations analysis. *Journal of Personality and Social Psychology, 50*, 713–719.

Miller, M. L., & Thayer, J. F. (1989). On the existence of discrete classes in personality: Is self-monitoring the correct joint to carve? *Journal of Personality and Social Psychology, 57*, 143–155.

Miller, N., & Campbell, D. (1959). Recency and primacy in persuasion as a function of the timing of speeches and measurements. *Journal of Abnormal and Social Psychology, 59*, 1–9.

Miller, N., Campbell, D., Twedt, H., & O'Connell, E. (1966). Similarity, contrast and complementarity in friendship choice. *Journal of Personality and Social Psychology, 3*, 3–12.

Miller, N., & Davidson-Podgorny, G. (1987). Theoretical models of intergroup relations and the use of cooperative terms as an intervention for desegregated settings. In C. Hendrick (Ed.), *Group process and intergroup relations.* (pp. 41–67). Newbury Park, Calif.: Sage.

Miller, N. E. (1948). Theory and experiments relating psychoanalytic displacement to stimulus-response generation. *Journal of Abnormal and Social Psychology, 43*, 155–178.

Miller, R. L., Brickman, P., & Bolen, D. (1975). Attribution versus persuasion as a means for modifying behavior. *Journal of Personality and Social Psychology, 31*, 430–441.

Minton, H. L. (1984). J. F. Brown's social psychology of the 1930's: A historical antecedent to the contemporary crisis in social psychology. *Personality and Social Psychology Bulletin, 10*, 7–30.

Mischel, W. (1968). *Personality and assessment.* New York: Wiley.

Mita, T. H., Dermer, M., & Knight, J. (1977). Reversed facial images and the mere-exposure hypothesis. *Journal of Personality and Social Psychology, 35*, 597–601.

Money, J., & Ehrhardt, A. (1972). *Man and woman, boy and girl.* Baltimore: Johns Hopkins University Press.

Montgomery, R. L. (1989). *Social influence and conformity: A transorientational model.* Unpublished manuscript, University of Missouri–Rolla.

Moreland, R. L. (1985). Social categorization and the assimilation of "new" group members. *Journal of Personality and Social Psychology, 48*, 1173–1190.

Moreland, R. L. (1987) The formation of small groups. In C. Hendrick (Ed.), *Group processes* (pp. 80–110). Newbury Park, Calif.: Sage.

Moreland, R. L., & Levine, J. M. (1982). Socialization in small groups: Temporal changes in individual group relations. In L. Berkowitz (Ed.), *Advances in experimental social psychology* (Vol. 15). New York: Academic Press.

Moreland, R. L., & Levine, J. M. (1988). Group dynamics over time: Development and socialization in small groups. In J. E. McGrath (Ed.), *The social psychology of time* (pp. 151–181). Newbury Park, Calif.: Sage.

Moretti, M. M., & Higgins, E. T. (1990). Relating self-discrepancy to self-esteem: The contribution of discrepancy beyond actual-self ratings. *Journal of Experimental Social Psychology, 26*, 108–123.

Morley, I. E., Webb, J., & Stephenson, G. M. (1988). Bargaining and attribution in the resolution of conflict. In W. Stroebe et al. (Eds.), *The social psychology of intergroup conflict* (pp. 117–134). Berlin: Springer-Verlag.

Morris, C. G., & Hackman, J. R. (1969). Behavioral correlates of perceived leadership. *Journal of Personality and Social Psychology, 13*, 350–361.

Morse, S. J., & Gergen, K. J. (1970). Social comparison, self-consistency, and the concept of self. *Journal of Personality and Social Psychology, 16*, 149–156.

Moscovici, S. (1976). *Social influence and social changes.* London: Academic Press.

Moscovici, S. (1985). Social influence and conformity. In G. Lindzey & E. Aronson (Eds.), *The handbook of social psychology* (3rd ed., Vol. 2, pp. 347–412). New York: Random House.

Moscovici, S. (1989). Preconditions for explanation in social psychology. *European Journal of Social Psychology, 19*, 407–430.

Moscovici, S., & Mugny, G. (1983). Minority influence. In P. Paulus (Ed.), *Basic group process.* New York: Springer-Verlag.

Moscovici, S., & Nemeth, C. J. (1974). Minority influence. In C. J. Nemeth (Ed.), *Social psychology: Classic and contemporary integrations.* Chicago: Rand McNally.

Moskowitz, D. S. (1988). Cross-situational generality in the laboratory: Dominance and friendliness. *Journal of Personality and Social Psychology, 54*, 829–839.

Moss, M. K., & Page, R. A. (1972). Reinforcement and helping behavior. *Journal of Applied Social Psychology, 2*, 360–371.

Moyer, K. E. (1971). *The physiology of hostility.* Chicago: Markham.

Mucchi-Faina, A. (1989, June). *Minority influence processes: Assimilation, reactive differentiation, active differentiation.* Paper presented at the 3rd Workshop on Minority Influence, Perugia, Italy.

Muhleman, J. T., Bruker, C., & Ingram, C. M. (1976). The generosity shift. *Journal of Personality and Social Psychology, 34*, 344–351.

Mullen, B. (1983). Operationalizing the effect of the group on the individual: A self-attention perspective. *Journal of Experimental Social Psychology, 19*, 295–322.

Mullen, B. (1986). Atrocity as a function of lynch mob composition: A self-attention perspective. *Personality and Social Psychology Bulletin, 12*, 187–197.

Mullen, B. (1987). Self-attention theory. In B. Mullen & G. R. Goethals (Eds.), *Theories of group behavior.* New York: Springer-Verlag.

Mullen B., Atkins, J. L., Champion, D. S., Edwards, C.,

Hardy, D., Story, J. E., and Vanderklok, M. (1985). The false consensus effect: A meta-analysis of 115 hypothesis tests. *Journal of Experimental Social Psychology, 21,* 262–283.

Mullen, B., & Goethals, G. R. (in press). Short note: Social projection, actual consensus, and valence. *British Journal of Social Psychology.*

Mummendey, A., & Otten, S. (1989). Perspective-specific differences in the segmentation and evaluation of aggressive interaction sequences. *European Journal of Social Psychology, 19,* 23–40.

Myer, T. (1972). The effect of sexually arousing and violent films on aggressive behavior. *Journal of Sex Research, 8,* 324–333.

Myers, D. G. (1982). Polarizing effects of social interaction. In H. Brandstatter, J. H. Davis, & G. Stocker-Kreichgauer (Eds.), *Group decision processes.* London: Academic Press.

Myers, D. G. (1983). *Social psychology.* New York: McGraw-Hill.

Nahemow, L., & Lawton, M. P. (1975). Similarity and propinquity in friendship formation. *Journal of Personality and Social Psychology, 32,* 205–213.

Napolitan, D. A., & Goethals, G. R. (1979). The attribution of friendliness. *Journal of Experimental Social Psychology, 15,* 105–113.

Nemeth, C. (1986). Differential contributions of majority and minority influence. *Psychological Review, 93,* 1–10, 23–32.

Nemeth, C. (1989, June). *The stimulating properties of dissent: The case of recall.* Paper presented at the 3rd Workshop on Minority Influence, Perugia, Italy.

Nemeth, C., & Chiles, C. (1988). Modeling courage: The role of dissent in fostering independence. *European Journal of Social Psychology, 18,* 275–280.

Nemeth, C., & Staw, B. M. (1989). The tradeoffs of social control and innovation in groups and organizations. In L. Berkowitz (Ed.), *Advances in experimental social psychology* (Vol. 23, pp. 175–210). Orlando, Fla.: Academic Press.

Neuberg, S. L. (1989). The goal of forming accurate impressions during social interactions: Attenuating the impact of negative expectancies. *Journal of Personality and Social Psychology, 56,* 374–386.

Newcomb, T. (1943). *Personality and social change.* Hinsdale, Ill.: Dryden.

Newcomb, T. (1953). An approach to the study of communicative acts. *Psychological Review, 60,* 393–404.

Newcomb, T. (1961). *The acquaintance process.* New York: Holt, Rinehart & Winston.

Newcomb, T. (1963). Persistence and repression of changed attitudes: Long-range studies. *Journal of Social Issues, 19,* 3–14.

Newcomb, T., Koenig, K., Flacks, R., & Warwick, D. (1967). *Persistence and change: Bennington College and its students after 25 years.* New York: Wiley.

Newcomb, T. A. (1947). Autistic hostility and social reality. *Human Relations, 1,* 69–86.

Newcomb, T. M. (1956). The prediction of interpersonal attraction. *American Psychologist, 11,* 575–586.

Newcomb, T. M. (1968). Interpersonal balance. In R. P. Abelson (Ed.), *Theories of cognitive consistency: A sourcebook.* Chicago: Rand McNally.

Newman, O. (1972). *Defensible space.* New York: Macmillan.

Nisbett, R. E., Caputo, C., Legant, P., & Marecek, J. (1973). Behavior as seen by the actor and as seen by the observer. *Journal of Personality and Social Psychology, 27,* 154–164.

Nisbett, R. E., & Ross, L. (1980). *Human inference: Strategies and shortcomings of social judgment.* Englewood Cliffs, N.J.: Prentice-Hall.

Nolen-Hoeksema, S., Seligman, M. E. P., & Girgus, J. S. (1986). Learned helplessness in children: A longitudinal study of depression, achievement, and explanatory style. *Journal of Personality and Social Psychology, 51,* 435–442.

Noller, P. (1980). Misunderstandings in marital communication: A study of couples' nonverbal communication. *Journal of Personality and Social Psychology, 39,* 1135–1148.

Norwood, J. L. (1982). *The female-male earning gap: A review of employment and earnings issues* (Report 673). Washington, D.C.: U.S. Department of Labor.

Nosanchuk, T. A. (1981). The way of the warrior: The effects of traditional martial arts training on aggressiveness. *Human Relations, 34,* 435–444.

Novak, D., & Lerner, M. (1968). Rejection as a consequence of perceived similarity. *Journal of Personality and Social Psychology, 9,* 147–152.

Novak, M. A., & Suomi, S. J. (1988). Psychological well-being of primates in captivity. *American Psychology, 43,* 765–773.

Nyquist, L. V., & Spence, J. T. (1986). Effects of dispositional dominance and sex role expectations on leadership behaviors. *Journal of Personality and Social Psychology, 50,* 87–93.

Oakes, P. J., & Turner, J. C. (1980). Social categorization and intergroup behavior: Does minimal intergroup discrimination make social identity more positive? *European Journal of Social Psychology, 10,* 295–301.

Ohbuchi, K., Kameda, M., & Agarie, N. (1989). Apology as aggression control: Its role in mediating appraisal of and response to harm. *Journal of Personality and Social Psychology 56,* 219–227.

Oldham, G. R. (1988). Effects of changes in workspace partitions and social density on employee reactions: A quasi experiment. *Journal of Applied Psychology, 73,* 253–258.

Olson, J. M., & Ross, M. (1988). False feedback about placebo effectiveness: Consequences for the misattribution of speech anxiety. *Journal of Experimental Social Psychology, 24,* 275–291.

Olszewski, D., Rotton, J., & Soler, E. (1976). *Conversation, conglomerate noise and behavioral aftereffects.* Paper presented at the meeting of the Midwestern Psychological Association, Chicago.

Orbell, J. M., van de Kragt, A. J., & Dawes, R. M. (1988). Explaining discussion-induced cooperation. *Journal of Personality and Social Psychology, 54,* 811–819.

Orive, R. (1988). Group consensus, action immediacy, and opinion confidence. *Personality and Social Psychology Bulletin, 14,* 573–577.

Orive, R. (1988). Social projection and social comparison of opinions. *Journal of Personality and Social Psychology, 54,* 953–964.

Orne, M. T. (1962). On the social psychology of the psychological experiment: With particular reference to demand characteristics and their implications. *American Psychologist, 17,* 776–783.

Orne, M. T., & Evans, F. J. (1965). Social control in the psychological experiment: Antisocial behavior and hypnosis. *Journal of Personality and Social Psychology, 1,* 189–200.

Orne, M. T., & Holland, C. C. (1968). On the ecological validity of laboratory deceptions. *International Journal of Psychiatry, 6,* 282–293.

Orvis, B. R., Kelley, H. H., & Butler, D. (1976). Attributional conflict in young couples. In J. H. Harvey, W. J. Ickes,

& R. E. Kidd (Eds.), *New directions in attribution research* (Vol. 2). Hillsdale, N.J.: Erlbaum.

Osgood, C. E. (1962). *An alternative to war or surrender*. Urbana: University of Illinois Press.

Osmond, H. (1957). Function as the basis of psychiatric ward design. *Mental Hospitals, 8,* 23–30.

Ostfeld, A., Kasl, S., D'Atri, D., & Fitzgerald, E. (1987). *Stress, crowding, and blood pressure in prison.* Hillsdale, N.J.: Erlbaum.

Overmier, J. B., & Seligman, M. E. P. (1967). Effects of inescapable shock upon subsequent escape and avoidance learning. *Journal of Comparative and Physiological Psychology, 63,* 28–33.

Page, M., & Scheidt, R. J. (1971). The elusive weapons effect: Demand awareness, valuation apprehension, and slightly sophisticated subjects. *Journal of Personality and Social Psychology, 20,* 304–318.

Pallak, M. S., & Pittman, T. S. (1972). General motivational effects of dissonance arousal. *Journal of Personality and Social Psychology, 21,* 349–358.

Papastamos, S., & Mugny, G. (1989, June). *Synchronic consistency and psychologization in minority influence.* Paper presented at the 3rd Workshop on Minority Influences, Perugia, Italy.

Parke, R., Berkowitz, L., Leyens, J. P., West, S. G., & Sebastian, R. J. (1977). Some effects of violent and nonviolent movies on the behavior of juvenile delinquents. In L. Berkowitz (Ed.), *Advances in experimental social psychology* (Vol. 10, pp. 139–169). New York: Academic Press.

Parker, R. D., Collmer, C. W. (1975). Child abuse: An interdisciplinary analysis. In M. E. Hetherington (Ed.), *Review of Child Development Research, Vol. 5.* Chicago: University of Chicago Press.

Patrick, C. J., Craig, K. D., & Prkachin, K. M. (1986). Observer judgements of acute pain: Facial action determinants. *Journal of Personality and Social Psychology, 50,* 1291–1298.

Patterson, M. L. (1977). Interpersonal distance, affect, and equilibrium theory. *Journal of Social Psychology, 101,* 205–214.

Paulhus, D. L., Shaffer, D. R., & Downing, L. L. (1977). Effects of making blood donor motives salient upon donor retention. *Personality and Social Psychology Bulletin, 3,* 99–102.

Paulus, P. (1983). Group influence on task performance and informational processing. In P. Paulus (Ed.), *Basic group processes.* New York: Springer.

Pavlov, I. P. (1927). *Conditional reflexes: An investigation of the physiological activity of the cerebral cortex.* London: Oxford University Press.

Pearl, D., & Bouthilet, L. (Eds.). (1982). *Television and behavior: Ten years of scientific progress and implications for the 80's.* Washington, D.C.: U.S. Government Printing Office.

Pelton, L. H. (1974). *The psychology of nonviolence.* Elmsford, N.Y.: Pergamon.

Pepitone, A. (1981). Lessons from the history of social psychology. *American Psychologist, 36,* 972–985.

Perez, J. A., & Mugny, G. (1987). Paradoxical effects of categorization in minority influence: When being an outgroup is an advantage. *European Journal of Social Psychology, 17,* 157–169.

Pessin, J., & Husband, R. (1933). Effects of social stimulation on human maze learning. *Journal of Abnormal and Social Psychology, 28,* 148–154.

Peters, L. H., Hartke, D., Pohlmann, J. T. (1985). Fiedler's contingency theory of leadership: An application of the

meta-analysis procedures of Schmidt and Hunter. *Psychological Bulletin, 97,* 274–285.

Peterson, C., & Barrett, L. C. (1987). Explanatory style and academic performance among college freshmen. *Journal of Personality and Social Psychology, 53,* 603–607.

Petrovsky, A. V. (1985). *Studies in psychology: The collective and the individual.* Moscow: Progress.

Pettigrew, T. F. (1958). The measurement and correlates of category width as a cognitive variable. *Journal of Personality, 26,* 532–544.

Pettigrew, T. F. (1959). Regional differences in anti-Negro prejudice. *Journal of Abnormal and Social Psychology, 59,* 28–36.

Petty, R. E., & Cacioppo, J. T. (1981). *Attitudes and persuasion: Classic and contemporary approaches.* Dubuque, Ia.: Wm. C. Brown.

Petty, R. E., & Cacioppo, J. T. (1986). The elaboration likelihood model of persuasion. In L. Berkowitz (Ed.), *Advances in experimental social psychology* (Vol. 19, pp. 123–205). New York: Academic Press.

Petty, R. E., Cacioppo, J. T., & Goldman, R. (1981). Personal involvement as a determinant of argument-based persuasion. *Journal of Personality and Social Psychology, 41,* 847–855.

Petty, R. E., Cacioppo, J. T., & Heesacker, M. (1981). The use of rhetorical questions in persuasion. *Journal of Personality and Social Psychology, 40,* 432–440.

Phares, E. J. (1984). *Introduction to personality.* Columbus, Oh.: Merrill.

Piaget, J. (1932). *The moral judgment of the child.* New York: Harcourt Brace Jovanovich.

Piliavin, I. M., Piliavin, J. A., & Rodin, J. (1975). Cost, diffusion, and the stigmatized victim. *Journal of Personality and Social Psychology, 32,* 429–438.

Piliavin, J. A., Dovidio, J. F., Gaertner, S. L., & Clark, R. D., III. (1982). Responsive bystanders: The process of intervention. In V. J. Derlega & J. Grzelak (Eds.), *Cooperation and helping behavior: Theories and research.* New York: Academic Press.

Porter, L. W., & Lawler, E. E. (1968). *Managerial attitudes and performances.* Pacific Grove, Calif.: Brooks/Cole.

Poulton, E. C. (1970). *Environment and human efficiency.* Springfield, Ill: Charles C Thomas.

Pratkanis, A. R., Greenwald, A. G., Leippe, M. R., & Baumgardner, M. H. (1988). In search of reliable persuasion effects. III. The sleeper effect is dead. Long live the sleeper effect. *Journal of Personality and Social Psychology, 54,* 203–215.

Provins, K. A., & Bell, C. R. (1970). Effects of heat stress on the performance of two tasks running concurrently. *Journal of Experimental Psychology, 85,* 40–44.

Pruitt, D. G. (1965). Definition of the situation as a determinant of international action. In H. C. Kelman (Ed.), *International behavior.* New York: Holt, Rinehart & Winston.

Pruitt, D. G. (1976). Power and bargaining. In B. Seidenberg & A. Snadowsky, *Social psychology: An introduction.* New York: Free Press.

Pruitt, D. G., & Johnson, D. F. (1970). Mediation as an aid to face saving in negotiation. *Journal of Personality and Social Psychology, 14,* 239–246.

Pyszczynski, T., Hamilton, J. C., Herring, F. H., & Greenberg, J. (1989). Depression, self-focused attention, and the negative memory bias. *Journal of Personality and Social Psychology, 57,* 351–357.

Pyszczynski, T., Holt, K., & Greenberg, J. (1987). Depression, self-focused attention, and expectancies for positive and negative future events for self and other. *Journal of Personality and Social Psychology, 52,* 994–1001.

Quattrone, G. A. (1986). On the perception of a group's variability. In S. Worchel & W. G. Austin (Eds.), *Psychology of intergroup relations* (pp. 25–48). Chicago: Nelson-Hall.

Quattrone, G. A., & Jones, E. E. (1978). Selective self-disclosure with and without correspondent performance. *Journal of Experimental Social Psychology, 14,* 511–526.

Quattrone, G. A., & Jones, E. E. (1980). The perception of variability with in-groups and out-groups: Implications for the law of small numbers. *Journal of Personality and Social Psychology, 38,* 141–152.

Rabbie, J. M., & Bekkers, F. (1976). Threatened leadership and intergroup competition. *Nederlands Tijdschrift voor de Psychologie en haar Grensaebieden, 31,* 269–283.

Rabbie, J. M., Brehm, J. W., & Cohen, A. R. (1959). Verbalization and reactions to cognitive dissonance. *Journal of Personality, 27,* 407–417.

Rabbie, J. M., Schot, J. C., & Visser, L. (1989). Social identity: A conceptual and empirical critique from the perspective of a behavioral interaction model. *European Journal of Social Psychology, 19,* 171–202.

Rada, J. B., & Rogers, R. W. (1973, October). *Obedience to authority: Presence of authority and command strength.* Paper presented at the meeting of the Southwestern Psychological Association, New Orleans.

Raloff, J. (1982). Occupational noise—the subtle pollutant. *Science News, 121,* 347–350.

Rands, M., Levinger, G., & Mellinger, G. (1981). Patterns of conflict resolution and marital satisfaction. *Journal of Family Issues, 2,* 297–321.

Rankin, R. E., & Campbell, D. T. (1955). Galvanic skin response to Negro and white experimenters. *Journal of Applied Social Psychology, 51,* 30–33.

Rappaport, A. (1967). A note on the "index for cooperation" for prisoner's dilemmas. *Journal of Personality and Social Psychology, 11,* 101–103.

Raven, B. H., Centers, R., & Rodrigues, A. (1969). *Social influence in the dyad: The basis of conjugal power* (Tech. Rep. 25, Nononr 233). Los Angeles: University of California at Los Angeles.

Raven, B. H., Centers, R., & Rodrigues, A. (1975). The bases of conjugal power. In Cromwell, R. E., & Olson, D. H. (Eds.), *Power in families* (pp. 217–234). Newbury Park, Calif.: Sage.

Raven, B. H., & French, J. R. (1958). Legitimate power, coercive power and observability in social influence. *Sociometry, 21,* 83–97.

Raven, B. H., & Kruglanski, A. (1970). Conflict and power. In P. Swingle (Ed.), *The structure of conflict.* New York: Academic Press.

Regan, D. T., & Fazio, R. (1977). On the consistency between attitudes and behavior: Look to the method of attitude formation. *Journal of Experimental Social Psychology, 13,* 28–45.

Reicher, S. D. (1984). The St. Paul riot: An explanation of the limits of crowd action in terms of social identity model. *European Journal of Social Psychology, 14,* 1–21.

Reinisch, J. M., & Sanders, S. A. (1986). A test of sex differences in aggressive response to hypothetical conflict situations. *Journal of Personality and Social Psychology, 50,* 1045–1049.

Reis, H. T., Nezlek, J., & Wheeler, L. (1980). Physical attractiveness in social interaction. *Journal of Personality and Social Psychology, 38,* 604–617.

Reizenstein, J. (1982). Hospital design and human behavior:

A review of recent literature. In A. Baum & J. Singer (Eds.), *Advances in environmental psychology* (Vol. 4). Hillsdale, N.J.: Erlbaum.

Rhodewalt, F., & Comer, R. (1982). Coronary-prone behavior and reactance: The attractiveness of an eliminated choice. *Personality and Social Psychology Bulletin, 8,* 152–158.

Rhodewalt, F., & Davison, J. (1986). Self-handicapping and subsequent performance: Role of outcome valence and attributional certainty. *Basic and Applied Social Psychology, 7,* 307–322.

Rhodewalt, F., Saltzman, A. T., & Wittmer, J. (1984). Self-handicapping among competitive athletes: The role of practice in self-esteem protection. *Basic and Applied Social Psychology, 5,* 197–210.

Rice, R. W., Bender, L. R., & Vitters, A. G. (1980). Leader sex, follower attitudes toward women, and leadership effectiveness: A laboratory study. *Organizational Behavior and Human Performance, 25,* 46–78.

Rice, R. W., Instone, D., & Adams, J. (1984). Leader sex, leader success, and leadership process: Two field studies. *Journal of Applied Psychology, 69,* 12–31.

Rice, R. W., & Kastenbaum, D. R. (1983). The contingency model of leadership: Some current issues. *Basic and Applied Social Psychology, 4,* 373–392.

Rickels, K., & Downing, R. (1967). Drug- and placebo-treated neurotic outpatients. *Archives of General Psychiatry, 16,* 369–372.

Riecken, H. W. (1958). The effect of talkativeness on ability to influence group solutions of problems. *Sociometry, 21,* 309–321.

Riess, M., Rosenfeld, R., Melburg, V., & Tedeschi, J. T. (1981). Self-preserving attributions: Biased private perceptions and distorted public descriptions. *Journal of Personality and Social Psychology, 41,* 224–231.

Riggio, R. E., Tucker, J., & Throckmorton, B. (1987). Social skills and deception ability. *Personality and Social Psychology Bulletin, 13,* 568–577.

Ringelmann, M. (l913). Recherches sur les moteurs animes: Travail de l'homme. *Annales de 1'Instint National Agronomigre, 2nd Series, 12,* 1–40.

Robertson, I. (1989). *Society: A brief introduction.* New York: Worth.

Rodin, J. (1976). Density, perceived choice, and response to controllable and uncontrollable outcomes. *Journal of Experimental Social Psychology, 12,* 564–578.

Rodin, J., & Baum, A. (1978). Crowding and helplessness: Potential consequences of density and loss of control. In A. Baum & Y. Epstein (Eds.), *Human response to crowding.* Hillsdale, N.J.: Erlbaum.

Roethlisberger, F., & Dickson, W. (1939). *Management and the worker.* Cambridge, Mass.: Harvard University Press.

Rogers, R. W., & Prentice-Dunn, S. (1981). Deindividuation and anger-mediated interracial aggression: Unmasking regressive racism. *Journal of Personality and Social Psychology, 41,* 63–73.

Rohles, F. J., Jr. (1981). Thermal comfort and strategies for energy conservation. *Journal of Social Issues, 37*(2), 132–149.

Rosch, E. (1978). Principles of categorization. In E. Rosch & B. B. Lloyd (Eds.), *Cognition and categorization.* Hillsdale, N.J.: Erlbaum.

Rosen, S., Bergman, M., Plester, D., El-Mofty, A. & Salti, M. (1962). Presbycusis study of a relative noise free population in the Sudan. *Annals of Otology, Rhinology, and Laryngology, 71,* 727–743.

Rosenbaum, L. L., & Rosenbaum, W. B. (1971). Morale and

productivity consequences of group leadership style, stress, and type of task. *Journal of Applied Psychology, 55,* 343–348.

Rosenbaum, M. E. (1986). The repulsion hypothesis: On the nondevelopment of relationships. *Journal of Personality and Social Psychology, 51,* 1156–1166.

Rosenberg, M. (1965). When dissonance fails: On eliminating evaluation apprehension from attitude measurement. *Journal of Personality and Social Psychology, 1,* 28–42.

Rosenblatt, P. C., & Budd, L. G. (1975). Territoriality and privacy in married and unmarried cohabiting couples. *Journal of Social Psychology, 97,* 67–76.

Rosenhan, D. L., Salovey, P., & Hargis, K. (1981). The joys of helping: Focus of attention mediates the impact of positive effect on altruism. *Journal of Personality and Social Psychology, 40,* 899–905.

Rosenthal, A. M. (1964). *Thirty-eight witnesses.* New York: McGraw-Hill.

Rosenthal, R. (1973). The Pygmalion effect lives. *Psychology Today, 7*(4), 56–63.

Rosenthal, R., & Benowitz, L. I. (1985). Sensitivity to nonverbal communication in normal, psychiatric, and brain-damaged samples. In P. D. Blanck, R. W. Buck, & R. Rosenthal (Eds.), *Nonverbal communication in the clinical context.* University Park: Pennsylvania State University Press.

Rosenthal, R., & Evans, J. (1968). Unpublished data, Harvard University.

Rosenthal, R., & Fode, K. L. (1963). Psychology of the scientist: V. Three experiments in experimenter bias. *Psychological Reports, 12,* 491–511.

Rosenthal, R., & Jacobson, L. (1968). *Pygmalion in the classroom: Teacher expectation and pupils' intellectual development.* New York: Holt, Rinehart & Winston.

Ross, E. A. (1908). *Social psychology: An outline and a source book.* New York: Macmillan.

Ross, L. (1977). The intuitive psychologist and his shortcomings: Distortions in the attribution process. In L. Berkowitz (Ed.), *Advances in experimental social psychology* (Vol. 10). New York: Academic Press.

Ross, L., Bierbrauer, G., & Hoffman, S. (1976). The role of attribution processes in conformity and dissent: Revisiting the Asch situation. *American Psychologist, 31,* 148–157.

Ross, L., Greene, D., & House, P. (1977). The "false consensus effect": An egocentric bias in social perception and attribution processes. *Journal of Experimental Social Psychology, 13,* 279–301.

Ross, L., Rodin, J., & Zimbardo, P. (1969). Toward an attribution therapy: The reduction of fear through induced cognitive-emotional misattribution. *Journal of Personality and Social Psychology, 12,* 279–288.

Ross, M. (1981). Self-centered biases in attribution of responsibility antecedents and consequences. In E. T. Higgens, C. P. Herman, & M. P. Zanna (Eds.), *Social cognition: The Ontario symposium* (Vol. 1). Hillsdale, N.J.: Erlbaum.

Ross, M., & Fletcher, G. J. O. (1985). Attribution and social perception. In G. Lindzey & E. Aronson (Eds.), *The handbook of social psychology* (3rd ed., Vol. 2). New York: Random House.

Ross, M., & Olson, J. M. (1981). An expectancy-attribution model of the effects of placebos. *Psychological Review, 88,* 408–437.

Ross, M., & Sicoly, F. (1979). Egocentric biases in availability and attribution. *Journal of Personality and Social Psychology, 37,* 322–336.

Roth, S., & Kubal, L. (1975). Effects of noncontingent rein-

forcement on tasks of differing importance: Facilitation and learned helplessness. *Journal of Personality and Social Psychology, 32,* 680–691.

Rothbart, M., Dawes, R., & Park, B. (1984). Stereotyping and sampling biases in intergroup perception. In R. Eiser (Ed.), *Attitudinal judgment* (pp. 109–134). New York: Springer-Verlag.

Rothbart, M., & Hallmark, W. (1988). In-group–out-group differences in the perceived efficacy of coercion and conciliation in resolving conflict. *Journal of Personality of Social Psychology, 55,* 248–257.

Rotter, J. B. (1966). Generalized expectancies for internal vs. external reinforcement. *Psychological Monographs, 80* (1, whole no. 609).

Rotter, J. B. (1971a, June). External and internal control. *Psychology Today,* pp. 37–42, 58–59.

Rotter, J. B. (1971b). Generalized expectancies for interpersonal trust. *American Psychologist, 26,* 443–452.

Rowles, G. (1984). Aging in rural environments. In I. Altman, M. Lawton, & J. Wohlwill (Eds.), *Elderly people and the environment.* New York: Plenum.

Rowles, G., & Ohta, R. S. (Eds.). (1983). *Aging and milieu: Environmental perspectives on growing old.* New York: Academic Press.

Ruback, R. B., & Innes, C. A. (1989). The relevance and irrelevance of psychological research: The example of prison crowding. *American Psychologist, 43,* 683–693.

Rubin, J. Z., Provenzano, F. J., & Luria, Z. (1974). The eye of the beholder: Parents' views on sex of newborns. *American Journal of Orthopsychiatry, 44,* 512–519.

Rubin, Z. (1970). Measurement of romantic love. *Journal of Personality and Social Psychology, 16,* 265–273.

Rubin, Z. (1973). *Liking and loving.* New York: Holt, Rinehart & Winston.

Rubin, Z., & Schenker, S. (1978). Friendship, proximity, and self-disclosure. *Journal of Personality, 46,* 1–22.

Ruble, D. (1987). The acquisition of self-knowledge: A self-socialization perspective. In N. Eisenberg (Ed.), *Contemporary topics in developmental psychology.* New York: Wiley.

Ruble, D. N., & Ruble, T. L. (1982). Sex stereotypes. In A. G. Miller (Ed.), *In the eye of the beholder: Contemporary issues in stereotyping* (pp. 188–252). New York: Praeger.

Rule, B. G., & Nesdale, A. R. (1976). Emotional arousal and aggressive behavior. *Psychological Bulletin, 83,* 851–863.

Rusboldt, C. E., & Zembrot, I. M. (1983). Responses to dissatisfaction in romantic involvement. *Journal of Experimental Social Psychology, 19,* 274–293.

Rushton, J. P., & Teachinan, G. (1978). The effects of positive reinforcement attributions and punishment on model-induced altruism in children. *Personality and Social Psychology Bulletin, 4,* 322–325.

Russel, J., & Snodgrass, J. (1987). Emotions and the environment. In D. Stokols, & I. Altman (Eds.), *Handbook of environmental psychology* (Vol. 1, pp. 245–280). New York: Wiley.

Russell, D., Cutrona, C. E., Rose, J., & Yurko, K. (1984). Social and emotional loneliness: An examination of Weiss's typology of loneliness. *Journal of Personality and Social Psychology, 46,* 1313–1321.

Russell, D., & Jones, W. H. (1980). When superstition fails: Reactions to disconfirmation of personal beliefs. *Personality and Social Psychology Bulletin, 6,* 83–88.

Ryan, W. (1971). *Blaming the victim.* New York: Vintage Books.

Saal, F. E., Downey, R. G., & Lahey, M. A. (1980). Rating the ratings: Assessing the psychometric quality of rating data. *Psychological Bulletin, 88,* 413–423.

Sabatelli, R. M., Buck, R., & Dreyer, A. (1982). Nonverbal

---

communication accuracy in married couples: Relationship with marital complaints. *Journal of Personality and Social Psychology, 43,* 1088–1097.

Sabatelli, R. M., & Cecil-Pigo, E. F. (1985). Relational interdependence and commitment in marriage. *Journal of Marriage and Family, 47,* 931–937.

Sadalla, E., & Montello, D. (1989). Remembering changes in direction. *Journal of Environment and Behavior, 21,* 346–363.

Sagar, H. A., & Schofield, J. W. (1980). Racial behavioral cues in black and white children's perceptions of ambiguously aggressive acts. *Journal of Personality and Social Psychology, 39,* 590–598.

Sanbonmatsu, D. M., Shavitt, S., Sherman, S. J., & Roskos-Ewoldsen, D. R. (1987). Illusory correlation in the perception of performance by self or a salient other. *Journal of Experimental Social Psychology, 23,* 518–543.

Sande, G. N., Goethals, G. R., Ferrari, L., & Worth, L. (1989). Value-guided attributions: Maintaining the moral self-image and the diabolical enemy-image. *Journal of Social Issues, 45,* 91–118.

Sande, G. N., Goethals, G. R., & Radloff, C. E. (1988). Perceiving one's own traits and others': The multifaceted self. *Journal of Personality and Social Psychology, 54,* 13–20.

Sanders, G. S. (1981). Driven by distraction: An integrative review of social facilitation theory and research. *Journal of Experimental Social Psychology, 17,* 227–251.

Sanders, G. S., & Baron, R. S. (1975). The motivating effects of distraction on task performance. *Journal of Personality and Social Psychology, 32,* 956–963.

Sanders, G. S., & Baron, R. S. (1977). Is social comparison irrelevant for producing choice shifts? *Journal of Experimental Social Psychology, 13,* 303–313.

Sansone, C. (1986). A question of competence: The effect of competence and task feedback on intrinsic interest. *Journal of Personality and Social Psychology, 51,* 918–931.

Sansone, C. (1989). Competence feedback, task feedback, and intrinsic interest: An examination of process and context. *Journal of Experimental and Social Psychology, 25,* 343–361.

Santayana, G. (1920). *Character and opinion in the United States.* New York: Scribner's.

Santee, R. T., & Maslach, C. (1982). To agree or not to agree: Personal dissent amid social pressure to conform. *Journal of Personality and Social Psychology, 42,* 690–701.

Savinar, J. (1975). The effect of ceiling height on personal space. *Man-Environment Systems, 5,* 321–324.

Scanzoni, J. (1979). Social exchange and behavioral interdependence. In R. Burgess & T. Huston (Eds.), *Social exchange in developing relationships.* New York: Academic Press.

Scarr, S., & McCartney, K. (1983). How people make their own environments: A theory of genotype → environment effects. *Child Development, 54,* 424–435.

Schachter, S. (1951). Deviation, rejection, and communication. *Journal of Abnormal and Social Psychology, 46,* 190–207.

Schachter, S. (1959). *The psychology of affiliation.* Palo Alto, Calif.: Stanford University Press.

Schachter, S. (1964). The interaction of cognitive and physiological determinants of emotional state. In L. Berkowitz (Ed.) *Advances in experimental social psychology* (Vol. 1). New York: Academic Press.

Schachter, S. (1971). *Emotion, obesity, and crime.* New York: Academic Press.

Schachter, S., & Singer, J. (1962). Cognitive, social and physiological determinants of emotional state. *Psychological Review, 69,* 379–399.

Schaller, M., & Maass, A. (1989). Illusory correlation and social categorization: Toward an integration of motivational and cognitive factors in stereotype formation. *Journal of Personality and Social Psychology, 56,* 709–721.

Schank, R. C., & Abelson, R. P. (1977). *Scripts, plans, goals and understanding: An inquiry into human knowledge structures.* Hillsdale, N.J.: Erlbaum.

Scheier, M. F. (1980). Effects of private and public self-consciousness on the public expression of personal beliefs. *Journal of Personality and Social Psychology, 39,* 514–521.

Schlenker, B. R. (1980). *Impression management: The self-concept, social identity, and interpersonal relations.* Pacific Grove, Calif.: Brooks/Cole.

Schlenker, B. R. (1982). Translating actions into attitudes: An identity-analytic approach to the explanation of social conduct. In L. Berkowitz (Ed.), *Advances in experimental social psychology* (Vol. 15). New York: Academic Press.

Schlenker, B. R., Helm, B., & Tedeschi, J. T. (1973). The effects of personality and situational variables on behavioral trust. *Journal of Personality and Social Psychology, 25,* 419–427.

Schlesinger, A. M., Jr. (1965). *The thousand days.* Boston: Houghton Mifflin.

Schmid, R. (1988). "Population could double in 40 years," Associated Press, April 28.

Schmidt, D., & Keating, J. (1979). Human crowding and personal control: An integration of the research. *Psychological Bulletin, 86,* 680–700.

Schmutte, G. T., & Taylor, S. P. (1980). Physical aggression as a function of alcohol and pain feedback. *Journal of Social Psychology, 110,* 235–245.

Schneider, F. W., & Harsvick, C. L. (1977). Gaze and distance as a function of changes in interpersonal gaze. *Social Behavior and Personality, 5*(1), 49–53.

Schopler, J., & Bateson, N. (1962). A dependence interpretation of the effects of a severe initiation. *Journal of Personality, 30,* 633–649.

Schreisheim, C. A., & Kerr, S. (1977a). R.I.P. LPC: A response to Fiedler. In J. F. Hunt & L. L. Larson (Eds.), *Leadership: The cutting edge* (pp. 51–56). Carbondale: Southern Illinois University Press.

Schreisheim, C. A., & Kerr, S. (1977b). Theories and measures of leadership: A critical appraisal of current and future directions. In J. G. Hunt & L. L. Larson (Eds.), *Leadership: The cutting edge* (pp. 9–45). Carbondale: Southern Illinois University.

Schroeder, D. A., Dovidio, J. F., Sibicky, M. E., Matthews, L.L., & Allen, J. L. (1988). Empathy concern and helping behavior: Egoism or altruism. *Journal of Experimental Social Psychology, 24,* 333–353.

Schuman, H., & Kalton, G. (1985). Survey methods. In G. Lindzey & E. Aronson (Eds.), *Handbook of social psychology* (3rd ed., Vol. 1, pp.1–46). New York: Random House.

Schwartz, S. H. (1977). Normative influences on altruism. In L. Berkowitz (Ed.), *Advances in experimental social psychology* (Vol. 10). New York: Academic Press.

Schwartz, S. H., & Gottlieb, A. (1980). Bystander anonymity and reactions to emergencies. *Journal of Personality and Social Psychology, 39,* 418–430.

Sears, D., & McConahay, J. (1973). *The politics on violence: The new urban blacks and the Watts riot.* Boston: Houghton Mifflin.

Sears, R. R., Whiting, J. W. M., Nowlis, J., & Sears, P. S. (1953). Child rearing antecedents of aggression and dependency in young children. *Genetic Psychology Monographs, 47,* 135–234.

Secord, P. F., & Backman, C. W. (1974). *Social psychology.* (2nd ed.). New York: McGraw-Hill.

Seeman, M., & Evans, J. W. (1962). Alienation and learning in a hospital setting. *American Sociological Review, 27,* 772–782.

Segall, M. H. (1988). Cultural roots of aggressive behavior. In M. H. Bond (Ed.), *The cross-cultural challenge to social psychology.* Newbury Park, Calif.: Sage.

Seligman, C. (1989). Environmental ethics. *Journal of Social Issues, 45,* 169–184.

Seligman, C., & Darley, J. (1977). Feedback as a means of decreasing residential energy consumption. *Journal of Applied Psychology, 62,* 363–368.

Seligman, M. E. P. (1975). *Helplessness: On depression, development, and death.* San Francisco: W. H. Freeman.

Shaver, P., Schwartz, J., Kirson, D., & O'Connor, C. (1987). Emotion knowledge: Further exploration of a prototype approach. *Journal of Personality and Social Psychology, 52,* 1061–1086.

Shaw, J. I., & Condelli, L. (1986). Effects of outcome and basis of power on the powerholder-target relationship. *Personality and Social Psychology Bulletin, 12,* 236–246.

Shaw, M. (1932). A comparison of individuals and small groups in the rational solution of complex problems. *American Journal of Psychology, 44,* 491–504.

Shaw, M. E. (1981). *Group dynamics: The psychology of small group behavior.* New York: McGraw-Hill.

Sheppard, B. (1985). Justice is no simple matter. Case for elaborating our model of procedural fairness. *Journal of Personality and Social Psychology, 49,* 953–962.

Sheppard, J. A., & Arkin, R. M. (1989a). Determinants of self-handicapping: Task importance and the effects of pre-existing handicaps on self-generated handicaps. *Personality and Social Psychology Bulletin, 15,* 101–112.

Sheppard, J. A., & Arkin, R. M. (1989b). Self-handicapping: The moderating roles of public self-consciousness and task importance. *Personality and Social Psychology Bulletin, 15,* 252–265.

Sherif, M. (1935). A study of some social factors in perception. *Archives of Psychology, 27*(187), 1–60.

Sherif, M., Harvey, O., White, B., Hood, W., & Sherif, C. (1961). *Intergroup conflict and cooperation: The Robber's Cove experiment.* Norman: Institute of Group Relations, University of Oklahoma.

Shiflett, S. C. (1981). Is there a problem with the LPC score in leader match? *Personnel Psychology, 34,* 765–769.

Shomer, R., Davis, A., & Kelley, H. (1966). Threats and the development of coordination: Further studies of the Deutsch and Krauss trucking game. *Journal of Personality and Social Psychology, 4,* 119–126.

Shotland, R. L., & Strau, M. K. (1976). Bystander response to an assault: When a man attacks a woman. *Journal of Personality and Social Psychology, 34,* 990–999.

Sigall, H., & Aronson, R. (1969). Liking for an evaluator as a function of her physical attractiveness and nature of the evaluations. *Journal of Experimental Social Psychology, 5,* 93–100.

Sigall, H., & Landy, D. (1973). Radiating beauty: Effects of attractive partner on person perception. *Journal of Social Psychology, 28,* 218–224.

Sigall, H., & Ostrove, N. (1975). Beautiful but dangerous: Effects of offender attractiveness and nature of the crime on juridic judgments. *Journal of Personality and Social Psychology, 31,* 410–414.

Sigall, H., & Page, R. (1971). Current stereotypes: A little fading, a little faking. *Journal of Personality and Social Psychology, 18,* 247–255.

Silvern, S. B., & Williamson, P. A. (1987). The effects of video game play on young children's aggression, fantasy, and prosocial behavior. *Journal of Applied Developmental Psychology, 8*(4), 453–462.

Silverthorne, C. P., & Mazmanian, L. (1975). The effects of heckling and media of presentation on the impact of a persuasive communication. *Journal of Social Psychology, 96,* 229–236.

Simmel, G. (1955). *Conflict.* New York: Free Press.

Simonton, D. K. (1986a). Dispositional attributions of (presidential) leadership: An experimental simulation of historiometric results. *Journal of Experimental Social Psychology, 22,* 389–418.

Simonton, D. K. (1986b). Presidential personality: Biographical use of the Gough Adjective Check List. *Journal of Personality and Social Psychology, 51,* 149–160.

Simonton, D. K. (1987). Presidential inflexibility and veto behavior: Two individual-situational interactions. *Journal of Personality, 55,* 1–18.

Sistrunk, F., & McDavid, J. W. (1971). Sex variables in conforming behavior. *Journal of Personality and Social Psychology, 17,* 200–207.

Sivacek, J., & Crano, W. D. (1982). Vested interest as a moderator of attitude-behavior consistency. *Journal of Personality and Social Psychology, 43,* 210–221.

Skinner, B. F. (1938). *The behavior of organisms.* New York: Appleton.

Skinner, B. F. (1953). *Science and human behavior.* New York: Macmillan.

Skolnick, P. (1971). Reactions to personal evaluations: A failure to replicate. *Journal of Personality and Social Psychology, 18,* 62–67.

Skrypnek, B. J., & Snyder, M. (1982). On the self-perpetuating nature of stereotypes about women and men. *Journal of Experimental Social Psychology, 18,* 277–291.

Slater, P. E. (1955). Role differentiation in small groups. *American Sociological Review, 67,* 300–310.

Slusher, M. P., & Anderson, C. A. (1987). When reality monitoring fails: The role of imagination in stereotype maintenance. *Journal of Personality and Social Psychology, 52,* 653–662.

Smith, K. D., Keating, J. P., & Stotland, E. (1989). Altruism reconsidered: The effect of denying feedback on a victim's status to empathetic witnesses. *Journal of Personality and Social Psychology, 57,* 641–650.

Smith, R. H., & Insko, C. A. (1987). Social comparison choice during ability evaluation: The effects of comparison publicity, performance feedback, and self-esteem. *Personality and Social Psychology Bulletin, 13,* 111–122.

Smith, T. W., Snyder, C. R., & Handelsman, M. M. (1982). On the self-serving function of an academic wooden leg: Test anxiety as a self-handicapping strategy. *Journal of Personality and Social Psychology, 42,* 314–321.

Smith, T. W., Snyder, C. R., & Perkins, S. C. (1983). The self-serving function of hypochondrical complaints: Physical symptoms as self-handicapping strategies. *Journal of Personality and Social Psychology, 44,* 787–797.

Snell, W. E. (1989). Willingness to self-disclose to female and male friends as a function of social anxiety and gender. *Personality and Social Psychology Bulletin, 15,* 113–125.

Snow, R. (1969). Unfinished Pygmalion. *Contemporary Psychology, 14,* 197–199.

Snyder, C. R., & Fromkin, H. L. (1980). *Uniqueness: The human pursuit of difference.* New York: Plenum.

Snyder, C. R., Lassgard, M., & Ford, C. (1986). Distancing after group success and failure: Basking in reflected glory and cutting off reflected failure. *Journal of Personality and Social Psychology, 51,* 683–689.

Snyder, M. (1974). Self-monitoring of expressive behavior. *Journal of Personality and Social Psychology, 30,* 526–537.

Snyder, M. (1979). Self-monitoring processes. In L. Berkowitz (Ed.), *Advances in experimental social psychology* (Vol. 12, pp. 85–128). New York: Academic Press.

Snyder, M. (1987). *Public appearances: Private realities.* New York: W. H. Freeman.

Snyder, M., Berscheid, E., & Glick, P. (1985). Focusing on the exterior and the interior: Two investigations of the initiation of personal relationships. *Journal of Personality and Social Psychology, 48,* 1427–1439.

Snyder, M., & Gangestad, S. (1982). Choosing social situations: Two investigations of self-monitoring processes. *Journal of Personality and Social Psychology, 43,* 123–135.

Snyder, M., & Gangestad, S. (1986). On the nature of self-monitoring: Matters of assessment, matters of validity. *Journal of Personality and Social Psychology, 51,* 125–139.

Snyder, M., & Kendzierski, D. (1982). Acting on one's attitudes: Procedures for linking attitude and behavior. *Journal of Experimental Social Psychology, 18,* 165–183.

Snyder, M., & Swann, W. B., Jr. (1976). When actions reflect attitudes: The politics of impression management. *Journal of Personality and Social Psychology, 34,* 1034–1042.

Snyder, M., Tanke, E. D., & Berscheid, E. (1977). Social perception and interpersonal behavior: On the self-fulfilling nature of social stereotypes. *Journal of Personality and Social Psychology, 35,* 656–666.

Snyder, M. L., Schulz, R., & Jones, E. E. (1974). Expectancy and apparent duration as determinants of fatigue. *Journal of Personality and Social Psychology, 29,* 426–434.

Solomon, M. R., & Schopler, J. (1982). Self-consciousness and clothing. *Personality and Social Psychology Bulletin, 8,* 508–514.

Sommer, R. (1969). *Personal space: The behavioral basis of design.* Englewood Cliffs, N.J.: Prentice-Hall.

Sommer, R., & Becker, F. D. (1969). Territorial defense and the good neighbor. *Journal of Personality and Social Psychology, 11,* 85–92.

Sommer, R., & Ross, H. (1958). Social interaction on a geriatric ward. *International Journal of Social Psychiatry, 4,* 128–133.

Sorrentino, R. M., & Boutillier, R. G. (1975). The effect of quantity and quality of verbal interaction on ratings of leadership ability. *Journal of Experimental Social Psychology, 11,* 403–411.

Sorrentino, R. M., & Field, N. (1986). Emergent leadership over time: The functional value of positive motivation. *Journal of Personality and Social Psychology, 50,* 1091–1099.

Spence, J. T., Helmreich, R. L., & Stapp, J. (1975). Ratings of self and peers on sex-role attributes and their relation to self-esteem and conceptions of masculinity and femininity. *Journal of Personality and Social Psychology, 32,* 29–39.

Spence, K. W., Farber, I. E., & McFann, H. H. (1956). The relation of anxiety (drive) level to performance in competitional and noncompetitional paried-associated learning. *Journal of Experimental Psychology, 52,* 296–305.

Staats, A. W., & Staats, C. K. (1958). Attitudes established by classical conditioning. *Journal of Abnormal and Social Psychology, 57,* 37–40.

Stagner, R. (1986). Reminiscences about the founding of SPSSI. *Journal of Social Issues, 42,* 35–42.

Stang, D. J. (1972). Conformity, ability, and self-esteem. *Representative Research in Social Psychology, 3,* 97–103.

Stasser, G., Taylor, L. A., & Hanna, C. (1989). Information sampling in structured and unstructured discussions in three- and six-person groups. *Journal of Personality and Social Psychology, 57,* 67–78.

Stasser, G., & Titus, W. (1985). Pooling of unshared information in group decision making: Biased information sampling during discussion. *Journal of Personality and Social Psychology, 48,* 1467–1478.

Staw, B. M. (1974). Attitudinal and behavioral consequences of changing a major organizational reward: A natural field experiment. *Journal of Personality and Social Psychology, 29,* 742–751.

Stech, F. J., & McClintock, C. G. (1981). Effects of communicating timing on duopoly bargaining outcomes. *Journal of Personality and Social Psychology, 40,* 664–674.

Steele, C. M. (1988). The psychology of self affirmation: Sustaining the integrity of the self. In L. Berkowitz (Ed.), *Advances in experimental social psychology* (Vol. 21, 261–302). Orlando, Fla.: Academic Press.

Steele, C. M., Hopp, H., & Gonzales, J. (1986). Dissonance and the lab coat: Self affirmation and the free choice paradigm. Unpublished manuscript, University of Washington.

Steele, C. M., & Liu, T. J. (1983). Dissonance process as self-affirmation. *Journal of Personality and Social Psychology, 45,* 5–19.

Steele, C. M., Southwick, L. L., & Critchlow, B. (1981). Dissonance and alcohol: Drinking your troubles away. *Journal of Personality and Social Psychology, 41,* 831–846.

Stein, A. H., & Friedrich, L. K. (1975). The impact of television on children and youth. In E. M. Hetherington (Ed.), *Review of Child Development Research.* Chicago: University of Chicago Press.

Steiner, I. D. (1972). *Group process and productivity.* New York: Academic Press.

Steiner, I. D. (1976). Task-performing groups. In J. Thibaut, J. Spence, & R. Carson (Eds.), *Contemporary trends in social psychology.* Morristown, N.J.: General Learning Press.

Stephan, W. (1985). Intergroup relations. In G. Lindzey & E. Aronson (Eds.), *Handbook of social psychology* (3rd ed., Vol. 2, pp. 599–648). New York: Random House.

Sterling, B., & Gaertner, S. L. (1984). The attribution of arousal and emergency helping: A bi-directional process. *Journal of Experimental Social Psychology, 6,* 586–596.

Sternberg, R. J. (1986). A triangular theory of love. *Psychological Review, 93,* 119–135.

Sternberg, R. J. (1987). Liking versus loving: A comparative evaluation of theories. *Psychological Bulletin, 102,* 331–345.

Sternberg, R. J., & Grajek, S. (1984). The nature of love. *Journal of Personality and Social Psychology, 47,* 312–329.

Stewart, R. (1965). Effects of continuous responding on the order effect in personality impression formation. *Journal of Personality and Social Psychology, 1,* 161–165.

Stogdill, R. (1948). Personal factors associated with leadership. *Journal of Psychology, 25,* 35–71.

Stokols, D. (1972). On the distinction between density and crowding: Some implications for future research. *Psychological Review, 79,* 275–278.

Stokols, D., & Altman, I. (1987). *Handbook of environmental psychology*. New York: Wiley.

Stoner, J. (1961). *A comparison of individual and group decisions, including risk*. Unpublished master's thesis. MIT, School of Industrial Management, Cambridge.

Storms, M. (1973). Videotape and the attribution process: Reversing actor's and observer's points of view. *Journal of Personality and Social Psychology, 27,* 165–175.

Storms, M., & Nisbett, R. E. (1970). Insomnia and the attribution process. *Journal of Personality and Social Psychology, 2,* 319–328.

Strack, F., Martin, L., & Stepper, S. (1988). Inhibiting and facilitating conditions of the human smile: A nonobstrusive test of the facial feedback hypothesis. *Journal of Personality and Social Psychology, 54,* 768–777.

Strauman, T. J., & Higgins, E. T. (1987). Automatic activation of self-discrepancies and emotional syndromes: When cognitive structures influence affect. *Journal of Personality and Social Psychology, 53,* 1004–1014.

Straus, M. A., Gelles, R. J., & Steinmetz, S. K. (1980). *Behind closed doors*. Garden City, N. Y.: Anchor Books.

Streufert, S., & Streufert, S. C. (1986). The development of internation conflict. In S. Worchel & W. G. Austin (Eds.), *The psychology of intergroup relations*. Chicago: Nelson-Hall.

Strickland, L. H. (1968). Changes in self-presentation in need for approval scores. *Perceptual and Motor Skills, 27,* 335–337.

Strom, P., & Buck, R. (1979). Staring and participants' sex: Physiological and subjective reactions. *Personality and Social Psychology Bulletin, 5,* 114–117.

Strong, S. R., Hills, H. J., Kilmartin, C. T., DeVries, H., Lanier, K., Nelson, B. N., Strickland, D., & Meyer, C.W. III (1988). The dynamic relations among interpersonal behaviors: A test of complementarity and anti-complementarity. *Journal of Personality and Social Psychology, 54,* 798–810.

Strube, R., & Werner, C. (1982). Interpersonal distance and personal space: A conceptual and methodological note. *Journal of Nonverbal Behavior, 6,* 163–170.

Struch, N., & Schwartz, S. H. (1989). Intergroup aggression: Its predictors and distinctness from in-group bias. *Journal of Personality and Social Psychology, 56,* 364–373.

Stryker, S., & Statham, A. (1986). Symbolic interaction and role theory. In G. Lindzey & E. Aronson (Eds.), *The handbook of social psychology* (3rd ed.). New York: Random House.

Stryphek, B. J., & Snyder, M. (1982). On the self-perpetuating nature of stereotypes about women and men. *Journal of Experimental Social Psychology, 18,* 277–291.

Sullivan, D. S., & Deiker, T. E. (1973). Subject-experimenter perceptions of ethical issues in human research. *American Psychologist, 28,* 587–591.

Sullivan, H. (1953). *Interpersonal theory of psychiatry*. New York: Norton.

Suls, J., Gaes, G., & Gastorf, J. (1979). Evaluating a sex-related ability: Comparison with same-, opposite-, and combined-sex norms. *Journal of Research in Personality, 13,* 294–304.

Suls, J., & Wills, T. A. (Eds.) (1990). *Social comparison: Contemporary theory and research*. Hillsdale, N.J.: Erlbaum.

Summers, A. (1986). *Goddess: The secret lives of Marilyn Monroe*. New York: New American Library.

Sumner, W. (1906). *Folkways*. Boston: Ginn.

Sundstrom, E. (1978). Crowding as a sequential process: Review of research on the effects of population density on humans. In A. Baum & Y. Epstein (Eds.), *Human response to crowding*. Hillsdale, N.J.: Erlbaum.

Sundstrom, E. (1986). *Workplaces: The psychology of the physical environment in offices and factories*. Cambridge, Mass.: Cambridge University Press.

Sundstrom, E. (1987). Work environments: Offices and factories. In D. Stokols & I. Altman (Eds.), *Handbook of environmental psychology* (Vol. 1, pp. 733–782). New York: Wiley.

Swann, W. B., & Read, S. J. (1981). Self-verification processes: How we sustain our self-conceptions. *Journal of Experimental Social Psychology, 17,* 351–372.

Sweeney, P. D., Anderson, K., & Bailey, S. (1986). Attributional style in depression: A meta-analytic review. *Journal of Personality and Social Psychology, 50,* 974–991.

Swingle, P. (1970). Exploitative behavior in non-zero-sum games. *Journal of Personality and Social Psychology, 16,* 121–132.

Swinth, R. L. (1976). A decision process model for predicting job preferences. *Journal of Applied Psychology, 61,* 242–245.

Syme, G., Seligman, C., & Macpherson, D. (1989). Environmental planning and management: An introduction. *Journal of Social Issues, 45,* 1–16.

Tagiuri, R., Blake, R., & Bruner, J. (1953). Some determinants of the perception of positive and negative feelings in others. *Journal of Abnormal and Social Psychology, 48,* 585–592.

Tajfel, H. (1970). Experiments in intergroup discrimination. *Scientific American, 223*(2), 96–102.

Tajfel, H. (1972). Experiments in a vacuum. In J. Israel & H. Tajfel (Eds.), *The context of social psychology: A critical assessment* (European Monographs in Social Psychology, No. 2). London: Academic Press.

Tajfel, H. (1979). Individuals and groups in social psychology. *British Journal of Social and Clinical Psychology, 18,* 183–190.

Tajfel, H. (1982). *Social identity and intergroup relations*. Cambridge, England: Cambridge University Press.

Tajfel, H., Flament, C., Bilig, M. G., & Bundy, F. F. (1971). Social categorization and intergroup behavior. *European Journal of Social Psychology, 1,* 149–177.

Tajfel, H., & Turner, J. C. (1986). The social identity theory of intergroup behavior. In S. Worchel & W. G. Austin (Eds.), *The psychology of intergroup relations*. Chicago: Nelson-Hall.

Tanford, S., & Penrod, S. (1984). Social influence model: A formal integration of research on majority and minority influence processes. *Psychological Bulletin, 95,* 189–225.

Tannenbaum, P. H., & Zillman, D. (1975). Emotional arousal in the facilitation of aggression through communication. In L. Berkowitz (Ed.), *Advances in experimental social psychology* (Vol. 8). New York: Academic Press.

Taormina, R. J., & Messick, D. M. (1983). Deservingness for foreign aid: Effects of need, similarity, and estimated effectiveness. *Journal of Applied Social Psychology, 13,* 371–391.

Taylor, D. A., Gould, R. J., & Brounstein, P. J. (1981). Effects of personalistic self-disclosure. *Personality and Social Psychology Bulletin, 7,* 487–492.

Taylor, R. B., & Lanni, J. C. (1981). Territorial dominance: The influence of the resident advantage in triadic decision making. *Journal of Personality and Social Psychology, 41*(S), 909–915.

Taylor, S. E. (1975). On inferring one's own attitudes from one's behavior: Some delimiting conditions. *Journal of Personality and Social Psychology, 31,* 126–131.

Taylor, S. E., & Fiske, S. T. (1975). Point of view and perceptions of causality. *Journal of Personality and Social Psychology, 32,* 439–445.

Taylor, S. E., & Fiske, S. T. (1978). Salience, attention and attribution: Top-of-the-head phenomena. In L. Berkowitz (Ed.), *Advances in experimental social psychology* (Vol. 11). New York: Academic Press.

Taylor, S. E., Fiske, S. T., Etcoff, N. L., & Ruderman, A. J. (1978). Categorical bases of person memory and stereotyping. *Journal of Personality and Social Psychology, 36,* 778–793.

Taylor, S. P., & Gammon, C. B. (1975). Effects of type and dose of alcohol on human physical aggression. *Journal of Personality and Social Psychology, 32,* 169–175.

Taylor, S. P., Gammon, C. B., & Capasso, D. R. (1976). Aggression as a function of the interaction of alcohol and threat. *Journal of Personality and Social Psychology, 34,* 938–941.

Taylor, S. P., Vardaris, R. M., Rawitch, A. G., Gammon, C. B., & Cranston, J. W. (1976). The effects of alcohol and delta-p-tetrahydrocannibol on human physical aggression. *Aggressive Behavior, 2,* 153–162.

Tedeschi, J. T. (1974). *Perspectives on social power.* Chicago: Aldine.

Tedeschi, J. T. (1979). Frustration, fantasy, aggression, and the exercise of coercive power. *Perceptual and Motor Skills, 48,* 215–219.

Tedeschi, J. T. (Ed.). (1981). *Impression management theory and social psychological research.* New York: Academic Press.

Tedeschi, J. T., Schlenker, B. R., & Bonoma, T. V. (1971). Cognitive dissonance: Private ratiocination or public spectacle? *American Psychologist, 26,* 685–695.

Tedeschi, J. T., Smith, R. O., & Brown, R. C. (1974). A reinterpretation of research and aggression. *Psychology Bulletin, 81,* 540–563.

Teger, A. (1980). *Too much invested to quit.* New York: Pergamon.

Tennen, H., & Eller, S. J. (1977). Attributional components of learned helplessness and facilitation. *Journal of Personality and Social Psychology, 35,* 265–271.

Tennen, H., & Herzberger, S. (1987). Depression, self-esteem, and the absence of self-protective attributional biases. *Journal of Personality and Social Psychology, 52,* 72–80.

Terborg, J. R., Castore, C., & DeNinno, J. A. (1976). A longitudinal field investigation of the impact of group composition on group performance and cohesion. *Journal of Personality and Social Psychology, 34,* 782–790.

Terman, L. (1904). A preliminary study in the psychology and pedagogy of leadership. *Pedagogical Seminary, 4,* 413–451.

Tesser, A. (1976). Attitude polarization as a function of thought and reality constraints. *Journal of Research in Personality, 10*(2), 183–194.

Tesser, A. (1988). Toward a self-evaluation maintenance model of social behavior. In L. Berkowitz (Ed.), *Advances in experimental social psychology* (Vol. 21, pp. 181–227). New York: Academic Press.

Tesser, A., & Conlee, M. C. (1975). Some effects of time and thought on attitude polarization. *Journal of Personality and Social Psychology, 31*(2), 262–270.

Tesser, A., & Leone, C. (1977). Cognitive schemas and thought as determinants of attitude change. *Journal of Experimental Social Psychology, 13*(4), 340–356.

Tesser, A., Leone, C., & Clary, E. G. (1978). Affect control: Process constraints versus catharsis. *Cognitive Therapy and Research, 2*(3), 265–274.

Tesser, A., Millar, M., & Moore, J. (1988). Some affective consequences of social comparison and reflection processes: The pain and pleasure of being close. *Journal of Personality and Social Psychology, 54,* 49–61.

Tesser, A., & Smith, J. (1980). Some effects of task relevance and friendship on helping: You don't always help the one you like. *Journal of Experimental Social Psychology, 16,* 582–590.

Tetlock, P. E., Skitka, L., & Boettger, R. (1989). Social and cognitive strategies for coping with accountability: Conformity, complexity, and bolstering. *Journal of Personality and Social Psychology, 57,* 632–640.

t'Hart, P. (1988, July). *Groupthink: Observations toward a theory.* Paper presented at the meeting of the International Society of Political Psychology, Meadowlands, N.J.

t'Hart, P., & Kroon, M. (1989, June). *Groupthink in context.* Paper presented at the meeting of the International Society of Political Psychology, Tel Aviv, Israel.

Thibaut, J. W. (1968). The development of contractual norms in bargaining replication and variation. *Journal of Conflict Resolution, 12,* 102–112.

Thibaut, J. W., & Kelley, H. H. (1959). *The social psychology of groups.* New York: Wiley.

Thibaut, J. W., & Walker, L. (1975). *Procedural justice: A psychological analysis.* Hillsdale, N.J.: Erlbaum.

Thibaut, J. W., & Walker, L. (1978). A theory of procedure. *California Law Review, 66,* 541–566.

Thompson, L. L., Manniz, E. A., & Bazerman, M. H. (1988). Group negotiation: Effects of decision role, agenda, and aspiration. *Journal of Personality and Social Psychology, 54,* 86–95.

Thompson, S. C., Check, P., & Graham, M. (1988). The other side of perceived control: Disadvantages and negative effects. In S. Spacapan & S. Oskamp (Eds.), *The social psychology of health* (pp. 69–94). Newbury Park, Calif.: Sage.

Thompson, W. C., Cowan, C. L., & Rosenhan, D. L. (1980). Focus of attention mediates the impact of negative effect on altruism. *Journal of Personality and Social Psychology, 39,* 291–300.

Thornton, B., Hogate, L., Moirs, K., Pinette, M., & Presby, W. (1986). Physiological evidence of an arousal-based motivational bias in the defensive attribution of responsibility. *Journal of Experimental Social Psychology, 22,* 148–162.

Thornton, J. W., & Jacobs, P. D. (1971). Learned helplessness in human subjects. *Journal of Experimental Psychology, 87*(3), 367–372.

Thurstone, L. L. (1946). Comment. *American Journal of Sociology, 52,* 39–40.

Thurstone, L. L., & Chave, E. J. (1929). *The measurement of attitudes.* Chicago: University of Chicago Press.

Tilker, H. A. (1970). Socially responsible behavior as a function of observer responsibility and victim feedback. *Journal of Personality and Social Psychology, 4,* 95–100.

Tobey, E. L., & Tunnell, G. (1981). Predicting our impressions on others: Effects of self-consciousness and acting, a self-monitoring subscale. *Personality and Social Psychology Bulletin, 7,* 661–669.

Topf, M. (1985). Personal and environmental predictors of patient disturbance due to hospital noise. *Journal of Applied Psychology, 70,* 22–28.

Torrance, E. P. (1954). The behavior of small groups under the stress of conditions of survival. *American Sociological Review, 19,* 751–755.

Touhey, J. C. (1972). Comparison of two dimensions of attitude similarity on heterosexual attraction. *Journal of Personality and Social Psychology, 23,* 8–10.

Travis, L. E. (1925). The effect of a small audience upon eye-hand coordination. *Journal of Abnormal and Social Psychology, 20,* 142–146.

Triandis, H. C., Bontempo, R., Villareal, M. J., Asai, M., & Lucca, N. (1988). Individualism and collectivism: Cross-cultural perspectives on self-ingroup relations. *Journal of Personality and Social Psychology, 54,* 323–338.

Triplett, N. (1897). The dynamogenic factors in pacemaking and competition. *American Journal of Psychology, 9,* 507–533.

Trope, Y., Cohen, O., & Moaz, Y. (1988). The perceptual and inferential effects of situational inducements on dispositional attribution. *Journal of Personality and Social Psychology, 55,* 165–177.

Tuan, Y. F. (1977). *Space and place: The perspective of experience.* Minneapolis: University of Minnesota.

Tucker, J. A., Vucinish, R. E., & Sobell, M. S. (1981). Alcohol consumption as a self-handicapping strategy. *Journal of Abnormal Psychology, 90,* 220–230.

Tuckman, B. W. (1965). Developmental sequence in small groups. *Psychological Bulletin, 63,* 384–399.

Turner, C. W., & Berkowitz, L. (1972). Identification with film aggressor (covert role taking) and reactions to film violence. *Journal of Personality and Social Psychology, 21,* 256–264.

Turner, J. C. (1987). *Rediscovering the social group: A self-categorization theory.* Oxford, England: Basil Blackwell.

Turner, J. C., & Brown, R. J. (1978). Social status, cognitive alternatives and intergroup relations. In H. Tajfel (Ed.), *Differentiation between social groups.* London: Academic Press.

Tversky, A., & Kahneman, D. (1973). Availability: A heuristic for judging frequency and probability. *Cognitive Psychology, 5,* 207–232.

Tyler, T. R., & Sears, D. O. (1977). Coming to like obnoxious people when we must live with them. *Journal of Personality and Social Psychology, 35,* 200–211.

U.S. Bureau of the Census (1981). *Statistical abstracts of the United States.* Washington, D.C.: U.S. Government Printing Office.

U.S. Department of State (1983). *Patterns of international terrorism: 1982.* Washington, D.C.: U.S. Government Printing Office.

Uleman, J. S. (1987). Consciousness and control: The case of spontaneous trait inferences. *Personality and Social Psychology Bulletin, 13,* 337–354.

Underwood, B., Berenson, J. F., Berenson, R. J., Cheng, K. K., Wilson, D., Kulik, J., Moore, B. S., & Wenzel, G. (1977). Attention, negative affect, and altruism: An ecological validation. *Personality and Social Psychology Bulletin, 3,* 51–53.

United States Holocaust Memorial Council. (1989). *Night of pogroms: "Kristallnacht."* Washington, D.C.: U. S. Government Printing Office.

Urruti, G., & Miller, C. E. (1984). Test of bargaining and equal access theories of coalition formation: Effects of experience, information about payoffs, and monetary stakes. *Journal of Personality and Social Psychology, 46,* 825–836.

Valins, S. (1966). Cognitive effects of false heart-rate feedback. *Journal of Personality and Social Psychology, 4,* 400–408.

Valins, S. (1972). Persistent effects of information about internal reactions: Ineffectiveness of debriefing. In H. London & R. E. Nisbett (Eds.), *The cognitive alteration of feeling states.* Chicago: Aldine.

Van Hook, E., & Higgins, E. T. (1988). Self-related problems beyond the self-concept: Motivational consequences of discrepant self-guides. *Journal of Personality and Social Psychology, 55,* 625–633.

Van Zelt, R. H. (1952). Sociometrically selected work teams increase production. *Personnel Psychology, 5,* 175–186.

Veitch, R., & Griffitt, W. (1976). Good news, bad news: Affective and interpersonal effects. *Journal of Applied Social Psychology, 6,* 69–75.

Viney, W. (1989). The cyclops and the twelve-eyed toad: William James and the unity-disunity problem in psychology. *American Psychologist, 44,* 1261–1265.

Vinokur, A., Burnstein, E., Sechrest, L., & Wortman, P. M. (1985). Group decision making by experts: A group problem solving approach. *Journal of Personality and Social Psychology, 49,* 70–84.

Vogel, S. F. (1979). Decurrant's comments symposium: Applications of androgyny to the theory and practice of psychotherapy. *Psychology of Women Quarterly, 3,* 255–258.

Voice. (1989, February 21). Short eyes: The Joel Steinberg we never saw.

Von Baeyer, C. L., Sherk, D. L., & Zanna, M. P. (1981). Impression management in the job interview: When the female applicant meets the male (chauvinist) interviewer. *Personality and Social Psychology Bulletin, 7,* 45–51.

Von Cranach, M., Ochsenbein, G., & Valach, L. (1987). The group as a self-active system: Outline of a theory of group action. *European Journal of Social Psychology, 16,* 193–229.

Wagner, H. L., MacDonald, C. J., & Manstead, A. S. R. (1986). Communication of individual emotions by spontaneous facial expressions. *Journal of Personality and Social Psychology, 50,* 737–743.

Walker, L. E. (1989). Psychology and violence against women. *American Psychology, 44,* 695–702.

Wallach, M., Kogan, N., & Bem, D. (1962). Group influence on individual risk taking. *Journal of Abnormal and Social Psychology, 65,* 75–86.

Walsh, R. H., Ferrell, M. A., & Tolone, W. L. (1976). Selection of reference group, perceived permissiveness of reference group and personal permissiveness attitudes and behavior. *Journal of Marriage and the Family, 38,* 495–507.

Walster, E. (1966). Assignment of responsibility for an accident. *Journal of Personality and Social Psychology, 3,* 73–79.

Walster, E., Aronson, V., Abrahams, D., & Rottman, L. (1966). The importance of physical attractiveness in dating behavior. *Journal of Personality and Social Psychology, 4,* 508–516.

Walster, E., Berscheid, E., & Walster, G. W. (1976). New directions in equity research. In L. Berkowitz (Ed.), *Advances in experimental social psychology* (Vol. 9). New York: Academic Press.

Walster, E., Berscheid, E., & Walster, G. W. (1978). *Equity: Theory and research.* Boston: Allyn & Bacon.

Walster, E., & Festinger, L. (1962). The effectiveness of "overheard" persuasive communications. *Journal of Abnormal and Social Psychology, 65,* 395–402.

Walster, E., & Walster, G. W. (1969). The matching hypothesis. *Journal of Personality and Social Psychology, 6,* 248–253.

Walster, E., & Walster, G. W. (1978). *Love.* Reading, Mass.: Addison-Wesley.

Walters, P. S., & Lindskold, S. (1982). *Intensity of conflict and response to conciliation.* Unpublished manuscript, Ohio University, Athens, Oh.

Walters, R., & Willows, D. (1968). Imitation behavior of disturbed children following exposure to aggressive and nonaggressive models. *Child Development, 39,* 79–91.

Waterman, C. K. (1969). The facilitating and interfering effects of cognitive dissonance on simple and complex paired-associate learning tasks. *Journal of Experimental Social Psychology, 5,* 31–42.

Waterman, C. K., & Katkin, E. S. (1967). The energizing (dynamogenic) effect of cognitive dissonance on task performance. *Journal of Personality and Social Psychology, 6,* 126–131.

Waters, H. F., & Malamud, P. (1975, March 10). "Drop that gun, Captain Video." *Newsweek,* pp. 81–82.

Watson, R. I. (1973). Investigation into deindividuation using a cross-cultural survey technique. *Journal of Personality and Social Psychology, 25,* 342–345.

Weaver, W. (1970, October 25). Nixon repudiates obscenity reports as morally void. *New York Times,* pp. 1, 71.

Webb, W., & Worchel, P. (1986). Trust and distrust. In S. Worchel & W. G. Austin (Eds.), *The psychology of intergroup relations.* Chicago: Nelson-Hall.

Webb, W., Worchel, S., Reichers, L., & Wayne, W. (1986). The influence of categorization on perceptions of crowding. *Personality and Social Psychology Bulletin, 12,* 539–546.

Weber, M. (1946). The sociology of charismatic authority. Reprinted in H. H. Gerth & C. W. Mills (Trans. and Eds.), *From Max Weber: Essay in sociology* (pp. 245–252). New York: Oxford University Press. (Originally published in 1921.)

Weiner, B. (1979). A theory of motivation for some classroom experiences. *Journal of Educational Psychology, 71,* 3–25.

Weiner, B. (1985). An attributional theory of achievement motivation and emotion. *Psychological Review, 92,* 548–573.

Weiner, B. (1986). *An attribution theory of motivation and emotion.* New York: Springer-Verlag.

Weiner, B., Frieze, I., Kukla, A., Reed, L., Rest, B., & Rosenbaum, R. M. (1971). *Perceiving the causes of success and failure.* Morristown, N.J.: General Learning Press.

Weiner, B., Perry, R. P., & Magnusson, J. (1988). An attributional analysis of reactions to stigmas. *Journal of Personality and Social Psychology, 55,* 738–748.

Weiss, R. S. (1973). *Loneliness: The experience of emotional and social isolation.* Cambridge, Mass.: MIT Press.

Weiss, R. S. (1974). The provisions of social relationships. In Z. Rubin (Ed.), *Doing unto others* (pp. 17–26). Englewood Cliffs, N.J.: Prentice-Hall.

Wells, B. (1972). The psycho-social influence of building environment: Sociometric findings in large and small office spaces. In R. Gutman (Ed.), *People and buildings.* New York: Basic Books.

Wells, G. L., & Petty, R. E. (1980). The effects of overt head-movements on persuasion, compatibility, and incompatibility of responses. *Journal of Basic and Applied Social Psychology, 1,* 219–230.

Wells, W. D., Goi, F. J., & Seader, S. (1958). A change in a product image. *Journal of Applied Psychology, 42,* 120–121.

Werner, G., & Latané, B. (1974). Interaction motivates attraction: Rats are fond of fondling. *Journal of Personality and Social Psychology, 29,* 328–334.

West, S. G., & Wicklund, R. A. (1980). *A primer of social psychological theories.* Pacific Grove, Calif.: Brooks/Cole.

Westin, A. F. (1967). *Privacy and freedom.* New York: Atheneum.

Westover, T. (1989). Perceived crowding in recreational settings, an environmental behavior model. *Journal of Environment and Behavior, 21,* 258–276.

Wexner, L. B. (1954). The degree to which colors (hues) are associated with mood tones. *Journal of Applied Psychology, 38,* 432–435.

Wheeler, L. (1966). Toward a theory of behavioral contagion. *Psychological Review, 73,* 179–192.

Wheeler, L., & Koestner, R. (1984). Performance evaluation: On choosing to know the related attributes of others when we know their performance. *Journal of Experimental Social Psychology, 20,* 263–271.

Wheeler, L., Koestner, R., & Driver, R. E. (1982). Related attributes in the choice of comparison others: It's there, but it isn't all there is. *Journal of Experimental Social Psychology, 18,* 489–500.

Wheeler, L., Reis, H., & Nezlek, J. (1983). Loneliness, social interaction, and sex roles. *Journal of Personality and Social Psychology, 45,* 943–953.

Whitcher, S. J., & Fisher, J. D. (1979). Multidimensional reaction to therapeutic touch in a hospital setting. *Journal of Personality and Social Psychology, 37,* 87–96.

White, G. L. (1980). Physical attractiveness and courtship progress. *Journal of Personality and Social Psychology, 39,* 660–668.

White, G. L. (1981). A model of romantic jealousy. *Motivation and Emotion, 5,* 295–310.

White, G. L., Fishbein, S., & Rutstein, J. (1981). Passionate love and the misattribution of arousal. *Journal of Personality and Social Psychology, 41,* 56–62.

White, M. (1975). Interpersonal distance as affected by room size, status, and sex. *Journal of Social Psychology, 95,* 241–249.

White, R. K. (1966). Misperception as a cause of two world wars. *Journal of Social Issues, 22*(3), 1–9.

White, R. K. (1985). Ten psychological contributions to the prevention of nuclear war. In S. Oskamp (Ed.), *International conflict and national policy issues: Applied Social Psychology Annual, 6,* 45–61.

Whyte, W., Jr. (1956). *The organization man.* New York: Simon & Schuster.

Wicker, A. (1969). Attitudes versus action: The relationship of verbal and overt behavioral responses to attitude objects. *Journal of Social Issues, 25,* 1–78.

Wicker, A. W. (1987). Behavior settings reconsidered: Temporal stages, resources, internal dynamics, context. In D. Stokols & I. Altman (Eds.), *Handbook of environmental psychology* (Vol. 1, pp. 613–654). New York: Wiley.

Wicker, A. W., Kirmeyer, S. L., Hanson, L., & Alexander, D. (1976). Effects of manning levels on subjective experiences, performance and verbal interactions in groups. *Organizational Behavior and Human Performance, 17,* 251–274.

Wicklund, R. A., & Brehm, J. W. (1976). *Perspectives on cognitive dissonance.* Hillsdale, N.J.: Erlbaum.

Wicklund, R. A., Cooper, J., & Linder, D. E. (1967). Effects of expected effort on attitude change prior to exposure. *Journal of Experimental Social Psychology, 3,* 416–428.

Wicklund, R. A., & Frey, D. (1980). Self-awareness theory: When the self makes a difference. In D. M. Wegner & R. R. Vallacher (Eds.), *The self in social psychology* (pp. 31–54). New York: Oxford University Press.

Wiggins, J. S. (1979). A psychological taxonomy of trait-descriptive terms: The interpersonal domain. *Journal of Personality and Social Psychology, 37,* 395–412.

Wilder, D. (1986). Cognitive factors affecting the success of intergroup contact. In S. Worchel & W. G. Austin (Eds.), *The psychology of intergroup relations.* Chicago: Nelson-Hall.

Wilder, D., & Shapiro, P. N. (1989). Role of competition-induced anxiety in limiting the beneficial impact of positive behavior by an out-group member. *Journal of Personality and Social Psychology, 56,* 60–69.

Wilder, D. A. (1977). Perception of groups, size of opposition, and social influence. *Journal of Experimental Social Psychology, 13,* 253–268.

Wilke, H., & Van Knippenberg, A. (1988). Group performance. In M. Hewstone, W. Stroebe, J. Codol, & G. Stephenson (Eds.), *Introduction to social psychology*. Oxford, England: Basil Blackwell.

Williams, K., Harkins, S., & Latané, B. (1981). Identifiability as a deterrent to social loafing: Two cheering experiments. *Journal of Personality and Social Psychology, 40*, 303–311.

Wills, T. A. (1981). Downward comparison principles in social psychology. *Psychological Bulletin, 90*, 245–271.

Wilson, G. D. (1966). Arousal properties of red versus green. *Perceptual and Motor Skills, 23*, 947–979.

Wilson, L., & Rogers, R. W. (1975). The fire this time: Effects of race of target, insult, and potential retaliation on black aggression. *Journal of Personality and Social Psychology, 32*, 857–864.

Wilson, T. D., & Lassiter, G. D. (1982). Increasing intrinsic interest with superfluous extrinsic constraints. *Journal of Personality and Social Psychology, 42*, 811–819.

Wilson, T. D., & Linville, P. W. (1982). Improving the academic performance of college freshmen: Attribution therapy revisited. *Journal of Personality and Social Psychology, 42*, 367–376.

Winch, R. (1958). *Mate-selection: A study of complementary needs*. New York: Harper & Row.

Winkler, J., & Taylor, S. E. (1979). Preference, expectations, and attributional bias: Two field studies. *Journal of Applied Social Psychology, 2*, 183–197.

Winter, D. G. (1987). Leader appeal, leader performance, and the motive profiles of leaders and followers: A study of American presidents and elections. *Journal of Personality and Social Psychology, 52*, 196–202.

Winter, L., & Uleman, J. S. (1984). When are social judgments made? Evidence for the spontaneousness of trait inferences. *Journal of Personality and Social Psychology, 47*, 237–252.

Wolfgang, M. E., & Fenacuti, F. (1967). *The subculture of violence*. London: Tavistock.

Wood, W. (1987). Meta-analytic review of sex differences in group performance. *Psychological Bulletin, 102*, 53–71.

Wood, W., & Eagly, A. H. (1981). Stages in the analysis of persuasive messages: The role of causal attributions and message comprehension. *Journal of Personality and Social Psychology, 40*, 246–259.

Worchel, S. (1974). The effect of three types of arbitrary thwarting on the instigation to aggression. *Journal of Personality, 42*, 300–318.

Worchel, S. (1984a). The darker side of helping: The social dynamics of helping and cooperation. In E. Staub et al. (Eds.), *The development and maintenance of prosocial behavior*. New York: Plenum.

Worchel, S. (1984b). *A model of achieving group independence*. Paper presented at the XXIII International Congress of Psychology, Acapulco, Mexico.

Worchel, S. (1986a). The influence of contextual variables on interpersonal spacing. *Journal of Nonverbal Behavior, 10*, 230–254.

Worchel, S. (1986b). The role of cooperation in reducing intergroup conflict. In S. Worchel and W. G. Austin (Eds.), *The psychology of intergroup relations* (pp. 153–176). Chicago: Nelson-Hall.

Worchel, S. (1989, June). *Minority influence in the group context: How group factors affect when the minority will be influential*. Paper presented at the 3rd Workshop on Minority Influence, Perugia, Italy.

Worchel, S., & Andreoli, V. (1978). Facilitation of social inter-

action through deindividuation of the target. *Journal of Personality and Social Psychology, 36*, 549–557.

Worchel, S., Andreoli, V., & Folger, R. (1977). Intergroup cooperation and intergroup attraction: The effect of previous interaction and outcome of combined effort. *Journal of Experimental Social Psychology, 13*, 131–140.

Worchel, S., & Arnold, S. (1973). The effects of censorship and attractiveness of the censor on attitude change. *Journal of Experimental Social Psychology, 9*, 365–377.

Worchel, S., Arnold, S., & Baker, M. (1975). The effects of censorship on attitude change: The influence of censor and communication characterisics. *Journal of Applied Social Psychology, 5*, 227–239.

Worchel, S., & Austin, W. G. (Eds.). (1986). *The psychology of intergroup relations*. Chicago: Nelson-Hall.

Worchel, S., & Brehm, J. W. (1970). Effect of threats to attitudinal freedom as a function of agreement with the communicator. *Journal of Personality and Social Psychology, 14*, 18–22.

Worchel, S., Coutant-Sasic, D., & Grossman, M. (in press). A model of group development and independence. In S. Worchel, W. Wood, & J. Simpson (Eds.), *Group process and productivity*. Newbury Park, Calif.: Sage.

Worchel, S., Hart, D., & Buttermeyer, J. (1989, April). *Is social loafing a group phenomenon?* Paper presented at the Southwestern Psychological Association Meeting, Houston.

Worchel, S., Lind, E., & Kaufman, K. (1975). Evaluations of group products as a function of expectations of group longevity, outcome of competition, and publicity of evaluations. *Journal of Personality and Social Psychology, 31*, 1089–1097.

Worchel, S., & Lollis, M. (1982). Reactions to territorial contamination as a function of culture. *Personality and Social Psychology Bulletin, 8*, 365–370.

Worchel, S., & Shackelford, S. (in press). Preparing groups for stress: The impact of environmental stress and group structure on performance. *Personality and Social Psychology Bulletin*.

Worchel, S., & Sigall, H. (1976). There is no place like home, unless . . . *The ACC Basketball Handbook*. Charlotte, N.C.: VMI Publications.

Worchel, S., & Teddlie, C. (1976). The experience of crowding: A two-factor theory. *Journal of Personality and Social Psychology, 34*, 30–40.

Worchel, S., Webb, W., & Reichers, L. (1989). The influence of expectancy and prior experience on environmental perceptions. *Midwestern Psychological Association*. Chicago.

Worchel, S., Wong, F., & Scheltema, K. (1989). Improving intergroup relations: Comparative effects of anticipated cooperation and helping in attraction for an aid-giver. *Social Psychology Quarterly, 52*, 213–219.

Word, C. H., Zanna, M. P., & Cooper, J. (1974). The nonverbal mediation of self-fulfilling prophecies in interracial interaction. *Journal of Experimental Social Psychology, 10*, 109–120.

Wortman, C. B., & Brehm, J. W. (1975). Responses to uncontrollable outcomes: An integration of reactance theory and the learned helplessness model. In L. Berkowitz (Ed.), *Advances in experimental social psychology* (Vol. 8, pp. 277–336). New York: Academic Press.

Wright, P., & Crawford, A. (1971). Agreement and friendship: A close look and some second thoughts. *Representative Research in Social Psychology, 2*, 52–69.

Wrightsman, L. S. (1964). Measurement of philosophies of human nature. *Psychological Reports, 14*, 743–751.

Wrightsman, L. S. (1969). Wallace supporters and adherence

to "law and order." *Journal of Personality and Social Psychology, 13,* 17–22.

Yancey, W. L. (1971). Architecture and social interaction: The case of a large-scale public housing project. *Environment and Behavior, 3,* 3–21.

Younger, J. C., Walker, L., & Arrowood, A. J. (1977). Postdecision dissonance at the fair. *Personality and Social Psychology Bulletin, 3,* 247–287.

Yukl, G. (1974). The effects of the opponent's initial offer, concession magnitude and concession frequency on bargaining behavior. *Journal of Personality and Social Psychology, 30,* 323–335.

Yukl, G. A., Malone, M., Hayslip, B., & Pamin, T. (1978). The effect of time pressure and issue settlement order on integrative bargaining. *Sociometry, 39,* 277–281.

Zajonc, R. B. (1965). Social facilitation. *Science, 149,* 269–274.

Zajonc, R. B. (1968). Attitudinal effects of mere exposure. *Journal of Personality and Social Psychology, 9,* monograph suppl. No. 2, pt. 2.

Zajonc, R. B. (1972). *Animal social behavior.* Morristown, N.J.: General Learning Press.

Zajonc, R. B. (1989). Styles of explanation in social psychology. *European Journal of Social Psychology, 19,* 345–368.

Zand, D. E. (1972). Trust and managerial problem-solving. *Administrative Science Quarterly, 17,* 229–239.

Zander, A. (1982). *Making groups effective.* San Francisco: Jossey-Bass.

Zanna, M. P., & Cooper, J. (1974). Dissonance and the pill: An attribution approach to studying the arousal properties of dissonance. *Journal of Personality and Social Psychology, 29,* 703–709.

Zanna, M. P., & Cooper, J. (1976). Dissonance and the attribution process. In J. H. Harvey, W. J. Ickes, & R. F. Kidd (Eds.), *New directions in attribution research* (Vol. 1). Hillsdale, N.J.: Erlbaum.

Zanna, M. P., & Fazio, R. H. (1982). The attitude-behavior relation: Moving toward a third generation of research. In M. P. Zanna, E. T. Higgins, & C. P. Herman (Eds.), *Consistency in social behavior: The Ontario symposium* (Vol. 2). Hillsdale, N.J.: Erlbaum.

Zanna, M., Goethals, G. R., & Hill, J. (1975). Evaluating a sex-rated ability: Social comparison with similar others and standard setters. *Journal of Experimental Social Psychology, 11,* 86–93.

Zeichner, A., & Pihl, P. O. (1979). Effects of alcohol and behavior contingencies on human aggression. *Journal of Abnormal Psychology, 88,* 153–160.

Zelditch, M. (1955). Role differentiation in the nuclear family: A comparative study. In T. Parsons & R. Bales (Eds.), *Family, socialization and interaction process.* Glencoe, Ill.: Free Press.

Zillmann, D. (1971). Excitation transfer in communication-mediated aggressive behavior. *Journal of Experimental Social Psychology, 7,* 419–434.

Zillmann, D. (1978). *Hostility and aggression.* Hillsdale, N.J.: Erlbaum.

Zillmann, D. (1983). Transfer of excitation in emotional behavior. In J. T. Cacioppo & R. E. Petty (Eds.), *Social psychophysiology: A sourcebook.* New York: Guilford.

Zillmann, D. (1984). *Connections between sex and aggression.* Hillsdale, N.J.: Erlbaum.

Zillmann, D., & Bryant, J. (1988). Pornography's impact on sexual satisfaction. *Journal of Applied Social Psychology, 18,* 438–453.

Zillmann, D., Bryant, J., & Carveth, R. A. (1981). The effect of erotica featuring sadomasochism and bestiality on motivated intermale aggression. *Personality and Social Psychology Bulletin, 7,* 153–159.

Zillmann, D., Bryant, J., Comisky, P. W., & Medoff, N. J. (1981). Excitation and hedonic valence in the effect of erotica on motivated intermale aggression. *European Journal of Social Psychology, 11,* 233–252.

Zillmann, D., & Johnson, R. C. (1973). Maternal aggressiveness perpetuated by exposure to aggressive films and reduced by exposure to nonaggressive films. *Journal of Research in Personality, 7,* 261–276.

Zimbardo, P. (1965). The effect of effort and improvisation in self-persuasion produced by role playing. *Journal of Experimental Social Psychology, 1,* 103–120.

Zimbardo, P. (1970). The human choice: Individuation, reason, and order versus individuation, impulse, and chaos. *Nebraska Symposium on Motivation.* Lincoln: University of Nebraska Press.

Zimbardo, P., Weisenberg, M., Firestone, I., & Levy, B. (1965). Communicator effectiveness in producing public conformity and private attitude change. *Journal of Personality, 33,* 233–255.

Zimring, C., Carpman, J., & Michelson, W. (1987). Design for special populations: Mentally retarded persons, children, hospital visitors. In D. Stokols & I. Altman (Eds.), *Handbook of environmental psychology* (Vol. 2, pp. 919–950). New York: Wiley.

Zimring, C., Weitzer, W., & Knight, R. C. (1982). Opportunity for control and the designed environment: The case of an institution for the developmentally disabled. In A. Baum & J. Singer (Eds.), *Advances in environmental psychology* (Vol. 4, pp. 170–210). Hillsdale, N.J.: Erlbaum.

Zuckerman, M., Amidon, M. D., Bishop, S. E., & Pomerantz, S. D. (1982). Face and tone of voice in the communication of deception. *Journal of Personality and Social Psychology, 43,* 347–357.

Zuckerman, M., DePaulo, B., & Rosenthal, R. (1981). Verbal and nonverbal communication of deception. In L. Berkowitz (Ed.), *Advances in experimental social psychology* (Vol. 14, pp. 1–59). New York: Academic Press.

Zukier, H., (1982). The role of the correlation and the dispersion of predictor variables in the use of nondiagnostic information. *Journal of Personality and Social Psychology, 43,* 1163–1175.

Zukier, H., & Pepitone, A. (1984). Social roles and strategies in prediction: Some determinants of the use of base-rate information. *Journal of Personality and Social Psychology, 47,* 349–360.

Name Index

Benoit, J., 68
Benowitz, L. I., 125, 126
Benson, P. L., 273
Berg, J. H., 229
Berger, S. M., 459
Berglas, S., 113, 114, 114
Berkowitz, L., 277, 298, 304, 305, 307, 313, 317, 367
Bernieri, F., 62
Berscheid, E., 121, 226, 228, 239, 240, 241, 245–246, 251, 252, 255, 256, 258, 259, 261, 346, 372
Bickman, L., 273
Bierbrauer, G., 422
Biggers, T., 157
Billig, M., 464
Biner, P., 499
Bird, A., 447
Bird, C., 362
Birdwhistell, R. L., 124
Bishop, J., 394
Black, R. H., 465
Blake, R. R., 248, 350, 423
Blanck, P. D., 125
Blaney, P. H., 119
Blaylock, B., 234
Block, J. H., 383
Block, L., 499
Bodenhausen, G. V., 372
Boettger, R., 426
Bogart, K., 78
Bolen, D., 71
Bonoma, T. V., 106, 216, 398
Booker, A., 304
Bootzin, R. R., 96
Bossard, J., 236
Boulding, K. E., 294–295
Bouthilet, L., 319
Boutillier, R. G., 407
Bowers, K. S., 62
Bowman, E., 445
Boye, D., 239
Bradley, G. W., 87
Brady, A., 480
Braiker, H. B., 257
Braly, K. W., 368, 369
Bray, R., 452
Brehm, J. W., 169–170, 196, 200, 207, 217, 219, 220, 426, 430, 491
Brehm, S. S., 217
Brewer, M. B., 23, 351
Brickman, P., 71, 234
Brickner, M., 460
Bridgeman, L., 352
Brier, J., 311
Briggs, S. R., 120
Broadbent, D. E., 494
Brock, T. C., 155, 198
Brockner, J., 331, 336
Broome, B., 341
Brophy, J. E., 62
Brounstein, P. J., 130
Brousseau, K. R., 440
Brown, B. B., 487, 488
Brown, B. R., 336
Brown, J. D., 92
Brown, J. F., 12
Brown, P., 308
Brown, R., 122, 125, 126, 129, 349, 366, 367, 428, 442, 457, 464, 466

Brown, R. C., 305
Brown, R. J., 351
Brown, V., 388
Bruins, J. J., 330
Bruker, C., 464
Bruner, J. S., 142, 248
Brunn, S., 460
Bryan, J., 275
Bryant, J., 311, 312
Buck, R., 123, 127
Budd, L. G., 486
Bulletin of the Atomic Scientists, 335
Burdick, M., 362
Burger, J. M., 75, 166
Burgess, M., 299
Burgess, R. L., 258
Burleson, J. A., 130
Burns, J. R., 402
Burns, L., 75
Burnstein, E., 464
Burt, M. R., 397
Busiek, R. D., 142
Buss, A. A., 294
Buss, A. H., 118, 120, 198, 304
Buss, D. M., 349
Buss, E., 304
Butler, D., 232
Butterfield, D. A., 388
Buttermeyer, J., 461
Byrne, D., 227, 233, 234, 480

Cacioppo, J. T., 139, 140–141, 151, 171, 174
Caldwell, D. F., 122
Caldwell, M. D., 340
Calhoun, J. B., 490
Callaway, M., 452
Campbell, B., 259
Campbell, D. T., 20, 140, 170–171, 176, 441
Campbell, J. D., 75, 419, 424, 426
Canavan, D., 332
Canavan-Gumpert, D., 399
Cann, A., 165, 166
Cannon, L. K., 494
Cantor, N., 374
Cantril, H., 5, 13, 14, 15, 301
Capasso, D. R., 310
Carli, L. L., 382, 427, 448, 449
Carlsmith, J. M., 23, 123, 163, 175, 194, 195, 197, 198, 199, 214
Carlson, M., 295
Carnegie, D., 109
Carnevale, P. J., 345, 349
Carp, F., 501
Carpman, J., 502
Carson, R. C., 127
Cartwright, D., 9, 145, 146, 397, 464
Carver, C. S., 115, 117, 119
Carveth, R. A., 312
Casella, D. F., 127
Cash, T. F., 246
Castore, C., 447
Castro, M. A. C., 288
Cavalli-Sforza, L. L., 141
Cavan, S., 484
Ceci, S. J., 31
Cecil-Pigo, E. F., 229
Centers, R., 400
Central Intelligence Agency, 334

Chaiken, S., 77, 151, 156, 160
Chave, E. J., 10
Check, J. V. P., 312
Check, P., 501
Cheek, J. M., 120
Chemers, M. M., 413, 414, 475
Chen, S. C., 458
Chertkoff, J. M., 344, 406
Chiles, C., 454
Chollar, S., 381
Cialdini, R. B., 88, 111, 152, 165–166, 270–271, 272
Clark, M. S., 229, 230, 231, 251, 274, 288
Clark, R. D., 454
Cleaver, E., 389
Clifford, M., 242
Clore, G. L., 227, 228, 233
Coch, L., 462
Cochran, C., 482
Coffman, J., 139, 369
Cohen, A. R., 195, 196, 198
Cohen, C. E., 374
Cohen, J., 287
Cohen, M. F., 299
Cohen, O., 40, 41
Cohen, S., 492, 494
Cohen, W., 494
Cohn, N. B., 130
Coleman, L. M., 369
Coll, J., 345
Collins, B. E., 199, 200
Collmer, C. W., 309
Comer, R., 212, 219, 220
Condelli, L., 398
Conlee, M. C., 172
Conley, M., 344
Conn, L. K., 62
Conolley, E. S., 423, 426
Consumer Reports, 165
Cook, S. W., 351
Cook, T. D., 154
Cooley, C. H., 70
Cooper, H., 62
Cooper, J., 62, 190, 198, 198, 199, 200, 201, 203, 204, 205, 210–212, 215, 234, 318, 387, 408
Cordes, B., 334
Costa, P. T., 127
Cotton, J. L., 81
Cottrell, N., 210, 459
Coutant-Sasic, D., 439, 457
Cowan, C. L., 275
Cowan, P. A., 306
Cox, V., 490, 508
Cozby, P. C., 130, 131
Craig, K. D., 123
Crano, W. D., 72, 116, 174
Crawford, A., 233
Crider, A. B., 52
Critchlow, B., 212, 213
Crocker, J., 53, 365
Crowne, D. P., 105
Croyle, R. T., 190, 212
Crutchfield, R. A., 418
Csikszentmihalyi, M., 477
Cunningham, J. D., 131
Curtis, R. C., 63

D'Agostino, P. R., 55
Damrad-Frye, R., 76

Danheiser, P. R., 121
Darley, J. M., 23, 50, 63, 72, 73, 226, 239, 276, 278, 280, 281, 282, 284, 285, 373, 388, 404, 429, 508
Darley, S. A., 385
Darwin, C., 123
Davidson, A. R., 184
Davidson, L. R., 131
Davidson-Podgorny, G., 352
Davies, J. C., 302
Davies, R. M., 260
Davis, A., 332
Davis, D., 238
Davis, J., 452
Davis, K. E., 12, 39, 41, 109, 199, 200, 226, 234, 255, 256
Davis, L., 256
Davis, M. H., 129
Davison, J., 114
Davitz, J. R., 297
Dawes, R. M., 149, 329, 330, 369
Dean, J., 483
Deaux, K., 273, 386, 387, 388
Deiker, T. E., 31
DeJong, P. F., 86
DeJong, W., 164–165, 282
Demare, D., 311
DeMorest, J. A., 122, 246
De Nicholas, M. E., 111
DeNinno, J. A., 447
DePaulo, B., 125
Dermer, M., 240, 251
Desselles, M. L., 445
Deutsch, M., 12, 330, 331, 332, 333, 340, 341, 346, 353, 419
Devine, P. G., 370, 373, 389
Dickoff, H., 236
Dickson, W., 440, 448
Diener, E., 466
Di Mento, J. F., 509
Dion, K. K., 241, 243
Doctor, R. M., 335
Dodson, J. A., 77
Dollard, J., 294, 297
Donnerstein, E., 312, 313, 314, 316
Donnerstein, M., 312, 316
Doob, A. N., 299
Dovidio, J. F., 375, 379
Downey, R. G., 403
Downing, L. L., 276, 466
Downing, R., 96
Dreyer, A., 127
Driscoll, R., 256
Driver, R. E., 73
Druckman, D., 341
Duberman, L., 131
Duclos, S. E., 77
Duffy, K., 349
Duncan, D. L., 372
Durkheim, E., 436
Dutton, D, G,, 254
Duval, S., 115, 117
Duval, V. H., 117
Dweck, C. S., 97

Eagly, A. H., 151, 154, 155, 296, 382, 388, 426, 427
Earle, W. B., 429
Earley, C., 464
Eaton, W. O., 382
Ebbinghaus, H., 170
Eckardt, G., 10

U.S. Bureau of the Census, 381, 504
U.S. Department of State, 334
U.S. Holocaust Memorial Council, 358

Valins, S., 82, 503
van de Kragt, A. J., 330
Vanderplas, N., 271
Van Hook, E., 94
van Knippenberg, A., 459
Van Treuren, R. R., 92
Van Zelt, R. H., 447
Veitch, R., 228, 233
Viney, W., 14
Vinokur, A., 450, 464
Vinsel, A. M., 479
Visser, L., 455
Vitters, A. G., 406
Volpato, C., 454
Von Baeyer, C. L., 109
Vucinish, R. E., 114

Wack, D., 210
Wackenhut, J., 376
Wagner, H. L., 126
Walker, L., 208, 209, 309, 347
Walker, M., 480
Wallach, M., 463
Wallston, B. S., 287
Walsh, R. H., 145
Walster, E., 50, 154, 228, 240, 242, 251, 252, 259, 346
Walster, G. W., 228, 241, 252, 259, 346
Walters, G., 139, 369
Walters, P. S., 343
Walters, R. H., 275, 305, 306, 307, 308
Waterman, C. K., 210
Waters, H. F., 315
Watson, R. I., 466
Watson, W. E., 465
Watts, J. C., 158
Weaver, W., 160
Webb, J., 341
Webb, W., 338, 339, 478, 491, 492
Weber, M., 408
Weber, R., 53
Weiby, M., 86
Weigold, M. F., 122
Weiner, B., 45, 46
Weintraub, M., 217
Weiss, J. A., 440
Weiss, R. S., 258, 259
Weiss, W., 152, 153, 175
Weitzer, W., 501
Wells, B., 499
Wells, G. L., 77
Wells, W. D., 368
Werner, C., 479
Werner, G., 238
West, S. G., 363, 430
Westin, A. F., 486
Westover, T., 491
Wexner, L. B., 498
Wheeler, L., 73, 244, 247, 258
White, G. L., 241, 254, 260
White, M., 482
White, R. K., 11, 342, 410, 456

Whyte, W., 463
Wicker, A. W., 182, 190, 446, 476, 478
Wicklund, R. A., 115, 117, 118, 198, 200, 203, 430
Wiggins, J. S., 127
Wilder, D. A., 351, 424, 425
Wilhelmy, R. A., 423, 426
Wilke, H. A., 330, 459
Willerman, B., 250
Williams, C. J., 189
Williams, D., 407
Williams, K., 460, 461
Williams, M. S., 465
Williamson, P. A., 318
Willits, J., 273
Willows, D., 307
Wills, T. A., 72, 74
Wilson, G. D., 498
Wilson, L., 378
Wilson, T. D., 79, 96, 98
Winch, R., 234, 235
Winer, B., 403
Winkler, J., 88
Winter, D. G., 407, 410
Winter, L., 48
Witcher, S. J., 126
Wittmer, J., 114
Wohlwill, J., 476, 506
Wolfgang, M. E., 306
Wong, F., 352
Wood, G. C., 457
Wood, L. E., 299
Wood, R., 477
Wood, W., 155, 426, 442, 448
Worchel, P., 235, 338, 339
Worchel, S., 160, 200, 201, 218, 219, 220, 288, 305, 349, 352, 353, 409, 439, 440, 456, 457, 461, 466, 478, 482, 485, 486, 491, 492
Word, C. H., 62, 387
Worth, L. T., 172
Wortman, C., 107, 109, 219, 236, 491
Wright, H., 476
Wright, P., 233
Wrightsman, L. S., 182, 339

Yalom, I. D., 403
Yamamoto, T., 485
Yancey, W. L., 500
Yates, S., 160
Younger, J. C., 208, 209
Yukl, G., 345

Zaccaro, S. J., 407
Zajonc, R., 12, 13, 56, 240, 459
Zand, D. E., 339
Zander, A., 397, 447
Zanna, M. P., 62, 73, 109, 190, 210–212, 385, 387
Zeichner, A., 311
Zelditch, M., 404, 442
Zembrot, I. M., 260
Zillmann, D., 81, 98, 311, 312, 316
Zimbardo, P., 81, 94, 98, 196, 198, 203, 466
Zimring, C., 501, 502
Zuckerman, M., 79, 125, 126
Zukier, H., 56

Subject Index

Gestures, 123–124
Glasnost, 402
Global attribution, 91
Globality of causes, 46
Gods Must Be Crazy, The, 472
Good feelings, persuasion and, 156–157
Good Samaritan parable, 275–276
Gorbachev, Mikhail, 402, 456
Graduated reciprocation in tension reduction (GRIT), 342–343, 354
"Great person" theory of leadership, 404
Greed, social dilemmas and, 329–330
Group
    defined, 435–437, 467
    development of a, 437–440
    influence on behavior, 418–420
Group behavior, self-attention perspective on, 118
Group dynamics, 434–469
    deindividuation in, 465–469
    development of groups and their members, 437–440
    group characteristics and productivity, 446–449
    group decision making, 449–455
    group influence on individual performance, 457–461
    group polarization, 463–465
    group productivity, 443–445
    groups' effects on individuals, 455–457
    groups' influence on individual decisions, 462–463
    structure of groups, 440–443
    task type and performance and, 445–446
Group needs, leadership and, 410
Group polarazation, 463–465, 469
Groupthink, 449–452, 468
    consequences of, 451

Halo error, 403
Handbook of Environmental Psychology, 501
Harwood Manufacturing Company study, 462–463
"Helper's dilemma," 288
Helping (*see also* Altruism)
    cost model of, 283–287
Heuristic processing model, 151, 175
Heyerdahl, Thor, 434–435
Hitler, Adolf, 358–360, 362–363, 408
Holocaust, events of, 358–360
Honesty, techniques to increase, 139–140
Hopkins, Ann, 381–382
Horizon House study, 78
Hormones, aggression and, 296
How to Win Friends and Influence People (Carnegie), 109, 248
Hypotheses, 14–15, 32

Idealized performances, 104, 105
Identification, 396, 397
Identification stage of a group, 439
Identity
    loss of in crowds, 466
    personal space and, 482
Idiosyncrasy credits, 426
Illusory correlations, 57, 64
    stereotypes and, 370–372
Images, creating, 156
Imagined arousal, 81–82
Imitation, aggression and, 306–307
Immediacy, 62
Impression
    consequences of forming impressions, 61–63

dilution effect and, 56–57
    importance of first impressions, 58–59
    schemata and, 52
Impression management, 104, 105, 216, 217
    aggression and, 320
Impression management theory, 106–107
Indefensible territory, 501
Independent variable, 18, 19, 32
Individual differences, 8
Individuation stage of a group, 439
Induced compliance, critical factors in, 198–202
Induced compliance paradigm, 193–202, 220
Influence (*see also* Social power)
    directionality of, 145
    of reference groups, 143–145
Informational power, 400, 401
Informational social influence, 418, 419, 431
Informed consent, 30, 31
Ingratiation, 131–132, 236, 237
    defined, 107
    power and, 106–112
    principles of, 107–108
Ingratiation tactics, 108–110
Ingratiator's dilemma, 107–108
In-group, perceptions of, 368–369
In-group favoritism, prejudice and, 364–365
Inoculation, 167–168, 176
Instinct theories of aggression, 295–296
Institutional design, 499–504
Institutionalization stage of a relationship, 258
Institutional review boards (IRBs), 30–31, 33
Institutional stage of a revolution, 303, 320
Instrumental aggression, 295
Instrumental conditioning, 147
Insults, interpersonal perception and, 248–249
Integrative problem solving, 341
Intelligence, leadership and, 406–407
Interaction distances, 479
Interactionist theories of leadership, 410
Interdependence, intergroup conflict and, 352
Intergroup conflict, 349–351, 354–355
    resolving, 351–352
Internal attribution, 38, 39, 63, 91
Internalization, 397
Internal locus of control, 89–90, 98
Internal validity, 20, 21
Interpersonal behavior, the self and, 103–104
Interpersonal conflict, 326, 327
Interpersonal style, 132
    classification of, 127–129
Interpersonal Trust Scale, 339
Intimacy
    as a component of love, 251
    personal space and, 482–483
Intimate distance, 479
Intimate relationships, self-monitoring and, 122
Intimidation, 110, 111, 132
Intrapersonal conflict, 326, 327
Invasion of privacy, ethics and, 30
Inverted U, 159, 175

Japanese business firms, 447
J-curve hypothesis, 302, 303
Jealousy, 260–261
Jews
    Nazi attacks on, 358–360

Public commitment, 164–168
Public distance, 479
Public self-consciousness, 115, 118
    effects of, 118–119
Public territory, 484, 485, 510

Quayle, Dan, 36–38

Racial ambivalence, 376–378
Racism
    aversive, 379–380
    defined, 360, 361
    modern, 374–381
    perspectives on, 361–368
    regressive, 378–379
    scope of, 360–361
Random assignment, 20, 21
Rape, incidence of, 381
Ray, Clifford, 136
Reactance, reactions to the arousal of, 217–218
Reactance theory, 430, 431
Reagan, Ronald, 324–325
Realistic conflict theory, 363
Recency effect, 60–61, 64
Reciprocity, 130, 131
Reciprocity norm, 277, 289
Reference groups, 175
    influence on attitudes, 143–145
Referent power, 400, 401
Reflected appraisal, 70–72, 97
Regressive racism, 378–379, 390
Reign-of-terror stage of a revolution, 303, 320
Reinforcement
    aggression and, 306, 320
    defined, 307
Reinforcement effect, 198, 199
Related attributes hypothesis, 73–74
Relationship Closeness Inventory (RCI), 255
Relationships (see also Personal relationships)
    long-term, 254–256
Relative deprivation, 300, 301, 320
Representativeness bias, 58, 59, 64
Research
    archival, 16
    on attitudes, 174
    becoming part of, 31
    in social psychology, 10
    on trust, 339
Research methods
    choosing, 27–28
    strengths and weaknesses of, 27
Responsibility
    dissonance motivation and, 215
    induced compliance and, 200–202, 220
Restlessness stage of a revolution, 302–303, 320
Revised learned helplessness (RLH) model, 91–92
Revolution
    frustration and, 300–305
    stages of, 302–303, 320
Reward model of attraction, 227–228, 229, 261
Reward power, 399
Reward/punishment systems, 330
Rewards
    altruism and, 273–274
    in-group evaluation and, 365
    propinquity and, 238

Rhetoric (Aristotle), 150
Risk taking, group influence and, 463–464
Risky shift, 464
Role ambiguity, 442, 443
Role conflict, 442, 443
Roles, in groups, 441–443
Romantic love, 252, 253 (see also Love relationships; Personal relationships)
Romeo and Juliet, 224, 226–227, 234, 235, 240, 256
"Romeo and Juliet effect," 256
ROTC study, 108–109

Saliency bias, 50, 51
Scapegoating, 390
    prejudice and, 366–368
Scapegoat theory, 367–368
Schema, 51–54, 64
Schemmel, Jerry, 266
Science, 32
    defined, 13
Script, 52, 53, 64
Seating arrangements, leadership and, 408–409
Secondary territories, 484, 485, 510
Self
    interpersonal behavior and, 103–104
    negative thoughts about, 93
    presentation of, 104–106
    "principled" versus "pragmatic," 121
Self-affirmation, dissonance theory and, 214–215
Self-attention, 115–120
    depression and, 119–120
Self-attribution, 75–84, 91–92
    applying, 94–97
    depression and, 92–93
Self-awareness, 115, 132
    escaping from, 116–117
Self-complexity, 93–94
Self-concept
    dissonance theory and, 214
    influence of groups on, 455
    self-presentation and, 106
    social interaction and, 70–75
Self-construction, 106, 107, 109
Self-disclosure, 129–131, 132
Self-discrepancy theory, 94, 95
Self-efficacy, 92, 93
Self-esteem
    attributional style and, 93
    in-group evaluation and, 365
Self-evaluation, social identity theory and, 364
Self-evaluation maintenance, 74, 75
Self-focused attention, 115
Self-fulfilling prophecy, 61–63, 64
    gender stereotypes and, 387
Self-guides, 94
Self-handicapping, 113–115, 132
Self-interested action, 330
Self-knowledge, 70
Self-monitoring, 120–122, 132
    measuring, 121
    physical attractiveness and, 244–246
Self-perception
    biases in, 84–88
    psychological well-being and, 89–97
Self-perception theory, 75, 76–77, 97, 215–216
Self-presentation approach to conformity, 427

Credits

CHAPTER ONE
21, 22, quote and Table 1-2 from *The Psychology of Affiliation,* by S. Schachter. Copyright © 1959 by Stanford University Press. Reprinted by permission.

CHAPTER TWO
41, Table 2-2 from "Role Playing Variations and Their Informational Value for Person Perception," by E. E. Jones, K. E. Davis, and K. Gergen, *Journal of Abnormal and Social Psychology,* 1961, *63,* 302–310. Copyright 1961 by the American Psychological Association. Reprinted by permission of the author. **45,** Table 2-3 from *Perceiving the Causes of Success and Failure,* by B. Weiner, I. Frieze, A. Kukla, L. Reed, B. Rest, and R. M. Rosenbaum. Copyright © 1971 by General Learning Press. Reprinted by permission of the author. **61,** Figure 2-1 from *Pygmalion in the Classroom: Teacher Expectation and Pupils' Intellectual Development,* by R. Rosenthal and L. Jacobson. Copyright © 1968 by Holt, Rinehart & Winston. Reprinted by permission.

CHAPTER THREE
84, Figure 3-1 from *Social Cognition,* by S. T. Fiske and S. E. Taylor. Copyright © 1984 by McGraw-Hill, Inc. Reprinted by permission. **87,** Figure 3-2 from "Some Determinants and Consequences of the Teacher's Perception of Causation," by R. L. Johnson, R. Feigenbaum, and M. Weiby, *Journal of Educational Psychology,* 1964, *55,* 237–246. Copyright 1964 by the American Psychological Association. Reprinted by permission of the author. **89,** Table 3-3 adapted from "External and Internal Control," by J. B. Rotter, *Psychology Today,* pp. 37–42, 58–59. Copyright © 1971 (PT Partners, L.P.). Reprinted with permission from *Psychology Today* magazine. **95,** Figure 3-3 adapted from "Insomnia and the Attribution Process," by M. Storms and R. E. Nisbett, *Journal of Personality and Social Psychology,* 1970, *2,* 319–328. Copyright 1970 by the American Psychological Association. Reprinted by permission of the author.

CHAPTER FOUR
112, Figure 4-1 adapted from "Self-Presentation by Association," by R. B. Cialdini and M. E. De Nicholas, *Journal of Personality and Social Psychology,* 1989, *57,* 626–631. Copyright 1989 by the American Psychological Association. Reprinted by permission of the author. **113,** excerpt courtesy of the *Globe* Newspaper. Copyright © 1990. **118,** Table 4-1 from *Self-Consciousness and Social Anxiety* by Arnold H. Buss. Copyright © 1980 by W. H. Freeman and Company. Reprinted with permission. **121,** Table 4-2 adapted from "Self-Monitoring of Expressive Behavior," by M. Snyder, *Journal of Personality and Social Psychology,* 1974, *30,* 526–537. Copyright 1974 by the American Psychological Association. Reprinted by permission of the author. **125,** Table 4-3 adapted with permission of The Free Press, a Division of Macmillan, Inc., from *Social Psychology,* Second Edition, by R. Brown. Copyright © 1986 by The Free Press. **128,** Figure 4-2 adapted from *Interpersonal Diagnosis of Personality,* by T. Leary. Copyright © 1957 by Ronald Press. Reprinted by permission of the author. **131,** Table 4-4 from the *The Transparent Self,* by S. M. Jourard. Copyright © 1971 by Van Nostrand Reinhold. Reprinted by permission.

CHAPTER FIVE
142, Figure 5-2 from "Assimilation in the Immediate Reproduction of Visually Perceived Figures," by J. S. Bruner, R. D. Busiek, and A. Minturn, *Journal of Experimental Psychology,* 1952, *44,* 151–155. Copyright 1952 by the American Psychological Association. Reprinted by permission of the author. **149,** Table 5-1 adapted from "Attitudes Established by Classical Conditioning," by A. W. Staats and C. K. Staats, *Journal of Abnormal and Social Psychology,* 1958, *57,* 37–40. Copyright 1958 by the American Psychological Association. Adapted by permission of the author. **153,** Figure 5-5 from "The Influence of Source Credibility on Communication Effectiveness," by C. I. Hovland and W. Weiss, *Public Opinion Quarterly,* 1952, *15,* 635–650. Copyright © 1952 by Public Opinion Quarterly. Reprinted by permission of University of Chicago Press. **157,** Figure 5-6 from "Facilitating Effects of 'Eating-while-Reading' on "Responsiveness to Persuasive Communications," by I. L. Janis, D. Kaye, and P. Kirschner, *Journal of Abnormal and Social Psychology,* 1965, *1,* 181–186. Copyright 1965 by the American Psychological Association. Reprinted by permission of the author. **158,** Table 5-2 adapted from "Effects of Fear-Arousing Communications," by I. L. Janis and S. Feshbach, *Journal of Abnormal and Social Psychology,* 1953, *48,* 78–92. Copyright 1953 by the American Psychological Association. Adapted by permission of the author. **166,** Figure 5-9 adapted from "Effects of Initial Request Size and Timing of a Second Request on Compliance: The Foot in the Door and the Door in the Face," by A. Cann, S. J. Sherman, and R. Elkes, *Journal of Personality and Social Psychology,* 1975, *32,* 774–782. Copyright 1975 by the American Psychological Association. Reprinted by permission of the author. **168,** Table 5-3 adapted from "The Relative Efficacy of Various Types of Prior Belief-Defense in Producing Immunity Against Persuasion," by W. J. McGuire and D. Papageorgis, *Journal of Abnormal and Social Psychology,* 1961, *62,* 317–337. Copyright 1961 by the American Psychological

ritoriality and Residential Crime: A Conceptual Framework," by B. Brown and I. Altman. In P. J. Brantingham and P. L. Brantingham, *Environmental Criminology.* Copyright © 1981 by Sage Publications, Inc. Reprinted by permission. **486,** Table 14-2 from "Reactions to Territorial Contamination as a Function of Culture," by S. Worchel and M. Lollis, *Personality and Social Psychology Bulletin,* 1982, *8,* 365–370. Copyright © 1982 by Sage Publications, Inc. Reprinted by permission. **496,** Figure 14-6 from "Ambient Temperature and Violent Crime," by C. A. Anderson and D. C. Anderson, *Journal of Personality and Social Psychology,* 1984, *46,* p. 196. Copyright 1984 by the American Psychological Association. Reprinted by permission. **496,** Figure 14-7 from "Aggression and Heat: The Influence of Ambient Temperature, Negative Affect, and a Cooling Drink on Physical Aggression," by R. A. Baron and P. A. Bell, *Journal of Personality and Social Psychology,* 1976, *33,* 245–255. Copyright 1976 by the American Psychological Association. Reprinted by permission of the author. **497,** Table 14-4 from *Environmental Psychology,* 2nd ed., by J. D. Fisher, P. A. Bell, and A. Baum. Copyright © 1984 by CBS College Publishing. Copyright © 1978 by W. B. Saunders Company. Reprinted by permission of Holt, Rinehart & Winston, Inc. **502,** Figure 14-8 from "Opportunity for Control and the Designed Environment: The Case of an Institution for the Developmentally Disabled, " by C. Zimring, W. Weitzer, and R. C. Knight. In A. Baum and J. Singer (Eds.), *Advances in Environmental Psychology,* Vol. 4, pp. 170–210. Copyright © 1982 by Lawrence Erlbaum Associates, Inc. Reprinted by permission. **503,** Figure 14-9 from *Architecture and Social Behavior: Psychological Studies in Social Density,* by A. Baum and S. Valins. Copyright © 1977 by Lawrence Erlbaum Associates, Inc. Reprinted by permission. **506,** Figure 14-10 from *Aging and Milieu: Environmental Perspectives on Growing Old,* by G. Roles and R. S. Ohta (Eds.). Copyright © 1983 by Academic Press, Inc. Reprinted by permission.

Photo credits

CHAPTER ONE
2, Georg Gerster/Comstock. **5,** The Bettmann Archive. **6,** UPI/The Bettmann Archive. **7,** Peter Menzel. **11,** Topham/The Image Works. **14,** UPI/Bettmann Newsphotos. **15,** Fred Ward/Black Star. **16,** Irv DeVore/Anthro Photo. **17,** Lester Sloan/Woodfin Camp & Associates. **26,** George Malave/Stock, Boston.

CHAPTER TWO
34, Mike Mazzaschi/Stock, Boston. **37,** Dirck Halstead/Gamma Liaison. **39,** PhotoEdit. **42,** Museum of the City of New York. **44,** © David Madison. **49,** Donna Ferrato/Black Star. **50,** © Spencer Grant/Stock, Boston. **53,** Steve Shapiro/Gamma Liaison. **54,** Elizabeth Crews. **57,** Tom McCarthy/Black Star.

CHAPTER THREE
66, Joseph Schuyler/Stock, Boston. **69,** © David Madison/Duomo Photography. **71,** Peter Menzel/Stock, Boston. **72,** Tim Davis/Photo Researchers. **77,** Jim Goodwin/Photo Researchers. **78,** Robert Brenner/PhotoEdit. **83,** Elizabeth Crews. **85,** © Lee Hocker. **86,** Nathaniel Antman/The Image Works. **90,** Rob Nelson/Black Star. **93,** © David M. Grossman.

CHAPTER FOUR
100, Suzanne Arms-Wimberley. **103,** Eric Robert/Sygma Photo News. **105,** Theo Westenberger/Sygma Photo News. **108,** © Charles Harbutt/Actuality, Inc. **110,** Setboun/Sipa Press. **116,** Gerard Fritz/Monkmeyer Press Photo Service. **121,** © Lee

Snyder/Photo Researchers. **124,** (top left and right) Ira Kirschenbaum/Stock, Boston; (bottom left) Eugene Gordon; (bottom right) George Rodger/Magnum Photos. **130,** The National Broadcasting Company.

CHAPTER FIVE
134, Suzanne Arms-Wimberley. **137,** (left) Patrick Chauvel/Sygma Photo News; (right) Walt Johnson/Picture Group. **138,** © 1988 Dennis Brack/Black Star. **141,** from "Facial Expression and Imagery in Depression: An Electromyographic Study," by G. Schwartz, P. L. Fair, P. Salt, M. R. Mandel and G. L. Kierman, *Psychosomatic Medicine,* Vol. 38, No. 5, September–October 1976. Copyright © by American Psychosomatic Society. Reprinted by permission. **144,** Henri Cartier-Bresson/Magnum Photos. **152,** New York State Health Department. **159,** (both) American Cancer Society. **161,** Photofest. **167,** © Catherine Noren/Stock, Boston. **173,** Barbara Rios/Photo Researchers.

CHAPTER SIX
178, Mark Antman/Stock, Boston. **181,** Photofest. **183,** UPI/Bettmann Newsphotos. **184,** Joe Viesti/Viesti Associates. **187,** Patrick Chauvel/Sygma Photo News. **189,** (left) Alon Reininger/Woodfin Camp & Associates; (right) Lester Sloan/Woodfin Camp & Associates. **203,** Jacques M. Chenet/Woodfin Camp & Associates. **206,** (left) MacDonald Photography/The Picture Cube; (right) Jonathan Rawle/Stock, Boston. **208,** Mimi Forsyth/Monkmeyer Press Photo Service. **218,** Richard Kalvar/Magnum Photos.

CHAPTER SEVEN
222, © Polly Brown/Actuality, Inc. **225,** Photofest. **227,** Elizabeth Crews. **229,** Chuck Fishman/Woodfin Camp & Associates. **238,** Reprinted from *Social Pressures in Informal Groups* by Leon Festinger, Stanley Schachter, and Kurt Back, with the permission of the publishers, Stanford University Press. Copyright 1950 by Leon Festinger, Stanley Schachter, and Kurt Back. **247,** Gamma Liaison. **252,** (top left) Jim Anderson/Woodfin Camp & Associates; (top right) Owen Franken/Stock, Boston; (bottom) Suzanne Arms-Wimberley. **258,** Frank Siteman/Stock, Boston.

CHAPTER EIGHT
262, © Spencer Grant/Photo Researchers. **265,** David Bentz/Contact Image Press/Woodfin Camp & Associates. **267,** Mary Ellen Mark/Library. **273,** Tony Jalandoni/Monkmeyer Press Photo Service. **278,** Wide World Photos. **280,** Alan Becker/Photo Researchers. **285,** Steve Goldberg/Monkmeyer Press Photo Service.

CHAPTER NINE
288, © Harry Wilks/Stock, Boston. **291,** Ari Mintz/© 1987 New York Newsday. **292,** © Jan Halaska/Photo Researchers. **296,** Reuters/Bettmann. **298,** Peter Turnley/Black Star. **302,** Handgun Control, Inc. **304,** © & ® 1990 Mirage Studios. All rights reserved. **308,** Eugene Richards/Magnum Photos. **309,** © B. Grunzweig/Photo Researchers. **317,** © Joan Liftin/Actuality, Inc.

CHAPTER TEN
322, © 1990 David Vance/The Image Bank West. **325,** Alain Nogues/Sygma Photo News. **326,** H. Armstrong Roberts. **327,** Bettye Lane/Photo Researchers. **330,** Suzanne Arms-Wimberley. **334,** Carlos Angel/Gamma Liaison. **336,** Alain Nogues/Sygma Photo News. **339,** Suzanne Arms-Wimberley. **342,** Eric Bouvet/Gamma Liaison. **344,** © Burk Uzzle/Picture Group. **348,** Wide World Photos.

To the owner of this book:

We hope that you have enjoyed *Understanding Social Psychology (Fifth Edition)* as much as we have enjoyed writing it. We'd like to know as much about your experiences with the book as you care to offer. Only through your comments and the comments of others can we learn how to make *Understanding Social Psychology* a better book for future readers.

School: _____ Your instructor's name: _____

1. What did you like most about *Understanding Social Psychology (Fifth Edition)*? _____

_____

_____

2. What did you like least about the book? _____

_____

3. Were all of the chapters of the book assigned for you to read? _____

   If not, which ones weren't? _____

4. If you used the Glossary, how helpful was it as an aid in understanding psychological concepts and terms?

_____

5. Did you use the Study Guide? _____

   If so, please tell us what component was most useful (terms, short answer questions, multiple-choice items, or other components):

_____

6. What is your reaction to the chapter opening incidents? _____

_____

_____

7. In the space below, or in a separate letter, please let us know what other comments about the book you'd like to make. (For example, were any chapters or concepts particularly difficult?) We'd be delighted to hear from you!

_____

_____

_____

_____

Basic Standard Deduction Amounts

Filing Status	2014	2015
Single	$ 6,200	$ 6,300
Married, filing jointly	12,400	12,600
Surviving spouse	12,400	12,600
Head of household	9,100	9,250
Married, filing separately	6,200	6,300

Amount of Each Additional Standard Deduction

Filing Status	2014	2015
Single	$1,550	$1,550
Married, filing jointly	1,200	1,250
Surviving spouse	1,200	1,250
Head of household	1,550	1,550
Married, filing separately	1,200	1,250

Personal and Dependency Exemption

2014	2015
$3,950	$4,000

Income Tax Rates—Corporations

Taxable Income		The Tax Is:	Of the Amount Over
Over	But not Over		
$ 0	$ 50,000	15%	$ 0
50,000	75,000	$ 7,500 + 25%	50,000
75,000	100,000	13,750 + 34%	75,000
100,000	335,000	22,250 + 39%*	100,000
335,000	10,000,000	113,900 + 34%	335,000
10,000,000	15,000,000	3,400,000 + 35%	10,000,000
15,000,000	18,333,333	5,150,000 + 38%**	15,000,000
18,333,333	....	35%	0

* Five percentage points of this rate represents a phaseout of the benefits of the lower tax rates on the first $75,000 of taxable income.

**Three percentage points of this rate represents a phaseout of the benefits of the lower tax rate (34% rather than 35%) on the first $10 million of taxable income.

Chapter 6

- Added a *Tax in the News* item about Notice 2014–21 and lost bitcoins.
- Simplified the discussion of NOLs.
- Added a Concept Summary on at-risk and passive loss limitation rules.

Chapter 7

- Added a discussion of the tax implications of virtual currency (bitcoin) and related IRS Notice 2014–21.
- Clarified discussion of the holding period for gifted property and property acquired from a decedent.
- Updated the *Tax in the News* item related to cost basis reporting.
- Simplified discussion and examples related to like-kind exchanges.
- Revised and clarified text and examples throughout the chapter.

Chapter 8

- Revised and clarified text and examples throughout the chapter.
- Modified or updated various *Global Tax Issues* and *Tax in the News* items.
- Revised and updated chapter Concept Summaries.

Chapter 9

- Made updates for inflation adjustments.
- Separated the discussion of tax determinations and filing procedures.
- Added a discussion on the basics of NIIT and the Additional Medicare Tax, as well as an example and exercise.

Chapter 10

- Made updates for inflation adjustments.
- Added a discussion on the basics of the Affordable Care Act's Premium Tax Credit and Individual Shared Responsibility Payment.

Chapter 11

- Updated materials to reflect inflation indexation.
- Revised and clarified text and examples throughout the chapter.
- Updated various computational formulas and amounts.

- Added a Concept Summary identifying and describing key employee fringe benefits.
- Added a Concept Summary about moving expenses.
- Simplified the summary dealing with the many tax provisions involving education.
- Added a Concept Summary comparing Traditional and Roth IRAs.
- Added a discussion of IRA rollovers and conversions.

Chapter 12

- Added a Concept Summary that illustrates the major shareholder consequences of a taxable property transaction as compared to one that is tax deferred under § 351.
- Added a Concept Summary that shows the tax rules that apply when liabilities are transferred in property transactions, including the special rules that apply in a § 351 transaction.
- Provided a new *Tax in the News* item that describes ways in which local and state jurisdictions compete to attract new businesses and employers in exchange for tax breaks.
- Revised and clarified text and examples throughout the chapter.

Chapter 13

- Updated statistics as to the amount of annual corporate distributions and the entities that make the distributions.
- Added an example illustrating regular tax and E & P timing and accounting method adjustments.
- Added an example clarifying the treatment given to § 179 under the regular tax and E & P rules.
- Revised a *Bridge to Finance* item and the stock redemption materials.

Chapter 14

- Added comments about the breadth and the use of pass-through entities in the U.S. economy.
- Revised the discussion of LLPs and LLCs and their advantages and disadvantages.
- Enhanced the discussion of the Medicare surtax and the net investment income tax (NIIT) applicable to certain higher-income taxpayers who have interests in partnerships and limited liability entities.

Chapter 15

- Updated statistics as to S corporation and LLC Federal income tax filings.
- Reorganized the discussion providing the overview and advantages of S corporation status.
- Clarified the discussion as to those entities that qualify as small business corporations.
- Enhanced coverage of *The Big Picture* scenario within the text discussion.
- Revised the discussion of entity-level taxes.

Chapter 16

- Revised and clarified text and examples throughout the chapter.
- Revised introductory statistics about the global economy and updated various indexed amounts and limitations.
- Updated statistics as to the combined income tax rates of various countries, including the United States.
- Expanded materials about how FATCA affects overseas investors and financial institutions.
- Updated statistics about the use of the foreign tax credit and about the tax returns of non-U.S. persons who generate U.S. taxable income.
- Updated statistics about the tax collections of the U.S. states.
- Modified the *Tax in the News* item "So Where Did You Work Today?"
- Added a new *Bridge to Economic Development and Political Science* feature.

Chapter 17

- Revised and clarified text and examples throughout the chapter.
- Added materials on small employer health insurance credit.
- Reordered AMT coverage and added discussion of circulation expenditures adjustment, intangible drilling costs preference, and AMT NOLs.
- Updated individual AMT information for inflation adjustments.

Chapter 18

- Reorganized the initial discussion about how to choose a tax-effective form of doing business, especially as to avoiding the double taxation of business income.
- Emphasized how nontax factors, especially limited liability, affect the entity choice.
- Reorganized the discussion of how the choices of entity differ as to the conduit and entity concepts of taxation.
- Expanded the material as to how best to distribute profits from an entity to its owners.
- Expanded the discussion of how the at-risk and passive activity rules can affect the entity choice.
- Expanded the discussion of differences of asset and entity sales when disposing of a business.
- Showed the effect of the net investment income tax (NIIT) on the choice of business entities.
- Simplified the Concept Summaries that compared the tax attributes of the different types of entities.

TAX LAW OUTLOOK

From your SWFT Series Editors:
Concerns about income inequity and job creation will keep income tax issues at the forefront of Congressional discussions throughout 2015 and 2016. Revenue raisers of all sorts will be considered as Federal budgets are crafted, including those to support the retirement and health care systems. Federal tax treatments of income from overseas sources also may be reviewed. While a comprehensive "tax reform" bill is not likely, there will be serious consideration of various proposals throughout the year involving broad-based tax changes. Expect provisions to be considered involving child tax credits and tax incentives for education, as well as other items to help middle-class taxpayers. Most likely the tax provisions that expired in 2014 will be extended to 2015 on a retroactive basis.

Congress may consider Federal corporate tax law changes during 2015–2016, including a decrease in the top tax rate and a move toward a territorial system in taxing income from overseas sources. Tax deferrals for unrepatriated global profits also may receive Congressional attention. State and local governments also have budget problems, and they are looking for new revenue sources, including an adoption of the unitary concept and a broadening of the income and sales/use tax bases.

SUPPLEMENTS SUPPORT STUDENTS AND INSTRUCTORS

Built around the areas students and instructors have identified as the most important, our integrated supplements package offers more flexibility than ever before to suit the way instructors teach and students learn.

Online and Digital Resources for Students

CengageNOW is a powerful course management and online homework tool that provides robust instructor control and customization to optimize the student learning experience and meet desired outcomes.

CengageNOW Instant Access Code ISBN:
978-1-305-39542-8

Contact your Cengage Learning Consultant about different bundle options.

Checkpoint® Student Edition from Thomson Reuters is the leading online tax research database used by professionals. There are three simple ways Checkpoint helps introduce students to tax research:

- Intuitive web-based design makes it fast and simple to find what you need.
- Checkpoint provides a comprehensive collection of primary tax law, cases, and rulings along with analytical insight you simply can't find anywhere else.
- Checkpoint has built-in productivity tools such as calculators to make research more efficient—a resource more tax pros use than any other.

Six months' access to Checkpoint Student Edition (after activation) is packaged automatically with every NEW copy of the textbook.*

More than software: Put the experience of H&R Block tax professionals on your side.

- A step-by-step interview guides you through a customized process.
- Accurate calculations and 100% satisfaction—guaranteed.

- Worry-free Audit Support™ and tax advice from an H&R Block tax professional.

A H&R Block® Premium & Business software CD is offered with each NEW copy of the textbook—at no additional cost to students*

CENGAGEbrain.com Students can use **CengageBrain.com** to select this textbook and access Cengage Learning content, empowering them to choose the most suitable format and giving them a better chance of success in the course. Buy printed materials, eBooks, and digital resources directly through Cengage Learning and save at **CengageBrain.com**.

Online Student Resources

Students can go to **www.cengagebrain.com** for free resources to help them study as well as the opportunity to purchase additional study aids. These valuable free study resources will help students earn a better grade:

- Flashcards use chapter terms and definitions to aid students in learning tax terminology for each chapter.
- Online glossary for each chapter provides terms and definitions from the text in alphabetical order for easy reference.
- Learning objectives can be downloaded for each chapter to help keep students on track.
- Tax tables used in the textbook are downloadable for reference.

Printed Resources for Students
Looseleaf Edition (978-1-305-39533-6)

This version provides all the pages of the text in an unbound, three-hole punched format for portability and ease of use. A H&R Block® Premium & Business software CD is included with every NEW textbook as well as Checkpoint® Student Edition from Thomson Reuters.*

---

* Checkpoint® Student Edition is not available with the Professional Editions of South-Western Federal Taxation texts. For all other editions, all NEW printed copies of the textbook are automatically packaged with Checkpoint Student Edition and H&R Block® tax software. If students purchase the eBook, they will not automatically receive access to Checkpoint Student Edition and H&R Block software. They must purchase the tax media pack offering both of these products. The ISBN is 978-1-285-44270-9 and can be purchased at **www.cengagebrain.com**.

Comprehensive Supplements Support Instructors' Needs

CengageNOW is a powerful course management and online homework tool that provides robust instructor control and customization to optimize the student learning experience and meet desired outcomes. In addition to the features and benefits mentioned earlier for students, CengageNOW includes these features for instructors:

- **Learning Outcomes Reporting** and the ability to analyze student work from the gradebook. Each exercise and problem is tagged by topic, learning objective, level of difficulty, estimated completion time, and business program standards to allow greater guidance in developing assessments and evaluating student progress.

- **Built-in Test Bank for online assessment**. The test bank files have been imported into CengageNOW so that they may be used as additional homework or tests.

Solutions Manual (978-1-305-39540-4)

Written by the South-Western Federal Taxation editors and authors, the Solutions Manual features solutions arranged in accordance with the sequence of chapter material.

Solutions to all homework items are tagged with their Estimated Time to Complete, Level of Difficulty, and Learning Objective(s), as well as the AACSB's and AICPA's core competencies—-giving instructors more control than ever in selecting homework to match the topics covered. The Solutions Manual also contains the lettered answers (only) to the end-of-chapter Roger CPA Review Questions. **Available in print and on Instructor Companion Website at www.cengage.com/login**.

PowerPoint® Lectures

The Instructor PowerPoint Lectures contain more than 30 slides per chapter, including outlines and instructor guides, concept definitions, alternate figures, and key points. **Available on Instructor Companion Website at www.cengage.com/login**.

Test Bank

Written by the **South-Western Federal Taxation** editors and authors, the Test Bank contains approximately 2,200 items and solutions arranged in accordance with the sequence of chapter material.

Each test item is tagged with its Estimated Time to Complete, Level of Difficulty, and Learning Objective(s), as well as the AACSB's and AICPA's core competencies—for easier instructor planning and test item selection. The 2016 Test Bank is available in Cengage's new test generator software, Cognero.

Cengage Learning Testing Powered by Cognero is a flexible, online system that allows you to:

- author, edit, and manage test bank content from multiple Cengage Learning solutions
- create multiple test versions in an instant
- deliver tests from your LMS, your classroom, or wherever you want
- create tests from school, home, the coffee shop—anywhere with Internet access. (No special installs or downloads needed.)

Test Bank files in Word format, along with versions to import into your LMS, available on Instructor Companion Website. Cognero Test Banks available via Single Sign-on account at www.cengage.com/login.

All instructor course materials are posted online at www.cengage.com/login. Once logged into the site, instructors should select this textbook to access the online Instructor Resources.

- Solutions Manual
- Detailed answer feedback for the end-of-chapter Roger CPA Review questions in Word format. (Lettered answers only are available in the Solutions Manual.)
- Additional Test Bank items and solutions
- PowerPoint Lectures

Custom Solutions

Cengage Learning Custom Solutions develops personalized solutions to meet your taxation education needs. Consider the following for your adoption of **South-Western Federal Taxation 2016 Edition**:

- Remove chapters you do not cover or rearrange their order to create a streamlined and efficient text.
- Add your own material to cover new topics or information.
- Add relevance by including sections from Smith's *Internal Revenue Code and Regulations*, Raabe/Whittenburg/Sanders/Sawyers' *Federal Tax Research*, or your state's tax laws and regulations.

---

* Checkpoint® Student Edition is not available with the Professional Editions of South-Western Federal Taxation.

ACKNOWLEDGMENTS

We want to thank all the adopters and non-adopters who participated in numerous online surveys as well as the following individuals who provided content reviews and feedback in the development of the ***South-Western Federal Taxation*** 2016 titles:

Deborah S. Adkins, *Nperspective, LLC*
Amy An, *University of Iowa*
Susan E. Anderson, *Elon University*
Henry M. Anding, *Woodbury University*
Jennifer A. Bagwell, *Ohio University*
George Barbi, *Lanier Technical College*
Terry W. Bechtel, *Texas A&M University-Texarkana*
Chris Becker, *LeMoyne College*
John G. Bell
Tamara Berges, *UCLA*
Ellen Best, *University of North Georgia*
Tim Biggart, *Berry College*
Rachel Birkey, *Illinois State University*
Chris E. Bjornson, *Indiana University Southeast*
Patrick M. Borja, *Citrus College / California State University, Los Angeles*
Dianne H. Boseman, *Nash Community College*
Cathalene Bowler, *University of Northern Iowa*
Darryl L. Brown, *Illinois Wesleyan University*
Timothy G. Bryan, *University of Southern Indiana*
Robert S. Burdette, *Salt Lake Community College*
Lisa Busto, *William Rainey Harper College*
Julia M. Camp, *Providence College*
Al Case, *Southern Oregon University*
Machiavelli W. Chao, *Merage School of Business University of California, Irvine*
Eric Chen, *University of Saint Joseph*
James Milton Christianson, *Southwestern University and Austin Community College*
Ann Burstein Cohen, *University at Buffalo, The State University of New York*
Ciril Cohen, *Fairleigh Dickinson University*
Dixon H. Cooper, *University of Arkansas*
Bradrick Cripe, *Northern Illinois University*
Rick L. Crosser, *Metropolitan State University of Denver*

Susan E.M. Davis, *South University*
Dwight E. Denman, *Newman University*
James M. DeSimpelare, *Ross School of Business at the University of Michigan*
John Dexter, *Northwood University*
Michael P. Donohoe, *University of Illinois at Urbana Champaign*
Deborah A. Doonan, *Johnson & Wales University*
Monique O. Durant, *Central Connecticut State University*
Wayne L. Edmunds, *Virginia Commonwealth University*
Dr. Rafi Efrat, *California State University, Northridge*
Elizabeth C. Ekmekjian, *William Paterson University*
Charles R. Enis, *The Pennsylvania State University*
Frank J. Faber
A. Anthony Falgiani, *University of South Carolina, Beaufort*
Jason Fiske, *Thomas Jefferson School of Law*
John Forsythe, *Eagle Gate College*
Alexander L. Frazin, *University of Redlands*
Carl J. Gabrini, *College of Coastal Georgia*
Kenneth W. Gaines, *East-West University, Chicago, Illinois*
Carolyn Galantine, *Pepperdine University*
Stephen C. Gara, *Drake University*
Sheri Geddes, *Hope College*
Alexander Gelardi, *University of St. Thomas*
Daniel J. Gibbons, *Waubonsee Community College*
Martie Gillen, *University of Florida*
Charles Gnizak, *Fort Hays State University*
Prof. J. David Golub, *Northeastern University*
George G. Goodrich, *John Carroll University*
Dr. Marina Grau, *Houston Community College – Houston TX*
Vicki Greshik, *University of Jamestown College*
Jeffrey S. Haig, *Santa Monica College*
Marcye S. Hampton, *University of Central Florida*
June Hanson, *Upper Iowa University*
Mary Ann Hofmann, *Appalachian State University*
Susanne Holloway, *Salisbury University*
Susan A. Honig, *Herbert H. Lehman College*

Christopher R. Hoyt, *University of Missouri (Kansas City) School of Law*
Marsha M. Huber, *Youngstown State University*
Carol Hughes, *Asheville-Buncombe Technical Community College*
Dr. Helen Hurwitz, *Saint Louis University*
Richard R. Hutaff, *Wingate University*
Zite Hutton, *Western Washington University*
Debra M. Johnson, *Montana State University Billings*
Brad Van Kalsbeek, *University of Sioux Falls*
John E. Karayan, *Woodbury University*
Cynthia Khanlarian, *Concord University*
Bob Kilpatrick, *Northern Arizona University*
Gordon Klein, *Lecturer, UCLA Anderson School*
Taylor Klett, *Sam Houston State University*
Aaron P. Knape, *Peru State College*
Ausher M. B. Kofsky, *Western New England University*
Emil Koren, *Saint Leo University*
Timothy R. Koski, *Middle Tennessee State University*
Sandra Kranz, *Bemidji State University*
Jack Lachman, *Brooklyn COLLEGE-CUNY*
Richard S. Leaman, *University of Denver*
Gene Levitt, *Mayville State University*
Stephanie Lewis, *The Ohio State University*
Teresa Lightner, *University of North Texas*
Sara Linton, *Roosevelt University*
Jane Livingstone, *Western Carolina University*
Mabel Machin, *Florida Institute of Technology*
Maria Alaina Mackin, *ECPI University*
Anne M. Magro, *George Mason University*
Richard B. Malamud, *California State University, Dominguez Hills*
Harold J. Manasa, *Winthrop University*
Barry R. Marks, *University of Houston-Clear Lake*
Anthony Masino, *East Tennessee State University*
Bruce W. McClain, *Cleveland State University*
Allison M. McLeod, *University of North Texas*
Meredith A. Menden, *Southern New Hampshire University*

John G. Miller, *Skyline College*

Lisa Nash, *CPA, MA, Vincennes University*

Mary E. Netzler, *Eastern Florida State College*

Joseph Malino Nicassio, *Westmoreland County Community College*

Mark R. Nixon, *Bentley University*

Garth Novack, *Pantheon Heavy Industries & Foundry*

Claude R. Oakley, *DeVry University, Georgia*

Al Oddo, *Niagara University*

Sandra Owen, *Indiana University – Bloomington*

Vivian J. Paige, *Old Dominion University*

Carolyn Payne, *University of La Verne*

Nichole L Pendleton, *Friends University*

Mark Persellin, *St. Mary's University*

Chuck Pier, *Angelo State University*

Lincoln M. Pinto, *DeVry University*

Sonja Pippin, *University of Nevada – Reno*

Steve Platau, *The University of Tampa*

Walfyette Powell, *Strayer University*

John S. Repsis, *University of Texas at Arlington*

John D. Rice, *Trinity University*

Randall Rinke, *Mercyhurst University*

Jennifer Hardwick Robinson, *Trident Technical College*

Shani N. Robinson, *Sam Houston State University*

Ray Rodriguez, *Murray State University*

Richard L. Russell, *Jackson State University*

Robert L. Salyer, *Northern Kentucky University*

Rhoda Sautner, *University of Mary*

Dr. Bunney L. Schmidt, *Keiser University*

Eric D. Schwartz, *LaRoche College*

Tony L. Scott, *Norwalk Community College*

Randy Serrett, *University of Houston – Downtown*

Paul Shoemaker, *University of Nebraska – Lincoln*

Kimberly Sipes, *Kentucky State University*

Georgi Smatrakalev, *Florida Atlantic University*

Leslie S. Sobol, *California State University Northridge*

Marc Spiegel, *University of California, Irvine*

Jason W. Stanfield, *Purdue University*

George Starbuck, *McMurry University*

Teresa Stephenson, *University of Wyoming*

Beth Stetson, *Oklahoma City University*

Frances A. Stott, *Bowling Green State University*

Todd S. Stowe, *Southwest Florida College*

Martin Stub, *DeVry University*

James Sundberg, *Eastern Michigan University*

Kent Swift, *University of Montana*

Robert L. Taylor, *Lees-McRae College*

Francis C. Thomas, *Richard Stockton College of New Jersey*

Randall R. Thomas, *Upper Iowa University*

Ronald R. Tidd, *Central Washington University*

MaryBeth Tobin, *Bridgewater State University*

Ralph Tower, *Wake Forest (Retired)*

James P. Trebby, *Marquette University*

Donald R. Trippeer, *State University of New York College at Oneonta*

James M. Turner, *Georgia Institute of Technology*

Anthony W. Varnon, *Southeast Missouri State University*

Adria Palacios Vasquez, *Texas A&M University – Kingsville*

Terri Walsh, *Seminole State College of Florida*

Marie Wang

Natasha R. Ware, *Southeastern University*

Sarah Webber, *University of Dayton*

Bill Weispfenning, *University of Jamestown (ND)*

Andrew Whitehair

Kent Williams, *Indiana Wesleyan University*

Marvin Williams, *University of Houston-Downtown*

Candace Witherspoon, *Valdosta State University*

Sheila Woods, *DeVry University, Houston, TX*

SPECIAL THANKS

We are grateful to the faculty members who have diligently worked through the problems and test questions to ensure the accuracy of the *South-Western Federal Taxation* homework, solutions manuals, test banks, comprehensive tax form problems, and practice sets. Their comments and corrections helped us focus on clarity as well as accuracy and tax law currency. They are **Sandra A. Augustine**, Hilbert College; **Chris E. Bjornson**, Indiana University Southeast; **Bradrick M. Cripe**, Northern Illinois University; **Eileen Eichler**, Farmingdale State College; **Elizabeth C. Ekmekjian**, William Paterson University; **Stephen C. Gara**, Drake University; **Mary Ann Hofmann**, Appalachian State University; **Debra M. Johnson**, Montana State University, Billings; **Timothy R. Koski**, Middle Tennessee State University; **Sandra J. Kranz**, Bemidji State University; **Stephanie Lewis**, The Ohio State University; **Joan M. Miller**, William Paterson University; **Randall Rinke**, Mercyhurst University – North East Campus; **Ray Rodriguez**, Southern Illinois University, Carbondale; **Lucia N. Smeal**, Georgia State University; **Eric Smith**, Weber State University; **Jason W. Stanfield**, Purdue University; **George R. Starbuck**, McMurry University; **Kent Swift**, University of Montana; **Ralph B. Tower**, Wake Forest University; **Donald R. Trippeer**, State University of New York College at Oneonta; **Raymond Wacker**, Southern Illinois University, Carbondale; **Sarah Webber**, University of Dayton; **Michael Weissenfluh**, Tillamook Bay Community College; **Marvin J. Williams**, University of Houston, Downtown; **Scott A. Yetmar**, Cleveland State University. We are grateful for their efforts.

We are also grateful for the editorial assistance of **Bonnie Hoffman**, CPA on many of the chapters. We also wish to thank Thomson Reuters for its permission to use Checkpoint with the text.

William A. Raabe / David M. Maloney / James C. Young / James E. Smith / Annette Nellen

The South-Western Federal Taxation Series

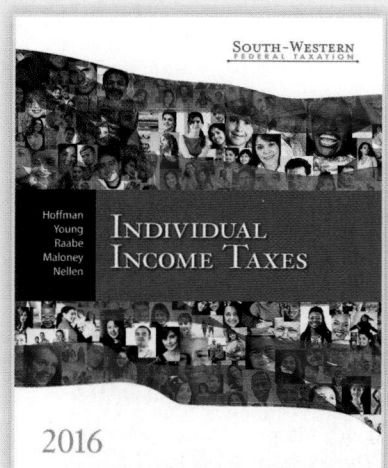

INDIVIDUAL INCOME TAXES, 2016 EDITION

(HOFFMAN, YOUNG, RAABE, MALONEY, NELLEN, Editors) provides accessible, comprehensive, and authoritative coverage of the relevant tax code and regulations as they pertain to the individual taxpayer, as well as coverage of all major developments in Federal taxation.

(ISBN 978-1-305-39330-1)

CORPORATIONS, PARTNERSHIPS, ESTATES & TRUSTS, 2016 EDITION

(HOFFMAN, RAABE, MALONEY, YOUNG, Editors) covers tax concepts as they affect corporations, partnerships, estates, and trusts. The authors provide accessible, comprehensive, and authoritative coverage of relevant tax code and regulations, as well as all major developments in Federal income taxation. This market-leading text is intended for students who have had a previous course in tax. The text includes **Chapter 14, "Taxes on the Financial Statements."**

(ISBN 978-1-305-39988-4)

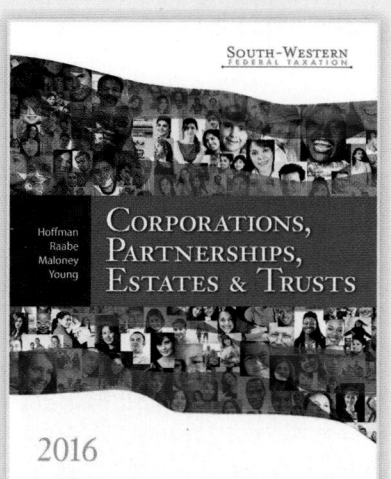

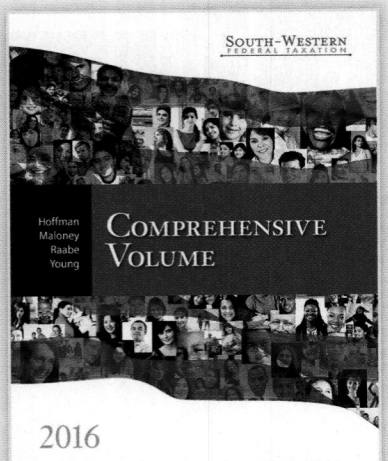

COMPREHENSIVE VOLUME, 2016 EDITION

(HOFFMAN, MALONEY, RAABE, YOUNG, Editors)
Combining the number one individual tax text with the number one corporations text, *Comprehensive Volume, 2016 Edition* is a true winner. An edited version of the first two ***South-Western Federal Taxation*** textbooks, this book is ideal for undergraduate or graduate levels. This text works for either a one-semester course in which an instructor wants to integrate coverage of individual and corporate taxation or for a two-semester sequence in which the use of only one book is desired.

(ISBN 978-1-305-39511-4)

ESSENTIALS OF TAXATION: INDIVIDUALS & BUSINESS ENTITIES, 2016 EDITION

(RAABE, MALONEY, YOUNG, SMITH, NELLEN, Editors)
emphasizes tax planning and the multidisciplinary aspects of taxation. Formerly titled *Taxation of Business Entities*, this text is designed with the AICPA Model Tax Curriculum in mind, presenting the introductory Federal taxation course from a business entity perspective. Its **Tax Planning Framework** helps users fit tax planning strategies into an innovative pedagogical framework. The text is an ideal fit for programs that offer only one course in taxation where users need to be exposed to individual taxation, as well as corporate and other business entity taxation. This text assumes no prior course in taxation has been taken.

(ISBN 978-1-305-39530-5)

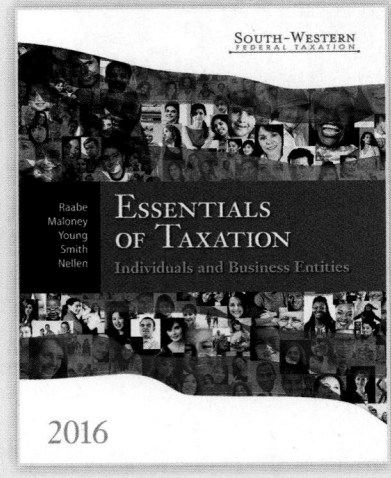

INTERNAL REVENUE CODE OF 1986 AND TREASURY REGULATIONS *Annotated and Selected, 2016 Edition*

(JAMES E. SMITH, MARK ALTIERI) An ideal alternative to the traditional, bulky, and expensive multivolume set of code and regulations, this single-volume reference provides a useful selection of code and regulations sections and clear annotations in the form of editorial summaries that explain, analyze, and cross-reference topics to help students fully understand the intricacies of the tax code. The text is a perfect supplement for any ***South-Western Federal Taxation*** text as well as an excellent primary text for a Federal taxation course that stresses a code and regulations approach.

2016 Edition coming in July 2015 (ISBN 978-1-305-66065-6)

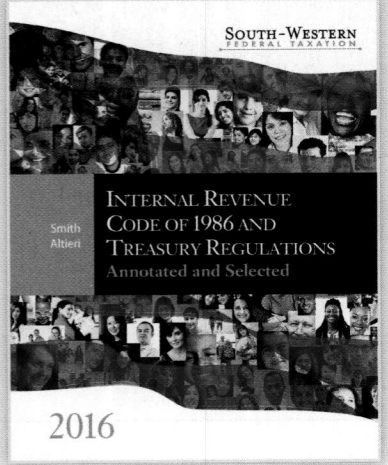

FEDERAL TAX RESEARCH, 10E
(RAABE, WHITTENBURG, SANDERS, AND SAWYERS)

Federal Tax Research, Tenth Edition, offers hands-on tax research analysis and fully covers computer-oriented tax research tools. The tenth edition offers a new chapter on Financial Accounting Research that, when combined with their study of tax research, will equip students with the valuable research skills they need to be marketable to future employers. Also included in this edition is coverage on international tax research, an expanded review of tax ethics, and many new real-life cases to help foster a true understanding of federal tax law.

(ISBN 978-1-285-43939-6)

ABOUT THE EDITORS

William A. Raabe, Ph.D., CPA, is the Distinguished Professor of Accounting in the College of Business and Economics of the University of Wisconsin–Whitewater. A graduate of Carroll University (Wisconsin) and the University of Illinois, Dr. Raabe's teaching and research interests include international and multistate taxation, technology in tax education, personal financial planning, and the economic impact of sports teams and fine arts groups. Dr. Raabe also writes *Federal Tax Research* and the PricewaterhouseCoopers Tax Case Studies. He has written extensively about book-tax differences in financial reporting. Dr. Raabe has been a visiting tax faculty member for a number of public accounting firms, bar associations, and CPA societies. He has received numerous teaching awards, including the Accounting Educator of the Year award from the Wisconsin Institute of CPAs. He has been the faculty adviser for student teams in the Deloitte Tax Case Competition (national finalists at three different schools) and the PricewaterhouseCoopers Extreme Tax policy competition (national finalist). For more information about Dr. Raabe, visit BillRaabeTax.com and BillRaabeTax on YouTube and Twitter.

David M. Maloney, Ph.D., CPA, is the Carman G. Blough Professor of Accounting Emeritus at the University of Virginia's McIntire School of Commerce. He completed his undergraduate work at the University of Richmond and his graduate work at the University of Illinois at Urbana-Champaign. Upon joining the Virginia faculty in January 1984, Dr. Maloney taught federal taxation in the graduate and undergraduate programs and was a recipient of major research grants from the Ernst & Young and KPMG Foundations. Dr. Maloney has published work in numerous professional journals, including *Journal of Taxation, The Tax Adviser, Tax Notes, Corporate Taxation, Accounting Horizons, Journal of Taxation of Investments,* and *Journal of Accountancy.*

James C. Young is the Crowe Horwath Professor of Accountancy at Northern Illinois University. A graduate of Ferris State University (B.S.) and Michigan State University (M.B.A. and Ph.D.), Jim's research focuses on taxpayer responses to the income tax using archival data. His dissertation received the PricewaterhouseCoopers/American Taxation Association Dissertation Award and his subsequent research has received funding from a number of organizations, including the Ernst & Young Foundation Tax Research Grant Program. His work has been published in a variety of academic and professional journals, including the *National Tax Journal, The Journal of the American Taxation Association,* and *Tax Notes.* Jim is a Northern Illinois University Distinguished Professor, received the Illinois CPA Society Outstanding Accounting Educator Award in 2012, and has received university teaching awards from Northern Illinois University, George Mason University, and Michigan State University.

James E. Smith is the John S. Quinn Professor of Accounting at the College of William and Mary. He has been a member of the Accounting Faculty for over 30 years. He received his Ph.D. degree from the University of Arizona. Professor Smith has served as a discussion leader for Continuing Professional Education programs for the AICPA, Federal Tax Workshops, and various state CPA societies. He has conducted programs in more than 40 states for approximately 25,000 CPAs. He has been the recipient of the AICPA's Outstanding Discussion Leader Award and the American Taxation Association/ Arthur Andersen Teaching Innovation Award. Among his other awards are the Virginia Society of CPAs' Outstanding Accounting Educator Award and the James Madison University's Outstanding Accounting Educator Award. He was the President of the Administrators of Accounting Programs Group (AAPG) in 1991–1992. He was the faculty adviser for the William and Mary teams that received first place in the Andersen Tax Challenge in 1994, 1995, 1997, 2000, and 2001 and in the Deloitte Tax Case Study Competition in 2002, 2004, 2005, 2006, 2008, and 2011.

Annette Nellen, CPA, CGMA, Esquire, directs San José State University's graduate tax program (MST) and teaches courses in tax research, tax fundamentals, accounting methods, property transactions, state taxation, employment tax, ethics, and tax policy. Professor Nellen is a graduate of CSU Northridge, Pepperdine (MBA), and Loyola Law School. Prior to joining SJSU in 1990, she was with a Big 4 firm and the IRS. At SJSU, Professor Nellen is a recipient of the Outstanding Professor and Distinguished Service Awards. Professor Nellen is an active member of the tax sections of the AICPA and American Bar Association. In 2013, she received the AICPA Arthur J. Dixon Memorial Award, the highest award given by the accounting profession in the area of taxation. Professor Nellen is the author of *BloombergBNA Tax Portfolio, Amortization of Intangibles,* and the *BloombergBNA Internet Law Resource Center, Overview of Internet Taxation Issues.* She has published numerous articles in the *AICPA Tax Insider, Tax Adviser, State Tax Notes,* and *The Journal of Accountancy.* She has testified before the House Ways & Means and Senate Finance Committees, and other committees on federal and state tax reform. Professor Nellen maintains the 21st Century Taxation website and blog (www.21stcenturytaxation.com) as well as websites on tax reform and state tax issues (www.cob.sjsu.edu/nellen_a/).

Brief Contents

Part 5: Business Entities

Part 6: Special Business Topics

Contents

Part 2: Structure of the Federal Income Tax

Part 3: Property Transactions

CHAPTER 7
PROPERTY TRANSACTIONS: BASIS, GAIN AND LOSS, AND NONTAXABLE EXCHANGES — 7-1

CHAPTER 8
PROPERTY TRANSACTIONS: CAPITAL GAINS AND LOSSES, SECTION 1231, AND RECAPTURE PROVISIONS — 8-1

Part 4: Taxation of Individuals

CHAPTER 9
INDIVIDUALS AS THE TAXPAYER   9-1

CHAPTER 10
INDIVIDUALS: INCOME, DEDUCTIONS, AND CREDITS   10-1

OVERVIEW OF INCOME PROVISIONS APPLICABLE TO INDIVIDUALS   10-2

Part 5: Business Entities

APPENDIXES

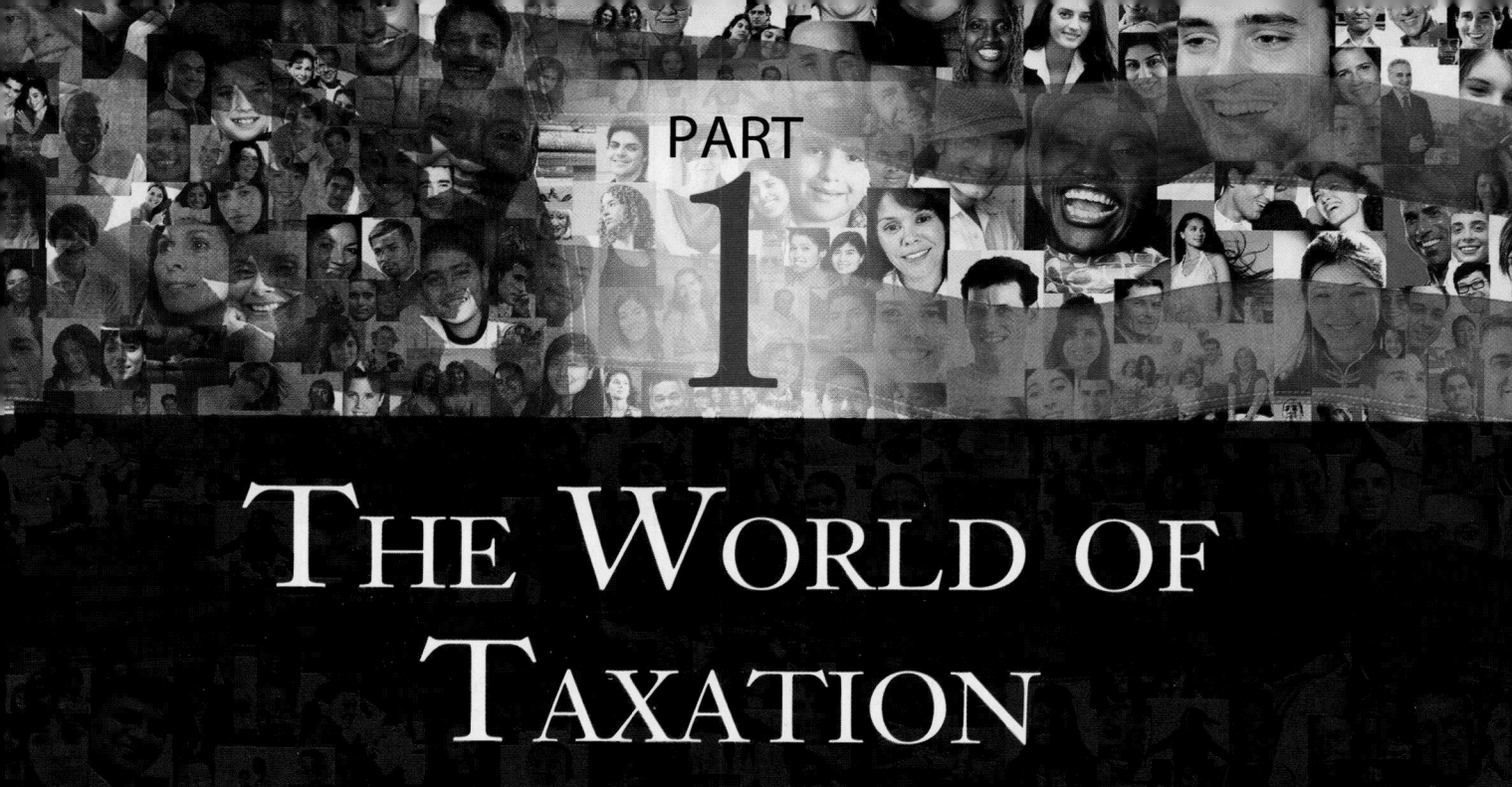

PART

1

THE WORLD OF TAXATION

CHAPTER **1**
Introduction to Taxation

CHAPTER **2**
Working with the Tax Law

CHAPTER **3**
Taxes on the Financial Statements

Part 1 provides an introduction to taxation in the United States. Various taxes imposed by Federal, state, and local governments are discussed. A unique tax planning framework is presented that is applied throughout the book in developing tax planning strategies for both business entities and individual taxpayers. The evolution of the Federal tax system is presented along with the influence of the IRS and the courts in that process. The tax research process, including the relevance of the legislative, administrative, and judicial sources of the tax law, is also discussed. Part 1 concludes with a chapter on accounting for income taxes, as a bridge to materials discussed in other accounting courses.

Introduction to Taxation

LEARNING OBJECTIVES: *After completing Chapter 1, you should be able to:*

LO.1 Define and illustrate the components of a tax.

LO.2 Identify the various taxes affecting business enterprises.

LO.3 Describe the basic tax formula for individuals and taxable business entities.

LO.4 State and explain the relationship between business entities and their owners.

LO.5 Identify tax planning opportunities and apply a general framework for tax planning.

LO.6 Explain the economic, social, equity, and political considerations that underlie the tax law.

LO.7 Describe the role played by the IRS and the courts in the evolution of the Federal tax system.

CHAPTER OUTLINE

TAX TALK *How many people were taxed, who was taxed, and what was taxed tell more about a society than anything else.* —CHARLES ADAMS

A TYPICAL TAX YEAR FOR A MODERN FAMILY

Travis and Betty Carter are married and live in a state that imposes both a sales tax and an income tax. They have two children, April (age 17) and Martin (age 18). Travis is a mining engineer who specializes in land reclamation. After several years with a mining corporation, Travis established a consulting practice that involves a considerable amount of travel.

Betty is a registered nurse who, until recently, was a homemaker. In November of the current year, she decided to reenter the job market and accepted a position with a medical clinic.

The Carters live only a few blocks from Ernest and Mary Walker, Betty Carter's parents. The Walkers are retired and live on interest, dividends, and Social Security benefits.

The following developments with current year and possible future tax ramifications occurred.

- The ad valorem property taxes on the Carters' residence increased, while those on the Walkers' residence decreased.

- When Travis registered an automobile that was purchased last year in another state, he had to pay a sales tax to his home state.

- As an anniversary present, the Carters gave the Walkers a recreational vehicle (RV).

- When Travis made a consulting trip to Chicago, the client withheld Illinois state income tax from the payment made to Travis for his services.

- Travis employed his children to draft blueprints and prepare scale models for use in his work. Both April and Martin have had training in drafting and topography.

- Early in the year, the Carters were audited by the state on an income tax return filed several years ago. Later in the year, they were audited by the IRS on a Form 1040 they filed for the same year. In each case, a tax deficiency and interest were assessed.

- The Walkers were audited by the IRS. Unlike the Carters, they did not have to deal with a revenue agent, but settled the matter by mail.

Explain these developments and resolve any tax issues raised.

Read the chapter and formulate your response.

Taxes have a pervasive impact on our lives. They affect every individual in the United States from birth to death, and even beyond death (through taxation of an individual's estate). Taxes likewise affect every business from formation of the business entity to its operations, distribution of profits to owners, and ultimate disposition or liquidation.

Despite the wide-ranging impact of taxes, most studies of the tax law overemphasize the provisions applying to individual taxpayers and ignore much of the tax law relevant to business. That approach fails to address the role of taxes in *business decisions*, and it fails to provide the broad knowledge base necessary to succeed in today's business environment. This text adopts a more balanced approach; it introduces the tax laws that apply to individuals, and those rules applicable to all business entities, and it surveys the tax rules specific to each type of taxpayer. It also recognizes that both tax and nontax considerations are important in personal and business affairs.

1-1 THE STRUCTURE OF TAXES

LO.1

Define and illustrate the components of a tax.

Most taxes have two components: a tax rate and a tax base (such as income, wages, value, or sales price). Tax liability is computed by multiplying these two components. Taxes vary by the structure of their rates and by the base subject to tax.

1-1a Tax Rates

Tax rates can be progressive, proportional, or regressive. A tax rate is *progressive* if it increases as the tax base increases. The Federal income tax is structured so as to be progressive. For example, the Federal income tax rates for corporations range from 15 to 39 percent. These rates increase with increases in taxable income.

Refer to the corporate tax rate schedule inside the front cover of this text. If Abel Corporation records taxable income of $5,000, its income tax is $750 and its average tax rate is 15% ($750/$5,000, or the ratio of tax liability to the tax base).

If, however, Abel's taxable income is $200,000, its income tax is $61,250 [$22,250 + .39 ($200,000 − $100,000)] and its average tax rate is 30.63% ($61,250/$200,000). The tax is progressive because the average tax rate increases with increases in the tax base (income).

A tax is *proportional* if the rate of tax is constant, regardless of the size of the tax base. State retail **sales taxes** are proportional. Proportional tax rates also underlie the various "flat tax" proposals recently in the news.[1]

Bob purchases an automobile for $6,000. If the sales tax on automobiles is 7% in Bob's state, he will pay a $420 tax. Alternatively, if Bob pays $20,000 for a car, his sales tax will be $1,400 (still 7% of the sales price). Because the average tax rate does not change with the tax base (sales price), the sales tax is proportional.

Finally, *regressive* tax rates decrease as the tax base increases. Federal **employment taxes**, such as FICA and FUTA, are regressive. When the tax base and the taxpayer's ability to pay generally are positively correlated (i.e., when they move in the same direction), many tax pundits view regressive tax rates as unfair. This is because the tax burden decreases as a *percentage* of the taxpayer's ability to pay.

In 2015, the combined Social Security and Medicare tax rate levied on the wages of employees is 7.65% up to a maximum of $118,500 and 1.45% on all wages over $118,500. Sarah earns a salary of $30,000. She pays FICA taxes of $2,295, an average tax rate of 7.65%. Alternatively, if Sarah earns $150,000, she pays $9,522 [(.0765 × $118,500) + .0145 × ($150,000 − $118,500)], an average tax rate of 6.35%.

Once the FICA base exceeds the maximum amount subject to the Social Security part of FICA, the FICA tax becomes regressive because the average tax rate decreases as the tax base increases.

---

[1]Flat tax proposals call for a new tax with one low proportional rate (usually between 15% and 20%). Such a tax would have a very broad base, taxing almost all forms of income with few deductions. To avoid taxing those with lower incomes, large personal exemptions would be provided (e.g., $50,000 for a family of four).

TAX FACT Carrying the Tax Burden

Data from the IRS indicate that the progressive nature of the Federal income tax, accelerated by laws passed under Presidents Bush I and Clinton, remains largely intact for U.S. individuals, even after the broad tax cuts issued under President George W. Bush in the early 2000s.

Annual median adjusted gross income (defining the upper and lower one-half of citizens) is about $34,250. Income of about $438,000 puts a taxpayer in the top 1 percent of filers, and effective Federal taxes for the top 10 percent of earners have increased faster than their incomes. The following table shows the share of taxes paid by various income categories.

Income Category	Share of Total Income (%)	Share of Federal Income Taxes Paid (%)
Top 1%	19	35
Top 5%	34	56
Bottom 50%	11	3

Additional observations include the following.

- Individuals earning less than $45,000 per year likely pay zero Federal income tax, and their payroll and gasoline taxes may be partly rebated through the earned income credit as well.

- When considering income, sales, payroll, property, and other taxes that are levied by U.S. governmental bodies of all sizes, taxpayers at nearly all income levels pay about 30 percent of their income in taxes.

- Due to additional taxes that are designated to pay for the Obamacare system, the degree of progressivity of the Federal income tax increases even further.

- The 400 individual Forms 1040 with the highest taxable income pay only about a 20 percent average Federal income tax rate, due chiefly to tax incentives that apply to investment income.

Under all three tax rate structures, the *amount* of taxes due increases as the tax base increases. The structure of tax rates only affects the *rate* of increase (i.e., progressive taxes increase at an increasing rate, proportional taxes increase at a constant rate, and regressive taxes increase at a decreasing rate).

1-1b Tax Bases

Most taxes are levied on one of four kinds of tax bases.

- Transactions [including sales or purchases of goods and services, and transfers of wealth (e.g., by gift or at death)].
- Property or wealth (including ownership of specific kinds of property).
- Privileges and rights (including the ability to do business as a corporation, the right to work in a certain profession, and the ability to move goods between countries).
- Income on a gross or net-of-expenses basis.

Because the Federal income tax usually has the most significant influence on business decisions, it is the principal focus of this text. Other taxes can play an important role, however, so it is important to have at least some familiarity with them. The next section introduces many of the taxes imposed on individuals and businesses in the United States.

In-depth coverage can be found on this book's companion website: www.cengagebrain.com   **1** DIGGING DEEPER

1-1c Incidence of Taxation

The degree to which various segments of society share the total tax burden is difficult to assess. Assumptions must be made concerning who absorbs the burden of paying the tax. For example, because dividend payments to shareholders are not deductible by a corporation and generally are taxable to shareholders, the same income is subject to a form of double taxation.

Concern over the potential for double taxation of the same income is valid to the extent that corporations are *not* able to shift the corporate tax to the consumer through higher prices and lower wages. But many research studies have shown that corporations are able to shift the corporate income tax burden (i.e., so that it is borne by both employees and the ultimate purchasers of goods), thereby avoiding any double taxation on the same income.

The progressiveness of the Federal income tax rate structure for individuals has varied over the years. In 1986, for example, there were 15 rates, ranging from 0 to 50 percent. These later were reduced to two rates of 15 and 28 percent. Currently, there are seven rates ranging from 10 to 39.6 percent.

1-2 TYPES OF TAXES

LO.2

Identify the various taxes affecting business enterprises.

After taxes on income, the various transaction taxes usually play the most important role in business (and personal) contexts. In many countries, transaction taxes are even more important than income taxes. There are three types of transaction taxes: sales and certain excise taxes , employment taxes, and taxes on the transfer of wealth (as gifts and at death).

1-2a Taxes on the Production and Sale of Goods

Sales tax and some excise taxes are imposed on the production, sale, or consumption of commodities or the use of services. Excise taxes and general sales taxes differ by the breadth of their bases. An excise tax base is limited to a specific kind of good or service, while a general sales tax is broad-based (e.g., it might be levied on all retail sales). All levels of government impose excise taxes, while state and local governments make heavy use of the general sales tax.

Federal Excise Taxes

Together with customs duties, excise taxes served as the principal source of revenue for the United States during its first 150 years of existence. Since World War II, the role of excise taxes in the Federal government's fund-raising efforts has steadily declined, falling from about 30 to 40 percent of revenues just prior to the war to about 3 percent now. During this time, the Federal government came to rely upon income and employment taxes as its principal sources of funds.

Despite the decreasing contribution of excise taxes to the Federal coffers, they continue to have a significant impact on specific industries. Currently, trucks, trailers, tires, liquor, tobacco, firearms, certain sporting equipment, and air travel all are subject to Federal excise taxes. In the past, the sale and manufacture of a variety of other goods, including furs, jewelry, boats, luxury automobiles, and theater tickets, have been taxed. Excise taxes extend beyond sales transactions. They are also levied on privileges and rights, as discussed below.

The bases used for Federal excise taxes are as diverse as the goods that are taxed. Fuels are taxed by the gallon, vaccines by the dose, telephone service and air travel by the price paid for the service, water travel by the passenger, coal by the ton extracted or by the sales price, insurance by the premiums paid, and the gas guzzler tax by the mileage rating on the automobile produced. Some of these taxes are levied on producers, some on resellers, and some on consumers. In almost every circumstance, the tax rate structure is proportional.

With the exception of Federal excise taxes on alcohol, tobacco, and firearms, Federal excise taxes are due at least quarterly, when the Federal excise tax return (Form 720) is filed.

State Excise Taxes

Many states levy excise taxes on the same items taxed by the Federal government. For example, most states have excise taxes on gasoline, liquor, and tobacco. However, the tax on specific goods can vary dramatically among states. Compare New York's $4.35 tax on each pack of 20 cigarettes to Georgia's $.37 tax. These differences at the state level provide ample incentive for smuggling between states and for state-line enterprises specializing in taxed goods.[2]

---

[2]Some excise taxes are referred to as "sin" taxes (because goods such as liquor and tobacco are subject to the tax). Although it is commonly believed that these taxes are imposed for the purpose of discouraging consumption, evidence frequently fails to show this effect. Because demand for alcohol products and gasoline tends to be relatively inelastic (insensitive to price), the increase in price caused by excise taxes has little to do with rates of consumption.

Other goods and services subject to state and local excise taxes include admission to amusement facilities; hotel occupancy; rental of other facilities; and sales of playing cards, oleomargarine products, and prepared foods. Most states impose a tax on transfers of property that require recording of documents (such as real estate sales and sales of stock and securities).

Local Excise Taxes

Over the last few years, two types of excise taxes imposed at the local level have become increasingly popular. These are the hotel occupancy tax and the rental car "surcharge." Because they tax the visitor who cannot vote, they are a political windfall and serve as a means of financing special projects that generate civic pride (e.g., convention centers and state-of-the-art sports arenas).

General Sales Tax

The broad-based general sales tax is a major source of revenue for most state and local governments. It is used in all but five states (Alaska, Delaware, Montana, New Hampshire, and Oregon). While specific rules vary from state to state, the sales tax typically employs a proportional tax rate and includes retail sales of tangible personal property (and occasionally personal services) in the base. Some states exempt medicine and food from the base, and sometimes tax rates vary with the good being sold (e.g., the sales tax rate for automobiles may differ from the rate on other goods). The sales tax is collected by the retailer and then paid to the state government.

Local general sales taxes, over and above those levied by the state, are common. It is not unusual to find taxpayers living in the same state who pay different general rates of sales taxes due to the location of their purchases.

For various reasons, some jurisdictions suspend the application of a general sales tax. The prevalent justification for these sales tax holidays involves the purchase of back-to-school items. Granted by approximately 20 states, the exemption typically is available in early August and covers modest expenditures for clothing and school supplies. Some states have used sales tax holidays to encourage the purchase of energy-conserving appliances (e.g., Maryland, Missouri, and Texas) and hurricane preparedness items (e.g., Louisiana and Virginia).

Use Taxes

One obvious approach to avoiding state and local sales taxes is to purchase goods in a state that has little or no sales tax and then transport the goods back to one's home state. **Use taxes** exist to prevent this tax reduction ploy. The use tax is a value-based

 **GLOBAL TAX ISSUES** **Why Is Gasoline Expensive? It Depends on Where You Live**

In recent years, increases in the cost of gasoline and fuel oil have sometimes aroused such a furor in the United States that supplies have been released from the national oil reserve. Whether such tactics reduce prices more than temporarily seems doubtful. But in the United States, unlike other countries, the price of gasoline largely is attributable to the cost of crude oil. In January 2015, the average price per gallon of gasoline in the United States was about $2.10.

In other countries, the real culprit is the amount of tax imposed. Consider the following situations.

Country	Price per Gallon (U.S. $)
United Kingdom	5.72
Germany	5.11
China	3.46
Saudi Arabia	0.48
Venezuela	0.06

While other factors may contribute to the various gasoline prices, the primary factor is the amount of tax charged in those countries. For example, in the United Kingdom, approximately 60 percent of the cost of gasoline is attributable to taxes.

tax, usually imposed at the same rate as the sales tax, on the use, consumption, or storage of tangible property. Every state that imposes a general sales tax levied on the consumer also applies a use tax.

The Big Picture

EXAMPLE 4

Return to the facts of *The Big Picture* on p. 1-1. The payment Travis made when he registered the car is probably a use tax. When the car was purchased in another state, likely no (or a lesser) sales tax was levied. The current payment makes up for the amount of sales tax he would have paid had the car been purchased in his home state.

The use tax is difficult to enforce for many purchases; therefore, the purchaser often does not pay it. Most of the states are taking steps to curtail this loss of revenue, especially by collecting use taxes that relate to sales conducted on the internet.

Value Added Tax

The **value added tax (VAT)** is a variation of a sales tax; it is levied at each stage of production on the value added by the producer. VAT is in widespread use in many countries around the world (most notably in the European Union and in Canada). The tax typically serves as a major source of revenue for governments that use it.[3]

EXAMPLE 5

Farmer Brown sells wheat to a flour mill for $100. If the wheat cost $65 for Brown to produce and if the VAT rate is 10%, then Brown will owe a VAT of $3.50 [.10($100 − $65)]. If the mill sells the flour for $200 to a baker, and if it cost the mill $120 to make the flour (including the cost of Brown's wheat), then it will pay a VAT of $8 [.10($200 − $120)]. If the baker sells the 200 loaves of bread he makes from the flour for $400, and if it cost the baker $280 to make the bread, then the baker pays a VAT of $12 [.10($400 − $280)].

The consumers who buy the bread will not pay any VAT directly. It is likely, however, that some or all of the total VAT paid of $23.50 ($3.50 + $8 + $12) will be paid by the consumers in the form of higher prices for the bread.

1-2b Employment Taxes

Both Federal and state governments tax the salaries and wages paid to employees. On the Federal side, employment taxes represent a major source of funds. For example, the **FICA tax** accounts for more than one-third of revenues in the Federal budget, second only to the income tax in its contribution.

The Federal government imposes two kinds of employment tax. The Federal Insurance Contributions Act (FICA) imposes a tax on self-employed individuals, employees, and employers. The proceeds of the tax are used to finance Social Security and Medicare benefits. The Federal Unemployment Tax Act (FUTA) imposes a tax on employers only. The **FUTA tax** provides funds to state unemployment benefit programs. Most state employment taxes are similar to the FUTA tax, with proceeds used to finance state unemployment benefit payments.

FICA Taxes

The FICA tax has two components: old age, survivors, and disability insurance payments (commonly referred to as Social Security) and Medicare health insurance payments. For 2015, the Social Security tax rate is 6.2 percent for the employee and 6.2 percent for the employer, and the Medicare tax rate is 1.45 percent for both the employer and the employee. The maximum base for the Social Security tax is $118,500 for 2015. There is no ceiling on the base amount for the Medicare tax. The employer withholds the FICA tax from an employee's wages.

---

[3]Some proposals to reduce the Federal government's reliance on the employment and income taxes have focused on VAT as an alternative tax system.

Payments usually are made through weekly or monthly electronic payments or deposits to a Federal depository. Employers must also file Form 941, Employer's Quarterly Federal Tax Return, by the end of the first month following each quarter of the calendar year (e.g., by July 31 for the quarter ending on June 30) and pay any remaining amount of employment taxes due for the previous quarter. Failure to pay can result in large and sometimes ruinous penalties.

FICA tax is not assessed on all wages paid. For example, wages paid to children under the age of 18 who are employed in a parent's trade or business are exempt from the tax.

The Big Picture

EXAMPLE 6

Return to the facts of *The Big Picture* on p. 1-1. Presuming that April and Martin perform meaningful services for Travis (which the facts seem to imply), they are legitimate employees. April is not subject to Social Security tax because she is under the age of 18. However, Martin is 18, and Travis needs to collect and pay FICA taxes for him.

Furthermore, recall that Betty Carter now is working and is subject to the Social Security and Medicare taxes. Travis, as an independent contractor, is subject to self-employment tax, discussed in the next section.

An additional .9 percent Medicare tax is imposed on earned income (including self-employment income) *above* $200,000 (single filers) or $250,000 (married filing jointly). Unlike the Social Security tax of 6.2 percent and the regular Medicare portion of 1.45 percent, an employer does not match the employees' .9 percent additional Medicare tax.

Similarly, an additional 3.8 percent Medicare tax is assessed on the investment income of individuals whose modified adjusted gross income exceeds $200,000 or $250,000, as above. For this purpose, investment income includes interest, dividends, net capital gains, and income for similar portfolio items.

The Big Picture

EXAMPLE 7

Return to the facts of *The Big Picture* on p. 1-1. The combined income of Travis and Betty Carter may be large enough to trigger one or both of the additional Medicare taxes. The marginal tax rate[4] of "upper income" taxpayers is higher than that of other individuals because of these taxes. Congress has designated these taxes to cover a portion of Federal health care costs. Betty would have considered these taxes when making her decision to re-enter the workforce.

Self-Employment Tax

Self-employed individuals also pay into the FICA system in the form of a self-employment (SE) tax (determined on Schedule SE, filed with Form 1040, U.S. Individual Income Tax Return). Self-employed individuals are required to pay both the employer and the employee portion of the FICA taxes. Therefore, the 2015 SE tax rate is 15.3 percent on self-employment income up to $118,500 and 2.9 percent on all additional self-employment income. Self-employed individuals deduct half of the SE tax—the amount normally deductible by an employer as a business expense. Self-employment income is discussed in more detail in Chapter 11.

Unemployment Taxes

For 2015, FUTA applies at a rate of 6.0 percent on the first $7,000 of covered wages paid during the year to each employee. As with FICA, this represents a regressive rate structure. The Federal government allows a credit for unemployment tax paid (or allowed

---

[4]A taxpayer's *marginal tax rate* (or *marginal tax bracket*) is the rate that would be paid on an additional dollar of taxable income.

under a merit rating system)[5] to the state. The credit cannot exceed 5.4 percent of the covered wages. Thus, the amount required to be paid to the IRS could be as low as .6 percent (6.0% − 5.4%).

FUTA and state unemployment taxes differ from FICA in that the tax is imposed only on the employer.

1-2c Taxes at Death

The transfer of property upon the death of the owner may be a taxable event. If the tax is imposed on the transferor at death, it is called an estate tax. If it taxes the recipient of the property, it is termed an inheritance tax. As is typical of other types of transaction taxes, the value of the property transferred provides the base for determining the amount of the tax at death.

The Federal government imposes an estate tax. A few state governments, however, levy their own additional inheritance taxes, estate taxes, or both.

At the time of her death, Wilma lived in a state that imposes an inheritance tax but not an estate tax. Mary, one of Wilma's heirs, lives in the same state. Wilma's estate is subject to the Federal estate tax, and Mary is subject to the state inheritance tax.

The Federal Estate Tax

Never designed to generate a large amount of revenue, the Federal estate tax was intended to prevent large concentrations of wealth from being kept within a family for many generations. Whether this objective has been accomplished is debatable, because estate taxes can be substantially reduced (or deferred for decades) through careful tax planning activities.

Determination of the estate tax base begins with the *gross estate*, which includes property the decedent owned at the time of death. It also includes property interests, such as life insurance proceeds paid to the estate or to a beneficiary other than the estate if the deceased-insured had any ownership rights in the policy. Most property included in the gross estate is valued at fair market value as of the date of death.

Deductions from the gross estate in arriving at the *taxable estate* include funeral and administration expenses, certain taxes, debts of the decedent, and transfers to charitable organizations. A *marital deduction* is available for amounts passing to a surviving spouse (a widow or widower).

When Luis died, he owned $10 million in various securities, real estate, and personal effects. Under his will, Luis paid $1 million to the local art museum and $2 million to his surviving wife Angelina. Luis's executor computes a Federal estate tax on the $7 million taxable estate.

Once the taxable estate has been determined and certain taxable gifts have been added to it, one must determine a tentative tax liability. The tentative liability is reduced by a variety of credits to arrive at the amount due.

In most cases, the first $5 million of a U.S. decedent's estate effectively is excluded from the estate tax, with a maximum 40 percent tax rate on any excess. Spouses can share a $10 million estate tax exclusion. The $5 million and $10 million amounts are indexed for inflation.[6]

State Taxes at Death

States usually levy an inheritance tax, an estate tax, or both. The two forms of tax differ according to whether the liability is imposed on the heirs or on the estate.

---

[5]States follow a policy of reducing unemployment tax on employers with stable employment. Thus, an employer with no employee turnover might face state unemployment tax rates as low as .1% or, in some cases, zero. This *merit rating system* explicitly accounts for the savings generated by steady employment.

[6]For 2015, the indexed exemption amount for each individual is $5.43 million, and spouses share a $10.86 million Federal estate tax exclusion.

Characteristically, an inheritance tax divides the heirs into classes based on their relationship to the decedent. The more closely related the heir, the lower the rates imposed and the greater the exemption allowed. Some states completely exempt amounts passing to a surviving spouse from taxation.

1-2d Gift Tax

Like estate and inheritance taxes, the Federal **gift tax** is an excise tax levied on the right to transfer property. In this case, however, the tax is imposed on transfers made during the owner's life rather than at death. The tax applies only to transferred amounts that are not supported by full and adequate consideration (i.e., gifts).

Carl sells property worth $20,000 to his daughter for $1,000. Although property worth $20,000 has been transferred, only $19,000 represents a gift, because this is the portion not supported by full and adequate consideration.

The Federal gift tax is intended to complement the estate tax. The gift tax base is the sum of all taxable gifts made *during one's lifetime*. Gifts are valued at the fair market value of the property on the date of the gift. To compute the tax due in a year, the tax rate schedule is applied to the sum of all lifetime taxable gifts. The resulting tax is then reduced by gift taxes paid in prior years.

The Federal gift tax and the Federal estate tax are *unified*.[7] The transfer of assets by a decedent at death effectively is treated as a final gift under the tax law. Thus, the $5 million exclusion (as indexed) and the 40 percent top tax rate for the estate tax also is available to calculate the tax liability generated by lifetime gifts. If the exclusion is exhausted during one's lifetime against taxable gifts, it is not available to reduce the estate tax liability. The same tax rate schedule applies to both lifetime gifts and the estate tax.

Before his death, Ben makes $5 million of taxable gifts. Ignore indexing of the exemption amounts. Because the unified transfer tax exclusion was used up during his life to offset the tax due on these gifts, no further amount is left to reduce Ben's estate tax liability.

Annual taxable gifts are determined by reducing the fair market value of gifts given by an *annual exclusion* of $14,000 per donee. A married couple can elect *gift splitting*, which enables them to transfer twice the annual exclusion ($28,000) per donee per year.

Taxable gifts are reduced by deductions for gifts to charity and to one's spouse (the *marital deduction*). Gifts for medical and educational purposes may be exempt from the gift tax as well.

Gift Tax Exclusion and Deductions

Marco made the following gifts: $500,000 to his wife Irena, $100,000 to their daughter Anita, and $100,000 to the San Mateo Church.

The marital and charitable deductions offset the gifts to Irena and the church. The $14,000 per donee annual exclusion reduces the taxable gift to Anita. Another $14,000 of the taxable gift could be eliminated if Irena agrees to a gift-splitting election.

On December 31, 2015, Vera gives $14,000 to each of her four married children, their spouses, and her eight grandchildren. On January 3, 2016, she repeats the procedure.

Due to the annual exclusion, Vera has *not* made a taxable gift, although she transferred $224,000 [$14,000 × 16 (the number of donees)] in each of the years, for a total of $448,000.

If Vera had been married, she could have given twice as much ($896,000) by electing gift splitting with her husband.

---
[7]§§ 2010 and 2505.

Unlike death, the timing of which usually is involuntary, the making of a gift is a voluntary parting of ownership. Thus, the ownership of a business or a plot of land can be transferred gradually without incurring drastic and immediate tax consequences.

1-2e Property Taxes

A property tax can be a tax on the ownership of property or a tax on wealth, depending on the base used. Any measurable characteristic of the property being taxed can be used as a base (e.g., weight, size, number, or value). Most property taxes in the United States are taxes on wealth; they use value as a base. These value-based property taxes are known as **ad valorem taxes**. Property taxes generally are administered by state and local governments, where they serve as a significant source of revenue.

Taxes on Realty

Property taxes on **realty** are used exclusively by states and their local political subdivisions such as cities, counties, and school districts. They represent a major source of revenue for local governments, but their importance at the state level is limited.

How realty is defined can have an important bearing on which assets are subject to tax. This is especially true in jurisdictions that do not impose ad valorem taxes on **personalty** (all assets that are not realty; discussed in the next section). Realty generally includes real estate and any capital improvements that are classified as fixtures. A fixture is something so permanently attached to the real estate that its removal will cause irreparable damage. A built-in bookcase might be a fixture, whereas a movable bookcase is not. Certain items such as electrical wiring and plumbing change from personalty to realty when installed in a building.

The following are some of the characteristics of ad valorem taxes on realty.

- Property owned by the Federal government is exempt from tax. Similar immunity usually is extended to property owned by state and local governments and by certain charitable organizations.

- Some states provide for lower valuations on property dedicated to agricultural use or other special uses (e.g., wildlife sanctuaries).

- Some states partially exempt the homestead, or personal residence, portion of property from taxation.

- Lower taxes may apply to a residence owned by a taxpayer age 65 or older.

- Some jurisdictions extend immunity from tax for a specified period of time (a tax holiday) to new or relocated businesses.

The Big Picture

EXAMPLE 14

Return to the facts of *The Big Picture* on p. 1-1. Why did the Walkers' taxes decrease while those of the Carters increased? A likely explanation is that one (or both) of the Walkers achieved senior citizen status. In the case of the Carters, the assessed value of their property probably increased. Perhaps they made significant home improvements (e.g., kitchen/bathroom renovation, addition of a sundeck).

Taxes on Personalty

Personalty includes all assets that are not realty. It may be helpful to distinguish between the classification of an asset (realty or personalty) and the use to which it is put. Realty and personalty can be either business-use or personal-use property. Examples include a residence (personal-use realty), an office building (business-use realty), surgical instruments (business-use personalty), and the family car (personal-use personalty).

Personalty can also be classified as tangible property or intangible property. For property tax purposes, intangible personalty includes stocks, bonds, and various other securities (e.g., bank shares).

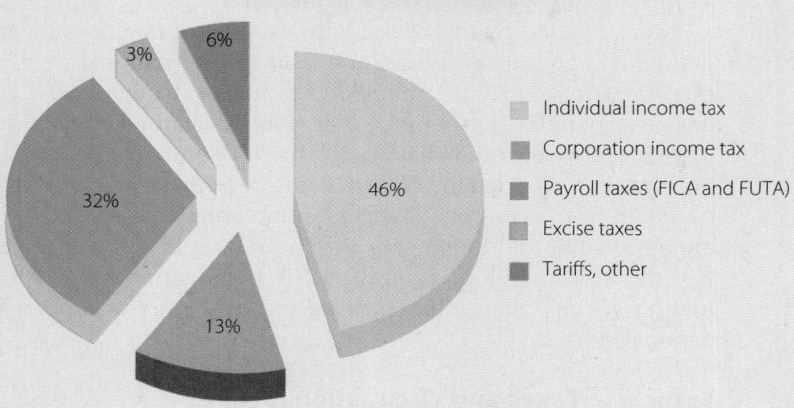

TAX FACT **A Profile of Tax Collections**

Federal budget receipts as estimated for fiscal 2015 indicate a dependence by the government on payroll and individual income taxes. Corporate income tax collections likely are far below what the general public might expect.

Federal Tax Collections

- Individual income tax
- Corporation income tax
- Payroll taxes (FICA and FUTA)
- Excise taxes
- Tariffs, other

The following generalizations may be made concerning the property taxes on personalty.

- Particularly with personalty devoted to personal use (e.g., jewelry, household furnishings), taxpayer compliance ranges from poor to zero. Some jurisdictions do not even attempt to enforce the tax on these items. For automobiles devoted to personal use, many jurisdictions have converted from value as the tax base to a tax based on the weight of the vehicle. Some jurisdictions also consider the vehicle's age (e.g., automobiles six years or older are not subject to the ad valorem tax because they are presumed to have little value).

- For personalty devoted to business use (e.g., inventories, trucks, machinery, equipment), taxpayer compliance and enforcement procedures are notably better.

- Some jurisdictions impose an ad valorem property tax on intangibles.

In-depth coverage can be found on this book's companion website: www.cengagebrain.com   **2 DIGGING DEEPER**

TAX IN THE NEWS **The Backdoor Tax Increase**

Can a landowner's property taxes increase even though the tax rate has not changed? Yes, if the assessed value of the property is increased! Known as a "backdoor tax increase," this procedure allows the taxing authority to generate additional revenue without having to secure voter approval for an increase in the tax rate.

Even more aggravating for the property owner is an increase in assessed value that is based on past market values and does not reflect the true current value. This kind of increase often occurs during periods of economic downturn (i.e., when real estate prices decline). Under these conditions, increases in assessed value are likely to cause considerable taxpayer dissatisfaction and lead to proposals for legislative relief, such as a freeze on upward property assessments.

1-2f **Taxes on Privileges and Rights**

Taxes on privileges and rights are usually considered excise taxes. The most important of these taxes are reviewed here.

Federal Customs Duties

Customs duties or tariffs can be characterized as a tax on the right to move goods across national borders. These taxes, together with selective excise taxes, provided most of the revenues needed by the Federal government during the nineteenth century. For example, tariffs and excise taxes alone paid off the national debt in 1835 and enabled the U.S. Treasury to pay a surplus of $28 million to the states. Today, however, customs duties account for only 1 percent of revenues in the Federal budget.

In recent years, tariffs have acted more as an instrument for carrying out protectionist policies than as a means of generating revenue. Thus, a particular U.S. industry might be saved from economic disaster, so the argument goes, by placing customs duties on the importation of foreign goods that can be sold at lower prices. Protectionists contend that the tariff therefore neutralizes the competitive edge held by the producer of the foreign goods.[8] But tariffs often lead to retaliatory action on the part of the nation or nations affected.

Franchise Taxes and Occupational Taxes

A franchise tax is a tax on the privilege of doing business in a state or local jurisdiction. Typically, the tax is imposed by states on corporations, but the tax base varies from state to state. While some states use a measure of corporate net income as part of the base, most states base the tax on the capitalization of the corporation (with or without certain long-term debt).

Closely akin to the franchise tax are occupational taxes applicable to various trades or businesses, such as a liquor store license, a taxicab permit, or a fee to practice a profession such as law, medicine, or accounting. Most of these are not significant revenue producers and fall more into the category of licenses than taxes. The revenue derived is used to defray the cost incurred by the jurisdiction to regulate the business or profession for the public good.

The Big Picture

EXAMPLE 15

Return to the facts of *The Big Picture* on p. 1-1. Although the facts do not mention the matter, both Travis and Betty will almost certainly pay occupational fees—Travis for engineering and Betty for nursing.

Severance Taxes

Severance taxes are based on the extraction of natural resources (e.g., oil, gas, iron ore, and coal). They are an important source of revenue for many states; Alaska does not levy either a state-level income or sales/use tax, because the collections from its severance taxes are so large.

1-2g **Income Taxes**

Income taxes are levied by the Federal government, most states, and some local governments. In recent years, the trend in the United States has been to place greater reliance on this method of taxation while other countries are relying more heavily on transactions taxes such as the VAT.

---

[8]The North American Free Trade Agreement (NAFTA) substantially reduces the tariffs on trade between Canada, Mexico, and the United States.

Income taxes generally are imposed on individuals, corporations, and certain fiduciaries (estates and trusts). Most jurisdictions attempt to ensure the collection of income taxes by requiring certain pay-as-you-go procedures, including withholding requirements for employees and estimated tax prepayments for all taxpayers.

The Structure of the Federal Income Tax

Although some variations exist, the basic Federal income tax formula is similar for all taxable entities. This formula is shown in Exhibit 1.1.

The income tax is based on the doctrine known as *legislative grace*: all income is subject to tax and no deductions are allowed unless specifically provided for in the law. Some types of income are excluded on the basis of various economic, social, equity, and political considerations. Examples of such exclusions from the income tax base include gifts, inheritances, life insurance proceeds received by reason of death, and interest income from state and local bonds.

All entities are allowed to deduct business expenses from gross income, but a number of limitations and exceptions are applied. A variety of credits against the tax are also allowed, again on the basis of economic, social, equity, or political goals of Congress.

Income tax rates for all entities are progressive. The corporate rates range from 15 percent on the lowest level of taxable income to 35 percent on the highest level. Individual rates range from 10 percent to 39.6 percent. Estates and trusts are also subject to income taxation, with rates ranging from 15 percent to 39.6 percent. Additional Medicare taxes (discussed previously) apply on top of these rates for certain upper-income taxpayers.

Partnerships, qualifying small business corporations, and some limited liability companies are not taxable entities, but must file information returns. Owners of these business entities then are taxed on the net taxable income of the enterprise, proportionate to their holdings.

For individuals, deductions are separated into two categories—deductions *for* adjusted gross income (AGI) and deductions *from* AGI. Generally, deductions *for* AGI are related to business activities, while deductions *from* AGI often are personal in nature (e.g., medical expenses, mortgage interest and property taxes on a personal residence, charitable contributions, and personal casualty losses) or are related to investment activities. Deductions *from* AGI take the form of *itemized deductions* and personal and dependency exemptions. Individuals may take a *standard deduction* (a specified amount based on filing status) rather than itemize actual deductions. An overview of the individual income tax formula is provided in Exhibit 1.2.

LO.3

Describe the basic tax formula for individuals and taxable business entities.

In-depth coverage can be found on this book's companion website: www.cengagebrain.com

3 DIGGING DEEPER

EXHIBIT 1.1	Basic Formula for Federal Income Tax	
Income (broadly defined)		$xxx,xxx
Less: Exclusions (income that is not subject to tax)		(xx,xxx)
Gross income (income that is subject to tax)		$xxx,xxx
Less: Deductions		(xx,xxx)
Taxable income		$xxx,xxx
Federal income tax on taxable income (see Tax Rate Schedules inside front cover of text)		$ xx,xxx
Less: Tax credits (including Federal income tax withheld and other prepayments of Federal income taxes)		(x,xxx)
Tax owed (or refund)		$ xxx

EXHIBIT 1.2	Federal Income Tax Formula for Individuals

Income (broadly defined)	$xx,xxx
Less: Exclusions (income that is not subject to tax)	(x,xxx)
Gross income (income that is subject to tax)	$xx,xxx
Less: Certain business and investment deductions (usually referred to as deductions *for* adjusted gross income)	(x,xxx)
Adjusted gross income	$xx,xxx
Less: The greater of certain personal and employee deductions (usually referred to as *itemized deductions*) *or* The standard deduction (including any *additional* standard deduction)	(x,xxx)
Less: Personal and dependency exemptions	(x,xxx)
Taxable income	$xx,xxx
Federal income tax on taxable income (see Tax Rate Schedules inside front cover of text)	$ x,xxx
Less: Tax credits (including Federal income tax withheld and other prepayments of Federal income taxes)	(xxx)
Tax owed (or refund)	$ xxx

State Income Taxes

Most states (except Alaska, Florida, Nevada, South Dakota, Texas, Washington, and Wyoming) impose a traditional income tax on individuals. Tennessee and New Hampshire tax only certain dividend and interest income. Most states also impose either a corporate income tax or a franchise tax based in part on corporate income. The following additional points can be made about state income taxes.

- State income tax usually relies on Federal income tax laws to some degree—the states use Federal taxable income as a base, with a few adjustments (e.g., a few allow a deduction for Federal income taxes paid and sometimes an exclusion on interest income earned on Federal securities).
- For individuals, a few states impose a flat rate on Federal AGI.
- Several states piggyback directly on the Federal income tax system by using the Federal income tax liability as a tax base.

TAX FACT   What Is the U.S. Tax Burden?

One popular measure of the burden of taxes in the U.S. economy is the Tax Foundation's "Tax Freedom Day." This statistic is a determination of the day upon which an individual has completed the entire year's obligation to governmental units (i.e., if all earnings were paid as taxes to this point, annual taxes would be paid up and one would now begin to "work for his or her own account").

Being "free from taxes" may bring about a feeling of relief, but in reality, tax burdens vary greatly from state to state. And as the U.S. economy has evolved and develops a more complex tax structure, adding emphasis on income and sales/use taxes and reducing the relative reliance on tariffs and excise taxes, year-to-year comparisons become difficult. Nonetheless, as a rough measure of the presence of government in our lives, Tax Freedom Day carries some importance.

If one is in need of consolation, Tax Freedom Day in Canada was June 9, 2014.

Year	Tax Freedom Day
1902	1/31
1930	2/12
1945	4/4
1960	4/15
1970	4/26
1990	5/1
1999	5/11
2000	5/3
2010	4/12
2014	4/21

- Most states also require withholding of state income tax from salaries and wages and estimated payments by corporations and self-employed individuals.
- Most states have their own set of rates, exemptions, and credits.
- Many states also allow a credit for taxes paid to other states.
- Virtually all state income tax returns provide checkoff boxes for donations to various causes. Many are dedicated to medical research and wildlife programs, but special projects are not uncommon. For example, Oklahoma uses a checkoff to retire the debt incurred for its capitol dome addition, while a Wisconsin checkoff financed part of the renovations of Lambeau Field (home of the Green Bay Packers). These checkoff boxes have been criticized as adding complexity to the returns and misleading taxpayers.

Local Income Taxes

Cities imposing an income tax include Baltimore, Cincinnati, Cleveland, Columbus, Denver, Detroit, Kansas City (MO), New York, Philadelphia, San Francisco, and St. Louis, among others. City income taxes usually apply to anyone who earns income in a city. They are designed to collect contributions for government services from those who live in the suburbs but work in the city as well as from local residents.

In-depth coverage can be found on this book's companion website: www.cengagebrain.com **4 DIGGING DEEPER**

1-3 INCOME TAXATION OF BUSINESS ENTITIES

LO.4
State and explain the relationship between business entities and their owners.

1-3a Proprietorships

The simplest form of business entity is a proprietorship, which is not a separate taxable entity. Instead, the proprietor reports the net profit of the business on his or her own individual tax return.

Individuals who own proprietorships (e.g., "Jenny's Fruit Stand") often have specific tax goals with regard to their financial interactions with the business. Because a proprietorship is, by definition, owned by an individual, the individual has great flexibility in structuring the entity's transactions in a way that will minimize his or her marginal income tax rate (or, in some cases, the marginal income tax rates of the family unit).

FINANCIAL DISCLOSURE INSIGHTS   What Do You Mean by "Income" Anyway?

Most business taxpayers keep at least "two sets of books," in that they report one amount of "income" for financial accounting purposes and another amount of "taxable income" as required by various taxing jurisdictions—the definition that will be used throughout this book. In fact, "income" might be defined in many different ways, depending on the recipient of the income reports of the enterprise. For instance, a business entity might prepare markedly different income reports for lenders, employee unions, managers in operating divisions, and international agencies.

Financial accounting income guidance is provided for U.S. businesses by the **Financial Accounting Standards Board (FASB)**, using the accumulated **Generally Accepted Accounting Principles (GAAP)** for the reporting period. When an entity conducts business outside the United States,

the **International Financial Reporting Standards (IFRS)** of the **International Accounting Standards Board (IASB)** also may apply.

Throughout this book, we point out some of the effects that Federal income tax provisions can have on the taxpayer's financial accounting results for the tax year. The vast majority of an entity's business transactions receive identical treatment under GAAP, IFRS, and the Federal tax law. But when the applicable provisions differ, "income" can be reported as different amounts—accounting professionals often refer to these as "book-tax differences."

A tax professional must be able to identify and explain the various constructs of "income" so that the business entity's operating results will be accurately reflected in its stock price, loan covenants, and cash-flow demands.

A proprietorship itself is not a taxpaying entity. The owner of the proprietorship reports the income and deductions of the business on a Schedule C (Profit or Loss from Business) and the net profit (or loss) of the proprietorship on his or her Form 1040 (U.S. Individual Income Tax Return). Specific issues related to the taxation of sole proprietorships are presented in detail in Chapter 11.

1-3b C Corporations

Some corporations pay tax on corporate taxable income, while others pay no tax at the corporate level. Corporations that are separate taxable entities are referred to as **C corporations**, because they are governed by Subchapter C of the Internal Revenue Code. C corporations are addressed in Chapters 12 and 13.

A C corporation is required to file a tax return (Form 1120) and is subject to the Federal income tax. The shareholders then pay income tax on the dividends they receive when the corporation distributes its profits. Thus, the profits of the corporation can be seen as subject to double taxation, first at the corporate level and then at the shareholder level.

EXAMPLE 16

Joseph is the president and sole shareholder of Falcon Corporation. Falcon's taxable income is $50,000, and its tax liability is $7,500. If Joseph has the corporation pay all of its after-tax income to him as a dividend, he will receive $42,500 and pay Federal income tax on that amount as an individual taxpayer. Most of Falcon's $50,000 income has been subjected to Federal income tax twice.

1-3c Partnerships

A partnership is not a separate taxable entity. The partnership is required to file a tax return (Form 1065) on which it summarizes the financial results of the business. Each partner then reports his or her share of the net income or loss and other special items that were reported on the partnership return.

EXAMPLE 17

Cameron and Connor form a partnership in which they are equal partners. The partnership reports a $100,000 net profit on its tax return, but is not subject to the Federal income tax. Cameron and Connor each report $50,000 net income from the partnership on their separate individual income tax returns.

1-3d S Corporations

Corporations that meet certain requirements and pay no tax at the corporate level are referred to as S corporations, because they are governed by Subchapter S of the Code. S corporations are discussed in detail in Chapter 15.

An S corporation is treated like a C corporation for all nontax purposes. Shareholders have limited liability, shares are freely transferable, the entity uses centralized management (vested in the board of directors), and there can be an unlimited continuity of life (i.e., the corporation continues to exist after the withdrawal or death of a shareholder).

With regard to tax factors, however, an S corporation is more like a partnership. The S corporation is not subject to the Federal *income tax*. Like a partnership, it does file a tax return (Form 1120S), but the shareholders report their share of net income or loss and other special items on their own tax returns.

Kay and Dawn form a corporation and elect to treat it as an S corporation. Kay owns 60% of the stock of the corporation, and Dawn owns 40%. The S corporation reports a $100,000 net profit on its tax return, but is not subject to the income tax. Kay reports $60,000 net income from the S corporation on her individual income tax return, and Dawn reports $40,000 on her tax return.

EXAMPLE 18

1-3e Limited Liability Companies and Limited Liability Partnerships

Limited liability companies (LLCs) and limited liability partnerships (LLPs) offer limited liability and some (but not all) of the other nontax features of corporations. Both forms usually are treated as partnerships for tax purposes.

The S corporation, limited liability company, and partnership forms of organization, which are referred to as *flow-through* entities, avoid the double taxation problem associated with the C corporation.

1-3f Dealings between Individuals and Entities

Many of the provisions in the tax law deal with the relationships between owners and the business entities they own. The following are some of the major interactions between owners and business entities.

- Owners put assets into a business when they establish a business entity (e.g., a proprietorship, partnership, or corporation).
- Owners take assets out of the business during its existence in the form of salary, dividends, withdrawals, redemptions of stock, etc.
- Through their entities, owner-employees set up retirement plans for themselves, including IRAs, Keogh plans, and qualified pension plans.
- Owners dispose of all or part of a business entity.

Every major transaction that occurs between an owner and a business entity has important tax ramifications. The following are a few of the many tax issues that arise.

- How to avoid taxation at both the owner level and the entity level (i.e., the multiple taxation problem).
- How to get assets into the business with the least adverse tax consequences.
- How to get accumulated profits and assets out of the business with the least adverse tax consequences.
- How to dispose of the business entity with the least adverse tax consequences.

When addressing these (and other) tax issues, a common set of tax planning tools can be applied. These tax planning fundamentals are introduced in the next section.

In-depth coverage can be found on this book's companion website: www.cengagebrain.com

5 DIGGING DEEPER

FINANCIAL DISCLOSURE INSIGHTS   **Book-Tax Differences**

"Income" is defined differently for Federal income tax and financial accounting purposes. Financial accounting income (FAI) is designed to indicate the profitability of the business entity for the reporting period, in a fair and understandable way, to shareholders, creditors, and other parties who are interested in the results. Taxable income is a device used by Congress to raise revenue; stimulate or stabilize the economy; and accomplish other economic, social, and political goals in an equitable manner. In general, FAI recognizes *revenue* and *expenses*, while taxable income includes *gross income* and *deductions*.

The taxable income of a business taxpayer is not identical to FAI to the extent that *temporary* and *permanent* book-tax differences exist. Broadly, book-tax differences result when:

- Tax benefits are accelerated or deferred relative to their recognition for book purposes, for example, when cost recovery deductions are claimed earlier than depreciation expenses are allowed.

- Tax benefits are not recognized at all for book purposes; for example, there is no book expense item corresponding to the domestic production activities deduction.

As a result of temporary book-tax differences, income tax payable (the amount due on the tax return, referred to by many tax professionals as the "cash tax") is not equal to the income tax expense on the book income statement. The income statement reflects the full income tax burden for the FAI of the reporting period, under the GAAP matching principle, but it is broken into the components *current income tax expense* and *deferred income tax expense*.

When a tax benefit is delayed for book purposes, such as for accelerated cost recovery deductions, a **deferred tax liability** is created on the entity's balance sheet. Taxable income will be greater than FAI in a subsequent year.

When a tax benefit is delayed for tax purposes, such as when a bad debt allowance is used for accounts receivable but is not permissible on the tax return, a **deferred tax asset** is created on the balance sheet. Taxable income will be less than FAI in a subsequent year.

Permanent book-tax differences, such as the exclusion for interest income from a state bond, do not affect the balance sheet. But because FAI and taxable income differ in this amount, the **effective tax rate** of the taxpayer is higher or lower than might be expected. The financial statement footnotes reconcile the statutory and effective tax rates of the entity, in dollar and/or percentage amounts.

The balance sheet accounts for deferred taxes can be sizable. For instance, in most years, Citigroup's deferred tax assets make up about one-third of its tangible equity capital.

LO.5

Identify tax planning opportunities and apply a general framework for tax planning.

1-4   **TAX PLANNING FUNDAMENTALS**

1-4a   **Overview of Tax Planning and Ethics**

Taxpayers generally attempt to minimize their tax liabilities, and it is perfectly acceptable to do so using legal means. It is a long-standing principle that taxpayers have no obligation to pay more than their fair share of taxes. The now-classic words of Judge Learned Hand in *Commissioner v. Newman* reflect the true values a taxpayer should have.

> Over and over again courts have said that there is nothing sinister in so arranging one's affairs as to keep taxes as low as possible. Everybody does so, rich or poor; and all do right, for nobody owes any public duty to pay more than the law demands; taxes are enforced exactions, not voluntary contributions. To demand more in the name of morals is mere cant.[9]

Tax Planning: Avoidance Versus Evasion

Minimizing taxes legally is referred to as **tax avoidance**. On the other hand, some taxpayers attempt to *evade* income taxes through illegal actions. There is a major distinction between tax avoidance and **tax evasion**. Although eliminating or reducing taxes is also a goal of tax evasion, the term *evasion* implies the use of subterfuge and fraud as a means to this end. Tax avoidance is legal, while tax evasion subjects the taxpayer to numerous civil and criminal penalties, including prison sentences.

---

[9]47–1 USTC ¶9175, 35 AFTR 857, 159 F.2d 848 (CA–2, 1947).

Clients expect tax practitioners to provide advice to help them minimize their tax costs. This part of the tax practitioner's practice is referred to as *tax planning*. To structure a sound tax minimization plan, a practitioner must have a thorough knowledge of the tax law. Tax planning skill is based on knowledge of tax saving provisions in the tax law, as well as provisions that contain costly pitfalls for the unwary.

Thorough study of the remainder of this text will provide a solid base of the knowledge required to recognize opportunities and avoid pitfalls. Tax planning requires the practitioner to have in mind both a framework for planning and an understanding of the tax planning implications of a client's situation.

The Ethics of Tax Planning

Tax planning (avoidance) is a fully ethical activity by the taxpayer and the tax professional, but tax evasion (fraud) is not. The tax adviser's actions are limited by the codes of conduct of various professional organizations, such as the American Institute of CPAs or the pertinent state bar association.

Other formal restrictions and directives concerning the conduct of the tax professional can be found in two broad forms.

- Penalties and interest may apply to the taxpayer when a tax liability is understated. Examples include penalties for filing a tax return after its due date, understating gross income amounts, and underpaying withholding or estimated taxes that are due.

- Sanctions are used for tax preparers who disregard the tax law. The Treasury issues a regulation known as *Circular 230* to provide guidance to tax return preparers. Tax penalties also apply when the tax preparer fails to sign a tax return that he or she has worked on or takes an improper filing position on a tax return.

In-depth coverage can be found on this book's companion website: www.cengagebrain.com

6 DIGGING DEEPER

1-4b A General Framework for Income Tax Planning

★ **Tax Planning Framework**

The primary goal of tax planning is to design a transaction so as to minimize its tax costs, while meeting the other nontax objectives of the client. Generally, this means that the client attempts to maximize the present value of its after-tax income and assets. Selecting a specific form of transaction solely for the sake of tax minimization often leads to a poor business decision. Effective tax planning requires careful consideration of the nontax issues involved in addition to the tax consequences.

Careful analysis of the tax formula (refer to Exhibit 1.1) reveals a series of tax minimization strategies. Through creative tax planning that also takes into consideration a client's nontax concerns, each component of the tax formula can be managed in a way that will help to minimize the client's tax liability. The General Framework for Income Tax Planning in Exhibit 1.3 lists each element in the income tax formula, develops tax planning strategies designed to minimize taxes, and provides brief summaries of specific examples of tax planning. The framework is followed by a discussion of the tax planning strategies, along with detailed examples of how the strategies can be applied. In Chapters 4 through 18 of this book, these strategies and their tax formula components provide the framework for Tax Planning Strategies features.

1-4c Tax Minimization Strategies Related to Income

➤ *Avoid Income Recognition.* Section 61(a) defines gross income as "all income from whatever source derived." However, the Code contains provisions that allow various types of income to be excluded from the tax base. Numerous exclusions are available for individuals, but very few are available for corporations. However, a corporation can provide excludible income for its owners at no tax cost to the corporation.

★ **Framework Focus: Income**

➤ *Tax Planning Strategy*

EXHIBIT 1.3	General Framework for Income Tax Planning	

Tax Formula	Tax Planning Strategy	Tax Planning Examples
Income and exclusions	➤ **Avoid income recognition.**	Compensate employees with nontaxable fringe benefits (see Example 19).
	➤ **Postpone recognition of income to achieve tax deferral.**	Postpone sale of assets (see Example 20).
− Deductions	➤ **Maximize deductible amounts.**	Invest in stock of another corporation (see Example 21).
	➤ **Accelerate recognition of deductions to achieve tax deferral.**	Elect to deduct charitable contribution in year of pledge rather than in year of payment (see Example 22).
= Taxable income		
× Tax rate	➤ **Shift net income from high-bracket years to low-bracket years.**	Postpone recognition of income to a low-bracket year (see Example 23).
		Postpone recognition of deductions to a high-bracket year (see Example 24).
	➤ **Shift net income from high-bracket taxpayers to low-bracket taxpayers.**	Pay children to work in the family business (see Example 25).
	➤ **Shift net income from high-tax jurisdictions to low-tax jurisdictions.**	Establish subsidiary operations in countries with low tax rates (see Examples 26 and 27).
	➤ **Control the character of income and deductions.**	Hold assets long enough to qualify for long-term capital gain rates before selling them (see Example 28).
		Invest in small business stock to obtain ordinary loss treatment under § 1244 (see Example 29).
	➤ **Avoid double taxation.**	Operate as a flow-through entity rather than a C corporation (see Example 30).
		Maximize deductible expenses paid by a C corporation to a shareholder/employee (see Example 31).
= Federal income tax		
− Tax credits	➤ **Maximize tax credits.**	Hire employees who qualify the business for the work opportunity tax credit (see Examples 32 and 33).
= Tax owed (or refund)		

EXAMPLE 19

The average employee of Penguin Corporation is a 25% bracket taxpayer. In negotiations with the employees' union, Penguin proposes that it will increase the amount it spends on nontaxable fringe benefits by an average of $3,000 per employee in lieu of granting a $3,000 average salary increase. The average employee will be better off by $750 if the union accepts Penguin's offer.

	Salary Increase	Fringe Benefit Increase
Value of compensation received	$3,000	$3,000
Tax on employee's compensation	(750)	(–0–)
After-tax increase in compensation	$2,250	$3,000

Although the average employee receives a $750 benefit, there is no tax cost to Penguin because both fringe benefits and salaries are deductible by the corporation.

➤ *Tax Planning Strategy*

➤ *Postpone Recognition of Income to Achieve Tax Deferral.* The tax law requires that both income and expenses be reported in the proper tax year. If not for this requirement, taxpayers could freely shift income and expenses from year to year to take advantage of tax rate differentials or could defer tax liabilities indefinitely. Although various rules limit the shifting of income and deductions across time periods, some opportunities still exist.

EXAMPLE 20

In 2010, Turquoise Corporation acquired land for investment purposes at a cost of $500,000. In November 2016, Turquoise is negotiating to sell the land to Aqua Corporation for $800,000. Aqua insists that the transaction be completed in 2016, but Turquoise wants to delay the sale until 2017 to defer the tax on the gain. In an effort to compromise, Turquoise agrees to sell the land in November 2016 and asks Aqua to pay for the land in two installments, $400,000 in December 2016 and $400,000 in January 2017. This enables Turquoise to use the installment method for recognizing the gain, under which Turquoise will report $150,000 of the gain in 2016 and the remaining $150,000 in 2017.

By electing the installment method, Turquoise defers the payment of tax on $150,000 of the gain for one year. If the marginal tax rate for Turquoise is 35%, this tax deferral strategy provides $52,500 ($150,000 × 35%) to be invested or used in the business for another year.

1-4d Tax Minimization Strategies Related to Deductions

★ **Framework Focus: Deductions**

➤ **Maximize Deductible Amounts.** A corporation that owns stock in another corporation is eligible for a *dividends received deduction (DRD)*. The DRD is equal to a specified percentage of the dividends received. The percentage is based on the amount of stock that the investor corporation owns in the investee corporation.

➤ *Tax Planning Strategy*

- 70 percent deduction for ownership of less than 20 percent.
- 80 percent deduction for ownership of 20 percent or more but less than 80 percent.
- 100 percent deduction for ownership of 80 percent or more.

EXAMPLE 21

Falcon Corporation invests in bonds of Sparrow Corporation and receives interest of $20,000. Red Hawk Corporation acquires 15% of the stock of Pheasant Corporation and receives a $20,000 dividend. Falcon's taxable income is increased by $20,000 of interest received. Red Hawk's income is increased by $20,000 in dividend income, but it is allowed a $14,000 dividends received deduction, thus increasing taxable income by only $6,000.

Example 21 demonstrates the *tax* advantage of dividend income versus interest income. However, it is also important to consider *nontax* factors. Is the investment in bonds safer than the investment in stock? Does the potential growth in the value of stock outweigh the possible risk of investing in stock versus bonds?

➤ **Accelerate Recognition of Deductions to Achieve Tax Deferral.** Both corporate and noncorporate taxpayers may deduct charitable contributions if the recipient is a qualified charitable organization. Generally, a deduction is allowed only for the year in which the payment is made. However, an important exception is available for *accrual basis corporations*. They may claim the deduction in the year *preceding* payment if two requirements are met. First, the contribution must be authorized by the board of directors by the end of that year. Second, the contribution must be paid on or before the fifteenth day of the third month of the next year.

➤ *Tax Planning Strategy*

EXAMPLE 22

Blue, Inc., a calendar year, accrual basis corporation, wants to make a $10,000 donation to the Atlanta Symphony Association (a qualified charitable organization), but does not have adequate funds to make the contribution in 2016. On December 28, 2016, Blue's board of directors *authorizes* a $10,000 contribution to the Association. The donation is made on March 14, 2017. Because Blue is an accrual basis corporation, it may claim the $10,000 donation as a deduction for tax year 2016, even though payment is not made until 2017.

Blue was able to take advantage of a tax provision and reduce 2016 taxable income by $10,000. If Blue is in the 35% marginal bracket, the corporation defers payment of $3,500 in Federal income tax. The $3,500 can be invested or used in the business for another tax year.

TAX FACT **The Rewards of Tax Planning**

Federal tax law does not fall equally on all taxpayers. Congress has allowed numerous tax incentives by which the taxpayer can manage long-term tax liabilities, when applying sound and ethical tax planning techniques. Here are some observations about the context in which the tax professional works with the taxpayer.

- The Federal income tax law provides over $1.4 trillion in credits, exemptions, exclusions, and deductions. The average individual reduces his or her tax liability by about $4,000 when these tax reductions are claimed.

- The most popular important Federal tax incentives for individuals include the following.

Tax Provision	Estimated Revenue Loss ($B)
Exclusions, deductions for health care costs	223
Exclusions for Social Security and retirement plan income	132
Earned income, child credits	131
Low tax rates on capital gains	96
Deduction for home mortgage interest	68
Deduction for gifts to charity	44

- The most important tax incentives for corporate taxpayers include the following. Corporations claim about 10 percent of all tax expenditures.

Tax Provision	Estimated Revenue Loss ($B)
Deferral of overseas income not repatriated	83
Accelerated depreciation deductions	25
Deduction for domestic manufacturing profits	12
Credit, deduction for research activities	11
Credit for providing low-income housing	7

★ **Framework Focus: Tax Rates**

➤ *Tax Planning Strategy*

1-4e **Tax Minimization Strategies Related to Tax Rates**

➤ *Shift Net Income from High-Bracket Years to Low-Bracket Years.* One objective of shifting income is to defer the payment of income tax (refer to Example 20). A second time-shifting strategy is to shift *net* income from high-tax to low-tax years. This can be accomplished by shifting income from high-bracket years to low-bracket years or by shifting deductions from low-bracket years to high-bracket years.

Shift Income to Low-Bracket Years

EXAMPLE 23

Egret Corporation, a calendar year taxpayer, is in the 34% bracket in 2016, but expects to be in the 25% bracket in 2017. The corporation, which is negotiating a $10,000 service contract with a client, decides to wait until 2017 to sign the contract and perform the services. The client is indifferent as to when the contract is completed. Thus, Egret saves $900 in income tax by deferring the service contract income to 2017, when it will be taxed at the 25% rate instead of the current 34% rate.

In this case, the income-shifting strategy is used to accomplish two tax planning objectives. First, shifting the income defers the payment of income tax from 2016 to 2017. Second, the shifting strategy results in the income being taxed at a rate of 25% rather than 34%.

EXAMPLE 24

Macaw Corporation has been sued for $125,000 damages by a customer, and the parties decided to settle out of court for $100,000. Macaw expects to be in the 25% bracket in 2016 and the 35% bracket in 2017. Macaw will save $10,000 in income tax if it finalizes the agreement in January 2017 rather than December 2016 [$100,000 × (35% − 25%)].

➤ *Tax Planning Strategy*

➤ *Shift Net Income from High-Bracket Taxpayers to Low-Bracket Taxpayers.* Individual income tax rates range from 10 to 35 percent (39.6 percent for certain high-income taxpayers). Although several provisions in the tax law prevent shifting income from high-bracket taxpayers to low-bracket taxpayers, many opportunities to do so remain. Business entities can be effective vehicles for shifting income to low-bracket taxpayers.

EXAMPLE 25

Bill Gregory is the president and sole shareholder of Grayhawk, Inc., an S corporation. He projects that Grayhawk will earn $400,000 this year. Bill is taxed on this income at a 35% marginal rate. Bill and his wife have four teenage children, all of whom are dependents. The Gregorys record no other taxable income; they file a joint return.

Bill employs the children as part-time workers throughout the year and pays them $11,000 each. This reduces Bill's income from Grayhawk by $44,000 and reduces his Federal income tax by $15,400 ($44,000 × 35%).

The salaries paid to the children will be subject to their lower Federal income tax rates. The salaries also might be exempt from the FICA and other payroll taxes; so the family unit's total tax liability has been reduced by shifting taxable income to the children.

> *Shift Net Income from High-Tax Jurisdictions to Low-Tax Jurisdictions.* A choice of the state or country where income is earned (or where a deduction is incurred) can have a large effect on an entity's overall tax liability. Hence, shifting income from high-tax jurisdictions to low-tax jurisdictions or shifting deductions from low-tax jurisdictions to high-tax jurisdictions is an important tax planning strategy.

> *Tax Planning Strategy*

Shifting Tax Jurisdictions

EXAMPLE 26

Gold International owns a sales subsidiary in Texas and a manufacturing subsidiary in Ireland (which imposes a 15% tax rate on certain types of business income). The Irish subsidiary makes drill presses and sells them for $4 million to the Texas subsidiary, which then modifies them and offers them for sale to businesses in the United States for $8.4 million. The cost of manufacturing and modifying each drill press is $3 million.

Of the $5.4 million of profit earned, $1 million is attributable to the Irish corporation (which is subject to a 15% tax rate), and $4.4 million is attributable to the U.S. corporation (which is subject to a 34% tax rate). Gold's total tax liability is $1,646,000 [($1,000,000 × 15%) + ($4,400,000 × 34%)].

EXAMPLE 27

Assume the same facts as in the previous example, except that $5 million of the profit is attributable to the Irish corporation and $400,000 is attributable to the U.S. corporation. In this case, Gold's total tax liability is $886,000 [($5,000,000 × 15%) + ($400,000 × 34%)]. Thus, by altering the amount of work done in each of the two subsidiaries and the amount of income generated by each, Gold's tax liability is decreased by $760,000 ($1,646,000 − $886,000).

> *Control the Character of Income and Deductions.* For various policy reasons, Congress has chosen to treat certain categories of income and losses more favorably than others. For instance, the provisions that apply to most individuals and tax long-term capital gains at a maximum rate of 20 percent, compared to a top 39.6 percent rate on ordinary income, were enacted to encourage individuals to make long-term investments of capital in the economy.

> *Tax Planning Strategy*

EXAMPLE 28

Lisa is the proprietor of Designer Enterprises. Because a proprietorship is a flow-through entity, Lisa reports all of Designer's transactions on her individual income tax return. On October 9, 2016, Lisa invested $25,000 of Designer's excess cash in Lavender Corporation stock. On October 1, 2017, the stock was worth $35,000.

Lisa's marginal tax rate is 33% for ordinary income and 15% for long-term capital gain. She has decided to sell the stock and use the cash to increase Designer's inventory. She must hold the stock until October 10, 2017, for the gain to qualify as long term (held more than a year). If Lisa sells the stock before October 10, 2017, the gain is taxed as short term and she pays 33% tax on the gain. If she sells the stock after October 9, 2017, the gain is long term and she will pay 15% tax on the gain.

To encourage investment in small businesses, Congress enacted the § 1244 provisions, which provide favorable Federal income tax treatment of losses incurred on the sale of qualifying small business stock. Generally, losses on the sale of stock are treated

TAX FACT The U.S. Federal Income Tax

The Federal income tax is pervasive throughout our lives, but how much do we know about where it came from and how it works?

- The current version of the Internal Revenue Code has surpassed its 100th birthday; it was first effective on March 1, 1913.

- A temporary Federal income tax was used to finance the Civil War and the Spanish-American War. The current Federal tax code was adopted after Britain, Germany, France, and other countries in Europe had adopted similar taxing systems.

- The first Form 1040 was four pages long.

- The tax return became Form 1040 because that was the next number sequentially in issued Federal forms.

- The first Form 1040 was due on March 1, 1914. The unextended due date became March 15 for 1919, and April 15 for 1955.

- Taxes largely are paid today using a withholding system, a creation made necessary to pay for World War II. But at first, no money was sent with the return. A field auditor checked every return and sent a bill to the taxpayer by June 1, payable by June 30.

- A majority of taxpayers at every income level engage paid tax professionals for assistance in preparing Federal income tax returns.

- Over 80 percent of all Forms 1040 are filed electronically. About 75 percent of Forms 1040 show a refund receivable by the taxpayer; the average refund is about $2,750.

as capital losses. Individuals with capital losses in excess of capital gains are permitted to deduct only $3,000 of such losses against ordinary income in a tax year.

To make small business stock more attractive as an investment, § 1244 allows up to $50,000 ($100,000 if married filing jointly) of losses on such stock to be treated as ordinary losses, thus exempting the § 1244 losses from being offset against capital gains and then from the $3,000 limit that would otherwise apply to any excess capital losses.

EXAMPLE 29

Roberto invested $80,000 in Mauve Corporation stock. He sold the stock this year for $40,000. He has no other capital asset transactions and does not expect to have any in future years. If the Mauve stock qualifies as § 1244 stock, Roberto may deduct the entire $40,000 as an ordinary loss. If the stock does not qualify as § 1244 stock, Roberto may deduct only $3,000 as a capital loss in the current tax year. He carries the remaining loss of $37,000 forward. In future years, the loss will continue to be subject to the annual $3,000 limitation unless there are offsetting capital gains.

> **Tax Planning Strategy**

> *Avoid Double Taxation.* The owners of a corporation can choose between two entity forms. A C corporation, also referred to as a regular corporation, is a taxable entity that pays tax on corporate profits. Shareholders also pay tax on dividends received from a C corporation, resulting in what is commonly referred to as *double taxation* (refer to Example 16). Note, however, as discussed in Chapter 4, that the dividends may be eligible for a beneficial tax rate.

Shareholders can avoid double taxation by electing that a corporate entity become an S corporation. Unlike a C corporation, an S corporation is not a taxable entity. Instead, the profits and losses of the S corporation flow through to the shareholders and are reported on their tax returns (see Chapter 15).

EXAMPLE 30

Chickadee, Inc., a C corporation with net income of $100,000, pays Carl, its sole shareholder, a $77,750 dividend. Chickadee must pay corporate income tax of $22,250 on the net income of $100,000, and Carl must pay tax on the $77,750 dividend. Sparrow, Inc., an S corporation, also earns $100,000. Sparrow is not a taxable entity, so it pays no income tax on the $100,000 net income. Sam, who is the sole shareholder of Sparrow, includes $100,000 in computing his taxable income.

Other entity choices can be used to avoid double taxation, including partnerships and limited liability companies. Partnerships and limited liability companies, like S corporations, are flow-through entities rather than taxable entities (see Chapter 14).

Choosing to operate as a **flow-through entity** is not the only way to avoid double taxation. Double taxation can be avoided or minimized by having the corporation make payments, such as salaries, rent, and interest to the shareholders.

EXAMPLE

31

Walt is the president and sole shareholder of Meadowlark, Inc., a C corporation. Meadowlark's taxable income before any payment to Walt is $600,000. Walt, a skilled manager, is primarily responsible for the profitability of the corporation. If Meadowlark pays Walt a dividend of $400,000, the corporation must pay Federal income tax on $600,000 and Walt must include the $400,000 dividend in gross income. However, if Meadowlark pays Walt a salary of $400,000, the salary is deductible and the corporation has only $200,000 of taxable income. Walt must include the $400,000 salary in gross income.

In either case, Walt includes $400,000 in gross income (the dividends may be eligible for a beneficial tax rate). Meadowlark, on the other hand, reports $400,000 less taxable income if the payment to Walt is a salary payment rather than a dividend payment.

In considering this plan, Meadowlark should examine the effects of employment taxes on Walt and the corporation as well.

1-4f **Tax Minimization Strategies Related to Credits**

> *Maximize Tax Credits.* Congress uses the tax credit provisions of the Internal Revenue Code liberally in implementing tax policy. It is important to understand the difference between a credit and a deduction, both of which reduce a taxpayer's tax liability. A deduction reduces taxable income, which results in a reduction of the tax paid. The tax benefit of the deduction depends on the amount of the qualifying expenditure and the taxpayer's tax rate. A tax credit reduces the tax liability dollar for dollar and is not affected by the taxpayer's tax rate.

★ **Framework Focus: Credits**

> *Tax Planning Strategy*

EXAMPLE

32

Oriole Corporation, which is in the 25% marginal bracket, has a $6,000 deduction for expenditures made to repair a machine. The deduction reduces taxable income by $6,000 and results in a tax liability reduction of $1,500 ($6,000 deduction × 25% marginal rate).

Oriole also incurred expenditures of $6,000 to rehabilitate a building, which qualifies the corporation for a tax credit of $600 ($6,000 rehabilitation expenditures × 10% rate for the credit). The rehabilitation expenditures credit results in a $600 reduction of Oriole's tax liability. In addition, Oriole's depreciable basis for the building increases by $5,400 ($6,000 expenditures − $600 credit).

One example of the use of credits to influence taxpayer behavior is the work opportunity tax credit, which was enacted to encourage employers to hire employees from several targeted and economically disadvantaged groups, including high-risk youths, summer youth employees, and military veterans. The employee is certified to be a member of a qualifying targeted group. The work opportunity tax credit is 40 percent of the first $6,000 of wages paid during the first 12 months of employment. For long-term family assistance recipients, the credit is even greater.

EXAMPLE

33

Robin Corporation hired a high-risk youth for four months at a cost of $6,000. Robin qualifies for the work opportunity tax credit and is allowed a credit of $2,400 ($6,000 wages × 40% credit rate) and a wage deduction of $3,600 ($6,000 wages − $2,400 credit). Robin is a 34% bracket taxpayer. The $3,600 deduction reduces Robin's income tax by $1,224 ($3,600 × 34%). The total tax saving thus is $3,624 ($1,224 from the deduction + $2,400 from the credit).

If the employee does not qualify Robin for the work opportunity tax credit, Robin is allowed a deduction of $6,000, which results in a tax saving of $2,040 ($6,000 × 34%). Thus, hiring an employee who qualifies Robin for the work opportunity tax credit saves an additional $1,584 in tax ($3,624 − $2,040).

1-4g **Thinking Outside the Framework**

Although the General Framework for Income Tax Planning in Exhibit 1.3 is broad and covers most tax planning strategies, some strategies fall outside the framework. In addition, other planning ideas can supplement the strategies in the framework. Some of these ideas are discussed below.

Determining the Tax Burden

To engage in effective tax planning, one must be able to identify the relevant tax rate that will be applied to a transaction. There are at least three kinds of tax rates to consider in making a financial decision. A taxpayer's *marginal* tax rate is paid on an additional dollar of taxable income. Referring to the corporate income tax rate schedule on the inside front cover of this text, a C corporation's marginal tax rate on its first dollar of income is 15 percent. Similarly, the marginal tax rate faced by a corporation with $100,001 of income is 39 percent.

The *average* tax rate is the ratio of taxes paid to the tax base. Thus, a corporation with $100,000 of taxable income is subject to an average tax rate of 22.25 percent ($22,250 in tax divided by $100,000 in taxable income).

A third kind of tax rate computation, the *effective* tax rate, can be seen as either (1) the ratio of taxes paid to financial net income before tax or (2) the sum of currently payable and deferred tax expense divided by the book net income before tax. Of these approaches to determining a taxpayer's tax rate, the marginal tax rate is most appropriate for tax planning purposes.

EXAMPLE 34

Azure Corporation reports taxable income of $80,000. Azure also received $10,000 of tax-free interest income from municipal bonds. Using the corporate tax rate schedule on the inside front cover of this text, one can determine that the company's tax liability is $15,450.

If Azure were to earn an additional dollar in taxable income, it would pay an extra $.34 in tax. Thus, the company's marginal tax rate is 34%. Azure's average tax rate is the ratio of taxes paid to book income, or 19.3% ($15,450/$80,000). Finally, the company has an effective rate of tax of 17.2% ($15,450/$90,000), the ratio of taxes paid to book net income before tax (here, the sum of taxable income and tax-free income).

The actual tax paid may not always be apparent. For example, the amount of taxes paid should include both current taxes and the present value of future taxes generated by a transaction. Present value and future value tables are included in Appendix F of this text.

EXAMPLE 35

Magenta Corporation is a publishing company that specializes in electronic media. It is a new corporation that was formed on January 1, 2015. During that year, it generated a net operating loss (NOL) of $300,000. The NOL can be carried forward to offset future years' taxable income and thereby reduce Magenta's future tax liabilities. Magenta expects to earn $100,000 of income each year over the next four years. The NOL should completely offset the company's taxable income for the first three of these years.

At the beginning of 2016, Magenta must decide whether to invest in a project that will earn an additional $40,000 of taxable income during 2016 or in a project that will generate $36,000 of tax-free income. The company's president reasons that because the company has an NOL carryforward, the applicable tax rate is 0%, so the taxable project should be chosen.

The president's reasoning is incorrect, because an additional $40,000 of income now will result in $40,000 of taxable income in 2018 (because there will be $40,000 less NOL available in that year).

	2016	2017	2018	2019
Alternative 1 (tax-free investment)				
Pre-NOL taxable income	$ 100,000	$ 100,000	$ 100,000	$100,000
NOL carryforward (from 2015)	(300,000)	(200,000)	(100,000)	–0–
Taxable income	$ –0–	$ –0–	$ –0–	$100,000
Alternative 2 (taxable investment)				
Pre-NOL taxable income	$ 140,000	$ 100,000	$ 100,000	$100,000
NOL carryforward (from 2015)	(300,000)	(160,000)	(60,000)	–0–
Taxable income	$ –0–	$ –0–	$ 40,000	$100,000

The tax cost of the $40,000 project equals the discounted value of the tax due for 2018. Assuming a 10% after-tax internal rate of return and a 15% corporate tax rate, the present value of taxes deferred for three years is $4,508 and the discounted tax rate is 11.27%. Thus, the after-tax proceeds on the taxable project are $35,492, or $508 *less* than the $36,000 earnings on the tax-free project.

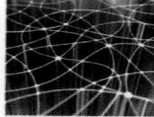

When the tax law is used to accomplish goals other than revenue collection, fiscal "winners" and "losers" can be created. The distribution is not equal across income levels for Federal tax expenditures and other Federal benefits. For this purpose, "Federal benefits" include retirement, health care, and poverty reduction programs that trigger payments to individuals.

"Federal tax breaks" usually do not involve an appropriation and payment by Congress. Instead, they represent tax reductions from individuals' exemptions, the standard deduction, itemized deductions (e.g., for payments of home mortgage interest), and lower tax rates on investment income.

Federal Benefits Received

Income Quintile	$ Received per Family Unit	% of Total Benefits Received	$B in Benefits Received
Lowest	18,007	33	666
2	17,755	27	551
3	13,003	17	349
4	10,780	12	246
Highest	10,087	10	203

Federal Tax Breaks Received

Income Quintile	$ Received per Family Unit	% of Total Benefits Received	$B in Benefits Received
Lowest	1,110	4	40
2	2,149	7	74
3	2,757	8	91
4	5,021	14	152
Highest	24,693	67	723

1-5 UNDERSTANDING THE FEDERAL TAX LAW

Explain the economic, social, equity, and political considerations that underlie the tax law.

The Federal tax law is a mosaic of statutory laws, administrative pronouncements, and court decisions. Anyone who has attempted to work with these provisions would admit to their complexity. For the person who has to trudge through a mass of rules to find the solution to a tax problem, it may be of some consolation to know that the law's complexity generally can be explained. Whether sound or not, there are reasons for the formulation of every rule. Recognizing these reasons, therefore, is an important step toward understanding the Federal tax law.

1-5a Revenue Needs

The foundation of the income tax system is the raising of revenue to cover the cost of government operations. Ideally, annual outlays should not exceed anticipated revenues, thereby leading to a balanced budget with no resulting deficit. Many states have achieved this objective by passing laws or constitutional amendments precluding deficit spending.

The U.S. Constitution allows deficit spending, and politicians often find it hard to resist the temptation to spend more than the tax system collects currently. Congress uses several approaches to reduce a tax bill's net revenue loss. When tax reductions are involved, the full impact of the legislation can be phased in over a period of years. Or as an alternative, the tax reduction can be limited to a period of years. When the period expires, Congress can then renew or not renew the provision in light of budget considerations.

1-5b Economic Considerations

Using the tax system in an effort to accomplish economic objectives has become increasingly popular in recent years. Generally, proponents of this approach use tax legislation to promote measures designed to help control the economy or encourage certain economic activities and businesses.

GLOBAL TAX ISSUES   Outsourcing of Tax Return Preparation

The use of foreign nationals to carry out certain job assignments for U.S. businesses is an increasingly popular practice. Outsourcing such activities as telemarketing to India, for example, usually produces the same satisfactory result but at a much lower cost.

Now outsourcing also is being applied to the preparation of tax returns. Not only can this practice be expected to continue, but it probably will increase in volume. Outsourcing tax return preparation does not violate Federal law, and the practice is compatible with accounting ethical guidelines as long as three safeguards are followed: First, the practitioner must make sure that client confidentiality is maintained. Second, the practitioner must verify the accuracy of the work that has been outsourced. Third, the practitioner must gain the consent of clients when any offshore third-party contractor is used to provide professional services.

Tax professionals justify tax preparation outsourcing as a means of conserving time and effort that can be applied toward more meaningful tax planning on behalf of their clients.

Sources: Reg. § 301.7216–2(c)(2); AICPA Ethics Ruling No. 1 (under Rule 301), see **www.aicpa.org/Research/standards/CodeofConduct/Pages/et_391.aspx**.

Encouragement of Certain Activities

Without passing judgment on the wisdom of any such choices, it is clear that the tax law encourages certain types of economic activity or segments of the economy. For example, the favorable treatment allowed research and development expenditures (immediate deduction vs. capitalization and amortization) can be explained by the desire to foster technological progress. Further, given the time value of money, the tax savings from a current deduction usually is preferable to capitalizing the cost with a write-off over the estimated useful life of the asset created.

Similarly, Congress has used depreciation deductions as a means of encouraging investment in business capital. Theoretically, shorter asset lives and accelerated methods should encourage additional investment in depreciable property acquired for business use. Conversely, longer asset lives and the required use of the straight-line method of depreciation dampen the tax incentive for capital outlays.

Part of the tax law addresses the global energy crisis—in terms of both our reliance on foreign oil and the need to ease the problem of global warming. Ecological considerations justify a tax provision that permits a more rapid expensing of the costs of installing pollution control facilities. Measures such as these that aid in maintaining a clean air environment and conserving energy resources also can be justified under social considerations.

Is it wise to stimulate U.S. exports of goods and services? Considering the pressing and continuing problem of a deficit in the U.S. balance of payments, the answer should be clear. In an international setting, Congress has deemed it advisable to establish incentives for U.S. citizens who accept employment overseas.

Is saving desirable for the economy? Saving leads to capital formation and thereby makes funds available to finance home construction and industrial expansion. The tax law encourages saving by according preferential treatment to private retirement plans. Not only are deductions allowed for contributions to certain retirement plans and Individual Retirement Accounts (IRAs), but income on the contributions might not be taxed until withdrawn.

Encouragement of Certain Industries

A sound agricultural base is necessary for a well-balanced national economy. Undoubtedly, this explains why farmers are accorded special treatment under the Federal income tax system. Among the benefits available to farmers are the election to expense rather than capitalize certain soil and water conservation expenditures and fertilizers and the election to defer the recognition of gain on the receipt of crop insurance proceeds.

To stimulate the manufacturing industry, Congress enacted the domestic production activities deduction. The provision creates a tax benefit in the form of a deduction for profits derived from manufacturing activities conducted within the United States. By restricting the deduction to manufacturing income attributable to wages reportable to the IRS, new U.S. jobs will result and the outsourcing of labor is discouraged. Thus, the tax system is used to encourage both domestic manufacturing and job growth.

Encouragement of Small Business

It seems that in the United States, a consensus exists that what is good for small business is good for the economy as a whole. This assumption has led to a definite bias in the tax law favoring small business. Several income tax provisions can be explained by the desire to benefit small business, including the low marginal tax rates applied to the first dollars of the entity's income.

1-5c Social Considerations

Some provisions of the Federal tax law, particularly those dealing with the income tax of individuals, can be explained by a desire to encourage certain social results.

- Certain benefits provided to employees through accident and health insurance plans financed by employers are nontaxable to employees. Encouraging such plans is considered socially desirable because they provide medical benefits in the event of an employee's illness or injury.

- A contribution made by an employer to a qualified pension or profit sharing plan for an employee may receive special treatment. The contribution and any income it generates are not taxed to the employee until the funds are distributed. Such an arrangement also benefits the employer by allowing a tax deduction when the contribution is made to the qualified plan. Various types of retirement plans are encouraged to supplement the subsistence income level the employee otherwise would obtain under the Social Security system.

- A deduction is allowed for contributions to qualified charitable organizations. The deduction attempts to shift some of the financial and administrative burden of socially desirable programs from the public (government) to the private (citizens) sector.

- Various tax credits, deductions, and exclusions are designed to encourage taxpayers to obtain or extend their level of education.

- A tax credit is allowed for amounts spent to furnish care for certain minor or disabled dependents to enable the taxpayer to seek or maintain gainful employment.

- A tax deduction is denied for certain expenditures deemed to be contrary to public policy. This disallowance extends to items such as fines, penalties, illegal kickbacks, bribes to government officials, and gambling losses in excess of gains. Social considerations dictate that the tax law should not encourage these activities by permitting a deduction.

1-5d Equity Considerations

The concept of equity is relative. Reasonable persons can, and often do, disagree about what is fair or unfair. In the tax area, moreover, equity is most often tied to a particular taxpayer's personal situation. To illustrate, compare the tax positions of those who rent their personal residences with those who own their homes. Renters may not take a Federal income tax deduction for the rent they pay. For homeowners, however, a large portion of the house payments they make may qualify for the Federal mortgage interest and property tax deductions. Although renters may have difficulty understanding this difference in tax treatment, the encouragement of home ownership can be justified on both economic and social grounds.

In many other parts of the law, however, equity concerns are evident. The concept of equity appears in tax provisions that alleviate the effect of multiple taxation and postpone the recognition of gain when the taxpayer lacks the ability or wherewithal to pay the tax. Provisions that mitigate the effect of the application of the annual accounting period concept also reflect equity considerations.

Alleviating the Effect of Multiple Taxation

The income earned by a taxpayer may be subject to taxes imposed by different taxing authorities. If, for example, the taxpayer is a resident of New York City, income might be subject to Federal, state of New York, and city of New York income taxes. To compensate for this apparent inequity, the Federal tax law allows a taxpayer to claim a deduction for state and local income taxes.

The deduction does not, however, neutralize the effect of multiple taxation because the benefit derived depends on the taxpayer's Federal income tax rate. Only a 100% rate tax credit, rather than a deduction, would completely eliminate the effects of multiple taxation on the same income. Equity considerations also can explain the Federal tax treatment of certain income from non-U.S. sources.

The Wherewithal to Pay Concept

The wherewithal to pay concept recognizes the inequity of taxing a transaction when the taxpayer lacks the means to pay the tax. The wherewithal to pay concept underlies a provision in the tax law dealing with the treatment of gain resulting from an involuntary conversion. An involuntary conversion occurs when property is destroyed by casualty or taken by a public authority through condemnation. If gain results from the conversion, it need not be recognized if the taxpayer replaces the property within a specified time period. The replacement property must be similar or related in service or use to that involuntarily converted.

EXAMPLE 36

Ron, a rancher, has some pasture land that is condemned by the state for use as a game preserve. The condemned pasture land cost Ron $120,000, but the state pays him $150,000 (its fair market value). Shortly thereafter, Ron buys more pasture land for $150,000.

Ron has a realized gain of $30,000 [$150,000 (condemnation award) − $120,000 (cost of land)]. It would be inequitable to require Ron to pay a tax on this gain for two reasons. First, without disposing of the property acquired (the new land), Ron would be hard-pressed to pay the tax. Second, his economic position has not changed.

What if Ron reinvests only $140,000 of the award in new pasture land? Now Ron recognizes a $10,000 taxable gain in the current year. Instead of ending up with only replacement property, Ron now holds land and $10,000 in cash.

Mitigating the Effect of the Annual Accounting Period Concept

Federal income tax returns are due for every tax year of the taxpayer. The application of this annual accounting period concept can lead to dissimilar tax treatment for taxpayers who are, from a long-range standpoint, in the same economic position.

EXAMPLE 37

José and Alicia, both unmarried sole proprietors, experienced the following results during the indicated tax years.

	Profit (or Loss)	
Year	José	Alicia
2015	$50,000	$150,000
2016	60,000	60,000
2017	60,000	(40,000)

continued

Although José and Alicia have the same total profit of $170,000 over the period from 2015 through 2017, the annual accounting period concept places Alicia at a disadvantage for tax purposes, both in terms of the time value of money and due to the higher tax rates that will apply to Alicia under the progressive rate structure.

However, the net operating loss deduction generated in 2017 offers Alicia some relief by allowing her to carry back some or all of her 2017 loss to the earlier profitable years (in this case, 2015). Thus, with an NOL carryback, Alicia can obtain an immediate refund for some of the taxes she paid on the $150,000 profit reported for 2015.

1-5e Political Considerations

A large segment of the Federal tax law is made up of statutory provisions. Because these statutes are enacted by Congress, is it any surprise that political considerations influence tax law?

Special Interest Legislation

Certain provisions of the tax law largely can be explained by the political influence some groups have had on Congress. For example, is there any other realistic reason that prepaid subscription and dues income is not taxed until earned, while prepaid rents are taxed to the landlord in the year received?

Special interest legislation is not necessarily to be condemned if it can be justified on economic, social, or some other utilitarian grounds. In most cases, however, it is objectionable in that it adds further complexity to an already cluttered tax law. It is, however, an inevitable product of our political system.

State and Local Government Influences

State law has had an influence in shaping our present Federal tax law. One example of this effect is the evolution of Federal tax law in response to states with community property systems. The states with community property systems are Louisiana, Texas, New Mexico, Arizona, California, Washington, Idaho, Nevada, and Wisconsin. Spouses in Alaska can elect community property treatment. The rest of the states are common law jurisdictions.

The difference between common law and community property systems centers around the property rights possessed by married persons. In a common law system, each spouse owns whatever he or she earns. Under a community property system, one-half of the earnings of each spouse is considered owned by the other spouse.

Al and Fran are husband and wife, and their only income is the $80,000 annual salary Al receives. If they live in New Jersey (a common law state), the $80,000 salary belongs to Al. If, however, they live in Arizona (a community property state), the $80,000 is divided equally, in terms of ownership, between Al and Fran.

EXAMPLE 38

At one time, the tax position of the residents of community property states was so advantageous that many common law states adopted community property systems. Needless to say, the political pressure placed on Congress to correct the disparity in tax treatment was considerable. To a large extent, this was accomplished in 1948 when the law extended many of the community property tax advantages to residents of common law jurisdictions.

The major advantage extended was the provision allowing married taxpayers to file joint returns and compute the tax liability as if one-half of the income had been earned by each spouse. This result is automatic in a community property state because half of the income earned by one spouse belongs to the other spouse. The income-splitting benefits of a joint return are incorporated as part of the tax rates applicable to married taxpayers. A similar motivation can be seen for the gift-splitting provisions of the Federal gift tax and the marital deduction of the Federal estate and gift taxes.

A tax system that is designed to accomplish so many, sometimes contradictory, goals is bound to be a complex animal. According to the Tax Foundation, the current system may actually be so complex as to be self-defeating.

By one estimate, the cost of compliance with Federal tax laws exceeds $425 billion per year. Roughly, this means that compliance costs act as an additional tax of about 30 cents for every tax dollar collected. This amount exceeds the annual costs of compensation for all of the workers at Walmart, UPS, IBM, McDonald's, and Citigroup combined.

For this study, the following items were counted as costs of tax compliance.

- The value of taxpayers' time spent record keeping, filing, planning, and otherwise complying with the tax laws.
- Tax collection costs (chiefly wages and benefits) of IRS employees.
- Expenditures made to professional tax preparers, consultants, and other preparers.

LO.7

Describe the role played by the IRS and the courts in the evolution of the Federal tax system.

1-5f **Influence of the Internal Revenue Service**

The influence of the IRS on tax law is apparent in many areas beyond its role in issuing the administrative pronouncements that make up a considerable portion of our tax law. The IRS has been instrumental in securing the passage of much legislation designed to curtail the most flagrant tax avoidance practices (to "close tax loopholes"). In addition, the IRS has sought and obtained legislation to make its own job easier (to attain administrative feasibility).

Closing Perceived Tax Loopholes

Certain tax provisions are intended to prevent a loophole from being used to avoid the tax consequences intended by Congress. Working within the letter of existing law, taxpayers and their advisers devise techniques that accomplish indirectly what cannot be accomplished directly. As a consequence, legislation is enacted to close the loopholes that taxpayers have located and exploited. Some tax law can be explained in this fashion and is discussed in the chapters to follow.

Administrative Feasibility

Some tax law is justified on the grounds that it simplifies the task of the IRS in collecting the revenue and administering the law. With regard to collecting the revenue, the IRS long ago realized the importance of placing taxpayers on a pay-as-you-go basis. Elaborate withholding procedures apply to wages, and accrual basis taxpayers often must pay taxes on prepaid income in the year received and not when earned. The approach may be contrary to generally accepted accounting principles, but it is consistent with the wherewithal to pay concept.

Of considerable aid to the IRS in collecting revenue are the numerous provisions that impose interest and penalties on taxpayers for noncompliance with the tax law. Provisions such as the penalties for failure to pay a tax or to file a return that is due, the negligence penalty for intentional disregard of Federal tax rules and regulations, and various penalties for civil and criminal fraud serve as deterrents to taxpayer noncompliance.

One of the keys to an effective administration of our tax system is the audit process conducted by the IRS. To carry out this function, the IRS is aided by provisions that reduce the chance of taxpayer error or manipulation and therefore reduce the audit effort that is necessary. An increase in the amount of the standard deduction, for example, reduces the number of individual taxpayers who will choose the alternative of itemizing their personal deductions. With fewer deductions to check, the audit function is simplified.

DIGGING DEEPER 7   In-depth coverage can be found on this book's companion website: www.cengagebrain.com

1-5g **Influence of the Courts**

In addition to interpreting statutory provisions and the administrative pronouncements issued by the IRS, the Federal courts have influenced tax law in two other respects. First, the courts have formulated certain judicial concepts that serve as guides in the application of various tax provisions. Second, certain key decisions have led to changes in the Internal Revenue Code.

Judicial Concepts Relating to Tax

Particularly in dealings between related parties, the courts test transactions by looking to whether the taxpayers acted in an arm's length manner. The question to be asked is: Would unrelated parties have handled the transaction in the same way?

Rex, the sole shareholder of Silver Corporation, leases property to the corporation for a yearly rent of $6,000. To test whether the corporation should be allowed a rent deduction for this amount, the IRS and the courts will apply the arm's length concept. Would Silver have paid $6,000 a year in rent if it had leased the same property from an unrelated party (rather than from Rex)?

Suppose it is determined that an unrelated third party would have charged an annual rent for the property of only $5,000. Under these circumstances, Silver can deduct only $5,000. The other $1,000 it paid for the use of the property represents a *nondeductible dividend*. Rex is treated as having received rent income of $5,000 and dividend income of $1,000.

Judicial Influence on Statutory Provisions

Some court decisions have been of such consequence that Congress has incorporated them into statutory tax law. For example, many years ago, the courts found that stock dividends distributed to the shareholders of a corporation were not taxable as income. This result largely was accepted by Congress, and a provision in the tax statutes now addresses the issue.

On occasion, however, Congress has reacted negatively to judicial interpretations of the tax law.

Nora leases unimproved real estate to Wade for 20 years. At a cost of $400,000, Wade erects a building on the land. The building is worth $150,000 when the lease terminates and Nora takes possession of the property. Does Nora have any gross income either when the improvements are made or when the lease terminates?

In a landmark decision, a court held that Nora must recognize income of $150,000 upon the termination of the lease.

Congress believed that the result reached in Example 40 was inequitable in that it was not consistent with the wherewithal to pay concept. Consequently, the tax law was amended to provide that a landlord does not recognize any income either when the improvements are made (unless made in lieu of rent) or when the lease terminates.

1-6 **SUMMARY**

Tax laws are pervasive in today's global economy. Individuals and businesses must contend with complex rules in planning their personal and professional activities. Taxes can fall on income, wealth, asset transfers, consumer expenditures, and other events.

Tax planning is a means by which to manage the amount and timing of tax liabilities to accomplish one's long-term objectives. The conduct of tax practitioners is regulated by professional associations, lawmakers, and the taxing agencies.

Taxing systems are designed to provide revenues for governments to accomplish the common goals of citizens. In addition to its necessary revenue-raising objective, the Federal tax law has developed in response to several other factors.

- *Economic considerations.* Tax provisions can help to regulate the economy and encourage certain activities and types of businesses.
- *Social considerations.* Some tax provisions are designed to encourage (or discourage) socially desirable (or undesirable) practices.
- *Equity considerations.* Tax provisions can alleviate the effect of multiple taxation, recognize the wherewithal to pay concept, and mitigate the effect of the annual accounting period concept.
- *Political considerations.* Tax provisions can represent special interest legislation and reflect the effect of state and local law.
- *Influence of the IRS.* Many tax provisions are intended to aid the IRS in the collection of revenue and the administration of the tax law.
- *Influence of the courts.* Court decisions have established a body of judicial concepts relating to tax law and have, on occasion, led Congress to enact statutory provisions to either clarify or negate their effect.

REFOCUS ON THE BIG PICTURE

A TYPICAL TAX YEAR FOR A MODERN FAMILY

The explanation given for the difference in the ad valorem property taxes—the Carters' increase and the Walkers' decrease—seems reasonable. It is not likely that the Carters' increase was due to a *general* upward assessment in valuation, as the Walkers' taxes on their residence (located nearby) dropped. More business use of the Carters' residence (presuming that Travis conducts his consulting practice from his home) might be responsible for the increase, but capital improvements appear to be a more likely cause.

The imposition of the use tax when Travis registered the new automobile illustrates one of the means by which a state can preclude the avoidance of its sales tax (see Example 4).

When gifts between family members are material in amount (e.g., an RV) and exceed the annual exclusion, a gift tax return needs to be filed. Even though no gift tax may be due because of the availability of the unified transfer tax exclusion ($5.43 million for 2015, as indexed), the filing of a return starts the running of the statute of limitations.

The imposition of the "jock tax" on nonathletes is unusual but not improper. The Carters must recognize that some of their income is subject to income taxes in two states and take advantage of whatever relief is available to mitigate the result.

Significant Federal income tax savings might be available if Travis were to hire the children to work in the consulting practice.

What If?

Because of the double audit (i.e., both state and Federal) and the deficiency assessed, the Carters need to make sure that future returns do not contain similar errors. As the text suggests, taxpayers with prior deficiencies are among those whose returns may be selected for audit.

Suggested Readings

Howard Gleckman, "The War on the IRS," **http://taxvox.taxpolicycenter.org/2014/12/16/war-irs/**.

Jill Lepore, "Tax Time: Why We Pay," *The New Yorker*, November 26, 2012.

Mark Robyn, Micah Cohen, and Joseph Henchman, "Sales Tax Holidays: Politically Expedient but Poor Tax Policy," July 24, 2013 working paper, **www.taxfoundation.org**.

Joseph J. Thorndike, "The Tenacity of Tax Complexity," December 2001 working paper, **www.taxhistory.org**.

Key Terms

Ad valorem taxes, 1-10

C corporations, 1-16

Deferred tax asset, 1-18

Deferred tax liability, 1-18

Effective tax rate, 1-18

Employment taxes, 1-2

Estate tax, 1-8

Excise taxes, 1-4

FICA tax, 1-6

Financial Accounting Standards Board (FASB), 1-16

Flow-through entity, 1-24

Franchise tax, 1-12

FUTA tax, 1-6

Generally Accepted Accounting Principles (GAAP), 1-16

Gift tax, 1-9

Inheritance tax, 1-8

International Accounting Standards Board (IASB), 1-16

International Financial Reporting Standards (IFRS), 1-16

Occupational taxes, 1-12

Personalty, 1-10

Proprietorship, 1-15

Realty, 1-10

S corporations, 1-17

Sales taxes, 1-2

Tax avoidance, 1-18

Tax evasion, 1-18

Use taxes, 1-5

Value added tax (VAT), 1-6

Wherewithal to pay, 1-30

Problems

1. **LO.1, 2, 5** James Corporation believes that it will have a better distribution location for its product if it relocates the corporation to another state. What considerations (both tax and nontax) should James weigh before making a decision on whether to make the move? — Issue ID

2. **LO.1** Distinguish between taxes that are *proportional* and those that are *progressive*.

3. **LO.2** Several years ago, Ethan purchased the former parsonage of St. James Church to use as a personal residence. To date, Ethan has not received any ad valorem property tax bills from either the city or the county tax authorities. — Issue ID
   a. What is a reasonable explanation for this oversight?
   b. What should Ethan do?

4. **LO.1, 6** In terms of Adam Smith's canon of economy, how does the Federal income tax fare? — Critical Thinking

5. **LO.2** Jim, a resident of Washington (which imposes a general sales tax), goes to Oregon (which does not impose a general sales tax) to purchase his automobile. Will Jim successfully avoid the Washington sales tax? Explain.

6. **LO.2** The Irontown Independent School District wants to sell a parcel of unimproved land that it does not need. Its three best offers are as follows: from the State Department of Public Safety (DPS), $4.3 million; from Trinity Lutheran Church, — Issue ID

$4.2 million; and from Baker Motors, $3.9 million. DPS would use the property for a new state highway patrol barracks, Trinity would start a church school, and Baker would open a car dealership. As the financial adviser for the school district, which offer would you prefer? Why?

Issue ID   7.   **LO.2** Eileen, a resident of Wyoming, goes to Montana to purchase her new automobile. She does this because Wyoming imposes a sales tax while Montana does not. Has Eileen successfully avoided the Wyoming sales tax? Explain.

Issue ID   8.   **LO.2** Sophia lives several blocks from her parents in the same residential subdivision. Sophia is surprised to learn that her ad valorem property taxes for the year were raised, while those of her parents were lowered. What is a possible explanation for the difference?

Decision Making   9.   **LO.4, 5** Marco and Cynthia have decided to go into business together. They will
Communications   operate a burrito delivery business. They expect to have a loss in the first and second years of the business and subsequently expect to make a substantial profit.

Marco and Cynthia are concerned about potential liability if a customer ever gets sick after eating one of their products. They have called your office and asked for advice about whether they should run their business as a partnership or as a corporation. Write a letter to Cynthia Clay, at 1206 Seventh Avenue, Fort Worth, TX 76101, describing the alternative forms of business they can select. In your letter, explain what form or forms of business you recommend and why.

Decision Making   10.   **LO.4, 5** Ashley runs a small business in Boulder, Colorado, that makes snow skis. She expects the business to grow substantially over the next three years. Because she is concerned about product liability and is planning to take the company public in 2016, she is currently considering incorporating the business. Financial data are as follows.

	2015	2016	2017
Sales revenue	$150,000	$320,000	$600,000
Tax-free interest income	5,000	8,000	15,000
Deductible cash expenses	30,000	58,000	95,000
Tax depreciation	25,000	20,000	40,000

Ashley expects her combined Federal and state marginal income tax rate to be 35% over the next three years before any profits from the business are considered. Her after-tax cost of capital is 12%.

a.   Compute the present value of the future cash flows for 2015 to 2017 assuming that Ashley incorporates the business and pays all after-tax income as dividends (for Ashley's dividends that qualify for the 15% rate).

b.   Compute the present value of the future cash flows for 2015 to 2017 assuming that Ashley continues to operate the business as a sole proprietorship.

c.   Should Ashley incorporate the business this year? Why or why not?

11.   **LO.3, 5** Mauve Supplies, Inc., reports total income of $120,000. The corporation's taxable income is $105,000. What are Mauve's marginal, average, and effective tax rates?

Issue ID   12.   **LO.2** Franklin County is in dire financial straits and is considering a number of sources for additional revenue. Evaluate the following possibilities in terms of anticipated taxpayer compliance.

a.   A property tax on business inventories.

b.   A tax on intangibles (i.e., stocks and bonds) held as investments.

c.   A property tax on boats used for recreational purposes.

13. **LO.6** Discuss the probable justification for each of the following provisions of the tax law.

    a. A tax credit allowed for electricity produced from renewable sources.

    b. A tax credit allowed for the purchase of a motor vehicle that operates on alternative energy sources (e.g., nonfossil fuels).

    c. A deduction for state and local income taxes.

    d. The deduction for personal casualty losses that is subject to computational limitations.

    e. Favorable treatment accorded to research and development expenditures.

    f. A deduction allowed for income resulting from U.S. production (manufacturing) activities.

    g. The deduction allowed for contributions to qualified charitable organizations.

    h. An election that allows certain corporations to avoid the corporate income tax and pass losses through to their shareholders.

14. **LO.6** Discuss the probable justification for each of the following aspects of the tax law.

    a. A tax credit is allowed for amounts spent to furnish care for minor children while the parent works.

    b. Deductions for interest on home mortgage and property taxes on one's personal residence.

    c. The income splitting benefits of filing a joint return.

    d. Gambling losses in excess of gambling gains.

    e. Net operating losses of a current year can be carried back to profitable years.

    f. A taxpayer who sells property on an installment basis can recognize gain on the sale over the period the payments are received.

    g. The exclusion from Federal tax of certain interest income from state and local bonds.

    h. Prepaid income is taxed to the recipient in the year it is received and not in the year it is earned.

15. **LO.2** Contrast a value added tax (VAT) with a national sales tax in terms of anticipated taxpayer compliance.
    Critical Thinking

16. **LO.2** Go to **www.taxfoundation.org**, and determine Tax Freedom Day for your state for 1950, 1960, 1970, 1980, 1990, 2000, and 2010. Report your results as a line graph.
    Critical Thinking Communications

17. **LO.5** Although the Federal income tax law is complex, most individual taxpayers are able to complete their tax returns without outside assistance. Gather data as to the accuracy of this statement. Summarize your comments in an e-mail to your instructor.
    Critical Thinking Communications

18. **LO.5** President Franklin D. Roosevelt once said, "I am wholly unable to figure out the amount of tax," and wrote to the Federal Commissioner of Revenue, "may I ask that [the agency] let me know the amount of the balance due."
    Ethics and Equity

    When a friend of FDR was ordered to pay $420,000 in tax penalties, the President called the Commissioner within earshot of reporters and told him to cut the penalties to $3,000. One listener, journalist David Brinkley, recalled years later: "Nobody seemed to think it was news or very interesting." Evaluate the President's comments and actions.

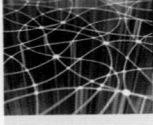

1. Discuss with respect to the Federal policy for reducing poverty:

   a. The individual income tax.

   b. The Social Security tax.

Communications

2. Prepare a two-page paper titled "How I Would Apply Federal Income Tax Law to Encourage the Availability of Universal Broadband in This Community" to submit to your economics professor.

Communications

3. Prepare an outline for a 10-minute speech to give to your government class. The speech is titled "If You Don't Pay Federal Taxes, You Can't Vote."

4. When taxes are "too high," taxpayers start to cheat on their taxes and dangerous consequences can result. Evaluate this statement. Give at least two examples to illustrate your conclusions.

5. Some tax rules can be justified on multiple grounds (e.g., economic or social). In this connection, comment on the possible justification for the rules governing the following.

   a. Pension plans.

   b. Education.

   c. Home ownership.

Working with the Tax Law

LEARNING OBJECTIVES: *After completing Chapter 2, you should be able to:*

LO.1 Describe the statutory, administrative, and judicial sources of the tax law and the purpose of each source.

LO.2 Locate and work with the tax law and explain the tax research process.

LO.3 Communicate the results of the tax research process in a client letter and a tax file memorandum.

LO.4 Employ a strategy of how best to use a computer when performing tax research and in taking the CPA exam.

CHAPTER OUTLINE

TAX TALK *The less people know about how sausages and laws are made, the better they'll sleep at night.* —Otto von Bismarck

© JHDT STOCK IMAGES LLC/SHUTTERSTOCK.COM

RESEARCHING TAX QUESTIONS

Early in December, Fred and Megan Samuels review their financial and tax situation with their son, Sam, and daughter-in-law, Dana. Currently, Sam and Dana live with Fred and Megan. Fred and Megan are in the 28% tax bracket. Both Sam and Dana are age 21.

Sam, a student at a nearby university, owns some publicly traded stock that he inherited from his grandmother. A current sale would result in approximately $8,000 of gross income ($19,000 amount realized − $11,000 adjusted basis).

At this point, Fred and Megan provide about 55% of Sam and Dana's support. Although neither is now employed, Sam earned $960 and Dana earned $900 earlier in the year. The problem: Should the stock be sold before the end of the year, and would the sale prohibit Fred and Megan from claiming Sam and Dana as dependents? Would the stock sale result in a tax liability for Sam and Dana?

Read the chapter and formulate your responses.

RANKING AUTHORITIES

REGULATIONS?

ADM. SOURCE?

Federal tax law is a mixture of statutory provisions, administrative pronouncements, and court decisions. Anyone who has attempted to work with this body of knowledge is familiar with its complexity. Tax research provides the vehicle by which one makes sense out of this complexity.

Describe the statutory, administrative, and judicial sources of the tax law and the purpose of each source.

2-1 TAX LAW SOURCES

Understanding taxation requires a mastery of the sources of the *rules of tax law*. These sources include not only legislative provisions in the form of the Internal Revenue Code but also congressional Committee Reports, Treasury Department Regulations, other Treasury Department pronouncements, and court decisions. Thus, the *primary sources* of tax information include pronouncements from all three branches of government: legislative, executive, and judicial.

In addition to being able to locate and interpret the sources of the tax law, a tax professional must understand the relative weight of authority within these sources. The tax law is of little significance, however, until it is applied to a set of facts and circumstances. This chapter, therefore, both introduces the statutory, administrative, and judicial sources of the tax law *and* explains how the law is applied to business and individual transactions. It also explains how to apply research techniques effectively.

Tax research is necessary because the application of the law to a specific situation sometimes is not clear. As complicated as the Internal Revenue Code is, it cannot clearly address every conceivable situation. Accordingly, the tax professional must search other sources (such as administrative rulings and judicial decisions) to determine the most likely tax treatment of a transaction.

Working with such knowledge, a tax professional then can advise the client about the tax consequences of several possible courses of action. Tax research, in other words, is of critical importance not only in properly characterizing completed events but also in planning proposed transactions.

2-1a Statutory Sources of the Tax Law

Statutory sources of law include the Constitution (Article I, Sections 7, 8, and 10), tax treaties (agreements between countries to mitigate the double taxation of taxpayers subject to the tax laws of those countries), and the Internal Revenue Code. The Constitution grants Congress the power to impose and collect taxes, and it authorizes the creation of treaties with other countries. The Internal Revenue Code is the statutory basis for arriving at solutions to all tax questions.

Origin of the Internal Revenue Code

Before 1939, the statutory provisions relating to taxation were contained in the individual revenue acts enacted by Congress every year or two. The inconvenience and confusion that resulted from dealing with many separate acts led Congress to codify all of the Federal tax laws in 1939. Known as the Internal Revenue Code of 1939, this codification arranged all Federal tax provisions in a logical sequence and placed them in a separate part of the Federal statutes. A further rearrangement took place in 1954 and resulted in the Internal Revenue Code of 1954, which continued in effect until it was replaced by the Internal Revenue Code of 1986.[1]

Statutory amendments to the tax law are integrated into the existing Code. Thus, subsequent tax legislation, such as the Patient Protection and Affordable Care Act of 2010 and the American Taxpayer Relief Act of 2012, became part of the Internal Revenue Code of 1986.

---

[1]Aside from changes due to a large tax act, the organization of the Internal Revenue Code of 1986 is not substantively different from the organization of the 1954 Code. In contrast, the numbering scheme of sections in the 1939 Code differs from that used in the 1954 Code.

TAX FACT Scope of the U.S. Tax System

Although it started out in 1913 as a tax on only the uppermost-income individuals, the tax system today is pervasive in our lives.

- In the typical tax year, the IRS receives about 20 million Forms 1040EZ and about 40 million Forms 1040A.
- The typical Form 1040 requires 7.25 hours to gather records and assemble the return, and 6.25 hours to prepare the form and attachments. The estimated cost of complying with tax rules is $425 billion per year.
- The Internal Revenue Code is about 4 million words (9,000 pages) long, and the Regulations require another 8 million words (165,000 pages). Combined, these documents are 12 times the length of Shakespeare's combined works and 15 times the length of the King James Bible.

The Legislative Process

Federal tax legislation generally originates in the House of Representatives, where it first is considered by the House Ways and Means Committee. It is also possible for tax bills to originate in the Senate if they are attached as riders to other legislative proposals. If acceptable to the committee, the proposed bill is referred to the entire House of Representatives for approval or disapproval. Approved bills are sent to the Senate, where they initially are considered by the Senate Finance Committee.

The next step is referral from the Senate Finance Committee to the entire Senate. Assuming no disagreement between the House and Senate, passage by the Senate means referral to the President for approval or veto. If the bill is approved or if the President's veto is overridden, the bill becomes law and part of the Internal Revenue Code.

When the Senate version of the bill differs from that passed by the House, the Conference Committee, which includes members of both the House Ways and Means Committee and the Senate Finance Committee, is called upon to resolve the differences.

House and Senate versions of major tax bills frequently differ. One reason bills often are changed in the Senate is that, under the usual rules of Congress, each senator has considerable latitude to make amendments when the Senate as a whole is voting on a bill referred to it by the Senate Finance Committee. In contrast, the entire House of Representatives either accepts or rejects what is proposed by the House Ways and Means Committee, and changes from the floor are rare.

The deliberations of the Conference Committee usually produce a compromise between the two versions, which is then voted on by both the House and the Senate. If both bodies accept the revised bill, it is referred to the President for approval or veto. The typical legislative process dealing with tax bills is summarized in Exhibit 2.1.

The role of the Conference Committee indicates the importance of compromise in the legislative process. As an example of the practical effect of the compromise process, consider what happened with amendments to the refundability provisions of the child tax credit (see Exhibit 2.2 on p. 2-5).

Referrals from the House Ways and Means Committee, the Senate Finance Committee, and the Conference Committee usually are accompanied by *Committee Reports*. These Committee Reports often explain the provisions of the proposed legislation and are a valuable source for ascertaining the *intent of Congress*. What Congress had in mind when it considered and enacted tax legislation is the key to interpreting legislation. Because Regulations interpreting new legislation normally are not issued immediately after a statute is enacted, taxpayers and the courts look to Committee Reports to determine congressional intent.

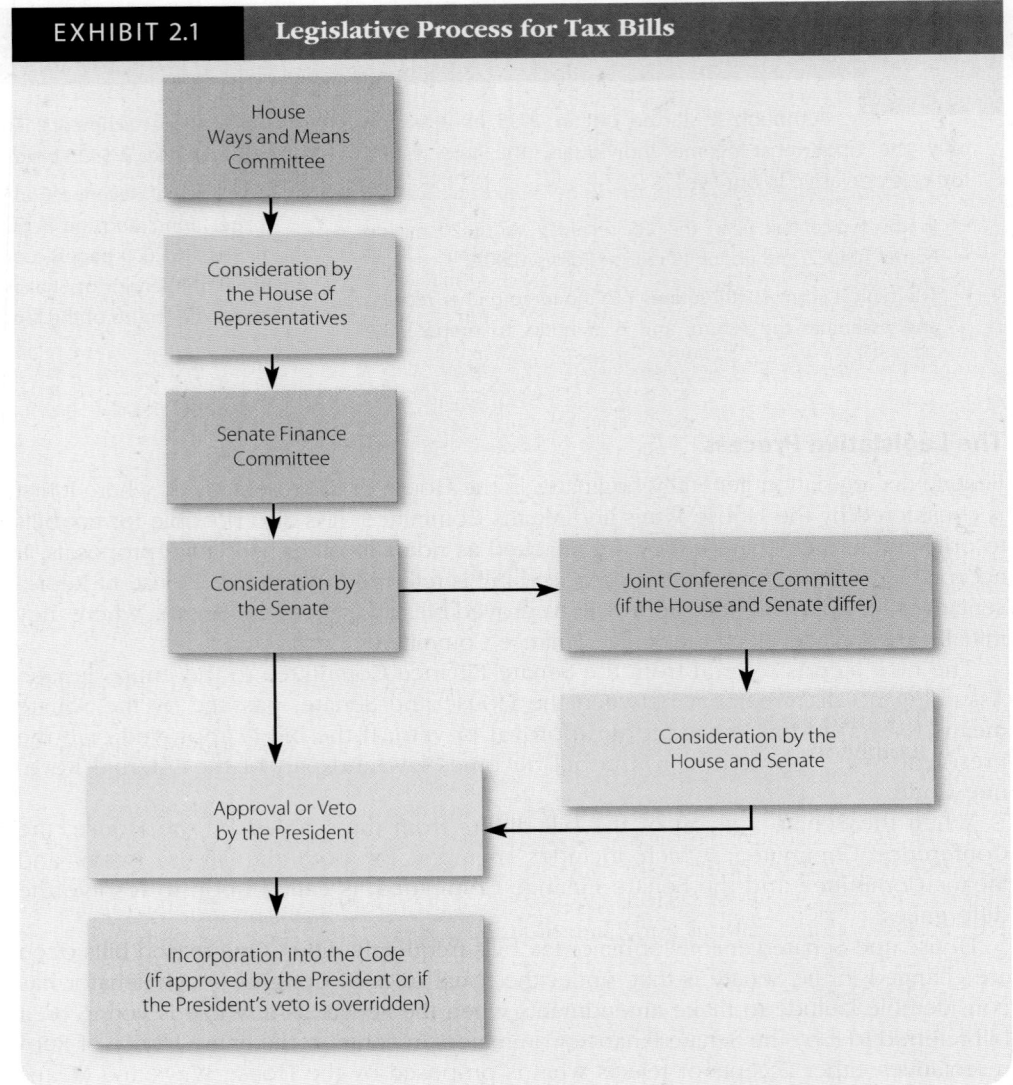

EXHIBIT 2.1   Legislative Process for Tax Bills

House Ways and Means Committee

Consideration by the House of Representatives

Senate Finance Committee

Consideration by the Senate

Joint Conference Committee (if the House and Senate differ)

Consideration by the House and Senate

Approval or Veto by the President

Incorporation into the Code (if approved by the President or if the President's veto is overridden)

Arrangement of the Code

The Internal Revenue Code is found in Title 26 of the U.S. Code. Here is a partial table of contents.

> Subtitle A. Income Taxes
> > Chapter 1. Normal Taxes and Surtaxes
> > > Subchapter A. Determination of Tax Liability
> > > > Part I. Tax on Individuals
> > > > > Sections 1–5
> > > > Part II. Tax on Corporations
> > > > > Sections 11–12

In referring to a provision of the Code, the tax professional usually cites the Section number. In referring to § 2(a) (dealing with the status of a surviving spouse), for example, it is unnecessary to include Subtitle A, Chapter 1, Subchapter A, and Part I. Merely mentioning § 2(a) suffices because the Section numbers run consecutively and do not begin again with each new Subtitle, Chapter, Subchapter, or Part. Not all Code Section

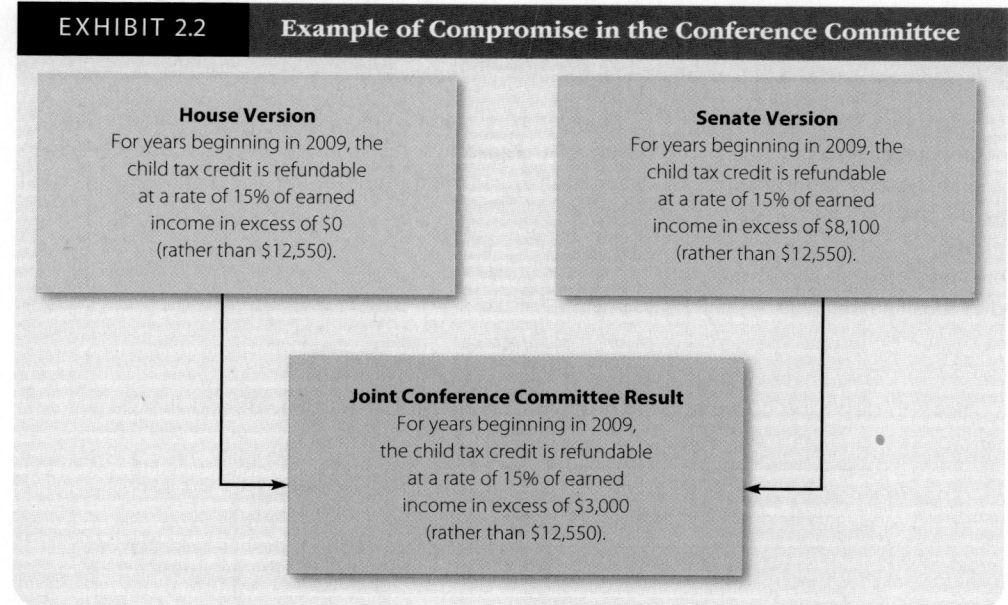

EXHIBIT 2.2   Example of Compromise in the Conference Committee

House Version
For years beginning in 2009, the child tax credit is refundable at a rate of 15% of earned income in excess of $0 (rather than $12,550).

Senate Version
For years beginning in 2009, the child tax credit is refundable at a rate of 15% of earned income in excess of $8,100 (rather than $12,550).

Joint Conference Committee Result
For years beginning in 2009, the child tax credit is refundable at a rate of 15% of earned income in excess of $3,000 (rather than $12,550).

numbers are used, however. Part I ends with § 5, and Part II starts with § 11 (at present, there are no §§ 6, 7, 8, 9, and 10).[2]

Tax practitioners commonly refer to certain areas of income tax law by Subchapter designation. Some of the more common Subchapter designations include Subchapter C ("Corporate Distributions and Adjustments"), Subchapter K ("Partners and Partnerships"), and Subchapter S ("Tax Treatment of S Corporations and Their Shareholders"). Particularly in the last situation, it is more convenient to describe the effect of the applicable Code provisions (§§ 1361–1379) as "Subchapter S" than as the "Tax Treatment of S Corporations and Their Shareholders."

Citing the Code

Code Sections often are broken down into subparts.[3] Section 2(a)(1)(A) serves as an example.

§   2   (a)   (1)   (A)

Abbreviation for "Section"

Section number

Subsection number[4]

Paragraph designation

Subparagraph designation

---

[2]When the Code was drafted, Section numbers were intentionally omitted so that later changes could be incorporated into the Code without disrupting its organization. When Congress does not leave enough space, subsequent Code Sections are given A, B, C, etc., designations. A good example is the treatment of §§ 280A through 280H.

[3]Some Code Sections do not have subparts. See, for example, §§ 211 and 241.

[4]Some Code Sections omit the subsection designation and use, instead, the paragraph designation as the first subpart. See, for example, §§ 212(1) and 1222(1).

Broken down by content, a citation for Code § 2(a)(1)(A) appears as follows.

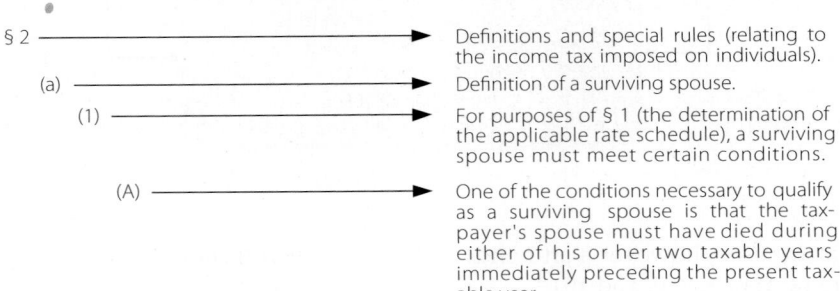

§ 2	Definitions and special rules (relating to the income tax imposed on individuals).
(a)	Definition of a surviving spouse.
(1)	For purposes of § 1 (the determination of the applicable rate schedule), a surviving spouse must meet certain conditions.
(A)	One of the conditions necessary to qualify as a surviving spouse is that the tax-payer's spouse must have died during either of his or her two taxable years immediately preceding the present taxable year.

Throughout the text, references to the Code Sections are in the form shown previously. The symbols "§" and "§§" are used in place of "Section" and "Sections," respectively. The following table illustrates the format used in the text.

Complete Reference	Text Reference
Section 2(a)(1)(A) of the Internal Revenue Code of 1986	§ 2(a)(1)(A)
Sections 1 and 2 of the Internal Revenue Code of 1986	§§ 1 and 2
Section 2 of the Internal Revenue Code of 1954	§ 2 of the Internal Revenue Code of 1954
Section 12(d) of the Internal Revenue Code of 1939[5]	§ 12(d) of the Internal Revenue Code of 1939

Effect of Treaties

The United States signs certain tax treaties (sometimes called tax conventions) with foreign countries to render mutual assistance in tax enforcement and to avoid double taxation. These treaties affect transactions involving U.S. persons and entities operating or investing in a foreign country, as well as persons and entities of a foreign country operating or investing in the United States. Although these bilateral agreements are not codified in any one source, they are published at **www.irs.gov**, as well as in various commercial tax services.

Neither a tax law nor a tax treaty automatically takes precedence. When there is a direct conflict, the most recent item prevails. With certain exceptions, a taxpayer must disclose on the tax return any filing position for which a treaty overrides a tax law.[6] There is a $1,000 per *failure to disclose* penalty for individuals and a $10,000 per failure to disclose penalty for C corporations.[7]

---

[5]Section 12(d) of the Internal Revenue Code of 1939 is the predecessor to § 2 of the Internal Revenue Codes of 1954 and 1986.

[6]§ 7852(d).

[7]§ 6712(a).

2-1b **Administrative Sources of the Tax Law**

The administrative sources of the Federal tax law can be grouped as follows: Treasury Department Regulations, Revenue Rulings and Revenue Procedures, and various other administrative pronouncements (see Exhibit 2.3). All are issued by either the U.S. Treasury Department or its subsidiary agency, the IRS.

Treasury Department Regulations

Regulations are issued by the U.S. Treasury Department under authority granted by Congress.[8] Usually interpretive by nature, they provide taxpayers with considerable guidance on the meaning and application of the Code and often include examples. Regulations carry considerable authority as the official interpretation of tax statutes. They are an important resource to consider in complying with the tax law.

Treasury Regulations are arranged in the same sequence as the Code. A number is added at the beginning, however, to indicate the type of tax or other matter to which they relate. For example, the prefix 1 designates the Regulations under the income tax law. Thus, the Regulations under Code § 2 would be cited as Reg. § 1.2, with subparts added for further identification. The numbering pattern of these subparts often has no correlation with the Code subsections. The prefix 20 designates estate tax Regulations, 25 addresses gift tax Regulations, 31 relates to employment taxes, and 301 refers to procedure and administration. This list is not all-inclusive. Reg. § 1.351–1(a)(2) is an example of such a citation.

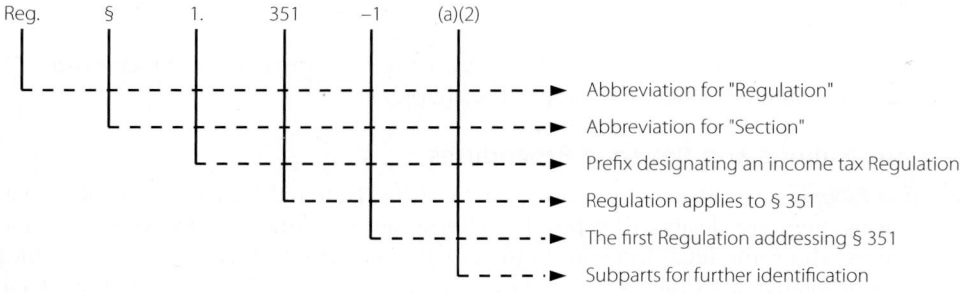

New Regulations and changes in existing Regulations usually are issued in proposed form before they are finalized. The interval between the proposal of a Regulation and its finalization permits taxpayers and other interested parties to comment on the propriety of the proposal. These comments usually are provided in writing, but oral comments can be offered at hearings held by the IRS on the Regulations in question pursuant to a public notice. This practice of notice-and-comment is a major distinction between Regulations and other forms of Treasury guidance such as Revenue Rulings, Revenue Procedures, and the like.

Proposed Regulations under Code § 2, for example, are cited as Prop.Reg. § 1.2. The Tax Court indicates that Proposed Regulations carry little weight in the litigation process.[9]

The Treasury Department issues **Temporary Regulations** relating to matters where immediate guidance is important. These Regulations are issued without the comment period required for Proposed Regulations. Temporary Regulations have the same authoritative value as final Regulations and may be cited as precedents. However, Temporary Regulations also are issued as Proposed Regulations and automatically expire within three years after the date of their issuance.[10]

Proposed, Temporary, and **Final Regulations** are published in the *Federal Register*, the *Internal Revenue Bulletin*, and major tax services.

---

[8]§ 7805.

[9]*F. W. Woolworth Co.*, 54 T.C. 1233 (1970); *Harris M. Miller*, 70 T.C. 448 (1978); and *James O. Tomerlin Trust*, 87 T.C. 876 (1986).

[10]§ 7805(e).

EXHIBIT 2.3	Administrative Sources	

Source	Location	Authority***
Regulations	*Federal Register** *Internal Revenue Bulletin*	Force and effect of law. May be cited as precedent.
Temporary Regulations	*Federal Register** *Internal Revenue Bulletin*	May be cited as a precedent.
Proposed Regulations	*Federal Register** *Internal Revenue Bulletin*	Preview of final Regulations. Not yet a precedent.
Revenue Rulings Revenue Procedures Treasury Decisions Actions on Decisions	*Internal Revenue Bulletin***	IRS interpretation only. Weak precedent.
Determination Letters Technical Advice Memoranda	Tax Analysts' *Tax Notes* RIA's *Internal Memoranda of the IRS* Commerce Clearing House's *IRS Position Reporter*	IRS interpretation only. Weak precedent.
Letter Rulings	Research Institute of America and Commerce Clearing House tax services**	Applicable only to taxpayer addressed. May not be cited as precedent.

*Final, Temporary, and Proposed Regulations are published in soft-cover form and online by several other publishers.
**Revenue Rulings, Revenue Procedures, and letter rulings also are published online by several other publishers.
***Each of these sources may be substantial authority for purposes of the accuracy-related penalty in § 6662.

Regulations may also be classified as *legislative, interpretive,* or *procedural*. This classification scheme is discussed later in the chapter.

Revenue Rulings and Revenue Procedures

Revenue Rulings are official pronouncements of the National Office of the IRS.[11] Like Regulations, they are designed to provide interpretation of the tax law. However, they do not carry the same legal force and effect as Regulations and usually deal with more restricted problems. In addition, Regulations are approved by the Secretary of the Treasury, whereas Revenue Rulings generally are not.

Both Revenue Rulings and Revenue Procedures serve an important function in providing *guidance* to IRS personnel and taxpayers in handling routine tax matters. Revenue Rulings and Revenue Procedures generally apply retroactively and may be revoked or modified by subsequent rulings or procedures, Regulations, legislation, or court decisions.

Revenue Rulings typically provide one or more examples of how the IRS would apply a law to specific fact situations. Revenue Rulings may arise from technical advice memoranda of the IRS, court decisions, suggestions from tax practitioner groups, and various tax publications. A Revenue Ruling also may arise from a specific taxpayer's request for a letter ruling. If the IRS believes that a taxpayer's request for a letter ruling deserves official publication due to its widespread effect, the letter ruling is converted into a Revenue Ruling and issued for the information and guidance of taxpayers, tax practitioners, and IRS personnel. Names, identifying descriptions, and money amounts are changed to conceal the identity of the requesting taxpayer.

Revenue Procedures are issued in the same manner as Revenue Rulings, but deal with the internal management practices and procedures of the IRS. Familiarity with these procedures increases taxpayer compliance and helps make the administration of the tax laws more efficient. The failure of a taxpayer to follow a Revenue Procedure can result in unnecessary delay or, in a discretionary situation, can cause the IRS to decline to act on behalf of the taxpayer.

---

[11]§ 7805(a).

Some recent Revenue Procedures dealt with the following matters.

- Procedures for issuing determination letters on the qualified status of employee pension plans.
- Procedures for requesting a filing date extension when electing S corporation status.
- Inflation-adjusted amounts for various Code provisions.

Revenue Rulings and Revenue Procedures are published weekly by the U.S. Government in the *Internal Revenue Bulletin* (I.R.B.).

The proper form for citing Revenue Rulings is as follows. Revenue Procedures are cited in the same manner, except that "Rev.Proc." is substituted for "Rev.Rul."

Rev.Rul. 2014–3, 2014–2 I.R.B. 259.

Explanation: Revenue Ruling Number 3, beginning at page 259 of the 2nd weekly issue of the *Internal Revenue Bulletin* for 2014.

Revenue Rulings and other tax resources may be found in the *Tax Almanac*, a free online resource at **www.taxalmanac.org**.[12]

Letter Rulings

Letter rulings are issued for a fee upon a taxpayer's request. They describe how the IRS will treat a *proposed* transaction for tax purposes. Letter rulings can be useful for taxpayers who want to be certain of how a transaction will be taxed before proceeding with it. Letter rulings allow taxpayers to avoid unexpected tax costs.

The procedure for requesting a ruling can be quite cumbersome, although it sometimes is the most effective way to carry out tax planning. The IRS limits the issuance of letter rulings to restricted, pre-announced areas of taxation; it generally will not rule on situations that are fact-intensive. Thus, a ruling may not be obtained on many of the problems that are particularly troublesome to taxpayers.[13]

The IRS makes letter rulings available for public inspection after identifying details are deleted.[14] Published digests of private letter rulings are found in RIA's *Private Letter Rulings*, Bloomberg BNA's *Daily Tax Reports*, and Tax Analysts' *Tax Notes*. *IRS Letter Rulings Reports* (published by Commerce Clearing House) contains both digests and full texts of all letter rulings. In addition, computerized databases of letter rulings are available through several commercial publishers.

Letter rulings are issued multidigit file numbers that indicate the year and week of issuance as well as the number of the ruling during that week. Consider, for example, Ltr.Rul. 201432030, which involves a request of a waiver for the rollover period of an IRA.

2014	32	030
Year 2014	32nd week of 2014	30th ruling issued during the 32nd week

Other Administrative Pronouncements

Treasury Decisions (TDs) are issued by the Treasury Department to promulgate new Regulations, amend or otherwise change existing Regulations, or announce the position of the Government on selected court decisions. Like Revenue Rulings and Revenue Procedures, TDs are published in the *Internal Revenue Bulletin*.

---

[12]Commercial sources for Revenue Rulings and Revenue Procedures are available, usually requiring a subscription fee. Older Revenue Rulings and Revenue Procedures are often cited as being published in the *Cumulative Bulletin* (C.B.) rather than the *Internal Revenue Bulletin* (I.R.B.).

[13]The first *Internal Revenue Bulletin* issued each year contains a list of areas in which the IRS will not issue advance rulings. This list may be modified throughout the year. See, for example, Rev.Proc. 2015–1, 2015–1 I.R.B. 1.

[14]§ 6110.

The IRS publishes other administrative communications in the *Internal Revenue Bulletin*, such as Announcements, Notices, Proposed Regulations, Termination of Exempt Organization Status, Practitioner Disciplinary Actions, and Prohibited Transaction Exemptions.

Like letter rulings, **determination letters** are issued at the request of taxpayers and provide guidance on the application of the tax law. They differ from letter rulings in that the issuing source is an IRS executive, rather than the National Office of the IRS. Further, determination letters usually involve *completed* (as opposed to proposed) transactions. Determination letters are not published regularly, and they are released officially only to the party making the request.

Difference between Letter Rulings and Determination Letters

EXAMPLE 1

The shareholders of Red Corporation and Green Corporation want assurance that the consolidation of their corporations into Blue Corporation will be a nontaxable reorganization. The proper approach is to ask the National Office of the IRS to issue a letter ruling concerning the income tax effect of the proposed transaction.

EXAMPLE 2

Chris operates a barbershop in which he employs eight barbers. To comply with the rules governing income tax and payroll tax withholdings, Chris wants to know whether the barbers working for him are employees or independent contractors. The proper procedure is to request a determination letter on their status from the IRS.

The National Office of the IRS releases **Technical Advice Memoranda (TAMs)** weekly. TAMs resemble letter rulings in that they give the IRS's determination of an issue. Letter rulings, however, are responses to requests by taxpayers, whereas TAMs are issued by the National Office of the IRS in response to questions raised by IRS field personnel during audits. TAMs deal with completed rather than proposed transactions and often are requested for questions relating to exempt organizations and employee plans.[15]

DIGGING DEEPER 1   In-depth coverage can be found on this book's companion website: www.cengagebrain.com

2-1c **Judicial Sources of the Tax Law**

After a taxpayer has exhausted some or all of the remedies available within the IRS (no satisfactory settlement has been reached at the agent level or at the Appeals Division level), a dispute can be taken to the Federal courts. The dispute first is considered by a **court of original jurisdiction** (known as a trial court), with any appeal (either by the taxpayer or the IRS) taken to the appropriate appellate court. In most situations, the taxpayer has a choice of four trial courts: a **District Court**, the **Court of Federal Claims**, the **Tax Court**, or the **Small Cases Division** of the Tax Court. The court system for Federal tax litigation is illustrated in Exhibit 2.4.

The broken line between the Tax Court and the Small Cases Division indicates that there is no appeal from the Small Cases Division, by either party to the case. Decisions from the Small Cases Division have no precedential value. Some of these cases are found on the U.S. Tax Court website. They may not be relied upon by other taxpayers, or even by the taxpayer itself in subsequent years. The jurisdiction of the

---

[15]Determination letters and technical advice memoranda may constitute substantial authority for purposes of the § 6662 accuracy-related penalty. Notice 90–20, 1990–1 C.B. 328.

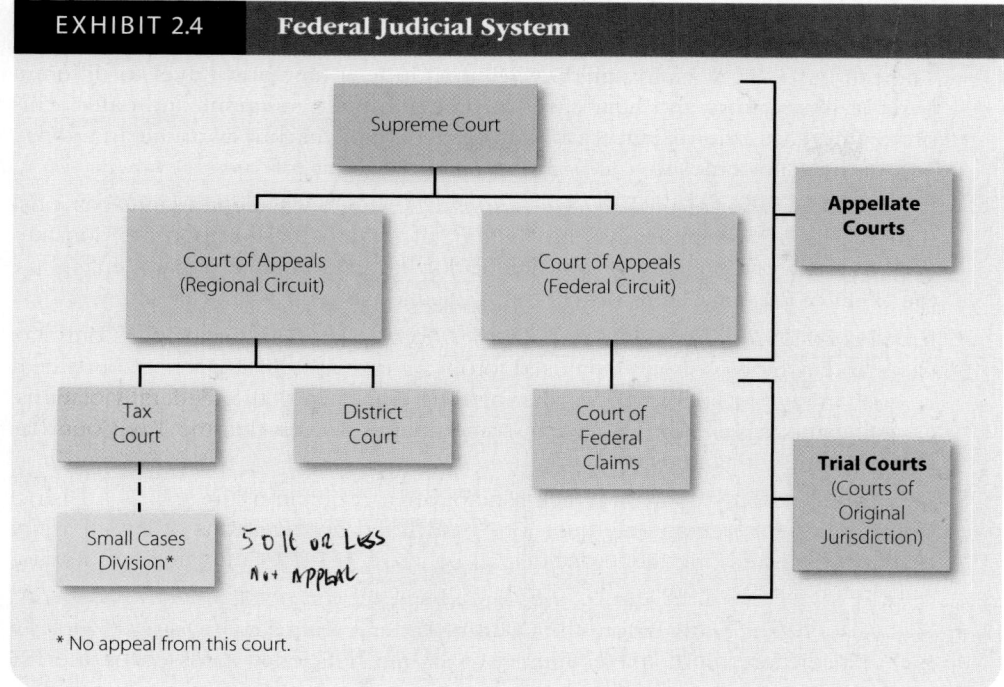

EXHIBIT 2.4   **Federal Judicial System**

* No appeal from this court.

Small Cases Division is limited to cases involving tax, interest, and penalty amounts of $50,000 or less.

In-depth coverage can be found on this book's companion website: www.cengagebrain.com   **2 DIGGING DEEPER**

Knowledge of several terms is important in understanding court decisions. The plaintiff is the party requesting action in a court, and the defendant is the party against whom the suit is brought. Sometimes a court uses the terms *petitioner* and *respondent*. In general, *petitioner* is a synonym for *plaintiff*, and *respondent* is a synonym for *defendant*. At the trial court level, a taxpayer usually is the plaintiff (or petitioner), and the government is the defendant (or respondent). If the taxpayer wins and the Government appeals as the new petitioner (or appellant), the taxpayer now is the respondent.

Trial Courts

The differences among the various trial courts (courts of original jurisdiction) can be summarized as follows.

- *Number of courts.* There is only one Court of Federal Claims and only one Tax Court, but there are many District Courts. The taxpayer does not select the District Court that will hear the dispute, but must sue in the one that has jurisdiction where the taxpayer resides.

- *Number of judges.* A case tried in a District Court is heard before only 1 judge. The Court of Federal Claims has 16 judges, and the Tax Court has 19 regular judges. The entire Tax Court, however, reviews a case (the case is heard *en banc*), thereby taking on a more compelling authority, when important or novel tax issues are involved. Most cases, though, are heard and decided by only 1 of the 19 regular judges.

- *Location.* The Court of Federal Claims meets most often in Washington, D.C., while a District Court meets at a prescribed seat for the particular district. Each state has at least one District Court, and many of the populous states have more than one. Choosing the District Court usually minimizes the inconvenience and expense of traveling for the taxpayer and his or her counsel. The Tax Court is based in Washington, D.C., but its judges regularly travel to different parts of the country and hear cases at predetermined locations and dates. This procedure eases the distance problem for the taxpayer, but it can mean a delay before the case comes to trial.

- *Jurisdiction of the Court of Federal Claims.* The Court of Federal Claims has jurisdiction over any claim against the United States that is based upon the Constitution, any Act of Congress, or any Regulation of an executive department. Thus, the Court of Federal Claims hears nontax litigation as well as tax cases.

- *Jurisdiction of the Tax Court and District Courts.* The Tax Court hears only tax cases and is the most frequently used forum for tax cases. The District Courts hear a wide variety of nontax cases, including drug crimes and other Federal violations, as well as tax cases. For this reason, some people suggest that the Tax Court has more expertise in tax matters.

- *Jury trial.* The only court in which a taxpayer can obtain a jury trial is a District Court. Juries can decide only questions of fact and not questions of law. If a jury trial is not elected, the judge decides all issues. A District Court decision applies only in the district in which the court has jurisdiction.

- *Payment of deficiency.* Before the Court of Federal Claims or a District Court can have jurisdiction, the taxpayer must pay the tax deficiency assessed by the IRS and then sue for a refund. If the taxpayer wins (assuming no successful appeal by the Government), the tax paid plus appropriate interest is recovered. Jurisdiction in the Tax Court, however, usually is obtained without first paying the assessed tax deficiency.

| DIGGING DEEPER 3 | In-depth coverage can be found on this book's companion website: www.cengagebrain.com |

- *Appeals.* Appeals from a District Court or a Tax Court decision go to the Court of Appeals for the circuit in which the taxpayer resides. Appeals from the Court of Federal Claims go to the Court of Appeals for the Federal Circuit. Few Tax Court cases are appealed, and when appeals are made, most are filed by the taxpayer rather than the IRS.

- *Bankruptcy.* When a taxpayer files a bankruptcy petition, the IRS, like other creditors, is prevented from taking action against the taxpayer. Sometimes a bankruptcy court settles a tax claim.

For a summary of several attributes of the Federal trial courts, see Concept Summary 2.1.

Concept Summary 2.1

Federal Judicial System: Trial Courts

Issue	Tax Court	District Court	Court of Federal Claims
Number of judges per court	19	1 per case	16
Payment of deficiency before trial	No	Yes	Yes
Jury trial available	No	Yes	No
Types of dispute	Tax cases only	Mostly criminal and civil issues	Claims against the United States
Jurisdiction	Nationwide	Location of taxpayer	Nationwide
IRS acquiescence policy	Yes	Yes	Yes
Appeal is to	U.S. Court of Appeals	U.S. Court of Appeals	Court of Appeals for the Federal Circuit

Appellate Courts

The losing party can appeal a trial court decision to a **Circuit Court of Appeals**. The 11 geographic circuits, the circuit for the District of Columbia, and the Federal Circuit[16] are shown in Exhibit 2.5.

Process and Outcomes If the government loses at the trial court level (District Court, Tax Court, or Court of Federal Claims), it need not (and frequently does not) appeal. The fact that an appeal is not made, however, does not indicate that the IRS agrees with the result and will not litigate similar issues in the future. The IRS may decide not to appeal for a number of reasons. First, its current litigation load may be heavy. As a consequence, the IRS may decide that available personnel should be assigned to other more important cases. Second, the IRS may not appeal for strategic reasons. For example, the taxpayer may be in a sympathetic position, or the facts may be particularly strong in his or her favor. In that event, the IRS may wait for a weaker case to test the legal issues involved. Third, if the appeal is from a District Court or the Tax Court, the Court of Appeals of jurisdiction could have some bearing on whether the IRS decides to pursue an appeal. Based on past experience and precedent, the IRS may conclude that the chance for success on a particular issue might be more promising in another Court of Appeals. If so, the IRS will wait for a similar case to arise in a different jurisdiction.

The role of appellate courts is limited to a review of the record of the case that was compiled by the trial courts. Thus, the appellate process usually involves a determination of whether the trial court applied the proper law in arriving at its decision, rather than a consideration of the trial court's factual findings.

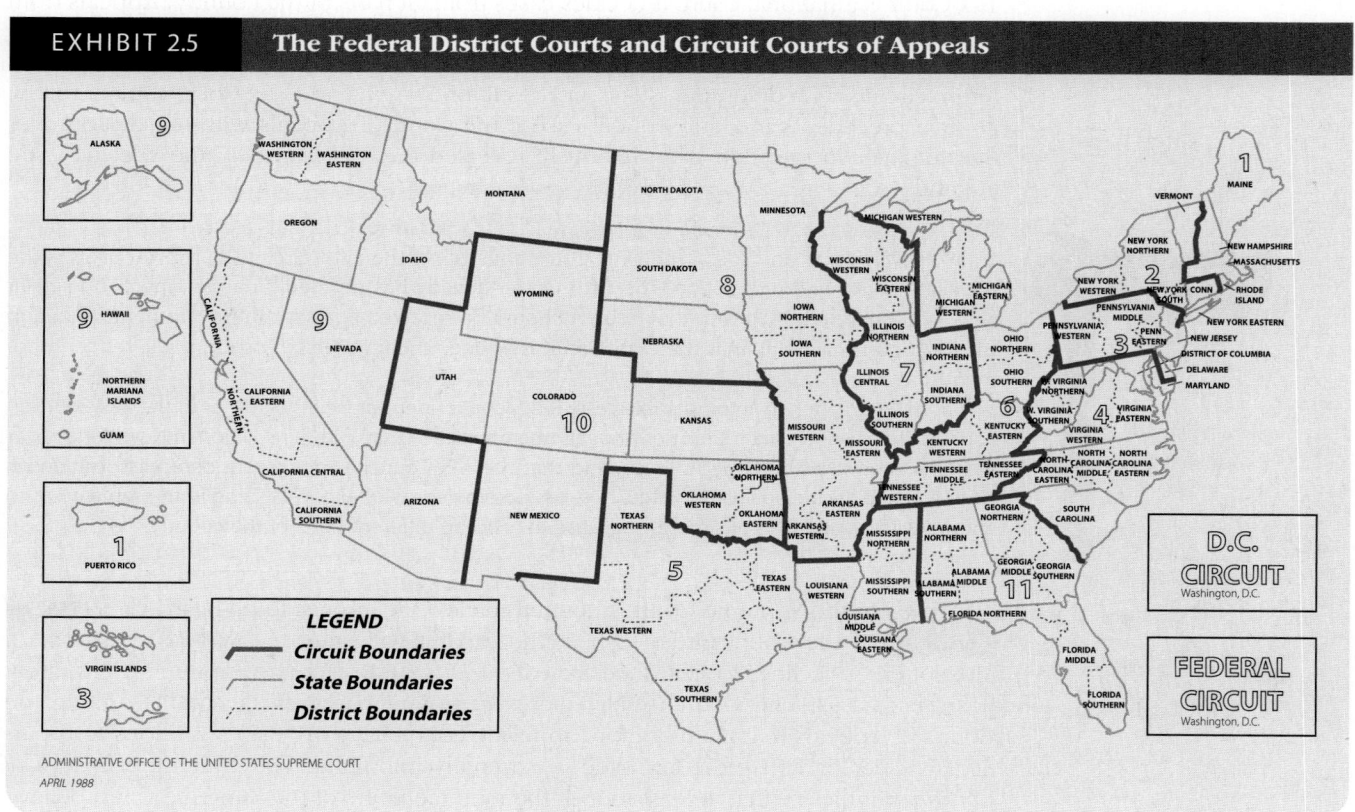

EXHIBIT 2.5 **The Federal District Courts and Circuit Courts of Appeals**

ADMINISTRATIVE OFFICE OF THE UNITED STATES SUPREME COURT
APRIL 1988

---

[16]The Court of Appeals for the Federal Circuit hears decisions appealed from the Court of Federal Claims.

An appeal can have any of a number of possible outcomes. The appellate court may let stand (affirm) or overturn (reverse) the lower court's finding, or it may send the case back for further consideration (remand). When many issues are involved, a mixed result is not unusual. Thus, the lower court may be affirmed (*aff'd.*) on Issue A and reversed (*rev'd.*) on Issue B, while Issue C is remanded (*rem'd.*) for additional fact finding.

When more than one judge is involved in the decision-making process, disagreements are not uncommon. In addition to the majority view, one or more judges may concur (agree with the result reached but not with some or all of the reasoning) or dissent (disagree with the result). In any one case, the majority view controls. But concurring and dissenting views can influence other courts or, at some subsequent date when the composition of the court has changed, even when involving the same court.

Other Rules and Strategies The Federal Circuit at the appellate level provides a taxpayer with an alternative forum to the Court of Appeals of his or her home circuit. When a particular circuit has issued an adverse decision for a case that is similar in facts, the taxpayer may prefer the Court of Federal Claims, because any appeal will be to the Court of Appeals for the Federal Circuit.

District Courts, the Tax Court, and the Court of Federal Claims must abide by the precedents set by the Court of Appeals of their jurisdiction. A particular Court of Appeals need not follow the decisions of another Court of Appeals. All courts, however, must follow decisions of the Supreme Court.

This pattern of appellate precedents raises an issue for the Tax Court. Because the Tax Court is a national court, it decides cases from all parts of the country. Appeals from its decisions, however, go to all of the Courts of Appeals except the Court of Appeals for the Federal Circuit. Accordingly, identical Tax Court cases might be appealed to different circuits with different results. As a result of *Golsen*,[17] the Tax Court will not follow its own precedents in a subsequent case if the Court of Appeals with jurisdiction over the taxpayer in question has previously reversed the Tax Court on the specific issue at hand.

EXAMPLE 3

Emily lives in Texas and sues in the Tax Court on Issue A. The Fifth Circuit Court of Appeals is the appellate court with jurisdiction. The Fifth Circuit already has decided, in a case involving similar facts but a different taxpayer, that Issue A should be resolved against the Government. Although the Tax Court maintains that the Fifth Circuit is wrong, under its *Golsen* policy, it will render judgment for Emily.

Shortly thereafter, in a comparable case, Rashad, a resident of New York, sues in the Tax Court on Issue A. The Second Circuit Court of Appeals, the appellate court with jurisdiction in New York, never has expressed itself on Issue A. Presuming that the Tax Court has not reconsidered its position on Issue A, it will decide against Rashad. Thus, it is possible for two taxpayers suing in the same court to end up with opposite results merely because they live in different parts of the country.

Appeal to the Supreme Court is not automatic. One applies to be heard via a Writ of Certiorari. If the Court agrees to hear the case, it will grant the Writ (*Cert. granted*). Most often, it declines to hear the case (*Cert. denied*). In fact, the Supreme Court rarely hears tax cases. The Court usually grants certiorari to resolve a conflict among the Courts of Appeals (e.g., two or more appellate courts have opposing positions on a particular issue) or where the tax issue is extremely important. The granting of a *Writ of Certiorari* indicates that at least four of the nine members of the Supreme Court believe that the issue is of sufficient importance to be heard by the full Court.

---
[17]*Jack E. Golsen*, 54 T.C. 742 (1970).

Judicial Citations

Court decisions are an important source of tax law. The ability to locate a case and to cite it is a must in working with the tax law. Judicial citations usually follow a standard pattern: case name, volume number, reporter series, page or paragraph number, court (where necessary), and year of decision.

Judicial Citations—The Tax Court The Tax Court issues two types of decisions: Regular and Memorandum. The Chief Judge decides whether the opinion is issued as a Regular or Memorandum decision. The distinction between the two involves both substance and form. In terms of substance, *Memorandum* decisions deal with situations necessitating only the application of already established principles of law. *Regular* decisions involve novel issues of the tax law that have not previously been resolved by the court. In actual practice, however, this distinction is not always so clear. Be that as it may, both Regular and Memorandum decisions represent the position of the Tax Court and, as such, can be relied on by others.

Regular and Memorandum decisions issued by the Tax Court also differ in form. Memorandum decisions are not published officially, while Regular decisions are published by the U.S. Government in a series called *Tax Court of the United States Reports* (T.C.). Each volume of these *Reports* covers a six-month period (January 1 through June 30 and July 1 through December 31) and is given a succeeding volume number. But there is usually a time lag between the date a decision is rendered and the date it appears in official form. A temporary citation often is used to help the researcher locate a recent Regular decision. Consider, for example, the temporary and permanent citations for *B.V. Belk, Jr.*, a decision filed on January 28, 2013.

Temporary Citation	{ *B.V. Belk, Jr.*, 140 T.C. ___, No. 1 (2013). { *Explanation:* Page number left blank because not yet known.
Permanent Citation	{ *B.V. Belk, Jr.*, 140 T.C. 1 (2013). { *Explanation:* Page number now available.

The temporary citation tells us that the case ultimately will appear in Volume 140 of the *Tax Court of the United States Reports*. Until this volume becomes available to the general public, however, the page number is left blank. Instead, the temporary citation identifies the case as being the 1st Regular decision issued by the Tax Court since Volume 139 ended. With this information, the decision easily can be located at the Tax Court website or in the Tax Court services published by Commerce Clearing House (CCH) and Research Institute of America (RIA). Once Volume 140 is released, the permanent citation is substituted, and the number of the case is dropped. Regular decisions and Memorandum decisions are published and searchable at **www.ustaxcourt.gov**.

Before 1943, the Tax Court was called the Board of Tax Appeals, and its decisions were published as the *United States Board of Tax Appeals Reports* (B.T.A.). These 47 volumes cover the period from 1924 to 1942. For example, the citation *Karl Pauli*, 11 B.T.A. 784 (1928) refers to the 11th volume of the *Board of Tax Appeals Reports*, page 784, issued in 1928.

If the IRS loses a decision, it may indicate whether or not it agrees or disagrees with the results reached by the court by publishing an acquiescence ("A" or "*Acq.*") or nonacquiescence ("NA" or "*Nonacq.*"), respectively. The acquiescence program is used where guidance is helpful, regardless of the court that issued the opinion.

The acquiescence or nonacquiescence is published in the *Internal Revenue Bulletin* as an *Action on Decision*. After the announcement is made by the IRS, the acquiescence status of the case is added to the citation for the decision. Examples of such announcements include A.O.D. 2012-007, 2013-25 I.R.B. (an acquiescence), and A.O.D. 2014-001, 2014-38 I.R.B. (a nonacquiescence). The IRS can revoke an acquiescence retroactively.

In-depth coverage can be found on this book's companion website: www.cengagebrain.com   **4 DIGGING DEEPER**

As noted earlier, Memorandum decisions are found at **www.ustaxcourt.gov**. Memorandum decisions also are published by CCH and RIA. Consider, for example, the three different ways that the *Nick R. Hughes* case can be cited.

Nick R. Hughes, T.C.Memo. 2009–94.
The 94th Memorandum decision issued by the Tax Court in 2009.

Nick R. Hughes, 97 TCM 1488 (2009).
Page 1488 of Volume 97 of the CCH *Tax Court Memorandum Decisions*.

Nick R. Hughes, RIA T.C.Memo. ¶2009,094.
Paragraph 2009,094 of the RIA *T.C. Memorandum Decisions*.

The second citation requires a parenthetical reference to the year in which the case was published. The other two citations do not need this reference, as the publication date is included elsewhere in the citation.

The citation to a decision changes when the IRS issues an acquiescence or a nonacquiescence. For example, the proper citation appears as follows for a case after the A.O.D. is issued.

James R. Dixon, 141 T.C. No. 3 (2013), *nonacq.*, A.O.D. 2014-001.

U.S. Tax Court Summary Opinions relate to decisions of the Tax Court's Small Cases Division. These opinions are published commercially, and on the U.S. Tax Court website, with the warning that they may not be treated as precedent for any other case. For example, *John Erwin Smith*, filed on February 19, 2014, is cited as follows.

John Erwin Smith, T.C. Summary Opinion 2014–13.

Judicial Citations—The District Courts, Court of Federal Claims, and Courts of Appeals

District Court, Court of Federal Claims, and Court of Appeals decisions dealing with Federal tax matters are reported in both the *U.S. Tax Cases* (USTC) and the *American Federal Tax Reports* (AFTR) series.

District Court decisions, dealing with *both* tax and nontax issues, are also published in the *Federal Supplement Series* (F.Supp.). Volume 999, published in 1998, was the last volume of the Federal Supplement Series. The *Federal Supplement Second Series* (F.Supp.2d) now is used. A District Court case can be cited in three different forms.

Turner v. U.S., 2004–1 USTC ¶60,478 (D.Ct. N.Tex.).

Explanation: Reported in the first volume of the *U.S. Tax Cases* (USTC) for calendar year 2004 (2004–1) and located at paragraph 60,478 (¶60,478).

Turner v. U.S., 93 AFTR 2d 2004–686 (D.Ct. N.Tex.).

Explanation: Reported in the 93rd volume of the second series of the *American Federal Tax Reports* (AFTR 2d) beginning on page 686.

Turner v. U.S., 306 F.Supp.2d 668 (D.Ct. N.Tex., 2004).

Explanation: Reported in the 306th volume of the *Federal Supplement Second Series* (F.Supp.2d) beginning on page 668. The date reference is needed, as it is not found elsewhere in the citation.

In all of the preceding citations, the names of both of the parties to the case are listed. This is a common practice in virtually all legal citations, with the name of the plaintiff or petitioner listed first. But in a Tax Court citation, because all such cases are brought by the taxpayer, no reference to the government is needed (i.e., "*v. Commissioner*" is omitted).

Decisions of the Courts of Appeals are published in the USTCs, the AFTRs, and the *Federal Second Series* (F.2d). Volume 999, published in 1993, was the last volume of the *Federal Second Series*. The *Federal Third Series* (F.3d) now is used. Decisions of

BRIDGE DISCIPLINE   **Bridge to Public Policy**

Sources of the Federal tax law reflect the general construct of the Federal government. The legislative branch issues the statutory tax law sources. The executive branch controls the administrative sources of the tax law, for the most part using the Department of the Treasury. The judicial branch issues various court decisions interpreting the tax law.

But the "checks and balances" called for by the U.S. Constitution are not so apparent in the implementation of the Federal tax law. Congressional committees often bury tax proposals that deserve greater disclosure and examination as sources of both revenue and public action. The "revenue neutrality" requirements that apply to many of the actions of Congress are avoided easily by applying "emergency" status to revenue and appropriation proposals. As a result, revenue-related language often is attached to numerous and diverse bills that are difficult for tax professionals to track.

Access to the judicial sources of the Federal tax law is prohibitively expensive for most taxpayers. And although the tendency to settle most litigation outside the court system may be cost-effective for all parties, it inhibits the abilities of tax researchers to identify trends in the evolution of the law. Further, the Supreme Court grants certiorari for tax cases so few times each year that the judicial system effectively includes only one trial court and then one appellate opportunity for the taxpayer.

Finally, the political process dictates that wide swings in enforcement initiatives and budgets will occur from year to year. Taxpayers must be able to predict how the law will be administered as they craft and execute their tax plans, but that becomes especially difficult when personnel turnover is common in the IRS and other tax-related agencies.

Federal tax law is a product of the rest of the governing process as it was designed long ago, but its current operations often make it a creature unto itself.

the Court of Federal Claims are published in the USTCs, the AFTRs, and the *Claims Court Reporter* (abbreviated as Cl.Ct.).

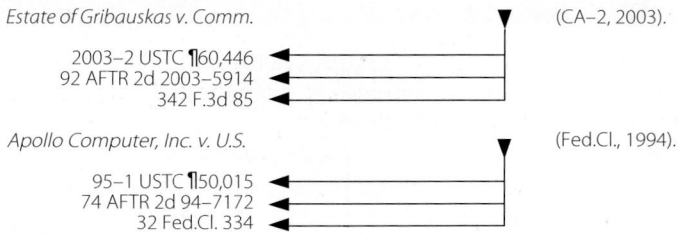

Gribauskas is a decision rendered by the Second Circuit Court of Appeals in 2003 (CA–2, 2003), while *Apollo Computer, Inc.* was issued by the Court of Federal Claims in 1994 (Fed.Cl., 1994), but not published in the USTC until 1995.

In-depth coverage can be found on this book's companion website: www.cengagebrain.com   **5 DIGGING DEEPER**

Judicial Citations—The Supreme Court Like all other Federal tax decisions (except those rendered by the Tax Court), Supreme Court decisions dealing with Federal tax matters are published by CCH in the USTCs and by RIA in the AFTRs. The U.S. Government Printing Office publishes all Supreme Court decisions in the *United States Supreme Court Reports* (U.S.). Such decisions also are found in the *Supreme Court Reporter* (S.Ct.) and the *United States Reports, Lawyer's Edition* (L.Ed.).

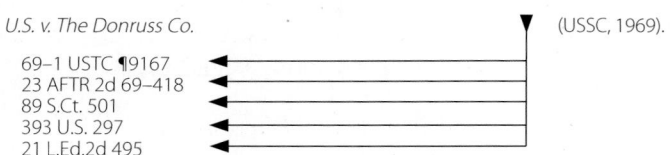

The parenthetical reference (USSC, 1969) identifies the decision as having been rendered by the U.S. Supreme Court in 1969. In this text, the citations of Supreme Court decisions are limited to the USTC, AFTR, and S.Ct. versions.

LO.2

Locate and work with the tax law and explain the tax research process.

2-2 WORKING WITH THE TAX LAW—TAX RESEARCH

Tax research is undertaken to determine the best available solution to a situation that has tax consequences. In the case of a completed transaction, the objective of the research is to determine the tax result of what has already taken place. For example, is the expenditure incurred by the taxpayer deductible or not deductible for tax purposes? When dealing with proposed transactions, tax research is concerned with the determination of possible alternative tax consequences to facilitate effective tax planning.

Tax research involves the following procedures.

- Identifying and refining the problem.
- Locating the appropriate tax law sources.
- Assessing the tax law sources.
- Arriving at the solution or at alternative solutions while giving due consideration to nontax factors.
- Effectively communicating the solution to the taxpayer or the taxpayer's representative.
- Following up on the solution (where appropriate) in light of new developments.

This process is depicted schematically in Exhibit 2.6. The broken lines indicate steps of particular interest when tax research is directed toward proposed, rather than completed, transactions.

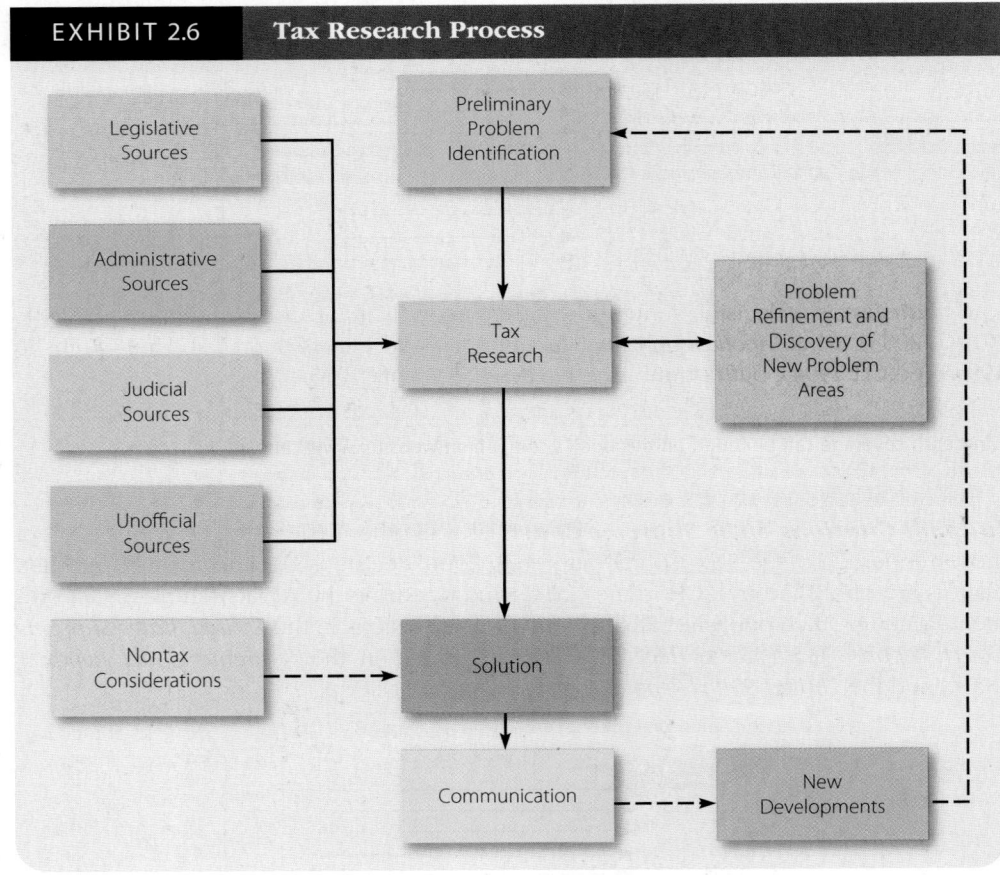

EXHIBIT 2.6   Tax Research Process

2-2a **Identifying the Problem**

Problem identification starts with a compilation of the relevant facts involved. In this regard, *all* of the facts that may have a bearing on the problem must be gathered, as any omission could modify the solution reached. To illustrate, consider what appears to be a very simple problem.

In reviewing their tax and financial situation, Joan and Richard, a married couple, notice that Joan's investment in Airways stock has declined from its purchase price of $8,000 to a current market value of $5,500. Joan wants to sell this stock now and claim the $2,500 loss ($5,500 value − $8,000 cost) as a deduction this year. Richard, however, believes that Airways will yet prosper and does not want to part with the stock. Their daughter Margaret suggests that they sell the Airways stock to Maple, Inc., a corporation owned equally by Joan and Richard. That way, they can claim the deduction this year but still hold the stock through their corporation. Will this suggestion work?

EXAMPLE 4

2-2b **Refining the Problem**

Joan and Richard in Example 4 face three choices.

1. Sell the Airways stock through their regular investment broker and get a deduction in the current year (Joan's plan).
2. Continue to hold the Airways stock (Richard's plan).
3. Sell the Airways stock to a corporation owned 50–50 by Joan and Richard (Margaret's suggestion).

The tax consequences of plans (1) and (2) are clear, but the question that Joan and Richard want to resolve is whether plan (3) will work as anticipated. Refining the problem further, can shareholders deduct a loss from the sale of an asset to a corporation that they control? Section 267(a)(1) indicates that losses from the sale of property between persons specified in § 267(b) are not deductible. This subsection lists 12 different relationships, including in § 267(b)(2): "an individual and a corporation more than 50 percent in value of the outstanding stock of which is owned, directly or indirectly, by or for such individual."

Thus, if Joan and Richard each own 50 percent of Maple, neither owns *more than* 50 percent, as § 267(b) requires. Accordingly, the loss disallowance rule would not apply to Joan, and Margaret's suggestion would appear to be sound.

The language of the statute, however, indicates that any stock owned *directly or indirectly* by an individual is counted toward the 50 percent test. Might Richard's stock be considered owned "indirectly" by Joan? Further research is necessary.

Section 267(c) contains rules for determining "constructive ownership of stock," or when stock owned by one person will be attributed to someone else. One of the rules in this subsection declares that an individual is considered to own any stock that is owned by that person's *family*, and family is defined in § 267(c)(4) as including a person's spouse, among others.

Therefore, Richard's stock will be attributed to Joan, so that Joan is treated as owning all of the stock of Maple, Inc. As a result, § 267(a) would indeed apply, and no loss would be deductible if Joan sells the Airways stock to Maple. In short, we must conclude that Margaret's suggestion will not work.

2-2c **Locating the Appropriate Tax Law Sources**

Once the problem is clearly defined, what is the next step? While it is a matter of individual judgment, most tax research begins with a keyword search of an online tax service. If the problem is not complex, the researcher may bypass the tax service and turn directly to the Internal Revenue Code and the Treasury Regulations. For the beginner, the latter procedure saves time and solves many of the more basic problems. If the researcher does not have a personal copy of the Code or Regulations, access to the

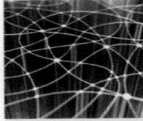

BRIDGE DISCIPLINE   **Bridge to Business Law**

U.S. income tax laws change daily by the action of Congress, tax administrators, and the courts. This process matches the three-branch structure of the rest of the government, with the legislative, executive, and judicial branches each having a say in making tax law. But this distinction among the functions of government is perhaps less clear when it involves the tax law.

- Presidential vetoes of tax legislation are rare.

- The Tax Court is a creation of the Congress in the Internal Revenue Code, not of the U.S. Constitution.

- The cost of tax litigation and the time it takes for a case to work its way through the judicial system render the courts unavailable to most taxpayers.

Under the U.S. Constitution, legislation involving government revenues must start in the House of Representatives. This provision likely was included so that the public would have greater control over those who want greater access to their pocketbooks. Several recent pieces of tax legislation, though, have been initiated as bills in the Senate. And most bills introduced in both houses of Congress are required to be "revenue-neutral" (i.e., they must include provisions by which the legislation's new programs will be paid for). In both houses, this has resulted in amendments to the Internal Revenue Code being attached to legislation involving clean air and water standards, child care programs, and product import and export limitations.

In a few cases, the courts considered a taxpayer challenge to the way this tax legislation was crafted. But so far the courts have failed to overturn any tax provisions solely because they were initiated in the Senate. The courts' rationale for this seemingly unconstitutional position is that (1) the House and its committees heard a full discussion of the proposal and (2) too much time has passed since adoption of the legislation to easily unwind it and undertake a refund procedure.

appropriate volume(s) of a tax service or an online service is necessary.[18] A partial list of the major tax services and their publishers are:

CCH IntelliConnect, Commerce Clearing House. Includes the *Standard Federal Tax Reporter*.

Thomson Reuters Checkpoint, Research Institute of America. Includes RIA's *United States Tax Reporter* and *Federal Tax Coordinator 2d*.

ATX/Kleinrock *Tax Expert*, CCH/Wolters Kluwer.

Tax Management Portfolios, Bloomberg BNA.

Westlaw services. Includes access to *Tax Management Portfolios* and *Federal Tax Coordinator 2d*.

TaxCenter, LexisNexis, primary law sources and various materials taken from CCH, Kleinrock, and Bloomberg BNA.

Federal Research Library, Tax Analysts (a nonprofit organization), primary law sources including treaties, with newsletters and commentaries.

DIGGING DEEPER 6   In-depth coverage can be found on this book's companion website: www.cengagebrain.com

Tax Services

In this text, it is not feasible to explain the use of any particular tax service—this ability can be obtained with further study and professional experience. However, several important observations about the use of tax services cannot be overemphasized. First, always check for current developments. Online tax services are updated several times a day, and tax newsletters often feature highlights of recent tax law developments. Second, there is no substitute for the original source. Do not base a conclusion solely on a tax service's commentary. If a Code Section, Regulation, or case is vital to the research, read it.

---

[18]Several of the major tax services publish paperback editions of the Code and Treasury Regulations that can be purchased at modest prices. These editions are usually revised twice each year. For an annotated and abridged version of the Code and Regulations that is published annually, see James E. Smith and Mark Altieri, *South-Western Federal Taxation: Internal Revenue Code of 1986 and Treasury Regulations: Annotated and Selected* (Cengage Learning, 2016).

Tax Commentary

Various tax publications are another source of relevant information. The use of tax editorial commentary in these publications often can shorten the research time needed to resolve a tax issue. If an article or a posting is relevant to the issue at hand, it may provide the references needed to locate the primary sources of the tax law that apply (e.g., citations to judicial decisions, Regulations, and other IRS pronouncements). Thus, the researcher obtains a "running start" in arriving at a solution to the problem.

The following are some of the more useful tax publications.

Journal of Taxation
Journal of International Taxation
Practical Tax Strategies
Estate Planning
Corporate Taxation
Business Entities
Taxation of Exempts
Real Estate Taxation
ria.thomsonreuters.com/journals

The Tax Executive
www.tei.org

The Tax Adviser
aicpa.org/pubs/taxadv

The Tax Lawyer
www.law.georgetown.edu/journals/tax

The ATA Journal of Legal Tax Research
aaajournals.org/loi/jltr

Trusts and Estates
wealthmanagement.com/te-home

Journal of Passthrough Entities
TAXES—The Tax Magazine
tax.cchgroup.com/books

Tax Notes
taxanalysts.com

2-2d Assessing Tax Law Sources

Once a source has been located, the next step is to assess it in light of the problem at hand. Proper assessment involves careful interpretation of the tax law and consideration of its relevance and significance.

Interpreting the Internal Revenue Code

The language of the Code often is difficult to comprehend fully. Contrary to many people's suspicions, the Code is not written deliberately to confuse its readers. Nevertheless, it often has that effect. The Code is intended to apply to more than 300 million citizens, most of whom are willing to exploit any linguistic imprecision to their benefit—to find a "loophole," in popular parlance. Moreover, many of the Code's provisions are limitations or restrictions involving two or more variables. Expressing such concepts algebraically would be more direct; using words to accomplish this task instead is often quite cumbersome.

Nevertheless, the Code is the governing law, the only source of tax law (other than treaties) that has received the actual approval of Congress and the President. Accordingly, it is usually the first source to be consulted, and often it is the only source needed.

Assessing the Significance of a Treasury Regulation

Treasury Regulations are the official interpretation of the Code and are entitled to great deference. Occasionally, however, a court will invalidate a Regulation or a portion thereof on the grounds that the Regulation is contrary to the intent of Congress. Usually, courts do not question the validity of Regulations because of the belief that "the first administrative interpretation of a provision as it appears in a new act often expresses the general understanding of the times or the actual understanding of those who played an important part when the statute was drafted."[19]

---

[19]*Augustus v. Comm.*, 41–1 USTC ¶9255, 26 AFTR 612, 118 F.2d 38 (CA–6, 1941).

Keep in mind the following observations when assessing the significance of a Regulation.

- IRS agents *must* give the Code and any related Regulations equal weight when dealing with taxpayers and their representatives.
- Proposed Regulations provide a preview of future final Regulations, but they are not binding on the IRS or taxpayers.
- In a challenge, the burden of proof is on the taxpayer to show that a Regulation varies from the language of the statute and has no support in the Committee Reports.
- Final Regulations can be classified as procedural, interpretive, or legislative. **Procedural Regulations** neither establish tax laws nor attempt to explain tax laws. Procedural Regulations often include procedural instructions, indicating information that taxpayers should provide the IRS, as well as information about the internal management and conduct of the IRS itself.
- **Interpretive Regulations** rephrase and elaborate what Congress stated in the Committee Reports that were issued when the tax legislation was enacted. If the language has gone through the public notice and comment procedures discussed earlier in the chapter, interpretive Regulations are *hard and solid* and almost impossible to overturn unless they do not clearly reflect the intent of Congress.
- In some Code Sections, Congress has given the *Treasury Secretary or a delegate* the specific authority to prescribe Regulations to carry out the details of administration or to otherwise create rules not included in the Code. Under such circumstances, Congress effectively is delegating its legislative powers to the Treasury Department. Regulations issued pursuant to this type of authority possess the force and effect of law and often are called **Legislative Regulations** [e.g., see § 385(a)].

DIGGING DEEPER 7 | **In-depth coverage can be found on this book's companion website: www.cengagebrain.com**

Assessing the Significance of Other Administrative Sources of the Tax Law

Revenue Rulings issued by the IRS carry much less weight than Treasury Department Regulations. Revenue Rulings are important, however, in that they reflect the position of the IRS on tax matters. In any dispute with the IRS on the interpretation of tax law, taxpayers should expect agents to follow the results reached in applicable Revenue Rulings. It is not unusual, however, for courts to overturn Revenue Rulings as incorrect applications of the law to the facts presented.

The Big Picture

EXAMPLE
5

Return to the facts of *The Big Picture* on p. 2-1. Tax law involving the sale of investment assets is found largely in the Internal Revenue Code. The Samuels family will find incontrovertible law for these transactions in the Code.

Rules concerning dependency exemptions chiefly are found in Regulations, Revenue Rulings, and instructions to IRS forms. With respect to these tax law sources, the authority of each is less than that of the Code, and the Regulations carry much more weight than the form instructions.

Assessing the Significance of Judicial Sources of the Tax Law

The judicial process as it relates to the formulation of tax law has been described. How much reliance can be placed on a particular decision depends upon the following factors.

- *The level of the court.* A decision rendered by a trial court (e.g., a District Court) carries less weight than one issued by an appellate court (e.g., the Fifth Circuit Court of Appeals). Until Congress changes the Code, decisions by the U.S. Supreme Court represent the last word on any tax issue.

- *The legal residence of the taxpayer.* If, for example, a taxpayer lives in Texas, a decision of the Fifth Circuit Court of Appeals means more than one rendered by the Second Circuit Court of Appeals. This is the case because any appeal from a District Court or the Tax Court would be to the Fifth Circuit and not to the Second Circuit.

- *The type of decision.* A Tax Court Regular decision carries more weight than a Memorandum decision; the Tax Court does not consider Memorandum decisions to have precedential value.[20]

- *The weight of the decision.* A decision that is supported by cases from other courts carries more weight than a decision that is not supported by other cases.

- *Subsequent events.* Was the decision affirmed or overruled on appeal?

In connection with the last two factors, a citator is helpful to tax research.[21] A **citator** provides the history of a case, including the authority relied on (e.g., other judicial decisions) in reaching the result. Reviewing the references listed in the citator discloses whether the decision was appealed and, if so, with what result (e.g., affirmed, reversed, remanded). It also reveals other cases with the same or similar issues and how they were decided. Thus, a citator reflects on the validity of a case and may lead to other relevant judicial material. If one plans to rely on a judicial decision to any significant degree, "running" the case through a citator is imperative.

The Big Picture

EXAMPLE 6

Return to the facts of *The Big Picture* on p. 2-1. Assume that on the Samuels' joint return a dependency exemption is claimed for both Sam and Dana. The IRS challenges these exemptions after an audit. The likelihood of a successful challenge to the IRS's position in this dispute will turn on several factors.

- Was an appellate court ruling in their favor issued by the Federal circuit in which they live? If so, that decision is controlling law. If not and the Samuels' circuit has not ruled to the contrary on the issue but another circuit has ruled in their favor in a parallel case, the taxpayers could use that decision as support for their side of the argument.

- Assume a Revenue Ruling also is found that supports the taxpayers' claim of the exemptions. But how long ago were the Revenue Ruling and appellate decision issued? A legal precedent generally is stronger if it was issued more recently.

- If the Samuels' circuit has ruled favorably, have other courts discussed the appellate court holding? Were those discussions favorable or unfavorable to the Samuels' position? The more courts that follow a holding and cite it favorably, the stronger the legal precedent of the holding. Information of this sort can be found by reviewing the case history of the decision or by consulting a citator.

Understanding Judicial Opinions

Reading judicial opinions can be more productive if certain conventions of usage are understood. Some courts, including the Tax Court, apply the terms *petitioner* and *respondent* to the plaintiff and defendant, respectively, particularly when the case does not involve an appellate proceeding. Appellate courts often use the terms *appellant* and *appellee* instead.

[20]*Severino R. Nico, Jr.,* 67 T.C. 647 (1977).

[21]The major citators are published by CCH, RIA, WESTLAW, and Shepard's Citations, Inc.

It is also important to distinguish between a court's final determination, or *holding*, and passing comments made in the course of its opinion. These latter remarks, examples, and analogies, often collectively termed *dicta*, are not part of the court's conclusion and do not have precedential value. Nevertheless, they often facilitate one's understanding of the court's reasoning and can enable a tax adviser to better predict how the court might resolve some future tax case.

DIGGING DEEPER 8 | In-depth coverage can be found on this book's companion website: www.cengagebrain.com

Assessing the Significance of Other Sources

Primary sources of tax law include the Constitution, legislative history materials (e.g., Committee Reports), statutes, treaties, Treasury Regulations, IRS pronouncements, and judicial decisions. In general, the IRS regards only primary sources as substantial authority. However, reference to *secondary materials* such as tax publications, treatises, legal opinions, and written determinations may be useful. In general, secondary sources do not constitute tax authority.

Although the statement that the IRS regards only primary sources as substantial authority is generally true, there is one exception. Substantial authority *for purposes of* the accuracy-related penalty in § 6662 includes a number of secondary materials (e.g., letter rulings).[22] "Authority" does not include conclusions reached in treatises, textbooks and Web postings by tax commentators, and written opinions rendered for compensation by tax professionals.

A letter ruling or determination letter can be relied upon *only* by the taxpayer to whom it is issued, except as noted previously with respect to the accuracy-related penalty.

DIGGING DEEPER 9 | In-depth coverage can be found on this book's companion website: www.cengagebrain.com

2-2e **Arriving at the Solution or at Alternative Solutions**

Example 4 raises the question of whether taxpayers would be denied a loss deduction from the sale of stock to a corporation that they own. The solution depends, in part, on the relationship of the corporation's shareholders to each other. Because Richard and Joan are married to each other, § 267(c)(2) attributes Richard's stock to Joan in applying the "more than 50 percent" test of § 267(b)(2). Accordingly, Joan and Maple, Inc., are considered related parties under § 267(a), and a sale between them does not produce a deductible loss. If Richard and Joan were not related to each other, the constructive stock ownership rules would not apply and a loss could be deducted on a sale by Joan to Maple.

If Maple, Inc., were a *partnership* instead of a corporation, § 267 would not apply.[23] However, a different Code Section, namely § 707, produces the same result: no deduction is allowed for the loss from a sale between a "more than 50 percent" partner and the partnership. This additional research prevents the couple from erroneously selling their Airways stock to a related partnership in hopes of obtaining a loss deduction from the sale. Accordingly, Joan still must sell the Airways stock to an unrelated party to deduct the loss.

Because Richard still wants to own Airways stock, he might consider purchasing new Airways Co. stock to replace the stock that Joan sells to the unrelated party. Additional research reveals that for the loss on the sale to be deductible, the "wash sale" rule requires that more than 30 days elapse between the purchase of the new stock and the sale of the old stock.[24] This rule applies to purchases and sales of *substantially identical*

---

[22]Reg. § 1.6661–3(b)(2).

[23]Reg. § 1.267(b)–1(b)(1).

[24]§ 1091.

stock or securities. As a result, to deduct the loss on the Airways stock, Richard either must wait more than 30 days after Joan sells the shares to buy new Airways stock or acquire stock in a different company at any time. This new company can even be in the same general business as Airways.[25]

2-2f Communicating Tax Research

LO.3

Communicate the results of the tax research process in a client letter and a tax file memorandum.

Once the problem has been researched adequately, a memorandum, a letter, or a speech setting forth the result may need to be prepared. The form the communication takes could depend on a number of considerations. For example, does an employer or instructor recommend a particular procedure or format for tax research memos? Is the memo to be given directly to the client, or will it first go to the preparer's employer? If the communication is a speech, who is the audience? How long should one speak?[26] Whatever form it takes, a good research communication should contain the following elements.

- A clear statement of the issue.
- In more complex situations, a short review of the fact pattern that raises the issue.
- A review of the pertinent tax law sources (e.g., Code, Regulations, Revenue Rulings, and judicial authority).
- Any assumptions made in arriving at the solution.
- The solution recommended and the logic or reasoning supporting it.
- The references consulted in the research process.

A memo to the tax file is a collection of thoughts resulting from a current tax research project. It is shared with others who have access to the memo files so that they do not need to duplicate the current work at a later date. The file memo is written by a tax professional, to be read by another tax professional, so it features citations in good form to the Code, Regulations, and other sources of the law, often hyperlinking directly to the underlying document. A file memo is organized so as to list the pertinent facts, open tax issues, a brief conclusion, and a discussion of the research findings and underlying tax logic. A file memo seldom exceeds two pages in length.

A letter to the client is written to convey the results of a research engagement and to identify the next steps for the taxpayer to consider. Because most clients have little knowledge or experience in working with tax source documents, citations typically are not used. If the recipient of the letter is a tax executive or other colleague, a more technical approach might be taken in the letter. The letter typically does not exceed a page or two, and it sometimes is supplemented with an attached spreadsheet or chart. It includes various social graces and any needed regulatory language.

Illustrations of the memo for the tax file and the client letter associated with Example 4 appear in Exhibits 2.7 and 2.8.

2-2g Following Up

Because tax research may involve a proposed (as opposed to a completed) transaction, a change in the tax law (legislative, administrative, or judicial) could alter the original conclusion. Additional research may be necessary to test the solution in light of current developments (refer to the broken lines at the right in Exhibit 2.6).

2-2h Conducting Online Tax Research

LO.4

Employ a strategy of how best to use a computer when performing tax research and in taking the CPA exam.

Computer-based tax research tools dominate the tax practice. Electronic tax resources allow the tax library to reflect the tax law's dynamic and daily changes. Nevertheless, using a computer to locate tax law sources cannot substitute for developing and maintaining a thorough knowledge of the tax law or for careful analysis when addressing tax research issues.

---

[25]Rev.Rul. 59–44, 1959–1 C.B. 205.

[26]See W. A. Raabe and G. E. Whittenburg, "Talking Tax: How to Make a Tax Presentation," *The Tax Adviser*, March 1997, pp. 179–182.

EXHIBIT 2.7	Tax File Memorandum

August 26, 2015

TAX FILE MEMORANDUM

FROM Gillian J. Jones

SUBJECT Joan and Richard Taxpayer
Engagement

Today I talked with Joan concerning her August 14, 2015 letter requesting tax assistance. Joan wants to know if she can sell some stock in Airways Co. to Maple, Inc., and deduct the $2,500 loss realized.

FACTS Maple, Inc., is owned 50% by Richard and 50% by Joan. Richard wants to continue holding Airways stock in anticipation of a rebound in its value, but Joan wants to sell her shares and deduct the realized loss. They have asked about a proposed sale of this stock to Maple.

ISSUE Can shareholders deduct a loss on the sale of an asset to a corporation, all of whose stock they own?

CONCLUSION Joan should *not* sell the Airways stock to Maple if the couple wants to deduct the realized loss in the current tax year. Instead, Joan should sell this stock to a third party. Then the couple should either acquire new Airways stock more than 30 days before or after the date of sale, or acquire stock of a similar company.

ANALYSIS Section 267(a) provides that no loss is deductible on a sale or exchange between certain related parties. One of these relationships involves a corporation and a shareholder who owns "more than 50 percent" of that corporation's stock [see § 267(b)(2)]. Although Richard owns only 50% of Maple, Inc., his wife, Joan, owns the other 50%. The constructive ownership rule of § 267(c)(2) attributes stock held by family members, and a spouse is part of a taxpayer's family for this purpose, according to § 267(c)(4). Consequently, Richard's stock is attributed to Joan, who is then treated as owning 100% of Maple, Inc. The related-party disallowance rule then applies to the loss from Joan's selling the Airways stock to Maple. Accordingly, Joan must sell this stock to an unrelated party to make the realized loss deductible.

Because Richard wants to retain an investment in Airways, he can purchase replacement stock either before or after Joan sells the original Airways stock. Section 1091(a), however, requires that more than 30 days elapse between the purchase and the sale, or the sale and the purchase, as the case may be. Moreover, for this purpose, an option to buy the stock is treated as equivalent to the stock itself. As a result, Richard must wait more than 30 days between transactions and cannot utilize stock options in the interim to minimize his stock price exposure.

A final alternative might be to replace the Airways stock with securities of a comparable company in the same industry. Although no two companies are exactly alike, there may be another company whose management philosophy, marketing strategy, and financial data are sufficiently similar to Airways to provide an equivalent return on investment. Under this alternative, Richard could acquire the new company's shares immediately, without waiting the 30 days mandated by § 1091(a). Despite the two companies' investment similarity, they would not be treated as "substantially identical" for this purpose (see Rev.Rul. 59–44, 1959–1 C.B. 205), and the Airways realized loss could be recognized.

Most computerized services allow a user to retrieve documents in order of relevance, or in the order listed by database sources. Although this can be useful, even though a document is placed high on the relevance list, it still may not constitute valid law. Reading the primary sources, validating their authority, and checking the citator are essential in reaching a correct answer.

Electronic Tax Services

Usually, tax professionals use one of the following strategies when performing computer-based tax research.

- *Search* various databases using keywords that are likely to be found in the underlying documents, as written by Congress, the judiciary, or administrative sources.

- *Link* to tax documents for which all or part of the proper citation is known.

- *Browse* the tax databases, examining various tables of contents and indexes in a traditional manner or using cross-references in the documents to jump from one tax law source to another.

Virtually all of the major commercial tax publishers and most of the primary sources of the law itself, such as the Supreme Court and some of the Courts of Appeals, provide tax material in a variety of electronic formats.

EXHIBIT 2.8	**Client Letter**

Raabe, Maloney, Young, & Nellen, CPAs
5191 Natorp Boulevard
Mason, OH 45040

August 30, 2015

Mr. and Ms. Richard Taxpayer
111 Tragg Boulevard
Williamsburg, VA 23185

Dear Joan and Richard:

It was good to see you last week at our firm's golf outing. I'm glad that your children are doing so well in college and that our work to build up their education funds was so effective in providing the needed cash flow!

I am responding to your request to review your family's financial and tax situation. Our conclusions are based upon the facts as outlined in your August 14 letter. Any change in the facts may affect our conclusions.

Joan owns stock in Airways Co. that has declined in value, but Richard would like to retain this stock in anticipation of a rebound in its value. You have proposed a sale of this stock at its current market value to Maple, Inc., a corporation owned 50–50 by the two of you. Such a sale, however, would not permit the loss to be deducted.

A better approach would be to sell the Airways stock to a third party before year-end and repurchase this stock in the market. Please understand that the loss will not be deductible unless more than 30 days elapse between the sale and the repurchase of the stock. You can sell the old stock first and then buy the new stock, or you can buy the new stock first and then sell the old stock; the ordering of the transactions does not change the result. However, it is essential that more than 30 days elapse between the sale and purchase transactions. Using options during this 30-day period is ineffective and also will prevent the loss from being deducted in the current taxable year.

If the 30-day requirement is unacceptable, you might consider replacing the Airways stock with securities of some other company, perhaps even a company in the same general business as Airways. In that situation, your loss on the Airways stock can be deducted without regard to when you buy the new stock.

Let's meet to discuss this some more—and to allow me to show you our new office. Please e-mail me if I can clarify any of these points or if you have more information for me to consider. My work on this engagement is regulated by Treasury Circular 230.

Sincerely yours,

Gillian J. Jones, CPA
Partner

Online Commercial Services

Online tax research systems allow practitioners to obtain virtually instantaneous use of tax law sources by accessing databases via the Internet. Some online services may employ price-per-search cost structures, which can be as much as $200 per hour. Thus, unless a practitioner who is subject to this pricing structure can pass along related costs to clients or others, online searching generally is limited to the most important issues and to the researchers with the most experience and training in search techniques.

Other Web Sources

The Internet provides a wealth of tax information in several popular forms, sometimes at no direct cost to the researcher. Many tax professionals begin a research task with a simple online search. Other sources include the following.

- *The Web* provides access to a number of sites maintained by accounting and consulting firms, publishers, tax academics and libraries, and governmental bodies. The best sites offer links to other sites and direct contact to the site providers. Exhibit 2.9 lists some of the websites that may be most useful to tax researchers and their Internet addresses as of press date.

EXHIBIT 2.9	Tax-Related Websites	
Website	**Web Address at Press Date**	**Description**
Internal Revenue Service	**irs.gov**	News releases, downloadable forms and instructions, tables, Circular 230, and filing advice.
Tax Analysts	**taxanalysts.com**	Policy-oriented readings on tax laws and proposals to change it, moderated bulletins on various tax subjects.
Tax laws online	**law.cornell.edu/cfr**	Treasury Regulations.
	law.cornell.edu/uscode	Internal Revenue Code.
	uscode.house.gov	
Commercial tax publishers	For example, **cchgroup.com**	Information about products and services available by subscription and newsletter excerpts.
Accounting firms and professional organizations	For example, the AICPA's page is at **aicpa.org**, Ernst & Young is at **ey.com**, and KPMG is at **kpmg.com**	Tax planning newsletters, descriptions of services offered and career opportunities, and exchange of data with clients and subscribers.
Cengage Learning	**cengagebrain.com**	Informational updates, newsletters, support materials for students and adopters, and continuing education.

Caution: Web addresses change frequently.

- *Blogs and newsletters* provide a means by which information related to the tax law can be exchanged among taxpayers, tax professionals, and others who subscribe to the group's services. The tax professional can read the exchanges among other members and offer replies and suggestions to inquiries as desired. Discussions address the interpretation and application of existing law, analysis of proposals and new pronouncements, and reviews of tax software.

While tax information on the Internet is plentiful, public domain information never should be relied upon without referring to other, more reliable sources. Always remember that anyone can set up a website and that quality control can be difficult for the tax professional to ascertain.

In many situations, solutions to research problems benefit from or require the use of various electronic tax research tools. A competent tax professional must become familiar and proficient with these tools and be able to use them effectively to meet the expectations of clients and the necessities of work in the modern world.[27]

2-3 TAX RESEARCH ON THE CPA EXAMINATION

The CPA examination is computer-based, and it emphasizes information technology and general business knowledge. The 14-hour exam has four sections, and taxation is included in the 3-hour Regulation section, which covers these topics.

- Federal tax procedures and accounting issues.
- Federal taxation of property transactions.
- Federal taxation—individuals.
- Federal taxation—entities.

Each exam section includes multiple-choice questions and case studies called simulations. About 60 multiple-choice tax questions appear in the Regulation section

---

[27]For a more detailed discussion of the use of electronic tax research in a tax practice, see R. B. Sawyers, W. A. Raabe, G. E. Whittenburg, and S. L. Gill, *Federal Tax Research*, 10th ed. (Cengage Learning, 2015).

FINANCIAL DISCLOSURE INSIGHTS **Where Does GAAP Come From?**

As this chapter has described, the tax law is developed by many entities, including Congress, the legislators of other countries, the courts, and the IRS. Accounting principles also have many sources. Consequently, in reconciling the tax and financial accounting reporting of a transaction, the tax professional will need to know the hierarchy of authority of accounting principles—in particular, the level of importance to assign to a specific GAAP document. The diagram below presents the sources of GAAP arranged in a general order of authority from highest to lowest.[28] Note how many of these GAAP sources parallel those that have been discussed with respect to the tax law.

Professional research is conducted to find and analyze the sources of accounting reporting standards, in much the same way a tax professional conducts research concerning an open tax question. In fact, many of the publishers that provide tax research materials also can be used to find GAAP and IFRS documents. These include Research Institute of America (RIA) and Commerce Clearing House (CCH). The Financial Accounting Standards Board (FASB) also makes its standards and interpretations available by subscription.

Highest Authority
- Financial Accounting Standards and Interpretations of the FASB.
- Pronouncements of bodies that preceded the FASB, such as the Accounting Principles Board (APB).

- FASB Technical Bulletins.
- Audit and Accounting Guides, prepared by the American Institute of CPAs (AICPA) and cleared by the FASB.
- Practice Bulletins, prepared by the American Institute of CPAs (AICPA) and cleared by the FASB.

- Interpretation Guides of the FASB Staff.
- Accounting Interpretations of the AICPA.
- IASB Accounting Standards.
- FASB Concepts Standards.
- Widely accepted accounting practices, professional journals, accounting textbooks, and treatises.

of the exam. All written communications tasks are placed in the Business Environment and Concepts section of the exam.

Simulations are small case studies designed to test a candidate's tax knowledge and skills using real-life work-related situations. Simulations include a four-function pop-up calculator, a blank spreadsheet with some elementary functionality, and authoritative literature for the candidate to research in completing the tax case study simulations (e.g., Internal Revenue Code, Regulations, IRS publications, and Federal tax forms). Examples of such simulations follow.

CPA Exam Simulation Example

EXAMPLE 7

The tax *citation type* simulation requires the candidate to research the Internal Revenue Code and enter a Code Section and subsection citation. For example, Amber Company is considering using the simplified dollar-value method of pricing its inventory for purposes of the LIFO method that is available to certain small businesses. What Internal Revenue Code Section is the relevant authority to which you should turn to determine whether the taxpayer is eligible to use this method? To be successful, the candidate needs to find § 474.

---

[28]See Chapter 10 of Sawyers, et al., cited in footnote 27, for a discussion of strategies and techniques used in conducting research with financial accounting resources.

BRIDGE DISCIPLINE   Bridge to Regulation and Oversight

The interests of the public are represented by Federal, state, and local governments, as they oversee the various economic transactions carried out by individuals and businesses. Control of the financial sector is assigned to the Treasury and the Securities and Exchange Commission, among other agencies.

Most citizens assume that attorneys and CPAs hold broad high-level skills in working with the tax laws. But the nature of today's economy dictates that professionals working in law and accounting instead develop narrower specialties that clients will find valuable in the marketplace. Only a subset of CPAs and attorneys practice regularly with the tax law, but all such professionals must hold and maintain broad-based skills in taxation.

Tax law is the subject of only one of the sections of the CPA exam, and only a portion of those questions relate to specific provisions of the tax law. The exam also tests the candidate's research and communication skills, and because it is administered with computer software, the candidate must have some technological facility as well.

The depth and variety of the skills that are required of an effective tax professional almost certainly are not measured well by the CPA or bar examinations. The integrity of the taxing system may be at risk when one can attain credible professional certification with only entry-level skills. It is likely that several further levels of specialty certifications, and rigorous, lifelong skill improvement, should be required of tax professionals.

CPA Exam Simulation Example

EXAMPLE 8

A *tax form completion* simulation requires the candidate to fill out a portion of a tax form. For example, Red is a limited liability company (LLC). Complete the income section of the Form 1065 for Red Company using the values found and calculated on previous tabs along with the following data.

Ordinary income from other partnerships	$ 5,200
Net gain (loss) from Form 4797	2,400
Management fee income	12,000

The candidate is provided with page 1 of Form 1065 on which to record the appropriate amounts.

Candidates can learn more about the CPA examination at **www.cpa-exam.org**. This online tutorial site reviews the exam's format, navigation functions, and tools. A 30- to 60-minute sample exam will familiarize a candidate with the types of questions on the examination.

REFOCUS ON THE BIG PICTURE

RESEARCHING TAX QUESTIONS

Fred and Megan will need you to conduct some rigorous tax research concerning the proper treatment of the stock sale and to determine the correct number of dependency exemptions for the year. Your work will entail a review of primary sources of the tax law and some computations for them, using a spreadsheet to illustrate your findings.

Communications with your clients will entail a variety of phone and e-mail exchanges; a memo for your tax file; and a letter to them, summarizing your findings and recommendations.

Your research likely will be complete using Code sections and several IRS rulings, but you must convey your results to the clients in a manner that is understandable to them, as they likely are untrained in the tax law.

What If?

It is not uncommon that you later will receive additional information from Fred and Megan about the affected transactions. This may occur if additional facts are discovered by them, if Fred and Megan gave you incomplete information because they did not understand which of the facts were relevant in determining the tax outcome, or if your original interviews and data collection from them were incomplete.

If this new information changes the conclusions and recommendations that you already had developed, you should make certain that the taxpayers understand that your original work no longer is valid and that they should not depend on it.

Suggested Readings

Sheldon I. Banoff and Richard M. Lipton, Editors' Shop Talk, "Is Wikipedia Good Authority in the Tax Court?" *Journal of Taxation*, April 2007.

"Can Treasury and the IRS Write Rules in 'Plain' Langauge?" *Journal of Taxation*, December 2010.

Alexandra Defelice, "Tax Research Comes in Many Flavors," *Accounting Today*, April 2009, **tinyurl.com/tax-research-flavors**.

T. S. Rose and J. Temares, "Tax Research Tips to Solve Tax Problems," *CPA Magazine*, **tinyurl.com/tax-research-tips**.

"Writing Skills for the Tax Professional," **www2.gsu.edu/~accerl/home.html**.

Key Terms

Acquiescence, 2-15	Interpretive Regulations, 2-22	Revenue Rulings, 2-8
Circuit Court of Appeals, 2-13	Legislative Regulations, 2-22	Small Cases Division, 2-10
Citator, 2-23	Letter rulings, 2-9	Supreme Court, 2-14
Court of Federal Claims, 2-10	Nonacquiescence, 2-15	Tax Court, 2-10
Court of original jurisdiction, 2-10	Precedents, 2-14	Technical Advice Memoranda (TAMs), 2-10
Determination letters, 2-10	Procedural Regulations, 2-22	Temporary Regulations, 2-7
District Court, 2-10	Proposed Regulations, 2-7	Writ of Certiorari, 2-14
Final Regulations, 2-7	Revenue Procedures, 2-8	

Problems

1. **LO.1** What precedents must each of these courts follow?
   a. U.S. Tax Court.
   b. U.S. Court of Federal Claims.
   c. U.S. District Court.

2. **LO.1, 3** Butch Bishop operates a small international firm named Tile, Inc. A new treaty between the United States and Spain conflicts with a Section of the Internal Revenue Code. Butch asks you for advice. If he follows the treaty position, does he need to disclose this on this year's tax return? If he is required to disclose, are there any penalties for failure to disclose? Prepare a letter in which you respond to Butch. Tile's address is 100 International Drive, Tampa, FL 33620.   Communications

3. **LO.1** Distinguish between the following.
   a. Treasury Regulations and Revenue Rulings.
   b. Revenue Rulings and Revenue Procedures.
   c. Revenue Rulings and letter rulings.
   d. Letter rulings and determination letters.

4. **LO.1, 2** Rank the following items from the lowest to the highest authority in the Federal tax law system.
   a. Interpretive Regulation. 3
   b. Legislative Regulation. 2
   c. Letter ruling. 6
   d. Revenue Ruling. 4
   e. Internal Revenue Code. 1
   f. Proposed Regulation. 5

5. **LO.1** Interpret each of the following citations.
   a. Temp.Reg. § 1.956–2T.
   b. Rev.Rul. 2012–15, 2012–23 I.R.B. 975.
   c. Ltr.Rul. 200204051.

6. **LO.1** List an advantage and a disadvantage of using the U.S. Court of Federal Claims as the trial court for Federal tax litigation.

Communications 7. **LO.1, 3** Eddy Falls is considering litigating a tax deficiency of approximately $229,030 in the court system. He asks you to provide him with a short description of his litigation alternatives, indicating the advantages and disadvantages of each. Prepare your response to Eddy in the form of a letter. His address is 200 Mesa Drive, Tucson, AZ 85714.

8. **LO.1** A taxpayer lives in Michigan. In a controversy with the IRS, the taxpayer loses at the trial court level. Describe the appeal procedure for each of the following trial courts.
   a. Small Cases Division of the Tax Court.
   b. Tax Court.
   c. District Court.
   d. Court of Federal Claims.

9. **LO.1** For the Tax Court, the District Court, and the Court of Federal Claims, indicate the following.
   a. Number of regular judges per court.
   b. Availability of a jury trial.
   c. Whether the deficiency must be paid before the trial.

10. **LO.1** A taxpayer living in the following states would appeal a decision of the U.S District Court to which Court of Appeals?
    a. Wyoming.
    b. Nebraska.
    c. Idaho.
    d. Louisiana.
    e. Illinois.

Critical Thinking 11. **LO.1** What is meant by the term *petitioner*?

12. **LO.1, 2** In assessing the validity of a prior court decision, discuss the significance of the following on the taxpayer's issue.
    a. The decision was rendered by the U.S. District Court of Wyoming. Taxpayer lives in Wyoming.
    b. The decision was rendered by the Court of Federal Claims. Taxpayer lives in Wyoming.
    c. The decision was rendered by the Second Circuit Court of Appeals. Taxpayer lives in California.
    d. The decision was rendered by the Supreme Court.
    e. The decision was rendered by the Tax Court. The IRS has acquiesced in the result.
    f. Same as (e), except that the IRS has nonacquiesced in the result.

13. **LO.1** What is the difference between a Regular decision, a Memorandum decision, and a Summary Opinion of the Tax Court?

14. **LO.1** Explain the following abbreviations.

a. CA–2.	f. *Cert. denied.*	k. F.3d.
b. Fed.Cl.	g. *acq.*	l. F.Supp.
c. *aff'd.*	h. B.T.A.	m. USSC.
d. *rev'd.*	i. USTC.	n. S.Ct.
e. *rem'd.*	j. AFTR.	o. D.Ct.

15. **LO.2** Referring to the citation only, determine which tax law source issued these documents.
    a. 716 F.2d 693 (CA–9, 1983).
    b. 92 T.C 400 (1998).
    c. 70 U.S. 224 (1935).
    d. 3 B.T.A. 1042 (1926).
    e. T.C.Memo. 1957–169.
    f. 50 AFTR 2d 92–6000 (Cl.Ct., 1992).
    g. Ltr.Rul. 9046036.
    h. 111 F.Supp.2d 1294 (S.D. N. Y., 2000).
    i. 98–50, 1998–1 C.B. 10.

16. **LO.2** Interpret each of the following citations.
    a. 14 T.C. 74 (1950).
    b. 592 F.2d 1251 (CA–5, 1979).
    c. 95–1 USTC ¶ 50,104 (CA–6, 1995).
    d. 75 AFTR 2d 95–110 (CA–6, 1995).
    e. 223 F.Supp. 663 (W.D. Tex., 1963).

17. **LO.2** Which of the following items may be found in the *Internal Revenue Bulletin*?
    a. Action on Decision.
    b. Small Cases Division of the Tax Court decision.
    c. Letter ruling.
    d. Revenue Procedure.
    e. Final Regulation.
    f. Court of Appeals decision.
    g. Acquiescences to Tax Court decisions.
    h. U.S. Circuit Court of Appeals decision.

18. **LO.2** Answer the following questions based upon this citation: *United Draperies, Inc. v. Comm.*, 340 F.2d 936 (CA–7, 1964), *aff'g* 41 T.C. 457 (1963), *cert. denied* 382 U.S. 813 (1965).
    a. In which court did this decision first appear?
    b. Did the appellate court uphold the trial court?
    c. Who was the plaintiff?
    d. Did the Supreme Court uphold the appellate court decision?

19. **LO.2, 4** For her tax class, Yvonne is preparing a research paper discussing the tax aspects of child support payments. Explain to Yvonne how she can research the provisions on this topic.   Issue ID

20. **LO.1, 2** Tom, an individual taxpayer, has been audited by the IRS and, as a result, has been assessed a substantial deficiency (which has not yet been paid) in additional income taxes. In preparing his defense, Tom advances the following possibilities.
    a. Although a resident of Kentucky, Tom plans to sue in a U.S. District Court in Oregon that appears to be more favorably inclined toward taxpayers.
    b. If (a) is not possible, Tom plans to take his case to a Kentucky state court where an uncle is the presiding judge.
    c. Because Tom has found a B.T.A. decision that seems to help his case, he plans to rely on it under alternative (a) or (b).
    d. If he loses at the trial court level, Tom plans to appeal either to the U.S. Court of Federal Claims or to the U.S. Second Circuit Court of Appeals because he has relatives in both Washington, D.C., and New York. Staying with these relatives could save Tom lodging expense while his appeal is being heard by the court selected.
    e. Whether or not Tom wins at the trial court or appeals court level, he feels certain of success on an appeal to the U.S. Supreme Court.

    Evaluate Tom's notions concerning the judicial process as it applies to Federal income tax controversies.

21. **LO.1** Using the legend provided, classify each of the following statements (more than one answer per statement may be appropriate).

Legend

D = Applies to the District Court
T = Applies to the Tax Court
C = Applies to the Court of Federal Claims
A = Applies to the Circuit Court of Appeals
U = Applies to the Supreme Court
N = Applies to none of the above

---

a. Decides only Federal tax matters.
b. Decisions are reported in the F.3d Series.
c. Decisions are reported in the USTCs.
d. Decisions are reported in the AFTRs.
e. Appeal is by *Writ of Certiorari.*
f. Court meets most often in Washington, D.C.
g. Offers the choice of a jury trial.
h. Is a trial court.
i. Is an appellate court.
j. Allows appeal to the Court of Appeals for the Federal Circuit and bypasses the taxpayer's own Circuit Court of Appeals.
k. Has a Small Cases Division.
l. Is the only trial court where the taxpayer does not have to first pay the tax assessed by the IRS.

22. **LO.1, 2** Using the legend provided, classify each of the following citations as to the type of court.

Legend

D = District Court
T = Tax Court
C = Court of Federal Claims
A = Circuit Court of Appeals
U = Supreme Court
N = None of the above

---

a. Rev.Rul. 2009–34, 2009–42 I.R.B. 502.
b. *Joseph R. Bolker*, 81 T.C. 782 (1983).
c. *Magneson*, 753 F.2d 1490 (CA–9, 1985).
d. *Lucas v. Ox Fibre Brush Co.*, 281 U.S. 115 (1930).
e. *Ashtabula Bow Socket Co.*, 2 B.T.A. 306 (1925).
f. *BB&T Corp.*, 97 AFTR 2d 2006–873 (D.Ct. Mid.N.Car., 2006).
g. *Choate Construction Co.*, T.C.Memo. 1997–495.
h. Ltr.Rul. 200940021.
i. *John and Rochelle Ray*, T.C. Summary Opinion 2006–110.

23. **LO.1, 2** Using the legend provided, classify each of the following tax sources.

Legend

P = Primary tax source
S = Secondary tax source
B = Both
N = Neither

---

a. Sixteenth Amendment to the U.S. Constitution.

b. Tax treaty between the United States and India.

c. Revenue Procedure.

d. Chief Counsel Advice (issued 2009).

e. U.S. District Court decision.

f. *Yale Law Journal* article.

g. Temporary Regulations (issued 2013).

h. U.S. Tax Court Memorandum decision.

i. Small Cases Division of the U.S. Tax Court decision.

j. House Ways and Means Committee report.

24. **LO.1** In which Subchapter of the Internal Revenue Code would one find information about corporate distributions?

a. Subchapter S.

b. Subchapter C.

c. Subchapter P.

d. Subchapter K.

e. Subchapter M.

25. **LO.1, 2** To locate an IRS Revenue Procedure that was issued during the past week, which source would you consult?

a. *Federal Register*.

b. *Internal Revenue Bulletin*.

c. Internal Revenue Code.

d. Some other source. Identify it.

26. **LO.1, 2** In the citation *Schuster's Express, Inc.*, 66 T.C. 588 (1976), *aff'd* 562 F.2d 39 (CA–2, 1977), *nonacq.*, to what do the 66, 39, and *nonacq.* refer?

27. **LO.1** Is there an automatic right to appeal to the U.S. Supreme Court? If so, what is the process?

28. **LO.2** An accountant friend of yours tells you that he "almost never" does any tax research because he believes that "research usually reveals that some tax planning idea has already been thought up and shot down." Besides, he points out, most tax returns are never audited by the IRS. Can a tax adviser who is dedicated to reducing his client's tax liability justify the effort to engage in tax research? Do professional ethics *demand* such efforts? Which approach would a client probably prefer?

Ethics and Equity

29. **LO.1, 4** Go to the U.S. Tax Court website.

Communications

a. What different types of cases can be found on the site?

b. What is a Summary Opinion? Find one.

c. What is a Memorandum decision? Find one.

d. Find the court's Rules of Practice and Procedures.

e. Is the site user-friendly? E-mail suggested improvements to the site's webmaster.

30. **LO.2, 3** Locate the following Code provisions, and give a brief description of each in an e-mail to your instructor.

Critical Thinking

Communications

a. § 61(a)(13).

b. § 643(a)(2).

c. § 2503(g)(2)(A).

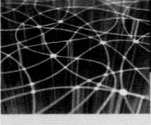

BRIDGE DISCIPLINE

1. Comment on these statements.
   a. The tax law is created and administered in the same way as other Federal provisions.
   b. Most taxpayers find it too expensive and time-consuming to sue the government in a tax dispute.

Communications   2. Using the title "The Federal Taxing System Operates Outside the U.S. Constitution," write a two-page paper to submit in your Government Policy course. Do not address "tax protester" issues (e.g., that the income tax is unconstitutional or that one's taxes should be measured using only the gold standard). Instead, concentrate on how Federal tax law is made and interpreted and how the process measures up to other governmental standards.

Communications   3. Develop an outline from which you will deliver a 10-minute talk to the local Chamber of Commerce, with the title "Regulation of the Tax Profession in the 21st Century." Use no more than four PowerPoint slides for your talk, and discuss what the business community now needs with respect to oversight of a stable, yet productive revenue-raising system. Include administrative developments of the last two years in your research.

Ethics and Equity   4. A friend of yours, who is a philosophy major, has overheard the conversation described in Problem 28 and declares that all tax research is "immoral." She says that tax research enables people with substantial assets to shift the burden of financing public expenditures to those who "get up every morning, go to work, play by the rules, and pay their bills." How do you respond?

Research Problems

**Note: Solutions to Research Problems can be prepared by using the Checkpoint®
Student Edition online research product, which is available to accompany this text. It
is also possible to prepare solutions to the Research Problems by using tax research
materials found in a standard tax library.**

Communications   **Research Problem 1.** Locate the following items, and e-mail to your professor a brief summary of the results.
   a. *Charles Y. Choi*, T.C. Memo. 2002–183.
   b. Ltr.Rul. 200231003.
   c. Action on Decision, 2000–004, May 10, 2000.

Research Problem 2. Locate the following Code citations, and give a brief topical description of each.
   a. § 708(a).
   b. § 1371(a).
   c. § 2503(a).

Communications   **Research Problem 3.** Locate the following Regulations, and give a brief topical description of each. Summarize your comments in an e-mail to your instructor.
   a. Reg. § 1.170A–4A(b)(2)(ii)(C).
   b. Reg. § 1.672(b)–1.
   c. Reg. § 20.2031–7(f).

Research Problem 4. Describe the material that is found in Subtitle E of the Code. Would you expect these provisions not to be addressed anywhere else in the Code? Explain.

Research Problem 5. Determine the missing data in these court decisions and rulings.

    a. *Higgins v. Comm.*, 312 U.S._____ (1941).

    b. *Talen v. U.S.*, 355 F.Supp.2d 22 (D.Ct. D.C., _____).

    c. Rev.Rul. 2008–18, 2008–13 I.R.B._____.

    d. *Pahl v. Comm.*, 150 F.3d 1124 (CA–9, _____).

    e. *Veterinary Surgical Consultants PC*, 117 T.C._____(2001).

    f. *Yeagle Drywall Co.*, T.C. Memo. 2001_____.

Research Problem 6. Locate the following Tax Court case: *Thomas J. Green, Jr.*, 59 T.C. 456 (1972). Briefly describe the issue in the case, and explain what the Tax Court said about using IRS publications to support a research conclusion.

Research Problem 7. Can a Tax Court Small Cases decision be treated as a precedent by other taxpayers? Explain.

Partial list of research aids:
§ 7463(b).
Maria Antionette Walton Mitchell, T.C. Summary Opinion 2004–160.

Research Problem 8. Find *Kathryn Bernal*, 120 T.C. 102 (2003), and answer the following questions.

    a. What was the docket number?

    b. When was the dispute filed?

    c. Who is the respondent?

    d. Who was the attorney for the taxpayers?

    e. Who was the judge who wrote the opinion?

    f. What was the disposition of the dispute?

Research Problem 9. This year, Frank lived with and supported Daisy, an unrelated 20-year-old woman to whom he was not married. Frank lives in a state that has a statute that makes cohabitation a misdemeanor for a man and a woman who are not married to each other. May Frank claim Daisy as a dependent, assuming that he meets all of the applicable tests to claim the exemption? Should Frank and Daisy move to another state? Describe your research path in a PowerPoint presentation for your classmates.

Decision Making

Communications

Partial list of research aids:
§ 152(f)(3).
John T. Untermann, 38 T.C. 93 (1962).

Use the tax resources of the Internet to address the following questions. Do not restrict your search to the Web, but include a review of newsgroups and general reference materials, practitioner sites and resources, primary sources of the tax law, chat rooms and discussion groups, and other opportunities.

Internet Activity

Research Problem 10. Go to **www.legalbitstream.com**, and find the case in which Mark Spitz, the Olympic gold medalist, is the petitioner. Answer the following questions.

    a. What tax years are at issue in the case?

    b. In what year was the case decided?

    c. What tax issues were involved? Did the court decide in favor of Spitz or the IRS?

    d. Were any penalties imposed on the taxpayer? Why or why not?

Communications   **Research Problem 11.** Find three blogs related to tax practice. On one PowerPoint slide, list the URLs for each blog and the general topical areas addressed at each. Send your slide to the others in your course.

Communications   **Research Problem 12.** Find one instance of each of the following using a nonsubscription site on the Web or an online library at your school. In an e-mail to your professor, give a full citation for the document and describe how you found it.

a. Letter Ruling.

b. Action on Decision.

c. IRS Notice.

d. Revenue Ruling.

e. Revenue Procedure.

f. Code Section.

g. Tax Regulation.

h. Tax treaty.

i. Tax Court Summary Opinion.

j. Tax Court Regular decision.

CHAPTER

3

Taxes on the Financial Statements

LEARNING OBJECTIVES: *After completing Chapter 3, you should be able to:*

LO.1 Enumerate the differences between book and tax methods of computing income tax expense.

LO.2 Compute a corporation's book income tax expense.

LO.3 Describe the purpose of the valuation allowance.

LO.4 Interpret the disclosure information contained in the financial statements.

LO.5 Identify the GAAP treatment concerning tax uncertainties and unrepatriated foreign earnings.

LO.6 Use financial statement income tax information to benchmark a company's tax position.

CHAPTER OUTLINE

TAX TALK *Truth is, figuring out how much tax a company actually pays is impossible.... Tax disclosure is just inscrutable.* —ROBERT WILLENS

© PUKHOV KONSTANTIN/SHUTTERSTOCK.COM

TAXES ON THE FINANCIAL STATEMENTS

Raymond Jones, the CEO of Arctic Corporation, would like some help reconciling the amount of income tax expense on Arctic's financial statements with the amount of income tax reported on the company's corporate income tax return for its first year of operations. Mr. Jones does not understand why he can't simply multiply the financial statement income by the company's 35 percent marginal tax rate to get the financial tax expense. While the financial statements show book income before tax of $25 million, the reported Federal tax expense is only $7.7 million. In addition, the corporate tax return reports taxable income of $19 million and Federal income taxes payable of $6.65 million ($19 million × 35%).

Without knowing the specifics of the company's financial statements, does Arctic's situation look reasonable? Why is Arctic's financial tax expense not equal to $8.75 million ($25 million × 35%)? What causes the $1.05 million difference between the taxes shown on the financial statements and the taxes due on the tax return?

Read the chapter and formulate your response.

The ultimate result of the many tax planning ideas, advice, and compliance efforts provided by tax professionals to their clients is captured in a simple summary number—income tax expense. A U.S. corporation's tax expense is reported in its annual Federal tax return, its financial statements, and other regulatory filings and is often the starting point for state and local tax returns. As it turns out, however, deriving a corporation's income tax expense is not so simple.

A corporation may report millions of dollars in tax expense in its financial statements and yet pay virtually nothing to the U.S., state, or foreign governments. Alternatively, a corporation may pay substantial amounts to the U.S., state, and foreign governments and report very little income tax expense in its financial statements. Why do such differences exist? Which income tax expense is the "correct" number? How can data regarding a corporation's income tax expense provide valuable information for the corporation, its competitors, and tax professionals assisting in the planning function? This chapter addresses these questions.

3-1 BOOK-TAX DIFFERENCES

LO.1

Enumerate the differences between book and tax methods of computing income tax expense.

A significant difference may exist between a corporation's Federal income tax liability as reported on its Form 1120 (tax) and the corporation's income tax expense as reported on its financial statements (book) prepared using generally accepted accounting principles (GAAP). This book-tax difference is caused by one or more of the following.

- Differences in reporting entities included in the calculation.
- Different definition of taxes included in the income tax expense amount.
- Different accounting methods.

A corporation's activities are captured in its accounting records, producing general ledger results. At the end of the year, these records are summarized to produce a trial balance. Adjustments to these accounting data may be necessary to produce both the corporation's financial statements and its corporate income tax return. These book and tax adjustments rarely match. Different entities may be included in the reports, and the book and tax rules can be quite different. For instance, GAAP includes a materiality principle, under which some items can be ignored if they are insignificant in amount. The tax law includes no similar materiality threshold: all items are material in computing taxable income.

On a tax return, Schedule M–1 or M–3 reconciles the differences between an entity's book income and its taxable income. See Exhibit 3.1.

3-1a Different Reporting Entities

A corporate group must consolidate all U.S. and foreign subsidiaries within a single financial statement for book purposes when the parent corporation controls more than 50 percent of the voting power of those subsidiaries.[1] In cases where the parent corporation owns between 20 and 50 percent of another corporation, the parent uses the equity method to account for the earnings of the subsidiary. Under the equity method, the parent currently records its share of the subsidiary's income or loss for the year.[2] Corporations that own less than 20 percent of other corporations typically use the *cost method* to account for income from these investments and include income only when actual dividends are received.

---

[1]*Consolidation*, ASC Topic 810 (formerly *Consolidation of All Majority Owned Subsidiaries*, Statement of Financial Accounting Standards No. 94). Certain adjustments are made to reduce book income for the after-tax income related to minority shareholders.

[2]*Investments—Equity Method and Joint Ventures*, ASC Topic 323 (formerly *The Equity Method of Accounting for Investments in Common Stock*, Accounting Principles Board Opinion No. 18).

EXHIBIT 3.1	Flow of Accounting Data

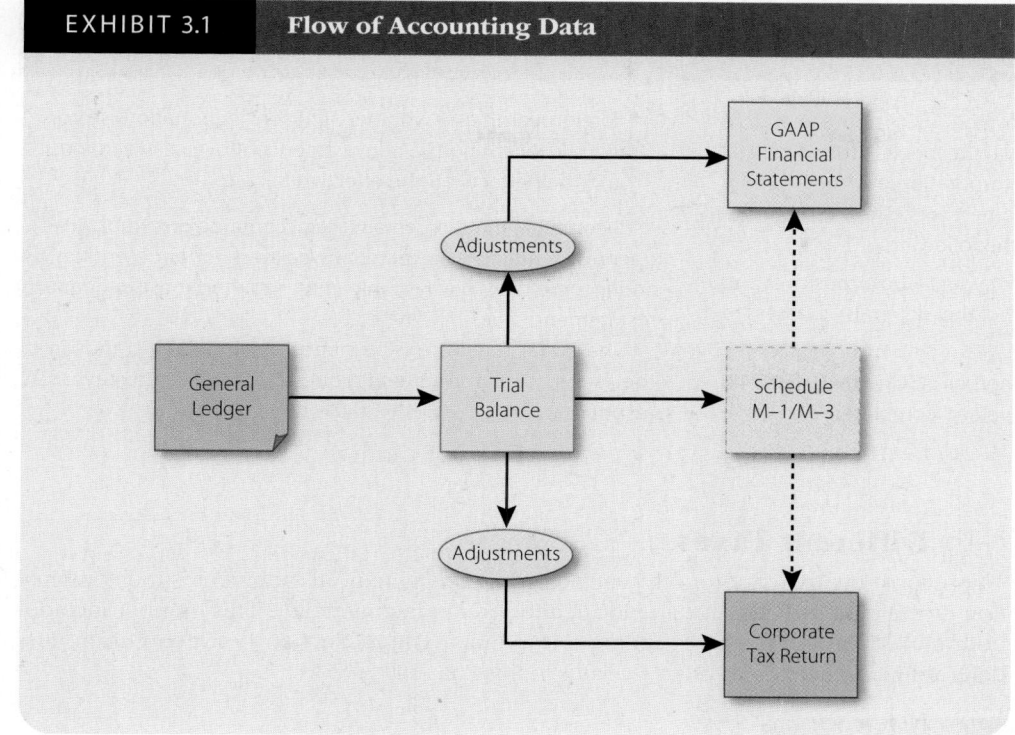

Return to the facts of *The Big Picture* on p. 3-1. Arctic Corporation owns 100% of Gator, Inc., a domestic corporation; 100% of Hurricane, Ltd., a foreign corporation; and 40% of Beach, Inc., a domestic corporation. Arctic's combined financial statement includes its own net income and the net income of both Gator and Hurricane. In addition, Arctic's financial statement includes its 40% share of Beach's net income. Arctic's financial statement includes the income of these subsidiaries regardless of whether Arctic receives any actual profit distributions from its subsidiaries.

EXAMPLE 1

For Federal income tax purposes, a U.S. corporation may elect to include in its consolidated U.S. tax return any *domestic* subsidiaries that are 80 percent or more owned.[3] On the other hand, the income of non-U.S. subsidiaries and less than 80 percent owned domestic subsidiaries is not included in the consolidated tax return.

Return to the facts of *The Big Picture* on p. 3-1. Also assume the facts presented in Example 1. If Arctic elects to include Gator as part of its consolidated Federal income tax return, Arctic's return includes its own taxable income and the taxable income generated by Gator. Hurricane's taxable income is not included in the consolidated return because it is a non-U.S. corporation. Beach, although a domestic corporation, cannot be consolidated with Arctic because Arctic owns only 40% of the stock. Income from Hurricane and Beach will be included in Arctic's U.S. taxable income only when Arctic receives actual or constructive dividends from those two companies.

EXAMPLE 2

[3]§§ 1501–1504. An election to consolidate an 80% or more owned subsidiary generally can be changed only with the permission of the IRS.

TAX IN THE NEWS   The Watchdog Is Watching

A recent report by the SEC listed the watchdog agency's areas of focus with respect to the financial statements of publicly traded corporations as they pertain to issues in accounting for income taxes. The most important of the focus areas include the following.

- Realizability of deferred tax assets—how positive and negative evidence supporting the deferrals is assessed by the taxpayer.

- Uncertain tax positions—whether ASC 740-10 (FIN 48) disclosures are comprehensive and complete.

- Foreign earnings—whether sufficient information is provided concerning the reinvestments of overseas earnings and their effects on the effective tax rate.

Income tax matters remain the accounting area most frequently identified as a material weakness for large entities, and income taxes always rank among the ten most frequent restatement issues.

The Edgar database is a good place to follow trends in the agency's information requests and the taxpayer's responses.

3-1b Different Taxes

The income tax expense reported on a corporation's financial statement is the combination of the entity's Federal, state, local, and foreign income taxes. This number includes both current and deferred tax expense amounts. The distinction between current and deferred income taxes is discussed later in this chapter.

The Big Picture

EXAMPLE 3

Return to the facts of *The Big Picture* on p. 3-1. Also assume the facts presented in Example 1. For book purposes, Arctic, Gator, and Hurricane combine their income and expenses into a single financial statement. The book tax expense for the year includes all Federal, state, local, and foreign income taxes paid or accrued by these three corporations. In addition, the book tax expense amount includes any future Federal, state, local, or foreign income tax expenses (or tax savings) on income reported in the current income statement.

The income tax expense computed on the Federal income tax return is only the U.S. *Federal* income tax expense. This amount is based on the U.S. corporation's taxable income. State and local income taxes are reported on the Federal tax return, but as deductions in arriving at taxable income.

The Big Picture

EXAMPLE 4

Return to the facts of *The Big Picture* on p. 3-1. Also assume the facts presented in Examples 1 and 2. Arctic and Gator file a consolidated Federal tax return. The tax expense reported on the Form 1120 is only the U.S. Federal income tax expense for the consolidated taxable income of Arctic and Gator. This tax expense does not include the income taxes that Arctic and its subsidiaries paid to state, local, or foreign governments.

3-1c Different Methods

Many differences exist between book and tax accounting methods. Some are **temporary differences**, with income and expenses appearing in both the financial statement and the tax return, but in different periods (i.e., a timing difference). Others are **permanent differences**, with items appearing in the financial statement or the tax return, but not both.

Temporary differences include the following.

- *Depreciation on fixed assets*. Taxpayers may use an accelerated depreciation method under the modified accelerated cost recovery system (MACRS) rules but a straight-line method for book purposes. Even if identical methods are used, the period over which the asset is depreciated may differ between book and tax.

- *Compensation-related expenses*. Generally, the tax law does not allow for the use of estimates or reserves, as is common under GAAP. For example, under GAAP, corporations accrue the future expenses related to providing postretirement benefits other than pensions (e.g., health insurance coverage). However, these expenses are deductible for tax purposes only when paid.

- *Accrued income and expenses*. Although most income and expense items are recognized for tax and book purposes in the same period, a number of items potentially appear in different periods. For example, warranty expenses are accrued for book purposes but are not deductible for tax purposes until incurred. Inventory write-offs are accrued for book but are not deductible for tax until incurred. On the income side, different methods regarding the timing of income recognition may create temporary differences. For instance, GAAP recognizes income and loss when the *fair value* of most investment assets changes during the year, while tax rules recognize such realized gain or loss only upon a sale or other taxable disposition of the asset.

- *Net operating losses*. Taxable income for the year cannot be less than zero; thus, operating losses from one tax year may be used to offset taxable income in another tax year. As a result, the losses incurred in one year for book purposes may be used as a deduction for tax purposes in a different year. No such loss carryovers are used under GAAP; GAAP losses are reported in the year incurred.

- *Intangible assets*. Goodwill and some other intangibles are not amortizable for book purposes. However, GAAP requires an annual determination of whether the intangible asset has suffered a reduction in value (i.e., impairment).[4] If an intangible has suffered an impairment, a current expense is required to reduce the asset's book value to the lower level. For tax purposes, certain intangibles (including goodwill) can be amortized over 15 years.[5]

Permanent differences include the following.

- *Nontaxable income*. A common example is municipal bond interest, which is income for book purposes but is not taxable.

- *Nondeductible expenses*. For example, the disallowed portion of meals and entertainment expense and certain penalties are not deductible for tax purposes, but they are expensed in arriving at book income.[6]

- *Special tax deductions*. GAAP does not allow expenses for certain income tax deductions, such as the domestic production activities deduction (DPAD) and the dividends-received deduction.

- *Tax credits*. Credits such as the research activities credit reduce Federal income tax liability but have no corresponding book treatment. Tax credits are discussed in Chapter 17.

In-depth coverage can be found on this book's companion website: www.cengagebrain.com   **1 DIGGING DEEPER**

---

[4]*Intangibles—Goodwill and Other*, ASC Topic 350 (formerly *Goodwill and Other Intangible Assets*, Statement of Financial Accounting Standards No. 142).

[5]§ 197.

[6]Federal income tax liabilities are another example of this type of permanent book-tax difference.

FINANCIAL DISCLOSURE INSIGHTS **Supersized Goodwill**

When a balance sheet includes an asset value for goodwill, the company's total valuation is seen to exceed the aggregate value of its physical assets, such as cash and equipment. Goodwill typically is created as the result of the takeover of a target entity in an acquisition transaction.

GAAP rules concerning goodwill and its impairment evolved in a context of stable market values and managed income. But when goodwill gets to be so large that it is a major asset in itself, are GAAP impairment write-downs sure to follow?

An impairment write-down often is an indication that an acquiror overpaid for the target entity in a takeover transaction. Thus, conglomerates that grow by a series of acquisitions may be doubly exposed to goodwill write-downs. Accordingly, goodwill and its impairment can

become an outsized element of the financial statements for many companies.

In a recent year, the following data concerning recorded goodwill were reported.

Company	Goodwill as a % of Total Value
Frontier Communications	165.7
Republic Services	108.8
Time Warner	80.8
Kraft Foods	54.3
Dow Chemical	34.2
Dr Pepper Snapple Group	32.2
Starbucks Corporation	0.8
Netflix	0.0

EXAMPLE 5

Wise, Inc., reported the following results for the current year.

Book income (before tax)	$ 685,000
Tax depreciation in excess of book	(125,000)
Nondeductible warranty expense	65,000
Municipal bond interest income	(35,000)
Taxable income (Form 1120)	$ 590,000

Wise reports net income before tax of $685,000 on its financial statement but must adjust this amount for differences between book and tax income.

Tax depreciation in excess of book is a tax deduction not currently expensed for book purposes, and warranty expense is deductible for book purposes but not yet deductible for tax. Both of these items are temporary differences, because they eventually reverse (with book depreciation eventually exceeding tax depreciation and the warranty expense ultimately deducted for tax when incurred).

The municipal bond interest is a permanent difference because this income will never be subject to tax.

3-1d **Tax Return Disclosures**

Book-tax differences are reported in the Federal income tax returns of most business entities.

Exhibit 3.2 contains the **Schedule M–1** from Form 1120, the corporate income tax return. The purpose of Schedule M–1 is to reconcile book income to the taxable income as reported on the tax return. Line 1 is the net income or loss per books, and line 2 adds back the book tax expense to get back to book income before tax.[7] The remainder of Schedule M–1 contains adjustments for both temporary and permanent differences, until arriving at taxable income on line 10.[8]

Schedule M–3 is required for a consolidated tax group with total year-end assets of $50 million or more. The Schedule M–3 provides the IRS with more detailed

---

[7]Line 1, "Net income (loss) per books," is not defined in the instructions to the form, and corporations can use various starting points in the Schedule M–1 (e.g., only the book income from U.S. members of the group). The Schedule M–3 is more specific in defining book income.

[8]Form 1120, page 1, line 28 represents corporate taxable income before subtracting the net operating loss and dividends-received deductions.

EXHIBIT 3.2	Schedule M–1

Schedule M–1   **Reconciliation of Income (Loss) per Books With Income per Return**

Note: The corporation may be required to file Schedule M-3 (see instructions).

1	Net income (loss) per books	
2	Federal income tax per books	
3	Excess of capital losses over capital gains .	
4	Income subject to tax not recorded on books this year (itemize):_____	
	_____	
5	Expenses recorded on books this year not deducted on this return (itemize):	
a	Depreciation . . . . $_____	
b	Charitable contributions . $_____	
c	Travel and entertainment . $_____	
	_____	
6	Add lines 1 through 5	

7	Income recorded on books this year not included on this return (itemize):	
	Tax-exempt interest $_____	
	_____	
	_____	
8	Deductions on this return not charged against book income this year (itemize):	
a	Depreciation . . $_____	
b	Charitable contributions $_____	
	_____	
	_____	
9	Add lines 7 and 8	
10	Income (page 1, line 28)—line 6 less line 9	

information than is provided in the Schedule M–1. In addition, the Schedule M–3 requires identification of whether a book-tax difference is temporary or permanent.

Schedule M–1 or M–3 typically is the starting point for IRS audits of corporations. Identifying large differences between book and taxable income may offer the IRS auditor insights into tax saving strategies (some perhaps questionable) employed by the taxpayer. See Chapter 12 for additional discussion of the Schedules M–1 and M–3. Concept Summary 3.1 summarizes the sources of typical corporate book-tax differences.

In-depth coverage can be found on this book's companion website: www.cengagebrain.com    **2   DIGGING DEEPER**

Concept Summary 3.1

Income Reporting: Book versus Tax

Financial Statement	U.S. Federal Income Tax Return
Reporting entities	**Reporting entities**
• 50% or more owned domestic and foreign subsidiaries *must* be consolidated.	• 80% or more owned domestic subsidiaries *may* be consolidated.
• Share of income from 20 to 50% owned domestic and foreign corporations included in current income.	• Share of income from other corporations reported only when actual or constructive dividends are received.
Income tax expense	**Income tax expense**
• Federal income taxes.	• Federal income taxes.
• State income taxes.	• Current only.
• Local income taxes.	
• Foreign income taxes.	
• Current and deferred.	
Methods	**Methods**
• Temporary differences.	• Temporary differences.
• Permanent differences.	• Permanent differences.
• Income tax note reconciliation.	• Schedule M–1 or M–3 reconciliation.

TAX FACT   The World of Schedule UTP

Some observations can be made about the Schedules UTP that large corporations file with the IRS.

Number of taxpayers filing a Schedule UTP for the tax year	About 2,300
Average number of tax positions reported on the Schedule UTP	2 per return
Percentage of uncertain positions that involved international tax issues	25%, most of which involved transfer pricing computations
Three most commonly encountered tax issues disclosed on Schedules UTP	(1) Research credit
	(2) Transfer pricing
	(3) Business deductions *vs.* capitalization
Uncertain tax positions of S&P 500 companies	Net Total: $200 billion
	Net Annual Increase: $ 20 billion

Uncertain Tax Positions

The IRS requires that large corporations list the tax return positions they have taken that may not be fully supported by the law. Schedule UTP ("uncertain tax positions") is added to the Form 1120 for all corporations with assets of at least $10 million.

Some tax professionals worry that the Schedule UTP alerts the IRS to specific items that will be most vulnerable to audit adjustments. Because tax returns are confidential documents, though, the public does not have access to a corporation's Schedule UTP.

Disclosures on the Schedule UTP include a list of tax return positions for the current and prior tax years where:

- The taxpayer or a related party recorded a reserve against the Federal income tax expense on its audited financial statements, or
- There was no recorded tax reserve based on its analysis of expected litigation with the IRS. This means that in the taxpayer's view, the probability of settling the issue with the IRS in the taxpayer's favor is less than 50 percent, and the taxpayer determines that it is *more likely than not* (a greater than 50 percent likelihood) to prevail on the merits of the issue in litigation.

Disclosures are not required for items that are immaterial under GAAP rules, or for which the filing position is sufficiently certain that no financial accounting reserve is required.

The IRS maintains that it will limit releases of the Schedule UTP to other taxing jurisdictions, and that it will not use Schedule UTP data to usurp the attorney-client and tax practitioner privileges of confidentiality or the work-product doctrine. Taxpayers are not required to disclose the amounts of any reserves or the precise nature of the tax planning technique that led to the reserve for the filing position.

For some taxpayers, income taxes reported on Schedules UTP are low, because they are "less aggressive" in making filing decisions, or because they negotiate with the IRS before filing a return as to certain deductions and credits. For other taxpayers, the uncertain positions are large enough to significantly reduce or eliminate altogether the tax liability for the year (i.e., if the IRS agrees in negotiations that the disputed deduction or credit is fully or largely to be allowed).

LO.2

Compute a corporation's book income tax expense.

3-2 INCOME TAXES IN THE FINANCIAL STATEMENTS

3-2a GAAP Principles

As mentioned earlier, a corporation's financial statements are prepared in accordance with GAAP. The purpose and objectives of these statements are quite different from the objective of the corporation's income tax return.

FINANCIAL DISCLOSURE INSIGHTS   **The Book-Tax Income Gap**

The corporate financial scandals of Enron and others have heightened interest in whether corporations are making appropriate disclosures (i.e., transparency) and in whether they are shouldering their fair share of the tax burden. In some years, the gap between book income and taxable income seems to be growing.

According to one study, 115 companies in the Standard and Poor's stock index incurred a Federal and state income tax rate of less than 20 percent. In fact, the rate for 39 of those companies was less than 10 percent.

At least 30 of the Fortune 500 companies paid zero or negative Federal corporate income taxes over a recent three-year period. These companies included General Electric, American Electric Power, FedEx, Honeywell, Pfizer, Verizon, Boeing, and PG&E. Pepco Holdings reported an effective Federal income tax rate of *negative* 57.6 percent!

The firms maintained that they had paid all of their required tax liabilities, and that a poor economy and effective income tax planning had resulted in their zero or negative effective tax rates.

Corporations further maintain that the large differences in book and tax income are a function of the different rules and objectives of GAAP for financial statements and the Internal Revenue Code for tax returns.

Low effective tax rates often are traceable to one or more of the following.

- Use of NOL carryovers.
- Large investments in depreciable assets.
- Use of state, local, federal, and international tax incentives (e.g., to encourage new companies and targeted industries such as high-tech, energy, and domestic manufacturing).
- Use of temporary tax provisions (e.g., stimulus, anti-recession, or other rules designed to stimulate the economy via tax cuts).
- Negotiations and settlements with revenue agencies.[9]
- Application of legal tax planning techniques.

The **ASC 740 (SFAS 109)** approach produces a total income tax expense (also called the **income tax provision**) for the income currently reported on a corporation's combined financial statement.[10] This approach follows the matching principle, where all of the expenses related to earning income are reported in the same period as the income without regard to when the expenses are actually paid.

EXAMPLE 6

PanCo, Inc., earns $100,000 in book income before tax and is subject to a 35% marginal Federal income tax rate. PanCo records a single temporary difference. Tax depreciation exceeds book depreciation by $20,000. Accordingly, PanCo's taxable income is $80,000 ($100,000 − $20,000 additional tax deduction).

On its income tax return, PanCo reports total Federal tax expense of $28,000 ($80,000 × 35%). On its financial statement, PanCo reports a total tax expense of $35,000 ($100,000 × 35%). This $7,000 book-tax difference is the difference between the book and tax basis of the depreciable asset times the current corporate tax rate ($7,000 = $20,000 × 35%).

Although PanCo did not actually pay the $7,000 tax this year, in future years when the book-tax depreciation difference reverses, the $7,000 eventually will be paid. Hence, the *future* income tax expense is matched to the related book income and is reported in the current year.

The total book tax expense under ASC 740 (SFAS 109) is made up of both current and deferred components. The **current tax expense** theoretically represents the taxes actually payable to (or refund receivable from) the governmental authorities for the current period.

---

[9]For instance, AstraZeneca recently reduced its effective tax rate after settling an audit with U.S. and U.K. tax authorities about its transfer pricing policies (see Chapter 16). The taxpayer's liability after the settlement was less than the tax reserve it had set aside on its GAAP statements with respect to the audit.

[10]*Income Taxes*, ASC Topic 740 (formerly *Accounting for Income Taxes*, Statement of Financial Accounting Standards No. 109).

GLOBAL TAX ISSUES   **Accounting for Income Taxes in International Standards**

The FASB and the International Accounting Standards Board (IASB) have worked to move the GAAP and IFRS treatment of income taxes closer together in light of the proposed convergence of GAAP and IFRS. Both ASC 740 (SFAS 109) and IAS 12 (the IFRS guidance for income taxes) are based on a balance sheet approach.

Nevertheless, several significant differences exist between the two standards. These include the thresholds for recognition and approach to valuation allowances, the treatment of foreign subsidiaries and undistributed earnings, and the measurement of uncertain tax positions.[11]

One might think of this amount as the actual check the taxpayer writes to the government (or refund received) for the current year. Exhibit 3.3 summarizes the computation of a corporation's current tax expense.

The deferred component of the book tax expense is called the **deferred tax expense** or **deferred tax benefit**. This component represents the future tax cost (or savings) connected with income reported in the current-period financial statement. Deferred tax expense or benefit is created as a result of temporary differences. More technically, ASC 740 (SFAS 109) adopts a **balance sheet approach** to measuring deferred taxes. Under this approach, the deferred tax expense or benefit is the change from one year to the next in the net **deferred tax liability** or **deferred tax asset**.

A deferred tax liability is the expected future tax liability related to current income (measured using enacted tax rates and rules). A deferred tax liability is created in the following situations.

- An item is deductible for tax in the current period but is not expensed for book until some future period.

- Income is includible currently for book purposes but is not includible in taxable income until a future period.

In essence, a deferred tax liability is created when the book basis of an asset exceeds its tax basis (the opposite condition creates a deferred tax asset).

EXHIBIT 3.3	Current Tax Expense*

	Pretax book income
±	Schedule M–1/M–3 adjustments
	Taxable income before NOLs
−	NOL carryforwards
	Taxable income
×	Applicable tax rate
	Current tax expense (provision) before tax credits
−	Tax credits
	Current tax expense (tax provision)

*Simplified calculation.

---

[11]One can keep up with the FASB and the IASB's work on the "Income Tax Project" by visiting the FASB website at **www.fasb.org** and searching for the "Technical Plan and Project Updates" section under "Projects."

Deferred Tax Expense

PJ Enterprises earns net income before depreciation of $500,000 in 2014 and $600,000 in 2015. PJ uses a single depreciable asset acquired in 2014 for $80,000. For tax purposes, PJ may deduct $60,000 in depreciation expense for the first year and $20,000 in depreciation expense for the second year (i.e., it uses an accelerated method). For book purposes, PJ depreciates the asset on a straight-line basis over two years ($40,000 depreciation expense per year).

EXAMPLE 7

2014

	Book	Tax
Income before depreciation	$500,000	$500,000
Depreciation	(40,000)	(60,000)
Income after depreciation	$460,000	$440,000
Corporate tax rate	× 35%	× 35%
Income tax expense/payable	$161,000	$154,000
Current tax expense	$154,000	
Deferred tax expense	$ 7,000	
Starting adjusted basis in depreciable asset	$ 80,000	$ 80,000
Ending adjusted basis in depreciable asset	(40,000)	(20,000)
Change in adjusted basis	$ 40,000	$ 60,000

Book-tax balance sheet difference	$20,000	
Corporate tax rate	× 35%	
Deferred tax liability	$ 7,000	

In this example, it is easy to "back into" the deferred tax expense amount of $7,000 by taking the difference between the tax payable per the tax return ($154,000) and the book tax expense ($161,000). This method is referred to as the "APB 11" approach, as it applies to the method used before ASC 740 (SFAS 109). Although this method may provide a quick check on the calculation in simple cases, it is not always correct. Be careful to calculate the deferred tax expense using the difference between the book and tax asset basis numbers ($20,000) at the enacted corporate tax rate (35%).

2015

	Book	Tax
Income before depreciation	$600,000	$600,000
Depreciation	(40,000)	(20,000)
Income after depreciation	$560,000	$580,000
Corporate tax rate	× 35%	× 35%
Income tax expense/payable	$196,000	$203,000
Current tax expense	$203,000	
Deferred tax expense	($ 7,000)	
Starting adjusted basis in depreciable asset	$ 40,000	$ 20,000
Ending adjusted basis in depreciable asset	(−0−)	(−0−)
Change in adjusted basis	$ 40,000	$ 20,000

Book-tax balance sheet difference	($20,000)	
Corporate tax rate	× 35%	
Deferred tax liability	($ 7,000)	

In 2015, the book-tax difference in the asset basis reverses, with a resulting reduction of the deferred tax liability account.

Deferred Tax Expense

EXAMPLE 8

Continue with the facts in Example 7. The following journal entries record the book tax expense (provision) for each year. The book total tax expense combines the current amount (income tax payable) and the future amount (deferred tax liability).

2014 Journal Entry

Income tax expense (provision)	$161,000	
Income tax payable		$154,000
Deferred tax liability		7,000

2015 Journal Entry

Income tax expense (provision)	$196,000	
Deferred tax liability	7,000	
Income tax payable		$203,000

At the end of 2014, the PJ balance sheet reflects a net deferred tax liability of $7,000. At the end of 2015, the balance sheet contains a zero deferred tax liability; the temporary difference that created the deferred tax liability has reversed itself.

A deferred tax asset is the expected future tax benefit related to current book income (measured using enacted tax rates and rules). A deferred tax asset is created in the following situations.

- An expense is claimed for book purposes in the current period but is not deductible for tax until some future period.
- Income is includible in taxable income currently but is not recorded as book income until a future period.

Deferred Tax Assets

EXAMPLE 9

MollCo, Inc., earns net income before warranty expense of $400,000 in 2014 and $450,000 in 2015. In 2014, MollCo deducts $30,000 in warranty expense for book purposes related to expected warranty repairs. This warranty expense is not deductible for tax purposes until actually incurred. Assume that the $30,000 warranty expense is paid in 2015, and that this is MollCo's only temporary difference.

2014

	Book	Tax
Income before warranty expense	$400,000	$400,000
Warranty expense	(30,000)	—
Income after warranty expense	$370,000	$400,000
Corporate tax rate	× 35%	× 35%
Income tax expense/payable	$129,500	$140,000
Current tax expense	$140,000	
Deferred tax expense	($ 10,500)	
Basis in warranty expense payable	$ 30,000	$ −0−
Book-tax balance sheet difference	($30,000)	
Corporate tax rate	× 35%	
Deferred tax asset	($10,500)	

Once again, it is easy to "back into" the deferred tax expense amount of $10,500 by taking the difference between the tax payable per the tax return ($140,000) and the book tax expense

continued

($129,500). However, the correct computation of the deferred tax expense is based on the difference between the book and tax basis in the balance sheet warranty expense payable ($30,000) at the corporate tax rate (35%).

2015	Book	Tax
Income before warranty expense	$450,000	$450,000
Warranty expense	—	(30,000)
Income after depreciation	$450,000	$420,000
Corporate tax rate	× 35%	× 35%
Income tax expense/payable	$157,500	$147,000
Current tax expense	$147,000	
Deferred tax expense	$ 10,500	
Basis in warranty expense payable	$ –0–	$ 30,000
Book-tax balance sheet difference		$30,000
Corporate tax rate		× 35%
Deferred tax asset		$10,500

In 2015, the book-tax difference in the warranty expense payable reverses, with a resulting elimination of the deferred tax asset account.

Deferred Tax Assets

EXAMPLE 10

Continue with the facts in Example 9. The following journal entries record the book tax expense (provision) for each year. Notice that the book total tax expense combines the current amount (income tax payable) and the future amount (deferred tax asset).

2014 Journal Entry

Income tax expense (provision)	$129,500	
Deferred tax asset	10,500	
Income tax payable		$140,000

2015 Journal Entry

Income tax expense (provision)	$157,500	
Deferred tax asset		$ 10,500
Income tax payable		147,000

At the end of 2014, the MollCo balance sheet reflects a net deferred tax asset of $10,500. At the end of 2015, the MollCo balance sheet contains a zero deferred tax asset; the temporary difference that created the deferred tax asset has reversed itself.

Deferred tax assets and liabilities are reported on the balance sheet just as any other asset or liability would be. However, the interpretation of these assets and liabilities is quite different. Typically, an asset is "good" because it represents a claim on something of value, and a liability is "bad" because it represents a future claim against the corporation's assets. In the case of deferred tax assets and liabilities, the interpretation is reversed. Deferred tax liabilities are "good" because they represent an amount that may be paid to the government in the future.

In essence, deferred tax liabilities are like an interest-free loan from the government with a due date perhaps many years in the future. Deferred tax assets, on the other hand, are future tax benefits and thus are similar to a receivable from the government that may not be received until many years in the future.

Describe the purpose of the valuation allowance.

3-2b Valuation Allowance

Much of GAAP is based on the conservatism principle . That is, accounting rules are designed to provide assurance that assets are not overstated and liabilities are not understated. Current recognition of deferred tax liabilities does not require significant professional judgment because future tax liabilities always are expected to be settled in full. However, under ASC 740 (SFAS 109), deferred tax assets are recognized only when it is *more likely than not* (a greater than 50 percent likelihood) that the future tax benefits will be realized.

EXAMPLE 11

Warren, Inc., reported book income before tax of $2 million in 2015. Warren's taxable income also is $2 million (i.e., there are no temporary or permanent differences). Warren reports a current U.S. income tax liability for 2015 of $700,000 before tax credits ($2 million × 35%). During 2015, Warren paid $100,000 in foreign income taxes that it is not able to use as a credit on its 2015 tax return because of the foreign tax credit (FTC) limitation (see Chapter 16).

Warren's auditors believe it is *more likely than not* that Warren will be able to use the $100,000 in FTCs within the next 10 years before they expire. Consequently, the future tax benefit of the FTCs is accounted for in the current-year book tax expense as a $100,000 future tax benefit.

The current and deferred tax expense are calculated as follows.

	Book	Tax
Income tax expense/payable	$600,000	$700,000
Current tax expense	$700,000	
Deferred tax expense (benefit)	($100,000)	

Warren records the following journal entry for the book income tax expense and deferred tax asset related to the expected use of the FTCs.

Income tax expense (provision)	$600,000	
Deferred tax asset	100,000	
Income tax payable		$700,000

Because Warren is able to record the benefit of the future FTCs, its effective tax rate is 30% ($600,000 tax expense/$2 million book income before tax).

When a deferred tax asset does not meet the *more likely than not* threshold for recognition, ASC 740 (SFAS 109) requires that a valuation allowance be created. The valuation allowance is a contra-asset account that offsets all or a portion of the deferred tax asset.

EXAMPLE 12

Assume that the auditors in Example 11 believe that Warren will be able to use only $40,000 of the FTCs, with the remaining $60,000 expiring. In this case, the future tax benefit recognized currently should be only $40,000 rather than the full $100,000. To implement this reduction in the deferred tax asset, Warren records a valuation allowance of $60,000, resulting in a book tax expense of $660,000.

	Book	Tax
Income tax expense/payable	$660,000	$700,000
Current tax expense	$700,000	
Deferred tax expense (benefit)	($ 40,000)	

continued

Warren records the following journal entry for the book income tax expense and deferred tax asset related to the expected use of the FTCs.

Income tax expense (provision)	$660,000	
Deferred tax asset	100,000	
Valuation allowance		$ 60,000
Income tax payable		700,000

Warren reduces the deferred tax asset by $60,000, which increases its effective tax rate to 33% ($660,000 tax expense/$2 million book income before tax), compared with the 30% effective tax rate in Example 11.

To determine whether a valuation allowance is required, both positive and negative evidence must be evaluated. Negative evidence (i.e., evidence suggesting that the deferred tax asset will not be realized) includes the following.

- History of losses.
- Expected future losses.
- Short carryback/carryforward periods.
- History of tax credits expiring unused.

Positive evidence (i.e., support for realizing the current benefit of future tax savings) includes the following.

- Strong earnings history.
- Existing contracts.
- Unrealized appreciation in assets.
- Sales backlog of profitable orders.

The valuation allowance is examined for appropriateness each year. The allowance may be increased or decreased in subsequent reporting periods if facts and circumstances change.

The Big Picture

EXAMPLE 13

Return to the facts of *The Big Picture* on p. 3-1. Arctic Corporation has recorded a $3 million deferred tax asset for an NOL carryforward. The deferred tax asset has been offset by a $1 million valuation allowance, due to doubts over the levels of future sales and profitability.

But this year, Arctic completed improvements to its inventory management system that are likely to increase the contribution margin of every product that Arctic sells. In addition, two of Arctic's largest customers have secured financing that will relieve the financial difficulties that have restricted them. In fact, Arctic just received purchase orders from those customers that will increase unit sales by 20% over the next 18 months. As a result, Arctic's auditors now support a release of $200,000 of the valuation allowance in the current quarter.

In-depth coverage can be found on this book's companion website: www.cengagebrain.com   **3 DIGGING DEEPER**

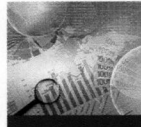

TAX PLANNING STRATEGIES **Releasing Valuation Allowances**

FRAMEWORK FOCUS: DEDUCTIONS

Strategy: Maximize Deductible Amounts.

When a corporation records a valuation allowance, it loses the ability to recognize the benefit of future tax savings in the current period. However, all is not lost if the taxpayer can demonstrate that facts and circumstances have changed. For example, if a taxpayer generates a net operating loss (NOL), it records a deferred tax asset for the future tax savings related to using the NOL. However, if the evidence suggests that it is *more likely than not* that the NOL will expire unused, a valuation allowance must be recorded.

To reduce this valuation allowance, the taxpayer must demonstrate that there will be future taxable income sufficient to absorb the NOL within the carryforward period. Sources of future taxable income include reversals of temporary differences that will produce future taxable income and other sources of future profits. Taxpayers also may demonstrate that the adoption of new tax planning strategies will allow the use of deferred tax assets.

For example, assume that Warren, Inc., from Example 12, adopts new planning strategies in 2016 that will allow it ultimately to use all $100,000 of its FTC carryforward. Warren earns $2.3 million in book income before tax and reports $2.3 million in taxable income in 2016 (i.e., no permanent or temporary differences). The current tax expense is $805,000 ($2.3 million × 35%).

Based on new evidence (implementation of tax planning strategies), the auditors determine that the entire $100,000

in FTCs will be used in the future before expiration. Accordingly, the $60,000 valuation allowance from 2015 is "released," and the tax benefit of this release affects the 2016 financial results as follows.

	Book	Tax
Income tax expense/payable	$745,000	$805,000
Current tax expense	$805,000	
Deferred tax expense	($ 60,000)	

Warren makes the following journal entry to record the book income tax expense and valuation allowance release related to the expected use of the FTCs.

Income tax expense (provision)	$745,000	
Valuation allowance	60,000	
Income tax payable		$805,000

Warren's effective tax rate for 2016 is 32.4 percent ($745,000/$2.3 million). Without the valuation allowance release, Warren's effective tax rate would have been 35 percent ($805,000/$2.3 million). This tax rate benefit is realized even though the $100,000 in FTC carryforwards have yet to be used in Warren's tax return.

LO.4

Interpret the disclosure information contained in the financial statements.

3-2c **Tax Disclosures in the Financial Statements**

As illustrated earlier, any temporary differences create deferred tax liabilities or deferred tax assets, and these amounts appear in the corporation's balance sheet.

FINANCIAL DISCLOSURE INSIGHTS **Tax Losses and the Deferred Tax Asset**

Although a current-year net operating loss (NOL) represents a failure of an entity's business model to some, others see it as an immediate tax refund. But when an NOL hits the balance sheet as a deferred tax asset, the story is not over. The NOL creates or increases a deferred tax asset that may or may not be used in future financial accounting reporting periods. The key question for a financial analyst is whether the entity will generate enough net revenue in future years to create a

positive tax liability that can be offset by the NOL carryover amount.

IFRS rules do not allow for a valuation allowance. Under IAS 12, a deferred tax asset is recorded only when it is "probable" (a higher standard than GAAP's "more likely than not") that the deferred tax amount will be realized, and then only to the extent of that probable amount. Thus, no offsetting valuation allowance is needed.

The Balance Sheet

As with any asset or liability, these accounts are classified as either current or noncurrent, based on the assets or liabilities that created the temporary difference. If the deferred tax liability or asset is not related to any asset, then the classification is based on the expected reversal period.

> **EXAMPLE 14**
>
> JenCo, Inc., holds a deferred tax liability generated because tax depreciation exceeds book depreciation on manufacturing equipment. Because the equipment is a noncurrent asset, the deferred tax liability also is noncurrent. JenCo also reports a deferred tax asset related to bad debt expenses deductible for book purposes but not yet deductible for tax purposes. Because the bad debt expense is related to accounts receivable, a current asset, the associated deferred tax asset is classified as current.
>
> If JenCo incurs an NOL, a deferred tax asset is created, because of the future tax benefit provided by the NOL deduction. The NOL is not related to any specific asset or liability. Accordingly, the deferred tax asset is classified based on when the corporation expects to use the NOL. If the expected use is more than one year in the future, the deferred tax asset is classified as noncurrent.

A corporation may hold both deferred tax assets and liabilities, current and noncurrent. The corporation reports the *net* current deferred tax assets or liabilities and the *net* noncurrent deferred tax assets or liabilities.

> **The Big Picture**
>
> **EXAMPLE 15**
>
> Return to the facts of *The Big Picture* on p. 3-1. Arctic Corporation holds the following deferred tax asset and liability accounts for the current year.
>
> | | |
> |---|---|
> | Current deferred tax assets | $50,000 |
> | Current deferred tax liabilities | 72,000 |
> | Noncurrent deferred tax assets | 93,000 |
> | Noncurrent deferred tax liabilities | 28,000 |
>
> On its balance sheet, Arctic reports a $22,000 current net deferred tax liability ($72,000 − $50,000) and a $65,000 noncurrent net deferred tax asset ($93,000 − $28,000).

FINANCIAL DISCLOSURE INSIGHTS   **Valuation Allowances for NOLs**

Financial analysts use the valuation allowance system to help them determine an entity's expected future cash flows. Some critics of the GAAP rules for valuation allowances maintain that the process allows management to manipulate profits and earnings per share in an arbitrary fashion.

Only a few of the largest business entities, supported by going-concern assumptions and access to worldwide debt and equity capital, need to record a sizable valuation allowance. But valuation allowances also often are found in the financial reports of smaller entities and those in volatile industries, whose future profitability is likely to present questions.

In a recent reporting year, for instance, the following telecommunications businesses reported a valuation allowance related to expectations that their NOLs (for Federal and/or state taxing jurisdictions) would expire unused.

	Deferred Tax Assets ($ in 000's)	Valuation Allowance ($ in 000's)
Verizon	$10,750	$2,700
Bell South	2,100	1,100
AT&T	11,400	1,050
SBC Communications	3,900	150

Establishing a valuation allowance does not affect the entity's internal cash balances, but it might have an effect on the stock price. Valuation allowances can be "released" by management when evidence develops that the carryforwards are more likely to be used in the future, for example, if profitability improves and appears to be sustainable. For instance, the homebuilder Toll Brothers created a large valuation allowance when the real estate market collapsed, but it will release the allowance when housing prices stabilize and increase.

TAX FACT   Effective Tax Rates for Selected Fortune 100 Companies

Here are some recent provisions for income taxes (state, federal, and international) made by selected major corporations, as a percentage of their book income before taxes. Recall that the top statutory Federal tax rate is 35%. State and local taxes generally add another 5 percentage points to that rate.

Aetna	34.9%	Disney	33.3%
Apple	24.2	ExxonMobil	44.0
Boeing	34.0	Ford	28.8
Chevron	43.2	General Electric	14.4
Citigroup	0.3	Google	19.4
		IBM	24.2
		JPMorgan Chase	24.6
		Pfizer	21.2
		United Health Group	35.9
		Wal-Mart	32.6
		Yahoo!	20.7

The Income Statement

In its income statement, a corporation reports a total income tax expense that consists of both the current tax expense (or benefit) and the deferred tax expense (or benefit). The tax expense is allocated among income from continuing operations, discontinued operations, extraordinary items, prior-period adjustments, and the cumulative effect of accounting changes. Additional disclosures are required for the tax expense allocated to income from continuing operations (e.g., current versus deferred, benefits of NOL deductions, and changes in valuation allowances).

Financial Statement Footnotes

The income tax note contains a wealth of information, including the following.

- Breakdown of income between domestic and foreign.
- Detailed analysis of the provision for income tax expense.
- Detailed analysis of deferred tax assets and liabilities.
- Effective tax rate reconciliation (dollar amount or percentage).
- Information on use of ASC 740-30 (APB 23) for the earnings of foreign subsidiaries.
- Discussion of significant tax matters.

The steps in determining a corporation's income tax expense for book purposes are summarized in Concept Summary 3.2.

Rate Reconciliation

The purpose of the rate reconciliation is to demonstrate how a corporation's actual book effective tax rate relates to its "hypothetical tax rate" as if the book income were taxed at the U.S. corporate rate of 35 percent. Although similar to Schedule M–1 or M–3, the tax note rate reconciliation generally reports only differences triggered by permanent differences. As discussed in the benchmarking section later in this chapter, an analysis of the rate reconciliation can provide substantial indicators as to the tax planning strategies adopted (or not adopted) by a company.

Concept Summary 3.2

Steps in Determining the Book Tax Expense

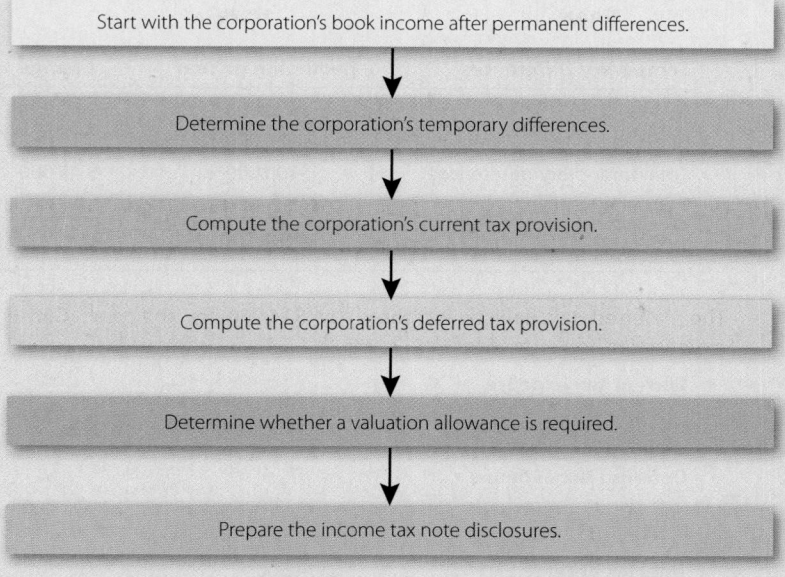

Start with the corporation's book income after permanent differences.

↓

Determine the corporation's temporary differences.

↓

Compute the corporation's current tax provision.

↓

Compute the corporation's deferred tax provision.

↓

Determine whether a valuation allowance is required.

↓

Prepare the income tax note disclosures.

Rate Reconciliations

EXAMPLE 16

BoxCo, Inc., a domestic corporation, owns 100% of PaperCo, Ltd., an Erasmus corporation. BoxCo's U.S. corporate tax rate is 35%, and its Erasmus rate is 10%. As discussed later in the chapter, BoxCo reports book but not taxable income for PaperCo's overseas profits, under ASC 740-30 (APB 23). Book income, permanent and temporary differences, and current tax expense are computed as follows.

	BoxCo	PaperCo
Book income before tax	$300,000	$200,000
Permanent differences		
Meals and entertainment expense	20,000	—
Municipal bond interest income	(50,000)	—
Book income after permanent differences	$270,000	$200,000
Temporary differences		
Tax > book depreciation	(50,000)	—
Book > tax bad debt expense	10,000	—
Taxable income	$230,000	$200,000
Tax rate	× 35%	× 10%
Current tax expense	$ 80,500	$ 20,000

Assume that the beginning-of-the-year difference between book and tax basis in the depreciable assets is $150,000, and that the beginning-of-the-year difference between book and tax basis in

continued

the bad debt expense is $50,000. Thus, the beginning-of-the-year deferred tax liability is $35,000 [($150,000 − $50,000) × 35%]. To determine the deferred tax expense (benefit) for the current year, the change in the balance sheet amounts for these temporary differences from the beginning to the end of the year must be determined and then multiplied by the appropriate tax rate.

Temporary Differences	Beginning of Year	Change	End of Year
Depreciation	$150,000	$ 50,000	$200,000
Bad debts	(50,000)	(10,000)	(60,000)
Total temporary differences	$100,000	$ 40,000	$140,000
Tax rate	× 35%	× 35%	× 35%
	$ 35,000	$ 14,000	$ 49,000

The deferred tax liability increased by $14,000 for the year. Consequently, BoxCo's total tax expense for book purposes is $114,500.

Current tax expense
    Domestic $ 80,500
    Foreign   20,000
Deferred tax expense
    Domestic   14,000
    Foreign   —
Total tax expense $114,500

The journal entry to record the book income tax expense is constructed as follows.

Income tax expense (provision) $114,500
    Income tax payable $100,500
    Deferred tax liability   14,000

BoxCo's book income is $500,000 (the combined book income of both BoxCo and PaperCo). The effective tax rate reconciliation is based on this book income, with the dollar amounts in the table representing the tax expense (benefit) related to the item and the percentage representing the tax expense (benefit) as a percentage of book income. For example, the municipal bond interest of $50,000 reduces tax liability by $17,500 ($50,000 × 35%). This $17,500 as a percentage of the $500,000 book income is 3.5%.

	Effective Tax Rate Reconciliation	
	$	%
Hypothetical tax at U.S. rate	$175,000	35.0
Disallowed meals and entertainment expense	7,000	1.4
Municipal bond interest	(17,500)	(3.5)
Foreign income taxed at less than U.S. rate	(50,000)*	(10.0)
Income tax expense (provision)	$114,500	22.9

*$200,000 × (35% − 10%)

Only permanent differences appear in the rate reconciliation. Temporary differences do not affect the *total* book income tax expense; they simply affect the amount of the tax expense that is current versus deferred.

TAX FACT **Effective Tax Rates Examined**

A U.S. Government Accountability Office (GAO) study examined the tax returns of profitable U.S. corporations for a recent tax year; the data came from an analysis of corporate Schedules M–3. Some of the most interesting findings from the study include the following.

- The effective tax rate for these entities was 12.6 percent of worldwide income. Including income tax obligations to state, local, and non-U.S. governments, the effective tax rate became 16.9 percent. The statutory Federal tax rate for these entities was 35 percent.

- Some of the largest reported book-tax differences included:
  - Interest deductions that were deferred for tax purposes.
  - Cost recovery deductions that were accelerated.
  - Retirement plan contributions that were accelerated.
  - Tax deductions for current non-U.S. income that were allowed.

Source: **www.gao.gov/assets/660/654957.pdf**

Rate Reconciliations

EXAMPLE 17

Assume the same facts as Example 16, except that a new income tax law is enacted before the end of the current year that will increase the U.S. corporate tax rate to 40% beginning next year. In this case, multiply the year-end total temporary differences of $140,000 by 40% rather than 35%. This results in an increase in the deferred tax liability of $21,000.

Temporary Differences	Beginning of Year	End of Year	Effect of Rate Change
Depreciation	$150,000	$200,000	
Bad debts	(50,000)	(60,000)	
Total temporary differences	$100,000	$140,000	
Tax rate	× 35%	× 40%	
Deferred tax liability	$ 35,000	$ 56,000	$21,000

The current-year deferred tax liability is a function of both the change in temporary differences at the enacted rate ($40,000 × 40%) and the additional 5% tax on the beginning temporary differences [$100,000 × (40% − 35%)].

This example illustrates the need for the "balance sheet" approach of ASC 740 (SFAS 109). Use of the APB 11 shortcut method would have produced the wrong answer.

EXAMPLE 18

LibbyCo, Inc., is a U.S. corporation that operates retail outlets selling eyeglasses. During the current year, LibbyCo reported pretax book income of $1,800. LibbyCo's U.S. corporate tax rate is 34%. It reports no NOLs, credits, or foreign or state income taxes. The entity is not subject to the alternative minimum tax.

LibbyCo's year-end tax and book balance sheet is summarized below, before accounting for tax deferrals. The statement highlights the book-tax basis differences for all assets and liabilities.

	Tax Debit/(Credit)	Book Debit/(Credit)	Difference
Assets			
Cash	$ 2,000	$ 2,000	$ —0—
Accounts receivable	5,400	5,400	—0—
Buildings	400,000	400,000	—0—
Accumulated depreciation	(315,000)	(330,000)	15,000
Furniture & fixtures	100,000	100,000	—0—
Accumulated depreciation	(70,000)	(45,000)	(25,000)
Total assets	$122,400	$132,400	($ 10,000)

continued

	Tax Debit/(Credit)	Book Debit/(Credit)	Difference
Liabilities			
Accrued vacation pay	$ —0—	($ 25,000)	$ 25,000
Note payable	(16,400)	(16,400)	—0—
Total liabilities	($ 16,400)	($ 41,400)	$ 25,000
Stockholders' Equity			
Paid-in capital	($ 6,000)	($ 6,000)	
Retained earnings	(100,000)	(85,000)	
Total liabilities and stockholders' equity	($122,400)	($132,400)	

The difference between the book and tax basis of these assets and liabilities is the cumulative difference from all prior years. To determine the temporary differences for the current year and any associated deferred tax liability or deferred tax asset, these differences are compared with the basis differences at the beginning of the year.

Assume the following beginning-of-the-year book-tax differences. The end-of-the-year differences are calculated above. The differences are classified based on whether they produce a future tax benefit (*deductible temporary differences*) or a future tax cost (*taxable temporary differences*).

	Beginning of Year	Current-Year Difference	End of Year
Deductible Temporary Differences			
Buildings—accumulated depreciation	$10,000	$ 5,000	$15,000
Accrued vacation pay	17,000	8,000	25,000
Subtotal	$27,000	$13,000	$40,000
Applicable tax rate	× 34%		× 34%
Gross deferred tax asset	$ 9,180		$13,600
Change in deferred tax asset		$ 4,420	
Taxable Temporary Differences			
Furniture & fixtures—accumulated depreciation	($22,000)	($ 3,000)	($25,000)
Subtotal	($22,000)	($ 3,000)	($25,000)
Applicable tax rate	× 34%		× 34%
Gross deferred tax liability	($ 7,480)		($ 8,500)
Change in deferred tax liability		($ 1,020)	
Net deferred tax asset / (deferred tax liability)	$ 1,700	$ 3,400	$ 5,100

The journal entry to record the deferred tax asset is constructed as follows.

Deferred tax asset	$3,400	
Income tax expense		$3,400

In addition to the temporary differences identified above, LibbyCo reported two permanent differences between book and taxable income. It earned $1,400 in tax-exempt municipal bond interest, and it incurred $2,000 in nondeductible meals and entertainment expense. With this information, the current tax expense is determined as follows.

continued

Pretax book income	$ 1,800
Book-tax adjustments	
Permanent items	
Tax-exempt income	(1,400)
Nondeductible meals and entertainment	2,000
Temporary differences	
Building depreciation	5,000
Accrued vacation pay	8,000
Furniture & fixtures depreciation	(3,000)
Taxable income	$12,400
Current tax expense (34%)	$ 4,216

The building depreciation for book purposes exceeds tax depreciation, the furniture and fixtures depreciation for tax purposes exceeds book depreciation, and the accrued vacation pay is deductible for book purposes but is not yet deductible for tax. These current-year temporary differences, combined with the two permanent items, also constitute the Schedule M–3 differences.

The journal entry to record the current tax expense is constructed as follows.

Income tax expense	$4,216	
Current income tax payable		$4,216

Assuming that no valuation allowance is required, the effect of these entries on the income statement is as follows. The current-year change in the deferred tax asset allows the book tax expense to be reduced by $3,400, producing a total book tax expense of $816 ($4,216 − $3,400).

Net income before tax	$1,800
Provision for income tax expense	(816)
Net income after tax	$ 984

The income tax footnote rate reconciliation is presented as follows.

Tax on book income at statutory rate	$ 612	34.00%
Tax-exempt income	(476)	(26.44)%
Nondeductible meals and entertainment	680	37.77%
Provision for income tax expense	$ 816	45.33%

With these facts, the shortcut APB 11 method illustrated below produces the same results as the ASC 740 (SFAS 109) method. The two methods would produce different results had there been changes to LibbyCo's applicable tax rate from the prior year, or if a valuation allowance had been required.

Pretax book income	$ 1,800
Permanent items	
Tax-exempt income	(1,400)
Nondeductible meals and entertainment	2,000
Book equivalent to taxable income	$ 2,400
Statutory tax rate	× 34%
Total book tax expense	$ 816

3-2d Special Issues

Financial Accounting for Tax Uncertainties

Companies take positions in their tax returns that may not ultimately survive the scrutiny of the IRS or other tax authorities. If a taxpayer loses the benefit of a favorable tax position after a future audit, there may be an unfavorable effect on the company's financial statement tax expense in that future year. The additional tax cost will become part of the

LO.5

Identify the GAAP treatment concerning tax uncertainties and unrepatriated foreign earnings.

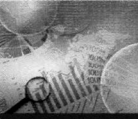

TAX PLANNING STRATEGIES   **Tax Savings Are Not Always Created Equal**

FRAMEWORK FOCUS: THINKING OUTSIDE THE FRAMEWORK

Many different types of tax planning strategies can produce tax savings. Yet, even when planning ideas produce identical current cash-flow effects, some ideas may have an edge. CEOs and CFOs of public companies are focused on the bottom line—the company's net income after tax and related earnings per share. A CFO is likely to be just as interested in an idea's effect on the company's bottom line income as on the cash tax savings.

For example, consider two tax planning ideas that each produce $700,000 of current tax savings. The first idea generates its $700,000 in tax savings by increasing tax depreciation relative to book depreciation by $2 million ($700,000 = $2 million × 35%). The second idea produces

research activities tax credits of $700,000, thus reducing current-year tax by $700,000.

Idea 1 produces its current tax savings via a temporary difference. Accordingly, the book tax expense will not reflect the $700,000 in tax savings. Instead, this $700,000 simply moves from the current tax category to the deferred tax category. Even if the book-tax difference is not expected to reverse in the next 30 years (effectively generating "permanent" savings), the book tax expense does not reflect this savings.

In contrast, idea 2 produces its current tax savings via a permanent difference. Thus, the book tax expense also declines by $700,000. This item appears in the income tax note rate reconciliation.

current tax expense, yet the income that this tax is related to would have been reported in the initial year. This result can wreak havoc with a company's effective tax rate.

To avoid such an increase in effective tax rate, companies may record a book reserve (or "cushion") for the uncertain tax position in the initial year. That is, rather than book the entire tax benefit (and thus reduce tax expense in the current year), the company may book only a portion (or none) of the tax benefit. If the company later loses the actual tax benefit upon audit, to the extent the additional tax imposed is charged against the reserve, the additional tax does not affect the future-year tax expense. If the company's tax position is not challenged in the future (or the company successfully defends any challenge), the reserve can be released. This release reduces the current tax expense in the future (release) year, and it lowers the company's effective tax rate in that year.

To add more structure to the accounting for tax reserves, the FASB released an interpretation, "Accounting for Uncertainty in Income Taxes" **[ASC 740-10 (FIN 48)]**. The approach required under this interpretation results in significantly more disclosure about uncertain tax positions by companies.

When ASC 740-10 (FIN 48) applies, uncertain tax positions effectively are defined as those material items not fully certain by the taxpayer to be sustainable upon a later review based on technical merits. Such tax positions result in a permanent reduction of income taxes payable, a deferral of income taxes otherwise currently payable to future years, or a change in the expected realizability of deferred tax assets.

Application of the ASC 740-10 (FIN 48) rules essentially is a two-step process—recognition and measurement. These steps are illustrated in Concept Summary 3.3.

First, a tax benefit from an uncertain tax position may be *recognized* in the financial statements only if it is *more likely than not* (a greater than 50 percent likelihood) that the position would be sustained on its technical merits. In this regard, audit or detection risk cannot be considered. This first step determines whether any of the tax benefit is recognized.

If the *more likely than not* standard is failed, no financial statement disclosure is required. If the uncertain tax position meets the *more likely than not* threshold, the second step is to determine the amount of the tax benefit to report.

Measurement of the amount of the tax benefit to be disclosed then occurs. This computation is based on the probabilities associated with the position not being challenged, or with it being challenged using a negotiated settlement or litigation.

The recognition and measurement of uncertain tax positions is reassessed at each reporting date. ASC 740-10 (FIN 48) requires a reconciliation of the beginning and

Concept Summary 3.3

Disclosures Under ASC 740-10 (FIN 48)

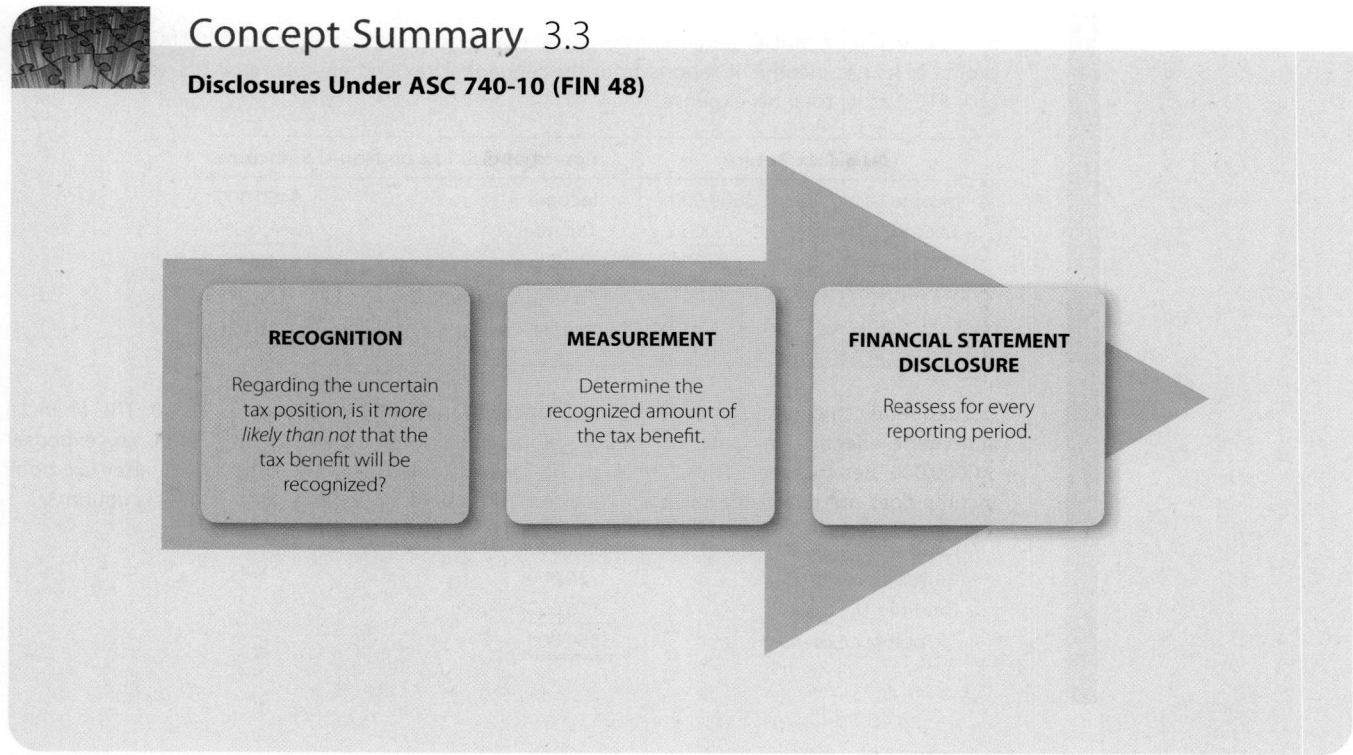

RECOGNITION	MEASUREMENT	FINANCIAL STATEMENT DISCLOSURE
Regarding the uncertain tax position, is it *more likely than not* that the tax benefit will be recognized?	Determine the recognized amount of the tax benefit.	Reassess for every reporting period.

ending balances of the unrecognized tax benefits and a discussion of potential changes in these unrecognized tax benefits that might occur over the next 12 months.

Earnings of Foreign Subsidiaries

As discussed earlier, a corporate group's financial statements include both domestic and foreign controlled subsidiaries. However, foreign corporations, even those controlled by U.S. shareholders, are not part of a U.S. consolidated tax return. Consequently, U.S. taxpayers can achieve deferral of current U.S. taxes on foreign income if they operate their overseas activities through foreign subsidiary corporations in jurisdictions with lower tax rates than those of the United States (see Chapter 16). Although the *actual* U.S. taxes on foreign corporations' profits are deferred, the reported effective tax rate for financial statement purposes may not reflect this deferral, because ASC 740 (SFAS 109) requires that a corporate group report both current and deferred income tax expense.

USCo, a domestic corporation, operates a manufacturing facility in Singapore through a Singapore corporation. USCo's U.S. tax rate is 35% and its Singapore tax rate is 6%. For the current year, USCo earns $600,000 in taxable income. The Singapore corporation earns $400,000 in taxable income from its operations, pays $24,000 in taxes to Singapore, and makes no distributions to its U.S. parent. The Singapore corporation is not taxed in the United States because it is not a U.S. entity, and it conducts no activities in the United States.

USCo is not taxed on the Singapore profits because it has not received any distributions of these profits. Accordingly, USCo has achieved deferral and reduced its worldwide cash tax costs.

EXAMPLE

19

continued

However, for financial statement purposes, the USCo group includes the $400,000 in Singapore profits in its net income. It reports both the Singapore tax and any *potential* U.S. tax (after allowable FTCs) as its total tax expense.

U.S. Tax Return		Potential U.S. Tax on Non-U.S. Income	
Income	$600,000	Income	$400,000
Tax rate	× 35%	Tax rate	× 35%
U.S. tax	$210,000	Total tax	$140,000
		Foreign tax credit	(24,000)
		Net U.S. tax	$116,000

Consequently, the total tax expense for financial statement purposes is $350,000. The financial statement effective tax rate on USCo's global income is 35% ($350,000 total tax expense/ $1,000,000 net income). Thus, although USCo paid only $234,000 in taxes, its after-tax book income does not reflect the savings generated from operating in Singapore, a low-tax country.

Current U.S. tax	$210,000
Current foreign tax	24,000
Deferred U.S. tax	116,000
Total tax expense	$350,000

ASC 740-30 (APB 23) provides an exception to ASC 740 (SFAS 109) for income from foreign subsidiaries.[12] If a corporation documents that it is **permanently reinvesting** the earnings of its foreign subsidiaries outside the United States, the corporation does not record as an expense any future U.S. income tax the corporation may pay on such earnings.

FINANCIAL DISCLOSURE INSIGHTS   Corporate Tax Rate Cuts: Be Careful What You Wish For

Many lawmakers, businesses, and think tanks are calling for a reform to the U.S. corporate income tax, including a cut in the top tax rate from the current 35 percent to perhaps 25 percent—a reduction in the top rate of almost 30 percent. The lower rate would match that used by most other developed countries, and a rate cut might make U.S. entities more competitive in the global marketplace. A rate cut would be paid for by repealing various deductions and credits that corporations use to reduce their average and effective tax rates.

But for those corporations that hold deferred tax assets (e.g., NOL and credit carryforwards), the corresponding GAAP results might not be so attractive. Deferred tax assets (DTAs) would be written down for book purposes (because lower tax rates will apply in the future, the deferred deductions and credits will produce lower tax savings). Such write-downs of the DTAs thus would reduce current book income—perhaps by dramatic amounts. That cannot be good for stock prices and executive bonuses.

A corporation's specific DTAs are not publicly disclosed, but a 30 percent cut in the U.S. corporate income tax rates would, on average, trigger a 30 percent DTA write-down. Could the GAAP consequences of a corporate income tax rate reduction be so negative as to move businesses to block the cut itself?

[12]Formerly *Opinion No. 23—Accounting for Income Taxes—Special Areas,* Accounting Principles Board.

USCo, in Example 19, uses ASC 740-30 (APB 23) to avoid reporting the $116,000 in deferred taxes. Because USCo plans to reinvest its Singapore earnings indefinitely outside the United States, it is not required to include the deferred U.S. taxes as part of its total tax expense.

USCo's total financial statement income remains $1 million, but its total tax expense is only $234,000 (the taxes currently paid to the United States and Singapore). The resulting financial statement effective tax rate is 23.4% ($234,000/$1,000,000), and the USCo group's after-tax book income reflects the Singapore tax savings.

EXAMPLE
20

ASC 740-30 (APB 23) is a major issue only when the foreign subsidiary is taxed at rates below the applicable U.S. tax rate. Otherwise, there is no potential for tax deferral.

Using ASC 740-30 (APB 23) is not an "all or nothing" decision. It can be adopted in some years and not others. Even within a year, it may be used for only a portion of foreign subsidiary earnings.

The Big Picture

Return to the facts of *The Big Picture* on p. 3-1. Recall from Example 1 that Arctic Corporation has a wholly owned foreign subsidiary, Hurricane, Ltd. Assume that Arctic also owns 100% of another foreign corporation, Typhoon, Ltd.

Arctic can choose to apply ASC 740-30 (APB 23) to both of its foreign subsidiaries in year 1 and to only Hurricane in year 2. In year 3, Arctic can choose to use ASC 740-30 (APB 23) for 40% of Hurricane's earnings and 80% of Typhoon's earnings.

EXAMPLE
21

An assertion by management that foreign earnings will remain overseas indefinitely converts a temporary book-tax difference into a permanent difference. This can result in a significant decrease in the entity's book effective tax rate.

Raven is a U.S. corporation that is subject to a 35% U.S. income tax rate. Its 100% owned subsidiary Cuervo operates in Despina, a country that does not levy an income tax. Cuervo makes no distributions to Raven during the tax year.

Raven's book-tax differences and effective tax rate are computed as follows. If Raven's management asserts that Cuervo's profits are to be permanently invested in Despina, the book effective tax rate decreases by about one-third.

EXAMPLE
22

	Cuervo Earnings Are "Permanently Reinvested" in Despina ($ in 000's)	Cuervo Earnings Are *Not* "Permanently Reinvested" in Despina ($ in 000's)
Pretax U.S. book income	$100,000	$100,000
Pretax Despina book income	50,000	50,000
Total pretax book income	$150,000	$150,000
Temporary book-tax difference: Despina earnings		(50,000)
Permanent book-tax difference: Despina earnings	(50,000)	
Taxable income	$100,000	$100,000
U.S. income tax	$ 35,000	$ 35,000
Deferred income tax expense		17,500
Total income tax expense	$ 35,000	$ 52,500
GAAP effective tax rate	23.3%	35.0%

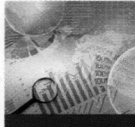

TAX PLANNING STRATEGIES   Reducing Effective Tax Rates with ASC 740-30 (APB 23) Can Backfire

FRAMEWORK FOCUS: DEDUCTIONS

Strategy: Maximize Deductible Amounts.

Because ASC 740-30 (APB 23) allows for higher reported book earnings (no deferred U.S. tax expense is recorded), its use may be reflected in higher stock prices and increased shareholder wealth. Many U.S. multinationals with foreign subsidiaries use ASC 740-30 (APB 23) to avoid reporting U.S. deferred taxes on foreign earnings.

The "permanent reinvestment" exception should not be employed unless the corporation truly expects to keep its foreign earnings outside the United States. Using ASC 740-30 (APB 23) and then repatriating foreign profits after all can cause extreme spikes in a corporation's effective tax rate.

EXAMPLE 23

USCo, a domestic corporation, owns 100% of Shamrock, Ltd., an Atlantis corporation. Its U.S. tax rate is 35%, and its Atlantis tax rate is 10%. In 2014, USCo earns $100,000 in taxable income and pays $35,000 to the United States. Shamrock earns $400,000 in taxable income and pays $40,000 in taxes to Atlantis. Shamrock makes no distributions to its U.S. parent and is not taxed in the United States because it is not a U.S. entity and has no activities in the United States.

USCo is not taxed on the Atlantis profits because it has not received any distributions of these profits. Furthermore, USCo uses ASC 740-30 (APB 23) to avoid recording any deferred U.S. income tax expense on its financial statements. Accordingly, USCo has achieved deferral and reduced its worldwide cash tax costs and book income tax expense.

USCo's total tax expense for financial statement purposes is $75,000.

Current U.S. tax	$35,000
Current foreign tax	40,000
Total tax expense	$75,000

The financial statement effective tax rate on USCo's global income is 15% ($75,000 total tax expense/$500,000 net income). Thus, the USCo group has achieved higher after-tax book income and earnings per share.

In 2015, USCo earns $200,000 in taxable income and pays $70,000 to the United States. Shamrock breaks even for the year and pays no taxes to Atlantis. At the same time, USCo decides that Shamrock should pay it a dividend of $360,000.

U.S. Tax Return	
U.S. income	$200,000
Foreign dividend*	400,000
Taxable income	$600,000
Tax rate	× 35%
	$210,000
FTC	(40,000)
Net U.S. tax	$170,000

* The total gross income is the $360,000 cash dividend grossed up by the $40,000 potential FTC (see Chapter 16).

For book purposes, USCo reports only $200,000 in net income (the $400,000 in Atlantis income was included in book income in 2014 and is not included again). The 2015 total tax expense for financial statement purposes is $170,000.

Current U.S. tax	$170,000
Current foreign tax	—0—
Total tax expense	$170,000

The financial statement effective tax rate on USCo's global income is 85% ($170,000 total tax expense/$200,000 net income). This extremely high effective rate is caused by the mismatching of the Atlantis income (reported in 2014) and the U.S. taxes on the Atlantis income (reported in 2015).

TAX IN THE NEWS The APB 23 Deferral

Multinational corporations tend to leave off-shore the cash resulting from their profitable overseas activities, deferring both book and tax income recognition thereof. This is not "idle cash" by any means, as the funds typically are used to finance growth in the non-U.S. operations of the entity. Furthermore, if the offshore cash were "brought home" to the United States (e.g., to create U.S. jobs or pay cash dividends to U.S. investors), book and taxable income would be triggered, and stock prices might suffer.

Here are recent estimates of the overseas cash holdings and the related deferred U.S. corporate income tax of several prominent entities.

Corporation	Overseas Cash ($ in billions)	Deferred Federal Corporate Income Tax ($ in billions)
Bank of America	$17.2	$ 4.3
Citigroup	42.6	11.5
Microsoft	60.8	4.5

In fact, when a U.S. corporation desires to make a dividend payment to its shareholders, it can borrow funds to provide the necessary liquidity, using the overseas cash as collateral for the loan; free cash results, but the tax deferral continues. Apple and other corporations have used this technique in the recent past.

eBay puzzled stock analysts, though, when it repatriated some of its overseas cash to make dividend payments and finance current operations. eBay's stock price fell by more than 4 percent on the day that it announced that it would repatriate $9 billion of its $12 billion of overseas cash balances, thereby triggering an immediate $3 billion in U.S. corporate income tax. The move dropped eBay's quarterly earnings from a $1 billion profit to a $2 billion deficit.

3-2e Summary

The tax department of a business often is charged with constructing the entity's tax strategies (*tax planning*) and filing all required tax returns (*tax compliance*) while preparing for subsequent audit and litigation activity (*tax controversy*). Tax professionals often work closely with those who prepare the entity's financial statements, especially concerning the tax footnote, tax deferral accounts, and tax rate reconciliations. Professional tax and accounting research underlies all of this work.

The efforts of a modern tax department are depicted in Exhibit 3.4. Tax professionals must be proficient in all of the indicated areas, so that they can meet the demands placed upon the entity by shareholders, regulators, and taxing agencies.

EXHIBIT 3.4	Functions of a Tax Department (by Percent of Time Spent)

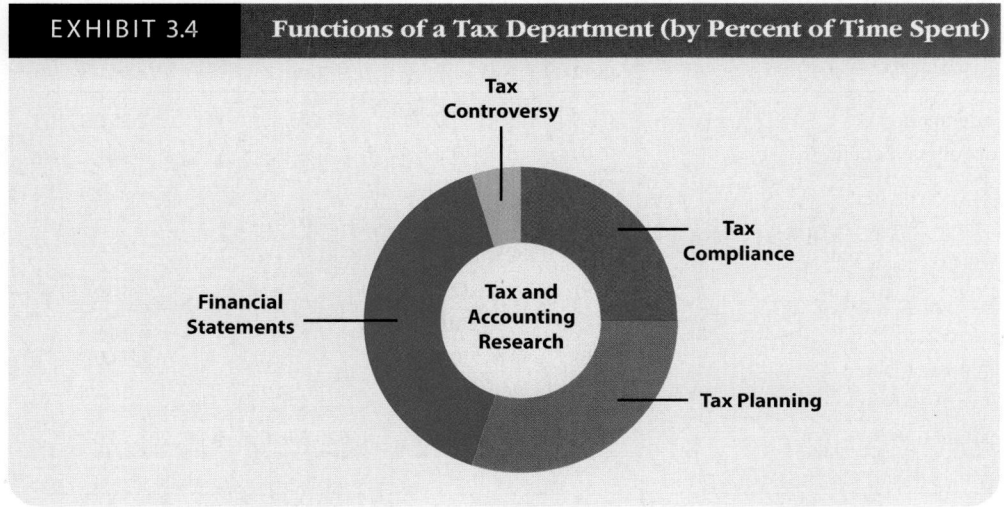

LO.6

Use financial statement income tax information to benchmark a company's tax position.

3-3 BENCHMARKING

An entity's income tax expense amount may appear to be of little interest to anyone beyond the taxpayer that makes the payment and the government agencies that collect it. The tax year is over, the transactions are completed, and the final costs have been tallied. Still, this historical tax information may prove valuable. A company's income tax expense is one of the single largest expense items on its income statement, and understanding the components of this expense is a critical activity for the tax professional.

Consider a typical baseball game. Two teams meet, interact following a specific set of rules, and ultimately complete the game, generating a final score. Of course, the final score is of immediate interest to the teams and the fans, but once the game is over, the score and associated statistics (runs, hits, and errors) are relegated to the history books. Yet, these statistics still can be quite useful. A team coach may use the game statistics to evaluate the strengths and weaknesses of the players to assist in improving performance. Other teams may use the statistics to develop strategies for upcoming games. Players can use the statistics to "benchmark" themselves against their own performance in prior games or against players on other teams. In short, there is a wealth of information in these historical data.

A taxpayer's reported income tax expense likewise is a valuable source of information for the company, its tax advisers, and its competitors. The reported information provides clues about a company's operational and tax planning strategies.

Companies may benchmark their tax situation to other years' results or to other companies in the same industry. The starting point for a **benchmarking** exercise usually is the data from the income tax note rate reconciliation.

3-3a Dynamic Benchmarking

Exhibit 3.5 shows the tax rate reconciliation information from the income tax notes for two recent years of Sears Holding Corporation (Sears) and Wal-Mart Stores, Inc. (Wal-Mart). Both companies are listed on the New York Stock Exchange, are in the same industry, and operate both inside and outside the United States. Although the income and tax expense amounts of both companies are quite different in magnitude, the tax amounts are converted to percentage of income numbers for comparability purposes. In year 1, Sears reported an effective tax rate that was 12 percentage points higher than Wal-Mart's rate. In year 2, Sears's effective tax rate was 4.9 points below

EXHIBIT 3.5	Tax Rate Reconciliation for Sears and Wal-Mart			
	Sears		**Wal-Mart**	
	Year 2	**Year 1**	**Year 2**	**Year 1**
Hypothetical tax (benefit) at U.S. Federal rate	35.0%	35.0%	35.0%	35.0%
State and local income taxes, net of Federal benefit	6.0	7.2	1.9	1.7
Tax credits	(3.0)	(6.3)		
Resolution of income tax matters	(6.2)	(6.8)		
Basis difference in domestic subsidiary	—	(30.2)		
Non-U.S. income taxed at different rates	(0.9)	(2.3)	(1.7)	(1.6)
Nondeductible goodwill	—	50.0		
Other	(1.6)	(0.4)	(1.0)	(1.0)
	29.3%	46.2%	34.2%	34.1%
Book income before tax (in millions)	$420.0	$184.0	$20,898.0	$20,158.0

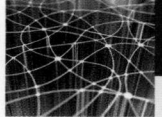

BRIDGE DISCIPLINE   **Bridge to Financial Analysis**

Financial analysts perform an important function for the capital markets in their detailed analyses of companies. The analyst combs through the financial reports and other information about a company to produce an informed opinion on how a company is performing. Analysts' earnings forecasts often constitute an important metric to examine when making decisions about investing in companies.

An experienced financial analyst typically will have a good handle on interpreting financial statement informa-

tion. However, even experienced analysts often will "punt" when it comes to interpreting the tax information contained in a financial statement, preferring to look at net income before taxes (or even EBITDA, earnings before interest, taxes, depreciation, and amortization).

A great deal of useful information about a business is contained in its tax footnote, and analysts might have an edge if they work at understanding the mysteries of taxes in the financial statements.

Wal-Mart's rate. What factors created these differences? Rate reconciliation information can provide clues.

Sears reported a higher effective tax rate in year 1 because its state and local income tax burden was higher, and because it suffered a goodwill impairment (the goodwill write-off is not tax deductible). These increase items were offset by reductions caused by certain basis differences in a domestic subsidiary, larger benefits from tax credits, and a larger benefit from a favorable resolution of tax matters.

When comparing effective tax rates, it is important to consider which components of the effective tax rate produce one-time effects, and which will be observed permanently. For example, for year 2, the effective tax rates of both companies were more similar (Sears was about 5 percentage points lower than Wal-Mart). In particular, without the large effects of nondeductible goodwill and the domestic subsidiary basis difference, Sears approaches the effective tax rate of Wal-Mart.

Consequently, it appears that there are no long-term structural differences in the tax burdens faced by the two companies. This is not surprising, given that both companies are incorporated in the United States, perform in the same industry, and operate in many of the same jurisdictions.

However, items such as the nondeductible goodwill difference do indicate that there may be potential fundamental differences in how Sears's management deals with growth via expansion rather than acquisitions. It is acquired goodwill rather than the homegrown sort that faces potential impairment. The Sears example shows that the results of past and current strategic decisions eventually may show up in the income tax footnote.

3-3b **Refining the Analysis**

In addition to comparing effective tax rates, companies can compare levels of deferred tax assets and liabilities.

EXAMPLE 24

Akiko Enterprises reports a net deferred tax liability of $280,000. Erde, Inc., a company in the same industry, reports a net deferred tax liability of $860,000. The presence of deferred tax liabilities on the balance sheet indicates that both companies are benefiting from deferring actual tax payments (essentially, an interest-free loan from the government).

At first glance, it may appear that Erde is doing better in this regard. However, what if Akiko holds total assets of $2.6 million and Erde's assets total $19.2 million? This information indicates that Akiko has 10.8% ($280,000/$2.6 million) of its total assets "financed" with an interest-free loan from the government, while Erde has only 4.5% ($860,000/$19.2 million) of its assets "financed" with its deferred tax liabilities.

A company may do a more refined benchmarking analysis by examining each component of its deferred tax assets and liabilities as a percentage of total assets. For example, an observer can examine how the deferred tax assets or liabilities related to property, plant, and equipment compare with those of its competitors. The nature of the components of deferred tax liabilities and deferred tax assets becomes quite important in a benchmarking analysis.

Benchmarking Financial Results

EXAMPLE
25

LinCo reports total book income before taxes of $10 million and a total tax expense of $3.2 million, producing a 32% effective tax rate. TuckCo also reports book income before taxes of $10 million. TuckCo's total tax expense is $3.1 million, producing an effective tax rate of 31%. At first glance, it appears that both companies are similar with regard to effective tax rates. The total tax expense divided between current and deferred is as follows.

	LinCo	TuckCo
Current tax expense	$4,100,000	$ 4,200,000
Deferred tax benefit	(900,000)	(1,100,000)
Total tax expense	$3,200,000	$ 3,100,000

Again, it appears that both companies have created deferred tax assets in the current year that are expected to produce tax savings in the future. Knowing the nature of the underlying deferred tax assets will add greatly to one's interpretation of the effective tax rates.

The deferred tax asset generating LinCo's $900,000 expected future tax savings is the use of an NOL. The deferred tax asset generating TuckCo's expected future tax savings is generated by different book and tax methods in accounting for warranty expense. This additional information reveals that LinCo previously has incurred losses, and it is critical that it earn future taxable income in order to use the NOL.

This is quite different from TuckCo's situation, which reveals only that common differences in accounting methods exist. Although the tax positions of LinCo and TuckCo seem very similar on the surface, a closer look reveals a striking difference.

EXAMPLE
26

WageCo and SalaryCo operate in the same industry, and they both report a 38% effective tax rate. Their book income and current, deferred, and total tax expense were reported as follows.

	WageCo	SalaryCo
Book income before tax	$1,500,000	$2,300,000
Current tax expense	$ 980,000	$ 24,000
Deferred tax expense (benefit)	(410,000)	850,000
Total tax expense	$ 570,000	$ 874,000
Effective tax rate	38%	38%

WageCo's total tax expense is highly dependent on the current recognition of future tax savings of $410,000. SalaryCo appears to be deferring a substantial portion of its tax expense to future years. Although both companies report a 38% effective tax rate, the details indicate that the two companies face very different tax situations.

3-3c Sustaining the Tax Rate

It is important in benchmarking exercises to remove the effect of one-time items in comparing sustainable effective tax rates across time or companies. Examples of one-time items include restructuring costs, legal settlements, and IRS or other tax liability settlements. A one-time item may seem beneficial or detrimental to a company's effective tax rate. But the very nature of such an item implies that it has little to do with the company's long-term sustainable tax costs.

MetalCo and IronCo operate in the same industry, and they report the following tax rate reconciliations in their tax footnotes.

	MetalCo	IronCo
Hypothetical tax at U.S. rate	35.0%	35.0%
State and local taxes	2.2	2.1
Foreign income taxed at less than U.S. rate	(6.2)	(6.1)
Tax Court settlement on disputed tax issue	(18.6)	—
Effective tax rate	12.4%	31.0%

Although it appears that MetalCo has a significantly lower effective tax rate (12.4%) than IronCo (31.0%), removing MetalCo's one-time item related to the court settlement indicates that both companies may operate under a 31% effective tax rate (12.4% + 18.6% = 31%).

3-3d Uses of Benchmarking Analysis

Benchmarking is part science and part art. A useful analysis requires both an accountant's knowledge of how the underlying financial statements are constructed, including arriving at the appropriate tax expense, and a detective's sense of where to look and what questions to ask. Concept Summary 3.4 summarizes the most typical uses of benchmarking in an analysis of an entity's financial results.

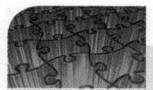

Concept Summary 3.4

Benchmarking Analysis

A benchmarking analysis can be helpful in comparing the tax positions of two or more business entities. One might consider the following aspects of the taxpayers' financial disclosures in this regard. This list is not all-inclusive; benchmarking also includes the judgment and experience of the parties conducting the analysis.

• Compare the effective tax rates of the entities.

• Explain the differences in effective rates. Are these differences sustainable over time?

• Apply the analysis to both the tax dollars involved and the underlying net assets of the entities.

• Discount (but do not ignore) any one-time tax benefits/detriments that are observed.

REFOCUS ON THE BIG PICTURE

TAXES ON THE FINANCIAL STATEMENTS

Raymond Jones should understand that the tax expense reported on the company's financial statements and the tax payable on the company's income tax returns often differ as a result of differences in the reporting entities used in the calculation and the different accounting methods used for book purposes and tax purposes. The use of different accounting methods may result in both temporary and permanent differences in financial statement income and taxable income. Examples of permanent differences include nontaxable income such as municipal bond interest and tax credits. Temporary differences include depreciation differences and other amounts that are affected by the timing of a deduction or an inclusion, but they ultimately result in the same amount being reflected in the financial statements and income tax returns.

Permanent differences such as municipal bond interest cause Arctic's book income to be greater than its taxable income. In calculating the tax expense shown on the financial statements, Arctic's book income must be adjusted for these permanent differences.

continued

This results in an effective tax rate for financial statement purposes (30.8 percent) that is below the top U.S. statutory corporate income tax rate of 35 percent.

In this case, Arctic's income tax expense of $7.7 million is higher than the current Federal income tax payable. This results from timing differences and creates a $1.05 million deferred tax liability that is reported on the company's balance sheet. Unlike other liabilities, deferred tax liabilities are "good" in the sense that they represent an amount that may be paid to the government in the future rather than today.

What If?

Mr. Jones is concerned about a newspaper article that said that companies reporting less tax on their tax returns than on their financial statements were cheating the IRS. Is this an accurate assessment?

While differences in income taxes payable to the IRS and financial tax expense can result from aggressive and illegal tax shelters, differences also result from different methods of accounting that are required for financial statement reporting using GAAP and tax laws enacted by Congress.

Suggested Readings

Cheryl Anderson, "Creating Value in the Corporate Tax Function Through Benchmarking," *AICPA Tax Adviser*, September 2008.

J. O. Everett, C. J. Hennig, and W. A. Raabe, *Schedule M–3 Compliance*, 2nd ed., Commerce Clearing House, 2008.

J. Richard Harvey, "Schedule UTP—Why So Few Disclosures?" *Tax Notes*, April 1, 2013.

C. J. Hennig, W. A. Raabe, and J. O. Everett, "FIN 48 Compliance," *AICPA Tax Adviser*, January 2008.

Floyd Norris, "The Islands Treasured by Offshore Tax Avoiders," *Wall Street Journal*, June 5, 2014.

Key Terms

ASC 740 (SFAS 109), 3-9	Deferred tax benefit, 3-10	Permanently reinvesting, 3-26
ASC 740-10 (FIN 48), 3-24	Deferred tax expense, 3-10	Rate reconciliation, 3-18
ASC 740-30 (APB 23), 3-26	Deferred tax liability, 3-10	Schedule M–1, 3-6
Balance sheet approach, 3-10	Equity method, 3-2	Schedule M–3, 3-6
Benchmarking, 3-30	Generally accepted accounting principles (GAAP), 3-2	Temporary differences, 3-4
Conservatism principle, 3-14		Valuation allowance, 3-14
Current tax expense, 3-9	Income tax provision, 3-9	
Deferred tax asset, 3-10	Permanent differences, 3-4	

Problems

1. **LO.2** Ovate, Inc., earns $140,000 in book income before tax and is subject to a 35% marginal Federal income tax rate. Ovate records a single temporary difference: Warranty expenses deducted for book purposes are $8,000, of which only $2,000 are deductible for tax purposes. Determine the amount of Ovate's deferred tax asset or liability.

2. **LO.3** Ion Corporation reports an income tax expense/payable for book purposes of $200,000 and $250,000 for tax purposes. According to Ion's management

and financial auditors, Ion will only be able to use $30,000 of any deferred tax asset, with the balance expiring. Determine the amount of Ion's deferred tax asset and valuation allowance from this year's activities.

3. **LO.4** RadioCo, a domestic corporation, owns 100% of TVCo, a manufacturing facility in the European country Adagio. TVCo has no operations or activities in the United States. The U.S. tax rate is 35%, and the Adagio tax rate is 15%.

   For the current year, RadioCo earns $200,000 in taxable income from its U.S. operations. TVCo earns $800,000 in taxable income from its operations, pays $120,000 in taxes to Adagio, and makes no distributions to RadioCo. Determine RadioCo's effective tax rate for book purposes with and without the permanent reinvestment assumption of ASC 740-30 (APB 23).

4. **LO.2** Prance, Inc., earns pretax book net income of $800,000 in 2014. Prance acquires a depreciable asset in 2014, and first-year tax depreciation exceeds book depreciation by $80,000. Prance reported no other temporary or permanent book-tax differences. The pertinent U.S. tax rate is 35%.
   a. Compute Prance's total income tax expense, current income tax expense, and deferred income tax expense.
   b. Determine the 2014 end-of-year balance in Prance's deferred tax asset and deferred tax liability balance sheet accounts.

5. **LO.1** Evaluate the following statement: For most business entities, book income differs from taxable income because "income" has different meanings for the users of the data in the income computation. — Ethics and Equity

6. **LO.1** Parent, a domestic corporation, owns 100% of Block, a foreign corporation, and Chip, a domestic corporation. Parent also owns 45% of Trial, a domestic corporation. Parent receives no distributions from any of these corporations. Which of these entities' net income is included in Parent's income statement for current-year financial reporting purposes?

7. **LO.1** Parent, a domestic corporation, owns 100% of Block, a foreign corporation, and Chip, a domestic corporation. Parent also owns 45% of Trial, a domestic corporation. Parent receives no distributions from any of these corporations. Which of these entities' taxable income is included in Parent's current-year Form 1120, U.S. income tax return? Parent consolidates all eligible subsidiaries.

8. **LO.1** Marcellus Jackson, the CFO of Mac, Inc., notices that the tax liability reported on Mac's tax return is less than the tax expense reported on Mac's financial statements. Provide a letter to Jackson outlining why these two tax expense numbers differ. Mac's address is 482 Linden Road, Paris, KY 40362. — Communications

9. **LO.1** Define the terms *temporary difference* and *permanent difference* as they pertain to the financial reporting of income tax expenses. Describe how these two book-tax differences affect the gap between book and taxable income. How are permanent and temporary differences alike? How are they different? — Issue ID

10. **LO.1** In no more than three PowerPoint slides, list several commonly encountered temporary and permanent book-tax differences. The slides will be used in your presentation next week to your school's Future CPAs Club. — Communications

11. **LO.2** Prance, in Problem 4, reports $600,000 of pretax book net income in 2015. Prance's book depreciation exceeds tax depreciation in this year by $20,000. Prance reports no other temporary or permanent book-tax differences. Assuming that the pertinent U.S. tax rate is 35%, compute Prance's total income tax expense, current income tax expense, and deferred income tax expense.

12. **LO.2** Using the facts of Problem 11, determine the 2015 end-of-year balance in Prance's deferred tax asset and deferred tax liability balance sheet accounts.

13. **LO.2** Mini, Inc., earns pretax book net income of $750,000 in 2014. Mini deducted $20,000 in bad debt expense for book purposes. This expense is not yet deductible for tax purposes. Mini records no other temporary or permanent differences. Assuming that the U.S. tax rate is 35%, compute Mini's total income tax expense, current income tax expense, and deferred income tax expense.

14. **LO.2** Using the facts of Problem 13, determine the 2014 end-of-year balance in Mini's deferred tax asset and deferred tax liability balance sheet accounts.

15. **LO.2** Mini, in Problem 13, reports $800,000 of pretax book net income in 2015. Mini did not deduct any bad debt expense for book purposes but did deduct $15,000 in bad debt expense for tax purposes. Mini records no other temporary or permanent differences. Assuming that the U.S. tax rate is 35%, compute Mini's total income tax expense, current income tax expense, and deferred income tax expense.

16. **LO.2** Using the facts of Problem 15, determine the 2015 end-of-year balance in Mini's deferred tax asset and deferred tax liability balance sheet accounts.

17. **LO.3** You saw on the online Business News Channel that YoungCo has "released one-third of its valuation allowances because of an upbeat forecast for sales of its tablet computers over the next 30 months." What effect does such a release likely have on YoungCo's current-year book effective tax rate? Be specific.

Decision Making
Communications

18. **LO.6** Jill is the CFO of PorTech, Inc. PorTech's tax advisers have recommended two tax planning ideas that will each provide $5 million of current-year cash tax savings. One idea is based on a timing difference and is expected to reverse in full 10 years in the future. The other idea creates a permanent difference that never will reverse.

    Determine whether these ideas will allow PorTech to reduce its reported book income tax expense for the current year. Illustrate in a table or timeline your preference for one planning strategy over the other. Which idea will you recommend to Jill?

Issue ID

19. **LO.4** Underwood, the CFO of TechCo, Inc., has used ASC 740-30 (APB 23) to avoid reporting any U.S. deferred tax expense on $50 million of the earnings of TechCo's foreign subsidiaries. All of these subsidiaries operate in countries with lower tax rates than in the United States. Underwood wants to bring to the United States $10 million in profits from these foreign subsidiaries in the form of dividends. How will this profit repatriation affect TechCo's book effective tax rate?

Issue ID

20. **LO.4** Jaime, the CFO of BuildCo, Inc., has used ASC 740-30 (APB 23) to avoid reporting any U.S. deferred tax expense on $100 million of the earnings of BuildCo's foreign subsidiaries. All of these subsidiaries operate in countries with higher tax rates than the ones that apply under U.S. law. Jaime wants to bring home $30 million in profits from these foreign subsidiaries in the form of dividends. How will this profit repatriation affect BuildCo's book effective tax rate?

21. **LO.6** RoofCo reports total book income before taxes of $20 million and a total tax expense of $8 million. FloorCo reports book income before taxes of $30 million and a total tax expense of $12 million. The companies' breakdown between current and deferred tax expense (benefit) is as follows.

	RoofCo	FloorCo
Current tax expense	$10.0	$13.0
Deferred tax benefit	(2.0)	(1.0)
Total tax expense	$ 8.0	$12.0

RoofCo's deferred tax benefit is from a deferred tax asset created because of differences in book and tax depreciation methods for equipment. FloorCo's deferred tax benefit is created by the expected future use of an NOL. Compare and contrast these two companies' effective tax rates. How are they similar? How are they different?

22. **LO.6** LawnCo and TreeCo operate in the same industry, and both report a 30% effective tax rate. Their book income and current, deferred, and total tax expense are reported below.

Communications

	LawnCo	TreeCo
Book income before tax	$500,000	$650,000
Current tax expense	$200,000	$ 20,000
Deferred tax expense (benefit)	(50,000)	175,000
Total tax expense	$150,000	$195,000
Effective tax rate	30%	30%

ShrubCo is a competitor of both of these companies. Prepare a letter to Laura Collins, VP-Taxation of ShrubCo, outlining your analysis of the other two companies' effective tax rates, using only the preceding information. ShrubCo's address is 9979 West Third Street, Peru, IN 46970.

23. **LO.6** HippCo and HoppCo operate in the same industry and report the following tax rate reconciliations in their tax footnotes. Compare and contrast the effective tax rates of these two companies.

	HippCo	HoppCo
Hypothetical tax at U.S. rate	35.0%	35.0%
State and local taxes	2.7	3.9
Foreign income taxed at less than U.S. rate	(12.5)	(7.8)
Tax Court settlement on disputed tax issue	6.0	—
Effective tax rate	31.2%	31.1%

24. **LO.6** In the current year, Dickinson, Inc., reports an effective tax rate of 36%, and Badger, Inc., reports an effective tax rate of 21%. Both companies are domestic and operate in the same industry. Your initial examination of the financial statements of the two companies indicates that Badger apparently is doing a better job with its tax planning, explaining the difference in effective tax rates. Consequently, all else being equal, you decide to invest in Badger.

Ethics and Equity

In a subsequent year, it comes to light that Badger had used some very aggressive tax planning techniques to reduce its reported tax expense. After an examination by the IRS, Badger loses the tax benefits and reports a very large tax expense in that year. Over this multiple-year period, it turns out that Dickinson had the lower effective tax rate after all.

Do you believe Badger was ethical in not fully disclosing the aggressiveness of its tax positions in its current financial statements? How does ASC 740-10 (FIN 48) affect Badger's disclosure requirement? Does ASC 740-10 (FIN 48) still leave room for ethical decision making by management in determining how to report uncertain tax positions? Explain.

25. **LO.2** Phillips, Inc., a cash basis C corporation, completes $100,000 in sales for year 1, but only $75,000 of this amount is collected during year 1. The remaining $25,000 from these sales is collected promptly during the first quarter of year 2. The applicable income tax rate for year 1 and thereafter is 30%. Compute Phillips's year 1 current and deferred income tax expense.

26. **LO.2** Continue with the results of Problem 25. Prepare the GAAP journal entries for Phillips's year 1 income tax expense.

27. **LO.2** Britton, Inc., an accrual basis C corporation, sells widgets on credit. Its book and taxable income for year 1 totals $60,000 before accounting for bad debts. Britton's book allowance for uncollectible accounts increased for year 1 by $10,000, but none of the entity's bad debts received a specific write-off for tax purposes. The applicable income tax rate for year 1 and thereafter is 30%. Compute Britton's year 1 current and deferred income tax expense.

28. **LO.2** Continue with the results of Problem 27. Prepare the GAAP journal entries for Britton's year 1 income tax expense.

29. **LO.2** Rubio, Inc., an accrual basis C corporation, reports the following amounts for the tax year. The applicable income tax rate is 30%. Compute Rubio's taxable income.

Book income, including the items below	$80,000
Increase in book allowance for anticipated warranty costs	5,000
Interest income from City of Westerville bonds	10,000
Bribes paid to Federal inspectors	17,000

30. **LO.2** Continue with the results of Problem 29. Determine Rubio's income tax expense and GAAP income for the year.

31. **LO.2** Willingham, Inc., an accrual basis C corporation, reports pretax book income of $1.6 million. At the beginning of the tax year, Willingham reported no deferred tax accounts on its balance sheet. It is subject to a 35% U.S. income tax rate in the current year and for the foreseeable future.

Willingham's book-tax differences include the following. Compute the entity's current and deferred income tax expense for the year.

Addition to the book reserve for uncollectible receivables (no specific write-offs occurred)	$4,000,000
Tax depreciation in excess of book	3,000,000
Book gain from installment sale of nonbusiness asset, deferred for tax	2,000,000
Interest income from school district bonds	200,000

32. **LO.2** Continue with the results of Problem 31. Prepare the GAAP journal entries for Willingham's income tax expense.

33. **LO.2** Relix, Inc., is a domestic corporation with the following balance sheet for book and tax purposes at the end of the year. Based on this information, determine Relix's net deferred tax asset or net deferred tax liability at year-end. Assume a 34% corporate tax rate and no valuation allowance.

	Tax Debit/(Credit)	Book Debit/(Credit)
Assets		
Cash	$ 500	$ 500
Accounts receivable	8,000	8,000
Buildings	750,000	750,000
Accumulated depreciation	(450,000)	(380,000)
Furniture & fixtures	70,000	70,000
Accumulated depreciation	(46,000)	(38,000)
Total assets	$ 332,500	$ 410,500
Liabilities		
Accrued litigation expense	$ −0−	($ 50,000)
Note payable	(78,000)	(78,000)
Total liabilities	($ 78,000)	($ 128,000)
Stockholders' Equity		
Paid-in capital	($ 10,000)	($ 10,000)
Retained earnings	(244,500)	(272,500)
Total liabilities and stockholders' equity	($ 332,500)	($ 410,500)

34. **LO.2** Based on the facts and results of Problem 33 and the beginning-of-the-year book-tax basis differences listed below, determine the change in Relix's deferred tax assets for the current year.

	Beginning of Year
Accrued litigation expense	$34,000
Subtotal	$34,000
Applicable tax rate	× 34%
Gross deferred tax asset	$11,560

35. **LO.2** Based on the facts and results of Problem 33 and the beginning-of-the-year book-tax basis differences listed below, determine the change in Relix's deferred tax liabilities for the current year.

	Beginning of Year
Building—accumulated depreciation	($57,000)
Furniture & fixtures—accumulated depreciation	(4,200)
Subtotal	($61,200)
Applicable tax rate	× 34%
Gross deferred tax liability	($20,808)

36. **LO.2** Based on the facts and results of Problems 33–35, determine Relix's change in net deferred tax asset or net deferred tax liability for the current year. Provide the journal entry to record this amount.

37. **LO.2** In addition to the temporary differences identified in Problems 33–36, Relix reported two permanent differences between book and taxable income. It earned $2,375 in tax-exempt municipal bond interest, and it incurred $780 in nondeductible meals and entertainment expense. Relix's book income before tax is $4,800. With this additional information, calculate Relix's current tax expense.

38. **LO.2** Provide the journal entry to record Relix's current tax expense as determined in Problem 37.

39. **LO.2** Based on the facts and results of Problems 33–38, calculate Relix's total provision for income tax expense reported in its financial statements and its book net income after tax.

40. **LO.2** Based on the facts and results of Problems 33–39, provide the income tax footnote rate reconciliation for Relix.

41. **LO.2** Kantner, Inc., is a domestic corporation with the following balance sheet for book and tax purposes at the end of the year. Based on this information, determine Kantner's net deferred tax asset or net deferred tax liability at year-end. Assume a 34% corporate tax rate and no valuation allowance.

	Tax Debit/(Credit)	Book Debit/(Credit)
Assets		
Cash	$ 1,000	$ 1,000
Accounts receivable	9,000	9,000
Buildings	850,000	850,000
Accumulated depreciation	(700,000)	(620,000)
Furniture & fixtures	40,000	40,000
Accumulated depreciation	(10,000)	(8,000)
Total assets	$190,000	$ 272,000

	Tax Debit/(Credit)	Book Debit/(Credit)
Liabilities		
Accrued warranty expense	$ —0—	($ 40,000)
Note payable	(16,000)	(16,000)
Total liabilities	($ 16,000)	($ 56,000)
Stockholders' Equity		
Paid-in capital	($ 50,000)	($ 50,000)
Retained earnings	(124,000)	(166,000)
Total liabilities and stockholders' equity	($190,000)	($ 272,000)

42. **LO.2** Based on the facts and results of Problem 41 and the beginning-of-the-year book-tax basis differences listed below, determine the change in Kantner's deferred tax assets for the current year.

	Beginning of Year
Accrued warranty expense	$30,000
Subtotal	$30,000
Applicable tax rate	× 34%
Gross deferred tax asset	$10,200

43. **LO.2** Based on the facts and results of Problem 41 and the beginning-of-the-year book-tax basis differences listed below, determine the change in Kantner's deferred tax liabilities for the current year.

	Beginning of Year
Building—accumulated depreciation	($62,000)
Furniture & fixtures—accumulated depreciation	(400)
Subtotal	($62,400)
Applicable tax rate	× 34%
Gross deferred tax liability	($21,216)

44. **LO.2** Based on the facts and results of Problems 41–43, determine Kantner's change in net deferred tax asset or net deferred tax liability for the current year. Provide the journal entry to record this amount.

45. **LO.2** In addition to the temporary differences identified in Problems 41–44, Kantner reported two permanent book-tax differences. It earned $7,800 in tax-exempt municipal bond interest, and it reported $850 in nondeductible meals and entertainment expense. Kantner's book income before tax is $50,000. With this additional information, calculate Kantner's current tax expense.

46. **LO.2** Provide the journal entry to record Kantner's current tax expense as determined in Problem 45.

47. **LO.2** Based on the facts and results of Problems 41–46, calculate Kantner's total provision for income tax expense reported on its financial statement and its book net income after tax.

48. **LO.2** Based on the facts and results of Problems 41–47, provide the income tax footnote rate reconciliation for Kantner.

BRIDGE DISCIPLINE

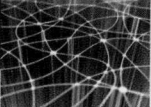

1. Using publicly available resources, locate summary financial information for two companies in the same industry. Compare and contrast the following items across the two companies: debt-to-equity ratio, return on assets, return on equity, inventory turnover ratio, and effective tax rate.

2. Using publicly available information, locate news or other items reporting financial analysts' forecasts or other information regarding two different companies. Determine whether the analyst appears to use any tax information in the report. For example, does the analyst use pretax or after-tax earnings in the analysis? Draft an e-mail to your instructor describing your findings.

    Communications

3. Using the annual reports or 10-Ks of two different public companies in the same industry, locate information regarding the compensation paid to their executives. Prepare a table comparing the compensation levels (cash and noncash) of top executives across the two companies, and send the table to your instructor. Illustrate the relationship between executive compensation and company performance by comparing the compensation to other company information such as net income.

    Communications

Research Problems

Use the tax resources of the Internet to address the following questions. Do not restrict your search to the Web, but include a review of newsgroups and general reference materials, practitioner sites and resources, primary sources of the tax law, chat rooms and discussion groups, and other opportunities.

Internet Activity

Research Problem 1. Locate the web page of Citizens for Tax Justice. Find the report "Corporate Taxpayers and Corporate Tax Dodgers, 2008-10." In no more than four PowerPoint slides for your classmates, summarize the following.

Communications

- Methodology, motivation, and background of the study.
- Five notable companies, their book income and their effective Federal income tax rates, and where those rates are zero or negative.
- Five industries, their effective tax rates, and the dollar amounts of the tax subsidies they receive.
- Five notable companies, their effective domestic effective Federal income tax rate, and the effective tax rate on their overseas profits.

Research Problem 2. Locate the most recent financial statements of two companies in the same industry using the companies' websites or the SEC's website (**www.sec.gov**). Perform a benchmarking analysis of the two companies' effective tax rates, components of the effective tax rate reconciliation, levels of deferred tax assets and liabilities, and other relevant data. Summarize this information in an e-mail to your instructor.

Research Problem 3. Locate articles or other discussions regarding the key differences between ASC 740 (SFAS 109) and International Accounting Standard No. 12 (related to income taxes). Summarize these key differences in an e-mail to your instructor. Make certain you have found the most current information for this comparison. Provide the URL for each of your sources.

Communications

Communications   **Research Problem 4.** Locate the financial statements of three different companies that report information in the income tax footnote regarding uncertain tax positions under ASC 740-10 (FIN 48). Create a schedule that compares and contrasts the changes in uncertain tax positions reported by the three companies. E-mail the schedule to your instructor.

Communications   **Research Problem 5.** Locate the financial statements of three different companies. Review the income tax footnote information on deferred tax assets (DTAs) and deferred tax liabilities (DTLs). Create a schedule that compares and contrasts the end-of-the year amounts of DTAs and DTLs, including any valuation allowances. E-mail the schedule to your instructor.

Research Problem 6. Using publicly available resources, locate summary financial information for two companies in the same industry. Compare and contrast the following items across the two companies: debt-to-equity ratio, return on assets, shareholder yield, return on equity, inventory turnover ratio, and effective tax rate. In your comparison, include the Federal, state/local, and international effective rates for the entities. Summarize in one paragraph the key reasons why the effective tax rates are similar (or different).

Roger CPA Review Questions

1. Identify the correct answer about the purposes of Schedules M-1 and M-3:

	Reconciles Book Income (Loss) with Income per Return	Distinguishes Between Permanent and Temporary Differences
a.	Both Schedule M-1 and Schedule M-3	Neither Schedule M-1 nor M-3
b.	Both Schedule M-1 and Schedule M-3	Schedule M-1 Only
c.	Schedule M-1 Only	Both Schedule M-1 and Schedule M-3
d.	Both Schedule M-1 and Schedule M-3	Schedule M-3 Only

2. Kelsey Corp. is an accrual-basis, calendar-year domestic corporation which is not part of a consolidated group. In the current tax year, Kelsey had over $10 million in gross receipts and ended the year with $9 million in total assets. Which reconciliation schedule—M-1 or M-3—should Kelsey file along with its corporate tax return for the current year?

   a.   Only Schedule M-1 can be filed.

   b.   Schedule M-3 is required.

   c.   Depends on how many years the corporation has been in existence.

   d.   Only Schedule M-1 is required, but Schedule M-3 may be elected instead.

3. Indicate for each of the following financial statement items whether it would cause no adjustment or whether its absolute value would be either added to or subtracted from net income per books when computing taxable income on the Schedule M-1:

	Municipal Bond Interest Earned	Excess of Capital Losses Over Capital Gains	Interest Expense Associated with Purchase of Municipal Bonds
a.	Subtracted from	No adjustment	No adjustment
b.	Added to	No adjustment	Subtracted from
c.	Subtracted from	Added to	Added to
d.	Subtracted from	No adjustment	Added to

4. Indicate for each of the following financial statement items whether it would cause no adjustment or whether its absolute value would be either added to or subtracted from net income per books when computing taxable income on the Schedule M-1:

	Premiums Paid on Key Employee Life Insurance	Excess of Book vs. Tax Depreciation	Accrued Warranty Expense
a.	No adjustment	No adjustment	No adjustment
b.	No adjustment	No adjustment	Subtracted from
c.	Subtracted from	Added to	Subtracted from
d.	Added to	Added to	Added to

5. Kookaburra Corp. reports net income per books of $575,000 for the current tax year. Included in this amount are the following items:

Item	Amount
Accrued vacation expense	$50,000
Meals and entertainment expense	40,000
Depreciation expense	35,000
Inventory shrinkage (accrual based on a percentage of total sales)	5,000

Depreciation reported on the current year tax return is $40,000.

Considering only the above information, what is Kookaburra Corp.'s taxable income for the current tax year?

a. $655,000   c. $640,000

b. $650,000   d. $645,000

PART 2

STRUCTURE OF THE FEDERAL INCOME TAX

CHAPTER **4**
Gross Income

CHAPTER **5**
Business Deductions

CHAPTER **6**
Losses and Loss Limitations

Part 2 introduces the components of the basic tax model. The gross income component, including the effect of exclusions, the accounting period, and accounting methods, is presented. This presentation is followed by an analysis of business deductions, including deductions that are allowed and disallowed and the proper timing for such deductions. Tax provisions are addressed concerning the amounts and timing of deductions that result from losses, including the use of carryovers and the proper financial accounting treatment of the resulting tax amounts.

Gross Income

LEARNING OBJECTIVES: *After completing Chapter 4, you should be able to:*

LO.1 Explain the concepts of gross income and realization and distinguish between the economic, accounting, and tax concepts of gross income.

LO.2 Explain when the cash, accrual, and hybrid methods of accounting are used and how they are applied.

LO.3 Identify who should pay the tax on an item of income.

LO.4 Apply the statutory authority as to when to exclude an item from gross income.

LO.5 Apply the tax provisions on loans made at below-market interest rates.

LO.6 Determine the extent to which receipts can be excluded under the tax benefit rule.

LO.7 Explain and apply the tax provision that excludes interest on state and local government obligations from gross income.

LO.8 Use the tax rules concerning the exclusion of leasehold improvements from gross income.

LO.9 Determine the extent to which life insurance proceeds are excluded from gross income.

LO.10 Describe when income must be reported from the discharge of indebtedness.

LO.11 Describe the general tax consequences of property transactions.

CHAPTER OUTLINE

TAX TALK *The first nine pages of the Internal Revenue Code define income. The remaining 1,100 pages spin the web of exceptions and preferences.* —WARREN G. MAGNUSON

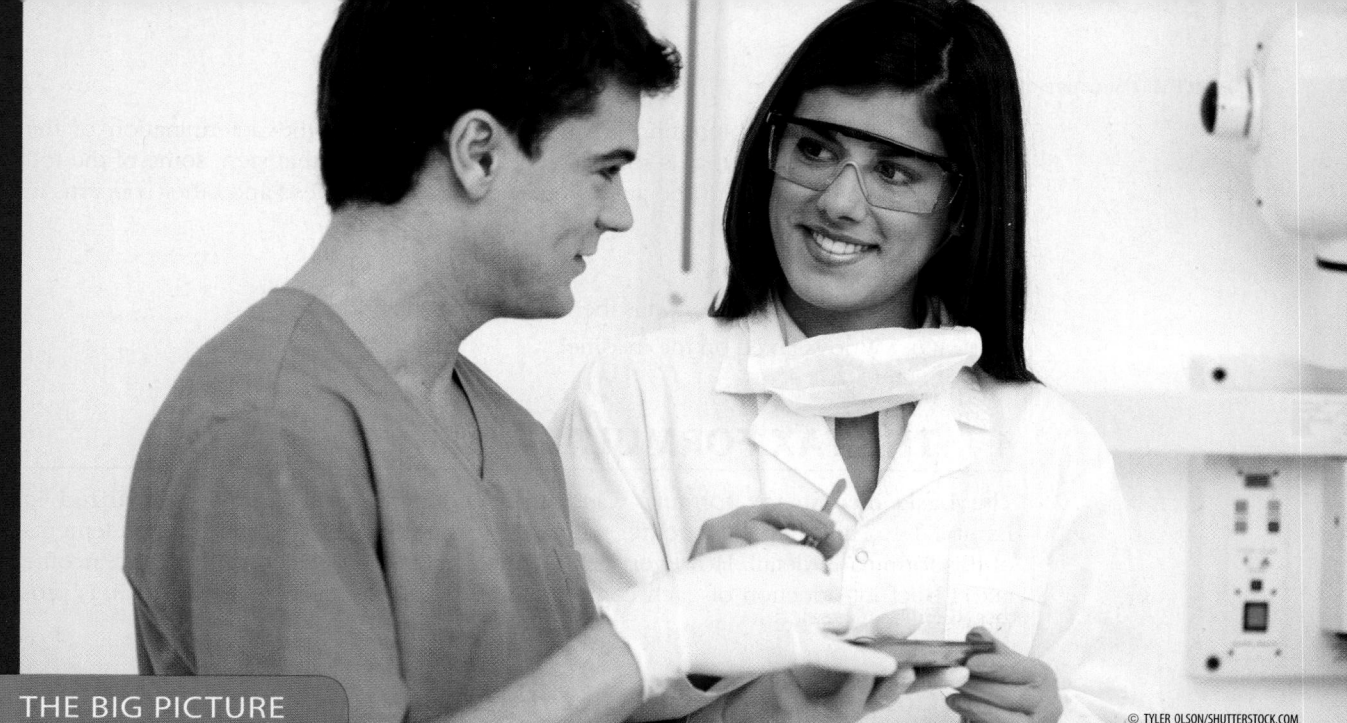

THE BIG PICTURE

JUST WHAT IS INCLUDED IN GROSS INCOME?

At the beginning of the year, Dr. Cliff Payne, age 27, opened his new dental practice as a personal service corporation. The entity uses a December 31 year-end and the accrual method of accounting. During the year, the corporation billed patients and insurance companies for $385,000 of dental services. At the end of the year, $52,000 of this amount had not been collected. The entity earned $500 interest on a money market account held at the local bank and another $500 interest on an investment in bonds issued by the Whitehall School District.

Dr. Payne's salary from his corporation is $10,000 per month. However, he did not cash his December payroll check until January. To help provide funds to invest in the new business, Dr. Payne's parents loaned him $150,000 and did not charge him any interest. He also owns stock that has increased in value from $7,000 at the beginning of the year to more than $25,000 at the end of the year.

Although Dr. Payne took several accounting classes in college, he would like your help in calculating the correct amounts of his own gross income and the gross income of the corporation.

Read the chapter and formulate your response.

The first step in computing an income tax liability is the determination of the amount of income that is subject to tax. In completing that step, some of the following questions must be answered. We will address these and other concerns in this chapter.

- *What:* What is income?
- *When:* In which tax period is the income recognized?
- *Who:* Who is taxed on the income?

4-1 THE TAX FORMULA

The basic income tax formula was introduced in Chapter 1 and summarized in Exhibit 1.1. This chapter, together with Chapters 5 through 8, examines the elements of this formula in detail. However, before embarking on a detailed study of the income tax, a brief introduction of each component of the tax formula, which follows, is provided as an overview.

4-1a Components of the Tax Formula

Income (Broadly Defined)

This includes all of the taxpayer's income, both taxable and nontaxable. Although it essentially is equivalent to gross receipts, it does not include a return of capital or borrowed funds.

Exclusions

For various reasons, Congress has chosen to exclude certain types of income from the income tax base. The principal income exclusions that apply to all entities (e.g., life insurance proceeds received by reason of death of the insured and state and local bond interest) are discussed later in this chapter, while exclusions that are unique to individuals are addressed in Chapters 9 through 11.

Gross Income

Section 61 of the Internal Revenue Code provides the following definition of gross income.

> Except as otherwise provided in this subtitle, gross income means all income from whatever source derived.

This language is based on the Sixteenth Amendment to the Constitution. The "except as otherwise provided" phrase refers to exclusions.

Supreme Court decisions have made it clear that *all* sources of income are subject to tax unless Congress specifically excludes the type of income received.

> The starting point in all cases dealing with the question of the scope of what is included in "gross income" begins with the basic premise that the purpose of Congress was to use the full measure of its taxing power.[1]

---

[1]*James v. U.S.*, 61–1 USTC ¶9449, 7 AFTR 2d 1361, 81 S.Ct. 1052 (USSC, 1961).

When § 61 refers to "income from whatever source derived," the taxing authorities are reaching far beyond the borders of the United States. Although one interpretation of "source" in this context is type of income (e.g., wages, interest, etc.), a broader interpretation revolves around the place where the income is generated. In this context, citizens and residents of the United States are subject to taxation on income earned from sources both inside and outside the country. This "worldwide income" tax base can cause potential double taxation problems, with other countries also taxing income earned within their borders, but mechanisms such as the foreign tax credit can alleviate these tax burdens.

Recently, a few prominent U.S. corporations have reorganized in other countries to avoid the higher U.S. tax rates on income earned abroad. About 3,000 individuals undergo a tax-motivated renunciation of U.S. citizenship every year. Chapter 16 discusses the Federal government's worldwide taxation of the income of a U.S. person.

While it is clear that income is to be broadly construed, the statutory law fails to provide a satisfactory definition of the term and lists only a small set of items that are specifically included in income, including:

- Compensation for services.
- Business income.
- Gains from sales and other disposition of property.
- Interest.
- Dividends.
- Rents and royalties.
- Certain income arising from discharge of indebtedness.
- Income from partnerships.

Deductions

Generally, all ordinary and necessary trade or business expenses are deductible by taxpaying entities. Such expenses include the cost of goods sold, salaries, wages, operating expenses (such as rent and utilities), research and development expenditures, interest, taxes, depreciation, amortization, and depletion.

As noted in Chapter 1, individuals can use two categories of deductions—deductions *for* AGI and deductions *from* AGI. In addition, individuals are unique among taxpaying entities in that they are permitted to deduct a variety of personal expenses (i.e., expenses unrelated to business or investment), they are allowed a standard deduction if this amount exceeds the deductible personal expenses, and they can claim a deduction for personal and dependency exemptions.

Determining the Tax

Taxable income is determined by subtracting deductions (after any applicable limitations) from gross income. The tax rates (located on the inside front cover of this text) then are applied to determine the tax. Finally, tax prepayments (such as Federal income tax withholding on salaries and estimated tax payments) and a wide variety of credits are subtracted from the tax to determine the amount due to the Federal government or the refund due to the taxpayer.

4-2 GROSS INCOME—WHAT IS IT?

4-2a Concepts of Income

As noted above, Congress failed to provide in the Code a clear definition of income. Instead, it was left to the judicial and administrative branches of government to determine the meaning of the term. As the income tax law developed, two competing

LO.1

Explain the concepts of gross income and realization and distinguish between the economic, accounting, and tax concepts of gross income.

FINANCIAL DISCLOSURE INSIGHTS   **What Does "Income" Mean to You?**

Accountants use a definition of income that relies on the realization principle.[2] **Accounting income** is not recognized until it is realized. For realization to occur:

- An exchange of goods or services must take place between the entity and some independent, external party, and

- The goods or services received by the entity must be capable of being objectively valued.[3]

Thus, an increase in the fair market value of an asset before its sale or other disposition is not sufficient to trigger the recognition of accounting income. Similarly, the imputed savings that arise when an entity creates assets for its own use (e.g., feed grown by a farmer for his or her livestock) do not constitute accounting income because no exchange has occurred.

Business taxpayers often reconcile their annual income computations for financial accounting and tax law purposes. Taxpayers required to prepare audited financial statements must explain in the footnotes to the statements (1) the most important accounting principles used in computing book income and (2) the most important tax elections and other consequences of the tax law on earnings per share.

models of income were considered by these agencies: economic income and accounting income.

The term **income** is used in the Code but is defined very broadly. Early in the history of our tax laws, the courts were required to interpret "the commonly understood meaning of the term which must have been in the minds of the people when they adopted the Sixteenth Amendment."[4]

Economists measure income (**economic income**) by determining the change (increase or decrease) in the fair market value of the entity's assets (net of liabilities) from the beginning to the end of the year. This focus on change in *net worth* as a measure of income (or loss) requires no disposition of assets. For *individual* taxpayers, one then adds the value of the year's personal consumption of goods and services (e.g., food, the rental value of owner-occupied housing, etc.).[5]

EXAMPLE 1

Trang's economic income is calculated by comparing her net worth at the end of the year (December 31) with her net worth at the beginning of the year (January 1) and adding her personal consumption.

Fair market value of Helen's assets on December 31	$220,000	
Less liabilities on December 31	(40,000)	
Net worth on December 31		$ 180,000
Fair market value of Helen's assets on January 1	$200,000	
Less liabilities on January 1	(80,000)	
Net worth on January 1		(120,000)
Increase in net worth		$ 60,000
Consumption		
Food, clothing, and other personal expenditures	$ 25,000	
Imputed rental value of the home Helen owns and occupies	12,000	
Total consumption		37,000
Economic income		$ 97,000

The tax law relies to some extent on net worth as a measure of income.[6] Potentially, anything that increases net worth is income, and anything that decreases net worth is

---

[2]See the American Accounting Association Committee Report on the "Realization Concept," *The Accounting Review* (April 1965): 312–322.

[3]Valuation is carried out in the local currency of the reporting entity.

[4]*Merchants Loan and Trust Co. v. Smietanka*, 1 USTC ¶42, 3 AFTR 3102, 41 S.Ct. 386 (USSC, 1921).

[5]See Henry C. Simons, *Personal Income Taxation* (Chicago: University of Chicago Press, 1933), Chapters 2–3.

[6]*Comm. v. Glenshaw Glass Co.*, 55–1 USTC ¶9308, 47 AFTR 162, 348 U.S. 426 (USSC, 1955).

deductible (if permitted by statute). Thus, *windfall income* such as buried treasure found in one's backyard is taxable, under the theory that net worth has increased.[7] Likewise, a lender does *not* recognize gross income on receipt of loan principal repayments. The lender's investment simply changes from a loan receivable to cash, so net worth does not change.

Because the strict application of a tax based on economic income would require taxpayers to determine the value of their assets annually, compliance would be burdensome. Controversies between taxpayers and the IRS inevitably would arise under an economic approach to income determination because of the subjective nature of valuation in many circumstances. In addition, using market values to determine income for tax purposes could result in liquidity problems. That is, a taxpayer's assets could increase in value but not be easily converted into the cash needed to pay the resulting tax (e.g., increases in the value of commercial real estate).[8] Thus, the IRS, Congress, and the courts have rejected broad application of the economic income concept as impractical.

The Big Picture

EXAMPLE 2

Return to the facts of *The Big Picture* on p. 4-1. Dr. Payne's portfolio has increased in value by more than 250% during the tax year, and that additional value constitutes economic income to him. But the Federal income tax law does not include the value increase in Dr. Payne's gross income, even though the taxpayer could convert some of those gains to cash through, say, a margin loan from his broker.

4-2b **Comparing Accounting and Tax Concepts of Income**

Although income tax rules frequently parallel financial accounting measurement concepts, differences do exist. Of major significance, for example, is the fact that unearned (prepaid) income received by an accrual basis taxpayer often is taxed in the year of receipt. For financial accounting purposes, such prepayments are not treated as income until earned. Because of this and other differences, many corporations report financial accounting income that is substantially different from the amounts reported for tax purposes.

The Supreme Court provided an explanation for some of the variations between accounting and taxable income in a decision involving inventory and bad debt adjustments.

> The primary goal of financial accounting is to provide useful information to management, shareholders, creditors, and others properly interested; the major responsibility of the accountant is to protect these parties from being misled. The primary goal of the income tax system, in contrast, is the equitable collection of revenue.... Consistently with its goals and responsibilities, financial accounting has as its foundation the principle of conservatism, with its corollary that "possible errors in measurement [should] be in the direction of understatement rather than overstatement of net income and net assets." In view of the Treasury's markedly different goals and responsibilities, understatement of income is not destined to be its guiding light....
>
> Financial accounting, in short, is hospitable to estimates, probabilities, and reasonable certainties; the tax law, with its mandate to preserve the revenue, can give no quarter to uncertainty.[9]

[7]*Cesarini v. U.S.*, 69–1 USTC ¶9270, 23 AFTR 2d 69–997, 296 F.Supp. 3 (D.Ct. N.Oh., 1969), *aff'd* 70–2 USTC ¶9509, 26 AFTR 2d 70–5107, 428 F.2d 812 (CA–6, 1970); Rev.Rul. 61, 1953–1 C.B. 17.

[8]In Chapter 1, this was identified as a justification of the wherewithal to pay concept.

[9]*Thor Power Tool Co. v. Comm.*, 79–1 USTC ¶9139, 43 AFTR 2d 79–362, 99 S.Ct. 773 (USSC, 1979).

4-2c **Form of Receipt**

Gross income is not limited to cash received. "It includes income realized in any form, whether in money, property, or services. Income may be realized [and recognized], therefore, in the form of services, meals, accommodations, stock or other property, as well as in cash."[10]

Ostrich Corporation allows Cameron, an employee, to use a company car for his vacation. Cameron realizes income equal to the rental value of the car for the time and mileage.

Donna is a CPA specializing in individual tax return preparation. Her neighbor, Jill, is a dentist. Each year, Donna prepares Jill's tax return in exchange for two dental checkups. Jill and Donna both have gross income equal to the fair market value of the services they provide.

Concept Summary 4.1

Gross Income Concepts

Taxable income is computed using a specific form of income statement, i.e., one created by Congress. Taxable income can be seen as similar but not identical to both economic income and the income computation that is required by generally accepted accounting principles (GAAP).

1. Economic income is not appropriate for computing taxable income. Economic income depends on annual measures of market value and consumption, both of which would be difficult to apply on a short tax-filing deadline.

2. Many of the same accounting methods that are allowed by GAAP also can be used in computing gross income and tax deductions, as the tax law largely follows the realization principle of financial accounting.

4-3 **YEAR OF INCLUSION**

4-3a **Taxable Year**

The annual accounting period or **taxable year** is a basic component of our tax system. Generally, a taxpayer uses the *calendar year* to report gross income. However, a *fiscal year* (a period of 12 months ending on the last day of any month other than December) can be adopted if the taxpayer maintains adequate books and records.[11] This fiscal year option generally is not available to partnerships, S corporations, and personal service corporations (i.e., one performing services in health, law, engineering, architecture, accounting, actuarial science, performing arts, or consulting).

Determining the tax year in which the income is recognized is important in determining the tax consequences of the income.

- With a progressive tax rate system, a taxpayer's marginal tax rate can change from year to year.
- Congress may change the tax rates.
- The relevant rates may change because of a change in the entity's status (e.g., a proprietorship may incorporate).
- Several provisions in the Code require computations using the taxpayer's income for the year (e.g., the charitable contribution deduction).
- The taxpayer wants to reduce the present value of any tax that is owed. In this regard, income recognition in a later year is preferred; the longer payment of the tax can be postponed, the lower the present value of the tax.

---

[10]Reg. § 1.61–1(a).

[11]§ 441; Reg. § 1.441–1.

4-3b Accounting Methods

The year in which an item of income is subject to tax often depends upon the accounting method the taxpayer employs. The three primary methods of accounting are (1) the cash receipts and disbursements method, (2) the accrual method, and (3) the hybrid method. Most individuals use the cash receipts and disbursements method of accounting, while most larger businesses use the accrual method. Because the Regulations require the accrual method for determining purchases and sales when inventory is an income-producing factor,[12] some businesses employ a hybrid method that is a combination of the cash and accrual methods.

In addition to these overall accounting methods, specialized tax accounting methods are available for certain items or transactions. For instance, a taxpayer may spread the gain from an installment sale of property over the collection period by using the *installment method* of income recognition. Contractors may either spread profits from contracts over the period in which the work is done (the *percentage of completion method*) or defer all profit until the year in which the project is completed (the *completed contract method*) in limited circumstances.[13]

The IRS can prescribe the accounting method to be used by the taxpayer. The IRS holds broad powers to determine whether an accounting method *clearly reflects income*.

> If no method of accounting has been regularly used by the taxpayer, or if the method used does not clearly reflect income, the computation of taxable income shall be made under such method as, in the opinion of the Secretary ... does clearly reflect income.[14]

Cash Receipts Method

Under the cash receipts method, property or services received are included in the taxpayer's gross income in the year of actual or constructive receipt by the taxpayer or agent, regardless of whether the income was earned in that year.[15] The income received need not be reduced to cash in the same year. All that is necessary for income recognition is that property or services received be measurable by a fair market value.[16]

Thus, a cash basis taxpayer that receives a note in payment for services recognizes gross income in the year of receipt equal to the fair market value of the note. However, a creditor's mere promise to pay (e.g., an account receivable), with no supporting note, usually is not considered to have a fair market value.[17] Thus, the cash basis taxpayer defers income recognition until the account receivable is collected.

LO.2

Explain when the cash, accrual, and hybrid methods of accounting are used and how they are applied.

---

[12]Reg. § 1.446–1(c)(2)(i).

[13]§§ 453 and 460.

[14]§ 446(b).

[15]*Julia A. Strauss*, 2 B.T.A. 598 (1925). The doctrine of *constructive receipt* holds that if income is unqualifiedly available although not physically in the taxpayer's possession, it is subject to the income tax. An example is accrued interest on a savings account. Under the doctrine of constructive receipt, the interest is taxed to a depositor in the year available, rather than the year actually withdrawn. The fact that the depositor uses the cash basis of accounting for tax purposes is irrelevant. Reg. § 1.451–2.

[16]Reg. §§ 1.446–1(a)(3) and (c)(1)(i).

[17]*Bedell v. Comm.*, 1 USTC ¶359, 7 AFTR 8469, 30 F.2d 622 (CA–2, 1929).

EXAMPLE 5

Finch & Thrush, a CPA firm, uses the cash receipts method of accounting. In 2014, the firm performs an audit for Orange Corporation and bills the client for $5,000, which is collected in 2015. In 2014, the firm also performs an audit for Blue Corporation. Because of Blue's precarious financial position, Finch & Thrush requires Blue to issue an $8,000 secured negotiable note in payment of the fee. The note has a fair market value of $6,000. The firm collects $8,000 on the note in 2015. Finch & Thrush reports the following gross income for the two years.

	2014	2015
Fair market value of note received from Blue	$6,000	
Cash received		
From Orange on account receivable		$ 5,000
From Blue on note receivable		8,000
Less: Recovery of capital	–0–	(6,000)
Total gross income	$6,000	$ 7,000

Generally, a cash basis taxpayer recognizes gross income when a check is received in payment for goods or services rendered in a business setting. This is true even if the taxpayer receives the check after banking hours. But if the person paying with the check requests that the check not be cashed until a subsequent date, the cash basis income is deferred until the date the check can be cashed.[18]

Certain taxpayers are not permitted to use the cash method of accounting. Specifically, the accrual basis must be used to report the income earned by (1) corporations (other than S corporations), (2) partnerships with a corporate partner (other than an S corporation), (3) business taxpayers that carry inventories, and (4) tax shelters. A number of other businesses still can use the cash method.[19]

- A farming business (other than certain corporations).
- A qualified personal service corporation (regardless of gross receipts level).
- A corporation or a partnership with a corporate partner that is not a tax shelter, whose average annual gross receipts for all prior three-year periods are $5 million or less.
- Certain small taxpayers that carry inventories.[20]

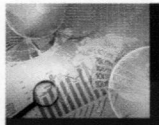

TAX PLANNING STRATEGIES   Cash Receipts Method

FRAMEWORK FOCUS: INCOME

Strategy: Postpone Recognition of Income to Achieve Tax Deferral.

FRAMEWORK FOCUS: TAX RATE

Strategy: Shift Net Income from High-Bracket Years to Low-Bracket Years.

The timing of income from services often can be controlled through the cash method of accounting. The usual lag between billings and collections (e.g., December's billings collected in January) can result in a deferral of some income until the last year of operations.

As another example, before rendering services, a corporate officer approaching retirement may contract with the corporation to defer a portion of his or her compensation to the lower tax bracket retirement years.

[18]*Charles F. Kahler*, 18 T.C. 31 (1952); *Bright v. U.S.*, 91–1 USTC ¶50,142, 67 AFTR 2d 91–673, 926 F.2d 383 (CA–5, 1991).
[19]§§ 441, 448(a), 448, 471.
[20]Rev.Procs. 2002-28, 2002-1 C.B. 815; 2001-10, 2001-1 C.B. 272.

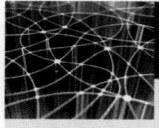

BRIDGE DISCIPLINE   **Bridge to Economics and Finance**

Nontaxable Economic Benefits

Home ownership is the prime example of economic income from capital that is not subject to tax. If the taxpayer uses his or her capital to purchase investments but pays rent on a personal residence, the taxpayer pays tax on the income from the investments but cannot deduct the rent payment.

However, if the taxpayer purchases a personal residence instead of the investments, he or she removes the investment income from the tax return but incurs no other form of gross income. A homeowner "pays rent to himself," but such rent is not subject to income tax. Thus, the homeowner has substituted nontaxable for taxable income.

Tax Deferral

Because deferred taxes are tantamount to interest-free loans from the government, the deferral of taxes is a worthy goal of the tax planner. However, the tax planner also must consider the tax rates for the years the income is shifted from and to. For example, a one-year deferral of income from a year in which the taxpayer's tax rate was 28 percent to a year in which the tax rate will be 35 percent would not be advisable if the taxpayer expects to earn less than a 7 percent after-tax return on the deferred tax dollars.

The taxpayer often can defer the recognition of income from appreciated property by postponing the event triggering realization (e.g., the final closing on a sale or exchange of property). If the taxpayer needs cash, obtaining a loan by using the appreciated property as collateral may be the least costly alternative. When the taxpayer anticipates reinvesting the proceeds, a sale may be inadvisable.

EXAMPLE

6

Ira owns 100 shares of Pigeon Company common stock with a cost of $20,000 and a fair market value of $50,000. Although the stock's value has increased substantially in the past three years, Ira thinks the growth cycle for the stock is over. If he sells the Pigeon stock, Ira will invest the proceeds from the sale in other common stock. Assuming that Ira's marginal tax rate on the sale is 20%, he keeps only $44,000 [$50,000 − .20($50,000 − $20,000)] to reinvest. The alternative investment must substantially outperform Pigeon in the future for the sale to be beneficial.

Accrual Method

Under the accrual method , an item generally is included in gross income for the year in which it is earned, regardless of when the income is collected. The income is earned when (1) all the events have occurred that fix the right to receive the income and (2) the amount to be received can be determined with reasonable accuracy.[21]

Generally, the taxpayer's rights to the income accrue when title to property passes to the buyer or the services are performed for the customer or client.[22] If the rights to the income have accrued but are subject to a potential refund claim (e.g., under a product warranty), the income is reported in the year of sale and a deduction is allowed in subsequent years when actual claims accrue.[23]

Where the taxpayer's rights to the income are being contested (e.g., when a contractor fails to meet specifications), gross income is recognized only when payment has been received.[24] If the payment is received before the dispute is settled, however, the

---

[21]Reg. § 1.451–1(a).

[22]*Lucas v. North Texas Lumber Co.*, 2 USTC ¶484, 8 AFTR 10276, 50 S.Ct. 184 (USSC, 1930).

[23]*Brown v. Helvering*, 4 USTC ¶1222, 13 AFTR 851, 54 S.Ct. 356 (USSC, 1933).

[24]*Burnet v. Sanford and Brooks*, 2 USTC ¶636, 9 AFTR 603, 51 S.Ct. 150 (USSC, 1931).

court-made claim of right doctrine requires the taxpayer to recognize the income in the year of receipt.[25]

If Finch & Thrush in Example 5 uses the accrual basis of accounting, it recognizes $13,000 ($8,000 + $5,000) income in 2014, the year its rights to the income accrue.

Tangerine Construction, Inc., completes construction of a building at the end of the year and presents a bill to the customer. The customer refuses to pay the bill and claims that Tangerine has not met specifications. A settlement with the customer is not reached until the next year.

No gross income accrues to Tangerine until the second year.

Hybrid Method

The accrual method is used to determine sales and cost of goods sold. To simplify record keeping, some taxpayers account for inventory using the accrual method but use the cash method for all other income and deduction items. This approach, called the hybrid method, is used primarily by small businesses when the cash method otherwise is not available.

4-3c Special Rules for Cash Basis Taxpayers

Constructive Receipt

Income that has not actually been received by the taxpayer is taxed as though it had been received—the income is constructively received—under the following conditions.

- The amount is made readily available to the taxpayer.
- The taxpayer's actual receipt is not subject to substantial limitations or restrictions.[26]

The rationale for the constructive receipt doctrine is that if the income is available, the taxpayer should not be allowed unilaterally to postpone income recognition. For instance, a taxpayer is not permitted to defer income for December services by refusing to accept payment until January.

Constructive Receipt

Rob, a physician, conducts his medical practice as a sole proprietorship. Rob is also a member of a barter club. This year, Rob provided medical care for other club members and earned 3,000 points. Each point entitles him to $1 in goods and services sold by other members of the club; the points can be used at any time. Rob exchanged his points for a new high-definition TV in the next year, but he recognizes $3,000 gross income in the first year, i.e. when the 3,000 points were credited to his account.[27]

On December 31, an employer issued a bonus check to an employee but asked her to hold it for a few days until the company could make deposits to cover the check. The income was not constructively received on December 31 because the issuer did not have sufficient funds in its account to pay the debt.[28]

Mauve, Inc., an S corporation, owned interest coupons that matured on December 31. The coupons can be converted to cash at any bank at maturity. Thus, the income was constructively received on December 31, even though Mauve failed to cash in the coupons until the following year.[29]

---

[25]*North American Oil Consolidated Co. v. Burnet*, 3 USTC ¶943, 11 AFTR 16, 52 S.Ct. 613 (USSC, 1932).

[26]Reg. § 1.451–2(a).

[27]Rev.Rul. 80–52, 1980–1 C.B. 100.

[28]*L. M. Fischer*, 14 T.C. 792 (1950).

[29]Reg. § 1.451–2(b).

TAX IN THE NEWS **Congress Rescues Lottery Winners from Constructive Receipt Problems**

Under the general rules of constructive receipt, a lottery winner who elected to receive the winnings in installments could face horrendous tax problems. If the winner had the right to receive the entire amount but elected to be paid in installments, tax could be due on the present value of the amounts to be received in the future as well as the amount received currently. Frequently, the winner made the election without being aware of the tax consequences.

To protect poorly advised, or unadvised, lottery winners, Congress changed the tax law so that the constructive receipt doctrine does not apply to "qualified prizes," a term crafted specifically to address the lottery and prize-winner's situation. Thus, lottery winnings can be received in installments and included in gross income as the installments are received.

Constructive Receipt

Flamingo Company mails dividend checks on December 31. The checks will not be received by the shareholders until January. The shareholders do not realize gross income until January.[30]

EXAMPLE 11

The constructive receipt doctrine does not reach income the taxpayer is not yet entitled to receive, even though the taxpayer could have contracted to receive the income

Murphy offers to pay Peach Corporation (a cash basis taxpayer) $100,000 for land in December 2015. Peach Corporation refuses, but offers to sell the land to Murphy on January 1, 2016, when the corporation will be in a lower tax bracket. If Murphy accepts Peach's offer, the gain is taxed to Peach in 2016, when the sale is completed.[31]

EXAMPLE 12

In-depth coverage can be found on this book's companion website: www.cengagebrain.com

1 DIGGING DEEPER

Original Issue Discount

Lenders frequently make loans that require a payment at maturity of more than the amount of the original loan. The difference between the amount due at maturity and the amount of the original loan is actually interest but is referred to as **original issue discount**. In these circumstances, the Code requires the original issue discount to be reported when it is earned, regardless of the taxpayer's accounting method.[32] The *interest earned* is calculated by the effective interest rate method.

On January 1, 2014, Blue and White, a cash basis partnership, pays $92,456 for a 24-month certificate of deposit. The certificate is priced to yield 4% (the effective interest rate) with interest compounded annually. No interest is paid until maturity, when Blue and White receives $100,000.

The partnership's gross income from the certificate is $7,544 ($100,000 − $92,456). Blue and White calculates income earned each year as follows.

EXAMPLE 13

2014 (.04 × $92,456) =	$3,698
2015 [.04($92,456 + $3,698)] =	3,846
	$7,544

[30]Reg. § 1.451–2(b).
[31]*Cowden v. Comm.*, 61–1 USTC ¶9382, 7 AFTR 2d 1160, 289 F.2d 20 (CA–5, 1961).
[32]§§ 1272(a)(3) and 1273(a).

The original issue discount rules do not apply to U.S. savings bonds or to obligations with a maturity date of one year or less from the date of issue.[33]

Amounts Received under an Obligation to Repay

The receipt of funds with an obligation to repay that amount in the future is the essence of borrowing. The taxpayer's assets and liabilities increase by the same amount, so no income is realized when the borrowed funds are received.

A landlord receives a damage deposit from a tenant. The landlord does not recognize income until the deposit is forfeited because the landlord has an obligation to repay the deposit if no damage occurs.[34] However, if the deposit is in fact a prepayment of rent, it is taxed in the year of receipt.

4-3d Special Rules for Accrual Basis Taxpayers

Prepaid Income

For financial reporting purposes, advance payments received from customers are reflected as prepaid income and as a liability of the seller. For tax purposes, however, the prepaid income often is taxed in the year of receipt.

In December 2014, Jared's sole proprietorship pays its January 2015 rent of $1,000. Jared's calendar-year, accrual basis landlord includes the $1,000 in 2014 gross income for tax purposes, although $1,000 unearned rent income is reported as a liability on the landlord's financial accounting balance sheet for December 31, 2014.

Deferral of Advance Payments for Goods

Generally, an accrual basis taxpayer can elect to defer recognition of income from advance payments for goods if the method of accounting for the sale is the same for tax and financial reporting purposes.[35]

Brown Company ships goods only after payment for the goods has been received. In December 2014, Brown receives a $10,000 payment for goods that are not shipped until January 2015. Assuming that a proper election is in place, Brown reports the income in 2015 for tax purposes, assuming that the company reports the income in 2015 for financial reporting purposes.

Deferral of Advance Payments for Services

When payments are received for services that will be performed in a later tax year, an accrual basis taxpayer can defer for one year the recognition of income for the services that will be performed later.[36] This method of accounting may also be used for advance payments received for goods, as well as licensing of intellectual property, and the sale, lease, or license of software.

Advance payments for prepaid rent or prepaid interest, however, always are taxed in the year of receipt, as illustrated in Example 15.

---

[33]§ 1272(a)(2).
[34]*John Mantell*, 17 T.C. 1143 (1952).

[35]Reg. § 1.451–5(b). The election covers the current and all future tax years, unless the IRS allows the taxpayer to terminate it. See Reg. § 1.451–5(c) for exceptions to this deferral opportunity.
[36]Rev.Proc. 2004–34, 2004–1 C.B. 991.

Yellow Corporation, an accrual basis calendar-year taxpayer, sells its computer consulting services under 12-month, 24-month, and 36-month contracts. The corporation provides services to each customer every month. On May 1, 2014, Yellow sold the following contracts.

EXAMPLE
17

Length of Contract	Total Proceeds
12 months	$3,000
24 months	4,800
36 months	7,200

Yellow may defer until 2015 all of the income that will be reported on its financial statements after 2014.

Length of Contract	Income Recorded in 2014	Income Recorded in 2015
12 months	$2,000 ($3,000 × 8/12)	$1,000 ($3,000 × 4/12)
24 months	1,600 ($4,800 × 8/24)	3,200 ($4,800 × 16/24)
36 months	1,600 ($7,200 × 8/36)	5,600 ($7,200 × 28/36)

TAX PLANNING STRATEGIES **Prepaid Income**

FRAMEWORK FOCUS: INCOME

Strategy: Postpone Recognition of Income to Achieve Tax Deferral.

The accrual basis taxpayer who receives advance payments from customers should adopt the available tax accounting income deferral methods. It then should structure the transactions using those rules, so as to avoid a payment of tax on income before the time the income actually is earned.

In addition, both cash and accrual basis taxpayers sometimes can defer income by stipulating that the payments are deposits rather than prepaid income. For example, a tax-savvy landlord might consider requiring an equivalent damage deposit rather than prepayment of the last month's rent.

Concept Summary 4.2

Income Tax Accounting

Tax accounting methods often parallel those used for financial accounting, especially those that affect the timing of the tax recognition of income and deduction items. Certain exceptions do exist, however.

1. Businesses may be able to adopt the cash, accrual, or hybrid method of accounting. The tax law allows certain businesses to use either the cash or hybrid method, while others may be required to use the accrual method. For instance, the accrual method typically is required if the taxpayer holds inventories or is a C corporation with over

$5 million of gross receipts (other than a qualified personal service corporation).

2. Other tax accounting methods parallel those of financial accounting, such as the installment method and the treatment of long-term contracts.

3. Special rules apply when the taxpayer has control, but not possession, of funds that have been earned.

4. Tax accounting method rules may allow the deferral of income recognition concerning prepayments for the sale of goods and services.

LO.3

Identify who should pay the tax on an item of income.

4-4 INCOME SOURCES

4-4a Personal Services

It is a well-established principle of taxation that income from personal services must be included in the gross income of the person who performs the services. This principle was first established in a Supreme Court decision, *Lucas v. Earl*.[37] Mr. Earl entered into a binding agreement with his wife under which Mrs. Earl was to receive one-half of Mr. Earl's salary. Justice Holmes used the celebrated fruit and tree metaphor to explain that the fruit (income) must be attributed to the tree from which it came (Mr. Earl's services). A mere assignment of income to another party does not shift the liability for the tax.

Services of an Employee

Services performed by an employee for the employer's customers are considered performed by the employer. Thus, the employer is taxed on the income from the services provided to the customer, and the employee is taxed on any compensation received from the employer.[38]

The Big Picture

EXAMPLE 18

Return to the facts of *The Big Picture* on p. 4-1. Dr. Payne has entered into an employment contract with his corporation and receives a salary. All patients contract to receive their dental services from the corporation, and those services are provided through the corporation's employee, Dr. Payne.

Thus, the corporation earned the income from patients' services and must include the patients' fees in its gross income. Payne includes his salary in his own gross income. The corporation claims a deduction for the reasonable salary paid to Payne.

DIGGING DEEPER 2   In-depth coverage can be found on this book's companion website: www.cengagebrain.com

4-4b Income from Property

Income earned from property (e.g., interest, dividends, rent) is included in the gross income of the owner of the property. If a shareholder clips interest coupons from bonds shortly before the interest payment date and transfers the coupons to his or her solely owned corporation, the interest still is taxed to the shareholder.

Often income-producing property is transferred after income from the property has accrued but before the income is recognized under the transferor's method of accounting. The IRS and the courts have developed rules to allocate the income between the transferor and the transferee. These allocation rules are addressed below. Other allocation rules address income in community property states.

DIGGING DEEPER 3   In-depth coverage can be found on this book's companion website: www.cengagebrain.com

Interest

According to the tax law, interest accrues daily. Therefore, the interest for the period that includes the date of an asset transfer is allocated between the transferor and the transferee based on the number of days during the period that each owned the property.

---

[37]2 USTC ¶496, 8 AFTR 10287, 50 S.Ct. 241 (USSC, 1930).

[38]*Sargent v. Comm.*, 91–1 USTC ¶50,168, 67 AFTR 2d 91–718, 929 F.2d 1252 (CA–8, 1991).

TAX FACT   How Much and What Type of Income?

Of the 145 million individual income tax returns filed for the 2012 tax year, 83 percent included wage or salary income, and about 37 percent included some amount of interest income. But except for these two categories, no other type of income was found in even a quarter of the returns filed. Sales of business assets were found on fewer than one-half percent of the returns, and about 4 percent of the returns included flow-through income or loss from partnerships and S corporations. Capital gains showed up on about 10 percent of the returns, but only when distributions from mutual fund investments were included.

EXAMPLE 19

Floyd, a cash basis taxpayer, gives his son, Seth, corporate bonds with a face amount of $12,000 and a 5% stated annual interest rate. The interest is payable on the last day of each quarter. Floyd makes the gift to Seth on February 28. Floyd recognizes $100 interest income at the time of the gift ($12,000 × 5% × 3/12 interest forthe quarter × 2/3 months in the quarter earned before the gift).

For the transferor, the timing of the recognition of gross income from the property depends upon the pertinent accounting method and the manner in which the property was transferred. In the case of a gift of income-producing property, the donor's share of the accrued income is recognized at the time it would have been recognized had the donor continued to own the property.[39] If the transfer is a sale, however, the transferor recognizes the accrued income at the time of the sale, because the accrued amount is included in the sales proceeds.

EXAMPLE 20

Mia purchased a corporate bond at its face amount on January 1 for $10,000. The bond paid 5% interest each December 31. On March 31, Mia sold the bond for $10,600. Mia recognizes $125 interest income, accrued as of the date of the sale (5% × $10,000 × 3/12 months before the sale). She also recognizes a $475 capital gain from the sale of the bond, computed as follows.

Amount received from sale	$ 10,600
Accrued interest income already recognized	(125)
Selling price of bond, less interest	$ 10,475
Less cost of the bond	(10,000)
Capital gain recognized on sale	$ 475

Dividends

A corporation is taxed on its earnings, and the shareholders are taxed on the dividends paid to them from the corporation's after-tax earnings.

Partial relief from the double taxation of dividends has been provided in that *qualified dividends* are taxed at the same marginal rate that is applicable to a net capital gain. Distributions that are not qualified dividends are taxed at the rates that apply to ordinary income.[40]

Tax Rate That Applies to the Taxpayer's Ordinary Income	Tax Rate That Applies to Dividend Income
0, 10, or 15%	0%
25, 28, 33, or 35%	15%
39.6%	20%

---

[39]Rev.Rul. 72–312, 1972–1 C.B. 22.

[40]§ 1(h)(11). Qualified dividends are not treated as capital gains in the gains and losses netting process; thus, they are *not* reduced by capital losses. For certain high-income individuals, the additional Medicare tax on net investment income also may apply to dividends, interest, net capital gains, and the like. See Chapter 9.

GLOBAL TAX ISSUES   **Which Foreign Dividends Get the Discounted Rate?**

A dividend from a non-U.S. corporation is eligible for qualified dividend status only if one of the following requirements is met: (1) the foreign corporation's stock is traded on an established U.S. securities market or (2) the foreign corporation is eligible for the benefits of a comprehensive income tax treaty or information-sharing agreement between its country of incorporation and the United States.[41]

Because the beneficial tax rate is intended to mitigate double taxation, only certain dividends are eligible for the beneficial treatment. Excluded are certain dividends from non-U.S. corporations, dividends from tax-exempt entities, and dividends that do not satisfy the holding period requirement.

Corporations that are shareholders (that is, they own stock in another corporation) may be allowed a deduction to offset some or all of their dividend income. See Chapter 12.

A holding period requirement must be satisfied for the lower tax rates to apply: the stock that paid the dividend must have been held for more than 60 days during the 121-day period beginning 60 days before the ex-dividend date.[42] The purpose of this requirement is to prevent the taxpayer from buying the stock shortly before the dividend is paid, receiving the dividend, and then selling the stock at a short-term capital loss after the stock goes ex-dividend. A stock's price often declines after the stock goes ex-dividend.

Qualified Dividends

EXAMPLE 21

Green Corporation pays a dividend of $1.50 on each share of its common stock. Madison and Daniel, two unrelated shareholders, each own 1,000 shares of the stock. Consequently, each receives a dividend of $1,500 (1,000 shares × $1.50). Assume that Daniel satisfies the 60/120-day holding period rule, but Madison does not.

The $1,500 that Daniel receives is subject to the lower rates on qualified dividends. The $1,500 that Madison receives, however, is not. Because Madison did not comply with the holding period rule, her dividend is not a *qualified dividend*; it is taxed at ordinary income rates.

EXAMPLE 22

Assume that both Madison and Daniel in Example 21 are in the 35% Federal income tax bracket. Consequently, Madison pays a tax of $525 (35% × $1,500) on her dividend, while Daniel pays a tax of $225 (15% × $1,500) on his. The $300 saving that Daniel enjoys underscores the advantages of receiving a qualified dividend.

A distribution by a corporation to its shareholders is classified as a dividend only if it is paid from the entity's *earnings and profits* (E&P). If the distribution is not made from E&P, it is treated as a return of the shareholder's investment and generally is not taxed at the time of the distribution. See Chapter 13.

Unlike interest, dividends do not accrue on a daily basis because the declaration of a dividend is at the discretion of the corporation's board of directors. Generally, dividends are taxed to the person who is entitled to receive them—the shareholder of record as of the corporation's record date.[43] Thus, if a taxpayer sells stock after a dividend has been declared but before the record date, the dividend generally is taxed to the purchaser.

If a donor makes a gift of stock to someone (e.g., a family member) after the declaration date but before the record date, the donor does not shift the dividend income to

---

[41]§§ 1(h)(11)(C)(i), (ii).

[42]The ex-dividend date is the date before the record date on which the corporation finalizes the list of shareholders who will receive the dividends.

[43]Reg. § 1.61–9(c). The record date is the cutoff for determining the shareholders who are entitled to receive the dividend.

TAX FACT Business Income and Loss

Sole proprietors reporting net business income or loss on Form 1040 constitute almost 16 percent of all returns filed. About 9 percent of all Forms 1040 show income from rentals or farming operations. And more than 1 percent of individuals report winnings from gambling activities!

the donee. The *fruit* has ripened sufficiently as of the declaration date to tax the dividend income to the donor of the stock.[44]

EXAMPLE 23

On June 20, the board of directors of Black Corporation declares a $10 per share dividend. The dividend is payable on June 30 to shareholders of record on June 25. As of June 20, Kathleen owns 200 shares of Black stock. On June 21, Kathleen sells 100 of the shares to Jon for their fair market value and gives 100 of the shares to Andrew (her son). Both Jon and Andrew are shareholders of record as of June 25.

Jon (the purchaser) is taxed on $1,000 because he is entitled to receive the dividend. However, Kathleen (the donor) is taxed on the $1,000 received by Andrew (the donee) because the gift was made after the declaration date but before the record date of the dividend.

In-depth coverage can be found on this book's companion website: www.cengagebrain.com

4 DIGGING DEEPER

4-4c Income Received by an Agent

Income received by the taxpayer's agent is considered to be received by the taxpayer. A cash basis principal must recognize the income at the time it is received by the agent.[45]

EXAMPLE 24

Longhorn, Inc., a cash basis corporation, delivers cattle to the auction barn in late December. The auctioneer, acting as the corporation's agent, sells the cattle and collects the proceeds in December. The auctioneer does not pay Longhorn until the following January. Longhorn includes the sales proceeds in its gross income in the year the auctioneer received the funds.

TAX PLANNING STRATEGIES Techniques for Reducing Investment Income

FRAMEWORK FOCUS: INCOME

Strategy: Postpone Recognition of Income to Achieve Tax Deferral.

FRAMEWORK FOCUS: TAX RATE

Strategy: Control the Character of Income

Because no tax is due until a gain has been recognized, the law favors investments that yield appreciation rather than annual income, and it favors capital gains over interest income.

EXAMPLE 25

Vera can buy a low-rated corporate bond or an acre of land for $10,000. The bond pays $1,000 of interest (10%) each year, and Vera expects the land to increase in value 10% each year for the next 10 years. She is in the 40% (combined Federal and state) tax bracket for ordinary income and 26% for qualifying capital gains. If the bond would mature or the land would be sold in 10 years and

continued

[44]*M. G. Anton*, 34 T.C. 842 (1960).　　　　[45]Rev.Rul. 79–379, 1979–2 C.B. 204.

Vera would reinvest the interest at a 10% before-tax return, she would accumulate the following amounts at the end of 10 years.

		Bond	Land
Original investment		$10,000	$10,000
Annual income	$ 1,000		
Less tax	(400)		
	$ 600		
Compound amount reinvested for 10 years at 6% after-tax	×13.18	7,908	
Future value		$17,908	
Compound amount, 10 years at 10%			× 2.59
			$25,900
Less tax on sale: 26%($25,900 − $10,000)			(4,134)
Future value			$21,766

Therefore, the value of the deferral that results from investing in the land rather than in the bond is $3,858 ($21,766 − $17,908). The income then would be subject to Vera's tax rates, namely, ordinary rates on interest income and capital gain rates on the land sale.

Apply the statutory authority as to when exclude an item from gross income.

4-5 SPECIFIC ITEMS OF GROSS INCOME

The all-inclusive principles of gross income determination as applied by the IRS and the courts have, on occasion, been expanded or modified by Congress through legislation. This legislation generally provides more specific rules for determining gross income from certain sources. Most of these special rules appear in §§ 71–90 of the Code.

In addition to provisions describing how specific sources of gross income are to be taxed, several specific rules *exclude* items from gross income. Authority for excluding specific items is provided in §§ 101–150 and in various other provisions in the Code.

Many statutory exclusions are unique to *individual taxpayers* (e.g., gifts and inheritances,[46] scholarships,[47] and a variety of fringe benefits paid to *employees*). These exclusions are discussed in Chapters 9 through 11. Other exclusions are broader and apply to all entities. These exclusions include interest on state and local bonds (§ 103), life insurance proceeds received by reason of death of the insured (§ 101), the fair market value of leasehold improvements received by the lessor when a lease is terminated (§ 109),[48] and income from discharge of indebtedness (§ 108).

Taxpayers can recognize gross income when there is a sale or other disposition of a nonbusiness asset. These transactions are discussed in more detail in Chapters 7 and 8, but this section includes an introduction to the tax rules that apply in the most common situations. Some of the broadly applied statutory rules describing inclusions and exclusions are discussed next.

---

[46]§ 102.
[47]§ 117.

[48]If the tenant made the improvements in lieu of rent payments, the value of the improvements is not eligible for exclusion.

Interest-free loans have become a popular form of compensation for executives. Several examples of multimillion-dollar loans have come to light as a result of recent bankruptcies by large corporations. The board of directors often justifies the loans as necessary to enable the executive to be able to purchase a residence or to buy stock in the company.

Loans by publicly held corporations to their executives generally are prohibited by Federal law. The Sarbanes-Oxley provisions generally prohibit loans by corporations to their executives. However, an exception permits corporate loans to finance the acquisition of a personal residence for an executive.

Interest-free loans also are subject to a special Federal income tax treatment. These rules are discussed in Section 4-5a.

4-5a **Imputed Interest on Below-Market Loans**

As discussed earlier in the chapter, generally, no income is recognized unless it is realized. Realization usually occurs when the taxpayer performs services or sells goods, thus becoming entitled to a payment from the other party. It follows that no income is realized if the goods or services are provided at no charge. Under this prior-law interpretation of the realization requirement, interest-free loans were used to shift income between taxpayers.

> Brown Corporation is in the 35% tax bracket and has $400,000 in a money market account earning 5% interest. Jack is the sole shareholder of Brown. He is in the 15% tax bracket and has no investment income. In view of the difference in tax rates, Jack believes that it would be better for him to receive and pay tax on the earnings from Brown's $400,000 investment. Jack does not want to receive the $400,000 from Brown as a dividend because that would trigger a tax.
>
> Under prior law, Jack could receive the money market account from Brown in exchange for a $400,000 non-interest-bearing note, payable on Brown's demand. As a result, Jack would receive the $20,000 annual earnings on the money market account, and the combined taxes of Brown and Jack would be decreased every year by $4,000.
>
> | | |
> |---|---|
> | Decrease in Brown's tax (.05 × $400,000) × .35 | ($7,000) |
> | Increase in Jack's tax (.05 × $400,000) × .15 | 3,000 |
> | Overall decrease in tax liability | ($4,000) |

EXAMPLE 26

The Code no longer allows this income-shifting result. Brown Corporation in the preceding example is deemed to have received an interest payment from Jack even though no interest was actually paid.[49] This payment of imputed interest is taxable to Brown. Jack may be able to deduct the imaginary interest payment on his return as investment interest if he itemizes deductions. Brown then is deemed to return the interest to Jack in the form of a taxable dividend.

Imputed interest is calculated using rates that the Federal government pays on new borrowings and is compounded semiannually. The Federal rates are adjusted monthly and are published by the IRS.[50] There are three Federal rates: short-term (not over three years and including demand loans), mid-term (over three years but not over nine years), and long-term (over nine years).

If interest is charged on the loan but is less than the Federal rate, the imputed interest is the difference between the amount that would have been charged at the Federal rate and the amount actually charged.

---

[49]§ 7872(a)(1).   [50]§§ 7872(b)(2) and (f)(2).

EXAMPLE 27

Assume that the Federal rate applicable to the loan in the preceding example is 3.5% through June 30 and 4% from July 1 through December 31. Brown Corporation made the loan on January 1, and the loan is still outstanding on December 31. Brown recognizes interest income of $15,140, and Jack reports interest expense of $15,140. Brown is deemed to have paid a $15,140 dividend to Jack.

Interest Calculations

January 1 to June 30 (.035 × $400,000) (½ year)	$ 7,000
July 1 to December 31 [.04($400,000 + $7,000)] (½ year)	8,140
	$15,140

If Brown had charged 3% interest under the terms of the note, compounded annually, the deemed interest amount would have been $3,140.

Interest at the Federal rate	$ 15,140
Less interest actually charged (.03 × $400,000)	(12,000)
Imputed interest	$ 3,140

The imputed interest rules apply to the following types of below-market loans.[51]

1. Gift loans (made out of love, respect, or generosity).
2. Compensation-related loans (employer loans to employees).
3. Corporation-shareholder loans (a corporation's loans to its shareholders, as in Example 26).

The effects of these loans on the borrower and lender are summarized in Exhibit 4.1.

Exceptions and Limitations

No interest is imputed on total outstanding *compensation-related loans* or *corporation-shareholder loans* of $10,000 or less unless the purpose of the loan is tax avoidance.[52] This vague tax avoidance standard exposes practically all compensation-related and corporation-shareholder loans to possible imputed interest problems. Nevertheless, the $10,000 exception should apply when an employee's borrowing was necessitated by personal needs (e.g., to meet unexpected expenses) rather than tax considerations.

EXHIBIT 4.1	Effect of Certain Below-Market Loans: Imputed Interest Income and Deductions		
Type of Loan		**Lender**	**Borrower**
Gift	Step 1	Interest income	Interest expense
	Step 2	Gift made*	Gift received
Compensation related	Step 1	Interest income	Interest expense
	Step 2	Compensation expense	Compensation income
Corporation to shareholder	Step 1	Interest income	Interest expense
	Step 2	Dividend paid	Dividend income

* The gift may be subject to the Federal gift tax (refer to Chapter 1).

[51]§ 7872(c). Additional situations exist where these rules apply. See, e.g., §§ 7872(c)(1)(D), (E).

[52]§ 7872(c)(3).

Similarly, no interest is imputed on outstanding *gift loans* of $10,000 or less between individuals, unless the loan proceeds are used to purchase income-producing property.[53] This exemption eliminates from these complex provisions immaterial amounts that do not result in sizable shifts of income.

On loans of $100,000 or less between individuals, the imputed interest cannot exceed the borrower's net investment income for the year (gross income from all investments less the related expenses).[54] Through the gift loan provision, the imputed interest rules are designed to prevent high-income individuals from shifting income to relatives in a lower marginal bracket. This shifting of investment income is considered to occur only to the extent that the borrower also recognizes net investment income. Thus, the income imputed to the lender is limited to the borrower's net investment income.

If the borrower's net investment income for the year does not exceed $1,000, no interest is imputed on loans of $100,000 or less. However, this exemption does not apply if a principal purpose of a loan is tax avoidance. In such a case, interest is imputed, and the imputed interest is not limited to the borrower's net investment income.[55]

These exceptions to the imputed interest rules are summarized in Exhibit 4.2.

The Big Picture

EXAMPLE 28

Return to the facts of *The Big Picture* on p. 4-1. Dr. Payne's loan from his parents likely is a *gift loan*, as his parents are not shareholders in the personal service corporation. Imputed interest must be computed annually with regard to this loan by both Dr. Payne and his parents, under two different tax rules: (1) the principal amount of the loan exceeds $100,000 and (2) the loan proceeds were invested in an income-producing asset.

EXAMPLE 29

Vicki made interest-free gift loans as follows.

Borrower	Amount	Borrower's Net Investment Income	Purpose
Susan	$ 8,000	$–0–	Education
Dan	9,000	500	Purchase of stock
Mai	25,000	–0–	Purchase of a business
Olaf	120,000	–0–	Purchase of a residence

Tax avoidance is not a principal purpose of any of the loans. The loan to Susan is not subject to the imputed interest rules because the $10,000 exception applies. The $10,000 exception does not apply to the loan to Dan because the proceeds were used to purchase income-producing assets. However, under the $100,000 exception, the imputed interest is limited to Dan's investment income ($500). Because the $1,000 exception also applies to this loan, no interest is imputed.

No interest is imputed on the loan to Mai because the $100,000 exception applies. None of the exceptions apply to the loan to Olaf because the loan was for more than $100,000; he recognizes imputed interest income related to his loan.

4-5b **Tax Benefit Rule**

Generally, if a taxpayer obtains a deduction for an item in one year and in a later year recovers all or a portion of the prior deduction, the recovery is included in gross income in the year received.[56]

LO.6

Determine the extent to which receipts can be excluded under the tax benefit rule.

---

[53]§ 7872(c)(2).

[54]§ 7872(d). The $100,000 provision applies only to gift loans.

[55]§ 7872 (d)(1)(B).

[56]§ 111(a).

EXHIBIT 4.2	Exceptions to the Imputed Interest Rules for Below-Market Loans	
Exception	**Eligible Loans**	**Ineligible Loans and Limitations**
De minimis—aggregate loans of $10,000 or less	Gift loans	Proceeds are used to purchase income-producing assets.
	Employer-employee	Principal purpose is tax avoidance.
	Corporation-shareholder	Principal purpose is tax avoidance.
Aggregate loans of $100,000 or less	Gift loans between individuals	Principal purpose is tax avoidance. For all other loans, interest is imputed to the extent of the borrower's net investment income if it exceeds $1,000.

MegaCorp deducted as a loss a $1,000 receivable from a customer when it appeared the amount would never be collected. The following year, the customer paid $800 on the receivable. Mega-Corp reports the $800 as gross income in the year it is received.

However, the tax benefit rule limits income recognition when a deduction does not yield a tax benefit in the year it is taken. If MegaCorp in Example 30 reported the same Federal income tax liability in the year that the loss occurred, the $800 receipt would be excluded from gross income in the year of the recovery.

Before deducting a $1,000 loss from an uncollectible business receivable, Tulip Company reported taxable income of $200. The business bad debt deduction yields only a $200 tax benefit (assuming no loss carryback is made). That is, taxable income is reduced by only $200 (to zero) as a result of the bad debt deduction. Therefore, if the customer makes a payment on the previously deducted receivable in the following year, only the first $200 is a taxable recovery of a prior deduction. Any additional amount collected is nontaxable because only $200 of the loss yielded a reduction in taxable income (i.e., a tax benefit).

Explain and apply the tax provision that excludes interest on state and local government obligations from gross income.

4-5c Interest on Certain State and Local Government Obligations

At the time the Sixteenth Amendment was ratified by the states, there was some question as to whether the Federal government possessed the constitutional authority to tax interest on state and local government obligations. Taxing such interest was thought to violate the doctrine of intergovernmental immunity because the tax would impair the ability of state and local governments to finance their operations.[57] Thus, interest on state and local government obligations was specifically exempted from Federal income taxation.[58] However, the Supreme Court has concluded that there is no constitutional prohibition against levying a nondiscriminatory Federal income tax on state and local government obligations.[59] Nevertheless, the statutory exclusion still exists.

The current exempt status applies solely to state and local government bonds. Thus, income received from the accrual of interest on a condemnation award or an overpayment of state tax is fully taxable.[60] Nor does the exemption apply to gains on the sale of tax-exempt securities.

---

[57]*Pollock v. Farmer's Loan & Trust Co.*, 3 AFTR 2602, 15 S.Ct. 912 (USSC, 1895).

[58]§ 103(a).

[59]*South Carolina v. Baker III*, 88–1 USTC ¶9284, 61 AFTR 2d 88–995, 108 S.Ct. 1355 (USSC, 1988).

[60]*Kieselbach v. Comm.*, 43–1 USTC ¶9220, 30 AFTR 370, 63 S.Ct. 303 (USSC, 1943); *U.S. Trust Co. of New York v. Anderson*, 3 USTC ¶1125, 12 AFTR 836, 65 F.2d 575 (CA–2, 1933).

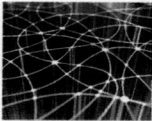

BRIDGE DISCIPLINE **Bridge to Public Economics**

The exclusion granted by the Federal government for interest paid on state and local bonds costs the U.S. Treasury approximately $35 billion per year, according to the Office of Management and Budget. Such forgone revenue is referred to as a "tax expenditure." However, if the capital markets are working properly, the exclusion should produce cost savings to the state and local governments.

If the exclusion were eliminated, state and local governments would pay higher interest rates on their bonds; the investor would demand a higher interest rate to produce the same after-tax yield as that received from taxable bonds of comparable risk. Therefore, the exclusion operates as a form of revenue sharing to the benefit of the state and local governments; it can be seen as a less-visible alternative to a direct grant from the Federal government to the state or local agency. It also is clear that this "expenditure" by the Federal government disproportionately is received by upper-income, high-wealth bondholders.

EXAMPLE 32

Macaw Corporation purchases State of Virginia bonds for $10,000 on July 1. The bonds pay $400 interest each June 30 and December 31. Macaw excludes from gross income the $400 interest received on December 31.

On March 31 of the next year, Macaw sells the bonds for $10,500 plus $200 of accrued interest. Macaw recognizes a $500 taxable gain ($10,500 − $10,000), but the $200 accrued interest is exempt from taxation.

In-depth coverage can be found on this book's companion website: www.cengagebrain.com

5 DIGGING DEEPER

The interest exclusion reduces the cost of borrowing for state and local governments. A taxpayer with a 35 percent marginal tax rate requires only a 5.2 percent yield on a tax-exempt bond to obtain the same after-tax income as a taxable bond paying 8 percent interest [5.2% ÷ (1 − .35) = 8%].

Although the Internal Revenue Code excludes from Federal gross income the interest on state and local government bonds, the interest paid on U.S. government bonds is not excluded from the Federal tax base. Congress has decided, however, that if the Federal government is not to tax state and local bond interest, the state and local governments are prohibited from taxing interest on U.S. government bonds.[61] While this parity between the Federal and state and local governments exists with regard to taxing each others' obligations, the states are free to tax another's obligations. Thus, some states exempt the interest on the bonds they issue, but tax the interest on bonds issued by other states.

The Big Picture

EXAMPLE 33

Return to the facts of *The Big Picture* on p. 4-1. Dr. Payne includes in gross income the $500 of interest income from the bank's money market account, but not the $500 that is earned on the Whitehall School District bonds.

4-5d **Improvements on Leased Property**

LO.8

Use the tax rules concerning the exclusion of leasehold improvements from gross income.

When a real property lease expires, the landlord regains control of both the real property and any improvements to the property (e.g., buildings and landscaping) made by the tenant during the term of the lease. Any improvements made to the leased property are excluded from the landlord's gross income unless the improvement is made to the property in lieu of rent.[62]

---

[61] 31 U.S.C.A. § 742.   [62] § 109.

TAX IN THE NEWS   **State Taxation of Other States' Interest**

Like many other states, Kentucky exempts from taxation interest earned on its own state bonds, but it taxes its own residents on interest income received from bonds issued by other states. A married couple residing in Kentucky challenged the law as unconstitutionally discriminating against interstate commerce by treating Kentucky bonds more favorably than the bonds issued by other states. The U.S. Supreme Court ruled in favor of Kentucky, thus permitting the state (and the 36 other states with similar laws) to tax the out-of-state bond interest while exempting Kentucky bond interest.

Many taxpayers invest in mutual funds that purchase bonds issued by several states. Although the interest from all of the state bonds generally is exempt from Federal income tax, the investor may owe state income tax to the state of residence on the interest received on the bonds of other states. Thus, a bond-oriented mutual fund must inform the investor of the amount of interest income earned from the bonds issued by the various states.

Source: *Department of Revenue of Kentucky v. Davis*, 128 S.Ct. 1801, 553 U.S. 328 (USSC, 2008).

EXAMPLE 34

Mahogany Corporation leases office space to Zink and Silver, Attorneys-at-Law. When the law firm took possession of the office space, it added wall partitions, a wireless computer network, and a variety of other improvements to the space. The improvements were not made in lieu of rent payments to Mahogany. When the lease expires and Mahogany regains possession of the space, the value of the improvements is excluded from Mahogany's gross income.

LO.9

Determine the extent to which life insurance proceeds are excluded from gross income.

4-5e Life Insurance Proceeds

Life insurance proceeds paid to the beneficiary because of the death of the insured are exempt from income tax.[63] Congress chose to exempt life insurance proceeds from gross income for several reasons, including the following.

- For family members, life insurance proceeds serve much the same purpose as a nontaxable inheritance.
- In a business context (as well as in a family situation), life insurance proceeds replace an economic loss suffered by the beneficiary.

Thus, Congress concluded that, in general, making life insurance proceeds exempt from income tax was a good policy.

EXAMPLE 35

Sparrow Corporation purchased an insurance policy on the life of its CEO and named itself as the beneficiary. Sparrow paid $24,000 in premiums. When the company's CEO died, Sparrow collected the insurance proceeds of $60,000. The $60,000 is excluded from Sparrow's gross income.

Exceptions to Exclusion Treatment

The income tax exclusion applies only when the insurance proceeds are received because of the death of the insured. If the owner cancels the policy and receives the cash surrender value, he or she must recognize gain to the extent of the excess of the amount received over the cost of the policy.[64]

Another exception to exclusion treatment applies if the policy is transferred after the insurance company issues it. If the policy is transferred for valuable consideration, the insurance proceeds are includible in the gross income of the transferee to the extent the proceeds received exceed the amount paid for the policy by the transferee plus any subsequent premiums paid.

---

[63]*Estate of D. R. Daly*, 3 B.T.A. 1042 (1926).

[64]*Landfield Finance Co. v. U.S.*, 69–2 USTC ¶9680, 24 AFTR 2d 69–5744, 418 F.2d 172 (CA–7, 1969).

Platinum Corporation pays premiums of $5,000 for an insurance policy with a face amount of $12,000 on the life of Beth, an officer of the corporation. Subsequently, Platinum sells the policy to Beth's husband, Jamal, for $5,500. On Beth's death, Jamal receives the proceeds of $12,000. Jamal excludes from gross income $5,500 plus any premiums he paid subsequent to the transfer. The remainder of the proceeds constitutes gross income to Jamal, as he acquired the policy for cash consideration.

The Code, however, provides several major exceptions to the consideration rule.[65] These exceptions permit exclusion treatment for transfers to the following parties. The first three exceptions facilitate the use of insurance contracts to fund **buy-sell agreements**.

1. A partner of the insured.
2. A partnership in which the insured is a partner.
3. A corporation in which the insured is an officer or shareholder.
4. A transferee whose basis in the policy is determined by reference to the transferor's basis, such as a gift or a transfer due to a divorce.
5. The insured party under the policy.

Rick and Sam are equal partners who have a buy-sell agreement that allows either partner to purchase the interest of a deceased partner for $500,000. Neither partner has sufficient cash to buy the other partner's interest, but each holds a life insurance policy on his own life in the amount of $500,000. Rick and Sam could exchange their policies (usually at little or no taxable gain), and upon the death of either partner, the surviving partner could collect tax-free insurance proceeds. The proceeds then could be used to purchase the decedent's interest in the partnership.

Investment earnings arising from the reinvestment of life insurance proceeds generally are subject to income tax. For example, the beneficiary may elect to collect the insurance proceeds in installments that include taxable interest income. The interest portion of each installment is included in gross income.[66]

In-depth coverage can be found on this book's companion website: www.cengagebrain.com   **6 DIGGING DEEPER**

TAX PLANNING STRATEGIES **Life Insurance**
FRAMEWORK FOCUS: INCOME AND EXCLUSION

Strategy: Avoid Income Recognition.

Life insurance is a tax-favored investment. The annual increase in the cash surrender value of the policy is not taxable because it is subject to substantial restrictions (no income has been actually or constructively received). By borrowing on the policy's cash surrender value, the owner can receive the policy's increase in value in cash without recognizing income.

4-5f **Income from Discharge of Indebtedness**

Gross income usually is generated when a creditor cancels a borrower's debt. Foreclosure by a creditor is also treated as a sale or exchange of the property.[67]

LO.10
Describe when income must be reported from the discharge of indebtedness.

[65]§ 101(a)(2).
[66]Reg. §§ 1.72-7(c)(1), 1.101-7T.
[67]*Estate of Delman v. Comm.*, 73 T.C. 15 (1979).

Juan owed State Bank $50,000 on a note secured by some investment land. When Juan's basis in the land was $20,000 and the land's fair market value was $50,000, the bank foreclosed on the loan and took title to the land. Juan recognizes a $30,000 gain on the foreclosure, as though he had sold the land directly to State Bank.

A creditor may cancel debt to ensure the viability of the debtor. In such cases, the debtor's net worth is increased by the amount of debt forgiven. Generally, the debtor recognizes gross income equal to the amount of debt canceled.[68]

Debt Cancellation and Gross Income

Brown Corporation is unable to meet the mortgage payments on its factory building. Both the corporation and the mortgage holder are aware of the depressed market for industrial property in the area. Foreclosure would only result in the creditor obtaining unsellable property.

To improve Brown's financial position and thus improve its chances of obtaining the additional credit necessary for survival from other lenders, the creditor agrees to forgive all amounts past due and to reduce the principal amount of the mortgage. Brown's gross income is increased by the amount of the debt that was forgiven *plus* the reduction in the remaining mortgage balance.

A corporation issues bonds with a face value of $500,000. Subsequently, the corporation repurchases the bonds in the market for $150,000. It has effectively canceled its $500,000 debt with a $150,000 payment, so it recognizes $350,000 in gross income.[69]

EXAMPLE 41

Keri borrowed $60,000 from National Bank to purchase a warehouse. Keri agreed to make monthly principal and interest payments for 15 years. The interest rate on the note was 3%.

When the balance on the note had been reduced through monthly payments to $48,000, the bank offered to accept $45,000 in full settlement of the note. The bank made the offer because interest rates had increased to 4.5%. Keri accepted the bank's offer. As a result, she recognizes $3,000 ($48,000 − $45,000) gross income.[70]

A discharge of indebtedness generally increases the taxpayer's gross income, but the reduction in debt is excluded in each of the following situations.[71]

1. Creditors' gifts.
2. Discharges that occur when the debtor is insolvent.
3. Discharges under Federal bankruptcy law.
4. Discharge of the farm debt of a solvent taxpayer.
5. Discharge of **qualified real property business indebtedness**.
6. A seller's cancellation of a buyer's indebtedness.
7. A shareholder's cancellation of a corporation's indebtedness.
8. Forgiveness of certain loans to students.
9. Discharge of acquisition indebtedness on the taxpayer's principal residence that occurs after 2006 and before 2015, and is the result of the financial condition of the debtor.

Creditors' Gifts

If the creditor reduces the debt as an act of *love, respect, or generosity*, the debtor has simply received a nontaxable gift (situation 1). Such motivations generally arise only on loans between friends or family members. Rarely will a gift be found to have occurred in a business context. A businessperson may settle a debt for less than the amount due,

---

[68]§ 61(a)(12).
[69]See *U.S. v. Kirby Lumber Co.*, 2 USTC ¶814, 10 AFTR 458, 52 S.Ct. 4 (USSC, 1931).
[70]Rev.Rul. 82–202, 1982–1 C.B. 35.
[71]§§ 108 and 1017.

but only as a matter of business expediency (e.g., high collection costs or disputes as to contract terms) rather than generosity.[72]

Insolvency and Bankruptcy

Cancellation of indebtedness income is excluded when the debtor is insolvent (i.e., the debtor's liabilities exceed the fair market value of the assets) or when the cancellation of debt results from a bankruptcy proceeding (situations 2 and 3). The insolvency exclusion is limited to the amount of insolvency. The tax law permits this exclusion to avoid imposing undue hardship on the debtor (wherewithal to pay) and the debtor's limited resources.

The law imposes a cost for the insolvency and bankruptcy exclusion. More specifically, the debtor must decrease certain tax benefits (capital loss carryforwards, net operating loss carryforwards, some tax credits, and suspended passive losses)[73] by the amount of income excluded. In addition, if the amount of excluded income exceeds these tax benefits, the debtor must then reduce the basis in assets.[74] Thus, excluded cancellation of indebtedness income either accelerates recognition of future income (by reducing tax benefit carryforwards) or is deferred until the debtor's assets are sold (or depreciated).

EXAMPLE 42

Before any debt cancellation, Maroon Corporation has assets with a fair market value of $500,000 and liabilities of $600,000. A creditor agrees to cancel $125,000 of liabilities. Maroon excludes $100,000 of the debt cancellation income (the amount of insolvency) and is taxed on $25,000. Maroon also reduces any tax benefits and the basis of its assets by $100,000 (the excluded income).

Qualified Real Property Indebtedness

Taxpayers (other than C corporations) can elect to exclude income from cancellation of indebtedness if the canceled debt is secured by real property used in a trade or business (situation 5). The debt must have been used to acquire or improve real property in a trade or business to qualify for the exclusion.[75]

The amount of the exclusion is limited to the *lesser of* (1) the excess of the debt over the fair market value of the real property or (2) the adjusted basis of all depreciable real property held. In addition, the basis of all depreciable real property held by the debtor is reduced by the excluded amount.

EXAMPLE 43

Blue, Inc., (an S corporation) owns a warehouse worth $5 million, with a $3 million basis. The warehouse is subject to a $7 million mortgage that was incurred in connection with the acquisition of the warehouse. In lieu of foreclosure, the lender decides that it will reduce the mortgage to $4.5 million. Blue may elect to exclude $2 million from gross income ($7 million − $5 million). If Blue makes the election, it reduces the aggregate basis of its depreciable realty by $2 million.

If the basis of the warehouse had been $1 million, and the warehouse was the only piece of depreciable realty that Blue owned, only $1 million of the debt cancellation income would be excluded.

Seller Cancellation

When a seller of property cancels debt previously incurred by a buyer in a purchase transaction, the cancellation generally does not trigger gross income to the buyer

---

[72]*Comm. v. Jacobson*, 49–1 USTC ¶9133, 37 AFTR 516, 69 S.Ct. 358 (USSC, 1949).

[73]See Chapter 6 for a discussion of net operating loss carryforwards and suspended passive losses. Chapter 8 discusses capital loss carryforwards. Chapter 17 discusses tax credits.

[74]§ 108(b).

[75]§ 108(a)(1)(D).

(situation 6). Instead, the reduction in debt is considered to be a reduction in the purchase price of the asset. Consequently, the basis of the asset is reduced in the hands of the buyer.[76]

Snipe, Inc., purchases a truck from Sparrow Autos for $10,000 in cash and a $25,000 note payable. Two days after the purchase, Sparrow announces a sale on the same model truck, with a sales price of $28,000. Snipe contacts Sparrow and asks to be given the sales price on the truck. Sparrow complies by canceling $7,000 of the note payable. The $7,000 is excluded from Snipe's gross income, and the basis of the truck to Snipe is $28,000.

Shareholder Cancellation

If a shareholder cancels the corporation's indebtedness to him or her (situation 7) and receives nothing in return, the cancellation usually is considered a contribution of capital to the corporation by the shareholder. Thus, the corporation recognizes no gross income. Instead, its paid-in capital is increased, and its liabilities are decreased by the same amount.[77]

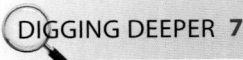

DIGGING DEEPER 7   In-depth coverage can be found on this book's companion website: www.cengagebrain.com

Student Loans

Many states make loans to students on the condition that the loan will be forgiven if the student practices a profession in the state upon completing his or her studies. The amount of the loan that is forgiven (situation 8) is excluded from gross income.[78]

4-5g Gains and Losses from Property Transactions

LO.11

Describe the general tax consequences of property transactions.

When property is sold or otherwise disposed of, gain or loss may result. Such gain or loss has an effect on the gross income of the party making the sale or other disposition when the gain or loss is *realized* and *recognized* for tax purposes. The concept of realized gain or loss is expressed as follows.

$$\text{Amount realized from the sale} - \text{Adjusted basis of the property} = \text{Realized gain (or loss)}$$

The *amount realized* is the selling price of the property less any costs of disposition (e.g., brokerage commissions) incurred by the seller. The *adjusted basis* of the property is determined as follows.

Cost (or other original basis) at date of acquisition[79]
Add: Capital additions
Subtract: Depreciation (if appropriate) and other capital recoveries (see Chapter 5)
Equals: Adjusted basis at date of sale or other disposition

Without realized gain or loss, generally, there can be no recognized (taxable) gain or loss. All realized gains are recognized unless some specific part of the tax law provides otherwise. Realized losses may or may not be recognized (deductible) for tax purposes, depending on the circumstances involved. For example, losses

---

[76]§ 108(e)(5).
[77]§ 108(e)(6).
[78]§ 108(f).

[79]Cost usually means purchase price plus expenses related to the acquisition of the property and incurred by the purchaser (e.g., brokerage commissions). For the basis of property acquired by gift or inheritance and other basis rules, see Chapter 7.

realized from the disposition of personal-use property (property held by individuals and not used for business or investment purposes) are not recognized.

During the current year, Ted sells his sailboat (adjusted basis of $4,000) for $5,500. Ted also sells one of his personal automobiles (adjusted basis of $8,000) for $5,000. Ted's realized gain of $1,500 from the sale of the sailboat is recognized. The $3,000 realized loss on the sale of the automobile, however, is not recognized. Thus, the gain is taxable, but the loss is not deductible.

Once it has been determined that the disposition of property results in a recognized gain or loss, the next step is to classify the gain or loss as capital or ordinary. Although ordinary gain is fully taxable and ordinary loss is fully deductible, the same is not true for capital gains and capital losses.

Capital Gains and Losses

Gains and losses from the disposition of capital assets receive special tax treatment. Capital assets are defined in the Code as any property held by the taxpayer *other than* property listed in § 1221. The list in § 1221 includes, among other things, inventory, accounts receivable, and depreciable property or real estate used in a business. The sale or exchange of assets in these categories usually results in ordinary income or loss treatment (see Chapter 8). The sale of any other asset generally creates a capital gain or loss.

Cardinal, Inc., owns a pizza parlor. During the current year, Cardinal sells an automobile. The automobile, which had been used as a pizza delivery car for three years, was sold at a loss of $1,000. Because this automobile was a depreciable asset used in its business, Cardinal reports an ordinary loss of $1,000, rather than a capital loss. Cardinal also sold securities held for investment during the current year. The securities were sold for a gain of $800. The securities are capital assets. Therefore, Cardinal has a capital gain of $800.

Computing the Net Capital Gain/Loss To ascertain the appropriate tax treatment of capital gains and losses, a netting process first is applied.

1. Capital gains and losses are classified as:
   a. short term, if the sold asset was held for one year or less, or
   b. long term, if the sold asset was held for more than one year.
2. Capital gains and losses then are netted within these two classifications. Specifically, short-term capital losses (STCL) are offset against short-term capital gains (STCG), resulting in either a net short-term capital loss (NSTCL) or a net short-term capital gain (NSTCG).
3. Similarly, long-term capital losses (LTCL) are offset against long-term capital gains (LTCG), resulting in either a net long-term capital gain (NLTCG) or a net long-term capital loss (NLTCL).
4. If the resulting amounts are of opposite signs (i.e., there remains a gain and a loss), those amounts are netted against each other. This produces the taxpayer's net capital gain or loss for the tax year. It is entirely long- or short-term, as dictated by the number that was larger in steps 2 and 3.

Colin is subject to a 35% marginal tax rate and reports the following capital gains (losses) from asset sales during the year.

Penguin Corporation stock (held for 7 months)	$ 1,000
Owl Corporation stock (held for 9 months)	(3,000)
Flamingo Corporation bonds (held for 14 months)	2,000
Land (held for 3 years)	4,000

continued

SHORT TERM: The Penguin gain of $1,000 is offset by the Owl loss of $3,000. This results in a $2,000 NSTCL.

LONG TERM: Netting the results of the sales of the bonds and the land, a $6,000 NLTCG is computed.

CONTINUE NETTING: Because there remains a gain and a loss, net these amounts against each other. A $4,000 net long-term capital gain results.

Taxing the Net Capital Gain/Loss Individuals and corporations are taxed differently on their net capital gains and losses. An individual's *net capital gain* is subject to the following *maximum* tax rates.[80] Certain upper-income taxpayers also may incur the additional Medicare tax on net investment income with respect to net capital gains. See Chapter 9.

	Maximum Rate[81]
Short-term gains	39.6%
Long-term gains	20%

A corporation's net capital gain does not receive any beneficial tax treatment. It is taxed as ordinary income.

The net capital losses of individuals can be used to offset up to $3,000 of ordinary income each year. Any remaining capital loss is carried forward indefinitely until it is exhausted.

Corporations may deduct capital losses only to the extent of capital gains. Capital losses of corporations in excess of capital gains may not be deducted against ordinary income. A corporation's unused capital losses can be carried back three years and then carried forward five years to offset capital gains in those years.[82]

EXAMPLE 48

Jones records a short-term capital loss of $5,000 during 2015 and no capital gains. If Jones is an individual, she can deduct $3,000 of this amount as an ordinary loss. The remaining $2,000 loss is carried forward to 2016 and thereafter, until it is fully deducted against ordinary income or netted against other capital gains and losses.

If Jones is a C corporation, none of the capital loss is deductible in 2015. All of the $5,000 loss is carried back and offset sequentially against capital gains in 2012, 2013, and 2014 (generating an immediate tax refund). Any remaining capital loss is carried forward and offset against capital gains in tax years 2016 to 2020.

DIGGING DEEPER 8   In-depth coverage can be found on this book's companion website: www.cengagebrain.com

[80]§ 1(h).

[81]Certain assets, such as collectibles (e.g., art, antiques, stamps, etc.) and some real estate, receive special treatment. When the 15% or 20% long-term capital gains tax rate otherwise applies, the collectibles gain is taxed at a maximum rate of 28%, and certain real estate gains are taxed at a maximum tax rate of 25%. See Chapter 8.

[82]§§ 1211 and 1212.

Concept Summary 4.3

Income Recognition Rules

Generally, realized income is recognized as gross income by the Federal tax law. Special rules apply for certain taxpayers and transactions.

1. Income from services and the use of property typically are taxed immediately as they are earned to the taxpayer that generated the income item.

2. Interest income is recognized as it is earned, and dividend income is taxed when the corporation makes a distribution to its shareholders from corporate E & P. Dividends can qualify for lower tax rates or offsetting deductions. Long-term capital gains also can qualify for lower tax rates.

3. Gross income may result when the taxpayer holds a debt investment that pays interest at a rate that is lower than the broader market would pay.

4. Income exclusions are available for certain types of income, including life insurance proceeds received and interest income received from the debt of U.S. government agencies at the state and local level.

5. Generally, gross income results for a borrower when a lender forgives an outstanding debt obligation. Certain taxpayers qualify for an exclusion of such income, though, e.g., in the context of a bankruptcy, a student loan, or a financially distressed residence.

REFOCUS ON THE BIG PICTURE

JUST WHAT IS INCLUDED IN GROSS INCOME?

Using the accrual method of accounting, the gross income recognized by Cliff Payne's corporation is $385,500. This includes the entire $385,000 of revenue earned from providing services to patients during the year and the $500 of interest income earned on the money market account. The $500 of school district bond interest is excluded from gross income.

Dr. Payne's own gross income includes $120,000 of salary earned during the year. Even though Cliff did not cash his December paycheck until January, he is considered to have constructively received the income, because it was readily available to him. Dr. Payne may be able to reduce his taxable income with a deduction in the amount of the imputed interest expense on the below-market loan from his parents. The increase in value on his stock does not result in gross income until he sells the stock and realizes a gain or loss.

What If?

Rather than electing the accrual method, what if Dr. Payne had chosen to use the cash method of accounting for his business? Using the cash method is acceptable for certain personal service corporations. While using the cash method would reduce the company's gross income from $385,000 to $333,000 ($385,000 amount billed less $52,000 still to be received), this is only part of the picture. Using the cash method also might result in some of the corporation's expenses not being deducted until they are paid in a future year.

Suggested Readings

Sheldon I. Banoff and Richard M. Lipton, "Tax Consequences of Recovering 'Mislaid Property,'" *Journal of Taxation*, July 2012.

"Delay in Cashing Not Delay in Taxing," *Practical Tax Strategies*, September 2005.

Todd D. Keator, "Rental Real Estate and the Net Investment Income Tax," *Journal of Taxation*, August 2013.

WWW   **For the latest in changes to tax legislation, visit www.cengagebrain.com.**

Richard Rubin and Carter Dougherty, "Bitcoin is Property, Not Currency, in Tax System: IRS," *Bloomberg.com*, March 25, 2014.

Key Terms

Accounting income, 4-4

Accounting method, 4-7

Accrual method, 4-9

Assignment of income, 4-14

Buy-sell agreements, 4-25

Cash receipts method, 4-7

Claim of right doctrine, 4-10

Constructive receipt, 4-10

Economic income, 4-4

Fruit and tree metaphor, 4-14

Gross income, 4-2

Hybrid method, 4-10

Income, 4-4

Life insurance proceeds, 4-24

Original issue discount, 4-11

Qualified real property business indebtedness, 4-26

Tax benefit rule, 4-22

Taxable year, 4-6

Computational Exercises

1. **LO.5** Lisbeth makes the following interest-free loans during the year. The relevant Federal interest rate is 5 percent, and none of the loans are motivated by tax avoidance. All of the loans were outstanding for the last six months of the tax year. Identify the Federal income tax effects of these loans.

Borrower	Amount	Borrower's Other Net Investment Income	Purpose of Loan
Richard	$ 5,000	$800	Gift
Woody	8,000	600	Stock purchase
Irene	105,000	0	Purchase principal residence

2. **LO.6** Leilei operates a sole proprietorship, using the accrual basis of tax accounting. Last year, she claimed a $10,000 bad debt deduction for a receivable from Jackie. But this year, Jackie sent her a check for $7,000, which Leilei accepted in full satisfaction of the receivable. How much gross income does Leilei record for the item this year?

3. **LO.3** Champ received a $10,000 distribution from NeatCo, a U.S. C corporation. NeatCo's earnings and profits for the year totaled $6,000. How much dividend income does Champ recognize? What Federal income tax rate applies to the dividend if Champ's ordinary income is subject to a 15 percent tax rate? A 33 percent rate?

4. **LO.11** Lefty completes the following capital asset transactions. Compute Lefty's recognized capital gain or loss from these transactions.

Long-term gain	$10,000
Short-term gain	4,000
Short-term loss	25,000

Problems

Issue ID

5. **LO.1** Howard buys wrecked cars and stores them on his property. Recently, he purchased a 1990 Ford Taurus for $400. If he can sell all of the usable parts, his total proceeds from the Taurus will be over $2,500. As of the end of the year, he has sold only the radio for $75, and he does not know how many, if any, of the remaining parts will ever be sold. What are Howard's income recognition issues?

6. **LO.1** Determine the taxpayer's current-year (1) economic income and (2) gross income for tax purposes from the following events.

   a. Sam's employment contract as chief executive of a large corporation was terminated, and he was paid $500,000 not to work for a competitor of the corporation for five years.

   b. Elliot, a 6-year-old child, was paid $5,000 for appearing in a television commercial. His parents put the funds in a savings account for the child's education.

   c. Valerie found a suitcase that contained $100,000. She could not determine who the owner was.

   d. Winn purchased a lottery ticket for $5 and won $750,000 from it.

   e. Larry spent $1,000 to raise vegetables that he and his family consumed. The cost of the vegetables in a store would have been $2,400.

   f. Dawn purchased an automobile for $1,500 that was worth $3,500. The seller was in desperate need of cash.

7. **LO.1** The roof of your corporation's office building recently suffered some damage as the result of a storm. You, the president of the corporation, are negotiating with a carpenter who has quoted two prices for the repair work: $600 if you pay in cash ("folding money") and $700 if you pay by check. The carpenter observes that the IRS can more readily discover his receipt of a check. Thus, he hints that he will report the receipt of the check (but not the cash).   **Ethics and Equity**

   The carpenter holds another full-time job and will do the work after hours and on the weekend. He comments that he should be allowed to keep all he earns after regular working hours. Evaluate what you should do.

8. **LO.1** Dolly is a college student who works as a part-time server in a restaurant. Her usual tip is 20% of the price of the meal. A customer ordered a piece of pie and said that he would appreciate prompt service. Dolly fulfilled the customer's request. The customer's bill was $8, but the customer left a $100 bill on the table and did not ask for a receipt. Dolly gave the cashier $8 and pocketed the $100 bill.

   Dolly concludes that the customer thought that he had left a $10 bill, although the customer did not return to correct the apparent mistake. The customer had commented about how much he appreciated Dolly's prompt service. Dolly thinks that a $2 tip would be sufficient and that the other $98 is like "found money." How much should Dolly include in her gross income?

9. **LO.2** Determine Amos's gross income in each of the following cases.

   a. In the current year, Amos purchased an automobile for $25,000. As part of the transaction, Amos received a $1,500 rebate from the manufacturer.

   b. Amos sold his business. In addition to the selling price of the stock, he received $50,000 for a covenant not to compete—an agreement that he will not compete directly with his former business for five years.

   c. Amos owned some land he held as an investment. As a result of a change in the zoning rules, the property increased in value by $20,000.

10. **LO.2** The Bluejay Apartments, a new development, is in the process of structuring its lease agreements. The company would like to set the damage deposits high enough that tenants will keep the apartments in good condition. The company actually is more concerned about such damage than about tenants not paying their rent.   **Decision Making**

    a. Discuss the tax effects of the following alternatives.

       • $500 damage deposit and $500 rent for the final month of the lease.

       • $1,000 rent for the final two months of the lease and no damage deposit.

       • $1,000 damage deposit with no rent prepayment.

    b. Which option do you recommend? Why?

Decision Making   11. **LO.2, 11** Julie is considering three alternative investments of $10,000. Julie is in the 28% marginal tax bracket for ordinary income and 15% for qualifying capital gains in all tax years. The selected investment will be liquidated at the end of five years. The alternatives are:

- A taxable corporate bond yielding 5% before tax and the interest reinvested at 5% before tax.
- A tax-favored bond that will have a maturity value of $12,200 (a 4% pretax rate of return).
- Land that will increase in value.

The gain on the land will be classified and taxed as a long-term capital gain. The interest from the bonds is taxed as ordinary income: the interest from the corporate bond as it is earned annually, but that from the tax-favored bond is recognized only upon redemption. How much must the land increase in value to yield a greater after-tax return than either of the bonds?

The compound amount of $1 and compound value of $1 annuity payments at the end of five years are given as:

Interest Rate	Future Value, $1 Compounded for 5 Years	Future Value, 5-Year Annuity of $1 Each
5%	$1.28	$5.53
4%	1.22	5.42
3.6%	1.19	5.37

12. **LO.1** Determine the taxpayer's gross income for tax purposes in each of the following situations.
   a. Deb, a cash basis taxpayer, traded a corporate bond with accrued interest of $300 for corporate stock with a fair market value of $12,000 at the time of the exchange. Deb's cost of the bond was $10,000. The value of the stock had decreased to $11,000 by the end of the year.
   b. Deb needed $10,000 to make a down payment on her house. She instructed her broker to sell some stock to raise the $10,000. Deb's cost of the stock was $3,000. Based on her broker's advice, instead of selling the stock, she borrowed the $10,000 using the stock as collateral for the debt.
   c. Deb's boss gave her two tickets to the Rabid Rabbits rock concert because Deb met her sales quota. At the time Deb received the tickets, each ticket had a face price of $200 and was selling on eBay for $300 each. On the date of the concert, the tickets were selling for $250 each. Deb and her son attended the concert.

13. **LO.2** Al is a medical doctor who conducts his practice as a sole proprietor. During 2015, he received cash of $280,000 for medical services. Of the amount collected, $40,000 was for services provided in 2014. At the end of 2015, Al held accounts receivable of $60,000, all for services rendered in 2015. In addition, at the end of the year, Al received $12,000 as an advance payment from a health maintenance organization (HMO) for services to be rendered in 2016. Compute Al's gross income for 2015:
   a. Using the cash basis of accounting.
   b. Using the accrual basis of accounting.

14. **LO.2** Selma operates a contractor's supply store. She maintains her books using the cash method. At the end of the year, her accountant computes her accrual basis income that is used on her tax return. For 2015, Selma reported cash receipts of $1.4 million, which included $200,000 collected on accounts receivable from 2014 sales. It also included the proceeds of a $100,000 bank loan. At the end of 2015, she held $250,000 in accounts receivable from customers, all from 2015 sales.

a. Compute Selma's accrual basis gross receipts for 2015.

b. Selma paid cash for all of the purchases. The total amount paid for merchandise in 2015 was $1.3 million. At the end of 2014, she had merchandise on hand with a cost of $150,000. At the end of 2015, the cost of merchandise on hand was $300,000. Compute Selma's gross income from merchandise sales for 2015.

15. **LO.2** Trip Garage, Inc. (459 Ellis Avenue, Harrisburg, PA 17111), is an accrual basis taxpayer that repairs automobiles. In late December 2015, the company repaired Samuel Mosley's car and charged him $1,000. Samuel did not think the problem had been fixed, so he refused to pay; thus, Trip refused to release the automobile.

Communications

In early January 2016, Trip made a few adjustments under the hood; Trip then convinced Samuel that the automobile was working properly. At that time, Samuel agreed to pay only $900 because he did not have the use of the car for a week. Trip said "fine," accepted the $900, and released the automobile to Samuel.

An IRS agent thinks Trip, as an accrual basis taxpayer, should report $1,000 of income in 2015, when the work was done, and then deduct a $100 business loss in 2016. Prepare a memo to Susan Apple, the treasurer of Trip, with your recommended treatment for the disputed income.

16. **LO.1, 4** Each Saturday morning, Ted makes the rounds of the local yard sales. He has developed a keen eye for bargains, but he cannot use all of the items he thinks are "real bargains." Ted has found a way to share the benefits of his talent with others. If Ted spots something priced at $40 that he knows is worth $100, for example, he will buy it and list it on eBay for $70.

Ethics and Equity

Ted does not include his gain in his gross income because he reasons that he is performing a valuable service for others (both the original sellers and the future buyers) and sacrificing profit he could receive. "Besides," according to Ted, "the IRS does not know about these transactions." Should Ted's ethical standards depend on his perception of his own generosity and the risk that his income-producing activities will be discovered by the IRS? Discuss.

17. **LO.2** Accounting students understand that the accrual method of accounting is superior to the cash method for measuring the income and expenses from an ongoing business for financial reporting purposes. Thus, CPAs advise their clients to use the accrual method of accounting. Yet, CPA firms generally use the cash method to prepare their own tax returns. Are the CPAs being hypocritical? Explain.

Ethics and Equity

18. **LO.2** Drake Appliance Company, an accrual basis taxpayer, sells home appliances and service contracts. Determine the effects of each of the following transactions on the company's 2015 gross income assuming that the company uses any available options to defer its taxes.

a. In December 2014, the company received a $1,200 advance payment from a customer for an appliance that Drake had special ordered from the manufacturer. The appliance did not arrive from the manufacturer until January 2015, and Drake immediately delivered it to the customer. The sale was reported in 2015 for financial accounting purposes.

b. In October 2015, the company sold a 6-month service contract for $240. The company also sold a 36-month service contract for $1,260 in July 2015.

c. On December 31, 2015, the company sold an appliance for $1,200. The company received $500 cash and a note from the customer for $700 and $260 interest, to be paid at the rate of $40 a month for 24 months. Because of the customer's poor credit record, the fair market value of the note was only $600. The cost of the appliance was $750.

19. **LO.2** Dr. Randolph, a cash basis taxpayer, knows that he will be in a lower marginal tax bracket next year. To take advantage of the expected decrease in

Ethics and Equity

his tax rate, Dr. Randolph instructs his office manager to delay filing the medical insurance claims for services performed in November and December until January of the following year. This will ensure that the receipts will not be included in his current gross income. Is Dr. Randolph abusing the cash method of accounting rules? Why or why not?

Decision Making

Communications

20. **LO.2** Your client is a new partnership, ARP Associates, which is an engineering consulting firm. Generally, ARP bills clients for services at the end of each month. Client billings are about $50,000 each month. On average, it takes 45 days to collect the receivables. ARP's expenses are primarily for salary and rent. Salaries are paid on the last day of each month, and rent is paid on the first day of each month.

The partnership has a line of credit with a bank, which requires monthly financial statements. These must be prepared using the accrual method. ARP's managing partner, Amanda Sims, has suggested that the firm also use the accrual method for tax purposes and thus reduce accounting fees by $600.

The partners are in the 35% (combined Federal and state) marginal tax bracket. Write a letter to your client explaining why you believe it would be worthwhile for ARP to file its tax return on the cash basis even though its financial statements are prepared on the accrual basis. ARP's address is 100 James Tower, Denver, CO 80208.

21. **LO.3** Alva received dividends on her stocks as follows.

Amur Corporation (a French corporation whose stock is traded on an established U.S. securities market)	$60,000
Blaze, Inc., a Delaware corporation	40,000
Grape, Inc., a Virginia corporation	22,000

a. Alva purchased the Grape stock three years ago, and she purchased the Amur stock two years ago. She purchased the Blaze stock 18 days before it went ex-dividend and sold it 20 days later at a $5,000 loss. Alva reported no other capital gains and losses for the year. She is in the 35% marginal tax bracket. Compute Alva's tax on her dividend income.

b. Alva's daughter, Veda, who is age 25 and who is not Alva's dependent, reported taxable income of $10,000, which included $1,000 of dividends on Grape stock. Veda purchased the stock two years ago. Compute Veda's tax liability on the dividends.

Decision Making

22. **LO.4, 5** Roy decides to buy a personal residence, and he goes to the bank for a $150,000 loan. The bank tells Roy that he can borrow the funds at 4% if his father will guarantee the debt. Roy's father, Hal, owns a $150,000 CD currently yielding 3.5%. The Federal rate is 3%. Hal agrees to either of the following.

- Roy borrows from the bank with Hal's guarantee provided to the bank.
- Cash in the CD (with no penalty) and lend Roy the funds at 2% interest.

Hal is in the 33% marginal tax bracket. Roy, whose only source of income is his salary, is in the 15% marginal tax bracket. The interest that Roy pays on the mortgage will be deductible by him. Which option will maximize the family's after-tax wealth?

Issue ID

23. **LO.5** Brad is the president of the Yellow Corporation. He and other members of his family control the corporation. Brad has a temporary need for $50,000, and the corporation has excess cash. He could borrow the money from a bank at 9%, and Yellow is earning 6% on its temporary investments. Yellow has made loans to other employees on several occasions. Therefore, Brad is considering borrowing $50,000 from the corporation. He will repay the loan principal in two years plus interest at 5%. Identify the relevant tax issues for Brad and Yellow Corporation.

24. **LO.5** Ridge is a generous individual. During the year, he made interest-free loans to various family members when the Federal interest rate was 3%. What are the Federal tax consequences of the following loans by Ridge?

    a. On June 30, Ridge loaned $12,000 to his cousin, Jim, to buy a used truck. Jim's only source of income was his wages on various construction jobs during the year.

    b. On August 1, Ridge loaned $8,000 to his niece, Sonja. The loan was meant to enable her to pay her college tuition. Sonja reported $1,200 interest income from CDs that her parents had given her.

    c. On September 1, Ridge loaned $25,000 to his brother, Al, to start a business. Al reported only $220 of dividends and interest for the year.

    d. On September 30, Ridge loaned $150,000 to his mother so that she could enter a nursing home. His mother's only income was $9,000 in Social Security benefits and $500 interest income received.

25. **LO.5** Indicate whether the imputed interest rules apply in the following situations.

    a. Mike loaned his sister $90,000 to buy a new home. Mike did not charge interest on the loan. The Federal rate was 5%. Mike's sister had $900 of investment income for the year.

    b. Sam's employer maintains an emergency loan fund for its employees. During the year, Sam's wife was very ill, and he incurred unusually large medical expenses. He borrowed $8,500 from his employer's emergency loan fund for six months. The Federal rate was 5.5%. Sam and his wife had no investment income for the year.

    c. Jody borrowed $25,000 from her controlled corporation for six months. She used the funds to pay her daughter's college tuition. The corporation charged Jody 4% interest. The Federal rate was 5%. Jody had $3,500 of investment income for the year.

    d. Kait loaned her son, Jake, $60,000 for six months. Jake used the $60,000 to pay off college loans. The Federal rate was 5%, and Kait did not charge Jake any interest. Jake had dividend and interest income of $2,100 for the tax year.

26. **LO.5** Vito is the sole shareholder of Vito, Inc. The corporation also employs him. On June 30, 2015, Vito borrowed $8,000 from Vito, Inc., and on July 1, 2016, he borrowed an additional $10,000. Both loans were due on demand. No interest was charged on the loans, and the Federal interest rate was 4% for all relevant dates.

    Vito used the money to purchase a boat. Elsewhere on his return, Vito recognized $2,500 of investment income. Determine the tax consequences to Vito and Vito, Inc., if:

    a. The loans are considered employer-employee loans.

    b. The loans are considered corporation-shareholder loans.

27. **LO.6** How does the tax benefit rule apply in the following cases?

    a. In 2013, the Orange Furniture Store, an accrual method taxpayer, sold furniture on credit for $1,000 to Sammy. Orange's cost of the furniture was $600. In 2014, Orange took a bad debt deduction for the $1,000 because Sammy would not pay his bill.

       In 2015, Sammy inherited some money and paid Orange the $1,000 he owed. Orange was in the 35% marginal tax bracket in 2013, the 15% marginal tax bracket in 2014, and the 35% marginal tax bracket in 2016.

    b. In 2014, Barb, a cash basis taxpayer, was in an accident and incurred $8,000 in medical expenses, which she claimed as an itemized deduction for medical expenses. Because of a limitation, though, the expense reduced her taxable income by only $3,000. In 2015, Barb successfully sued the person who caused the physical injury and collected $8,000 to reimburse her for the cost of her medical expenses. Barb was in the 15% marginal tax bracket in all tax years.

28. **LO.7** Determine Hazel's Federal gross income from the following receipts for the year.

Gain on sale of Augusta County bonds	$800
Interest on U.S. government savings bonds	400
Interest on state income tax refund	200
Interest on Augusta County bonds	700

Decision Making   29. **LO.7** Tammy, a resident of Virginia, is considering whether to purchase a North Carolina bond that yields 4.6% before tax. She is in the 35% Federal marginal tax bracket and the 5% state marginal tax bracket.

Tammy is aware that State of Virginia bonds of comparable risk are yielding 4.5%. Virginia bonds are exempt from Virginia tax, but the North Carolina bond interest is taxable in Virginia.

Which of the two options will provide the greater after-tax return to Tammy? Tammy can deduct all state taxes paid on her Federal income tax return.

Decision Making   30. **LO.7** Tonya, a Virginia resident, inherited a $100,000 State of Virginia bond this year. Her marginal Federal income tax rate is 35%, and her marginal state tax rate is 5%. The Virginia bond pays 3.3% interest, which is not subject to Virginia income tax. Alternatively, Tonya can purchase a corporate bond of comparable risk that will yield 5.2% or a U.S. government bond that pays 4.6% interest. Tonya does not itemize her deductions. Which investment provides the greatest after-tax yield?

Decision Making   31. **LO.9** The Egret Company has a 40% combined Federal and state marginal tax rate. Egret's board estimates that, if its current president should die, the company would incur $200,000 in costs to find a suitable replacement. In addition, profits on various projects the president is responsible for would likely decrease by $300,000. The president has recommended that Egret purchase a $500,000 life insurance policy.

How much insurance should the company carry on the life of its president to compensate for the after-tax loss that would result from the president's death? Assume that the $200,000 costs of finding a president are deductible and the lost profits would have been taxable.

32. **LO.9** Ray and Carin are partners in an accounting firm. The partners have entered into an arm's length agreement requiring Ray to purchase Carin's partnership interest from Carin's estate if she dies before Ray. The price is set at 120% of the book value of Carin's partnership interest at the time of her death.

Ray purchased an insurance policy on Carin's life to fund this agreement. After Ray had paid $45,000 in premiums, Carin was killed in an automobile accident, and Ray collected $800,000 of life insurance proceeds. Ray used the life insurance proceeds to purchase Carin's partnership interest.

What amount should Ray include in his gross income from receiving the life insurance proceeds?

Critical Thinking   33. **LO.9** Laura recently was diagnosed with cancer and has begun chemotherapy
Decision Making   treatments. A cancer specialist has given Laura less than one year to live. She has incurred sizable medical bills and other general living expenses and is in need of cash. Therefore, Laura is considering selling stock that cost her $35,000 in 2005 and now has a fair market value of $50,000. This amount would be sufficient to pay her medical bills.

However, she has read about a company (VitalBenefits.com) that would purchase her life insurance policy for $50,000. To date, Laura has paid $30,000 in premiums on the policy.

a.   Considering only the Federal income tax effects, would selling the stock or selling the life insurance policy result in more beneficial tax treatment?

b. Assume that Laura is a dependent child and that her mother owns the stock and the life insurance policy, which is on the mother's life. Which of the alternative means of raising the cash would result in more beneficial tax treatment?

34. **LO.10** Vic, who was experiencing financial difficulties, was able to adjust his debts as follows. Determine the Federal income tax consequences to Vic.

a. Vic is an attorney. Vic owed his uncle $25,000. The uncle told Vic that if he serves as the executor of the uncle's estate, Vic's debt will be canceled in the uncle's will.

b. Vic borrowed $80,000 from First Bank. The debt was secured by land that Vic purchased for $100,000. Vic was unable to pay, and the bank foreclosed when the liability was $80,000, which was also the fair market value of the property.

c. The Land Company, which had sold land to Vic for $80,000, reduced the mortgage principal on the land by $12,000.

35. **LO.11** During the year, Olivia recorded the following transactions involving capital assets.

Gain on the sale of unimproved land (held as an investment for 4 years)	$ 4,000
Loss on the sale of a camper (purchased 2 years ago and used for family vacations)	(5,000)
Loss on the sale of IBM stock (purchased 9 months ago as an investment)	(1,000)
Gain on the sale of a fishing boat and trailer (acquired 11 months ago at an auction and used for recreational purposes)	2,000

a. If Olivia is in the 33% bracket, how much Federal income tax results?

b. If Olivia is in the 15% bracket, how much Federal income tax results?

36. **LO.11** Andy reported the following gains and losses from the sale of capital assets.   Critical Thinking

Loss on Pigeon Corporation stock (held 9 months)	($14,000)
Gain on painting (held for 2 years as an investment)	5,000
Gain on unimproved land (held for 3 years as an investment)	3,000

a. If Andy is in the 35% tax bracket, determine the Federal income tax consequences of these transactions.

b. What if Andy is in the 15% tax bracket?

c. What if Andy is a C corporation in the 35% tax bracket?

37. **LO.11** Liz and Doug were divorced on July 1 of the current year after 10 years   Critical Thinking
of marriage. Their current year's income received before the divorce included:

Doug's salary	$41,000
Liz's salary	55,000
Rent on apartments purchased by Liz 15 years ago	8,000
Dividends on stock Doug inherited from his mother 4 years ago	1,900
Interest on a savings account in Liz's name funded with her salary	2,400

Allocate the income to Liz and Doug assuming that they live in:

a. California.

b. Texas.

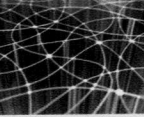

BRIDGE DISCIPLINE

1. Find the audited financial statements of a major U.S. corporation.
   a. Summarize its most important financial accounting policies.
   b. Describe two elements of the Federal income tax law that significantly affected the corporation's earnings per share for the operating year.

Communications

2. For the same corporation, summarize three key tax accounting applications, and point out how they differ from book income principles. Summarize your findings, and present them to your classmates in no more than five PowerPoint slides.

3. The exclusion of state and local bond interest from Federal income tax often is criticized as creating a tax haven for the wealthy. Critics, however, often fail to take into account the effect of market forces. In recent months, the long-term tax-exempt interest rate has been 3.5%, while the long-term taxable rate for bonds of comparable risk was approximately 4.7%. On the other hand, state and local governments do enjoy a savings in interest costs because of the tax-favored status of their bonds.

   To date, Congress has concluded that the benefits gained by the states and municipalities and their residents, such as the access to capital and the creation of jobs to construct and maintain critical infrastructure, outweigh any damages to our progressive income tax system. Do you agree with the proponents of the exclusion? Why or why not?

Critical Thinking

Communications

4. In a two-page paper, separately evaluate each of the following alternative proposals for taxing the income from property.
   a. All assets would be valued at the end of the year, any increase in value that occurred during the year would be included in gross income, and any decrease in value would be deductible from gross income.
   b. No gain or loss would be recognized until the taxpayer sold or exchanged the property.
   c. Increases or decreases in the value of property traded on a national exchange (e.g., the New York Stock Exchange) would be reflected in gross income for the years in which the changes in value occur. For all other assets, no gain or loss would be recognized until the owner disposes of the property.

Communications

5. Various Federal stimulus provisions were designed to assist state and local governments in borrowing funds, leveraging the gross income exclusion for such bond interest so that such jurisdictions would have increased access to funds. One of the justifications for these provisions was that state and local governments cannot run budget deficits and cannot "print money," so the recent recession put them in a difficult cash-flow position.

   Audits of the use of these borrowed funds showed that some of the bond proceeds were used by the jurisdictions to participate in "public-private partnerships," where government funds were used to assist private entities in expanding in or relocating to the jurisdiction. Specifically, bond proceeds were found to have been used to provide targeted road-building and utility-construction projects to benefit large commercial entities.

   Is this an appropriate use of the gross income exclusion for state and local bond interest? Summarize your comments in an e-mail to your instructor.

Research Problems

THOMSON REUTERS
CHECKPOINT®
Student Edition

Note: Solutions to Research Problems can be prepared by using the Checkpoint® Student Edition online research product, which is available to accompany this text. It is also possible to prepare solutions to the Research Problems by using tax research materials found in a standard tax library.

Research Problem 1. Tranquility Funeral Home, Inc., your client, is an accrual basis taxpayer that sells "pre-need" funeral contracts. Under these contracts, the customer pays in advance for goods and services to be provided at the contract beneficiary's death. These payments are refundable at the contract purchaser's request, pursuant to state law, at any time until the goods and services are furnished. Tranquility, consistent with its financial accounting reporting, includes the payments in income for the year the funeral service is provided.

    An IRS agent insists that the contract payments constitute prepaid income subject to tax in the year of receipt. Your client believes the amounts involved are tax-deferred customer deposits.

    Write a letter to Tranquility that contains your tax advice about how the issue should be resolved. The client's address is 400 Rock Street, Memphis, TN 38152.

Communications

Research Problem 2. Clint, your client, owns a life insurance policy on his own life. He has paid $6,800 in premiums, and the cash surrender value of the policy is $30,000. Clint borrowed $30,000 from the insurance company, using the cash surrender value as collateral. He is considering canceling the policy in payment of the loan. Clint would like to know the Federal income tax consequences of canceling his policy. Summarize your findings in a brief research memo.

Communications

Research Problem 3. Your client, New Shoes Ltd., is a retailer that often issues store gift (debit) cards to customers in lieu of a cash refund. You recall that the IRS issued a revenue procedure that provided that the prepaid income rules in Revenue Procedure 2004–34 could be applied to the income from the gift cards. Locate a more recent revenue procedure that authorizes the deferral of gross income from gift cards. Outline the key points of this document, and send the outline to your instructor.

Communications

Research Problem 4. Your friend Hui is an investor in bitcoin. Indicate whether and how she is subject to Federal income taxation in the following circumstances.

   a. Earns $1,000 in bitcoin from mining.
   b. Purchases $1,000 in bitcoin from another friend.
   c. Sells the purchase in part (b) in the market to a third party for $1,400.
   d. Spends $1,000 of bitcoin to acquire an asset worth $1,500.
   e. Spends $1,000 of bitcoin to acquire an asset worth $750.
   f. Holds bitcoin that she bought in February for $1,000. On December 31, the bitcoin is worth $1,200.

Use the tax resources of the Internet to address the following questions. Do not restrict your search to the Web, but include a review of newsgroups and general reference materials, practitioner sites and resources, primary sources of the tax law, chat rooms and discussion groups, and other opportunities.

Internet Activity

Research Problem 5. Construct a chart for your state and four of its neighboring states. Provide "Yes/No" entries for each state in the following categories. Send the chart to your classmates by e-mail.

Communications

   • Does the state exclude interest income from U.S. Treasury bonds?
   • Does the state exclude interest income from Fannie Mae bonds?

- Does the state exclude interest income from bonds issued by governments in its own state?
- Does the state exclude interest income from bonds issued by governments in other states?

Communications   **Research Problem 6.** Determine the applicable Federal interest rate as of today for purposes of § 7872 below-market loans. In an e-mail to your professor, describe how the rate is determined and how you discovered the pertinent rules.

Research Problem 7. Go to the web page for a securities broker or mutual fund. Use a "calculator" provided there to indicate the following.

Taxable Interest Rate	Your Marginal Tax Rate	Break-Even Exempt Interest Rate
5%	35%	?
5%	15%	?
8%	28%	?
8%	33%	?

Communications   **Research Problem 8.** Lottery winnings are taxable for Federal income tax purposes. What many lottery hopefuls forget, though, is that lottery winnings are also taxable in many states. Determine if lottery winnings are taxable for California residents, as well as residents of your own state. Does your state tax the winnings of one of its residents who won a prize in the lottery of another state? If your state does not have an income tax, find the answer to this question for California.

Roger CPA Review Questions

1. Stephen purchased a video game console five years ago for $500. In order to raise money for the "latest and greatest" console, Stephen sold his original console for $100. Because of advances in technology, Stephen can purchase the new console for $400. What is the tax treatment of Stephen's sale of his console?
   a. Stephen recognizes a $400 loss
   b. Stephen does not report the sale
   c. Stephen recognizes a $300 loss
   d. Stephen recognizes a $100 gain

2. Which of the following is excluded from gross income on an individual's 20X14 tax return?
   a. January 20X15 rent received in December 20X14
   b. Value arising from personal use of company vehicle in 20X14
   c. Dividends announced by a C Corporation in December 20X13 and received in January 20X14
   d. Refundable security deposit received in January 20X14 for a lease ending in July 20X15

Business Deductions

LEARNING OBJECTIVES: *After completing Chapter 5, you should be able to:*

LO.1 Articulate the meaning and application of the ordinary, necessary, and reasonableness requirements for the deduction of business expenses.

LO.2 Describe the cash and accrual methods of accounting for business deductions.

LO.3 Apply a variety of Internal Revenue Code deduction disallowance provisions.

LO.4 Indicate the limitations applicable to the charitable contribution deduction for corporations.

LO.5 State and apply the alternative tax treatments for research and experimental expenditures and identify several other common business deductions.

LO.6 Determine the amount of cost recovery under MACRS and apply the § 179 expensing election and the deduction limitations on listed property and automobiles when making the MACRS calculation.

LO.7 Identify intangible assets that are eligible for amortization and calculate the amount of the deduction.

LO.8 Determine the amount of depletion expense and specify the alternative tax treatments for intangible drilling and development costs.

CHAPTER OUTLINE

TAX TALK *Last year I had difficulty with my income tax. I tried to take my analyst off as a business deduction. The Government said it was entertainment. We compromised finally and made it a religious contribution.* —WOODY ALLEN

THE BIG PICTURE

CALCULATING DEDUCTIBLE EXPENSES

Michael Forney, owner of a small engine service and repair business, operates his business as a C corporation with a December 31 year-end. Using the accrual method of accounting, Mr. Forney reports the following expense information along with $435,500 of gross income.

Salaries and wages (including Michael's salary of $55,000 and Terry's salary of $3,000)	$150,000
Building rent	24,000
Depreciation of machinery and equipment*	13,000
Insurance (coverage for all assets of the business)	6,000
Consulting fees	6,000
Utilities	12,000
Taxes and licenses	6,000
Fine paid to city	2,500
Advertising	3,000
Interest expense	3,000
Charitable contributions	3,000
Dues paid to Small Engine Repair Institute	10,000
Political contributions	2,000

*$130,000 of new machinery and equipment were purchased this year. The financial reporting system depreciation is based on straight-line depreciation over 10 years. The MACRS cost recovery period for tax purposes is 7 years. Assume for purposes of this scenario that no depreciation may be claimed this year for assets acquired in prior years because they have been fully depreciated.

Michael would like to know the amount of his deductible expenses for tax purposes.

Mr. Forney owns 80 percent of the corporation's stock, while his wife (Kathleen) and his mother (Terry) each own 10 percent of the stock. Michael is a full-time employee at his business, and his mother helps out with the books for about two hours a week. At this time, Kathleen does not work at the business.

Michael would also like your advice on another matter. Because his business has been very profitable over the years, it has built up large cash reserves, and its cash flow continues to be strong. Even with the high levels of cash in the business, it has never paid any dividends to the shareholders. For next year, he is

continued

considering paying himself a salary of $140,000 and his mother a salary of $30,000. This would give them more cash to spend for planned vacations and home improvements.

Finally, during the year, Michael purchased another personal residence for $300,000 and converted his original residence to rental property. The original residence cost $250,000 five years ago and has a current market value of $180,000. Also during the year, he purchased a condo for $170,000, which he will rent to tenants. Michael holds these rental properties outside his small engine service and repair business. He would like to know the tax implications, if any, of these transactions.

Read the chapter and formulate your response.

The tax law has an all-inclusive definition of income; that is, income from whatever source derived is includible in gross income. Income cannot be excluded unless there is a specific statement to that effect in the Internal Revenue Code.

Conversely, deductions are disallowed unless a specific provision in the tax law permits them. The inclusive definition of income and the exclusive definition of deductions may not seem fair to taxpayers, but it is the structure of the law. This chapter discusses many of the common business deductions encountered by taxpayers that are specified in the Code.

LO.1

Articulate the meaning and application of the ordinary, necessary, and reasonableness requirements for the deduction of business expenses.

5-1 OVERVIEW OF BUSINESS DEDUCTIONS

As just noted, an income tax deduction is not allowed under Federal law unless Congress creates a specific provision allowing it. For businesses, trade or business deductions are allowed by statute, but only if they are both *ordinary and necessary* and *reasonable* in amount.

5-1a Ordinary and Necessary Requirement

Section 162(a) permits a deduction for all <mark>ordinary and necessary</mark> expenses paid or incurred in carrying on a trade or business. To understand the scope of this provision, it is critical to understand the meanings of the terms *ordinary* and *necessary*.

Neither ordinary nor necessary is defined in the Code or Regulations. However, the courts have had to deal with these terms on numerous occasions and have held that an expense is necessary if a prudent businessperson would incur the same expense and the expense is expected to be appropriate and helpful in the taxpayer's business.[1] But as Example 1 shows, no deduction will be allowed unless the expense is also ordinary.

EXAMPLE

1

Pat purchased a business that had just been adjudged bankrupt. Because the business had a poor financial rating, Pat wanted to restore its financial reputation. Consequently, he paid off some of the debts owed by the former owners that had been cancelled by the bankruptcy court. Because Pat had no legal obligation to make these payments, the U.S. Supreme Court found he has trying to generate goodwill. Although the payments were necessary (i.e., appropriate and helpful), they were *not* ordinary and their deduction *was not* allowed.[2]

An expense is ordinary if it is normal, usual, or customary in the type of business conducted by the taxpayer and is not capital in nature.[3] However, an expense need not

---

[1] *Welch v. Helvering*, 3 USTC ¶1164, 12 AFTR 1456, 54 S.Ct. 8 (USSC, 1933).

[2] *Welch v. Helvering*, cited in footnote 1.

[3] *Deputy v. DuPont*, 40–1 USTC ¶9161, 23 AFTR 808, 60 S.Ct. 363 (USSC, 1940).

be recurring to be deductible as ordinary. For example, a business may be in a situation that is a very rare occurrence and incur an expense. If other businesses in a similar situation are likely to incur a similar expense, then the expense can be ordinary, even though it is not recurring.

Zebra Corporation engaged in a mail-order business. The post office judged that Zebra's advertisements were false and misleading. Under a fraud order, the post office stamped "fraudulent" on all letters addressed to Zebra's business and returned them to the senders. Zebra spent $30,000 on legal fees in an unsuccessful attempt to force the post office to stop. The legal fees (although not recurring) were ordinary business expenses because they were normal, usual, or customary under the circumstances.[4]

5-1b **Reasonableness Requirement**

Although § 162 is intended to allow taxpayers to deduct a broad range of trade or business expenses, the Code applies a **reasonableness requirement** solely to salaries and other compensation for services.[5] However, the courts have held that for *any* business expense to be ordinary and necessary, it must also be reasonable in amount.[6]

What constitutes reasonableness is a question of fact.[7] If an expense is unreasonable, the excess amount is not allowed as a deduction. The question of reasonableness usually arises with respect to closely held corporations where there is no separation of ownership and management.

Transactions between shareholders and a closely held corporation may result in the disallowance of deductions for excessive salaries, rent, and other expenses paid by the corporation to the shareholders. The courts will view an unusually large salary in light of all relevant circumstances and may find that the salary is reasonable despite its size. If excessive payments for salaries, rent, and other expenses are closely related to the percentage of stock owned by the recipients, the payments are generally treated as dividends.[8] Because dividends are not deductible by the corporation, the disallowance results in an increase in corporate taxable income. Deductions for reasonable salaries will not be disallowed solely because the corporation has paid insubstantial portions of its earnings as dividends to its shareholders.

Return to the facts of *The Big Picture* on p. 5-1. The small engine service and repair business, a closely held C corporation, is owned by Michael Forney, his wife (Kathleen) and his mother (Terry). The company has been highly profitable over the years and has never paid dividends. Michael is the key employee of the business, while his mother plays a very minor role. Assume that their current salaries of $55,000 and $3,000 are comparable to what they could earn at similar companies for the work they do.

If Mr. Forney's plan to more than double his salary and increase his mother's salary by tenfold is implemented, the amounts in excess of their current salaries may be deemed unreasonable; if that is the case, the excess would be disallowed as deductible salary. The disallowed amounts would then be treated as dividends rather than salary income to Michael and Terry. Salaries are deductible by the corporation, but dividends are not. Note, however, that the shareholders may benefit from this reclassification. Salaries would be taxed at ordinary income rates and are subject to payroll taxes. However, dividend income would be taxed at long-term capital gain rates if the dividends are qualified (see Chapter 13).

---

[4]*Comm. v. Heininger*, 44–1 USTC ¶9109, 31 AFTR 783, 64 S.Ct. 249 (USSC, 1943).

[5]§ 162(a)(1).

[6]*Comm. v. Lincoln Electric Co.*, 49–2 USTC ¶9388, 38 AFTR 411, 176 F.2d 815 (CA–6, 1949).

[7]*Kennedy, Jr. v. Comm.*, 82–1 USTC ¶9186, 49 AFTR 2d 82–628, 671 F.2d 167 (CA–6, 1982), *rev'g* 72 T.C. 793 (1979).

[8]Reg. § 1.162–8.

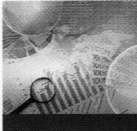

TAX PLANNING STRATEGIES   **Unreasonable Compensation**

FRAMEWORK FOCUS: TAX RATE

Strategy: Avoid Double Taxation.

In substantiating the reasonableness of a shareholder-employee's compensation, an internal comparison test is sometimes useful. If it can be shown that nonshareholder-employees and shareholder-employees in comparable positions receive comparable compensation, it is indicative that compensation is not unreasonable.

Another possibility is to demonstrate that the shareholder-employee has been underpaid in prior years. For example, the shareholder-employee may have agreed to take a less-than-adequate salary during the unprofitable formative years of the business. He or she would expect the "postponed"

compensation to be paid in later, more profitable years. The agreement should be documented, if possible, in the corporate minutes.

Keep in mind that in testing for reasonableness, the total pay package must be considered. Compensation includes all fringe benefits or perquisites, such as contributions by the corporation to a qualified pension plan, regardless of when the funds are available to the employee.

For additional discussion of the meaning of reasonable compensation, see Chapter 13.

Common Business Deductions

The language of § 162 is broad enough to permit the deduction of many different types of ordinary and necessary business expenses. Some of the more common deductions are listed in Exhibit 5.1.

LO.2

Describe the cash and accrual methods of accounting for business deductions.

5-2   TIMING OF EXPENSE RECOGNITION

A taxpayer's accounting method is a major factor in determining taxable income. The method used determines *when* an item is includible in income and *when* an item is deductible on the tax return. Usually, the taxpayer's regular method of record keeping is used for income tax purposes.[9] The taxing authorities require that the method used clearly reflect income and that items be handled consistently.[10] The most common methods of accounting are the cash method and the accrual method. If a taxpayer owns multiple businesses, it may be possible to use the cash method for some and the accrual method for others.

Throughout the portions of the Code dealing with deductions, the phrase *paid or incurred* is used. A cash basis taxpayer is allowed a deduction only in the year an expense is *paid*. An accrual basis taxpayer is allowed a deduction in the year in which the liability for the expense is *incurred* (becomes certain).

EXHIBIT 5.1	Partial List of Business Deductions
Advertising	Pension and profit sharing plans
Bad debts	Rent or lease payments
Commissions and fees	Repairs and maintenance
Depletion	Salaries and wages
Depreciation	Supplies
Employee benefit programs	Taxes and licenses
Insurance	Travel and transportation
Interest	Utilities

[9]§ 446(a).   [10]§§ 446(b) and (e); Reg. § 1.446–1(a)(2).

5-2a Cash Method Requirements

The expenses of cash basis taxpayers are deductible only when they are actually paid with cash or other property. Promising to pay or issuing a note does not satisfy the actually paid requirement.[11] However, the payment can be made with borrowed funds. Thus, taxpayers are allowed to claim the deduction at the time they charge expenses on credit cards. They are deemed to have simultaneously borrowed money from the credit card issuer and constructively paid the expenses.[12]

Although the cash basis taxpayer must have actually or constructively paid the expense, payment does not ensure a current deduction. The Regulations require capitalization of any expenditure that creates an asset having a useful life that extends substantially beyond the end of the tax year.[13] Thus, cash basis and accrual basis taxpayers cannot take a current deduction for capital expenditures except through amortization, depletion, or depreciation over the tax life of the asset.

EXAMPLE 4

Redbird, Inc., a calendar year and cash basis taxpayer, rents property from Bluejay, Inc. On July 1, 2015, Redbird pays $24,000 rent for the 24 months ending June 30, 2017.

The prepaid rent extends 18 months after the close of the tax year—substantially beyond the year of payment. Therefore, Redbird must capitalize the prepaid rent and amortize the expense on a monthly basis. Redbird's deduction for 2015 is $6,000.

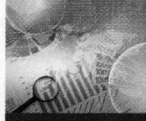

TAX PLANNING STRATEGIES Time Value of Tax Deductions

FRAMEWORK FOCUS: DEDUCTIONS

Strategy: Accelerate Recognition of Deductions to Achieve Tax Deferral.

Cash basis taxpayers often have the ability to make early payments for their expenses at the end of the tax year. This may permit the payments to be deducted in the year of payment instead of in the following tax year. In view of the time value of money, a tax deduction this year may be worth more than the same deduction next year.

Before employing this strategy, the taxpayer must consider what next year's expected income and tax rates will be and whether a cash-flow problem may develop from early payments. Thus, a variety of considerations must be taken into account when planning the timing of tax deductions.

In-depth coverage can be found on this book's companion website: www.cengagebrain.com

1 DIGGING DEEPER

5-2b Accrual Method Requirements

The period in which an accrual basis taxpayer can deduct an expense is determined by applying the *all events test* and the *economic performance test*. That is, a deduction cannot be claimed until (1) all of the events have occurred to create the taxpayer's liability and (2) the amount of the liability can be determined with reasonable accuracy. Once these requirements are satisfied, the deduction is permitted only if economic performance has occurred. The economic performance test is met only when the service, property, or use of property giving rise to the liability is actually performed for, provided to, or used by the taxpayer.[14]

---

[11]*Page v. Rhode Island Trust Co., Exr.*, 37–1 USTC ¶9138, 19 AFTR 105, 88 F.2d 192 (CA–1, 1937).

[12]Rev.Rul. 78–39, 1978–1 C.B. 73. See also Rev.Rul. 80–335, 1980–2 C.B. 170, which applies to pay-by-phone arrangements.

[13]Reg. § 1.461–1(a).

[14]§ 461(h).

EXAMPLE 5

Robin, Inc., an entertainment business, sponsored a jazz festival in a rented auditorium at City College. Robin is responsible for cleaning up after the festival, which took place on December 22, 2015, and reinstalling the auditorium seats. Because the college is closed over the Christmas holidays, the company hired by Robin to perform the work did not begin these activities until January 3, 2016. Robin cannot deduct its $1,200 labor cost until 2016, when the services are performed.

DIGGING DEEPER 2

In-depth coverage can be found on this book's companion website: www.cengagebrain.com

As illustrated in Examples 6 and 7, an exception to the economic performance requirement allows some *recurring* items to be deducted if certain conditions are met.[15]

Exceptions to Economic Performance Rules

EXAMPLE 6

Towhee Company, an accrual basis, calendar year taxpayer, entered into a monthly maintenance contract during the year. Towhee makes a monthly accrual at the end of every month for this service and pays the fee sometime between the first and fifteenth of the following month when services are performed. The December 2015 accrual is deductible in 2015 even though the service is performed on January 12, 2016.

EXAMPLE 7

Tanager, Inc., an accrual basis, calendar year taxpayer, shipped merchandise sold on December 30, 2015, via Greyhound Van Lines on January 3, 2016, and paid the freight charges at that time. Because Tanager reported the sale of the merchandise in 2015, the shipping charge should also be deductible in 2015. This procedure results in a better matching of income and expenses.

Reserves for estimated expenses (frequently employed for financial accounting purposes) generally are not allowed for tax purposes because the economic performance test cannot be satisfied.

EXAMPLE 8

Oriole Airlines is required by Federal law to test its engines after 3,000 flying hours. Aircraft cannot return to flight until the tests have been conducted. An unrelated aircraft maintenance company does all of the company's tests for $1,500 per engine.

For financial reporting purposes, the company accrues an expense based upon $.50 per hour of flight and credits an allowance account. The actual amounts paid for maintenance are offset against the allowance account.

For tax purposes, the economic performance test is not satisfied until the work has been done. Therefore, the reserve method cannot be used for tax purposes.

LO.3

Apply a variety of Internal Revenue Code deduction disallowance provisions.

5-3 DISALLOWANCE POSSIBILITIES

While most ordinary and necessary business expenses are deductible, the tax law contains provisions that disallow a deduction for certain expenditures. The most frequently encountered disallowance provisions are discussed next.

5-3a Public Policy Limitations

Certain disallowance provisions are a codification or extension of prior court decisions. For example, after the courts denied deductions for payments considered to be in violation of public policy, the tax law was changed to provide specific authority for the disallowance of these deductions.

---

[15]§ 461(h)(3)(A).

Justification for Denying Deductions

The courts developed the principle that a payment in violation of public policy is not a necessary expense and is not deductible.[16] Although a bribe or fine may be helpful and may even contribute to the profitability of an activity, allowing a deduction for such expenses would be contrary to public policy. A deduction would, in effect, represent an indirect governmental subsidy for taxpayer wrongdoing.

Under legislation enacted based on this principle, the following deductions are disallowed for specific types of expenditures that are considered contrary to public policy:

- Bribes and kickbacks illegal under either Federal or state law, including those associated with Medicare or Medicaid.
- Two-thirds of the treble damage payments made to claimants resulting from violation of antitrust law.[17]
- Fines and penalties paid to a government for violation of law.

Refer to the facts of *The Big Picture* on p. 5-1. Michael Forney had not instituted proper procedures for disposing of used motor oil and other engine fluids from his business. During the current tax year, he was fined $2,500 by the city. Mr. Forney believes the fine should be deducted as an ordinary business expense. However, because the fine was due to a violation of public policy, the $2,500 is not deductible.

In-depth coverage can be found on this book's companion website: www.cengagebrain.com **3 DIGGING DEEPER**

Legal Expenses Incurred in Defense of Civil or Criminal Penalties

To deduct legal expenses as trade or business expenses, the taxpayer must be able to show that the origin and character of the claim are directly related to a trade or business. Personal legal expenses are not deductible. Thus, legal fees incurred in connection with a criminal defense are deductible only if the crime is associated with the taxpayer's trade or business.[18]

Debra, a majority shareholder and chief financial officer of Blue Corporation, incurs legal expenses in connection with her defense in a criminal indictment for evasion of Blue's income taxes. Debra may deduct her legal expenses because she is deemed to be in the trade or business of being an executive. The legal action impairs her ability to conduct this business activity.[19]

Expenses Related to an Illegal Business

The usual expenses of operating an illegal business (e.g., a money laundering operation) are deductible.[20] While allowing deductions for illegal activity may seem inappropriate, recall that the law taxes net income from a business operation, not gross revenue. However, § 162 disallows a deduction for fines, bribes to public officials, illegal kickbacks, and other illegal payments without regard to whether these payments are part of a legal or illegal business.

---

[16]*Tank Truck Rentals, Inc. v. Comm.*, 58–1 USTC ¶9366, 1 AFTR 2d 1154, 78 S.Ct. 507 (USSC, 1958).
[17]§§ 162(c), (f), and (g).
[18]*Comm. v. Tellier*, 66–1 USTC ¶9319, 17 AFTR 2d 633, 86 S.Ct. 1118 (USSC, 1966).
[19]Rev.Rul. 68–662, 1968–2 C.B. 69.
[20]*Comm. v. Sullivan*, 58–1 USTC ¶9368, 1 AFTR 2d 1158, 78 S.Ct. 512 (USSC, 1958).

GLOBAL TAX ISSUES   Overseas Gun Sales Result in Large Fines

The Foreign Corrupt Practices Act (FCPA) is intended to punish taxpayers who make illegal payments to foreign officials to obtain economic advantages. Not only are such payments (usually improperly recorded as business expenses) nondeductible for income tax purposes, but serious and consistent violations can lead to the imposition of fines. Severe consequences can result from violating the bribery provisions of the FCPA, as Smith & Wesson recently discovered.

Smith & Wesson is a Massachusetts-based firearms manufacturer that wanted to begin selling firearms in India, Pakistan, and other foreign countries. As a small player in

this international market, company officials decided to provide gifts to government officials in these countries to encourage them to do business with Smith & Wesson.

This turned out to be a costly mistake. Smith & Wesson had profits of only $100,000 from this scheme before it was uncovered, and in 2014, it agreed to pay the Securities and Exchange Commission fines of more than $2 million. Of course, the fines are not deductible because they are a violation of public policy.

Source: **www.sec.gov/News/PressRelease/Detail/PressRelease/1370542384677#**
.VDM-3RbuqKI.

EXAMPLE 11

Grizzly, Inc., owns and operates a restaurant. In addition, Grizzly operates an illegal gambling establishment out of the restaurant's back room. In connection with the illegal activity, Grizzly has the following expenses during the year:

Rent	$ 60,000
Payoffs to police	40,000
Depreciation on equipment	100,000
Wages	140,000
Interest	30,000
Criminal fines	50,000
Illegal kickbacks	10,000
Total	$430,000

All of the usual expenses (rent, depreciation, wages, and interest) are deductible; payoffs, fines, and kickbacks are not deductible. Of the $430,000 spent, $330,000 is deductible and $100,000 is not.

An exception applies to expenses incurred in illegal trafficking in drugs.[21] Drug dealers are not allowed a deduction for ordinary and necessary business expenses incurred in their business. In arriving at gross income from the business, however, dealers may reduce total sales by the cost of goods sold.[22]

5-3b Political Contributions and Lobbying Activities

Political Contributions

Generally, no business deduction is permitted for direct or indirect payments for political purposes.[23] Historically, the government has been reluctant to extend favorable tax treatment to political expenditures by businesses. Allowing deductions might encourage abuses and enable businesses to have undue influence on the political process.

---

[21]§ 280E.

[22]Reg. § 1.61–3(a). Gross income is defined as sales minus cost of goods sold. Thus, while § 280E prohibits any deductions for drug dealers, it does not modify the normal definition of gross income.

[23]§ 276.

The Big Picture

EXAMPLE 12

Refer to the facts of *The Big Picture* on p. 5-1. Michael Forney's business made political contributions to the State Senate campaigns of Tom Smith and Virginia White. Mr. Forney made these contributions to encourage these candidates to support a new bill that is beneficial to the state's small businesses. Therefore, he assumed that these would be deductible business expenses. However, political contributions are not deductible, so he will receive no tax benefit from them.

Lobbying Expenditures

The Code places severe restrictions on the deductibility of expenses incurred in connection with lobbying activities.[24] These provisions deny deductions for expenditures incurred in connection with attempting to influence:

- State or Federal legislation and
- The actions of certain high-ranking public officials.

The disallowance also applies to a pro rata portion of the membership dues of trade associations and other groups that are involved in lobbying activities. There are three exceptions to the disallowance provisions. First, an exception is provided for influencing *local* legislation (e.g., city and county governments). Second, the disallowance provision does not apply to activities devoted solely to *monitoring* legislation. Third, a *de minimis* exception allows the deduction of up to $2,000 of annual *in-house expenditures* incurred by the taxpayer if the expenditures are not otherwise disallowed under the provisions discussed above. In-house lobbying expenditures do not include expenses paid to professional lobbyists or any portion of dues used by associations for lobbying. If in-house expenditures exceed $2,000, none of the in-house expenditures can be deducted.

The Big Picture

EXAMPLE 13

Refer to the facts of *The Big Picture* on p. 5-1. Mr. Forney's business made contributions to the Small Engine Repair Institute, a trade association for owners of similar-type businesses. The trade association estimates that 70% of its dues are allocated to lobbying activities. Thus, the deduction on the corporate tax return is limited to $3,000 ($10,000 × 30%).

5-3c Excessive Executive Compensation

The Code contains a *millionaires' provision* that applies to compensation paid by *publicly held* corporations.[25] The provision does not limit the amount of compensation that can be *paid* to an employee. Instead, it limits the amount the employer can *deduct* for the taxable compensation of a covered executive to $1 million annually. Covered employees as defined by the SEC are the principal executive officer (PEO), the principal financial officer (PFO), and the three other most highly compensated executives. This disallowance does not apply to commissions based on individual performance and performance-based compensation tied to overall company performance.

5-3d Disallowance of Deductions for Capital Expenditures

The Code specifically disallows a deduction for "any amount paid out for new buildings or for permanent improvements or betterments made to increase the value of any property or estate."[26] Incidental repairs and maintenance of the property are not capital expenditures and can be deducted as ordinary and necessary business expenses. Repairing a roof is a deductible expense, but replacing a roof is a capital expenditure subject to

---

[24]§ 162(e).
[25]§ 162(m).

[26]§ 263(a)(1).

TAX IN THE NEWS   Do Deduction Limits Affect Executive Compensation?

Only $1 million of compensation can be deducted for the CEO, CFO, and three other highest-compensated executives of publicly traded companies. However, as noted previously, this limitation does not apply to performance-based compensation. One interesting issue is whether this exception is broad enough to allow publicly traded companies to pay substantial compensation to executives and still receive a tax deduction. The answer is clearly yes.

For example, in 2012, the CEO of eBay received base salary of $970,353, which is just under the $1 million limitation. However, he received bonuses and stock incentives of over $28.5 million, which are deductible under the performance-based exception. The CEO of Textron had salary of exactly $1 million, and performance-based compensation was over

$10 million. The biggest payday was for Robert Iger, CEO of Walt Disney, who had salary of $2.5 million and performance-based compensation of almost $34 million.

Of 170 S&P 500 CEO salaries that were analyzed by *USA TODAY*, only two had a base salary greater than $2 million, and many had a base salary at or very close to $1 million. This indicates that the $1 million limit does have an influence on the base salary of CEOs. However, because of the performance-based exception, this tax law appears to have had very little impact on the escalation of executive salaries.

Source: Based on Matt Krantz and Barbara Hansen, "CEO Pay Rockets As Economy, Stocks Recover," *USA TODAY*, April 1, 2013, **www.usatoday.com/story/money/business/2013/03/27/ceo-pay-executive-compensation-2012/2006203/**.

depreciation deductions over a prescribed period. The tune-up of a delivery truck is an expense; a complete overhaul probably is a capital expenditure. Adding new gravel to a gravel parking lot is a repair, but paving what was a gravel parking lot is a capital expenditure because this is doing more than restoring the asset to its original condition.

New Regulations took effect January 1, 2014, which provide additional guidance on whether expenditures to acquire, produce, or improve tangible property must be capitalized or deducted.[27]

DIGGING DEEPER 4   In-depth coverage can be found on this book's companion website: **www.cengagebrain.com**

Capitalization versus Expense

When an expenditure is capitalized rather than expensed, the deduction is at best deferred and at worst lost forever. Although an immediate tax benefit for a large cash expenditure is lost, the cost may be deductible in increments over a longer period of time as the asset provides utility to the taxpayer.

For example, if the expenditure is for a tangible asset that has an ascertainable life, it is capitalized and may be deducted as depreciation over the life of the asset or as a cost recovery allowance over its depreciable life. (Depreciation and cost recovery allowances are discussed later in this chapter.) Land is not subject to depreciation (or cost recovery) because it does not have an ascertainable life.

 **EXAMPLE 14**   Buffalo Corporation purchases an old but usable apartment building and land located in an apartment-zoned area. Buffalo pays $500,000 for the property and immediately has the building demolished at a cost of $100,000. The $500,000 purchase price and the $100,000 demolition costs must be capitalized, and the tax basis of the land becomes $600,000. Because land is a nondepreciable asset, no deduction is allowed.

5-3e Investigation of a Business

Investigation expenses are paid or incurred to determine the feasibility of entering a new business or expanding an existing business. They include costs such as travel, engineering and architectural surveys, marketing reports, and various legal and accounting

---

[27]Reg. § 1.263(a)–3.

services. How such expenses are treated for tax purposes depends on a number of variables, including the following:

- The current business, if any, of the taxpayer.
- The nature of the business being investigated.
- Whether the acquisition actually takes place.

If the taxpayer is in a business that is the *same as or similar* to that being investigated, all investigation expenses are deductible in the year paid or incurred. The tax result is the same whether or not the taxpayer acquires the business being investigated.[28]

The Big Picture

EXAMPLE 15

Return to the facts of *The Big Picture* on p. 5-1. Michael Forney believes that his mechanical and business skills can be used to turn around other small engine businesses whose revenues have been declining. He investigates Southside Small Engine Services LLC, a nearby competitor that is for sale. Expenses paid to consultants and accountants as part of this investigation totaled $6,000. He determined that Southside Small Engine Services would not be a good investment, so he did not buy it.

The $6,000 spent to investigate this business is deductible as a business expense because Mr. Forney is already in the small engine service and repair business. Investigating new business opportunities in one's current trade or business is an ordinary and necessary business expense.

When the taxpayer is *not* in a business that is the same as or similar to the one being investigated, the tax result depends on whether the new business is acquired. If the business is not acquired, all investigation expenses generally are nondeductible.[29]

EXAMPLE 16

Lynn, president and sole shareholder of Marmot Corporation, incurs expenses when traveling from Rochester, New York, to California to investigate the feasibility of acquiring several auto care centers. Marmot is in the residential siding business. If no acquisition takes place, Marmot may not deduct any of the expenses.

If the taxpayer is *not* in a business that is the same as or similar to the one being investigated and actually acquires the new business, the expenses must be capitalized as **startup expenditures**. Startup expenditures are not deductible under § 162 because they are incurred *before* a business begins rather than in the course of operating a trade or business. The first $5,000 of the expenses is immediately deducted. Any excess of expenses is amortized over a period of 180 months (15 years). In arriving at the $5,000 immediate deduction allowed, a dollar-for-dollar reduction must be made for those expenses in excess of $50,000.[30] An election can be made by the taxpayer to not deduct or amortize any portion of the startup costs. In that case, this intangible asset will remain on the balance sheet until the business is sold.

EXAMPLE 17

Tina, a sole proprietor, owns and operates 10 restaurants located in various cities throughout the Southeast. She travels to Atlanta to discuss the acquisition of an auto dealership. In addition, she incurs legal and accounting costs associated with the potential acquisition. After incurring total investigation costs of $52,000, she acquires the auto dealership on October 1, 2015.

Tina may immediately deduct $3,000 [$5,000 − ($52,000 − $50,000)] and amortize the balance of $49,000 ($52,000 − $3,000) over a period of 180 months. For calendar year 2015, therefore, Tina can deduct $3,817 [$3,000 + ($49,000 × 3/180)].

In-depth coverage can be found on this book's companion website: www.cengagebrain.com | **5 DIGGING DEEPER**

---

[28]*York v. Comm.*, 58–2 USTC ¶9952, 2 AFTR 2d 6178, 261 F.2d 421 (CA–4, 1958).

[29]Rev.Rul. 57–418, 1957–2 C.B. 143; *Morton Frank*, 20 T.C. 511 (1953); and *Dwight A. Ward*, 20 T.C. 332 (1953).

[30]§ 195(b).

5-3f **Transactions between Related Parties**

The Code places restrictions on the recognition of gains and losses from related-party transactions. Without these restrictions, relationships created by birth, marriage, and business would provide endless possibilities for engaging in financial transactions that produce tax savings with no real economic substance or change. For example, to create an artificial loss, a corporation could sell investment property to its sole shareholder at a loss and deduct the loss on the corporate return. The shareholder could then hold the asset indefinitely. Although title to the property has changed, there has been no real economic loss if the shareholder and corporation are considered an economic unit. A complex set of laws has been designed to eliminate such possibilities.

Relationships and Constructive Ownership

Before reviewing the tax consequences of related party transactions, it is important to know the individuals and business entities that are considered to be related parties. *Related parties* include the following:

- Brothers and sisters (whether whole, half, or adopted), spouse, ancestors (parents and grandparents), and lineal descendants (children and grandchildren) of the taxpayer.
- A corporation owned more than 50 percent (directly or indirectly) by the taxpayer.
- Two corporations that are members of a controlled group.
- A series of other complex relationships between trusts, corporations, and individual taxpayers.

Constructive ownership provisions are applied to determine whether the taxpayers are related. Under these provisions, stock owned by certain relatives or related entities is *deemed* to be owned by the taxpayer for purposes of applying the loss and expense deduction disallowance provisions. For example, a taxpayer is deemed to own not only his or her stock but also the stock owned by his or her lineal descendants, ancestors, brothers and sisters or half-brothers and half-sisters, and spouse.

EXAMPLE 18

The stock of Sparrow Corporation is owned 20% by Ted, 30% by Ted's father, 30% by Ted's mother, and 20% by Ted's sister. On July 1 of the current year, Ted loaned $10,000 to Sparrow Corporation at 6% annual interest, principal and interest payable on demand. For tax purposes, Sparrow uses the accrual basis and Ted uses the cash basis. Both report on a calendar year basis.

Through constructive ownership, Ted is deemed also to own the 80% held by his parents and sister. Thus, he actually and constructively owns 100% of Sparrow. As discussed on the next page, if the corporation accrues the interest within the taxable year, no deduction can be taken until payment is made to Ted.

Losses

The Code provides for the disallowance of any losses from sales or exchanges of property directly or indirectly between related parties.[31] A right of offset is created equal to the disallowed loss. When the property is subsequently sold to an unrelated party, any gain recognized is reduced by the right of offset. However, the right of offset cannot create or increase a loss. Any right of offset not used by the related-party buyer to offset some or all of the recognized gain on a subsequent sale or exchange to an unrelated party is permanently lost.

---

[31]§ 267(a)(1).

EXAMPLE
19

Return to the facts of *The Big Picture* on p. 5-1. Assume that Michael Forney, the 80% shareholder in his small engine service and repair business, sells a stock investment in his personal portfolio with a basis of $10,000 to his corporation for its fair market value of $8,000. Michael's $2,000 loss from the sale of the stock is disallowed because the sale is to a related party. The disallowed loss creates a $2,000 right of offset.

   Michael's business sells the stock several years later for $11,000. However, only $1,000 of gain ($11,000 selling price − $8,000 basis − $2,000 right of offset) is taxable to the business upon the subsequent sale.

EXAMPLE
20

Assume the same facts as Example 19, except that the corporation sells the stock for $9,000 to an unrelated party. The corporation's gain of $1,000 ($9,000 selling price − $8,000 basis) is not recognized because of the right of offset of $2,000 from Michael's sale.

   The offset may result in only a partial tax benefit upon the subsequent sale (as in this case). If Michael originally had sold the stock to an unrelated party rather than to his corporation, he could have recognized a $2,000 loss. However, aggregating the effect to Michael and his corporation, they can benefit from only $1,000 of loss.

Unpaid Expenses and Interest

The law prevents related taxpayers from engaging in tax avoidance schemes where one related taxpayer uses the accrual method of accounting and the other uses the cash basis. The accrual basis allows the deduction of expenses when incurred, while the cash method requires that income be reported when received. In the absence of restrictions, an accrual basis, closely held corporation, for example, could borrow funds from a cash basis individual shareholder. At the end of the year, the corporation would accrue and deduct the interest expense, but the cash basis lender would not recognize interest income because no interest had been paid. Section 267 specifically defers the accrual of an interest deduction until the lender is required to include the interest in income; that is, when it is actually received by the cash basis taxpayer. This matching provision also applies to other expenses, such as salaries and bonuses. While this provision applies to related parties as previously defined, note that it also applies to transactions between any partner (shareholder) and a partnership (S corporation), regardless of the ownership interest held by the partner or shareholder.

   The deduction deferral provision does not apply if both of the related taxpayers use the accrual method or both use the cash method. Likewise, it does not apply if the related party reporting income uses the accrual method and the related party taking the deduction uses the cash method.

5-3g Lack of Adequate Substantiation

The tax law is built on a voluntary compliance system. Taxpayers file their tax returns, report income and take deductions to which they are entitled, and pay their taxes through withholding or estimated tax payments during the year. The taxpayer has the burden of proof for substantiating expenses deducted on the returns and must retain adequate records. Upon audit, the IRS can disallow any undocumented or unsubstantiated deductions. These requirements have resulted in numerous conflicts between taxpayers and the IRS.

5-3h Expenses and Interest Related to Tax-Exempt Income

Certain income, such as interest on municipal bonds, is tax-exempt.[32] The law also allows the taxpayer to deduct expenses incurred for the production of income.[33]

---

[32]§ 103.   [33]§ 212.

However, the law does not permit a taxpayer to profit at the expense of the government by excluding interest income and deducting any related interest expense.[34]

EXAMPLE 21

Oriole, Inc., a corporation in the 35% income tax bracket, purchased $100,000 of 6% municipal bonds. At the same time, Oriole used the bonds as collateral on a bank loan of $100,000 at 8% interest. A positive cash flow would result from the tax benefit as follows:

Cash paid out on loan	($8,000)
Cash received from bonds	6,000
Net negative cash flow	($2,000)

Had the deduction of $8,000 been allowed for interest expense, this would have resulted in a tax benefit of $2,800 (35% × $8,000). In that case, a positive cash flow of $800 ($6,000 + $2,800 − $8,000) would have resulted.

To eliminate the possibility illustrated in the preceding example, the Code specifically disallows a deduction for the expenses of producing tax-exempt income. Interest on any indebtedness incurred or continued to purchase or carry tax-exempt obligations also is disallowed.

EXAMPLE 22

In January of the current year, Crane Corporation borrowed $100,000 at 8% interest. Crane used the loan proceeds to purchase 5,000 shares of stock in White Corporation. In July, Crane sold the stock for $120,000 and reinvested the proceeds in City of Denver bonds, the income from which is tax-exempt.

Assuming that the $100,000 loan remained outstanding throughout the entire year, Crane cannot deduct the interest attributable to the period when it held the bonds.

DIGGING DEEPER 6 In-depth coverage can be found on this book's companion website: www.cengagebrain.com

5-4 CHARITABLE CONTRIBUTIONS

LO.4

Indicate the limitations applicable to the charitable contribution deduction for corporations.

Corporations and individuals are allowed to deduct contributions made to qualified domestic charitable organizations.[35] Qualified organizations include:[36]

- A state or possession of the United States or any subdivisions thereof.
- A corporation, trust, or community chest, fund, or foundation that is situated in the United States and is organized and operated exclusively for religious, charitable, scientific, literary, or educational purposes or for the prevention of cruelty to children or animals.

DIGGING DEEPER 7 In-depth coverage can be found on this book's companion website: www.cengagebrain.com

Generally, a deduction for a **charitable contribution** will be allowed only for the year in which the payment is made. However, an *accrual basis corporation* may claim the deduction in the year preceding payment if two requirements are met. First, the contribution must be *authorized* by the board of directors by the end of that year. Second, it must be *paid* on or before the fifteenth day of the third month of the following year.

[34]§ 265.
[35]§ 170.
[36]§ 170(c).

On December 29, 2015, Blue Company, a calendar year, accrual basis partnership, authorizes a $5,000 donation to the Atlanta Symphony Association (a qualified charitable organization). The donation is made on March 11, 2016. Because Blue Company is a partnership, the contribution can be deducted only in 2016.[37]

However, if Blue Company is a corporation and the December 29, 2015 authorization was made by its board of directors, Blue may claim the $5,000 donation as a deduction for calendar year 2015.

5-4a Property Contributions

The amount that can be deducted for a noncash charitable contribution depends on the type of property contributed. For this purpose, property must be identified as capital gain property or ordinary income property. **Capital gain property** is property that, if sold, would result in long-term capital gain or § 1231 gain for the taxpayer. Such property generally must be a capital asset and must be held for the long-term holding period (more than one year). **Ordinary income property** is property that, if sold, would result in ordinary income for the taxpayer. Examples of ordinary income property include inventory and capital assets held short term (one year or less). Refer to Chapter 4 for a brief introduction to the distinction between capital and ordinary assets and Chapter 8 for a complete discussion of the nature of capital and § 1231 assets.

The deduction for a charitable contribution of capital gain property is generally measured by the property's *fair market value*.

During the current year, Mallard Corporation donates a parcel of land (a capital asset) to Oakland Community College. Mallard acquired the land five years ago for $60,000, and the fair market value on the date of the contribution is $100,000.

The corporation's charitable contribution deduction (subject to a percentage limitation discussed later) is measured by the asset's fair market value of $100,000, even though the $40,000 of appreciation on the land has never been included in Mallard's income.

In two situations, a charitable contribution of capital gain property is measured by the basis of the property, rather than fair market value. If a corporation contributes *tangible personal property* and the charitable organization puts the property to an *unrelated use*, the deduction is limited to the basis of the property. Unrelated use is defined as use that is not related to the purpose or function that qualifies the organization for exempt status.

Contributions of Tangible Personal Property

White Corporation donates a painting worth $200,000 to Western States Art Museum (a qualified charity), which exhibits the painting. White had acquired the painting in 2000 for $90,000.

Because the museum put the painting to a related use, White is allowed to deduct $200,000, the fair market value of the painting.

Assume the same facts as in the previous example, except that White Corporation donates the painting to the American Cancer Society, which sells the painting and deposits the $200,000 proceeds in the organization's general fund.

White's deduction is limited to the $90,000 basis because it contributed tangible personal property that was put to an unrelated use by the charitable organization.

---

[37]Each partner will report an allocable portion of the charitable contribution deduction as of December 31, 2016 (the end of the partnership's tax year). See Chapter 14.

The deduction for charitable contributions of capital gain property to certain private nonoperating foundations (defined in §§ 4942 and 509) is also limited to the basis of the property.

As a general rule, the deduction for a contribution of ordinary income property is limited to the *basis* of the property. On certain contributions of inventory by *corporations*, however, the amount of the deduction is equal to the lesser of (1) the sum of the property's basis plus 50 percent of the appreciation on the property or (2) twice the property's basis. The following contributions of inventory qualify for this increased contribution amount.

- A contribution of property to a charitable organization for use that is related to the organization's exempt function and such use is solely for the care of the ill, needy, or infants.

- A contribution of tangible personal research property constructed by the corporation to a qualified educational or scientific organization that uses the property for research or experimentation or for research training. (The property must be contributed within two years from the date of its construction by the donor, and its original use must begin with the donee.)[38]

EXAMPLE 27

Lark Corporation, a clothing retailer, donates children's clothing to the Salvation Army to be used to attire homeless children. Lark's basis in the clothes is $2,000, and the fair market value (the sales price to customers) is $3,000. Lark's deduction is $2,500 [$2,000 basis + 50% × ($3,000 − $2,000)].

If, instead, the fair market value of the clothes is $7,000, Lark's deduction is $4,000 (2 × $2,000 basis).

5-4b Limitations Imposed on Charitable Contribution Deductions

Both corporations and individuals are subject to percentage limitations on the charitable contribution deduction.[39] The complex limitations for individual taxpayers are covered in Chapter 10.

For any tax year, a corporate taxpayer's contribution deduction is limited to 10 percent of taxable income. For this purpose, taxable income is computed without regard to the charitable contribution deduction, any net operating loss carryback or capital loss carryback, the dividends received deduction, and the domestic production activities deduction. Any contributions in excess of the 10 percent limitation may be carried forward to the five succeeding tax years. Any carryforward must be added to subsequent contributions and will be subject to the 10 percent limitation. In applying this limitation, the current year's contributions must be deducted first, with carryover amounts from previous years deducted in order of time.[40]

Annual Limitation and Carryover Rules Illustrated

EXAMPLE 28

During 2015, Orange Corporation (a calendar year taxpayer) had the following income and expenses.

Income from operations	$140,000
Expenses from operations	110,000
Dividends received	10,000
Charitable contributions made in May 2015	6,000

For purposes of the 10% limitation only, Orange Corporation's taxable income is $40,000 ($140,000 − $110,000 + $10,000). Consequently, the allowable charitable contribution deduction for 2015 is $4,000 (10% × $40,000). The $2,000 unused portion of the contribution can be carried forward to 2016, 2017, 2018, 2019, and 2020 (in that order) until exhausted.

---

[38]These conditions are set forth in §§ 170(e)(3) and (4).

[39]The percentage limitations applicable to individuals and corporations are set forth in § 170(b).

[40]The carryover rules relating to all taxpayers are in § 170(d).

Annual Limitation and Carryover Rules Illustrated

Assume the same facts as in the previous example. In 2016, Orange Corporation has taxable income (for purposes of the 10% limitation) of $50,000 and makes a charitable contribution of $4,500. The maximum deduction allowed for 2016 is $5,000 (10% × $50,000). The entire 2016 contribution of $4,500 and $500 of the 2015 charitable contribution carryforward are currently deductible. The remaining $1,500 of the 2015 carryforward may be carried over to 2017 (and later years, if necessary).

EXAMPLE 29

5-5 RESEARCH AND EXPERIMENTAL EXPENDITURES

Section 174 covers the treatment of research and experimental expenditures. The Regulations define research and experimental expenditures as follows:

> all such costs incident to the development or improvement of a product (including an experimental or pilot model, a plant process, a product, a formula, an invention, or similar property). The term includes the costs of obtaining a patent, such as attorneys' fees expended in making and perfecting a patent application. Expenditures represent research and development costs in the experimental or laboratory sense if they are for activities intended to discover information that would eliminate uncertainty concerning the development or improvement of a product. The term does not include expenditures such as those for the ordinary testing or inspection of materials or products for quality control or those for efficiency surveys, management studies, consumer surveys, advertising, or promotions.[41]

LO.5
State and apply the alternative tax treatments for research and experimental expenditures and identify several other common business deductions.

The law permits *three alternatives* for handling research and experimental expenditures.

- Deduct in the year paid or incurred.
- Defer and amortize.
- Capitalize.

If the costs are capitalized, a deduction is not available until the research project is abandoned or is deemed worthless. Because many products resulting from research projects do not have a definite and limited useful life, a taxpayer should ordinarily opt to write off (deduct) the expenditures immediately or to defer and amortize them. It is generally preferable to elect an immediate write-off of the research expenditures because of the time value of the tax savings related to the deduction.

The law also provides a credit for increasing research expenses over what the expense amount was in a base year or years. Two different formulas are available for computing the credit.[42]

5-5a Expense Method

A taxpayer can deduct all of the research and experimental expenditures incurred in the current year and all subsequent years. The consent of the IRS is not required if the method is adopted for the first taxable year in which such expenditures were paid or incurred. Once this method is adopted, the taxpayer must continue to deduct all qualifying expenditures unless a request for a change is made to, and approved by, the IRS. In certain instances, a taxpayer may incur research and experimental expenditures before actually engaging in any trade or business activity. In such instances, the Supreme Court has applied the liberal standard of deductibility crafted by Congress in § 174 and permitted a deduction in the year of incurrence.[43]

---

[41]Reg. § 1.174–2(a)(1), (2), and (3).

[42]§ 41. See Chapter 17 for a more detailed discussion of the research activities credit. Congress is expected to extend this credit, which expired on December 31, 2014.

[43]*Snow v. Comm.*, 74–1 USTC ¶9432, 33 AFTR 2d 74–1251, 94 S.Ct. 1876 (USSC, 1974).

5-5b **Deferral and Amortization Method**

Alternatively, research and experimental expenditures may be deferred and amortized if the taxpayer makes an election.[44] Under the election, research and experimental expenditures are amortized ratably over a period of not less than 60 months. A deduction is allowed beginning with the month in which the taxpayer first realizes benefits from the research and experimental expenditures. The election is binding, and a change requires permission from the IRS.

EXAMPLE 30

Gold Corporation decides to develop a new line of adhesives. The project begins in 2015. Gold incurs the following expenses in 2015 and 2016 in connection with the project.

	2015	2016
Salaries	$25,000	$18,000
Materials	8,000	2,000
Depreciation on machinery	6,500	5,700

The benefits from the project will be realized starting in March 2017. If Gold Corporation elects a 60-month deferral and amortization period, there is no deduction prior to March 2017, the month benefits from the project begin to be realized. The deduction for 2017 is $10,867, computed as follows:

Salaries ($25,000 + $18,000)	$43,000
Materials ($8,000 + $2,000)	10,000
Depreciation ($6,500 + $5,700)	12,200
Total	$65,200
2017: $65,200 × (10 months/60 months)	$10,867

The option to treat research and experimental expenditures as a deferred expense is usually employed when a company does not have sufficient income to offset the research and experimental expenses. Rather than create net operating loss carryovers that might not be utilized because of the 20-year limitation on such carryovers, the deferral and amortization method may be used. The deferral of research and experimental expenditures should also be considered if the taxpayer expects higher tax rates in the future.

5-6 **OTHER EXPENSE RULES**

In addition to the provisions related to charitable contributions and research and experimental expenditures, a variety of other expenses are subject to special rules and limitations. Some of these rules are noted briefly in the paragraphs that follow.

5-6a **Interest Expense**

Generally, corporations are not limited in the amount of interest expense they may deduct. However, the deductibility of expenses (including interest) from certain activities may be limited.[45] In contrast, individuals generally may not deduct interest expense on loans used for personal purposes. However, if the loan is secured by the taxpayer's personal residence, the related interest may be deductible. Furthermore, individuals may deduct interest expense associated with investments to the extent of net investment income and interest on qualified student loans.[46]

Because the deductibility of interest expense associated with certain activities is limited, the IRS provides rules for allocating interest expense among activities. Under these rules, interest is allocated in the same manner as the debt with respect to which the

---

[44]§ 174(b)(2).

[45]See, for example, the discussion of the passive activity limits in Chapter 6.

[46]See Chapter 10 for a more detailed discussion of the deductibility of interest by individuals.

interest is paid, and debt is allocated by tracing disbursements of the debt proceeds to specific expenditures. The interest tracing rules are complex and depend on whether loan proceeds are commingled with other cash and the length of time the loan proceeds are held before they are spent.

5-6b **Taxes**

As with interest expense, tax payments in a business or investment context are generally deductible. However, most Federal taxes are not deductible. Individuals may also deduct tax payments, subject to limitations (discussed in Chapter 10). One unique problem associated with determining the deductibility of taxes relates to real estate taxes paid during a year when the real estate is sold.

Real estate taxes for the entire year are apportioned between the buyer and seller based on the number of days the property was held by each during the real property tax year. This apportionment is required whether the tax is paid by the buyer or the seller or is prorated according to the purchase agreement. The apportionment determines who is entitled to deduct the real estate taxes in the year of sale. The required apportionment prevents the shifting of the deduction for real estate taxes from buyer to seller, or vice versa. In making the apportionment, the assessment date and the lien date are disregarded. The date of sale counts as a day the property is owned by the buyer.

A county's real property tax year runs from January 1 to December 31. Nuthatch Corporation, the owner on January 1 of real property located in the county, sells the real property to Crane, Inc., on June 30. Crane owns the real property from June 30 through December 31. The tax for the real property tax year, January 1 through December 31, is $3,650.

Assuming that this is not a leap year, the portion of the real property tax treated as imposed upon Nuthatch, the seller, is $1,800 [(180/365) × $3,650, January 1 through June 29], and $1,850 [(185/365) × $3,650, June 30 through December 31] of the tax is treated as imposed upon Crane, the purchaser.

If the actual real estate taxes are not prorated between the buyer and seller as part of the purchase agreement, adjustments are required. The adjustments are necessary to determine the amount realized by the seller and the basis of the property to the buyer. If the buyer pays the entire amount of the tax, it effectively has paid the seller's portion of the real estate tax and has therefore paid more for the property than the actual purchase price. Thus, the amount of real estate tax that is apportioned to the seller (for Federal income tax purposes) and paid by the buyer is added to the buyer's basis. The seller must increase the amount realized on the sale by the same amount.

Seth sells real estate on October 3 for $400,000. The buyer, Winslow Company, pays the real estate taxes of $3,650 for the calendar year, which is the real estate property tax year. Assuming that this is not a leap year, $2,750 (for 275 days) is apportioned to and is deductible by the seller, Seth, and $900 (for 90 days) of the taxes is deductible by Winslow. The buyer has paid Seth's real estate taxes of $2,750 and has therefore paid $402,750 for the property. Winslow's basis is increased to $402,750, and the amount realized by Seth from the sale is increased to $402,750.

The opposite result occurs if the seller (rather than the buyer) pays the real estate taxes. In this case, the seller reduces the amount realized from the sale by the amount that has been apportioned to the buyer. The buyer is required to reduce his or her basis by a corresponding amount.

5-6c **Domestic Production Activities Deduction**

A number of years ago, Congress replaced certain tax provisions that our world trading partners regarded as allowing unfair advantage to U.S. exports. As part of these changes, Congress created a deduction based on the income from U.S. manufacturing activities (designated as *production activities*). The domestic production activities deduction (DPAD) is contained in § 199. Form 8903 is used to report the calculation of the domestic production activities deduction.

Calculation of the Domestic Production Activities Deduction

The DPAD is based on the following formula:[47]

$$9\% \times \text{Lesser of} \begin{cases} \text{Qualified production activities income (QPAI)} \\ \text{Taxable (or modified adjusted gross) income or alternative minimum taxable income} \end{cases}$$

For this computation, taxable income is determined without regard to the DPAD. In the case of an individual (a sole proprietorship or an owner of a flow-through entity), modified adjusted gross income is substituted for taxable income.[48]

The taxable income limitation is determined after the application of any net operating loss (NOL) deduction for the tax year (NOLs are explained in Chapter 6). Thus, a company with an NOL carryforward for a tax year is ineligible for the DPAD if the carryforward eliminates current taxable income. Further, a taxpayer that has an NOL carryback may lose part or all of the DPAD benefit for that year. If qualified production activities income (QPAI) cannot be used in a particular year due to the taxable income limitation (see the preceding formula), it is lost forever. (The calculation of QPAI is explained in the next section.)

DPAD: Calculation Using QPAI and Taxable Income

 **EXAMPLE 33**

Opal, Inc., manufactures and sells costume jewelry. It also sells costume jewelry purchased from other manufacturers. During 2015, Opal had a *profit* of $200,000 (QPAI) from the sale of its own manufactured jewelry and a *loss* of $50,000 from the sale of the purchased jewelry.

Based on this information, Opal's QPAI is $200,000 and its taxable income is $150,000 ($200,000 − $50,000). Opal's DPAD becomes $13,500 [9% of the lesser of $200,000 (QPAI) or $150,000 (taxable income)].

EXAMPLE 34

Assume the same facts as in the previous example, except that Opal also has an NOL carryover from 2014 of $300,000.

As taxable income for 2015 is zero ($200,000 − $50,000 − $300,000), there is no DPAD.

Another important limitation is that the amount of the DPAD cannot exceed 50 percent of certain W–2 wages paid by the taxpayer during the tax year.[49] If no W-2 wages are paid, no DPAD will be allowed. So, part of the rationale behind this limitation is to preserve U.S. manufacturing jobs and discourage their outsourcing.

An employer's W–2 wages include the sum of the aggregate amount of wages and elective deferrals required to be included on the W–2 wage statements for certain employees during the employer's taxable year. Elective deferrals include those amounts deferred under § 457 plans and Roth IRA contributions. An employer previously included wages paid to all workers during a tax year and not just the wages of the employees engaged in qualified production activities. However, as a result of a recent statutory change, an employer is permitted to include only those W–2 wages paid to employees engaged in qualified production activities.

---

[47]§ 199(a).

[48]§ 199(d)(2). Generally, modified AGI is AGI prior to the effect of § 199.

[49]§ 199(b).

DPAD: W–2 Limitation

In 2015, Red, Inc., a calendar year taxpayer, has QPAI of $2 million and taxable income of $2.1 million. Because Red outsources much of its work to independent contractors, its W–2 wage base, which for Red is related entirely to production activities, is $80,000.

Although Red's DPAD normally would be $180,000 [9% of the lesser of $2 million (QPAI) or $2.1 million (taxable income)], it is limited to $40,000 [50% of $80,000 (W–2 wages)].

EXAMPLE 35

Assume the same facts as in the previous example, except that Red also pays salaries of $50,000 related to its *nonproduction* activities.

Because these wages are not paid to employees engaged in production activities, the wage limitation on the DPAD remains at $40,000 [50% of $80,000 ($80,000 + $0)].

EXAMPLE 36

Calculation of Qualified Production Activities Income

Qualified production activities income (QPAI) is the excess of **domestic production gross receipts (DPGR)** over the sum of:

- The cost of goods sold allocated to such receipts.
- Other deductions, expenses, or losses directly allocated to such receipts.
- The ratable portion of deductions, expenses, and losses not directly allocable to such receipts or another class of income.[50]

QPAI is determined on an item-by-item basis—not on a division-by-division or a transaction-by-transaction basis. Because all items must be netted in the calculation, the final QPAI amount can be either positive or negative. The effect of the netting rule is to preclude taxpayers from selecting only profitable product lines or profitable transactions when calculating QPAI.

A taxpayer manufactures pants and shirts with the following QPAI results: $5 for one pair of pants and a negative $2 for one shirt. Because the two items are netted, the QPAI amount that controls is $3 ($5 − $2).

EXAMPLE 37

Five specific categories of DPGR qualify for the DPAD.[51]

- The lease, license, sale, exchange, or other disposition of qualified production property (QPP) that was manufactured, produced, grown, or extracted (MPGE) in the United States.
- Qualified films (i.e., motion picture film or video tape) largely created in the United States.
- The production of electricity, natural gas, or potable water.
- Construction (but not self-construction) performed in the United States.
- Engineering and architectural services for domestic construction.

The sale of food and beverages prepared by a taxpayer at a retail establishment and the transmission or distribution of electricity, natural gas, or potable water are specifically excluded from the definition of DPGR.

Eligible Taxpayers

The deduction is available to a variety of taxpayers, including individuals, partnerships, S corporations, C corporations, cooperatives, estates, and trusts. For a pass-through entity (e.g., partnerships and S corporations), the deduction flows through to the owners. In the case of a sole proprietor, a deduction *for* AGI results and is claimed on Form 1040, line 35 on page 1.

---

[50]§ 199(c).   [51]§ 199(c)(4).

TAX FACT   **Cost Recovery by Any Other Name**

Of the more than $1.097 trillion of corporate cost recovery deductions claimed in a recent tax year, the three most familiar types of these asset-related tax incentives were reported as shown in the table to the right.

	Percentage of Total Deductions Claimed
Amortization	17.88
Cost recovery or depreciation	79.69
Depletion	2.43
	100.00

Source: 2011 Corporation Returns—Returns of Active Corporations, Table 2—Balance Sheet, Income Statement and Selected Other Items by Size of Total Assets; Internal Revenue Service, 2014.

LO.6

Determine the amount of cost recovery under MACRS and apply the § 179 expensing election and the deduction limitations on listed property and automobiles when making the MACRS calculation.

5-7 COST RECOVERY ALLOWANCES

5-7a Overview

Taxpayers may "write off" (deduct) the cost of certain assets that are used in a trade or business or held for the production of income. A write-off may take the form of a *cost recovery allowance* (depreciation under prior law), depletion, or amortization. Tangible assets, other than natural resources, are written off through cost recovery allowances. Natural resources, such as oil, gas, coal, and timber, are *depleted*. Intangible assets, such as copyrights and patents, are *amortized*. Generally, no write-off is allowed for an asset that does not have a determinable useful life.

The tax rules for writing off the cost of business assets differ from the accounting rules. Several methods are available for determining depreciation for accounting purposes, including the straight-line, declining-balance, and sum-of-the-years' digits methods. Historically, *depreciation* for tax purposes was computed using variations of these accounting methods. Congress completely overhauled the depreciation rules in 1981 by creating the accelerated cost recovery system (ACRS), which shortened depreciable lives and allowed accelerated depreciation methods. In 1986, Congress made substantial modifications to ACRS, which resulted in the modified accelerated cost recovery system (MACRS). Tax professionals use the terms depreciation and cost recovery interchangably.

The statutory changes that have taken place since 1980 have widened the gap that exists between the accounting and tax versions of depreciation. The tax rules that existed prior to 1981 were much more compatible with generally accepted accounting principles. This chapter focuses on the MACRS rules because they cover current acquisitions (i.e., after 1986).

5-7b Depreciation and Cost Recovery

Depreciation or cost recovery is available only with respect to qualifying assets held for business use or for the production of income. Thus, identifying the particular assets that qualify and their basis is critical to determining the appropriate depreciation or cost recovery deduction.

Nature of Property

Property includes both realty (real property) and personalty (personal property). *Realty* generally includes land and buildings permanently affixed to the land. *Personalty* is defined as any asset that is not realty. Personalty includes furniture, machinery, equipment,

For many business entities, success in producing goods for sale is dependent on the efficient use of fixed assets, such as machinery and equipment. An important question for such businesses to resolve is how they should gain access to the required complement of fixed assets: that is, whether the assets should be purchased or leased. To answer this question, the taxpayer must determine which alternative is more cost-effective. Critical to this assessment is quantifying the after-tax cost (including the associated tax benefits) of each option.

Purchasing productive assets for business use often necessitates an immediate cash outflow. However, the tax savings resulting from the available depreciation expense deductions mitigate the impact of that outflow by reducing the taxpayer's taxable income and the income tax paid for the year. Consequently, the tax savings from the depreciation calculation associated with the purchase of an asset reduce the after-tax cost of employing the asset. The analysis can be refined further by evaluating the tax savings from the depreciation deductions in present value terms by quantifying the tax savings from the depreciation expense over the life of the asset. The asset's purchase also can be financed with debt.

Taxpayers who lease rather than buy an asset benefit by not giving up the use of funds that otherwise would have gone to purchase the asset. Lessees also forgo the opportunity to claim depreciation deductions; however, they reduce the cost of the leasing option by claiming the lease expense as a deduction against their tax base.

and many other types of assets. Do not confuse personalty (or personal property) with personal-use property. Personal-use property is any property (realty or personalty) that is held for personal use rather than for use in a trade or business or an income-producing activity. Cost recovery deductions are not allowed for personal-use assets.

In summary, both realty and personalty can be either business-use/income-producing property or personal-use property. Examples include:

- A residence (realty that is personal use),
- An office building (realty that is business use),
- A dump truck (personalty that is business use), and
- Common wearing apparel (personalty that is personal use).

It is imperative that this distinction between the classification of an asset (realty or personalty) and the use to which the asset is put (business or personal) be understood.

Assets used in a trade or business or for the production of income (e.g., an automobile that the taxpayer rents to third parties) are eligible for cost recovery if they are subject to wear and tear, decay or decline from natural causes, or obsolescence. Assets that do not decline in value on a predictable basis or that do not have a determinable useful life (e.g., land, stock, and antiques) are not eligible for cost recovery.

Placed in Service Requirement

The key date for the commencement of depreciation is the date an asset is placed in service. This date, and not the purchase date of an asset, is the relevant date. This distinction is particularly important for an asset that is purchased near the end of the tax year, but not placed in service until after the beginning of the following tax year.

Cost Recovery Allowed or Allowable

The basis of cost recovery property is reduced by the cost recovery *allowed* (and by not less than the *allowable* amount). The allowed cost recovery is the cost recovery actually deducted, whereas the allowable cost recovery is the amount that could have been taken under the applicable cost recovery method. If the taxpayer does not claim any cost recovery on property during a particular year, the basis of the property still is reduced by the amount of cost recovery that should have been deducted (the *allowable* cost recovery).

EXAMPLE
38

On March 15 in Year 1, Heron, Inc., purchased, for $10,000, a copier, to use in its business. The copier is 5-year property, and Heron elected to use the straight-line method of cost recovery. Heron made the election because its business was new, and Heron reasoned that in the first few years of the business, a large cost recovery deduction was not needed.

Because the business was doing poorly, Heron did not even claim any cost recovery deductions in Years 3 and 4. In Years 5 and 6, Heron deducted the proper amount of cost recovery. Therefore, the allowed cost recovery (cost recovery actually deducted) and the allowable cost recovery are computed as follows:[52]

	Cost Recovery Allowed	Cost Recovery Allowable
Year 1	$1,000	$ 1,000
Year 2	2,000	2,000
Year 3	–0–	2,000
Year 4	–0–	2,000
Year 5	2,000	2,000
Year 6	1,000	1,000
Totals	$6,000	$10,000

The adjusted basis of the copier at the end of Year 6 is $0 ($10,000 cost − $10,000 *allowable* cost recovery). If Heron sells the copier for $800 in Year 7, it will recognize an $800 gain ($800 amount realized − $0 adjusted basis).

Cost Recovery Basis for Personal-Use Assets Converted to Business or Income-Producing Use

If personal-use assets are converted to business or income-producing use, the basis for cost recovery and for loss is the lower of the adjusted basis or the fair market value at the time the property was converted. As a result of this basis rule, losses that occurred while the property was personal-use property are not recognized for tax purposes through the cost recovery of the property.

The Big Picture

EXAMPLE
39

Return to the facts of *The Big Picture* on p. 5-1. Five years ago, Michael Forney purchased a personal residence for $250,000. In the current year, with the housing market down, Michael found an attractively priced larger home that he acquired for his personal residence. Because of the downturn in the housing market, however, he was not able to sell his original residence and recover his purchase price of $250,000. The residence was appraised at $180,000.

Instead of continuing to try to sell the original residence, he converted it to rental property. The basis for cost recovery of the rental property is $180,000 because the fair market value is less than the adjusted basis. The $70,000 decline in value is deemed to be personal (because it occurred while the property was held for Michael's personal use) and therefore nondeductible.

5-7c Modified Accelerated Cost Recovery System (MACRS)

MACRS provides separate cost recovery periods and methods for realty (real property) and personalty (personal property). Cost recovery allowances for real property, other than land, are based on recovery lives specified in the law. The IRS provides tables that specify cost recovery allowances for personalty and for realty. Concept Summary 5.1 provides an overview of the various conventions that apply under MACRS.

[52]The cost recovery allowances are based on the half-year convention, which allows a half-year's cost recovery in the first and last years of the recovery period.

Concept Summary 5.1

Statutory Percentage Method under MACRS

	Personal Property	Real Property*
Convention	Half-year or mid-quarter	Mid-month
Cost recovery deduction in the year of disposition	Half-year for year of disposition or half-quarter for quarter of disposition	Half-month for month of disposition

*Straight-line method must be used.

5-7d Cost Recovery for Personal Property

MACRS provides that the cost recovery basis of eligible personalty (and certain realty) is recovered over 3, 5, 7, 10, 15, or 20 years.[53] Examples of property in the different cost recovery categories are shown in Exhibit 5.2.[54]

Accelerated depreciation is allowed for these six MACRS classes of property. The appropriate computational methods and conventions are built into the tables; so in general, it is not necessary to perform any calculations. To determine the amount of the cost recovery allowance, simply identify the asset by class and go to the appropriate table.[55] The MACRS percentages for personalty are shown in Exhibit 5.5 (MACRS tables are located at the end of the chapter prior to the problem materials).

EXHIBIT 5.2	Cost Recovery Periods: MACRS Personalty

Class	Examples
3-year	Tractor units for use over-the-road
	Any horse that is not a racehorse and is more than 12 years old at the time it is placed in service
	Special tools used in the manufacturing of motor vehicles, such as dies, fixtures, molds, and patterns
5-year	Automobiles and taxis
	Light and heavy general-purpose trucks
	Calculators and copiers
	Computers and peripheral equipment
7-year	Office furniture, fixtures, and equipment
	Agricultural machinery and equipment
10-year	Vessels, barges, tugs, and similar water transportation equipment
	Assets used for petroleum refining or for the manufacture of grain and grain mill products, sugar and sugar products, or vegetable oils and vegetable oil products
	Single-purpose agricultural or horticultural structures
15-year	Land improvements
	Assets used for industrial steam and electric generation and/or distribution systems
	Assets used in the manufacture of cement
20-year	Farm buildings except single-purpose agricultural and horticultural structures
	Water utilities

---

[53]Property is classified by recovery period under MACRS based on asset depreciation range (ADR) midpoint lives provided by the IRS. Rev.Proc. 87–56, 1987–2 C.B. 674 is the source for the ADR midpoint lives.

[54]§ 168(e).

[55]§ 168(b).

Taxpayers may *elect* the straight-line method to compute cost recovery allowances for each of these classes of property. Certain property is not eligible for accelerated cost recovery and must be depreciated under an alternative depreciation system (ADS). Both the straight-line election and ADS are discussed later in the chapter.

MACRS views personal property as placed in service in the middle of the asset's first year and allows a half-year of cost recovery in the year of acquisition and in the final year of cost recovery (the **half-year convention**).[56] Thus, for example, the statutory recovery period for property with a life of three years begins in the middle of the year the asset is placed in service and ends three years later. In practical terms, this means that the actual write-offs are claimed over 4, 6, 8, 11, 16, and 21 tax years. MACRS also allows for a half-year of cost recovery in the year of disposition or retirement.

Half-Year Convention

Robin Corporation acquires a 5-year class asset on April 10, 2015, for $30,000. Robin's cost recovery deduction for 2015 is computed as follows:

MACRS calculation based on Exhibit 5.5 ($30,000 × .20) $6,000

Assume the same facts as in the previous example. Robin disposes of the asset on March 5, 2017. Robin's cost recovery deduction for 2017 is $2,880 [$30,000 × 1/2 × .192 (Exhibit 5.5)].

Mid-Quarter Convention

The half-year convention arises from the simplifying presumption that assets generally will be acquired evenly throughout the tax year. However, Congress was concerned that taxpayers might override that presumption by placing large amounts of property in service during the last quarter of the taxable year (and, by doing so, receive a half-year's depreciation on those large, fourth-quarter acquisitions).

To inhibit this behavior, Congress added the **mid-quarter convention** that applies if more than 40 percent of the value of property other than eligible real estate[57] is placed in service during the last quarter of the year.[58] Under the convention, property acquisitions are grouped by the quarter they were acquired for cost recovery purposes. Acquisitions during the first quarter are allowed 10.5 months (three and one-half quarters) of cost recovery; the second quarter, 7.5 months (two and one-half quarters); the third quarter, 4.5 months (one and one-half quarters); and the fourth quarter, 1.5 months. The percentages are shown in Exhibit 5.6.

Silver Corporation puts into service the following new 5-year class property in 2015.

Acquisition Dates	Cost
February 15	$ 200,000
July 10	400,000
December 5	600,000
Total	$1,200,000

Under the statutory percentage method, Silver's cost recovery allowances for the first two years are computed as follows. Because more than 40% ($600,000/$1,200,000 = 50%) of the acquisitions are in the last quarter, the mid-quarter convention applies.

continued

---

[56]§ 168(d)(4)(A).

[57]See Cost Recovery for Real Estate on the following page for a discussion of eligible real estate.

[58]§ 168(d)(3).

2015

	Mid-Quarter Convention Depreciation (Exhibit 5.6)		Total Depreciation
February 15	$200,000 × .35	=	$ 70,000
July 10	$400,000 × .15	=	60,000
December 5	$600,000 × .05	=	30,000
Total			$160,000

2016

February 15	$200,000 × .26	=	$ 52,000
July 10	$400,000 × .34	=	136,000
December 5	$600,000 × .38	=	228,000
Total			$416,000

Without the mid-quarter convention, Silver's 2015 MACRS deduction would have been $240,000 [$1,200,000 × .20 (Exhibit 5.5)]. The mid-quarter convention slows down the taxpayer's available cost recovery deductions.

When property to which the mid-quarter convention applies is disposed of, the property is treated as though it were disposed of at the midpoint of the quarter. Hence, in the quarter of disposition, cost recovery is allowed for one-half of the quarter.

EXAMPLE 43

Assume the same facts as in the previous example, except that Silver Corporation sells the $400,000 asset on November 30, 2016. The cost recovery allowance for 2016 is computed as follows (Exhibit 5.6):

February 15	$200,000 × .26	=	$ 52,000
July 10	$400,000 × .34 × (3.5/4)	=	119,000
December 5	$600,000 × .38	=	228,000
Total			$399,000

5-7e Cost Recovery for Real Estate

Under MACRS, the cost recovery period for residential rental real estate is 27.5 years, and the straight-line method is used for computing the cost recovery allowance. **Residential rental real estate** includes property where 80 percent or more of the gross rental revenues are from nontransient dwelling units (e.g., an apartment building). Hotels, motels, and similar establishments are not residential rental property. Nonresidential real estate uses a recovery period of 39 years; it also is depreciated using the straight-line method.[59]

Some items of real property are not treated as real estate for purposes of MACRS. For example, single-purpose agricultural structures are in the 10-year MACRS class. Land improvements are in the 15-year MACRS class. See Exhibit 5.2.

All eligible real estate placed in service after June 22, 1984 (under both ACRS and MACRS) is depreciated using the **mid-month convention**.[60] Regardless of when the property is placed in service, it is deemed to have been placed in service at the middle of the month. This allows for one-half month's cost recovery for the month the property is placed in service. If the property is disposed of before the end of the recovery period, one-half month's cost recovery is permitted for the month of disposition regardless of the specific date of disposition.

---

[59]§§ 168(b), (c), and (e). A 31.5-year life is used for such property placed in service before May 13, 1993.

[60]§ 168(d)(1).

Cost recovery is computed by multiplying the applicable rate (taken from a table) by the cost recovery basis. The MACRS real property rates are provided in Exhibit 5.7.

Real Estate Cost Recovery

EXAMPLE 44

Badger Rentals, Inc., acquired a building on April 1, 1998, for $800,000. If the building is classified as residential real estate, the cost recovery deduction for 2015 is $29,088 (.03636 × $800,000).

If the building is sold on October 7, 2015, the cost recovery deduction for 2015 is $23,028 [.03636 × (9.5/12) × $800,000].

If the building is acquired on March 2, 1993, for $1 million and is classified as nonresidential real estate, the cost recovery deduction for 2015 is $31,740 (.03174 × $1,000,000).

If the building is sold on January 5, 2015, the cost recovery deduction for 2015 is $1,323 [.03174 × (.5/12) × $1,000,000]. (See the first two sections of Exhibit 5.7 for the percentages.)

EXAMPLE 45

Oakenwood Properties, Inc., acquired a building on November 19, 2015, for $1.2 million. If the building is classified as nonresidential real estate, the cost recovery deduction for 2015 is $3,852 (.00321 × $1,200,000). The cost recovery deduction for 2016 is $30,768 (.02564 × $1,200,000).

If the building is sold on May 21, 2016, the cost recovery deduction for 2016 is $11,538 [.02564 × (4.5/12) × $1,200,000]. (See the last section of Exhibit 5.7 for the percentages.)

5-7f Straight-Line Election

Although MACRS requires straight-line depreciation for all eligible real estate, the taxpayer may *elect* to use the straight-line method for depreciable personal property.[61] The property is depreciated using the class life (recovery period) of the asset with a half-year convention or a mid-quarter convention, whichever applies. The election is available on a class-by-class and year-by-year basis. The percentages for the straight-line election with a half-year convention appear in Exhibit 5.8.

Straight-Line Election

EXAMPLE 46

Terry puts into service a new 10-year class asset on August 4, 2015, for $100,000. He elects the straight-line method of cost recovery. Terry's cost recovery deduction for 2015 is $5,000 ($100,000 × .05). His cost recovery deduction for 2016 is $10,000 ($100,000 × .10). (See Exhibit 5.8 for the percentages.)

EXAMPLE 47

Assume the same facts as in the previous example, except that Terry sells the asset on November 21, 2016. His cost recovery deduction for 2016, which is subject to the half-year convention, is $5,000 [$100,000 × .10 × 1/2 (Exhibit 5.8)].

5-7g Additional First-Year Depreciation

As noted in Chapter 1, Congress uses the tax system to stimulate the economy—especially in challenging economic times. Such is the case with **additional first-year depreciation** (also referred to as "bonus depreciation"). Under this provision, taxpayers can take an additional 50 percent cost recovery in the year qualified property is placed in service.[62]

---

[61] § 168(b)(5).

[62] § 168(k). The 50% additional first-year depreciation is allowed for qualified property placed in service after 2011 and before 2015. Congress is expected to extend this provision and the text, examples, and problems assume this will occur. Different rules applied between 2008 and 2011.

FINANCIAL DISCLOSURE INSIGHTS Tax and Book Depreciation

A common book-tax difference relates to the depreciation amounts that are reported for GAAP and Federal income tax purposes. Typically, tax depreciation deductions are accelerated; that is, they are claimed in earlier reporting periods than is the case for financial accounting purposes.

Almost every tax law change since 1980 has included depreciation provisions that accelerate the related deductions relative to the expenses allowed under GAAP.

Accelerated cost recovery deductions represent a means by which the taxing jurisdiction infuses the business with cash flow created by the reduction in the year's tax liabilities.

For instance, recently, about one-quarter of General Electric's deferred tax liabilities related to depreciation differences. For Toyota's and Ford's depreciation differences, that amount was about one-third. And for the trucking firm Ryder Systems, depreciation differences accounted for all but 1 percent of the deferred tax liabilities.

Qualified property includes most *new* depreciable assets other than buildings. *New* means original or first use of the property. Property that is used but newly acquired by the taxpayer does not qualify.

The additional first-year depreciation is taken in the year in which the qualifying property is placed in service. This amount may be claimed in addition to otherwise available depreciation deductions. After the additional first-year depreciation is calculated, the standard MACRS cost recovery allowance is calculated by multiplying the cost recovery basis (original cost recovery basis less additional first-year depreciation) by the percentage that reflects the applicable cost recovery method and convention.

A taxpayer may elect *not* to claim additional first-year depreciation. Examples 48 and 49 reflect the tax treatment for 2015 assuming Congress extends this provision.

Bonus Depreciation

EXAMPLE 48

Morgan acquires, for $50,000, and places in service a 5-year class asset on March 20, 2015. Morgan's total 2015 cost recovery deduction is:

50% additional first-year depreciation ($50,000 × .50)	$25,000
MACRS cost recovery [($50,000 − $25,000) × .20 (Exhibit 5.5)]	5,000
Total cost recovery	$30,000

EXAMPLE 49

Assume the same facts as in the previous example. Morgan disposes of the asset on October 22, 2016. Morgan's 2016 cost recovery deduction for the asset is $4,000 [$25,000 × ½ year × .32 (Exhibit 5.5)].

5-7h Election to Expense Assets (§ 179)

Section 179 (Election to Expense Certain Depreciable Business Assets) permits a taxpayer to elect to deduct up to $500,000 of the acquisition cost of *tangible personal property* used in a trade or business.[63] Amounts that are expensed under § 179 may not be capitalized and depreciated.

The **§ 179 expensing election** is an annual election that applies to the acquisition cost of property placed in service that year. The immediate expense election generally is not available for real property or for property used for the production of income.[64]

---

[63]The annual expense and phaseout amounts ($500,000 and $2 million, respectively) apply to 2014 and prior years. However, Congress is expected to extend these amounts to 2015 and the text, examples, and problems assume this will occur. If this does not occur, the annual expense and phaseout amounts will be $25,000 and $200,000, respectively.

[64]§§ 179(b) and (d). Generally, property used for the production of income is property that is held in a capacity or function where income is generated, but where it is not used by a trade or business.

TAX IN THE NEWS   **Cost Segregation**

Cost segregation identifies certain assets within a commercial property that can qualify for shorter depreciation schedules than the building itself. The identified assets are classified as 5-, 7-, or 15-year property, rather than 39-year property, as part of the building. This allows for greater accelerated depreciation, which reduces taxable income and hence the tax liability.

For instance, a telecommunications system might be segregated from the building in which it is installed. This allows the system to be depreciated over 5 or 7 years, instead of 39 years.

Any elected § 179 expense is taken *before* additional first-year and any other depreciation is computed. The base for calculating both any additional first-year cost recovery and the standard MACRS deduction is determined net of the § 179 expense.

EXAMPLE 50

Kodiak Corporation acquires and places in service equipment (5-year class asset) on February 1, 2015, at a cost of $525,000. It elects to expense $500,000 under § 179. Kodiak also claims the 50 percent additional first-year cost recovery deduction for 2015. As a result, the total deduction for the year is calculated as follows:

§ 179 expense	$500,000
50% additional first-year depreciation [($525,000 − $500,000) × 50%]	12,500
Standard MACRS amount [($525,000 − $500,000 − $12,500) × .20]	2,500
Total cost recovery claimed	$515,000

Annual Limitations

Two additional limitations apply to the amount deductible under § 179. First, the ceiling amount on the deduction is reduced dollar for dollar when § 179 property placed in service during the taxable year exceeds a maximum amount ($2 million). Second, the § 179 deduction cannot exceed the taxpayer's trade or business taxable income, computed without regard to the § 179 amount.

Any § 179 deduction in excess of taxable income is carried forward to future taxable years and added to other amounts eligible for expensing. The § 179 amount eligible for expensing in a carryforward year is limited to the *lesser* of (1) the appropriate statutory dollar amount ($500,000) reduced by the cost of § 179 property placed in service in excess of $2 million in the carryforward year or (2) business taxable income in the carryforward year.

EXAMPLE 51

Jill owns a computer service and operates it as a sole proprietorship. In 2015, taxable income is $138,000 before considering any § 179 deduction. If Jill spends $2.3 million on new equipment, her § 179 expense deduction for the year is computed as follows:

§ 179 deduction before adjustment	$ 500,000
Less: Dollar limitation reduction ($2,300,000 − $2,000,000)	(300,000)
Remaining § 179 deduction	$ 200,000
Business income limitation	$ 138,000
§ 179 deduction allowed	$ 138,000
§ 179 deduction carryforward ($200,000 − $138,000)	$ 62,000

Effect on Basis

The basis of the property for cost recovery purposes is reduced by the § 179 amount after accounting for the current-year amount of property placed in service in excess of $2 million). This adjusted amount does not reflect any business income limitation.

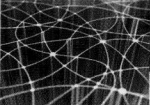

Bridge to Economics and the Business Cycle

Congress has passed several stimulus packages intended to stabilize and accelerate the economy. One provision increased the amount of certain fixed asset acquisition costs that could be expensed rather than depreciated. Given that some sectors of the economy are still struggling, however, many companies are not able to take

advantage of the increased deductions because they cannot afford to purchase new assets. Businesses do not purchase assets simply to save on taxes.

Source: Based on Joyce Rosenberg, "Deduction Dilemma Hits Companies," *Telegraph Herald* (Dubuque, Iowa), November 9, 2008, p. B2.

5-7i Business and Personal Use of Automobiles and Other Listed Property

Limits exist on MACRS deductions for automobiles and other listed property used for both personal and business purposes.[65] These limits would apply, for example, to an automobile used by a sole proprietor partly for business purposes and partly for personal use.

If the listed property is *predominantly* used for business, the taxpayer can use the MACRS tables to recover the cost. In cases where the property is *not predominantly* used for business, the cost is recovered using the *straight-line method*. The statutory percentage method results in a faster recovery of cost than the straight-line method. Listed property includes:[66]

- Any passenger automobile.
- Any other property used as a means of transportation.
- Any property of a type generally used for purposes of entertainment, recreation, or amusement.
- Any computer or peripheral equipment, with the exception of equipment used exclusively at a regular business establishment, including a qualifying home office.
- Any other property specified in the Regulations.

Automobiles and Other Listed Property Used Predominantly in Business

For listed property to be considered as predominantly used in business, its *business usage* must exceed 50 percent.[67] The use of listed property for production of income does not qualify as business use for purposes of the more-than-50% test. However, both production-of-income and business-use percentages are used to compute the cost recovery deduction.

EXAMPLE

52

On September 1, 2015, Emma acquires and places in service listed 5-year recovery property. The property cost $10,000. Emma does not claim any available additional first-year cost recovery.

If Emma uses the property 40% for business and 25% for the production of income, the property is not considered as predominantly used for business. The asset cost is recovered using the straight-line method. Emma's cost recovery allowance for the year is $650 ($10,000 × .10 × .65).

If, however, Emma uses the property 60% for business and 25% for the production of income, the property is considered as used predominantly for business. Therefore, she may use the MACRS tables. Emma's cost recovery allowance for the year is $1,700 ($10,000 × .20 × .85).

In determining the percentage of business usage for listed property, a mileage-based percentage is used for automobiles. For other listed property, one employs the most appropriate unit of time (e.g., hours) for which the property actually is used (rather than its availablility for use).[68]

---

[65]§ 280F.

[66]§ 280F(d)(4).

[67]§ 280F(b)(3).

[68]Reg. § 1.280F–6T(e).

Limits on Cost Recovery for Automobiles

The law places special limitations on cost recovery deductions for *passenger automobiles*.[69] These statutory dollar limits were imposed on passenger automobiles because of the belief that the tax system was being used to underwrite automobiles whose cost and luxury features far exceeded what was needed for the taxpayer's business use.

The following "luxury auto" depreciation limits apply.[70]

Date Placed in Service	First Year	Second Year	Third Year	Fourth and Later Years
2014*	$3,160	$5,100	$3,050	$1,875
2012–2013	$3,160	$5,100	$3,050	$1,875
2010–2011	$3,060	$4,900	$2,950	$1,775
2009	$2,960	$4,800	$2,850	$1,775

*Because the 2015 indexed amounts are not yet available, the 2014 amounts are used in the examples and end-of-chapter problem materials.

For an automobile placed in service prior to 2009, the limitation for subsequent years' cost recovery is based on the limits for the year the automobile was placed in service.[71] If a new passenger automobile otherwise qualifies for additional first-year depreciation, the *luxury auto* limitation increases by $8,000 for aquisitions made in 2014 (i.e., to $11,160).

There are also separate cost recovery limitations for trucks and vans and for electric automobiles. Because these limitations are applied in the same manner as those imposed on passenger automobiles, these additional limitations are not discussed further in this chapter.

The luxury auto limits are imposed before any percentage reduction for personal use. In addition, the limitation in the first year includes any amount the taxpayer elects to expense under § 179.[72] If the passenger automobile is used partly for personal use, the personal-use percentage is ignored for the purpose of determining the unrecovered cost available for deduction in later years.

EXAMPLE 53

On July 1, 2015, Dan acquires and places in service a new automobile that cost $40,000. He does not elect § 179 expensing and he elects not to take any available additional first-year depreciation. The car is used 80% for business and 20% for personal purposes in each tax year. Dan chooses the MACRS 200% declining-balance method of cost recovery (the auto is a 5-year asset; see Exhibit 5.5).

The depreciation computation for 2015 through 2020 is summarized in the table below. The cost recovery allowed is the lesser of the MACRS amount or the recovery limitation.

Year	MACRS Amount	Recovery Limitation	Depreciation Allowed
2015	$6,400 ($40,000 × .2000 × 80%)	$2,528 ($3,160 × 80%)	$2,528
2016	$10,240 ($40,000 × .3200 × 80%)	$4,080 ($5,100 × 80%)	$4,080
2017	$6,144 ($40,000 × .1920 × 80%)	$2,440 ($3,050 × 80%)	$2,440
2018	$3,686 ($40,000 × .1152 × 80%)	$1,500 ($1,875 × 80%)	$1,500
2019	$3,686 ($40,000 × .1152 × 80%)	$1,500 ($1,875 × 80%)	$1,500
2020	$1,843 ($40,000 × .0576 × 80%)	$1,500 ($1,875 × 80%)	$1,500

continued

---

[69]§ 280F(d)(5).

[70]§ 280F(a)(1); Rev.Proc. 2014-21, 2014–11 I.R.B.641.

[71]Cost recovery limitations for years prior to 2009 are found in IRS Publication 463.

[72]§ 280F(d)(1).

If Dan continues to use the car after 2020, his cost recovery is limited to the lesser of the recoverable basis or the recovery limitation (i.e., $1,875 × business-use percentage). For this purpose, the recoverable basis is computed as if the full cost recovery limitation was allowed, even if the full deduction was not claimed. Thus, the recoverable basis as of January 1, 2020, is $23,065 ($40,000 − $3,160 − $5,100 − $3,050 − $1,875 − $1,875 − $1,875).

If Dan takes additional first-year depreciation in 2015, the calculated amount of additional first-year depreciation is $16,000 ($40,000 × 80% × 50%). However, the deduction would be limited to $8,928 [($8,000 + $3,160) × 80%].

The cost recovery limitations are maximum amounts. If the regular MACRS calculation produces a lesser amount of cost recovery, the lesser amount is used.

On April 2, 2015, Gail places in service a pre-owned automobile that cost $10,000. The car is always used 70% for business and 30% for personal use.

The cost recovery allowance for 2015 is $1,400 ($10,000 × .20 × 70%), and not $2,212 (the $3,160 passenger auto maximum × 70%).

EXAMPLE 54

The luxury auto limitations apply *only* to passenger automobiles and not to other listed property.

Limitation for SUVs

A $25,000 limit applies to the § 179 deduction when the luxury auto limits do not apply. The limit is in effect for sport utility vehicles (SUVs) with an unloaded gross vehicle weight (GVW) rating of more than 6,000 pounds and not more than 14,000 pounds.[73]

During 2015, Jay acquires and places in service a new SUV that cost $70,000 and has a GVW of 8,000 pounds. Jay uses the vehicle 100% of the time for business purposes. The total deduction for 2015 with respect to the SUV is computed as follows:

§ 179 expense, as limited	$25,000
50% additional first-year depreciation [($70,000 − $25,000) × 50%]	22,500
Standard MACRS amount [($70,000 − $25,000 − $22,500) × .20 (Exhibit 5.5)]	4,500
Total cost recovery claimed	$52,000

EXAMPLE 55

Automobiles and Other Listed Property Not Used Predominantly in Business

For automobiles and other listed property not used predominantly in business in the year of acquisition (i.e., 50 percent or less), the straight-line method under the alternative depreciation system is required (see Section 5-7k).[74] Under this system, the straight-line recovery period for automobiles is five years. However, the cost recovery allowance for any passenger automobile cannot exceed the luxury auto amount.

The straight-line method is used even if, at some later date, the business usage of the property increases to more than 50 percent. In that case, the amount of cost recovery reflects the increase in business usage.

Change from Predominantly Business Use

If the business-use percentage of listed property falls to 50 percent or less after the year the property is placed in service, the property is subject to *cost recovery recapture*. The amount required to be recaptured and included in the taxpayer's return as ordinary income is the excess cost recovery. *Excess cost recovery* is the excess of the cost recovery deduction taken in prior years using the statutory percentage method over the amount that would have been allowed if the straight-line method had been used since the property was placed in service.[75]

After the business usage of the listed property drops below the more-than-50% level, the straight-line method must be used for the remaining life of the property.

---

[73]§ 179(b)(6).

[74]§ 280F(b)(1).

[75]§ 280F(b)(2).

Concept Summary 5.2 illustrates the cost recovery rules for various types of listed property.

Concept Summary 5.2

Listed Property Cost Recovery

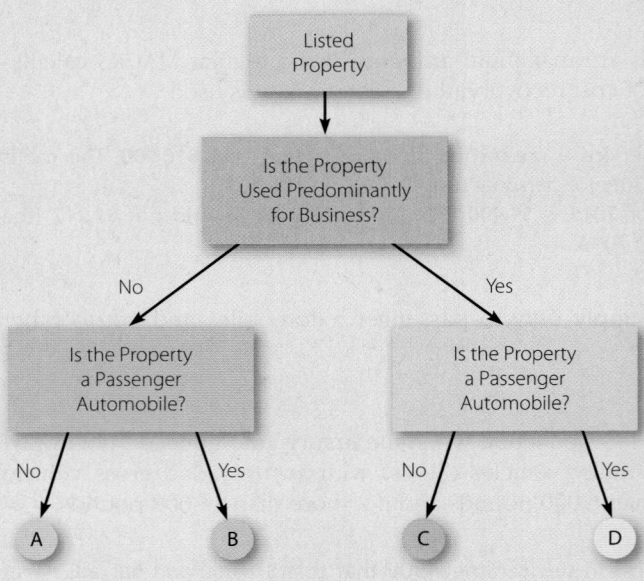

Legend to Tax Treatment

A   Straight-line cost recovery reduced by the personal use percentage.

B   Straight-line cost recovery subject to the recovery limitations that apply (based on the year placed in service) and reduced by the personal use percentage.

C   Statutory percentage cost recovery reduced by the personal use percentage.

D   Statutory percentage cost recovery subject to the recovery limitations that apply (based on the year placed in service) and reduced by the personal use percentage.

Leased Automobiles

A taxpayer who leases a passenger automobile for business purposes reports an *inclusion amount* in gross income. The inclusion amount is computed from an IRS table for each taxable year for which the taxpayer leases the automobile. The purpose of this provision is to prevent taxpayers from circumventing the luxury auto and other limitations by leasing, instead of purchasing, an automobile.

The inclusion amount is based on the fair market value of the automobile; it is prorated for the number of days the auto is used during the taxable year. The prorated dollar amount then is multiplied by the business and income-producing usage percentage.[76] The taxpayer deducts the lease payments, multiplied by the business and income-producing usage percentage. In effect, the taxpayer's annual deduction for the lease payment is reduced by the inclusion amount.

---

[76]Reg. § 1.280F–7(a).

A new car, on average, loses a much larger portion of its value during the first five years through economic depreciation than it loses during later years. Depreciation accounts for about 35 percent of the ownership costs of a car during this five-year period.

Leasing a car will not eliminate the problem because the monthly lease payments are determined, in part, by the projected value of the car at the end of the lease. Because a new car loses its value faster in the earlier years, the shorter the lease, the higher the economic cost of depreciation.

EXAMPLE

56

On April 1, 2015, Jim leases and places in service a passenger automobile worth $52,400. The lease is to be for a period of five years. During the taxable years 2015 and 2016, Jim uses the automobile 70% for business and 30% for personal use.

Assuming that the inclusion amounts from the IRS table for 2015 and 2016 are $32 and $70, respectively, Jim includes in gross income:

2015: $32 × (275/365) × .70 = $17
2016: $70 × (366/366) × .70 = $49

In each year, Jim still can deduct 70% of the lease payments made, related to his business use of the auto.

Substantiation Requirements

Listed property is subject to the substantiation requirements of § 274. This means that the taxpayer must prove for any business usage the amount of expense or use, the time and place of use, the business purpose for the use, and the business relationship to the taxpayer of persons using the property.

Substantiation requires adequate records or sufficient evidence corroborating the taxpayer's statement. However, these substantiation requirements do not apply to vehicles that, by reason of their nature, are not likely to be used more than a *de minimis* amount for personal purposes.[77]

5-7j **Farm Property**

A farming business is defined as the trade or business of farming, which includes operating a nursery or sod farm and the raising or harvesting of trees bearing fruit, nuts, or other crops, or ornamental trees.[78] When tangible personal property is used in a farming business, the cost of the asset generally is recovered under MACRS using the 150 percent declining-balance method.[79] However, the MACRS straight-line method is required for any tree or vine bearing fruits or nuts.[80]

In general, the cost of real property used in the farming business is recovered over the usual recovery periods (27.5 years and 39 years) using the straight-line method. Exhibit 5.3 shows examples of cost recovery periods for some typical farming assets.

Special rules are used if the uniform capitalization rules apply to the farming business.[81] Under the uniform capitalization rules, the costs of property produced or acquired for resale must be capitalized.

Alternatively, a farmer can elect to not have the uniform capitalization rules apply. In this case, the alternative depreciation system (ADS) straight-line method must be used (see Section 5-7k). Section 179 expensing can be used even when the ADS is in effect.[82]

---

[77]§§ 274(d) and (i).
[78]§ 263A(e)(4).
[79]§ 168(b)(2)(B).

[80]§§ 168(b)(3)(E) and 168(e)(3)(D)(ii).
[81]§ 263A(d)(3)(A).
[82]Reg. § 1.263A–4(d)(4)(ii).

EXHIBIT 5.3	**Cost Recovery Periods for Farming Assets**	

	Recovery Period in Years	
Assets	**MACRS**	**ADS**
Agricultural structures (single purpose)	10	15
Cattle (dairy or breeding)	5	7
Farm buildings	20	25
Farm machinery and equipment	7	10
Fences (agricultural)	7	10
Horticultural structures (single purpose)	10	15
Trees or vines bearing fruit or nuts	10	20
Truck (heavy-duty, unloaded weight 13,000 pounds or more)	5	6
Truck (actual weight less than 13,000 pounds)	5	5

Farm Property

EXAMPLE 57

Redberry Farms, Inc., purchased new farm equipment on July 10, 2015, for $80,000.
If Redberry does not elect to expense any of the cost under § 179, its cost recovery deduction for 2015 is $8,568 [(.1071 × $80,000) (Exhibit 5.9)].

EXAMPLE 58

Assume the same facts as in the previous example, except that Redberry Farms, Inc., has made an election not to have the uniform capitalization rules apply.
Redberry's 2015 cost recovery deduction is $4,000 [(.05 × $80,000) (Exhibit 5.10)].

5-7k Alternative Depreciation System (ADS)

The **alternative depreciation system (ADS)** must be used in lieu of MACRS:[83]

- To calculate the portion of depreciation treated as an alternative minimum tax (AMT) adjustment (see Chapter 17).[84]
- To compute depreciation allowances for property:
  - Used predominantly outside the United States.
  - Leased or otherwise used by a tax-exempt entity.
  - Financed with the proceeds of tax-exempt bonds.
  - Imported from foreign countries that maintain discriminatory trade practices or otherwise engage in discriminatory acts.
- To compute depreciation allowances as part of earnings and profits (see Chapter 13).

Exhibits 5.9, 5.10, and 5.11 provide cost recovery rates under the ADS method. Generally, personal property is depreciated under the ADS using the appropriate asset class life (e.g., 5- or 7-year) and the 150 percent declining-balance method. ADS uses straight-line depreciation for all realty, over a 40-year class life.

---

[83]§ 168(g).

[84]This AMT adjustment applies for real and personal property placed in service before 1999. However, it continues to apply for personal property placed in service after 1998 if the taxpayer uses the 200% declining-balance method for regular income tax purposes. See Chapter 17.

5-8 AMORTIZATION

LO.7
Identify intangible assets that are eligible for amortization and calculate the amount of the deduction.

Taxpayers can claim an **amortization** deduction on certain intangible assets. The amount of the deduction is determined by amortizing the adjusted basis of such intangibles ratably over a 15-year period beginning in the month in which the intangible is acquired.[85]

An *amortizable § 197 intangible* is any § 197 intangible acquired after August 10, 1993, and held in connection with the conduct of a trade or business or for the production of income. Section 197 intangibles include goodwill and going-concern value, franchises, trademarks, and trade names. Covenants not to compete, copyrights, and patents also are included if they are acquired in connection with the acquisition of a business. Generally, self-created intangibles are not § 197 intangibles.

The 15-year amortization period applies regardless of the actual useful life of an amortizable § 197 intangible. No other depreciation or amortization deduction is permitted with respect to any amortizable § 197 intangible except those permitted under the 15-year amortization rules.

On June 1, Sally purchased and began operating the Falcon Café. Of the purchase price, $90,000 is allocated to goodwill.

The year's § 197 amortization deduction is $3,500 [($90,000 ÷ 15) × (7/12)].

EXAMPLE 59

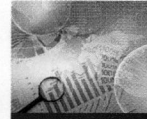

TAX PLANNING STRATEGIES **Structuring the Sale of a Business**

FRAMEWORK FOCUS: TAX RATE

Strategy: Control the Character of Income and Deductions.

On the sale of a sole proprietorship where the sales price exceeds the fair market value of the tangible assets and stated intangible assets, a planning opportunity may exist for both the seller and the buyer.

The seller's preference is for the excess amount to be allocated to *goodwill* because goodwill is a capital asset whose sale may result in favorably taxed long-term capital gain. Amounts received for a *covenant not to compete,* however, produce ordinary income, which is not subject to favorable long-term capital gain rates.

Because a covenant and goodwill both are amortized over a statutory 15-year period, the tax results of a covenant

not to compete versus goodwill are the same for the *buyer*. However, the buyer should recognize that an allocation to goodwill rather than a covenant may provide a tax benefit to the seller. Therefore, the buyer, in negotiating the purchase price, should factor in the tax benefit to the seller of having the excess amount labeled goodwill rather than a covenant not to compete. Of course, if the noncompetition aspects of a covenant are important to the buyer, a portion of the excess amount can be assigned to a covenant.

5-9 DEPLETION

LO.8
Determine the amount of depletion expense and specify the alternative tax treatments for intangible drilling and development costs.

Natural resources (e.g., oil, gas, coal, gravel, and timber) are subject to **depletion**, which can be seen as a form of depreciation applicable to natural resources. Land generally cannot be depleted.

The owner of an interest in the natural resource is entitled to deduct depletion. An owner is one who has an economic interest in the property.[86] An economic interest

---

[85]§ 197(a).　　　　　[86]Reg. § 1.611–1(b).

requires the acquisition of an interest in the resource in place and the receipt of income from the extraction or severance of that resource. Although all natural resources are subject to depletion, oil and gas wells are used as an example in the following paragraphs to illustrate the related costs and issues.

In developing an oil or gas well, the producer typically makes four types of expenditures:

- Natural resource costs.
- Intangible drilling and development costs.
- Tangible asset costs.
- Operating costs.

Natural resources are physically limited, and the costs to acquire them (e.g., oil under the ground) are, therefore, recovered through depletion. Costs incurred in making the property ready for drilling, such as the cost of labor in clearing the property, erecting derricks, and drilling the hole, are **intangible drilling and development costs (IDCs)**. These costs generally have no salvage value and are a lost cost if the well is not productive (dry).

Costs for tangible assets such as tools, pipes, and engines are capitalized and recovered through depreciation (cost recovery). Costs incurred after the well is producing are operating costs. These costs include expenditures for items such as labor, fuel, and supplies. Operating costs are deductible as trade or business expenses. Intangible drilling and development costs and depletable costs receive different treatment.

5-9a **Intangible Drilling and Development Costs (IDCs)**

Intangible drilling and development costs can be handled in one of two ways at the option of the taxpayer. They can be either charged off as an expense in the year in which they are incurred or capitalized and written off through depletion. The taxpayer makes the election in the first year such expenditures are incurred, either by taking a deduction on the return or by adding them to the depletable basis.

Once made, the election is binding on both the taxpayer and the IRS for all such expenditures in the future. If the taxpayer fails to elect to expense IDCs, on the original timely filed return for the first year in which such expenditures are incurred, an irrevocable election to capitalize them has been made.

As a general rule, it is more advantageous to expense IDCs. The obvious benefit of an immediate write-off (as opposed to a deferred write-off through depletion) is not the only advantage. Because a taxpayer can use percentage depletion, which is calculated without reference to basis, the IDCs may be completely lost as a deduction if they are capitalized.

5-9b **Depletion Methods**

There are two methods of calculating depletion. *Cost depletion* can be used on any wasting asset (and is the only method allowed for timber). *Percentage depletion* is subject to a number of limitations, particularly for oil and gas deposits. Depletion should be calculated both ways, and the method that results in the larger deduction should be used. The choice between cost depletion and percentage depletion is an annual decision; the taxpayer can use cost depletion in one year and percentage depletion in the following year.

Cost Depletion

Cost depletion is determined by using the adjusted basis of the asset.[87] The basis is divided by the estimated recoverable units of the asset (e.g., barrels and tons) to arrive at the depletion per unit. This amount then is multiplied by the number of units sold (not

---

[87] § 612.

the units produced) during the year to arrive at the cost depletion allowed. Cost depletion, therefore, resembles the units-of-production method of calculating depreciation.

On January 1, 2015, Pablo purchases the rights to a mineral interest for $1 million. At that time, the remaining recoverable units in the mineral interest are estimated to be 200,000. The depletion per unit is $5 [$1,000,000 (adjusted basis) ÷ 200,000 (estimated recoverable units)].

If 60,000 units are mined and 25,000 are sold, the cost depletion is $125,000 [$5 (depletion per unit) × 25,000 (units sold)].

If the taxpayer later discovers that the original estimate was incorrect, the depletion per unit for future calculations is redetermined, using the revised estimate.[88]

Assume the same facts as in the previous example. In 2016, Pablo realizes that an incorrect estimate was made. The remaining recoverable units now are determined to be 400,000. Based on this new information, the revised depletion per unit is $2.1875 [$875,000 (adjusted basis) ÷ 400,000 (estimated recoverable units)]. The adjusted basis is the original cost ($1,000,000) reduced by the depletion claimed in 2015 ($125,000).

If 30,000 units are sold in 2016, the depletion for the year is $65,625 [$2.1875 (depletion per unit) × 30,000 (units sold)].

Percentage Depletion

Percentage depletion (also referred to as statutory depletion) uses a specified percentage provided by the Code. The percentage varies according to the type of mineral interest involved. A sample of these percentages is shown in Exhibit 5.4. The rate is applied to the gross income from the property, but in no event may percentage depletion exceed 50 percent of the taxable income from the property before the allowance for depletion.[89]

CarrolCo reports gross income of $100,000 and other property-related expenses of $60,000 and uses a depletion rate of 22%. CarrollCo's depletion allowance is determined as follows:

Gross income	$100,000
Less: Other expenses	(60,000)
Taxable income before depletion	$ 40,000
Depletion allowance [the lesser of $22,000 (22% × $100,000) or $20,000 (50% × $40,000)]	(20,000)
Taxable income after depletion	$ 20,000

The adjusted basis of CarrollCo's property is reduced by $20,000, the depletion deduction allowed. If the other expenses had been only $55,000, the full $22,000 could have been deducted, and the adjusted basis would have been reduced by $22,000.

Note that percentage depletion is based on a percentage of the gross income from the property and makes no reference to cost. All other cost recovery deductions detailed in this chapter are a function of the adjusted basis (cost) of the property. Thus, when percentage depletion is used, it is possible to claim aggregate depletion deductions that exceed the original cost of the property. If percentage depletion is used, however, the adjusted basis of the property (for computing cost depletion in a future tax year) is reduced by any depletion deducted, until the basis reaches zero.

---

[88]§ 611(a).

[89]§ 613(a). Special rules apply for certain oil and gas wells (e.g., the 50% ceiling is replaced with a 100% ceiling, and the percentage depletion may not exceed 65% of the taxpayer's taxable income from all sources before the allowance for depletion). § 613A.

EXHIBIT 5.4	**Sample of Percentage Depletion Rates**

22% Depletion

Cobalt	Sulfur
Lead	Tin

15% Depletion

Copper	Oil and gas
Gold	Silver

10% Depletion

Coal	Perlite

5% Depletion

Gravel	Sand

TAX PLANNING STRATEGIES   Switching Depletion Methods

FRAMEWORK FOCUS: DEDUCTIONS

Strategy: Maximize Deductible Amounts.

As long as the basis of a depletable asset remains above zero, cost depletion or percentage depletion, whichever method the taxpayer elects, is used. When the basis of the asset is exhausted, percentage depletion still can be taken.

EXAMPLE 63

Warbler Company reports the following related to its sulfur mine:

Remaining depletable basis	$ 11,000
Gross income (10,000 units)	100,000
Expenses (other than depletion)	30,000
Percentage depletion rate	22%

Because cost depletion is limited to the remaining depletable basis of $11,000, Warbler would choose percentage depletion of $22,000 [lesser of ($100,000 × 22%) or ($70,000 × 50%)]. The basis in the mine then becomes zero.

In future years, however, Warbler can continue to use percentage depletion; percentage depletion is computed without reference to the remaining asset basis.

5-10 COST RECOVERY TABLES

Summary of Cost Recovery Tables

Exhibit 5.5   MACRS statutory percentage table for personalty.
Applicable depreciation methods: 200 or 150 percent declining-balance switching to straight-line.
Applicable recovery periods: 3, 5, 7, 10, 15, 20 years.
Applicable convention: half-year.

Exhibit 5.6   MACRS statutory percentage table for personalty.
Applicable depreciation method: 200 percent declining-balance switching to straight-line.
Applicable recovery periods: 3, 5, 7 years.
Applicable convention: mid-quarter.

Summary of Cost Recovery Tables (continued)

Exhibit 5.7 MACRS straight-line table for realty.
Applicable depreciation method: straight-line.
Applicable recovery periods: 27.5, 31.5, 39 years.
Applicable convention: mid-month.

Exhibit 5.8 MACRS optional straight-line table for personalty.
Applicable depreciation method: straight-line.
Applicable recovery periods: 3, 5, 7, 10, 15, 20 years.
Applicable convention: half-year.

Exhibit 5.9 ADS for Alternative Minimum Tax: 150 percent declining-balance table for personalty.
Applicable depreciation method: 150 percent declining-balance switching to straight-line.
Applicable recovery periods: 3, 5, 7, 9.5, 10, 12 years.
Applicable convention: half-year.

Exhibit 5.10 ADS straight-line table for personalty.
Applicable depreciation method: straight-line.
Applicable recovery periods: 5, 10, 12 years.
Applicable convention: half-year.

Exhibit 5.11 ADS straight-line table for realty.
Applicable depreciation method: straight-line.
Applicable recovery period: 40 years.
Applicable convention: mid-month.

EXHIBIT 5.5	MACRS Accelerated Depreciation for Personal Property Assuming Half-Year Convention					

For Property Placed in Service after December 31, 1986

Recovery Year	3-Year (200% DB)	5-Year (200% DB)	7-Year (200% DB)	10-Year (200% DB)	15-Year (150% DB)	20-Year (150% DB)
1	33.33	20.00	14.29	10.00	5.00	3.750
2	44.45	32.00	24.49	18.00	9.50	7.219
3	14.81*	19.20	17.49	14.40	8.55	6.677
4	7.41	11.52*	12.49	11.52	7.70	6.177
5		11.52	8.93*	9.22	6.93	5.713
6		5.76	8.92	7.37	6.23	5.285
7			8.93	6.55*	5.90*	4.888
8			4.46	6.55	5.90	4.522
9				6.56	5.91	4.462*
10				6.55	5.90	4.461
11				3.28	5.91	4.462
12					5.90	4.461
13					5.91	4.462
14					5.90	4.461
15					5.91	4.462
16					2.95	4.461
17						4.462
18						4.461
19						4.462
20						4.461
21						2.231

*Switchover to straight-line depreciation.

EXHIBIT 5.6	**MACRS Accelerated Depreciation for Personal Property Assuming Mid-Quarter Convention**

For Property Placed in Service after December 31, 1986 (Partial Table*)

	3-Year			
Recovery Year	First Quarter	Second Quarter	Third Quarter	Fourth Quarter
1	58.33	41.67	25.00	8.33
2	27.78	38.89	50.00	61.11

	5-Year			
Recovery Year	First Quarter	Second Quarter	Third Quarter	Fourth Quarter
1	35.00	25.00	15.00	5.00
2	26.00	30.00	34.00	38.00

	7-Year			
Recovery Year	First Quarter	Second Quarter	Third Quarter	Fourth Quarter
1	25.00	17.85	10.71	3.57
2	21.43	23.47	25.51	27.55

*The figures in this table are taken from the official tables that appear in Rev.Proc. 87–57, 1987–2 C.B. 687. Because of their length, the complete tables are not presented.

EXHIBIT 5.7	**MACRS Straight-Line Depreciation for Real Property Assuming Mid-Month Convention***

For Property Placed in Service after December 31, 1986: 27.5-Year Residential Real Property

Recovery Year(s)	The Applicable Percentage Is (Use the Column for the Month in the First Year the Property Is Placed in Service):											
	1	2	3	4	5	6	7	8	9	10	11	12
1	3.485	3.182	2.879	2.576	2.273	1.970	1.667	1.364	1.061	0.758	0.455	0.152
2–18	3.636	3.636	3.636	3.636	3.636	3.636	3.636	3.636	3.636	3.636	3.636	3.636
19–27	3.637	3.637	3.637	3.637	3.637	3.637	3.637	3.637	3.637	3.637	3.637	3.637
28	1.970	2.273	2.576	2.879	3.182	3.485	3.636	3.636	3.636	3.636	3.636	3.636
29	0.000	0.000	0.000	0.000	0.000	0.000	0.152	0.455	0.758	1.061	1.364	1.667

For Property Placed in Service after December 31, 1986, and before May 13, 1993: 31.5-Year Nonresidential Real Property

Recovery Year(s)	The Applicable Percentage Is (Use the Column for the Month in the First Year the Property Is Placed in Service):											
	1	2	3	4	5	6	7	8	9	10	11	12
1	3.042	2.778	2.513	2.249	1.984	1.720	1.455	1.190	0.926	0.661	0.397	0.132
2–19	3.175	3.175	3.175	3.175	3.175	3.175	3.175	3.175	3.175	3.175	3.175	3.175
20–31	3.174	3.174	3.174	3.174	3.174	3.174	3.174	3.174	3.174	3.174	3.174	3.174
32	1.720	1.984	2.249	2.513	2.778	3.042	3.175	3.175	3.175	3.175	3.175	3.175
33	0.000	0.000	0.000	0.000	0.000	0.000	0.132	0.397	0.661	0.926	1.190	1.455

For Property Placed in Service after May 12, 1993: 39-Year Nonresidential Real Property

Recovery Year(s)	The Applicable Percentage Is (Use the Column for the Month in the First Year the Property Is Placed in Service):											
	1	2	3	4	5	6	7	8	9	10	11	12
1	2.461	2.247	2.033	1.819	1.605	1.391	1.177	0.963	0.749	0.535	0.321	0.107
2–39	2.564	2.564	2.564	2.564	2.564	2.564	2.564	2.564	2.564	2.564	2.564	2.564
40	0.107	0.321	0.535	0.749	0.963	1.177	1.391	1.605	1.819	2.033	2.247	2.461

*The official tables contain a separate row for each year. For ease of presentation, certain years are grouped in these tables. In some instances, this will produce a difference of .001 for the last digit when compared with the official tables.

EXHIBIT 5.8	MACRS Straight-Line Depreciation for Personal Property Assuming Half-Year Convention*

For Property Placed in Service after December 31, 1986

MACRS Class	% First Recovery Year	Other Recovery Years		Last Recovery Year	
		Years	%	Year	%
3-year	16.67	2–3	33.33	4	16.67
5-year	10.00	2–5	20.00	6	10.00
7-year	7.14	2–7	14.29	8	7.14
10-year	5.00	2–10	10.00	11	5.00
15-year	3.33	2–15	6.67	16	3.33
20-year	2.50	2–20	5.00	21	2.50

*The official table contains a separate row for each year. For ease of presentation, certain years are grouped in this table. In some instances, this will produce a difference of .01 for the last digit when compared with the official table.

EXHIBIT 5.9	ADS for Alternative Minimum Tax: 150% Declining-Balance for Personal Property Assuming Half-Year Convention

For Property Placed in Service after December 31, 1986 (Partial Table*)

Recovery Year	3-Year 150%	5-Year 150%	7-Year 150%	9.5-Year 150%	10-Year 150%	12-Year 150%
1	25.00	15.00	10.71	7.89	7.50	6.25
2	37.50	25.50	19.13	14.54	13.88	11.72
3	25.00**	17.85	15.03	12.25	11.79	10.25
4	12.50	16.66**	12.25**	10.31	10.02	8.97
5		16.66	12.25	9.17**	8.74**	7.85
6		8.33	12.25	9.17	8.74	7.33**
7			12.25	9.17	8.74	7.33
8			6.13	9.17	8.74	7.33
9				9.17	8.74	7.33
10				9.16	8.74	7.33
11					4.37	7.32
12						7.33
13						3.66

*The figures in this table are taken from the official table that appears in Rev.Proc. 87–57, 1987–2 C.B. 687. Because of its length, the complete table is not presented.
**Switchover to straight-line depreciation.

EXHIBIT 5.10	ADS Straight-Line for Personal Property Assuming Half-Year Convention

For Property Placed in Service after December 31, 1986 (Partial Table*)

Recovery Year	5-Year Class	10-Year Class	12-Year Class
1	10.00	5.00	4.17
2	20.00	10.00	8.33
3	20.00	10.00	8.33
4	20.00	10.00	8.33
5	20.00	10.00	8.33
6	10.00	10.00	8.33
7		10.00	8.34
8		10.00	8.33
9		10.00	8.34
10		10.00	8.33
11		5.00	8.34
12			8.33
13			4.17

*The figures in this table are taken from the official table that appears in Rev.Proc. 87–57, 1987–2 C.B. 687. Because of its length, the complete table is not presented. The tables for the mid-quarter convention also appear in Rev.Proc. 87–57.

EXHIBIT 5.11	ADS Straight-Line for Real Property Assuming Mid-Month Convention

For Property Placed in Service after December 31, 1986

Recovery Year(s)	Month Placed in Service											
	1	2	3	4	5	6	7	8	9	10	11	12
1	2.396	2.188	1.979	1.771	1.563	1.354	1.146	0.938	0.729	0.521	0.313	0.104
2–40	2.500	2.500	2.500	2.500	2.500	2.500	2.500	2.500	2.500	2.500	2.500	2.500
41	0.104	0.312	0.521	0.729	0.937	1.146	1.354	1.562	1.771	1.979	2.187	2.396

REFOCUS ON THE BIG PICTURE

CALCULATING DEDUCTIBLE EXPENSES

In general, the expenses incurred in Michael Forney's small engine service and repair business are deductible as long as they are ordinary and necessary expenses. In addition, the salaries and wages paid must be reasonable. However, his plan to increase salaries radically next year for himself and his mother probably should not be pursued, because most or all of the increase could be considered unreasonable. Charitable contributions generally are limited to 10 percent of taxable income before the charitable contribution deduction, and political contributions and the fine are not deductible. The dues paid to Small Engine Repair Institute are not fully deductible because 70 percent of the organization's efforts relate to lobbying activities. However, the amount paid to consultants to investigate a new business opportunity is fully deductible as an ordinary and necessary business expense.

Michael can elect to expense the costs of the machinery and equipment under the provisions of § 179. For the current year, assume the § 179 deduction is limited to $500,000 and cannot exceed the taxable income derived from the business (before the § 179 deduction). In this case, the entire purchase price of $130,000 is deductible.

continued

Gross income	$ 435,500
Less: Salaries and wages	(150,000)
Building rent	(24,000)
§ 179 deduction	(130,000)
Insurance	(6,000)
Consulting fees	(6,000)
Utilities	(12,000)
Taxes and licenses	(6,000)
Advertising	(3,000)
Interest expense	(3,000)
Dues paid to Small Engine Repair Institute	(3,000)
Taxable income before the charitable contribution deduction	$ 92,500
Less: Charitable contributions	(3,000)
Taxable income	$ 89,500

As to Michael's rental properties, he will be required to report all associated rent income and expenses, including depreciation on the house he converted from personal use to rental use and on the rental condo he purchased.

What If?

Instead assume that Mr. Forney purchased and placed in service this year $142,000 of new machinery and equipment of the type that qualifies for the § 179 deduction. In addition, Michael thinks that he can justify increasing his salary to $115,500 because of special expertise he developed recently, which will increase total salaries and wages to $210,500. Michael still can elect to expense all $142,000 of the cost of the machinery and equipment under § 179. In other words, the machinery and equipment will not be depreciated using the additional first-year depreciation or regular MACRS rules. As a result of the increased salary and § 179 deductions, the charitable contribution deduction now is limited to $2,000. The remainder ($1,000) is carried over to the next tax year.

Gross income	$ 435,500
Less: Salaries and wages	(210,500)
Building rent	(24,000)
§ 179 deduction	(142,000)
Insurance	(6,000)
Consulting fees	(6,000)
Utilities	(12,000)
Taxes and licenses	(6,000)
Advertising	(3,000)
Interest expense	(3,000)
Dues paid to Small Engine Repair Institute	(3,000)
Taxable income before the charitable contribution deduction	$ 20,000
Less: Charitable contributions (limited to 10% of taxable income)	(2,000)
Taxable income	$ 18,000

Suggested Readings

Bradley T. Borden and Cali A. Lieberman, "Section 179(f) Deductions and Recapture of Costs of Qualified Real Property," *Journal of Taxation,* January 2014.

Wilton B. Hyman, "Finding Breaks for Business in the American Taxpayer Relief Act of 2012," *Business Entities*, July/August 2013.

Robert W. Jamison and Christopher W. Hesse, "Controlled Groups and the Sec. 179 Election for S Corporations," *The Tax Adviser*, November 2013.

John M. Malloy, Craig J. Langstraat, and James M. Plečnik, "Major Developments in Cost Segregation," *The Tax Adviser*, April 2014.

Kreig D. Mitchell, "The R&D Tax Credit for Start-Up Companies," *Practical Tax Strategies*, February 2012.

Debra T. Sinclair and Britton A. McKay, "Excess Compensation and the Independent Investor Test," *Practical Tax Strategies*, April 2013.

Key Terms

Accelerated cost recovery system (ACRS), 5-22	Domestic production gross receipts (DPGR), 5-21	Percentage depletion, 5-39
Additional first-year depreciation, 5-28	Half-year convention, 5-26	Qualified production activities income (QPAI), 5-21
Alternative depreciation system (ADS), 5-36	Intangible drilling and development costs (IDCs), 5-38	Reasonableness requirement, 5-3
Amortization, 5-37	Listed property, 5-31	Related-party transactions, 5-12
Capital gain property, 5-15	Mid-month convention, 5-27	Research and experimental expenditures, 5-17
Charitable contribution, 5-14	Mid-quarter convention, 5-26	Residential rental real estate, 5-27
Cost depletion, 5-38	Modified accelerated cost recovery system (MACRS), 5-22	Section 179 expensing election, 5-29
Cost recovery, 5-22		Startup expenditures, 5-11
Depletion, 5-37	Modified adjusted gross income, 5-20	W–2 wages, 5-20
Depreciation, 5-22	Ordinary and necessary, 5-2	
Domestic production activities deduction (DPAD), 5-20	Ordinary income property, 5-15	

Computational Exercises

1. **LO.2** Glenda, a calendar year and cash basis taxpayer, rents property from Janice. As part of the rental agreement, Glenda pays $8,400 rent on April 1, 2015 for the 12 months ending March 31, 2016.

   a. How much is Glenda's deduction for rent expense in 2015?

   b. Assume the same facts, except that the $8,400 is for 24 months rent ending March 31, 2017. How much is Glenda's deduction for rent expense in 2015?

2. **LO.3** Vella owns and operates an illegal gambling establishment. In connection with this activity, he has the following expenses during the year:

Rent	$ 24,000
Bribes	40,000
Travel expenses	4,000
Utilities	18,000
Wages	230,000
Payroll taxes	13,800
Property insurance	1,600
Illegal kickbacks	22,000

   What are Vella's total deductible expenses for tax purposes?

3. **LO.3** Stanford owns and operates two dry cleaning businesses. He travels to Boston to discuss acquiring a restaurant. Later in the month, he travels to New York to discuss acquiring a bakery. Stanford does not acquire the restaurant but does purchase the bakery on November 1, 2015. Stanford incurred the following expenses:

Total investigation costs related to the restaurant	$28,000
Total investigation costs related to the bakery	51,000

   What is the maximum amount Stanford can deduct in 2015 for investigation expenses?

4. **LO.5** Tabitha sells real estate on March 2 for $260,000. The buyer, Ramona, pays the real estate taxes of $5,200 for the calendar year, which is the real estate property tax year. Assume that this is not a leap year.

   a. Determine the real estate taxes apportioned to and deductible by the seller, Tabitha, and the amount of taxes deductible by Ramona.

   b. Calculate Ramona's basis in the property and the amount realized by Tabitha from the sale.

5. **LO.5** Sandstorm Corporation decides to develop a new line of paints. The project begins in 2015. Sandstorm incurs the following expenses in 2015 in connection with the project:

Salaries	$85,000
Materials	30,000
Depreciation on equipment	12,500

   The benefits from the project will be realized starting in July 2016. If Sandstorm Corporation chooses to defer and amortize its research and experimental expenditures over a period of 60 months, what are its related deductions in 2015 and 2016?

6. **LO.6** Hamlet acquires a 7-year class asset on November 23, 2015, for $100,000. Hamlet does not elect immediate expensing under § 179. He does not claim any available additional first-year depreciation. Calculate Hamlet's cost recovery deductions for 2015 and 2016.

7. **LO.6** Lopez acquired a building on June 1, 2010, for $1 million. Calculate Lopez's cost recovery deduction for 2015 if the building is:

   a. Classified as residential rental real estate.

   b. Classified as nonresidential real estate.

8. **LO.6** In 2015, McKenzie purchased qualifying equipment for his business that cost $212,000. The taxable income of the business for the year is $5,600 before consideration of any § 179 deduction. Calculate McKenzie's § 179 expense deduction for 2015 and any carryover to 2016.

9. **LO.6** On April 5, 2015, Kinsey places in service a new automobile that cost $36,000. He does not elect § 179 expensing, and he elects not to take any available additional first-year depreciation. The car is used 70% for business and 30% for personal use in each tax year.

   Kinsey chooses the MACRS 200% declining-balance method of cost recovery (the auto is a 5-year asset). Assume the following luxury automobile limitations: year 1: $3,160; year 2: $5,100. Compute the total depreciation allowed for 2015 and 2016.

10. **LO.8** Jebali Company reports gross income of $340,000 and other property-related expenses of $229,000 and uses a depletion rate of 14%. Calculate Jebali's depletion allowance for the current year.

Problems

11. **LO.2** Duck, an accrual basis corporation, sponsored a rock concert on December 29, 2015. Gross receipts were $300,000. The following expenses were incurred and paid as indicated:

Expense		Payment Date
Rental of coliseum	$ 25,000	December 21, 2015
Cost of goods sold:		
Food	30,000	December 30, 2015
Souvenirs	60,000	December 30, 2015

Expense		Payment Date
Performers	100,000	January 5, 2016
Cleaning of coliseum	10,000	February 1, 2016

Because the coliseum was not scheduled to be used again until January 15, the company with which Duck had contracted did not perform the cleanup until January 8–10, 2016.

Calculate Duck's net income from the concert for tax purposes for 2015.

Issue ID   12. **LO.3** Ted, an agent for Waxwing Corporation, which is an airline manufacturer, is negotiating a sale with a representative of the U.S. government and with a representative of a developing country. Waxwing has sufficient capacity to handle only one of the orders. Both orders will have the same contract price. Ted believes that if Waxwing authorizes a $500,000 payment to the representative of the foreign country, he can guarantee the sale. He is not sure that he can obtain the same result with the U.S. government. Identify the relevant tax issues for Waxwing.

13. **LO.3** Linda operates an illegal gambling operation and incurs the following expenses. Which of these expenses can reduce her taxable income?

   a.   Bribes paid to city employees.
   b.   Salaries to employees.
   c.   Security cameras.
   d.   Kickbacks to police.
   e.   Rent on an office.
   f.   Depreciation on office furniture and equipment.
   g.   Tenant's casualty insurance.
   h.   Utilities.

Ethics and Equity   14. **LO.3** Cardinal Corporation is a trucking firm that operates in the Mid-Atlantic states. One of Cardinal's major customers frequently ships goods between Charlotte and Baltimore. Occasionally, the customer sends last-minute shipments that are outbound for Europe on a freighter sailing from Baltimore. To satisfy the delivery schedule in these cases, Cardinal's drivers must substantially exceed the speed limit. Cardinal pays for any related speeding tickets. During the past year, two drivers had their licenses suspended for 30 days each for driving at such excessive speeds. Cardinal continues to pay each driver's salary during the suspension periods.

Cardinal believes that it is necessary to conduct its business in this manner if it is to be profitable, maintain the support of the drivers, and maintain the goodwill of customers. Evaluate Cardinal's business practices.

15. **LO.3** Quail Corporation anticipates that being positively perceived by the individual who is elected mayor will be beneficial for business. Therefore, Quail contributes to the campaigns of both the Democratic and Republican candidates. The Republican candidate is elected mayor. Can Quail deduct any of the political contributions it made? Explain.

16. **LO.3** Melissa, the owner of a sole proprietorship, does not provide health insurance for her 20 employees. She plans to spend $1,500 lobbying in opposition to legislation that would require her to provide such insurance. Discuss the tax advantages and disadvantages of paying the $1,500 to a professional lobbyist rather than spending the $1,500 on in-house lobbying expenditures.

Issue ID   17. **LO.3** Ella owns 60% of the stock of Peach, Inc. The stock has declined in value since she purchased it five years ago. She is going to sell 5% of the stock to a relative. Ella is also going to make a gift of 10% of the stock to another relative. Identify the relevant tax issues for Ella.

18. **LO.3** Jarret owns City of Charleston bonds with an adjusted basis of $190,000. During the year, he receives interest payments of $3,800. Jarret partially financed the purchase of the bonds by borrowing $100,000 at 5% interest. Jarret's interest payments on the loan this year are $4,900, and his principal payments are $1,100.

    a. Should Jarret report any interest income this year? Explain.

    b. Can Jarret deduct any interest expense this year? Explain.

19. **LO.3** Nancy, the owner of a very successful hotel chain in the Southeast, is exploring the possibility of expanding the chain into a city in the Northeast. She incurs $35,000 of expenses associated with this investigation. Based on the regulatory environment for hotels in the city, she decides not to expand. During the year, she also investigates opening a restaurant that will be part of a national restaurant chain. Her expenses for this are $53,000. The restaurant begins operations on September 1. Determine the amount Nancy can deduct in the current year for investigating these two businesses.

20. **LO.3** Brittany Callihan sold stock (basis of $184,000) to her son, Ridge, for $160,000, the fair market value.   *Decision Making*

    Communications

    a. What are the tax consequences to Brittany?

    b. What are the tax consequences to Ridge if he later sells the stock for $190,000? For $152,000? For $174,000?

    c. Write a letter to Brittany in which you inform her of the tax consequences if she sells the stock to Ridge for $160,000. Explain how a sales transaction could be structured that would produce better tax consequences for her. Brittany's address is 32 Country Lane, Lawrence, KS 66045.

21. **LO.3** For each of the following independent transactions, calculate the recognized gain or loss to the seller and the adjusted basis to the buyer.

    a. Bonnie sells Parchment, Inc. stock (adjusted basis $17,000) to Phillip, her brother, for its fair market value of $12,000.

    b. Amos sells land (adjusted basis $85,000) to his nephew, Boyd, for its fair market value of $70,000.

    c. Susan sells a tax-exempt bond (adjusted basis $20,000) to her wholly owned corporation for its fair market value of $19,000.

    d. Ron sells a business truck (adjusted basis $20,000) that he uses in his sole proprietorship to his cousin, Agnes, for its fair market value of $18,500.

    e. Martha sells her partnership interest (adjusted basis $175,000) in Pearl Partnership to her adult daughter, Kim, for $220,000.

22. **LO.4** In 2015, Gray Corporation, a calendar year C corporation, holds a $75,000   *Decision Making* charitable contribution carryover from a gift made in 2010. Gray is contemplating a gift of land to a qualified charity in either 2015 or 2016. Gray purchased the land as an investment five years ago for $100,000 (current fair market value is $250,000).

    Before considering any charitable deduction, Gray projects taxable income of $1 million for 2015 and $1.2 million for 2016. Should Gray make the gift of the land to charity in 2015 or in 2016? Provide support for your answer.

23. **LO.4** Dan Simms is the president and sole shareholder of Simms Corporation, 1121   *Decision Making* Madison Street, Seattle, WA 98121. Dan plans for the corporation to make a   *Communications* charitable contribution to the University of Washington, a qualified public charity. He will have the corporation donate Jaybird Corporation stock, held for five years, with a basis of $11,000 and a fair market value of $25,000. Dan projects a $310,000 net profit for Simms Corporation in 2015 and a $100,000 net profit in 2016. Dan calls you on December 11, 2015, and asks whether Simms should make the contribution in 2015 or 2016. Write a letter advising Dan about the timing of the contribution.

24. **LO.5** Blue Corporation, a manufacturing company, decided to develop a new line of merchandise. The project began in 2015. Blue had the following expenses in connection with the project.

	2015	2016
Salaries	$500,000	$600,000
Materials	90,000	70,000
Insurance	8,000	11,000
Utilities	6,000	8,000
Cost of inspection of materials for quality control	7,000	6,000
Promotion expenses	11,000	18,000
Advertising	–0–	20,000
Equipment depreciation	15,000	14,000
Cost of market survey	8,000	–0–

The new product will be introduced for sale beginning in July 2017. Determine the amount of the deduction for research and experimental expenditures for 2015, 2016, and 2017 if:

a. Blue Corporation elects to expense the research and experimental expenditures.

b. Blue Corporation elects to amortize the research and experimental expenditures over 60 months.

25. **LO.5** Sarah Ham, operating as a sole proprietor, manufactures printers in the United States. For 2015, the proprietorship has QPAI of $400,000. Sarah's modified AGI was $350,000. The W–2 wages paid by the proprietorship to employees engaged in the qualified domestic production activity were $60,000. Calculate Sarah's DPAD for 2015.

Decision Making   26. **LO.5** In 2015, Rose, Inc., has QPAI of $4 million and taxable income of $3 million. Rose pays independent contractors $500,000. Rose's W–2 wages are $600,000, but only $400,000 of the wages are paid to employees engaged in qualified domestic production activities.

a. Calculate the DPAD for Rose, Inc., for 2015.

b. What suggestions could you make to enable Rose to increase its DPAD?

27. **LO.6** On November 4, 2013, Blue Company acquired an asset (27.5-year residential real property) for $200,000 for use in its business. In 2013 and 2014, respectively, Blue took $642 and $5,128 of cost recovery. These amounts were incorrect; Blue applied the wrong percentages (i.e., those for 39-year rather than 27.5-year property). Blue should have taken $910 and $7,272 of cost recovery in 2013 and 2014, respectively.

On January 1, 2015, the asset was sold for $180,000. Calculate the gain or loss on the sale of the asset for that year.

28. **LO.6** Juan, a sole proprietor, acquires a new 5-year class asset on March 14, 2015, for $200,000. This is the only asset Juan acquired during the year. He does not elect immediate expensing under § 179. Juan does not claim any available additional first-year depreciation. On July 15, 2016, Juan sells the asset.

a. Determine Juan's cost recovery for 2015.

b. Determine Juan's cost recovery for 2016.

29. **LO.6** Debra acquired the following new assets during 2015.

Date	Asset	Cost
April 11	Furniture	$40,000
July 28	Trucks	40,000
November 3	Computers	70,000

Determine Debra's cost recovery deductions for the current year. Debra does not elect immediate expensing under § 179. She does not claim any available additional first-year depreciation.

30. **LO.6** On May 5, 2015, Christy purchased and placed in service a hotel. The hotel cost $10.8 million. Calculate Christy's cost recovery deductions for 2015 and for 2025.

31. **LO.6** Janice acquired an apartment building on June 4, 2015, for $1.6 million. The value of the land is $300,000. Janice sold the apartment building on November 29, 2021.

    a. Determine Janice's cost recovery deduction for 2015.

    b. Determine Janice's cost recovery deduction for 2021.

32. **LO.6** During March 2015, Sam constructed new agricultural fences on his farm. The cost of the fencing was $80,000. Sam does not elect immediate expensing under § 179 and he does not claim any available additional first-year depreciation. However, an election not to have the uniform capitalization rules apply is in effect. Compute Sam's cost recovery deduction for 2015. Sam wants to maximize his cost recovery deductions.

33. **LO.6** Lori, who is single, purchased 5-year class property for $200,000 and 7-year class property for $400,000 on May 20, 2015. Lori expects the taxable income derived from her business (without regard to the amount expensed under § 179) to be about $800,000. Lori wants to elect immediate § 179 expensing, but she doesn't know which asset she should expense under § 179. Lori does not claim any available additional first-year depreciation.

    Decision Making

    a. Determine Lori's total deduction if the § 179 expense is first taken with respect to the 5-year class asset.

    b. Determine Lori's total deduction if the § 179 expense is first taken with respect to the 7-year class asset.

    c. What is your advice to Lori?

34. **LO.6** Olga is the proprietor of a small business. In 2015, the business's income, before consideration of any cost recovery or § 179 deduction, is $250,000.

    Olga spends $600,000 on new 7-year class assets and elects to take the § 179 deduction on them. She does not claim any available additional first-year depreciation. Olga's cost recovery deduction for 2015, except for the cost recovery with respect to the new 7-year assets, is $95,000. Determine Olga's total cost recovery for 2015 with respect to the 7-year class assets and the amount of any § 179 carryforward.

35. **LO.6** On June 5, 2014, Dan purchased and placed in service a 7-year class asset costing $550,000. Determine the maximum deductions that Dan can claim with respect to this asset in 2014 and 2015.

36. **LO.6** Jabari Johnson is considering acquiring an automobile at the beginning of 2015 that he will use 100% of the time as a taxi. The purchase price of the automobile is $35,000. Johnson has heard of cost recovery limits on automobiles and wants to know the maximum amount of the $35,000 he can deduct in the first year.

    Communications

    Write a letter to Jabari in which you present your calculations. Also prepare a memo for the tax files, summarizing your analysis. Johnson's address is 100 Morningside, Clinton, MS 39058.

37. **LO.6** On October 15, 2015, Jon purchased and placed in service a used car. The purchase price was $25,000. This was the only business-use asset Jon acquired in 2015. He used the car 80% of the time for business and 20% for personal use. Jon used the MACRS statutory percentage method. Calculate the total deduction Jon may take for 2015 with respect to the car.

38. **LO.6** On June 5, 2014, Leo purchased and placed in service a new car that cost $20,000. The business-use percentage for the car is always 100%. Leo claims any available additional first-year depreciation. Compute Leo's cost recovery deduction for 2014 and 2015.

Critical Thinking   39. **LO.6** On May 28, 2015, Mary purchased and placed in service a new $20,000 car. The car was used 60% for business, 20% for production of income, and 20% for personal use in 2015. In 2016, the usage changed to 40% for business, 30% for production of income, and 30% for personal use. Mary did not elect immediate expensing under § 179. She did not claim any available additional first-year depreciation. Compute Mary's cost recovery deduction and any cost recovery recapture in 2016.

40. **LO.6** In 2015, Muhammad purchased a new computer for $16,000. The computer is used 100% for business. Muhammad did not make a § 179 election with respect to the computer. He does not claim any available additional first-year depreciation. If Muhammad uses the MACRS statutory percentage method, determine his cost recovery deduction for 2015 for computing taxable income and for computing his alternative minimum tax.

Decision Making   41. **LO.6** Jamie purchased $100,000 of new office furniture for her business in June of the current year. Jamie understands that if she elects to use ADS to compute her regular income tax, there will be no difference between the cost recovery for computing the regular income tax and the AMT. Jamie wants to know the *regular* income tax cost, after three years, of using ADS rather than MACRS. Assume that Jamie does not elect § 179 limited expensing and that her marginal tax rate is 28%. She does not claim any available additional first-year depreciation.

Decision Making   42. **LO.7** Mike Saxon is negotiating the purchase of a business. The final purchase
Communications   price has been agreed upon, but the allocation of the purchase price to the assets is still being discussed. Appraisals on a warehouse range from $1,200,000 to $1,500,000. If a value of $1,200,000 is used for the warehouse, the remainder of the purchase price, $800,000, will be allocated to goodwill. If $1,500,000 is allocated to the warehouse, goodwill will be $500,000.

   Mike wants to know what effect each alternative will have on cost recovery and amortization during the first year. Under the agreement, Mike will take over the business on January 1 of next year. Write a letter to Mike in which you present your calculations and recommendation. Also prepare a memo for the tax files. Mike's address is 200 Rolling Hills Drive, Shavertown, PA 18708.

Ethics and Equity   43. **LO.8** Sam Jones owns a granite stone quarry. When he acquired the land, Sam allocated $800,000 of the purchase price to the quarry's recoverable mineral reserves, which were estimated at 10 million tons of granite stone. Based on these estimates, the cost depletion was $.08 per ton. In April of the current year, Sam received a letter from the State Department of Highways notifying him that part of his property was being condemned so that state could build a new road. At that time, the recoverable mineral reserves had an adjusted basis of $600,000 and 7.5 million tons of granite rock. Sam estimates that the land being condemned contains about 2 million tons of granite. Therefore, for the current year, Sam has computed his cost depletion at $.11 per ton [$600,000/(7,500,000 − 2,000,000)]. Evaluate the appropriateness of what Sam is doing.

44. **LO.8** Wes acquired a mineral interest during the year for $10 million. A geological survey estimated that 250,000 tons of the mineral remained in the deposit. During the year, 80,000 tons were mined, and 45,000 tons were sold for $12 million. Other related expenses amounted to $5 million. Assuming that the mineral depletion rate is 22%, calculate Wes's lowest taxable income, after any depletion deductions.

BRIDGE DISCIPLINE

1. Sparrow Corporation is considering the acquisition of an asset for use in its business over the next five years. However, Sparrow must decide whether it would be better served by leasing the asset or buying it. An appropriate asset could be purchased for $15,000, and it would qualify as a three-year asset under the MACRS classification. Assume that the election to expense assets under § 179 is not available, that any available additional first-year depreciation is not claimed, and that the asset is not expected to have a salvage value at the end of its use by Sparrow. Alternatively, Sparrow could lease the asset for a $3,625 annual cost over the five-year period. If Sparrow is in the 34% tax bracket, would you recommend that Sparrow buy or lease the asset? In your calculations, assume that 10% is an appropriate discount factor. — Decision Making

2. Lark Corporation is considering the acquisition of an asset for use in its business over the next five years. However, Lark must decide whether it would be better served by leasing the asset or buying it. An appropriate asset could be purchased for $15,000, and it would qualify as a three-year asset under the MACRS classification. Assume that the election to expense assets under § 179 is made, but any available additional first-year depreciation is not claimed, and that the asset is not expected to have a salvage value at the end of its use by Lark. Alternatively, Lark could lease the asset for a $3,625 annual cost over the five-year period. If Lark is in the 34% tax bracket, would you recommend that Lark buy or lease the asset? In your calculations, assume that 10% is an appropriate discount factor. — Decision Making

3. Wayside Fruit Company is a sole proprietorship owned by Neil Stephenson. The company's records reflect the following:

Sales revenue	$185,000
Operating expenses	125,000
Depreciation expense for book	13,000
Cost recovery allowance for tax	17,500
Loss on the sale of delivery truck to Neil's brother	5,000
Amount paid to fruit inspector to overlook below-standard fruit shipped to various vendors	3,000

Compute the net income before tax for book purposes and the amount of taxable income for Wayside Fruit Company.

Research Problems

Note: Solutions to Research Problems can be prepared by using the Checkpoint® Student Edition online research product, which is available to accompany this text. It is also possible to prepare solutions to the Research Problems by using tax research materials found in a standard tax library.

THOMSON REUTERS
CHECKPOINT
Student Edition

Research Problem 1. Gray Chemical Company manufactured pesticides that were toxic. Over the course of several years, the toxic waste contaminated the air and water around the company's plant. Several employees suffered toxic poisoning, and the Environmental Protection Agency cited the company for violations. In court, the judge found Gray guilty and imposed fines of $15 million. The company voluntarily set up a charitable fund for the purpose of bettering the environment and funded it with — Communications

$8 million. The company incurred legal expenses in setting up the foundation and defending itself in court. The court reduced the fine from $15 million to $7 million.

Gray deducted the $8 million paid to the foundation and the legal expenses incurred. The IRS disallowed both deductions on the grounds that the payment was, in fact, a fine and in violation of public policy.

Gray's president, Ted Jones, has contacted you regarding the deductibility of the $7 million fine, the $8 million payment to the foundation, and the legal fees. Write a letter to Mr. Jones that contains your advice, and prepare a memo for the tax files. Gray's address is 200 Lincoln Center, Omaha, NE 68182.

Partial list of research aids:
§§ 162(a) and (f).
Reg. § 1.162–21(b).

Research Problem 2. In 2011, Jed James began planting a vineyard. The costs of the land preparation, labor, rootstock, and planting were capitalized. The land preparation costs do not include any nondepreciable land costs. In 2015, when the plants became viable, Jed placed the vineyard in service. Jed wants to know whether he can claim a deduction under § 179 on his 2015 income tax return for the 2011 costs for planting the vineyard.

Communications **Research Problem 3.** Juan owns a business that acquires exotic automobiles that are high-tech, state-of-the-art vehicles with unique design features or equipment. The exotic automobiles are not licensed, nor are they set up to be used on the road. Rather, the cars are used exclusively for car shows or related promotional photography. With respect to the exotic automobiles, can Juan take a cost recovery deduction on his Federal income tax return? Prepare an outline for your classmates addressing this issue.

Partial list of research aids:
Bruce Selig, 70 TCM 1125, T.C.Memo. 1995–519.

Internet Activity

Use the tax resources of the Internet to address the following questions. Do not restrict your search to the Web, but include a review of newsgroups and general reference materials, practitioner sites and resources, primary sources of the tax law, chat rooms and discussion groups, and other opportunities.

Research Problem 4. Many states that have corporate income taxes "piggyback" onto the Federal corporate income tax calculation. In other words, these states' corporate income tax calculations incorporate many of the Federal calculations and deductions to make both compliance and verification of tax liability easier. However, some state legislatures were concerned that the domestic production activities deduction, if allowed for state tax purposes, would result in significant revenue losses. Determine whether states with corporate income taxes allow or disallow the domestic production activities deduction in the calculation of the state's corporate income tax liability. Be sure to state the sources for your answer.

Communications **Research Problem 5.** Changes to depreciation systems often are discussed by policymakers and observers of the tax system. Outline the terms and policy objectives of one of the changes currently proposed by the Treasury, a member of Congress, or a tax policy think tank.

Roger CPA Review Questions

1. Regarding the tax treatment of a business's research and experimental (R&E) expenditures, which of the following statements is true?
   a. A common reason for electing tax deferral for such expenses is the expectation of lower tax rates in the future.
   b. Expenses associated with the acquisition of land upon which a purpose-built R&E facility is constructed are considered R&E expenditures for tax purposes.

   c. Companies generally prefer to expense R&E costs immediately, but may elect instead to defer and amortize such costs over a minimum of 60 months.

   d. Companies may elect to immediately expense R&E costs incurred in the first applicable taxable year and all future years through an appropriate filing with the IRS.

2. Identify the correct statement below regarding the Domestic Production Activities Deduction (DPAD).

   a. Qualified Production Activities Income (QPAI) is calculated by applying a percentage to net income from an IRS rate table based on specific criteria.

   b. The DPAD cannot exceed attributable W-2 wages paid.

   c. A sole proprietorship cannot claim the DPAD, but a partnership or S corporation with more than one shareholder can.

   d. Taxable income for the purposes of calculating or amending the DPAD includes any net operating loss (NOL) deduction, such as an NOL carryforward or NOL carryback.

3. Newton, a business owner, signed a ten-year lease beginning in July of 20X14, and immediately paid rent for the remainder of 20X14, all of 20X15, and all of 20X16. How much of the rent paid at the lease signing can be declared as a business expense on Schedule C of Newton's 20X14 tax return?

   a. All of it

   b. The July 20X14 – June 20X15 portion only

   c. None of it

   d. The 20X14 portion only

4. A sale between which of the following could trigger a gain or a loss for federal tax purposes?

   a. Husband and wife   c. Majority shareholder and corporation

   b. Cousin and cousin   d. Ancestor and descendent

5. Quanti Co., a calendar-year taxpayer, purchased equipment for $5,000 on December 21, 20X14, representing the company's **only** purchase of tangible personal property that took place during 20X14. On its 20X14 tax return, how many months of MACRS depreciation may Quanti Co. claim on the tools?

   a. One-and-a-half months   c. Six months

   b. One month   d. None

6. Which of the following is **correct** about depreciation under federal tax law?

   I. The recovery period is longer than the useful life of the asset.
   II. There are different recovery periods for new and used property.
   III. Salvage values are ignored.

   a. I and II only   c. III only

   b. II only   d. I, II, and III

7. Joe purchased a van on February 1, 20X4 for use in his business, Crew Airport Transport. The van was purchased for $30,000, has an estimated useful life of 10 years, and a salvage value of $2,000. No other assets were put into service that year. What is Joe's MACRS depreciation for the van in 20X4?

   a. $2,567   c. $10,500

   b. $6,000   d. $10,267

8. Dolly purchased and placed into service qualifying depreciable property in 20X4 at a total cost of $2,250,000. Dolly has elected to take the Section 179 deduction. What is Dolly's Section 179 deduction for 20X4?

   a. $0

   b. $250,000

   c. $500,000

   d. $1,750,000

9. Christa purchased and placed into service five-year assets at a total cost of $2,250,000. If Christa elects both the Section 179 deduction and additional first-year bonus depreciation, but does not elect the straight-line method, what is Christa's depreciation expense for tax purposes for the year, assuming a half-year convention?

   a. $250,000

   b. $500,000

   c. $1,250,000

   d. $1,450,000

10. Orange, Inc., a calendar-year C corporation, has $800,000 of qualified production activities income (QPAI) and $950,000 of total taxable income in 20X14. All of the QDPAI was produced by Orange's manufacturing plant, which relies mainly on a temporary employment agency for its workforce, employing only two W-2 employees who in aggregate earned $140,000 in 20X14. Orange also has an office in Mexico, which is unrelated to its domestic manufacturing plant and which employs one W-2 employee, who earned $75,000 in 20X14. What amount of Domestic Production Activities Deduction may Orange claim on its 20X14 corporate tax return?

   a. $73,350

   b. $72,000

   c. Depends on wages paid by employment agency

   d. $70,000

CHAPTER

6

Losses and Loss Limitations

LEARNING OBJECTIVES: *After completing Chapter 6, you should be able to:*

LO.1 Determine the amount, classification, and timing of the bad debt deduction.

LO.2 State and illustrate the tax treatment of worthless securities, including § 1244 stock.

LO.3 Identify a casualty and determine the amount, classification, and timing of casualty and theft losses.

LO.4 Describe the impact of the net operating loss carryback and carryover provisions on previous and subsequent years' taxable income.

LO.5 Explain the tax shelter problem and the reasons for at-risk and passive loss limitations.

LO.6 Describe how the at-risk limitation and the passive loss rules limit deductions for losses and identify taxpayers subject to these restrictions.

LO.7 Discuss the definitions of activity, material participation, and rental activity under the passive loss rules.

LO.8 Determine the relationship between the at-risk and passive loss limitations.

LO.9 Explain the special treatment available to real estate activities.

LO.10 Determine the consequences of the disposition of passive activities.

TAX TALK *The income tax has made more liars out of the American people than golf has. Even when you make a tax form out on the level, you don't know when it's through if you are a crook or a martyr.* —WILL ROGERS

RECEIVING TAX BENEFITS FROM LOSSES

Robyn, an unmarried, cash basis and calendar year taxpayer, is nearing the end of a year that she would like to forget. Several years ago, she loaned $25,000 to her friend Jamil to enable him to start a business. Jamil had made scheduled payments of $7,000 (including $1,000 of interest) when he suddenly died in January. At the time of his death, he was insolvent, and Robyn's attempts to collect the debt were fruitless.

Last year, Robyn invested $60,000 by purchasing stock in Owl Corporation, a closely held small business corporation started by her brother. However, the company declared bankruptcy in May of this year, and Robyn was notified by the bankruptcy trustee that she can expect to receive nothing from the company.

Robyn has owned and operated a bookstore as a sole proprietorship for the past 10 years. The bookstore has been profitable and produced annual taxable income of approximately $75,000. However, due to the growth of online vendors and e-books, the business lost $180,000 this year.

In September, a tornado caused a large oak tree to blow over onto Robyn's house. The cost of removing the tree and making repairs to the house was $32,000. Robyn received a check for $25,000 from her insurance company. Her adjusted basis for the house was $280,000.

Finally, Robyn invested $20,000 for a 10 percent interest in a limited partnership that owns and operates orange groves in Florida. Due to a hard freeze that damaged much of the fruit, the partnership lost $200,000 and allocated $20,000 of ordinary loss to Robyn.

Robyn has come to you for tax advice and would like to know the tax ramifications of each of the events and transactions listed above.

Read the chapter and formulate your response.

hapter 5 introduced rules governing the deductibility of trade or business expenses. This chapter extends the notion of deductibility to losses occurring in the course of business operations. In particular, special rules concerning the tax treatment of bad debts, casualty losses, and operating losses are reviewed. In addition, tax shelters and the rules that limit their usefulness as tax avoidance devices are discussed.

6-1 BAD DEBTS

Determine the amount, classification, and timing of the bad debt deduction.

If a taxpayer lends money or purchases a debt instrument and the debt is not repaid, a **bad debt** deduction is allowed. Similarly, if an accrual basis taxpayer sells goods or provides services on credit and the account receivable subsequently becomes worthless, a bad debt deduction is permitted.[1] No deduction is allowed, however, for a bad debt arising from the sale of a product or service when the taxpayer is on the cash basis because no income is reported until the cash has been collected. Permitting a bad debt deduction for a cash basis taxpayer would amount to a double deduction because the expenses of the product or service rendered are deducted when payments are made to suppliers and to employees or when the sale is made.

> **EXAMPLE 1**
>
> Ella, a sole proprietor, operates a business named Executive Accounting and Tax Services. Last year, Pat hired Ella to help him with the accounting for his small business. Ella also prepared the S corporation income tax return for the business and Pat's personal income tax return. Ella billed Pat $8,000 for the services she performed. Pat has never paid the bill, his business no longer exists, and his whereabouts are unknown.
>
> If Ella is an accrual basis taxpayer, she includes the $8,000 in income when the services are performed. When she determines that Pat's account will not be collected, she deducts the $8,000 as a bad debt.
>
> If Ella is a cash basis taxpayer, she does not include the $8,000 in income until payment is received. When she determines that Pat's account will not be collected, she cannot deduct the $8,000 as a bad debt expense because it was never recognized as income.

> **The Big Picture**
>
> **EXAMPLE 2**
>
> Return to the facts of *The Big Picture* on p. 6-1. Because Robyn is a cash basis taxpayer, she cannot take as a bad debt deduction any unpaid accrued interest on the loan to her friend, Jamil, because it was never recognized as income.

6-1a Specific Charge-Off Method

Most taxpayers are required to use the **specific charge-off method** when accounting for bad debts. However, some financial institutions are permitted to use an alternative **reserve method** for computing bad debt deductions.

A taxpayer using the specific charge-off method may claim a deduction when a specific *business* debt becomes either partially or wholly worthless or when a specific *nonbusiness* debt becomes wholly worthless.[2] For a business debt, the taxpayer must satisfy the IRS that the debt is partially worthless and must demonstrate the amount of worthlessness.

If a business debt previously deducted as partially worthless becomes totally worthless in a future year, only the remainder not previously deducted can be deducted in the future year.

In the case of total worthlessness, a deduction is allowed for the entire amount in the year that the debt becomes worthless. The amount of the deduction depends on the taxpayer's basis in the bad debt. If the debt arose from the sale of services or products and the face amount was previously included in income, that amount is deductible. If the

---

[1]Reg. § 1.166–1(e).   [2]§ 166(a).

taxpayer purchased the debt, the deduction equals the amount the taxpayer paid for the debt instrument.

Determining when a bad debt becomes worthless can be a difficult task. Legal proceedings need not be initiated against the debtor when the surrounding facts indicate that such action will not result in collection.

In 2013, Partridge Company lent $1,000 to Kay, who agreed to repay the loan in two years. In 2015, Kay disappeared after the note became delinquent. If a reasonable investigation by Partridge indicates that Kay cannot be found or that a suit against Kay would not result in collection, Partridge can deduct the $1,000 in 2015.

EXAMPLE 3

Bankruptcy is generally an indication of at least partial worthlessness of a debt. Bankruptcy may create worthlessness before the settlement date. If this is the case, the deduction may be taken in the year of worthlessness.

In Example 3, assume that Kay filed for personal bankruptcy in 2014 and that the debt is a business debt. At that time, Partridge learned that unsecured creditors (including Partridge) were ultimately expected to receive 20 cents on the dollar. In 2015, settlement is made, and Partridge receives only $150. Partridge should deduct $800 ($1,000 loan − $200 expected settlement) in 2014 and $50 in 2015 ($200 balance − $150 proceeds).

EXAMPLE 4

If a receivable is written off (deducted) as uncollectible and is subsequently collected during the same tax year, the write-off entry is reversed. If a receivable has been written off (deducted) as uncollectible, collection in a later tax year may result in income being recognized. Income will result if the deduction yielded a tax benefit in the year it was taken (the tax benefit rule).

See Concept Summary 6.1 for a review of the tax treatment given to business and nonbusiness bad debts.

Concept Summary 6.1

The Tax Treatment of Bad Debts Using the Specific Charge-Off Method

	Business Bad Debts	Nonbusiness Bad Debts
Timing of deduction	A deduction is allowed when the debt becomes either partially or wholly worthless.	A deduction is allowed *only* when the debt becomes wholly worthless.
Character of deduction	The bad debt may be deducted as an ordinary loss.	The bad debt is classified as a short-term capital loss, subject to the $3,000 capital loss limitation for individuals.
Recovery of amounts previously deducted	If the account recovered was written off during the current tax year, the write-off entry is reversed. If the account was written off in a previous tax year, income is created subject to the tax benefit rule.	If the account recovered was written off during the current tax year, the write-off entry is reversed. If the account was written off in a previous tax year, income is created subject to the tax benefit rule.

6-1b **Business versus Nonbusiness Bad Debts**

The nature of a debt depends upon whether the lender is engaged in the business of lending money or whether there is a proximate relationship between the creation of the debt and the *lender's* trade or business. Where either of these conditions is true, a bad debt is classified as a **business bad debt**. If these conditions are not met, a bad debt is classified as a **nonbusiness bad debt**. The use to which the borrowed funds are put is of no consequence when making this classification decision.

EXAMPLE 5

The Big Picture

Return to the facts of *The Big Picture* on p. 6-1. Robyn loaned her friend Jamil $25,000. Jamil used the money to start a business, which subsequently failed. When Jamil died after having made principal payments of $6,000 on the loan, he was insolvent.

Even though the proceeds of the loan were used in a business, the loan is a nonbusiness bad debt because the business was Jamil's, not Robyn's, and Robyn is not in the business of lending money.

EXAMPLE 6

Horace operates a sole proprietorship that sells premium electronic equipment. Horace uses the accrual method to account for sales of the electronic equipment. During the year, he sold $4,000 of equipment to Herbie on credit. Later that year, the account receivable becomes worthless. The loan is a business bad debt, because the debt was related to Horace's business.

Generally, nonbusiness bad debts are incurred only by individuals. It is assumed that any loans made by a corporation are related to its trade or business. Therefore, any bad debts resulting from loans made by a corporation are automatically business bad debts.

The distinction between a business bad debt and a nonbusiness bad debt is important. A business bad debt is deductible as an ordinary loss in the year incurred, whereas a nonbusiness bad debt is always treated as a short-term capital loss. Thus, regardless of the age of a nonbusiness bad debt, the deduction may be of limited benefit due to the $3,000 capital loss limitation for individuals (refer to the discussion in Chapter 4).

6-1c **Loans between Related Parties**

Loans between related parties raise the issue of whether the transaction was a *bona fide* loan or some other type of transfer, such as a gift, a disguised dividend payment, or a contribution to capital. The Regulations state that a bona fide debt arises from a debtor-creditor relationship based on a valid and enforceable obligation to pay a fixed or determinable sum of money. Thus, individual circumstances must be examined to determine whether advances between related parties are loans. Some considerations are these:

- Was a note properly executed?
- Was there a reasonable rate of interest?
- Was collateral provided?
- What collection efforts were made?
- What was the intent of the parties?

EXAMPLE 7

Ted, who is the sole shareholder of Penguin Corporation, lends the corporation $10,000 so that it can continue business operations. The note specifies a 2% interest rate and is payable on demand. Penguin has shown losses in each year of its five-year existence. The corporation also has liabilities greatly in excess of its assets. It is likely that Ted's transfer to the corporation would be treated as a contribution to capital rather than a liability. Consequently, no bad debt deduction would be allowed upon default by Penguin.

DIGGING DEEPER 1   **In-depth coverage can be found on this book's companion website: www.cengagebrain.com**

6-2 WORTHLESS SECURITIES

A loss is allowed for securities that become *completely* worthless during the year (worthless securities).[3] Such securities are shares of stock, bonds, notes, or other evidence of indebtedness issued by a corporation or government. The losses generated are treated as capital losses (refer to Chapter 4) deemed to have occurred on the *last day* of the tax year. By treating losses as having occurred on the last day of the tax year, a loss that would otherwise have been classified as short term (if the date of worthlessness were used) may be classified as long term.

LO.2

State and illustrate the tax treatment of worthless securities, including § 1244 stock.

The Big Picture

EXAMPLE 8

Return to the facts of *The Big Picture* on p. 6-1. Robyn owned stock in Owl Corporation that she acquired as an investment on October 1, 2014, at a cost of $60,000. On May 31, 2015, the stock became worthless when the company declared bankruptcy.

Because the stock is deemed to have become worthless as of December 31, 2015, Robyn has a capital loss from an asset held for 15 months (a long-term capital loss). Alternatively, if the stock is § 1244 small business stock (see the following section), she has a $50,000 ordinary loss and a $10,000 long-term capital loss.

6-2a Small Business Stock (§ 1244)

The general rule is that shareholders receive capital loss treatment for losses from the sale or exchange of corporate stock. As noted in Chapter 4, the deductibility of capital losses is limited. However, it is possible to avoid capital loss limitations if the loss is sustained on small business stock (§ 1244 stock) . Such a loss could arise from a sale of the stock or from the stock becoming worthless. Only *individuals*[4] who acquired the stock *from* the issuing corporation are eligible to receive ordinary loss treatment under § 1244. The ordinary loss treatment is limited to $50,000 ($100,000 for married individuals filing jointly) per year. Losses on § 1244 stock in excess of the statutory limits are treated as capital losses.

The issuing corporation must meet certain requirements under § 1244 for the loss on the stock to be treated as an *ordinary*—rather than a capital—loss. The principal requirement is that the total capitalization of the corporation is limited to a maximum of $1 million. This capital limit includes all money and other property received by the corporation for stock and all capital contributions made to the corporation. The $1 million test is made at the time the stock is issued. There are no requirements regarding the kind of stock issued. Section 1244 stock can be either common or preferred.

Section 1244 applies only to losses. If § 1244 stock is sold at a gain, the provision does not apply and the gain is capital gain (which, for individuals, may be subject to preferential tax treatment, as discussed in Chapter 4).

EXAMPLE 9

Iris, a single individual, was looking for an investment that would give some diversification to her stock portfolio. A friend suggested that she acquire some stock in Eagle Corporation, a new startup company. On July 1, 2013, Iris purchased 100 shares of Eagle Corporation for $100,000. At the time Iris acquired her stock from Eagle Corporation, the corporation had $700,000 of paid-in capital. As a result, the stock qualified as § 1244 stock. On June 20, 2015, Iris sold all of her Eagle stock to Michael for $20,000. Because the Eagle stock is § 1244 stock, Iris has a $50,000 ordinary loss and a $30,000 long-term capital loss.

If Michael were to sell the stock later for $8,000 in a taxable transaction, the $12,000 loss would not qualify for ordinary loss treatment under §1244 because Eagle Corporation had not issued the stock to him.

---

[3]§ 165(g).

[4]The term *individuals* for this purpose does not include a trust or an estate (but could include a partnership or an LLC).

TAX PLANNING STRATEGIES   **Maximizing the Benefits of § 1244**

FRAMEWORK FOCUS: TAX RATE

Strategy: Control the Character of Income and Deductions.

Because § 1244 limits the amount of loss classified as ordinary loss on a yearly basis, a taxpayer might maximize the benefits of § 1244 by selling the stock in more than one taxable year.

Mitch, a single individual, acquired small business stock in 2013 for $150,000 (150 shares at $1,000 per share). On December 20, 2015, the stock is worth $60,000 (150 shares at $400 per share). Mitch wants to sell the stock at this time. He earns a salary of $80,000 a year, has no other capital transactions, and does not expect any in the future.

If Mitch sells all of the small business stock in 2015, his recognized loss will be $90,000 ($60,000 selling price − $150,000 cost). The loss will be characterized as a $50,000 ordinary loss and a $40,000 long-term capital loss. In computing taxable income for 2015, Mitch could deduct the $50,000 ordinary loss but could deduct only $3,000 of the capital loss (assuming that he has no capital gains). The remainder of the capital loss could be carried over and used in future years subject to the capital loss limitations.

Alternatively, if Mitch sells 82 shares in 2015, he will recognize an ordinary loss of $49,200 [82 × ($400 − $1,000)]. If Mitch then sells the remainder of the shares in 2016, he will recognize an ordinary loss of $40,800 [68 × ($400 − $1,000)], successfully avoiding the capital loss limitation. Mitch could deduct the $49,200 ordinary loss in computing 2015 taxable income and the $40,800 ordinary loss in computing 2016 taxable income.

LO.3

Identify a casualty and determine the amount, classification, and timing of casualty and theft losses.

6-3 **CASUALTY AND THEFT LOSSES**

Losses on business property are deductible, whether attributable to casualty, theft, or some other cause (e.g., rust, termite damage). While all *business* property losses are generally deductible, the amount and timing of casualty and theft losses are determined using special rules. Furthermore, for individual taxpayers, who may deduct casualty losses on personal-use (nonbusiness) property as well as on business and investment property (held in partnerships and S corporations or in an individual capacity), a set of special limitations applies. Casualty gains are also afforded special consideration in the tax law.

6-3a **Definition of Casualty**

The term *casualty* generally includes *fire, storm, shipwreck,* and *theft.* In addition, losses from *other casualties* are deductible. Such losses generally include any loss resulting from an event that is (1) identifiable; (2) damaging to property; and (3) sudden, unexpected, and unusual in nature. The term also includes accidental loss of property provided the loss qualifies under the same rules as any other casualty.

A *sudden event* is an event that is swift and precipitous and not gradual or progressive. An *unexpected event* is one that is ordinarily unanticipated and occurs without the intent of the taxpayer who suffers the loss. An *unusual event* is an event that is extraordinary and nonrecurring and does not commonly occur during the activity in which the taxpayer was engaged when the destruction occurred.[5] Examples include auto accidents, sonic booms, vandalism, and mine cave-ins. A taxpayer can take a deduction for a casualty loss from an automobile accident if the accident is not attributable to the taxpayer's willful act or willful negligence. Weather that causes damage (e.g., drought) must be unusual and severe for the particular region to qualify as a casualty. Furthermore, damage must be to the *taxpayer's* property to be deductible.

---

[5]Rev.Rul. 72–592, 1972–2 C.B. 101.

Events That Are Not Casualties

Not all acts of nature are treated as casualty losses for income tax purposes. Because a casualty must be sudden, unexpected, and unusual, progressive deterioration (such as erosion due to wind or rain) is not a casualty because it does not meet the suddenness test.

An example of an event that generally does not qualify as a casualty is insect damage. When termites caused damage over a period of several years, some courts have disallowed a casualty loss deduction.[6] On the other hand, some courts have held that termite damage over periods of up to 15 months after infestation constituted a sudden event and was, therefore, deductible as a casualty loss.[7] Despite the existence of some judicial support for the deductibility of termite damage as a casualty loss, the current position of the IRS is that termite damage is not deductible.[8]

Other examples of events that are not casualties are losses resulting from a decline in value rather than an actual loss of the property. For example, a taxpayer was allowed a loss for the actual flood damage to his property but not for the decline in market value due to the property being in a flood-prone area.[9] Similarly, a decline in value of an office building due to fire damage to nearby buildings is not deductible as a casualty.

6-3b Deduction of Casualty Losses

Generally, a casualty loss is deducted in the year the loss occurs. However, no casualty loss is permitted if a reimbursement claim with a reasonable *prospect of full recovery* exists.[10] If the taxpayer has a partial claim, only part of the loss can be claimed in the year of the casualty and the remainder is deducted in the year the claim is settled.

Fuchsia Corporation's new warehouse was completely destroyed by fire in 2015. Its cost and fair market value were $250,000. Fuchsia's only claim against the insurance company was on a $70,000 policy and was not settled by year-end. The following year, 2016, Fuchsia settled with the insurance company for $60,000. Fuchsia is entitled to a $180,000 deduction in 2015 and a $10,000 deduction in 2016.

If a taxpayer receives reimbursement for a casualty loss sustained and deducted in a previous year, an amended return is not filed for that year. Instead, the taxpayer must include the reimbursement in gross income on the return for the year in which it is received to the extent the previous deduction resulted in a tax benefit (refer to Chapter 4).

Golden Hawk, Inc., had a deductible casualty loss of $15,000 on its 2014 tax return. Golden Hawk's taxable income for 2014 was $60,000 after deducting the $15,000 loss. In June 2015, the corporation is reimbursed $13,000 for the prior year's casualty loss.

Golden Hawk includes the entire $13,000 in gross income for 2015 because the deduction in 2014 produced a tax benefit.

Disaster Area Losses

An exception to the general rule for the time of deduction is allowed for disaster area losses, which are casualties or disaster-related business losses sustained in an area designated as a disaster area by the President of the United States.[11] In such cases, the taxpayer may *elect* to treat the loss as having occurred in the taxable year immediately *preceding* the taxable year in which the disaster actually occurred. The rationale for this exception is to provide immediate relief to disaster victims in the form of accelerated tax benefits.

If the due date, plus extensions, for the prior year's return has not passed, a taxpayer makes the election to claim the disaster area loss on the prior year's tax return. If a disaster area is designated after the prior year's return has been filed, it is necessary to file

---

[6]*Fay v. Helvering*, 41–2 USTC ¶9494, 27 AFTR 432, 120 F.2d 253 (CA–2, 1941); *U.S. v. Rogers*, 41–1 USTC ¶9442, 27 AFTR 423, 120 F.2d 244 (CA–9, 1941).

[7]*Rosenberg v. Comm.*, 52–2 USTC ¶9377, 42 AFTR 303, 198 F.2d 46 (CA–8, 1952); *Shopmaker v. U.S.*, 54–1 USTC ¶9195, 45 AFTR 758, 119 F.Supp. 705 (D.Ct. Mo., 1953).

[8]Rev.Rul. 63–232, 1963–2 C.B. 97.

[9]*S. L. Solomon*, 39 TCM 1282, T.C.Memo. 1980–87.

[10]Reg. § 1.165–1(d)(2)(i).

[11]§ 165(h).

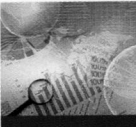

TAX PLANNING STRATEGIES   Documentation of Related-Taxpayer Loans, Casualty Losses, and Theft Losses

FRAMEWORK FOCUS: DEDUCTIONS

Strategy: Maximize Deductible Amounts.

Because the validity of loans between related taxpayers might be questioned, adequate documentation is needed to substantiate a bad debt deduction if the loan subsequently becomes worthless. Documentation should include proper execution of the note (legal form) and the establishment of a bona fide purpose for the loan. In addition, it is desirable to stipulate a reasonable rate of interest and a fixed maturity date.

Because a theft loss deduction is not permitted for misplaced items, a police report and evidence of the value of the property (e.g., appraisals, pictures of the property, and purchase receipts) are necessary to document a theft.

Similar documentation of the value of property should be provided to support a casualty loss deduction because the amount of loss is measured, in part, by the decline in fair market value of the property.

Casualty loss deductions must be reported on Form 4684.

either an amended return or a refund claim. In any case, the taxpayer must show clearly that such an election is being made.

The Big Picture

EXAMPLE 13

Return to the facts of *The Big Picture* on p. 6-1. On September 28, 2015, Robyn's personal residence was damaged when a tornado caused an oak tree to fall on the house. The amount of her uninsured casualty loss was $7,000 ($32,000 − $25,000 insurance recovery). Due to the extent of the damage in the area, the President of the United States designated the area a disaster area. Because Robyn's loss is a disaster area loss, she may elect to file an amended return for 2014 and take the loss in that year.

If Robyn elects this course of action, the amount of the loss will be reduced first by $100 (the materiality amount in 2014) and then by 10% of her 2014 AGI.

If Robyn forgoes the election, she may take the loss on her 2015 income tax return. The amount of the loss will be reduced first by $100 (the materiality amount in 2015) and then by 10% of her 2015 AGI. The advantage to Robyn of claiming the deduction in the earlier year is to receive the tax relief sooner.

6-3c Definition of Theft

Theft includes, but is not necessarily limited to, larceny, embezzlement, and robbery.[12] Theft does not include misplaced items.[13]

Theft losses are treated like other casualty losses, but the *timing* of recognition of the loss differs. A theft loss is deducted in the *year of discovery*, which may not be the same as the year of the theft. If in the year of the discovery a claim exists (e.g., against an insurance company) and there is a reasonable expectation of recovering the adjusted basis of the asset from the insurance company, no deduction is permitted.[14] If in the year of settlement the recovery is less than the asset's adjusted basis, a deduction may be available. If the recovery is greater than the asset's adjusted basis, *casualty gain* may be recognized.

EXAMPLE 14

Sakura, Inc., owned a computer that was stolen from its offices in December 2014. The theft was discovered on June 3, 2015, and the corporation filed a claim with its insurance company that was settled on January 30, 2016.

Assuming that there is a reasonable expectation of full recovery, no deduction is allowed in 2015. A deduction may be available in 2016 if the actual insurance proceeds are less than the adjusted basis of the asset. (Loss measurement rules are discussed later in this chapter.)

---

[12]Reg. § 1.165–8(d).

[13]*Mary Francis Allen*, 16 T.C. 163 (1951).

[14]Reg. §§ 1.165–1(d)(2) and 1.165–8(a)(2).

TAX IN THE NEWS   **The Tax Consequences of Lost Bitcoins**

In Notice 2014–21 (2014–16 I.R.B. 938), the Internal Revenue Service provided initial guidance on transactions involving virtual currency (including bitcoins). Specifically, the IRS indicates that bitcoin is *not* currency; rather, it is property. As such, gain and losses on the disposition of bitcoins cannot be "exchange gain or loss." This may come as a disappointment to taxpayers who lost money in bitcoin investments and may have hoped that the losses would be classified as exchange losses (and, as such, ordinary losses). Taxpayers who have disposed of appreciated investment positions in bitcoins may enjoy capital gains treatment. Taxpayers who hold bitcoin as inventory will be subject to ordinary gains and losses upon disposition.

But what happens if the hard drive on which bitcoins are stored crashes and the data are not recoverable? Is this a "sudden, unexpected, and unusual event" that could qualify for a casualty loss? One might argue that failure to back up the data on the hard drive might be deemed carelessness (and so none of the loss would be allowed). And, certainly,

no loss would be allowed until the taxpayer could confirm that there was no chance of recovery.

What if the taxpayer inadvertently deletes keys to bitcoins he or she previously mined? In general, one cannot take a loss for lost or misplaced property. In this case, no loss would be allowed due to carelessness on the part of the taxpayer. So the bottom line is this: Always back up your digital files.

What about losses in the 2013 collapse of Mt. Gox? Suppose a taxpayer lost $20,000 worth of bitcoins in his or her Mt. Gox trading accounts (with a basis of $12,000). Is this a loss due to theft? If the loss is a result of theft or embezzlement, the taxpayer would be entitled to claim a loss in the tax year that he or she discovers the loss. Further, at this point, it isn't clear whether any of the "lost" Mt. Gox bitcoins have been stolen or are even unrecoverable. If there is a "reasonable chance of recovery," the taxpayer might not even be able to write off the Mt. Gox loss (and given that more than 25 percent of the "lost" bitcoins at Mt. Gox were subsequently located, there appears to be such a "reasonable chance of recovery").

6-3d   **Loss Measurement**

The rules for determining the amount of a loss depend in part on whether business, investment, or personal-use (nonbusiness) property was involved. Another factor that must be considered is whether the property was partially or completely destroyed.

If business property or investment property (e.g., rental property) is *completely destroyed*, the loss is equal to the adjusted basis[15] (typically cost less depreciation) of the property at the time of destruction.

A different measurement rule applies for *partial destruction* of business and investment property and for *partial* or *complete destruction* of personal-use property held by individuals. In these situations, the loss is the *lesser* of:

- The adjusted basis of the property, or
- The difference between the fair market value of the property before the event and the fair market value immediately after the event.

EXAMPLE

15

Wynd and Rain, a law firm, owned an airplane that was used only for business purposes. The airplane was damaged in an accident. On the date of the accident, the fair market value of the plane was $52,000, and its adjusted basis was $32,000. After the accident, the plane was appraised at $24,000.

The law firm's loss deduction is $28,000 (the lesser of the adjusted basis or the decrease in fair market value). If instead the airplane had been completely destroyed in the accident, the loss deduction would have been $32,000 (the adjusted basis of the airplane).

Any insurance recovery reduces the loss for business, investment, and personal-use losses. In fact, a taxpayer may realize a gain if the insurance proceeds exceed the adjusted basis of the property. Chapter 8 discusses the treatment of net gains and losses on business property and income-producing property.

A special rule on insurance recovery applies to *personal-use property*. In particular, individuals are not permitted to deduct a casualty loss for damage to insured personal-use property unless an insurance claim is filed. This rule applies, whether the insurance provides partial or full reimbursement for the loss.[16]

---

[15]See Chapter 7 for a detailed discussion of basis rules.   [16]§ 165(h)(5)(E).

Generally, an appraisal before and after the casualty is needed to measure the amount of loss. However, the *cost of repairs* to the damaged property generally is acceptable as a method of establishing the loss in value.[17]

DIGGING DEEPER 2 | In-depth coverage can be found on this book's companion website: **www.cengagebrain.com**

Multiple Losses

When multiple casualty losses occur during the year, the amount of each loss is computed separately. The rules for computing loss deductions where multiple losses have occurred are illustrated in Example 16.

EXAMPLE

16

During the year, Swan Enterprises had the following business casualty losses:

| Asset | Adjusted Basis | Fair Market Value of the Asset | | Insurance Recovery |
		Before the Casualty	After the Casualty	
A	$900	$600	$–0–	$400
B	300	800	250	150

The following losses are allowed:

- Asset A: $500. The complete destruction of a business asset results in a deduction of the adjusted basis of the property (reduced by any insurance recovery), regardless of the asset's fair market value.

- Asset B: $150. The partial destruction of a business asset results in a deduction equal to the lesser of the adjusted basis ($300) or the decline in value ($550), reduced by any insurance recovery ($150).

6-3e Casualty and Theft Losses of Individuals

Recall from Chapters 1 and 4 that the individual income tax formula distinguishes between deductions *for* AGI and deductions *from* AGI. Casualty and theft losses incurred by an individual in connection with a business or with rental and royalty activities are deductible *for* AGI and are limited only by the rules previously discussed.[18] Losses from most other investment activities and personal-use losses are generally deducted *from* AGI. Investment casualty and theft losses (e.g., the theft of a security) are classified as other miscellaneous itemized deductions (not subject to a 2 percent-of-AGI floor as explained in Chapter 10). Casualty and theft losses of personal-use property are subject to special limitations discussed next.

Personal-Use Property

In addition to the valuation rules discussed previously, casualty and theft loss deductions from personal-use property must be reduced by a $100 *per event* floor and a 10 percent-of-AGI *aggregate* floor.[19] The $100 floor applies separately to each casualty or theft and applies to the entire loss from each casualty or theft (e.g., if a storm damages both a taxpayer's residence and automobile, only $100 is subtracted from the total amount of the loss). All personal-use losses incurred during the year (net of the $100 floor for each event) are then added together, and the total is reduced by 10 percent of the taxpayer's AGI. The resulting amount is the taxpayer's itemized deduction for personal-use casualty and theft losses.

---

[17]Reg. § 1.165–7(a)(2)(ii).
[18]§ 62(a)(1).

[19]§§ 165(c)(3) and (h).

Rocky, who had AGI of $30,000, was involved in a motorcycle accident in 2015. His motorcycle, which was used only for personal use and had a fair market value of $12,000 and an adjusted basis of $9,000, was completely destroyed. He received $5,000 from his insurance company.

Rocky's casualty loss deduction is $900 [$9,000 basis − $5,000 insurance recovery − $100 floor − $3,000 (.10 × $30,000 AGI)]. The $900 casualty loss is an itemized deduction (*from* AGI).

EXAMPLE
17

Where there are both casualty and theft gains and losses from personal-use property, special netting rules apply. Generally, if casualty and theft gains exceed losses during the year, the gains and losses are treated as capital gains and losses. Alternatively, if losses exceed gains, the casualty and theft gains (and losses to the extent of gains) are treated as ordinary gains and losses. Any excess losses are deductible as personal-use casualty and theft losses.

See Concept Summary 6.2 for a review of the tax treatment of casualty gains and losses.

Concept Summary 6.2

Casualty Gains and Losses

	Business-Use or Income-Producing Property	Personal-Use Property
Event creating the loss	Any event.	Casualty or theft.
Amount	The lesser of the decline in fair market value or the adjusted basis, but always the adjusted basis if the property is totally destroyed.	The lesser of the decline in fair market value or the adjusted basis.
Insurance	Insurance proceeds received reduce the amount of the loss.	Insurance proceeds received (or for which there is an unfiled claim) reduce the amount of the loss.
$100 floor	Not applicable.	Applicable per event.
Gains and losses	Gains and losses are netted (see detailed discussion in Chapter 8).	Personal casualty and theft gains and losses are netted.
Gains exceeding losses		The gains and losses are treated as gains and losses from the sale of capital assets.
Losses exceeding gains		The gains—and the losses to the extent of gains—are treated as ordinary items in computing AGI. The losses in excess of gains, to the extent that they exceed 10% of AGI, are itemized deductions (*from* AGI).

In-depth coverage can be found on this book's companion website: www.cengagebrain.com   **3** DIGGING DEEPER

6-4 NET OPERATING LOSSES

A net operating loss (NOL) in a particular tax year would produce no tax benefits if the Code did not provide for the carryback and carryforward of such losses to profitable years.

6-4a Introduction

The requirement that every taxpayer file an annual income tax return (whether on a calendar year or a fiscal year) can lead to inequities for taxpayers who experience uneven income over a series of years. These inequities result from the application of progressive tax rates to taxable income determined on an annual basis.

LO.4

Describe the impact of the net operating loss carryback and carryover provisions on previous and subsequent years' taxable income.

EXAMPLE

18

Orange, Inc., realizes the following taxable income or loss over a five-year period: year 1, $50,000; year 2, ($30,000); year 3, $100,000; year 4, ($200,000); and year 5, $380,000. Blue Corporation has taxable income of $60,000 every year. Note that both corporations have total taxable income of $300,000 over the five-year period. Assume that there is no provision for carryback or carryover of net operating losses. Orange and Blue would have the following five-year tax liabilities:

Year	Orange's Tax	Blue's Tax
1	$ 7,500	$10,000
2	–0–	10,000
3	22,250	10,000
4	–0–	10,000
5	129,200	10,000
	$158,950	$50,000

Note: The computation of tax is made without regard to any
NOL benefit. Rates applicable to 2015 are used to compute the tax.

Even though Orange and Blue realized the same total taxable income ($300,000) over the five-year period, Orange would have to pay taxes of $158,950, while Blue would pay taxes of only $50,000.

To provide partial relief from this inequitable tax treatment, a deduction is allowed for net operating losses (NOLs).[20] This provision permits an NOL for any one year to offset taxable income in other years. The NOL provision provides relief only for losses from the operation of a trade or business or from casualty and theft.

Only C corporations and individuals are permitted an NOL deduction because losses of partnerships and S corporations pass through to their owners. For C corporations, the NOL equals any negative taxable income for the year, with an adjustment for the dividends received deduction (see Chapter 12). In addition, deductions for prior-year NOLs are not allowed when determining a current-year NOL.

6-4b Carryback and Carryover Periods

The mechanism providing a tax benefit from the NOL is the provision that allows a loss deduction in profitable years of the business activity. The loss may be carried back to earlier years and/or carried over to future years.

General Rules

A current-year NOL is usually carried back and deducted against income over the two preceding tax years.[21] It is carried back first to the second year before the loss year and then to the year immediately preceding the loss year (until it fully offsets income). If the loss is not completely used against income in the carryback period, it is carried forward for 20 years following the loss year. NOLs that are not used within the 20-year carryforward period are lost. Thus, an NOL sustained in 2015 is used first in 2013 and then 2014. Then the loss is carried forward and offsets income in 2016 through 2035.

When an NOL is carried back, the taxpayer requests an immediate refund of prior years' taxes by filing an amended return for the previous two years. Alternatively, a form for a quick refund may be filed (Form 1139 for corporations or Form 1045 for individuals). When an NOL is carried forward, the current return shows an NOL deduction for the prior year's loss. Thus, a struggling business with an NOL can receive rapid cash-flow assistance.

---

[20]§ 172.

[21]A three-year carryback period is available for any portion of an individual's NOL resulting from a casualty or theft loss. The three-year carryback rule also applies to NOLs that are attributable to presidentially declared disaster areas that are incurred by a small business. For purposes of this provision, a small business is a business whose average annual gross receipts for a three-year period are $5 million or less. See § 172(b)(1)(F).

NOLs from Multiple Tax Years

When the taxpayer has NOLs in two or more years, the earliest year's loss is used first. Later years' losses can then be used until they offset income or are lost. Thus, one year's return could show NOL carryovers from two or more years. Each loss is computed and applied separately.

Election to Forgo Carryback

A taxpayer can *irrevocably elect* not to carry back an NOL. The election is made on a corporate tax return (Form 1120) by checking the appropriate box. Individuals can make the election by attaching a statement to their tax return. If the election is made, the loss can *only* be carried forward for 20 years. This election may be desirable in circumstances where marginal tax rates in future years are expected to exceed rates in prior years.

6-5 THE TAX SHELTER PROBLEM

LO.5

Explain the tax shelter problem and the reasons for at-risk and passive loss limitations.

Before Congress enacted legislation to reduce their effectiveness, tax shelters provided a popular way to avoid or defer taxes, as they could generate losses and other benefits to offset income from other sources. Because of the tax avoidance potential of many tax shelters, they were attractive to wealthy taxpayers with high marginal tax rates. Many tax shelters merely provided an opportunity for "investors" to buy deductions and credits in ventures that were not expected to generate a profit, even in the long run.

Although it may seem odd that a taxpayer would intentionally invest in an activity that was designed to produce losses, there is a logical explanation. The typical tax shelter operated as a partnership and relied heavily on nonrecourse financing.[22] Accelerated depreciation and interest expense deductions generated large losses in the early years of the activity. At the very least, the tax shelter deductions deferred the recognition of any net income from the venture until the activity was sold. In the best of situations, the investor could realize additional tax savings by offsetting other income (e.g., salary, interest, dividends) with losses flowing from the tax shelter. Ultimately, the sale of the investment would result in *tax-favored* capital gain. The following example illustrates what was possible *before* Congress enacted legislation to curb tax shelter abuses.

EXAMPLE

19

Bob, who earned a salary of $400,000 as a business executive and dividend income of $15,000, invested $20,000 for a 10% interest in a cattle-breeding tax shelter. He did not participate in the operation of the business. Through the use of $800,000 of nonrecourse financing and available cash of $200,000, the partnership acquired a herd of an exotic breed of cattle costing $1 million. Depreciation, interest, and other deductions related to the activity resulted in a loss of $400,000, of which Bob's share was $40,000. Bob was allowed to deduct the $40,000 loss even though he had invested and stood to lose only $20,000 if the investment became worthless. The net effect of the $40,000 deduction from the partnership was that a portion of Bob's salary and dividend income was "sheltered," and as a result, he was required to calculate his tax liability on only $375,000 of income [$415,000 (salary and dividends) − $40,000 (deduction)] rather than $415,000. If this deduction were available under current law and if Bob was in a combined Federal and state income tax bracket of 40%, a tax savings of $16,000 ($40,000 × 40%) would be generated in the first year alone!

---

[22]Nonrecourse debt is an obligation for which the borrower is not personally liable. An example of nonrecourse debt is a liability on real estate acquired by a partnership without the partnership or any of the partners assuming any liability for the mortgage. The acquired property generally is pledged as collateral for the loan.

BRIDGE DISCIPLINE   **Bridge to Finance**

An overarching requirement to maximizing wealth is to reduce the present value cost of taxation. One way to reduce the cost of taxation in present value terms is to defer the payment of a tax into the future for as long as possible. This can be accomplished by reducing the taxpayer's tax base (i.e., taxable income) either by deferring the recognition of income or by accelerating the timing of deductions. As a result, to the extent that the tax cost associated with an investment alternative is reduced, the after-tax benefit from that investment and the investor's wealth position are enhanced.

For example, a common attribute of many tax-advantaged investments is the availability of tax losses that investors may claim on their own income tax returns. Many times, these tax losses are the result of investment-level deductions, such as interest and depreciation expenses, that are bunched in the early years of the life of the investment rather than being due to economic woes of the investment itself.

Through the at-risk limitations and the passive loss rules, the tax law works to scale back the ability of taxpayers to claim tax losses flowing from certain investments. These limitations have a direct impact on *when* investors can claim loss deductions flowing from affected investments. The typical result of these provisions is that the loss deductions are deferred. Therefore, when evaluating competing investment alternatives, taxpayers must address the impact of these tax limitations in projecting the after-tax benefits that can be expected to follow.

A review of Example 19 shows that the taxpayer took a two-for-one write-off ($40,000 deduction, $20,000 amount invested). In the heyday of these types of tax shelters, promoters often promised tax deductions for the investor well in excess of the amount invested.

The first major provision aimed at tax shelters is the at-risk limitation. Its objective is to limit a taxpayer's deductions to the amount that the taxpayer could actually lose from the investment (the amount "at risk") if it becomes worthless. Thus, in Example 19, the at-risk rule limits Bob's loss to $20,000—the amount at risk.

The second major attack on tax shelters came with the passage of the passive loss rules. The passive loss rules require the taxpayer to segregate all income and losses into three categories: active, portfolio, and passive. (These categories are defined in Section 6-7.) In general, the passive loss limits *disallow* the deduction of passive losses *against active or portfolio income* even when the taxpayer is at risk to the extent of the loss. In general, passive losses can only offset passive income.

Thus, in Example 19, the passive loss rules disallow a current deduction for any of the loss. The loss from the tax shelter is a passive loss because Bob does not materially participate in the activity. Therefore, the $20,000 loss that is allowed under the at-risk rules is disallowed under the passive loss rules because Bob does not report any passive income for the year—he reports only active and portfolio income. Consequently, Bob's current-year income must reflect his nonpassive income of $415,000. As explained later in the chapter, the disallowed $20,000 passive loss is suspended and may be deducted in a future year under certain conditions.

The following two sections explore the nature of the at-risk limits and the passive activity loss rules and their impact on investors. Congress intentionally structured these rules so that investors evaluating potential investments must consider mainly the *economics* of the venture instead of the *tax benefits* or tax avoidance possibilities that an investment may generate.

LO.6

Describe how the at-risk limitation and the passive loss rules limit deductions for losses and identify taxpayers subject to these restrictions.

6-6 AT-RISK LIMITATIONS

The at-risk provisions limit the deductibility of losses from business and income-producing activities. These provisions, which apply to individuals and closely held corporations, are designed to prevent taxpayers from deducting losses in excess of their actual economic investment in an activity. In the case of an S corporation or a partnership, the at-risk limits apply at the owner level. Under the at-risk rules, a taxpayer's deductible loss from an activity for any taxable year is limited to the amount the taxpayer has at risk at the end of the taxable year (i.e., the amount the taxpayer could actually lose in the activity).

While the amount at risk generally vacillates over time, the initial amount considered at risk consists of the following:[23]

- The amount of cash and the adjusted basis of property contributed to the activity by the taxpayer.
- Amounts borrowed for use in the activity for which the taxpayer is personally liable.
- The adjusted basis of property pledged as security that is not used in the activity.

This amount usually is increased each year by the taxpayer's share of income and is decreased by the taxpayer's share of deductible losses and withdrawals from the activity. In addition, because *general partners* are jointly and severally liable for recourse debts of the partnership, their at-risk amounts are increased when the partnership increases its debt and are decreased when the partnership reduces its debt. However, a taxpayer generally is not considered at risk with respect to borrowed amounts if either of the following is true:

- The taxpayer is not personally liable for repayment of the debt (e.g., non-recourse debt).
- The lender has an interest (other than as a creditor) in the activity.

An important exception provides that in the case of an activity involving the holding of real property, a taxpayer is considered at risk for his or her share of any *qualified nonrecourse financing* that is secured by real property used in the activity.[24]

Subject to the passive loss rules discussed later in the chapter, a taxpayer may deduct a loss as long as the at-risk amount is positive. However, once the at-risk amount is exhausted, any remaining loss cannot be deducted until a later year. Any losses disallowed for any given taxable year by the at-risk rules may be deducted in the first succeeding year in which the rules do not prevent the deduction—that is, when there is, and to the extent of, a positive at-risk amount.

EXAMPLE 20

In 2015, Sue invests $40,000 in an oil partnership. The partnership incurs a first-year net loss, of which $60,000 is her share. Assume that Sue's interest in the partnership is subject to the at-risk limits but is not subject to the passive loss limits. Because Sue has only $40,000 of capital at risk, she cannot deduct more than $40,000 against her other income and must reduce her at-risk amount to zero ($40,000 at-risk amount − $40,000 loss deducted). The nondeductible loss of $20,000 ($60,000 loss generated − $40,000 loss allowed) can be carried over to 2016.

In 2016, Sue has taxable income of $15,000 from the oil partnership and invests an additional $10,000 in the venture. Her at-risk amount is now $25,000 ($0 beginning balance + $15,000 taxable income + $10,000 additional investment). This enables Sue to deduct the $20,000 carryover loss and requires her to reduce her at-risk amount to $5,000 ($25,000 at-risk amount − $20,000 carryover loss allowed).

Complicating the at-risk rule is the fact that previously allowed losses must be recaptured as income to the extent the at-risk amount is reduced below zero.[25] This rule applies in situations such as those when the amount at risk is reduced below zero by distributions to the taxpayer or when the status of indebtedness changes from recourse to nonrecourse.

Calculation of at-risk amount is reviewed in Concept Summary 6.3.

---

[23]§ 465(b)(1).

[24]Section 465(b)(6) defines *qualified nonrecourse financing*. See also the related discussion in Chapter 14.

[25]§ 465(e).

Concept Summary 6.3

Calculation of At-Risk Amount

Increases to a taxpayer's at-risk amount:

- Cash and the adjusted basis of property contributed to the activity.
- Amounts borrowed for use in the activity for which the taxpayer is personally liable.
- The adjusted basis of property pledged as security that is not used in the activity.
- Taxpayer's share of amounts borrowed for use in the activity that are qualified nonrecourse financing.
- Taxpayer's share of the activity's income.

Decreases to a taxpayer's at-risk amount:

- Withdrawals from the activity.
- Taxpayer's share of the activity's deductible loss.
- Taxpayer's share of any reductions of debt for which recourse against the taxpayer exists or any reductions of qualified nonrecourse debt.

6-7 PASSIVE LOSS LIMITS

This section identifies and explains a number of key issues that are pertinent when applying the passive loss limits.

- The limits apply only to passive losses incurred by certain types of taxpayers.
- Losses are limited under these rules only if they are generated by a passive activity.
- Special rules exist for interests in real estate activities.
- Benefits may arise when a disposition of a passive activity occurs.

6-7a Classification and Impact of Passive Income and Loss

The passive loss rules operate by requiring taxpayers to classify their income and losses into various categories. Then the rules limit the extent to which losses in the passive category can be used to offset income in the other categories.

Classification

The passive loss rules require income and loss to be classified into one of three categories: *active, portfolio,* or *passive.* Active income includes the following:

- Wages, salary, commissions, bonuses, and other payments for services rendered by the taxpayer.
- Profit from a trade or business in which the taxpayer is a material participant (material participation is described later in the chapter).

Portfolio income includes the following:

- Interest, dividends, annuities, and royalties not derived in the ordinary course of a trade or business.
- Gain or loss from the disposition of property that produces portfolio income or is held for investment purposes.

Section 469 provides that passive income or loss arises from activities that are treated as passive, which include:

- Any trade or business or income-producing activity in which the taxpayer does not materially participate.
- Subject to certain exceptions (discussed later in the chapter), all rental activities, whether or not the taxpayer materially participates.

General Impact

Losses or expenses generated by passive activities can only be deducted to the extent of income from passive activities. Any excess loss may not be used to offset income

from active or portfolio income. Instead, any unused passive losses are suspended and carried forward to future years to offset passive income generated in those years. Otherwise, suspended losses may be used only when a taxpayer disposes of his or her entire interest in an activity. In that event, generally, all current and suspended losses related to the activity may offset active and portfolio income.

The Big Picture

EXAMPLE 21

Return to the facts of *The Big Picture* on p. 6-1. Recall that Robyn invested $20,000 in the Florida orange grove limited partnership, which produced an allocable $20,000 loss for her this year. Assume that Robyn earns a salary of $100,000 along with $12,000 in dividends and interest from various portfolio investments. Because her at-risk basis in the partnership is $20,000, the current $20,000 loss is not limited by the at-risk rules. However, because the loss is a passive loss, it is not deductible against her other income. The loss is suspended and is carried over to the future. If Robyn has passive income from this investment or from other passive activities in the future, she can offset the suspended loss against that passive income. If she does not have passive income to offset this suspended loss in the future, she will be allowed to offset the loss against other types of income when she eventually disposes of her investment in the passive activity.

Impact of Suspended Losses

The actual economic gain or loss from a passive investment (including any suspended losses) can be determined when a taxpayer disposes of his or her entire interest in the investment. As a result, under the passive loss rules described above, upon a fully taxable disposition, any overall loss realized from the taxpayer's activity is recognized and can be offset against passive, active, and portfolio income.

A fully taxable disposition generally involves a sale of the property to a third party at arm's length and thus, presumably, for a price equal to the property's fair market value. As presented in the following example, a gain recognized upon the transfer of an interest in a passive activity generally is treated as passive and is first offset by the suspended passive losses from that activity.

EXAMPLE 22

Rex sells an apartment building, a passive activity, with an adjusted basis of $100,000 for $180,000. In addition, he has suspended passive losses of $60,000 associated with the building. His total gain, $80,000, and his taxable gain, $20,000, are calculated as follows:

Net sales price	$ 180,000
Less: Adjusted basis	(100,000)
Total gain	$ 80,000
Less: Suspended losses	(60,000)
Taxable gain (passive)	$ 20,000

If current and suspended losses of the passive activity exceed the gain realized from the sale or if the sale results in a realized loss, the amount of

- any loss from the activity for the tax year (including losses suspended in the activity disposed of)

in excess of

- net income or gain for the tax year from all passive activities (without regard to the activity disposed of)

is treated as a loss that is not from a passive activity. In computing the loss from the activity for the year of disposition, any gain or loss recognized is included in the calculation.

Dean sells an apartment building, a passive activity, with an adjusted basis of $100,000 for $150,000. In addition, he has current and suspended passive losses of $60,000 associated with the building and has no other passive activities. His total gain of $50,000 and his deductible loss of $10,000 are calculated as follows:

Net sales price	$ 150,000
Less: Adjusted basis	(100,000)
Total gain	$ 50,000
Less: Suspended losses	(60,000)
Deductible loss (not passive)	($ 10,000)

The $10,000 loss can be deducted against Dean's active and portfolio income. Even if the building is sold for a loss (i.e., the adjusted basis exceeds the sales price), the total loss, including the suspended losses, is deductible as a nonpassive loss.

Carryovers of Suspended Losses

The preceding examples assumed that the taxpayer had an interest in only one passive activity; as a result, the suspended loss was related exclusively to the activity that was disposed of. However, taxpayers often own more than one passive activity, in which case any suspended losses must be allocated among those passive activities that generated losses. The allocation to an activity is made by multiplying the disallowed passive activity loss from all activities using the following fraction:

$$\frac{\text{Loss from one passive activity}}{\text{Sum of losses for taxable year from all passive activities having losses}}$$

Diego has investments in three passive activities with the following income and losses for 2014:

Activity A	($30,000)
Activity B	(20,000)
Activity C	25,000
Net passive loss	($25,000)
Net passive loss of $25,000 allocated to:	
Activity A [$25,000 × ($30,000/$50,000)]	($15,000)
Activity B [$25,000 × ($20,000/$50,000)]	(10,000)
Total suspended losses	($25,000)

Suspended losses are carried over indefinitely and are offset in the future, first against any passive income from the activities to which they relate and then against passive income from other passive activities.[26] Taxpayers subject to the passive loss limitation rule must maintain records to track the suspended losses and the activities to which they belong.

---

[26]§ 469(b).

Assume that the facts are the same as in the preceding example and that in 2015, Activity A produces $10,000 of income. Diego may use $10,000 of Activity A's suspended loss of $15,000 from 2014 to offset the $10,000 income from this activity. If Diego sells Activity A in early 2016, the remaining $5,000 suspended loss is used to offset any income from the activity reported by Diego in 2016 and to determine his final gain or loss.

EXAMPLE 25

Passive Credits

Credits (such as the low-income housing credit and rehabilitation credit—discussed in Chapter 17) that arise from passive activities are limited in much the same way as passive losses. Passive credits can be utilized only against regular tax attributable to passive income,[27] which is calculated by comparing the tax on all income (including passive income) with the tax on income excluding passive income.

Sam owes $50,000 of tax, disregarding net passive income, and $80,000 of tax, considering both net passive and other taxable income (disregarding the credits in both cases). The amount of tax attributable to the passive income is $30,000.

EXAMPLE 26

In the preceding example, Sam can claim a maximum of $30,000 of passive activity credits; the excess credits are carried over. These passive activity credits can be used only against the *regular* tax attributable to passive income. If a taxpayer has a net loss from passive activities during a given year, no credits can be used.

Carryovers of Passive Credits

Tax credits attributable to passive activities can be carried forward indefinitely, much like suspended passive losses. Unlike passive losses, however, passive credits are lost forever when the activity is disposed of in a taxable transaction where loss is recognized. Credits are allowed on dispositions only when there is sufficient tax on passive income to absorb them.

Use of Passive Credits upon Disposition of an Activity

Alicia sells a passive activity for a gain of $10,000. The activity had suspended losses of $40,000 and suspended credits of $15,000. The $10,000 gain is offset by $10,000 of the suspended losses, and the remaining $30,000 of suspended losses is deductible against Alicia's active and portfolio income. The suspended credits are lost forever because the sale of the activity did not generate any tax after the effect of the suspended losses was considered.

EXAMPLE 27

If Alicia in the preceding example had realized a $100,000 gain on the sale of the passive activity, the suspended credits could have been used to the extent of the regular tax attributable to the net passive income.

EXAMPLE 28

Gain on sale	$100,000
Less: Suspended losses	(40,000)
Net gain	$ 60,000

If the tax attributable to the net gain of $60,000 is $15,000 or more, the entire $15,000 of suspended credits can be used. If the tax attributable to the gain is less than $15,000, the excess of the suspended credits over the tax attributable to the gain is lost forever.

When a taxpayer has sufficient regular tax liability from passive activities to trigger the use of suspended credits, the credits lose their character as passive credits. They are reclassified as regular tax credits and made subject to the same limits as other credits (see Chapter 17).

---

[27]§ 469(d)(2).

Passive Activity Changes to Active

If a formerly passive activity becomes active, suspended losses are allowed to the extent of income from the now active business.[28] If any of the suspended loss remains, it continues to be treated as a loss from a passive activity. The excess suspended loss can be deducted against passive income or carried over to the next tax year and deducted to the extent of income from the now active business in the succeeding year(s).

EXAMPLE 29

For several years, Rebecca has owned an interest in a passive activity that has produced losses of $80,000 during that period. Because she did not have passive income from other sources, she could not deduct any of the activity's passive losses. In the current year, she has become a material participant in the activity and her share of the business profits total $25,000. As a result, she may use $25,000 of the suspended passive loss to offset the current business profits. Rebecca's remaining suspended passive loss from the activity is $55,000 ($80,000 − $25,000), which is carried over to future years and used to offset income from the formerly passive activity or income from other passive activities.

6-7b Taxpayers Subject to the Passive Loss Rules

The passive loss rules apply to individuals, estates, trusts, personal service corporations, and closely held C corporations.[29] Passive income or loss from investments in partnerships or S corporations (see Chapters 14 and 15) flows through to the owners, and the passive loss rules are applied at the owner level. Consequently, it is necessary to understand how the passive activity rules apply to both entities *and* their owners (including individual taxpayers).

Personal Service Corporations

Determination of whether a corporation is a **personal service corporation** is based on rather broad definitions. A personal service corporation is a regular (or C) corporation that meets both of the following conditions:

• The principal activity is the performance of personal services.
• Such services are substantially performed by owner-employees.

[28]§ 469(f).   [29]§ 469(a).

Generally, personal service corporations include those in the fields of health, law, engineering, architecture, accounting, actuarial science, performing arts, and consulting.[30]

Application of the passive loss limitations to personal service corporations is intended to prevent taxpayers from sheltering personal service income by creating personal service corporations and acquiring passive activities at the corporate level.

EXAMPLE

30

Two tax accountants who earn an aggregate of $200,000 a year in their individual practices agree to work together in a newly formed personal service corporation. Shortly after its formation, the corporation invests in a passive activity that produces a $200,000 loss during the year. Because the passive loss rules apply to personal service corporations, the corporation may not deduct the $200,000 passive loss against the $200,000 of active income.

In-depth coverage can be found on this book's companion website: www.cengagebrain.com   **4 DIGGING DEEPER**

Closely Held C Corporations

Application of the passive loss rules to closely held (nonpersonal service) C corporations is also intended to prevent individuals from incorporating to avoid the passive loss limitations. A corporation is classified as a **closely held C corporation** if at any time during the taxable year, more than 50 percent of the value of its outstanding stock is owned, directly or indirectly, by or for five or fewer individuals. Closely held C corporations (other than personal service corporations) may use passive losses to offset *active* income but *not portfolio* income.

EXAMPLE

31

Silver Corporation, a closely held (nonpersonal service) C corporation, has a $500,000 passive loss from a rental activity, $400,000 of active income, and $100,000 of portfolio income. The corporation may offset $400,000 of the $500,000 passive loss against the $400,000 of active business income but may not offset the remainder against the $100,000 of portfolio income. Thus, $100,000 of the passive loss is suspended ($500,000 passive loss − $400,000 offset against active income).

Application of the passive loss limitations to closely held C corporations prevents shareholders from transferring their portfolio investments to such corporations to offset passive losses against portfolio income.

6-7c Rules for Determining Passive Activities

Identifying what constitutes an activity is a necessary first step in applying the passive loss limitation. The rules used to delineate an activity state that in general, a taxpayer can treat one or more trade or business activities or rental activities as a single activity if those activities form an *appropriate economic unit* for measuring gain or loss. The Regulations provide guidelines for identifying appropriate economic units.[31] These guidelines are designed to prevent taxpayers from arbitrarily combining different businesses in an attempt to circumvent the passive loss limitation. For example, combining a profitable active business and a passive business generating losses into one activity would allow the taxpayer to offset passive losses against active income.

LO.7

Discuss the definitions of activity, material participation, and rental activity under the passive loss rules.

In-depth coverage can be found on this book's companion website: www.cengagebrain.com   **5 DIGGING DEEPER**

To determine which ventures form an appropriate economic unit, all of the relevant facts and circumstances must be considered. However, special rules restrict the grouping of rental and nonrental activities.[32] The following example, adapted from the Regulations, illustrates the application of the activity grouping rules.[33]

---

[30]§ 448(d)(2)(A).

[31]Reg. § 1.469–4.

[32]Reg. § 1.469–4(d).

[33]Reg. § 1.469–4(c)(3).

EXAMPLE 32

George owns a men's clothing store and an Internet café in Chicago. He also owns a men's clothing store and an Internet café in Milwaukee. Reasonable methods of applying the facts and circumstances test may result in any of the following groupings:

- All four businesses may be grouped into a single activity because of common ownership and control.

- The clothing stores may be grouped into an activity, and the Internet cafés may be grouped into an activity.

- The Chicago businesses may be grouped into an activity, and the Milwaukee businesses may be grouped into an activity.

- Each of the four businesses may be treated as a separate activity.

Once a set of activities has been grouped by the taxpayer using the above rules, the grouping cannot be changed unless a material change in the facts and circumstances occurs or the original grouping was clearly inappropriate. In addition, the Regulations also grant the IRS the right to regroup activities when one of the primary purposes of the taxpayer's grouping is to avoid the passive loss limitation and the grouping fails to reflect an appropriate economic unit.[34]

6-7d Material Participation

As indicated previously, if a taxpayer materially participates in a nonrental trade or business activity, any loss from that activity is treated as an active loss that can offset active or portfolio income. (Participation is defined later in the chapter.) If a taxpayer does not materially participate, however, the loss is treated as a passive loss, which can only offset passive income. Therefore, controlling whether a particular activity is treated as active or passive is an important part of the tax strategy of a taxpayer who owns an interest in one or more businesses. Consider the following examples.

Implications of Material Participation Status

EXAMPLE 33

Cameron, a corporate executive, earns a salary of $600,000 per year. In addition, he owns a separate business in which he participates. The business produces a loss of $100,000 during the year. If Cameron materially participates in the business, the $100,000 loss is an active loss that may offset his active income from his corporate employer. If he does not materially participate, the loss is passive and is suspended unless he has other passive income. Cameron may use the suspended loss in the future only when he has passive income or disposes of the activity.

EXAMPLE 34

Connor, an attorney, earns $350,000 a year in his law practice. In addition, he owns interests in two activities, A and B, in which he participates. Activity A, in which he does not *materially* participate, produces a loss of $50,000. Connor has not yet met the material participation standard, described below, for Activity B, which produces income of $80,000. However, he can meet the material participation standard if he spends an additional 50 hours in Activity B during the year. Should Connor attempt to meet the material participation standard for Activity B? If he continues working in Activity B and becomes a material participant, the $80,000 of income from the activity is active and the $50,000 passive loss from Activity A must be suspended. A more favorable tax strategy is for Connor *not to meet* the material participation standard for Activity B, thus making the income from that activity passive. This enables him to offset the $50,000 passive loss from Activity A against most of the passive income from Activity B.

It is possible to devise numerous scenarios in which the taxpayer could control the tax outcome by increasing or decreasing participation in different activities. Examples 33 and 34 demonstrate two of the possibilities. The conclusion reached in most analyses of

---

[34]Reg. § 1.469–4(f).

this type is that taxpayers will benefit by having profitable activities classified as passive so that any passive losses can be used to offset that passive income. If the activity produces a loss, however, the taxpayer will benefit if it is classified as active so that the loss is not subject to the passive loss limitations.

Temporary Regulations[35] provide seven tests (listed in Concept Summary 6.4) that serve to determine when **material participation** is achieved.

Concept Summary 6.4

Tests to Determine Material Participation

Tests Based on Current Participation

1. The individual participates in the activity for more than 500 hours during the year.

2. The individual's participation in the activity for the taxable year constitutes substantially all of the participation in the activity of all individuals (including nonowner employees) for the year.

3. The individual participates in the activity for more than 100 hours during the year, and this participation is not less than that participation of any other individual (including nonowner employees) for the year.

4. The activity is a **significant participation activity** (where the person's participation *exceeds* 100 hours during the year), and the hours for all significant participation activities during the year is more than 500 hours.

Tests Based on Prior Participation

5. The individual materially participated in the activity for any 5 taxable years during the 10 taxable years that immediately precede the current taxable year.

6. The activity is a personal service activity, and the individual materially participated in the activity for any three preceding taxable years.

Test Based on Facts and Circumstances

7. Based on all of the facts and circumstances, the individual participates in the activity on a regular, continuous, and substantial basis during the year.

In-depth coverage can be found on this book's companion website: www.cengagebrain.com **6 DIGGING DEEPER**

Participation Defined

Participation generally includes any work done by an individual in an activity that he or she owns. Participation does not include work if it is of a type not customarily done by owners *and* if one of its principal purposes is to avoid the disallowance of passive losses or credits. Work done in an individual's capacity as an investor (e.g., reviewing financial reports in a nonmanagerial capacity) is not counted in applying the material participation tests. However, participation by an owner's spouse counts as participation by the owner.[36]

EXAMPLE 35

Tom, a partner in a CPA firm, owns a computer store that operated at a loss during the year. To offset this loss against the income from his CPA practice, Tom would like to avoid having the computer business classified as a passive activity. During the year, he worked 480 hours in the business in management and selling activities and 30 hours doing janitorial chores. In addition, Tom's wife participated 40 hours as a salesperson. It is likely that Tom's 480 hours of participation in management and selling activities will count as participation in work customarily done by owners, but the 30 hours spent doing janitorial chores will not. However, the 40 hours of participation by his wife will count. Assuming none of the participation's principal purposes is to avoid the allowance of passive losses or credits, Tom will qualify as a material participant under the more-than-500-hour rule (480 + 40 = 520).

---

[35]Temp.Reg. § 1.469–5T(a).

[36]§ 469(h)(5) and Temp.Reg. § 1.469–5T(f)(3).

TAX IN THE NEWS   **The Passive Loss Rules Are a Trap for the Novice Landlord**

Most sophisticated investors are well aware of the passive loss rules. Such investors are not surprised when the rules apply and have learned how to minimize their negative effect.

The "trap" of the passive loss rules often falls on taxpayers who have never heard of them and hold passive activities "on the side" only as secondary ventures. Suppose, for example, that Taylor just inherited her aunt's furnished residence. Rather than sell the house in a depressed market, she is attracted by the regular cash flow provided by rent income. Although Taylor knows to expect a tax benefit from the paper loss that may result from rental property, does she know about the passive loss limitations? Unlike the professional, most novice landlords are surprised by these rules on an after-the-fact basis.

Limited Partners

A *limited* partner is a partner whose liability to third-party creditors of the partnership is limited to the amount the partner has invested in the partnership. Such a partnership must have at least one *general* partner, who is fully liable in an individual capacity for the debts of the partnership to third parties. Generally, a *limited partner* is not considered a material participant unless he or she qualifies under Test 1, 5, or 6 as shown in Concept Summary 6.4. However, a *general partner* may qualify as a material participant by meeting any of the seven tests. If a general partner also owns a limited interest in the same limited partnership, all interests are treated as a general interest.[37]

Corporations

Personal service corporations and closely held C corporations cannot directly participate in an activity. However, a corporation is deemed to materially participate if its owners materially participate in an activity of the corporation. Together, the participating owners must own directly or indirectly more than 50 percent of the value of the outstanding stock of the corporation.[38] Alternatively, a closely held C corporation may be deemed to materially participate in an activity if, during the entire year, it has at least one full-time employee actively managing the business and at least three full-time nonowner employees working for the business. In addition, the corporation's trade or business expenses must exceed, by 15 percent, the gross income from that business for the year.[39]

6-7e **Rental Activities**

Subject to certain exceptions, all rental activities are treated as passive activities.[40] A **rental activity** is defined as any activity where payments are received principally for the use of tangible (real or personal) property.[41] Importantly, an activity classified as a rental activity is subject to the passive loss rules even if the taxpayer meets a material participation test.

---

[37]§ 469(h)(2) and Temp.Reg. § 1.469–5T(e)(3)(ii). Under Prop.Reg. § 1.469–5, however, material participation status for owners of LLCs and LLPs is dependent on the taxpayer's general involvement in the business.
[38]Temp.Reg. § 1.469–1T(g)(3)(i)(A).

[39]Temp.Reg. § 1.469–1T(g)(3)(i)(B).
[40]§ 469(c)(2).
[41]§ 469(j)(8).

Sarah owns a fleet of automobiles that are held for rent, and she spends an average of 60 hours a week in the activity. Assuming that her automobile business is classified as a rental activity, it is automatically subject to the passive activity rules even though Sarah spends more than 500 hours a year in its operation.

EXAMPLE
36

Certain rentals of real and personal property might be classified under the passive loss rules as nonrental activities.[42] In these situations, assuming the activity is a trade or business, the material participation tests shown in Concept Summary 6.4 must be applied to determine whether the activity is a passive activity.

In-depth coverage can be found on this book's companion website: www.cengagebrain.com   **7 DIGGING DEEPER**

Dan owns a bicycle rental business at a nearby resort. Because the average period of customer use is seven days or less, Dan's business is not treated as a rental activity.

EXAMPLE
37

This exception to the definition of a rental activity is based on the presumption that a person who rents property for seven days or less is generally required to provide significant services to the customer. Providing such services supports a conclusion that the person is engaged in a service business rather than a rental business.

If Dan is a material participant, the business is treated as active. If he is not a material participant, it is treated as a passive activity. For additional discussion of the rental exceptions, see IRS Publication 925 (*Passive Activity and At-Risk Rules*).

The general rules relating to passive activity losses are reviewed in Concept Summary 6.5.

Concept Summary 6.5

Passive Activity Loss Rules: Key Issues and Answers

What is the fundamental passive activity rule?	Passive activity losses may be deducted only against passive activity income and gains. Losses not allowed are suspended and used in future years.
Who is subject to the passive activity rules?	Individuals.
	Estates.
	Trusts.
	Personal service corporations.
	Closely held C corporations.
What is a passive activity?	Trade or business or income-producing activity in which the taxpayer does not materially participate during the year or rental activities, subject to certain exceptions, regardless of the taxpayer's level of participation.
What is an activity?	One or more trades or businesses or rental activities that comprise an appropriate economic unit.
How is an appropriate economic unit determined?	Based on a reasonable application of the relevant facts and circumstances.
What is material participation?	In general, the taxpayer participates on a regular, continuous, and substantial basis. More specifically, when the taxpayer meets the conditions of one of the seven tests provided in the Regulations.
What is a rental activity?	In general, an activity where payments are received for the use of tangible property. Special rules apply to rental real estate.

---

[42]Temp.Reg. § 1.469–1T(e)(3).

LO.8

Determine the relationship between the at-risk and passive loss limitations.

6-7f Interaction of At-Risk and Passive Loss Limits

The determination of whether a loss is suspended under the passive loss rules is made *after* application of the at-risk rules, as well as other provisions relating to the measurement of taxable income. A loss that is not allowed for the year because the taxpayer is not at risk with respect to it is suspended under the at-risk provisions, not under the passive loss rules. Further, a taxpayer's at-risk basis is reduced by the losses (but not below zero) even if the deductions are not currently usable because of the passive loss rules. The following examples illustrate these points.

At-Risk and Passive Loss Interactions

Jack's adjusted basis in a passive activity is $10,000 at the beginning of 2014. His loss from the activity in 2014 is $4,000. Because Jack has no passive activity income, the $4,000 cannot be deducted. At year-end, Jack has an adjusted basis and an at-risk amount of $6,000 in the activity and a suspended passive loss of $4,000.

Jack in the preceding example has a loss of $9,000 in the activity in 2015. Because the $9,000 exceeds his at-risk amount ($6,000) by $3,000, that $3,000 loss is disallowed by the at-risk rules. If Jack has no passive activity income, the remaining $6,000 is suspended under the passive activity rules. At year-end, he has:

- A $3,000 loss suspended under the at-risk rules.

- $10,000 of suspended passive losses ($4,000 from 2014 and $6,000 from 2015).

- An adjusted basis and at-risk amount in the activity of zero.

Jack in Example 39 realizes $1,000 of passive income from the activity in 2016. Because the $1,000 increases his at-risk amount, $1,000 of the $3,000 unused loss from 2015 is reclassified as a passive loss. If he has no other passive income, the $1,000 income is offset by $1,000 of suspended passive losses. At the end of 2016, Jack has:

- No taxable passive income.

- $2,000 ($3,000 − $1,000) of suspended losses under the at-risk rules.

- $10,000 of (reclassified) suspended passive losses ($10,000 + $1,000 of reclassified suspended at-risk losses − $1,000 of passive losses offset against passive income).

- An adjusted basis and an at-risk amount in the activity of zero.

EXAMPLE 41

In 2017, Jack has no gain or loss from the activity in Example 40. He contributes $5,000 more to the passive activity. Because the $5,000 contribution increases his at-risk amount, the $2,000 of losses suspended under the at-risk rules is reclassified as passive. Jack gets no passive loss deduction in 2017. At year-end, he has:

- No suspended losses under the at-risk rules.

- $12,000 of suspended passive losses ($10,000 + $2,000 of reclassified suspended at-risk losses).

- An adjusted basis and an at-risk amount of $3,000 ($5,000 additional investment − $2,000 of reclassified losses).

See Concept Summary 6.6 for the interactions of the at-risk and passive loss limits.

Concept Summary 6.6

Treatment of Losses Subject to the At-Risk and Passive Activity Loss Limitations

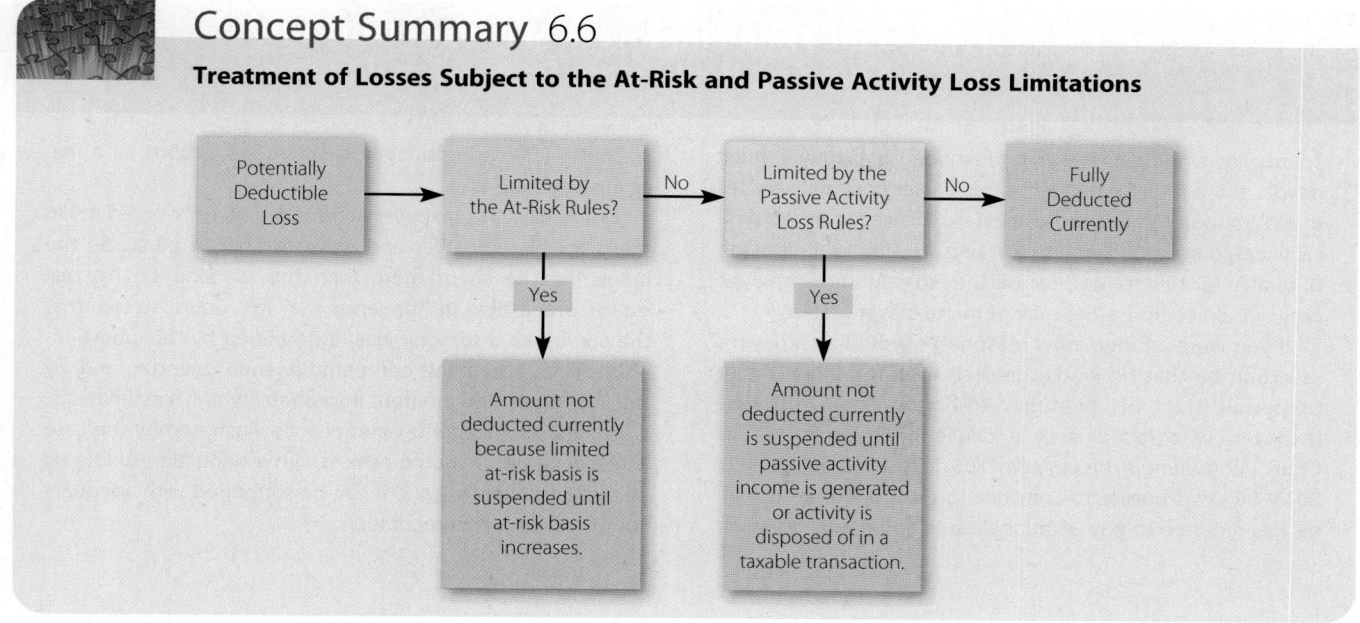

6-7g Special Rules for Real Estate

The passive loss rules contain two exceptions related to real estate activities. These exceptions allow all or part of real estate rental losses to offset active or portfolio income even though the activity otherwise is defined as a passive activity.

LO.9

Explain the special treatment available to real estate activities.

Real Estate Professionals

The first exception allows certain real estate professionals to avoid passive loss treatment for losses from real estate rental activities.[43] To qualify for nonpassive treatment, a taxpayer must satisfy both of the following requirements:

- More than half of the personal services that the taxpayer performs in trades or businesses are performed in real property trades or businesses in which the taxpayer materially participates.
- The taxpayer performs more than 750 hours of services in these real property trades or businesses as a material participant.

Taxpayers who do not satisfy the above requirements must continue to treat income and losses from real estate rental activities as passive income and losses.

EXAMPLE

42

During the current year, Della performs personal service activities as follows: 900 hours as a personal financial planner, 550 hours in a real estate development business, and 600 hours in a real estate rental activity. Any loss Della incurs in either real estate activity will not be subject to the passive loss rules. Being a nonrental business, the real estate development business is deemed active under the more-than-500-hour material participation test. The real estate rental activity is active because Della meets the two requirements to be a real estate professional [more than 50% of her personal services are devoted to real property trades or businesses (i.e., the development and rental) and these hours exceed 750]. Thus, she is allowed to apply the material participation tests to the real estate rental, and she meets one of these tests (the more than 500 hours test). Hence, any losses from either real estate activity can offset active and portfolio income. Likewise, any income from these activities is nonpassive (active) income.

As discussed earlier, a spouse's work is taken into consideration in satisfying the material participation requirement. However, the hours worked by a spouse are not

---
[43]§ 469(c)(7).

TAX IN THE NEWS · Full-Time Employees May Face Difficulty Showing Real Estate Professional Status

To qualify as a real estate professional, a taxpayer must devote more than 50 percent of his or her personal services to real property trades or businesses. This requirement typically would make it difficult for a person with a full-time job to qualify for this status because the efforts as an employee likely would comprise the bulk of the taxpayer's labor.

If you were a judge, how reasonable would a taxpayer's assertion be that he worked more time on his real estate properties than his full-time, 40-hour-a-week job? One taxpayer, who faced such a challenge before the Tax Court (*Mohammad Hassanipour* 105 TCM 1542, T.C. Memo. 2013–88), was unable to convince the judge. Consequently, he was required to pay additional taxes and penalties—over

$45,000—for inappropriately claiming deductions as a real estate professional.

Essentially, the taxpayer reported that he worked 1,936 hours for his employer and was not able to persuade the judge that he spent more than this working on his real estate properties. In the end, the Tax Court stated that the taxpayer's testimony was undermined by "his questionable claims about the contemporaneous calendar, and by the vagueness and inherent improbability of his estimates."

A basic premise of tax compliance illustrated by the case is that a taxpayer should never claim a deduction unless he or she is entitled to it and it can be supported with adequate and convincing documentation.

taken into account when ascertaining whether a taxpayer has worked for more than 750 hours in real property trades or businesses during a year. Services performed by an employee are not treated as being related to a real estate trade or business unless the employee performing the services owns more than a 5 percent interest in the employer. In addition, a closely held C corporation may also qualify for the passive loss relief if more than 50 percent of its gross receipts for the year are derived from real property trades or businesses in which it materially participates.[44]

Rental Real Estate with Active Participation

The second exception to the passive loss limits is more significant in that it is not restricted to real estate professionals. This exception allows individuals to deduct up to $25,000 of losses from real estate rental activities against active and portfolio income.[45] The potential annual $25,000 deduction is reduced by 50 percent of the taxpayer's adjusted gross income (AGI) in excess of $100,000. Thus, the entire deduction is phased out at $150,000 of AGI. If married individuals file separately, the $25,000 deduction is reduced to zero unless they lived apart for the entire year, in which case the loss amount is $12,500 each and the phaseout begins at $50,000.

To qualify for the $25,000 exception, a taxpayer must meet both of the following requirements:[46]

- *Actively participate* in the real estate rental activity.
- Own 10 percent or more (in value) of all interests in the activity during the entire taxable year (or shorter period during which the taxpayer held an interest in the activity).

The difference between *active participation* and *material participation* is that the former can be satisfied without regular, continuous, and substantial involvement in operations as long as the taxpayer participates in making management decisions in a significant and bona fide sense. In this context, relevant management decisions include decisions such as approving new tenants, deciding on rental terms, and approving capital or repair expenditures.

The $25,000 allowance is available after all active participation rental losses and gains are netted and applied to other passive income. If a taxpayer has a real estate

[44]§ 469(c)(7)(B) and Reg. § 1.469–9. In *Frank Aragona Trust*, 142 T.C. No. 9 (2014), the Tax Court found that a trust also could qualify for the real estate professional rule.

[45]§ 469(i).
[46]§ 469(i)(6).

rental loss in excess of the amount that can be deducted under the real estate rental exception, that excess is treated as a passive loss, usable in future years.

Brad has $90,000 of AGI before considering rental activities. Brad also has $85,000 of losses from a real estate rental activity in which he actively participates. He also actively participates in another real estate rental activity from which he has $30,000 of income. He has other passive income of $36,000. Of the net rental loss of $55,000 ($30,000 − $85,000), $36,000 is absorbed by the passive income, leaving $19,000 that can be deducted against active or portfolio income because of the availability of the $25,000 allowance.

The $25,000 offset allowance is an aggregate of both deductions and credits in deduction equivalents. The deduction equivalent of a passive activity credit is the amount of deductions that reduces the tax liability for the taxable year by an amount equal to the credit.[47] A taxpayer with $5,000 of credits and a marginal tax rate of 25 percent would have a deduction equivalent of $20,000 ($5,000/25%).

If total deductions and deduction equivalents exceed $25,000, the taxpayer must allocate the benefit on a pro rata basis. First, the allowance must be allocated among the losses (including real estate rental activity losses suspended in prior years) and then to credits.

Deduction Equivalent Considerations

Kevin is an active participant in a real estate rental activity that produces $8,000 of income, $26,000 of deductions, and $1,500 of credits. Kevin, whose marginal tax rate is 25%, may deduct the net passive loss of $18,000 ($8,000 − $26,000). After deducting the loss, he has an available deduction equivalent of $7,000 ($25,000 − $18,000 passive loss). Because the actual credits produce a deduction equivalent ($1,500 ÷ 25% = $6,000) that is less than $7,000, Kevin may claim the entire $1,500 credit.

Kelly, whose marginal tax rate is 25%, actively participates in three separate real estate rental activities. The relevant tax results for each activity are as follows:

- Activity A: $20,000 of losses.
- Activity B: $10,000 of losses.
- Activity C: $4,200 of credits.

Kelly's deduction equivalent from the credits is $16,800 ($4,200/25%). Therefore, the total passive deductions and deduction equivalents are $46,800 ($20,000 + $10,000 + $16,800), which exceeds the maximum allowable amount of $25,000. Consequently, Kelly must allocate pro rata first from among losses and then from among credits. Deductions from losses are limited as follows:

- Activity A: $25,000 × [$20,000/($20,000 + $10,000)] = $16,667.
- Activity B: $25,000 × [$10,000/($20,000 + $10,000)] = $8,333.

Because the amount of passive deductions exceeds the $25,000 maximum, the deduction balance of $5,000 and passive credits of $4,200 must be carried forward. Kelly's suspended losses and credits by activity are as follows:

	Total	Activity A	Activity B	Activity C
Allocated losses	$ 30,000	$ 20,000	$10,000	$ –0–
Allocated credits	4,200	–0–	–0–	4,200
Utilized losses	(25,000)	(16,667)	(8,333)	–0–
Suspended losses	5,000	3,333	1,667	–0–
Suspended credits	4,200	–0–	–0–	4,200

---

[47]§ 469(j)(5).

LO.10

Determine the consequences
of the disposition of passive
activities.

6-7h **Disposition of Passive Activities**

Recall from an earlier discussion that if a taxpayer disposes of an entire interest in a passive activity, any suspended losses (and in certain cases, suspended credits) may be utilized when calculating the final economic gain or loss on the investment. In addition, if a loss ultimately results, that loss can offset other types of income. However, the consequences may differ if the activity is disposed of in a transaction that is not fully taxable. The following sections discuss the treatment of suspended passive losses in two such dispositions.

Disposition of a Passive Activity at Death

When a transfer of a taxpayer's interest occurs because of the taxpayer's death, suspended losses are allowed (to the decedent) to the extent they exceed the amount, if any, of the allowed step-up in basis.[48] Suspended losses that are equal to or less than the amount of the basis increase are, however, lost. The losses allowed generally are reported on the final return of the deceased taxpayer.

Disposition of Suspended Losses at Death

Alyson dies with passive activity property having an adjusted basis of $40,000, suspended losses of $10,000, and a fair market value at the date of her death of $75,000. The increase (i.e., step-up) in basis (see Chapter 7) is $35,000 (fair market value at date of death in excess of adjusted basis). None of the $10,000 suspended loss is deductible on Alyson's final return or by the beneficiary. The suspended losses ($10,000) are lost because they do not exceed the step-up in basis ($35,000).

Assume the same facts as in the previous example except that the property's fair market value at the date of Alyson's death is $47,000. Because the step-up in basis is only $7,000 ($47,000 − $40,000), the suspended losses allowed are limited to $3,000 ($10,000 suspended loss at time of death − $7,000 increase in basis). The $3,000 loss available to Alyson is reported on her final income tax return.

Disposition of a Passive Activity by Gift

In a disposition of a taxpayer's interest in a passive activity by gift, the suspended losses are added to the basis of the property.[49]

As such, the suspended losses become permanently nondeductible to both the donor and the donee. Nonetheless, a tax *benefit* may be available to the donee for another reason. Due to the increase in the property's basis, greater depreciation deductions can result and there will be less gain (or more loss) on a subsequent sale of the property. The side benefits of increased basis do not materialize if the recipient is a charity, as such organizations generally are not subject to income taxation.

EXAMPLE 48

Carlton makes a gift to Yolanda of passive activity property having an adjusted basis of $40,000, suspended losses of $10,000, and a fair market value at the date of the gift of $100,000. Carlton cannot deduct the suspended losses in the year of the disposition. However, the suspended losses of $10,000 transfer with the property and are added to the adjusted basis of the property, thus becoming $50,000 in Yolanda's hands. Assuming Yolanda is able to sell the property for $105,000 soon after she receives the gift, her taxable gain would be $55,000 ($105,000 − $50,000), which reflects the benefit from the increased basis.

---

[48]§ 469(g)(2).   [49]§ 469(j)(6).

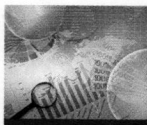

TAX PLANNING STRATEGIES **Utilizing Passive Losses**

FRAMEWORK FOCUS: TAX RATE

Strategy: Control the Character of Income and Deductions.

Perhaps the biggest challenge individuals face with the passive loss rules is to recognize the potential impact of the rules and then to structure their affairs to minimize this impact. Taxpayers who have passive activity losses (PALs) should adopt a strategy of generating passive activity income that can be sheltered by existing passive losses. One approach is to buy an interest in a passive activity that is generating income (referred to as a passive income generator, or PIG). Then the PAL can offset income from the PIG. From a tax perspective, it would be foolish to buy a loss-generating passive activity unless one has passive income to shelter or the activity is rental real estate that can qualify for the $25,000 exception or the exception available to real estate professionals.

If a taxpayer does invest in an activity that produces losses subject to the passive loss rules, the following strategies may help minimize the loss of current deductions:

- If money is borrowed to finance the purchase of a passive activity, the associated interest expense is generally treated as part of any passive loss. Consequently, by using more available (i.e., not borrowed) cash to purchase the passive investment, the investor will need less debt and will incur less interest expense. By incurring less interest expense, a possible suspended passive loss deduction is reduced.

- If the investor does not have sufficient cash readily available for the larger down payment, cash can be obtained by borrowing against the equity in his or her personal residence. The interest expense on such debt will be deductible under the qualified residence interest provisions (see Chapter 10) and will not be subject to the passive loss limitations. Thus, the taxpayer avoids the passive loss limitation and secures a currently deductible interest expense.

As explained earlier, unusable passive losses often accumulate and provide no current tax benefit because the taxpayer has no passive income. When the taxpayer disposes of the entire interest in a passive activity, however, any suspended losses from that activity are used to reduce the taxable gain. If any taxable gain still remains, it can be offset by losses from other passive activities. As a result, the taxpayer should carefully select the year in which to dispose of a passive activity. It is to the taxpayer's advantage to wait until sufficient passive losses have accumulated to offset any gain recognized on the asset's disposition.

EXAMPLE
49

Bill, a calendar year taxpayer, owns interests in two passive activities: Activity A, which he plans to sell in December of this year at a gain of $100,000, and Activity B, which he plans to keep indefinitely. Current and suspended losses associated with Activity B total $60,000, and Bill expects losses from the activity to be $40,000 next year. If Bill sells Activity A this year, the $100,000 gain can be offset by the current and suspended losses of $60,000 from Activity B, producing a net taxable gain of $40,000. However, if Bill delays the sale of Activity A until January of next year, the $100,000 gain will be fully offset by the $100,000 of losses generated by Activity B ($60,000 current and prior losses + $40,000 next year's loss). Consequently, by postponing the sale by one month, he could avoid recognizing $40,000 of gain that would otherwise result.

Taxpayers with passive losses should consider the level of their involvement in all other trades or businesses in which they have an interest. If they show that they do not materially participate in a profitable activity, the activity becomes a passive activity. Current and suspended passive losses then could shelter any income generated by the profitable business. Family partnerships in which certain members do not materially participate would qualify. The silent partner in any general partnership engaged in a trade or business would also qualify.

continued

EXAMPLE 50

Gail has an investment in a limited partnership that produces annual passive losses of approximately $25,000. She also owns a newly acquired interest in a convenience store where she works. Her share of the store's income is $35,000. If she works enough to be classified as a material participant, her $35,000 share of income is treated as active income. This results in $35,000 being subject to tax every year, while her $25,000 loss is suspended. However, if Gail reduces her involvement at the store so that she is not a material participant, the $35,000 of income receives passive treatment. Consequently, the $35,000 of income can be offset by the $25,000 passive loss, resulting in only $10,000 being subject to tax. Thus, by reducing her involvement, Gail ensures that the income from the profitable trade or business receives passive treatment and can then be used to absorb passive losses from other passive activities.

The passive loss rules can have a dramatic effect on a taxpayer's ability to claim passive losses currently. As a result, it is important to keep accurate records of all sources of income and losses, particularly any suspended passive losses and credits and the activities to which they relate, so that their potential tax benefit will not be lost.

The passive activity rules can also affect planning for individuals subject to the Net Investment Income Tax (Chapter 9).

REFOCUS ON THE BIG PICTURE

RECEIVING TAX BENEFITS FROM LOSSES

While Robyn's circumstances were unfortunate, the good news is that she will be able to receive some tax benefits from the losses.

- *Bad debt.* Based on the facts provided, it appears that Robyn's loan to her friend, Jamil, was a bona fide nonbusiness bad debt. The amount of the loss deduction is the unpaid principal balance of $19,000 ($25,000 − $6,000). As a nonbusiness bad debt, the loss is classified as a short-term capital loss (see Example 5).

- *Loss from stock investment.* Likewise, the $60,000 loss on the Owl Corporation stock investment is deductible. If Robyn purchased the stock directly from the company, the stock may qualify as small business stock under § 1244. If this is the case, the first $50,000 of the loss is an ordinary loss and the remaining $10,000 loss is treated as a long-term capital loss. If the stock is not § 1244 stock, the entire $60,000 loss is treated as a long-term capital loss (see Example 8).

- *Loss from bookstore.* The $180,000 loss from the bookstore is reported on Schedule C of Robyn's Form 1040. It is an ordinary loss and qualifies for net operating loss (NOL) treatment if she does not have enough other taxable income this year against which the loss could be offset. Any NOL can be carried back 2 years or carried forward for the next 20 years to produce refunds of taxes paid from prior years or to reduce taxes owed on taxable income earned in the future.

- *Casualty loss.* The loss from the damage to Robyn's personal residence is a personal casualty loss. Using the cost of repairs method, the amount of the casualty loss is $7,000 ($32,000 loss − $25,000 insurance recovery). However, this amount must be reduced by the statutory amount of $100 and 10 percent of AGI (see Example 13).

- *Passive activity loss.* The $20,000 loss on the limited partnership is not deductible currently due to the passive loss limitation. However, the loss can be carried forward and utilized in the future to offset any passive income generated from the venture or other passive activities (see Example 21).

continued

© G. BADEN/FLIRT/CORBIS

What If?

What if instead of operating orange groves, the partnership was a general partnership that owns and rents apartments to college students and Robyn actively participates in the venture? In this case, Robyn may qualify for a $20,000 ordinary loss deduction under the rental real estate with active participation exception.

Suggested Readings

John O. Everett, Cherie J. Hennig, William A. Raabe, and Blaise M. Sonnier, "How Effective Planning Can Increase the Tax Benefits of Corporate NOLs," *Journal of Taxation*, February 2014.

James R. Hamill, "The Section 1411 Surtax and the Real Estate Professional," *Practical Tax Strategies*, March 2014.

William C. Hood, "Deducting Ponzi Losses," *Practical Tax Strategies*, March 2014.

Daniel Rowe, "Activity Grouping: The Impact of Recent Developments," *The Tax Adviser*, February 2013.

John H. Skarbnik, "Real Estate Professionals: Avoiding the Passive Activity Loss Rules," *The Tax Adviser*, July 2014.

Key Terms

Active income, 6-16

Material participation, 6-23

Reserve method, 6-2

At-risk limitation, 6-14

Net operating loss (NOL), 6-11

Significant participation activity, 6-23

Bad debt, 6-2

Nonbusiness bad debt, 6-4

Small business stock (§ 1244 stock), 6-5

Business bad debt, 6-4

Passive loss, 6-14

Specific charge-off method, 6-2

Casualty losses, 6-7

Personal service corporation, 6-20

Tax shelters, 6-13

Closely held C corporation, 6-21

Portfolio income, 6-16

Theft losses, 6-8

Disaster area losses, 6-7

Rental activity, 6-24

Worthless securities, 6-5

Computational Exercises

1. **LO.1** During the past tax year, Jane identified $50,000 as a nonbusiness bad debt. In that tax year, Jane had $100,000 of taxable income, of which $5,000 consisted of short-term capital gains. During the current tax year, Jane collected $10,000 of the amount she had previously identified as a bad debt. Determine Jane's tax treatment of the $10,000 received in the current tax year.

2. **LO.1** Bob owns a collection agency. He purchases uncollected accounts receivable from other businesses at 60% of their face value and then attempts to collect these accounts. During the current year, Bob collected $60,000 on an account with a face value of $80,000. Determine the amount of Bob's bad debt deduction.

3. **LO.2** On May 9, 2013, Calvin acquired 250 shares of stock in Aero Corporation, a new startup company, for $68,750. Calvin acquired the stock directly from Aero, and it is classified as § 1244 stock (at the time Calvin acquired his stock, the corporation had $900,000 of paid-in capital). On January 15, 2015, Calvin sold all of his Aero stock for $7,000. Assuming that Calvin is single, determine his tax consequences as a result of this sale.

4. **LO.3** Mary's diamond ring was stolen in 2014. She originally paid $8,000 for the ring, but it was worth considerably more at the time of the theft. Mary filed an insurance claim for the stolen ring, but the claim was denied. Because the insurance claim was denied, Mary took a casualty loss deduction for the stolen ring on her 2014 tax return. In 2014, Mary had AGI of $40,000. In 2015, the insurance company had a "change of heart" and sent Mary a check for $5,000 for the stolen ring. Determine the proper tax treatment of the $5,000 Mary received from the insurance company in 2015.

5. **LO.3** Determine the treatment of a loss on rental property under the following facts:

Basis	$650,000
FMV before the loss	800,000
FMV after the loss	200,000

6. **LO.6** In the current year, Ed invests $30,000 in an oil partnership. He has taxable income for the current year of $2,000 from the oil partnership and withdraws $10,000. What is Ed's at-risk amount at the end of the year?

7. **LO.6** Lucy sells her partnership interest, a passive activity, with an adjusted basis of $305,000 for $330,000. In addition, she has current and suspended losses of $28,000 associated with the partnership and has no other passive activities. Calculate Lucy's total gain and her current deductible loss. Describe the type of income that the deductible loss may offset.

8. **LO.8** Rhonda has an adjusted basis and an at-risk amount of $7,500 in a passive activity at the beginning of the year. She also has a suspended passive loss of $1,500 carried over from the prior year. During the current year, she has a loss of $12,000 from the passive activity. Rhonda has no passive income from other sources this year. Determine the following items relating to Rhonda's passive activity as of the end of the year.
   a. Adjusted basis and at-risk amount in the passive activity.
   b. Loss suspended under the at-risk rules.
   c. Suspended passive loss.

9. **LO.9** Noah, who has $62,000 of AGI before considering rental activities, has $70,000 of losses from a real estate rental activity in which he actively participates. He also actively participates in another real estate rental activity from which he has $33,000 of income. He has other passive income of $20,000. What amount of rental loss can Noah use to offset active or portfolio income in the current year?

10. **LO.10** Rose dies with passive activity property having an adjusted basis of $65,000, suspended losses of $13,000, and a fair market value at the date of her death of $90,000. Of the $13,000 suspended loss existing at the time of Rose's death, how much is deductible on her final return or by the beneficiary?

Problems

Communications   11. **LO.1** Several years ago, Loon Finance Company, which is in the lending business, loaned Sara $30,000 to purchase an automobile to be used for personal purposes. In August of the current year, Sara filed for bankruptcy, and Loon was notified that it could not expect to receive more than $4,000. As of the end of the current year, Loon has received $1,000. Loon has contacted you about the possibility of taking a bad debt deduction for the current year.

Write a letter to Loon Finance Company that contains your advice as to whether it can claim a bad debt deduction for the current year. Also prepare a memo for the tax files. Loon's address is 100 Tyler Lane, Erie, PA 16563.

12. **LO.1** Monty loaned his friend Ned $20,000 three years ago. Ned signed a note and made payments on the loan. Last year, when the remaining balance was $11,000, Ned filed for bankruptcy and notified Monty that he would be unable to pay the balance on the loan. Monty treated the $11,000 as a nonbusiness bad debt. Last year, Monty had capital gains of $4,000 and taxable income of $20,000. During the current year, Ned paid Monty $10,000 in satisfaction of the debt. Determine Monty's tax treatment for the $10,000 received in the current year.

13. **LO.2** Many years ago, Jack purchased 400 shares of Canary stock. During the current year, the stock became worthless. It was determined that the company "went under" because several corporate officers embezzled a large amount of company funds. Identify the relevant tax issues for Jack.

    Issue ID

14. **LO.1** Jake and Mary Snow are residents of the state of New York. They are cash basis taxpayers and file a joint return for the calendar year. Jake is a licensed master plumber. Two years ago, Jake entered into a contract with New York City to perform plumbing services. During the current year, Jake was declared to be in breach of the contract, and he ceased performing plumbing services. Jake received a Form W–2 that reported $50,000 for wages paid. He also maintains that the city has not paid him $35,000 for work he performed. Jake is considering claiming a $35,000 business bad debt on his tax return. Evaluate Jake's plan.

    Ethics and Equity

15. **LO.1, 2** Mable and Jack file a joint return. For the current year, they had the following items:

Salaries	$120,000
Loss on sale of § 1244 stock acquired two years ago	105,000
Gain on sale of § 1244 stock acquired six months ago	20,000
Nonbusiness bad debt	19,000

    Determine the impact of the above items on Mable and Jack's income for the current year.

16. **LO.2** Mary, a single taxpayer, purchased 10,000 shares of § 1244 stock several years ago at a cost of $20 per share. In November of the current year, Mary receives an offer to sell the stock for $12 per share. She has the option of either selling all of the stock now or selling half of the stock now and half of the stock in January of next year. Mary's salary is $80,000 for the current year, and it will be $90,000 next year. Mary has long-term capital gains of $8,000 for the current year and will have $10,000 next year. If Mary's goal is to minimize her AGI for the two years, determine whether she should sell all of her stock this year or half of her stock this year and half next year.

    Decision Making

17. **LO.3** Olaf lives in the state of Minnesota. A tornado hit the area and damaged his home and automobile. Applicable information is as follows:

    Decision Making

Item	Adjusted Basis	FMV before	FMV after	Insurance Proceeds
Home	$350,000	$500,000	$100,000	$280,000
Auto	60,000	40,000	10,000	20,000

Because of the extensive damage caused by the tornado, the President designated the area a disaster area.

Olaf and his wife, Anna, always file a joint return. Their 2014 tax return shows AGI of $180,000 and taxable income of $140,000. In 2015, their return shows AGI of $300,000 and taxable income (exclusive of the casualty loss deduction) of $215,000.

Determine the amount of Olaf and Anna's loss and the year in which they should take the loss.

Issue ID
18. **LO.3** In 2012, John opened an investment account with Randy Hansen, who held himself out to the public as an investment adviser and securities broker. John contributed $200,000 to the account in 2012. John provided Randy with a power of attorney to use the $200,000 to purchase and sell securities on John's behalf. John instructed Randy to reinvest any gains and income earned. In 2012, 2013, and 2014, John received statements of the amount of income earned by his account and included these amounts in his gross income for these years. In 2015, it was discovered that Randy's purported investment advisory and brokerage activity was in fact a fraudulent investment arrangement known as a Ponzi scheme. In reality, John's account balance was zero, the money having been used by Randy in his scheme. Identify the relevant tax issues for John.

Critical Thinking
19. **LO.4** Mary, a single taxpayer with two dependent children, has the following items of income and expense during 2015:

Gross receipts from business	$144,000
Business expenses	180,000
Alimony received	22,000
Interest income	3,000
Itemized deductions (no casualty or theft)	24,000

   a. Determine Mary's taxable income for 2015.
   b. Determine Mary's NOL for 2015.

20. **LO.6** In 2014, Fred invested $50,000 in a general partnership. Fred's interest is not considered to be a passive activity. If his share of the partnership losses is $35,000 in 2014 and $25,000 in 2015, how much can he deduct in each year?

Communications
21. **LO.6** In the current year, Bill Parker (54 Oak Drive, St. Paul, MN 55164) is considering making an investment of $60,000 in Best Choice Partnership. The prospectus provided by Bill's broker indicates that the partnership investment is not a passive activity and that Bill's share of the entity's loss in the current year will likely be $40,000, while his share of the partnership loss next year will probably be $25,000. Write a letter to Bill in which you indicate how the losses would be treated for tax purposes in the current year and the following year.

22. **LO.6** A number of years ago, Kay acquired an interest in a partnership in which she is not a material participant. Kay's basis in her partnership interest at the beginning of 2014 is $40,000. Kay's share of the partnership loss is $35,000 in 2014, while her share of the partnership income is $15,000 in 2015. How much may Kay deduct in 2014 and 2015, assuming she owns no other passive activities?

Decision Making
23. **LO.6** Jorge owns two passive investments, Activity A and Activity B. He plans to dispose of Activity A in the current year or next year. Juanita has offered to buy Activity A this year for an amount that would produce a taxable passive gain to Jorge of $115,000. However, if the sale, for whatever reason, is not made to Juanita, Jorge believes that he could find a buyer who would pay about $7,000 less than Juanita. Passive losses and gains generated (and expected to be generated) by Activity B follow:

Two years ago	($35,000)
Last year	(35,000)
This year	(8,000)
Next year	(30,000)
Future years	Minimal profits

All of Activity B's losses are suspended. Should Jorge close the sale of Activity A with Juanita this year, or should he wait until next year and sell to another buyer? Jorge is in the 28% tax bracket.

24. **LO.6** Sarah has investments in four passive activity partnerships purchased several years ago. Last year, the income and losses were as follows:

Activity	Income (Loss)
A	$ 30,000
B	(30,000)
C	(15,000)
D	(5,000)

In the current year, she sold her interest in Activity D for a $10,000 gain. Activity D, which had been profitable until last year, had a current loss of $1,500. How will the sale of Activity D affect Sarah's taxable income in the current year?

25. **LO.6** Leon sells his interest in a passive activity for $100,000. Determine the tax effect of the sale based on each of the following independent facts:

a. Adjusted basis in this investment is $35,000. Losses from prior years that were not deductible due to the passive loss restrictions total $40,000.

b. Adjusted basis in this investment is $75,000. Losses from prior years that were not deductible due to the passive loss restrictions total $40,000.

c. Adjusted basis in this investment is $75,000. Losses from prior years that were not deductible due to the passive loss restrictions total $40,000. In addition, suspended credits total $10,000.

26. **LO.6** In the current year, White, Inc., earns $400,000 from operations and receives $36,000 in dividends and interest from various portfolio investments. White also pays $150,000 to acquire a 20% interest in a passive activity that produces a $200,000 loss.

a. Assuming that White is a personal service corporation, how will these transactions affect its taxable income?

b. Same as (a), except that White is closely held but not a personal service corporation.

27. **LO.7** John, an engineer, operates a separate business that he acquired eight years ago. If he participates 85 hours in the business and it incurs a loss of $34,000, under what circumstances can John claim an active loss?

28. **LO.7** Rene retired from public accounting after a long and successful career of 45 years. As part of her retirement package, she continues to share in the profits and losses of the firm, albeit at a lower rate than when she was working full-time. Because Rene wants to stay busy during her retirement years, she has invested and works in a local hardware business, operated as a partnership. Unfortunately, the business has recently gone through a slump and has not been generating profits. Identify relevant tax issues for Rene.

Issue ID

29. **LO.6, 8** Kristin Graf (123 Baskerville Mill Road, Jamison, PA 18929) is trying to decide how to invest a $10,000 inheritance. One option is to make an additional investment in Rocky Road Excursions in which she has an at-risk basis of $0, suspended losses under the at-risk rules of $7,000, and suspended passive losses of $1,000. If Kristin makes this investment, her share of the expected profits this year will be $8,000. If her investment stays the same, her share of profits from Rocky Road Excursions will be $1,000. Another option is to invest $10,000 as a limited partner in the Ragged Mountain Winery; this investment will produce passive income of $9,000. Write a letter to Kristin to review the tax consequences of each alternative. Kristin is in the 28% tax bracket.

Decision Making

Communications

30. **LO.8** The end of the year is approaching, and Maxine has begun to focus on ways of minimizing her income tax liability. Several years ago, she purchased an

Decision Making

investment in Teal Limited Partnership, which is subject to the at-risk and the passive activity loss rules. (Last year, Maxine sold a different investment that was subject to these rules and that produced passive income.) She believes that her investment in Teal has good long-term economic prospects. However, it has been generating tax losses for several years in a row. In fact, when she was discussing last year's income tax return with her tax accountant, he said that unless "things change" with respect to her investments, she would not be able to deduct losses this year.

a. What was the accountant referring to in his comment?

b. You learn that Maxine's current at-risk basis in her investment is $1,000 and that her share of the current loss is expected to be $13,000. Based on these facts, how will her loss be treated?

c. After reviewing her situation, Maxine's financial adviser suggests that she invest at least an additional $12,000 in Teal to ensure a full loss deduction in the current year. How do you react to his suggestion?

d. What would you suggest Maxine consider as she attempts to maximize her current-year deductible loss?

31. **LO.8** A number of years ago, Lee acquired a 20% interest in the BlueSky Partnership for $60,000. The partnership was profitable through 2014, and Lee's amount at risk in the partnership interest was $120,000 at the beginning of 2015. BlueSky incurred a loss of $400,000 in 2015 and reported income of $200,000 in 2016. Assuming that Lee is not a material participant, how much of his loss from BlueSky Partnership is deductible in 2015 and 2016? Consider the at-risk and passive loss rules, and assume Lee owns no other investments.

32. **LO.6** Grace acquired an activity four years ago. The loss from the activity is $50,000 in the current year (at-risk basis of $40,000 as of the beginning of the year). Without considering the loss from the activity, she has gross income of $140,000. If the activity is a convenience store and Grace is a material participant, what is the effect of the activity on her taxable income?

33. **LO.5, 6, 8** Jonathan, a physician, earns $200,000 from his practice. He also receives $18,000 in dividends and interest from various portfolio investments. During the year, he pays $45,000 to acquire a 20% interest in a partnership that produces a $300,000 loss. Compute Jonathan's AGI assuming that:

a. He does not participate in the operations of the partnership.

b. He is a material participant in the operations of the partnership.

34. **LO.5, 6, 8** Five years ago, Gerald invested $150,000 in a passive activity, his sole investment venture. On January 1, 2014, his amount at risk in the activity was $30,000. His shares of the income and losses were as follows:

Year	Income (Loss)
2014	($40,000)
2015	(30,000)
2016	50,000

Gerald holds no suspended at-risk or passive losses at the beginning of 2014. How much can Gerald deduct in 2014 and 2015? What is his taxable income from the activity in 2016? Consider the at-risk rules as well as the passive loss rules.

Ethics and Equity

Communications

35. **LO.5, 6, 7** You have just met with Scott Myers (603 Pittsfield Drive, Champaign, IL 61821), a successful full-time real estate developer and investor. During your meeting, you discussed his tax situation because you are starting to prepare his current Federal income tax return. During your meeting, Scott mentioned that he and his wife, Susan, went to great lengths to maximize their participation in an apartment complex that they own and manage. In particular, Scott included the following activities in the 540 hours of participation for the current year:

- Time spent thinking about the rentals.
- Time spent by Susan on weekdays visiting the apartment complex to oversee operations of the buildings (i.e., in a management role).
- Time spent by both Scott and Susan on weekends visiting the apartment complex to assess operations. Scott and Susan always visited the complex together on weekends, and both counted their hours (i.e., one hour at the complex was two hours of participation).
- Time spent on weekends driving around the community looking for other potential rental properties to purchase. Again, both Scott's hours and Susan's hours were counted, even when they drove together.

After reviewing Scott's records, you note that the apartment complex generated a significant loss this year. Prepare a letter to Scott describing your position on the deductibility of the loss.

36. **LO.6, 9** Bonnie and Jake (ages 35 and 36, respectively) are married with no dependents and live in Montana (not a community property state). Because Jake has large medical expenses, they seek your advice about filing separately to save taxes. Their income and expenses for 2015 are as follows:

Decision Making

Bonnie's salary	$ 42,500
Jake's salary	26,000
Interest income (joint)	1,500
Rental loss from actively managed rental property	(23,000)
Jake's unreimbursed medical expenses	8,500
All other itemized deductions:*	
Bonnie	9,000
Jake	3,400

*None subject to limitations.

Determine whether Bonnie and Jake should file jointly or separately for 2015.

37. **LO.9** During the current year, Gene, a CPA, performs services as follows: 1,800 hours in his tax practice and 50 hours in an apartment leasing operation in which he has a 15% interest. Because of his oversight duties, Gene is considered to be an active participant. He expects that his share of the loss realized from the apartment leasing operation will be $30,000 and that his tax practice will show a profit of approximately $80,000. Gene is single and has no other income. Discuss the character and treatment of the income and losses generated by these activities.

38. **LO.9** Ida, who has AGI of $80,000 before considering rental activities, is active in three separate real estate rental activities. Ida has a marginal tax rate of 28%. She has $12,000 of losses from Activity A, $18,000 of losses from Activity B, and income of $10,000 from Activity C. She also has $2,100 of tax credits from Activity A. Calculate the deductions and credits that she is allowed and the suspended losses and credits.

39. **LO.9** Ella has $105,000 of losses from a real estate rental activity in which she actively participates. She has other rent income of $25,000 and other passive income of $32,000. Her AGI before considering these items of income and loss is $95,000. How much rental loss can Ella deduct against active and portfolio income (ignoring the at-risk rules)? Does she have any suspended losses to carry over? Explain.

40. **LO.5, 6, 10** In the current year, Abe gives an interest in a passive activity to his daughter, Andrea. The value of the interest at the date of the gift is $25,000, and its adjusted basis to Abe is $13,000. During the time that Abe owned the investment, losses of $3,000 could not be deducted because of the passive loss limitations. What is the tax treatment of the suspended passive activity losses to Abe and Andrea?

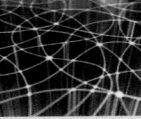

BRIDGE DISCIPLINE

1. Marketplace, Inc., has recognized over time that a certain percentage of its customer accounts receivable will not be collected. To ensure the appropriate matching of revenues and expenditures in its financial reports, Marketplace uses the reserve method for bad debts. Records show the following pertaining to its treatment of bad debts.

Beginning allowance for bad debts	$120,000
Ending allowance for bad debts	123,000
Bad debts written off during the year	33,000

   a. What was the bad debt expense for financial accounting purposes during the year?

   b. What was the bad debt expense for income tax purposes during the year?

   c. Assuming that the before-tax net income for financial accounting purposes was $545,000, what is the taxable income for the year if the treatment of bad debts is the only book-tax difference?

Decision Making 2. Heather wants to invest $40,000 in a relatively safe venture and has discovered two alternatives that would produce the following ordinary income and loss over the next three years:

Year	Alternative 1 Income (Loss)	Alternative 2 Income (Loss)
1	($20,000)	($48,000)
2	(28,000)	32,000
3	72,000	40,000

   She is interested in the after-tax effects of these alternatives over a three-year horizon. Assume that:

   - Heather's investment portfolio produces sufficient passive income to offset any potential passive loss that may arise from these alternatives.

   - Heather's marginal tax rate is 25% and her cost of capital is 6% (the present value factors are .9434, .8900, and .8396).

   - Each investment alternative possesses equal growth potential and comparable financial risk.

   - In the loss years for each alternative, there is no cash flow from or to the investment (i.e., the loss is due to depreciation), while in those years when the income is positive, cash flows to Heather equal the amount of the income.

   Based on these facts, compute the present value of these two investment alternatives and determine which option Heather should choose.

Decision Making 3. Emily has $100,000 that she wants to invest and is considering the following two options:

   - Option A: Investment in Redbird Mutual Fund, which is expected to produce interest income of $8,000 per year.

- Option B: Investment in Cardinal Limited Partnership (buys, sells, and operates wine vineyards). Emily's share of the partnership's ordinary income and loss over the next three years would be as follows:

Year	Income (Loss)
1	($ 8,000)
2	(2,000)
3	34,000

Emily is interested in the after-tax effects of these alternatives over a three-year horizon. Assume that Emily's investment portfolio produces ample passive income to offset any passive losses that may be generated. Her cost of capital is 8% (the present value factors are .92593, .85734, and .79383), and she is in the 28% tax bracket. The two investment alternatives possess equal growth potential and comparable financial risk. Based on these facts, compute the present value of these two investment alternatives and determine which option Emily should choose.

Research Problems

Note: Solutions to Research Problems can be prepared by using the Checkpoint® Student Edition online research product, which is available to accompany this text. It is also possible to prepare solutions to the Research Problems by using tax research materials found in a standard tax library.

THOMSON REUTERS
CHECKPOINT®
Student Edition

Research Problem 1. Esther owns a large home on the East Coast. Her home is surrounded by large, mature oak trees that significantly increase the value of her home. In August 2014, a hurricane damaged many of the trees surrounding her home. In September 2014, Esther engaged a local arborist to evaluate and treat the trees, but five of the largest trees were seriously weakened by the storm. These trees died from disease in 2015. Esther has ascertained that the amount of the casualty loss from the death of the five trees is $25,000; however, she is uncertain in which year to deduct this loss. Discuss whether the casualty loss should be deducted in the calculation of Esther's 2014 or 2015 taxable income.

Partials list of research aids:
Reg. § 1.165–1.
Oregon Mesabi Corporation, 39 B.T.A. 1033 (1939).

Research Problem 2. Five years ago, Bridget decided to purchase a limited partnership interest in a fast-food restaurant conveniently located near the campus of Southeast State University. The general partner of the restaurant venture promised her that the investment would prove to be a winner. During the process of capitalizing the business, $2 million was borrowed from Northside Bank; however, each of the partners was required to pledge personal assets as collateral to satisfy the bank loan in the event that the restaurant defaulted. Bridget pledged shares of publicly traded stock (worth $200,000, basis of $75,000) to satisfy the bank's requirement.

The restaurant did a good business until just recently, when flagrant health code violations were discovered and widely publicized by the media. As a result, business has declined to a point where the restaurant's continued existence is doubtful. In addition, the $2 million loan is now due for payment. Because the restaurant cannot pay, the bank has called for the collateral provided by the partners to be used to satisfy the debt. Bridget sells the pledged stock for $200,000 and forwards the proceeds to the bank. Bridget believes that her share of the restaurant's current and suspended passive losses can offset the $125,000 gain from the stock sale. As a result, after netting the passive losses against the gain, none of the gain is subject to tax.

How do you react to Bridget's position?

Research Problem 3. During 2015, John was the chief executive officer and a shareholder of Maze, Inc. He owned 60% of the outstanding stock of Maze. In 2012, John and Maze, as co-borrowers, obtained a $100,000 loan from United National Bank. This loan was secured by John's personal residence. Although Maze was listed as a co-borrower, John repaid the loan in full in 2015. On Maze's Form 1120 tax returns, no loans from shareholders were reported. Discuss whether John is entitled to a bad debt deduction for the amount of the payment on the loan.

Partial list of research aids:
U.S. v. Generes, 405 U.S. 93 (1972).
Dale H. Sundby, T.C.Memo. 2003–204.
Arrigoni v. Comm., 73 T.C. 792 (1980).
Estate of Herbert M. Rapoport, T.C.Memo. 1982–584.
Clifford L. Brody and Barbara J. DeClerk, T.C. Summary Opinion, 2004–149.

Internet
Activity

Use the tax resources of the Internet to address the following questions. Do not restrict your search to the Web, but include a review of newsgroups and general reference materials, practitioner sites and resources, primary sources of the tax law, chat rooms and discussion groups, and other opportunities.

Research Problem 4. Find a newspaper article that discusses tax planning for casualty losses when a disaster area designation is made. Does the article convey the pertinent tax rules correctly? Then list all of the locations identified by the President as Federal disaster areas in the last two years.

Research Problem 5. Investment advisers and tax professionals are continuously striving to create sophisticated transactions and investment vehicles (i.e., tax-advantaged investments) that are designed to provide economic benefits to investors by reducing their taxes. These professionals might like to patent such schemes. Identify whether patenting a tax shelter is a legal possibility.

Roger CPA Review Questions

1. Glenn and Mary's house was damaged by a hurricane in 20X4. The fair value of their home before the hurricane was $150,000. After the hurricane, the fair value of their home was $125,000. They received $10,000 from their homeowner's insurance policy. What is their casualty loss deduction for 20X4, if their adjusted gross income was $40,000?

   a. $10,900   c. $14,900
   b. $11,000   d. $15,000

2. Hank's home is burglarized on December 22, 20X14. Personal property with a fair market value of $40,000 and an adjusted basis to Hank of $25,000 is stolen. Hank paid an independent appraiser $700 on December 29 to determine the fair market value of the property at the time of the break-in. Hank's homeowner's insurance policy leads him to believe he is entitled to receive $15,000 in reimbursement for the event, but no settlement has been made with the insurance company by year-end. Hank's AGI in 20X14 is $30,000. How much may Hank deduct from AGI as a result of these facts on his 20X14 tax return? Assume Hank itemizes and assume there has still been no settlement with the insurance company at the time of filing.

   a. $7,000   c. $6,900
   b. $21,900   d. $22,000

3. On the night of October 14, 20X14, a hurricane caused serious damage to Paige's personal vehicle and to the roof of her personal residence, a townhome. Just prior to the hurricane, Paige had a $200,000 basis in her home and a $12,000 basis in her vehicle, which had a fair market value just prior to the hurricane of $10,000. The damage to the roof is appraised at $7,000, and the fair market value of the vehicle immediately after the hurricane is appraised at $5,000. Paige is uninsured and has a 20X14 AGI of $40,000. What amount of casualty loss deduction may Paige claim on her 20X14 tax return as a result of the hurricane?

    a. $9,800
    b. $7,900
    c. $9,900
    d. $7,800

4. In 20X14, Adams, an individual, changed residences and converted her former residence into a passive rental activity. In 20X14, Adams lived in the former residence for 60 days; incurred $7,000 in qualifying expenses preparing the property for rental; and rented it to a tenant for 90 days, receiving $3,000 in rent. Before considering the rental activity, Adams's adjusted gross income for 20X14 is $120,000. After considering the rental activity, what should Adams's 20X14 adjusted gross income be?

    a. $120,000
    b. $116,000
    c. $118,500
    d. $123,000

5. Lee, a married individual, is an employee with three rental properties in which Lee does not actively participate. In 20X14, Property 1 had a net loss of $10,000, Property 2 had a net gain of $25,000, and Property 3 had a net loss of $5,000. Lee's W-2 income in 20X14 was $110,000. Considering only the foregoing facts, what is Lee's 20X14 adjusted gross income?

    a. $120,000
    b. $125,000
    c. $110,000
    d. $135,000

6. Anscomb is an employee who also solely owns and actively participates in a rental activity which produced a $20,000 loss in the current year. Anscomb's W-2 income in the current year is $115,000. Considering only the foregoing facts, what should Anscomb's adjusted gross income be for the current year?

    a. $97,500
    b. $115,000
    c. $107,500
    d. $102,500

7. Lewis is not an active participant in three rental activities which have turned profits in recent years. The following profit and losses apply to the current year for Lewis:

	Gain or (Loss)
Rental Activity 1	($10,000)
Rental Activity 2	12,000
Rental Activity 3	(8,000)
Total	($ 6,000)

    What amount of the suspended loss should Lewis allocate to Rental Activity 3?

    a. $4,500
    b. $2,667
    c. $0
    d. Suspended losses may be allocated according to the taxpayer's preference

8. Smith bought a rental property in Year 1 for $100,000. In Year 1, Smith's Adjusted Gross Income (AGI) was $125,000, and Smith sustained a $30,000 loss on the property. In Year 2, Smith's AGI was $175,000, and Smith sustained a $20,000 loss on the property. In Year 3, Smith sold the property for $155,000. What amount of gain or loss must Smith report on Smith's Year 3 tax return as a result of the sale? Assume

Smith actively participated in the rental activity in all three years but is not considered a real estate professional for tax purposes.

a. $17,500 gain   c. $22,500 gain

b. $0 (no gain or loss)   d. $20,000 gain

9. Patel bought a rental property in Year 1 for $150,000. In Year 1, Patel's Adjusted Gross Income (AGI) was $100,000, and Patel sustained a $15,000 loss on the property. In Year 2, Patel's AGI was $140,000, and Patel sustained a $10,000 loss on the property. In Year 3, Patel sold the property for $175,000. What amount of gain or loss must Patel report on Patel's Year 3 tax return as a result of the sale? Assume Patel did not actively participate in the rental activity in any of the three years.

a. $25,000   c. $5,000

b. $0 (no income or loss)   d. $20,000

10. The following chart applies to Bettelli, an investor who owns two rental activities, Property A and Property B, and has no other involvement in passive activities:

	Property	Income (Loss)
Year 1	A	($12,000)
	B	5,000
Year 2	A	(6,000)
	B	1,000

Bettelli met the requirements for active participation in Year 1 but not in Year 2. Bettelli's AGI in Year 1 was $140,000; in Year 2, $180,000.

In Year 3, Bettelli sells Property A for a $15,000 gain. How much of the gain must Bettelli report on Bettelli's Year 3 tax return?

a. $0   c. $8,000

b. $3,000   d. $13,000

PART 3

PROPERTY TRANSACTIONS

CHAPTER **7**

Property Transactions: Basis, Gain and Loss, and Nontaxable Exchanges

CHAPTER **8**

Property Transactions: Capital Gains and Losses, Section 1231, and Recapture Provisions

Part 3 presents the tax treatment of sales, exchanges, and other dispositions of property. Topics discussed include the determination of the realized gain or loss, recognized gain or loss, and the classification of the recognized gain or loss as capital or ordinary. The topic of basis is evaluated both in terms of its effect on the calculation of the gain or loss and in terms of the determination of the basis of any contemporaneous or related subsequent acquisitions of property.

Property Transactions: Basis, Gain and Loss, and Nontaxable Exchanges

LEARNING OBJECTIVES: *After completing Chapter 7, you should be able to:*

LO.1 State and explain the computation of realized gain or loss on property dispositions.

LO.2 Distinguish between realized and recognized gain or loss.

LO.3 Understand and illustrate how basis is determined for various methods of asset acquisition.

LO.4 Describe various loss disallowance provisions.

LO.5 Apply the nonrecognition provisions and basis determination rules for like-kind exchanges.

LO.6 Explain the nonrecognition provisions available on the involuntary conversion of property.

LO.7 Identify other nonrecognition provisions contained in the Code.

CHAPTER OUTLINE

TAX TALK *To base all of your decisions on tax consequences is not necessarily to maintain the proper balance and perspective on what you are doing.* —BARBER CONABLE

CALCULATING BASIS AND RECOGNIZED GAIN FOR PROPERTY TRANSACTIONS

Alice owns land that she received from her father 10 years ago as a gift. The land was purchased by her father in 1992 for $2,000 and was worth $10,000 at the time of the gift. Alice's father did not owe gift taxes upon making the transfer. The property is currently worth about $50,000. Alice is considering selling the land and purchasing a piece of undeveloped property in the mountains.

Alice also owns 500 shares of AppleCo stock, 300 of which were acquired as an inheritance when her grandfather died in 1996. Alice's grandfather paid $12,000 for the shares, and the shares were worth $30,000 at the time of his death. The other 200 shares of AppleCo were purchased by Alice two months ago for $28,000. The stock is currently worth $120 per share, and Alice is considering selling the shares.

In addition, Alice owns a house that she inherited from her grandmother two years ago. Her grandmother lived in the house for over 50 years. Alice has many fond memories associated with the house because she spent many summer vacations there, and she has been reluctant to sell the house. However, a developer has recently purchased several homes in the area and has offered Alice $600,000 for the property. Based on the estate tax return, the fair market value of the house at the date of her grandmother's death was $475,000. According to her grandmother's attorney, her grandmother's basis for the house was $275,000. Alice is considering selling the house. She expects any selling expenses to be minimal because she already has identified a buyer for the property.

The building Alice used in her business was destroyed by a fire on October 5, 2015. Fortunately, the building (adjusted basis of $50,000) was insured and on November 17, 2015, she receives an insurance reimbursement of $100,000 for the loss. Alice intends to invest $80,000 in a new building and use the other $20,000 of insurance proceeds to pay off credit card debt.

Alice has come to you for tax advice with respect to the property she owns. What is the recognized gain or loss for the land, stock, and house if they are sold? What tax consequences arise with respect to the involuntary conversion of her business building? Can Alice avoid paying taxes on any of the sales? Alice's objectives are to minimize the recognition of any realized gain and to maximize the recognition of any realized loss.

Read the chapter and formulate your response.

This chapter and the following chapter explain the income tax consequences of property transactions, including the sale or other disposition of property. To begin with, the following questions are considered:

- Is there a realized gain or loss?
- If so, is that gain or loss recognized for tax purposes?
- If that gain or loss is recognized, is it ordinary or capital?
- What is the basis of any replacement property that is acquired?

This chapter discusses the determination of realized and recognized gain or loss and the basis of property. The next chapter covers the classification of recognized gain or loss as ordinary or capital.

For the most part, the rules discussed in Chapters 7 and 8 apply to all types of taxpayers. Individuals, partnerships, closely held corporations, limited liability companies, and publicly held corporations all own assets for use in business activities or as investments in entities that themselves conduct business activities. Individuals, however, are unique among taxpayers because they also own assets that are used in daily life and have no significant business or investment component. Because of that possibility, some property transaction concepts may apply somewhat differently to individual taxpayers. Thus, the material that follows pertains to taxpayers generally, except where otherwise noted.

7-1 DETERMINATION OF GAIN OR LOSS

To determine the tax consequences of a property transaction, the taxpayer must first determine the amount of gain or loss realized.

7-1a Realized Gain or Loss

LO.1

State and explain the computation of realized gain or loss on property dispositions.

For tax purposes, gain or loss is the difference between the *amount realized* from the sale or other disposition of property and the property's *adjusted basis* on the date of disposition. If the amount realized exceeds the property's adjusted basis, the result is a realized gain. Conversely, if the property's adjusted basis exceeds the amount realized, the result is a realized loss.[1]

Lavender, Inc., sells Swan Corporation stock with an adjusted basis of $3,000 for $5,000. Lavender's realized gain is $2,000. If Lavender had sold the stock for $2,000, it would have had a realized loss of $1,000.

Sale or Other Disposition

The term *sale or other disposition* is defined broadly to include virtually any disposition of property. Thus, trade-ins, casualties, condemnations, thefts, and bond retirements are all treated as dispositions of property. The most common disposition of property is a sale or an exchange. Usually, the key factor in determining whether a disposition has taken place is whether an identifiable event has occurred[2] as opposed to a mere fluctuation in the value of the property.[3]

Heron & Associates owns Tan Corporation stock that cost $3,000. The stock has appreciated in value by $2,000 since Heron purchased it. Heron has no realized gain because mere fluctuation in value is not a disposition or an identifiable event for tax purposes. Nor would Heron have a realized loss had the stock declined in value.

---

[1]§ 1001(a) and Reg. § 1.1001–1(a).
[2]Reg. § 1.1001–1(c)(1).

[3]*Lynch v. Turrish*, 1 USTC ¶18, 3 AFTR 2986, 38 S.Ct. 537 (USSC, 1918).

Amount Realized

The amount realized from a sale or other disposition of property is the sum of any money received plus the fair market value of other property received. The amount realized also includes any real property taxes treated as imposed on the seller that are actually paid by the buyer.[4] The reason for including these taxes in the amount realized is that by paying the taxes, the purchaser is, in effect, paying an additional amount to the seller for the property.

The amount realized also includes any liability on the property disposed of, such as a mortgage debt, if the buyer assumes the mortgage or the property is sold subject to the mortgage.[5] The amount of the liability is included in the amount realized, even if the debt is nonrecourse and even if the amount of the debt is greater than the fair market value of the mortgaged property.[6]

EXAMPLE 3

Bunting & Co. sells property to Orange, Inc., for $50,000 cash. There is a $20,000 mortgage on the property. Bunting's amount realized from the sale is $70,000 if Orange assumes the mortgage or takes the property subject to the mortgage.

The fair market value of property received in a sale or other disposition has been defined by the courts as the price at which the property will change hands between a willing seller and a willing buyer when neither is compelled to sell or buy.[7] Fair market value is determined by considering the relevant factors in each case.[8] An expert appraiser is often required to evaluate these factors in arriving at fair market value. When the fair market value of the property received cannot be determined, the value of the property given up by the taxpayer may be used.[9]

In calculating the amount realized, selling expenses (such as advertising, commissions, and legal fees) relating to the disposition are deducted. The amount realized is the net amount the taxpayer received directly or indirectly, in the form of cash or anything else of value, from the disposition of the property.

Adjusted Basis

The adjusted basis of property disposed of is the property's original basis adjusted to the date of disposition.[10] Original basis is the cost or other basis of the property on the date the property is acquired by the taxpayer. Considerations involving original basis are discussed later in this chapter. *Capital additions* increase and *recoveries of capital* decrease the original basis so that on the date of disposition, the adjusted basis reflects the unrecovered cost or other basis of the property.[11] Adjusted basis is determined as follows:

Cost (or other adjusted basis) on date of acquisition
+ Capital additions
− Capital recoveries
= Adjusted basis on date of disposition

Capital Additions

Capital additions include the cost of capital improvements and betterments made to the property by the taxpayer. These expenditures are distinguishable from expenditures for the ordinary repair and maintenance of the property, which are neither capitalized nor added to the original basis (refer to Chapter 5). The latter expenditures are deductible in

---

[4]§ 1001(b) and Reg. § 1.1001–1(b). Refer to Example 32 in Chapter 5 for a discussion of this subject.

[5]*Crane v. Comm.*, 47–1 USTC ¶9217, 35 AFTR 776, 67 S.Ct. 1047 (USSC, 1947). Although a legal distinction exists between the direct assumption of a mortgage and the taking of property subject to a mortgage, the tax consequences in calculating the amount realized are the same.

[6]*Comm. v. Tufts*, 83–1 USTC ¶9328, 51 AFTR 2d 83–1132, 103 S.Ct. 1826 (USSC, 1983).

[7]*Comm. v. Marshman*, 60–2 USTC ¶9484, 5 AFTR 2d 1528, 279 F.2d 27 (CA–6, 1960).

[8]*O'Malley v. Ames*, 52–1 USTC ¶9361, 42 AFTR 19, 197 F.2d 256 (CA–8, 1952).

[9]*U.S. v. Davis*, 62–2 USTC ¶9509, 9 AFTR 2d 1625, 82 S.Ct. 1190 (USSC, 1962).

[10]§ 1011(a) and Reg. § 1.1011–1.

[11]§ 1016(a) and Reg. § 1.1016–1.

the current taxable year if they are related to business or income-producing property. Amounts representing real property taxes treated as imposed on the seller but paid or assumed by the buyer are part of the cost of the property.[12] Any liability on property that is assumed by the buyer is also included in the buyer's original basis of the property. The same rule applies if property is acquired subject to a liability. In a similar fashion, amortization of the discount on bonds increases the adjusted basis of the bonds.[13]

Bluebird Corporation purchased some manufacturing equipment for $25,000. Whether Bluebird uses $25,000 from the business's cash account to pay for this equipment or uses $5,000 from that account and borrows the remaining $20,000, the basis of this equipment will be the same—namely, $25,000. Moreover, it does not matter whether Bluebird borrowed the $20,000 from the equipment's manufacturer, from a local bank, or from any other lender.

Capital Recoveries

Capital recoveries decrease the adjusted basis of property. The prominent types of capital recoveries are discussed below.

Depreciation and Cost Recovery Allowances The original basis of depreciable property is reduced by the annual depreciation charges (or cost recovery allowances) while the property is held by the taxpayer. The amount of depreciation that is subtracted from the original basis is the greater of the *allowed* or *allowable* depreciation calculated on an annual basis.[14] In most circumstances, the allowed and allowable depreciation amounts are the same (refer to Chapter 5).

Casualties and Thefts A casualty or theft may result in the reduction of the adjusted basis of property.[15] The adjusted basis is reduced by the amount of the deductible loss. In addition, the adjusted basis is reduced by the amount of insurance proceeds received. However, the receipt of insurance proceeds may result in a recognized gain rather than a deductible loss. The gain increases the adjusted basis of the property.[16]

Capital Recoveries: Casualties and Thefts

An insured truck owned by Falcon Corporation is destroyed in an accident. At the time of the accident, the adjusted basis was $8,000, and the fair market value was $6,500. Falcon receives insurance proceeds of $6,500.

The amount of the casualty *loss* is $1,500 ($6,500 insurance insurance proceeds − $8,000 adjusted basis). The truck's adjusted basis becomes $0 ($8,000 pre-accident adjusted basis − $1,500 casualty loss − $6,500 of insurance proceeds received).

Osprey, Inc., owned an insured truck that was destroyed in an accident. At the time of the accident, the adjusted basis and fair market value of the truck were $6,500 and $8,000, respectively. Osprey receives insurance proceeds of $8,000.

The amount of the casualty *gain* is $1,500 ($8,000 insurance proceeds − $6,500 adjusted basis). The truck's adjusted basis is increased by the $1,500 casualty gain and is reduced by the $8,000 of insurance proceeds received ($6,500 basis before casualty + $1,500 casualty gain − $8,000 insurance proceeds = $0 ending adjusted basis).

---

[12]Reg. §§ 1.1001–1(b)(2) and 1.1012–1(b). Refer to Chapter 5 for a discussion of this subject.

[13]See Chapter 4 for a discussion of bond discount and the related amortization.

[14]§ 1016(a)(2) and Reg. § 1.1016–3(a)(1)(i).

[15]Refer to Chapter 6 for the discussion of casualties and thefts.

[16]Reg. § 1.1016–6(a).

BRIDGE DISCIPLINE **Bridge to Financial Accounting**

Certain property transactions discussed later in this chapter are treated differently for tax purposes than for financial accounting purposes. For example, the category of transactions generally referred to as "nontaxable exchanges," such as like-kind exchanges and involuntary conversions, gives taxpayers the opportunity to defer the recognition of gain on the disposition of property in qualifying transactions. The gains or losses deferred under tax law, however, are not deferred for financial reporting purposes. Instead, the actual gain or loss realized is reflected in the entity's financial reports.

Identifying and calculating the book-tax differences that arise from *taxable* dispositions of certain other property may not be so easy. For example, as discussed in Chapter 5, cost

recovery (i.e., depreciation) rules provided by the tax law specify various ways in which an asset's cost may be recovered over time. These methods often differ from the methods used to depreciate an asset for book purposes. Consequently, the annual book-tax differences in these depreciation expense calculations are noted in the financial reports. But in addition, these cumulative differences, as reflected in the accumulated depreciation account, will also produce a book-tax difference on the asset's disposition. That is, because an asset's accumulated depreciation may differ for book and tax purposes, its adjusted basis will also differ. Consequently, when the asset is sold, the amount of gain or loss for book purposes will differ from that recognized for tax purposes.

Certain Corporate Distributions A corporate distribution to a shareholder that is not taxable is treated as a return of capital, and it reduces the basis of the shareholder's stock in the corporation.[17] Once the basis of the stock is reduced to zero, the amount of any subsequent distributions is a capital gain if the stock in the hands of the shareholder is a capital asset. See Chapter 13.

Amortizable Bond Premium The basis in a bond purchased at a premium is reduced by the amortizable portion of the bond premium.[18] Investors in taxable bonds may *elect* to amortize the bond premium.[19] The amount of the amortized premium on taxable bonds is allowed as an interest deduction. Therefore, the election enables the taxpayer to take an annual interest deduction to offset ordinary income in exchange for a larger capital gain or smaller capital loss on the disposition of the bond (due to the basis reduction).

In-depth coverage can be found on this book's companion website: **www.cengagebrain.com**   **1 DIGGING DEEPER**

In contrast to the treatment of taxable bonds, the premium on tax-exempt bonds *must* be amortized, and no interest deduction is permitted. Furthermore, the basis of tax-exempt bonds is reduced even though the amortization is not allowed as a deduction. No amortization deduction is permitted on tax-exempt bonds because the interest income is exempt from tax, and the amortization of the bond premium merely represents an adjustment of the effective amount of such income.

EXAMPLE 7

Navy, Inc., purchases Eagle Corporation taxable bonds with a face value of $100,000 for $110,000, thus paying a premium of $10,000. The annual interest rate is 7%, and the bonds mature 10 years from the date of purchase. The annual interest income is $7,000 (7% × $100,000).

If Navy elects to amortize the bond premium, the $10,000 premium is deducted over the 10-year period. Navy's basis for the bonds is reduced each year by the amount of the amortization deduction.

If the bonds were tax-exempt, amortization of the bond premium and the basis adjustment would be mandatory and no deduction would be allowed for the amortization.

---

[17]§ 1016(a)(4) and Reg. § 1.1016–5(a).
[18]§ 1016(a)(5) and Reg. § 1.1016–5(b). The accounting treatment of bond premium amortization is the same as for tax purposes. The amortization results in a decrease in the bond investment account.

[19]§ 171(c).

TAX IN THE NEWS   Tax Implications of Virtual Currency (Bitcoin)

On March 25, 2014, the Internal Revenue Service (IRS) issued Notice 2014-21 (2014-16 I.R.B. 938), which, through a series of questions and answers, "describes how existing tax principles apply to transactions using virtual currency."

Background. Bitcoin is a decentralized virtual store of value that is beginning to gain greater acceptance as a medium of exchange in the mainstream marketplace. Notice 2014-21 describes virtual currencies such as Bitcoin as follows:

"[A] digital representation of value that functions as a medium of exchange, a unit of account, and/or a store of value .... Virtual currency that has an equivalent value in real currency, or that acts as a substitute for real currency, is referred to as 'convertible' virtual currency...."

Bitcoin derives value not from governmental backing or a link to an underlying commodity, but purely from its finite nature, the effort required to generate new Bitcoin, and the value its users place on it and its acceptance as a medium of exchange in certain segments of the market. Bitcoin supply is finite (the maximum number of Bitcoin that will ever exist is approximately 21 million). A good summary of fundamental questions and answers surrounding Bitcoin can be found at **http://bitcoin.org/en/faq**.

IRS Guidance. Notice 2014-21 provides answers to frequently asked questions (FAQs) on virtual currency such as Bitcoin. These FAQs provide basic information on the U.S. Federal tax implications of transactions in, or transactions that use, virtual currency. In some environments, virtual currency operates like "real" currency (e.g., the coin and paper money of the United States) but it does not have legal tender status in any jurisdiction.

In its guidance, the IRS indicates that Bitcoin is *not* currency; rather, virtual currency is treated as *property* for U.S. Federal tax purposes. General tax principles that apply to property transactions apply to transactions using virtual currency. Among other things, this means that:

- Wages paid to employees using virtual currency are taxable to the employee, must be reported by an employer on a Form W–2, and are subject to Federal income tax withholding and payroll taxes.

- Payments using virtual currency made to independent contractors and other service providers are taxable, and self-employment tax rules generally apply. Payers are subject to the same information reporting requirements as any other payer (so, for example, a Form 1099–MISC must be issued to an independent contractor if Bitcoin payments exceed $600 per year).

- The character of gain or loss from the sale or exchange of virtual currency depends on whether the virtual currency is a capital asset in the hands of the taxpayer.

- A payment made using virtual currency is subject to information reporting to the same extent as any other payment made in property.

The full set of 16 questions and answers provided by the IRS can be found at **www.irs.gov/pub/irs-drop/n-14-21.pdf**.

Easements An easement is the legal right to use another's land for a special purpose. Historically, easements were commonly used to obtain rights-of-way for utility lines, roads, and pipelines. In recent years, grants of conservation easements have become a popular means of obtaining charitable contribution deductions and reducing the value of real estate for transfer tax (i.e., estate and gift) purposes. Likewise, scenic easements are used to reduce the value of land as assessed for ad valorem property tax purposes.

If the taxpayer does not retain any right to the use of the land, all of the basis is assigned to the easement. However, if the use of the land is only partially restricted, an allocation of some of the basis to the easement is appropriate.

7-1b Recognized Gain or Loss

LO.2

Distinguish between realized and recognized gain or loss.

Recognized gain is the amount of the realized gain that is included in the taxpayer's gross income.[20] A **recognized loss**, on the other hand, is the amount of a realized loss that is deductible for tax purposes.[21] As a general rule, the entire amount of a realized gain or loss is recognized when it is realized.[22]

---

[20]§ 61(a)(3) and Reg. § 1.61–6(a).

[21]§ 165(a) and Reg. § 1.165–1(a).

[22]§ 1001(c) and Reg. § 1.1002–1(a).

Concept Summary 7.1 summarizes the realized gain or loss and recognized gain or loss concepts.

Concept Summary 7.1

Recognized Gain or Loss

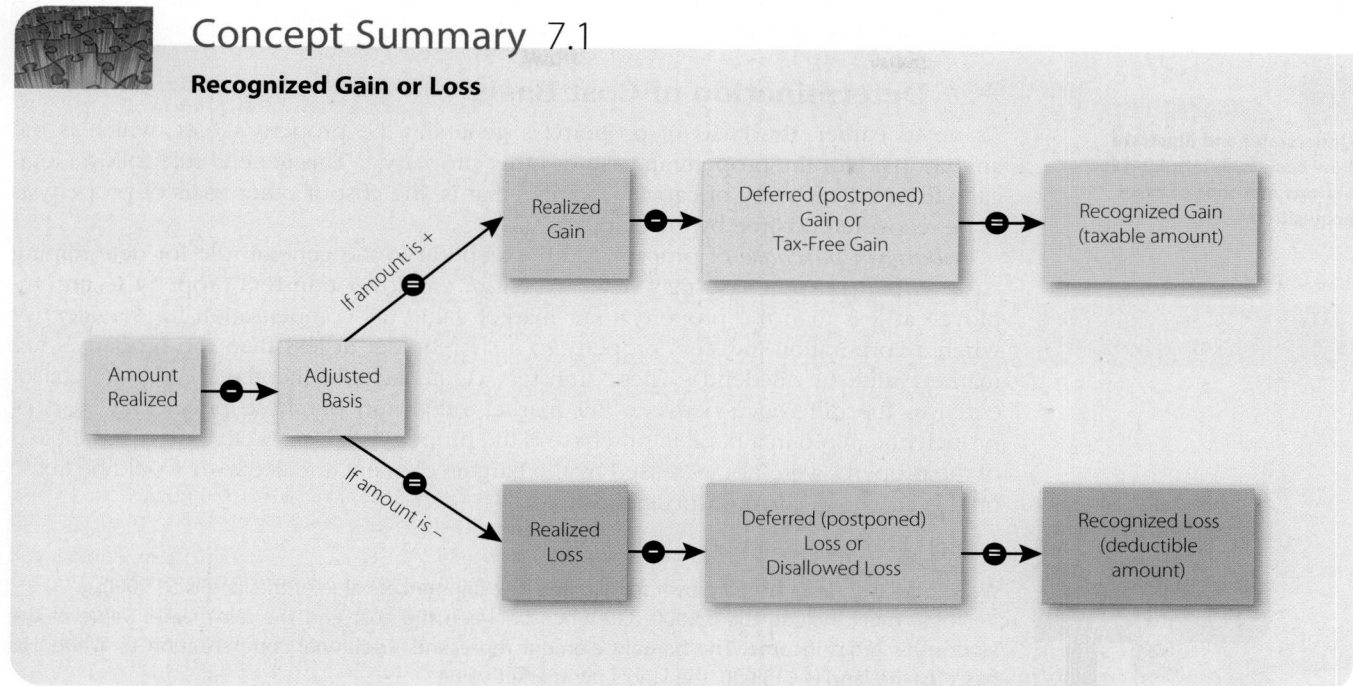

7-1c **Nonrecognition of Gain or Loss**

In certain cases, a realized gain or loss is not recognized upon the sale or other disposition of property. One such case involves nontaxable exchanges, which are covered later in this chapter. In addition, realized losses from the sale or exchange of property between certain related parties are not recognized.[23]

Dispositions of Personal-Use Assets

For individual taxpayers, special rules apply to *personal-use* assets (i.e., assets such as a residence or an automobile that are not used in any business or investment activity). A loss from the sale, exchange, or condemnation of such assets is not recognized for tax purposes. An exception exists for casualty or theft losses from personal-use assets (refer to Chapter 6). In contrast, any gain realized from the disposition of personal-use assets is generally taxable.

Freda sells an automobile, which she has held exclusively for personal use, for $6,000. The basis of the automobile is $5,000. Freda has a realized and recognized gain of $1,000.

    If she sold this automobile for $4,500, she would have a realized loss of $500, but the loss would not be recognized for tax purposes.

EXAMPLE

8

In-depth coverage can be found on this book's companion website: **www.cengagebrain.com**   **2 DIGGING DEEPER**

---

[23]§ 267(a)(1).

7-2 BASIS CONSIDERATIONS

A key element in calculating gain or loss from a property transaction is the asset's basis at the time of the transaction. Various methods for determining basis apply, depending on how the asset was acquired.

LO.3

Understand and illustrate how basis is determined for various methods of asset acquisition.

7-2a Determination of Cost Basis

As noted earlier, the basis of property is generally the property's cost, which is the amount paid for the property in cash or other property.[24] This general rule follows logically from the recovery of capital doctrine; that is, the cost or other basis of property is to be recovered tax-free by the taxpayer.

A *bargain purchase* of property is an exception to the general rule for determining basis. A bargain purchase may result when an employer transfers property to an employee at less than the property's fair market value (as compensation for services) or when a corporation transfers property to a shareholder at less than the property's fair market value (a dividend). These transfers create taxable income for the purchaser equal to the difference between fair market value and purchase price. The basis of property acquired in a bargain purchase is the property's fair market value.[25] If the basis of the property were not increased by the bargain element, the taxpayer would be taxed on this amount again at disposition.

EXAMPLE 9

Wade buys land from his employer for $10,000. The fair market value of the land is $15,000.

Wade must include the $5,000 difference between the cost and the fair market value of the land in his gross income. The bargain element represents additional compensation to Wade. His basis for the land is $15,000, the land's fair market value.

Identification Problems

Sometimes, it can be difficult to determine the cost of an asset being sold. This problem is frequently encountered in sales of corporate stock, because a taxpayer may purchase separate lots of a company's stock on different dates and at different prices. When the stock is sold, if the taxpayer cannot identify the specific shares being sold (specific identification), the stock sold is determined on a first-in, first-out (FIFO) basis. Thus, the holding period and cost of the stock sold are determined by referring to the purchase date and cost of the first lot of stock acquired.[26] But if the stock being sold can be adequately identified, then the basis and holding period of the specific stock sold are used in determining the nature and amount of gain or loss.[27] Thus, to avoid FIFO treatment when the sold securities are held by a broker, it is often necessary to provide specific instructions and receive written confirmation of the securities being sold.

EXAMPLE 10

Pelican, Inc., purchases 100 shares of Olive Corporation stock on July 1, 2013, for $5,000 ($50 a share) and another 100 shares of Olive stock on July 1, 2014, for $6,000 ($60 a share). Pelican sells 50 shares of the stock on January 2, 2015.

The cost of the stock sold, assuming that Pelican cannot adequately identify the shares, is $50 a share (from shares purchased on July 1, 2013), or $2,500. This is the cost Pelican will compare with the amount realized in determining the gain or loss from the sale.

---

[24]§ 1012 and Reg. § 1.1012–1(a).

[25]Reg. §§ 1.61–2(d)(2)(i) and 1.301–1(j). See the discussion in Chapter 11 of the circumstances under which what appears to be a taxable bargain purchase is an excludible qualified employee discount.

[26]*Kluger Associates, Inc.*, 69 T.C. 925 (1978).

[27]Reg. § 1.1012–1(c)(1).

Allocation Problems

When a taxpayer acquires *several assets in a lump-sum purchase*, the total cost must be allocated among the individual assets.[28] Allocation is necessary for several reasons:

- Some of the assets acquired may be depreciable (e.g., buildings), while others may not be (e.g., land).
- Only a portion of the assets acquired may be sold.
- Some of the assets may be capital or depreciable assets that receive special tax treatment upon subsequent sale or other disposition.

The lump-sum cost is allocated on the basis of the fair market values of the individual assets acquired.

EXAMPLE
11

Magenta Corporation purchases a building and land for $800,000. Because of the depressed nature of the industry in which the seller was operating, Magenta was able to negotiate a very favorable purchase price. Appraisals of the individual assets indicate that the fair market value of the building is $600,000 and that of the land is $400,000.

Magenta's basis for the building is $480,000 [($600,000/$1,000,000) × $800,000], and its basis for the land is $320,000 [($400,000/$1,000,000) × $800,000].

If a business is purchased and **goodwill** is involved, a special allocation applies. Initially, the purchase price is assigned to the assets, excluding goodwill, to the extent of their total fair market value. This assigned amount is allocated among the assets on the basis of the fair market value of the individual assets acquired. Goodwill is then assigned the residual amount of the purchase price. The resultant allocation is applicable to both the buyer and the seller.[29]

EXAMPLE
12

Roadrunner, Inc., sells its business to Coyote Corporation. The two companies agree that the values of the specific assets are as follows:

Marketable securities	$ 5,000
Inventory	35,000
Building	500,000
Land	200,000

After negotiations, Roadrunner and Coyote agree on a sales price of $1 million. Applying the residual method, the residual purchase price is allocated to goodwill, resulting in the following basis of assets to Coyote Corporation:

Marketable securities	$ 5,000
Inventory	35,000
Building	500,000
Land	200,000
Goodwill	260,000

In the case of *nontaxable stock dividends*, the allocation depends on whether the dividend is a common stock dividend on common stock or a preferred stock dividend on common stock. If the stock dividend is common on common, the cost of the original common shares is allocated to the total shares owned after the dividend.[30]

EXAMPLE
13

Yellow, Inc., owns 100 shares of Sparrow Corporation common stock for which it paid $1,100. Yellow receives a 10% common stock dividend, giving it a new total of 110 shares. Before the stock dividend, Yellow's basis was $11 per share ($1,100 ÷ 100 shares). The basis of each share after the stock dividend is $10 ($1,100 ÷ 110 shares).

---

[28]Reg. § 1.61–6(a).

[29]§ 1060. The classification of the seller's recognized gain associated with the goodwill is discussed in Chapter 8.

[30]§§ 305(a) and 307(a). The holding period of the new shares includes the holding period of the old shares. § 1223(5) and Reg. § 1.1223–1(e). See Chapter 8 for a discussion of the importance of the holding period.

TAX IN THE NEWS   Brokers Provide Cost Basis Data to Taxpayers (and the IRS)

Brokers and others in similar enterprises are now required to provide investors with an annual report on the cost basis of their stocks sold during the year (to be included on Form 1099–B and reported to the IRS).

The primary reason for the requirement is to enable taxpayers to use the correct basis in calculating the gain or loss on the sale of the stock (perhaps many years after the initial purchase). Nontaxable stock dividends, stock splits, and spin-offs may create confusion and result in unreliable data being used to determine the basis. For the investor who has multiple lots of the same stock, the likelihood of making an incorrect determination of cost basis is even greater.

A secondary reason for the reporting requirement is to generate more revenue for the Treasury. The Treasury

believes that it will collect an additional $6 billion to $9 billion per year as a result of this requirement. Tax professionals will also benefit by providing consulting related to the requirements—some estimate the related compliance costs will exceed $500 million per year.

Although the primary burden for determining cost basis is placed on the broker, the ultimate responsibility for reporting the information correctly remains on the taxpayer (and his or her tax adviser).

Sources: Based on "Cost Basis Reporting: Why Corporate Issuers (and Not Just Brokers) Should Care," *A&M Tax Advisor Weekly*, **www.taxand.com**, July 14, 2011; Laura Saunders, "When Your Broker 'Outs' You," *Wall Street Journal*, March 2, 2013, p. D3; Tara Siegel Bernard, "New Tax Laws Take Guesswork Out of Investment Tax Liability," *New York Times*, March 15, 2013.

If the nontaxable stock dividend is preferred stock on common, the cost of the original common shares is allocated between the common and preferred shares on the basis of their relative fair market values on the date of distribution.[31]

EXAMPLE 14

Brown Company owns 100 shares of Cardinal Corporation common stock for which it paid $1,000. Brown receives a nontaxable stock dividend of 50 shares of preferred stock on the Cardinal common stock. The fair market values on the date of distribution of the preferred stock dividend are $30 a share for common stock and $40 a share for preferred stock.

Fair market value of common ($30 × 100 shares)	$3,000
Fair market value of preferred ($40 × 50 shares)	2,000
	$5,000
Basis of common: 3/5 × $1,000	$ 600
Basis of preferred: 2/5 × $1,000	$ 400

The basis per share for the common stock is $6 ($600/100 shares). The basis per share for the preferred stock is $8 ($400/50 shares).

7-2b Gift Basis

Although business entities can neither make nor receive gratuitous transfers, ownership interests in such entities are frequently the subject of lifetime and testamentary gifts. Partnership interests, stock in closely or publicly held corporations, and other assets are regularly passed from one generation of owners to another for a variety of family and business reasons. Special basis rules apply to such transfers.

When a taxpayer receives property as a gift, there is no cost to the donee (recipient). Thus, under the cost basis provision, the donee's basis would be zero. With a zero basis, if the donee sold the property, the entire amount realized would be treated as taxable gain. Instead, the Code[32] assigns a basis to the property received that depends upon the following:

- The date of the gift.
- The basis of the property to the donor.
- The fair market value of the property.
- The amount of the gift tax paid, if any.

---

[31]Reg. § 1.307–1(a).   [32]§ 1015(a).

Gift Basis Rules If No Gift Tax Is Paid

If a property's fair market value on the date of the gift exceeds the donor's basis in the property, the donor's basis carries over to the new owner.[33] This basis is called a *carryover basis* and is used in determining the donee's gain or loss.

The Big Picture

EXAMPLE 15

Return to the facts of *The Big Picture* on p. 7-1. Alice's father purchased the land in 1992 for $2,000. He gave the land to Alice 10 years ago, when the fair market value was $10,000. No gift tax was paid on the transfer. Alice is considering selling the land, which is currently worth $50,000.

If she sells the property for $50,000, Alice will have a realized gain of $48,000 ($50,000 amount realized − $2,000 basis in the land).

If the property's fair market value on the date of the gift is *lower* than the donor's basis in the property, the donee's basis cannot be determined until the donee disposes of the property. For the purpose of determining *gain*, the donor's basis will carry over, as in the preceding example. But for determining *loss*, the property's basis will be its fair market value when the gift was made.

The Big Picture

EXAMPLE 16

Return to the facts of *The Big Picture* on p. 7-1. Instead, assume that Alice's father had purchased the land in 1992 for $12,000. He gave the land to Alice 10 years ago, when the fair market value was $10,000. No gift tax was paid on the transfer.

If Alice sells the property for $50,000, she has a realized gain of $38,000 ($50,000 amount realized − $12,000 basis in the land).

However, if the property has declined in value because of the discovery of contaminants on the property and Alice is able to sell the land for only $8,000, she will realize a loss of $2,000 ($8,000 amount realized − $10,000 basis in the land).

Note that this loss basis rule prevents the donee from receiving a tax benefit from a decline in value that occurred while the donor held the property. Therefore, in the preceding example, Alice has a loss of only $2,000 rather than a loss of $4,000 ($8,000 − $12,000). The $2,000 difference represents the decline in value that occurred while Alice's father held the property. Ironically, however, a donee might be subject to income tax on the appreciation that occurred while the donor held the property, as illustrated in Example 15.

In any case, the operation of this dual basis rule produces a curious anomaly: if the sales proceeds fall *between* the donor's adjusted basis and the property's fair market value at the date of gift, no gain or loss is recognized.

The Big Picture

EXAMPLE 17

Return to the facts of *The Big Picture* on p. 7-1. Instead, assume that Alice's father had purchased the land in 1992 for $12,000. He gave the land to Alice 10 years ago, when the fair market value was $10,000. No gift tax was paid on the transfer. Now Alice plans to sell the property for $11,000. To calculate gain, she would use a basis of $12,000, her father's basis. But when a $12,000 basis is compared with the $11,000 sales proceeds, a *loss* is produced. Yet in determining loss, Alice must use the property's fair market value at the date of gift—namely, $10,000. When a $10,000 basis is compared to sales proceeds of $11,000, a *gain* is produced. Accordingly, no gain or loss is recognized on this transaction.

Adjustment for Gift Tax

Because of the size of the unified estate and gift tax exemption ($5.43 million in 2015), basis adjustments for gift taxes paid are rare. If, however, gift taxes are paid by the

---

[33]§ 1015(a) and Reg. § 1.1015–1(a)(1). See Reg. § 1.1015–1(a)(3) for cases in which the facts necessary to determine the donor's adjusted basis are unknown. See Example 18 for the effect of depreciation deductions by the donee.

TAX PLANNING STRATEGIES Gift Planning

FRAMEWORK FOCUS: TAX RATE

Strategy: Shift Net Income from High-Bracket Taxpayers to Low-Bracket Taxpayers.

FRAMEWORK FOCUS: DEDUCTIONS

Strategy: Maximize Deductible Amounts.

Gifts of *appreciated property* can produce tax savings if the donee is in a lower tax bracket than the donor. The carryover basis rule effectively shifts the tax on the property's appreciation to the new owner, even if all of the appreciation arose while the property was owned by the donor.

On the other hand, donors should generally avoid making gifts of property that are worth less than the donor's adjusted basis (loss property). The operation of the basis rule for losses may result in either (1) a realized loss that is not deductible by either the donor or the donee or (2) reduced tax benefits when the loss is recognized by a donee facing lower marginal tax rates. Unless the property is expected to rebound in value before it is sold, a donor would be better advised to sell the property that has declined in value, deduct the resulting loss, and then transfer the proceeds to the prospective donee.

donor, the portion of the gift tax paid that is related to any appreciation is taken into account in determining the donee's gain basis.[34]

For *gifts made before 1977*, the full amount of the gift tax paid is added to the donor's basis, with basis capped at the donor's fair market value at the date of the gift.

Holding Period

The **holding period** for property acquired by gift begins on the date the donor acquired the property,[35] unless the special circumstance requiring use of the property's fair market value at the date of gift applies. If so, the holding period starts on the date of the gift.[36] The significance of the holding period for capital assets is discussed in Chapter 8.

Basis for Depreciation

The basis for depreciation on depreciable gift property is the donee's basis for determining gain.[37] This rule is applicable even if the donee later sells the property at a loss and uses the property's fair market value at the date of gift in calculating the amount of the realized loss.

EXAMPLE 18

Vito gave a machine to Tina earlier this year. At that time, the adjusted basis was $32,000 (cost of $40,000 — accumulated depreciation of $8,000), and the fair market value was $26,000. No gift tax was due. Tina's basis for determining gain is $32,000, and her loss basis is $26,000. During this year, Tina deducts depreciation (cost recovery) of $6,400 ($32,000 × 20%). (Refer to Chapter 5 for the cost recovery tables.) At the end of this year, Tina's basis determinations are calculated as follows:

	Gain Basis	Loss Basis
Donor's basis or fair market value	$32,000	$26,000
Depreciation	(6,400)	(6,400)
	$25,600	$19,600

[34]§ 1015(d)(6) and Reg. § 1.1015–5(c)(2). Examples illustrating these rules can be found in Reg. § 1.1015–5(c)(5) and IRS Publication 551 (*Basis of Assets*), p. 9.

[35]§ 1223(2) and Reg. § 1.1223–1(b).

[36]Rev.Rul. 59–86, 1959–1 C.B. 209.

[37]§ 1011 and Reg. §§ 1.1011–1 and 1.167(g)–1.

7-2c **Property Acquired from a Decedent**

For a taxpayer who has received property from a deceased individual (i.e., decedent) and later disposes of that property, the property's basis must be determined. Typically, a favorable rule may be applied.

General Rules

The basis of property acquired from a decedent is generally the property's fair market value at the date of death (referred to as the *primary valuation amount*).[38] The property's basis is the fair market value six months after the date of death if the executor or administrator of the estate *elects* the alternate valuation date for estate tax purposes. This amount is referred to as the *alternate valuation amount*.

| In-depth coverage can be found on this book's companion website: www.cengagebrain.com | **3** DIGGING DEEPER |

EXAMPLE

19

Linda and various other family members inherited stock in a closely held corporation from Linda's father, who died earlier this year. At the date of death, her father's basis for the stock Linda inherited was $35,000. The stock's fair market value at the date of death was $50,000. The alternate valuation date was not elected. Linda's basis for income tax purposes is $50,000. This is commonly referred to as a *stepped-up basis*.

If, instead, the stock's fair market value at the date of death was $20,000, Linda's basis would be $20,000. This is commonly referred to as a *stepped-down basis*.

The Big Picture

EXAMPLE

20

Return to the facts of *The Big Picture* on p. 7-1. Alice owns 500 shares of AppleCo stock, 300 of which were inherited from her grandfather. Her grandfather's cost basis in the stock was $12,000 (i.e., its purchase price), but the shares were worth $30,000 at the time of his death. Alice purchased the other 200 shares for $28,000.

Therefore, the basis in her 500 AppleCo shares is $58,000: the 300 shares received as an inheritance take a stepped-up basis of $30,000, and the 200 shares purchased take a cost basis of $28,000.

The alternate valuation date and amount are only available to estates for which an estate tax return must be filed [generally, estates with a valuation in excess of $5.43 million in 2015 ($5.34 million in 2014)]. Even if an estate tax return is filed and the executor elects the alternate valuation date, the six-months-after-death date is available only for property that the executor has not distributed before this date.[39]

The alternate valuation date can be elected *only if*, as a result of the election, *both* the value of the gross estate and the estate tax liability are lower than they would have been if the primary valuation date had been used.[40]

| In-depth coverage can be found on this book's companion website: www.cengagebrain.com | **4** DIGGING DEEPER |

---

[38]§ 1014(a) and § 1022.

[39]§ 2032(a)(1) and Rev.Rul. 56–60, 1956–1 C.B. 443. For any property distributed by the executor during the six-month period preceding the alternate valuation date, the basis to the beneficiary will equal the fair market value on the date of distribution.

[40]§ 2032(c). This provision prevents the alternate valuation election from being used to increase the basis of the property to the beneficiary for income tax purposes without simultaneously increasing the estate tax liability (because of estate tax deductions or credits).

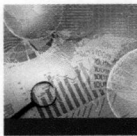

TAX PLANNING STRATEGIES **Property from a Decedent**

FRAMEWORK FOCUS: INCOME

Strategy: Avoid Income Recognition.

FRAMEWORK FOCUS: DEDUCTIONS

Strategy: Maximize Deductible Amounts.

If a taxpayer *retains appreciated property* until death, the property's basis will be "stepped up" to its fair market value at that time. Thus, no income tax will be paid on the property's appreciation by either the former owner (the decedent) or the new owner (the heir).

On the other hand, *depreciated property should be sold* prior to death. Otherwise, the property's basis in the heir's hands will be its declined fair market value, and neither the decedent nor the heir will be able to deduct the loss that occurred while the property was owned by the decedent.

Holding Period of Property Acquired from a Decedent

The holding period of property acquired from a decedent is *deemed to be long term* (held for the required long-term holding period). This provision applies regardless of whether the property is disposed of at a gain or at a loss.[41]

7-2d Disallowed Losses

In certain situations, losses that normally would be recognized are disallowed. Such disallowance commonly occurs in transactions between related parties and in wash sales.

Related Taxpayers

LO.4

Describe various loss disallowance provisions.

Section 267 provides that realized losses from sales or exchanges of property between certain related parties are not recognized. This loss disallowance provision applies to several types of related-party transactions.[42] The most common involve (1) members of a family and (2) an individual and a corporation in which the individual owns, directly or indirectly, more than 50 percent in value of the corporation's outstanding stock. Section 707 provides a similar loss disallowance provision where the related parties are a partner and a partnership in which the partner owns, directly or indirectly, more than 50 percent of the capital interests or profits interests in the partnership. Neither provision, however, prevents the recognition of *gains* between related parties. The rules governing the relationships covered by § 267 were discussed in Chapter 5.

If income-producing or business property is transferred to a related party and a loss is disallowed, the basis of the property to the recipient is the property's cost to the transferee. However, if a subsequent sale or other disposition of the property by the original transferee results in a realized gain, the amount of gain is reduced by the loss that was previously disallowed. This *right of offset* is not applicable if the original sale involved the sale of a personal-use asset (e.g., a personal residence). Furthermore, the right of offset is available only to the original transferee (the related-party buyer). See Examples 19 and 20 in Chapter 5.

 DIGGING DEEPER **5**   In-depth coverage can be found on this book's companion website: www.cengagebrain.com

Wash Sales

Section 1091 stipulates that in certain cases, a realized loss on the sale or exchange of stock or securities is not recognized. Specifically, if a taxpayer sells or exchanges stock

---

[41]§ 1223(11).   [42]§ 267(b).

or securities and within 30 days before *or* after the date of the sale or exchange acquires *substantially identical* stock or securities, any loss realized from the sale or exchange is not recognized because the transaction is a wash sale.[43] The term *acquire* means acquire by purchase or in a taxable exchange and includes an option to purchase substantially identical securities. *Substantially identical* means the same in all important particulars. Corporate bonds and preferred stock normally are not considered substantially identical to a corporation's common stock. However, if the bonds and preferred stock are convertible into common stock, they may be considered substantially identical under certain circumstances.[44] Attempts to avoid the application of the wash sale rules by having a related taxpayer repurchase the securities have been unsuccessful.[45] The wash sale provisions do *not* apply to gains.

Recognition of the loss is disallowed because the taxpayer is considered to be in substantially the same economic position after the sale and repurchase as before. This disallowance rule does not apply to taxpayers engaged in the business of buying and selling securities.[46] Investors, however, are not allowed to create losses through wash sales to offset income for tax purposes.

A realized loss that is not recognized is added to the *basis* of the substantially identical stock or securities whose acquisition resulted in the nonrecognition of loss.[47] In other words, the basis of the replacement stock or securities is increased by the amount of the unrecognized loss. If the loss were not added to the basis of the newly acquired stock or securities, the taxpayer would never recover the entire basis of the old stock or securities. As a result, the wash sale rule operates to *defer* the recognition of the taxpayer's loss.

EXAMPLE 21

Oriole Manufacturing Company sold 50 shares of Green Corporation stock (basis of $10,000) for $8,000. Ten days later, Oriole purchased 50 shares of the same stock for $7,000.

Oriole's realized loss of $2,000 ($8,000 amount realized − $10,000 basis) is not recognized because it resulted from a wash sale. Oriole's basis in the newly acquired stock is $9,000 ($7,000 purchase price + $2,000 unrecognized loss from the wash sale).

The basis of the new stock or securities includes the unrecovered portion of the basis of the formerly held stock or securities. Therefore, the *holding period* of the new stock or securities begins on the date of acquisition of the old stock or securities.[48]

A taxpayer may acquire fewer shares than the number sold in a wash sale. In this case, the loss from the sale is prorated between recognized and unrecognized loss on the basis of the ratio of the number of shares acquired to the number of shares sold.[49]

TAX PLANNING STRATEGIES **Avoiding Wash Sales**

FRAMEWORK FOCUS: DEDUCTIONS

Strategy: Maximize Deductible Amounts.

The wash sale restriction can be avoided by replacing the sold security with a *similar* but not "substantially identical" security. For example, if IBM common stock is sold to claim an unrealized loss, the taxpayer could immediately acquire Dell common stock without triggering the wash sale rule, even though both entities are computer companies.

Nontax considerations must also come into play, however, because IBM and Dell are two different companies with different investment prospects. Although both securities will be affected by many of the same factors, they will also be subject to different factors that may be even more significant than the ones they share.

---

[43]§ 1091(a) and Reg. §§ 1.1091–1(a) and (f).
[44]Rev.Rul. 56–406, 1956–2 C.B. 523.
[45]*McWilliams v. Comm.*, 47–1 USTC ¶9289, 35 AFTR 1184, 67 S.Ct. 1477 (USSC, 1947).
[46]Reg. § 1.1091–1(a).

[47]§ 1091(d) and Reg. § 1.1091–2(a).
[48]§ 1223(4) and Reg. § 1.1223–1(d).
[49]§ 1091(b) and Reg. § 1.1091–1(c).

7-2e Conversion of Property from Personal Use to Business or Income-Producing Use

As discussed previously, losses from the sale of personal-use assets are not recognized for tax purposes, but losses from the sale of business and income-producing assets are deductible. Can a taxpayer convert a personal-use asset that has declined in value to business or income-producing use and then sell the asset to recognize a business or income-producing loss? The tax law prevents this practice by specifying that the *basis for determining loss* on personal-use assets converted to business or income-producing use is the *lower* of the property's adjusted basis or its fair market value on the date of conversion.[50] The *gain basis* for converted property is the property's adjusted basis on the date of conversion, regardless of whether the property's use is business, income-producing, or personal in nature.

EXAMPLE 22

Diane's personal residence has an adjusted basis of $175,000 and a fair market value of $160,000. When she converts the personal residence to residential rental property on January 1, her basis for determining loss is $160,000 (lower of $175,000 adjusted basis and fair market value of $160,000). The $15,000 decline in value is a personal loss and can never be recognized for tax purposes. Diane's basis for determining gain is $175,000.

The basis for determining loss is also the *basis for depreciating* the converted property.[51] This is an exception to the general rule that the basis for depreciation is the basis for determining gain (e.g., property received by gift). This exception prevents the taxpayer from recovering a personal loss indirectly through depreciation of the higher original basis. Once property is converted, both its basis for loss and its basis for gain are adjusted for depreciation deductions from the date of conversion to the date of disposition.

EXAMPLE 23

Assume the same facts as in Example 22. The MACRS cost recovery deduction for the current year is $5,576 ($160,000 × 3.485%). Thus, at the end of the current year, Diane's adjusted basis for gain for the rental property is $169,424 ($175,000 − $5,576), and her adjusted basis for loss is $154,424 ($160,000 − $5,576).

DIGGING DEEPER 6, 7   In-depth coverage can be found on this book's companion website: www.cengagebrain.com

7-2f Summary of Basis Adjustments

Some of the more common items that either increase or decrease the basis of an asset appear in Concept Summary 7.2.

[50]Reg. § 1.165–9(b)(2).   [51]Reg. § 1.167(g)–1.

Concept Summary 7.2

Adjustments to Basis

Item	Effect	Refer to Chapter	Explanation
Amortization of bond discount	Increase	7	Amortization is mandatory for certain taxable bonds and elective for tax-exempt bonds.
Amortization of bond premium	Decrease	7	Amortization is mandatory for tax-exempt bonds and elective for taxable bonds.
Amortization of covenant not to compete	Decrease	5	Covenant must be for a definite and limited time period. The amortization period is a statutory period of 15 years.
Amortization of intangibles	Decrease	5	Intangibles are amortized over a 15-year period.
Bad debts	Decrease	6	Most taxpayers must use the specific charge-off method.
Capital additions	Increase	7	Certain items, at the taxpayer's election, can be capitalized or deducted.
Casualty	Decrease	7	For a casualty loss, the amount of the adjustment is the sum of the deductible loss and the insurance proceeds received. For a casualty gain, the amount of the adjustment is the insurance proceeds received reduced by the recognized gain.
Condemnation	Decrease	7	See casualty explanation.
Cost recovery	Decrease	5	Section 168 is applicable to tangible assets placed in service after 1980 whose useful life is expressed in terms of years.
Depletion	Decrease	5	Use the greater of cost or percentage depletion. Percentage depletion can be deducted even when the basis is zero.
Depreciation	Decrease	5	Section 167 is applicable to tangible assets placed in service before 1981 and to tangible assets not depreciated in terms of years.
Easement	Decrease	7	If the taxpayer does not retain any use of the land, all of the basis is allocable to the easement transaction. However, if only part of the land is affected by the easement, only part of the basis is allocable to the easement transaction.
Improvements by lessee to lessor's property	Increase	4	Adjustment occurs only if the lessor is required to include the fair market value of the improvements in gross income under § 109.
Imputed interest	Decrease		Amount deducted is not part of the cost of the asset.
Inventory: lower of cost or market	Decrease		Not available if the LIFO method is used.
Limited expensing under § 179	Decrease	5	Occurs only if the taxpayer elects § 179 treatment.
Medical capital expenditure deducted as a medical expense	Decrease	10	Adjustment is the amount of the deduction (the effect on basis is to increase it by the amount of the capital expenditure net of the deduction).
Real estate taxes: apportionment between the buyer and seller	Increase or decrease	5	To the extent the buyer pays the seller's pro rata share, the buyer's basis is increased. To the extent the seller pays the buyer's pro rata share, the buyer's basis is decreased.
Rebate from manufacturer	Decrease		Because the rebate is treated as an adjustment to the purchase price, it is not included in the buyer's gross income.
Stock dividend	Decrease	7	Adjustment occurs only if the stock dividend is nontaxable. While the basis per share decreases, the total stock basis does not change.
Stock rights	Decrease	13	Adjustment to stock basis occurs only for nontaxable stock rights and only if the fair market value of the rights is at least 15% of the fair market value of the stock, or if less than 15%, the taxpayer elects to allocate the basis between the stock and the rights.
Theft	Decrease	6	See casualty explanation.

In discussing the topic of basis, a number of specific techniques for determining basis have been presented. Although the various techniques are responsive to and mandated by transactions occurring in the marketplace, they possess enough common characteristics to be categorized as follows:

- The basis of the asset may be determined by its cost.
- The basis of the asset may be determined by the basis of another asset.
- The basis of the asset may be determined by its fair market value.
- The basis of the asset may be determined by the basis of the asset in the hands of another taxpayer.

7-3 GENERAL CONCEPT OF A NONTAXABLE EXCHANGE

A taxpayer who is going to replace a productive asset (e.g., machinery) used in a trade or business may structure the transaction as a sale of the old asset and the purchase of a new asset. When this approach is used, any realized gain or loss on the sale of the old asset is recognized. The basis of the new asset is its cost. Alternatively, the taxpayer may be able to trade the old asset for the new asset. This exchange of assets may produce beneficial tax consequences as a nontaxable exchange.

The tax law recognizes that nontaxable exchanges result in a change in the *form* but not the *substance* of a taxpayer's relative economic position. The replacement property received in the exchange is viewed as essentially a continuation of the old investment.[52] Additional justification for nontaxable treatment is that this type of transaction does not provide the taxpayer with the wherewithal to pay the tax on any realized gain.

The nonrecognition provisions for nontaxable exchanges do not apply to realized losses from the sale or exchange of personal-use assets. Such losses are never recognized (i.e., they are disallowed) because they are personal in nature.

In contrast, in a nontaxable exchange, recognition of gains or losses is *postponed* (i.e., deferred) until the new property received in the nontaxable exchange is subsequently disposed of in a taxable transaction. This is accomplished by assigning a carryover basis to the replacement property.

EXAMPLE 24

Starling Management Company completes a *nontaxable exchange* of property with an adjusted basis of $10,000 and a fair market value of $12,000 for property with a fair market value of $12,000.

Starling has a realized gain of $2,000 ($12,000 amount realized − $10,000 adjusted basis). Its recognized gain is $0. Starling's basis in the replacement property is a carryover basis of $10,000.

Assume that the replacement property is nondepreciable and that Starling subsequently sells it for $12,000. The realized and recognized gain will be the $2,000 gain that was postponed (deferred) in the nontaxable transaction. If the replacement property is depreciable, the carryover basis of $10,000 is used in calculating depreciation.

In some nontaxable exchanges, only some of the property involved in the transaction qualifies for nonrecognition treatment. If the taxpayer receives cash or other nonqualifying property, part or all of the realized gain from the exchange is recognized. In these situations, gain is recognized because the taxpayer has changed or improved its relative economic position and has the wherewithal to pay income tax to the extent of cash or other property received.

It is important to distinguish between a nontaxable disposition (or nonrecognition transaction, as the term is used in the statute) and a tax-free transaction. As previously mentioned, the term *nontaxable* refers to postponement of recognition via some version of carryover basis. In a *tax-free* transaction, the nonrecognition is permanent (e.g.,

---

[52]Reg. § 1.1002–1(c).

see the discussion later in this chapter of the exclusion of gain from the sale of a principal residence).

Either way, nontaxable and tax-free transactions must be understood as exceptions to the Code's general rule that gains and losses are recognized when they are realized. These exceptions have their own sets of requirements, limitations, and restrictions, all of which must be satisfied for a transaction to be characterized as nontaxable or tax-free. Otherwise, the general rule of recognition applies to the gain or loss at hand.

7-4 LIKE-KIND EXCHANGES—§ 1031

Apply the nonrecognition provisions and basis determination rules for like-kind exchanges.

Section 1031 provides for nontaxable exchange treatment if the following requirements are satisfied:[53]

- The form of the transaction is an exchange.
- Both the property transferred and the property received are held either for productive use in a trade or business or for investment.
- The property is like-kind property.

Qualifying like-kind exchanges include exchanges of business for business, business for investment, investment for business, and investment for investment property. Property held for personal use does not qualify under the like-kind exchange provisions. Thus, the purpose for which the property is held by the taxpayer in question is critical. For example, if Janet uses a small truck in her trade or business, it may qualify for like-kind treatment, but if she uses this truck as her personal-use vehicle, it is ineligible for nonrecognition treatment under § 1031.

Some assets are excluded from like-kind treatment by statute. These excluded assets include a taxpayer's inventory or "stock in trade," as well as most forms of investment other than real estate. Thus, stocks, bonds, partnership interests (whether general or limited), and other securities, even though held for investment, do not qualify for like-kind exchange treatment.

The nonrecognition provision for like-kind exchanges is *mandatory* rather than elective. A taxpayer who wants to recognize a realized gain or loss will have to structure the transaction in a form that does not satisfy the statutory requirements for a like-kind exchange.

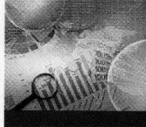

TAX PLANNING STRATEGIES   **Like-Kind Exchanges**

FRAMEWORK FOCUS: DEDUCTIONS

Strategy: Maximize Deductible Amounts.

Because nonrecognition of gain or loss is mandatory in like-kind exchanges, a taxpayer must affirmatively *avoid such exchanges* if nonrecognition treatment is not desired. If an asset is worth less than its adjusted basis, a *loss would result* from its disposition. Accordingly, the taxpayer should sell this property outright to ensure the deductibility of the loss, assuming it would otherwise be deductible.

Even if *disposition would result in a gain*, a taxpayer might want to recognize this gain in the current taxable year. If so,

a like-kind exchange should be avoided. Circumstances suggesting this strategy include:

- Unused capital loss carryovers, especially if the taxpayer is a corporation for which such carryovers are limited in duration (see Chapters 4 and 8).
- Unused net operating loss carryovers (see Chapter 6).
- Unused general business credit carryovers (see Chapter 17).
- Suspended or current passive activity losses (see Chapter 6).

---

[53]§ 1031(a) and Reg. § 1.1031(a)–1(a).

7-4a **Like-Kind Property**

The term *like-kind* is explained in the Regulations as follows: "The words 'like-kind' refer to the nature or character of the property and not to its grade or quality. One kind or class of property may not … be exchanged for property of a different kind or class."[54] The Regulations go on to explain that although real estate can be exchanged only for other real estate, the definition of real estate is quite broad. *Real estate* (or realty) includes principally rental buildings, office and store buildings, manufacturing plants, warehouses, and land. It is immaterial whether real estate is improved or unimproved. Thus, unimproved land can be exchanged for an apartment house. On the other hand, real property located in the United States exchanged for foreign real property (and vice versa) does not qualify as like-kind property. A similar provision applies to exchanges of foreign and domestic personalty.

In any case, real estate cannot be exchanged in a like-kind transaction for personalty. *Personalty* includes tangible assets other than real estate, such as machinery, equipment, trucks, automobiles, furniture, and fixtures. Thus, an exchange of a machine (personalty) for a small office building (realty) is not a like-kind exchange. Finally, the Code mandates that livestock of different sexes are not like-kind property.

EXAMPLE 25

Pheasant, Inc., made the following exchanges during the taxable year:

a. Inventory for a machine used in business.
b. Land held for investment for a building used in business.
c. Stock held for investment for equipment used in business.
d. A light-duty business truck for a light-duty business truck.
e. Livestock for livestock of a different sex.
f. Land held for investment in New York for land held for investment in London.

Exchanges (b), investment real property for business real property, and (d), business personalty for business personalty, qualify as exchanges of like-kind property.

The other exchanges do not qualify because they involve (a), inventory; (c), stock; (e), livestock of different sexes; and (f), U.S. and foreign real estate.

DIGGING DEEPER 8 | In-depth coverage can be found on this book's companion website: www.cengagebrain.com

Special Rule for Depreciable Tangible Personal Property

The Regulations dealing with § 1031 like-kind exchanges provide greater specificity when determining whether depreciable tangible personalty is of a like kind. Such property held for productive use in a business is of like kind only if the exchanged property is within the same *general business asset class* (as specified by the IRS in Rev.Proc. 87–57 or as subsequently modified) or the same *product class* (as specified by the Department of Commerce). Property included in a general business asset class is evaluated exclusively under the Revenue Procedure, rather than under the product class system. (See Chapter 2 for a discussion of the nature and authority of Revenue Procedures.)

The following are examples of general business asset classes:

- Office furniture, fixtures, and equipment.
- Information systems (computers and peripheral equipment).
- Airplanes.
- Automobiles and taxis.
- Buses.
- Light general-purpose trucks.
- Heavy general-purpose trucks.

---
[54]Reg. § 1.1031(a)–1(b).

These Regulations narrow the range of depreciable tangible personalty subject to § 1031 like-kind exchange treatment. For example, the exchange of office equipment for a computer does not qualify as an exchange of like-kind property. Even though both assets are depreciable tangible personalty, they are not like-kind property because they are in different general business asset classes. Accordingly, any realized *gain or loss* on the office equipment would be recognized currently.

In-depth coverage can be found on this book's companion website: www.cengagebrain.com   **9** DIGGING DEEPER

7-4b Exchange Requirement

The transaction must generally involve a direct exchange of property to qualify as a like-kind exchange. The sale of old property and the purchase of new property, even though like kind, is not an exchange. However, the Code does provide a limited procedure for real estate to be exchanged for qualifying property that is acquired subsequent to the exchange.[55]

Of course, the taxpayer may want to avoid nontaxable exchange treatment. Recognition of gain gives the taxpayer a higher basis for depreciation. To the extent that such gains would, if recognized, either receive favorable capital gain treatment or be passive activity income that could be offset by passive activity losses, it might be preferable to avoid the nonrecognition provisions through an indirect exchange transaction. For example, a taxpayer may sell property to one company, recognize the gain, and subsequently purchase similar property from another company. The taxpayer may also want to avoid nontaxable exchange treatment so that a realized loss can be recognized.

In-depth coverage can be found on this book's companion website: www.cengagebrain.com   **10** DIGGING DEEPER

7-4c Boot

If the taxpayer in a like-kind exchange gives or receives some property that is not like-kind property, recognition may occur. Property that is not like-kind property, including cash, is often referred to as **boot**. Although the term *boot* does not appear in the Code, tax practitioners commonly use it rather than saying "property that does not qualify as like-kind property."

The *receipt* of boot will trigger recognition of gain if there is realized gain. The amount of the recognized gain is the *lesser* of the boot received or the realized gain (realized gain serves as the ceiling on recognition).

Implications of Boot Received

EXAMPLE 26

Blue, Inc., and White Corporation exchange machinery, and the exchange qualifies as like kind under § 1031. Because Blue's machinery (adjusted basis of $20,000) is worth $24,000 and White's machine has a fair market value of $19,000, White also gives Blue cash of $5,000.

Blue's recognized gain is $4,000, the lesser of the realized gain of $4,000 ($24,000 amount realized − $20,000 adjusted basis) or the fair market value of the boot received of $5,000.

EXAMPLE 27

Assume the same facts as in the preceding example, except that White's machine is worth $21,000 (not $19,000). Under these circumstances, White gives Blue cash of $3,000 to make up the difference.

Blue's recognized gain is $3,000, the lesser of the realized gain of $4,000 ($24,000 amount realized − $20,000 adjusted basis) or the fair market value of the boot received of $3,000.

---

[55]§ 1031(a)(3).

The receipt of boot does not result in recognition if there is realized loss.

Implications of Boot Received

EXAMPLE 28

Assume the same facts as in Example 26, except that the adjusted basis of Blue's machine is $30,000. Blue's realized loss is $6,000 ($24,000 amount realized − $30,000 adjusted basis). The receipt of the boot of $5,000 does not trigger recognition of Blue's loss.

The *giving* of boot does not trigger recognition if the boot consists solely of cash.

Implications of Boot Given

EXAMPLE 29

Flicker, Inc., and Gadwall Corporation exchange equipment in a like-kind exchange. Flicker receives equipment with a fair market value of $75,000 and transfers equipment worth $63,000 (adjusted basis of $45,000) and cash of $12,000.

Flicker's realized gain is $18,000 ($75,000 amount realized − $45,000 adjusted basis of equipment transferred − $12,000 cash), none of which is recognized.

If, however, the boot given is appreciated or depreciated property, gain or loss is recognized to the extent of the difference between the adjusted basis and the fair market value of the boot. For this purpose, *appreciated or depreciated property* is property with an adjusted basis that differs from fair market value.

Implications of Boot Given

EXAMPLE 30

Assume the same facts as in the preceding example, except that Flicker transfers equipment worth $30,000 (adjusted basis of $36,000) and boot worth $45,000 (adjusted basis of $27,000). Flicker's net gain on this exchange is $12,000 [$75,000 amount realized − adjusted basis of $63,000 ($36,000 + $27,000)]. But Flicker is transferring two pieces of property: equipment (like-kind property) with a built-in realized loss of $6,000 ($30,000 fair market value − $36,000 adjusted basis) and non-like-kind property (boot) with a built-in realized gain of $18,000 ($45,000 fair market value − $27,000 adjusted basis).

In this case, the $6,000 realized loss on the like-kind property is *deferred* (not recognized) and the $18,000 realized gain on the non-like-kind property is recognized. In other words, the realized loss on the like-kind property *cannot* be used to offset the realized gain on the boot given up as part of the transaction.

7-4d Basis and Holding Period of Property Received

If an exchange does not qualify as nontaxable under § 1031, gain or loss is recognized and the basis of property received in the exchange is the property's fair market value. If the exchange qualifies for nonrecognition, the basis of property received must be adjusted to reflect any postponed (deferred) gain or loss. The *basis of like-kind property* received in the exchange is the property's fair market value less postponed gain or plus postponed loss. The *basis* of any *boot* received is the boot's fair market value.

Basis of Like-Kind Property Received

EXAMPLE 31

Vireo Property Management Company exchanges a building (used in its business) with an adjusted basis of $300,000 and a fair market value of $380,000 for land with a fair market value of $380,000. The land is to be held as an investment. The exchange qualifies as like kind (an exchange of business real property for investment real property). Thus, the basis of the land is $300,000 (land's fair market value of $380,000 − $80,000 postponed gain on the building). If the land is later sold for its fair market value of $380,000, the $80,000 postponed gain is recognized.

Basis of Like-Kind Property Received

Assume the same facts as in the preceding example, except that the building has an adjusted basis of $480,000 and a fair market value of only $380,000. The basis in the newly acquired land is $480,000 (fair market value of $380,000 + $100,000 postponed loss on the building). If the land is later sold for its fair market value of $380,000, the $100,000 postponed loss is recognized.

The Code provides an alternative approach for determining the basis of like-kind property received:

Adjusted basis of like-kind property surrendered
+ Adjusted basis of boot given
+ Gain recognized
− Fair market value of boot received
− Loss recognized
= *Basis of like-kind property received*

This approach accords with the recovery of capital doctrine. That is, the unrecovered cost or other basis is increased by additional cost (boot given) or decreased by cost recovered (boot received). Any gain recognized is included in the basis of the new property. The taxpayer has been taxed on this amount and is now entitled to recover it tax-free. Any loss recognized is deducted from the basis of the new property because the taxpayer has already received a tax benefit on that amount.

The holding period of the property surrendered in the exchange carries over and *tacks on* to the holding period of the like-kind property received.[56] This rule derives from the basic concept that the new property is a continuation of the old investment. The boot received has a new holding period (from the date of exchange) rather than a carryover holding period.

Depreciation recapture potential carries over to the property received in a like-kind exchange.[57] See Chapter 8 for a discussion of this topic.

In-depth coverage can be found on this book's companion website: www.cengagebrain.com   **11 DIGGING DEEPER**

If the taxpayer either assumes a liability or takes property subject to a liability, the amount of the liability is treated as boot given. For the taxpayer whose liability is assumed or whose property is taken subject to the liability, the amount of the liability is treated as boot received. The following example illustrates the effect of such a liability. In addition, the example illustrates the tax consequences for both parties involved in the like-kind exchange.

Jaeger & Company and Lark Enterprises, Inc., exchange real estate investments. Jaeger gives up property with an adjusted basis of $250,000 (fair market value of $420,000) that is subject to a mortgage of $80,000 (assumed by Lark). In return for this property, Jaeger receives property with a fair market value of $340,000 (Lark's adjusted basis in the property is $200,000). Jaeger's and Lark's realized and recognized gains and their basis in the like-kind property received are computed as follows:[58]

continued

[56]§ 1223(1) and Reg. § 1.1223–1(a). For like-kind exchanges after March 1, 1954, the tacked-on holding period applies only if the like-kind property surrendered was either a capital asset or § 1231 property.
[57]Reg. §§ 1.1245–2(a)(4) and 1.1250–2(d)(1).

[58]Example (2) of Reg. § 1.1031(d)–2 illustrates a special situation in which both the buyer and the seller transfer liabilities that are assumed by the other party or both parties acquire property that is subject to a liability.

	Jaeger	Lark
Amount realized:		
Like-kind property received	$ 340,000	$ 420,000
Boot received:		
Cash		
Mortgage assumed	80,000	
	$ 420,000	$ 420,000
Adjusted basis:		
Like-kind property given	(250,000)	(200,000)
Boot given:		
Cash		
Mortgage assumed		(80,000)
Realized gain	$ 170,000	$ 140,000
Recognized gain	80,000*	–0–**
Deferred gain	$ 90,000	$ 140,000
Basis of property transferred:		
Like-kind property	$ 250,000	$ 200,000
Cash		
Mortgage assumed		80,000
	$ 250,000	$ 280,000
Plus: Gain recognized	80,000	
Less: Boot received	(80,000)	
Basis of new property	$ 250,000	$ 280,000

*Lesser of boot received ($80,000 mortgage assumed) or realized gain ($170,000).
**No boot received. Therefore, no gain is recognized.

BRIDGE DISCIPLINE   **Bridge to Economics**

One can assert that the "tax variable" is neutralized in nontaxable exchanges when taxable gains or losses do not arise. Neutralizing potential tax consequences can have a positive result given that tax costs tend to dampen economic activity. For example, in a like-kind exchange, a taxpayer can exchange one asset for another asset of like kind without having to recognize a gain or pay a tax. The justification for the tax deferral is that the taxpayer is viewed as having an equivalent economic investment after the transaction as before the transaction. But the tax-neutral result changes when the taxpayer receives property that is not "like kind" because the taxpayer's economic standing has changed.

If, for example, the taxpayer receives investment land *and* cash in exchange for investment land, her ownership in the land given up has, at least in part, been converted to cash, and to that degree, her investment has substantively changed. That is, the taxpayer's economic investment has changed from an ownership exclusively in land to ownership in land *and* cash. Alternatively, if the taxpayer gives up her investment in land for corporate stock in a high-tech venture, the nature of her investment also would substantively change as a result of the transaction. These differences in the taxpayer's economic position after the transaction lead to the transactions being taxed.

LO.6

Explain the nonrecognition provisions available on the involuntary conversion of property.

7-5 INVOLUNTARY CONVERSIONS—§ 1033

Section 1033 provides that a taxpayer who suffers an involuntary conversion of property may postpone recognition of *gain* realized from the conversion. The objective of this provision is to provide relief to the taxpayer who has suffered hardship and does not have the wherewithal to pay the tax on any gain realized from the conversion. Postponement of realized gain is permitted to the extent that the taxpayer *reinvests* the amount realized from the conversion in replacement property. If the amount reinvested in replacement property is *less than* the amount realized, realized gain *is recognized* to the extent of the deficiency.

By its terms, § 1033 generally is *elective*. A taxpayer need not postpone recognition of gain, even if replacement property is acquired. In essence, a taxpayer has three options:

- Reinvest the proceeds and elect § 1033's nonrecognition of gain.
- Reinvest the proceeds and not elect § 1033, thereby triggering recognition of realized gain under the usual rules applicable to property transactions.
- Not reinvest the proceeds and recognize the realized gain accordingly.

If a *loss* occurs on an involuntary conversion, § 1033 does not apply and the general rules for loss recognition are effective. See Chapter 6 for the discussion of the deduction of losses.

7-5a Involuntary Conversion Defined

An **involuntary conversion** results from the destruction (complete or partial), theft, seizure, requisition or condemnation, or sale or exchange under threat or imminence of requisition or condemnation of the taxpayer's property.[59] This description includes fires (other than arson),[60] tornadoes, hurricanes, earthquakes, floods, and other natural disasters. In these circumstances, *gain* can result from insurance proceeds received in an amount that exceeds the taxpayer's historical cost of the property, especially if depreciation deductions have lowered the property's adjusted basis.

For requisitions and condemnations, the amount realized includes the compensation paid by the public authority acquiring the taxpayer's property. To prove the existence of a threat or imminence of condemnation, the taxpayer must obtain confirmation that there has been a decision to acquire the property for public use. In addition, the taxpayer must have reasonable grounds to believe the property will be taken.[61] The property does not have to be sold to the authority threatening to condemn it to qualify for § 1033 postponement. If the taxpayer satisfies the confirmation and reasonable grounds requirements, he or she can sell the property to another party.[62] Likewise, the sale of property to a condemning authority by a taxpayer who acquired the property from its former owner with the knowledge that the property was under threat of condemnation also qualifies as an involuntary conversion under § 1033.[63]

In-depth coverage can be found on this book's companion website: www.cengagebrain.com   **12 DIGGING DEEPER**

7-5b Replacement Property

The requirements for replacement property under the involuntary conversion rules generally are more restrictive than those for like-kind property under § 1031. The basic requirement is that the replacement property be similar or related in service or use to the involuntarily converted property.[64]

Different interpretations of the phrase *similar or related in service or use* apply depending on whether the involuntarily converted property is held by an *owner-user* or by an *owner-investor* (e.g., lessor). For an owner-investor, the *taxpayer use test* applies, and for an owner-user, the *functional use test* applies. Furthermore, a special test applies in the case of involuntary conversions that result from condemnations.

[59]§ 1033(a) and Reg. §§ 1.1033(a)–1(a) and –2(a).
[60]Rev.Rul. 82–74, 1982–1 C.B. 110.
[61]Rev.Rul. 63–221, 1963–2 C.B. 332, and *Joseph P. Balistrieri*, 38 TCM 526, T.C.Memo. 1979–115.
[62]Rev.Rul. 81–180, 1981–2 C.B. 161.
[63]Rev.Rul. 81–181, 1981–2 C.B. 162.
[64]§ 1033(a) and Reg. § 1.1033(a)–1.

Functional Use Test

Under this test, a taxpayer's use of the replacement property and of the involuntarily converted property must be the same. Replacing a manufacturing plant with a wholesale grocery warehouse does not meet this test. Instead, the plant must be replaced with another facility of similar functional use.

Taxpayer Use Test

The taxpayer use test for owner-investors provides the taxpayer with more flexibility in terms of what qualifies as replacement property than does the functional use test for owner-users. Essentially, the properties must be used by the taxpayer (the owner-investor) in similar endeavors. For example, rental property held by an owner-investor qualifies if replaced by other rental property, regardless of the type of rental property involved. The test is met when an investor replaces a manufacturing plant with a wholesale grocery warehouse if both properties are held for the production of rental income.[65] The replacement of a rental residence with a personal residence does not meet the test.[66]

Special Rule for Condemnations

In addition to the functional and taxpayer use tests, the Code provides a special rule for business or investment real property *that is condemned*. This rule applies the broad like-kind classification for real estate to such circumstances. Accordingly, improved real property can be replaced with unimproved real property.

The rules concerning the nature of replacement property are illustrated in Concept Summary 7.3.

Concept Summary 7.3

Involuntary Conversions: Replacement Property Tests

Type of Property and User	Taxpayer Use Test	Functional Use Test	Special Rule for Condemnations*
An investor's rented shopping mall is destroyed by fire; the mall may be replaced with other rental properties (e.g., an apartment building).	X		
A manufacturing plant is destroyed by fire; replacement property must consist of another manufacturing plant that is functionally the same as the property converted.		X	
Personal residence of a taxpayer is condemned by a local government authority; replacement property must consist of another personal residence.		X	
Land used by a manufacturing company is condemned by a local government authority.			X
Apartment and land held by an investor are sold due to the threat or imminence of condemnation.			X

*Applies the same test as in the case of like-kind exchanges.

7-5c Time Limitation on Replacement

The taxpayer normally has a two-year period after the close of the taxable year in which gain is realized from an involuntary conversion to replace the property.[67] This rule

---

[65]*Loco Realty Co. v. Comm.*, 62–2 USTC ¶9657, 10 AFTR 2d 5359, 306 F.2d 207 (CA–8, 1962).

[66]Rev.Rul. 70–466, 1970–2 C.B. 165.

[67]§§ 1033(a)(2)(B) and (g)(4) and Reg. § 1.1033(a)–2(c)(3). The two-year period is extended to a four-year period if the property is located in a Presidentially-declared disaster area.

affords as much as three years from the date of realization of gain to replace the property if the realization of gain took place on the first day of the taxable year.[68]

Magpie, Inc.'s building is destroyed by fire on December 16, 2014. The adjusted basis is $325,000. Magpie receives $400,000 from the insurance company on January 10, 2015. The company is a calendar year and cash method taxpayer. The latest date for replacement is December 31, 2017 (the end of the taxable year in which realized gain occurred plus two years). The critical date is not the date the involuntary conversion occurred, but rather the date of gain realization (when the insurance proceeds are received).

In the case of a condemnation of real property used in a trade or business or held for investment, the Code substitutes a three-year period for the normal two-year period. In this case, a taxpayer might have as many as four years from the date of realization of gain to replace the property.

Assume the same facts as in the preceding example, except that Magpie's building is condemned. On November 1, 2014, Magpie receives notification of the future condemnation, which occurs on December 16, 2014. The condemnation proceeds are received on January 10, 2015. The latest date for replacement is December 31, 2018 (the end of the taxable year in which realized gain occurred plus three years).

The *earliest date* for replacement typically is the date the involuntary conversion occurs. However, if the property is condemned, it is possible to replace the condemned property before this date. In this case, the earliest date is the date of the threat or imminence of requisition or condemnation of the property. The purpose of this provision is to enable the taxpayer to make an orderly replacement of the condemned property.

7-5d Nonrecognition of Gain

Nonrecognition of gain can be either mandatory or elective, depending on whether the conversion is direct (into replacement property) or indirect (into money).

Direct Conversion

If the conversion is directly into replacement property rather than into money, nonrecognition of realized gain is *mandatory*. In this case, the basis of the replacement property is the same as the adjusted basis of the converted property. Direct conversion is rare in practice and usually involves condemnations.

Oak, Inc.'s property, with an adjusted basis of $20,000, is condemned by the state. Oak receives property with a fair market value of $50,000 as compensation for the property taken. Because the nonrecognition of realized gain is mandatory for direct conversions, Oak's realized gain of $30,000 is not recognized and the basis of the replacement property is $20,000 (adjusted basis of the condemned property).

Conversion into Money

If the conversion is into money, the realized gain is recognized only to the extent the amount realized from the involuntary conversion exceeds the cost of the qualifying replacement property.[69] This is the usual case, and nonrecognition (postponement) is *elective*. If the election is not made, the realized gain is recognized.

The basis of the replacement property is the property's cost less any postponed (deferred) gain.[70] If the election to postpone gain is made, the holding period of the replacement property includes the holding period of the converted property.

---

[68]A taxpayer can apply for an extension of this time period anytime before its expiration [Reg. § 1.1033(a)–2(c)(3)]. Also, the period for filing the application for extension can be extended if a taxpayer shows reasonable cause.

[69]§ 1033(a)(2)(A) and Reg. § 1.1033(a)–2(c)(1).
[70]§ 1033(b).

Section 1033 applies *only to gains* and *not to losses*. Losses from involuntary conversions are recognized if the property is held for business or income-producing purposes. Personal casualty losses are recognized, but condemnation losses related to personal use assets (e.g., a personal residence) are neither recognized nor postponed.

The Big Picture

EXAMPLE 37

Return to the facts of *The Big Picture* on p. 7-1. Alice's building (used in her trade or business), with an adjusted basis of $50,000, is destroyed by a fire on October 5, 2015. Alice is a calendar year taxpayer. On November 17, 2015, she receives an insurance reimbursement of $100,000 for the loss. Assume that Alice goes ahead with her plan to invest $80,000 in a new building and to use the other $20,000 of insurance proceeds to pay off credit card debt.

- Alice has until December 31, 2017, to make the new investment and qualify for the nonrecognition election.

- Alice's realized gain is $50,000 ($100,000 insurance proceeds received − $50,000 adjusted basis of old building).

- Assuming that the replacement property qualifies as similar or related in service or use, Alice's recognized gain is $20,000. Because she reinvested $20,000 less than the insurance proceeds received ($100,000 proceeds − $80,000 reinvested), her realized gain is recognized to that extent.

- Alice's basis in the new building is $50,000. This is the building's cost of $80,000 less the postponed gain of $30,000 (realized gain of $50,000 − recognized gain of $20,000).

The Big Picture

EXAMPLE 38

Return to the facts of *The Big Picture* on p. 7-1. Assume the same facts as in the previous example, except that Alice receives only $45,000 of insurance proceeds. She has a realized and recognized loss of $5,000. The basis of the new building is the building's cost of $80,000.

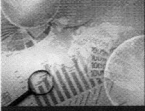

TAX PLANNING STRATEGIES   Recognizing Involuntary Conversion Gains

FRAMEWORK FOCUS: TAX RATE

Strategy: Shift Net Income from High-Bracket Years to Low-Bracket Years.

FRAMEWORK FOCUS: DEDUCTIONS

Strategy: Maximize Deductible Amounts.

Sometimes, a taxpayer may prefer to *recognize a gain from an involuntary conversion* and will choose not to elect § 1033, even though replacement property is acquired. Circumstances suggesting this strategy would include:

- The taxpayer realized the gain in a low-bracket tax year, quite possibly because of the events that caused the involuntary conversion, such as a flood and its aftermath that seriously disrupted the business.

- The taxpayer has an expiring net operating loss carryover that can offset most, if not all, of the gain from the involuntary conversion.

- The replacement property is depreciable, and the taxpayer would prefer an unreduced basis for this asset to maximize depreciation deductions in future years.

Nontax considerations might also come into play, perhaps suggesting that the property not be replaced at all. Even before the event that produced the involuntary conversion, the taxpayer might have been wanting to downsize the business or terminate it outright. In any case, the taxpayer might prefer to recognize the gain, pay the tax involved, and thereby free up the remaining proceeds for other uses—business, investment, or even personal—especially if the gain is small compared to the amount of proceeds received.

7-6 OTHER NONRECOGNITION PROVISIONS

LO.7

Identify other nonrecognition provisions contained in the Code.

Several additional nonrecognition provisions are treated briefly in the remainder of this chapter.

7-6a Transfer of Assets to Business Entity—§§ 351 and 721

Taxpayers can transfer assets to corporations in exchange for stock without recognizing gain or loss on the transfer according to § 351. See Chapter 12 for the applicable restrictions and corresponding basis adjustments for the stock acquired. A similar provision (§ 721) allows the nontaxable transfer of assets to a partnership in exchange for an interest in that partnership. See Chapter 14 for a description of § 721.

7-6b Exchange of Stock for Property—§ 1032

Under § 1032, a corporation does not recognize gain or loss on the receipt of money or other property in exchange for its stock (including treasury stock). In other words, a corporation does not recognize gain or loss when it deals in its own stock. This provision accords with the accounting treatment of such transactions. See Chapter 12 for additional discussion.

7-6c Certain Exchanges of Insurance Policies—§ 1035

Under § 1035, no gain or loss is recognized from the exchange of certain insurance contracts or policies. The rules relating to exchanges not solely in kind (i.e., with boot) and the basis of the property acquired are the same as under § 1031. Exchanges qualifying for nonrecognition include the following:

- The exchange of life insurance contracts.
- The exchange of a life insurance contract for an endowment or annuity contract.
- The exchange of an endowment contract for another endowment contract that provides for regular payments beginning at a date not later than the date payments would have begun under the contract exchanged.
- The exchange of an endowment contract for an annuity contract.
- The exchange of annuity contracts.

7-6d Exchange of Stock for Stock of the Same Corporation—§ 1036

Section 1036 provides that a shareholder does not recognize gain or loss on the exchange of common stock solely for common stock in the same corporation or from the exchange of preferred stock for preferred stock in the same corporation. Exchanges between individual shareholders as well as between a shareholder and the corporation are included under this nonrecognition provision. The rules relating to exchanges not solely in kind and the basis of the property acquired are the same as under § 1031. For example, a nonrecognition exchange occurs when common stock with different rights, such as voting for nonvoting, is exchanged. A shareholder usually recognizes gain or loss from the exchange of common for preferred or preferred for common even though the stock exchanged is in the same corporation.

7-6e Rollovers into Specialized Small Business Investment Companies—§ 1044

Section 1044 provides a postponement opportunity associated with the sale of publicly traded securities. If the amount realized is reinvested in the common stock or partnership interest of a specialized small business investment company (SSBIC), the realized gain is not recognized. Gain will be recognized, however, to the extent of any amount not reinvested. To qualify, the taxpayer must reinvest the proceeds within 60 days of the date of sale.

7-6f Sale of a Principal Residence—§ 121

Section 121 allows individual taxpayers to exclude gain from the sale of a *principal residence*. This provision applies to the first $250,000 of realized gain, or $500,000 on certain joint returns. For this purpose, the residence must have been owned and used by the taxpayer as the primary residence for at least two of the five years preceding the date of sale. In addition, the exclusion is not available for sales occurring within two years of its last use. This exclusion can be prorated, however, if a taxpayer failed to meet one or more of these time period requirements due to a change in his or her place of employment or health. Moreover, a surviving spouse counts the ownership and usage periods of the decedent spouse in meeting the two-year test. This provision applies only to gains; losses on residences, like those of other personal-use assets, are not recognized for tax purposes.

DIGGING DEEPER 13, 14, 15   **In-depth coverage can be found on this book's companion website: www.cengagebrain.com**

7-6g Transfers of Property between Spouses or Incident to Divorce—§ 1041

Section 1041 provides for nontaxable exchange treatment on property transfers *between spouses during marriage*. The basis to the recipient spouse is a carryover basis.

Section 1041 also provides that transfers of property *between spouses or former spouses incident to divorce* are nontaxable transactions. Therefore, the basis to the recipient is a carryover basis. To be treated as incident to the divorce, the transfer must be related to the cessation of marriage or must occur within one year after the date on which the marriage ceases.

REFOCUS ON THE BIG PICTURE

CALCULATING BASIS AND RECOGNIZED GAIN FOR PROPERTY TRANSACTIONS

Alice's basis in the land acquired as a gift is a carryover basis of $2,000. If Alice sells the land outright, she will realize and recognize a gain of $48,000. However, if she replaces the property with other real property, she should be able to qualify for favorable like-kind exchange treatment under § 1031 and defer the gain on the property disposition. However, if Alice receives any cash from the exchange, realized gain would be recognized to the extent of the cash (boot) received.

Alice's basis in the 300 shares of stock received as an inheritance is the property's $30,000 fair market value at the date of death. If Alice sells the 300 shares, she will realize and recognize a $6,000 gain [$36,000 sales price (300 shares × $120) − $30,000 basis].

Alice's basis in the 200 shares of stock purchased is her purchase price of $28,000. Those shares are currently worth $24,000 (200 shares × $120). Consequently, if she sells those shares, she will realize and recognize a $4,000 loss.

continued

You advise Alice that her basis in the house is its $475,000 fair market value on the date of her grandmother's death. If Alice sells the house for $600,000, her realized and recognized gain would be $125,000.

Regarding the fire-related involuntary conversion of Alice's business building, a $50,000 realized gain occurs upon the receipt of the $100,000 of insurance proceeds. Because she intends to invest only $80,000 of the insurance proceeds in a qualifying property, Alice's recognized gain will be $20,000 ($100,000 proceeds − $80,000 reinvested). Therefore, her realized gain would be recognized to that extent (see Example 37).

What If?

Alice is leaning toward selling the house. However, she knows that her grandmother would not want her to have to pay income taxes on the sale. Alice asks whether there is any way she could avoid paying taxes on the sale.

You inform Alice of the exclusion provision under § 121. Alice can qualify for this exclusion of up to $250,000 of realized gain if she owns and occupies the house as her principal residence for at least two of the five years prior to a sale.

From a tax planning perspective, what can Alice do so that none of the $50,000 of realized gain from the involuntary conversion is recognized? To have full postponement of the $50,000 realized gain, Alice would have to reinvest all of the $100,000 of insurance proceeds received in another qualified building. Under this circumstance, the basis of the replacement building would be $50,000 ($100,000 cost of replacement building − $50,000 deferred gain).

Suggested Readings

Mary Cunningham, "Accomplishing Section 1031 Tax-Deferred Exchanges," *Practical Tax Strategies*, August 2014.

James R. Hamill, "Preserving the Residence Sale Exclusion for Mixed Use Property," *Practical Tax Strategies*, June 2013.

Katherine M. Hetherington and Timothy R. Hurley, "Selling Principal Residence When Debt Exceeds Fair Market Value," *Practical Tax Strategies*, February 2013.

Christian J. Kenefick, "What Is a $10 Gold Coin Worth? Basis, FMV, and Realization Issues Abound," *Journal of Taxation*, February 2013.

Edward J. Schnee, "Like-Kind Exchange Rules: Continued Evolution," *The Tax Adviser*, July 2014.

Jay A. Soled, Leonard Goodman, and Anthony Pochesci, "Penalty Exposure for Incorrect Tax Basis Reporting on Information Returns," *Journal of Taxation*, August 2013.

Key Terms

Adjusted basis, 7-3	Holding period, 7-12	Realized loss, 7-2
Amount realized, 7-3	Involuntary conversion, 7-25	Recognized gain, 7-6
Boot, 7-21	Like-kind exchanges, 7-19	Recognized loss, 7-6
Fair market value, 7-3	Nontaxable exchange, 7-18	Wash sale, 7-15
Goodwill, 7-9	Realized gain, 7-2	

Computational Exercises

1. **LO.3** Luciana, a nonshareholder, purchases a condominium from her employer for $85,000. The fair market value of the condominium is $120,000. What is Luciana's basis in the condominium and the amount of any income as a result of this purchase?

2. **LO.3** Sebastian purchases two pieces of equipment for $100,000. Appraisals of the equipment indicate that the fair market value of the first piece of equipment is $72,000 and that of the second piece of equipment is $108,000. What is Sebastian's basis in these two assets?

3. **LO.2, 4** Lisa sells business property with an adjusted basis of $130,000 to her son, Alfred, for its fair market value of $100,000.
   a. What is Lisa's realized and recognized gain or loss?
   b. What is Alfred's recognized gain or loss if he subsequently sells the property for $138,000? For $80,000?

4. **LO.4** Arianna's personal residence has an adjusted basis of $230,000 and a fair market value of $210,000. Arianna converts the personal residence to rental property. What is Arianna's gain basis? What is her loss basis?

Critical Thinking 5. **LO.1, 4** Peyton sells an office building and the associated land on May 1, 2015. Under the terms of the sales contract, Peyton is to receive $1,600,000 in cash. The purchaser is to assume Peyton's mortgage of $950,000 on the property. To enable the purchaser to obtain adequate financing, Peyton is to pay the $9,000 in points charged by the lender. The broker's commission on the sale is $75,000. The purchaser agrees to pay the $24,000 in property taxes for the entire year. What is Peyton's amount realized?

6. **LO.2, 5** Logan and Johnathan exchange land, and the exchange qualifies as like kind under § 1031. Because Logan's land (adjusted basis of $85,000) is worth $100,000 and Johnathan's land has a fair market value of $80,000, Johnathan also gives Logan cash of $20,000.
   a. What is Logan's recognized gain?
   b. Assume instead that Johnathan's land is worth $90,000 and he gives Logan $10,000 cash. Now what is Logan's recognized gain?

7. **LO.2, 6** Camilo's property, with an adjusted basis of $155,000, is condemned by the state. Camilo receives property with a fair market value of $180,000 as compensation for the property taken.
   a. What is Camilo's realized and recognized gain?
   b. What is the basis of the replacement property?

Critical Thinking 8. **LO.2, 7** Constanza, who is single, sells her current personal residence (adjusted basis of $165,000) for $450,000. She has owned and lived in the house for 30 years. Her selling expenses are $22,500. What is Constanza's realized and recognized gain?

Problems

9. **LO.1** If a taxpayer sells property for cash, the amount realized consists of the net proceeds from the sale. For each of the following, indicate the effect on the amount realized:
   a. The property is sold on credit.
   b. A mortgage on the property is assumed by the buyer.

c. A mortgage on the property of the buyer is assumed by the seller.

d. The buyer acquires the property subject to a mortgage of the seller.

e. Stock that has a basis to the purchaser of $6,000 and a fair market value of $10,000 is received by the seller as part of the consideration.

10. **LO.1, 2** Pam owns a personal-use boat that has a fair market value of $35,000 and an adjusted basis of $45,000. Pam's AGI is $100,000. Calculate the realized and recognized gain or loss if:

a. Pam sells the boat for $35,000.

b. Pam exchanges the boat for another boat worth $35,000.

c. The boat is stolen and Pam receives insurance proceeds of $35,000.

d. Would your answer in (a) change if the fair market value and the selling price of the boat were $48,000?

11. **LO.1, 2** Yancy's personal residence is condemned as part of an urban renewal project. His adjusted basis for the residence is $480,000. He receives condemnation proceeds of $460,000 and invests the proceeds in stocks and bonds.

a. Calculate Yancy's realized and recognized gain or loss.

b. If the condemnation proceeds are $505,000, what are Yancy's realized and recognized gain or loss?

c. What are Yancy's realized and recognized gain or loss in (a) if the house was rental property?

12. **LO.1, 2, 3** Finch, Inc., purchases 1,000 shares of Bluebird Corporation stock on October 3, 2015, for $300,000. On December 12, 2015, Finch purchases an additional 750 shares of Bluebird stock for $210,000. According to market quotations, Bluebird stock is selling for $285 per share on December 31, 2015. Finch sells 500 shares of Bluebird stock on March 1, 2016, for $162,500.

a. What is the adjusted basis of Finch's Bluebird stock on December 31, 2015?

b. What is Finch's recognized gain or loss from the sale of Bluebird stock on March 1, 2016, assuming the shares sold are from the shares purchased on December 12, 2015?

c. What is Finch's recognized gain or loss from the sale of Bluebird stock on March 1, 2016, assuming Finch cannot adequately identify the shares sold?

13. **LO.2, 3** Rod Clooney purchases Agnes Mitchell's sole proprietorship for $990,000 on August 15, 2015. The assets of the business are as follows:

Communications

Asset	Agnes's Adjusted Basis	FMV
Accounts receivable	$ 70,000	$ 70,000
Inventory	90,000	100,000
Equipment	150,000	160,000
Furniture and fixtures	95,000	130,000
Building	190,000	250,000
Land	25,000	75,000
Total	$620,000	$785,000

Rod and Agnes agree that $50,000 of the purchase price is for Agnes's five-year covenant not to compete.

a. Calculate Agnes's realized and recognized gain.

b. Determine Rod's basis for each of the assets.

c. Write a letter to Rod informing him of the tax consequences of the purchase. His address is 300 Riverview Drive, Delaware, OH 43015.

14. **LO.1, 2, 3** Roberto has received various gifts over the years. He has decided to dispose of the following assets he received as gifts:

   a. In 1951, he received land worth $32,000. The donor's adjusted basis was $35,000. Roberto sells the land for $95,000 in 2015.

   b. In 1956, he received stock in Gold Company. The donor's adjusted basis was $19,000. The fair market value on the date of the gift was $34,000. Roberto sells the stock for $40,000 in 2015.

   c. In 1962, he received land worth $15,000. The donor's adjusted basis was $20,000. Roberto sells the land for $9,000 in 2015.

   d. In 2003, he received stock worth $30,000. The donor's adjusted basis was $42,000. Roberto sells the stock for $38,000 in 2015.

   What is the recognized gain or loss from each of the preceding transactions? Assume for each of the gift transactions that no gift tax was paid.

15. **LO.1, 2, 3** Nicky receives a car from Sam as a gift. Sam paid $48,000 for the car. He had used it for business purposes and had deducted $10,000 for depreciation up to the time he gave the car to Nicky. The fair market value of the car is $33,000.

   a. Assuming that Nicky uses the car for business purposes, what is her basis for depreciation?

   b. Assume that Nicky deducts depreciation of $6,500 and then sells the car for $32,500. What is her recognized gain or loss?

   c. Assume that Nicky deducts depreciation of $6,500 and then sells the car for $20,000. What is her recognized gain or loss?

Issue ID   16. **LO.3** Simon owns stock that has declined in value since acquired. He has decided either to give the stock to his nephew, Fred, or to sell it and give Fred the proceeds. If Fred receives the stock, he will sell it to obtain the proceeds. Simon is in the 15% tax bracket, while Fred's bracket is 25%. In either case, the holding period for the stock will be short-term. Identify the tax issues relevant to Simon in deciding whether to give the stock or the sale proceeds to Fred.

17. **LO.3** On September 18, 2015, Gerald received land and a building from Frank as a gift. Frank's adjusted basis and the fair market value at the date of the gift are as follows:

Asset	Adjusted Basis	FMV
Land	$100,000	$212,000
Building	80,000	100,000

   No gift tax was paid on the transfer.

   a. Determine Gerald's adjusted basis for the land and building.

   b. Assume instead that the fair market value of the land was $87,000 and that of the building was $65,000. Determine Gerald's adjusted basis for the land and building.

18. **LO.3** Dan bought a hotel for $2,600,000 in January 2011. In May 2015, he died and left the hotel to Ed. While Dan owned the hotel, he deducted $289,000 of cost recovery. The fair market value in May 2015 was $2,800,000. The fair market value six months later was $2,850,000.

   a. What is the basis of the property to Ed?

   b. What is the basis of the property to Ed if the fair market value six months later was $2,500,000 (not $2,850,000) and the objective of the executor was to minimize the estate tax liability?

19. **LO.4** Sheila sells land to Elane, her sister, for the fair market value of $40,000. Six months later when the land is worth $45,000, Elane gives it to Jacob, her son. (No gift tax resulted.) Shortly thereafter, Jacob sells the land for $48,000.

    a. Assuming that Sheila's adjusted basis for the land is $24,000, what are Sheila's and Jacob's recognized gain or loss on the sales?

    b. Assuming that Sheila's adjusted basis for the land is $60,000, what are Sheila's and Jacob's recognized gain or loss on the sales?

20. **LO.1, 2, 3, 4** Tyneka inherited 1,000 shares of Aqua, Inc. stock from Joe. Joe's basis was $35,000, and the fair market value on July 1, 2015 (the date of death), was $45,000. The shares were distributed to Tyneka on July 15, 2015. Tyneka sold the stock on July 30, 2016, for $33,000. After giving the matter more thought, she decides that Aqua is a good investment and purchases 1,000 shares for $30,000 on August 20, 2016.   *Decision Making*

    a. What is Tyneka's basis for the 1,000 shares purchased on August 20, 2016?

    b. Could Tyneka have obtained different tax consequences in (a) if she had sold the 1,000 shares on December 27, 2015, and purchased the 1,000 shares on January 5, 2016? Explain.

21. **LO.4** Sam owns 1,500 shares of Eagle, Inc. stock that he purchased over 10 years ago for $80,000. Although the stock has a current market value of $52,000, Sam still views the stock as a solid long-term investment. He has sold other stock during the year with overall gains of $30,000, so he would like to sell the Eagle stock and off-set the $28,000 loss against these gains—but somehow keep his Eagle investment. He has devised a plan to keep his Eagle investment by using funds in his traditional IRA to purchase 1,500 Eagle shares immediately after selling the shares he currently owns. Evaluate Sam's treatment of these stock transactions. Can his plan work? Explain.   *Ethics and Equity*

22. **LO.1, 2, 4** Abby's home had a basis of $360,000 ($160,000 attributable to the land) and a fair market value of $340,000 ($155,000 attributable to the land) when she converted 70% of it to business use by opening a bed-and-breakfast. Four years after the conversion, Abby sells the home for $500,000 ($165,000 attributable to the land).

    a. Calculate Abby's basis for gain, loss, and cost recovery for the portion of her personal residence that was converted to business use.

    b. Calculate the cost recovery deducted by Abby during the four-year period of business use assuming that the bed-and-breakfast is opened on January 1 of year 1 and the house is sold on December 31 of year 4.

    c. What is Abby's recognized gain or loss on the sale of the business-use portion?

23. **LO.4** Surendra's personal residence originally cost $340,000 (ignore land). After living in the house for five years, he converts it to rental property. At the date of conversion, the fair market value of the house is $320,000. As to the rental property, calculate Surendra's basis for: *Critical Thinking* *Decision Making*

    a. Loss.

    b. Depreciation.

    c. Gain.

    d. Could Surendra have obtained better tax results if he had sold his personal residence for $320,000 and then purchased another house for $320,000 to hold as rental property? Explain.

24. **LO.5** Sue exchanges a sport utility vehicle (adjusted basis of $16,000; fair market value of $19,500) for cash of $2,000 and a pickup truck (fair market value of $17,500). Both vehicles are for business use. Sue believes that her basis for the truck is $17,500. In calculating her basis, what has Sue failed to consider?

Issue ID   25. **LO.6** A warehouse owned by M&S (a partnership) and used in its business (i.e., to store inventory) is being condemned by the city to provide a right-of-way for a highway. The warehouse has appreciated by $180,000 based on an estimate of fair market value. In the negotiations, the city is offering $35,000 less than what M&S believes the property is worth. Alan, a real estate broker, has offered to purchase the property for $20,000 more than the city's offer. The partnership plans to invest the proceeds it will receive in an office building that it will lease to various tenants.

   a.   Identify the relevant tax issues for M&S.

   b.   Would the answer in (a) change if M&S's warehouse was property being held for investment rather than being used in its business? Explain.

Decision Making   26. **LO.5** Tanya Fletcher owns undeveloped land (adjusted basis of $80,000 and fair market value of $92,000) on the East Coast. On January 4, 2015, she exchanges it with Martin (an unrelated party) for undeveloped land on the West Coast and $3,000 cash. Martin has an adjusted basis of $72,000 for his land, and its fair market value is $89,000. As the real estate market on the East Coast is thriving, on September 1, 2016, Martin sells the land he acquired for $120,000.

Communications

   a.   What are Tanya's recognized gain or loss and adjusted basis for the West Coast land on January 4, 2015?

   b.   What are Martin's recognized gain or loss and adjusted basis for the East Coast land on January 4, 2015?

   c.   What is Martin's recognized gain or loss from the September 1, 2016 sale?

   d.   What effect does Martin's 2016 sale have on Tanya?

   e.   Write a letter to Tanya advising her of the tax consequences of this exchange. Her address is The Corral, El Paso, TX 79968.

27. **LO.5** Starling Corporation exchanges a yellow bus (used in its business) for Robin Corporation's gray bus and some garage equipment (used in its business). The assets have the following characteristics:

	Adjusted Basis	Fair Market Value
Yellow bus	$6,000	$15,000
Gray bus	3,000	11,000
Equipment	2,000	4,000

   a.   What are Starling's recognized gain or loss and basis for the gray bus and garage equipment?

   b.   What are Robin's recognized gain or loss and basis for the yellow bus?

28. **LO.5** Maple Company owns a machine (adjusted basis of $90,000; fair market value of $125,000) that it uses in its business. Maple exchanges it for another machine (worth $100,000) and stock (worth $25,000). Determine Maple's:

   a.   Realized and recognized gain or loss on the exchange.

   b.   Basis in the new machine.

   c.   Basis in the stock Maple received.

Issue ID   29. **LO.5** Tulip, Inc., would like to dispose of some land it acquired four years ago because the land will not continue to appreciate. Its value has increased by $50,000 over the four-year period. The company also intends to sell stock that has declined in value by $50,000 during the six months since its purchase. Tulip has four offers to acquire the stock and land:

   Buyer 1:   Exchange land.
   Buyer 2:   Purchase land for cash.
   Buyer 3:   Exchange stock.
   Buyer 4:   Purchase stock for cash.

Identify the tax issues relevant to Tulip in disposing of this land and stock.

30. **LO.5** What is the basis of the new property in each of the following exchanges?
   a. Apartment building held for investment (adjusted basis of $145,000) for office building to be held for investment (fair market value of $225,000).
   b. Land and building used as a barbershop (adjusted basis of $190,000) for land and building used as a grocery store (fair market value of $350,000).
   c. Office building (adjusted basis of $45,000) for bulldozer (fair market value of $42,000), both held for business use.
   d. IBM common stock (adjusted basis of $20,000) for ExxonMobil common stock (fair market value of $28,000).
   e. Rental house (adjusted basis of $90,000) for mountain cabin to be held for personal use (fair market value of $225,000).
   f. General partnership interest (adjusted basis of $400,000) for a limited partnership interest (fair market value of $580,000).

31. **LO.1, 2, 5** Rose Company owns Machine A (adjusted basis of $12,000 and fair market value of $15,000), which it uses in its business. Rose sells Machine A for $15,000 to Aubry (a dealer) and then purchases Machine B for $15,000 from Joan (also a dealer). Machine B would normally qualify as like-kind property.
   a. What are Rose Company's realized and recognized gain on the sale of Machine A?
   b. What is Rose's basis for Machine B?
   c. What factors would motivate Rose to sell Machine A and purchase Machine B rather than exchange one machine for the other?
   d. Assume that the adjusted basis of Machine A is $15,000 and the fair market value of both machines is $12,000. Respond to (a) through (c).

32. **LO.5** Cardinal Properties, Inc., exchanges real estate used in its business along with stock for real estate to be held for investment. The stock transferred has an adjusted basis of $45,000 and a fair market value of $50,000. The real estate transferred has an adjusted basis of $85,000 and a fair market value of $190,000. The real estate acquired has a fair market value of $240,000.
   a. What is Cardinal's realized gain or loss?
   b. Its recognized gain or loss?
   c. The basis of the newly acquired real estate?

33. **LO.5** Tom and Frank are brothers. Each owns investment property in the other's hometown. To make their lives easier, they decide to legally exchange the investment properties. Under the terms of the exchange, Frank will transfer realty (adjusted basis of $52,000; fair market value of $80,000) and Tom will exchange realty (adjusted basis of $60,000; fair market value of $92,000). Tom's property is subject to a mortgage of $12,000 that will be assumed by Frank.   Decision Making
   a. What are Frank's and Tom's recognized gains?
   b. What are their adjusted bases?
   c. As an alternative, Frank has proposed that rather than assuming the mortgage, he will transfer cash of $12,000 to Tom. Tom would use the cash to pay off the mortgage. Advise Tom on whether this alternative would be beneficial to him from a tax perspective.

34. **LO.5** Determine the realized, recognized, and postponed gain or loss and the new basis for each of the following like-kind exchanges:

	Adjusted Basis of Old Asset	Boot Given	Fair Market Value of New Asset	Boot Received
a.	$ 7,000	$ –0–	$12,000	$4,000
b.	14,000	2,000	15,000	–0–
c.	3,000	7,000	8,000	500
d.	15,000	–0–	29,000	–0–
e.	10,000	–0–	11,000	1,000
f.	17,000	–0–	14,000	–0–

35. **LO.5** Turquoise Realty Company owns an apartment house that has an adjusted basis of $760,000 but is subject to a mortgage of $192,000. Turquoise transfers the apartment house to Dove, Inc., and receives from Dove $120,000 in cash and an office building with a fair market value of $780,000 at the time of the exchange. Dove assumes the $192,000 mortgage on the apartment house.

   a. What is Turquoise's realized gain or loss?

   b. What is its recognized gain or loss?

   c. What is the basis of the newly acquired office building?

Critical Thinking

Ethics and Equity

36. **LO.5** Randall owns an office building (adjusted basis of $250,000) that he has been renting to a group of physicians. During negotiations over a new seven-year lease, the physicians offer to purchase the building for $900,000. Randall accepts the offer with the stipulation that the sale be structured as a delayed § 1031 transaction. Consequently, the sales proceeds are paid to a qualified third-party intermediary on the closing date of September 30, 2015. On October 2, 2015, Randall properly identifies an office building that he would like to acquire. Unfortunately, on November 10, 2015, the property Randall selected is withdrawn from the market. Working with the intermediary, on November 12, 2015, Randall identifies another office building that meets his requirements. The purchase of this property closes on December 15, 2015, and the title is transferred to Randall. Randall treats the transaction as a § 1031 like-kind exchange. Even though the original office building identified was not acquired, Randall concludes that in substance, he has satisfied the 45-day rule. He identified the acquired office building as soon as the negotiations ceased on his first choice. Should the IRS accept Randall's attempt to comply? Explain.

37. **LO.6** Howard's roadside vegetable stand (adjusted basis of $275,000) is destroyed by a tractor-trailer accident. He receives insurance proceeds of $240,000 ($300,000 fair market value – $60,000 coinsurance). Howard immediately uses the proceeds plus additional cash of $45,000 to build another roadside vegetable stand at the same location. What are the tax consequences to Howard?

38. **LO.6** For each of the following involuntary conversions, indicate whether the property acquired qualifies as replacement property, the recognized gain, and the basis for the property acquired.

   a. A warehouse is destroyed by a tornado. The space in the warehouse was rented to various tenants. The adjusted basis was $470,000. The owner of the warehouse uses all of the insurance proceeds of $700,000 to build a shopping mall in a neighboring community where no property has been damaged by tornadoes. The shopping mall is rented to various tenants.

   b. A warehouse is destroyed by fire. The adjusted basis is $300,000. Because of economic conditions in the area, the owner decides not to rebuild the warehouse. Instead, it uses all of the insurance proceeds of $400,000 to build a warehouse in another state.

c. Ridge's personal residence is condemned as part of a local government project to widen the highway from two lanes to four lanes. The adjusted basis is $170,000. Ridge uses all of the condemnation proceeds of $200,000 to purchase another personal residence.

d. Swallow Fashions, Inc., owns a building that is destroyed by a hurricane. The adjusted basis is $250,000. Because of an economic downturn in the area caused by the closing of a military base, Swallow decides to rent space for its retail outlet rather than replace the building. It uses all of the insurance proceeds of $300,000 to buy a four-unit apartment building in another city. A realtor in that city will handle the rental of the apartments.

e. Susan and Rick's personal residence is destroyed by a tornado. They had owned it for 15 months. The adjusted basis was $170,000. Because they would like to travel, they decide not to acquire a replacement residence. Instead, they invest all of the insurance proceeds of $200,000 in a duplex, which they rent to tenants.

f. Ellen and Harry's personal residence (adjusted basis of $245,000) is destroyed in a flood. They had owned it for 18 months. Of the insurance proceeds of $350,000, they reinvest $342,000 in a replacement residence four months later.

39. **LO.6** Edith's warehouse (adjusted basis of $450,000) is destroyed by a hurricane in October 2015. Edith, a calendar year taxpayer, receives insurance proceeds of $525,000 in January 2016. Calculate Edith's realized gain or loss, recognized gain or loss, and basis for the replacement property if she:

a. Acquires a new warehouse for $550,000 in January 2016.

b. Acquires a new warehouse for $500,000 in January 2016.

c. Does not acquire replacement property.

40. **LO.7** Wesley, who is single, listed his personal residence with a real estate agent on March 3, 2015, at a price of $390,000. He rejected several offers in the $350,000 range during the summer. Finally, on August 16, 2015, he and the purchaser signed a contract to sell for $363,000. The sale (i.e., closing) took place on September 7, 2015. The closing statement showed the following disbursements: *Critical Thinking*

Real estate agent's commission	$ 21,780
Appraisal fee	600
Exterminator's certificate	300
Recording fees	800
Mortgage to First Bank	305,000
Cash to seller	34,520

Wesley's adjusted basis for the house is $200,000. He owned and occupied the house for seven years. On October 1, 2015, Wesley purchases another residence for $325,000.

a. Calculate Wesley's recognized gain on the sale.

b. What is Wesley's adjusted basis for the new residence?

c. Assume instead that the selling price is $800,000. What is Wesley's recognized gain? His adjusted basis for the new residence?

41. **LO.7** Roby and James have been married for nine years. Roby sells Plum, Inc. stock that she has owned for four years to James for its fair market value of $180,000. Her adjusted basis is $200,000.   *Critical Thinking* *Decision Making*

a. Calculate Roby's recognized gain or recognized loss.

b. Calculate James's adjusted basis for the stock.

c. How would the tax consequences in (a) and (b) differ if Roby had made a gift of the stock to James? Which form of the transaction would you recommend?

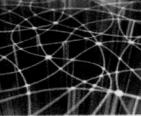

BRIDGE DISCIPLINE   Bridge Discipline

1. In April of the current year, Blue Corporation purchased an asset to be used in its manufacturing operations for $100,000. Blue's management expects the asset to ratably provide valuable services in the production process for eight years and have a salvage value of $12,000. The asset is a five-year asset for tax purposes. Blue has adopted the half-year convention for book purposes in the year of acquisition and disposition; Blue uses MACRS for tax purposes.
   a. Compute the depreciation expense in the year of acquisition for book and tax purposes.
   b. Identify the book-tax difference related to the depreciation expense in the year of acquisition.

2. Refer to the facts in the preceding problem. Assume that Blue Corporation disposes of the manufacturing asset at the beginning of year 7 for $40,000. Compute the amount of gain or loss recognized for book and tax purposes. What is the book-tax difference in the year of disposition?

3. Identify whether the taxpayer's economic position has changed in the following exchanges such that they are subject to current taxation. That is, identify whether the following qualify as like-kind exchanges under § 1031.
   a. Improved for unimproved real estate.
   b. Vending machine (used in business) for inventory.
   c. Rental house for personal residence.
   d. Business equipment for securities.
   e. Warehouse for office building (both used for business).
   f. Truck for computer (both used in business).
   g. Rental house for land (both held for investment).
   h. Ten shares of stock in Blue Corporation for 10 shares of stock in Red Corporation.
   i. Office furniture for office equipment (both used in business).
   j. Unimproved land in Jackson, Mississippi, for unimproved land in Toledo, Spain.
   k. General partnership interest for a general partnership interest.

Research Problems

Note: Solutions to Research Problems can be prepared by using the Checkpoint® Student Edition online research product, which is available to accompany this text. It is also possible to prepare solutions to the Research Problems by using tax research materials found in a standard tax library.

Communications   **Research Problem 1.** Ruth Ames died on January 10, 2015. In filing the estate tax return, her executor, Melvin Sims, elects the primary valuation date and amount (fair market value on the date of death). On March 12, 2015, Melvin invests $30,000 of cash that Ruth had in her money market account in acquiring 1,000 shares of Orange, Inc. ($30 per share). On January 10, 2015, Orange was selling for $29 per share. The stock is distributed to a beneficiary, Annette Rust, on June 1, 2015, when it is selling for $33 per share. Melvin wants you to determine the amount at which the Orange shares should appear on the estate tax return and the amount of Annette's adjusted basis for the stock. Write a letter to Melvin in which you respond to his inquiry, and prepare a memo for the tax files. His address is 100 Center Lane, Miami, FL 33124.

Research Problem 2. Terry owns real estate with an adjusted basis of $600,000 and a fair market value of $1.1 million. The amount of the nonrecourse mortgage on the property is $2.5 million. Because of substantial past and projected future losses associated with the real estate development (occupancy rate of only 37% after three years), Terry deeds the property to the creditor.

a. What are the tax consequences to Terry?

b. Assume that the data are the same, except that the fair market value of the property is $2,525,000. Therefore, when Terry deeds the property to the creditor, she also receives $25,000 from the creditor. What are the tax consequences to Terry?

Research Problem 3. Ted and Marvin Brown purchased an apartment building in 2004 as equal tenants in common. After a hectic decade of co-ownership, the brothers decided that their business association should be terminated. This led to the sale of the apartment building and a division of the proceeds.

Critical Thinking

The realized gain on the sale of the apartment building for each brother was $350,000. Ted recognized gain on his share and used the net proceeds to invest in stock. Marvin wanted to defer any recognized gain, so he worked with a realtor to identify property that would be eligible for § 1031 like-kind exchange treatment. After one prospect failed, the realtor identified a single-family home on Lake Tahoe that was currently being rented by the owner. Marvin agreed with the choice and acquired the single-family house, using the proceeds from the apartment building. Because the single-family house qualified as like-kind property, Marvin deferred all of his realized gain.

After attempting to rent the property for eight months without success, Marvin concluded that he could not continue to make the mortgage payments on his primary residence and this rental property. To ease his financial liquidity problem, Marvin sold his principal residence for a realized gain of $190,000 and moved into the Lake Tahoe house. He reported no recognized gain on the sale of his principal residence as the sale qualified for § 121 exclusion treatment.

The IRS issued a deficiency notice to Marvin associated with the sale of the apartment building. The position of the IRS was that Marvin did not hold the single-family residence for investment purposes as required by § 1031. Instead, his intention was personal—to use it as a replacement for his current residence that he planned on selling.

Who should prevail?

Use the tax resources of the Internet to address the following questions. Do not restrict your search to the Web, but include a review of newsgroups and general reference materials, practitioner sites and resources, primary sources of the tax law, chat rooms and discussion groups, and other opportunities.

Internet Activity

Research Problem 4. Many see the "step-up in basis at death" rule of § 1014 as an expensive tax loophole enjoyed by the wealthy. Find the latest estimates of the revenue loss to the Treasury that is attributable to this rule.

Communications

a. How does Canada's tax law determine the basis of property acquired from a decedent?

b. Send an e-mail to a member of the House Ways and Means Committee expressing a preference for the preservation of the current § 1014 rule or the modifications made to it by the Tax Relief Reconciliation Act of 2001 and the Tax Relief Act of 2010.

Research Problem 5. In general, the 45-day identification period and the 180-day exchange period for like-kind exchanges cannot be extended. Does this rule change if the like-kind property or the taxpayer involved in the exchange is located in a Presidentially declared disaster area? Use the IRS's website (**www.irs.gov**) to find the answer.

Roger CPA Review Questions

1. Kellye purchased her home in 20X4 for $140,000. After living in it for five years, she sold it in 20X9 for $170,000, its market value. What is the tax treatment of the sale of Kellye's home?
   a. A $30,000 gain is recognized, but not reported.
   b. A $30,000 gain is recognized and reported.
   c. A $30,000 gain is carried forward.
   d. The transaction is not reported.

2. Ike, a single taxpayer, is reassigned for his job and must move to a new state. While searching for a place to live, he encounters a person who is selling their home in order to move to Ike's current city. The two agree to trade their properties to each other without any further consideration. Ike's house has a fair market value of $200,000 and basis of $130,000. He has lived in the house for one year. The house he is acquiring in the trade has a fair market value of $300,000. What gain will Ike recognize for federal tax purposes?
   a. $50,000   c. $0
   b. $100,000   d. $300,000

3. Mikhail owns real estate with a basis of $400,000 and a fair market value of $650,000. He exchanges it for other real estate with a fair market value of $480,000. In addition, Mikhail is relieved of a mortgage on the old property of $200,000, assumes a mortgage on the new property of $100,000, and receives $70,000 in cash. Under Code Section 1031, what is Mikhail's recognized gain on the exchange?
   a. $170,000   c. $70,000
   b. $270,000   d. $350,000

4. Stephen purchased a video game console five years ago for $500. In order to raise money for the "latest and greatest" console, Stephen sold his console for $100. Because of advances in technology, Stephen can purchase the new console for $400. What is the tax treatment of Stephen's sale of his console?
   a. Stephen recognizes a $400 loss.
   b. Stephen does not report the sale.
   c. Stephen recognizes a $300 loss.
   d. Stephen recognizes a $100 gain.

5. Uncle Ubb gave his nephew, Leroy Lamprey, a gift of stock worth $10,000. Uncle Ubb's basis in the stock was $15,000. Leroy sold the stock to an unrelated party for $11,000. What amount of gain or loss should Leroy report as a result of this sale?
   a. $0   c. $200 gain
   b. $4,000 loss   d. $1,000 gain

6. On June 1, 20X13, Gary gave Gertrude a gift of stock worth $10,000, paying no gift tax on the transaction. Gary had purchased the stock for $7,500 in 20X11. On October 1, 20X13, Gertrude sold the stock to an unrelated party for $11,000. What is the amount and character of Gertrude's gain upon the sale?
   a. $1,000 short-term capital gain
   b. $3,500 long-term capital gain
   c. $1,000 long-term capital gain
   d. $3,500 short-term capital gain

7. Shomit purchases 100 shares of stock in Classy Corporation for $500 in Year 1. On December 20 of Year 2, he purchases an additional 100 shares in the company for $400. On December 27 of Year 2, Shomit sells the 100 shares acquired in Year 1 for $410. What is Shomit's resulting basis in the shares acquired on December 20 of Year 2?

    a. $400
    b. $500
    c. $490
    d. $410

8. Sengupta died on February 1, 20X14, and bequeathed two different assets to a beneficiary, Roberts. Asset One was distributed to Roberts on April 24, 20X14; Asset Two was distributed to Roberts on October 25, 20X14. The executor of Sengupta's estate makes a qualified alternate valuation date election. The basis of each bequeathed asset will thus be the fair market value on which date?

	Asset One	Asset Two
a.	August 1, 20X14	August 1, 20X14
b.	April 24, 20X14	August 1, 20X14
c.	April 24, 20X14	October 25, 20X14
d.	August 1, 20X14	October 25, 20X14

Property Transactions: Capital Gains and Losses, Section 1231, and Recapture Provisions

LEARNING OBJECTIVES: *After completing Chapter 8, you should be able to:*

LO.1 Explain the general scheme of taxation for capital gains and losses and distinguish capital assets from ordinary assets.

LO.2 State and explain the relevance of a sale or exchange to classification as a capital gain or loss.

LO.3 Determine the applicable holding period for a capital asset.

LO.4 Describe the tax treatment of capital gains and losses for noncorporate taxpayers.

LO.5 Describe the tax treatment of capital gains and losses for corporate taxpayers.

LO.6 Distinguish § 1231 assets from ordinary and capital assets and calculate § 1231 gain or loss.

LO.7 Determine when recapture provisions apply and derive their effects.

TAX TALK *Governments likely to confiscate wealth are unlikely to find much wealth to confiscate in the long run.* —THOMAS SOWELL

© MONKEY BUSINESS IMAGES/SHUTTERSTOCK.COM

Capital Gains and Losses, § 1231 Gains and Losses, and Recapture

Alice owns land that she received from her father 10 years ago as a gift. The land was purchased by her father in 1992 for $2,000 and was worth $10,000 at the time of the gift. The property is currently worth about $50,000. If Alice sells the land, you previously determined in Chapter 7 that she would have a taxable gain of $48,000.

Alice also owns 500 shares of AppleCo stock, 300 of which were acquired as an inheritance when Alice's grandfather died in 1996. Alice's grandfather paid $12,000 for the AppleCo shares, and they were worth $30,000 at the time of his death. If Alice sells those shares for $120 each, you previously determined that she would have a $6,000 taxable gain. The other 200 shares were purchased by Alice two months ago for $28,000. If Alice sells those shares for $120 each, you determined that she would have a recognized loss of $4,000.

Nine months ago, Alice purchased 100 shares of Eagle Company stock for $5,000. Also on the same day, Alice invested $50,000 in a 50 percent interest in a patent that Kathy, a former college roommate who is an unemployed inventor, had obtained for a special battery she had developed to power "green" cars. To date, Kathy has been unable to market the battery to an auto manufacturer or supplier, but she has high hopes of doing so in the future.

In addition, Alice purchased a franchise from Orange, Inc., for $100,000, which she subsequently sells to Maurve, Inc. for $101,000 nine months later.

Alice also owns a house that she inherited from her grandmother two years ago. Based on the estate tax return, the fair market value of the house at the date of her grandmother's death was $475,000, and Alice will recognize a $125,000 gain on the sale of the property.

Finally Alice's new husband, Jeff, sold depreciable equipment used in his sole proprietorship. The business purchased the equipment for $50,000 and deducted $35,000 of depreciation before selling it for $60,000.

Now Alice would like to know more about the gains and losses and the tax liability she and her husband can expect from these transactions.

Read the chapter and formulate your response.

Historically, for Federal income tax purposes, gains from capital assets have received preferential treatment in the form of either partial exclusion, lower rates, or a maximum tax rate. Losses from capital assets, however, have received less desirable treatment than losses from other assets. In addition, the Code has imposed limitations on when capital losses can be deducted to prevent taxpayers from manipulating their tax liability excessively.

During World War II, capital asset treatment was extended to other assets. These assets are now called "§ 1231 assets" after the Code Section that prescribes their special treatment. Later, Congress believed that this special treatment was no longer entirely warranted. Instead of repealing § 1231, however, Congress left that section in place but eroded many—but not all—of its benefits through *recapture provisions* in § 1245 and § 1250. Together, these Code Sections constitute one of the most complicated areas of tax law affecting both individual taxpayers and business entities.

Because taxpayers can time the realization of gains and losses by choosing when or even whether to sell the asset in question, preferential treatment is given for capital gains. The nature of this preferential treatment is discussed later in this chapter, but the essential point for now is that preferential treatment is confined to the excess of net long-term capital gains over net short-term capital losses. In addition, the tax law requires taxpayers to separate their capital asset transactions from their transactions involving noncapital assets. It further requires taxpayers to separate their long-term (i.e., more than one year) transactions from their short-term (i.e., one year or less) transactions. Moreover, certain types of capital assets (principally real estate and "collectibles") receive specific treatment apart from the rates generally applicable to capital assets.

LO.1

Explain the general scheme of taxation for capital gains and losses and distinguish capital assets from ordinary assets.

8-1 GENERAL SCHEME OF TAXATION

Recognized gains and losses must be properly classified. Proper classification depends upon three characteristics.

- The tax status of the property, including the specific type of asset.
- The manner of the property's disposition.
- The holding period of the property.

The three possible tax statuses are capital asset, § 1231 asset, and ordinary asset. Property disposition may be by sale, exchange, casualty, theft, or condemnation. The two relevant holding periods are one year or less (short-term) and more than one year (long-term).

8-2 CAPITAL ASSETS

Investments comprise the most typical category of capital assets and include corporate stocks and bonds, mutual funds, partnership interests, government securities, and vacant land. These assets can be held by any type of taxpayer—individuals; partnerships; limited liability companies; and corporations, whether closely held or publicly held. In addition, individuals own certain capital assets that are part of their daily life, such as residences, automobiles, furniture, and artwork. The classification of these *personal-use* assets as capital assets is relevant only when their disposition produces a recognized gain. Losses from the disposition of personal-use assets are not recognized for tax purposes, as explained in the preceding chapter. For businesses, goodwill is often the only capital asset.

DIGGING DEEPER 1   In-depth coverage can be found on this book's companion website: www.cengagebrain.com

8-2a **Definition of a Capital Asset (§ 1221)**

Capital assets are not directly defined in the Code. Instead, § 1221(a) defines what is *not* a capital asset. A capital asset is property held by the taxpayer that is *not* any of the following.

- Inventory or property held primarily for sale to customers in the ordinary course of a business. The Supreme Court, in *Malat v. Riddell*,[1] defined *primarily* as meaning "of first importance or principally."

- Accounts and notes receivable acquired from the sale of inventory or acquired for services rendered in the ordinary course of business.

- Depreciable property or real estate used in a business.

- Certain copyrights; literary, musical, or artistic compositions; or letters, memoranda, or similar property held by (1) a taxpayer whose efforts created the property; (2) in the case of a letter, memorandum, or similar property, a taxpayer for whom it was produced; or (3) a taxpayer who received the property as a lifetime gift from someone described in (1) or (2). When a sale or exchange involves musical compositions or copyrights in musical works either (1) created by the taxpayer's personal efforts or (2) having a basis determined by reference to the basis in the hands of a taxpayer whose personal efforts created the compositions or copyrights, the taxpayer may elect to treat the sale or exchange as the disposition of a capital asset.[2]

- U.S. government publications that are (1) received by a taxpayer from the U.S. government other than by purchase at the price at which they are offered for sale to the public or (2) held by a taxpayer who received the publication as a lifetime gift from someone described in (1).

- Supplies of a type regularly used or consumed in the ordinary course of a business.

Inventory

What constitutes inventory is determined by reference to the taxpayer's business.

Inventory Determination

Green Company buys and sells used automobiles. Its automobiles are inventory. Therefore, Green's gains from the sale of the cars are ordinary income.

Soong sells her personal-use automobile at a $500 gain. The automobile is a personal-use asset and, therefore, a capital asset. Soong's gain is a capital gain.

No asset is inherently capital or ordinary. If Soong in Example 2 sells her capital asset automobile to Green Company in Example 1, that very same automobile loses its capital asset status, because it is inventory to Green Company. Similar transformations can occur if, for example, an art dealer sells a painting (inventory, *not* a capital asset) to a private collector (now a capital asset). Whether an asset is capital or ordinary, therefore, depends entirely on the relationship of *that asset* to the taxpayer who sold it. This classification dilemma is but one feature of capital asset treatment that makes this area so confusing and perennially complicated.

---

[1]66–1 USTC ¶9317, 17 AFTR 2d 604, 86 S.Ct. 1030 (USSC, 1966).   [2]§ 1221(b)(3).

Accounts and Notes Receivable

Collection of an accrual basis account receivable usually does not result in a gain or loss because the amount collected equals the receivable's basis. The *sale* of an account or note receivable may generate a gain or loss, however, because it will probably be sold for more or less than its basis. That gain or loss will be ordinary because the receivable is not a capital asset. A cash basis account receivable has no basis; so sale of such a receivable generates a gain, and that gain is ordinary income. Collection of a cash basis receivable also generates ordinary income.

Oriole Company, an accrual basis taxpayer, has accounts receivable of $100,000. Gross income of $100,000 was recorded, and a $100,000 basis was established when the receivable was created. Because Oriole needs working capital, it sells the receivables for $83,000 to a financial institution. Accordingly, it has a $17,000 ordinary loss.

If Oriole is a cash basis taxpayer, it has $83,000 of ordinary income because it would not have recorded any income earlier and the receivable would have no tax basis. ■

Business Fixed Assets

Depreciable personal property and real estate (both depreciable and nondepreciable) used by a business are not capital assets. Thus, *business fixed assets* are not capital assets. Business fixed assets can sometimes be treated as capital assets pursuant to § 1231, however, as discussed later in this chapter.

Copyrights and Creative Works

Generally, the person whose efforts led to the copyright or creative work has an ordinary asset, not a capital asset. This rule makes the creator comparable to a taxpayer whose customary activity (salary, business profits) is taxed as ordinary income. *Creative works* include the works of authors, composers, and artists. Also, the person for whom a letter, a memorandum, or another similar property was created has an ordinary asset. Finally, a person receiving a copyright, creative work, a letter, a memorandum, or similar property by lifetime gift from the creator or the person for whom the work was created also has an ordinary asset. Note the exception mentioned earlier that permits the taxpayer to elect to treat the sale or exchange of a musical composition or a copyright of a musical work as the disposition of a capital asset.

Creative Works

Wanda is a part-time music composer. A music publisher purchases one of her songs for $5,000. Wanda has a $5,000 ordinary gain from the sale of an ordinary asset unless she elects to treat the gain as a capital gain. ■

Ed received a letter from the President of the United States in 1994. In the current year, Ed sells the letter to a collector for $300. Ed has a $300 ordinary gain from the sale of an ordinary asset (because the letter was created for Ed). ■

Isabella gives a song she composed to her son. Her son sells the song to a music publisher for $5,000. Her son has a $5,000 ordinary gain from the sale of an ordinary asset unless he elects to treat the gain as a capital gain.

If he inherits the song from Isabella, his basis for the song is its fair market value at Isabella's death. In this situation, the song is a capital asset because the son's basis is not related to Isabella's basis for the song (i.e., the song was not a *lifetime* gift). ■

U.S. Government Publications

U.S. government publications received from the U.S. government (or its agencies) for a reduced price (i.e., below that at which it is available to the general public) are not capital assets. This prevents a taxpayer from later donating the publications to charity and claiming a charitable contribution deduction equal to the fair market value of the publications. A charitable contribution of a capital asset generally yields a deduction equal to the asset's fair market value. If such property is received by gift from the original purchaser, the property is not a capital asset to the donee. (For a more comprehensive explanation of charitable contributions of property, refer to Chapter 5.)

In-depth coverage can be found on this book's companion website: www.cengagebrain.com   **2** DIGGING DEEPER

8-2b **Statutory Expansions**

Because of the uncertainty often associated with capital asset status, Congress has occasionally enacted Code Sections to clarify the definition in particular circumstances. These statutory expansions of the capital asset definition are discussed in this section.

Dealers in Securities

As a general rule, securities (stocks, bonds, and other financial instruments) held by a dealer are considered to be inventory and are, therefore, not subject to capital gain or loss treatment. A *dealer in securities* is a merchant (e.g., a brokerage firm) that regularly engages in the purchase and resale of securities to customers. However, under the following circumstances, a dealer will have capital gain or capital loss. If a dealer clearly identifies certain securities as held for investment purposes by the close of business on the acquisition date, gain from the securities' sale will be capital gain. The gain will be ordinary if the dealer ceases to hold the securities for investment prior to the sale. Losses are capital losses if at any time the securities have been clearly identified by the dealer as held for investment.

In-depth coverage can be found on this book's companion website: www.cengagebrain.com   **3** DIGGING DEEPER

Real Property Subdivided for Sale (§ 1237)

Substantial real property development activities may result in the owner being considered a dealer for tax purposes. If so, income from the sale of real estate property lots will be treated as the sale of inventory and therefore will be taxed as ordinary income. However, § 1237 allows real estate investors to claim capital gain treatment if they engage *only* in *limited* development activities. To be eligible for § 1237 treatment, the following requirements must be met.

- The taxpayer is not a corporation.
- The taxpayer is not a real estate dealer.
- No substantial improvements have been made to the lots sold. *Substantial* generally means more than a 10 percent increase in the value of a lot. Shopping centers and other commercial or residential buildings are considered substantial, while filling, draining, leveling, and clearing operations are not.
- The taxpayer has held the lots sold for at least 5 years, except for inherited property. The substantial improvements test is less stringent if the property is held at least 10 years.

If the preceding requirements are met, all gain is capital gain until the taxable year in which the *sixth* lot is sold. Sales of contiguous lots to a single buyer in the same transaction count as the sale of one lot. Beginning with the taxable year in which the *sixth* lot is sold, 5 percent of the revenue from lot sales is potential ordinary income. That potential ordinary income is offset by any selling expenses from the lot sales. Practically, sales commissions often are at least 5 percent of the sales price, so usually none of the gain is treated as ordinary income.

Section 1237 does not apply to losses. A loss from the sale of subdivided real property is ordinary loss unless the property qualifies as a capital asset under § 1221. The following example illustrates the application of § 1237.

EXAMPLE 7

Ahmed owns a large tract of land and subdivides it for sale. Assume that Ahmed meets all of the requirements of § 1237 and during the tax year sells the first 10 lots to 10 different buyers for $10,000 each. Ahmed's basis in each lot sold is $3,000, and he incurs total selling expenses of $4,000 on the sales. Ahmed's gain is computed as follows.

Selling price (10 × $10,000)	$100,000	
Less: Selling expenses	(4,000)	
Amount realized		$ 96,000
Basis (10 × $3,000)		(30,000)
Realized and recognized gain		$ 66,000
Classification of recognized gain:		
Ordinary income		
Five percent of selling price (5% × $100,000)	$ 5,000	
Less: Selling expenses	(4,000)	
Ordinary gain		1,000
Capital gain		$ 65,000

Note that a portion of the gain recognized is given ordinary treatment because the *sixth* lot is sold in the current year.

8-3 SALE OR EXCHANGE

LO.2

State and explain the relevance of a sale or exchange to classification as a capital gain or loss.

Recognition of capital gain or loss usually requires a **sale or exchange** of a capital asset. The Code uses the term *sale or exchange*, but does not define it. Generally, a property sale involves the receipt of money by the seller and/or the assumption by the purchaser of the seller's liabilities. An exchange involves the transfer of property for other property. Thus, an involuntary conversion (casualty, theft, or condemnation) is not a sale or exchange. In several situations, the determination of whether or when a sale or exchange has taken place has been clarified by the enactment of Code Sections that specifically provide for sale or exchange treatment. These situations are discussed below.

Recognized gains or losses from the cancellation, lapse, expiration, or any other termination of a right or obligation with respect to personal property (other than stock) that is or would be a capital asset in the hands of the taxpayer are capital gains or losses.[3] See the discussion under Options (below) for more details.

8-3a Worthless Securities and § 1244 Stock

Occasionally, securities such as stocks and bonds may become worthless due to the insolvency of their issuer. If the security is a capital asset, the loss is deemed to have occurred as the result of a sale or exchange on the *last day* of the tax year.[4] This last-day rule may have the effect of converting a short-term capital loss into a long-term capital loss. (See Capital Losses later in this chapter.) Worthless securities are discussed in Chapter 6.

Section 1244 allows an *ordinary* deduction on disposition of stock at a loss. The stock must be that of a small business corporation, and the ordinary deduction is limited to $50,000 ($100,000 for married individuals filing jointly) per year.

---

[3]§ 1234A.   [4]§ 165(g)(1).

TAX IN THE NEWS Bankruptcy and Worthless Stock

During 2009, General Motors went into bankruptcy, was reorganized, and emerged from bankruptcy. However, the common shareholders of the General Motors that went into bankruptcy were not the common shareholders of the General Motors that emerged from bankruptcy.

The original common shareholders lost their entire investment because their stock became worthless. The holding period of their stock ended for tax purposes on December 31, 2009, because of the worthless stock rules. They had a capital loss equal to whatever their basis was for the worthless shares.

The debtors of General Motors accepted common shares in the General Motors that emerged from bankruptcy. Generally, the exchange of debt for common shares in a bankruptcy reorganization is not a taxable transaction, and the basis of the debt becomes the basis for the shares.

8-3b Retirement of Corporate Obligations

A debt obligation (e.g., a bond or note payable) may have a tax basis different from its redemption value because it may have been acquired at a premium or discount (see Chapter 7 for a discussion of bond amortization). Consequently, the collection of the redemption value may result in a loss or a gain. Generally, the collection of a debt obligation is treated as a sale or exchange.[5] Therefore, any loss or gain is capital because a sale or exchange has taken place.

EXAMPLE 8

Osprey, Inc., purchases $1,000 of Golden Eagle Corporation bonds for $1,020 in the open market.

If the bonds are held to maturity and the bond premium is not amortized, the $20 difference between Osprey's collection of the $1,000 redemption value and its cost of $1,020 is treated as capital loss.

4 DIGGING DEEPER

In-depth coverage can be found on this book's companion website: www.cengagebrain.com

8-3c Options

Frequently, a potential buyer of property wants to defer a final purchase decision, but wants to control the sale and/or the sale price in the meantime. **Options** are used to achieve such control. The potential purchaser (grantee) pays the property owner (grantor) for an option on the property. The grantee then becomes the option holder. An option, which usually sets the price at which a grantee can buy the property, expires after a specified period of time.

Sale of an Option

In addition to exercising an option or letting it expire, a grantee can often arrange for its sale or exchange. Such a sale or exchange generally results in capital gain or loss if the option property is (or would be) a capital asset to the grantee.[6]

EXAMPLE 9

Robin & Associates wants to buy some vacant land for investment purposes, but currently cannot afford the full purchase price. Instead, Robin & Associates (grantee) pays the landowner (grantor) $3,000 for an option to buy the land for $100,000 anytime in the next two years. The option is a capital asset to Robin because if the firm actually purchased the land (the option property), the land would be a capital asset.

Three months after purchasing the option, Robin sells it for $7,000. The firm has a $4,000 ($7,000 − $3,000) capital gain on this sale.

---

[5]§ 1271.

[6]§ 1234(a) and Reg. § 1.1234–1(a)(1).

Failure to Exercise Options

If an option holder (grantee) fails to exercise the option, the lapse of the option is considered a sale or exchange on the option expiration date. Thus, the resulting loss is a capital loss if the property subject to the option is (or would be) a capital asset in the hands of the grantee.

The grantor of an option on *stocks, securities, commodities, or commodity futures* receives short-term capital gain treatment upon the expiration of the option.[7] For example, an individual investor who owns stock (a capital asset) may sell a call option, entitling the buyer of the option to acquire the stock at a specified price higher than the stock's value at the date the option is granted. The writer of the call (the grantor) receives a premium for writing the option. If the price of the stock does not increase during the option period, the option will expire unexercised. Upon the expiration of the option, the grantor must recognize a short-term capital gain equal to the premium received (whereas the grantee recognizes a loss, the character of which depends on the underlying asset). These provisions do not apply to options held for sale to customers (the inventory of a securities dealer).

Options on property *other than* stocks, securities, commodities, or commodity futures (for instance, vacant land) result in ordinary income to the grantor when the option expires. For instance, the landowner in the preceding example would have ordinary income of $3,000 if Robin (the grantee) had allowed the option to expire.

Exercise of Options by Grantee

If an option is exercised, the amount paid for the option is added to the optioned property's selling price. This increases the gain (or reduces the loss) to the grantor resulting from the sale of the property. The grantor's gain or loss is capital or ordinary depending on the tax status of the property. The grantee adds the cost of the option to the basis of the property purchased.

The Big Picture

EXAMPLE 10

Return to the facts of *The Big Picture* on p. 8-1. On February 1, 2015, Alice purchases 100 shares of Eagle Company stock for $5,000. On April 1, 2015, she writes a call option on the stock, giving the grantee the right to buy the stock for $6,000 during the following six-month period. Alice (the grantor) receives a call premium of $500 for writing the call.

- If the call is exercised by the grantee on August 1, 2015, Alice has $1,500 ($6,000 + $500 − $5,000) of short-term capital gain from the sale of the stock. The grantee has a $6,500 ($500 option premium + $6,000 purchase price) basis for the stock.

- Investors sometimes get nervous and want to "lock in" gains or losses. Assume that, prior to the grantee's exercise of the call, Alice decides to sell her stock for $6,000 and enters into a closing transaction by purchasing a call on 100 shares of Eagle Company stock for $5,000. Because the Eagle stock is selling for $6,000, Alice must pay a call premium of $1,000. She recognizes a $500 short-term capital loss [$500 (call premium received) − $1,000 (call premium paid)] on the closing transaction. On the actual sale of the Eagle stock, Alice has a short-term capital gain of $1,000 [$6,000 (selling price) − $5,000 (cost)]. The original grantee is not affected by Alice's closing transaction. The original option is still in existence, and the grantee's tax consequences depend on what action the grantee takes—exercising the option, letting the option expire, or selling the option.

- Assume that the original option expired unexercised. Alice has a $500 short-term capital gain equal to the call premium received for writing the option. This gain is not recognized until the option expires. The grantee has a loss from expiration of the option. The nature of the loss will depend upon whether the option was a capital asset or an ordinary asset.

---

[7]§ 1234(b)(1).

Concept Summary 8.1 sets out the consequences of various transactions involving options, to both the grantor and grantee.

Concept Summary 8.1

Options: Consequences to the Grantor and Grantee

Event	Effect on	
	Grantor	**Grantee**
Option is granted.	Receives value and has a contract obligation (a liability).	Pays value and has a contract right (an asset).
Option expires.	Has a short-term capital gain if the option property is stocks, securities, commodities, or commodity futures. Otherwise, gain is ordinary income.	Has a loss (capital loss if option property would have been a capital asset for the grantee).
Option is exercised.	Amount received for option increases proceeds from sale of the option property.	Amount paid for option becomes part of the basis of the option property purchased.
Option is sold or exchanged by grantee.	Result depends upon whether option later expires or is exercised (see above).	Could have gain or loss (capital gain or loss if option property would have been a capital asset for the grantee).

8-3d Patents

Transfer of a patent is treated as the sale or exchange of a long-term capital asset when *all substantial rights* to the patent (or an undivided interest that includes all such rights) are transferred by a *holder*.[8] The transferor/holder may receive payment in virtually any form. Lump-sum or periodic payments are most common. The amount of the payments may also be contingent on the transferee/purchaser's productivity, use, or disposition of the patent. If the transfer meets these requirements, any gain or loss is *automatically a long-term* capital gain or loss. Whether the asset was a capital asset for the transferor, whether a sale or exchange occurred, and how long the transferor held the patent are all irrelevant. Copyrights for authors, composers, and artists are not capital assets, as discussed earlier. Example 11 illustrates the special treatment for patents.

Substantial Rights

As noted previously, to receive favorable capital gain treatment, all *substantial rights* to the patent (or an undivided interest in it) must be transferred. All substantial rights to a patent means all rights that are valuable at the time the patent rights (or an undivided interest in the patent) are transferred. All substantial rights have not been transferred when the transfer is limited geographically within the issuing country or when the transfer is for a period less than the remaining legal life of the patent. The circumstances of the entire transaction, rather than merely the language used in the transfer instrument, are to be considered in deciding whether all substantial rights have been transferred.[9]

---

[8]§ 1235. [9]Reg. § 1.1235–2(b)(1).

EXAMPLE 11

Return to the facts of *The Big Picture* on p. 8-1. Kathy transfers her remaining 50% share of the rights in the battery patent to the Green Battery Company in exchange for a lump-sum payment of $1 million plus $.50 for each battery sold.

Assuming that Kathy has transferred all substantial rights, the question of whether the transfer is a sale or exchange of a capital asset is not relevant. Kathy automatically has a long-term capital gain from both the lump-sum payment received and the per battery royalty to the extent that those proceeds exceed her basis for the patent. Kathy also had an automatic long-term capital gain when she sold the other 50% of her rights in the patent to Alice, because Kathy transferred an undivided interest that included all substantial rights in the patent.

Whether Alice gets long-term capital gain treatment on a transfer to Green Battery will depend on whether she is a holder (see the following discussion and Example 12).

Holder Defined

The *holder* of a patent must be an *individual* and is usually the invention's creator. A holder may also be an individual who purchases the patent rights from the creator before the patented invention has been reduced to practice. However, the creator's employer and certain parties related to the creator do not qualify as holders. Thus, in the common situation where an employer has all rights to an employee's inventions, the employer is not eligible for long-term capital gain treatment. More than likely, the employer will have an ordinary asset because the patent was developed as part of its business.

The Big Picture

EXAMPLE 12

Continuing with the facts of Example 11, Kathy is clearly a holder of the patent because she is the inventor and was not an employee when she invented the battery. When Alice purchased a 50% interest in the patent nine months ago, she became a holder if the patent had not yet been reduced to practice. Because batteries were apparently not being manufactured at the time of the purchase, the patent had not been reduced to practice.

Consequently, Alice is also a holder, and she has an automatic long-term capital gain or loss when she transfers all substantial rights in her interest in the patent to Green Battery Company. Alice's basis for her share of the patent is $50,000, and the proceeds from the transfer of her share of the patent are $1 million plus $.50 for each battery sold. Thus, Alice will have a long-term capital gain even though she has not held her interest in the patent for more than one year.

8-3e Franchises, Trademarks, and Trade Names (§ 1253)

A mode of operation, a widely recognized brand name (trade name), and a widely known business symbol (trademark) are all valuable assets. These assets may be licensed (commonly known as *franchising*) by their owner for use by other businesses. Many fast-food restaurants (such as McDonald's and Taco Bell) are franchises. The franchisee usually pays the owner (franchisor) an initial fee plus a contingent fee. The contingent fee is often based upon the franchisee's sales volume.

For Federal income tax purposes, a franchise is an agreement that gives the franchisee the right to distribute, sell, or provide goods, services, or facilities within a specified area.[10] A franchise transfer includes the grant of a franchise, a transfer by one franchisee to another person, or the renewal of a franchise.

[10]§ 1253(b)(1).

Section 1253 provides that a transfer of a franchise, trademark, or trade name is *not* a sale or exchange of a capital asset when the transferor retains any significant power, right, or continuing interest in the property transferred.

| In-depth coverage can be found on this book's companion website: www.cengagebrain.com | 5 DIGGING DEEPER |

Significant Power, Right, or Continuing Interest

Significant powers, rights, or continuing interests include control over assignment of the franchise, trademark, or trade name, as well as the quality of the transferee's products or services. The following rights also are included.

- Right to require the transferee to sell or advertise *only* the transferor's products or services.
- Right to require the transferee to purchase substantially all supplies and equipment from the transferor.
- Right to receive substantial contingent payments.
- Right to terminate the franchise, trademark, or trade name at will.

In the unusual case where no significant power, right, or continuing interest is retained by the transferor, a sale or exchange may occur, and capital gain or loss treatment may be available. For capital gain or loss treatment to be available, the asset transferred must still qualify as a capital asset.

The Big Picture

EXAMPLE 13

Return to the facts of *The Big Picture* on p. 8-1. Alice sells for $101,000 to Mauve, Inc., the franchise purchased from Orange, Inc., nine months ago. The $101,000 received by Alice is not contingent, and all significant powers, rights, and continuing interests are transferred. The $1,000 gain ($101,000 proceeds − $100,000 basis) is a short-term capital gain because Alice has held the franchise for only nine months.

Noncontingent Payments

When the transferor retains a significant power, right, or continuing interest, the transferee's noncontingent payments to the transferor are ordinary income to the transferor. The franchisee capitalizes the payments and amortizes them over 15 years. If the franchise is sold, amortization is subject to recapture under § 1245, as discussed later in this chapter.

EXAMPLE 14

Grey Company signs a 10-year franchise agreement with DOH Donuts. Grey (the franchisee) makes payments of $3,000 per year for the first 8 years of the franchise agreement—a total of $24,000. Grey cannot deduct $3,000 per year as the payments are made. Instead, Grey must amortize the $24,000 total over 15 years. Thus, Grey may deduct $1,600 per year for each of the 15 years of the amortization period.

The same result would occur if Grey had made a $24,000 lump-sum payment at the beginning of the franchise period. Assuming that DOH Donuts (the franchisor) retains significant powers, rights, or a continuing interest, it will have ordinary income when it receives the payments from Grey.

Contingent Payments

The contingent franchise payments are ordinary income for the franchisor and an ordinary deduction for the franchisee when the transferor retains a significant power, right, or continuing interest.

EXAMPLE 15

TAK, a spicy chicken franchisor, transfers an 8-year franchise to Egret Corporation. TAK retains a significant power, right, or continuing interest. Egret, the franchisee, agrees to pay TAK 15% of sales. This contingent payment is ordinary income to TAK and a business deduction for Egret as the payments are made.

Concept Summary 8.2 reviews the effects of transactions involving franchises on both the franchisor and franchisee.

Concept Summary 8.2

Franchises: Consequences to the Franchisor and Franchisee

Event	Effect on	
	Franchisor	**Franchisee**
Franchisor Retains Significant Powers and Rights		
Noncontingent payment	Ordinary income.	Capitalized and amortized over 15 years as an ordinary deduction; if franchise is sold, amortization is subject to recapture under § 1245.
Contingent payment	Ordinary income.	Ordinary deduction.
Franchisor Does _Not_ Retain Significant Powers and Rights		
Noncontingent payment	Ordinary income if franchise rights are an ordinary asset; capital gain if franchise rights are a capital asset (unlikely).	Capitalized and amortized over 15 years as an ordinary deduction; if the franchise is sold, amortization is subject to recapture under § 1245.
Contingent payment	Ordinary income.	Ordinary deduction.

8-3f Lease Cancellation Payments

The tax treatment of payments received for canceling a lease depends on whether the recipient of the payments is the **lessor** or the **lessee** and whether the lease is a capital asset.

Lessee Treatment

Lease cancellation payments received by a lessee (the tenant) are treated as an exchange.[11] Thus, these payments are capital gains if the lease is a capital asset. Generally, a lessee's lease is a capital asset if the property (either personalty or realty) is used for the lessee's personal use (e.g., his or her residence). A lease held one year or less is an ordinary income asset if the property is used in the lessee's trade or business.[12]

EXAMPLE 16

Merganser, Inc., owns an apartment building that it is going to convert into an office building. Vicki is one of the apartment tenants who receives $1,000 from Merganser to cancel the lease. Vicki has a capital gain of $1,000 (which is long term or short term depending upon how long she has held the lease). Merganser has an ordinary deduction of $1,000.

---

[11]§ 1241 and Reg. § 1.1241–1(a).

[12]Reg. § 1.1221–1(b) and PLR 200045019. If the lease was held for more than one year before cancellation, it is a § 1231 asset.

Lessor Treatment

Payments received by a lessor (the landlord) for a lease cancellation are always ordinary income because they are considered to be in lieu of rental payments.[13]

Finch & Company owns an apartment building near a university campus. Hui-Fen is one of the tenants. Hui-Fen is graduating early and offers Finch $800 to cancel the apartment lease. Finch accepts the offer. Finch has ordinary income of $800. Hui-Fen has a nondeductible payment because the apartment was personal-use property.

EXAMPLE 17

8-4 HOLDING PERIOD

LO.3

Determine the applicable holding period for a capital asset.

Property must be held more than one year to qualify for long-term capital gain or loss treatment.[14] Property not held for the required long-term period results in short-term capital gain or loss. To compute the **holding period**, start counting on the day after the property was acquired and include the day of disposition.

The Big Picture

Return to the facts of *The Big Picture* on p. 8-1. Assume that Alice purchased the 200 shares of AppleCo stock on January 15, 2014. If she sells them on January 16, 2015, Alice's holding period is more than one year and the gain or loss is long term.

If instead Alice sells the stock on January 15, 2015, the holding period is exactly one year and the gain or loss is short term.

EXAMPLE 18

To be held for more than one year, a capital asset acquired on the last day of any month must not be disposed of until on or after the first day of the thirteenth succeeding month.[15]

Purple, Inc., purchases a capital asset on March 31, 2014. If Purple sells the asset on March 31, 2015, the holding period is one year and Purple will have a short-term capital gain or loss.

If Purple sells the asset on April 1, 2015, the holding period is more than one year and it will have a long-term capital gain or loss.

EXAMPLE 19

8-4a Special Holding Period Rules

There are several special holding period rules.[16] The application of these rules varies depending upon the type of asset involved and how it was acquired.

Nontaxable Exchanges

The holding period of property received in a like-kind exchange (and certain other qualified nontaxable exchanges) includes the holding period of the former asset if the property that was exchanged was either a capital asset or a § 1231 asset.

Holding Period Rules

Red Manufacturing Corporation exchanges some vacant real estate it owns (a capital asset) for land closer to its factory.

The transaction is a like-kind exchange, so the holding period of the new land includes the holding period of the old land.

EXAMPLE 20

A lightning strike destroyed Vireo Company's generator (a § 1231 asset) in March. Vireo uses all of the insurance proceeds it received to acquire a comparable generator.

The holding period of the new generator includes the holding period of the old generator because this is a nontaxable involuntary conversion.

EXAMPLE 21

---

[13]Reg. § 1.61–8(b).
[14]§ 1222(3).

[15]Rev.Rul. 66–7, 1966–1 C.B. 188.
[16]§ 1223.

Nontaxable Transactions Involving Carryover of Another Taxpayer's Basis

If a transaction is nontaxable and the former owner's basis carries over to the present owner, the former owner's holding period is included in (tacked on to) the present owner's holding period. See the discussion of nontaxable transactions in Chapter 7.

Carryover Basis

Kareem acquired 100 shares of Robin Corporation stock for $1,000 on December 31, 2011. He transferred the shares by gift to Megan on December 31, 2014, when the stock was worth $2,000. Kareem's basis of $1,000 becomes the basis for determining gain or loss on a subsequent sale by Megan. Megan's holding period begins with the date the stock was acquired by Kareem.

Assume the same facts as in the preceding example, except that the fair market value of the shares was only $800 on the date of the gift. If Megan sells the stock for a loss, its value on the date of the gift is her basis. Accordingly, the tacked-on holding period rule does not apply, and Megan's holding period begins with the date of the gift.

So if she sells the shares for $500 on April 1, 2015, Megan has a $300 recognized capital loss, the holding period is from December 31, 2014, to April 1, 2015, and the loss is short term.

Disallowed Loss Transactions

Under several Code provisions, realized losses are disallowed. When a loss is disallowed, there is no carryover of holding period. Losses can be disallowed under § 267 (sale or exchange between related taxpayers) and § 262 (sale or exchange of personal-use assets) as well as other Code Sections. Taxpayers who acquire property in a disallowed loss transaction begin a new holding period and have a basis equal to the purchase price.

Janet sells her personal automobile at a loss. She may not deduct the loss because it arises from the sale of personal-use property. Janet purchases a replacement automobile for more than the selling price of her former automobile. Janet has a basis equal to the cost of the replacement automobile, and her holding period begins when she acquires the replacement automobile.

Inherited Property

The holding period for inherited property is treated as long term no matter how long the property is actually held by the heir. The holding period of the decedent or the decedent's estate is not relevant to the heir's holding period.

Shonda inherits Blue Company stock from her father, who died in 2015. She receives the stock on April 1, 2015, and sells it on November 1, 2015. Even though Shonda did not hold the stock for more than one year, she receives long-term capital gain or loss treatment on the sale.

8-4b Short Sales

A short sale occurs when a taxpayer sells borrowed property and repays the lender with substantially identical property either held on the date of the sale or purchased after the sale. Short sales typically involve corporate stock. The seller's objective is to make a profit in anticipation of a decline in the stock's price. If the price declines, the seller in a short sale recognizes a profit equal to the difference between the sales price of the borrowed stock and the price paid for its replacement.

Section 1233 provides that a short sale gain or loss is a capital gain or loss to the extent the short sale property constitutes a capital asset of the taxpayer. This gain or loss is not recognized until the short sale is closed. Generally, the holding period of the short sale property is determined by how long the property used to close the short sale was held.

Short Sales

On January 4, Green & Associates sold short 100 shares of Osprey Corporation for $1,500. Green closed the transaction on July 28 of the same year by purchasing 100 shares of Osprey for $1,000 and delivering them to the broker from whom the securities were borrowed. Because this stock was held less than one year (actually, less than a day), Green's $500 gain ($1,500 sale price − $1,000 basis) is short term.

EXAMPLE
26

Assume the same facts as in the preceding example, except that the January 4 short sale was not closed until January 28 of the *following* year. The result is the same, because the stock was acquired and used to close the transaction on the same day; that is, it was not held more than a year.

EXAMPLE
27

If a taxpayer owns securities that are "substantially identical" to those sold short, § 1259 subjects the short sale to potential *constructive sale treatment*, and the taxpayer recognizes gain (but not loss) as of that date. If the taxpayer has not closed the short sale by delivering the short sale securities to the broker from whom the securities were borrowed before January 31 of the year following the short sale, the short sale is deemed to have closed on the short sale date. The holding period in such circumstances is determined by how long the securities in question were held.

Assume the same facts as in Example 26, except that Green & Associates owned 100 shares of Osprey Corporation when it sold short 100 shares on January 4. Green does not close the short sale before January 31 of the following year. Green must recognize any gain on its 100 shares of Osprey as of January 4 of the current year. If Green owned those shares more than one year as of that date, the gain is long term.

EXAMPLE
28

TAX PLANNING STRATEGIES   **Timing Capital Gains**

FRAMEWORK FOCUS: INCOME AND EXCLUSIONS

Strategy: Postpone Recognition of Income to Achieve Tax Deferral.

FRAMEWORK FOCUS: DEDUCTIONS

Strategy: Maximize Deductible Amounts.

Taxpayers have considerable control over the timing of their capital gains through the mechanism of realization. Accordingly, a taxpayer might want to defer recognizing a large capital gain in a year with *substantial itemized deductions*, such as large personal casualty losses or miscellaneous itemized deductions. In so doing, the taxpayer minimizes the loss of such deductions due to AGI limitations. See additional discussion in Chapter 10.

Nontax considerations, of course, often dictate when assets are sold. If a particular stock is peaking in popularity, selling it might be a wise investment strategy, even if the taxpayer's current tax situation is not optimal.

Similarly, if a taxpayer needs cash to start a business, purchase a home, or pay for a child's education or medical costs, the capital asset might need to be sold at a time when investment *and* tax considerations counsel otherwise. In these circumstances, however, a taxpayer might choose to *borrow* the money required and use the capital asset as collateral for the loan, rather than sell the asset. A loan does not trigger tax consequences, and the taxpayer can continue to hold the asset until a more opportune time—albeit at the cost of paying interest, which may be nondeductible.

In-depth coverage can be found on this book's companion website: www.cengagebrain.com

6 DIGGING DEEPER

LO.4

Describe the tax treatment
of capital gains and losses
for noncorporate taxpayers.

8-5 TAX TREATMENT OF CAPITAL GAINS AND LOSSES OF NONCORPORATE TAXPAYERS

This section discusses how capital gains and losses are taxed to noncorporate taxpayers; that is, individuals, trusts, and estates. The rules applicable to corporations are considered in the following section of this chapter.

8-5a Capital Gains

Gains from the sale or exchange of capital assets are taxed at various rates, depending upon the holding period, the taxpayer's regular tax rate, and the type of asset involved.

Short-Term Gains

Gains on capital assets held one year or less are taxed as *ordinary income*. Accordingly, the applicable tax rates vary from 10 percent to 39.6 percent. Although short-term capital gains receive no preferential tax treatment compared to ordinary income, they do have one advantage: they can absorb capital losses without limit. As discussed later in this section, *capital losses* are deducted first against capital gains (without limit) and then against ordinary income, but only up to $3,000 per year.[17] Thus, someone with a large capital loss will find short-term capital gains attractive, even though such gains do not qualify for lower tax rates.

Long-Term Gains

Gains on capital assets held more than one year are classified as *long-term* gains and are eligible for a special 20 percent tax rate (for taxpayers in the 39.6 percent bracket), 15 percent tax rate (for taxpayers in the 25, 28, 33, or 35 percent tax bracket), or 0 percent rate (for taxpayers in the 10 or 15 percent tax bracket). Thus, the benefit of these long-term capital gain tax rates can be significant, with as much as a 20 percentage point tax rate differential (i.e., for a taxpayer whose ordinary rate is 35 percent and who benefits from the 15 percent capital gains rate).

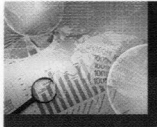

TAX PLANNING STRATEGIES **Gifts of Appreciated Securities**

FRAMEWORK FOCUS: TAX RATE

Strategy: Shift Net Income from High-Bracket Taxpayers to Low-Bracket Taxpayers.

Persons with appreciated securities that have been held over one year may reduce the tax due on their sale by giving the securities to someone (often a child) who is in the *lowest tax bracket*. The donor's holding period carries over, along with his or her basis, and the donee's lower tax rate applies when the securities are sold. As a result, the gain could be taxed at the donee's 0 percent, rather than the donor's 15 or 20 percent. The donee should be at least age 19 (or 24 in the case of a full-time student) by year-end,

however, or the *kiddie tax* will nullify most of the tax advantage being sought. The kiddie tax subjects the gain to the parents' tax rate. See Chapter 9.

Such gifts usually bear no gift tax due to the annual $14,000 exclusion. But once the property is transferred by the donor, it belongs to the donee. It is not available to the donor, nor may it be used to pay a parent's essential support obligations. Moreover, these assets may affect a child's eligibility for need-based financial aid when applying to college.

In point of fact, relatively few capital gains are realized by persons in the 10 or 15 percent tax bracket. In addition, there are relatively few taxpayers who are in the highest

---

[17]§ 1211(b).

GLOBAL TAX ISSUES · **Capital Gain Treatment in the United States and Other Countries**

Few other countries apply an alternative tax rate or other incentive to long-term capital gains. Instead, those gains are taxed in the same manner as other income. Consequently, even though the U.S. system of identifying and taxing capital assets is complex, it may be preferable because of the lower tax rates and because the lower rates are available to taxpayers in all tax brackets.

income tax bracket and subject to the 20 percent rate. Thus, the tax rate that generally applies to long-term capital gains is 15 percent.

There are two major exceptions, however, to this general treatment. The first exception relates to so-called *28% property*, which consists of the following items.

- **Collectibles** (works of art, rugs, antiques, gems, coins, stamps, and alcoholic beverages) held more than one year.[18]
- The taxable portion of the gain on sales of *qualified small business stock* (see the end of this section).

These assets are labeled *28% property*, because the gains they produce are taxed at 28 percent. But this 28 percent rate is a *maximum* rate, so a taxpayer in a lower tax bracket would pay at that lower rate. As a result, the benefit of the applicable tax rates for gains on 28% property is as follows.

Ordinary Income Tax Rates	Applicable Tax Rates	Differential (Percentage Points)
10%	10%	None
15	15	None
25	25	None
28	28	None
33	28	5
35	28	7
39.6	28	11.6

Note that gains on 28% property receive preferential tax treatment only when realized by taxpayers in the top three tax brackets.

The second major exception involves depreciable real estate that has been held more than one year. Some—but not all—of the gain attributable to depreciation deductions on real estate such as apartments, office buildings, shopping centers, and warehouses is taxable at 25 percent rather than 0, 15, or 20 percent. The amount that is taxed in this manner depends upon how much depreciation is "recaptured" as ordinary income under § 1250, as explained later in this chapter. Accordingly, these gains are called *unrecaptured § 1250 gain*. In any case, the 25 percent rate is a *maximum* rate; so the benefit of the applicable tax rates for gains from the sale of depreciable real estate really only impacts those in the 28% to 39.6% tax brackets by saving them 3% to as much as 14.6%.

Concept Summary 8.3 reviews the tax treatment given to capital gains recognized by noncorporate taxpayers.

[18]§ 408(m) and Reg. § 1.408–10(b).

Concept Summary 8.3

Capital Gains of Noncorporate Taxpayers

Type of Asset	Applicable Rate
Held not more than one year (short-term).	10%–39.6%, same as ordinary income.
Collectibles held more than one year (28% property).	10%/15%/25% for lowest-bracket taxpayers, 28% for all others.
Taxable portion (50%, 25%, or 0%) of gain on qualified small business stock held more than five years (28% property; see Section 8-5d for a detailed explanation of the special treatment given to "qualfiied small business stock").	10%/15%/25% for lowest-bracket taxpayers, 28% for all others.
Unrecaptured § 1250 gain on depreciable real estate held more than one year.	10%/15% for two lowest-bracket taxpayers, 25% for all others.
Other capital assets held more than one year (regular long-term).	0% for two lowest-bracket taxpayers, 20% for taxpayers in the highest bracket, 15% for all others.

8-5b Capital Losses

As explained previously, capital gains can be classified into four general categories.

- Short term—taxed as ordinary income.
- 28% property—taxed at no more than 28 percent.
- Unrecaptured § 1250 gain—taxed at no more than 25 percent.
- Regular long term—taxed at 0 percent, 15 percent, or 20 percent.

A taxpayer can also have losses from capital assets in *three* of these four categories. The *unrecaptured* § 1250 *gain* category applies only to gain.

8-5c Capital Gain and Loss Netting Process

When both gains and losses occur in the year, they must be netted against each other in the following order.

Step 1. Group all gains and losses into short-term, 28% property, unrecaptured § 1250, and regular long-term categories.

Step 2. Net the gains and losses within each category to obtain net short-term, 28% property, unrecaptured § 1250, and regular long-term gain or loss.

Step 3. Offset the net 28% property and unrecaptured § 1250 amounts if they are of opposite sign. Add them if they have the same sign. Then offset the resulting amount against the regular net long-term amount if they are of opposite sign, or add the amounts if they have the same sign.

Step 4. Offset the result of step 3 with the net short-term gain *or loss* from step 2 if they are of opposite sign.

These netting rules offset net short-term capital loss against the *highest-taxed gain first*. Consequently, if there is a net short-term capital loss, it first offsets any net 28% property gain, any remaining loss offsets unrecaptured § 1250 gain, and then any remaining loss offsets regular long-term gain.

If the result of step 4 is *only* a short-term capital gain, the taxpayer is not eligible for a reduced tax rate. If the result of step 4 is a loss, a **net capital loss** exists and the taxpayer may be eligible for a *capital loss deduction* (discussed later in this chapter). If there was no offsetting in step 4 because the short-term and step 3 results were both gains *or* if the result of the offsetting is a 28% property, an unrecaptured § 1250 property, and/or a regular long-term gain, a **net capital gain** exists and the taxpayer may be eligible for a reduced tax rate. The net capital gain may consist of regular *long-term gain*, *unrecaptured § 1250 gain*, and/or *28% property gain*. Each of these gains may be taxed at a different rate.

Special Tax Rates and Capital Gain and Loss Netting Process

Joe is in the 35% Federal income tax bracket. He is taxed as follows.

Ordinary income	35%
Unrecaptured § 1250 gain	25%
28% gain	28%
Short-term capital gain	35%
Other long-term capital gain	15%

EXAMPLE 29

This example shows how a *net long-term capital loss* is applied.

Step	Short-Term	28% Gain	Unrecaptured § 1250 Gain	Regular Long-Term	Comment
1	$ 3,000	$ 1,000		$ 3,000	
				(8,000)	
2	$ 3,000	$ 1,000		($ 5,000)	
3		(1,000)	→	1,000	Netted because of opposite sign.
		$ –0–		($ 4,000)	
4	(3,000)	→	→	3,000	The net short-term gain is netted against the net regular long-term loss, and the remaining loss is eligible for the capital loss deduction.
	$ –0–			($ 1,000)	

EXAMPLE 30

This example shows how *net short-term* and *regular long-term capital losses* are applied.

Step	Short-Term	28% Gain	Unrecaptured § 1250 Gain	Regular Long-Term	Comment
1	$ 3,000	$15,000	$4,000	$ 3,000	
	(5,000)	(7,000)		(8,000)	
2	($ 2,000)	$ 8,000	$4,000	($ 5,000)	
3		(5,000)	←	5,000	Net regular long-term loss is netted against 28% gain first.
		$ 3,000		$ –0–	
4	2,000 →	(2,000)			Short-term loss is netted against 28% gain next.
	$ –0–	$ 1,000	$4,000		
		Net 28% gain	Net 25% gain		

EXAMPLE 31

If a net loss remains after applying these rules for offsetting losses, a noncorporate taxpayer may deduct up to $3,000 of that loss against ordinary income.[19] Losses in excess of $3,000 are carried over to future years where they are applied first against capital gains and then deducted up to $3,000 per year. Capital loss carryovers expire, however, when the taxpayer dies.

---

[19]§ 1211(b)(1). Married persons filing separate returns are limited to a $1,500 deduction per tax year.

Use of Capital Loss Carryovers

James incurred a $10,000 loss on his only capital asset transaction in 2015. If he has no other capital asset transactions from that point on, his $10,000 loss is deducted as follows.

Year	Deduction
2015	$3,000
2016	3,000
2017	3,000
2018	1,000

Assume the same facts as in the preceding example, except that James realizes a capital gain of $4,500 in 2017. At that time, his remaining capital loss carryover is $4,000 ($10,000 − $6,000 deducted previously). Because his capital gain in 2017 (i.e., $4,500) exceeds this loss carryforward, James can deduct the entire $4,000 against that year's capital gain.

EXAMPLE 34

Assume the same facts as in Example 32, except that James died in late 2016. His remaining capital loss carryforward of $4,000 ($10,000 − $6,000 deducted in 2015 and 2016) expires unused.

When a taxpayer's capital loss exceeds $3,000 and derives from more than one category, it is used in the following order: first, short-term; then, 28% property; then, unrecaptured § 1250 property; and finally, regular long-term. Unused losses are carried forward as follows: short-term losses carry forward as short-term losses, and long-term losses carry forward as long-term losses.

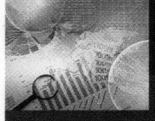

TAX PLANNING STRATEGIES **Matching Gains with Losses**

FRAMEWORK FOCUS: INCOME AND EXCLUSIONS

Strategy: Avoid Income Recognition.

A taxpayer who has already realized a large capital gain may want to *match this gain* with an *offsetting capital loss*. Doing so will shelter the capital gain from taxation and will also free up an asset that has declined in value. Without the capital gain, after all, the taxpayer might hesitate to sell a loss asset, because the resulting capital loss may be deductible only in $3,000 annual increments.

Similarly, a taxpayer with a large realized capital loss might use the occasion to sell some appreciated assets. Doing so would enable the taxpayer to use the capital loss immediately and at the same time realize the benefit of the asset appreciation at little or no tax cost.

On the other hand, matching capital losses and long-term capital gains means that the taxpayer utilizes the capital loss against income that would otherwise qualify for a preferential tax rate of 0, 15, or 20 percent. If the taxpayer's ordinary income is taxed at a higher rate, he or she might prefer to deduct the loss against that higher taxed income, even on a schedule of $3,000 per year. However, the *time value of money* must be considered; a current-year deduction at 0, 15, or 20 percent might be worth more than a series of annual deductions at higher rates spread over several years.

Nontax considerations, such as investment prospects for the assets in question, are also important. Future investment prospects are often unknowable or at least highly speculative, while tax effects can be determined with relative certainty—which explains some of the late December selling activity in publicly traded securities and mutual funds.

Nancy incurs a long-term capital loss of $8,500 this year, of which $3,000 is deducted against her ordinary income. The remaining $5,500 ($8,500 loss − $3,000 deducted) carries forward as a long-term capital loss.

EXAMPLE 35

In-depth coverage can be found on this book's companion website: www.cengagebrain.com

7 DIGGING DEEPER

8-5d Small Business Stock

A special 50 percent *exclusion* is available to noncorporate taxpayers who derive capital gains from the sale or exchange of qualified small business stock.[20] Thus, half of the gain is excluded from the taxpayer's gross income, and the other half is subjected to a maximum tax rate of 28 percent, as noted earlier. However, for a period during the recent economic downturn, the exclusion increased to 75 percent for qualified small business stock acquired after February 17, 2009. And later, the exclusion increased to 100 percent for qualified stock acquired after September 27, 2010, and before 2015. Thus, the effective tax rate on gains from such stock is 14 percent (28% × 50%), 7 percent (28% × 25%), or 0 percent (28% × 0%), respectively. However, beginning in 2015, the exclusion amount reverted to 50 percent of the gain.

Yolanda realized a $100,000 gain on the sale of qualified small business stock that she acquired in 2004. Yolanda is subject to the 33% marginal tax rate without considering this gain. So $50,000 of this gain is excluded from her gross income, and the other $50,000 is taxed at a maximum tax rate of 28%. Thus, Yolanda owes income tax of $14,000 ($50,000 × 28%), an effective tax rate of 14% on the entire $100,000 capital gain.

EXAMPLE 36

This treatment is more favorable than the capital gain tax treatment explained previously. Accordingly, Congress imposed additional restrictions to ensure that the gains receiving this treatment were derived in the circumstances Congress intended to promote. These restrictions include the following.

- The stock must have been newly issued *after* August 10, 1993.

- The taxpayer must have held the stock *more than five years*.

- The issuing corporation must use at least 80 percent of its assets, determined by their value, in the *active conduct* of a trade or business.

- When the stock was issued, the issuing corporation's assets must not have exceeded $50 million, at adjusted basis, including the proceeds of the stock issuance.

- The corporation does not engage in banking, financing, insurance, investing, leasing, farming, mineral extraction, hotel or motel operations, restaurant operations, or any business whose principal asset is the *reputation or skill* of its employees (such as accounting, architecture, health, law, engineering, or financial services).

Even if each of these requirements is met, the amount of gain eligible for the exclusion is limited to the *greater* of 10 times the taxpayer's basis in the stock or $10 million per taxpayer per company,[21] computed on an aggregate basis.

---

[20]§ 1202(a).

[21]For married persons filing separately, the limitation is $5 million.

Vanita purchased $100,000 of qualified small business stock when it was first issued in October 2000. This year, she sold the stock for $4 million. Her gain is $3.9 million ($4,000,000 − $100,000). Although this amount exceeds 10 times her basis ($100,000 × 10 = $1,000,000), it is *less* than $10 million; so the entire $3.9 million gain is eligible for the 50% exclusion.

Transactions that fail to satisfy *any one* of the applicable requirements are taxed as capital gains (and losses) realized by noncorporate taxpayers generally.

Gains are also eligible for *nonrecognition* treatment if the sale proceeds are invested in other qualified small business stock within 60 days.[22] To the extent that the sale proceeds are not so invested, gain is recognized, but the exclusion still applies. To be eligible for this treatment, the stock sold must have been held more than six months.

Assume the same facts as in the preceding example, except that Vanita sold her stock in January 2016 and used $3.5 million of the sale proceeds to purchase other qualified small business stock one month later. Vanita's gain is recognized to the extent that the sale proceeds were not reinvested—namely, $500,000 ($4,000,000 sale proceeds − $3,500,000 reinvested). The 50% exclusion will apply, however, to the $500,000.

DIGGING DEEPER 8   **In-depth coverage can be found on this book's companion website: www.cengagebrain.com**

8-6 TAX TREATMENT OF CAPITAL GAINS AND LOSSES OF CORPORATE TAXPAYERS

The treatment of a corporation's net capital gain or loss differs dramatically from the rules for noncorporate taxpayers discussed in the preceding section. Briefly, the differences are as follows.

- Capital gains are taxed at the ordinary income tax rates.[23]
- Capital losses offset only capital gains. No deduction of capital losses is permitted against ordinary taxable income.
- There is a three-year carryback and a five-year carryforward period for net capital losses.[24] Capital loss carrybacks and carryforwards are always treated as short-term, regardless of their original nature.

Note that with the treatment given to corporate capital gains and losses, no substantive advantage results to the taxpayer. In fact, capital asset designation often can lead to a detriment (e.g., a delay or the ultimate loss of capital loss deduction).

Sparrow Corporation has a $15,000 long-term capital loss for the current year and $57,000 of ordinary taxable income. Sparrow may not offset the $15,000 long-term capital loss against its ordinary income by taking a capital loss deduction. The $15,000 long-term capital loss becomes a $15,000 short-term capital loss for carryback and carryforward purposes. This amount may offset capital gains in the three-year carryback period or, if not absorbed there, offset capital gains in the five-year carryforward period. Any amount remaining after this carryforward period expires is permanently lost.

---

[22]§ 1045(a).

[23]§ 1201. The alternative tax rate of 35% produces no beneficial results.

[24]§ 1212(a)(1).

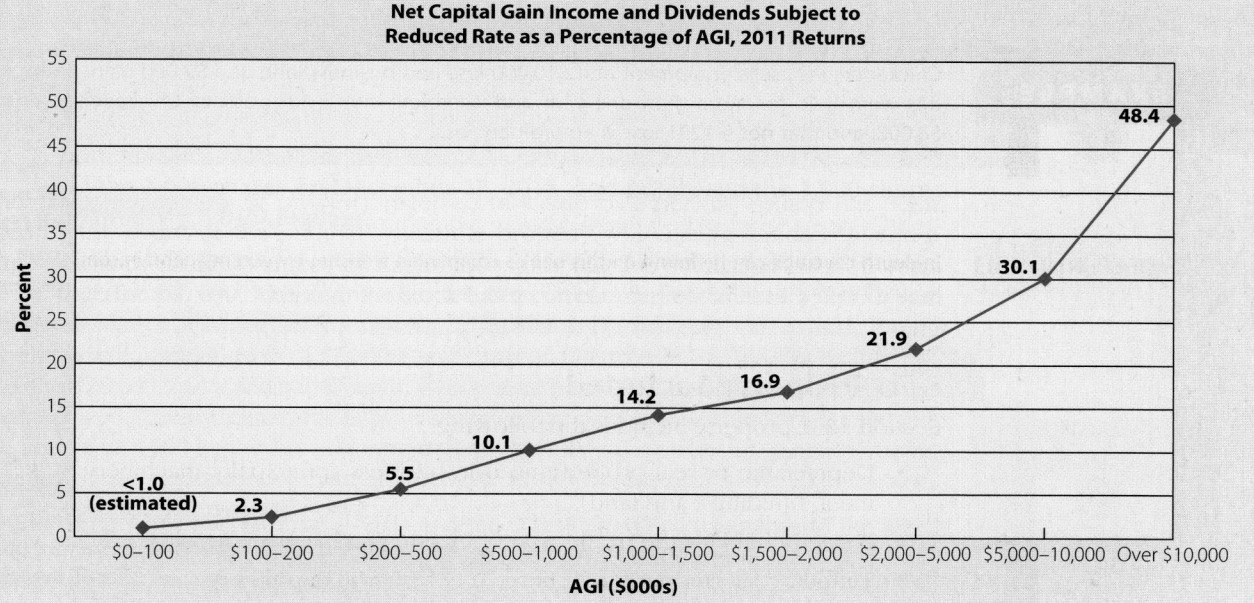

TAX FACT Capital Gains for the Wealthy?

Economists and other observers of society often accuse the Code of favoring those with higher levels of income and wealth, despite a fairly substantial progressivity in the Federal income tax rate structure. The claim is that the wealthy are the primary owners of capital assets and that capital gains and dividends from those assets are subject to highly favorable tax treatment. Current tax return data may confirm those assertions.

Source: Based on Justin Bryan, "Individual Income Tax Returns, 2011," *SOI Bulletin,* Fall 2013, Figure F.

Net Capital Gain Income and Dividends Subject to Reduced Rate as a Percentage of AGI, 2011 Returns

(Chart: Percent vs. AGI ($000s))

Data points:
- $0–100: <1.0 (estimated)
- $100–200: 2.3
- $200–500: 5.5
- $500–1,000: 10.1
- $1,000–1,500: 14.2
- $1,500–2,000: 16.9
- $2,000–5,000: 21.9
- $5,000–10,000: 30.1
- Over $10,000: 48.4

8-7 SECTION 1231 ASSETS

LO.6

Distinguish § 1231 assets from ordinary and capital assets and calculate § 1231 gain or loss.

Businesses own many assets that are used in the business rather than held for resale. In financial accounting, such assets are known as "fixed assets." For example, a foundry's 30,000-pound stamping machine is a fixed asset. It is also a depreciable asset. The building housing the foundry is another fixed asset. The remainder of this chapter largely deals with how to *classify* the gains and losses from the disposition of fixed assets. Chapter 5 discussed how to depreciate such assets. Chapter 7 discussed how to determine the adjusted basis and the amount of gain or loss from their disposition.

8-7a Relationship to Capital Assets

At first glance, the *classification of fixed assets* ought to be straightforward. Section 1221(a)(2) specifically excludes from the capital asset definition any property that is depreciable or that is real estate "used in a trade or business." Accordingly, the foundry's stamping machine and the building housing the foundry described earlier are not capital assets. Therefore, one would expect gains to be taxed as ordinary income and losses to be deductible as ordinary losses. Since World War II, however, certain business assets have received more favorable treatment.

Section 1231 provides that business assets held for more than one year can receive the best of both worlds: capital gain treatment on gains and ordinary loss treatment on losses. More specifically, this provision requires that gains and losses from **§ 1231 property** be aggregated at the end of the taxable year; the *net result* is then classified as capital gain if a net gain is produced, or as ordinary loss if a net loss is produced. As a result, a particular disposition's character as capital or ordinary is not determined until the taxable year has concluded and all of the taxpayer's **§ 1231 gains and losses** are tabulated.

Section 1231 Treatment

EXAMPLE 40

Brown & Co. sells a building at a $5,000 gain and equipment at a $3,000 loss. Both properties were § 1231 assets because they were used in Brown's trade or business and held for more than one year. Brown's net gain is $2,000, and that net gain may be treated as a long-term capital gain under § 1231.

EXAMPLE 41

Chickadee, Inc., sells equipment at a $10,000 loss and business land at a $2,000 gain. Both properties were held for more than one year and, therefore, are § 1231 assets. Chickadee's net loss is $8,000, and that net § 1231 loss is an ordinary loss.

DIGGING DEEPER 9   In-depth coverage can be found on this book's companion website: www.cengagebrain.com

8-7b Property Included

Section 1231 property includes the following.

- Depreciable or real property used in business (principally machinery and equipment, buildings, and land).
- Property held for the production of income if it has been involuntarily converted.
- Timber, coal, or domestic iron ore to which § 631 applies.
- Livestock held for draft, breeding, dairy, or sporting purposes.
- Unharvested crops on land used in business.
- Certain *purchased* intangible assets (such as patents and goodwill) that are eligible for amortization.

DIGGING DEEPER 10, 11   In-depth coverage can be found on this book's companion website: www.cengagebrain.com

8-7c Property Excluded

Section 1231 property generally does *not* include the following.

- Property not held more than one year. Livestock must be held at least 12 months (24 months in some cases). Unharvested crops do not have to be held for more than one year, but the land must be so held.
- Business-use property, where casualty losses exceed casualty gains for the taxable year. If a taxpayer has a net casualty loss, the casualty gains and losses are treated as ordinary gains and losses.
- Inventory and property held primarily for sale to customers.
- Copyrights; literary, musical, or artistic compositions, etc.; and certain U.S. government publications.
- Accounts receivable and notes receivable arising in the ordinary course of the trade or business.

TAX IN THE NEWS   **Loss from Cattle Rustling**

A newspaper in "cattle country" reported that rustlers had stolen 20 head of prime milk cows from a local ranch. The rancher never recovered the cows. According to the article, the rancher had no insurance on the cows and was upset because he had no way of recovering his loss.

A CPA might advise the rancher that he could be entitled to a special "theft loss" for tax purposes because the theft loss rules apply to § 1231 assets such as cattle held for 24 months or more.

8-7d Casualty or Theft and Nonpersonal-Use Capital Assets

When § 1231 assets are disposed of by casualty or theft, a special netting rule is applied. For simplicity, the term *casualty* is used to mean both casualty and theft dispositions. First, the casualty gains and losses from § 1231 assets *and* the casualty gains and losses from long-term nonpersonal-use capital assets are determined. For business entities, virtually any capital asset is a nonpersonal-use capital asset, because partnerships, limited liability companies, and corporations are incapable of using assets *personally*. This classification, therefore, is most significant to individual taxpayers who might use certain capital assets as part of their daily life.

Casualties and thefts are *involuntary conversions*, it should be recalled, and gains from such conversions need not be recognized if the proceeds are timely reinvested in similar property. Thus, the netting process described in the next section would not consider any casualty and theft gains that are being deferred because insurance proceeds were reinvested according to the requirements of § 1033 (see Chapter 7). Section 1231, in other words, has no effect on whether a *realized* gain or loss is recognized. Instead, § 1231 merely dictates how a *recognized* gain will be classified.

This special netting process for casualties and thefts does not apply to *condemnation* gains and losses. As a result, if a § 1231 asset is disposed of by condemnation, any resulting gain or loss will get § 1231 treatment.

8-7e General Procedure for § 1231 Computation

To determine the tax treatment of § 1231 gains and losses specific steps of a rather complex *netting* procedure must be followed. See Concept Summary 8-4 on page 8-26, which may be used as a guide to better understand these netting rules.

Step 1: Casualty Netting

Net all recognized long-term gains and losses from casualties of § 1231 assets and non-personal-use capital assets. This casualty netting is beneficial because if there is a net gain, the gain may receive long-term capital gain treatment. If there is a net loss, it receives ordinary loss treatment.

a. If the casualty gains exceed the casualty losses, add the net gain to the other § 1231 gains for the taxable year.
b. If the casualty losses exceed the casualty gains, exclude all casualty losses and gains from further § 1231 computation. The casualty gains are ordinary income, and the casualty losses are deductible. For individual taxpayers, the casualty losses must be classified further. For individual taxpayers, § 1231 asset casualty losses are deductible *for* AGI, while other casualty losses are deductible *from* AGI (see Chapter 10).

Step 2: § 1231 Netting

After adding any net casualty gain from step 1a on the previous page to the other § 1231 gains and losses (including *recognized* § 1231 asset condemnation gains and losses), net all § 1231 gains and losses.

a. If the gains exceed the losses, the net gain is offset by the "lookback" nonrecaptured § 1231 losses (see step 3).

b. If the losses exceed the gains, the net loss is deducted against ordinary income. For individual taxpayers only, the gains are ordinary income, the § 1231 asset losses are deductible *for* AGI, and the other casualty losses are deductible *from* AGI.

Concept Summary 8.4

Section 1231 Netting Procedure (Discussed in Section 8-7e)

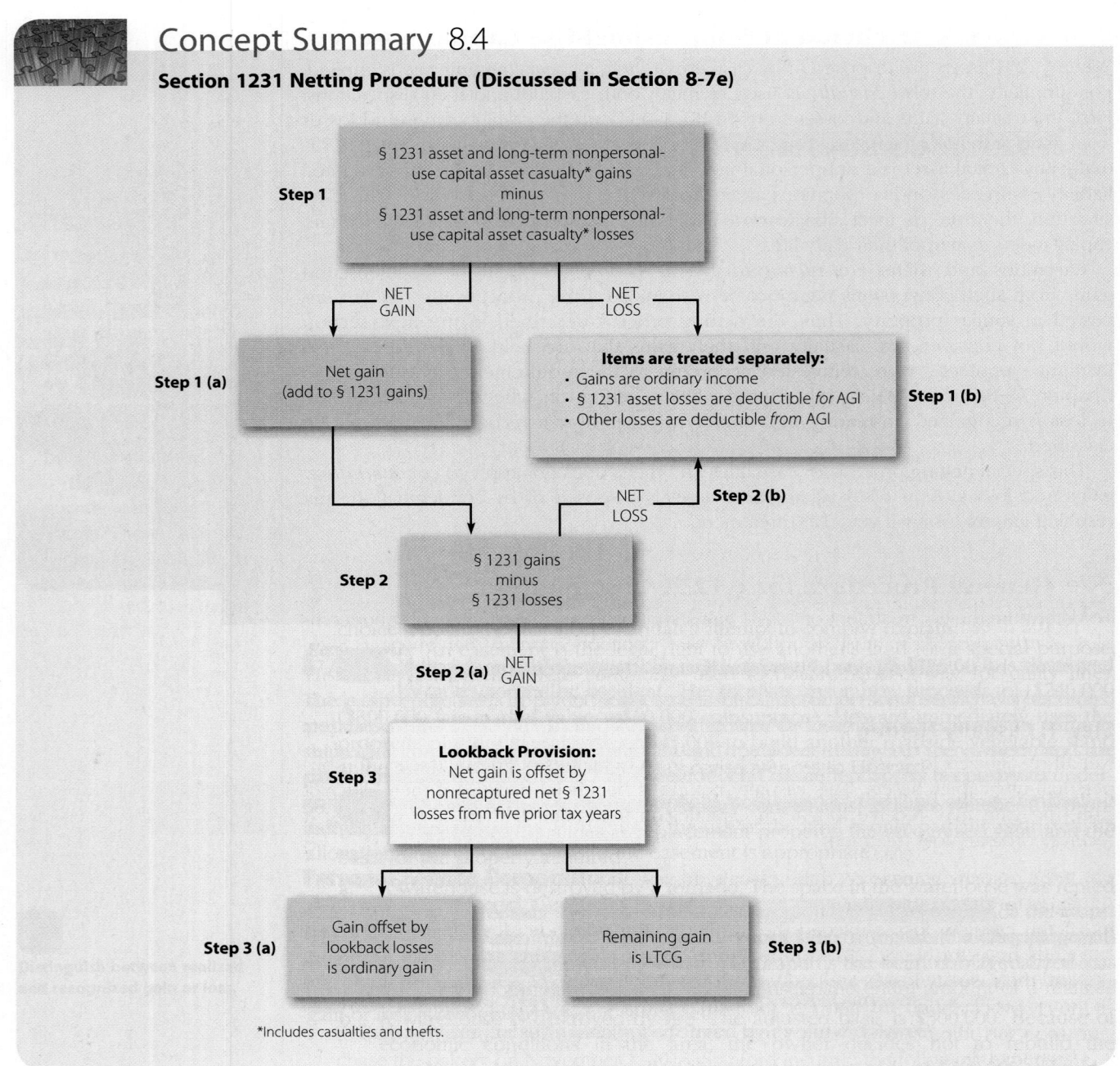

*Includes casualties and thefts.

Section 1231 Computations

EXAMPLE

42

Falcon Management, Inc., recognized the following gains and losses this year.

Capital Gains and Losses	
Long-term capital gain	$3,000
Long-term capital loss	(400)
Short-term capital gain	1,000
Short-term capital loss	(200)

Casualties	
Gain from insurance recovery on fire loss to building, owned five years	$ 1,200
Loss from theft of computer (uninsured), owned two years	(1,000)

§ 1231 Gains and Losses from Sale of Depreciable Business Assets Held Long Term	
Asset A	$ 300
Asset B	1,100
Asset C	(500)

Gains and Losses from Sale of Depreciable Business Assets Held Short Term	
Asset D	$ 200
Asset E	(300)

Falcon had no net § 1231 losses in prior tax years.

Disregarding the recapture of depreciation (discussed later in this chapter), Falcon's gains and losses receive the following tax treatment.

- **Step 1:** The casualty netting of the § 1231 and nonpersonal-use capital assets contains two items—the $1,200 gain from the business building and the $1,000 loss from the computer. Consequently, there is a $200 net gain and that gain is treated as a § 1231 gain (added to the § 1231 gains).

- **Step 1 (a):** The gains from § 1231 transactions (Assets A and B and the § 1231 asset casualty gain) exceed the losses (Asset C) by $1,100 ($1,600 − $500). This excess is a long-term capital gain and is added to Falcon's other long-term capital gains.

- **Step 2:** Falcon's net long-term capital gain is $3,700 ($3,000 + $1,100 from § 1231 transactions − $400 long-term capital loss). Its net short-term capital gain is $800 ($1,000 − $200). The result is capital gain income of $4,500, which will be taxed at ordinary rates. If Falcon were an individual rather than a corporation, the $3,700 net long-term capital gain portion would be eligible for preferential capital gain treatment and the $800 net short-term capital gain would be taxed as ordinary income.

- Falcon treats the gain and loss from Assets D and E as ordinary gain and loss, because § 1231 does not apply unless the assets have been held more than one year.[25]

Results of the Gains and Losses on Falcon's Tax Computation	
Net long-term capital gain	$3,700
Net short-term capital gain	800
Ordinary gain from sale of Asset D	200
Ordinary loss from sale of Asset E	(300)
Gross income	$4,400

---

[25]§ 1231(b)(1).

Section 1231 Computations

EXAMPLE
43

Assume the same facts as in the preceding example, except that the loss from Asset C was $1,700 instead of $500.

- The treatment of the casualty gains and losses is the same.

- **Step 1 (b):** The losses from § 1231 transactions now exceed the gains by $100 ($1,700 − $1,600). As a result, the net loss is deducted in full as an ordinary loss.

- Capital gain income is $3,400 ($2,600 long-term + $800 short-term).

Results of the Gains and Losses on Falcon's Tax Computation	
Net long-term capital gain	$2,600
Net short-term capital gain	800
Net ordinary loss on Assets A, B, and C and § 1231 casualty gain	(100)
Ordinary gain from sale of Asset D	200
Ordinary loss from sale of Asset E	(300)
Gross income	$3,200

Step 3: § 1231 Lookback Provision

The net § 1231 gain from step 2a on p. 8-26 is offset by the nonrecaptured net § 1231 losses for the five preceding taxable years.[26] For transactions in 2015, the lookback years are 2010, 2011, 2012, 2013, and 2014.

a.   To the extent of the nonrecaptured net § 1231 loss, the current-year net § 1231 gain is ordinary income. The *nonrecaptured* net § 1231 losses are losses that have not already been used to offset net § 1231 gains.

b.   Only the net § 1231 gain exceeding this net § 1231 loss carryforward is given long-term capital gain treatment. The **§ 1231 lookback** provision reduces the taxpayer's ability to gain a tax advantage by "timing" sales artificially.

Section 1231 Lookback Provision

EXAMPLE
44

Komodo Manufacturing Corporation sold used equipment and some business real estate during 2015 for a net § 1231 gain of $25,000. During 2014, Komodo had no § 1231 transactions, but in 2013, it had a net § 1231 loss of $17,000. This loss causes $17,000 of the 2015 gain to be classified as ordinary income. The remaining 2015 gain of $8,000 ($25,000 of § 1231 gain − $17,000 nonrecaptured loss) is § 1231 gain.

EXAMPLE
45

Assume the same facts as in the preceding example, except that Komodo had a net § 1231 loss of $37,000 in 2013 and a net § 1231 gain of $10,000 in 2014.

- The 2013 net § 1231 loss of $37,000 would cause the net § 1231 gain of $10,000 in 2014 to be classified as ordinary income, and $27,000 ($37,000 loss − $10,000 recaptured) would carry over to 2015.

- The remaining nonrecaptured § 1231 loss of $27,000 from 2013 completely offsets the § 1231 gain of $25,000 from 2015, making that entire gain ordinary income.

- The remaining nonrecaptured § 1231 loss from 2013 is $2,000 ($27,000 nonrecaptured § 1231 loss carried to 2015 − $25,000 recaptured in 2015). This recapture potential carries over to 2016.

---

[26]§ 1231(c).

8-8 SECTION 1245 RECAPTURE

As explained earlier, when Congress determined that § 1231 was unduly generous, it chose to *recapture* some of § 1231's benefits rather than repeal that section altogether. This recapture phenomenon applies exclusively to the gain side of § 1231; the ordinary loss feature applicable to § 1231 property is not affected by the Code's recapture provisions. In essence, recapture takes part—often all—of the gain from the sale or exchange of a § 1231 asset and classifies it as *ordinary income* before the netting process of § 1231 begins. Accordingly, recaptured gain is computed *first*, without considering the other § 1231 transactions that occurred during the taxable year. This section discusses the § 1245 recapture rules, and the next section discusses the § 1250 recapture rules.

Section 1245 requires taxpayers to treat all gain as ordinary gain unless the property is sold for more than its original cost. This result is accomplished by requiring that all gain be treated as ordinary gain to the extent of the depreciation taken on the property disposed of. Section 1231 gain results only if the property is disposed of for more than its original cost. The excess of the sales price over the original cost is § 1231 gain. As described more completely in the next section, § 1245 applies primarily to personalty such as machinery, trucks, and office furniture.

The Big Picture

EXAMPLE 46

Return to the facts of *The Big Picture* on p. 8-1. Recall that Alice's husband, Jeff, had purchased, for $50,000, depreciable equipment for use in his business and had deducted $35,000 of depreciation.

If Jeff sold the equipment for $45,000, his gain would be $30,000 [$45,000 amount realized − $15,000 adjusted basis ($50,000 cost − $35,000 depreciation taken)]. Section 1245 treats as ordinary income (not as § 1231 gain) any gain to the extent of depreciation taken. In this example, the entire $30,000 gain would be ordinary income.

The Big Picture

EXAMPLE 47

Continue with the facts of *The Big Picture* on p. 8-1. If Jeff sold the business equipment for $60,000, he would have a gain of $45,000 ($60,000 amount realized − $15,000 adjusted basis). The § 1245 gain would be $35,000 (equal to the depreciation taken), and the remaining gain of $10,000 (equal to the excess of the sales price over the original cost) would be § 1231 gain.

The Big Picture

EXAMPLE 48

Continue with the facts of Example 47, except that Jeff sold the equipment for $8,000 instead of $45,000. Jeff would have a loss of $7,000 ($8,000 amount realized − $15,000 adjusted basis). Because there is a loss, there is no depreciation recapture. All of the loss is § 1231 loss.

Section 1245 recapture applies to the portion of *recognized* gain from the sale or other disposition of § 1245 property that represents depreciation, including § 167 depreciation, § 168 cost recovery, § 179 immediate expensing, § 168(k) additional first-year depreciation, and § 197 amortization. Section 1245 merely *classifies* gain as ordinary income; it does not cause gain to be recognized. Thus, in Example 46, Jeff recaptures as ordinary income only the $30,000 of actual gain, not the entire $35,000 of depreciation taken. In other words, § 1245 recaptures the *lesser* of the depreciation taken or the gain recognized.

The method of depreciation (e.g., accelerated or straight-line) does not matter. All depreciation taken is potentially subject to recapture. Thus, § 1245 recapture is often referred to as *full recapture*. Any remaining gain after subtracting the amount recaptured as ordinary income will usually be § 1231 gain. The remaining gain is casualty

BRIDGE DISCIPLINE   **Bridge to Financial Accounting**

The essence of much of the tax code is to create definitions that discriminate among certain types of income or expenditures so that special tax treatment can be afforded to one of the definitional groups. For instance, municipal bond interest might be favored over corporate bond interest income, long-term capital gains over short-term capital gains or ordinary income, and processing fees to bribes. In each case, the former generally allows a reduction of taxable income or the tax liability and helps the taxpayer meet its goal of maximizing the available after-tax income that it generates.

Maximizing net income also is a goal of financial accounting, at least from the viewpoint of current and potential shareholders. In the long run, stock prices may advance solely because of the positive earnings that the corporation generates relative to the rest of the capital markets. The greater the net earnings, the greater the increase in stock price and private wealth.

But financial accounting makes far fewer distinctions when classifying the reporting entity's revenues and expenses. Most of the tax code's definitions and distinctions are politically or economically motivated means designed to reduce the effective tax rate of the taxpayer, perhaps without affecting its nominal rate.

The preferential treatment of long-term capital gains is one of the most long-lived of these tax fictions. The "best of both worlds" § 1231 treatment is over 70 years old itself. Whereas the gain or loss generated by the sale of a business or investment asset is merely included in the body of the income statement of the reporting entity, § 1221 and § 1231 can reduce the taxpayer's effective tax rate and § 1245 and § 1250 can increase it.

Differences in classification of income and deductions created solely by the tax code constitute most of the items to be reconciled in the Schedule M–1 or M–3 of the C corporation, S corporation, partnership, and limited liability entity. Many of these items must be reported as permanent or temporary differences in the Deferred Tax Liability account regulated by ASC 740 (SFAS 109).

gain, however, if the asset is disposed of in a casualty event. For example, if the equipment in Example 47 had been disposed of by casualty and the $60,000 received had been an insurance recovery, Jeff would still have a gain of $45,000, and $35,000 of that gain would still be recaptured by § 1245 as ordinary gain. The other $10,000 of gain, however, would be casualty gain.

If § 1245 property is disposed of in a transaction other than a sale, exchange, or involuntary conversion, the maximum amount recaptured is the excess of the property's fair market value over its adjusted basis. See the discussion under Exceptions to §§ 1245 and 1250 later in this chapter.

8-8a   Section 1245 Property

Generally, § 1245 property includes all depreciable personal property (e.g., machinery and equipment), including livestock. Buildings and their structural components usually are not § 1245 property. The following property is *also* subject to § 1245 treatment.

- Amortizable personal property such as goodwill, patents, copyrights, and leaseholds of § 1245 property.

- Professional baseball and football player contracts.

- Expensed costs to remove architectural and transportation barriers that restrict the handicapped and/or elderly.

- Section 179 immediately expensed depreciable tangible personal property.

- Certain depreciable tangible real property (other than buildings and their structural components) employed as an integral part of certain activities such as manufacturing and production. For example, a natural gas storage tank where the gas is used in the manufacturing process is § 1245 property.

- Pollution control facilities, railroad grading and tunnel bores, on-the-job training facilities, and child care facilities on which amortization is taken.

- Single-purpose agricultural and horticultural structures and petroleum storage facilities (e.g., a greenhouse or silo).

8-8b Observations on § 1245

- In most instances, the total depreciation taken will exceed the recognized gain. Therefore, the disposition of § 1245 property usually results in ordinary income rather than § 1231 gain (refer to Example 46).

- Recapture applies to the total amount of depreciation allowed or allowable regardless of the depreciation method used (i.e., full recapture).

- Recapture applies regardless of the holding period of the property. Of course, the entire recognized gain would be ordinary income if the property was not held more than one year, because then § 1231 would not apply.

- Section 1245 does not apply to losses, which receive § 1231 treatment.

- Gains from the disposition of § 1245 assets may also be treated as passive activity gains (refer to Chapter 6).

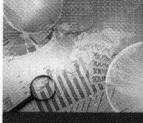

TAX PLANNING STRATEGIES   Depreciation Recapture and § 179

FRAMEWORK FOCUS: DEDUCTIONS

Strategy: Accelerate Recognition of Deductions to Achieve Tax Deferral.

Section 1245 recapture applies to all types of depreciation, including § 179 *immediate expensing*. Expensing under § 179, however, is elective and entirely within the discretion of the taxpayer. Choosing this option accelerates depreciation on the affected property but increases the potential recapture as well. Therefore, if a taxpayer anticipates that an asset will generate a gain when it is sold and that such sale will occur in the early years of the asset's life, the taxpayer might decide to forgo electing the additional depreciation under § 179.

On the other hand, electing § 179 remains attractive if little or no gain is anticipated upon an asset's disposition. After all, § 1245 recapture applies only to the extent gain is actually realized. Moreover, even if a substantial gain is anticipated upon an asset's disposition, the *time value of money* might suggest that § 179 be elected if the disposition is expected to be many years away. In any case, the taxpayer can usually control when an asset is sold or exchanged and can thereby extend the time before the taxes saved by electing § 179 must be returned as § 1245 recapture.

8-9 SECTION 1250 RECAPTURE

Some depreciable property that is not subject to § 1245 recapture faces a separate recapture computation mechanism in § 1250. For the most part, § 1250 applies to *depreciable real property* (principally buildings and their structural components), such as apartments, office buildings, factories, stores, and warehouses. Intangible real property, such as leaseholds of § 1250 property, also is included.

Section 1250 recapture is less onerous than § 1245 recapture. Section 1250 recaptures only a property's *additional depreciation*, which is the excess of the depreciation actually deducted over the amount that would have been allowed under the straight-line method of depreciation. For this reason, § 1250 recapture is often referred to as *partial recapture*, in contrast to § 1245's full recapture.

Because § 1250 recaptures only the excess over straight-line depreciation, the concept does not apply to properties that were depreciated using the straight-line method (unless they were held for one year or less). Real property placed in service *after 1986* can only be depreciated using the straight-line method, so there is *no § 1250 recapture* upon the disposition of such properties that are held for longer than one year. Finally, § 1250 does not affect the § 1231 treatment of realized losses.

TAX IN THE NEWS   Building or Tangible Personal Property?

Many taxpayers have "cost-segregated" their buildings. This means that an engineering study is done to determine whether some of a building's cost can be segregated into tangible personal property (generally a 5-year or 7-year MACRS life with accelerated depreciation) rather than real property (a 27.5-year or 39-year MACRS life with straight-line depreciation). The faster depreciation for the tangible personal property yields significant tax savings.

However, there is a downside. When the property is sold, the tangible personal property gains are taxable as ordinary income due to § 1245 depreciation recapture, whereas the gain from the sale of the building is not subject to full recapture, is a § 1231 gain, and may receive long-term capital gain treatment.

EXAMPLE 49

Sanjay Enterprises, Ltd., acquires a residential rental building on January 1, 2014, for $300,000. Sanjay receives an offer of $450,000 for the building and sells it on December 23, 2015.

- Sanjay takes $20,909 [($300,000 × .03485) + ($300,000 × .03636 × $^{11.5}/_{12}$) = $20,909] of total depreciation for 2014 and 2015. The adjusted basis of the property is $279,091 ($300,000 − $20,909).
- Sanjay's recognized gain is $170,909 ($450,000 − $279,091).
- All of the gain is § 1231 gain.

Concept Summary 8.5 compares and contrasts the § 1245 and § 1250 depreciation recapture rules.

Concept Summary 8.5

Comparison of § 1245 and § 1250 Depreciation Recapture

	§ 1245	§ 1250
Property affected	All depreciable personal property, including items such as § 179 expense and § 197 amortization of intangibles such as goodwill, patents, and copyrights.	Nonresidential real property acquired after 1969 and before 1981, on which accelerated depreciation was taken. Residential rental real property acquired after 1975 and before 1987, on which accelerated depreciation was taken.
Depreciation recaptured	Potentially all depreciation taken. If the selling price is greater than or equal to the original cost, all depreciation is recaptured. If the selling price is between the adjusted basis and the original cost, only some depreciation is recaptured.	Normally, there is no depreciation recapture, but in the special situations listed above, there can be § 1250 depreciation recapture of additional depreciation (the excess of accelerated depreciation over straight-line depreciation). All depreciation taken if property disposed of in first year.
Limit on recapture	Lesser of depreciation taken or gain recognized.	Lesser of additional depreciation or gain recognized.
Treatment of gain exceeding recapture gain	Usually § 1231 gain.	Usually § 1231 gain.
Treatment of loss	No depreciation recapture; loss is usually § 1231 loss.	No depreciation recapture; loss is usually § 1231 loss.

8-9a Unrecaptured § 1250 Gain (Real Estate 25% Gain)

As noted previously in the chapter, *noncorporate taxpayers* pay tax at a maximum rate of 25 percent on their **unrecaptured § 1250 gain**. This gain represents that part of the gain on § 1250 property that is attributable to depreciation that was not recaptured by § 1250.

The procedure for computing this amount involves three distinct steps.

Step 1. Determine the part of the recognized gain that is attributable to *depreciation deductions* claimed in prior years.

Step 2. Apply § 1250 to determine the portion of the gain calculated in step 1 that is recaptured as ordinary income (if any).

Step 3. Subtract the gain recaptured under § 1250 (step 2) from the gain derived in step 1. This amount is the *unrecaptured § 1250 gain.*

Recall that for property placed in service after 1986, § 1250 generally does not apply, because such property is depreciated using the straight-line method under MACRS. As a result, *all* of the gain attributable to depreciation on such assets is unrecaptured § 1250 gain.

EXAMPLE 50

Linda placed two apartment buildings in service at a cost of $100,000 each. On each building, she claimed depreciation deductions of $78,000. Thus, her adjusted basis for each building is $22,000 ($100,000 cost − $78,000 depreciation deducted). Because the buildings were depreciated using the straight-line method, there is no § 1250 recapture. She now sells these buildings for $96,000 and $110,000, respectively, and computes her gain as follows.

	Building A	Building B
Amount realized	$ 96,000	$110,000
Adjusted basis	(22,000)	(22,000)
Recognized gain	$ 74,000	$ 88,000
Depreciation recaptured by § 1250	(–0–)	(–0–)
Remaining gain	$ 74,000	$ 88,000
Unrecaptured § 1250 gain	(74,000)	(78,000)
§ 1231 gain	None	$ 10,000

8-9b **Additional Recapture for Corporations**

Although depreciation recapture is generally the same for all taxpayers, corporations that sell depreciable real estate face an additional amount of depreciation recapture. Section 291(a)(1) requires recapture of 20 percent of the excess of the amount that would be recaptured under § 1245 (had § 1245 applied) over the amount actually recaptured under § 1250.

EXAMPLE 51

Red Corporation purchases nonresidential real property on May 1, 2000, for $800,000. Straight-line depreciation is taken in the amount of $316,239 before the property is sold on October 8, 2015, for $1.2 million.

First, determine the recognized gain:

Sales price		$1,200,000
Less: Adjusted basis—		
Cost of property	$ 800,000	
Less: Cost recovery	(316,239)	(483,761)
Recognized gain		$ 716,239

Second, determine the § 1245 recapture potential. This is the lesser of $716,239 (recognized gain) or $316,239 (cost recovery claimed).

Third, determine the normal § 1250 recapture amount:

Cost recovery taken	$ 316,239
Less: Straight-line cost recovery	(316,239)
§ 1250 ordinary income	$ –0–

continued

Fourth, because the taxpayer is a corporation, determine the additional § 291 amount:

§ 1245 recapture potential	$ 316,239
Less: § 1250 recapture amount	(–0–)
Excess § 1245 recapture potential	$ 316,239
Apply § 291 percentage	× 20%
Additional ordinary income under § 291	$ 63,248

Red Corporation's recognized gain of $716,239 is accounted for as follows:

Ordinary income under § 1250	$ –0–
Ordinary income under § 291	63,248
§ 1231 gain	652,991
Total recognized gain	$ 716,239

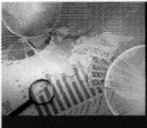

TAX PLANNING STRATEGIES **Selling Depreciable Real Estate**

FRAMEWORK FOCUS: DEDUCTIONS

Strategy: Maximize Deductible Amounts.

FRAMEWORK FOCUS: TAX RATE

Strategy: Control the Character of Income and Deductions.

A building depreciated on an accelerated method eventually generates annual allowances that are smaller than the amount the straight-line method would have produced. Beyond that "cross-over" point, the *cumulative* amount of "additional depreciation" is reduced every year the asset is used. Doing so effectively converts gain for an individual taxpayer that would otherwise be subject to § 1250 recapture into "unrecaptured § 1250 gain," enabling the taxpayer to save the difference between the applicable tax rate on ordinary income and 25 percent.

Continuing to use the building, however, brings forth an array of important *nontax considerations*. Each year a building is used subjects it to additional maintenance expenses to keep it in operating condition. Moreover, a building's appeal to current and prospective tenants tends to decline over time as newer structures appear offering more modern amenities, such as wireless high-speed Internet access, and other conveniences. Finally, local real estate developments might produce lower resale prices that offset much, if not all, of the tax advantage obtained by holding the property for the additional time.

8-10 **EXCEPTIONS TO §§ 1245 AND 1250**

Recapture under §§ 1245 and 1250 does not apply to the following transactions.

8-10a **Gifts**

Depreciation recapture potential carries over to the donee.[27]

EXAMPLE 52

Wade gives his daughter, Helen, § 1245 property with an adjusted basis of $1,000. The amount of recapture potential is $700. Helen uses the property in her business and claims further depreciation of $100 before selling it for $1,900.

Helen's recognized gain is $1,000 [$1,900 amount realized − $900 adjusted basis ($1,000 carryover basis − $100 depreciation taken by Helen)], of which $800 is recaptured as ordinary income ($100 depreciation taken by Helen + $700 recapture potential carried over from Wade). The remaining gain of $200 is § 1231 gain. Even if Helen had used the property for personal purposes, the $700 recapture potential would have carried over.

---

[27]§§ 1245(b)(1) and 1250(d)(1) and Reg. §§ 1.1245–4(a)(1) and 1.1250–3(a)(1).

8-10b Death

Although not an attractive tax planning approach, death eliminates all recapture potential.[28] Depreciation recapture potential does not carry over from a decedent to an estate or an heir.

Assume the same facts as in the preceding example, except that Helen receives the property as a result of Wade's death and the property has a fair market value of $1,700 when Wade dies. The $700 recapture potential from Wade is extinguished at his death. Helen has a basis in the property equal to its fair market value at Wade's death ($1,700).

Helen will have a $300 gain when the property is sold because the selling price ($1,900) exceeds the property's adjusted basis of $1,600 ($1,700 basis to Helen − $100 depreciation) by $300. Because of § 1245, Helen has ordinary income of $100. The remaining gain of $200 is § 1231 gain.

8-10c Charitable Transfers

Depreciation recapture potential reduces the amount of any charitable contribution deduction.[29]

Bullfinch Corporation donates to a museum § 1245 property with a fair market value of $10,000 and an adjusted basis of $7,000. Assume that the depreciation recapture potential associated with this property is $2,000 (the amount of recapture that would occur if the property were sold).

The company's charitable contribution deduction (subject to the limitations discussed in Chapter 5) is $8,000 ($10,000 fair market value − $2,000 recapture potential).

8-10d Certain Nontaxable Transactions

In certain transactions, the transferor's adjusted basis for the property carries over to the transferee. Then depreciation recapture potential also carries over to the transferee.[30] Included in this category are transfers of property pursuant to the following.

- Nontaxable incorporations under § 351 (see Chapter 12).
- Certain liquidations of subsidiary corporations under § 332 (see Chapter 13).
- Nontaxable contributions to a partnership under § 721 (see Chapter 14).
- Nontaxable corporate reorganizations.

Gain may be recognized in these transactions if boot is received. If gain is recognized, it is treated as ordinary income to the extent of the recapture potential or the recognized gain, whichever is lower.[31]

8-10e Like-Kind Exchanges and Involuntary Conversions

As explained in Chapter 7, realized gain is recognized to the extent of boot received in a like-kind exchange. Realized gain is also recognized to the extent the proceeds from an involuntary conversion are not reinvested in similar property. Such recognized gain is subject to recapture as ordinary income under §§ 1245 and 1250. Any remaining recapture potential carries over to the property received in the exchange.

---

[28]§§ 1245(b)(2) and 1250(d)(2).

[29]§ 170(e)(1)(A) and Reg. § 1.170A–4(b)(1). In certain circumstances, § 1231 gain also reduces the amount of the charitable contribution. See § 170(e)(1)(B).

[30]§§ 1245(b)(3) and 1250(d)(3). Reg. §§ 1.1245–2(a)(4) and (c)(2), 1.1245–4(c), 1.1250–2(d)(1) and (3).

[31]§§ 1245(b)(3) and 1250(d)(3) and Reg. §§ 1.1245–4(c) and 1.1250–3(c).

EXAMPLE 55

Crane Corporation exchanges § 1245 property with an adjusted basis of $300 for § 1245 property with a fair market value of $6,000 plus $1,000 cash (boot). The exchange qualifies as a like-kind exchange under § 1031. Crane's realized gain is $6,700 ($7,000 amount realized − $300 adjusted basis of property).

Because Crane received boot of $1,000, it recognizes gain to this extent. Assuming that the recapture potential is $7,500, Crane recognizes § 1245 gain of $1,000. The remaining recapture potential of $6,500 carries over to the like-kind property received.

DIGGING DEEPER 12   In-depth coverage can be found on this book's companion website: www.cengagebrain.com

8-11 REPORTING PROCEDURES

Noncapital gains and losses are reported on Form 4797, Sales of Business Property. However, before Form 4797 is filled out, Part B of Form 4684 (Casualties and Thefts) must be completed to determine whether any casualties will enter into the § 1231 computation procedure. Recall that recognized gains from § 1231 asset casualties may be recaptured by § 1245 or § 1250. These gains do not appear on Form 4684. The § 1231 gains and nonpersonal-use long-term capital gains are netted against § 1231 and nonpersonal-use long-term capital losses on Form 4684 to determine whether there is a net gain to transfer to Form 4797, Part I.

DIGGING DEEPER 13   In-depth coverage can be found on this book's companion website: www.cengagebrain.com

TAX PLANNING STRATEGIES   Timing of Recapture

FRAMEWORK FOCUS: TAX RATE

Strategy: Shift Net Income from High-Bracket Years to Low-Bracket Years.
Shift Net Income from High-Bracket Taxpayers to Low-Bracket Taxpayers.

Because recapture is usually not triggered until the property is sold or disposed of, it may be possible to plan for recapture in low-bracket or loss years. If a taxpayer has net operating loss carryovers that are about to expire, the recognition of ordinary income from recapture may be advisable to absorb the loss carryovers.

EXAMPLE 56

Angel Corporation has a $15,000 net operating loss carryover that will expire this year. It owns a machine that it plans to sell in the early part of next year. The expected gain of $17,000 from the sale of the machine will be recaptured as ordinary income under § 1245. Angel sells the machine before the end of this year and offsets $15,000 of the ordinary income by the net operating loss carryover.

It is also possible to postpone recapture or to shift the burden of recapture to others. For example, recapture is avoided upon the disposition of a § 1231 asset if the taxpayer replaces the property by entering into a like-kind exchange. In this instance, recapture potential is merely carried over to the newly acquired property (refer to Example 55).

Recapture can be shifted to others through the gratuitous transfer of § 1245 or § 1250 property to family members. A subsequent sale of such property by the donee will trigger recapture to the donee rather than the donor (refer to Example 52). This technique is advisable when the donee is in a lower income tax bracket than the donor.

REFOCUS ON THE BIG PICTURE

CAPITAL GAINS AND LOSSES, § 1231 GAINS AND LOSSES, AND RECAPTURE

The land, stock, franchise, and home owned by Alice are all capital assets and will produce capital gain or loss when sold. Accordingly, Alice will have a long-term capital gain of $48,000 from the sale of the land, a long-term capital gain of $6,000 from the sale of 300 shares of inherited AppleCo stock, a short-term capital loss of $4,000 from the sale of the other 200 shares of AppleCo stock, a short-term capital gain of $1,000 from the sale of the franchise, and a $125,000 long-term capital gain from the sale of the house. The treatment given to the Eagle stock will depend on the nature of its disposition (see Example 10).

For the patent, because Alice is a "holder" of the patent, it will qualify for the beneficial capital gain rate regardless of the holding period if the patent should produce income in excess of her $50,000 investment. However, if Alice loses money on the investment, she will be able to deduct only $3,000 of the loss per year against her ordinary income (assuming that there are no offsetting capital gains in the year of a sale).

The depreciable property owned by Alice's husband is § 1231 property. The $45,000 gain from the sale of the property ($60,000 amount realized − $15,000 adjusted basis) is subject to depreciation recapture under § 1245. Accordingly, the first $35,000 of the gain (up to the amount of depreciation taken on the property) is taxed as ordinary income. The remaining $10,000 is § 1231 gain and is given long-term capital gain treatment.

As a result of these transactions where the amount of gain or loss is determined, Alice and her husband have a net long-term capital gain of $189,000 ($48,000 + $6,000 + $125,000 + $10,000) and a net short-term capital loss of $3,000 ($1,000 gain − $4,000 loss). The long-term capital gain and short-term capital loss are netted, so the final result is a net capital gain of $186,000, which is taxed at the 15 or 20 percent tax rate. Alice and her husband also report $35,000 of ordinary income on their joint income tax return because of the depreciation recapture provisions.

What If?

What if the depreciable business property was worth only $10,000 when it was sold? In this case, there is no depreciation recapture, and the $5,000 loss is deductible as an ordinary loss under § 1231.

Suggested Readings

Tom Crice, "The Perils of Winning: Settlement Payments, Trade Secrets, and Taxes," *Practical Tax Strategies*, September 2012.

Melanie James, "Factors Influencing Reduction in Value for Potential Capital Gains Tax," *Practical Tax Strategies*, April 2014.

Timothy R. Koski, "Bitcoin—Tax Planning in the Uncertain World of Virtual Currency," *Practical Tax Strategies*, December 2014.

"LLC Members Received Capital Gains Income from Sale of LLC's Assets," *Practical Tax Strategies*, October 2012.

Patrick J. Smith, Francois Hechinger, John M. Nuckolls, "Capital Gain Exclusion on Small Business Stock," *The Tax Adviser*, May 2011.

Key Terms

Computational Exercises

1. **LO.1** Dexter owns a large tract of land and subdivides it for sale. Assume that Dexter meets all of the requirements of § 1237 and during the tax year sells the first eight lots to eight different buyers for $22,000 each. Dexter's basis in each lot sold is $15,000, and he incurs total selling expenses of $900 on each sale. What is the amount of Dexter's capital gain and ordinary income?

Critical Thinking   2. **LO.2** Shelia purchases $50,000 of newly issued Gingo Corporation bonds for $45,000. The bonds have original issue discount (OID) of $5,000. After Shelia amortized $2,300 of OID and held the bonds for four years, she sold the bonds for $48,000. What is the amount and character of her gain or loss?

3. **LO.2** Olivia wants to buy some vacant land for investment purposes. She currently cannot afford the full purchase price. Instead, Olivia pays the landowner $8,000 to obtain an option to buy the land for $175,000 anytime in the next four years. Fourteen months after purchasing the option, Olivia sells the option for $10,000. What is the amount and character of Olivia's gain or loss?

4. **LO.4** Coline has the following capital gain and loss transactions for 2015.

Short-term capital gain	$ 5,000
Short-term capital loss	(2,100)
Long-term capital gain (28%)	6,000
Long-term capital gain (15%)	2,000
Long-term capital loss (28%)	(10,500)

After the capital gain and loss netting process, what is the amount and character of Coline's gain or loss?

5. **LO.4** Elliott has the following capital gain and loss transactions for 2015.

Short-term capital gain	$ 1,500
Short-term capital loss	(3,600)
Long-term capital gain (28%)	12,000
Long-term capital gain (25%)	4,800
Long-term capital gain (15%)	6,000
Long-term capital loss (28%)	(4,500)
Long-term capital loss (15%)	(9,000)

After the capital gain and loss netting process, what is the amount and character of Elliott's gain or loss?

6. **LO.6,7** Renata Corporation purchased equipment in 2013 for $180,000 and has taken $83,000 of regular MACRS depreciation. Renata Corporation sells the equipment in 2015 for $110,000. What is the amount and character of Renata's gain or loss?

7. **LO.6,7** Jacob purchased business equipment for $56,000 in 2012 and has taken $35,000 of regular MACRS depreciation. Jacob sells the equipment in 2015 for $26,000. What is the amount and character of Jacob's gain or loss?

8. **LO.6,7** Sissie owns two items of business equipment. Both were purchased in 2011 for $100,000, both have a 7-year MACRS recovery period, and both have an adjusted basis of $37,490. Sissie is considering selling these assets in 2015. One of them is worth $60,000, and the other is worth $23,000. Because both items were used in her business, Sissie simply assumes that the loss on one will offset the gain from the other and that the net gain or loss will increase or reduce her business income. What is the amount and character of Sissie's gain or loss?

9. **LO.7** An apartment building was acquired in 2006. The depreciation taken on the building was $123,000, and the building was sold for a $34,000 gain. What is the maximum amount of 25% gain?

10. **LO.7** In a § 1031 like-kind exchange, Rafael exchanges equipment that originally cost $200,000. On the date of the exchange, the equipment given up has an adjusted basis of $85,000 and a fair market value of $110,000. Rafael pays $15,000 and receives equipment with a fair market value of $125,000. What is the amount and character of Rafael's gain or loss?

11. **LO.7** Gaston Corporation distributes § 1245 property as a dividend to its share-holders. The property's fair market value is $580,000, and the adjusted basis is $560,000. In addition, the amount of the recapture potential is $55,000. What is the amount and character of Gaston's gain or loss?

Critical Thinking

Problems

12. **LO.1** An individual taxpayer sells some used assets at a garage sale. Why are none of the proceeds taxable in most situations?

Issue ID

13. **LO.1** Alison owns a painting that she received as a gift from her aunt 10 years ago. The aunt created the painting. Alison has displayed the painting in her home and has never attempted to sell it. Recently, a visitor noticed the painting and offered Alison $5,000 for it. If Alison decides to sell the painting, what tax issues does she face?

Issue ID

14. **LO.1** During the year, Eugene had the four property transactions summarized below. Eugene is a collector of antique glassware and occasionally sells a piece to get funds to buy another. What are the amount and nature of the gain or loss from each of these transactions?

Property	Date Acquired	Date Sold	Adjusted Basis	Sales Price
Antique vase	06/18/04	05/23/15	$37,000	$42,000
Blue Growth Fund (100 shares)	12/23/06	11/22/15	22,000	38,000
Orange bonds	02/12/07	04/11/15	34,000	42,000*
Green stock (100 shares)	02/14/15	11/23/15	11,000	13,000

*The sales price included $750 of accrued interest income.

15. **LO.1** Rennie owns a video game arcade. He buys vintage video games from estates, often at much less than the retail value of the property. He usually installs the vintage video games in a special section of his video game arcade that appeals to players of "classic" video games. Recently, Rennie sold a classic video game that a

Decision Making

customer "just had to have." Rennie paid $11,250 for it, owned it for 14 months, and sold it for $18,000. Rennie had suspected that this particular classic video game would be of interest to collectors; so he had it refurbished, put it on display in his video arcade, and listed it for sale on the Internet. No customers in the arcade had played it other than those testing it before considering it for purchase. Rennie would like the gain on the sale of the classic video game to be a long-term capital gain. Did he achieve that objective? Why or why not?

16. **LO.1** George is the owner of numerous classic automobiles. His intention is to hold the automobiles until they increase in value and then sell them. He rents the automobiles for use in various events (e.g., antique automobile shows) while he is holding them. In 2015, he sold a classic automobile for $1.5 million. He had held the automobile for five years, and it had a tax basis of $750,000. Was the automobile a capital asset? Why or why not?

Communications   17. **LO.1** Hyacinth, Inc., is a dealer in securities. The firm has spotted a fast-rising company and would like to buy and hold its stock for investment. The stock is currently selling for $2 per share, and Hyacinth thinks it will climb to $40 a share within two years. How can Hyacinth ensure that any gain it realizes will be taxed as long-term capital gain? Draft a letter responding to Hyacinth's inquiry. The firm's address is 200 Catamon Drive, Great Falls, MT 59406.

18. **LO.1** Eagle Partners meets all of the requirements of § 1237 (subdivided realty). In 2015, Eagle Partners begins selling lots and sells four separate lots to four different purchasers. Eagle Partners also sells two contiguous lots to another purchaser. The sales price of each lot is $30,000. The partnership's basis for each lot is $15,000. Selling expenses are $500 per lot.
   a. What are the realized and recognized gain?
   b. Explain the nature of the gain (i.e., ordinary income or capital gain).
   c. Would your answers change if, instead, the lots sold to the fifth purchaser were not contiguous? If so, how?

Critical Thinking   19. **LO.1, 2** Benny purchased $400,000 of Peach Corporation face value bonds for $320,000 on November 13, 2014. The bonds had been issued with $80,000 of original issue discount because Peach was in financial difficulty in 2014. On December 3, 2015, Benny sold the bonds for $283,000 after amortizing $1,000 of the original issue discount. What are the nature and amount of Benny's gain or loss?

20. **LO.2** Carla was the owner of vacant land that she was holding for investment. She paid $2 million for the land in 2013. Raymond was an investor in vacant land. He thought Carla's land might be the site of an exit ramp from a new freeway. Raymond gave Carla $836,000 for an option on her land in 2014. The option was good for two years and gave Raymond the ability to purchase Carla's land for $4,765,000. The freeway was not approved by the government, and Raymond's option expired in 2015. Does Carla have $836,000 of long-term capital gain upon the expiration of the option? Explain.

Decision Making   21. **LO.2, 3, 4** Mac, an inventor, obtained a patent on a chemical process to clean old aluminum siding so that it can be easily repainted. Mac has a $50,000 tax basis in the patent. Mac does not have the capital to begin manufacturing and selling this product, so he has done nothing with the patent since obtaining it two years ago.
   Now a group of individuals has approached him and offered two alternatives. Under one alternative, they will pay Mac $600,000 (payable evenly over the next 15 years) for the exclusive right to manufacture and sell the product. Under the other, they will form a business and contribute capital to it to begin manufacturing and selling the product; Mac will receive 20% of the company's shares of stock in exchange for all of his patent rights. Discuss which alternative is better for Mac.

22. **LO.2** Blue Corporation and Fuchsia Corporation are engaged in a contract negotiation over the use of Blue's trademarked name, DateSiteForSeniors. For a one-time payment of $45,000, Blue licensed Fuchsia to use the name DateSiteForSeniors, and the license requires that Fuchsia pay Blue a royalty every time a new customer signs up on Fuchsia's website. Blue is a developer of "website ideas" that it then licenses to other companies such as Fuchsia. Did Fuchsia purchase a franchise right from Blue, or did Fuchsia purchase the name DateSiteForSeniors from Blue?

23. **LO.2** Freys, Inc., sells a 12-year franchise to Red Company. The franchise contains many restrictions on how Red may operate its store. For instance, Red cannot use less than Grade 10 Idaho potatoes; must fry the potatoes at a constant 410 degrees; must dress store personnel in Freys-approved uniforms; and must have a Freys sign that meets detailed specifications on size, color, and construction. When the franchise contract is signed, Red makes a noncontingent $160,000 payment to Freys. During the same year, Red pays Freys $300,000—14% of Red's sales. How does Freys treat each of these payments? How does Red treat each of the payments?

24. **LO.3** Maria held vacant land that qualified as an investment asset. She purchased the vacant land on April 10, 2011. She exchanged the vacant land for a rental house in a qualifying like-kind exchange on January 22, 2015. Maria was going to hold the house for several years and then sell it. However, she got an "offer she could not refuse" and sold it on November 22, 2015, for a substantial gain. What was Maria's holding period for the house?

25. **LO.3** Thrasher Corporation sells short 100 shares of ARC stock at $20 per share on January 15, 2015. It buys 200 shares of ARC stock on April 1, 2015, at $25 per share. On May 2, 2015, Thrasher closes the short sale by delivering 100 of the shares purchased on April 1.
    a. What are the amount and nature of Thrasher's loss upon closing the short sale?
    b. When does the holding period for the remaining 100 shares begin?
    c. If Thrasher sells (at $27 per share) the remaining 100 shares on January 20, 2016, what will be the nature of its gain or loss?

Critical Thinking

26. **LO.1, 3, 4** Elaine Case (single with no dependents) has the following transactions in 2015:

Communications

AGI (exclusive of capital gains and losses)	$240,000
Long-term capital gain	22,000
Long-term capital loss	(8,000)
Short-term capital gain	19,000
Short-term capital loss	(23,000)

What is Elaine's net capital gain or loss? Draft a letter to Elaine describing how the net capital gain or loss will be treated on her tax return. Assume that Elaine's income from other sources puts her in the 39.6% bracket. Elaine's address is 300 Ireland Avenue, Shepherdstown, WV 25443.

27. **LO.4** Sally has taxable income of $160,000 as of November 30 of this year. She wants to sell a Rodin sculpture that has appreciated $90,000 since she purchased it six years ago, but she does not want to pay more than $15,000 of additional tax on the transaction. Sally also owns various stocks, some of which are currently worth less than their basis. How can she achieve her desired result?

Decision Making

28. **LO.5** Platinum, Inc., has determined its taxable income as $215,000 before considering the results of its capital gain or loss transactions. Platinum has a short-term capital loss of $24,000, a long-term capital loss of $38,000, and a short-term capital gain of $39,000. What is Platinum's taxable income? What (if any) are the amount and nature of its capital loss carryover?

Ethics and Equity   29. **LO.1, 4** The taxpayer is an antiques collector and is going to sell an antique purchased many years ago for a large gain. The facts and circumstances indicate that the taxpayer might be classified as a dealer rather than an investor in antiques. The taxpayer will save $40,000 in taxes if the gain is treated as long-term capital gain rather than as ordinary income. The taxpayer is considering the following options as ways to ensure the $40,000 tax savings.

- Give the antique to his daughter, who is an investment banker, to sell.
- Merely assume that he has held the antique as an investment.
- Exchange the antique in a like-kind exchange for another antique he wants.

One of the tax preparers the taxpayer has contacted has said that he would be willing to prepare the return under the second option. Would you? Why or why not? Evaluate the other options.

Communications   30. **LO.1, 4** In 2015, Bertha Jarow (head of household with three dependents) had a $28,000 loss from the sale of a personal residence. She also purchased from an individual inventor for $7,000 (and resold in two months for $18,000) a patent on a rubber bonding process. The patent had not yet been reduced to practice. Bertha purchased the patent as an investment. In addition, she had the following capital gains and losses from stock transactions:

Long-term capital loss	($ 6,000)
Long-term capital loss carryover from 2014	(12,000)
Short-term capital gain	21,000
Short-term capital loss	(7,000)

What is Bertha's net capital gain or loss? Draft a letter to Bertha explaining the tax treatment of all of these transactions. Assume that Bertha's income from other sources puts her in the 28% bracket. Bertha's address is 1120 West Street, Ashland, OR 97520.

Issue ID   31. **LO.1, 3, 4** Bridgette is known as the "doll lady." She started collecting dolls as a child, always received one or more dolls as gifts on her birthday, never sold any dolls, and eventually owned 600 dolls. She is retiring and moving to a small apartment and has decided to sell her collection. She lists the dolls on an Internet auction site and, to her great surprise, receives an offer from another doll collector of $45,000 for the entire collection. Bridgette sells the entire collection, except for five dolls she purchased during the last year. She had owned all of the dolls sold for more than a year. What tax factors should Bridgette consider in deciding how to report the sale?

Critical Thinking   32. **LO.1, 2, 4** Two years ago, Harriet Company (an unincorporated entity) developed
Decision Making   a process for preserving doughnuts that gives the doughnuts a much longer shelf life. The process is not patented or copyrighted, and only Harriet knows how it works. A conglomerate has approached Harriet with an offer to purchase the formula for the process. Specifically, the offer allows Harriet to choose between the following. Which option should Harriet accept?

- $650,000 cash for the formula and a 10-year covenant not to compete, paying Harriet $65,000 per year for 10 years.
- $650,000 cash for a 10-year covenant not to compete, and an annual $65,000 royalty for the formula, payable for 10 years.

Communications   33. **LO.6** A sculpture that Tulip & Co. held for investment was destroyed in a flood. The sculpture was insured, and Tulip had a $60,000 gain from this casualty. It also had a $17,000 loss from an uninsured antique vase that was destroyed by the flood. The vase was also held for investment. Tulip had no other property transactions during the year and has no nonrecaptured § 1231 losses from prior years. Both the sculpture and the vase had been held for more than one year when the flood occurred. Compute Tulip's net gain or loss, and identify how it would be treated. Write a letter to Tulip, explaining the nature of the gain or loss. Tulip's address is 2367 Meridian Road, Hannibal, MO 63401.

34. **LO.6** Harold, a CPA, has a new client who recently moved to town. Harold prepares the client's current-year tax return, which shows a net § 1231 gain. Harold calls the client to request copies of the returns for the preceding five years to determine if there are any § 1231 lookback losses. The client says that the returns are "still buried in the moving mess somewhere" and cannot be found. The client also says that he does not remember any § 1231 net losses on the prior year returns. What should Harold do? Justify your answer.

Ethics and Equity

35. **LO.6** Geranium, Inc., has the following net § 1231 results for each of the years shown. What is the nature of the net gain in 2014 and 2015?

Tax Year	Net § 1231 Loss	Net § 1231 Gain
2010	$18,000	
2011	33,000	
2012	42,000	
2013		$41,000
2014		30,000
2015		41,000

36. **LO.6** Delphinium Company owns two parcels of land (§ 1231 assets). One parcel can be sold at a loss of $60,000, and the other parcel can be sold at a gain of $70,000. The company has no nonrecaptured § 1231 losses from prior years. The parcels could be sold at any time because potential purchasers are abundant. The company has a $35,000 short-term capital loss carryover from a prior tax year and no capital assets that could be sold to generate long-term capital gains. Both land parcels have been held more than one year. What should Delphinium do based upon these facts? (Assume that tax rates are constant, and ignore the present value of future cash flows.)

Decision Making

37. **LO.6, 7** Siena Industries (a sole proprietorship) sold three § 1231 assets on October 10, 2015. Data on these property dispositions are as follows.

Asset	Cost	Acquired	Depreciation	Sold for
Rack	$100,000	10/10/11	$62,000	$85,000
Forklift	35,000	10/16/12	23,000	5,000
Bin	87,000	03/12/14	34,000	60,000

a. Determine the amount and the character of the recognized gain or loss from the disposition of each asset in 2015.

b. Assuming that Siena has no nonrecaptured net § 1231 losses from prior years, how much of the recognized gains are treated as long-term capital gains?

38. **LO.6, 7** On December 1, 2013, Lavender Manufacturing Company (a corporation) purchased another company's assets, including a patent. The patent was used in Lavender's manufacturing operations; $49,500 was allocated to the patent, and it was amortized at the rate of $275 per month. On July 30, 2015, Lavender sold the patent for $95,000. Twenty months of amortization had been taken on the patent. What are the amount and nature of the gain Lavender recognizes on the disposition of the patent? Write a letter to Lavender, discussing the treatment of the gain. Lavender's address is 6734 Grover Street, Boothbay Harbor, ME 04538. The letter should be addressed to Bill Cubit, Controller.

Communications

39. **LO.6, 7** Larry is the sole proprietor of a trampoline shop. During 2015, the following transactions occurred.

- Unimproved land adjacent to the store was condemned by the city on February 1. The condemnation proceeds were $15,000. The land, acquired in 1986, had an allocable basis of $40,000. Larry has additional parking across the street and plans to use the condemnation proceeds to build his inventory.

- A truck used to deliver trampolines was sold on January 2 for $3,500. The truck was purchased on January 2, 2011, for $6,000. On the date of sale, the adjusted basis was zero.

- Larry sold an antique rowing machine at an auction. Net proceeds were $4,900. The rowing machine was purchased as used equipment 17 years ago for $5,200 and is fully depreciated.

- Larry sold an apartment building for $300,000 on September 1. The rental property was purchased on September 1, 2012, for $150,000 and was being depreciated over a 27.5-year MACRS life using the straight-line method. At the date of sale, the adjusted basis was $124,783.

- Larry's personal yacht was stolen on September 5. The yacht had been purchased in August at a cost of $25,000. The fair market value immediately preceding the theft was $19,600. Larry was insured for 50% of the original cost, and he received $12,500 on December 1.

- Larry sold a Buick on May 1 for $9,600. The vehicle had been used exclusively for personal purposes. It was purchased on September 1, 2011, for $20,800.

- Larry's trampoline stretching machine (owned two years) was stolen on May 5, but the business's insurance company will not pay any of the machine's value because Larry failed to pay the insurance premium. The machine had a fair market value of $8,000 and an adjusted basis of $6,000 at the time of theft.

- Larry had AGI of $102,000 from sources other than those described above.

- Larry has no nonrecaptured § 1231 lookback losses.

    a. For each transaction, what are the amount and nature of recognized gain or loss?

    b. What is Larry's 2015 AGI?

Critical Thinking 40. **LO.6, 7** A business building on which straight-line depreciation of $13,000 was taken is sold on the installment basis for $100,000 with $20,000 down and four yearly installments of $20,000 plus interest. The adjusted basis for the building is $35,000 at the time of the sale. The building had been held for more than 12 months. What are the amount and nature of the recognized gain?

41. **LO.7** Nicholas owns business equipment with a $155,000 adjusted basis; he paid $200,000 for the equipment, and it is currently worth $173,000. Nicholas dies suddenly, and his son Alvin inherits the property. What is Alvin's basis for the property? What happens to the § 1245 depreciation recapture potential?

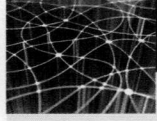

BRIDGE DISCIPLINE

1. Using an online research service, find the audited financial statements of a major U.S. corporation.
    a. List some of the items that the corporation reports as having different treatment for tax and financial accounting purposes. These items often are mentioned in the footnotes to the statements.
    b. List two or more such items that seem to increase the taxpayer's after-tax income and two or more that seem to decrease it.

Research Problems

Note: Solutions to Research Problems can be prepared by using the Checkpoint® Student Edition online research product, which is available to accompany this text. It is also possible to prepare solutions to the Research Problems by using tax research materials found in a standard tax library.

Research Problem 1. Clyde had worked for many years as the chief executive of Red Industries, Inc., and had been a major shareholder. Clyde and the company had a falling out, and Clyde was terminated. Clyde and Red executed a document under which Clyde's stock in Red would be redeemed and Clyde would agree not to compete against Red in its geographic service area. After extensive negotiations between the parties, Clyde agreed to surrender his Red stock in exchange for $600,000. Clyde's basis in his shares was $143,000, and he had held the shares for 17 years. The agreement made no explicit allocation of any of the $600,000 to Clyde's agreement not to compete against Red. How should Clyde treat the $600,000 payment on his 2015 tax return?

Research Problem 2. Ali owns 100 shares of Brown Corporation stock. He purchased the stock at five different times and at five different prices per share as indicated.

Decision Making

Share Block	Number of Shares	Per Share Price	Purchase Date
A	10	$60	10/10/1998
B	20	20	08/11/1999
C	15	15	10/24/2000
D	35	30	04/23/2001
E	20	25	07/28/2002

On April 28, 2015, Ali will sell 40 shares of Brown stock for $40 per share. All of Ali's shares are held by his stockbroker. The broker's records track when the shares were purchased. May Ali designate the shares he sells? If so, which shares should he sell? Assume that Ali wants to maximize his gain because he has a capital loss carryforward.

Research Problem 3. Siva Nathaniel owns various plots of land in Fulton County, Georgia. He acquired the land at various times during the last 20 years. About every fourth year, Siva subdivides into lots one of the properties he owns. He then has water, sewer, natural gas, and electricity hookups put in each lot and paves new streets. Siva has always treated his sales of such lots as sales of capital assets. His previous tax returns were prepared by an accountant whose practice you recently purchased. Has the proper tax treatment been used on the prior tax returns? Explain.

Partial list of research aids:
§§ 1221 and 1237.
Jesse W. and Betty J. English, 65 TCM 2160, T.C.Memo. 1993–111.

Use the tax resources of the Internet to address the following questions. Do not restrict your search to the Web, but include a review of newsgroups and general reference materials, practitioner sites and resources, primary sources of the tax law, chat rooms and discussion groups, and other opportunities.

Internet Activity

Research Problem 4. Find a website, other than the IRS website, that discusses the taxation of short sales of securities.

Research Problem 5. Perform a Google search to find information about capital gains tax rates worldwide (and across U.S. states). Try searching for: "capital gains rate by country (state)." What jurisdiction has the highest capital gains tax rate? What U.S. states have high capital gains tax rates?

Roger CPA Review Questions

1. Identify which of the following is a capital asset:

   I.   A canvas painting of a portrait client, in the painter's hands
   II. Depreciable fixtures in a business parking lot
   III. Treasury stock

   a. II only
   b. II and III only
   c. III only
   d. None of the above

2. On January 15 of the current year, Kreutzer, an individual, inherited from Gladstone shares of stock worth $25,000. Gladstone had purchased the shares in June of the previous year for $20,000, and the shares were worth $23,000 at Gladstone's date of death. The executor of Gladstone's estate did not elect to use the alternate valuation date. In March of the current year, Kreutzer sold the shares for $27,000. As a result of the sale, what will be the amount and type of gain reported by Kreutzer?

   a. $4,000 long-term capital gain
   b. $2,000 short-term capital gain
   c. $7,000 short-term capital gain
   d. $2,000 long-term capital gain

3. In 20X14, Colossus Corporation incurred a net capital loss in the amount of $25,000. Colossus had the following net capital gains in the previous five years:

   20X13 - $7,000
   20X12 - $2,000
   20X11 - $5,000
   20X10 - $4,000
   20X09 - $3,000

   How much of the 20X14 net capital loss may Colossus carry over to 20X15?

   a. $0
   b. $8,000
   c. $11,000
   d. $1,000

4. The following facts apply to Eliot, an individual, in the current year:

   April 1: Sold shares of stock, purchased on April 1 of the previous year, for a $2,000 gain

   May 15: Sold equipment used in Eliot's business, which had been purchased in July of the previous year, for a $2,000 gain.

   July 12: Sold shares of stock, purchased in February of the previous year, for a $7,000 gain.

   November 3: Sold equipment used in Eliot's business, which had been purchased in January of the current year, for a $1,000 loss.

   December 9: Sold shares of stock, purchased on February 22 of the current year, for a $3,000 loss.

   Considering only the above facts, what is Eliot's net capital gain for the current year?

   a. $7,000 long-term capital gain
   b. $9,000 long-term capital gain
   c. $5,000 long-term capital gain
   d. $6,000 long-term capital gain

5. Joe purchased a van for $30,000 on February 1, 20X4, for use with his business, Crew Airport Transport. Joe elected to take the Section 179 deduction. On January 1, 20X6, Joe sold the van for $20,000. What were the tax effects of this transaction?
   a. $10,000 loss
   b. $20,000 capital gain
   c. $20,000 ordinary gain
   d. $10,000 capital gain, $10,000 ordinary gain

6. In Year 3, Daniels, an individual, sold Section 1245 property for $21,000 that had an adjusted basis of $12,000, resulting in a $9,000 gain. The property had cost Daniels $20,000 when purchased in Year 1, and $8,000 of MACRS depreciation had been taken. How should Daniels report the gain on Daniels' Year 3 tax return?
   a. As a long-term capital gain of $9,000
   b. As an ordinary gain of $1,800 and a long-term capital gain of $7,200
   c. As an ordinary gain of $8,000 and a long-term capital gain of $1,000
   d. As an ordinary gain of $7,200 and a long-term capital gain of $1,800

7. Cowabunga Corp. had a highly profitable Year 4, during which it purchased $1,000,000 in tangible personal property and elected to claim the highest depreciation expense allowed for tax purposes under Code Section 179. In Year 6, Cowabunga sells the tangible personal property, which now has an adjusted basis of $200,000 as a result of the heavy depreciation taken in Years 4 and 5. Had only MACRS depreciation been taken on the property, its adjusted basis at the time of sale would have been $800,000. At a sales price of $930,000, how much of the $730,000 realized gain must be reported as ordinary gain for tax purposes?
   a. $720,000
   b. $600,000
   c. $0
   d. $730,000

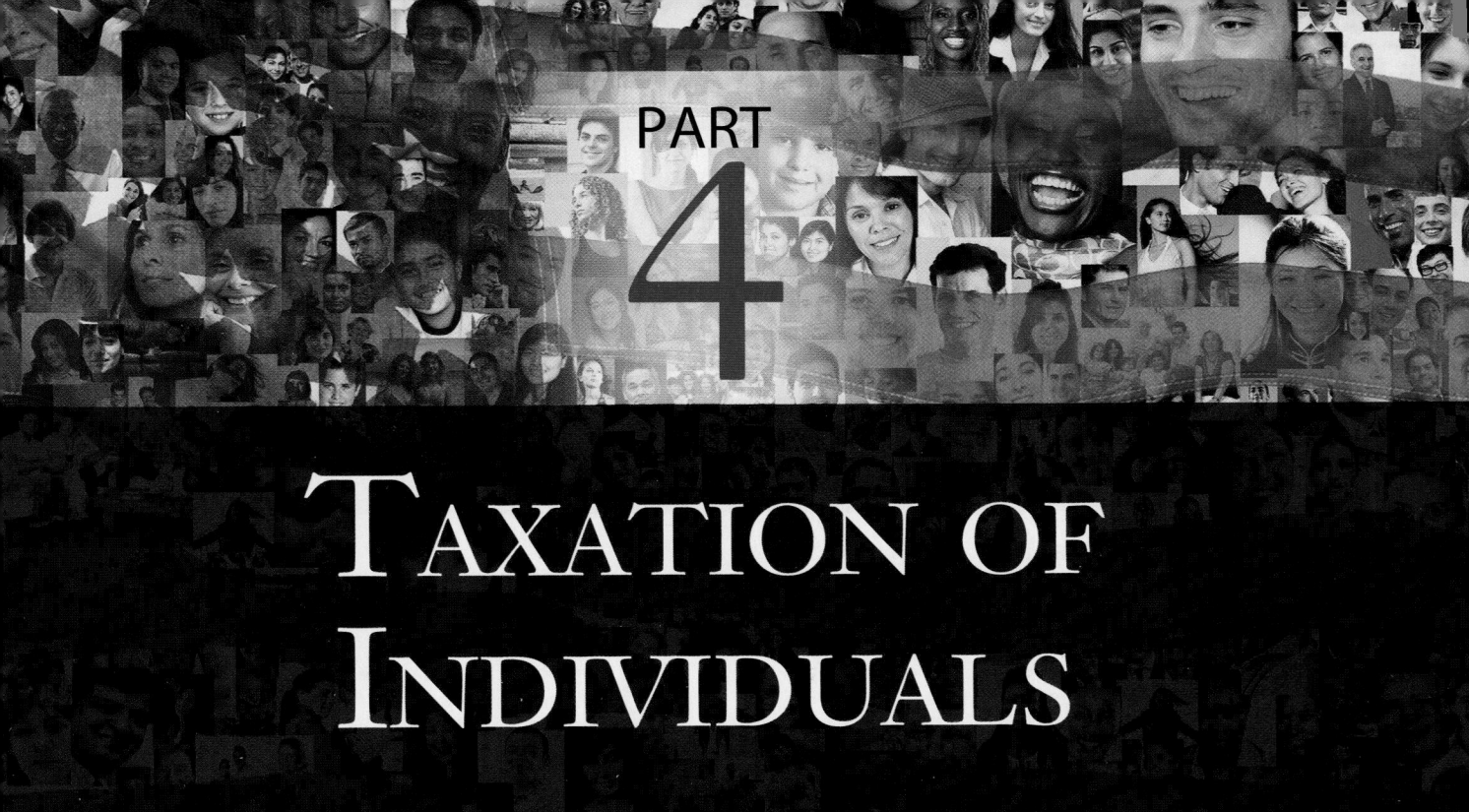

PART 4

TAXATION OF INDIVIDUALS

CHAPTER **9**
Individuals as the Taxpayer

CHAPTER **10**
Individuals: Income, Deductions, and Credits

CHAPTER **11**
Individuals as Employees and Proprietors

Part 4 focuses on numerous tax concepts and rules for individuals. The topics are ones unique to individual taxpayers, including personal exemptions, filing status, itemized deductions, sole proprietorship provisions, the kiddie tax, education credits, the earned income credit, and relevant provisions of the Affordable Care Act. These rules all serve to complete the tax formula for Federal income tax liability of individuals, for purposes of tax compliance and planning.

CHAPTER

9

Individuals as the Taxpayer

LEARNING OBJECTIVES: *After completing Chapter 9, you should be able to:*

LO.1 Describe and apply the components of the Federal income tax formula for individuals.

LO.2 Explain the standard deduction and evaluate its choice in arriving at taxable income.

LO.3 Apply the rules for arriving at personal exemptions.

LO.4 Explain the rules for determining dependency exemptions.

LO.5 List the filing requirements and choose the proper filing status.

LO.6 Demonstrate the proper procedures for determining the tax liability.

LO.7 Identify and report kiddie tax situations.

CHAPTER OUTLINE

TAX TALK *I'm proud of paying taxes in the United States. The only thing is—I could be just as proud for half the money.* —ARTHUR GODFREY

© MICHAEL DEFREITAS CARIBBEAN/ALAMY

A Divided Household

Polly maintains a household in which she lives with her unemployed husband (Nick), stepdaughter (Paige), and a family friend (Maude). She provides more than one-half of the support for both Paige and Maude. Maude was fatally injured in an automobile accident in February, and Polly paid for her hospitalization and funeral expenses. Paige, an accomplished gymnast, graduated from high school last year. Paige has a part-time job but spends most of her time training and looking for an athletic scholarship to the "right" college. In March, Nick left for parts unknown and has not been seen or heard from since. Polly was more surprised than distressed over Nick's unexpected departure.

Based on these facts, what are Polly's income tax concerns for the current year?

Read the chapter and formulate your response.

T he individual income tax accounts for approximately 38 percent of Federal budget receipts, compared with approximately 8 percent for the corporate income tax. The tax laws affecting individuals have become increasingly complex in recent years as the government adds new laws to protect or increase this important source of revenue. Taxpayers respond to each new tax act with techniques to exploit loopholes, and the government responds with loophole-closing provisions, making the individual income tax law even more complex.[1]

Describe and apply the components of the Federal income tax formula for individuals.

9-1 THE INDIVIDUAL TAX FORMULA

Individuals are subject to Federal income tax based on taxable income. This chapter explains how taxable income and the income tax of an individual taxpayer are determined. To compute taxable income, it is necessary to understand the tax formula in Concept Summary 9.1.

Concept Summary 9.1

Individual Income Tax Formula

Income (broadly defined)	$xx,xxx
Less: Exclusions	(x,xxx)
Gross income	$xx,xxx
Less: Deductions *for* adjusted gross income	(x,xxx)
Adjusted gross income (AGI)	$xx,xxx
Less: The greater of—	
Total itemized deductions *or* standard deduction	(x,xxx)
Less: Personal and dependency exemptions	(x,xxx)
Taxable income	$xx,xxx
Tax on taxable income (see Tax Tables or Tax Rate Schedules)	$ x,xxx
Less: Tax credits (including income taxes withheld and prepaid)	(xxx)
Tax due (or refund)	$ xxx

Although this formula is rather simple, determining an individual's taxable income can be quite complex because of the numerous provisions that govern the determination of gross income and allowable deductions.

After taxable income is computed, the appropriate tax rates must be applied. This requires a determination of the individual's filing status because different rates apply for single taxpayers, married taxpayers, and heads of household. The individual tax rate structure is progressive, with rates for 2015 ranging from 10 percent to 39.6 percent.[2] For comparison, the lowest rate structure, which was in effect from 1913 to 1915, ranged from 1 to 7 percent, and the highest, in effect during 1944 to 1945, ranged from 23 to 94 percent.

Once the individual's tax has been computed, prepayments and credits are subtracted to determine whether the taxpayer owes additional tax or is entitled to a refund.

9-1a Components of the Tax Formula

Before the application of the tax formula is illustrated, a brief discussion of each of its components is helpful.

---

[1]Refer to the discussion of tax complexity in Chapter 1.

[2]The current Tax Rate Schedules that apply to individuals are shown on the inside front cover of the text.

Income (Broadly Defined)

In the tax formula, "income" is broadly defined and includes all of the taxpayer's income, both taxable and nontaxable. In general, the courts have defined "income" as any increase in wealth.[3] As a result, it does not include a return of capital or receipt of borrowed funds. Nor does gross income include unrealized appreciation in the value of a taxpayer's assets.

Dan decides to quit renting and buy a new house. Consequently, the owner of the apartment building returns to Dan the $600 damage deposit he previously made. To make a down payment on the house, Dan sells stock for $20,000 (original cost of $8,000) and borrows $150,000 from a bank.

Only the $12,000 gain from the sale of the stock is income to Dan. The $600 damage deposit and the $8,000 cost of the stock are a return of capital. The $150,000 bank loan is not income as Dan has an obligation to repay that amount (and it does not increase his wealth).

Exclusions

For various reasons, Congress has chosen to exclude certain types of income from the income tax base. The principal income exclusions are listed in Exhibit 9.1. The exclusions most commonly encountered by individual taxpayers (employee fringe benefits) are discussed in detail in Chapter 11.

Gross Income

The Internal Revenue Code defines gross income broadly as "except as otherwise provided …, all income from whatever source derived."[4] The "except as otherwise provided" phrase refers to exclusions. Gross income includes, but is not limited to, the items in Exhibit 9.2.

EXHIBIT 9.1	Partial List of Exclusions from Gross Income

Accident and health insurance proceeds

Annuity payments (to the extent proceeds represent a recovery of the taxpayer's investment)

Child support payments

Damages for personal injury or sickness

Fringe benefits of employees:

- Educational assistance payments provided by employer
- Employer-provided accident and health insurance
- Group term life insurance (for coverage up to $50,000)
- Meals and lodging (if furnished for convenience of employer)
- Tuition reductions for employees of educational institutions
- Miscellaneous benefits

Gains from sale of principal residence (subject to statutory ceiling)

Gifts and inheritances received

Interest from state and local bonds

Life insurance paid upon death of insured

Scholarship grants (to a limited extent)

Social Security benefits (to a limited extent)

Workers' compensation benefits

---

[3]*Comm. v. Glenshaw Glass Co.*, 55–1 USTC ¶9308, 47 AFTR 162, 348 U.S. 426 (USSC, 1955).

[4]§ 61(a).

EXHIBIT 9.2	Partial List of Gross Income Items

Alimony	Interest
Bargain purchase from employer	Jury duty fees
Bonuses	Partnership income
Breach of contract damages	Pensions
Business income	Prizes (with some exceptions)
Commissions	Professional fees
Compensation for services	Punitive damages
Debts forgiven (with some exceptions)	Rents
Dividends	Rewards
Embezzled funds	Royalties
Farm income	Salaries
Fees	Severance pay
Gains from illegal activities	Strike and lockout benefits
Gains from sale of property	Tips and gratuities
Gambling winnings	Treasure trove (found property)
Hobby income	Wages

EXAMPLE 2

Beth received the following amounts during the year:

Salary	$30,000
Interest on savings account	900
Gift from her aunt	10,000
Prize won in state lottery	1,000
Alimony from ex-husband	12,000
Child support from ex-husband	6,000
Damages for injury in auto accident	25,000
Ten $50 bills in an unmarked envelope found in an airport lounge (airport authorities could not locate anyone who claimed ownership)	500
Federal income tax refund for last year's tax overpayment	120

In addition, her stock investments increased in value by $5,000.
Review Exhibits 9.1 and 9.2 to determine the amount Beth must include in the computation of taxable income and the amount she may exclude. Then check your answer in footnote 5.[5]

Deductions *for* Adjusted Gross Income

Individual taxpayers have two categories of deductions: (1) deductions *for* adjusted gross income (deductions from gross income to arrive at adjusted gross income) and (2) deductions *from* adjusted gross income. Deductions *for* adjusted gross income (AGI) include the following:[6]

- Ordinary and necessary expenses incurred in a trade or business.
- Part of the self-employment tax paid.
- Alimony paid.

---

[5]Beth must include $44,400 in computing taxable income ($30,000 salary + $900 interest + $1,000 lottery prize + $12,000 alimony + $500 found property). She can exclude $41,000 ($10,000 gift from aunt + $6,000 child support + $25,000 damages). The $120 Federal income tax refund is excluded because it represents an adjustment (i.e., overpayment) of a nondeductible expenditure made in the previous year. The unrealized gain of $5,000 on the stock held for investment is not included in gross income. Such gain will be included in gross income only when it is realized upon disposition of the stock.

[6]See § 62 for a comprehensive list of items that are deductible *for* AGI. Deductions *for* AGI are sometimes known as *above-the-line* deductions because on the tax return, they are taken before the "line" designating AGI.

- Certain payments to traditional Individual Retirement Accounts and Health Savings Accounts.
- Moving expenses.
- The capital loss deduction (limited to $3,000).

The effect on AGI of deductions *for* AGI is illustrated below.

Mason, age 45, earned a salary of $78,000 in the current year. He contributed $4,000 to his traditional Individual Retirement Account (IRA), sold stock held as an investment for a short-term capital loss of $2,000, and paid $4,600 in alimony to his ex-wife. His AGI is determined as follows:

Gross income		
Salary		$ 78,000
Less: Deductions *for* AGI		
IRA contribution	$4,000	
Capital loss	2,000	
Alimony paid	4,600	(10,600)
AGI		$ 67,400

Deductions *from* Adjusted Gross Income

As a general rule, personal expenditures are disallowed as deductions in arriving at taxable income. However, Congress allows specified personal expenses as deductions *from* AGI (commonly referred to as itemized deductions). Itemized deductions are discussed in Chapter 10.

AGI is an important subtotal that serves as the basis for computing percentage limitations on certain itemized deductions such as medical expenses, charitable contributions, and certain casualty losses. For example, medical expenses are deductible only to the extent they exceed 10 percent (or 7.5 percent through 2016 if either spouse is age 65 or older) of AGI, and charitable contribution deductions may not exceed 50 percent of AGI. These limitations might be described as a percentage *floor* under the medical expense deduction and a 50 percent *ceiling* on the charitable contribution deduction.

Assume the same facts as in Example 3, except that Mason also had unreimbursed medical expenses of $8,000. Medical expenses may be included in his itemized deductions to the extent they exceed 10% of AGI. In computing his itemized deductions, Mason may include medical expenses of $1,260 [$8,000 medical expenses − $6,740 (10% × $67,400 AGI)].

Trade or business expenses, which are deductions *for* AGI, must be incurred in connection with a trade or business. Nonbusiness expenses, on the other hand, are expenses incurred in connection with an income-producing activity that does not qualify as a trade or business. Such expenses are itemized deductions.

Leo is the owner and operator of a video game arcade. All allowable expenses that he incurs in connection with the arcade business are deductions *for* AGI. In addition, Leo paid mortgage interest, state income tax, and charitable contributions. These personal expenses are allowable as itemized deductions.

Standard Deduction

In lieu of claiming itemized deductions, taxpayers will use the standard deduction. As discussed later in the chapter, the standard deduction amount varies depending on filing status, age, and blindness. Each year, as required by law, the IRS adjusts the standard deduction amount for the effects of inflation.

Personal and Dependency Exemptions

Exemptions are allowed for the taxpayer, the taxpayer's spouse, and each dependent of the taxpayer. Like the standard deduction, personal and dependency exemptions (discussed later) are adjusted each year for inflation. The exemption amount for 2015 is $4,000 (up from $3,950 in 2014).

Taxable Income

The determination of taxable income is illustrated in Example 6.

Grace, age 25, is single and has her disabled and dependent mother living with her. This qualifies Grace for head-of-household filing status and a standard deduction of $9,250 in 2015. In 2015, Grace earned a $42,000 salary as a high school teacher. Her other income consisted of $1,100 interest on a certificate of deposit (CD) and $500 of nontaxable interest on municipal bonds she had received as a graduation gift in 2010. During 2015, she sustained a deductible capital loss of $1,000. Her itemized deductions are $9,500. Grace's taxable income for the year is computed as follows:

Income (broadly defined)		
Salary		$42,000
Interest on a CD		1,100
Interest on municipal bonds		500
Total income		$43,600
Less: Exclusion—		
Interest on municipal bonds		(500)
Gross income		$43,100
Less: Deduction *for* adjusted gross income—capital loss		(1,000)
Adjusted gross income (AGI)		$42,100
Less: The *greater* of—		
Total itemized deductions	$9,500	
or the standard deduction for head of household	9,250	(9,500)
Less: Personal and dependency exemptions (2 × $4,000)		(8,000)
Taxable income		$24,600

Note that the exclusion of $500 (i.e., interest from municipal bonds) is subtracted in determining gross income. The loss of $1,000 from a property transaction is classified as a deduction *for* AGI. Grace chose to itemize her deductions *from* AGI as they exceed the standard deduction (see Exhibit 9.3 for the derivation of the $9,250 amount). Grace's income tax is determined later in this chapter in Example 36.

9-2 STANDARD DEDUCTION

LO.2

Explain the standard deduction and evaluate its choice in arriving at taxable income.

A major component of the tax formula is the standard deduction. The effect of the standard deduction is to exempt part of a taxpayer's income from Federal income tax liability. In the past, Congress has attempted to set the tax-free amount represented by the standard deduction approximately equal to an estimated poverty level,[7] but it has not always been consistent in doing so.

9-2a Basic and Additional Standard Deduction

The standard deduction is the sum of two components: the *basic* standard deduction and the *additional* standard deduction.[8] Exhibit 9.3 lists the basic standard deduction allowed for taxpayers in each filing status. All taxpayers allowed a *full* standard

[7]S.Rep. No. 92–437, 92nd Cong., 1st Sess., 1971, p. 54. Another purpose of the standard deduction was discussed in Chapter 1 under Influence of the Internal Revenue Service—Administrative Feasibility. The size of the standard deduction has a direct bearing on the number of taxpayers who are in a position to itemize deductions. Reducing the number of taxpayers who itemize also reduces the audit effort required from the IRS.

[8]§ 63(c)(1).

EXHIBIT 9.3	Basic Standard Deduction Amounts	
Filing Status	**2014**	**2015**
Single	$ 6,200	$ 6,300
Married, filing jointly	12,400	12,600
Surviving spouse	12,400	12,600
Head of household	9,100	9,250
Married, filing separately	6,200	6,300

deduction are entitled to the applicable amount listed in Exhibit 9.3. The standard deduction amounts are subject to adjustment for inflation each year.

Certain taxpayers are not allowed to claim *any* standard deduction, and the standard deduction is *limited* for others. These provisions are discussed later in the chapter.

A taxpayer who is age 65 or over *or* blind in 2015 qualifies for an *additional standard deduction* of $1,250 or $1,550, depending on filing status (see amounts in Exhibit 9.4).Two additional standard deductions are allowed for a taxpayer who is age 65 or over *and* blind. The additional standard deduction provisions also apply for a qualifying spouse who is age 65 or over or blind, but a taxpayer may not claim an additional standard deduction for a dependent.

To determine whether to itemize, the taxpayer compares the *total* standard deduction (the sum of the basic standard deduction and any additional standard deductions) with total itemized deductions. Taxpayers are allowed to deduct the *greater* of itemized deductions or the standard deduction. The choice is elective. Undoubtedly, some taxpayers claim the standard deduction because they do not want to bother completing the Schedule A required for itemizing deductions *from* AGI. Likewise, the choice is an annual one, and a taxpayer is not bound by what was done on returns filed for past years. For example, many taxpayers who have previously claimed the standard deduction will switch to itemizing after purchasing a home (because of the mortgage interest and property tax deductions). In other circumstances, the reverse could be true—the taxpayer will switch from itemizing to taking the standard deduction. As illustrated in the next example, age can make a difference.

Prior to 2015, Sara, who is single, had always chosen to itemize. In 2015, however, she reaches age 65. Her itemized deductions for 2015 are $6,500, but her total standard deduction is $7,850 [$6,300 (basic standard deduction) + $1,550 (additional standard deduction)].

Sara should compute her taxable income for 2015 using the standard deduction ($7,850) because it exceeds her itemized deductions ($6,500).

EXAMPLE

7

In-depth coverage can be found on this book's companion website: **www.cengagebrain.com**   **1** DIGGING DEEPER

EXHIBIT 9.4	Amount of Each Additional Standard Deduction	
Filing Status	**2014**	**2015**
Single	$1,550	$1,550
Married, filing jointly	1,200	1,250
Surviving spouse	1,200	1,250
Head of household	1,550	1,550
Married, filing separately	1,200	1,250

9-2b **Special Limitations on the Standard Deduction for Dependents**

Special rules apply to the standard deduction and personal exemption of an individual who can be claimed as a dependent on another person's tax return.

When filing his or her own tax return, a *dependent's* basic standard deduction in 2015 is limited to the greater of $1,050 or the sum of the individual's earned income for the year plus $350.[9] However, if the sum of the individual's earned income plus $350 exceeds the normal standard deduction, the standard deduction is limited to the appropriate amount shown in Exhibit 9.3. These limitations apply only to the basic standard deduction. A dependent who is 65 or over or blind or both is also allowed the additional standard deduction amount on his or her own return (refer to Exhibit 9.4).

Dependent Standard Deduction

Susan, who is 17 years old and single, is claimed as a dependent on her parents' tax return. During 2015, she received $1,200 of interest (unearned income) on a savings account. She also earned $400 from a part-time job. When Susan files her own tax return, her standard deduction is $1,050 (the greater of $1,050 or the sum of earned income of $400 plus $350).

Assume the same facts as in Example 8, except that Susan is 67 years old and is claimed as a dependent on her son's tax return. In this case, when Susan files her own tax return, her standard deduction is $2,600 [$1,050 (the greater of $1,050 or the sum of earned income of $400 plus $350) + $1,550 (the additional standard deduction allowed because Susan is age 65 or over)].

Peggy, who is 16 years old and single, earned $800 from a summer job and had no unearned income during 2015. She is claimed as a dependent on her parents' tax return. Her standard deduction is $1,150 (the greater of $1,050 or the sum of earned income of $800 plus $350).

EXAMPLE 11

Jack, who is 20 years old, single, and a full-time college student, is claimed as a dependent on his parents' tax return. He worked as a musician during the summer of 2015, earning $6,500. Jack's standard deduction is $6,300 (the greater of $1,050 or the sum of earned income of $6,500 plus $350, but limited to the $6,300 standard deduction for a single taxpayer).

LO.3

Apply the rules for arriving at personal exemptions.

9-3 **PERSONAL EXEMPTIONS**

The use of exemptions in the tax system is based in part on the idea that a taxpayer with a small amount of income should be exempt from income taxation. An exemption frees a specified amount of income from tax ($4,000 in 2015 and $3,950 in 2014). The exemption amount is adjusted annually for inflation.

Exemptions that are allowed for the taxpayer and spouse are designated as **personal exemptions** . Those exemptions allowed for the care and maintenance of other persons are called dependency exemptions and are discussed in the next section.

An individual cannot claim a personal exemption if he or she is claimed as a dependent by another.

---

[9]§ 63(c)(5). Both the $1,050 amount and the $350 amount are subject to adjustment for inflation each year. In 2014, the amounts were $1,000 and $350.

EXAMPLE 12

Assume the same facts as in Example 11. On his own income tax return,[10] Jack's taxable income is determined as follows:

Gross income	$ 6,500
Less: Standard deduction	(6,300)
Personal exemption	(—0—)
Taxable income	$ 200

Jack is not allowed a personal exemption because he is claimed as a dependent by his parents.

When a husband and wife file a joint return, they may claim two personal exemptions. However, when separate returns are filed, a married taxpayer cannot claim an exemption for his or her spouse *unless* the spouse has no gross income and is not claimed as the dependent of another taxpayer.[11]

The determination of marital status generally is made at the end of the taxable year, except when a spouse dies during the year. Spouses who enter into a legal separation under a decree of divorce or separate maintenance before the end of the year are considered to be unmarried at the end of the taxable year.

The amount of the exemption is not reduced due to the taxpayer's death. The same rule applies to dependency exemptions. As long as an individual qualified as a dependent at the time of death, the full amount of the exemption can be claimed.

9-4 DEPENDENCY EXEMPTIONS

LO.4

Explain the rules for determining dependency exemptions.

As is the case with personal exemptions, a taxpayer is permitted to claim an exemption of $4,000 in 2015 ($3,950 in 2014) for each person who qualifies as a dependent. A **dependency exemption** is available for either a qualifying child or a qualifying relative and must not run afoul of certain other rules (i.e., joint return or nonresident alien prohibitions).

9-4a Qualifying Child

In the interest of uniformity and simplicity, Congress has tried to establish a uniform definition of a qualifying child. The qualifying child definition applies to the following tax provisions:

- Dependency exemption.
- Head-of-household filing status.
- Earned income tax credit.
- Child tax credit.
- Credit for child and dependent care expenses.

A **qualifying child** must meet the relationship, abode, age, and support tests.[12] For dependency exemption purposes, a qualifying child must also satisfy the joint return test and the citizenship or residency test (see Other Rules for Dependency Exemptions later in the chapter).

Relationship Test

The relationship test includes a taxpayer's child (son or daughter), adopted child, stepchild, eligible foster child, brother, sister, half brother, half sister, stepbrother, stepsister, or a *descendant* of any of these parties (e.g., grandchild, nephew, and niece). Note that *ancestors* of any of these parties (e.g., uncles and aunts) and in-laws (e.g., son-in-law and brother-in-law) *are not included*.

An adopted child includes a child lawfully placed with the taxpayer for legal adoption even though the adoption is not final. An eligible foster child is a child who is placed with the taxpayer by an authorized placement agency or by a judgment decree or other order of any court of competent jurisdiction.

---

[10]As noted on p. 9-17 (Filing Requirements for Dependents), Jack will be required to file an income tax return.

[11]§ 151(b).

[12]§ 152(c).

Abode Test

A qualifying child must live with the taxpayer for more than half of the year. For this purpose, temporary absences (e.g., school, vacation, medical care, military service, detention in a juvenile facility) are disregarded. Special rules apply in the case of certain kidnapped children.[13]

Age Test

A qualifying child must be under age 19 or under age 24 in the case of a student by the end of the tax year. A student is a child who, during any part of five months of the year, is enrolled full-time at a school or government-sponsored on-farm training course.[14] Also, an individual cannot be older than the taxpayer claiming him or her as a qualifying child (e.g., a brother cannot claim his older sister as a qualifying child). The age test does not apply to a child who is disabled during any part of the year.[15]

The Big Picture

EXAMPLE 13

Return to the facts of *The Big Picture* on p. 9-1. Does Paige meet the requirements of a qualifying child as to Polly? Paige satisfies the relationship and abode tests, but the answer to the age test remains unclear. Because she is not a full-time student or disabled, she must be under 19 to meet the age test. Unfortunately, the facts given do not provide Paige's age.

Support Test

To be a qualifying child, the individual must not be self-supporting (i.e., provide more than one-half of his or her own support). In the case of a child who is a full-time student, scholarships are not considered to be support.[16]

EXAMPLE 14

Shawn, age 23, is a full-time student and lives with his parents and an older cousin. During 2015, Shawn receives his support from the following sources: 30% from a part-time job, 30% from a scholarship, 20% from his parents, and 20% from the cousin.

Shawn is not self-supporting and can be claimed by his parents as a dependent even though his parents contribute only 20% of his support. (Note: Shawn cannot be a qualifying child as to his cousin due to the relationship test.)

Tiebreaker Rules

In some situations, a child may be a qualifying child to more than one person. In this event, the tax law specifies which person has priority in claiming the dependency exemption.[17] Called "tiebreaker rules," these rules are summarized in Concept Summary 9.2.

Concept Summary 9.2

Tiebreaker Rules for Claiming Qualifying Child

Persons Eligible to Claim Exemption	Person Prevailing
One of the persons is the parent.	Parent
Both persons are the parents, and the child lives longer with one parent.	Parent with the longer period of residence
Both persons are the parents, and the child lives with each the same period of time.	Parent with the higher adjusted gross income (AGI)
None of the persons are the parent.	Person with highest AGI

---

[13]§ 152(f)(6).
[14]§ 152(f)(2).
[15]Within the meaning of § 22(e)(3) for purposes of the credit for the elderly or disabled.
[16]§ 152(f)(5).
[17]§ 152(c)(4).

In-depth coverage can be found on this book's companion website: www.cengagebrain.com

2 DIGGING DEEPER

9-4b Qualifying Relative

In addition to the category of a qualifying child, there is a second category of dependency exemption designated as the qualifying relative .

A qualifying relative must meet the following relationship, gross income, and support tests.[18] As in the case of the qualifying child category, qualifying relative status also requires that the joint return and nonresident alien restrictions be avoided (see Other Rules for Dependency Exemptions later in the chapter).

Relationship Test

The relationship test for a qualifying relative is more expansive than for a qualifying child. Also included are the following relatives:

- Lineal ascendants (e.g., parents and grandparents).
- Collateral ascendants (e.g., uncles and aunts).
- Certain in-laws (e.g., son-, daughter-, father-, mother-, brother-, and sister-in-law).[19]

Children who do not satisfy the qualifying child definition may meet the qualifying relative criteria.

Inez provides more than half of the support of her son, age 20, who is neither disabled nor a full-time student. The son is not a qualifying child due to the age test, but is a qualifying relative if the gross income test is met. Consequently, Inez may claim a dependency exemption for her son.

EXAMPLE 15

The relationship test also includes unrelated parties who live with the taxpayer all year (i.e., are members of the household). Member-of-the-household status is not available for anyone whose relationship with the taxpayer violates local law or anyone who was a spouse during any part of the year.[20] However, an ex-spouse can qualify as a member of the household in a year following the divorce.

As the relationship test indicates, the category designation of "qualifying relative" is somewhat misleading. As just noted, persons other than relatives can qualify as dependents. Furthermore, not all relatives will qualify—notice the absence of "cousin" (although a cousin could be a member of the household).

The Big Picture

Return to the facts of *The Big Picture* on p. 9-1. Although Maude is unrelated to Polly, she qualifies as Polly's dependent by being a member of the household. Because Maude is a dependent, Polly can also claim the medical expenses she paid on Maude's behalf. The funeral expenses are not deductible. Although Maude lived for only two months, the full amount of the dependency exemption is allowed and does not have to be apportioned.

EXAMPLE 16

Gross Income Test

A dependent's gross income must be *less* than the exemption amount—$4,000 in 2015 and $3,950 in 2014. Gross income is determined by the income that is taxable. In the

---

[18]§ 152(d).

[19]Once established by marriage, in-law status continues to exist and survives divorce.

[20]§§ 152(d)(2)(H) and (f)(3).

case of scholarships, for example, include the taxable portion (e.g., amounts received for room and board) and exclude the nontaxable portion (e.g., amounts received for books and tuition). See the discussion of scholarships in Chapter 10.

Gross Income Test

EXAMPLE 17

Elsie provides more than half of the support of her son, Tom, who does not live with her. Tom, age 26, is a full-time student in medical school, earns $3,000 from a part-time job, and receives a $12,000 scholarship covering his tuition.

Elsie may claim Tom as a dependent because he meets the gross income test and is a qualifying relative. (Note: Tom is not a qualifying child due to either the abode or the age test.)

EXAMPLE 18

Aaron provides more than half of the support of his widowed aunt, Myrtle, who does not live with him. Myrtle's income for the year is as follows: dividend income of $1,100, earnings from pet sitting of $1,200, nontaxable Social Security benefits of $6,000, and nontaxable interest from City of Milwaukee bonds of $8,000.

Because Myrtle's gross income is only $2,300 ($1,100 + $1,200), she meets the gross income test and can be claimed as Aaron's dependent.

The Big Picture

EXAMPLE 19

Return to the facts of *The Big Picture* on p. 9-1. Assuming that Paige is not a qualifying child (see Example 13), can she be a qualifying relative for dependency exemption purposes? She meets the relationship and support tests, but what about the gross income test? If her income from her part-time job is less than $4,000, she does qualify and can be claimed by Polly as a dependent.

Support Test

Over one-half of the support of the qualifying relative must be furnished by the taxpayer. Support includes food, shelter, clothing, toys, medical and dental care, and education. However, a scholarship (both taxable and nontaxable portions) received by a student is not included for purposes of determining whether the taxpayer furnished more than half of the relative's support.

EXAMPLE 20

Hal contributed $3,400 (consisting of food, clothing, and medical care) toward the support of his nephew, Sam, who lives with him. Sam earned $1,300 from a part-time job and received $2,000 from a student loan to attend a local university. Assuming that the other dependency tests are met, Hal can claim Sam as a dependent because Hal has contributed more than half of Sam's support (i.e., Hal contributed $3,400 and Sam contributed $3,300).

If an individual does not spend funds that have been received from any source, the unspent amounts are not counted for purposes of the support test.

EXAMPLE 21

Emily contributed $3,000 to her father's support during the year. In addition, her father received $2,400 in Social Security benefits, $200 of interest, and wages of $600. Her father deposited the Social Security benefits, interest, and wages in his own savings account and did not use any of the funds for his support. Thus, the Social Security benefits, interest, and wages are not considered to be support provided by Emily's father. Emily may claim her father as a dependent if the other tests are met.

An individual's own funds, however, must be taken into account if applied toward support. In this regard, the source of the funds so used is not relevant.

Frank contributes $8,000 toward his parents' total support of $20,000. The parents, who do not live with Frank, obtain the other $12,000 from savings and a home equity loan on their residence. Although the parents have no income, their use of savings and borrowed funds are counted as part of their support. Because Frank does not satisfy the support test, he cannot claim his parents as dependents.

EXAMPLE 22

Capital expenditures for items such as furniture, appliances, and automobiles are included for purposes of the support test if the item does, in fact, constitute support.

Norm purchased a television costing $950 and gave it to his mother, who lives with him. The television was placed in the mother's bedroom and was used exclusively by her. Norm should include the cost of the television in determining the support of his mother.

EXAMPLE 23

Multiple Support Agreements An exception to the support test involves a `multiple support agreement`. A multiple support agreement permits one of a group of taxpayers who furnish support for a qualifying relative to claim a dependency exemption for that individual even if no one person provides more than 50 percent of the support.[21] The group together must provide more than 50 percent of the support. Any person who contributed *more than 10 percent* of the support is entitled to claim the exemption if each person in the group who contributed more than 10 percent files a written consent. This provision frequently enables one of the children of aged dependent parents to claim an exemption when none of the children meets the 50 percent support test.

Each person who is a party to the multiple support agreement must meet all other requirements (except the support requirement) for claiming the exemption. A person who does not meet the relationship or member-of-the-household test, for instance, cannot claim the dependency exemption under a multiple support agreement. It does not matter if he or she contributes more than 10 percent of the individual's support.

Wanda, who resides with her son, Adam, received $12,000 from various sources during the year. This constituted her entire support for the year. She received support from the following individuals:

EXAMPLE 24

	Amount	Percentage of Total
Adam, a son	$ 5,760	48
Bob, a son	1,200	10
Carol, a daughter	3,600	30
Diane, a friend	1,440	12
	$12,000	100

If Adam and Carol file a multiple support agreement, either may claim the dependency exemption for Wanda. Bob may not claim Wanda because he did not contribute *more than 10%* of her support. Bob's consent is not required for Adam and Carol to file a multiple support agreement. Diane does not meet the relationship or member-of-the-household test and cannot be a party to the agreement. The decision as to who claims Wanda rests with Adam and Carol. It is possible for Carol to claim Wanda, even though Adam furnished more of Wanda's support.

In-depth coverage can be found on this book's companion website: www.cengagebrain.com   **3** DIGGING DEEPER

---

[21]§ 152(d)(3).

TAX PLANNING STRATEGIES   Multiple Support Agreements and the Medical Expense Deduction

FRAMEWORK FOCUS: DEDUCTIONS

Strategy: Maximize Deductible Amounts.

Generally, medical expenses are deductible only if they are paid on behalf of the taxpayer, his or her spouse, and their dependents.[22] Because deductibility may rest on dependency status, planning is important in arranging multiple support agreements.

During the year, Suzanne will be supported by her two sons (Gary and Alan) and her daughter (Maria). Each will furnish approximately one-third of the required support. If the parties decide that the dependency exemption should be claimed by Maria under a multiple support agreement, any medical expenses incurred by Suzanne should be paid by Maria.

In planning a multiple support agreement, take into account which of the parties is most likely to have total medical expenses that exceed the 10 percent (7.5 percent if at least 65) of AGI limitation. In Example 25, for instance, Maria might be a poor choice if she and her family do not expect to incur many medical expenses of their own.

Children of Divorced or Separated Parents Another exception to the support test applies when parents with children are divorced or separated under a decree of separate maintenance. For unmarried parents, living apart (for the last six months of the year) will suffice. Special rules apply if the parents meet the following conditions:

- They would have been entitled to the dependency exemption(s) had they been married and filed a joint return.
- They have custody (either jointly or singly) of the child (or children) for more than half of the year.

Under the general rule, the parent having custody of the child (children) for the greater part of the year (i.e., the custodial parent) is entitled to the dependency exemption(s). The general rule does not apply if a multiple support agreement is in effect. It also does not apply if the custodial parent issues a waiver in favor of the noncustodial parent.[23]

 DIGGING DEEPER 4   **In-depth coverage can be found on this book's companion website: www.cengagebrain.com**

9-4c Other Rules for Dependency Exemptions

In addition to fitting into either the qualifying child or the qualifying relative category, a dependent must meet the joint return and the citizenship or residency tests.

Joint Return Test

If a dependent is married, the supporting taxpayer (e.g., the parent of a married child) generally is not permitted a dependency exemption if the married individual files a joint return with his or her spouse.[24] The joint return rule does not apply, however, if the following conditions are met:

- The reason for filing is to claim a refund for tax withheld.
- No tax liability would exist for either spouse on separate returns.
- Neither spouse is required to file a return.

---

[22]See the discussion of medical expenses in Chapter 10.
[23]See Reg. § 1.152–4T and §§ 152(e)(2) and (5).
[24]§ 152(b)(2).

Paul provides over half of the support of his son, Quinn. He also provides over half of the support of Vera, who is Quinn's wife. During the year, both Quinn and Vera had part-time jobs. To recover the taxes withheld, they file a joint return. If Quinn and Vera have income low enough that they are not *required* to file a return, Paul is allowed to claim both as dependents.

EXAMPLE 26

TAX PLANNING STRATEGIES **Problems with a Joint Return**

FRAMEWORK FOCUS: DEDUCTIONS

Strategy: Maximize Deductible Amounts.

A married person who files a joint return generally cannot be claimed as a dependent by another taxpayer. If a joint return has been filed, the damage may be undone if separate returns are substituted on a timely basis (on or before the due date of the return).

While preparing a client's 2014 income tax return on April 2, 2015, a tax practitioner discovered that the client's daughter had filed a joint return with her husband in late January 2015. Presuming that the daughter otherwise qualifies as the client's dependent, the exemption is not lost if she and her husband file separate returns on or before April 15, 2015.

EXAMPLE 27

Citizenship or Residency Test

To be a dependent, the individual must be a U.S. citizen, a U.S. resident, or a resident of Canada or Mexico for some part of the calendar year in which the taxpayer's tax year begins.[25]

9-4d Comparison of Categories for Dependency Exemptions

Concept Summary 9.3 identifies the tests for the two categories of dependency exemptions. In contrasting the two categories, the following observations are in order:

- As to the relationship tests, the qualifying relative category is considerably more expansive. Besides including those prescribed under the qualifying child grouping, other relatives are added. Nonrelated persons who are members of the household are also included.

Concept Summary 9.3

Tests for Dependency Exemption

Category	
Qualifying Child	**Qualifying Relative**
Relationship[1]	Support
Abode	Relationship[2] or member of household
Age	Gross income
Support	Joint return[3]
Joint return[3]	Citizenship or residency[3]
Citizenship or residency[3]	

[1] Children and their descendants, and siblings and stepsiblings and their descendants.
[2] Children and their descendants, siblings and their children, parents and their ascendants, uncles and aunts, stepparents and stepsiblings, and certain in-laws.
[3] The joint return rules and the citizenship or residency rules are the same for each category.

---

[25] § 152(b)(3).

- The support tests are entirely different. In the case of a qualifying child, support is not necessary. What is required is that the child not be self-supporting.
- The qualifying child category has no gross income limitation, whereas the qualifying relative category has no age restriction.

9-4e **Phaseout of Exemptions**

Several provisions of the tax law are intended to increase the tax liability of more affluent taxpayers who might otherwise enjoy some benefit from having some of their taxable income subject to the lower income tax brackets (e.g., 10 percent, 15 percent, 25 percent). One such provision phases out certain itemized deductions and is discussed in Chapter 10. Another provision phases out personal and dependency exemptions.[26] The exemption phaseout occurs as AGI exceeds specified threshold amounts (indexed annually for inflation). The phaseout begins when AGI exceeds the following:

Filing Status	2014	2015
Married, filing jointly	$305,050	$309,900
Head of household	279,650	284,050
Single	254,200	258,250
Married, filing separately	152,525	154,950

Exemptions are phased out by 2 percent for each $2,500 (or fraction thereof) by which the taxpayer's AGI exceeds the threshold amounts. For a married taxpayer filing separately, the phaseout is 2 percent for each $1,250 (or fraction thereof). The allowable exemption amount can be determined with the following steps:

1. AGI − threshold amount = excess amount.
2. Excess amount ÷ $2,500 = reduction factor [rounded up to the next whole number (e.g., 18.1 = 19)] × 2 = phaseout percentage.
3. Phaseout percentage (from step 2) × exemption amount = phaseout amount.
4. Exemption amount − phaseout amount = allowable exemption deduction.

EXAMPLE 28

Brad files as a single individual in 2015. His AGI is $290,900. He is entitled to one personal exemption. Brad's allowable exemption amount is determined as follows:

1. $290,900 − $258,250 = $32,650 excess amount.
2. [($32,650 ÷ $2,500) = 13.06; rounded to 14]; 14 × 2 = 28% (phaseout percentage).
3. 28% × $4,000 = $1,120 phaseout amount.
4. $4,000 − $1,120 = $2,880 allowable exemption deduction.

LO.5

List the filing requirements and choose the proper filing status.

9-5 **TAX DETERMINATION—FILING CONSIDERATIONS**

Once taxable income has been ascertained, a two-step process is used in determining income tax due (or refund available). First, certain procedural matters must be resolved. Second, the tax has to be computed and adjusted for available tax credits—see Concept Summary 9.1 and the tax formula. This section deals with the procedural aspects—designated as filing considerations. The next section covers the computation procedures.

Under the category of filing considerations, the following questions need to be resolved:

- Is the taxpayer required to file an income tax return?
- If so, which form should be used?
- When and how should the return be filed?
- What is the taxpayer's filing status?

---

[26]§ 151(d)(3).

No government likes to admit that it is enacting new taxes or even raising the rates on existing taxes. Needless to say, this is particularly true of the U.S. Congress. But there are more subtle ways to raise revenue (or to curtail revenue loss). The most popular way is to use a so-called *stealth tax*. A stealth tax is not really a tax at all. Instead, it is a means of reducing the benefits of certain tax provisions to higher-income taxpayers.

The heart and soul of the stealth tax is the phaseout approach. As income increases, the tax benefit thought to be derived from a particular provision decreases. Because the phaseout usually is gradual and not drastic, many affected taxpayers are unaware of what has happened.

The tax law is rampant with phaseouts. One of the most prominent phaseouts limits the deductibility of personal and dependency exemptions (which was discussed on the previous page). In addition, here are some other examples of these stealth taxes, each of which is discussed in Chapter 10:

- Child tax credit.
- Social Security benefits.
- Interest deduction on student loans.
- Itemized deductions.
- Education tax credits.
- Earned income credit.
- Premium tax credit.

9-5a Filing Requirements

General Rules

An individual must file a tax return if certain minimum amounts of gross income have been received. The general rule is that a tax return is required for every individual who has gross income that equals or exceeds the sum of the exemption amount plus the applicable standard deduction.[27] For example, a single taxpayer under age 65 must file a tax return in 2015 if gross income equals or exceeds $10,300 ($4,000 exemption plus $6,300 standard deduction).[28]

In-depth coverage can be found on this book's companion website: www.cengagebrain.com   **5 DIGGING DEEPER**

The additional standard deduction for being age 65 or older is considered in determining the gross income filing requirements. For example, the 2015 filing requirement for a single taxpayer age 65 or older is $11,850 ($6,300 basic standard deduction + $1,550 additional standard deduction + $4,000 exemption).

A self-employed individual with net earnings of $400 or more from a business or profession must file a tax return regardless of the amount of gross income.

Even though an individual has gross income below the filing level amounts and therefore does not owe any tax, he or she must file a return to obtain a tax refund of amounts withheld. A return is also necessary to obtain the benefits of the earned income credit (see Chapter 10) allowed to taxpayers with little or no tax liability. In addition, an individual who needs to reconcile the amount of premium tax credit received in advance during the year or owed to them (to help pay for health insurance obtained through the Marketplace) must file a return (see Chapter 10).

Filing Requirements for Dependents

Computation of the gross income filing requirement for an individual who can be claimed as a dependent on another person's tax return is subject to more complex rules. For example, such an individual must file a return if he or she has earned income

---

[27]Because the exemption and standard deduction amounts are subject to an annual inflation adjustment, the gross income amounts for determining whether a tax return must be filed normally change each year.

[28]§ 6012(a)(1).

only and gross income that is more than the total standard deduction (including any additional standard deduction) the individual is allowed for the year.

 DIGGING DEEPER 6 | In-depth coverage can be found on this book's companion website: www.cengagebrain.com

9-5b **Filing Status**

The amount of tax will vary considerably depending on the filing status that is used. This is illustrated in the following example.

EXAMPLE 29

The following amounts of tax are computed using the 2015 Tax Rate Schedules for a taxpayer (or taxpayers in the case of a joint return) with $60,000 of taxable income (see Appendix A).

Filing Status	Amount of Tax
Single	$10,794
Married, filing jointly	8,078
Married, filing separately	10,794
Head of household	9,323

Besides the effect from the tax rates that will apply, filing status also has an impact on the amount of the standard deduction that is allowed—see Exhibits 9.3 and 9.4 earlier in the chapter.

Single Taxpayers

A taxpayer who is unmarried or separated from his or her spouse by a decree of divorce or separate maintenance and does not qualify for another filing status must use the rates for single taxpayers. Marital status is determined as of the last day of the tax year, except when a spouse dies during the year. In that case, marital status is determined as of the date of death.

Married Individuals

The joint return was originally enacted to establish equity between married taxpayers in common law states and those in community property states. Before the joint return rates were enacted, taxpayers in community property states were in an advantageous position relative to taxpayers in common law states because they could split their income.

Taxpayers in common law states did not have this income-splitting option, so their taxable income was subject to higher marginal rates. This inconsistency in treatment was remedied by the joint return provisions. The progressive rates in the joint return Tax Rate Schedule are constructed based on the assumption that income is earned equally by the two spouses.

A same-sex couple who is legally married in a state or jurisdiction that recognizes same-sex marriage is treated as married for Federal tax purposes (no matter where they live). According to the IRS, registered domestic partners, though, are not "spouses" under Federal law. Therefore, they cannot file Federal tax returns using married filing jointly or married filing separately status. The same rule applies to same-sex partners in civil unions.[29]

If married individuals elect to file separate returns, each reports only his or her own income, exemptions, deductions, and credits, and each must use the Tax Rate

[29]Rev.Rul. 2013–17, 2013–38 I.R.B. 201 and *U.S. v. Windsor*, 2013–2 USTC ¶50,400, 111 AFTR 2d 2013–2385, 133 S.Ct. 2675; **www.irs.gov/uac/** **Answers-to-Frequently-Asked-Questions-for-Registered-Domestic-Partners-and-Individuals-in-Civil-Unions**.

BRIDGE DISCIPLINE **Bridge to Equity or Fairness**

Much has been made in the press and in political circles over the years concerning the so-called marriage penalty tax. This marriage penalty refers to the additional income tax that married couples pay over and above the aggregate amount two single individuals would pay with equal amounts of income. The marriage penalty arose because of the nature of the income tax rate structure that applies to individual taxpayers.

Relevant policy and ethical issues related to this dilemma are:

• Should the income tax system contain a bias against marriage?

• Should the income tax system require two people of economic means equal to that of two other people to pay a different amount of income taxes?

• Should the income tax system encourage two individuals to cohabit outside the commitment of marriage?

Long aware of the inequity of the marriage penalty, Congress reduced the effect of the problem by increasing the standard deduction available to married filers to 200 percent of that applicable to single persons and increasing the 15 percent bracket for joint filers to 200 percent of the size of that bracket applicable to single filers.

Schedule applicable to married taxpayers filing separately. In a community property state, each individual must report his or her half of the community property income.[30] It is generally advantageous for married individuals to file a joint return because the combined amount of tax is lower. However, special circumstances (e.g., significant medical expenses incurred by one spouse subject to the 10 percent limitation) may warrant the election to file separate returns. It may be necessary to compute the tax under both assumptions to determine the most advantageous filing status. Filing a joint return carries the potential disadvantage of joint and several liability. This means that the IRS can pursue the collection of the tax due for that year against either spouse.

Marriage Penalty When Congress enacted the rate structure available to those filing joint returns, it generally favored married taxpayers. In certain situations, however, the parties would incur less tax if they were not married and filed separate returns. The additional tax that a joint return caused, commonly called the **marriage penalty**, usually developed when *both* spouses had large taxable incomes.

In-depth coverage can be found on this book's companion website: www.cengagebrain.com   **7 DIGGING DEEPER**

Surviving Spouse The joint return rates also apply for two years following the death of one spouse if the surviving spouse maintains a household for a dependent child. The child must be a son, stepson, daughter, or stepdaughter who qualifies as a dependent of the taxpayer. This is referred to as **surviving spouse** status.[31]

Head of Household

Unmarried individuals who maintain a household for a dependent (or dependents) are generally entitled to use the **head-of-household** rates.[32] The tax liability using the head-of-household rates falls between the liability using the joint return Tax Rate Schedule and the liability using the Tax Rate Schedule for single taxpayers.

To qualify for head-of-household rates, a taxpayer must pay more than half the cost of maintaining a household as his or her home. The household must also be the principal

---

[30]Form 8958 (Allocation of Tax Amounts Between Certain Individuals in Community Property States) is used for this purpose.

[31]§ 2(a). The IRS label for surviving spouse status is "qualifying widow(er) with dependent child."

[32]§ 2(b).

John Garth is a U.S. citizen and resident, but he spends much of his time in London, where his employer sends him on frequent assignments. John is married to Victoria, a citizen and resident of the United Kingdom.

Can John and Victoria file a joint return for U.S. Federal income tax purposes? Although § 6013(a)(1) specifically precludes the filing of a joint return if one spouse is a nonresident alien, another Code provision permits an exception. Under § 6013(g), the parties can elect to treat the nonqualifying spouse as a "resident" of the United States. This election would allow John and Victoria to file jointly.

But should John and Victoria make this election? If Victoria has considerable income of her own (from non-U.S. sources), the election could be ill-advised. As a nonresident alien, Victoria's non-U.S. source income *would not* be subject to the U.S. income tax. If she is treated as a U.S. resident, however, her non-U.S. source income *will be subject to U.S. tax*. Under the U.S. worldwide approach to taxation, all income (regardless of where earned) of anyone who is a *resident* or *citizen* of the United States is subject to tax.

home of a dependent. Except for temporary absences (e.g., school, hospitalization), the dependent must live in the taxpayer's household for over half the year.

The Big Picture

EXAMPLE 30

Return to the facts of *The Big Picture* on p. 9-1. Assuming that Polly can be treated as single (i.e., not married), can Maude qualify Polly for head-of-household filing status? The answer is no. Even though Maude can be claimed as Polly's dependent (see Example 16), she does not meet the relationship test.

DIGGING DEEPER 8   In-depth coverage can be found on this book's companion website: www.cengagebrain.com

Abandoned Spouse Rules

Congress has enacted provisions that allow married taxpayers, commonly referred to as abandoned spouses, to file as a head of household if the following conditions are satisfied:

- The taxpayer does not file a joint return.
- The taxpayer paid more than one-half the cost of maintaining his or her home for the tax year.
- The taxpayer's spouse did not live in the home during the last six months of the tax year.
- The home was the principal residence of the taxpayer's son, daughter, stepson, stepdaughter, foster child, or adopted child for more than half the year, and the child can be claimed as a dependent.[33]

The resulting tax burden using the relatively favorable head-of-household status is lower than when using the married filing separately rate schedule.

The Big Picture

EXAMPLE 31

Return to the facts of *The Big Picture* on p. 9-1. Can Polly qualify as an abandoned spouse? Yes, if she can claim Paige as a dependent—either as a qualifying child (see Example 13) or as a qualifying relative (see Example 19). If so, Polly can use head-of-household filing status. If not, her filing status is married filing separately.

[33]§ 7703(b).

9-6 TAX DETERMINATION—COMPUTATION PROCEDURES

LO.6

Demonstrate the proper procedures for determining the tax liability.

The computation of income tax due (or refund) involves applying the proper set of tax rates to taxable income and then adjusting the liability for available credits. In certain cases, however, the application of the kiddie tax will cause a modification of the means by which the tax is determined.

9-6a Tax Table Method

The tax liability is computed using either the Tax Table method or the Tax Rate Schedule method. Most taxpayers compute their tax using the **Tax Table**. Eligible taxpayers compute taxable income (as shown in Concept Summary 9.1) and *must* determine their tax by reference to the Tax Table.

In-depth coverage can be found on this book's companion website: www.cengagebrain.com

9 DIGGING DEEPER

Although the Tax Table is derived from the Tax Rate Schedules (discussed next), the tax calculated using the two methods may vary slightly. This variation occurs because the tax for a particular income range in the Tax Table is based on the midpoint amount.

Linda is single and has taxable income of $30,000 for calendar year 2014. To determine Linda's tax using the Tax Table (see Appendix A),[34] find the $30,000 to $30,050 income line. The tax of $4,050 is actually the tax the Tax Rate Schedule for 2014 (see Appendix A) would yield on taxable income of $30,025 (i.e., the midpoint amount between $30,000 and $30,050).

EXAMPLE

32

9-6b Tax Rate Schedule Method

Taxpayers who do not use the Tax Tables use the **Tax Rate Schedules**. The 2015 rate schedule for single taxpayers is reproduced in Exhibit 9.5.[35] This schedule is used to illustrate the tax computations in Examples 33 and 34.

Pat is single and had $5,870 of taxable income in 2015. His tax is $587 ($5,870 × 10%).

EXAMPLE

33

EXHIBIT 9.5	2015 Tax Rate Schedule for Single Taxpayers		

If Taxable Income Is			
Over	**But Not Over**	**The Tax Is:**	**Of the Amount Over**
$ –0–	$ 9,225	10%	$ –0–
9,225	37,450	$ 922.50 + 15%	9,225
37,450	90,750	5,156.25 + 25%	37,450
90,750	189,300	18,481.25 + 28%	90,750
189,300	411,500	46,075.25 + 33%	189,300
411,500	413,200	119,401.25 + 35%	411,500
413,200		119,996.25 + 39.6%	413,200

---

[34]The 2015 Tax Table was not available from the IRS at the date of publication of this text. The Tax Table for 2014 is located at **www.irs.gov** and is used to illustrate this computation.

[35]Individual tax rates are found in § 1.

Several terms are used to describe tax rates. The rates in the Tax Rate Schedules are often referred to as *statutory* (or nominal) rates. The *marginal* rate is the tax rate that would be assessed on the next dollar of income for a particular taxpayer. In Example 33, the statutory rate and the marginal rate are both 10 percent.

EXAMPLE 34

Chris is single and had taxable income of $92,000 in 2015. Her tax is $18,831.25 [$18,481.25 + 28% ($92,000 − $90,750)].

The *average* rate is equal to the tax liability divided by taxable income. In Example 34, Chris has statutory rates of 10 percent, 15 percent, 25 percent, and 28 percent and a marginal rate of 28 percent. Chris's average rate is 20.5 percent ($18,831.25 tax liability ÷ $92,000 taxable income).

A tax is *progressive* (or graduated) if a higher rate of tax applies as the tax base increases. The progressive nature of the Federal income tax on individuals is illustrated by computing the tax in Example 34 utilizing each rate bracket.

Tax on first $9,225 at 10%	$ 922.50
Tax on $37,450 − $9,225 at 15%	4,233.75
Tax on $90,750 − $37,450 at 25%	13,325.00
Tax on $92,000 − $90,750 at 28%	350.00
Total tax on taxable income of $92,000	$18,831.25

A special computation limits the effective tax rate on qualified dividends (see Chapter 4) and net long-term capital gains (see Chapter 8).

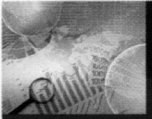

TAX PLANNING STRATEGIES Shifting Income and Deductions across Time

FRAMEWORK FOCUS: TAX RATE

Strategy: Shift Net Income from High-Bracket Years to Low-Bracket Years.

It is natural for taxpayers to be concerned about the tax rates that apply to them. What might a tax practitioner suggest to clients about tax rate planning? There are several possibilities. For example, a taxpayer who is in the 15 percent bracket this year and expects to be in the 28 percent bracket next year should, if possible, defer payment of deductible expenses until next year to maximize the tax benefit of the deduction.

A note of caution is in order with respect to shifting income and expenses between years. Congress has recognized the tax planning possibilities of such shifting and has enacted many provisions to limit a taxpayer's ability to do so. Some of these limitations on the shifting of income and deductions are discussed in Chapters 4 through 6.

9-6c Computation of Net Taxes Payable or Refund Due

The pay-as-you-go feature of the Federal income tax system requires payment of all or part of the taxpayer's income tax liability during the year. These payments take the form of Federal income tax withheld by employers or estimated tax paid by the taxpayer or both.[36] The payments are applied against the tax from the Tax Table or Tax Rate Schedules to determine whether the taxpayer will get a refund or pay additional tax.

---

[36]See § 3402 for withholding and § 6654 for estimated payments.

TAX IN THE NEWS **Same-Sex Couples May Face a Tax Filing Nightmare**

In *U.S. v. Windsor*, the Supreme Court struck down portions of the Defense of Marriage Act. Specifically, this decision invalidated a Federal definition of marriage as between one man and one woman. Recent guidance from the IRS (Rev.Rul. 2013–17) provides that a same-sex couple possessing a marriage license from any U.S. state or other jurisdiction will be considered married for Federal income tax purposes (no matter where they live). However, this interpretation of marriage does not extend to "domestic partnerships" or "civil unions." Couples in these relationships are still regarded as *single* by the IRS.

As far as income taxes are concerned, have these new rules resolved the prior difficulties of same-sex couples? The answer depends on where they live and whether such location imposes an income tax. Consider the following possibilities as to residence.

1. No state or local income taxes imposed.
2. State and local income taxes imposed and jurisdiction recognizes same-sex marriages.
3. State and local income taxes imposed but jurisdiction does not recognize same-sex marriages.

Category (1) was never a problem and category (2) has largely been resolved. Thus, the filing status used for state and local purposes (e.g., married filing jointly) will also be available for Federal purposes. Category (3), moreover, continues to yield divergent results. For example, married persons in Category 3 are generally treated as "single" under state law.

For persons in a domestic partnership or civil union, a different inconsistency comes about. They could be treated as married for state purposes but single in terms of Federal tax law.

Employers are required to withhold income tax on compensation paid to their employees and to pay this tax to the government. The employer notifies the employee of the amount of income and income tax withheld on Form W–2 (Wage and Tax Statement). The employee should receive this form by January 31 after the year in which the income tax is withheld.

If taxpayers receive income that is not subject to withholding or income from which insufficient tax is withheld, they may have to pay estimated tax. These individuals must file Form 1040–ES (Estimated Tax for Individuals) and pay in quarterly installments the income tax and self-employment tax estimated to be due.

The income tax from the Tax Table or the Tax Rate Schedules also is reduced by the individual's tax credits. There is an important distinction between tax credits and tax deductions. Tax credits (including tax withheld) reduce the tax liability dollar for dollar. Tax deductions reduce taxable income on which the tax liability is based.

EXAMPLE 35

Gail is a taxpayer in the 25% tax bracket. As a result of incurring $1,000 in child care, she is entitled to a $200 credit for child and dependent care expenses ($1,000 child care expenses × 20% credit rate). She also contributed $1,000 to the American Cancer Society and included this amount in her itemized deductions.

The credit for child and dependent care expenses results in a $200 reduction of Gail's tax liability for the year. The contribution to the American Cancer Society reduces taxable income by $1,000 and results in a $250 reduction in Gail's tax liability ($1,000 reduction in taxable income × 25% tax rate).

Selected tax credits for individuals are discussed in Chapter 10. Following are some of the more common credits available to individuals:

- Child tax credit.
- Credit for child and dependent care expenses.
- Earned income credit.
- Premium tax credit.

The computation of net taxes payable or refund due can be illustrated by returning to the facts of Example 6.

EXAMPLE 36

Grace is single and has her disabled and dependent mother living with her. Recall that Example 6 established that Grace has taxable income of $24,600. Further assume that she has the following income tax withheld, $2,500; estimated tax payments, $600; and a credit for dependent care expenses, $200. Grace's net tax payable (refund due) is computed as follows:

Income tax (from 2015 Tax Rate Schedule for head of household)		$3,033 (rounded)
Less: Tax credits and prepayments—		
Credit for dependent care expenses	$ 200	
Income tax withheld	2,500	
Estimated tax payments	600	(3,300)
Net taxes payable (refund due if negative)		($ 267)

9-6d Additional Taxes for Certain Individuals

A review of page 2 of Form 1040 shows that an individual may owe taxes in addition to the income tax. These other taxes include the following:

- Alternative minimum tax (see discussion in Chapter 17)
- Self-employment tax (see discussion in Chapter 11)
- Taxes from Forms 8959 and 8960 (discussed below)

The taxes computed on Forms 8959 and 8960 were created as part of the Affordable Care Act. The tax reported on Form 8959 is the Additional Medicare Tax. This tax is computed at a rate of 0.9 percent on wages and self-employment income in excess of threshold amounts. For married taxpayers the threshold amount is $250,000 ($125,000 if married filing separately), and $200,000 for all other taxpayers. An employer must withhold the 0.9% tax on wages paid to any employee that exceed $200,000 for the year (regardless of the employee's filing status). The Additional Medicare Tax is imposed only on the employee, not also the employer.

Form 8960 reports an individual's Net Investment Income Tax (NIIT). This tax is imposed at a rate of 3.8 percent of the lesser of:

- Net investment income, or
- The excess of modified adjusted gross income (MAGI) over $250,000 for married taxpayers filing a joint return ($125,000 if married filing separately) and $200,000 for all other taxpayers.

In general, "net investment income" includes interest, dividends, annuities, royalties, rents, income from passive activities, and net gains from the sale of investment property, reduced by deductions allowed in generating such income. For purposes of computing the NIIT, MAGI is defined as AGI increased by any foreign earned income exclusion (adjusted for related deductions). See Chapter 11 for discussion of the foreign earned income exclusion.

A high income individual may be subject to both the 3.8 percent NIIT as well as the 0.9 percent Additional Medicare Tax on wages or self-employment income. The effect of the NIIT and Additional Medicare Tax is to increase the individual's marginal tax rate.

EXAMPLE 37

Rajiv is single and has the following income for 2015: wages of $220,000, interest income of $6,000, and capital gain of $28,000. Rajiv owes Additional Medicare Tax of $180 (0.9% × [$220,000 − $200,000]). In addition, he owes NIIT of $1,292 computed as follows:

3.8% × the lesser of:

- Net investment income of $34,000 ($6,000 + $28,000), or
- Modified adjusted gross income of $254,000 ($220,000 + $6,000 + $28,000) over $200,000, or $54,000

Unlike many threshold amounts, the ones for the NIIT and the Additional Medicare Tax are not adjusted annually for inflation. These additional taxes must be paid during the year through income tax withholdings or estimated tax payments.

9-6e Kiddie Tax—Unearned Income of Children Taxed at Parents' Rate

LO.7

Identify and report kiddie tax situations.

Most individuals compute taxable income using the tax formula shown in Concept Summary 9.1. Special provisions govern the computation of taxable income and the tax liability for certain children who have unearned income in excess of specified amounts.

Recall that individuals who are claimed as dependents by other taxpayers cannot claim an exemption on their own return. This prevents parents from shifting the tax on investment income (such as interest and dividends) to a child by transferring ownership of the assets producing the income. Without this provision, the child would pay no tax on the income to the extent it was sheltered by the child's exemption and standard deduction amounts.

Current tax law also reduces or eliminates the possibility of saving taxes by shifting income from parents to children by taxing the net unearned income of these children as if it were the parents' income. Unearned income includes income such as taxable interest, dividends, capital gains, rents, royalties, pension and annuity income, and income (other than earned income) received as the beneficiary of a trust.

This provision, commonly referred to as the kiddie tax, applies to any child who is under age 19 (or under age 24 if a full-time student) and has unearned income of more than $2,100 in 2015 ($2,000 in 2014).[37] The kiddie tax does not apply if the child has earned income that exceeds half of his or her support, if the child is married and files a joint return, or if both parents are deceased.

Net Unearned Income

In 2015, net unearned income of a dependent child is computed as follows:

> Unearned income
> Less: $1,050
> Less: The *greater* of
>> $1,050 of the standard deduction *or*
>> The amount of allowable itemized deductions directly connected with the production of the unearned income
> Equals: Net unearned income

If net unearned income is not a positive amount, the child's tax is computed without using the parents' rate. If the amount of net unearned income (regardless of source) is positive, the net unearned income will be taxed at the parents' rate. The child's remaining taxable income (known as nonparental source income) is taxed at the child's rate. The $1,050 amounts in the preceding formula are subject to adjustment for inflation each year.

In-depth coverage can be found on this book's companion website: www.cengagebrain.com   **10 DIGGING DEEPER**

Election to Report Certain Unearned Income on Parents' Return

In 2015, if a child who is subject to the kiddie tax is required to file a tax return and meets all of the following requirements, the parents may elect to report the child's unearned income that exceeds $2,100 ($2,000 in 2014) on the parents' own tax return.

- Gross income is from interest and dividends only.

- Gross income is more than $1,050 but less than $10,500 (for 2014, these amounts are $1,000 and $10,000).

- No estimated tax has been paid in the name and Social Security number of the child, and the child is not subject to backup withholding.

---

[37]§ 1(g)(2).

If the parental election is made, the child is treated as having no gross income and is not required to file a tax return. In this case, Form 8814 (Parents' Election to Report Child's Interest and Dividends) must be filed as part of the parents' tax return.

The parent(s) must also pay an additional tax equal to the smaller of $105 or 10 percent of the child's gross income over $1,050. Parents who have substantial itemized deductions based on AGI may find that making the parental election increases total taxes for the family unit. Taxes should be calculated both with and without the parental election to determine the appropriate choice.

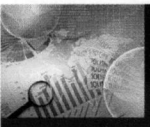

TAX PLANNING STRATEGIES **Income of Certain Children**

FRAMEWORK FOCUS: TAX RATE

Strategy: Shift Net Income from High-Bracket Taxpayers to Low-Bracket Taxpayers.

Taxpayers can use several strategies to avoid or minimize the effect of the rules that tax the unearned income of certain children at the parents' rate. With the cutoff age being 19 (under 24 for full-time students), many children are vulnerable to the application of the kiddie tax. Parents should consider giving a younger child assets that defer the inclusion in gross income until the child reaches a nonvulnerable age. For example, U.S. government Series EE savings bonds can be used to defer income until the bonds are cashed in.

Growth stocks typically pay little in the way of dividends. However, the unrealized appreciation on an astute investment may more than offset the lack of dividends. The child can hold the growth stock until he or she reaches a safe age. If the stock is sold then at a profit, the profit is taxed at the child's low rates.

Taxpayers in a position to do so can employ their children in their business and pay them a reasonable wage for the work they actually perform (e.g., light office help such as filing). The child's earned income is sheltered by the standard deduction, and the parents' business is allowed a deduction for the wages. The kiddie tax rules have no effect on earned income, even if it is earned from the parents' business.

9-7 TAX RETURN FILING PROCEDURES

9-7a Selecting the Proper Form

Although a variety of forms are available to individual taxpayers, the use of some of these forms is restricted. For example, Form 1040–EZ cannot be used if:

- Taxpayer claims any dependents,
- Taxpayer (or spouse) is 65 or older or blind,
- Taxable income is $100,000 or more, or
- Taxpayer claims the premium tax credit.

Taxpayers who want to itemize deductions *from* AGI cannot use Form 1040–A, but must file Form 1040 (the so-called long form).

TAX FACT **What Form of Tax Compliance Is Right for You?**

Based on recent projections from the IRS, when preparing about 152 million individual income tax returns expected to be filed in 2016, taxpayers will be using relatively fewer paper Forms 1040, 1040A, and 1040–EZ. As a result, the IRS expects the level of electronically filed returns to be at or near an all-time high.

	Percentage
Paper individual returns	14
Electronically filed individual returns	86
	100

Source: Fiscal Year Return Projections for the United States: 2014–2021, IRS, Document 6292, Spring 2014 Update, Table 1.

9-7b **The E-File Approach**

The e-file program is an increasingly popular approach (and is mandatory for most tax return preparers). The required tax information is transmitted to the IRS electronically either directly from the taxpayer (i.e., an "e-file online return") or indirectly through an electronic return originator (ERO). EROs are tax professionals who have been accepted into the electronic filing program by the IRS. Such parties hold themselves out to the general public as "authorized IRS e-file providers." Providers often are the preparers of the return as well.

Through prearrangement with the IRS, approximately 15 software providers offer free e-filing services. These services generally are available only to taxpayers who have AGI of $57,000 or below. A list of these providers and their eligibility requirements can be obtained through the IRS website.

The e-file approach has two major advantages over paper filing. First, compliance with the format required by the IRS eliminates many errors that would otherwise occur. Second, the time required for processing a refund usually is reduced to three weeks or less.

9-7c **When and Where to File**

Tax returns of individuals are due on or before the fifteenth day of the fourth month following the close of the tax year. For the calendar year taxpayer, the usual filing date is on or before April 15 of the following year.[38] When the due date falls on a Saturday, Sunday, or legal holiday, the last day for filing falls on the next business day.

If a taxpayer is unable to file the return by the specified due date, a six-month extension of time can be obtained by filing Form 4868 (Application for Automatic Extension of Time to File U.S. Individual Income Tax Return).[39]

Although obtaining an extension excuses a taxpayer from a penalty for failure to file, it does not insulate against the penalty for failure to pay. If more tax is owed, the filing of Form 4868 should be accompanied by an additional remittance to cover the balance due. The return should be sent or delivered to the Regional Service Center listed in the instructions for each type of return or contained in software applications.[40]

9-7d **Modes of Payment**

Usually, payment is made by check. However, the IRS has approved the use of Master-Card, American Express, Discover, and Visa to pay Federal taxes through a card service provider. The use of a credit card or debit card to pay taxes will result in a fee charged against the cardholder by the credit card company and service provider.

REFOCUS ON THE BIG PICTURE

A DIVIDED HOUSEHOLD

© MICHAEL DEFREITAS CARIBBEAN/ALAMY

Of major concern to Polly is her filing status. If she qualifies as an abandoned spouse, she is entitled to file as head of household. If not, she is considered to be a married person filing separately. Moreover, to be an abandoned spouse, Polly must be able to claim Paige as a dependent. To be a dependent, Paige must meet the requirements of a qualifying child or a qualifying relative.

For qualifying child purposes, Paige must meet either the age (i.e., under age 19) or the full-time student (under age 24) test. (A disabled child exception seems highly unlikely.) Because Paige currently is not a full-time student, is she under age 19? If so, she is a qualifying child (see Example 13). If Paige is not a qualifying child, is she a qualifying relative? Here, the answer depends on meeting the gross income test (see Example 19). How much did Paige earn from her part-time job? If her

continued

---

[38]§ 6072(a).

[39]Reg. § 1.6081–4. See also *Your Federal Income Tax* (IRS Publication 17).

[40]The appropriate Regional Service Center address can be found at **www.irs.gov/uac/Where-To-File-Addresses-for-Tax-Professionals**.

earnings are under $4,000, she satisfies the gross income test. Thus, if Paige can be claimed as a dependent under either the qualifying child or the qualifying relative category, Polly is an abandoned spouse entitled to head-of-household filing status (see Example 31). If not, she is a married person filing separately.

Maude can be claimed as Polly's dependent because she is a member of the household. It does not matter that she died in February, and the dependency exemption amount need not be apportioned and is allowed in full. Because Maude is her dependent, Polly can claim the medical expenses she paid on Maude's behalf. The funeral expenses, however, are not deductible (see Example 16).

Does Maude qualify Polly for head-of-household filing status? No—although she is a dependent, Maude does not meet the relationship test (see Example 30).

What If?

Assume that Nick left for parts unknown in August (not March). Now Polly cannot qualify as an abandoned spouse. Her spouse lived in the home during part of the last six months of the year. Consequently, Polly is treated as married and cannot qualify for head-of-household filing status. She must file as a married person filing separately. The change in when Nick left will not affect the dependency issue regarding Paige, however.

Suggested Readings

David R. Baldwin, Lawrence H. Carlton, Donna Haim, Jonathan Horn, Susanne Morrow, Kenneth L. Rubin, Kaye F. Sheridan, Amy M. Vega, and Donald J. Zidik Jr., "New Directions in Individual Taxation," *The Tax Adviser*, September 2014.

Robin Clark and Darlene Pulliam, "Innocent Spouse Relief Under Rev. Proc. 2013-34," *The Tax Adviser*, November 2014.

Reed W. Easton, "Tax Planning Opportunities for Nontraditional Families after *Windsor*," *Practical Tax Strategies*, September 2013.

Andrew Lafond and Bruce A. Leauby, "Help Wanted: Hire Your Kids for Tax Savings," *Practical Tax Strategies*, October 2013.

M. Jill Lockwood, Britton McKay, and Michael Wiggins, "Tax Planning for Divorce: Avoiding the Pitfalls," *Practical Tax Strategies,* September 2012.

Key Terms

Dependency exemption, 9-9	Marriage penalty, 9-19	Standard deduction, 9-5
E-file, 9-27	Multiple support agreement, 9-13	Surviving spouse, 9-19
Head-of-household, 9-19	Personal exemptions, 9-8	Tax Rate Schedules, 9-21
Itemized deductions, 9-5	Qualifying child, 9-9	Tax Table, 9-21
Kiddie tax, 9-25	Qualifying relative, 9-11	Unearned income, 9-25

Computational Exercises

Issue ID 1. **LO.2** Sam and Abby are dependents of their parents, and each has income of $2,100 for the year. Sam's standard deduction for the year is $1,050, while Abby's is $2,450. As their income is the same, what causes the difference in the amount of the standard deduction?

2. **LO.2** Compute the 2015 standard deduction for the following taxpayers.   Critical Thinking
   a. Margie is 15 and claimed as a dependent by her parents. She has $800 in dividend income and $1,400 in wages from a part-time job.
   b. Ruby and Woody are married and file a joint tax return. Ruby is age 66 and Woody is 69. Their taxable retirement income is $10,000.
   c. Shonda is age 68 and single. She is claimed by her daughter as a dependent. Her earned income is $500 and her interest income is $125.
   d. Frazier, age 55, is married but is filing a separate return. His wife itemizes her deductions.

3. **LO.4** In 2015, Dominique and Felix are married and file a joint tax return. Their AGI is $312,650 and they claim three exemptions. Determine their total exemption amount for 2015.

4. **LO.5** Paul and Sonja, who are married, had itemized deductions of $8,200 and   Issue ID
   $400, respectively, during 2015. Paul suggests that they file separately—he will itemize his deductions *from* AGI, and she will claim the standard deduction.
   a. Evaluate Paul's suggestion.
   b. What should they do?

5. **LO.6** Compute the 2015 tax liability and the marginal and average tax rates for the following taxpayers (use the 2015 tax rate schedules in Appendix A for this purpose).
   a. Chandler, who files as a single taxpayer, has taxable income of $91,000.
   b. Lazare, who files as a head of household, has taxable income of $56,000.

6. **LO.6** George and Aimee are married. George has wage income of $190,000 and Aimee has a sole proprietorship that generated net income of $85,000. They also have interest and dividend income of $21,000. Compute any NIIT and Additional Medicare Tax they owe for the current year.

7. **LO.7** In 2015, Simon, age 12, has interest income of $800 and dividend income of   Critical Thinking
   $4,000. He has no investment expenses. His parents have taxable income of $80,200 and file a joint tax return. Assume that no parental election is made. Determine Simon's net unearned income, allocable parental tax, and total tax liability.

Problems

8. **LO.1, 5** During the year, Addison is involved in the following transactions: Issue ID
   • Lost money gambling on a recent trip to a casino.
   • Helped pay for her neighbor's dental bills. The neighbor is a good friend who is unemployed.
   • Received from the IRS a tax refund due to Addison's overpayment of last year's Federal income taxes.
   • Paid a traffic ticket received while double parking to attend a business meeting.
   • Contributed to the mayor's reelection campaign. The mayor had promised Addison to have some of her land rezoned. The mayor was reelected and got Addison's land rezoned.
   • Borrowed money from a bank to make a down payment on an automobile.
   • Sold a houseboat and a camper on eBay. Both were personal use items, and the gain from one offset the loss from the other.
   • Her dependent grandfather died on June 3 of the year.
   • Paid for dependent grandfather's funeral expenses.
   • Paid premiums on her dependent son's life insurance policy.
   What are the possible income tax ramifications of these transactions?

9. **LO.1** Which of the following items are *inclusions* in gross income?

  a. During the year, stock the taxpayer purchased as an investment doubled in value.

  √ b. Amount an off-duty motorcycle police officer received for escorting a funeral procession.

  √ c. While his mother was in the hospital, the taxpayer sold her jewelry and gave the money to his girlfriend.

  d. Child support payments received.

  e. A damage deposit the taxpayer recovered when he vacated the apartment he had rented.

  √ f. Interest received by the taxpayer on an investment in general purpose bonds issued by IBM.

  √ g. Amounts received by the taxpayer, a baseball "Hall of Famer," for autographing sports equipment (e.g., balls and gloves).

  √ h. Tips received by a bartender from patrons. (Taxpayer is paid a regular salary by the cocktail lounge that employs him.)

  √ i. Taxpayer sells his Super Bowl tickets for three times what he paid for them.

  j. Taxpayer receives a new BMW from his grandmother when he passes the CPA exam.

10. **LO.1** Which of the following items are *exclusions* from gross income?

  a. Alimony payments received.

  √ b. Damages award received by the taxpayer for personal physical injury—none were for punitive damages.

  c. A new golf cart won in a church raffle.

  √ d. Amount collected on a loan previously made to a college friend.

  √ e. Insurance proceeds paid to the taxpayer on the death of her uncle—she was the designated beneficiary under the policy.

  √ f. Interest income on City of Chicago bonds.

  g. Jury duty fees.

  h. Stolen funds the taxpayer had collected for a local food bank drive.

  i. Reward paid by the IRS for information provided that led to the conviction of the taxpayer's former employer for tax evasion.

  j. An envelope containing $8,000 found (and unclaimed) by the taxpayer in a bus station.

Decision Making 11. **LO.1** In late 2015, the Polks come to you for tax advice. They are considering selling some stock investments for a loss and making a contribution to a traditional IRA. In reviewing their situation, you note that they have large medical expenses and a casualty loss, neither of which is covered by insurance. What advice would you give the Polks?

12. **LO.1, 2, 3, 4** Compute the taxable income for 2015 in each of the following independent situations:

  a. Drew and Meg, ages 40 and 41, respectively, are married and file a joint return. In addition to four dependent children, they have AGI of $65,000 and itemized deductions of $15,000.

  b. Sybil, age 40, is single and supports her dependent parents, who live with her, as well as her grandfather, who is in a nursing home. She has AGI of $80,000 and itemized deductions of $8,000.

  c. Scott, age 49, is a surviving spouse. His household includes two unmarried stepsons who qualify as his dependents. He has AGI of $75,000 and itemized deductions of $10,100.

d. Amelia, age 33, is an abandoned spouse who maintains a household for her three dependent children. She has AGI of $58,000 and itemized deductions of $9,500.

e. Dale, age 42, is divorced but maintains the home in which he and his daughter, Jill, live. Jill is single and qualifies as Dale's dependent. Dale has AGI of $64,000 and itemized deductions of $9,900.

13. **LO.1, 2, 3, 4** Compute the taxable income for 2015 for Emily on the basis of the following information. Her filing status is single.

Salary	$85,000
Interest income from bonds issued by Xerox	1,100
Alimony payments received	6,000
Contribution to traditional IRA	5,500
Gift from parents	25,000
Short-term capital gain from stock investment	2,000
Amount lost in football office pool	500
Number of potential dependents (two cousins, who live in Canada)	?
Age	40

14. **LO.1, 2, 3, 4** Compute the taxable income for 2015 for Aiden on the basis of the following information. Aiden is married but has not seen or heard from his wife since 2013.

Salary	$ 80,000
Interest on bonds issued by the City of Boston	3,000
Interest on CD issued by Wells Fargo Bank	2,000
Cash dividend received on Chevron common stock	2,200
Life insurance proceeds paid on death of aunt (Aiden was the designated beneficiary of the policy)	200,000
Inheritance received upon death of aunt	100,000
Jackson (a cousin) repaid a loan Aiden made to him in 2009 (no interest was provided for)	5,000
Itemized deductions (state income tax, property taxes on residence, interest on home mortgage, and charitable contributions)	9,700
Number of dependents (children, ages 17 and 18, and mother-in-law, age 70)	3
Age	43

15. **LO.2** In choosing between the standard deduction and itemizing deductions *from* AGI, what effect, if any, does each of the following have?   Issue ID

a. The age of the taxpayer(s).

b. The health (i.e., physical condition) of the taxpayer.

c. Whether taxpayers rent or own their residence.

d. Taxpayer's filing status (e.g., single, married, filing jointly).

e. Whether married taxpayers decide to file separate returns.

f. The taxpayer's uninsured personal residence was recently destroyed by fire.

g. The number of personal and dependency exemptions the taxpayer can claim.

16. **LO.2, 3, 5** David is age 78, is a widower, and is being claimed as a dependent by his son. How does this situation affect the following?

a. David's own individual filing requirement.

b. David's personal exemption.

c. The standard deduction allowed to David.

d. The availability of any additional standard deduction.

17. **LO.2** Determine the amount of the standard deduction allowed for 2015 in the following independent situations. In each case, assume that the taxpayer is claimed as another person's dependent.

    a. Curtis, age 18, has income as follows: $700 interest from a certificate of deposit and $6,100 from repairing cars.

    b. Mattie, age 18, has income as follows: $600 cash dividends from a stock investment and $4,700 from handling a paper route.

    c. Mel, age 16, has income as follows: $675 interest on a bank savings account and $800 for painting a neighbor's fence.

    d. Lucy, age 15, has income as follows: $400 cash dividends from a stock investment and $500 from grooming pets.

    e. Sarah, age 67 and a widow, has income as follows: $500 from a bank savings account and $3,200 from babysitting.

18. **LO.4** Using the legend provided below, classify each statement as to the taxpayer for dependency exemption purposes.

Legend	
QC =	Could be a qualifying child
QR =	Could be a qualifying relative
B =	Could satisfy the definition of *both* a qualifying child *and* a qualifying relative
N =	Could not satisfy the definition of *either* a qualifying child *or* a qualifying relative

    a. Taxpayer's son has gross income of $7,000.

    b. Taxpayer's niece has gross income of $3,000.

    c. Taxpayer's uncle lives with him.

    d. Taxpayer's daughter is age 25 and disabled.

    e. Taxpayer's daughter is age 18, has gross income of $8,000, and does not live with him.

    f. Taxpayer's cousin does not live with her.

    g. Taxpayer's brother does not live with her.

    h. Taxpayer's sister has dropped out of school, is age 17, and lives with him.

    i. Taxpayer's older nephew is age 23 and a full-time student.

    j. Taxpayer's grandson lives with her and has gross income of $7,000.

19. **LO.4** Caden and Lily are divorced on March 3, 2014. For financial reasons, however, Lily continues to live in Caden's apartment and receives her support from him. Caden does not claim Lily as a dependent on his 2014 Federal income tax return but does so on his 2015 return. Explain.

20. **LO.3, 4** For tax year 2015, determine the number of personal and dependency exemptions in each of the following independent situations:

    a. Leo and Amanda (ages 48 and 46, respectively) are husband and wife and furnish more than 50% of the support of their two children, Elton (age 18) and Trista (age 24). During the year, Elton earns $4,500 providing transportation for elderly persons with disabilities, and Trista receives a $5,000 scholarship for tuition at the law school she attends.

    b. Audry (age 45) was divorced this year. She maintains a household in which she, her ex-husband (Clint), and his mother (Olive) live and furnishes more than 50% of their support. Olive is age 91 and blind.

    c. Crystal, age 45, furnishes more than 50% of the support of her married son, Andy (age 18), and his wife, Paige (age 19), who live with her. During the year, Andy earned $8,000 from a part-time job. All parties live in Iowa (a common law state).

    d. Assume the same facts as in (c), except that all parties live in Washington (a community property state).

21. **LO.3, 4** Sam and Elizabeth Jefferson file a joint return and have three children—all of whom qualify as dependents. If the Jeffersons have AGI of $332,000, what is their allowable deduction for personal and dependency exemptions for 2015?

22. **LO.4** Wesley and Myrtle (ages 90 and 88, respectively) live in an assisted care facility and for 2014 and 2015 received their support from the following sources:

	Percentage of Support
Social Security benefits	16%
Son	20
Niece	29
Cousin	12
Brother	11
Family friend (not related)	12

    a. Which persons are eligible to claim the dependency exemptions under a multiple support agreement?

    b. Must Wesley and Myrtle be claimed by the same person(s) for both 2014 and 2015? Explain.

    c. Who, if anyone, can claim their medical expenses?

23. **LO.2, 7** Taylor, age 18, is claimed as a dependent by her parents. For 2015, she has the following income: $4,000 of wages from a summer job, $1,800 of interest from a money market account, and $2,000 of interest from City of Boston bonds.   **Critical Thinking**

    a. What is Taylor's taxable income for 2015?

    b. What is Taylor's tax for 2015? [Her parents file a joint return and have taxable income of $130,000 (no dividends or capital gains).]

24. **LO.4** Walter and Nancy provide 60% of the support of their daughter (age 18) and son-in-law (age 22). The son-in-law (John) is a full-time student at a local university, while the daughter (Irene) holds various part-time jobs from which she earns $11,000. Walter and Nancy engage you to prepare their tax return for 2015. During a meeting with them in late March 2016, you learn that John and Irene have filed a joint return. What tax advice would you give based on the following assumptions: **Issue ID**

    Decision Making

    a. All parties live in Louisiana (a community property state).

    b. All parties live in New Jersey (a common law state).

25. **LO.1, 4, 6** Charlotte (age 40) is a surviving spouse and provides all of the support of her four minor children who live with her. She also maintains the household in which her parents live and furnished 60% of their support. Besides interest on City of Miami bonds in the amount of $5,500, Charlotte's father received $2,400 from a part-time job. Charlotte has a salary of $80,000, a short-term capital loss of $2,000, a cash prize of $4,000 from a church raffle, and itemized deductions of $10,500. Using the Tax Rate Schedules, compute the 2015 tax liability for Charlotte.

26. **LO.1, 2, 3, 4, 5, 6** Morgan (age 45) is single and provides more than 50% of the support of Rosalyn (a family friend), Flo (a niece, age 18), and Jerold (a nephew, age 18). Both Rosalyn and Flo live with Morgan, but Jerold (a French citizen) lives in Canada. Morgan earns a salary of $95,000, contributes $5,000 to a traditional IRA, and receives sales proceeds of $15,000 for an RV that cost $60,000 and was used for vacations. She has $8,200 in itemized deductions. Using the Tax Rate Schedules, compute the 2015 tax liability for Morgan.

Ethics and Equity   27. **LO.5** Bob and Carol have been in and out of marital counseling for the past few years. Early in 2015, they decide to separate. However, because they are barely able to get by on their current incomes, they cannot afford separate housing or the legal costs of a divorce. So, Bob moves out of their house in March and takes up residence in their detached garage (which has an enclosed workshop and bathroom). Carol stays in the house with their two children and pays more than half of the costs of maintaining their residence. Bob does not enter the house for the remainder of the year. Can Carol qualify as an abandoned spouse?

Critical Thinking   28. **LO.5** Which of the following individuals are required to file a tax return for 2015? Should any of these individuals file a return even if filing is not required? Why or why not?

a.   Patricia, age 19, is a self-employed single individual with gross income of $5,200 from an unincorporated business. Business expenses amounted to $4,900.

b.   Mike is single and is 67 years old. His gross income from wages was $10,800.

c.   Ronald is a dependent child under age 19 who received $6,500 in wages from a part-time job.

d.   Sam is married and files a joint return with his spouse, Lana. Both Sam and Lana are 67 years old. Their combined gross income was $24,250.

e.   Quinn, age 20, is a full-time college student who is claimed as a dependent by his parents. For 2015, Quinn has taxable interest and dividends of $2,500.

Decision Making   29. **LO.5, 6** Roy and Brandi are engaged and plan to get married. During 2015, Roy is a full-time student and earns $9,000 from a part-time job. With this income, student loans, savings, and nontaxable scholarships, he is self-supporting. For the year, Brandi is employed and has wages of $61,000. How much income tax, if any, can Brandi save if she and Roy marry in 2015 and file a joint return?

30. **LO.6** Jayden calculates his 2015 income tax by using both the Tax Tables and the Tax Rate Schedules. Because the Tax Rate Schedules yield a slightly lower tax liability, he plans to pay this amount.

a.   Why is there a difference?

b.   Is Jayden's approach permissible? Why or why not?

Critical Thinking   31. **LO.1, 3, 7** Paige, age 17, is claimed as a dependent on her parents' 2015 return, on which they report taxable income of $120,000 (no qualified dividends or capital gains). Paige earned $3,900 pet sitting and $4,100 in interest on a savings account. What are Paige's taxable income and tax liability for 2015?

Critical Thinking   32. **LO.1, 3, 7** Terri, age 16, is claimed as a dependent on her parents' 2015 return. During the year, Terri earned $5,000 in interest income and $3,000 from part-time jobs.

a.   What is Terri's taxable income?

b.   How much of Terri's income is taxed at her rate? At her parents' rate?

c.   Can the parental election be made? Why or why not?

Comprehensive Tax Return Problems

Tax Return Problem   1.   Lance H. and Wanda B. Dean are married and live at 431 Yucca Drive, Santa Fe, NM 87501. Lance works for the convention bureau of the local Chamber of Commerce, while Wanda is employed part-time as a paralegal for a law firm.

During 2014, the Deans had the following receipts:

Salaries ($60,000 for Lance, $41,000 for Wanda)		$101,000
Interest income—		
City of Albuquerque general purpose bonds	$1,000	
Ford Motor Company bonds	1,100	
Ally Bank certificate of deposit	400	2,500
Child support payments from John Allen		7,200
Annual gifts from parents		26,000
Settlement from Roadrunner Touring Company		90,000
Lottery winnings		600
Federal income tax refund (for tax year 2013)		400

Wanda was previously married to John Allen. When they divorced several years ago, Wanda was awarded custody of their two children, Penny and Kyle. (Note: Wanda has never issued a Form 8332 waiver.) Under the divorce decree, John was obligated to pay alimony and child support—the alimony payments were to terminate if Wanda remarried.

In July, while going to lunch in downtown Santa Fe, Wanda was injured by a tour bus. As the driver was clearly at fault, the owner of the bus, Roadrunner Touring Company, paid her medical expenses (including a one-week stay in a hospital). To avoid a lawsuit, Roadrunner also transferred $90,000 to her in settlement of the personal injuries she sustained.

The Deans had the following expenditures for 2014:

Medical expenses (not covered by insurance)		$7,200
Taxes—		
Property taxes on personal residence	$3,600	
State of New Mexico income tax (includes amount		
withheld from wages during 2014)	4,200	7,800
Interest on home mortgage		6,000
Paid church pledge		3,600
Life insurance premiums (policy on Lance's life)		1,200
Contribution to traditional IRA (on Wanda's behalf)		5,000
Traffic fines		300
Contribution to the reelection campaign fund of the		
mayor of Santa Fe		500
Funeral expenses for Wayne Boyle		6,300

The life insurance policy was taken out by Lance several years ago and designates Wanda as the beneficiary. As a part-time employee, Wanda is excluded from coverage under her employer's pension plan. Consequently, she provides for her own retirement with a traditional IRA obtained at a local trust company. Because the mayor is a member of the local Chamber of Commerce, Lance felt compelled to make the political contribution.

The Deans' household includes the following, for whom they provide more than half of the support:

	Social Security Number*	Birth Date
Lance Dean (age 42)	123-45-6786	12/16/1972
Wanda Dean (age 40)	123-45-6787	08/08/1974
Penny Allen (age 19)	123-45-6788	10/09/1995
Kyle Allen (age 17)	123-45-6789	05/03/1997
Wayne Boyle (age 75)	123-45-6785	06/15/1939

*In the interest of privacy and to protect against taxpayer identification misuse, Social Security numbers used throughout the textbook have been replaced with fictitious numbers.

Penny graduated from high school on May 9, 2014, and is undecided about college. During 2014, she earned $8,500 (placed in a savings account) playing a harp in the lobby of a local hotel. Wayne is Wanda's widower father, who died on January 20, 2014. For the past few years, Wayne qualified as a dependent of the Deans.

Federal income tax withheld is $5,200 (Lance) and $3,100 (Wanda). The proper amount of Social Security and Medicare tax was withheld.

Determine the Federal income tax for 2014 for the Deans on a joint return by completing the appropriate forms. They do not want to contribute to the Presidential Election Campaign Fund. All members of the family had health care coverage for all of 2014. If an overpayment results, it is to be refunded to them. Suggested software: H&R BLOCK Tax Software.

Tax Return Problem

Decision Making

Communications

TAX SOFTWARE

2. Logan B. Taylor is a widower whose wife, Sara, died on June 6, 2012. He lives at 4680 Dogwood Lane, Springfield, MO 65801. He is employed as a paralegal by a local law firm. During 2014, he had the following receipts:

Salary		$ 80,000
Interest income—		
Money market account at Omni Bank	$ 300	
Savings account at Boone State Bank	1,100	
City of Springfield general purpose bonds	3,000	4,400
Inheritance from Daniel		60,000
Life insurance proceeds		200,000
Amount from sale of St. Louis lot		80,000
Proceeds from estate sale		9,000
Federal income tax refund (for 2013 tax overpayment)		700

Logan inherited securities worth $60,000 from his uncle, Daniel, who died in 2014. Logan also was the designated beneficiary of an insurance policy on Daniel's life with a maturity value of $200,000. The lot in St. Louis was purchased on May 2, 2009, for $85,000 and held as an investment. As the neighborhood has deteriorated, Logan decided to cut his losses and sold the lot on January 5, 2014, for $80,000. The estate sale consisted largely of items belonging to Sara and Daniel (e.g., camper, boat, furniture, and fishing and hunting equipment). Logan estimates that the property sold originally cost at least twice the $9,000 he received and has declined or stayed the same in value since Sara and Daniel died.

Logan's expenditures for 2014 include the following:

Medical expenses (including $10,500 for dental)		$11,500
Taxes—		
State of Missouri income tax (includes withholdings during 2014)	$3,200	
Property taxes on personal residence	4,500	7,700
Interest on home mortgage		4,600
Contribution to church (paid pledges for 2014 and 2015)		4,800

Logan and his dependents are covered by his employer's health insurance policy for all of 2014. However, he is subject to a deductible, and dental care is not included. The $10,500 dental charge was for Helen's implants. Helen is Logan's widowed mother, who lives with him (see below). Logan normally pledges $2,400 ($200 per month) each year to his church. On December 5, 2014, upon the advice of his pastor, he prepaid his pledge for 2015.

Logan's household, all of whom he supports, includes the following:

	Social Security Number	Birth Date
Logan Taylor (age 48)	123-45-6787	08/30/1966
Helen Taylor (age 70)	123-45-6780	01/13/1944
Asher Taylor (age 23)	123-45-6783	07/18/1991
Mia Taylor (age 22)	123-45-6784	02/16/1992

Helen receives a modest Social Security benefit. Asher, a son, is a full-time student in dental school and earns $4,500 as a part-time dental assistant. Mia, a daughter, does not work and is engaged to be married.

Part 1—Tax Computation
Using the appropriate forms and schedules, compute Logan's income tax for 2014. Federal income tax of $5,500 was withheld from his wages. If Logan has any over-payment on his income tax, he wants the refund sent to him. Assume that the proper amounts of Social Security and Medicare taxes were withheld. Logan does not want to contribute to the Presidential Election Campaign Fund. Suggested soft-ware: H&R BLOCK Tax Software.

Part 2—Follow-Up Advice
In early 2015, the following take place:

- Helen decides she wants to live with one of her daughters and moves to Arizona.
- Asher graduates from dental school and joins an existing practice in St. Louis.
- Mia marries, and she and her husband move in with his parents.
- Using the insurance proceeds he received on Daniel's death, Logan pays off the mortgage on his personal residence.

Logan believes these events may have an effect on his tax position for 2015. Therefore, he requests your advice.

Write a letter to Logan explaining in general terms the changes that will occur for tax purposes. Assume that Logan's salary and other factors not mentioned (e.g., property and state income taxes) will remain the same. Use the Tax Rate Schedules in projecting Logan's tax for 2015.

Research Problems

Note: Solutions to Research Problems can be prepared by using the Checkpoint® Student Edition online research product, which is available to accompany this text. It is also possible to prepare solutions to the Research Problems by using tax research materials found in a standard tax library.

THOMSON REUTERS
CHECKPOINT®
Student Edition

Research Problem 1. Kathy and Brett Ouray married in 1997. They began to experience marital difficulties in 2011 and, in the current year, although they are not legally sepa-rated, consider themselves completely estranged. They have contemplated getting a divorce. However, because of financial concerns and because they both want to remain involved in the lives of their three sons, they have not yet filed for divorce. In addition, their financial difficulties have meant that Kathy and Brett cannot afford to live in sepa-rate residences. So although they consider themselves emotionally estranged, they and their three sons all reside in a single-family home in Chicago, Illinois.

Although Brett earns significantly more than Kathy, both contribute financially to maintaining their home and supporting their teenage sons. In one of their few and brief conversations this year, they determined that Brett had contributed far more than Kathy to the maintenance of their home and the support of their sons. Thus, Brett has decided that for the current tax year, they will file separate Federal income tax returns and that he will claim head-of-household filing status. While they live under the same roof, Brett believes that he and Kathy should maintain separate households. Given this fact and the fact that he provides significantly more for the support of his and Kathy's sons, he believes he is eligible for head-of-household fil-ing status. Advise Brett on which filing status is most appropriate for him in the cur-rent year. His address is 16 Lahinch, Chicago, IL 60608.

Communications

Decision Making

Research Problem 2. John and Janet Baker are husband and wife and maintain a household in which the following persons live: Calvin and Florence Carter and Darin, Andrea, and Morgan Baker.

- Calvin and Florence are Janet's parents, who are retired. During the year, they receive $19,000 in nontaxable funds (e.g., disability income, interest on municipal bonds, and Social Security benefits). Of this amount, $8,000 is spent equally between them for clothing, transportation, and recreation (e.g., vacation) and the balance of $11,000 is invested in tax-exempt securities. Janet paid $1,000 for her mother's dental work and paid the $1,200 premium on an insurance policy her father owned on his own life. Calvin also had medical expenses, but he insisted on paying for them with his own funds.

- Darin is the Bakers' 18-year-old son who is not a student but operates a pool-cleaning service on a part-time basis. During the year, he earns $14,000 from the business, which he places in a savings account for later college expenses.

- Andrea is the Bakers' 19-year-old daughter who does not work or go to school. Tired of the inconvenience of borrowing and sharing the family car, during the year, she purchased a Camaro for $21,000. Andrea used funds from a savings account she had established several years ago with an inheritance from her paternal grandfather.

- Morgan is the Bakers' 23-year-old daughter. To attend graduate school at a local university, she applied for and obtained a student loan of $20,000. She uses the full amount to pay her college tuition.

The Bakers' fair rental value of their residence, including utilities, is $14,000, while their total food expense for the household is $10,500.

a. How many dependency exemptions are the Bakers entitled to claim for the year? Explain your answer.

b. From a planning standpoint, how might the Bakers have improved the tax result?

Partial list of research aids:
Reg. §§ 1.152–1(a) and –1(c).
Your Federal Income Tax (IRS Publication 17), Chapter 3.

Internet Activity

Use the tax resources of the Internet to address the following questions. Do not restrict your search to the Web, but include a review of newsgroups and general reference materials, practitioner sites and resources, primary sources of the tax law, chat rooms and discussion groups, and other opportunities.

Research Problem 3. Locate IRS Form 2120 (at **www.irs.gov**), and answer the following questions.

a. Who must sign the form?

b. Who must file the form?

c. Can it be used for someone who is not related to the taxpayer? Explain.

Research Problem 4. What purpose is served by Form 8857? Read the directions to the form, and see IRS Publication 971 for additional information.

Research Problem 5. A nonresident alien earns money in the United States that is subject to Federal income tax. What guidance does the IRS provide about what tax form needs to be used and when it should be filed? In terms of the proper filing date, does it matter whether the earnings were subject to income tax withholding? Explain.

Roger CPA Review Questions

1. Keller is a single individual who in 20X14 qualified for a foreign earned income exclusion of $80,000. Keller's 20X14 net investment income was $25,000, and Keller's 20X14 Adjusted Gross Income prior to the foreign earned income exclusion was $220,000. Given a 3.8% Unearned Income Medicare Contribution Tax rate, what is Keller's 20X14 liability for this surtax?

   a. $760
   b. $0
   c. $950
   d. $570

2. Walters, an individual, received the following in 20X13:

W-2 income	$10,000
Federal tax refund for 20X12	1,250
Scholarship stipend, in return for teaching assistant duties performed	25,000
Cash inheritance from deceased great-uncle	5,000

   Considering only the above, what is Walters' 20X13 gross income?

   a. $35,000
   b. $36,250
   c. $15,000
   d. $16,250

3. For "qualifying widow(er)" filing status, which of the following requirements must be met?

   I.   The surviving spouse does not remarry before the end of the current year.
   II. The surviving spouse was eligible to file a joint tax return in the year of the spouse's death.
   III. The surviving spouse maintains the cost of the principal residence for six months.

   a. I, II, and III
   b. I and II, but not III
   c. I and III, but not II
   d. I only

4. Parker and his wife Marie would have been filing a joint tax return for 20X1; however, Marie died in October of 20X1. Parker has not remarried and continues to maintain a home for himself and his two children during 20X1, 20X2, 20X3, and 20X4. Parker's filing statuses for 20X1, 20X2, 20X3, and 20X4 are as follows:

	20X1	20X2	20X3	20X4
a.	Qualifying widower	Married filing joint return	Qualifying widower	Head of household
b.	Married filing joint return	Married filing joint return	Head of household	Qualifying widower
c.	Married filing joint return	Qualifying widower	Qualifying widower	Head of household
d.	Qualifying widower	Qualifying widower	Head of household	Qualifying widower

CHAPTER

10

Individuals: Income, Deductions, and Credits

LEARNING OBJECTIVES: *After completing Chapter 10, you should be able to:*

LO.1 Identify specific income inclusions and exclusions applicable to individuals.

LO.2 Determine an individual's allowable itemized deductions.

LO.3 Explain and illustrate the adoption expenses credit, child tax credit, education tax credits, credit for child and dependent care expenses, and earned income credit.

LO.4 Explain some of the key tax provisions of the Affordable Care Act.

CHAPTER OUTLINE

TAX TALK *A tax loophole is something that benefits the other guy. If it benefits you, it is tax reform.* –RUSSELL B. LONG

THE TAX IMPLICATIONS OF LIFE!

Donna and David Steele, ages 35 and 37, respectively, recently married and have come to you for tax advice. They have several questions about their tax situation. Both are employed, and they expect to have combined wages from all sources of $70,000 for the current year.

During the year, Donna worked as an intern in the compliance area at a CPA firm. She was paid well enough for her work that she was able to save some money for school. The CPA firm was so pleased with Donna's work that, at the conclusion of her internship, she was given a bonus of $1,500 more than the firm had agreed to pay her. The extra amount was intended to help with her graduate school expenses in the masters of accounting program at State University. Because of her excellent academic record, the university awarded Donna a graduate assistantship that waived her tuition of $6,000 per semester and paid her $400 per month. In exchange, Donna was required to teach a principles of accounting course each semester. She used the cash she received each month for books and incidental fees. Donna also paid $250 of interest during the year on student loans still outstanding from her undergraduate years.

Donna and David received a wedding gift of $10,000 from her grandmother, and the couple earned $250 of interest on a savings account they opened with the money. David sold stock for $1,000 that was purchased two years ago for $5,000.

Late in the year, Donna was crossing a street in the pedestrian crosswalk when a delivery van struck her. The driver of the truck had a blood alcohol level of .12. She suffered a severe injury to her right arm that required her to miss work for a month or so. The delivery company's insurance company settled the case by paying damages as follows:

Compensatory damages:	
Medical expenses	$ 30,000
Injury to Donna's right arm	100,000
Pain and suffering	50,000
Loss of income	10,000
Legal fees	25,000
Punitive damages	160,000
	$375,000

continued

This is David's second marriage, and he pays alimony to his ex-wife. He has custody of his 15-year-old son, Stephen, who lives with Donna and David for nine months each year. The Steeles rent their home, paid $3,500 of state income taxes, paid an $412 motor vehicle registration tax on their personal car, incurred additional medical expenses of $25,000, and made $2,500 of charitable contributions.

Without calculating Donna and David's tax liability, what are the tax implications of the transactions noted above? Are there other tax deductions or credits for which they may qualify or other tax issues about which they should be made aware?

Read the chapter and formulate your response.

T his chapter focuses on the computation of taxable income for individual taxpayers. Recall that taxable income is the base on which the tax liability is calculated. In the simplest of terms, taxable income is determined by reducing *gross income* by allowable *tax deductions*. Prior chapters provided discussions where the meanings of these terms were explored in a general sense. However, this chapter describes special rules that apply to individual taxpayers, with respect to both income and deduction items. In addition, the chapter discusses key individual tax credits that may further reduce an individual's tax liability. Finally, the chapter concludes by describing key components of the Affordable Care Act that could impact an individual's tax computation.

10-1 OVERVIEW OF INCOME PROVISIONS APPLICABLE TO INDIVIDUALS

LO.1

Identify specific income inclusions and exclusions applicable to individuals.

As indicated in Chapter 9, the definition of gross income is broad enough to include almost all receipts of money, property, or services. However, the tax law provides for exclusion of many types of income.[1] The following income provisions, which apply to all taxpayers (including individuals), were discussed in Chapter 4:

- Interest from state and local bonds.
- Life insurance paid on death of the insured.
- Imputed interest on below-market loans.
- Income from discharge of indebtedness.
- Income included under the tax benefit rule.

Most *exclusions* available only to individuals are for *fringe benefits* received by *employees* (refer to Exhibit 9.1 in Chapter 9). Fringe benefits are discussed in Chapter 11. Other specific inclusions and exclusions for individuals are discussed next.

10-2 SPECIFIC INCLUSIONS APPLICABLE TO INDIVIDUALS

As discussed earlier, the general principles of gross income determination have occasionally yielded results that Congress found unacceptable. Thus, Congress has provided more specific rules for determining the amount of gross income from certain sources.

---

[1] See §§ 101–140.

BRIDGE DISCIPLINE   **Bridge to Economics and Finance**

As is the case for business entities, a primary financial goal for individual taxpayers should entail maximizing the *after-tax value* of their assets over time. This approach requires not only selecting the best investment alternatives but also choosing those investments with the most favorable tax attributes. Fundamental to this notion is recognizing the key role the government plays in all economic activity through its taxing authority. As a result, an investor should consider economically sound strategies that minimize the extent to which the government can stake a claim to his or her success. For example, taxpayers can reduce the government's share of their wealth accumulations by deferring the payment of taxes until future years and by taking advantage of investment strategies for which tax incentives are available. Taxpayers should choose the investment alternatives that provide the best after-tax return over time and not necessarily the ones that lead to the least amount of taxation.

These points can be illustrated by examining two classic strategies. One of the best ways for individuals to maximize their personal wealth is to invest to the extent possible in qualified retirement savings programs [e.g., traditional Individual Retirement Accounts, § 401(k) accounts]. Not only do current additions to such accounts provide a current tax deduction, but earnings in the account are not subject to taxation until they are withdrawn, which, in most cases, is during the retirement years of the owner. Postponing the tax in these two ways reduces the present value of the tax cost, which increases the after-tax value of the investment. Another strategy involves investing in tax-free municipal bonds, which produce interest income that is free of Federal income tax. The returns from such investments, however, should be compared with the after-tax returns flowing from available taxable debt securities. For example, a relevant question is how the implicit tax (see Chapter 1) associated with a municipal bond compares with the explicit tax associated with a taxable bond.

Some of these special rules appear in §§ 71–90 of the Code. The following provisions applicable to individuals are covered in this chapter:

- Alimony and separate maintenance payments.
- Prizes and awards.
- Unemployment compensation.
- Social Security benefits.

10-2a **Alimony and Separate Maintenance Payments**

When a married couple divorces or become legally separated, state law generally requires a division of the property accumulated during the marriage. In addition, one spouse may have a legal obligation to support the other spouse. The Code distinguishes between the support payments (alimony or separate maintenance) and the property division in terms of the tax consequences. Further, if payments are made that are intended to provide for the support of a child, the law is clear that these payments are distinguishable from both alimony and property settlements.

Alimony and separate maintenance payments are deductible by the party making the payments and are includible in the gross income of the party receiving the payments.[2] Thus, taxation of the income is shifted from the income earner to the income beneficiary.

Pete and Tina are divorced, and Pete is required to pay Tina $15,000 of alimony each year. Pete earns $61,000 a year. Therefore, Tina must include the $15,000 in her gross income, and Pete is allowed to deduct $15,000 from his gross income.

EXAMPLE

1

Property Settlements

A transfer of property other than cash to a former spouse under a divorce decree or agreement is not a taxable event. The transferor is not entitled to a deduction and does

---

[2]§§ 71 and 215.

not recognize gain or loss on the transfer. The transferee does not recognize income and takes a basis equal to the transferor's basis.[3]

EXAMPLE 2

Paul transfers stock to Rosa this year as part of a divorce settlement. The cost of the stock to Paul was $12,000, and the stock's fair market value at the time of the transfer is $15,000. Rosa later sells the stock for $16,000. Paul is not required to recognize gain from the transfer of the stock to Rosa, and Rosa has a realized *and* recognized gain of $4,000 ($16,000 − $12,000) when she sells the stock.

Requirements for Alimony

To classify payments as support obligations (alimony), as opposed to property of the other spouse (property settlements) or child support obligations, Congress developed the following objective rules. Payments made under agreements and decrees are *classified as alimony* only if the following conditions are satisfied:

- The payments are in cash. (This clearly distinguishes alimony from a property division.)
- The agreement or decree does not specify that the payments are not alimony. (This allows the parties to determine by agreement whether the payments will be alimony.)
- The payor and payee are not members of the same household at the time the payments are made. (This ensures the payments are for maintaining two households.)
- There is no liability to make the payments for any period after the death of the payee.[4]

DIGGING DEEPER 1   In-depth coverage can be found on this book's companion website: www.cengagebrain.com

Child Support

While alimony is taxable, a taxpayer does *not* report income from the receipt of child support payments made by his or her former spouse. This result occurs because the money is received subject to the duty to use the money for the child's benefit. The payor is not allowed to deduct the child support payments because the payments are made to satisfy the payor's legal obligation to support the child.

In many cases, it may be difficult to determine whether the payments are intended to be alimony or child support. The tax law resolves this issue in many cases with the following rule: If the amount of the payments would be reduced upon the happening of a contingency related to a child (e.g., the child attains age 21 or dies), the amount of the future reduction in the payment is deemed child support.[5] The rule is applied even though the divorce agreement specifies other amounts for the support of the child.[6]

EXAMPLE 3

Under the divorce agreement, Matt is required to make periodic alimony payments of $500 per month to Grace. However, when Matt and Grace's child reaches age 21, marries, or dies (whichever occurs first), the payments will be reduced to $300 per month. Because the required contingency is the cause for the reduction in the payments, from $500 to $300, child support payments are $200 per month and alimony is $300 per month.

---

[3]Section 1041 was added to the Code in 1984 to repeal the rule of *U.S. v. Davis*, 62–2 USTC ¶9509, 9 AFTR 2d 1625, 82 S.Ct. 1190 (USSC, 1962). Under the *Davis* rule, which applied to pre-1985 divorces, a property transfer incident to divorce was a taxable event.

[4]See *Divorced or Separated Individuals* (IRS Publication 504) for additional information on alimony.
[5]§ 71(c)(2).
[6]*Johnson v. Comm.*, T.C.Memo. 2014–67.

TAX IN THE NEWS   **Social Security Benefits as a Source of Federal Revenue**

Recipients' Social Security benefits are indexed for inflation, but the base amounts used in the formula to calculate the taxable portion of the benefits are not indexed. (For a complete discussion of this formula, see the materials associated with Digging Deeper 2.) The $25,000 and $32,000 base amounts were established in 1984. If they were indexed for inflation, these nontaxable amounts would have doubled by 2010. Thus, as income and Social Security benefits rise with inflation, taxable income increases more than the related increase in "real" benefits.

10-2b **Prizes and Awards**

The fair market value of prizes and awards must be included in gross income.[7] Therefore, TV giveaway prizes, magazine publisher prizes, door prizes, and awards from an employer to an employee in recognition of performance are fully taxable to the recipient.

A narrow exception permits a prize or an award to be excluded from gross income if *all* of the following requirements are satisfied:

- The prize or award is received in recognition of religious, charitable, scientific, educational, artistic, literary, or civic achievement (e.g., Nobel Prize, Pulitzer Prize, or faculty teaching award).

- The recipient was selected without taking any action to enter the contest or proceeding.

- The recipient is not required to render substantial future services as a condition for receiving the prize or award.[8]

- The recipient arranges for the prize or award to be paid *directly* to a qualified governmental unit or nonprofit organization.

A taxpayer can avoid including prizes and awards in gross income by refusing to accept the prize or award.[9]

Another exception is provided to allow exclusion of certain employee achievement awards in the form of tangible personal property (e.g., a gold watch). The awards must be made in recognition of length of service or safety achievement. Generally, the ceiling on the excludible amount for an employee is $400 per taxable year. However, if the award is a *qualified plan award,* the ceiling on the exclusion is $1,600 per taxable year.[10]

10-2c **Unemployment Compensation**

The unemployment compensation program is sponsored and operated by the states and Federal government to provide a source of income for people who have been employed and are temporarily out of work. In a series of rulings over a period of 40 years, the IRS exempted unemployment benefits from tax. These payments were considered social benefit programs for the promotion of the general welfare. After experiencing dissatisfaction with the IRS's treatment of unemployment compensation, Congress amended the Code to make the benefits taxable.[11]

10-2d **Social Security Benefits**

If a taxpayer's income exceeds a specified base amount, as much as 50 or 85 percent of Social Security retirement benefits must be included in gross income. The taxable

---

[7]§ 74.
[8]§ 74(b).
[9]See Rev.Rul. 57–374, 1957–2 C.B. 69 and Rev.Proc. 87–54, 1987–2 C.B. 669.

[10]§§ 74(c) and 274(j).
[11]§ 85.

amount of benefits is determined through the application of one of two complex formulas described in § 86.

DIGGING DEEPER 2 | **In-depth coverage can be found on this book's companion website: www.cengagebrain.com**

10-3 SPECIFIC EXCLUSIONS APPLICABLE TO INDIVIDUALS

If an income item is within the all-inclusive definition of gross income, the item can be excluded only if the taxpayer can locate specific authority for doing so. The discussion that follows focuses on common exclusion items provided in the law that are available to individual taxpayers.

10-3a Gifts and Inheritances

Beginning with the Income Tax Act of 1913 and continuing to the present, Congress has allowed the recipient of a gift to exclude the value of the property from gross income. The exclusion applies to gifts made during the life of the donor (*inter vivos* gifts) and transfers that take effect upon the death of the donor (bequests and inheritances).[12] However, the recipient of a gift of income-producing property is subject to tax on the income subsequently earned from the property. Also, as discussed in Chapter 1, the donor or the decedent's estate may be subject to gift or estate taxes on such transfers.

In numerous cases, "gifts" are made in a business setting. For example, a salesperson gives a purchasing agent free samples, an employee receives cash from his or her employer upon retirement, or a corporation makes payments to employees who were victims of a natural disaster. In these and similar instances, it is frequently unclear whether the payment was a gift or represents compensation for past, present, or future services.

The courts have defined a gift as "a voluntary transfer of property by one to another without adequate consideration or compensation therefrom."[13] If the payment is intended to be for services rendered, it is not a gift, even though the payment is made without legal or moral obligation and the payor receives no economic benefit from the transfer. To qualify as a gift, the payment must be made "out of affection, respect, admiration, charity or like impulses."[14] Thus, the cases on this issue have been decided on the basis of the donor's intent.[15]

In the case of cash or other property received by an employee from his or her employer, Congress has eliminated any ambiguity. Transfers from an employer to an employee cannot be excluded as a gift.[16]

The Big Picture

EXAMPLE 4

Return to the facts of *The Big Picture* on p. 10-1. The $1,500 bonus paid to Donna by the CPA firm was compensation for her services rather than a gift, even though the employer had not contracted to pay this additional amount. This results because the payment was most likely not motivated by the employer's generosity, but rather was made as a result of business considerations. Even if the payment had been made out of generosity, because the payment was received from her employer, Donna could not exclude the "gift."

---

[12]§ 102.

[13]*Estate of D. R. Daly*, 3 B.T.A. 1042 (1926).

[14]*Robertson v. U.S.*, 52–1 USTC ¶9343, 41 AFTR 1053, 72 S.Ct. 994 (USSC, 1952).

[15]See, for example, *Comm. v. Duberstein*, 60–2 USTC ¶9515, 5 AFTR 2d 1626, 80 S.Ct. 1190 (USSC, 1960).

[16]§ 102(c). But see § 139 for qualified disaster situations.

TAX IN THE NEWS **Begging as a Tax-Disfavored Occupation**

The Tax Court has ruled that amounts received from begging are nontaxable gifts. In a reversal of the normal roles, the beggars contended that the amounts received were earned income while the IRS argued that the taxpayers had merely received gifts. The beggars wanted the fruit of their efforts to be treated as earned income to qualify them for the earned income credit (see

discussion later in this chapter). In all cases addressing the issue, the taxpayers were incarcerated and received the money from relatives and friends who had few prospects for being repaid.

Source: John Walter Wolf, 78 TCM 488, T.C.Memo. 1990–320.

In-depth coverage can be found on this book's companion website: www.cengagebrain.com

3 DIGGING DEEPER

10-3b Scholarships

General Information

Payments or benefits received by a student at an educational institution may be (1) compensation for services, (2) a gift, or (3) a scholarship. If the payments or benefits are received as compensation for services (past or present), the fact that the recipient is a student generally does not render the amounts received nontaxable.[17] Thus, a university teaching or research assistant is usually considered an employee, and his or her stipend is taxable compensation for services rendered. On the other hand, athletic scholarships largely are nontaxable when the individual is not required to participate in the sport.[18] In general, amounts received to be used for educational purposes (other than amounts received from family members) cannot be excluded as gifts because conditions attached to the receipt of the funds mean that the payments were not made out of "detached generosity."

As an exception to the compensation for services, nonprofit educational institutions can provide qualified tuition reduction plans for their employees and the employees can exclude the tuition from their gross income. The exclusion also applies to tuition reductions granted to the employee's spouse and the employee's dependent children.[19]

The scholarship rules are intended to provide exclusion treatment for education-related benefits that cannot qualify as gifts but are not compensation for services. According to the Regulations, "a scholarship is an amount paid or allowed to, or for the benefit of, an individual to aid such individual in the pursuit of study or research."[20] The recipient must be a candidate for a degree at an educational institution.[21]

The Big Picture

Return to the facts of *The Big Picture* on p. 10-1. State University waives tuition for all graduate teaching assistants. The tuition waived is intended as compensation for services and is therefore included in the graduate assistants' gross income. Therefore, the $6,000 Donna received in the form of a tuition waiver each semester is compensation for her services. The $400 she received each month also is compensation for services. The fact that she used the funds for educational expenses does not change the tax treatment of the compensation.

EXAMPLE 5

---

[17]Reg. § 1.117–2(a). See *C. P. Bhalla*, 35 T.C. 13 (1960), for a discussion of the distinction between a scholarship and compensation. See also *Bingler v. Johnson*, 69–1 USTC ¶9348, 23 AFTR 2d 1212, 89 S.Ct. 1439 (USSC, 1969). For potential exclusion treatment, see the discussion of qualified tuition reductions in Chapter 11.

[18]Rev.Rul. 77–263, 1977–2 C.B. 47.
[19]§ 117(d).
[20]Prop.Reg. § 117–6(c)(3)(i).
[21]§ 117(a).

Terry enters a contest sponsored by a local newspaper. Each contestant is required to submit an essay on local environmental issues. The prize is one year's tuition at State University. Terry wins the contest. The newspaper has a legal obligation to Terry (as the contest winner). Thus, the benefit is not a gift. However, because the tuition payment aids Terry in pursuing her studies and is not compensation for services, the payment is a scholarship.

A scholarship recipient may exclude from gross income the amount used for tuition and related expenses (fees, books, supplies, and equipment required for courses), provided the conditions of the grant do not require that the funds be used for other purposes.[22]

Kelly receives a scholarship of $9,500 from State University to be used to pursue a bachelor's degree. She spends $4,000 on tuition, $3,000 on books and supplies, and $2,500 for room and board. Kelly may exclude $7,000 ($4,000 + $3,000) from gross income. The $2,500 spent for room and board is includible in Kelly's gross income.

Timing Issues

Frequently, the scholarship recipient is a cash basis taxpayer who receives the money in one tax year but pays the educational expenses in a subsequent year. The amount eligible for exclusion may not be known at the time the money is received. In that case, the transaction is held open until the educational expenses are paid.[23]

In August 2015, Sanjay received $10,000 as a scholarship for the academic year 2015–2016. Sanjay's expenditures for tuition, books, and supplies were as follows:

August–December 2015	$3,000
January–May 2016	4,500
	$7,500

Sanjay's gross income for 2016 includes $2,500 ($10,000 − $7,500) that is not excludible as a scholarship. None of the scholarship is included in his gross income in 2015.

Disguised Compensation

Some employers make scholarships available solely to the children of key employees. The tax objective of these plans is to provide a nontaxable fringe benefit to the executives by making the payment to the child in the form of an excludible scholarship. However, the IRS has ruled that the payments are generally includible by the parent-employee as compensation for services.[24]

10-3c Damages

A person who suffers harm caused by another is often entitled to **compensatory damages**. The tax consequences of the receipt of damages depend on the type of harm the taxpayer has experienced. The taxpayer may seek recovery for (1) a loss of income, (2) expenses incurred, (3) property destroyed, or (4) personal injury.

Generally, reimbursement for a loss of income is taxed in the same manner as the income replaced (see the exception under Personal Injury below). Damages that are a recovery of expenses previously deducted by the taxpayer are generally taxable under the tax benefit rule (refer to Chapter 4).

---

[22]§ 117(b).

[23]Prop.Reg. § 1.117–6(b)(2).

[24]Rev.Rul. 75–448, 1975–2 C.B. 55 and *Richard T. Armantrout*, 67 T.C. 996 (1977).

A payment for damaged or destroyed property is treated as an amount received in a sale or exchange of the property. Thus, the taxpayer has a realized gain if the damages payments received exceed the property's basis. Damages for personal injuries receive special treatment under the Code.

Personal Injury

The legal theory of personal injury damages is that the amount received is intended "to make the plaintiff (the injured party) whole as before the injury."[25] It follows that if the damages payments received were subject to tax, the after-tax amount received would be less than the actual damages incurred and the injured party would not be "whole as before the injury." With regard to personal injury damages, a distinction is made between compensatory damages and punitive damages .

Compensatory damages are intended to compensate the taxpayer for the damages incurred. Only those compensatory damages received on account of *physical personal injury or sickness* can be excluded from gross income.[26] Such exclusion treatment includes amounts received for loss of income associated with the physical personal injury or physical sickness. Compensatory damages awarded on account of emotional distress are not received on account of physical injury or sickness and thus cannot be excluded from gross income (except to the extent of any amount received for medical care). Likewise, any amounts received for age discrimination or injury to one's reputation cannot be excluded.

Punitive damages are amounts the party that caused the harm must pay to the victim as punishment for outrageous conduct. Punitive damages are not intended to compensate the victim, but rather to punish the party that caused the harm. Thus, it follows that amounts received as punitive damages may actually place the victim in a better economic position than before the harm was experienced. Thus, punitive damages are included in gross income.

These rules are set forth in Concept Summary 10.1.

 ## Concept Summary 10.1

Taxation of Damages

Type of Claim	Taxation of Award or Settlement
Breach of contract (generally loss of income)	Taxable.
Property damages	Recovery of cost; gain to the extent of the excess over basis. A loss is deductible for business property and investment property to the extent of basis over the amount realized. A loss may be deductible for personal-use property (see discussion of casualty losses in Chapter 6).
Personal injury	
Physical	All compensatory amounts are excluded unless previously deducted (e.g., medical expenses). Amounts received as punitive damages are included in gross income.
Nonphysical	Compensatory damages and punitive damages are included in gross income.

The Big Picture

Return to the facts of *The Big Picture* on p. 10-1. The damages Donna received were awarded as a result of a physical personal injury. Therefore, all of the compensatory damages can be excluded. Note that even the compensation for the loss of income of $10,000 can be excluded. The punitive damages Donna received, however, must be included in her gross income.

EXAMPLE
9

---

[25]*C. A. Hawkins*, 6 B.T.A. 1023 (1928).   [26]§ 104(a)(2).

10-3d **Workers' Compensation**

State workers' compensation laws require the employer to pay fixed amounts for specific job-related injuries. The state laws were enacted so that the employee will not have to go through the ordeal of a lawsuit (and possibly not collect damages because of some defense available to the employer) to recover the damages. Although the payments are intended, in part, to compensate for a loss of future income, Congress has specifically exempted workers' compensation benefits from inclusion in gross income.[27]

10-3e **Accident and Health Insurance Benefits**

The income tax treatment of accident and health insurance benefits depends on whether the policy providing the benefits was purchased by the taxpayer or the taxpayer's employer. Benefits collected under an accident and health insurance policy purchased by the taxpayer are excludible even though the payments are a substitute for income.[28]

Bonnie purchases a medical and disability insurance policy. The insurance company pays Bonnie $1,000 per week to replace wages she loses while in the hospital. Although the payments serve as a substitute for income, the amounts received are tax-exempt benefits collected under Bonnie's insurance policy.

A different set of rules applies if the accident and health insurance protection was purchased by the individual's employer, as discussed in Chapter 11.

10-3f **Educational Savings Bonds**

The cost of a college education has risen dramatically during the past several decades. According to U.S. Department of Education estimates, the cost of attending a publicly supported university for four years now commonly exceeds $60,000. For a private university, the cost often exceeds $200,000. Consequently, Congress has attempted to assist low- to middle-income parents in saving for their children's college education.

One of the ways that Congress assists such families is through an interest income exclusion on educational savings bonds.[29] The interest on U.S. government Series EE savings bonds may be excluded from gross income if the bond proceeds are used to pay qualified higher education expenses.

Qualified higher education expenses consist of tuition and fees paid to an eligible educational institution for the taxpayer, spouse, or dependent. If the redemption proceeds (both principal and interest) exceed the qualified higher education expenses, only a pro rata portion of the interest will qualify for exclusion treatment.

Tracy's redemption proceeds from qualified savings bonds during the taxable year are $6,000 (principal of $4,000 and interest of $2,000). Tracy's qualified higher education expenses are $5,000. Because the redemption proceeds exceed the qualified higher education expenses, only $1,667 [($5,000/$6,000) × $2,000] of the interest is excludible.

The exclusion is limited by the application of the wherewithal to pay concept. That is, once the *modified AGI (MAGI)* exceeds a threshold amount, the phaseout of the exclusion begins. The threshold amounts are adjusted for inflation each year. For 2015, the phaseout begins at $77,200 ($115,750 on a joint return).[30] The phaseout is completed when MAGI exceeds the threshold amount by more than $15,000 ($30,000 on a joint return). The otherwise excludible interest is reduced by the amount calculated as follows:

$$\frac{\text{MAGI} - \$77,200}{\$15,000} \times \begin{array}{c}\text{Excludible interest} \\ \text{before phaseout}\end{array} = \begin{array}{c}\text{Reduction in} \\ \text{excludible interest}\end{array}$$

---

[27]§ 104(a)(1).

[28]§ 104(a)(3).

[29]§ 135.

[30]The indexed amounts for 2014 were $76,000 and $113,950.

On a joint return, $115,750 is substituted for $77,200 (in 2015), and $30,000 is substituted for $15,000.

Assume the same facts as in Example 11, except that Tracy's MAGI for 2015 is $80,000. Tracy is single. The phaseout results in Tracy's interest exclusion being reduced by $311 {[($80,000 − $77,200)/$15,000] × $1,667}. Therefore, Tracy's exclusion is $1,356 ($1,667 − $311).

10-4 ITEMIZED DEDUCTIONS

Determine an individual's allowable itemized deductions.

Taxpayers are allowed to deduct *from* AGI specified expenditures as itemized deductions. Itemized deductions, which are reported on Schedule A, can be classified as follows:

- Expenses that are purely *personal* in nature.
- Expenses incurred by *employees* in connection with their employment activities.
- Expenses related to (1) the *production or collection of income* and (2) the *management of property* held for the production of income.[31]

Expenses in the third category, sometimes referred to as *nonbusiness expenses*, differ from trade or business expenses (discussed previously). Trade or business expenses, which are deductions *for* AGI, must be incurred in connection with a trade or business. Nonbusiness expenses, on the other hand, are expenses incurred in connection with an income-producing activity that does not qualify as a trade or business. If the nonbusiness expense is incurred in connection with rent or royalty property, it is classified as a deduction *for* AGI. Otherwise, it is classified as a deduction *from* AGI. Itemized deductions include, but are not limited to, the expenses listed in Exhibit 10.1.

EXHIBIT 10.1	Partial List of Itemized Deductions

Personal Expenditures

Medical expenses in excess of 10% (7.5% if at least age 65) of AGI

State and local income taxes or sales taxes

Real estate taxes

Personal property taxes

Interest on home mortgage

Charitable contributions (limited to a maximum of 50% of AGI)

Casualty and theft losses (in excess of 10% of AGI)

Tax return preparation fee (in excess of 2% of AGI)

Expenditures Related to Employment (in Excess of 2% of AGI)

Union dues

Professional dues and subscriptions

Certain educational expenses

Unreimbursed employee business expenses

Expenditures Related to Income-Producing Activities

Investment interest (to the extent of net investment income)

Investment counsel fees (in excess of 2% of AGI)

Other investment expenses (in excess of 2% of AGI)

---

[31]§ 212.

The election to itemize is appropriate when total itemized deductions exceed the standard deduction based on the taxpayer's filing status (see Chapter 9). The more important itemized deductions are discussed next.

10-4a Medical Expenses

Medical expenses paid for the care of the taxpayer, spouse, and dependents are allowed as an itemized deduction to the extent the expenses are not reimbursed. The medical expense deduction is limited to the amount by which such expenses exceed a threshold percentage of the taxpayer's AGI. Under current law, the threshold percentage is 10 percent for most taxpayers. For taxpayers age 65 and older, however, the threshold is 7.5 percent of AGI until 2017, when it increases to 10 percent.[32]

The Big Picture

EXAMPLE 13

Return to the facts of *The Big Picture* on p. 10-1. In addition to the medical expenses incurred associated with Donna's accident that were later reimbursed by the delivery company's insurance company, the Steeles had other qualifying medical expenses. Assuming that their AGI for the year is $200,000, they will need to itemize their deductions and have more than $20,000 ($200,000 × 10%) in unreimbursed medical expenses to receive a tax benefit from those expenses. Thus, the deductible amount would be whatever qualifying medical expenses were incurred that exceeded the $20,000 threshold.

Medical Expenses Defined

The term *medical care* includes expenditures incurred for the "diagnosis, cure, mitigation, treatment, or prevention of disease, or for the purpose of affecting any structure or function of the body."[33] Medical expense also includes premiums paid for health care insurance, prescribed drugs and insulin, and lodging while away from home for the purpose of obtaining medical care. Examples of deductible and nondeductible medical expenses appear in Exhibit 10.2.

EXHIBIT 10.2	Examples of Deductible and Nondeductible Medical Expenses Paid by Taxpayer

Deductible	Nondeductible
Medical (including dental, mental, and hospital) care	Funeral, burial, or cremation expenses
Prescription drugs and insulin	Nonprescription drugs (except insulin)
Special equipment	Bottled water
Wheelchairs	Diaper service, maternity clothes
Crutches	Programs for the general improvement of health
Artificial limbs	Weight reduction
Eyeglasses (including contact lenses)	Health spas
Hearing aids	Social activities (e.g., dancing and swimming lessons)
Transportation for medical care	Unnecessary cosmetic surgery
Medical and hospital insurance premiums	
Long-term care insurance premiums (subject to limitations)	
Cost of alcohol and drug rehabilitation	
Certain costs to stop smoking	
Weight reduction programs related to obesity	

[32]Prior to 2013, the percentage threshold for regular income tax purposes was 7.5 percent of AGI for all taxpayers.

[33]§ 213(d).

Cosmetic Surgery

Amounts paid for unnecessary cosmetic surgery are not deductible medical expenses. However, if cosmetic surgery is deemed necessary, it is deductible as a medical expense. Cosmetic surgery is necessary when it improves the effects of (1) a deformity arising from a congenital abnormality, (2) a personal injury, or (3) a disfiguring disease.

Nursing Home Care

The cost of care in a nursing home or home for the aged, including meals and lodging, can be included in deductible medical expenses if the primary reason for being in the home is to get medical care. If the primary reason for being there is personal, any costs for medical or nursing care can be included in deductible medical expenses, but the cost of meals and lodging must be excluded.

Capital Expenditures

When capital expenditures are incurred for medical purposes, they must be deemed medically necessary by a physician, the facility must be used primarily by the patient alone, and the expense must be reasonable. Examples of such expenditures include dust elimination systems,[34] elevators,[35] and vans specially designed for wheelchair-bound taxpayers. Other examples of expenditures that may qualify are swimming pools if the taxpayer does not have access to a neighborhood pool and air conditioners if they do not become permanent improvements (e.g., window units).[36]

Both a capital expenditure for a permanent improvement and expenditures made for the operation or maintenance of the improvement may qualify as medical expenses. The allowable cost of such qualified medical expenditures is deductible in the year incurred. Although depreciation is required for most other capital expenditures, it is not required for those qualifying for medical purposes.

Medical Expenses for Spouse and Dependents

In computing the medical expense deduction, a taxpayer may include medical expenses for a spouse and for a person who was a dependent at the time the expenses were paid or incurred. Of the requirements that normally apply in determining dependency status, neither the gross income nor the joint return test applies in determining dependency status for medical expense deduction purposes.

Transportation and Lodging

Payments for transportation to and from a hospital or other medical facility for medical care are deductible as medical expenses (subject to the AGI 10% or 7.5% floor). These costs include bus, taxi, train, or plane fare; charges for ambulance service; and out-of-pocket expenses for the use of an automobile. A mileage allowance of 23 cents per mile for 2015 may be used instead of actual out-of-pocket automobile expenses.[37] Whether the taxpayer chooses to claim out-of-pocket automobile expenses or the 23 cents per mile automatic mileage option, related parking fees and tolls can also be deducted. Also included are transportation expenditures for someone such as a parent or nurse who must accompany the patient. The cost of meals while en route to obtain medical care is not deductible.

In-depth coverage can be found on this book's companion website: www.cengagebrain.com   **4** DIGGING DEEPER

---

[34]Ltr.Rul. 7948029.

[35]*Riach v. Frank*, 62–1 USTC ¶9419, 9 AFTR 2d 1263, 302 F.2d 374 (CA–9, 1962).

[36]Reg. § 1.213–1(e)(1)(iii).

[37]This amount is adjusted periodically. The amount was 23.5 cents per mile for 2014.

TAX IN THE NEWS   **Medical Expense Deductions Are Now Harder to Come By**

For taxpayers under age 65, being in a position to claim a medical expense deduction is more challenging than ever because of a recent increase in the AGI threshold that limits a medical expense's deductibility. Currently, the threshold is 10 percent of AGI for most taxpayers, an increase from 7.5 percent under prior law. For example, if a taxpayer's AGI is $100,000, only those medical expenses in excess of $10,000 are deductible ($100,000 × 10%—an increase of $2,500 from the prior threshold).

This means that to protect a medical expense deduction, taxpayers must have a better grasp on what qualifies as a medical expense and do a better job of documenting these costs. IRS Publication 502, *Medical and Dental Expenses*, includes a long list of qualifying expenses as well as expenses that do not qualify.

For example, the travel costs to see a doctor or dentist count, as well as fees paid to a chiropractor or psychologist for medical care. Contact lenses, pregnancy test kits, and even doctor-prescribed weight loss programs may qualify. However, the law is not liberal enough to allow for the deductibility of health club dues or for the purchase of substances that are illegal under Federal law, such as medical marijuana.

Health Savings Accounts

Qualifying individuals may make deductible contributions to a **Health Savings Account (HSA)** . An HSA is a qualified trust or custodial account administered by a qualified HSA trustee, which can be a bank, an insurance company, or another IRS-approved trustee.[38] A taxpayer can use an HSA in conjunction with a high-deductible medical insurance policy to help reduce the overall cost of medical coverage. The high-deductible policy provides coverage for extraordinary medical expenses (in excess of the deductible), and expenses not covered by the policy can be paid with funds withdrawn tax-free from the HSA.

EXAMPLE 14

Sanchez, who is married and has three dependent children, carries a high-deductible medical insurance policy with a deductible of $4,400. He establishes an HSA and contributes the maximum allowable amount to the HSA in 2015. During 2015, the Sanchez family incurs medical expenses of $7,000. The high-deductible policy covers $2,600 of the expenses ($7,000 expenses − $4,400 deductible). Sanchez may withdraw $4,400 from the HSA to pay the medical expenses not covered by the high-deductible policy.

High-Deductible Plans   High-deductible policies are less expensive than low-deductible policies, so taxpayers with low medical costs can benefit from the lower premiums and use funds from the HSA to pay costs not covered by the high-deductible policy. A plan must meet two requirements to qualify as a high-deductible plan.[39]

1. The annual deductible in 2015 is not less than $1,300 for self-only coverage ($2,600 for family coverage).
2. The annual limit in 2015 on total out-of-pocket costs (excluding the premiums) under the plan does not exceed $6,450 for self-only coverage ($12,900 for family coverage).

Tax Treatment of HSA Contributions and Distributions   To establish an HSA, a taxpayer contributes funds to a tax-exempt trust.[40] As illustrated in the preceding example, funds can be withdrawn from an HSA to pay medical expenses that are not covered by the high-deductible policy. The following general tax rules apply to HSAs:

1. Contributions made by the taxpayer to an HSA are deductible from gross income to arrive at AGI (deduction *for* AGI). Thus, the taxpayer does not need to itemize to take the deduction.

---

[38]§ 223.
[39]§ 223(c)(2).

[40]§ 223(d).

2. Earnings on HSAs are not subject to taxation unless distributed, in which case taxability depends on the way the funds are used.[41]

    • Distributions from HSAs are excluded from gross income if they are used to pay for medical expenses not covered by the high-deductible policy.

    • Distributions that are not used to pay for medical expenses are included in gross income and are subject to an additional 20 percent penalty if made before age 65, death, or disability. Such distributions made by reason of death or disability and distributions made after the HSA beneficiary becomes eligible for Medicare are taxed but not penalized.

HSAs have at least two other attractive features. First, an HSA is portable. Taxpayers who switch jobs can take their HSAs with them. Second, anyone under age 65 who has a high-deductible plan and is not covered by another policy that is not a high-deductible plan can establish an HSA.

Deductible Amount The annual deduction for contributions to an HSA is limited to the sum of the monthly limitations. The monthly limitation is calculated for each month the individual is an eligible individual. The monthly deduction is not allowed after the individual becomes eligible for Medicare coverage.

The amount of the monthly limitation for an individual who has self-only coverage in 2015 is one-twelfth of $3,350, while the monthly limitation for an individual who has family coverage in 2015 is one-twelfth of $6,650. These amounts are subject to annual cost-of-living adjustments.[42] An eligible taxpayer who has attained the age of 55 by the end of the tax year may make an additional annual contribution in 2015 of up to $1,000.

Determining the Maximum HSA Contribution Deduction

Liu (age 45), who is married and self-employed, carries a high-deductible medical insurance policy with family coverage and an annual deductible of $4,000. In addition, he has established an HSA. Liu's maximum annual contribution to the HSA in 2015 is $6,650.

EXAMPLE
15

During 2015, Adam, who is self-employed, made 12 monthly payments of $1,200 for an HSA contract that provides medical insurance coverage with a $3,600 deductible. The plan covers Adam, his wife, and their two children. Of the $1,200 monthly fee, $675 was for the high-deductible policy, and $525 was deposited into an HSA. The monthly deductible contribution to the HSA is calculated as follows:

EXAMPLE
16

Maximum annual deduction for family coverage	$6,650.00
Monthly limitation (1/12 of $6,650)	554.17

Because Adam is *self-employed*, he can deduct $8,100 of the amount paid for the high-deductible policy ($675 per month × 12 months) as a deduction *for* AGI (refer to Chapter 11). In addition, he can deduct the $6,300 ($525 × 12) paid to the HSA as a deduction *for* AGI. Note that the $6,300 HSA deduction does not exceed the $6,650 ceiling.

10-4b **Taxes**

A deduction is allowed for certain state and local taxes paid or accrued by a taxpayer.[43] The deduction was created to relieve the burden of multiple taxation upon the same source of revenue.

Deductible taxes must be distinguished from nondeductible fees. Fees for special privileges or services are not deductible as itemized deductions if personal in nature.

---

[41]§ 223(f).

[42]§ 223(b)(2). The annual limits were $3,300 and $6,550 in 2014.

[43]Most deductible taxes are listed in § 164, while the nondeductible items are included in § 275.

Examples include fees for dog licenses, automobile inspections, automobile titles and registration, hunting and fishing licenses, bridge and highway tolls, drivers' licenses, parking meter deposits, and postage. These items, however, could be deductible if incurred as a business expense or for the production of income (refer to Chapter 5). Deductible and nondeductible taxes for purposes of computing itemized deductions are summarized in Exhibit 10.3.

Personal Property Taxes

Deductible personal property taxes must be *ad valorem* (assessed in relation to the value of the property). Therefore, a motor vehicle tax based on weight, model, year, or horsepower is not an ad valorem tax. In contrast, a motor vehicle tax based on the value of the car is deductible.

The Big Picture

EXAMPLE 17

Return to the facts of *The Big Picture* on p. 10-1. In Donna and David Steele's state, assume that the government imposes a motor vehicle registration tax equal to 2% of the value of the vehicle plus 40 cents per hundredweight. The Steeles own a car having a value of $20,000 and weighing 3,000 pounds. They pay an annual registration tax of $412. Of this amount, $400 (2% × $20,000 of value) is deductible as a personal property tax if they itemize their deductions. The remaining $12, based on the weight of the car, is not deductible.

Real Estate Taxes

Real estate taxes of individuals are generally deductible. Taxes on personal-use property and investment property are deductible as itemized deductions. Taxes on business property are deductible as business expenses. Real property taxes on property that is sold during the year must be allocated between the buyer and the seller (refer to Chapter 5).

State and Local Income Taxes and Sales Taxes

The position of the IRS is that state and local *income* taxes imposed upon an individual are deductible only as itemized deductions, even if the taxpayer's sole source of income is from a business, rents, or royalties.

Cash basis taxpayers are entitled to deduct state income taxes withheld by the employer in the year the taxes are withheld. In addition, estimated state income tax payments are deductible in the year the payment is made by cash basis taxpayers even if the payments relate to a prior or subsequent year.[44] If the taxpayer overpays state

EXHIBIT 10.3	**Deductible and Nondeductible Taxes**

Deductible	Nondeductible
State, local, and foreign real property taxes	Federal income taxes
State and local personal property taxes	FICA taxes imposed on employees
State and local income taxes *or* sales/use taxes*	Employer FICA taxes paid on domestic household workers
Foreign income taxes	Estate, inheritance, and gift taxes
	Federal, state, and local excise taxes (e.g., gasoline, tobacco, and spirits)
	Taxes on real property to the extent such taxes are to be apportioned and treated as imposed on another taxpayer
	Special assessments for streets, sidewalks, curbing, and other similar improvements

*The sales/use tax alternative is available through 2014. Many tax professionals expect Congress to extend this provision.

[44]Rev.Rul. 71–190, 1971–1 C.B. 70. See also Rev.Rul. 82–208, 1982–2 C.B. 58, where a deduction is not allowed when the taxpayer cannot, in good faith, reasonably determine that there is additional state income tax liability.

income taxes because of excessive withholdings or estimated tax payments, the refund received is included in gross income of the following year to the extent the deduction reduced the taxable income in the prior year.

EXAMPLE

18

Leona, a cash basis, unmarried taxpayer, had $800 of state income tax withheld during 2015. Also in 2015, Leona paid $100 that was due when she filed her 2014 state income tax return in 2015 and made estimated payments of $300 toward her 2015 state income tax liability. When Leona files her 2015 Federal income tax return in April 2016, she elects to itemize deductions, which amount to $7,500, including the $1,200 of state income tax payments and withholdings. The itemized deductions reduce her taxable income.

As a result of overpaying her 2015 state income tax, Leona receives a refund of $200 early in 2016. She will include this amount in her 2016 gross income in computing her Federal income tax. It does not matter whether Leona received a check from the state for $200 or applied the $200 toward her 2016 state income tax.

Individuals can elect to deduct either their state and local income taxes *or* their sales/use taxes paid as an itemized deduction on Schedule A of Form 1040. The annual election can reflect actual sales/use tax payments *or* an amount from an IRS table. The amount from the table may be increased by sales tax paid on the purchase of motor vehicles, boats, and other specified items. Most likely, the sales tax deduction will be elected by those living in states with no individual income tax. At present, this deduction alternative is available only through 2014. However, many tax professionals believe that Congress will extend this provision.

TAX PLANNING STRATEGIES   **Timing the Payment of Deductible Taxes**

FRAMEWORK FOCUS: DEDUCTIONS

Strategy: Accelerate Recognition of Deductions to Achieve Tax Deferral.

It is sometimes possible to defer or accelerate the payment of certain deductible taxes, such as state income tax, real property tax, and personal property tax. For instance, the final installment of estimated state income tax is generally due after the end of a given tax year. However, accelerating the payment of the final installment could result in larger itemized deductions for the current year.

10-4c   Interest

For Federal income tax purposes, interest must be divided into five categories: business interest, personal interest, interest on qualified student loans, investment interest, and qualified residence interest. Business interest is fully deductible as an ordinary and necessary expense. Currently, personal (consumer) interest is not deductible. This includes credit card interest; interest on car loans; and other types of interest. However, interest on qualified student loans, investment interest, and qualified residence (home mortgage) interest are deductible, subject to the limits discussed below.

Interest on Qualified Student Loans

Taxpayers who pay interest on a qualified student loan may be able to deduct the interest as a deduction *for* AGI. The deduction is allowable only to the extent the proceeds of the loan are used to pay qualified education expenses. The maximum annual deduction is $2,500. However, in 2015, the deduction is phased out for taxpayers with modified AGI (MAGI) between $65,000 and $80,000 ($130,000 and $160,000 on joint returns). The deduction is not available for taxpayers who are claimed as dependents or for married taxpayers filing separately.[45]

In 2015, Curt and Rita, who are married and file a joint return, paid $3,000 of interest on a qualified student loan. Their MAGI was $137,500. Their maximum potential deduction for qualified student loan interest is $2,500, but it must be reduced by $625 as a result of the phaseout rules.

$$\text{\$2,500 interest} \times (\text{\$137,500 MAGI} - \text{\$130,000 phaseout floor})/$$
$$\text{\$30,000 phaseout range} = \text{\$625 reduction}$$

Curt and Rita are allowed a student loan interest deduction of $1,875 ($2,500 maximum deduction − $625 reduction = $1,875 deduction *for* AGI).

Investment Interest

Years ago, well-to-do taxpayers used the interest deduction in the tax law to create wealth. By borrowing to purchase investments that would appreciate in the future, the interest on the debt was claimed as an ordinary deduction when paid. Later, when the asset was sold at a gain, only a capital gains tax was due on the appreciation. Thus, today's interest deduction could lead to tomorrow's capital gain.

In response, Congress has limited the deductibility of **investment interest**, which is interest paid on debt borrowed for the purpose of purchasing or continuing to hold investment property. The deduction for investment interest allowed during the tax year is limited to the lesser of the investment interest paid or net investment income.[46]

Net investment income, which serves as the ceiling on the deductibility of investment interest, is the excess of investment income over investment expenses. Investment income includes gross income from interest, annuities, and royalties not derived in the ordinary course of a trade or business.

Investment expenses are those deductible expenses directly connected with the production of investment income, such as brokerage and investment counsel fees. Investment expenses do not include interest expense.

After net investment income is determined, the allowable deductible investment interest expense is calculated.

Ethan's financial records for the year reflect the following:

Interest income from bank savings account	$10,000
Taxable annuity receipts	5,500
Investment counsel fee	1,100
Safe deposit box rental (to hold annuity documents)	200
Investment interest expense	17,000

Ethan's investment income amounts to $15,500 ($10,000 + $5,500), and investment expenses total $1,300 ($1,100 + $200). Therefore, his net investment income is $14,200 ($15,500 − $1,300). Consequently, the investment interest deduction is limited to $14,200, the lesser of investment interest paid or net investment income.

The amount of investment interest disallowed is carried over to future years. No limit is placed on the length of the carryover period.

DIGGING DEEPER 5   In-depth coverage can be found on this book's companion website: www.cengagebrain.com

---

[45]§ 221. See § 221(b)(2)(C) for the definition of MAGI. For 2014, the MAGI threshold amounts also were $65,000 and $80,000 ($130,000 and $160,000 on joint returns).

[46]§ 163(d)(1).

Qualified Residence Interest

Qualified residence interest is interest paid or accrued during the taxable year on indebtedness (subject to limitations) secured by any property that is a qualified residence of the taxpayer. Qualified residence interest falls into two categories: (1) interest on acquisition indebtedness and (2) interest on home equity loans . Before each of these categories is discussed, however, the term *qualified residence* must be defined.

A qualified residence includes the taxpayer's principal residence and one other residence of the taxpayer or spouse. The principal residence is one that meets the requirement for nonrecognition of gain upon sale under § 121 (see Chapter 7). The one other residence, or second residence, refers to one that is used as a residence if not rented or, if rented, meets the requirements for a personal residence under the complex rental of vacation home rules of § 280A. A taxpayer who has more than one second residence can make the selection each year as to which one is the qualified second residence. A residence includes, in addition to a house in the ordinary sense, cooperative apartments, condominiums, and mobile homes and boats that have living quarters (sleeping accommodations and toilet and cooking facilities).

Although in most cases interest paid on a home mortgage is fully deductible, there are limitations.[47] Interest paid or accrued during the tax year on aggregate acquisition indebtedness of $1 million or less ($500,000 for married persons filing separate returns) is deductible as qualified residence interest. *Acquisition indebtedness* refers to amounts incurred in acquiring, constructing, or substantially improving a qualified residence of the taxpayer.

Qualified residence interest also includes interest on home equity loans. These loans utilize the personal residence of the taxpayer as security, typically in the form of a second mortgage. Because the funds from home equity loans can be used for personal purposes (e.g., auto purchases and medical expenses), what would otherwise have been nondeductible personal interest becomes deductible qualified residence interest. However, interest is deductible only on the portion of a home equity loan that does not exceed the lesser of:

- The fair market value of the residence, reduced by the acquisition indebtedness, or

- $100,000 ($50,000 for married persons filing separate returns).

EXAMPLE

21

Larry owns a personal residence with a fair market value of $450,000 and an outstanding first mortgage of $420,000. Therefore, his equity in his home is $30,000 ($450,000 − $420,000). Larry issues a second mortgage on the residence and in return borrows $15,000 to purchase a new family automobile. All interest on the $435,000 of first and second mortgage debt is treated as qualified residence interest.

Under current law, mortgage insurance premiums paid by the taxpayer on a qualified residence may be deducted (treated as qualified residence interest). However, the deduction begins to phase out for taxpayers with AGI in excess of $100,000 ($50,000 for married taxpayers filing separately). The deduction is fully phased out when AGI exceeds $109,000 ($54,500 for married taxpayers filing separately).[48]

Interest Paid for Services Mortgage loan companies commonly charge a fee, often called a loan origination fee, for finding, placing, or processing a mortgage loan. Loan origination fees are typically nondeductible amounts included in the basis of the acquired property. Other fees, sometimes called points and expressed as a percentage of the loan amount, are paid to reduce the interest rate charged over the term of the loan. Essentially, the payment of points is a prepayment of interest and is considered

---

[47]§ 163(h)(3).

[48]§§ 163(h)(3)(E)(i) and (ii). This provision expired at the end of 2014. However, many tax professionals expect that Congress will extend this provision.

compensation to a lender solely for the use or forbearance of money. To be deductible, points must be in the nature of interest and cannot be a form of service charge or payment for specific services.[49]

Points must be capitalized and are amortized and deductible ratably over the life of the loan. A special exception, however, permits the purchaser of a principal residence to deduct qualifying points in the year of payment.[50] The exception also covers points paid to obtain funds for home improvements.

Points paid to refinance an existing home mortgage cannot be immediately deducted, but must be capitalized and amortized as an interest deduction over the life of the new loan.[51]

EXAMPLE 22

Sandra purchased her residence many years ago, obtaining a 30-year mortgage at an annual interest rate of 8%. In the current year, Sandra refinances the mortgage to reduce the interest rate to 4%. To obtain the refinancing, she has to pay points of $2,600. Therefore, the $2,600, which is considered prepayment of interest, must be capitalized and amortized over the life of the mortgage.

Prepayment Penalty

When a mortgage or loan is paid off in full in a lump sum before its term, the lending institution may require an additional payment of a certain percentage applied to the unpaid amount at the time of prepayment. This is known as a prepayment penalty and is considered to be interest (e.g., personal, investment, qualified residence) in the year paid. The general rules for deductibility of interest also apply to prepayment penalties.

Interest Paid to Related Parties

Nothing prevents the deduction of interest paid to a related party as long as the payment actually took place and the interest meets the requirements for deductibility. However, a special rule applies for related taxpayers when the debtor uses the accrual basis and the related creditor is on the cash basis. If this rule is applicable, interest that has been accrued but not paid at the end of the debtor's tax year is not deductible until payment is made and the income is reportable by the cash basis recipient.

Tax-Exempt Securities

The tax law provides that no deduction is allowed for interest on debt incurred to purchase or carry tax-exempt securities.[52] A major problem for the courts has been to determine what is meant by the words *to purchase or carry*. Refer to Chapter 5 for a detailed discussion of these issues.

Prepaid Interest

Accrual method reporting is imposed on cash basis taxpayers for interest prepayments that extend beyond the end of the taxable year.[53] Such payments must be allocated to the tax years to which the interest payments relate. These provisions are intended to prevent cash basis taxpayers from *manufacturing* tax deductions before the end of the year by prepaying interest.

Classification of Interest Expense

Whether interest is deductible *for* AGI or as an itemized deduction (*from* AGI) depends on whether the indebtedness has a business, investment, or personal purpose. If the indebtedness is incurred in relation to a business (other than performing services as an employee) or for the production of rent or royalty income, the interest is deductible *for* AGI. If the indebtedness is incurred for personal use, such as qualified residence interest, any deduction allowed is taken *from* AGI and is reported on Schedule A of Form 1040 if

---

[49]Rev.Rul. 69–188, 1969–1 C.B. 54.
[50]§ 461(g)(2).
[51]Rev.Rul. 87–22, 1987–1 C.B. 146.

[52]§ 265(a)(2).
[53]§ 461(g)(1).

the taxpayer elects to itemize. Note, however, that interest on a student loan is deductible *for* AGI. If the taxpayer is an employee who incurs debt in relation to his or her employment, the interest is considered to be personal, or consumer, interest and is not deductible. Business expenses appear on Schedule C of Form 1040, and expenses related to rents or royalties are reported on Schedule E. Concept Summary 10.2 reviews the tax treatment given to the various types of interest expense incurred by individual taxpayers.

Concept Summary 10.2

Deductibility of Personal, Education, Investment, and Mortgage Interest

Type	Deductible	Comments
Personal (consumer) interest	No	Includes any interest that is not qualified residence interest, interest on qualified student loans, investment interest, or business interest. Examples include interest on car loans and credit card debt.
Qualified student loan interest	Yes	Deduction *for* AGI; subject to limitations.
Investment interest (*not* related to rental or royalty property)	Yes	Itemized deduction; limited to net investment income for the year; disallowed interest can be carried over to future years.
Investment interest (related to rental or royalty property)	Yes	Deduction *for* AGI; limited to net investment income for the year; disallowed interest can be carried over to future years.
Qualified residence interest on acquisition indebtedness	Yes	Deductible as an itemized deduction; limited to indebtedness of $1 million.
Qualified residence interest on home equity indebtedness	Yes	Deductible as an itemized deduction; limited to indebtedness equal to lesser of $100,000 or FMV of residence minus acquisition indebtedness.

10-4d **Charitable Contributions**

As noted in Chapter 5, § 170 allows individuals to deduct contributions made to qualified domestic organizations. Contributions to qualified charitable organizations serve certain social welfare needs and thus relieve the government of the cost of providing these needed services to the community.

Criteria for a Gift

A **charitable contribution** is defined as a gift made to a qualified organization.[54] The major elements needed to qualify a contribution as a gift are a donative intent, the absence of consideration, and acceptance by the donee. Consequently, the taxpayer has the burden of establishing that the transfer was made from motives of disinterested generosity as established by the courts.[55] This test is quite subjective and has led to problems of interpretation (refer to the discussion of gifts earlier in this chapter).

Benefit Received Rule

When a donor derives a tangible benefit from a contribution, he or she cannot deduct the value of the benefit.

Ralph purchases a ticket at $100 for a special performance of the local symphony (a qualified charity). If the price of a ticket to a symphony concert is normally $35, Ralph is allowed only $65 as a charitable contribution. Even if Ralph does not attend the concert, his deduction is limited to $65.

If, however, he does *not* accept the ticket from the symphony (or returns it prior to the event), he can deduct the full $100.

EXAMPLE
23

---

[54] § 170(c).

[55] *Comm. v. Duberstein*, 60–2 USTC ¶9515, 5 AFTR 2d 1626, 80 S.Ct. 1190 (USSC, 1960).

An exception to this benefit rule provides for the deduction of an automatic percentage of the amount paid for the right to purchase athletic tickets from colleges and universities.[56] Under this exception, 80 percent of the amount paid to or for the benefit of the institution qualifies as a charitable contribution deduction.

Janet donates $1,000 to State University's athletic department. The payment guarantees that she will have preferred seating on the 50-yard line at football games. Subsequently, Janet buys four $50 game tickets. Under the exception to the benefit rule, she is allowed an $800 (80% × $1,000) charitable contribution deduction for the taxable year.

Contribution of Services

No deduction is allowed for the value of one's services contributed to a qualified charitable organization. However, unreimbursed expenses related to the services rendered may be deductible. For example, the cost of a uniform (without general utility) that is required to be worn while performing services may be deductible, as are certain out-of-pocket transportation costs incurred for the benefit of the charity. In lieu of these out-of-pocket costs for an automobile, a standard mileage rate of 14 cents per mile is allowed.[57] Deductions are permitted for transportation, reasonable expenses for lodging, and the cost of meals while away from home that are incurred in performing the donated services. The travel expenses are not deductible if the travel involves a significant element of personal pleasure, recreation, or vacation.[58]

Nondeductible Items

In addition to the benefit received rule and the restrictions placed on the contribution of services, the following items may not be deducted as charitable contributions:

- Dues, fees, or bills paid to country clubs, lodges, fraternal orders, or similar groups.
- Cost of raffle, bingo, or lottery tickets.
- Cost of tuition.
- Value of blood given to a blood bank.
- Donations to homeowners associations.
- Gifts to individuals.
- Rental value of property used by a qualified charity.

Time of Deduction

A charitable contribution generally is deducted in the year the payment is made. This rule applies to both cash and accrual basis individuals. A contribution is ordinarily deemed to have been made on the date of delivery of the property to the donee. A contribution made by check is considered delivered on the date of mailing. Thus, a check mailed on December 31, 2015, is deductible on the taxpayer's 2015 tax return. If the contribution is charged on a credit card, the date the charge is made determines the year of deduction.

Record-Keeping Requirements

No deduction is allowed for a charitable contribution made to a qualified organization unless the taxpayer gathers (and, in some cases, supplies to the IRS) the appropriate documentation and substantiation. The specific type of documentation required depends on the amount of the contribution and whether the contribution is made in

---

[56]§ 170(l).
[57]§ 170(i).

[58]§ 170(j).

cash or noncash property.[59] For example, written acknowledgment from the charity is required to deduct a single cash or property contribution of $250 or more. In addition, special rules may apply to gifts of certain types of property (e.g., used automobiles) where Congress has noted taxpayer abuse in the past. Further, for certain gifts of non-cash property, Form 8283 (Noncash Charitable Contributions) must be attached to the taxpayer's return.

The required substantiation must be obtained before the earlier of (1) the due date (including extensions) of the return for the year the contribution is claimed or (2) the date the return is filed. Failure to comply with the reporting rules may result in disallowance of the charitable contribution deduction. In addition, significant overvaluation exposes the taxpayer to stringent penalties.

Valuation Requirements

Property donated to a charity is generally valued at fair market value at the time the gift is made. The Code and Regulations give very little guidance on the measurement of the fair market value except to say, "The fair market value is the price at which the property would change hands between a willing buyer and a willing seller, neither being under any compulsion to buy or sell and both having reasonable knowledge of relevant facts."

Generally, charitable organizations do not attest to the fair market value of the donated property. Nevertheless, the taxpayer must maintain reliable written evidence as to its value.

In-depth coverage can be found on this book's companion website: www.cengagebrain.com   **6** DIGGING DEEPER

Limitations on Charitable Contribution Deduction

The potential charitable contribution deduction is the total of all donations, both money and property, that qualify for the deduction. After this determination is made, the actual amount of the charitable contribution deduction that is allowed for individuals for the tax year is limited as follows:

- If the qualifying contributions for the year total 20 percent or less of AGI, they are fully deductible.

- If the qualifying contributions are more than 20 percent of AGI, the deductible amount may be limited to 20 percent, 30 percent, or 50 percent of AGI, depending on the type of property given and the type of organization to which the donation is made.

- In any case, the maximum charitable contribution deduction may not exceed 50 percent of AGI for the tax year.

The following sections explain when the 50 percent, 30 percent, and 20 percent limitations apply.

---

[59]The specific documentation thresholds and requirements are provided in § 170(f).

To understand the complex rules for computing the amount of a charitable contribution deduction, it is necessary to understand the distinction between **capital gain property** and **ordinary income property**. These rules, which were discussed in Chapter 5, are summarized in Concept Summary 10.3.

Concept Summary 10.3

Determining the Deduction for Contributions of Property by Individuals

If the Type of Property Contributed Is:	And the Property Is Contributed to:	The Contribution Is Measured by:	But the Deduction Is Limited to:
Capital gain property	A 50% organization	Fair market value of the property	30% of AGI
Ordinary income property	A 50% organization	The basis of the property*	50% of AGI
Capital gain property (and the property is tangible personal property put to an unrelated use by the donee)	A 50% organization	The basis of the property*	50% of AGI
Capital gain property	A private nonoperating foundation that is not a 50% organization	The basis of the property*	The lesser of: 1. 20% of AGI 2. 50% of AGI minus other contributions to 50% organizations

*If the FMV of the property is less than the adjusted basis (i.e., the property has declined in value instead of appreciating), the FMV is used.

Fifty Percent Ceiling

Contributions made to public charities may not exceed 50 percent of an individual's AGI for the year. The 50 percent ceiling on contributions applies to public charities such as churches; schools; hospitals; and Federal, state, or local governmental units. The 50 percent ceiling also applies to contributions to private operating foundations and certain private nonoperating foundations.

In the remaining discussion of charitable contributions, public charities and private foundations (both operating and nonoperating) that qualify for the 50 percent ceiling will be referred to as 50 percent organizations.

Thirty Percent Ceiling

A 30 percent ceiling applies to contributions of cash and ordinary income property to private nonoperating foundations that are not 50 percent organizations. The 30 percent ceiling also applies to contributions of appreciated capital gain property to 50 percent organizations.[60]

In the event the contributions for any one tax year involve both 50 percent and 30 percent property, the allowable deduction comes first from the 50 percent property.

EXAMPLE 25

During the year, Lisa makes the following donations to her church: cash of $2,000 and unimproved land worth $30,000. Lisa had purchased the land four years ago for $22,000 and held it as an investment. Therefore, it is capital gain property. Lisa's AGI for the year is $60,000. Disregarding percentage limitations, Lisa's potential deduction is $32,000 [$2,000 (cash) + $30,000 (fair market value of land)].

continued

---

[60]Under a special election, a taxpayer may choose to permanently forgo a deduction of the appreciation on capital gain property. Referred to as the reduced deduction election, this enables the taxpayer to move from the 30% limitation to the 50% limitation. See § 170(b)(1)(C)(iii).

In applying the percentage limitations, however, the current deduction for the land is limited to $18,000 [30% (limitation applicable to capital gain property) × $60,000 (AGI)]. Thus, the total current deduction is $20,000 ($2,000 cash + $18,000 land). Note that the total deduction does not exceed $30,000, which is 50% of Lisa's AGI.

Twenty Percent Ceiling

A 20 percent ceiling applies to contributions of appreciated capital gain property to private nonoperating foundations that are not 50 percent organizations. Also recall from Chapter 5 that only the basis of the contributed property is allowed as a deduction.

In-depth coverage can be found on this book's companion website: www.cengagebrain.com	 7 DIGGING DEEPER

Contribution Carryovers

Contributions that exceed the percentage limitations for the current year can be carried over for five years.[61] In the carryover process, such contributions do not lose their identity for limitation purposes. Thus, if the contribution originally involved 30 percent property, the carryover will continue to be classified as 30 percent property in the carryover year.

Assume the same facts as in Example 25. Because only $18,000 of the $30,000 value of the land is deducted in the current year, the balance of $12,000 may be carried over to the following year. But the carryover will still be treated as capital gain property and will be subject to the 30%-of-AGI limitation.

EXAMPLE 26

In applying the percentage limitations, current charitable contributions must be claimed first before any carryovers can be considered. If carryovers involve more than one year, they are utilized in a first-in, first-out order.

10-4e Miscellaneous Itemized Deductions Subject to 2 Percent Floor

In general, no deduction is allowed for personal, living, or family expenses.[62] However, a taxpayer may incur a number of deductible expenditures related to employment. If an employee or outside salesperson incurs unreimbursed business expenses or expenses that are reimbursed under a nonaccountable plan (see Chapter 11), including travel and transportation, the expenses are deductible as **miscellaneous itemized deductions**.[63] Certain other expenses also fall into the special category of miscellaneous itemized deductions. Some are deductible only to the extent they exceed 2 percent of the taxpayer's AGI. These miscellaneous itemized deductions include the following:

- Professional dues to membership organizations.
- Cost of uniforms or other clothing that cannot be used for normal wear.
- Fees incurred for the preparation of one's tax return or fees incurred for tax litigation before the IRS or the courts.
- Job-hunting costs.
- Fee paid for a safe deposit box used to store papers and documents relating to taxable income-producing investments.
- Investment expenses that are deductible under § 212 as discussed previously in this chapter.

---

[61]§ 170(d); Reg. § 1.170A–10.
[62]§ 262.

[63]Actors and performing artists who meet certain requirements are not subject to this rule. See § 62(a)(2)(B).

- Appraisal fees to determine the amount of a casualty loss or the fair market value of donated property.
- Hobby losses up to the amount of hobby income (see Chapter 11).
- Unreimbursed employee expenses (refer to Chapter 11).

Certain employee business expenses that are reimbursed are not itemized deductions, but are deducted *for* AGI. Employee business expenses are discussed in depth in Chapter 11.

10-4f Other Miscellaneous Deductions

Certain expenses and losses do not fall into any category of itemized deductions already discussed but are nonetheless deductible. The following expenses and losses are deductible on Schedule A as Other Miscellaneous Deductions. These are not subject to the 2%-of-AGI floor.

- Gambling losses up to the amount of gambling winnings.
- Impairment-related work expenses of a handicapped person.
- Federal estate tax on income in respect of a decedent.
- Deduction for repayment of amounts under a claim of right (but only if more than $3,000; see Chapter 4).

10-4g Overall Limitation on Certain Itemized Deductions

Similar in effect to the exemption phaseout described in Chapter 9, high-income taxpayers also are subject to a limitation on the tax benefits from certain itemized deductions. In 2015, the phaseout of itemized deductions (also referred to as a *cutback adjustment*) applies to married taxpayers filing jointly whose AGI exceeds $309,900 ($258,250 for single filers).[64] Phaseouts of this type are sometimes referred to as "stealth taxes."

The limitation applies to the following frequently encountered itemized deductions:

- Taxes.
- Home mortgage interest, including points.
- Charitable contributions.
- Unreimbursed employee expenses subject to the 2%-of-AGI floor.
- All other expenses subject to the 2%-of-AGI floor.

The following are *not* subject to the limitation on itemized deductions:

- Medical expenses.
- Investment interest expense.
- Nonbusiness casualty and theft losses.
- Gambling losses.

Taxpayers subject to the limitation must reduce itemized deductions by the *lesser* of:

- 3 percent of the amount by which AGI exceeds $309,900 ($258,250 if single).
- 80 percent of itemized deductions that are affected by the limit.

The overall limitation is applied after applying all other limitations to those itemized deductions that are affected by the overall limitation. For example, other limitations apply to charitable contributions, certain meals and entertainment expenses, and certain miscellaneous itemized deductions.

---

[64]§ 68. The AGI thresholds are $284,050 for heads of household and $154,950 for married taxpayers filing separately. In 2014, the phaseouts applied to married taxpayers filing jointly whose AGI exceeded $305,050 ($254,200 for single taxpayers, $279,650 for heads of household, and $152,525 for married taxpayers filing separately).

Gavin, who is single and age 45, had AGI of $275,000 for 2015. He incurred the following expenses and losses during the year:

EXAMPLE
27

Medical expenses before 10%-of-AGI limitation	$29,500
State and local income taxes	3,200
Real estate taxes	2,800
Home mortgage interest	7,200
Charitable contributions	2,000
Casualty loss before 10% limitation (after $100 floor)	29,000
Unreimbursed employee expenses (subject to 2%-of-AGI limitation)	5,800
Gambling losses (Gavin had $3,000 of gambling income)	7,000

Gavin's itemized deductions *before* the overall limitation are computed as follows:

Medical expenses [$29,500 − (10% × $275,000)]	$ 2,000
State and local income taxes	3,200
Real estate taxes	2,800
Home mortgage interest	7,200
Charitable contributions	2,000
Casualty loss [$29,000 − (10% × $275,000)]	1,500
Unreimbursed employee expenses [$5,800 − (2% × $275,000)]	300
Gambling losses ($7,000 loss limited to $3,000 of gambling income)	3,000
Total itemized deductions before overall limitation	$22,000

Gavin's itemized deductions subject to the overall limitation are as follows:

State and local income taxes	$ 3,200
Real estate taxes	2,800
Home mortgage interest	7,200
Charitable contributions	2,000
Unreimbursed employee expenses	300
Total	$15,500

Gavin must reduce the amount by the lesser of the following:

• 3% × ($275,000 AGI − $258,250)	$ 503
• 80% of itemized deductions subject to limitation ($15,500 × .80)	12,400

Therefore, the amount of the reduction is $503, and Gavin has $21,497 of deductible itemized deductions, computed as follows:

Deductible itemized deductions subject to overall limitation ($15,500 − $503)	$14,997
Itemized deductions not subject to overall limitation:	
Medical expenses	2,000
Casualty loss	1,500
Gambling losses	3,000
Deductible itemized deductions	$21,497

TAX PLANNING STRATEGIES   **Effective Utilization of Itemized Deductions**

FRAMEWORK FOCUS: DEDUCTIONS

Strategy: Maximize Deductible Amounts.

An individual may use the standard deduction in one year and itemize deductions in another year. Therefore, it is frequently possible to obtain maximum benefit by shifting itemized deductions from one year to another. For example, if a taxpayer's itemized deductions and the standard deduction are approximately the same for each year of a two-year period, the taxpayer should use the standard deduction in one year and shift itemized deductions (to the extent permitted by law) to the other year. The individual could, for example, prepay a church pledge for a particular year or avoid paying end-of-the-year medical expenses to shift the deduction to the following year.

10-5 INDIVIDUAL TAX CREDITS

LO.3

Explain and illustrate the adoption expenses credit, child tax credit, education tax credits, credit for child and dependent care expenses, and earned income credit.

A tax credit should not be confused with an income tax deduction. Recall from the discussion of the individual income tax formula in Chapter 1 that the tax benefit received from a tax deduction depends on the taxpayer's tax rate, while a tax credit is not affected by the tax rate. Instead, a credit is a dollar-for-dollar reduction in a taxpayer's tax liability. Several commonly encountered tax credits available to individuals are discussed in this section.

10-5a Adoption Expenses Credit

Adoption expenses paid or incurred by a taxpayer may give rise to the **adoption expenses credit**.[65] The provision is intended to assist taxpayers who incur nonrecurring costs directly associated with the adoption process, such as adoption fees, attorney fees, court costs, social service review costs, and transportation costs.

In 2015, up to $13,400 of costs incurred to adopt an eligible child qualify for the credit. An eligible child is one who is:

- Under 18 years of age at the time of the adoption, or
- Physically or mentally incapable of taking care of himself or herself.

A taxpayer may claim the credit in the year qualifying expenses were paid or incurred if they were paid or incurred during or after the tax year in which the adoption was finalized. For qualifying expenses paid or incurred in a tax year prior to the year the adoption was finalized, the credit must be claimed in the tax year following the tax year during which the expenses are paid or incurred. A married couple must file a joint return to claim the credit.

In late 2014, Sam and Martha pay $4,000 in legal fees, adoption fees, and other expenses directly related to the adoption of an infant daughter, Susan. In 2015, the year in which the adoption becomes final, they pay an additional $10,000. Sam and Martha are eligible for a $13,400 credit in 2015 (for expenses of $14,000, limited by the $13,400 ceiling, paid in 2014 and 2015).

The amount of the credit that is otherwise available is subject to phaseout for taxpayers whose AGI (modified for this purpose) exceeds $201,010 in 2015, and it is phased out completely when AGI reaches $241,010. The resulting credit is calculated by reducing the allowable credit (determined without this reduction) by the amount determined using the following formula:

$$\text{Allowable credit} \times \frac{\text{AGI} - \$201,010}{\$40,000}$$

Assume the same facts as in the previous example, except that Sam and Martha's AGI is $226,010 in 2015. As a result, their available credit in 2015 is reduced from $13,400 to $5,025 {$13,400 − [$13,400 × ($25,000/$40,000)]}.

The credit is nonrefundable and is available to taxpayers only in a year in which this credit and the other nonrefundable credits do not exceed the taxpayer's tax liability. However, any unused adoption expenses credit may be carried over for up to five years, being utilized on a first-in, first-out basis.

10-5b Child Tax Credit

The **child tax credit** provision allows individual taxpayers to take a tax credit based solely on the *number* of their qualifying children. This credit is one of several "family-friendly" provisions that currently are part of our tax law. To be eligible for the credit, the child must be under age 17, must be a U.S. citizen, and must be claimed as a dependent on the taxpayer's return.

---

[65]§ 23.

Maximum Credit and Phaseouts

Under current law, the maximum credit available is $1,000 per child.[66] The available credit is phased out for higher-income taxpayers beginning when AGI reaches $110,000 for joint filers ($55,000 for married taxpayers filing separately) and $75,000 for single taxpayers. The credit is phased out by $50 for each $1,000 (or part thereof) of AGI above the threshold amounts.[67] Because the maximum credit available to taxpayers depends on the number of qualifying children, the income level at which the credit is phased out completely also depends on the number of children qualifying for the credit.[68]

EXAMPLE

30

Juanita and Alberto are married and file a joint tax return claiming their two children, ages 6 and 8, as dependents. Their AGI is $122,400. Juanita and Alberto's maximum child tax credit is $2,000 ($1,000 × 2 children). Because Juanita and Alberto's AGI is in excess of the $110,000 threshold, the maximum credit must be reduced by $50 for every $1,000 (or part thereof) above the threshold amount {$50 × [($122,400 − $110,000)/$1,000]}. Thus, the credit reduction equals $650 [$50 × 13 (rounded up from 12.4)]. Therefore, Juanita and Alberto's child tax credit is $1,350 ($2,000 − $650).

10-5c Credit for Child and Dependent Care Expenses

The credit for child and dependent care expenses mitigates the inequity felt by working taxpayers who must pay for child care services to work outside the home.[69] This credit is a specified percentage of expenses incurred to enable the taxpayer to work or to seek employment. Expenses on which the credit for child and dependent care expenses is based are subject to limitations.

Eligibility

To be eligible for the credit, an individual must have either of the following:

- A dependent under age 13.
- A dependent or spouse who is physically or mentally incapacitated and who lives with the taxpayer for more than one-half of the year.

Generally, married taxpayers must file a joint return to obtain the credit.

Eligible Employment-Related Expenses

Eligible expenses include amounts paid for household services and care of a qualifying individual that are incurred to enable the taxpayer to be employed. Child and dependent care expenses include expenses incurred in the home, such as payments for a housekeeper. Out-of-the-home expenses incurred for the care of a dependent under the age of 13 also qualify for the credit.

Out-of-the-home expenses incurred for an older dependent or spouse who is physically or mentally incapacitated qualify for the credit if that person regularly spends at least eight hours each day in the taxpayer's household. This makes the credit available to taxpayers who keep handicapped older children and elderly relatives in the home instead of institutionalizing them.

Out-of-the-home expenses incurred for services provided by a dependent care center qualify only if the center complies with all applicable laws and regulations of a state or unit of local government.

Child care payments to a relative are eligible for the credit unless the relative is a child (under age 19) of the taxpayer.

---

[66]§ 24. The maximum credit per child is scheduled to remain at $1,000 through 2017.

[67]AGI is modified for purposes of this calculation. The threshold amounts are *not* indexed for inflation. See §§ 24(a) and (b).

[68]The child tax credit generally is refundable to the extent of 15% of the taxpayer's earned income in excess of $3,000.

[69]§ 21.

Earned Income Ceiling

Qualifying employment-related expenses are limited to an individual's earned income. For married taxpayers, this limitation applies to the spouse with the lesser amount of earned income. Special rules are provided for taxpayers with nonworking spouses who are disabled or are full-time students. If a nonworking spouse is physically or mentally disabled or is a full-time student, he or she is deemed to have earned income for purposes of this limitation. The deemed amount is $250 per month if there is one qualifying individual in the household (e.g., a dependent child under age 13) or $500 per month if there are two or more qualifying individuals in the household. In the case of a student-spouse, the student's income is deemed to be earned only for the months the student is enrolled on a full-time basis at an educational institution.[70]

Calculation of the Credit

In general, the credit is equal to a percentage of unreimbursed employment-related expenses up to $3,000 for one qualifying individual and $6,000 for two or more individuals. The credit rate varies between 20 percent and 35 percent, depending on the taxpayer's AGI (see Exhibit 10.4).

EXAMPLE 31

Nancy, who has two children under age 13, worked full-time while her spouse, Ron, attended college for 10 months during the year. Nancy earned $22,000 and incurred $6,200 of child care expenses. Ron is deemed to be fully employed and to have earned $500 for each of the 10 months (or a total of $5,000).

Because Nancy and Ron report AGI of $22,000, they are allowed a credit rate of 31%. Nancy and Ron are limited to $5,000 in qualified child care expenses ($6,000 maximum expenses, limited to Ron's deemed earned income of $5,000). Therefore, they are entitled to a tax credit of $1,550 (31% × $5,000) for the year.

EXHIBIT 10.4	Child and Dependent Care Credit Computations	
Adjusted Gross Income		
Over	**But Not Over**	**Applicable Rate of Credit**
$ 0	$15,000	35%
15,000	17,000	34%
17,000	19,000	33%
19,000	21,000	32%
21,000	23,000	31%
23,000	25,000	30%
25,000	27,000	29%
27,000	29,000	28%
29,000	31,000	27%
31,000	33,000	26%
33,000	35,000	25%
35,000	37,000	24%
37,000	39,000	23%
39,000	41,000	22%
41,000	43,000	21%
43,000	No limit	20%

[70]§ 21(d).

10-5d **Education Tax Credits**

Two credits, the American Opportunity credit and the lifetime learning credit,[71] are available to help qualifying low- and middle-income individuals defray the cost of higher education. The credits are available for qualifying tuition and related expenses incurred by students pursuing undergraduate or graduate degrees or vocational training. Books and other course materials are eligible for the American Opportunity credit (but not the lifetime learning credit).[72] Room and board are ineligible for both credits.

Maximum Credit

The American Opportunity credit permits a maximum credit of $2,500 per year (100 percent of the first $2,000 of tuition expenses plus 25 percent of the next $2,000 of tuition expenses) for the *first four years* of postsecondary education. The lifetime learning credit permits a credit of 20 percent of qualifying expenses (up to $10,000 per year) incurred in a year in which the American Opportunity credit is not claimed with respect to a given student. Generally, the lifetime learning credit is used for individuals who are beyond the first four years of postsecondary education.

Eligible Individuals

Both education credits are available for qualified expenses incurred by a taxpayer, taxpayer's spouse, or taxpayer's dependent. The American Opportunity credit is available per eligible student, while the lifetime learning credit is calculated per taxpayer. To be eligible for the American Opportunity credit, a student must take at least one-half of the full-time course load for at least one academic term at a qualifying educational institution. No comparable requirement exists for the lifetime learning credit. Therefore, taxpayers who are seeking new job skills or maintaining existing skills through graduate training or continuing education are eligible for the lifetime learning credit. Taxpayers who are married must file a joint return to claim either education credit.

Income Limitations and Refundability

Both education credits are subject to income limitations. In addition, the American Opportunity credit is partially refundable and may be used to offset a taxpayer's alternative minimum tax (AMT) liability (the lifetime learning credit is neither refundable nor an AMT liability offset).

The American Opportunity credit amount is phased out beginning when the taxpayer's AGI (modified for this purpose) reaches $80,000 ($160,000 for married taxpayers filing jointly).[73] The reduction is equal to the extent to which AGI exceeds $80,000 ($160,000 for married taxpayers filing jointly) as a percentage of a $10,000 phaseout range ($20,000 for married taxpayers filing jointly). As a result, the credit is completely eliminated when modified AGI reaches $90,000 ($180,000 for married taxpayers filing jointly). The entire credit allowed may be used to reduce a taxpayer's AMT liability. In addition, 40 percent of the American Opportunity credit is refundable.[74]

In 2015, the lifetime learning credit amount is phased out beginning when the taxpayer's AGI (modified for this purpose) reaches $55,000 ($110,000 for married taxpayers

---

[71]§ 25A.

[72]§ 25A(i)(3).

[73]These amounts are not adjusted for inflation.

[74]If the credit is claimed for a taxpayer subject to § 1(g) (the "kiddie tax"), the credit is not refundable.

filing jointly). The reduction is equal to the extent to which AGI exceeds $55,000 ($110,000 for married filing jointly) as a percentage of a $10,000 ($20,000 for married filing jointly) phaseout range. The credit is completely eliminated when AGI reaches $65,000 ($130,000 for married filing jointly).

American Opportunity Credit: Calculation and Limitation

EXAMPLE 32

Tom and Jennifer are married; file a joint tax return; have modified AGI of $158,000; and have two children, Lora and Sam. Tom and Jennifer paid $7,500 of tuition and $8,500 for room and board for Lora (a freshman) and $8,100 of tuition plus $7,200 for room and board for Sam (a junior). Both Lora and Sam are full-time students and are Tom and Jennifer's dependents.

Lora's tuition and Sam's tuition are qualified expenses for the American Opportunity credit. For 2015, Tom and Jennifer may claim a $2,500 American Opportunity credit for both Lora's and Sam's expenses [(100% × $2,000) + (25% × $2,000)]. So, in total, they qualify for a $5,000 American Opportunity credit.

EXAMPLE 33

Assume the same facts as in Example 32, except that Tom and Jennifer's modified AGI for 2015 is $172,000, instead of $158,000. In this case, Tom and Jennifer are eligible to claim a $2,000 American Opportunity credit for 2015 (rather than a $5,000 credit).

The potential $5,000 American Opportunity credit must be reduced because their modified AGI exceeds the $160,000 limit for married taxpayers. The percentage reduction is computed as the amount by which modified AGI exceeds the limit, expressed as a percentage of the phaseout range, or [($172,000 − $160,000)/$20,000], resulting in a 60% reduction. Therefore, the maximum available credit for 2015 is $2,000 ($5,000 × 40% allowable portion).

Restrictions on Double Tax Benefit

Taxpayers are prohibited from receiving a double tax benefit associated with qualifying educational expenses. Therefore, taxpayers who claim an education credit may not deduct the expenses, nor may they claim the credit for amounts that are otherwise excluded from gross income (e.g., scholarships and employer-paid educational assistance).

10-5e Earned Income Credit

The **earned income credit**, which has been a part of the law for many years, has been justified as a means of providing tax equity to the working poor. In addition, the credit has been designed to help offset regressive taxes, such as the gasoline tax, that impose a relatively larger burden on low-income taxpayers. Further, the credit is intended to encourage economically disadvantaged individuals to become contributing members of the workforce.[75]

Eligibility Requirements

Eligibility for the credit depends not only on whether the taxpayer meets the earned income and AGI thresholds but also on whether he or she has a qualifying child. The term *qualifying child* generally has the same meaning here as it does for purposes of determining who qualifies as a dependent.

In addition to being available for taxpayers with qualifying children, the earned income credit is also available to certain workers without children. However, this

---

[75]§ 32. This credit is subject to indexation.

provision is available only to such taxpayers ages 25 through 64 who cannot be claimed as a dependent on another taxpayer's return.

Amount of the Credit

The earned income credit is determined by multiplying a maximum amount of earned income by the appropriate credit percentage. Generally, earned income includes employee compensation and net earnings from self-employment but excludes items such as interest, dividends, pension benefits, nontaxable employee compensation, and alimony. If a taxpayer has children, the credit percentage used in the calculation depends on the number of qualifying children. For 2009 through 2017, Congress has increased the credit percentage for families with three or more children and has increased the phaseout threshold amounts for married taxpayers filing joint returns. Thus, in 2015, the maximum earned income credit is $3,359 ($9,880 × 34%) for a taxpayer with one qualifying child, $5,548 ($13,870 × 40%) for a taxpayer with two qualifying children, and $6,242 ($13,870 × 45%) for a taxpayer with three or more qualifying children. However, the maximum earned income credit is phased out completely if the taxpayer's earned income or AGI exceeds certain thresholds. To the extent the greater of earned income or AGI exceeds $23,630 in 2015 for married taxpayers filing a joint return ($18,110 for other taxpayers), the difference, multiplied by the appropriate phaseout percentage, is subtracted from the maximum earned income credit.

It is not necessary for the taxpayer to actually compute the earned income credit. To simplify the compliance process, the IRS issues an Earned Income Credit Table for determining the appropriate amount of the credit. This table and a worksheet are included in the instructions available to individual taxpayers.

10-6 AFFORDABLE CARE ACT PROVISIONS

LO.4

Explain some of the key tax provisions of the Affordable Care Act.

Some of the most sweeping new legislation in the last decade is known as the Affordable Care Act (ACA) or "ObamaCare." The Affordable Care Act was enacted to increase the quality and affordability of health insurance, reduce the number of uninsured individuals in the United States by expanding public and private insurance coverage, and lower health care costs for individuals and the government. Included in the ACA are a number of tax provisions, two of which are discussed briefly below. The Net Investment Income Tax (NIIT) and Additional Medicare tax, also part of the ACA, were covered in Chapter 9.

10-6a Individual Shared Responsibility Payment

The ACA's "individual mandate"—which has been deemed a "tax" by the U.S. Supreme Court[76]—requires all individuals not covered by an employer-sponsored health plan, Medicare, Medicaid, or other public insurance programs to secure a private insurance policy or pay a penalty for each month they do not have health coverage. The penalty is the individual shared responsibility payment (ISRP).[77]

Under this provision, individuals without coverage in 2016 will pay an ISRP of the greater of (1) $695 per year up to a maximum of three times that amount ($2,085) per family or (2) 2.5 percent of household income. The ISRP is phased in over several years (the penalty is the greater of $95 or 1.0 percent of household income in 2014 and $325 or 2.0 percent of household income in 2015). After 2016, $695 amount will be increased

---

[76]*National Federation of Independent Business v. Sebelius*, 132 S.Ct. 2566 (2012).   [77]§ 5000A.

annually by a cost-of-living adjustment. The ISRP cannot be higher than the national average cost of a bronze-level health plan ($207 per month per individual for 2015 and $204 per month for 2014).[78]

Exemptions are granted for financial hardship, religious objections, Native Americans, those without coverage for less than three consecutive months, undocumented immigrants, incarcerated individuals, those for whom the lowest cost plan option exceeds a specified percentage of household income, and those with incomes below the tax filing threshold (in 2015, the percentage is 8.05 percent and the income threshold for taxpayers under age 65 is $10,300 for singles and $20,600 for couples).[79]

10-6b **Premium Tax Credit**

Individuals and families whose household incomes are at least 100 percent but no more than 400 percent of the federal poverty level (also called the federal poverty line; FPL) may be eligible to receive a federal subsidy [the **premium tax credit (PTC)**] if they purchase insurance via the Health Insurance Marketplace (the Marketplace).[80] Individuals whose income exceeds 400 percent of the FPL are not eligible for a PTC. For 2015 tax returns, the FPL for claiming a PTC is $11,670 for a single person (an additional $4,060 is added to that amount for each person in the household).[81]

Income Relative to FPL	Premiums Limited To
100–133% of FPL	2.01% of income
133–150% of FPL	3.02–4.02% of income
150–200% of FPL	4.02–6.34% of income
200–250% of FPL	6.34–8.10% of income
250–300% of FPL	8.10–9.56% of income
300–400% of FPL	9.56% of income

Individuals can choose to receive their PTC in advance, and the Marketplace will send the money directly to the insurer to reduce the monthly insurance payments. Alternatively, individuals can receive the PTC as a refundable credit when they file their tax return for the year. Most individuals choose to receive their PTC in advance. In either case, however, taxpayers will be required to complete Form 8962 (Premium Tax Credit) when their tax return is filed. Taxpayers who claim the premium tax credit cannot use Form 1040EZ (they must use either Form 1040A or Form 1040).

Taxpayers who enrolled in health care coverage via the Marketplace will receive information necessary to complete Form 8962 by the end of January each year [Form 1095–A (Health Insurance Marketplace Statement)]. Included in this information statement are monthly health insurance premium payments and any premium tax credit received in advance. This information also is reported to the IRS.

Taxpayers who received the credit in advance must reconcile the actual credit based on actual income that year with the amounts that were subsidized through the Marketplace. They will receive a refund (if the advance credit was too low) or owe an additional tax obligation (if the advance credit was too large).

---

[78]Rev.Proc. 2014–46, 2014–33 I.R.B. 367, and Rev.Proc. 2015–15, 2015–5 I.R.B. 564.

[79]Rev.Proc. 2014–37, 2014–33 I.R.B. 363. Individuals eligible for an exemption are to report it on Form 8965 (Health Coverage Exemptions). This form also includes worksheets for calculating any ISRP owed.

[80]§ 36B. Also see Rev.Proc. 2014–37, 2014–33 I.R.B. 363.

[81]80 FR 3236. Different amounts apply for Alaska and Hawaii. For 2014 tax returns, these amounts were $11,490 and $4,020, respectively. For 2016 tax returns, these amounts will be $11,770 and $4,160, respectively.

THE TAX IMPLICATIONS OF LIFE!

While Donna and David's wages and salaries of $70,000 are taxable, they should be aware that their employers may have provided them with a number of tax-free fringe benefits. In addition, if Donna and David paid monthly premiums for accident and health care plans or contributed to a flexible spending account, those amounts may reduce their taxable income (these items are discussed more fully in Chapter 11). The good news is that the $10,000 gift received from Donna's grandmother can be excluded from gross income. However, the $250 of interest earned on the money is taxable, as is the $1,500 bonus Donna earned at the CPA firm.

Donna's tuition waiver of $6,000 and the related payments of $400 per month are intended as a form of compensation. Therefore, she must include both of these in her gross income. However, insofar as the damages awards are concerned, all of the compensatory damages of $215,000 can be excluded from gross income because they relate to personal physical injury or sickness. However the punitive damages of $160,000 must be included in Donna's gross income.

Donna and David have several deductions *for* adjusted gross income. In addition to the alimony paid by David, $3,000 of the capital loss from the stock sale is deductible *for* AGI and interest on the qualified student loan is deductible *for* AGI (subject to a phaseout).

While medical expenses, state income taxes, personal property taxes, and charitable contributions are deductible *from* AGI, Donna and David should claim the standard deduction for a married couple as it appears to exceed their itemized deductions.

Donna and David will claim three personal and dependency exemptions—one for each spouse and one for David's son. They will determine their tax liability using the tax rate schedule for married couples filing a joint return.

Donna and David may be eligible for one or more tax credits, including the child tax credit and an education tax credit related to the tuition paid by Donna. If Stephen has unearned income in excess of certain thresholds, Donna and David should be made aware of the potential "kiddie" tax problem.

What If?

What if Donna and David purchase a house in the current year? What are the likely tax implications of owning a new home? If Donna and David purchase a new home, mortgage interest and property taxes paid on the home are treated as additional itemized deductions. Depending on the amount of these deductions, Donna and David's itemized deductions might then exceed the standard deduction amount, giving them a larger tax deduction and reducing their tax liability even more.

Suggested Readings

J. Russell Hardin and Thomas G. Noland, "The Tax Impact of Home Mortgage Modification Programs," *Practical Tax Strategies,* August 2014.

David J. Hess and Lois D. Bryan, "Using An IRA for A Planned Charitable Gift," *Practical Tax Strategies,* March 2012.

Mark Jackson, "Unintended Consequences of the Earned Income Tax Credit," *Practical Tax Strategies*, February 2013.

M. Jill Lockwood, Britton McKay, and Michael Wiggins, "Tax Planning for Divorce: Avoiding the Pitfalls," *Practical Tax Strategies,* September 2012.

Eric Smith, "Distinguishing 'Live-Burn' and 'Deconstruction' Donations," *Practical Tax Strategies,* April 2014.

Key Terms

Accident and health insurance benefits, 10-10

Acquisition indebtedness, 10-19

Adoption expenses credit, 10-28

Alimony and separate maintenance payments, 10-3

American Opportunity credit, 10-31

Capital gain property, 10-24

Charitable contribution, 10-21

Child tax credit, 10-28

Compensatory damages, 10-8

Credit for child and dependent care expenses, 10-29

Earned income credit, 10-32

Educational savings bonds, 10-10

Health Savings Account (HSA), 10-14

Home equity loans, 10-19

Investment interest, 10-18

Individual shared responsibility payment (ISRP), 10-33

Lifetime learning credit, 10-31

Medical expenses, 10-12

Miscellaneous itemized deductions, 10-25

Net investment income, 10-18

Ordinary income property, 10-24

Points, 10-19

Premium tax credit (PTC), 10-34

Punitive damages, 10-9

Qualified residence interest, 10-19

Scholarship, 10-7

Computational Exercises

1. **LO.1** Casper and Cecile are divorced this year. As part of the divorce settlement, Casper transferred stock to Cecile. Casper purchased the stock for $25,000, and it had a market value of $43,000 on the date of the transfer. Cecile sold the stock for $40,000 a month after receiving it. In addition Casper is required to pay Cecile $1,500 a month in alimony. He made five payments to her during the year. What are the tax consequences for Casper and Cecile regarding these transactions?

   a. How much gain or loss does Casper recognize on the transfer of the stock?

   b. Does Casper receive a deduction for the $7,500 alimony paid?

   c. How much income does Cecile have from the $7,500 alimony received?

   d. When Cecile sells the stock, how much gain or loss does she report?

Critical Thinking 2. **LO.1** Compute the taxable Social Security benefits in each of the following situations:

   a. Erwin and Eleanor are married and file a joint tax return. They have adjusted gross income of $46,000, no tax-exempt interest, and $12,400 of Social Security benefits.

   b. Erwin and Eleanor have adjusted gross income of $12,000, no tax-exempt interest, and $16,000 of Social Security benefits.

3. **LO.1** Jarrod receives a scholarship of $18,500 from Riggers University to be used to pursue a bachelor's degree. He spends $12,000 on tuition, $1,500 on books and supplies, $4,000 for room and board, and $1,000 for personal expenses. How much may Jarrod exclude from his gross income?

4. **LO.2** Pierre, a cash basis, unmarried taxpayer, had $1,400 of state income tax withheld during 2015. Also in 2015, Pierre paid $455 that was due when he filed his 2014 state income tax return and made estimated payments of $975 toward his 2015 state income tax liability. When Pierre files his 2015 Federal income tax return in April 2016, he elects to itemize deductions, which amount to $10,650, including the state income tax payments and withholdings, all of which reduce his taxable income.

a. What is Pierre's 2015 state income tax deduction?

b. As a result of overpaying his 2015 state income tax, Pierre receives a refund of $630 early in 2016. The standard deduction for single taxpayers for 2015 was $6,300. How much of the $630 will Pierre include in his 2016 gross income?

5. **LO.2** Troy's financial records for the year reflect the following:

Interest income from bank savings account	$ 900
Taxable annuity receipts	1,800
Safe deposit box rental (to hold annuity documents)	125
Investment interest expense	3,200

Calculate Troy's net investment income and his current investment interest deduction. Assume that Troy does not itemize his personal deductions. How is any potential excess investment interest deduction treated?

6. **LO.2** Miller owns a personal residence with a fair market value of $195,000 and an outstanding first mortgage of $157,500. Miller gets a second mortgage on the residence and in return borrows $10,000 to purchase new jet skis. How much of the first and second mortgage debt is treated as qualified residence indebtedness?

7. **LO.2** Donna donates stock in Chipper Corporation to the American Red Cross on September 10, 2015. She purchased the stock for $18,100 on December 28, 2014, and it had a fair market value of $27,000 when she made the donation.

a. What is Donna's charitable contribution deduction?

b. Assume instead that the stock had a fair market value of $15,000 (rather than $27,000) when it was donated to the American Red Cross. What is Donna's charitable contribution deduction?

8. **LO.2** Issac has AGI of $73,400 and incurred the following expenses. How much of the business and personal expenditures are deductible (after any limitation) either as miscellaneous itemized deductions or as other itemized deductions?

Cost of uniforms	$ 535
Tax return preparation fees	600
Fee paid for a safe deposit box used to store papers and documents relating to taxable income-producing investments	65
Job-hunting costs	1,100

9. **LO.2** Pedro, who is a single taxpayer, had AGI of $328,000 for 2015. He incurred the following expenses during the year:

Medical expenses before 10%-of-AGI limitation	$12,000
State and local income taxes	8,900
Real estate taxes	1,600
Home mortgage interest	16,000
Charitable contributions	2,200
Deductible investment interest expense	1,700

Compute the amount of Pedro's itemized deductions after any applicable reductions.

10. **LO.3** In late 2014, Randy and Rachel Erwin paid $7,000 in legal fees, adoption fees, and other expenses directly related to the adoption of an infant son, Jameson. In 2015, the year in which the adoption becomes final, they pay an additional $8,000. Their AGI in 2015 is $135,000.

a. Determine the amount of the Erwins' adoption tax credit in 2015.

b. Instead, assume that the Erwins' 2015 AGI is $210,000. Determine the amount of the Erwins' adoption tax credit in 2015.

11. **LO.3** Santiago and Amy are married and file a joint tax return claiming their three children, ages 12, 14, and 18, as dependents. Their AGI is $140,000. Determine the amount of the couple's child tax credit.

12. **LO.3** Paola and Isidora are married, file a joint tax return, report modified AGI of $148,000, and have one dependent child, Dante. The couple paid $12,000 of tuition and $10,000 for room and board for Dante (a freshman). Dante is a full-time student. Determine the amount of the American Opportunity credit for the year.

Problems

Issue ID

13. **LO.1** William and Abigail, who live in San Francisco, have been experiencing problems with their marriage. They have a 3-year-old daughter, April, who stays with William's parents during the day because both William and Abigail are employed. Abigail worked to support William while he attended medical school, and now she has been accepted by a medical school in Mexico. Abigail has decided to divorce William and attend medical school. April will stay in San Francisco because of her strong attachment to her grandparents and because they can provide her with excellent day care. Abigail knows that William will expect her to contribute to the cost of raising April. Abigail also believes that to finance her education, she must receive cash for her share of the property they accumulated during their marriage. In addition, she believes that she should receive some reimbursement for her contribution to William's support while he was in medical school. She expects the divorce proceedings to take several months. Identify the relevant tax issues for Abigail.

Decision Making

14. **LO.1** Alicia and Rafel are in the process of negotiating a divorce agreement. They both worked during the marriage and contributed an equal amount to the marital assets. They own a home with a fair market value of $400,000 (cost of $300,000) that is subject to a mortgage of $250,000. They have lived in the home for 12 years. They also have investment assets with a cost of $160,000 and a fair market value of $410,000. Thus, the net worth of the couple is $560,000 ($400,000 − $250,000 + $410,000). The holding period for the investments is longer than one year. Alicia would like to continue to live in the house. Therefore, she has proposed that she receive the residence subject to the mortgage, a net value of $150,000. In addition, she would receive $17,600 each year for the next 10 years, which has a present value (at 6% interest) of $130,000. Rafel would receive the investment assets. If Rafel accepts this plan, he must sell one-half of the investments so that he can purchase a home. Assume that you are counseling Alicia. Explain to Alicia whether the proposed agreement would be "fair" on an after-tax basis.

15. **LO.1** For each of the following, determine the amount that should be included in gross income:

    a. Peyton was selected the most valuable player in the Super Bowl. In recognition of this, he was awarded an automobile with a value of $60,000. Peyton did not need the automobile, so he asked that the title be put in his parents' names.

    b. Jacob was awarded the Nobel Peace Prize. When he was presented the check for $1.4 million, Jacob said, "I do not need the money. Give it to the United Nations to use toward the goal of world peace."

    c. Linda won the Craig County Fair beauty pageant. She received a $10,000 scholarship that paid her $6,000 for tuition and $4,000 for meals and housing for the academic year.

Critical Thinking
Decision Making

16. **LO.1** Linda and Don are married and file a joint return. In 2015, they received $12,000 in Social Security benefits and $35,000 in taxable pension benefits and interest.

a. Compute the couple's adjusted gross income on a joint return.

b. Don would like to know whether they should sell for $100,000 (at no gain or loss) a corporate bond that pays 8% in interest each year and use the proceeds to buy a $100,000 nontaxable State of Virginia bond that will pay $6,000 in interest each year.

c. If Linda in (a) works part-time and earns $30,000, how much will Linda and Don's adjusted gross income increase?

17. **LO.1** Adrian was awarded an academic scholarship to State University for the 2015–2016 academic year. He received $6,500 in August and $7,200 in December 2015. Adrian had enough personal savings to pay all expenses as they came due. Adrian's expenditures for the relevant period were as follows:

Tuition, August 2015	$3,700
Tuition, January 2016	3,750
Room and board	
August–December 2015	2,800
January–May 2016	2,500
Books and educational supplies	
August–December 2015	1,000
January–May 2016	1,200

Determine the effect on Adrian's gross income for 2015 and 2016.

18. **LO.1** Leigh sued an overzealous bill collector and received the following settlement:

Damage to her automobile that the collector attempted to repossess	$ 3,300
Physical damage to her arm caused by the collector	15,000
Loss of income while her arm was healing	6,000
Punitive damages	80,000

a. What effect does the settlement have on Leigh's gross income?

b. Assume that Leigh also collected $25,000 of damages for slander to her personal reputation caused by the bill collector misrepresenting the facts to Leigh's employer and other creditors. Is this $25,000 included in Leigh's gross income? Explain.

19. **LO.2** Emma Doyle, age 55, is employed as a corporate attorney. For calendar year 2015, she had AGI of $100,000 and paid the following medical expenses: Communications

Medical insurance premiums	$3,700
Doctor and dentist bills for Bob and April (Emma's parents)	6,800
Doctor and dentist bills for Emma	5,200
Prescription medicines for Emma	400
Nonprescription insulin for Emma	350

Bob and April would qualify as Emma's dependents, except that they file a joint return. Emma's medical insurance policy does not cover them. Emma filed a claim for reimbursement of $2,800 of her own expenses with her insurance company in December 2015 and received the reimbursement in January 2016. What is Emma's maximum allowable medical expense deduction for 2015? Prepare a memo for your firm's tax files in which you document your conclusions.

20. **LO.2** Michael has always been overweight, and now he has decided to do something about it. He recently read in a news story that the IRS allows a medical expense deduction for the cost of certain weight reduction programs. He scheduled an appointment with his doctor to discuss enrolling in the clinic's weight reduction   Ethics and Equity

program and mentioned that he was happy that he would be able to deduct the cost. His doctor, who was familiar with the IRS's position, informed Michael that he was 10 pounds below the weight considered obese under the IRS guidelines and would not be able to take the medical expense deduction. Michael scheduled another appointment and proceeded to eat much more than usual for the next month. He returned 20 pounds heavier than at the first appointment and joked with the doctor that he now qualified for the medical expense deduction. Discuss whether Michael is justified in deducting the cost of the weight reduction program.

21. **LO.2** Paul, age 62, suffers from emphysema and severe allergies and, upon the recommendation of his physician, has a dust elimination system installed in his personal residence. In connection with the system, Paul incurs and pays the following amounts during 2015.

Doctor and hospital bills	$ 2,500
Dust elimination system	10,000
Increase in utility bills due to the system	450
Cost of certified appraisal	300

In addition, Paul pays $750 for prescribed medicines.

   The system has an estimated useful life of 20 years. The appraisal was to determine the value of Paul's residence with and without the system. The appraisal states that his residence was worth $350,000 before the system was installed and $356,000 after the installation. Paul's AGI for the year was $50,000. How much of the medical expenses qualify for the medical expense deduction in 2015?

22. **LO.2** Norma, who uses the cash method of accounting, lives in a state that imposes an income tax. In April 2015, she files her state income tax return for 2014 and pays an additional $1,000 in state income taxes. During 2015, her withholdings for state income tax purposes amount to $7,400, and she pays estimated state income tax of $700. In April 2016, she files her state income tax return for 2015, claiming a refund of $1,800. Norma receives the refund in August 2016.

   a. Assuming that Norma itemized deductions in 2015, how much may she claim as a deduction for state income taxes on her Federal return for calendar year 2015 (filed in April 2016)?

   b. Assuming that Norma itemized deductions in 2015, how will the refund of $1,800 that she received in 2016 be treated for Federal income tax purposes?

   c. Assume that Norma itemized deductions in 2015 and that she elects to have the $1,800 refund applied toward her 2016 state income tax liability. How will the $1,800 be treated for Federal income tax purposes?

   d. Assuming that Norma did not itemize deductions in 2015, how will the refund of $1,800 received in 2016 be treated for Federal income tax purposes?

Decision Making

Communications

Critical Thinking

23. **LO.2** In 2015, Kathleen Tweardy incurs $30,000 of interest expense related to her investments. Her investment income includes $7,500 of interest, $6,000 of qualified dividends, and a $12,000 net capital gain on the sale of securities. Kathleen asks you to compute the amount of her deduction for investment interest, taking into consideration any options she might have. In addition, she wants your suggestions as to any tax planning alternatives that are available. Write a letter to her that contains your advice. Kathleen lives at 11934 Briarpatch Drive, Midlothian, VA 23113.

Critical Thinking

24. **LO.2** Helen borrowed $150,000 to acquire a parcel of land to be held for investment purposes. During 2015, she paid interest of $12,000 on the loan. She had AGI of $90,000 for the year. Other items related to Helen's investments include the following:

Investment income	$11,000
Long-term capital gain on sale of stock	3,500
Investment counsel fees	200

Helen is unmarried and does not itemize her deductions.

a. Determine Helen's investment interest deduction for 2015.

b. Discuss the treatment of the portion of Helen's investment interest that is disallowed in 2015.

25. **LO.2** In 2006, Liam, who is single, purchased a personal residence for $340,000 and took out a mortgage of $200,000 on the property. In May of the current year, when the residence had a fair market value of $440,000 and Liam owed $140,000 on the mortgage, he took out a home equity loan for $220,000. He used the funds to purchase a recreational vehicle, which he uses 100% for personal use. What is the maximum amount on which Liam can deduct home equity interest?

26. **LO.2** In December of each year, Eleanor Young contributes 10% of her gross income to the United Way (a 50% organization). Eleanor, who is in the 28% marginal tax bracket, is considering the following alternatives for satisfying the contribution.

Decision Making

Communications

Critical Thinking

	Fair Market Value
(1) Cash donation	$23,000
(2) Unimproved land held for six years ($3,000 basis)	23,000
(3) Blue Corporation stock held for eight months ($8,000 basis)	23,000
(4) Gold Corporation stock held for two years ($28,000 basis)	23,000

Eleanor has asked you to help her decide which of the potential contributions listed above will be most advantageous taxwise. Evaluate the four alternatives, and write a letter to Eleanor to communicate your advice to her. Her address is 2622 Bayshore Drive, Berkeley, CA 94709.

27. **LO.2** Ramon had AGI of $180,000 in 2015. He is considering making a charitable contribution this year to the American Heart Association, a qualified charitable organization. Determine the current allowable charitable contribution deduction in each of the following independent situations, and indicate the treatment for any amount that is not deductible currently.

Decision Making

Critical Thinking

a. A cash gift of $95,000.

b. A gift of OakCo stock worth $95,000 on the contribution date. Ramon acquired the stock as an investment two years ago at a cost of $84,000.

c. A gift of a painting worth $95,000 that Ramon purchased three years ago for $60,000. The charity has indicated that it would sell the painting to generate cash to fund medical research.

28. **LO.2** Linda, age 37, who files as a single taxpayer, had AGI of $280,000 for 2015. She incurred the following expenses and losses during the year:

Medical expenses (before the 10%-of-AGI limitation)	$33,000
State and local income taxes	4,500
State sales tax	1,300
Real estate taxes	4,000
Home mortgage interest	5,000
Automobile loan interest	750
Credit card interest	1,000
Charitable contributions	7,000
Casualty loss (before 10% limitation but after $100 floor)	34,000
Unreimbursed employee expenses subject to the 2%-of-AGI limitation	7,600

Calculate Linda's allowable itemized deductions for the year.

29. **LO.3** Ann and Bill were on the list of a local adoption agency for several years, seeking to adopt a child. Finally, in 2014, good news came their way, and an adoption seemed imminent. They paid qualified adoption expenses of $5,000 in 2014 and $11,000 in 2015. Assume that the adoption becomes final in 2015. Ann and Bill always file a joint income tax return.

    a. Determine the amount of the adoption expenses credit available to Ann and Bill, assuming that their combined annual income is $120,000. In what year(s) will they benefit from the credit?

    b. Assuming that Ann and Bill's modified AGI in 2014 and 2015 is $220,000, calculate the amount of the adoption expenses credit.

30. **LO.3** Paul and Karen are married, and both are employed (Paul earns $44,000 and Karen earns $9,000 during 2015). Paul and Karen have two dependent children, both under the age of 13. So they can work, Paul and Karen pay $3,800 to various unrelated parties to care for their children while they are working. Assuming that Paul and Karen file a joint return, what, if any, is their tax credit for child and dependent care expenses?

31. **LO.3** Jim and Mary Jean are married and have two dependent children under the age of 13. Both parents are gainfully employed and during 2015 earn salaries as follows: $16,000 (Jim) and $5,200 (Mary Jean). To care for their children while they work, they pay Eleanor (Jim's mother) $5,600. Eleanor does not qualify as a dependent of Jim and Mary Jean. Assuming that Jim and Mary Jean file a joint tax return, what, if any, is their credit for child and dependent care expenses?

Communications 32. **LO.3** Bernadette, a longtime client of yours, is an architect and the president of the local Rotary chapter. To keep up to date with the latest developments in her profession, she attends continuing education seminars offered by the architecture school at State University. During 2015, Bernadette spends $2,000 on course tuition to attend such seminars. She also spends another $400 on architecture books during the year.

    Bernadette's son, Pablo, is a senior majoring in engineering at the University of the Midwest. During the 2015 calendar year, Pablo incurs the following expenses: $8,200 for tuition ($4,100 per semester) and $750 for books and course materials. Pablo, who Bernadette claims as a dependent, lives at home while attending school full-time. Bernadette is married, files a joint return, and reports a combined AGI with her husband of $112,000.

    a. Calculate Bernadette's education tax credit for 2015.

    b. In her capacity as president of the local Rotary chapter, Bernadette has asked you to make a 30- to 45-minute speech outlining the different ways the tax law helps defray (1) the cost of higher education and (2) the cost of continuing education once someone is in the workforce. Prepare an outline of possible topics for presentation. A tentative title for your presentation is "How Can the Tax Law Help Pay for College and Continuing Professional Education?"

Issue ID 33. **LO.3** Mark and Lisa are approaching an exciting time in their lives as their oldest son, Austin, graduates from high school and moves on to college. What are some of the tax issues Mark and Lisa should consider as they think about paying for Austin's college education?

Ethics and Equity 34. **LO.3** For many years, Loretta Johnson, a single mother of three children, has been struggling to make ends meet by working at two jobs that pay barely the minimum wage and together provide just over $15,000. Fortunately, her housing and food costs have been partially subsidized through various government programs. In addition, she has been able to take advantage of the earned income credit, which has provided around $3,000 annually to help her with living expenses. The credit has truly made a difference in the lives of Loretta and her family by helping them keep their creditors at bay. She is proud that she has worked hard and provided for her family for many years without having to accept welfare.

Now, however, Loretta faces a problem as her children have grown up and moved out of her home. With no qualifying children in her household, she no longer qualifies for the earned income credit. Although she will continue working at her two jobs, such a significant loss to her household budget cuts into her ability to be self-reliant. As a survival strategy and as a way of keeping the earned income credit, Loretta arranges to have one of her grandchildren live with her for just over six months every year. This enables a significant percentage of her household budget to be secure. How do you react to Loretta's strategy?

35. **LO.3** Joyce, a widow, lives in an apartment with her two minor children (ages 8 and 10), whom she supports. Joyce earns $33,000 during 2015. She uses the standard deduction.

Critical Thinking
Decision Making

a. Calculate the amount, if any, of Joyce's earned income credit.

b. During the year, Joyce is offered a new job that has greater future potential than her current job. If she accepts the job offer, her earnings for the year will be $39,000; however, she is afraid she will not qualify for as much of the earned income credit. Using after-tax cash-flow calculations, determine whether Joyce should accept the new job offer.

Comprehensive Tax Return Problems

1. Alice J. and Bruce M. Byrd are married taxpayers who file a joint return. Their Social Security numbers are 123-45-6789 and 111-11-1111, respectively. Alice's birthday is September 21, 1967, and Bruce's is June 27, 1966. They live at 473 Revere Avenue, Lowell, MA 01850. Alice is the office manager for Lowell Dental Clinic, 433 Broad Street, Lowell, MA 01850 (employer identification number 98-765432). Bruce is the manager of a Super Burgers fast-food outlet owned and operated by Plymouth Corporation, 1247 Central Avenue, Hauppauge, NY 11788 (employer identification number 11-1111111).

Tax Return Problem
Decision Making

The following information is shown on their Wage and Tax Statements (Form W–2) for 2014.

Line	Description	Alice	Bruce
1	Wages, tips, other compensation	$58,000	$62,100
2	Federal income tax withheld	4,500	6,300
3	Social Security wages	58,000	62,100
4	Social Security tax withheld	3,596	3,850
5	Medicare wages and tips	58,000	62,100
6	Medicare tax withheld	841	900
15	State	Massachusetts	Massachusetts
16	State wages, tips, etc.	58,000	62,100
17	State income tax withheld	2,950	3,100

The Byrds provide over half of the support of their two children, Cynthia (born January 25, 1990, Social Security number 123-45-6788) and John (born February 7, 1994, Social Security number 123-45-6786). Both children are full-time students and live with the Byrds except when they are away at college. Cynthia earned $4,200 from a summer internship in 2014, and John earned $3,800 from a part-time job.

During 2014, the Byrds provided 60% of the total support of Bruce's widower father, Sam Byrd (born March 6, 1938, Social Security number 123-45-6787). Sam lived alone and covered the rest of his support with his Social Security benefits. Sam died in November, and Bruce, the beneficiary of a policy on Sam's life, received life insurance proceeds of $800,000 on December 28.

The Byrds had the following expenses relating to their personal residence during 2014:

Property taxes	$5,000
Qualified interest on home mortgage	8,700
Repairs to roof	5,750
Utilities	4,100
Fire and theft insurance	1,900

The Byrds had the following medical expenses for 2014:

Medical insurance premiums	$4,500
Doctor bill for Sam incurred in 2013 and not paid until 2014	7,600
Operation for Sam	8,500
Prescription medicines for Sam	900
Hospital expenses for Sam	3,500
Reimbursement from insurance company, received in 2014	3,600

The medical expenses for Sam represent most of the 60% that Bruce contributed toward his father's support.

Other relevant information follows:

- When they filed their 2013 state return in 2014, the Byrds paid additional state income tax of $900.
- During 2014, Alice and Bruce attended a dinner dance sponsored by the Lowell Police Disability Association (a qualified charitable organization). The Byrds paid $300 for the tickets. The cost of comparable entertainment would normally be $50.
- The Byrds contributed $5,000 to Lowell Presbyterian Church and gave used clothing (cost of $1,200 and fair market value of $350) to the Salvation Army. All donations are supported by receipts, and the clothing is in very good condition.
- In 2014, the Byrds received interest income of $2,750, which was reported on a Form 1099–INT from Second National Bank.
- Alice's employer requires that all employees wear uniforms to work. During 2014, Alice spent $850 on new uniforms and $566 on laundry charges.
- Bruce paid $400 for an annual subscription to the *Journal of Franchise Management* and $741 for annual membership dues to his professional association.
- Neither Alice's nor Bruce's employer reimburses for employee expenses.
- The Byrds do not keep the receipts for the sales taxes they paid and had no major purchases subject to sales tax.
- Everyone in the Byrd family had health care coverage for all months of 2014.
- Alice and Bruce paid no estimated Federal income tax. Neither Alice nor Bruce wants to designate $3 to the Presidential Election Campaign Fund.

Part 1—Tax Computation
Compute net tax payable or refund due for Alice and Bruce Byrd for 2014. If they have overpaid, they want the amount to be refunded to them. If you use tax forms for your computations, you will need Forms 1040 and 2106 and Schedules A and B. Suggested software: H&R BLOCK Tax Software.

Part 2—Tax Planning
Alice and Bruce are planning some significant changes for 2015. They have provided you with the following information and asked you to project their taxable income and tax liability for 2015.

The Byrds will invest the $800,000 of life insurance proceeds in short-term certificates of deposit (CDs) and use the interest for living expenses during 2015. They expect to earn total interest of $32,000 on the CDs.

Bruce has been promoted to regional manager, and his salary for 2015 will be $88,000. He estimates that state income tax withheld will increase by $4,000 and the Social Security tax withheld will be $5,456.

Alice, who has been diagnosed with a serious illness, will take a leave of absence from work during 2015. The estimated cost for her medical treatment is $15,400, of which $6,400 will be reimbursed by their insurance company in 2015. Their medical insurance premium will increase to $9,769. Property taxes on their residence are expected to increase to $5,100. The Byrds' home mortgage interest expense and charitable contributions are expected to be unchanged from the prior year.

John will graduate from college in December 2014 and will take a job in New York City in January 2015. His starting salary will be $46,000.

Assume that all of the information reported in 2014 will be the same in 2015 unless other information has been presented.

2. Paul and Donna Decker are married taxpayers, ages 44 and 42, respectively, who file a joint return for 2015. The Deckers live at 1121 College Avenue, Carmel, IN 46032. Paul is an assistant manager at Carmel Motor Inn, and Donna is a teacher at Carmel Elementary School. They present you with W–2 forms that reflect the following information:

Tax Computation Problem

	Paul	Donna
Salary	$68,000	$56,000
Federal tax withheld	6,770	6,630
State income tax withheld	900	800
FICA (Social Security and Medicare) withheld	5,202	4,284
Social Security numbers*	111-11-1111	123-45-6789

*In the interest of privacy and to protect against taxpayer identification misuse, Social Security numbers used throughout the textbook have been replaced with fictitious numbers.

Donna is the custodial parent of two children from a previous marriage who reside with the Deckers through the school year. The children, Larry and Jane Parker, reside with their father, Bob, during the summer. Relevant information for the children follows:

	Larry	Jane
Age	17	18
Social Security numbers	123-45-6788	123-45-6787
Months spent with Deckers	9	9

Under the divorce decree, Bob pays child support of $150 per month per child during the nine months the children live with the Deckers. Bob says that he spends $200 per month per child during the three summer months they reside with him. Donna and Paul can document that they provide $2,000 of support per child per year. The divorce decree is silent as to which parent can claim the exemptions for the children.

In August, Paul and Donna added a suite to their home to provide more comfortable accommodations for Hannah Snyder (Social Security number 123-45-6786), Donna's mother, who had moved in with them in February 2014 after the death of Donna's father. Not wanting to borrow money for this addition, Paul sold 300 shares of Acme Corporation stock for $50 per share on May 3, 2015, and used the proceeds of $15,000 to cover construction costs. The Deckers had purchased the stock on April 29, 2010, for $25 per share. They received dividends of $750 on the jointly owned stock a month before the sale.

Hannah, who is 66 years old, received $7,500 in Social Security benefits during the year, of which she gave the Deckers $2,000 to use toward household expenses and deposited the remainder in her personal savings account. The Deckers determine that they have spent $2,500 of their own money for food, clothing, medical expenses, and other items for Hannah. They do not know what the rental value of Hannah's suite would be, but they estimate it would be at least $300 per month.

Interest paid during the year included the following:

Home mortgage interest (paid to Carmel Federal Savings and Loan)	$7,890
Interest on an automobile loan (paid to Carmel National Bank)	1,660
Interest on Citibank Visa card	620

In July, Paul hit a submerged rock while boating. Fortunately, he was uninjured after being thrown from the boat and landing in deep water. However, the boat, which was uninsured, was destroyed. Paul had paid $25,000 for the boat in June 2014, and its value was appraised at $18,000 on the date of the accident.

The Deckers paid doctor and hospital bills of $10,700 and were reimbursed $2,000 by their insurance company. They spent $640 for prescription drugs and medicines and $5,904 for premiums on their health insurance policy. They have filed additional claims of $1,200 with their insurance company and have been told they will receive payment for that amount in January 2016. Included in the amounts paid for doctor and hospital bills were payments of $380 for Hannah and $850 for the children. All members of the Decker family had health insurance coverage for all of 2015.

Additional information of potential tax consequence follows:

Real estate taxes paid	$3,850
Sales taxes paid (per table)	1,379
Contributions to church	1,950
Appraised value of books donated to public library	740
Paul's unreimbursed employee expenses to attend hotel management convention:	
Airfare	340
Hotel	170
Meals	95
Registration fee	340
Refund of state income tax for 2014 (the Deckers itemized on their 2014 Federal tax return)	1,520

Compute net tax payable or refund due for the Deckers for 2015. Ignore the child tax credit in your computations. If the Deckers have overpaid, the amount is to be credited toward their taxes for 2016.

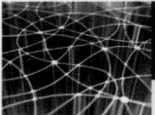

BRIDGE DISCIPLINE

1. George comes to you asking for your advice. He wants to invest $10,000 either in a debt security or in an equity investment. His choices are shown below.

   - Redbreast Corporation bond, annual coupon rate of 7.50%.
   - City of Philadelphia general obligation bond, coupon rate of 6.00%.
   - Blue Corporation 7.50% preferred stock (produces qualified dividend income).

   These alternatives are believed to carry comparable risk. Assuming that George is in the 35% marginal tax bracket, which investment alternative could be expected to produce the superior annual after-tax rate of return?

2. Assume the same facts as in Problem 1, except that George is a C corporation rather than an individual and is in the 34% marginal tax bracket. Which investment strategy would maximize George, Inc.'s annual return?

Research Problems

Note: Solutions to Research Problems can be prepared by using the Checkpoint® Student Edition online research product, which is available to accompany this text. It is also possible to prepare solutions to the Research Problems by using tax research materials found in a standard tax library.

THOMSON REUTERS
CHECKPOINT®
Student Edition

Research Problem 1. Aubrey Brown is a decorated veteran of the Vietnam War. As a result of his exposure to Agent Orange during the war, Aubrey developed lung cancer and is unable to work. He received $12,000 of Social Security disability payments in the current year. He reasons that the payments should be excluded from his gross income because the payments are compensation for the physical injury he suffered as a result of his service in the armed forces. Is Aubrey correct? Explain.

Partial list of research aids:
Rev.Rul. 77–318, 1977–2 C.B. 45.
Reimels v. Comm., 2006–1 USTC ¶50,147, 97 AFTR 2d 2006–820, 436 F.3d 344 (CA–2, 2006).

Research Problem 2. Ken and Mary Jane Blough, your neighbors, have asked you for advice after receiving correspondence in the mail from the IRS. You learn that the IRS is asking for documentation in support of the itemized deductions the Bloughs claimed on a recent tax return. The Bloughs tell you that their income in the year of question was $75,000. Because their record-keeping habits are poor, they felt justified in claiming itemized deductions equal to the amounts that represent the average claimed by other taxpayers in their income bracket. These averages are calculated and reported by the IRS annually based on actual returns filed in an earlier year. Accordingly, they claimed medical expenses of $7,102, taxes of $6,050, interest of $10,659, and charitable contributions of $2,693. What advice do you give the Bloughs?

Partial list of research aids:
Cheryl L. de Werff, T.C. Summary Opinion, 2011–29.

Research Problem 3. Ashby and Curtis, a professional couple, have a 2-year-old son, Jason. Curtis works full-time as an electrical engineer, but Ashby has not worked outside the home since Jason was born. As Jason is getting older, Ashby thinks that Jason would benefit from attending nursery school several times a week, which would give her an opportunity to reinvigorate her love of painting at a nearby art studio. Ashby thinks that if she is lucky, the proceeds from the sale of her paintings will pay for the nursery school tuition. But in addition, she is planning to claim the credit for child and dependent care expenses because the care provided Jason at the nursery school is required for her to pursue her art career. Can Ashby and Curtis claim the credit for child and dependent care expenses for the nursery school expenditure? Why or why not?

Use the tax resources of the Internet to address the following questions. Do not restrict your search to the Web, but include a review of newsgroups and general reference materials, practitioner sites and resources, primary sources of the tax law, chat rooms and discussion groups, and other opportunities.

Internet
Activity

Research Problem 4. Go to the web page of a consulting firm that offers counseling services to individuals as they negotiate the terms of a divorce. What specific tax-related services do these firms offer? Suggest a new tax-related service the consulting firm could offer.

Research Problem 5. The cutback adjustment that limits the amount of itemized deductions for some taxpayers is otherwise known as the Pease limitation. This limitation is named after former Congressman Donald Pease and was first in effect for tax years after December 31, 1990. The purpose of this limitation is to raise additional tax revenue by limiting some popular and common itemized deductions incurred by high-income taxpayers. One such deduction is the charitable contribution deduction. Search Google or a business press database to see what tax law analysts speculated the consequences would be of limiting charitable contribution deductions. Also determine whether such speculation has materialized.

Research Problem 6. In March 2015, the U.S. Supreme Court heard oral arguments in *King v. Burwell* involving an issue about the Premium Tax Credit. Identify the issue, the holding, and the response of the Secretary of Health and Human Services or the Secretary of the Treasury.

Roger CPA Review Questions

1. Walters, an individual, received the following in 20X13:

W-2 income	$10,000
Federal tax refund for 20X12	1,250
Scholarship stipend, in return for teaching assistant duties performed	25,000
Cash inheritance from deceased great-uncle	5,000

Considering only the above, what is Walters' 20X13 gross income?

a. $35,000   c. $15,000
b. $36,250   d. $16,250

2. The following pertain to Joyce in 20X14:

Medical insurance premiums paid by employer	$4,800
Teacher of the Year Award, in the form of gift cards redeemable at local businesses	500
Jewelry box, received from employer for 25 years of service (FMV)	100
20X14 holiday bonus awarded in December 20X14, to be paid in January 20X15	250

What total amount from the above may be excluded from Joyce's 20X14 gross income?

a. $5,650   c. $5,150
b. $350   d. $850

3. Pierce, a married individual, received the following in 20X14:

Worker's compensation award	$25,000
W-2 income	20,000
Unemployment compensation	4,800
Damages awarded for emotional distress experienced as a result of workplace bodily injury	10,000

Considering only the above, what is Pierce's 20X14 gross income?

a. $49,800   c. $30,000
b. $34,800   d. $24,800

4. Kellye, a teacher, volunteers for eight hours per week at a school for high-risk children, a qualified charitable organization. Kellye's normal rate for teaching is $30 per hour. Kellye's out-of-pocket costs in 20X4 were $250 for supplies, and she spent $20 each week in transportation getting to and from the school. Kellye had no cash

contributions to charity in 20X4. If Kellye volunteered every week in 20X4, what is her charitable contributions deduction?

a. $0

b. $250

c. $1,290

d. $13,770

5. Aaron, age 55, has an adjusted gross income in 20X4 of $30,000. His expenses are as follows:

Non-prescription medicine	$ 100
Prescription medicine	500
Doctor visits	500
Weekly meal preparation for a diet plan	2,000
Removal of a benign facial mole	400
Contact lenses	500
Eyeglasses	200
Dental services	300

What is Aaron's itemized deduction for medical expenses?

a. $0

b. $1,500

c. $2,000

d. $4,500

6. Which of the following deductions for taxes paid may be taken in the same year?

a. Real estate taxes, state income taxes, state sales taxes

b. Real estate taxes, property taxes, state income taxes

c. Property taxes, state income taxes, state sales taxes

d. Real estate taxes, property taxes, state income taxes, state sales taxes

7. Zunilda is a 77-year-old individual with an AGI of $25,000 in 2014. She began living in a nursing home in 2014 upon the recommendation of her primary care physician in order to receive medical care for a specific condition. She had the following unreimbursed expenses in 2014:

Expense	Amount
Nursing home health care costs	$5,000
Nursing home meal and lodging costs	8,000
Prescription drugs	1,500

As a result of these unreimbursed expenses, how much may Zunilda deduct from AGI on her 2014 tax return? Assume Zunilda elects to itemize deductions.

a. $12,000

b. $4,000

c. $12,625

d. $4,625

8. Which of the following credits is *not* refundable?

a. Child Tax Credit

b. Child and Dependent Care Credit

c. American Opportunity Tax Credit

d. Earned Income Credit

9. Which of the following credits is refundable?

a. Child Tax Credit

b. Child and Dependent Care Credit

c. Lifetime Learning Credit

d. Foreign Tax Credit

10. Which of the following education-related expenses can be used to claim an education credit?

	Tuition	Fees	Room & Board	Meals
a.	Yes	Yes	Yes	Yes
b.	Yes	Yes	Yes	No
c.	Yes	Yes	No	Yes
d.	Yes	Yes	No	No

11. Michael and Kathy have one dependent, Dustin, who is in his third year of college. Additionally, Michael is taking classes in the evening towards an MBA. What credits are Michael and Kathy allowed to claim?

   I. American Opportunity Tax Credit
   II. Lifetime Learning Credit

   a. I only
   b. II only
   c. I and II
   d. I or II

12. Which of the following best describes the effect of a tax credit?
   a. It reduces a person's gross income.
   b. It reduces a person's adjusted gross income.
   c. It reduces a person's taxable income.
   d. It reduces a person's tax liability.

Individuals as Employees and Proprietors

LEARNING OBJECTIVES: *After completing Chapter 11, you should be able to:*

LO.1 Distinguish between employee and self-employed status.

LO.2 State and explain the exclusions from income available to employees who receive fringe benefits.

LO.3 Apply the rules for computing deductible expenses of employees, including transportation, travel, moving, education, and entertainment expenses.

LO.4 Explain the difference between accountable and nonaccountable employee plans.

LO.5 Understand the opportunities available to build wealth through Individual Retirement Accounts.

LO.6 State and explain the tax provisions applicable to proprietors.

LO.7 Distinguish between business and hobby activities and apply the rules limiting the deduction of hobby losses.

CHAPTER OUTLINE

TAX TALK *The taxpayer—that's someone who works for the Federal government but doesn't have to take a civil service examination.* —RONALD REAGAN

THE BIG PICTURE

SELF-EMPLOYED VERSUS EMPLOYEE—WHAT'S THE DIFFERENCE?

Mark and Mary Herman come to you for tax advice. Mark Herman is a self-employed consultant. Last year, Mark's business generated revenue of $165,000 and incurred expenses of $18,000 for rent and utilities for an office. Mark also spent $8,000 purchasing depreciable equipment used in the business and paid a part-time secretary $12,000 for administrative work performed during the year. He hired Ellen, an assistant to help him in his consulting practice, and paid her $40,000. Mark paid $3,000 for his own health insurance and $500 for term life insurance; he did not contribute to any retirement plans. Mary (Mark's wife) also works as a consultant, but is employed by a large firm. Her salary last year was $85,000. Mary's employer paid $3,000 of premiums for her health insurance and provided $50,000 of group term life insurance to each of its employees. Mary is not covered by a qualified retirement plan at work, but she contributed $5,500 to a traditional IRA. Mary routinely travels for her job and was reimbursed by her employer for all travel expenses. In addition, Mary spent $500 on other employee business expenses that were not reimbursed by her employer.

What are the tax consequences of these items? Can Mark and Mary deduct the expenses they incurred? Are there other tax planning opportunities the couple may be missing or tax issues of which they should be aware?

Read the chapter and formulate your response.

Generally, individuals earn business income as employees or through self-employment. Self-employed individuals are variously described as freelancers, independent contractors, external consultants, micro-business owners, entrepreneurs, and proprietors. In many cases, properly categorizing an individual as an employee or as self-employed for tax purposes is a complex determination. This chapter begins with a discussion of the factors that must be considered in determining whether an individual is an employee or is self-employed. This is followed by a discussion of tax provisions applicable to employees and then by a discussion of tax provisions related to self-employed individuals.

11-1 EMPLOYEE VERSUS SELF-EMPLOYED

LO.1

Distinguish between employee and self-employed status.

When one person performs services for another person or for an entity, the person performing the services either is an employee or is self-employed (i.e., an independent contractor). Globalization, advances in technology, and economic factors have led to increases in self-employment. Some individuals view self-employment as a way to be their own boss, have a flexible work schedule, and do work they truly love. Employers often see hiring self-employed individuals (rather than employees) as a means to achieve greater workforce flexibility and control costs. As a result, the proper determination of employment status is important and is often scrutinized.

From an employer's perspective, misclassification of an individual as self-employed rather than as an employee is not uncommon. This misclassification can be unintentional, resulting from the difficulty in applying a complex set of rules related to employee versus independent contractor status. However, misclassification may be an intentional strategy to avoid certain costs that are associated with having employees. Unlike employees, self-employed individuals do not have to be included in various fringe benefit programs and retirement plans. Furthermore, employers are not required to pay FICA and unemployment taxes (refer to Chapter 1) on compensation paid to independent contractors.

From an individual's perspective, categorization as an employee may avoid certain risks associated with self-employment that employees generally do not assume. For example, a self-employed individual assumes responsibility for employment-related tax obligations and assumes the legal responsibilities associated with performing the job. From a tax perspective, a self-employed individual is responsible for both the employee and the employer share of FICA and unemployment taxes. However, allowable business expenses of self-employed taxpayers are generally classified as deductions *for* AGI and are reported on Schedule C (Profit or Loss from Business) of Form 1040.[1] With the exception of reimbursement under an accountable plan (covered later in the chapter), expenses of employees are deductions *from* AGI. They are reported on Form 2106 (Employee Business expenses) and Schedule A (Itemized Deductions) of Form 1040.[2]

The IRS is aware that businesses can improperly classify workers as self-employed rather than as employees. Failure to properly categorize an individual's work status correctly can have serious tax consequences; tax deficiencies as well as interest and penalties may result for the employer and the employee. The next section discusses those factors that are considered in the proper classification of an individual as an employee or as a self-employed person.

11-1a Factors Considered in Classification

The pivotal issue in classifying an individual as an independent contractor or an employee is whether an employer-employee relationship exists. The common law definition of an employee originated in judicial case law and is summarized in various IRS

---

[1] §§ 62(a)(1) and 162(a). In simple situations, a Schedule C–EZ can be substituted. Also, a Schedule SE (Self-Employment Tax) must be filed.

[2] § 67(a). In simple situations, a Form 2106–EZ (Unreimbursed Employee Business Expenses) can be substituted.

BRIDGE DISCIPLINE **Bridge to Equity or Fairness and Business Law**

Max performs services for Calico, Inc. Amy performs services for Amber, Inc. They perform basically the same service. Yet, Max is classified as an employee, and Amy is classified as an independent contractor. Does such a legal classification produce equitable results in terms of the effects it has on Max and Amy?

Employee status produces a number of potential perks. Included are coverage in the employer's fringe benefits programs such as medical insurance, group term life insurance, and § 132 fringe benefits. For an employee, the current tax rate for Social Security is 6.2 percent and for Medicare, the rate is 1.45 percent (i.e., the employer is responsible for matching the employee amounts). For a self-employed person, the tax rates for Social Security and Medicare are 12.4 percent and 2.9 percent, respectively.

In distinguishing between an employee and an independent contractor, the overriding theme of common law is that the employee is subject to the will and control of the employer as to what is to be done and how it is to be done. Put in tax law terminology, an employer has the right to control and direct the individual who performs the services,

not only as to the result to be accomplished by the work but also as to the details and means by which the result is accomplished. Among the factors generally considered in determining whether this right exists are the following:

- Degree of control exercised over the details of the work.
- Provision of facilities used in the work.
- Opportunity for profit or loss.
- Right to discharge.
- Whether work is part of regular business.
- Permanency of the relationship.
- Relationship that the parties believe they are creating.
- Manner of payment, by the job or by the hour.
- Skill required.
- Offering of the services to the general public rather than to one individual or entity.
- Distinct occupation or recognized trade or calling involved.
- Custom in the trade.

pronouncements. For example, Revenue Ruling 87–41 lists 20 factors that can be used in determining whether a worker is a common law employee or an independent contractor (and, thus, self-employed).[3]

A common law employee-employer relationship exists when the employer has the right to specify the end result and the ways and means by which that result is to be attained.[4] An employee is subject to the will and control of the employer with respect not only to what shall be done but also to how it shall be done. If the individual is subject to the direction or control of another only to the extent of the end result but not as to the means of accomplishment, an employee-employer relationship does not exist.

Certain factors indicate a common law employee-employer relationship. These include the performance of the following by the employer:

- Furnishing tools or equipment and a place to work.
- Providing support services, including the hiring of assistants to help do the work.
- Making training available to provide needed job skills.
- Allowing participation in various workplace fringe benefits (e.g., accident and health plans, group life insurance, and retirement plans).
- Paying for services based on time rather than the task performed.

Each case is tested on its own merits, and the right to control the means and methods of accomplishment is the definitive test. Generally, physicians, lawyers, dentists, contractors, subcontractors, and others who offer services to the public are not classified as employees.

In-depth coverage can be found on this book's companion website: www.cengagebrain.com | **1** DIGGING DEEPER

---

[3]1987–1 C.B. 296.   [4]Reg. § 31.3401(c)–1(b).

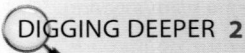

The Big Picture

EXAMPLE 1

Return to the facts of *The Big Picture* on p. 11-1. Mark is a consultant whose major client accounts for 60% of his billings. He does the routine consulting work at the client's request. He is paid a monthly retainer in addition to amounts charged for extra work. Mark is a self-employed individual. Even though most of his income comes from one client, he still has the right to determine *how* the end result of his work is attained.

The Big Picture

EXAMPLE 2

Return to the facts of *The Big Picture* on p. 11-1. Ellen is a recent MBA graduate hired by Mark to assist him in the performance of services for the client mentioned in Example 1. Ellen is under Mark's supervision; he reviews her work and pays her an hourly fee. Ellen is Mark's employee.

DIGGING DEEPER 2   In-depth coverage can be found on this book's companion website: www.cengagebrain.com

---

TAX PLANNING STRATEGIES   Self-Employed Individuals

FRAMEWORK FOCUS: DEDUCTIONS

Strategy: Maximize Deductible Amounts.

Some taxpayers, such as real estate agents and consultants, have the flexibility to be classified as either employees or self-employed individuals. These taxpayers should carefully consider all factors and not automatically assume that self-employed status is preferable.

It is advantageous to deduct one's business expenses *for* AGI and avoid the 2 percent floor for miscellaneous itemized deductions. However, a self-employed individual may incur additional expenses such as local gross receipts taxes, license fees, franchise fees, personal property taxes, and occupation taxes. Record-keeping and filing requirements can also be quite burdensome.

One of the most expensive considerations is the **self-employment tax** imposed on independent contractors

and other self-employed individuals. A self-employed person is required to pay twice the amount of Social Security and Medicare taxes that are imposed on an employee with the same amount of earned income (wages). Even though a deduction *for* AGI is allowed for one-half of the self-employment tax paid, an employee and a self-employed individual are not in the same tax position on equal amounts of earnings. For the applicability of these taxes to workers, see Chapter 1.

After analyzing all of these factors, taxpayers in many cases may decide that employee status is preferable to self-employed status.

LO.2

State and explain the exclusions from income available to employees who receive fringe benefits.

11-2 EXCLUSIONS AVAILABLE TO EMPLOYEES

Several exclusions that are available to *all taxpayers* were discussed in Chapter 4; these include interest income on obligations of state and local governments, life insurance proceeds, and income from discharge of indebtedness. Other exclusions, available only to *individuals*, were discussed in Chapter 10; these exclusions include gifts and inheritances, scholarships, and compensation for injuries and sickness. Exclusions available only to *employees* are generally referred to as qualified fringe benefits. The popularity of fringe benefits is attributable to the fact that the cost of such benefits is deductible by employers and excludible from income by employees. The next sections discuss several of the most popular fringe benefits available to employees.

TAX IN THE NEWS Same-Sex Marriage and Employer-Provided Insurance

Now that same-sex marriages are recognized in most states, those marriages are recognized for Federal income tax purposes. As a result of the 2013 Supreme Court decision in *United States v. Windsor* [133 S.Ct. 2675 (USSC, 2013)], the IRS recognizes marriages validly entered into in a state or country whose laws authorize the marriage of two individuals of the same sex even if the married couple is domiciled in a state that does not recognize the validity of same-sex marriages. As a result, when a same-sex spouse is provided coverage under a spouse's employee health insurance, the premiums may be excluded from the employee's gross income. This was not allowed prior to *Windsor*, resulting in the employee having taxable income from the benefit.

Source: Rev.Rul. 2013–17, 2013–38 I.R.B. 201.

EXAMPLE 3

Cardinal Corporation, which has a marginal tax rate of 35%, provides health insurance coverage to employees at a cost of $1,000 per employee. Because Cardinal can deduct the health insurance premiums paid to provide this coverage, the net cost to the corporation is $650 per employee ($1,000 cost − $350 tax savings). The employee is allowed to exclude the value of this fringe benefit, so there is no tax cost to the employee.

The average employee of Cardinal Corporation is in the 28% bracket. If Cardinal did not provide the health insurance coverage and the employee paid a $1,000 premium, the employee would have to use after-tax dollars to acquire the coverage. The employee would have to earn $1,389 to pay for the coverage [$1,389 wages − ($1,389 × 28% tax)]. The after-tax cost to the corporation of $1,389 in wages is $903 ($1,389 wages − $486 corporate tax savings). Thus, the cost of health insurance coverage is $253 less per employee ($903 − $650) because it is both deductible by the corporation and excludible by the employee.

11-2a Employer-Sponsored Accident and Health Plans

Congress encourages employers to provide employees, retired former employees, and their dependents with accident and health benefits, disability insurance, and long-term care plans. The *premiums* are deductible by the employer and are excluded from the employee's gross income.[5] Although § 105(a) provides the general rule that the employee has includible income when he or she collects the insurance *benefits*, two exceptions are provided.

Section 105(b) generally excludes payments received for medical care of the employee, spouse, and dependents. However, if the payments are for expenses that do not meet the Code's definition of medical care,[6] the amount received must be included in gross income. In addition, the taxpayer must include in gross income any amounts received for medical expenses that were deducted by the taxpayer on a prior return.

EXAMPLE 4

In 2015, Tab's employer-sponsored health insurance plan paid $4,000 for hair transplants that did not meet the Code's definition of medical care. Tab must include the $4,000 in his gross income in 2015.

Section 105(c) excludes payments for the permanent loss or the loss of the use of a member or function of the body or the permanent disfigurement of the employee, the spouse, or a dependent. However, payments that are a substitute for salary (e.g., related to the period of time absent from work) are included in income.

---

[5] § 106, Reg. § 1.106–1, and Rev.Rul. 82–196, 1982–2 C.B. 53.

[6] See the discussion of medical care in Chapter 10.

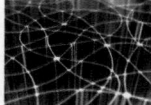

BRIDGE DISCIPLINE **Bridge to Economic and Societal Needs**

The media frequently report on challenges facing senior citizens. Organizations such as the AARP effectively lobby for the rights of senior citizens through direct lobbying in Washington and through grassroots efforts throughout the country. With the graying of America, these concerns and lobbying efforts are likely to be magnified.

Congress, in the 1930s, enacted Social Security to partially provide for the retirement needs of senior citizens. In the 1960s, Congress enacted Medicare to partially provide for the medical needs of senior citizens.

The Internal Revenue Code contains a number of provisions that are "senior citizen friendly." Among these are the following:

- General exclusion, except for taxpayers above certain income levels, of Social Security benefits from gross income (§ 86).
- Exclusion of life insurance proceeds from the gross income of the recipient (§ 101).
- Exclusion of medical insurance premiums and benefits from gross income (§ 105 and § 106).
- Limited exclusion from gross income of gain on the sale of a principal residence (§ 121).
- Limited exclusion from gross income of long-term care insurance premiums and benefits (§ 7702B).
- Beneficial treatment of retirement plans (§§ 401–436).

EXAMPLE 5

Jill loses an eye in an automobile accident unrelated to her work. As a result of the accident, Jill incurs $2,000 of medical expenses, which she deducts on her return. She collects $10,000 from an accident insurance policy carried by her employer. The benefits are paid according to a schedule of amounts that varies with the part of the body injured (e.g., $10,000 for loss of an eye and $20,000 for loss of a hand). Because the payment is for loss of a *member or function of the body*, the $10,000 is excluded from Jill's gross income. Jill was absent from work for a week as a result of the accident. Her employer also provides her with insurance for the loss of income due to illness or injury. Jill collects $500, which is includible in her gross income.

11-2b **Medical Reimbursement Plans**

In lieu of providing an employee with insurance coverage for hospital and medical expenses, the employer may agree to reimburse the employee for these expenses. The amounts received through the insurance coverage (insured plan benefits) are excluded from gross income under § 105 (as previously discussed). Unfortunately, because of cost considerations, the insurance companies that issue this type of policy usually require a broad coverage of employees. An alternative is to have a plan that is not funded with insurance (a self-insured arrangement). Under a self-insured plan, the employer reimburses employees directly for any medical expenses. The benefits received under a self-insured plan can be excluded from the employee's gross income if the plan does not discriminate in favor of highly compensated employees.[7]

There is also an alternative means of accomplishing a medical reimbursement plan. The employer can purchase a medical insurance plan with a high deductible (e.g., the employee is responsible for the first $2,600 of the family's medical expenses) and then make contributions to the employee's **Health Savings Account (HSA)**.[8] The employer can make contributions each month up to the maximum contribution of 100 percent of the deductible amount. The monthly deductible amount is limited to one-twelfth of $3,350 under a high-deductible plan for self-only coverage. The monthly amount for an individual who has family coverage is limited to one-twelfth of $6,650 under a high-deductible plan. Withdrawals from the HSA must be used to reimburse the employee for the medical expenses paid by the employee that are not covered under the high-deductible plan. The employee is not taxed on the employer's contributions to the HSA, the earnings on the funds in the account, or the withdrawals made for medical expenses.[9]

---

[7]§ 105(h).

[8]§§ 106(d) and 223. See additional coverage in Chapter 10.

[9]§§ 106(d), 223(b), and 223(d).

11-2c Long-Term Care Benefits

Generally, long-term care insurance, which covers expenses such as the cost of care in a nursing home, is treated the same as accident and health insurance benefits. Thus, the employee does not recognize income when the employer pays the premiums. Also, the individual who purchases his or her own policy can exclude the benefits from gross income. However, statutory limitations (indexed for inflation) exist for the following amounts:

- Premiums paid by the employer.
- Benefits collected under the employer's plan.
- Benefits collected from the individual's policy.

The employer or insurance company generally provides the employee with information on the amount of his or her taxable benefits. The maximum amount excluded must be reduced by any amount received from other third parties (e.g., Medicare, Medicaid).[10]

EXAMPLE 6

Hazel, who suffers from Alzheimer's disease, is a patient in a nursing home for the last 30 days of 2015. While in the nursing home, she incurs total costs of $7,600. Medicare pays $3,200 of the costs. Hazel receives $7,000 from her long-term care insurance policy, which pays while she is in the facility.

The amount Hazel may exclude is calculated as follows:

Greater of:		
Daily statutory amount in 2015 ($330 × 30 days)	$9,900	
Actual cost of the care	7,600	$ 9,900
Less: Amount received from Medicare		(3,200)
Amount of exclusion		$ 6,700

Therefore, Hazel must include $300 ($7,000 − $6,700) of the long-term care benefits received in her gross income.

The exclusion for long-term care insurance is not available if it is provided as part of a cafeteria plan or a flexible spending plan (discussed later in this chapter).

11-2d Meals and Lodging Furnished for the Convenience of the Employer

Income can take any form, including meals and lodging. However, § 119 excludes from gross income the value of meals and lodging provided to the employee and the employee's spouse and dependents under the following conditions:[11]

- The meals and/or lodging are *furnished by the employer*, on the employer's *business premises*, for the *convenience of the employer*.
- In the case of lodging, the *employee is required* to accept the lodging as a condition of employment.

The courts have interpreted both of these requirements strictly, as discussed below.

Furnished by the Employer

The following two questions have been raised with regard to the *furnished by the employer* requirement:

- Who is considered an *employee*?
- What is meant by *furnished*?

---

[10]§ 7702B and § 213(d)(10). See IRS Publication 525 for the taxable and nontaxable amounts that the employer is required to report on the employee's Form W–2.

[11]§ 119(a). The value of meals and lodging is also excluded from FICA and FUTA tax. *Rowan Companies, Inc. v. U.S.*, 81–1 USTC ¶9479, 48 AFTR 2d 81–5115, 101 S.Ct. 2288 (USSC, 1981).

The IRS and some courts have reasoned that because a partner is not an employee, the exclusion does not apply to a partner. However, the Tax Court and the Fifth Circuit Court of Appeals have ruled in favor of the taxpayer on this issue.[12]

The Supreme Court held that a *cash meal allowance* was ineligible for the exclusion because the employer did not actually furnish the meals.[13] Similarly, one court denied the exclusion where the employer paid for the food and supplied the cooking facilities but the employee prepared the meal.[14]

On the Employer's Business Premises

The *on the employer's business premises* requirement, applicable to both meals and lodging, has resulted in much litigation. The Regulations define business premises as simply "the place of employment of the employee."[15] Thus, the Sixth Circuit Court of Appeals held that a residence, owned by the employer and occupied by an employee, located two blocks from the motel that the employee managed was not part of the business premises.[16] However, the Tax Court considered an employer-owned house located across the street from the hotel that was managed by the taxpayer to be on the business premises of the employer.[17] Perhaps these two cases can be reconciled by comparing the distance from the lodging facilities to the place where the employer's business was conducted. Apparently, the closer the lodging is to the business operations, the more likely the convenience of the employer is served.

For the Convenience of the Employer

The *convenience of the employer* test is intended to focus on the employer's motivation for furnishing the meals and lodging rather than on the benefits received by the employee. If the employer furnishes the meals and lodging primarily to enable the employee to perform his or her duties properly, it does not matter that the employee considers these benefits to be a part of his or her compensation.

The Regulations give the following examples in which the tests for excluding meals are satisfied:[18]

- A restaurant requires its service staff to eat their meals on the premises during the busy lunch and breakfast hours.
- A bank furnishes meals on the premises for its tellers to limit the time the employees are away from their booths during the busy hours.
- A worker is employed at a construction site in a remote part of Alaska. The employer must furnish meals and lodging due to the inaccessibility of other facilities.

Required as a Condition of Employment

The *employee is required to accept test* applies only to lodging. If the employee's use of the housing would serve the convenience of the employer but the employee is not required to use the housing, the exclusion is not available.

 **EXAMPLE 7**

VEP, a utilities company, has all of its service personnel on 24-hour call for emergencies. The company encourages its employees to live near the plant so that they can respond quickly to emergency calls. Company-owned housing is available rent-free. Only 10 of the employees live in company housing because it is not suitable for families.

continued

[12]Rev.Rul. 80, 1953–1 C.B. 62; *Comm. v. Doak*, 56–2 USTC ¶9708, 49 AFTR 1491, 234 F.2d 704 (CA–4, 1956); but see *G. A. Papineau*, 16 T.C. 130 (1951); *Armstrong v. Phinney*, 68–1 USTC ¶9355, 21 AFTR 2d 1260, 394 F.2d 661 (CA–5, 1968).

[13]*Comm. v. Kowalski*, 77–2 USTC ¶9748, 40 AFTR 2d 77–6128, 98 S.Ct. 315 (USSC, 1977).

[14]*Tougher v. Comm.*, 71–1 USTC ¶9398, 27 AFTR 2d 71–1301, 441 F.2d 1148 (CA–9, 1971).

[15]Reg. § 1.119–1(c)(1).

[16]*Comm. v. Anderson*, 67–1 USTC ¶9136, 19 AFTR 2d 318, 371 F.2d 59 (CA–6, 1966).

[17]*J. B. Lindeman*, 60 T.C. 609 (1973).

[18]Reg. § 1.119–1(f).

Although the company-provided housing serves the convenience of the employer, it is not required. Therefore, the employees who live in company housing must include its value in gross income.

In addition, if the employee has the option of cash or lodging, the employer-required test is not satisfied.

EXAMPLE
8

Khalid is the manager of a large apartment complex. The employer requires Khalid to live on the premises but does not charge him rent. The rental value of his apartment is $9,600 a year. Although Khalid considers the rent-free housing a significant benefit, he is not required to include the value of the housing in his gross income.

Other housing exclusions are available for certain employees of educational institutions, ministers of the gospel, and military personnel.

11-2e Group Term Life Insurance

For many years, the IRS did not attempt to tax the value of life insurance protection provided to an employee by the employer. Some companies took undue advantage of the exclusion by providing large amounts of insurance protection for key executives. In response, Congress enacted § 79, which created a limited exclusion for group term life insurance. The premiums on the first $50,000 of group term life insurance protection are excludible from the employee's gross income.

The benefits of this exclusion are available only to employees. Proprietors and partners are not considered employees. Moreover, the Regulations generally require broad-scale coverage of employees to satisfy the group requirement (e.g., shareholder-employees would not constitute a qualified group). The exclusion applies only to term insurance (protection for a period of time but with no cash surrender value) and not to ordinary life insurance (lifetime protection plus a cash surrender value that can be drawn upon before death).

As mentioned, the exclusion applies to the first $50,000 of group term life insurance protection. For each $1,000 of coverage in excess of $50,000, the employee must include the amounts indicated in Exhibit 11.1 in gross income.[19]

| In-depth coverage can be found on this book's companion website: www.cengagebrain.com | **3** DIGGING DEEPER |

EXAMPLE
9

Finch Corporation has a group term life insurance policy with coverage equal to the employee's annual salary. Keith, age 52, is president of the corporation and receives an annual salary of $350,000. Keith must include $828 in gross income from the insurance protection for the year.

$$[(\$350{,}000 - \$50{,}000) \div \$1{,}000] \times \$.23 \times 12 \text{ months} = \$828$$

If the plan discriminates in favor of certain key employees (e.g., officers), the key employees are not eligible for the exclusion. In such a case, the key employees must include in gross income the *greater* of actual premiums paid by the employer or the amount calculated from the Uniform Premiums table in Exhibit 11.1. The other employees are still eligible for the $50,000 exclusion and continue to use the Uniform Premiums table to compute the income from excess insurance protection.[20]

11-2f Qualified Tuition Reduction Plans

Employees (including retired and disabled former employees) of nonprofit educational institutions are allowed to exclude a tuition waiver from gross income if the waiver is

---

[19]Reg. § 1.79–3(d)(2).   [20]§ 79(d).

EXHIBIT 11.1	Uniform Premiums for $1,000 of Group Term Life Insurance Protection

Attained Age on Last Day of Employee's Tax Year	Cost of $1,000 of Protection for a One-Month Period*
Under 25	$ .05
25–29	.06
30–34	.08
35–39	.09
40–44	.10
45–49	.15
50–54	.23
55–59	.43
60–64	.66
65–69	1.27
70 and above	2.06

*Reg. § 1.79–3, effective for coverage after June 30, 1999.

pursuant to a qualified tuition reduction plan. The exclusion applies to tuition reductions granted to the employee, the employee's spouse, and the employee's dependent children.[21]

A scholarship recipient may exclude from gross income the amount used for tuition and related expenses (fees, books, supplies, and equipment required for courses), provided the conditions of the grant do not require that the funds be used for other purposes.[22]

EXAMPLE 10

Kelly receives a scholarship of $9,500 from State University to be used to pursue a bachelor's degree. She spends $4,000 on tuition, $3,000 on books and supplies, and $2,500 for room and board. Kelly may exclude $7,000 ($4,000 + $3,000) from gross income. The $2,500 spent for room and board is included in Kelly's gross income.

11-2g Other Employee Fringe Benefits

Congress has dealt specifically with some other fringe benefits, which are summarized below.

- The employee does not have to include in gross income the value of child and dependent care services paid for by the employer and incurred to enable the employee to work. The exclusion cannot exceed $5,000 per year ($2,500 if married and filing separately). For a married couple, the annual exclusion cannot exceed the earned income of the spouse who has the lesser amount of earned income. For an unmarried taxpayer, the exclusion cannot exceed the taxpayer's earned income.[23]

- The value of the use of a gymnasium or other athletic facilities by employees, their spouses, and their dependent children may be excluded from an employee's gross income. The facilities must be on the employer's premises, and substantially all of the use of the facilities must be by employees and their family members.[24]

---

[21]§ 117(d).
[22]§ 117(b).

[23]§ 129. The exclusion applies to the same types of expenses that, if paid by the employee (and not reimbursed by the employer), would be eligible for the credit for child and dependent care expenses, discussed in Chapter 10.
[24]§ 132(j)(4).

TAX IN THE NEWS **Providing a Feel-Good Fringe Benefit at a Low Cost**

Employers can provide employees with a variety of fringe benefits that are eligible for exclusion treatment. One such benefit is the adoption expense exclusion (subject to a statutory indexed ceiling amount).

Adoption assistance programs offered by employers to employees enjoy a family-friendly image and are inexpensive to provide from a total labor force perspective. According to Hewitt Associates, a benefits consulting firm, only about .1 percent of eligible workers use the exclusion each year. Nevertheless, in the current economic environment, employers are reducing such programs as a way to cut costs. In 2009, employers offering adoption assistance programs fell to 10 percent, down from 22 percent in 2006,

according to a survey of 522 employers by the Society for Human Resource Management. General Motors suspended its adoption assistance program five months before filing for bankruptcy.

International adoptions by U.S. parents have fallen 24 percent since 2004, with only 17,438 of such adoptions taking place in 2008. At the same time adoption assistance programs are being cut, costs for international adoptions are increasing and now range between $15,000 and $40,000.

Source: Based on Sue Shellenbarger, "Targeting 'Feel-Good' Benefits," *Wall Street Journal*, July 8, 2009, p. D1.

- Qualified employer-provided educational assistance (tuition, fees, books, and supplies) at the undergraduate and graduate levels is excludible from gross income. The exclusion does not cover meals, lodging, and transportation costs. In addition, it does not cover educational payments for courses involving sports, games, or hobbies. The exclusion is subject to an annual employee statutory ceiling of $5,250.[25]

- The employee can exclude from gross income up to $13,400 of expenses incurred to adopt a child where the adoption expenses are paid or reimbursed by the employer under a qualified adoption assistance program.[26] The limit on the exclusion is the same even if the child has special needs (is not physically or mentally capable of caring for himself or herself). However, for a child with special needs, the $13,400 exclusion from gross income applies even if the actual adoption expenses are less than that amount. For 2015, the exclusion is phased out as adjusted gross income increases from $201,010 to $241,010.

11-2h **Cafeteria Plans**

Generally, if an employee is offered a choice between cash and some other form of compensation, the employee is deemed to have constructively received the cash even when the noncash option is elected. Thus, the employee has gross income regardless of the option chosen.

An exception to this constructive receipt treatment is provided under the cafeteria plan rules. Under such a plan, the employee is permitted to choose between cash and nontaxable benefits (e.g., group term life insurance, health and accident protection, child care). If the employee chooses the otherwise nontaxable benefits, the cafeteria plan rules allow the benefits to be excluded from the employee's gross income.[27] Cafeteria plans provide tremendous flexibility in tailoring the employee pay package to fit individual needs. Some employees (usually the younger group) prefer cash, while others (usually the older group) will opt for the fringe benefit program. However, long-term care insurance cannot be part of a cafeteria plan. Thus, an employer that wants to provide long-term care benefits must provide such benefits separate from the cafeteria plan.[28]

---

[25]§ 127.
[26]§ 137.

[27]§ 125.
[28]§ 125(f).

EXAMPLE
11

Hawk Corporation offers its employees (on a nondiscriminatory basis) a choice of any one or all of the following benefits:

Benefit	Cost
Group term life insurance	$ 200
Hospitalization insurance for family members	2,400
Child care payments	1,800
	$4,400

If a benefit is not selected, the employee receives cash equal to the cost of the benefit. Kay, an employee, has a spouse who works for another employer that provides hospitalization insurance but no child care payments. Kay elects to receive the group term life insurance, the child care payments, and $2,400 of cash. Only the $2,400 must be included in Kay's gross income.

11-2i Flexible Spending Plans

Flexible spending plans (often referred to as flexible benefit plans) operate much like cafeteria plans. Under these plans, the employee accepts lower cash compensation (as much as $2,550 in 2015) in return for the employer's agreement to pay certain costs the employer can pay without the employee recognizing gross income. For example, assume that the employer's health insurance policy does not cover dental expenses. The employee could estimate his or her dental expenses for the upcoming year and agree to a salary reduction equal to the estimated dental expenses. The employer then pays or reimburses the employee for the actual dental expenses incurred, up to the amount of the salary reduction. If the employee's actual dental expenses are less than the reduction in cash compensation, the employee cannot recover the difference. Hence, these plans are often referred to as *use or lose* plans. To avoid forfeiture of unpaid amounts, the IRS allows a payment until March 15 of the following year to count. As is the case for cafeteria plans, flexible spending plans cannot be used to pay long-term care insurance premiums.

Concept Summary 11.1 reviews the exclusions discussed to this point in the chapter.

Concept Summary 11.1

Employee Fringe Benefits

Type of Benefit	Exclusion
Accident, health, and long-term care insurance and medical reimbursement (§§ 105 and 106)	Insurance premiums paid by the employer and benefits received
High-deductible health insurance and contributions to employee's Health Savings Account (§§ 106 and 223)	Employer premiums on high-deductible medical insurance plus contributions to Health Savings Account (statutory limits, indexed for inflation)
Meals and lodging furnished for the convenience of the employer (§ 119)	Value of meals and lodging on the employer's premises
Group term life insurance (§ 79)	Premiums on up to $50,000 of protection
Qualified tuition reduction (§ 117(d))	Value of tuition waiver
Child care provided by the employer or reimbursement of employee's cost (§ 129)	Services provided or reimbursement of expenses up to $5,000 a year
Athletic facilities on the employer's premises (§ 132)	Value of services
Educational assistance for tuition, fees, books, and supplies (§ 127)	Limited to $5,250 annually
Adoption assistance (§ 137)	Expenses up to $13,400
Flexible spending plans (§ 125)	Limited to $2,550 annually

11-2j General Classes of Excluded Benefits

An employer can provide a variety of economic benefits to employees. Under the all-inclusive concept of income, the benefits are taxable unless one of the provisions previously discussed specifically excludes the item from gross income. The amount of the income is the fair market value of the benefit. This reasoning can lead to results that Congress considers unacceptable, as illustrated in the following example.

Ryan is employed in New York as a ticket clerk for Trans National Airlines. He has a sick mother, who lives in Miami, Florida, but he has no money for plane tickets. Trans National has daily flights from New York to Miami that often leave with empty seats. The cost of a round-trip ticket is $400. If Trans National allows Ryan to fly without charge to Miami, under the general gross income rules, Ryan has income equal to the value of a ticket. Therefore, Ryan must include $400 in gross income for the value of a trip to Miami.

Because Congress believed that taxing fringe benefits often yielded harsh results, § 132 was enacted to provide exclusion treatment. This provision established seven broad classes of nontaxable employee benefits:[29]

- No-additional-cost services.
- Qualified employee discounts.
- Working condition fringes.
- *De minimis* fringes.
- Qualified transportation fringes.
- Qualified moving expense reimbursements.
- Qualified retirement planning services.

No-Additional-Cost Services

Return to Example 12. This illustrates the reason for the **no-additional-cost service** type of fringe benefit. The value of the services received is excluded from an employee's gross income if all of the following conditions are satisfied:

- The employee receives services, as opposed to property.
- The employer does not incur substantial additional costs, including forgone revenue, in providing the services to the employee.
- The services are offered to customers in the ordinary course of the business in which the employee works.[30]

In Example 12, although the airplane may burn slightly more fuel because Ryan is aboard and Ryan may receive the same meal or snacks as paying customers, the additional costs to the airline would not be substantial. Thus, the trip could qualify as a no-additional-cost service.

On the other hand, assume that Ryan is given a reserved seat on a flight that is frequently full. The employer would be forgoing revenue to allow Ryan to fly. This forgone revenue would be a substantial additional cost, and thus the benefit would be taxable to Ryan.

In-depth coverage can be found on this book's companion website: www.cengagebrain.com   **4 DIGGING DEEPER**

The no-additional-cost exclusion extends to the employee's spouse and dependent children and to retired and disabled former employees.[31] However, the exclusion is not extended to highly compensated employees unless the benefit is available on a nondiscriminatory basis.

---

[29]See, generally, § 132.
[30]Reg. § 1.132–2.

[31]Reg. § 1.132–1(b).

Qualified Employee Discounts

When the employer sells goods or services (other than no-additional-cost benefits just discussed) to the employee for a price that is less than the price charged regular customers, the employee realizes income equal to the discount. However, the discount, referred to as a **qualified employee discount**, can be excluded from the gross income of the employee, subject to the following conditions and limitations:

- The exclusion is not available for discounted sales of real property (e.g., a house) or for personal property of the type commonly held for investment (e. g., common stocks).
- The property or services must be from the same line of business in which the employee works.
- In the case of *property*, the exclusion is limited to the *gross profit component* of the price to customers.
- In the case of *services*, the exclusion is limited to 20 percent of the customer price.

EXAMPLE 14

Silver Corporation, which operates a department store, sells a television to a store employee for $300. The regular customer price is $500, and the gross profit rate is 25%. The corporation also sells the employee a service contract for $120. The regular customer price for the contract is $150. The employee must recognize income of $75.

Customer price for property	$ 500	
Less: Gross profit (25%)	(125)	
	$ 375	
Employee price	(300)	
Excess discount recognized as income		$75
Customer price for service	$ 150	
Less: 20%	(30)	
	$ 120	
Employee price	(120)	
Excess discount recognized as income		0
Total income recognized		$75

As in the case of no-additional-cost benefits, the exclusion applies to employees (including service partners), their spouses and dependent children, and retired and disabled former employees.

Working Condition Fringes

Generally, an employee may exclude the cost of property or services provided by the employer if the employee could deduct the cost of those items if he or she had actually paid for them. These benefits are called **working condition fringes**.

EXAMPLE 15

Mitch is a CPA employed by an accounting firm. The employer pays Mitch's annual dues to professional organizations. Mitch is not required to include the payment of the dues in gross income because if he had paid the dues, he would have been allowed to deduct the amount as an employee business expense (as discussed later in this chapter).

In many cases, this exclusion merely avoids reporting income and an offsetting deduction. Also note that unlike the other fringe benefits discussed previously, working condition fringes can be made available on a discriminatory basis and still qualify for the exclusion.

De Minimis Fringes

As the term suggests, **de minimis fringe benefits** are so small that accounting for them is impractical. Examples of *de minimis* fringes include the following:

- Occasional personal use of a company copying machine, occasional company cocktail parties or picnics for employees, occasional supper money or taxi fare for employees because of overtime work, and certain holiday gifts of property with a low fair market value are excluded.

- The value of meals consumed in a subsidized eating facility (e.g., an employees' cafeteria) operated by the employer is excluded if the facility is located on or near the employer's business premises, if revenue equals or exceeds direct operating costs, and if nondiscrimination requirements are met.

When taxpayers venture beyond established norms, there is obviously room for disagreement as to what is *de minimis*.

In Notice 2011–72, the IRS addressed the question of whether cell phones provided by the employer could be excluded from gross income as a working condition fringe benefit. Generally, the value of the cell phone can be excluded if it is provided for business reasons such as to enable the employee to be in contact with clients when the employee is away from the office. When the primary purpose test is satisfied, any personal use of the employer-provided cell phone will be excluded as a *de minimis* fringe benefit.

Qualified Transportation Fringes

The intent of the exclusion for **qualified transportation fringes** is to encourage the use of mass transit for commuting to and from work. Qualified transportation fringes encompass the following transportation benefits provided by the employer to the employee:

1. Transportation in a commuter highway vehicle between the employee's residence and the place of employment.
2. A transit pass.
3. Qualified parking.
4. Qualified bicycle commuting reimbursement.

Statutory dollar limits are placed on the amount of the exclusion. Categories (1) and (2) above are combined for purposes of applying the limit. In this case, the limit on the exclusion for 2015 is $130 per month. Category (3) has a separate limit. For qualified parking, the limit on the exclusion for 2015 is $250 per month. Both of these dollar limits are indexed annually for inflation.

A commuter highway vehicle is any highway vehicle with a seating capacity of at least six adults (excluding the driver). In addition, at least 80 percent of the vehicle's use must be for transporting employees between their residences and place of employment.

Qualified parking includes the following:

- Parking provided to an employee on or near the employer's business premises.

- Parking provided to an employee on or near a location from which the employee commutes to work via mass transit, in a commuter highway vehicle, or in a carpool.

The *qualified bicycle commuting reimbursement* enables an employee to exclude up to $20 per month received from an employer as reimbursement for the cost of commuting by bicycle (i.e., bicycle purchase, improvement, repair, and storage).

Qualified transportation fringes may be provided directly by the employer or may be in the form of cash reimbursements.

Gray Corporation's offices are located in the center of a large city. The company pays for parking spaces to be used by the company officers. Steve, a vice president, receives $300 of such benefits each month. The parking space rental qualifies as a qualified transportation fringe. Of the $300 benefit received each month by Steve, $250 is excludible from gross income. The balance of $50 is included in his gross income. The same result would occur if Steve paid for the parking and was reimbursed by his employer.

Qualified Moving Expense Reimbursements

Qualified moving expenses that are reimbursed or paid by the employer are excludible from gross income. A qualified moving expense is an expense that would be deductible under § 217. See the discussion of moving expenses later in this chapter.

Qualified Retirement Planning Services

Qualified retirement planning services include any retirement planning advice or information that an employer who maintains a qualified retirement plan provides to an employee or the employee's spouse. Congress decided to exclude the value of such services from gross income because they are a key part of retirement income planning. Such an exclusion should motivate more employers to provide retirement planning services to their employees.

Nondiscrimination Provisions

For no-additional-cost services, qualified employee discounts, and qualified retirement planning services that are discriminatory in favor of *highly compensated employees*, exclusion treatment is denied. However, any non-highly compensated employees who receive these benefits can still enjoy exclusion treatment.[32]

Dove Company's officers are allowed to purchase goods from the company at a 25% discount. All other employees are allowed only a 15% discount. The company's gross profit margin on these goods is 30%. Because the officers receive more favorable discounts, the plan is discriminatory in favor of the officers. In regard to all other employees, the discount is "qualified" because it is available to all employees (other than the officers who receive a more favorable discount) and the discount is less than the company's gross profit.

Peggy, an officer in the company, purchased goods from the company for $750 when the price charged to customers was $1,000. Peggy must include $250 in gross income because the plan is discriminatory.

Mason, an employee of the company who is not an officer, purchased goods for $850 when the customer price was $1,000. Mason is not required to recognize gross income because he received a qualified employee discount.

De minimis fringe benefits (except for subsidized eating facilities) and working condition fringe benefits can be provided on a discriminatory basis. Likewise, the qualified transportation fringe and the qualified moving expense reimbursement can be provided on a discriminatory basis.

If fringe benefits cannot qualify for any of the specific exclusions or do not fit into any of the general classes of excluded benefits, the employee must recognize gross income equal to the fair market value of the benefits received.

A review of employee fringe benefits is set forth in Concept Summary 11.2.

DIGGING DEEPER 5 | In-depth coverage can be found on this book's companion website: www.cengagebrain.com

---

[32]§§ 132(j)(1) and 132(m)(2).

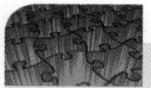

Concept Summary 11.2

General Classes of Fringe Benefits

Benefit	Description and Examples	Coverage Allowed	Effect of Discrimination
1. No-additional-cost services	The employee takes advantage of the employer's excess capacity (e.g., free passes for airline employees).	Current, retired, and disabled employees; their spouses and dependent children; spouses of deceased employees. Partners are treated as employees.	No exclusion for highly compensated employees.
2. Qualified discounts on goods	The employee is allowed a discount no greater than the gross profit margin on goods sold to customers.	Same as (1) above.	Same as (1) above.
3. Qualified discounts on services	The employee is allowed a discount (maximum of 20%) on services the employer offers to customers.	Same as (1) above.	Same as (1) above.
4. Working condition fringes	Expenses paid by the employer that would be deductible if paid by the employee (e.g., a mechanic's tools). Also includes auto salesperson's use of a car held for sale.	Current employees, partners, directors, and independent contractors.	No effect.
5. *De minimis* items	Expenses so immaterial that accounting for them is not warranted (e.g., occasional supper money, personal use of the copy machine).	Any recipient of a fringe benefit.	No effect.
6. Qualified transportation fringes	Transportation benefits provided by the employer to employees, including a commute in a commuter highway vehicle, a transit pass, qualified parking, and qualified bicycle commuting.	Current employees.	No effect.
7. Qualified moving expense reimbursements	Qualified moving expenses that are paid or reimbursed by the employer. A qualified moving expense is one that would be deductible under § 217.	Current employees.	No effect.
8. Qualified retirement planning services	Qualified retirement planning services that are provided by the employer.	Current employees and spouses.	Same as (1) above.

11-2k Foreign Earned Income

The United States uses a global tax system as opposed to a territorial system. Under this global system, a U.S. citizen is generally subject to U.S. tax on his or her income regardless of the income's geographic origin. As a result, a U.S. citizen who earns income in another country could experience double taxation: the same income would be taxed in the United States and in the foreign country. Out of a sense of fairness and so as not to discourage U.S. citizens from working abroad, Congress has provided alternative forms of relief from taxes on foreign earned income. The taxpayer can elect *either* (1) to include the foreign income in his or her taxable income and then claim a credit for foreign taxes paid or (2) to exclude the foreign earnings from his or her U.S. gross income (the **foreign earned income exclusion**).[33] The foreign tax credit option is discussed in Chapter 17, but as is apparent from the following discussion, most taxpayers choose the exclusion.

---

[33]§ 911.

Foreign earned income consists of the earnings from the individual's personal services rendered in a foreign country (other than as an employee of the U.S. government). To qualify for the exclusion, the taxpayer must be either of the following:

- A bona fide resident of the foreign country (or countries).
- Present in a foreign country (or countries) for at least 330 days during any 12 consecutive months.

EXAMPLE 18

Sandra's trip to and from a foreign country in connection with her work encompassed the following dates:

Arrived in Foreign Country	Returned to the United States
March 10, 2014	February 15, 2015

During the 12 consecutive months ending on March 10, 2015, Sandra was present in the foreign country for at least 330 days (365 days less 13 days in February and 10 days in March 2015). Therefore, all income earned in the foreign country through March 10, 2015, is eligible for the exclusion.

The exclusion is *limited* to an indexed amount of $100,800 for 2015 ($99,200 in 2014). For married persons, both of whom have foreign earned income, the exclusion is computed separately for each spouse. If all of the days in the tax year are not qualifying days (i.e., days present in the foreign country), the taxpayer must compute the maximum exclusion on a daily basis ($100,800 divided by the number of days in the entire year and multiplied by the number of qualifying days).

EXAMPLE 19

Keith qualifies for the foreign earned income exclusion. He was present in France for all of 2015. Keith's salary for 2015 is $120,000. Because all of the days in 2015 are qualifying days, Keith can exclude $100,800 of his $120,000 salary.

Assume instead that only 335 days were qualifying days. Then Keith's exclusion is limited to $92,515, computed as follows:

$$\$100,800 \times \frac{335 \text{ days in foreign country}}{365 \text{ days in the year}} = \$92,515$$

LO.3

Apply the rules for computing deductible expenses of employees, including transportation, travel, moving, education, and entertainment expenses.

11-3 EMPLOYEE EXPENSES

Once the employment relationship is established, employee expenses fall into one of the following categories:

- Transportation.
- Travel.
- Moving.
- Education.
- Entertainment.
- Other.

The deductions for these expenses are discussed next in the order presented. Keep in mind, however, that these expenses are not necessarily limited to employees. A deduction for business transportation, for example, is equally available to taxpayers who are self-employed.

11-3a Transportation Expenses

Qualified Expenditures

An employee may deduct unreimbursed employment-related **transportation expenses** as an itemized deduction *from* AGI. Transportation expenses include only the cost of transporting the employee from one place to another in the course of employment when the employee is not away from home in travel status. Such costs include taxi fares, automobile expenses, tolls, and parking.

Commuting Expenses

Commuting between home and one's place of employment is a personal, nondeductible expense. The fact that one employee drives 30 miles to work and another employee walks six blocks is of no significance.[34] However, the expenses of getting from one job to another job or from one workstation to another workstation are deductible transportation expenses rather than nondeductible commuting expenses.

In-depth coverage can be found on this book's companion website: www.cengagebrain.com

6 DIGGING DEEPER

EXAMPLE 20

In the current year, Cynthia holds two jobs, a full-time job with Blue Corporation and a part-time job with Wren Corporation. Cynthia customarily leaves home at 7:30 A.M. and drives 30 miles to the Blue Corporation plant, where she works until 5:00 P.M. After dinner at a nearby café, Cynthia drives 20 miles to Wren Corporation and works from 7:00 to 11:00 P.M. The distance from the second job to Cynthia's home is 40 miles. Her deduction is based on 20 miles (the distance between jobs).

Referring back to Example 20, assume that Cynthia has an office in the home that qualifies as a principal place of business. Thus, the transportation between home and various work locations is not a commuting expense. That is, any transportation from her home office to and from business sites will not be disallowed as a commuting expense.

Computation of Automobile Expenses

A taxpayer has two choices in computing deductible automobile expenses. The first alternative is to use the actual operating cost, which includes depreciation (refer to Chapter 5), gas, oil, repairs, licenses, and insurance costs. Records must be kept that document the automobile's personal and business use. Only the percentage allocable to business transportation and travel is allowed as a deduction.

The second alternative is the **automatic mileage method**. For 2015, the deduction is based on 57.5 cents per mile for business miles.[35] Parking fees and tolls are allowed in addition to expenses computed using the automatic mileage method.

Generally, a taxpayer may elect either method for any particular year. However, the following restrictions apply:

- The vehicle must be owned or leased by the taxpayer.
- The vehicle is not used for hire (e.g., taxicab).
- If five or more vehicles are in use (for business purposes) at the *same* time (not alternately), a taxpayer may not use the automatic mileage method.
- Use of the automatic mileage method in the first year the auto is placed in service is considered an election not to use the MACRS method of depreciation (refer to Chapter 5).
- A taxpayer may not switch to the automatic mileage method if the MACRS statutory percentage method or the election to expense under § 179 has been used.

In-depth coverage can be found on this book's companion website: www.cengagebrain.com

7 DIGGING DEEPER

---

[34]*Tauferner v. U.S.*, 69–1 USTC ¶9241, 23 AFTR 2d 69–1025, 407 F.2d 243 (CA–10, 1969).

[35]Notice 2014–79, 2014–53 I.R.B 1001. For 2014, the rate was 56 cents.

11-3b **Travel Expenses**

Definition of Travel Expenses

An itemized deduction is allowed for *unreimbursed* travel expenses related to a tax-payer's employment. Travel expenses are more broadly defined in the Code than are transportation expenses. Travel expenses include transportation expenses and meals and lodging while away from home in the pursuit of a trade or business. Meals cannot be lavish or extravagant. A deduction for meals and lodging is available only if the tax-payer is away from his or her tax home. Deductible travel expenses also include reasonable laundry and incidental expenses.

DIGGING DEEPER 8	In-depth coverage can be found on this book's companion website: www.cengagebrain.com

Away-from-Home Requirement

The crucial test for the deductibility of travel expenses is whether the employee is away from home overnight. "Overnight" need not be a 24-hour period, but it must be a period substantially longer than an ordinary day's work and must require rest, sleep, or a relief-from-work period.[36] A one-day business trip is not travel status, and meals and lodging for such a trip are not deductible.

Temporary Assignments

The employee must be away from home for a temporary period. If the taxpayer-employee is reassigned to a new post for an indefinite period of time, that new post becomes his or her tax home. Temporary indicates that the assignment's termination is expected within a reasonably short period of time. The position of the IRS is that the tax home is the business location, post, or station of the taxpayer. Thus, travel expenses are not deductible if a taxpayer is reassigned for an indefinite period and does not move his or her place of residence to the new location.

Temporary Becomes Permanent

EXAMPLE 21

Malcolm's employer opened a branch office in San Diego. Malcolm was assigned to the new office for three months to train a new manager and to assist in setting up the new office. He tried commuting from his home in Los Angeles for a week and decided that he could not continue driving several hours a day. He rented an apartment in San Diego, where he lived during the week. He spent weekends with his wife and children at their home in Los Angeles. Malcolm's rent, meals, laundry, incidentals, and automobile expenses in San Diego are deductible. To the extent Malcolm's transportation expense related to his weekend trips home exceeds what his cost of meals and lodging would have been, the excess is personal and nondeductible.

EXAMPLE 22

Assume that Malcolm in Example 21 was transferred to the new location to become the new manager permanently. His wife and children continued to live in Los Angeles until the end of the school year. Malcolm is no longer "away from home" because the assignment is not temporary. His travel expenses are not deductible.

To curtail controversy in this area, the Code specifies that a taxpayer "shall not be treated as temporarily away from home during any period of employment if such period exceeds 1 year."[37]

DIGGING DEEPER 9	In-depth coverage can be found on this book's companion website: www.cengagebrain.com

---

[36]*U.S. v. Correll*, 68–1 USTC ¶9101, 20 AFTR 2d 5845, 88 S.Ct 445 (USSC, 1967); Rev.Rul. 75–168, 1975–1 C.B. 58.

[37]§ 162(a).

Determining the Tax Home

Under ordinary circumstances, determining the location of a taxpayer's tax home does not present a problem. The tax home is the area in which the taxpayer derives his or her principal source of income; when the taxpayer has more than one place of employment, the tax home is based on the amount of time spent in each location.

It is possible for a taxpayer never to be away from his or her tax home. In other words, the tax home follows the taxpayer.[38] Under such circumstances, all meals and lodging remain personal and are not deductible.

EXAMPLE
23

Jim is single and works full-time as a long-haul truck driver. He lists his mother's home as his address and stays there during holidays. However, he contributes nothing toward its maintenance. Because Jim has no regular place of duty or place where he regularly lives, his tax home is where he works (i.e., on the road). As an itinerant (transient), he is never away from home, and all of his meals and lodging while on the road are personal and not deductible.

The result reached in Example 23 is justified on the grounds that there is no duplication of living expenses in the case of itinerant taxpayers.[39]

Combined Business and Pleasure Travel

To be deductible, travel expenses need not be incurred in the performance of specific job functions. Travel expenses incurred to attend a professional convention are deductible by an employee if attendance is connected with services as an employee. For example, an employee of a law firm can deduct travel expenses incurred to attend a meeting of the American Bar Association.

In order to limit the possibility of a taxpayer claiming a tax deduction for what is essentially a personal vacation, several provisions have been enacted to restrict deductions associated with combined business and pleasure trips. If the business/pleasure trip is from one point in the United States to another point in the United States (*domestic travel*), the transportation expenses are deductible only if the trip is primarily for business.[40] Meals, lodging, and other expenses are allocated between business and personal days. If the trip is primarily for pleasure, no transportation expenses qualify as a deduction.

In-depth coverage can be found on this book's companion website: www.cengagebrain.com   **10** DIGGING DEEPER

EXAMPLE
24

In the current year, Hana travels from Seattle to New York primarily for business. She spends five days conducting business and three days sightseeing and attending shows. Her plane and taxi fare amounts to $1,160. Her meals amount to $200 per day, and lodging and incidental expenses are $350 per day. She can deduct the transportation expenses of $1,160 because the trip is primarily for business (five days of business versus three days of sightseeing). Deductible meals are limited to five days and are subject to the 50% cutback (discussed later in the chapter) for a total of $500 [5 days × ($200 × 50%)], and other deductions are limited to $1,750 (5 days × $350). If Hana is an employee, the unreimbursed travel expenses are miscellaneous itemized deductions subject to the 2%-of-AGI floor.

When the trip is outside the United States (*foreign travel*), special rules apply.[41] Transportation expenses must be allocated between business and personal days *unless* (1) the taxpayer is away from home for seven days or less or (2) less than 25 percent of the time was for personal purposes. No allocation is required if the taxpayer has no

---

[38]*Moses Mitnick*, 13 T.C. 1 (1949).

[39]Rev.Rul. 73–539, 1973–2 C.B. 201 and *James O. Henderson*, 70 TCM 1407, T.C.Memo. 1995–559, *aff'd* by 98–1 USTC ¶50,375, 81 AFTR 2d 98–1748, 143 F.3d 497 (CA–9, 1998).

[40]Reg. § 1.162–2(b)(1).

[41]§ 274(c) and Reg. § 1.274–4. For purposes of the seven-days-or-less exception, the departure travel day is not counted.

substantial control over arrangements for the trip or the desire for a vacation is not a major factor in taking the trip. If the trip is primarily for pleasure, no transportation charges are deductible. Days devoted to travel are considered business days. Weekends, legal holidays, and intervening days are considered business days, provided that both the preceding and succeeding days were business days.

 DIGGING DEEPER 11 | In-depth coverage can be found on this book's companion website: www.cengagebrain.com

EXAMPLE

25

In the current year, Robert takes a trip from New York to Japan primarily for business purposes. He is away from home from June 10 through June 19. He spends three days vacationing and seven days (including two travel days) conducting business. His airfare is $4,000, his meals amount to $200 per day, and lodging and incidental expenses are $300 per day. Because Robert is away from home for more than seven days and more than 25% of his time is devoted to personal purposes, only 70% (7 days business/10 days total) of the transportation is deductible. His deductions are as follows:

Transportation (70% × $4,000)		$2,800
Lodging ($300 × 7)		2,100
Meals ($200 × 7)	$1,400	
Less: 50% cutback (discussed later in this chapter)	(700)	700
Total deductions		$5,600

Note that if Robert was gone the same period of time but spent only two days vacationing, no allocation of transportation would be required. Because the pleasure portion of the trip was less than 25% of the total, all of the airfare would qualify for the travel deduction.

The foreign convention rules do not operate to bar a deduction to an employer if the expense is *compensatory* in nature. For example, a trip to Rome won by a top salesperson is included in the gross income of the employee and is fully deductible by the employer.

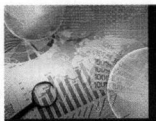

TAX PLANNING STRATEGIES   **Transportation and Travel Expenses**

FRAMEWORK FOCUS: DEDUCTIONS

Strategy: Maximize Deductible Amounts.

Adequate detailed records of all transportation and travel expenses should be kept. Because the automatic (standard) mileage allowance often is modest in amount, a new, expensive automobile used primarily for business may generate a higher expense based on actual cost. The election to expense part of the cost of the automobile under § 179, MACRS depreciation, insurance, repairs and maintenance, automobile club dues, and other related costs may result in

automobile expenses greater than the automatic mileage allowance.

If a taxpayer wants to sightsee or vacation on a business trip, it would be beneficial to schedule business on both a Friday and a Monday to turn the weekend into business days for allocation purposes. It is especially crucial to schedule appropriate business days when foreign travel is involved.

11-3c **Moving Expenses**

Moving expenses are deductible for moves in connection with the commencement of work at a new principal workplace.[42] Both employees and self-employed individuals

---
[42]§ 217(a).

can deduct these expenses. To be eligible for a moving expense deduction, a taxpayer must meet two basic tests: distance and time.

Distance Test

To meet the distance test, the taxpayer's new job location must be at least 50 miles farther from the taxpayer's old residence than the old residence was from the former place of employment. In this regard, the location of the new residence is not relevant. This eliminates a moving expense deduction for (1) taxpayers who purchase a new home in the same general area without changing their place of employment and (2) taxpayers who accept a new job in the same area as their old job.

If an individual is not employed before the move, the new job must be at least 50 miles from the former residence. Concept Summary 11.3 illustrates the application of the distance test.

Concept Summary 11.3

Meeting and Not Meeting the Distance Test

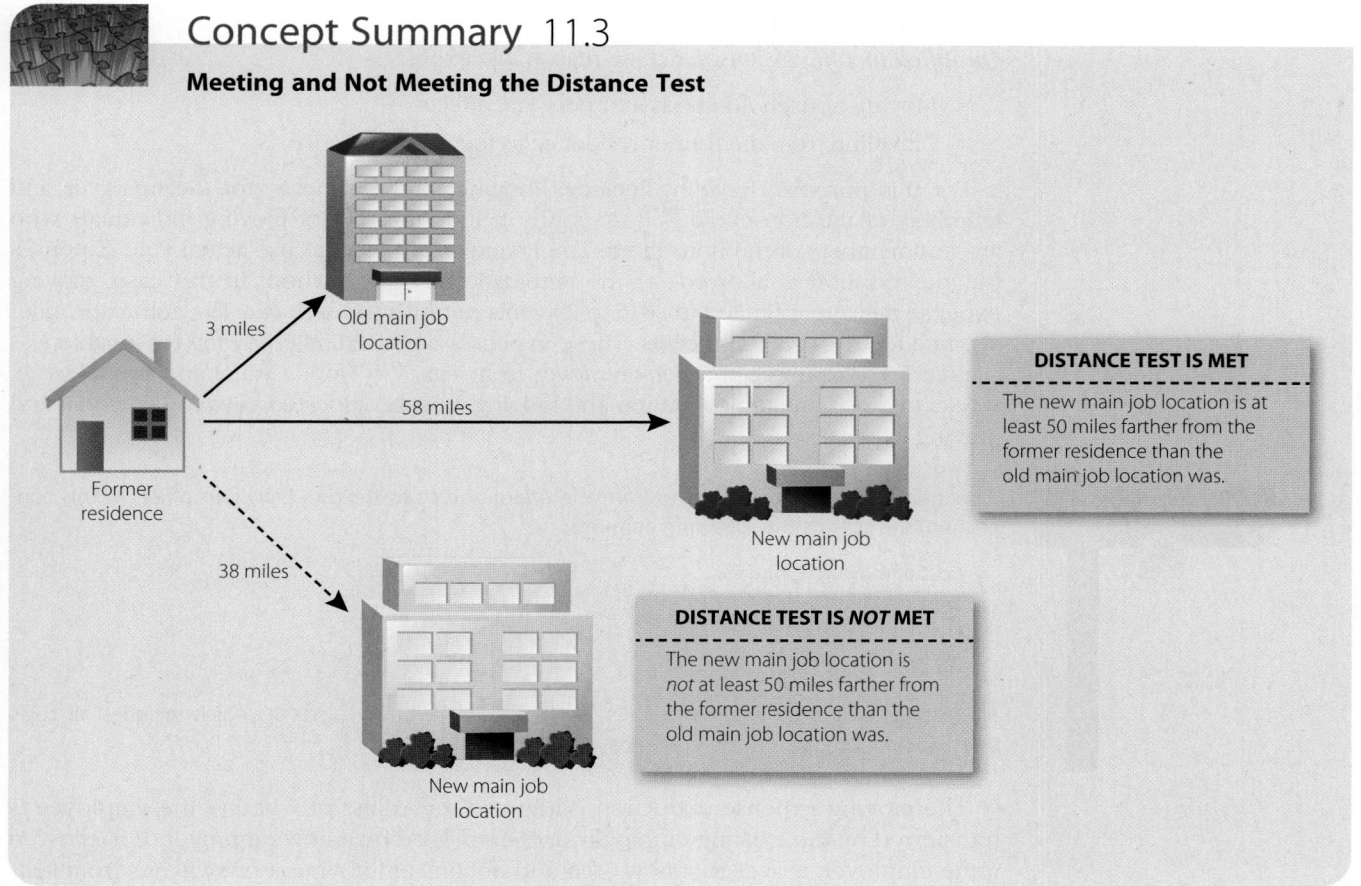

3 miles — Old main job location

58 miles — New main job location

DISTANCE TEST IS MET
The new main job location is at least 50 miles farther from the former residence than the old main job location was.

Former residence

38 miles — New main job location

DISTANCE TEST IS *NOT* MET
The new main job location is *not* at least 50 miles farther from the former residence than the old main job location was.

Time Test

To meet the time test, an employee must be employed on a full-time basis at the new location for 39 weeks in the 12-month period following the move. If the taxpayer is a self-employed individual, he or she must work in the new location for 78 weeks during the 24 months following the move. The first 39 weeks must be in the first 12 months. The time test is disregarded if the taxpayer dies, becomes disabled, or is discharged (other than for willful misconduct) or transferred by the employer.

Treatment of Moving Expenses

Qualified moving expenses include reasonable expenses of:

- Moving household goods and personal effects.
- Traveling from the former residence to the new residence.

For this purpose, traveling includes lodging, but not meals, for the taxpayer and members of the household.[43] It does not include the cost of moving individuals who are not members of the household. The taxpayer can elect to use actual auto expenses (no depreciation is allowed) or the automatic mileage method. In this case, moving expense mileage is limited in 2015 to 23 cents per mile for each car. The automatic mileage rate for 2014 was 23.5 cents. These expenses are also limited by the reasonableness standard. For example, if a person moves from Texas to Florida via Maine and takes six weeks to do so, the transportation and lodging must be allocated between personal and moving expenses.

EXAMPLE 26

Jill is transferred by her employer from the Atlanta office to the San Francisco office. In this connection, she spends the following amounts:

Cost of moving furniture	$4,800
Transportation	700
Meals	450
Lodging	600

Jill's total qualified moving expense is $6,100 ($4,800 + $700 + $600), which includes all costs listed above except for the cost of meals.

The moving expense deduction is allowed regardless of whether the employee is transferred by the existing employer or is employed by a new employer. It is allowed if the employee moves to a new area and obtains employment or switches from self-employed status to employee status (and vice versa). The moving expense deduction is also allowed if an individual is unemployed before obtaining employment in a new area.

What Is Not Included

In addition to meals while en route, the moving expense deduction does *not* include the following costs:

- New car tags and driver's licenses.
- Loss on the sale of a residence or penalty for breaking a lease.

[43]§ 217(b).

- Forfeiture of security deposits and loss from disposing of club memberships.
- Pre-move house-hunting expenses.
- Temporary living expenses.

In-depth coverage can be found on this book's companion website: www.cengagebrain.com **13** DIGGING DEEPER

TAX PLANNING STRATEGIES Moving Expenses

FRAMEWORK FOCUS: DEDUCTIONS

Strategy: Maximize Deductible Amounts.

Persons who retire and move to a new location incur personal nondeductible moving expenses. If the retired person accepts a full-time job in the new location before moving and meets the time and distance requirements, the moving expenses are deductible.

At the time of his retirement from the national office of a major accounting firm, Gordon had an annual salary of $480,000. He moves from New York City to Seattle to retire and accepts a full-time teaching position at a Seattle junior college at an annual salary of $22,000. If Gordon satisfies the 39-week test, his moving expenses are deductible. The disparity between the two salaries (previous and current) is of no consequence.

EXAMPLE
27

11-3d Education Expenses

Employees *and* self-employed individuals can deduct expenses incurred for education as ordinary and necessary business expenses, provided the expenses are incurred to maintain or improve existing skills required in the present job. An employee can also deduct expenses incurred to meet the express requirements of the employer or the requirements imposed by law to retain his or her employment status.

Education expenses are not deductible if the education is for either of the following purposes (except as discussed under A Limited Deduction Approach, which follows):

- To meet the minimum educational standards for qualification in the taxpayer's existing job.
- To qualify the taxpayer for a new trade or business.[44]

Thus, fees incurred for professional exams (the bar exam, for example) and fees for review courses (such as a CPA review course) are not deductible.[45] If the education incidentally results in a promotion or raise, the deduction still can be taken as long as the education maintained and improved existing skills and did not qualify the person for a new trade or business. A change in duties is not always fatal to the deduction if the new duties involve the same general work. For example, the IRS has ruled that a practicing dentist's education expenses incurred to become an orthodontist are deductible.[46]

Requirements Imposed by Law or by the Employer for Retention of Employment

Taxpayers are permitted to deduct education expenses if additional courses are required by the employer or are imposed by law. Many states require a minimum of a

---

[44]Reg. §§ 1.162–5(b)(2) and (3).

[45]Reg. § 1.212–1(f) and Rev.Rul. 69–292, 1969–1 C.B. 84.

[46]Rev.Rul. 74–78, 1974–1 C.B. 44.

TAX IN THE NEWS   **Is an MBA Degree Deductible?**

Education that maintains or improves existing skills is deductible, but education that qualifies a taxpayer for a new field is not. But how do these basic rules apply to a conventional (i.e., nonspecialized) MBA degree? Does being a manager or a consultant require an MBA degree? Generally, the answer has always been that it does not. In this regard, therefore, the education does not create a new skill; so its cost should be deductible.

Several recent holdings, however, have found that an MBA degree can lead to qualifying for a new trade or business. But these holdings involved situations where the education resulted in a job change and satisfied different minimum requirements set by the employer. In one case, for example, the taxpayer moved from the position of investment analyst to become an investment banker, and the latter position required an MBA degree. Under these circumstances, the cost of the education was held to be nondeductible.

But barring a change to a job where the degree is required, the cost of an MBA degree should be deductible as merely improving existing managerial skills.

Source: *Daniel R. Allemeier, Jr., 90 TCM 197, T.C.Memo. 2005–207.*

bachelor's degree and a specified number of additional courses to retain a teaching job. In addition, some public school systems have imposed a master's degree requirement and require teachers to make satisfactory progress toward a master's degree to keep their positions. If the required education is the minimum degree required for the job, no deduction is allowed.

Professionals (e.g., physicians, attorneys, and CPAs) may deduct expenses incurred to meet continuing professional education requirements imposed by states as a condition for retaining a license to practice.

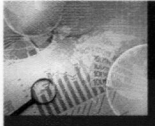

DIGGING DEEPER 14 | In-depth coverage can be found on this book's companion website: **www.cengagebrain.com**

Maintaining or Improving Existing Skills

The *maintaining or improving existing skills* requirement in the Code has been difficult for both taxpayers and the courts to interpret. For example, a business executive is permitted to deduct the costs of obtaining an MBA on the grounds the advanced management education is undertaken to maintain and improve existing management skills. The executive is eligible to deduct the costs of specialized, nondegree management courses that are taken for continuing education or for maintaining or improving existing skills. Expenses incurred by the executive to obtain a law degree are not deductible, however, because the education constitutes training for a new trade or business. The Regulations specifically deny a self-employed accountant a deduction for expenses relating to law school.[47]

TAX PLANNING STRATEGIES   **Education Expenses**

FRAMEWORK FOCUS: DEDUCTIONS

Strategy: Maximize Deductible Amounts.

Education expenses are treated as nondeductible personal items unless the individual is employed or is engaged in a trade or business. A temporary leave of absence for further education is one way to ensure that the taxpayer is still treated as being engaged in a trade or business. An individual was permitted to deduct education expenses even

continued

---

[47]Reg. § 1.162–5(b)(3)(ii) Example (1).

though he resigned from his job, returned to school full-time for two years, and accepted another job in the same field upon graduation. The court held that the student had merely suspended active participation in his field.[48]

If the time out of the field is too long, education expense deductions will be disallowed. For example, a teacher who left the field for four years to raise her child and curtailed her employment searches and writing activities was denied a deduction for education expenses. She was no longer actively engaged in the trade or business of being an educator.[49]

To secure the deduction, an individual should arrange his or her work situation to preserve employee or business status.

As discussed below under *A Limited Deduction Approach*, a limited exception is available for taxpayers who do not meet the preceding requirements.

Classification of Specific Items

Education expenses include books, tuition, supplies, transportation (e.g., from the office to night school), and travel (e.g., meals and lodging while away from home at summer school).

EXAMPLE 28

Bill, who holds a bachelor of education degree, is a secondary education teacher in the Charleston school system. The school board recently raised its minimum education requirement for new teachers from four years of college training to five. A grandfather clause allows teachers with only four years of college to continue to qualify if they show satisfactory progress toward a graduate degree. Bill enrolls at the University of South Carolina during the summer and takes two graduate courses. His unreimbursed expenses for this purpose are as follows:

Books and tuition	$3,600
Lodging while in travel status (June–August)	2,150
Meals while in travel status	1,100
Laundry while in travel status	220
Transportation	900

Bill has an itemized deduction as follows:

Books and tuition	$3,600
Lodging	2,150
Meals less 50% cutback (discussed later in this chapter)	550
Laundry	220
Transportation	900
	$7,420

11-3e A Limited Deduction Approach

One of the major shortcomings of the education deduction, discussed previously, is that it is unavailable for taxpayers obtaining a basic skill (i.e., to meet the minimum standards required for the taxpayer's current job). This shortcoming has been partly resolved with the  **deduction for qualified tuition and related expenses** .

A deduction *for* AGI is allowed for qualified tuition and related expenses involving higher education (i.e., postsecondary). The deduction is the lesser of the qualifying amount spent or the maximum amount allowed by § 222. The maximum deductions allowed are shown in Exhibit 11.2. Note that the limitations are based on the taxpayer's MAGI and filing status.[50] Although a phaseout is provided for, note its short and drastic

---

[48]*Stephen G. Sherman*, 36 TCM 1191, T.C.Memo. 1977–301.

[49]*Brian C. Mulherin*, 42 TCM 834, T.C.Memo. 1981–454; *George A. Baist*, 56 TCM 778, T.C.Memo. 1988–554.

[50]MAGI is modified adjusted gross income as defined in § 222(b)(2). Examples of some of these modifications include adding back to regular AGI the

foreign earned income exclusion and the domestic production activities deduction. This provision expired after December 31, 2014, but it is expected to be extended.

EXHIBIT 11.2	Limitations for Qualified Tuition Deduction

Filing Status	MAGI Limit	Maximum Deduction Allowed
Single	$ 65,000	$4,000
Married	130,000	
Single	65,001 to 80,000*	2,000
Married	130,001 to 160,000*	2,000

*No deduction is available if MAGI exceeds this amount.

effect. Only two steps are involved ($65,000/$80,000 for single and $130,000/$160,000 for married), and the benefit of § 222 *disappears completely* after the second step. Thus, a married couple with MAGI of $160,000 would lose the entire deduction if they earned an additional $1. The § 222 limitations are not indexed for inflation.

Various aspects of the higher education tuition deduction are summarized as follows:

- *Qualified tuition and related expenses* include whatever is required for enrollment at the institution. Usually, student activity fees, books, and room and board are not included.[51]
- The expense need not be employment-related, although it can be.
- The deduction is available for a taxpayer's spouse or anyone who can be claimed as a dependent and is an eligible student.
- The deduction is not available for married persons who file separate returns.[52]
- To avoid a "double benefit," the deduction must be coordinated with other education provisions (e.g., American Opportunity and lifetime learning credits as discussed in Chapter 10). Along this same line, no deduction is allowed for a taxpayer who qualifies as another's dependent.[53]
- The deduction *for* AGI classification avoids the 2%-of-AGI floor on miscellaneous itemized deductions. See Chapter 10.

EXAMPLE 29

Tina is single and a full-time employee of a CPA firm. During the current year, she attends law school at night and incurs the following expenses: $4,200 for tuition and $340 for books and supplies. Presuming that she satisfies the MAGI limitation (see Exhibit 11.2), she can claim $4,000 as a deduction *for* AGI. If she itemizes her deductions for the year, can she claim the $540 not allowed under § 222 ($200 tuition in excess of $4,000 + $340 for books and supplies) as an education expense eligible for itemized deduction treatment? No, because obtaining a law degree leads to a new trade or business.

The deduction for qualified tuition and related expenses can be determined by completing Form 8917 (Tuition and Fees Deduction). The form should be attached to Form 1040 (or Form 1040A).

---

[51]Section 222(d) refers to § 25A(f), which deals with the American Opportunity and lifetime learning credits (see Chapter 10). Student activity fees and prescribed course-related books may be allowed if they are a condition for enrollment.

[52]§ 222(d)(4).

[53]§ 222(c).

Another deduction item relating to education is the limited deduction of interest on student loans, which is covered in Chapter 10.[54]

11-3f Entertainment Expenses

Many taxpayers attempt to deduct personal entertainment expenses as business expenses. For this reason, the tax law restricts the deductibility of entertainment expenses. The Code contains strict record-keeping requirements and provides restrictive tests for the deduction of certain types of entertainment expenses.

The Fifty Percent Cutback

Only 50 percent of meal and entertainment expenses is deductible.[55] The limitation applies to employees, employers, and self-employed individuals. Although the 50 percent cutback can apply to either the employer or the employee, it will not apply twice. The cutback applies to the one who really pays (economically) for the meals or entertainment.

In-depth coverage can be found on this book's companion website: www.cengagebrain.com

Jane, an employee of Pato Corporation, entertains one of her clients. If Pato Corporation does not reimburse Jane, her expenses are subject to the cutback. If, however, Pato Corporation reimburses Jane (or pays for the entertainment directly), Pato suffers the cutback.

EXAMPLE 30

Transportation expenses are not affected by the cutback rule—only meals and entertainment expenses are reduced. The cutback also applies to taxes and tips relating to meals and entertainment. Cover charges, parking fees at an entertainment location, and room rental fees for a meal or cocktail party are also subject to the 50 percent cutback.

In-depth coverage can be found on this book's companion website: www.cengagebrain.com

Joe pays a $40 cab fare to meet his client for dinner. The meal costs $150, and Joe leaves a $30 tip. His deduction is $130 [($150 meal costs + $30 tip) × 50% + $40 cab fare].

EXAMPLE 31

Classification of Expenses

Entertainment expenses are classified either as *directly related* to business or *associated with* business.[56] Directly related expenses are related to an actual business meeting or discussion. These expenses are distinguished from entertainment expenses that are incurred to promote goodwill, such as maintaining existing customer relations. To obtain a deduction for directly related entertainment, it is not necessary to show that actual benefit resulted from the expenditure as long as there was a reasonable expectation of benefit. To qualify as directly related, the expense should be incurred in a business setting. If there is little possibility of engaging in the active conduct of a trade or business due to the nature of the social facility, it is difficult to qualify the expenditure as directly related to business.

Expenses associated with, rather than directly related to, business entertainment must serve a specific business purpose, such as obtaining new business or continuing existing business. These expenditures qualify only if the expenses directly precede or follow

---

[54]§ 221.

[55]§ 274(n).

[56]§ 274(a)(1)(A).

a bona fide business discussion. Entertainment occurring on the same day as the business discussion is considered associated with business.

Jerry, a manufacturer's representative, took his client to play a round of golf during the afternoon. They had dinner the same evening, during which time business was discussed. After dinner, they went to a nightclub to have drinks and listen to a jazz band. The business dinner qualifies as directly related entertainment. The golf outing and the visit to the nightclub qualify as associated with entertainment.

TAX PLANNING STRATEGIES Entertainment Expenses

FRAMEWORK FOCUS: DEDUCTIONS

Strategy: Maximize Deductible Amounts.

Taxpayers should maintain detailed records of amounts, time, place, business purpose, and business relationships. A credit card receipt details the place, date, and amount of the expense. A notation made on the receipt of the names of the person(s) attending, the business relationship, and the topic of discussion should constitute sufficient documentation.[57] Failure to provide sufficient documentation could lead to disallowance of entertainment expense deductions.

Associated with or goodwill entertainment requires a business discussion to be conducted immediately before or after the entertainment. Furthermore, a business purpose must exist for the entertainment. Taxpayers should arrange for a business discussion before or after such entertainment. They also must document the business purpose, such as obtaining new business from a prospective customer.

Restrictions upon Deductibility of Business Meals

Business meals are deductible only if:[58]

- The meal is directly related to or associated with the active conduct of a trade or business,
- The expense is not lavish or extravagant under the circumstances, and
- The taxpayer (or an employee) is present at the meal.

A business meal with a business associate or customer is not deductible unless business is discussed before, during, or after the meal. This requirement does not apply to meals consumed while away from home in travel status.

Taxpayer Presence at Business Meals

Lacy travels to San Francisco for a business convention. She pays for dinner with three colleagues and is not reimbursed by her employer. They do not discuss business. She can deduct 50% of the cost of her meal. However, she cannot deduct the cost of her colleagues' meals.

Lance, a party to a contract negotiation, buys dinner for other parties to the negotiation but does not attend the dinner. No deduction is allowed because Lance was not present.

Restrictions upon Deductibility of Club Dues

The Code provides that "No deduction shall be allowed ... for amounts paid or incurred for membership in any club organized for business, pleasure, recreation, or other social purpose."[59] Although this prohibition seems quite broad, it does not apply to clubs

---

[57]*Kenneth W. Guenther,* 54 TCM 382, T.C.Memo. 1987–440.
[58]§ 274(k).
[59]§ 274(a)(3).

whose primary purpose is public service and community volunteerism (e.g., Kiwanis, Lions, and Rotary). Although *dues* are not deductible, actual entertainment at a club may qualify.

During the current year, Vincent spent $1,400 on business lunches at the Lakeside Country Club. The annual membership fee was $6,000, and Vincent used the facility 60% of the time for business. Presuming that the lunches meet the business meal test, Vincent may claim $700 (50% cutback × $1,400) as a deduction. None of the club dues are deductible.

EXAMPLE

35

In-depth coverage can be found on this book's companion website: www.cengagebrain.com

17 DIGGING DEEPER

Business Gifts

Although not subject to a cutback adjustment, business gifts are deductible only to the extent of $25 per donee per year.[60] An exception is made for gifts costing $4 or less (e.g., pens with the employee's or company's name on them) or promotional materials. Such items are not treated as business gifts subject to the $25 limitation. In addition, incidental costs such as engraving of jewelry and nominal charges for gift-wrapping, mailing, and delivery are not included in the cost of the gift in applying the limitation. Gifts to superiors and employers are not deductible. The $25 limitation on business gifts cannot be circumvented by having the donor's spouse join in the gift or by making multiple gifts that include the customer's family. Records must be maintained to substantiate business gifts.

11-3g Other Employee Expenses

In addition to those expenses discussed previously, the Code provides for the deduction of a number of other job-related expenses. The home office deduction, educator expenses, miscellaneous employee expenses, and job hunting expenses are discussed in this section.

Office in the Home

Employees and self-employed individuals are not allowed a deduction for office in the home expenses unless a portion of the residence is used *exclusively and on a regular basis* as either:

- The principal place of business for any trade or business of the taxpayer.
- A place of business used by clients, patients, or customers.

Employees must meet an additional test: the use must be for the convenience of the employer rather than merely being "appropriate and helpful."[61]

The precise meaning of "principal place of business" has been the subject of considerable controversy.[62] Congress ultimately resolved the controversy by amending the Code.[63]

The term *principal place of business* now includes a place of business that satisfies the following requirements:

- The office is used by the taxpayer to conduct administrative or management activities of a trade or business.
- There is no other fixed location of the trade or business where the taxpayer conducts these activities.

---

[60]§ 274(b)(1).

[61]§ 280A(c)(1).

[62]See the restrictive interpretation arrived at in *Comm. v. Soliman*, 93–1 USTC ¶50,014, 71 AFTR 2d 93–463, 113 S.Ct. 701 (USSC, 1993).

[63]§ 280A(c)(1).

EXAMPLE 36

Dr. Smith is a self-employed anesthesiologist. During the year, he spends 30 to 35 hours per week administering anesthesia and postoperative care to patients in three hospitals, none of which provides him with an office. He also spends two or three hours per day in a room in his home that he uses exclusively as an office. He does not meet patients there, but he performs a variety of tasks related to his medical practice (e.g., contacting surgeons, doing bookkeeping, and reading medical journals). A deduction will be allowed because Dr. Smith uses the office in the home to conduct administrative or management activities of his trade or business and there is no other fixed location where these activities can be carried out.

The exclusive use requirement means that a specific part of the home must be used solely for business purposes. A deduction, if permitted, requires an allocation of total expenses of operating the home between business and personal use based on floor space or number of rooms.

Even if the taxpayer meets the above requirements, the allowable home office expenses cannot exceed the gross income from the business less all other business expenses attributable to the activity. That is, the home office deduction cannot create a loss. Furthermore, the home office expenses that are allowed as itemized deductions anyway (e.g., mortgage interest and real estate taxes) must be deducted first. All home office expenses of an employee are miscellaneous itemized deductions, except those (such as interest and taxes) that qualify as other personal itemized deductions. Home office expenses of a self-employed individual are trade or business expenses and are deductible *for* AGI. Any disallowed home office expenses are carried forward and used in future years subject to the same limitations.

DIGGING DEEPER 18 | **In-depth coverage can be found on this book's companion website: www.cengagebrain.com**

EXAMPLE 37

Rick is a certified public accountant employed by a regional CPA firm as a tax manager. He operates a separate business in which he refinishes furniture in his home. For this business, he uses two rooms in the basement of his home exclusively and regularly. The floor space of the two rooms is 240 square feet, which constitutes 10% of the total floor space of his 2,400-square-foot residence. Gross income from the business totals $8,000. Expenses of the business (other than home office expenses) are $6,500. Rick incurs the following home office expenses:

Real property taxes on residence	$ 4,000
Interest expense on residence	7,500
Operating expenses of residence (including homeowners insurance)	2,000
Depreciation on residence (based on 10% business use)	350

Rick's deductions are determined as follows:

Business income		$ 8,000
Less: Other business expenses		(6,500)
Net income from the business (before the office in the home deduction)		$ 1,500
Less: Allocable taxes ($4,000 × 10%)	$400	
Allocable interest ($7,500 × 10%)	750	(1,150)
		$ 350
Less: Allocable operating expenses of the residence ($2,000 × 10%)		(200)
		$ 150
Less: Allocable depreciation ($350, limited to remaining income)		(150)
		$ –0–

Rick has a carryover deduction of $200 (the unused excess depreciation). Because he is self-employed, the allocable taxes and interest ($1,150), the other deductible office expenses ($200 + $150), and $6,500 of other business expenses are deductible *for* AGI.

Educator Expenses

Many teachers purchase school supplies for classroom use and are not reimbursed by their employer. Such teachers may deduct the costs they incur for books, supplies, computer equipment and related software and services, other equipment, and supplementary materials they use in the classroom. The annual statutory ceiling on the deduction *for* AGI classification is $250.[64]

Miscellaneous Employee Expenses

Deductible miscellaneous employee expenses include special clothing and its upkeep, union dues, and professional expenses. Also deductible are professional dues, professional meetings, and employment agency fees for seeking new employment in the taxpayer's current trade or business, whether or not a new job is secured.

To be deductible, *special clothing* must be both specifically required as a condition of employment and not adaptable for regular wear. For example, a police officer's uniform is not suitable for off-duty activities. An exception is clothing used to the extent it takes the place of regular clothing (e.g., some military uniforms).

Captain Roberts is on active duty in the U.S. Army. The cost of his regular uniforms is not deductible because such clothing is suitable for regular wear. Captain Roberts, however, spends over $1,100 to purchase "dress blues." Under military regulations, dress uniforms may be worn only during ceremonial functions (e.g., official events, parades). The $1,100 cost, to the extent it exceeds any clothing allowance, qualifies as a deduction.

EXAMPLE
38

Job Hunting

The current position of the IRS is that expenses incurred in *seeking employment* are deductible if the taxpayer is seeking employment in the same trade or business. The deduction is allowed whether or not the attempts to secure employment are successful. No deduction is allowed for persons seeking their first job or seeking employment in a new trade or business.

11-3h Classification of Employee Expenses

The classification of employee expenses depends on whether they are reimbursed by the employer under an accountable plan. If so, then they are not reported by the employee at all. In effect, this result is equivalent to reporting the reimbursement as income and treating the expenses as deductions *for* AGI.[65] Alternatively, if the expenses are reimbursed under a nonaccountable plan or are not reimbursed at all, they are classified as deductions *from* AGI and can be claimed only if the employee-taxpayer itemizes (subject to the 2%-of-AGI floor). Exceptions are made for moving expenses and the employment-related expenses of a qualified performing artist, where a deduction *for* AGI is allowed. Thus, the tax treatment of reimbursements under accountable and nonaccountable plans differs significantly.

LO.4

Explain the difference between accountable and nonaccountable employee plans.

Accountable Plans

An accountable plan requires the employee to:

- Adequately account for (substantiate) the expenses. An employee renders an *adequate accounting* by submitting a record, with receipts and other substantiation, to the employer.[66]
- Return any excess reimbursement or allowance. An "excess reimbursement or allowance" is any amount the employee does not adequately account for as an ordinary and necessary business expense.

---

[64]§ 62(a)(2)(D). This provision expired at the end of 2014, but it is expected to be extended.

[65]§ 62(a)(2).

[66]Reg. § 1.162–17(b)(4).

The law provides that no deduction is allowed for any travel, entertainment, business gift, or listed property (automobiles and computers) expenditure unless properly substantiated by adequate records. The records should contain the following information:[67]

- The amount of the expense.
- The time and place of travel or entertainment (or date of gift).
- The business purpose of the expense.
- The business relationship of the taxpayer to the person entertained (or receiving the gift).

This means that the taxpayer must maintain an account book or diary in which the above information is recorded at the time of the expenditure. Documentary evidence such as an itemized receipt is required to support any expenditure for lodging while traveling away from home and for any other expenditure of $75 or more. If a taxpayer fails to keep adequate records, each expense must be established by a written or oral statement of the exact details of the expense and by other corroborating evidence.[68]

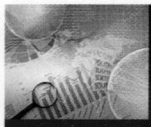 DIGGING DEEPER 19 | In-depth coverage can be found on this book's companion website: www.cengagebrain.com

Nonaccountable Plans

A **nonaccountable plan** is a plan in which an adequate accounting or return of excess amounts, or both, is not required. All reimbursements of expenses are reported in full as wages on the employee's Form W–2. Any allowable expenses are deductible in the same manner as unreimbursed expenses.

An employer may have an accountable plan and require employees to return excess reimbursements or allowances, but an employee may fail to follow the rules of the plan. In that case, the expenses and reimbursements are also subject to nonaccountable plan treatment.

Unreimbursed Employee Expenses

Unreimbursed employee expenses are treated in a straightforward manner. Meals and entertainment expenses are subject to the 50 percent limit. Total unreimbursed employee business expenses are usually reported as miscellaneous itemized deductions subject to the 2%-of-AGI floor (refer to Chapter 10). If the employee could have received, but did not seek, reimbursement for whatever reason, none of the employment-related expenses are deductible.

TAX PLANNING STRATEGIES   Unreimbursed Employee Business Expenses

FRAMEWORK FOCUS: DEDUCTIONS

Strategy: Maximize Deductible Amounts.

The 2 percent floor for unreimbursed employee business expenses offers a tax planning opportunity for married couples. If one spouse has high miscellaneous expenses subject to the floor, it may be beneficial for the couple to file separate returns. If they file jointly, the 2 percent floor is based on the adjusted gross incomes of both. Filing separately lowers the reduction to 2 percent of only one spouse's adjusted gross income.

Other provisions of the law should be considered, however. For example, filing separately could cost a couple

losses of up to $25,000 from self-managed rental units under the passive activity loss rules (discussed in Chapter 6).

Another possibility is to negotiate a salary reduction with one's employer in exchange for the 100 percent reimbursement of employee expenses. The employee is better off because the 2 percent floor does not apply. The employer is better off because certain expense reimbursements are not subject to Social Security and other payroll taxes.

---

[67]§ 274(d).

[68]Reg. § 1.274–5T(c)(3).

In-depth coverage can be found on this book's companion website: www.cengagebrain.com **20** DIGGING DEEPER

11-3i **Contributions to Individual Retirement Accounts**

Traditional and Roth Individual Retirement Accounts, or IRAs, are fairly well-known types of retirement plans. They can be simple to create and maintain. The tax rules that govern deductible contributions, taxable distributions, age requirements, and possible penalties for early withdrawals or excess contributions are discussed in the following section.

LO.5

Understand the opportunities available to build wealth through Individual Retirement Accounts.

Traditional IRAs

An individual can contribute to a traditional **Individual Retirement Account (IRA)** assuming that the person (or spouse) has earned income and is under age $70\frac{1}{2}$. These contributions may be deductible, depending upon income level and access to another work-related retirement plan. For 2015, the contribution ceiling is the lesser of $5,500 (or $11,000 for spousal IRAs) or 100 percent of compensation.[69] The contribution ceiling applies to all types of IRAs (traditional deductible, traditional nondeductible, and Roth). An individual who attains the age of 50 by the end of the tax year can make an additional catch-up IRA contribution of up to $1,000 in 2015.

If the taxpayer is an active participant in a qualified plan, the traditional IRA deduction limitation is phased out *proportionately* between certain AGI ranges, as shown in Exhibit 11.3.[70] If AGI is above the phaseout range, no IRA deduction is allowed.

AGI is calculated taking into account any passive losses and taxable Social Security benefits and ignoring any foreign income exclusion, savings bonds interest exclusion, and the IRA deduction. There is a $200 floor on the IRA deduction limitation for individuals whose AGI is not above the phaseout range.

IRA Deduction Calculation

EXAMPLE 39

Dan, who is single, has compensation income of $67,000 in 2015. He is an active participant in his employer's qualified retirement plan. Dan contributes $5,500 to a traditional IRA. The deductible amount is reduced from $5,500 by $3,300 because of the phaseout mechanism (see Exhibit 11.3):

$$\frac{\$6,000}{\$10,000} \times \$5,500 = \$3,300 \text{ reduction}$$

Therefore, of the $5,500 contribution, Dan can deduct only $2,200 ($5,500 − $3,300).

EXAMPLE 40

Ben, an unmarried individual, is an active participant in his employer's qualified retirement plan in 2015. With AGI of $70,800, he would normally have an IRA deduction limit of $110 {$5,500 − [($70,800 − $61,000)/$10,000 × $5,500]}. However, because of the special floor provision, Ben is allowed a $200 IRA deduction.

An individual is not considered an active participant in a qualified plan merely because the individual's spouse is an active participant in such a plan for any part of a plan year. Thus, even when filing jointly, the nonparticipating individual may take a full $5,500 deduction regardless of the participation status of his or her spouse, unless the couple has AGI above $183,000. If their AGI is above $183,000, the phaseout of the deduction begins at $183,000 and ends at $193,000 (phaseout over the $10,000 range) rather than beginning and ending at the phaseout amounts in Exhibit 11.3.[71]

---

[69]§§ 219(b)(1) and (c)(2). The limit is adjusted annually for inflation in $500 increments.

[70]§ 219(g).

[71]§ 219(g)(7).

Filing Status	Phaseout Begins*	Phaseout Ends*
Single and head of household	$61,000	$ 71,000
Married, filing joint return	98,000	118,000
Married, filing separate return	–0–	10,000

EXHIBIT 11.3   Phaseout of Traditional IRA Deduction of an Active Participant in 2015

*These AGI amounts are indexed annually for inflation.

EXAMPLE 41

Nell is covered by a qualified employer retirement plan at work. Her husband, Nick, is not an active participant in a qualified plan. If Nell and Nick's combined AGI is $135,000, Nell cannot make a deductible IRA contribution because she exceeds the income threshold for an active participant. However, because Nick is not an active participant and their combined AGI does not exceed $183,000, he can make a fully deductible contribution of $5,500 to an IRA.

To the extent an individual is ineligible to make a deductible contribution to an IRA, *nondeductible contributions* can be made to separate accounts. The nondeductible contributions are subject to the same dollar limits as deductible contributions ($5,500 of earned income, $11,000 for a spousal IRA). Income in the account accumulates tax-free until distributed. Only the account earnings are taxed upon distribution because the account basis equals the contributions made by the taxpayer. A taxpayer may elect to treat deductible IRA contributions as nondeductible. If an individual has no taxable income for the year after taking into account other deductions, the election would be beneficial. The election is made on the individual's tax return for the taxable year to which the designation relates.

Roth IRAs

A Roth IRA is a *nondeductible* alternative to the traditional deductible IRA. Introduced by Congress to encourage individual savings, earnings inside a Roth IRA are not taxable, and all qualified distributions from a Roth IRA are tax-free.[72] The maximum allowable annual contribution to a Roth IRA for 2015 is the lesser of $5,500 ($11,000 for spousal IRAs) or 100 percent of the individual's compensation for the year. Contributions to a Roth IRA must be made by the due date (excluding extensions) of the taxpayer's tax return. Roth IRAs are not subject to the minimum distribution rules that apply to traditional IRAs. Contributions to a Roth IRA (unlike a traditional IRA) may continue beyond age $70\frac{1}{2}$ so long as the person generates compensation income and is not barred by the AGI limits.

A taxpayer can make tax-free withdrawals from a Roth IRA after an initial five-year holding period if any of the following requirements are satisfied:

- The distribution is made on or after the date on which the participant attains age $59\frac{1}{2}$.
- The distribution is made to a beneficiary (or the participant's estate) on or after the participant's death.
- The participant becomes disabled.
- The distribution is used to pay for qualified first-time homebuyer's expenses (statutory ceiling of $10,000).

[72]§ 408A.

Edith establishes a Roth IRA at age 42 and contributes $5,000 per year for 20 years. The account is now worth $149,400, consisting of $100,000 of nondeductible contributions and $49,400 in accumulated earnings that have not been taxed. Edith may withdraw the $149,400 tax-free from the Roth IRA because she is over age 59$\frac{1}{2}$ and has met the five-year holding period requirement.

If the taxpayer receives a distribution from a Roth IRA and does not satisfy the aforementioned requirements, the distribution may be taxable. If the distribution represents a return of capital, it is not taxable. Conversely, if the distribution represents a payout of earnings, it is taxable. Under the ordering rules for Roth IRA distributions, distributions are treated as first made from contributions (return of capital).

Assume the same facts as in the previous example, except that Edith is only age 50 and receives a distribution of $55,000. Because her basis for the Roth IRA is $100,000 (contributions made), the distribution is tax-free and her basis is reduced to $45,000 ($100,000 − $55,000).

Roth IRAs are subject to income limits. In 2015, the maximum annual contribution of $5,500 is phased out beginning at AGI of $116,000 for single taxpayers and $183,000 for married couples who file a joint return. The phaseout range is $10,000 for married taxpayers filing jointly and $15,000 for single taxpayers. For a married taxpayer filing separately, the contribution is phased out over a range beginning with AGI of $0 and ending with $10,000.

Bev, who is single, would like to contribute $5,500 to her Roth IRA. Her AGI in 2015 is $126,000. As a result, her contribution is limited to $1,833 ($5,500 − $3,667), calculated as follows:

$$\frac{\$10,000}{\$15,000} \times \$5,500 = \$3,667 \text{ reduction}$$

| In-depth coverage can be found on this book's companion website: www.cengagebrain.com | 21 DIGGING DEEPER |

Rollovers and Conversions

Often when employees change jobs, they do not want to leave their retirement savings with their former employer. As a result, retirement savings in a qualified plan may be directly transferred from that plan to an IRA or may be "rolled over" into an IRA. Amounts that are directly transferred will not be included in the owner's gross income. Rollover distributions will not be included in gross income as long as the funds received are transferred to an IRA within 60 days of receipt.[73]

In addition, a traditional IRA may be rolled over or converted to a Roth IRA. The tax consequences depend on whether the contributions made to the traditional IRA were deductible or nondeductible. If deductible, the basis for the IRA is zero. Thus, the entire amount of the rollover or conversion is included in gross income. If nondeductible, the basis for the IRA is equal to the sum of the contributions. Thus, only the IRA earnings included in the rollover or conversion are included in gross income.

One benefit from rolling over or converting a traditional IRA to a Roth IRA arises because traditional IRAs require withdrawals beginning at age 70$\frac{1}{2}$, while there are no required withdrawals from a Roth IRA. Thus, amounts in a Roth IRA can be accumulated over the taxpayer's lifetime and then passed to heirs without income tax consequences.

See Concept Summary 11.4 for an overview of some of the primary differences between traditional and Roth IRAs.

---

[73]§ 203(d)(3).

Concept Summary 11.4

Traditional IRAs and Roth IRAs Compared

	Traditional IRA	Roth IRA
Contribution limit	$5,500 or 100% of compensation, pre-tax dollars.	$5,500 or 100% of compensation, after-tax dollars.
Deduction limit	$5,500 or 100% of compensation.	No deduction.
Tax benefits	Tax-deferred growth of earnings.	Tax-free growth of earnings.
Taxation at withdrawal in retirement	Deductible contributions and earnings taxed as ordinary income.	Contributions and earnings withdrawn tax-free.
Taxation of withdrawals prior to retirement	10% penalty for withdrawals before 59$\frac{1}{2}$, except for withdrawals to pay for certain medical expenses and health insurance, qualified education expenses, and qualified first-time homebuyer expenses.	10% penalty on for earnings withdrawn before age 59$\frac{1}{2}$. No penalty on contributions withdrawn after 5 years or where the distribution is used to pay for qualified first-time homebuyer's expenses (statutory ceiling of $10,000).
Timing of contribution	Grace period up to due date of tax return (not including extensions).	Grace period up to due date of tax return (not including extensions).
Minimum required distribution	Must begin at 70$\frac{1}{2}$.	None.

LO.6

State and explain the tax provisions applicable to proprietors.

11-4 INDIVIDUALS AS PROPRIETORS

11-4a The Proprietorship as a Business Entity

A sole proprietorship is *not* a taxable entity separate from the individual who owns the proprietorship. The owner reports the results of business operations of the proprietorship on Schedule C of Form 1040. The net profit or loss reported on the Schedule C is then transferred to the first page of the Form 1040. The proprietor reports all of the net profit or net loss from the business, regardless of the amount actually withdrawn from the proprietorship during the year.

Income and expenses of the proprietorship retain their character when reported by the proprietor. For example, ordinary income of the proprietorship is treated as ordinary income when reported by the proprietor, and capital gain of the proprietorship is treated as capital gain by the proprietor.

EXAMPLE 45

George is the sole proprietor of George's Bicycle Shop. Gross income of the business in 2015 is $200,000, and operating expenses are $110,000. George also sells a capital asset held by the business for a $10,000 long-term capital gain. During 2015, he withdraws $60,000 from the business for living expenses. George reports the operating income and expenses of the business on Schedule C, resulting in net profit (ordinary income) of $90,000 ($200,000 − $110,000). Even though he withdrew only $60,000, George reports all of the $90,000 net profit from the business on Form 1040, where he computes taxable income and the tax liability for the year. He also reports a $10,000 long-term capital gain on his personal tax return (Schedule D of Form 1040).

11-4b Income of a Proprietorship

The broad definition of gross income in § 61(a) applies equally to individuals and business entities, including proprietorships, corporations, and partnerships. Thus, asset inflows into a proprietorship are to be treated as income unless a Code section provides for an exclusion from income (e.g., interest on state and local bonds, appreciation on investments). Refer to Chapter 4 for a detailed discussion of gross income.

11-4c Deductions Related to a Proprietorship

The provisions that govern business deductions also are general and not entity-specific. The § 162 requirement that trade or business expenses be *ordinary and necessary* (refer to Chapter 5) applies to proprietorships as well as corporations, partnerships, and other business entities. However, certain specific deductions are available only to self-employed taxpayers. These deductions are addressed next.

Health Insurance Premiums

A self-employed taxpayer may deduct 100 percent of insurance premiums paid for medical coverage as a deduction *for* AGI.[74] The deduction is allowed for premiums paid on behalf of the taxpayer, the taxpayer's spouse, and dependents of the taxpayer. The deduction is not allowed to any taxpayer who is eligible to participate in a subsidized health plan maintained by any employer of the taxpayer or of the taxpayer's spouse.

This deduction is reported in the Adjusted Gross Income section of Form 1040 rather than on Schedule C. Premiums paid for medical coverage of the *employees* of a self-employed taxpayer are deductible as business expenses on Schedule C, however.

Ellen, a sole proprietor of a restaurant, has two dependent children. During 2015, she paid health insurance premiums of $8,800 for her own coverage and $8,000 for coverage of her two children. Ellen can deduct $16,800 as a deduction *for* AGI.

EXAMPLE
46

Self-Employment Tax

The tax on self-employment income is levied to provide Social Security and Medicare benefits (old age, survivors, and disability insurance and hospital insurance) for self-employed individuals. Individuals with net earnings of $400 or more from self-employment are subject to the self-employment tax.[75] For 2015, the combined self-employment tax rate is 15.3 percent (12.4 percent for Social Security and 2.9 percent for Medicare). For 2015, the ceiling amount is $118,500, and for 2014, the ceiling amount is $117,000. The ceiling amount is adjusted annually for inflation.

For purposes of computing the *self-employment tax,* self-employed taxpayers are allowed a deduction from net earnings equal to one-half of the self-employment tax rate.[76] This deduction of 7.65 percent (one-half of the 15.3 percent rate) is reflected by

---

TAX IN THE NEWS   The Tax Gap Includes $58 Billion in Payroll Taxes

The "tax gap"—the difference between what taxpayers owe to the Federal government in taxes and what they pay—is approaching $400 billion annually. A significant portion of that amount consists of delinquent payroll taxes—the money withheld from employees' salaries by employers for FICA taxes (Social Security and Medicare taxes).

According to a study by the Government Accountability Office (GAO), more than 1.6 million businesses together owe in excess of $58 billion related to delinquent payroll taxes. Of that amount, $26 billion represents actual taxes owed, $18 billion is for interest, and $14 billion is for penalties. In contrast, businesses owe only $24 billion in delinquent corporate income taxes. Businesses in the construction, profes-

sional services, and health care industries have the largest payroll tax delinquencies.

Collecting payroll taxes seems to be a perennial problem. The GAO study pointed out that delinquencies today are about the same as they were a decade ago when 1.8 million businesses owed about $49 billion. Today, though, debts are more likely to be long-standing. About 500 employers owe at least 10 years' worth of taxes, and nearly 15,000 owe 5 years' worth. About half of the $58 billion owed is from 2002 or earlier. Since then, the IRS has stepped up its enforcement efforts through the use of liens and levies on businesses that fail to pay over the taxes withheld. And additional employment tax audits will provide the IRS with a better understanding of overall employment tax compliance.

---

[74] § 162(l).

[75] § 6017.

[76] § 1402(a)(12).

multiplying net earnings from self-employment by 92.35 percent (100% − 7.65%), as shown in Example 47. For purposes of computing *taxable income,* an income tax deduction is allowed for part (currently, one-half) of the amount of self-employment tax paid.[77]

Example 47 illustrates the computation of the self-employment tax, as well as the income tax deduction for one-half of the self-employment tax paid. For income tax purposes, the amount to be reported on Schedule C is net earnings from self-employment *before* the deduction for one-half of the self-employment tax. The deduction of one-half of the self-employment tax paid is reported separately on Form 1040 as a deduction *for* AGI.

EXAMPLE 47

Computation of the self-employment tax is determined using the steps below. The self-employment tax is determined for two taxpayers with net earnings from self-employment for 2015 as follows: Ned, $55,000 and Terry, $135,000.

Ned's Self-Employment Tax Worksheet

1. Net earnings	$55,000.00
2. Multiply line 1 by 92.35%.	$50,792.50
3. If the amount on line 2 is $118,500 or less, multiply the line 2 amount by 15.3%. This is the self-employment tax.	$ 7,771.25
4. If the amount on line 2 is more than $118,500, multiply the excess over $118,500 by 2.9% and add $18,130.50. This is the self-employment tax.	

Terry's Self-Employment Tax Worksheet

1. Net earnings	$135,000.00
2. Multiply line 1 by 92.35%.	$124,672.50
3. If the amount on line 2 is $118,500 or less, multiply the line 2 amount by 15.3%. This is the self-employment tax.	
4. If the amount on line 2 is more than $118,500, multiply the excess over $118,500 by 2.9% and add $18,130.50. This is the self-employment tax.	$ 18,309.50

For income tax purposes, Ned has net earnings from self-employment of $55,000 and a deduction *for* AGI of $3,885.63 ($7,771.25 × 50%). Terry has net earnings from self-employment of $135,000 and a deduction *for* AGI of $9,154.75 ($18,309.50 × 50%). Both taxpayers benefit from the deduction for one-half of the self-employment tax paid.

If an individual who is self-employed also receives wages subject to the FICA tax from working as an employee of another organization, the ceiling amount of the Social Security portion on which the self-employment tax is computed is reduced. However, a combination of FICA wages and self-employment earnings will not reduce the Medicare component of the self-employment tax, as there is no ceiling on this component of the tax.

EXAMPLE 48

In 2015, Kelly recorded $76,000 of net earnings from a data imaging services business she owns. During the year, she also received wages of $54,000 as an employee of a small accounting firm. The amount of Kelly's self-employment income subject to the Social Security portion (12.4%) is $64,500 ($118,500 − $54,000), producing a tax of $7,998 ($64,500 × 12.4%); note that $64,500 is less than $70,186 of net self-employment income.

continued

---

[77]§ 164(f).

	Social Security Portion
Ceiling amount	$118,500
Less: FICA wages	(54,000)
Net ceiling	$ 64,500
Net self-employment income ($76,000 × 92.35%)	$ 70,186
Lesser of net ceiling or net self-employment income	$ 64,500

Although there is a limit on Social Security taxes ($118,500 maximum base in 2015), no such limit exists for the Medicare portion of the self-employment tax. Therefore, all of Kelly's net self-employment income ($76,000 × .9235 = $70,186) is subject to the 2.9% Medicare portion of the self-employment tax. Thus, the self-employment tax on this portion is $2,035.39 ($70,186 × 2.9%).

If Kelly's wages were only $30,000, then the net ceiling in the table above would be $88,500. Because her net self-employment income ($70,186) is less than this amount, she would compute her self-employment tax following the approach in the previous example.

Net earnings from self-employment include gross income from a trade or business less allowable trade or business deductions, the distributive share of any partnership income or loss derived from a trade or business activity, and net income from rendering personal services as an independent contractor. Gain or loss from the disposition of property (including involuntary conversions) is excluded from the computation of self-employment income unless the property involved is inventory.

11-4d Retirement Plans for Self-Employed Individuals

Self-employed individuals have several options for retirement funding. Individual Retirement Accounts (discussed earlier in this chapter) are available to both employees and self-employed individuals. Other options for self-employed individuals include, but are not limited to, H.R. 10 (Keogh) plans and SIMPLE plans, both of which are discussed next.

Keogh Plans

Self-employed individuals (e.g., partners and sole proprietors) are eligible to establish and receive qualified retirement benefits under Keogh plans (also known as H.R. 10 plans). Self-employed individuals who establish Keogh plans for themselves are also required to cover their *employees* under the plan.

Keogh investments can include a variety of funding vehicles, such as mutual funds, annuities, real estate shares, certificates of deposit, debt instruments, commodities, securities, and personal properties. When an individual decides to make all investment decisions, a *self-directed retirement plan* is established. Investment in most collectibles (e.g., coins or art) is not allowed in a self-directed plan.

A Keogh plan may be either a *defined contribution* plan or a *defined benefit* plan. In a defined contribution plan, the amount that can be contributed each year is subject to limitations. Retirement benefits depend on the amount contributed and the amount earned by the plan. In a defined benefit plan, the amount of retirement income is fixed and is determined on the basis of the employee's compensation while working, the number of years in the plan, and age upon retirement.

A self-employed individual may annually contribute the smaller of $53,000 (in 2015) or 100 percent of earned income to a defined contribution Keogh plan.[78] If the defined contribution plan is a profit sharing plan or stock bonus plan, however, a 25 percent deduction limit applies. Under a defined benefit Keogh plan, the annual benefit is limited to the smaller of $210,000 (in 2015) or 100 percent of the average compensation for the three highest years.[79]

[78]§ 415(c)(1).

[79]§ 415(b)(1). The amount is indexed annually.

Earned income refers to net earnings from self-employment.[80] Net earnings from self-employment means the gross income derived by an individual from any trade or business carried on by that individual, less appropriate deductions, plus the distributive share of income or loss from a partnership.[81] Earned income is reduced by contributions to a Keogh plan on the individual's behalf and by 50 percent of any self-employment tax.[82]

EXAMPLE 49

Pat, a partner, has earned income of $150,000 in 2015 (after the deduction for one-half of self-employment tax, but before any Keogh contribution). The maximum contribution Pat may make to a defined contribution Keogh plan is $53,000, the lesser of $150,000 or $53,000.

For discrimination purposes, the 25 percent limitation on the employee contribution to a profit sharing plan or stock bonus plan is computed on the first $265,000 (in 2015) of earned income. Thus, the maximum contribution in 2015 is $53,000 ($265,000 − .25X = X; X = $212,000). Therefore, $265,000 − $212,000 = $53,000. Alternatively, this can be calculated by multiplying $265,000 by 20 percent.

EXAMPLE 50

Terry, a self-employed accountant, has a profit sharing plan with a contribution rate of 15% of compensation. Terry's earned income after the deduction of one-half of self-employment tax, but before the Keogh contribution, is $265,000. Terry's contribution is limited to $34,565 ($265,000 − .15X = X), because X = $230,435 and .15 × $230,435 = $34,565.

Although a Keogh plan must be established before the end of the year in question, contributions may be made up to the unextended filing date for that year.

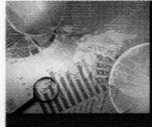

TAX PLANNING STRATEGIES **Important Dates Related to IRAs and Keogh Plans**

FRAMEWORK FOCUS: DEDUCTIONS

Strategy: Accelerate Recognition of Deductions to Achieve Tax Deferral.

A Keogh or IRA participant may make a deductible contribution for a tax year up to the time prescribed for filing the individual's tax return for that tax year. A Keogh plan must have been *established* by the end of the *prior* tax year (e.g., December 31, 2015) to obtain a deduction on the 2015 income tax return for the contribution made in the *current* year (2016). An individual can establish an IRA during the *current* tax year (up to the normal filing date) and still receive a deduction on the prior-year income tax return for the contribution made in the *current* year.

SIMPLE Plans

Employers with 100 or fewer employees who do not maintain another qualified retirement plan may establish a *savings incentive match plan for employees* (SIMPLE plan).[83] The plan can be in the form of a § 401(k) plan or an IRA. A SIMPLE § 401(k) plan is not subject to the nondiscrimination rules that are normally applicable to § 401(k) plans.

All employees who received at least $5,000 in compensation from the employer during any two preceding years and who reasonably expect to receive at least $5,000 in compensation during the current year must be eligible to participate in the plan. The decision to participate is up to the employee. A *self-employed individual* also may participate in the plan.

The contributions made by the employee (a salary reduction approach) must be expressed as a percentage of compensation rather than as a fixed dollar amount. The

---

[80]§ 401(c)(2).
[81]§ 1402(a).

[82]§§ 401(c)(2)(A)(v) and 164(f).
[83]§ 408(p).

SIMPLE plan must not permit the elective employee contribution for the year to exceed $12,500 (in 2015).[84] The SIMPLE elective deferral limit is increased under the catch-up provision for employees age 50 and over. The amount is $3,000 in 2015 and is indexed for inflation in $500 increments.

Generally, the employer must either match elective employee contributions up to 3 percent of the employee's compensation or provide nonmatching contributions of 2 percent of compensation for each eligible employee. Thus, for an employee under age 50, the maximum amount that may be contributed to the plan for 2015 is $20,450 [$12,500 employee contributions + $7,950 ($265,000 compensation ceiling × 3%) employer match].

No other contributions may be made to the plan other than the employee elective contribution and the required employer matching contribution (or nonmatching contribution under the 2 percent rule). All contributions are fully vested. An employer is required to make the required matching or nonmatching contributions to a SIMPLE § 401(k) plan once it is established, whereas an employer's contributions to a traditional § 401(k) plan generally may be discretionary.

An employer's deduction for contributions to a SIMPLE § 401(k) plan is limited to the greater of 25 percent of the compensation paid or accrued or the amount the employer is required to contribute to the plan. Thus, an employer may deduct contributions to a SIMPLE § 401(k) plan in excess of 25 percent of the $265,000 salary cap. A traditional § 401(k) plan is limited to 25 percent of the total compensation of plan participants for the year (excluding age 50 catch-ups).

An employer is allowed a deduction for matching contributions only if the contributions are made by the due date (including extensions) for the employer's tax return. Contributions to a SIMPLE plan are excludible from the employee's gross income, and the SIMPLE plan is tax-exempt.

The Mauve Company has a SIMPLE plan for its employees under which it provides nonmatching contributions of 2% of compensation for each eligible employee. The maximum amount that can be added to each participant's account in 2015 is $17,800, composed of the $12,500 employee salary reduction plus an employer contribution of $5,300 ($265,000 × 2%).

Distributions from a SIMPLE plan are taxed under the IRA rules. Tax-free rollovers can be made from one SIMPLE account to another. A SIMPLE account can be rolled over to an IRA tax-free after the expiration of a two-year period since the individual first participated in the plan. Withdrawals of contributions during the two-year period beginning on the date an employee first participates in the SIMPLE plan are subject to a 25 percent early withdrawal penalty rather than the 10 percent early withdrawal penalty that otherwise would apply.

TAX PLANNING STRATEGIES   **Factors Affecting Retirement Plan Choices**

FRAMEWORK FOCUS: DEDUCTIONS

Strategy: Maximize Deductible Amounts.

An IRA might not be the best retirement plan option for many self-employed taxpayers. The maximum amount that can be deducted is $5,500 per year ($11,000 for a spousal plan), which may be too low to provide funding for an adequate level of retirement income. Other options such as Keogh plans and SIMPLE plans allow larger contributions and larger deductions. However, a self-employed individual who establishes either a Keogh or a SIMPLE plan is required to cover employees under such plans. This can result in substantial expenditures, not only for the required contributions but also for expenses of administering the plan. An advantage of an IRA is that coverage of employees is not required.

---

[84]For 2014, the amount was $12,000.

11-4e **Accounting Periods and Methods**

Proprietors may choose among various accounting methods, just as other business entities do (refer to Chapters 4 and 5). The cash method is commonly used by proprietorships that provide services, while the accrual or hybrid method generally is required if inventory is a material income-producing factor.

The accounting period rules for proprietorships generally are much simpler than the rules for partnerships and S corporations. Because a proprietorship is not an entity separate from the proprietor, the proprietorship must use the same tax year-end as the proprietor. This does not preclude the use of a fiscal year for a proprietorship, but most proprietorships use the calendar year.

11-4f **Estimated Tax Payments**

Although the following discussion largely centers on self-employed taxpayers, some of the procedures may be applicable to employed persons. In many cases, for example, employed persons may be required to pay estimated tax if they have income that is not subject to withholding (e.g., income from consulting work, rental property, dividends, or interest).

Estimated Tax for Individuals

Estimated tax is the amount of tax (including alternative minimum tax and self-employment tax) an individual expects to owe for the year after subtracting tax credits and income tax withheld. Any individual who has estimated tax for the year of $1,000 or more and whose withholding does not equal or exceed the required annual payment (discussed below) must make quarterly payments.[85] Otherwise, a penalty may be assessed. No quarterly payments are required and no penalty will apply on an underpayment if the taxpayer's estimated tax is under $1,000. No penalty will apply if the taxpayer had no tax liability for the preceding tax year, the preceding tax year was a taxable year of 12 months, and the taxpayer was a citizen or resident for the entire preceding tax year. In this regard, having no tax liability is not the same as having no additional tax to pay.

The required annual payment must first be computed. This is the smaller of the following amounts:

- Ninety percent of the tax shown on the current year's return.
- One hundred percent of the tax shown on the preceding year's return (the return must cover the full 12 months of the preceding year). If the AGI on the preceding year's return exceeds $150,000 ($75,000 if married filing separately), the 100 percent requirement is increased to 110 percent.

In general, one-fourth of this required annual payment is due on April 15, June 15, and September 15 of the tax year and January 15 of the following year. Thus, the quarterly installment of the required annual payment reduced by the applicable withholding is the estimated tax to be paid. An equal part of withholding is deemed paid on each due date, even if a taxpayer's earnings fluctuate widely during the year. Payments are to be accompanied by the payment voucher from Form 1040–ES for the appropriate date.

Penalty on Underpayments

A nondeductible penalty is imposed on the amount of underpayment of estimated tax. The rate for this penalty is adjusted quarterly to reflect changes in the average prime rate.

An *underpayment* occurs when any quarterly payment (the sum of estimated tax paid and income tax withheld) is less than 25 percent of the required annual payment.

---

[85]§§ 6654(c)(1) and 6654(e)(1).

The penalty is applied to the amount of the underpayment for the period of the under-payment.[86]

Marta made the following payments of estimated tax for 2015 and had no income tax withheld:

April 15, 2015	$1,400
June 15, 2015	2,300
September 15, 2015	1,500
January 15, 2016	1,800

Marta's actual tax for 2015 is $8,000, and her tax in 2014 was $10,000. Therefore, each installment should have been at least $1,800 [($8,000 × 90%) × 25%]. Of the payment on June 15, $400 will be credited to the unpaid balance of the first quarterly installment due on April 15,[87] thereby effectively stopping the underpayment penalty for the first quarterly period. Of the remaining $1,900 payment on June 15, $100 is credited to the September 15 payment, resulting in this third quarterly payment being $200 short. Then $200 of the January 15, 2016 payment is credited to the September 15 shortfall, ending the period of underpayment for that portion due. The January 15, 2016 installment is now underpaid by $200, and a penalty will apply from January 15, 2016, to April 15, 2016 (unless some tax is paid sooner). Marta's underpayments for the periods of under-payment are as follows:

1st installment due:	$400 from April 15, 2015, to June 15, 2015
2nd installment due:	Paid in full
3rd installment due:	$200 from September 15, 2015, to January 15, 2016
4th installment due:	$200 from January 15, 2016, to April 15, 2016

If a possible underpayment of estimated tax is indicated, Form 2210 should be filed to compute the penalty due or to justify that no penalty applies.

11-5 HOBBY LOSSES

Distinguish between business and hobby activities and apply the rules limiting the deduction of hobby losses.

Employee deductions and deductions related to a proprietorship were discussed in previous sections of this chapter. Employees are allowed to deduct certain expenditures incurred in connection with their work activities. Expenses incurred by a self-employed taxpayer are deductible only if the taxpayer can show that the activity was entered into for the purpose of making a profit.

Certain activities can have attributes that make it difficult to determine if the primary motivation for the activity is to make a profit or is for personal pleasure. Examples include raising horses and operating a farm that is also used as a weekend residence. While personal losses are not deductible, losses attributable to profit-seeking activities may be deducted and used to offset a taxpayer's other income. Activities that have both personal and profit-seeking motives are classified as hobbies, and the tax law limits the deductibility of hobby losses.

The income and deductions from a hobby are reported separately on the tax return. Whether deductions related to a hobby generate a tax benefit, the revenue for the hobby is always reported as other income on page 1 of Form 1040. The reporting of deductions is discussed below.

11-5a General Rules

If an individual can show that an activity has been conducted with the intent to earn a profit, losses from the activity are fully deductible. The hobby loss rules apply only if the activity is not engaged in for profit. Hobby expenses are deductible only to the extent of hobby income.[88]

---

[86]§ 6654(b)(2).

[87]Payments are credited to unpaid installments in the order in which the installments are required to be paid. § 6654(b)(3).

[88]§ 183(b)(2).

The Regulations stipulate that the following nine factors should be considered in determining whether an activity is profit seeking or a hobby:[89]

- Whether the activity is conducted in a businesslike manner.
- The expertise of the taxpayers or their advisers.
- The time and effort expended.
- The expectation that the assets of the activity will appreciate in value.
- The taxpayer's previous success in conducting similar activities.
- The history of income or losses from the activity.
- The relationship of profits earned to losses incurred.
- The financial status of the taxpayer (e.g., if the taxpayer does not have substantial amounts of other income, this may indicate that the activity is engaged in for profit).
- Elements of personal pleasure or recreation in the activity.

The presence or absence of a factor is not by itself determinative of whether the activity is profit-seeking or is a hobby. Rather, the decision is a subjective one that is based on an analysis of the facts and circumstances.

11-5b **Presumptive Rule of § 183**

The Code provides a rebuttable presumption that an activity is profit-seeking if the activity shows a profit in at least three of the previous five tax years.[90] If the activity involves horses, a profit in at least two of the previous seven tax years meets the presumptive rule. If these profitability tests are met, the activity is presumed to be a trade or business rather than a personal hobby. In this situation, the burden of proof shifts from the taxpayer to the IRS. That is, the IRS bears the burden of proving that the activity is personal rather than trade- or business-related.

EXAMPLE 53

Camille and Walter are married taxpayers who enjoy a busy lifestyle. Camille, who is an executive for a large corporation, is paid a salary of $800,000. Walter is a collector of antiques. Several years ago he opened an antique shop in a local shopping center and spends most of his time buying and selling antiques. He occasionally earns a small profit from this activity but more frequently incurs substantial losses. If Walter's losses are business-related, they are fully deductible against Camille's salary income on a joint return. In resolving this issue, consider the following:

- Initially determine whether Walter's antique activity has met the three-out-of-five-years profit test.
- If the presumption is not met, the activity may nevertheless qualify as a business if Walter can show that the intent is to engage in a profit-seeking activity. It is not necessary to show actual profits.
- Attempt to fit the operation within the nine criteria prescribed in the Regulations listed previously.

11-5c **Determination of the Deductible Amount**

If an activity is deemed to be a hobby, the expenses are deductible only to the extent of the gross income from the hobby. These expenses must be deducted in the following order:

1. Amounts deductible under other Code sections without regard to the nature of the activity, such as property taxes and home mortgage interest.

---

[89]Reg. §§ 1.183–2(b)(1) through (9).   [90]§ 183(d).

2. Amounts deductible under other Code sections if the activity had been engaged in for profit, but only if those amounts do not affect adjusted basis. Examples include maintenance, utilities, and supplies.
3. Amounts that affect adjusted basis and would be deductible under other Code sections if the activity had been engaged in for profit.[91] Examples include depreciation, amortization, and depletion.

The last two categories of deductions are deductible *from* AGI as itemized deductions to the extent they exceed 2 percent of AGI.[92] If the taxpayer uses the standard deduction rather than itemizing, the hobby loss deductions generate no tax benefit. Even if this is the case, the revenue from a hobby must still be reported on page 1 of Form 1040.

EXAMPLE 54

Jim, the vice president of an oil company, has AGI of $80,000. He decides to pursue painting in his spare time. He uses a home studio, comprising 10% of the home's square footage. During the current year, Jim incurs the following expenses:

Frames	$ 1,800
Art supplies	900
Fees paid to models	4,000
Home studio expenses:	
Total home property taxes	2,000
Total home mortgage interest	10,000
Total home maintenance and utilities	4,600
Calculated depreciation on 10% of home	500

During the year, Jim sold paintings for a total of $8,660. If the activity is held to be a hobby, Jim is allowed deductions as follows:

Gross income		$ 8,660
Deduct: Taxes and interest (10% of $12,000)		(1,200)
Remainder		$ 7,460
Deduct: Frames	$1,800	
Art supplies	900	
Models' fees	4,000	
Maintenance and utilities (10%)	460	(7,160)
Remainder		$ 300
Depreciation ($500, but limited to $300)		(300)
Net income		$ –0–

Jim includes the $8,660 of income in AGI, making his AGI $88,660. The taxes and interest are itemized deductions, deductible in full. The remaining $7,460 of expenses are reduced by 2% of his AGI (2% x $88,660 = $1,773), so the net deduction is $5,687. All of these deductions are reported as itemized deductions on Schedule A. Because the property taxes and home mortgage interest are deductible even without the hobby, the net effect is a $2,973 ($8,660 − $5,687) increase in taxable income.

---

[91]Reg. § 1.183–1(b)(1). [92]Reg. § 1.67–1T(a)(1)(iv) and Rev.Rul. 75–14, 1975–1 C.B. 90.

REFOCUS ON THE BIG PICTURE

SELF-EMPLOYED VERSUS EMPLOYEE—WHAT'S THE DIFFERENCE?

Mark may deduct the ordinary and necessary business expenses incurred by his proprietorship. This includes the $18,000 for rent and utilities, the $12,000 paid to his secretary, and the $40,000 paid to Ellen, his assistant. The $8,000 paid for equipment can be depreciated or may qualify for immediate expensing under § 179. As a self-employed taxpayer, Mark may deduct 100 percent of the $3,000 of health insurance premiums paid, but only if he is not eligible to participate in the subsidized health plan maintained by Mary's employer. On the other hand, Mark cannot deduct the premiums of $500 paid for his life insurance policy. Mark may want to consider contributing to his own IRA or establishing a Keogh plan or SIMPLE plan to allow for greater retirement contributions. Mark should be aware that in addition to paying income tax on the net income earned by his business, he also owes self-employment tax at a combined rate of 15.3 percent and will be able to claim an income tax deduction for half of the self-employment tax paid.

While Mary will owe income tax on her $85,000 salary, the health insurance premiums of $3,000 and group term life insurance premiums paid by her employer qualify as tax-free fringe benefits. In addition, as long as Mary is required to substantiate her travel expenses as part of an accountable plan, none of the travel-related reimbursements need to be included in Mary's gross income. Because Mary is not covered by a qualified retirement plan at work, she can also deduct the entire $5,500 contribution made to her traditional IRA. While the $500 of employee business expenses are technically deductible, they provide a tax benefit to Mary only if they exceed 2 percent of the couple's AGI. While Mary is not subject to self-employment tax, she still incurred a 7.65 percent payroll tax related to Social Security and Medicare. Her employer paid an additional 7.65 percent.

What If?

In order to improve her skills in her current job, Mary is considering entering an MBA program at a local college. At the same time, to save money while Mary is in school, Mark is considering moving his office into a vacant room in their home. Are Mary's education expenses deductible? Can Mark deduct expenses associated with his home office? As long as the new degree is not required to meet the minimum requirements of her existing job and the degree does not qualify Mary for a new trade or business, Mary's books, tuition, and other related educational expenses are deductible as a miscellaneous itemized deduction. However, like the $500 of other employee business expenses mentioned earlier, the expenses provide a tax benefit only to the extent they exceed 2 percent of the couple's AGI. As a self-employed individual, Mark is allowed to deduct the costs of a home office as long as the office is used exclusively and on a regular basis as either the principal place of business or a place of business used by his clients and customers. Deductible expenses would include a portion of mortgage interest and property taxes paid on the home; a portion of utilities, repairs and maintenance, and other household expenses; and depreciation on the business portion of the home.

Suggested Readings

Thomas Dalton and Shreesh Deshpande, "Quantifying the Choice Between a Roth and Traditional IRA," *Practical Tax Strategies*, September 2011.

David J. Hess and Lois D. Bryan, "Using an IRA for a Planned Charitable Contribution," *Practical Tax Strategies*, March 2012.

Melanie James, "When are Commuting Costs Deductible?" *Practical Tax Strategies*, November 2014.

David L. Keligian, "Winning Independent Contractor Status," *Journal of Taxation*, November 2011.

Susan L. Megaard and Michael M. Megaard, "When Should the New Safe Harbor Method for Deducting Home-Office Expenses be Elected," *Journal of Taxation*, July 2013.

Matthew A. Melone, "Tax Court Upholds Deductions for MBA Tuition," *Practical Tax Strategies*, March 2010.

Key Terms

Accountable plan, 11-2

Automatic mileage method, 11-19

Cafeteria plans, 11-11

De minimis fringe benefits, 11-15

Deduction for qualified tuition and related expenses, 11-27

Education expenses, 11-25

Entertainment expenses, 11-29

Estimated tax, 11-44

Flexible spending plans, 11-12

Foreign earned income exclusion, 11-17

Health Savings Account (HSA), 11-6

Hobby losses, 11-45

Independent contractor, 11-2

Individual Retirement Account (IRA), 11-35

Keogh plans, 11-41

Moving expenses, 11-22

No-additional-cost service, 11-13

Nonaccountable plan, 11-34

Office in the home expenses, 11-31

Qualified employee discount, 11-14

Qualified transportation fringes, 11-15

Self-employment tax, 11-4

Transportation expenses, 11-18

Travel expenses, 11-20

Working condition fringes, 11-14

Computational Exercises

1. **LO.2** Valentino is a patient in a nursing home for 45 days in 2015. While in the nursing home, he incurs total costs of $13,500. Medicare pays $8,000 of the costs. Valentino receives $15,000 from his long-term care insurance policy, which pays while he is in the facility. Assume that the daily Federal statutory amount for Valentino is $330. Of the $15,000, what amount may Valentino exclude from his gross income?

2. **LO.2** Mio was transferred from New York to Germany. He lived and worked in Germany for 340 days in 2015. Mio's salary for 2015 is $190,000. What is Mio's foreign earned income exclusion?

3. **LO.3** Michael holds a full-time job with Brown Company and a part-time job with Tan Corporation. During a workday, he drives 20 miles to Brown, returns home, has a meal, and then drives 15 miles to Tan. Tan is located 12 miles from Brown. What is Michael's deductible mileage?

4. **LO.3** Fred travels from Denver to Miami primarily on business. He spends five days conducting business and two days sightseeing. His expenses are $400 (airfare), $150 per day (meals), and $300 per night (lodging). What are Fred's deductible expenses?

5. **LO.3** After accepting his first job upon graduating from college, Christian has the following moving expenses:

Rental of moving van	$450
Meals	200
Lodging	250

Presuming no reimbursement, what is Christian's moving expense deduction?

6. **LO.3** Samantha was recently employed by an accounting firm. During the year, she spends $2,500 for a CPA exam review course and begins working on a law degree in night school. Her law school expenses were $4,200 for tuition and $450 for books. Assuming no reimbursement, how much can Samantha deduct for the:
   a. CPA exam review course?
   b. Law school expenses?

7. **LO.3** Robert entertains four key clients and their spouses at a nightclub. Expenses were $200 (limo charge), $120 (cover charge), $700 (drinks and dinner), and $140 (tips to servers). If Robert is self-employed, how much can he deduct for this event?

8. **LO.3** Andrew sends Godiva chocolates to 10 of his key clients at Christmas. The chocolates cost $50 a box not including $4 for gift wrapping and shipping. How much can Andrew deduct?

9. **LO.5** In 2015, Miranda records net earnings from self-employment of $146,000. She has no other income. Determine the amount of Miranda's self-employment tax and her *for* AGI income tax deduction.

10. **LO.5** Myers, who is single, has compensation income of $68,000 in 2015. He is an active participant in his employer's qualified retirement plan. Myers contributes $5,500 to a traditional IRA. Of the $5,500 contribution, how much can Myers deduct? See Exhibit 11.3, Phaseout of Traditional IRA Deduction of an Active Participant in 2015.

11. **LO.5** Meredith, who is single, would like to contribute $5,500 to her Roth IRA. What is the maximum amount that Meredith can contribute if her AGI is $117,000?

Problems

12. **LO.1** Mason performs services for Isabella. In determining whether Mason is an employee or an independent contractor, comment on the relevance of each of the factors listed below.
    a. Mason performs services only for Isabella and does not work for anyone else.
    b. Mason sets his own work schedule.
    c. Mason reports his job-related expenses on a Schedule C.
    d. Mason obtained his job skills from Isabella's training program.
    e. Mason performs the services at Isabella's business location.
    f. Mason is paid based on time worked rather than on task performed.

13. **LO.2** Rex, age 55, is an officer of Blue Company, which provides him with the following nondiscriminatory fringe benefits in 2015:
    • Hospitalization insurance premiums for Rex and his dependents. The cost of the coverage for Rex is $2,900 per year, and the additional cost for his dependents is $3,800 per year. The plan has a $2,000 deductible, but his employer contributed $1,500 to Rex's Health Savings Account (HSA). Rex withdrew only $800 from the HSA, and the account earned $50 of interest during the year.

- Insurance premiums of $840 for salary continuation payments. Under the plan, Rex will receive his regular salary in the event he is unable to work due to illness. Rex collected $4,500 on the policy to replace lost wages while he was ill during the year.

- Rex is a part-time student working on his bachelor's degree in engineering. His employer reimbursed his $5,200 tuition under a plan available to all full-time employees.

Determine the amount Rex must include in gross income.

14. **LO.2** Casey is in the 15% marginal tax bracket, and Jean is in the 35% marginal tax bracket. Their employer is experiencing financial difficulties and cannot continue to pay for the company's health insurance plan. The annual premiums are approximately $8,000 per employee. The employer has proposed to either (1) require the employee to pay the premiums or (2) reduce each employee's pay by $10,000 per year with the employer paying the premium. Which option is less objectionable to Casey, and which is less objectionable to Jean?   Decision Making

15. **LO.2** Belinda spent the last 60 days of 2015 in a nursing home. The cost of the services provided to her was $18,000 ($300 per day). Medicare paid $8,500 toward the cost of her stay. Belinda also received $5,500 of benefits under a long-term care insurance policy she had purchased. What is the effect on Belinda's gross income?

16. **LO.2** Does the taxpayer recognize gross income in the following situations? Explain.

a. Ava is a filing clerk at a large insurance company. She is permitted to leave the premises for her lunch, but she usually eats in the company's cafeteria because it is quick and she is on a tight schedule. On average, she pays $2 for a lunch that would cost $12 at a restaurant. However, if the prices in the cafeteria were not so low and the food was not so delicious, she would probably bring her lunch at a cost of $3 per day.

b. Scott is an executive for an international corporation located in New York City. Often he works late, taking telephone calls from the company's European branch. Scott often stays in a company-owned condominium when he has a late-night work session. The condominium is across the street from the company office.

c. Ira recently moved to take a new job. For the first month on the new job, Ira was searching for a home to purchase or rent. During this time, his employer permitted Ira to live in an apartment the company maintains for customers during the buying season. The month that Ira occupied the apartment was not during the buying season, however, and the apartment would not otherwise have been occupied.

17. **LO.2** Tim is the vice president of western operations for Maroon Oil Company and is stationed in San Francisco. He is required to live in an employer-owned home, which is three blocks from his company office. The company-provided home is equipped with high-speed Internet access and several telephone lines. Tim receives telephone calls and e-mails that require immediate attention any time of day or night because the company's business is spread all over the world. A full-time administrative assistant resides in the house to assist Tim with the urgent business matters. Tim often uses the home for entertaining customers, suppliers, and employees. The fair market value of comparable housing is $9,000 per month. Tim is also provided with free parking at his company's office. The value of the parking is $350 per month. Calculate the amount associated with the company-provided housing and free parking that Tim must include in his gross income.

Communications   18. **LO.1,4** Finch Construction Company provides the carpenters it employs with all of the required tools. However, the company believes that this has led to some employees not taking care of the tools and to the mysterious disappearance of some of the tools. The company is considering requiring all of its employees to provide their own tools. Employees' salaries would be increased by $1,500 to compensate for the additional costs. Write a letter to Finch's management, explaining the tax consequences of this plan to the carpenters. Finch's address is 300 Harbor Drive, Vermillion, SD 57069.

Decision Making   19. **LO.2** Rosa's employer has instituted a flexible benefits program. Rosa will use the plan to pay for her daughter's dental expenses and other medical expenses that are not covered by health insurance. Rosa is in the 28% marginal tax bracket and estimates that the medical and dental expenses not covered by health insurance will be within the range of $4,000 to $5,000. Her employer's plan permits her to set aside as much as $5,000 in the flexible benefits account. Rosa does not itemize her deductions.

a. Rosa puts $4,000 in her flexible benefits account, and her actual expenses are $5,000. What is her cost of underestimating the expenses?

b. Rosa puts $5,000 in her flexible benefits account, and her actual expenses are only $4,000. What is her cost of overestimating her expenses?

c. What is Rosa's cost of underfunding as compared with the cost of overfunding the flexible benefits account?

d. Does your answer in part (c) suggest that Rosa should fund the account closer to the low end or to the high end of her estimates?

20. **LO.2** Sparrow Corporation would like you to review its employee fringe benefits program with regard to the tax consequences of the plan for the company's president (Polly), who is also the majority shareholder.

a. The company has a qualified retirement plan. The company pays the cost of employees attending a retirement planning seminar. The employee must be within 10 years of retirement, and the cost of the seminar is $1,500 per attendee.

b. The company owns a parking garage that is used by customers, employees, and the general public. Only the general public is required to pay for parking. The charge to the general public for Polly's parking for the year would have been $3,600 (a $300 monthly rate).

c. All employees are allowed to use the company's fixed charge long-distance telephone services as long as the privilege is not abused. Although no one has kept track of the actual calls, Polly's use of the telephone had a value (what she would have paid on her personal telephone) of approximately $600.

d. The company owns a condominium at the beach, which it uses to entertain customers. Employees are allowed to use the facility without charge when the company has no scheduled events. Polly used the facility 10 days during the year. Her use had a rental value of $1,000.

e. The company is in the household moving business. Employees are allowed to ship goods without charge whenever there is excess space on a truck. Polly purchased a dining room suite for her daughter. Company trucks delivered the furniture to the daughter. Normal freight charges would have been $750.

f. The company has a storage facility for household goods. Officers are allowed a 20% discount on charges for storing their goods. All other employees are allowed a 10% discount. Polly's discounts for the year totaled $900.

21. **LO.2** Ted works for Azure Motors, an automobile dealership. All employees can buy a car at the company's cost plus 2%. The company does not charge employees the $300 dealer preparation fee that nonemployees must pay. Ted purchased an automobile for $29,580 ($29,000 + $580). The company's cost was

$29,000. The price for a nonemployee would have been $33,900 ($33,600 + $300 preparation fee). What is Ted's gross income from the purchase of the automobile?

22. **LO.2** Several of Egret Company's employees have asked the company to create a hiking trail that employees could use during their lunch hour. The company owns vacant land that is being held for future expansion, but would have to spend approximately $50,000 if it were to make a trail. Nonemployees would be allowed to use the facility as part of the company's effort to build strong community support. What are the relevant tax issues for the employees?

Issue ID

23. **LO.2** Bluebird, Inc., does not provide its employees with any tax-exempt fringe benefits. The company is considering adopting a hospital and medical benefits insurance plan that will cost approximately $9,000 per employee. To adopt this plan, the company may have to reduce salaries and/or lower future salary increases. Bluebird is in the 35% (combined Federal and state rates) bracket. Bluebird is also responsible for matching the Social Security and Medicare taxes withheld on employees' salaries (at the full 7.65% rate). The hospital and medical benefits insurance plan will not be subject to the Social Security and Medicare taxes, and the company is not eligible for the small business credit for health insurance. The employees generally fall into two marginal tax rate groups:

Income Tax	Social Security and Medicare Tax	Total
.15	.0765	.2265
.35	.0145	.3645

The company has asked you to assist in its financial planning for the hospital and medical benefits insurance plan by computing the following:

a. How much taxable compensation is the equivalent of $9,000 of exempt compensation for each of the two classes of employees?

b. What is the company's after-tax cost of the taxable compensation computed in part (a)?

c. What is the company's after-tax cost of the exempt compensation?

d. Briefly explain your conclusions from the preceding analysis.

24. **LO.2** George is a U.S. citizen who is employed by Hawk Enterprises, a global company. Beginning on June 1, 2015, George began working in London. He worked there until January 31, 2016, when he transferred to Paris. He worked in Paris the remainder of 2016. His salary for the first five months of 2015 was $100,000, and it was earned in the United States. His salary for the remainder of 2015 was $175,000, and it was earned in London. George's 2016 salary from Hawk was $300,000, with part being earned in London and part being earned in Paris. What is George's gross income in 2015 and 2016 (assume that the 2016 indexed amount is the same as the 2015 indexed amount)?

25. **LO.3** William is employed by an accounting firm and uses his automobile in connection with his work. During the month of October 2015, he works at the office for 3 days and participates in the audit of a key client for 19 days. In the audit situation, William goes directly from his home to the client's office. On all other days, he drives to his employer's office. On four Saturdays in October, he drives from his home to a local university, where he attends classes in a part-time MBA program. Relevant mileage is as follows:

Critical Thinking

Home to office	12
Office to audit client	13
Home to audit client	14
Home to university	10

Using the automatic mileage method, what is William's deduction for the month?

26. **LO.3** Kristen, the regional manager for a national hardware chain, is based in Atlanta. During March and April of this year, she has to replace temporarily the district manager in Jackson (Mississippi). During this period, Kristen flies to Jackson on Sunday night, spends the week at the district office, and returns home to Atlanta on Friday afternoon. The cost of returning home is $550, while the cost of spending the weekend in Jackson would have been $490.

    a. Presuming no reimbursement by her employer, how much, if any, of these weekend expenses may Kristen deduct?

    b. Would your answer in (a) change if the amounts involved were reversed (i.e., the trip home cost $490; staying in Jackson would have been $550)? Explain.

27. **LO.3** In June of this year, Dr. and Mrs. Bret Spencer traveled to Denver to attend a three-day conference sponsored by the American Society of Implant Dentistry. Bret, a practicing oral surgeon, participated in scheduled technical sessions dealing with the latest developments in surgical procedures. On two days, Mrs. Spencer attended group meetings where various aspects of family tax planning were discussed. On the other day, she went sightseeing. Mrs. Spencer does not work for her husband, but she does their tax returns and handles the family investments. Expenses incurred in connection with the conference are summarized as follows:

Airfare (two tickets)	$2,000
Lodging (single and double occupancy are the same rate—$250 each day)	750
Meals ($200 × 3 days)*	600
Conference registration fee (includes $120 for Family Tax Planning sessions)	620
Car rental	300

    *Split equally between Dr. and Mrs. Spencer.

    How much, if any, of these expenses can the Spencers deduct?

28. **LO.3** On Thursday, Justin flies from Baltimore (his home office) to Cadiz (Spain). He conducts business on Friday and Tuesday; vacations on Saturday, Sunday, and Monday (a legal holiday in Spain); and returns to Baltimore on Thursday. Justin was scheduled to return home on Wednesday, but all flights were canceled due to bad weather. Therefore, he spent Wednesday watching floor shows at a local casino.

    a. For tax purposes, what portion of Justin's trip is regarded as being for business?

    b. Suppose Monday had not been a legal holiday. Would this change your answer to (a)? Explain.

    c. Under either (a) or (b), how much of Justin's airfare qualifies as a deductible business expense?

Ethics and Equity   29. **LO.3** Veronica is a key employee of Perdiz Corporation, an aerospace engineering concern located in Seattle. Perdiz would like to establish an office on the east coast of Florida and wants Veronica to be in charge of the branch. Veronica is hesitant about making the move because she fears she will have to sell her residence in Seattle at a loss. Perdiz buys the house from Veronica for $420,000, its cost to her. She has owned and occupied the house as her principal residence for eight years. One year later, Perdiz resells the property for $370,000. Nothing regarding the sale of the residence is ever reflected on Veronica's income tax returns. Needless to say, Perdiz absorbs all of Veronica's moving expenses. Do you have any qualms as to the way these matters have been handled for income tax purposes? Explain.

30. **LO.3** Upon losing his job as a plant manager in Quincy, Massachusetts, Anthony incurs $6,200 in job search expenses. Having no success in finding new employment in the same type of work, Anthony moves to Clearwater, Florida, in 2015 and begins a charter boat business. His expenses in connection with the move are summarized below.

Penalty for breaking lease on Quincy rented residence	$2,800
Forfeiture of membership in Quincy Country Club	2,200
Packing and moving van charges	7,100
Lodging during move (3 nights)	380
Meals during move	360
Mileage (total for two automobiles)	2,400 miles

How much of these expenses may Anthony deduct?

31. **LO.3** Elijah is employed as a full-time high school teacher. The school district for which   Issue ID
      he works recently instituted a policy requiring all of its teachers to start working
on a master's degree. Pursuant to this new rule, Elijah spent most of the summer of
2015 taking graduate courses at an out-of-town university. His expenses are as follows:

Tuition	$6,600
Books and course materials	1,500
Lodging	1,700
Meals	2,200
Laundry and dry cleaning	200
Campus parking	300

In addition, Elijah drove his personal automobile 2,200 miles in connection with the
education. He uses the automatic mileage method.
   a.   How much, if any, of these expenses might qualify as a deduction *for* AGI?
   b.   How much, if any, of these expenses might qualify as a deduction *from* AGI?

32. **LO.3** In each of the following independent situations, determine how much, if any,   Issue ID
      qualifies as a deduction *for* AGI under § 222 (qualified tuition and related
expenses).
   a.   Lily is single and is employed as an architect. During 2015, she spent $4,100 in
        tuition to attend law school at night. Her MAGI is $64,000.
   b.   Liam is single and is employed as a pharmacist. During 2015, he spent $2,400
        ($2,100 for tuition and $300 for books) to take a course in herbal supplements
        at a local university. His MAGI is $81,000.
   c.   Hailey is married and is employed as a bookkeeper. She spends $5,200 for tui-
        tion and $900 for books and supplies to pursue a bachelor's degree in account-
        ing. Her MAGI is $40,000 on the separate return she files.
   d.   John spends $6,500 of his savings for tuition to attend Carmine State College.
        John is claimed as a dependent by his parents.
   e.   How much, if any, of the preceding amounts *not allowed under § 222* might
        otherwise qualify as a deduction *from* AGI?

33. **LO.3** During the year, Brenda has the following expenses related to her employment: Decision Making

Airfare	$8,500
Meals	4,000
Lodging	4,900
Transportation while in travel status (taxis and limos)	940
Entertainment of clients	8,000

Although Brenda renders an adequate accounting to her employer, she is reimbursed for only $12,000 of the above expenses. What are Brenda's tax consequen-
ces based on the following assumptions?
   a.   The $12,000 reimbursement does not designate which expenses are covered.
   b.   The reimbursement specifically covers only the meals and entertainment expenses.
   c.   The reimbursement covers any of the expenses other than meals and entertainment.
   d.   If Brenda has a choice of reimbursement procedures [parts (a), (b), or (c)
        above], which should she select? Why?

Critical Thinking   34. **LO.3, 4** Charles has AGI of $94,000 during the year and the following expenses related to his employment:

Lodging while in travel status	$5,000
Meals during travel	4,000
Business transportation	6,000
Entertainment of clients	3,800
Professional dues and subscriptions	800

Charles is reimbursed $14,000 under his employer's accountable plan. What are his deductions *for* and *from* AGI?

35. **LO.5** Janet, age 29, is unmarried and is an active participant in a qualified retirement plan. Her modified AGI is $63,000 in 2015.

   a.   Calculate the amount Janet can contribute to a traditional IRA and the amount she can deduct.

   b.   Assume instead that Janet is a participant in a SIMPLE IRA and that she elects to contribute 4% of her compensation to the account, while her employer contributes 3%. What amount will be contributed for 2015? What amount will be vested?

36. **LO.5** Carri and Dane, ages 34 and 32, respectively, have been married for 11 years, and both are active participants in employer qualified retirement plans. Their total AGI in 2015 is $186,000, and they earn salaries of $87,000 and $95,000, respectively. What amount may Carri and Dane:

   a.   Contribute to regular IRAs?

   b.   Deduct for their contributions in (a)?

   c.   Contribute to Roth IRAs?

   d.   Deduct for their contributions in (c)?

Critical Thinking   37. **LO.5** Dana, age 54, has a traditional deductible IRA with an account balance of $107,600, of which $77,300 represents contributions and $30,300 represents earnings. In 2015, she converts her traditional IRA into a Roth IRA. What amount must Dana include in her gross income for 2015?

38. **LO.6** In 2015, Susan's sole proprietorship earns $300,000 of self-employment net income (after the deduction for one-half of self-employment tax).

   a.   Calculate the maximum amount Susan can deduct for contributions to a defined contribution Keogh plan.

   b.   Suppose Susan contributes more than the allowable amount to the Keogh plan. What are the tax consequences to her?

   c.   Can Susan retire and begin receiving Keogh payments at age 58 without incurring a penalty? Explain.

39. **LO.6** Harvey is a self-employed accountant with earned income from the business of $120,000 (after the deduction for one-half of his self-employment tax). He has a profit sharing plan (e.g., defined contribution Keogh plan). What is the maximum amount Harvey can contribute to his retirement plan in 2015?

Critical Thinking   40. **LO.6** In each of the following *independent* situations, determine the amount of FICA (Social Security and Medicare) the employer should withhold from the employee's 2015 salary.

   a.   Harry earns a $50,000 salary, files a joint return, and claims four withholding allowances.

   b.   Hazel earns a $115,000 salary, files a joint return, and claims four withholding allowances.

   c.   Tracy earns a $190,000 salary, files a joint return, and claims four withholding allowances.

41. **LO.6** In 2015, Maria records self-employed earnings of $135,000. Following the format illustrated in the example in the text, compute Maria's self-employment tax liability and the allowable income tax deduction for the self-employment tax paid.

42. **LO.7** Samantha, an executive, has AGI of $100,000 before considering income or loss from her miniature horse business. Her outside income comes from prizes for winning horse shows, stud fees, and sales of yearlings. Samantha's home is on 20 acres, half of which she uses for the horse activity (i.e., stables, paddocks, fences, tack houses, and other related improvements).

    Samantha's office in her home is 10% of the square footage of the house. She uses the office exclusively for maintaining files and records on the horse activities. Her books show the following income and expenses for the current year:

Income from fees, prizes, and sales		$22,000
Expenses		
Entry fees		1,000
Feed and veterinary bills		4,000
Supplies		900
Publications and dues		500
Travel to horse shows (no meals)		2,300
Salaries and wages of employees		8,000
Depreciation—		
Horse equipment	$3,000	
Horse farm improvements	7,000	
On 10% of personal residence	1,000	11,000
Total home mortgage interest		24,000
Total property taxes on home		2,200
Total property taxes on horse farm improvements		800

The mortgage interest is only on her home because the horse farm improvements are not mortgaged.

a. What are Samantha's tax consequences if the miniature horse activity is a hobby?

b. If it is a business?

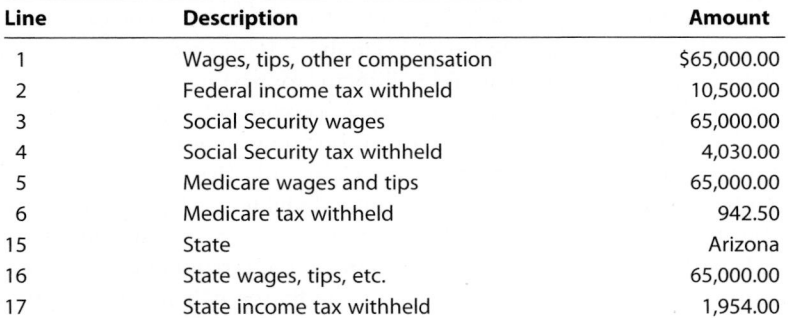

Comprehensive Tax Return Problems

1. Beth R. Jordan lives at 2322 Skyview Road, Mesa, AZ 85201. She is a tax accountant with Mesa Manufacturing Company, 1203 Western Avenue, Mesa, AZ 85201 (employer identification number 11-1111111). She also writes computer software programs for tax practitioners and has a part-time tax practice. Beth is single and has no dependents. Beth's birthday is July 4, 1972, and her Social Security number is 123-45-6789. She wants to contribute $3 to the Presidential Election Campaign Fund.

Tax Return Problem

TAX SOFTWARE

    The following information is shown on Beth's Wage and Tax Statement (Form W–2) for 2014.

Line	Description	Amount
1	Wages, tips, other compensation	$65,000.00
2	Federal income tax withheld	10,500.00
3	Social Security wages	65,000.00
4	Social Security tax withheld	4,030.00
5	Medicare wages and tips	65,000.00
6	Medicare tax withheld	942.50
15	State	Arizona
16	State wages, tips, etc.	65,000.00
17	State income tax withheld	1,954.00

During the year, Beth received interest of $1,300 from Arizona Federal Savings and Loan and $400 from Arizona State Bank. Each financial institution reported the interest income on a Form 1099–INT. She received qualified dividends of $800 from Blue Corporation, $750 from Green Corporation, and $650 from Orange Corporation. Each corporation reported Beth's dividend payments on a Form 1099–DIV.

Beth received a $1,100 income tax refund from the state of Arizona on April 29, 2014. On her 2013 Federal income tax return, she reported total itemized deductions of $8,200, which included $2,200 of state income tax withheld by her employer.

Fees earned from her part-time tax practice in 2014 totaled $3,800. She paid $600 to have the tax returns processed by a computerized tax return service.

On February 8, 2014, Beth bought 500 shares of Gray Corporation common stock for $17.60 a share. On September 12, 2014, she sold the stock for $14 a share.

Beth bought a used sports utility vehicle for $6,000 on June 5, 2014. She purchased the vehicle from her brother-in-law, who was unemployed and was in need of cash. On November 2, 2014, she sold the vehicle to a friend for $6,500.

On January 2, 2014, she acquired 100 shares of Blue Corporation common stock for $30 a share. She sold the stock on December 19, 2014, for $55 a share.

During the year, Beth records revenues of $16,000 from the sale of a software program she developed. She incurred the following expenditures in connection with her software development business.

Cost of personal computer	$7,000
Cost of printer	2,000
Furniture	3,000
Supplies	650
Fee paid to computer consultant	3,500

Beth elected to expense the maximum portion of the cost of the computer, printer, and furniture allowed under the provisions of § 179. These items were placed in service on January 15, 2014, and used 100% in her business.

Although her employer suggested that Beth attend a convention on current developments in corporate taxation, she was not reimbursed for the travel expenses of $1,420 she incurred in attending the convention. The $1,420 included $200 for the cost of meals.

During the year, Beth paid $300 for prescription medicines and $2,875 for doctor bills and hospital bills. Medical insurance premiums were paid for her by her employer. Beth paid real property taxes of $1,766 on her home. Interest on her home mortgage was $3,845, and interest to credit card companies was $320. She contributed $30 each week to her church and $10 each week to the United Way. Professional dues and subscriptions totaled $350. Beth paid estimated Federal income taxes of $1,000.

Part 1—Tax Computation

Compute the net tax payable or refund due for Beth R. Jordan for 2014. If you use tax forms for your solution, you will need Forms 1040, 2106-EZ, and 4562 and Schedules A, B, C, D, and SE. Suggested software: H&R BLOCK Tax Software.

Part 2—Tax Planning

Beth is anticipating significant changes in her life in 2015, and she has asked you to estimate her taxable income and tax liability for 2015. She just received word that she has been qualified to adopt a 2-year-old daughter. Beth expects that the adoption will be finalized in 2015 and that she will incur approximately $2,000 of adoption expenses. In addition, she expects to incur approximately $3,500 of child and dependent care expenses relating to the care of her new daughter, which will enable her to keep her job at Mesa Manufacturing Company. However, with the additional demands on her time because of her daughter, she has decided to discontinue her two part-time jobs (i.e., the part-time tax practice and her software business), and she will cease making estimated income tax payments. In your computations, assume that all other income and expenditures will remain at approximately the same levels as in 2014.

2. David R. and Ella M. Cole (ages 39 and 38, respectively) are husband and wife who live at 1820 Elk Avenue, Denver, CO 80202. David is a regional sales manager for Wren Industries, a national wholesaler of plumbing and heating supplies, and Ella is a part-time dental hygienist for a chain of dental clinics.

Tax Computation Problem

Communications

TAX SOFTWARE

- David is classified by Wren as a statutory employee with compensation for 2014 (based on commissions) of $95,000. He is expected to maintain his own office and pay for all business expenses from this amount. Wren does not require him to render any accounting as to the use of these funds. It does not withhold Federal and state income taxes but does withhold and account for the payroll taxes incurred (e.g., Social Security and Medicare). The Coles are adequately covered by Wren's noncontributory medical plan but have chosen not to participate in its § 401(k) retirement plan.

   David's employment-related expenses for 2014 are summarized below.

Airfare	$8,800
Lodging	5,000
Meals (during travel status)	4,800
Entertainment	3,600
Ground transportation (e.g., limos, rental cars, and taxis)	800
Business gifts	900
Office supplies (includes postage, overnight delivery, and copying)	1,500

   The entertainment involved business meals for purchasing agents, store owners, and building contractors. The business gifts consisted of $50 gift certificates to a national restaurant. These were sent by David during the Christmas holidays to 18 of his major customers.

   In addition, David drove his 2012 Ford Expedition 11,000 miles for business and 3,000 for personal use during 2014. He purchased the Expedition on August 15, 2011, and has always used the automatic (standard) mileage method for tax purposes. Parking and tolls relating to business use total $340 in 2014.

- When the Coles purchased their present residence in April 2011, they devoted 450 of the 3,000 square feet of living space to an office for David. The property cost $440,000 ($40,000 of which is attributable to the land) and has since appreciated in value. Expenses relating to the residence in 2014 (except for mortgage interest and property taxes; see below) are as follows:

Insurance	$2,600
Repairs and maintenance	900
Utilities	4,700
Painting office area; area rugs and plants (in the office)	1,800

   In terms of depreciation, the Coles use the MACRS percentage tables applicable to 39-year nonresidential real property. As to depreciable property (e.g., office furniture), David tries to avoid capitalization and uses whatever method provides the fastest write-off for tax purposes.

- Ella works part-time as a substitute for whichever hygienist is ill or on vacation or when one of the clinics is particularly busy (e.g., prior to the beginning of the school year). Besides her transportation, she must provide and maintain her own uniforms. Her expenses for 2014 appear below.

Uniforms	$690
State and city occupational licenses	380
Professional journals and membership dues in the American Dental Hygiene Association	340
Correspondence study course (taken online) dealing with teeth whitening procedures	420

Ella's salary for the year is $42,000, and her Form W–2 for the year shows income tax withholdings of $4,000 (Federal) and $1,000 (state) and the proper amount of Social Security and Medicare taxes. Because Ella is a part-time employee, she is not included in her employer's medical or retirement plans.

- In addition to those items already mentioned, the Coles had the following receipts during 2014.

Interest income—		
State of Colorado general purpose bonds	$2,500	
IBM bonds	800	
Wells Fargo Bank CD	1,200	$ 4,500
Federal income tax refund for year 2013		510
Life insurance proceeds paid by Eagle Assurance Corporation		200,000
Inheritance of savings account from Sarah Cole		50,000
Sales proceeds from two ATVs		9,000

For several years, the Coles's household has included David's divorced mother, Sarah, who has been claimed as their dependent. In late November 2014, Sarah unexpectedly died of coronary arrest in her sleep. Unknown to Ella and David, Sarah had a life insurance policy and a savings account (with David as the designated beneficiary of each). In 2013, the Coles purchased two ATVs for $14,000. After several near mishaps, they decided that the sport was too dangerous. In 2014, they sold the ATVs to their neighbor.

- Additional expenditures for 2014 include:

Funeral expenses for Sarah		$ 4,500
Taxes—		
Real property taxes on personal residence	$6,400	
Colorado state income tax due (paid in April 2014 for tax year 2013)	310	6,710
Mortgage interest on personal residence		6,600
Paid church pledge		2,400
Contributions to traditional IRAs for Ella and David ($5,500 + $5,500)		11,000

In 2014, the Coles made quarterly estimated tax payments of $1,400 (Federal) and $500 (state) for a total of $5,600 (Federal) and $2,000 (state).

Part 1—Tax Computation

Using the appropriate forms and schedules, compute the Coles's Federal income tax for 2014. Disregard the alternative minimum tax (AMT) and various education credits. Education credits were discussed in Chapter 10, and the AMT is discussed in Chapter 17. Relevant Social Security numbers are:

David Cole	123-45-6788
Ella Cole	123-45-6787
Sarah Cole	123-45-6799

The Coles do not want to contribute to the Presidential Election Campaign Fund. Also, they want any overpayment of tax refunded to them and *not* applied toward next year's tax liability. Suggested software: H&R BLOCK Tax Software.

Part 2—Follow-Up Advice

Ella has always wanted to pursue a career in nursing. To this end, she has earned a substantial number of college credits on a part-time basis. With Sarah no longer requiring home care, Ella believes that she can now complete her degree by attending college on a full-time basis.

    David would like to know how Ella's plans will affect their income tax position. Specifically, he wants to know:

- How much Federal income tax they will save if Ella quits her job.
- Any tax benefits that might be available from the cost of the education.

Write a letter to David, addressing these concerns. Note: In making your projections, assume that David's salary and expenses remain the same. Also disregard any consideration of the educational tax credits (i.e., American Opportunity and lifetime learning).

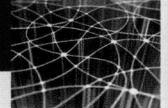

BRIDGE DISCIPLINE

1. Justin performs services for Partridge, Inc., and receives compensation of $85,000 for the year. Determine the tax consequences of Social Security and Medicare on Justin's take-home pay if:
   a. Justin is classified as an employee of Partridge.
   b. Justin is classified as an independent contractor.

2. The Code contains provisions that are "friendly" to specific groups of taxpayers. Among these are the following:

   • Senior citizens.

   • Married taxpayers.

   • Employed taxpayers.

   • Taxpayers with children.

   • Self-employed taxpayers.

   Provide justification for the special treatment for each of the above groups, and give an example of such special treatment for each group.

Research Problems

Note: Solutions to Research Problems can be prepared by using the Checkpoint® Student Edition online research product, which is available to accompany this text. It is also possible to prepare solutions to the Research Problems by using tax research materials found in a standard tax library.

Research Problem 1. The employees of the city of Greenville must make mandatory contributions to the city's postretirement health benefit plan. The employees' contributions are placed in a trust and are used exclusively for the employees' benefits. The employees believe that because they are required to make the contributions from their base salaries, the result should be the same as if the employer made the contribution and had reduced their salaries by the amount of the contributions. Therefore, the employees believe they should be permitted to exclude the payments from gross income. The employees have asked you to research the issue.

Research Problem 2. Rick Beam has been an independent sales representative for various textile manufacturers for many years. His products consist of soft goods such as tablecloths, curtains, and drapes. Rick's customers are clothing store chains, department stores, and smaller specialty stores. The employees of these companies who are responsible for purchasing merchandise are known as buyers. These companies generally prohibit their buyers from accepting gifts from manufacturers' sales representatives.

Communications

Each year, Rick gives cash gifts (never more than $25) to most of the buyers who are his customers. Generally, he cashes a large check in November and gives the money personally to the buyers around Christmas. Rick says, "This is one of the ways that I maintain my relationship with my buyers." He maintains adequate substantiation of all of the gifts.

Rick's deductions for these gifts have been disallowed by the IRS based on § 162(c)(2). Rick is confused and comes to you, a CPA, for advice.

a. Write a letter to Rick concerning his tax position on this issue. Rick's address is 948 Octavia Street, Baton Rouge, LA 70821.

b. Prepare a memo for your files supporting the advice you have given.

Research Problem 3. Aaron, a resident of Minnesota, has been a driver for Green Delivery Service for the past six years. For this purpose, he leases a truck from Green, and his compensation is based on a percentage of the income resulting from his pickup and delivery services. Green allows its drivers to choose their 10-hour shifts and does not exercise any control on how these services are carried out (e.g., the route to be taken or the order in which parcels are delivered or picked up). Under Green's operating agreement with its drivers, Green can terminate the arrangement after 30 days' notice. In practice, however, Green allows its truckers to quit immediately without giving advance notice. The agreement also labels the drivers as independent contractors. Green maintains no health or retirement plans for its drivers, and each year it reports their income by issuing Forms 1099–MISC (and not Forms W–2). Green requires its drivers to maintain a commercial driver's license and be in good standing with the state highway law enforcement division.

Citing the employment tax Regulations in §§ 31.3121(d)–1(c)(2) and 31.3306(i)–1(b), an IRS agent contends that Aaron is an independent contractor and, therefore, is subject to the self-employment tax. Based on *Peno Trucking, Inc.* (93 TCM 1027, T.C.Memo. 2007–66), Aaron disagrees and contends that he is an employee (i.e., not self-employed). Who is correct? Why?

Internet Activity

Use the tax resources of the Internet to address the following questions. Do not restrict your search to the Web, but include a review of newsgroups and general reference materials, practitioner sites and resources, primary sources of the tax law, chat rooms and discussion groups, and other opportunities.

Research Problem 4. Search the Internet for a U.S. 801(k) plan. Explain what it is.

Research Problem 5. Sarah was contemplating making a contribution to her traditional IRA in 2014. She determined she would contribute $5,000 in December 2014, but forgot about making the contribution until she was preparing her 2014 tax return in February 2015. Use the website of any well-known IRA provider (e.g., Fidelity, Vanguard, T. Rowe Price) to determine if Sarah can make a 2014 contribution to her IRA after the tax year has ended.

Research Problem 6. In reporting the transactions of a self-employed taxpayer, when can a Schedule C–EZ be used instead of the regular Schedule C of Form 1040?

Roger CPA Review Questions

1. The following facts pertain to Catch Ewe Later, a sole proprietorship owned by Shepherd:

20X09 net profit or (loss)	($ 3,000)
20X10 net profit or (loss)	10,000
20X11 net profit or (loss)	1,000
20X12 net profit or (loss)	1,700
20X13 net profit or (loss)	5,000

In 20X14 Shepherd gave out 50 livestock vests to prospective clients, at a cost of $10 per vest. What amount of business expense can Shepherd include, as a result of the vests, on Shepherd's 20X14 Schedule C?

a. $500

b. $200

c. $0

d. $1,000

2. On February 15 of the current year, Young received a $10,000 lump-sum payment from a qualified profit-sharing plan, the full amount of which Young rolled over into an IRA 46 days later. How much of this lump-sum payment may Young exclude from current year gross income?

a. $0

b. $10,000

c. Depends on contribution limit

d. $8,000

3. Claire is a self-employed individual who owns and runs Claire's Creations LLC. In 20X14 she had $225,000 in net self-employment earnings, including a deduction for 50% of the self-employment tax, prior to any Keogh deduction. Claire has a defined contribution stock bonus Keogh plan. What is the highest deductible Keogh contribution Claire can make for the 20X14 tax year? Assume no excess contribution carry-over from prior years.

a. $56,250

b. $225,000

c. $52,000

d. $45,000

PART 5

BUSINESS ENTITIES

Part 5 focuses on the different types of business entities and includes an analysis of the life cycle of a business, from formation, to the taxation of business activities, through the termination of the entity. The specific business entities covered are the C corporation, the S corporation, the partnership, and the LLC. Rules also are reviewed as to the Federal income tax treatment of distributions from a C corporation.

CHAPTER

12

Corporations: Organization, Capital Structure, and Operating Rules

LEARNING OBJECTIVES: *After completing Chapter 12, you should be able to:*

LO.1 Identify major tax and nontax considerations associated with the corporate form of business.

LO.2 Explain the tax consequences of incorporating and transferring assets to controlled corporations.

LO.3 Describe the special rules that apply when a corporation assumes a shareholder's liability.

LO.4 Identify the basis issues relevant to the shareholder and the corporation.

LO.5 Explain the tax aspects of the capital structure of a corporation.

LO.6 Characterize the tax differences between debt and equity investments.

LO.7 List and apply the tax rules unique to corporations.

LO.8 Compute the corporate income tax.

LO.9 Explain the rules unique to computing the tax of related corporations.

LO.10 Describe the reporting process for corporations.

CHAPTER OUTLINE

TAX TALK *Taxes owing to the Government ... are the price that business has to pay for protection and security.* —BENJAMIN N. CARDOZO

THE BIG PICTURE

GROWING INTO THE CORPORATE FORM

Amber has operated her business as a sole proprietorship since it was formed 10 years ago. Now, however, she has decided to incorporate the business as Garden, Inc., because the corporate form offers several important nontax advantages, including limited liability. Also, the incorporation would enable her husband, Jimmy, to become a part owner in the business. Amber expects to transfer her business assets in exchange for Garden stock, while Jimmy will provide accounting and legal services for an equity interest. Amber's sole proprietorship assets available for transfer to the new corporation are as follows:

	Adjusted Basis	Fair Market Value
Accounts receivable	$ –0–	$ 50,000
Building	100,000	400,000
Other assets	300,000	550,000
	$400,000	$1,000,000

Aware of the problem of double taxation associated with operating as a regular corporation, Amber is considering receiving some corporate debt at the time of the incorporation. The interest expense on the debt will then provide a deduction for Garden, Inc. Amber's main concern is whether the incorporation will be a taxable transaction. Can the transaction be structured to avoid tax?

Read the chapter and formulate your response.

Business operations may be conducted in a number of different forms. As with many business decisions, consideration must be given to the tax consequences of choosing a particular business entity. This chapter deals with the unique tax consequences of operating an entity as a regular corporation, including:

- Classification of the entity as a corporation.
- The tax consequences to the shareholders and the corporation upon the formation of the corporation.
- The capital structure of the corporation.
- Determination of the corporate income tax liability.
- Corporate tax filing requirements.

12-1 AN INTRODUCTION TO CORPORATE TAX

LO.1

Identify major tax and nontax considerations associated with the corporate form of business.

Corporations are governed by Subchapter C or Subchapter S of the Internal Revenue Code. Those governed by Subchapter C are referred to as **C corporations** or **regular corporations**. Corporations governed by Subchapter S are referred to as **S corporations**.

S corporations, which generally do not pay Federal income tax, are similar to partnerships in that ordinary business income (loss) flows through to the shareholders to be reported on their separate returns. Also like partnerships, S corporations do not aggregate all income and expense items in computing ordinary business income (loss). Certain items flow through to the shareholders and retain their separate character when reported on the shareholders' returns. The S corporation ordinary business income (loss) and the separately reported items are allocated to the shareholders according to their stock ownership interests. See Chapter 15 for detailed coverage of S corporations.

12-1a Double Taxation of Corporate Income

Unlike proprietorships, partnerships, and S corporations, C corporations are subject to an entity-level Federal income tax. This results in what is known as a *double taxation* effect. A C corporation reports its income and expenses on Form 1120. The corporation computes tax on the taxable income reported on Form 1120 using the rate schedule applicable to corporations (refer to the rate schedule inside the front cover of this text). When a corporation distributes its income, the corporation's shareholders report dividend income on their own tax returns. Thus, income that has already been taxed at the corporate level is also taxed at the shareholder level. The effects of double taxation are illustrated in Examples 1 and 2.

Double Taxation Illustrated

EXAMPLE 1

Lavender Corporation has taxable income of $100,000 in 2015. It pays corporate tax of $22,250. This leaves $77,750, all of which is distributed as a dividend to Mike, a 43-year-old single individual and the corporation's sole shareholder. Mike has no income sources other than Lavender Corporation.

Mike has taxable income of $67,450 ($77,750 − $6,300 standard deduction − $4,000 personal exemption). He pays tax at the preferential rate applicable to qualified dividends received by individuals. His tax is $4,500 [($37,450 × 0%) + ($30,000 × 15%)].

The combined tax on the corporation's net profit is $26,750 ($22,250 paid by the corporation + $4,500 paid by the shareholder).

EXAMPLE 2

Assume the same facts as in Example 1, except that the business is organized as a sole proprietorship. Mike reports the $100,000 profit from the business on his tax return.

Mike has taxable income of $89,700 ($100,000 − $6,300 standard deduction − $4,000 personal exemption) and pays tax of $18,219. Therefore, operating the business as a sole proprietorship results in a tax *savings* of $8,531 in 2015 [$26,750 (combined tax from Example 1) − $18,219].

When the management of a corporation decides to expand its business by establishing a presence in a foreign market, the new business venture may take one of several organizational forms. As each form comes with its respective advantages and disadvantages, making the best choice can be difficult.

One common approach is to conduct the foreign activity as a *branch* operation of the U.S. corporation. The foreign branch is not a separate legal entity, but a division of the U.S. corporation established overseas. As a result, any gains and losses produced by the foreign unit are included in the corporation's overall financial results.

Another possibility is to organize the foreign operations as a *subsidiary* of the U.S. parent corporation. If this route is chosen, the subsidiary can be either a *domestic* subsidiary (i.e., organized in the United States) or a *foreign* subsidiary (organized under the laws of a foreign country).

One fundamental tax difference between these two approaches is that the gains and losses of a domestic subsidiary may be consolidated with the operations of the U.S. parent, while the operations of a foreign subsidiary cannot. Thus, the use of a domestic subsidiary to conduct foreign operations yields generally the same final result as the use of a branch. With both approaches, the financial statements of the U.S. parent reflect the results of its worldwide operations.

Taxation of Dividends

Double taxation stems, in part, from the fact that dividend distributions are not deductible by a C corporation. Shareholders of closely held corporations frequently attempt to circumvent this disallowance by disguising a dividend distribution as some other purported transaction. One of the more common ways of disguising dividend distributions is to pay excessive compensation to shareholder-employees of a closely held corporation. The IRS scrutinizes compensation and other economic transactions (e.g., loans, leases, and sales) between shareholders and closely held corporations to ensure that payments are reasonable in amount. (See Chapter 13 for more discussion on constructive dividends.)

To alleviate some of the double taxation effect, Congress reduced the tax rate applicable to the dividend income of individuals. Qualified dividend income is currently taxed at the same preferential rate as long-term capital gains—20 percent, 15 percent, or 0 percent depending on the taxpayer's regular income tax bracket. The 20 percent rate applies when the taxpayer's regular tax rate is 39.6 percent; the 0 percent rate applies when the taxpayer's regular tax rate is 15 percent or less.

In addition, a 3.8 percent Medicare surtax applies to net investment income in excess of modified adjusted gross income of $200,000 ($250,000 if married filing jointly), thus increasing the double taxation of dividend income for high-income taxpayers.

12-1b **Comparison of Corporations and Other Forms of Doing Business**

Chapter 18 presents a detailed comparison of sole proprietorships, partnerships, S corporations, and C corporations as forms of doing business. However, it is appropriate at this point to consider some of the major tax and nontax factors that favor corporations over other business entities.

Consideration of tax factors requires an examination of the corporate rate structure. The marginal tax rates for corporations range from 15 percent to 39 percent. In comparison, the marginal tax rates for individuals range from 10 percent to 35 percent (assuming the taxpayer is not a high-income taxpayer to whom the 39.6 percent rate applies). In many cases, the tax burden will be greater if a business is operated as a corporation (as in Example 1). However, the corporate form of doing business presents tax savings opportunities when the applicable corporate marginal rate is lower than the applicable individual marginal rate.

TAX FACT **Corporations' Reporting Responsibilities**

Like individuals, corporations are required to report their taxable income and other financial information to the IRS on an annual basis. The forms used depend on the type and size of the corporation. Based on projections, the IRS expects to receive approximately 6.7 million corporate income tax returns during the 2016 filing season.

Interestingly, nearly 77 percent of C and S corporations are expected to submit their returns electronically.

Type of Corporation	Form	Percentage
C Corporation	1120	26.1%
C Corporation	Others	5.0
S Corporation	1120S	68.9
		100.0%

Source: Fiscal Year Return Projections for the United States: 2014–2021, IRS, Document 6292, Spring 2014 Update, Table 1.

EXAMPLE 3

Susanna, an individual taxpayer in the 39.6% marginal tax rate bracket, can generate $100,000 of additional taxable income in the current year. If the income is taxed to Susanna, the associated tax is $39,600 ($100,000 × 39.6%).

If, however, Susanna is able to shift the income to a newly created corporation, the corporate tax is $22,250. Thus, by taking advantage of the lower corporate marginal tax rates, a tax *savings* of $17,350 ($39,600 − $22,250) is achieved.

Any attempt to take advantage of the difference between the corporate and individual marginal tax rates also must consider the double taxation effect. When the preferential rate for dividend income is considered, however, tax savings opportunities still exist.

EXAMPLE 4

Assume in Example 3 that the corporation distributes all of its after-tax earnings to Susanna as a dividend. The dividend results in income tax of $15,550 [($100,000 − $22,250) × 20%] to Susanna.

Thus, even when the double taxation effect is considered, the combined tax burden of $37,800 ($22,250 paid by the corporation + $15,550 paid by the shareholder) represents an income tax *savings* of $1,800 when compared to the $39,600 of tax that results when the $100,000 of income is subject to Susanna's 39.6% marginal rate.

Examples 3 and 4 ignore other tax issues that also must be considered in selecting the proper form of doing business, but they illustrate the tax savings that can be achieved by taking advantage of tax rate differentials. In addition to the 3.8 percent Medicare surtax (mentioned above), some of the other tax considerations that could affect the selection of a business form include the character of business income, the expectation of business losses, employment taxes, and state taxes.

Unlike other forms of business, the tax attributes of income and expense items of a C corporation do not pass through the corporate entity to the shareholders. As a result, if the business is expected to generate tax-favored income (e.g., tax-exempt income or long-term capital gains), one of the other (non-C corporation) forms of business may be desirable.

Losses of a C corporation are treated differently than losses of a proprietorship, a partnership, or an S corporation. A loss incurred by a proprietorship may be deductible by the owner, because all income and expense items are reported by the proprietor. Partnership and S corporation losses are passed through the entity and may be deductible by the partners or shareholders. C corporation losses, however, have no effect on the taxable income of the shareholders. Therefore, one of the non-C corporation forms of business may be desirable if business losses are anticipated.

BRIDGE DISCIPLINE **Bridge to Finance**

Investment brokers and promoters often try to entice individuals to invest their disposable income in ventures designed to produce handsome returns. In most situations, the type of business entity in which the funds are invested takes the form of a "flow-through" entity, such as a limited partnership. Such investment ventures rarely operate as regular corporations.

A limited partnership is the favored investment vehicle for several reasons. One of the most significant reasons is that the investors who become limited partners are protected from exposure to unlimited liability. In addition, any operating losses of the entity (which may be expected in the venture's early years) flow through to the partners and, as a result, may provide an immediate tax benefit on the partners' returns. Another major advantage of the partnership form, in contrast to the corporate form, is that the business earnings are subject to only one level of tax—at the partner or investor level. If the investments were housed in a corporation, a tax would be levied first on the corporate earnings and then at the investor level when the corporation makes distributions to the shareholders.

Franco plans to start a business this year. He expects that the business will incur operating losses for the first three years and then become highly profitable. Franco decides to operate as an S corporation during the loss period because the losses will flow through and be deductible on his personal return. When the business becomes profitable, he intends to switch to C corporation status.

EXAMPLE

5

The net income of a proprietorship is subject to the self-employment tax, as are some partnership allocations of income to partners. In the alternative, wages paid to a shareholder-employee of a corporation (C or S) are subject to payroll taxes. The combined corporation-employee payroll tax burden should be compared with the self-employment tax associated with the proprietorship and partnership forms of business. This analysis should include the benefit of the deduction available to a corporation for payroll taxes paid, as well as the deduction available to an individual for one-half of the self-employment taxes paid.

At the entity level, state corporate income taxes and/or franchise taxes are applicable for businesses formed as corporations. Although no entity-level Federal income tax is typically assessed on S corporations, limited liability companies (LLCs), or partnerships, a few states impose a corporate income tax or franchise tax on such business forms. Consideration of state taxation when selecting a business form is particularly relevant for businesses that operate in more than one state. (See Chapter 16 for a discussion of the taxation of multistate corporations.) At the owner level, the income of sole proprietorships, S corporations, and partnerships (including most LLCs) is subject to state individual income taxation. Similarly, dividend income from corporate distributions is subject to state income taxation without any rate preference for such income.

12-1c **Nontax Considerations**

Nontax considerations will sometimes override tax considerations and lead to the conclusion that a business should be operated as a corporation. The following are some of the more important nontax considerations:

- Sole proprietors and general partners in partnerships face the danger of *unlimited liability*. That is, creditors of the business may file claims not only against the assets of the business but also against the *personal* assets of proprietors or general partners. State corporate law protects shareholders from claims against their personal assets for corporate debts.

- The corporate form of business can provide a vehicle for raising large amounts of capital through widespread stock ownership. Most major businesses in the United States are operated as corporations.

- Shares of stock in a corporation are freely transferable, whereas a partner's sale of his or her partnership interest is subject to approval by the other partners.

- Shareholders may come and go, but a corporation can continue to exist. Death or withdrawal of a partner, on the other hand, may terminate the existing partnership and cause financial difficulties that result in dissolution of the entity. Thus, *continuity of life* is a distinct advantage of the corporate form of doing business.

- Corporations have *centralized management*. All management responsibility is assigned to a board of directors, which appoints officers to carry out the corporation's business. Partnerships, by contrast, may have decentralized management, in which every partner has a right to participate in the organization's business decisions. Limited partnerships, though, may have centralized management. Centralized management is essential for the smooth operation of a widely held business.

12-1d Limited Liability Companies

The limited liability company (LLC) has proliferated greatly in recent years, particularly since 1988 when the IRS first ruled that it would treat qualifying LLCs as partnerships for tax purposes. All 50 states and the District of Columbia have passed laws that allow LLCs, and thousands of companies have chosen LLC status. As with a corporation, operating as an LLC allows its owners ("members") to avoid unlimited liability, which is a primary *nontax* consideration in choosing this form of business organization. The tax advantage of LLCs is that qualifying businesses may be treated as proprietorships or partnerships for tax purposes, thereby avoiding the problem of double taxation associated with regular corporations.

Some states allow an LLC to have centralized management, but not continuity of life or free transferability of interests. Other states allow LLCs to adopt any or all of the corporate characteristics of centralized management, continuity of life, and free transferability of interests. The comparison of business entities in Chapter 18 includes a discussion of LLCs.

12-1e Entity Classification

In 1996, the IRS issued its so-called check-the-box Regulations.[1] The Regulations enable taxpayers to choose the tax status of a business entity without regard to its corporate (or noncorporate) characteristics. These rules simplified tax administration considerably and eliminated much of the litigation that arose under prior law.

Under the check-the-box Regulations, an unincorporated entity with *more than one* owner is, by default, classified as a partnership. An unincorporated entity with *only one* owner is, by default, classified as a disregarded entity (or DRE). A DRE is treated as a sole proprietorship if it is owned by an individual taxpayer or as a branch or a division of a corporate owner. If the entity wants to use its default status, it simply files the appropriate tax return. If it wants to use a different status or change its status, it does so by "checking a box" on Form 8832. Thus, an LLC (single or multi-member) can choose to be taxed as a C corporation and, if otherwise qualifies, even elect S corporation status. See Chapter 15 for more on S corporations.

The status election is not available to entities that are incorporated under state law or to entities that are required to be taxed as corporations under Federal law (e.g., certain publicly traded partnerships). LLCs are not treated as being incorporated under state law, so they default to either partnership or DRE status. Although an LLC does not typically pay Federal income taxes, LLCs are obligated to report and pay employment and excise taxes.

DIGGING DEEPER 1   **In-depth coverage can be found on this book's companion website: www.cengagebrain.com**

---

[1] Reg. §§ 301.7701–1 through –4, and –7.

12-2 ORGANIZATION OF AND TRANSFERS TO CONTROLLED CORPORATIONS

LO.2

Explain the tax consequences of incorporating and transferring assets to controlled corporations.

Property transactions normally produce tax consequences if a gain or loss is realized. As a result, unless special provisions in the Code apply, a transfer of property to a corporation in exchange for stock is a taxable transaction. The amount of gain or loss is measured by the difference between the fair market value of the stock received and the tax basis of the property transferred.

12-2a General Rules

In contrast to the typical result of full gain or loss recognition, the Code permits nonrecognition of gain or loss in limited circumstances. For example, with both § 1031 (like-kind exchanges—see Chapter 7) and § 351 (transfers of property to controlled corporations), gain or loss is postponed until a substantive change in the taxpayer's investment occurs (e.g., a sale of property or ownership shares to outsiders). When a taxpayer exchanges some of his or her property for other property of a like kind, § 1031 provides that gain (or loss) realized on the exchange is not recognized because a substantive change in the taxpayer's investment has not occurred. The deferral of gain or loss is accomplished by calculating a substituted basis for the like-kind property received. With this substituted basis, the realized gain or loss associated with the property given up is ultimately recognized when the property received in the exchange is sold.

In a similar fashion, § 351, which deals with transfers to *controlled corporations* (defined later in the chapter), provides that gain or loss is not recognized upon the transfer of property to a corporation in exchange for stock. For example, when a business is incorporated, the owner's economic status remains the same; only the *form* of the investment has changed. The investment in the business assets carries over to an investment in corporate stock. When only stock in the corporation is received, the shareholder is hardly in a position to pay a tax on any realized gain. Thus, this approach is justified under the wherewithal to pay concept discussed in Chapter 1. As noted later, however, when the taxpayer receives property other than stock (i.e., cash or other "boot") from the corporation, some or all of the realized gain is recognized.

A further justification for the nonrecognition of gain or loss provisions under § 351 is that Congress believes tax rules should not impede the exercise of sound business judgment (e.g., choice of the corporate form of doing business).

EXAMPLE

6

Ron is considering incorporating his sole proprietorship. He is concerned about his personal liability for the obligations of the business. Ron realizes that if he incorporates, depending on state law, he will be liable only for the debts of the business that he has personally guaranteed. If Ron incorporates his business, the following assets will be transferred to the corporation:

	Tax Basis	Fair Market Value
Cash	$ 10,000	$ 10,000
Furniture and fixtures	20,000	60,000
Land and building	240,000	300,000
	$270,000	$370,000

In exchange, Ron will receive stock in the newly formed corporation worth $370,000. Without the nonrecognition provisions of § 351, Ron would recognize a taxable gain of $100,000 ($370,000 − $270,000) on the transfer. Under § 351, however, Ron does not recognize any gain because his economic status has not changed. Ron's investment in the assets of his sole proprietorship ($270,000) carries over to his investment in the incorporated business, which is now represented by his ownership of stock in the corporation. Thus, § 351 provides for tax neutrality on the initial incorporation of Ron's sole proprietorship.

In a manner similar to a like-kind exchange, if a taxpayer transfers property to a corporation and receives "boot" (money or property other than stock), § 351(b) provides that gain is recognized to the extent of the lesser of the gain realized or the boot received (the amount of money and the fair market value of other property received). Gain is characterized (e.g., ordinary, capital) according to the type of asset transferred.[2] Loss on a § 351 transaction is never recognized. The nonrecognition of gain or loss is accompanied by a substituted basis in the shareholder's stock.[3] The major shareholder consequences of a taxable property transaction versus one that is tax deferred are identified in Concept Summary 12.1.

EXAMPLE 7

Abby and Bill form White Corporation. Abby transfers property with an adjusted basis of $30,000 and a fair market value of $60,000 for 50% of White's stock. Bill transfers property with an adjusted basis of $70,000 and a fair market value of $60,000 for the remaining 50% of the stock. The transfers qualify under § 351.

Abby has a deferred gain of $30,000, and Bill has a deferred loss of $10,000. Both have a substituted basis in the stock of White Corporation. Abby has a basis of $30,000 in her stock, and Bill has a basis of $70,000 in his stock. Therefore, if either Abby or Bill later disposes of the White stock in a taxable transaction (e.g., a sale), this deferred gain/loss will then be fully recognized—a $30,000 gain to Abby and a $10,000 loss to Bill.

Alternatively, if Abby and Bill each had received White stock worth $50,000 and cash of $10,000, a gain would be recognized by Abby, but a loss would not be recognized by Bill. Specifically, Abby would recognize $10,000 of the $30,000 realized gain because she receives boot of $10,000, while Bill's receipt of boot would not trigger the recognition of a loss (i.e., recognition of loss never occurs in a § 351 transaction on the receipt of boot). Additional discussion of gain/loss recognition and the basis of stock received appears later in the chapter.

Concept Summary 12.1

Shareholder Consequences: Taxable Corporate Formation versus Tax-Deferred § 351 Transaction

Amount realized – adjusted basis of consideration transferred.

Gain Realized
- Taxable → Gain recognized; basis of stock received equals its FMV.
- Tax Deferred → Gain deferred under § 351; basis of stock received equals its FMV – deferred gain.

Loss Realized
- Taxable → Loss recognized; basis of stock received equals its FMV.
- Tax Deferred → Loss deferred under § 351; basis of stock received equals its FMV + deferred loss.

Section 351 is *mandatory* if a transaction satisfies the provision's requirements. There are three requirements for nonrecognition of gain or loss: (1) *property* is transferred (2) in exchange for *stock* and (3) the transferors must be in *control* of the transferee corporation immediately after the transfer. These three requirements are discussed next.

12-2b Transfer of Property

Questions have arisen concerning what constitutes **property** for purposes of § 351. The Code specifically excludes services rendered from the definition of property. With this exception, the definition of property is comprehensive. For example, along with plant and equipment, unrealized receivables held by a cash basis taxpayer and installment notes are considered property.[4] The transfer of an installment note in a transaction qualifying under § 351 is not a disposition of the installment note. Thus, gain is not recognized to the transferor. Proprietary processes and formulas as well as proprietary information in the general nature of a patentable invention also qualify as property under § 351.[5]

As demonstrated below, a taxpayer must report as income the fair market value of any consideration received as compensation for services because § 351 specifically excludes services from the definition of property.[6] Thus, if a taxpayer receives stock as consideration for rendering services to the corporation, the taxpayer recognizes ordinary income. In this case, the amount of income recognized by the taxpayer is equal to the fair market value of the stock received. As a consequence, the taxpayer's basis in the stock received is its fair market value.

EXAMPLE

8

Ann and Bob form Brown Corporation and transfer the following consideration:

	Consideration Transferred		
	Basis to Transferor	**Fair Market Value**	**Number of Shares Issued**
From Ann:			
Personal services rendered to Brown Corporation	$ –0–	$20,000	200
From Bob:			
Installment note receivable	5,000	40,000	
Inventory	10,000	30,000	800
Proprietary process	–0–	10,000	

The value of each share in Brown Corporation is $100.[7] Ann has ordinary income of $20,000 on the transfer because services do not qualify as "property." She has a basis of $20,000 in her 200 shares of stock in Brown (i.e., Ann is treated as having bought some of the Brown stock by rendering services). Bob recognizes no gain on the transfer because all of the consideration he transferred to Brown qualifies as "property" and he has "control" of Brown after the transfer. (See the discussion concerning control on the next page.) Bob has a substituted basis of $15,000 in the Brown stock.

As mentioned earlier, if property is transferred to a corporation in exchange for any property other than stock, the property received constitutes boot. The boot is taxable to the transferor-shareholder to the extent of any realized gain.[8]

---

[4]*Hempt Brothers, Inc. v. U.S.*, 74–1 USTC ¶9188, 33 AFTR 2d 74–570, 490 F.2d 1172 (CA–3, 1974), and Reg. § 1.453–9(c)(2).

[5]Rev.Rul. 64–56, 1964–1 C.B. 133; Rev.Rul. 71–564, 1971–2 C.B. 179.

[6]§§ 61 and 83.

[7]The value of closely held stock normally is presumed to be equal to the value of the property transferred.

[8]§ 351(b).

12-2c **Stock**

Generally, the term *stock* needs no clarification. It includes common stock and most preferred stock. However, the Regulations state that the term *stock* does not include stock rights and stock warrants.[9] In addition, it does not include "nonqualified preferred stock," which possesses many of the attributes of debt.[10]

Thus, any corporate debt or **securities** (i.e., long-term debt such as bonds) are treated as boot because they do not qualify as stock. Therefore, the receipt of debt in exchange for the transfer of appreciated property to a controlled corporation causes recognition of gain.

The Big Picture

EXAMPLE 9

Return to the facts of *The Big Picture* on p. 12-1. Assume that the proposed transaction qualifies under § 351, but Amber decides to receive some corporate debt along with the stock.

If Amber receives Garden stock worth $900,000 and Garden debt of $100,000 in exchange for the property transferred, Amber realizes a gain of $600,000 [$1,000,000 (value of consideration received) − $400,000 (basis in the transferred property)]. However, because the transaction qualifies under § 351, only $100,000 of the gain is recognized (this is becuase the $100,000 of Garden debt is treated as boot). The remaining realized gain of $500,000 is deferred.

12-2d **Control of the Corporation**

For a transaction to qualify as nontaxable under § 351, the transferor(s) of the property must be in **control** of the corporation immediately after the exchange. That is, the person or persons transferring *property* must have at least an 80 percent stock ownership in the corporation, resulting in the entity being a controlled corporation. The property transferors must own stock possessing at least 80 percent of the total combined voting power of all classes of stock entitled to vote *and* at least 80 percent of the total *number* of shares of all other classes of stock.[11]

Control Immediately after the Transfer

Control after the exchange can apply to a single person or to several taxpayers if they are all parties to an integrated transaction. To satisfy the timing requirement, the Regulations provide that when more than one person is involved, the exchange does not necessarily require simultaneous exchanges by two or more persons. The Regulations do, however, require that the rights of the parties (i.e., those transferring property to the corporation) be previously set out and determined. Also, the agreement to transfer property should be executed "with an expedition consistent with orderly procedure," and the transfers should occur close together in time.[12]

The Point at Which Control Is Determined

EXAMPLE 10

Jack exchanges property with a basis of $60,000 and a fair market value of $100,000 for 70% of the stock of Gray Corporation. The other 30% is owned by Jane, who acquired it several years ago. The fair market value of Jack's stock is $100,000.

Jack recognizes a taxable gain of $40,000 on the transfer because he does not have control immediately after the exchange and his transaction cannot be integrated with Jane's for purposes of the control requirement.

---

[9]Reg. § 1.351–1(a)(1)(ii).

[10]§ 351(g). Examples of nonqualified preferred stock include preferred stock that is redeemable within 20 years of issuance and whose dividend rate is based on factors other than corporate performance. See also Reg. § 1.351–1(a)(1)(ii).

[11]§ 368(c). Nonqualified preferred stock is treated as stock, not boot, for purposes of this control test.

[12]Reg. § 1.351–1(a)(1).

The Point at Which Control Is Determined

Lana, Leo, and Lori incorporate their respective businesses by forming Green Corporation. Lana exchanges her property for 300 shares in Green on January 7, 2015. Leo exchanges his property for 400 shares in Green on January 14, 2015, and Lori exchanges her property for 300 shares in Green on March 5, 2015.

The three exchanges are part of a prearranged plan, so the control requirement is met. The nonrecognition provisions of § 351 apply to all of the exchanges.

Stock need not be issued to the property transferors in the same proportion as the relative value of the property transferred by each. However, when stock received is not proportionate to the value of the property transferred, the actual effect of the transaction must be properly characterized. For example, in such situations, one transferor may actually be making a gift to another transferor.

Ron and Shelia, father and daughter, form Oak Corporation. Ron transfers property worth $50,000 in exchange for 100 shares of stock, while Shelia transfers property worth $50,000 for 400 shares of stock.

The transfers qualify under § 351 because Ron and Shelia have control of the Oak stock immediately after the transfers of property. However, the implicit gift of 150 shares by Ron to Shelia must be recognized and appropriately characterized. As such, the value of the gift might be subject to the gift tax.

Once control has been achieved, it is not necessarily lost if, shortly after the transaction, stock received by shareholders in a § 351 exchange is sold or given to persons who are not parties to the exchange.[13]

Mark and Carl form Black Corporation. They transfer appreciated property to the corporation with each receiving 50 shares of Black stock. Shortly after the formation, Mark gives 25 shares to his son.

Because Mark was not committed to making the gift, he is considered to own his original shares of Black Corporation stock and, along with Carl, to control Black Corporation "immediately after the exchange." The requirements of § 351 are met, and neither Mark nor Carl is taxed on the exchange.

A different result might materialize if a plan for the ultimate disposition of the stock existed *before* the exchange.

Assume the same facts as in Example 13, except that Mark immediately gives 25 shares to a business associate pursuant to a plan to satisfy an outstanding obligation.

In this case, the formation of Black would be taxable to Mark and Carl because of their lack of control (i.e., Mark and Carl, the property transferors, would have owned only 75% of the stock).

---

[13]*Wilgard Realty Co. v. Comm.*, 42–1 USTC ¶9452, 29 AFTR 325, 127 F.2d 514 (CA–2, 1942).

TAX PLANNING STRATEGIES   Utilizing § 351

FRAMEWORK FOCUS: INCOME AND EXCLUSIONS

Strategy: Avoid Income Recognition.

When using § 351, ensure that all parties transferring property (including cash) receive control of the corporation. Simultaneous transfers are not necessary, but a long period of time between transfers makes the transaction vulnerable to taxation if the transfers are not properly documented as part of a single plan. To do this, the parties should document and preserve evidence of their intentions. Also, it is helpful to have some reasonable explanation for any delay in the transfers.

To meet the requirements of § 351, mere momentary control on the part of the transferor may not suffice if loss of control is compelled by a prearranged agreement.[14]

EXAMPLE 15

For many years, Todd operated a business as a sole proprietor employing Linda as manager. To dissuade Linda from quitting and going out on her own, Todd promised her a 30% interest in the business. To fulfill this promise, Todd transferred the business to newly formed Green Corporation in return for all of its stock. Immediately thereafter, Todd transfers 30% of the stock to Linda. As a consequence, he no longer meets the 80% control requirement. Section 351 probably does not apply to Todd's transfer to Green Corporation. It appears that Todd was under an obligation to relinquish control. If this preexisting obligation exists, § 351 will not be available to Todd because, as the sole property transferor, he does not have control of Green Corporation. If there is no obligation and the loss of control was voluntary on Todd's part, momentary control would suffice.[15]

Make sure that later transfers of property to an existing corporation satisfy the 80 percent control requirement if recognition of gain is to be avoided. Also with respect to later transfers, a transferor's interest cannot be counted if the value of stock received is relatively small compared with the value of stock already owned. Further, the primary purpose of the transfer may not be to qualify other transferors for § 351 treatment.[16] (For a complete discussion of this issue, see "Transfers to Existing Corporations" on p. 12-14).

For contributions of property by a partner to a partnership, at formation or subsequent to formation, § 721 is available to provide nonrecognition treatment. This partnership provision generally resembles § 351. However, in such situations, any partner can make a tax-deferred contribution without regard to a control test. Thus, the 80 percent control requirement, which serves as a high threshold to be met if tax-deferred treatment is desired in a corporate setting, contrasts to the treatment given in partnership taxation where no such control test applies. See Chapters 14 and 18 for additional discussion.

Transfers for Property and Services

Section 351 treatment is lost if stock is transferred to persons who did not contribute property, causing those who did to lack control immediately after the exchange.

The Big Picture

EXAMPLE 16

Return to the facts of *The Big Picture* on p. 12-1. Assume that Amber transfers her $1,000,000 of property to Garden, Inc., and receives 50% of its stock. Jimmy receives the other 50% of the stock for services rendered (worth $1,000,000).

Both Amber and Jimmy have tax consequences from the transfers. Jimmy has ordinary income of $1,000,000 because he does not exchange property for stock. Amber has a taxable gain of $600,000 [$1,000,000 (fair market value of the stock in Garden) − $400,000 (basis in the transferred property)]. As the sole transferor of property, she receives only 50% of Garden's stock.

---

[14]Rev.Rul. 54–96, 1954–1 C.B. 111.

[15]Compare *Fabs v. Florida Machine and Foundry Co.*, 48–2 USTC ¶9329, 36 AFTR 1161, 168 F.2d 957 (CA–5, 1948), with *John C. O'Connor*, 16 TCM 213, T.C.Memo. 1957–50, *aff'd* in 58–2 USTC ¶9913, 2 AFTR 2d 6011, 260 F.2d 358 (CA–6, 1958).

[16]Reg. § 1.351–1(a)(1)(ii).

As noted earlier, a person receiving stock in exchange for services and for property transferred is taxed on the stock value related to those services but not on the stock issued for property. In addition, such a person can still be treated as a "property transferor" and in such a case, all stock received by the person transferring both property and services is counted in determining whether the transferors acquired control of the corporation.[17]

The Big Picture

EXAMPLE 17

Assume the same facts as in Example 16, except that Jimmy transfers property worth $800,000 (basis of $260,000) in addition to services rendered to Garden, Inc. (valued at $200,000).

Now Jimmy becomes a part of the control group. Amber and Jimmy, as property transferors, together receive 100% of the corporation's stock. Consequently, § 351 is applicable to the exchanges. Amber has no recognized gain. Jimmy does not recognize gain on the transfer of the property, but he recognizes ordinary income to the extent of the value of the shares issued for services rendered. Thus, Jimmy recognizes $200,000 of ordinary income currently.

Transfers for Services and Nominal Property

Note that to be part of the group meeting the 80 percent control test, the person contributing services must transfer property having more than a "relatively small value" compared to the value of services performed. Section 351 will not apply when a small amount of property is transferred and the primary purpose of the transfer is to qualify the transaction under § 351 for concurrent transferors.[18]

The IRS generally requires that before a transferor who receives stock for both property and services can be included in the control group, the value of the property transferred must be at least 10 percent of the value of the services provided.[19] If the value of the property transferred is less than this amount, the IRS will not issue an advance ruling that the exchange meets the requirements of § 351.

Determining Control Group Membership When Services Are Rendered

EXAMPLE 18

Sara and Rick form Grouse Corporation. Sara transfers land (worth $100,000, basis of $20,000) for 50% of the stock in Grouse. Rick transfers equipment (worth $50,000, adjusted basis of $10,000) and provides services worth $50,000 for 50% of the stock.

Because the value of the property Rick transfers is not small relative to the value of the services he renders, his stock in Grouse Corporation is counted in determining control for purposes of § 351; thus, the transferors own 100% of the stock in Grouse. In addition, all of Rick's stock, not just the shares received for the equipment, is counted in determining control.

As a result, Sara does not recognize gain on the transfer of the land. Rick, however, must recognize income of $50,000 on the transfer of services. Even though the transfer of the equipment qualifies under § 351, his transfer of services for stock does not.

EXAMPLE 19

Assume the same facts as in Example 18 except the value of Rick's property is $2,000 and the value of his services is $98,000.

In this situation, the value of the property is small relative to the value of the services (and well below the 10 percent threshold provided by the IRS); therefore, Rick will not be considered a property transferor. Consequently, the control requirement is not met and the transaction is fully taxable to both Sara and Rick. None of Rick's stock is counted in determining control because the property he transfers has a nominal value in comparison to the value of the services he renders.

As a result, Sara recognizes $80,000 of gain on the transfer of the land. She has a basis of $100,000 in her Grouse stock. Rick must recognize income of $98,000 on the transfer for services rendered, and any realized gain or loss is recognized on the property transferred. Rick also has a $100,000 basis in his Grouse stock.

---

[17]Reg. § 1.351–1(a)(2), Ex. 3.

[18]Reg. § 1.351–1(a)(1)(ii).

[19]Rev.Proc. 77–37, 1977–2 C.B. 568.

Transfers to Existing Corporations

Once a corporation is in operation, § 351 also applies to any later transfers of property for stock by either new or existing shareholders.

EXAMPLE 20

Sam and Beth formed Blue Corporation three years ago. Both Sam and Beth transferred appreciated property to Blue in exchange for 500 shares each in the corporation. The original transfers qualified under § 351, and neither Sam nor Beth was taxed on the exchange. In the current year, Sam transfers property (worth $100,000, adjusted basis of $5,000) for 500 additional Blue shares.

Sam has a taxable gain of $95,000 on the transfer. The exchange does not qualify under § 351 because Sam does not have 80% control of Blue Corporation immediately after the transfer; he owns 1,000 shares of the 1,500 shares outstanding, or a 66⅔% interest.

If current shareholders transfer property with a small value relative to the value of stock already owned, a special rule applies (similar to the nominal property rule noted previously). In particular, if the purpose of the transfer is to qualify a transaction under § 351, the ownership of the current shareholders is not counted when determining control. Thus, in the preceding example, if Beth had contributed $200 for one share of stock at the time of Sam's contribution, Beth's ownership would not have counted toward the 80 percent control requirement and Sam would still have had a taxable exchange.

LO.3

Describe the special rules that apply when a corporation assumes a shareholder's liability.

12-2e Assumption of Liabilities—§ 357

Without a provision to the contrary, the transfer of mortgaged property to a controlled corporation could require recognition of gain by the transferor if the corporation took over the mortgage. This would be consistent with the treatment given in like-kind exchanges under § 1031. Liabilities assumed by the other party are considered the equivalent of cash and treated as boot received. Section 357(a) provides, however, that when the acquiring corporation assumes a liability in a § 351 transaction, the liability is not treated as boot received for gain recognition purposes. Nevertheless, liabilities assumed by the transferee corporation are treated as boot in determining the basis of the stock received. As a result, the basis of the stock received is reduced by the amount of the liabilities assumed by the corporation.

The Big Picture

EXAMPLE 21

Return to the facts of *The Big Picture* on p. 12-1. Assume that you learn that Amber's husband, Jimmy, becomes disinterested in becoming a stockholder in Garden, Inc., and that Amber's building is subject to a liability of $70,000 that Garden assumes. Consequently, Amber receives 100% of the Garden stock and is relieved of the $70,000 liability in exchange for property with an adjusted basis of $400,000 and fair market value of $1,000,000.

The exchange is tax-free under § 351 because the release of a liability is not treated as boot under § 357(a). However, the basis to Amber of the Garden stock is $330,000 [$400,000 (basis of property transferred) − $70,000 (amount of the liability assumed by Garden)].

The general rule of § 357(a) has two exceptions: (1) § 357(b) provides that if the principal purpose of the assumption of the liabilities is to avoid tax *or* if there is no bona fide business purpose behind the exchange, the liabilities are treated as boot; (2) § 357(c) provides that if the sum of the liabilities exceeds the adjusted basis of the properties transferred, the excess is taxable gain.

Exception (1): Tax Avoidance or No Bona Fide Business Purpose

Satisfying the bona fide business purpose under § 357(b) is not difficult if the liabilities are incurred in connection with the transferor's normal course of conducting a trade or business. But the bona fide business purpose requirement can cause difficulty if the

liability is taken out shortly before the property is transferred and the proceeds are utilized for personal purposes.[20] This type of situation is analogous to a cash distribution by the corporation, which is taxed as boot.

Dan transfers real estate (basis of $140,000 and fair market value of $190,000) to a controlled corporation in return for stock in the corporation. Shortly before the transfer, Dan mortgages the real estate and uses the $20,000 of proceeds to meet personal obligations. Thus, along with the real estate, the mortgage is transferred to the corporation. In this case, the assumption of the mortgage lacks a bona fide business purpose. Consequently, the release of the liability is treated as boot received, and Dan has a taxable gain on the transfer of $20,000, computed as follows:[21]

EXAMPLE 22

Stock	$ 170,000
Release of liability—treated as boot	20,000
Total amount realized	$ 190,000
Less: Basis of real estate	(140,000)
Realized gain	$ 50,000
Recognized gain	$ 20,000

The effect of the application of § 357(b) is to taint *all* liabilities transferred, even if *some* are supported by a bona fide business purpose.

Tim, an accrual basis taxpayer, incorporates his sole proprietorship. Among the liabilities transferred to the new corporation are trade accounts payable of $100,000 and a credit card bill of $5,000. Tim had used the credit card to purchase an anniversary gift for his wife. Under these circumstances, the *entire* $105,000 of liabilities is boot and triggers the recognition of gain to the extent gain is realized.

EXAMPLE 23

Exception (2): Liabilities in Excess of Basis

Section 357(c) states that if the amount of a shareholder's liabilities assumed *exceeds* the total of the adjusted bases of the properties transferred by that shareholder, the excess is taxable gain. Without this provision, if liabilities exceed the basis in the property exchanged, a taxpayer would have a negative basis in the stock received in the controlled corporation.[22] Section 357(c) precludes the negative basis possibility by treating the excess over basis as gain to the transferor.

---

[20]See, for example, *Campbell, Jr. v. Wheeler*, 65–1 USTC ¶9294, 15 AFTR 2d 578, 342 F.2d 837 (CA–5, 1965).

[21]§ 351(b).

[22]*Jack L. Easson*, 33 T.C. 963 (1960), *rev'd* in 61–2 USTC ¶9654, 8 AFTR 2d 5448, 294 F.2d 653 (CA–9, 1961).

EXAMPLE 24

Andre transfers land and equipment with adjusted bases of $350,000 and $50,000, respectively, to a newly formed corporation in exchange for 100% of the stock. The corporation assumes $500,000 of liabilities on the transferred land. Without § 357(c), Andre's basis in the stock of the new corporation would be negative $100,000 [$400,000 (bases of properties transferred) + $0 (gain recognized) − $0 (boot received) − $500,000 (liabilities assumed)]. Section 357(c), however, causes Andre to recognize a gain of $100,000 ($500,000 liabilities assumed − $400,000 bases of assets transferred). As a result, the stock has a zero basis in Andre's hands, determined as follows:

Bases in the properties transferred ($350,000 + $50,000)	$ 400,000
Plus: Gain recognized	100,000
Less: Boot received	(–0–)
Less: Liabilities assumed	(500,000)
Basis in the stock received	$ –0–

Thus, Andre recognizes $100,000 of gain, and a negative stock basis is avoided.

The definition of liabilities under § 357(c) excludes obligations that would have been deductible to the transferor had those obligations been paid before the transfer. Thus, accounts payable of a cash basis taxpayer that give rise to a deduction are not considered liabilities for purposes of § 357(c). In addition, they are not considered in the computation of the shareholder's stock basis.

EXAMPLE 25

Tina, a cash basis taxpayer, incorporates her sole proprietorship. In return for all of the stock of the new corporation, she transfers the following items:

	Adjusted Basis	Fair Market Value
Cash	$10,000	$10,000
Unrealized accounts receivable (amounts due to Tina but not yet received by her)	–0–	40,000
Trade accounts payable	–0–	30,000
Note payable	5,000	5,000

Unrealized accounts receivable and trade accounts payable have a zero basis. Under the cash method of accounting, no income is recognized until the receivables are collected and no deduction materializes until the payables are satisfied. The note payable has a basis because it was issued for consideration received.

In this situation, the trade accounts payable are disregarded for gain recognition purposes and for the determination of Tina's stock basis. Thus, because the balance of the note payable does not exceed the basis of the assets transferred, Tina does not have a problem of liabilities in excess of basis (i.e., the note payable of $5,000 does not exceed the aggregate basis in the cash and accounts receivable of $10,000).

If §§ 357(b) and (c) both apply to the same transfer, § 357(b) dominates.[23] This could be significant because § 357(b) does not create gain on the transfer, as does § 357(c), but merely converts the liability to boot. Thus, the realized gain limitation continues to apply to § 357(b) transactions.

EXAMPLE 26

Chris owns land with a basis of $100,000 and a fair market value of $1 million. The land is subject to a mortgage of $300,000. One month prior to transferring the land to Robin Corporation, Chris borrows an additional $200,000 for personal purposes and gives the lender a second mortgage on the land. Therefore, upon the incorporation, Robin Corporation issues stock worth $500,000 to Chris and assumes the mortgages on the land.

continued

---

[23]§ 357(c)(2)(A).

Both § 357(c) and § 357(b) apply to the transfer. The mortgages on the property exceed the basis of the property. Thus, Chris has a gain of $400,000 under § 357(c). Chris borrowed $200,000 just prior to the transfer and used the loan proceeds for personal purposes. Under § 357(b), Chris has boot of $500,000 in the amount of the liabilities, which triggers $500,000 of recognized gain. Note that *all* of the liabilities are treated as boot, not just the "tainted" $200,000 liability.

	§ 357(b) Result	§ 357(c) Result
Amount realized:		
Robin Corporation stock	$ 500,000	$ 500,000
Release of mortgage on land	300,000	300,000
Release of second mortgage—personal purposes	200,000	200,000
Total amount realized	$1,000,000	$1,000,000
Basis of land	(100,000)	(100,000)
Realized gain	$ 900,000	$ 900,000
Gain recognized under § 357(b) ($300,000 + $200,000)	$ 500,000	
Gain recognized under § 357(c) [($300,000 + $200,000) − $100,000]		$ 400,000

Unfortunately for Chris, the relatively more onerous rule of § 357(b) dominates over § 357(c).

Concept Summary 12.2 summarizes the tax rules that apply when liabilities are transferred in property transactions, including the special rules that apply in § 351 transactions.

Concept Summary 12.2

Tax Consequences of Liability Assumption

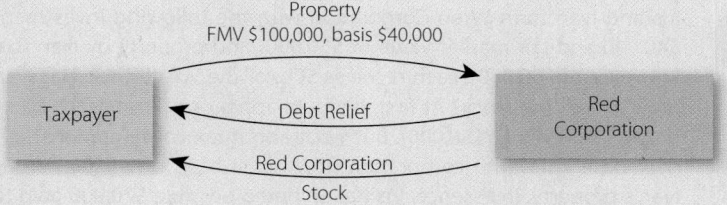

Property
FMV $100,000, basis $40,000

Taxpayer → Red Corporation

Debt Relief

Red Corporation Stock

General rule: (§ 1001)	If Red Corporation takes property subject to Taxpayer's liability or assumes Taxpayer's liability, Taxpayer is treated as having received cash. Therefore, if the liability is $20,000, Taxpayer is treated as receiving Red stock of $80,000 and cash of $20,000 in a fully taxable transaction. Gain realized and recognized is $60,000.
Special rule in a § 351 transaction: [§ 357(a)]	Assume the same facts as above, except that the transfer is a § 351 transaction. Taxpayer is not treated as receiving cash of $20,000 for gain recognition purposes (the debt relief is *not* treated as boot). Therefore, gain recognition is avoided. The debt relief will, however, reduce the Taxpayer's basis in Red Corporation stock.
Exception to § 351 transaction rule—Tax avoidance or no bona fide business purpose: [§ 357(b)]	Assume the same facts as above, except that the transfer is a § 351 transaction and the liability does *not* have a business purpose. Taxpayer is treated as receiving cash of $20,000 for gain recognition purposes (the debt relief *is* treated as boot). Therefore, $20,000 of the realized gain is recognized.
Exception to § 351 transaction rule—Liabilities in excess of basis: [§ 357(c)]	Assume the same facts as above, except that the transfer is a § 351 transaction, the liability is $45,000 and the Red stock is worth $55,000, and § 357(b) does not apply. Taxpayer recognizes a $5,000 gain (excess of $45,000 liability over $40,000 property basis).

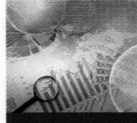

TAX PLANNING STRATEGIES **Avoiding § 351**

FRAMEWORK FOCUS: TAX RATE

Strategy: Shift Net Income from High-Bracket Years to Low-Bracket Years.
Control the Character of Income and Deductions.

Section 351(a) provides for the nonrecognition of gain on transfers to controlled corporations. As such, it is often regarded as a relief provision favoring taxpayers. In some situations, however, avoiding § 351(a) may produce a more advantageous tax result. The transferors might prefer to recognize gain on the transfer of property if the tax cost is low. For example, they may be in low tax brackets, or the gain may be a capital gain that could be neutralized by available capital losses. Also, recognition of gain will lead to a stepped-up basis in the transferred property in the corporation.

Another reason a particular transferor might want to avoid § 351 concerns possible loss recognition. Recall that § 351 refers to the nonrecognition of both gains and losses. Section 351(b)(2) specifically states: "No loss to such recipient shall be recognized." A transferor who wants to recognize loss has several alternatives:

- Sell the property to the corporation for its stock. The IRS could attempt to collapse the "sale," however, by taking the approach that the transfer really falls under § 351(a).[24]

- Sell the property to the corporation for other property or boot. Because the transferor receives no stock, § 351 is inapplicable.

- Transfer the property to the corporation in return for securities or nonqualified preferred stock. Recall that § 351 does not apply to a transferor who receives securities or nonqualified preferred stock. In both this and the previous alternatives, watch for the possible disallowance of the loss under the related-party rules.

Suppose loss property is to be transferred to the corporation and no loss is recognized by the transferor due to § 351(a). This could present an interesting problem in terms of assessing the economic realities involved.

EXAMPLE 27

Iris and Ivan form Wren Corporation with the following investments: property by Iris (basis of $40,000 and fair market value of $50,000) and property by Ivan (basis of $60,000 and fair market value of $50,000). Each receives 50% of the Wren stock. Has Ivan acted wisely in settling for only 50% of the stock? At first, it would appear so because Iris and Ivan each invested property of the same value ($50,000). But what about tax considerations? By applying the general carryover basis rules, the corporation now has a basis of $40,000 in Iris's property and $60,000 in Ivan's property. In essence, Iris has shifted a possible $10,000 gain to the corporation while Ivan has transferred a $10,000 potential loss. Thus, an equitable allocation of the Wren stock would call for Ivan to receive a greater percentage interest than Iris would receive.

This issue is further complicated by the special basis adjustment required when a shareholder such as Ivan contributes property with a built-in loss to a corporation. (See the discussion of this basis adjustment for loss property in the next section.) In this situation, if Wren is to take a carryover basis in Ivan's property, Ivan must reduce his stock basis by the $10,000 built-in loss. This reduced stock basis, of course, could lead to a greater tax burden on Ivan when he sells the Wren stock. This may suggest additional support for Ivan having a greater percentage interest than Iris has.

LO.4

Identify the basis issues relevant to the shareholder and the corporation.

12-2f **Basis Determination and Other Issues**

Recall that § 351(a) postpones gain or loss recognition until the taxpayer's investment changes substantively. By virtue of the basis rules described next, the postponed gain or loss is recognized when the stock is disposed of in a taxable transaction.

[24]*U.S. v. Hertwig*, 68–2 USTC ¶9495, 22 AFTR 2d 5249, 398 F.2d 452 (CA–5, 1968).

Basis of Stock to Shareholder

For a taxpayer transferring property to a corporation in a § 351 transaction, the basis of *stock* received in the transaction is the same as the basis the taxpayer had in the property transferred, increased by any gain recognized on the exchange of property and decreased by boot received. For basis purposes, boot received includes liabilities transferred by the shareholder to the corporation. Also note that if the shareholder receives *other property* (i.e., boot) along with the stock, that property takes a basis equal to its fair market value.[25] In Exhibit 12.1, the reference to gain recognized does not consider any income resulting from the performance of personal services. See the discussion that follows relating to an elective stock basis reduction that may be taken when a shareholder contributes property with a net built-in loss.

Basis of Property to Corporation

The basis of property received by the corporation generally is the basis of the exchanged property in the hands of the transferor increased by the amount of any gain recognized on the transfer by the transferor-shareholder.[26]

These basis rules are illustrated in Examples 28 and 29.

Calculating Basis: Shareholder Stock and Corporate Property

EXAMPLE
28

Maria and Ned form Brown Corporation. Maria transfers land (basis of $30,000 and fair market value of $70,000); Ned invests cash ($60,000). They each receive 50 shares in Brown Corporation, worth $1,200 per share, but Maria also receives $10,000 of cash from Brown. The transfers of property, the realized and recognized gain on the transfers, and the basis of the stock in Brown Corporation to Maria and Ned are as follows:

	A	B	C	D	E	F
	Basis of Property Transferred	FMV of Stock Received	Boot Received	Realized Gain (B + C − A)	Recognized Gain (Lesser of C or D)	Basis of Stock in Brown (A − C + E)
From Maria:						
Land	$30,000	$60,000	$10,000	$40,000	$10,000	$30,000
From Ned:						
Cash	60,000	60,000	–0–	–0–	–0–	60,000

Brown Corporation has a basis of $40,000 in the land (Maria's basis of $30,000 plus her recognized gain of $10,000).

EXHIBIT 12.1	Shareholder's Basis of Stock Received in Exchange for Property

Adjusted basis of property transferred	$xx,xxx
Plus: Gain recognized	xxx
Minus: Boot received (including any liabilities transferred)	(xxx)
Minus: Adjustment for loss property (if elected)	(xxx)
Equals: Basis of stock received	$xx,xxx

[25]§ 358(a). Recall from earlier discussions that the basis of stock received for services equals its fair market value.

[26]§ 362(a).

Calculating Basis: Shareholder Stock and Corporate Property

EXAMPLE
29

Assume the same facts as in Example 28, except that Maria's basis in the land is $68,000 (instead of $30,000). Because recognized gain cannot exceed realized gain, the transfer generates only $2,000 of gain to Maria. The realized and recognized gain and the basis of the stock in Brown Corporation to Maria are as follows:

	A	B	C	D	E	F
	Basis of Property Transferred	FMV of Stock Received	Boot Received	Realized Gain (B + C − A)	Recognized Gain (Lesser of C or D)	Basis of Stock in Brown (A − C + E)
Land	$68,000	$60,000	$10,000	$2,000	$2,000	$60,000

Brown's basis in the land is $70,000 ($68,000 basis to Maria + $2,000 gain recognized by Maria).

Exhibit 12.2 summarizes the basis calculation for property received by a corporation. Concept Summary 12.3 shows the shareholder and corporate consequences of a transfer of property to a corporation for stock, with and without the application of § 351. The facts applicable to shareholder Maria's transfer in Example 28 are used to illustrate the differences between the transaction being tax-deferred and taxable.

EXHIBIT 12.2	Corporation's Basis in Property Received
Adjusted basis of property transferred	$xx,xxx
Plus: Gain recognized by transferor-shareholder	xxx
Minus: Adjustment for loss property (if required)	(xxx)
Equals: Basis of property to corporation	$xx,xxx

Concept Summary 12.3

Tax Consequences to the Shareholders and Corporation: With and Without the Application of § 351 (Based on the Facts of Example 28)

	With § 351			Without § 351		
Shareholder	Gain/Loss Recognized	Stock Basis	Other Property Basis	Gain/Loss Recognized	Stock Basis	Other Property Basis
Maria	Realized gain recognized to extent of boot received; loss not recognized.	Substituted (see Exhibit 12.1).	FMV	All realized gain or loss recognized.	FMV	FMV
	$10,000	$30,000	$10,000	$40,000	$60,000	$10,000

	With § 351		Without § 351	
Corporation	Gain/Loss Recognized	Property Basis	Gain/Loss Recognized	Property Basis
Brown	No gain or loss recognized on the transfer of corporate stock for property.	Carryover (see Exhibit 12.2).	No gain or loss recognized on the transfer of corporate stock for property.	FMV
	$0	$40,000	$0	$70,000

Note that the benefit to Maria of deferring $30,000 of gain under § 351 comes with a cost: her stock basis is $30,000 (rather than $60,000), and the corporation's basis in the property received is $40,000 (rather than $70,000).

Basis Adjustment for Loss Property

A corporation's basis for property received in a § 351 transaction is carried over from the shareholder. As a result, the corporation's basis has no correlation to the property's fair market value. However, in certain situations when **built-in loss property** is contributed to a corporation, the aggregate basis of the assets transferred by a shareholder exceeds their fair market value. When this built-in loss situation exists, an anti-loss duplication rule requires the basis in the loss properties to be stepped down by allocating the built-in loss proportionately among the assets.[27] This basis adjustment is necessary to prevent the parties from obtaining a double benefit from the losses involved.

EXAMPLE 30

In a transaction qualifying under § 351, Charles transfers the following assets to Gold Corporation in exchange for all of its stock:

	Tax Basis	Fair Market Value	Built-In Gain/(Loss)
Equipment	$100,000	$ 90,000	($10,000)
Land	200,000	230,000	30,000
Building	150,000	100,000	(50,000)
	$450,000	$420,000	($30,000)

Charles's stock basis is $450,000 [$450,000 (basis of the property transferred) + $0 (gain recognized) − $0 (boot received)]. However, Gold's basis for the loss assets transferred must be reduced by the amount of the net built-in loss ($30,000) in proportion to each asset's share of the loss.

	Unadjusted Tax Basis	Adjustment	Adjusted Tax Basis
Equipment	$100,000	($ 5,000)*	$ 95,000
Land	200,000		200,000
Building	150,000	(25,000)**	125,000
	$450,000	($30,000)	$420,000

* $\frac{\$10,000 \text{ (loss attributable to equipment)}}{\$60,000 \text{ (total built-in loss)}} \times \$30,000 \text{ (net built-in loss)} = \$5,000 \text{ (adjustment to basis in equipment)}.$

** $\frac{\$50,000 \text{ (loss attributable to building)}}{\$60,000 \text{ (total built-in loss)}} \times \$30,000 \text{ (net built-in loss)} = \$25,000 \text{ (adjustment to basis in building)}.$

Note the end result of Example 30:

- Charles still has a built-in loss in his stock basis. Thus, if he sells the Gold Corporation stock, he will recognize a loss of $30,000 [$420,000 (selling price based on presumed value of the stock) − $450,000 (basis in the stock)].

- Gold Corporation can no longer recognize any loss on the sale of *all* of its assets [$420,000 (selling price based on value of assets) − $420,000 (adjusted basis in assets) = $0 (gain or loss)].

In the event a corporation is subject to the built-in loss adjustment, an alternative approach is available. If both the shareholder and the corporation elect, the basis reduction can be made to the shareholder's stock rather than to the corporation's property.

---

[27]§ 362(e)(2). This adjustment is determined separately with respect to each property transferor. This adjustment also is required in the case of a contribution to capital by a shareholder.

EXAMPLE 31

Assume the same facts as in the previous example. If Charles and Gold elect, Charles can reduce his stock basis to $420,000 ($450,000 − $30,000). As a result, Gold's aggregate basis in the assets it receives is $450,000. If Charles has no intention of selling his stock, this election could be desirable as it benefits Gold by giving the corporation a higher depreciable basis in the equipment and building.

Note the end result of Example 31:

- Charles has no built-in loss. Thus, if he sells the Gold Corporation stock, he will recognize no gain or loss [$420,000 (presumed value of the stock) − $420,000 (basis in the stock)].
- Gold Corporation has a built-in loss. Thus, if it sells *all* of its assets [$420,000 (selling price based on value of assets) − $450,000 (basis in assets)], it recognizes a loss of $30,000.

Consequently, as shown in the two previous examples, the built-in loss adjustment places the loss with either the shareholder or the corporation but not both.

Stock Issued for Services Rendered

A corporation's transfer of its stock for property is not a taxable exchange.[28] A transfer of shares for services is also not a taxable transaction to a corporation.[29] Can a corporation deduct as a business expense the fair market value of the stock it issues in consideration of services? Yes, unless the services are such that the payment is characterized as a capital expenditure.[30]

The Big Picture

EXAMPLE 32

Return to the facts of *The Big Picture* on p. 12-1. Amber transfers her $1,000,000 of property to Garden, Inc., and receives 50% of the stock. In addition, assume that Jimmy transfers property worth $800,000 (basis of $260,000) and agrees to serve as manager of the corporation for one year (services worth $200,000) for 50% of the stock.

Amber's and Jimmy's transfers qualify under § 351. Neither Amber nor Jimmy is taxed on the transfer of his or her property. However, Jimmy has income of $200,000, the value of the services he will render to Garden, Inc. Garden has a basis of $260,000 in the property it acquired from Jimmy, and it may claim a compensation expense deduction under § 162 for $200,000. Jimmy's stock basis is $460,000 [$260,000 (basis of property transferred) + $200,000 (income recognized for services rendered)].

The Big Picture

EXAMPLE 33

Assume in the preceding example that Jimmy receives the Garden stock as consideration for the appreciated property and for providing legal services in organizing the corporation. The value of Jimmy's legal services is $200,000.

Jimmy has no gain on the transfer of the property but has income of $200,000 for the value of the services rendered. Garden, Inc., has a basis of $260,000 in the property it acquired from Jimmy and must capitalize the $200,000 as an organizational expenditure. Jimmy's stock basis is $460,000 [$260,000 (basis of property transferred) + $200,000 (income recognized for services rendered)].

Holding Period for Shareholder and Transferee Corporation

The shareholder's holding period for stock received for a capital asset or for § 1231 property includes the holding period of the property transferred to the corporation. The holding period of the property is *tacked on* to the holding period of the stock. The holding period for stock received for any other property (e.g., inventory) begins on the day after the exchange. The transferee corporation's holding period for property acquired in a § 351 transfer is the holding period of the transferor-shareholder regardless of the character of the property to the transferor. For instance, whether the

---

[28]§ 1032.

[29]Reg. § 1.1032–1(a).

[30]Rev.Rul. 62–217, 1962–2 C.B. 59, modified by Rev.Rul. 74–503, 1974–2 C.B. 117.

property transferred is an ordinary asset (e.g., inventory), a § 1231 asset, or a capital asset, the corporation's holding period is the same as the transferor's.[31]

12-2g Recapture Considerations

In a § 351 nontaxable transfer (no boot involved) to a controlled corporation, the depreciation recapture rules do not apply.[32] Instead, any recapture potential of the property carries over to the corporation as it steps into the shoes of the transferor-shareholder for purposes of basis determination. However, to the extent gain is recognized, the recapture rules are applied.

EXAMPLE

34

Paul transfers equipment (adjusted basis of $30,000, original cost of $120,000, and fair market value of $100,000) to a controlled corporation in return for stock. If Paul had sold the equipment, it would have yielded a gain of $70,000, all of which would have been recaptured as ordinary income under § 1245.

If the transfer comes within § 351, Paul has no recognized gain and no depreciation to recapture. If the corporation later disposes of the equipment in a taxable transaction, it must take into account the § 1245 recapture potential originating with Paul. So, for example, if the corporation were to sell the asset shortly after incorporation for $100,000, all of the $70,000 gain recognized would be given ordinary treatment because of the depreciation recapture rules.

Alternatively, if Paul had received boot of $60,000 on the transfer, all of the recognized gain would have been recaptured as ordinary income. The remaining $30,000 ($90,000 − $60,000) of recapture potential would have carried over to the corporation.

TAX PLANNING STRATEGIES **Other Considerations When Incorporating a Business**

FRAMEWORK FOCUS: TAX RATE

Strategy: Control the Character of Income and Deductions.
    Shift Net Income from High-Bracket Taxpayers to Low-Bracket Taxpayers.

FRAMEWORK FOCUS: DEDUCTIONS

Strategy: Maximize Deductible Amounts.

FRAMEWORK FOCUS: INCOME AND EXCLUSIONS

Strategy: Avoid Income Recognition.

When a business is incorporated, the organizers must determine which assets and liabilities should be transferred to the corporation. A transfer of assets that produce passive income (rents, royalties, dividends, and interest) can cause the corporation to be a personal holding company in a tax year when operating income is low. Thus, the corporation could be subject to the personal holding company penalty tax (see the discussion in Chapter 13).

A transfer of the accounts payable of a cash basis taxpayer may prevent the organizer from taking a tax deduction if the accounts are paid by the corporation. Therefore, the parties should decide who will receive the greatest benefit from the deduction and then plan accordingly.

Leasing property to the corporation may be a more attractive alternative than transferring ownership. Leasing provides the taxpayer with the opportunity of withdrawing money from the corporation in a deductible form without the payment being characterized as a nondeductible dividend. If the property is donated to a family member in a lower tax bracket, the lease income can be shifted as well. If the depreciation and other deductions available in connection with the property are larger than the lease income, a high-tax-rate taxpayer could retain the property until the income exceeds the deductions.

continued

---

[31]§§ 1223(1) and (2).   [32]§§ 1245(b)(3) and 1250(d)(3).

The Big Picture

EXAMPLE 35

Return to the facts of *The Big Picture* on p. 12-1. If Amber decides to retain the $50,000 of cash basis accounts receivable rather than transfer them to the newly formed Garden, Inc., she will recognize $50,000 of ordinary income upon their collection.

Alternatively, if the receivables are transferred to Garden as the facts suggest, the corporation will recognize the ordinary income. However, a subsequent corporate distribution to Amber of the cash collected could be subject to double taxation as a dividend (see Chapter 13 for further discussion). Given the alternatives available, Amber needs to evaluate which approach is better for the parties involved.

Another way to shift income to other taxpayers is by the use of corporate debt. Shareholder debt in a corporation can be given to family members with low marginal tax rates. This technique also shifts income without a loss of control of the corporation.

LO.5

Explain the tax aspects of the capital structure of a corporation.

12-3 CAPITAL STRUCTURE OF A CORPORATION

When forming or expanding a corporation, the transaction can be financed with capital contributions or debt proceeds or a combination of the two. Evaluating the relative advantages and disadvantages of these two basic elements in the capital structure of a corporation can involve various considerations, including the tax aspects of each.

12-3a Capital Contributions

When money or property is received in exchange for capital stock (including treasury stock), the corporation does not recognize any gain or loss.[33] Also, it does not include in gross income any shareholders' contributions of money or property to the capital of the corporation or through voluntary pro rata transfers. This is the case even though there is no increase in the number of outstanding shares of stock of the corporation. The payments represent an additional price paid for the shares held by the shareholders (increasing their basis) and are treated as additions to the operating capital of the corporation.[34]

Contributions by nonshareholders, such as land contributed to a corporation by a civic group or a governmental group to induce the corporation to locate in a particular community, are also excluded from the gross income of a corporation.[35] However, property that is transferred to a corporation by a nonshareholder in exchange for goods or services rendered is taxable income to the corporation.[36]

EXAMPLE 36

A cable company charges its customers an initial fee to hook up to a new cable system installed in the area. These payments are used to finance the total cost of constructing the cable company's infrastructure. The customers will make monthly payments for the cable service. The initial payments are used for capital expenditures, but they represent payments for services to be rendered by the cable company. As such, they are taxable income and not contributions to capital by nonshareholders.

The basis of property received by a corporation from a shareholder as a capital contribution is equal to the basis of the property in the hands of the shareholder, although the basis may be subject to a downward adjustment when loss property is

---

[33]§ 1032.

[34]§ 118 and Reg. § 1.118–1.

[35]See *Edwards v. Cuba Railroad Co.*, 1 USTC ¶139, 5 AFTR 5398, 45 S.Ct. 614 (USSC, 1925).

[36]Reg. § 1.118–1. See also *Teleservice Co. of Wyoming Valley*, 27 T.C. 722 (1957), *aff'd* in 58–1 USTC ¶9383, 1 AFTR 2d 1249, 254 F.2d 105 (CA–3, 1958), *cert. den.* 78 S.Ct. 1360 (USSC, 1958).

contributed. The basis of property transferred to a corporation by a nonshareholder as a contribution to capital is zero.

If a corporation receives *money* as a contribution to capital from a nonshareholder, a special rule applies. The basis of any property acquired with the money during a 12-month period beginning on the day the contribution was received is reduced by the amount of the cash contribution. The excess of money received over the cost of new property is used to reduce the basis of other property held by the corporation and is applied in the following order:

1. Depreciable property.
2. Property subject to amortization.
3. Property subject to depletion.
4. All other remaining properties.

The basis of property within each category is reduced in proportion to the relative bases of the properties.[37]

> **EXAMPLE**
>
> **37**
>
> A city donates land worth $400,000 to Cardinal Corporation as an inducement for Cardinal to locate in the city. The receipt of the land produces no taxable income to Cardinal, and the land's basis to the corporation is zero. If, in addition, the city gives the corporation $100,000 in cash, the money is not taxable income to the corporation. However, if the corporation purchases property with the $100,000 in cash within the next 12 months, the basis of the property is reduced by $100,000. Any excess cash that is retained and not used by Cardinal is handled according to the ordering rules noted previously. So, for example, if Cardinal purchases only $70,000 of property during the following year, the basis of Cardinal's other depreciable property is reduced by $30,000.

12-3b Debt in the Capital Structure

LO.6

Characterize the tax differences between debt and equity investments.

Various tax and nontax considerations are relevant when developing the capital structure of a corporation. The relative amounts of debt and equity and their characteristics are of primary importance.

Advantages of Debt

Significant tax differences exist between debt and equity in the capital structure, and shareholders must be aware of these differences. The advantages of issuing long-term

---

[37]§ 362(c); Reg. §§ 1.362–2(b) and 1.118–1.

debt are numerous. Interest on debt is deductible by the corporation, while dividend payments are not. Further, the shareholders are not taxed on debt repayments unless the repayments exceed basis. An investment in stock usually cannot be withdrawn tax-free as long as a corporation has earnings and profits. Withdrawals will be deemed to be taxable dividends to the extent of earnings and profits of the distributing corporation. (The concept of earnings and profits is discussed in Chapter 13.)

Another distinction between debt and equity relates to the taxation of dividend and interest income. Dividend income on equity holdings is taxed to individual investors at the low capital gains rates, while interest income on debt is taxed at the higher ordinary income rates.

EXAMPLE 38

Wade transfers cash of $100,000 to a newly formed corporation for 100% of the stock. In the first year of operations, the corporation has net income of $40,000. If the corporation distributes $9,500 to Wade, the distribution is a taxable dividend with no corresponding deduction to the corporation. Assume, instead, that Wade transfers to the corporation cash of $50,000 for stock. In addition, he lends the corporation $50,000. The note is payable in equal annual installments of $5,000 and bears interest at the rate of 9%. At the end of the year, the corporation pays Wade interest of $4,500 ($50,000 × 9%) and a note repayment of $5,000. The interest payment is taxable to Wade and a deductible expense to the corporation. The $5,000 principal repayment on the loan is neither taxed to Wade nor deductible by the corporation. Based on the tax rates as noted, the after-tax impact to Wade and the corporation under each alternative is illustrated below.

	If the Distribution Is	
	$9,500 Dividend	**$5,000 Note Repayment and $4,500 Interest**
After-tax benefit to Wade*		
[$9,500 × (1 − 15%)]	$8,075	
{$5,000 + [$4,500 × (1 − 35%)]}		$7,925
After-tax cost to corporation**		
No deduction to corporation	$9,500	
{$5,000 + [$4,500 × (1 − 35%)]}		$7,925

  *Assumes that Wade's dividend income is taxed at the 15% capital gains rate and that his interest income is taxed at the 35% ordinary income rate.
  **Assumes that the corporation is in the 35% marginal tax bracket.

Reclassification of Debt as Equity (Thin Capitalization Problem)

In situations where the corporation is said to be thinly capitalized, the IRS contends that debt is an equity interest and denies the corporation the tax advantages of debt financing. **Thin capitalization** occurs when shareholder debt is high relative to shareholder equity. If a debt instrument has too many features of stock, it may be treated as a form of stock by the IRS. As a result, the principal and interest payments are considered dividends. Under § 385, the IRS has the authority to characterize corporate debt wholly as equity or as part debt and part equity. In the current environment, however, the IRS may be less inclined to raise the thin capitalization issue because the conversion of interest income to dividend income would produce a tax benefit to individual investors.

For the most part, the principles used to classify debt as equity developed in connection with closely held corporations where the holders of the debt are often shareholders. The rules have often proved inadequate for dealing with large, publicly traded corporations.

Section 385 lists several factors that *may* be used to determine whether a debtor-creditor relationship or a shareholder-corporation relationship exists. The thrust of § 385 is to authorize the Treasury to prescribe Regulations that provide more definite guidelines for determining when debt should be reclassified as equity. To date, the Treasury Department has not drafted final Regulations. Consequently, taxpayers must rely on judicial decisions to determine whether a true debtor-creditor relationship exists.

TAX IN THE NEWS **A Careful Evaluation May Be Required to Distinguish Debt from Equity**

While the tax advantages of debt over equity may be clear (i.e., interest payments on debt are deductible but dividend payments on capital contributions are not), being able to distinguish debt from equity may not be as obvious. In arm's-length, market-based transactions between unrelated parties, the debt versus equity question most likely would never arise. However, the difficulty of distinguishing debt and equity is particularly acute in situations where the parties involved are closely connected or related. To assist taxpayers in distinguishing debt financing and equity financing, the courts have developed a number of factors (noted below) to be considered in such an analysis.

In *NA General Partnership & Subsidiaries* (103 TCM 1916; T.C.Memo. 2012–172), the Tax Court evaluated the nature of

advances made by a parent entity to NA General Partnership & Subsidiaries (treated as a corporation for Federal tax purposes) in light of the court-developed factors. The court noted that the substance of a transaction is controlling, and not merely its form, and that none of the factors is decisive but they should be considered in light of the facts and circumstances of the case.

Based on an exhaustive evaluation of 11 factors in the taxpayer's situation, the court concluded that the advances were debt. Happily for the taxpayer, the court's decision paved the way for $932 million of payments to be treated as deductible interest rather than nondeductible dividend payments.

The courts have identified the following factors to be considered when classifying a security as debt or equity:

- Whether the debt instrument is in proper form. An open account advance is more easily characterized as a contribution to capital than a loan evidenced by a properly written note executed by the shareholder.[38]

- Whether the debt instrument bears a reasonable rate of interest and has a definite maturity date. When a shareholder advance does not provide for interest, the return expected is that inherent in an equity interest (e.g., a share of the profits or an increase in the value of the shares).[39] Likewise, a lender unrelated to the corporation will usually be unwilling to commit funds to the corporation for an indefinite period of time (i.e., no definite due date).

- Whether the debt is paid on a timely basis. A lender's failure to insist upon timely repayment (or satisfactory renegotiation) indicates that the return sought does not depend upon interest income and the repayment of principal.

- Whether payment is contingent upon earnings. A lender ordinarily will not advance funds that are likely to be repaid only if the venture is successful.

- Whether the debt is subordinated to other liabilities. Subordination tends to eliminate a significant characteristic of the creditor-debtor relationship. Creditors should have the right to share with other general creditors in the event of the corporation's dissolution or liquidation. Subordination also destroys another basic attribute of creditor status—the power to demand payment at a fixed maturity date.[40]

- Whether holdings of debt and stock are proportionate (e.g., each shareholder owns the same percentages of debt and stock). When debt and equity obligations are held in the same proportion, shareholders are, apart from tax considerations, indifferent as to whether corporate distributions are in the form of interest or dividends.

- Whether funds loaned to the corporation are used to finance initial operations or capital asset acquisitions. Funds used to finance initial operations or to acquire

---

[38]*Estate of Mixon, Jr. v. U.S.*, 72–2 USTC ¶9537, 30 AFTR 2d 72–5094, 464 F.2d 394 (CA–5, 1972).

[39]*Slappey Drive Industrial Park v. U.S.*, 77–2 USTC ¶9696, 40 AFTR 2d 77–5940, 561 F.2d 572 (CA–5, 1977).

[40]*Fin Hay Realty Co. v. U.S.*, 68–2 USTC ¶9438, 22 AFTR 2d 5004, 398 F.2d 694 (CA–3, 1968).

capital assets the corporation needs to operate are generally obtained through equity investments.

- Whether the corporation has a high ratio of shareholder debt to shareholder equity. Thin capitalization indicates that the corporation lacks reserves to pay interest and principal on debt when corporate income is insufficient to meet current needs.[41] In determining a corporation's debt-equity ratio, courts look at the relation of the debt both to the book value of the corporation's assets and to their actual fair market value.[42]

Section 385 also authorizes the Treasury to issue Regulations classifying an instrument as *wholly* debt or equity or as *part* debt and *part* equity. This flexible approach is important because some instruments cannot readily be classified either wholly as stock or wholly as debt. It may also provide an avenue for the IRS to address problems in publicly traded corporations.

LO.7

List and apply the tax rules unique to corporations.

12-4 CORPORATE OPERATIONS

The rules related to gross income, deductions, and losses discussed in previous chapters of this text generally apply to corporations. In a few instances, it was noted that corporations face unique limitations such as the 10 percent of taxable income limitation for charitable contributions and the limitation allowing corporate capital losses to be deductible only against capital gains. Corporations also are permitted some deductions not generally available to other entities. These special deductions and other special rules regarding the determination of the corporate income tax liability are discussed in the following pages.

12-4a Deductions Available Only to Corporations

Certain deductions are specific to corporate taxpayers. These provisions include the dividends received deduction and the organizational expenditures deduction.

Dividends Received Deduction

The purpose of the **dividends received deduction** is to mitigate multiple taxation of corporate income. Without the deduction, dividends paid between corporations could be subject to several levels of tax. For example, if Corporation A pays Corporation B a dividend and B passes the dividend on to its shareholders, the dividend is taxed at three levels: Corporation A, Corporation B, and Corporation B's shareholders. The dividends received deduction alleviates this inequity by limiting or eliminating the amount of dividend income taxable to corporations.

As the following table illustrates, the amount of the dividends received deduction depends on the percentage of ownership (voting power and value) the recipient corporate shareholder holds in a *domestic corporation* making the dividend distribution.[43]

Percentage of Ownership by Corporate Shareholder	Deduction Percentage
Less than 20%	70%
20% or more (but less than 80%)	80%
80% or more*	100%

*The payor corporation must be a member of an affiliated group with the recipient corporation.

---

[41]A court held that a debt-equity ratio of approximately 14.6:1 was not excessive. See *Tomlinson v. 1661 Corp.*, 67–1 USTC ¶9438, 19 AFTR 2d 1413, 377 F.2d 291 (CA–5, 1967). A 26:1 ratio was found acceptable in *Delta Plastics, Inc.*, 85 TCM 940, T.C.Memo. 2003–54.

[42]In *Bauer v. Comm.*, 84–2 USTC ¶9996, 55 AFTR 2d 85–433, 748 F.2d 1365 (CA–9, 1984), a debt-equity ratio of 92:1 resulted when book value was

used. But the ratio ranged from 2:1 to 8:1 when equity included both paid-in capital and accumulated earnings.

[43]§ 243(a). Dividends from foreign corporations generally do not qualify for a dividends received deduction. But see § 245.

The dividends received deduction cannot exceed the taxable income limitation. This limitation is equal to the corporation's taxable income multiplied by the percentage that corresponds with the deduction percentage. Thus, if a corporate shareholder owns less than 20 percent of the stock in the distributing corporation, the dividends received deduction is limited to 70 percent of taxable income. For this purpose, taxable income is computed without regard to the net operating loss (NOL) deduction, the domestic production activities deduction, the dividends received deduction, and any capital loss carryback. However, the taxable income limitation does not apply if the corporation has an NOL for the current taxable year.[44]

The following steps are useful in the computation of the deduction:

1. Multiply the dividends received by the deduction percentage.
2. Multiply the taxable income by the deduction percentage.
3. The deduction is limited to the lesser of step 1 or step 2, unless deducting the amount derived in step 1 results in an NOL. If it does, the amount derived in step 1 is used. This is referred to as the *NOL rule*.

EXAMPLE 39

Red, White, and Blue Corporations, three unrelated calendar year corporations, report the following information for the year:

	Red Corporation	White Corporation	Blue Corporation
Gross income from operations	$ 400,000	$ 320,000	$ 260,000
Expenses from operations	(340,000)	(340,000)	(340,000)
Dividends received from domestic corporations (less than 20% ownership)	200,000	200,000	200,000
Taxable income before the dividends received deduction	$ 260,000	$ 180,000	$ 120,000

In determining the dividends received deduction, use the three-step procedure described above.

	Red Corporation	White Corporation	Blue Corporation
Step 1 (70% × $200,000)	$140,000	$140,000	$140,000
Step 2			
70% × $260,000 (taxable income)	$182,000		
70% × $180,000 (taxable income)		$126,000	
70% × $120,000 (taxable income)			$ 84,000
Step 3			
Lesser of step 1 or step 2	$140,000	$126,000	
Step 1 amount results in an NOL			$140,000

White Corporation is subject to the 70% of taxable income limitation (step 2). The NOL rule does not apply because subtracting $140,000 (step 1) from $180,000 (taxable income before the dividends received deduction) does not yield a negative figure. Blue Corporation qualifies under the NOL rule because subtracting $140,000 (step 1) from $120,000 (taxable income before the dividends received deduction) yields a negative figure.

In summary, each corporation has a dividends received deduction for the year as follows: $140,000 for Red Corporation, $126,000 for White Corporation, and $140,000 for Blue Corporation.

No dividends received deduction is allowed unless the corporation has held the stock for more than 45 days.[45] This restriction was enacted to close a tax loophole

---

[44]Further, the limitation does not apply in the case of the 100% deduction available to members of an affiliated group. § 246(b)(2).

[45]The stock must be held more than 45 days during the 91-day period beginning on the date that is 45 days before the ex-dividend date (or in the case of preferred stock, more than 90 days during the 181-day period beginning on the date that is 90 days before the ex-dividend date). § 246(c).

involving dividends on stock that is held only briefly. When stock is purchased shortly before a dividend record date and soon thereafter sold ex-dividend, a capital loss corresponding to the amount of the dividend often results (ignoring other market valuation changes). If the dividends received deduction was allowed in such cases, the capital loss resulting from the stock sale would exceed the taxable portion of the related dividend income.

EXAMPLE 40

On October 1, 2015, Pink Corporation declares a $1 per share dividend for shareholders of record as of November 1, 2015, and payable on December 1, 2015. Black Corporation purchases 10,000 shares of Pink stock on October 29, 2015, for $25,000 and sells those 10,000 shares ex-dividend on November 5, 2015, for $15,000. (It is assumed that there is no fluctuation in the market price of the Pink stock other than the dividend element.) The sale results in a short-term capital loss of $10,000 ($15,000 amount realized − $25,000 basis). On December 1, Black receives a $10,000 dividend from Pink. Without the holding period restriction, Black Corporation would recognize a $10,000 deduction (subject to the capital loss limitation) but only $3,000 of income [$10,000 dividend − $7,000 dividends received deduction ($10,000 × 70%)], or a $7,000 net loss. However, because Black did not hold the Pink stock for more than 45 days, no dividends received deduction is allowed.

DIGGING DEEPER 2   In-depth coverage can be found on this book's companion website: www.cengagebrain.com

Organizational Expenditures Deduction

Expenses incurred in connection with the organization of a corporation normally are chargeable to a capital account. That they benefit the corporation during its existence seems clear. But over what period should organizational expenses be amortized? The lack of a determinable and limited estimated useful life makes such a determination difficult. Section 248 was enacted to solve this problem.

Under § 248, a corporation may *elect* to amortize **organizational expenditures** over the 180-month period beginning with the month in which the corporation begins business.[46] Organizational expenditures include:

- Legal services incident to organization (e.g., drafting the corporate charter and bylaws, minutes of organizational meetings, and terms of original stock certificates).
- Necessary accounting services.
- Expenses of temporary directors and of organizational meetings of directors or shareholders.
- Fees paid to the state of incorporation.

Expenditures that *do not qualify* as organizational expenditures include those connected with issuing or selling shares of stock or other securities (e.g., commissions, professional fees, and printing costs) or with transferring assets to a corporation. These expenditures reduce the amount of capital raised and are not deductible.

The first $5,000 of organizational costs is immediately expensed, with any remaining amount of organizational costs amortized over a 180-month period. However, the $5,000 expensing amount is phased out on a dollar-for-dollar basis when these costs exceed $50,000. For example, a corporation with $52,000 of organizational costs would expense $3,000 [$5,000 − ($52,000 − $50,000)] of this amount and amortize the $49,000 balance ($52,000 − $3,000) over 180 months.

To qualify for the election, the expenditure must be *incurred* before the end of the tax year in which the corporation begins business. In this regard, the corporation's method of accounting is of no consequence. Thus, an expense incurred by a cash basis corporation in its first tax year qualifies even though the expense is not paid until a subsequent year.

---

[46]The month in which a corporation begins business may not be immediately apparent. Ordinarily, a corporation begins business when it starts the business operations for which it was organized. Reg. § 1.248–1(d). For a similar problem in the Subchapter S area, see Chapter 15.

A corporation is deemed to have made the election to amortize organizational expenditures for the taxable year in which it begins business. No separate statement or specific identification of the deducted amount as organizational expenditures is required. A corporation can elect to forgo the deemed election by clearly electing to capitalize organizational expenditures on a timely filed return for its first taxable year. In that case, the capitalized amount will be deductible by the corporation at such time as it ceases to do business and liquidates.

EXAMPLE 41

Black Corporation, an accrual basis, calendar year taxpayer, was formed and began operations on April 1, 2015. The following expenses were incurred during its first year of operations (April 1– December 31, 2015):

Expenses of temporary directors and of organizational meetings	$15,500
Fee paid to the state of incorporation	2,000
Accounting services incident to organization	18,000
Legal services for drafting the corporate charter and bylaws	32,000
Expenses incident to the printing and sale of stock certificates	48,000

Black Corporation elects to amortize the $67,500 of organizational costs under § 248. Because of the dollar cap (i.e., dollar-for-dollar reduction for amounts in excess of $50,000), none of the $5,000 expensing allowance is available. The monthly amortization is $375 [($15,500 + $2,000 + $18,000 + $32,000) ÷ 180 months], and $3,375 ($375 × 9 months) is deductible for tax year 2015.

Note that the $48,000 of expenses incident to the printing and sale of stock certificates does not qualify for the election. These expenses cannot be deducted. Instead, they reduce the amount of the capital realized from the sale of stock.

Organizational expenditures are distinguished from *startup expenditures*.[47] Startup expenditures include various investigation expenses involved in entering a new business (e.g., travel, market surveys, financial audits, and legal fees) and operating expenses such as rent and payroll that are incurred by a corporation before it actually begins to produce any gross income. At the election of the taxpayer, such expenditures are deductible in the same manner as organizational expenditures. Thus, up to $5,000 can be immediately expensed (subject to the phaseout) and any remaining amounts amortized over a period of 180 months. The same rules that apply to the deemed election (and election to forgo the deemed election) for organizational expenditures also apply to startup expenditures.

TAX PLANNING STRATEGIES **Organizational Expenditures**

FRAMEWORK FOCUS: DEDUCTIONS

Strategy: Maximize Deductible Amounts.

To qualify for the 180-month amortization procedure of § 248, only organizational expenditures incurred in the first taxable year of the corporation can be considered. This rule could prove to be an unfortunate trap for corporations formed late in the year.

EXAMPLE 42

Thrush Corporation is formed in December 2015. Qualified organizational expenditures are incurred as follows: $62,000 in December 2015 and $30,000 in January 2016. If Thrush uses the calendar year for tax purposes, only $62,000 of the organizational expenditures qualify for amortization.

One solution to the problem posed by this example may be for Thrush Corporation to adopt a fiscal year that ends on or beyond January 31. All organizational expenditures will then have been incurred before the close of the first tax year. Alternatively, the corporation could wait to be formed until January 2016.

---

[47]§ 195.

LO.8

Compute the corporate income tax.

12-4b Determining the Corporate Income Tax Liability

Corporate income tax rates have fluctuated over the years, with the current rate structure reflecting a significant reduction that occured in 1986. For example, the top statutory corporate income tax rate was reduced from 46 percent to 35 percent. Refer to the inside front cover of the text for a schedule of current corporate income tax rates. Unlike the individual income tax rate brackets, the corporate income tax brackets are *not* indexed for inflation.

The Big Picture

EXAMPLE 43

Return to the facts of *The Big Picture* on p. 12-1. Assume that Amber incorporates her business as a calendar year C corporation and that for 2015, the corporation has taxable income of $51,500. Its income tax liability is $7,875, determined as follows:

Tax on $50,000 at 15%	$7,500
Tax on $1,500 at 25%	375
Tax liability	$7,875

For taxable income in excess of $100,000, the amount of the tax is increased by the lesser of (1) 5 percent of the excess or (2) $11,750. In effect, the additional tax means a 39 percent rate for every dollar of taxable income from $100,000 to $335,000.

EXAMPLE 44

Silver Corporation, a calendar year taxpayer, has taxable income of $335,000 for the current year. Its income tax liability is $113,900, determined as follows:

Tax on $100,000	$ 22,250
Tax on $235,000 × 39%	91,650
Tax liability	$113,900

Note that the tax liability of $113,900 is 34% of $335,000. Thus, due to the 39% rate (34% normal rate + 5% additional tax on taxable income between $100,000 and $335,000), the benefit of the lower rates on the first $75,000 of taxable income completely phases out at $335,000. The tax rate drops back to 34% on taxable income between $335,000 and $10 million.

Section 11(b)(2) provides that qualified **personal service corporations (PSCs)** are taxed at a flat 35 percent rate on all taxable income. Thus, PSCs do not enjoy the tax savings of the 15 percent to 34 percent brackets applicable to other corporations. For this purpose, a PSC is a corporation that is substantially employee-owned. Also, it must engage in one of the following activities: health, law, engineering, architecture, accounting, actuarial science, performing arts, or consulting.

LO.9

Explain the rules unique to computing the tax of related corporations.

12-4c Tax Liability of Related Corporations

Members of a controlled group of corporations (**related corporations**) are subject to special rules for computing the income tax, the AMT exemption, and the § 179 election to expense certain depreciable assets.[48] If these restrictions did not exist, the shareholders of a corporation could gain significant tax advantages by splitting a single corporation into *multiple* corporations. The next two examples illustrate the potential *income tax* advantage of multiple corporations.

---

[48]§§ 1561(a) and 179(d)(6).

Tax Savings from Multiple Corporations

Gray Corporation annually yields taxable income of $300,000. The corporate tax on $300,000 is $100,250, computed as follows:

Tax on $100,000	$ 22,250
Tax on $200,000 × 39%	78,000
Tax liability	$100,250

Assume that Gray Corporation in the previous example is divided equally into four corporations. Each corporation would have taxable income of $75,000, and the tax for each (absent the special provisions for related corporations) would be computed as follows:

Tax on $50,000	$ 7,500
Tax on $25,000 × 25%	6,250
Tax liability	$13,750

The total liability for the four corporations would be $55,000 ($13,750 × 4). Consequently, the savings would be $45,250 ($100,250 − $55,000).

To preclude the advantages that could be gained by using multiple corporations, the tax law requires special treatment for *controlled groups* of corporations. A comparison of Examples 45 and 46 reveals that the income tax savings that could be achieved by using multiple corporations result from having more of the total taxable income taxed at lower marginal rates. To close this potential loophole, the law limits a controlled group's taxable income in the tax brackets below 35 percent to the amount the corporations in the group would have if they were one corporation. Thus, in Example 46, under the controlled corporation rules, only $12,500 (one-fourth of the first $50,000 of taxable income) for each of the four related corporations would be taxed at the 15 percent rate. The 25 percent rate would apply to the next $6,250 (one-fourth of the next $25,000) of taxable income of each corporation. This equal allocation of the $50,000 and $25,000 amounts is required unless all members of the controlled group consent to an apportionment plan providing for an unequal allocation.

Similar limitations apply to controlled groups with respect to the § 179 expense election (see Chapter 5) and to the $40,000 AMT exemption amount (see Chapter 17).

12-4d Controlled Groups

A controlled group of corporations includes parent-subsidiary groups, brother-sister groups, combined groups, and certain insurance companies. Parent-subsidiary controlled groups are discussed in the following section.

Parent-Subsidiary Controlled Group

A parent-subsidiary controlled group consists of one or more *chains* of corporations connected through stock ownership with a common parent corporation. The ownership connection can be established through either a *voting power test* or a *value test*. The voting power test requires ownership of stock possessing at least 80 percent of the total voting power of all classes of stock entitled to vote. The value test requires ownership of at least 80 percent of the total value of all shares of all classes of stock of each of the corporations, except the parent corporation, by one or more of the other corporations.[49]

---

[49]§ 1563(a)(1).

Aqua Corporation owns 80% of White Corporation. Aqua and White Corporations are members of a parent-subsidiary controlled group. Aqua is the parent corporation, and White is the subsidiary.

The parent-subsidiary relationship described in Example 47 is easy to recognize because Aqua Corporation is the direct owner of White Corporation. Real-world business organizations are often more complex, sometimes including numerous corporations with chains of ownership connecting them. In these complex corporate structures, determining whether the controlled group classification is appropriate becomes more difficult. The ownership requirements can be met through direct ownership (refer to Example 47) or through indirect ownership, as illustrated in the following example.

Red Corporation owns 80% of the voting stock of White Corporation, and White Corporation owns 80% of the voting stock of Blue Corporation.

Red, White, and Blue Corporations constitute a controlled group in which Red is the common parent and White and Blue are subsidiaries. This parent-subsidiary relationship is diagrammed in Exhibit 12.3. The same result would occur if Red Corporation, rather than White Corporation, owned the Blue Corporation stock.

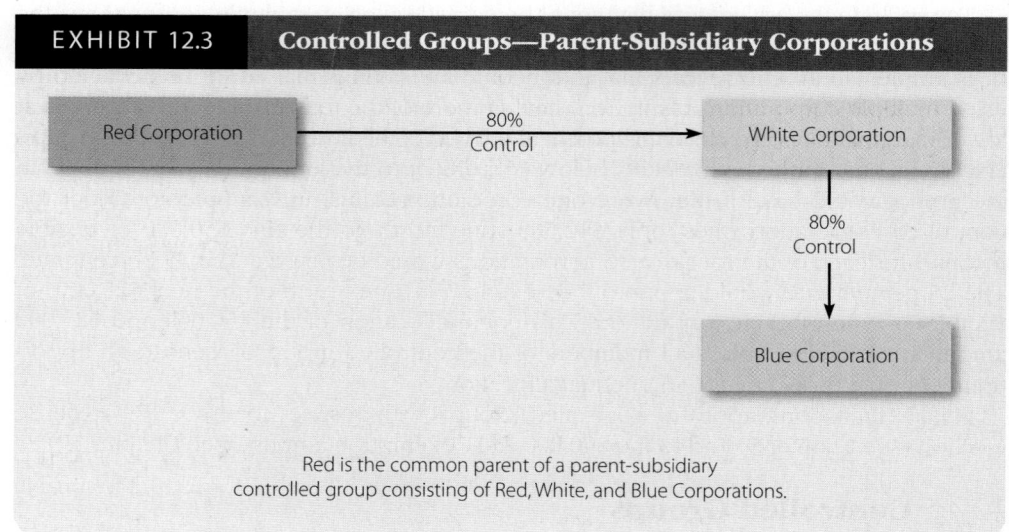

EXHIBIT 12.3 **Controlled Groups—Parent-Subsidiary Corporations**

Red is the common parent of a parent-subsidiary controlled group consisting of Red, White, and Blue Corporations.

DIGGING DEEPER 3 In-depth coverage can be found on this book's companion website: www.cengagebrain.com

Application of § 482

Congress has recognized that a parent corporation has the power to shift income among its subsidiaries. Likewise, shareholders who control other related groups of corporations can shift income and deductions among the related corporations.

When the true taxable income of a subsidiary or other related corporation has been understated or overstated, the IRS can reallocate the income and deductions of the related corporations under § 482. Section 482 permits the IRS to allocate gross income, deductions, and credits between any two or more organizations, trades, or businesses that are owned or controlled by the same interests. This is appropriate when the allocation is necessary to prevent avoidance of taxes or to reflect income correctly. Controlled groups of corporations, especially multinational corporations, are particularly vulnerable to § 482.

12-5 PROCEDURAL MATTERS

LO.10

Describe the reporting process for corporations.

This section covers various aspects of the corporate income tax return, including filing requirements, estimated tax payments, and special disclosure schedules on the return.

12-5a Filing Requirements for Corporations

A corporation must file a Federal income tax return (Form 1120) whether or not it has taxable income. A corporation that was not in existence throughout an entire annual accounting period is required to file a return for the portion of the year during which it was in existence. In addition, a corporation must file a return even though it has ceased to do business if it has valuable claims for which it will bring suit. A corporation is relieved of filing income tax returns only when it ceases to do business and retains no assets.[50]

The return must be filed on or before the fifteenth day of the third month following the close of a corporation's tax year. Corporations with assets of $10 million or more generally are required to file electronically. A C corporation, other than a PSC, can use either a calendar year or a fiscal year to report its taxable income. The tax year of the shareholders has no effect on the corporation's tax year.

12-5b Estimated Tax Payments

A corporation must make payments of estimated tax unless its tax liability can reasonably be expected to be less than $500. The required annual payment (which includes any estimated AMT liability) is the *lesser* of (1) 100 percent of the corporation's tax for the current year or (2) 100 percent of the tax for the preceding year (if that was a 12-month tax year, the return filed showed a tax liability, and the corporation involved is not a *large corporation*). Estimated payments can be made in four installments due on or before the fifteenth day of the fourth month, the sixth month, the ninth month, and the twelfth month of the corporate taxable year.[51] The full amount of the unpaid tax is due on the due date of the return without regard to extensions. A corporation failing to pay its required estimated tax payments will be subjected to a nondeductible penalty on the amount by which the installments are less than the tax due.

12-5c Schedule M–1—Reconciliation of Income (Loss) per Books with Income per Return

Schedule M–1 of Form 1120 is used to *reconcile* net income as computed for financial accounting purposes with taxable income reported on the corporation's income tax return (commonly referred to as book-tax differences). Schedule M–1 is used by corporations with less than $10 million of total assets.

The starting point on Schedule M–1 is net income (loss) per books. Additions and subtractions are entered for items that affect financial accounting net income and taxable income differently. The following items are entered as additions (see lines 2 through 5 of Schedule M–1 on the next page):

- Federal income tax expense per books (deducted in computing net income per books but not deductible in computing taxable income).

- The excess of capital losses over capital gains (deducted for financial accounting purposes but not deductible by corporations for income tax purposes).

- Income that is reported in the current year for tax purposes but is not reported in computing net income per books (e.g., prepaid income).

- Various expenses that are deducted in computing net income per books but are not deducted in computing taxable income (e.g., charitable contributions in excess of the 10 percent ceiling applicable to corporations).

---

[50]§ 6012(a)(2) and Reg. § 1.6012–2(a).

[51]§ 6655. If the due date falls on a Saturday, Sunday, or legal holiday, the due date is the next business day. See § 6655(g)(2) for the definition of a *large corporation*.

The following subtractions are entered on lines 7 and 8 of Schedule M–1:

- Income reported for financial accounting purposes but not included in taxable income (e.g., tax-exempt interest).
- Deductions taken on the tax return but not expensed in computing net income per books (e.g., domestic production activities deduction).

The result is taxable income (before the NOL deduction and the dividends received deduction).

EXAMPLE 49

During the current year, Tern Corporation had the following transactions:

Net income per books (after tax)	$ 92,400
Taxable income	50,000
Federal income tax expense per books	7,500
Interest income from tax-exempt bonds	5,000
Interest paid on loan, the proceeds of which were used to purchase the tax-exempt bonds	500
Life insurance proceeds received as a result of the death of a key employee	50,000
Premiums paid on key employee life insurance policy	2,600
Excess of capital losses over capital gains	2,000

For book and tax purposes, Tern Corporation determines depreciation under the straight-line method. Tern's Schedule M–1 for the current year is as follows:

Schedule M-1   Reconciliation of Income (Loss) per Books With Income per Return
Note: The corporation may be required to file Schedule M-3 (see instructions).

1	Net income (loss) per books	92,400	7	Income recorded on books this year not included on this return (itemize):	
2	Federal income tax per books	7,500		Tax-exempt interest $5,000	
3	Excess of capital losses over capital gains	2,000		Life insurance proceeds on key employee $50,000	55,000
4	Income subject to tax not recorded on books this year (itemize):		8	Deductions on this return not charged against book income this year (itemize):	
5	Expenses recorded on books this year not deducted on this return (itemize):			a Depreciation $	
a	Depreciation $			b Charitable contributions $	
b	Charitable contributions $				
c	Travel and entertainment $				
	Prem.–life ins. $2,600; Int.–exempt bonds $500	3,100	9	Add lines 7 and 8	55,000
6	Add lines 1 through 5	105,000	10	Income (page 1, line 28)—line 6 less line 9	50,000

12-5d Schedule M–2—Analysis of Unappropriated Retained Earnings per Books

Schedule M–2 reconciles unappropriated retained earnings at the beginning of the year with unappropriated retained earnings at year-end. The beginning balance plus net income per books, as entered on line 1 of Schedule M–1, less dividend distributions during the year equals ending retained earnings. Other sources of increases or decreases in retained earnings are also listed on Schedule M–2.

EXAMPLE 50

Assume the same facts as in the preceding example. Tern Corporation's beginning balance in unappropriated retained earnings is $125,000. During the year, Tern distributed a cash dividend of $30,000 to its shareholders. Based on these further assumptions, Tern's Schedule M–2 for the current year is as follows:

Schedule M-2   Analysis of Unappropriated Retained Earnings per Books (Line 25, Schedule L)

1	Balance at beginning of year	125,000	5	Distributions: a Cash	30,000
2	Net income (loss) per books	92,400		b Stock	
3	Other increases (itemize):			c Property	
			6	Other decreases (itemize):	
			7	Add lines 5 and 6	30,000
4	Add lines 1, 2, and 3	217,400	8	Balance at end of year (line 4 less line 7)	187,400

DIGGING DEEPER 4   In-depth coverage can be found on this book's companion website: www.cengagebrain.com

BRIDGE DISCIPLINE   **Bridge to Financial Accounting**

Measures of corporate income for financial reporting and income tax purposes differ because the objectives of these measures differ. Income measures for financial reporting purposes are intended to help various stakeholders have a clear view of the corporation's financial position and operational results. Income measures for Federal income tax purposes, on the other hand, must comply with the relevant provisions of the Internal Revenue Code. The tax law is intended not only to raise revenues to fund government operations but also to reflect the objectives of government fiscal policy.

As a consequence of these differing objectives, revenue and expense measurements used to determine taxable income may differ from those used in financial reporting. In most cases, differences between book and tax measurements are temporary in nature. Two such temporary differences relate to the different methods of calculating depreciation expense and the limits placed on the deductibility of net capital losses for tax purposes. Permanent differences between book and tax income, such as the dividends received deduction and the domestic production activities deduction, also may exist.

Accounting standards for reporting income tax expenses and liabilities require that the tax impact of *temporary* differences be recognized currently in the financial statements. Because many temporary differences allow a firm to postpone its tax payments to later years, the financial statements must show the amount of the expense that is paid currently and that portion that is to be paid in a later period. The portion of the taxes to be paid in a later period is shown as a liability for such future income taxes. The liability for future income taxes is referred to as a deferred income tax liability.

See Chapter 3 for a complete discussion of this topic.

12-5e Schedule M–3—Net Income (Loss) Reconciliation for Corporations with Total Assets of $10 Million or More

Corporate taxpayers with total assets of $10 million or more are required to report much greater detail relative to differences between income (loss) reported for financial accounting purposes and income (loss) reported for tax purposes. This expanded reconciliation of book and taxable income (loss) is reported on Schedule M–3. Corporations that are not required to file Schedule M–3 may do so voluntarily. Any corporation that files Schedule M–3 is not allowed to file Schedule M–1. Corporations (and partnerships) with $10 million to $50 million of total assets may elect to file Schedule M–1 in lieu of Schedule M–3, Parts II and III. Electing entities must still file Schedule M–3, Part I (lines 1–12). Entities with less than $10 million of assets that voluntarily file Schedule M–3 also may elect the reduced Schedule M–3 filing requirements.

Schedule M–3 is a response, at least in part, to financial reporting scandals such as Enron and WorldCom. One objective of Schedule M–3 is to create greater transparency between corporate financial statements and tax returns. Another objective is to identify corporations that engage in aggressive tax practices by requiring that transactions that create book-tax differences be disclosed on corporate tax returns. The increase in transparency and disclosure comes at a cost, however, as the IRS estimates that, on average, almost 89 hours are needed to comply with the requirements of Schedule M–3.

Total assets for purposes of the $10 million test and the income and expense amounts required by Schedule M–3 are determined from the taxpayer's financial reports. If the taxpayer files Form 10–K with the Securities and Exchange Commission (SEC), that statement is used. If no 10–K is filed, information from another financial source is used, in the following order: certified financial statements, prepared financial statements, or the taxpayer's books and records.

In-depth coverage can be found on this book's companion website: www.cengagebrain.com   **5, 6** DIGGING DEEPER

12-5f Effect of Taxes on Financial Statements

Given the differences between taxable income and net income per books, what effect do these differences have on an entity's financial statements? How are income tax accruals arrived at and reported for accounting purposes? What other types of disclosures regarding present and potential tax liabilities are required to satisfy the accounting standards? Recall that these and other questions were answered and discussed at length in Chapter 3.

For 2014 tax returns, a corporation with total assets of $10 million or more must file Schedule UTP (Uncertain Tax Position Statement) with its Form 1120. In general, a corporation is required to report tax positions taken on a current or prior year's Federal income tax return and for which the corporation recorded a reserve for Federal income tax in its audited financial statements (or for which no reserve was recorded because of an expectation to litigate). Financial reporting of tax positions is discussed in Chapter 3.

REFOCUS ON THE BIG PICTURE

GROWING INTO THE CORPORATE FORM

Amber, the sole property transferor, must acquire at least 80 percent of the stock issued by Garden, Inc., for the transaction to qualify for tax-deferred treatment under § 351. Otherwise, she will recognize $600,000 of taxable gain as a result of the transfer. As a corollary, Jimmy must not receive more than 20 percent of Garden's stock in exchange for services (see Example 16). Even if the requirements of § 351 are met, any debt issued by the corporation will be treated as boot and will result in at least some gain recognition to Amber (see Example 9). Therefore, Amber must evaluate the cost of recognizing gain now versus the benefit of Garden obtaining an interest deduction later.

What If?

Can the § 351 transaction be modified to further reduce personal and business tax costs, both at the time of formation and in the future? Several strategies may be worth considering.

- Have Jimmy transfer some property along with the services rendered to Garden, Inc. As long as Jimmy transfers property with more than a relatively small value compared to the value of services performed, Jimmy will be considered part of the control group. This would allow Amber to own less than 80 percent of the new corporation and still have the transaction qualify under § 351.

- Instead of having Garden issue debt on formation, Amber might withhold certain assets. For example, if the building is not transferred, it can be leased to the corporation. The resulting rent payment would mitigate the double taxation problem by reducing Garden's taxable income via a rent deduction.

- An additional benefit results if Amber does not transfer the cash basis receivables to Garden. This approach avoids a tax at the corporate level when they are collected by the corporation and another tax on Amber when the receipts are distributed as a dividend (see Example 35).

- If Amber's sole proprietorship has any accounts payable outstanding at the time of the corporate formation, it might be wise to transfer those to Garden. The subsequent corporate payment of the liability produces a deduction that will reduce any corporate income tax.

Suggested Readings

Wei-Chih Chiang and Jianjn Du, "The Debt-Equity Debate in the *Castle Harbour* Case," *Practical Tax Strategies*, March 2013.

David B. Friedel, J.D., and Yaw O. Awuah, "Sec. 351 Control Requirement: Opportunities and Pitfalls," *The Tax Adviser*, July 2014.

Janel Greiman and Thomas J. Nash, "Did Averting Fiscal Cliff Allow C Corporations to Overtake Passthroughs?," *Practical Tax Strategies*, August 2013.

William Hood, "Deducting Start-Up Costs and Organizational Costs," *Practical Tax Strategies*, April 2012.

Jeffrey L. Rubinger and Nadia E. Kruler, "Service Applies Substance Over Form Doctrine to Disallow Dividends-Received Deduction," *Journal of Taxation*, July 2013.

Edward J. Schnee and W. Eugene Seago, "Taxing the Transfer of Debts Between Debtors and Creditors," The *Tax Adviser*, July 2012.

Key Terms

Built-in loss property, 12-21

C corporations, 12-2

Capital contribution, 12-24

Check-the-box Regulations, 12-6

Control, 12-10

Controlled group, 12-33

Disregarded entity, 12-6

Dividends received deduction, 12-28

Limited liability company (LLC), 12-6

Limited partnerships, 12-6

Organizational expenditures, 12-30

Parent-subsidiary controlled group, 12-33

Personal service corporations (PSCs), 12-32

Property, 12-9

Regular corporations, 12-2

Related corporations, 12-32

S corporations, 12-2

Schedule M–1, 12-35

Schedule M–3, 12-37

Securities, 12-10

Thin capitalization, 12-26

Computational Exercises

1. **LO.2** Marie and Ethan form Roundtree Corporation with the transfer of the following. Marie performs personal services for the corporation with a fair market value of $80,000 in exchange for 400 shares of stock. Ethan contributes an installment note receivable (basis $25,000; fair market value $30,000), land (basis $50,000; fair market value $170,000), and inventory (basis $100,000; fair market value $120,000) in exchange for 1,600 shares. Determine Marie and Ethan's current income, gain, or loss; calculate the basis that each takes in the Roundtree stock.

2. **LO.2** Grady exchanges qualified property, basis of $12,000 and fair market value of $18,000, for 60% of the stock of Eadie Corporation. The other 40% of the stock is owned by Pedro, who acquired it five years ago. Calculate Grady 's current income, gain, or loss and the basis he takes in his shares of Eadie stock as a result of this transaction.

3. **LO.3** Jocelyn contributes land with a basis of $60,000 and fair market value of $90,000 and inventory with a basis of $5,000 and fair market value of $8,000 in exchange for 100% of Zion Corporation stock. The land is subject to a $15,000 mortgage. Determine Jocelyn's recognized gain or loss and the basis in the Zion stock received.

4. **LO.3** Martin transfers real estate with an adjusted basis of $260,000 and fair market value of $350,000 to a newly formed corporation in exchange for 100% of the stock. The corporation assumes the liability on the transferred real estate in the amount of $300,000. Determine Martin's recognized gain on the transfer and the basis for his stock.

5. **LO.4** Yvonne and Simon form Ion Corporation. Yvonne transfers equipment (basis of $110,000 and fair market value of $165,000). Simon invests $130,000 of cash. They each receive 100 shares in Ion Corporation, worth $130,000, but Yvonne also receives $35,000 of cash from Ion. Calculate Ion Corporation's basis in the equipment. In addition, determine Yvonne and Simon's basis in the Ion stock.

6. **LO.6** Chaz transfers cash of $60,000 to a newly formed corporation for 100% of the stock. In its initial year, the corporation has net income of $15,000. The income is credited to the earnings and profits account of the corporation. The corporation distributes $5,000 to Chaz.

   a. How do Chaz and the corporation treat the $5,000 distribution?

   b. Assume, instead, that Chaz transfers to the corporation cash of $30,000 for stock and cash of $30,000 for a note of the same amount. The note is payable in equal annual installments of $3,000 each (beginning at the end of the corporation's initial year of operations) and bears interest at the rate of 6%. At the end of the year, the corporation pays an amount to meet this obligation. Determine the total amount of the payment and its tax treatment to Chaz and the corporation.

7. **LO.7** Crane and Loon Corporations, two unrelated C corporations, have the following transactions for 2015:

	Crane	Loon
Gross income from operations	$180,000	$300,000
Expenses from operations	255,000	310,000
Dividends received from domestic corporations (15% ownership)	100,000	230,000

   a. Compute the dividends received deduction for Crane Corporation.

   b. Compute the dividends received deduction for Loon Corporation.

8. **LO.7** Cherry Corporation, a calendar year C corporation, is formed and begins business on April 1, 2015. In connection with its formation, Cherry incurs organizational expenditures of $54,000. Determine Cherry Corporation's deduction for organizational expenditures for 2015.

9. **LO.8** Compute the income tax liability for each of the following unrelated C corporations.

   a. Darter Corporation has taxable income of $68,000.

   b. Owl Corporation has taxable income of $10,800,000.

   c. Toucan Corporation, a personal service corporation, has taxable income of $170,000.

Problems

10. **LO.1** Janice is the sole owner of Catbird Company. In the current year, Catbird had operating income of $100,000, a long-term capital gain of $15,000, and a charitable contribution of $5,000. Janice withdrew $70,000 of profit from Catbird. How should Janice report this information on her individual tax return if Catbird Company is:

    a. An LLC?

    b. An S corporation?

    c. A C corporation?

11. **LO.1** Can a sole proprietor form as a single-member limited liability company (LLC)? If so, how would such an LLC be taxed?

12. **LO.1** In the current year, Riflebird Company had operating income of $220,000, operating expenses of $175,000, and a long-term capital loss of $10,000. How

do Riflebird Company and Roger, the sole owner of Riflebird, report this information on their respective Federal income tax returns for the current year under the following assumptions?

a. Riflebird Company is a proprietorship (Roger did not make any withdrawals from the business).

b. Riflebird Company is a C corporation (no dividends were paid during the year).

13. **LO.1** Ellie and Linda are equal owners in Otter Enterprises, a calendar year business. During the current year, Otter Enterprises has $320,000 of gross income and $210,000 of operating expenses. In addition, Otter has a long-term capital gain of $15,000 and makes distributions to Ellie and Linda of $25,000 each. Discuss the impact of this information on the taxable income of Otter, Ellie, and Linda if Otter is:

a. A partnership.

b. An S corporation.

c. A C corporation.

14. **LO.1** In the current year, Azure Company has $350,000 of net operating income before deducting any compensation or other payments to its sole owner, Sasha. In addition, Azure has interest on municipal bonds of $25,000. Sasha has significant income from other sources and is in the 39.6% marginal tax bracket. Based on this information, determine the income tax consequences to Azure Company and to Sasha during the year for each of the following independent situations.

a. Azure is a C corporation and pays no dividends or salary to Sasha.

b. Azure is a C corporation and distributes $75,000 of dividends to Sasha.

c. Azure is a C corporation and pays $75,000 of salary to Sasha.

d. Azure is a sole proprietorship, and Sasha withdraws $0.

e. Azure is a sole proprietorship, and Sasha withdraws $75,000.

15. **LO.2** Sarah incorporates her small business but does not transfer the machinery and equipment used by the business to the corporation. Instead, the machinery and equipment are leased to the corporation for an annual rent. What tax reasons might Sarah have for not transferring the machinery and equipment to the corporation when the business was incorporated?   Issue ID

16. **LO.2, 4** Seth, Pete, Cara, and Jen form Kingfisher Corporation with the following consideration:

	Consideration Transferred		
	Basis to Transferor	Fair Market Value	Number of Shares Issued
From Seth—			
Inventory	$30,000	$96,000	30*
From Pete—			
Equipment ($30,000 of depreciation taken by Pete in prior years)	45,000	99,000	30**
From Cara—			
Proprietary process	15,000	90,000	30
From Jen—			
Cash	30,000	30,000	10

*Seth receives $6,000 in cash in addition to the 30 shares.
**Pete receives $9,000 in cash in addition to the 30 shares.

Assume that the value of each share of Kingfisher stock is $3,000. As to these transactions, provide the following information:

a. Seth's recognized gain or loss. Identify the nature of any such gain or loss.

b. Seth's basis in the Kingfisher Corporation stock.

c. Kingfisher Corporation's basis in the inventory.

d. Pete's recognized gain or loss. Identify the nature of any such gain or loss.

e. Pete's basis in the Kingfisher Corporation stock.

f. Kingfisher Corporation's basis in the equipment.

g. Cara's recognized gain or loss.

h. Cara's basis in the Kingfisher Corporation stock.

i. Kingfisher Corporation's basis in the proprietary process.

j. Jen's recognized gain or loss.

k. Jen's basis in the Kingfisher stock.

17. **LO.2, 4** Tom and Gail form Owl Corporation with the following consideration:

	Consideration Transferred		
	Basis to Transferor	Fair Market Value	Number of Shares Issued
From Tom—			
Cash	$ 50,000	$ 50,000	
Installment note	240,000	350,000	40
From Gail—			
Inventory	$ 60,000	$ 50,000	
Equipment	125,000	250,000	
Patentable invention	15,000	300,000	60

The installment note has a face amount of $350,000 and was acquired last year from the sale of land held for investment purposes (adjusted basis of $240,000). As to these transactions, provide the following information:

a. Tom's recognized gain or loss.

b. Tom's basis in the Owl Corporation stock.

c. Owl Corporation's basis in the installment note.

d. Gail's recognized gain or loss.

e. Gail's basis in the Owl Corporation stock.

f. Owl Corporation's basis in the inventory, equipment, and patentable invention.

g. How would your answers to the preceding questions change if Tom received common stock and Gail received preferred stock?

h. How would your answers change if Gail was a partnership?

Decision Making   18. **LO.2** Jane, Jon, and Clyde incorporate their respective businesses and form Starling Corporation. On March 1 of the current year, Jane exchanges her property (basis of $50,000 and value of $150,000) for 150 shares in Starling Corporation. On April 15, Jon exchanges his property (basis of $70,000 and value of $500,000) for 500 shares in Starling. On May 10, Clyde transfers his property (basis of $90,000 and value of $350,000) for 350 shares in Starling.

a. If the three exchanges are part of a prearranged plan, what gain will each of the parties recognize on the exchanges?

b. Assume that Jane and Jon exchanged their property for stock four years ago, while Clyde transfers his property for 350 shares in the current year. Clyde's transfer is not part of a prearranged plan with Jane and Jon to incorporate their businesses. What gain will Clyde recognize on the transfer?

c. Returning to the original facts, if the property that Clyde contributes has a basis of $490,000 (instead of $90,000), how might the parties otherwise structure the transaction?

19. **LO.2** Dan and Patricia form Crane Corporation. Dan transfers land (worth   Issue ID
$200,000, basis of $60,000) for 50% of the stock in Crane. Patricia transfers
machinery (worth $150,000, adjusted basis of $30,000) and provides services worth
($50,000) for 50% of the stock.
   a. Will the transfers qualify under § 351? Explain.
   b. What are the tax consequences to Dan and Patricia?
   c. What is Crane Corporation's basis in the land and the machinery?

20. **LO.2** John organized Toucan Corporation 10 years ago. He contributed property
worth $1 million (basis of $200,000) for 2,000 shares of stock in Toucan (representing 100% ownership). John later gave each of his children, Julie and Rachel,
500 shares of the stock. In the current year, John transfers property worth $350,000
(basis of $170,000) to Toucan for 1,000 more of its shares. What gain, if any, will
John recognize on the transfer?

21. **LO.2** Rhonda owns 50% of the stock of Peach Corporation. She and the other 50%   Decision Making
shareholder, Rachel, have decided that additional contributions of capital are
needed if Peach is to remain successful in its competitive industry. The two shareholders
have agreed that Rhonda will contribute assets having a value of $200,000 (adjusted ba-
sis of $15,000) in exchange for additional shares of stock. After the transaction, Rhonda
will hold 75% of Peach Corporation and Rachel's interest will fall to 25%.
   a. What gain is realized on the transaction? How much of the gain will be recognized?
   b. Rhonda is not satisfied with the transaction as proposed. How will the consequences change if Rachel agrees to transfer $1,000 of cash in exchange for addi-
   tional stock? In this case, Rhonda would own slightly less than 75% of Peach,
   and Rachel's interest would be slightly more than 25%.
   c. If Rhonda still is not satisfied with the result, what should be done to avoid any
   gain recognition?

22. **LO.2,3,4** Adam transfers property with an adjusted basis of $50,000 (fair market
value of $400,000) to Swift Corporation for 90% of the stock. The prop-
erty is subject to a liability of $60,000, which Swift assumes.
   a. What is the basis of the Swift stock to Adam?
   b. What is the basis of the property to Swift Corporation?

23. **LO.2,3,4** Allie forms Broadbill Corporation by transferring land (basis of $125,000,
fair market value of $775,000), which is subject to a mortgage of $375,000.
One month prior to incorporating Broadbill, Allie borrows $100,000 for personal rea-
sons and gives the lender a second mortgage on the land. Broadbill Corporation issues
stock worth $300,000 to Allie and assumes the mortgages on the land.
   a. What are the tax consequences to Allie and to Broadbill Corporation?
   b. How would the tax consequences to Allie differ if she had not borrowed the
   $100,000?

24. **LO.2,4** Rafael transfers the following assets to Crane Corporation in exchange for   Decision Making
all of its stock. (Assume that neither Rafael nor Crane plans to make any
special tax elections at the time of incorporation.)

Assets	Rafael's Adjusted Basis	Fair Market Value
Inventory	$ 60,000	$100,000
Equipment	150,000	105,000
Shelving	80,000	65,000

   a. What is Rafael's recognized gain or loss?
   b. What is Rafael's basis in the stock?
   c. What is Crane's basis in the inventory, equipment, and shelving?

d. If Rafael has no intentions of selling his Crane stock for at least 15 years, what action would you recommend that Rafael and Crane Corporation consider? How does this change the previous answers?

25. **LO.2, 3, 4** Kesha, a sole proprietor, is engaged in a cash basis service business. In the current year, she incorporates the business to form Kiwi Corporation. She transfers assets with a basis of $500,000 (fair market value of $1.2 million), a bank loan of $450,000 (which Kiwi assumes), and $80,000 in trade payables in return for all of Kiwi's stock. What are the tax consequences of the incorporation of the business?

Issue ID 26. **LO.2** Nancy and her daughter, Kathleen, have been working together in a cattery called "The Perfect Cat." Nancy formed the business in 2000 as a sole proprietorship, and it has been very successful. Assets have a fair market value of $450,000 and a basis of $180,000. On the advice of their tax accountant, Nancy decides to incorporate "The Perfect Cat." Because of Kathleen's participation, Nancy would like her to receive shares in the corporation. What are the relevant tax issues?

Ethics and Equity 27. **LO.2** Early in the year, Charles, Lane, and Tami form the Harrier Corporation for the express purpose of developing a shopping center. All parties are experienced contractors, and they transfer various business assets (e.g., building materials, land) to Harrier in exchange for all of its stock. Three months after it is formed, Harrier purchases two cranes from Lane for their fair market value of $400,000 by issuing four annual installment notes of $100,000 each. Because the adjusted basis of the cranes is $550,000, Lane plans to recognize a § 1231 loss of $150,000 in the year of the sale. Does Lane have any potential income tax problem with this plan? Explain.

28. **LO.2, 4** Alice and Jane form Osprey Corporation. Alice transfers property, basis of $25,000 and fair market value of $200,000, for 50 shares in Osprey Corporation. Jane transfers property, basis of $50,000 and fair market value of $165,000, and agrees to serve as manager of Osprey for one year; in return, Jane receives 50 shares in Osprey. The value of Jane's services to Osprey is $35,000.
a. What gain or income will Alice and Jane recognize on the exchange?
b. What basis will Osprey Corporation have in the property transferred by Alice and Jane? How should Osprey treat the value of the services that Jane renders?

29. **LO.2, 4** Assume in Problem 28 that Jane receives the 50 shares of Osprey Corporation stock in consideration for the appreciated property and for the provision of accounting services in organizing the corporation. The value of Jane's services is $35,000.
a. What gain or income does Jane recognize?
b. What is Osprey Corporation's basis in the property transferred by Jane? How should Osprey treat the value of the services that Jane renders?

30. **LO.2, 4** In January 2015, Wanda transferred machinery worth $200,000 (adjusted basis of $30,000) to a controlled corporation, Oriole, Inc. The transfer qualified under § 351. Wanda had deducted $165,000 of depreciation on the machinery while it was used in her proprietorship. Later in 2015, Oriole sells the machinery for $190,000. What are the tax consequences to Wanda and to Oriole on the sale of the machinery?

31. **LO.5** Red Corporation wants to set up a manufacturing facility in a midwestern state. After considerable negotiations with a small town in Ohio, Red accepts the following offer: land (fair market value of $3 million) and cash of $1 million.
a. How much gain or income, if any, must Red Corporation recognize?
b. What basis will Red Corporation have in the land?
c. Within one year of the contribution, Red constructs a building for $800,000 and purchases inventory for $200,000. What basis will Red Corporation have in each of those assets?

32. **LO.6** Emily Patrick (36 Paradise Road, Northampton, MA 01060) formed Teal Corporation a number of years ago with an investment of $200,000 of cash, for which she received $20,000 in stock and $180,000 in bonds bearing interest of 8% and maturing in nine years. Several years later, Emily lent the corporation an additional $50,000 on open account. In the current year, Teal Corporation becomes insolvent and is declared bankrupt. During the corporation's existence, Emily was paid an annual salary of $60,000. Write a letter to Emily in which you explain how she should treat her losses for tax purposes.

Critical Thinking

Communications

33. **LO.7** In each of the following independent situations, determine the dividends received deduction. Assume that none of the corporate shareholders owns 20% or more of the stock in the corporations paying the dividends.

	Almond Corporation	Blond Corporation	Cherry Corporation
Income from operations	$ 700,000	$ 800,000	$ 900,000
Expenses from operations	(600,000)	(850,000)	(910,000)
Qualifying dividends	100,000	100,000	100,000

34. **LO.7** Gull Corporation, a cash method, calendar year C corporation, was formed and began business on November 1, 2015. Gull incurred the following expenses during its first year of operations (November 1, 2015–December 31, 2015):

Expenses of temporary directors and organizational meetings	$21,000
Fee paid to state of incorporation	3,000
Expenses for printing and sale of stock certificates	11,000
Legal services for drafting the corporate charter and bylaws (not paid until January 2016)	19,000

   a. Assuming that Gull Corporation elects under § 248 to expense and amortize organizational expenditures, what amount may be deducted in 2015?
   b. Assume the same facts as above, except that the amount paid for the legal services was $28,000 (instead of $19,000). What amount may be deducted as organizational expenditures in 2015?

35. **LO.7** Egret Corporation, a calendar year C corporation, was formed on March 6, 2015, and opened for business on July 1, 2015. After its formation but prior to opening for business, Egret incurred the following expenditures:

Accounting	$ 7,000
Advertising	14,500
Employee payroll	11,000
Rent	8,000
Utilities	1,000

What is the maximum amount of these expenditures that Egret can deduct in 2015?

36. **LO.8** In each of the following *independent* situations, determine the corporation's income tax liability. Assume that all corporations use a calendar year for tax purposes and that the tax year involved is 2015.

	Taxable Income
Purple Corporation	$ 65,000
Azul Corporation	290,000
Pink Corporation	12,350,000
Turquoise Corporation	19,000,000
Teal Corporation (a personal service corporation)	130,000

Critical Thinking 37. **LO.9** The outstanding stock in Red, Blue, and Green Corporations, each of which has only one class of stock, is owned by the following unrelated individuals:

	Corporations		
Shareholders	**Red**	**Blue**	**Green**
Marrin	20%	10%	30%
Murray	10%	50%	20%
Moses	50%	30%	35%

a.   Determine whether Red, Blue, and Green Corporations constitute a brother-sister controlled group.

b.   Assume that Murray does not own stock in any of the corporations. Would a brother-sister controlled group exist? Explain.

38. **LO.10** Emerald Corporation, a calendar year and accrual method taxpayer, provides the following information and asks you to prepare Schedule M–1 for 2015:

Net income per books (after-tax)	$257,950
Federal income tax per books	41,750
Tax-exempt interest income	15,000
Life insurance proceeds received as a result of death of corporate president	150,000
Interest on loan to purchase tax-exempt bonds	1,500
Excess of capital losses over capital gains	6,000
Premiums paid on life insurance policy on life of Emerald's president	7,800

39. **LO.10** The following information for 2015 relates to Sparrow Corporation, a calendar year, accrual method taxpayer.

Net income per books (after-tax)	$174,100
Federal income tax per books	86,600
Tax-exempt interest income	4,500
MACRS depreciation in excess of straight-line depreciation used for financial accounting purposes	7,200
Excess of capital loss over capital gains	9,400
Nondeductible meals and entertainment	5,500
Interest on loan to purchase tax-exempt bonds	1,100

Based on the above information, use Schedule M–1 of Form 1120, which is available on the IRS website, to determine Sparrow's taxable income for 2015.

Critical Thinking 40. **LO.10** In the current year, Woodpecker, Inc., a C corporation with $8.5 million in assets, deducted amortization of $40,000 on its financial statements and $55,000 on its Federal tax return. Is Woodpecker required to file Schedule M–3? If a Schedule M–3 is filed by Woodpecker, how is the difference in amortization amounts treated on that schedule?

Critical Thinking 41. **LO.10** Dove Corporation, a calendar year C corporation, had the following information for 2015:

Net income per books (after-tax)	$386,250
Taxable income	120,000
Federal income tax per books	30,050
Cash dividend distributions	150,000
Unappropriated retained earnings as of January 1, 2015	796,010

Based on the above information, use Schedule M–2 of Form 1120 (see Example 50 in the text) to determine Dove's unappropriated retained earnings balance as of December 31, 2015.

42. **LO.10** In the current year, Pelican, Inc., incurs $50,000 of nondeductible fines and penalties. Its depreciation expense is $245,000 for financial statement purposes and $310,000 for tax purposes. How is this information reported on Schedule M–3?   Critical Thinking

43. **LO.10** In January 2015, Pelican, Inc., established an allowance for uncollectible accounts (bad debt reserve) of $70,000 on its books and increased the allowance by $120,000 during the year. As a result of a client's bankruptcy, Pelican, Inc., decreased the allowance by $60,000 in November 2015. Pelican, Inc., deducted the $190,000 of increases to the allowance on its 2015 income statement, but was not allowed to deduct that amount on its tax return. On its 2015 tax return, the corporation was allowed to deduct the $60,000 actual loss sustained because of its client's bankruptcy. On its financial statements, Pelican, Inc., treated the $190,000 increase in the bad debt reserve as an expense that gave rise to a temporary difference. On its 2015 tax return, Pelican, Inc., took a $60,000 deduction for bad debt expense. How is this information reported on Schedule M–3?   Critical Thinking

Comprehensive Tax Return Problem

1. On November 1, 2005, Janet Morton and Kim Wong formed Pet Kingdom, Inc., to sell pets and pet supplies. Pertinent information regarding Pet Kingdom is summarized as follows:

   Tax Return Problem

   TAX SOFTWARE

   • Pet Kingdom's business address is 1010 Northwest Parkway, Dallas, TX 75225; its telephone number is (214) 555-2211; and its e-mail address is petkingdom@pki.com.
   • The employer identification number is 11-1111111, and the principal business activity code is 453910.
   • Janet and Kim each own 50% of the common stock; Janet is president and Kim is vice president of the company. No other class of stock is authorized.
   • Both Janet and Kim are full-time employees of Pet Kingdom. Janet's Social Security number is 123-45-6789, and Kim's Social Security number is 987-65-4321.
   • Pet Kingdom is an accrual method, calendar year taxpayer. Inventories are determined using FIFO and the lower of cost or market method. Pet Kingdom uses the straight-line method of depreciation for book purposes and accelerated depreciation (MACRS) for tax purposes.
   • During 2014, the corporation distributed cash dividends of $250,000.

   Pet Kingdom's financial statements for 2014 follow.

Income Statement

Income		
Gross sales		$5,750,000
Sales returns and allowances		(200,000)
Net sales		$5,550,000
Cost of goods sold		(2,300,000)
Gross profit		$3,250,000
Dividends received from stock investments in less-than-20%-owned U.S. corporations		43,750
Interest income:		
State bonds	$15,000	
Certificates of deposit	20,000	35,000
Total income		$3,328,750
		(*continued*)

Expenses

Salaries—officers:		
Janet Morton	$262,500	
Kim Wong	262,500	$525,000
Salaries—clerical and sales		725,000
Taxes (state, local, and payroll)		238,000
Repairs and maintenance		140,000
Interest expense:		
Loan to purchase state bonds	$ 9,000	
Other business loans	207,000	216,000
Advertising		58,000
Rental expense		109,000
Depreciation*		106,000
Charitable contributions		38,000
Employee benefit programs		60,000
Premiums on term life insurance policies on lives of Janet Morton and Kim Wong; Pet Kingdom is the designated beneficiary		40,000
Total expenses		(2,255,000)
Net income before taxes		$1,073,750
Federal income tax		(356,023)
Net income per books		$ 717,727

*Depreciation for tax purposes is $136,000. You are not provided enough detailed data to complete a Form 4562 (depreciation). If you solve this problem using H&R BLOCK Tax Software, enter the amount of depreciation on line 20 of Form 1120.

Balance Sheet

Assets	January 1, 2014	December 31, 2014
Cash	$ 1,200,000	$ 1,037,750
Trade notes and accounts receivable	2,062,500	2,147,000
Inventories	2,750,000	3,030,000
Stock investment	1,125,000	1,125,000
State bonds	375,000	375,000
Certificates of deposit	400,000	400,000
Prepaid Federal tax	–0–	3,977
Buildings and other depreciable assets	5,455,000	5,455,000
Accumulated depreciation	(606,000)	(712,000)
Land	812,500	812,500
Other assets	140,000	128,500
Total assets	$13,714,000	$13,802,727

Liabilities and Equity	January 1, 2014	December 31, 2014
Accounts payable	$ 2,284,000	$ 1,975,000
Other current liabilities	175,000	155,000
Mortgages	4,625,000	4,575,000
Capital stock	2,500,000	2,500,000
Retained earnings	4,130,000	4,597,727
Total liabilities and equity	$13,714,000	$13,802,727

During 2014, Pet Kingdom made estimated tax payments of $90,000 each quarter to the IRS. Prepare a Form 1120 for Pet Kingdom for tax year 2014. Suggested software: H&R BLOCK Tax Software.

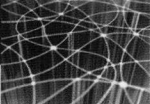

BRIDGE DISCIPLINE

1. Charles is planning to invest $10,000 in a venture whose management is undecided as to whether it should be structured as a regular corporation or as a partnership. Charles will hold a 10% interest in the entity. Determine the treatment to Charles if the entity is a corporation and if it is a partnership. In the analysis, assume that Charles is in the 35% marginal tax bracket and that the entity, if operating as a corporation, is in the 34% marginal tax bracket. Also assume that the passive activity rules do not apply to Charles.

   a. If the entity incurs an $80,000 operating loss in year 1, what is Charles's cash outflow if the entity is a corporation? A partnership? Do not consider the 3.8% Medicare surtax in the analysis.

   b. In year 2, the entity earns operating income of $200,000 and makes no distributions to any of the owners. What is the Federal income tax burden on Charles if the investment is a corporation? A partnership?

   c. In year 3, the entity earns operating income of $200,000 and distributes all of that year's after-tax proceeds to the owners. What amount of cash is available to Charles if the entity operates as a corporation (assume that any distribution is a qualified dividend)? A partnership?

2. On your review of the books and records of Ridge Corporation, you note the following information pertaining to its tax provision:

Net income per books	$525,400
Book income tax expense	234,600
Dividends received deduction	70,000
Capital gains	50,000
Capital losses	(60,000)
MACRS depreciation	80,000
Book depreciation	65,000

   a. Calculate Ridge's taxable income and Federal income tax liability for the year.
   b. Calculate Ridge's deferred income tax liability.

Research Problems

Note: Solutions to Research Problems can be prepared by using the Checkpoint® Student Edition online research product, which is available to accompany this text. It is also possible to prepare solutions to the Research Problems by using tax research materials found in a standard tax library.

THOMSON REUTERS
CHECKPOINT®
Student Edition

Research Problem 1. Tim is a real estate broker who specializes in commercial real estate. Although he usually buys and sells on behalf of others, he also maintains a portfolio of property of his own. He holds this property, mainly unimproved land, either as an investment or for sale to others.

In early 2013, Irene and Al contact Tim regarding a tract of land located just outside the city limits. Tim bought the property, which is known as the Moore farm, several years ago for $600,000. At that time, no one knew that it was located on a geological fault line. Irene, a well-known architect, and Al, a building contractor, want Tim to join them in developing the property for residential use. They are aware of the fault line but believe that they can circumvent the problem by using newly developed design and construction technology. Because of the geological flaw, however, they regard the Moore farm as being worth only $450,000. Their intent is to organize a corporation to build the housing project, and each party will receive stock commensurate to the property or services contributed.

After consulting his tax adviser, Tim agrees to join the venture if certain modifications to the proposed arrangement are made. The transfer of the land would be structured as a sale to the corporation. Instead of receiving stock, Tim would receive a note from the corporation. The note would be interest-bearing and be due in five years. The maturity value of the note would be $450,000—the amount that even Tim concedes is the fair market value of the Moore farm.

What income tax consequences ensue from Tim's suggested approach? Compare this result with what would happen if Tim merely transferred the Moore farm in return for stock in the new corporation.

Communications

Research Problem 2. A new client, John Dobson, recently formed John's Premium Steakhouse, Inc., to operate a new restaurant. The restaurant will be a first-time business venture for John, who recently retired after 30 years of military service. John transferred cash to the corporation in exchange for 100% of its stock, and the corporation is considering leasing a building and restaurant equipment. John has asked you for guidance on the tax treatment of various expenses (e.g., licensing, training, advertising) he expects the corporation to incur during the restaurant's pre-opening period. Research the tax treatment of startup expenditures, including the point at which a business begins for purposes of determining what expenses are included. Prepare a memo for the client files describing the results of your research.

Partial list of research aids:
§ 195.
Reg. § 1.195–1.

Decision Making

Communications

Research Problem 3. Lynn Jones, Shawn, Walt, and Donna are trying to decide whether they should organize a corporation and transfer their shares of stock in several corporations to this new corporation. All of their shares are listed on the New York Stock Exchange and are readily marketable. Lynn would transfer shares in Brown Corporation, Shawn would transfer stock in Rust Corporation, Walt would transfer stock in White Corporation, and Donna would transfer stock in several corporations. The stock would be held by the newly formed corporation for investment purposes. Lynn asks you, her tax adviser, whether she would have gain on the transfer of her substantially appreciated shares in Brown Corporation if she transferred the shares to a newly formed corporation. Your input will be critical as they make their decision. Prepare a letter to your client, Lynn Jones, and a memo for the firm's files. Lynn's address is 1540 Maxwell Avenue, Highland, KY 41099.

Internet Activity

Use the tax resources of the Internet to address the following questions. Do not restrict your search to the Web, but include a review of newsgroups and general reference materials, practitioner sites and resources, primary sources of the tax law, chat rooms and discussion groups, and other opportunities.

Communications

Research Problem 4. On November 21, 2013, Max Baucus, Chairman of the Senate Finance Committee, released a proposal to change several provisions related to the taxation of business income including, but not limited to, that earned by corporations. The proposal deals primarily with cost recovery and tax accounting methods. Many of the proposed changes are similar to ones contained in House Ways and Means Committee Chairman Dave Camp's small business tax reform discussion draft released earlier in the year. Locate the staff discussion draft of Chairman Baucus's proposal, and prepare a PowerPoint presentation of no more than five slides highlighting the major reforms contained in the proposal.

Research Problem 5. Limited liability company (LLC) status has become a popular form of operating a business in the United States. Investigate how the growth of LLC status has affected the relative number of new businesses that have chosen to operate as corporations.

Roger CPA Review Questions

1. What is the filing deadline for a C Corporation?

   a. March 15

   b. April 15

   c. The 15th day of the 3rd month after year end

   d. The 15th day of the 4th month after year end

2. Crimson Corp. was organized as a calendar-year corporation in January 20X14, incurring $51,000 in qualified organizational expenses, and began business in March 20X14. What is the maximum amount Crimson may deduct for organizational expenditures on its 20X14 corporate tax return?

   a. $4,000   c. $6,350

   b. $6,611   d. $7,133

3. Kellye and Becky formed Whoop! Shotz Corporation by contributing property with a fair market value of $50,000 and $70,000 cash, respectively, each for a 50% owner-ship in the newly formed company. What is Kellye's taxable gain in this situation if the adjusted basis in the property is $25,000 and the company is valued at $120,000?

   a. $0   c. $25,000

   b. $10,000   d. $35,000

4. Kellye, Becky, and Emily formed Whoop! Shotz Corporation on 1/1/20X4 with the following contributions:

Kellye	$50,000 cash
Becky	$50,000 cash
Emily	Legal services

   Each was given a one-third ownership in Whoop! Shotz. What amount of income will Emily recognize if the company is valued at $150,000 after formation?

   a. $50,000   c. $0

   b. $33,333   d. $40,000

5. Kellye and Becky create Whoop! Shotz Corporation by contributing property with a fair market value of $50,000 and cash of $70,000, respectively. Each receives a 50% share in the company, which is valued at $150,000 immediately after the formation. The property has an adjusted basis of $25,000 and is subject to a $10,000 mortgage, which is assumed by the company. What gain will Kellye recognize in this situation?

   a. $0   c. $15,000

   b. $10,000   d. $25,000

CHAPTER 13

Corporations: Earnings & Profits and Distributions

LEARNING OBJECTIVES: *After completing Chapter 13, you should be able to:*

LO.1 Explain the role that earnings and profits play in determining the tax treatment of distributions.

LO.2 Compute a corporation's earnings and profits (E & P).

LO.3 Apply the rules for assigning earnings and profits to distributions.

LO.4 Evaluate the tax effects of noncash dividends on the recipient shareholder and the corporation making the distribution.

LO.5 Identify the nature and treatment of constructive dividends.

LO.6 Distinguish between taxable and nontaxable stock dividends.

LO.7 Discuss the tax treatment of stock redemptions and corporate liquidations.

CHAPTER OUTLINE

TAX TALK *The relative stability of profits after taxes is evidence that the corporation profits tax is, in effect, almost entirely shifted; the government simply uses the corporation as a tax collector.* —K. E. BOULDING

TAXING CORPORATE DISTRIBUTIONS

Lime Corporation, an ice cream manufacturer, has had a very profitable year. To share its profits with its two shareholders, Orange Corporation and Gustavo, it distributes cash of $200,000 to Orange and real estate worth $300,000 (adjusted basis of $20,000) to Gustavo. The real estate is subject to a mortgage of $100,000, which Gustavo assumes. The distribution is made on December 31, Lime's year-end.

Lime Corporation has had both good and bad years in the past. More often than not, however, it has lost money. Despite this year's banner profits, the GAAP-based balance sheet for Lime indicates a year-end deficit in retained earnings. Consequently, for financial reporting purposes, the distribution of cash and land is treated as a liquidating distribution, resulting in a reduction of Lime's paid-in capital account.

The tax consequences of the distributions to Lime Corporation and its shareholders depend on a variety of factors that are not directly related to the financial reporting treatment. Identify these factors, and explain the tax effects of the distributions to both Lime Corporation and its two shareholders.

Read the chapter and formulate your response.

Generally, a corporation cannot deduct distributions made to its shareholders. In contrast, shareholders may be required to treat distributions as fully subject to tax, a nontaxable recovery of capital, or capital gain.

Because distributions provide no deduction to the paying corporation and often require income recognition by the shareholders, a double tax seemingly results (i.e., at both the corporate and shareholder levels). Because of the possibility of a double tax when dealing with corporations, the tax treatment of distributions often raises issues such as the following.

- The availability of earnings to be distributed.
- The basis of the shareholder's stock.
- The character of the property being distributed.
- Whether the shareholder gives up ownership in return for the distribution.
- Whether the distribution is liquidating or nonliquidating.

13-1 CORPORATE DISTRIBUTIONS—OVERVIEW

LO.1

Explain the role that earnings and profits play in determining the tax treatment of distributions.

To the extent a distribution is made from corporate earnings and profits (E & P), the shareholder is deemed to receive a dividend , usually taxed in a preferential manner.[1] Generally, corporate distributions are presumed to be paid out of E & P (defined later in this chapter) and are treated as dividends, *unless* the parties to the transaction can show otherwise.

The portion of a corporate distribution that is not taxed as a dividend (because of insufficient E & P) is nontaxable to the extent of the shareholder's basis in the stock. The stock basis is reduced accordingly. The excess of the distribution over the shareholder's basis is treated as a gain from the sale or exchange of the stock.[2]

EXAMPLE 1

At the beginning of the year, Amber Corporation (a calendar year taxpayer) holds accumulated E & P of $30,000. The corporation reports no current E & P. During the year, the corporation distributes $40,000 to its *equal* shareholders, Bob and Bonnie (i.e., each receives $20,000). Only $30,000 of the $40,000 distribution is a taxable dividend.

Suppose Bob's basis in his stock is $8,000, while Bonnie's basis is $4,000. Under these conditions, Bob recognizes a taxable dividend of $15,000 and reduces the basis of his stock from $8,000 to $3,000. The $20,000 Bonnie receives from Amber Corporation is accounted for as follows.

- Taxable dividend of $15,000.
- Reduction in stock basis from $4,000 to zero.
- Taxable gain of $1,000.

13-2 EARNINGS AND PROFITS (E & P)

The notion of earnings and profits is similar in many respects to the financial accounting concept of retained earnings. Both are measures of the firm's accumulated capital. However, these two concepts differ in a fundamental way. The computation of retained earnings is based on financial accounting rules, while E & P is determined using rules specified in the tax law.

E & P fixes the upper limit on the amount of dividend income shareholders must recognize as a result of a distribution by the corporation. In this sense, E & P represents the corporation's economic ability to pay a dividend without impairing its capital. Thus, the effect of a specific transaction on the E & P account often can be determined by considering whether the transaction increases or decreases the corporation's capacity to pay a dividend.

---

[1] §§ 301(c)(1) and 316(a). Corporate shareholders claim a dividends received deduction. Others typically pay a tax on dividends at a maximum 15% or 20% rate.

[2] § 301(c).

TAX FACT   **Who Pays Dividends?**

The vast majority of dividends paid by C corporations come from the very largest enterprises (measured by size of total assets) as reported on Forms 1120 for the latest tax year for which data are available. About 80 percent of the members of the Standard & Poor's 500 pay an annual dividend, distributing less than 40 percent of annual profits. Only about 9 percent of all dividend payments during a tax year are made by C corporations with less than $500 million in total assets.

Percentage of Dividends Paid, by Size of Corporate Assets

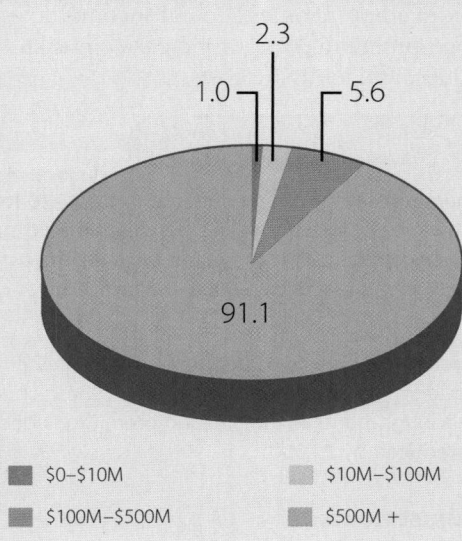

2.3
1.0 —   — 5.6
91.1

- $0–$10M
- $10M–$100M
- $100M–$500M
- $500M +

13-2a   **Computation of E & P**

LO.2

Compute a corporation's earnings and profits (E & P).

The Code does not explicitly define the term *earnings and profits*. Instead, a series of adjustments to taxable income are identified to provide a measure of the corporation's economic income.[3] In general, E & P determinations are applied in the same manner for cash and accrual basis taxpayers.

Accumulated E & P is fixed as of the beginning of the tax year; it is the sum of the undistributed earnings of the entity since the later of its incorporation date or February 28, 1913. Current E & P is that portion of E & P attributable to the current tax year's operations. It is computed by using the corporation's Federal taxable income and then applying a series of adjustments to more closely approximate the cash flow of the entity.[4]

Additions to Taxable Income

To determine current E & P, one must add certain previously excluded income items back to taxable income. Included among these positive adjustments are interest income on municipal bonds, excluded life insurance proceeds (in excess of cash surrender value), and Federal income tax refunds from taxes paid in prior years.

In addition to excluded income items, the dividends received deduction and the domestic production activities deduction (DPAD) are added back to taxable income to determine E & P. Neither of these deductions decreases the corporation's assets. They are added back because they do not impair the corporation's ability to pay dividends: they do not reduce E & P.

---

[3]Reg. § 1.312–6(a).

[4]Section 312 describes many of the adjustments to taxable income necessary to determine E & P. Regulation § 1.312–6 addresses the effect of accounting methods on E & P.

Eagle Corporation collects $100,000 on a key employee life insurance policy (Eagle is the owner and beneficiary of the policy). At the time the policy matured on the death of the insured employee, it possessed a cash surrender value of $30,000. None of the $100,000 is included in Eagle's taxable income, but $70,000 is added to its taxable income when computing current E & P.

Subtractions from Taxable Income

Some of the corporation's nondeductible expenditures are subtracted from taxable income to arrive at E & P. These negative adjustments include the nondeductible portion of meals and entertainment expenses; related-party losses; expenses incurred to produce tax-exempt income; Federal income taxes paid; nondeductible key employee life insurance premiums (net of increases in cash surrender value); and nondeductible fines, penalties, and lobbying costs.

E & P Subtraction Modifications

Joseph Corporation sells property (basis of $10,000) to its sole shareholder for $8,000. Because of § 267 (disallowance of losses on sales between related parties), Joseph cannot deduct the $2,000 loss in computing its taxable income. But because the overall economic effect of the transaction is a decrease in Joseph's assets by $2,000, the loss reduces current E & P for the year of the sale.

Jacquie Corporation pays a $10,000 premium on a key employee life insurance policy covering the life of its president. As a result of the payment, the cash surrender value of the policy is increased by $7,000. Although none of the $10,000 premium is deductible by Jacquie for tax purposes, current E & P is reduced by $3,000.

Timing Adjustments

Some E & P adjustments shift the effect of a transaction from the year of its inclusion in or deduction from taxable income to the year in which it has an economic effect on the corporation. Charitable contribution carryovers, net operating loss carryovers, and capital loss carryovers all give rise to this kind of adjustment.

During 2014, Raven Corporation makes charitable contributions, $12,000 of which cannot be deducted in arriving at its taxable income for the year because of the 10% taxable income limitation. Consequently, the $12,000 is carried forward to 2015 and fully deducted in that year. The excess charitable contribution reduces Raven's 2014 current E & P by $12,000 and increases its current E & P for 2015, when the deduction is allowed, by a like amount. The increase in 2015 E & P is necessary because the charitable contribution carryover reduces the taxable income for that year (the starting point for computing E & P) but already has been taken into account in determining 2014 current E & P.

Gains and losses from property transactions generally affect the determination of E & P only to the extent they are recognized for tax purposes. Thus, gains and losses deferred under the like-kind exchange provision and deferred involuntary conversion gains do not affect E & P until recognized. Accordingly, no timing adjustment is required for these items.

Accounting Method Adjustments

In addition to the above adjustments, accounting methods used for determining E & P generally are more conservative than those allowed for calculating taxable income. For example, the installment method is not permitted for E & P purposes even though, in some cases, it is allowed when computing taxable income. Thus, an adjustment is required for the deferred gain attributable to sales of property made during the year under the installment method. Specifically, all principal payments are treated as having been received in the year of sale.[5]

---

[5]§ 312(n)(5).

EXAMPLE 6

In 2014, Cardinal Corporation, a calendar year taxpayer, sells unimproved real estate (basis of $20,000) for $100,000. Under the terms of the sale, Cardinal will receive two annual payments of $50,000 beginning in 2015, each with interest of 9%. Cardinal does not elect out of the installment method.

Because Cardinal's 2014 taxable income will not reflect any of the gain from the sale, the corporation must make an $80,000 positive adjustment for that year (the deferred gain from the sale) in computing current E & P. Then $40,000 negative adjustments are required in 2015 and 2016 when the deferred gain is recognized under the installment method.

Treatment of the gain for regular tax and E & P purposes can be summarized as follows. A similar analysis can be used for most of the timing and accounting method adjustments.

Tax Year	Regular Tax	E & P Treatment	E & P Adjustment
2014	$ –0–	$80,000	+$80,000
2015	40,000	–0–	–40,000
2016	40,000	–0–	–40,000

The alternative depreciation system (ADS) is used in computing E & P.[6] This method requires straight-line depreciation with a half-year convention, over a recovery period equal to the Asset Depreciation Range (ADR) midpoint life.[7] If MACRS cost recovery is used for income tax purposes, a positive or negative adjustment equal to the difference between MACRS and ADS must be made each year. Finally, no additional first-year depreciation is allowed under the ADS.[8]

Likewise, when assets are disposed of, an additional adjustment to taxable income is required to allow for the difference in gain or loss resulting from the difference in income tax basis and E & P basis.[9] The adjustments arising from depreciation are illustrated in the following example.

EXAMPLE 7

On January 2, 2014, White Corporation purchased equipment with an ADR midpoint life of 10 years for $30,000. The equipment was then depreciated over its 7-year MACRS class life. No § 179 or additional first-year depreciation was claimed. The asset was sold on July 2, 2016, for $27,000. For purposes of determining taxable income and E & P, cost recovery claimed on the equipment is summarized below.

Year	Cost Recovery Computation	MACRS	ADS	E & P Adjustment
2014	$30,000 × 14.29%	$ 4,287		
	$30,000 ÷ 10-year ADR recovery period × ½ (half-year for first year of service)		$1,500	$2,787
2015	$30,000 × 24.49%	7,347		
	$30,000 ÷ 10-year ADR recovery period		3,000	4,347
2016	$30,000 × 17.49% × ½ (half-year for year of disposal)	2,624		
	$30,000 ÷ 10-year ADR recovery period × ½ (half-year for year of disposal)		1,500	1,124
Total cost recovery		$14,258	$6,000	$8,258

Each year, White Corporation increases its taxable income by the adjustment amount indicated above to determine E & P. In addition, when computing 2016 E & P, White reduces taxable income by $8,258 to account for the excess gain recognized for income tax purposes.

continued

---

[6]§ 312(k)(3)(A).

[7]See § 168(g)(2). The ADR midpoint life for most assets is set out in Rev.Proc. 87–56, 1987–2 C.B. 674. The recovery period is 5 years for automobiles and light-duty trucks and 40 years for real property. For assets with no class life, the recovery period is 12 years.

[8]§ 168(k)(2). Under the MACRS provisions, additional first-year cost recovery is available for certain assets placed in service from 2008 through 2014.

[9]§ 312(f)(1).

	Income Tax	E & P
Amount realized	$ 27,000	$ 27,000
Adjusted basis for income tax ($30,000 cost − $14,258 MACRS)	(15,742)	
Adjusted basis for E & P ($30,000 cost − $6,000 ADS)		(24,000)
Gain on sale	$ 11,258	$ 3,000
Adjustment amount ($3,000 − $11,258)	($ 8,258)	

In addition to more conservative depreciation methods, the E & P rules impose limitations on the deductibility of § 179 expense.[10] In particular, this expense is deducted over a period of five years for E & P purposes. Thus, in any year that § 179 is elected, 80 percent of the resulting expense is added back to taxable income to determine current E & P. In each of the following four years, a subtraction from taxable income equal to 20 percent of the § 179 expense is made.

EXAMPLE 8

On January 2, 2014, LarsonCo placed in service a five-year depreciable asset. The acquisition price of the asset was $50,000, and LarsonCo claimed a § 179 deduction for the full amount. Treatment of the § 179 amounts for regular tax and E & P purposes can be summarized as follows.

Tax Year	Regular Tax	E & P Treatment	E & P Adjustment
2014	$50,000	$10,000	+$40,000
2015	–0–	10,000	−10,000
2016	–0–	10,000	−10,000
2017	–0–	10,000	−10,000
2018	–0–	10,000	−10,000

The E & P rules also require specific accounting methods in various situations, making adjustments necessary when certain methods are used for income tax purposes. For example, E & P requires cost depletion rather than percentage depletion. When accounting for long-term contracts, E & P rules specify the percentage of completion method rather than the completed contract method. As the E & P determination does not allow for the amortization of organizational expenses, any such expense deducted when computing taxable income must be added back.

To account for income deferral under the LIFO inventory method, the E & P computation requires an adjustment for changes in the LIFO recapture amount (the excess of FIFO over LIFO inventory value) during the year. Increases in the LIFO recapture amount are added to taxable income and decreases are subtracted, to the extent of prior-year increases.

E & P rules also specify that intangible drilling costs and mine exploration and development costs be amortized over a period of 60 months and 120 months, respectively.[11] For income tax purposes, however, these costs can be deducted currently.

13-2b **Summary of E & P Adjustments**

E & P serves as a measure of the earnings of the corporation that are available for distribution as taxable dividends to the shareholders. Current E & P is determined by making a series of adjustments to the corporation's taxable income. These adjustments are reviewed in Concept Summary 13.1.

LO.3

Apply the rules for assigning earnings and profits to distributions.

13-2c **Allocating E & P to Distributions**

When a positive balance exists in both the current and accumulated E & P accounts, corporate distributions are deemed to be made first from current E & P and then from

---

[10]§ 312(k)(3)(B).   [11]§ 312(n).

Concept Summary 13.1

Computing E & P

Transaction	Adjustment to Taxable Income to Determine Current E & P	
	Addition	**Subtraction**
Tax-exempt income	X	
Dividends received deduction	X	
Collection of proceeds from insurance policy on life of corporate officer (in excess of cash surrender value)	X	
Deferred gain on installment sale (all of the gain is added to E & P in year of sale)	X	
Future recognition of installment sale gross profit		X
Excess capital loss		X
Excess charitable contribution (over 10% limitation) in year incurred		X
Deduction of charitable contribution, NOL, or capital loss carryovers in succeeding taxable years (increase E & P because deduction reduces taxable income while E & P was reduced in a prior year)	X	
Federal income taxes paid		X
Federal income tax refund	X	
Loss on sale between related parties		X
Nondeductible fines, penalties, lobbying costs, meals, and entertainment		X
Payment of premiums on insurance policy on life of corporate officer (in excess of increase in cash surrender value of policy)		X
Realized gain (not recognized) on an involuntary conversion	No effect	
Realized gain or loss (not recognized) on a like-kind exchange	No effect	
Excess percentage depletion (only cost depletion can reduce E & P)	X	
Accelerated depreciation (E & P is reduced only by straight-line, units-of-production, or machine hours depreciation)	X	X
Additional first-year depreciation	X	
Domestic production activities deduction	X	
§ 179 expense in year elected (80%)	X	
§ 179 expense in four years following election (20% each year)		X
Increase (decrease) in LIFO recapture amount	X	X
Intangible drilling costs deducted currently (reduce E & P in future years by amortizing costs over 60 months)	X	
Mine exploration and development costs (reduce E & P in future years by amortizing costs over 120 months)	X	

accumulated E & P. When distributions exceed the amount of current E & P, it becomes necessary to allocate current and accumulated E & P to each distribution made during the year. First, dollars of current E & P are applied on a pro rata basis to each distribution. Then accumulated E & P is applied in chronological order, beginning with the earliest distribution. This allocation is important if any shareholder sells stock during the year.

EXAMPLE

9

On January 1 of the current year, Black Corporation holds accumulated E & P of $10,000. Current E & P for the year amounts to $30,000, earned evenly throughout the year. Megan and Matt are the sole *equal* shareholders of Black from January 1 to July 31.

On August 1, Megan sells all of her stock to Helen. Black makes two distributions to shareholders during the year: $40,000 to Megan and Matt ($20,000 to each) on July 1 and $40,000 to Matt and Helen ($20,000 to each) on December 1. Current and accumulated E & P are applied to the two distributions as follows.

	Source of Distribution		
	Current E & P	Accumulated E & P	Return of Capital
July 1 distribution ($40,000)	$15,000	$10,000	$15,000
December 1 distribution ($40,000)	15,000	–0–	25,000

Because 50% of the total distributions are made on July 1 and December 1, respectively, one-half of current E & P is assigned to each of the two distributions. Accumulated E & P is applied in chronological order, so the entire amount attaches to the July 1 distribution. The tax consequences to the shareholders follow.

	Shareholder		
	Megan	Matt	Helen
July distribution ($40,000)			
Dividend income—			
From current E & P ($15,000)	$ 7,500	$ 7,500	$ –0–
From accumulated E & P ($10,000)	5,000	5,000	–0–
Return of capital ($15,000)	7,500	7,500	–0–
December distribution ($40,000)			
Dividend income—			
From current E & P ($15,000)	–0–	7,500	7,500
From accumulated E & P ($0)	–0–	–0–	–0–
Return of capital ($25,000)	–0–	12,500	12,500
Total distribution	$20,000	$40,000	$20,000
Total dividend income	$12,500	$20,000	$ 7,500
Nontaxable return of capital (assuming sufficient basis in the stock investment)	$ 7,500	$20,000	$12,500

Because the balance in the accumulated E & P account is exhausted when it is applied to the July 1 distribution, Megan has more dividend income than Helen does, even though both receive equal distributions during the year. In addition, each shareholder's basis is reduced by the nontaxable return of capital; any excess over basis results in taxable gain.

When the tax years of the corporation and its shareholders are not the same, it may be impossible to determine the amount of current E & P on a timely basis. For example, if shareholders use a calendar year and the corporation uses a fiscal year, current E & P may not be ascertainable until after the shareholders' tax returns have been filed. To address this timing issue, the allocation rules presume that current E & P is sufficient to cover every distribution made during the year until the parties can show otherwise.

EXAMPLE
10

Green Corporation uses a June 30 fiscal year for tax purposes. Carol, Green's only shareholder, uses a calendar year. On July 1, 2014, Green has a zero balance in its accumulated E & P account. For fiscal year 2014–2015, the corporation incurs a $5,000 deficit in current E & P. On August 1, 2014, Green distributed $10,000 to Carol. The distribution is dividend income to Carol and is reported when she files her income tax return for the 2014 calendar year, on or before April 15, 2015.

Because Carol cannot prove until June 30, 2015, at the earliest, that the corporation has generated a deficit for the fiscal year, she must assume that the $10,000 distribution is fully drawn from a positive current E & P. When Carol learns of the deficit, she can file an amended return for 2014 showing the $10,000 as a return of capital. Alternatively, Carol can file for an extension for her 2014 return while she awaits Green Corporation's fiscal year-end.

Additional difficulties arise when either the current or the accumulated E & P account has a deficit balance. In particular, when current E & P is positive and accumulated E & P has a deficit balance, accumulated E & P is *not* netted against current E & P. Instead, the distribution is deemed to be a taxable dividend to the extent of the positive current E & P balance.

The Big Picture

Return to the facts of *The Big Picture* on p. 13-1. Recall that Lime Corporation had a deficit in GAAP-based retained earnings at the start of the year and banner profits during the year. Assume that these financial results translate into an $800,000 deficit in accumulated E & P at the start of the year and current E & P of $600,000. In addition, for purposes of this example, assume that there is no mortgage on the real estate.

In this case, current E & P would exceed the total cash and property distributed to the shareholders. The distributions are treated as taxable dividends; they are deemed to be paid from current E & P even though Lime still has a deficit in accumulated E & P at the end of the year.

In contrast to the previous rule, when a deficit exists in current E & P and a positive balance exists in accumulated E & P, the accounts are netted at the date of distribution. If the resulting balance is zero or negative, the distribution is a return of capital. If a positive balance results, the distribution is a dividend to the extent of the balance. Any loss in current E & P is deemed to accrue ratably throughout the year unless the parties can show otherwise. Various E & P rules are indicated in Concept Summary 13.2.

At the beginning of the current year, Gray Corporation (a calendar year taxpayer) has accumulated E & P of $10,000. During the year, the corporation incurs a $15,000 deficit in current E & P that accrues ratably. On July 1, Gray distributes $6,000 in cash to Hal, its sole shareholder. To determine how much of the $6,000 cash distribution represents dividend income to Hal, the balances of both accumulated and current E & P as of July 1 are determined and netted. This occurs because of the deficit in current E & P.

	Source of Distribution	
	Current E & P	**Accumulated E & P**
January 1		$10,000
July 1 (1/2 of $15,000 deficit in current E & P)	($7,500)	2,500
July 1 distribution of $6,000:		
Dividend income: $2,500		
Return of capital: $3,500		

The balance in E & P just before the July 1 distribution is $2,500. Thus, of the $6,000 distribution, $2,500 is taxed as a dividend, and $3,500 represents a return of capital.

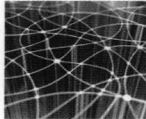

BRIDGE DISCIPLINE   **Bridge to Finance**

Investors often have tried to read the dividend policies of a corporation as indicators of the strength of the entity: constant dividend payments indicated a stable financial structure for the corporation, while dividend increases were a predictor of good times and triggered stock price increases. Reductions in historic dividend payment patterns foreshadowed financial difficulties and often caused a quick and sizable drop in share price.

Nobel Prize winners Merton Miller, University of Chicago, and Franco Modigliani, MIT, saw things differently. They viewed dividends as a remnant of various financing sources available to the corporation: if it was cheaper to finance future growth by retaining profits and decreasing or eliminating dividend payments, so be it. The entity must reduce

its cost of capital wherever possible, and under this interpretation, a dividend decrease might indicate the internal financial strength of the corporation. Conversely, the payment of a dividend reduces the capital available to the entity, thereby forcing the entity to finance its operations and growth from some third-party source and risking future weakness if the cost of that capital increases.

Miller and Modigliani found that stock price and dividend policy were unrelated, and that changes in dividend patterns should not affect the capitalized value of the business. Even with lower tax rates on dividends, few shareholders complain that the typical growth stock rarely pays dividends. Nevertheless, shares of companies that pay dividends outperform those that don't pay dividends.

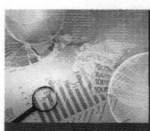

TAX PLANNING STRATEGIES   **Corporate Distributions**

FRAMEWORK FOCUS: INCOME AND EXCLUSIONS

Strategy: Avoid Income Recognition.

In connection with the discussion of corporate distributions, the following points need reinforcement.

- Because E & P is the measure of dividend income, its periodic determination is essential to corporate planning. Thus, an E & P account should be established and maintained, particularly if the possibility exists that a corporate distribution might be a return of capital.

- Accumulated E & P is the sum of all past years' current E & P. Because there is no statute of limitations on the computation of E & P, the IRS can redetermine a corporation's current E & P for a tax year long since passed. Such a change affects accumulated E & P and has a direct impact on the taxability of current distributions to shareholders.

- Distributions can be planned to avoid or minimize dividend exposure.

EXAMPLE 13

Flicker Corporation has accumulated E & P of $100,000 as of January 1 of the current year. During the year, it expects to generate earnings from operations of $80,000 and to sell an asset for a loss of $100,000. Thus, it anticipates a current E & P deficit of $20,000. Flicker also expects to make a cash distribution of $60,000.

A tax-effective approach is to recognize the loss as soon as possible and immediately thereafter make the cash distribution to the shareholders. Suppose these two steps take place on January 1. Because the current E & P has a deficit, the accumulated E & P account must be brought up to date (refer to Example 12). Thus, at the time of the distribution, the combined E & P balance is zero [$100,000 (beginning balance in accumulated E & P) − $100,000 (existing deficit in current E & P)], and the $60,000 distribution to the shareholders constitutes a return of capital. Current deficits are deemed to accrue pro rata throughout the year unless the parties can prove otherwise. Here they can.

continued

EXAMPLE 14

After several unprofitable years, Darter Corporation has a deficit in accumulated E & P of $100,000 as of January 1, 2014. Starting in 2014, Darter expects to generate annual E & P of $50,000 for the next four years and would like to distribute this amount to its shareholders. The corporation's cash position (for dividend purposes) will correspond to the current E & P generated. Compare the following possibilities.

1. On December 31 of 2014, 2015, 2016, and 2017, Darter Corporation distributes cash of $50,000.
2. On December 31 of 2015 and 2017, Darter Corporation distributes cash of $100,000.

The two alternatives are illustrated as follows.

Year	Accumulated E & P (First of Year)	Current E & P	Distribution	Amount of Dividend
	Alternative 1			
2014	($100,000)	$50,000	$50,000	$50,000
2015	(100,000)	50,000	50,000	50,000
2016	(100,000)	50,000	50,000	50,000
2017	(100,000)	50,000	50,000	50,000
	Alternative 2			
2014	($100,000)	$50,000	$ –0–	$ –0–
2015	(50,000)	50,000	100,000	50,000
2016	(50,000)	50,000	–0–	–0–
2017	–0–	50,000	100,000	50,000

Alternative 1 produces $200,000 of dividend income because each $50,000 distribution is fully paid from current E & P. Alternative 2, however, produces only $100,000 of dividend income to the shareholders. The remaining $100,000 is a return of capital. Why?

At the time Darter made its first distribution of $100,000 on December 31, 2015, it had a deficit of $50,000 in accumulated E & P (the original deficit of $100,000 is reduced by the $50,000 of current E & P from 2014). Consequently, the $100,000 distribution yields a $50,000 dividend (the current E & P for 2015), and $50,000 is treated as a return of capital. As of January 1, 2016, Darter's accumulated E & P now has a deficit balance of $50,000, because a distribution cannot increase a deficit in E & P. Adding the remaining $50,000 of current E & P from 2016, the balance as of January 1, 2017, is zero. Thus, the second distribution of $100,000 made on December 31, 2017, also yields $50,000 of dividends (the current E & P for 2017) and a $50,000 return of capital.

Concept Summary 13.2

Allocating E & P to Distributions

1. Current E & P is applied first to distributions on a pro rata basis; then accumulated E & P is applied (as necessary) in chronological order beginning with the earliest distribution. See Example 9.

2. Until the parties can show otherwise, it is presumed that current E & P covers all distributions. See Example 10.

3. When a deficit exists in accumulated E & P and a positive balance exists in current E & P, distributions are regarded as dividends to the extent of current E & P. See Example 11.

4. When a deficit exists in current E & P and a positive balance exists in accumulated E & P, the two accounts are netted at the date of distribution. If the resulting balance is zero or a deficit, the distribution is treated as a return of capital, first reducing the basis of the stock to zero, then generating taxable gain. If a positive balance results, the distribution is a dividend to the extent of the balance. Any loss in current E & P is deemed to accrue ratably throughout the year unless the corporation can show otherwise. See Example 12.

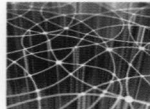

BRIDGE DISCIPLINE **Bridge to Investments**

Most investors look to the stocks of utilities, real estate investment trusts, and tobacco companies as the source of steady dividend payments. This is a prudent decision on the investor's part, as the typical S&P 500 stock offers a dividend yield of about 2 percent. But an investor could put together an effective portfolio using only stocks and mutual funds that regularly produce higher dividend yields.

Dividends can be important to the investor because:

• They can be used in a tax-sheltered account, like a § 401(k) plan, such that the tax inefficiency of the dividends is not recognized immediately by the investor.

• Even today, about 40 percent of the total return from an investment can be traced to holding stocks that make regular distributions.

• Generally, a dividend-paying company is a profitable company, and corporate profits often are hard to come by.

• Earning and reinvesting dividends is an easy way to put into place an investment policy of dollar-cost averaging, a technique that forces the investor to buy more shares when prices are low and fewer shares when prices are high. Dollar-cost averaging often implements a contrarian investment strategy.

LO.4

Evaluate the tax effects of noncash dividends on the recipient shareholder and the corporation making the distribution.

13-3 NONCASH DIVIDENDS

The previous discussion assumed that all distributions by a corporation to its shareholders are in the form of cash. Although most corporate distributions are paid in cash, a corporation may distribute a noncash, or property dividend for various reasons. For example, the shareholders may want a particular asset that is held by the corporation. Or a corporation that is strapped for cash may want to distribute a dividend to its shareholders.

Distributions of noncash assets are treated for tax purposes the same as distributions of cash, except for effects attributable to any difference between the basis and the fair market value of the distributed property. Distributions of property with a basis that differs from fair market value raise several tax questions.

• For the shareholder:
  • What is the amount of the distribution?
  • What is the basis of the property in the shareholder's hands?
• For the corporation:
  • Is a gain or loss recognized as a result of the distribution?
  • What is the effect of the distribution on E & P?

13-3a Noncash Dividends—Effect on the Shareholder

When a corporation distributes property rather than cash to a shareholder, the amount distributed is measured by the fair market value of the property on the date of distribution.[12] As with a cash distribution, the portion of a property distribution covered by existing E & P is a dividend, and any excess is treated as a return of capital. If the fair market value of the property distributed exceeds the corporation's E & P and the shareholder's basis in the stock investment, a capital gain usually results.

The amount distributed is reduced by any liabilities to which the distributed property is subject immediately before and immediately after the distribution and by any liabilities of the corporation assumed by the shareholder. The basis in the distributed property to the shareholder is the fair market value of the property on the date of the distribution.

---

[12]§ 301.

The Big Picture

Return to the facts of *The Big Picture* on p. 13-1. Lime Corporation distributed property with a $300,000 fair market value and $20,000 adjusted basis to Gustavo, one of its shareholders. The property was subject to a $100,000 mortgage, which Gustavo assumed. As a result, Gustavo reports a distribution of $200,000 [$300,000 (fair market value) − $100,000 (liability)], which is taxed as a dividend. The basis of the property to Gustavo is $300,000, its fair market value.

EXAMPLE 15

Red Corporation owns 10% of Tan Corporation. Tan has ample E & P to cover any distributions made during the year. One distribution made to Red consists of a vacant lot with a basis of $50,000 and a fair market value of $30,000. Red recognizes dividend income of $30,000 (before the dividends received deduction), and its basis in the lot becomes $30,000.

EXAMPLE 16

Distributing property that has depreciated in value as a property dividend may reflect poor income tax planning. Note what happens in Example 16. Basis of $20,000 disappears due to the loss (Tan's basis $50,000, fair market value $30,000). As an alternative, if Tan Corporation sells the lot, it can use the $20,000 loss to reduce its taxes. Then Tan can distribute the $30,000 cash proceeds to its shareholders.

13-3b Noncash Dividends—Effect on the Corporation

As noted earlier, the distribution of a property dividend raises two questions related to the corporation's tax position: Is a gain or loss recognized? What is the effect on E & P?

Recognition of Gain or Loss

All distributions of appreciated property trigger a recognized gain to the distributing corporation.[13] In effect, a corporation that distributes appreciated property is treated as if it had sold the property to the shareholder for its fair market value. However, the distributing corporation does *not* recognize any realized loss on the distributed property.

The Big Picture

Return to the facts of *The Big Picture* on p. 13-1. Lime Corporation distributed property with a fair market value of $300,000 and an adjusted basis of $20,000 to Gustavo, one of its shareholders. As a result, Lime recognizes a $280,000 gain on the distribution.

EXAMPLE 17

A corporation distributes land with a basis of $30,000 and a fair market value of $10,000. The corporation does not recognize a loss on the distribution.

EXAMPLE 18

If the distributed property is subject to a liability in excess of basis or the shareholder assumes such a liability, a special rule applies. For purposes of determining gain on the distribution, the fair market value of the property is treated as being at least the amount of the liability.[14]

Assume that the land in Example 18 is subject to a liability of $35,000, which is assumed by the shareholder who receives the land. The corporation recognizes gain of $5,000 on the distribution ($35,000 liability − $30,000 basis in the land).

EXAMPLE 19

Effect of Corporate Distributions on E & P

Corporate distributions reduce E & P by the amount of money distributed and by the greater of the fair market value or the adjusted basis of property distributed, less the amount of any liability on the property.[15] E & P is increased by gain recognized when appreciated property is distributed as a property dividend.

---

[13]§ 311.
[14]§ 311(b)(2).
[15]§§ 312(a), (b), and (c).

Effects of Noncash Distributions

Crimson Corporation distributes property (basis $10,000 and fair market value $20,000) to Brenda, its shareholder. Crimson recognizes a $10,000 gain, which is added to its E & P. E & P then is reduced by $20,000, the fair market value of the distributed property. Brenda reports dividend income of $20,000 (presuming sufficient E & P).

Assume the same facts as in Example 20, except that the property's adjusted basis to Crimson is $25,000. Crimson's E & P is reduced by $25,000, the property's adjusted basis, which is greater than the property's fair market value. Brenda reports dividend income of $20,000 (the fair market value of the property received).

Assume the same facts as in Example 21, except that the property is subject to a liability of $6,000, which Brenda assumes. E & P is now reduced by $19,000 [$25,000 (adjusted basis) − $6,000 (liability)]. Brenda records a dividend of $14,000 [$20,000 (amount of the distribution) − $6,000 (liability)], and her basis in the property is $20,000, its fair market value.

Under no circumstances can a distribution, whether cash or property, either generate a deficit in E & P or add to a deficit in E & P. Deficits can arise only through recognized corporate losses.

EXAMPLE 23

Teal Corporation holds accumulated E & P of $10,000 at the beginning of the current tax year. During the year, it records current E & P of $15,000. At the end of the year, it distributes cash of $30,000 to its sole shareholder, Walter.

Teal's E & P at the end of the year is reduced to zero by the dividend distribution. The remaining $5,000 of the distribution to Walter cannot generate a deficit in E & P.

Source of Distribution	Effects
Current E & P	($15,000)
Accumulated E & P	(10,000)
Return of Capital	5,000

BRIDGE DISCIPLINE **Bridge to Finance**

The double tax on corporate income always has been controversial. Arguably, taxing dividends twice creates several undesirable economic distortions, including:

- An incentive to invest in noncorporate rather than corporate entities.

- An incentive for corporations to finance operations with debt rather than with equity because interest payments are deductible. Notably, this behavior increases the vulnerability of corporations in economic downturns because of higher leverage.

- An incentive for corporations to retain earnings and structure distributions of profits to avoid the double tax.

Collectively, these distortions raise the cost of capital for corporate investments. In addition, elimination of the double tax would make the United States more competitive globally, as a majority of U.S. trading partners assess only one tax on corporate income.

While many support a reduced or zero tax rate on dividends, others contend that the double tax should remain in place to rein in the concentration of economic power held by publicly traded corporations. Those favoring retention of the double tax also note that the benefits of reduced tax rates on dividends flow disproportionately to the wealthy.

DIGGING DEEPER **1** | **In-depth coverage can be found on this book's companion website: www.cengagebrain.com**

13-4 CONSTRUCTIVE DIVIDENDS

Any measurable economic benefit conveyed by a corporation to its shareholders can be treated as a dividend for Federal income tax purposes even though it is not formally declared or designated as a dividend. A so-called constructive dividend typically is not issued pro rata to all shareholders.[16] Nor must the distribution satisfy the legal requirements of a dividend as set forth by applicable state law.

Constructive dividends usually arise in the context of closely held corporations. Here the dealings between the parties are less structured, and frequently, formalities are not preserved. The constructive dividend might be seen as a substitute for actual distributions. Usually, it is intended to accomplish some tax objective not available through the direct payment of dividends. The shareholders may be attempting to distribute corporate profits in a form, such as compensation, that is deductible to the corporation. Alternatively, the shareholders may be seeking benefits for themselves while avoiding the recognition of income.

Some constructive dividends are, in reality, disguised dividends. But not all constructive dividends are deliberate attempts to avoid actual and formal dividends; many are inadvertent. Thus, an awareness of the various constructive dividend situations is essential to protect the parties from unanticipated, undesirable tax consequences.

13-4a Types of Constructive Dividends

The most frequently encountered types of constructive dividends are summarized below and on the following pages.

Shareholder Use of Corporate-Owned Property

A constructive dividend can occur when a shareholder uses the corporation's property for personal purposes at no cost. Personal use of corporate-owned automobiles, airplanes, yachts, fishing camps, hunting lodges, and other entertainment facilities is commonplace in some closely held corporations. The shareholder has dividend income to the extent of the fair rental value of the property for the period of its personal use.[17]

Bargain Sale of Corporate Property to a Shareholder

Shareholders often purchase property from a corporation at a cost below the fair market value of the property. These bargain sales produce dividend income to the extent the property's fair market value on the date of sale differs from the amount the shareholder paid for the property.[18] These situations might be avoided by appraising the property on or about the date of the sale. The appraised value should become the price to be paid by the shareholder.

Bargain Rental of Corporate Property

A bargain rental of corporate property by a shareholder also produces dividend income. Here the measure of the constructive dividend is the excess of the property's fair rental value over the rent actually paid. Again, appraisal data should be used to avoid any questionable situations.

Payments for the Benefit of a Shareholder

If a corporation pays an obligation of a shareholder, the payment is treated as a constructive dividend. The obligation involved need not be legally binding on the shareholder; it may, in fact, be a moral obligation.[19] Forgiveness of shareholder indebtedness

---

[16]See *Lengsfield v. Comm.*, 57–1 USTC ¶9437, 50 AFTR 1683, 241 F.2d 508 (CA–5, 1957).

[17]*Daniel L. Reeves*, 94 TCM 287, T.C.Memo. 2007–273.

[18]Reg. § 1.301–1(j).

[19]*Montgomery Engineering Co. v. U.S.*, 64–2 USTC ¶9618, 13 AFTR 2d 1747, 230 F.Supp. 838 (D.Ct. N.J., 1964), *aff'd* in 65–1 USTC ¶9368, 15 AFTR 2d 746, 344 F.2d 996 (CA–3, 1965).

GLOBAL TAX ISSUES   **A Worldwide View of Dividends**

From an international perspective, U.S. double taxation of dividends is unusual. Most developed countries have adopted a policy of corporate integration, which imposes a single tax on corporate profits. Corporate integration takes several forms. One popular approach is to impose a tax at the corporate level, but allow shareholders to claim a credit for corporate-level taxes paid when dividends are received. A second alternative is to allow a corporate-level deduction for dividends paid to shareholders. A third approach is to allow shareholders to exclude corporate dividends from income. A fourth alternative is the adoption of a "comprehensive business income tax," which excludes both dividend and interest income while disallowing deductions for interest expense.

Facing trade-offs between equity and the economic distortions introduced by the double tax and the prevalence of corporate integration throughout the world, the United States continues to struggle with the issue of how corporate distributions should be taxed.

by the corporation creates an identical problem.[20] Excessive rentals paid by a corporation for the use of shareholder property also are treated as constructive dividends.

Unreasonable Compensation

A salary payment to a shareholder-employee that is deemed to be **unreasonable compensation** is frequently treated as a constructive dividend. As a consequence, it is not deductible by the corporation. In determining the reasonableness of salary payments, the following factors are considered.

- The employee's qualifications.
- A comparison of salaries with dividend distributions.
- The prevailing rates of compensation for comparable positions in comparable business concerns.
- The nature and scope of the employee's work.
- The size and complexity of the business.
- A comparison of salaries paid with both gross and net income.
- The taxpayer's salary policy toward all employees.
- For small corporations with a limited number of officers, the amount of compensation paid to the employee in question in previous years.
- For large corporations, whether a "reasonable investor" would have agreed to the level of compensation paid.[21]

Loans to Shareholders

Advances to shareholders that are not bona fide loans usually are reclassified as constructive dividends. Whether an advance qualifies as a bona fide loan is a question of fact to be determined in light of the particular circumstances. Factors considered in determining whether the advance is a bona fide loan include the following.[22]

- Whether the advance is on open account or is evidenced by a written instrument.
- Whether the shareholder furnished collateral or other security for the advance.
- How long the advance has been outstanding.
- Whether any repayments have been made.

---

[20]Reg. § 1.301–1(m).

[21]*Mayson Manufacturing Co. v. Comm.*, 49–2 USTC ¶9467, 38 AFTR 1028, 178 F.2d 115 (CA–6, 1949) and *Alpha Medical v. Comm.*, 99–1 USTC ¶50,461, 83 AFTR 2d 99–697, 172 F.3d 942 (CA–6, 1999).

[22]*Fin Hay Realty Co. v. U.S.*, 68–2 USTC ¶9438, 22 AFTR 2d 5004, 398 F.2d 694 (CA–3, 1968).

TAX IN THE NEWS **Hard Work Pays Off!**

By 1985, William Rogers, a pharmacist with 25 years of experience in health care, had successfully developed and sold two businesses—a pharmacy chain and a medical supply company. In 1986, after turning down a $1 million offer to manage the home health care division of a large corporation, Rogers founded Alpha Medical, Inc., with a $1,000 contribution. Over the next four years, Rogers built Alpha Medical into a business with 60 employees, a taxable income of almost $7 million, and a 1990 return on equity of almost 100 percent. The business provided both financial management and medical consulting services to hospitals and home health care companies.

Rogers was the company's sole shareholder and president. He regularly worked 12 hours a day and was on call 24 hours a day. Rogers made all major decisions for Alpha Medical, acquired all of the company's clients, and personally negotiated all of the company's contracts. In addition, he personally developed many of the company's products and collaborated with programmers to develop proprietary software used by the company.

In 1986, Rogers received only $67,000 in compensation. The amount increased to $431,000 in 1988 and $928,000 in 1989. In 1990, Rogers was paid over $4.4 million, 64 percent of the company's taxable income, while the company paid only a $1,500 dividend.

During an audit of Alpha Medical, the IRS argued that only $400,000 of Rogers' compensation in 1990 was reasonable and that the remaining $4 million was not deductible. As a result, the IRS assessed a $1.3 million tax deficiency and an accuracy-related penalty.

The Tax Court split the difference between the IRS and the taxpayer, holding that $2.3 million of Rogers' pay was reasonable. On appeal, however, the Sixth Circuit Court of Appeals ruled that all $4.4 million of the compensation paid to Rogers was reasonable. In its decision, the Court of Appeals said that "in light of Rogers' record of accomplishment, risks he assumed, and amazing growth, reasonable shareholders would have gladly agreed to Rogers' level of compensation."

The Court of Appeals also explicitly noted that Rogers had been undercompensated in prior years and that he had incurred a substantial opportunity cost when he refused the $1 million job offer so that he could start Alpha Medical.

- The shareholder's ability to repay the advance.
- The shareholder's use of the funds (e.g., payment of routine bills versus nonrecurring, extraordinary expenses).
- The regularity of the advances.
- The dividend-paying history of the corporation.

Even when a corporation makes a bona fide loan to a shareholder, a constructive dividend may be triggered, equal to the amount of any imputed (forgone) interest on the loan.[23] Imputed interest equals the amount of interest (using the rate the Federal government pays on new borrowings, compounded semiannually) that exceeds the interest charged on the loan. The corporation reports both interest income and a nondeductible dividend payment, and the shareholder records taxable dividend income and an interest payment.

EXAMPLE 24

Mallard Corporation lends its principal shareholder, Henry, $100,000 on January 2 of the current year. The loan is interest-free and payable on demand. On December 31, the imputed interest rules are applied. Assuming that the Federal interest rate is 3%, compounded semiannually, the amount of imputed interest is $3,045. This amount is deemed paid by Henry to Mallard in the form of interest. Mallard then is deemed to return the amount to Henry as a constructive dividend.

Thus, Henry reports dividend income of $3,045 and perhaps a deduction for the interest deemed paid to Mallard. Mallard records interest income of $3,045 for the amount that it was deemed to have received, with no deduction for the dividend payment.

---

[23]See § 7872. A more detailed discussion of imputed interest is found in Chapter 4.

13-4b **Tax Treatment of Constructive Dividends**

For tax purposes, constructive distributions are treated the same as actual distributions.[24] Thus, a corporate shareholder is entitled to the dividends received deduction (refer to Chapter 12). The constructive distribution is taxable as a dividend only to the extent of the corporation's current and accumulated E & P. The burden rests with the taxpayer to prove that a distribution constitutes a return of capital because of a zero balance in E & P.[25]

 DIGGING DEEPER 2 | **In-depth coverage can be found on this book's companion website: www.cengagebrain.com**

TAX PLANNING STRATEGIES **Constructive Dividends**

FRAMEWORK FOCUS: INCOME AND EXCLUSIONS

Strategy: Avoid Income Recognition.

Tax planning can be particularly effective in avoiding constructive dividend situations. Shareholders should try to structure their dealings with the corporation on an arm's length basis. For example, reasonable rent should be paid for the use of corporate property, and a fair price should be paid for its purchase. The parties should make every effort to support the amount involved with appraisal data or market information obtained from reliable sources at or near the time of the transaction.

Dealings between shareholders and a closely held corporation should be as formal as possible. In the case of loans to shareholders, for example, the parties should provide for an adequate rate of interest and written evidence of the debt. Shareholders also should establish and follow a realistic repayment schedule.

If shareholders want to distribute corporate profits in a form deductible to the corporation, a balanced mix of the possible alternatives lessens the risk of constructive dividend treatment. Rent for the use of shareholder property, interest on amounts borrowed from shareholders, or salaries for services rendered by shareholders are all feasible substitutes for dividend distributions. But overdoing any one approach may attract the attention of the IRS. Too much interest, for example, may mean that the corporation is thinly capitalized, and some of the debt may be reclassified as equity.

Much can be done to protect against the disallowance of unreasonable compensation. Example 25 is an illustration, all too common in a family corporation, of what *not* to do.

 EXAMPLE 25

Bob Cole wholly owns Eagle Corporation. Corporate employees and annual salaries include Rebecca, Bob's wife ($120,000); Sam, Bob's son ($80,000); Bob ($640,000); and Ed, an unrelated longtime friend ($320,000). The operation of Eagle is shared about equally between Bob and Ed. Rebecca performed significant services for Eagle during its formative years but now merely attends the annual meeting of the board of directors. Sam is a full-time student and occasionally signs papers for the corporation in his capacity as treasurer.

Eagle has not made a cash distribution for 10 years, although it has accumulated substantial E & P. Rebecca, Sam, and Bob run the risk of a finding of unreasonable compensation, based on the following factors.

- Rebecca's salary is vulnerable unless proof is available that some or all of her $120,000 annual salary is payment for services rendered to the corporation in prior years and that she was underpaid for those years.[26]

continued

---

[24]*Simon v. Comm.*, 57–2 USTC ¶9989, 52 AFTR 698, 248 F.2d 869 (CA–8, 1957).

[25]*DiZenzo v. Comm.*, 65–2 USTC ¶9518, 16 AFTR 2d 5107, 348 F.2d 122 (CA–2, 1965).

[26]See, for example, *R. J. Nicoll Co.*, 59 T.C. 37 (1972).

- Sam's salary also is vulnerable; he does not appear to earn the $80,000 paid to him by the corporation. Although neither Sam nor Rebecca is a shareholder, each one's relationship to Bob is enough of a tie-in to raise the unreasonable compensation issue.

- Bob's salary appears susceptible to challenge. Why is he receiving $320,000 more than Ed when it appears that they share equally in the operation of the corporation?

- The fact that Eagle has not distributed any cash over the past 10 years, even though it is capable of doing so, increases the likelihood of a constructive dividend.

What could have been done to improve the tax position of the parties in Example 25? Rebecca and Sam are not entitled to a significant salary, as neither seems to be performing any services for the corporation. Bob probably should reduce his compensation to correspond to that paid to Ed. He then can attempt to distribute corporate earnings to himself in some other form.

Paying some dividends to Bob also would help alleviate the problems raised in Example 25. The IRS has been successful in denying a deduction for salary paid to a shareholder-employee, even when the payment was reasonable, in a situation where the corporation had not distributed any dividends.[27] Most courts, however, have not denied deductions for compensation solely because a dividend was not paid. A better approach is to compare an employee's compensation with the level of compensation prevalent in the particular industry.

The corporation can substitute *indirect* compensation for Bob by paying expenses that benefit him personally but are nevertheless deductible to the corporation. For example, premiums paid by the corporation for sickness, accident, and hospitalization insurance for Bob are deductible to the corporation and generally nontaxable to him.[28] Any payments under the policy are not taxable to Bob unless they exceed his medical expenses.[29]

The corporation also can pay for travel and entertainment expenses incurred by Bob on behalf of the corporation. If these expenditures are primarily for the benefit of the corporation, Bob recognizes no taxable income, and the corporation claims a deduction.[30] The tax treatment of these benefits is discussed in more detail in Chapter 11.

When testing for reasonableness, the IRS looks at the total compensation package, including indirect compensation payments to a shareholder-employee. Thus, indirect payments must not be overlooked.

What Is the Employee's Compensation?

EXAMPLE 26

Cora, the president and sole shareholder of Willet Corporation, is paid an annual salary of $100,000 by the corporation. Cora would like to draw funds from the corporation but is concerned that additional salary payments might cause the IRS to contend that her salary is unreasonable.

Cora does not want Willet to pay any dividends. She also wants to donate $50,000 to her alma mater to establish scholarships for needy students. Willet Corporation could make the contribution on Cora's behalf. The payment clearly benefits Cora, but the amount of the contribution is not taxed to her.[31] Willet claims a charitable contribution deduction for the payment.

EXAMPLE 27

Assume in Example 26 that Cora has made an individual pledge to the university to provide $50,000 for scholarships for needy students. Willet Corporation satisfies Cora's pledge by paying the $50,000 to the university. The $50,000 will be taxed to Cora. In this context, the $50,000 payment to the university may be treated as *indirect* compensation to Cora.[32]

continued

---

[27]*McCandless Tile Service v. U.S.*, 70–1 USTC ¶9284, 25 AFTR 2d 70–870, 422 F.2d 1336 (Ct.Cls., 1970). The court in *McCandless* concluded that a return on equity of 15% of net profits was reasonable.

[28]Reg. § 1.162–10.

[29]The medical reimbursement plan must meet certain nondiscrimination requirements. § 105(h)(2).

[30]Reg. § 1.62–2(c)(4).

[31]*Henry J. Knott*, 67 T.C. 681 (1977).

[32]*Schalk Chemical Co. v. Comm.*, 62–1 USTC ¶9496, 9 AFTR 2d 1579, 304 F.2d 48 (CA–9, 1962).

In determining whether Cora's salary is unreasonable, both the *direct* payment of $100,000 and the *indirect* $50,000 payment are considered. Cora's total compensation package is $150,000. Cora may be eligible for a charitable contribution deduction of up to 50% of her adjusted gross income (see Chapter 10).

Certain activities can combine both business and personal dimensions (e.g., a business trip to Hawaii). A country club membership can generate both business and personal use. Such items can be attractive as forms of indirect compensation, but disentangling the business and personal use of business assets can be a challenge.

In fact, many companies have policies that allow for the "limited personal use" of certain corporate assets (such as computers, telephones, mobile devices, copy machines, conference rooms, and vehicles). This "limited personal use" exception is normally provided as long as the use is occasional, is not for outside employment, does not result in excessive costs, and does not interfere with work responsibilities. Ultimately, whether a constructive dividend exists when indirect compensation is used often depends on the employer's policies and related documentation substantiating some business justification for the usage.

13-5 **STOCK DIVIDENDS**

LO.6

Distinguish between taxable and nontaxable stock dividends.

On occasion, a C corporation issues a dividend in the form of its own stock (i.e., instead of using cash or other property). This may occur because the entity is short of cash or because it wants to dispose of some treasury stock that it holds. A **stock dividend** is triggered by a board directive. Stock dividends are rare events; about 2 percent of all C corporation distributions during a typical tax year involve the corporation's own shares.

As a general rule, stock dividends are excluded from income if they are pro rata distributions of stock or stock rights paid on common stock.[33] However, there are exceptions to this general rule.

DIGGING DEEPER 3 | In-depth coverage can be found on this book's companion website: www.cengagebrain.com

---

FINANCIAL DISCLOSURE INSIGHTS   **Dividend Payments React to Tax Law Changes**

Recurring dividend payments are rare, but U.S. C corporations can pay dividends when they want to. A decade ago, when the tax law allowed a one-time exclusion for 85 percent of dividends repatriated from overseas subsidiaries, suddenly large corporate taxpayers responded. About 1,000 U.S. C corporations increased their dividend payments for the year by more than $300 billion over their average annual payments to shareholders. As a result, attributable Federal corporate income tax revenues increased by about $16 billion.

Some politicians are calling for adoption of another *tax holiday* of this sort, as a means of increasing U.S. jobs and decreasing the country's budget deficits. Estimates are that

Apple, Cisco, Google, and Microsoft alone have about $325 billion of cash overseas, and similar cash stockpiles can be found in the pharmaceutical, energy, and financial industries. Could a second tax holiday on dividends paid from offshore act as another economic stimulus and create thousands of new jobs, as some expect?

Some observers maintain that strings should be attached to the repatriated funds if the corporation is to enjoy the tax holiday. Oversight measures should be enacted, they say, to make certain the funds are not used for executive compensation or stock buybacks, as it appears was the case with the first tax holiday. The funds should be traceable to hiring, research, and infrastructure spending.

---

[33]Companies often issue stock dividends or authorize stock splits to keep the stock price in an affordable range. Stock splits do not change the total value of an investment. For example, 100 shares at $100 will become 200 shares at $50 after the split. However, some studies show that a stock split often leads to an upward price trend over the year following the split.

If a stock dividend is not taxable, the corporation's E & P is not reduced.[34] If a stock dividend is taxable, the distributing corporation treats the distribution in the same manner as any other taxable distribution.

If a stock dividend is taxable, the shareholder's basis of the newly received shares is fair market value and the holding period starts on the date of receipt. If a stock dividend is not taxable, the basis of the stock on which the dividend is distributed is reallocated.[35]

If the dividend shares are identical to these formerly held shares, basis in the old stock is reallocated by dividing the taxpayer's cost in the old stock by the total number of shares. If the dividend stock is not identical to the underlying shares (e.g., a stock dividend of preferred on common), basis is determined by allocating the basis of the formerly held shares between the old and new stock according to the fair market value of each. The holding period includes the holding period of the previously held stock.[36]

Stock Dividends

EXAMPLE 28

Gail bought 1,000 shares of common stock two years ago for $10,000. In the current tax year, Gail receives 10 shares of common stock as a nontaxable stock dividend. Gail's basis of $10,000 is divided by 1,010. Consequently, each share of stock has a basis of $9.90 instead of the pre-dividend $10 basis.

EXAMPLE 29

Assume instead that Gail received a nontaxable preferred stock dividend of 100 shares. The preferred stock has a fair market value of $1,000, and the common stock, on which the preferred is distributed, has a fair market value of $19,000. After the receipt of the stock dividend, the basis of the common stock is $9,500, and the basis of the preferred is $500, computed as follows.

Fair market value of common	$19,000
Fair market value of preferred	1,000
	$20,000
Basis of common: $19/20 \times \$10,000$	$ 9,500
Basis of preferred: $1/20 \times \$10,000$	$ 500

In-depth coverage can be found on this book's companion website: www.cengagebrain.com   **4 DIGGING DEEPER**

BRIDGE DISCIPLINE **Bridge to Finance**

Stock buybacks are popular among U.S. corporations as a means to manipulate share prices. If a buyback is executed properly, all shareholders retain their respective levels of control over the entity, but because fewer shares now are available on the market, an artificial increase in share price occurs. Often, the market temporarily "overcorrects" for the buyback, probably because of the publicity the transaction attracts in the press, and the corporation's total capitalized value actually increases.

Most stock buybacks result in dividend income to the shareholders. Stock redemptions of this type generally do not qualify for capital gain/loss treatment under the tax law. Thus, parties must measure the costs associated with an effective distribution of retained earnings in this way. If dividend income is subject to a favorable tax rate or if the corporate owner of the redeemed shares qualifies for the dividends received deduction, there are few impediments to the plans for the buyback.

Some analysts see an increase in stock buyback activity as a sign of an increasingly healthy economy. A combination of large corporate cash balances and low market interest rates also can accelerate the buyback market.

---

[34]§ 312(d)(1).

[35]§ 307(a).

[36]§ 1223(5).

LO.7

Discuss the tax treatment of stock redemptions and corporate liquidations.

13-6 STOCK REDEMPTIONS

Many investors are tempted to use a "no dividends" strategy in working with a healthy corporation whose accumulated profits and market value continue to rise over time.

EXAMPLE 30

Sally invests $100,000 in the new Cream Corporation. Cream is successful in generating operating profits, and it reinvests its accumulated profits in the business rather than paying dividends. Fifteen years later, Sally's shares are worth $300,000, and her share of Cream's E & P exceeds $1 million. Sally sells the shares for a $200,000 long-term capital gain, taxed at a rate of only 20%. By selling her stock to a third party, Sally can reduce the sales proceeds by her stock basis, resulting in a significant tax savings to her, at no detriment to Cream.

A similar strategy would seem to work where several shareholders can act in concert. Using a **stock redemption** to carry out this strategy, the corporation buys back shares from its shareholders in a market transaction. Stock redemptions occur for numerous reasons, including the following.

- To acquire the holdings of a retiring or deceased shareholder.
- To carry out a property settlement related to a divorce.
- To increase the per-share price of the stock as it trades in a market.
- To implement a business succession plan (e.g., using a buy-sell agreement to transfer shares from one generation of shareholders to a younger one).

Stock redemptions, generally result in dividend income for the shareholder whose stock is redeemed, rather than a capital gain or loss, unless the shareholder surrenders significant control in the entity as a result of the redemption. Capital gain/loss treatment largely is restricted to stock buybacks where either:

- All of the shareholder's stock is redeemed.[37]
- After the redemption, the investor is a minority shareholder and owns less than 80 percent of the interest owned in the corporation before the redemption.[38]

DIGGING DEEPER 5   In-depth coverage can be found on this book's companion website: www.cengagebrain.com

In measuring the investor's stock holdings before and after the redemption, shares owned by related taxpayers also are counted.[39]

DIGGING DEEPER 6   In-depth coverage can be found on this book's companion website: www.cengagebrain.com

EXAMPLE 31

Mike and Cheryl are husband and wife, and each owns 100 shares in Mauve Corporation, the total of all of Mauve's outstanding stock. Mauve's operations have produced a sizable aggregated operating profit over the years, such that its E & P exceeds $5 million. Mike and Cheryl have realized appreciation of $600,000 on their original investment of $100,000 each, and they would like to enjoy some of the cash that Mauve has accumulated during their holding period.

At Mike's request, instead of paying a dividend, Mauve buys back one-half of Mike's shares for $350,000. This seems to produce a $300,000 long-term capital gain [$350,000 (sales proceeds)− $50,000 (basis in 50 shares of Mauve stock)], but it results in a $350,000 dividend for Mike, as the redemption did not reduce the control of Mauve that Mike and Cheryl can exercise.

---

[37]§ 302(b)(3).
[38]§ 302(b)(2).

[39]Section 318 is used for this purpose.

GLOBAL TAX ISSUES Non-U.S. Shareholders Prefer Capital Gain Treatment in Stock Redemptions

As a general rule, non-U.S. shareholders of U.S. corporations are subject to U.S. income tax on dividend income but not on capital gains. In some situations, a nonresident alien or business entity is taxed on a capital gain from the disposition of stock in a U.S. corporation, but only if the stock was effectively connected with the conduct of a U.S. trade or business of the individual.

Whether a stock redemption qualifies for capital gain treatment therefore takes on added significance for non-U.S. shareholders. If one of the qualifying stock redemption rules can be satisfied, the foreign shareholder typically will avoid U.S. income tax on the transaction. If, instead, dividend income is the result, a 30 percent withholding tax typically applies.

When the transaction is treated as a dividend, the investor's basis in the redeemed shares *does not disappear*; rather, it attaches to any remaining shares that he or she owns. Corporate E & P is reduced by the amount of any recognized dividend.

Stock redemptions also can result in capital gain/loss treatment when the shareholder dies or when the corporation downsizes.[40] Other tax consequences for the redeeming corporation are summarized as follows.

- If noncash property is used to acquire the redeemed shares, the corporation recognizes any realized gain (but not loss) on the distributed assets.[41]

- When the shareholder is taxed as having received a capital gain, E & P of the redeeming corporation *disappears* to the extent of the percentage of shares redeemed relative to the shares outstanding before the buyback.[42]

TAX PLANNING STRATEGIES Stock Redemptions

FRAMEWORK FOCUS: TAX RATES

Strategy: Control the Character of Income and Deductions.

Stock redemptions offer several possibilities for tax planning.

- Usually a stock redemption triggers dividend treatment. A preferential tax rate on dividend income reduces some of the adverse consequences of a nonqualified stock redemption for noncorporate shareholders.

- Dividend treatment for a stock redemption may be preferable to a redemption that produces a capital gain if the distributing corporation has little or no E & P or where the distributee-shareholder is another C corporation. In the latter situation, dividend treatment may be preferred due to the availability of the dividends received deduction.

- Stock redemptions are particularly well suited for purchasing the interest of a retiring or deceased shareholder. Rather than the remaining shareholders buying the stock of the retiring or deceased shareholder, corporate funds are used to redeem the stock from the retiring shareholder or from the decedent shareholder's estate. A corporate buy-sell agreement can be used to effect a redemption of a retiring or deceased shareholder's stock. The ability to use the corporation's funds to buy out a shareholder's interest also can be advantageous in property settlements between divorcing taxpayers.

13-7 CORPORATE LIQUIDATIONS

When a corporation makes a nonliquidating distribution (e.g., a cash dividend or a stock redemption), the entity typically continues as a going concern. With a complete

---

[40]For example, see §§ 302(b)(4) and 303.
[41]§ 311.

[42]The E & P reduction cannot exceed the amount of the redemption proceeds. § 312(n)(7).

liquidation, however, corporate existence terminates, as does the shareholder's ownership interest. A complete liquidation, like a qualifying stock redemption, produces sale or exchange treatment to the *shareholder*. However, the tax effects of a liquidation to the *corporation* vary somewhat from those of a redemption. Gain/loss treatment is the general rule for the liquidating corporation, although some losses are disallowed.

13-7a **The Liquidation Process**

A corporate liquidation exists when a corporation ceases to be a going concern. The corporation continues solely to wind up its affairs, pay debts, and distribute any remaining assets to its shareholders. Legal dissolution under state law is not required for a liquidation to be complete for tax purposes. A liquidation can exist even if the corporation retains a nominal amount of assets to pay remaining debts and preserve legal status.[43]

Shareholders may decide to liquidate a corporation for one or more reasons, including the following.

- The corporate business has been unsuccessful.
- The shareholders want to acquire the corporation's assets.
- Another person or entity wants to purchase the corporation's assets. The purchaser may buy the shareholders' stock and then liquidate the corporation to acquire the assets. Alternatively, the purchaser may buy the assets directly from the corporation. After the assets are sold, the corporation distributes the sales proceeds to its shareholders and liquidates.

13-7b **Liquidating and Nonliquidating Distributions Compared**

As noted previously, a *nonliquidating* property distribution, whether in the form of a dividend or a stock redemption, triggers gain (but not loss) to the distributing corporation. For the shareholder, the receipt of cash or property produces dividend income to the extent of the corporation's E & P or, in the case of a qualifying stock redemption, results in sale or exchange treatment.

Like a qualifying stock redemption, a complete *liquidation* typically generates capital gain/loss for the shareholders. E & P has no effect on the gain or loss to be recognized by the shareholder in either type of distribution.[44] However, a complete liquidation produces different tax consequences to the liquidating corporation. With certain exceptions, a liquidating corporation recognizes gain *and* loss upon the distribution of its assets. Thus, a liquidation usually results in income tax for both the corporation and the shareholders; this can be seen as a form of double taxation.

EXAMPLE 32

Goose Corporation, with an E & P balance of $40,000, makes a cash distribution of $50,000 to one of its shareholders. The shareholder's basis in the Goose stock is $24,000. If the distribution is not a qualifying stock redemption or in complete liquidation, the shareholder recognizes dividend income of $40,000 (the amount of Goose's E & P) and treats the remaining $10,000 of the distribution as a return of capital (i.e., stock basis is reduced to $14,000).

If the distribution is a qualifying stock redemption or is pursuant to a complete liquidation, the shareholder recognizes a capital gain of $26,000 ($50,000 distribution − $24,000 stock basis).

DIGGING DEEPER 7 | In-depth coverage can be found on this book's companion website: www.cengagebrain.com

---

[43]Reg. § 1.332–2(c).   [44]§ 331.

TAX PLANNING STRATEGIES Corporate Liquidations

FRAMEWORK FOCUS: TAX RATES

Strategy: Avoid Double Taxation.

Usually, distributions in liquidation are taxed at both the corporate level and the shareholder level. When a corporation liquidates, it can, as a general rule, claim losses on assets that have depreciated in value. These assets should not be distributed in the form of a property dividend or stock redemption, because losses are not recognized on nonliquidating distributions.

Shareholders faced with large prospective gains in a liquidation may consider shifting part or all of that gain to other taxpayers. One approach is to donate the liquidating

corporation's stock to charity. A charitable contribution of the stock can produce a deduction equal to the stock's fair market value.

Alternatively, the stock may be transferred by gift to family members. Some or all of the later capital gain on liquidation could be taxed at a lower tax rate on long-term capital gains. However, possible gift tax issues on the stock transfer must be considered (see Chapter 1). Effective planning for stock transfers in the context of a liquidation therefore is crucial in arriving at the desired tax result.

13-8 RESTRICTIONS ON CORPORATE ACCUMULATIONS

Two provisions of the Code are designed to prevent corporations and their shareholders from avoiding the double tax on dividend distributions. Both provisions impose a penalty tax on undistributed income retained by the corporation. The rules underlying these provisions are complex and beyond the scope of this text. However, a brief description is provided as an introduction.

The *accumulated earnings tax*[45] imposes a 20 percent tax on the current year's corporate earnings that have been accumulated without a reasonable business need. The burden of proving what constitutes a reasonable need is borne by the taxpayer. In determining the excessive accumulated income, most businesses are allowed a $250,000 minimum exemption. Thus, most corporations can accumulate $250,000 in earnings over a series of years without fear of an accumulated earnings tax. Beyond the exemption amount, a C corporation's earnings can be accumulated, without incurring the penalty tax, for:

* Working capital needs (e.g., to purchase inventory or pay salaries and taxes),

* Retirement of debt incurred in connection with the business,

* Investment or loans to suppliers or customers (if necessary to maintain the corporation's business), or

* Realistic business contingencies, including lawsuits or self-insurance.

The *personal holding company (PHC) tax*[46] was enacted to discourage the sheltering of certain kinds of passive income in corporations owned by individuals with high marginal tax rates. The PHC tax is applied at a 20 percent rate; in any single year, the IRS cannot impose both the PHC tax and the accumulated earnings tax on the same corporation. Generally, an entity is considered a PHC and may be subject to the tax if:

* More than 50 percent of the value of the outstanding stock was owned by five or fewer individuals at any time during the last half of the year, and

* A substantial portion (60 percent or more) of the corporation's income is comprised of passive types of income, including dividends, interest, rents, royalties, or certain personal service income.

---

[45]§§ 531–537.   [46]§§ 541–547.

REFOCUS ON THE BIG PICTURE

TAXING CORPORATE DISTRIBUTIONS

A number of factors affect the tax treatment of Lime Corporation's distributions. The amount of current and accumulated E & P (which differs from the financial reporting concept of retained earnings) partially determines the tax effect on the shareholders. Given that Lime had a highly profitable year, it is possible that current E & P equals or exceeds the amount of the distributions. If so, they are dividends to the shareholders rather than a return of capital.

Orange Corporation receives $200,000 of dividend income that is mostly offset by the dividends received deduction. The amount of the offsetting deduction depends on the ownership percentage that Orange holds in Lime. In this situation, Orange likely would qualify for a dividends received deduction of $160,000 ($200,000 × 80%). Gustavo has $200,000 of dividend income (i.e., $300,000 value of the real estate less the $100,000 mortgage). Assuming that Lime is a domestic corporation and that Gustavo has held his stock for the entire year, the distribution is a qualified dividend. As a result, the dividend is subject to reduced income tax rates. Gustavo's basis in the real estate is its fair market value at distribution, or $300,000.

From Lime's perspective, the distribution of the appreciated property triggers a recognized gain, equal to $280,000 ($300,000 fair market value less $20,000 adjusted basis). While the gain increases Lime's E & P, the distributions to the shareholders reduce it by $200,000 for the cash and $200,000 for the real estate ($300,000 fair market value reduced by the $100,000 mortgage).

What If?

What if the balance of current E & P is less than the combined value of the cash and real estate distributed to the shareholders? Current E & P is applied pro rata to the cash and the real estate. Because the amounts received by the two shareholders are equal ($200,000 each), the current E & P applied is taxed as a dividend and is treated as described above.

To the extent the distributions are not paid from current E & P, accumulated E & P is applied in a pro rata fashion (both distributions were made on December 31). However, if Lime reports a deficit in accumulated E & P, the remaining amounts distributed to the two shareholders are first a tax-free recovery of stock basis, and any excess is taxed as a sale of the stock (probably classified as capital gain).

Suggested Readings

Julie Allen, et al., "The Forgotten Impact of Accounting Methods When Computing E & P," *Corporate Taxation*, September/October 2010.

John C. Ramirez, "Reasonable Compensation for Corporate Owner/Employees," *Valuation Strategies*, July/August 2012.

Edward J. Schnee and W. Eugene Seago, "Constructive Dividends from Related Entities: The Distributing Corporation's Issues," *Journal of Taxation*, March 2010.

John Waggoner, "Stock Buybacks Surge: Is That a Good Thing?," **USAToday.com**, May 29, 2014.

Key Terms

Accumulated E & P, 13-3

Constructive dividend, 13-15

Corporate liquidation, 13-24

Current E & P, 13-3

Dividend, 13-2

Earnings and profits, 13-2

Property dividend, 13-12

Stock dividend, 13-20

Stock redemption, 13-22

Unreasonable compensation, 13-16

Computational Exercises

1. **LO.1** At the beginning of the year, Myrna Corporation (a calendar year taxpayer) holds E & P of $32,000. The corporation generates no additional E & P during the year. On December 31, the corporation distributes $50,000 to its sole shareholder, Abby, whose stock basis is $10,000. How does the Federal income tax law treat this distribution?

2. **LO.3** On January 1 of the current year, Rhondell Corporation holds accumulated E & P of $13,000. Current E & P for the year is $84,000, earned evenly throughout the year. Elizabeth and Jonathan are the sole equal shareholders of Rhondell from January 1 to April 30. On May 1, Elizabeth sells all of her stock to Marshall.

   Rhondell makes two distributions to shareholders during the year, as indicated below. Analyze the distributions by completing the table that follows. Assume that the shareholders have sufficient basis in their stock for any amount that is treated as return of capital.

Total Distribution	From Current E & P	From Accumulated E & P	Return of Capital
April 30, $42,000 cash	$_____	$_____	$_____
December 31, $58,000 cash	_____	_____	_____

3. **LO.5** Global Corporation distributed property with an $850,000 fair market value and a $415,000 adjusted basis to Kang, one of its shareholders. The property was subject to a $230,000 mortgage, which Kang assumed. Global's accumulated E & P totals $3 million.

   What is the amount of Kang's dividend income on the distribution? What is Kang's basis in the property received?

4. **LO.5** Fargo Corporation holds $5 million in accumulated E & P. It distributes to Leilei, one of its shareholders, land worth $310,000; basis of the land to Fargo is $260,000. Determine the Federal income tax consequences of the distribution to Fargo.

5. **LO.7** During the current year, Gnatcatcher, Inc. (E & P of $1 million), distributed $200,000 each to Brandi and Yuen in redemption of some of their Gnatcatcher stock. The two shareholders are not related; they acquired their shares five years ago. Brandi and Yuen are in the 33% income tax bracket, and each had a $45,000 basis in her redeemed stock.

   a. Assume that the distribution to Brandi is a qualifying stock redemption. Determine Brandi's tax liability on the distribution.

   b. Assume that the distribution to Yuen is a nonqualified stock redemption. Determine Yuen's tax liability on the distribution.

6. **LO.7** Rosalie owns 50% of the outstanding stock of Salmon Corporation. In a qualifying stock redemption, Salmon distributes $80,000 to Rosalie in exchange for one-half of her shares, which have a basis of $100,000. Compute Rosalie's recognized loss, if any, on the redemption.

Critical Thinking   7.   **LO.7** Derk owns 250 shares of stock in Rose Corporation. The remaining 750 shares of Rose are owned as follows: 150 by Derk's daughter Rosalie, 200 by Derk's aunt Penelope, and 400 by a partnership in which Derk holds an 80% interest. Determine the number of shares that Derk owns (directly and indirectly) in Rose Corporation.

8.   **LO.7** Caramel Corporation has 5,000 shares of stock outstanding. In a qualifying stock redemption, Caramel distributes $145,000 in exchange for 1,000 of its shares. At the time of the redemption, Caramel has recorded paid-in capital of $800,000 and E & P of $300,000. Calculate the reduction to Caramel's E & P as a result of the distribution.

Problems

9.   **LO.1, 3** At the start of the current year, Blue Corporation (a calendar year taxpayer) holds accumulated E & P of $100,000. Blue's current E & P is $60,000. At the end of the year, it distributes $200,000 ($100,000 each) to its equal shareholders, Pam and Jon. Their basis in the stock is $11,000 for Pam and $26,000 for Jon. How is the distribution treated for tax purposes?

10.   **LO.2** Cardinal Corporation, a calendar year taxpayer, receives dividend income of $250,000 from a corporation in which it holds a 10% interest. Cardinal also receives interest income of $35,000 from municipal bonds. (The municipality used the proceeds from the bond issue to construct a public library.) Cardinal borrowed funds to purchase the municipal bonds and pays $20,000 of interest on the loan. Excluding these items, Cardinal's taxable income is $500,000.
   a.   What is Cardinal's taxable income after these items are taken into account?
   b.   What is Cardinal's accumulated E & P at the start of next year if its beginning balance this year is $150,000?

11.   **LO.2** Compute current E & P for Sparrow Corporation (a calendar year, accrual basis taxpayer). Sparrow reported the following transactions during 2015, its second year of operation.

Taxable income	$330,000
Federal income tax liability paid	112,000
Tax-exempt interest income	5,000
Meals and entertainment expenses (total)	3,000
Premiums paid on key employee life insurance	3,500
Increase in cash surrender value attributable to life insurance premiums	700
Proceeds from key employee life insurance policy	130,000
Cash surrender value of life insurance policy at distribution	20,000
Excess of capital losses over capital gains	13,000
MACRS deduction	26,000
Straight-line depreciation using ADS lives	16,000
Section 179 expense elected during 2014	25,000
Dividends received from domestic corporations (less than 20% owned)	25,000

• Sparrow uses the LIFO inventory method, and its LIFO recapture amount increased by $10,000 during 2015.
• Sparrow sold some property on installments during 2014. The property was sold for $40,000 and had an adjusted basis then of $32,000. During 2015, Sparrow received a $15,000 payment on the installment sale.

12. **LO.1, 2, 3** On September 30, Silver Corporation, a calendar year taxpayer, sold a parcel of land (basis of $400,000) for a $1 million note. The note is payable in five installments, with the first payment due next year. Because Silver did not elect out of the installment method, none of the $600,000 gain is taxed this year.

    Silver Corporation had a $300,000 deficit in accumulated E & P at the beginning of the year. Before considering the effect of the land sale, Silver had a deficit in current E & P of $50,000.

    Sam, the sole shareholder of Silver, has a basis of $200,000 in his stock. If Silver distributes $900,000 to Sam on December 31, how much income must he report for tax purposes?

13. **LO.2** In determining Blue Corporation's current E & P for this tax year, how should taxable income be adjusted as a result of the following transactions?
    a. A capital loss carryover from two years ago, fully used this year.
    b. Nondeductible meal expenses.
    c. Interest income on municipal bonds.
    d. Nondeductible lobbying expenses.
    e. Loss on a sale between related parties.
    f. Federal income tax refund from last year's return, received this year.

14. **LO.1, 3** Sparrow Corporation is a calendar year taxpayer. At the beginning of the current year, Sparrow holds accumulated E & P of $33,000. The corporation incurs a deficit in current E & P of $46,000 that accrues ratably throughout the year. On June 30, Sparrow distributes $20,000 to its sole shareholder, Libby. If Libby's stock has a basis of $4,000, how is she taxed on the distribution?

15. **LO.1, 3** Complete the following schedule for each case. Unless otherwise indicated, assume that the shareholders have ample basis in the stock investment. All taxpayers use a calendar tax year.

	Accumulated E & P Beginning of Year	Current E & P	Cash Distributions (All on Last Day of Year)	Dividend Income	Return of Capital
a.	($200,000)	$ 70,000	$130,000	$_____	$_____
b.	150,000	(120,000)	210,000	_____	_____
c.	90,000	70,000	150,000	_____	_____
d.	120,000	(60,000)	130,000	_____	_____
e.	Same as (d), except that the distribution of $130,000 is made on June 30.			_____	_____

16. **LO.1, 3** Larry, the sole shareholder of Brown Corporation, sold his stock to Ed on July 30 for $270,000. Larry's basis in the stock was $200,000 at the beginning of the year. Brown had accumulated E & P of $120,000 on January 1 and current E & P of $240,000. During the year, Brown made the following distributions: $450,000 cash to Larry on July 1 and $150,000 cash to Ed on December 30. How will Larry and Ed be taxed on the distributions? How much gain will Larry recognize on the sale of his stock to Ed?

17. **LO.1, 2** In each of the following independent situations, indicate the effect on taxable income and E & P, stating the amount of any increase (or decrease) in each as a result of the transaction. Assume that E & P has already been increased by taxable income.

Transaction	Taxable Income Increase (Decrease)	E & P Increase (Decrease)
a. Realized gain of $80,000 on involuntary conversion of building ($10,000 of gain is recognized).	_____	_____
b. Mining exploration costs incurred on May 1 of current year; $24,000 is deductible from current-year taxable income.	_____	_____
c. Sale of equipment to unrelated third party for $240,000; basis is $120,000 (no election out of installment method; no payments are received in current year).	_____	_____
d. Dividends of $20,000 received from 5% owned corporation, together with dividends received deduction (assume that the taxable income limit does not apply).	_____	_____
e. Domestic production activities deduction of $45,000 claimed in current year.	_____	_____
f. Section 179 expense deduction of $25,000 in current year.	_____	_____
g. Continue with the facts of (f) for the next tax year.	_____	_____
h. MACRS depreciation of $80,000. ADS depreciation would have been $90,000.	_____	_____
i. Federal income taxes of $80,000 paid in current year.	_____	_____

18. **LO.2** Penguin Corporation (a cash basis, calendar year taxpayer) recorded the following income and expenses in the current year.

Income from services	$400,000
Salaries paid to employees	70,000
Tax-exempt interest income	24,000
Dividends from a corporation in which Penguin holds a 12% interest	40,000
Short-term capital loss on the sale of stock	17,000
Estimated Federal income taxes paid	110,000

Penguin purchased seven-year MACRS property in the current year for $80,000; it did not claim any § 179 or additional first-year depreciation. The property has a 10-year ADR midpoint life. Determine Penguin's taxable income and current E & P.

19. **LO.1, 3** At the beginning of the year, Teal Corporation held accumulated E & P of $225,000. On March 30, Teal sold an asset at a loss of $225,000. For the calendar year, Teal incurred a deficit in current E & P of $305,000, which includes the $225,000 loss on the sale of the asset. If Teal made a distribution of $50,000 to its sole shareholder on April 1, how is the shareholder taxed?

20. **LO.1, 3** Green Corporation (a calendar year taxpayer) had a deficit in accumulated E & P of $250,000 at the beginning of the current year. Its net profit for the period January 1 through July 30 was $300,000, but its E & P for the entire taxable year was only $40,000. If Green made a distribution of $60,000 to its sole shareholder on August 1, how will the shareholder be taxed?

21. **LO.1, 3** Black Corporation and Tom each own 50% of Tan Corporation's common stock. On January 1, Tan holds a deficit in accumulated E & P of $200,000. Its current E & P is $90,000. During the year, Tan makes cash distributions of $40,000 each to Black and Tom.

   a. How are the two shareholders taxed on the distribution?

   b. What is Tan's accumulated E & P at the end of the year?

22. **LO.1, 4** Heather, an individual, owns all of the outstanding stock in Silver Corporation. Heather purchased her stock in Silver nine years ago, and her basis is $56,000. At the beginning of this year, the corporation has $76,000 of accumulated E & P and no current E & P (before considering the effect of the distributions as noted below). What are the tax consequences to Heather (amount and type of income and basis in property received) and Silver Corporation (gain or loss and effect on E & P) in each of the following situations?

    a. Silver distributes land to Heather. The land was held as an investment and has a fair market value of $54,000 and an adjusted basis of $42,000.

    b. Assume that Silver has no current or accumulated E & P prior to the distribution. How would your answer to (a) change?

    c. Assume that the land distributed in (a) is subject to a $46,000 mortgage (which Heather assumes). How would your answer change?

    d. Assume that the land has a fair market value of $54,000 and an adjusted basis of $62,000 on the date of the distribution. How would your answer to (a) change?

23. **LO.1, 4** Lime Corporation, with E & P of $500,000, distributes land (worth $300,000, adjusted basis of $350,000) to Harry, its sole shareholder. The land is subject to a liability of $120,000, which Harry assumes. What are the tax consequences to Lime and to Harry?

24. **LO.4** Raven Corporation owns three machines that it uses in its business. It no longer needs two of these machines and is considering distributing them to its two shareholders as a property dividend. The machines have a fair market value of $20,000 each. The basis of each machine is as follows: A, $27,000; B, $20,000; and C, $12,000. Raven has asked you for advice. What do you recommend?

    Decision Making

25. **LO.1, 2, 3, 4** Cerulean Corporation has two equal shareholders, Eloise and Olivia. Eloise acquired her Cerulean stock three years ago by transferring property worth $700,000, basis of $300,000, for 70 shares of the stock. Olivia acquired 70 shares in Cerulean Corporation two years ago by transferring property worth $660,000, basis of $110,000. Cerulean Corporation's accumulated E & P as of January 1 of the current year is $350,000.

    Issue ID

    On March 1 of the current year, the corporation distributed to Eloise property worth $120,000, basis to Cerulean of $50,000. It distributed cash of $220,000 to Olivia. On July 1 of the current year, Olivia sold her stock to Magnus for $820,000. On December 1 of the current year, Cerulean distributed cash of $90,000 each to Magnus and Eloise. What are the tax issues?

26. **LO.1, 2, 4** Petrel Corporation has accumulated E & P of $85,000 at the beginning of the year. Its current-year taxable income is $320,000. On December 31, Petrel distributed business property (worth $140,000, adjusted basis of $290,000) to Juan, its sole shareholder. Juan assumes a $70,000 liability on the property.

    Decision Making

    Included in the determination of Petrel's current taxable income is $16,000 of income recognized from an installment sale in a previous year. In addition, the corporation incurred a Federal income tax liability of $112,000, paid life insurance premiums of $4,500, and received term life insurance proceeds of $150,000 on the death of an officer.

    a. What is Juan's gross income from the distribution?

    b. What is Petrel's E & P after the property distribution?

    c. What is Juan's tax basis in the property received?

    d. How would your answers to (a) and (b) change if Petrel had sold the property at its fair market value, used $70,000 of the proceeds to pay off the liability, and distributed the remaining cash and any tax savings to Juan?

27. **LO.5** Parrot Corporation is a closely held company with accumulated E & P of $300,000 and current E & P of $350,000. Tom and Jerry are brothers; each owns a 50% share in Parrot, and they share management responsibilities equally. What are the tax consequences of each of the following independent transactions involving Parrot, Tom, and Jerry? How does each transaction affect Parrot's E & P?

    a. Parrot sells an office building (adjusted basis of $350,000; fair market value of $300,000) to Tom for $275,000.

    b. Parrot lends Jerry $250,000 on March 31 of this year. The loan is evidenced by a note that is payable on demand. No interest is charged on the loan (the current applicable Federal interest rate is 7%).

    c. Parrot owns an airplane that it leases to others for a specified rental rate. Tom and Jerry also use the airplane for personal use and pay no rent. During the year, Tom used the airplane for 120 hours, and Jerry used it for 160 hours. The rental value of the airplane is $350 per hour, and its maintenance costs average $80 per hour.

    d. Tom leases equipment to Parrot for $20,000 per year. The same equipment can be leased from another company for $9,000 per year.

Decision Making   28. **LO.5** Robin Corporation would like to transfer excess cash to its sole shareholder, Adam, who is also an employee. Adam is in the 28% tax bracket, and Robin is in the 34% bracket.

    Because Adam's contribution to Robin's profit is substantial, Robin believes that a $25,000 bonus in the current year is reasonable compensation and should be deductible in full. However, Robin is considering paying Adam a $25,000 dividend because Adam's tax rate on dividends is lower than his tax rate on compensation. Is Robin correct in believing that a dividend is the better choice? Why or why not?

Critical Thinking   29. **LO.6** Your client, Raptor Corporation, declares a dividend permitting its common shareholders to elect to receive 9 shares of cumulative preferred stock or 3 additional shares of Raptor common stock for every 10 shares of common stock held. Raptor has only common stock outstanding (fair market value of $45 per share). One shareholder elects to receive preferred stock, while the remaining shareholders choose the common stock.

Communications

    Raptor asks you whether the shareholders recognize any taxable income on the receipt of the stock. Prepare a letter to Raptor or a memo for the tax research file regarding this matter. Raptor's address is 1812 S. Camino Seco, Tucson, AZ 85710.

Critical Thinking   30. **LO.6** Ken purchased 10,000 shares of Gold Corporation common stock six years ago for $160,000. In the current year, Ken received a preferred stock dividend of 800 shares, while the other holders of common stock received a common stock dividend. The preferred stock that Ken received is worth $80,000, and his common stock has a fair market value of $240,000. Assume that Gold holds ample E & P to cover any distributions made during the year. What is Ken's basis in the preferred and common stock after the dividend is received? When does his holding period commence for the preferred stock?

Critical Thinking   31. **LO.6** Denim Corporation declares a nontaxable dividend payable in rights to subscribe to common stock. One right and $60 entitle the holder to subscribe to one share of stock. One right is issued for every two shares of stock owned. At the date of distribution of the rights, the market value of the stock is $110 per share, and the market value of the rights is $55 each. Lauren owns 300 shares of stock that she purchased two years ago for $9,000. Lauren receives 150 rights, of which she exercises 105 to purchase 105 additional shares. She sells the remaining 45 rights for $2,475. What are the tax consequences of this transaction to Lauren?

Critical Thinking   32. **LO.6** Jacob Corcoran bought 10,000 shares of Grebe Corporation stock two years ago for $24,000. Last year, Jacob received a nontaxable stock dividend of 2,000 shares in Grebe. In the current tax year, Jacob sold all of the stock received as

Communications

a dividend for $18,000. Prepare a letter to Jacob or a memo for the tax research file describing the tax consequences of the stock sale. Jacob's address is 925 Arapahoe Street, Boulder, CO 80304.

33. **LO.7** Joseph and Erica, husband and wife, jointly own all of the stock in Velvet   Issue ID
Corporation. The two are currently involved in divorce proceedings, and pursuant to those negotiations, they have agreed that only one of them will remain a shareholder in Velvet after the divorce. Because Erica has been more involved in Velvet's management and operations over the years, the parties have agreed that Joseph's ownership should be acquired by either Erica or Velvet. What issues should be considered in determining whether Erica or Velvet should acquire Joseph's shares in the corporation?

34. **LO.1, 7** Julio is in the 33% tax bracket. He acquired 2,000 shares of stock in Gray Corporation seven years ago at a cost of $50 per share. In the current year, Julio received a payment of $150,000 from Gray Corporation in exchange for 1,000 of his shares in Gray. Gray has E & P of $1 million. What tax liability would Julio incur on the payment in each of the following situations? Assume that Julio has no capital losses.
    a. The stock redemption qualifies for sale or exchange treatment.
    b. The stock redemption does not qualify for sale or exchange treatment.

35. **LO.1, 7** How would your answer to Problem 34 differ if Julio were a corporate shareholder (in the 34% tax bracket) rather than an individual shareholder and the stock ownership in Gray Corporation represented a 25% interest?

36. **LO.1, 7** Assume in Problem 34 that Julio has a capital loss carryover of $50,000 in   Decision Making
the current tax year. Julio has no other capital gain transactions during the year. What amount of the capital loss may Julio deduct in the current year in the following situations?
    a. The payment from Gray Corporation is a qualifying stock redemption for tax purposes (i.e., receives sale or exchange treatment).
    b. The payment from Gray does not qualify as a stock redemption for tax purposes (i.e., does not receive sale or exchange treatment).
    c. If Julio had the flexibility to structure the transaction as described in either (a) or (b), which form would he choose?

37. **LO.1, 7** How would your answer to parts (a) and (b) of Problem 36 differ if Julio were a corporate shareholder (in the 34% tax bracket) rather than an individual shareholder and the stock ownership in Gray Corporation represented a 25% interest?

38. **LO.7** Silver Corporation has 2,000 shares of common stock outstanding. Howard   Critical Thinking
owns 600 shares, Howard's grandfather owns 300 shares, Howard's mother owns 300 shares, and Howard's son owns 100 shares. In addition, Maroon Corporation owns 500 shares. Howard owns 70% of the stock of Maroon.
    a. Applying the stock attribution rules, how many shares does Howard own in Silver?
    b. Assume that Howard owns only 40% of the stock in Maroon. How many shares does Howard own, directly and indirectly, in Silver?
    c. Assume the same facts as in (a) above, but in addition, Howard owns a 25% interest in the Yellow Partnership. Yellow owns 200 shares in Silver. How many shares does Howard own, directly and indirectly, in Silver?

39. **LO.7** Shonda owns 1,000 of the 1,500 shares outstanding in Rook Corporation   Critical Thinking
(E & P of $1 million). Shonda paid $50 per share for the stock seven years

ago. The remaining stock in Rook is owned by unrelated individuals. What are the tax consequences to Shonda in the following independent situations?

a.   Rook redeems 450 shares of Shonda's stock for $225,000.

b.   Rook redeems 600 shares of Shonda's stock for $300,000.

Critical Thinking   40. **LO.7** Broadbill Corporation (E & P $650,000) has 1,000 shares of common stock outstanding. The shares are owned by the following individuals: Tammy, 300 shares; Yvette, 400 shares; and Jeremy, 300 shares. Each of the shareholders paid $50 per share for the Broadbill stock four years ago.

In the current year, Broadbill distributes $75,000 to Tammy in redemption of 150 of her shares. Determine the tax consequences of the redemption to Tammy and to Broadbill under the following independent circumstances.

a.   Tammy and Jeremy are grandmother and grandson.

b.   The three shareholders are siblings.

Critical Thinking   41. **LO.7** For the last 11 years, Lime Corporation has owned and operated four different trades or businesses. Lime also owns stock in several corporations that it purchased for investment purposes.

The stock of Lime is held equally by Sultan, an individual, and by Turquoise Corporation. Sultan and Turquoise each own 1,000 shares in Lime, purchased 9 years ago at a cost of $200 per share.

Determine whether either of the following independent transactions qualify as partial liquidations under § 302(b)(4). In each transaction, determine the tax consequences to Lime, to Turquoise, and to Sultan. Lime holds E & P of $2.1 million on the date of the distribution. Lime redeems 250 shares from each shareholder.

a.   Lime sells one of its business lines (basis $500,000, fair market value $700,000) and distributes the proceeds equally to Sultan and Turquoise.

b.   Lime equally distributes stock (basis $425,000, fair market value $700,000) that it holds in other corporations to Sultan and Turquoise.

Critical Thinking   42. **LO.7** Compare the tax treatment of liquidating and redemption distributions in terms of the following.

a.   Recognition of gain or loss by the shareholder.

b.   Basis of property received by the shareholder.

Critical Thinking   43. **LO.7** Dove Corporation (E & P of $800,000) has 1,000 shares of stock outstanding. The shares are owned as follows: Julia, 600 shares; Maxine (Julia's sister), 300 shares; and Janine (Julia's daughter), 100 shares. Dove owns land (basis $300,000, fair market value $260,000) that it purchased as an investment seven years ago.

Dove distributes the land to Julia in exchange for all of her shares in the corporation. Julia had a basis of $275,000 in the shares. What are the tax consequences for both Dove and Julia if the distribution is:

a.   A qualifying stock redemption?

b.   A liquidating distribution?

Issue ID   44. **LO.5** Pink Corporation has several employees. Their names and salaries are listed below.

Judy	$470,000
Holly (Judy's daughter)	100,000
Terry (Judy's son)	100,000
John (an unrelated third party)	320,000

Holly and Terry are the only shareholders of Pink. Judy and John share equally in the management of the company's operations. Holly and Terry are both full-time college students at a university 200 miles away. Pink has substantial E & P and never has distributed a dividend. Discuss any income tax issues related to Pink's salary arrangement.

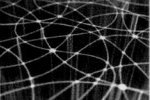

BRIDGE DISCIPLINE

1. Find the audited financial statements of five major U.S. corporations, each in a different operating industry (e.g., manufacturing, energy, financial services, health care).
   a. Compute the total return on each corporation's stock for the past two years.
   b. Compute the dividend yield of the stock for the past two years.

2. Find a report involving the buyback of common stock by a publicly traded U.S. corporation. In no more than four PowerPoint slides, summarize the transaction, and discuss the tax and finance motivations for the redemption presented in the article.   Communications

3. A dividend is declared by the corporation's board of directors, and it is paid to each shareholder in an equal fashion. Evaluate this statement from an accounting and Federal income tax standpoint. Summarize your position in no more than four PowerPoint slides in preparation for a presentation to your classmates in Business Law I.   Communications

Research Problems

Note: Solutions to Research Problems can be prepared by using the Checkpoint® Student Edition online research product, which is available to accompany this text. It is also possible to prepare solutions to the Research Problems by using tax research materials found in a standard tax library.

THOMSON REUTERS
CHECKPOINT®
Student Edition

Research Problem 1. Kenny Merinoff and his son, John, own all of the outstanding stock of Flamingo Corporation. John and Kenny are officers in the corporation and, together with their uncle, Ira, comprise the entire board of directors. Flamingo uses the cash method of accounting and adopted a calendar year-end.

Communications

In late 2008, the board of directors adopted the following legally enforceable resolution (agreed to in writing by each of the officers).

> Salary payments made to an officer of the corporation that are disallowed in whole or in part as a deductible expense for Federal income tax purposes shall be reimbursed by such officer to the corporation to the full extent of the disallowance. It shall be the duty of the board of directors to enforce the collection of each such amount.

In 2013, Flamingo paid Kenny $800,000 in compensation. John received $650,000. As part of an audit in late 2014, the IRS found the compensation of both officers to be excessive. It disallowed deductions for $400,000 of the payment to Kenny and $350,000 of the payment to John. The IRS recharacterized the disallowed payments as constructive dividends. Complying with the resolution by the board of directors, both Kenny and John repaid the disallowed compensation to Flamingo Corporation in 2015.

John and Kenny have asked you to determine how their repayments are treated for Federal income tax purposes. John still is working as a highly compensated executive for Flamingo, while Kenny is retired and living off of his savings. Prepare a memo for your firm's tax research files describing the results of your review.

Partial list of research aids:
§ 1341.
Vincent E. Oswald, 49 T.C. 645 (1968).

Research Problem 2. Your client, White Corporation, has done well since its formation 20 years ago. This year, it recognized a $50 million capital gain from the sale of a subsidiary. White's CEO has contacted you to discuss a proposed transaction to reduce the tax on the capital gain. Under the proposal, White will purchase all of the common stock in Purple Corporation for $200 million. Purple is a profitable corporation that has $63 million in cash and marketable securities, $137 million in operating assets, and approximately $280 million in E & P.

After its acquisition, Purple will distribute $50 million in cash and marketable securities to White. Due to the 100% dividends received deduction, no taxable income results to White from the dividend. White then will resell Purple for $150 million.

The subsequent sale of Purple generates a $50 million capital loss [$150 million (sale price) − $200 million (stock basis)]. The loss from the stock sale can then be used to offset the preexisting $50 million capital gain. Will the proposed plan work? Why or why not?

Partial list of research aids:
§ 1059.

Communications **Research Problem 3.** Emerald Corporation must change its method of accounting for Federal income tax purposes. The change will require that an adjustment to income be made over three tax periods. Jonas, the sole shareholder of Emerald, wants to better understand the implications of this adjustment for E & P purposes, as he anticipates a distribution from Emerald in the current year. Prepare a memo for your firm's files describing the results of your research.

Partial list of research aids:
§ 481(a).
Rev.Proc. 97–27, 1997–1 C.B. 680.

 Internet Activity

Use the tax resources of the Internet to address the following questions. Do not restrict your search to the Web, but include a review of newsgroups and general reference materials, practitioner sites and resources, primary sources of the tax law, chat rooms and discussion groups, and other opportunities.

Research Problem 4. In July 2013, Windstream Corp. (Nasdaq: WIN), a Fortune 500 and S&P 500 company, made an announcement regarding the taxation of a recent distribution. It also made a projection regarding the anticipated tax consequences of future distributions.

Locate articles or press releases regarding Windstream's announcement and related distribution. What might have led Windstream to make the announcement? What implications might the information contained in the announcement have had for investors' expectations regarding the company's future earnings? On what might the predictions regarding the taxation of future distributions have been based?

Communications **Research Problem 5.** Write an e-mail query to two tax consultants who practice in your state. Ask each for an example or two of a constructive dividend that a client recently paid. Give your instructor copies of your query and the responses you receive.

Communications **Research Problem 6.** Publicly traded corporations reacquire their own shares for various reasons. Through the use of a tender offer, a corporation can purchase a substantial percentage of the company's stock. Prepare an outline discussing (1) why publicly traded corporations reacquire their own shares and (2) how the tender offer process works for both corporations and shareholders. E-mail your outline to your tax professor.

1. Candy Corp. is a C Corporation that began operations in Year 1. Candy Corp.'s Year 1 through Year 3 taxable earnings and profits (E & P) are as follows:

Year	E & P
1	($25,000)
2	5,000
3	10,000

   On the last day of Year 3, Candy Corp. makes a $12,500 cash shareholder distribution, distributed equally among its two shareholders, Goode and Plenteau. How much of Goode's distribution is a nontaxable return of capital? Assume sufficient basis in Goode's stock investment.

   a. $5,000
   b. $0
   c. $1,250
   d. $6,250

2. As of December 31, 20X14, Eliot Corp. has net income per books of $100,000, which includes municipal bond interest of $4,000, a deduction for business meals of $5,000, a deduction for a net capital loss of $5,000, and a deduction for Federal income taxes of $22,000. What is Eliot Corp.'s current earnings and profits (E & P) for 20X14?

   a. $98,500
   b. $107,500
   c. $125,500
   d. $102,500

3. As of December 31, 20X15, Hardy Corp. has net income per books of $120,000, which includes straight-line depreciation expense of $5,000. Hardy Corp. claimed accelerated depreciation of $15,000 for tax purposes. Also included in book income were lobbying expenses of $4,000 and a Federal income tax refund of $5,000. What is Hardy Corp.'s current earnings and profits (E & P) for 20X15?

   a. $119,000
   b. $109,000
   c. $124,000
   d. $114,000

4. As of December 31, 20X15, Caledonia Corp. has taxable income of $150,000, which includes a $20,000 accelerated depreciation deduction; had straight-line depreciation been used, the deduction would have been $6,000. Also included in taxable income is an operating loss carryforward from a prior year of $3,000. Additionally, Caledonia earned $4,000 in municipal bond interest during the year. What is Caledonia Corp.'s current earnings and profits (E & P) for 20X15?

   a. $164,000
   b. $171,000
   c. $157,000
   d. $168,000

5. At the beginning of the year, Crispin, a C corporation, had a deficit of $35,000 in accumulated earnings and profits (E & P). For the current year, Crispin reported E & P of $12,000. Crispin distributed $10,000 during the year. What was the amount of Crispin's accumulated E & P deficit at year-end?

   a. $23,000
   b. $33,000
   c. $27,000
   d. $37,000

6. On January 1 of the current year, Quail Corp., an accrual-basis, calendar-year C corporation, had accumulated earnings and profits (E & P) of $20,000. On December 31 of the current year, Quail Corp. has current E & P of $24,000, earned evenly throughout

the year. Ray and Devi were sole equal shareholders of Quail throughout the year. Quail made two distributions to the shareholders during the year: $30,000 on July 1 and $30,000 on December 31. How much of the December 31 distribution is taxable dividend income for Devi?

   a. $7,000   c. $6,000
   b. $11,000   d. $1,000

7. Compendium Corp. distributed cash and personal property to its sole shareholder. Considering the following facts, what is the amount of gain that would be recognized by Compendium as the result of making this distribution to its shareholder?

Item	Amount
Cash	$25,000
Personal property	
Fair market value	10,000
Adjusted basis	4,000
Liability on property assumed by shareholder	12,000

   a. $4,000   c. $8,000
   b. $6,000   d. $29,000

8. Calvin owns 40% of the outstanding shares of Copernicus Corp., which has accumulated earnings and profits of $100,000 as of December 31, Year 1. The outstanding shares not owned by Calvin are owned by parties unrelated to Calvin. On January 1 of Year 2, Calvin, wishing to pursue another business opportunity, sells his stock back to Copernicus Corp. Copernicus distributes cash of $250,000 in redemption of all of Calvin's stock. If Calvin's adjusted basis for the stock on the date of redemption is $125,000, what will be the tax effect of the redemption to Calvin?

   a. $125,000 capital gain   c. $125,000 dividend
   b. $25,000 dividend   d. $150,000 dividend

9. Katsu Corp. distributes property to its shareholders as part of a complete liquidation. The fair market value of the property is $500,000, Katsu's adjusted basis in the property is $150,000, and the property is subject to a liability of $200,000. What amount of gain will Katsu recognize as a result of the transaction?

   a. $150,000   c. $300,000
   b. $550,000   d. $350,000

10. Close Corp. distributed cash and a parcel of land in a nonliquidating distribution to its sole shareholder. The following facts apply to this distribution:

Item	Amount
Cash	$50,000
Land	
Fair market value	30,000
Adjusted basis	40,000

Based on these facts, what amount of gain or loss should be recognized by Close Corp. as a result of this distribution?

   a. $60,000 loss
   b.   No gain or loss should be recognized
   c. $10,000 loss
   d. $40,000 gain

11. Callow Corp. has 400 shares of stock outstanding. Callow exchanges $150,000 cash for 100 of the shares in a qualifying stock redemption. Just prior to the redemption, Callow had earnings and profits (E & P) of $300,000. By what amount will Callow Corp.'s E & P be reduced as a result of this redemption? Assume a sufficiently large additional paid-in capital account balance.

 a. $150,000

 b. E & P will not be reduced

 c. $75,000

 d. Depends on balance in Additional Paid-In Capital

Partnerships and Limited Liability Entities

LEARNING OBJECTIVES: *After completing Chapter 14, you should be able to:*

LO.1 Identify governing principles and theories of partnership taxation.

LO.2 Apply the tax rules regarding the formation of a partnership with cash and property contributions.

LO.3 Determine the tax treatment of expenditures of a newly formed partnership and identify elections available to the partnership.

LO.4 Calculate partnership taxable income and describe how partnership items affect a partner's income tax liability.

LO.5 Determine a partner's basis in the partnership interest.

LO.6 Apply the limitations on deducting partnership losses.

LO.7 Apply the tax laws regarding transactions between a partner and the partnership.

LO.8 Explain how LLPs and LLCs differ, and list the tax advantages and disadvantages of using an LLC.

CHAPTER OUTLINE

TAX TALK *If you are truly serious about preparing your child for the future, don't teach him to subtract—teach him to deduct.* —Fran Lebowitz

THE TAX CONSEQUENCES OF PARTNERSHIP FORMATION AND OPERATIONS

For 15 years, Maria has owned and operated a seaside bakery and café called The Beachsider. Each morning, customers line up on the boardwalk in front of the building and enjoy fresh coffee and croissants while waiting for a table. "The building is too small," Maria commented to her landlord, Kyle. "Is there any way we can expand?" The Beachsider is one of several older buildings on 3 acres of a 10-acre parcel that Kyle inherited 30 years ago. The remaining 7 acres are undeveloped.

Kyle and Maria talked to Josh, a real estate developer, and he proposed an expansion to The Beachsider and upgrades to the other buildings. The improvements would preserve the character of the original retail center, and the remaining acreage would be available for future expansion. Kyle and Maria were impressed with Josh's vision and excited about the plans to upgrade the property and expand Maria's business.

The parties agreed to form a partnership to own and operate The Beachsider and to improve and lease the other buildings. Josh summarized the plan as follows: "Kyle and Maria will each contribute one-half of the capital we need. Kyle's real estate is valued at about $2 million. Maria's bakery equipment and the café furnishings are valued at about $500,000. The improvements will cost about $1.5 million, which Maria has agreed to contribute to the partnership."

Josh continued, "You have agreed that I do not need to contribute any capital to the partnership. I will oversee the construction, and when it is complete, I will vest in a 5 percent interest in the partnership's capital. On an ongoing basis, I will oversee the partnership's operations in exchange for a fixed salary and 20 percent of the partnership's ongoing profits. The construction is estimated to be completed in June of this year, and my capital interest is estimated to be valued at $200,000 at that time."

What are the tax consequences if the trio forms Beachside Properties as a limited liability company (LLC) to own and operate the retail center? What issues might arise later in the life of the entity?

Read the chapter and formulate your response.

Much of the new business in today's world of commerce is conducted through what the Internal Revenue Code would classify as *partnerships*. As evidence of their popularity, more than 3 million partnership tax returns are filed with the IRS annually.

Whether termed a *joint venture* or some other designation, a partnership is formed when individuals or separate business entities get together for the specific purpose of earning profits by jointly operating a trade or business. For example, a group can limit its goals to a specific list of agreed-to projects or to a given time period, or businesses can work together without altering any of their underlying capital structures. In many service professions, such as law, medicine, and accounting, state laws prohibit the owners from using a corporation to limit their liability to clients or patients; there, the partnership form prevails.

14-1 OVERVIEW OF PARTNERSHIP TAXATION

LO.1

Identify governing principles and theories of partnership taxation.

There are several types of partnership entities, each suited for different situations. Partnerships are used in almost every imaginable industry, and their popularity among business owners continues to rise.

The tax law addressing the transactions of partners and partnerships is found in Subchapter K of the Internal Revenue Code. These provisions comprise only a few short pages in the Code, however. Most of the details of partnership tax law have evolved through extensive Regulations and a healthy number of court cases.

14-1a Forms of Doing Business—Federal Tax Consequences

This chapter and the next chapter analyze business forms that offer certain advantages over C corporations. These entities are partnerships and S corporations, which are called *flow-through* or *pass-through* entities because the owners of the trade or business elect to avoid treating the enterprise as a separate taxable entity. Instead, the owners are taxed on a proportionate share of the firm's taxable income at the end of each of its taxable years, regardless of the amount of cash or property distributions the owners receive during the year. The entity serves as an information provider to the IRS and its owners with respect to the proportionate income shares, and the tax falls directly upon the owners of those shares.

A partnership may be especially advantageous in many cases. A partnership's income is subject to only a single level of taxation, whereas C corporation income can be subject to *double taxation*. Corporate income is taxed at the entity level at rates up to 35 percent. Any after-tax corporate income that is distributed to the entity's owners may be taxed again as a dividend at the owner level.

In addition, the entity offers certain planning opportunities not available to other entities. Both C and S corporations are subject to rigorous allocation and distribution requirements (generally, each allocation or distribution is proportionate to the ownership interest of the shareholder). A partnership, though, may adjust its allocations of income and cash flow among the partners each year according to their needs, as long as certain standards are met. Any previously unrealized income (such as appreciation of corporate assets) of a C corporation is recognized at the entity level when the corporation liquidates, but a partnership generally may liquidate tax-free. Finally, many states impose reporting and licensing requirements on corporate entities, including S corporations. These include franchise or capital stock tax returns that may require annual assessments and costly professional preparation assistance. Partnerships, on the other hand, often have no reporting requirements beyond Federal and state informational tax returns.

Although partnerships may avoid many of the income tax and reporting burdens faced by other entities, they are subject to all other taxes in the same manner as any other business. Thus, the partnership files returns and pays the outstanding amount of pertinent sales taxes, property taxes, and payroll taxes.

TAX FACT **Partnership Power**

Partnerships and limited liability entities represent a sizable number of business enterprises, and they generate a significant part of the net income of the economy, especially in the investment sectors. The table at the right presents some statistics about the activities of these entities from the most recent year for which data are available.

Number of partnerships	3,100,000
Number of partners	20,650,000
Reported partnership net income—total	$410 billion
Number of limited partnerships	395,000
Number of limited liability entities	2,500,000

In summary, partnerships offer advantages to both large and small businesses. For smaller business operations, a partnership enables several owners to combine their resources at low cost. For larger business operations, a partnership offers a unique ability to raise capital with low filing and reporting costs (compared to corporate bond issuances, for example).

14-1b **Definition of a Partnership**

A partnership is an association of two or more persons formed to carry on a trade or business, with each contributing money, property, labor, or skill, and with all expecting to share in profits and losses. A "person" can be an individual, a corporation, or another partnership. For Federal income tax purposes, a partnership includes a syndicate, a group, a pool, a joint venture, or another unincorporated organization through which any business, financial operation, or venture is carried on. The entity must not otherwise be classified as a corporation, trust, or estate.[1]

An eligible noncorporate entity can "check the box" on the partnership tax return, indicating that the entity wants to be taxed as a partnership.[2] A partnership must have at least two owners, so a sole proprietor or one-owner limited liability entity cannot "check the box" and be taxed as a partnership.[3]

Businesses operating in several forms are taxed as partnerships. Provisions controlling these legal forms of doing business typically are dictated by the laws of the states in which the businesses operate.

- In a **general partnership**, the partners share profits and losses in some specified manner, as dictated by the partnership agreement. Creditors can reach the assets of the business and the personal assets of the general partners to satisfy any outstanding debts. A general partner can be bankrupted by a judgment against the entity, even though the partner did not cause the violation triggering the damages.

- In a **limited partnership**, profits and losses are shared as the partners agree, but ownership interests are either general (creditors can reach the personal assets of the partner) or limited (a partner's exposure to entity liabilities is limited to the partner's own capital contributions). Usually, the general partners conduct most of the partnership business, and they have a greater say in making decisions that affect the entity operations.

- The **limited liability partnership (LLP)** is used chiefly in the service professions, such as accounting, medicine, law, and consulting. The primary difference between an LLP and a general partnership is that an LLP partner is not personally liable for acts of negligence, fraud, or malpractice committed by other partners.

---

[1]§ 7701(a)(2).
[2]Reg. §§ 301.7701–1 to –3, as discussed in Chapter 12.

[3]§ 761(a).

As movies have become more expensive to produce, many production studios have turned to limited partnerships or LLCs as a lucrative source of investment capital. For example, several well-known studios have sold limited partnership or LLC interests in entities formed to produce specific movies.

The sponsoring studio usually injects capital for a small (1–5 percent) general partnership interest, and the limited partners contribute the remaining capital—millions of dollars in most cases.

These film-financing partnerships are not necessarily private operations. A layperson with a well-connected tax or investment adviser can become a partner in the next Channing Tatum project, perhaps financed by Silver Screen Partners. Partnership shares sell for multiples of $100,000 or more, and in return, the investor can become part-owner in an entity that is certain to throw off operating losses for many years to come.

Especially interested in movie financing of this type can be non-U.S. investors. The use of partnerships and limited liability entities is a common way to attract cross-border investment, as many developed countries treat such joint ventures favorably under their tax laws, allowing deferral of income recognition and lower tax withholding on the income of these entities.

U.S. investors are attracted to joint venture financing of film projects in several countries, including Germany and Canada, and U.S. states, including Illinois and Louisiana, that offer generous tax credits for projects that are filmed and processed chiefly within their borders. The partnership tax regime can offer an immediate flow-through of these tax benefits.

The next time you go to a movie, watch the credits and think about the large number of people who invested cash in the movie, all benefiting from the partnership tax laws!

- The **limited liability company (LLC)** is discussed in more detail later in this chapter. This entity is taxed as a partnership, but its capital structure resembles that of a corporation, with shares for sale and an owner's liability limited almost strictly to the extent of capital contributions. Most states allow LLCs to be owned solely by one person.

14-1c Partnership Taxation and Reporting

A partnership is not a taxable entity.[4] Rather, the taxable income or loss of the partnership flows through to the partners at the end of the entity's tax year.[5] Partners report their allocable share of the partnership's income or loss for the year on their tax returns. As a result, the partnership itself pays no Federal income tax on its income; instead, the partners' individual tax liabilities are affected by the activities of the entity.

Partnership Flow-Throughs

Adam is a 40% partner in the ABC Partnership. Both Adam's and the partnership's tax years end on December 31. This year, the partnership generates $200,000 of ordinary taxable income. However, because the partnership needs capital for expansion and debt reduction, Adam makes no cash withdrawals during the year. He meets his living expenses by reducing his investment portfolio. Adam is taxed on his $80,000 allocable share of the partnership's income ($200,000 × 40%), even though he received no distributions from the entity during the year. This allocated income is included in Adam's gross income.

Assume the same facts as in Example 1, except that the partnership realizes a taxable loss of $100,000. Adam's $40,000 proportionate share of the loss flows through to him from the partnership, and he can deduct the loss. (Note: Loss limitation rules discussed later in the chapter may result in some or all of this loss being deducted by Adam in a later year.)

---

[4]§ 701. [5]§ 702.

Separately Stated Items

Many items of partnership income, expense, gain, or loss retain their tax identity as they flow through to the partners. These **separately stated items** include those items that may affect any two partners' tax liability computations differently.[6] For example, the § 179 expense of a partnership is separately stated because one partner might be able to deduct his or her share of the expense completely, while another's deduction might be limited.

Separately stated items include recognized gains and losses from property transactions, dividend income, preferences and adjustments for the alternative minimum tax (see Chapter 17), foreign tax payments, and expenditures that individual partners would treat as itemized deductions (e.g., charitable contributions).

Items that are not separately stated, because all partners treat them the same on their income tax returns, are aggregated and form the *ordinary income* of the partnership. Thus, profits from product sales, advertising expenses, and depreciation recapture amounts are combined to form the entity's ordinary income. This amount then is allocated among the partners and flows through to their tax returns. The ordinary income that flows through to a general partner, as well as any salary-like guaranteed payments (discussed in a later section) received, usually is subject to self-employment tax, as well as Federal income tax.[7]

EXAMPLE 3

Beth is a 25% partner in the BR Partnership. The cash basis entity collected sales income of $60,000 and incurred $15,000 in business expenses. In addition, it sold a corporate bond for a $9,000 long-term capital gain. Finally, the partnership made a $1,000 contribution to the local Performing Arts Fund. The fund is a qualifying charity. BR and all of its partners use a calendar tax year.

Beth is allocated ordinary taxable income of $11,250 [($60,000 − $15,000) × 25%] from the partnership. She also reports her allocated share of the entity's long-term capital gain ($2,250) and charitable contributions ($250).

The ordinary income increases Beth's gross income, and is subject to both income and self-employment taxes. Beth's share of BR's capital gain and charitable contribution are combined with her other similar activities for the year as though she had incurred them herself. These items could be treated differently on the tax returns of the various partners (e.g., because a partner may be subject to a percentage limitation on charitable contribution deductions), so they are not included in the computation of ordinary partnership income. Instead, the items flow through to the partners separately.

Tax Reporting Rules

Even though it is not a taxpaying entity, the partnership files an information tax return, Form 1065. This return is due by the fifteenth day of the fourth month following the end of the tax year. For a calendar year partnership, this deadline is April 15.

An automatic five-month extension is available (to September 15 for a calendar year partnership) for filing the Form 1065. As part of the Form 1065, the partnership prepares a Schedule K–1 for each partner that shows that partner's share of partnership items.

The partnership incurs a penalty if it fails to file a timely (by the extended due date) Form 1065. The penalty is $195 per month times the numbers of partners, up to a maximum of 12 months.

Look at Form 1065 in Appendix B, and refer to it during the following discussion. The ordinary income and expense items generated by the partnership's trade or business activities are netted to produce a single income or loss amount. The partnership reports this ordinary income or loss from its trade or business activities on Form 1065, page 1. Schedule K (page 4 of Form 1065) accumulates all items that must be separately reported to the partners, including net trade or business income or loss (from page 1). The

[6]§ 703(a)(1). [7]§ 1402(a).

amounts on Schedule K are allocated among and reported by the partners on each owner's Schedule K–1; in Appendix B, the Schedule K-1 immediately follows Form 1065.

EXAMPLE 4

The BR Partnership in Example 3 reports its $60,000 of sales income on Form 1065, page 1, line 1. The $15,000 of business expenses are reported in the appropriate amounts on page 1, line 2 or lines 9–20. Partnership ordinary income of $45,000 is shown on page 1, line 22, and on Schedule K, line 1. The $9,000 capital gain and the $1,000 charitable contribution are reported only on Schedule K, on lines 9a and 13a, respectively.

Beth receives a Schedule K–1 from the partnership that shows her shares of partnership ordinary income of $11,250, long-term capital gain of $2,250, and charitable contributions of $250 on lines 1, 9a, and 13 (Code A), respectively.

She combines these amounts with similar items from other sources on her personal tax return. For example, if she has a $5,000 long-term capital loss from a stock transaction during the year, her overall net capital loss is $2,750. She then evaluates this net amount to determine the amount she may deduct on her Form 1040.

The partnership reconciles book income with its tax return data on Schedule M–1 or Schedule M–3. This reconciliation is similar to the book-tax reconciliation prepared by a C corporation, as discussed in Chapter 12 (see section 12-5).

Schedule M–3 generally is required in lieu of Schedule M–1 if the partnership owns $50 million or more in assets at the end of the year or it reports gross receipts of at least $35 million. The net taxable income calculated on the Analysis of Net Income (Loss) schedule should agree with the reconciled taxable income on Schedule M–1 or Schedule M–3. Schedule L shows an accounting-basis balance sheet, and Schedule M–2 reconciles partners' beginning and ending capital accounts.

14-1d **Partner's Ownership Interest in a Partnership**

Each partner typically owns both a **capital interest** and a **profits (loss) interest** in the partnership. A capital interest is measured by a partner's **capital sharing ratio**, which is the partner's percentage ownership of the capital of the partnership. A partner's capital interest can be determined in several ways. The most widely accepted method measures the capital interest as the percentage of net asset value (asset value remaining after payment of all partnership liabilities) a partner would receive upon immediate liquidation of the partnership.

A profits (loss) interest relates to the partner's percentage allocation of current partnership operating results. **Profit and loss sharing ratios** usually are specified in the partnership agreement. They are used to determine each partner's allocation of partnership ordinary taxable income (loss) and separately stated items.[8] The partnership can change its profit and loss allocations at any time by amending the partnership agreement.

---

[8]§ 704(a).

BRIDGE DISCIPLINE Bridge to Business Law

Although a written partnership agreement is not required by most U.S. states, many rules governing the tax consequences to partners and their partnerships refer to such an agreement. Remember that a partner's distributive share of income, gain, loss, deduction, or credit is determined in accordance with the partnership agreement. Consequently, if taxpayers operating a business in partnership form want a measure of certainty as to the tax consequences of their activities, a carefully drafted partnership agreement is crucial.

An agreement that sets forth the obligations, rights, and powers of the partners should prove invaluable in settling controversies among them and provide some degree of certainty as to the tax consequences of the partners' actions.

The partnership agreement may provide for a **special allocation** of certain items to specified partners, or it may allocate items in a different proportion from the general profit and loss sharing ratios. These items are reported separately to the partner receiving the allocation. For a special allocation to be recognized for tax purposes, it must produce nontax economic consequences to the partners receiving the allocation.[9]

Partnership Special Allocations

When the George-Helen Partnership was formed, George contributed cash and Helen contributed some City of Boise bonds that she had held for investment purposes. The partnership agreement allocates all of the tax-exempt interest income from the bonds ($15,000 this year) to Helen as an inducement for her to remain a partner.

This is an acceptable special allocation for income tax purposes; it reflects the differing economic circumstances that underlie the partners' contributions to the capital of the entity. Because Helen would have received the tax-exempt income if she had not joined the partnership, she can retain the tax-favored treatment via the special allocation.

EXAMPLE 5

Assume the same facts as in Example 5. Three years after it was formed, the George-Helen Partnership purchased some City of Butte bonds. The municipal bond interest income of $15,000 flows through to the partners as a separately stated item, so it retains its tax-exempt status.

The partnership agreement allocates all of this income to George because he is subject to a higher marginal income tax rate than is Helen. The partnership then allocates $15,000 more of the partnership's ordinary income to Helen than to George. These allocations are not effective for income tax purposes because they have no purpose other than a reduction of the partners' combined income tax liability.

EXAMPLE 6

A partner has a **basis in the partnership interest**, just as he or she would have a tax basis in any asset owned. When income flows through to a partner from the partnership, the partner's basis in the partnership interest increases accordingly. When a loss flows through to a partner, basis is reduced.[10] A partner's basis is important when determining the treatment of distributions from the partnership to the partner, establishing the deductibility of partnership losses, and calculating gain or loss on the disposition of the partnership interest.

The Philly Clinic contributes $20,000 of cash to acquire a 30% capital and profits interest in the Red Robin LLC. In its first year of operations, the LLC earns ordinary income of $40,000 and makes no distributions to its members. The Clinic's initial basis is the $20,000 it paid for the interest. Philly recognizes ordinary income of $12,000 (30% interest × $40,000 ordinary income). Philly increases its basis in Red Robin by the same amount, to $32,000.

EXAMPLE 7

---

[9]§ 704(b).

[10]§§ 705, 722, and 723.

The Code provides for increases and decreases in a partner's basis so that the income or loss from partnership operations is taxed only once. In Example 7, if the Philly Clinic sold its interest at the end of the first year for $32,000, it would recognize no gain or loss. If the Code did not provide for an adjustment to the owner's basis for flow-through amounts, Philly's basis still would be $20,000. In that case, Philly would recognize a gain of $12,000 in addition to being taxed on its $12,000 share of the flow-through income from Red Robin.

DIGGING DEEPER 1 | **In-depth coverage can be found on this book's companion website: www.cengagebrain.com**

LO.2

Apply the tax rules regarding the formation of a partnership with cash and property contributions.

14-2 FORMATION OF A PARTNERSHIP: TAX EFFECTS

14-2a Gain or Loss on Contributions to the Partnership

When a taxpayer transfers property to an entity in exchange for valuable consideration, a taxable exchange usually results. Typically, both the taxpayer and the entity realize and recognize gain or loss on the exchange.[11] The gain or loss recognized by the transferor is the difference between the fair market value of the consideration received and the adjusted basis of the property transferred.[12]

In most situations, however, neither the partner nor the partnership recognizes the gain or loss that is realized when a partner contributes property to a partnership in exchange for a partnership interest. Instead, recognition of any realized gain or loss is deferred under § 721.[13] Section 721 applies whenever an owner makes a contribution to the capital of the partnership or LLC, not just when the entity is formed.

There are two reasons for this nonrecognition treatment. First, forming a partnership allows investors to combine their assets toward greater economic goals than could be achieved separately. Only the form of ownership, rather than the amount owned by each investor, has changed. Requiring that gain be recognized on such transfers would make the formation of some partnerships economically unfeasible. Second, because the partnership interest received is typically not a liquid asset, the partner may not be able to generate the cash with which to pay the tax. Thus, deferral of the gain recognizes the economic realities of the business world and follows the wherewithal to pay principle. This treatment is similar to the treatment of assets transferred to a controlled corporation and the treatment of like-kind exchanges.[14]

Creating a Partnership

EXAMPLE
8

In exchange for a 60% profits and loss interest worth $60,000, Alicia transfers two assets to the Wren LLC on the day the entity is created. She contributes cash of $40,000 and retail display equipment (basis to her as a sole proprietor, $8,000; fair market value, $20,000). Because an exchange has occurred between two parties, Alicia *realizes* a $12,000 gain on this transaction. The gain realized is the fair market value of the LLC interest of $60,000 less the basis of the assets that Alicia surrendered to the entity [$40,000 (cash) + $8,000 (equipment)].

Under § 721, Alicia *does not recognize* the $12,000 realized gain in the year of contribution. Alicia might not have had sufficient cash if she had been required to pay tax on the $12,000 gain. All that she received from the entity was an illiquid LLC interest; she received no cash with which to pay any resulting tax liability.

---

[11]§ 1001(c).
[12]§ 1001(a).

[13]§ 721.
[14]§§ 351 and 1031.

Creating a Partnership

Assume the same facts as in Example 8, except that the equipment Alicia contributes to the LLC has an adjusted basis of $25,000. She has incurred a $5,000 *realized* loss [$60,000− ($40,000 + $25,000)], but she cannot deduct the loss. Realized losses, as well as realized gains, are deferred by § 721.

Unless it was essential that the entity receive Alicia's display equipment rather than similar equipment purchased from an outside supplier, Alicia should have considered selling the equipment to a third party. This would have allowed her to deduct a $5,000 loss in the year of the sale. Alicia then could have contributed $60,000 of cash (including the proceeds from the sale) for her interest in the entity, and Wren would have had funds to purchase similar equipment.

Five years after Wren (Examples 8 and 9) was created, Alicia contributes another piece of equipment to the entity. This property has a basis of $35,000 and a fair market value of $50,000. Alicia defers the recognition of the $15,000 realized gain. Section 721 is effective *whenever* an owner makes a contribution to the capital of the partnership or LLC, not just when the entity is formed.

Concept Summary 14.1

Partnership/LLC Taxation

1. Compared with a C corporation, a partnership may offer some advantages, including a single level of taxation, the availability of certain planning opportunities, and simplified administration and reporting.

2. Entities treated as a partnership for tax purposes include general partnerships, limited partnerships, limited liability companies (LLCs), and limited liability partnerships (LLPs).

3. Partnership income and losses flow through to the partners and are reported on the partners' tax returns. The partnership reports ordinary income or loss as well as *separately stated items* to the partners. Under certain conditions, items may be *specially allocated* to specified partners.

4. The partnership files Form 1065 as an information return and prepares a Schedule K–1 to report each partner's share of income and deductions.

14-2b Exceptions to Nonrecognition

Contributions to the capital of a partnership or limited liability entity sometimes trigger recognized gain or loss. Realized gain or loss may be recognized when:

- The transaction is essentially a taxable exchange of properties,
- The transaction is the equivalent of a taxable sale of properties, or
- The partnership interest is received in exchange for services rendered to the partnership by the partner.[15]

Disguised Exchange

If a transaction is essentially a taxable exchange of properties, tax on the gain is not deferred under the nonrecognition provisions of § 721.[16]

---

[15]§ 721(b). A few other exceptions to § 721 treatment also exist.

[16]Reg. § 1.731–1(c)(3).

EXAMPLE 11

Sara owns land, and Bob owns stock. Sara would like to have Bob's stock, and Bob wants Sara's land. If Sara and Bob both contribute their property to newly formed SB Partnership in exchange for interests in the partnership, the tax on the transaction appears to be deferred under § 721. The tax on a subsequent distribution by the partnership of the land to Bob and the stock to Sara also appears to be deferred under partnership distribution rules.

Not so! Tax law disregards the passage of the properties through the partnership and holds, instead, that Sara and Bob exchanged the land and stock directly. Thus, the transaction is treated as any other taxable exchange.

Disguised Sale

Immediate gain recognition also occurs in the context of a **disguised sale** of property or of a partnership interest. A disguised sale occurs when a partner contributes property to a partnership and soon thereafter receives a distribution from the partnership. This distribution could be viewed as a payment by the partnership for purchase of the property.[17]

EXAMPLE 12

Kim transfers property to the existing KLM Partnership. The property has an adjusted basis of $10,000 and a fair market value of $30,000. Two weeks later, the partnership distributes $30,000 of cash to Kim. Lacking an exception under the distribution rules, the $30,000 of cash received would not be taxable to Kim if the basis for her partnership interest prior to the distribution was greater than the amount distributed.

However, the transaction appears to be a disguised purchase-sale transaction, rather than an asset contribution and distribution. Therefore, Kim recognizes gain of $20,000 on transfer of the property, and the partnership is deemed to have purchased the property for $30,000.

A disguised sale is presumed to exist when a contribution by one partner is followed within two years by a specified distribution to him or her from the partnership.

Services

Another exception to the nonrecognition provision of § 721 occurs when a partner receives a capital interest in the partnership as compensation for services rendered to the partnership. This is not a tax-deferred transaction because services are not treated as "property" that can be transferred to a partnership on a tax-free basis. Instead, the partner performing the services recognizes ordinary compensation income equal to the fair market value of the partnership interest received.[18]

The partnership may deduct the amount included in the *service partner's* income if the services are of a deductible nature. If the services are not deductible by the partnership, they are capitalized. For example, architectural plans created by a partner are capitalized into the basis of a structure built with those plans. Alternatively, day-to-day management services performed by a partner for the partnership usually are deductible by the partnership.

EXAMPLE 13

Bill, Carol, and Dave form the BCD Partnership, with each receiving a one-third capital and profits interest in the entity. Dave receives his one-third interest as compensation for the accounting and tax planning services he rendered to the partnership. The value of a one-third capital interest in the partnership (for each of the parties) is $20,000.

The partnership deducts $20,000 for Dave's services in computing ordinary income. Dave recognizes $20,000 of compensation income, and he takes a $20,000 basis in his partnership interest. The same result would occur if the partnership had paid Dave $20,000 for his services and he immediately contributed that amount to the entity for a one-third ownership interest.

---

[17]§ 707(a)(2)(B).

[18]§ 83(a).

In-depth coverage can be found on this book's companion website: www.cengagebrain.com

2 DIGGING DEEPER

14-2c **Tax Issues Related to Contributed Property**

When a partner makes a tax-deferred contribution of an asset to the capital of a partnership, the entity assigns a *carryover basis* to the property.[19] The partnership's basis in the asset (the asset's "inside basis") is equal to the basis the partner held in the property prior to its transfer to the partnership. The partner's basis in the new partnership interest (the owner's "outside basis") equals the prior basis in the contributed asset. The tax term for this basis concept is *substituted basis*. Thus, two assets are created out of one when a partnership is formed, namely, the property in the hands of the new entity and the new asset (the partnership interest) in the hands of the partner. Both assets are assigned a basis that is derived from the partner's basis in the contributed property.

The holding period of a partner's interest includes that of the contributed property when the property was a § 1231 asset or capital asset in the partner's hands. When other assets, including cash, are contributed, the holding period starts on the day the interest is acquired.

EXAMPLE 14

On June 1, José transfers property to the JKL LLC in exchange for a one-third interest in the entity. The property has an adjusted basis to José of $10,000 and a fair market value of $30,000. José incurs a $20,000 realized gain on the exchange ($30,000 − $10,000), but he does not recognize any of the gain. Jose's basis for his interest in JKL is the amount necessary to recognize the $20,000 deferred gain if his interest later is sold for its $30,000 fair market value. This amount, $10,000, is the substituted basis.

The basis of the property contributed to JKL is the amount necessary to allow for the recognition of the $20,000 deferred gain if the property later is sold for its $30,000 fair market value. This amount, also $10,000, is the carryover basis.

The holding period for the contributed asset also carries over to the entity. Thus, JKL's holding period for the asset includes the period during which José owned the asset individually.

Depreciation Method and Period

If depreciable property is contributed to the partnership, the partnership usually is required to use the same cost recovery method and life as had been used by the partner. The partnership merely "steps into the shoes" of the partner and continues the same cost recovery calculations.

Intangible Assets

If a partner contributes an existing "§ 197" intangible asset to the partnership, the partnership generally will "step into the shoes" of the partner in determining future amortization deductions. Section 197 intangible assets include purchased goodwill, going-concern value, information systems, customer- or supplier-related intangible assets, patents, licenses obtained from a governmental unit, franchises, trademarks, covenants not to compete, and other items.

---

[19]§ 723.

Receivables, Inventory, and Built-In Losses

To prevent ordinary income from being converted into capital gain, gain or loss is treated as ordinary when the partnership disposes of either of the following.[20]

- Contributed receivables that were unrealized in the contributing partner's hands at the contribution date. Such receivables include the right to receive payment for goods or services.
- Contributed property that was inventory in the contributor's hands on the contribution date, if the partnership disposes of the property within *five years of the contribution*. For this purpose, inventory includes all tangible property except capital and real or depreciable business assets.

A similar rule is designed to prevent a capital loss from being converted into an ordinary loss. Under the rule, if contributed property is disposed of at a loss and the property had a "built-in" capital loss on the contribution date, the loss is treated as a capital loss if the partnership disposes of the property *within five years of the contribution*. The capital loss is limited to the "built-in" loss on the date of contribution.[21]

The Big Picture

EXAMPLE 15

Return to the facts of *The Big Picture* on p. 14-1. Recall that Kyle, Maria, and Josh decide to structure their venture as an LLC. Assume that Kyle has a basis of $600,000 in the $2 million of real estate he contributed, and that Maria has a $0 basis in the bakery equipment and the café furnishings.

When Beachside Properties LLC is formed, no tax results for the LLC or for Kyle or Maria. Kyle does not recognize his $1.4 million realized gain, nor does Maria recognize her $500,000 realized gain.

Kyle takes a substituted basis of $600,000 for his interest, and Maria takes a substituted basis of $1.5 million ($1.5 million for contributed cash + $0 for contributed property). Beachside Properties assumes a carryover basis of $600,000 for the real estate contributed by Kyle and $0 for the property contributed by Maria. To the extent the buildings and other land improvements are depreciable, the LLC "steps into Kyle's shoes" in calculating depreciation deductions.

When Josh vests in his 5% capital interest in the LLC, the $200,000 value of the interest is taxable to him, because it is a capital interest received in exchange for services. Beachside Properties probably will capitalize this amount because it relates to construction activities. Josh's 20% share of the future profits of the LLC are taxed to him as they flow through from the LLC.

14-2d Inside and Outside Bases

Reference has been made previously to the partnership's inside basis and the partners' outside basis. **Inside basis** refers to the adjusted basis of each partnership asset, as determined from the partnership's tax accounts. **Outside basis** represents each partner's basis in the partnership interest. Each partner "owns" a share of the partnership's inside basis for all of its assets, and all partners should maintain a record of their respective outside bases.

LO.3

Determine the tax treatment of expenditures of a newly formed partnership and identify elections available to the partnership.

14-2e Tax Accounting Elections

Numerous tax accounting elections must be made when a new partnership is formed. These elections are formal decisions on how a particular transaction or tax attribute should be handled. Most of these elections must be made by the partnership rather than

---

[20]§ 724. For this purpose, § 724(d)(2) waives the holding period requirement in defining § 1231 property.

[21]§ 724(c).

Concept Summary 14.2

Partnership Formation and Basis Computation

1. Generally, partners or partnerships do not recognize gain or loss when property is contributed in exchange for capital interests.

2. Partners contributing property in exchange for partnership interests take the contributed property's adjusted basis for their *outside basis* in their partnership interest. The partners are said to take a substituted basis in their partnership interest.

3. The partnership keeps the contributing partner's basis as the *inside basis* in property it receives. The contributed property is said to take a carryover basis.

4. The partnership's holding period for contributed property may include the contributing partner's holding period.

5. Income or gain is recognized by a contributing partner when services are contributed or when the capital contribution is a disguised sale or exchange.

6. Special rules may apply when the partnership disposes of contributed receivables, inventory, or loss assets.

by the partners individually.[22] For example, the *partnership* makes the elections involving the following tax accounting items.

- Inventory methods.
- Tax year and accounting method (cash, accrual, or hybrid).
- Cost recovery methods and assumptions.
- First-year cost recovery deductions for certain tangible personal property.
- Treatment (i.e., deduction or credit) of research and experimentation costs.
- Amortization of organizational costs and amortization period.
- Cost allocation methods to compute the domestic production activities deduction.

Each partner is bound by the decisions made by the partnership relative to these elections. If the partnership fails to make an election, a partner cannot make the election individually.

Although most elections are made by the partnership, each *partner* separately makes a specific election for the following relatively narrow tax accounting issues.

- Whether to take a deduction or a credit for taxes paid to foreign countries.
- Whether to claim the cost or percentage depletion method for oil and gas wells.
- Whether to reduce the basis of depreciable property first when excluding income from discharge of indebtedness.

14-2f Initial Costs of a Partnership

In its initial stages, a partnership incurs expenses relating to some or all of the following: forming the partnership (organizational costs), admitting partners to the partnership, marketing and selling partnership units to prospective partners **(syndication costs)**, acquiring assets, starting business operations (startup costs), negotiating contracts, and dealing with other items.

Many of these expenditures are not currently deductible. However, the Code permits a deduction or ratable (straight-line) amortization of "organizational" and "startup" costs. Costs incurred to acquire tangible assets are included in the initial basis of the acquired assets, leading to depreciation deductions. "Syndication costs" may be neither amortized nor deducted.[23]

---

[22]§ 703(b).

[23]§ 709(a).

Organizational Costs

Organizational costs are incurred incident to the creation of the partnership and are capital in nature. Such costs include accounting and legal fees associated with the partnership formation.[24] Costs incurred for the following purposes are *not* organizational costs.

- Acquiring assets for the partnership.
- Transferring assets to the partnership.
- Admitting partners, other than at formation.
- Removing partners, other than at formation.
- Negotiating operating contracts.

A partnership may deduct up to $5,000 of organizational costs in the year in which it begins business. This amount is reduced, however, by these organizational costs that exceed $50,000. Any organizational costs that cannot be deducted under this provision are amortizable over 180 months beginning with the month in which the partnership begins business.

The election to deduct organizational costs is made by entering the proper amounts on the first partnership return. Lacking such a computation, no deduction or amortization of the organizational costs is allowed until the entity is liquidated.

EXAMPLE 16

The Bluejay LLC, which was formed on March 1, incurs $52,000 in organizational costs. Bluejay uses a calendar tax year. On its first tax return for the period March–December, Bluejay can deduct $5,722 for these items. This deduction is the sum of:

- $5,000 reduced by the $2,000 ($52,000 − $50,000) amount by which the organizational costs exceed $50,000 = $3,000.
- $2,722 ($49,000 × 10/180) amortization of the remaining $49,000 ($52,000 − $3,000) of organizational costs for 10 months.

If Bluejay had failed to make a proper election to deduct or amortize the organizational costs, none of these costs would have been deductible until the entity liquidated.

Startup Costs

Operating costs that are incurred after the entity is formed but before it begins business are known as startup costs. Like organizational costs, startup costs are capitalized and may be immediately expensed and/or amortized.[25] Such costs include marketing surveys prior to conducting business, pre-operating advertising expenses, costs of establishing an accounting system, and salaries paid to executives and employees before the start of business.

A partnership may deduct up to $5,000 of startup costs in the year in which it begins business. This amount is reduced, however, by the startup costs that exceed $50,000.

Costs that are not deductible under this provision are amortizable over 180 months beginning with the month in which the partnership begins business. If the deduction for startup costs is not claimed, no deduction or amortization of the startup costs is allowed until the partnership is liquidated.

DIGGING DEEPER **3**   In-depth coverage can be found on this book's companion website: www.cengagebrain.com

---

[24]§ 709(b)(2).   [25]§ 195.

14-3 OPERATIONS OF THE PARTNERSHIP

A key consideration in the taxation of partnerships is that a variety of entities can be partners and each may be affected differently by the partnership's operations. In particular, any combination of individuals, corporations, trusts, estates, or other partnerships may be partners. Furthermore, at the end of each year, every partner receives a share of the partnership's income, deductions, credits, and alternative minimum tax (AMT) preferences and adjustments.[26]

These flow-through items ultimately may be reported and taxed on a wide variety of income tax returns [e.g., Forms 1040 (Individuals), 1041 (Fiduciaries), 1120 (C corporations), and 1120S (S corporations)], each facing different limitations and rules. Thus, the ultimate tax treatment of partnership operations is directly affected by how the partnership reports its operating results.

14-3a Schedules K and K-1

A partnership measures and reports two kinds of income: separately stated items and nonseparately stated ordinary (operating) income. A separately stated item is any item with tax attributes that could affect partners differently. Separately stated items are segregated and reported separately on the partnership's Schedule K and each partner's Schedule K–1. All other (nonseparately stated) income and expenses are reported as income from operations on page 1 of the partnership's Form 1065; the net amount then is allocated to the partners on Schedules K and K–1. Items passed through separately include the following.[27]

- Net short-term and net long-term capital gains or losses.
- Section 1231 gains and losses.
- Charitable contributions.
- Portfolio income items (qualified and ordinary dividends, interest, and royalties).
- Expenses related to portfolio income.
- Immediately expensed tangible personal property (§ 179).
- Data used by partners to compute their deduction for domestic production activities.[28]
- AMT preference and adjustment items.
- Self-employment income.
- Passive activity items (e.g., rental real estate income or loss).
- Intangible drilling and development costs.
- Taxes paid to other countries.

A partnership is not allowed to claim the following deductions.

- Net operating loss (NOL).
- Dividends received deduction.
- Items that are allowed only to individuals, such as standard deductions or personal exemptions.

---

[26]§ 702(a).
[27]§ 702(b).

[28]§ 199.

The Big Picture

EXAMPLE
17

Return to the facts of *The Big Picture* on p. 14-1. In its second year of operations, Beachside Properties LLC reports income and expenses from operating the café as well as rent income and expenses from leasing the other buildings. Beachside's activities are summarized as follows.

Sales revenue	$2,000,000
Cost of sales	800,000
Salaries to employees	500,000
Cost recovery deductions	91,984
Utilities, supplies, and other expenses	128,016
Taxes and licenses (including payroll taxes)	60,000
Contribution to charity	6,000
Short-term capital gain	12,000
Net income from rental real estate	300,000
Qualified dividends received	4,000
Tax-exempt income (bond interest)	2,100
AMT adjustment (cost recovery)	18,224
Payment of medical expenses on behalf of Kyle	4,000
Net operating loss (NOL) from last year's operations	250,000
Cash distribution to Maria	20,000

Refer to Form 1065 in Appendix B. Beachside's ordinary income is determined and reported on the partnership return as follows.

Nonseparately Stated Items (Ordinary Income)	
Sales revenue	$2,000,000
Cost of sales	(800,000)
Salaries to employees	(500,000)
Cost recovery deductions	(91,984)
Utilities, supplies, and other expenses	(128,016)
Taxes and licenses (including payroll taxes)	(60,000)
Ordinary income [Form 1065, page 1, line 22, and Form 1065, page 4 (Schedule K), line 1]	$ 420,000

Beachside's separately stated income and deduction items are:

Separately Stated Income and Deductions (Schedule K)	
Net income from rental real estate (line 2)	$300,000
Qualified dividends received (line 6b)	4,000
Short-term capital gain (line 8)	12,000
Contribution to charity (line 13a)	(6,000)

Beachside is not allowed a deduction for last year's NOL—this item was passed through to the owners in the previous year. Moreover, the LLC is not allowed a deduction for payment of Kyle's medical expenses. This payment probably is handled as a distribution to Kyle, who may report it as a medical expense on his Form 1040, Schedule A in determining itemized deductions.

Maria's distribution is not deducted by Beachside. That amount instead reduces Maria's basis in her LLC interest.

The AMT adjustment is not a separate component of Beachside's ordinary income. It is reported to Beachside's members so that they can properly calculate any AMT liability of their own.

Beachside reports the following additional information the members may utilize in preparing their own income tax returns.

continued

Additional Information (Schedule K)	
AMT adjustment—cost recovery (line 17a)	$18,224
Tax-exempt income—bond interest (line 18a)	2,100
Distributions (line 19a)	24,000
Investment income (line 20a)	4,000

The LLC members' pass-through income represents net earnings (loss) from self-employment and is reported on line 14a.

The Big Picture

EXAMPLE 18

Continue with the facts in Example 17, but now consider the entity's book-tax reconciliation. Beachside Properties LLC must prepare the Analysis of Net Income (Loss) and Schedule M–1 on Form 1065, page 5. In preparing these schedules, the LLC combines the ordinary income of $420,000 and the four separately stated income and deduction amounts in Example 17 to arrive at "net income" of $730,000. This amount is shown on line 1 of the Analysis of Net Income (Loss) and is the amount to which book income is reconciled on Schedule M–1, line 9.

The Big Picture

EXAMPLE 19

Assume the same facts as in Example 17, but now consider the effect of the LLC's operations on one of its members. Maria, a 40% owner, will receive a Schedule K–1 from Beachside Properties, on which she is allocated a 40% share of ordinary income and separately stated items. Thus, on her Form 1040, Maria includes $168,000 of ordinary income, a $2,400 charitable contribution, a $4,800 short-term capital gain, $120,000 of passive rent income, and $1,600 of qualified dividend income. Maria's Schedule K-1 also reports the $20,000 cash distribution received.

Maria discloses her $840 share of tax-exempt interest on the first page of Form 1040. In determining her AMT liability (if any), Maria will take into account a $7,290 positive adjustment ($18,224 × 40%).

Domestic Production Activities Deduction (§ 199)

As noted in Chapter 5, the conduct of certain businesses, usually manufacturing activities, can yield a domestic production activities deduction (DPAD). To determine the base for the deduction, domestic production gross receipts (DPGR) is computed. Then related cost of goods sold and direct and indirect expenses are subtracted to arrive at qualified production activities income (QPAI). The deduction (or DPAD) generally is 9 percent of the lesser of QPAI or taxable income.[29] When the taxpayer is not a corporation, modified AGI is substituted for taxable income. In no event, however, may the DPAD exceed 50 percent of the W–2 wages paid that are attributable to domestic production activities.[30]

When pass-through entities are involved (i.e., partnerships, S corporations, estates, and trusts), special rules apply.[31] Specifically, in the case of partnerships and limited liability entities, the following rules govern the DPAD computation and allowance.

- Whether an activity qualifies for the DPAD is determined at the entity level.
- Each partner is allocated its share of QPAI and W–2 wages related to domestic production activities. The appropriate amounts are listed on Schedule K–1 of Form 1065.

[29]§ 199(a).
[30]§ 199(b).

[31]The rules applicable to pass-through entities are contained in § 199(d)(1) and Reg. § 1.199–5.

- The partner combines the partnership pass-through items with those from other sources (e.g., if the partner operates a separate factory).
- The deduction then is computed at the partner level.
- Guaranteed payments, discussed in detail in a later section, are not W–2 wages for DPAD purposes.[32]

DIGGING DEEPER 4   In-depth coverage can be found on this book's companion website: www.cengagebrain.com

Distributions, Withdrawals

Asset distributions and withdrawals by partners during the year do not affect the partnership's income determination.[33] These items usually are treated as made on the last day of the partnership's tax year. Such distributions reduce the partner's outside basis in the entity by the amount of the cash received, or by the inside basis of the asset to the entity, but not below zero. The entity's inside basis in assets is similarly reduced. The partner usually assigns to the received property a basis equal to the entity's inside basis in the distributed asset.

EXAMPLE 20

Bueno Company is a partner in the BB Partnership. The basis in Bueno's partnership interest is $10,000. The partnership distributes $3,000 cash to Bueno at the end of the year. Bueno does not recognize any gain on the distribution. It reduces its basis in BB by $3,000 (the amount of the distribution) to $7,000. Bueno's basis in the cash received is $3,000, and the partnership's inside basis for its assets is reduced by the $3,000 of cash distributed.

BB also distributes to Bueno a plot of land worth $5,000, with a $2,000 basis to BB. Neither BB nor Bueno recognizes a gain from this distribution. Bueno assigns the land a $2,000 basis, and it reduces its basis in BB by the same amount.

The result in Example 20 arises whether or not a similar distribution is made to other partners. In a partnership, all partners need not receive a pro rata distribution at the same time, as long as capital account balances are maintained appropriately.

DIGGING DEEPER 5   In-depth coverage can be found on this book's companion website: www.cengagebrain.com

[32]Reg. § 1.199–5(b)(1)(i).   [33]§ 731(a).

Concept Summary 14.3

Tax Reporting of Partnership Activities

Item	Partnership Level (Form 1065)	Partner Level (Schedule K–1)
1. Compute partnership ordinary income.	Page 1, line 22. Schedule K, line 1.	Line 1. Each partner's share is passed through for separate reporting. Each partner's basis is increased.
2. Compute partnership ordinary loss.	Page 1, line 22. Schedule K, line 1.	Line 1. Each partner's share is passed through for separate reporting. Each partner's basis is decreased. The amount of a partner's loss deduction may be limited. Losses that may not be deducted are carried forward for use in future years.
3. Separately reported income and deduction items such as portfolio income, capital gain and loss, AMT and foreign tax items, and § 179 deductions.	Schedule K, various lines.	Various lines. Each partner's share of each item is passed through for separate reporting.
4. Net earnings from self-employment.	Schedule K, line 14a, Code A.	Line 14, Code A.

14-3b Partnership Allocations

After ordinary income, separately stated items, and other related information are determined at the partnership level, those amounts are allocated among the partners and reported on their tax returns. Allocations are made as required by the partnership agreement, using the profit and loss sharing ratios agreed to by the owners.

Alternatively, two key special allocation rules also can affect a partner's Schedule K–1 results.[34]

Economic Effect

The partnership agreement can provide that any partner may share capital, profits, and losses in ratios that are tailored to their needs.[35] For example, a partner could have a 25 percent capital sharing ratio, yet be allocated 30 percent of the profits and 20 percent of the losses of the partnership, or, as in Examples 5 and 6, a partner could be allocated a specific amount or items of income, deduction, gain, or loss. Such special allocations are permissible if they meet the **economic effect test**.[36] The rules prevent partners from shifting income and loss items merely to reduce current taxes.

In-depth coverage can be found on this book's companion website: www.cengagebrain.com   **6** DIGGING DEEPER

Precontribution Gain or Loss

Certain income, gain, loss, and deductions relative to contributed property may not be allocated under the economic effect rules.[37] Instead, **precontribution gain or loss** is allocated among the partners to take into account the variation between the basis of the

---

[34]The Code requires or allows certain other allocations not discussed here.   [36]Reg. § 1.704–1(b).
[35]§ 704(a).   [37]§ 704(b).

property and its fair market value on the date of contribution.[38] For nondepreciable property, this means that *built-in* gain or loss on the date of contribution is allocated to the contributing partner when the property eventually is disposed of by the partnership in a taxable transaction.

The Big Picture

EXAMPLE

21

Return to the facts of *The Big Picture* on p. 14-1. When Beachside Properties LLC was formed, among other items, Kyle contributed land (value of $800,000 and basis of $600,000) and buildings (value of $1,200,000 and basis of $0). Maria contributed equipment and furnishings (value of $500,000 and basis of $0).

For book purposes, Beachside records the land and other properties at their fair market values. For tax purposes, the LLC takes carryover bases in the properties. The LLC must keep track of the differences between the basis in each property and the value at the contribution date. If any of this property is sold, the gain is allocated to the contributing partner to the extent of any previously unrecognized built-in gain.

For example, if Beachside sells the land contributed by Kyle for $1.1 million, the gain is calculated and allocated as follows.

	Book	Tax
Amount realized	$1,100,000	$1,100,000
Less: Adjusted basis	(800,000)	(600,000)
Gain realized	$ 300,000	$ 500,000
Built-in gain allocated solely to Kyle	(—0—)	(200,000)
Remaining gain (allocated among members)	$ 300,000	$ 300,000

For Federal income tax purposes, Kyle recognizes $320,000 of the gain [($300,000 × 40%) + $200,000], Maria recognizes $120,000 ($300,000 × 40%), and Josh recognizes $60,000 ($300,000 × 20%).

LO.5

Determine a partner's basis in the partnership interest.

14-3c Basis of a Partnership Interest

A partner's basis in the partnership interest is important for determining the treatment of distributions from the partnership to the partner, establishing the deductibility of partnership losses, and calculating gain or loss on the partner's disposition of the partnership interest.

A partner's basis is not reflected anywhere on the Schedule K–1. Instead, each partner maintains a personal record of the basis in the partnership interest.

Initial Basis in the Partnership Interest

A partner's basis in a newly formed partnership usually equals (1) the adjusted basis in any cash or other property contributed to the partnership plus (2) the fair market value of any services the partner performed for the partnership (i.e., the amount of ordinary income reported by the partner for services rendered to the partnership).

A partnership interest also can be acquired after the partnership has been formed. The method of acquisition controls how the partner's initial basis is computed. If the partnership interest is purchased from another partner, the purchasing partner's basis is the amount paid (cost basis) for the partnership interest. The basis of a partnership interest acquired by gift is the donor's basis for the interest plus, in certain cases, some or all of the transfer (gift) tax paid by the donor. The basis of a partnership interest acquired through inheritance generally is the fair market value of the interest on the date the partner dies.

---

[38]§ 704(c)(1)(A).

The equivalent in financial accounting to the partner's basis in his or her partnership interest is the **capital account**. A partner's ending balance in the capital account is not required to be the same as his or her basis in the partnership interest. Just as the tax and accounting bases of a specific asset may differ, a partner's capital account and basis in the partnership interest usually are not equal.

Whereas contributions and most distributions from the partnership do not create financial accounting income, the capital account is "written up or down" to aggregate fair market value when the entity is formed. For most partnerships with simple financial transactions, *changes* to the capital account parallel closely the annual changes to the partner's basis in the partnership. Basis in one's partnership interest cannot be a negative number, but the capital account can become negative.

Oddly, the Schedules K–1 for the partners require an accounting for their capital accounts, but there is no required reconciliation for the partner's tax basis on the Schedule K–1. As a result, the tax adviser may find that a new partnership client has poor records with respect to the basis amounts of the partners, and a reconstruction must take place so that future computations will be correct. Sometimes, lacking adequate information with which to make this computation, the capital account is used because it is "close enough" and forms a good surrogate for the partner's basis in the partnership.

Basis Adjustments Due to Entity Operations

After the partnership begins its activities, or after a new partner is admitted to the partnership, the partner's basis is adjusted for numerous items. The following operating results *increase* a partner's basis.

- The partner's proportionate share of partnership income (including capital gains and tax-exempt income).
- The partner's proportionate share of any increase in partnership liabilities.

The following operating results *decrease* the partner's basis in the partnership. A partner's basis in the partnership interest cannot be reduced below zero.

- The partner's proportionate share of partnership deductions and losses (including capital losses).
- The partner's proportionate share of nondeductible expenses.
- The partner's proportionate share of any reduction in partnership liabilities.[39]

Increasing the basis for the partner's share of partnership taxable income is logical, because the partner already has been taxed on the income. By increasing the partner's basis, the partner is not taxed again on the income when he or she sells the interest or receives a distribution from the partnership.

It also is logical that tax-exempt income should increase the partner's basis. If the income is tax-exempt in the current period, it should not contribute to the recognition of gain when the partner either sells the interest or receives a distribution from the partnership. Decreasing the basis for the partner's share of deductible losses, deductions, and noncapitalizable, nondeductible expenditures is done for the same reasons.

Yuri is a one-third member in the XYZ LLC. His proportionate share of operations during the current year consists of $20,000 of ordinary taxable income and $10,000 of tax-exempt income. None of the income is distributed to Yuri.

The basis of Yuri's LLC interest before adjusting for his share of income is $35,000, and the fair market value of the interest before considering the income items is $50,000.

The unrealized gain inherent in Yuri's investment in XYZ is $15,000 ($50,000 − $35,000). Yuri's proportionate share of the income items should increase the fair market value of the interest to

EXAMPLE

22

continued

---

[39]§§ 705 and 752.

$80,000 ($50,000 + $20,000 + $10,000). When the basis of Yuri's interest is increased to $65,000 ($35,000 + $20,000 + $10,000), the unrealized gain inherent in Yuri's investment remains at $15,000.

Thus, $20,000 of ordinary taxable income is taxed to Yuri this year and should not be taxed again when Yuri either sells his interest or receives a distribution. Similarly, the tax-exempt income is exempt this year and should not increase Yuri's gain when he either sells his interest or receives a distribution from XYZ.

TAX FACT   What Do Partnerships Do?

Partnerships report over $20 trillion in assets on their Form 1065 balance sheets. The partnership form seems to be especially popular for businesses operating in the financial services and real estate industries. Manufacturing assets tend not to be found as frequently in these entities.

Assets of Partnerships, by Industry

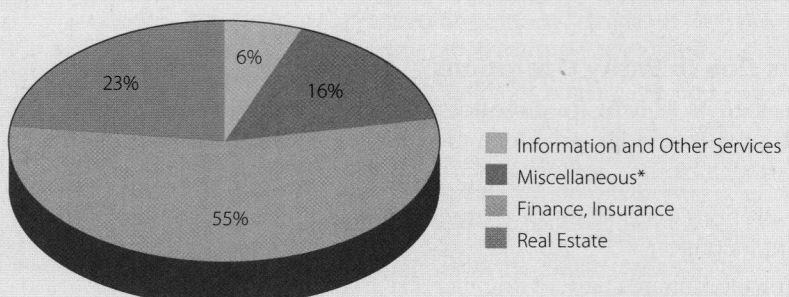

6%
16%
23%
55%

- Information and Other Services
- Miscellaneous*
- Finance, Insurance
- Real Estate

*Includes aggregated amounts from the agriculture, health care, construction, manufacturing, wholesale and retail trade, education, and arts and entertainment sectors.

Partnership Liabilities

A partner's basis includes the partner's share of partnership debt.[40] Partnership debt includes most debt that is considered a liability under financial accounting rules. However, partnership debt for this purpose does *not* include the accounts payable of a cash basis partnership and certain contingent liabilities.

Partnership debt is classified as either recourse or nonrecourse.[41] For **recourse debt**, the partnership or at least one of the partners is personally liable. This liability can exist, for example, through the operation of state law or through personal guarantees that a partner makes to the creditor. If the entity defaults on the loan, the lender can pursue the other assets of the borrower, including personal-use property.

For **nonrecourse debt**, no partner is personally liable. Lenders of nonrecourse debt generally require that collateral be pledged against the loan. Upon default, the lender can claim only the collateral, not the partners' personal assets.

Liabilities and Partnership Interest Basis

EXAMPLE 23

The Bay Partnership financed its asset acquisitions with debt. If the partnership defaults on the debt, the lender can place a lien on the partners' salaries and personal assets. This constitutes recourse debt.

---

[40]§ 752.

[41]Reg. § 1.752–1(a). All of the debts of an LLC generally are treated as nonrecourse debt for its members, because it is the entity, and not the members, that is ultimately liable for repayment.

Liabilities and Partnership Interest Basis

The Tray LLC financed its asset acquisitions with debt. If the entity defaults on the debt, the lender can repossess the equipment purchased with the loan proceeds. This constitutes nonrecourse debt.

When Ray bought into the Sleigh LLC, the entity was in the midst of settling litigation as to its liability to those who had purchased its products and were making warranty claims against the entity. Ray's basis in his Sleigh interest does not include his share of these contingent liabilities.

A partner's share of entity-level debt usually increases as a result of increases in outstanding partnership debt. This creates additional basis in the partnership for the partner, against which flow-through losses can be deducted.

Jim and Becky contribute property to form the JB Partnership. Jim contributes cash of $30,000. Becky contributes land with an adjusted basis and fair market value of $45,000, subject to a liability of $15,000. The partnership borrows $50,000 to finance construction of a building on the contributed land. At the end of the first year, the accrual basis partnership owes $3,500 in trade accounts payable to various vendors. No other operating activities occurred. If Jim and Becky share equally in liabilities, the partners' bases in their partnership interests are determined as follows.

Jim's Basis		Becky's Basis	
Contributed cash	$30,000	Basis in contributed land	$ 45,000
		Less: Debt assumed by partnership	(15,000)
Share of debt on land (assumed by partnership)	7,500	Share of debt on land (assumed by partnership)	7,500
Share of construction loan	25,000	Share of construction loan	25,000
Share of trade accounts payable	1,750	Share of trade accounts payable	1,750
Basis, end of year 1	$64,250	Basis, end of year 1	$ 64,250

A decrease in a partner's share of partnership debt is treated as a cash distribution and decreases the partner's basis. This limits the partner's ability to deduct current-year flow-through losses.

In-depth coverage can be found on this book's companion website: www.cengagebrain.com | **7 DIGGING DEEPER**

14-3d Partner's Basis, Gain, and Loss

The partner's basis also is affected by (1) postacquisition contributions of cash or property to the partnership and (2) postacquisition distributions of cash or property from the partnership.

Ed is a one-third member in ERM LLC. On January 1, Ed's basis in his interest was $50,000. The calendar year, accrual basis entity generated ordinary taxable income of $210,000. It also received $60,000 of tax-exempt interest income from City of Buffalo bonds. It paid $3,000 in nondeductible fines and penalties.

On July 1, Ed contributed $20,000 cash and a computer (zero basis to him) to ERM. Ed's monthly cash draw from the LLC is $3,000; this is not a guaranteed payment. The only entity liabilities are trade accounts payable. On January 1, the trade accounts payable totaled $45,000; this account balance was $21,000 on December 31. Ed shares in one-third of the entity's liabilities for basis purposes.

continued

Ed's basis in the LLC on December 31 is $115,000, computed as follows.

Beginning basis in the LLC interest	$ 50,000
Share of ordinary income	70,000
Share of tax-exempt income	20,000
Share of nondeductible fines and penalties	(1,000)
Ed's basis in noncash capital contribution (computer)	–0–
Additional cash contributions	20,000
Capital withdrawal ($3,000 per month)	(36,000)
Share of net decrease in ERM liabilities [$1/3 \times$ ($45,000 − $21,000)]	(8,000)
Ending basis in the LLC interest	$115,000

If Ed withdraws cash of $115,000 from ERM the next year, the withdrawal is tax-free to him and reduces his basis to zero. The distribution is tax-free because Ed has recognized his share of net income throughout his association with the entity via the annual flow-through of his share of the ERM income and expense items to his personal tax return.

If Ed receives a $20,000 cash withdrawal of his share of the municipal bond interest income, that amount retains its nontaxable character; his basis was increased when ERM received the interest income.

Noncash Distributions

When a distribution involves something other than cash, the recipient partner (1) reduces the basis in the partnership interest and (2) assigns a basis to the asset received, both by the amount of the inside basis of the distributed asset. When cash and another asset are distributed at the same time, the partner first accounts for the cash received.

Loss never is recognized when a partnership makes a distribution other than possibly in its own liquidation. A partner recognizes gain only when receiving *cash* in an amount in excess of the basis in the partnership.

Distributions of Noncash Assets

EXAMPLE 28

Pert Corporation has a $100,000 basis in the PQR Partnership. Pert receives a distribution from PQR in the form of a plot of land (basis to PQR of $40,000, fair market value of $50,000). Pert does not recognize gain from the distribution. Pert's basis in the land is $40,000 (i.e., a carryover basis), and its basis in PQR now is $60,000 ($100,000 − $40,000).

EXAMPLE 29

Pert Corporation has a $100,000 basis in the PQR Partnership. Pert receives a distribution from PQR in the form of a plot of land (basis to PQR of $40,000, fair market value of $50,000) and $75,000 of cash.

Pert does not recognize any gain from the distribution because the cash received ($75,000) does not exceed Pert's partnership basis ($100,000). Pert's basis in the land is $25,000, the basis in PQR remaining after accounting for the cash ($100,000 partnership basis − $75,000 cash = $25,000 basis assigned to land). Pert's basis in the partnership now is zero ($25,000 basis after accounting for the cash − $25,000 assigned to the land).

EXAMPLE 30

Pert Corporation has a $100,000 basis in the PQR Partnership. Pert receives a distribution from PQR in the form of a plot of land (basis to PQR of $40,000, fair market value of $50,000) and $125,000 of cash. Pert recognizes $25,000 of gain from the distribution ($125,000 cash received − $100,000 basis in PQR). Pert's basis in the land is $0, as there is no basis in PQR remaining after accounting for the cash. Pert's basis in the partnership also is zero.

Capital Changes

When a partnership interest is sold, exchanged, or retired, the partner must compute the basis as of the date the transaction occurs. The partner recognizes gain or loss on the disposition of the partnership interest, and this usually is a capital gain or loss. Income "bunching" may occur if the partner recognizes the pass-through of operating income in the same tax year during which the sale of the interest occurs. To the extent the partner is allocated a share of ordinary income items (i.e., "hot assets") that have yet to be recognized by the partnership, some of the capital gain is converted to ordinary income.[42]

When its basis in the TUV Partnership is $100,000, taking into account all earnings to date and the sale-date liabilities of the partnership, Kurt Corporation sells its interest in the entity to Gloria for $120,000. Kurt recognizes a $20,000 capital gain [$120,000 (amount realized) − $100,000 (basis in partnership interest)].

EXAMPLE 31

When its basis in the TUV Partnership is $100,000, taking into account all earnings to date and the sale-date liabilities of the partnership, Kurt Corporation sells its interest in the entity to Gloria for $120,000. At the time of the sale, Kurt's share of the TUV hot assets is $8,000. Kurt recognizes $8,000 of ordinary income and $12,000 of capital gain (i.e., the total gain of $20,000 is comprised of $8,000 of ordinary income and $12,000 of capital gain).

EXAMPLE 32

When its basis in the TUV Partnership is $100,000, taking into account all earnings to date and the sale-date liabilities of the partnership, Kurt Corporation sells its interest in the entity to Gloria for $120,000. At the time of the sale, Kurt's share of the TUV hot assets is $28,000. Kurt recognizes $28,000 of ordinary income and $8,000 of capital loss (i.e., the total gain of $20,000 is comprised of $28,000 of ordinary income and $8,000 of capital loss).

EXAMPLE 33

14-3e Loss Limitations

Partnership losses flow through to the partners for use on their tax returns. However, the amount and nature of the partner's deductible losses may be limited. When limitations apply, all or some of the losses are suspended and carried forward until the rules allow them to be used. Only then can the losses decrease the partner's tax liability.

Three different limitations may apply to partnership losses that are passed through to a partner. The first allows the deduction of *losses* only to the extent the partner has a positive basis in the partnership interest. Losses that are deductible under this basis limitation may then be subject to the *at-risk* limitations. Losses are deductible under this provision only to the extent the partner is at risk for the partnership interest. Any losses that survive this second limitation may be subject to a third limitation, the *passive* loss rules. Only losses that make it through all three of these applicable limitations are eligible to be deducted on the partner's tax return.

Apply the limitations on deducting partnership losses.

---

[42]Partnership items that hold unrecognized ordinary income are known as *hot assets*. Hot assets include the unrealized receivables of a cash basis partnership and a broadly defined concept of inventory. §§ 751(a) and (d).

EXAMPLE 34

Meg is a 50% member in MQ Telecomm Services LLC. On January 1, Meg's basis in her LLC interest is $50,000, and her at-risk amount is $35,000. Her share of losses from MQ for the year is $60,000, all of which is passive. Meg owns another income-producing investment that generated $25,000 of passive income during the year. Meg can deduct $25,000 of the MQ losses on her Form 1040.

Applicable Provision	Deductible Loss	Suspended Loss
Basis limitation	$50,000	$10,000
At-risk limitation	35,000	15,000
Passive loss limitation	25,000	10,000

Meg can deduct only $50,000 under the basis limitation rule. Of this $50,000, only $35,000 is deductible under the at-risk limitation. Under the passive loss limitation, passive losses can only be deducted against passive income. Thus, Meg can deduct only $25,000 on her return. The remaining $35,000 of losses is suspended.

Basis Limitation

A partner may deduct losses and deductions flowing through from the partnership only to the extent of the partner's basis in the partnership.[43] Items that cannot be deducted because of this rule are suspended and carried forward (never back) for use against future increases in the partner's basis. Such increases might result from additional capital contributions, from sharing in additional partnership debts, or from future partnership income.

EXAMPLE 35

Carol and Dan do business as the CD Partnership, sharing profits and losses equally. All parties use the calendar year. At the start of the current year, the basis of Carol's partnership interest is $25,000. The partnership sustains an operating loss of $80,000 in the current year. Only $25,000 of Carol's $40,000 allocable share of the partnership loss can be deducted under the basis limitation. As a result, the basis of Carol's partnership interest is zero as of January 1 of the following year, and Carol must carry forward the remaining $15,000 of partnership losses.

Now assume that CD earns a profit of $70,000 for the next calendar year. Carol reports net partnership income of $20,000 ($35,000 share of income − $15,000 carryforward loss). The basis of Carol's partnership interest becomes $20,000.

Concept Summary 14.4 later in the chapter shows that contributions to capital, partnership income items, and distributions from the partnership are taken into account before loss items. This *losses last* rule can produce some unusual results in taxation of partnership distributions and deductibility of losses.

TAX PLANNING STRATEGIES **Make Your Own Tax Shelter**

FRAMEWORK FOCUS: DEDUCTIONS

Strategy: Maximize Deductible Amounts.

In Example 35, Carol's entire $40,000 share of the current-year partnership loss could have been deducted under the basis limitation in the current year if she had contributed an additional $15,000 or more to the entity's capital by December 31 of the first tax year. Alternatively, if the partnership had incurred additional debt by the end of the first tax year, Carol's basis might have

been increased to permit some or all of the loss to be deducted in that year.

Thus, if partnership losses are projected for a given year, careful tax planning can ensure their deductibility under the basis limitation. Note, however, that the effects of the at-risk and passive activity limitations as discussed below also must be considered.

---

[43]§ 704(d).

EXAMPLE
36

The Basis Limitation on Losses

The Ellen-Glenn Partnership is owned equally by two partners: Ellen and the Glenn Hospital. At the beginning of the year, Ellen's basis in her partnership interest is $0. Her share of partnership income is $12,000 for the year, and she receives a $10,000 distribution from the partnership.

Under the basis adjustment ordering rules of Concept Summary 14.4, Ellen's basis first is increased by the $12,000 of partnership income; then it is decreased by her $10,000 distribution. She reports her $12,000 share of partnership taxable income on her personal tax return. Her basis in the partnership at the end of the year is $2,000 ($0 beginning basis + $12,000 income − $10,000 distribution).

Assume the same facts as in Example 36, except that Ellen's share of partnership operating results is a $12,000 loss instead of $12,000 income. She again receives a $10,000 distribution.

A distribution of cash in excess of basis in the partnership interest results in a gain to the distributee partner to the extent of the excess. Ellen's distribution is considered before the deductibility of the loss is evaluated under the basis limitation.

Therefore, Ellen recognizes gain on the $10,000 distribution because she has a $0 basis in her partnership interest. Unfortunately for Ellen, the operating loss cannot be deducted under the basis limitation rule, because Ellen still holds a $0 basis in her partnership interest. The loss is suspended, and Ellen carries it forward to a future tax year.

At-Risk Limitation

Under the at-risk rules (see Chapter 6), a partner's deductions for certain pass-through losses are limited to amounts that are economically invested in the partnership. Invested amounts include the cash and the adjusted basis of property contributed by the partner and the partner's share of partnership earnings that has not been distributed.[44]

Losses that are not deductible under the at-risk rules are suspended. When a positive at-risk amount arises in a future tax year, the suspended loss is allowed.

When some or all of the partners are personally liable for partnership recourse debt, that debt is included in the basis of the partnership for those partners. Usually, those partners also include the debt in their amount at risk.

No partner, however, carries any financial risk on nonrecourse debt. Therefore, as a general rule, partners cannot include nonrecourse debt in their amount at risk even though that debt is included in the basis of their partnership interest. This rule has an important exception, however. Real estate nonrecourse financing provided by a bank, retirement plan, or similar party or by a Federal, state, or local government generally is deemed to be at risk.[45] Such debt is termed **qualified nonrecourse debt**.

Losses and At-Risk Amounts

Kelly invests $5,000 in the Kelly Green Limited Partnership as a 5% general partner. Shortly thereafter, the partnership acquires the master recording of a well-known vocalist for $250,000 ($50,000 from the partnership and $200,000 secured from a local bank via *recourse* debt). Kelly's share of the recourse debt is $10,000, and her basis in the interest is $15,000 ($5,000 cash investment + $10,000 debt share).

Because the debt is recourse, Kelly's at-risk amount also is $15,000. Kelly's share of partnership losses in the first year of operations is $11,000. Kelly can deduct the full $11,000 of partnership losses under both the basis and the at-risk limitations because this amount is less than both her outside basis and at-risk amount.

---

[44]§ 465(a).   [45]§ 465(b)(6).

EXAMPLE 39

Assume the same facts as in Example 38, except that the bank loan is nonrecourse. Kelly's basis in the partnership interest still is $15,000, but she can deduct only $5,000 of the flow-through loss. The amount she has at risk in the partnership does not include the nonrecourse debt. (The debt does not relate to real estate, so it cannot be qualified nonrecourse debt.)

The $6,000 suspended loss ($11,000 loss pass-through − $5,000 deduction) is deducted in a future tax year when a positive at-risk amount exists. This might occur because the entity has generated an undistributed net profit, or due to a capital contribution by Kelly.

Passive Activity Rules

A partnership loss pass-through also may be disallowed under the passive activity rules. Recall from Chapter 6 that an activity is considered passive if the taxpayer (in this case, a partner) does not materially participate or if the activity is considered a rental activity.

Losses from passive partnership activities are aggregated by each partner with his or her other passive income and losses. Any net passive loss is suspended and carried forward to future years, unless the partner also has generated net passive income for the tax year. The passive activity limitation applies after the owner's basis and at-risk limitations.

Concept Summary 14.4

Partner's Basis in Partnership Interest

Basis generally is adjusted in the following order.

Initial basis: Amount paid for partnership interest, or gift or inherited basis (including share of partnership debt).

+ Partner's subsequent asset contributions and allocable debt increases.
+ Since interest acquired, partner's share of the partnership's:
  - Income items.
  - Tax-exempt income items.
  - Excess of depletion deductions over adjusted basis of property subject to depletion.
− Partner's distributions and withdrawals and allocable debt decreases.

− Since interest acquired, partner's share of the partnership's:
  - Separately stated deductions.
  - Nondeductible items not chargeable to a capital account.
  - Special depletion deduction for oil and gas wells.
  - Loss items.

The basis of a partner's interest never can be negative.

Entity-level liabilities, and thus a partner's basis in the partnership, may change from day to day, but the partner's basis generally needs to be computed only once or twice a year.

LO.7

Apply the tax laws regarding transactions between a partner and the partnership.

14-4 TRANSACTIONS BETWEEN PARTNER AND PARTNERSHIP

Many types of transactions occur between a partnership and its partners. A partner may contribute property to the partnership, perform services for the partnership, or receive distributions from the partnership. A partner may borrow money from or lend money to the partnership. Property may be bought and sold between a partner and the partnership. Several of these transactions were discussed earlier in the chapter. The remaining types of partner-partnership transactions are the focus of this section.

14-4a Guaranteed Payments

A **guaranteed payment** is a payment for services performed by the partner or for the use of the partner's capital. The payment is not determined by reference to partnership income. Guaranteed payments usually are expressed as a fixed-dollar amount or as a percentage of capital the partner has invested in the partnership. Whether the partnership deducts or capitalizes the guaranteed payment depends on the nature of the payment.

Donna, Deepak, and Dale formed the accrual basis DDD Partnership. DDD and each of the partners are calendar year taxpayers. According to the partnership agreement, Donna is to manage the partnership and receive a $21,000 distribution from the entity every year, payable in 12 monthly installments. Deepak is to receive an amount that is equal to 18% of his capital account, as it is computed by the firm's accountant at the beginning of the year, payable in 12 monthly installments. Dale is DDD's advertising specialist. She withdraws 4% of the partnership's net income for personal use. Donna and Deepak receive guaranteed payments from the partnership, but Dale does not.

Guaranteed payments resemble the salary or interest payments of other businesses and receive somewhat similar income tax treatment.[46] In contrast to the provision that usually applies to withdrawals of assets by partners from their partnerships, guaranteed payments are deductible (or capitalized) by the entity. Deductible guaranteed payments, like any other deductible expenses of a partnership, can create an ordinary loss for the entity.

The partner's guaranteed payment is reported as a separately stated item on Schedules K and K–1. The partner uses this information (in lieu of a Form W–2 or 1099) to report the income on the partner's tax return. Partners receiving a guaranteed payment report ordinary income and treat it as paid on the last day of the entity's tax year.

Guaranteed Payments: Income and Deductions

Continue with the situation introduced in Example 40. For calendar year 2014, Donna receives the $21,000 as provided by the partnership agreement, Deepak's guaranteed payment is $17,000, and Dale withdraws $20,000 under the personal expenditures clause. Before considering these amounts, the partnership's ordinary income for the year is $650,000.

DDD can deduct its payments to Donna and Deepak, so the final amount of its ordinary income is $612,000 ($650,000 − $21,000 − $17,000). Thus, each of the equal partners is allocated $204,000 of ordinary partnership income ($612,000 ÷ 3). In addition, Donna reports the $21,000 guaranteed payment as gross income, and Deepak includes the $17,000 guaranteed payment in his gross income.

Dale's partnership draw is a distribution from her interest basis and is not taxed separately to her.

Assume the same facts as in Example 41, except that the partnership uses a "natural business" tax year that ends on March 31, 2015. Thus, even though Donna received 9 of her 12 payments for fiscal 2015 in the 2014 calendar year, all of Donna's guaranteed payments are taxable to her in 2015. Similarly, all of Deepak's guaranteed payments are taxable to him in 2015, rather than when they are received.

The deduction for, and the gross income from, guaranteed payments is allowed on the same date that all of the other income and expense items relative to the partnership are allocated to the partners (i.e., on the last day of the entity's tax year).

14-4b Other Transactions between a Partner and a Partnership

Many common transactions between a partner and the partnership are treated as if the partner were an outsider, dealing with the partnership at arm's length.[47] Loan transactions, rental payments, and sales of property between the partner and the partnership generally are treated in this manner.

---

[46]§ 707(c). [47]§ 707(a).

EXAMPLE 43

The Eastside Co-op, a one-third partner in the ABC Partnership, owns a tract of land the partnership wants to purchase. The land has a fair market value of $30,000 and an adjusted basis to Eastside of $17,000. If Eastside sells the land to ABC, Eastside recognizes a $13,000 gain on the sale, and ABC takes a $30,000 cost basis in the land. If the land has a fair market value of $10,000 on the sale date, Eastside recognizes a $7,000 loss.

DIGGING DEEPER 8

In-depth coverage can be found on this book's companion website: www.cengagebrain.com

Sales of Property

No loss is recognized on a sale of property between a person and a partnership when the person owns, directly or indirectly, more than 50 percent of partnership capital or profits.[48] The disallowed loss may not vanish entirely, however. If the person later sells the property at a gain, the disallowed loss reduces the gain that would otherwise be recognized.[49]

EXAMPLE 44

Barry sells land (adjusted basis, $30,000; fair market value, $45,000) to the BCD LLC, of which he controls a 60% capital interest. BCD pays him only $20,000 for the land. Barry cannot deduct his $10,000 realized loss. Barry and the LLC are related parties, and the loss is disallowed.

When BCD sells the land to an outsider at a later date, it receives a sales price of $44,000. The entity can offset the recognition of its $24,000 realized gain on the subsequent sale ($44,000 sales proceeds − $20,000 adjusted basis) by the amount of the $10,000 prior disallowed loss ($20,000 − $30,000). Thus, BCD recognizes a $14,000 gain on its sale of the land.

Using a similar rationale, any gain that is realized on a sale or exchange between a partner and a partnership in which the partner controls a capital or profits interest of more than 50 percent is recognized as ordinary income, unless the asset is a capital asset to both the seller and the purchaser.[50]

EXAMPLE 45

The Kent School purchases some land (adjusted basis, $30,000; fair market value, $45,000) for $45,000 from the JJ Realty LLC, in which Kent controls a 90% profits interest. The land was a capital asset to JJ. If Kent holds the land as a capital asset, the LLC recognizes a $15,000 capital gain. However, if the school also is a land developer and the property is not a capital asset to it, JJ recognizes $15,000 of ordinary income from the sale, even though it held the property as a capital asset.

14-4c **Partners as Employees**

A partner usually does not qualify as an employee under Federal tax law, specifically for purposes of payroll taxes (e.g., FICA or FUTA). Moreover, because a partner is not an employee, the partnership cannot deduct its payments for the partner's fringe benefits, and the partner reports as gross income the value of the fringe benefits received. Nonetheless, a general partner's share of ordinary partnership income and guaranteed payments for services generally are classified as Federal self-employment (SE) income.[51]

The partner pays an SE tax in addition to the Federal income tax on pass-through items, and the additional Medicare taxes also may apply. The combination of these tax obligations can become expensive. Tax liabilities on SE income of a partner include:

- A 12.4 percent tax on the first $118,500 (for 2015) of SE income, for the individual's account in the FICA retirement system.
- A 2.9 percent tax on all SE income, to support the Medicare system.

---

[48]§ 707(b).
[49]This is similar to treatment under § 267.
[50]§ 707(b)(2).
[51]§ 1402(a).

TAX PLANNING STRATEGIES **Transactions between Partners and Partnerships**

FRAMEWORK FOCUS: DEDUCTIONS

Strategy: Maximize Deductible Amounts.

To ensure that no negative tax results occur, partners should be careful when engaging in transactions with the partnership. A partner who owns a majority of the partnership generally should not sell property at a loss to the partnership because the loss is disallowed. Similarly, a majority partner should not sell a capital asset to the partnership at a gain if the asset is to be used by the partnership as other than a capital asset. The gain on this transaction is taxed as ordinary income to the selling partner rather than as capital gain.

As an alternative to selling property to a partnership, a partner may lease it to the partnership. The partner recognizes rent income, and the partnership has a rent expense. A partner who needs more cash immediately can sell the property to an outside third party; then the third party can lease the property to the partnership for a fair rental.

A partner who is an individual may be subject to additional taxes that support the Federal Medicare system, on flow-through items from the entity. Certain upper-income taxpayers must pay:

- A .9 percent tax on SE income,[52] and
- A 3.8 percent tax on flow-through net investment income (NII), including interest and dividend income, passive income, and capital gains. NII does not include tax-exempt interest income, but it does include the share of pass-through operating income for a passive or limited partner.[53]

In-depth coverage can be found on this book's companion website: www.cengagebrain.com   **9** DIGGING DEEPER

Concept Summary 14.5

Partner-Partnership Transactions

1. Partners can transact business with their partnerships in a nonpartner capacity. These transactions include the sale and exchange of property, rentals, and loans of funds.

2. A payment to a partner may be classified as a guaranteed payment if it is for services or use of the partner's capital and is not based on partnership income. A guaranteed payment usually is deductible by the partnership and is included in the partner's income on the last day of the partnership's tax year.

3. Losses are disallowed between a partner or related party and a partnership when the partner or related party owns more than a 50% interest in the partnership's capital or profits.

4. Income from a related-party sale is treated as ordinary income if the property is not a capital asset to both the transferor and the transferee.

5. Partners are not employees of their partnership, so the entity cannot deduct payments for partner fringe benefits, nor need it withhold or pay any payroll tax for payments to partners.

6. A partner may be subject to self-employment and the additional Medicare taxes on guaranteed payments received, and on a distributive share of flow-through income.

---

[52]§ 1401(b)(2)(A). Form 8959 is used to compute this tax.

[53]§ 1411. Form 8960 is used to compute this tax.

LO.8

Explain how LLPs and LLCs differ, and list the tax advantages and disadvantages of using an LLC.

14-5 LIMITED LIABILITY COMPANIES

The *limited liability company (LLC)* combines partnership taxation with limited personal liability for all owners of the entity. All states and the District of Columbia have passed legislation permitting the establishment of LLCs. The following sections explain the taxation, advantages, and disadvantages of using LLCs.

14-5a Taxation of LLCs

A properly structured LLC is taxed as a partnership. Because LLC members are not personally liable for the debts of the entity, the LLC effectively is treated as a limited partnership with no general partners. This may result in an unusual application of partnership taxation rules. The IRS has not specifically ruled on most aspects of LLC taxation, so several of the following comments apply rules as to how a limited partner would be taxed.

- Formation of a new LLC is treated in the same manner as formation of a partnership. Generally, no gain or loss is recognized by the LLC member or the LLC, the member takes a substituted basis in the LLC interest, and the LLC takes a carryover basis in the assets it receives.

- An LLC's income and losses are allocated proportionately. Special allocations are permitted, as long as they are supported by a nontax economic effect.

- An LLC member contributing property with built-in gains can be subject to tax on certain distributions within seven years of the contribution.

- A loss must meet the basis, at-risk, and passive loss requirements to be currently deductible. Because debt of an LLC is considered nonrecourse to each of the members, it is not included in the at-risk limitation unless it is "qualified nonrecourse financing."

- The initial accounting period and accounting method elections are available to an LLC.

- Property takes a carryover or substituted basis when distributed from an LLC.

14-5b Advantages of an LLC

An LLC offers certain advantages over a limited partnership.

- Generally, none of the members of an LLC is personally liable for the entity's debts. In contrast, general partners in a limited partnership have personal liability for partnership recourse debts.

- Limited partners cannot participate in the management of a partnership. All owners of an LLC have the legal right to participate in the entity's management.

An LLC also offers certain advantages over an S corporation (see Chapter 15), including the following.

- An LLC can have an unlimited number of owners, while an S corporation is limited to 100 shareholders.

- Any taxpayers, including corporations, nonresident aliens, other partnerships, and trusts, can be owners of an LLC. S corporation shares can be held only by specified parties.

- The transfer of property to an LLC in exchange for an ownership interest in the entity is governed by partnership tax provisions rather than corporate tax provisions. Thus, the transfers need not satisfy the 80 percent control requirement needed for tax-free treatment under the corporate tax statutes (see Chapter 12).

- The S corporation taxes on built-in gains and passive income do not apply to LLCs.
- An owner's basis in an LLC includes the owner's share of almost all LLC liabilities under the law. Only certain entity liabilities are included in the S corporation shareholder's basis.
- An LLC may make special allocations, whereas S corporations must allocate income, loss, etc., only on a per-share/per-day basis.

14-5c **Disadvantages of an LLC**

Only a limited body of case law interprets the various state statutes, so the application of specific provisions in a specific state may be uncertain. An additional uncertainty for LLCs that operate in more than one jurisdiction pertains to which state's law will prevail and how it will be applied.

Among other factors, statutes differ from state to state as to the type of business an LLC can conduct—primarily the extent to which a service-providing firm can operate as an LLC. Special rules also may apply where the LLC has only one member.

Despite these uncertainties and limitations, LLCs are being formed at increasing rates, and the ranks of multistate LLCs also are rising quickly.

Concept Summary 14.6

Advantages and Disadvantages of the Partnership Form

The partnership form may be attractive when one or more of the following factors is present.

- The entity is generating net taxable losses and/or valuable tax credits, which will be of use to the owners.
- The owners want to avoid complex corporate administrative and filing requirements.
- The owners want to make special allocations of certain income or deduction items that are not possible under the C or S corporation forms.
- Other means of reducing the effects of the double taxation of corporate business income (e.g., compensation to owners, interest, and rental payments) have been exhausted.
- The entity does not generate material amounts of tax preference and adjustment items, which increase the AMT liabilities of its owners.
- The entity is generating net passive income, which its owners can use to claim immediate deductions for net passive losses they have generated from other sources.
- The owners hold adequate bases in their ownership interests to facilitate the deduction of flow-through losses and the assignment of an adequate basis to assets distributed in kind to the owners.

The partnership form may be less attractive when one or more of the following factors is present.

- The tax paid by the owners on the entity's income is greater than that payable by the entity as a C corporation, and the income is not expected to be distributed soon. (If distributed by a C corporation, double taxation would likely occur.)
- The entity is generating net taxable income without distributing any cash to the owners. The owners may not have sufficient cash with which to pay the tax on the entity's earnings.
- The type of income the entity is generating (e.g., business and portfolio income) is not as attractive to its owners as net passive income would be, because the owners could use net passive income to offset the net passive losses they have generated on their own.
- The entity is in a high-exposure business, and the owners want protection from personal liability. An LLC or LLP structure may be available, however, to limit personal liability.
- The owners want to reduce exposure to Federal self-employment and additional Medicare taxes.
- Partnership operations are complex (indicating that Form 1065 might not be filed until near the due date for the return), but partners with the same tax year need to file their returns as early as possible for personal reasons (e.g., to meet debt requirements or to receive a tax refund).

14-6 SUMMARY

Partnerships and LLCs are popular among business owners because formation of the entity is relatively simple and tax-free. The Code places very few restrictions on who can be a partner. Partnerships are especially attractive when operating losses are anticipated or when marginal rates that would apply to partnership income are less than those that would be paid by a C corporation. Partnerships do not offer the limited liability of a corporate entity, but the use of limited partnerships, LLCs, and LLPs can offer some protection to the owners.

Partnerships are tax-reporting, not taxpaying, entities. Distributive shares of ordinary income and separately stated items are taxed to the partners on the last day of the tax year. Special allocations and guaranteed payments are allowed and offer partners the ability to tailor the cash-flow and taxable amounts that are distributed by the entity to its owners. Deductions for flow-through losses may be limited by the related-party, passive activity, and at-risk rules, as well as by the partner's basis in the partnership. The flexibility of the partnership rules makes this form continually attractive to new businesses, especially in a global setting.

REFOCUS ON THE BIG PICTURE

THE TAX CONSEQUENCES OF PARTNERSHIP FORMATION AND OPERATIONS

© RODERICK PAUL WALKER/ALAMY

After considering the various types of partnerships, Kyle, Maria, and Josh decided to form Beachside Properties as an LLC. Upon formation of the entity, there was no gain or loss recognized by the LLC or any of its members (see Example 15). Beachside Properties computes its income as shown in Example 17 and allocates the income as illustrated in Example 19. The LLC's income affects the members' bases and capital accounts. An important consideration for the LLC members is whether their distributive shares and guaranteed payments will be treated as self-employment income.

What If?

What happens in the future when the LLC members decide to expand or renovate Beachside's facilities? At that time, the existing members can contribute additional funds, the entity can receive capital from new members, or the entity can borrow money. A partnership or limited liability entity is not subject to the 80 percent control requirement applicable to the formation of a corporation and subsequent transfers to it. Therefore, new investors can contribute cash or other property in exchange for interests in the entity—and the transaction will qualify for tax-deferred treatment.

Suggested Readings

J. Everett, W. Raabe, and C. Hennig, "Planning Considerations When Converting a C Corporation to an LLC," *The Tax Adviser*, February 2011.

Susan L. Megaard and Michael M. Megaard, "Reducing Self-Employment Taxes on Owners of LLPs and LLCs," *Business Entities*, March/April 2012.

W. E. Seago, K. Orbach, and E. Schnee, "Working with the Unearned Income Medicare Tax," *Journal of Taxation*, March 2013.

Patrick H. Smith, "Taxation by States of Single-Member LLCs," *Business Entities*, September/October 2007.

Key Terms

Basis in the partnership interest, 14-7
Capital account, 14-21
Capital interest, 14-6
Capital sharing ratio, 14-6
Disguised sale, 14-10
Economic effect test, 14-19
General partnership, 14-3
Guaranteed payment, 14-28

Inside basis, 14-12
Limited liability company (LLC), 14-4
Limited liability partnership (LLP), 14-3
Limited partnership, 14-3
Nonrecourse debt, 14-22
Organizational costs, 14-14
Outside basis, 14-12
Precontribution gain or loss, 14-19

Profit and loss sharing ratios, 14-6
Profits (loss) interest, 14-6
Qualified nonrecourse debt, 14-27
Recourse debt, 14-22
Separately stated items, 14-5
Special allocation, 14-7
Syndication costs, 14-13

Computational Exercises

1. **LO.4** Enerico contributes $100,000 cash in exchange for a 40% interest in the calendar year ABC LLC. This year, ABC generates $80,000 of ordinary taxable income. Enerico withdraws $10,000 cash from the partnership at the end of the tax year.

   a. Compute Enerico's gross income from ABC's ordinary income for the tax year.

   b. Compute Enerico's gross income from the LLC's cash distribution.

2. **LO.2** Henrietta transfers cash of $75,000 and equipment with a fair market value of $25,000 (basis to her as a sole proprietor, $10,000) in exchange for a 40% profit and loss interest worth $100,000 in the XYZ Partnership.

   a. Compute Henrietta's realized and recognized gains from the asset transfers.

   b. Compute Henrietta's basis in her interest in XYZ.

   c. What is XYZ's basis in the equipment that it now holds?

3. **LO.2** Wozniacki and Wilcox form Jewel LLC, with each investor receiving a one-half interest in the capital and profits of the LLC. Wozniacki receives his one-half interest as compensation for tax planning services that he rendered prior to the formation of the LLC. Wilcox contributes $50,000 cash. The value of a one-half capital interest in the LLC (for each of the parties) is $50,000.

   a. Compute Wozniacki's realized and recognized gain from joining Jewel.

   b. Compute Wozniacki's basis in his interest in Jewel.

   c. How does Jewel treat the services that Wozniacki has rendered?

4. **LO.5** At the beginning of the tax year, Barnaby's basis in the BBB Partnership was $50,000, including his $5,000 share of partnership debt. At the end of the tax year, his share of the entity's debt was $8,000.

   Barnaby's share of BBB's ordinary income for the year was $20,000, and he received cash distributions totaling $12,000. In addition, his share of the partnership's tax-exempt income was $1,000. Determine Barnaby's basis at the end of the tax year.

5. **LO.3** Candlewood LLC began its business on September 1; it uses a calendar tax and accounting year. Candlewood incurred $6,500 in legal fees for drafting the LLC's operating agreement and $3,000 in accounting fees for tax advice of an organizational nature, for a total of $9,500 of organizational costs.

   Candlewood also incurred $30,000 of preopening advertising expenses and $24,500 of salaries and training costs for new employees before opening for business, for a total of $54,500 of startup costs. The LLC desires to take the largest deduction available for these costs. Compute Candlewood's deductions for the first year of its operations for:

   a.   Organizational expenses.

   b.   Startup expenses.

6.   **LO.4** Franco owns a 60% interest in the Dulera LLC. On December 31 of the current tax year, his basis in the LLC interest is $128,000. The fair market value of the interest is $140,000. Dulera then distributes to Franco $30,000 cash and equipment with an adjusted basis of $5,000 and a fair market value of $8,000.

   a.   Compute Franco's basis in Dulera after the distribution.

   b.   Compute Franco's basis in the equipment that he received from Dulera.

Critical Thinking   7.   **LO.4** When Bruno's basis in his interest in the MNO LLC is $150,000, he receives cash of $55,000, a proportionate share of inventory, and land in a distribution that liquidates MNO and his interest in the LLC. The inventory has a basis to the entity of $45,000 and a fair market value of $48,000. The land's basis is $70,000, and its fair market value is $60,000. Compute Bruno's recognized gain or loss from the liquidating distribution.

Problems

Issue ID   8.   **LO.2** Janda and Kelsey contributed $1 million each to the JKL LLC in exchange for 45% capital and profits interests in the entity. Lilli will contribute no cash, but has agreed to manage the LLC's business operations in exchange for an $80,000 annual salary and a 10% interest in the LLC's capital and profits (valued at $200,000). What are the consequences of the entity formation and Lilli's compensation arrangement to the LLC members? To the LLC itself?

9.   **LO.2** Emma and Laine form the equal EL Partnership. Emma contributes cash of $100,000. Laine contributes property with an adjusted basis of $40,000 and a fair market value of $100,000.

   a.   How much gain, if any, must Emma recognize on the transfer? Must Laine recognize any gain? If so, how much?

   b.   What is Emma's basis in her partnership interest?

   c.   What is Laine's basis in her partnership interest?

   d.   What basis does the partnership take in the property transferred by Laine?

Decision Making   10.   **LO.2** Kenisha and Shawna form the equal KS LLC with a cash contribution of $360,000 from Kenisha and a property contribution (adjusted basis of $380,000, fair market value of $360,000) from Shawna.

   a.   How much gain or loss, if any, does Shawna realize on the transfer? Does Shawna recognize any gain or loss? If so, how much?

   b.   What is Kenisha's basis in her LLC interest?

   c.   What is Shawna's basis in her LLC interest?

   d.   What basis does the LLC take in the property transferred by Shawna?

   e.   Are there more effective ways to structure the formation? Explain.

11.   **LO.2** Liz and John formed the equal LJ Partnership on January 1 of the current year. Liz contributed $80,000 of cash and land with a fair market value of $90,000 and an adjusted basis of $75,000. John contributed equipment with a fair market value of $170,000 and an adjusted basis of $20,000. John previously used the equipment in his sole proprietorship.

   a.   How much gain or loss will Liz, John, and LJ realize?

   b.   How much gain or loss will Liz, John, and LJ recognize?

c.   What bases will Liz and John take in their partnership interests?

d.   What bases will LJ take in the assets it receives?

e.   How will LJ depreciate any assets it receives from the partners?

12. **LO.2, 5** Sam and Drew are equal members of the SD LLC, formed on June 1 of the current year. Sam contributed land that he inherited from his uncle in 2007. Sam's uncle purchased the land in 1982 for $30,000. The land was worth $100,000 when Sam's uncle died. The fair market value of the land was $200,000 at the date it was contributed to SD.

    Drew has significant experience developing real estate. After SD is formed, he will prepare a plan for developing the property and secure zoning approvals for the LLC. Drew normally would bill a third party $50,000 for these efforts. Drew will also contribute $150,000 of cash in exchange for his 50% interest in SD. The value of Drew's 50% interest is $200,000.

a.   How much gain or income does Sam recognize on his contribution of the land to SD? What is the character of any gain or income recognized?

b.   What basis does Sam take in his LLC interest?

c.   How much gain or income will Drew recognize on the formation of SD? What is the character of any gain or income recognized?

d.   What basis will Drew take in his LLC interest?

13. **LO.2** Continue with the facts presented in Problem 12. At the end of the first year, SD distributes $100,000 cash to Sam. No distribution is made to Drew.

a.   How does Sam treat the payment?

b.   How much income or gain would Sam recognize as a result of the payment?

c.   Under general tax rules, what basis would SD take in the land Sam contributed?

14. **LO.3** On July 1 of the current year, the R&R Partnership was formed to operate a bed-and-breakfast inn. The partnership paid $3,000 in legal fees for drafting the partnership agreement and $5,000 for accounting fees related to organizing the entity. It also paid $10,000 in syndication costs to locate and secure investments from limited partners.

    In addition, before opening the inn for business, the entity paid $15,500 for advertising and $36,000 in costs related to an open house just before the grand opening of the property. The partnership opened the inn for business on October 1.

a.   How are these expenses classified?

b.   How much may the partnership deduct in its initial year of operations?

c.   How are costs treated that are not deducted currently?

15. **LO.2, 4** Phoebe and Parker are equal members of Phoenix Investors LLC. They are real estate investors who formed the entity several years ago with equal cash contributions. Phoenix then purchased a parcel of land.

    On January 1 of the current year, to acquire a one-third interest in the entity, Reece contributed to Phoenix some land she had held for investment. Reece purchased the land five years ago for $75,000; its fair market value at the contribution date was $90,000. No special allocation agreements were in effect before or after Reece was admitted to the LLC. Phoenix holds all land for investment.

    Immediately before Reece's property contribution, the Phoenix balance sheet was as follows.

	Basis	FMV		Basis	FMV
Land	$30,000	$180,000	Phoebe, capital	$15,000	$ 90,000
			Parker, capital	15,000	90,000
	$30,000	$180,000		$30,000	$180,000

a. At the contribution date, what is Reece's basis in her interest in Phoenix?

b. When does the LLC's holding period begin for the contributed land?

c. On June 30 of the current year, the LLC sold the land contributed by Reece for $90,000. How much is the recognized gain or loss? How is it allocated among the LLC members?

d. Prepare a balance sheet reflecting basis and fair market value for the entity immediately after the land sale.

16. **LO.4, 5** Amy and Mitchell are equal partners in the accrual basis AM Partnership. At the beginning of the current tax year, Amy's capital account has a balance of $300,000, and the partnership has recourse debts of $200,000 payable to unrelated parties. All partnership recourse debt is shared equally between the partners.

The following information about AM's operations for the current year is obtained from the partnership's records.

Ordinary income	$400,000
Interest income from P&G bond	4,000
Long-term capital loss	6,000
Short-term capital gain	12,000
Charitable contribution	4,000
Cash distribution to Amy	20,000

Year-end partnership debt payable to unrelated parties is $140,000. If all transactions are reflected in her beginning capital and basis in the same manner:

a. What is Amy's basis in the partnership interest at the beginning of the year?

b. What is Amy's basis in the partnership interest at the end of the current year?

17. **LO.4, 5** Assume the same facts as in Problem 16. What income, gains, losses, and deductions does Amy report on her income tax return? Based on the information provided, what other calculations is she required to make?

18. **LO.4, 5** Continue with the same facts of Problem 16. Consider Amy's tax-basis capital account.

a. What is Amy's capital account at the beginning of the year?

b. What is Amy's capital account at the end of the year?

c. How do the capital account balances differ from her basis amounts in Problem 16?

Critical Thinking   19. **LO.3** Cerulean, Inc., Coral, Inc., and Crimson, Inc., form the Three Cs Partnership on January 1 of the current year. Cerulean is a 50% partner, and Crimson and Coral are 25% partners. For reporting purposes, Crimson uses a fiscal year with an October 31 year-end, Coral uses the calendar year, and Cerulean uses a fiscal year with a February 28/29 year-end. What is the required tax year for Three Cs under the least aggregate deferral method?

20. **LO.2, 4, 5** The JM Partnership was formed to acquire land and subdivide it as residential housing lots. On March 1, 2015, Jessica contributed land valued at $600,000 to the partnership in exchange for a 50% interest. She had purchased the land in 2007 for $420,000 and held it for investment purposes (capital asset). The partnership holds the land as inventory.

On the same date, Matt contributed land valued at $600,000 that he had purchased in 2005 for $720,000. He became a 50% owner. Matt is a real estate developer, but he held this land personally for investment purposes. The partnership holds this land as inventory.

In 2016, the partnership sells the land contributed by Jessica for $620,000. In 2017, the partnership sells the real estate contributed by Matt for $580,000.

a. What is each partner's initial basis in his or her partnership interest?

b. What is the amount of gain or loss recognized on the sale of the land contributed by Jessica? What is the character of this gain or loss?

c. What is the amount of gain or loss recognized on the sale of the land contributed by Matt? What is the character of this gain or loss?

d. How would your answer in (c) change if the property were sold in 2022?

21. **LO.2, 5** Lee, Brad, and Rick form the LBR Partnership on January 1 of the current year. In return for a 25% interest, Lee transfers property (basis of $15,000, fair market value of $17,500) subject to a nonrecourse liability of $10,000. The liability is assumed by the partnership. Brad transfers property (basis of $16,000, fair market value of $7,500) for a 25% interest, and Rick transfers cash of $15,000 for the remaining 50% interest.

a. How much gain must Lee recognize on the transfer?

b. What is Lee's basis in his interest in the partnership?

c. How much loss may Brad recognize on the transfer?

d. What is Brad's basis in his interest in the partnership?

e. What is Rick's basis in his interest in the partnership?

f. What basis does the LBR Partnership take in the property transferred by Lee?

g. What is the partnership's basis in the property transferred by Brad?

22. **LO.2, 5** Assume the same facts as in Problem 21, except that the property contributed by Lee has a fair market value of $27,500 and is subject to a nonrecourse mortgage of $20,000.

Critical Thinking

a. What is Lee's basis in his partnership interest?

b. How much gain must Lee recognize on the transfer?

c. What is Brad's basis in his partnership interest?

d. What is Rick's basis in his partnership interest?

e. What basis does the LBR Partnership take in the property transferred by Lee?

23. **LO.5, 6** The BCD Partnership plans to distribute cash of $20,000 to partner Barb at the end of the tax year. The partnership reported a loss for the year, and Barb's share of the loss is $10,000. Barb holds a basis of $15,000 in the partnership interest, including her share of partnership liabilities. The partnership expects to report substantial income in future years.

Issue ID

Decision Making

a. How does Barb calculate the ending basis in the BCD partnership interest?

b. How much income or loss must Barb report for the tax year?

c. Will the deduction for any of the $10,000 loss be suspended? Why or why not?

d. Could any planning opportunities be used to minimize the tax ramifications of the distribution? Explain.

24. **LO.2, 3** The Pelican Partnership was formed on August 1 of the current year and admitted Morlan and Merriman as equal partners on that date. The partners both contributed $300,000 of cash to establish a children's clothing store in the local mall. The partners spent August and September buying inventory, equipment, supplies, and advertising for their "Grand Opening" on October 1. The partnership will use the accrual method of accounting. The following are some of the costs incurred during Pelican's first year of operations.

Legal fees to form partnership	$ 8,000
Advertising for "Grand Opening"	18,000
Advertising after opening	30,000
Consulting fees for establishing accounting system	20,000
Rent, at $2,000 per month	10,000
Utilities, at $1,000 per month	5,000
Salaries to salesclerks (beginning in October)	50,000
Payments to Morlan and Merriman for services ($6,000 per month each for three months)	36,000
Tax return preparation expense	12,000

In addition, on October 1, Pelican purchased all of the assets of Granny Newcombs, Inc. Of the total purchase price for these assets, $200,000 was allocated to the Granny Newcombs trade name and logo.

Determine how each of the listed costs is treated by Pelican, and identify the period over which the costs can be deducted, if any.

25. **LO.7** Four GRRLs Partnership is owned by four unrelated friends. Lacy holds a 40% interest; each of the others owns 20%. Lacy sells investment property to the partnership for its fair market value of $200,000. Her tax basis in the property was $250,000.

a. How much loss, if any, may Lacy recognize?

b. If Four GRRLs later sells the property for $260,000, how much gain must it recognize?

c. How would your answers in (a) and (b) change if Lacy owned a 60% interest in the partnership?

d. If Lacy's basis in the investment property was $120,000 (instead of $250,000) and she was a 60% partner, how much, if any, gain would she recognize on the sale of the property to Four GRRLs? How is it characterized?

26. **LO.7** Burgundy, Inc., and Violet Gomez are equal partners in the calendar year BV LLC. Burgundy uses a fiscal year ending April 30, and Violet uses a calendar year. Burgundy receives an annual guaranteed payment of $100,000 for use of capital contributed by Burgundy. BV's taxable income (after deducting the payment to Burgundy) is $80,000 for 2015 and $90,000 for 2016.

a. How much income from BV must Burgundy report for its tax year ending April 30, 2016?

b. How much income from BV must Violet report for her tax year ending December 31, 2016?

Critical Thinking   27. **LO.4, 7** Mona and Denise, mother and daughter, operate a local restaurant as an LLC. The MD LLC earned a profit of $200,000 in the current year. Denise's equal LLC interest was acquired by gift from Mona. Assume that capital is a material income-producing factor and that Mona manages the day-to-day operations of the restaurant without any help from Denise. Reasonable compensation for Mona's services is $50,000.

a. How much of the MD income is allocated to Mona?

b. What is the maximum amount of LLC income that can be allocated to Denise?

c. Assuming that Denise is 15 years old, has no other income, and is claimed as a dependent by Mona, how is Denise's income from the restaurant taxed?

Critical Thinking   28. **LO.5** In each of the following independent cases in which the partnership owns no hot assets, indicate the following. All of the partners received proportionate distributions.

- Whether the partner recognizes gain or loss.
- Whether the partnership recognizes gain or loss.
- The partner's adjusted basis for the property distributed.
- The partner's outside basis in the partnership after the distribution.

a. Kim receives $20,000 of cash in partial liquidation of her interest in the partner-ship. Kim's outside basis for her partnership interest immediately before the distribution is $3,000.

b. Kourtni receives $40,000 of cash and land with a $30,000 inside basis to the partnership (value $50,000) in partial liquidation of her interest. Kourtni's outside basis for her partnership interest immediately before the distribution is $80,000.

c. Assume the same facts as in (b), except that Kourtni's outside basis for her partnership interest immediately before the distribution is $60,000.

d. Klois receives $50,000 of cash and inventory with a basis of $30,000 and a fair market value of $50,000 in partial liquidation of her partnership interest. Her basis was $90,000 before the distribution.

29. **LO.4, 5, 7** At the beginning of the tax year, Melodie's basis in the MIP LLC was $60,000, including Melodie's $40,000 share of the LLC's liabilities. At the end of the year, MIP distributed to Melodie cash of $10,000 and inventory (basis of $6,000, fair market value of $10,000). MIP repaid all of its liabilities by the end of the year.

    Critical Thinking

a. If this is a proportionate nonliquidating distribution, what is the tax effect of the distribution to Melodie and MIP? After the distribution, what is Melodie's basis in the inventory and in her MIP interest?

b. Would your answers to (a) change if this had been a proportionate liquidating distribution? Explain.

30. **LO.2, 4, 5** Suzy contributed assets valued at $360,000 (basis of $200,000) in exchange for her 40% interest in Suz-Anna GP (a general partnership). Anna contributed land and a building valued at $640,000 (basis of $380,000) in exchange for the remaining interest. Anna's property was encumbered by a qualified nonrecourse debt of $100,000, which was assumed by the partnership. The partnership reports the following income and expenses for the current tax year.

    Critical Thinking

Sales	$560,000
Utilities, salaries, and other operating expenses	360,000
Short-term capital gain	10,000
Tax-exempt interest income	4,000
Charitable contributions	8,000
Distribution to Suzy	10,000
Distribution to Anna	20,000

At the end of the year, Suz-Anna held recourse debt of $100,000 for partnership accounts payable and qualified nonrecourse debt of $200,000.

a. What is Suzy's basis after formation of the partnership? Anna's basis?

b. What income and separately stated items does Suz-Anna report on Suzy's Schedule K–1? What items does Suzy report on her tax return?

c. All partnership debts are shared proportionately. At the end of the tax year, what are Suzy's basis and amount at risk in her partnership interest?

Critical Thinking
Issue ID

31. **LO.2, 4, 5, 8** Continue with the facts presented in Problem 30, except that Suz-Anna was formed as an LLC instead of a general partnership.

a. How would Suz-Anna's ending liabilities be treated?

b. How would Suzy's basis and amount at risk be different? Explain.

Ethics and Equity
Communications

32. **LO.4** The Sparrow Partnership plans to distribute $200,000 cash to its partners at the end of the year. Marjorie is a 40% partner and would receive $80,000. Her basis in the partnership is only $10,000, however, so she would recognize a $70,000 gain if she receives the proposed cash distribution.

Marjorie has asked Sparrow instead to purchase a parcel of land that she has found, on which she will build her retirement residence. The partnership then will distribute that land to her. Under the partnership distribution rules, Marjorie would take a $10,000 basis in the land worth $80,000. Her basis in the partnership would be reduced to $0, but recognition of the $70,000 gain is deferred.

Do you think this is an appropriate transaction? Explain your conclusion in an e-mail to your instructor.

Comprehensive Tax Return Problem

Tax Return Problem

TAX SOFTWARE

1. Ryan Ross (111-11-1111), Oscar Omega (222-22-2222), Clark Carey (333-33-3333), and Kim Kardigan (444-44-4444) are equal active members in ROCK the Ages LLC. ROCK serves as agent and manager for prominent musicians in the Los Angeles area. The LLC's Federal ID number is 55-5555555. It uses the cash basis and a calendar tax year, and it began operations on January 1, 2003. Its current address is 6102 Wilshire Boulevard, Suite 2100, Los Angeles, CA 90036.

ROCK was the force behind such music icons as Rhiannon, Elena Gomez, Tyler Quick, and Conjuring Dragons, and it has had a very profitable year. The following information was taken from the LLC's income statement for the current year.

Revenues

Fees and commissions	$4,800,000
Taxable interest income from bank deposits	1,600
Tax-exempt interest	3,200
Net gains on stock sales	4,000
Total revenues	$4,808,800

Expenses

Advertising and public relations	$ 380,000
Charitable contributions	28,000
Section 179 expense	20,000
Employee salaries and wages	1,000,000
Guaranteed payment (services), Ryan Ross, office manager	800,000
Guaranteed payment (services), other members	600,000
Entertainment, subject to 50% disallowance	200,000
Travel	320,000
Legal and accounting fees	132,000
Office rentals paid	80,000
Interest expense on line of credit for operations	10,000
Insurance premiums	52,000
Office expense	200,000
Payroll taxes	92,000
Utilities	54,800
Total expenses	$3,968,800

During the past few years, ROCK has taken advantage of bonus depreciation and §179 deductions and fully remodeled the premises and upgraded its lease-hold improvements. This year, ROCK wrapped up its remodeling with the purchase of $20,000 of office furniture, for which it will claim a §179 deduction. ROCK uses the same cost recovery methods for both tax and financial purposes. There is no depreciation adjustment for alternative minimum tax purposes.

ROCK invests much of its excess cash in non-dividend-paying growth stocks and tax-exempt securities. During the year, the LLC sold two securities. On June 15, 2014, ROCK purchased 1,000 shares of Tech, Inc. stock for $100,000; it sold those shares on December 15, 2014, for $80,000. On March 15, 2013, ROCK purchased 2,000 shares of BioLabs, Inc. stock for $136,000; it sold those shares for $160,000 on December 15, 2014. These transactions were reported to the IRS on Forms 1099–B; ROCK's basis in these shares was reported on the form.

Net income per books for 2014 is $840,000. The firm's activities do not constitute "qualified production activities" for purposes of the § 199 deduction. On January 1, the members' capital accounts equaled $200,000 each. No additional capital contributions were made. In addition to their guaranteed payments, each member withdrew $250,000 cash during the year.

ROCK's book balance sheet as of December 31, 2014, is as follows.

	Beginning	Ending
Cash	$ 444,000	$??
Tax-exempt securities	120,000	120,000
Marketable securities	436,000	300,000
Leasehold improvements, furniture, and equipment	960,000	980,000
Accumulated depreciation	(960,000)	(980,000)
Total assets	$1,000,000	$??
Line of credit for operations	$ 200,000	$ 160,000
Capital, Ross	200,000	??
Capital, Omega	200,000	??
Capital, Carey	200,000	??
Capital, Kardigan	200,000	??
Total liabilities and capital	$1,000,000	$??

All debt is shared equally by the members. Each member has personally guaranteed the debt of the LLC.

The business code for "Agents and Managers for Artists, Athletes, Entertainers, and Other Public Figures" is 711410. The LLC's Form 1065 was prepared by Ryan Ross and sent to the Ogden, UT IRS Service Center. All of the owners are active in ROCK's operations.

a. Prepare pages 1, 4, and 5 of the Form 1065 for ROCK the Ages LLC.

b. If you are using tax return preparation software, prepare Form 4562 and Schedule D.

c. Prepare Schedule K-1 for Ryan Ross, 15520 W. Earlson Street, Pacific Palisades, CA 90272.

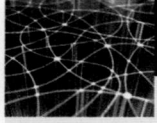

BRIDGE DISCIPLINE

1. What is the function of a partner's capital account under the rules of generally accepted accounting principles (GAAP)? What is the partner's initial balance in the capital account? How and when does the capital account increase and decrease? What is the GAAP treatment of distributions to a partner?

2. Jim Dunn, Amy Lauersen, and Tony Packard have agreed to form a partnership. In return for a 30% capital interest, Dunn transferred machinery (basis $268,000, fair market value $400,000) subject to a liability of $100,000. The liability was assumed by the partnership. Lauersen transferred land (basis $450,000, fair market value $300,000) for a 30% capital interest. Packard transferred cash of $400,000 for the remaining 40% interest. Compute the initial values of Dunn's:
   a. Basis in his partnership interest for tax purposes.
   b. Capital account for financial reporting purposes.

3. To what extent are the personal assets of a general partner, limited partner, or member of an LLC subject to (a) contractual liability claims, such as trade accounts payable, and (b) malpractice claims against the entity? Answer the question for partners or members in a general partnership, an LLP, a nonprofessional LLC, and a limited partnership.

Research Problems

THOMSON REUTERS
CHECKPOINT®
Student Edition

Note: Solutions to Research Problems can be prepared by using the Checkpoint® Student Edition online research product, which is available to accompany this text. It is also possible to prepare solutions to the Research Problems by using tax research materials found in a standard tax library.

Research Problem 1. Fredstone Consolidated, Inc., and Gradison Enterprises, Inc. are both real estate developers. Each entity owns a 50% general partner interest in Realty Partners, GP, a general partnership.

Fredstone and Gradison each contributed $15,000 to form the partnership. The partnership uses the $30,000 contributed by the partners and a recourse loan of $100,000 obtained from an unrelated third-party lender to acquire $130,000 of rental properties. (All amounts are in thousands.)

The partners believe that they will generate extensive tax losses in the first year due to depreciation expense and initial cash-flow requirements. Fredstone and Gradison agreed to share losses equally. To make sure that the losses can be allocated as intended, they included a provision in the partnership agreement requiring each partner to restore any deficit balance in their partnership capital account upon liquidation of the partnership.

Fredstone also was willing to include a provision that requires it to make up any deficit balance within 90 days of liquidation of the partnership. This provision does not apply to Gradison; instead, it must restore any deficit balance in its capital account within two years of liquidation of the partnership. No interest accrues on the deferred restoration payment.

Can Realty allocate the $100,000 recourse debt equally to the two partners, so that they can deduct their respective shares of partnership losses? Explain.

Critical Thinking   **Research Problem 2.** Barney Chang and Aldrin, Inc., a domestic C corporation, have decided to form BA LLC. The new entity will produce a product that Barney recently developed and patented. Barney and Aldrin each will own a 50% capital and profits interest in the LLC. Barney is a calendar year taxpayer, while Aldrin is taxed using a June 30 fiscal year end. BA does not have a "natural business year" and elects to be taxed as a partnership.

a. Determine the taxable year of the LLC under the Code and Regulations.

b. Two years after formation of BA, Barney sells half of his interest (25%) to Aldrin. Can BA retain the taxable year determined in part (a)? Why or why not?

Use the tax resources of the Internet to address the following questions. Do not restrict your search to the Web, but include a review of newsgroups and general reference materials, practitioner sites and resources, primary sources of the tax law, chat rooms and discussion groups, and other opportunities.

Internet Activity

Research Problem 3. Find an article posted by a law firm that comments on pitfalls to avoid in drafting partnership agreements. Ideally, use the home page of a firm that has offices in your state. Summarize the posting in no more than four PowerPoint slides, and send your file to your instructor.

Communications

Research Problem 4. Find a blog that concentrates on the taxation of partners and partnerships. Post a message defining the terms *inside basis* and *outside basis* and illustrating why the distinction between them is important. Respond to any replies you receive. Print your message and one or two of the replies.

Communications

Research Problem 5. Determine the statutory tax treatment in your state of a one-member LLC. Write an e-mail to your professor, comparing this rule with Federal tax law.

Communications

Research Problem 6. Graph the increases in the numbers of LLCs and LLPs filing Federal tax returns for five-year periods beginning with 1970. Explain any trends in the data that you identify. Send your report as an e-mail to your instructor.

Communications

Roger CPA Review Questions

1. Which of the following is (are) correct about the holding period of the property acquired by a partnership as a contribution to the contributing partner's capital account?

   I. The holding period begins on the date the partner's holding period of the contributed asset began
   II. The holding period depends on the character of the property transferred
   III. The holding period excludes the period during which the property was held by the contributing partner

   a. I and II
   b. II and III
   c. I only
   d. None of the above

2. Guaranteed payments made by a partnership to partners for services rendered to the partnership include which of the following?

   a. Sales of partners' assets to the partnership at guaranteed amounts regardless of market values
   b. A salary of $170,000 annually without regard to partnership income
   c. Payments of principal on secured notes honored at maturity
   d. Net long-term capital gains earned by the partnership

3. Properly reported guaranteed payments have the following effect(s):

   I. The guaranteed payment increases the receiving partner's ordinary income by the entire amount paid during the tax year

  II. The guaranteed payment decreases every partner's tax basis in the partnership by the entire amount paid during the tax year

  III. The guaranteed payment is deductible by the partnership in computing its ordinary income or loss for the tax year

  a. All of the above   c. I and II, but not III

  b. I and III, but not II   d. None of the above

4. On March 17, 20X4, Packer became a partner in Cats & Dogs Co., an already formed partnership. Packer does not have property to contribute and thus contributes services in exchange for his 5% interest in Cats & Dogs. Cats & Dogs' net assets are as follows:

	Basis	Fair Market Value
January 1, 20X4	$150,000	$150,000
March 17, 20X4	150,000	170,000
December 31, 20X4	150,000	175,000

On Packer's 20X4 tax return, what amount must Packer include as ordinary income from the receipt of the partnership interest?

  a. $0   c. $8,500

  b. $7,500   d. $8,750

5. On a partnership tax return, all of the following are subject to special limitations and must be separately passed through to the partners, except:

  a. Charitable contributions c. Long-term capital gains

  b. Guaranteed payments   d. Dividend income

6. Prairee partnership has four equal partners, Dodd, Crank, Pick, and Mack. Each of the partners had a tax basis of $320,000 as of January 1, 20X5. Prairee's 20X5 net business income was $152,000. During 20X5, Prairee paid Mack guaranteed payments of $4,000 for deductible services rendered, which were not included in determining Prairee's net business income. During 20X5, each of the four partners took a distribution of $50,000. What amount from Prairee should be included on Dodd's 20X5 tax return?

  a. $152,000   c. $38,000

  b. $42,000   d. $37,000

7. Prairee partnership has four equal partners, Dodd, Crank, Pick, and Mack. Each of the partners had a tax basis of $320,000 as of January 1, 20X5. Prairee's 20X5 net business income was $152,000. During 20X5, Prairee paid Mack guaranteed payments of $4,000 for deductible services rendered. During 20X5, each of the four partners took a distribution of $50,000. What is Mack's tax basis in Prairee on December 31, 20X5?

  a. $307,000   c. $422,000

  b. $358,000   d. $472,000

8. Osha, a cash basis calendar-year partnership, began business on April 1, 20X5. Osha incurred and paid the following during 20X5:

Legal work associated with formation of the partnership	$15,260
Accounting work associated with raising additional capital	10,000

What is the maximum amount of deductible organizational costs on Osha's 20X5 partnership return?

  a. $5,000   c. $5,684

  b. $5,513   d. $6,013

9. Catherine has a $100,000 basis in her partnership interest. On April 28 of the current tax year, the partnership distributes to her cash of $32,000, cash basis receivables with an inside basis of $0 and a fair market value of $12,000, and a parcel of land with a fair market value of $75,000 and a basis to the partnership of $65,000. After accounting for this distribution, what is Catherine's basis in the land?

    a. $65,000   c. $63,000
    b. $53,000   d. $56,000

S Corporations

LEARNING OBJECTIVES: *After completing Chapter 15, you should be able to:*

LO.1 Explain the tax effects associated with S corporation status.

LO.2 Identify corporations that qualify for the S election.

LO.3 Explain how to make and terminate an S election.

LO.4 Compute nonseparately stated income and allocate income, deductions, and credits to shareholders.

LO.5 Determine how distributions to S corporation shareholders are taxed.

LO.6 Calculate a shareholder's basis in S corporation stock.

LO.7 Explain the tax effects of losses on S shareholders.

LO.8 Compute the entity-level taxes on S corporations.

CHAPTER OUTLINE

TAX TALK *In levying taxes and in shearing sheep it is well to stop when you get down to the skin.* —Austin O'Malley

CONVERTING A C CORPORATION TO AN S CORPORATION

Fowle, Inc., has been operating as a C corporation for a number of years, consistently earning taxable income of less than $100,000 per year. The company has accumulated its earnings for a variety of business needs and has not paid dividends to date. Thus, the corporation has been able to take advantage of lower C corporation tax rates and has avoided double taxation problems so far.

Fowle receives some tax-exempt income, generates a small domestic production activities deduction (DPAD), and holds about $200,000 of C corporation earnings and profits. The company's sole owner, David, currently draws a salary of $92,000. Fowle has issued two classes of stock, voting common and non-voting preferred.

The company now is facing increased competition as a result of cheaper imports from China. David expects very large operating losses for the next few years. David would like to know if there is a way that he can deduct the anticipated losses.

Read the chapter and formulate your response.

LO.1

Explain the tax effects associated with S corporation status.

An individual establishing a business has a number of choices as to the form of business entity under which to operate. Chapters 12 and 13 outline many of the rules, advantages, and disadvantages of operating as a regular C corporation. Chapter 14 discusses the partnership entity, as well as the limited liability company (LLC) and limited liability partnership (LLP) forms.

Another alternative, the **S corporation**, provides many of the benefits of partnership taxation and at the same time gives the owners limited liability protection from creditors. The S corporation rules, which are contained in **Subchapter S** of the Internal Revenue Code (§§ 1361–1379), were enacted to allow flexibility in the entity choice that businesspeople face. Thus, S status combines the legal environment of C corporations with taxation similar to that applying to partnerships.

15-1 AN OVERVIEW OF S CORPORATIONS

S corporations (like C corporations) are organized as corporations under state law. Other than for income tax purposes, they are recognized as separate legal entities and generally provide shareholders with the same liability protection afforded by C corporations. As a rule, where the S corporation provisions are silent, C corporation rules apply.

The S corporation rules should be seen as supplementary to the Federal income tax rules for all C corporations (see Chapters 12 and 13) and to those for partnerships and limited liability entities (contained in Code Subchapter K; see Chapter 14). Some provisions apply only to electing S corporations (addressed throughout this chapter), but S corporations also must apply certain tax rules of Code Subchapters C and K.

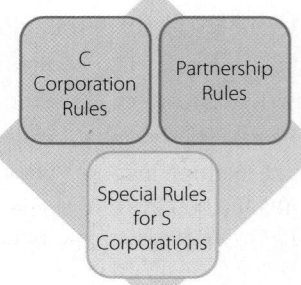

Today, the choice of a flow-through entity for a closely held business often is between an S corporation (a Federal tax entity) and an LLC (a state tax entity). Both are flow-through entities for Federal income tax purposes and provide limited liability for the owners under nontax state law. In the typical year, over 4 million S corporations file Federal income tax returns, and filings are received from over 2 million LLCs.

S Corporation Advantages

EXAMPLE 1

An S corporation earns $300,000, and all after-tax income is distributed currently. The marginal individual tax rate applicable to the entity's shareholders is 39.6% for ordinary income and 20% for dividend income. The marginal corporate tax rate is 34%. The entity's available after-tax earnings, compared with those of a similar C corporation, are computed below.

	C Corporation	S Corporation
Earnings	$ 300,000	$ 300,000
Less: Corporate income tax	(102,000)	(—0—)
Amount available for distribution	$ 198,000	$ 300,000
Less: Income tax at owner level	(39,600)*	(118,800)**
Available after-tax earnings	$ 158,400	$ 181,200

*$198,000 × 20% dividend income tax rate.
**$300,000 × 39.6% ordinary income tax rate.

continued

The S corporation generates an extra $22,800 of after-tax earnings ($181,200 − $158,400) when compared with a similar C corporation. The C corporation might be able to reduce this disadvantage, however, by paying out its earnings as compensation, rents, or interest to its owners. In addition, tax at the owner level is deferred or avoided by not distributing after-tax earnings.

S Corporation Advantages

A new corporation elects S status and incurs a net operating loss (NOL) of $300,000. The shareholders may use their proportionate shares of the NOL to offset other taxable income in the current year, providing an immediate tax savings. In contrast, a newly formed C corporation is required to carry the NOL forward for up to 20 years and receives no tax benefit in the current year. Hence, an S corporation can accelerate the use of NOL deductions and thereby provide a greater present value for the tax savings generated by the loss.

EXAMPLE

2

BRIDGE DISCIPLINE **Bridge to Business Law**

An S corporation is a corporation for all purposes other than its Federal and state income tax law treatment. The entity registers as a corporation with the secretary of state of the state of its incorporation. It issues shares and may hold some treasury stock. Dealings in its own stock are not taxable to the S corporation.

The corporation itself is attractive as a form of business ownership because it offers limited liability to all shareholders from the claims of customers, employees, and others. This is not the case for any type of partnership, where there always is at least one general partner bearing the ultimate personal liability for the operations of the entity (except in the new limited liability limited partnership). Forming an entity as an S corporation facilitates the raising of capital for the business, as an infinite number of shares can be divided in any way imaginable, so as to pass income and deductions, gains, losses, and

credits through to the owners, assuming that the fairly generous "type of shareholder" requirements continue to be met.

An S corporation must comply with all licensing and registration requirements of its home state under the rules applicable to corporate entities. Some states levy privilege taxes on the right to do business in the corporate form, and the S corporation typically is not exempted from this tax.

Because an S corporation is a separate legal entity from its owners, shareholders can be treated as employees and receive qualified retirement and fringe benefits under the Code, as well as unemployment and worker's compensation protection through the corporation. Some limitations apply to the deductibility of fringe benefits, though.

The tax fiction of the S corporation is attractive to investors, as well over one-half of all U.S. corporations have an S election in effect.

TAX FACT **The Business of S Corporations**

S corporations file more than 4 million tax returns every year, concentrated in the service and financial industries.

S Corporation Returns Filed (%), 2011 Tax Year

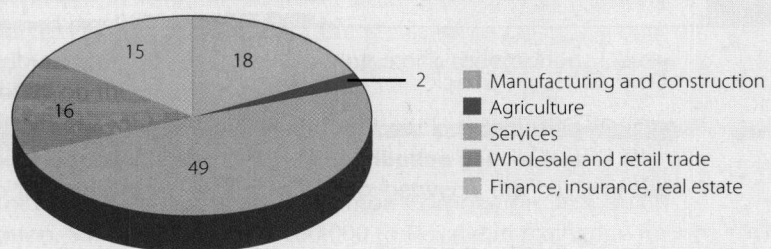

- Manufacturing and construction
- Agriculture
- Services
- Wholesale and retail trade
- Finance, insurance, real estate

LO.2

Identify corporations that qualify for the S election.

15-2 QUALIFYING FOR S CORPORATION STATUS

There are certain conditions that a corporation must meet before S corporation status is available.

15-2a Definition of a Small Business Corporation

To achieve S corporation status, a corporation *first* must qualify as a **small business corporation**. A small business corporation:

- Is a domestic corporation (incorporated and organized in the United States).
- Is eligible to elect S corporation status.
- Issues only one class of stock.
- Is limited to a maximum of 100 shareholders.
- Has only individuals, estates, and certain trusts and exempt organizations as shareholders.
- Has no nonresident alien shareholders.

Thus, foreign corporations do not qualify. S status is also not permitted for certain banks or insurance companies. S corporations are permitted to have wholly owned C and S corporation subsidiaries.[1] No maximum or minimum dollar sales or capitalization restrictions apply to S corporations.

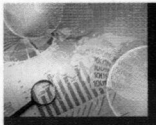

TAX PLANNING STRATEGIES **When to Elect S Corporation Status**

FRAMEWORK FOCUS: DEDUCTIONS

Strategy: Maximize Deductible Amounts.

FRAMEWORK FOCUS: TAX RATE

Strategy: Shift Net Income from High-Bracket Taxpayers to Low-Bracket Taxpayers.
Shift Net Income from High-Tax Jurisdictions to Low-Tax Jurisdictions.

A number of considerations will affect a decision to make an S election.

- Avoid the S election if shareholders have high marginal income tax rates relative to C corporation rates.
- If corporate losses are anticipated and there is unlikely to be corporate taxable income soon, S corporation status is advisable.
- If a C corporation holds an NOL carryover from prior years, the losses cannot be used in an S corporation year.

- There may be tax advantages to the S shareholder who receives a flow-through of passive income or the domestic production activities deduction.
- Some states treat S corporations as C corporations and apply a corporate income tax to them.
- Tax-exempt income at the S level does not lose its special tax treatment for shareholders.
- An S corporation avoids the corporate ACE adjustment, personal holding company tax, and accumulated earnings tax.

One Class of Stock

A small business corporation may have only one class of stock issued and outstanding.[2] This restriction permits differences in voting rights, but not differences in distribution or liquidation rights.[3] Thus, two classes of common stock that are identical except that one

---

[1]Other eligibility rules exist. § 1361(b).
[2]§ 1361(b)(1)(D).

[3]§ 1361(c)(4).

class is voting and the other is nonvoting are treated as a single class of stock for S corporation purposes.

In contrast, voting common stock and voting preferred stock (with a preference on dividends) are treated as two classes of stock. Authorized and unissued stock or treasury stock of another class does not disqualify the corporation. Likewise, unexercised stock options, phantom stock, stock appreciation rights, warrants, and convertible debentures usually do not constitute a second class of stock.[4]

In-depth coverage can be found on this book's companion website: **www.cengagebrain.com**   **1 DIGGING DEEPER**

Although the one-class-of-stock requirement seems straightforward, it is possible for debt to be reclassified as stock, resulting in an unexpected loss of S corporation status.[5] To mitigate concern over possible reclassification of debt as a second class of stock, the law provides a set of *safe harbor* provisions. Neither straight debt[6] nor short-term advances[7] constitute a second class of stock.

The Big Picture

EXAMPLE 3

Return to the facts of *The Big Picture* on p. 15-1. Fowle, Inc., could elect to be an S corporation, except that one class of stock is voting common and the other class is nonvoting preferred. If S status is desired, a recapitalization of the Fowle stock is required, perhaps issuing nonvoting common in place of the preferred stock, which would satisfy the one-class-of-stock requirement.

In-depth coverage can be found on this book's companion website: **www.cengagebrain.com**   **2 DIGGING DEEPER**

Shareholder Limitations

As S corporation is limited to 100 shareholders. If shares of stock are owned jointly by two individuals, they generally are treated as separate shareholders. However, family members (e.g., ancestors, descendants, spouses, and former spouses) of the investor can be counted as one shareholder for purposes of determining the number of shareholders.[8]

EXAMPLE 4

Fred and Wilma (husband and wife) jointly own 10 shares in Oriole, Inc., an S corporation, with the remaining 90 shares outstanding owned by 99 other shareholders. Fred and Wilma are divorced. Both before and after the divorce, the 100-shareholder limit is met, and Oriole can qualify as a small business corporation.

S corporation shareholders may be individuals, estates, or certain trusts and exempt organizations.[9] This limitation prevents partnerships, corporations, most LLCs, LLPs, and most IRAs from owning S corporation stock. Without this rule, partnerships and corporate shareholders could easily circumvent the 100-shareholder limitation.

EXAMPLE 5

Paul and 200 other individuals want to form an S corporation. Paul reasons that if the group forms a partnership, the partnership can then form an S corporation and act as a single shareholder, thereby avoiding the 100-shareholder rule. Paul's plan will not work, because partnerships cannot own stock in an S corporation.

---

[4]Reg. § 1.1361–1(l)(1).
[5]Refer to the discussion of debt-versus-equity classification in Chapter 12.
[6]§ 1361(c)(5)(A).
[7]Reg. § 1.1361–1(l)(1).

[8]§§ 1361(c)(1)(A)(ii) and (B)(i). TD 9422, 2008–42 I.R.B. 898.
[9]§ 1361(b)(1)(B). A one-member LLC typically is an eligible S shareholder.

Nonresident aliens cannot own stock in an S corporation.[10] Thus, individuals who are not U.S. citizens *must live in the United States* to own S corporation stock. Shareholders who live in community property states and are married to a nonresident alien[11] cannot own S corporation stock, because the nonresident alien spouse is treated as owning half of the stock.[12] Similarly, if a resident alien shareholder moves outside the United States, the S election is terminated.

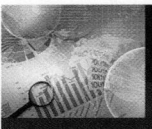

TAX PLANNING STRATEGIES **Beating the 100-Shareholder Limit**

FRAMEWORK FOCUS: TAX RATE

Strategy: Avoid Double Taxation.

Although partnerships and corporations cannot own small business corporation stock, S corporations themselves can be partners in a partnership or shareholders in a corporation. In this way, the 100-shareholder requirement can be bypassed in a limited sense. For example, if two S corporations, each

with 80 shareholders, form a partnership, the shareholders of both corporations can enjoy the limited liability conferred by S corporation status and a single level of tax on the resulting profits.

LO.3

Explain how to make and terminate an S election.

15-2b **Making the Election**

To become an S corporation, the entity must file a valid election with the IRS. The election is made on Form 2553. For the election to be valid, it should be filed on a timely basis and all shareholders must consent. For S corporation status to apply in the current tax year, the election must be filed either in the previous year or on or before the fifteenth day of the third month of the current year.[13]

The Big Picture

EXAMPLE

6

Return to the facts of *The Big Picture* on p. 15-1. Suppose that in 2016, David decides to elect that Fowle, Inc., become an S corporation beginning January 1, 2017. Fowle's S election can be made at any time in 2016 or by March 15, 2017. An election after March 15, 2017, will not be effective until the 2018 calendar tax year.

Even if the 2½-month deadline is met, an S election is not valid unless the corporation qualifies as a small business corporation for the *entire* tax year. Otherwise, the election is effective for the following tax year. Late elections, filed after the 2½-month deadline, may be considered timely if there is reasonable cause for the late filing.

A corporation that does not yet exist cannot make an S corporation election.[14] Thus, for new corporations, a premature election may not be effective. A new corporation's

---

[10]§ 1362(b)(1)(C).

[11]Assets acquired by a married couple are generally considered community property in these states: Alaska (by election), Arizona, California, Idaho, Louisiana, Nevada, New Mexico, Texas, Washington, and Wisconsin.

[12]See *Ward v. U.S.*, 81–2 USTC ¶9674, 48 AFTR 2d 81–5942, 661 F.2d 226 (Ct.Cls., 1981), where the court found that the stock was owned as community property. Because the taxpayer-shareholder (a U.S. citizen) was married to a citizen and resident of Mexico, the nonresident alien prohibi-

tion was violated. If the taxpayer-shareholder had held the stock as separate property, the S election would have been valid.

[13]§ 1362(b). Extensions of time to file Form 2553 may be possible in certain situations; see Rev.Proc. 2007–62, 2007–41 I.R.B. 786.

[14]See, for example, *T.H. Campbell & Bros., Inc.*, 34 TCM 695, T.C.Memo. 1975–149; Ltr.Rul. 8807070.

2¹/₂-month election period begins at the earliest occurrence of any of the following events.

- When the corporation has shareholders.
- When it acquires assets.
- When it begins doing business.[15]

15-2c **Shareholder Consent**

A qualifying election requires the consent of all of the corporation's shareholders.[16] Consent must be in writing, and it generally must be filed by the election deadline. Both husband and wife must consent if they own their stock jointly (as joint tenants, tenants in common, tenants by the entirety, or community property).[17] In certain circumstances (e.g., a shareholder is out of the country when the consent form is due), one may receive an extension of time to file a consent.

TAX PLANNING STRATEGIES **Making a Proper Election**

FRAMEWORK FOCUS: TAX RATE

Strategy: Avoid Double Taxation.

- Because S corporation status is *elected*, strict compliance with the requirements is demanded by both the IRS and the courts. Any failure to meet a condition in the law may lead to loss of the S election and raise the specter of double tax.

- Make sure all shareholders consent. If any doubt exists concerning the shareholder status of an individual, it would be wise to request that he or she sign a consent

anyway.[18] Missing consents are fatal to the election, whereas there is no problem with submitting too many consents.

- Make sure the election is timely and properly filed. Either deliver the election to an IRS office in person or send it by certified or registered mail or via a major overnight delivery service. The date used to determine timeliness is the postmark date, not the date the IRS receives the election.

In-depth coverage can be found on this book's companion website: www.cengagebrain.com **3** DIGGING DEEPER

15-2d **Loss of the Election**

An S election remains in force until it is revoked or lost. Election or consent forms are not required for future years. However, an S election can terminate if any of the following occurs.[19]

- Shareholders owning a majority of shares (voting and nonvoting) voluntarily revoke the election.
- A new shareholder owning more than one-half of the stock affirmatively refuses to consent to the election.
- The corporation no longer qualifies as a small business corporation.
- The corporation does not meet the passive investment income limitation.

---

[15]Reg. § 1.1372–2(b)(1). Also see, for example, *Nick A. Artukovich*, 61 T.C. 100 (1973).

[16]§ 1362(a)(2).

[17]Rev.Rul. 60–183, 1960–1 C.B. 625; *William Pestcoe*, 40 T.C. 195 (1963); Reg. § 1.1362–6(b)(3)(iii). This rule likely also applies to all family members who are being treated as one shareholder.

[18]See *William B. Wilson*, 34 TCM 463, T.C.Memo. 1975–92.

[19]§ 1362(d).

Voluntary Revocation

A `voluntary revocation` of the S election requires the consent of shareholders owning a majority of shares on the day the revocation is to be made.[20] A revocation filed up to and including the fifteenth day of the third month of the tax year is effective for the entire tax year, unless a later date is specified. Similarly, unless an effective date is specified, a revocation made after the first $2\frac{1}{2}$ months of the current tax year is effective for the following tax year.

The shareholders of Petunia Corporation, a calendar year S corporation, voluntarily revoke the S election on January 5, 2016. They do not specify a future effective date in the revocation. If the revocation is properly executed and timely filed, Petunia will be a C corporation for the entire 2016 tax year. If the revocation is not made until June 2016, Petunia remains an S corporation in 2016 and becomes a C corporation at the beginning of 2017.

A corporation can revoke its S status *prospectively* by specifying a future date when the revocation is to be effective. A revocation that designates a future effective date splits the corporation's tax year into a short S corporation year and a short C corporation year. The day on which the revocation occurs is treated as the first day of the C corporation year. The corporation allocates income or loss for the entire year on a pro rata basis using the number of days in each short year.

Assume the same facts as in the preceding example, except that Petunia designates July 1, 2016, as the revocation date. Accordingly, June 30 is the last day of the S corporation's tax year. The C corporation's tax year runs from July 1, 2016, to December 31, 2016. Income or loss for the 12-month period is allocated between the two short years (i.e., 184/366 to the C corporation year).

Rather than allocating on a pro rata basis, the corporation can elect to compute the actual income or loss attributable to the two short years. This election requires the consent of everyone who was a shareholder at any time during the S corporation's short year and everyone who owns stock on the first day of the C corporation's year.[21]

Loss of S Corporation Status

If an S corporation fails to qualify as a small business corporation at any time after the election has become effective, its status as an S corporation ends. The termination occurs on the day the corporation ceases to be a small business corporation.[22] Thus, if the corporation ever has more than 100 shareholders, a second class of stock, or a nonqualifying shareholder or it otherwise fails to meet the definition of a small business corporation, the S election is terminated immediately.

Peony Corporation has been a calendar year S corporation for three years. On August 13, one of its 100 shareholders sells *some* of her stock to an outsider. Peony now has 101 shareholders, and it ceases to be a small business corporation. Peony is an S corporation through August 12 and a C corporation from August 13 to December 31.

Passive Investment Income Limitation

The Code provides a `passive investment income (PII)` limitation for some S corporations that previously were C corporations, or for S corporations that have merged with

---

[20] § 1362(d)(1)(B).
[21] § 1362(e)(3).

[22] § 1362(d)(2)(B).

C corporations. If an S corporation holds C corporation earnings and profits (E & P) and it generates passive investment income in excess of 25 percent of its gross receipts for three consecutive tax years, the S election is terminated as of the beginning of the fourth year.[23]

For 2013, 2014, and 2015, Chrysanthemum Corporation, a calendar year S corporation, derived passive investment income in excess of 25% of its gross receipts. If Chrysanthemum holds accumulated E & P from years in which it was a C corporation, its S election is terminated as of January 1, 2016.

EXAMPLE 10

PII includes dividends, interest, rents, gains and losses from sales of capital assets, and royalties net of investment deductions. Rents are not considered PII if the corporation renders significant personal services to the occupant.

Violet Corporation owns and operates an apartment building. The corporation provides utilities for the building, maintains the lobby, and furnishes trash collection for tenants. These activities are not considered significant personal services, so any rent income earned by the corporation will be considered PII.

Alternatively, if Violet also provides maid services to its tenants (personal services beyond what normally would be expected from a landlord in an apartment building), the rent income would no longer be PII.

EXAMPLE 11

Reelection after Termination

After an S election has been terminated, the corporation must wait five years before reelecting S corporation status. The five-year waiting period is waived if:

- There is a more-than-50-percent change in ownership of the corporation after the first year for which the termination is applicable, or
- The event causing the termination was not reasonably within the control of the S corporation or its majority shareholders.

TAX PLANNING STRATEGIES **Preserving the S Election**

FRAMEWORK FOCUS: TAX RATE

Strategy: Avoid Double Taxation.

Unexpected loss of S corporation status can be costly to a corporation and its shareholders. Given the complexity of the rules facing these entities, constant vigilance is necessary to preserve the S election.

- As a starting point, the corporation's management and shareholders should be made aware of the various transactions that can lead to the loss of an election.
- Prevent violations of the small business corporation limitations. Because most such violations result from transfers

of stock, the corporation and its shareholders should consider adopting a set of stock transfer restrictions.

A carefully designed set of restrictions could prevent sale of stock to nonqualifying entities or violation of the 100-shareholder rule. Similarly, stock could be repurchased by the corporation under a buy-sell agreement upon the death of a shareholder, thereby preventing nonqualifying trusts from becoming shareholders.[24]

---

[23]§ 1362(d)(3)(A)(ii).

[24]Most such agreements do not create a second class of stock. Rev.Rul. 85–161, 1985–2 C.B. 191; *Portage Plastics Co. v. U.S.*, 72–2 USTC ¶9567, 30 AFTR 2d 72–5229, 470 F.2d 308 (CA–7, 1973).

LO.4

Compute nonseparately stated income and allocate income, deductions, and credits to shareholders.

15-3 OPERATIONAL RULES

S corporations are treated much like partnerships for tax purposes. Each year, the S corporation determines nonseparately stated income or loss and separately stated income, deductions, and credits. These items are taxed only once, as they pass through to shareholders. All items are allocated to each shareholder based on average ownership of stock throughout the year.[25] The flow-through of each item of income, deduction, and credit from the corporation to the shareholder is illustrated in Exhibit 15.1.

15-3a Computation of Taxable Income

An S corporation's taxable income or loss is determined in a manner similar to the tax rules that apply to partnerships, except that S corporations recognize gains (but not losses) on distributions of appreciated property to shareholders.[26] With a few exceptions, S corporations generally make tax accounting and other elections at the corporate level.[27] Other special provisions affecting only the computation of C corporation income, such as the dividends received deduction, do not extend to S corporations.[28]

In general, S corporation items are divided into (1) nonseparately stated income or loss and (2) separately stated income, losses, deductions, and credits that could

| EXHIBIT 15.1 | Flow-Through of Items of Income and Loss to S Corporation Shareholders |

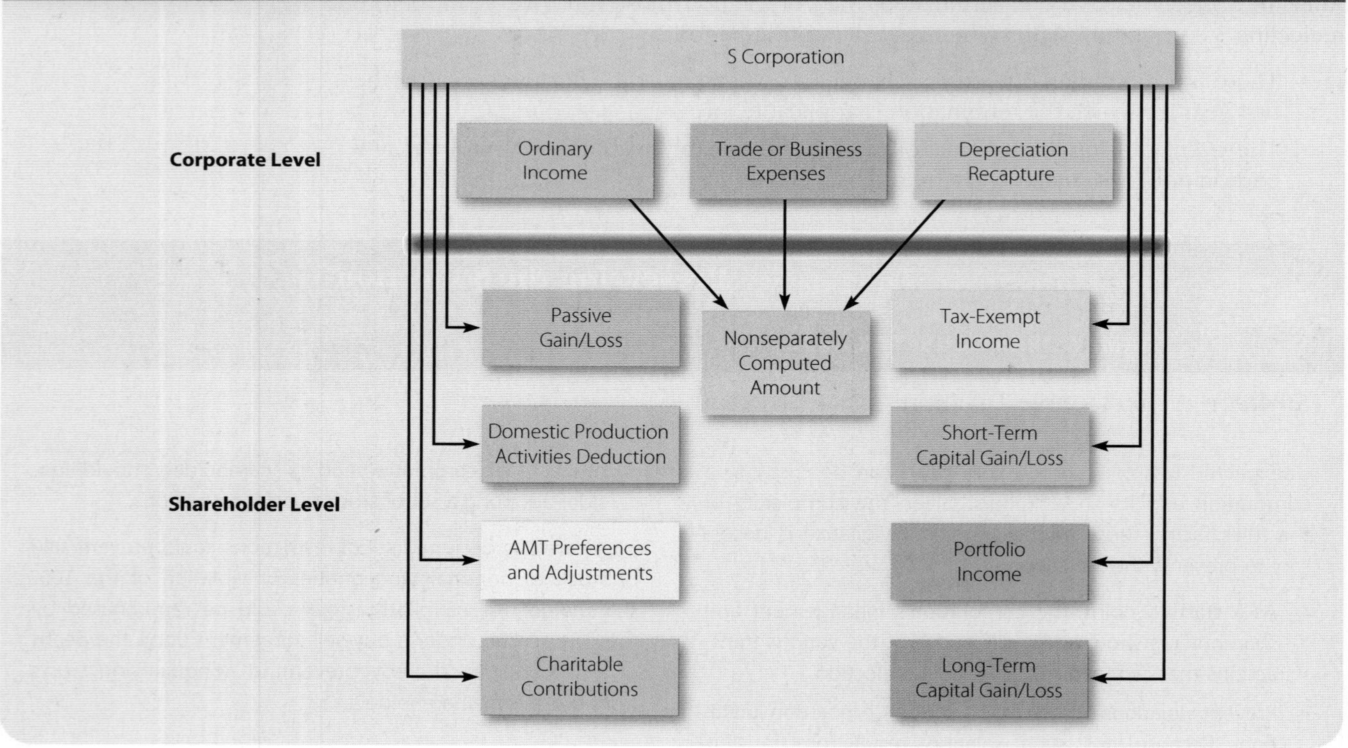

S Corporation

Corporate Level

Ordinary Income

Trade or Business Expenses

Depreciation Recapture

Passive Gain/Loss

Nonseparately Computed Amount

Tax-Exempt Income

Domestic Production Activities Deduction

Short-Term Capital Gain/Loss

Shareholder Level

AMT Preferences and Adjustments

Portfolio Income

Charitable Contributions

Long-Term Capital Gain/Loss

---

[25]§§ 1366(a), (b), and (c).

[26]§ 1363(b).

[27]Certain elections are made at the shareholder level (e.g., the choice between a foreign tax deduction or credit).

[28]§ 703(a)(2).

uniquely affect the tax liability of any shareholder. In essence, nonseparate items are aggregated into an undifferentiated amount that constitutes Subchapter S ordinary income or loss.

EXAMPLE

12

The following is the income statement for Larkspur, Inc., an S corporation.

Sales		$ 40,000
Less: Cost of goods sold		(23,000)
Gross profit on sales		$ 17,000
Less: Interest expense	$1,200	
Charitable contributions	400	
Advertising expenses	1,500	
Other operating expenses	2,000	(5,100)
Book income from operations		$ 11,900
Add: Tax-exempt interest income	$ 300	
Dividend income	200	
Long-term capital gain	500	1,000
Less: Short-term capital loss		(150)
Net income per books		$ 12,750

Larkspur's ordinary income (i.e., nonseparately stated income) is calculated as follows, using net income for book purposes as the starting point.

Net income per books		$12,750
Separately stated items		
Deduct: Tax-exempt interest income	$300	
Dividend income	200	
Long-term capital gain	500	(1,000)
Add: Charitable contributions	$400	
Short-term capital loss	150	550
Ordinary income		$12,300

The $12,300 of Larkspur's nonseparately stated income, as well as each of the five separately stated items, is divided among the shareholders based upon their stock ownership.

An S corporation reports details as to the differences between book income and pass-through items on its Form 1120S, Schedule M–1 or M–3.

15-3b **Allocation of Income and Loss**

Each shareholder is allocated a pro rata portion of nonseparately stated income or loss and all separately stated items. The pro rata allocation method assigns an equal amount of each of the S items to each day of the year.[29] If a shareholder's stock holding changes during the year, this allocation assigns the shareholder a pro rata share of each item for each day the stock is owned. On the date of transfer, the transferor (not the transferee) is considered to own the stock.[30]

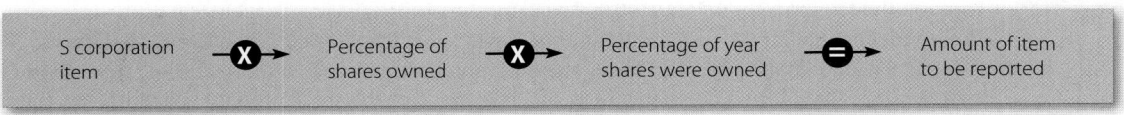

| S corporation item | X | Percentage of shares owned | X | Percentage of year shares were owned | = | Amount of item to be reported |

---

[29]§§ 1366(a)(1) and 1377(a)(1).   [30]Reg. § 1.1377–1(a)(2)(ii).

TAX FACT   A "Small" Business Corporation

The majority of S corporations have only one shareholder.

Returns Filed by Number of S Corporation Shareholders, 2011 Tax Year

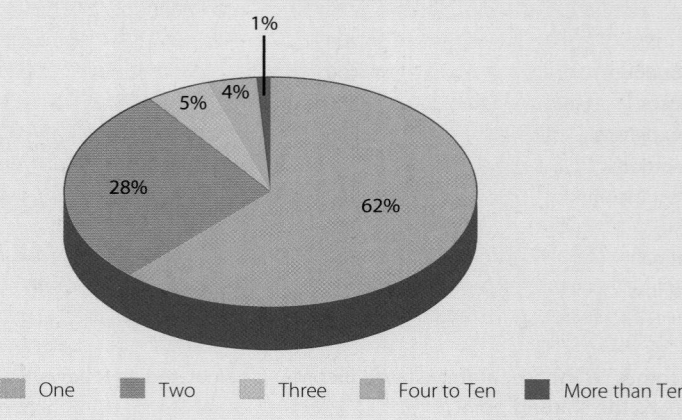

Shareholders: ■ One   ■ Two   ■ Three   ■ Four to Ten   ■ More than Ten

EXAMPLE 13

Pat, a shareholder, owned 10% of Larkspur's stock (from Example 12) for 100 days and 12% for the remaining 265 days. Using the required per-day allocation method, Pat's share of the Subchapter S ordinary income is the total of $12,300 \times [10\% \times (100/365)]$ plus $12,300 \times [12\% \times (265/365)]$, or $1,409. All of Pat's Schedule K–1 totals flow through to the corresponding lines on his individual income tax return (Form 1040).

The Short-Year Election

If a shareholder's interest is completely terminated during the tax year by a sale or by a disposition following death, all shareholders owning stock during the year and the corporation may elect to treat the S taxable year as two taxable years. The first year ends on the date of the termination. Under this election, an interim closing of the books is undertaken, and the shareholders report their shares of the S corporation items as they occurred during the short tax year.[31]

The short-year election provides an opportunity to shift income, losses, and credits among shareholders. The election is desirable in circumstances where more loss can be allocated to taxpayers with higher marginal tax rates.

DIGGING DEEPER 4   In-depth coverage can be found on this book's companion website: www.cengagebrain.com

EXAMPLE 14

Alicia, the owner of all of the shares of an S corporation, transfers her stock to Cindy halfway through the tax year. There is a $100,000 NOL for the entire tax year, but $30,000 of the loss occurs during the first half of the year. Without a short-year election, $50,000 of the loss is allocated to Alicia and $50,000 is allocated to Cindy. If the corporation makes the short-year election, Cindy is allocated $70,000 of the loss. In this case, the sales price of the stock probably would be increased to recognize the tax benefits being transferred from Alicia to Cindy.

---

[31]§ 1377(a)(2).

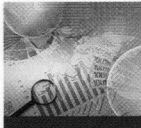

TAX PLANNING STRATEGIES **Salary Structure**

FRAMEWORK FOCUS: TAX RATE

Strategy: Shift Net Income from High-Bracket Taxpayers to Low-Bracket Taxpayers. Avoid Double Taxation.

The amount of any salary paid to a shareholder-employee of an S corporation can have varying tax consequences and should be considered carefully. Larger amounts might be advantageous if the maximum contribution allowed under the employee's retirement plan has not been reached. Smaller amounts may be beneficial if the parties are trying to shift taxable income to lower-bracket shareholders, reduce payroll taxes, curtail a reduction of Social Security benefits, or restrict losses that do not pass through because of the basis limitation.

A strategy of decreasing compensation and correspondingly increasing distributions to shareholder-employees often results in substantial savings in employment taxes. However, a shareholder of an S corporation cannot always perform substantial services and arrange to receive distributions rather than compensation so that the corporation may avoid paying employment taxes. The shareholder may be deemed an employee, and any distributions will be recharacterized as wages subject to FICA and FUTA taxes.[32] For planning purposes, some level of compensation should be paid to all shareholder-employees to avoid any recharacterization of distributions as deductible salaries—especially in personal service corporations.

Use of S corporations as an income-shifting device within a family (e.g., through a gift of stock from a high-marginal-rate taxpayer to a low-marginal-rate taxpayer) may be ineffective. The IRS can ignore such transfers unless the stock is purchased at fair market value.[33] Effectively, the IRS can require that reasonable compensation be paid to family members who render services or provide capital to the S corporation.

15-3c **Tax Treatment of Distributions to Shareholders**

LO.5

Determine how distributions to S corporation shareholders are taxed.

S corporations do not generate E & P while the S election is in effect. Indeed, all profits are taxed in the year earned, as though they were distributed on a pro rata basis to the shareholders. Thus, distributions from S corporations do not constitute dividends in the traditional sense—there is no corporate E & P to distribute.

It is possible, however, for S corporations to have an accumulated E & P (AEP) account. This can occur when:

- The S corporation was previously a C corporation, or
- A C corporation with its own AEP merged into the S corporation.

Distributions from S corporations are measured as the cash received plus the fair market value of any other distributed property. The tax treatment of distributions differs, depending upon whether the S corporation has AEP.

S Corporation with No AEP

If the S corporation has no AEP, the distribution is a tax-free recovery of capital to the extent it does not exceed the basis of the shareholder's stock. When the amount of the distribution exceeds the stock basis, the excess is treated as a gain from the sale or exchange of property (capital gain in most cases). The vast majority of S corporations fall into this favorable category.

Hyacinth, Inc., a calendar year S corporation, has no AEP. During the year, Juan, an individual shareholder of the corporation, receives a cash distribution of $12,200 from Hyacinth. Juan's basis in his stock is $9,700. Juan recognizes a capital gain of $2,500, the excess of the distribution over the stock basis ($12,200 − $9,700). The remaining $9,700 is tax-free, but it reduces Juan's basis in his stock to zero.

EXAMPLE

15

---

[32]Rev.Rul. 74–44, 1974–1 C.B. 287; *Spicer Accounting, Inc. v. U.S.*, 91–1 USTC ¶50,103, 66 AFTR 2d 90–5806, 918 F.2d 90 (CA–9, 1990); *Radtke v. U.S.*, 90–1 USTC ¶50,113, 65 AFTR 2d 90–1155, 895 F.2d 1196 (CA–7, 1990); *Joseph M. Grey Public Accountant, P.C.*, 119 T.C. 121 (2002); *David E. Watson, P.C. v. U.S.*, 2010–1 USTC ¶50,444, 105 AFTR 2d 2010-2624,

714 F. Supp.2d 954 (D.C. S.IA). The IRS uses salary surveys and other statistical methods to determine the appropriate compensation level. *McAlary Ltd.*, T.C. Summary Opinion 2013–62.

[33]§ 1366(e) and Reg. § 1.1373–1(a).

TAX IN THE NEWS   Some Guidelines for S Corporation Shareholder-Employee Compensation

Shareholder compensation issues differ between C and S corporations. Usually, a C corporation guards against shareholder salaries being "too high," so as to avoid IRS charges of unreasonable compensation and the conversion of a salary into a nondeductible dividend distribution. An S corporation must make certain that its shareholder salaries are not "too low," to counter potential IRS assertions that the compensation structure was designed to avoid payroll tax liabilities.

An IRS fact sheet provides taxpayers with these factors to determine reasonable compensation for an S shareholder.

- Training, education, and experience.
- Duties and responsibilities.
- Time and effort devoted to business.
- Dividend history.
- Payments to nonshareholders-employees.
- Timing and manner of paying bonuses to key employees.
- What comparable businesses pay for similar services.
- Compensation agreements.
- Use of a formula to determine compensation.

Source: FS-2008-25, Wage Compensation for S Corporation Officers, August 2008.

S Corporation with AEP

For S corporations that hold AEP, a more complex set of rules applies. These rules treat distributions of pre-election (C corporation) and postelection (S corporation) earnings differently. Distributions of AEP are taxed as dividends, while distributions of previously taxed S corporation earnings are tax-free to the extent of the shareholder's basis in the stock.

Distributions are deemed to be first from previously taxed, undistributed earnings of the S corporation. Such distributions are tax-free and are determined by reference to a special account, the **accumulated adjustments account (AAA)**.[34] Next, AEP is distributed as taxable dividends (i.e., as payments from AEP). After AEP is depleted, tax-free distributions are made from the **other adjustments account (OAA)**, as discussed below. Remaining amounts of the distribution are received tax free until the shareholder's stock basis reaches zero,[35] with any excess being treated typically as capital gain.

Ordering Rules for Distributions

EXAMPLE 16

Short, a calendar year S corporation, distributes $1,300 of cash to its only shareholder, Otis, on December 31. Otis's basis in his stock is $1,400, AAA is $500, and Short holds $750 of AEP before the distribution.

The first $500 of the distribution is a tax-free recovery of basis from the AAA. The next $750 is a taxable dividend distribution from AEP. The remaining $50 of cash is a tax-free recovery of basis. Immediately after the distribution, Short records a zero balance in AAA and AEP. Otis's stock basis now is $850.

	Corporate AAA	Corporate AEP	Otis's Stock Basis
Beginning balance	$ 500	$ 750	$1,400
Distribution from AAA	(500)		(500)
Distribution from AEP		(750)	
Distribution from stock basis			(50)
Ending balance	$ –0–	$ –0–	$ 850

---

[34]For S corporations in existence prior to 1983, an account similar to the AAA was used. This account, called *previously taxed income* (PTI), can be distributed in cash tax free to shareholders after AAA has been distributed. See §§ 1368(c)(1) and (e)(1).

[35]§ 1368(c).

Ordering Rules for Distributions

Assume the same facts as in the preceding example. The next year, Short's income totals zero. It distributes $1,000 to Otis. Of the distribution, $850 is a tax-free recovery of the stock basis, and $150 is taxed to Otis as a capital gain.

EXAMPLE 17

With the consent of all of its shareholders, an S corporation can elect to have a distribution treated as if it were made from AEP rather than from the AAA. This mechanism is known as an **AAA bypass election** . This election may be desirable when making distributions to move the entity to the no-AEP system of accounting for distributions, at a maximum tax cost of 20 percent of the AEP (i.e., the maximum income tax rate applied to dividends for most shareholders).

Rotor, an S corporation, has $50 of AEP. An AAA bypass election for Rotor's next shareholder distribution would eliminate the need to track the AAA and would greatly simplify the accounting for future distributions. The cost for this simplification is the tax on $50 of dividend income.

EXAMPLE 18

Accumulated Adjustments Account

The AAA is the cumulative total of undistributed nonseparately and separately stated income and deduction items for S corporation years beginning after 1982. As noted, it provides a mechanism to ensure that earnings of an S corporation are taxed only once. Changes to the AAA are reported annually in Schedule M–2 on page 4 of the Form 1120S.

The initial AAA balance is zero when an S election is made. AAA then is computed at the end of each tax year rather than at the time of a distribution. First, add to the year's beginning balance any current nonseparately computed income and positive separately stated items (except tax-exempt income). Next, account for distributions *prior* to subtracting the negative items.

Concept Summary 15.1

Distributions from an S Corporation

Where Earnings and Profits Exist	Where No Earnings and Profits Exist
1. Distributions are tax-free to the extent of the accumulated adjustments account (AAA).*	
2. Next, the distribution constitutes dividend income to the extent of accumulated E & P (AEP).†	
3. Distributions are tax-free to the extent of the other adjustments account (OAA).*	
4. Any residual distribution is nontaxable to the extent of the shareholder's basis in stock.*	1. Distributions are nontaxable to the extent of shareholder's basis in stock.*
5. Excess is treated as gain from a sale or exchange of stock (capital gain in virtually all cases).	2. Excess is treated as gain from a sale or exchange of stock (capital gain in virtually all cases).

*The distribution reduces the shareholder's stock basis. A shareholder's stock basis serves as the upper limit on the amount that may be received tax free.
†The AAA bypass election is available to pay out AEP before reducing the AAA [§ 1368 (e) (3)].

AAA is applied to the distributions made during the year on a pro rata basis (in a fashion similar to the application of current E & P, discussed in Chapter 13). The determination of AAA is summarized in Exhibit 15.2.

EXHIBIT 15.2   Adjustments to the Corporate AAA

Increase by:

1. Schedule K income items other than tax-exempt income.
2. Nonseparately computed income.

Decrease by:

3. Distribution(s) from AAA (but not below zero).
4. Negative Schedule K items other than distributions (e.g., losses, deductions).

Although adjustments to AAA and stock basis adjustments are similar, there are some important differences between the two amounts. In particular,

- The AAA is not affected by tax-exempt income and related expenses.
- The AAA can have a negative balance. All losses decrease the AAA balance, even those in excess of the shareholder's basis. However, distributions may not make the AAA negative or increase a negative balance in the account.
- Every shareholder has a proportionate interest in the AAA, regardless of the amount of his or her stock basis.[36] In fact, AAA is a corporate account, so there is no connection between the amount and any specific shareholder.[37] Thus, the benefits of AAA can be shifted from one shareholder to another. For example, when an S corporation shareholder sells stock to another party, any AAA balance on the purchase date can be distributed tax free to the purchaser.

Other Adjustments Account

The OAA tracks the entity's net items that affect basis but not the AAA, such as tax-exempt income and any related nondeductible expenses. Distributions from this account are tax-free.

Schedule M–2

Page 4 of the Form 1120S includes Schedule M–2, a reconciliation of beginning and ending balances in the AAA and OAA accounts. Most tax professionals recommend that the Schedule M–2 be kept current even if the entity has retained no AEP so that if future events require the use of these amounts, they need not be reconstructed after the fact.

EXAMPLE 19

Poinsettia, an S corporation, records the following items.

AAA, beginning of year	$ 8,500
OAA, beginning of year	–0–
Ordinary income	25,000
Tax-exempt interest income	4,000
Key employee life insurance proceeds received	5,000
Payroll penalty expense	2,000
Charitable contributions	3,000
Unreasonable compensation	5,000
Premiums on key employee life insurance	2,100
Distributions to shareholders	16,000

continued

---

[36]§ 1368(c).   [37]§ 1368(e)(1)(A).

Poinsettia's Schedule M–2 appears as follows.

Schedule M-2	Analysis of Accumulated Adjustments Account, Other Adjustments Account, and Shareholders' Undistributed Taxable Income Previously Taxed (see instructions)		(a) Accumulated adjustments account	(b) Other adjustments account	(c) Shareholders' undistributed taxable income previously taxed
1	Balance at beginning of tax year		8,500	0	
2	Ordinary income from page 1, line 21 . . .		25,000		
3	Other additions			9,000**	
4	Loss from page 1, line 21		( )		
5	Other reductions		(10,000*)	(2,100)	
6	Combine lines 1 through 5		23,500	6,900	
7	Distributions other than dividend distributions		16,000		
8	Balance at end of tax year. Subtract line 7 from line 6		7,500	6,900	

*$2,000 (payroll penalty) + $3,000 (charitable contributions) + $5,000 (unreasonable compensation).
**$4,000 (tax-exempt interest income) + $5,000 (life insurance proceeds).

In-depth coverage can be found on this book's companion website: www.cengagebrain.com | **5 DIGGING DEEPER**

Effect of Terminating the S Election

Normally, distributions to shareholders from a C corporation are taxed as dividends to the extent of E & P. However, any distribution of *cash* by a C corporation to shareholders during a one-year period[38] following an S election termination receives special treatment. Such a distribution is treated as a tax-free recovery of stock basis to the extent that it does not exceed the AAA.[39] Because *only* cash distributions reduce the AAA during this *postelection termination period*, a corporation should not make property distributions during this time. Instead, the entity should sell property and distribute the proceeds to shareholders.

The Big Picture

EXAMPLE
20

Return to the facts of *The Big Picture* on p. 15-1. Assume that Fowle has operated as an S corporation for many years and that the entity turned profitable once it mastered the pricing methods of its import markets. Then David decides to terminate the S election as of the end of the year. On December 31 of that year, Fowle's AAA balance totals $1.3 million. David can receive a nontaxable distribution of cash during the next year, to the full extent of the entity's AAA balance. Any cash distributions so received reduce the basis of David's Fowle stock, but not below zero.

TAX PLANNING STRATEGIES   **The Accumulated Adjustments Account**

FRAMEWORK FOCUS: TAX RATE

Strategy: Avoid Double Taxation.

The AAA is needed to determine the tax treatment of distributions from S corporations with AEP *and* distributions made during the post-termination election period. Therefore, it is important for all S corporations (even those with no AEP) to maintain a current AAA (and OAA) balance. Without an accurate AAA balance, distributions could needlessly be classified as taxable dividends. Alternatively, it will be costly to reconstruct the AAA after the S election terminates.

Distributions should be made when AAA is positive. If future years bring operating losses, AAA is reduced and shareholder exposure to AEP and taxable dividends increases.

---

[38]§ 1377(b).

[39]§ 1371(e). Termination-period distributions from the OAA are not exempt.

15-3d Tax Treatment of Noncash Distributions by the Corporation

An S corporation recognizes a gain on any distribution of appreciated property as if the asset were sold to the shareholder at its fair market value.[40] The corporate gain is passed through to the shareholders. There is an important reason for this rule. Without it, property might be distributed tax free (other than for certain recapture items) and later sold without income recognition to the shareholder because the shareholder's basis equals the asset's fair market value. The character of the gain—capital gain or ordinary income—depends upon the type of asset being distributed.

The S corporation does not recognize a loss when distributing assets that are worth less than their basis. As with gain property, the shareholder's basis is equal to the asset's fair market value. Thus, the potential loss is postponed until the shareholder sells the stock of the S corporation. Because loss property receives a step-down in basis without any loss recognition by the S corporation, distributions of loss property should be avoided. See Concept Summary 15.2.

Noncash Distributions by an S Corporation

EXAMPLE 21

Yarrow, Inc., an S corporation for 12 years, distributes to Xiang, one of its shareholders, a tract of land held as an investment. The land was purchased for $22,000 many years ago and is currently worth $82,000. Yarrow recognizes a capital gain of $60,000, which increases the AAA by $60,000. The gain flows through proportionately to all of Yarrow's shareholders and is taxed to them.

Such a tax-free property distribution reduces AAA and Xiang's S stock basis by $82,000 (fair market value). The tax consequences are the same for appreciated property whether (a) it is distributed to shareholders and they dispose of it or (b) the corporation sells the property and distributes the proceeds to its shareholders.

EXAMPLE 22

Continue with the facts of Example 21. If the land had been purchased for $82,000 and was currently worth $22,000, Xiang would take a $22,000 basis in the land. The $60,000 realized loss is not recognized at the corporate level. The loss does not reduce Yarrow's AAA. However, if the S corporation sells the asset to an unrelated party, it does recognize the loss and reduces AAA.

EXAMPLE 23

Assume the same facts as in Examples 21 and 22, except that Yarrow is a C corporation (E & P balance of $1 million) or a partnership. Assume that Xiang's basis before the distribution in her corporate stock or partnership interest is $100,000, and ignore any corporate-level taxes. Compare the results.

	Appreciated Property		
	S Corporation	C Corporation	Partnership
Entity gain/loss	$60,000	$60,000	$ –0–
Owner's gain/loss/dividend	60,000	82,000	–0–
Owner's basis in land	82,000	82,000	22,000

	Property That Has Declined in Value		
	S Corporation	C Corporation	Partnership
Entity gain/loss	$ –0–	$ –0–	$ –0–
Owner's gain/loss/dividend	–0–	22,000	–0–
Owner's basis in land	22,000	22,000	82,000

---

[40]§ 311(b).

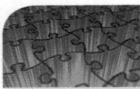

Concept Summary 15.2

Consequences of Noncash Distributions

	Appreciated Property	Depreciated Property
S corporation	Realized gain is recognized by the corporation, which passes it through to the shareholders. Such gain increases a shareholder's stock basis, generating a basis in the property equal to FMV. On the distribution, the shareholder's stock basis is reduced by the FMV of the property (but not below zero).	Realized loss is not recognized. The shareholder takes an FMV basis in the property.
C corporation	Realized gain is recognized under § 311(b) and increases E & P (net of tax). The shareholder reports a taxable dividend to the extent of corporate E & P, equal to the property's FMV (reduced by any liabilities assumed). The shareholder takes a basis in the asset equal to its FMV.	Realized loss is not recognized. The shareholder takes an FMV basis in the property.
Partnership	No gain to the partnership or partner. The partner takes a carryover basis in the asset, but the asset basis is limited to the partner's basis in the partnership.	Realized loss is not recognized. The partner takes a carryover basis in the asset, but the asset basis is limited to the partner's basis in the partnership.

15-3e Shareholder's Basis in S Stock

The calculation of the initial tax basis of stock in an S corporation is similar to that for the basis of stock in a C corporation and depends upon the manner in which the shares are acquired (e.g., gift, inheritance, purchase, exchange under § 351). Once the initial tax basis is determined, various transactions during the life of the corporation affect the shareholder's basis in the stock. Although each shareholder is required to compute his or her own basis in the S shares, neither Form 1120S nor Schedule K–1 provides a place for tracking this amount.

A shareholder's basis is increased by stock purchases and capital contributions. Operations during the year cause the following additional upward adjustments to basis.[41]

- Nonseparately computed income.
- Separately stated income items (e.g., tax-exempt income).

Basis then is reduced by distributions not reported as income by the shareholder (e.g., an AAA distribution). Next, the following items reduce basis (but not below zero).

- Nondeductible expenses of the corporation (e.g., fines, penalties, and illegal kickbacks).
- Nonseparately computed loss.
- Separately stated loss and deduction items.

As under the partnership rules, basis first is increased by income items; then it is decreased by distributions and finally by losses.[42] In most cases, this *losses last* rule is advantageous to the S shareholder.

LO.6

Calculate a shareholder's basis in S corporation stock.

In its first year of operation, Iris, Inc., a calendar year S corporation, earns income of $2,000. Before accounting for the entity's operating results, assume the stock basis of Iris's sole shareholder, Marty, is zero. Therefore, Marty's stock basis is increased to $2,000. On February 2 in its second year of operation, Iris distributes $2,000 to Marty. During the remainder of the second year, the corporation incurs a $2,000 loss.

Under the S corporation ordering rules, the $2,000 distribution is tax-free AAA to Marty. The distribution is accounted for before the loss. The $2,000 loss is suspended until Marty generates additional stock basis (e.g., from capital contributions or future entity profits).

EXAMPLE

24

---

[41]§ 1367(a).   [42]Reg. § 1.1367–1(f).

A shareholder's basis in S corporation stock never is reduced below zero. Once stock basis reaches zero, any additional basis reductions (losses or deductions, but *not* distributions) decrease (but not below zero) the shareholder's basis in loans made to the S corporation. Any excess of losses or deductions over both stock and loan bases is not deductible in the current year. Losses can be deducted only to the extent they offset stock or loan basis. Thus, until additional basis is created due to capital contributions or flow-through income, the loss deductions are suspended.

When there is a capital contribution or an item of flow-through income, basis first is restored to the shareholder loans, up to the original principal amount.[43] Then basis in the stock is restored.

EXAMPLE 25

Stacey, a sole shareholder, holds a $7,000 stock basis and a $2,000 basis in a loan that she made to Romulus, a calendar year S corporation with zero AEP. At the beginning of the year, the corporation's AAA and OAA balances are zero. Ordinary income for the year is $8,200. During the year, the corporation also received $2,000 of tax-exempt interest income.

Cash of $17,300 is distributed to Stacey on November 15. As a result, Stacey recognizes only a $100 capital gain.

	Corporate AAA	Corporate OAA	Stacey's Stock Basis	Stacey's Loan Basis
Beginning balance	$ –0–	$ –0–	$ 7,000	$2,000
Ordinary income	8,200		8,200	
Tax-exempt income		2,000	2,000	
Subtotal	$ 8,200	$ 2,000	$17,200	$2,000
Distribution ($17,300)				
From AAA	(8,200)		(8,200)	
From OAA		(2,000)	(2,000)	
From stock basis			(7,000)	
Ending balance	$ –0–	$ –0–	$ –0–	$2,000
Distribution in excess of stock basis (capital gain)			$ 100	

Pass-through losses can reduce loan basis, but distributions do not. Stock basis cannot be reduced below zero, and the $100 excess distribution does not reduce Stacey's loan basis.

The basis rules for S corporation stock are similar to the rules for determining a partner's basis in a partnership interest. However, a partner's basis in the partnership interest includes the partner's direct investment plus a *ratable share* of partnership liabilities.[44] If a partnership borrows from a partner, the partner receives a basis increase as if the partnership had borrowed from an unrelated third party.[45] In contrast, corporate borrowing has no effect on the stock basis of an S corporation shareholder. Loans from a shareholder to the S corporation have a tax basis only for the shareholder making the loan.

If a loan's basis has been reduced and is not restored, income is recognized when the corporation repays the loan. If the corporation issued a note as evidence of the debt, repayment constitutes an amount received in exchange for a capital asset and the amount that exceeds the shareholder's basis is capital gain.[46] However, if the loan is

[43]§ 1367(b)(2); Reg. § 1.1367–2(e).

[44]§ 752(a).

[45]Reg. § 1.752–1(e).

[46]*Joe M. Smith*, 48 T.C. 872 (1967), *aff'd* and *rev'd* in 70–1 USTC ¶9327, 25 AFTR 2d 70–936, 424 F.2d 219 (CA–9, 1970); Rev.Rul. 64–162, 1964–1 C.B.

304. An open account loan is treated as evidenced by a note if the shareholder's net payable at the end of the tax year exceeds $25,000. Reg. § 1.1367–2.

made on open account, the repayment constitutes ordinary income to the extent it exceeds the shareholder's basis in the loan. Thus, a written note should be given to ensure capital gain treatment for the income that results from a loan's repayment.

The Big Picture

EXAMPLE

26

Return to the facts of *The Big Picture* on p. 15-1. Assume that Fowle has made an S election. At the beginning of 2016, David's basis in his Fowle stock was $90,000. During the year, he made a $40,000 loan to the corporation, using a written debt instrument and market interest rates.

Fowle generated a $93,000 taxable loss for 2016. Thus, at the beginning of 2017, David's stock basis was zero, and the basis in his loan to Fowle was $37,000.

Fowle repaid the loan in full on March 1, 2017. David recognizes a $3,000 capital gain on the repayment.

In-depth coverage can be found on this book's companion website: **www.cengagebrain.com**

6 DIGGING DEEPER

TAX PLANNING STRATEGIES Working with Suspended Losses

FRAMEWORK FOCUS: INCOME AND EXCLUSION

Strategy: Avoid Income Recognition.

Distributions made to shareholders with suspended losses usually create capital gain income because there is no stock basis to offset. Usually, distributions should be deferred until the shareholder creates stock basis in some form. In this way, no gross income is recognized until the suspended losses are fully used.

The Big Picture

EXAMPLE

27

Continue with the facts of Example 26, except that Fowle's loss cannot be deducted by David because he has a zero basis in both the stock and debt of the entity. David purchases $5,000 of additional stock in Fowle. David gets an immediate deduction for his investment, due to his $93,000 in suspended losses. Alternatively, if Fowle shows a $5,000 profit for the year, David pays no tax on the flow-through income, as it is offset by the suspended losses.

However, if Fowle distributes $5,000 to David in 2015 without earning any profit for the year, and prior to any capital contribution by him, David recognizes a $5,000 capital gain, because the distribution exceeds the zero stock basis.

15-3f **Treatment of Losses**

LO.7

Explain the tax effects of losses on S shareholders.

Net Operating Loss

One major advantage of an S election is the ability to pass through net operating losses (NOLs) of the corporation directly to the shareholders. A shareholder can deduct an NOL for the year in which the S corporation's tax year ends. The corporation does not deduct the NOL. A shareholder's basis in the stock is reduced by any NOL pass-through, but not below zero. The entity's AAA is reduced by the same deductible amount.[47]

---

[47]§§ 1368(a)(1)(A) and (e)(1)(A).

Deductions for an S corporation's pass-throughs (e.g., NOL, capital loss, and charitable contributions) cannot exceed a shareholder's stock basis *plus* the basis of any loans made by the shareholder to the corporation.[48] A shareholder is entitled to carry forward a loss pass-through to the extent the loss for the year exceeds basis. Any pass-through carried forward may be deducted *only* by the *same* shareholder if and when the basis in the stock of or loans to the corporation is restored.[49]

EXAMPLE 28

Ginny owns 10% of the stock of Pilot, a calendar year S corporation. Her basis in the shares is $10,000 at the beginning of 2013. The indicated events are accounted for under the S corporation rules as follows.

Tax Year	Event	Tax Consequences
2013	Ginny's share of Pilot's operating loss is $15,000.	Ginny deducts $10,000. Her stock basis is reduced to zero. She holds a $5,000 suspended loss.
2014	Ginny's share of Pilot's operating loss is $4,000.	No current deduction allowed for the loss, as Ginny has no stock basis to offset. Her suspended loss is now $9,000.
2015	Ginny's share of Pilot's operating loss is $7,000. She purchases an additional $10,000 of stock from Pilot.	The purchase creates $10,000 of stock basis. Ginny deducts $10,000—the current $7,000 loss and $3,000 of the suspended loss. Stock basis again is zero, and the new suspended loss is $6,000.
2016	Ginny sells all of her Pilot shares to Christina on January 1.	The $6,000 suspended loss disappears—it cannot be transferred to Christina.

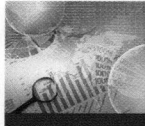

TAX PLANNING STRATEGIES **Loss Considerations**

FRAMEWORK FOCUS: DEDUCTIONS

Strategy: Maximize Deductible Amounts.

A net loss in excess of tax basis may be carried forward and deducted only by the same shareholder in succeeding years. Thus, before disposing of the stock, a shareholder should increase stock/loan basis to flow through the loss. The next shareholder cannot acquire the loss carryover.

The NOL provisions create a need for sound tax planning during the last election year and the post-termination transition period. If it appears that the S corporation is going to sustain an NOL or use up any loss carryover, each shareholder's basis should be analyzed to determine whether it can absorb the owner's share of the loss. If basis is insufficient to absorb the loss, further investments should be considered before the end of the post-termination period. Such investments can be accomplished through additional stock purchases from the corporation or from other shareholders to increase basis.

EXAMPLE 29

A calendar year C corporation records a $20,000 NOL in 2014. The corporation makes a valid S election in 2015 and incurs another $20,000 NOL in that year. At all times during 2015, the stock of the corporation was owned by the same 10 shareholders, each of whom owned 10% of the stock.

Tim, one of the shareholders, holds a stock basis of $1,800 at the beginning of 2015. None of the 2014 NOL may be carried forward into the S year. Although Tim's share of the 2015 NOL is $2,000, his deduction for the loss is limited to $1,800 in 2015 with a $200 carryover to 2016.

---

[48]See *Donald J. Sauvigne*, 30 TCM 123, T.C.Memo. 1971–30.   [49]§ 1366(d).

Concept Summary 15.3

Treatment of S Corporation Losses

Step 1. Allocate total loss to the shareholder on a daily basis, based upon stock ownership.

Step 2. If the shareholder's loss exceeds his or her stock basis, apply any excess to the basis of corporate indebtedness to the shareholder. Loss allocations do not reduce stock or loan basis below zero.

Step 3. Where a flow-through loss exceeds the stock and loan basis, any excess is suspended and carried over to succeeding tax years.

Step 4. In succeeding tax years, any net increase in basis restores the debt basis first, up to its original amount.

Step 5. Once debt basis is restored, any remaining net increase restores stock basis.

If the S election terminates, any suspended loss carryover may be deducted during the post-termination period to the extent of the stock basis at the end of this period. Any loss remaining at the end of this period is lost forever.

At-Risk Rules

As discussed in Chapters 6 and 14, S corporation shareholders, like partners, are limited in the amount of loss they may deduct by their "at-risk" amounts.

An amount at risk is determined separately for each shareholder. The amount of the corporate losses that are passed through and deductible by the shareholders is not affected by the amount the corporation has at risk. A shareholder usually is considered at risk with respect to an activity to the extent of cash and the adjusted basis of other property contributed to the electing corporation, any amount borrowed for use in the activity for which the taxpayer has personal liability for payment from personal assets, and the net fair market value of personal assets that secure nonrecourse borrowing.

Any losses that are suspended under the at-risk rules are carried forward to future tax years. The S stock basis limitations and at-risk limitations are applied before the passive activity limitations (see below).

Carl has a basis of $35,000 in his S corporation stock. He takes a $15,000 nonrecourse loan from a relative and lends the proceeds to the S corporation. Carl now has a stock basis of $35,000 and a loan basis of $15,000. However, due to the at-risk limitation, he can deduct only $35,000 of losses from the S corporation.

EXAMPLE
30

Passive Losses and Credits

S corporations are not directly subject to the passive activity limits, but corporate rental activities are inherently passive, and other activities of an S corporation may be passive unless the shareholder(s) materially participate(s) in operating the business.

If the corporate activity involves rentals or the shareholders do not materially participate, the shareholders can apply such losses or credits only against income from other passive activities. An S shareholder's stock basis is reduced by passive losses that flow through to the shareholder, even though the shareholder may not be entitled to a current deduction due to the passive loss limitations.

15-3g Other Operational Rules

Several other points may be made about the possible effects of various Code provisions on S corporations.

- An S corporation must make estimated tax payments with respect to any recognized built-in gain and excess passive investment income tax (discussed next).

- Any family member who renders services or furnishes capital to an S corporation must be paid reasonable compensation. Otherwise, the IRS can make adjustments to reflect the value of the services or capital. This rule may make it more difficult for related parties to shift Subchapter S taxable income to children or other family members.

BRIDGE DISCIPLINE Bridge to Public Finance

Proceeds from the Federal self-employment tax are used by the Federal government to fund retirement and health care entitlements. Any shortfalls in these funds mean that the following may occur.

- Citizens needing retirement annuities and/or health care services will receive less than is needed. This may not be a desirable result in a moral or ethical sense, as life will be more difficult than it otherwise might be for those of modest means.

- Retirement income and health care services must be funded from general revenues, meaning almost exclusively funds from the Federal income tax. This represents a mismatch of payor and payee, an income redistribution result that would not be attractive to some. In a zero-sum sense, benefits of this sort reduce funding for other budgetary needs of the Federal government (e.g., for defense, transportation, or research).

- The flow-through of S items to a shareholder is not self-employment income and is not subject to the self-employment tax.[50] Compensation for services rendered to an S corporation is, however, subject to FICA taxes. This treatment of earned income of S corporations is attractive compared to the treatment of a proprietorship or a partnership, whose income is taxed as self-employment income to the owners.

- A number of qualified fringe benefits, which typically are received by employees on a tax-free basis, are subject to tax when received by a more-than-2 percent shareholder-employee of an S corporation. Such benefits include the value of group term life insurance, medical insurance, and meals and lodging furnished for the convenience of the employer. These items are treated as wages and are subject to most payroll taxes. The employee can deduct medical insurance premiums on his or her Form 1040.

- An S corporation is liable for a penalty if it does not file its Form 1120S on a timely basis. The penalty is $195 per month times the number of S shareholders, for up to 12 months.[51]

- An accrual basis S corporation uses the cash method of accounting for purposes of deducting business expenses and interest owed to a cash basis related party.[52] Thus, the timing of the shareholder's income and the corporate deduction must match.

- With respect to the domestic production activities deduction (DPAD), the S corporation passes through the various amounts needed, and the deduction is computed at the shareholder level. For instance, domestic production gross receipts (DPGR), the corresponding cost of goods sold, and attributable W–2 wages, among other items, are separately stated items reported to the shareholders on a pro rata basis.

- The S election is not recognized by the District of Columbia and several states, including Connecticut, Michigan, and Tennessee. Thus, some or all of the entity's income may be subject to a state-level income tax.

- An S corporation may issue § 1244 stock to its shareholders to obtain ordinary loss treatment.

- Loss deductions may be disallowed due to a lack of a profit motive. If the activities at the corporate level are not profit-motivated, the losses may be disallowed under the hobby loss rules (see Chapter 11).[53]

---

[50]Rev.Rul. 59–221, 1959–1 C.B. 225.

[51]§ 6699. The penalty is waived if the entity can show reasonable cause for the failure to file.

[52]§ 267(b).

[53]§183; *Michael J. Houston*, 69 TCM 2360, T.C.Memo. 1995–159; *Mario G. De Mendoza, III*, 68 TCM 42, T.C.Memo. 1994–314.

15-4 **ENTITY-LEVEL TAXES**

15-4a **Tax on Pre-Election Built-In Gain**

Normally, an S corporation does *not* pay an income tax, because all items flow through to the shareholders. But an S corporation that previously was a C corporation may be required to pay a built-in gains tax, a LIFO recapture tax, a general business credit recapture, or a passive investment income tax.

Without the built-in gains tax , it would be possible to avoid the corporate double tax on a disposition of appreciated property by electing S corporation status.

LO.8

Compute the entity-level taxes on S corporations.

> **EXAMPLE**
> **31**
>
> Zinnia, Inc., a C corporation, owns a single asset with a basis of $100,000 and a fair market value of $500,000. If Zinnia sells this asset and distributes the cash to its shareholders, there are two levels of tax, one at the corporate level and one at the shareholder level. Alternatively, if Zinnia distributes the asset to its shareholders as a dividend, a double tax still results.
>
> In an attempt to avoid the double tax, Zinnia elects S corporation status. It then sells the asset and distributes the proceeds to shareholders. Without the built-in gains tax, the gain would be taxed only once, at the shareholder level. The distribution of the sales proceeds would be a tax-free reduction of the stock basis and the AAA. However, the built-in gains tax assures that Zinnia would not avoid the double tax. (See Example 32.)

The built-in gains tax generally applies to C corporations converting to S status. It is a *corporate-level* tax on any built-in gain recognized when the S corporation disposes of an asset in a taxable disposition within 10 calendar years after the date on which the S election took effect. The 10-year holding period is reduced to 7 years for tax years beginning in 2009 and 2010, and to 5 years for 2011 through 2014.[54]

General Rules

The base for the built-in gains tax includes any unrealized gain on appreciated assets (e.g., real estate, cash basis receivables, goodwill) held by a corporation on the day it elects S status. The highest corporate tax rate (currently 35 percent) is applied to the unrealized gain when any of the assets are sold. Any gain from the sale (net of the built-in gains tax)[55] also passes through as a taxable gain to shareholders.

> **EXAMPLE**
> **32**
>
> Assume the same facts as in the preceding example. A corporate-level built-in gains tax must be paid by Zinnia if it sells the asset after electing S status. Upon sale of the asset, the corporation owes a tax of $140,000 ($400,000 × 35%). In addition, the shareholders report a $260,000 taxable flow-through gain ($400,000 − $140,000). Hence, the built-in gains tax effectively imposes a double tax on Zinnia and its shareholders, as would have been the case had Zinnia remained a C corporation.

In-depth coverage can be found on this book's companion website: www.cengagebrain.com

7 DIGGING DEEPER

The amount of built-in gain recognized in any year is limited to an *as if* taxable income for the year, computed as if the corporation were a C corporation. Any built-in gain that escapes taxation due to the taxable income limitation is carried forward and recognized in future tax years. Thus, a corporation can defer a built-in gain tax liability whenever it has a low or negative taxable income.

---

[54]§ 1374(d)(7)(B). Not all of the states followed this temporary reduction of the recognition period. After 2014, the holding period returned to ten 12-month years.

[55]§ 1366(f)(2).

Vinca's recognized built-in gain for 2015 is $400,000. If Vinca were a C corporation, its 2015 taxable income would be $300,000. Thus, the amount of built-in gain subject to tax in 2015 is $300,000. The excess built-in gain of $100,000 is carried forward and taxed in 2016 (assuming adequate C corporation taxable income in that year).

There is no statutory limit on the carryforward period, but the gain would effectively expire at the end of the 5-, 7-, or 10-year recognition period applicable to all built-in gains.[56]

An S corporation can offset built-in gains with unexpired NOLs or capital losses from C corporation years.

Yowler, an S corporation, reports a built-in gain of $100,000 and taxable income of $90,000. Yowler's built-in gains tax liability is calculated as follows, applying the indicated loss carryforwards.

Lesser of taxable income or built-in gain	$ 90,000
Less: NOL carryforward from C year	(12,000)
Capital loss carryforward from C year	(8,000)
Tax base	$ 70,000
Highest corporate income tax rate	× .35
Tentative tax	$ 24,500
Less: Business credit carryforward from C year	(4,000)
Built-in gains tax liability	$ 20,500

The $10,000 realized (but not taxed) built-in gain in excess of taxable income is carried forward to the next year, as long as the next year is within the 5-, 7-, or 10-year recognition period.

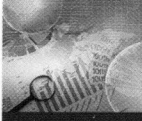

TAX PLANNING STRATEGIES **Managing the Built-In Gains Tax**

FRAMEWORK FOCUS: INCOME AND EXCLUSION

Strategy: Avoid Income Recognition.
Postpone Recognition of Income to Achieve Tax Deferral.

Although limitations exist on contributions of loss property to the corporation before S status is elected, it still is possible for a corporation to minimize built-in gains and maximize built-in losses prior to the S election. A cash basis S corporation can accomplish this by reducing receivables, accelerating payables, and accruing compensation costs.

To further reduce or defer the tax, the corporation may take advantage of the taxable income limitation by shifting income and deductions to minimize taxable income in years when built-in gain is recognized. Although the postponed built-in gain is carried forward to future years, the time value of money makes the postponement beneficial. For example, paying compensation to shareholder-employees in place of a distribution creates a deduction that reduces taxable income and postpones the built-in gains tax.

Giving built-in gain property to a charitable organization does not trigger the built-in gains tax.

Built-in *loss* property may be sold in the same year built-in gain property is sold to reduce or eliminate the built-in gains tax. Generally, the taxpayer should sell built-in loss property in a year when an equivalent amount of built-in gain property is sold. Otherwise, the built-in loss could be wasted.

Tulip, Inc., an S corporation, holds a built-in gain of $110,000 and reports current taxable income of $120,000 before payment of salaries to its shareholders. If Tulip pays at least $120,000 in salaries to the shareholders (rather than making a distribution), its taxable income drops to zero and the built-in gains tax is postponed. Thus, Tulip may want to keep the salaries as high as possible to postpone the built-in gains tax in future years and reap a benefit from the time value of money. Of course, paying the salaries may increase the associated payroll tax liabilities.

[56]§ 1374(d)(7); Notice 90–27, 1990–1 C.B. 336.

TAX FACT **No Double Taxation?**

S corporations paid over $300 million in Federal corporate-level taxes for tax year 2011, a significant level of collections from "tax-exempt" entities.

In the typical tax year, corporate-level Federal income taxes are reported by about 7,000 S corporations, about .20 percent of all S returns filed.

LIFO Recapture Tax

When a C corporation uses the FIFO method for its last year before making the S election, any built-in gain is recognized and taxed as the inventory is sold. A LIFO-basis corporation would not recognize this gain unless the corporation invaded the LIFO layer during the built-in gains tax period. To preclude a deferral of gain recognition by a C corporation that is electing S status, any LIFO recapture amount at the time of the S election is subject to a corporate-level tax.

The taxable LIFO recapture amount equals the excess of the inventory's value under FIFO over the LIFO value. The resulting tax is payable in four equal installments, with the first payment due on or before the due date for the corporate return for the last C corporation year (without regard to any extensions). The remaining three installments are paid on or before the due dates of the succeeding corporate returns. No interest is due if payments are made by the due dates, and no estimated taxes are due on the four tax installments. No refund is allowed if the LIFO value is higher than the FIFO value.

EXAMPLE 36

Daffodil Corporation converts from a C corporation to an S corporation at the beginning of 2015. Daffodil used the LIFO inventory method in 2014 and had an ending LIFO inventory of $110,000 (FIFO value of $190,000).

Daffodil adds the $80,000 LIFO recapture amount to its 2014 taxable income, resulting in an increased tax liability of $28,000 ($80,000 × 35%). Daffodil pays one-fourth of the tax ($7,000) with its 2014 (final) C corporation tax return. The three succeeding installments of $7,000 each are paid with Daffodil's 2015–2017 S corporation tax returns.

15-4b Passive Investment Income Penalty Tax

A tax is imposed on the excess passive income of S corporations that possess AEP from C corporation years. The tax rate is the highest corporate income tax rate for the year (currently 35 percent). The rate is applied to excess net passive income (ENPI), which is determined using the following formula.

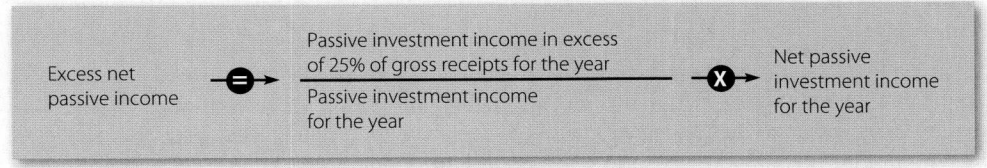

Passive investment income (PII) includes gross receipts derived from royalties, rents, dividends, interest, and annuities. Only the net gain from the disposition of capital assets is taken into account in computing PII gross receipts.[57] Net passive income is passive income reduced by any deductions directly connected with the production of that income. Any passive income tax reduces the amount the shareholders must take into income.

---

[57]§§ 1362(d)(3)(B) and (C).

TAX IN THE NEWS   **The Self-Employment Income Advantage**

A significant advantage of an S corporation involves the current definition of self-employment income. Although compensation for services rendered to an S corporation is subject to FICA taxes, a shareholder's share of income from an S corporation is not self-employment income. The rationale for this S corporation loophole is that the S shareholder does not personally carry on the entity's trade or business. In contrast, the earned income of a partnership or proprietorship is treated as self-employment income to the partner or proprietor.

The choice between a salary and pass-through income is not clear-cut, however.

- Although a salary is subject to payroll tax and pass-through income is not [*P.B. Ding v. Comm.*, 2000–1 USTC

¶50137, 84 AFTR 2d 99–7517, 200 F.3d 587 (CA–9, 1999)], this income does not accrue Social Security benefits for its recipient.

- S corporation income distributions do not count as compensation for computing an employee's contribution formula for a qualified retirement plan.

- The IRS and the courts require an S shareholder to take a reasonable salary (see footnote 32).

- If a partner or proprietor reports salary income from other sources and the aggregate salaries exceed the annual FICA ceiling, the partnership or proprietorship may provide tax savings compared to those of an S corporation.

The excess net passive income cannot exceed a hypothetical C corporate taxable income for the year, before considering special C corporation deductions (e.g., the dividends received deduction) or an NOL carryover.[58]

EXAMPLE 37

Lilac Corporation, an electing S corporation, records gross receipts totaling $264,000 (of which $110,000 is PII). Expenditures directly connected to the production of the PII total $30,000. Therefore, Lilac reports net PII of $80,000 ($110,000 − $30,000), and its PII exceeds 25% of its gross receipts by $44,000 [$110,000 PII − (25% × $264,000)]. Excess net passive income (ENPI) is $32,000, calculated as follows.

$$\text{ENPI} = \frac{\$44,000}{\$110,000} \times \$80,000 = \$32,000$$

Lilac's PII tax is $11,200 ($32,000 × 35%).

TAX PLANNING STRATEGIES   **Avoid PII Pitfalls**

FRAMEWORK FOCUS: TAX RATE

Strategy: Avoid Double Taxation.

Watch for a possible violation of the PII limitation. Avoid a consecutive third year with excess passive income when the corporation has accumulated E & P from C corporation years. In this connection, assets that produce passive income (e.g., stocks and bonds, certain rental assets) might be retained by the shareholders in their individual capacities and kept out of the corporation.

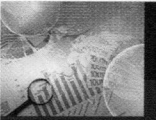

DIGGING DEEPER 8 | **In-depth coverage can be found on this book's companion website: www.cengagebrain.com**

---

[58]§§ 1374(d)(4) and 1375(a) and (b).

15-5 SUMMARY

The S corporation rules are elective and can be used to benefit a number of owners of small businesses.

- When the business is profitable, the S corporation election removes the threat of double taxation on corporate profits.
- When the business is generating losses, deductions for allocable losses are immediately available to the shareholders.

More than two-thirds of all U.S. corporations operate under the S rules. Flow-through income is taxed to the shareholders, who increase basis in their corporate stock accordingly. In this manner, subsequent distributions to shareholders can be made tax free. Flow-through losses reduce stock and debt basis, but loss deductions are suspended when basis reaches zero. Flow-through items that could be treated differently by various shareholders are separately stated on Schedule K–1 of the Form 1120S.

The S rules are designed for the closely held business with a simple capital structure. Eligibility rules are not oppressive, and they do not include any limitations on the corporation's capitalization value, sales, number or distribution of employees, or other operating measures. Accounting for an S corporation's shareholder distributions can be complex, though, and maintenance of S status must be monitored on an ongoing basis.

Corporate-level taxes seldom are assessed on S corporations, but they guard against abuses of the S rules, such as shifting appreciated assets from higher C corporation rates to lower individual rates (the built-in gains tax) or doing the same with investment assets (the tax on excessive PII).

REFOCUS ON THE BIG PICTURE

CONVERTING A C CORPORATION TO AN S CORPORATION

As long as Fowle, Inc., is a C corporation, David cannot deduct on his individual tax return the losses the business incurs. However, the corporation can carry any net operating losses (NOLs) back and claim refunds for prior taxes paid and carry any remaining NOLs forward to reduce taxes paid if the company becomes profitable again.

If David wants to deduct the losses on his individual return, the corporation should make an S election or possibly become an LLC. Assuming that Fowle meets the one class of stock requirement, an S election may be appropriate. The election should be made before any losses are incurred because any regular corporate NOLs do not flow through to an S shareholder.

Fowle should make a timely election on Form 2553, and David must consent to the election in writing. For the S election to be effective this year, it should be made on or before the fifteenth day of the third month of the current year.

continued

© WAVEBREAKMEDIA LTD/SHUTTERSTOCK.COM

The S corporation's DPAD computations flow through to David, as does Fowle's tax-exempt interest income. The entity may want to reconsider its salary and fringe benefits levels for David, so as to minimize the creation of a payroll tax burden, and to manage the restrictions on deductions for fringe benefits provided to an S shareholder. Fowle's tax-exempt interest can be distributed to David tax free only after all of the entity's AEP has been accounted for.

What If?

What if David expects the loss years to be followed by increased profitability as the company shifts some of its manufacturing to other countries with cheaper labor and material costs? In this case, David expects that the corporation will make significant distributions to him. How might this affect David's decision about whether the corporation should make an S election?

David should be aware of several rules that may result in income tax being paid by the S corporation or by him as the shareholder. First, distributions from an S corporation may be treated as taxable dividends to a shareholder to the extent the S corporation has earnings and profits dating to its years as a C corporation. While distributions are deemed to be made first from accumulated net S corporation earnings (i.e., the balance in AAA), distributions in excess of that amount may be treated as a taxable dividend, being paid from AEP (accumulated E & P).

In addition, David should be aware that an S corporation that has been a C corporation in the past may be required to pay a built-in gains tax or LIFO recapture tax. The base for the built-in gains tax includes any unrealized gain on appreciated assets held by Fowle, Inc., on the day the company becomes an S corporation. The highest Federal corporate income tax rate is applied to the unrealized gains when any of the assets are sold within a specified number of years. If Fowle uses the LIFO inventory method, any LIFO recapture amount at the time of the S election also is subject to a corporate-level tax.

Suggested Readings

"Benefits of Using an S Corporation for Trading," **forbes.com**, May 13, 2014.

"Forming an S Corporation to Reduce Self-Employment Taxes," **www.mymoneyblog.com**.

Christopher W. Hesse, "Five-Year Built-In Gain Recognition Period," *The Tax Adviser*, December 2013.

Tony Nitti, "S Corporation Shareholder Compensation: How Much Is Enough?" *The Tax Adviser*, August 2011.

Ryan H. Pace, "Debunking the Notion That S Corporations Are Taxed 'Just Like' Partnerships," *Business Entities*, July/August 2007.

Key Terms

AAA bypass election, 15-15

Accumulated adjustments account (AAA), 15-14

Built-in gains tax, 15-25

Other adjustments account (OAA), 15-14

Passive investment income (PII), 15-8

S corporation, 15-2

Small business corporation, 15-4

Subchapter S, 15-2

Voluntary revocation, 15-8

Computational Exercises

1. **LO.4** Dion, a shareholder, owned 20% of MeadowBrook's stock for 292 days and 25% for the remaining 73 days in the year. Using the per-day allocation method, compute Dion's share of the following S corporation items.

	Schedule K Totals	Dion's Schedule K–1 Totals
Ordinary income	$60,000	$_____
Tax-exempt interest	1,000	$_____
Charitable contributions	3,400	$_____

2. **LO.4, 6** Greiner, Inc., a calendar year S corporation, holds no AEP. During the year, Chad, an individual shareholder, receives a $30,000 cash distribution from Greiner. Prior to the distribution, Chad's basis in his Greiner stock is $25,000.
   a. Determine Chad's ordinary income and capital gain, if any, from the distribution.
   b. What is the basis of Chad's Greiner stock after accounting for the distribution?

3. **LO.5, 6** Holbrook, a calendar year S corporation, distributes $15,000 cash to its only shareholder, Cody, on December 31. Cody's basis in his stock is $20,000, Holbrook's AAA balance is $8,000, and Holbrook holds $2,500 AEP before the distribution. Complete the chart below.

	Distribution from Account	Effect on Stock Basis	Balance after Distribution
From AAA Account	$_____	$_____	$_____
From AEP Account	$_____	$_____	$_____
From Cody's stock basis	$_____	$_____	$_____

4. **LO.5** Ten years ago, Vogel Inc., an S corporation, purchased a plot of investment land for $45,000. This year, Vogel distributed the land, now worth $120,000, to Jamari, its majority shareholder.
   a. Determine the effects of the distribution on the gross income of Vogel and Jamari, and on Vogel's AAA balance.
   b. How would your responses change if the land had been purchased for $120,000 and now was worth $45,000?

5. **LO.7** Kaiwan, Inc., a calendar year S corporation, is partly owned by Sharrod, whose beginning stock basis is $32,000. During the year, Sharrod's share of a Kaiwan long-term capital gain (LTCG) is $5,000, and his share of an ordinary loss is $18,000. Sharrod then receives a $20,000 cash distribution. Compute the following.
   a. Sharrod's deductible loss.
   b. Sharrod's suspended loss.
   c. Sharrod's new basis in the Kaiwan stock.

Problems

6. **LO.2** Which of the following can be a shareholder of an S corporation?
   a. Resident alien.
   b. Partnership.
   c. IRA.
   d. C corporation.

7. **LO.2** Isaac and 121 of his close friends want to form an S corporation. Isaac reasons that if he and his friends form a partnership, the partnership then can

establish an S corporation and act as a single shareholder, thereby avoiding the 100 shareholder rule. Will Isaac's plan work? Why or why not?

8. **LO.2** Joey lives in North Carolina, a common law state. He is a shareholder in an S corporation. If he marries a nonresident alien, will the S election terminate? Would your answer change if he lived in Louisiana? Explain.

Issue ID   9. **LO.3** On March 2, the two 50% shareholders of a calendar year corporation decide to elect S status. One of the shareholders, Terry, purchased her stock from a previous shareholder (a nonresident alien) on January 18 of the same year. Identify any potential problems for Terry or the corporation.

Communications   10. **LO.5, 6** Scott Tyrney owns 21% of an S corporation. He is confused with respect to the amounts of the corporate AAA and his stock basis. Write a memo to the tax research file, identifying the key differences between AAA and an S shareholder's stock basis.

11. **LO.6** For each of the following independent statements, indicate whether the transaction will increase (+), decrease (−), or have no effect (*NE*) on the basis of a shareholder's stock in an S corporation.

   a.   Expenses related to tax-exempt income.
   b.   Short-term capital gain.
   c.   Nonseparately computed loss.
   d.   Section 1231 gain.
   e.   Depletion *not* in excess of basis.
   f.   Separately computed income.
   g.   Nontaxable return-of-capital distribution by the corporation.
   h.   Advertising expenses.
   i.   Business gifts in excess of $25.
   j.   Depreciation recapture income.
   k.   Dividends received by the S corporation from an investment in ExxonMobil stock.
   l.   LIFO recapture tax paid.
   m. Long-term capital loss.
   n.   Cash distribution to shareholder out of AAA.

Issue ID   12. **LO.6, 7** Junie's share of her S corporation's net operating loss is $50,000, but her stock basis is only $30,000. Point out the Federal income tax consequences that Junie must face.

13. **LO.5, 6** Mary is a shareholder in CarrollCo, a calendar year S corporation. At the beginning of the year, her stock basis is $10,000, her share of the AAA is $2,000, and her share of corporate AEP is $6,000. At the end of the year, Mary receives a $6,000 cash distribution from CarrollCo.

   Mary's share of S corporation items includes a $2,000 long-term capital gain and a $10,000 ordinary loss. Determine the effects of these events on Mary's share of CarrollCo's AAA, on CarrollCo's AEP, and on Mary's stock basis.

14. **LO.4** The profit and loss statement of Kitsch Ltd., an S corporation, shows $100,000 book income. Kitsch is owned equally by four shareholders. From supplemental data, you obtain the following information about items that are included in book income.

Selling expenses	($21,200)
Tax-exempt interest income	3,000
Dividends received	9,000
§1231 gain	7,000
Depreciation recapture income	11,000
Collected bad debts previously deducted	5,000
Long-term capital loss	(6,000)
Salary paid to owners (each)	(12,000)
Cost of goods sold	(91,000)

a. Compute Kitsch's nonseparately stated income or loss for the tax year.

b. What would be the share of this year's nonseparately stated income or loss items for James Billings, one of the Kitsch shareholders?

15. **LO.4** Maul, Inc., a calendar year S corporation, incurred the following items.

Tax-exempt interest income	$ 7,000
Sales	140,000
Depreciation recapture income	12,000
Long-term capital gain	20,000
§1231 gain	7,000
Cost of goods sold	(42,000)
Administrative expenses	(15,000)
Depreciation expense (MACRS)	(17,000)
Charitable contributions	(7,000)

a. Calculate Maul's nonseparately computed income or loss.

b. If Carl is a 40% shareholder of Maul, what is Carl's share of Maul's long-term capital gain?

16. **LO.4** Zebra, Inc., a calendar year S corporation, incurred the following items this year. Sammy is a 40% Zebra shareholder throughout the year.

Operating income	$100,000
Cost of goods sold	(40,000)
Depreciation expense (MACRS)	(10,000)
Administrative expenses	(5,000)
§1231 gain	21,000
Depreciation recapture income	25,000
Short-term capital loss from stock sale	(6,000)
Long-term capital loss from stock sale	(4,000)
Long-term capital gain from stock sale	15,000
Charitable contributions	(4,500)

a. Calculate Sammy's share of Zebra's nonseparately computed income or loss.

b. Calculate Sammy's share of any Zebra long-term capital gain.

17. **LO.4** On January 1, Bobby and Alicia own equally all of the stock of an electing S corporation called Prairie Dirt Delight. The company has a $60,000 loss for the year (not a leap year). On the 219th day of the year, Bobby sells his half of the stock to his son, Bubba. How much of the $60,000 loss, if any, is allocated to Bubba?

18. **LO.4, 5** McLin, Inc., a calendar year S corporation, holds $90,000 of AEP. Tobias, the sole McLin shareholder, has an $80,000 basis in his stock with a zero balance in the AAA.   *Decision Making*

a. Determine the tax aspects if a $90,000 salary is paid to Tobias.

b. Same as (a), except that Tobias receives a cash distribution of $90,000 from AEP.

19. **LO.4, 5** Tiger, Inc., a calendar year S corporation, is owned equally by four shareholders: Ann, Becky, Chris, and David. Tiger owns investment land that was purchased for $160,000 four years ago. On September 14, when the land is worth $240,000, it is distributed to David. Assuming that David's basis in his S corporation stock is $270,000 on the distribution date, discuss any Federal income tax ramifications.

20. **LO.4, 5, 6** Spence, Inc., a calendar year S corporation, generates an ordinary loss of $110,000 and makes a distribution of $140,000 to its sole shareholder, Storm Nelson. Nelson's stock basis and AAA at the beginning of the year both total $200,000. Write a memo to your senior manager, Aaron McMullin, discussing the tax treatment of Spence's activities.   *Communications*

21. **LO.5** Polly has been the sole shareholder of a calendar year S corporation since its inception. Polly's stock basis is $15,500, and she receives a distribution of $19,000. Corporate-level accounts are as follows. How is Polly taxed on the distribution?

| AAA | .... | $6,000 | AEP | .... | $500 |

Communications

22. **LO.4, 7** Sweetie, a calendar year S corporation, reports an ordinary loss of $80,000 and a capital loss of $20,000. Mei Freiberg owns 30% of the corporate stock and holds a $24,000 basis in the stock. Determine the amounts of the ordinary loss and capital loss, if any, that flow through to Freiberg. Prepare a memo for the tax research files explaining your computations.

23. **LO.4, 5, 6** Valence Corporation's Form 1120S shows ordinary income of $88,000 for the year. Daniel owns 40% of the Valence stock throughout the year. The following information is obtained from the corporate records.

Salary paid to Daniel	($40,000)
Tax-exempt interest income	5,000
Charitable contributions	(6,000)
Dividends received from a non-U.S. corporation	5,000
Long-term capital loss	(6,000)
Depreciation recapture income	11,000
Refund of prior-year state income taxes	5,000
Cost of goods sold	(80,000)
Short-term capital loss	(7,000)
Administrative expenses	(18,000)
Short-term capital gain	14,000
Selling expenses	(11,000)
Daniel's beginning stock basis	32,000
Daniel's additional stock purchases	9,000
Beginning AAA	45,000
Daniel's loan to corporation	20,000

a. Compute Valence's book income or loss.
b. Compute Daniel's ending stock basis.
c. Calculate ending corporate AAA.

24. **LO.5** If the beginning balance in Swan, Inc.'s OAA is $6,700 and the following transactions occur, what is Swan's ending OAA balance?

Depreciation recapture income	$ 21,600
Payroll tax penalty	(4,200)
Tax-exempt interest income	4,012
Nontaxable life insurance proceeds	100,000
Life insurance premiums paid (nondeductible)	(3,007)

25. **LO.5, 6** Cougar, Inc., is a calendar year S corporation. Cougar's Form 1120S shows nonseparately stated ordinary income of $80,000 for the year. Johnny owns 40% of the Cougar stock throughout the year. The following information is obtained from Cougar's corporate records.

Tax-exempt interest income	$ 3,000
Salary paid to Johnny	(52,000)
Charitable contributions	(6,000)
Dividends received from a non-U.S. corporation	5,000
Short-term capital loss	(6,000)
Depreciation recapture income	11,000
Refund of prior state income taxes	5,000
Cost of goods sold	(72,000)

Long-term capital loss	($ 7,000)
Administrative expenses	(18,000)
Long-term capital gain	14,000
Selling expenses	(11,000)
Johnny's beginning stock basis	32,000
Johnny's additional stock purchases	9,000
Beginning AAA	31,000
Johnny's loan to corporation	20,000

a. Compute Cougar's book income or loss.

b. Compute Johnny's ending stock basis.

c. Calculate Cougar's ending AAA balance.

26. **LO.6** Maple, Inc., is an S corporation with a single shareholder, Bob Maple. Bob believes that his stock basis in the entity is $50,000, but he has lost some of the records to substantiate this amount. Maple reports an ordinary loss for the year of $80,000. What are the Federal income tax aspects to consider? — Issue ID

27. **LO.6, 7** Orange, Inc., a calendar year corporation in Clemson, South Carolina, elects S corporation status for 2015. The company generated a $74,000 NOL in 2014 and another NOL of $43,000 in 2015. — Issue ID

Orange stock always is owned by the same four shareholders, each owning 25% of the stock. Pete, one of the shareholders, holds a $6,020 basis in this Orange stock at the beginning of 2015. Identify the Federal income tax issues that Pete faces.

28. **LO.7** Samuel Reese sold 1,000 shares of his stock in Maroon, Inc., an S corporation. He sold the stock for $15,700 after he had owned it for six years. Samuel had paid $141,250 for the stock, which was issued under § 1244. Samuel is married and separately owns the 1,000 shares. Determine the appropriate Federal income tax treatment of any gain or loss on the stock sale. — Critical Thinking

29. **LO.7** Blue is the owner of all of the shares of Blue Bell, an S corporation. Blue is considering receiving a salary of $110,000 from the business. She will pay the 7.65% FICA taxes on the salary, and the S corporation will pay the same amount of FICA tax. If Blue reduces her salary to $50,000 and takes an additional $60,000 as a cash distribution from AAA, how would her Federal income tax liabilities change? — Critical Thinking / Decision Making

30. **LO.1** One of your clients, Texas, Inc., is considering electing S status. Both of Texas's equal shareholders paid $30,000 for their stock. As of the beginning of 2013, Texas's Subchapter C NOL carryforward is $110,000. Its taxable income projections for the next few years are as follows. Will you counsel Texas to make the S election? Explain. — Critical Thinking / Decision Making

2013	$40,000
2014	25,000
2015	25,000
2016	25,000

31. **LO.6, 7** C&C Properties is an S corporation that owns two rental real estate undertakings: Carrot Plaza and Cantaloupe Place. Both properties produce an annual $10,000 operating loss. C&C's Schedule K aggregates the results of the two locations into one number. — Critical Thinking

Dan and Marta, C&C's two equal shareholders, both hold a $7,000 stock basis in C&C as of the beginning of the year. Marta actively participates in the Cantaloupe location, but not at Carrot. Dan actively participates at neither location. Determine the amount of the available loss pass-throughs for both shareholders.

Tax Return Problem

Tax Return Problem

TAX SOFTWARE

1. John Parsons (123-45-6781) and George Smith (123-45-6782) are 70% and 30% owners, respectively, of Premium, Inc. (11-1111111), a candy company located at 1005 16th Street, Cut and Shoot, TX 77303. Premium's S election was made on January 15, 2008, its date of incorporation. The following information was taken from the company's 2014 income statement. Premium's book income for the year was $704,574.

Interest income	$ 100,000
Gross sales receipts	2,410,000
Beginning inventory	9,607
Direct labor	(203,102)
Direct materials purchased	(278,143)
Direct other costs	(249,356)
Ending inventory	3,467
Salaries and wages	(442,103)
Officers' salaries	(150,000)
Repairs	(206,106)
Depreciation expense	(15,254)
Interest expense	(35,222)
Rent expense (operating)	(40,000)
Taxes	(65,101)
Charitable contributions (cash)	(20,000)
Advertising expenses	(20,000)
Payroll penalties	(15,000)
Other deductions	(59,899)

A 2014 comparative balance sheet appears below.

	January 1	December 31
Cash	$ 47,840	$?
Accounts receivable	93,100	123,104
Inventories	9,607	3,467
Prepaid expenses	8,333	17,582
Building and equipment	138,203	185,348
Accumulated depreciation	(84,235)	(?)
Land	2,000	2,000
Total assets	$214,848	$844,422
Accounts payable	$ 42,500	$ 72,300
Notes payable (less than 1 year)	4,500	2,100
Notes payable (more than 1 year)	26,700	24,300
Capital stock	30,000	30,000
Retained earnings	111,148	?
Total liabilities and capital	$214,848	$844,422

Premium's accounting firm provides the following additional information.

Cash distributions to shareholders	$100,000
Beginning balance, accumulated adjustments account	$111,148

Using the preceding information, prepare a complete Form 1120S and Schedule K–1s for John Parsons and George Smith, both of whom live at 5607 20th Street, Cut and Shoot, TX 77303. Do not complete the Form 4562. If any information is missing, make realistic assumptions.

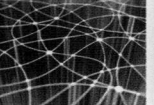

BRIDGE DISCIPLINE

1. Using an online research service, determine whether your state:
   a. Allows flow-through treatment for Federal S corporations.
   b. Requires any state-specific form to elect or elect out of S treatment at the state level.
   c. Places any additional withholding tax burdens on out-of-state U.S. shareholders or on non-U.S. shareholders of an S corporation.
   d. Requires any additional information disclosures or compliance deadlines for S corporations operating in the state *other than* to the revenue department (e.g., a report that must be filed with the secretary of state).
   e. Accepts "composite" or "block" income tax returns.

2. Using no more than five slides, at least two of which include a chart or graphic to illustrate your observations, prepare a presentation for your fellow students at the annual Pay It Forward conference at the university student union. In your talk, discuss the societal implications of the rule that excludes from the self-employment tax any flow-through income (other than salary and wages) that is assigned to a shareholder in an S corporation, while taxing that of the owners of a partnership or an LLC.

Communications

Research Problems

Note: Solutions to Research Problems can be prepared by using the Checkpoint® Student Edition online research product, which is available to accompany this text. It is also possible to prepare solutions to the Research Problems by using tax research materials found in a standard tax library.

Research Problem 1. Eel Corporation, in Spivey Corners, North Carolina, has filed a Form 1120S for six years, and the local office of the IRS has sent the company a letter requesting an audit next month. Carrie, who is in charge of tax matters at Eel, cannot find a copy of the original S election, Form 2553.

Decision Making

The original shareholders and officers all agree that a local accountant filed the form, but he passed away last year. Several of the shareholders instruct Carrie to prepare a backdated Form 2553, which they will sign. Carrie could then copy the form and tell the agent that this was a copy of the original Form 2553. What should Carrie do? She estimates that any proposed deficiency would be in the range of $625,000.

Partial list of research aids:
§§ 1362(b)(5) and (f).
Rev.Proc. 97–48, 1997–2 C.B. 521.
Ltr.Rul. 9748033.

Research Problem 2. Sean Moon is president, secretary, treasurer, sole director, and sole shareholder of Streetz, an S corporation real estate company. He manages all aspects of the company's operations, and he is the only person working at the company that holds a real estate broker's license. Sean works 12-hour days and takes few days off. Corporate records indicate the following.

Year	Gross Receipts	Net Income
2014	$376,453	$122,605
2015	405,244	161,660
2016	518,189	231,454

Moon and his wife, Kim, filed joint Federal income tax returns, but they did not report any wages or salaries on their returns. During 2016, Moon transferred $240,000 from Streetz to his personal account.

You are an expert witness for the IRS. Identify the items that you would present to the U.S. Tax Court with respect to the amount of Moon's compensation that is subject to employment taxes and any other taxes due for 2016 (especially the additional Medicare net investment income tax). *Hint:* This is a reasonable compensation issue.

Internet Activity

Use the tax resources of the Internet to address the following questions. Do not restrict your search to the Web, but include a review of newsgroups and general reference materials, practitioner sites and resources, primary sources of the tax law, chat rooms and discussion groups, and other opportunities.

Communications

Research Problem 3. Use spreadsheet software to graph the growth in the number of S corporation returns filed. Obtain data for these years: 1975, 1980, 1985, 1990, 1995, 2000, and 2005. In a note to your instructor, explain the trends that you found in S returns filed.

Communications

Research Problem 4. Summarize the trends in court decisions concerning salaries paid to shareholders of small S corporations. Title your essay "S Corporation Salaries: Too Much or Too Little?" Send your essay in an e-mail to your instructor.

Communications

Research Problem 5. Summarize in no more than five slides the purpose and provisions of the S Corporation Modernization Act of 2009.

Roger CPA Review Questions

1. Mindy, an individual, owns 100% of Markee, an S corporation and has an initial stock basis of $10,000. 20X4 is the first year of Markee's operations. Additional items reported by Markee during the current year are:

Municipal bond interest	$10,000
Ordinary income	3,400
Shareholder distributions	5,000

   What was Mindy's basis in Markee at the end of 20X4?

   a. $5,000   c. $15,000
   b. $8,400   d. $18,400

2. Mindy, an individual, owns 100% of Markee, an S corporation and has an initial stock basis of $10,000. 20X4 is the first year of Markee's operations. Additional items reported by Markee during the current year are:

Municipal bond interest	$10,000
Ordinary income	3,400
Shareholder distributions	5,000

   What amount of the $5,000 distribution is taxable to Mindy?

   a. $0   c. $3,400
   b. $1,600   d. $5,000

3. Monie, an individual taxpayer, owns 50% of Monie & Co, an S corporation. At the beginning of 20X4, Monie's basis in Monie & Co stock was $55,000. During 20X4, Monie & Co realized ordinary loss in the amount of $45,000 and a short-term capital loss of $15,000. Monie & Co made total distributions of $70,000 to its shareholders during this taxable year. What amount of the $70,000 distribution is taxable to Monie?

   a. $70,000   c. $25,000
   b. $35,000   d. $10,000

4. Which of the following would cause a revocation of S status for an already formed S corporation?

   I.   A partnership becomes a shareholder of an S corporation
   II. An S corporation becomes a partner in a partnership
   III. An S corporation becomes a shareholder in a C corporation
   IV. A nonresident alien becomes a shareholder of an S corporation

   a. None of the above
   b. II and III
   c. I and IV
   d. All of the above

5. Rocket Co, an S corporation, pays single coverage health insurance premiums of $17,000 per year. Philip is a 1% shareholder-employee in Rocket. On Philip's behalf, Rocket pays Philip's family coverage under the health insurance plan. What amount of insurance premiums is includible in Philip's gross income?

   a. $17,000
   b. $170
   c. $17
   d. $0

6. Shareholders of Rayle Co, a calendar year corporation whose S status was terminated during 20X4, are looking to re-apply for the S status as soon as possible. What is the earliest year a new S election can be made, in the absence of IRS consent to an earlier election?

   a. 20X9
   b. 20X8
   c. 20X7
   d. 20X4

7. Pankee Inc., was originally formed as a C corporation and made an S election 5 years ago. Which of the following statements correctly describes the taxability of Pankee's distributions to its shareholders?

   a. A distribution to the shareholders will be taxable to the shareholders, if it is treated as coming from the S corporation's accumulated adjusted account and represents an amount already taxed to the shareholders
   b. A distribution to the shareholders will be nontaxable to the shareholders, if it is treated as coming from the S corporation's accumulated adjusted account and represents an amount already taxed to the shareholders
   c. A distribution to the shareholders will be nontaxable to the shareholders, if it is treated as coming from the S corporation's accumulated earnings and profits, earned during its years as a C corporation
   d. A distribution to the shareholders will be nontaxable to the shareholders regardless of whether it is treated as coming from the S corporation's accumulated adjusted account or its accumulated earnings and profits

8. As of January 1, 20X4, Kirk owed all 300 shares of Cork Inc., a calendar year S corporation. On September 1, 20X4 (243 days after January 1), Kirk sold 50 shares each to Steve and Moe and kept the remaining 200 shares for himself. For the year ended December 31, 20X4, Cork reported nonseparately computed income of $109,500 and made no distributions to its shareholders. What amount of nonseparately stated income from Cork should Kirk report on his 20X4 tax return?

   a. $97,300
   b. $109,500
   c. $73,000
   d. $36,500

PART 6

SPECIAL BUSINESS TOPICS

CHAPTER **16**
Multijurisdictional Taxation

CHAPTER **17**
Business Tax Credits and Corporate Alternative Minimum Tax

CHAPTER **18**
Comparative Forms of Doing Business

Part 6 covers several topics that are relevant to all types of business entities. Business entities operate in both the international arena and state arenas. Therefore, multijurisdictional taxation is addressed from both a multinational business perspective and a multistate business perspective. A review then follows of tax credits allowed to reduce the Federal income tax liability on business income. This is followed by a discussion of the alternative tax system applicable to certain C corporations, that is, the AMT. Part 6 concludes with a comparative analysis of the different types of business entities previously discussed. This analysis recognizes the relevance of each of the life cycle components in selecting a business entity form.

Multijurisdictional Taxation

LEARNING OBJECTIVES: *After completing Chapter 16, you should be able to:*

LO.1 Discuss the computational and compliance issues that arise when a taxpayer operates in more than one taxing jurisdiction.

LO.2 Identify the sources of tax law applicable to a taxpayer operating in more than one country.

LO.3 Outline the U.S. tax effects related to the offshore operations of a U.S. taxpayer.

LO.4 Describe the tax effects related to the U.S. operations of a non-U.S. taxpayer.

LO.5 Identify the sources of tax law applicable to a taxpayer operating in more than one U.S. state.

LO.6 Apply computational principles designed to compute state taxable income for a taxpayer operating in more than one U.S. state.

LO.7 Synthesize the international and multistate tax systems and identify common issues faced by both systems.

CHAPTER OUTLINE

TAX TALK *Don't tax you, don't tax me; tax the fellow behind the tree.* —RUSSELL B. LONG

Don't tax you, don't tax me; tax the companies across the sea. —DAN ROSTENKOWSKI

GOING INTERNATIONAL

VoiceCo, a domestic corporation, designs, manufactures, and sells specialty microphones for use in theaters. All of its activities take place in Florida, although it ships products to customers all over the United States. When it received inquiries about its products from foreign customers, VoiceCo decided to test the foreign market and placed ads in foreign trade journals. Soon it was taking orders from foreign customers.

VoiceCo is concerned about its potential foreign income tax exposure. Although it has no assets or employees in the foreign jurisdictions, it now is involved in international commerce. Is VoiceCo subject to income taxes in foreign countries? Must it pay U.S. income taxes on the profits from its foreign sales? What if VoiceCo pays taxes to other countries? Does it receive any benefit from these payments on its U.S. tax return?

VoiceCo has established a manufacturing plant in Ireland to meet the European demand for its products. VoiceCo incorporated the Irish operation as a controlled foreign corporation (CFC) named VoiceCo-Ireland. So long as VoiceCo-Ireland does not distribute profits to VoiceCo, will the profits escape U.S. taxation? What are the consequences to VoiceCo of being the owner of the CFC?

Read the chapter and formulate your response.

One of the tax planning principles that has been discussed throughout this text relates to the use of favorable tax jurisdictions—moving income into lower-taxed districts and deductions into higher-taxed ones. Many individuals dream of moving all of their income and wealth to a tax-friendly state or a proverbial island in the tropics, never to be taxed again. This chapter examines the temptations that attract taxpayers to this idea and various ways in which this goal can and cannot be accomplished.

16-1 THE MULTIJURISDICTIONAL TAXPAYER

LO.1

Discuss the computational and compliance issues that arise when a taxpayer operates in more than one taxing jurisdiction.

Companies large and small must deal with the consequences of earning income through activities in different jurisdictions. A small business may have its center of operations in a single city but have customers in many states and countries. Consider the typical U.S. multinational corporation. Its assets, employees, customers, suppliers, lenders, and owners are located in numerous locations, crossing city, county, state, national, and even "virtual" borders.

EXAMPLE 1

RobotCo, a corporation created and organized in Delaware, produces and sells robotic manufacturing equipment. It holds its valuable patents and intangible property in Delaware and Bermuda. The company has manufacturing operations in Ireland, Singapore, Germany, Texas, and New Jersey. It has distribution centers in Canada, the United Kingdom, Germany, Hong Kong, Texas, New Jersey, Georgia, California, Illinois, and Arizona. RobotCo's sales force spends time in Europe, Asia, Mexico, Canada, and almost every state in the union. RobotCo's engineers likewise provide technical service to customers wherever they may be located. And in recent years, RobotCo has developed a substantial Web presence.

RobotCo must determine its potential exposure to tax in each of these jurisdictions. Such exposure usually is based on RobotCo's nexus (or economic connection) to the various locations. Unfortunately for all concerned, each of these taxing jurisdictions uses a different taxing system and methods, imposes taxes under differing structures, and even defines the tax base differently. How does RobotCo divide its income among the various jurisdictions that want a piece of the tax pie, determine its tax costs, mitigate any potential double taxation, and file the appropriate information returns with this diverse set of taxing authorities? Such questions and more must be addressed by modern-day businesses.

Thousands of state and local jurisdictions are involved in the taxation of interstate transactions through income, property, sales, or other taxes. State and local taxes make up over one-third of all taxes collected in the United States. Global trade also represents a major portion of the U.S. economy. In a recent year, U.S. exports of goods and services amounted to $2.25 trillion, with imports reaching $2.75 trillion. U.S. companies hold direct investments abroad exceeding $3 trillion, and foreign companies had invested over $2 trillion in U.S. businesses. Hundreds of countries and many more political subdivisions participated in the taxation of these transactions. These interstate and international trade flows, along with cross-state and cross-country investments, create significant Federal, state, and local tax consequences for both U.S. and foreign entities.

16-2 U.S. TAXATION OF MULTINATIONAL TRANSACTIONS

Cross-border transactions create the need for special tax considerations for both the United States and its trading partners. From a U.S. perspective, international tax laws should promote the global competitiveness of U.S. enterprises and at the same time

BRIDGE DISCIPLINE **Bridge to International Law**

Many of the provisions of the U.S. tax law relating to international transactions are thinly disguised extensions of a principle of international law—the ability of sovereign countries to protect the safety and privacy of their citizens abroad.

For instance, U.S. tax auditors often have difficulty obtaining or reviewing the documentation supporting deductions claimed by U.S. taxpayers operating overseas. Banking, credit card, and other records that are available (in the course of business or forcibly by summons) for strictly U.S. transactions are not available once those same transactions cross national borders.

How could the U.S. tax base include rental and royalty income of a U.S. investor operating through a corporation in another country when property ownership and taxation records are not available for substantiation or audit outside the country of the investment? Perhaps this explains why the U.S. tax base typically excludes such items.

Conversely, when the taxing agencies of multiple countries are allowed by law to trade among themselves information about business operations and taxpayers, the fairness and completeness of the taxing process may improve. But such lengthening of the reach of the taxing authorities results from diplomatic negotiations among the countries, not from the passage of legislation.

protect the tax revenue base of the United States. These two objectives sometimes conflict, however. The need to deal with both objectives contributes to the complexity of the rules governing the U.S. taxation of cross-border transactions.

U.S. persons engage in activities outside the United States for many different reasons. Consider two U.S. corporations that have established sales subsidiaries in foreign countries. Dedalus, Inc., operates in Germany, a high-tax country, because customers demand local attention from sales agents. Mulligan, Inc., operates in the Cayman Islands, a tax haven country, simply to shift income outside the United States. U.S. tax law must fairly address both situations with the same law.

EXAMPLE

2

U.S. international tax provisions are concerned primarily with two types of potential taxpayers: U.S. persons earning income from outside the United States and non-U.S. persons earning income from inside the United States.[1] U.S. persons earning income only from inside the United States do not create any international tax issues and are taxed under the purely domestic provisions of the Internal Revenue Code. Non-U.S. persons earning income from outside the United States are not within the taxing jurisdiction of the United States (unless this income is somehow directly connected to U.S. operations).

The U.S. taxation of international transactions can be organized in terms of "outbound" and "inbound" taxation. **Outbound taxation** refers to the U.S. taxation of foreign-source income earned by U.S. taxpayers. **Inbound taxation** refers to the U.S. taxation of U.S.-source income earned by foreign taxpayers. Exhibit 16.1 summarizes these concepts.

U.S. taxpayers often "internationalize" gradually over time. A U.S. business may operate on a strictly domestic basis for several years, then explore offshore markets by exporting its products abroad, and later license its products to a foreign manufacturer or enter into a joint venture with a foreign partner. If its forays into non-U.S. markets are successful, the U.S. business may create a foreign subsidiary and move a portion of its operations abroad by establishing a sales or manufacturing facility.

---

[1]The term *person* includes an individual, corporation, partnership, trust, estate, or association. § 7701(a)(1). The terms *domestic* and *foreign* are defined in §§ 7701(a)(4) and (5).

EXHIBIT 16.1   **U.S. Taxation of Cross-Border Transactions**

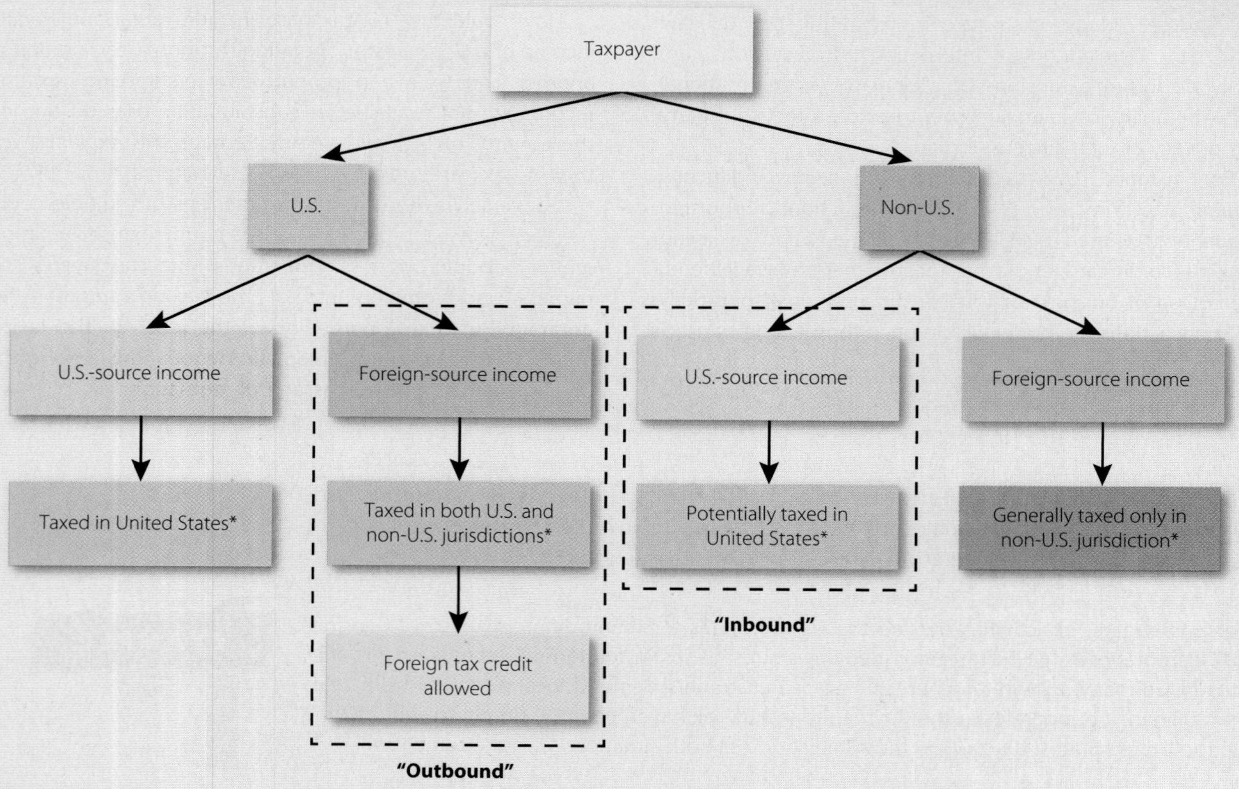

```
                                    ┌──────────────┐
                                    │   Taxpayer    │
                                    └──────────────┘
                              ┌───────────┴───────────┐
                        ┌──────────┐              ┌──────────┐
                        │   U.S.   │              │ Non-U.S. │
                        └──────────┘              └──────────┘
```

U.S.-source income	Foreign-source income	U.S.-source income	Foreign-source income
Taxed in United States*	Taxed in both U.S. and non-U.S. jurisdictions*	Potentially taxed in United States*	Generally taxed only in non-U.S. jurisdiction*
	Foreign tax credit allowed		

"Inbound"

"Outbound"

*Income may or may not be subject to tax in the non-U.S. jurisdiction, depending on local country tax law.
Some U.S.-source income is exempt from tax in the United States for both U.S. and non-U.S. persons.

For the U.S. owners, a domestically controlled foreign corporation can have significant U.S. tax consequences, including potential deferrals of income recognition from offshore activities. Non-U.S. businesses likewise enter the U.S. market in stages. In either case, each step generates increasingly significant international tax consequences. Exhibit 16.2 shows a typical timeline for "going global."

DIGGING DEEPER 1   In-depth coverage can be found on this book's companion website: www.cengagebrain.com

---

EXHIBIT 16.2   **Global Activities Timeline**

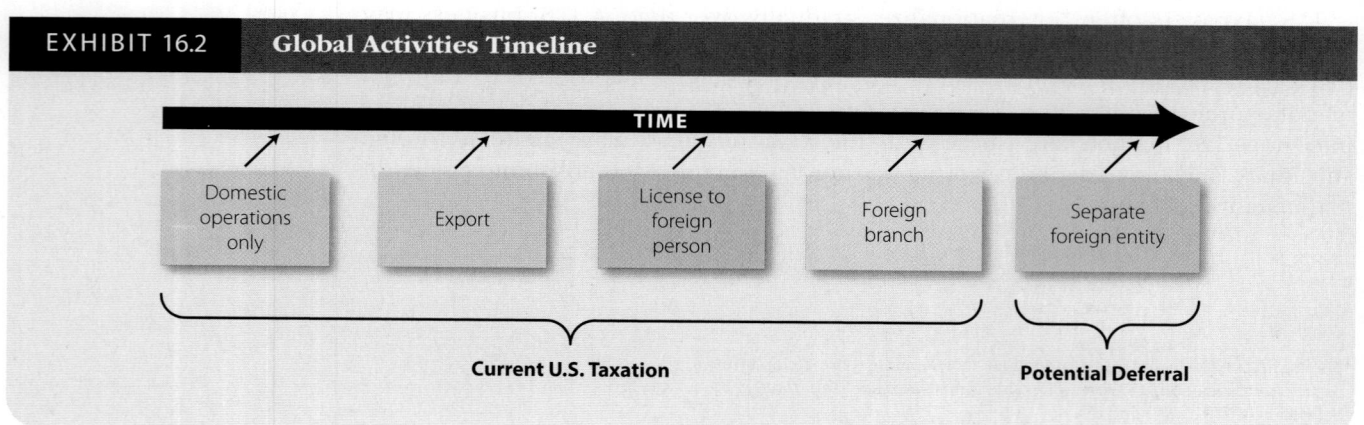

Domestic operations only	Export	License to foreign person	Foreign branch	Separate foreign entity

Current U.S. Taxation   **Potential Deferral**

16-2a **Sources of Law**

U.S. individuals and companies operating across national borders are subject to the laws of every jurisdiction in which they operate or invest. Accordingly, the source of law depends on the nature of a taxpayer's connection with a particular country.

For U.S. persons, the Internal Revenue Code addresses the tax consequences of earning income anywhere in the world. However, U.S. persons also must comply with the local tax law of the other nations in which they operate.

For non-U.S. persons, U.S. statutory law is relevant to income they earn that is connected to U.S. income-producing activities, whether those activities involve a passive investment or an active trade or business. Whether non-U.S. persons also are subject to potential tax in their home countries on their U.S. income depends on their own local tax law.

It is difficult for the United States (or any country) to craft local tax laws that equitably address all of the potential issues that arise when two countries attempt to tax the same income. Furthermore, any uncertainty as to tax consequences can be an impediment to global business investment. Consequently, countries enter into income tax treaties with each other to provide more certainty to taxpayers.

Tax treaties are the result of specific negotiations with a treaty partner, so each treaty is unique. Nevertheless, all tax treaties are organized in the same way and address similar issues. For example, all treaties include provisions regarding the taxation of investment income, business profits from a permanent establishment (PE), personal service income, and exceptions for certain persons (e.g., athletes, entertainers, students, and teachers).

Permanent establishment (PE) is an important concept that is defined in all income tax treaties. A person has a PE within a country when its activities within that country rise beyond a minimal level. Tax treaties outline the activities that create a PE, including an office, plant, or other fixed place of business. Treaties also specify certain activities that do not create a PE (e.g., a temporary construction project). Once a person has a PE within a country, the business profits associated with the PE become subject to tax in that country.

Amelia, Inc., a U.S. corporation, sells boating supplies to customers in the United States and Canada. Amelia has no assets in Canada. All Canadian sales transactions are conducted via the Internet or telephone from Amelia's Florida office. Because Amelia does not have any assets in Canada or conduct any activities within Canada, it does not have a Canadian PE. Consequently, Canada does not impose an income tax on the profit associated with Amelia's Canadian sales. However, if Amelia opens a sales office in Canada, a PE will exist, and Canada will tax the profits associated with the PE.

Although the United States has entered into almost 70 income tax treaties, many jurisdictions where U.S. taxpayers operate are not covered by a treaty. Where there is no tax treaty, the more subjective test of whether a person is "engaged in a trade or business" within a country replaces the PE determination. Both the PE concept and the engaged in a trade or business concept are closely related to the determination of whether a person has nexus within a jurisdiction for state and local tax purposes (discussed later in this chapter).

16-2b **Tax Issues**

Authority to Tax

The United States taxes the *worldwide* income of U.S. taxpayers.[2] The United States claims the right to tax all of a U.S. person's income because of the protection of

---

[2]Gross income for a U.S. person includes all income from whatever source derived. "Source" in this context means not only type of income (e.g., wages or interest) but also geographic source (e.g., the United States or Belgium). § 61.

TAX FACT **U.S. Income Tax Treaties in Force**

The United States has entered into income tax treaties with the following nations.

Armenia	France	Lithuania	South Africa
Australia	Georgia	Luxembourg	Spain
Austria	Germany	Malta	Sri Lanka
Azerbaijan	Greece	Mexico	Sweden
Bangladesh	Hungary	Moldova	Switzerland
Barbados	Iceland	Morocco	Tajikistan
Belarus	India	Netherlands	Thailand
Belgium	Indonesia	New Zealand	Trinidad
Bulgaria	Ireland	Norway	Tunisia
Canada	Israel	Pakistan	Turkey
China	Italy	Philippines	Turkmenistan
Cyprus	Jamaica	Poland	Ukraine
Czech Republic	Japan	Portugal	United Kingdom
Denmark	Kazakhstan	Romania	Uzbekistan
Egypt	Korea	Russia	Venezuela
Estonia	Kyrgyzstan	Slovak Republic	
Finland	Latvia	Slovenia	

U.S. law provided to a person connected to the United States through citizenship, residency, or place of organization.

Because non-U.S. governments also may tax some of the U.S. person's income when it is earned within the other country's borders, U.S. taxpayers may be subjected to double taxation. There are two broad methods of mitigating this double taxation problem. Under the *territorial* approach, a country simply exempts from tax the income derived from sources outside its borders. Most European and Asian countries have adopted this approach.[3] The second approach, and the one adopted by the United States, is to tax the *worldwide* income of all domestic persons and then provide a **foreign tax credit** (FTC) against home country taxes for taxes paid to other countries on the same income. The United States allows its taxpayers to reduce their U.S. tax liability by some or all of the foreign income taxes paid on income earned outside the United States.

EXAMPLE 4

Gator Enterprises, Inc., a U.S. corporation, operates a manufacturing branch in Italy because of customer demand there, local availability of raw materials, and the high cost of shipping finished goods. This branch income is taxed in the United States as part of Gator's worldwide income, but it also is taxed in Italy. Without the availability of a foreign tax credit to mitigate this double taxation, Gator Enterprises would suffer an excessive tax burden and could not compete with local Italian companies.

The United States does adopt the territorial approach in taxing non-U.S. persons. Such inbound taxpayers generally are subject to tax only on income earned within U.S. borders.

EXAMPLE 5

Purdie, Ltd., a corporation based in the United Kingdom, operates in the United States. Although it is not a U.S. person, Purdie is taxed in the United States on its U.S.-source business income. If Purdie, Ltd., could operate free of U.S. tax, its U.S.-based competitors would face a serious disadvantage.

---

[3]In some cases, countries allow the territorial exemption from home country taxation only if the income has been subject to tax in another country. Other countries, however, exempt such income even if no source country tax is imposed.

FINANCIAL DISCLOSURE INSIGHTS   **Effective Tax Strategies Using Overseas Operations**

In a global economy, publicly traded business entities can operate in many taxing jurisdictions. For instance, General Electric reports that it files current-year tax returns with more than 250 countries, amounting to over 7,000 income tax returns at the Federal and local levels worldwide. Note that this tax activity does not take into account the sales, value added, property, and other tax returns that are required by the U.S. states and localities.

The financial reports of profitable U.S. companies indicate that overseas operations can produce tax benefits of their own, not taking into account the effects of increased market share and financial stability. For instance, the trucking firm Ryder Systems recently reported current tax refunds of about $235,000 and deferred tax savings of about $500,000 on non-U.S. profits of about $11.5 million.

In a recent period, Eli Lilly reduced its effective tax rate by about one-third due to overseas operations. And General Electric recently reduced its effective tax rate to a negative amount because of various income deferrals related to overseas earnings. These deferral techniques are discussed later in the chapter.

Income Sourcing

Determining the source of net income is a critical component in calculating the U.S. tax consequences to both U.S. and foreign persons. A number of specific provisions contained in §§ 861 through 865 address the income-sourcing rules for all types of income, including interest, dividends, rents, royalties, services, and sales of assets. Although sometimes complex and subject to various special exceptions, these sourcing rules generally assign income to a geographic source based on the location where the economic activity producing the income took place. In some cases, this relationship is clear, and in others, the connection is more obscure.

Sourcing Rules

Wickless, Inc., a U.S. corporation, provides scuba diving lessons to customers in Florida and in the Bahamas. These services are sourced based on the place where the activity is performed. The services performed in Florida are U.S.-source income, and those performed in the Bahamas are foreign-source income. Because Wickless, Inc., is a U.S. person, all the income, U.S. and foreign, is subject to U.S. taxation. But the foreign-source portion is important in determining any available foreign tax credits for Wickless.

Brown, Inc., a U.S. corporation, receives dividend income from Takeda Corporation, a Japanese corporation, based on its ownership of Takeda common stock. Brown purchased the stock in the United States and receives all payments in the United States. At first glance, it appears that all of the activities related to earning the dividend income take place in the United States. Nevertheless, the dividend income is treated as foreign source because it is paid by a foreign corporation.[4]

In addition to sourcing income, the U.S. rules require taxpayers to assign deductions to U.S.- or foreign-source categories. Deductions that are directly related to an activity or property are first allocated to classes of income to which they directly relate (e.g., sales, services, rentals). This is followed by an apportionment between the U.S. and foreign groupings using some reasonable basis (e.g., revenue, gross profit, assets, units sold, time spent). If a deduction is not definitely related to any class of gross income, the deduction is first assigned to all classes of gross income and then apportioned between U.S.- and foreign-source income.

---

[4]Section 861(a)(2) establishes that only dividends from domestic corporations are U.S.-source income.

TAX FACT **Where Do We Stand?**

The drastic reductions in marginal tax rates brought about in the United States in 1981 and 1986, and the ongoing effort by Congress to make the Federal corporate income tax neutral as to the business decisions of U.S. entities operating in the global economy, have rippled through the rest of the world. Even perpetually high-tax countries such as Sweden and the United Kingdom were forced to cut back marginal tax rate structures to remain competitive and often had to change the tax base to match the revisions of the U.S. tax law.

As a result of this dramatic evolution in international tax rates, the average marginal business income tax rate in developed countries now lies between 30 and 35 percent, down from perhaps 50 percent in the 1960s. This description does not take into account, though, the dependence of many U.S. trading partners on transaction taxes, such as the value added tax and wealth-based taxes, which make difficult an apples-to-apples comparison of rates alone. Further, each country treats payroll taxes and entitlements differently, and these are increasingly expensive components of the tax structure. After taking these other taxes into account, the United States may be closer to the worldwide average.

But U.S. corporate income tax law has not changed much since the 1980s, and the rest of the world appears to be continuing the rate-cutting the United States started. The United States may need another round of rate cuts to stay in the game. By one measure, at least, after significant rate cuts by Japan and the United Kingdom, the United States applies the highest corporate income tax rate in the developed world.

Top Statutory Corporate Income Tax Rates for Selected Countries	
Bermuda	0.0%
France	37.0%
Germany	30.2%
Ireland	12.5%
Japan	37.0%
Mexico	30.0%
Sweden	22.0%
United Kingdom	21.0%
United States	39.1%

Note: Includes additional taxes on corporate taxable income levied by states, cities, provinces, cantons, and other smaller jurisdictions.

The Big Picture

EXAMPLE 8

Return to the facts of *The Big Picture* on p. 16-1. Assume that VoiceCo makes an overseas investment and generates $2 million of gross income and a $50,000 expense, all related to its microphone manufacturing and sales. The expense is allocated and apportioned on the basis of gross income.

	Gross Income			Apportionment	
	Foreign	U.S.	Allocation	Foreign	U.S.
Sales	$1,000,000	$500,000	$37,500*	$25,000	$12,500**
Manufacturing	400,000	100,000	12,500	10,000	2,500***
Totals			$50,000	$35,000	$15,000

* $50,000 × ($1,500,000/$2,000,000) = $37,500.
** $37,500 × ($500,000/$1,500,000) = $12,500.
*** $12,500 × ($100,000/$500,000) = $2,500.

If VoiceCo could show that $45,000 of the expense was directly related to its sales income, the $45,000 would be allocated directly to that class of gross income, with the remainder allocated and apportioned between U.S. and foreign source ratably.

		Apportionment	
	Allocation	Foreign	U.S.
Sales	$45,000	$30,000	$15,000
Manufacturing	5,000	4,000	1,000
Totals	$50,000	$34,000	$16,000

GLOBAL TAX ISSUES   **Deferral and Repatriation**

U.S. taxpayers with foreign operations have a choice as to how they structure such operations for U.S. tax purposes. If the U.S. taxpayer operates through an unincorporated foreign branch, the net profits from the foreign branch are subject to current taxation in the U.S. tax return of the U.S. taxpayer.

If instead the U.S. taxpayer operates abroad through a separate wholly owned foreign corporation, the income from the foreign operation is deferred from U.S. taxation until the profits are repatriated back to the United States (via a dividend or similar distribution) or when they are treated as repatriated through the operation of the Subpart F deemed dividend provisions (as discussed later). This option can have a significant effect on a U.S. taxpayer's current-period tax burden, particularly if the foreign operations are in a lower-tax jurisdiction.

As discussed in Chapter 3, under ASC 740 (APB 23), this deferral of taxes also can reduce the financial statement tax expense if the offshore profits are indefinitely reinvested outside the United States.

Many deductions may be allocated and apportioned based on any reasonable method the taxpayer chooses.[5] However, the U.S. tax rules impose a specific method for certain types of deductions, including interest and research and experimentation expenses. Interest expense is allocated and apportioned based on the theory that money is fungible. For example, if a taxpayer borrows to support its manufacturing activity, this frees up other funds for use to support its investment activities. Accordingly, the tax rules require that interest expense be allocated and apportioned to all activities and property of the taxpayer, regardless of the specific purpose for incurring the debt on which interest is paid. Taxpayers must allocate and apportion interest expense on the basis of asset location, using either the fair market value or the tax book value of the assets.

TAX IN THE NEWS   **The IRS Watches from Abroad**

Taxpayers long have tried to shield information from the IRS about assets and income (e.g., in the proverbial Swiss bank account). Computing resources and cooperation among government taxing authorities make it more difficult to do so than ever before.

The IRS stations agents in Beijing, Hong Kong, Sydney, the British Virgin Islands (BVI), and other jurisdictions where it perceives that taxpayers are shifting financial resources with tax evasion motives. For instance, the Treasury pays attention when it learns that the profits of U.S. corporations entail over 1,000 percent of the GDP of the Cayman Islands and of the BVI. When U.S. profits constitute 38 percent of Ireland's GDP, and 15 percent of that of the Netherlands, something more than just business decisions likely are involved.

It often takes many years to put together a case to show the tax evasion activities of a U.S. person. Typical IRS weapons include information-sharing agreements among governments and/or taxing agencies, whistleblower programs, and litigation.

The U.S. Foreign Account Tax Compliance Act (FATCA) requires that a bank (even one organized outside the United States) provide the IRS with certain identifying information about all U.S. persons with an account at the bank. Lacking such compliance information, the bank must pay a fine if it wants to hold assets in the United States.

FATCA, along with other efforts to disclose holdings in non-U.S. banks, can be an effective revenue-raiser for the United States. But as Switzerland starts to cooperate with other countries and discloses information about secret bank accounts, some investors move money to similar accounts in less cooperative countries such as Singapore and Hong Kong.

---

[5]Reg. § 1.861–8.

The Big Picture

EXAMPLE

9

Return to the facts of *The Big Picture* on p. 16-1. Assume that VoiceCo makes an overseas investment and generates both U.S.-source and foreign-source gross income for the current year. VoiceCo's assets (measured at tax book value) are as follows.

Assets generating U.S.-source income	$18,000,000
Assets generating foreign-source income	5,000,000
	$23,000,000

VoiceCo incurs interest expense of $800,000 for the current year. Using the tax book value method, interest expense is apportioned to foreign-source income as follows.

$$\frac{\$5,000,000 \text{ (foreign assets)}}{\$23,000,000 \text{ (total assets)}} \times \$800,000 \text{ (interest expense)} = \$173,913$$

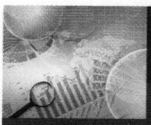

TAX PLANNING STRATEGIES   **Sourcing Income from Sales of Inventory**

FRAMEWORK FOCUS: TAX RATE

Strategy: Control the Character of Income and Deductions.

Generally, income from the sale of personal property is sourced according to the residence of the seller under § 865. Several important exceptions exist for inventory. Income from the sale of purchased inventory is sourced in the country in which the sale takes place under the "title passage" rule. This rule provides the taxpayer with flexibility regarding the sourcing of income and deductions, and it allows for the creation of zero-taxed foreign-source income.

USCo, a domestic corporation, purchases inventory for resale from unrelated parties and sells the inventory to customers in the United States and Brazil. If title on the Brazilian sales passes in the United States (i.e., risks of loss shift to the Brazilian customers at the shipping point), the inventory income is U.S. source. If title passes outside the United States (e.g., at the customer's warehouse in Brazil), the inventory income is foreign source.

Although the Code identifies the income item as foreign source, this income likely is not subject to any Brazilian tax because USCo has no employees, assets, or activities in Brazil. Although the income is subject to U.S. tax in either case (as it represents taxable income to a U.S. person), in the latter case, USCo has generated foreign-source income with no corresponding foreign income tax. This will prove very useful in managing USCo's ability to use foreign tax credits, as discussed later in this chapter.

When a taxpayer both produces and sells inventory, the income is apportioned between the country of production and the country of sale. Taxpayers often elect a 50–50 allocation method as allowed by § 863(b), where 50 percent of the profits from the sale are automatically assigned to the location of the production assets and 50 percent of the profits are assigned to the location where title passes.

Assume that USCo manufactures inventory in its Texas plant and sells the inventory to customers in Mexico. Regardless of the actual economic profit relationship between the manufacturing and selling activities, 50 percent of the profit on the Mexican sales can be assigned to foreign-source income by simply passing title outside the United States.

Foreign Tax Credit

As discussed earlier, the United States retains the right to tax its citizens and residents on their worldwide taxable income. To reduce the possibility of double taxation, Congress created the foreign tax credit (FTC).

A qualified taxpayer is allowed a tax credit for foreign income taxes paid or accrued. All of the taxes paid by the taxpayer to various countries on its operations are combined to compute the FTC. The credit is a dollar-for-dollar reduction of U.S. income tax liability.

TAX FACT Corporate Use of the Foreign Tax Credit

Information from recent Forms 1120 indicates that the foreign tax credit is used by a small number of corporate taxpayers, but that the credit spans a very large portion of the global economy.

Of foreign tax payments reported on Forms 1118 and 1120, more than 40 percent were paid to European countries, with the most going to the United Kingdom, Luxembourg, Norway, and the Netherlands. Tax payments to Canada accounted for 7 percent of the total. Pacific Rim countries received over 11 percent of total foreign tax payments, and all of Africa totaled only about 3 percent.

Tax returns claiming a foreign tax credit	6,700
Total assets of corporations claiming the credit	$31.7 trillion
Taxable income of corporations claiming the credit	$735 billion
U.S. income tax liability of corporations claiming the credit	$259 billion
Foreign tax credit claimed	$107 billion
Foreign income taxes available for the credit	$192 billion

Applying the FTC

EXAMPLE 10

Caulkin Tools, Inc., a U.S. corporation, operates a branch operation in Mexico from which it earns taxable income of $750,000 for the current year. Caulkin pays income tax of $150,000 on these earnings to the Mexican tax authorities. Caulkin also includes the $750,000 in gross income for U.S. tax purposes.

Before considering the FTC, Caulkin owes $255,000 in U.S. income taxes on this foreign-source income. Thus, total taxes on the $750,000 could equal $405,000 ($150,000 + $255,000), a 54% effective rate.

But Caulkin takes an FTC of $150,000 against its U.S. tax liability on the foreign-source income. Caulkin's total taxes on the $750,000 now are $255,000 ($150,000 + $105,000), a 34% effective rate.

EXAMPLE 11

MettCo, Inc., a domestic corporation, receives a $5,000 dividend from DeanCo, Ltd., a foreign corporation owned less than 5% by MettCo. The foreign country imposes a 20% withholding tax on dividend payments to nonresidents. Accordingly, DeanCo withholds $1,000 ($5,000 × 20%) from the dividend and remits this tax to the local country tax authorities. DeanCo pays the remaining $4,000 to MettCo.

Although MettCo did not directly pay the $1,000 in foreign tax, the entire amount is allowed as a direct tax to MettCo for FTC purposes. MettCo reports $5,000 in dividend income on its U.S. tax return (the gross amount of the dividend), but it receives an FTC against any U.S. tax for the $1,000 in foreign withholding tax.

The FTC is elective for the tax year. Lacking an election to take the FTC, a deduction is claimed for foreign taxes paid or incurred. One cannot take a credit and a deduction for the same foreign income taxes, and in most situations, the FTC is more valuable to the taxpayer.

FTC Limits The United States does not grant an FTC for all foreign taxes paid, and there are limits on the amount of foreign taxes that can be taken as a credit. First, only foreign *income* taxes are potentially creditable. Second, the FTC allowed in any tax year is limited to the U.S. tax imposed on the foreign-source income included on the U.S. tax return.[6] Thus, taxpayers are allowed a credit for the lesser of the foreign income taxes paid or accrued or the following limitation.

$$\text{FTC limit} = \frac{\text{Foreign-source taxable income}}{\text{Worldwide taxable income}} \times \text{U.S. tax liability before FTC}$$

[6]Sections 901, 902, and 903 provide definitions of creditable foreign taxes. Section 904 contains the FTC limitation rules.

Worldwide taxable income is the total taxable income reported on the taxpayer's U.S. tax return, not the total worldwide income of a group of related domestic and foreign entities. Any potential FTCs disallowed because of the FTC limitation may be carried back 1 year or forward 10 years, subject to the FTC limits in those tax years.

Lassaline, Inc., a domestic corporation, invests in the bonds of non-U.S. corporations. Lassaline's worldwide taxable income for the tax year is $1.2 million, consisting of $1 million of profits from U.S. sales and $200,000 of interest income from foreign sources. Foreign taxes of $90,000 were withheld on these interest payments.

Lassaline's U.S. tax before the FTC is $408,000. Its FTC is limited to $68,000 [($200,000/$1,200,000) × $408,000]. Thus, Lassaline's net U.S. tax liability is $340,000 after allowing the $68,000 FTC. The remaining $22,000 of FTCs ($90,000 − $68,000) may be carried back or forward.

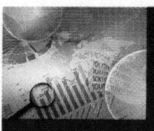

TAX PLANNING STRATEGIES   **Utilizing the Foreign Tax Credit**

FRAMEWORK FOCUS: TAX CREDITS

Strategy: Maximize Tax Credits.

The FTC limitation can prevent the total amount of foreign taxes paid in high-tax jurisdictions from being credited. Taxpayers can overcome this problem by generating additional foreign-source income that is subject to no or low foreign taxation.

A U.S. taxpayer's ability to use FTCs is directly related to its level of foreign-source income relative to its total taxable income. To the extent a U.S. taxpayer can keep the average tax rate on its foreign-source income at or below the U.S. tax rate on such income, the foreign taxes will be fully creditable. Consequently, combining high- and low-tax foreign-source income is an important planning objective.

Compare the following scenarios where Genius, a U.S. corporation, incurs FTC situations that differ depending on its ability to mix high- and low-taxed income. In the first scenario, Genius earns only $500,000 of highly taxed foreign-source income. In the second scenario, it also generates $100,000 of low-taxed foreign-source income.

	Only Highly Taxed Income	With Low-Taxed Income
Foreign-source income	$500,000	$600,000
Foreign taxes	275,000	280,000
U.S.-source income	700,000	700,000
U.S. taxes (34%)	408,000	442,000
FTC limitation	170,000*	204,000**

* ($500,000/$1,200,000) × $408,000 = $170,000.
** ($600,000/$1,300,000) × $442,000 = $204,000.

When the low-taxed income is added, Genius's actual foreign taxes increase by only $5,000 ($280,000 versus $275,000), but its FTC limitation increases by $34,000 (from $170,000 to $204,000). The ability to "cross-credit" high- and low-taxed foreign income is available, though, only when all of the foreign-source income is classified in the same income basket.

To limit the ability of U.S. taxpayers to cross-credit foreign taxes, the FTC rules provide for two **separate foreign tax credit income categories** (or baskets): passive and general. In any tax year, taxpayers are allowed to credit the lesser of foreign income taxes paid or accrued or the FTC limit only *within each separate basket*. The separate FTC limitation categories for different types of income each use this same basic FTC limitation formula. The separate limitation categories affect the amount of FTC that can be taken by generally segregating income subject to a high level of foreign tax from lower-taxed foreign income.

EXAMPLE 14

BenCo, Inc., a U.S. corporation, operates a foreign branch in Germany that earns taxable income of $1.5 million from manufacturing operations and $600,000 from passive activities. BenCo pays foreign taxes of $600,000 (40%) and $100,000 ($16^2/_3$%), respectively, on this foreign-source income.

The corporation earns $4 million of U.S.-source taxable income, resulting in worldwide taxable income of $6.1 million. BenCo's U.S. taxes before the FTC are $2,074,000 (at 34%). The following table illustrates the effect of the separate limitation baskets on cross-crediting.

Separate Foreign Income Category	Net Taxable Amount	Foreign Taxes	U.S. Tax before FTC at 34%	FTC Allowed with Separate Limits
General	$1,500,000	$600,000	$510,000	$510,000
Passive	600,000	100,000	204,000	100,000
Total	$2,100,000	$700,000	$714,000	$610,000

Without the separate limitation provisions, the FTC would be the lesser of (1) $700,000 foreign taxes or (2) $714,000 share of U.S. tax [($2,100,000/$6,100,000) × $2,074,000]. The "basket" provisions reduce the FTC by $90,000 ($700,000 versus $610,000). In this way, the foreign-source income taxed at the foreign tax rate of 40% cannot be aggregated with foreign-source income taxed at only $16^2/_3$%.

Direct and Indirect FTCs U.S. taxpayers may claim FTCs for foreign taxes they pay directly or through withholding as so-called direct credits. In addition, U.S. corporate taxpayers may claim FTCs for foreign taxes paid indirectly. If a U.S. corporation operates in a foreign country through a branch, the direct credit is available to the U.S. parent for foreign taxes paid.

If, however, a U.S. corporation operates in a country through a foreign subsidiary, the direct credit is not available for foreign taxes paid by the foreign corporation. An indirect or **deemed-paid credit** is available to U.S. corporate taxpayers that receive actual or constructive dividends from foreign corporations that have paid foreign income taxes.[7] These foreign taxes are deemed paid by the corporate shareholders in the same proportion as the dividends actually or constructively received bear to the foreign corporation's undistributed E & P.

$$\text{Deemed-paid credit} = \frac{\text{Actual or constructive dividend}}{\text{Undistributed E \& P}} \times \text{Foreign taxes paid}$$

If a U.S. taxpayer claims a deemed-paid credit, § 78 requires the corporation to *gross up* (add to income) the dividend income by the amount of the deemed-paid credit. If the FTC is not claimed, the income gross-up is not required.

EXAMPLE 15

Wren, Inc., a domestic corporation, owns 50% of Finch, Inc., a foreign corporation. Wren receives a dividend of $120,000 from Finch. Finch paid foreign taxes of $500,000 on its E & P, which totals $1.2 million. Wren's deemed-paid foreign taxes for FTC purposes are $50,000.

Cash dividend from Finch	$120,000
Deemed-paid foreign taxes [($120,000/$1,200,000) × $500,000]	50,000
Gross income to Wren	$170,000

Wren includes $170,000 in gross income for the year. As a result of the dividend received, Wren can claim a credit for the $50,000 in deemed-paid foreign taxes.

---

[7]U.S. corporations must meet certain minimum ownership requirements under § 902 to claim a deemed-paid credit. In the formula for the indirect credit, only foreign taxes paid and E & P generated after 1986 are used.

FINANCIAL DISCLOSURE INSIGHTS   **Overseas Operations and Book-Tax Differences**

Non-U.S. operations account for a large portion of the permanent book-tax differences of U.S. business entities. These differences may relate to different tax bases, different tax rate structures, or special provisions concerning tax-based financing with the other country. For instance, lower tax rates applied by Ireland, Bermuda, and the Netherlands recently reduced Cisco's current-year tax liabilities by about $1 billion per year.

Tax planning strategies using non-U.S. operations also are found in the deferred tax asset and liability accounts. Tax deferrals allowed under current U.S. tax rules and carryforwards of the foreign tax credit can be substantial for some businesses. For example, IBM recently reported a deferred tax asset relating to delays in using its FTCs amounting to about $500 million. For the operating arm of General Electric, that amount was about $2 billion.

DIGGING DEEPER 2   **In-depth coverage can be found on this book's companion website: www.cengagebrain.com**

Controlled Foreign Corporations

Foreign corporations—even those controlled by U.S. shareholders—generally are not included in a U.S. consolidated income tax return. Consequently, in the absence of some other provision, the income of a foreign corporation is included on the U.S. shareholder's U.S. income tax return only when dividend income is received. To minimize current U.S. tax liability, taxpayers often attempt to defer the recognition of taxable income. One way to do this is to shift the income-generating activity to a foreign entity; then the income earned will not be subject to U.S. tax until it is repatriated.

For example, a U.S. person can create a foreign holding company to own the stock of foreign operating affiliates or intangible assets, such as patents and trademarks. Thus, the income generated by these foreign holdings would escape current U.S. taxation. A non-U.S. corporation also can be used to accumulate income from sales or service activities by acting as an intermediary between the U.S. corporation and an offshore customer. The offshore subsidiary corporation would be used to purchase goods from the U.S. parent or domestic affiliates and then resell the goods to foreign customers or provide services on behalf of the U.S. parent or affiliates.

In some cases, the use of intermediate overseas subsidiaries is based on a substantive business purpose. In other cases, they are employed only to reduce tax costs. Because of this potential for abuse, Congress has enacted various provisions to limit the availability of deferral.

The most important of these antideferral provisions are those affecting **controlled foreign corporations (CFCs)**. Subpart F of the Code provides that certain types of "tainted" income generated by CFCs are included in current-year gross income by the U.S. shareholders, without regard to actual distributions. U.S. shareholders must include in gross income their pro rata share of **Subpart F income**. This rule applies to U.S. shareholders who own stock in the corporation on the last day of the tax year or on the last day the foreign corporation is a CFC.

EXAMPLE

16

Jordan, Ltd., a calendar year foreign corporation, is a CFC for the entire tax year. Taylor, Inc., a U.S. corporation, owns 60% of Jordan's one class of stock for the entire year. Jordan earned $100,000 of Subpart F income for the year and makes no actual distributions during the year. Taylor, a calendar year taxpayer, includes $60,000 in gross income as a constructive dividend for the tax year.

To the extent Jordan has paid any foreign income taxes, Taylor may claim an indirect foreign tax credit for the portion of the foreign taxes related to the $60,000 constructive dividend.

What Is a CFC? A CFC is any non-U.S. corporation in which more than 50 percent of the total combined voting power of all classes of voting stock, or the total value of the stock of the corporation, is owned by U.S. shareholders on any day during the taxable year of the foreign corporation. The offshore subsidiaries of most multinational U.S. parent corporations are CFCs.

For the purposes of determining whether a foreign corporation is a CFC, a **U.S. shareholder** is a U.S. person who owns, or is considered to own, 10 percent or more of the total combined voting power of all classes of voting stock of the foreign corporation. Stock owned directly, indirectly, and constructively is counted. Indirect ownership involves stock held through a foreign entity, such as a foreign corporation, foreign partnership, or foreign trust. This stock is considered to be actually owned proportionately by the shareholders, partners, or beneficiaries.

Constructive ownership rules, with certain modifications, apply in determining whether a U.S. person is a U.S. shareholder, in determining whether a foreign corporation is a CFC, and for certain related-party provisions of Subpart F.

Subpart F Income A U.S. shareholder of a CFC does not necessarily lose the ability to defer U.S. taxation of income earned by the CFC. Only certain income earned by the CFC triggers immediate U.S. taxation as a constructive dividend. This tainted income, often referred to as Subpart F income, can be characterized as income that is easily shifted or has little or no economic connection with the CFC's country of incorporation. Examples include:

- Passive income such as interest, dividends, rents, and royalties.
- Sales income where neither the manufacturing activity nor the customer base is in the CFC's country and either the property supplier or the customer is related to the CFC.
- Service income where the CFC is providing services on behalf of its U.S. owners outside the CFC's country.

Subpart F Income

EXAMPLE

17

Collins, Inc., a domestic corporation, sells $1 million of its products to customers in Europe. All manufacturing and sales activities take place in the United States. Collins has no employees, assets, or operations in Europe and thus is not subject to income tax in any European jurisdiction.

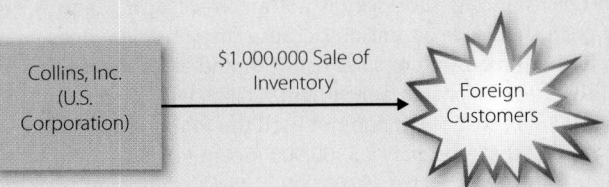

Collins reported the following tax consequences from these inventory sales.

Sales revenue	$1,000,000
Cost of goods sold	(600,000)
Net income	$ 400,000
U.S. tax at 35%	$ 140,000

Assume that Collins instead creates a wholly owned foreign subsidiary in the Cayman Islands, where no income taxes are imposed on corporate income. Collins then sells the inventory to the subsidiary at an intercompany transfer price of $700,000, and the subsidiary sells the inventory to the ultimate European customers for $1 million. The subsidiary does not further process the inventory and is only minimally involved in the sales function, as Collins's employees arrange the transactions with the ultimate customers. In essence, the sale to the subsidiary is simply a "paper" transaction.

continued

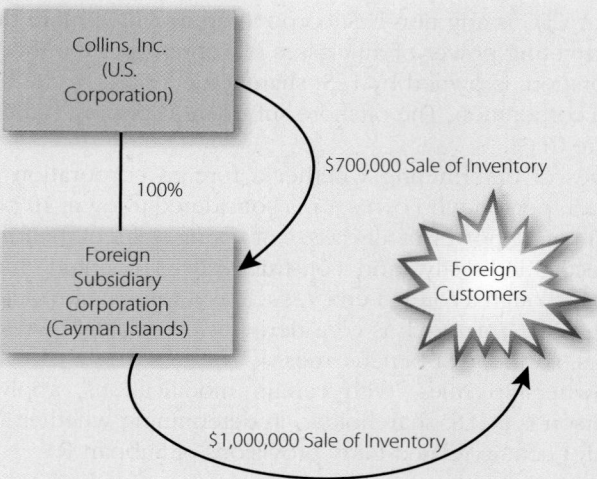

If there were no tax law restrictions, this structure would create the following tax consequences.

	Collins, Inc.	Foreign Subsidiary
Sales revenue	$ 700,000	$1,000,000
Cost of goods sold	(600,000)	(700,000)
Net income	$ 100,000	$ 300,000
U.S. tax at 35%	$ 35,000	
Foreign tax at 0%		$ –0–

Because the Cayman subsidiary is not engaged in a U.S. trade or business, it is not subject to any U.S. tax on its income. So long as the subsidiary's profits are kept outside the United States, Collins believes it can avoid any U.S. income tax on these profits (i.e., the deferral privilege). Thus, at first glance, it appears that using the foreign subsidiary significantly reduces Collins's current tax cost from $140,000 to $35,000.

However, Collins will find this strategy attacked by the U.S. taxing authorities on two fronts, either of which results in the loss of all or most of the tax savings.

First, the IRS may use the transfer pricing rules of § 482 to claim that the $700,000 intercompany transfer price between Collins and its subsidiary is not a correct **arm's length price**. The IRS may claim that the transfer price should be $1 million because the subsidiary does not add any value to the inventory through further processing or sales activities and all of the risks of the transaction are borne by Collins. With this transfer pricing adjustment, Collins will have a $400,000 profit from the sales and the same $140,000 tax cost as if it had not used the foreign subsidiary as an intermediary.

Under the Subpart F rules, the subsidiary's $300,000 income creates a constructive dividend for Collins, thus producing a $105,000 tax cost ($300,000 × 35%). Combined with its original $35,000 tax, Collins's total tax cost for the sales is $140,000 ($35,000 + $105,000), and the use of the foreign subsidiary does not achieve any tax savings.

EXAMPLE 18

Assume that, in Example 17, Collins's foreign subsidiary instead was incorporated in Ireland, where the tax rate on such sales income is 12.5%. The subsidiary purchases raw materials from Collins and performs substantial manufacturing activity in Ireland before selling the inventory to customers in Hong Kong.

In this case, the sales income is not Subpart F income. Because of the substantial activity provided by the Ireland subsidiary, there is economic substance to the non-U.S. entity that generates the income.

The fact that the Irish subsidiary pays a substantially lower tax rate than the U.S. parent does not by itself trigger a constructive dividend. However, Collins must still document the appropriateness of its intercompany transfer price on raw material sales to its Irish subsidiary.

TAX PLANNING STRATEGIES Avoiding Constructive Dividends

FRAMEWORK FOCUS: TAX CREDITS

Strategy: Maximize Deductible Amounts.

To defer U.S. taxes on foreign income, U.S. taxpayers often create separate foreign subsidiaries to hold their offshore operations. This approach is successful so long as the foreign subsidiaries do not pay dividends to the U.S. owners and do not earn Subpart F income that creates constructive dividends. U.S. companies often set up foreign holding companies in tax-favorable jurisdictions to hold the foreign operating subsidiaries.

For example, a U.S. parent might create a CFC holding company with two operating subsidiaries. The subsidiaries both pay interest to the holding company on intercompany loans. The interest is deductible by the operating subsidiaries at a high tax rate (providing tax savings in those countries) and is taxed to the holding company at a relatively low tax rate. This approach provides a net tax savings to the foreign group. However, the interest payments to the holding company may constitute Subpart F income and trigger a constructive dividend back to the U.S. parent. If so, the tax savings related to the intercompany loans are offset by the U.S. taxes on the Subpart F income.

A mechanism exists that allows the holding company to avoid Subpart F treatment for the interest income. The **check-the-box Regulations** provide a great deal of flexibility for U.S.-based multinational corporations. For example, corporations are allowed to elect (i.e., check the box on a form) to treat certain foreign subsidiaries as unincorporated branches for U.S. purposes rather than separate legal entities. This election does not change the treatment of the entities under local tax law.

Using the check-the-box rules, the U.S. parent can elect to treat the foreign subsidiaries as branches for U.S. purposes. In this case, the two foreign subsidiaries are treated as mere divisions of the holding company. Accordingly, the intercompany loans do not exist from a U.S. perspective, and there is no interest income because the interest payments are treated as simply fund transfers within a single corporation. Without the interest income, there is no Subpart F income and thus no constructive dividends. However, the foreign tax savings still exist because the interest payments do exist from a foreign tax perspective, and they continue to provide interest deductions at the subsidiary level.

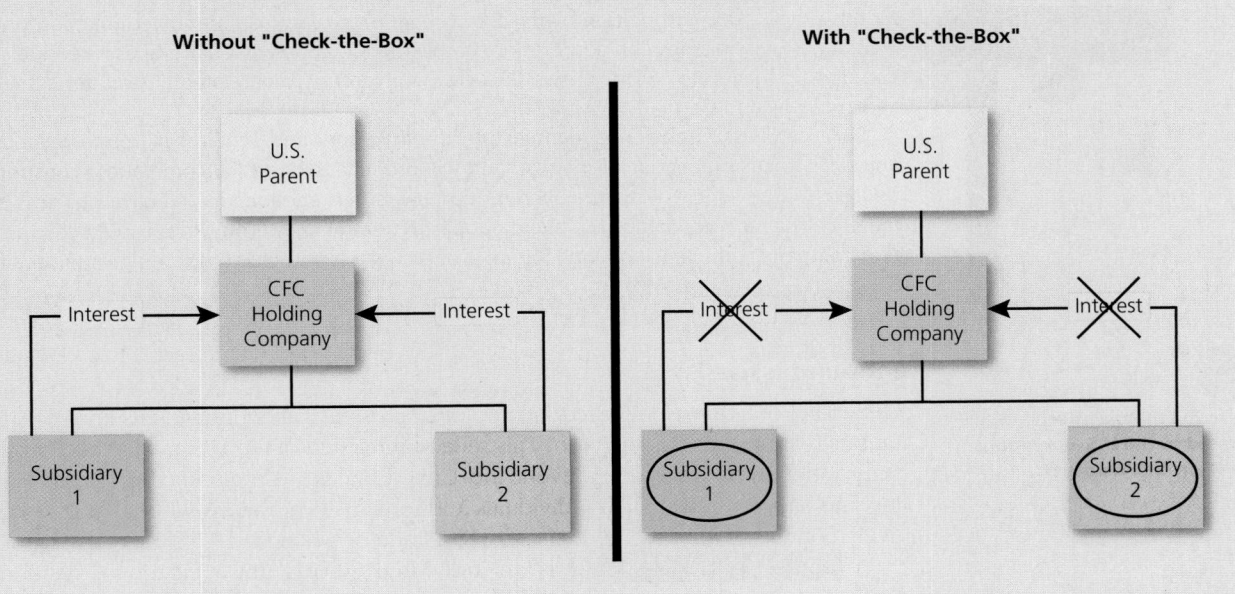

Subpart F Income—Summary The Subpart F provisions are quite complex and subject to numerous exceptions. Still, in general, any time a CFC earns income that has little economic connection to its local country, the income potentially can create a constructive dividend to the CFC's U.S. shareholders. Alternatively, if the CFC is actively generating the income, it likely is not Subpart F income.

TAX IN THE NEWS   Taxes Take a Smaller Bite Out of Apple

Apple, Inc., is a good case study for how effective tax planning can make a successful tech company even more profitable after taxes are considered. The company's business model produces plenty of free cash flow, but it operates in an industry that is based as much on intellectual property as physical plant and employee productivity. As the current tax laws largely were drafted to operate in a manufacturing and merchandising economy, Apple and other similar companies can exploit to their tax advantage a number of items that a more current tax code might address.

Apple's tax planning appears to follow the letter and the spirit of current tax law. Even though most of Apple's executives, engineers, and designers work in the United States, much of the company's profit is taxed elsewhere. Here are some highlights of how Apple uses current tax laws effectively.

- Over time, the company moves its physical plant to low-tax jurisdictions such as Nevada, Ireland, and the Netherlands.

- The company lobbies for and then uses tax incentives (e.g., for research and experimentation activities) that are offered by the Federal, state, and local governments.

- Apple uses tax planning arrangements that create subsidiaries in low-tax countries (e.g., in the British Virgin

Islands). Using proper transfer pricing techniques, sales transactions are routed through the low-tax jurisdictions, and more profits are left after tax for corporate growth and development.

- Another tax-shifting strategy employs so-called commissionaires, who arrange sales of the company's goods but never take possession of any inventory. Thus, Apple's profit derived from the work distributors in high-tax countries is taxed in a low-tax country such as Singapore.

In response to criticism surrounding its tax planning, Apple counters that the company and its employees still pay billions of dollars in payroll, sales, property, and individual income taxes. And Apple's retail stores certainly draw customer traffic that benefits other tenants in shopping malls.

One downside of these tax-shifting strategies is that Apple can defer the Federal income tax on such profits only as long as the related cash remains overseas; a repatriation would trigger high-rate U.S. taxes. The U.S. Treasury might have a good argument if Apple's offshore cash was "idle," but surely most of it is used to grow the business as it operates in a global environment.

EXAMPLE

19

Murphy, Inc., a U.S. corporation owns all of GreenCo, Ltd., an Irish manufacturing corporation, and SwissCo, a Swiss distribution corporation. Both GreenCo and SwissCo are CFCs. GreenCo sells its inventory production to SwissCo. SwissCo sells the inventory to unrelated customers located in Switzerland, Italy, and Germany.

Because SwissCo does not manufacture the inventory and acquires it from a related supplier, any sales to customers outside Switzerland will produce Subpart F income and a constructive dividend to Murphy, Inc. This is true even though SwissCo is engaged in an active business and is not merely a "paper" corporation. To avoid Subpart F treatment, Murphy, Inc., should create a distribution company within each country where it operates to sell to customers only within that country.

LO.4

Describe the tax effects related to the U.S. operations of a non-U.S. taxpayer.

Inbound Issues

Generally, only the U.S.-source income of nonresident alien individuals and foreign corporations is subject to U.S. taxation. This reflects the reach of the U.S. tax jurisdiction. This constraint, however, does not prevent the United States from also taxing the foreign-source income of nonresident alien individuals and foreign corporations when that income is effectively connected with the conduct of a U.S. trade or business.

A nonresident alien (NRA) is an individual who is not a citizen or resident of the United States. *Citizenship* is determined under the immigration and naturalization laws of the United States. A person is treated as a *resident* of the United States for income tax purposes if he or she meets either the green card test or the substantial presence test. If either of these tests is met for the calendar year, the individual is deemed a U.S. resident for the year.

TAX FACT The Inbound Sector

Inbound corporate operations produce a small but significant portion of U.S. income tax collections.

With an average U.S. income tax rate of about 37 percent on inbound commerce, perhaps some of the other countries in the world look at the United States as a high-tax jurisdiction.

Number of Forms 1120-F filed	20,000
Taxable income reported	$9.1 billion
Net tax liability	$3.4 billion

Two important definitions determine the U.S. tax consequences to foreign persons with U.S.-source income: "the conduct of a U.S. trade or business" and "**effectively connected income**." Specifically, for a foreign person's noninvestment income to be subject to U.S. taxation, the non-U.S. person must be considered engaged in a U.S. trade or business and must earn income effectively connected with that business.

General criteria for determining whether a U.S. trade or business exists include the location of production activities, management, distribution activities, and other business functions. The Code does not explicitly define a U.S. trade or business, but case law has described the concept as activities carried on in the United States that are regular, substantial, and continuous.

Once a non-U.S. person is considered engaged in a U.S. trade or business, all U.S.-source income other than investment and capital gain income is considered effectively connected to that trade or business and is therefore subject to U.S. taxation. Effectively connected income is taxed at the same rates that apply to U.S. persons, and deductions for expenses attributable to that income are allowed.

Certain U.S.-source income that is *not* effectively connected with the conduct of a U.S. trade or business is subject to a flat 30 percent tax. This income includes dividends; certain interest; rents; royalties; certain compensation; premiums; annuities; and other income of this type from fixed, determinable, annual or periodic (**FDAP**) sources. This tax generally is levied by a withholding mechanism that requires the payors of the income to withhold 30 percent of gross amounts (or a lower rate as established by a treaty). This method improves the collectability of Federal taxes from nonresidents and non-U.S. corporations.

EXAMPLE 20

Robert, a citizen and resident of New Zealand, produces wine for export. During the current year, Robert earns $500,000 from exporting wine to unrelated wholesalers in the United States. The title to the wine passes to the U.S. wholesalers in New York. Robert has no offices or employees in the United States. The income from the wine sales is U.S.-source income, but because Robert is not engaged in a U.S. trade or business, the income is not subject to taxation in the United States.

Robert begins operating a hot dog cart in New York City. This activity constitutes a U.S. trade or business. Consequently, all U.S.-source income other than FDAP or capital gain income is taxed in the United States as income effectively connected with a U.S. trade or business. Thus, both the hot dog cart profits and the $500,000 in wine income are taxed in the United States.

Several exceptions exempt non-U.S. persons from U.S. taxation on their U.S. investment income that is not connected with a U.S. business. For example, certain U.S.-sourced portfolio debt investments and capital gains (other than gains on U.S. real property investments) are exempt from U.S. tax for most non-U.S. investors. Gains from investments in U.S. real property (held directly or indirectly through other entities) are subject to U.S. taxation. Concept Summary 16.1 summarizes the U.S. taxation of non-U.S. persons.

FINANCIAL DISCLOSURE INSIGHTS   Tax Rates in Non-U.S. Jurisdictions

When Congress changes the U.S. tax law, it seldom applies tax rate changes retroactively or prospectively—the rate changes usually are applicable on the date the tax bill is effective. Other countries do not always enact tax law changes in this way. Sometimes a country will adopt a schedule of tax rate increases or decreases to go into effect over a period of years.

Tax legislation of this sort can have an important effect on the U.S. taxpayer's effective tax rate as computed in the footnotes to the financial statements. When another country adopts prospective tax rate changes, an increase or decrease in the effective tax rate is reported with respect to the deferred tax accounts for GAAP purposes. Specifically, the effective tax rate decreases when a tax rate cut is scheduled in a country that does business with the U.S. party, and the rate increases when a tax rate increase is adopted for future tax years. In the last three decades, most developed countries have been cutting business income tax rates.

A recent effective tax rate computation for Berkshire Hathaway showed a decrease of about 1 percentage point due to scheduled tax rate cuts in Germany and the United Kingdom. Allied Healthcare Products showed a similar adjustment of about 2 percentage points. In contrast, the effective tax rate increased by about 1 percentage point for American Travellers Life Insurance Company.

Concept Summary 16.1

U.S. Tax Treatment of a Non-U.S. Person's Income*

Type of Income	Tax Rate
U.S.-source fixed, determinable, annual, or periodic (FDAP) income (not effectively connected to a U.S. business)	Generally 30% withholding on gross amount (or lower treaty rate) with certain limited exceptions.
U.S.-source income effectively connected with a U.S. trade or business	Regular individual or corporate rates applied against net income (after deductions).
Gain on U.S. real property (direct or indirect interest)	Taxed as if effectively connected to a U.S. trade or business.
Capital gains (other than on U.S. real property) not effectively connected to a U.S. trade or business	Foreign corporation: Not subject to U.S. tax. Individual: Generally not taxed but may be subject to a 30% U.S. tax if taxpayer is physically present in the United States for 183 days or more in a taxable year.
Foreign-source business income	Generally not subject to U.S. taxation unless attributable to a U.S. office or fixed place of business.

*Subject to change under treaty provisions.

16-3 CROSSING STATE LINES: STATE AND LOCAL INCOME TAXATION IN THE UNITED STATES

Very few taxpayers sell goods and services solely in the U.S. state in which they are based. Sales in other states are attractive for a variety of business reasons, including the expansion of market share and the achievement of economies of scale. By extending its operations into other states, a firm may be able to lower its labor and distribution costs, obtain additional sources of long-term debt and equity, and perhaps find a more favorable tax climate.

Many of the same issues discussed earlier in the chapter concerning international operations are encountered when a multistate operation is in place. Both international and multistate operations raise basic questions such as where did the transaction occur and who is liable for the collection of the tax.

TAX FACT   **State Tax Revenue Sources**

The corporate income tax accounts for only a small portion of total tax revenues of the states. For 2013, over $850 billion in taxes was collected by the states (i.e., more than $2,700 per U.S. individual).

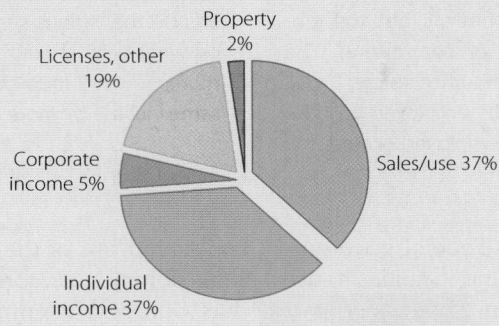

Property 2%
Licenses, other 19%
Corporate income 5%
Individual income 37%
Sales/use 37%

However, as state and local income taxation has evolved in the United States, differences in terminology, definitions, and scope of the tax have arisen. Although prior knowledge of the U.S. international tax regime can be helpful in studying the state and local income tax structure, there still is much to learn. In addition, the sheer number of income taxing districts at the state and local level make an encounter with the state and local income tax laws of the United States a challenging experience.

16-3a **Sources of Law**

Think of how complicated a tax professional's work would be if there were several hundred different Internal Revenue Codes, each with its own Regulations, rulings, and court decisions. That description is hardly an exaggeration of the state and local income tax law faced by a taxpayer operating in more than one jurisdiction. Unless a firm's salable goods or services are designed, made, and sold strictly within one taxing jurisdiction, the multistate regime comes into effect.

Almost every U.S. state taxes the recognized income of proprietors, corporations, and other entities that have a presence in the state.[8] All of those states have constitutional provisions allowing an income tax and aggregated legislation defining the tax base, specifying when the tax is due and from whom, and otherwise administering the tax. A separate revenue department interprets the law and administers the annual taxing process.

Every one of these systems is distinct and different in multiple ways—the name and location of the chief tax official, the definitions of what is taxable and deductible and what is not, the due dates and filing requirements applicable to the tax, and the taxpayer-friendliness of the audit and appeals system.

Despite the no-new-taxes pledge of many politicians on election day, income taxes are still popular in the United States. Income taxes are levied by states, cities, counties, villages, commuter districts, stadium boards, and numerous other bodies that have been granted taxing authority by their states. And politicians think that they can gain economic development advantages over their neighbors by granting special tax breaks—"Locate your assembly plant here, and we'll exempt one-half of your employees' wages from the state income tax"—so the laws are constantly changing. By one estimate, a business taxpayer might be exposed to almost 500 different income taxing jurisdictions in the United States.

LO.5

Identify the sources of tax law applicable to a taxpayer operating in more than one U.S. state.

---

[8]Some states tax the investment income of individuals, but those taxes are not addressed in this chapter. Nevada, South Dakota, Washington, and Wyoming do not have a corporate income tax. Washington uses a business and occupation tax; several states impose a tax on the gross receipts (not on the net income) of a business.

TAX IN THE NEWS   So Where Did You Work Today?

The dream of many intellectual-property employees is to work at home with the employer's computer and communications equipment. Not only is the dress code there targeted to the worker's comfort, but the employee can avoid the time and cost of commuting. The employer saves by not having to provide office space.

But what are the tax effects when the employee or independent contractor submits work to an employer located in a different state? The general rule has been that state income taxes fall in full in the state where the work is done. Is this still the rule, or must the employee apportion the hours of the day among the various states that receive the work product? If so, on what basis should such apportionment be made? Furthermore, how will the worker reduce any potential taxation of the same income by more than one state?

The Federal government has stayed out of the fray and has not attempted to force states and localities to use a single common tax formula and administrative organization. Only in **Public Law 86–272** has Congress attempted to bring order to the multistate income tax process. This 1957 pro-interstate commerce provision exempts from state and local taxation a sale of tangible personal property where the only contact with the state was the **solicitation** activity of the taxpayer.

In the past 20 or 30 years, the states have taken some steps to coordinate their activities. Several groups of states exchange information as to the seller and purchase price for cross-border sales so that income and sales/use tax obligations can be computed and collected properly. A few states have reciprocity arrangements with their neighbors to straighten out the complications that can arise when an employee lives in one jurisdiction but works in another.

EXAMPLE 21

Harry works at the Illinois plant of Big Corporation, but he lives in Iowa. His wages are subject to Iowa tax. If Illinois and Iowa had a reciprocity agreement in place, either (1) Big would collect and remit income tax at Iowa's rates and remit the tax to the Iowa revenue department or (2) Big would collect Illinois tax, and that state would keep the withholdings paid, in full satisfaction of Harry's Iowa tax obligations for the year.

About half of the states are members of the **Multistate Tax Commission (MTC)**, a body that proposes legislation to the states and localities and issues its own regulations and informational materials. A majority of the non-MTC members follow the agency's rules virtually without exception. The Uniform Division of Income for Tax Purposes Act (UDITPA) is made available to states and localities interested in a coherent set of income assignment rules, and it forms the basis for the income tax statutes in most of the MTC member states.

The MTC, which provides very specific formulas and definitions to be used in computing state taxable income, is as close as the states have come so far to a multilateral tax treaty process. If all states and localities followed all of the MTC rules, taxpayers would be unable to gain any "border advantages" or disadvantages. But political concerns likely will keep this coordinated result from ever happening.

16-3b Tax Issues

The key issues facing a state or locality in drafting and implementing an income tax model are the same as those facing the international tax community. The results of the deliberative process, though, have produced somewhat different sets of rules and terminology.

Authority to Tax

A business is taxable in the state in which it is resident, organized, or incorporated. Tax liabilities also arise in other jurisdictions where **nexus** exists; that is, a sufficient presence in the other state has been established on an ongoing basis. Such presence might come about because the corporation was organized there, the proprietor lives there, an in-state customer made a purchase, or the business employed people or equipment within the borders of the state. The precise activities that create nexus vary from jurisdiction to jurisdiction, although most of the taxing states follow the broad rules of Public Law 86–272 and the regulations of the MTC.[9]

When a taxpayer operates in more than one state, total taxable income for the year is split among the jurisdictions in which the operations take place. Portions of the total income amount are assigned to each of the business locations, so several tax returns and payments will be due. For a taxpayer considering an expansion of operations, the tax adviser can make an important contribution in helping to decide with which state(s) nexus will be created.

The nexus rules of state/local taxation serve much the same function as do the permanent establishment provisions of international taxation. The PE standards are based in the language of the applicable tax treaty and interpretive court decisions. They look for real estate holdings and manufacturing equipment. Permanent establishment is found when an office in the host country participates significantly in the making of a sales or service contract.

In-depth coverage can be found on this book's companion website: www.cengagebrain.com	**4 DIGGING DEEPER**

Income Sourcing

The multistate business, like its international counterpart, must divide the taxable income generated for the year among the states in which it operates. Then tax liability is computed for the states in which nexus has been established. The computational template illustrated in Exhibit 16.3 indicates how most states derive their shares of the entity's aggregate taxable income. Usually, the starting point for this computation is Federal taxable income.

State modification items come about because each state creates its own tax base in the legislative process, and some of the rules adopted may differ from those used in the Internal Revenue Code. The modification items reflect such differences in the tax base. For example, modifications might be created to reflect the following differences between state and Federal taxable income.

LO.6

Apply computational principles designed to compute state taxable income for a taxpayer operating in more than one U.S. state.

EXHIBIT 16.3	**Computing State Income Tax Liability**

	Federal taxable income
±	State modification items
	State tax base
±	Nonbusiness income/loss (for allocation)
	Business income (for apportionment)
×	Apportionment percentage for the state
	Taxable income apportioned to the state
±	Taxable income/loss allocated to the state
	State taxable income/loss
	State tax, per tax table or rate schedule
−	State's tax credits
	Net state tax liability

---

[9]Income and sales/use tax regimes use different nexus standards. Generally, it has been "easier" to establish nexus for sales/use tax purposes; most states have a separate set of rules to determine the taxability of income or a transaction. But recent U.S. Supreme Court cases apply a "physical presence" test for the sales/use tax, a somewhat stricter test than the income tax nexus rules of the MTC. This chapter concentrates on income tax nexus provisions.

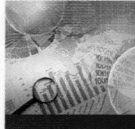

TAX PLANNING STRATEGIES Nexus: To Have or Have Not

FRAMEWORK FOCUS: TAX RATE

Strategy: Shift Net Income from High-Tax Jurisdictions to Low-Tax Jurisdictions.

Most taxpayers try to avoid establishing nexus in a new state, for example, by providing a sales representative with a cash auto allowance rather than a company car, by restricting the location of inventory to only a few states, or by limiting a salesperson's activities to those that are protected by the solicitation standard of Public Law 86–272. This effort to avoid nexus stems in part from the additional compliance burden that falls upon the taxpayer when a new set of income tax returns, information forms, and deadlines must be dealt with in the new state.

Another concern is that the marginal tax rate that applies to the net taxable income generated by the taxpayer may increase. Such a tax increase occurs, of course, only when the applicable tax rate in the new state is higher than the rate that would apply in the home state. If a business already is based in a tax-friendly state such as Florida or Texas or in a no-tax state such as Nevada, its aggregate tax liability is sure to increase.

Still, nexus is not necessarily a bad thing. Consider what happens if a business based in California, Maryland, Wisconsin, or another high-tax jurisdiction purposely creates nexus in a low- or no-tax state. If the new state applies a lower marginal rate than is available in the home state or offers special exemptions or exclusions that match the taxpayer's operations, the aggregate tax bill can decrease. Then the planning efforts include determining which activities will *create* nexus in the new jurisdiction and meeting or maintaining that standard.

For instance, an entertainer based in Manhattan is subject to the high income taxes of New York City and New York State. By establishing a permanent office in Tennessee, nexus will be created, and some portion of the taxpayer's income will be subject to taxation there, instead of New York. These are permanent savings, accruing immediately to after-tax income and the share price of the stock of the taxpayer.

- The state might allow a different cost recovery schedule.
- The state might tax interest income from its own bonds or from those of other states.
- The state might allow a deduction for Federal income taxes paid.
- The state might disallow a deduction for payment of its own income taxes.
- The state might allow a net operating loss (NOL) deduction only for losses generated in the state.
- The state's NOL deduction might reflect different carryover periods than Federal law allows.

State tax modifications are made even if the taxpayer operates only in its home state.

Allocation and Apportionment The next step in computing state taxable income is to allocate items of nonbusiness income and loss to the states in which such items are derived. For instance, a Kansas entity might recognize some net income from the rental of a Missouri office building to a tenant. The net rental amount is in Federal taxable income, but it must appear only and fully in Missouri taxable income. So by means of the modification process, the rents are removed from the taxable income for both states and then added back into Missouri taxable income. The allocation process is very much like the income-sourcing procedures employed in international taxation.

EXAMPLE

22

HammerCo reports $400,000 in taxable income for the year from its sales operations based exclusively in Mississippi and Arkansas. HammerCo recognized net rent income of $60,000 from a building it owns in Mississippi. It earned $20,000 in interest income from Arkansas bonds. This amount is excluded from Federal taxable income, and it is taxed under Mississippi law, but not by Arkansas. HammerCo also claimed a Federal NOL carryforward of $75,000 from a prior period. Mississippi follows Federal law for NOLs, but Arkansas does not allow such carryovers. Thus, Federal taxable income totals $385,000 ($400,000 + $60,000 − $75,000).

continued

HammerCo's modifications to determine the state tax base, after starting with Federal taxable income, are as follows.

Mississippi		Arkansas	
Amount	**Modification**	**Amount**	**Modification**
− $60,000	Total nonbusiness income	− $60,000	Total nonbusiness income
+ $20,000	Municipal bond interest income	+ $75,000	Remove Federal NOL deduction
+ $60,000	Net rent income from Mississippi rentals		

The business income of the taxpayer is **apportioned** among the states in which it operates. The apportionment percentage for the state is multiplied times the apportionable income of the taxpayer to measure the extent of the taxpayer's exposure to the state's income tax. The application of the apportionment percentage is illustrated in Exhibit 16.3.

Most states apply an apportionment procedure involving three factors, each meant to estimate the taxpayer's relative activities in the state.

- The **sales factor** = In-state sales/total sales.
- The **payroll factor** = In-state payroll/total payroll.
- The **property factor** = In-state property/total property.

The state's apportionment percentage is the average of these three factors. This three-factor apportionment can be traced to the earliest days of state income taxation. Today, most states add additional weight to the sales factor, believing it to be the most accurate and measurable reflection of the taxpayer's in-state activities. It is common to "double-weight" the sales factor. A few states use only the sales factor in the apportionment procedure.

 TAX IN THE NEWS   **State Deficits Change How Revenue Departments Work**

The current crunch in state budget making has lasted for several years, and new sources of revenue and new attitudes toward enforcement are prime goals of state and local operations.

Much of this budget squeeze has been felt in the increased attention toward sales and use taxes, with many states now dedicating more resources toward those taxes than toward the individual and corporate income taxes. Collecting unpaid use taxes on Internet and mail-order sales and finding new taxpayers to add to the income and sales/use tax rolls are prime enforcement targets for many states.

But a sustained revenue shortfall tends to make some revenue departments more desperate or more creative. In either event, we can observe the use of new or recycled approaches to tax enforcement that can surprise the taxpayer who has not been paying attention. Some of the techniques observed lately include the following.

- Applying local business and occupation taxes, payroll taxes, and license fees to telecommuters and work-at-home entrepreneurs and creative workers.

- Increasing audit staff and travel resources, resulting in increased and better-targeted auditing of returns.

- Temporary increases in underpayment and nonfiling fines and penalties and reductions in grace periods for late filing or payment.

- Adding "unpaid use tax" lines to the income tax return. This does result in some revenue collected from taxpayers who have guilty consciences or high levels of integrity, but mainly it sets up the taxpayer for penalties on a later audit, when the sworn-to-be-complete income tax return shows a zero balance on the use tax line.

- Refusing legislatively to adopt certain Federal tax breaks, such as special cost recovery elections or the increases in deductible or tax-deferred retirement and education allowances.

- Increased use of private collection agencies to find delinquent taxpayers and produce dollars for the state treasury.

EXAMPLE
23

LinkCo, Inc., operates in two states. It reports the following results for the year. LinkCo's apportionment percentages for both states are computed as shown. Amounts are stated in millions of dollars.

	State A	State B	Totals
Sales	$30	$20	$50
Payroll	40	20	60
Property	45	5	50
Sales factor	$30/$50 = .6	$20/$50 = .4	
Payroll factor	$40/$60 = .67	$20/$60 = .33	
Property factor	$45/$50 = .9	$5/$50 = .1	
Apportionment percentage	(.6 + .67 + .9) ÷ 3 = .72	(.4 + .33 + .1) ÷ 3 = .28	

Note that 100% of LinkCo's income is apportioned between the two states: 72% to State A and 28% to State B.

Now assume that State A double-weights the sales factor. LinkCo's apportionment percentages are computed as follows.

	State A	State B	Totals
Sales	$30	$20	$50
Payroll	40	20	60
Property	45	5	50
Sales factor	$30/$50 = .6	$20/$50 = .4	
Payroll factor	$40/$60 = .67	$20/$60 = .33	
Property factor	$45/$50 = .9	$5/$50 = .1	
Apportionment percentage	(.6 + .6 + .67 + .9) ÷ 4 = .69	(.4 + .33 + .1) ÷ 3 = .28	

State B's apportionment computations are not affected by A's double-weighting of the sales factor. The percentages now do not total 100%. The effect of the special weighting is to reduce LinkCo's tax liability in A. This is likely LinkCo's "home state" given the location of its personnel and plant and equipment.

Finally, assume that State B uses a "sales-factor-only" weighting. The A apportionment percentage is .69, and the B percentage is .4. Now the apportionment percentages *exceed* 100%.

Most states follow the regulations of the MTC and the outline of the UDITPA in defining and applying the apportionment factors. But because the states do not follow identical rules in the makeup of the factors, the apportionment percentages seldom total precisely to 100 percent. Some other aspects of the three-factor approach include the following.

- Sales are assigned using the tax accounting methods of the taxpayer. Sales are assigned using the "ultimate destination" concept; that is, a sale is usually assigned to the state of the purchaser.

- If a sale is made into a state with no income tax or a state with which the taxpayer has not established nexus, tax is likely escaped. But over a third of the states apply a **throwback rule** that causes the sale to be sourced to the state of the seller (i.e., by overriding the "ultimate destination" rule).

- Payroll is assigned to the state in which the employee's services primarily are performed. Payroll includes wages, bonuses, commissions, and taxable fringe benefits. Some states exclude officer compensation because it can distort the computations. Some states exclude contributions to a § 401(k) plan.

- The property factor uses an average historical cost basis, net of accumulated depreciation. Idle property is ignored, but construction in progress is included. Property in transit is assigned to the state of its presumed destination.

- Property leased but not owned by the taxpayer is included in the property factor at eight times the annual rentals paid.

FINANCIAL DISCLOSURE INSIGHTS **State/Local Taxes and the Tax Expense**

In applying GAAP principles for a business entity, state and local tax expenses are found in several places in the taxpayer's financial reports. In the tax footnote, the state/local tax costs often are reported in dollar and/or percentage terms, in both current and deferred components. The following are examples of state/local tax expenses that were reported in a recent year.

	Current State/Local Tax Expense ($ million)	Deferred State/Local Tax Expense ($ million)
Eli Lilly	$ 49	($ 1)
ExxonMobil	340	221
Ryder Systems	6	3
Ford Motor	7	(59)

Corporations also report permanent book-tax differences in determining the effective tax rate for the reporting period. In a recent year, Berkshire Hathaway reported that state/local permanent book-tax differences reduced its effective income tax rate by about 1.5 percentage points. Ford Motor reported a similar rate reduction, but Ryder Systems's effective tax rate increased by about 6 percentage points for the year due to such permanent book-tax differences.

Many states use specialized apportionment percentages for industries whose sales and asset profile is not properly reflected in the traditional three-factor formula. For instance, the airline industry might divide its income based on passenger-miles beginning and ending in the state. Truckers might be able to divide taxable income among the states based on in-state vehicle-trips or tons-per-day. Communications companies might use the in-state miles of cable or number of wireless devices to make up an apportionment formula.

In-depth coverage can be found on this book's companion website: www.cengagebrain.com   **5 DIGGING DEEPER**

The Unitary Theory About 30 states use a unitary approach in computing the apportionment factors. Conglomerates are required, or can elect, to base their computations on the data for all of their affiliated corporations, not just the legal entities that do business with the state. Affiliates included under the unitary theory share a majority ownership with a parent or group of shareholders. They also often share data processing, sales force, and marketing resources.

The *combined return* that the unitary business files includes much more data than might be expected on a separate-entity basis, but the taxing jurisdictions often believe that the unitary figures offer a more accurate reflection of the taxpayer's activity within the state and that, therefore, a more accurate tax liability can be derived.

Unitary Taxation

Kipp Industries is a holding company for three subsidiaries: GrapeCo operating in California, PotatoCo operating in Idaho, and BratCo operating in Germany. Only GrapeCo has nexus with California. But because California is a unitary state, the California apportionment percentage is computed also using PotatoCo and BratCo data.

EXAMPLE 24

Return to the facts of Example 24. If Kipp Industries files a waters'-edge election, the unitary group that files a California income tax return can be limited to GrapeCo and PotatoCo since BratCo operates outside the United States.

EXAMPLE 25

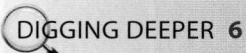 DIGGING DEEPER 6 | In-depth coverage can be found on this book's companion website: www.cengagebrain.com

Concept Summary 16.2 sets out some of the key issues in corporate multistate income taxation.

Concept Summary 16.2
Corporate Multistate Income Taxation

1. A taxpayer is subject to income tax in the state in which it resides or is organized.

2. A taxpayer is subject to income tax in states where it has a business presence and enjoys the resources of the host state in conducting its operations.

3. A multistate taxpayer must divide its aggregate taxable income for the year among the states in which it conducts business.

4. Nonbusiness income is allocated to the state in which it is generated.

5. Business income is apportioned among the states in which the taxpayer has nexus.

6. Apportionment usually is conducted using a formula based on the relative sales, employment, and asset holdings in the various states.

7. The sales factor uses a destination test, while the payroll and property factors use a source test.

8. Most states weight the sales factor higher than the other apportionment factors.

9. Some states apply a special apportionment formula for certain industries when the traditional three-factor formula could distort the income division procedure in some way.

10. About 30 states employ the unitary theory in deriving the apportionment factors, using the data from a group of corporations to compute the apportionment formula. Other states allow or require a consolidated return from a conglomerate.

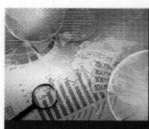

TAX PLANNING STRATEGIES   Where Should My Income Go?

FRAMEWORK FOCUS: TAX RATE

Strategy: Shift Net Income from High-Tax Jurisdictions to Low-Tax Jurisdictions.

Every state defines its apportionment factors in a slightly different manner. The multistate taxpayer needs to keep track of these differences and place activities in the state that will serve them best.

Planning with the sales factor includes a detailed analysis of the destination point of the product shipments for the year, especially when the firm has customers in low- and no-tax states. The property factor should include only assets that are used in the taxpayer's trade or business, not the investment, leasing, or research functions. Permanently idle property is excluded from the property factor as well. The payroll factor can be manipulated by hiring independent contractors to carry out certain sales and distribution work or by relocating highly paid managers to low-tax states.

By setting up an investment holding company in a no- or low-tax state such as Delaware or Nevada and transferring

income-producing securities and intangible assets to that entity, significant tax reductions can be obtained. When the net investment income is paid back to the parent corporation, the dividends received deduction eliminates the tax liability there.

The unitary system does not always result in a tax increase, although the additional record-keeping burden of operating in a unitary state cannot be understated. If the affiliates make available less profitable operations or a presence in low- or no-tax states or countries, the current tax liability may be reduced. The record-keeping burden can be reduced if the taxpayer makes a waters'-edge election, which allows it to include only affiliate data from within the boundaries of the United States.

16-4 **COMMON CHALLENGES**

LO.7

Synthesize the international and multistate tax systems and identify common issues faced by both systems.

Practical and policy issues facing the U.S. states, developed countries, and the taxpayers operating in all of them show a great degree of similarity between the multistate and international tax regimes. Terminology may differ, and the evolution of tax solutions may take radically different paths, but the key issues that face the multijurisdictional community are at once challenging and rewarding.

16-4a **Authority to Tax**

The old-economy orientation of the nexus and permanent establishment rules presents great difficulty in today's economy, as jurisdictions attempt to describe the income and sales/use tax base fairly. An electronic presence also exploits the resources of the host country and should trigger a tax in the visited jurisdiction. Mathematically, the apportionment and sourcing rules should result in only a modest tax liability in the host jurisdiction, but it is improper to maintain that no presence exists and no tax should be paid in the context of a toll-free telephone number or Internet sale.

But perhaps the notion of *presence* is becoming less important over time, and the level of resource usage in the host jurisdiction also is declining. For example, just-in-time manufacturing and purchasing strategies reduce the need for warehousing by some taxpayers. Human capital can be dispersed through telecommuting, video conferencing, and project rotation using work-group software that provides acceptable levels of data security. If the future is to a great degree wireless, perhaps the standard of presence will diminish, as the buyer and the seller are both "everywhere."

16-4b **Division of Income**

The multistate apportionment procedure could use an overhaul. The fact that a majority of states change the weighting of the sales factor indicates that some other income division method might better serve taxpayers and governments. Three-factor apportionment was designed for an age of traveling sales representatives and sales of built, grown, and manufactured goods. Sales reps were assigned territories they could drive through on short notice, so they usually lived close to their customer base. In that case, the sales and payroll factors could be highly redundant.

Today, with communication and distribution systems more highly developed, the sales factor appears incrementally to be the preferred income-sourcing device. Sales of goods and services should be assigned based on a destination test so that the transaction is assigned to the state of the purchaser.

The three-factor formula further breaks down for income derived from specialized industries, as evidenced by the special computational methods allowed by many states. Perhaps the economy is so specialized today that income simply cannot be assigned by the use of one simple formula. Nonetheless, more uniformity among the states as to definitions and computational rules for the factors would be welcome.

The U.S. Treasury has held hearings in the last decade concerning the adoption of an apportionment approach to the sourcing of international taxable income. Although a formulary apportionment would represent a more reliable and predictable method of dividing multinational income and deduction amounts, the data collection burden that such a system would create may be too much to expect from most of the trading partners in the short term. Moreover, the model treaties developed by the United States and the Organization for Economic Cooperation and Development (OECD) include language relating to the income-sourcing rules and transfer pricing at arm's length, not an apportionment approach.

16-4c **Transfer Pricing**

The transfer pricing system used in international trade requires the taxpayer to keep a database of comparable prices and transactions, even though often no such comparability

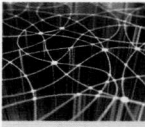

BRIDGE DISCIPLINE   Bridge to Cost Accounting and Executive Compensation

Multijurisdictional companies operate across state and country borders. The transfer price used by a company can have a significant effect on the amount of profits subject to taxation within a particular taxing jurisdiction. Companies face other concerns when establishing transfer pricing policies. For example, the internal determination of how a division of the company is performing may be based on transfer pricing between related entities within the global group. Furthermore, the compensation of the managers within those divisions may be tied directly to divisional performance.

If an intercompany price is set in a manner that optimizes the global tax position, a separate cost accounting policy may be required to determine an entity's profitability for purposes of compensating employees. Tax advisers often face resistance from operations managers when suggesting improved transfer pricing methods, because such improvements often change the traditional division of profits among different parts of the business.

exists. Especially when dealing with proprietary goods and design, it may be impossible to find comparable goods and, therefore, an acceptable transfer price for them. One solution to this situation would be to allow additional definitions of comparable goods, or of ranges of acceptable transfer prices, perhaps subjected to audit on a rotating five-year basis. The use of advance pricing agreements further allows a greater degree of control by the governments in data collection and analysis, ideally prior to the undertaking of the sales or manufacturing transactions.

DIGGING DEEPER 7   In-depth coverage can be found on this book's companion website: www.cengagebrain.com

16-4d Tax Havens

When taxpayers perceive effective tax rates as too high, planning usually includes seeking out a **tax haven** . If income-producing securities or profitable service operations can be moved to another jurisdiction, ideally one with significantly lower marginal tax rates on that type of income, permanent tax savings can be achieved. A tax haven usually applies minimal rules for a taxpayer to establish residency, and it adopts little or no cooperation in international exchanges of tax and financial information. The Bahamas, Monaco, and Panama, among other countries, often are seen as tax havens.

When a government witnesses a loss of its tax base due to the transfer of assets and income out of the jurisdiction, anti-tax-haven legislation is discussed, but it seldom is effective. The U.S. international tax regime shows several distinct attempts to find and tax income moved offshore, but those taxes collect only nominal revenues in the typical tax year. Income-shifting devices currently used by multistate taxpayers have been attacked by the states in various ways, but legislators hesitate to be too aggressive, probably out of fear of the state being branded "anti-business."

Perhaps a separate set of nexus rules could be created to address the most portable types of income, such as that from interest and dividends. But this difficult problem likely needs a multilateral solution, which is unlikely to be found in the short term among states and countries, each with unique revenue shortfalls and political profiles.

DIGGING DEEPER 8   In-depth coverage can be found on this book's companion website: www.cengagebrain.com

FINANCIAL DISCLOSURE INSIGHTS **Deferred Tax Assets Overseas**

U.S. corporations are not the only entities that can have balance sheets with excessive deferred tax accounts. Restrictive regulatory rules as to how non-U.S. banks compute their capital amounts tend to create large deferred tax assets for them.

Deferred tax assets do not affect the entity's actual cash balances, but they can affect the stock price in the short term. Even professional equity analysts can have difficulty understanding announcements of tax adjustments to the balance sheet. Regulations limit the level of deferred tax assets that banks can hold in a given country, and political pressure to increase those limits is appearing as the proportion of shareholder equity that is made up of deferred tax assets has grown significantly in the last five years.

The following are estimates from JPMorgan Chase of the magnitude of deferred tax asset balances for selected banks overseas and banks in the United States.

	Percentage of Shareholder Equity Constituted by Deferred Tax Assets
Dexia	44%
Deutsche Bank	24
Monte dei Paschi	23
UBS	21
Credit Suisse	20
U.S. banks, average	11

16-4e Interjurisdictional Agreements

Treaties are documents that address many issues other than the taxable income computation. They involve several players within the governmental structure, and they take several years to draft and adopt. Treaties involving the United States tend to be only bilateral, meaning that it is difficult to anticipate and coordinate the interaction of several treaties as they apply to a single taxpayer.

At the multistate level, the Federal government has been slow to take up issues involving a synchronization of the income tax systems used by the states. Although this reluctance may be partly for strictly constitutional reasons, it is largely because of the

BRIDGE DISCIPLINE **Bridge to Economic Development and Political Science**

The tax professional occasionally is in a position to negotiate with a state or city taxing jurisdiction to garner tax relief for a client as an incentive to locate a plant or distribution center in that geographic area. In times when construction budgets are high and interstate competition is fierce to attract or retain businesses that are making location decisions, such tax concessions can be significant.

For instance, to encourage a business to build a large distribution center in the area, community leaders might be agreeable to:

- Paying for roads, sewer, water, and other improvements through taxpayer bonds;

- Reducing property taxes by 50 percent for the first 10 years of the center's operations; and

- Permanently excluding any distribution-related vehicles and equipment from the personal property tax.

An incentive-granting community provides the concessions even though the influx of new workers will place a great strain on public school facilities and likely necessitate improvements in traffic patterns and other infrastructure.

Consider the position of a large employer that has been located in the area for more than 50 years. By how much should it be willing to absorb the tax increases that result when economic development concessions are used to attract new, perhaps temporary, businesses to the area? Should the employer challenge the constitutionality of the grant of such sizable tax breaks to some, but not all, business taxpayers in the jurisdiction? Should higher "impact fees" be assessed on new developments?

Does your analysis change if the new business competes with the longtime resident for sales? For employees? For political power?

difficulties presented by the lack of uniformity among the states' tax laws and enforcement efforts.

But the future must hold a greater degree of cooperation among various taxing jurisdictions, at least in the trading of information and the coordination of enforcement efforts. The United States must create additional treaties or information-sharing agreements with countries in South America and Africa. And the future of the European Union probably holds a series of revised agreements addressing tax issues with the United States.

Procedural developments may accomplish the same result. For instance, block filing by S corporations and their shareholders with various states accomplishes a number of income division and information-sharing goals. In this context and others, sharing data, while still respecting the confidentiality needs of the taxpayer and requirements of the governments, represents a technologically sound method of collecting taxes in today's multijurisdictional economy.

DIGGING DEEPER 9   In-depth coverage can be found on this book's companion website: www.cengagebrain.com

REFOCUS ON THE BIG PICTURE

GOING INTERNATIONAL

Simply selling into a foreign jurisdiction probably will not trigger any overseas income tax consequences. However, income earned from foreign sales is taxed currently to VoiceCo in the United States. By establishing a CFC in Ireland, VoiceCo benefits from income tax deferral. As long as the income is not distributed to VoiceCo and as long as the income is not Subpart F income, VoiceCo can avoid taxes on the profits of VoiceCo-Ireland. If VoiceCo receives dividends from its foreign subsidiary, it can claim foreign tax credits, which help alleviate the double taxation that would otherwise result.

What If?

VoiceCo is considering building a new manufacturing facility in another state in the United States. How will VoiceCo's expansion decision be affected by state tax considerations? In making the decision to expand, VoiceCo should consider a variety of state tax issues including whether the state imposes a corporate income tax at all and, if so, whether the state requires unitary reporting. Other relevant issues affecting the tax calculation in the state include what apportionment formula is used by the state and whether the state has a throwback rule.

Suggested Readings

Grant Gross, "Internet Tax Moratorium Extended Again," **www.pcworld.com**, December 15, 2014.

Albena Peters, "Controlled Foreign Corporation Rules in the United States, Canada, and Germany," *Corporate Taxation*, March/April 2012.

Michael S. Schadewald and William A. Raabe, "Present and Future Directions in Federal and State Taxation of Income from Cross Border Trade," *TAXES*, April 1997.

Brett R. Wilkinson and Katherine Wilkinson, "The Creditability of Foreign Taxes," *The Tax Adviser*, January 2014.

Key Terms

Allocate, 16-24

Apportioned, 16-25

Arm's length price, 16-16

Check-the-box Regulations, 16-17

Controlled foreign corporations (CFCs), 16-14

Deemed-paid credit, 16-13

Effectively connected income, 16-19

FDAP, 16-19

Foreign tax credit, 16-6

Inbound taxation, 16-3

Income tax treaties, 16-5

Multistate Tax Commission (MTC), 16-22

Nexus, 16-22

Nonresident alien (NRA), 16-18

Outbound taxation, 16-3

Payroll factor, 16-25

Permanent establishment (PE), 16-5

Property factor, 16-25

Public Law 86–272, 16-22

Sales factor, 16-25

Separate foreign tax credit income categories, 16-12

Solicitation, 16-22

Subpart F income, 16-14

Tax haven, 16-30

Throwback rule, 16-26

Unitary approach, 16-27

U.S. shareholder, 16-15

Waters'-edge election, 16-28

Computational Exercises

1. **LO.3** Cordero, Inc., is a calendar-year taxpayer and a CFC for the entire tax year. Vance Company, a U.S. corporation, owns 75% of Cordero's one class of stock for the entire year. Cordero's Subpart F income for the year is $450,000, and no distributions were made to the parent. Determine Vance's gross income from the Subpart F constructive dividend from Cordero.

2. **LO.3** Enders, Inc., a domestic corporation, reports $290,000 total taxable income for the year, consisting of $208,800 in U.S.-source business profits and $81,200 of income from foreign investment securities. Overseas tax authorities withheld $24,000 in income taxes on the investment income. Enders's U.S. tax before the FTC is $78,000. Compute Enders's foreign tax credit for the year.

3. **LO.6** Castle Corporation conducts business and has nexus in states A, B, and C. All of the states use a three-equal-factors apportionment formula, with the factors evenly weighted. Castle generates $555,000 apportionable income and $75,000 allocable income related to state C activities. Castle's sales, payroll, and property are divided evenly among the three states. Compute taxable income for:
   a. State A.
   b. State B.
   c. State C.

4. **LO.6** Fillon operates manufacturing facilities in states A and B. Fillon has nexus with both states; apportionment factors are .70 for A and .30 for B. Taxable income for the year totaled $150,000, with a $200,000 A profit and a $50,000 B loss. Calculate taxable income for the year for:
   a. State A.
   b. State B.

5. **LO.6** Beckett Corporation has nexus with states A and B. Apportionable income for the year totals $800,000. Beckett's apportionment factors for the year use the following data. Compute Beckett's B taxable income for the year; B uses a three-factor apportionment formula, with a double-weighted sales factor.

	State A	State B	Totals
Sales	$960,000	$640,000	$1,600,000
Property	180,000	–0–	180,000
Payroll	220,000	–0–	220,000

6. **LO.6** Chirp Corporation owns two subsidiaries. Song, located in State A, generated $500,000 taxable income this year. Bird, located in State B, generated a $100,000 loss for the period.

   a.   Determine Song's taxable income in States A and B, assuming that the subsidiaries constitute independent corporations under the tax law.

   b.   How does your answer change if the companies constitute a unitary business?

Problems

7. **LO.3** BlueCo, a domestic corporation, incorporates GreenCo, a new wholly owned entity in Germany. Under both German and U.S. legal principles, this entity is a corporation. BlueCo faces a 35% U.S. tax rate.

    GreenCo earns $1,500,000 in net profits from its German activities, and GreenCo makes no dividend distributions to BlueCo. How much Federal income tax will BlueCo pay for the current year as a result of GreenCo's earnings, assuming that there is no deemed dividend under Subpart F? Ignore any foreign tax credit (FTC) implications.

8. **LO.3** Evaluate this statement: It is unfair that the United States taxes its citizens and residents on their worldwide income.

9. **LO.3** Describe the different approaches used by countries to tax the earnings of their citizens and residents generated outside the borders of the country.

Decision Making   10. **LO.3** Create, Inc., produces inventory in its foreign manufacturing plants for sale in the United States. Its foreign manufacturing assets have a tax book value of $5 million and a fair market value of $15 million. Its assets related to the sales activity have a tax book value of $2 million and a fair market value of $5 million. Create's interest expense totaled $400,000 for the current year.

   a.   What amount of interest expense is allocated and apportioned to foreign-source income using the tax book value method? What amount of Create's interest expense is allocated and apportioned to foreign-source income using the fair market value method?

   b.   If Create wants to maximize its FTC, which method should it use?

11. **LO.3** Chock, a U.S. corporation, purchases inventory for resale from distributors within the United States and resells this inventory at a $1 million profit to customers outside the United States. Title to the goods passes outside the United States. What is the source of Chock's inventory sales income?

12. **LO.3** Willa, a U.S. corporation, owns the rights to a patent related to a medical device. Willa licenses the rights to use the patent to IrishCo, which uses the patent in its manufacturing facility located in Ireland. What is the source of the $1 million royalty income received by Willa from IrishCo for the use of the patent?

13. **LO.3** USCo incurred $100,000 in interest expense for the current year. The tax book value of USCo's assets generating foreign-source income is $5 million. The tax book value of USCo's assets generating U.S.-source income is $45 million. How much of the interest expense is allocated and apportioned to foreign-source income?

14. **LO.3** QuinnCo could not claim all of the income taxes it paid to Japan as a foreign tax credit (FTC) this year. What computational limit probably kept QuinnCo from taking its full FTC? Explain.

15. **LO.3** FoldIt, a U.S. business, paid income taxes to Mexico relative to profitable sales of shipping boxes it made in that country. Can it claim a deduction for these taxes in computing U.S. taxable income? A tax credit? Both? Explain.

16. **LO.3** Klein, a domestic corporation, receives a $10,000 dividend from ForCo, a wholly owned foreign corporation. The deemed-paid (indirect) foreign tax credit associated with this dividend is $3,000. What is the total gross income included in Klein's tax return as a result of this dividend?

17. **LO.3** ABC, Inc., a domestic corporation, reports $50 million of taxable income, including $15 million of general limitation foreign-source taxable income, on which ABC paid $5 million in foreign income taxes. The U.S. tax rate is 35%. What is ABC's foreign tax credit?

18. **LO.3** Mary, a U.S. citizen, is the sole shareholder of CanCo, a Canadian corporation. During its first year of operations, CanCo earns $14 million of foreign-source taxable income, pays $6 million of Canadian income taxes, and distributes a $2 million dividend to Mary. Can Mary claim a deemed-paid (indirect) foreign tax credit on her Form 1040 with respect to receipt of a dividend distribution from CanCo? Why or why not?

19. **LO.3** ABC, Inc., a domestic corporation, owns 100% of HighTax, a foreign corporation. HighTax has $50 million of undistributed E & P, all of which is attributable to general limitation income, and $30 million of foreign income taxes paid. HighTax distributes a $5 million dividend to ABC. The dividend, which is subject to a 5% foreign withholding tax, is ABC's only item of income during the year. ABC's marginal U.S. tax rate is 35%. How much foreign tax credit and carryover is produced by the dividend?

20. **LO.3** USCo, a domestic corporation, reports worldwide taxable income of $1.5 million, including a $400,000 dividend from ForCo, a wholly owned foreign corporation. ForCo's undistributed E & P totals $16 million, and it has paid $10 million of foreign income taxes attributable to these earnings. All foreign income is in the general limitation basket. What is USCo's deemed-paid (indirect) foreign tax credit related to the dividend received (before consideration of any limitation)?

21. **LO.3** USCo, a domestic corporation, reports worldwide taxable income of $500,000, including a $300,000 dividend from ForCo, a wholly owned foreign corporation. ForCo's undistributed E & P totals $1 million, and it has paid $200,000 of foreign income taxes attributable to these earnings. All foreign income is in the general limitation basket. What is USCo's deemed-paid (indirect) foreign tax credit related to the dividend received (before consideration of any limitation)?

22. **LO.3** Fleming, Inc., a domestic corporation, operates in both Canada and the United States. This year, the business generated taxable income of $400,000 from foreign sources and $300,000 from U.S. sources. All of Fleming's foreign-source income is in the general limitation basket. Fleming's total worldwide taxable income is $700,000. Fleming pays Canadian taxes of $152,000. What is Fleming's allowed FTC for the tax year? Assume a 35% U.S. income tax rate.

23. **LO.3** Drake, Inc., a U.S. corporation, operates a branch sales office in Turkey. During the current year, Drake earned $500,000 in taxable income from U.S. sources and $100,000 in taxable income from sources in Turkey. Drake paid $40,000 in income taxes to Turkey. All of the income is characterized as general limitation income. Compute Drake's U.S. income tax liability after consideration of any foreign tax credit. Drake's U.S. tax rate is 35%.

24. **LO.3** Crank, Inc., a U.S. corporation, operates a branch sales office in Ghana. During the current year, Crank earned $200,000 in taxable income from U.S. sources and $50,000 in taxable income from sources in Ghana. Crank paid $5,000 in income taxes to Ghana. All of the income is characterized as general limitation income. Compute Crank's U.S. income tax liability after consideration of any foreign tax credit. Crank's U.S. tax rate is 35%.

Decision Making   25. **LO.3** Harold, Inc., a domestic corporation, earned $500,000 from foreign manufacturing activities on which it paid $150,000 of foreign income taxes. Harold's foreign sales income is taxed at a 45% foreign tax rate. Both sales and manufacturing income are assigned to the general limitation basket. What amount of foreign sales income can Harold earn without generating any excess FTCs for the current year? Assume a 35% U.S. rate.

26. **LO.3** Food, Inc., a domestic corporation, owns 70% of the stock of Drink, Inc., a foreign corporation. For the current year, Food receives a dividend of $20,000 from Drink. Drink's E & P (after taxes) and foreign taxes are $6 million and $800,000, respectively. What is Food's total gross income from receipt of this dividend if it elects to claim the FTC for deemed-paid foreign taxes?

27. **LO.3** Orion, Inc., a U.S. corporation, reports foreign-source income and pays foreign taxes for the tax year as follows.

	Income	Taxes
Passive category	$150,000	$ 13,000
General category	300,000	150,000

Orion's worldwide taxable income is $600,000, and U.S. taxes before the FTC are $210,000 (assume a 35% rate). What is Orion's U.S. tax liability after the FTC?

Issue ID   28. **LO.3** Discuss the policy reasons for the existence of the Subpart F rules. Give two examples of Subpart F income.

29. **LO.3** USCo owns 65% of the voting stock of LandCo, a Country X corporation. Terra, an unrelated Country Y corporation, owns the other 35% of LandCo. LandCo owns 100% of the voting stock of OceanCo, a Country Z corporation. Assuming that USCo is a U.S. shareholder, do LandCo and OceanCo meet the definition of a CFC? Explain.

30. **LO.3** Is a foreign corporation owned equally by 100 unrelated U.S. citizens considered to be a controlled foreign corporation (CFC)? Explain.

31. **LO.3** Hart Enterprises, a domestic corporation, owns 100% of OK, Ltd., an Irish corporation. OK's gross income for the year is $10 million. Determine whether any of the following transactions produce Subpart F gross income for the current year.

a.   OK earned $600,000 from sales of products purchased from Hart and sold to customers outside Ireland.

b.   OK earned $1 million from sales of products purchased from Hart and sold to customers in Ireland.

c.   OK earned $400,000 from sales of products purchased from unrelated suppliers and sold to customers in Germany.

d.   OK purchased raw materials from Hart, used these materials to manufacture finished goods, and sold these goods to customers in Italy. OK earned $300,000 from these sales.

e.   OK earned $50,000 in dividend income from Canada and Mexico passive investments.

32. **LO.3** HiramCo, a U.S. entity, operates a manufacturing business in both Mexico and Costa Rica, and it holds its investment portfolio in Sweden. How many foreign tax credit computations must HiramCo make? Be specific, and use the term *basket* in your answer.

33. **LO.4** Give a simple answer to Andre's question: "If I move to the United States, how will the Federal government tax my widget sales and capital gains?" Andre will be living in New York City, where state and local taxes are very high. Ignore the effects of tax treaties in your answer.

34. **LO.3** Skills, Inc., a U.S. corporation, reports current foreign-source income classi-fied in two different FTC income baskets. It earns $50,000 in passive foreign-source income, and it suffers a net loss of $30,000 in the general limitation basket. What is the numerator of Skills's FTC limitation formula for the passive basket in the current year? Explain.

35. **LO.3** Night, Inc., a domestic corporation, earned $300,000 from foreign manufactur-ing activities, on which it paid $90,000 of foreign income taxes. Night's foreign sales income is taxed at a 50% foreign tax rate. What amount of foreign sales income can Night earn without generating any excess FTCs for the current year? Assume a 34% U.S. tax rate.

Decision Making

36. **LO.4** Evaluate the following statement: Foreign persons never are subject to U.S. taxation on U.S.-source investment income so long as they are not engaged in a U.S. trade or business.

37. **LO.3** Lili, Inc., a domestic corporation, operates a branch in France. The earnings record of the branch is as follows.

Critical Thinking

Year	Taxable Income (Loss)	Foreign Taxes Paid
2013	($ 25,000)	$ –0–
2014	(40,000)	–0–
2015	(10,000)	–0–
2016	120,000	40,000

For 2013–2016, Lili, Inc., reports U.S.-source taxable income of $500,000 each year. What is the allowed FTC for 2016? Assume a 35% U.S. tax rate.

38. **LO.3, 4** Write a memo for the tax research file on the difference between "inbound" and "outbound" activities in the context of U.S. taxation of international income.

Communications

39. **LO.3** Warwick, Inc., a U.S. corporation, owns 100% of NewGrass, Ltd., a foreign corporation. NewGrass earns only general limitation income. During the cur-rent year, NewGrass paid Warwick a $10,000 dividend. The deemed-paid foreign tax credit associated with this dividend is $3,000. The foreign jurisdiction requires a withholding tax of 10%, so Warwick received only $9,000 in cash as a result of the dividend. What is Warwick's total U.S. gross income reported as a result of the cash dividend?

40. **LO.5** Evaluate this statement: A state can tax only its resident individuals and the corporations and partnerships that are organized in-state.

41. **LO.5** You are working with the top management of one of your clients in selecting the U.S. location for a new manufacturing operation. Craft a plan for the CEO to use in discussions with the economic development representatives of each of the top candidate states. In no more than two PowerPoint slides, list some of the tax incentives the CEO should request from a particular state during the bilateral nego-tiations between the parties. Your list should be both creative and aggressive in its requests.

Issue ID

Communications

42. **LO.5** Considering only the aggregate state income tax liability, how should a tax-payer who is a resident in State A selling widgets deploy its sales force? The states that entail the taxpayer's entire customer base use the following flat income tax rates.

Decision Making

State A	5%
State B	3
State C	6
State D	0

Ethics and Equity   43. **LO.5** Continue to consider the case of the taxpayer in Problem 42. Is it acceptable to you if the taxpayer purposely shifts its sales force among the states to reduce its tax liabilities?

44. **LO.6** Compute state taxable income for HippCo, Inc. Its Federal taxable income for the year is $1 million. Its operations are confined to Oregon and Montana. HippCo generates only business and interest income for the year.

- Federal cost recovery deductions totaled $200,000. Montana used this amount, but Oregon allowed only $120,000.
- Interest income of $25,000 from Oregon bonds was excluded from Federal taxable income. Oregon taxes all municipal bond income, while Montana taxes all such interest except that from its own bonds.
- Interest income from Treasury bonds that was recognized on the Federal return came to $11,000. Neither state taxes such income.

45. **LO.6** Continue with the facts of Problem 44. Using the format of Exhibit 16.3, compute state taxable income for HippCo, assuming also that the taxpayer recognized $225,000 of net rent income during the year from a warehouse building in Montana. Federal taxable income still is $1 million.

46. **LO.6** PinkCo, Inc., operates in two states. It reports the following results for the year. Compute the apportionment percentage for both states. Amounts are stated in millions of dollars.

	State A	**State B**	**Totals**
Sales	$25	$ 75	$100
Payroll	20	30	50
Property	0	100	100

47. **LO.6** Repeat the computations of Problem 46, but now assume that State B uses a double-weighted sales factor in its apportionment formula.

48. **LO.6** Repeat the computations of Problem 46, but now assume that State A is a sales-factor-only state and that State B uses the following weights: sales .70, payroll .15, and property .15.

Issue ID   49. **LO.6** State A enjoys a prosperous economy, with high real estate values and compensation levels. State B's economy has seen better days—property values are depressed, and unemployment is higher than in other states. Most consumer goods are priced at about 10% less in B as compared with prices in A. Both A and B apply unitary income taxation on businesses that operate in-state. Does unitary taxation distort the assignment of taxable income between A and B? Explain.

Critical Thinking   50. **LO.6** Hernandez, which has been an S corporation since inception, is subject to tax
Communications   in States Y and Z. On Schedule K of its Federal Form 1120S, Hernandez reported ordinary income of $500,000 from its business, taxable interest income of $10,000, capital loss of $30,000, and $40,000 of dividend income from a corporation in which it owns 30%.

Both states apportion income by use of a three-factor formula that equally weights sales, payroll, and the average cost of property; both states treat interest and dividends as business income. In addition, both Y and Z follow Federal provisions with respect to the determination of corporate taxable income. Y recognizes S status, but Z does not.

Based on the following information, write a memo to the shareholders of Hernandez, detailing the amount of taxable income on which Hernandez will pay tax in Y and Z. Hernandez corporate offices are located at 5678 Alabaster Circle, Bowling Green, KY 42103.

	State Y	State Z
Sales	$1,000,000	$800,000
Property (average cost)	500,000	100,000
Payroll	800,000	200,000

51. **LO.6** Prepare a PowerPoint presentation (maximum of six slides) entitled "Planning Principles for Our Multistate Clients." The slides will be used to lead a 20-minute discussion with colleagues in the corporate tax department. Keep the outline general, but assume that your colleagues already work with clients operating in at least 15 states. Address only income tax issues.

Issue ID
Communications

52. **LO.3, 7** Miha Ohua is the CFO of a U.S. company that has operations in Europe and Asia. The company has several manufacturing subsidiaries in low-tax foreign countries where the tax rate averages 6%. These subsidiaries purchase raw materials used in the production process from related subsidiaries located in countries where the tax rate averages 33%.

Miha is considering establishing a transfer price for the raw materials so that the higher-tax subsidiaries charge a low price for the raw materials. In this way, little of the profit is left in these subsidiaries, and most of the profits end up in the low-tax subsidiaries. This approach might reduce the U.S. company's overall global tax rate. Write a memo to Miha, outlining the issues with this plan.

Issue ID
Communications

BRIDGE DISCIPLINE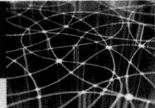

1. What type of information-sharing agreements does the IRS have with the revenue agency of the Bahamas? Canada? Germany? Israel? Argentina?

2. Write a paper of no more than two pages discussing the treatment of state and local taxes that is found in the text of U.S. income tax treaties with two other countries.

Communications

3. Several U.S. states finance their operations without the benefit of a corporate income tax. Prepare five to seven PowerPoint slides, and make a presentation to your school's Accounting Club. In your presentation, discuss the public economic and policy effects of using nontraditional revenue sources to fund state operating and infrastructure projects. Compare the taxing and expenditure process used in your state with at least two of these jurisdictions: Alaska; Hawaii; Michigan; Texas; Washington, D.C.; and Washington State.

Communications

4. The trend in state income taxation is to move to an apportionment formula that places extra weight on the sales factor. Several states now use sales-factor-only apportionment. Explain why this development is attractive to the taxing states.

Research Problems

Note: Solutions to Research Problems can be prepared by using the Checkpoint® Student Edition online research product, which is available to accompany this text. It is also possible to prepare solutions to the Research Problems by using tax research materials found in a standard tax library.

Communications

Research Problem 1. Jerry Jeff Keen, the CFO of Boots Unlimited, a Texas corporation, has come to you regarding a potential restructuring of business operations. Boots long has manufactured its western boots in plants in Texas and Oklahoma.

Recently, Boots has explored the possibility of setting up a manufacturing subsidiary in Ireland, where manufacturing profits are taxed at 10%. Jerry Jeff sees this as a great idea, given that the alternative is to continue all manufacturing in the United States, where profits are taxed at 34%. Boots plans to continue all of the cutting, sizing, and hand tooling of leather in its U.S. plants. This material will be shipped to Ireland for final assembly, with the finished product shipped to retail outlets all over Europe and Asia. Your initial concern is whether the income generated by the Irish subsidiary will be considered foreign base company income. Address this issue in a research memo, along with any planning suggestions.

Partial list of research aids:
§ 954(d).
Reg. § 1.954–3(a).
Bausch & Lomb, 71 TCM 2031, T.C.Memo. 1996–57.

Research Problem 2. Polly Ling is a successful professional golfer. She is a resident of a country that does not have a tax treaty with the United States. Ling plays matches around the world, about one-half of which are in the United States. Ling's reputation is without blemish; in fact, she is known as being exceedingly honest and upright, and many articles discuss how she is a role model for young golfers due to her tenacious and successful playing style and her favorable character traits. Every year, she reports the most penalty strokes on herself among the participants in women's matches, and this is seen as reinforcing her image as an honest and respectful competitor.

This combination of quality play and laudable reputation has brought many riches to Ling. She comes to you with several Federal income tax questions. She knows that as a non-U.S. resident, any of her winnings from tournament play that occurs in the United States are subject to U.S. income taxation. But what about each of the following items? How does U.S. tax law affect Ling? Apply the sourcing rules in this regard, and determine whether the graduated U.S. Federal income tax rate schedules apply.

- Endorsement income from YourGolf, for wearing clothing during matches with its logo prominently displayed. Ling must play in at least 10 tournaments per year that are televised around the world. She also must participate in photo sessions and in blogs and tweets associated with the tournaments. Payment to Ling is structured as a flat fee, with bonuses paid if she finishes in the top five competitors for each match. This is known as an *on-court endorsement.*

- Endorsement income from GolfZone, for letting the company use her likeness in a video game that simulates golf tournaments among known golfers and other players that the (usually middle-aged men and women) gamers identify. In this way, the gamer seems to be playing against Ling on famous golf courses. Two-thirds of all dollar sales of the game licenses are to U.S. customers.

- Endorsement income from Eliteness, for appearing in print and Internet ads that feature Ling wearing the company's high-end watches. One-fifth of all dollar sales of the watches are to U.S. customers. The latter two items are known as *off-court endorsements.*

Internet Activity

Use the tax resources of the Internet to address the following questions. Do not restrict your search to the Web, but include a review of newsgroups and general reference materials, practitioner sites and resources, primary sources of the tax law, chat rooms and discussion groups, and other opportunities.

Research Problem 3. Supervise and Wager Company produces consumer goods that are distributed and sold primarily in North America, Europe, and Asia. The business includes a U.S. parent company, S&W, Inc., and separate operating subsidiaries in each region in which the company conducts significant business.

The company's board is considering a structural reorganization to reduce the global tax costs. Options include reorganizing the parent company in either Bermuda or Ireland. Under any option, current shareholders will contribute their stock in the U.S. parent company in return for an equivalent amount of stock in the new parent. The U.S. parent will be liquidated, and the new corporation then will be the sole shareholder of the operating subsidiaries.

a. What might S&W be trying to achieve with the proposed organizational restructuring?

b. What insight can you provide regarding the immediate and longer-term tax consequences of the reorganization? *Hint:* Use the word *inversion* in your search term.

Research Problem 4. Make a list of the countries with which the United States currently is negotiating an income tax treaty. Include the date on which negotiations started and the current status of the negotiations. Then list five countries with which the United States does *not* have in force a bilateral income tax treaty.

Research Problem 5. For your analysis, choose 10 countries, one of which is the United States. Create a table showing whether each country applies a worldwide or territorial approach to international income taxation. Then list the country's top income tax rate on business profits. Send a copy of this table to your instructor.

Communications

Research Problem 6. Locate data on the size of the international economy, including data on international trade, foreign direct investment of U.S. firms, and investments in the United States by foreign firms. Useful Web locations include **www.census.gov** and **www.bea.gov**. Prepare an analysis of these data for a three-year period, using spreadsheet and graphing software, and e-mail your findings to your instructor.

Communications

Research Problem 7. Read the "tax footnote" of five publicly traded U.S. corporations. Find the effective state/local income tax rates of each. Create a PowerPoint presentation (maximum of five slides) for your instructor, summarizing the search and reporting your findings.

Communications

Research Problem 8. Identify three states considered to be in the same economic region as your own. For each of the three states, answer the following questions. Answers to most can be found at **www.taxadmin.org**.

• What is the overall tax burden per capita, and where does it rank among all states?

• What is the overall tax burden as a percentage of personal income, and where does it rank among all states?

• From what source(s) does it raise most of its revenues (e.g., sales/use tax, highway tolls)?

• What is the highest marginal tax rate on corporate income?

• What is its apportionment formula, including factors and weights?

What advice or insight might you provide to your state legislature regarding your state's tax system, based on your responses to the above?

CHAPTER

17

Business Tax Credits and Corporate Alternative Minimum Tax

LEARNING OBJECTIVES: *After completing Chapter 17, you should be able to:*

LO.1 Explain the difference in the use of credits and deductions as a Federal tax policy tool.

LO.2 Apply various business-related tax credits.

LO.3 Explain the reason for the alternative minimum tax.

LO.4 Identify and calculate AMT adjustments.

LO.5 Identify and calculate the tax preferences that are included in determining the AMT.

LO.6 State and explain the function of adjusted current earnings (ACE).

LO.7 Compute the AMT liability for corporations and individuals.

CHAPTER OUTLINE

TAX TALK *A government which robs Peter to pay Paul can always count on the support of Paul.* —GEORGE BERNARD SHAW

THE BIG PICTURE

DEALING WITH TAX CREDITS AND THE AMT

Mike, the CEO of Progress Corporation, is committed to helping revitalize the crumbling downtown area in his hometown. The area has experienced high unemployment as companies have left for the suburbs, and Mike is considering expanding his business and purchasing an old office building in a historic section of downtown. The building will require substantial renovations, and Mike has heard that there are tax credits that might help reduce his costs. He would also like to hire inner-city workers and help working families by providing on-site child care. He is interested in learning whether his company might take advantage of any other tax credits offered by the Federal government that might reduce his costs.

Read the chapter and formulate your response.

LO.1

Explain the difference in the use of credits and deductions as a Federal tax policy tool.

Federal tax law often serves other purposes besides merely raising revenue for the government. Evidence of equity, social, and economic considerations, among others, is found throughout the tax law. These considerations also have considerable import in the area of tax credits . Congress has generally used tax credits to promote social or economic objectives or to work toward greater tax equity among different types of taxpayers. For example, the disabled access credit was enacted to accomplish a social objective: to encourage taxpayers to renovate older buildings so that they would be accessible to the disabled and be in compliance with the Americans with Disabilities Act. As another example, the foreign tax credit, which has been a part of the law for decades, has as its chief purpose the economic and equity objectives of mitigating the burden of multiple taxation on a single stream of income.

A tax credit should not be confused with an income tax deduction. Certain expenditures (e.g., business expenses) are permitted as deductions from gross income in arriving at taxable income. While the tax benefit received from a tax deduction depends on the tax rate, a tax credit is not affected by the tax rate of the taxpayer. All taxpayers can benefit equally when a tax credit is used.

EXAMPLE

1

Assume that Congress wants to encourage a certain type of expenditure. One way to accomplish this objective is to allow a tax credit of 25% for such expenditures. Another way is to allow a deduction for the expenditures. Assume that Red Corporation's tax rate is 15%, while Blue Corporation's tax rate is 34%. The following tax benefits are available to each corporation for a $1,000 expenditure.

	Red	Blue
Tax benefit if a 25% credit is allowed	$250	$250
Tax benefit if a deduction is allowed	150	340

As these results indicate, tax credits can provide benefits on a more equitable basis than tax deductions often do.

In order to prevent taxpayers with high income from completely avoiding a Federal income tax liability, the alternative minimum tax (AMT) was introduced in 1969 and has since been amended on multiple occasions. Many of the adjustments and tax preference items necessary to arrive at alternative minimum taxable income (AMTI) are the same for individuals and corporations. Other items such as the tax rates and exemptions are different between individuals and corporations, but the objective is identical—to force taxpayers that are more profitable than their regular taxable income reflects to pay additional income taxes.

LO.2

Apply various business-related tax credits.

17-1 BUSINESS-RELATED TAX CREDIT PROVISIONS

Congress has generally used tax credits to achieve social or economic objectives or to promote equity among different types of taxpayers. This section of the chapter describes the operation of the general business credit along with the most common types of credits that affect a business.

17-1a General Business Credit

The general business credit is comprised of a number of other credits, each of which is computed separately under its own set of rules. The general business credit combines these credits into one amount to limit the annual credit that can be used to offset a taxpayer's income tax liability.

Two special rules apply to the general business credit. First, any unused credit is carried back 1 year, then forward 20 years. Second, for any tax year, the general business credit is limited to the taxpayer's *net income tax* reduced by the greater of:[1]

- The *tentative minimum tax* [see the discussion of the alternative minimum tax (AMT) later in this chapter].
- 25 percent of *net regular tax liability* that exceeds $25,000.[2]

Net regular tax liability is the regular tax liability reduced by certain nonrefundable credits (e.g., foreign tax credit).

EXAMPLE 2

Tanager Corporation's general business credit for the current year is $70,000. Tanager's net income tax is $150,000, tentative minimum tax is $130,000, and net regular tax liability is $150,000. Tanager has no other tax credits. The general business credit allowed for the tax year is computed as follows.

Net income tax	$ 150,000
Less: The greater of—	
• $130,000 (tentative minimum tax)	
• $31,250 [25% × ($150,000 − $25,000)]	(130,000)
Amount of general business credit allowed for tax year	$ 20,000

Tanager then has $50,000 ($70,000 − $20,000) of unused general business credits that may be carried back or forward.

Treatment of Unused General Business Credits

Unused general business credits are initially carried back one year and reduce the tax liability of that year. Thus, the taxpayer may receive a tax refund as a result of the carryback. Any remaining unused credits are then carried forward 20 years.[3]

A FIFO method is applied to the carryback, carryovers, and utilization of credits earned during a particular year. The oldest credits are used first in determining the amount of the general business credit. The FIFO method minimizes the potential for loss of a general business credit benefit due to the expiration of credit carryovers and generally works to the taxpayer's benefit.

---

[1] § 38(c). This rule works to keep the general business credit from completely eliminating the tax liability for many taxpayers.

[2] § 38(c)(3)(B). The $25,000 amount is apportioned among the members of a controlled group.

[3] § 39(a)(1).

EXAMPLE 3

This example illustrates the use of general business credit carryovers for the taxpayer's 2015 tax year.

General business credit carryovers (unused in prior tax years)		
2012	$ 4,000	
2013	6,000	
2014	2,000	
Total carryovers	$12,000	
2015 general business credit		$ 40,000
Total credit allowed in 2015 (based on tax liability)	$50,000	
Less: Carryovers used		
2012	(4,000)	
2013	(6,000)	
2014	(2,000)	
Remaining credit allowed in 2015	$38,000	
2015 general business credit used		(38,000)
2015 unused amount carried forward to 2016		$ 2,000

Each component of the general business credit is determined separately under its own set of rules. Some of the more important credits that make up the general business credit are explained here in the order listed in Exhibit 17.1.

EXHIBIT 17.1   **Principal Components of the General Business Credit**

The general business credit combines (but is not limited to) the following.

- Tax credit for rehabilitation expenditures
- Work opportunity tax credit
- Research activities credit
- Various energy credits
- Low-income housing credit
- Disabled access credit
- Credit for small employer pension plan startup costs
- Credit for employer-provided child care

BRIDGE DISCIPLINE **Bridge to Finance**

When calculating the cash-flow benefit of particular tax attributes and making a decision based on this analysis, an inappropriate decision can be made unless present value analysis is incorporated into the calculation.

The general business credit and the related carryback and carryover provisions can be used to illustrate the cash-flow impact.

Blonde, Inc.'s general business credit for 2015 is $400,000. However, the amount that may be used to reduce the current-year tax liability is only $280,000. None can be used in 2014 (the carryback year), so the $120,000 is carried forward. The $120,000 of unused general business credit is expected to offset Blonde's future tax liability as follows.

2016	$20,000
2017	40,000
2018	60,000

It appears that the cash-flow benefit to Blonde is $400,000. In nominal dollars, this result is correct. However, when the present value concept is applied, the cash-flow benefit is only $376,280 (assuming that Blonde's discount rate is 4 percent).

2015	$280,000 × 1.000	=	$280,000
2016	20,000 × .9615	=	19,230
2017	40,000 × .9246	=	36,984
2018	60,000 × .8890	=	53,340
			$389,554

The carryforward period for the general business credit is 20 years. Using a 4 percent discount rate, one dollar in 20 years is worth about 46 cents ($1 × .4564) today. So taxpayers should use the general business credit to offset tax liability as rapidly as possible.

17-1b **Tax Credit for Rehabilitation Expenditures**

Taxpayers are allowed a tax credit for expenditures incurred to rehabilitate older industrial and commercial buildings and certified historic structures. The **rehabilitation expenditures credit** is intended to discourage businesses from moving from economically distressed areas (e.g., an inner city) to outlying locations and to encourage the preservation of historic structures. The current operating features of this credit follow.[4]

Rate of the Credit for Rehabilitation Expenses	Nature of the Property
10%	Nonresidential buildings and residential rental property, other than certified historic structures, originally placed in service before 1936
20%	Nonresidential and residential certified historic structures

Taxpayers who claim the rehabilitation credit must reduce the basis of the rehabilitated building by the credit allowed.[5]

The Big Picture

Return to the facts of *The Big Picture* on p. 17-1. Assume that Progress spends $60,000 to rehabilitate a building (adjusted basis of $40,000) that had been placed in service in 1932.

Progress is allowed a credit of $6,000 (10% × $60,000) for rehabilitation expenditures. The corporation then increases the basis of the building by $54,000 [$60,000 (rehabilitation expenditures) − $6,000 (credit allowed)].

If the building were a historic structure, the credit allowed would be $12,000 (20% × $60,000) and the building's depreciable basis would increase by $48,000 [$60,000 (rehabilitation expenditures) − $12,000 (credit allowed)].

EXAMPLE

4

---

[4]§ 47.

[5]§ 50(c).

To qualify for the credit, buildings must be substantially rehabilitated. A building has been *substantially rehabilitated* if qualified rehabilitation expenditures exceed the *greater of*:

- The adjusted basis of the property before the rehabilitation expenditures, or
- $5,000.

Qualified rehabilitation expenditures do not include the cost of acquiring a building, the cost of facilities related to a building (such as a parking lot), and the cost of enlarging an existing building. Stringent rules apply concerning the retention of the building's original internal and external walls.

Recapture of Tax Credit for Rehabilitation Expenditures

The rehabilitation credit taken is recaptured if the rehabilitated property is disposed of prematurely or if it ceases to be qualifying property. The **rehabilitation expenditures credit recapture** is added to the taxpayer's regular tax liability in the recapture year. The recapture amount also is *added* to the adjusted basis of the building.

The portion of the credit recaptured is a specified percentage of the credit that was taken by the taxpayer. This percentage is based on the period the property was held by the taxpayer, as shown in Exhibit 17.2. If the property is held at least five years, no recapture can result.

EXAMPLE 5

On March 15, 2012, Chickadee Corporation rehabilitated a building qualifying for the 10% credit. The company spent $30,000 in qualifying rehabilitation expenditures and claimed a $3,000 credit ($30,000 × 10%). The basis of the building was increased by $27,000 ($30,000 − $3,000).

Chickadee sold the building on December 15, 2015. Chickadee recaptures a portion of the rehabilitation credit based on the schedule in Exhibit 17.2. Because Chickadee held the rehabilitated property for more than three years but less than four, 40% of the credit, or $1,200, is added to the company's 2015 income tax liability. In addition, the adjusted basis of the building is increased by the $1,200 recapture amount.

17-1c Work Opportunity Tax Credit

The **work opportunity tax credit**[6] was enacted to encourage employers to hire individuals from a variety of targeted and economically disadvantaged groups. Examples of such targeted persons include qualified ex-felons, high-risk youths, food stamp recipients, veterans, summer youth employees, and long-term family assistance recipients.

EXHIBIT 17.2	Recapture Calculation for Rehabilitation Expenditures Credit

If the Property Is Held for	The Recapture Percentage Is
Less than 1 year	100
One year or more but less than 2 years	80
Two years or more but less than 3 years	60
Three years or more but less than 4 years	40
Four years or more but less than 5 years	20

---

[6] § 51. The credit is available only if qualifying employees start work by December 31, 2014; Congress is expected to extend this credit, and the examples and end-of-chapter materials that follow assume this is the case.

Computation of the Work Opportunity Tax Credit: General

The credit generally is equal to 40 percent of the first $6,000 of wages (per eligible employee) for the first 12 months of employment. The credit is not available for wages paid to an employee after the *first year* of employment. If the employee's first year overlaps two of the employer's tax years, however, the employer may take the credit over two tax years. If the credit is claimed, the employer's tax deduction for wages is reduced by the amount of the credit.

To qualify an employer for the 40 percent credit, the employee must (1) be certified by a designated local agency as being a member of one of the targeted groups and (2) have completed at least 400 hours of service to the employer. If an employee meets the first condition but not the second, the credit is reduced to 25 percent, provided the employee has completed a minimum of 120 hours of service to the employer.

In-depth coverage can be found on this book's companion website: www.cengagebrain.com   **1 DIGGING DEEPER**

The Big Picture

Return to the facts of *The Big Picture* on p. 17-1. In January 2015, Progress Corporation hires four individuals who are certified to be members of a qualifying targeted group. Each employee works 1,000 hours and is paid wages of $8,000 during the year.

Progress's work opportunity credit is $9,600 [($6,000 × 40%) × 4 employees]. If the tax credit is taken, Progress reduces its deduction for wages paid by $9,600. No credit is available for wages paid to these employees after their first year of employment.

On June 1, 2015, Maria, a calendar year taxpayer, hires Joe, a member of a certified group, and obtains the required certification to qualify Maria for the work opportunity credit. During his seven months of work in 2015, Joe is paid $3,500 for 500 hours of work. Maria is allowed a credit of $1,400 ($3,500 × 40%) for 2015.

Joe continues to work for Maria in 2016 and is paid $7,000 through May 31, 2016. Because up to $6,000 of first-year wages are eligible for the credit, Maria is also allowed a 40% credit on $2,500 [$6,000 − $3,500 (wages paid in 2015)] of 2016 wages paid. The credit is $1,000 ($2,500 × 40%). None of Joe's wages paid after May 31, 2016, the end of the first year of employment, are eligible for the credit.

Computation of the Work Opportunity Tax Credit: Long-Term Family Assistance Recipient

The credit[7] is available to employers hiring individuals who have been long-term recipients of family assistance welfare benefits. In general, *long-term recipients* are those individuals who are certified by a designated local agency as being members of a family receiving assistance under a public aid program for the 18-month period ending on the hiring date. Unlike the work opportunity credit for other targeted groups, which applies only to first-year wages paid to qualified individuals, this credit is available for qualified wages paid in the first *two years* of employment. If an employee's first and second work years overlap two or more of the employer's tax years, the employer may take the credit during the applicable tax years.

The credit is equal to 40 percent of the first $10,000 of qualified wages paid to an employee in the first year of employment plus 50 percent of the first $10,000 of

---

[7]Prior to 2007, this component of the work opportunity tax credit was called the welfare-to-work credit, provided for under § 51A. Under current law, long-term family assistance recipients are a designated targeted group under the work opportunity tax credit, and the maximum credit is now slightly more generous than under prior law. § 51(d)(1)(I).

qualified wages in the second year of employment, resulting in a maximum credit per qualified employee of $9,000 [$4,000 (year 1) + $5,000 (year 2)]. The credit rate is higher for second-year wages to encourage employers to retain qualified individuals, thereby promoting the overall welfare-to-work goal.

In April 2015, Blue Company hires three individuals who are certified as long-term family assistance recipients. Each employee is paid $12,000 during 2015. Two of the three individuals continue to work for Blue in 2016, earning $9,000 each during the year.

Blue's work opportunity tax credit is $12,000 [(40% × $10,000) × 3 employees] for 2015 and $9,000 [(50% × $9,000) × 2 employees] for 2016. In each year, Blue must reduce its deduction for wages paid by the amount of the credit for that year.

17-1d Research Activities Credit

To encourage research and development (R & D) in the U.S. business community, a credit is allowed for certain qualifying expenditures paid or incurred by a taxpayer. The research activities credit is the *sum* of three components: (1) an incremental research activities credit, (2) a basic research credit, and (3) an energy research credit.[8]

Incremental Research Activities Credit

The incremental research activities credit applies at a 20 percent rate to the *excess* of qualified research expenses for the taxable year (the credit year) over a base amount.[9] Determining the *base amount* involves a relatively complex series of computations meant to approximate recent historical levels of research activity by the taxpayer. Thus, the credit is allowed only for increases in research expenses.

In general, *research expenditures* qualify if the research relates to discovering technological information that is intended for use in the development of a new or improved business component of the taxpayer. Such expenses qualify fully if the research is performed in-house (by the taxpayer or its employees). If the research is conducted by persons outside the taxpayer's business (under contract), only 65 percent of the amount paid qualifies for the credit.[10]

Bobwhite Company incurs the following research expenditures.

In-house wages, supplies, computer time	$135,000
Payment to Cutting Edge Scientific Foundation for research	100,000

Bobwhite's qualified research expenditures are $200,000 [$135,000 + ($100,000 × 65%)]. If the base amount is $100,000, the incremental research activities credit is $20,000 [($200,000 − $100,000) × 20%].

Beyond the general guidelines described above, the Code does not give specific examples of qualifying research. However, the credit is *not* allowed for research that falls into certain categories, including the following.[11]

- Research conducted after the beginning of commercial production of the business component.
- Surveys and studies such as market research, testing, or routine data collection.

---

[8]§ 41. Each component of the research credit is available only if qualifying expenditures are paid or incurred by December 31, 2014; Congress is expected to extend this credit, and the examples and end-of-chapter materials that follow assume this is the case.

[9]In lieu of determining the incremental research credit as described here, a taxpayer may elect to calculate the credit using an alternative simplified credit procedure. See §§ 41(c)(4) and (5).

[10]§ 41(b)(3)(A). In the case of payments to a qualified research consortium, § 41(b)(3)(A) provides that 75% of the amount paid qualifies for the credit. In contrast, for amounts paid to an energy research consortium, § 41(b)(3)(D) allows the full amount to qualify for the credit.

[11]§ 41(d).

- Research conducted *outside* the United States (other than research undertaken in Puerto Rico or possessions of the United States).
- Research in the social sciences, arts, or humanities.

Qualified research and experimentation expenditures not only are eligible for the 20 percent credit but also can be *expensed* in the year incurred. In this regard, a taxpayer has two choices.[12]

- Use the full credit and reduce the expense deduction for research expenses by 100 percent of the credit.
- Retain the full expense deduction and reduce the credit by the product of the full credit times the maximum corporate tax rate (35 percent).

As an alternative to the expense deduction, the taxpayer may *capitalize* the research expenses and *amortize* them over 60 months or more. In this case, the amount capitalized and subject to amortization is reduced by the full amount of the credit *only* if the credit exceeds the amount allowable as a deduction.

EXAMPLE 10

Assume the same facts as in Example 9, which shows that the potential incremental research activities credit is $20,000. In the current year, the amounts Bobwhite can deduct and the credit amount under each of the three choices are computed as follows.

	Credit Amount	Deduction Amount
• Full credit and reduced deduction		
$20,000 − $0	$20,000	
$200,000 − $20,000		$180,000
• Reduced credit and full deduction		
$20,000 − [(100% × $20,000) × 35%]	13,000	
$200,000 − $0		200,000
• Full credit and capitalize and elect to amortize costs over 60 months		
$20,000 − $0	20,000	
($200,000/60) × 12		40,000

The value of the deduction depends on Bobwhite's marginal tax rates.

Basic Research Credit

Corporations (other than S corporations or personal service corporations) are allowed an additional 20 percent credit for basic research expenditures incurred, in *excess* of a base amount.[13] This credit is not available to individual taxpayers. *Basic research expenditures* are defined as amounts paid in cash to a qualified basic research organization, such as a college or university or a tax-exempt organization operated primarily to conduct scientific research.

Basic research is defined generally as any original investigation for the advancement of scientific knowledge not having a specific commercial objective. The definition excludes basic research conducted outside the United States and basic research in the social sciences, arts, or humanities.

Energy Research Credit

This component of the research credit is intended to stimulate additional energy research. The calculation of the credit is relatively straightforward; it is equal to

---

[12]§§ 174 and 280C(c). Recall the discussion of rules for deducting research and experimental expenditures in Chapter 5.

[13]§ 41(e).

20 percent of the amounts paid or incurred by a taxpayer to an energy research consortium for energy research.

17-1e Energy Credits

The Internal Revenue Code contains a variety of credits for businesses and individuals to encourage the conservation of natural resources and the development of energy sources other than oil and gas. The primary goals of the tax provisions are to improve energy-related infrastructure and encourage higher levels of energy conservation. Most of these credits are temporary in nature, and many of them expired in 2014, although Congress will likely extend some of these credits in 2015.

Some of the more widely applicable provisions include credits for:

- Builders who construct energy-efficient homes.
- Individuals who make energy-saving improvements to their residences.
- Businesses that buy fuel cell and microturbine power plants.
- Taxpayers who purchase alternative power motor vehicles and refueling property.

Like many other tax credits, the **energy credits** have been designed to modify taxpayer behavior. More specifically, in this case, Congress's intention is that these credits will lead to greater conservation and more efficient use of energy.

17-1f Disabled Access Credit

The **disabled access credit** is designed to encourage small businesses to make their facilities more accessible to disabled individuals. The credit is available for any eligible access expenditures paid or incurred by an eligible small business. The credit is calculated at the rate of 50 percent of the eligible expenditures that exceed $250 but do not exceed $10,250. Thus, the maximum amount for the credit is $5,000 ($10,000 × 50%).[14]

An *eligible small business* is a business that during the previous year either had gross receipts of $1 million or less or had no more than 30 full-time employees. A sole proprietorship, a partnership, a regular corporation, or an S corporation can qualify as such an entity.

Eligible access expenditures generally include any reasonable and necessary amounts that are paid or incurred to make certain changes to facilities. These changes must involve the removal of architectural, communication, physical, or transportation barriers that would otherwise make a business inaccessible to disabled and handicapped individuals. Examples of qualifying projects include installing ramps, widening doorways, and adding raised markings on elevator control buttons. The facility must have been placed in service prior to November 5, 1990 for any improvements to be eligible for the credit.

To the extent a disabled access credit is available, the asset's adjusted basis is reduced by the amount of the credit. This ensures that no additional deduction or credit is allowed under any other provision of the tax law.

EXAMPLE 11

This year, Red, Inc., an eligible business, makes $11,000 of capital improvements to business realty that had been placed in service in June 1990. The expenditures are intended to make Red's business more accessible to the disabled and are considered eligible expenditures for purposes of the disabled access credit.

The amount of the credit is $5,000 [($10,250 maximum − $250 floor) × 50%]. The depreciable basis of the capital improvement is $6,000 [$11,000 (cost) − $5,000 (amount of the credit)].

17-1g Credit for Small Employer Pension Plan Startup Costs

Small businesses are entitled to a nonrefundable credit for administrative costs associated with establishing and maintaining certain qualified retirement plans.[15] While such costs (e.g., payroll system changes and consulting fees) generally are deductible as

---

[14]§ 44.   [15]§ 45E.

ordinary and necessary business expenses, the credit is intended to lower the after-tax cost of establishing a qualified retirement program and thereby to encourage qualifying businesses to offer retirement plans for their employees.

The credit for small employer pension plan startup costs is available for eligible employers at the rate of 50 percent of qualified startup costs. An eligible employer is one with fewer than 100 employees who have earned at least $5,000 of compensation. The maximum credit is $500 (based on a maximum $1,000 of qualifying expenses), and the deduction for the startup costs incurred is reduced by the amount of the credit. The credit can be claimed for qualifying costs incurred in each of the three years beginning with the tax year in which the retirement plan becomes effective (maximum total credit of $1,500).

EXAMPLE 12

Maple Company decides to establish a qualified retirement plan for its employees. In the process, it pays consulting fees of $1,200 to a firm that will provide educational seminars to Maple's employees and will assist the payroll department in making necessary changes to the payroll system.

Maple may claim a credit for the pension plan startup costs of $500 ($1,200 of qualifying costs, limited to $1,000 × 50%), and its deduction for these expenses is reduced to $700 ($1,200 − $500).

17-1h Credit for Employer-Provided Child Care

An employer can deduct expenditures incurred to provide for the care of children of employees as ordinary and necessary business expenses. Alternatively, employers may claim a credit for qualifying expenditures incurred while providing child care facilities to their employees during normal working hours.[16]

The credit for employer-provided child care, limited annually to $150,000, is composed of the aggregate of two components: 25 percent of qualified child care expenses and 10 percent of qualified child care resource and referral services. *Qualified child care expenses* include the costs of acquiring, constructing, rehabilitating, expanding, and operating a child care facility. *Child care resource and referral services* include amounts paid or incurred under a contract to provide child care resource and referral services to an employee.

Any qualifying expenses otherwise deductible by the taxpayer are reduced by the amount of the credit. In addition, the taxpayer's basis for any property acquired or constructed and used for qualifying purposes is reduced by the amount of the credit. If within 10 years of being placed in service a child care facility ceases to be used for a qualified use, the taxpayer recaptures a portion of the credit previously claimed.[17]

The Big Picture

EXAMPLE 13

Return to the facts of *The Big Picture* on p. 17-1. During the year, Progress Corporation constructs a child care facility for $400,000 to be used by its employees who have preschool-aged children in need of child care services while their parents are at work. In addition, Progress incurs salary costs for child care workers and other administrative costs associated with the facility of $100,000 during the year.

As a result, Progress's credit for employer-provided child care is $125,000 [($400,000 + $100,000) × 25%]. Correspondingly, the basis of the facility is reduced to $300,000 ($400,000 − $100,000), and the deduction for salaries and administrative costs is reduced to $75,000 ($100,000 − $25,000).

In-depth coverage can be found on this book's companion website: **www.cengagebrain.com**   **2 DIGGING DEEPER**

---

[16]§ 45F.   [17]§ 45F(d).

GLOBAL TAX ISSUES Sourcing Income in Cyberspace—Getting It Right When Calculating the Foreign Tax Credit

The overall limitation on the foreign tax credit plays a critical role in restricting the amount of the credit available to a taxpayer. In the overall limitation formula, the taxpayer must characterize the year's taxable income as either earned (or sourced) inside or outside the United States. As a general rule, a relatively greater percentage of foreign-source income in the formula leads to a larger foreign tax credit. But classifying income as either foreign or U.S. source is not always a simple matter.

The existing income-sourcing rules were developed long before the existence of the Internet, and taxing authorities are finding it challenging to apply these rules to Internet transactions. Where does a sale take place when the web server is in Scotland, the seller is in India, and the customer is in Illinois? Where is a service performed when all activities take place over the Net? These questions and more must be answered by the United States and its trading partners as the Internet economy grows in size and importance.

17-1i **Foreign Tax Credit**

Both individual taxpayers and corporations may claim a credit (see Chapter 16 for more details) for foreign income tax paid on income earned and subject to tax in another country or a U.S. possession.[18] The purpose of the **foreign tax credit (FTC)** is to reduce the possibility of double taxation of foreign income.

EXAMPLE 14

Ace Tools, Inc., a U.S. corporation, has a branch operation in Mexico, from which it earns taxable income of $750,000 for the current year. Ace pays income tax of $150,000 on these earnings to the Mexican tax authorities. Ace must also include the $750,000 in gross income for U.S. tax purposes.

Before considering the FTC, Ace owes $255,000 in U.S. income taxes on this foreign-source income. Thus, total taxes on the $750,000 could equal $405,000 ($150,000 + $255,000), a 54% effective rate. But Ace takes the FTC of $150,000 against its U.S. tax liability on the foreign-source income. Ace Tools' total taxes on the $750,000 now are $255,000 ($150,000 + $105,000), a 34% effective rate.

The tax year's FTC equals the *lesser* of the foreign taxes imposed or the *overall limitation* determined according to the following formula. Thus, where applicable foreign tax rates exceed those of the United States, the credit offsets no more than the marginal U.S. tax on the double-taxed income.

$$\frac{\text{Foreign-source taxable income}}{\text{Worldwide taxable income}} \times \text{U.S. tax before FTC}$$

Foreign taxes paid but not allowed as a credit due to the overall limitation are carried back 1 tax year and then forward 10 years.[19]

EXAMPLE 15

Oriole, Inc., a U.S. corporation, conducts business in a foreign country. Oriole's worldwide taxable income for the tax year is $120,000, consisting of $100,000 in income from U.S. operations and $20,000 of income from the foreign source. Foreign tax of $6,000 was paid to foreign tax authorities on the $20,000. Before the FTC, Oriole's U.S. tax on the $120,000 is $30,050.

The corporation's FTC is $5,008 {lesser of $6,000 paid or $5,008 limitation [$30,050 × ($20,000/$120,000)]}. Oriole's net U.S. tax liability is $25,042 ($30,050 − $5,008).

Thus, Oriole carries over (back 1 year and forward 10 years) a $992 FTC ($6,000 − $5,008) because of the overall limitation.

---

[18]§ 27 provides for the credit, but the qualifications and calculation procedure for the credit are contained in §§ 901–908. Alternatively, the taxpayer can *deduct* the foreign taxes paid.

[19]§ 904(c).

17-1j Small Employer Health Insurance Credit

Under the Affordable Care Act of 2010, a tax credit is provided for a qualified small employer for nonelective contributions to purchase health insurance for its employees.[20] To qualify for the credit in 2015, the employer must have no more than 25 full-time equivalent employees whose annual full-time wages average no more than $51,600 ($50,800 in 2014). The employer must pay at least half the cost of the health insurance premiums.[21] The credit is 50 percent of the health insurance premiums paid. It is subject to a phaseout if the employer has more than 10 full-time equivalent employees and/or has annual full-time wages that average more than $25,800 ($25,400 in 2014).[22]

Concept Summary 17.1 provides an overview of the tax credits discussed in this chapter.

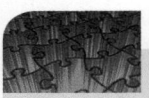

Concept Summary 17.1

Tax Credits

Credit	Computation	Comments
General business (§ 38)	May not exceed net income tax minus the greater of tentative minimum tax or 25% of net regular tax liability that exceeds $25,000.	Components include tax credit for rehabilitation expenditures, work opportunity tax credit, research activities credit, low-income housing credit, disabled access credit, credit for small employer pension plan startup costs, and credit for employer-provided child care.
		Unused credit may be carried back 1 year and forward 20 years. FIFO method applies to carrybacks, carryovers, and credits earned during current year.
Rehabilitation expenditures (§ 47)	Qualifying investment times rehabilitation percentage, depending on type of property. Regular rehabilitation rate is 10%; rate for certified historic structures is 20%.	Part of general business credit and therefore subject to same carryback, carryover, and FIFO rules. Purpose is to discourage businesses from moving from economically distressed areas to new locations.
Work opportunity (§ 51)	Credit is limited to 40% of the first $6,000 of wages paid to each eligible employee. For long-term family assistance recipients, credit is limited to 40% of first $10,000 of wages paid to each eligible employee in first year of employment, plus 50% of first $10,000 of wages paid to same employee in second year of employment.	Part of the general business credit and therefore subject to the same carryback, carryover, and FIFO rules. Purpose is to encourage employment of members of economically disadvantaged groups.
Research activities (§ 41)	Incremental credit is 20% of excess of computation-year expenditures over a base amount. Basic research credit is allowed to certain corporations for 20% of cash payments to qualified organizations that exceed a specially calculated base amount. An energy research credit is allowed for 20% of qualifying payments made to an energy research consortium.	Part of general business credit and therefore subject to same carryback, carryover, and FIFO rules. Purpose is to encourage high-tech and energy research in the United States.
Low-income housing (§ 42)	Appropriate rate times eligible basis (portion of project attributable to low-income units).	Part of general business credit and therefore subject to same carryback, carryover, and FIFO rules. Recapture may apply. Purpose is to encourage construction of housing for low-income individuals. Credit is available each year for 10 years.

continued

---

[20]§ 45R.

[21]§§ 45R(d)(1) and (4). The wage amount is indexed for inflation beginning in 2014.

[22]§ 45R(c). The credit percentage for tax-exempt employers is 35%.

Tax Credits—(Continued)

Credit	Computation	Comments
Energy credits	Various items to encourage individuals and businesses to "go green."	Part of general business credit and therefore subject to same carryback, carryover, and FIFO rules.
Disabled access (§ 44)	Credit is 50% of eligible access expenditures that exceed $250 but do not exceed $10,250. Maximum credit is $5,000.	Part of general business credit and therefore subject to same carryback, carryover, and FIFO rules. Purpose is to encourage small businesses to become more accessible to disabled individuals. Available only to eligible small businesses.
Credit for small employer pension plan startup costs (§ 45E)	The credit equals 50% of qualified startup costs incurred by eligible employers. Maximum annual credit is $500. Deduction for related expenses is reduced by the amount of the credit.	Part of general business credit and therefore subject to same carryback, carryover, and FIFO rules. Purpose is to encourage small employers to establish qualified retirement plans for their employees.
Credit for employer-provided child care (§ 45F)	Credit is equal to 25% of qualified child care expenses plus 10% of qualified expenses for child care resource and referral services. Maximum credit is $150,000. Deduction for related expenses or basis must be reduced by the amount of the credit.	Part of general business credit and therefore subject to same carryback, carryover, and FIFO rules. Purpose is to encourage employers to provide child care for their employees' children during normal working hours.
Foreign tax (§ 27)	Foreign taxable income/total worldwide taxable income × U.S. tax = overall limitation. Lesser of foreign taxes imposed or overall limitation.	Unused credits may be carried back 1 year and forward 10 years. Purpose is to reduce double taxation of foreign income.
Small Employer Health Insurance Credit (§ 45R)	The credit is 50% of the health insurance premiums paid (subject to a phaseout).	To qualify for the credit in 2015, the employer must have no more than 25 full-time equivalent employees whose annual full-time wages average no more than $51,600.

LO.3

Explain the reason for the alternative minimum tax.

17-2 CORPORATE ALTERNATIVE MINIMUM TAX

A perception that many large corporations were not paying their fair share of Federal income tax was especially widespread in the early 1980s. A study released in 1986 reported that 130 of the 250 largest corporations in the United States (e.g., Reynolds Metals, General Dynamics, Georgia Pacific, and Texas Commerce Bankshares) paid no Federal tax, or received refunds, in at least one year between 1981 and 1985. Political pressure subsequently led to the adoption of an **alternative minimum tax (AMT)** to ensure that corporations with substantial economic income pay at least a minimum amount of Federal taxes.

The AMT limits the tax savings for some taxpayers who are seen as gaining "too much" from exclusions, deductions, and credits available under the law. A separate tax system with a proportional tax rate is applied each year to a corporation's economic income. If the tentative AMT is greater than the regular corporate income tax, then the corporation must pay the regular tax plus this excess, the AMT.

Since its inception, the AMT has been vulnerable to criticisms that it is too complex. Smaller corporations especially find that the imposition of a second tax structure unduly increases their compliance burdens. Thus, under current rules, most smaller corporations are not subject to the AMT at all. A C corporation is exempted from the AMT if it meets the following tests:

- It was treated as a small corporation exempt from the AMT for all prior years beginning after 1997.
- Its annual average gross receipts for the three-year period (or portion thereof during which the corporation was in existence) ending before its current tax year did not exceed $7.5 million ($5 million if the corporation had only one prior tax year).

This provision exempts up to 95 percent of all C corporations from the AMT. A corporation *automatically* is classified as a small corporation in the first tax year of existence. A corporation that fails these tests for any year will be subject to the AMT rules for that year and all future years.

17-2a **The AMT Formula**

The AMT is imposed in addition to the regular corporate income tax, but is computed in a manner separate from it.[23] Typically for the AMT, more items are subject to tax under AMT rules, some gross income items are accelerated, and some deductions are deferred.

The formula for determining the AMT liability of corporate taxpayers appears in Exhibit 17.3 and follows the format of Form 4626 (Alternative Minimum Tax—Corporations).

The base for the AMT, alternative minimum taxable income (AMTI), begins with regular taxable income before any deductions for net operating losses (NOLs). A series of additions and subtractions is then made. Most AMT adjustments relate to *timing differences* that arise because of different regular income tax and AMT treatments. Adjustments that are caused by timing differences eventually reverse; that is, positive adjustments are offset by negative adjustments in the future, and vice versa. A common AMT adjustment is depreciation; AMT depreciation is determined using longer lives than those used for regular MACRS. Preference items always increase alternative minimum taxable income (AMTI).

AMT Adjustments: Timing Differences

EXAMPLE 16

In 2015, Bobwhite, Inc. deducted depreciation expense of $30,000 for regular income tax purposes. For AMT purposes, assume that the depreciation is spread evenly over the next three years ($10,000 per year). The AMT adjustment for 2015 is computed as follows.

Depreciation deducted for regular income tax purposes	$ 30,000
Depreciation deducted for AMT purposes	(10,000)
AMT adjustment (positive)	$ 20,000

EXAMPLE 17

Assume the same facts as in Example 16. The timing difference that gave rise to the positive adjustment in 2015 will reverse in the future. For AMT purposes, Bobwhite will deduct $10,000 in 2016 and $10,000 in 2017. The regular income tax deduction in each of those years will be $0, because the entire $30,000 expenditure was deducted in 2015. This results in a negative AMT adjustment of $10,000 each in 2016 and 2017. The AMT adjustments over the three-year period are summarized below.

Year	Regular Income Tax Deduction	AMT Deduction	AMT Adjustment
2015	$30,000	$10,000	$ 20,000
2016	–0–	10,000	(10,000)
2017	–0–	10,000	(10,000)
Totals	$30,000	$30,000	$ –0–

Timing differences eventually reverse. Thus, positive AMT adjustments can be offset later by negative adjustments.

---

[23]The AMT provisions are contained in §§ 55 through 59.

EXHIBIT 17.3	AMT Formula for Corporations

Regular taxable income before NOL deduction

Plus/minus:		AMT adjustments (except ACE adjustment)
Plus:		Tax preferences
	Equals:	AMTI before AMT NOL deduction and ACE adjustment
Plus/minus:		ACE adjustment
	Equals:	AMTI before AMT NOL deduction
Minus:		AMT NOL deduction (limited to 90%)
	Equals:	Alternative minimum taxable income (AMTI)
Minus:		Exemption
	Equals:	AMT base
Times:		20% rate
	Equals:	Tentative AMT before credits
Minus:		AMT foreign tax credit and other credits
	Equals:	Tentative minimum tax (TMT)
Minus:		Regular income tax liability before credits minus regular foreign tax credit
	Equals:	Alternative minimum tax (AMT) if positive

LO.4

Identify and calculate AMT adjustments.

17-2b AMT Adjustments

As Exhibit 17.3 indicates, the starting point for computing AMTI is the taxable income of the corporation before any NOL deduction. Certain *adjustments* must be made to this amount. Unlike tax preference items, which always increase AMTI, the adjustments may be either increases or decreases to taxable income.

Although NOLs are listed separately in Exhibit 17.3, they are actually adjustments that reduce taxable income. They are listed separately in Exhibit 17.3 and on the AMT tax form because they may not exceed more than 90 percent of AMTI. Thus, the NOL adjustment cannot be determined until all other adjustments and tax preference items are considered.

Computing Adjustments

It is necessary to determine not only the amount of an adjustment but also whether the adjustment is positive or negative. Careful study of Examples 16 and 17 reveals the following pattern with regard to *deductions*.

- If the deduction allowed for regular income tax purposes exceeds the deduction allowed for AMT purposes, the difference is a positive adjustment.
- If the deduction allowed for AMT purposes exceeds the deduction allowed for regular income tax purposes, the difference is a negative adjustment.

Conversely, the direction of an adjustment attributable to an *income* item can be determined as follows.

- If the income reported for regular income tax purposes exceeds the income reported for AMT purposes, the difference is a negative adjustment.
- If the income reported for AMT purposes exceeds the income reported for regular income tax purposes, the difference is a positive adjustment.

The principal AMT adjustments are discussed next. The adjustment for circulation expenditures was discussed previously.

Depreciation of Post-1986 Real Property

Tax legislation enacted in 1997 eliminated the AMT depreciation adjustment for real property by providing that the MACRS recovery periods (see Exhibit 5.7) used in calculating the regular income tax apply in calculating the AMT. Note, however, that this AMT recovery period conformity provision applies only to property placed in service after 1998.[24] Thus, the AMT depreciation adjustment discussed below applies only for real property placed in service before 1999.

For real property placed in service after 1986 (MACRS property) and before 1999, AMT depreciation is computed under the alternative depreciation system (ADS), which uses the straight-line method over a 40-year life. The depreciation lives for regular income tax purposes are 27.5 years for residential rental property and 39 years for all other real property.[25] The difference between AMT depreciation and regular income tax depreciation is treated as an adjustment in computing the AMT. The differences will be positive during the asset's regular income tax life because the cost is written off over a shorter period for regular income tax purposes. For example, during the 27.5-year income tax life of residential real property, the regular income tax depreciation will exceed the AMT depreciation because AMT depreciation is computed over a 40-year period.

Exhibit 5.7 is used to compute regular income tax depreciation on real property placed in service after 1986. For AMT purposes, depreciation on real property placed in service after 1986 and before 1999 is computed under the ADS (refer to Exhibit 5.11).

EXAMPLE

18

In January 1998, Robin Rentals placed in service a residential building that cost $100,000. Regular income tax depreciation, AMT depreciation, and the AMT adjustment are as follows.

| | Depreciation | | |
Year	Regular Income Tax	AMT	AMT Adjustment
1998	$ 3,485[1]	$ 2,396[2]	$ 1,089
1999–2014	58,176[3]	40,000[4]	18,176
2015	3,636	2,500	1,136
Total	$65,297	$44,896	$20,401

[1] $100,000 cost × 3.485% (Exhibit 5.7) = $3,485
[2] $100,000 cost × 2.396% (Exhibit 5.11) = $2,396
[3] $100,000 cost × 3.636% (Exhibit 5.7) = $3,636 for 16 years
[4] $100,000 cost × 2.500% (Exhibit 5.11) = $2,500 for 16 years

If the building had been placed in service after 1998, there would have been no AMT depreciation adjustment for the tax year it was placed in service or for subsequent years. The depreciation for the tax year the building was placed in service for both regular income tax purposes and AMT purposes would have been $3,485 ($100,000 × 3.485%).

After real property placed in service before 1999 has been held for the entire depreciation period for regular income tax purposes, the asset is fully depreciated. However, the depreciation period under the ADS is 41 years due to application of the mid-month convention, so depreciation will continue for AMT purposes. This causes negative adjustments after the property has been fully depreciated for regular income tax purposes.

EXAMPLE

19

Assume the same facts as in the previous example for the building placed in service in 1998. Regular income tax depreciation in the year 2027 (the thirtieth year of the asset's life) is zero (refer to Exhibit 5.7). AMT depreciation is $2,500 ($100,000 cost × 2.500% from Exhibit 5.11).

Therefore, Robin has a negative AMT adjustment of $2,500 ($0 regular income tax depreciation − $2,500 AMT depreciation).

---

[24]§ 56(a)(1)(A)(i).

[25]The 39-year life generally applies to nonresidential real property placed in service on or after May 13, 1993.

After real property is fully depreciated for both regular income tax and AMT purposes, the positive and negative adjustments that have been made for AMT purposes will net to zero.

Depreciation of Post-1986 Personal Property

For most personal property placed in service after 1986 (MACRS property), the MACRS deduction for regular income tax purposes is based on the 200 percent declining-balance method with a switch to straight-line when that method produces a larger depreciation deduction for the asset. Refer to Exhibit 5.5 for computing regular income tax depreciation.

For AMT purposes, the taxpayer must use the ADS for such property placed in service before 1999. This method is based on the 150 percent declining-balance method with a similar switch to straight-line for all personal property.[26] Refer to Exhibit 5.9 for percentages to be used in computing AMT depreciation.

The MACRS deduction for personal property is larger than the ADS deduction in the early years of an asset's life. However, the ADS deduction is larger in the later years. This is so because ADS lives are sometimes longer than MACRS lives and use less accelerated depreciation methods.[27] Over the ADS life of the asset, the same aggregate amount of depreciation is deducted for both regular income tax and AMT purposes. In the same manner as other timing adjustments, the AMT adjustments for depreciation will net to zero over the ADS life of the asset.

The taxpayer may elect to use the ADS for regular income tax purposes. If this election is made, no AMT adjustment is required because the depreciation deduction is the same for regular income tax and for the AMT. The election eliminates the burden of maintaining two sets of tax depreciation records at the cost of a higher regular tax liability.

For personal property placed in service after 1998, MACRS recovery periods are used in calculating AMT depreciation, but the 150 percent declining-balance method still is used. Thus, if the taxpayer elects to use the 150 percent declining-balance method for regular income tax purposes, there are no AMT adjustments. Conversely, if the taxpayer uses the 200 percent declining-balance method for regular income tax purposes, there is an AMT adjustment for depreciation.

As discussed in Chapter 5, for regular tax purposes, an additional first-year depreciation deduction equal to 50 percent of the unadjusted depreciable basis of qualified property is available for property placed in service after 2011, and before 2015. For property to which this additional first-year depreciation deduction (also known as bonus depreciation) is elected, no depreciation adjustment for AMT purposes is required. This is true both in the year the asset is placed in service and in all succeeding years in which the asset is depreciated.

Pollution Control Facilities

For regular income tax purposes, the cost of certified pollution control facilities may be amortized over a period of 60 months. For AMT purposes, the cost of these facilities placed in service after 1986 and before 1999 is depreciated under the ADS over the appropriate class life, determined as explained previously for depreciation of post-1986 property.[28] The required adjustment for AMTI is the difference between the amortization deduction allowed for regular income tax purposes and the depreciation deduction computed under the ADS. The adjustment may be positive or negative.

The AMT adjustment for pollution control facilities is reduced for property placed in service after 1998. This reduction is achieved by providing conformity in

---

[26]§ 56(a)(1).

[27]Class lives and recovery periods are established for all assets in Rev.Proc. 87–56, 1987–2 C.B. 674.

[28]§ 56(a)(5).

the recovery periods used for regular income tax purposes and AMT purposes (MACRS recovery periods).

In-depth coverage can be found on this book's companion website: www.cengagebrain.com	**3** DIGGING DEEPER

Circulation Expenditures

Circulation expenditures are expenses incurred to establish, maintain, or increase the circulation of a newspaper, a magazine, or another periodical. For regular income tax purposes, circulation expenditures, other than those the taxpayer elects to charge to a capital account, may be expensed in the year incurred.[29] For AMT purposes, circulation expenditures are not deductible in the year incurred. In computing AMTI, these expenditures must be capitalized and amortized ratably over the three-year period beginning in the year the expenditures were made.[30]

Completed Contract Method of Accounting

For a long-term contract, taxpayers are required to use the percentage of completion method for AMT purposes.[31] However, in limited circumstances, taxpayers can use the completed contract method for regular income tax purposes.[32] The resulting AMT adjustment is equal to the difference between income reported under the percentage of completion method and the amount reported using the completed contract method.[33] The adjustment can be either positive or negative, depending on the amount of income recognized under the different methods.

A taxpayer can avoid an AMT adjustment on long-term contracts by using the percentage of completion method for regular income tax purposes rather than the completed contract method.

Adjusted Gain or Loss

When a sale or disposition of property occurs, gain or loss reported for regular income tax may differ from gain or loss determined for the AMT. This difference occurs because the adjusted basis of the property for AMT purposes must reflect any current and prior AMT adjustments for the following.[34]

- Depreciation.
- Circulation expenditures.
- Amortization of certified pollution control facilities.

A negative gain or loss adjustment is required if:

- The gain for AMT purposes is less than the gain for regular income tax purposes,
- The loss for AMT purposes is more than the loss for regular income tax purposes, or
- A loss is computed for AMT purposes and a gain is computed for regular income tax purposes.

Otherwise, the AMT gain or loss adjustment is positive.

---

[29]§ 173(a).

[30]§ 56(b)(2)(A)(i).

[31]§ 56(a)(3).

[32]See Chapter 18 of *South-Western Federal Taxation: Individual Income Taxes* for a detailed discussion of the completed contract and percentage of completion methods of accounting.

[33]§ 56(a)(3).

[34]§ 56(a)(6).

EXAMPLE 20

In January 1998, Cardinal Corporation paid $100,000 for a duplex acquired for rental purposes. Regular income tax depreciation, AMT depreciation, and the AMT adjustment are as follows.

| | Depreciation | | |
Year	Regular Income Tax	AMT	AMT Adjustment
1998	$ 3,485[1]	$ 2,396[2]	$ 1,089
1999	3,636[3]	2,500[4]	1,136
2000–2013	50,904[5]	35,000[6]	15,904
2014	3,636	2,500	1,136

[1] $100,000 cost × 3.485% (Exhibit 5.7) = $3,485
[2] $100,000 cost × 2.396% (Exhibit 5.11) = $2,396
[3] $100,000 cost × 3.636% (Exhibit 5.7) = $3,636
[4] $100,000 cost × 2.500% (Exhibit 5.11) = $2,500
[5] $3,636 each year for 14 years (2000 through 2013)
[6] $2,500 each year for 14 years (2000 through 2013)

Cardinal then sold the duplex on December 20, 2015, for $105,000. Regular income tax depreciation for 2015 is $3,485 [($100,000 cost × 3.636% from Exhibit 5.7) × ($11.5/12$)]. AMT depreciation for 2015 is $2,396 [($100,000 cost × 2.500% from Exhibit 5.11) × ($11.5/12$)]. Cardinal's positive AMT adjustment for 2015 is $1,089 ($3,485 regular income tax depreciation − $2,396 AMT depreciation).

Because depreciation on the duplex differs for regular income tax and AMT purposes, Cardinal's adjusted basis for the property is different for regular income tax and AMT purposes. Consequently, the gain or loss on disposition of the duplex is different for regular income tax and AMT purposes.

The adjusted basis for Cardinal's duplex is $34,854 for regular income tax purposes and $55,208 for AMT purposes.

	Regular Income Tax	AMT
Cost	$100,000	$100,000
Depreciation:		
1998	(3,485)	(2,396)
1999	(3,636)	(2,500)
2000–2013	(50,904)	(35,000)
2014	(3,636)	(2,500)
2015	(3,485)	(2,396)
Adjusted basis	$ 34,854	$ 55,208

The regular income tax gain is $70,146, and the AMT gain is $49,792.

	Regular Income Tax	AMT
Amount realized	$105,000	$105,000
Adjusted basis	(34,854)	(55,208)
Recognized gain	$ 70,146	$ 49,792

Because the regular income tax and AMT gain on the sale of the duplex differ, Cardinal makes a negative AMT adjustment of $20,354 ($70,146 regular income tax gain − $49,792 AMT gain). The negative adjustment matches the $20,354 total of the 18 positive adjustments for depreciation ($1,089 in 1998 + $1,136 in 1999 + $15,904 from 2000 through 2013 + $1,136 in 2014 + $1,089 in 2015).

Passive Activity Losses

Net losses on passive activities are not deductible in computing either the regular income tax or the AMT for closely held C corporations (cannot offset portfolio income) and personal service corporations (cannot offset either active income or portfolio income).[35] This does not, however, eliminate the possibility of adjustments attributable to passive activities.

The rules for computing taxable income differ from the rules for computing AMTI. It follows, then, that the rules for computing such a loss for regular income tax purposes differ from the AMT rules for computing such a loss. Therefore, any *passive loss* computed for regular income tax purposes may differ from the passive loss computed for AMT purposes.

EXAMPLE 21

Robin, Inc., a personal service corporation, acquired two passive activities in 2015. Robin received net passive income of $10,000 from Activity A and had no AMT adjustments or preferences in connection with the activity. Activity B had gross income of $27,000 and operating expenses (not affected by AMT adjustments or preferences) of $19,000. Robin claimed MACRS depreciation of $20,000 for Activity B; depreciation under the ADS would have been $15,000. In addition, Robin deducted $10,000 of percentage depletion in excess of basis. The following comparison illustrates the differences in the computation of the passive loss for regular income tax and AMT purposes for Activity B.

	Regular Income Tax	AMT
Gross income	$27,000	$27,000
Deductions:		
Operating expenses	($19,000)	($19,000)
Depreciation	(20,000)	(15,000)
Depletion	(10,000)	–0–
Total deductions	($49,000)	($34,000)
Passive loss	($22,000)	($ 7,000)

Because the adjustment for depreciation ($5,000) applies and the preference for depletion ($10,000) is not taken into account in computing AMTI, the regular income tax passive activity loss of $22,000 for Activity B is reduced by these amounts, resulting in a passive activity loss of $7,000 for AMT purposes.

For regular income tax purposes, Robin would offset the $10,000 of net passive income from Activity A with $10,000 of the passive loss from Activity B. For AMT purposes, the corporation would offset the $10,000 of net passive income from Activity A with the $7,000 passive activity loss allowed from Activity B, resulting in passive activity income of $3,000. Thus, in computing AMTI, Robin makes a positive passive loss adjustment of $3,000 [$10,000 (passive activity loss allowed for regular income tax) − $7,000 (passive activity loss allowed for the AMT)].[36]

For regular income tax purposes, Robin, Inc., has a suspended passive loss of $12,000 [$22,000 (amount of loss) − $10,000 (used in 2015)]. This suspended passive loss can offset passive income in the future or can offset active or portfolio income when the corporation disposes of the loss activity (refer to Chapter 6). For AMT purposes, Robin's suspended passive loss is $0 [$7,000 (amount of loss) − $7,000 (amount used in 2015)].

17-2c **Tax Preferences**

AMTI includes designated tax preference items. Tax preferences always increase AMTI. Some of the principal tax preferences are discussed on the following pages.

Percentage Depletion

Congress enacted the percentage depletion rules to provide taxpayers with incentives to invest in the development of specified natural resources. Percentage depletion is computed by multiplying a rate specified in the Code times the gross income from the property (refer to Chapter 5). The percentage rate is based on the type of mineral involved. The basis of the property is reduced by the amount of depletion taken until

LO.5

Identify and calculate the tax preferences that are included in determining the AMT.

---

[35]§ 469(a).

[36]The depreciation adjustment and depletion preference are combined as part of the passive loss adjustment and are *not* reported separately.

the basis reaches zero. However, once the basis of the property reaches zero, taxpayers are allowed to continue taking percentage depletion deductions. Thus, over the life of the property, depletion deductions may greatly exceed the cost of the property.

For AMT purposes, percentage depletion can never exceed the basis of the property. The percentage depletion preference is equal to the excess of the regular income tax deduction for percentage depletion over the adjusted basis of the property at the end of the taxable year.[37] Basis is determined without regard to the depletion deduction for the taxable year. This preference item is figured separately for each piece of property for which the taxpayer is claiming depletion.

EXAMPLE 22

Finch, Inc., owns a mineral property that qualifies for a 22% depletion rate. The basis of the property at the beginning of the year is $10,000. Gross income from the property for the year is $100,000. For regular income tax purposes, Finch's percentage depletion deduction (assume that it is not limited by taxable income from the property) is $22,000. For AMT purposes, Finch has a tax preference of $12,000 ($22,000 − $10,000).

Interest on Private Activity Bonds

Income from private activity bonds is not included in taxable income, and expenses related to carrying such bonds are not deductible for regular income tax purposes. However, interest on private activity bonds usually is included as a preference in computing AMTI. Expenses incurred in carrying the bonds are offset against the interest income in computing the tax preference.[38] As a result of special legislation, interest on private activity bonds issued in 2009 or 2010 is not a tax preference.

The Code contains a lengthy, complex definition of **private activity bonds**.[39] In general, such debt is issued by states or municipalities, but more than 10 percent of the proceeds are used to benefit private business. For example, a bond issued by a city whose proceeds are used to construct a factory that is leased to a private business at a favorable rate is a private activity bond. Interest from municipal bonds that are not private activity bonds is not a tax preference item.

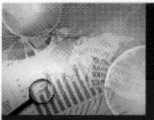

TAX PLANNING STRATEGIES Avoiding Preferences and Adjustments

FRAMEWORK FOCUS: TAX RATE

Strategy: Control the Character of Income and Deductions.

Investments in state and local bonds are attractive for income tax purposes because the interest is not included in gross income. Some of these bonds (most private activity bonds) are issued to generate funds that are not used for an essential function of the government (e.g., to provide infrastructure for shopping malls or industrial parks or to build sports facilities). The interest on such bonds is a tax preference item (except for private activity bonds issued in 2009 and 2010) and could lead to the imposition of the AMT. When the AMT applies, an investment in regular tax-exempt bonds or even fully taxed private-sector bonds might yield a higher after-tax rate of return.

If the security is a private activity bond, the interest usually is a tax preference for AMT purposes. According to the

Bond Market Association, interest from almost 8.7 percent of the $1.9 trillion municipal bond market is subject to the AMT. The association's website (**www.investinginbonds.com**) provides a primer on the AMT's effect on municipal bonds and explains how to determine whether the related interest is subject to the AMT.

For a corporation anticipating AMT problems, capitalizing rather than expensing certain costs can avoid generating preferences and adjustments. The decision should be based on the present discounted value of after-tax cash flows under the available alternatives. Costs that may be capitalized and amortized, rather than expensed, include circulation expenditures, mining exploration and development costs, and research and experimentation expenditures.

---

[37] § 57(a)(1). Percentage depletion on oil and gas wells taken by independent producers and royalty owners does not create an AMT preference. See § 613A(c).

[38] § 57(a)(5).

[39] § 141.

Intangible Drilling Costs

In computing regular taxable income, taxpayers can deduct certain intangible drilling and development costs in the year incurred, although such costs are normally capital in nature. The deduction is allowed for costs incurred in connection with oil and gas wells and geothermal wells. For AMT purposes, excess intangible drilling costs (IDC) for the year are treated as a preference.[40] The excess IDC preference is computed as follows:

IDC expensed in the year incurred
Minus: Deduction if IDC were capitalized and amortized over 10 years
Equals: Excess of IDC expense over amortization
Minus: 65% of net oil and gas or geothermal income
Equals: Tax preference item

The IDC preference is computed separately for oil and gas wells and geothermal wells. A taxpayer can avoid the preference for IDC by electing to write off the expenditures over a 10-year period for regular income tax purposes.

Ben, who incurred IDC of $50,000 during the year, elected to expense that amount. His net oil and gas income for the year was $60,000. Currently, Ben has no income from geothermal wells. Ben's preference for IDC is $6,000 [($50,000 IDC − $5,000 amortization) − (65% × $60,000 income)].

EXAMPLE

23

17-2d Adjusted Current Earnings (ACE)

The **adjusted current earnings (ACE)** rules make up a third measure of income, in addition to AMT income and taxable income. S corporations, real estate investment trusts, regulated investment companies, and real estate mortgage investment conduits are not subject to the ACE provisions. ACE represents another attempt by Congress to ensure that large corporations with significant financial accounting income pay a fair share of Federal corporate income tax. ACE is computed by adjusting AMT income for items that are often treated differently for taxable income versus financial accounting income.

The ACE adjustment can be negative or positive. AMTI is increased by 75 percent of the excess of ACE over unadjusted AMTI, or AMTI is reduced by 75 percent of the excess of unadjusted AMTI over ACE. Any negative ACE adjustment is limited to the aggregate of the positive adjustments under ACE for prior years reduced by the previously claimed negative adjustments (see Concept Summary 17.2).[41] Any unused negative adjustment is lost forever.

LO.6

State and explain the function of adjusted current earnings (ACE).

A calendar year corporation reports the following.

	2014	2015	2016
Unadjusted AMTI	$3,000,000	$3,000,000	$3,100,000
Adjusted current earnings	4,000,000	3,000,000	2,000,000

In 2014, because ACE exceeds unadjusted AMTI by $1 million, the positive ACE adjustment is $750,000 (75% × $1,000,000). No adjustment is necessary for 2015. Unadjusted AMTI exceeds ACE by $1,100,000 in 2016, so there is a potential negative ACE adjustment of $825,000. Because the total increases to AMTI for prior years equal $750,000 (and there are no negative adjustments), only $750,000 of the potential negative ACE adjustment reduces AMTI for 2016. Further, $75,000 of negative ACE is lost forever.

EXAMPLE

24

---

[40]42 §57(a)(2).

[41]§§ 56(g)(1) and (2). *Unadjusted AMTI* is AMTI before the ACE adjustment and the AMT NOL deduction; the IRS refers to this item as "pre-adjustment AMTI."

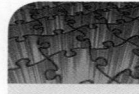

Concept Summary 17.2

Determining the ACE Adjustment*

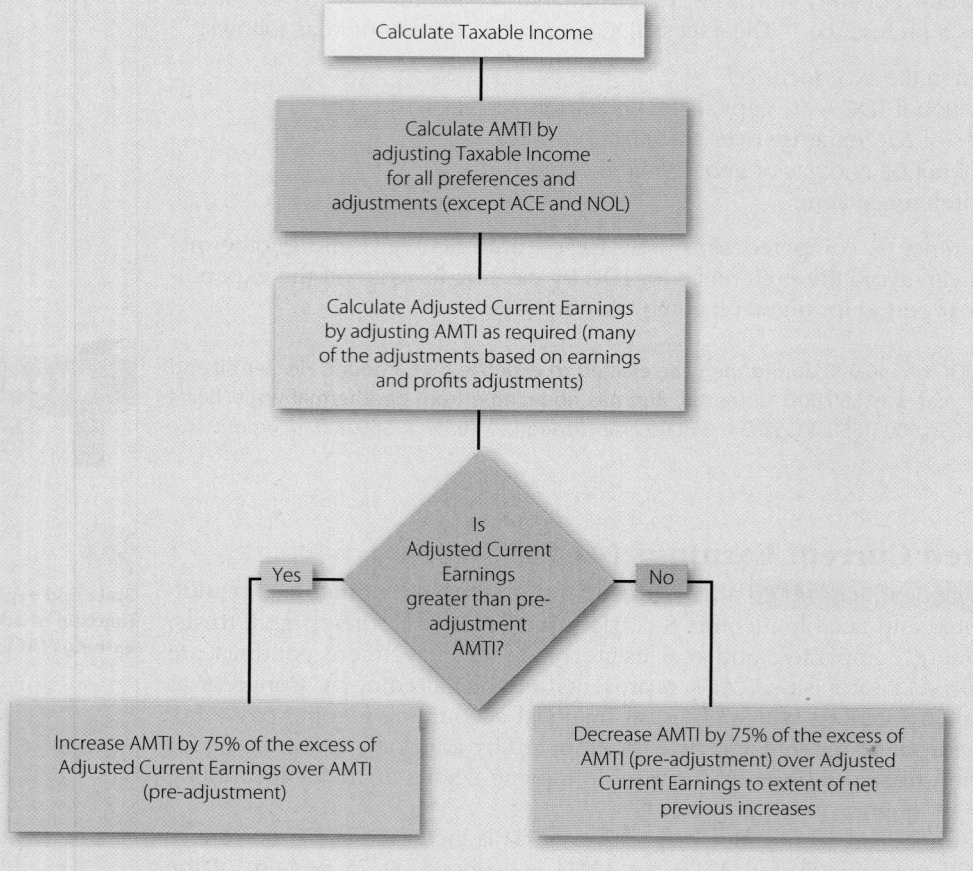

*Reprinted (with edits) from *Oil and Gas Tax Quarterly* with permission. Copyright 1989 Matthew Bender & Company, Inc., a part of LexisNexis. All rights reserved.

The starting point for computing ACE is AMTI, which is regular taxable income after AMT adjustments (other than the NOL and ACE adjustments) and tax preferences.[42] Pre-NOL AMTI is adjusted for certain items to determine ACE.

 DIGGING DEEPER 4   **In-depth coverage can be found on this book's companion website: www.cengagebrain.com**

EXAMPLE

25

Crimson Corporation makes the ACE adjustment calculation as follows.

AMTI		$ 5,780,000
Plus:		
Municipal bond interest	$210,000	
Installment gain	140,000	
70% dividends received deduction	300,000	
Income element in cash surrender life insurance	60,000	
Organization expense amortization	70,000	780,000
Subtotal		$ 6,560,000
		continued

[42]§ 56(g)(3).

Less:		
Life insurance premiums paid	$240,000	(240,000)
Adjusted current earnings		$ 6,320,000
AMTI		(5,780,000)
Base amount		$ 540,000
Times 75%		× .75
ACE adjustment (positive)		$ 405,000

ACE should not be confused with current Earnings & Profits (E & P). Many items are treated in the same manner, but certain items that are deductible in computing E & P (but are not deductible in calculating taxable income) generally are not deductible in computing ACE (e.g., Federal income taxes). Concept Summary 17.3 compares the effects that various transactions have on the determination of ACE and E & P.

Concept Summary 17.3

How Various Transactions Affect ACE and E & P

	Effect on Unadjusted AMTI in Arriving at ACE	Effect on Taxable Income in Arriving at Corporate E & P
Tax-exempt income (net of expenses)	Add	Add
Federal income tax	No effect	Subtract
Dividends received deduction (80% and 100% rules)	No effect	Add
Dividends received deduction (70% rule)	Add	Add
Exemption amount ($40,000)	No effect	No effect
Excess charitable contribution	No effect	Subtract
Excess capital losses	No effect	Subtract
Disallowed meals and entertainment expenses	No effect	Subtract
Penalties and fines	No effect	Subtract
Intangible drilling costs deducted currently	Add	Add
Deferred gain on installment sales	Add	Add
Realized (not recognized) gain (e.g., involuntary conversion, like-kind exchanges)	No effect	No effect
Loss on sale between related parties	No effect	Subtract
Key employee insurance proceeds	Add	Add
Premiums paid on key employee life insurance	Subtract	Subtract
Cash surrender value increase on life insurance policy	Add	Add
Organization expense amortization	Add	Add

17-2e Alternative Tax Net Operating Loss Deduction

In computing taxable income, taxpayers are allowed to deduct net operating loss (NOL) carryovers and carrybacks. While the NOL deduction is allowed for AMT purposes, the regular income tax NOL must be modified to correctly compute AMTI. The starting point in computing the alternative tax NOL deduction (ATNOLD) is the NOL computed for regular income tax purposes. The regular income tax NOL is then modified for AMT adjustments and tax preferences with the result being the ATNOLD. Thus, preferences and adjustment items that have benefited the taxpayer in computing the regular income tax NOL (in other words, the adjustments and preferences that have increased the regular tax NOL) are added back, thereby reducing or eliminating the ATNOLD.[43]

In 2015, Sparrow Corporation incurred an NOL of $400,000. Sparrow owns an item of MACRS five-year property, placed in service on March 15, 2015, at a cost of $1,000,000. Regular tax depreciation is $200,000 ($1,000,000 × 20%), and AMT depreciation is $150,000 ($1,000,000 × 15%). Sparrow's deductions also include tax preferences of $80,000. Its ATNOLD carryback to 2013 is $320,000 ($400,000 regular income tax NOL − $80,000 tax preferences deducted in computing the NOL). Because the adjustment for depreciation was positive, the depreciation adjustment does not affect the ATNOLD.

In keeping with the goal of ensuring that taxpayers with economic income pay some minimum amount of tax, a ceiling exists on the amount of the ATNOLD that can be deducted in the carryback or carryforward year. The deduction is limited to 90 percent of AMTI (before the ATNOLD) for the carryback or carryforward year.[44]

Assume the same facts as in the previous example, except that Sparrow's AMTI (before the ATNOLD) in 2013 is $190,000. Therefore, of the $320,000 ATNOLD carried back to 2013 from 2014, only $171,000 ($190,000 × 90%) can be used in recalculating the 2013 AMT. The unused $149,000 of 2015 ATNOLD is now carried to 2014 for use in recalculating the 2014 AMT.

A taxpayer who has an ATNOLD that is carried back or over to another year must use the ATNOLD against AMTI in the carryback or carryforward year even if the taxpayer is not subject to the AMT. This can result in the loss of an ATNOLD, even when the taxpayer does not have an AMT liability.

Swan's ATNOLD for 2015 (carried over from 2014) is $10,000. AMTI in 2015, before considering the ATNOLD, is $25,000. If Swan's regular income tax exceeds the tentative minimum tax (TMT), the AMT does not apply. Nevertheless, Swan's ATNOLD of $10,000 is "used up" in 2015 and is not available for carryover to a later year.

For regular income tax purposes, the NOL generally can be carried back 2 years and forward 20 years. However, the taxpayer may elect to forgo the 2-year carryback. These rules generally apply to the ATNOLD as well, except that the election to forgo the 2-year carryback is available for the ATNOLD only if the taxpayer elected it for the regular income tax NOL.

Compute the AMT liability for corporations and individuals.

17-2f **Computation of Alternative Minimum Taxable Income**

The following example illustrates the effect of tax preferences and adjustments in arriving at AMTI.

Tan Corporation (a calendar year company) recorded the following transactions:

Taxable income	$4,250,000
Income deferred by using completed contract method (versus percentage of completion method)	450,000
Percentage depletion claimed (the property has a zero adjusted basis)	1,575,000
Interest on City of Elmira (Michigan) 2007 private activity bonds	1,175,000

continued

---

[43]§ 56(a)(4).

[44]§ 56(d)(1)(A)(i)(II).

Tan Corporation is not a small corporation for AMT purposes. Its AMTI is determined as follows:

Taxable income		$4,250,000
Adjustments		
Income deferred by using completed contract method (versus percentage of completion method)		450,000
Tax preferences		
Excess depletion deduction	$1,575,000	
Interest on private activity municipal bonds	1,175,000	2,750,000
AMTI		$7,450,000

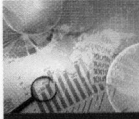

TAX PLANNING STRATEGIES Optimum Use of the AMT and Regular Corporate Income Tax Rate Difference

FRAMEWORK FOCUS: TAX RATE

Strategy: Shift Net Income from High-Bracket Years to Low-Bracket Years.

A corporation that cannot avoid the AMT in a particular year often can save taxes by taking advantage of the difference between the AMT and the regular income tax rates. In general, a corporation that expects to be subject to the AMT should consider accelerating income and deferring deductions for the remainder of the year. Because the difference between the regular income tax rate and the AMT rate may be as much as 15 percentage points, this strategy may result in the income being taxed at less than it would be if reported in the next year (a non-AMT year). If the same corporation expects to be subject to the AMT for the next year (or years) and is not subject to AMT this year, this technique should be reversed.

EXAMPLE 30

Falcon Corporation expects to be in the 34% regular income tax bracket in 2016, but is subject to the AMT in 2015. In late 2015, Falcon is contemplating selling a tract of unimproved land (basis of $200,000 and fair market value of $1 million), which is classified as inventory. Under these circumstances, it may be preferable to sell the land in 2015. The gain of $800,000 ($1,000,000 − $200,000) generates a tax of $160,000 [$800,000 (recognized gain) × 20% (AMT rate)].

If, however, the land is sold in 2016, the resulting tax is $272,000 [$800,000 (recognized gain) × 34% (regular corporate income tax rate)]. A nominal savings of $112,000 ($272,000 − $160,000) materializes by making the sale in 2015.

Whenever one accelerates income or defers deductions, a present value analysis should be conducted. This technique to accelerate gross income is attractive only if it reduces the present value of tax liabilities.

17-2g AMT Rate and Exemption

The AMT rate is 20 percent. The rate is applied to the *AMT base*, which is AMTI reduced by the *AMT exemption*. The exemption amount for a corporation is $40,000 reduced by 25 percent of the amount by which AMTI exceeds $150,000. The exemption phases out entirely when AMTI reaches $310,000.

EXAMPLE 31

Beige Corporation has AMTI of $180,000. Because the exemption amount is reduced by $7,500 [25% × ($180,000 − $150,000)], the exemption amount remaining is $32,500 ($40,000 − $7,500). Thus, Beige Corporation's alternative minimum tax base (refer to Exhibit 17.3) is $147,500 ($180,000 − $32,500).

17-2h **Minimum Tax Credit**

The minimum tax credit acts to make the AMT merely a *prepayment of tax* for corporations. Essentially, the AMT paid in one tax year may be carried forward indefinitely and used as a credit against the corporation's future *regular* tax liability that exceeds its tentative minimum tax. The minimum tax credit may not be carried back and may not be offset against any future AMT liability.

EXAMPLE 32

Return to the facts of Example 29. As Tan Corporation's AMTI exceeds $310,000, there is no AMT exemption amount. The tentative minimum tax is $1,490,000 (20% of $7,450,000).

Tan's regular income tax liability is $1,445,000 ($4,250,000 × 34%). As a result, its AMT liability is $45,000 ($1,490,000 − $1,445,000). The minimum tax credit carried forward is $45,000, the current year's AMT. The credit can be used to reduce regular income tax liability in a future tax year (but not below the tentative minimum tax for that year).

17-2i **Other Aspects of the AMT**

Form 4626 (Alternative Minimum Tax—Corporations) is the form corporations use to report AMT amounts to the IRS. Any AMT calculated is carried over to Schedule J of Form 1120 (U.S. Corporation Income Tax Return). In addition to paying their regular income tax liability, corporations must make estimated tax payments of the AMT liability. Even corporations that prepare quarterly financial statements may find that this requirement adds to compliance costs.

In a year in which the corporation is subject to the AMT, the AMT amount creates a minimum tax credit available for carryover to future years. This credit can be used in the future to the extent the regular tax liability exceeds the tentative minimum tax for a year. This credit can be carried forward indefinitely. Certain small corporations can use specified tax credits to reduce the AMT liability. For all other corporations, only the foreign tax credit can be claimed in an AMT year.[45]

---

[45]§ 38(c)(5)(A).

Often, the tax law is changed to prevent or reduce certain perceived abuses. Such was the case when the AMT was enacted in 1969. The identifiable perceived abuse was that 155 individual taxpayers had zero Federal income tax liability despite having incomes in excess of $200,000.

Thus, the original idea behind the AMT was one of fairness, based on the premise that taxpayers with significant economic income should pay at least a minimum amount of tax. Although this idea has not changed, the tax is fast becoming anything but fair, according to most observers. That same concept of fairness later led Nina Olsen, the IRS's Taxpayer Advocate, to identify the expanding scope of the AMT as the number one problem facing taxpayers that needs to be legislatively addressed. The American Taxpayer Relief Act of 2012 addressed a portion of the concerns raised by increasing the individual AMT exemption amounts and adjusting them for inflation.

Yet, the AMT still applies to a large number of taxpayers—about 4 million in 2013. What has caused this shift in what is deemed fair? The idea that taxpayers with significant economic income should pay at least a minimum amount of tax has not changed. Thus, a tax that was perceived as fair when it affected only a "few" now is perceived as unfair because it affects "many."

17-3 INDIVIDUAL ALTERNATIVE MINIMUM TAX

The AMT applicable to individuals is similar to the corporate AMT. Most of the adjustments and preferences discussed previously apply equally to individuals and corporations. However, there are several important differences.

- The individual AMT rate is slightly progressive, with rates at 26 percent on the first $185,400 ($92,700 for married, filing separately) of AMTI and at 28 percent on any additional AMTI.

- The alternative rate on net capital gain of 0, 15, or 20 percent applies.

- The AMT exemption and phaseout amounts are tied to the individual's filing status for the year. The exemption phases out at a rate of $1 for every $4 of AMTI.[46] The exemption amounts for 2015 are listed in the table below.

| | | Phaseout Range | |
Filing Status	Exemption Amount	Begins at	Ends at
Married, joint	$83,400	$158,900	$492,500
Married, separate	41,700	79,450	246,250
Single or Head of household	53,600	119,200	333,600

- Individuals make no AMT adjustment for ACE.

- Some additional adjustments apply to individual taxpayers. Taxes and miscellaneous itemized deductions subject to the 2 percent-of-AGI floor are not allowed as deductions for AMTI. Medical expenses are allowed only to the extent they exceed 10 percent of AGI (instead of a 7.5 percent limitation for regular income tax purposes if at least age 65). Interest expense deductions are limited to qualified residence interest, interest on certain student loans, and investment interest (subject to limitations). The 3 percent phaseout of itemized deductions that applies to certain high-income taxpayers (refer to Chapter 9) does *not* apply in computing the individual AMT. Finally, the standard deduction and personal and dependency exemptions are not allowed as deductions when computing AMTI. Other individual-specific adjustments also exist, including an adjustment accelerating the taxation of incentive stock options. Personal nonrefundable credits can offset any AMT liability.

- Determination of the minimum tax credit is more complex for individual taxpayers. The credit usually applies only to AMT generated as a result of *timing* differences.

---

[46]AMT exemption amounts for 2014 were $82,100, $41,050, and $52,800, respectively.

In most years, the disallowance of a deduction for state and local income taxes and for personal and dependency exemptions accounts for 85 percent of the AMT revenue collected from individuals.

The individual AMT and the corporate AMT have the same objective: to force taxpayers who have more economic income than that reflected in taxable income to pay a fair share of Federal income tax.

REFOCUS ON THE BIG PICTURE

DEALING WITH TAX CREDITS AND THE AMT

Tax credits are used by the Federal government to promote certain social and economic objectives. Credits are dollar-for-dollar reductions in tax liability. While tax credits may have strict qualification requirements, taking advantage of available credits may significantly reduce a business's tax liability. Progress Corporation qualifies for a 10 percent tax credit for rehabilitating a building that was placed in service before 1936 (see Example 4). In addition, Progress hires workers from economically disadvantaged groups, so it qualifies for the work opportunity tax credit (see Example 6).

The company also qualifies for the credit for employer-provided child care, equal to 25 percent of qualified child care expenses (see Example 13). Mike and his CPA might also want to explore taking advantage of the disabled access credit, which is designed to encourage small businesses to make their facilities accessible to disabled individuals.

What If?

Mike has heard horror stories about the alternative minimum tax (AMT) and is concerned about its potential impact on his company. What if Mike's company is subject to the AMT?

If Progress Corporation is subject to the AMT, the company's general business credits (including the tax credit for rehabilitation expenditures, the work opportunity tax credit, the disabled access credit, and the credit for employer-provided child care) are limited to the taxpayer's regular income tax reduced by the greater of the company's tentative minimum tax or 25 percent of the regular income tax liability exceeding $25,000. Accordingly, much of the tax benefit may be lost or require a carryback or carryover to another tax year. However, small corporations with average gross receipts under certain thresholds may be exempt from the AMT. Before Mike proceeds with his plans, his exposure to the AMT should be determined.

Suggested Readings

Beth Henricks, "Enlist Human Resources to Screen for Employment Tax Credits," *Practical Tax Strategies*, April 2008.

Thomas Horan and Margaret Horan, "Strategies for Reducing the Alternative Minimum Tax Liability," *The CPA Journal*, March 2013.

Kreig D. Mitchell, "The R&D Tax Credit for Start-Up Companies," *Practical Tax Strategies*, February 2012.

Tom Prieto, "AMT Planning with Listed Options," *Practical Tax Strategies*, October 2010.

William R. Swindle, "Recent Cases Provide Relief for Substantiating Research Tax Credit Claims," *Practical Tax Strategies*, June 2010.

Dean Zerbe, Benjamin Yaker, and David Ji, "New Law Opens Door for Businesses to Take R&D Tax Credit," *Practical Tax Strategies*, April 2011.

Key Terms

Adjusted current earnings (ACE), 17-23

Alternative minimum tax (AMT), 17-14

Alternative minimum taxable income (AMTI), 17-15

Credit for employer-provided child care, 17-11

Credit for small employer pension plan startup costs, 17-11

Disabled access credit, 17-10

Energy credits, 17-10

Foreign tax credit (FTC), 17-12

General business credit, 17-2

Minimum tax credit, 17-28

Private activity bonds, 17-22

Rehabilitation expenditures credit, 17-5

Rehabilitation expenditures credit recapture, 17-6

Research activities credit, 17-8

Tax credits, 17-2

Tax preference items, 17-21

Work opportunity tax credit, 17-6

Computational Exercises

1. **LO.2** Carlson's general business credit for the current year is $84,000 His net income tax is $190,000, tentative minimum tax is $175,000, and net regular tax liability is $185,000. He has no other tax credits. Determine the amount of Carlson's general business credit for the year.

2. **LO.2** Emily spent $135,000 to rehabilitate a building (adjusted basis of $90,000) that originally had been placed in service in 1935.

   a. What is Emily's rehabilitation expenditures tax credit?

   b. What would be your answer if the building was a historic structure?

3. **LO.2** During 2015, Lincoln Company hires seven individuals who are certified to be members of a qualifying targeted group. Each employee works in excess of 600 hours and is paid wages of $7,500 during the year. Determine the amount of Lincoln's work opportunity credit.

4. **LO.2** Dorcas incurs the following research expenditures.

In-house wages	$60,000
In-house supplies	5,000
Paid to ABC, Inc., for research	80,000

   a. Determine the amount of qualified research expenditures.

   b. Assuming that the base amount is $50,000, determine Dorcas's incremental research activities credit.

5. **LO.3** Siga, Inc., a calendar year corporation, records the following gross receipts and taxable income for 2013 through 2015.

Year	Gross Receipts	Taxable Income
2013	$4,200,000	$ 900,000
2014	7,000,000	1,600,000
2015	7,700,000	1,900,000

   Siga's first year of operations was 2013. Is Siga exempt from AMT in 2013, 2014, or 2015?

6. **LO.4** In 2015, Brennen sold a machine used in his business for $180,000. The machine was purchased eight years ago for $340,000. Depreciation up to the date of the sale for regular income tax purposes was $210,000 and $190,000 for AMT purposes.

   What, if any, AMT adjustment arises as a result of the sale of the machine?

7. **LO.4** Pineview Corporation placed an asset (three-year MACRS class life) costing $5,000 in service on June 1, 2015. Complete the table below by providing the AMT adjustment and indicate whether the adjustment increases or decreases taxable income.

Year	Tax Deduction	AMT Deduction	AMT Adjustment	Increases or Decreases
2015	$1,667	$1,250	$ _____	_____
2016	2,222	1,875	$ _____	_____
2017	740	1,250	$ _____	_____
2018	371	625	$ _____	_____

8. **LO.6** Given the following information, determine the ACE adjustment for each year.

	2015	2016	2017
Unadjusted AMTI	$ 800,000	$2,000,000	$1,500,000
Adjusted current earnings	1,200,000	2,000,000	900,000

Problems

9. **LO.2** Charles has a tentative general business credit of $42,000 for the current year. His net regular tax liability before the general business credit is $107,000, and his tentative minimum tax is $88,000. Compute Charles's allowable general business credit for the year.

10. **LO.2** Oak Corporation holds the following general business credit carryovers.

2011	$ 5,000
2012	15,000
2013	6,000
2014	19,000
Total carryovers	$45,000

If the general business credit generated by activities during 2015 equals $36,000 and the total credit allowed during the current year is $60,000 (based on tax liability), what amounts of the current general business credit and carryovers are utilized against the 2015 income tax liability? What is the amount of the unused credit carried forward to 2016?

11. **LO.2** In January 2014, Iris Corporation purchased and placed in service a 1933 building that houses retail businesses. The cost was $300,000, of which $25,000 applied to the land. In modernizing the facility, Iris Corporation incurred $312,000 of renovation costs of the type that qualify for the rehabilitation credit. These improvements were placed in service in October 2015.
    a. Compute Iris Corporation's rehabilitation tax credit for 2015.
    b. Calculate the cost recovery deductions for the building and the renovation costs for 2015.

Decision Making

Communications

12. **LO.2** In the current year, Paul Chaing (4522 Fargo Street, Geneva, IL 60134) acquires a qualifying historic structure for $350,000 (excluding the cost of the land) and plans to substantially rehabilitate the structure. He is planning to spend either $320,000 or $380,000 on rehabilitation expenditures. Write a letter to Paul and a memo for the tax files explaining, for the two alternative expenditures, (1) the computation that determines the rehabilitation expenditures tax credit available to Paul,

(2) the effect of the credit on Paul's adjusted basis in the property, and (3) the cash-flow differences as a result of the tax consequences related to his expenditure choice.

13. **LO.2** The tax credit for rehabilitation expenditures is available to help offset the costs related to substantially rehabilitating certain buildings. The credit is calculated on the rehabilitation expenditures incurred and not on the acquisition cost of the building itself.

Ethics and Equity

You are a developer who buys, sells, and does construction work on real estate in the inner city of your metropolitan area. A potential customer approaches you about acquiring one of your buildings that easily could qualify for the 20% rehabilitation credit on historic structures. The stated sales price of the structure is $100,000 (based on appraisals ranging from $80,000 to $120,000), and the rehabilitation expenditures, if the job is done correctly, would be about $150,000.

Your business has been slow recently due to the sluggish real estate market in your area, and the potential customer makes the following proposal: if you reduce the sales price of the building to $75,000, he will pay you $175,000 to perform the rehabilitation work. Although the buyer's total expenditures would be the same, he would benefit from this approach by obtaining a larger tax credit ($25,000 increased rehabilitation costs × 20% = $5,000).

It has been a long time since you have sold any of your real estate. How will you respond?

14. **LO.2** Green Corporation hires six individuals on January 4, 2015, all of whom qualify for the work opportunity credit. Three of these individuals receive wages of $8,500 during 2015, and each individual works more than 400 hours during the year. The other three individuals each work 300 hours and receive wages of $5,000 during the year.
   a. Calculate the amount of Green's work opportunity credit for 2015.
   b. If Green pays total wages of $140,000 to its employees during the year, how much of this amount is deductible in 2015 assuming that the work opportunity credit is taken?

15. **LO.2** In March 2015, Sparrow Corporation hired three individuals—Austin, Adam, and Angela—all of whom are certified as long-term family assistance recipients. Each of these individuals earned $11,000 during 2015. Only Adam continued to work for Sparrow in 2016, and he earned $13,500 then. In March 2016, Sparrow hired Sam, who also is certified as a long-term family assistance recipient. During 2016, Sam earned $12,000.
   a. Compute Sparrow Corporation's work opportunity credit for 2015 and 2016.
   b. If Sparrow pays total wages to its employees of $325,000 in 2015 and $342,000 in 2016, what is its wage deduction in each of those years?

16. **LO.2** Tom, a calendar year taxpayer, informs you that during the year, he incurs expenditures of $40,000 that qualify for the incremental research activities credit. In addition, it is determined that his research-credit base amount for the year is $32,800.
   a. Determine Tom's incremental research activities credit for the year.
   b. Tom is in the 25% tax bracket. Determine which approach to the research expenditures and the research activities credit (other than capitalization and subsequent amortization) would provide the greater tax benefit to Tom.

Decision Making

17. **LO.2** Ahmed Zinna (16 Southside Drive, Charlotte, NC 28204), one of your clients, owns two retail establishments in downtown Charlotte and has come to you seeking advice concerning the tax consequences of complying with the Americans with Disabilities Act. He understands that he needs to install various features at his

Communications

stores (e.g., ramps, doorways, and restrooms that are handicapped-accessible) to make them more accessible to disabled individuals.

Ahmed asks whether any tax credits will be available to help offset the cost of the necessary changes. He estimates the cost of the planned changes to his facilities as follows.

Location	Projected Cost
Calvin Street	$22,000
Stowe Avenue	8,500

Ahmed reminds you that the Calvin Street store was constructed in 2004, while the Stowe Avenue store is in a building that was constructed in 1947. Ahmed operates his business as a sole proprietorship and has approximately eight employees at each location. Write a letter to Ahmed in which you summarize your conclusions concerning the tax consequences of the proposed capital improvements.

18. **LO.2** Blue Horizons, Inc., a U.S. corporation, is a manufacturing concern that sells most of its products in the United States. It also does some business in the European Union through various branches. During the current year, Blue Horizons has taxable income of $700,000, of which $500,000 is U.S.-sourced and $200,000 is foreign-sourced. Foreign income taxes paid amounted to $45,000. Blue Horizons's U.S. income tax liability is $238,000. What is its U.S. income tax liability net of the allowable foreign tax credit?

19. **LO.3** Aqua, Inc., a calendar year corporation, has the following gross receipts and taxable income for 2012 through 2015:

Year	Gross Receipts	Taxable Income
2012	$6,000,000	$1,400,000
2013	7,000,000	1,312,000
2014	7,500,000	985,000
2015	7,200,000	1,002,000

Aqua's first year of operations was 2012.

a. When is Aqua first exempt from the AMT as a small corporation?

b. Is Aqua subject to the AMT for 2015? Explain.

20. **LO.4** Falcon, Inc., owns a silver mine that it purchased several years ago for $925,000. The adjusted basis at the beginning of the year is $400,000. For the year, Falcon deducts depletion of $700,000 (greater of cost depletion of $290,000 or percentage depletion of $700,000) for regular income tax purposes.

a. Calculate Falcon's AMT preference.

b. Calculate Falcon's adjusted basis for regular income tax purposes.

c. Calculate Falcon's adjusted basis for AMT purposes.

Decision Making

Communications

21. **LO.5** In March 2015, Grackle, Inc., acquired used equipment for its business at a cost of $300,000. The equipment is five-year class property for regular income tax purposes and for AMT purposes. Grackle does not claim any available additional first-year depreciation.

a. If Grackle depreciates the equipment using the method that will produce the greatest deduction for 2015 for regular income tax purposes, what is the amount of the AMT adjustment? Grackle does not elect §179 limited expensing.

b. How can Grackle reduce the AMT adjustment to $0? What circumstances would motivate Grackle to do so?

c. Draft a letter to Helen Carlon, Grackle's controller, regarding the choice of depreciation methods. Helen's address is 500 Monticello Avenue, Glendale, AZ 85306.

22. **LO.5** Rust Company is a real estate construction business with average annual gross receipts of $3 million. Rust uses the completed contract method on a particular contract that requires 16 months to complete. The contract is for $500,000, with estimated costs of $300,000. At the end of 2015, $180,000 of costs had been incurred. The contract is completed in 2016, with the total cost being $295,000. Determine the amount of adjustments for AMT purposes for 2015 and 2016.

23. **LO.5** Allie, who was an accounting major in college, is the controller of a medium-size construction corporation. She prepares the corporate tax return each year. Due to reporting a home construction contract using the completed contract method, the corporation is subject to the AMT in 2015. Allie files the 2015 corporate tax return in early February 2016. The total tax liability is $58,000 ($53,000 regular income tax liability + $5,000 AMT).

    In early March, Allie reads an article on minimizing income taxes. Based on this article, she decides that it would be beneficial for the corporation to report the home construction contract using the percentage of completion method on its 2015 return. Although this will increase the corporation's 2015 income tax liability, it will minimize the total income tax liability over the two-year construction period. Therefore, Allie files an amended return on March 14, 2016. Evaluate Allie's actions from both a tax avoidance and an ethical perspective.

Ethics and Equity

24. **LO.5** Buford sells an apartment building for $720,000. His adjusted basis is $500,000 for regular income tax purposes and $550,000 for AMT purposes. Calculate Buford's:
    a. Gain for regular income tax purposes.
    b. Gain for AMT purposes.
    c. AMT adjustment, if any.

25. **LO.5** Pheasant, Inc., is going to be subject to the AMT in 2015. The corporation owns an investment building and is considering disposing of it and investing in other realty. Based on an appraisal of the building's value, the realized gain would be $85,000. Ed has offered to purchase the building from Pheasant with a December 29, 2015 closing date.

Issue ID

    Ed wants to close the transaction in 2015 because he will receive certain beneficial tax consequences only if the transaction is closed prior to 2016. Abby has offered to purchase the building with a January 2, 2016 closing date. The adjusted basis of the building is $95,000 greater for AMT purposes than for the regular income tax. Pheasant expects to be in the 34% regular income tax bracket.

    What are the relevant Federal income tax issues that Pheasant faces in making its decision?

26. **LO.5** Flicker, Inc., a closely held corporation, acquired a passive activity this year. Gross income from operations of the activity was $160,000. Operating expenses, not including depreciation, were $122,000. Regular income tax depreciation of $49,750 was computed under MACRS. AMT depreciation, computed using the ADS, was $41,000. Compute Flicker's passive loss deduction and passive loss suspended for regular income tax purposes. Then determine the same amounts for AMT purposes.

27. **LO.6** Maize Corporation (a calendar year corporation) reports the following information for the years listed.

	2014	2015	2016
Adjusted current earnings	$5,000,000	$5,000,000	$7,000,000
Unadjusted AMTI	8,000,000	5,000,000	3,000,000

Compute the ACE adjustment for each year.

28. **LO.6** Based on the following facts, calculate adjusted current earnings (ACE).

Alternative minimum taxable income (AMTI before ACE adjustment)	$5,120,000
Municipal bond interest	630,000
Expenses related to municipal bonds	50,000
Key employee life insurance proceeds in excess of cash surrender value	2,000,000
Organization expense amortization	100,000
Cost of goods sold	6,220,000
Advertising expenses	760,000
Loss between related parties	260,000
Life insurance premiums paid	300,000

29. **LO.6** Purple Corporation, a calendar year taxpayer, began operations in 2013. It reported the following amounts for its first four tax years. Calculate Purple's positive and negative ACE adjustments for each year.

	Unadjusted AMTI	ACE
2013	$85,000,000	$70,000,000
2014	70,000,000	90,000,000
2015	54,000,000	40,000,000
2016	60,000,000	20,000,000

30. **LO.4, 5, 6** Determine whether each of the following transactions is a preference (P), is an adjustment (A), or is not applicable (NA) for purposes of the corporate AMT.
    a.   Depletion in excess of basis taken by Giant Oil Company.
    b.   Accelerated depreciation on property.
    c.   Charitable contributions of cash.
    d.   Adjusted current earnings.
    e.   Untaxed appreciation on property donated to charity.
    f.   Dividends received deduction.

31. **LO.7** In each of the following *independent* situations, determine the tentative minimum tax. Assume that the company is not in small corporation status.

	AMTI (before the Exemption Amount)
Quincy Corporation	$150,000
Redland Corporation	160,000
Tanzen Corporation	320,000

32. **LO.7** Peach Corporation (a calendar year company) recorded the following transactions.

Taxable income	$5,000,000
Regular tax depreciation on realty in excess of ADS (placed in service in 1991)	1,700,000
Amortization of certified pollution control facilities (in excess of ADS amortization)	200,000
Tax-exempt interest on private activity bonds issued in 2006	300,000
Percentage depletion in excess of the property's adjusted basis	700,000

    a.   Determine Peach Corporation's AMTI.
    b.   Determine the alternative minimum tax base (refer to Exhibit 17.3).
    c.   Determine the tentative minimum tax.
    d.   What is the amount of the AMT?

33. **LO.7** Included in Alice's regular taxable income and in her AMT base is a $300,000 capital gain on the sale of stock she owned for three years. Alice is in the 35%

tax bracket for regular income tax purposes. In calculating her regular income tax liability, she uses the appropriate alternative tax rate on net capital gain of 20%.

a. What rate should Alice use in calculating her tentative AMT?

b. What is Alice's AMT adjustment?

c. How would your answers in (a) and (b) change if the taxpayer were a C corporation in the 34% tax bracket for regular income tax purposes?

34. **LO.7** Calculate the AMT for the following cases in 2015. The individual taxpayer reports regular taxable income of $450,000 and no tax credits.

	Tentative Minimum Tax	
Filing Status	**Case 1**	**Case 2**
Single	$200,000	$100,000
Married, filing jointly	200,000	100,000

35. **LO.4, 5** Jane and Robert Brown are married and have eight children, all of whom are eligible to be claimed as the couple's dependents. Robert earns $94,000 working as an accountant, and Jane earns $35,000 as a teaching aide. Given their large family, they live in a frugal manner. The family maintains a large garden and some fruit trees from which they get most of their produce, and the children take family and consumer science classes so that they can help make their clothing. The couple has no other income besides their salaries (all of their investment income is earned in retirement savings), and their itemized deductions are less than the standard deduction. In addition, they have no additional adjustments or preferences for AMT purposes.

a. What is the couple's 2015 regular tax liability?

b. What is the couple's 2015 AMT?

BRIDGE DISCIPLINE

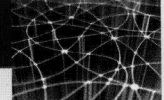

1. Balm, Inc., has a general business credit for 2015 of $90,000. Balm's regular income tax liability before credits is $140,000, and its tentative AMT is $132,000.

   a. Calculate the amount of general business credit Balm can use in 2015, and calculate its general business credit carryback and carryforward, if any.

   b. Balm projects a $140,000 regular 2016 income tax liability. Its tentative AMT will be $132,000. Balm is considering making an investment early in 2016 that annually will produce $45,000 of tax-exempt income. Balm is trying to decide between two alternatives. The first alternative is a tax-exempt bond that is a 2013 private activity bond. The second alternative is a tax-exempt bond that is not a private activity bond. Advise Balm on the preferable investment.

2. Cooper Partnership, a calendar year partnership, made qualifying rehabilitation expenditures to a building that it has used in its business for eight years. These improvements were placed in service on January 5, 2014. The amount of the rehabilitation expenditures credit was $40,000.

   Cooper is negotiating to sell the building in either December 2015 or January 2016. The sales price will be $600,000, and the recognized gain will be $100,000. Provide support for the CFO's position that Cooper should delay the sale until 2016.

3. For many years, Saul's sole proprietorship and his related Form 1040 have had a number of AMT tax preferences and AMT adjustments. He has made the AMT calculation each year, but the calculated amount always has been $0. Saul's regular taxable income and the AMT adjustments and preferences for 2015 are the same as for last year. Yet, he must pay AMT this year. Explain how this could happen.

Research Problems

THOMSON REUTERS
CHECKPOINT®
Student Edition

Note: Solutions to Research Problems can be prepared by using the Checkpoint® Student Edition online research product, which is available to accompany this text. It is also possible to prepare solutions to the Research Problems by using tax research materials found in a standard tax library.

Research Problem 1. During a recent Sunday afternoon excursion, Miriam, an admirer of early twentieth-century architecture, discovers a 1920s-era house in the country-side outside Mobile, Alabama, during a recent Sunday excursion. She wants not only to purchase and renovate this particular house but also to move the structure into Mobile so that her community can enjoy its architectural features.

Being aware of the availability of the tax credit for rehabilitation expenditures, she wants to maximize her use of the provision, if it is available in this case, once the renovation work begins in Mobile. However, Miriam also informs you that she will pursue the purchase, relocation, and renovation of the house only if the tax credit is available.

Comment on Miriam's decision and on whether any renovation expenditures incurred will qualify for the tax credit for rehabilitation expenditures.

Partial list of research aids:
George S. Nalle III v. Comm., 72 AFTR 2d 93–5705, 997 F.2d 1134, 93–2 USTC ¶50,468 (CA–5, 1993).

Communications

Research Problem 2. Your ophthalmologist, Dr. Hunter Francis (55 Wheatland Drive, Hampton, CT 06247), has been very pleased with the growth of his practice in the 15 years he has been in business. This growth has resulted, at least in part, because he has aggressively marketed his services and tried to accommodate clients with various needs. This year, Dr. Francis purchased a sophisticated piece of equipment that enables him to diagnose persons with mental handicaps, hearing impairments, and physical disabilities without having to go through a series of questions. In addition, he can treat his patients who are not disabled more accurately and efficiently by using this equipment.

Since purchasing the machine this year for $9,500, Dr. Francis has used it on many occasions. Unfortunately, he has not been able to attract any patients with disabilities, even though previously he referred such people to other ophthalmologists who owned the necessary equipment. Therefore, the primary purpose for acquiring the equipment (i.e., to attract patients with disabilities) has not been realized, but he has put it to good use in treating other patients. Write a letter to Dr. Francis explaining whether he may claim the disabled access credit for this acquisition.

Research Problem 3. Teal, Inc., owns two warehouses that were placed in service before 1987. This year, accelerated depreciation on Warehouse A is $36,000 (straight-line depreciation would have been $30,000). On Warehouse B, accelerated depreciation was $16,000 (straight-line depreciation would have been $20,000). What is the amount of Teal's AMT tax preference for excess depreciation?

Internet Activity

Use the tax resources of the Internet to address the following questions. Do not restrict your search to the Web, but include a review of newsgroups and general reference materials, practitioner sites and resources, primary sources of the tax law, chat rooms and discussion groups, and other opportunities.

Research Problem 4. The foreign tax credit is especially valuable when a U.S. business earns income in a country whose income tax rates exceed those of the United States. List five countries whose tax rates on business income exceed those of the United States and five where the corresponding U.S. rates are higher.

Research Problem 5. Ascertain whether your state's income tax has an AMT component. If your state does not levy an income tax, choose a contiguous state that does. List the AMT tax rate for corporations, and describe if or how the AMT tax base follows Federal AMTI.

Roger CPA Review Questions

1. When an entity is responsible for paying the alternative minimum tax (AMT) due to adjustments related to the timing of income, how might that excess tax be recovered?
    a. File a claim for a refund in the year paid.
    b. Carryforward to offset against a future AMT liability **only**.
    c. Carryforward to offset against future AMT **or** regular tax liabilities.
    d. Carryforward to offset against a future regular tax liability **only**.

2. Identify any item or items below which are added to Alternative Minimum Taxable Income (AMTI) in order to compute the Adjusted Current Earnings (ACE) adjustment.

    I.   Dividends-received deduction on dividends received from a 20%-owned corporation.
    II. Municipal bond interest, excluding any municipal bond interest already included in AMTI.
    III. Life insurance proceeds on the death of a key employee.

    a. I and III only
    c. I and II only
    b. I, II and III
    d. II and III only

3. Mary, a 65 year-old taxpayer, had an adjusted gross income of $150,000 in 20X4. In the same year, Mary also incurred $20,000 in medical expenses. In computing Mary's alternative minimum tax, what will be the adjustment for Mary's medical expenses?

    a. $3,750
    c. $8,750
    b. $5,000
    d. $11,250

4. Which of the following will increase a taxpayer's alternative minimum taxable income (AMTI)?

	Personal Exemption	Property Taxes	Medical Expenses Over 10% of AGI
a.	Yes	Yes	Yes
b.	Yes	Yes	No
c.	No	Yes	Yes
d.	Yes	No	Yes

5. Which of the following best describes the effect of a tax credit?
    a. It reduces a person's gross income.
    b. It reduces a person's adjusted gross income.
    c. It reduces a person's taxable income.
    d. It reduces a person's tax liability.

Comparative Forms of Doing Business

LEARNING OBJECTIVES: *After completing Chapter 18, you should be able to:*

LO.1 Identify the principal legal and tax forms for conducting a business.

LO.2 Apply nontax factors in the choice among alternative organizational forms.

LO.3 Identify which organizational forms result in the double taxation of business income.

LO.4 Identify techniques for avoiding double taxation.

LO.5 Identify the influence of the conduit and entity concepts on the tax treatment of an entity's operations and the entity's relation to its owners.

LO.6 Analyze the effects of the disposition of a business on the owners and the entity for each of the forms for conducting a business.

LO.7 Compare the tax consequences of the choice among the most common forms of doing business.

CHAPTER OUTLINE

TAX TALK *[My firm] had a rule—at least it seemed to be a rule—that everybody that came had to spend at least a year working on taxes. The general rationale for the rule as I could understand it was that taxes were so important to everything that you do, whatever the kind of case you are handling, you have to know something about the tax consequences of things.* —CHARLES A. HORSKY

CHOOSING A BUSINESS FORM AND OTHER INVESTMENTS

Bill and George are going to start a new business and have come to you for advice on the most appropriate organizational form for the business. They have narrowed the choice to a C corporation, an S corporation, or an LLC but would like you to advise them as to the primary advantages and disadvantages of the different forms. They have an adequate amount in savings to finance the business initially. Limited liability is a significant concern as is limiting the amount of taxes paid. Bill and George anticipate that the company will lose money in the first two years of operation. After that, however, they expect to earn $200,000 in before-tax profit and distribute any after-tax profit to the owners. Bill and George are both single, and both are subject to a 28 percent marginal tax rate.

George also is considering investing $10,000 in a limited partnership. As a way of leveraging the risks and rewards associated with his investments, Bill earlier had acquired a 30 percent interest in a boutique retail coffee franchise outlet. Bill now is considering selling this investment, which has experienced rapid appreciation. Because he is considering cashing out the gain, he needs to know the adjusted basis of his ownership interest.

Read the chapter and formulate your response.

A variety of factors, both tax and nontax, can affect the choice of the form of business entity. The form that is appropriate at one point in the life of an entity and its owners may not be appropriate at a different time.

This chapter provides the basis for comparing and contrasting the tax consequences of several business decisions across different types of tax and legal forms. Understanding the comparative tax consequences of those decisions for the different types of entities and being able to apply them effectively to specific fact patterns will facilitate effective tax planning, including the initial choice of an organizational form in which to conduct a business.

18-1 FORMS OF DOING BUSINESS

LO.1

Identify the principal legal and tax forms for conducting a business.

The principal legal forms for conducting a business are the sole proprietorship, partnership, limited liability company, and corporation. A limited liability company (LLC) possesses the corporate characteristic of limited liability (i.e., the owners are shielded from the debts of the entity), but it lacks at least some of the other characteristics typically associated with corporations, such as centralized management, free transferability of ownership interests, and/or unlimited life. The specific legal attributes of each of these organizational forms, including their relations to their owners and non-owners, are determined by the laws of the state in which they are organized.

These same forms generally are recognized for Federal income tax purposes as well, with the tax treatment determined by the legal form. However, three major exceptions exist. First, the "check-the-box" Regulations provide for LLCs to generally be treated either as sole proprietorships or partnerships for tax purposes, depending on the number of owners. An LLC with only one owner is a disregarded entity for tax purposes. A disregarded entity is treated as a sole proprietorship if the owner is an individual or as a division of a corporate owner. An LLC with more than one owner is treated as a partnership.

Second, the same Regulations allow most unincorporated entities to elect to be treated as corporations for Federal income tax purposes.[1] Therefore, an entity may be taxed as a corporation even though it is not organized as such under state law. Finally, a corporation may elect to be treated as an S corporation for tax purposes.[2] The income of an S corporation is taxed similarly to that of a partnership. However, the designation has no effect on the corporation for state law purposes.

An individual conducting a sole proprietorship reports the taxable income of the proprietorship by filing Schedule C along with his or her individual Form 1040. If more than one trade or business is conducted, a separate Schedule C is filed for each trade or business. A partnership reports its taxable income by filing Form 1065. A corporation that has not made an S election files Form 1120, and an S corporation files Form 1120S.

About 7 million corporations file U.S. income tax returns every year, and about 4.4 million of these use S corporation status. About 3.4 million partnership returns are filed every year, with over 60 percent of those being filed by LLCs. More than 21 million individual returns report sole proprietorship activities on Schedule C in a typical tax year. The business entity forms that are growing in number the fastest are the sole proprietorship (twice as many as 15 years ago) and the partnership (perhaps due to the popularity of limited liability companies).

18-2 NONTAX FACTORS AFFECTING THE CHOICE OF BUSINESS FORM

LO.2

Apply nontax factors in the choice among alternative organizational forms.

Taxes are only one of many factors to consider when making a business decision. Above all, any business decision should make economic sense.

---

[1]Reg. §§ 301.7701–1 through –4, and –6.   [2]§§ 1361 and 1362. See Chapter 15.

TAX IN THE NEWS   Should You Check That Box?

The check-the-box rules have been evolving since their introduction into the Regulations in late 1996. They are designed to remove tax considerations from the owners' choice of the legal form in which to conduct business. These provisions act to reduce the owners' exposure to the double taxation of taxable business profits. But taxpayers considering the use of these rules have run into several complications.

• Changing tax entity classifications from year to year comes at a cost. Changing the business form from a corporation to a partnership might trigger taxes for both the entity and its owners, defeating the purpose of the entity change.

• State income tax laws do not always match those of the Federal tax code. Several states have been slow to adopt the check-the-box rules, and others have modified the rules in some way. For instance, in several states, a one-member limited liability company does not receive the expected tax treatment of a partnership; it is reclassified as a corporation or sole proprietorship. Uncertainty as to the state income tax treatment of a check-the-box selection alone may keep the owners from exercising their supposed freedom of choice of tax entity.

The Big Picture

Return to the facts of *The Big Picture* on p. 18-1. George is considering investing $10,000 in a limited partnership. The partnership is expected to generate losses for two years before generating any profits. George projects that he will be able to deduct his share of the losses up to his $10,000 capital contribution within the next two years. Because George's marginal tax rate is 28%, the investment will produce tax savings of $2,800 ($10,000 × 28%).

However, there is a substantial risk that he will not recover any of his original investment. If this occurs, his negative cash flow from the investment in the limited partnership is $7,200 ($10,000 − $2,800). The tax savings cannot make up for the loss of the investment itself. George must decide whether the investment makes economic sense.

EXAMPLE 1

18-2a **Limited Liability**

A corporation offers its owners limited liability under state law. This absence of personal liability on the part of the owners is the most frequently cited advantage of the corporate form.

Ed, Fran, and Gabriella each invest $25,000 for all of the shares of stock of Brown Corporation. Brown obtains creditor financing of $100,000. Brown is the defendant in a personal injury suit resulting from an accident involving one of its delivery trucks. The court awards a judgment of $2.5 million to the plaintiff. The award exceeds Brown's insurance coverage by $1.5 million. Even though the judgment probably will result in Brown's bankruptcy, the shareholders will have no personal liability for the unpaid corporate debts.

EXAMPLE 2

Limited liability is not available to all corporations. For many years, state laws did not permit professional individuals (e.g., accountants, attorneys, architects, and physicians) to incorporate. Even though professionals now are allowed to incorporate, the statutes do not provide limited liability for the performance of professional services.

Even if state law provides for limited liability, the shareholders of small corporations may be forced to forgo this benefit. Quite often, a corporation may be unable to obtain external financing (e.g., a bank loan) at reasonable interest rates unless the shareholders guarantee the loan.

The limited partnership form provides limited liability to the limited partners. Their liability is limited to the amount invested plus any additional amount they agree to invest. In contrast, a general partner has unlimited liability.

TAX FACT   Revenue Relevance of Corporate versus Individual Taxpayers

Federal income taxes (FIT) provide over half of the Federal budget receipts. As indicated in the table to the right, the portion provided by individual taxpayers (which includes the effect of flow-through entities) far exceeds that provided by corporate taxpayers.

	2015	2014
% of budget receipts from FIT	59%	57%
% of FIT from individual taxpayers	78%	81%
% of FIT from corporate taxpayers	23%	19%

Source: Federal Budget of the United States.

EXAMPLE 3

Hazel, the general partner, invests $250,000 in HIJ, a limited partnership. Iris and Jane, the limited partners, each invest $50,000. While the potential loss for Iris and Jane is limited to $50,000 each, Hazel's liability is unlimited.

It may be possible to provide the general partner with limited liability indirectly by establishing a corporation as the general partner (see Exhibit 18.1). When a venture is structured this way, the general partner (the corporation) has limited its liability under the corporate statutes. In the figure, individual A is protected from personal liability by being merely the shareholder of Corporation A.

Like corporations, LLCs provide liability protection to all of its owners. This, coupled with the ability to be taxed as a partnership, is the most frequently cited benefit of an LLC. However, as discussed below, other corporate characteristics often are missing from LLCs. Limited liability partnerships (LLPs) also provide liability protection to all of their owners, but only for liabilities arising from the negligence or wrongdoing of the other owners. Partners in an LLP are not protected from the entity's contractual liabilities.

18-2b Other Factors

Other nontax factors may be significant in selecting an organization form. For example, in addition to limited liability, the corporation generally is characterized by unlimited life (i.e., the existence of the corporation is unaffected by a change in its ownership), separation of ownership and management, and the free transferability of interests. One or more of these characteristics is usually absent in other business forms.

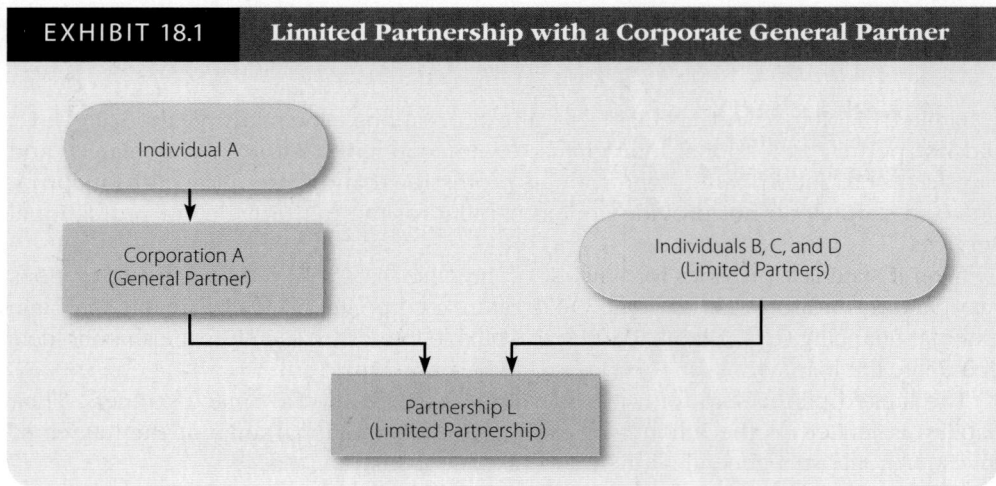

EXHIBIT 18.1   Limited Partnership with a Corporate General Partner

Many professional service firms (e.g., accountants, architects, attorneys) have chosen to become limited liability partnerships. In the accounting profession, this includes all of the Big 4 (i.e., Deloitte, EY, KPMG, and PwC) and most regional and local accounting firms.

An LLP helps to provide protection for the purely personal assets of the partners. Under the LLP organizational structure, the only partners whose personal assets are at risk to pay a judgment are those actually involved in the negligence or wrongdoing at issue. Note, however, that the entity is still responsible for the full judgment. Thus, the capital of the entity is still at risk.

18-2c Capital Formation

The combination of liability exposure with other nontax factors may significantly affect an entity's ability to raise capital. A sole proprietorship is limited to the capital that can be provided, or raised, by the proprietor. A partnership has a greater opportunity to raise funds through the pooling of owner resources.

Adam and Beth decide to form a partnership, AB. Adam contributes cash of $200,000, and Beth contributes land with an adjusted basis of $60,000 and a fair market value of $200,000. The partnership is going to construct an apartment building at a cost of $800,000. AB pledges the land and the building to secure a loan of $700,000.

EXAMPLE
4

A limited partnership offers even greater potential than a general partnership, because a limited partnership can secure funds from investors without exposing them to the liabilities related to the venture or involving them in the management of the business (i.e., future limited partners).

Carol and Dave form a limited partnership, CD. Carol contributes cash of $200,000, and Dave contributes land with an adjusted basis of $60,000 and a fair market value of $200,000. The partnership is going to construct a shopping center at a cost of $5 million. Included in this cost is the purchase price of $800,000 for land adjacent to that contributed by Dave. Thirty limited partnership interests are sold for $100,000 each to raise $3 million. CD then pledges the shopping center (including the land) and obtains nonrecourse creditor financing of another $2 million.

EXAMPLE
5

Of the different business entities, the corporate form offers the greatest ease and potential for obtaining owner financing because it can offer investors a combination of liability protection and liquidity that other business forms cannot. The ultimate examples of this form are the large public companies that are listed on the stock exchanges.

18-3 SINGLE VERSUS DOUBLE TAXATION

LO.3

Identify which organizational forms result in the double taxation of business income.

Forming a new legal entity in which to conduct a business may also lead to additional income tax. If the entity itself is taxed on its earnings and the owners, as taxpayers distinct from the entity, are taxed again when those earnings are distributed, double taxation of the entity's income results.

18-3a Overall Effect on Entity and Owners

The sole proprietorship, partnership, and LLC are subject to a *single* level of Federal income taxation. This result occurs because the owner(s) and the business generally are not considered separate entities for tax purposes. The tax liability is levied at the owner level rather than at the entity level.

BRIDGE DISCIPLINE **Bridge to Business Law and Financial Accounting**

When a business entity is created and assets are transferred to the business entity by the owners, the tax balance sheet and the financial accounting balance sheet generally show different amounts for the assets. The balance sheet amounts reflect the extent to which the *conduit theory* or *entity theory* is applied.

Conduit theory, also referred to as aggregate theory or proprietary theory, assumes that the business entity is merely an extension of the owners. Therefore, the transfer of the assets by the owners to the entity is not a taxable event. The owners' basis for their ownership interests is a carryover basis. The business entity's basis for its assets is a carryover basis.

Entity theory assumes that the business entity is separate and apart from the owners. Therefore, the transfer of assets by the owners to the entity is a taxable event. The owners' basis for their ownership interests is a new basis (i.e., fair market value). The business entity's basis for its assets is a new basis (i.e., fair market value).

Financial accounting uses a form of the entity theory. Thus, the critical value is the fair market value of each asset contributed by an owner to the business entity. Tax law generally applies the conduit theory. Thus, the critical value for income tax computations is the owner's adjusted basis for the contributed assets.

In contrast, a corporation and its owners can be subject to *double* taxation. This is frequently cited as the major tax disadvantage of the corporate form. The corporation is taxed on the income when it is initially earned, and the owners are taxed on distributions to the extent they are made from corporate earnings.[3]

The S corporation provides a way for certain corporations and their shareholders to avoid double taxation. However, the ownership structure of an S corporation is restricted in both the number and type of shareholders. Further, the distribution policy of the S corporation, as well as the tax rates of the shareholders, may mitigate the extent of the double taxation problem. Finally, taxing the shareholders on corporate earnings, regardless of whether distributions are made, may create difficulties under the *wherewithal to pay* concept.[4]

EXAMPLE 6

Hawk Corporation has been operating as an S corporation since it began its business two years ago. For both of the prior years, Hawk incurred a tax loss. Hawk has taxable income of $75,000 this year and expects that its earnings will increase each year in the foreseeable future. Part of this earnings increase results from Hawk's expansion into other communities in the state. Because most of this expansion will be financed internally, no dividend distributions will be made to Hawk's shareholders.

Assuming that all of Hawk's shareholders are in the 33% tax bracket, their tax liability on corporate earnings will be $24,750 ($75,000 × 33%). Even though Hawk will not distribute any cash to the shareholders, they still will be required to pay the tax liability. This creates a wherewithal to pay problem. In addition, the corporate tax liability would have been less if Hawk had not been an S corporation [(15% × $50,000) + (25% × $25,000) = $13,750].

The shareholders' wherewithal to pay problem could be resolved by terminating the S corporation election. The tax liability would then be imposed at the corporate level. Because Hawk does not intend to make any dividend distributions, double taxation at the present time would be avoided. Terminating the election also reduces the overall tax liability by $11,000 ($24,750 − $13,750).[5]

In making the decision about the form of business entity, Hawk's shareholders should consider more than the current taxable year. If the S election is terminated, another election might not be available for five years. Thus, the decision to revoke the election should be made using at least a five-year planning horizon. Perhaps a better solution would be to retain the election and distribute enough dividends to the S corporation shareholders to enable them to pay the shareholder tax liability.

---

[3]If the corporation is a personal service corporation (see Chapter 12), the corporation is subject to a flat tax rate of 35%.

[4]Recall the Chapter 15 discussions of the taxes on an S corporation's built-in gains, LIFO recapture, and investment income. These taxes ensure that income earned before a corporation elects S corporation status remains subject to double taxation.

[5]The absence of distributions to shareholders could create an accumulated earnings tax (AET) problem under § 531. However, as long as earnings are used to finance expansion, the "reasonable needs" provision will be satisfied, and the corporation will avoid any AET. Refer to the discussion of the AET in Chapter 13.

GLOBAL TAX ISSUES Do Corporations Pay Taxes?

A disadvantage of being a C corporation is the potential for double taxation. This potential disappears, however, if the taxable income of the corporation is zero or negative.

A Government Accountability Office (GAO) study indicates that for the period 1996–2000, more than 60 percent of U.S. corporations did not owe or pay any Federal income taxes. Neither did 70 percent of foreign-owned corporations doing business in the United States. By 2003,

corporate tax receipts had fallen to 7.4 percent of overall Federal receipts, the lowest percentage since 1983.

Another GAO study released in early 2009 found that 83 of the largest publicly traded corporations maintain subsidiaries in 50 tax havens. Senator Carl Levin (who requested the GAO study) along with Senator Byron Dorgan (now retired), concluded that "too many corporations are finagling ways to dodge paying Uncle Sam, despite the benefits they receive from doing business in this country."

Two other variables that relate to the adverse effect of double taxation are the timing and form of corporate distributions. First, double taxation is not triggered until corporate earnings are distributed.[6] To the extent that double taxation does occur in the future, the cash-flow effect should be discounted to its present value.

Second, when the distribution is made, the tax will depend on whether the distribution is treated as a dividend or as a sale of the shareholders' stock. In either case, the tax burden may be lower than it might otherwise have been. A qualified dividend is eligible for the lower tax rates applicable to long-term capital gains (see Chapter 4). A distribution treated as a sale of stock (a qualified redemption or complete liquidation) also allows the shareholder to recover tax-free the original investment in the stock (see Chapter 13).[7]

18-3b Alternative Minimum Tax

All of the forms of business are directly or indirectly subject to the alternative minimum tax (AMT).[8] For the sole proprietorship and the C corporation, the effect is direct (the AMT liability calculation is attached to the tax form that reports the entity's taxable income—Form 1040 or Form 1120). For the partnership, limited liability company, and S corporation, the effect is indirect; the tax preferences and adjustments pass through from the entity to the owners, and the AMT liability calculation is *not* assessed on the tax form that reports the entity's taxable income—Form 1065 or Form 1120S.

When compared with other entities, the C corporation appears to have a slight advantage. The corporate AMT rate of 20 percent is less than the individual AMT rates of 26 and 28 percent.

An even better perspective is provided by comparing the maximum AMT rate with the maximum regular rate for both the individual and the corporation. For the individual, the AMT rate is 71 percent (28%/39.6%) of the maximum regular rate. The AMT rate for the corporation is 57 percent (20%/35%) of the maximum regular rate. Therefore, on the basis of comparative rates, the C corporation appears to offer lower AMT tax burdens. In addition, as discussed below, under certain circumstances, a C corporation is exempt from the AMT.

The apparent corporate AMT rate advantage may be more than offset by the ACE adjustment, which applies only to C corporations.[9] If the ACE adjustment continually causes the C corporation to be subject to the AMT, the owners should consider electing S corporation status (if eligibility requirements can be satisfied). Because the S corporation does not compute an ACE adjustment, it may be possible to reduce the tax liability.

---

[6]This assumes that there is no accumulated earnings tax problem.
[7]See § 302 and Chapter 13.
[8]§ 55.

[9]§§ 56(c)(1) and (f). Refer to the discussion of the corporate AMT (and ACE) in Chapter 17.

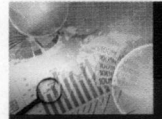

TAX IN THE NEWS   **Who Pays Corporate AMT?**

One of the issues often raised in debates over tax legislation is whether the corporate AMT should be repealed. Among the topics discussed are the revenue generated, the related compliance costs, and the number of corporations subject to the AMT.

According to the IRS, nearly 6 million corporate tax returns were filed in 2011. Of these returns, under 12,000 included any AMT liability.

Proponents of the corporate AMT argue that these statistics show that the AMT is being paid by corporations targeted by the law (i.e., large corporations). Opponents argue

that the same statistics show that the compliance costs borne by the mass of corporations do not justify the continuation of this tax system.

The exemption from the AMT for small corporations may be providing the needed solution. Large corporations must make minimal Federal income tax payments when the AMT applies. Most C corporations no longer need to compute the tax.

_____

Source: IRS *Tax Stats.*

The AMT does not apply to modest-sized C corporations. To be exempt from the tax, the corporation must meet both of the following tests.

- Average annual gross receipts of not more than $5 million for its first two years of existence after 1993.
- Average annual gross receipts of not more than $7.5 million for every subsequent three-tax-year period.

A corporation automatically is classified as a small corporation in the first year of existence. About 95 percent of all C corporations are likely to meet these tests and be exempt from the AMT in the future.

TAX PLANNING STRATEGIES   **Planning for the AMT**

FRAMEWORK FOCUS: TAX RATE

Strategy: Shift Net Income from High-Bracket Years to Low-Bracket Years.

If the AMT will apply in the current year, the entity should consider accelerating income and delaying deductions, so that current-year taxable income is taxed at the lower AMT rate.

For a C corporation, the potential rate differential is 15 percentage points (20 percent AMT rate versus 35 percent top regular tax rate). For an individual (i.e., as a sole

proprietor, as a partner, or as an S corporation shareholder), the potential tax rate differential is 11.6 percentage points (28 percent highest AMT rate versus 39.6 percent top regular tax rate).

A present value analysis should be used to make such decisions about any income acceleration and deduction deferrals.

18-3c **State Taxation**

In selecting a form for doing business, the determination of the tax consequences should not be limited to Federal income taxes. Consideration also should be given to state income taxes and, if applicable, local income taxes.

The S corporation provides a good illustration of this point. Suppose that the owners of a new venture are considering how to organize their new business. The business is expected to generate losses in its first few years of operation. The owners' main concerns are personal protection from the venture's liabilities and the ability to recognize its losses immediately against their individual taxable incomes. They narrow their choices to an LLC and S corporation.

Believing the choices equally able to meet their objectives, the investors choose the S corporation because of their relative familiarity with the corporate form. However, they later learn that the state in which they incorporate does not recognize the Federal S election. Therefore, the losses are not deductible by the owners when they calculate their state taxable incomes, leading to a greater state income tax liability than if they had chosen to operate as an LLC.

18-4 MINIMIZING DOUBLE TAXATION

LO.4

Identify techniques for avoiding double taxation.

As explained earlier, only the corporate form is potentially subject to double taxation. However, the lower tax rates that apply to qualified dividends can reduce the burden of double taxation. Several other planning techniques also are available for further reducing, or eliminating, the second layer of taxation.

- Making distributions to the shareholders that are deductible to the corporation.
- Deferring distributions to the shareholders.
- Making distributions that qualify for return of capital treatment at the shareholder level.
- Making the S corporation election.

18-4a Deductible Distributions

Corporations often make distributions to their owners in a form that results in a deduction to the corporation. Structuring their affairs such that distributions from a corporation to its shareholders are deductible represents good tax planning. Common examples of such deductible distributions include:

- Salary payments to shareholder-employees.
- Lease or rental payments to shareholder-lessors.
- Interest payments to shareholder-creditors.

Recognizing the potential for abuse, the IRS scrutinizes these types of distributions carefully. All three forms are evaluated in terms of *reasonableness*.[10] In addition, shareholder loans that lack a sufficient number of the characteristics usually associated with debt may be reclassified as equity.[11] IRS success with either approach raises the specter of double taxation.

Using Deductible Distributions to Avoid Double Taxation

EXAMPLE

7

Donna owns all the stock of Green Corporation and is the chief executive officer. Green's taxable income before salary payments to Donna is as follows.

Year 1	Year 2	Year 3
$80,000	$50,000	$250,000

Donna receives a monthly salary of $3,000. In December of each year, Donna reviews the operations for the year and determines the year-end bonus she is to receive. Donna's yearly bonuses are as follows.

continued

---

[10]§ 162(a)(1). *Mayson Manufacturing Co. v. Comm.*, 49–2 USTC ¶9467, 38 AFTR 1028, 178 F.2d 115 (CA–6, 1949); *Harolds Club v. Comm.*, 65–1 USTC ¶9198, 15 AFTR 2d 241, 340 F.2d 861 (CA–9, 1965).

[11]§ 385; Rev.Rul. 83–98, 1983–2 C.B. 40; *Bauer v. Comm.*, 84–2 USTC ¶9996, 55 AFTR 2d 85–433, 748 F.2d 1365 (CA–9, 1984).

Year 1	Year 2	Year 3
$44,000	$14,000	$214,000

The apparent purpose of Green's bonus program is to reduce the corporate taxable income to zero and thereby avoid double taxation. An examination of Green's tax return by the IRS would likely result in a deduction disallowance for **unreasonable compensation**.

Using Deductible Distributions to Avoid Double Taxation

EXAMPLE 8

Tom and Vicki each contribute $20,000 to TV Corporation for all of its stock. In addition, they each lend $80,000 to TV. The loan is documented by formal notes, the interest rate is 8%, and the maturity date is 10 years from the date of the loan.

The notes provide the opportunity for the corporation to make payments of $6,400 each year to both Tom and Vicki, and for the payments not to be subject to double taxation. This happens because the interest payments are includible in the gross income of Tom and Vicki, but are deductible by TV in calculating its taxable income. At the time of repayment in 10 years, neither Tom nor Vicki recognizes gross income from the repayment; the $80,000 amount realized is equal to the basis for the note of $80,000.

If the IRS succeeded in reclassifying the notes as equity, Tom and Vicki still would recognize gross income of $6,400, but the interest would be reclassified as dividend income (which may be taxed at the 15% rate). Because dividend payments are not deductible by TV, the corporation's taxable income would increase by $12,800 ($6,400 × 2). To make matters worse, the repayment of the notes in 10 years would not qualify as a recovery of capital, resulting in additional dividend income for Tom and Vicki.

18-4b **Deferring Distributions**

Double taxation will not occur unless the corporation makes (actual or deemed) distributions to the shareholders. A policy of deferring distributions to shareholders can postpone the second layer of taxation on corporate earnings. The retained earnings will drive the value of the shares upward, equal to the accumulated after-tax cash. Further tax savings can occur if the shares are held until the investor's death. Under the basis step-up rule, the basis of the stock for the beneficiaries will be the fair market value at the date of the decedent's death rather than the decedent's basis, and any gain realized during the decedent's lifetime will disappear.

DIGGING DEEPER 1 | In-depth coverage can be found on this book's companion website: www.cengagebrain.com

18-4c **Return-of-Capital Distributions**

The exposure to double taxation can be reduced if the corporate distributions to the shareholders can qualify for return of capital rather than dividend treatment. This can occur when the corporation's earnings and profits (E & P) are low or negative in amount (see discussion in Chapter 13). The stock redemption and liquidation provisions offer an opportunity to avoid dividend treatment altogether. Under these rules, the distribution may be treated as a sale of the shareholder's stock, resulting in a tax-free recovery of basis and then recognition of low-tax long-term capital gain.

TAX IN THE NEWS   Changing the Tax Treatment of Debt

Interest payments made by a business on entity debt are deductible. Dividend payments made by a business on entity equity are not deductible. The same tax results as to these payments could be achieved by either of the following changes.

- Make the dividend payments deductible.
- Make the interest payments nondeductible.

Although only at the embryonic stage, serious analysis is under way with respect to the latter approach. A proposal by the panel appointed by President Obama considered the change in the current tax treatment of debt among one of the main aspects of a corporate tax overhaul.

Congress and legislative advisers have requested a study on the issue by the Joint Committee on Taxation. Among the factors supporting such an analysis are the following.

- Curtailing the interest deductions would generate revenue.
- Limiting such interest deductions could help discourage another buildup of leverage by financial firms, which many people believe contributed to the 2008 U.S. financial meltdown.
- The present advantage of debt financing when compared with equity financing would disappear.
- The problems arising from thin capitalizations would be eliminated.

Of course, with any change in the tax law, there are winners and losers. Perceived losers would include Wall Street, big manufacturers, and small businesses that do not have access to equity markets.

Source: Based on John D. McKinnon, "Potential Tax Change Is Red Flag for Some Firms," *Wall Street Journal*, April 4, 2011, p. A2.

18-4d S Corporation Status

Electing S corporation status generally eliminates double taxation. Several factors should be considered when making this election.

- Are all of the shareholders willing to consent to the election?
- Can the qualification requirements under § 1361 be satisfied at the time of the election?
- Can the S corporation requirements continue to be satisfied?
- For what period will the conditions that make the election beneficial continue to prevail?
- Will the corporate distribution policy create wherewithal to pay problems at the shareholder level?

BRIDGE DISCIPLINE   Bridge to Economics

Corporations such as Coca-Cola, IBM, Microsoft, Walmart, and Exxon-Mobil are major players not only in their industries but also in the world economy. However, some people also are attracted to "mom-and-pop stores," which cumulatively play a major role in the economy.

In recognition of the important role of small businesses and their size competitive disadvantage at times, Congress has provided small businesses with beneficial tax treatment that is not available to major business entities. Included among such beneficial treatments are the following.

- § 11 – beneficial tax rates.
- § 44 – disabled access credit.
- § 55(e) – exemption from the AMT for small corporations.

- § 179 – limited expensing for tangible personal property.
- § 1045 – deferral of gain for qualified small business stock.
- § 1202 – partial exclusion of gain for certain small business stock.
- § 1244 – ordinary loss treatment.

Each of these provisions defines "small" in a different way. Sometimes, however, when beneficial tax treatment is provided for a business entity, *small* may be used inappropriately. The classic example is the small business corporation of Subchapter S. Some S corporations hold billions of dollars of assets. They are "small" chiefly in the sense that the number of shareholders cannot exceed 100 unrelated shareholders.

TAX FACT Income Tax Returns Filed by Business Entities

Type of Taxpayer	Tax Returns Filed (millions)			
	1980	1990	2000	2012
Individual	93.1	112.3	126.9	146.2
Partnership	1.4	1.8	2.1	3.3
C corporation	2.1	2.3	2.2	2.3
S corporation	.5	1.5	2.8	4.1

The number of S corporation returns has increased dramatically since 1980. LLCs usually file using the Federal income tax partnership rules, and the popularity of this entity form has led to a notable increase in the number of partnership returns filed.

Source: IRS Tax Stats.

EXAMPLE 9

Emerald Corporation commenced business in January 2014. The two shareholders, Diego and Jaime, are both in the 28% tax bracket. The following operating results are projected for the first five years of operations.

2014	2015	2016	2017	2018
($50,000)	$400,000	$600,000	$800,000	$1,000,000

The corporation plans to expand rapidly. Therefore, no distributions will be made to shareholders. In addition, beginning in 2015, preferred stock will be offered to a substantial number of investors to help finance the expansion.

If the S corporation election is made for 2014, the $50,000 loss can be passed through to Diego and Jaime. The loss will generate a positive cash-flow effect of $14,000 ($50,000 × 28%). Assume that the election is either revoked or involuntarily terminated at the beginning of 2015 as a result of the issuance of the preferred stock. The C corporation tax liability for 2015 is $136,000 ($400,000 × 34%).

If the S corporation election is not made for 2014, the $50,000 loss is a net operating loss. The amount can be carried forward to reduce the 2015 corporate taxable income to $350,000 ($400,000 − $50,000). The resultant tax liability is $119,000 ($350,000 × 34%).

Should the S corporation election be made for just the one-year period? The answer is unclear. With an assumed after-tax rate of return to Diego and Jaime of 10%, the value of the $14,000 one year hence is $15,400 ($14,000 × 110%). Even considering the time value of money, the combined corporation-shareholder negative cash-flow effect of $120,600 ($136,000 − $15,400) in the case of an S election is not significantly different from the $119,000 corporate tax liability that would result for a C corporation.

Another benefit of electing S corporation status is that the corporation is not subject to the accumulated earnings or personal holding company taxes.

LO.5

Identify the influence of the conduit and entity concepts on the tax treatment of an entity's operations and the entity's relation to its owners.

18-5 CONDUIT VERSUS ENTITY TREATMENT

Under the **conduit concept**, the entity is viewed as merely an extension of the owners. Under the **entity concept**, the entity is regarded as being separate and distinct from its owners. The effects of the conduit and entity concepts extend to a variety of tax issues, including the following.

- Recognition at time of contribution of assets.
- Basis of ownership interest.
- Results of operations.
- Recognition at time of distribution.
- Application of the at-risk and passive activity loss rules.
- Use of special allocations.

The taxation of corporations is influenced almost entirely by the entity concept. The tax law's approach to partnerships and LLCs is less consistent. Although the Federal income tax treatment of partnerships and LLCs is primarily influenced by the conduit concept, several provisions clearly reflect the entity concept.

The sole proprietorship is not analyzed separately here because the owner and the business are the same legal and tax entity. In one circumstance, however, a tax difference can result. Income recognition does not occur when an owner contributes an asset to a sole proprietorship. Thus, the business generally takes a carryover basis. However, if the asset is a personal-use asset, the sole proprietorship's basis is the *lower of* the adjusted basis or the fair market value at the date of contribution. If a personal-use asset is contributed to a partnership or corporation, this same *lower-of* rule applies.

18-5a **Effect on Recognition at Time of Contribution of Assets**

Because the conduit approach applies to partnerships, § 721 provides for no recognition on the contribution of property to a partnership in exchange for a partnership interest. Section 721 protects both contributions associated with the formation of the partnership and later contributions. The partnership takes a carryover basis in the contributed property, and the partners have a carryover basis in their partnership interests.[12]

Because the entity approach applies to corporations, the transfer of property to a corporation in exchange for its stock is a taxable event. However, if the § 351 control requirement (80 percent) is satisfied, no gain or loss is recognized. In this case, both the corporate property and the shareholders' stock take a carryover basis.[13] This control requirement increases the likelihood of gain recognition for shareholders who contribute appreciated property to the corporation *after* its formation.

18-5b **Effect on Basis of Ownership Interest**

Because the contribution of property to a partnership or an LLC in exchange for an ownership interest is not a taxable event under § 721, the owner's basis for the ownership interest carries over from the contributed property. The same is true of contributions to C and S corporations if the 80 percent control requirement of § 351 is satisfied. If the control requirement is not satisfied, any realized gain or loss on a contribution of property to a corporation is recognized by the shareholder, and the investor's stock basis is equal to the fair market value of the contributed property.

In a partnership or an LLC, because the owner is the taxpayer, profits and losses of the entity also affect the owner's basis in the entity interest. Likewise, the owner's basis is increased by the share of entity liability increases and is decreased by the share of liability decreases. Accordingly, ownership basis changes frequently.[14]

Because a C corporation is a taxpaying entity, the shareholder's basis for the stock is not affected by corporate profits and losses or corporate liability changes.

The treatment of an S corporation shareholder falls between that of the partner and the C corporation shareholder. The S corporation shareholder's stock basis is increased by the share of profits and decreased by the share of losses, but it usually is not affected by corporate liability increases or decreases.[15]

---

[12]Refer to the pertinent discussion in Chapter 14.

[13]Refer to the pertinent discussion in Chapter 12.

[14]§§ 705 and 752.

[15]Recall from Chapter 15 that pass-through S corporation losses can reduce a *shareholder's* basis in loans to the entity.

The Big Picture

EXAMPLE

10

Return to the facts of *The Big Picture* on p. 18-1. Bill contributed cash of $100,000 to an entity for a 30% ownership interest in the franchise. The entity borrowed $50,000 and repaid $20,000 of this amount by the end of the taxable year. The profits for the year are $90,000.

If the entity is a partnership or LLC, Bill's basis at the end of the period is $136,000 ($100,000 investment + $9,000 share of net liability increase + $27,000 share of profits). If Bill is a C corporation shareholder instead, his stock basis is $100,000 ($100,000 original investment). If the corporation is an S corporation, Bill's stock basis is $127,000 ($100,000 + $27,000).

18-5c Effect on Results of Operations

The entity concept can produce double taxation of the income earned by a C corporation (the corporation is taxed on its earnings, and the shareholders are taxed on the distribution of those earnings). Thus, from the perspective of taxing the results of operations, the entity concept appears to be a disadvantage in using C corporations. However, whether the entity concept actually produces disadvantageous results depends on the following.

- The generation of positive taxable income by the corporation.
- The relative tax rates applicable to the corporation and its shareholders.
- The distribution policy of the corporation.

As discussed previously, techniques exist for getting cash out of the profitable corporation to the shareholders without incurring double taxation (e.g., compensation payments to shareholder-employees, lease payments to shareholder-lessors, and interest payments to shareholder-creditors). Because these payments are deductible to the corporation, they reduce corporate taxable income. If the payments can be used to reduce corporate taxable income to zero, the corporation will have no tax liability.

Income that cannot be distributed in deductible form will be subject to tax at the corporate level. The maximum individual tax rate (39.6 percent) exceeds the maximum C corporation tax rate (35 percent), potentially reducing the tax that would have been due on the income if the entity had not incorporated. However, it is possible that the maximum marginal tax rate does not apply to either the corporation or some of its shareholders. Therefore, the effect of incorporation on the tax rate applicable to current income will vary among situations.

Regardless of the tax rate applicable to corporate income, that income potentially is subject to double taxation. As discussed earlier, however, double taxation occurs only if distributions (actual or constructive) are made to the shareholders. Thus, if no distributions (actual or constructive) are made in the current year, only one current level of taxation will occur. If and when distributions are made, double taxation can be mitigated if the distribution qualifies as a recovery of capital (a qualified redemption or liquidation). Finally, taxation of the earnings at the shareholder level can be avoided permanently if the stock passes through the decedent shareholder's estate.[16]

Application of the entity concept also causes income and deductions to lose any unique tax characteristics when they are passed through to shareholders in the form of dividends. This may produce a negative result for capital gains. Because capital gains lose their identity when passed through in the form of dividends, they cannot be used to offset capital losses at the shareholder level. An even more negative result is produced when dividends are paid out of tax-exempt income. Tax-exempt income is excludible in calculating corporate taxable income, but is included in calculating current

---

[16]Recall Chapter 7's analysis of the basis step-up rules for property acquired from a decedent.

earnings and profits. Thus, income that was excludible when initially earned becomes taxable because of the entity concept.

The tax treatment of the income of partnerships, LLCs, and S corporations is influenced primarily by the conduit concept. Any item that is subject to special treatment at the taxpayer level is reported separately to the owner. Other items are aggregated and reported as ordinary taxable income.[17]

Many of the problems the entity concept may produce for the C corporation form are not present in pass-through entities. In particular, pass-through entities are not subjected to double taxation, problems with the reasonableness requirement, or loss of identity of the income or expense item at the owner level.

Partnerships, LLCs, and S corporations do not represent complete and consistent applications of the conduit concept. For example, these entities may employ accounting periods and methods that differ from those of their owners. Further, the characterization of income, gains, and losses generally is determined at the entity level. For example, whether a gain qualifies as a long-term capital gain depends on the nature of the asset in the hands of the entity and how long the entity held it. S corporations that operated as C corporations prior to making the S election also may be subject to entity-level tax on a portion of their incomes (see discussion in Chapter 15). This limited application of the entity concept necessitates additional planning to minimize any corporate-level tax.

18-5d Effect on Recognition at Time of Distribution

The application of the conduit concept results in distributions not being taxed to the owners. The application of the entity concept produces the opposite result: distributions that would be tax-free if made to partners would be taxable to shareholders of C corporations.

A combination entity/conduit concept applies to property distributions from S corporations. The entity concept generally applicable to corporations leads to the recognition of gain for any appreciation attributable to the distributed property.[18] However, the conduit concept leads to the gain being taxed also at the shareholder level.

EXAMPLE 11

Tan, an S corporation, is equally owned by Leif and Matt. Tan distributes two parcels of land to Leif and Matt. Tan has a basis of $10,000 for each parcel. Each parcel has a fair market value of $15,000. The distribution results in a $10,000 ($30,000 − $20,000) recognized gain for Tan. Leif and Matt each report $5,000 of the gain on their individual income tax returns.

Stock redemptions and complete liquidations receive identical treatment whether a C or S corporation is involved.[19]

18-5e Effect of the At-Risk and Passive Activity Loss Rules

The at-risk and passive activity loss rules prevent certain taxpayers from recognizing losses that might otherwise be available to them. The at-risk rules prevent affected taxpayers from recognizing losses for which they are not at a risk of economic loss. The passive activity loss rules generally allow affected taxpayers to recognize losses from passive activities only to offset income from passive activities. The at-risk and passive activity loss rules apply to individuals and closely held C corporations. The passive activity loss rules apply to personal service corporations as well. Although neither set of rules applies to flow-through entities directly, the rules are especially relevant to the individual owners of these entities who may not be at risk for all of the losses that may pass through to them from the entity, or may not actively participate in the entity's activities. See Chapter 6 for a detailed discussion.

The at-risk rules are particularly relevant to partners who may have nonrecourse debt included in the basis of their partnership interest (see discussion in Chapter 14).

---

[17]§§ 701, 702, 1363, and 1366.

[18]§ 311(b).

[19]§§ 302, 331, and 336.

Note that the exclusion of the debt from a partner's amount at risk, in spite of it being included in the basis of the partnership interest, will cause a partner to be treated similarly to a shareholder in an S corporation who may not include the debt in the basis of his or her stock at all. However, as partnership recourse debt may also be included in a partner's basis in the partnership interest, taxpayers may be able to recognize more losses generated by a pass-through entity by organizing the entity as a partnership rather than an S corporation. Of course, this will expose the owners to a greater risk of economic loss.

EXAMPLE 12

Walt is the general partner and Ira and Vera are the limited partners in the WIV limited partnership. Walt contributes land with an adjusted basis of $40,000 and a fair market value of $50,000 for his partnership interest, and Ira and Vera each contribute cash of $100,000 for their partnership interests. They agree to share profits and losses equally. To finance construction of an apartment building, the partnership obtains $600,000 of nonrecourse financing (not qualified nonrecourse financing; see chapter 14), using the land and the building as the pledged assets. Each partner's basis for the partnership interest is as follows.

	Walt	**Ira**	**Vera**
Contribution	$ 40,000	$100,000	$100,000
Share of nonrecourse debt	200,000	200,000	200,000
Basis	$240,000	$300,000	$300,000

Without the at-risk rules, Ira and Vera could recognize losses up to $300,000 each even though they invested only $100,000 and have no personal liability for the nonrecourse debt. However, the at-risk rules limit loss recognition to the at-risk basis, which is $100,000 for Ira and $100,000 for Vera.

The at-risk rules also affect the general partner. Because Walt is not at risk for the nonrecourse debt, his at-risk basis is $40,000. If the mortgage were recourse debt, his at-risk basis would be $640,000 ($40,000 + $600,000), as the general partner.

If, instead, the entity were an S corporation and Walt received 20% of the stock and Ira and Vera each received 40%, the basis for their stock would be as follows.

Walt	**Ira**	**Vera**
$40,000	$100,000	$100,000

Note that the at-risk rules prevent any nonrecourse debt included in basis of a partner's interest from increasing the ability to recognize losses over what would be available if the owners had organized as an S corporation. Whether WIV had organized as a partnership or an S corporation, Walt would be able only to recognize losses up to $40,000, while Ira and Vera would only be able to recognize losses up to $100,000.

If the debt were recourse debt, however, it would be included in the at-risk basis of Walt's partnership interest, allowing him to recognize losses up to $640,000. It would not, however, affect the basis of his stock if WIV had organized as an S corporation.

The passive activity loss rules generally allow individuals and personal service corporations to recognize losses from passive activities only to offset income from passive activities. The passive activity losses of a closely held corporation, however, also can be used to offset active income.

Neither the at-risk nor the passive activity loss rules apply to larger C corporations. Therefore, C corporations that are not closely held can recognize losses for which they may not be at risk or from activities in which they do not materially participate.

As discussed above, the at-risk and passive activity loss rules apply to individuals and closely held C corporations. A *closely held C corporation* exists when more than

50 percent of the value of the outstanding stock at any time during the last half of the taxable year is owned by or for not more than five individuals.

The general passive loss rules apply to personal service corporations. Therefore, passive activity losses can be offset only against passive activity income. For closely held C corporations, the application of the passive activity rules is less harsh. Passive activity losses can be offset against both active and passive income.

A corporation is classified as a *personal service corporation* if the following requirements are satisfied.[20]

- The principal activity of the corporation is the performance of personal services.
- The services are substantially performed by owner-employees.
- Owner-employees own more than 10 percent in value of the stock of the corporation.

Because the conduit concept applies to partnerships, S corporations, and limited liability entities, passive activity income and losses are separately stated at the entity level and are passed through to the owners with their passive character maintained.

18-5f Effect on the Ability to Use Special Allocations

An advantage of the conduit concept over the entity concept is the flexibility in allocating income among its owners by using special allocations. Partnerships and limited liability companies have many occasions to use special allocations, including the following (refer to Chapter 14).

- A desire to share profits and losses differently from the share in capital.
- A desire to share profits and losses differently from year to year.
- A requirement to allocate a built-in gain or loss on contributed property to the contributing partner.

To the extent that the fair market value of property contributed to the entity at the time of formation is not equal to the property's adjusted basis, the entity might want to make a special allocation associated with the subsequent sale of the contributed property. With a special allocation, the owner contributing the property receives the tax benefit or detriment for any recognized gain or loss that subsequently results because of the initial difference between the adjusted basis and the fair market value. For a partnership, this special allocation treatment is mandatory.

Special allocations are not permitted in C corporations. Indirectly, however, the corporate form may be able to achieve results similar to those produced by special allocations through payments to owners (e.g., salary payments, lease rental payments, and interest payments) and through different classes of stock (e.g., preferred and common). However, even in these cases, the breadth of the treatment and the related flexibility are far less than that available under the conduit concept.

Although S corporations generally operate as conduits, they are treated more like C corporations than partnerships with respect to special allocations. This treatment results from the application of the per-share and per-day allocation rule in § 1377(a). Although S corporations are limited to one class of stock, they still can use salary, interest, and rental payments to owners to shift income to the desired recipient.

In-depth coverage can be found on this book's companion website: www.cengagebrain.com   **2 DIGGING DEEPER**

---

[20]§ 469, derived from the definition in § 269A.

TAX FACT Profitability of Partnerships

Since 1980, the number of partnership income tax returns has more than doubled (i.e., from 1.4 million returns to 3.4 million returns). The beneficial tax treatment of LLCs is expected to cause this trend to continue. While the partnership provides a tax shelter opportunity by passing losses through to the partner, a majority of partnerships are profitable.

	1985	1990	1995	2000	2010	2011
% of returns with profits	53%	56%	63%	60%	50%	52%
% of returns with losses	47%	44%	37%	40%	50%	48%

Source: IRS *Tax Stats.*

EXAMPLE 13

Khalid contributes land with an adjusted basis of $10,000 and a fair market value of $50,000 for a 50% ownership interest in Maple Company. At the same time, Tracy contributes cash of $50,000 for the remaining 50% ownership interest. Because Maple is unable to obtain the desired zoning, it subsequently sells the land for $50,000.

Khalid holds a realized gain of $40,000 ($50,000 − $10,000) and a recognized gain of $0 resulting from the contribution. His basis in his ownership interest in Maple is $10,000, and Maple takes a basis in the land of $10,000. Maple realizes and recognizes a gain of $40,000 ($50,000 − $10,000) when it sells the land.

If Maple is a corporation, the appreciation of the land attributable to the time it was owned by Khalid becomes part of the corporation's taxable income, the resulting tax is paid by the corporation, and the tax burden is indirectly shared equally by both shareholders. There is no way by which the corporation can allocate the recognized gain, and the related tax burden, directly to Khalid.

If Maple is a partnership, the entire $40,000 recognized gain on the sale is allocated to Khalid, regardless of his profits or equity interest. Note that although S corporations are taxed similarly to partnerships, the S corporation provisions do not allow special allocations. If the entity were an S corporation, Khalid and Tracy would each include $20,000 of the recognized gain in their taxable income.

LO.6

Analyze the effects of the disposition of a business on the owners and the entity for each of the forms for conducting a business.

18-6 DISPOSITION OF A BUSINESS OR AN OWNERSHIP INTEREST

A key factor in evaluating the tax consequences of a business disposition is whether the disposition is viewed as the sale of an ownership interest or as a sale of assets. Generally, the tax consequences are more favorable to the seller if the transaction is treated as a sale of the ownership interest.

18-6a Sole Proprietorships

Regardless of the form of the transaction, the sale of a sole proprietorship is treated as the sale of individual assets. Thus, gains and losses must be calculated separately for each asset. Classification as capital gain or ordinary income depends on the nature and holding period of the individual assets. Ordinary income property such as inventory will result in ordinary gains and losses. Section 1231 property such as land, buildings, and machinery used in the business will produce § 1231 gains and losses (subject to depreciation recapture under §§ 1245 and 1250). Capital assets such as investment land and stocks qualify for capital gain or loss treatment.

If the amount realized exceeds the fair market value of the identifiable assets, the excess is allocated to goodwill, which generates capital gain for the seller. If instead the excess payment is allocated to a covenant not to compete, the related gain is classified

as ordinary income rather than capital gain. Both goodwill and covenants are amortized by the purchaser over a 15-year statutory period.[21]

> **EXAMPLE 14**
>
> Seth, who is in the 35% tax bracket, sells his sole proprietorship to Wilma for $600,000. The identifiable assets are as follows.
>
> | | Adjusted Basis | Fair Market Value |
> |---|---|---|
> | Inventory | $ 20,000 | $ 25,000 |
> | Accounts receivable | 40,000 | 40,000 |
> | Machinery and equipment* | 125,000 | 150,000 |
> | Buildings** | 175,000 | 250,000 |
> | Land | 40,000 | 100,000 |
> | | $400,000 | $565,000 |
>
> *Potential § 1245 recapture of $50,000.
> **Potential § 1250 recapture of $20,000.
>
> The sale produces the following results for Seth.
>
> | | Gain (Loss) | Ordinary Income | § 1231 Gain | Capital Gain |
> |---|---|---|---|---|
> | Inventory | $ 5,000 | $ 5,000 | | |
> | Accounts receivable | –0– | | | |
> | Machinery and equipment | 25,000 | 25,000 | | |
> | Buildings | 75,000 | 20,000 | $ 55,000 | |
> | Land | 60,000 | | 60,000 | |
> | Goodwill | 35,000 | | | $35,000 |
> | | $200,000 | $50,000 | $115,000 | $35,000 |
>
> If the sale is structured this way, Wilma can deduct the $35,000 paid for goodwill over a 15-year period. If instead Wilma paid the $35,000 to Seth for a covenant not to compete for a period of seven years, Seth's $35,000 gain would be taxed to him as ordinary income. If the covenant has no legal relevance to Wilma, in exchange for treating the payment as a goodwill payment, she should negotiate for a price reduction that reflects Seth's benefit from the lower capital gains tax.

18-6b Partnerships and Limited Liability Companies

The sale of a partnership or LLC can be structured as the sale of assets or as the sale of an ownership interest. If the transaction takes the form of an asset sale, it is treated the same as for a sole proprietorship (described previously).

The sale of an ownership interest generally is treated as the sale of a capital asset. Therefore, structuring a transaction as a sale of an ownership interest may be preferable to structuring it as a sale of the partnership assets. However, this benefit is severely curtailed by the need to recognize gain related to appreciation of many of the partnership's ordinary income-producing assets as ordinary gain, even on the sale of an ownership interest.[22]

From a buyer's perspective, tax consequences are not affected by the form of the transaction. If the transaction is an asset purchase, the basis for the assets equals the amount paid. If a buyer intends to continue to operate as an LLC or a partnership, the assets can be contributed to the entity under § 721. Therefore, the owner's basis in the entity interest is equal to the purchase price for the assets. Likewise, if ownership interests are purchased, the owner's basis is the purchase price paid. The partnership's basis for the assets is the purchase price because the original partnership was terminated.[23]

---

[21]§ 197.
[22]§ 751.

[23]§ 708(b)(1)(B).

A problem may arise when a taxpayer purchases a partnership or LLC interest from another owner. In such a case, the amount paid for the interest may not be equal to the new owner's share of the entity's basis in its assets. Put another way, the basis of the assets inside the entity may not reflect the amount paid for them by the new owner. To help prevent this problem, the entity may make an election to adjust its basis in its assets to reflect the amount paid by the new owner. This basis adjustment is allocable entirely to the new owner (see Chapter 14), ensuring the new owner can recover the (indirect) cost of the underlying assets.

EXAMPLE 15

Roz buys a one-third interest in the RST Partnership for $50,000 (outside basis). All of the entity's assets are depreciable, and their basis to the partnership (inside basis) is $90,000. If a § 754 election is in effect, the partnership can step up the basis of its depreciable assets by $20,000, the difference between Roz's outside and inside basis amounts [$50,000 − (1/3 × $90,000)]. All of the "new" asset basis is allocated to Roz.

Such an election, once made, is binding on the entity and applies to all subsequent exchanges of ownership interests. Therefore, while it may benefit a new owner if the entity's assets have appreciated prior to the acquisition date, creating a positive basis adjustment for the acquiring owner, it may be detrimental to a future acquirer if assets are depreciated at the time of acquisition, resulting in a negative basis adjustment for the new owner.[24]

18-6c C Corporations

The sale of a business held by a C corporation can be structured as either an asset sale or a stock sale. The stock sale has the dual advantage to the seller of being less complex both as a legal transaction and as a tax transaction. It also has the advantage of providing a way to avoid double taxation. Finally, any gain or loss on the sale of the stock is treated as a capital gain or loss to the shareholder.

EXAMPLE 16

Jane and Zina each own 50% of the stock of Purple Corporation. They have owned the business for 10 years. Jane's basis in her stock is $40,000, and Zina's basis in her stock is $60,000. They agree to sell the stock to Rex for $300,000. Jane recognizes a long-term capital gain of $110,000 ($150,000 − $40,000), and Zina recognizes a long-term capital gain of $90,000 ($150,000 − $60,000). Rex takes a basis in his stock of $300,000. Purple's basis in its assets does not change as a result of the stock sale.

18-6d S Corporations

Because the S corporation is a corporation under state law, it is subject to the provisions for a C corporation discussed in the prior section. An asset sale at the corporate level or a liquidating distribution of assets produces gain or loss recognition at the corporate level. However, under the conduit concept applicable to the S corporation, the recognized amount is taxed at the shareholder level. Therefore, double taxation is avoided directly (only the shareholder is involved) for a stock sale and indirectly (the conduit concept ignores the involvement of the corporation) for an asset sale.

Double taxation might seem to be avoided by making an S corporation election prior to the liquidation of a C corporation, but the built-in gains tax eliminates this opportunity; taxation occurs at the corporate level, and double taxation results.

Concept Summary 18.1 reviews the tax consequences of business dispositions.

[24]§§ 743 and 754.

TAX PLANNING STRATEGIES **Selling Stock or Assets**

FRAMEWORK FOCUS: TAX RATE

Strategy: Avoid Double Taxation.

Structuring the transfer of the business as a stock sale may produce detrimental tax results for the purchaser. As Example 16 illustrates, the basis of the corporation's assets is not affected by the stock sale. If the fair market value of the stock exceeds the corporation's adjusted basis for its assets, the purchaser is denied the opportunity to step up the basis of the assets to reflect the amount in effect paid for them through the stock acquisition—no § 754 election is available to C corporations.

If an asset sale is used, the seller of the business can be either the corporation or its shareholders. If the seller is the corporation, the corporation sells the business (the assets), pays any debts not transferred, and makes a liquidating distribution to the shareholders. If the sellers are the shareholders, the corporation pays any debts that will not be transferred and makes a liquidating distribution to the shareholders; then the shareholders sell the business.

Regardless of the approach used for an asset sale, double taxation occurs. The corporation is taxed on the actual sale

of the assets, and it is taxed as if it had sold the assets when it makes the liquidating distribution to the shareholders. The shareholders are taxed when they receive cash or assets distributed in kind by the corporation.

An asset sale resolves the purchaser's problem of not being able to step up the basis of the assets to their fair market value. The basis for each asset is its purchase price. Then the purchaser needs to transfer the property to a corporation in a § 351 transaction.

From the perspective of the seller, the ideal form of the transaction is a stock sale. Conversely, from the purchaser's perspective, the ideal form is an asset purchase. Thus, a conflict exists between the buyer's and the seller's objectives regarding the form of the transaction. Therefore, the bargaining ability of the seller and the purchaser to structure the sale as a stock sale or an asset sale, respectively, is critical.

Concept Summary 18.1

Tax Treatment of Disposition of a Business

Form of Entity	Form of Transaction	Tax Consequences	
		Seller	**Buyer**
Sole proprietorship	Sale of individual assets.	Gain or loss is calculated separately for the individual assets. Classification as capital or ordinary depends on the nature and holding period of the individual assets. If amount realized exceeds the fair market value of the identifiable assets, the excess is allocated to goodwill (except to the extent identified with a covenant not to compete), which is a capital asset.	Basis for individual assets is the allocated cost. Prefers that any excess of purchase price over the fair market value of identifiable assets be identified with a covenant not to compete. Otherwise, the buyer is neutral, because both goodwill and covenants are amortized over a 15-year statutory period.
	Sale of the business.	Treated as a sale of the individual assets (as above).	Treated as a purchase of the individual assets (as above).
Partnership and limited liability company	Sale of individual assets.	Treatment is the same as for the sole proprietorship.	Treatment is the same as for the sole proprietorship. If the intent is to operate in partnership form, the assets can be contributed to a partnership under § 721.
	Sale of ownership interest.	Entity interest is treated as the sale of a capital asset (subject to ordinary income potential for unrealized receivables and substantially appreciated inventory).	Basis for new owner's ownership interest is the cost. The new entity's basis for the assets is also the pertinent cost (i.e., contributed to the entity under § 721), because the original entity will have terminated.

continued

Tax Treatment of Disposition of a Business—(Continued)

Form of Entity	Form of Transaction	Tax Consequences	
		Seller	**Buyer**
C corporation	Sale of corporate assets by corporation (i.e., corporation sells assets, pays debts, and makes liquidating distribution to the shareholders).	Double taxation occurs. Corporation is taxed on the sale of the assets with the gain or loss determination and the classification as capital or ordinary treated the same as for the sole proprietorship. Shareholders calculate gain or loss as the difference between the stock basis and the amount received from the corporation in the liquidating distribution. Capital gain or loss usually results, because stock typically is a capital asset.	Basis for individual assets is the allocated cost. If the intent is to operate in corporate form, the assets can be contributed to a corporation in a tax-deferred manner under § 351.
	Sale of corporate assets by the shareholders (i.e., corporation pays debts and makes liquidating distribution to the shareholders).	Double taxation occurs. At the time of the liquidating distribution to the shareholders, the corporation is taxed as if it had sold the assets. Shareholders calculate gain or loss as the difference between the stock basis and the fair market value of the assets received from the corporation in the liquidating distribution. Capital gain or loss usually results, because stock typically is a capital asset.	Same as corporate asset sale.
	Sale of corporate stock.	Enables double taxation to be avoided. Because the corporation is not a party to the transaction, there are no tax consequences at the corporate level. Shareholders calculate gain or loss as the difference between the stock basis and the amount received for the stock. Capital gain or loss usually results, because stock typically is a capital asset.	Basis for the stock is its cost. The basis for the corporate assets is not affected by the stock purchase.
S corporation	Sale of corporate assets by corporation.	Recognition occurs at the corporate level on the sale of the assets, with the gain or loss determination and the classification as capital or ordinary treated the same as for the sole proprietorship. Conduit concept applicable to the S corporation results in the recognized amount being taxed at the shareholder level. Double taxation associated with the asset sale is avoided, because the shareholder's stock basis is increased by the amount of gain recognition and decreased by the amount of loss recognition. Shareholders calculate gain or loss as the difference between the stock basis and the amount received from the corporation in the liquidating distribution. Capital gain or loss usually results, because stock typically is a capital asset.	Basis for individual assets is the allocated cost. If the intent is to operate in corporate form (i.e., as an S corporation), the assets can be contributed to a corporation in a tax-deferred manner under § 351.
	Sale of corporate assets by the shareholders.	At the time of the liquidating distribution to the shareholders, recognition occurs at the corporation level as if the corporation had sold the assets. The resulting tax consequences for the shareholders and the corporation are the same as for the sale of corporate assets by the S corporation.	Same as corporate asset sale by the S corporation.
	Sale of corporate stock.	Same as the treatment for the sale of stock of a C corporation.	Same as the treatment for the purchase of stock of a C corporation.

18-7 CONVERSION TO OTHER ENTITY TYPES

As the owners' tax and nontax goals change, they may decide to convert the tax entity form to a different tax or legal form. This raises three primary issues.

- Does the conversion result in the recognition of gain or loss?
- What is the basis for the ownership interest in the new entity form?
- What is the basis of the assets of the new entity form?

18-7a Sole Proprietorship

The conversion of a sole proprietorship into another entity form can be achieved without any recognition of gain or loss at the entity or owner level. This result occurs regardless of the choice of the new entity form. If the proprietorship is converted into a partnership or an LLC, nonrecognition can be achieved.[25] If the business is converted into either an S corporation or a C corporation, nonrecognition also is available.[26]

If the proprietorship converts into a partnership or an LLC, the owner's basis in the ownership interest carries over from the contributed property.[27] Similarly, if the proprietorship converts into a corporation, the shareholder's basis for the stock received carries over from the shareholder's basis in the contributed property.[28]

After a conversion, the partnership or LLC takes a carryover basis for its assets.[29] Similarly, a corporation takes a carryover basis for its assets.[30]

18-7b C Corporation

A C corporation can convert into any of the following entity forms.

- Sole proprietorship.
- Partnership or LLC.
- S corporation.

Converting to an S corporation merely requires the election of S status.[31] As discussed in Chapter 15, the S election can be made only if all shareholders consent to the election and if the S corporation qualification requirements are satisfied.[32] These qualification requirements become maintenance requirements that must be met to retain the S election.

The election of S status produces the following tax consequences.

- No recognition of gain or loss.
- Carryover basis for the shareholders' stock.
- Carryover basis for the assets of the corporation.

If a C corporation converts into a sole proprietorship, a partnership, or an LLC, the corporation must be liquidated. This produces the following tax consequences.

- Recognition of gain or loss at the corporate level.[33]
- Recognition of gain or loss at the shareholder level.[34]
- Fair market value basis for the assets distributed in liquidation.[35]

---

[25]§ 721(a).
[26]§ 351(a).
[27]§ 722.
[28]§ 358(a).
[29]§ 723.
[30]§ 362(a).

[31]§ 1362(a).
[32]§§ 1361(a), 1361(b), and 1362(a)(2).
[33]§ 336(a).
[34]§ 331(a).
[35]§ 334(a).

After liquidation, the C corporation's former shareholders contribute the assets to the new entity. The tax consequences to the owners and to the entity are the same as those discussed earlier.

18-7c **Partnership**

A partnership or an LLC can convert into either of the following entity forms, both of which permit having multiple owners.

- C corporation.
- S corporation.

The owners can transfer their interests to the C corporation or S corporation in exchange for the stock of the entity. Because the transfer likely satisfies the § 351 requirements, any realized gain or loss is not recognized.[36] If, however, the 80 percent control requirement is not satisfied, the realized gain or loss is recognized by the owners.[37]

Assuming that the § 351 requirements for nonrecognition are satisfied, the following tax results occur.

- The basis of the stock to the shareholders is a carryover basis.[38]
- The basis of the assets to the corporation is a carryover basis.[39]

LO.7

Compare the tax consequences of the choice among the most common forms of doing business.

18-8 **OVERALL COMPARISON OF BUSINESS FORMS**

Concept Summary 18.2 provides a detailed comparison of the tax consequences of the choice among the most common forms of doing business.

Concept Summary 18.2

Tax Attributes of Different Forms of Doing Business (Assume That Partners and Shareholders Are All Individuals)

	Sole Proprietorship	Partnership/Limited Liability Company	S Corporation	C Corporation
Restrictions on type or number of owners	One owner. The owner must be an individual.	Must have at least 2 owners.	Only individuals, estates, certain trusts, and certain tax-exempt entities can be owners. Maximum number of shareholders limited to 100.*	None, except some states require a minimum of two shareholders.
Incidence of tax	Sole proprietorship's income and deductions are reported on Schedule C of the individual's Form 1040. A separate Schedule C is prepared for each business.	Entity not subject to Federal income tax. Owners in their separate capacity subject to tax on their distributive share of income. Entity files Form 1065.	Except for certain built-in gains and passive investment income when earnings and profits are present from C corporation tax years, entity not subject to Federal income tax. S corporation files Form 1120S. Shareholders are subject to tax on income attributable to their stock ownership.	Income subject to double taxation. Entity subject to tax, and shareholder subject to tax on any corporate dividends received. Corporation files Form 1120.

*Spouses and family members can be treated as one shareholder.

continued

---

[36]§ 351(a).
[37]§ 368(c).

[38]§ 358(a).
[39]§ 362(a).

Tax Attributes of Different Forms of Doing Business—(Continued)

	Sole Proprietorship	Partnership/Limited Liability Company	S Corporation	C Corporation
Highest tax rate (before additional Medicare taxes)	39.6% at individual level.	39.6% at owner level.	39.6% at shareholder level.	35% at corporate level plus 20%/15%/0% on any corporate dividends at shareholder level (if qualified dividends; otherwise 39.6%).
Choice of tax year	Same tax year as owner.	Selection generally restricted to coincide with tax year of majority owners or principal owners or to tax year determined under the least aggregate deferral method.	Restricted to a calendar year unless IRS approves a different year for business purposes or other exceptions apply.	Unrestricted selection allowed at time of filing first tax return.
Timing of taxation	Based on owner's tax year.	Owners report their share of income in their tax year within which the entity's tax year ends. Owners in their separate capacities are subject to payment of estimated taxes.	Shareholders report their shares of income in their tax year within which the corporation's tax year ends. Shareholders may be subject to payment of estimated taxes.	Corporation subject to tax at close of its tax year. May be subject to payment of estimated taxes. Dividends are subject to tax at the shareholder level in the tax year received.
Basis for allocating income to owners	Not applicable (only one owner).	Profit and loss sharing agreement. Cash basis items of cash basis entities are allocated on a daily basis. Other entity items are allocated after considering varying interests of owners.	Pro rata share based on stock ownership. Shareholder's pro rata share is determined on a daily basis, according to the number of shares of stock held on each day of the corporation's tax year.	Not applicable.
Contribution of property to the entity	Not a taxable transaction.	Generally not a taxable transaction.	Is a taxable transaction unless the § 351 requirements are satisfied.	Is a taxable transaction unless the § 351 requirements are satisfied.
Character of income taxed to owners	Retains source characteristics.	Conduit—retains source characteristics.	Conduit—retains source characteristics.	All source characteristics are lost when income is distributed to owners.
Basis for allocating a net operating loss to owners	Not applicable (only one owner).	Profit and loss sharing agreement. Cash basis items of cash basis entities are allocated on a daily basis. Other entity items are allocated after considering varying interests of owners.	Prorated among shareholders on a daily basis.	Not applicable.
Limitation on losses deductible by owners	Investment in business assets.	Owner's investment plus share of liabilities.	Shareholder's investment plus loans made by shareholder to corporation.	Not applicable.
Subject to at-risk rules?	Yes, at the owner level. Indefinite carryover of excess loss.	Yes, at the owner level. Indefinite carryover of excess loss.	Yes, at the shareholder level. Indefinite carryover of excess loss.	Yes, for closely held corporations. Indefinite carryover of excess loss.
Subject to passive activity loss rules?	Yes, at the owner level. Indefinite carryover of excess loss.	Yes, at the owner level. Indefinite carryover of excess loss.	Yes, at the shareholder level. Indefinite carryover of excess loss.	Yes, for closely held corporations and personal service corporations. Indefinite carryover of excess loss.

continued

Tax Attributes of Different Forms of Doing Business—(Continued)

	Sole Proprietorship	Partnership/Limited Liability Company	S Corporation	C Corporation
Tax consequences of earnings retained by entity	Taxed to owner when earned and increases his or her investment in the sole proprietorship.	Taxed to owners when earned and increases interest bases in the entity.	Taxed to shareholders when earned and increases interest bases in stock.	Taxed to corporation when earned and may be subject to penalty tax if accumulated unreasonably.
Nonliquidating distributions to owners	Not taxable.	Not taxable unless money received exceeds recipient owner's basis in entity interest. Existence of § 751 assets may cause recognition of ordinary income.	Generally not taxable unless the distribution exceeds the shareholder's AAA or stock basis. Existence of accumulated earnings and profits could cause some distributions to be dividends.	Taxable in year of receipt to extent of earnings and profits or if exceeds basis in stock.
Capital gains (before additional Medicare taxes)	Taxed at owner level using maximum rate of 0%, 15%, 20%, 25%, or 28%.	Conduit—owners must account for their respective shares. Taxed at owner level.	Conduit, with certain exceptions (a possible penalty tax)—shareholders must account for their respective shares. Tax treatment determined at shareholder level.	Taxed at corporate level with a maximum 35% rate. No other benefits.
Capital losses	Only $3,000 of capital losses can be offset each tax year against ordinary income. Indefinite carryover.	Conduit—owners must account for their respective shares. Tax treatment determined at owner level.	Conduit—shareholders must account for their respective shares. Tax treatment determined at shareholder level.	Carried back three years and carried forward five years. Deductible only to offset other entity capital gains.
§ 1231 gains and losses	Taxable or deductible at owner level. Five-year lookback rule for § 1231 losses.	Conduit—owners must account for their respective shares. Tax treatment determined at owner level.	Conduit—shareholders must account for their respective shares. Tax treatment determined at shareholder level.	Taxable or deductible at corporate level only. Five-year lookback rule for § 1231 losses.
Foreign tax credits	Available at owner level.	Conduit—tax payments passed through to owners.	Generally conduit—tax payments passed through to shareholders.	Available at corporate level only.
§ 1244 treatment of loss on sale of interest	Not applicable.	Not applicable.	Available.	Available.
Basis treatment of entity liabilities	Not applicable.	Includible in interest basis.	Not includible in stock basis.	Not includible in stock basis.
Special tax on built-in gains	Not applicable.	Not applicable.	Possible corporate tax.	Not applicable.
Special allocations to owners	Not applicable (only one owner).	Available if supported by substantial economic effect.	Not available.	Not applicable.
Deduction for fringe benefits to owners	None.	None.	None unless a 2% or less shareholder.	Available within antidiscrimination rules.
Effect of liquidation/ redemption/ reorganization on basis of entity assets	Not applicable.	Usually carried over from entity to owner.	Taxable step-up to fair market value.	Taxable step-up to fair market value.

continued

Tax Attributes of Different Forms of Doing Business—(Continued)

	Sole Proprietorship	Partnership/Limited Liability Company	S Corporation	C Corporation
Sale of ownership interest	Treated as the sale of individual assets. Classification of recognized gain or loss depends on the nature of the individual assets.	Treated as the sale of an entity interest. Recognized gain or loss is classified as capital, although appreciated inventory and receivables are subject to ordinary income treatment.	Treated as the sale of corporate stock. Recognized gain is classified as capital gain. Recognized loss is classified as capital loss, subject to ordinary loss treatment under § 1244.	Treated as the sale of corporate stock. Recognized gain is classified as capital gain. Recognized loss is classified as capital loss, subject to ordinary loss treatment under § 1244.
Distribution of appreciated property	Not taxable.	No recognition at the entity level.	Gain or loss recognition at the corporate level to the extent of the appreciation. Conduit—amount of recognized gain is passed through to shareholders.	Taxable at the corporate level to the extent of any realized appreciation.
Splitting of income among family members	Not applicable (only one owner).	Difficult—IRS will not recognize a family member as an owner unless certain requirements are met.	Rather easy—gift of stock will transfer tax on a pro rata share of income to the donee. However, IRS can make adjustments to reflect adequate compensation for services.	Same as an S corporation, except that donees will be subject to tax only on earnings distributed to them. Other than unreasonable compensation, IRS generally cannot make adjustments to reflect adequate compensation for services and capital.
Organizational costs	Startup expenditures are eligible for $5,000 limited expensing (subject to phaseout) and amortizing balance over 180 months.	Organizational and startup expenditures each are eligible for $5,000 limited expensing (subject to phaseout) and amortizing balance over 180 months.	Same as partnership.	Same as partnership.
Charitable contributions	Various limitations apply at owner level.	Conduit—owners are subject to deduction limitations in their own capacities.	Conduit—shareholders are subject to deduction limitations in their own capacities.	Limited to 10% of taxable income before certain deductions.
Alternative minimum tax	Applies at owner level. AMT rates are 26% and 28%.	Applies at the owner level rather than at the entity level. AMT preferences and adjustments are passed through from the entity to the owners.	Applies at the shareholder level rather than at the corporate level. AMT preferences and adjustments are passed through from the S corporation to the shareholders.	Applies at the corporate level. AMT rate is 20%. Smaller C corporations are exempt.
ACE adjustment to AMTI	Does not apply.	Does not apply.	Does not apply.	The adjustment is made in calculating AMTI. The adjustment is 75% of the excess of adjusted current earnings over unadjusted AMTI. In certain cases, the adjustment may be negative.

REFOCUS ON THE BIG PICTURE

CHOOSING A BUSINESS FORM AND OTHER INVESTMENTS

Conducting their business as a C corporation, an S corporation, or an LLC would meet Bill and George's objectives of providing limited liability. From a tax perspective, both the S corporation and the LLC would allow the early-year losses to be passed through to the owners. This cannot be achieved with a C corporation, in which the losses are trapped until future years when the company is profitable. Once the entity turns profitable, the tax consequences are as follows.

- As a C corporation, the entity would pay income tax of $61,250 on taxable earnings of $200,000. If the remaining after-tax earnings of $138,750 are distributed equally to Bill and George (each owner would receive a taxable dividend of $69,375), each shareholder pays an additional income tax of $10,406 ($69,375 × 15%). The combined entity/owner tax liability is $82,062, resulting in after-tax cash flows of $117,938.

- If the entity is operated as an S corporation or an LLC, no tax is paid at the entity level. However, the entire $200,000 is taxed as ordinary income at the owner level, resulting in each owner paying $28,000 ($100,000 × 28%) income tax. The combined entity/owner tax liability is $56,000, resulting in after-tax cash flows of $144,000.

It appears that either the S corporation or the LLC meets Bill and George's objectives of having limited liability and minimizing tax liability. The LLC form offers an additional advantage in that an LLC need not satisfy the numerous statutory qualification requirements to elect and maintain S corporation status. However, based on the facts in this situation, it is unlikely that satisfying the requirements would create any difficulty for Bill and George.

The results of George's investing in a limited partnership appear in Example 1. While beneficial tax results are expected to occur, George needs to be aware of the economic risk of losing his $10,000 investment.

For Bill, the recognized gain on the sale of his investment in the retail coffee franchise outlet is dependent on that entity's form. If the franchise was a pass-through entity, the recognized gain would be different than if the entity were a C corporation: entity profits increase the owner's interest basis in a pass-through entity, whereas entity profits have no effect on a shareholder's basis in C corporation stock.

What If?

Assume instead that Bill and George decide to expand the business and reinvest the annual $200,000 before-tax earnings instead of paying out dividends to the owners. If the business is organized as a C corporation, it can accumulate the earnings—as long as the company has reasonable business needs—and avoid the additional tax that is paid by Bill and George when the company makes taxable dividend distributions. Although the entity-level tax of $61,250 still must be paid, after-tax cash flows increase to $138,750. While the S corporation or LLC with after-tax cash flows of $144,000 still would be preferred in this situation, the double tax problem of the C corporation can be minimized with effective planning.

Suggested Readings

John O. Everett, Cherie J. Hennig, and William A. Raabe, "Converting a C Corporation into an LLC: Quantifying the Tax Costs and Benefits," *Journal of Taxation*, August 2010.

Janel Grieman and Thomas J. Nash, "Did Averting Fiscal Cliff Allow C Corporations to Overtake Passthroughs?" *Practical Tax Strategies*, August 2013.

"Payments to a Taxpayer for the Sale of Business Were Ordinary Income," *Practical Tax Strategies*, November 2010.

W. Eugene Seago and Edward J. Schnee, "Double Deductions Resulting from Transfers to Controlled Corporations" *Journal of Taxation*, March 2011.

Key Terms

Conduit concept, 18-12	Entity concept, 18-12	Unreasonable compensation, 18-10

Computational Exercises

1. **LO.5** Roscoe contributes a personal-use asset, adjusted basis $15,000 and fair market value $28,000, to a new business in which he is an owner. Determine Roscoe's recognized gain on the transfer, and the basis of the asset to the business, if the new operation is a:

   a. Sole proprietorship.

   b. Partnership, where Roscoe holds a 10% interest.

   c. Corporation, where Roscoe holds a 25% interest and all shareholders contribute assets for stock in the transaction.

2. **LO.5** Mira and Lemma are equal owners of a business entity. Each contributed $25,000 cash to the business. Then the entity acquired a $100,000 loan from a bank. This year, operating profits totaled $30,000. Determine Lemma's interest basis at the end of the tax year, assuming that the entity is:

   a. A partnership.

   b. A C corporation.

   c. An S corporation.

3. **LO.5** Castle and Dorabella formed an S corporation; Castle owns 75% of the outstanding shares, and Dorabella owns the rest. When the entity's AAA balance is $1 million, it distributes an asset to each shareholder; the basis of each asset to the corporation is $45,000. Castle's asset is worth $90,000, and Dorabella's is worth $50,000. Determine the indicated amounts that result from the distribution.

   a. The corporation's recognized gain, if any.

   b. Dorabella's recognized gross income.

   c. Castle's recognized gross income.

Problems

4. **LO.2, 3, 4, 5, 6, 7** Using the legend provided, indicate which form of business entity each of the following characteristics describes. Some of the characteristics may apply to more than one form of business entity.

Legend	
SP	= Applies to sole proprietorship
P	= Applies to partnership and LLC
S	= Applies to S corporation
C	= Applies to C corporation
N	= Applies to none

   a. Has limited liability.
   b. Greatest ability to raise capital.
   c. Subject to double taxation.
   d. Subject to the ACE adjustment in computing AMT income.
   e. Limit on types and number of shareholders.
   f. Has unlimited liability.
   g. Sale of the business can be subject to double taxation.
   h. Contribution of property to the entity in exchange for an ownership interest can result in the nonrecognition of realized gain.
   i. Profits and losses affect the basis for an ownership interest.
   j. Entity liabilities affect the basis for an ownership interest.
   k. Distributions of earnings are taxed as dividend income to the owners.
   l. Total invested capital cannot exceed $1 million.
   m. AAA is an account that relates to this entity.

5. **LO.5** Using the legend provided, indicate which form of business entity each of the following characteristics describes. Some of the characteristics may apply to more than one form of business entity.

Legend	
P	= Applies to partnership and LLC
S	= Applies to S corporation
C	= Applies to C corporation

   a. Basis for an ownership interest is increased by an investment by the owner.
   b. Basis for an ownership interest is decreased by a distribution to the owner.
   c. Basis for an ownership interest is increased by entity profits.
   d. Basis for an ownership interest is decreased by entity losses.
   e. Basis for an ownership interest is increased as the entity's liabilities increase.
   f. Basis for an ownership interest is decreased as the entity's liabilities decrease.

6. **LO.2** Sea Green Enterprises reports the following assets and liabilities on its balance sheet.

	Net Book Value	Fair Market Value
Assets	$600,000	$925,000
Liabilities	200,000	200,000

Sea Green has just lost a product liability suit with damages of $10 million being awarded to the plaintiff. Although Sea Green will appeal the judgment, legal counsel indicates that the judgment is highly unlikely to be overturned by the appellate court. The product liability insurance carried by Sea Green includes a payout ceiling of $6 million. What is the amount of liability of the entity and its owners if Sea Green is:

a. A sole proprietorship?

b. A partnership or an LLC?

c. A C corporation?

d. An S corporation?

7. **LO.3, 4** Bryan operates his business as a C corporation. He is the only shareholder. **Ethics and Equity** The accumulated E & P is $800,000. Starting next year, Bryan will distribute $200,000 cash per year, plus all of the annual current-year earnings. Recognizing that the distribution would be taxed as dividend income, he has developed the following tax strategy.

- Sell the corporate assets to himself for the fair market value.
- Have the corporation invest the sales proceeds in a mutual fund.
- Contribute the assets to an LLC and operate his business in this legal form.

Evaluate Bryan's proposal to avoid double taxation.

8. **LO.3** Red, White, Blue, and Orange report taxable income as follows.

Corporation	Taxable Income
Red	$ 99,000
White	330,000
Blue	900,000
Orange	40,000,000

a. Calculate the marginal tax rate and the effective tax rate for each of the C corporations.

b. Explain why the marginal tax rate for a C corporation can exceed 35% but the effective tax rate cannot.

9. **LO.1, 2, 3** Amy and Jeff Barnes will operate their florist shop as a partnership or as **Decision Making** an S corporation. Their mailing address is 5700 Richmond Highway, **Communications** Alexandria, VA 22301. After paying salaries of $100,000 to each of the owners, the shop's annual earnings are projected to be about $150,000. The earnings are to be invested in the growth of the business. Write a letter to Amy and Jeff, advising them of which of the two entity forms they should select.

10. **LO.3** Gerald is an entrepreneur who likes to be actively involved in his business **Decision Making** ventures. He is going to invest $500,000 in a business that he projects will produce a tax loss of approximately $125,000 per year in the short run. However, Gerald is confident that, once consumers become aware of the new product being sold by the business and the quality of the service it provides, the business will generate a profit of at least $200,000 per year. Gerald generates substantial other income (from both business ventures and investment activities) each year. Advise Gerald on the business form he should select for the short run. He will be the sole owner of the business.

11. **LO.2, 3** Duke and Jacquie Coleman, married filing jointly, will establish a manufac- **Decision Making** turing business. The couple anticipates that the business will be profitable immediately due to a patent that Jacquie holds; profits for the first year will be about $300,000 and will increase at a rate of about 20% per year for the foreseeable future. Advise the Colemans as to the form of business entity that they should select. The Colemans are in the 39.6% Federal income tax bracket.

Decision Making   12. **LO.3** Plum Corporation will begin operations on January 1. Earnings for the next five years are projected to be relatively stable at about $80,000 per year. The shareholders of Plum are in the 33% tax bracket.

    a.   Plum will reinvest its after-tax earnings in the growth of the company. Should Plum operate as a C corporation or as an S corporation?

    b.   Plum will distribute its after-tax earnings each year to its shareholders. Should Plum operate as a C corporation or as an S corporation?

13. **LO.3** Mabel and Alan, who are in the 35% tax bracket, recently acquired a fast-food franchise. Both of them will work in the business and receive a salary of $175,000. They anticipate that the annual profits of the business, after deducting salaries, will be approximately $450,000. The entity will distribute enough cash each year to Mabel and Alan to cover their Federal income taxes associated with any flow-through income from the franchise.

    a.   What amount will the entity distribute if the franchise operates as a C corporation?

    b.   What amount will the entity distribute if the franchise operates as an S corporation?

    c.   What will be the amount of the combined entity/owner tax liability in (a) and (b)?

14. **LO.3** Owl is a closely held corporation owned by eight shareholders (each has 12.5% of the stock). Selected financial information provided by Owl follows.

Taxable income	$6,250,000
Positive AMT adjustments (excluding ACE adjustment)	600,000
Negative AMT adjustments	(30,000)
Tax preferences	5,000,000
Retained earnings	900,000
Accumulated E & P	2,000,000
ACE adjustment	750,000

    a.   Calculate Owl's regular Federal income tax liability and AMT if it is a C corporation.

    b.   Calculate Owl's regular Federal income tax liability and AMT if it is an S corporation.

    c.   How would your answers in (a) and (b) change if Owl was not closely held (e.g., 5,000 shareholders with no shareholder owning more than 2% of the stock)?

Decision Making   15. **LO.3** Falcon Corporation, a calendar year taxpayer, is a deepwater offshore drilling company that is planning to sell drilling equipment that it no longer needs. The drilling equipment has an adjusted basis of $400,000 ($700,000 − $300,000 depreciation) and a fair market value of $500,000. The AMT adjusted basis of the equipment is $425,000.

The buyer of the drilling equipment would like to close the transaction prior to the end of the calendar year. Falcon is considering the following options.

- $500,000 in cash payable on December 31, 2015.
- The sale is closed on December 31, 2015; the consideration is a $500,000 note issued by the buyer. The maturity date of the note is January 2, 2016, with the equipment pledged as security.

Falcon projects that its taxable income for 2015 and 2016 will be $400,000 (gross receipts of about $9.5 million) without the sale. Falcon has other AMT adjustments and tax preferences of $425,000 in 2015, which will not recur in 2016. Determine the tax consequences to Falcon under both options, and recommend the option that is preferable.

16. **LO.4** Heron Corporation has been in operation for 10 years. Since Heron's creation, all of its stock has been owned by Andy, who initially invested $200,000 in the corporation. Heron has been successful far beyond Andy's expectations, and the current fair market value of the stock is $10 million. While he has been paid a salary of $200,000 per year by the corporation, all of Heron's earnings have been reinvested in the growth of the corporation.

Heron currently is being audited by the IRS. One of the issues raised by the IRS agent is the possibility of the assessment of the accumulated earnings tax. Andy is not concerned about this issue because he believes Heron can easily justify the accumulations based on its past rapid expansion by opening new outlets. The expansion program is fully documented in the minutes of Heron's board of directors. Andy has provided this information to the IRS agent.

Two years ago, Andy decided that he would curtail any further expansion into new markets by Heron. In his opinion, further expansion would exceed his ability to manage the corporation effectively. Because the tax year under audit is three years in the past, Andy sees no reason to provide the IRS agent with this information.

Heron will continue its policy of no dividend payments into the foreseeable future. Andy believes that if the accumulated earnings issue is satisfactorily resolved on this audit, it probably will not be raised again on any subsequent audits. Thus, double taxation in the form of the tax on dividends at the shareholder level or the accumulated earnings tax at the corporate level can be avoided.

What is Heron's responsibility to disclose to the IRS agent the expected change in its growth strategy? Are Andy's beliefs regarding future accumulated earnings tax issues realistic? Explain.

Ethics and Equity
Critical Thinking

17. **LO.4** Two sisters and their brother, all unmarried, own and operate a dairy farm. They live on the farm and take their meals there for the "convenience of the employer." The fair market value of their lodging is $45,000, and the fair market value of their meals is $18,000. The meals are prepared by the farm cook, who provides their meals along with those of the eight other farm employees.

a. Determine the tax consequences of the meals and lodging to the sisters and their brother if the farm is incorporated.

b. Determine the tax consequences of the meals and lodging to the sisters and their brother if the farm is not incorporated.

Critical Thinking

18. **LO.4** A business entity has four equal owners. Its taxable income before the cost of certain fringe benefits paid to owners and other employees is $400,000. The amounts paid for these fringe benefits are reported as follows.

Critical Thinking

	Owners	Other Employees
Group term life insurance	$20,000	$ 40,000
Meals and lodging incurred for the convenience of the employer	50,000	75,000
Qualified retirement plan	30,000	90,000

a. Calculate the Federal taxable income of the entity, assuming that it is a(n):
- Partnership.
- C corporation.
- S corporation.

b. Determine the Federal income effects on the owners, assuming the use of each of the three business forms.

19. **LO.4** Turtle, a C corporation, reports taxable income of $300,000 before paying salaries to the three equal shareholder-employees, Britney, Shania, and Alan. Turtle follows a policy of distributing all after-tax earnings to the shareholders.

a. Determine the tax consequences for Turtle, Britney, Shania, and Alan if the corporation pays salaries to Britney, Shania, and Alan as follows.

Option 1		Option 2	
Britney	$135,000	Britney	$67,500
Shania	90,000	Shania	45,000
Alan	75,000	Alan	37,500

b. Is Turtle likely to encounter any tax problems associated with either option? Explain.

20. **LO.4** Parrott, Inc., a C corporation, is owned by Abner (60%) and Deanna (40%). Abner is the president, and Deanna is the vice president for sales. Parrott, Abner, and Deanna are cash basis taxpayers. Late in the year, Parrott encounters working capital difficulties. Therefore, Abner loans the corporation $810,000 and Deanna loans the corporation $540,000. Each loan uses a 5% note that is due in five years with interest payable annually.

a. Determine the tax consequences to Parrott, Abner, and Deanna if the notes are classified as debt.

b. Determine the tax consequences to Parrott, Abner, and Deanna if the notes are classified as equity.

Decision Making
Communications

21. **LO.4** Laurie Gladin owns land and a building that she has been using in her sole proprietorship. She is going to incorporate her sole proprietorship as a C corporation. Laurie must decide whether to contribute the land and building to the corporation or to lease them to the corporation. The net income of the sole proprietorship for the past five years has averaged $250,000. Advise Laurie on the tax consequences. Summarize your analysis in a memo for the tax file.

Decision Making

22. **LO.4** Marci and Jennifer each own 50% of the stock of Lavender, a C corporation. After each of them is paid a "reasonable" salary of $150,000, the taxable income of Lavender typically is about $800,000.

The corporation is about to purchase a $2 million shopping mall ($1,500,000 allocated to the building and $500,000 allocated to the land). The mall will be rented to tenants at a net rental rate (including rental commissions, depreciation, etc.) of $600,000 annually. Marci and Jennifer will contribute $1 million each to the corporation to provide the cash required for the acquisition.

Their CPA has suggested that Marci and Jennifer purchase the shopping mall as individuals and lease it to Lavender for a fair rental of $400,000. Both Marci and Jennifer are in the 35% tax bracket. The acquisition will occur on January 2 next year. Determine whether the shopping mall should be acquired by Lavender or by Marci and Jennifer in accordance with their CPA's recommendation. Depreciation on the shopping mall for the year is $37,000.

Decision Making

23. **LO.4** Since Garnet Corporation was formed five years ago, its stock has been held as follows: 525 shares by Frank and 175 shares by Grace. Their basis in the stock is $350,000 for Frank and $150,000 for Grace. As part of a stock redemption, Garnet redeems 125 of Frank's shares for $175,000 and 125 of Grace's shares for $175,000.

a. What are the tax consequences of the stock redemption to Frank and Grace?

b. How would the tax consequences to Frank and Grace be different if, instead of the redemption, they each sell 125 shares to Chuck (an unrelated party)?

c. What factors should influence their decision on whether to redeem or sell the 250 shares of stock?

Issue ID

24. **LO.4** Oscar created Lavender Corporation four years ago. The C corporation has paid Oscar as president a salary of $200,000 each year. Annual earnings after taxes approximate $700,000 each year. Lavender has not paid any dividends, nor

does it intend to do so in the future. Instead, Oscar wants his heirs to receive the stock with a step-up in stock basis when he dies. Identify the relevant tax issues.

25. **LO.4** Tammy and Willy own 40% of the stock of Roadrunner, an S corporation. The other 60% is owned by 99 other shareholders, all of whom are single and unrelated. Tammy and Willy have agreed to a divorce and are in the process of negotiating a property settlement. Identify the relevant tax issues for Tammy and Willy.

Issue ID

26. **LO.4** Clay Corporation has been an S corporation since its incorporation 10 years ago. During the first three years of operations, it incurred total losses of $250,000. Since then, Clay has generated earnings of approximately $180,000 each year. None of the earnings have been distributed to the three equal shareholders, Claire, Lynn, and Todd, because the corporation has been in an expansion mode.

Decision Making

At the beginning of this year, Claire sells her stock to Nell for $400,000. Nell has reservations about the utility of the S election. Therefore, Lynn, Todd, and Nell are discussing whether the election should be continued. They expect the earnings to remain at approximately $180,000 each year. However, because they perceive that the company's expansion period is over and Clay has adequate working capital, they may start distributing the earnings to the shareholders. All of the shareholders are in the 33% tax bracket.

Advise the three shareholders as to whether Clay's S election should be maintained.

27. **LO.5** Phillip and Evans form a business entity. Each contributes the following property.

Decision Making

	Phillip	**Evans**
Cash	$600,000	
Land		$600,000*

*Fair market value. Evans's adjusted basis is $200,000.

Three months later, the entity sells the land for $652,000 because of unexpected zoning problems. The proceeds are to be applied toward the purchase of another parcel of land, to be used for real estate development. Determine the Federal income tax consequences to the entity and to the owners upon both the formation and the later sale of the land. Perform your analysis assuming that the entity is:

a. A partnership.

b. An S corporation.

c. A C corporation.

How could the parties structure the transaction so as to defer any recognized tax gain? Be specific.

28. **LO.5** Agnes, Becky, and Carol form a business entity with each contributing the following.

	Adjusted Basis	**Fair Market Value**
Agnes: Cash	$100,000	$100,000
Becky: Land	60,000	120,000
Carol: Services		50,000

Their ownership percentages will be as follows.

Agnes	40%
Becky	40%
Carol	20%

Becky's land has a $20,000 mortgage that is assumed by the entity. Carol is an attorney who receives her ownership interest in exchange for legal services. Determine the recognized gain to the owners, the basis for their ownership interests, and the entity's basis for its assets if the entity is organized as:

a.   A partnership.

b.   A C corporation.

c.   An S corporation.

29. **LO.5** Eloise contributes $40,000 to MeldCo in exchange for a 30% ownership interest. During the first year of operations, MeldCo earns a profit of $200,000. At the end of that year, MeldCo holds liabilities of $75,000.

a.   Calculate Eloise's basis for her stock if MeldCo is a C corporation.

b.   Calculate Eloise's basis for her stock if MeldCo is an S corporation.

c.   Calculate Eloise's basis for her partnership interest if MeldCo is a partnership.

30. **LO.5** ListCo reports the following income for the current tax year.

Operations	$92,000
Tax-exempt interest income	19,000
Long-term capital gain	60,000

ListCo holds earnings and profits (AAA for an S corporation) of $900,000 at the beginning of the year. Then ListCo distributes $200,000 in total to the owners.

a.   Calculate the taxable income if ListCo is (1) a C corporation and (2) an S corporation.

b.   Determine the effect of the distribution on the shareholders if ListCo is (1) a C corporation and (2) an S corporation.

Ethics and Equity   31. **LO.5** For many years, Sophie has owned and operated several apartment buildings. In 2011 and upon the advice of her attorney, Sophie transferred the apartment buildings to a newly created corporation. Her main reason for incorporating the business was to achieve the legal protection of limited liability.

Every year since 2011, Sophie has prepared and filed a Form 1120 for the corporation. No corporate income tax has been paid because, after the deduction of various expenses (including Sophie's "management fee"), the corporation reports zero taxable income.

This year, Sophie decides that filing Form 1120 is a waste of time and serves no useful purpose. Instead, she plans to report all of the financial activities of the apartment business on her own individual Form 1040.

Comment on the propriety of what Sophie plans to do.

32. **LO.5** The Coffee Company engages in the following transactions during the taxable year.

• Sells stock held for three years as an investment for $30,000 (adjusted basis of $20,000).

• Sells land used in the business for $65,000. The land has been used as a parking lot and originally cost $40,000.

• Receives tax-exempt interest on municipal bonds of $5,000.

• Receives dividends on IBM stock of $80,000.

Describe the effect of these transactions on the entity and its owners if the entity is organized as:

a.   A partnership.

b.   A C corporation.

c.   An S corporation.

33. **LO.5** Swift Corporation distributes land (basis of $55,000 and fair market value of $120,000) to Sam and cash ($240,000) to Allison in exchange for part of their stock. Other shareholders do not redeem any of their stock. Sam surrenders shares of stock that have a basis of $25,000. Prior to the stock redemption, Sam owned 20% of the Swift stock, and after the redemption, he owns 15%.

    At the same time, Swift distributes cash to Allison, and she surrenders shares of stock with a basis of $40,000. Prior to the stock redemption, Allison owned 70% of the Swift stock, and after the redemption, she owns 60%.

    Determine the tax consequences to Swift, Sam, and Allison if Swift is:

    a.   A C corporation.
    b.   An S corporation.

34. **LO.5** Indigo, Inc., a personal service corporation, incurs the following income and losses.

Active income	$325,000
Portfolio income	49,000
Passive activity loss	333,000

    a.   Calculate Indigo's taxable income.
    b.   Assume that instead of being a personal service corporation, Indigo is a closely held C corporation. Calculate Indigo's taxable income.
    c.   Would the answer in (b) change if the passive loss was $320,000 rather than $333,000? Explain.

35. **LO.5** Rosa contributes $50,000 to FlipCo in exchange for a 10% ownership interest. Rosa materially participates in FlipCo's business.

    FlipCo incurs a loss of $900,000 for the current tax year. Entity liabilities at the end of the year are $700,000. Of this amount, $150,000 is for recourse debt, and $550,000 is for nonrecourse debt.

    a.   Assume that FlipCo is a partnership. How much of Rosa's share of the loss can she deduct for the year on her individual tax return? What is Rosa's basis for her partnership interest at the end of the year?
    b.   Assume that FlipCo is a C corporation. How much of Rosa's share of the loss can she deduct for the year on her individual tax return? What is Rosa's basis for her stock at the end of the year?

36. **LO.5** Bishop contributes undeveloped land to a business entity in January for a 40% ownership interest. Bishop's basis for the land is $140,000, and the fair market value is $600,000. The business entity was formed three years ago by Petula and Rene, who have equal ownership. The entity is successful in getting the land rezoned from agricultural to residential use, but the owners decide to sell the land so that the entity can invest in another project.

    In August, the land is sold for $650,000. Determine the tax consequences of the sale of the undeveloped land for the business entity and the three owners if the entity is organized as:

    a.   A C corporation.
    b.   An S corporation.
    c.   A partnership.
    d.   An LLC.

37. **LO.5** Jo and Velma are equal owners of the JV Partnership. Jo invests $500,000 cash in the partnership. Velma contributes land and a building (basis to her of $125,000, fair market value of $500,000). The entity then borrows $250,000 cash using recourse financing and $100,000 using nonrecourse financing.

    a.   Compute the outside basis in the partnership interest for Jo and Velma.
    b.   Compute the at-risk amount for Jo and Velma.

38. **LO.5** Megan owns 55% and Vern owns 45% of a business entity. The owners would like to use the entity to share profits (55% for Megan and 45% for Vern) and to share losses (80% for Vern and 20% for Megan). Determine the tax consequences if the entity has a tax loss of $160,000 and is organized as:

  a.   A partnership.

  b.   A C corporation.

  c.   An S corporation.

39. **LO.5** Sanjay contributes land to a business entity in January of the current year for a 30% ownership interest. Sanjay's basis for the land is $60,000, and the fair market value is $100,000. The business entity was formed three years ago by Polly and Rita, who have equal ownership. The entity is unsuccessful in getting the land rezoned from agricultural to residential. In October of the current year, the land is sold for $110,000.

  Determine the tax consequences of the sale of the land for the entity and its owners if the entity is organized as:

  a.   A C corporation.

  b.   An S corporation.

  c.   A partnership.

40. **LO.7** Emily and Freda are negotiating with George to purchase the business he operates as Pelican, Inc. The assets of Pelican, Inc., a C corporation, are recorded as follows.

Asset	Basis	FMV
Cash	$ 20,000	$ 20,000
Accounts receivable	50,000	50,000
Inventory	100,000	110,000
Furniture and fixtures	150,000	170,000*
Building	200,000	250,000**
Land	40,000	150,000

*Potential depreciation recapture is $45,000.
**The straight-line method was used to depreciate the building. Accumulated depreciation is $340,000.

George's basis for the Pelican stock is $560,000. George is subject to a 35% marginal tax rate, and Pelican faces a 34% marginal tax rate.

  a.   Emily and Freda purchase the *stock* of Pelican from George for $908,000. Determine the tax consequences to Emily and Freda, Pelican, and George.

  b.   Emily and Freda purchase the *assets* from Pelican for $908,000. Determine the tax consequences to Emily and Freda, Pelican, and George.

  c.   The purchase price is $550,000 because the fair market value of the building is $150,000, and the fair market value of the land is $50,000. No amount is assigned to goodwill. Emily and Freda purchase the *stock* of Pelican from George. Determine the tax consequences to Emily and Freda, Pelican, and George.

Decision Making   41. **LO.7** Linda is the owner of a sole proprietorship. The entity has the following assets.

Asset	Basis	FMV
Cash	$10,000	$10,000
Accounts receivable	–0–	25,000
Office furniture and fixtures*	15,000	17,000
Building**	75,000	90,000
Land	60,000	80,000

*Potential depreciation recapture is $5,000.
**The straight-line method has been used to depreciate the building.

Linda sells the business for $260,000 to Juan.

a. Determine the tax consequences to Linda, including the classification of any recognized gain or loss.

b. Determine the tax consequences to Juan.

c. Advise Juan on how the purchase agreement could be modified to produce more beneficial tax consequences for him.

42. **LO.7** Gail and Harry own the GH Partnership. They have conducted the business as a partnership for 10 years. The bases for their partnership interests are as follows.

Decision Making

Gail	Harry
$100,000	$150,000

GH Partnership holds the following assets.

Asset	Basis	FMV
Cash	$ 10,000	$ 10,000
Accounts receivable	30,000	28,000
Inventory	25,000	26,000
Building*	100,000	150,000
Land	250,000	400,000

*The straight-line method has been used to depreciate the building. Accumulated depreciation is $70,000.

Gail and Harry sell their partnership interests to Keith and Liz for $307,000 each.

a. Determine the tax consequences of the sale to Gail, Harry, and GH Partnership.

b. From a tax perspective, should it matter to Keith and Liz whether they purchase Gail and Harry's partnership interests or the partnership assets from GH Partnership? Explain.

43. **LO.7** Hector and Walt are purchasing the Copper Partnership from Jan and Gail for $700,000; Hector and Walt will be equal partners. During the negotiations, Jan and Gail succeeded in having the transaction structured as the purchase of the partnership rather than as a purchase of the individual assets. The adjusted basis of the individual assets of Copper is $580,000.

Decision Making

a. What are Hector's and Walt's bases for their partnership interests (i.e., outside bases)?

b. What is Copper's adjusted basis for its assets after the transaction? Would an optional adjustment-to-basis election be helpful? Why or why not?

44. **LO.7** Vladimir owns all of the stock of Ruby Corporation. The fair market value of the stock (and Ruby's assets) is about four times his adjusted basis for the stock. Vladimir is negotiating with an investor group for the sale of the corporation. Identify the relevant tax issues for Vladimir.

Issue ID

45. **LO.7** Maurice Allred is going to purchase either the stock or the assets of Jewel Corporation. All of the Jewel stock is owned by Charley. Maurice and Charley agree that Jewel is worth $700,000. The tax basis for Jewel's assets is $500,000.

Decision Making

Communications

Write a letter to Maurice, advising him on whether he should negotiate to purchase the stock or the assets. Prepare a memo for the tax research file on this matter. Maurice's address is 100 Aspen Green, Chattanooga, TN 37403.

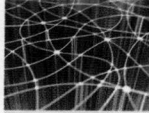

BRIDGE DISCIPLINE

1. Parchment, Inc., is created with the following asset and liability contributions. Jake and Fran each receive 100 shares of Parchment common stock.

Shareholder	Assets	Basis	Fair Market Value
Jake	Cash	$100,000	$100,000
Fran	Land	40,000	120,000*

*The land is subject to a mortgage of $20,000 that Parchment assumes.

   a. Prepare a financial accounting balance sheet for Parchment. Discuss the relevance of conduit theory and entity theory in the creation of Parchment.
   b. Prepare a tax balance sheet for Parchment. Discuss the relevance of conduit theory and entity theory in the creation of Parchment.
   c. Assume that Parchment sells the land for $150,000 four months after Parchment was created. Discuss the effect of the sale on the financial accounting balance sheet and the tax balance sheet.

2. Assume that Parchment in (1) elects S corporation status at the time of its creation. Respond to (a), (b), and (c).

3. Assume that Parchment in (1) is a general partnership rather than a corporation. Respond to (a), (b), and (c). Would your answer change if Parchment were an LLC that "checked the box" to be taxed as a partnership? Explain.

4. Teal, Inc., owns total assets of $100 million, and it reports annual revenues of $700 million. Lavender, Inc., owns total assets of $12 million, and it reports annual revenues of $900,000. Both corporations have been in existence for three years.
   a. Explain why neither Teal nor Lavender computes an AMT liability for its first tax year.
   b. Explain why, in later years, Teal computes an AMT liability and Lavender is not required to do so.
   c. Do you think that this different tax treatment for Teal and Lavender is equitable? Explain your position.

Research Problems

THOMSON REUTERS
Student Edition

Note: Solutions to Research Problems can be prepared by using the Checkpoint® Student Edition online research product, which is available to accompany this text. It is also possible to prepare solutions to the Research Problems by using tax research materials found in a standard tax library.

Research Problem 1. The Turnaround LLC was formed several years ago. It incurred losses for several years, reducing many of its members' bases in their interests to zero. However, the business recently obtained some new and promising contracts, and there is an expectation of profits in the coming years.

Turnaround then admitted several new members, who each made capital contributions for their interests. The new owners anticipate that it will be necessary to reinvest any profits back into the business for some time. As there no longer will be losses to pass through, and any double taxation of profits will be delayed for some time, the owners of Turnaround are considering converting the business to a C corporation.

The business controls the following assets. There is no § 754 election in effect.

	Fair Market Value	Adjusted Basis
Cash	$ 500,000	$500,000
PP&E	500,000	500,000
Customer contracts	1,000,000	0

The original owners of Turnaround now hold a 50% capital and profits interest. They have come to you for advice regarding the potential tax consequences of the conversion for them, as well as for the new corporation.

Partial list of research aids:
Rev.Rul. 70–239, 1970–1 C.B. 74.
Rev.Rul. 84–111, 1984–2 C.B. 88.
Rev.Rul. 2004–59, 2004–24 I.R.B 1050.
Treas. Reg. § 301.7701–3(g)(i).

Research Problem 2. Crane is a partner in the Cardinal Partnership. A dispute arose with the partnership regarding Crane's share of current earnings. The partnership contends that the amount is $75,000, while Crane believes his share is $100,000.

Crane ceased being a partner on November 1. As a result of the dispute, the partnership distributed only $75,000 to Crane. It placed the disputed $25,000 in escrow. However, Crane's Schedule K–1 from the partnership included the full $100,000. Crane believes that the K–1 should include only the $75,000 that is not in dispute. Is Crane correct? Explain.

Use the tax resources of the Internet to address the following questions. Do not restrict your search to the Web, but include a review of newsgroups and general reference materials, practitioner sites and resources, primary sources of the tax law, chat rooms and discussion groups, and other opportunities.

Internet Activity

Research Problem 3. Find a blog posting or discussion thread with comments from tax professionals about Federal income tax consequences that occur when a business converts from an LLC to an S corporation or when a C corporation converts to a pass-through entity. Summarize the comments and suggestions that you find in these discussions in a one-page memo to your instructor.

Communications

Research Problem 4. For your state, list the forms that are required to be filed when a pass-through entity incorporates or when a corporation converts to a pass-through entity. Give statutory citations for the conversion rules, due dates for any required forms, and addresses for where the forms are to be sent. Attach a copy of one of the forms to a memo summarizing your findings, and send the documents to your instructor.

Communications

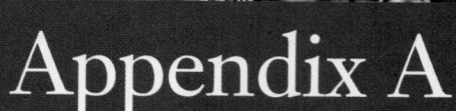

Appendix A

Tax Rate Schedules and Tables

2014 Tax Rate Schedules

Single—Schedule X

If taxable income is: Over—	But not over—	The tax is:	of the amount over—
$ 0	$ 9,075	.........10%	$ 0
9,075	36,900	$ 907.50 + 15%	9,075
36,900	89,350	5,081.25 + 25%	36,900
89,350	186,350	18,193.75 + 28%	89,350
186,350	405,100	45,353.75 + 33%	186,350
405,100	406,750	117,541.25 + 35%	405,100
406,750	....	118,118.75 + 39.6%	406,750

Head of household—Schedule Z

If taxable income is: Over—	But not over—	The tax is:	of the amount over—
$ 0	$ 12,950	.........10%	$ 0
12,950	49,400	$ 1,295.00 + 15%	12,950
49,400	127,550	6,762.50 + 25%	49,400
127,550	206,600	26,300.00 + 28%	127,550
206,600	405,100	48,434.00 + 33%	206,600
405,100	432,200	113,939.00 + 35%	405,100
432,200	....	123,424.00 + 39.6%	432,200

Married filing jointly or Qualifying widow(er)—Schedule Y–1

If taxable income is: Over—	But not over—	The tax is:	of the amount over—
$ 0	$ 18,150	.........10%	$ 0
18,150	73,800	$ 1,815.00 + 15%	18,150
73,800	148,850	10,162.50 + 25%	73,800
148,850	226,850	28,925.00 + 28%	148,850
226,850	405,100	50,765.00 + 33%	226,850
405,100	457,600	109,587.50 + 35%	405,100
457,600	....	127,962.50 + 39.6%	457,600

Married filing separately—Schedule Y–2

If taxable income is: Over—	But not over—	The tax is:	of the amount over—
$ 0	$ 9,075	.........10%	$ 0
9,075	36,900	$ 907.50 + 15%	9,075
36,900	74,425	5,081.25 + 25%	36,900
74,425	113,425	14,462.50 + 28%	74,425
113,425	202,550	25,382.50 + 33%	113,425
202,550	228,800	54,793.75 + 35%	202,550
228,800	....	63,981.25 + 39.6%	228,800

2015 Tax Rate Schedules

Single—Schedule X

If taxable income is: Over—	But not over—	The tax is:	of the amount over—
$ 0	$ 9,225	.........10%	$ 0
9,225	37,450	$ 922.50 + 15%	9,225
37,450	90,750	5,156.25 + 25%	37,450
90,750	189,300	18,481.25 + 28%	90,750
189,300	411,500	46,075.25 + 33%	189,300
411,500	413,200	119,401.25 + 35%	411,500
413,200	....	119,996.25 + 39.6%	413,200

Head of household—Schedule Z

If taxable income is: Over—	But not over—	The tax is:	of the amount over—
$ 0	$ 13,150	.........10%	$ 0
13,150	50,200	$ 1,315.00 + 15%	13,150
50,200	129,600	6,872.50 + 25%	50,200
129,600	209,850	26,722.50 + 28%	129,600
209,850	411,500	49,192.50 + 33%	209,850
411,500	439,000	115,737.00 + 35%	411,500
439,000	....	125,362.00 + 39.6%	439,000

Married filing jointly or Qualifying widow(er)—Schedule Y–1

If taxable income is: Over—	But not over—	The tax is:	of the amount over—
$ 0	$ 18,450	.........10%	$ 0
18,450	74,900	$ 1,845.00 + 15%	18,450
74,900	151,200	10,312.50 + 25%	74,900
151,200	230,450	29,387.50 + 28%	151,200
230,450	411,500	51,577.50 + 33%	230,450
411,500	464,850	111,324.00 + 35%	411,500
464,850	....	129,996.50 + 39.6%	464,850

Married filing separately—Schedule Y–2

If taxable income is: Over—	But not over—	The tax is:	of the amount over—
$ 0	$ 9,225	.........10%	$ 0
9,225	37,450	$ 922.50 + 15%	9,225
37,450	75,600	5,156.25 + 25%	37,450
75,600	115,225	14,693.75 + 28%	75,600
115,225	205,750	25,788.75 + 33%	115,225
205,750	232,425	55,662.00 + 35%	205,750
232,425	....	64,998.25 + 39.6%	232,425

2014 Tax Table

See the instructions for line 44 to see if you must use the Tax Table below to figure your tax.

Example. Mr. and Mrs. Brown are filing a joint return. Their taxable income on Form 1040, line 43, is $25,300. First, they find the $25,300-25,350 taxable income line. Next, they find the column for married filing jointly and read down the column. The amount shown where the taxable income line and filing status column meet is $2,891. This is the tax amount they should enter on Form 1040, line 44.

Sample Table

At Least	But Less Than	Single	Married filing jointly*	Married filing separately	Head of a house-hold
			Your tax is—		
25,200	25,250	3,330	2,876	3,330	3,136
25,250	25,300	3,338	2,884	3,338	3,144
25,300	25,350	3,345	(2,891)	3,345	3,151
25,350	25,400	3,353	2,899	3,353	3,159

If line 43 (taxable income) is— At least	But less than	And you are— Single	Married filing jointly *	Married filing sepa-rately	Head of a house-hold
		Your tax is—			
0	5	0	0	0	0
5	15	1	1	1	1
15	25	2	2	2	2
25	50	4	4	4	4
50	75	6	6	6	6
75	100	9	9	9	9
100	125	11	11	11	11
125	150	14	14	14	14
150	175	16	16	16	16
175	200	19	19	19	19
200	225	21	21	21	21
225	250	24	24	24	24
250	275	26	26	26	26
275	300	29	29	29	29
300	325	31	31	31	31
325	350	34	34	34	34
350	375	36	36	36	36
375	400	39	39	39	39
400	425	41	41	41	41
425	450	44	44	44	44
450	475	46	46	46	46
475	500	49	49	49	49
500	525	51	51	51	51
525	550	54	54	54	54
550	575	56	56	56	56
575	600	59	59	59	59
600	625	61	61	61	61
625	650	64	64	64	64
650	675	66	66	66	66
675	700	69	69	69	69
700	725	71	71	71	71
725	750	74	74	74	74
750	775	76	76	76	76
775	800	79	79	79	79
800	825	81	81	81	81
825	850	84	84	84	84
850	875	86	86	86	86
875	900	89	89	89	89
900	925	91	91	91	91
925	950	94	94	94	94
950	975	96	96	96	96
975	1,000	99	99	99	99

1,000

At least	But less than	Single	Married filing jointly *	Married filing sepa-rately	Head of a house-hold
1,000	1,025	101	101	101	101
1,025	1,050	104	104	104	104
1,050	1,075	106	106	106	106
1,075	1,100	109	109	109	109
1,100	1,125	111	111	111	111
1,125	1,150	114	114	114	114
1,150	1,175	116	116	116	116
1,175	1,200	119	119	119	119
1,200	1,225	121	121	121	121
1,225	1,250	124	124	124	124
1,250	1,275	126	126	126	126
1,275	1,300	129	129	129	129
1,300	1,325	131	131	131	131
1,325	1,350	134	134	134	134
1,350	1,375	136	136	136	136
1,375	1,400	139	139	139	139
1,400	1,425	141	141	141	141
1,425	1,450	144	144	144	144
1,450	1,475	146	146	146	146
1,475	1,500	149	149	149	149
1,500	1,525	151	151	151	151
1,525	1,550	154	154	154	154
1,550	1,575	156	156	156	156
1,575	1,600	159	159	159	159
1,600	1,625	161	161	161	161
1,625	1,650	164	164	164	164
1,650	1,675	166	166	166	166
1,675	1,700	169	169	169	169
1,700	1,725	171	171	171	171
1,725	1,750	174	174	174	174
1,750	1,775	176	176	176	176
1,775	1,800	179	179	179	179
1,800	1,825	181	181	181	181
1,825	1,850	184	184	184	184
1,850	1,875	186	186	186	186
1,875	1,900	189	189	189	189
1,900	1,925	191	191	191	191
1,925	1,950	194	194	194	194
1,950	1,975	196	196	196	196
1,975	2,000	199	199	199	199

2,000

At least	But less than	Single	Married filing jointly *	Married filing sepa-rately	Head of a house-hold
2,000	2,025	201	201	201	201
2,025	2,050	204	204	204	204
2,050	2,075	206	206	206	206
2,075	2,100	209	209	209	209
2,100	2,125	211	211	211	211
2,125	2,150	214	214	214	214
2,150	2,175	216	216	216	216
2,175	2,200	219	219	219	219
2,200	2,225	221	221	221	221
2,225	2,250	224	224	224	224
2,250	2,275	226	226	226	226
2,275	2,300	229	229	229	229
2,300	2,325	231	231	231	231
2,325	2,350	234	234	234	234
2,350	2,375	236	236	236	236
2,375	2,400	239	239	239	239
2,400	2,425	241	241	241	241
2,425	2,450	244	244	244	244
2,450	2,475	246	246	246	246
2,475	2,500	249	249	249	249
2,500	2,525	251	251	251	251
2,525	2,550	254	254	254	254
2,550	2,575	256	256	256	256
2,575	2,600	259	259	259	259
2,600	2,625	261	261	261	261
2,625	2,650	264	264	264	264
2,650	2,675	266	266	266	266
2,675	2,700	269	269	269	269
2,700	2,725	271	271	271	271
2,725	2,750	274	274	274	274
2,750	2,775	276	276	276	276
2,775	2,800	279	279	279	279
2,800	2,825	281	281	281	281
2,825	2,850	284	284	284	284
2,850	2,875	286	286	286	286
2,875	2,900	289	289	289	289
2,900	2,925	291	291	291	291
2,925	2,950	294	294	294	294
2,950	2,975	296	296	296	296
2,975	3,000	299	299	299	299

* This column must also be used by a qualifying widow(er).

(Continued)

2014 Tax Table—*Continued*

3,000

At least	But less than	Single	Married filing jointly *	Married filing separately	Head of a household
3,000	3,050	303	303	303	303
3,050	3,100	308	308	308	308
3,100	3,150	313	313	313	313
3,150	3,200	318	318	318	318
3,200	3,250	323	323	323	323
3,250	3,300	328	328	328	328
3,300	3,350	333	333	333	333
3,350	3,400	338	338	338	338
3,400	3,450	343	343	343	343
3,450	3,500	348	348	348	348
3,500	3,550	353	353	353	353
3,550	3,600	358	358	358	358
3,600	3,650	363	363	363	363
3,650	3,700	368	368	368	368
3,700	3,750	373	373	373	373
3,750	3,800	378	378	378	378
3,800	3,850	383	383	383	383
3,850	3,900	388	388	388	388
3,900	3,950	393	393	393	393
3,950	4,000	398	398	398	398

4,000

At least	But less than	Single	Married filing jointly *	Married filing separately	Head of a household
4,000	4,050	403	403	403	403
4,050	4,100	408	408	408	408
4,100	4,150	413	413	413	413
4,150	4,200	418	418	418	418
4,200	4,250	423	423	423	423
4,250	4,300	428	428	428	428
4,300	4,350	433	433	433	433
4,350	4,400	438	438	438	438
4,400	4,450	443	443	443	443
4,450	4,500	448	448	448	448
4,500	4,550	453	453	453	453
4,550	4,600	458	458	458	458
4,600	4,650	463	463	463	463
4,650	4,700	468	468	468	468
4,700	4,750	473	473	473	473
4,750	4,800	478	478	478	478
4,800	4,850	483	483	483	483
4,850	4,900	488	488	488	488
4,900	4,950	493	493	493	493
4,950	5,000	498	498	498	498

5,000

At least	But less than	Single	Married filing jointly *	Married filing separately	Head of a household
5,000	5,050	503	503	503	503
5,050	5,100	508	508	508	508
5,100	5,150	513	513	513	513
5,150	5,200	518	518	518	518
5,200	5,250	523	523	523	523
5,250	5,300	528	528	528	528
5,300	5,350	533	533	533	533
5,350	5,400	538	538	538	538
5,400	5,450	543	543	543	543
5,450	5,500	548	548	548	548
5,500	5,550	553	553	553	553
5,550	5,600	558	558	558	558
5,600	5,650	563	563	563	563
5,650	5,700	568	568	568	568
5,700	5,750	573	573	573	573
5,750	5,800	578	578	578	578
5,800	5,850	583	583	583	583
5,850	5,900	588	588	588	588
5,900	5,950	593	593	593	593
5,950	6,000	598	598	598	598

6,000

At least	But less than	Single	Married filing jointly *	Married filing separately	Head of a household
6,000	6,050	603	603	603	603
6,050	6,100	608	608	608	608
6,100	6,150	613	613	613	613
6,150	6,200	618	618	618	618
6,200	6,250	623	623	623	623
6,250	6,300	628	628	628	628
6,300	6,350	633	633	633	633
6,350	6,400	638	638	638	638
6,400	6,450	643	643	643	643
6,450	6,500	648	648	648	648
6,500	6,550	653	653	653	653
6,550	6,600	658	658	658	658
6,600	6,650	663	663	663	663
6,650	6,700	668	668	668	668
6,700	6,750	673	673	673	673
6,750	6,800	678	678	678	678
6,800	6,850	683	683	683	683
6,850	6,900	688	688	688	688
6,900	6,950	693	693	693	693
6,950	7,000	698	698	698	698

7,000

At least	But less than	Single	Married filing jointly *	Married filing separately	Head of a household
7,000	7,050	703	703	703	703
7,050	7,100	708	708	708	708
7,100	7,150	713	713	713	713
7,150	7,200	718	718	718	718
7,200	7,250	723	723	723	723
7,250	7,300	728	728	728	728
7,300	7,350	733	733	733	733
7,350	7,400	738	738	738	738
7,400	7,450	743	743	743	743
7,450	7,500	748	748	748	748
7,500	7,550	753	753	753	753
7,550	7,600	758	758	758	758
7,600	7,650	763	763	763	763
7,650	7,700	768	768	768	768
7,700	7,750	773	773	773	773
7,750	7,800	778	778	778	778
7,800	7,850	783	783	783	783
7,850	7,900	788	788	788	788
7,900	7,950	793	793	793	793
7,950	8,000	798	798	798	798

8,000

At least	But less than	Single	Married filing jointly *	Married filing separately	Head of a household
8,000	8,050	803	803	803	803
8,050	8,100	808	808	808	808
8,100	8,150	813	813	813	813
8,150	8,200	818	818	818	818
8,200	8,250	823	823	823	823
8,250	8,300	828	828	828	828
8,300	8,350	833	833	833	833
8,350	8,400	838	838	838	838
8,400	8,450	843	843	843	843
8,450	8,500	848	848	848	848
8,500	8,550	853	853	853	853
8,550	8,600	858	858	858	858
8,600	8,650	863	863	863	863
8,650	8,700	868	868	868	868
8,700	8,750	873	873	873	873
8,750	8,800	878	878	878	878
8,800	8,850	883	883	883	883
8,850	8,900	888	888	888	888
8,900	8,950	893	893	893	893
8,950	9,000	898	898	898	898

9,000

At least	But less than	Single	Married filing jointly *	Married filing separately	Head of a household
9,000	9,050	903	903	903	903
9,050	9,100	908	908	908	908
9,100	9,150	915	913	915	913
9,150	9,200	923	918	923	918
9,200	9,250	930	923	930	923
9,250	9,300	938	928	938	928
9,300	9,350	945	933	945	933
9,350	9,400	953	938	953	938
9,400	9,450	960	943	960	943
9,450	9,500	968	948	968	948
9,500	9,550	975	953	975	953
9,550	9,600	983	958	983	958
9,600	9,650	990	963	990	963
9,650	9,700	998	968	998	968
9,700	9,750	1,005	973	1,005	973
9,750	9,800	1,013	978	1,013	978
9,800	9,850	1,020	983	1,020	983
9,850	9,900	1,028	988	1,028	988
9,900	9,950	1,035	993	1,035	993
9,950	10,000	1,043	998	1,043	998

10,000

At least	But less than	Single	Married filing jointly *	Married filing separately	Head of a household
10,000	10,050	1,050	1,003	1,050	1,003
10,050	10,100	1,058	1,008	1,058	1,008
10,100	10,150	1,065	1,013	1,065	1,013
10,150	10,200	1,073	1,018	1,073	1,018
10,200	10,250	1,080	1,023	1,080	1,023
10,250	10,300	1,088	1,028	1,088	1,028
10,300	10,350	1,095	1,033	1,095	1,033
10,350	10,400	1,103	1,038	1,103	1,038
10,400	10,450	1,110	1,043	1,110	1,043
10,450	10,500	1,118	1,048	1,118	1,048
10,500	10,550	1,125	1,053	1,125	1,053
10,550	10,600	1,133	1,058	1,133	1,058
10,600	10,650	1,140	1,063	1,140	1,063
10,650	10,700	1,148	1,068	1,148	1,068
10,700	10,750	1,155	1,073	1,155	1,073
10,750	10,800	1,163	1,078	1,163	1,078
10,800	10,850	1,170	1,083	1,170	1,083
10,850	10,900	1,178	1,088	1,178	1,088
10,900	10,950	1,185	1,093	1,185	1,093
10,950	11,000	1,193	1,098	1,193	1,098

11,000

At least	But less than	Single	Married filing jointly *	Married filing separately	Head of a household
11,000	11,050	1,200	1,103	1,200	1,103
11,050	11,100	1,208	1,108	1,208	1,108
11,100	11,150	1,215	1,113	1,215	1,113
11,150	11,200	1,223	1,118	1,223	1,118
11,200	11,250	1,230	1,123	1,230	1,123
11,250	11,300	1,238	1,128	1,238	1,128
11,300	11,350	1,245	1,133	1,245	1,133
11,350	11,400	1,253	1,138	1,253	1,138
11,400	11,450	1,260	1,143	1,260	1,143
11,450	11,500	1,268	1,148	1,268	1,148
11,500	11,550	1,275	1,153	1,275	1,153
11,550	11,600	1,283	1,158	1,283	1,158
11,600	11,650	1,290	1,163	1,290	1,163
11,650	11,700	1,298	1,168	1,298	1,168
11,700	11,750	1,305	1,173	1,305	1,173
11,750	11,800	1,313	1,178	1,313	1,178
11,800	11,850	1,320	1,183	1,320	1,183
11,850	11,900	1,328	1,188	1,328	1,188
11,900	11,950	1,335	1,193	1,335	1,193
11,950	12,000	1,343	1,198	1,343	1,198

* This column must also be used by a qualifying widow(er).

(Continued)

2014 Tax Table—*Continued*

If line 43 (taxable income) is— At least	But less than	Single	Married filing jointly *	Married filing separately	Head of a household
			Your tax is—		
12,000					
12,000	12,050	1,350	1,203	1,350	1,203
12,050	12,100	1,358	1,208	1,358	1,208
12,100	12,150	1,365	1,213	1,365	1,213
12,150	12,200	1,373	1,218	1,373	1,218
12,200	12,250	1,380	1,223	1,380	1,223
12,250	12,300	1,388	1,228	1,388	1,228
12,300	12,350	1,395	1,233	1,395	1,233
12,350	12,400	1,403	1,238	1,403	1,238
12,400	12,450	1,410	1,243	1,410	1,243
12,450	12,500	1,418	1,248	1,418	1,248
12,500	12,550	1,425	1,253	1,425	1,253
12,550	12,600	1,433	1,258	1,433	1,258
12,600	12,650	1,440	1,263	1,440	1,263
12,650	12,700	1,448	1,268	1,448	1,268
12,700	12,750	1,455	1,273	1,455	1,273
12,750	12,800	1,463	1,278	1,463	1,278
12,800	12,850	1,470	1,283	1,470	1,283
12,850	12,900	1,478	1,288	1,478	1,288
12,900	12,950	1,485	1,293	1,485	1,293
12,950	13,000	1,493	1,298	1,493	1,299
13,000					
13,000	13,050	1,500	1,303	1,500	1,306
13,050	13,100	1,508	1,308	1,508	1,314
13,100	13,150	1,515	1,313	1,515	1,321
13,150	13,200	1,523	1,318	1,523	1,329
13,200	13,250	1,530	1,323	1,530	1,336
13,250	13,300	1,538	1,328	1,538	1,344
13,300	13,350	1,545	1,333	1,545	1,351
13,350	13,400	1,553	1,338	1,553	1,359
13,400	13,450	1,560	1,343	1,560	1,366
13,450	13,500	1,568	1,348	1,568	1,374
13,500	13,550	1,575	1,353	1,575	1,381
13,550	13,600	1,583	1,358	1,583	1,389
13,600	13,650	1,590	1,363	1,590	1,396
13,650	13,700	1,598	1,368	1,598	1,404
13,700	13,750	1,605	1,373	1,605	1,411
13,750	13,800	1,613	1,378	1,613	1,419
13,800	13,850	1,620	1,383	1,620	1,426
13,850	13,900	1,628	1,388	1,628	1,434
13,900	13,950	1,635	1,393	1,635	1,441
13,950	14,000	1,643	1,398	1,643	1,449
14,000					
14,000	14,050	1,650	1,403	1,650	1,456
14,050	14,100	1,658	1,408	1,658	1,464
14,100	14,150	1,665	1,413	1,665	1,471
14,150	14,200	1,673	1,418	1,673	1,479
14,200	14,250	1,680	1,423	1,680	1,486
14,250	14,300	1,688	1,428	1,688	1,494
14,300	14,350	1,695	1,433	1,695	1,501
14,350	14,400	1,703	1,438	1,703	1,509
14,400	14,450	1,710	1,443	1,710	1,516
14,450	14,500	1,718	1,448	1,718	1,524
14,500	14,550	1,725	1,453	1,725	1,531
14,550	14,600	1,733	1,458	1,733	1,539
14,600	14,650	1,740	1,463	1,740	1,546
14,650	14,700	1,748	1,468	1,748	1,554
14,700	14,750	1,755	1,473	1,755	1,561
14,750	14,800	1,763	1,478	1,763	1,569
14,800	14,850	1,770	1,483	1,770	1,576
14,850	14,900	1,778	1,488	1,778	1,584
14,900	14,950	1,785	1,493	1,785	1,591
14,950	15,000	1,793	1,498	1,793	1,599

If line 43 (taxable income) is— At least	But less than	Single	Married filing jointly *	Married filing separately	Head of a household
			Your tax is—		
15,000					
15,000	15,050	1,800	1,503	1,800	1,606
15,050	15,100	1,808	1,508	1,808	1,614
15,100	15,150	1,815	1,513	1,815	1,621
15,150	15,200	1,823	1,518	1,823	1,629
15,200	15,250	1,830	1,523	1,830	1,636
15,250	15,300	1,838	1,528	1,838	1,644
15,300	15,350	1,845	1,533	1,845	1,651
15,350	15,400	1,853	1,538	1,853	1,659
15,400	15,450	1,860	1,543	1,860	1,666
15,450	15,500	1,868	1,548	1,868	1,674
15,500	15,550	1,875	1,553	1,875	1,681
15,550	15,600	1,883	1,558	1,883	1,689
15,600	15,650	1,890	1,563	1,890	1,696
15,650	15,700	1,898	1,568	1,898	1,704
15,700	15,750	1,905	1,573	1,905	1,711
15,750	15,800	1,913	1,578	1,913	1,719
15,800	15,850	1,920	1,583	1,920	1,726
15,850	15,900	1,928	1,588	1,928	1,734
15,900	15,950	1,935	1,593	1,935	1,741
15,950	16,000	1,943	1,598	1,943	1,749
16,000					
16,000	16,050	1,950	1,603	1,950	1,756
16,050	16,100	1,958	1,608	1,958	1,764
16,100	16,150	1,965	1,613	1,965	1,771
16,150	16,200	1,973	1,618	1,973	1,779
16,200	16,250	1,980	1,623	1,980	1,786
16,250	16,300	1,988	1,628	1,988	1,794
16,300	16,350	1,995	1,633	1,995	1,801
16,350	16,400	2,003	1,638	2,003	1,809
16,400	16,450	2,010	1,643	2,010	1,816
16,450	16,500	2,018	1,648	2,018	1,824
16,500	16,550	2,025	1,653	2,025	1,831
16,550	16,600	2,033	1,658	2,033	1,839
16,600	16,650	2,040	1,663	2,040	1,846
16,650	16,700	2,048	1,668	2,048	1,854
16,700	16,750	2,055	1,673	2,055	1,861
16,750	16,800	2,063	1,678	2,063	1,869
16,800	16,850	2,070	1,683	2,070	1,876
16,850	16,900	2,078	1,688	2,078	1,884
16,900	16,950	2,085	1,693	2,085	1,891
16,950	17,000	2,093	1,698	2,093	1,899
17,000					
17,000	17,050	2,100	1,703	2,100	1,906
17,050	17,100	2,108	1,708	2,108	1,914
17,100	17,150	2,115	1,713	2,115	1,921
17,150	17,200	2,123	1,718	2,123	1,929
17,200	17,250	2,130	1,723	2,130	1,936
17,250	17,300	2,138	1,728	2,138	1,944
17,300	17,350	2,145	1,733	2,145	1,951
17,350	17,400	2,153	1,738	2,153	1,959
17,400	17,450	2,160	1,743	2,160	1,966
17,450	17,500	2,168	1,748	2,168	1,974
17,500	17,550	2,175	1,753	2,175	1,981
17,550	17,600	2,183	1,758	2,183	1,989
17,600	17,650	2,190	1,763	2,190	1,996
17,650	17,700	2,198	1,768	2,198	2,004
17,700	17,750	2,205	1,773	2,205	2,011
17,750	17,800	2,213	1,778	2,213	2,019
17,800	17,850	2,220	1,783	2,220	2,026
17,850	17,900	2,228	1,788	2,228	2,034
17,900	17,950	2,235	1,793	2,235	2,041
17,950	18,000	2,243	1,798	2,243	2,049

If line 43 (taxable income) is— At least	But less than	Single	Married filing jointly *	Married filing separately	Head of a household
			Your tax is—		
18,000					
18,000	18,050	2,250	1,803	2,250	2,056
18,050	18,100	2,258	1,808	2,258	2,064
18,100	18,150	2,265	1,813	2,265	2,071
18,150	18,200	2,273	1,819	2,273	2,079
18,200	18,250	2,280	1,826	2,280	2,086
18,250	18,300	2,288	1,834	2,288	2,094
18,300	18,350	2,295	1,841	2,295	2,101
18,350	18,400	2,303	1,849	2,303	2,109
18,400	18,450	2,310	1,856	2,310	2,116
18,450	18,500	2,318	1,864	2,318	2,124
18,500	18,550	2,325	1,871	2,325	2,131
18,550	18,600	2,333	1,879	2,333	2,139
18,600	18,650	2,340	1,886	2,340	2,146
18,650	18,700	2,348	1,894	2,348	2,154
18,700	18,750	2,355	1,901	2,355	2,161
18,750	18,800	2,363	1,909	2,363	2,169
18,800	18,850	2,370	1,916	2,370	2,176
18,850	18,900	2,378	1,924	2,378	2,184
18,900	18,950	2,385	1,931	2,385	2,191
18,950	19,000	2,393	1,939	2,393	2,199
19,000					
19,000	19,050	2,400	1,946	2,400	2,206
19,050	19,100	2,408	1,954	2,408	2,214
19,100	19,150	2,415	1,961	2,415	2,221
19,150	19,200	2,423	1,969	2,423	2,229
19,200	19,250	2,430	1,976	2,430	2,236
19,250	19,300	2,438	1,984	2,438	2,244
19,300	19,350	2,445	1,991	2,445	2,251
19,350	19,400	2,453	1,999	2,453	2,259
19,400	19,450	2,460	2,006	2,460	2,266
19,450	19,500	2,468	2,014	2,468	2,274
19,500	19,550	2,475	2,021	2,475	2,281
19,550	19,600	2,483	2,029	2,483	2,289
19,600	19,650	2,490	2,036	2,490	2,296
19,650	19,700	2,498	2,044	2,498	2,304
19,700	19,750	2,505	2,051	2,505	2,311
19,750	19,800	2,513	2,059	2,513	2,319
19,800	19,850	2,520	2,066	2,520	2,326
19,850	19,900	2,528	2,074	2,528	2,334
19,900	19,950	2,535	2,081	2,535	2,341
19,950	20,000	2,543	2,089	2,543	2,349
20,000					
20,000	20,050	2,550	2,096	2,550	2,356
20,050	20,100	2,558	2,104	2,558	2,364
20,100	20,150	2,565	2,111	2,565	2,371
20,150	20,200	2,573	2,119	2,573	2,379
20,200	20,250	2,580	2,126	2,580	2,386
20,250	20,300	2,588	2,134	2,588	2,394
20,300	20,350	2,595	2,141	2,595	2,401
20,350	20,400	2,603	2,149	2,603	2,409
20,400	20,450	2,610	2,156	2,610	2,416
20,450	20,500	2,618	2,164	2,618	2,424
20,500	20,550	2,625	2,171	2,625	2,431
20,550	20,600	2,633	2,179	2,633	2,439
20,600	20,650	2,640	2,186	2,640	2,446
20,650	20,700	2,648	2,194	2,648	2,454
20,700	20,750	2,655	2,201	2,655	2,461
20,750	20,800	2,663	2,209	2,663	2,469
20,800	20,850	2,670	2,216	2,670	2,476
20,850	20,900	2,678	2,224	2,678	2,484
20,900	20,950	2,685	2,231	2,685	2,491
20,950	21,000	2,693	2,239	2,693	2,499

* This column must also be used by a qualifying widow(er).

(Continued)

2014 Tax Table—Continued

21,000

If line 43 (taxable income) is—		And you are—			
At least	But less than	Single	Married filing jointly *	Married filing separately	Head of a household
		Your tax is—			
21,000	21,050	2,700	2,246	2,700	2,506
21,050	21,100	2,708	2,254	2,708	2,514
21,100	21,150	2,715	2,261	2,715	2,521
21,150	21,200	2,723	2,269	2,723	2,529
21,200	21,250	2,730	2,276	2,730	2,536
21,250	21,300	2,738	2,284	2,738	2,544
21,300	21,350	2,745	2,291	2,745	2,551
21,350	21,400	2,753	2,299	2,753	2,559
21,400	21,450	2,760	2,306	2,760	2,566
21,450	21,500	2,768	2,314	2,768	2,574
21,500	21,550	2,775	2,321	2,775	2,581
21,550	21,600	2,783	2,329	2,783	2,589
21,600	21,650	2,790	2,336	2,790	2,596
21,650	21,700	2,798	2,344	2,798	2,604
21,700	21,750	2,805	2,351	2,805	2,611
21,750	21,800	2,813	2,359	2,813	2,619
21,800	21,850	2,820	2,366	2,820	2,626
21,850	21,900	2,828	2,374	2,828	2,634
21,900	21,950	2,835	2,381	2,835	2,641
21,950	22,000	2,843	2,389	2,843	2,649

22,000

At least	But less than	Single	Married filing jointly *	Married filing separately	Head of a household
22,000	22,050	2,850	2,396	2,850	2,656
22,050	22,100	2,858	2,404	2,858	2,664
22,100	22,150	2,865	2,411	2,865	2,671
22,150	22,200	2,873	2,419	2,873	2,679
22,200	22,250	2,880	2,426	2,880	2,686
22,250	22,300	2,888	2,434	2,888	2,694
22,300	22,350	2,895	2,441	2,895	2,701
22,350	22,400	2,903	2,449	2,903	2,709
22,400	22,450	2,910	2,456	2,910	2,716
22,450	22,500	2,918	2,464	2,918	2,724
22,500	22,550	2,925	2,471	2,925	2,731
22,550	22,600	2,933	2,479	2,933	2,739
22,600	22,650	2,940	2,486	2,940	2,746
22,650	22,700	2,948	2,494	2,948	2,754
22,700	22,750	2,955	2,501	2,955	2,761
22,750	22,800	2,963	2,509	2,963	2,769
22,800	22,850	2,970	2,516	2,970	2,776
22,850	22,900	2,978	2,524	2,978	2,784
22,900	22,950	2,985	2,531	2,985	2,791
22,950	23,000	2,993	2,539	2,993	2,799

23,000

At least	But less than	Single	Married filing jointly *	Married filing separately	Head of a household
23,000	23,050	3,000	2,546	3,000	2,806
23,050	23,100	3,008	2,554	3,008	2,814
23,100	23,150	3,015	2,561	3,015	2,821
23,150	23,200	3,023	2,569	3,023	2,829
23,200	23,250	3,030	2,576	3,030	2,836
23,250	23,300	3,038	2,584	3,038	2,844
23,300	23,350	3,045	2,591	3,045	2,851
23,350	23,400	3,053	2,599	3,053	2,859
23,400	23,450	3,060	2,606	3,060	2,866
23,450	23,500	3,068	2,614	3,068	2,874
23,500	23,550	3,075	2,621	3,075	2,881
23,550	23,600	3,083	2,629	3,083	2,889
23,600	23,650	3,090	2,636	3,090	2,896
23,650	23,700	3,098	2,644	3,098	2,904
23,700	23,750	3,105	2,651	3,105	2,911
23,750	23,800	3,113	2,659	3,113	2,919
23,800	23,850	3,120	2,666	3,120	2,926
23,850	23,900	3,128	2,674	3,128	2,934
23,900	23,950	3,135	2,681	3,135	2,941
23,950	24,000	3,143	2,689	3,143	2,949

24,000

At least	But less than	Single	Married filing jointly *	Married filing separately	Head of a household
24,000	24,050	3,150	2,696	3,150	2,956
24,050	24,100	3,158	2,704	3,158	2,964
24,100	24,150	3,165	2,711	3,165	2,971
24,150	24,200	3,173	2,719	3,173	2,979
24,200	24,250	3,180	2,726	3,180	2,986
24,250	24,300	3,188	2,734	3,188	2,994
24,300	24,350	3,195	2,741	3,195	3,001
24,350	24,400	3,203	2,749	3,203	3,009
24,400	24,450	3,210	2,756	3,210	3,016
24,450	24,500	3,218	2,764	3,218	3,024
24,500	24,550	3,225	2,771	3,225	3,031
24,550	24,600	3,233	2,779	3,233	3,039
24,600	24,650	3,240	2,786	3,240	3,046
24,650	24,700	3,248	2,794	3,248	3,054
24,700	24,750	3,255	2,801	3,255	3,061
24,750	24,800	3,263	2,809	3,263	3,069
24,800	24,850	3,270	2,816	3,270	3,076
24,850	24,900	3,278	2,824	3,278	3,084
24,900	24,950	3,285	2,831	3,285	3,091
24,950	25,000	3,293	2,839	3,293	3,099

25,000

At least	But less than	Single	Married filing jointly *	Married filing separately	Head of a household
25,000	25,050	3,300	2,846	3,300	3,106
25,050	25,100	3,308	2,854	3,308	3,114
25,100	25,150	3,315	2,861	3,315	3,121
25,150	25,200	3,323	2,869	3,323	3,129
25,200	25,250	3,330	2,876	3,330	3,136
25,250	25,300	3,338	2,884	3,338	3,144
25,300	25,350	3,345	2,891	3,345	3,151
25,350	25,400	3,353	2,899	3,353	3,159
25,400	25,450	3,360	2,906	3,360	3,166
25,450	25,500	3,368	2,914	3,368	3,174
25,500	25,550	3,375	2,921	3,375	3,181
25,550	25,600	3,383	2,929	3,383	3,189
25,600	25,650	3,390	2,936	3,390	3,196
25,650	25,700	3,398	2,944	3,398	3,204
25,700	25,750	3,405	2,951	3,405	3,211
25,750	25,800	3,413	2,959	3,413	3,219
25,800	25,850	3,420	2,966	3,420	3,226
25,850	25,900	3,428	2,974	3,428	3,234
25,900	25,950	3,435	2,981	3,435	3,241
25,950	26,000	3,443	2,989	3,443	3,249

26,000

At least	But less than	Single	Married filing jointly *	Married filing separately	Head of a household
26,000	26,050	3,450	2,996	3,450	3,256
26,050	26,100	3,458	3,004	3,458	3,264
26,100	26,150	3,465	3,011	3,465	3,271
26,150	26,200	3,473	3,019	3,473	3,279
26,200	26,250	3,480	3,026	3,480	3,286
26,250	26,300	3,488	3,034	3,488	3,294
26,300	26,350	3,495	3,041	3,495	3,301
26,350	26,400	3,503	3,049	3,503	3,309
26,400	26,450	3,510	3,056	3,510	3,316
26,450	26,500	3,518	3,064	3,518	3,324
26,500	26,550	3,525	3,071	3,525	3,331
26,550	26,600	3,533	3,079	3,533	3,339
26,600	26,650	3,540	3,086	3,540	3,346
26,650	26,700	3,548	3,094	3,548	3,354
26,700	26,750	3,555	3,101	3,555	3,361
26,750	26,800	3,563	3,109	3,563	3,369
26,800	26,850	3,570	3,116	3,570	3,376
26,850	26,900	3,578	3,124	3,578	3,384
26,900	26,950	3,585	3,131	3,585	3,391
26,950	27,000	3,593	3,139	3,593	3,399

27,000

At least	But less than	Single	Married filing jointly *	Married filing separately	Head of a household
27,000	27,050	3,600	3,146	3,600	3,406
27,050	27,100	3,608	3,154	3,608	3,414
27,100	27,150	3,615	3,161	3,615	3,421
27,150	27,200	3,623	3,169	3,623	3,429
27,200	27,250	3,630	3,176	3,630	3,436
27,250	27,300	3,638	3,184	3,638	3,444
27,300	27,350	3,645	3,191	3,645	3,451
27,350	27,400	3,653	3,199	3,653	3,459
27,400	27,450	3,660	3,206	3,660	3,466
27,450	27,500	3,668	3,214	3,668	3,474
27,500	27,550	3,675	3,221	3,675	3,481
27,550	27,600	3,683	3,229	3,683	3,489
27,600	27,650	3,690	3,236	3,690	3,496
27,650	27,700	3,698	3,244	3,698	3,504
27,700	27,750	3,705	3,251	3,705	3,511
27,750	27,800	3,713	3,259	3,713	3,519
27,800	27,850	3,720	3,266	3,720	3,526
27,850	27,900	3,728	3,274	3,728	3,534
27,900	27,950	3,735	3,281	3,735	3,541
27,950	28,000	3,743	3,289	3,743	3,549

28,000

At least	But less than	Single	Married filing jointly *	Married filing separately	Head of a household
28,000	28,050	3,750	3,296	3,750	3,556
28,050	28,100	3,758	3,304	3,758	3,564
28,100	28,150	3,765	3,311	3,765	3,571
28,150	28,200	3,773	3,319	3,773	3,579
28,200	28,250	3,780	3,326	3,780	3,586
28,250	28,300	3,788	3,334	3,788	3,594
28,300	28,350	3,795	3,341	3,795	3,601
28,350	28,400	3,803	3,349	3,803	3,609
28,400	28,450	3,810	3,356	3,810	3,616
28,450	28,500	3,818	3,364	3,818	3,624
28,500	28,550	3,825	3,371	3,825	3,631
28,550	28,600	3,833	3,379	3,833	3,639
28,600	28,650	3,840	3,386	3,840	3,646
28,650	28,700	3,848	3,394	3,848	3,654
28,700	28,750	3,855	3,401	3,855	3,661
28,750	28,800	3,863	3,409	3,863	3,669
28,800	28,850	3,870	3,416	3,870	3,676
28,850	28,900	3,878	3,424	3,878	3,684
28,900	28,950	3,885	3,431	3,885	3,691
28,950	29,000	3,893	3,439	3,893	3,699

29,000

At least	But less than	Single	Married filing jointly *	Married filing separately	Head of a household
29,000	29,050	3,900	3,446	3,900	3,706
29,050	29,100	3,908	3,454	3,908	3,714
29,100	29,150	3,915	3,461	3,915	3,721
29,150	29,200	3,923	3,469	3,923	3,729
29,200	29,250	3,930	3,476	3,930	3,736
29,250	29,300	3,938	3,484	3,938	3,744
29,300	29,350	3,945	3,491	3,945	3,751
29,350	29,400	3,953	3,499	3,953	3,759
29,400	29,450	3,960	3,506	3,960	3,766
29,450	29,500	3,968	3,514	3,968	3,774
29,500	29,550	3,975	3,521	3,975	3,781
29,550	29,600	3,983	3,529	3,983	3,789
29,600	29,650	3,990	3,536	3,990	3,796
29,650	29,700	3,998	3,544	3,998	3,804
29,700	29,750	4,005	3,551	4,005	3,811
29,750	29,800	4,013	3,559	4,013	3,819
29,800	29,850	4,020	3,566	4,020	3,826
29,850	29,900	4,028	3,574	4,028	3,834
29,900	29,950	4,035	3,581	4,035	3,841
29,950	30,000	4,043	3,589	4,043	3,849

* This column must also be used by a qualifying widow(er).

(Continued)

2014 Tax Table—*Continued*

30,000

At least	But less than	Single	Married filing jointly *	Married filing separately	Head of a household
30,000	30,050	4,050	3,596	4,050	3,856
30,050	30,100	4,058	3,604	4,058	3,864
30,100	30,150	4,065	3,611	4,065	3,871
30,150	30,200	4,073	3,619	4,073	3,879
30,200	30,250	4,080	3,626	4,080	3,886
30,250	30,300	4,088	3,634	4,088	3,894
30,300	30,350	4,095	3,641	4,095	3,901
30,350	30,400	4,103	3,649	4,103	3,909
30,400	30,450	4,110	3,656	4,110	3,916
30,450	30,500	4,118	3,664	4,118	3,924
30,500	30,550	4,125	3,671	4,125	3,931
30,550	30,600	4,133	3,679	4,133	3,939
30,600	30,650	4,140	3,686	4,140	3,946
30,650	30,700	4,148	3,694	4,148	3,954
30,700	30,750	4,155	3,701	4,155	3,961
30,750	30,800	4,163	3,709	4,163	3,969
30,800	30,850	4,170	3,716	4,170	3,976
30,850	30,900	4,178	3,724	4,178	3,984
30,900	30,950	4,185	3,731	4,185	3,991
30,950	31,000	4,193	3,739	4,193	3,999

31,000

At least	But less than	Single	Married filing jointly *	Married filing separately	Head of a household
31,000	31,050	4,200	3,746	4,200	4,006
31,050	31,100	4,208	3,754	4,208	4,014
31,100	31,150	4,215	3,761	4,215	4,021
31,150	31,200	4,223	3,769	4,223	4,029
31,200	31,250	4,230	3,776	4,230	4,036
31,250	31,300	4,238	3,784	4,238	4,044
31,300	31,350	4,245	3,791	4,245	4,051
31,350	31,400	4,253	3,799	4,253	4,059
31,400	31,450	4,260	3,806	4,260	4,066
31,450	31,500	4,268	3,814	4,268	4,074
31,500	31,550	4,275	3,821	4,275	4,081
31,550	31,600	4,283	3,829	4,283	4,089
31,600	31,650	4,290	3,836	4,290	4,096
31,650	31,700	4,298	3,844	4,298	4,104
31,700	31,750	4,305	3,851	4,305	4,111
31,750	31,800	4,313	3,859	4,313	4,119
31,800	31,850	4,320	3,866	4,320	4,126
31,850	31,900	4,328	3,874	4,328	4,134
31,900	31,950	4,335	3,881	4,335	4,141
31,950	32,000	4,343	3,889	4,343	4,149

32,000

At least	But less than	Single	Married filing jointly *	Married filing separately	Head of a household
32,000	32,050	4,350	3,896	4,350	4,156
32,050	32,100	4,358	3,904	4,358	4,164
32,100	32,150	4,365	3,911	4,365	4,171
32,150	32,200	4,373	3,919	4,373	4,179
32,200	32,250	4,380	3,926	4,380	4,186
32,250	32,300	4,388	3,934	4,388	4,194
32,300	32,350	4,395	3,941	4,395	4,201
32,350	32,400	4,403	3,949	4,403	4,209
32,400	32,450	4,410	3,956	4,410	4,216
32,450	32,500	4,418	3,964	4,418	4,224
32,500	32,550	4,425	3,971	4,425	4,231
32,550	32,600	4,433	3,979	4,433	4,239
32,600	32,650	4,440	3,986	4,440	4,246
32,650	32,700	4,448	3,994	4,448	4,254
32,700	32,750	4,455	4,001	4,455	4,261
32,750	32,800	4,463	4,009	4,463	4,269
32,800	32,850	4,470	4,016	4,470	4,276
32,850	32,900	4,478	4,024	4,478	4,284
32,900	32,950	4,485	4,031	4,485	4,291
32,950	33,000	4,493	4,039	4,493	4,299

33,000

At least	But less than	Single	Married filing jointly *	Married filing separately	Head of a household
33,000	33,050	4,500	4,046	4,500	4,306
33,050	33,100	4,508	4,054	4,508	4,314
33,100	33,150	4,515	4,061	4,515	4,321
33,150	33,200	4,523	4,069	4,523	4,329
33,200	33,250	4,530	4,076	4,530	4,336
33,250	33,300	4,538	4,084	4,538	4,344
33,300	33,350	4,545	4,091	4,545	4,351
33,350	33,400	4,553	4,099	4,553	4,359
33,400	33,450	4,560	4,106	4,560	4,366
33,450	33,500	4,568	4,114	4,568	4,374
33,500	33,550	4,575	4,121	4,575	4,381
33,550	33,600	4,583	4,129	4,583	4,389
33,600	33,650	4,590	4,136	4,590	4,396
33,650	33,700	4,598	4,144	4,598	4,404
33,700	33,750	4,605	4,151	4,605	4,411
33,750	33,800	4,613	4,159	4,613	4,419
33,800	33,850	4,620	4,166	4,620	4,426
33,850	33,900	4,628	4,174	4,628	4,434
33,900	33,950	4,635	4,181	4,635	4,441
33,950	34,000	4,643	4,189	4,643	4,449

34,000

At least	But less than	Single	Married filing jointly *	Married filing separately	Head of a household
34,000	34,050	4,650	4,196	4,650	4,456
34,050	34,100	4,658	4,204	4,658	4,464
34,100	34,150	4,665	4,211	4,665	4,471
34,150	34,200	4,673	4,219	4,673	4,479
34,200	34,250	4,680	4,226	4,680	4,486
34,250	34,300	4,688	4,234	4,688	4,494
34,300	34,350	4,695	4,241	4,695	4,501
34,350	34,400	4,703	4,249	4,703	4,509
34,400	34,450	4,710	4,256	4,710	4,516
34,450	34,500	4,718	4,264	4,718	4,524
34,500	34,550	4,725	4,271	4,725	4,531
34,550	34,600	4,733	4,279	4,733	4,539
34,600	34,650	4,740	4,286	4,740	4,546
34,650	34,700	4,748	4,294	4,748	4,554
34,700	34,750	4,755	4,301	4,755	4,561
34,750	34,800	4,763	4,309	4,763	4,569
34,800	34,850	4,770	4,316	4,770	4,576
34,850	34,900	4,778	4,324	4,778	4,584
34,900	34,950	4,785	4,331	4,785	4,591
34,950	35,000	4,793	4,339	4,793	4,599

35,000

At least	But less than	Single	Married filing jointly *	Married filing separately	Head of a household
35,000	35,050	4,800	4,346	4,800	4,606
35,050	35,100	4,808	4,354	4,808	4,614
35,100	35,150	4,815	4,361	4,815	4,621
35,150	35,200	4,823	4,369	4,823	4,629
35,200	35,250	4,830	4,376	4,830	4,636
35,250	35,300	4,838	4,384	4,838	4,644
35,300	35,350	4,845	4,391	4,845	4,651
35,350	35,400	4,853	4,399	4,853	4,659
35,400	35,450	4,860	4,406	4,860	4,666
35,450	35,500	4,868	4,414	4,868	4,674
35,500	35,550	4,875	4,421	4,875	4,681
35,550	35,600	4,883	4,429	4,883	4,689
35,600	35,650	4,890	4,436	4,890	4,696
35,650	35,700	4,898	4,444	4,898	4,704
35,700	35,750	4,905	4,451	4,905	4,711
35,750	35,800	4,913	4,459	4,913	4,719
35,800	35,850	4,920	4,466	4,920	4,726
35,850	35,900	4,928	4,474	4,928	4,734
35,900	35,950	4,935	4,481	4,935	4,741
35,950	36,000	4,943	4,489	4,943	4,749

36,000

At least	But less than	Single	Married filing jointly *	Married filing separately	Head of a household
36,000	36,050	4,950	4,496	4,950	4,756
36,050	36,100	4,958	4,504	4,958	4,764
36,100	36,150	4,965	4,511	4,965	4,771
36,150	36,200	4,973	4,519	4,973	4,779
36,200	36,250	4,980	4,526	4,980	4,786
36,250	36,300	4,988	4,534	4,988	4,794
36,300	36,350	4,995	4,541	4,995	4,801
36,350	36,400	5,003	4,549	5,003	4,809
36,400	36,450	5,010	4,556	5,010	4,816
36,450	36,500	5,018	4,564	5,018	4,824
36,500	36,550	5,025	4,571	5,025	4,831
36,550	36,600	5,033	4,579	5,033	4,839
36,600	36,650	5,040	4,586	5,040	4,846
36,650	36,700	5,048	4,594	5,048	4,854
36,700	36,750	5,055	4,601	5,055	4,861
36,750	36,800	5,063	4,609	5,063	4,869
36,800	36,850	5,070	4,616	5,070	4,876
36,850	36,900	5,078	4,624	5,078	4,884
36,900	36,950	5,088	4,631	5,088	4,891
36,950	37,000	5,100	4,639	5,100	4,899

37,000

At least	But less than	Single	Married filing jointly *	Married filing separately	Head of a household
37,000	37,050	5,113	4,646	5,113	4,906
37,050	37,100	5,125	4,654	5,125	4,914
37,100	37,150	5,138	4,661	5,138	4,921
37,150	37,200	5,150	4,669	5,150	4,929
37,200	37,250	5,163	4,676	5,163	4,936
37,250	37,300	5,175	4,684	5,175	4,944
37,300	37,350	5,188	4,691	5,188	4,951
37,350	37,400	5,200	4,699	5,200	4,959
37,400	37,450	5,213	4,706	5,213	4,966
37,450	37,500	5,225	4,714	5,225	4,974
37,500	37,550	5,238	4,721	5,238	4,981
37,550	37,600	5,250	4,729	5,250	4,989
37,600	37,650	5,263	4,736	5,263	4,996
37,650	37,700	5,275	4,744	5,275	5,004
37,700	37,750	5,288	4,751	5,288	5,011
37,750	37,800	5,300	4,759	5,300	5,019
37,800	37,850	5,313	4,766	5,313	5,026
37,850	37,900	5,325	4,774	5,325	5,034
37,900	37,950	5,338	4,781	5,338	5,041
37,950	38,000	5,350	4,789	5,350	5,049

38,000

At least	But less than	Single	Married filing jointly *	Married filing separately	Head of a household
38,000	38,050	5,363	4,796	5,363	5,056
38,050	38,100	5,375	4,804	5,375	5,064
38,100	38,150	5,388	4,811	5,388	5,071
38,150	38,200	5,400	4,819	5,400	5,079
38,200	38,250	5,413	4,826	5,413	5,086
38,250	38,300	5,425	4,834	5,425	5,094
38,300	38,350	5,438	4,841	5,438	5,101
38,350	38,400	5,450	4,849	5,450	5,109
38,400	38,450	5,463	4,856	5,463	5,116
38,450	38,500	5,475	4,864	5,475	5,124
38,500	38,550	5,488	4,871	5,488	5,131
38,550	38,600	5,500	4,879	5,500	5,139
38,600	38,650	5,513	4,886	5,513	5,146
38,650	38,700	5,525	4,894	5,525	5,154
38,700	38,750	5,538	4,901	5,538	5,161
38,750	38,800	5,550	4,909	5,550	5,169
38,800	38,850	5,563	4,916	5,563	5,176
38,850	38,900	5,575	4,924	5,575	5,184
38,900	38,950	5,588	4,931	5,588	5,191
38,950	39,000	5,600	4,939	5,600	5,199

* This column must also be used by a qualifying widow(er).

(Continued)

2014 Tax Table—*Continued*

If line 43 (taxable income) is—		And you are—			
At least	But less than	Single	Married filing jointly *	Married filing separately	Head of a household
		Your tax is—			

39,000

At least	But less than	Single	Married filing jointly *	Married filing separately	Head of a household
39,000	39,050	5,613	4,946	5,613	5,206
39,050	39,100	5,625	4,954	5,625	5,214
39,100	39,150	5,638	4,961	5,638	5,221
39,150	39,200	5,650	4,969	5,650	5,229
39,200	39,250	5,663	4,976	5,663	5,236
39,250	39,300	5,675	4,984	5,675	5,244
39,300	39,350	5,688	4,991	5,688	5,251
39,350	39,400	5,700	4,999	5,700	5,259
39,400	39,450	5,713	5,006	5,713	5,266
39,450	39,500	5,725	5,014	5,725	5,274
39,500	39,550	5,738	5,021	5,738	5,281
39,550	39,600	5,750	5,029	5,750	5,289
39,600	39,650	5,763	5,036	5,763	5,296
39,650	39,700	5,775	5,044	5,775	5,304
39,700	39,750	5,788	5,051	5,788	5,311
39,750	39,800	5,800	5,059	5,800	5,319
39,800	39,850	5,813	5,066	5,813	5,326
39,850	39,900	5,825	5,074	5,825	5,334
39,900	39,950	5,838	5,081	5,838	5,341
39,950	40,000	5,850	5,089	5,850	5,349

40,000

At least	But less than	Single	Married filing jointly *	Married filing separately	Head of a household
40,000	40,050	5,863	5,096	5,863	5,356
40,050	40,100	5,875	5,104	5,875	5,364
40,100	40,150	5,888	5,111	5,888	5,371
40,150	40,200	5,900	5,119	5,900	5,379
40,200	40,250	5,913	5,126	5,913	5,386
40,250	40,300	5,925	5,134	5,925	5,394
40,300	40,350	5,938	5,141	5,938	5,401
40,350	40,400	5,950	5,149	5,950	5,409
40,400	40,450	5,963	5,156	5,963	5,416
40,450	40,500	5,975	5,164	5,975	5,424
40,500	40,550	5,988	5,171	5,988	5,431
40,550	40,600	6,000	5,179	6,000	5,439
40,600	40,650	6,013	5,186	6,013	5,446
40,650	40,700	6,025	5,194	6,025	5,454
40,700	40,750	6,038	5,201	6,038	5,461
40,750	40,800	6,050	5,209	6,050	5,469
40,800	40,850	6,063	5,216	6,063	5,476
40,850	40,900	6,075	5,224	6,075	5,484
40,900	40,950	6,088	5,231	6,088	5,491
40,950	41,000	6,100	5,239	6,100	5,499

41,000

At least	But less than	Single	Married filing jointly *	Married filing separately	Head of a household
41,000	41,050	6,113	5,246	6,113	5,506
41,050	41,100	6,125	5,254	6,125	5,514
41,100	41,150	6,138	5,261	6,138	5,521
41,150	41,200	6,150	5,269	6,150	5,529
41,200	41,250	6,163	5,276	6,163	5,536
41,250	41,300	6,175	5,284	6,175	5,544
41,300	41,350	6,188	5,291	6,188	5,551
41,350	41,400	6,200	5,299	6,200	5,559
41,400	41,450	6,213	5,306	6,213	5,566
41,450	41,500	6,225	5,314	6,225	5,574
41,500	41,550	6,238	5,321	6,238	5,581
41,550	41,600	6,250	5,329	6,250	5,589
41,600	41,650	6,263	5,336	6,263	5,596
41,650	41,700	6,275	5,344	6,275	5,604
41,700	41,750	6,288	5,351	6,288	5,611
41,750	41,800	6,300	5,359	6,300	5,619
41,800	41,850	6,313	5,366	6,313	5,626
41,850	41,900	6,325	5,374	6,325	5,634
41,900	41,950	6,338	5,381	6,338	5,641
41,950	42,000	6,350	5,389	6,350	5,649

42,000

At least	But less than	Single	Married filing jointly *	Married filing separately	Head of a household
42,000	42,050	6,363	5,396	6,363	5,656
42,050	42,100	6,375	5,404	6,375	5,664
42,100	42,150	6,388	5,411	6,388	5,671
42,150	42,200	6,400	5,419	6,400	5,679
42,200	42,250	6,413	5,426	6,413	5,686
42,250	42,300	6,425	5,434	6,425	5,694
42,300	42,350	6,438	5,441	6,438	5,701
42,350	42,400	6,450	5,449	6,450	5,709
42,400	42,450	6,463	5,456	6,463	5,716
42,450	42,500	6,475	5,464	6,475	5,724
42,500	42,550	6,488	5,471	6,488	5,731
42,550	42,600	6,500	5,479	6,500	5,739
42,600	42,650	6,513	5,486	6,513	5,746
42,650	42,700	6,525	5,494	6,525	5,754
42,700	42,750	6,538	5,501	6,538	5,761
42,750	42,800	6,550	5,509	6,550	5,769
42,800	42,850	6,563	5,516	6,563	5,776
42,850	42,900	6,575	5,524	6,575	5,784
42,900	42,950	6,588	5,531	6,588	5,791
42,950	43,000	6,600	5,539	6,600	5,799

43,000

At least	But less than	Single	Married filing jointly *	Married filing separately	Head of a household
43,000	43,050	6,613	5,546	6,613	5,806
43,050	43,100	6,625	5,554	6,625	5,814
43,100	43,150	6,638	5,561	6,638	5,821
43,150	43,200	6,650	5,569	6,650	5,829
43,200	43,250	6,663	5,576	6,663	5,836
43,250	43,300	6,675	5,584	6,675	5,844
43,300	43,350	6,688	5,591	6,688	5,851
43,350	43,400	6,700	5,599	6,700	5,859
43,400	43,450	6,713	5,606	6,713	5,866
43,450	43,500	6,725	5,614	6,725	5,874
43,500	43,550	6,738	5,621	6,738	5,881
43,550	43,600	6,750	5,629	6,750	5,889
43,600	43,650	6,763	5,636	6,763	5,896
43,650	43,700	6,775	5,644	6,775	5,904
43,700	43,750	6,788	5,651	6,788	5,911
43,750	43,800	6,800	5,659	6,800	5,919
43,800	43,850	6,813	5,666	6,813	5,926
43,850	43,900	6,825	5,674	6,825	5,934
43,900	43,950	6,838	5,681	6,838	5,941
43,950	44,000	6,850	5,689	6,850	5,949

44,000

At least	But less than	Single	Married filing jointly *	Married filing separately	Head of a household
44,000	44,050	6,863	5,696	6,863	5,956
44,050	44,100	6,875	5,704	6,875	5,964
44,100	44,150	6,888	5,711	6,888	5,971
44,150	44,200	6,900	5,719	6,900	5,979
44,200	44,250	6,913	5,726	6,913	5,986
44,250	44,300	6,925	5,734	6,925	5,994
44,300	44,350	6,938	5,741	6,938	6,001
44,350	44,400	6,950	5,749	6,950	6,009
44,400	44,450	6,963	5,756	6,963	6,016
44,450	44,500	6,975	5,764	6,975	6,024
44,500	44,550	6,988	5,771	6,988	6,031
44,550	44,600	7,000	5,779	7,000	6,039
44,600	44,650	7,013	5,786	7,013	6,046
44,650	44,700	7,025	5,794	7,025	6,054
44,700	44,750	7,038	5,801	7,038	6,061
44,750	44,800	7,050	5,809	7,050	6,069
44,800	44,850	7,063	5,816	7,063	6,076
44,850	44,900	7,075	5,824	7,075	6,084
44,900	44,950	7,088	5,831	7,088	6,091
44,950	45,000	7,100	5,839	7,100	6,099

45,000

At least	But less than	Single	Married filing jointly *	Married filing separately	Head of a household
45,000	45,050	7,113	5,846	7,113	6,106
45,050	45,100	7,125	5,854	7,125	6,114
45,100	45,150	7,138	5,861	7,138	6,121
45,150	45,200	7,150	5,869	7,150	6,129
45,200	45,250	7,163	5,876	7,163	6,136
45,250	45,300	7,175	5,884	7,175	6,144
45,300	45,350	7,188	5,891	7,188	6,151
45,350	45,400	7,200	5,899	7,200	6,159
45,400	45,450	7,213	5,906	7,213	6,166
45,450	45,500	7,225	5,914	7,225	6,174
45,500	45,550	7,238	5,921	7,238	6,181
45,550	45,600	7,250	5,929	7,250	6,189
45,600	45,650	7,263	5,936	7,263	6,196
45,650	45,700	7,275	5,944	7,275	6,204
45,700	45,750	7,288	5,951	7,288	6,211
45,750	45,800	7,300	5,959	7,300	6,219
45,800	45,850	7,313	5,966	7,313	6,226
45,850	45,900	7,325	5,974	7,325	6,234
45,900	45,950	7,338	5,981	7,338	6,241
45,950	46,000	7,350	5,989	7,350	6,249

46,000

At least	But less than	Single	Married filing jointly *	Married filing separately	Head of a household
46,000	46,050	7,363	5,996	7,363	6,256
46,050	46,100	7,375	6,004	7,375	6,264
46,100	46,150	7,388	6,011	7,388	6,271
46,150	46,200	7,400	6,019	7,400	6,279
46,200	46,250	7,413	6,026	7,413	6,286
46,250	46,300	7,425	6,034	7,425	6,294
46,300	46,350	7,438	6,041	7,438	6,301
46,350	46,400	7,450	6,049	7,450	6,309
46,400	46,450	7,463	6,056	7,463	6,316
46,450	46,500	7,475	6,064	7,475	6,324
46,500	46,550	7,488	6,071	7,488	6,331
46,550	46,600	7,500	6,079	7,500	6,339
46,600	46,650	7,513	6,086	7,513	6,346
46,650	46,700	7,525	6,094	7,525	6,354
46,700	46,750	7,538	6,101	7,538	6,361
46,750	46,800	7,550	6,109	7,550	6,369
46,800	46,850	7,563	6,116	7,563	6,376
46,850	46,900	7,575	6,124	7,575	6,384
46,900	46,950	7,588	6,131	7,588	6,391
46,950	47,000	7,600	6,139	7,600	6,399

47,000

At least	But less than	Single	Married filing jointly *	Married filing separately	Head of a household
47,000	47,050	7,613	6,146	7,613	6,406
47,050	47,100	7,625	6,154	7,625	6,414
47,100	47,150	7,638	6,161	7,638	6,421
47,150	47,200	7,650	6,169	7,650	6,429
47,200	47,250	7,663	6,176	7,663	6,436
47,250	47,300	7,675	6,184	7,675	6,444
47,300	47,350	7,688	6,191	7,688	6,451
47,350	47,400	7,700	6,199	7,700	6,459
47,400	47,450	7,713	6,206	7,713	6,466
47,450	47,500	7,725	6,214	7,725	6,474
47,500	47,550	7,738	6,221	7,738	6,481
47,550	47,600	7,750	6,229	7,750	6,489
47,600	47,650	7,763	6,236	7,763	6,496
47,650	47,700	7,775	6,244	7,775	6,504
47,700	47,750	7,788	6,251	7,788	6,511
47,750	47,800	7,800	6,259	7,800	6,519
47,800	47,850	7,813	6,266	7,813	6,526
47,850	47,900	7,825	6,274	7,825	6,534
47,900	47,950	7,838	6,281	7,838	6,541
47,950	48,000	7,850	6,289	7,850	6,549

* This column must also be used by a qualifying widow(er).

(Continued)

2014 Tax Table—*Continued*

48,000

At least	But less than	Single	Married filing jointly *	Married filing separately	Head of a household
48,000	48,050	7,863	6,296	7,863	6,556
48,050	48,100	7,875	6,304	7,875	6,564
48,100	48,150	7,888	6,311	7,888	6,571
48,150	48,200	7,900	6,319	7,900	6,579
48,200	48,250	7,913	6,326	7,913	6,586
48,250	48,300	7,925	6,334	7,925	6,594
48,300	48,350	7,938	6,341	7,938	6,601
48,350	48,400	7,950	6,349	7,950	6,609
48,400	48,450	7,963	6,356	7,963	6,616
48,450	48,500	7,975	6,364	7,975	6,624
48,500	48,550	7,988	6,371	7,988	6,631
48,550	48,600	8,000	6,379	8,000	6,639
48,600	48,650	8,013	6,386	8,013	6,646
48,650	48,700	8,025	6,394	8,025	6,654
48,700	48,750	8,038	6,401	8,038	6,661
48,750	48,800	8,050	6,409	8,050	6,669
48,800	48,850	8,063	6,416	8,063	6,676
48,850	48,900	8,075	6,424	8,075	6,684
48,900	48,950	8,088	6,431	8,088	6,691
48,950	49,000	8,100	6,439	8,100	6,699

49,000

At least	But less than	Single	Married filing jointly *	Married filing separately	Head of a household
49,000	49,050	8,113	6,446	8,113	6,706
49,050	49,100	8,125	6,454	8,125	6,714
49,100	49,150	8,138	6,461	8,138	6,721
49,150	49,200	8,150	6,469	8,150	6,729
49,200	49,250	8,163	6,476	8,163	6,736
49,250	49,300	8,175	6,484	8,175	6,744
49,300	49,350	8,188	6,491	8,188	6,751
49,350	49,400	8,200	6,499	8,200	6,759
49,400	49,450	8,213	6,506	8,213	6,769
49,450	49,500	8,225	6,514	8,225	6,781
49,500	49,550	8,238	6,521	8,238	6,794
49,550	49,600	8,250	6,529	8,250	6,806
49,600	49,650	8,263	6,536	8,263	6,819
49,650	49,700	8,275	6,544	8,275	6,831
49,700	49,750	8,288	6,551	8,288	6,844
49,750	49,800	8,300	6,559	8,300	6,856
49,800	49,850	8,313	6,566	8,313	6,869
49,850	49,900	8,325	6,574	8,325	6,881
49,900	49,950	8,338	6,581	8,338	6,894
49,950	50,000	8,350	6,589	8,350	6,906

50,000

At least	But less than	Single	Married filing jointly *	Married filing separately	Head of a household
50,000	50,050	8,363	6,596	8,363	6,919
50,050	50,100	8,375	6,604	8,375	6,931
50,100	50,150	8,388	6,611	8,388	6,944
50,150	50,200	8,400	6,619	8,400	6,956
50,200	50,250	8,413	6,626	8,413	6,969
50,250	50,300	8,425	6,634	8,425	6,981
50,300	50,350	8,438	6,641	8,438	6,994
50,350	50,400	8,450	6,649	8,450	7,006
50,400	50,450	8,463	6,656	8,463	7,019
50,450	50,500	8,475	6,664	8,475	7,031
50,500	50,550	8,488	6,671	8,488	7,044
50,550	50,600	8,500	6,679	8,500	7,056
50,600	50,650	8,513	6,686	8,513	7,069
50,650	50,700	8,525	6,694	8,525	7,081
50,700	50,750	8,538	6,701	8,538	7,094
50,750	50,800	8,550	6,709	8,550	7,106
50,800	50,850	8,563	6,716	8,563	7,119
50,850	50,900	8,575	6,724	8,575	7,131
50,900	50,950	8,588	6,731	8,588	7,144
50,950	51,000	8,600	6,739	8,600	7,156

51,000

At least	But less than	Single	Married filing jointly *	Married filing separately	Head of a household
51,000	51,050	8,613	6,746	8,613	7,169
51,050	51,100	8,625	6,754	8,625	7,181
51,100	51,150	8,638	6,761	8,638	7,194
51,150	51,200	8,650	6,769	8,650	7,206
51,200	51,250	8,663	6,776	8,663	7,219
51,250	51,300	8,675	6,784	8,675	7,231
51,300	51,350	8,688	6,791	8,688	7,244
51,350	51,400	8,700	6,799	8,700	7,256
51,400	51,450	8,713	6,806	8,713	7,269
51,450	51,500	8,725	6,814	8,725	7,281
51,500	51,550	8,738	6,821	8,738	7,294
51,550	51,600	8,750	6,829	8,750	7,306
51,600	51,650	8,763	6,836	8,763	7,319
51,650	51,700	8,775	6,844	8,775	7,331
51,700	51,750	8,788	6,851	8,788	7,344
51,750	51,800	8,800	6,859	8,800	7,356
51,800	51,850	8,813	6,866	8,813	7,369
51,850	51,900	8,825	6,874	8,825	7,381
51,900	51,950	8,838	6,881	8,838	7,394
51,950	52,000	8,850	6,889	8,850	7,406

52,000

At least	But less than	Single	Married filing jointly *	Married filing separately	Head of a household
52,000	52,050	8,863	6,896	8,863	7,419
52,050	52,100	8,875	6,904	8,875	7,431
52,100	52,150	8,888	6,911	8,888	7,444
52,150	52,200	8,900	6,919	8,900	7,456
52,200	52,250	8,913	6,926	8,913	7,469
52,250	52,300	8,925	6,934	8,925	7,481
52,300	52,350	8,938	6,941	8,938	7,494
52,350	52,400	8,950	6,949	8,950	7,506
52,400	52,450	8,963	6,956	8,963	7,519
52,450	52,500	8,975	6,964	8,975	7,531
52,500	52,550	8,988	6,971	8,988	7,544
52,550	52,600	9,000	6,979	9,000	7,556
52,600	52,650	9,013	6,986	9,013	7,569
52,650	52,700	9,025	6,994	9,025	7,581
52,700	52,750	9,038	7,001	9,038	7,594
52,750	52,800	9,050	7,009	9,050	7,606
52,800	52,850	9,063	7,016	9,063	7,619
52,850	52,900	9,075	7,024	9,075	7,631
52,900	52,950	9,088	7,031	9,088	7,644
52,950	53,000	9,100	7,039	9,100	7,656

53,000

At least	But less than	Single	Married filing jointly *	Married filing separately	Head of a household
53,000	53,050	9,113	7,046	9,113	7,669
53,050	53,100	9,125	7,054	9,125	7,681
53,100	53,150	9,138	7,061	9,138	7,694
53,150	53,200	9,150	7,069	9,150	7,706
53,200	53,250	9,163	7,076	9,163	7,719
53,250	53,300	9,175	7,084	9,175	7,731
53,300	53,350	9,188	7,091	9,188	7,744
53,350	53,400	9,200	7,099	9,200	7,756
53,400	53,450	9,213	7,106	9,213	7,769
53,450	53,500	9,225	7,114	9,225	7,781
53,500	53,550	9,238	7,121	9,238	7,794
53,550	53,600	9,250	7,129	9,250	7,806
53,600	53,650	9,263	7,136	9,263	7,819
53,650	53,700	9,275	7,144	9,275	7,831
53,700	53,750	9,288	7,151	9,288	7,844
53,750	53,800	9,300	7,159	9,300	7,856
53,800	53,850	9,313	7,166	9,313	7,869
53,850	53,900	9,325	7,174	9,325	7,881
53,900	53,950	9,338	7,181	9,338	7,894
53,950	54,000	9,350	7,189	9,350	7,906

54,000

At least	But less than	Single	Married filing jointly *	Married filing separately	Head of a household
54,000	54,050	9,363	7,196	9,363	7,919
54,050	54,100	9,375	7,204	9,375	7,931
54,100	54,150	9,388	7,211	9,388	7,944
54,150	54,200	9,400	7,219	9,400	7,956
54,200	54,250	9,413	7,226	9,413	7,969
54,250	54,300	9,425	7,234	9,425	7,981
54,300	54,350	9,438	7,241	9,438	7,994
54,350	54,400	9,450	7,249	9,450	8,006
54,400	54,450	9,463	7,256	9,463	8,019
54,450	54,500	9,475	7,264	9,475	8,031
54,500	54,550	9,488	7,271	9,488	8,044
54,550	54,600	9,500	7,279	9,500	8,056
54,600	54,650	9,513	7,286	9,513	8,069
54,650	54,700	9,525	7,294	9,525	8,081
54,700	54,750	9,538	7,301	9,538	8,094
54,750	54,800	9,550	7,309	9,550	8,106
54,800	54,850	9,563	7,316	9,563	8,119
54,850	54,900	9,575	7,324	9,575	8,131
54,900	54,950	9,588	7,331	9,588	8,144
54,950	55,000	9,600	7,339	9,600	8,156

55,000

At least	But less than	Single	Married filing jointly *	Married filing separately	Head of a household
55,000	55,050	9,613	7,346	9,613	8,169
55,050	55,100	9,625	7,354	9,625	8,181
55,100	55,150	9,638	7,361	9,638	8,194
55,150	55,200	9,650	7,369	9,650	8,206
55,200	55,250	9,663	7,376	9,663	8,219
55,250	55,300	9,675	7,384	9,675	8,231
55,300	55,350	9,688	7,391	9,688	8,244
55,350	55,400	9,700	7,399	9,700	8,256
55,400	55,450	9,713	7,406	9,713	8,269
55,450	55,500	9,725	7,414	9,725	8,281
55,500	55,550	9,738	7,421	9,738	8,294
55,550	55,600	9,750	7,429	9,750	8,306
55,600	55,650	9,763	7,436	9,763	8,319
55,650	55,700	9,775	7,444	9,775	8,331
55,700	55,750	9,788	7,451	9,788	8,344
55,750	55,800	9,800	7,459	9,800	8,356
55,800	55,850	9,813	7,466	9,813	8,369
55,850	55,900	9,825	7,474	9,825	8,381
55,900	55,950	9,838	7,481	9,838	8,394
55,950	56,000	9,850	7,489	9,850	8,406

56,000

At least	But less than	Single	Married filing jointly *	Married filing separately	Head of a household
56,000	56,050	9,863	7,496	9,863	8,419
56,050	56,100	9,875	7,504	9,875	8,431
56,100	56,150	9,888	7,511	9,888	8,444
56,150	56,200	9,900	7,519	9,900	8,456
56,200	56,250	9,913	7,526	9,913	8,469
56,250	56,300	9,925	7,534	9,925	8,481
56,300	56,350	9,938	7,541	9,938	8,494
56,350	56,400	9,950	7,549	9,950	8,506
56,400	56,450	9,963	7,556	9,963	8,519
56,450	56,500	9,975	7,564	9,975	8,531
56,500	56,550	9,988	7,571	9,988	8,544
56,550	56,600	10,000	7,579	10,000	8,556
56,600	56,650	10,013	7,586	10,013	8,569
56,650	56,700	10,025	7,594	10,025	8,581
56,700	56,750	10,038	7,601	10,038	8,594
56,750	56,800	10,050	7,609	10,050	8,606
56,800	56,850	10,063	7,616	10,063	8,619
56,850	56,900	10,075	7,624	10,075	8,631
56,900	56,950	10,088	7,631	10,088	8,644
56,950	57,000	10,100	7,639	10,100	8,656

* This column must also be used by a qualifying widow(er).

(Continued)

2014 Tax Table—Continued

57,000

At least	But less than	Single	Married filing jointly *	Married filing separately	Head of a household
57,000	57,050	10,113	7,646	10,113	8,669
57,050	57,100	10,125	7,654	10,125	8,681
57,100	57,150	10,138	7,661	10,138	8,694
57,150	57,200	10,150	7,669	10,150	8,706
57,200	57,250	10,163	7,676	10,163	8,719
57,250	57,300	10,175	7,684	10,175	8,731
57,300	57,350	10,188	7,691	10,188	8,744
57,350	57,400	10,200	7,699	10,200	8,756
57,400	57,450	10,213	7,706	10,213	8,769
57,450	57,500	10,225	7,714	10,225	8,781
57,500	57,550	10,238	7,721	10,238	8,794
57,550	57,600	10,250	7,729	10,250	8,806
57,600	57,650	10,263	7,736	10,263	8,819
57,650	57,700	10,275	7,744	10,275	8,831
57,700	57,750	10,288	7,751	10,288	8,844
57,750	57,800	10,300	7,759	10,300	8,856
57,800	57,850	10,313	7,766	10,313	8,869
57,850	57,900	10,325	7,774	10,325	8,881
57,900	57,950	10,338	7,781	10,338	8,894
57,950	58,000	10,350	7,789	10,350	8,906

58,000

At least	But less than	Single	Married filing jointly *	Married filing separately	Head of a household
58,000	58,050	10,363	7,796	10,363	8,919
58,050	58,100	10,375	7,804	10,375	8,931
58,100	58,150	10,388	7,811	10,388	8,944
58,150	58,200	10,400	7,819	10,400	8,956
58,200	58,250	10,413	7,826	10,413	8,969
58,250	58,300	10,425	7,834	10,425	8,981
58,300	58,350	10,438	7,841	10,438	8,994
58,350	58,400	10,450	7,849	10,450	9,006
58,400	58,450	10,463	7,856	10,463	9,019
58,450	58,500	10,475	7,864	10,475	9,031
58,500	58,550	10,488	7,871	10,488	9,044
58,550	58,600	10,500	7,879	10,500	9,056
58,600	58,650	10,513	7,886	10,513	9,069
58,650	58,700	10,525	7,894	10,525	9,081
58,700	58,750	10,538	7,901	10,538	9,094
58,750	58,800	10,550	7,909	10,550	9,106
58,800	58,850	10,563	7,916	10,563	9,119
58,850	58,900	10,575	7,924	10,575	9,131
58,900	58,950	10,588	7,931	10,588	9,144
58,950	59,000	10,600	7,939	10,600	9,156

59,000

At least	But less than	Single	Married filing jointly *	Married filing separately	Head of a household
59,000	59,050	10,613	7,946	10,613	9,169
59,050	59,100	10,625	7,954	10,625	9,181
59,100	59,150	10,638	7,961	10,638	9,194
59,150	59,200	10,650	7,969	10,650	9,206
59,200	59,250	10,663	7,976	10,663	9,219
59,250	59,300	10,675	7,984	10,675	9,231
59,300	59,350	10,688	7,991	10,688	9,244
59,350	59,400	10,700	7,999	10,700	9,256
59,400	59,450	10,713	8,006	10,713	9,269
59,450	59,500	10,725	8,014	10,725	9,281
59,500	59,550	10,738	8,021	10,738	9,294
59,550	59,600	10,750	8,029	10,750	9,306
59,600	59,650	10,763	8,036	10,763	9,319
59,650	59,700	10,775	8,044	10,775	9,331
59,700	59,750	10,788	8,051	10,788	9,344
59,750	59,800	10,800	8,059	10,800	9,356
59,800	59,850	10,813	8,066	10,813	9,369
59,850	59,900	10,825	8,074	10,825	9,381
59,900	59,950	10,838	8,081	10,838	9,394
59,950	60,000	10,850	8,089	10,850	9,406

60,000

At least	But less than	Single	Married filing jointly *	Married filing separately	Head of a household
60,000	60,050	10,863	8,096	10,863	9,419
60,050	60,100	10,875	8,104	10,875	9,431
60,100	60,150	10,888	8,111	10,888	9,444
60,150	60,200	10,900	8,119	10,900	9,456
60,200	60,250	10,913	8,126	10,913	9,469
60,250	60,300	10,925	8,134	10,925	9,481
60,300	60,350	10,938	8,141	10,938	9,494
60,350	60,400	10,950	8,149	10,950	9,506
60,400	60,450	10,963	8,156	10,963	9,519
60,450	60,500	10,975	8,164	10,975	9,531
60,500	60,550	10,988	8,171	10,988	9,544
60,550	60,600	11,000	8,179	11,000	9,556
60,600	60,650	11,013	8,186	11,013	9,569
60,650	60,700	11,025	8,194	11,025	9,581
60,700	60,750	11,038	8,201	11,038	9,594
60,750	60,800	11,050	8,209	11,050	9,606
60,800	60,850	11,063	8,216	11,063	9,619
60,850	60,900	11,075	8,224	11,075	9,631
60,900	60,950	11,088	8,231	11,088	9,644
60,950	61,000	11,100	8,239	11,100	9,656

61,000

At least	But less than	Single	Married filing jointly *	Married filing separately	Head of a household
61,000	61,050	11,113	8,246	11,113	9,669
61,050	61,100	11,125	8,254	11,125	9,681
61,100	61,150	11,138	8,261	11,138	9,694
61,150	61,200	11,150	8,269	11,150	9,706
61,200	61,250	11,163	8,276	11,163	9,719
61,250	61,300	11,175	8,284	11,175	9,731
61,300	61,350	11,188	8,291	11,188	9,744
61,350	61,400	11,200	8,299	11,200	9,756
61,400	61,450	11,213	8,306	11,213	9,769
61,450	61,500	11,225	8,314	11,225	9,781
61,500	61,550	11,238	8,321	11,238	9,794
61,550	61,600	11,250	8,329	11,250	9,806
61,600	61,650	11,263	8,336	11,263	9,819
61,650	61,700	11,275	8,344	11,275	9,831
61,700	61,750	11,288	8,351	11,288	9,844
61,750	61,800	11,300	8,359	11,300	9,856
61,800	61,850	11,313	8,366	11,313	9,869
61,850	61,900	11,325	8,374	11,325	9,881
61,900	61,950	11,338	8,381	11,338	9,894
61,950	62,000	11,350	8,389	11,350	9,906

62,000

At least	But less than	Single	Married filing jointly *	Married filing separately	Head of a household
62,000	62,050	11,363	8,396	11,363	9,919
62,050	62,100	11,375	8,404	11,375	9,931
62,100	62,150	11,388	8,411	11,388	9,944
62,150	62,200	11,400	8,419	11,400	9,956
62,200	62,250	11,413	8,426	11,413	9,969
62,250	62,300	11,425	8,434	11,425	9,981
62,300	62,350	11,438	8,441	11,438	9,994
62,350	62,400	11,450	8,449	11,450	10,006
62,400	62,450	11,463	8,456	11,463	10,019
62,450	62,500	11,475	8,464	11,475	10,031
62,500	62,550	11,488	8,471	11,488	10,044
62,550	62,600	11,500	8,479	11,500	10,056
62,600	62,650	11,513	8,486	11,513	10,069
62,650	62,700	11,525	8,494	11,525	10,081
62,700	62,750	11,538	8,501	11,538	10,094
62,750	62,800	11,550	8,509	11,550	10,106
62,800	62,850	11,563	8,516	11,563	10,119
62,850	62,900	11,575	8,524	11,575	10,131
62,900	62,950	11,588	8,531	11,588	10,144
62,950	63,000	11,600	8,539	11,600	10,156

63,000

At least	But less than	Single	Married filing jointly *	Married filing separately	Head of a household
63,000	63,050	11,613	8,546	11,613	10,169
63,050	63,100	11,625	8,554	11,625	10,181
63,100	63,150	11,638	8,561	11,638	10,194
63,150	63,200	11,650	8,569	11,650	10,206
63,200	63,250	11,663	8,576	11,663	10,219
63,250	63,300	11,675	8,584	11,675	10,231
63,300	63,350	11,688	8,591	11,688	10,244
63,350	63,400	11,700	8,599	11,700	10,256
63,400	63,450	11,713	8,606	11,713	10,269
63,450	63,500	11,725	8,614	11,725	10,281
63,500	63,550	11,738	8,621	11,738	10,294
63,550	63,600	11,750	8,629	11,750	10,306
63,600	63,650	11,763	8,636	11,763	10,319
63,650	63,700	11,775	8,644	11,775	10,331
63,700	63,750	11,788	8,651	11,788	10,344
63,750	63,800	11,800	8,659	11,800	10,356
63,800	63,850	11,813	8,666	11,813	10,369
63,850	63,900	11,825	8,674	11,825	10,381
63,900	63,950	11,838	8,681	11,838	10,394
63,950	64,000	11,850	8,689	11,850	10,406

64,000

At least	But less than	Single	Married filing jointly *	Married filing separately	Head of a household
64,000	64,050	11,863	8,696	11,863	10,419
64,050	64,100	11,875	8,704	11,875	10,431
64,100	64,150	11,888	8,711	11,888	10,444
64,150	64,200	11,900	8,719	11,900	10,456
64,200	64,250	11,913	8,726	11,913	10,469
64,250	64,300	11,925	8,734	11,925	10,481
64,300	64,350	11,938	8,741	11,938	10,494
64,350	64,400	11,950	8,749	11,950	10,506
64,400	64,450	11,963	8,756	11,963	10,519
64,450	64,500	11,975	8,764	11,975	10,531
64,500	64,550	11,988	8,771	11,988	10,544
64,550	64,600	12,000	8,779	12,000	10,556
64,600	64,650	12,013	8,786	12,013	10,569
64,650	64,700	12,025	8,794	12,025	10,581
64,700	64,750	12,038	8,801	12,038	10,594
64,750	64,800	12,050	8,809	12,050	10,606
64,800	64,850	12,063	8,816	12,063	10,619
64,850	64,900	12,075	8,824	12,075	10,631
64,900	64,950	12,088	8,831	12,088	10,644
64,950	65,000	12,100	8,839	12,100	10,656

65,000

At least	But less than	Single	Married filing jointly *	Married filing separately	Head of a household
65,000	65,050	12,113	8,846	12,113	10,669
65,050	65,100	12,125	8,854	12,125	10,681
65,100	65,150	12,138	8,861	12,138	10,694
65,150	65,200	12,150	8,869	12,150	10,706
65,200	65,250	12,163	8,876	12,163	10,719
65,250	65,300	12,175	8,884	12,175	10,731
65,300	65,350	12,188	8,891	12,188	10,744
65,350	65,400	12,200	8,899	12,200	10,756
65,400	65,450	12,213	8,906	12,213	10,769
65,450	65,500	12,225	8,914	12,225	10,781
65,500	65,550	12,238	8,921	12,238	10,794
65,550	65,600	12,250	8,929	12,250	10,806
65,600	65,650	12,263	8,936	12,263	10,819
65,650	65,700	12,275	8,944	12,275	10,831
65,700	65,750	12,288	8,951	12,288	10,844
65,750	65,800	12,300	8,959	12,300	10,856
65,800	65,850	12,313	8,966	12,313	10,869
65,850	65,900	12,325	8,974	12,325	10,881
65,900	65,950	12,338	8,981	12,338	10,894
65,950	66,000	12,350	8,989	12,350	10,906

* This column must also be used by a qualifying widow(er).

(Continued)

2014 Tax Table—*Continued*

66,000

At least	But less than	Single	Married filing jointly *	Married filing separately	Head of a household
66,000	66,050	12,363	8,996	12,363	10,919
66,050	66,100	12,375	9,004	12,375	10,931
66,100	66,150	12,388	9,011	12,388	10,944
66,150	66,200	12,400	9,019	12,400	10,956
66,200	66,250	12,413	9,026	12,413	10,969
66,250	66,300	12,425	9,034	12,425	10,981
66,300	66,350	12,438	9,041	12,438	10,994
66,350	66,400	12,450	9,049	12,450	11,006
66,400	66,450	12,463	9,056	12,463	11,019
66,450	66,500	12,475	9,064	12,475	11,031
66,500	66,550	12,488	9,071	12,488	11,044
66,550	66,600	12,500	9,079	12,500	11,056
66,600	66,650	12,513	9,086	12,513	11,069
66,650	66,700	12,525	9,094	12,525	11,081
66,700	66,750	12,538	9,101	12,538	11,094
66,750	66,800	12,550	9,109	12,550	11,106
66,800	66,850	12,563	9,116	12,563	11,119
66,850	66,900	12,575	9,124	12,575	11,131
66,900	66,950	12,588	9,131	12,588	11,144
66,950	67,000	12,600	9,139	12,600	11,156

67,000

At least	But less than	Single	Married filing jointly *	Married filing separately	Head of a household
67,000	67,050	12,613	9,146	12,613	11,169
67,050	67,100	12,625	9,154	12,625	11,181
67,100	67,150	12,638	9,161	12,638	11,194
67,150	67,200	12,650	9,169	12,650	11,206
67,200	67,250	12,663	9,176	12,663	11,219
67,250	67,300	12,675	9,184	12,675	11,231
67,300	67,350	12,688	9,191	12,688	11,244
67,350	67,400	12,700	9,199	12,700	11,256
67,400	67,450	12,713	9,206	12,713	11,269
67,450	67,500	12,725	9,214	12,725	11,281
67,500	67,550	12,738	9,221	12,738	11,294
67,550	67,600	12,750	9,229	12,750	11,306
67,600	67,650	12,763	9,236	12,763	11,319
67,650	67,700	12,775	9,244	12,775	11,331
67,700	67,750	12,788	9,251	12,788	11,344
67,750	67,800	12,800	9,259	12,800	11,356
67,800	67,850	12,813	9,266	12,813	11,369
67,850	67,900	12,825	9,274	12,825	11,381
67,900	67,950	12,838	9,281	12,838	11,394
67,950	68,000	12,850	9,289	12,850	11,406

68,000

At least	But less than	Single	Married filing jointly *	Married filing separately	Head of a household
68,000	68,050	12,863	9,296	12,863	11,419
68,050	68,100	12,875	9,304	12,875	11,431
68,100	68,150	12,888	9,311	12,888	11,444
68,150	68,200	12,900	9,319	12,900	11,456
68,200	68,250	12,913	9,326	12,913	11,469
68,250	68,300	12,925	9,334	12,925	11,481
68,300	68,350	12,938	9,341	12,938	11,494
68,350	68,400	12,950	9,349	12,950	11,506
68,400	68,450	12,963	9,356	12,963	11,519
68,450	68,500	12,975	9,364	12,975	11,531
68,500	68,550	12,988	9,371	12,988	11,544
68,550	68,600	13,000	9,379	13,000	11,556
68,600	68,650	13,013	9,386	13,013	11,569
68,650	68,700	13,025	9,394	13,025	11,581
68,700	68,750	13,038	9,401	13,038	11,594
68,750	68,800	13,050	9,409	13,050	11,606
68,800	68,850	13,063	9,416	13,063	11,619
68,850	68,900	13,075	9,424	13,075	11,631
68,900	68,950	13,088	9,431	13,088	11,644
68,950	69,000	13,100	9,439	13,100	11,656

69,000

At least	But less than	Single	Married filing jointly *	Married filing separately	Head of a household
69,000	69,050	13,113	9,446	13,113	11,669
69,050	69,100	13,125	9,454	13,125	11,681
69,100	69,150	13,138	9,461	13,138	11,694
69,150	69,200	13,150	9,469	13,150	11,706
69,200	69,250	13,163	9,476	13,163	11,719
69,250	69,300	13,175	9,484	13,175	11,731
69,300	69,350	13,188	9,491	13,188	11,744
69,350	69,400	13,200	9,499	13,200	11,756
69,400	69,450	13,213	9,506	13,213	11,769
69,450	69,500	13,225	9,514	13,225	11,781
69,500	69,550	13,238	9,521	13,238	11,794
69,550	69,600	13,250	9,529	13,250	11,806
69,600	69,650	13,263	9,536	13,263	11,819
69,650	69,700	13,275	9,544	13,275	11,831
69,700	69,750	13,288	9,551	13,288	11,844
69,750	69,800	13,300	9,559	13,300	11,856
69,800	69,850	13,313	9,566	13,313	11,869
69,850	69,900	13,325	9,574	13,325	11,881
69,900	69,950	13,338	9,581	13,338	11,894
69,950	70,000	13,350	9,589	13,350	11,906

70,000

At least	But less than	Single	Married filing jointly *	Married filing separately	Head of a household
70,000	70,050	13,363	9,596	13,363	11,919
70,050	70,100	13,375	9,604	13,375	11,931
70,100	70,150	13,388	9,611	13,388	11,944
70,150	70,200	13,400	9,619	13,400	11,956
70,200	70,250	13,413	9,626	13,413	11,969
70,250	70,300	13,425	9,634	13,425	11,981
70,300	70,350	13,438	9,641	13,438	11,994
70,350	70,400	13,450	9,649	13,450	12,006
70,400	70,450	13,463	9,656	13,463	12,019
70,450	70,500	13,475	9,664	13,475	12,031
70,500	70,550	13,488	9,671	13,488	12,044
70,550	70,600	13,500	9,679	13,500	12,056
70,600	70,650	13,513	9,686	13,513	12,069
70,650	70,700	13,525	9,694	13,525	12,081
70,700	70,750	13,538	9,701	13,538	12,094
70,750	70,800	13,550	9,709	13,550	12,106
70,800	70,850	13,563	9,716	13,563	12,119
70,850	70,900	13,575	9,724	13,575	12,131
70,900	70,950	13,588	9,731	13,588	12,144
70,950	71,000	13,600	9,739	13,600	12,156

71,000

At least	But less than	Single	Married filing jointly *	Married filing separately	Head of a household
71,000	71,050	13,613	9,746	13,613	12,169
71,050	71,100	13,625	9,754	13,625	12,181
71,100	71,150	13,638	9,761	13,638	12,194
71,150	71,200	13,650	9,769	13,650	12,206
71,200	71,250	13,663	9,776	13,663	12,219
71,250	71,300	13,675	9,784	13,675	12,231
71,300	71,350	13,688	9,791	13,688	12,244
71,350	71,400	13,700	9,799	13,700	12,256
71,400	71,450	13,713	9,806	13,713	12,269
71,450	71,500	13,725	9,814	13,725	12,281
71,500	71,550	13,738	9,821	13,738	12,294
71,550	71,600	13,750	9,829	13,750	12,306
71,600	71,650	13,763	9,836	13,763	12,319
71,650	71,700	13,775	9,844	13,775	12,331
71,700	71,750	13,788	9,851	13,788	12,344
71,750	71,800	13,800	9,859	13,800	12,356
71,800	71,850	13,813	9,866	13,813	12,369
71,850	71,900	13,825	9,874	13,825	12,381
71,900	71,950	13,838	9,881	13,838	12,394
71,950	72,000	13,850	9,889	13,850	12,406

72,000

At least	But less than	Single	Married filing jointly *	Married filing separately	Head of a household
72,000	72,050	13,863	9,896	13,863	12,419
72,050	72,100	13,875	9,904	13,875	12,431
72,100	72,150	13,888	9,911	13,888	12,444
72,150	72,200	13,900	9,919	13,900	12,456
72,200	72,250	13,913	9,926	13,913	12,469
72,250	72,300	13,925	9,934	13,925	12,481
72,300	72,350	13,938	9,941	13,938	12,494
72,350	72,400	13,950	9,949	13,950	12,506
72,400	72,450	13,963	9,956	13,963	12,519
72,450	72,500	13,975	9,964	13,975	12,531
72,500	72,550	13,988	9,971	13,988	12,544
72,550	72,600	14,000	9,979	14,000	12,556
72,600	72,650	14,013	9,986	14,013	12,569
72,650	72,700	14,025	9,994	14,025	12,581
72,700	72,750	14,038	10,001	14,038	12,594
72,750	72,800	14,050	10,009	14,050	12,606
72,800	72,850	14,063	10,016	14,063	12,619
72,850	72,900	14,075	10,024	14,075	12,631
72,900	72,950	14,088	10,031	14,088	12,644
72,950	73,000	14,100	10,039	14,100	12,656

73,000

At least	But less than	Single	Married filing jointly *	Married filing separately	Head of a household
73,000	73,050	14,113	10,046	14,113	12,669
73,050	73,100	14,125	10,054	14,125	12,681
73,100	73,150	14,138	10,061	14,138	12,694
73,150	73,200	14,150	10,069	14,150	12,706
73,200	73,250	14,163	10,076	14,163	12,719
73,250	73,300	14,175	10,084	14,175	12,731
73,300	73,350	14,188	10,091	14,188	12,744
73,350	73,400	14,200	10,099	14,200	12,756
73,400	73,450	14,213	10,106	14,213	12,769
73,450	73,500	14,225	10,114	14,225	12,781
73,500	73,550	14,238	10,121	14,238	12,794
73,550	73,600	14,250	10,129	14,250	12,806
73,600	73,650	14,263	10,136	14,263	12,819
73,650	73,700	14,275	10,144	14,275	12,831
73,700	73,750	14,288	10,151	14,288	12,844
73,750	73,800	14,300	10,159	14,300	12,856
73,800	73,850	14,313	10,169	14,313	12,869
73,850	73,900	14,325	10,181	14,325	12,881
73,900	73,950	14,338	10,194	14,338	12,894
73,950	74,000	14,350	10,206	14,350	12,906

74,000

At least	But less than	Single	Married filing jointly *	Married filing separately	Head of a household
74,000	74,050	14,363	10,219	14,363	12,919
74,050	74,100	14,375	10,231	14,375	12,931
74,100	74,150	14,388	10,244	14,388	12,944
74,150	74,200	14,400	10,256	14,400	12,956
74,200	74,250	14,413	10,269	14,413	12,969
74,250	74,300	14,425	10,281	14,425	12,981
74,300	74,350	14,438	10,294	14,438	12,994
74,350	74,400	14,450	10,306	14,450	13,006
74,400	74,450	14,463	10,319	14,463	13,019
74,450	74,500	14,475	10,331	14,477	13,031
74,500	74,550	14,488	10,344	14,491	13,044
74,550	74,600	14,500	10,356	14,505	13,056
74,600	74,650	14,513	10,369	14,519	13,069
74,650	74,700	14,525	10,381	14,533	13,081
74,700	74,750	14,538	10,394	14,547	13,094
74,750	74,800	14,550	10,406	14,561	13,106
74,800	74,850	14,563	10,419	14,575	13,119
74,850	74,900	14,575	10,431	14,589	13,131
74,900	74,950	14,588	10,444	14,603	13,144
74,950	75,000	14,600	10,456	14,617	13,156

Note: If line 43 (taxable income) is. And you are—. Your tax is—

* This column must also be used by a qualifying widow(er).

(Continued)

2014 Tax Table—Continued

75,000

If line 43 (taxable income) is—		Single	Married filing jointly *	Married filing separately	Head of a household
At least	But less than		Your tax is—		
75,000	75,050	14,613	10,469	14,631	13,169
75,050	75,100	14,625	10,481	14,645	13,181
75,100	75,150	14,638	10,494	14,659	13,194
75,150	75,200	14,650	10,506	14,673	13,206
75,200	75,250	14,663	10,519	14,687	13,219
75,250	75,300	14,675	10,531	14,701	13,231
75,300	75,350	14,688	10,544	14,715	13,244
75,350	75,400	14,700	10,556	14,729	13,256
75,400	75,450	14,713	10,569	14,743	13,269
75,450	75,500	14,725	10,581	14,757	13,281
75,500	75,550	14,738	10,594	14,771	13,294
75,550	75,600	14,750	10,606	14,785	13,306
75,600	75,650	14,763	10,619	14,799	13,319
75,650	75,700	14,775	10,631	14,813	13,331
75,700	75,750	14,788	10,644	14,827	13,344
75,750	75,800	14,800	10,656	14,841	13,356
75,800	75,850	14,813	10,669	14,855	13,369
75,850	75,900	14,825	10,681	14,869	13,381
75,900	75,950	14,838	10,694	14,883	13,394
75,950	76,000	14,850	10,706	14,897	13,406

76,000

At least	But less than	Single	Married filing jointly *	Married filing separately	Head of a household
76,000	76,050	14,863	10,719	14,911	13,419
76,050	76,100	14,875	10,731	14,925	13,431
76,100	76,150	14,888	10,744	14,939	13,444
76,150	76,200	14,900	10,756	14,953	13,456
76,200	76,250	14,913	10,769	14,967	13,469
76,250	76,300	14,925	10,781	14,981	13,481
76,300	76,350	14,938	10,794	14,995	13,494
76,350	76,400	14,950	10,806	15,009	13,506
76,400	76,450	14,963	10,819	15,023	13,519
76,450	76,500	14,975	10,831	15,037	13,531
76,500	76,550	14,988	10,844	15,051	13,544
76,550	76,600	15,000	10,856	15,065	13,556
76,600	76,650	15,013	10,869	15,079	13,569
76,650	76,700	15,025	10,881	15,093	13,581
76,700	76,750	15,038	10,894	15,107	13,594
76,750	76,800	15,050	10,906	15,121	13,606
76,800	76,850	15,063	10,919	15,135	13,619
76,850	76,900	15,075	10,931	15,149	13,631
76,900	76,950	15,088	10,944	15,163	13,644
76,950	77,000	15,100	10,956	15,177	13,656

77,000

At least	But less than	Single	Married filing jointly *	Married filing separately	Head of a household
77,000	77,050	15,113	10,969	15,191	13,669
77,050	77,100	15,125	10,981	15,205	13,681
77,100	77,150	15,138	10,994	15,219	13,694
77,150	77,200	15,150	11,006	15,233	13,706
77,200	77,250	15,163	11,019	15,247	13,719
77,250	77,300	15,175	11,031	15,261	13,731
77,300	77,350	15,188	11,044	15,275	13,744
77,350	77,400	15,200	11,056	15,289	13,756
77,400	77,450	15,213	11,069	15,303	13,769
77,450	77,500	15,225	11,081	15,317	13,781
77,500	77,550	15,238	11,094	15,331	13,794
77,550	77,600	15,250	11,106	15,345	13,806
77,600	77,650	15,263	11,119	15,359	13,819
77,650	77,700	15,275	11,131	15,373	13,831
77,700	77,750	15,288	11,144	15,387	13,844
77,750	77,800	15,300	11,156	15,401	13,856
77,800	77,850	15,313	11,169	15,415	13,869
77,850	77,900	15,325	11,181	15,429	13,881
77,900	77,950	15,338	11,194	15,443	13,894
77,950	78,000	15,350	11,206	15,457	13,906

78,000

At least	But less than	Single	Married filing jointly *	Married filing separately	Head of a household
78,000	78,050	15,363	11,219	15,471	13,919
78,050	78,100	15,375	11,231	15,485	13,931
78,100	78,150	15,388	11,244	15,499	13,944
78,150	78,200	15,400	11,256	15,513	13,956
78,200	78,250	15,413	11,269	15,527	13,969
78,250	78,300	15,425	11,281	15,541	13,981
78,300	78,350	15,438	11,294	15,555	13,994
78,350	78,400	15,450	11,306	15,569	14,006
78,400	78,450	15,463	11,319	15,583	14,019
78,450	78,500	15,475	11,331	15,597	14,031
78,500	78,550	15,488	11,344	15,611	14,044
78,550	78,600	15,500	11,356	15,625	14,056
78,600	78,650	15,513	11,369	15,639	14,069
78,650	78,700	15,525	11,381	15,653	14,081
78,700	78,750	15,538	11,394	15,667	14,094
78,750	78,800	15,550	11,406	15,681	14,106
78,800	78,850	15,563	11,419	15,695	14,119
78,850	78,900	15,575	11,431	15,709	14,131
78,900	78,950	15,588	11,444	15,723	14,144
78,950	79,000	15,600	11,456	15,737	14,156

79,000

At least	But less than	Single	Married filing jointly *	Married filing separately	Head of a household
79,000	79,050	15,613	11,469	15,751	14,169
79,050	79,100	15,625	11,481	15,765	14,181
79,100	79,150	15,638	11,494	15,779	14,194
79,150	79,200	15,650	11,506	15,793	14,206
79,200	79,250	15,663	11,519	15,807	14,219
79,250	79,300	15,675	11,531	15,821	14,231
79,300	79,350	15,688	11,544	15,835	14,244
79,350	79,400	15,700	11,556	15,849	14,256
79,400	79,450	15,713	11,569	15,863	14,269
79,450	79,500	15,725	11,581	15,877	14,281
79,500	79,550	15,738	11,594	15,891	14,294
79,550	79,600	15,750	11,606	15,905	14,306
79,600	79,650	15,763	11,619	15,919	14,319
79,650	79,700	15,775	11,631	15,933	14,331
79,700	79,750	15,788	11,644	15,947	14,344
79,750	79,800	15,800	11,656	15,961	14,356
79,800	79,850	15,813	11,669	15,975	14,369
79,850	79,900	15,825	11,681	15,989	14,381
79,900	79,950	15,838	11,694	16,003	14,394
79,950	80,000	15,850	11,706	16,017	14,406

80,000

At least	But less than	Single	Married filing jointly *	Married filing separately	Head of a household
80,000	80,050	15,863	11,719	16,031	14,419
80,050	80,100	15,875	11,731	16,045	14,431
80,100	80,150	15,888	11,744	16,059	14,444
80,150	80,200	15,900	11,756	16,073	14,456
80,200	80,250	15,913	11,769	16,087	14,469
80,250	80,300	15,925	11,781	16,101	14,481
80,300	80,350	15,938	11,794	16,115	14,494
80,350	80,400	15,950	11,806	16,129	14,506
80,400	80,450	15,963	11,819	16,143	14,519
80,450	80,500	15,975	11,831	16,157	14,531
80,500	80,550	15,988	11,844	16,171	14,544
80,550	80,600	16,000	11,856	16,185	14,556
80,600	80,650	16,013	11,869	16,199	14,569
80,650	80,700	16,025	11,881	16,213	14,581
80,700	80,750	16,038	11,894	16,227	14,594
80,750	80,800	16,050	11,906	16,241	14,606
80,800	80,850	16,063	11,919	16,255	14,619
80,850	80,900	16,075	11,931	16,269	14,631
80,900	80,950	16,088	11,944	16,283	14,644
80,950	81,000	16,100	11,956	16,297	14,656

81,000

At least	But less than	Single	Married filing jointly *	Married filing separately	Head of a household
81,000	81,050	16,113	11,969	16,311	14,669
81,050	81,100	16,125	11,981	16,325	14,681
81,100	81,150	16,138	11,994	16,339	14,694
81,150	81,200	16,150	12,006	16,353	14,706
81,200	81,250	16,163	12,019	16,367	14,719
81,250	81,300	16,175	12,031	16,381	14,731
81,300	81,350	16,188	12,044	16,395	14,744
81,350	81,400	16,200	12,056	16,409	14,756
81,400	81,450	16,213	12,069	16,423	14,769
81,450	81,500	16,225	12,081	16,437	14,781
81,500	81,550	16,238	12,094	16,451	14,794
81,550	81,600	16,250	12,106	16,465	14,806
81,600	81,650	16,263	12,119	16,479	14,819
81,650	81,700	16,275	12,131	16,493	14,831
81,700	81,750	16,288	12,144	16,507	14,844
81,750	81,800	16,300	12,156	16,521	14,856
81,800	81,850	16,313	12,169	16,535	14,869
81,850	81,900	16,325	12,181	16,549	14,881
81,900	81,950	16,338	12,194	16,563	14,894
81,950	82,000	16,350	12,206	16,577	14,906

82,000

At least	But less than	Single	Married filing jointly *	Married filing separately	Head of a household
82,000	82,050	16,363	12,219	16,591	14,919
82,050	82,100	16,375	12,231	16,605	14,931
82,100	82,150	16,388	12,244	16,619	14,944
82,150	82,200	16,400	12,256	16,633	14,956
82,200	82,250	16,413	12,269	16,647	14,969
82,250	82,300	16,425	12,281	16,661	14,981
82,300	82,350	16,438	12,294	16,675	14,994
82,350	82,400	16,450	12,306	16,689	15,006
82,400	82,450	16,463	12,319	16,703	15,019
82,450	82,500	16,475	12,331	16,717	15,031
82,500	82,550	16,488	12,344	16,731	15,044
82,550	82,600	16,500	12,356	16,745	15,056
82,600	82,650	16,513	12,369	16,759	15,069
82,650	82,700	16,525	12,381	16,773	15,081
82,700	82,750	16,538	12,394	16,787	15,094
82,750	82,800	16,550	12,406	16,801	15,106
82,800	82,850	16,563	12,419	16,815	15,119
82,850	82,900	16,575	12,431	16,829	15,131
82,900	82,950	16,588	12,444	16,843	15,144
82,950	83,000	16,600	12,456	16,857	15,156

83,000

At least	But less than	Single	Married filing jointly *	Married filing separately	Head of a household
83,000	83,050	16,613	12,469	16,871	15,169
83,050	83,100	16,625	12,481	16,885	15,181
83,100	83,150	16,638	12,494	16,899	15,194
83,150	83,200	16,650	12,506	16,913	15,206
83,200	83,250	16,663	12,519	16,927	15,219
83,250	83,300	16,675	12,531	16,941	15,231
83,300	83,350	16,688	12,544	16,955	15,244
83,350	83,400	16,700	12,556	16,969	15,256
83,400	83,450	16,713	12,569	16,983	15,269
83,450	83,500	16,725	12,581	16,997	15,281
83,500	83,550	16,738	12,594	17,011	15,294
83,550	83,600	16,750	12,606	17,025	15,306
83,600	83,650	16,763	12,619	17,039	15,319
83,650	83,700	16,775	12,631	17,053	15,331
83,700	83,750	16,788	12,644	17,067	15,344
83,750	83,800	16,800	12,656	17,081	15,356
83,800	83,850	16,813	12,669	17,095	15,369
83,850	83,900	16,825	12,681	17,109	15,381
83,900	83,950	16,838	12,694	17,123	15,394
83,950	84,000	16,850	12,706	17,137	15,406

* This column must also be used by a qualifying widow(er).

(Continued)

2014 Tax Table—*Continued*

84,000

At least	But less than	Single	Married filing jointly *	Married filing separately	Head of a household
					Your tax is—
84,000	84,050	16,863	12,719	17,151	15,419
84,050	84,100	16,875	12,731	17,165	15,431
84,100	84,150	16,888	12,744	17,179	15,444
84,150	84,200	16,900	12,756	17,193	15,456
84,200	84,250	16,913	12,769	17,207	15,469
84,250	84,300	16,925	12,781	17,221	15,481
84,300	84,350	16,938	12,794	17,235	15,494
84,350	84,400	16,950	12,806	17,249	15,506
84,400	84,450	16,963	12,819	17,263	15,519
84,450	84,500	16,975	12,831	17,277	15,531
84,500	84,550	16,988	12,844	17,291	15,544
84,550	84,600	17,000	12,856	17,305	15,556
84,600	84,650	17,013	12,869	17,319	15,569
84,650	84,700	17,025	12,881	17,333	15,581
84,700	84,750	17,038	12,894	17,347	15,594
84,750	84,800	17,050	12,906	17,361	15,606
84,800	84,850	17,063	12,919	17,375	15,619
84,850	84,900	17,075	12,931	17,389	15,631
84,900	84,950	17,088	12,944	17,403	15,644
84,950	85,000	17,100	12,956	17,417	15,656

85,000

At least	But less than	Single	Married filing jointly *	Married filing separately	Head of a household
85,000	85,050	17,113	12,969	17,431	15,669
85,050	85,100	17,125	12,981	17,445	15,681
85,100	85,150	17,138	12,994	17,459	15,694
85,150	85,200	17,150	13,006	17,473	15,706
85,200	85,250	17,163	13,019	17,487	15,719
85,250	85,300	17,175	13,031	17,501	15,731
85,300	85,350	17,188	13,044	17,515	15,744
85,350	85,400	17,200	13,056	17,529	15,756
85,400	85,450	17,213	13,069	17,543	15,769
85,450	85,500	17,225	13,081	17,557	15,781
85,500	85,550	17,238	13,094	17,571	15,794
85,550	85,600	17,250	13,106	17,585	15,806
85,600	85,650	17,263	13,119	17,599	15,819
85,650	85,700	17,275	13,131	17,613	15,831
85,700	85,750	17,288	13,144	17,627	15,844
85,750	85,800	17,300	13,156	17,641	15,856
85,800	85,850	17,313	13,169	17,655	15,869
85,850	85,900	17,325	13,181	17,669	15,881
85,900	85,950	17,338	13,194	17,683	15,894
85,950	86,000	17,350	13,206	17,697	15,906

86,000

At least	But less than	Single	Married filing jointly *	Married filing separately	Head of a household
86,000	86,050	17,363	13,219	17,711	15,919
86,050	86,100	17,375	13,231	17,725	15,931
86,100	86,150	17,388	13,244	17,739	15,944
86,150	86,200	17,400	13,256	17,753	15,956
86,200	86,250	17,413	13,269	17,767	15,969
86,250	86,300	17,425	13,281	17,781	15,981
86,300	86,350	17,438	13,294	17,795	15,994
86,350	86,400	17,450	13,306	17,809	16,006
86,400	86,450	17,463	13,319	17,823	16,019
86,450	86,500	17,475	13,331	17,837	16,031
86,500	86,550	17,488	13,344	17,851	16,044
86,550	86,600	17,500	13,356	17,865	16,056
86,600	86,650	17,513	13,369	17,879	16,069
86,650	86,700	17,525	13,381	17,893	16,081
86,700	86,750	17,538	13,394	17,907	16,094
86,750	86,800	17,550	13,406	17,921	16,106
86,800	86,850	17,563	13,419	17,935	16,119
86,850	86,900	17,575	13,431	17,949	16,131
86,900	86,950	17,588	13,444	17,963	16,144
86,950	87,000	17,600	13,456	17,977	16,156

87,000

At least	But less than	Single	Married filing jointly *	Married filing separately	Head of a household
87,000	87,050	17,613	13,469	17,991	16,169
87,050	87,100	17,625	13,481	18,005	16,181
87,100	87,150	17,638	13,494	18,019	16,194
87,150	87,200	17,650	13,506	18,033	16,206
87,200	87,250	17,663	13,519	18,047	16,219
87,250	87,300	17,675	13,531	18,061	16,231
87,300	87,350	17,688	13,544	18,075	16,244
87,350	87,400	17,700	13,556	18,089	16,256
87,400	87,450	17,713	13,569	18,103	16,269
87,450	87,500	17,725	13,581	18,117	16,281
87,500	87,550	17,738	13,594	18,131	16,294
87,550	87,600	17,750	13,606	18,145	16,306
87,600	87,650	17,763	13,619	18,159	16,319
87,650	87,700	17,775	13,631	18,173	16,331
87,700	87,750	17,788	13,644	18,187	16,344
87,750	87,800	17,800	13,656	18,201	16,356
87,800	87,850	17,813	13,669	18,215	16,369
87,850	87,900	17,825	13,681	18,229	16,381
87,900	87,950	17,838	13,694	18,243	16,394
87,950	88,000	17,850	13,706	18,257	16,406

88,000

At least	But less than	Single	Married filing jointly *	Married filing separately	Head of a household
88,000	88,050	17,863	13,719	18,271	16,419
88,050	88,100	17,875	13,731	18,285	16,431
88,100	88,150	17,888	13,744	18,299	16,444
88,150	88,200	17,900	13,756	18,313	16,456
88,200	88,250	17,913	13,769	18,327	16,469
88,250	88,300	17,925	13,781	18,341	16,481
88,300	88,350	17,938	13,794	18,355	16,494
88,350	88,400	17,950	13,806	18,369	16,506
88,400	88,450	17,963	13,819	18,383	16,519
88,450	88,500	17,975	13,831	18,397	16,531
88,500	88,550	17,988	13,844	18,411	16,544
88,550	88,600	18,000	13,856	18,425	16,556
88,600	88,650	18,013	13,869	18,439	16,569
88,650	88,700	18,025	13,881	18,453	16,581
88,700	88,750	18,038	13,894	18,467	16,594
88,750	88,800	18,050	13,906	18,481	16,606
88,800	88,850	18,063	13,919	18,495	16,619
88,850	88,900	18,075	13,931	18,509	16,631
88,900	88,950	18,088	13,944	18,523	16,644
88,950	89,000	18,100	13,956	18,537	16,656

89,000

At least	But less than	Single	Married filing jointly *	Married filing separately	Head of a household
89,000	89,050	18,113	13,969	18,551	16,669
89,050	89,100	18,125	13,981	18,565	16,681
89,100	89,150	18,138	13,994	18,579	16,694
89,150	89,200	18,150	14,006	18,593	16,706
89,200	89,250	18,163	14,019	18,607	16,719
89,250	89,300	18,175	14,031	18,621	16,731
89,300	89,350	18,188	14,044	18,635	16,744
89,350	89,400	18,201	14,056	18,649	16,756
89,400	89,450	18,215	14,069	18,663	16,769
89,450	89,500	18,229	14,081	18,677	16,781
89,500	89,550	18,243	14,094	18,691	16,794
89,550	89,600	18,257	14,106	18,705	16,806
89,600	89,650	18,271	14,119	18,719	16,819
89,650	89,700	18,285	14,131	18,733	16,831
89,700	89,750	18,299	14,144	18,747	16,844
89,750	89,800	18,313	14,156	18,761	16,856
89,800	89,850	18,327	14,169	18,775	16,869
89,850	89,900	18,341	14,181	18,789	16,881
89,900	89,950	18,355	14,194	18,803	16,894
89,950	90,000	18,369	14,206	18,817	16,906

90,000

At least	But less than	Single	Married filing jointly *	Married filing separately	Head of a household
90,000	90,050	18,383	14,219	18,831	16,919
90,050	90,100	18,397	14,231	18,845	16,931
90,100	90,150	18,411	14,244	18,859	16,944
90,150	90,200	18,425	14,256	18,873	16,956
90,200	90,250	18,439	14,269	18,887	16,969
90,250	90,300	18,453	14,281	18,901	16,981
90,300	90,350	18,467	14,294	18,915	16,994
90,350	90,400	18,481	14,306	18,929	17,006
90,400	90,450	18,495	14,319	18,943	17,019
90,450	90,500	18,509	14,331	18,957	17,031
90,500	90,550	18,523	14,344	18,971	17,044
90,550	90,600	18,537	14,356	18,985	17,056
90,600	90,650	18,551	14,369	18,999	17,069
90,650	90,700	18,565	14,381	19,013	17,081
90,700	90,750	18,579	14,394	19,027	17,094
90,750	90,800	18,593	14,406	19,041	17,106
90,800	90,850	18,607	14,419	19,055	17,119
90,850	90,900	18,621	14,431	19,069	17,131
90,900	90,950	18,635	14,444	19,083	17,144
90,950	91,000	18,649	14,456	19,097	17,156

91,000

At least	But less than	Single	Married filing jointly *	Married filing separately	Head of a household
91,000	91,050	18,663	14,469	19,111	17,169
91,050	91,100	18,677	14,481	19,125	17,181
91,100	91,150	18,691	14,494	19,139	17,194
91,150	91,200	18,705	14,506	19,153	17,206
91,200	91,250	18,719	14,519	19,167	17,219
91,250	91,300	18,733	14,531	19,181	17,231
91,300	91,350	18,747	14,544	19,195	17,244
91,350	91,400	18,761	14,556	19,209	17,256
91,400	91,450	18,775	14,569	19,223	17,269
91,450	91,500	18,789	14,581	19,237	17,281
91,500	91,550	18,803	14,594	19,251	17,294
91,550	91,600	18,817	14,606	19,265	17,306
91,600	91,650	18,831	14,619	19,279	17,319
91,650	91,700	18,845	14,631	19,293	17,331
91,700	91,750	18,859	14,644	19,307	17,344
91,750	91,800	18,873	14,656	19,321	17,356
91,800	91,850	18,887	14,669	19,335	17,369
91,850	91,900	18,901	14,681	19,349	17,381
91,900	91,950	18,915	14,694	19,363	17,394
91,950	92,000	18,929	14,706	19,377	17,406

92,000

At least	But less than	Single	Married filing jointly *	Married filing separately	Head of a household
92,000	92,050	18,943	14,719	19,391	17,419
92,050	92,100	18,957	14,731	19,405	17,431
92,100	92,150	18,971	14,744	19,419	17,444
92,150	92,200	18,985	14,756	19,433	17,456
92,200	92,250	18,999	14,769	19,447	17,469
92,250	92,300	19,013	14,781	19,461	17,481
92,300	92,350	19,027	14,794	19,475	17,494
92,350	92,400	19,041	14,806	19,489	17,506
92,400	92,450	19,055	14,819	19,503	17,519
92,450	92,500	19,069	14,831	19,517	17,531
92,500	92,550	19,083	14,844	19,531	17,544
92,550	92,600	19,097	14,856	19,545	17,556
92,600	92,650	19,111	14,869	19,559	17,569
92,650	92,700	19,125	14,881	19,573	17,581
92,700	92,750	19,139	14,894	19,587	17,594
92,750	92,800	19,153	14,906	19,601	17,606
92,800	92,850	19,167	14,919	19,615	17,619
92,850	92,900	19,181	14,931	19,629	17,631
92,900	92,950	19,195	14,944	19,643	17,644
92,950	93,000	19,209	14,956	19,657	17,656

* This column must also be used by a qualifying widow(er).

(Continued)

2014 Tax Table—*Continued*

If line 43 (taxable income) is—		And you are—			
At least	But less than	Single	Married filing jointly *	Married filing separately	Head of a household
		Your tax is—			

93,000

At least	But less than	Single	Married filing jointly *	Married filing separately	Head of a household
93,000	93,050	19,223	14,969	19,671	17,669
93,050	93,100	19,237	14,981	19,685	17,681
93,100	93,150	19,251	14,994	19,699	17,694
93,150	93,200	19,265	15,006	19,713	17,706
93,200	93,250	19,279	15,019	19,727	17,719
93,250	93,300	19,293	15,031	19,741	17,731
93,300	93,350	19,307	15,044	19,755	17,744
93,350	93,400	19,321	15,056	19,769	17,756
93,400	93,450	19,335	15,069	19,783	17,769
93,450	93,500	19,349	15,081	19,797	17,781
93,500	93,550	19,363	15,094	19,811	17,794
93,550	93,600	19,377	15,106	19,825	17,806
93,600	93,650	19,391	15,119	19,839	17,819
93,650	93,700	19,405	15,131	19,853	17,831
93,700	93,750	19,419	15,144	19,867	17,844
93,750	93,800	19,433	15,156	19,881	17,856
93,800	93,850	19,447	15,169	19,895	17,869
93,850	93,900	19,461	15,181	19,909	17,881
93,900	93,950	19,475	15,194	19,923	17,894
93,950	94,000	19,489	15,206	19,937	17,906

94,000

At least	But less than	Single	Married filing jointly *	Married filing separately	Head of a household
94,000	94,050	19,503	15,219	19,951	17,919
94,050	94,100	19,517	15,231	19,965	17,931
94,100	94,150	19,531	15,244	19,979	17,944
94,150	94,200	19,545	15,256	19,993	17,956
94,200	94,250	19,559	15,269	20,007	17,969
94,250	94,300	19,573	15,281	20,021	17,981
94,300	94,350	19,587	15,294	20,035	17,994
94,350	94,400	19,601	15,306	20,049	18,006
94,400	94,450	19,615	15,319	20,063	18,019
94,450	94,500	19,629	15,331	20,077	18,031
94,500	94,550	19,643	15,344	20,091	18,044
94,550	94,600	19,657	15,356	20,105	18,056
94,600	94,650	19,671	15,369	20,119	18,069
94,650	94,700	19,685	15,381	20,133	18,081
94,700	94,750	19,699	15,394	20,147	18,094
94,750	94,800	19,713	15,406	20,161	18,106
94,800	94,850	19,727	15,419	20,175	18,119
94,850	94,900	19,741	15,431	20,189	18,131
94,900	94,950	19,755	15,444	20,203	18,144
94,950	95,000	19,769	15,456	20,217	18,156

95,000

At least	But less than	Single	Married filing jointly *	Married filing separately	Head of a household
95,000	95,050	19,783	15,469	20,231	18,169
95,050	95,100	19,797	15,481	20,245	18,181
95,100	95,150	19,811	15,494	20,259	18,194
95,150	95,200	19,825	15,506	20,273	18,206
95,200	95,250	19,839	15,519	20,287	18,219
95,250	95,300	19,853	15,531	20,301	18,231
95,300	95,350	19,867	15,544	20,315	18,244
95,350	95,400	19,881	15,556	20,329	18,256
95,400	95,450	19,895	15,569	20,343	18,269
95,450	95,500	19,909	15,581	20,357	18,281
95,500	95,550	19,923	15,594	20,371	18,294
95,550	95,600	19,937	15,606	20,385	18,306
95,600	95,650	19,951	15,619	20,399	18,319
95,650	95,700	19,965	15,631	20,413	18,331
95,700	95,750	19,979	15,644	20,427	18,344
95,750	95,800	19,993	15,656	20,441	18,356
95,800	95,850	20,007	15,669	20,455	18,369
95,850	95,900	20,021	15,681	20,469	18,381
95,900	95,950	20,035	15,694	20,483	18,394
95,950	96,000	20,049	15,706	20,497	18,406

96,000

At least	But less than	Single	Married filing jointly *	Married filing separately	Head of a household
96,000	96,050	20,063	15,719	20,511	18,419
96,050	96,100	20,077	15,731	20,525	18,431
96,100	96,150	20,091	15,744	20,539	18,444
96,150	96,200	20,105	15,756	20,553	18,456
96,200	96,250	20,119	15,769	20,567	18,469
96,250	96,300	20,133	15,781	20,581	18,481
96,300	96,350	20,147	15,794	20,595	18,494
96,350	96,400	20,161	15,806	20,609	18,506
96,400	96,450	20,175	15,819	20,623	18,519
96,450	96,500	20,189	15,831	20,637	18,531
96,500	96,550	20,203	15,844	20,651	18,544
96,550	96,600	20,217	15,856	20,665	18,556
96,600	96,650	20,231	15,869	20,679	18,569
96,650	96,700	20,245	15,881	20,693	18,581
96,700	96,750	20,259	15,894	20,707	18,594
96,750	96,800	20,273	15,906	20,721	18,606
96,800	96,850	20,287	15,919	20,735	18,619
96,850	96,900	20,301	15,931	20,749	18,631
96,900	96,950	20,315	15,944	20,763	18,644
96,950	97,000	20,329	15,956	20,777	18,656

97,000

At least	But less than	Single	Married filing jointly *	Married filing separately	Head of a household
97,000	97,050	20,343	15,969	20,791	18,669
97,050	97,100	20,357	15,981	20,805	18,681
97,100	97,150	20,371	15,994	20,819	18,694
97,150	97,200	20,385	16,006	20,833	18,706
97,200	97,250	20,399	16,019	20,847	18,719
97,250	97,300	20,413	16,031	20,861	18,731
97,300	97,350	20,427	16,044	20,875	18,744
97,350	97,400	20,441	16,056	20,889	18,756
97,400	97,450	20,455	16,069	20,903	18,769
97,450	97,500	20,469	16,081	20,917	18,781
97,500	97,550	20,483	16,094	20,931	18,794
97,550	97,600	20,497	16,106	20,945	18,806
97,600	97,650	20,511	16,119	20,959	18,819
97,650	97,700	20,525	16,131	20,973	18,831
97,700	97,750	20,539	16,144	20,987	18,844
97,750	97,800	20,553	16,156	21,001	18,856
97,800	97,850	20,567	16,169	21,015	18,869
97,850	97,900	20,581	16,181	21,029	18,881
97,900	97,950	20,595	16,194	21,043	18,894
97,950	98,000	20,609	16,206	21,057	18,906

98,000

At least	But less than	Single	Married filing jointly *	Married filing separately	Head of a household
98,000	98,050	20,623	16,219	21,071	18,919
98,050	98,100	20,637	16,231	21,085	18,931
98,100	98,150	20,651	16,244	21,099	18,944
98,150	98,200	20,665	16,256	21,113	18,956
98,200	98,250	20,679	16,269	21,127	18,969
98,250	98,300	20,693	16,281	21,141	18,981
98,300	98,350	20,707	16,294	21,155	18,994
98,350	98,400	20,721	16,306	21,169	19,006
98,400	98,450	20,735	16,319	21,183	19,019
98,450	98,500	20,749	16,331	21,197	19,031
98,500	98,550	20,763	16,344	21,211	19,044
98,550	98,600	20,777	16,356	21,225	19,056
98,600	98,650	20,791	16,369	21,239	19,069
98,650	98,700	20,805	16,381	21,253	19,081
98,700	98,750	20,819	16,394	21,267	19,094
98,750	98,800	20,833	16,406	21,281	19,106
98,800	98,850	20,847	16,419	21,295	19,119
98,850	98,900	20,861	16,431	21,309	19,131
98,900	98,950	20,875	16,444	21,323	19,144
98,950	99,000	20,889	16,456	21,337	19,156

99,000

At least	But less than	Single	Married filing jointly *	Married filing separately	Head of a household
99,000	99,050	20,903	16,469	21,351	19,169
99,050	99,100	20,917	16,481	21,365	19,181
99,100	99,150	20,931	16,494	21,379	19,194
99,150	99,200	20,945	16,506	21,393	19,206
99,200	99,250	20,959	16,519	21,407	19,219
99,250	99,300	20,973	16,531	21,421	19,231
99,300	99,350	20,987	16,544	21,435	19,244
99,350	99,400	21,001	16,556	21,449	19,256
99,400	99,450	21,015	16,569	21,463	19,269
99,450	99,500	21,029	16,581	21,477	19,281
99,500	99,550	21,043	16,594	21,491	19,294
99,550	99,600	21,057	16,606	21,505	19,306
99,600	99,650	21,071	16,619	21,519	19,319
99,650	99,700	21,085	16,631	21,533	19,331
99,700	99,750	21,099	16,644	21,547	19,344
99,750	99,800	21,113	16,656	21,561	19,356
99,800	99,850	21,127	16,669	21,575	19,369
99,850	99,900	21,141	16,681	21,589	19,381
99,900	99,950	21,155	16,694	21,603	19,394
99,950	100,000	21,169	16,706	21,617	19,406

$100,000
or over
use the Tax
Computation
Worksheet

* This column must also be used by a qualifying widow(er).

Income Tax Rates—Estates and Trusts

Tax Year 2014

Taxable Income		The Tax Is:	Of the Amount Over—
Over—	But not Over—		
$ 0	$ 2,500	15%	$ 0
2,500	5,800	$ 375.00 + 25%	2,500
5,800	8,900	1,200.00 + 28%	5,800
8,900	12,150	2,068.00 + 33%	8,900
12,150	....	3,140.50 + 39.6%	12,150

Tax Year 2015

Taxable Income		The Tax Is:	Of the Amount Over—
Over—	But not Over—		
$ 0	$ 2,500	15%	$ 0
2,500	5,900	$ 375.00 + 25%	2,500
5,900	9,050	1,225.00 + 28%	5,900
9,050	12,300	2,107.00 + 33%	9,050
12,300	....	3,179.50 + 39.6%	12,300

Income Tax Rates—Corporations

Taxable Income		The Tax Is:	Of the Amount Over—
Over—	But not Over—		
$ 0	$ 50,000	15%	$ 0
50,000	75,000	$ 7,500 + 25%	50,000
75,000	100,000	13,750 + 34%	75,000
100,000	335,000	22,250 + 39%	100,000
335,000	10,000,000	113,900 + 34%	335,000
10,000,000	15,000,000	3,400,000 + 35%	10,000,000
15,000,000	18,333,333	5,150,000 + 38%	15,000,000
18,333,333	....	35%	0

Unified Transfer Tax Rates

For Gifts Made and for Deaths in 2007–2009

If the Amount with Respect to Which the Tentative Tax to Be Computed Is:	The Tentative Tax Is:
Not over $10,000	18 percent of such amount.
Over $10,000 but not over $20,000	$1,800, plus 20 percent of the excess of such amount over $10,000.
Over $20,000 but not over $40,000	$3,800, plus 22 percent of the excess of such amount over $20,000.
Over $40,000 but not over $60,000	$8,200, plus 24 percent of the excess of such amount over $40,000.
Over $60,000 but not over $80,000	$13,000, plus 26 percent of the excess of such amount over $60,000.
Over $80,000 but not over $100,000	$18,200, plus 28 percent of the excess of such amount over $80,000.
Over $100,000 but not over $150,000	$23,800, plus 30 percent of the excess of such amount over $100,000.
Over $150,000 but not over $250,000	$38,800, plus 32 percent of the excess of such amount over $150,000.
Over $250,000 but not over $500,000	$70,800, plus 34 percent of the excess of such amount over $250,000.
Over $500,000 but not over $750,000	$155,800, plus 37 percent of the excess of such amount over $500,000.
Over $750,000 but not over $1,000,000	$248,300, plus 39 percent of the excess of such amount over $750,000.
Over $1,000,000 but not over $1,250,000	$345,800, plus 41 percent of the excess of such amount over $1,000,000.
Over $1,250,000 but not over $1,500,000	$448,300, plus 43 percent of the excess of such amount over $1,250,000.
Over $1,500,000	$555,800, plus 45 percent of the excess of such amount over $1,500,000.

Gift Tax Rates

For Gifts Made Only in 2010

If the Amount with Respect to Which the Tentative Tax to Be Computed Is:	The Tentative Tax Is:
Not over $10,000	18 percent of such amount.
Over $10,000 but not over $20,000	$1,800, plus 20 percent of the excess of such amount over $10,000.
Over $20,000 but not over $40,000	$3,800, plus 22 percent of the excess of such amount over $20,000.
Over $40,000 but not over $60,000	$8,200, plus 24 percent of the excess of such amount over $40,000.
Over $60,000 but not over $80,000	$13,000, plus 26 percent of the excess of such amount over $60,000.
Over $80,000 but not over $100,000	$18,200, plus 28 percent of the excess of such amount over $80,000.
Over $100,000 but not over $150,000	$23,800, plus 30 percent of the excess of such amount over $100,000.
Over $150,000 but not over $250,000	$38,800, plus 32 percent of the excess of such amount over $150,000.
Over $250,000 but not over $500,000	$70,800, plus 34 percent of the excess of such amount over $250,000.
Over $500,000	$155,800, plus 35 percent of the excess of such amount over $500,000.

Unified Transfer Tax Rates

For Gifts Made and for Deaths in 2011–2012

If the Amount with Respect to Which the Tentative Tax to Be Computed Is:	The Tentative Tax Is:
Not over $10,000	18 percent of such amount.
Over $10,000 but not over $20,000	$1,800, plus 20 percent of the excess of such amount over $10,000.
Over $20,000 but not over $40,000	$3,800, plus 22 percent of the excess of such amount over $20,000.
Over $40,000 but not over $60,000	$8,200, plus 24 percent of the excess of such amount over $40,000.
Over $60,000 but not over $80,000	$13,000, plus 26 percent of the excess of such amount over $60,000.
Over $80,000 but not over $100,000	$18,200, plus 28 percent of the excess of such amount over $80,000.
Over $100,000 but not over $150,000	$23,800, plus 30 percent of the excess of such amount over $100,000.
Over $150,000 but not over $250,000	$38,800, plus 32 percent of the excess of such amount over $150,000.
Over $250,000 but not over $500,000	$70,800, plus 34 percent of the excess of such amount over $250,000.
Over $500,000	$155,800, plus 35 percent of the excess of such amount over $500,000.

Unified Transfer Tax Rates

For Gifts Made and for Deaths after 2012

If the Amount with Respect to Which the Tentative Tax to Be Computed Is:	The Tentative Tax Is:
Not over $10,000	18 percent of such amount.
Over $10,000 but not over $20,000	$1,800, plus 20 percent of the excess of such amount over $10,000.
Over $20,000 but not over $40,000	$3,800, plus 22 percent of the excess of such amount over $20,000.
Over $40,000 but not over $60,000	$8,200, plus 24 percent of the excess of such amount over $40,000.
Over $60,000 but not over $80,000	$13,000, plus 26 percent of the excess of such amount over $60,000.
Over $80,000 but not over $100,000	$18,200, plus 28 percent of the excess of such amount over $80,000.
Over $100,000 but not over $150,000	$23,800, plus 30 percent of the excess of such amount over $100,000.
Over $150,000 but not over $250,000	$38,800, plus 32 percent of the excess of such amount over $150,000.
Over $250,000 but not over $500,000	$70,800, plus 34 percent of the excess of such amount over $250,000.
Over $500,000 but not over $750,000	$155,800, plus 37 percent of the excess of such amount over $500,000.
Over $750,000 but not over $1,000,000	$248,300, plus 39 percent of the excess of such amount over $750,000.
Over $1,000,000	$345,800, plus 40 percent of the excess of such amount over $1,000,000.

2014 OPTIONAL SALES TAX TABLES

When Used

The election to deduct state and local general sales taxes requires that the taxpayer forgo any deduction for state and local income taxes. Whether this is advisable or not depends on a comparison of the amounts involved. In making the choice, however, the outcome could be influenced by the additional sales tax incurred due to certain "big ticket" purchases that were made. For example, a taxpayer who chose to deduct state and local income taxes for 2013 might well prefer the sales tax deduction in 2014 if a new boat was purchased or home improvements were made during the year. To make the sales tax election, the taxpayer must enter the amount on Schedule A, line 5, and check box b. Unless extended by Congress, the sales tax deduction will expire as to tax years after 2014.

If the sales tax election is made, the amount of the deduction can be determined by use of the *actual expense method* or the *optional sales tax tables* issued by the IRS. The actual expense method can be used only when the taxpayer has actual receipts to support the deduction claimed. In the absence of receipts, the usual case with most taxpayers, resorting to the optional sales tax tables is necessary. Under neither method, however, is the purchase of items used in a taxpayer's trade or business to be considered.

Adjustments Necessary

The optional sales tax tables are based on a number of assumptions that require adjustments to be made. As the starting point for the use of the tables is AGI, nontaxable receipts have not been included. Examples of receipts that should be added include: tax-exempt interest, veterans' benefits, nontaxable combat pay, public assistance payments, workers' compensation, nontaxable Social Security, and other retirement benefits. They do not include any large nontaxable items that are not likely to be spent. For example, a $100,000 inheritance should not be added if it was invested in a certificate of deposit.

The tables represent the sales tax on the average (and recurring) expenditures based on level of income by family size and do not include exceptional purchases. Therefore, add to the table amount any sales taxes on major purchases (such as motor vehicles, aircraft, boats, and home building materials, etc.).

When the optional sales tax tables are utilized, special adjustments may be needed when a taxpayer has lived in more than one taxing jurisdiction (e.g., state, county, city) during the year. The adjustments involve apportionment of taxes based on days involved and are illustrated in Instructions for Schedule A (Form 1040), pages A-3 to A-6.

Local Sales Taxes

Local sales taxes (i.e., those imposed by counties, cities, transit authorities) may or may not require a separate determination. In those states where they are not imposed, no further computations are necessary. This is also the case where the local taxes are uniform and are incorporated into the state sales tax table. In other situations, another step is necessary to arrive at the optional sales tax table deduction. Depending on where the taxpayer lives, one of two procedures needs to be used. In one procedure, the local sales tax is arrived at by using the **state table** amount—see the Example 1 worksheet. In the other procedure, special **local tables** issued by the IRS for enumerated state and local jurisdictions are modified (if necessary) and used—see the Example 2 worksheet.

Use Illustrated

EXAMPLE 1 The Archers file a joint return for 2014 reflecting AGI of $88,000 and claiming three exemptions. They have tax-exempt interest of $3,000, and during the year they incurred sales tax of $1,650 on the purchase of an automobile for their dependent teenage son. They live in Bellaire, Texas, where the general sales tax rates are 6.25% for state and 2% for local. Since the IRS *has not issued* optional local sales tax tables for Texas, use the Worksheet below to arrive at the Archers' general sales tax deduction of $3,086.

Sales Tax Deduction Worksheet

(To be used when *no* IRS Optional Local Sales Tax Table Available)

Adjusted Gross Income (AGI) as listed on line 38 of Form 1040		$88,000
Add nontaxable items		3,000
Table income to be used for purposes of line 1 below		$91,000
1. Use table income to determine table amount—go to state of residence and find applicable range of table income and exemption column* for *state* sales tax		$ 1,088
2a. Enter local general sales tax rate	2.0	
2b. Enter state general sales tax rate	6.25	
2c. Divide 2a by 2b	0.32	
2d. Multiply line 1 by line 2c for the local sales tax		348
3. Enter general sales tax on large purchases		1,650
4. Deduction for general sales tax (add lines 1 + 2d + 3) and report on line 5 of Schedule A of Form 1040		$ 3,086

*Use total of personal and dependency exemptions as reported in item 6d of Form 1040.

EXAMPLE 2 The Hardys file a joint return for 2014, reporting AGI of $40,000 and claiming four exemptions (two personal and two dependency). They received $30,000 in nontaxable pension benefits. Although the Hardys do not keep sales tax receipts, they can prove that they paid $4,800 in sales tax on the purchase of a new boat in 2014. The Hardys are residents of Georgia and live in a jurisdiction that imposes a 2% local sales tax. Since the IRS *has issued* optional local sales tax tables for Georgia, use the Worksheet below to arrive at the Hardys' general sales tax deduction of $5,666.

Sales Tax Deduction Worksheet

(To be used for Alaska, Arizona, Arkansas,
Colorado, Georgia, Illinois, Louisiana, Missouri, New York, North Carolina,
South Carolina, Tennessee, Utah, Virginia, and West Virginia)

Adjusted Gross Income (AGI) as listed on line 38 of Form 1040		$40,000
Add nontaxable income		30,000
Table income to be used for purposes of line 1 below		$70,000
1. Use the table income to determine *state* sales tax amount—go to table for state of residence and find applicable income range and exemption column*		$ 540
2a. Enter local general sales tax rate	2.0	
2b. Enter IRS *local* sales tax table amount (based on 1%)	$163	
2c. Multiply line 2b by 2a for the local sales tax		326
3. Enter general sales tax on large purchases		4,800
4. Deduction for general sales tax (add lines 1 + 2c + 3) and report on line 5 of Schedule A of Form 1040		$ 5,666

*Use total of personal and dependency exemptions as reported in item 6d of Form 1040.

2014 Optional State Sales Tax Tables *(State Sales Tax Rate Shown Next to State Name)*

Alabama 1 4.0000%

Income At	But less than	1	2	3	4	5	Over 5
$0	$20,000	223	263	290	310	328	352
$20,000	$30,000	329	387	426	456	481	517
$30,000	$40,000	384	451	496	531	560	601
$40,000	$50,000	431	505	556	595	628	673
$50,000	$60,000	473	554	609	652	687	737
$60,000	$70,000	510	598	657	703	741	795
$70,000	$80,000	545	638	701	750	790	847
$80,000	$90,000	577	675	742	793	836	896
$90,000	$100,000	607	710	780	834	879	942
$100,000	$120,000	647	757	831	888	936	1003
$120,000	$140,000	699	817	896	958	1010	1082
$140,000	$160,000	747	873	957	1023	1078	1155
$160,000	$180,000	792	924	1013	1083	1141	1222
$180,000	$200,000	833	972	1066	1139	1200	1285
$200,000	$225,000	877	1023	1121	1198	1261	1351
$225,000	$250,000	924	1077	1180	1260	1327	1421
$250,000	$275,000	968	1127	1235	1319	1389	1487
$275,000	$300,000	1009	1176	1288	1375	1448	1550
$300,000	or more	1256	1461	1598	1705	1794	1919

Arizona 2 5.6000%

Income At	But less than	1	2	3	4	5	Over 5
$0	$20,000	214	237	251	262	271	283
$20,000	$30,000	364	403	428	446	462	482
$30,000	$40,000	448	496	527	550	569	595
$40,000	$50,000	524	580	616	644	666	696
$50,000	$60,000	594	658	699	730	755	789
$60,000	$70,000	658	729	775	809	837	875
$70,000	$80,000	719	797	847	884	915	956
$80,000	$90,000	777	861	915	955	988	1033
$90,000	$100,000	832	922	979	1023	1058	1106
$100,000	$120,000	906	1004	1067	1115	1153	1206
$120,000	$140,000	1005	1114	1184	1237	1279	1338
$140,000	$160,000	1099	1218	1295	1353	1399	1464
$160,000	$180,000	1187	1316	1399	1462	1512	1582
$180,000	$200,000	1272	1411	1499	1566	1621	1695
$200,000	$225,000	1362	1510	1605	1677	1735	1815
$225,000	$250,000	1460	1618	1721	1798	1860	1945
$250,000	$275,000	1553	1722	1831	1913	1979	2070
$275,000	$300,000	1643	1822	1937	2024	2094	2191
$300,000	or more	2199	2439	2594	2711	2805	2935

Arkansas 2 6.5000%

Income At	But less than	1	2	3	4	5	Over 5
$0	$20,000	283	315	335	350	363	380
$20,000	$30,000	460	513	546	572	592	620
$30,000	$40,000	558	621	662	693	718	753
$40,000	$50,000	644	718	765	801	830	869
$50,000	$60,000	722	805	859	899	931	976
$60,000	$70,000	794	886	945	989	1025	1074
$70,000	$80,000	862	961	1025	1073	1112	1165
$80,000	$90,000	925	1032	1100	1152	1194	1251
$90,000	$100,000	985	1099	1172	1227	1272	1333
$100,000	$120,000	1066	1189	1269	1328	1377	1443
$120,000	$140,000	1173	1309	1396	1462	1515	1588
$140,000	$160,000	1274	1421	1516	1588	1646	1726
$160,000	$180,000	1368	1526	1628	1705	1768	1853
$180,000	$200,000	1457	1627	1736	1818	1884	1976
$200,000	$225,000	1552	1732	1848	1936	2007	2104
$225,000	$250,000	1654	1847	1970	2064	2140	2244
$250,000	$275,000	1751	1955	2087	2186	2266	2376
$275,000	$300,000	1845	2060	2198	2303	2387	2504
$300,000	or more	2413	2696	2878	3015	3126	3279

California 3 7.5000%

Income At	But less than	1	2	3	4	5	Over 5
$0	$20,000	267	292	308	321	330	344
$20,000	$30,000	446	488	515	536	552	574
$30,000	$40,000	546	598	631	656	676	703
$40,000	$50,000	635	695	734	763	787	818
$50,000	$60,000	716	785	829	861	888	924
$60,000	$70,000	792	867	916	952	981	1021
$70,000	$80,000	862	945	998	1037	1069	1112
$80,000	$90,000	929	1018	1075	1117	1152	1198
$90,000	$100,000	992	1088	1148	1194	1230	1280
$100,000	$120,000	1078	1182	1248	1297	1337	1391
$120,000	$140,000	1192	1306	1379	1434	1478	1538
$140,000	$160,000	1299	1424	1504	1564	1612	1677
$160,000	$180,000	1400	1535	1621	1685	1737	1808
$180,000	$200,000	1497	1641	1733	1802	1857	1933
$200,000	$225,000	1599	1753	1851	1924	1984	2064
$225,000	$250,000	1709	1874	1979	2058	2121	2207
$250,000	$275,000	1815	1990	2101	2185	2252	2344
$275,000	$300,000	1917	2102	2219	2307	2379	2476
$300,000	or more	2540	2785	2942	3059	3153	3282

Colorado 2 2.9000%

Income At	But less than	1	2	3	4	5	Over 5
$0	$20,000	111	124	133	139	144	151
$20,000	$30,000	174	194	207	217	225	236
$30,000	$40,000	208	232	247	259	268	281
$40,000	$50,000	237	264	282	295	306	320
$50,000	$60,000	264	294	313	328	339	356
$60,000	$70,000	288	320	341	357	370	388
$70,000	$80,000	310	345	368	385	399	418
$80,000	$90,000	331	368	392	410	425	446
$90,000	$100,000	350	390	415	435	450	472
$100,000	$120,000	377	419	447	467	484	507
$120,000	$140,000	411	457	487	510	528	553
$140,000	$160,000	444	493	525	550	569	596
$160,000	$180,000	474	526	561	586	607	636
$180,000	$200,000	502	558	594	621	644	674
$200,000	$225,000	532	591	629	658	682	714
$225,000	$250,000	564	626	667	698	722	757
$250,000	$275,000	594	660	703	735	761	797
$275,000	$300,000	623	692	737	771	798	836
$300,000	or more	798	885	942	985	1020	1068

Connecticut 4 6.3500%

Income At	But less than	1	2	3	4	5	Over 5
$0	$20,000	263	289	305	317	327	340
$20,000	$30,000	432	475	502	522	539	561
$30,000	$40,000	526	578	611	636	656	683
$40,000	$50,000	609	670	708	737	760	792
$50,000	$60,000	685	753	797	829	856	891
$60,000	$70,000	755	830	878	914	943	983
$70,000	$80,000	820	902	955	994	1025	1068
$80,000	$90,000	882	970	1027	1069	1103	1149
$90,000	$100,000	940	1035	1095	1140	1176	1226
$100,000	$120,000	1019	1122	1187	1236	1276	1329
$120,000	$140,000	1124	1237	1309	1363	1407	1466
$140,000	$160,000	1222	1346	1425	1484	1531	1596
$160,000	$180,000	1315	1448	1533	1596	1647	1717
$180,000	$200,000	1403	1545	1636	1704	1758	1833
$200,000	$225,000	1496	1648	1745	1817	1875	1955
$225,000	$250,000	1597	1759	1863	1940	2002	2087
$250,000	$275,000	1693	1865	1975	2057	2123	2213
$275,000	$300,000	1785	1967	2083	2170	2240	2335
$300,000	or more	2350	2591	2744	2859	2951	3078

District of Columbia 4 5.7500%

Income At	But less than	1	2	3	4	5	Over 5
$0	$20,000	168	181	189	195	200	207
$20,000	$30,000	284	307	322	332	341	353
$30,000	$40,000	350	379	397	410	421	436
$40,000	$50,000	409	443	464	480	493	510
$50,000	$60,000	464	502	526	544	559	579
$60,000	$70,000	514	556	583	604	620	642
$70,000	$80,000	561	608	638	660	678	702
$80,000	$90,000	606	657	689	713	732	759
$90,000	$100,000	649	704	738	764	784	813
$100,000	$120,000	708	767	804	833	855	886
$120,000	$140,000	785	851	893	924	949	984
$140,000	$160,000	858	931	977	1011	1039	1077
$160,000	$180,000	928	1006	1056	1093	1123	1164
$180,000	$200,000	994	1078	1132	1172	1204	1248
$200,000	$225,000	1064	1155	1212	1255	1290	1337
$225,000	$250,000	1141	1238	1300	1346	1383	1434
$250,000	$275,000	1214	1318	1384	1433	1473	1527
$275,000	$300,000	1285	1395	1465	1517	1559	1617
$300,000	or more	1721	1870	1965	2036	2093	2171

Florida 1 6.0000%

Income At	But less than	1	2	3	4	5	Over 5
$0	$20,000	238	261	276	287	296	308
$20,000	$30,000	396	434	459	478	493	513
$30,000	$40,000	483	531	561	584	602	627
$40,000	$50,000	561	616	651	678	699	729
$50,000	$60,000	632	695	734	764	789	822
$60,000	$70,000	698	767	811	844	871	907
$70,000	$80,000	759	834	882	918	948	988
$80,000	$90,000	817	898	950	989	1020	1063
$90,000	$100,000	873	959	1014	1056	1090	1136
$100,000	$120,000	947	1041	1101	1147	1183	1233
$120,000	$140,000	1046	1150	1216	1266	1307	1362
$140,000	$160,000	1139	1253	1325	1380	1424	1484
$160,000	$180,000	1227	1349	1427	1486	1533	1599
$180,000	$200,000	1310	1441	1525	1588	1639	1708
$200,000	$225,000	1399	1538	1628	1695	1749	1824
$225,000	$250,000	1494	1644	1739	1811	1869	1949
$250,000	$275,000	1586	1744	1846	1922	1984	2068
$275,000	$300,000	1674	1841	1949	2029	2094	2184
$300,000	or more	2211	2434	2576	2683	2770	2889

Georgia 2 4.0000%

Income At	But less than	1	2	3	4	5	Over 5
$0	$20,000	151	168	179	187	194	203
$20,000	$30,000	241	267	284	297	308	322
$30,000	$40,000	289	321	341	357	369	387
$40,000	$50,000	332	368	391	409	423	443
$50,000	$60,000	370	411	437	456	472	494
$60,000	$70,000	405	449	478	499	517	541
$70,000	$80,000	438	486	516	540	558	584
$80,000	$90,000	468	519	552	577	597	625
$90,000	$100,000	497	551	586	613	634	663
$100,000	$120,000	536	594	632	660	683	715
$120,000	$140,000	587	651	692	723	748	783
$140,000	$160,000	635	704	748	782	809	846
$160,000	$180,000	680	753	801	836	865	905
$180,000	$200,000	722	800	850	888	919	961
$200,000	$225,000	766	849	903	943	975	1020
$225,000	$250,000	814	902	959	1002	1036	1084
$250,000	$275,000	860	952	1012	1057	1094	1144
$275,000	$300,000	903	1001	1064	1111	1149	1202
$300,000	or more	1166	1292	1372	1433	1482	1550

Hawaii 1,7 4.0000%

Income At	But less than	1	2	3	4	5	Over 5
$0	$20,000	220	255	279	297	312	333
$20,000	$30,000	356	414	452	482	507	542
$30,000	$40,000	430	501	548	584	614	656
$40,000	$50,000	496	578	632	674	708	757
$50,000	$60,000	556	647	708	755	794	849
$60,000	$70,000	611	711	779	830	873	933
$70,000	$80,000	662	771	844	900	947	1012
$80,000	$90,000	711	828	906	966	1016	1086
$90,000	$100,000	756	881	964	1029	1082	1156
$100,000	$120,000	818	953	1043	1113	1170	1250
$120,000	$140,000	899	1047	1147	1223	1287	1375
$140,000	$160,000	975	1136	1244	1328	1396	1493
$160,000	$180,000	1047	1220	1335	1425	1499	1602
$180,000	$200,000	1115	1299	1422	1518	1597	1707
$200,000	$225,000	1186	1383	1514	1616	1699	1817
$225,000	$250,000	1263	1473	1613	1721	1811	1936
$250,000	$275,000	1337	1559	1707	1822	1916	2049
$275,000	$300,000	1407	1641	1798	1918	2018	2158
$300,000	or more	1836	2142	2347	2505	2636	2819

Idaho 1 6.0000%

Income At	But less than	1	2	3	4	5	Over 5
$0	$20,000	337	396	436	467	493	529
$20,000	$30,000	501	588	647	692	730	783
$30,000	$40,000	586	687	756	809	852	914
$40,000	$50,000	660	773	849	908	957	1026
$50,000	$60,000	725	849	932	997	1051	1126
$60,000	$70,000	784	917	1007	1077	1135	1216
$70,000	$80,000	838	980	1076	1150	1212	1298
$80,000	$90,000	888	1038	1140	1218	1283	1375
$90,000	$100,000	935	1093	1199	1282	1351	1447
$100,000	$120,000	998	1166	1279	1367	1440	1542
$120,000	$140,000	1080	1260	1382	1477	1556	1666
$140,000	$160,000	1155	1348	1478	1579	1663	1781
$160,000	$180,000	1225	1429	1567	1673	1762	1886
$180,000	$200,000	1291	1506	1650	1762	1855	1986
$200,000	$225,000	1360	1585	1737	1855	1952	2090
$225,000	$250,000	1433	1670	1830	1953	2056	2200
$250,000	$275,000	1503	1750	1917	2046	2154	2305
$275,000	$300,000	1569	1826	2000	2135	2247	2404
$300,000	or more	1959	2277	2492	2658	2796	2990

Illinois 2 6.2500%

Income At	But less than	1	2	3	4	5	Over 5
$0	$20,000	251	281	301	316	329	346
$20,000	$30,000	389	434	465	488	507	533
$30,000	$40,000	462	516	551	578	601	632
$40,000	$50,000	525	586	626	657	682	718
$50,000	$60,000	582	649	694	728	756	795
$60,000	$70,000	634	707	755	792	822	864
$70,000	$80,000	681	760	812	851	884	929
$80,000	$90,000	726	809	864	907	941	989
$90,000	$100,000	768	856	914	959	995	1046
$100,000	$120,000	824	919	981	1028	1067	1122
$120,000	$140,000	898	1000	1068	1119	1162	1221
$140,000	$160,000	967	1076	1149	1204	1250	1313
$160,000	$180,000	1030	1147	1224	1283	1331	1398
$180,000	$200,000	1091	1214	1295	1357	1409	1480
$200,000	$225,000	1154	1284	1369	1435	1489	1564
$225,000	$250,000	1221	1359	1449	1519	1576	1655
$250,000	$275,000	1285	1429	1525	1598	1658	1741
$275,000	$300,000	1347	1497	1597	1673	1736	1823
$300,000	or more	1713	1902	2028	2124	2203	2312

Indiana 4 7.0000%

Income At	But less than	1	2	3	4	5	Over 5
$0	$20,000	288	322	343	360	373	391
$20,000	$30,000	448	500	533	558	579	607
$30,000	$40,000	533	595	634	664	688	721
$40,000	$50,000	607	677	722	756	783	821
$50,000	$60,000	674	751	801	839	869	911
$60,000	$70,000	734	818	873	914	947	992
$70,000	$80,000	790	881	939	983	1019	1068
$80,000	$90,000	842	939	1001	1048	1086	1138
$90,000	$100,000	891	994	1060	1109	1149	1205
$100,000	$120,000	957	1067	1138	1191	1234	1293
$120,000	$140,000	1043	1163	1240	1298	1345	1409
$140,000	$160,000	1123	1252	1335	1398	1448	1518
$160,000	$180,000	1198	1335	1424	1490	1544	1618
$180,000	$200,000	1269	1414	1508	1578	1635	1714
$200,000	$225,000	1342	1496	1595	1670	1730	1813
$225,000	$250,000	1422	1585	1689	1768	1832	1920
$250,000	$275,000	1497	1668	1779	1862	1929	2021
$275,000	$300,000	1569	1748	1864	1951	2022	2118
$300,000	or more	1998	2226	2373	2484	2574	2697

Iowa 1 6.0000%

Income At	But less than	1	2	3	4	5	Over 5
$0	$20,000	246	273	291	304	315	330
$20,000	$30,000	407	453	483	506	524	549
$30,000	$40,000	497	554	590	618	640	671
$40,000	$50,000	577	644	686	718	744	780
$50,000	$60,000	651	726	774	810	840	880
$60,000	$70,000	718	801	855	895	927	972
$70,000	$80,000	782	872	930	974	1010	1059
$80,000	$90,000	842	939	1002	1049	1088	1140
$90,000	$100,000	899	1003	1070	1121	1162	1218
$100,000	$120,000	976	1089	1162	1217	1262	1323
$120,000	$140,000	1078	1203	1284	1345	1395	1463
$140,000	$160,000	1175	1312	1400	1467	1521	1595
$160,000	$180,000	1265	1413	1508	1580	1638	1719
$180,000	$200,000	1352	1510	1612	1689	1751	1837
$200,000	$225,000	1443	1612	1722	1804	1871	1962
$225,000	$250,000	1542	1724	1840	1928	2000	2098
$250,000	$275,000	1637	1830	1954	2047	2123	2228
$275,000	$300,000	1728	1932	2063	2162	2243	2353
$300,000	or more	2288	2559	2734	2866	2973	3120

Kansas 1 6.1500%

Income At	But less than	1	2	3	4	5	Over 5
$0	$20,000	354	413	453	483	509	545
$20,000	$30,000	546	637	698	746	785	840
$30,000	$40,000	648	756	828	884	931	996
$40,000	$50,000	736	859	941	1005	1057	1131
$50,000	$60,000	815	951	1042	1113	1171	1253
$60,000	$70,000	887	1035	1134	1211	1274	1363
$70,000	$80,000	953	1112	1219	1301	1369	1465
$80,000	$90,000	1015	1184	1298	1386	1458	1560
$90,000	$100,000	1074	1252	1372	1465	1542	1649
$100,000	$120,000	1152	1343	1472	1571	1654	1769
$120,000	$140,000	1253	1462	1602	1710	1800	1925
$140,000	$160,000	1348	1573	1723	1839	1936	2071
$160,000	$180,000	1436	1675	1835	1959	2062	2205
$180,000	$200,000	1520	1772	1942	2073	2181	2333
$200,000	$225,000	1607	1873	2053	2191	2306	2466
$225,000	$250,000	1700	1982	2172	2318	2440	2610
$250,000	$275,000	1788	2085	2284	2439	2566	2745
$275,000	$300,000	1873	2184	2392	2554	2687	2874
$300,000	or more	2376	2770	3034	3239	3408	3645

Kentucky 4 6.0000%

Income At	But less than	1	2	3	4	5	Over 5
$0	$20,000	235	262	279	293	303	318
$20,000	$30,000	371	414	441	462	479	502
$30,000	$40,000	445	496	529	553	573	601
$40,000	$50,000	509	567	605	633	656	688
$50,000	$60,000	568	632	674	705	731	766
$60,000	$70,000	621	691	736	771	799	837
$70,000	$80,000	670	746	795	832	862	903
$80,000	$90,000	716	797	850	889	921	965
$90,000	$100,000	760	846	901	943	977	1024
$100,000	$120,000	818	911	970	1015	1052	1103
$120,000	$140,000	895	996	1061	1110	1150	1205
$140,000	$160,000	967	1076	1146	1199	1243	1302
$160,000	$180,000	1034	1150	1226	1282	1328	1392
$180,000	$200,000	1098	1221	1301	1361	1410	1477
$200,000	$225,000	1165	1295	1380	1443	1495	1566
$225,000	$250,000	1237	1375	1464	1532	1587	1662
$250,000	$275,000	1305	1451	1545	1616	1674	1754
$275,000	$300,000	1371	1523	1622	1697	1758	1841
$300,000	or more	1764	1960	2086	2182	2260	2367

(Continued)

2014 Optional State Sales Tax Tables *(Continued)*

Income		Louisiana			2	4.0000%		Maine			4	5.5000%		Maryland			4	6.0000%		Massachusetts			4	6.2500%	
$0	$20,000	161	175	184	191	196	204	146	159	167	173	178	184	208	229	244	255	264	276	201	219	230	239	246	255
$20,000	$30,000	267	291	306	318	327	339	246	267	281	291	299	310	343	380	404	422	437	458	317	345	363	376	387	402
$30,000	$40,000	326	356	374	388	399	415	302	328	345	358	368	381	419	464	493	515	533	559	379	413	434	450	463	481
$40,000	$50,000	379	413	435	451	464	482	352	383	402	417	429	445	486	538	572	598	619	648	434	472	496	514	529	549
$50,000	$60,000	427	466	490	509	523	544	398	433	455	472	485	503	547	606	644	673	697	731	483	525	552	573	589	611
$60,000	$70,000	471	514	541	562	578	600	441	479	504	522	537	557	604	668	711	743	770	806	528	574	603	626	643	668
$70,000	$80,000	513	560	589	612	629	654	480	523	550	570	586	608	656	727	773	808	837	877	569	619	651	675	694	720
$80,000	$90,000	552	603	635	659	678	704	518	564	593	615	632	656	706	782	832	870	901	944	608	661	695	721	741	769
$90,000	$100,000	590	644	678	703	724	752	554	603	634	657	676	701	754	835	888	929	962	1008	645	701	737	764	786	815
$100,000	$120,000	640	699	736	764	786	817	603	656	690	715	736	763	818	906	964	1008	1044	1093	694	755	793	822	846	877
$120,000	$140,000	707	772	813	844	868	902	668	727	764	792	815	845	902	1000	1064	1112	1152	1207	759	825	867	899	924	959
$140,000	$160,000	771	841	886	919	946	983	729	793	834	865	889	923	982	1088	1158	1211	1254	1314	819	891	936	970	997	1035
$160,000	$180,000	830	906	954	990	1020	1059	786	856	900	933	960	996	1057	1171	1247	1304	1350	1415	875	952	1000	1036	1066	1106
$180,000	$200,000	887	968	1020	1058	1090	1132	842	916	963	999	1027	1066	1129	1251	1331	1392	1442	1511	929	1009	1061	1099	1130	1173
$200,000	$225,000	946	1033	1089	1130	1163	1209	900	980	1030	1068	1099	1140	1204	1335	1420	1486	1539	1613	985	1070	1125	1165	1198	1243
$225,000	$250,000	1011	1104	1164	1208	1243	1292	963	1049	1103	1143	1176	1220	1286	1426	1517	1587	1644	1723	1045	1136	1193	1236	1271	1319
$250,000	$275,000	1073	1172	1235	1282	1320	1371	1024	1114	1172	1215	1250	1297	1364	1512	1609	1683	1744	1828	1102	1197	1258	1304	1341	1391
$275,000	$300,000	1133	1237	1304	1353	1393	1448	1082	1178	1239	1285	1321	1371	1439	1596	1698	1776	1840	1929	1157	1257	1321	1368	1407	1460
$300,000	or more	1498	1637	1725	1791	1844	1917	1440	1569	1650	1711	1760	1827	1898	2105	2241	2345	2429	2546	1485	1613	1695	1756	1805	1872

Income		Michigan			4	6.0000%		Minnesota			1	6.8750%		Mississippi			1	7.0000%		Missouri			2	4.2250%	
$0	$20,000	226	251	266	278	288	301	235	254	265	274	281	291	414	476	518	550	576	613	172	195	211	223	233	247
$20,000	$30,000	357	395	419	437	452	473	394	426	446	461	473	489	642	739	803	853	893	950	272	309	334	353	368	390
$30,000	$40,000	427	472	501	523	541	565	483	522	547	566	581	601	763	878	955	1014	1062	1129	325	370	400	422	441	466
$40,000	$50,000	488	540	573	598	618	646	562	609	638	660	677	701	868	1000	1087	1154	1209	1285	373	424	457	483	504	534
$50,000	$60,000	543	601	638	665	688	719	636	688	722	746	766	793	963	1109	1205	1279	1340	1425	415	472	509	538	562	594
$60,000	$70,000	594	656	697	727	751	785	703	762	799	826	848	878	1048	1207	1313	1393	1460	1552	454	516	557	588	614	650
$70,000	$80,000	641	708	751	784	810	847	767	831	871	901	925	958	1128	1299	1412	1499	1570	1670	490	557	601	635	663	701
$80,000	$90,000	685	757	803	837	866	904	827	896	940	972	998	1034	1202	1384	1505	1598	1674	1780	524	595	643	679	708	749
$90,000	$100,000	726	802	851	888	918	959	885	959	1005	1040	1068	1106	1272	1465	1593	1690	1771	1883	556	632	682	720	751	794
$100,000	$120,000	782	863	916	956	988	1032	962	1043	1094	1132	1162	1204	1366	1573	1710	1815	1901	2021	599	680	734	775	809	855
$120,000	$140,000	854	944	1001	1044	1079	1127	1065	1155	1212	1254	1288	1333	1488	1713	1862	1977	2071	2202	655	744	803	847	884	935
$140,000	$160,000	923	1019	1081	1127	1165	1217	1163	1262	1324	1370	1407	1457	1602	1845	2005	2129	2230	2371	708	804	867	915	955	1010
$160,000	$180,000	986	1089	1155	1204	1245	1300	1255	1361	1428	1478	1518	1572	1708	1966	2138	2269	2377	2527	757	859	927	979	1021	1080
$180,000	$200,000	1047	1155	1225	1278	1320	1379	1343	1457	1529	1583	1625	1684	1808	2082	2263	2402	2517	2676	804	912	984	1039	1083	1146
$200,000	$225,000	1110	1225	1299	1355	1400	1462	1436	1559	1636	1693	1739	1801	1913	2202	2394	2541	2662	2831	853	968	1043	1101	1149	1215
$225,000	$250,000	1178	1300	1378	1437	1485	1551	1537	1669	1751	1813	1862	1929	2025	2332	2535	2691	2819	2997	905	1027	1108	1169	1220	1290
$250,000	$275,000	1242	1371	1453	1516	1566	1635	1634	1774	1862	1927	1980	2051	2132	2454	2668	2832	2967	3155	955	1084	1169	1233	1287	1360
$275,000	$300,000	1304	1439	1526	1591	1644	1716	1728	1876	1969	2038	2094	2169	2234	2572	2796	2968	3109	3305	1003	1138	1227	1295	1351	1428
$300,000	or more	1676	1848	1959	2042	2109	2202	2303	2502	2627	2720	2795	2896	2842	3272	3557	3775	3955	4205	1292	1464	1578	1665	1737	1836

Income		Nebraska			1	5.5000%		Nevada			5	6.8500%		New Jersey			4,6	7.0000%		New Mexico			1	5.1250%	
$0	$20,000	223	247	262	273	282	294	265	293	311	324	335	350	248	266	278	286	293	302	195	217	231	241	250	262
$20,000	$30,000	371	410	436	455	470	491	412	455	482	503	520	543	413	443	463	477	489	505	337	375	400	419	434	455
$30,000	$40,000	453	502	533	556	575	601	490	541	574	598	618	646	504	542	566	584	599	618	419	467	498	522	541	567
$40,000	$50,000	527	583	619	647	669	699	558	616	653	681	704	735	586	631	659	680	696	719	492	550	587	614	637	668
$50,000	$60,000	594	658	699	730	755	789	619	683	725	755	780	815	661	712	743	767	786	812	561	626	669	701	727	762
$60,000	$70,000	656	727	772	806	834	872	675	745	789	823	850	888	730	786	822	848	869	898	625	698	745	781	810	850
$70,000	$80,000	714	792	841	878	908	949	727	802	850	886	915	955	795	856	895	924	947	978	685	766	818	857	889	933
$80,000	$90,000	769	853	906	946	979	1023	775	855	906	944	975	1018	857	923	964	995	1020	1054	743	831	887	930	965	1013
$90,000	$100,000	822	911	968	1011	1046	1093	821	905	959	999	1032	1077	915	986	1030	1063	1090	1126	798	892	954	1000	1037	1089
$100,000	$120,000	892	990	1052	1098	1136	1188	881	972	1030	1073	1108	1157	994	1071	1119	1155	1184	1224	873	977	1044	1094	1136	1192
$120,000	$140,000	986	1094	1163	1214	1256	1314	961	1059	1122	1170	1208	1260	1098	1184	1238	1278	1310	1353	973	1089	1165	1221	1267	1331
$140,000	$160,000	1075	1193	1268	1324	1370	1433	1036	1141	1209	1260	1301	1357	1197	1291	1349	1393	1428	1476	1069	1197	1280	1343	1393	1463
$160,000	$180,000	1158	1285	1366	1427	1477	1544	1105	1217	1289	1343	1387	1447	1290	1391	1454	1502	1540	1591	1159	1299	1389	1457	1512	1588
$180,000	$200,000	1238	1374	1461	1526	1579	1651	1171	1289	1365	1423	1469	1533	1379	1487	1555	1606	1646	1702	1247	1397	1494	1568	1627	1709
$200,000	$225,000	1322	1467	1560	1630	1687	1764	1239	1365	1445	1506	1555	1622	1473	1588	1661	1716	1759	1818	1340	1502	1606	1685	1750	1838
$225,000	$250,000	1414	1569	1669	1744	1804	1887	1313	1446	1531	1595	1647	1718	1575	1698	1776	1835	1881	1945	1441	1616	1729	1814	1883	1978
$250,000	$275,000	1501	1666	1772	1852	1916	2004	1383	1522	1612	1679	1734	1808	1672	1803	1887	1948	1998	2066	1538	1725	1846	1937	2012	2113
$275,000	$300,000	1585	1760	1872	1956	2024	2117	1450	1596	1690	1760	1817	1895	1766	1905	1993	2058	2111	2182	1633	1832	1960	2057	2136	2245
$300,000	or more	2100	2334	2483	2596	2686	2811	1850	2035	2154	2243	2315	2414	2340	2526	2644	2731	2802	2897	2222	2496	2672	2806	2915	3064

Income		New York			2	4.0000%		North Carolina			2	4.7500%		North Dakota			1	5.0000%		Ohio			1	5.7500%	
$0	$20,000	144	154	161	166	170	175	221	250	270	285	297	314	188	210	225	237	246	259	225	245	258	268	275	286
$20,000	$30,000	238	256	268	276	283	292	350	398	429	452	472	498	295	330	353	370	385	405	371	404	426	442	455	472
$30,000	$40,000	291	313	327	338	346	357	420	477	514	543	566	598	352	394	421	442	459	483	452	493	519	538	554	576
$40,000	$50,000	338	364	380	392	402	415	481	547	589	622	648	685	402	449	481	505	524	552	523	571	601	624	642	667
$50,000	$60,000	382	411	429	443	454	468	536	609	657	693	723	764	447	500	534	561	583	613	589	642	677	702	723	751
$60,000	$70,000	421	453	474	489	501	518	587	667	719	759	791	836	488	545	583	612	636	669	649	708	746	774	797	828
$70,000	$80,000	459	494	516	532	546	564	634	720	777	819	855	903	527	588	628	660	685	721	705	770	811	841	866	900
$80,000	$90,000	494	532	556	573	588	607	678	770	830	876	914	966	562	628	671	704	731	769	758	828	872	905	932	968
$90,000	$100,000	527	568	593	613	628	649	719	817	881	930	970	1025	596	665	711	746	775	815	809	883	930	965	994	1033
$100,000	$120,000	572	617	645	665	682	705	775	881	950	1002	1045	1104	641	715	764	802	833	876	877	958	1009	1047	1078	1120
$120,000	$140,000	632	681	712	735	754	779	848	964	1039	1097	1144	1209	700	781	835	876	909	956	967	1056	1112	1155	1189	1235
$140,000	$160,000	689	743	776	802	822	849	917	1042	1124	1186	1236	1307	755	842	900	944	981	1031	1052	1149	1210	1256	1294	1344
$160,000	$180,000	742	800	837	864	886	915	981	1114	1202	1268	1323	1398	806	899	961	1008	1047	1101	1132	1236	1302	1352	1392	1446
$180,000	$200,000	793	855	894	923	947	978	1041	1183	1276	1347	1404	1484	855	954	1019	1069	1110	1167	1208	1319	1390	1443	1485	1544
$200,000	$225,000	847	913	955	986	1011	1045	1105	1256	1354	1429	1490	1575	906	1010	1079	1132	1176	1236	1288	1407	1482	1539	1584	1646
$225,000	$250,000	905	976	1021	1054	1081	1117	1174	1334	1438	1518	1583	1673	961	1071	1144	1201	1247	1311	1375	1501	1582	1642	1691	1758
$250,000	$275,000	961	1036	1084	1119	1148	1186	1239	1407	1518	1602	1671	1766	1013	1129	1206	1265	1314	1381	1457	1592	1677	1741	1793	1864
$275,000	$300,000	1014	1094	1144	1182	1212	1253	1301	1478	1594	1683	1755	1855	1063	1185	1265	1327	1378	1448	1537	1679	1769	1837	1891	1966
$300,000	or more	1342	1449	1516	1566	1607	1661	1676	1905	2054	2168	2261	2390	1362	1517	1619	1698	1763	1853	2023	2210	2330	2419	2491	2589

2014 Optional State Sales Tax Tables

Income	Oklahoma			1	4.5000%	
$0 $20,000	243	279	303	322	338	359
$20,000 $30,000	379	435	473	502	526	560
$30,000 $40,000	452	519	564	598	627	667
$40,000 $50,000	515	591	642	682	714	760
$50,000 $60,000	572	657	713	757	793	844
$60,000 $70,000	624	716	778	826	865	920
$70,000 $80,000	672	771	838	889	931	990
$80,000 $90,000	717	823	894	948	993	1056
$90,000 $100,000	760	871	946	1004	1052	1119
$100,000 $120,000	817	936	1017	1079	1130	1202
$120,000 $140,000	891	1022	1109	1177	1233	1311
$140,000 $160,000	960	1101	1195	1268	1328	1412
$160,000 $180,000	1025	1175	1275	1353	1417	1507
$180,000 $200,000	1086	1245	1351	1433	1501	1596
$200,000 $225,000	1150	1318	1431	1518	1589	1690
$225,000 $250,000	1219	1397	1516	1608	1684	1790
$250,000 $275,000	1284	1471	1597	1694	1774	1886
$275,000 $300,000	1347	1543	1674	1776	1860	1977
$300,000 or more	1721	1970	2137	2266	2373	2522

Income	Pennsylvania			1	6.0000%	
$0 $20,000	194	210	220	228	234	243
$20,000 $30,000	319	346	363	376	386	400
$30,000 $40,000	388	421	442	458	471	488
$40,000 $50,000	449	488	512	530	545	566
$50,000 $60,000	505	548	576	597	614	637
$60,000 $70,000	557	605	635	658	677	702
$70,000 $80,000	605	657	690	715	736	763
$80,000 $90,000	650	707	743	770	791	821
$90,000 $100,000	693	754	792	821	844	876
$100,000 $120,000	752	817	859	890	916	950
$120,000 $140,000	829	901	947	982	1010	1048
$140,000 $160,000	901	980	1031	1068	1099	1141
$160,000 $180,000	969	1054	1109	1150	1182	1228
$180,000 $200,000	1034	1125	1183	1227	1262	1311
$200,000 $225,000	1103	1200	1262	1309	1346	1398
$225,000 $250,000	1177	1281	1347	1397	1438	1493
$250,000 $275,000	1248	1358	1429	1482	1524	1583
$275,000 $300,000	1316	1432	1507	1563	1608	1670
$300,000 or more	1731	1886	1985	2059	2119	2201

Income	Rhode Island			4	7.0000%	
$0 $20,000	255	278	293	304	313	325
$20,000 $30,000	397	433	455	472	486	504
$30,000 $40,000	472	515	541	562	578	600
$40,000 $50,000	537	586	616	639	658	683
$50,000 $60,000	596	650	684	709	730	758
$60,000 $70,000	650	708	745	773	795	825
$70,000 $80,000	699	762	802	832	855	888
$80,000 $90,000	745	812	855	886	912	947
$90,000 $100,000	789	860	905	938	965	1002
$100,000 $120,000	847	923	971	1007	1036	1076
$120,000 $140,000	923	1006	1059	1098	1130	1173
$140,000 $160,000	994	1084	1140	1182	1216	1263
$160,000 $180,000	1060	1155	1216	1261	1297	1346
$180,000 $200,000	1123	1224	1287	1335	1374	1426
$200,000 $225,000	1188	1295	1362	1413	1453	1509
$225,000 $250,000	1258	1371	1443	1496	1539	1598
$250,000 $275,000	1325	1444	1519	1575	1620	1682
$275,000 $300,000	1388	1513	1592	1651	1698	1763
$300,000 or more	1768	1926	2027	2102	2162	2245

Income	South Carolina			2	6.0000%	
$0 $20,000	234	257	272	284	293	305
$20,000 $30,000	386	425	450	469	484	505
$30,000 $40,000	470	519	549	572	591	616
$40,000 $50,000	545	601	637	664	685	715
$50,000 $60,000	614	677	718	748	772	805
$60,000 $70,000	677	747	792	825	852	888
$70,000 $80,000	736	812	861	897	926	966
$80,000 $90,000	792	874	926	965	997	1040
$90,000 $100,000	845	933	988	1030	1064	1110
$100,000 $120,000	917	1012	1072	1118	1154	1204
$120,000 $140,000	1011	1117	1183	1233	1274	1329
$140,000 $160,000	1101	1216	1288	1343	1387	1447
$160,000 $180,000	1185	1308	1387	1445	1493	1557
$180,000 $200,000	1265	1397	1481	1544	1594	1663
$200,000 $225,000	1350	1490	1580	1647	1701	1775
$225,000 $250,000	1441	1592	1687	1759	1817	1896
$250,000 $275,000	1528	1688	1790	1866	1927	2011
$275,000 $300,000	1613	1781	1889	1969	2034	2122
$300,000 or more	2127	2350	2492	2599	2684	2801

Income	South Dakota			1	4.0000%	
$0 $20,000	235	271	296	314	330	351
$20,000 $30,000	366	423	461	490	514	548
$30,000 $40,000	437	505	550	584	613	653
$40,000 $50,000	498	575	627	666	699	744
$50,000 $60,000	553	639	696	740	776	827
$60,000 $70,000	603	697	759	807	846	901
$70,000 $80,000	649	750	817	869	911	971
$80,000 $90,000	693	800	872	927	972	1035
$90,000 $100,000	733	848	923	982	1030	1097
$100,000 $120,000	788	911	992	1055	1106	1178
$120,000 $140,000	860	993	1082	1151	1207	1285
$140,000 $160,000	927	1071	1167	1240	1301	1385
$160,000 $180,000	989	1143	1245	1323	1388	1478
$180,000 $200,000	1048	1211	1319	1402	1471	1566
$200,000 $225,000	1109	1282	1396	1485	1557	1658
$225,000 $250,000	1175	1358	1480	1573	1650	1757
$250,000 $275,000	1238	1431	1559	1657	1738	1851
$275,000 $300,000	1298	1500	1634	1737	1822	1941
$300,000 or more	1657	1915	2086	2218	2326	2478

Income	Tennessee			2	7.0000%	
$0 $20,000	366	416	450	475	496	525
$20,000 $30,000	579	658	711	751	784	830
$30,000 $40,000	693	789	852	900	940	995
$40,000 $50,000	793	903	975	1030	1075	1138
$50,000 $60,000	884	1006	1086	1147	1198	1268
$60,000 $70,000	967	1099	1187	1254	1309	1386
$70,000 $80,000	1043	1187	1281	1354	1413	1495
$80,000 $90,000	1115	1268	1369	1447	1510	1598
$90,000 $100,000	1183	1345	1453	1535	1602	1695
$100,000 $120,000	1274	1449	1564	1652	1725	1825
$120,000 $140,000	1393	1584	1710	1807	1886	1996
$140,000 $160,000	1505	1712	1848	1952	2037	2156
$160,000 $180,000	1609	1830	1975	2086	2178	2305
$180,000 $200,000	1708	1942	2096	2214	2311	2446
$200,000 $225,000	1812	2060	2223	2348	2451	2594
$225,000 $250,000	1923	2186	2360	2493	2602	2753
$250,000 $275,000	2029	2307	2490	2630	2745	2904
$275,000 $300,000	2131	2422	2614	2761	2882	3049
$300,000 or more	2740	3114	3361	3550	3705	3920

Income	Texas			1	6.2500%	
$0 $20,000	254	283	301	315	326	342
$20,000 $30,000	419	466	497	520	539	565
$30,000 $40,000	510	568	606	634	657	688
$40,000 $50,000	591	658	702	735	762	799
$50,000 $60,000	664	741	790	828	858	899
$60,000 $70,000	732	817	872	913	946	992
$70,000 $80,000	796	888	948	993	1029	1079
$80,000 $90,000	856	956	1020	1068	1107	1161
$90,000 $100,000	913	1020	1088	1140	1181	1239
$100,000 $120,000	991	1106	1180	1236	1282	1344
$120,000 $140,000	1092	1220	1302	1364	1414	1483
$140,000 $160,000	1189	1328	1417	1485	1540	1615
$160,000 $180,000	1279	1429	1525	1598	1657	1739
$180,000 $200,000	1365	1525	1629	1707	1770	1857
$200,000 $225,000	1456	1627	1738	1821	1888	1981
$225,000 $250,000	1555	1738	1856	1945	2017	2116
$250,000 $275,000	1649	1843	1968	2063	2139	2245
$275,000 $300,000	1739	1944	2077	2177	2258	2369
$300,000 or more	2292	2564	2740	2872	2979	3127

Income	Utah			2	4.7000%	
$0 $20,000	236	267	288	304	317	335
$20,000 $30,000	376	426	459	484	504	533
$30,000 $40,000	452	512	551	581	606	640
$40,000 $50,000	518	587	632	666	695	734
$50,000 $60,000	578	655	705	743	775	819
$60,000 $70,000	633	717	772	814	848	896
$70,000 $80,000	684	774	834	879	917	968
$80,000 $90,000	732	829	892	941	981	1036
$90,000 $100,000	777	880	947	999	1041	1100
$100,000 $120,000	838	948	1021	1077	1123	1186
$120,000 $140,000	917	1039	1118	1179	1229	1299
$140,000 $160,000	992	1123	1210	1276	1330	1404
$160,000 $180,000	1062	1202	1294	1365	1423	1503
$180,000 $200,000	1128	1277	1375	1450	1511	1596
$200,000 $225,000	1197	1356	1460	1539	1604	1695
$225,000 $250,000	1272	1440	1551	1635	1705	1800
$250,000 $275,000	1343	1521	1638	1727	1800	1901
$275,000 $300,000	1412	1598	1721	1814	1891	1997
$300,000 or more	1822	2063	2221	2342	2441	2578

Income	Vermont			1	6.0000%	
$0 $20,000	163	174	181	186	190	195
$20,000 $30,000	253	270	281	288	294	303
$30,000 $40,000	301	321	334	343	350	360
$40,000 $50,000	343	366	380	390	399	410
$50,000 $60,000	380	406	422	433	442	455
$60,000 $70,000	415	442	459	472	482	496
$70,000 $80,000	446	476	494	508	519	533
$80,000 $90,000	476	507	527	541	553	569
$90,000 $100,000	503	537	558	573	585	602
$100,000 $120,000	540	576	599	615	628	646
$120,000 $140,000	589	628	652	670	685	704
$140,000 $160,000	634	677	703	722	738	758
$160,000 $180,000	676	721	749	770	786	809
$180,000 $200,000	716	764	793	815	833	856
$200,000 $225,000	758	808	840	863	881	906
$225,000 $250,000	803	856	889	914	933	959
$250,000 $275,000	845	901	936	962	982	1010
$275,000 $300,000	886	944	981	1008	1029	1059
$300,000 or more	1128	1203	1249	1283	1311	1348

Income	Virginia			2	4.3000%	
$0 $20,000	178	203	218	230	240	254
$20,000 $30,000	274	310	334	352	367	388
$30,000 $40,000	324	367	395	417	434	459
$40,000 $50,000	368	416	448	472	492	520
$50,000 $60,000	407	460	495	522	544	574
$60,000 $70,000	442	500	538	567	591	624
$70,000 $80,000	475	537	578	609	634	670
$80,000 $90,000	506	572	615	648	675	712
$90,000 $100,000	534	604	650	685	713	753
$100,000 $120,000	573	647	696	733	764	806
$120,000 $140,000	623	704	757	797	830	876
$140,000 $160,000	670	757	813	857	892	941
$160,000 $180,000	714	805	866	912	949	1001
$180,000 $200,000	755	852	915	964	1003	1058
$200,000 $225,000	798	900	967	1018	1060	1118
$225,000 $250,000	844	952	1022	1076	1121	1182
$250,000 $275,000	887	1001	1075	1132	1178	1242
$275,000 $300,000	929	1047	1125	1184	1233	1300
$300,000 or more	1178	1326	1424	1498	1559	1643

Income	Washington			1	6.5000%	
$0 $20,000	260	287	304	316	327	341
$20,000 $30,000	431	476	504	526	543	567
$30,000 $40,000	526	581	616	642	663	693
$40,000 $50,000	611	674	715	746	770	804
$50,000 $60,000	688	760	806	840	868	907
$60,000 $70,000	760	839	889	928	959	1001
$70,000 $80,000	826	912	968	1009	1043	1090
$80,000 $90,000	890	982	1042	1087	1123	1173
$90,000 $100,000	950	1049	1112	1160	1199	1252
$100,000 $120,000	1030	1138	1207	1259	1302	1360
$120,000 $140,000	1138	1257	1333	1391	1437	1502
$140,000 $160,000	1239	1369	1452	1515	1566	1636
$160,000 $180,000	1334	1474	1563	1631	1686	1762
$180,000 $200,000	1424	1574	1670	1743	1801	1882
$200,000 $225,000	1520	1680	1783	1860	1923	2009
$225,000 $250,000	1624	1795	1905	1987	2055	2147
$250,000 $275,000	1723	1904	2021	2109	2180	2278
$275,000 $300,000	1818	2010	2133	2226	2301	2405
$300,000 or more	2401	2655	2819	2942	3042	3179

Income	West Virginia			2	6.0000%	
$0 $20,000	250	279	297	311	323	338
$20,000 $30,000	413	461	492	516	535	561
$30,000 $40,000	503	563	601	630	653	686
$40,000 $50,000	584	653	697	731	758	796
$50,000 $60,000	657	735	786	824	855	897
$60,000 $70,000	725	811	867	909	943	991
$70,000 $80,000	789	883	943	989	1027	1078
$80,000 $90,000	849	950	1016	1065	1105	1161
$90,000 $100,000	906	1014	1084	1137	1180	1239
$100,000 $120,000	983	1101	1177	1234	1281	1345
$120,000 $140,000	1085	1215	1299	1363	1415	1486
$140,000 $160,000	1181	1323	1415	1485	1541	1619
$160,000 $180,000	1271	1425	1524	1599	1660	1744
$180,000 $200,000	1358	1522	1628	1708	1773	1863
$200,000 $225,000	1449	1624	1738	1823	1893	1989
$225,000 $250,000	1548	1735	1857	1948	2023	2125
$250,000 $275,000	1642	1841	1970	2068	2147	2256
$275,000 $300,000	1733	1944	2080	2183	2266	2381
$300,000 or more	2289	2569	2750	2886	2998	3151

Income	Wisconsin			1	5.0000%	
$0 $20,000	212	233	247	257	266	277
$20,000 $30,000	347	382	405	422	436	455
$30,000 $40,000	421	465	493	513	530	553
$40,000 $50,000	487	538	570	594	614	640
$50,000 $60,000	547	604	641	668	690	720
$60,000 $70,000	603	666	706	736	760	793
$70,000 $80,000	654	723	767	799	826	862
$80,000 $90,000	703	777	824	859	888	927
$90,000 $100,000	750	828	878	916	946	988
$100,000 $120,000	812	898	952	993	1026	1071
$120,000 $140,000	895	989	1049	1094	1130	1180
$140,000 $160,000	973	1075	1141	1190	1229	1283
$160,000 $180,000	1046	1156	1226	1279	1322	1380
$180,000 $200,000	1115	1233	1308	1365	1410	1472
$200,000 $225,000	1189	1314	1395	1455	1503	1570
$225,000 $250,000	1268	1402	1488	1552	1604	1675
$250,000 $275,000	1344	1486	1577	1645	1700	1776
$275,000 $300,000	1416	1567	1663	1735	1793	1872
$300,000 or more	1860	2059	2186	2281	2357	2462

Income	Wyoming			1	4.0000%	
$0 $20,000	160	175	184	191	197	204
$20,000 $30,000	266	290	305	317	326	339
$30,000 $40,000	324	354	372	387	398	414
$40,000 $50,000	376	410	432	449	462	480
$50,000 $60,000	423	462	487	506	520	541
$60,000 $70,000	467	510	537	558	574	597
$70,000 $80,000	508	555	585	607	625	649
$80,000 $90,000	547	597	629	653	673	699
$90,000 $100,000	583	637	671	697	718	746
$100,000 $120,000	633	691	729	757	779	810
$120,000 $140,000	698	763	804	835	860	894
$140,000 $160,000	760	831	876	909	937	974
$160,000 $180,000	818	894	943	979	1008	1048
$180,000 $200,000	874	955	1007	1046	1077	1119
$200,000 $225,000	932	1019	1074	1116	1149	1195
$225,000 $250,000	996	1089	1148	1192	1227	1276
$250,000 $275,000	1056	1155	1217	1264	1302	1354
$275,000 $300,000	1114	1219	1285	1334	1374	1429
$300,000 or more	1470	1608	1696	1762	1815	1887

Note. Residents of **Alaska** do not have a state sales tax, but should follow the instructions on the next pages to determine their local sales tax amount.

1. Use the Ratio Method to determine your local sales tax deduction, then add that to the appropriate amount in the state table. Your state sales tax rate is provided next to the state name.
2. Follow the instructions on the next pages to determine your local sales tax deduction, then add that to the appropriate amount in the state table.
3. The California table includes the 1.25% uniform local sales tax rate in addition to the 6.25% state sales tax rate for a total of 7.50%. Some California localities impose a larger local sales tax. Taxpayers who reside in those jurisdictions should use the Ratio Method to determine their local sales tax deduction, then add that to the appropriate amount in the state table. The denominator of the correct ratio is 7.50%, and the numerator is the total sales tax rate minus the 7.50% tax rate.
4. This state does not have a local general sales tax, so the amount in the state table is the only amount to be deducted.
5. The Nevada table includes the 2.25% uniform local sales tax rate in addition to the 4.6000% state sales tax rate for a total of 6.85%. Some Nevada localities impose a larger local sales tax. Taxpayers who reside in those jurisdictions should use the Ratio Method to determine their local sales tax deduction, then add that to the appropriate amount in the state table. The denominator of the correct ratio is 6.85%, and the numerator is the total sales tax rate minus the 6.85% tax rate.
6. Residents of Salem County, New Jersey should deduct only half of the amount in the state table.
7. The 4.0% rate for Hawaii is actually an excise tax but is treated as a sales tax for purpose of this deduction.

Which Optional Local Sales Tax Table Should I Use?

IF you live in the state of...	AND you live in...	THEN use Local Table...
Alaska	Any locality	C
Arizona	Chandler, Glendale, Gilbert, Mesa, Peoria, Phoenix, Scottsdale, Tempe, Tucson, Yuma, or any other locality	B
Arkansas	Any locality	B
Colorado	Adams County, Arapahoe County, Boulder County, Centennial, Colorado Springs, Denver City/Denver County, El Paso County, Larimer County, Pueblo County, or any other locality	A
	Greeley, Jefferson County, Lakewood, Longmont or Pueblo City	B
	Arvada, Boulder, Fort Collins, Thornton, or Westminster	C
Georgia	Any locality	B
Illinois	City of Aurora	B
	Any other locality	A
Louisiana	Ascension Parish, Bossier Parish, Caddo Parish, Calcasieu Parish, East Baton Rouge Parish, Iberia Parish, Jefferson Parish, Lafayette Parish, Lafourche Parish, Livingston Parish, Orleans Parish, Ouachita Parish, Rapides Parish, St. Bernard Parish, St. Landry Parish, St. Tammany Parish, Tangipahoa Parish, or Terrebonne Parish	C
	Any other locality	B
Missouri	Any locality	B
New York	Counties: Albany, Allegany, Broome, Cattaraugus, Cayuga, Chautauqua, Chemung, Chenango, Clinton, Columbia, Cortland, Delaware, Dutchess, Erie, Essex, Franklin, Fulton, Genesee, Greene, Hamilton, Herkimer, Jefferson, Lewis, Livingston, Madison, Monroe, Montgomery, Nassau, Niagara, Oneida, Onondaga, Ontario, Orange, Orleans, Oswego, Otsego, Putnam, Rensselaer, Rockland, St. Lawrence, Saratoga, Schenectady, Schoharie, Schuyler, Seneca, Steuben, Suffolk, Sullivan, Tioga, Tompkins, Ulster, Warren, Washington, Wayne, Westchester, Wyoming, or Yates New York City or Norwich City	B
	Any other locality	D*
North Carolina	Any locality	A
South Carolina	Aiken County, Horry County, Lexington County, Newberry County, Orangeburg County, York County, or Myrtle Beach	A
	Bamberg County, Charleston County, Cherokee County, Chesterfield County, Darlington County, Dillon County, Florence County, Hampton County, Jasper County, Lee County, Marion County, Marlboro County, or any other locality	B
Tennessee	Any locality	B
Utah	Any locality	A
Virginia	Any locality	B
West Virginia	Any locality	B

2014 Optional Local Sales Tax Tables for Certain Local Jurisdictions

Income (At least)	But less than	A: 1	A: 2	A: 3	A: 4	A: 5	A: Over 5	B: 1	B: 2	B: 3	B: 4	B: 5	B: Over 5
		Local Table A						**Local Table B**					
$0	$20,000	38	43	46	48	50	52	47	53	58	62	64	68
20,000	30,000	60	66	71	74	77	81	71	82	89	94	99	105
30,000	40,000	71	79	84	88	91	96	84	97	105	111	117	124
40,000	50,000	81	90	96	100	104	109	96	110	119	126	132	140
50,000	60,000	89	99	106	111	115	121	106	122	132	140	146	155
60,000	70,000	97	108	115	121	125	131	115	132	143	152	159	169
70,000	80,000	105	117	124	130	135	141	124	142	154	163	170	181
80,000	90,000	112	124	132	139	144	150	132	151	164	173	181	192
90,000	100,000	118	131	140	147	152	159	139	159	173	183	192	203
100,000	120,000	127	141	150	157	163	171	149	171	185	196	205	218
120,000	140,000	138	154	164	171	178	186	162	186	201	213	223	237
140,000	160,000	149	166	176	184	191	200	175	200	216	229	240	254
160,000	180,000	159	176	188	197	204	213	186	212	230	244	255	271
180,000	200,000	168	187	199	208	216	226	196	225	243	258	270	286
200,000	225,000	178	198	210	220	228	239	208	237	257	272	285	302
225,000	250,000	189	209	223	233	241	253	220	251	272	288	301	319
250,000	275,000	199	220	234	245	254	266	231	264	286	303	316	336
275,000	300,000	208	231	246	257	266	279	242	276	299	317	331	351
300,000	or more	265	294	313	327	338	354	306	349	378	400	418	444

Income (At least)	But less than	C: 1	C: 2	C: 3	C: 4	C: 5	C: Over 5	D: 1	D: 2	D: 3	D: 4	D: 5	D: Over 5
		Local Table C						**Local Table D**					
$0	$20,000	56	64	69	73	77	81	36	39	40	42	43	44
20,000	30,000	87	100	108	114	120	127	60	64	67	69	71	73
30,000	40,000	104	119	129	136	143	151	73	78	82	85	87	89
40,000	50,000	119	136	147	156	163	173	85	91	95	98	101	104
50,000	60,000	132	151	163	173	181	192	96	103	107	111	114	117
60,000	70,000	144	164	178	189	197	209	105	113	119	122	125	130
70,000	80,000	155	177	192	203	212	225	115	124	129	133	137	141
80,000	90,000	165	189	205	217	227	240	124	133	139	143	147	152
90,000	100,000	175	200	217	230	240	255	132	142	148	153	157	162
100,000	120,000	188	215	233	247	258	274	143	154	161	166	171	176
120,000	140,000	205	235	254	269	282	299	158	170	178	184	189	195
140,000	160,000	221	253	274	290	304	322	172	186	194	201	206	212
160,000	180,000	236	270	293	310	324	344	186	200	209	216	222	229
180,000	200,000	250	286	310	328	343	364	198	214	224	231	237	245
200,000	225,000	265	303	329	348	364	386	212	228	239	247	253	261
225,000	250,000	281	322	348	369	385	409	226	244	255	264	270	279
250,000	275,000	296	339	367	388	406	431	240	259	271	280	287	297
275,000	300,000	311	355	385	407	426	452	254	274	286	296	303	313
300,000	or more	397	454	492	520	544	577	336	362	379	392	402	415

Appendix B

Tax Forms

(Tax forms can be obtained from the IRS website: **www.irs.gov**)

Form **1040**

Department of the Treasury—Internal Revenue Service   (99)

U.S. Individual Income Tax Return   **2014**   OMB No. 1545-0074   IRS Use Only—Do not write or staple in this space.

For the year Jan. 1–Dec. 31, 2014, or other tax year beginning _____ , 2014, ending _____ , 20____   See separate instructions.

| Your first name and initial | Last name | Your social security number |

| If a joint return, spouse's first name and initial | Last name | Spouse's social security number |

| Home address (number and street). If you have a P.O. box, see instructions. | Apt. no. | ▲ Make sure the SSN(s) above and on line 6c are correct. |

City, town or post office, state, and ZIP code. If you have a foreign address, also complete spaces below (see instructions).

| Foreign country name | Foreign province/state/county | Foreign postal code |

Presidential Election Campaign
Check here if you, or your spouse if filing jointly, want $3 to go to this fund. Checking a box below will not change your tax or refund.   ☐ You   ☐ Spouse

Filing Status

Check only one box.

1 ☐ Single
2 ☐ Married filing jointly (even if only one had income)
3 ☐ Married filing separately. Enter spouse's SSN above and full name here. ▶
4 ☐ Head of household (with qualifying person). (See instructions.) If the qualifying person is a child but not your dependent, enter this child's name here. ▶
5 ☐ Qualifying widow(er) with dependent child

Exemptions

6a ☐ **Yourself.** If someone can claim you as a dependent, **do not** check box 6a . . . . . }
b ☐ **Spouse** . . . .

c Dependents:

(1) First name Last name	(2) Dependent's social security number	(3) Dependent's relationship to you	(4) ✓ if child under age 17 qualifying for child tax credit (see instructions)
			☐
			☐
			☐
			☐

If more than four dependents, see instructions and check here ▶ ☐

Boxes checked on 6a and 6b ____
No. of children on 6c who:
• lived with you ____
• did not live with you due to divorce or separation (see instructions) ____
Dependents on 6c not entered above ____
Add numbers on lines above ▶ ____

d Total number of exemptions claimed . . . .

Income

Attach Form(s) W-2 here. Also attach Forms W-2G and 1099-R if tax was withheld.

If you did not get a W-2, see instructions.

7	Wages, salaries, tips, etc. Attach Form(s) W-2	7	
8a	**Taxable** interest. Attach Schedule B if required	8a	
b	**Tax-exempt** interest. **Do not** include on line 8a . . .	8b	
9a	Ordinary dividends. Attach Schedule B if required	9a	
b	Qualified dividends	9b	
10	Taxable refunds, credits, or offsets of state and local income taxes	10	
11	Alimony received	11	
12	Business income or (loss). Attach Schedule C or C-EZ	12	
13	Capital gain or (loss). Attach Schedule D if required. If not required, check here ▶ ☐	13	
14	Other gains or (losses). Attach Form 4797	14	
15a	IRA distributions . 15a ____ b Taxable amount . . .	15b	
16a	Pensions and annuities 16a ____ b Taxable amount . . .	16b	
17	Rental real estate, royalties, partnerships, S corporations, trusts, etc. Attach Schedule E	17	
18	Farm income or (loss). Attach Schedule F	18	
19	Unemployment compensation	19	
20a	Social security benefits 20a ____ b Taxable amount . . .	20b	
21	Other income. List type and amount _____	21	
22	Combine the amounts in the far right column for lines 7 through 21. This is your **total income** ▶	22	

Adjusted Gross Income

23	Educator expenses	23		
24	Certain business expenses of reservists, performing artists, and fee-basis government officials. Attach Form 2106 or 2106-EZ	24		
25	Health savings account deduction. Attach Form 8889 .	25		
26	Moving expenses. Attach Form 3903	26		
27	Deductible part of self-employment tax. Attach Schedule SE .	27		
28	Self-employed SEP, SIMPLE, and qualified plans . .	28		
29	Self-employed health insurance deduction	29		
30	Penalty on early withdrawal of savings	30		
31a	Alimony paid b Recipient's SSN ▶ _____	31a		
32	IRA deduction	32		
33	Student loan interest deduction	33		
34	Tuition and fees. Attach Form 8917	34		
35	Domestic production activities deduction. Attach Form 8903	35		
36	Add lines 23 through 35	36	
37	Subtract line 36 from line 22. This is your **adjusted gross income** . . . . . ▶	37	

For Disclosure, Privacy Act, and Paperwork Reduction Act Notice, see separate instructions.   Cat. No. 11320B   Form **1040** (2014)

Form 1040 (2014)   Page **2**

	38	Amount from line 37 (adjusted gross income)	38	
Tax and Credits	39a	Check if: ☐ **You** were born before January 2, 1950, ☐ **Spouse** was born before January 2, 1950, ☐ Blind. ☐ Blind. } **Total boxes** checked ▶ **39a**		
	b	If your spouse itemizes on a separate return or you were a dual-status alien, check here▶ **39b**☐		

Standard Deduction for—
- People who check any box on line 39a or 39b **or** who can be claimed as a dependent, see instructions.
- All others:
Single or Married filing separately, $6,200
Married filing jointly or Qualifying widow(er), $12,400
Head of household, $9,100

	40	**Itemized deductions** (from Schedule A) **or** your **standard deduction** (see left margin) . .	40	
	41	Subtract line 40 from line 38	41	
	42	**Exemptions.** If line 38 is $152,525 or less, multiply $3,950 by the number on line 6d. Otherwise, see instructions	42	
	43	**Taxable income.** Subtract line 42 from line 41. If line 42 is more than line 41, enter -0- . .	43	
	44	**Tax** (see instructions). Check if any from: **a** ☐ Form(s) 8814 **b** ☐ Form 4972 **c** ☐	44	
	45	**Alternative minimum tax** (see instructions). Attach Form 6251	45	
	46	Excess advance premium tax credit repayment. Attach Form 8962	46	
	47	Add lines 44, 45, and 46 . . . . ▶	47	
	48	Foreign tax credit. Attach Form 1116 if required . . .	**48**	
	49	Credit for child and dependent care expenses. Attach Form 2441	**49**	
	50	Education credits from Form 8863, line 19	**50**	
	51	Retirement savings contributions credit. Attach Form 8880	**51**	
	52	Child tax credit. Attach Schedule 8812, if required . .	**52**	
	53	Residential energy credits. Attach Form 5695	**53**	
	54	Other credits from Form: **a** ☐ 3800 **b** ☐ 8801 **c** ☐	**54**	
	55	Add lines 48 through 54. These are your **total credits**	55	
	56	Subtract line 55 from line 47. If line 55 is more than line 47, enter -0- . . . . . ▶	56	
Other Taxes	57	Self-employment tax. Attach Schedule SE	57	
	58	Unreported social security and Medicare tax from Form: **a** ☐ 4137 **b** ☐ 8919 . .	58	
	59	Additional tax on IRAs, other qualified retirement plans, etc. Attach Form 5329 if required . .	59	
	60a	Household employment taxes from Schedule H	60a	
	b	First-time homebuyer credit repayment. Attach Form 5405 if required	60b	
	61	Health care: individual responsibility (see instructions) Full-year coverage ☐	61	
	62	Taxes from: **a** ☐ Form 8959 **b** ☐ Form 8960 **c** ☐ Instructions; enter code(s)	62	
	63	Add lines 56 through 62. This is your **total tax** . . . . ▶	63	
Payments	64	Federal income tax withheld from Forms W-2 and 1099 . .	**64**	
	65	2014 estimated tax payments and amount applied from 2013 return	**65**	
	66a	**Earned income credit (EIC)**	**66a**	
	b	Nontaxable combat pay election **66b**		
	67	Additional child tax credit. Attach Schedule 8812	**67**	
	68	American opportunity credit from Form 8863, line 8 . . .	**68**	
	69	Net premium tax credit. Attach Form 8962	**69**	
	70	Amount paid with request for extension to file	**70**	
	71	Excess social security and tier 1 RRTA tax withheld	**71**	
	72	Credit for federal tax on fuels. Attach Form 4136	**72**	
	73	Credits from Form: **a** ☐ 2439 **b** ☐ Reserved **c** ☐ Reserved **d** ☐	**73**	
	74	Add lines 64, 65, 66a, and 67 through 73. These are your **total payments** . . . . . ▶	74	
Refund	75	If line 74 is more than line 63, subtract line 63 from line 74. This is the amount you **overpaid**	75	
	76a	Amount of line 75 you want **refunded to you.** If Form 8888 is attached, check here . ▶☐	76a	
	b	Routing number ☐☐☐☐☐☐☐☐☐ ▶**c** Type: ☐ Checking ☐ Savings		
	d	Account number ☐☐☐☐☐☐☐☐☐☐☐☐☐☐☐☐☐		
	77	Amount of line 75 you want **applied to your 2015 estimated tax** ▶ **77**		
Amount You Owe	78	**Amount you owe.** Subtract line 74 from line 63. For details on how to pay, see instructions ▶	78	
	79	Estimated tax penalty (see instructions) **79**		

If you have a qualifying child, attach Schedule EIC.

Direct deposit? See instructions. ▶

Third Party Designee	Do you want to allow another person to discuss this return with the IRS (see instructions)? ☐ **Yes.** Complete below. ☐ **No**		
	Designee's name ▶	Phone no. ▶	Personal identification number (PIN) ▶ ☐☐☐☐☐

Sign Here

Joint return? See instructions. Keep a copy for your records.

Under penalties of perjury, I declare that I have examined this return and accompanying schedules and statements, and to the best of my knowledge and belief, they are true, correct, and complete. Declaration of preparer (other than taxpayer) is based on all information of which preparer has any knowledge.

Your signature	Date	Your occupation	Daytime phone number
Spouse's signature. If a joint return, **both** must sign.	Date	Spouse's occupation	If the IRS sent you an Identity Protection PIN, enter it here (see inst.) ☐☐☐☐☐☐

Paid Preparer Use Only

Print/Type preparer's name	Preparer's signature	Date	Check ☐ if self-employed	PTIN
Firm's name ▶			Firm's EIN ▶	
Firm's address ▶			Phone no.	

SCHEDULE C (Form 1040) Department of the Treasury Internal Revenue Service (99)	**Profit or Loss From Business** (Sole Proprietorship) ▶ Information about Schedule C and its separate instructions is at *www.irs.gov/schedulec*. ▶ **Attach to Form 1040, 1040NR, or 1041; partnerships generally must file Form 1065.**	OMB No. 1545-0074 **2014** Attachment Sequence No. **09**

Name of proprietor	Social security number (SSN)

A Principal business or profession, including product or service (see instructions)

B Enter code from instructions ▶

C Business name. If no separate business name, leave blank.

D Employer ID number (EIN), (see instr.)

E Business address (including suite or room no.) ▶ _____

   City, town or post office, state, and ZIP code

F Accounting method: **(1)** ☐ Cash   **(2)** ☐ Accrual   **(3)** ☐ Other (specify) ▶ _____

G Did you "materially participate" in the operation of this business during 2014? If "No," see instructions for limit on losses   ☐ Yes   ☐ No

H If you started or acquired this business during 2014, check here   .   .   .   .   ▶ ☐

I Did you make any payments in 2014 that would require you to file Form(s) 1099? (see instructions)   .   .   .   .   .   ☐ Yes   ☐ No

J If "Yes," did you or will you file required Forms 1099?   .   .   .   .   ☐ Yes   ☐ No

Part I   Income

1	Gross receipts or sales. See instructions for line 1 and check the box if this income was reported to you on Form W-2 and the "Statutory employee" box on that form was checked . . . . ▶ ☐	**1**	
2	Returns and allowances	**2**	
3	Subtract line 2 from line 1	**3**	
4	Cost of goods sold (from line 42)	**4**	
5	**Gross profit.** Subtract line 4 from line 3	**5**	
6	Other income, including federal and state gasoline or fuel tax credit or refund (see instructions) . . .	**6**	
7	**Gross income.** Add lines 5 and 6 . . . . ▶	**7**	

Part II   Expenses. Enter expenses for business use of your home **only** on line 30.

8	Advertising	**8**		**18** Office expense (see instructions)	**18**	
9	Car and truck expenses (see instructions). . . .	**9**		**19** Pension and profit-sharing plans .	**19**	
10	Commissions and fees .	**10**		**20** Rent or lease (see instructions):		
11	Contract labor (see instructions)	**11**		**a** Vehicles, machinery, and equipment	**20a**	
12	Depletion . . .	**12**		**b** Other business property . . .	**20b**	
13	Depreciation and section 179 expense deduction (not included in Part III) (see instructions). . . .	**13**		**21** Repairs and maintenance . . .	**21**	
				22 Supplies (not included in Part III) .	**22**	
				23 Taxes and licenses	**23**	
				24 Travel, meals, and entertainment:		
14	Employee benefit programs (other than on line 19). .	**14**		**a** Travel	**24a**	
15	Insurance (other than health)	**15**		**b** Deductible meals and entertainment (see instructions) .	**24b**	
16	Interest:			**25** Utilities	**25**	
a	Mortgage (paid to banks, etc.)	**16a**		**26** Wages (less employment credits). .	**26**	
b	Other	**16b**		**27a** Other expenses (from line 48) . .	**27a**	
17	Legal and professional services	**17**		**b** **Reserved for future use** . . .	**27b**	

28	**Total expenses** before expenses for business use of home. Add lines 8 through 27a . . . . . ▶	**28**	
29	Tentative profit or (loss). Subtract line 28 from line 7	**29**	
30	Expenses for business use of your home. Do not report these expenses elsewhere. Attach Form 8829 unless using the simplified method (see instructions). **Simplified method filers only:** enter the total square footage of: (a) your home: _____ and (b) the part of your home used for business: _____ . Use the Simplified Method Worksheet in the instructions to figure the amount to enter on line 30	**30**	
31	**Net profit or (loss).** Subtract line 30 from line 29. • If a profit, enter on both **Form 1040, line 12** (or **Form 1040NR, line 13**) and on **Schedule SE, line 2.** (If you checked the box on line 1, see instructions). Estates and trusts, enter on **Form 1041, line 3.** • If a loss, you **must** go to line 32.	**31**	
32	If you have a loss, check the box that describes your investment in this activity (see instructions). • If you checked 32a, enter the loss on both **Form 1040, line 12,** (or **Form 1040NR, line 13**) and on **Schedule SE, line 2.** (If you checked the box on line 1, see the line 31 instructions). Estates and trusts, enter on **Form 1041, line 3.** • If you checked 32b, you **must** attach **Form 6198.** Your loss may be limited.	**32a** ☐ All investment is at risk. **32b** ☐ Some investment is not at risk.

For Paperwork Reduction Act Notice, see the separate instructions.   Cat. No. 11334P   Schedule C (Form 1040) 2014

| **Part III** | **Cost of Goods Sold** (see instructions) |

33 Method(s) used to
value closing inventory: **a** ☐ Cost   **b** ☐ Lower of cost or market   **c** ☐ Other (attach explanation)

34 Was there any change in determining quantities, costs, or valuations between opening and closing inventory?
If "Yes," attach explanation . . . .   ☐ **Yes**   ☐ **No**

35 Inventory at beginning of year. If different from last year's closing inventory, attach explanation . . .	**35**	
36 Purchases less cost of items withdrawn for personal use	**36**	
37 Cost of labor. Do not include any amounts paid to yourself	**37**	
38 Materials and supplies	**38**	
39 Other costs	**39**	
40 Add lines 35 through 39	**40**	
41 Inventory at end of year	**41**	
42 **Cost of goods sold.** Subtract line 41 from line 40. Enter the result here and on line 4	**42**	

| **Part IV** | **Information on Your Vehicle.** Complete this part **only** if you are claiming car or truck expenses on line 9 and are not required to file Form 4562 for this business. See the instructions for line 13 to find out if you must file Form 4562. |

43 When did you place your vehicle in service for business purposes? (month, day, year)   ▶ _____ / _____ / _____

44 Of the total number of miles you drove your vehicle during 2014, enter the number of miles you used your vehicle for:

a Business _____   **b** Commuting (see instructions) _____   **c** Other _____

45 Was your vehicle available for personal use during off-duty hours? . . . .   ☐ **Yes**   ☐ **No**

46 Do you (or your spouse) have another vehicle available for personal use?. . . . .   ☐ **Yes**   ☐ **No**

47a Do you have evidence to support your deduction? . . . .   ☐ **Yes**   ☐ **No**

b If "Yes," is the evidence written? . . . .   ☐ **Yes**   ☐ **No**

| **Part V** | **Other Expenses.** List below business expenses not included on lines 8–26 or line 30. |

---	
48 **Total other expenses.** Enter here and on line 27a **48**	

SCHEDULE D
(Form 1040)

Department of the Treasury
Internal Revenue Service (99)

Capital Gains and Losses

▶ Attach to Form 1040 or Form 1040NR.
▶ Information about Schedule D and its separate instructions is at *www.irs.gov/scheduled*.
▶ Use Form 8949 to list your transactions for lines 1b, 2, 3, 8b, 9, and 10.

OMB No. 1545-0074

2014

Attachment
Sequence No. 12

Name(s) shown on return

Your social security number

Part I   Short-Term Capital Gains and Losses—Assets Held One Year or Less

See instructions for how to figure the amounts to enter on the lines below. This form may be easier to complete if you round off cents to whole dollars.	(d) Proceeds (sales price)	(e) Cost (or other basis)	(g) Adjustments to gain or loss from Form(s) 8949, Part I, line 2, column (g)	(h) Gain or (loss) Subtract column (e) from column (d) and combine the result with column (g)
1a Totals for all short-term transactions reported on Form 1099-B for which basis was reported to the IRS and for which you have no adjustments (see instructions). However, if you choose to report all these transactions on Form 8949, leave this line blank and go to line 1b .				
1b Totals for all transactions reported on Form(s) 8949 with **Box A** checked				
2 Totals for all transactions reported on Form(s) 8949 with **Box B** checked				
3 Totals for all transactions reported on Form(s) 8949 with **Box C** checked				

4 Short-term gain from Form 6252 and short-term gain or (loss) from Forms 4684, 6781, and 8824 .	**4**	
5 Net short-term gain or (loss) from partnerships, S corporations, estates, and trusts from Schedule(s) K-1	**5**	
6 Short-term capital loss carryover. Enter the amount, if any, from line 8 of your **Capital Loss Carryover Worksheet** in the instructions	**6**	( )
7 **Net short-term capital gain or (loss).** Combine lines 1a through 6 in column (h). If you have any long-term capital gains or losses, go to Part II below. Otherwise, go to Part III on the back	**7**	

Part II   Long-Term Capital Gains and Losses—Assets Held More Than One Year

See instructions for how to figure the amounts to enter on the lines below. This form may be easier to complete if you round off cents to whole dollars.	(d) Proceeds (sales price)	(e) Cost (or other basis)	(g) Adjustments to gain or loss from Form(s) 8949, Part II, line 2, column (g)	(h) Gain or (loss) Subtract column (e) from column (d) and combine the result with column (g)
8a Totals for all long-term transactions reported on Form 1099-B for which basis was reported to the IRS and for which you have no adjustments (see instructions). However, if you choose to report all these transactions on Form 8949, leave this line blank and go to line 8b .				
8b Totals for all transactions reported on Form(s) 8949 with **Box D** checked				
9 Totals for all transactions reported on Form(s) 8949 with **Box E** checked				
10 Totals for all transactions reported on Form(s) 8949 with **Box F** checked.				

11 Gain from Form 4797, Part I; long-term gain from Forms 2439 and 6252; and long-term gain or (loss) from Forms 4684, 6781, and 8824	**11**	
12 Net long-term gain or (loss) from partnerships, S corporations, estates, and trusts from Schedule(s) K-1	**12**	
13 Capital gain distributions. See the instructions	**13**	
14 Long-term capital loss carryover. Enter the amount, if any, from line 13 of your **Capital Loss Carryover Worksheet** in the instructions	**14**	( )
15 **Net long-term capital gain or (loss).** Combine lines 8a through 14 in column (h). Then go to Part III on the back	**15**	

For Paperwork Reduction Act Notice, see your tax return instructions.   Cat. No. 11338H   Schedule D (Form 1040) 2014

Part III	**Summary**

16   Combine lines 7 and 15 and enter the result . . . . | **16** |

- If line 16 is a **gain,** enter the amount from line 16 on Form 1040, line 13, or Form 1040NR, line 14. Then go to line 17 below.
- If line 16 is a **loss,** skip lines 17 through 20 below. Then go to line 21. Also be sure to complete line 22.
- If line 16 is **zero,** skip lines 17 through 21 below and enter -0- on Form 1040, line 13, or Form 1040NR, line 14. Then go to line 22.

17   Are lines 15 and 16 **both** gains?
  ☐ **Yes.** Go to line 18.
  ☐ **No.** Skip lines 18 through 21, and go to line 22.

18   Enter the amount, if any, from line 7 of the **28% Rate Gain Worksheet** in the instructions . . ▶ | **18** |

19   Enter the amount, if any, from line 18 of the **Unrecaptured Section 1250 Gain Worksheet** in the instructions . . . . ▶ | **19** |

20   Are lines 18 and 19 **both** zero or blank?
  ☐ **Yes.** Complete the **Qualified Dividends and Capital Gain Tax Worksheet** in the instructions for Form 1040, line 44 (or in the instructions for Form 1040NR, line 42). **Do not** complete lines 21 and 22 below.

  ☐ **No.** Complete the **Schedule D Tax Worksheet** in the instructions. **Do not** complete lines 21 and 22 below.

21   If line 16 is a loss, enter here and on Form 1040, line 13, or Form 1040NR, line 14, the **smaller** of:

- The loss on line 16 or
- ($3,000), or if married filing separately, ($1,500) } . . . . | **21** ( ) |

  Note. When figuring which amount is smaller, treat both amounts as positive numbers.

22   Do you have qualified dividends on Form 1040, line 9b, or Form 1040NR, line 10b?

  ☐ **Yes.** Complete the **Qualified Dividends and Capital Gain Tax Worksheet** in the instructions for Form 1040, line 44 (or in the instructions for Form 1040NR, line 42).

  ☐ **No.** Complete the rest of Form 1040 or Form 1040NR.

Form **1065**		**U.S. Return of Partnership Income**	OMB No. 1545-0123
Department of the Treasury Internal Revenue Service		For calendar year 2014, or tax year beginning _____ , 2014, ending _____ , 20 _____ . ▶ Information about Form 1065 and its separate instructions is at *www.irs.gov/form1065.*	20**14**

A Principal business activity	Type or Print	Name of partnership	D Employer identification number
B Principal product or service		Number, street, and room or suite no. If a P.O. box, see the instructions.	E Date business started
C Business code number		City or town, state or province, country, and ZIP or foreign postal code	F Total assets (see the instructions) $

G Check applicable boxes: **(1)** ☐ Initial return **(2)** ☐ Final return **(3)** ☐ Name change **(4)** ☐ Address change **(5)** ☐ Amended return
      (6) ☐ Technical termination - also check (1) or (2)

H Check accounting method: **(1)** ☐ Cash **(2)** ☐ Accrual **(3)** ☐ Other (specify) ▶ _____

I Number of Schedules K-1. Attach one for each person who was a partner at any time during the tax year ▶ _____

J Check if Schedules C and M-3 are attached . . . . ☐

Caution. Include **only** trade or business income and expenses on lines 1a through 22 below. See the instructions for more information.

Income

1a	Gross receipts or sales	1a	
b	Returns and allowances	1b	
c	Balance. Subtract line 1b from line 1a	1c	
2	Cost of goods sold (attach Form 1125-A)	2	
3	Gross profit. Subtract line 2 from line 1c	3	
4	Ordinary income (loss) from other partnerships, estates, and trusts (attach statement) . .	4	
5	Net farm profit (loss) (attach Schedule F (Form 1040))	5	
6	Net gain (loss) from Form 4797, Part II, line 17 (attach Form 4797)	6	
7	Other income (loss) (attach statement)	7	
8	**Total income (loss).** Combine lines 3 through 7	8	

Deductions (see the instructions for limitations)

9	Salaries and wages (other than to partners) (less employment credits)	9	
10	Guaranteed payments to partners	10	
11	Repairs and maintenance	11	
12	Bad debts	12	
13	Rent	13	
14	Taxes and licenses	14	
15	Interest	15	
16a	Depreciation (if required, attach Form 4562)	16a	
b	Less depreciation reported on Form 1125-A and elsewhere on return	16b	16c
17	Depletion **(Do not deduct oil and gas depletion.)**	17	
18	Retirement plans, etc.	18	
19	Employee benefit programs	19	
20	Other deductions (attach statement)	20	
21	**Total deductions.** Add the amounts shown in the far right column for lines 9 through 20 .	21	
22	**Ordinary business income (loss).** Subtract line 21 from line 8	22	

Sign Here

Under penalties of perjury, I declare that I have examined this return, including accompanying schedules and statements, and to the best of my knowledge and belief, it is true, correct, and complete. Declaration of preparer (other than general partner or limited liability company member manager) is based on all information of which preparer has any knowledge.

▶ _____ Signature of general partner or limited liability company member manager	▶ _____ Date	May the IRS discuss this return with the preparer shown below (see instructions)? ☐ **Yes** ☐ **No**

Paid Preparer Use Only

Print/Type preparer's name	Preparer's signature	Date	Check ☐ if self-employed	PTIN
Firm's name ▶			Firm's EIN ▶	
Firm's address ▶			Phone no.	

For Paperwork Reduction Act Notice, see separate instructions.   Cat. No. 11390Z   Form **1065** (2014)

Form 1065 (2014)   Page **2**

Schedule B	Other Information

		Yes	No
1	What type of entity is filing this return? Check the applicable box:		
a	☐ Domestic general partnership **b** ☐ Domestic limited partnership		
c	☐ Domestic limited liability company **d** ☐ Domestic limited liability partnership		
e	☐ Foreign partnership **f** ☐ Other ▶		
2	At any time during the tax year, was any partner in the partnership a disregarded entity, a partnership (including an entity treated as a partnership), a trust, an S corporation, an estate (other than an estate of a deceased partner), or a nominee or similar person?		
3	At the end of the tax year:		
a	Did any foreign or domestic corporation, partnership (including any entity treated as a partnership), trust, or tax-exempt organization, or any foreign government own, directly or indirectly, an interest of 50% or more in the profit, loss, or capital of the partnership? For rules of constructive ownership, see instructions. If "Yes," attach Schedule B-1, Information on Partners Owning 50% or More of the Partnership		
b	Did any individual or estate own, directly or indirectly, an interest of 50% or more in the profit, loss, or capital of the partnership? For rules of constructive ownership, see instructions. If "Yes," attach Schedule B-1, Information on Partners Owning 50% or More of the Partnership		
4	At the end of the tax year, did the partnership:		
a	Own directly 20% or more, or own, directly or indirectly, 50% or more of the total voting power of all classes of stock entitled to vote of any foreign or domestic corporation? For rules of constructive ownership, see instructions. If "Yes," complete (i) through (iv) below		

(i) Name of Corporation	(ii) Employer Identification Number (if any)	(iii) Country of Incorporation	(iv) Percentage Owned in Voting Stock

b	Own directly an interest of 20% or more, or own, directly or indirectly, an interest of 50% or more in the profit, loss, or capital in any foreign or domestic partnership (including an entity treated as a partnership) or in the beneficial interest of a trust? For rules of constructive ownership, see instructions. If "Yes," complete (i) through (v) below . .

(i) Name of Entity	(ii) Employer Identification Number (if any)	(iii) Type of Entity	(iv) Country of Organization	(v) Maximum Percentage Owned in Profit, Loss, or Capital

		Yes	No
5	Did the partnership file Form 8893, Election of Partnership Level Tax Treatment, or an election statement under section 6231(a)(1)(B)(ii) for partnership-level tax treatment, that is in effect for this tax year? See Form 8893 for more details		
6	Does the partnership satisfy **all four** of the following conditions?		
a	The partnership's total receipts for the tax year were less than $250,000.		
b	The partnership's total assets at the end of the tax year were less than $1 million.		
c	Schedules K-1 are filed with the return and furnished to the partners on or before the due date (including extensions) for the partnership return.		
d	The partnership is not filing and is not required to file Schedule M-3		
	If "Yes," the partnership is not required to complete Schedules L, M-1, and M-2; Item F on page 1 of Form 1065; or Item L on Schedule K-1.		
7	Is this partnership a publicly traded partnership as defined in section 469(k)(2)?		
8	During the tax year, did the partnership have any debt that was cancelled, was forgiven, or had the terms modified so as to reduce the principal amount of the debt?		
9	Has this partnership filed, or is it required to file, Form 8918, Material Advisor Disclosure Statement, to provide information on any reportable transaction?		
10	At any time during calendar year 2014, did the partnership have an interest in or a signature or other authority over a financial account in a foreign country (such as a bank account, securities account, or other financial account)? See the instructions for exceptions and filing requirements for FinCEN Form 114, Report of Foreign Bank and Financial Accounts (FBAR). If "Yes," enter the name of the foreign country. ▶		

Form **1065** (2014)

Form 1065 (2014)   Page **3**

Schedule B	**Other Information** *(continued)*	Yes	No

11 At any time during the tax year, did the partnership receive a distribution from, or was it the grantor of, or transferor to, a foreign trust? If "Yes," the partnership may have to file Form 3520, Annual Return To Report Transactions With Foreign Trusts and Receipt of Certain Foreign Gifts. See instructions . . . .

12a Is the partnership making, or had it previously made (and not revoked), a section 754 election? . . . . . .
See instructions for details regarding a section 754 election.

   b Did the partnership make for this tax year an optional basis adjustment under section 743(b) or 734(b)? If "Yes," attach a statement showing the computation and allocation of the basis adjustment. See instructions . . . .

   c Is the partnership required to adjust the basis of partnership assets under section 743(b) or 734(b) because of a substantial built-in loss (as defined under section 743(d)) or substantial basis reduction (as defined under section 734(d))? If "Yes," attach a statement showing the computation and allocation of the basis adjustment. See instructions

13 Check this box if, during the current or prior tax year, the partnership distributed any property received in a like-kind exchange or contributed such property to another entity (other than disregarded entities wholly owned by the partnership throughout the tax year) . . . . ▶ ☐

14 At any time during the tax year, did the partnership distribute to any partner a tenancy-in-common or other undivided interest in partnership property? . . . .

15 If the partnership is required to file Form 8858, Information Return of U.S. Persons With Respect To Foreign Disregarded Entities, enter the number of Forms 8858 attached. See instructions ▶

16 Does the partnership have any foreign partners? If "Yes," enter the number of Forms 8805, Foreign Partner's Information Statement of Section 1446 Withholding Tax, filed for this partnership. ▶

17 Enter the number of Forms 8865, Return of U.S. Persons With Respect to Certain Foreign Partnerships, attached to this return. ▶

18a Did you make any payments in 2014 that would require you to file Form(s) 1099? See instructions . . . . .

   b If "Yes," did you or will you file required Form(s) 1099? . . . .

19 Enter the number of Form(s) 5471, Information Return of U.S. Persons With Respect To Certain Foreign Corporations, attached to this return. ▶

20 Enter the number of partners that are foreign governments under section 892. ▶

Designation of Tax Matters Partner (see instructions)
Enter below the general partner or member-manager designated as the tax matters partner (TMP) for the tax year of this return:

Name of designated TMP ▶		Identifying number of TMP ▶	
If the TMP is an entity, name of TMP representative ▶		Phone number of TMP ▶	
Address of designated TMP ▶			

Form **1065** (2014)

Form 1065 (2014)

Page **4**

Schedule K	Partners' Distributive Share Items		Total amount

Income (Loss)

1	Ordinary business income (loss) (page 1, line 22)		1	
2	Net rental real estate income (loss) (attach Form 8825)		2	
3a	Other gross rental income (loss)	3a		
b	Expenses from other rental activities (attach statement)	3b		
c	Other net rental income (loss). Subtract line 3b from line 3a		3c	
4	Guaranteed payments		4	
5	Interest income		5	
6	Dividends: **a** Ordinary dividends		6a	
	b Qualified dividends	6b		
7	Royalties		7	
8	Net short-term capital gain (loss) (attach Schedule D (Form 1065))		8	
9a	Net long-term capital gain (loss) (attach Schedule D (Form 1065))		9a	
b	Collectibles (28%) gain (loss)	9b		
c	Unrecaptured section 1250 gain (attach statement)	9c		
10	Net section 1231 gain (loss) (attach Form 4797)		10	
11	Other income (loss) (see instructions) Type ▶		11	

Deductions

12	Section 179 deduction (attach Form 4562)		12	
13a	Contributions		13a	
b	Investment interest expense		13b	
c	Section 59(e)(2) expenditures: **(1)** Type ▶ _____ **(2)** Amount ▶		13c(2)	
d	Other deductions (see instructions) Type ▶		13d	

Self-Employment

14a	Net earnings (loss) from self-employment		14a	
b	Gross farming or fishing income		14b	
c	Gross nonfarm income		14c	

Credits

15a	Low-income housing credit (section 42(j)(5))		15a	
b	Low-income housing credit (other)		15b	
c	Qualified rehabilitation expenditures (rental real estate) (attach Form 3468, if applicable)		15c	
d	Other rental real estate credits (see instructions) Type ▶		15d	
e	Other rental credits (see instructions) Type ▶		15e	
f	Other credits (see instructions) Type ▶		15f	

Foreign Transactions

16a	Name of country or U.S. possession ▶			
b	Gross income from all sources		16b	
c	Gross income sourced at partner level		16c	
	Foreign gross income sourced at partnership level			
d	Passive category ▶ _____ **e** General category ▶ _____ **f** Other ▶		16f	
	Deductions allocated and apportioned at partner level			
g	Interest expense ▶ _____ **h** Other ▶		16h	
	Deductions allocated and apportioned at partnership level to foreign source income			
i	Passive category ▶ _____ **j** General category ▶ _____ **k** Other ▶		16k	
l	Total foreign taxes (check one): ▶ Paid ☐ Accrued ☐		16l	
m	Reduction in taxes available for credit (attach statement)		16m	
n	Other foreign tax information (attach statement)			

Alternative Minimum Tax (AMT) Items

17a	Post-1986 depreciation adjustment		17a	
b	Adjusted gain or loss		17b	
c	Depletion (other than oil and gas)		17c	
d	Oil, gas, and geothermal properties—gross income		17d	
e	Oil, gas, and geothermal properties—deductions		17e	
f	Other AMT items (attach statement)		17f	

Other Information

18a	Tax-exempt interest income		18a	
b	Other tax-exempt income		18b	
c	Nondeductible expenses		18c	
19a	Distributions of cash and marketable securities		19a	
b	Distributions of other property		19b	
20a	Investment income		20a	
b	Investment expenses		20b	
c	Other items and amounts (attach statement)			

Form **1065** (2014)

Form 1065 (2014)

Analysis of Net Income (Loss)

1 Net income (loss). Combine Schedule K, lines 1 through 11. From the result, subtract the sum of Schedule K, lines 12 through 13d, and 16l **1**

2 Analysis by partner type:

	(i) Corporate	**(ii)** Individual (active)	**(iii)** Individual (passive)	**(iv)** Partnership	**(v)** Exempt Organization	**(vi)** Nominee/Other
a General partners						
b Limited partners						

Schedule L — Balance Sheets per Books

Assets	Beginning of tax year (a)	(b)	End of tax year (c)	(d)
1 Cash				
2a Trade notes and accounts receivable				
b Less allowance for bad debts				
3 Inventories				
4 U.S. government obligations				
5 Tax-exempt securities				
6 Other current assets (attach statement)				
7a Loans to partners (or persons related to partners)				
b Mortgage and real estate loans				
8 Other investments (attach statement)				
9a Buildings and other depreciable assets				
b Less accumulated depreciation				
10a Depletable assets				
b Less accumulated depletion				
11 Land (net of any amortization)				
12a Intangible assets (amortizable only)				
b Less accumulated amortization				
13 Other assets (attach statement)				
14 Total assets				
Liabilities and Capital				
15 Accounts payable				
16 Mortgages, notes, bonds payable in less than 1 year				
17 Other current liabilities (attach statement)				
18 All nonrecourse loans				
19a Loans from partners (or persons related to partners)				
b Mortgages, notes, bonds payable in 1 year or more				
20 Other liabilities (attach statement)				
21 Partners' capital accounts				
22 Total liabilities and capital				

Schedule M-1 — Reconciliation of Income (Loss) per Books With Income (Loss) per Return

Note. The partnership may be required to file Schedule M-3 (see instructions).

1 Net income (loss) per books . . . .

2 Income included on Schedule K, lines 1, 2, 3c, 5, 6a, 7, 8, 9a, 10, and 11, not recorded on books this year (itemize): _____

3 Guaranteed payments (other than health insurance) . . . .

4 Expenses recorded on books this year not included on Schedule K, lines 1 through 13d, and 16l (itemize):

a Depreciation $ _____

b Travel and entertainment $ _____

5 Add lines 1 through 4 . . . . . .

6 Income recorded on books this year not included on Schedule K, lines 1 through 11 (itemize):

a Tax-exempt interest $ _____

7 Deductions included on Schedule K, lines 1 through 13d, and 16l, not charged against book income this year (itemize):

a Depreciation $ _____

8 Add lines 6 and 7 . . . .

9 Income (loss) (Analysis of Net Income (Loss), line 1. Subtract line 8 from line 5 .

Schedule M-2 — Analysis of Partners' Capital Accounts

1 Balance at beginning of year . . .

2 Capital contributed: **a** Cash . . .
b Property . .

3 Net income (loss) per books . . . .

4 Other increases (itemize): _____

5 Add lines 1 through 4 . . . . . .

6 Distributions: **a** Cash . . . . .
b Property . . . . .

7 Other decreases (itemize): _____

8 Add lines 6 and 7 . . . .

9 Balance at end of year. Subtract line 8 from line 5

Form **1065** (2014)

651113

☐ Final K-1   ☐ Amended K-1   OMB No. 1545-0123

Schedule K-1
(Form 1065)

Department of the Treasury
Internal Revenue Service

20**14**

For calendar year 2014, or tax

year beginning _____ , 2014

ending _____ , 20 ____

Partner's Share of Income, Deductions, Credits, etc.

► See back of form and separate instructions.

Part I	Information About the Partnership

A   Partnership's employer identification number

B   Partnership's name, address, city, state, and ZIP code

C   IRS Center where partnership filed return

D   ☐ Check if this is a publicly traded partnership (PTP)

Part II	Information About the Partner

E   Partner's identifying number

F   Partner's name, address, city, state, and ZIP code

G ☐ General partner or LLC   ☐ Limited partner or other LLC
       member-manager   member

H ☐ Domestic partner   ☐ Foreign partner

I1 What type of entity is this partner? _____

I2 If this partner is a retirement plan (IRA/SEP/Keogh/etc.), check here
· ☐

J   Partner's share of profit, loss, and capital (see instructions):

	Beginning		Ending
Profit	%		%
Loss	%		%
Capital	%		%

K   Partner's share of liabilities at year end:

Nonrecourse · · · · · · $ _____

Qualified nonrecourse financing · $ _____

Recourse · · · · · · $ _____

L   Partner's capital account analysis:

Beginning capital account · · · $ _____

Capital contributed during the year $ _____

Current year increase (decrease) · $ _____

Withdrawals & distributions · · $ (_____)

Ending capital account · · · · $ _____

☐ Tax basis   ☐ GAAP   ☐ Section 704(b) book
☐ Other (explain)

M   Did the partner contribute property with a built-in gain or loss?
☐ **Yes**   ☐ **No**
If "Yes," attach statement (see instructions)

Part III	Partner's Share of Current Year Income, Deductions, Credits, and Other Items

1	Ordinary business income (loss)	15	Credits
2	Net rental real estate income (loss)		
3	Other net rental income (loss)	16	Foreign transactions
4	Guaranteed payments		
5	Interest income		
6a	Ordinary dividends		
6b	Qualified dividends		
7	Royalties		
8	Net short-term capital gain (loss)		
9a	Net long-term capital gain (loss)	17	Alternative minimum tax (AMT) items
9b	Collectibles (28%) gain (loss)		
9c	Unrecaptured section 1250 gain		
10	Net section 1231 gain (loss)	18	Tax-exempt income and nondeductible expenses
11	Other income (loss)		
		19	Distributions
12	Section 179 deduction		
13	Other deductions	20	Other information
14	Self-employment earnings (loss)		

*See attached statement for additional information.

For IRS Use Only

For Paperwork Reduction Act Notice, see Instructions for Form 1065.   IRS.gov/form1065   Cat. No. 11394R   **Schedule K-1 (Form 1065) 2014**

Form **1120**		**U.S. Corporation Income Tax Return**		OMB No. 1545-0123
Department of the Treasury Internal Revenue Service		For calendar year 2014 or tax year beginning _____ , 2014, ending _____ , 20 _____		**2014**

► Information about Form 1120 and its separate instructions is at *www.irs.gov/form1120.*

A Check if:		**TYPE OR PRINT**	Name	**B** Employer identification number
1a Consolidated return (attach Form 851) ☐				
b Life/nonlife consolidated return . . ☐			Number, street, and room or suite no. If a P.O. box, see instructions.	**C** Date incorporated
2 Personal holding co. (attach Sch. PH) . . ☐				
3 Personal service corp. (see instructions) . ☐			City or town, state, or province, country and ZIP or foreign postal code	**D** Total assets (see instructions) $
4 Schedule M-3 attached ☐				

E Check if: **(1)** ☐ Initial return   **(2)** ☐ Final return   **(3)** ☐ Name change   **(4)** ☐ Address change

Income	**1a**	Gross receipts or sales	**1a**	
	b	Returns and allowances	**1b**	
	c	Balance. Subtract line 1b from line 1a	**1c**	
	2	Cost of goods sold (attach Form 1125-A)	**2**	
	3	Gross profit. Subtract line 2 from line 1c	**3**	
	4	Dividends (Schedule C, line 19)	**4**	
	5	Interest	**5**	
	6	Gross rents	**6**	
	7	Gross royalties	**7**	
	8	Capital gain net income (attach Schedule D (Form 1120))	**8**	
	9	Net gain or (loss) from Form 4797, Part II, line 17 (attach Form 4797)	**9**	
	10	Other income (see instructions—attach statement)	**10**	
	11	**Total income.** Add lines 3 through 10 . . . . ►	**11**	

Deductions (See instructions for limitations on deductions.)	**12**	Compensation of officers (see instructions—attach Form 1125-E) . . . . ►	**12**	
	13	Salaries and wages (less employment credits)	**13**	
	14	Repairs and maintenance	**14**	
	15	Bad debts	**15**	
	16	Rents	**16**	
	17	Taxes and licenses	**17**	
	18	Interest	**18**	
	19	Charitable contributions	**19**	
	20	Depreciation from Form 4562 not claimed on Form 1125-A or elsewhere on return (attach Form 4562) .	**20**	
	21	Depletion	**21**	
	22	Advertising	**22**	
	23	Pension, profit-sharing, etc., plans	**23**	
	24	Employee benefit programs	**24**	
	25	Domestic production activities deduction (attach Form 8903)	**25**	
	26	Other deductions (attach statement)	**26**	
	27	**Total deductions.** Add lines 12 through 26 . . . . ►	**27**	
	28	Taxable income before net operating loss deduction and special deductions. Subtract line 27 from line 11.	**28**	
	29a	Net operating loss deduction (see instructions)	**29a**	
	b	Special deductions (Schedule C, line 20)	**29b**	
	c	Add lines 29a and 29b	**29c**	

Tax, Refundable Credits, and Payments	**30**	**Taxable income.** Subtract line 29c from line 28 (see instructions)	**30**	
	31	Total tax (Schedule J, Part I, line 11)	**31**	
	32	Total payments and refundable credits (Schedule J, Part II, line 21)	**32**	
	33	Estimated tax penalty (see instructions). Check if Form 2220 is attached . . . . . ► ☐	**33**	
	34	**Amount owed.** If line 32 is smaller than the total of lines 31 and 33, enter amount owed	**34**	
	35	**Overpayment.** If line 32 is larger than the total of lines 31 and 33, enter amount overpaid	**35**	
	36	Enter amount from line 35 you want: **Credited to 2015 estimated tax ►** **Refunded ►**	**36**	

Sign Here
Under penalties of perjury, I declare that I have examined this return, including accompanying schedules and statements, and to the best of my knowledge and belief, it is true, correct, and complete. Declaration of preparer (other than taxpayer) is based on all information of which preparer has any knowledge.

► _____   _____   ► _____
Signature of officer   Date   Title

May the IRS discuss this return with the preparer shown below (see instructions)? ☐ Yes ☐ No

Paid Preparer Use Only

Print/Type preparer's name	Preparer's signature	Date	Check ☐ if self-employed	PTIN
Firm's name ►			Firm's EIN ►	
Firm's address ►			Phone no.	

For Paperwork Reduction Act Notice, see separate instructions.   Cat. No. 11450Q   Form **1120** (2014)

Form 1120 (2014)   Page **2**

Schedule C	Dividends and Special Deductions (see instructions)	(a) Dividends received	(b) %	(c) Special deductions (a) × (b)
1	Dividends from less-than-20%-owned domestic corporations (other than debt-financed stock)		70	
2	Dividends from 20%-or-more-owned domestic corporations (other than debt-financed stock)		80	
3	Dividends on debt-financed stock of domestic and foreign corporations		see instructions	
4	Dividends on certain preferred stock of less-than-20%-owned public utilities . . .		42	
5	Dividends on certain preferred stock of 20%-or-more-owned public utilities		48	
6	Dividends from less-than-20%-owned foreign corporations and certain FSCs . . .		70	
7	Dividends from 20%-or-more-owned foreign corporations and certain FSCs . . .		80	
8	Dividends from wholly owned foreign subsidiaries		100	
9	**Total.** Add lines 1 through 8. See instructions for limitation			
10	Dividends from domestic corporations received by a small business investment company operating under the Small Business Investment Act of 1958		100	
11	Dividends from affiliated group members		100	
12	Dividends from certain FSCs		100	
13	Dividends from foreign corporations not included on lines 3, 6, 7, 8, 11, or 12 . . .			
14	Income from controlled foreign corporations under subpart F (attach Form(s) 5471) .			
15	Foreign dividend gross-up			
16	IC-DISC and former DISC dividends not included on lines 1, 2, or 3			
17	Other dividends			
18	Deduction for dividends paid on certain preferred stock of public utilities			
19	**Total dividends.** Add lines 1 through 17. Enter here and on page 1, line 4 . . . ▶			
20	**Total special deductions.** Add lines 9, 10, 11, 12, and 18. Enter here and on page 1, line 29b . . . . ▶			

Form **1120** (2014)

Form 1120 (2014) Page 3

Schedule J Tax Computation and Payment (see instructions)

Part I–Tax Computation

1	Check if the corporation is a member of a controlled group (attach Schedule O (Form 1120)) . . . . ▶ ☐		
2	Income tax. Check if a qualified personal service corporation (see instructions) . . . . ▶ ☐	2	
3	Alternative minimum tax (attach Form 4626)	3	
4	Add lines 2 and 3	4	
5a	Foreign tax credit (attach Form 1118)	5a	
b	Credit from Form 8834 (see instructions)	5b	
c	General business credit (attach Form 3800)	5c	
d	Credit for prior year minimum tax (attach Form 8827) . . .	5d	
e	Bond credits from Form 8912	5e	
6	**Total credits.** Add lines 5a through 5e	6	
7	Subtract line 6 from line 4	7	
8	Personal holding company tax (attach Schedule PH (Form 1120))	8	
9a	Recapture of investment credit (attach Form 4255)	9a	
b	Recapture of low-income housing credit (attach Form 8611)	9b	
c	Interest due under the look-back method—completed long-term contracts (attach Form 8697)	9c	
d	Interest due under the look-back method—income forecast method (attach Form 8866)	9d	
e	Alternative tax on qualifying shipping activities (attach Form 8902)	9e	
f	Other (see instructions—attach statement)	9f	
10	**Total.** Add lines 9a through 9f	10	
11	**Total tax.** Add lines 7, 8, and 10. Enter here and on page 1, line 31	11	

Part II–Payments and Refundable Credits

12	2013 overpayment credited to 2014	12	
13	2014 estimated tax payments	13	
14	2014 refund applied for on Form 4466	14 (	)
15	Combine lines 12, 13, and 14	15	
16	Tax deposited with Form 7004	16	
17	Withholding (see instructions)	17	
18	**Total payments.** Add lines 15, 16, and 17	18	
19	Refundable credits from:		
a	Form 2439	19a	
b	Form 4136	19b	
c	Form 8827, line 8c	19c	
d	Other (attach statement—see instructions).	19d	
20	**Total credits.** Add lines 19a through 19d	20	
21	**Total payments and credits.** Add lines 18 and 20. Enter here and on page 1, line 32	21	

Schedule K Other Information (see instructions)

		Yes	No
1	Check accounting method: **a** ☐ Cash **b** ☐ Accrual **c** ☐ Other (specify) ▶ _____		
2	See the instructions and enter the:		
a	Business activity code no. ▶ _____		
b	Business activity ▶ _____		
c	Product or service ▶ _____		
3	Is the corporation a subsidiary in an affiliated group or a parent-subsidiary controlled group?		
	If "Yes," enter name and EIN of the parent corporation ▶ _____		
4	At the end of the tax year:		
a	Did any foreign or domestic corporation, partnership (including any entity treated as a partnership), trust, or tax-exempt organization own directly 20% or more, or own, directly or indirectly, 50% or more of the total voting power of all classes of the corporation's stock entitled to vote? If "Yes," complete Part I of Schedule G (Form 1120) (attach Schedule G)		
b	Did any individual or estate own directly 20% or more, or own, directly or indirectly, 50% or more of the total voting power of all classes of the corporation's stock entitled to vote? If "Yes," complete Part II of Schedule G (Form 1120) (attach Schedule G) .		

Form **1120** (2014)

Form 1120 (2014)   Page **4**

Schedule K	**Other Information** *continued* (see instructions)

				Yes	**No**

5   At the end of the tax year, did the corporation:

a   Own directly 20% or more, or own, directly or indirectly, 50% or more of the total voting power of all classes of stock entitled to vote of any foreign or domestic corporation not included on **Form 851,** Affiliations Schedule? For rules of constructive ownership, see instructions. If "Yes," complete (i) through (iv) below.

(i) Name of Corporation	**(ii)** Employer Identification Number (if any)	**(iii)** Country of Incorporation	**(iv)** Percentage Owned in Voting Stock

b   Own directly an interest of 20% or more, or own, directly or indirectly, an interest of 50% or more in any foreign or domestic partnership (including an entity treated as a partnership) or in the beneficial interest of a trust? For rules of constructive ownership, see instructions. If "Yes," complete (i) through (iv) below.

(i) Name of Entity	**(ii)** Employer Identification Number (if any)	**(iii)** Country of Organization	**(iv)** Maximum Percentage Owned in Profit, Loss, or Capital

6   During this tax year, did the corporation pay dividends (other than stock dividends and distributions in exchange for stock) in excess of the corporation's current and accumulated earnings and profits? (See sections 301 and 316.)   .   .   .   .

If "Yes," file **Form 5452,** Corporate Report of Nondividend Distributions.

If this is a consolidated return, answer here for the parent corporation and on Form 851 for each subsidiary.

7   At any time during the tax year, did one foreign person own, directly or indirectly, at least 25% of **(a)** the total voting power of all classes of the corporation's stock entitled to vote or **(b)** the total value of all classes of the corporation's stock?   .   .   .   .

For rules of attribution, see section 318. If "Yes," enter:

(i) Percentage owned ▶ _____   and   **(ii)** Owner's country ▶ _____

(c) The corporation may have to file **Form 5472,** Information Return of a 25% Foreign-Owned U.S. Corporation or a Foreign Corporation Engaged in a U.S. Trade or Business. Enter the number of Forms 5472 attached ▶ _____

8   Check this box if the corporation issued publicly offered debt instruments with original issue discount   .   .   .   .   .   .   ▶ ☐

If checked, the corporation may have to file **Form 8281,** Information Return for Publicly Offered Original Issue Discount Instruments.

9   Enter the amount of tax-exempt interest received or accrued during the tax year ▶ $ _____

10   Enter the number of shareholders at the end of the tax year (if 100 or fewer) ▶ _____

11   If the corporation has an NOL for the tax year and is electing to forego the carryback period, check here   .   .   .   .   .   ▶ ☐

If the corporation is filing a consolidated return, the statement required by Regulations section 1.1502-21(b)(3) must be attached or the election will not be valid.

12   Enter the available NOL carryover from prior tax years (do not reduce it by any deduction on line 29a.) ▶ $ _____

13   Are the corporation's total receipts (page 1, line 1a, plus lines 4 through 10) for the tax year **and** its total assets at the end of the tax year less than $250,000?   .   .   .   .

If "Yes," the corporation is not required to complete Schedules L, M-1, and M-2. Instead, enter the total amount of cash distributions and the book value of property distributions (other than cash) made during the tax year ▶ $ _____

14   Is the corporation required to file Schedule UTP (Form 1120), Uncertain Tax Position Statement (see instructions)?   .   .   .   .

If "Yes," complete and attach Schedule UTP.

15a   Did the corporation make any payments in 2014 that would require it to file Form(s) 1099?   .   .   .   .

b   If "Yes," did or will the corporation file required Forms 1099?   .   .   .   .

16   During this tax year, did the corporation have an 80% or more change in ownership, including a change due to redemption of its own stock?   .   .   .   .

17   During or subsequent to this tax year, but before the filing of this return, did the corporation dispose of more than 65% (by value) of its assets in a taxable, non-taxable, or tax deferred transaction?   .   .   .   .

18   Did the corporation receive assets in a section 351 transfer in which any of the transferred assets had a fair market basis or fair market value of more than $1 million?   .   .   .   .

Form **1120** (2014)

Form 1120 (2014)   Page **5**

Schedule L — Balance Sheets per Books

		Beginning of tax year		End of tax year	
	Assets	**(a)**	**(b)**	**(c)**	**(d)**
1	Cash				
2a	Trade notes and accounts receivable				
b	Less allowance for bad debts	( )		( )	
3	Inventories				
4	U.S. government obligations				
5	Tax-exempt securities (see instructions)				
6	Other current assets (attach statement)				
7	Loans to shareholders				
8	Mortgage and real estate loans				
9	Other investments (attach statement)				
10a	Buildings and other depreciable assets				
b	Less accumulated depreciation	( )		( )	
11a	Depletable assets				
b	Less accumulated depletion	( )		( )	
12	Land (net of any amortization)				
13a	Intangible assets (amortizable only)				
b	Less accumulated amortization	( )		( )	
14	Other assets (attach statement)				
15	Total assets				
	Liabilities and Shareholders' Equity				
16	Accounts payable				
17	Mortgages, notes, bonds payable in less than 1 year				
18	Other current liabilities (attach statement)				
19	Loans from shareholders				
20	Mortgages, notes, bonds payable in 1 year or more				
21	Other liabilities (attach statement)				
22	Capital stock: **a** Preferred stock				
	b Common stock				
23	Additional paid-in capital				
24	Retained earnings—Appropriated (attach statement)				
25	Retained earnings—Unappropriated				
26	Adjustments to shareholders' equity (attach statement)				
27	Less cost of treasury stock		( )		( )
28	Total liabilities and shareholders' equity				

Schedule M-1 — Reconciliation of Income (Loss) per Books With Income per Return

Note: The corporation may be required to file Schedule M-3 (see instructions).

1	Net income (loss) per books		7	Income recorded on books this year not included on this return (itemize):
2	Federal income tax per books			Tax-exempt interest $ _____
3	Excess of capital losses over capital gains			
4	Income subject to tax not recorded on books this year (itemize): _____			
	_____		8	Deductions on this return not charged against book income this year (itemize):
5	Expenses recorded on books this year not deducted on this return (itemize):		**a**	Depreciation . . $ _____
			b	Charitable contributions $ _____
a	Depreciation . . . $ _____			_____
b	Charitable contributions . $ _____			
c	Travel and entertainment . $ _____		9	Add lines 7 and 8
6	Add lines 1 through 5		10	Income (page 1, line 28)—line 6 less line 9

Schedule M-2 — Analysis of Unappropriated Retained Earnings per Books (Line 25, Schedule L)

1	Balance at beginning of year		5	Distributions: **a** Cash
2	Net income (loss) per books			**b** Stock
3	Other increases (itemize): _____			**c** Property
	_____		6	Other decreases (itemize): _____
	_____		7	Add lines 5 and 6
4	Add lines 1, 2, and 3		8	Balance at end of year (line 4 less line 7)

Form **1120** (2014)

Form **1120S**

Department of the Treasury
Internal Revenue Service

U.S. Income Tax Return for an S Corporation

▶ Do not file this form unless the corporation has filed or is attaching Form 2553 to elect to be an S corporation.
▶ Information about Form 1120S and its separate instructions is at *www.irs.gov/form1120s*.

OMB No. 1545-0123

20**14**

For calendar year 2014 or tax year beginning _____ , 2014, ending _____ , 20____

A S election effective date	**TYPE OR PRINT** — Name	**D** Employer identification number
B Business activity code number (see instructions)	Number, street, and room or suite no. If a P.O. box, see instructions.	**E** Date incorporated
C Check if Sch. M-3 attached ☐	City or town, state or province, country, and ZIP or foreign postal code	**F** Total assets (see instructions) $

G Is the corporation electing to be an S corporation beginning with this tax year? ☐ Yes ☐ No   If "Yes," attach Form 2553 if not already filed

H Check if: **(1)** ☐ Final return **(2)** ☐ Name change **(3)** ☐ Address change **(4)** ☐ Amended return **(5)** ☐ S election termination or revocation

I Enter the number of shareholders who were shareholders during any part of the tax year . . . . ▶

Caution. Include **only** trade or business income and expenses on lines 1a through 21. See the instructions for more information.

Income

1a Gross receipts or sales	**1a**	
b Returns and allowances	**1b**	
c Balance. Subtract line 1b from line 1a	**1c**	
2 Cost of goods sold (attach Form 1125-A)	**2**	
3 Gross profit. Subtract line 2 from line 1c	**3**	
4 Net gain (loss) from Form 4797, line 17 (attach Form 4797)	**4**	
5 Other income (loss) (see instructions—attach statement)	**5**	
6 **Total income (loss).** Add lines 3 through 5 . . . . ▶	**6**	

Deductions (see instructions for limitations)

7 Compensation of officers (see instructions—attach Form 1125-E) . . .	**7**	
8 Salaries and wages (less employment credits)	**8**	
9 Repairs and maintenance	**9**	
10 Bad debts	**10**	
11 Rents	**11**	
12 Taxes and licenses	**12**	
13 Interest	**13**	
14 Depreciation not claimed on Form 1125-A or elsewhere on return (attach Form 4562) . . .	**14**	
15 Depletion (**Do not deduct oil and gas depletion.**)	**15**	
16 Advertising	**16**	
17 Pension, profit-sharing, etc., plans	**17**	
18 Employee benefit programs	**18**	
19 Other deductions (attach statement)	**19**	
20 **Total deductions.** Add lines 7 through 19 . . . . ▶	**20**	
21 **Ordinary business income (loss).** Subtract line 20 from line 6	**21**	

Tax and Payments

22a Excess net passive income or LIFO recapture tax (see instructions) . .	**22a**	
b Tax from Schedule D (Form 1120S)	**22b**	
c Add lines 22a and 22b (see instructions for additional taxes)	**22c**	
23a 2014 estimated tax payments and 2013 overpayment credited to 2014	**23a**	
b Tax deposited with Form 7004	**23b**	
c Credit for federal tax paid on fuels (attach Form 4136)	**23c**	
d Add lines 23a through 23c	**23d**	
24 Estimated tax penalty (see instructions). Check if Form 2220 is attached . . . . ▶ ☐	**24**	
25 **Amount owed.** If line 23d is smaller than the total of lines 22c and 24, enter amount owed . .	**25**	
26 **Overpayment.** If line 23d is larger than the total of lines 22c and 24, enter amount overpaid . .	**26**	
27 Enter amount from line 26 **Credited to 2015 estimated tax** ▶ _____ **Refunded** ▶	**27**	

Sign Here

Under penalties of perjury, I declare that I have examined this return, including accompanying schedules and statements, and to the best of my knowledge and belief, it is true, correct, and complete. Declaration of preparer (other than taxpayer) is based on all information of which preparer has any knowledge.

▶ _____ Signature of officer   Date

▶ _____ Title

May the IRS discuss this return with the preparer shown below (see instructions)? ☐ Yes ☐ No

Paid Preparer Use Only

Print/Type preparer's name	Preparer's signature	Date	Check ☐ if self-employed	PTIN
Firm's name ▶			Firm's EIN ▶	
Firm's address ▶			Phone no.	

For Paperwork Reduction Act Notice, see separate instructions.   Cat. No. 11510H   Form **1120S** (2014)

Form 1120S (2014)   Page **2**

Schedule B	**Other Information** (see instructions)	**Yes**	**No**

1 Check accounting method: **a** ☐ Cash **b** ☐ Accrual
  c ☐ Other (specify) ▶ _____

2 See the instructions and enter the:
  a Business activity ▶ _____ **b** Product or service ▶ _____

3 At any time during the tax year, was any shareholder of the corporation a disregarded entity, a trust, an estate, or a nominee or similar person? If "Yes," attach Schedule B-1, Information on Certain Shareholders of an S Corporation . .

4 At the end of the tax year, did the corporation:

a Own directly 20% or more, or own, directly or indirectly, 50% or more of the total stock issued and outstanding of any foreign or domestic corporation? For rules of constructive ownership, see instructions. If "Yes," complete (i) through (v) below . . . .

(i) Name of Corporation	(ii) Employer Identification Number (if any)	(iii) Country of Incorporation	(iv) Percentage of Stock Owned	(v) If Percentage in (iv) is 100%, Enter the Date (if any) a Qualified Subchapter S Subsidiary Election Was Made

b Own directly an interest of 20% or more, or own, directly or indirectly, an interest of 50% or more in the profit, loss, or capital in any foreign or domestic partnership (including an entity treated as a partnership) or in the beneficial interest of a trust? For rules of constructive ownership, see instructions. If "Yes," complete (i) through (v) below . . . .

(i) Name of Entity	(ii) Employer Identification Number (if any)	(iii) Type of Entity	(iv) Country of Organization	(v) Maximum Percentage Owned in Profit, Loss, or Capital

5 a At the end of the tax year, did the corporation have any outstanding shares of restricted stock? . . . .
  If "Yes," complete lines (i) and (ii) below.
  (i)   Total shares of restricted stock . . . . ▶ _____
  (ii)   Total shares of non-restricted stock . . . . ▶ _____

b At the end of the tax year, did the corporation have any outstanding stock options, warrants, or similar instruments? .
  If "Yes," complete lines (i) and (ii) below.
  (i)   Total shares of stock outstanding at the end of the tax year ▶ _____
  (ii)   Total shares of stock outstanding if all instruments were executed ▶ _____

6 Has this corporation filed, or is it required to file, **Form 8918,** Material Advisor Disclosure Statement, to provide information on any reportable transaction? . . . .

7 Check this box if the corporation issued publicly offered debt instruments with original issue discount . . . . ▶ ☐
  If checked, the corporation may have to file **Form 8281,** Information Return for Publicly Offered Original Issue Discount Instruments.

8 If the corporation: **(a)** was a C corporation before it elected to be an S corporation **or** the corporation acquired an asset with a basis determined by reference to the basis of the asset (or the basis of any other property) in the hands of a C corporation **and (b)** has net unrealized built-in gain in excess of the net recognized built-in gain from prior years, enter the net unrealized built-in gain reduced by net recognized built-in gain from prior years (see instructions) . . . . ▶ $ _____

9 Enter the accumulated earnings and profits of the corporation at the end of the tax year. $ _____

10 Does the corporation satisfy **both** of the following conditions?
  a The corporation's total receipts (see instructions) for the tax year were less than $250,000 . . . .
  b The corporation's total assets at the end of the tax year were less than $250,000 . . . .
    If "Yes," the corporation is not required to complete Schedules L and M-1.

11 During the tax year, did the corporation have any non-shareholder debt that was canceled, was forgiven, or had the terms modified so as to reduce the principal amount of the debt? . . . .
    If "Yes," enter the amount of principal reduction $ _____

12 During the tax year, was a qualified subchapter S subsidiary election terminated or revoked? If "Yes," see instructions .

13 a Did the corporation make any payments in 2014 that would require it to file Form(s) 1099? . . . .
  b If "Yes," did the corporation file or will it file required Forms 1099? . . . .

Form **1120S** (2014)

Form 1120S (2014)   Page **3**

Schedule K		Shareholders' Pro Rata Share Items		Total amount	
	1	Ordinary business income (loss) (page 1, line 21)	**1**		
	2	Net rental real estate income (loss) (attach Form 8825)	**2**		
	3a	Other gross rental income (loss)	3a		
	b	Expenses from other rental activities (attach statement) . .	3b		
	c	Other net rental income (loss). Subtract line 3b from line 3a	**3c**		
	4	Interest income	**4**		
	5	Dividends: **a** Ordinary dividends	**5a**		
		b Qualified dividends	5b		
	6	Royalties	**6**		
	7	Net short-term capital gain (loss) (attach Schedule D (Form 1120S))	**7**		
	8a	Net long-term capital gain (loss) (attach Schedule D (Form 1120S))	**8a**		
	b	Collectibles (28%) gain (loss)	8b		
	c	Unrecaptured section 1250 gain (attach statement)	8c		
	9	Net section 1231 gain (loss) (attach Form 4797)	**9**		
	10	Other income (loss) (see instructions) . . Type ▶	**10**		
	11	Section 179 deduction (attach Form 4562)	**11**		
	12a	Charitable contributions	**12a**		
	b	Investment interest expense	**12b**		
	c	Section 59(e)(2) expenditures **(1)** Type ▶ _____ **(2)** Amount ▶	12c(2)		
	d	Other deductions (see instructions) . . . Type ▶	**12d**		
	13a	Low-income housing credit (section 42(j)(5))	**13a**		
	b	Low-income housing credit (other)	**13b**		
	c	Qualified rehabilitation expenditures (rental real estate) (attach Form 3468, if applicable) . .	**13c**		
	d	Other rental real estate credits (see instructions) Type ▶ _____	**13d**		
	e	Other rental credits (see instructions) . . Type ▶ _____	**13e**		
	f	Biofuel producer credit (attach Form 6478)	**13f**		
	g	Other credits (see instructions) . . . . . Type ▶	**13g**		
	14a	Name of country or U.S. possession ▶ _____			
	b	Gross income from all sources	**14b**		
	c	Gross income sourced at shareholder level	**14c**		
		Foreign gross income sourced at corporate level			
	d	Passive category	**14d**		
	e	General category	**14e**		
	f	Other (attach statement)	**14f**		
		Deductions allocated and apportioned at shareholder level			
	g	Interest expense	**14g**		
	h	Other	**14h**		
		Deductions allocated and apportioned at corporate level to foreign source income			
	i	Passive category	**14i**		
	j	General category	**14j**		
	k	Other (attach statement)	**14k**		
		Other information			
	l	Total foreign taxes (check one): ▶ ☐ Paid ☐ Accrued	**14l**		
	m	Reduction in taxes available for credit (attach statement)	**14m**		
	n	Other foreign tax information (attach statement)			
	15a	Post-1986 depreciation adjustment	**15a**		
	b	Adjusted gain or loss	**15b**		
	c	Depletion (other than oil and gas)	**15c**		
	d	Oil, gas, and geothermal properties—gross income	**15d**		
	e	Oil, gas, and geothermal properties—deductions	**15e**		
	f	Other AMT items (attach statement)	**15f**		
	16a	Tax-exempt interest income	**16a**		
	b	Other tax-exempt income	**16b**		
	c	Nondeductible expenses	**16c**		
	d	Distributions (attach statement if required) (see instructions)	**16d**		
	e	Repayment of loans from shareholders	**16e**		

Row group labels (left margin, top to bottom): Income (Loss); Deductions; Credits; Foreign Transactions; Alternative Minimum Tax (AMT) Items; Items Affecting Shareholder Basis

Form **1120S** (2014)

Form 1120S (2014)

Schedule K	Shareholders' Pro Rata Share Items (continued)		Total amount		
Other Information	**17a** Investment income	**17a**			
	b Investment expenses	**17b**			
	c Dividend distributions paid from accumulated earnings and profits	**17c**			
	d Other items and amounts (attach statement)				
Reconciliation	**18** **Income/loss reconciliation.** Combine the amounts on lines 1 through 10 in the far right column. From the result, subtract the sum of the amounts on lines 11 through 12d and 14l	**18**			

Schedule L	Balance Sheets per Books	Beginning of tax year		End of tax year	
	Assets	(a)	(b)	(c)	(d)
1	Cash				
2a	Trade notes and accounts receivable . . .				
b	Less allowance for bad debts	( )		( )	
3	Inventories				
4	U.S. government obligations				
5	Tax-exempt securities (see instructions) . .				
6	Other current assets (attach statement) . . .				
7	Loans to shareholders				
8	Mortgage and real estate loans				
9	Other investments (attach statement) . . .				
10a	Buildings and other depreciable assets . . .				
b	Less accumulated depreciation	( )		( )	
11a	Depletable assets				
b	Less accumulated depletion	( )		( )	
12	Land (net of any amortization)				
13a	Intangible assets (amortizable only)				
b	Less accumulated amortization	( )		( )	
14	Other assets (attach statement)				
15	Total assets				
	Liabilities and Shareholders' Equity				
16	Accounts payable				
17	Mortgages, notes, bonds payable in less than 1 year				
18	Other current liabilities (attach statement) . .				
19	Loans from shareholders				
20	Mortgages, notes, bonds payable in 1 year or more				
21	Other liabilities (attach statement)				
22	Capital stock				
23	Additional paid-in capital				
24	Retained earnings				
25	Adjustments to shareholders' equity (attach statement)				
26	Less cost of treasury stock		( )		( )
27	Total liabilities and shareholders' equity . .				

Form **1120S** (2014)

Form 1120S (2014)

Schedule M-1	Reconciliation of Income (Loss) per Books With Income (Loss) per Return

Note. The corporation may be required to file Schedule M-3 (see instructions)

1	Net income (loss) per books			5	Income recorded on books this year not included on Schedule K, lines 1 through 10 (itemize):	
2	Income included on Schedule K, lines 1, 2, 3c, 4, 5a, 6, 7, 8a, 9, and 10, not recorded on books this year (itemize) _____			a	Tax-exempt interest $ _____	
3	Expenses recorded on books this year not included on Schedule K, lines 1 through 12 and 14I (itemize):			6	Deductions included on Schedule K, lines 1 through 12 and 14I, not charged against book income this year (itemize):	
a	Depreciation $ _____			a	Depreciation $ _____	
b	Travel and entertainment $ _____					
	_____			7	Add lines 5 and 6	
4	Add lines 1 through 3			8	Income (loss) (Schedule K, line 18). Line 4 less line 7	

Schedule M-2	Analysis of Accumulated Adjustments Account, Other Adjustments Account, and Shareholders' Undistributed Taxable Income Previously Taxed (see instructions)

		(a) Accumulated adjustments account	(b) Other adjustments account	(c) Shareholders' undistributed taxable income previously taxed
1	Balance at beginning of tax year			
2	Ordinary income from page 1, line 21 . . .			
3	Other additions			
4	Loss from page 1, line 21	( )		
5	Other reductions	( )	( )	
6	Combine lines 1 through 5			
7	Distributions other than dividend distributions			
8	Balance at end of tax year. Subtract line 7 from line 6			

Form **1120S** (2014)

671113

☐ Final K-1   ☐ Amended K-1   OMB No. 1545-0123

Schedule K-1
(Form 1120S)
Department of the Treasury
Internal Revenue Service

2014

For calendar year 2014, or tax
year beginning _____ , 2014
ending _____ , 20 ____

Shareholder's Share of Income, Deductions, Credits, etc.
▶ See back of form and separate instructions.

Part I	**Information About the Corporation**

A   Corporation's employer identification number

B   Corporation's name, address, city, state, and ZIP code

C   IRS Center where corporation filed return

Part II	**Information About the Shareholder**

D   Shareholder's identifying number

E   Shareholder's name, address, city, state, and ZIP code

F   Shareholder's percentage of stock
ownership for tax year . . . . _____ %

For IRS Use Only

Part III **Shareholder's Share of Current Year Income, Deductions, Credits, and Other Items**

1	Ordinary business income (loss)	13	Credits
2	Net rental real estate income (loss)		
3	Other net rental income (loss)		
4	Interest income		
5a	Ordinary dividends		
5b	Qualified dividends	14	Foreign transactions
6	Royalties		
7	Net short-term capital gain (loss)		
8a	Net long-term capital gain (loss)		
8b	Collectibles (28%) gain (loss)		
8c	Unrecaptured section 1250 gain		
9	Net section 1231 gain (loss)		
10	Other income (loss)	15	Alternative minimum tax (AMT) items
11	Section 179 deduction	16	Items affecting shareholder basis
12	Other deductions		
		17	Other information

* See attached statement for additional information.

For Paperwork Reduction Act Notice, see Instructions for Form 1120S.   IRS.gov/form1120s   Cat. No. 11520D   **Schedule K-1 (Form 1120S) 2014**

Form **2553**
(Rev. December 2013)

Department of the Treasury
Internal Revenue Service

Election by a Small Business Corporation
(Under section 1362 of the Internal Revenue Code)

▶ See Parts II and III on page 3.
▶ **You can fax this form to the IRS (see separate instructions).**
▶ **Information about Form 2553 and its separate instructions is at** *www.irs.gov/form2553.*

OMB No. 1545-0123

Note. This election to be an S corporation can be accepted only if all the tests are met under *Who May Elect* in the instructions, all shareholders have signed the consent statement, an officer has signed below, and the exact name and address of the corporation (entity) and other required form information have been provided.

Part I	Election Information

Type or Print

Name (see instructions)	**A** Employer identification number
Number, street, and room or suite no. (If a P.O. box, see instructions.)	**B** Date incorporated
City or town, state, and ZIP code	**C** State of incorporation

D   Check the applicable box(es) if the corporation (entity), after applying for the EIN shown in **A** above, changed its ☐ name or ☐ address

E   Election is to be effective for tax year beginning (month, day, year) (see instructions) . . . . . . ▶ _____
   Caution. A corporation (entity) making the election for its first tax year in existence will usually enter the beginning date of a short tax year that begins on a date other than January 1.

F   Selected tax year:
   (1) ☐   Calendar year
   (2) ☐   Fiscal year ending (month and day) ▶ _____
   (3) ☐   52-53-week year ending with reference to the month of December
   (4) ☐   52-53-week year ending with reference to the month of ▶ _____
   If box (2) or (4) is checked, complete Part II.

G   If more than 100 shareholders are listed for item J (see page 2), check this box if treating members of a family as one shareholder results in no more than 100 shareholders (see test 2 under *Who May Elect* in the instructions) ▶ ☐

H   Name and title of officer or legal representative who the IRS may call for more information | **I** Telephone number of officer or legal representative

If this S corporation election is being filed late, I declare that I had reasonable cause for not filing Form 2553 timely, and if this late election is being made by an entity eligible to elect to be treated as a corporation, I declare that I also had reasonable cause for not filing an entity classification election timely and that the representations listed in Part IV are true. See below for my explanation of the reasons the election or elections were not made on time and a description of my diligent actions to correct the mistake upon its discovery (see instructions).

Sign Here

Under penalties of perjury, I declare that I have examined this election, including accompanying documents, and, to the best of my knowledge and belief, the election contains all the relevant facts relating to the election, and such facts are true, correct, and complete.

▶ _____
Signature of officer

_____
Title

_____
Date

For Paperwork Reduction Act Notice, see separate instructions.   Cat. No. 18629R   Form **2553** (Rev. 12-2013)

Form 2553 (Rev. 12-2013)

Page **2**

Part I	Election Information (continued) **Note.** If you need more rows, use additional copies of page 2.

J Name and address of each shareholder or former shareholder required to consent to the election. (see instructions)	K **Shareholder's Consent Statement** Under penalties of perjury, I declare that I consent to the election of the above-named corporation (entity) to be an S corporation under section 1362(a) and that I have examined this consent statement, including accompanying documents, and, to the best of my knowledge and belief, the election contains all the relevant facts relating to the election, and such facts are true, correct, and complete. I understand my consent is binding and may not be withdrawn after the corporation (entity) has made a valid election. If seeking relief for a late filed election, I also declare under penalties of perjury that I have reported my income on all affected returns consistent with the S corporation election for the year for which the election should have been filed (see beginning date entered on line E) and for all subsequent years.		L Stock owned or percentage of ownership (see instructions)		M Social security number or employer identification number (see instructions)	N Shareholder's tax year ends (month and day)
	Signature	Date	Number of shares or percentage of ownership	Date(s) acquired		

Form **2553** (Rev. 12-2013)

Form **4562**

Department of the Treasury
Internal Revenue Service   (99)

Depreciation and Amortization
(Including Information on Listed Property)
▶ Attach to your tax return.
▶ Information about Form 4562 and its separate instructions is at *www.irs.gov/form4562*.

OMB No. 1545-0172

20**14**

Attachment
Sequence No. **179**

Name(s) shown on return	Business or activity to which this form relates	Identifying number

Part I   **Election To Expense Certain Property Under Section 179**
Note: *If you have any listed property, complete Part V before you complete Part I.*

1 Maximum amount (see instructions)	**1**	
2 Total cost of section 179 property placed in service (see instructions)	**2**	
3 Threshold cost of section 179 property before reduction in limitation (see instructions)	**3**	
4 Reduction in limitation. Subtract line 3 from line 2. If zero or less, enter -0-	**4**	
5 Dollar limitation for tax year. Subtract line 4 from line 1. If zero or less, enter -0-. If married filing separately, see instructions	**5**	

6	**(a)** Description of property	**(b)** Cost (business use only)	**(c)** Elected cost	

7 Listed property. Enter the amount from line 29	**7**	
8 Total elected cost of section 179 property. Add amounts in column (c), lines 6 and 7	**8**	
9 Tentative deduction. Enter the **smaller** of line 5 or line 8	**9**	
10 Carryover of disallowed deduction from line 13 of your 2013 Form 4562	**10**	
11 Business income limitation. Enter the smaller of business income (not less than zero) or line 5 (see instructions)	**11**	
12 Section 179 expense deduction. Add lines 9 and 10, but do not enter more than line 11	**12**	
13 Carryover of disallowed deduction to 2015. Add lines 9 and 10, less line 12 ▶	**13**	

Note: *Do not use Part II or Part III below for listed property. Instead, use Part V.*

Part II   **Special Depreciation Allowance and Other Depreciation (Do not** include listed property.**)** (See instructions.)

14 Special depreciation allowance for qualified property (other than listed property) placed in service during the tax year (see instructions)	**14**	
15 Property subject to section 168(f)(1) election	**15**	
16 Other depreciation (including ACRS)	**16**	

Part III   **MACRS Depreciation (Do not** include listed property.**)** (See instructions.)

Section A

17 MACRS deductions for assets placed in service in tax years beginning before 2014	**17**	
18 If you are electing to group any assets placed in service during the tax year into one or more general asset accounts, check here . . . . ▶ ☐		

Section B—Assets Placed in Service During 2014 Tax Year Using the General Depreciation System

(a) Classification of property	**(b)** Month and year placed in service	**(c)** Basis for depreciation (business/investment use only—see instructions)	**(d)** Recovery period	**(e)** Convention	**(f)** Method	**(g)** Depreciation deduction
19a 3-year property						
b 5-year property						
c 7-year property						
d 10-year property						
e 15-year property						
f 20-year property						
g 25-year property			25 yrs.		S/L	
h Residential rental property			27.5 yrs.	MM	S/L	
			27.5 yrs.	MM	S/L	
i Nonresidential real property			39 yrs.	MM	S/L	
				MM	S/L	

Section C—Assets Placed in Service During 2014 Tax Year Using the Alternative Depreciation System

20a Class life					S/L	
b 12-year			12 yrs.		S/L	
c 40-year			40 yrs.	MM	S/L	

Part IV   **Summary** (See instructions.)

21 Listed property. Enter amount from line 28	**21**	
22 **Total.** Add amounts from line 12, lines 14 through 17, lines 19 and 20 in column (g), and line 21. Enter here and on the appropriate lines of your return. Partnerships and S corporations—see instructions .	**22**	
23 For assets shown above and placed in service during the current year, enter the portion of the basis attributable to section 263A costs	**23**	

For Paperwork Reduction Act Notice, see separate instructions.   Cat. No. 12906N   Form **4562** (2014)

Form 4562 (2014)

Part V | **Listed Property** (Include automobiles, certain other vehicles, certain aircraft, certain computers, and property used for entertainment, recreation, or amusement.)

Note: *For any vehicle for which you are using the standard mileage rate or deducting lease expense, complete **only** 24a, 24b, columns (a) through (c) of Section A, all of Section B, and Section C if applicable.*

Section A—Depreciation and Other Information (Caution: *See the instructions for limits for passenger automobiles.***)**

24a Do you have evidence to support the business/investment use claimed? ☐ Yes ☐ No   **24b** If "Yes," is the evidence written? ☐ Yes ☐ No

(a) Type of property (list vehicles first)	(b) Date placed in service	(c) Business/ investment use percentage	(d) Cost or other basis	(e) Basis for depreciation (business/investment use only)	(f) Recovery period	(g) Method/ Convention	(h) Depreciation deduction	(i) Elected section 179 cost
25 Special depreciation allowance for qualified listed property placed in service during the tax year and used more than 50% in a qualified business use (see instructions) . **25**								
26 Property used more than 50% in a qualified business use:								
		%						
		%						
		%						
27 Property used 50% or less in a qualified business use:								
		%			S/L –			
		%			S/L –			
		%			S/L –			
28 Add amounts in column (h), lines 25 through 27. Enter here and on line 21, page 1 . **28**								
29 Add amounts in column (i), line 26. Enter here and on line 7, page 1 . . . . **29**								

Section B—Information on Use of Vehicles

Complete this section for vehicles used by a sole proprietor, partner, or other "more than 5% owner," or related person. If you provided vehicles to your employees, first answer the questions in Section C to see if you meet an exception to completing this section for those vehicles.

		(a) Vehicle 1		(b) Vehicle 2		(c) Vehicle 3		(d) Vehicle 4		(e) Vehicle 5		(f) Vehicle 6	
30	Total business/investment miles driven during the year (**do not** include commuting miles) .												
31	Total commuting miles driven during the year												
32	Total other personal (noncommuting) miles driven												
33	Total miles driven during the year. Add lines 30 through 32												
34	Was the vehicle available for personal use during off-duty hours?	Yes	No	Yes	No	Yes	No	Yes	No	Yes	No	Yes	No
35	Was the vehicle used primarily by a more than 5% owner or related person? . .												
36	Is another vehicle available for personal use?												

Section C—Questions for Employers Who Provide Vehicles for Use by Their Employees

Answer these questions to determine if you meet an exception to completing Section B for vehicles used by employees who **are not** more than 5% owners or related persons (see instructions).

		Yes	No
37	Do you maintain a written policy statement that prohibits all personal use of vehicles, including commuting, by your employees?		
38	Do you maintain a written policy statement that prohibits personal use of vehicles, except commuting, by your employees? See the instructions for vehicles used by corporate officers, directors, or 1% or more owners . .		
39	Do you treat all use of vehicles by employees as personal use?		
40	Do you provide more than five vehicles to your employees, obtain information from your employees about the use of the vehicles, and retain the information received?		
41	Do you meet the requirements concerning qualified automobile demonstration use? (See instructions.) . . .		

Note: *If your answer to 37, 38, 39, 40, or 41 is "Yes," do not complete Section B for the covered vehicles.*

Part VI | **Amortization**

(a) Description of costs	(b) Date amortization begins	(c) Amortizable amount	(d) Code section	(e) Amortization period or percentage	(f) Amortization for this year
42 Amortization of costs that begins during your 2014 tax year (see instructions):					
43 Amortization of costs that began before your 2014 tax year **43**					
44 **Total.** Add amounts in column (f). See the instructions for where to report **44**					

Form **4562** (2014)

Form **4626**

Department of the Treasury
Internal Revenue Service

Alternative Minimum Tax—Corporations

▶ Attach to the corporation's tax return.
▶ Information about Form 4626 and its separate instructions is at *www.irs.gov/form4626.*

OMB No. 1545-0123

20**14**

Name	Employer identification number

Note: *See the instructions to find out if the corporation is a small corporation exempt from the alternative minimum tax (AMT) under section 55(e).*

1	Taxable income or (loss) before net operating loss deduction	**1**	
2	**Adjustments and preferences:**		
a	Depreciation of post-1986 property	**2a**	
b	Amortization of certified pollution control facilities.	**2b**	
c	Amortization of mining exploration and development costs	**2c**	
d	Amortization of circulation expenditures (personal holding companies only)	**2d**	
e	Adjusted gain or loss	**2e**	
f	Long-term contracts	**2f**	
g	Merchant marine capital construction funds.	**2g**	
h	Section 833(b) deduction (Blue Cross, Blue Shield, and similar type organizations only)	**2h**	
i	Tax shelter farm activities (personal service corporations only)	**2i**	
j	Passive activities (closely held corporations and personal service corporations only)	**2j**	
k	Loss limitations	**2k**	
l	Depletion	**2l**	
m	Tax-exempt interest income from specified private activity bonds	**2m**	
n	Intangible drilling costs	**2n**	
o	Other adjustments and preferences	**2o**	
3	Pre-adjustment alternative minimum taxable income (AMTI). Combine lines 1 through 2o.	**3**	

4 **Adjusted current earnings (ACE) adjustment:**

a	ACE from line 10 of the ACE worksheet in the instructions	**4a**	
b	Subtract line 3 from line 4a. If line 3 exceeds line 4a, enter the difference as a negative amount (see instructions).	**4b**	
c	Multiply line 4b by 75% (.75). Enter the result as a positive amount	**4c**	
d	Enter the excess, if any, of the corporation's total increases in AMTI from prior year ACE adjustments over its total reductions in AMTI from prior year ACE adjustments (see instructions). **Note:** *You* **must** *enter an amount on line 4d (even if line 4b is positive).*	**4d**	
e	ACE adjustment. • If line 4b is zero or more, enter the amount from line 4c • If line 4b is less than zero, enter the **smaller** of line 4c or line 4d as a negative amount	**4e**	
5	Combine lines 3 and 4e. If zero or less, stop here; the corporation does not owe any AMT	**5**	
6	Alternative tax net operating loss deduction (see instructions).	**6**	
7	**Alternative minimum taxable income.** Subtract line 6 from line 5. If the corporation held a residual interest in a REMIC, see instructions	**7**	

8 **Exemption phase-out** (if line 7 is $310,000 or more, skip lines 8a and 8b and enter -0- on line 8c):

a	Subtract $150,000 from line 7 (if completing this line for a member of a controlled group, see instructions). If zero or less, enter -0-	**8a**	
b	Multiply line 8a by 25% (.25).	**8b**	
c	Exemption. Subtract line 8b from $40,000 (if completing this line for a member of a controlled group, see instructions). If zero or less, enter -0-	**8c**	
9	Subtract line 8c from line 7. If zero or less, enter -0-	**9**	
10	Multiply line 9 by 20% (.20)	**10**	
11	Alternative minimum tax foreign tax credit (AMTFTC) (see instructions)	**11**	
12	Tentative minimum tax. Subtract line 11 from line 10.	**12**	
13	Regular tax liability before applying all credits except the foreign tax credit	**13**	
14	**Alternative minimum tax.** Subtract line 13 from line 12. If zero or less, enter -0-. Enter here and on Form 1120, Schedule J, line 3, or the appropriate line of the corporation's income tax return	**14**	

Form **4797**

Department of the Treasury
Internal Revenue Service

Sales of Business Property
(Also Involuntary Conversions and Recapture Amounts
Under Sections 179 and 280F(b)(2))

► Attach to your tax return.
► Information about Form 4797 and its separate instructions is at *www.irs.gov/form4797.*

OMB No. 1545-0184

20**14**

Attachment
Sequence No. **27**

Name(s) shown on return

Identifying number

1 Enter the gross proceeds from sales or exchanges reported to you for 2014 on Form(s) 1099-B or 1099-S (or substitute statement) that you are including on line 2, 10, or 20 (see instructions) . . . . | **1** |

Part I **Sales or Exchanges of Property Used in a Trade or Business and Involuntary Conversions From Other Than Casualty or Theft—Most Property Held More Than 1 Year** (see instructions)

2	**(a)** Description of property	**(b)** Date acquired (mo., day, yr.)	**(c)** Date sold (mo., day, yr.)	**(d)** Gross sales price	**(e)** Depreciation allowed or allowable since acquisition	**(f)** Cost or other basis, plus improvements and expense of sale	**(g)** Gain or (loss) Subtract (f) from the sum of (d) and (e)

3 Gain, if any, from Form 4684, line 39 . . . . | **3** |
4 Section 1231 gain from installment sales from Form 6252, line 26 or 37 . . . . | **4** |
5 Section 1231 gain or (loss) from like-kind exchanges from Form 8824 . . . . | **5** |
6 Gain, if any, from line 32, from other than casualty or theft. . . . . | **6** |
7 Combine lines 2 through 6. Enter the gain or (loss) here and on the appropriate line as follows: . . . . | **7** |

Partnerships (except electing large partnerships) and S corporations. Report the gain or (loss) following the instructions for Form 1065, Schedule K, line 10, or Form 1120S, Schedule K, line 9. Skip lines 8, 9, 11, and 12 below.

Individuals, partners, S corporation shareholders, and all others. If line 7 is zero or a loss, enter the amount from line 7 on line 11 below and skip lines 8 and 9. If line 7 is a gain and you did not have any prior year section 1231 losses, or they were recaptured in an earlier year, enter the gain from line 7 as a long-term capital gain on the Schedule D filed with your return and skip lines 8, 9, 11, and 12 below.

8 Nonrecaptured net section 1231 losses from prior years (see instructions) . . . . | **8** |
9 Subtract line 8 from line 7. If zero or less, enter -0-. If line 9 is zero, enter the gain from line 7 on line 12 below. If line 9 is more than zero, enter the amount from line 8 on line 12 below and enter the gain from line 9 as a long-term capital gain on the Schedule D filed with your return (see instructions) . . . . | **9** |

Part II **Ordinary Gains and Losses** (see instructions)

10 Ordinary gains and losses not included on lines 11 through 16 (include property held 1 year or less):

11 Loss, if any, from line 7 . . . . | **11** ( ) |
12 Gain, if any, from line 7 or amount from line 8, if applicable . . . . | **12** |
13 Gain, if any, from line 31 . . . . | **13** |
14 Net gain or (loss) from Form 4684, lines 31 and 38a . . . . | **14** |
15 Ordinary gain from installment sales from Form 6252, line 25 or 36 . . . . | **15** |
16 Ordinary gain or (loss) from like-kind exchanges from Form 8824. . . . . | **16** |
17 Combine lines 10 through 16 . . . . | **17** |
18 For all except individual returns, enter the amount from line 17 on the appropriate line of your return and skip lines a and b below. For individual returns, complete lines a and b below:

a If the loss on line 11 includes a loss from Form 4684, line 35, column (b)(ii), enter that part of the loss here. Enter the part of the loss from income-producing property on Schedule A (Form 1040), line 28, and the part of the loss from property used as an employee on Schedule A (Form 1040), line 23. Identify as from "Form 4797, line 18a." See instructions . . | **18a** |
b Redetermine the gain or (loss) on line 17 excluding the loss, if any, on line 18a. Enter here and on Form 1040, line 14 | **18b** |

For Paperwork Reduction Act Notice, see separate instructions.   Cat. No. 13086I   Form **4797** (2014)

Form 4797 (2014)
Page **2**

Part III   Gain From Disposition of Property Under Sections 1245, 1250, 1252, 1254, and 1255
(see instructions)

19	(a) Description of section 1245, 1250, 1252, 1254, or 1255 property:	(b) Date acquired (mo., day, yr.)	(c) Date sold (mo., day, yr.)
A			
B			
C			
D			

	These columns relate to the properties on lines 19A through 19D. ▶		**Property A**	**Property B**	**Property C**	**Property D**
20	Gross sales price (**Note:** *See line 1 before completing.*)	20				
21	Cost or other basis plus expense of sale	21				
22	Depreciation (or depletion) allowed or allowable. . .	22				
23	Adjusted basis. Subtract line 22 from line 21. . . .	23				
24	Total gain. Subtract line 23 from line 20	24				
25	**If section 1245 property:**					
a	Depreciation allowed or allowable from line 22 . . .	25a				
b	Enter the **smaller** of line 24 or 25a	25b				
26	**If section 1250 property:** If straight line depreciation was used, enter -0- on line 26g, except for a corporation subject to section 291.					
a	Additional depreciation after 1975 (see instructions) .	26a				
b	Applicable percentage multiplied by the **smaller** of line 24 or line 26a (see instructions)	26b				
c	Subtract line 26a from line 24. If residential rental property **or** line 24 is not more than line 26a, skip lines 26d and 26e	26c				
d	Additional depreciation after 1969 and before 1976. .	26d				
e	Enter the **smaller** of line 26c or 26d	26e				
f	Section 291 amount (corporations only)	26f				
g	Add lines 26b, 26e, and 26f.	26g				
27	**If section 1252 property:** Skip this section if you did not dispose of farmland or if this form is being completed for a partnership (other than an electing large partnership).					
a	Soil, water, and land clearing expenses	27a				
b	Line 27a multiplied by applicable percentage (see instructions)	27b				
c	Enter the **smaller** of line 24 or 27b	27c				
28	**If section 1254 property:**					
a	Intangible drilling and development costs, expenditures for development of mines and other natural deposits, mining exploration costs, and depletion (see instructions)	28a				
b	Enter the **smaller** of line 24 or 28a	28b				
29	**If section 1255 property:**					
a	Applicable percentage of payments excluded from income under section 126 (see instructions)	29a				
b	Enter the **smaller** of line 24 or 29a (see instructions) .	29b				

Summary of Part III Gains. Complete property columns A through D through line 29b before going to line 30.

30	Total gains for all properties. Add property columns A through D, line 24	30	
31	Add property columns A through D, lines 25b, 26g, 27c, 28b, and 29b. Enter here and on line 13	31	
32	Subtract line 31 from line 30. Enter the portion from casualty or theft on Form 4684, line 33. Enter the portion from other than casualty or theft on Form 4797, line 6	32	

Part IV   Recapture Amounts Under Sections 179 and 280F(b)(2) When Business Use Drops to 50% or Less
(see instructions)

			(a) Section 179	(b) Section 280F(b)(2)
33	Section 179 expense deduction or depreciation allowable in prior years.	33		
34	Recomputed depreciation (see instructions)	34		
35	Recapture amount. Subtract line 34 from line 33. See the instructions for where to report . .	35		

Form **4797** (2014)

Form **6251**

Department of the Treasury
Internal Revenue Service (99)

Alternative Minimum Tax—Individuals

▶ Information about Form 6251 and its separate instructions is at *www.irs.gov/form6251.*
▶ **Attach to Form 1040 or Form 1040NR.**

OMB No. 1545-0074

2014

Attachment
Sequence No. **32**

Name(s) shown on Form 1040 or Form 1040NR

Your social security number

Part I Alternative Minimum Taxable Income (See instructions for how to complete each line.)

1	If filing Schedule A (Form 1040), enter the amount from Form 1040, line 41, and go to line 2. Otherwise, enter the amount from Form 1040, line 38, and go to line 7. (If less than zero, enter as a negative amount.)	**1**
2	Medical and dental. If you or your spouse was 65 or older, enter the **smaller** of Schedule A (Form 1040), line 4, **or** 2.5% (.025) of Form 1040, line 38. If zero or less, enter -0-	**2**
3	Taxes from Schedule A (Form 1040), line 9	**3**
4	Enter the home mortgage interest adjustment, if any, from line 6 of the worksheet in the instructions for this line	**4**
5	Miscellaneous deductions from Schedule A (Form 1040), line 27.	**5**
6	If Form 1040, line 38, is $152,525 or less, enter -0-. Otherwise, see instructions	**6** ( )
7	Tax refund from Form 1040, line 10 or line 21	**7** ( )
8	Investment interest expense (difference between regular tax and AMT).	**8**
9	Depletion (difference between regular tax and AMT)	**9**
10	Net operating loss deduction from Form 1040, line 21. Enter as a positive amount	**10**
11	Alternative tax net operating loss deduction	**11** ( )
12	Interest from specified private activity bonds exempt from the regular tax	**12**
13	Qualified small business stock (7% of gain excluded under section 1202)	**13**
14	Exercise of incentive stock options (excess of AMT income over regular tax income)	**14**
15	Estates and trusts (amount from Schedule K-1 (Form 1041), box 12, code A)	**15**
16	Electing large partnerships (amount from Schedule K-1 (Form 1065-B), box 6)	**16**
17	Disposition of property (difference between AMT and regular tax gain or loss)	**17**
18	Depreciation on assets placed in service after 1986 (difference between regular tax and AMT)	**18**
19	Passive activities (difference between AMT and regular tax income or loss)	**19**
20	Loss limitations (difference between AMT and regular tax income or loss)	**20**
21	Circulation costs (difference between regular tax and AMT)	**21**
22	Long-term contracts (difference between AMT and regular tax income)	**22**
23	Mining costs (difference between regular tax and AMT)	**23**
24	Research and experimental costs (difference between regular tax and AMT)	**24**
25	Income from certain installment sales before January 1, 1987	**25** ( )
26	Intangible drilling costs preference	**26**
27	Other adjustments, including income-based related adjustments	**27**
28	**Alternative minimum taxable income.** Combine lines 1 through 27. (If married filing separately and line 28 is more than $242,450, see instructions.)	**28**

Part II Alternative Minimum Tax (AMT)

29 Exemption. (If you were under age 24 at the end of 2014, see instructions.)

IF your filing status is . . .	AND line 28 is not over . . .	THEN enter on line 29 . . .
Single or head of household	$117,300	$52,800
Married filing jointly or qualifying widow(er)	156,500	82,100
Married filing separately	78,250	41,050

If line 28 is **over** the amount shown above for your filing status, see instructions.

29

30	Subtract line 29 from line 28. If more than zero, go to line 31. If zero or less, enter -0- here and on lines 31, 33, and 35, and go to line 34	**30**
31	• If you are filing Form 2555 or 2555-EZ, see instructions for the amount to enter. • If you reported capital gain distributions directly on Form 1040, line 13; you reported qualified dividends on Form 1040, line 9b; **or** you had a gain on both lines 15 and 16 of Schedule D (Form 1040) (as refigured for the AMT, if necessary), complete Part III on the back and enter the amount from line 64 here. • **All others:** If line 30 is $182,500 or less ($91,250 or less if married filing separately), multiply line 30 by 26% (.26). Otherwise, multiply line 30 by 28% (.28) and subtract $3,650 ($1,825 if married filing separately) from the result.	**31**
32	Alternative minimum tax foreign tax credit (see instructions)	**32**
33	Tentative minimum tax. Subtract line 32 from line 31	**33**
34	Add Form 1040, line 44 (minus any tax from Form 4972), and Form 1040, line 46. Subtract from the result any foreign tax credit from Form 1040, line 48. If you used Schedule J to figure your tax on Form 1040, line 44, refigure that tax without using Schedule J before completing this line (see instructions)	**34**
35	**AMT.** Subtract line 34 from line 33. If zero or less, enter -0-. Enter here and on Form 1040, line 45	**35**

For Paperwork Reduction Act Notice, see your tax return instructions.   Cat. No. 13600G   Form **6251** (2014)

Form 6251 (2014)   Page **2**

Part III   Tax Computation Using Maximum Capital Gains Rates

Complete Part III only if you are required to do so by line 31 or by the Foreign Earned Income Tax Worksheet in the instructions.

36 Enter the amount from Form 6251, line 30. If you are filing Form 2555 or 2555-EZ, enter the amount from line 3 of the worksheet in the instructions for line 31 . . . . **36**

37 Enter the amount from line 6 of the Qualified Dividends and Capital Gain Tax Worksheet in the instructions for Form 1040, line 44, or the amount from line 13 of the Schedule D Tax Worksheet in the instructions for Schedule D (Form 1040), whichever applies (as refigured for the AMT, if necessary) (see instructions). If you are filing Form 2555 or 2555-EZ, see instructions for the amount to enter **37**

38 Enter the amount from Schedule D (Form 1040), line 19 (as refigured for the AMT, if necessary) (see instructions). If you are filing Form 2555 or 2555-EZ, see instructions for the amount to enter **38**

39 If you did not complete a Schedule D Tax Worksheet for the regular tax or the AMT, enter the amount from line 37. Otherwise, add lines 37 and 38, and enter the **smaller** of that result or the amount from line 10 of the Schedule D Tax Worksheet (as refigured for the AMT, if necessary). If you are filing Form 2555 or 2555-EZ, see instructions for the amount to enter **39**

40 Enter the **smaller** of line 36 or line 39 . . . . **40**

41 Subtract line 40 from line 36 . . . . **41**

42 If line 41 is $182,500 or less ($91,250 or less if married filing separately), multiply line 41 by 26% (.26). Otherwise, multiply line 41 by 28% (.28) and subtract $3,650 ($1,825 if married filing separately) from the result . . . ▶ **42**

43 Enter:
• $73,800 if married filing jointly or qualifying widow(er),
• $36,900 if single or married filing separately, or } **43**
• $49,400 if head of household.

44 Enter the amount from line 7 of the Qualified Dividends and Capital Gain Tax Worksheet in the instructions for Form 1040, line 44, or the amount from line 14 of the Schedule D Tax Worksheet in the instructions for Schedule D (Form 1040), whichever applies (as figured for the regular tax). If you did not complete either worksheet for the regular tax, enter the amount from Form 1040, line 43; if zero or less, enter -0-. If you are filing Form 2555 or 2555-EZ, see instructions for the amount to enter **44**

45 Subtract line 44 from line 43. If zero or less, enter -0- **45**

46 Enter the **smaller** of line 36 or line 37 . . . . **46**

47 Enter the **smaller** of line 45 or line 46. This amount is taxed at 0% **47**

48 Subtract line 47 from line 46 . . . . **48**

49 Enter:
• $406,750 if single
• $228,800 if married filing separately } **49**
• $457,600 if married filing jointly or qualifying widow(er)
• $432,200 if head of household

50 Enter the amount from line 45 . . . . **50**

51 Enter the amount from line 7 of the Qualified Dividends and Capital Gain Tax Worksheet in the instructions for Form 1040, line 44, or the amount from line 19 of the Schedule D Tax Worksheet, whichever applies (as figured for the regular tax). If you did not complete either worksheet for the regular tax, enter the amount from Form 1040, line 43; if zero or less, enter -0-. If you are filing Form 2555 or Form 2555-EZ, see instructions for the amount to enter **51**

52 Add line 50 and line 51 . . . . **52**

53 Subtract line 52 from line 49. If zero or less, enter -0- **53**

54 Enter the smaller of line 48 or line 53 . . . . **54**

55 Multiply line 54 by 15% (.15) . . . . ▶ **55**

56 Add lines 47 and 54 . . . . **56**

If lines 56 and 36 are the same, skip lines 57 through 61 and go to line 62. Otherwise, go to line 57.

57 Subtract line 56 from line 46 . . . . **57**

58 Multiply line 57 by 20% (.20) . . . . ▶ **58**

If line 38 is zero or blank, skip lines 59 through 61 and go to line 62. Otherwise, go to line 59.

59 Add lines 41, 56, and 57 . . . . **59**

60 Subtract line 59 from line 36 . . . . **60**

61 Multiply line 60 by 25% (.25) . . . . ▶ **61**

62 Add lines 42, 55, 58, and 61 . . . . **62**

63 If line 36 is $182,500 or less ($91,250 or less if married filing separately), multiply line 36 by 26% (.26). Otherwise, multiply line 36 by 28% (.28) and subtract $3,650 ($1,825 if married filing separately) from the result **63**

64 Enter the **smaller** of line 62 or line 63 here and on line 31. If you are filing Form 2555 or 2555-EZ, do not enter this amount on line 31. Instead, enter it on line 4 of the worksheet in the instructions for line 31 . . . **64**

Form **6251** (2014)

Form **8949**	**Sales and Other Dispositions of Capital Assets**	OMB No. 1545-0074

Form **8949**

Department of the Treasury
Internal Revenue Service

Sales and Other Dispositions of Capital Assets

▶ Information about Form 8949 and its separate instructions is at *www.irs.gov/form8949*.
▶ File with your Schedule D to list your transactions for lines 1b, 2, 3, 8b, 9, and 10 of Schedule D.

OMB No. 1545-0074

20**14**

Attachment
Sequence No. **12A**

Name(s) shown on return

Social security number or taxpayer identification number

Before you check Box A, B, or C below, see whether you received any Form(s) 1099-B or substitute statement(s) from your broker. A substitute statement will have the same information as Form 1099-B. Either may show your basis (usually your cost) even if your broker did not report it to the IRS. Brokers must report basis to the IRS for most stock you bought in 2011 or later (and for certain debt instruments you bought in 2014 or later).

Part I **Short-Term.** Transactions involving capital assets you held 1 year or less are short term. For long-term transactions, see page 2.

Note. You may aggregate all short-term transactions reported on Form(s) 1099-B showing basis was reported to the IRS and for which no adjustments or codes are required. Enter the total directly on Schedule D, line 1a; you are not required to report these transactions on Form 8949 (see instructions).

You *must* check Box A, B, *or* C below. Check only one box. If more than one box applies for your short-term transactions, complete a separate Form 8949, page 1, for each applicable box. If you have more short-term transactions than will fit on this page for one or more of the boxes, complete as many forms with the same box checked as you need.

- ☐ **(A)** Short-term transactions reported on Form(s) 1099-B showing basis was reported to the IRS (see **Note** above)
- ☐ **(B)** Short-term transactions reported on Form(s) 1099-B showing basis was **not** reported to the IRS
- ☐ **(C)** Short-term transactions not reported to you on Form 1099-B

1 (a) Description of property (Example: 100 sh. XYZ Co.)	(b) Date acquired (Mo., day, yr.)	(c) Date sold or disposed (Mo., day, yr.)	(d) Proceeds (sales price) (see instructions)	(e) Cost or other basis. See the **Note** below and see *Column (e)* in the separate instructions	Adjustment, if any, to gain or loss. If you enter an amount in column (g), enter a code in column (f). See the separate instructions. (f) Code(s) from instructions	(g) Amount of adjustment	(h) Gain or (loss). Subtract column (e) from column (d) and combine the result with column (g)

2 Totals. Add the amounts in columns (d), (e), (g), and (h) (subtract negative amounts). Enter each total here and include on your Schedule D, **line 1b** (if **Box A** above is checked), **line 2** (if **Box B** above is checked), or **line 3** (if **Box C** above is checked) ▶

Note. If you checked Box A above but the basis reported to the IRS was incorrect, enter in column (e) the basis as reported to the IRS, and enter an adjustment in column (g) to correct the basis. See *Column (g)* in the separate instructions for how to figure the amount of the adjustment.

For Paperwork Reduction Act Notice, see your tax return instructions.   Cat. No. 37768Z   Form **8949** (2014)

Form 8949 (2014)

Name(s) shown on return. Name and SSN or taxpayer identification no. not required if shown on other side	Social security number or taxpayer identification number

Before you check Box D, E, or F below, see whether you received any Form(s) 1099-B or substitute statement(s) from your broker. A substitute statement will have the same information as Form 1099-B. Either may show your basis (usually your cost) even if your broker did not report it to the IRS. Brokers must report basis to the IRS for most stock you bought in 2011 or later (and for certain debt instruments you bought in 2014 or later).

Part II   **Long-Term.** Transactions involving capital assets you held more than 1 year are long term. For short-term transactions, see page 1.

Note. You may aggregate all long-term transactions reported on Form(s) 1099-B showing basis was reported to the IRS and for which no adjustments or codes are required. Enter the total directly on Schedule D, line 8a; you are not required to report these transactions on Form 8949 (see instructions).

You *must* check Box D, E, or F below. Check only one box. If more than one box applies for your long-term transactions, complete a separate Form 8949, page 2, for each applicable box. If you have more long-term transactions than will fit on this page for one or more of the boxes, complete as many forms with the same box checked as you need.

- ☐ **(D)** Long-term transactions reported on Form(s) 1099-B showing basis was reported to the IRS (see **Note** above)
- ☐ **(E)** Long-term transactions reported on Form(s) 1099-B showing basis was **not** reported to the IRS
- ☐ **(F)** Long-term transactions not reported to you on Form 1099-B

1 **(a)** Description of property (Example: 100 sh. XYZ Co.)	**(b)** Date acquired (Mo., day, yr.)	**(c)** Date sold or disposed (Mo., day, yr.)	**(d)** Proceeds (sales price) (see instructions)	**(e)** Cost or other basis. See the **Note** below and see *Column (e)* in the separate instructions	Adjustment, if any, to gain or loss. If you enter an amount in column (g), enter a code in column (f). See the separate instructions.		**(h)** Gain or (loss). Subtract column (e) from column (d) and combine the result with column (g)
					(f) Code(s) from instructions	**(g)** Amount of adjustment	
2 Totals. Add the amounts in columns (d), (e), (g), and (h) (subtract negative amounts). Enter each total here and include on your Schedule D, **line 8b** (if **Box D** above is checked), **line 9** (if **Box E** above is checked), or **line 10** (if **Box F** above is checked) ▶							

Note. If you checked Box D above but the basis reported to the IRS was incorrect, enter in column (e) the basis as reported to the IRS, and enter an adjustment in column (g) to correct the basis. See *Column (g)* in the separate instructions for how to figure the amount of the adjustment.

Form **8949** (2014)

Appendix C

Glossary

The key terms in this glossary have been defined to reflect their conventional use in the field of taxation. The definitions may therefore be incomplete for other purposes.

A

AAA bypass election. In the context of a distribution by an S corporation, an election made by the entity to designate that the distribution is first from accumulated earnings and profits (AEP) and only then from the accumulated adjustments account (AAA).

Abandoned spouse. The abandoned spouse provision enables a married taxpayer with a dependent child whose spouse did not live in the taxpayer's home during the last six months of the tax year to file as a head of household rather than as married filing separately.

Accelerated cost recovery system (ACRS). A method in which the cost of tangible property is recovered (depreciated) over a prescribed period of time. This depreciation approach disregards salvage value, imposes a period of cost recovery that depends upon the classification of the asset into one of various recovery periods, and prescribes the applicable percentage of cost that can be deducted each year. A modified system is currently the default cost recovery method; it is referred to as MACRS. § 168.

Accelerated death benefits. The amount received from a life insurance policy by the insured who is terminally ill or chronically ill. Any realized gain may be excluded from the gross income of the insured if the policy is surrendered to the insurer or is sold to a licensed viatical settlement provider. § 101(g).

Acceleration rule. Treatment of an intercompany transaction on a consolidated return, when a sold asset leaves the group.

Accident and health benefits. Employee fringe benefits provided by employers through the payment of health and accident insurance premiums or the establishment of employer-funded medical reimbursement plans. Employers generally are entitled to a deduction for such payments, whereas employees generally exclude such fringe benefits from gross income. §§ 105 and 106.

Accident and health insurance benefits. See *accident and health benefits.*

Accountable plan. A type of expense reimbursement plan that requires an employee to render an adequate accounting to the employer and return any excess reimbursement or allowance. If the expense qualifies, it will be treated as a deduction *for* AGI.

Accounting income. The accountant's concept of income is generally based upon the realization principle. Financial accounting income may differ from taxable income (e.g., accelerated depreciation might be used for Federal income tax and straight-line depreciation for financial accounting purposes). Differences are included in a reconciliation of taxable and accounting income on Schedule M–1 or Schedule M–3 of Form 1120 for corporations.

Accounting method. The method under which income and expenses are determined for tax purposes. Important accounting methods include the cash basis and the accrual basis. Special methods are available for the reporting of gain on installment sales, recognition of income on construction projects (the completed contract and percentage of completion methods), and the valuation of inventories (last-in, first-out and first-in, first-out). §§ 446–474.

Accounting period. The period of time, usually a year, used by a taxpayer for the determination of tax liability. Unless a fiscal year is chosen, taxpayers must determine and pay their income tax liability by using the calendar year (January 1 through December 31) as the period of measurement. An example of a fiscal year is July 1 through June 30. A change in accounting period (e.g., from a calendar year to a fiscal year) generally requires the consent of the IRS. Usually, taxpayers are free to select either an initial calendar or a fiscal year without the consent of the IRS. §§ 441–444.

Accrual method. A method of accounting that reflects expenses incurred and income earned for any one tax year. In contrast to the cash basis of accounting, expenses need not be paid to be deductible, nor need income be received to be taxable. Unearned income (e.g., prepaid interest and rent) generally is taxed in the year of receipt regardless of the method of accounting used by the taxpayer. § 446(c)(2).

Accumulated adjustments account (AAA). An account that aggregates an S corporation's post-1982 income, loss, and deductions for the tax year (including nontaxable income and nondeductible losses and expenses). After the year-end income and expense adjustments are made, the account is reduced by distributions made during the tax year.

Accumulated E & P. See *accumulated earnings and profits.*

Accumulated earnings and profits. Net undistributed tax-basis earnings of a corporation aggregated from March 1, 1913, to the end of the prior tax year. Used to determine the amount of dividend income associated with a distribution to shareholders. § 316 and Reg. § 1.316–2.

Accumulated earnings credit. A reduction allowed in arriving at accumulated taxable income, in determining the accumulated earnings tax.

Accumulated earnings tax. A special tax imposed on C corporations that accumulate (rather than distribute) their earnings beyond the reasonable needs of the business. The accumulated earnings tax and related interest are imposed on accumulated taxable income in addition to the corporate income tax. §§ 531–537.

Accumulated taxable income (ATI). The base upon which the accumulated earnings tax is imposed. Generally, it is the taxable income of the corporation as adjusted for certain items (e.g., the Federal income tax, excess charitable contributions, the dividends received deduction) less the dividends paid deduction and the accumulated earnings credit. § 535.

Accuracy-related penalty. Major civil taxpayer penalties relating to the accuracy of tax return data, including misstatements stemming from taxpayer negligence and improper valuation of income and deductions, are coordinated under this umbrella term. The penalty usually equals 20 percent of the understated tax liability.

ACE adjustment. An adjustment in computing corporate alternative minimum taxable income (AMTI), computed at 75 percent of the excess of adjusted current earnings (ACE) over unadjusted AMTI. ACE computations reflect longer and slower cost recovery deductions and other restrictions on the timing of certain recognition events. Exempt interest, life insurance proceeds, and other receipts that are included in earnings and profits but not in taxable income also increase the ACE adjustment. If unadjusted AMTI exceeds ACE, the ACE adjustment is negative. The negative adjustment is limited to the aggregate of the positive adjustments under ACE for prior years, reduced by any previously claimed negative adjustments.

Acquiescence. Agreement by the IRS on the results reached in certain judicial decisions; sometimes abbreviated *Acq.* or *A.*

Acquisition indebtedness. Debt incurred in acquiring, constructing, or substantially improving a qualified residence of the taxpayer. The interest on such loans is deductible as qualified residence interest. However, interest on such debt is deductible only on the portion of the indebtedness that does not exceed $1,000,000 ($500,000 for married persons filing separate returns). § 163(h)(3).

Acquisitive reorganization. A "Type D" reorganization where substantially all of the acquiring corporation's property is transferred to the target and the acquiring corporation's shareholders own at least 50 percent of the target after the restructuring. The acquiring liquidates after the restructuring.

Active income. Wages, salary, commissions, bonuses, profits from a trade or business in which the taxpayer is a material participant, gain on the sale or other disposition of assets used in an active trade or business, and income from intangible property if the taxpayer's personal efforts significantly contributed to the creation of the property. The passive activity loss rules require classification of income and losses into three categories with active income being one of them.

Ad valorem tax. A tax imposed on the value of property. The most common ad valorem tax is that imposed by states, counties, and cities on real estate. Ad valorem taxes can be imposed on personal property as well.

Additional first-year depreciation. See *fifty percent additional first-year depreciation* and *one hundred percent additional first-year depreciation.*

Additional Medicare Tax. A tax created as part of the Affordable Care Act that went into effect starting in 2013. This tax is imposed at 0.9% on an individual's wage and self-employment income in excess of a threshold amount. For married individuals, the threshold is $250,000 ($125,000 if married filing separately). For other individuals the threshold is $200,000. These dollar amounts are not adjusted annually for inflation. If an employer pays an employee more than $200,000 during the year, then regardless of filing status, the employer is required to withhold the Additional Medicare Tax on the excess paid over $200,000 and reports the tax on the employee's Form W-2. The tax is reported on Form 8959 (Additional Medicare Tax), filed with the individual's Form 1040. § 3101(b) and § 1401(b).

Adjusted basis. The cost or other basis of property reduced by depreciation allowed or allowable and increased by capital improvements. Other special adjustments are provided in § 1016 and the related Regulations.

Adjusted current earnings (ACE). Used to determine an adjustment in computing corporate alternative minimum taxable income (AMTI). ACE reflects restrictions on the timing of certain recognition events. Exempt interest, life insurance proceeds, and other receipts that are included in earnings and profits but not in taxable income also increase ACE.

Adjustments. See *AMT adjustments.*

Adoption expenses credit. A provision intended to assist taxpayers who incur nonrecurring costs directly associated with the adoption process, such as legal costs, social service review costs, and transportation costs. Up to $13,400 ($13,400 for a child with special needs regardless of the actual adoption expenses) of costs incurred to adopt an eligible child qualify for the credit. A taxpayer may claim the credit in the year qualifying expenses are paid or incurred if the expenses are paid during or after the year in which the adoption is finalized. For qualifying expenses paid or incurred in a tax year prior to the year the adoption is finalized, the credit must be claimed in the tax year following the tax year during which the expenses are paid or incurred. § 23.

Affiliated group. A parent-subsidiary group of corporations that is eligible to elect to file on a consolidated basis. Eighty percent ownership of the voting power and value of all of the corporations must be achieved every day of the tax year, and an identifiable parent corporation must exist (i.e., it must own at least 80 percent of another group member without applying attribution rules).

Aggregate (conduit) concept. The theory of partnership taxation under which, in certain cases, a partnership is treated as a mere collection of the activities of each partner. See also *entity concept*.

Alimony and separate maintenance payments. Alimony deductions result from the payment of a legal obligation arising from the termination of a marital relationship. Payments designated as alimony generally are included in the gross income of the recipient and are deductible *for* AGI by the payor.

Alimony recapture. The amount of alimony that previously has been included in the gross income of the recipient and deducted by the payor that now is deducted by the recipient and included in the gross income of the payor as the result of front-loading. § 71(f).

All events test. For accrual method taxpayers, income is earned when (1) all of the events have occurred that fix the right to receive the income and (2) the amount can be determined with reasonable accuracy. Accrual of income cannot be postponed simply because a portion of the income may have to be returned in a subsequent period. The all events test also is utilized to determine when expenses can be deducted by an accrual basis taxpayer. The application of the test could cause a variation between the treatment of an item for accounting and for tax purposes. For example, a reserve for warranty expense may be properly accruable under generally accepted accounting principles but not be deductible under the Federal income tax law. Because of the application of the all events test, the deduction becomes available in the year the warranty obligation becomes fixed and the amount is determinable with reasonable certainty. Reg. §§ 1.446–1(c)(1)(ii) and 1.461–1(a)(2).

Allocate. The assignment of income for various tax purposes. A multistate corporation's nonbusiness income usually is allocated to the state where the nonbusiness assets are located; it is not apportioned with the rest of the entity's income. The income and expense items of an estate or a trust are allocated between income and corpus components. Specific items of income, expense, gain, loss, and credit can be allocated to specific partners if a substantial economic nontax purpose for the allocation is established.

Alternate valuation date. Property passing from a decedent by death may be valued for estate tax purposes as of the date of death or the alternate valuation date. The alternate valuation date is six months after the date of death or the date the property is disposed of by the estate, whichever comes first. To use the alternate valuation date, the executor or administrator of the estate must make an affirmative election. Election of the alternate valuation date is not available unless it decreases the amount of the gross estate and reduces the estate tax liability.

Alternative depreciation system (ADS). A cost recovery system that produces a smaller deduction than would be calculated under ACRS or MACRS. The alternative system

must be used in certain instances and can be elected in other instances. § 168(g).

Alternative minimum tax (AMT). The AMT is a fixed percentage of alternative minimum taxable income (AMTI). AMTI generally starts with the taxpayer's adjusted gross income (for individuals) or taxable income (for other taxpayers). To this amount, the taxpayer (1) adds designated preference items (e.g., tax-exempt interest income on private activity bonds), (2) makes other specified adjustments (e.g., to reflect a longer, straight-line cost recovery deduction), (3) adjusts certain AMT itemized deductions for individuals (e.g., interest incurred on housing but not taxes paid), and (4) subtracts an exemption amount. The taxpayer must pay the greater of the resulting AMT (reduced for larger corporations by only the foreign tax credit) or the regular income tax (reduced by all allowable tax credits). The AMT does not apply at all to certain small C corporations. AMT preferences and adjustments are assigned to partners, LLC members, and S corporation shareholders.

Alternative minimum tax credit. The AMT can result from timing differences that give rise to positive adjustments in calculating the AMT base. To provide equity for the taxpayer when these timing differences reverse, the regular tax liability may be reduced by a tax credit for a prior year's minimum tax liability attributable to timing differences. § 53.

Alternative minimum taxable income (AMTI). The base (prior to deducting the exemption amount) for computing a taxpayer's alternative minimum tax. This consists of the taxable income for the year modified for AMT adjustments and AMT preferences. § 55(b)(2).

Alternative tax. An option that is allowed in computing the tax on net capital gain. For the corporate taxpayer, the rate is 35 percent (the same as the highest regular corporate tax rate). Thus, for corporate taxpayers, the alternative tax does not produce a beneficial result. For noncorporate taxpayers, the rate is usually 15 percent (but is 25 percent for unrecaptured § 1250 gain and 28 percent for collectibles and § 1202 gain). However, if the noncorporate taxpayer is in either the 10 percent or the 15 percent tax bracket, the alternative tax rate is 0 percent (rather than 15 percent). Certain high-income taxpayers (i.e., in the 39.6 percent tax bracket) have an alternative tax rate of 20 percent. §§ 1(h) and 1201.

Alternative tax NOL deduction (ATNOLD). In calculating the AMT, the taxpayer is allowed to deduct NOL carryovers and carrybacks. However, for this purpose, a special calculation is required that is referred to as the ATNOLD. The regular income tax is modified for AMT adjustments and preferences to produce the ATNOLD. § 56(d).

American Opportunity credit. This credit replaces the HOPE scholarship credit for 2009 through 2017 and applies for qualifying expenses for the first four years of postsecondary education. Qualified expenses include tuition and related expenses and books and other course materials. Room and board are ineligible for the credit. The maximum credit available per student is $2,500 (100 percent of the first $2,000 of qualified expenses and 25 percent of the next $2,000 of qualified expenses). Eligible students include the taxpayer, taxpayer's spouse, and taxpayer's dependents. To qualify for the credit, a student must take at least one-half of the full-time course load for at least one academic term at a qualifying educational institution. The credit is phased out for higher-income taxpayers. § 25A.

Amortization. The tax deduction for the cost or other basis of an intangible asset over the asset's estimated useful life. Examples of amortizable intangibles include patents, copyrights, and leasehold interests. Most purchased intangible assets (e.g., goodwill) can be amortized for income tax purposes over a 15-year period.

Amount realized. The amount received by a taxpayer upon the sale or exchange of property. Amount realized is the sum of the cash and the fair market value of any property or services received by the taxpayer plus any related debt assumed by the buyer. Determining the amount realized is the starting point for arriving at realized gain or loss. § 1001(b).

AMT adjustments. In calculating AMTI, certain adjustments are added to or deducted from taxable income. These adjustments generally reflect timing differences. § 56.

AMT exemption. An amount deducted from alternative minimum taxable income in deriving alternative minimum tax base. The exemption amount is phased out when AMTI exceeds specified threshold amounts.

AMT preferences. In calculating alternative minimum taxable income (AMTI), certain preference items are added to taxable income. AMT preferences generally reflect differences between the regular tax and the alternative minimum tax (AMT) computational bases. For instance, interest income from certain state and local bonds may be an AMT preference item.

Annual exclusion. In computing the taxable gifts for the year, each donor excludes the first $14,000 (for 2015) of a gift to each donee. Usually, the annual exclusion is not available for gifts of future interests. § 2503(b).

Annuity. A fixed sum of money payable to a person at specified times for a specified period of time or for life. If the party making the payment (i.e., the obligor) is regularly engaged in this type of business (e.g., an insurance company), the arrangement is classified as a commercial annuity. A so-called private annuity involves an obligor that is not regularly engaged in selling annuities (e.g., a charity or family member).

Apportion. The assignment of the business income of a multi-state corporation to specific states for income taxation. Usually, the apportionment procedure accounts for the property, payroll, and sales activity levels of the various states, and a proportionate assignment of the entity's total income is made using a three-factor apportionment formula. These activities indicate the commercial domicile of the corporation relative to that income. Some states exclude nonbusiness income from the apportionment procedure; they allocate nonbusiness income to the states where the nonbusiness assets are located.

Appreciated inventory. In partnership taxation, appreciated inventory is a hot asset, and a partner's share of its ordinary income potential must be allocated. If a partner sells an interest in the partnership, ordinary income is recognized to the extent of the partner's share in the partnership's inventory and unrealized receivables. The definition of "inventory" here is broad enough to include any accounts receivable, including unrealized receivables.

Arm's length. See *arm's length transaction.*

Arm's length price. See *arm's length transaction.*

Arm's length transaction. The standard under which unrelated parties would determine an exchange price for a transaction. Suppose, for example, Cardinal Corporation sells property to its sole shareholder for $10,000. In testing whether the $10,000 is an "arm's length" price, one would ascertain the price that would have been negotiated between the corporation and an unrelated party in a bargained exchange.

ASC 740 (SFAS 109). Under Generally Accepted Accounting Principles, the rules for the financial reporting of the tax expense of an enterprise. Permanent differences affect the enterprise's effective tax rate. Temporary differences create a deferred tax asset or a deferred tax liability on the balance sheet.

ASC 740-10 (FIN 48). An interpretation by the Financial Accounting Standards Board. When an uncertain tax return position exists, this interpretation is used to determine the financial reporting treatment, if any, for the taxpayer. If it is more likely than not (i.e., a greater than 50 percent probability) that the uncertain return position will be sustained (e.g., by the courts) on its technical merits, it must be reported on the financial statements. The amount to be reported then is computed based on the probabilities of the outcome of the technical review, and the amounts at which the dispute would be resolved. If the more-likely-than-not test is failed, no current financial disclosure of the results of the return position is required.

ASC 740-30 (APB 23). Under Generally Accepted Accounting Principles, the rules for the financial reporting of the tax expense relative to a U.S. corporation's non-U.S. subsidiary. If the parent documents that it is permanently reinvesting the non-U.S. earnings of a non-U.S. subsidiary, the parent does not record as an expense any U.S. income tax the parent might pay on such earnings (i.e., the book tax expense is deferred until such earnings are, if ever, repatriated to the United States).

Asset use test. In the context of a corporate reorganization, a means by which to determine if the continuity of business enterprise requirement is met. The acquiring corporation must continue to use the target entity's assets in the acquiror's business going forward; if this is not the case, the requirement is failed.

Assignment of income. A taxpayer attempts to avoid the recognition of income by assigning to another the property that generates the income. Such a procedure will not avoid income recognition by the taxpayer making the assignment if the income was earned at the point of the transfer. In this case, the income is taxed to the person who earns it.

At-risk limitation. Generally, a taxpayer can deduct losses related to a trade or business, S corporation, partnership, or investment asset only to the extent of the at-risk amount. The taxpayer has an amount at risk in a business or investment venture to the extent that personal assets have been subjected to the risks of the business. Typically, the taxpayer's at-risk amount includes (1) the amount of money or other property that the investor contributed to the venture for the investment, (2) the amount of any of the entity's liabilities for which the taxpayer personally is liable and that relate to the investment, and (3) an allocable share of nonrecourse debts incurred by the venture from third parties in arm's length transactions for real estate investments.

Attribution. Under certain circumstances, the tax law applies attribution (constructive ownership) rules to assign to one taxpayer the ownership interest of another taxpayer. If, for example, the stock of Gold Corporation is held 60 percent by Marsha and 40 percent by Sidney, Marsha may be deemed to own 100 percent of Gold Corporation if Marsha and Sidney are mother and child. In that case, the stock owned by Sidney is attributed to Marsha. Stated differently, Marsha has a 60 percent direct and a 40 percent indirect interest in Gold Corporation. It can also be said that Marsha is the constructive owner of Sidney's interest.

Automatic mileage method. Automobile expenses are generally deductible only to the extent the automobile is used in business or for the production of income. Personal commuting expenses are not deductible. The taxpayer may deduct actual expenses (including depreciation and insurance), or the standard (automatic) mileage rate may be used (57.5 cents per mile for 2015 and 56 cents per mile for 2014). Automobile expenses incurred for medical purposes or in connection with job-related moving expenses are deductible to the extent of actual out-of-pocket expenses or at the rate of 23 cents per mile for 2015 and 23.5 cents per mile for 2014. For charitable activities, the rate is 14 cents per mile.

B

Bad debts. A deduction is permitted if a business account receivable subsequently becomes partially or completely worthless, providing the income arising from the debt previously was included in income. Available methods are the specific charge-off method and the reserve method. However, except for certain financial institutions, TRA of 1986 repealed the use of the reserve method for 1987 and thereafter. If the reserve method is used, partially or totally worthless accounts are charged to the reserve. A nonbusiness bad debt deduction is allowed as a short-term capital loss if the loan did not arise in connection with the creditor's trade or business activities. Loans between related parties (family members) generally are classified as nonbusiness. § 166.

Balance sheet approach. The process under ASC 740 (SFAS 109) by which an entity's deferred tax expense or deferred tax benefit is determined as a result of the reporting period's changes in the balance sheet's deferred tax asset and deferred tax liability accounts.

Basis in partnership interest. The acquisition cost of the partner's ownership interest in the partnership. Includes purchase price and associated debt acquired from other partners and in the course of the entity's trade or business.

Benchmarking. The tax professional's use of two or more entities' effective tax rates and deferred tax balance sheet accounts. Used chiefly to compare the effectiveness of the entities' tax planning techniques, and to suggest future tax-motivated courses of action.

Blockage rule. A factor to be considered in valuing a large block of corporate stock. Application of this rule generally justifies a discount in the asset's fair market value, because the disposition of a large amount of stock at any one time may depress the value of the shares in the marketplace.

Boot. Cash or property of a type not included in the definition of a tax-deferred exchange. The receipt of boot causes an otherwise tax-deferred transfer to become immediately taxable to the extent of the lesser of the fair market value of the boot or the realized gain on the transfer. For example, see transfers to controlled corporations under § 351(b) and like-kind exchanges under § 1031(b).

Branch profits tax. A tax on the effectively connected earnings and profits of the U.S. branch of a foreign corporation. The tax is levied in addition to the usual § 11 tax in an amount equal to 30 percent of the dividend equivalent amount. Treaties can override the tax or reduce the withholding percentage. Earnings reinvested in the U.S. operations of the entity are not subject to the tax until repatriation.

Built-in gains tax. A penalty tax designed to discourage a shift of the incidence of taxation on unrealized gains from a C corporation to its shareholders, via an S election. Under this provision, any recognized gain during the first 10 (or 7 or 5) years of S status generates a corporate-level tax on a base not to exceed the aggregate untaxed built-in gains brought into the S corporation upon its election from C corporation taxable years.

Built-in loss property. Property contributed to a corporation under § 351 or as a contribution to capital that has a basis in excess of its fair market value. An adjustment is necessary to step down the basis of the property to its fair market value. The adjustment prevents the corporation and the contributing shareholder from obtaining a double tax benefit. The corporation allocates the adjustment proportionately among the assets with the built-in loss. As an alternative to the corporate adjustment, the shareholder may elect to reduce the basis in the stock.

Business bad debt. A tax deduction allowed for obligations obtained in connection with a trade or business that have become either partially or completely worthless. In contrast to nonbusiness bad debts, business bad debts are deductible as business expenses. § 166.

Business purpose. A justifiable business reason for carrying out a transaction. Mere tax avoidance is not an acceptable business purpose. The presence of a business purpose is crucial in the area of corporate reorganizations and certain liquidations.

Buy-sell agreement. An arrangement, particularly appropriate in the case of a closely held corporation or a partnership, whereby the surviving owners (shareholders or partners) or the entity agrees to purchase the interest of a withdrawing owner. The buy-sell agreement provides for an orderly disposition of an interest in a business and may aid in setting the value of the interest for estate tax purposes.

Bypass amount. The amount that can be transferred by gift or at death free of any unified transfer tax. For 2015, the bypass amount is $5.43 million for estate tax and $5.43 million for gift tax.

Bypass election. In the context of a distribution by an S corporation, an election made by the entity to designate that the distribution is first from accumulated earnings and profits and only then from the accumulated adjustments account (AAA).

C

C corporation. A separate taxable entity subject to the rules of Subchapter C of the Code. This business form may create a double taxation effect relative to its shareholders. The entity is subject to the regular corporate tax and a number of penalty taxes at the Federal level.

Cafeteria plan. An employee benefit plan under which an employee is allowed to select from among a variety of employer-provided fringe benefits. Some of the benefits may be taxable, and some may be statutory nontaxable benefits (e.g., health and accident insurance and group term life insurance). The employee is taxed only on the taxable benefits selected. A cafeteria benefit plan is also referred to as a flexible benefit plan. § 125.

Capital account. The financial accounting analog of a partner's tax basis in the entity.

Capital asset. Broadly speaking, all assets are capital except those specifically excluded from that definition by the Code. Major categories of noncapital assets include property held for resale in the normal course of business (inventory), trade accounts and notes receivable, and depreciable property and real estate used in a trade or business (§ 1231 assets). § 1221.

Capital contribution. Various means by which a shareholder makes additional funds available to the corporation (placed at the risk of the business), sometimes without the receipt of additional stock. If no stock is received, the contributions are added to the basis of the shareholder's existing stock investment and do not generate gross income to the corporation. § 118.

Capital gain. The gain from the sale or exchange of a capital asset.

Capital gain property. Property contributed to a charitable organization that if sold rather than contributed, would have resulted in long-term capital gain to the donor.

Capital interest. Usually, the percentage of the entity's net assets that a partner would receive on liquidation. Typically determined by the partner's capital sharing ratio.

Capital loss. The loss from the sale or exchange of a capital asset.

Capital sharing ratio. A partner's percentage ownership of the entity's capital.

Cash balance plan. A hybrid form of pension plan similar in some aspects to a defined benefit plan. Such a plan is funded by the employer, and the employer bears the investment risks and rewards. But like defined contribution plans, a cash balance plan establishes allocations to individual employee accounts, and the payout for an employee depends on investment performance.

Cash equivalent doctrine. Generally, a cash basis taxpayer does not report income until cash is constructively or actually received. Under the cash equivalent doctrine, cash basis taxpayers are required to report income if they receive the equivalent of cash (e.g., property is received) in a taxable transaction.

Cash method. See *cash receipts method.*

Cash receipts method. A method of accounting that reflects deductions as paid and income as received in any one tax year. However, deductions for prepaid expenses that benefit more than one tax year (e.g., prepaid rent and prepaid interest) usually are spread over the period benefited rather than deducted in the year paid. § 446(c)(1).

Casualty loss. A casualty is defined as "the complete or partial destruction of property resulting from an identifiable event of a sudden, unexpected or unusual nature" (e.g., floods, storms, fires, auto accidents). Individuals may deduct a casualty loss only if the loss is incurred in a trade or business or in a transaction entered into for profit or arises from fire, storm, shipwreck, or other casualty or from theft. Individuals usually deduct personal casualty losses as itemized deductions subject to a $100 nondeductible amount and to an annual floor equal to 10 percent of adjusted gross income that applies after the $100 per casualty floor has been applied. Special rules are provided for the netting of certain casualty gains and losses.

Certiorari. Appeal from a U.S. Court of Appeals to the U.S. Supreme Court is by Writ of Certiorari. The Supreme Court does not have to accept the appeal and usually does not (cert. den.) unless there is a conflict among the lower courts that needs to be resolved or a constitutional issue is involved.

Charitable contributions. Contributions are deductible (subject to various restrictions and ceiling limitations) if made to qualified nonprofit charitable organizations. A cash basis taxpayer is entitled to a deduction solely in the year of payment. Accrual basis corporations may accrue contributions at year-end if payment is properly authorized before the end of the year and payment is made within two and one-half months after the end of the year. § 170.

Check-the-box Regulations. By using the check-the-box rules prudently, an entity can select the most attractive tax results offered by the Code, without being bound by legal forms. By default, an unincorporated entity with more than one owner is taxed as a partnership; an unincorporated entity with one owner is a disregarded entity, taxed as a sole proprietorship or corporate division. No action is necessary by the taxpayer if the legal form or default status is desired. Form 8832 is used to "check a box" and change the tax status. Not available if the entity is incorporated under state law.

Child tax credit. A tax credit based solely on the number of qualifying children under age 17. The maximum credit available is $1,000 per child through 2017. A qualifying child must be claimed as a dependent on a parent's tax return to qualify for the credit. Taxpayers who qualify for the child tax credit may also qualify for a supplemental credit. The supplemental credit is treated as a component of the earned income credit and is therefore refundable. The credit is phased out for higher-income taxpayers. § 24.

Circuit Court of Appeals. Any of 13 Federal courts that consider tax matters appealed from the U.S. Tax Court, a U.S. District Court, or the U.S. Court of Federal Claims. Appeal from a U.S. Court of Appeals is to the U.S. Supreme Court by Certiorari.

Circular 230. A portion of the Federal tax Regulations that describes the levels of conduct at which a tax preparer must operate. Circular 230 dictates, for instance, that a tax preparer may not charge an unconscionable fee or delay the execution of a tax audit with inappropriate delays. Circular

230 requires that there be a reasonable basis for a tax return position and that no frivolous returns be filed.

Citator. A tax research resource that presents the judicial history of a court case and traces the subsequent references to the case. When these references include the citating cases' evaluations of the cited case's precedents, the research can obtain some measure of the efficacy and reliability of the original holding.

Claim of right doctrine. A judicially imposed doctrine applicable to both cash and accrual basis taxpayers that holds that an amount is includible in income upon actual or constructive receipt if the taxpayer has an unrestricted claim to the payment. For the tax treatment of amounts repaid when previously included in income under the claim of right doctrine, see § 1341.

Closely held C corporation. A regular corporation (i.e., the S election is not in effect) for which more than 50 percent of the value of its outstanding stock is owned, directly or indirectly, by five or fewer individuals at any time during the tax year. The term is relevant in identifying C corporations that are subject to the passive activity loss provisions. § 469.

Closely held corporation. A corporation where stock ownership is not widely dispersed. Rather, a few shareholders are in control of corporate policy and are in a position to benefit personally from that policy.

Closing agreement. In a tax dispute, the parties sign a closing agreement to spell out the terms under which the matters are settled. The agreement is binding on both the Service and the taxpayer.

Collectibles. A special type of capital asset, the gain from which is taxed at a maximum rate of 28 percent if the holding period is more than one year. Examples include art, rugs, antiques, gems, metals, stamps, some coins and bullion, and alcoholic beverages held for investment.

Combined return. In multistate taxation, a group of unitary corporations may elect or be required to file an income tax return that includes operating results for all of the affiliates, not just those with nexus in the state. Thus, apportionment data is reported for the group's worldwide or water's edge operations.

Community property. Louisiana, Texas, New Mexico, Arizona, California, Washington, Idaho, Nevada, and Wisconsin have community property systems. Alaska residents can elect community property status for assets. The rest of the states are common law property jurisdictions. The difference between common law and community property systems centers around the property rights possessed by married persons. In a common law system, each spouse owns whatever he or she earns. Under a community property system, one-half of the earnings of each spouse is considered owned by the other spouse. Assume, for example, that Jeff and Alice are husband and wife and that their only income is the $50,000 annual salary Jeff receives. If they live in New York (a common law state), the $50,000 salary belongs to Jeff. If, however, they live in Texas (a community property state), the $50,000 salary is owned one-half each by Jeff and Alice.

Compensatory damages. Damages received or paid by the taxpayer can be classified as compensatory damages or as punitive damages. Compensatory damages are paid to compensate one for harm caused by another. Compensatory damages are excludible from the recipient's gross income.

Complete termination redemption. Sale or exchange treatment is available relative to this type of redemption. The shareholder must retire all of his or her outstanding shares in the corporation (ignoring family attribution rules) and cannot hold an interest, other than that of a creditor, for the 10 years following the redemption. § 302(b)(3).

Completed contract method. A method of reporting gain or loss on certain long-term contracts. Under this method of accounting, all gross income and expenses are recognized in the tax year in which the contract is completed. Reg. § 1.451–3.

Complex trust. Not a simple trust. Such trusts may have charitable beneficiaries, accumulate income, and distribute corpus. §§ 661–663.

Composite return. In multistate taxation, an S corporation may be allowed to file a single income tax return that assigns pass-through items to resident and nonresident shareholders. The composite or "block" return allows the entity to remit any tax that is attributable to the nonresident shareholders.

Conduit concept. An approach assumed by the tax law in the treatment of certain entities and their owners. Specific tax characteristics pass through the entity without losing their identity. For example, items of income and expense, capital gains and losses, tax credits, etc., realized by a partnership pass through the partnership (a conduit) and are subject to taxation at the partner level. Also, in an S corporation, certain items pass through and are reported on the returns of the shareholders.

Conservation easement. An interest in real property that maintains its natural or pristine condition. Most often it restricts the development of the property. Properly structured, the grant of such an easement can generate an income tax deduction for the donor. If the grant takes place after the owner's death, a § 2055 charitable contribution deduction results, and a portion of the property's value is excluded from the gross estate. § 2031(c).

Conservatism principle. The theory behind much of Generally Accepted Accounting Principles, under which assurance is provided that an entity's balance sheet assets are not overstated, nor liabilities understated. For instance, under ASC 740 (SFAS 109), a deferred tax asset is not recorded until it is more likely than not that the future tax benefit will be realized.

Consolidated return. A procedure whereby certain affiliated corporations may file a single return, combine the tax transactions of each corporation, and arrive at a single income tax liability for the group. The election to file a consolidated return usually is binding on future years. §§ 1501–1505 and related Regulations.

Consolidation. The combination of two or more corporations into a newly created corporation. Thus, Apt Corporation and Bye Corporation combine to form Cart Corporation. A consolidation may qualify as a nontaxable reorganization if certain conditions are satisfied. §§ 354 and 368(a)(1)(A).

Constructive dividend. A taxable benefit derived by a shareholder from his or her corporation that is not actually initiated by the board of directors as a dividend. Examples include unreasonable compensation, excessive rent payments, bargain purchases of corporate property, and shareholder use of corporate property. Constructive dividends generally are found in closely held corporations.

Constructive liquidation scenario. The means by which recourse debt is shared among partners in basis determination.

Constructive receipt. If income is unqualifiedly available although not physically in the taxpayer's possession, it still is subject to the income tax. An example is accrued interest on a savings account. Under the constructive receipt concept, the interest is taxed to a depositor in the year available, rather than the year actually withdrawn. The fact that the depositor uses the cash basis of accounting for tax purposes is irrelevant. See Reg. § 1.451–2.

Continuity of business enterprise. In a tax-favored reorganization, a shareholder or corporation that has substantially the same investment after an exchange as before should not be taxed on the transaction. Specifically, the transferee corporation must continue the historic business of the transferor or use a significant portion of the transferor's assets in the new business.

Continuity of interest. In a tax-favored reorganization, a shareholder or corporation that has substantially the same investment after an exchange as before should not be taxed on the transaction. Specifically, the seller must acquire an equity interest in the acquiring corporation equal in value to at least 50 percent of all formerly outstanding stock of the acquired entity.

Control. Holding a specified level of stock ownership in a corporation. For § 351, the new shareholder(s) must hold at least 80 percent of the total combined voting power of all voting classes of stock and at least 80 percent of the shares of all nonvoting classes. Other tax provisions require different levels of control to bring about desired effects, such as 50 or 100 percent.

Controlled foreign corporation (CFC). A non-U.S. corporation in which more than 50 percent of the total combined voting power of all classes of stock entitled to vote or the total value of the stock of the corporation is owned by U.S. shareholders on any day during the taxable year of the foreign corporation. For purposes of this definition, a U.S. shareholder is any U.S. person who owns, or is considered to own, 10 percent or more of the total combined voting power of all classes of voting stock of the foreign corporation. Stock owned directly, indirectly, and constructively is used in this measure. See *U.S. shareholder.*

Controlled group. A controlled group of corporations is required to share the lower corporate tax rates and various other tax benefits among the members of the group. A controlled group may be either a brother-sister or a parent-subsidiary group.

Corporate liquidation. Occurs when a corporation distributes its net assets to its shareholders and ceases to be a going concern. Generally, a shareholder recognizes capital gain or loss upon the liquidation of the entity, regardless of the corporation's balance in its earnings and profits account. The liquidating corporation recognizes gain and loss on assets that it sells during the liquidation period and on assets that it distributes to shareholders in kind.

Corpus. The body or principal of a trust. Suppose, for example, Grant transfers an apartment building into a trust, income payable to Ruth for life, remainder to Shawn upon Ruth's death. Corpus of the trust is the apartment building.

Correspondence audit. An audit conducted by the IRS by the U.S. mail. Typically, the IRS writes to the taxpayer requesting the verification of a particular deduction or exemption. The remittance of copies of records or other support is requested of the taxpayer.

Cost depletion. Depletion that is calculated based on the adjusted basis of the asset. The adjusted basis is divided by the expected recoverable units to determine the depletion per unit. The depletion per unit is multiplied by the units sold during the tax year to calculate cost depletion.

Cost recovery. The portion of the cost of an asset written off under ACRS (or MACRS), which replaced the depreciation system as a method for writing off the cost of an asset for most assets placed in service after 1980 (after 1986 for MACRS). § 168.

Court of Federal Claims. A trial court (court of original jurisdiction) that decides litigation involving Federal tax matters. Appeal from this court is to the Court of Appeals for the Federal Circuit.

Court of original jurisdiction. The Federal courts are divided into courts of original jurisdiction and appellate courts. A dispute between a taxpayer and the IRS is first considered by a court of original jurisdiction (i.e., a trial court). The four Federal courts of original jurisdiction are the U.S. Tax Court, the U.S. District Court, the Court of Federal Claims, and the Small Cases Division of the U.S. Tax Court.

Credit for certain retirement plan contributions. A nonrefundable credit is available based on eligible contributions of up to $2,000 to certain qualified retirement plans, such as traditional and Roth IRAs and § 401(k) plans. The benefit provided by this credit is in addition to any deduction or exclusion that otherwise is available resulting from the qualifying contribution. The amount of the credit depends on the taxpayer's AGI and filing status. § 25B.

Credit for child and dependent care expenses. A tax credit ranging from 20 percent to 35 percent of employment-related expenses (child and dependent care expenses) for amounts of up to $6,000 is available to individuals who are employed (or deemed to be employed) and maintain a household for a dependent child under age 13, disabled spouse, or disabled dependent. § 21.

Credit for employer-provided child care. A nonrefundable credit is available to employers who provide child care facilities to their employees during normal working hours. The credit, limited to $150,000, is comprised of two components. The portion of the credit for qualified child care expenses is equal to 25 percent of these expenses, while the portion of the credit for qualified child care resource and referral services is equal to 10 percent of these expenses. Any qualifying expenses otherwise deductible by the taxpayer must be reduced by the amount of the credit. In addition, the taxpayer's basis for any property used for qualifying purposes is reduced by the amount of the credit. § 45F.

Credit for small employer pension plan startup costs. A nonrefundable credit available to small businesses based on administrative costs associated with establishing and maintaining certain qualified plans. While such qualifying costs generally are deductible as ordinary and necessary business expenses, the availability of the credit is intended to lower the costs of starting a qualified retirement program and therefore encourage qualifying businesses to establish retirement plans for their employees. The credit is available for eligible employers at the rate of 50 percent of qualified startup costs. The maximum credit is $500 (based on a maximum $1,000 of qualifying expenses). § 45E.

Crop insurance proceeds. The proceeds received when an insured crop is destroyed. Section 451(d) permits the farmer to defer reporting the income from the insurance proceeds until the tax year following the taxable year of the destruction.

Crop method. A method of accounting for agricultural crops that are planted in one year but harvested in a subsequent year. Under this method, the costs of raising the crop are accumulated as inventory and are deducted when the income from the crop is realized.

Cross-purchase buy-sell agreement. Under this arrangement, the surviving owners of the business agree to buy out the withdrawing owner. Assume, for example, Ron and Sara are equal shareholders in Tip Corporation. Under a cross-purchase buy-sell agreement, Ron and Sara would contract to purchase the other's interest, should that person decide to withdraw from the business.

Current E & P. See *current earnings and profits.*

Current earnings and profits. Net tax-basis earnings of a corporation aggregated during the current tax year. A corporate distribution is deemed to be first from the entity's current earnings and profits and then from accumulated earnings and profits. Shareholders recognize dividend income to the extent of the earnings and profits of the corporation. A dividend results to the extent of current earnings and profits, even if there is a larger negative balance in accumulated earnings and profits.

Current tax expense. Under ASC 740 (SFAS 109), the book tax expense that relates to the current reporting period's net income and is actually payable (or creditable) to the appropriate governmental agencies for the current period. Also known as "cash tax" or "tax payable."

D

De minimis fringe. Benefits provided to employees that are too insignificant to warrant the time and effort required to account for the benefits received by each employee and the value of those benefits. Such amounts are excludible from the employee's gross income. § 132.

De minimis fringe benefit. See *de minimis fringe.*

Death benefit. A payment made by an employer to the beneficiary or beneficiaries of a deceased employee on account of the death of the employee.

Debt-financed income. Included in computations of the unrelated business income of an exempt organization, the gross income generated from debt-financed property.

Deceased spouse's unused exclusion (DSUE). In computing the Federal estate tax, the decedent uses the exclusion amount to shelter an amount of the gross estate from taxa-tion. When the first spouse to die fails to use a portion of his/her exclusion amount, the unused portion is "portable," and becomes available to the surviving spouse. The surviving spouse can use the DSUE only of his/her last spouse to predecease.

Deduction for qualified tuition and related expenses. Taxpayers are allowed a deduction of up to $4,000 for higher education expenses. Certain taxpayers are not eligible for the deduction: those whose gross AGI exceeds a specified amount and those who can be claimed as a dependent by another taxpayer. These expenses are classified as a deduction *for* AGI, and they need not be employment-related. § 222.

Deductions *for* adjusted gross income. The Federal income tax is not imposed upon gross income. Rather, it is imposed upon taxable income. Congressionally identified deductions for individual taxpayers are subtracted either from gross income to arrive at adjusted gross income or from adjusted gross income to arrive at the tax base, taxable income.

Deductions *from* adjusted gross income. See *deductions for adjusted gross income.*

Deductions in respect of a decedent. Deductions accrued at the moment of death but not recognizable on the final income tax return of a decedent because of the method of accounting used. Such items are allowed as deductions on the estate tax return and on the income tax return of the estate (Form 1041) or the heir (Form 1040). An example of a deduction in respect of a decedent is interest expense accrued to the date of death by a cash basis debtor.

Deemed-paid credit. A foreign tax credit allowed to a U.S. taxpayer that has received an actual or constructive dividend from a non-U.S. corporation that has paid foreign income taxes. The credit is computed using the proportion of foreign income taxes paid by the payor corporation to its post-1986 undistributed earnings. Under § 78, the U.S. taxpayer claiming a deemed-paid credit includes the same amount in gross income for the tax year.

Deferred compensation. Compensation that will be taxed when received or upon the removal of certain restrictions on receipt and not when earned. Contributions by an employer to a qualified pension or profit sharing plan on behalf of an employee are an example. The contributions will not be taxed to the employee until the funds are made available or distributed to the employee (e.g., upon retirement).

Deferred tax asset. Under ASC 740 (SFAS 109), an item created on an enterprise's balance sheet by a temporary book-tax difference, such that a tax benefit is not recognized until a later date, although it already has been reported in the financial statements (e.g., the carryforward of a disallowed deduction).

Deferred tax benefit. Under ASC 740 (SFAS 109), a reduction in the book tax expense that relates to the current reporting period's net income but will not be realized until a future reporting period. Creates or adds to the entity's deferred tax asset balance sheet account. For instance, the carryforward of a net operating loss is a deferred tax benefit.

Deferred tax expense. Under ASC 740 (SFAS 109), a book tax expense that relates to the current reporting period's net income but will not be realized until a future reporting period. Creates or adds to the entity's deferred tax liability balance sheet account. For instance, a deferred tax expense is created when tax depreciation deductions for the period are "accelerated" and exceed the corresponding book depreciation expense.

Deferred tax liability. As determined under the rules of ASC 740 (SFAS 109), an item created on an enterprise's balance sheet by a temporary book-tax difference, such that a tax benefit is recognized earlier for tax purposes than it is in the financial accounting records (e.g., the use of an accelerated cost recovery deduction).

Defined benefit plan. Qualified plans can be dichotomized into defined benefit plans and defined contribution plans. Under a defined benefit plan, a formula defines the benefits employees are to receive. The formula usually includes years of service, employee compensation, and some stated percentage. The employer must make annual contributions based on actuarial computations that will be sufficient to pay the vested retirement benefits.

Defined contribution pension plan. Qualified plans can be dichotomized into defined benefit plans and defined contribution plans. Under a defined contribution plan, a separate account is maintained for each covered employee. The employee's benefits under the plan are based solely on (1) the amount contributed and (2) income from the fund that accrues to the employee's account. The plan defines the amount the employer is required to contribute (e.g., a flat dollar amount, an amount based on a special formula, or an amount equal to a certain percentage of compensation).

Dependency exemption. See *personal and dependency exemptions.*

Depletion. The process by which the cost or other basis of a natural resource (e.g., an oil or gas interest) is recovered upon extraction and sale of the resource. The two ways to determine the depletion allowance are the cost and percentage (or statutory) methods. Under cost depletion, each unit of production sold is assigned a portion of the cost or other basis of the interest. This is determined by dividing the cost or other basis by the total units expected to be recovered. Under percentage (or statutory) depletion, the tax law provides a special percentage factor for different types of minerals and other natural resources. This percentage is multiplied by the gross income from the interest to arrive at the depletion allowance. §§ 613 and 613A.

Depreciation. The deduction for the cost or other basis of a tangible asset over the asset's estimated useful life.

Determination letter. Upon the request of a taxpayer, the IRS will comment on the tax status of a completed transaction. Determination letters frequently are used to determine whether a retirement or profit sharing plan qualifies under the Code, and to determine the tax-exempt status of certain nonprofit organizations.

Disabled access credit. A tax credit designed to encourage small businesses to make their facilities more accessible to disabled individuals. The credit is equal to 50 percent of the eligible expenditures that exceed $250 but do not exceed $10,250. Thus, the maximum amount for the credit is $5,000. The adjusted basis for depreciation is reduced by the

amount of the credit. To qualify, the facility must have been placed in service before November 6, 1990. § 44.

Disaster area loss. A casualty sustained in an area designated as a disaster area by the President of the United States. In such an event, the disaster loss may be treated as having occurred in the taxable year immediately preceding the year in which the disaster actually occurred. Thus, immediate tax benefits are provided to victims of a disaster. § 165(i).

Disclaimers. Rejections, refusals, or renunciations of claims, powers, or property. Section 2518 sets forth the conditions required to avoid gift tax consequences as the result of a disclaimer.

Disguised sale. When a partner contributes property to the entity and soon thereafter receives a distribution from the partnership, the transactions are collapsed and the distribution is seen as a purchase of the asset by the partnership. § 707(a)(2)(B).

Disproportionate distribution. A distribution from a partnership to one or more of its partners in which at least one partner's interest in partnership hot assets is increased or decreased. For example, a distribution of cash to one partner and hot assets to another changes both partners' interest in hot assets and is disproportionate. The intent of rules for taxation of disproportionate distributions is to ensure that each partner eventually recognizes his or her proportionate share of partnership ordinary income.

Disproportionate redemption. Sale or exchange treatment is available relative to this type of redemption. After the exchange, the shareholder owns less than 80 percent of his or her pre-redemption interest in the corporation and only a minority interest in the entity. § 302(b)(2).

Disregarded entity. The Federal income tax treatment of business income usually follows the legal form of the taxpayer (i.e., an individual's sole proprietorship is reported on the Form 1040); a C corporation's taxable income is computed on Form 1120. The check-the-box Regulations are used if the unincorporated taxpayer wants to use a different tax regime. Under these rules, a disregarded entity is taxed as an individual or a corporate division; other tax regimes are not available. For instance, a one-member limited liability company is a disregarded entity.

Distributable net income (DNI). The measure that determines the nature and amount of the distributions from estates and trusts that the beneficiaries must include in income. DNI also limits the amount that estates and trusts can claim as a deduction for such distributions. § 643(a).

District Court. See *Federal District Court.*

Dividend. A nondeductible distribution to the shareholders of a corporation. A dividend constitutes gross income to the recipient if it is paid from the current or accumulated earnings and profits of the corporation.

Dividend equivalent amount (DEA). The amount subject to the branch profits tax, it is equal to the effectively connected E & P of the U.S. branch of a foreign corporation, reduced/(increased) by an increase/(reduction) in U.S. net equity.

Dividends received deduction. A deduction allowed a shareholder that is a corporation for dividends received from a domestic corporation. The deduction usually is 70 percent of the dividends received, but it could be 80 or 100 percent depending upon the ownership percentage held by the recipient corporation. §§ 243–246.

Divisive reorganization. A "Type D" spin-off, split-off or split-up reorganization in which the original corporation divides its active business (in existence for at least five years) assets among two or more corporations. The stock received by the original corporation shareholders must be at least 80 percent of the other corporations.

Dock sale. A purchaser uses its owned or rented vehicles to take possession of the product at the seller's shipping dock. In most states, the sale is apportioned to the operating state of the purchaser, rather than the seller. See also *apportion* and *sales factor*.

Dollar-value LIFO. An inventory technique that focuses on the dollars invested in the inventory rather than the particular items on hand each period. Each inventory item is assigned to a pool. A pool is a collection of similar items and is treated as a separate inventory. At the end of the period, each pool is valued in terms of prices at the time LIFO was adopted (base period prices), whether or not the particular items were actually on hand in the year LIFO was adopted, to compare with current prices to determine if there has been an increase or decrease in inventories.

Domestic production activities deduction (DPAD). A deduction based on 9 percent of the lesser of qualified production activities income (QPAI) or modified adjusted gross income but not to exceed 50 percent of the W–2 production wages paid. In the case of a corporate taxpayer, taxable income is substituted for modified AGI. § 199.

Domestic production gross receipts (DPGR). A key component in computing the domestic production activities deduction (DPAD). Includes receipts from the sale and other disposition of qualified production property produced in significant part within the United States. DPGR is defined in § 199(c)(4).

E

Earned income credit. A tax credit designed to provide assistance to certain low-income individuals who generally have a qualifying child. This is a refundable credit. To receive the most beneficial treatment, the taxpayer must have qualifying children. However, it is possible to qualify for the credit without having a child. See Chapter 12 for the computation procedure required in order to determine the amount of the credit allowed.

Earnings and profits (E & P). Measures the economic capacity of a corporation to make a distribution to shareholders that is not a return of capital. Such a distribution results in dividend income to the shareholders to the extent of the corporation's current and accumulated earnings and profits.

Economic effect test. Requirements that must be met before a special allocation may be used by a partnership. The premise behind the test is that each partner who receives an allocation of income or loss from a partnership bears the economic benefit or burden of the allocation.

Economic income. The change in the taxpayer's net worth, as measured in terms of market values, plus the value of the assets the taxpayer consumed during the year. Because of the impracticality of this income model, it is not used for tax purposes.

Economic performance test. One of the requirements that must be satisfied for an accrual basis taxpayer to deduct an expense. The accrual basis taxpayer first must satisfy the all events test. That test is not deemed satisfied until economic performance occurs. This occurs when property or services are provided to the taxpayer, or in the case in which the taxpayer is required to provide property or services, whenever the property or services are actually provided by the taxpayer.

Education expenses. Employees may deduct education expenses that are incurred either (1) to maintain or improve existing job-related skills or (2) to meet the express requirements of the employer or the requirements imposed by law to retain employment status. The expenses are not deductible if the education is required to meet the minimum educational standards for the taxpayer's job or if the education qualifies the individual for a new trade or business. Reg. § 1.162–5.

Educational savings bonds. U.S. Series EE bonds whose proceeds are used for qualified higher educational expenses for the taxpayer, the taxpayer's spouse, or a dependent. The interest may be excluded from gross income, provided the taxpayer's adjusted gross income does not exceed certain amounts. § 135.

Effective tax rate. The financial statements for an entity include several footnotes, one of which reconciles the expected (statutory) income tax rate (e.g., 35 percent for a C corporation) with the effective tax rate (i.e., total tax expense as a percentage of book income). The reconciliation often is done in dollar and/or percentage terms.

Effectively connected income. Income of a nonresident alien or foreign corporation that is attributable to the operation of a U.S. trade or business under either the asset-use or the business-activities test.

E-file. The electronic filing of a tax return. The filing is either direct or indirect. As to direct, the taxpayer goes online using a computer and tax return preparation software. Indirect filing occurs when a taxpayer utilizes an authorized IRS e-file provider. The provider often is the tax return preparer.

E-filing. See *E-file*.

Employment taxes. Taxes that an employer must pay on account of its employees. Employment taxes include FICA (Federal Insurance Contributions Act) and FUTA (Federal Unemployment Tax Act) taxes. Employment taxes are paid to the IRS in addition to income tax withholdings at specified intervals. Such taxes can be levied on the employees, the employer, or both.

Energy credits. See *energy tax credits*.

Energy tax credits. Various tax credits are available to those who invest in certain energy property. The purpose of the credit is to create incentives for conservation and to develop alternative energy sources.

Enrolled agent (EA). A tax practitioner who has gained admission to practice before the IRS by passing an IRS examination and maintaining a required level of continuing professional education.

Entertainment expenses. Expenses that are deductible only if they are directly related to or associated with a trade or business. Various restrictions and documentation requirements have been imposed upon the deductibility of entertainment expenses to prevent abuses by taxpayers. See, for example, the provision contained in § 274(n) that disallows 50 percent (20 percent prior to 1994) of entertainment expenses. § 274.

Entity accounting income. Entity accounting income is not identical to the taxable income of a trust or estate, nor is it determined in the same manner as the entity's financial accounting income would be. The trust document or will determines whether certain income, expenses, gains, or losses are allocated to the corpus of the entity or to the entity's income beneficiaries. Only the items that are allocated to the income beneficiaries are included in entity accounting income.

Entity buy-sell agreement. An arrangement whereby the entity is to purchase a withdrawing owner's interest. When the entity is a corporation, the agreement generally involves a stock redemption on the part of the withdrawing shareholder. See also *buy-sell agreement* and *cross-purchase buy-sell agreement*.

Entity concept. The theory of partnership taxation under which a partnership is treated as a separate and distinct entity from the partners and has its own tax attributes.

Equity method. Under Generally Accepted Accounting Principles, the method of financial reporting for the operations of a subsidiary when the parent corporation owns between 20 and 50 percent of the subsidiary's stock. Creates a book-tax difference, as the two entities' operating results are combined for book purposes, but a Federal income tax consolidated return cannot be filed.

Estate freeze. Procedures directed toward fixing and stabilizing the value of an interest retained in a business, while transferring the growth portion to family members. In the case of a closely held corporation, the estate freeze usually involves keeping the preferred stock and giving away the common stock. The ultimate objective is to reduce estate value when the original owner-donor dies.

Estate tax. A tax imposed on the right to transfer property by death. Thus, an estate tax is levied on the decedent's estate and not on the heir receiving the property.

Estimated tax. The amount of tax (including alternative minimum tax and self-employment tax) a taxpayer expects to owe for the year after subtracting tax credits and income tax withheld. The estimated tax must be paid in installments at designated intervals (e.g., for the individual taxpayer, by April 15, June 15, September 15, and January 15 of the following year).

Excess lobbying expenditure. An excise tax is applied on otherwise tax-exempt organizations with respect to the excess of total lobbying expenditures over grass roots lobbying expenditures for the year.

Excess loss account. When a subsidiary has generated more historical losses than its parent has invested in the entity, the parent's basis in the subsidiary is zero, and the parent records additional losses in an excess loss account. This treatment allows the parent to continue to deduct losses of the subsidiary, even where no basis reduction is possible, while avoiding the need to show a negative stock basis on various financial records. If the subsidiary stock is sold while an excess loss account exists, capital gain income usually is recognized to the extent of the balance in the account.

Excise tax. A tax on the manufacture, sale, or use of goods; on the carrying on of an occupation or activity; or on the transfer of property. Thus, the Federal estate and gift taxes are, theoretically, excise taxes.

Exclusion amount. The value of assets that is exempt from transfer tax due to the credit allowed for gifts or transfers by death. For gifts and deaths in 2015, the exclusion amount is $5.43 million. An exclusion amount unused by a deceased spouse may be used by the surviving spouse. See also *exemption equivalent amount*.

Exempt organization. An organization that is either partially or completely exempt from Federal income taxation. § 501.

Exemption amount. See *AMT exemption*.

Exemption equivalent. The maximum value of assets that can be transferred to another party without incurring any Federal gift or estate tax because of the application of the unified tax credit. See also *exemption equivalent amount*.

Exemption equivalent amount. The nontaxable amount (in 2015, $5.43 million for gift tax and estate tax) that is the equivalent of the unified transfer tax credit allowed.

Expanded affiliated group (EAG). For purposes of the domestic production activities deduction (DPAD), all members of an expanded affiliated group (EAG) are treated as a single corporation. Thus, the activities of any member of the group are attributed to the other members. An EAG must meet the requirements for filing a consolidated return with ownership levels lowered to 50 percent. § 199(d)(4)(B).

F

Fair market value. The amount at which property would change hands between a willing buyer and a willing seller, neither being under any compulsion to buy or to sell and both having reasonable knowledge of the relevant facts. Reg. §§ 1.1001–1(a) and 20.2031–1(b).

Farm price method. A method of accounting for agricultural crops. The inventory of crops is valued at its market price less the estimated cost of disposition (e.g., freight and selling expense).

FDAP. Income of a nonresident alien or non-U.S. corporation that is received in the form of dividends, interest, rents, royalties, certain compensation, premiums, annuities, and other "fixed, determinable, annual, or periodic" forms. FDAP income usually is subject to U.S. income taxation at a flat 30 percent tax rate.

Federal District Court. A trial court for purposes of litigating Federal tax matters. It is the only trial court in which a jury trial can be obtained.

Feeder organization. An entity that carries on a trade or business for the benefit of an exempt organization. However, such a relationship does not result in the feeder organization itself being tax-exempt. § 502.

FICA tax. An abbreviation that stands for Federal Insurance Contributions Act, commonly referred to as the Social Security tax. The FICA tax is comprised of the Social Security tax (old age, survivors, and disability insurance) and the Medicare tax (hospital insurance) and is imposed on both employers and employees. The employer is responsible for withholding from the employee's wages the Social Security tax at a rate of 6.2 percent on a maximum wage base and the Medicare tax at a rate of 1.45 percent (no maximum wage base). The maximum Social Security wage base for 2015 is $118,500 and for 2014 is $117,000.

Field audit. An audit conducted by the IRS on the business premises of the taxpayer or in the office of the tax practitioner representing the taxpayer.

Fifty percent additional first-year depreciation. This provision, which was effective for property acquired after December 31, 2007, and placed in service before January 1, 2015, provided for an additional cost recovery deduction of 50 percent in the tax year the qualified property is placed in service. Qualified property included most types of new property other than buildings. The taxpayer can elect to forgo this bonus depreciation. See also *one hundred percent additional first-year depreciation.*

Final Regulation. See *finalized Regulation.*

Finalized Regulation. The U.S. Treasury Department Regulations (abbreviated Reg.) represent the position of the IRS as to how the Internal Revenue Code is to be interpreted. Their purpose is to provide taxpayers and IRS personnel with rules of general and specific application to the various provisions of the tax law. Regulations are published in the *Federal Register* and in all tax services.

Financial Accounting Standards Board (FASB). See *Generally Accepted Accounting Principles (GAAP).*

Fiscal year. A 12-month period ending on the last day of a month other than December. In certain circumstances, a taxpayer is permitted to elect a fiscal year instead of being required to use a calendar year.

Flat tax. In its pure form, a flat tax would eliminate all exclusions, deductions, and credits and impose a one-rate tax on gross income.

Flexible spending plan. An employee benefit plan that allows the employee to take a reduction in salary in exchange for the employer paying benefits that can be provided by the employer without the employee being required to recognize income (e.g., medical and child care benefits).

Flow-through entity. The entity is a tax reporter rather than a taxpayer. The owners are subject to tax. Examples are partnerships, S corporations, and limited liability companies.

Foreign earned income exclusion. The Code allows exclusions for earned income generated outside the United States to alleviate any tax base and rate disparities among countries. In addition, the exclusion is allowed for housing expenditures incurred by the taxpayer's employer with respect to the non-U.S. assignment, and self-employed individuals can deduct foreign housing expenses incurred in a trade or business. The exclusion is limited to $100,800 per year for 2015 ($99,200 in 2014). § 911.

Foreign Investment in Real Property Tax Act (FIRPTA). Under the Foreign Investment in Real Property Tax Act, gains or losses realized by nonresident aliens and non-U.S. corporations on the disposition of U.S. real estate creates U.S. source income and are subject to U.S. income tax.

Foreign tax credit (FTC). A U.S. citizen or resident who incurs or pays income taxes to a foreign country on income subject to U.S. tax may be able to claim some of these taxes as a credit against the U.S. income tax. §§ 27 and 901–905.

Franchise. An agreement that gives the transferee the right to distribute, sell, or provide goods, services, or facilities within a specified area. The cost of obtaining a franchise may be amortized over a statutory period of 15 years. In general, the franchisor's gain on the sale of franchise rights is an ordinary gain because the franchisor retains a significant power, right, or continuing interest in the subject of the franchise. §§ 197 and 1253.

Franchise tax. A tax levied on the right to do business in a state as a corporation. Although income considerations may come into play, the tax usually is based on the capitalization of the corporation.

Fraud. Tax fraud falls into two categories: civil and criminal. Under civil fraud, the IRS may impose as a penalty an amount equal to as much as 75 percent of the underpayment [§ 6651(f)]. Fines and/or imprisonment are prescribed for conviction of various types of criminal tax fraud (§§ 7201–7207). Both civil and criminal fraud involve a specific intent on the part of the taxpayer to evade the tax; mere negligence is not enough. Criminal fraud requires the additional element of willfulness (i.e., done deliberately and with evil purpose). In practice, it becomes difficult to distinguish between the degree of intent necessary to support criminal, rather than civil, fraud. In either situation, the IRS has the burden of proof to show the taxpayer committed fraud.

Fringe benefit. Compensation or other benefit received by an employee that is not in the form of cash. Some fringe benefits (e.g., accident and health plans, group term life insurance) may be excluded from the employee's gross income and therefore are not subject to the Federal income tax.

Frivolous return. A tax return that included a position that has no more than a 5 percent chance of being sustained upon review. Taxpayer and tax preparer penalties are assessed if a frivolous position is included in a filed tax return.

Fruit and tree metaphor. The courts have held that an individual who earns income from property or services cannot assign that income to another. For example, a father cannot assign his earnings from commissions to his child and escape income tax on those amounts.

Functional currency. The currency of the economic environment in which the taxpayer carries on most of its activities and in which the taxpayer transacts most of its business.

FUTA tax. An employment tax levied on employers. Jointly administered by the Federal and state governments, the tax provides funding for unemployment benefits. FUTA applies at a rate of 6.0 percent on the first $7,000 of covered wages paid during the year for each employee in 2015. The Federal government allows a credit for FUTA paid (or allowed under a merit rating system) to the state. The credit cannot exceed 5.4 percent of the covered wages.

Future interest. An interest that will come into being at some future time. It is distinguished from a present interest, which already exists. Assume that Dan transfers securities to a newly created trust. Under the terms of the trust instrument, income from the securities is to be paid each year to Wilma for her life, with the securities passing to Sam upon Wilma's death. Wilma has a present interest in the trust because she is entitled to current income distributions. Sam has a future interest because he must wait for Wilma's death to benefit from the trust. The annual exclusion of $14,000 (in 2015) is not allowed for a gift of a future interest. § 2503(b).

G

General business credit. The summation of various nonrefundable business credits, including the tax credit for rehabilitation expenditures, business energy credit, work opportunity credit, research activities credit, low-income housing credit, and disabled access credit. The amount of general business credit that can be used to reduce the tax liability is limited to the taxpayer's net income tax reduced by the greater of (1) the tentative minimum tax or (2) 25 percent of the net regular tax liability that exceeds $25,000. Unused general business credits can be carried back 1 year and forward 20 years. § 38.

General partner. A partner who is fully liable in an individual capacity for the debts of the partnership to third parties. A general partner's liability is not limited to the investment in the partnership. See also *limited partner.*

General partnership (GP). A partnership that is owned by one or more general partners. Creditors of a general partnership can collect amounts owed them from both the partnership assets and the assets of the partners individually.

Generally Accepted Accounting Principles (GAAP). Guidelines relating to how to construct the financial statements of enterprises doing business in the United States. Promulgated chiefly by the Financial Accounting Standards Board (FASB).

Gift tax. A tax imposed on the transfer of property by gift. The tax is imposed upon the donor of a gift and is based on the fair market value of the property on the date of the gift.

Golden parachute payment. A severance payment to employees that meets the following requirements: (1) the payment is contingent on a change of ownership of a corporation through a stock or asset acquisition and (2) the aggregate present value of the payment equals or exceeds three times the employee's average annual compensation. To the extent the severance payment meets these conditions, a deduction is disallowed to the employer for the excess of the payment over a statutory base amount (a five-year average of compensation if the taxpayer was an employee for the entire five-year period). In addition, a 20 percent excise tax is imposed on the employee who receives the excess severance pay. §§ 280G and 4999.

Goodwill. The reputation and built-up business of a company. For accounting purposes, goodwill has no basis unless it is purchased. In the purchase of a business, goodwill generally is the difference between the purchase price and the fair market value of the assets acquired. The intangible asset goodwill can be amortized for tax purposes over a 15-year period. Reg. § 1.167(a)–3.

Grantor. A transferor of property. The creator of a trust is usually referred to as the grantor of the entity.

Grantor trust. A trust under which the grantor retains control over the income or corpus (or both) to such an extent that he or she is treated as the owner of the property and its income for income tax purposes. Income from a grantor trust is taxable to the grantor and not to the beneficiary who receives it. §§ 671–679.

Grass roots expenditures. Exempt organizations are prohibited from engaging in political activities, but spending incurred to influence the opinions of the general public relative to specific legislation is permitted by the law.

Gross estate. The property owned or previously transferred by a decedent that is subject to the Federal estate tax. The gross estate can be distinguished from the probate estate, which is property actually subject to administration by the administrator or executor of an estate. §§ 2031–2046.

Gross income. Income subject to the Federal income tax. Gross income does not include all economic income. That is, certain exclusions are allowed (e.g., interest on municipal bonds). For a manufacturing or merchandising business, gross income usually means gross profit (gross sales or gross receipts less cost of goods sold). § 61 and Reg. § 1.61–3(a).

Group term life insurance. Life insurance coverage provided by an employer for a group of employees. Such insurance is renewable on a year-to-year basis, and typically no cash surrender value is built up. The premiums paid by the employer on the insurance are not taxed to the employees on coverage of up to $50,000 per person. § 79 and Reg. § 1.79–1(b).

Guaranteed payments. Payments made by a partnership to a partner for services rendered or for the use of capital to the extent the payments are determined without regard to the income of the partnership. The payments are treated as though they were made to a nonpartner and thus are deducted by the entity.

H

Half-year convention. A cost recovery convention that assumes that all property is placed in service at mid-year and thus provides for a half-year's cost recovery for that year.

Head of household. An unmarried individual who maintains a household for another and satisfies certain conditions set forth in § 2(b). This status enables the taxpayer to use a set of income tax rates that are lower than those applicable to other unmarried individuals but higher than those applicable to surviving spouses and married persons filing a joint return.

Health Savings Account (HSA). A medical savings account created in legislation enacted in December 2003 that is designed to replace and expand Archer Medical Savings Accounts.

Highly compensated employee. The employee group is generally divided into two categories for fringe benefit (including pension and profit sharing plans) purposes. These are (1) highly compensated employees and (2) non-highly compensated employees. For most fringe benefits, if the fringe benefit plan discriminates in favor of highly compensated employees, it will not be a qualified plan with respect, at a minimum, to the highly compensated employees.

Historic business test. In a corporate reorganization, a means by which to determine if the continuity of business enterprise requirement is met. The acquiring corporation must continue to operate the target entity's existing business(es) going forward; if this is not the case, the requirement is failed.

Hobby loss. Losses from an activity not engaged in for profit. The Code restricts the amount of losses that an individual can deduct for hobby activities so that these transactions cannot be used to offset income from other sources. § 183.

Holding period. The period of time during which property has been held for income tax purposes. The holding period is significant in determining whether gain or loss from the sale or exchange of a capital asset is long-term or short-term. § 1223.

Home equity loans. Loans that utilize the personal residence of the taxpayer as security. The interest on such loans is deductible as qualified residence interest. However, interest is deductible only on the portion of the loan that does not exceed the lesser of (1) the fair market value of the residence, reduced by the acquisition indebtedness, or (2) $100,000 ($50,000 for married persons filing separate returns). A major benefit of a home equity loan is that there are no tracing rules regarding the use of the loan proceeds. § 163(h)(3).

Hot assets. Unrealized receivables and substantially appreciated inventory under § 751. When hot assets are present, the sale of a partnership interest or the disproportionate distribution of the assets can cause ordinary income to be recognized.

H.R. 10 plans. See *Keogh plans.*

Hybrid method. A combination of the accrual and cash methods of accounting. That is, the taxpayer may account for some items of income on the accrual method (e.g., sales and cost of goods sold) and other items (e.g., interest income) on the cash method.

I

Imputed interest. For certain long-term sales of property, the IRS can convert some of the gain from the sale into interest income if the contract does not provide for a minimum rate of interest to be paid by the purchaser. The seller recognizes less long-term capital gain and more ordinary income (interest income). § 483 and the related Regulations.

Inbound taxation. U.S. tax effects when a non-U.S. person begins an investment or business activity in the United States.

Incentive stock option (ISO). A type of stock option that receives favorable tax treatment. If various qualification requirements can be satisfied, there are no recognition tax consequences when the stock option is granted. However, the spread (the excess of the fair market value at the date of exercise over the option price) is a tax preference item for purposes of the alternative minimum tax. The gain on disposition of the stock resulting from the exercise of the stock option will be classified as long-term capital gain if certain holding period requirements are met (the employee must not dispose of the stock within two years after the option is granted or within one year after acquiring the stock). § 422.

Income. For tax purposes, an increase in wealth that has been realized.

Income in respect of a decedent (IRD). Income earned by a decedent at the time of death but not reportable on the final income tax return because of the method of accounting that appropriately is utilized. Such income is included in the gross estate and is taxed to the eventual recipient (either the estate or heirs). The recipient is, however, allowed an income tax deduction for the estate tax attributable to the income. § 691.

Income tax provision. Under ASC 740 (SFAS 109), a synonym for the book tax expense of an entity for the financial reporting period. Following the "matching principle," all book tax expense that relates to the net income for the reporting period is reported on that period's financial statements, including not only the current tax expense, but also any deferred tax expense and deferred tax benefit.

Income tax treaties. See *tax treaty.*

Independent contractor. A self-employed person as distinguished from one who is employed as an employee.

Indexation. A procedure whereby adjustments are made by the IRS to key tax components (e.g., standard deduction, tax brackets, personal and dependency exemptions) to reflect inflation. The adjustments usually are made annually and are based on the change in the consumer price index.

Individual Retirement Account (IRA). A type of retirement plan to which an individual with earned income can contribute a statutory maximum of $5,500 in 2015. IRAs can be classified as traditional IRAs or Roth IRAs. With a traditional IRA, an individual can contribute and deduct a maximum of $5,500 per tax year in 2015. The deduction is a deduction *for* AGI. However, if the individual is an active participant in another qualified retirement plan, the deduction is phased out proportionally between certain AGI ranges (note that the phaseout limits the amount of the deduction and not the amount of the contribution). With a Roth IRA, an individual can contribute a maximum of $5,500 per tax year in 2015. No deduction is permitted. However, if a five-year holding period requirement is satisfied and if the distribution is a qualified distribution, the taxpayer can make tax-free withdrawals from a Roth IRA. The maximum annual contribution is phased out proportionally between certain AGI ranges. §§ 219 and 408A.

Individual Shared Responsibility Payment (ISRP). A mandate or penalty tax that individuals owe starting in 2014 for any month in which they do not have health coverage and do not qualify for an exemption. This mandate was created as part of the Affordable Care Act to encourage individuals to obtain health care coverage. If owed, the penalty is the greater of a "flat dollar amount" or a percentage of household income less the filing threshold. When fully in effect in 2016, the flat dollar amount is $695 and the percent applied to household income is 2.5%. For a family, the flat dollar amount cannot exceed three times the flat dollar amount. After 2016, the $695 amount is adjusted annually. The overall cap on the penalty is the national average cost of a bronze level plan (this amount is published by the IRS). Worksheets for computing the penalty are included in the instructions to Form 8965 (Health Coverage Exemptions). § 5000A.

Inheritance tax. A tax imposed on the right to receive property from a decedent. Thus, theoretically, an inheritance tax is imposed on the heir. The Federal estate tax is imposed on the estate.

Inside basis. A partnership's basis in the assets it owns.

Installment method. A method of accounting enabling certain taxpayers to spread the recognition of gain on the sale of property over the collection period. Under this procedure, the seller arrives at the gain to be recognized by computing the gross profit percentage from the sale (the gain divided by the contract price) and applying it to each payment received. § 453.

Intangible drilling and development costs (IDC). Taxpayers may elect to expense or capitalize (subject to amortization) intangible drilling and development costs. However, ordinary income recapture provisions apply to oil and gas properties on a sale or other disposition if the expense method is elected. §§ 263(c) and 1254(a).

Intermediate sanctions. The IRS can assess excise taxes on disqualified persons and organization management associated with so-called public charities engaging in excess benefit transactions. An excess benefit transaction is one in which a disqualified person engages in a non-fair market value transaction with the exempt organization or receives unreasonable compensation. Prior to the idea of intermediate sanctions, the only option available to the IRS was to revoke the organization's exempt status.

International Accounting Standards Board (IASB). The body that promulgates International Financial Reporting Standards (IFRS). Based in London, representing accounting standard setting bodies in over 100 countries, the IASB develops accounting standards that can serve as the basis for harmonizing conflicting reporting standards among nations.

International Financial Reporting Standards (IFRS). Produced by the International Accounting Standards Board (IASB), guidelines developed since 2001 as to revenue recognition, accounting for business combinations, and a conceptual framework for financial reporting. IFRS provisions are designed so that they can be used by all entities, regardless of where they are based or conduct business. IFRS have gained widespread acceptance throughout the world, and the SEC is considering how to require U.S. entities to use IFRS in addition to, or in lieu of, the accounting rules of the Financial Accounting Standards Board.

Interpretive Regulation. A Regulation issued by the Treasury Department that purports to explain the meaning of a particular Code Section. An interpretive Regulation is given less deference than a legislative Regulation.

Investment income. Consisting of virtually the same elements as portfolio income, a measure by which to justify a deduction for interest on investment indebtedness.

Investment interest. Payment for the use of funds used to acquire assets that produce investment income. The deduction for investment interest is limited to net investment income for the tax year.

Investor losses. Losses on stock and securities. If stocks and bonds are capital assets in the hands of the holder, a capital loss materializes as of the last day of the taxable year in which the stocks or bonds become worthless. Under certain circumstances involving stocks and bonds of affiliated corporations, an ordinary loss is permitted upon worthlessness.

Involuntary conversion. The loss or destruction of property through theft, casualty, or condemnation. Gain realized on an involuntary conversion can, at the taxpayer's election, be deferred for Federal income tax purposes if the owner reinvests the proceeds within a prescribed period of time in property that is similar or related in service or use. § 1033.

Itemized deductions. Personal and employee expenditures allowed by the Code as deductions from adjusted gross income. Examples include certain medical expenses, interest on home mortgages, state income taxes, and charitable contributions. Itemized deductions are reported on Schedule A of Form 1040. Certain miscellaneous itemized deductions are reduced by 2 percent of the taxpayer's adjusted gross income. In addition, a taxpayer whose adjusted gross income exceeds a certain level (indexed annually) must reduce the itemized deductions by 3 percent of the excess of adjusted gross income over that level. Medical, casualty and theft, and investment interest deductions are not subject to the 3 percent reduction. The 3 percent reduction may not reduce itemized deductions that are subject to the reduction to below 20 percent of their initial amount.

J

Joint tenants. Two or more persons having undivided ownership of property with the right of survivorship. Right of survivorship gives the surviving owner full ownership of the property. Suppose Bob and Tami are joint tenants of a tract of land. Upon Bob's death, Tami becomes the sole owner of the property. For the estate tax consequences upon the death of a joint tenant, see § 2040.

K

Keogh plans. Retirement plans available to self-employed taxpayers. They are also referred to as H.R. 10 plans. Under such plans, a taxpayer may deduct each year up to 100 percent of net earnings from self-employment or $53,000 for 2015, whichever is less. If the plan is a profit sharing plan, the percentage is 25 percent.

Kiddie tax. Passive income, such as interest and dividends, that is recognized by a child under age 19 (or under age 24 if a full-time student) is taxed to him or her at the rates that would have applied had the income been incurred by the child's parents, generally to the extent the income exceeds $2,100 for 2015. The additional tax is assessed regardless of the source of the income or the income's underlying property. If the child's parents are divorced, the custodial parent's rates are used. The parents' rates reflect any applicable alternative minimum tax and the phaseouts of lower tax brackets and other deductions. § 1(g).

L

Least aggregate deferral method. An algorithm set forth in the Regulations to determine the tax year for a partnership or an S corporation with owners whose tax years differ.

The tax year selected is the one that produces the least aggregate deferral of income for the owners.

Least aggregate deferral rule. See *least aggregate deferral method.*

Legislative Regulation. Some Code Sections give the Secretary of the Treasury or his delegate the authority to prescribe Regulations to carry out the details of administration or to otherwise complete the operating rules. Regulations issued pursuant to this type of authority truly possess the force and effect of law. In effect, Congress is almost delegating its legislative powers to the Treasury Department.

Lessee. One who rents property from another. In the case of real estate, the lessee is also known as the tenant.

Lessor. One who rents property to another. In the case of real estate, the lessor is also known as the landlord.

Letter ruling. The written response of the IRS to a taxpayer's request for interpretation of the revenue laws with respect to a proposed transaction (e.g., concerning the tax-free status of a reorganization). Not to be relied on as precedent by other than the party who requested the ruling.

Liabilities in excess of basis. On the contribution of capital to a corporation, an investor recognizes gain on the exchange to the extent contributed assets carry liabilities with a face amount in excess of the tax basis of the contributed assets. This rule keeps the investor from holding the investment asset received with a negative basis. § 357(c).

Life insurance proceeds. A specified sum (the face value or maturity value of the policy) paid to the designated beneficiary of the policy by the life insurance company upon the death of the insured.

Lifetime learning credit. A tax credit for qualifying expenses for taxpayers pursuing education beyond the first two years of postsecondary education. Individuals who are completing their last two years of undergraduate studies, pursuing graduate or professional degrees, or otherwise seeking new job skills or maintaining existing job skills are all eligible for the credit. Eligible individuals include the taxpayer, taxpayer's spouse, and taxpayer's dependents. The maximum credit is 20 percent of the first $10,000 of qualifying expenses and is computed per taxpayer. The credit is phased out for higher-income taxpayers. § 25A.

Like-kind exchange. An exchange of property held for productive use in a trade or business or for investment (except inventory and stocks and bonds) for other investment or trade or business property. Unless non-like-kind property (boot) is received, the exchange is fully tax-deferred. § 1031.

Limited liability company (LLC). A legal entity allowed by all of the states. The entity is subject to Federal income tax treatment as though it were a partnership in which all members or owners of the LLC are treated much like limited partners. There are no restrictions on ownership, all members may participate in management, and none has personal liability for the entity's debts.

Limited liability limited partnership (LLLP). A limited partnership for which the general partners are also protected from entity liabilities. An LLLP—or "triple LP"—can be formed in about 20 states. In those states, a limited partnership files with the state to adopt LLLP status.

Limited liability partnership (LLP). A legal entity allowed by many of the states, where a general partnership registers with the state as an LLP. Owners are general partners, but a partner is not liable for any malpractice committed by other partners. The personal assets of the partners are at risk for the entity's contractual liabilities, such as accounts payable. The personal assets of a specific partner are at risk for his or her own professional malpractice and tort liability and for malpractice and torts committed by those whom he or she supervises.

Limited partner. A partner whose liability to third-party creditors of the partnership is limited to the amounts invested in the partnership. See also *general partner* and *limited partnership.*

Limited partnership (LP). A partnership in which some of the partners are limited partners. At least one of the partners in a limited partnership must be a general partner.

Liquidating distribution. A distribution by a partnership or corporation that is in complete liquidation of the entity's trade or business activities. Typically, such distributions generate capital gain or loss to the investors without regard, for instance, to the earnings and profits of the corporation or to the partnership's basis in the distributed property. They can, however, lead to recognized gain or loss at the corporate level.

Listed property. Property that includes (1) any passenger automobile; (2) any other property used as a means of transportation; (3) any property of a type generally used for purposes of entertainment, recreation, or amusement; (4) any computer or peripheral equipment (with an exception for exclusive business use); (5) any cellular telephone (or other similar telecommunications equipment); and (6) any other property of a type specified in the Regulations. If listed property is predominantly used for business, the taxpayer is allowed to use the statutory percentage method of cost recovery. Otherwise, the straight-line cost recovery method must be used. § 280F.

Living trust. A revocable trust. Often touted as a means of avoiding some probate costs.

Lobbying expenditure. An expenditure made for the purpose of influencing legislation. Such payments can result in the loss of the exempt status of, and the imposition of Federal income tax on, an exempt organization.

Long-term care insurance. Insurance that helps pay the cost of care when the insured is unable to care for himself or herself. Such insurance is generally thought of as insurance against the cost of an aged person entering a nursing home. The employer can provide the insurance, and the premiums may be excluded from the employee's gross income. § 7702B.

Long-term contract. A building, installation, construction, or manufacturing contract that is entered into but not completed within the same tax year. A manufacturing contract is a long-term contract only if the contract is to manufacture (1) a unique item not normally carried in finished goods inventory or (2) items that normally require more than 12 calendar months to complete. The two available methods to account for long-term contracts are the percentage of completion method and the completed contract method. The completed contract method can be used only in limited circumstances. § 460.

Long-term nonpersonal use capital assets. Includes investment property with a long-term holding period. Such property disposed of by casualty or theft may receive § 1231 treatment.

Long-term tax-exempt rate. Used in deriving net operating loss limitations in the context of an equity structure shift. The highest of the Federal long-term interest rates in effect for any of the last three months. § 382.

Lower of cost or market (replacement cost). An elective inventory method, whereby the taxpayer may value inventories at the lower of the taxpayer's actual cost or the current replacement cost of the goods. This method cannot be used in conjunction with the LIFO inventory method.

Low-income housing credit. Beneficial treatment to owners of low-income housing is provided in the form of a tax credit. The calculated credit is claimed in the year the building is placed in service and in the following nine years. § 42.

Lump-sum distribution. Payment of the entire amount due at one time rather than in installments. Such distributions often occur from qualified pension or profit sharing plans upon the retirement or death of a covered employee. The recipient of a lump-sum distribution may recognize both long-term capital gain and ordinary income upon the receipt of the distribution. The ordinary income portion may be subject to a special 10-year income averaging provision. § 402(e).

M

Majority interest partners. Partners who have more than a 50 percent interest in partnership profits and capital, counting only those partners who have the same taxable year. The term is of significance in determining the appropriate taxable year of a partnership. § 706(b).

Marital deduction. A deduction allowed against the taxable estate or taxable gifts upon the transfer of property from one spouse to another.

Marriage penalty. The additional tax liability that results for a married couple when compared with what their tax liability would be if they were not married and filed separate returns.

Matching rule. Treatment of an intercompany transaction on a consolidated return, when a sold asset remains within the group.

Material participation. If an individual taxpayer materially participates in a nonrental trade or business activity, any loss from that activity is treated as an active loss that can be offset against active income. Material participation is achieved by meeting any one of seven tests provided in the Regulations. § 469(h).

Meaningful reduction test. A decrease in the shareholder's voting control. Used to determine whether a stock redemption qualifies for sale or exchange treatment.

Medical expenses. Medical expenses of an individual, a spouse, and dependents are allowed as an itemized deduction to the extent such amounts (less insurance reimbursements) exceed 10 percent (or 7.5 percent if at least age 65) of adjusted gross income. § 213.

Merger. The absorption of one corporation by another with the corporation being absorbed losing its legal identity. Flow Corporation is merged into Jobs Corporation, and the shareholders of Flow receive stock in Jobs in exchange for their stock in Flow. After the merger, Flow ceases to exist as a separate legal entity. If a merger meets certain conditions, it is not currently taxable to the parties involved. § 368(a)(1).

Mid-month convention. A cost recovery convention that assumes that property is placed in service in the middle of the month that it is actually placed in service.

Mid-quarter convention. A cost recovery convention that assumes that property placed in service during the year is placed in service at the middle of the quarter in which it is actually placed in service. The mid-quarter convention applies if more than 40 percent of the value of property (other than eligible real estate) is placed in service during the last quarter of the year.

Minimum tax credit (AMT). See *alternative minimum tax credit.*

Miscellaneous itemized deductions. A special category of itemized deductions that includes expenses such as professional dues, tax return preparation fees, job-hunting costs, unreimbursed employee business expenses, and certain investment expenses. Such expenses are deductible only to the extent they exceed 2 percent of adjusted gross income. § 67.

Modified accelerated cost recovery system (MACRS). A method in which the cost of tangible property is recovered over a prescribed period of time. Enacted by the Economic Recovery Tax Act (ERTA) of 1981 and substantially modified by the Tax Reform Act (TRA) of 1986 (the modified system is referred to as MACRS), the approach disregards salvage value, imposes a period of cost recovery that depends upon the classification of the asset into one of various recovery periods, and prescribes the applicable percentage of cost that can be deducted each year. § 168.

Modified adjusted gross income. A key determinant in computing the domestic production activities deduction (DPAD) and certain other tax provisions (e.g., deduction for higher education tuition, exclusion of interest on education savings bonds). §§ 135, 144, and 199.

Moving expenses. A deduction *for* AGI is permitted to employees and self-employed individuals provided certain tests are met. The taxpayer's new job must be at least 50 miles farther from the old residence than the old residence was from the former place of work. In addition, an employee must be employed on a full-time basis at the new location for 39 weeks in the 12-month period following the move. Deductible moving expenses include the cost of moving the household and personal effects, transportation, and lodging expenses during the move. The cost of meals during the move is not deductible. Qualified moving expenses that are paid (or reimbursed) by the employer can be excluded from the employee's gross income. In this case, the related deduction by the employee is not permitted. §§ 62(a)(15), 132(a)(6), and 217.

Multiple support agreement. To qualify for a dependency exemption, the support test must be satisfied. This requires that over 50 percent of the support of the potential dependent be provided by the taxpayer. Where no one person provides more than 50 percent of the support, a multiple support agreement enables a taxpayer to still qualify for the dependency exemption. Any person who contributed more than 10 percent of the support is entitled to claim the exemption if each person in the group who contributed more than 10 percent files a written consent (Form 2120). Each person who is a party to the multiple support agreement must meet all of the other requirements for claiming the dependency exemption. § 152(c).

Multistate Tax Commission (MTC). A regulatory body of the states that develops operating rules and regulations for the implementation of the UDITPA and other provisions that assign the total taxable income of a multistate corporation to specific states.

N

National sales tax. Intended as a replacement for the current Federal income tax. Unlike a value added tax (VAT), which is levied on the manufacturer, it would be imposed on the consumer upon the final sale of goods and services. To keep the tax from being regressive, low-income taxpayers would be granted some kind of credit or exemption.

Negligence. Failure to exercise the reasonable or ordinary degree of care of a prudent person in a situation that results in harm or damage to another. A penalty is assessed on taxpayers who exhibit negligence or intentional disregard of rules and Regulations with respect to the underpayment of certain taxes.

Net capital gain (NCG). The excess of the net long-term capital gain for the tax year over the net short-term capital loss. The net capital gain of an individual taxpayer is eligible for the alternative tax. § 1222(11).

Net capital loss (NCL). The excess of the losses from sales or exchanges of capital assets over the gains from sales or exchanges of such assets. Up to $3,000 per year of the net capital loss may be deductible by noncorporate taxpayers against ordinary income. The excess net capital loss carries over to future tax years. For corporate taxpayers, the net capital loss cannot be offset against ordinary income, but it can be carried back three years and forward five years to offset net capital gains. §§ 1211, 1212, and 1221(10).

Net investment income. The excess of investment income over investment expenses. Investment expenses are those deductible expenses directly connected with the production of investment income. Investment expenses do not include investment interest. The deduction for investment interest for the tax year is limited to net investment income. § 163(d).

Net Investment Income Tax (NIIT). A tax created as part of the Affordable Care Act that went into effect starting in 2013. This tax is imposed on individuals, estates, and trusts at a rate of 3.8% of the lesser of (i) net investment income, or (ii) modified AGI less a threshold amount. For married individuals, the threshold is $250,000 ($125,000 if married filing separately). For other individuals the threshold is $200,000. For estates and trusts, the threshold amount is equal to the amount where the 39.6% tax bracket begins for that year. For individuals, the dollar amounts are not adjusted for inflation. The tax is reported on Form 8960 (Net Investment Income Tax—Individuals, Estates, and Trusts), filed with the individual's Form 1040. § 1411.

Net operating loss (NOL). To mitigate the effect of the annual accounting period concept, § 172 allows taxpayers to use an excess loss of one year as a deduction for certain past or future years. In this regard, a carryback period of 2 (or more) years and a carryforward period of 20 years currently are allowed.

Nexus. A multistate corporation's taxable income can be apportioned to a specific state only if the entity has established a sufficient presence, or nexus, with that state. State law, which often follows the Uniform Division of Income for Tax Purposes Act (UDITPA), specifies various activities that lead to nexus in various states.

Ninety-day letter. This notice is sent to a taxpayer upon request, upon the expiration of the 30-day letter, or upon exhaustion by the taxpayer of his or her administrative remedies before the IRS. The notice gives the taxpayer 90 days in which to file a petition with the U.S. Tax Court. If a petition is not filed, the IRS will demand payment of the assessed deficiency. §§ 6211–6216.

No-additional-cost services. Services the employer may provide the employee at no additional cost to the employer. Generally, the benefit is the ability to utilize the employer's excess capacity (e.g., vacant seats on an airliner). Such amounts are excludible from the recipient's gross income.

Nonaccountable plan. An expense reimbursement plan that does not have an accountability feature. The result is that employee expenses must be claimed as deductions *from* AGI. An exception is moving expenses that are deductions *for* AGI.

Nonacquiescence. Disagreement by the IRS on the result reached in certain judicial decisions. *Nonacq.* or *NA*.

Nonbusiness bad debt. A bad debt loss that is not incurred in connection with a creditor's trade or business. The loss is classified as a short-term capital loss and is allowed only in the year the debt becomes entirely worthless. In addition to family loans, many investor losses are nonbusiness bad debts. § 166(d).

Nonliquidating distribution. A payment made by a partnership or corporation to the entity's owner when the entity's legal existence does not cease thereafter. If the payor is a corporation, such a distribution can result in dividend income to the shareholders. If the payor is a partnership, the partner usually assigns a basis in the distributed property that is equal to the lesser of the partner's basis in the partnership interest or the basis of the distributed asset to the partnership. In this regard, the partner first assigns basis to any cash that he or she receives in the distribution. The partner's remaining basis, if any, is assigned to the noncash assets according to their relative bases to the partnership.

Nonqualified deferred compensation (NQDC). Compensation arrangements that are frequently offered to executives. Such plans may include stock options, restricted stock, etc. Often, an executive may defer the recognition of taxable income. The employer, however, does not receive a tax deduction until the employee is required to include the compensation in income.

Nonqualified stock option (NQSO). A type of stock option that does not satisfy the statutory requirements of an incentive stock option. If the NQSO has a readily ascertainable fair market value (e.g., the option is traded on an established exchange), the value of the option must be included in the employee's gross income at the date of the grant. Otherwise, the employee does not recognize income at the grant date. Instead, ordinary income is recognized in the year of exercise of the option.

Nonrecourse debt. Debt secured by the property that it is used to purchase. The purchaser of the property is not personally liable for the debt upon default. Rather, the creditor's recourse is to repossess the related property. Nonrecourse debt generally does not increase the purchaser's at-risk amount.

Nonrefundable credit. A credit that is not paid if it exceeds the taxpayer's tax liability. Some nonrefundable credits qualify for carryback and carryover treatment.

Nonresident alien (NRA). An individual who is neither a citizen nor a resident of the United States. Citizenship is determined under the immigration and naturalization laws of the United States. Residency is determined under § 7701(b) of the Internal Revenue Code.

Nontaxable exchange. A transaction in which realized gains or losses are not recognized. The recognition of gain or loss is postponed (deferred) until the property received in the nontaxable exchange is subsequently disposed of in a taxable transaction. Examples are § 1031 like-kind exchanges and § 1033 involuntary conversions.

Not essentially equivalent redemption. Sale or exchange treatment is given to this type of redemption. Although various safe-harbor tests are failed, the nature of the redemption is such that dividend treatment is avoided, because it represents a meaningful reduction in the shareholder's interest in the corporation. § 302(b)(1).

O

Occupational fee. A tax imposed on various trades or businesses. A license fee that enables a taxpayer to engage in a particular occupation.

Occupational taxes. See *occupational fee.*

Offer in compromise. A settlement agreement offered by the IRS in a tax dispute, especially where there is doubt as to the collectibility of the full deficiency. Offers in compromise can include installment payment schedules, as well as reductions in the tax and penalties owed by the taxpayer.

Office audit. An audit conducted by the IRS in the agent's office.

Office in the home expenses. Employment and business-related expenses attributable to the use of a residence (e.g., den or office) are allowed only if the portion of the residence is exclusively used on a regular basis as a principal place of business of the taxpayer or as a place of business that is used by patients, clients, or customers. If the expenses are incurred by an employee, the use must be for the convenience of the employer as opposed to being merely appropriate and helpful. In computing the office-in-the-home expenses, a taxpayer can use either the regular method or simplified method. As a general rule, the regular method requires more effort and recordkeeping but results in a larger deduction. § 280A.

One hundred percent additional first-year depreciation. The Tax Relief Act of 2010 provides for a cost recovery deduction of 100 percent in the tax year qualified property is placed in service. Qualified property includes most types of new property other than buildings. This provision is effective for property acquired after December 31, 2010, and placed in service before January 1, 2012. See also *fifty percent additional first-year depreciation.*

One-year rule for prepaid expenses. Taxpayers who use the cash method are required to use the accrual method for deducting certain prepaid expenses (i.e., must capitalize the item and can deduct only when used). If a prepayment will not be consumed or expire by the end of the tax year following the year of payment, the prepayment must be capitalized and prorated over the benefit period. Conversely, if the prepayment will be consumed by the end of the tax year following the year of payment, it can be expensed when paid. To obtain the current deduction under the one-year rule, the payment must be a required payment rather than a voluntary payment.

Operating agreement. The governing document of a limited liability company. This document is similar in structure, function, and purpose to a partnership agreement.

Optional adjustment election. See *Section 754 election.*

Options. The sale or exchange of an option to buy or sell property results in capital gain or loss if the property is a capital asset. Generally, the closing of an option transaction results in short-term capital gain or loss to the writer of the call and the purchaser of the call option. § 1234.

Ordinary and necessary. An ordinary expense is common and accepted in the general industry or type of activity in which the taxpayer is engaged. It comprises one of the tests for the deductibility of expenses incurred or paid in connection with a trade or business; for the production or collection of income; for the management, conservation, or maintenance of property held for the production of income; or in connection with the determination, collection, or refund of any tax. §§ 162(a) and 212. A necessary expense is appropriate and helpful in furthering the taxpayer's business or income-producing activity. §§ 162(a) and 212.

Ordinary income property. Property contributed to a charitable organization that, if sold rather than contributed, would have resulted in other than long-term capital gain to the donor (i.e., ordinary income property and short-term capital gain property). Examples are inventory and capital assets held for less than the long-term holding period.

Organizational costs. See *organizational expenditures.*

Organizational expenditures. Items incurred early in the life of a corporate entity that are eligible for a $5,000 limited expensing (subject to phaseout) and an amortization of the balance over 180 months. Organizational expenditures exclude those incurred to obtain capital (underwriting fees) or assets (subject to cost recovery). Typically, eligible expenditures include legal and accounting fees and state incorporation payments. Such items must be incurred by the end of the entity's first tax year. § 248.

Original issue discount (OID). The difference between the issue price of a debt obligation (e.g., a corporate bond) and the maturity value of the obligation when the issue price is less than the maturity value. OID represents interest and must be amortized over the life of the debt obligation using the effective interest method. The difference is not considered to be original issue discount for tax purposes when it is less than one-fourth of 1 percent of the redemption price at maturity multiplied by the number of years to maturity. §§ 1272 and 1273(a)(3).

Other adjustments account (OAA). Used in the context of a distribution from an S corporation. The net accumulation of the entity's exempt income (e.g., municipal bond interest).

Other property. In a corporate reorganization, any property in the exchange that is not stock or securities, such as cash or inventory. This amount usually constitutes boot. This result is similar to that in a like-kind exchange.

Outbound taxation. U.S. tax effects when a U.S. person begins an investment or business activity outside the United States.

Outside basis. A partner's basis in his or her partnership interest.

Ownership change. An event that triggers a § 382 limitation for the acquiring corporation.

P

Parent-subsidiary controlled group. A controlled or affiliated group of corporations where at least one corporation is at least 80 percent owned by one or more of the others. The affiliated group definition is more difficult to meet.

Partial liquidation. A stock redemption where noncorporate shareholders are permitted sale or exchange treatment. In certain cases, an active business must have existed for at least five years. Only a portion of the outstanding stock in the entity is retired.

Partnership. For income tax purposes, a partnership includes a syndicate, group, pool, or joint venture, as well as ordinary partnerships. In an ordinary partnership, two or more parties combine capital and/or services to carry on a business for profit as co-owners. § 7701(a)(2).

Partnership agreement. The governing document of a partnership. A partnership agreement should describe the rights and obligations of the partners; the allocation of entity income, deductions, and cash flows; initial and future capital contribution requirements; conditions for terminating the partnership; and other matters.

Passive investment company. A means by which a multistate corporation can reduce the overall effective tax rate by isolating investment income in a low- or no-tax state.

Passive investment income (PII). Gross receipts from royalties, certain rents, dividends, interest, annuities, and gains from the sale or exchange of stock and securities. When earnings and profits (E & P) also exists, if the passive investment income of an S corporation exceeds 25 percent of the corporation's gross receipts for three consecutive years, S status is lost.

Passive loss. Any loss from (1) activities in which the taxpayer does not materially participate or (2) rental activities (subject to certain exceptions). Net passive losses cannot be used to offset income from nonpassive sources. Rather, they are suspended until the taxpayer either generates net passive income (and a deduction of such losses is allowed) or disposes of the underlying property (at which time the loss deductions are allowed in full). One relief provision allows landlords who actively participate in the rental activities to deduct up to $25,000 of passive losses annually. However, a phaseout of the $25,000 amount commences when the landlord's AGI exceeds $100,000. Another relief provision applies for material participation in a real estate trade or business.

Patent. An intangible asset that may be amortized over a statutory 15-year period as a § 197 intangible. The sale of a patent usually results in favorable long-term capital gain treatment. §§ 197 and 1235.

Payroll factor. The proportion of a multistate corporation's total payroll that is traceable to a specific state. Used in determining the taxable income that is to be apportioned to that state.

Pension plan. A type of deferred compensation arrangement that provides for systematic payments of definitely determinable retirement benefits to employees who meet the requirements set forth in the plan.

Percentage depletion. Depletion based on a statutory percentage applied to the gross income from the property. The taxpayer deducts the greater of cost depletion or percentage depletion. § 613.

Percentage of completion method. A method of reporting gain or loss on certain long-term contracts. Under this method of accounting, the gross contract price is included in income as the contract is completed. Reg. § 1.451–3.

Permanent and total disability. A person is considered permanently and totally disabled if he or she is unable to engage in any substantial gainful activity due to a physical or mental impairment. In addition, this impairment must be one that can be expected to result in death or that has lasted or can be expected to last for a continuous period of not less than 12 months. The taxpayer generally must provide the IRS a physician's statement documenting this condition.

Permanent differences. Under ASC 740 (SFAS 109), tax-related items that appear in the entity's financial statements or its tax return but not both. For instance, interest income from a municipal bond is a permanent book-tax difference.

Permanent establishment (PE). A level of business activity, as defined under an income tax treaty, that subjects the taxpayer to taxation in a country other than that in which the taxpayer is based. Often evidenced by the presence of a plant, an office, or other fixed place of business. Inventory storage and temporary activities do not rise to the level of a PE. PE is the treaty's equivalent to nexus.

Permanently reinvesting. Under ASC 740-30 (APB 23) of Generally Accepted Accounting Principles, a special rule that relates to the book tax expense of non-U.S. subsidiaries. If a parent corporation documents that it is permanently reinvesting the non-U.S. earning of a non-U.S. subsidiary, the parent does not record as an expense any U.S. income tax that the parent might pay on such earnings, i.e., the book tax expense is deferred until such earnings are (if ever) repatriated to the United States.

Personal and dependency exemptions. The tax law provides an exemption for each individual taxpayer and an additional exemption for the taxpayer's spouse if a joint return is filed. An individual may also claim a dependency exemption for each dependent, provided certain tests are met. The amount of the personal and dependency exemptions is $4,000 in 2015 ($3,950 in 2014). The exemption is subject to phaseout once adjusted gross income exceeds certain statutory threshold amounts.

Personal casualty gain. The recognized gain from any involuntary conversion of personal use property arising from fire, storm, shipwreck, or other casualty, or from theft.

Personal casualty loss. The recognized loss from any involuntary conversion of personal use property arising from fire, storm, shipwreck, or other casualty, or from theft.

Personal exemption. See *personal and dependency exemptions.*

Personal holding company tax. A penalty tax imposed on certain closely held corporations with excessive investment income. Assessed at the top individual tax rate on personal holding company income, reduced by dividends paid and other adjustments. § 541.

Personal residence. If a residence has been owned and used by the taxpayer as the principal residence for at least two years during the five-year period ending on the date of sale, up to $250,000 of realized gain is excluded from gross income. For a married couple filing a joint return, the $250,000 is increased to $500,000 if either spouse satisfies the ownership requirement and both spouses satisfy the use requirement. § 121.

Personal service corporation (PSC). A corporation whose principal activity is the performance of personal services (e.g., health, law, engineering, architecture, accounting, actuarial science, performing arts, or consulting) and where such services are substantially performed by the employee-owners. The 35 percent statutory income tax rate applies to PSCs.

Personalty. All property that is not attached to real estate (realty) and is movable. Examples of personalty are machinery, automobiles, clothing, household furnishings, and personal effects.

Points. Loan origination fees that may be deductible as interest by a buyer of property. A seller of property who pays points reduces the selling price by the amount of the points paid for the buyer. While the seller is not permitted to deduct this amount as interest, the buyer may do so.

Portfolio income. Income from interest, dividends, rentals, royalties, capital gains, or other investment sources. Net passive losses cannot be used to offset net portfolio income.

Power of appointment. A legal right granted to someone by a will or other document that gives the holder the power to dispose of property or the income from property. When the holder may appoint the property to his or her own benefit, the power usually is called a general power of appointment. If the holder cannot benefit himself or herself but may only appoint to certain other persons, the power is a special power of appointment. Assume Gary places $500,000 worth of securities in trust granting Donna the right to determine each year how the trustee is to divide the income between Ann and Babs. Under these circumstances, Donna has a special power of appointment. If Donna had the further right to appoint the income to herself, she probably possesses a general power of appointment. For the estate tax and gift tax effects of powers of appointment, see §§ 2041 and 2514.

Precedent. A previously decided court decision that is recognized as authority for the disposition of future decisions.

Precontribution gain or loss. Partnerships allow for a variety of special allocations of gain or loss among the partners, but gain or loss that is "built in" on an asset contributed to the partnership is assigned specifically to the contributing partner. § 704(c)(1)(A).

Preferences. See *AMT preferences.*

Preferred stock bailout. A process where a shareholder used the issuance and sale, or later redemption, of a preferred stock dividend to obtain long-term capital gains, without any loss of voting control over the corporation. In effect, the shareholder received corporate profits without suffering the consequences of dividend income treatment. This procedure led Congress to enact § 306, which, if applicable, converts the prior long-term capital gain on the sale or redemption of the tainted stock to dividend income.

Premium Tax Credit (PTC). A tax credit that is refundable and available in advance of filing a return for the year. The PTC serves to reduce the cost of health coverage obtained on the Marketplace (Exchange). A PTC is available to individuals who purchase coverage on the Exchange and have household income equal to or greater than 100% of the Federal poverty line (FPL) and no greater than 400% of the FPL. Also, an individual must not have been able to obtain affordable coverage from his or her employer. If obtained in advance, the PTC is given to the insurance provider to lower the monthly premium cost to the individual. The PTC is reconciled on Form 8962 (Premium Tax Credit) filed with Form 1040 or 1040-A (not Form 1040-EZ). Individuals who obtain insurance through the Marketplace receive Form 1095-A (Health Insurance Marketplace Statement) by January 31 of the following year. This form provides information necessary to claim or reconcile the PTC, including the monthly cost of premiums and the amount of PTC received in advance each month. § 36B.

Previously taxed income (PTI). Under prior law, the undistributed taxable income of an S corporation was taxed to the shareholders as of the last day of the corporation's tax year and usually could be withdrawn by the shareholders without tax consequences at some later point in time. The role of PTI has been taken over by the accumulated adjustments account. See also *accumulated adjustments account (AAA).*

Principal partner. A partner with a 5 percent or greater interest in partnership capital or profits. § 706(b)(3).

Private activity bond. Interest on state and local bonds is excludible from gross income. § 103. Certain such bonds are labeled private activity bonds. Although the interest on such bonds is excludible for regular income tax purposes, it is treated as a tax preference in calculating the AMT.

Private foundation. An exempt organization that is subject to additional statutory restrictions on its activities and on contributions made to it. Excise taxes may be levied on certain prohibited transactions, and the Code places more stringent restrictions on the deductibility of contributions to private foundations. § 509.

Probate costs. The costs incurred in administering a decedent's estate.

Probate estate. The property of a decedent that is subject to administration by the executor or administrator of an estate.

Procedural Regulation. A Regulation issued by the Treasury Department that is a housekeeping-type instruction indicating information that taxpayers should provide the IRS as well as information about the internal management and conduct of the IRS itself.

Profit and loss sharing ratios. Specified in the partnership agreement and used to determine each partner's allocation of ordinary taxable income and separately stated items. Profits and losses can be shared in different ratios. The ratios can be changed by amending the partnership agreement or by using a special allocation. § 704(a).

Profit sharing plan. A deferred compensation plan established and maintained by an employer to provide for employee participation in the company's profits. Contributions are paid from the employer's current or accumulated profits to a trustee. Separate accounts are maintained for each participant employee. The plan must provide a definite, predetermined formula for allocating the contributions among the participants. It also must include a definite, predetermined formula for distributing the accumulated funds after a fixed number of years, on the attainment of a stated age, or on the occurrence of certain events such as illness, layoff, or retirement.

Profits (loss) interest. A partner's percentage allocation of partnership operating results, determined by the profit and loss sharing ratios.

Property. Assets defined in the broadest legal sense. Property includes the unrealized receivables of a cash basis taxpayer, but not services rendered. § 351.

Property dividend. Generally treated in the same manner as a cash distribution, measured by the fair market value of the property on the date of distribution. Distribution of appreciated property causes the distributing C or S corporation to recognize gain. The distributing corporation does not recognize loss on property that has depreciated in value.

Property factor. The proportion of a multistate corporation's total property that is traceable to a specific state. Used in determining the taxable income that is to be apportioned to that state.

Proportionate distribution. A distribution in which each partner in a partnership receives a pro rata share of hot assets being distributed. For example, a distribution of $10,000 of hot assets equally to two 50 percent partners is a proportionate distribution.

Proposed Regulation. A Regulation issued by the Treasury Department in proposed, rather than final, form. The interval between the proposal of a Regulation and its finalization permits taxpayers and other interested parties to comment on the propriety of the proposal.

Proprietorship. A business entity for which there is a single owner. The net profit of the entity is reported on the owner's Federal income tax return (Schedule C of Form 1040).

Public Law 86–272. A congressional limit on the ability of the state to force a multistate corporation to assign taxable income to that state. Under P.L. 86–272, where orders for tangible personal property are both filled and delivered outside the state, the entity must establish more than the mere solicitation of such orders before any income can be apportioned to the state.

Punitive damages. Damages received or paid by the taxpayer can be classified as compensatory damages or as punitive damages. Punitive damages are those awarded to punish the defendant for gross negligence or the intentional infliction of harm. Such damages are includible in gross income. § 104.

Q

Qualified ABLE program. A state program that allows funds to be set aside for the benefit of an individual who became disabled or blind before age 26. Cash may be put into the fund annually up to the annual gift tax exclusion amount. Distributions to the designated beneficiary are not taxable provided they do not exceed qualified disability expenses for the year. § 529A.

Qualified business unit (QBU). A subsidiary, branch, or other business entity that conducts business using a currency other than the U.S. dollar.

Qualified dividend income. See *qualified dividends*.

Qualified dividends. Distributions made by domestic (and certain non-U.S.) corporations to noncorporate shareholders that are subject to tax at the same rates as those applicable to net long-term capital gains (i.e., 0 percent, 15 percent, or 20 percent). The 20 percent rate applies to certain high-income taxpayers (i.e., whose tax bracket is 39.6 percent). The dividend must be paid out of earnings and profits, and the shareholders must meet certain holding period requirements as to the stock. §§ 1(h)(1) and (11).

Qualified employee discounts. Discounts offered employees on merchandise or services that the employer ordinarily sells or provides to customers. The discounts must be generally available to all employees. In the case of property, the discount cannot exceed the employer's gross profit (the sales price cannot be less than the employer's cost). In the case of services, the discounts cannot exceed 20 percent of the normal sales price. § 132.

Qualified nonrecourse debt. Debt issued on realty by a bank, retirement plan, or governmental agency. Included in the at-risk amount by the investor. § 465(b)(6).

Qualified production activities income (QPAI). A key determinant in computing the domestic production activities deduction (DPAD). It consists of domestic production gross receipts (DPGR) reduced by cost of goods sold and other assignable expenses. Thus, QPAI represents the profit derived from domestic production activities. § 199.

Qualified real property business indebtedness. Indebtedness that was incurred or assumed by the taxpayer in connection with real property used in a trade or business and is secured by such real property. The taxpayer must not be a C corporation. For qualified real property business indebtedness, the taxpayer may elect to exclude some or all of the income realized from cancellation of debt on qualified real property. If the election is made, the basis of the property must be reduced by the amount excluded. The amount excluded cannot be greater than the excess of the principal amount of the outstanding debt over the fair market value (net of any other debt outstanding on the property) of the property securing the debt. § 108(c).

Qualified residence interest. A term relevant in determining the amount of interest expense the individual taxpayer may deduct as an itemized deduction for what otherwise would be disallowed as a component of personal interest (consumer interest). Qualified residence interest consists of interest paid on qualified residences (principal residence and one other residence) of the taxpayer. Debt that qualifies as qualified residence interest is limited to $1 million of debt to acquire, construct, or substantially improve qualified residences (acquisition indebtedness) plus $100,000 of other debt secured by qualified residences (home equity indebtedness). The home equity indebtedness may not exceed the fair market value of a qualified residence reduced by the acquisition indebtedness for that residence. § 163(h)(3).

Qualified small business corporation. For purposes of computing an exclusion upon the sale of qualified small business stock, a C corporation that has aggregate gross assets not exceeding $50 million and that is conducting an active trade or business. § 1202.

Qualified small business stock. Stock in a qualified small business corporation, purchased as part of an original issue after August 10, 1993. The shareholder may exclude from gross income 50 (or 75 or 100) percent of the realized gain on the sale of the stock if he or she held the stock for more than five years. § 1202.

Qualified terminable interest property (QTIP). Generally, the marital deduction (for gift and estate tax purposes) is not available if the interest transferred will terminate upon the death of the transferee spouse and pass to someone else. Thus, if Jim (the husband) places property in trust, life estate to Mary (the wife), and remainder to their children upon Mary's death, this is a terminable interest that will not provide Jim (or Jim's estate) with a marital deduction. If, however, the transfer in trust is treated as qualified terminable interest property (the QTIP election is made), the terminable interest restriction is waived and the marital deduction becomes available. In exchange for this deduction, the surviving spouse's gross estate must include the value of the QTIP election assets, even though he or she has no control over the ultimate disposition of the asset. Terminable interest property qualifies for this election if the donee (or heir) is the only beneficiary of the asset during his or her lifetime and receives income distributions relative to the property at least annually. For gifts, the donor spouse is the one who makes the QTIP election. For property transferred by death, the executor of the estate of the deceased spouse makes the election. §§ 2056(b)(7) and 2523(f).

Qualified transportation fringes. Transportation benefits provided by the employer to the employee. Such benefits include (1) transportation in a commuter highway vehicle between the employee's residence and the place of employment, (2) a transit pass, and (3) qualified parking. Qualified transportation fringes are excludible from the employee's gross income to the extent categories (1) and (2) above do not exceed $130 per month in 2015 and category (3) does not exceed $250 per month in 2015. These amounts are indexed annually for inflation. § 132.

Qualified tuition program. A program that allows college tuition to be prepaid for a beneficiary. When amounts in the plan are used, nothing is included in gross income provided they are used for qualified higher education expenses. § 529.

Qualified tuition reduction plan. A type of fringe benefit plan that is available to employees of nonprofit educational institutions. Such employees (and the spouse and dependent children) are allowed to exclude from gross income a tuition waiver pursuant to a qualified tuition reduction plan. The exclusion applies to undergraduate tuition. In limited circumstances, the exclusion also applies to the graduate tuition of teaching and research assistants. § 117(d).

Qualifying child. An individual who, as to the taxpayer, satisfies the relationship, abode, and age tests. To be claimed as a dependent, such individual must also meet the citizenship and joint return tests and not be self-supporting. §§ 152(a)(1) and (c).

Qualifying relative. An individual who, as to the taxpayer, satisfies the relationship, gross income, support, citizenship, and joint return tests. Such an individual can be claimed as a dependent of the taxpayer. §§ 152(a)(2) and (d).

R

Rate reconciliation. Under Generally Accepted Accounting Principles, a footnote to the financial statements often includes a table that accounts for differences in the statutory income tax rate that applies to the entity (say, 35 percent) and the higher or lower effective tax rate that the entity realized for the reporting period. The rate reconciliation includes only permanent differences between the book tax expense and the entity's income tax provision. The rate reconciliation table often is expressed in dollar and/or percentage terms.

Realized gain. See *realized gain or loss*.

Realized gain or loss. The difference between the amount realized upon the sale or other disposition of property and the adjusted basis of the property. § 1001.

Realized loss. See *realized gain or loss*.

Realty. Real estate.

Reasonable cause. Relief from taxpayer and preparer penalties often is allowed where reasonable cause is found for the taxpayer's actions. For example, reasonable cause for the late filing of a tax return might be a flood that damaged the taxpayer's record-keeping systems and made a timely completion of the return difficult.

Reasonable needs of the business. A means of avoiding the penalty tax on an unreasonable accumulation of earnings. In determining the base for this tax (accumulated taxable income), § 535 allows a deduction for "such part of earnings and profits for the taxable year as are retained for the reasonable needs of the business." § 537.

Reasonableness. See *reasonableness requirement*.

Reasonableness requirement. The Code includes a reasonableness requirement with respect to the deduction of salaries and other compensation for services. What constitutes reasonableness is a question of fact. If an expense is unreasonable, the amount that is classified as unreasonable is not allowed as a deduction. The question of reasonableness generally arises with respect to closely held corporations where there is no separation of ownership and management. § 162(a)(1).

Recapitalization. An "E" reorganization, constituting a major change in the character and amount of outstanding equity of a corporation. For instance, common stock exchanged for preferred stock can qualify for tax-free "E" reorganization treatment.

Recognized gain. See *recognized gain or loss.*

Recognized gain or loss. The portion of realized gain or loss subject to income taxation.

Recognized loss. See *recognized gain or loss.*

Recourse debt. Debt for which the lender may both foreclose on the property and assess a guarantor for any payments due under the loan. A lender also may make a claim against the assets of any general partner in a partnership to which debt is issued, without regard to whether the partner has guaranteed the debt.

Recovery of capital doctrine. When a taxable sale or exchange occurs, the seller may be permitted to recover his or her investment (or other adjusted basis) in the property before gain or loss is recognized.

Redemption to pay death taxes. Sale or exchange treatment is available relative to this type of stock redemption, to the extent of the proceeds up to the total amount paid by the estate or heir for estate/inheritance taxes and administration expenses. The stock value must exceed 35 percent of the value of the decedent's adjusted gross estate. In meeting this test, shareholdings in corporations where the decedent held at least 20 percent of the outstanding shares are combined.

Refundable credit. A credit that is paid to the taxpayer even if the amount of the credit (or credits) exceeds the taxpayer's tax liability.

Regular corporation. See *C corporation.*

Rehabilitation expenditures credit. A credit that is based on expenditures incurred to rehabilitate industrial and commercial buildings and certified historic structures. The credit is intended to discourage businesses from moving from older, economically distressed areas to newer locations and to encourage the preservation of historic structures. § 47.

Rehabilitation expenditures credit recapture. When property that qualifies for the rehabilitation expenditures credit is disposed of or ceases to be used in the trade or business of the taxpayer, some or all of the tax credit claimed on the property may be recaptured as additional tax liability. The amount of the recapture is the difference between the amount of the credit claimed originally and what should have been claimed in light of the length of time the property was actually held or used for qualifying purposes. § 50.

Related corporation. See *controlled group.*

Related party. Various Code Sections define related parties and often include a variety of persons within this (usually detrimental) category. Generally, related parties are accorded different tax treatment from that applicable to other taxpayers who enter into similar transactions. For instance, realized losses that are generated between related parties are not recognized in the year of the loss. However, these deferred losses can be used to offset recognized gains that occur upon the subsequent sale of the asset to a nonrelated party. Other uses of a related-party definition include the conversion of gain upon the sale of a depreci-able asset into all ordinary income (§ 1239) and the identification of constructive ownership of stock relative to corporate distributions, redemptions, liquidations, reorganizations, and compensation.

Related-party transactions. The tax law places restrictions upon the recognition of gains and losses between related parties because of the potential for abuse. For example, restrictions are placed on the deduction of losses from the sale or exchange of property between related parties. In addition, under certain circumstances, related-party gains that would otherwise be classified as capital gain are classified as ordinary income. §§ 267, 707(b), and 1239.

Rental activity. Any activity where payments are received principally for the use of tangible property is a rental activity. Temporary Regulations provide that in certain circumstances, activities involving rentals of real and personal property are not to be treated as rental activities. The Temporary Regulations list six exceptions.

Reorganization. Occurs, among other instances, when one corporation acquires another in a merger or an acquisition, a single corporation divides into two or more entities, a corporation makes a substantial change in its capital structure, or a corporation undertakes a change in its legal name or domicile. The exchange of stock and other securities in a corporate reorganization can be effected favorably for tax purposes if certain statutory requirements are followed strictly. Tax consequences include the nonrecognition of any gain that is realized by the shareholders except to the extent of boot received.

Required taxable year. A partnership or limited liability company must use a required tax year as its tax accounting period, or one of three allowable alternative tax year ends. The required tax year is determined using the least aggregate deferral rule. But if there is a common tax year used by owners holding a majority of the entity's capital or profits interests, or used by all of the owners who hold 5 percent or more of the capital or profits interests, then that tax year end is used by the entity.

Research activities credit. A tax credit whose purpose is to encourage research and development. It consists of three components: the incremental research activities credit, the basic research credit, and the energy credit. The incremental research activities credit is equal to 20 percent of the excess qualified research expenditures over the base amount. The basic research credit is equal to 20 percent of the excess of basic research payments over the base amount. § 41.

Research and experimental expenditures. The Code provides three alternatives for the tax treatment of research and experimentation expenditures. They may be expensed in the year paid or incurred, deferred subject to amortization, or capitalized. If the taxpayer does not elect to expense such costs or to defer them subject to amortization (over 60 months), the expenditures must be capitalized. § 174. Three types of research activities credits are available: the basic research credit, the incremental research activities credit, and the energy credit. The rate for each type is 20 percent. § 41.

Reserve method. A method of accounting whereby an allowance is permitted for estimated uncollectible accounts.

Actual write-offs are charged to the reserve, and recoveries of amounts previously written off are credited to the reserve. The Code permits only certain financial institutions to use the reserve method. § 166.

Residential rental real estate. Buildings for which at least 80 percent of the gross rents are from dwelling units (e.g., an apartment building). This type of building is distinguished from nonresidential (commercial or industrial) buildings in applying the recapture of depreciation provisions. The term also is relevant in distinguishing between buildings that are eligible for a 27.5-year life versus a 39-year life for MACRS purposes. Generally, residential buildings receive preferential treatment.

Restricted property plan. An arrangement whereby an employer transfers property (usually stock) to an employee at a bargain price (for less than the fair market value). If the transfer is accompanied by a substantial risk of forfeiture and the property is not transferable, no compensation results to the employee until the restrictions disappear. An example of a substantial risk of forfeiture would be a requirement that the employee return the property if his or her employment is terminated within a specified period of time. § 83.

Revenue Agent's Report (RAR). A Revenue Agent's Report (RAR) reflects any adjustments made by the agent as a result of an audit of the taxpayer. The RAR is mailed to the taxpayer along with the 30-day letter, which outlines the appellate procedures available to the taxpayer.

Revenue neutrality. A description that characterizes tax legislation when it neither increases nor decreases the total revenue collected by the taxing jurisdiction. Thus, any tax revenue losses are offset by tax revenue gains.

Revenue Procedure. A matter of procedural importance to both taxpayers and the IRS concerning the administration of the tax laws is issued as a Revenue Procedure (abbreviated Rev.Proc.). A Revenue Procedure is published in an *Internal Revenue Bulletin* (I.R.B.).

Revenue Ruling. A Revenue Ruling (abbreviated Rev.Rul.) is issued by the National Office of the IRS to express an official interpretation of the tax law as applied to specific transactions. It is more limited in application than a Regulation. A Revenue Ruling is published in an *Internal Revenue Bulletin* (I.R.B.).

Reversionary interest. The trust property that reverts to the grantor after the expiration of an intervening income interest. Assume that Phil places real estate in trust with income to Junior for 11 years, and upon the expiration of this term, the property returns to Phil. Under these circumstances, Phil holds a reversionary interest in the property. A reversionary interest is the same as a remainder interest, except that, in the latter case, the property passes to someone other than the original owner (e.g., the grantor of a trust) upon the expiration of the intervening interest.

Roth IRAs. See *Individual Retirement Account (IRA)*.

S

S corporation. The designation for a small business corporation. See also *Subchapter S*.

Sale or exchange. A requirement for the recognition of capital gain or loss. Generally, the seller of property must receive money or relief from debt to have sold the property. An exchange involves the transfer of property for other property. Thus, collection of a debt is neither a sale nor an exchange. The term *sale or exchange* is not defined by the Code.

Sales factor. The proportion of a multistate corporation's total sales that is traceable to a specific state. Used in determining the taxable income that is to be apportioned to that state.

Sales tax. A state- or local-level tax on the retail sale of specified property. Generally, the purchaser pays the tax, but the seller collects it, as an agent for the government. Various taxing jurisdictions allow exemptions for purchases of specific items, including certain food, services, and manufacturing equipment. If the purchaser and seller are in different states, a use tax usually applies.

Schedule K–1. A tax information form prepared for each partner in a partnership, each shareholder of an S corporation, and some beneficiaries of certain trusts. The Schedule K–1 reports the owner's share of the entity's ordinary income or loss from operations, as well as the owner's share of separately stated items.

Schedule M–1. On the Form 1120, a reconciliation of book net income with Federal taxable income. Accounts for temporary and permanent differences in the two computations, such as depreciation differences, exempt income, and nondeductible items. On Forms 1120S and 1065, the Schedule M–1 reconciles book income with the owners' aggregate ordinary taxable income.

Schedule M–3. An *expanded* reconciliation of book net income with Federal taxable income (see *Schedule M–1*). Required of C and S corporations and partnerships/LLCs with total assets of $10 million or more.

Scholarships. Scholarships are generally excluded from the gross income of the recipient unless the payments are a disguised form of compensation for services rendered. However, the Code imposes restrictions on the exclusion. The recipient must be a degree candidate. The excluded amount is limited to amounts used for tuition, fees, books, supplies, and equipment required for courses of instruction. Amounts received for room and board are not eligible for the exclusion. § 117.

Section 121 exclusion. If a residence has been owned and used by the taxpayer as the principal residence for at least two years during the five-year period ending on the date of sale, up to $250,000 of realized gain is excluded from gross income. For a married couple filing a joint return, the $250,000 is increased to $500,000 if either spouse satisfies the ownership requirement and both spouses satisfy the use requirement.

Section 179 expensing. The ability to deduct a capital expenditure in the year an asset is placed in service rather than over the asset's useful life or cost recovery period. The annual ceiling on the deduction is $25,000 for 2015 ($500,000 for 2014). However, the deduction is reduced dollar for dollar when § 179 property placed in service during the taxable year exceeds $200,000 in 2015 ($2 million in 2014). In addition, the amount expensed under § 179 cannot exceed the aggregate amount of taxable income derived from the conduct of any trade or business by the taxpayer.

Section 179 expensing election. See *Section 179 expensing.*

Section 338 election. When a corporation acquires at least 80 percent of a subsidiary within a 12-month period, it can elect to treat the acquisition of such stock as an asset purchase. The acquiring corporation's basis in the subsidiary's assets then is the cost of the stock. The subsidiary is deemed to have sold its assets for an amount equal to the grossed-up basis in its stock.

Section 382 limitation. When one corporation acquires another, the acquiror's ability to use the loss and credit carryovers of the target may be limited, in an anti-abuse provision specified in the Code. Generally, for instance, the maximum NOL deduction available to the acquiror is the takeover-date value of the target times the tax-exempt interest rate on that date.

Section 401(k) plan. A cash or deferred arrangement plan that allows participants to elect to receive up to $18,000 in 2015 in cash (taxed currently) or to have a contribution made on their behalf to a profit sharing or stock bonus plan (excludible from gross income). The plan may also be in the form of a salary reduction agreement between the participant and the employer.

Section 754 election. An election that may be made by a partnership to adjust the basis of partnership assets to reflect a purchasing partner's outside basis in interest or to reflect a gain, loss, or basis adjustment of a partner receiving a distribution from a partnership. The intent of the election is to maintain the equivalence between outside and inside basis for that partner. Once the election is made, the partnership must make basis adjustments for all future transactions, unless the IRS consents to revoke the election.

Section 1231 gains and losses. If the combined gains and losses from the taxable dispositions of § 1231 assets plus the net gain from business involuntary conversions (of both § 1231 assets and long-term capital assets) is a gain, the gains and losses are treated as long-term capital gains and losses. In arriving at § 1231 gains, however, the depreciation recapture provisions (e.g., § 1245) are applied first to produce ordinary income. If the net result of the combination is a loss, the gains and losses from § 1231 assets are treated as ordinary gains and losses. § 1231(a).

Section 1231 lookback. For gain to be classified as § 1231 gain, the gain must survive the § 1231 lookback. To the extent of nonrecaptured § 1231 losses for the five prior tax years, the gain is classified as ordinary income. § 1231(c).

Section 1231 property. Depreciable assets and real estate used in trade or business and held for the required long-term holding period. § 1231(b).

Section 1244 stock. Stock issued under § 1244 by qualifying small business corporations. If § 1244 stock becomes worthless, the shareholders may claim an ordinary loss rather than the usual capital loss, within statutory limitations.

Section 1245 property. Property that is subject to the recapture of depreciation under § 1245. For a definition of § 1245 property, see § 1245(a)(3).

Section 1245 recapture. Upon a taxable disposition of § 1245 property, all depreciation claimed on the property is recaptured as ordinary income (but not to exceed any recognized gain from the disposition).

Section 1250 property. Real estate that is subject to the recapture of depreciation under § 1250. For a definition of § 1250 property, see § 1250(c).

Section 1250 recapture. Upon a taxable disposition of § 1250 property, accelerated depreciation or cost recovery claimed on the property may be recaptured as ordinary income.

Securities. Generally, stock, debt, and other financial assets. To the extent securities other than the stock of the transferee corporation are received in a § 351 exchange, the new shareholder realizes a gain.

Self-employment tax. A tax of 12.4 percent is levied on individuals with net earnings from self-employment (up to $118,500 in 2015) to provide Social Security benefits (i.e., the old age, survivors, and disability insurance portion) for such individuals. In addition, a tax of 2.9 percent is levied on individuals with net earnings from self-employment (with no statutory ceiling) to provide Medicare benefits (i.e., the hospital insurance portion) for such individuals. If a self-employed individual also receives wages from an employer that are subject to FICA, the self-employment tax will be reduced. A partial deduction is allowed in calculating the self-employment tax. Individuals with net earnings of $400 or more from self-employment are subject to this tax. §§ 1401 and 1402.

Separate foreign tax credit limitation category. The foreign tax credit of a taxpayer is computed for each of several types of income sources, as specified by the Code to limit the results of tax planning. FTC income "baskets" include general and passive. The FTC for the year is the sum of the credits as computed within all of the taxpayer's separate FTC baskets used for the tax year.

Separate return limitation year (SRLY). A series of rules limits the amount of an acquired corporation's net operating loss carryforwards that can be used by the acquiror. Generally, a consolidated return can include the acquiree's net operating loss carryforward only to the extent of the lesser of the subsidiary's (1) current-year or (2) cumulative positive contribution to consolidated taxable income.

Separately stated item. Any item of a partnership or an S corporation that might be taxed differently to any two owners of the entity. These amounts are not included in the ordinary income of the entity, but are instead reported separately to the owners; tax consequences are determined at the owner level.

Severance tax. A tax imposed upon the extraction of natural resources.

Short period. See *short taxable year.*

Short sale. A sale that occurs when a taxpayer sells borrowed property (usually stock) and repays the lender with substantially identical property either held on the date of the short sale or purchased after the sale. No gain or loss is recognized until the short sale is closed, and such gain or loss is generally short-term. § 1233.

Short taxable year. A tax year that is less than 12 months. A short taxable year may occur in the initial reporting period, in the final tax year, or when the taxpayer changes tax years.

Significant participation activity. Seven tests determine whether an individual has achieved material participation in an activity, one of which is based on more than 500 hours of participation in significant participation activities. A significant participation activity is one in which the individual's participation exceeds 100 hours during the year. Temp.Reg. § 1.469–5T.

Simple trust. Trusts that are not complex trusts. Such trusts may not have a charitable beneficiary, accumulate income, or distribute corpus.

Simplified employee pension (SEP) plan. An employer may make contributions to an employee's IRA in amounts not exceeding the lesser of 15 percent of compensation or $53,000 per individual in 2015. These employer sponsored simplified employee pensions are permitted only if the contributions are nondiscriminatory and are made on behalf of all employees who have attained age 21 and have worked for the employer during at least three of the five preceding calendar years. § 219(b).

Small business corporation. A corporation that satisfies the definition of § 1361(b), § 1244(c), or both. Satisfaction of § 1361(b) permits an S election, and satisfaction of § 1244 enables the shareholders of the corporation to claim an ordinary loss on the worthlessness of stock.

Small business stock. See *Section 1244 stock.*

Small Cases Division. A division within the U.S. Tax Court where jurisdiction is limited to claims of $50,000 or less. There is no appeal from this court.

Sole proprietorship. An individual who operates a business activity reports the results of the business on Form 1040 for the year, usually on Schedule C or F. Federal income tax liabilities are computed using individual tax rates.

Solicitation. A level of activity brought about by the taxpayer within a specific state. Under Public Law 86-272, certain types of solicitation activities do not create nexus with the state. Exceeding mere solicitation, though, creates nexus.

Special allocation. Any amount for which an agreement exists among the partners of a partnership outlining the method used for spreading the item among the partners.

Special use value. Permits the executor of an estate to value, for estate tax purposes, real estate used in a farming activity or in connection with a closely held business at its current use value rather than at its most suitable or optimal use value. Under this option, a farm is valued for farming purposes even though, for example, the property might have a higher potential value as a shopping center. For the executor of an estate to elect special use valuation, the conditions of § 2032A must be satisfied.

Specific charge-off method. A method of accounting for bad debts in which a deduction is permitted only when an account becomes partially or completely worthless.

Spin-off. A type of reorganization where, for example, Ace Corporation transfers some assets to Bow Corporation in exchange for enough Bow stock to represent control. Ace then distributes the Bow stock to its shareholders.

Split-off. A type of reorganization where, for example, Arc Corporation transfers some assets to Bond Corporation in exchange for enough Bond stock to represent control. Arc then distributes the Bond stock to its shareholders in exchange for some of their Arc stock.

Split-up. A type of reorganization where, for example, Ally Corporation transfers some assets to Bar Corporation and the remainder to Zip Corporation. In return, Ally receives enough Bar and Zip stock to represent control of each corporation. Ally then distributes the Bar and Zip stock to its shareholders in return for all of their Ally stock. The result of the split-up is that Ally is liquidated, and its shareholders now have control of Bar and Zip.

Sprinkling trust. When a trustee has the discretion to either distribute or accumulate the entity accounting income of the trust and to distribute it among the trust's income beneficiaries in varying magnitudes. The trustee can "sprinkle" the income of the trust.

Standard deduction. The individual taxpayer can either itemize deductions or take the standard deduction. The amount of the standard deduction depends on the taxpayer's filing status (single, head of household, married filing jointly, surviving spouse, or married filing separately). For 2015, the amount of the standard deduction ranges from $6,300 (for single) to $12,600 (for married, filing jointly). Additional standard deductions of either $1,250 (for married taxpayers) or $1,550 (for single taxpayers) are available if the taxpayer is blind or age 65 or over. Limitations exist on the amount of the standard deduction of a taxpayer who is another taxpayer's dependent. The standard deduction amounts are adjusted for inflation each year. § 63(c).

Startup expenditures. Expenditures paid or incurred prior to the beginning of the business that would have been deductible as an ordinary and necessary business expense if business operations had begun. Examples of such expenditures include advertising; salaries and wages; travel and other expenses incurred in lining up prospective distributors, suppliers, or customers; and salaries and fees to executives, consultants, and professional service providers. A taxpayer will immediately expense the first $5,000 (subject to phaseout) of startup expenditures and amortize the balance over a period of 180 months, unless the taxpayer elects to not do so.

Statute of limitations. Provisions of the law that specify the maximum period of time in which action may be taken concerning a past event. Code §§ 6501–6504 contain the limitation periods applicable to the IRS for additional assessments, and §§ 6511–6515 relate to refund claims by taxpayers.

Statutory employee. Statutory employees are considered self-employed independent contractors for purposes of reporting income and expenses on their tax returns. Generally, a statutory employee must meet three tests:

- It is understood from a service contract that the services will be performed by the person.

- The person does not have a substantial investment in facilities (other than transportation used to perform the services).

- The services involve a continuing relationship with the person for whom they are performed.

For further information on statutory employees, see Circular E, *Employer's Tax Guide* (IRS Publication 15).

Step transaction. Disregarding one or more transactions to arrive at the final result. Assume, for example, that the shareholders of Clue Corporation liquidate the corporation and receive cash and operating assets. Immediately after the liquidation, the shareholders transfer the operating assets to newly formed Blue Corporation. Under these circumstances, the IRS may contend that the liquidation of Clue should be disregarded (thereby depriving the shareholders of capital gain treatment). What may really have happened is a reorganization of Clue with a distribution of boot (ordinary income) to Clue's shareholders. If so, there will be a carryover of basis in the assets transferred from Clue to Blue.

Step-down in basis. A reduction in the tax basis of property.

Step-up in basis. An increase in the income tax basis of property. A step-up in basis occurs when a decedent dies owning appreciated property. Since the estate or heir acquires a basis in the property equal to the property's fair market value on the date of death (or alternate valuation date if available and elected), any appreciation is not subject to the income tax. Thus, a step-up in basis is the result, with no immediate income tax consequences.

Stock bonus plan. A type of deferred compensation plan in which the employer establishes and maintains the plan and contributes employer stock to the plan for the benefit of employees. The contributions need not be dependent on the employer's profits. Any benefits of the plan are distributable in the form of employer stock, except that distributable fractional shares may be paid in cash.

Stock dividend. Not taxable if pro rata distributions of stock or stock rights on common stock. Section 305 governs the taxability of stock dividends and sets out five exceptions to the general rule that stock dividends are nontaxable.

Stock option. The right to purchase a stated number of shares of stock from a corporation at a certain price within a specified period of time. §§ 421 and 422.

Stock redemption. A corporation buys back its own stock from a specified shareholder. Typically, the corporation recognizes any realized gain on the noncash assets that it uses to effect a redemption, and the shareholder obtains a capital gain or loss upon receipt of the purchase price.

Stock rights. Assets that convey to the holder the power to purchase corporate stock at a specified price, often for a limited period of time. Stock rights received may be taxed as a distribution of earnings and profits. After the right is exercised, the basis of the acquired share includes the investor's purchase price or gross income, if any, to obtain the right. Disposition of the right also can be taxable.

Subchapter S. Sections 1361–1379 of the Internal Revenue Code. An elective provision permitting certain small business corporations (§ 1361) and their shareholders (§ 1362) to elect to be treated for income tax purposes in accordance with the operating rules of §§ 1363–1379. However, some S corporations usually avoid the corporate income tax, and corporate losses can be claimed by the shareholders.

Subpart F. Identifies the current tax treatment of income earned by a controlled foreign corporation. Certain types of income are included in U.S. gross income by U.S. shareholders of such an entity as they are generated, not when they are repatriated.

Subpart F income. See *Subpart F.*

Substance over form. A standard used when one must ascertain the true reality of what has occurred. Suppose, for example, a father sells stock to his daughter for $1,000. If the stock is really worth $50,000 at the time of the transfer, the substance of the transaction is probably a gift to her of $49,000.

Substantial authority. Taxpayer and tax preparer understatement penalties are waived where substantial authority existed for the disputed position taken on the return.

Substantial risk of forfeiture (SRF). A term that is associated with a restricted property plan. Generally, an employee who receives property (e.g., stock of the employer-corporation) from the employer at a bargain price or at no cost must include the bargain element in gross income. However, the employee currently does not have to do so if there is a substantial risk of forfeiture. A substantial risk of forfeiture exists if a person's rights to full enjoyment of property are conditioned upon the future performance, or the refraining from the performance, of substantial services by the individual. § 83.

Sunset provision. A provision attached to new tax legislation that will cause such legislation to expire at a specified date. Sunset provisions are attached to tax cut bills for long-term budgetary reasons to make their effect temporary. Once the sunset provision comes into play, the tax cut is rescinded and former law is reinstated. An example of a sunset provision is contained in the Tax Relief Reconciliation Act of 2001 that related to the estate tax. After the estate tax was phased out in 2010, a sunset provision called for the reinstatement of the estate tax as of January 1, 2011.

Supreme Court. See *U.S. Supreme Court.*

Surviving spouse. When a husband or wife predeceases the other spouse, the survivor is known as a surviving spouse. Under certain conditions, a surviving spouse may be entitled to use the income tax rates in § 1(a) (those applicable to married persons filing a joint return) for the two years after the year of death of his or her spouse. § 2. With respect to the Federal estate tax, this term describes the second spouse to die of a married couple, for the period between the two dates of death.

Syndication costs. Incurred in promoting and marketing partnership interests for sale to investors. Examples include legal and accounting fees, printing costs for prospectus and placement documents, and state registration fees. These items are capitalized by the partnership as incurred, with no amortization thereof allowed.

T

Tax avoidance. The minimization of one's tax liability by taking advantage of legally available tax planning opportunities. Tax avoidance can be contrasted with tax evasion, which entails the reduction of tax liability by illegal means.

Tax benefit rule. A provision that limits the recognition of income from the recovery of an expense or a loss properly deducted in a prior tax year to the amount of the deduction that generated a tax saving. Assume that last year Gary had medical expenses of $4,000 and adjusted gross income of $30,000. Because of the AGI limitation, Gary could deduct only $1,000 of these expenses [$4,000 − (10% × $30,000)]. If this year Gary is reimbursed in full by his insurance company for the $4,000 of expenses, the tax benefit rule limits the amount of income from the reimbursement to $1,000 (the amount previously deducted with a tax saving).

Tax Court. See *U.S. Tax Court.*

Tax credit for the elderly or disabled. An elderly (age 65 and over) or disabled taxpayer may receive a tax credit amounting to 15 percent of $5,000 ($7,500 for qualified married individuals filing jointly). This amount is reduced by Social Security benefits, excluded pension benefits, and one-half of the taxpayer's adjusted gross income in excess of $7,500 ($10,000 for married taxpayers filing jointly). § 22.

Tax credits. Amounts that directly reduce a taxpayer's tax liability. The tax benefit received from a tax credit is not dependent on the taxpayer's marginal tax rate, whereas the benefit of a tax deduction or exclusion is dependent on the taxpayer's tax bracket.

Tax evasion. The reduction of taxes by the use of subterfuge or fraud or other nonlegal means. For example, a cash basis taxpayer tries to increase his or her charitable contribution deduction by prepaying next year's church pledge with a pre-dated check issued in the following year.

Tax haven. A country in which either locally sourced income or residents of the country are subject to a low rate of taxation.

Tax preferences items. See *AMT preferences.*

Tax preparer. One who prepares tax returns for compensation. A tax preparer must register with the IRS and receive a special ID number to practice before the IRS and represent taxpayers before the agency in tax audit actions. The conduct of a tax preparer is regulated under Circular 230. Tax preparers also are subject to penalties for inappropriate conduct when working in the tax profession.

Tax Rate Schedules. Rate schedules that are used by upper-income taxpayers and those not permitted to use the tax table. Separate rate schedules are provided for married individuals filing jointly, heads of households, single taxpayers, estates and trusts, and married individuals filing separate returns. § 1.

Tax research. The method used to determine the best available solution to a situation that possesses tax consequences. Both tax and nontax factors are considered.

Tax shelters. The typical tax shelter generated large losses in the early years of the activity. Investors would offset these losses against other types of income and therefore avoid paying income taxes on this income. These tax shelter investments could then be sold after a few years and produce capital gain income, which is taxed at a lower rate compared to ordinary income. The passive activity loss rules and the at-risk rules now limit tax shelter deductions.

Tax Table. A table that is provided for taxpayers with less than $100,000 of taxable income. Separate columns are provided for single taxpayers, married taxpayers filing jointly, heads of households, and married taxpayers filing separately. § 3.

Tax treaty. An agreement between the U.S. Department of State and another country designed to alleviate double taxation of income and asset transfers and to share administra-

tive information useful to tax agencies in both countries. The United States has income tax treaties with almost 70 countries and transfer tax treaties with about 20.

Taxable estate. The taxable estate is the gross estate of a decedent reduced by the deductions allowed by §§ 2053–2057 (e.g., administration expenses, marital and charitable deductions). The taxable estate is subject to the unified transfer tax at death. § 2051.

Taxable gift. The amount of a gift that is subject to the unified transfer tax. Thus, a taxable gift has been adjusted by the annual exclusion and other appropriate deductions (e.g., marital and charitable). § 2053.

Taxable year. The annual period over which income is measured for income tax purposes. Most individuals use a calendar year, but many businesses use a fiscal year based on the natural business year.

Technical Advice Memoranda (TAM). TAMs are issued by the IRS in response to questions raised by IRS field personnel during audits. They deal with completed rather than proposed transactions and are often requested for questions related to exempt organizations and employee plans.

Technical termination of a partnership. The entity is treated for tax purposes as though it has terminated, even though it continues in its activities. When there has been a sale or exchange of more than 50 percent of the capital interests of the partnership within 12 months, the partnership is deemed to have terminated when the 50 percent threshold is crossed. A new partnership immediately is formed through asset contributions by the partners. These activities can affect the entity's tax year and its bases in the assets it holds.

Temporary differences. Under ASC 740 (SFAS 109), tax-related items that appear in the entity's financial statements and its tax return, but in different time periods. For instance, doubtful accounts receivable often create a temporary book-tax difference, as a bad debt reserve is used to compute an expense for financial reporting purposes, but a bad debt often is deductible only under the specific write-off rule for tax purposes, and the difference observed for the current period creates a temporary difference.

Temporary Regulation. A Regulation issued by the Treasury Department in temporary form. When speed is critical, the Treasury Department issues Temporary Regulations that take effect immediately. These Regulations have the same authoritative value as Final Regulations and may be cited as precedent for three years. Temporary Regulations are also issued as proposed Regulations.

Tenants by the entirety. Essentially, a joint tenancy between husband and wife.

Tenants in common. A form of ownership where each tenant (owner) holds an undivided interest in property. Unlike a joint tenancy or a tenancy by the entirety, the interest of a tenant in common does not terminate upon that individual's death (there is no right of survivorship). Assume that Tim and Cindy acquire real estate as equal tenants in common. Upon Tim's death, his one-half interest in the property passes to his estate or heirs, not automatically to Cindy.

Terminable interest. An interest in property that terminates upon the death of the holder or upon the occurrence of some other specified event. The transfer of a terminable interest by one spouse to the other may not qualify for the marital deduction. §§ 2056(b) and 2523(b).

Theft loss. A loss from larceny, embezzlement, or robbery. It does not include misplacement of items.

Thin capitalization. When debt owed by a corporation to the shareholders becomes too large in relation to the corporation's capital structure (i.e., stock and shareholder equity), the IRS may contend that the corporation is thinly capitalized. In effect, some or all of the debt is reclassified as equity. The immediate result is to disallow any interest deduction to the corporation on the reclassified debt. To the extent of the corporation's earnings and profits, interest payments and loan repayments on the reclassified debt are treated as dividends to the shareholders.

Thirty-day letter. A letter that accompanies an RAR (Revenue Agent's Report) issued as a result of an IRS audit of a taxpayer (or the rejection of a taxpayer's claim for refund). The letter outlines the taxpayer's appeal procedure before the IRS. If the taxpayer does not request any such procedures within the 30-day period, the IRS issues a statutory notice of deficiency (the 90-day letter).

Throwback rule. If there is no income tax in the state to which a sale otherwise would be apportioned, the sale essentially is exempt from state income tax, even though the seller is domiciled in a state that levies an income tax. Nonetheless, if the seller's state has adopted a throwback rule, the sale is attributed to the seller's state and the transaction is subjected to a state-level tax.

Traditional IRA. See *Individual Retirement Account (IRA)*.

Transfer pricing. The process of setting internal prices for transfers of goods and services among related taxpayers. For example, what price should be used when Subsidiary purchases management services from Parent? The IRS can adjust transfer prices when it can show that the taxpayers were attempting to avoid tax by, say, shifting losses, deductions, or credits from low-tax to high-tax entities or jurisdictions.

Transportation expenses. Transportation expenses for an employee include only the cost of transportation (e.g., taxi fares and automobile expenses) in the course of employment when the employee is not away from home in travel status. Commuting expenses are not deductible.

Travel expenses. Expenses that include meals (generally subject to a 50 percent disallowance) and lodging and transportation expenses while away from home in the pursuit of a trade or business (including that of an employee).

Treaty shopping. An international investor attempts to use the favorable aspects of a tax treaty to his or her advantage, often elevating the form of the transaction over its substance (e.g., by establishing only a nominal presence in the country offering the favorable treaty terms).

U

UDITPA. The Uniform Division of Income for Tax Purposes Act has been adopted in some form by many of the states. The Act develops criteria by which the total taxable income of a multistate corporation can be assigned to specific states.

Unclaimed property. A U.S. state may have the right to acquire property that has been made available to an individual or legal entity for a fixed period of time, where the claimant has not taken possession of the property after a notice period. Examples of such property that a state could acquire are an uncashed payroll check, or an unused gift card.

Undistributed personal holding company income. The tax base for the personal holding company tax. § 545.

Unearned income. Income received but not yet earned. Normally, such income is taxed when received, even for accrual basis taxpayers.

Unified transfer tax. Rates applicable to transfers by gift and death made after 1976. § 2001(c).

Unified transfer tax credit. A credit allowed against any unified transfer tax. §§ 2010 and 2505.

Uniform capitalization (UNICAP) rules. Under § 263A, the Regulations provide a set of rules that all taxpayers (regardless of the particular industry) can use to determine the items of cost (and means of allocating those costs) that must be capitalized with respect to the production of tangible property.

Unitary approach. See *unitary theory*.

Unitary theory. Sales, property, and payroll of related corporations are combined for nexus and apportionment purposes, and the worldwide income of the unitary entity is apportioned to the state. Subsidiaries and other affiliated corporations found to be part of the corporation's unitary business (because they are subject to overlapping ownership, operation, or management) are included in the apportionment procedure. This approach can be limited if a water's edge election is in effect.

Unit-livestock-price method. A method of accounting for the cost of livestock. The livestock are valued using a standard cost of raising an animal with the characteristics of the animals on hand to the same age as those animals.

Unrealized receivables. Amounts earned by a cash basis taxpayer but not yet received. Because of the method of accounting used by the taxpayer, these amounts have a zero income tax basis. When unrealized receivables are distributed to a partner, they generally convert a transaction from nontaxable to taxable or an otherwise capital gain to ordinary income (i.e., as a "hot asset").

Unreasonable compensation. A deduction is allowed for "reasonable" salaries or other compensation for personal services actually rendered. To the extent compensation is "excessive" ("unreasonable"), the distribution could be treated as a dividend, such that no deduction is allowed. The problem of unreasonable compensation usually is limited to closely held corporations, where the motivation is to pay out profits in some form that is deductible to the corporation.

Unreasonable position. A tax preparer penalty is assessed regarding the understatement of a client's tax liability due to a tax return position that is found to be too aggressive. The penalty is avoided if there is substantial authority for the position or if the position is disclosed adequately on the tax return. The penalty equals the greater of $1,000 or one-half of the tax preparer's fee that is traceable to the aggressive position.

Unrecaptured § 1250 gain. Gain from the sale of depreciable real estate held more than one year. The gain is equal to or less than the depreciation taken on such property and is reduced by § 1245 and § 1250 gain.

Unrelated business income (UBI). Income recognized by an exempt organization that is generated from activities not related to the exempt purpose of the entity. For instance, the gift shop located in a hospital may generate unrelated business income. § 511.

Unrelated business income tax (UBIT). Levied on the unrelated business income of an exempt organization.

U.S. Court of Federal Claims. A trial court (court of original jurisdiction) that decides litigation involving Federal tax matters. Appeal from this court is to the Court of Appeals for the Federal Circuit.

U.S. shareholder. For purposes of classification of an entity as a controlled foreign corporation, a U.S. person who owns, or is considered to own, 10 percent or more of the total combined voting power of all classes of voting stock of a foreign corporation. Stock owned directly, indirectly, and constructively is counted for this purpose.

U.S. Supreme Court. The highest appellate court or the court of last resort in the Federal court system and in most states. Only a small number of tax decisions of the U.S. Courts of Appeal are reviewed by the U.S. Supreme Court under its certiorari procedure. The Supreme Court usually grants certiorari to resolve a conflict among the Courts of Appeal (e.g., two or more appellate courts have assumed opposing positions on a particular issue) or when the tax issue is extremely important (e.g., size of the revenue loss to the Federal government).

U.S. Tax Court. One of four trial courts of original jurisdiction that decides litigation involving Federal income, death, or gift taxes. It is the only trial court where the taxpayer must not first pay the deficiency assessed by the IRS. The Tax Court will not have jurisdiction over a case unless a statutory notice of deficiency (90-day letter) has been issued by the IRS and the taxpayer files the petition for hearing within the time prescribed.

U.S. trade or business. A set of activities that is carried on in a regular, continuous, and substantial manner. A non-U.S. taxpayer is subject to U.S. tax on the taxable income that is effectively connected with a U.S. trade or business.

Use tax. A sales tax that is collectible by the seller where the purchaser is domiciled in a different state.

V

Vacation home. The Code places restrictions upon taxpayers who rent their residences or vacation homes for part of the tax year. The restrictions may result in a scaling down of expense deductions for the taxpayers. § 280A.

Valuation allowance. Under ASC 740 (SFAS 109), a tax-related item is reported for book purposes only when it is more likely than not that the item actually will be realized. When the "more likely than not" test is failed, a contra-asset account is created to offset some or all of the related deferred tax asset. For instance, if the entity projects that it will not be able to use all of its net operating loss carryforward due to a lack of future taxable income, a valuation allowance is created to reduce the net deferred tax asset

that corresponds to the carryforward. If income projections later change and it appears that the carryforward will be used, the valuation allowance is reversed or "released." Creation of a valuation allowance usually increases the current tax expense and thereby reduces current book income, and its release often increases book income in the later reporting period.

Value added tax (VAT). A national sales tax that taxes the increment in value as goods move through the production process. A VAT is much used in other countries but has not yet been incorporated as part of the U.S. Federal tax structure.

Vesting requirements. A qualified deferred compensation arrangement must satisfy a vesting requirement. Under this provision, an employee's right to accrued plan benefits derived from employer contributions must be nonforfeitable in accordance with one of two vesting time period schedules (or two required alternate vesting schedules for certain employer matching contributions).

Voluntary revocation. The owners of a majority of shares in an S corporation elect to terminate the S status of the entity as of a specified date. The day on which the revocation is effective is the first day of the corporation's C tax year.

W

W–2 wages. The domestic production activities deduction (DPAD) cannot exceed 50 percent of the W–2 wages paid for any particular year. Prop.Reg. § 199–2(f)(2) provides several methods for calculating the W–2 wages, but the payments must involve common law employees. To qualify, employees need to be involved in the production process. § 199.

Wash sale. A loss from the sale of stock or securities that is disallowed because the taxpayer, within 30 days before or after the sale, has acquired stock or securities substantially identical to those sold. § 1091.

Water's edge. A limitation on the worldwide scope of the unitary theory. If a corporate water's edge election is in effect, the state can consider in the apportionment procedure only the activities that occur within the boundaries of the United States.

Water's-edge election. See *water's edge.*

Wherewithal to pay. This concept recognizes the inequity of taxing a transaction when the taxpayer lacks the means with which to pay the tax. Under it, there is a correlation between the imposition of the tax and the ability to pay the tax. It is particularly suited to situations in which the taxpayer's economic position has not changed significantly as a result of the transaction.

Whistleblower Program. An IRS initiative that offers special rewards to informants who provide evidence regarding tax evasion activities of businesses or high-income individuals. More than $2 million of tax, interest, and penalty must be at stake. The reward can reach 30 percent of the tax recovery that is attributable to the whistleblower's information.

Withholding allowances. The number of withholding allowances serves as the basis for determining the amount of income taxes withheld from an employee's salary or wages. The more withholding allowances claimed, the less income tax withheld by an employer. An employee may claim withholding allowances for personal exemptions for self and spouse (unless claimed as a dependent of another person), dependency exemptions, and special withholding allowances.

Work opportunity tax credit. Employers are allowed a tax credit equal to 40 percent of the first $6,000 of wages (per eligible employee) for the first year of employment. Eligible employees include certain hard-to-employ individuals (e.g., qualified ex-felons, high-risk youth, food stamp recipients, and veterans). The employer's deduction for wages is reduced by the amount of the credit taken. For qualified summer youth employees, the 40 percent rate is applied to the first $3,000 of qualified wages.

Working condition fringe. A type of fringe benefit received by the employee that is excludible from the employee's gross income. It consists of property or services provided (paid or reimbursed) by the employer for which the employee could take a tax deduction if the employee had paid for them. § 132.

Worthless securities. A loss (usually capital) is allowed for a security that becomes worthless during the year. The loss is deemed to have occurred on the last day of the year. Special rules apply to securities of affiliated companies and small business stock. § 165.

Writ of Certiorari. Appeal from a U.S. Court of Appeals to the U.S. Supreme Court is by Writ of Certiorari. The Supreme Court need not accept the appeal, and it usually does not (*cert. den.*) unless a conflict exists among the lower courts that must be resolved or a constitutional issue is involved.

Appendix D-1

Table of Code Sections Cited

Appendix D-2

Table of Regulations Cited

Appendix D-3

Table of Revenue Procedures and Revenue Rulings Cited

Appendix E

Table of Cases Cited

Appendix F

Present Value and Future Value Tables

Present Value of $1

N/R	4%	5%	6%	7%	8%	9%	10%	11%	12%	13%	14%
1	0.9615	0.9524	0.9434	0.9346	0.9259	0.9174	0.9091	0.9009	0.8929	0.8850	0.8772
2	0.9246	0.9070	0.8900	0.8734	0.8573	0.8417	0.8264	0.8116	0.7972	0.7831	0.7695
3	0.8890	0.8638	0.8396	0.8163	0.7938	0.7722	0.7513	0.7312	0.7118	0.6931	0.6750
4	0.8548	0.8227	0.7921	0.7629	0.7350	0.7084	0.6830	0.6587	0.6355	0.6133	0.5921
5	0.8219	0.7835	0.7473	0.7130	0.6806	0.6499	0.6209	0.5935	0.5674	0.5428	0.5194
6	0.7903	0.7462	0.7050	0.6663	0.6302	0.5963	0.5645	0.5346	0.5066	0.4803	0.4556
7	0.7599	0.7107	0.6651	0.6227	0.5835	0.5470	0.5132	0.4817	0.4523	0.4251	0.3996
8	0.7307	0.6768	0.6274	0.5820	0.5403	0.5019	0.4665	0.4339	0.4039	0.3762	0.3506
9	0.7026	0.6446	0.5919	0.5439	0.5002	0.4604	0.4241	0.3909	0.3606	0.3329	0.3075
10	0.6756	0.6139	0.5584	0.5083	0.4632	0.4224	0.3855	0.3522	0.3220	0.2946	0.2697
11	0.6496	0.5847	0.5268	0.4751	0.4289	0.3875	0.3505	0.3173	0.2875	0.2607	0.2366
12	0.6246	0.5568	0.4970	0.4440	0.3971	0.3555	0.3186	0.2858	0.2567	0.2307	0.2076
13	0.6006	0.5303	0.4688	0.4150	0.3677	0.3262	0.2897	0.2575	0.2292	0.2042	0.1821
14	0.5775	0.5051	0.4423	0.3878	0.3405	0.2992	0.2633	0.2320	0.2046	0.1807	0.1597
15	0.5553	0.4810	0.4173	0.3624	0.3152	0.2745	0.2394	0.2090	0.1827	0.1599	0.1401
16	0.5339	0.4581	0.3936	0.3387	0.2919	0.2519	0.2176	0.1883	0.1631	0.1415	0.1229
17	0.5134	0.4363	0.3714	0.3166	0.2703	0.2311	0.1978	0.1696	0.1456	0.1252	0.1078
18	0.4936	0.4155	0.3503	0.2959	0.2502	0.2120	0.1799	0.1528	0.1300	0.1108	0.0946
19	0.4746	0.3957	0.3305	0.2765	0.2317	0.1945	0.1635	0.1377	0.1161	0.0981	0.0829
20	0.4564	0.3769	0.3118	0.2584	0.2145	0.1784	0.1486	0.1240	0.1037	0.0868	0.0728

Present Value of an Ordinary Annuity of $1

N/R	4%	5%	6%	7%	8%	9%	10%	11%	12%	13%	14%
1	0.9615	0.9524	0.9434	0.9346	0.9259	0.9174	0.9091	0.9009	0.8929	0.8850	0.8772
2	1.8861	1.8594	1.8334	1.8080	1.7833	1.7591	1.7355	1.7125	1.6901	1.6681	1.6467
3	2.7751	2.7232	2.6730	2.6243	2.5771	2.5313	2.4869	2.4437	2.4018	2.3612	2.3216
4	3.6299	3.5460	3.4651	3.3872	3.3121	3.2397	3.1699	3.1024	3.0373	2.9745	2.9137
5	4.4518	4.3295	4.2124	4.1002	3.9927	3.8897	3.7908	3.6959	3.6048	3.5172	3.4331
6	5.2421	5.0757	4.9173	4.7665	4.6229	4.4859	4.3553	4.2305	4.1114	3.9975	3.8887
7	6.0021	5.7864	5.5824	5.3893	5.2064	5.0330	4.8684	4.7122	4.5638	4.4226	4.2883
8	6.7327	6.4632	6.2098	5.9713	5.7466	5.5348	5.3349	5.1461	4.9676	4.7988	4.6389
9	7.4353	7.1078	6.8017	6.5152	6.2469	5.9952	5.7590	5.5370	5.3282	5.1317	4.9464
10	8.1109	7.7217	7.3601	7.0236	6.7101	6.4177	6.1446	5.8892	5.6502	5.4262	5.2161
11	8.7605	8.3064	7.8869	7.4987	7.1390	6.8052	6.4951	6.2065	5.9377	5.6869	5.4527
12	9.3851	8.8633	8.3838	7.9427	7.5361	7.1607	6.8137	6.4924	6.1944	5.9176	5.6603
13	9.9856	9.3936	8.8527	8.3577	7.9038	7.4869	7.1034	6.7499	6.4235	6.1218	5.8424
14	10.5631	9.8986	9.2950	8.7455	8.2442	7.7862	7.3667	6.9819	6.6282	6.3025	6.0021
15	11.1184	10.3797	9.7122	9.1079	8.5595	8.0607	7.6061	7.1909	6.8109	6.4624	6.1422
16	11.6523	10.8378	10.1059	9.4466	8.8514	8.3126	7.8237	7.3792	6.9740	6.6039	6.2651
17	12.1657	11.2741	10.4773	9.7632	9.1216	8.5436	8.0216	7.5488	7.1196	6.7291	6.3729
18	12.6593	11.6896	10.8276	10.0591	9.3719	8.7556	8.2014	7.7016	7.2497	6.8399	6.4674
19	13.1339	12.0853	11.1581	10.3356	9.6036	8.9501	8.3649	7.8393	7.3658	6.9380	6.5504
20	13.5903	12.4622	11.4699	10.5940	9.8181	9.1285	8.5136	7.9633	7.4694	7.0248	6.6231

Future Value of $1

N/R	4%	5%	6%	7%	8%	9%	10%	11%	12%	13%	14%
1	1.0400	1.0500	1.0600	1.0700	1.0800	1.0900	1.1000	1.1100	1.1200	1.1300	1.1400
2	1.0816	1.1025	1.1236	1.1449	1.1664	1.1881	1.2100	1.2321	1.2544	1.2769	1.2996
3	1.1249	1.1576	1.1910	1.2250	1.2597	1.2950	1.3310	1.3676	1.4049	1.4429	1.4815
4	1.1699	1.2155	1.2625	1.3108	1.3605	1.4116	1.4641	1.5181	1.5735	1.6305	1.6890
5	1.2167	1.2763	1.3382	1.4026	1.4693	1.5386	1.6105	1.6851	1.7623	1.8424	1.9254
6	1.2653	1.3401	1.4185	1.5007	1.5869	1.6771	1.7716	1.8704	1.9738	2.0820	2.1950
7	1.3159	1.4071	1.5036	1.6058	1.7138	1.8280	1.9487	2.0762	2.2107	2.3526	2.5023
8	1.3686	1.4775	1.5938	1.7182	1.8509	1.9926	2.1436	2.3045	2.4760	2.6584	2.8526
9	1.4233	1.5513	1.6895	1.8385	1.9990	2.1719	2.3579	2.5580	2.7731	3.0040	3.2519
10	1.4802	1.6289	1.7908	1.9672	2.1589	2.3674	2.5937	2.8394	3.1058	3.3946	3.7072
11	1.5395	1.7103	1.8983	2.1049	2.3316	2.5804	2.8531	3.1518	3.4785	3.8359	4.2262
12	1.6010	1.7959	2.0122	2.2522	2.5182	2.8127	3.1384	3.4985	3.8960	4.3345	4.8179
13	1.6651	1.8856	2.1329	2.4098	2.7196	3.0658	3.4523	3.8833	4.3635	4.8980	5.4924
14	1.7317	1.9799	2.2609	2.5785	2.9372	3.3417	3.7975	4.3104	4.8871	5.5348	6.2613
15	1.8009	2.0789	2.3966	2.7590	3.1722	3.6425	4.1772	4.7846	5.4736	6.2543	7.1379
16	1.8730	2.1829	2.5404	2.9522	3.4259	3.9703	4.5950	5.3109	6.1304	7.0673	8.1372
17	1.9479	2.2920	2.6928	3.1588	3.7000	4.3276	5.0545	5.8951	6.8660	7.9861	9.2765
18	2.0258	2.4066	2.8543	3.3799	3.9960	4.7171	5.5599	6.5436	7.6900	9.0243	10.5752
19	2.1068	2.5270	3.0256	3.6165	4.3157	5.1417	6.1159	7.2633	8.6128	10.1974	12.0557
20	2.1911	2.6533	3.2071	3.8697	4.6610	5.6044	6.7275	8.0623	9.6463	11.5231	13.7435

Future Value of an Ordinary Annuity of $1

N/R	4%	5%	6%	7%	8%	9%	10%	11%	12%	13%	14%
1	1.0000	1.0000	1.0000	1.0000	1.0000	1.0000	1.0000	1.0000	1.0000	1.0000	1.0000
2	2.0400	2.0500	2.0600	2.0700	2.0800	2.0900	2.1000	2.1100	2.1200	2.1300	2.1400
3	3.1216	3.1525	3.1836	3.2149	3.2464	3.2781	3.3100	3.3421	3.3744	3.4069	3.4396
4	4.2465	4.3101	4.3746	4.4399	4.5061	4.5731	4.6410	4.7097	4.7793	4.8498	4.9211
5	5.4163	5.5256	5.6371	5.7507	5.8666	5.9847	6.1051	6.2278	6.3528	6.4803	6.6101
6	6.6330	6.8019	6.9753	7.1533	7.3359	7.5233	7.7156	7.9129	8.1152	8.3227	8.5355
7	7.8983	8.1420	8.3938	8.6540	8.9228	9.2004	9.4872	9.7833	10.0890	10.4047	10.7305
8	9.2142	9.5491	9.8975	10.2598	10.6366	11.0285	11.4359	11.8594	12.2997	12.7573	13.2328
9	10.5828	11.0266	11.4913	11.9780	12.4876	13.0210	13.5795	14.1640	14.7757	15.4157	16.0853
10	12.0061	12.5779	13.1808	13.8164	14.4866	15.1929	15.9374	16.7220	17.5487	18.4197	19.3373
11	13.4864	14.2068	14.9716	15.7836	16.6455	17.5603	18.5312	19.5614	20.6546	21.8143	23.0445
12	15.0258	15.9171	16.8699	17.8885	18.9771	20.1407	21.3843	22.7132	24.1331	25.6502	27.2707
13	16.6268	17.7130	18.8821	20.1406	21.4953	22.9534	24.5227	26.2116	28.0291	29.9847	32.0887
14	18.2919	19.5986	21.0151	22.5505	24.2149	26.0192	27.9750	30.0949	32.3926	34.8827	35.5811
15	20.0236	21.5786	23.2760	25.1290	27.1521	29.3609	31.7725	34.4054	37.2797	40.4175	43.8424
16	21.8245	23.6575	25.6725	27.8881	30.3243	33.0034	35.9497	39.1899	42.7533	46.6717	50.9804
17	23.6975	25.8404	28.2129	30.8402	33.7502	36.9737	40.5447	44.5008	48.8837	53.7391	59.1176
18	25.6454	28.1324	30.9057	33.9990	37.4502	41.3013	45.5992	50.3959	55.7497	61.7251	68.3941
19	27.6712	30.5390	33.7600	37.3790	41.4463	46.0185	51.1591	56.9395	63.4397	70.7494	78.9692
20	29.7781	33.0660	36.7856	40.9955	45.7620	51.1601	57.2750	64.2028	72.0524	80.9468	91.0249

Appendix G

Tax Formulas

AMT Formula for Individuals

Regular Taxable Income (before standard deduction and exemptions)

Plus or minus:	AMT Adjustments
Plus:	AMT preferences
Equals:	Alternative minimum taxable income (AMTI)
Minus:	AMT Exemption
Equals:	Tentative minimum tax (TMT) base
Times:	26% and 28% AMT rates
Equals:	Tentative minimum tax before foreign tax credit
Minus:	AMT foreign tax credit
Equals:	Tentative minimum tax
Minus:	Regular income tax liability (after foreign tax credit)
Equals:	Alternative minimum tax (if TMT > Regular tax liability)

AMT Exemption Phaseout for Individuals for 2015

		Phaseout	
Filing Status	**Exemption**	**Begins at**	**Ends at**
Married, filing jointly	$83,400	$158,900	$492,500
Single or head of household	53,600	119,200	333,600
Married, filing separately	41,700	79,450	246,250

AMT Formula for Corporations

Regular Taxable Income before NOL Deduction

Plus or minus:	AMT Adjustments (except ACE adjustment)
Plus:	AMT preferences
Equals:	AMTI before AMT NOL deduction and ACE adjustment
Plus or minus:	ACE adjustment
Equals:	AMTI before AMT NOL deduction
Minus:	AMT NOL deduction (limited to 90% of amount from prior line)
Equals:	Alternative minimum taxable income (AMTI)
Minus:	AMT Exemption
Equals:	Tentative minimum tax base
Times:	20% AMT rate
Equals:	Tentative minimum tax before AMT foreign tax credit
Minus:	AMT foreign tax credit
Equals:	Tentative minimum tax (TMT)
Minus:	Regular income tax liability (after foreign tax credit)
Equals:	Alternative minimum tax (if TMT > Regular tax liability)

Tax Formula for Corporate Taxpayers

Income (broadly defined)	$xxx,xxx
Less: Exclusions (income that is not subject to tax)	(xx,xxx)
Gross income	$xxx,xxx
Less: Certain business deductions	(xx,xxx)
Taxable income	$xxx,xxx
Federal income tax (see Tax Rate Schedule inside front cover of text)	$ xx,xxx
Less: Tax credits (including prepayments of Federal income taxes)	(x,xxx)
Tax due (or refund)	$ xx,xxx

Tax Formula for Individuals

Income (broadly defined)	$xx,xxx
Less: Exclusions (income that is not subject to tax)	(x,xxx)
Gross income	$xx,xxx
Less: Deductions *for* adjusted gross income	(x,xxx)
Adjusted gross income	$xx,xxx
Less: The greater of—	
Total itemized deductions	
or standard deduction	(x,xxx)
Less: Personal and dependency exemptions	(x,xxx)
Taxable income	$xx,xxx
Tax on taxable income	$ x,xxx
Less: Tax credits (including Federal income tax withheld and	
other prepayments of Federal income taxes)	(xxx)
Tax due (or refund)	$ xxx

Index

T

AMT Formula for Individuals

Regular Taxable Income (before standard deduction and exemptions)

Plus or minus:	AMT Adjustments
Plus:	AMT preferences
Equals:	Alternative minimum taxable income (AMTI)
Minus:	AMT Exemption
Equals:	Tentative minimum tax (TMT) base
Times:	26% and 28% AMT rates
Equals:	Tentative minimum tax before foreign tax credit
Minus:	AMT foreign tax credit
Equals:	Tentative minimum tax
Minus:	Regular income tax liability (after foreign tax credit)
Equals:	Alternative minimum tax (if TMT > Regular tax liability)

AMT Exemption Phaseout for Individuals for 2015

		Phaseout	
Filing Status	**Exemption**	**Begins at**	**Ends at**
Married, filing jointly	$83,400	$158,900	$492,500
Single or head of household	53,600	119,200	333,600
Married, filing separately	41,700	79,450	246,250

AMT Formula for Corporations

Regular Taxable Income before NOL Deduction

Plus or minus:	AMT Adjustments (except ACE adjustment)
Plus:	AMT preferences
Equals:	AMTI before AMT NOL deduction and ACE adjustment
Plus or minus:	ACE adjustment
Equals:	AMTI before AMT NOL deduction
Minus:	AMT NOL deduction (limited to 90% of amount from prior line)
Equals:	Alternative minimum taxable income (AMTI)
Minus:	AMT Exemption
Equals:	Tentative minimum tax base
Times:	20% AMT rate
Equals:	Tentative minimum tax before AMT foreign tax credit
Minus:	AMT foreign tax credit
Equals:	Tentative minimum tax (TMT)
Minus:	Regular income tax liability (after foreign tax credit)
Equals:	Alternative minimum tax (if TMT > Regular tax liability)